Parts of a Dictionary Entry

entry word — pronunciation — definition — example — picture

entry

meg·a·phone (meg′ə fōn′) a large horn used to increase the loudness of the voice: *The cheer leader at the football game yelled through a megaphone.* *n.*

☛ **Megaphone** comes from the Greek words *megas* meaning 'great' and *phōnē* meaning 'sound'; **microphone** comes from the Greek words *micros* meaning 'small' and *phōnē* meaning 'sound'.

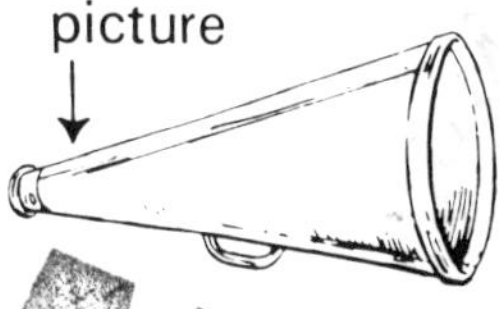

A megaphone

fistnote (word history)

definition number — usage label

mad (mad) **1** out of one's mind; crazy; insane: *A man must be mad to cut himself on purpose.* **2** *Informal.* very angry: *The insult made him mad.* **3** much excited; wild: *The dog made mad efforts to catch up with the automobile.* **4** foolish, unwise: *a mad undertaking.* **5** very lively: *a mad party.* **6** blindly and unreasonably fond: *Some girls are mad about going to dances.* **7** having rabies or hydrophobia: *A mad dog foams at the mouth and may bite people.* *adj.,* **mad·der, mad·dest.**
—mad′ly, *adv.*

special forms — part-of-speech label — run-on entry

idiom →

like mad, *Informal.* furiously; very hard or fast: *I ran like mad to catch the train.*

☛ **Mad, crazy, insane** have similar meanings. **Insane** is the proper word to describe someone suffering from severe mental illness: *The man was so worried that he became insane.* **Mad** is used in the same way but often just means very reckless, or foolish: *Crossing the Pacific on a raft seems a mad thing to do.* **Crazy** suggests a more wild or disturbed state: *She is nearly crazy with fear.*

fistnote (synonyms)

man·ner (man′ər) **1** the way something happens or is done: *The trouble arose in a curious manner.* **2** a person's way of acting or behaving; a style or fashion: *She has a kind manner. He dresses in a strange manner.* **3** kind or kinds: *He saw all manner of birds in the forest.* **4 manners,** *pl.* **a** ways or customs: *Books and movies show us the manners of other times and places.* **b** ways of behaving towards others: *bad manners.* **c** polite behavior: *It is nice to see a child with manners.* *n.*

hidden entry (def. 4)

☛ **Manner** and **manor** are pronounced the same.

↑ fistnote (homonyms)

may·be (mā′bē) possibly or perhaps; it may be so. *adv.*

☛ **Maybe** as an adverb is one word: *Maybe it will rain tomorrow.* **May be** as a verb phrase is two words: *He may be home soon.*

fistnote (usage)

Canadian Junior Dictionary

A book in the
DICTIONARY OF
CANADIAN ENGLISH
series

Canadian Junior Dictionary

W. S. Avis

R. J. Gregg

M. H. Scargill

Gage Educational Publishing Limited

Illustrations by *Lazare and Parker*

Consultants

Heather Hooper, Consultant, North Bay, Ontario
Dorothy Balfour Hutton, Educational Consultant, Edmonton, Alberta
J. E. Parsons, teacher and writer, Toronto, Ontario
Vivian Theberge, Reading Clinician, Catholic School Centre, Calgary, Alberta

ISBN 0-7715-1988-5

3 4 5 6 7 8 9 GL 80 79 78

Printed and bound in Canada

Contents

Introduction

Since 1962 the *Dictionary of Canadian English* series has become a valued source of linguistic information for students in elementary and secondary schools across Canada. *The Beginning Dictionary* especially has established itself both as a reference work suited to the needs of young children and as a teaching dictionary, admirably suited to the learning and practising of dictionary skills.

The *Canadian Junior Dictionary* is a revision and expansion of *The Beginning Dictionary*. Over two thousand new entries and numerous additional meanings have brought the dictionary up to date and have broadened its scope to meet the needs of today's children. In addition, the whole text, including definitions and examples, has been checked and, where necessary, revised to make the coverage sufficient and the tone contemporary.

An important aspect of the revision involves metrication. New entries have been added to cover the basic terms of the International System of Units (SI), and metric measurements are used in example sentences and phrases throughout the dictionary. Entries have been retained for the units of measure in the imperial system, but the basic imperial units are related to metric measurements. The assumption is that the terms of both systems will remain in use in Canada for some time, but that children's prime system of measurement will be SI.

New typesetting and layout make the pages of the dictionary more readable and more inviting to the student. Moreover, approximately five hundred and fifty pictures have been specially drawn for the *Canadian Junior Dictionary* by a group of Canadian artists. Overall, there is an average of slightly more than one picture to a page.

A new feature of this dictionary is the use of fistnotes. Placed at the end of many entries, these provide additional aid and encouragement to the student in four distinct ways: by indicating homonyms, by distinguishing between synonyms, by giving advice on usage, and by supplying simple but interesting histories of words. These fistnotes are designed not only to help the student put the dictionary to practical use when reading or writing, but also to stimulate an abiding interest in language.

Above all, the *Canadian Junior Dictionary* is a teaching dictionary. The many aids to the student, including a simplified pronunciation key, make this a book that fosters both skill and confidence in the use of a dictionary. Furthermore, the following forty-two-page section, entitled "Inside the *Canadian Junior Dictionary*," systematically introduces the main parts and features of the dictionary and at the same time provides material for teaching the basic dictionary skills. There are numerous student exercises and, as far as possible, each page has been set up to constitute a separate lesson.

Throughout the *Canadian Junior Dictionary*, the editors have sought to represent the English language as it is used in Canada today. They have, moreover, followed the traditions of the *Dictionary of Canadian English* series by concentrating on the special needs and levels of understanding of the students for whom this particular dictionary is intended.

Inside the *Canadian Junior Dictionary*

Inside the dictionary are facts about nearly 30 000 words. These are only a few of the words in the English language, but they are the ones you are most likely to use when you speak, write, listen, or read.

The following pages provide information and activities that will help you to know what kinds of facts about words are inside the dictionary and how best to find and make use of them. These pages will also give you practice in looking up words for different purposes. As you use your dictionary more and more, you will find it becomes both easier to use and more helpful. You will also discover many interesting and surprising things about words and their uses.

The information and activities that follow are grouped under these four headings:

It is a good idea to work through the sections in this same order. As you get into each new section, you will find you are discovering new kinds of information that are given in the dictionary. You will also be finding new ways of using the dictionary.

The charts printed on the endpapers inside the front and back covers contain a handy collection of facts to help you understand the dictionary entries. Inside the front cover are the complete Pronunciation Key and the chart of Parts of a Dictionary Entry from page xlv. Inside the back cover are a Grammar Key, a Word History Key, and another copy of the Pronunciation Key. These endpaper charts are easy to find, so remember to use them whenever you need their help.

Words and Meanings

Read the following sentences and think about each of the italicized words. Do you know the meaning of any of these words? If not, can you guess what each one means?

1. The damaged helicopter landed safely at the *heliport*.
2. A person chokes if food goes down the windpipe instead of the *esophagus*.
3. The raindrop was a shimmering *globule* of water on the leaf.
4. The puppet show ended when the strings of the *marionettes* got twisted.
5. The ground was soaked, and heavy *gumbo* stuck to our rubbers.

Talk about the meaning of each italicized word. What clues in the context of the sentence or in the word itself can help you guess its meaning? If you are still uncertain about any of the meanings, look these words up in the dictionary.

The main purpose of a dictionary is to explain the meanings of words. However, you don't have to use the dictionary every time you meet a word that seems new to you. The dictionary is not meant to keep you from thinking about words. It is meant to *help* you think about them.

Sometimes it is difficult to tell the exact meaning of a new word, though it is quite easy to guess its general idea. Look at the following examples:

6. A *caragana* hedge sheltered the farmhouse from the prairie winds.
7. He liked eating *filberts*, and he cracked their shells with his teeth.
8. Nobody believed that the *zircons* on her ring were diamonds.
9. The Eskimo cut up the sealskin with her *ooloo*.
10. The vegetables were served in china *tureens*.

Talk about the meaning of each italicized word. If you are not sure what each one means, guess as much of the meaning as you can. Then look up each of the italicized words in the dictionary. What does the dictionary definition tell you that you were not able to guess?

The meanings of the italicized words in the following sentences are harder to guess. Think and talk about them. Then look up each one that you don't know in the dictionary.

1. Can you imagine what boiling *magma* looks like?
2. He was fascinated by the flight of the *grebe*.
3. Some famous people like to travel *incognito*.
4. She was sure she had broken her *patella*.
5. His story was a long piece of *rigmarole*.

FINDING AN ENTRY

Each word that is explained or defined in a dictionary is called an *entry word*. Everything that is said about a particular word makes up a complete *entry*. Did you have any difficulty in finding the dictionary entries for the words you looked up while working on the previous section? This new section is designed to help you find dictionary entries quickly and easily. More speed will come with more practice.

Alphabetical Order

a b c d e f g h i j k l m
n o p q r s t u v w x y z

All the entries in the *Canadian Junior Dictionary* are in alphabetical order – they are *alphabetized*. Write down the following words in the order in which they appear as dictionary entries:

I you will car boat lake key rain

When a group of words all have the same first letter, they have to be alphabetized by the second letter. Write the following six words in alphabetical order:

cease czar coal chain case cry

When the first two letters are the same, alphabetize by the third letter:

chain church chasm chrysalis choose chestnut

When the first three letters are the same, alphabetize by the fourth letter:

quarter quay quack quantity quaver quaint

Try making up some alphabetizing exercises for your group or partner to work on. How many words can you think of that have to be alphabetized by the fifth letter? List as many as you can.

Arrange the following words in alphabetical order. You will then be able to write them down as a complete sentence.

David A Park clawed on cat yesterday bad Street.

(If you make up an exercise like this, write down your sentence first and then write down the words in scrambled order on another piece of paper. Perhaps your group would like to try unscrambling a sentence of twenty-six words, each word beginning with a different letter of the alphabet.)

The following words make sense when the words are put in alphabetical order. How quickly can you write down the unscrambled sentence?

eight storeroom jugs wrestled empty All night when tiles landed on our last William.

One way of doing this exercise would be to draw three columns, like this:

a to f	g to q	r to z

Words starting with *a* to *f* go into the first column, words starting with *g* to *q* go into the middle column, and words starting with *r* to *z* go into the last one.

When you have put each word of the scrambled sentence in the proper column, it will be quite easy to alphabetize the words in the first column, then those in the second, and then those in the third.

Use the three-column method to put the following words in order, and then write them as a sentence.

Fred's telling John if A mystery dinner locates notes where barbecue hike ends lost us.

Whenever you want to look up a word in the dictionary, decide if the first letter of the word comes in the beginning (*a* to *f*), the middle (*g* to *q*), or the end (*r* to *z*) of the alphabet. Then try to open the dictionary at approximately the right part.

At which part (beginning, middle, or end) would you open the dictionary to look up each of the following words?

electrode smithereens quasar jalopy bonanza yodel

Guidewords

At the top of the outside column of each page of the dictionary, on either side of the page number, are two words in heavy, bold type. For example:

blameless	**51**	**blight**

These words are called *guidewords.* They indicate which entries are on that particular page. The guideword on the left is the first entry word to appear on the page. The one on the right is the last entry word to appear on the page. Therefore all the entry words that come alphabetically between the two guidewords will appear on the same page.

By looking at the guidewords shown above, decide which of the following will appear as entry words on page 51:

bland	**black**	**bleach**
blaze	**bless**	**bloat**
blind	**blood**	**blast**

The following are the guidewords for four pages of the dictionary:

clog	**99**	**cloverleaf**
clown	**100**	**coat**
coating	**101**	**code**
codfish	**102**	**collar**

On which page will each of the following words be entered? Write each word with the correct page number beside it.

coach	**coin**	**cocoa**
coddle	**cog**	**coal**
cloud	**club**	**coat of arms**
clutter	**cloth**	**cluck**

Remember

Entry words in the dictionary are printed in bold type and arranged in alphabetical order.

Guidewords are printed in bold type and set at the top of a dictionary page to show the first and last entry words on that page. So guidewords help to guide you to the right page for whatever word you wish to look up.

Homographs

He gave the boy a cuff and walked away.

Do you know the meaning of *cuff* in the above sentence? If you look the word up in the dictionary, you will find not one entry but two:

> **cuff**[1] (kuf) **1** the part of the sleeve of a shirt, blouse, etc. that goes around the wrist. **2** the turned-up fold around the bottom of a sleeve or of a trouser leg. *n.*
> **cuff**[2] (kuf) **1** hit with the hand; slap. **2** a slap, usually on the head or face. 1 *v.*, 2 *n.*

These two words have the same spelling, but they have different origins and very different meanings, so they are treated as separate entries. The small raised number after each entry is a signal that there is another entry word with the same spelling. Words with the same spelling but different origins and meanings are called *homographs.*

Read the two entries for *cuff* and decide whether *cuff*[1] or *cuff*[2] gives the right meaning for the sentence at the top of this page.

Now look at the italicized words in the following sentences. Look these words up in the dictionary. Then write down the entry (entry word plus small raised number) that covers the meaning of each word in its sentence. The first one is done for you as an example.

1. She went out in the rain to *post* a letter. *post*[3]
2. He told me to *post* the sign on the door.
3. The fur trapper finally reached the trading *post.*
4. She covered the turkey with *foil* and put it in the oven.
5. He thrust with his *foil* but couldn't score a hit.
6. The police set a trap to *foil* the thieves.

How many entries for *cricket* are there in the dictionary? Write down the one that might be illustrated by this picture.

The dictionary has three main ways of helping its readers to understand the meanings of words: definitions (explanations), examples (phrases or sentences), and pictures.

Definitions

Here is the dictionary entry for a word that you may have looked up earlier:

> **glob·ule** (glob′yůl) a very small ball; a tiny drop: *Globules of sweat stood out on his forehead. n.*

The entry tells you that *globule* means "a very small ball; a tiny drop." This part of the entry is called the *definition.* Actually these are two statements of meaning. "A very small ball" and "a tiny drop" could each be substituted for "globule" in the following sentence.

> A globule of water shimmered on the leaf.
> A very small ball of water shimmered on the leaf.
> A tiny drop of water shimmered on the leaf.

Look up the italicized words in the following sentences. Then replace each of these words with all or part of its definition. The first one is done for you as an example.

1. Terry told us how to play *dodgeball.*
   Terry told us how to play a game in which players forming a circle or two opposite lines try to hit opponents in the centre with a large ball.
2. My uncle is looking for *ore* in the North.
3. On rainy days Dad *putters* in the basement.
4. Leslie and a *pal* will meet us.
5. A *pudgy* child can't crawl under this fence.
6. Here are rules and *explicit* instructions for the new game.

Sometimes a definition cannot easily be substituted for the entry word without the wording being shortened or changed around. For example:

> **ma·rine** (mə rēn′) **1** of the sea; found in the sea; produced by the sea: *Seals and whales are marine animals.*

As a substitute for "Seals and whales are marine animals," we would not normally say, "Seals and whales are found in the sea animals." But we could change the wording and say, "Seals and whales are animals found in the sea."

Rewrite the following sentences, replacing each italicized word with its definition. Change the order and grouping of words where necessary to make the sentence sound right.

1. Pirates often attacked *maritime* cities.
2. There was an *audible* reaction from the audience.
3. Our teacher wants us to ask *pertinent* questions.

Often other changes have to be made in order to fit a definition into a context. Here, for example, is the dictionary entry for *brief*, followed by additional sentences illustrating definitions 2, 3, and 4.

> **brief** (brēf) **1** lasting only a short time: *a brief meeting.* **2** using few words: *a brief letter. Be as brief as you can.* **3** a formal statement or request: *Our community association presented a brief to the local council.* **4** give detailed information to: *The commanding officer briefed the pilots just before they took off.* 1, 2 *adj.,* 3 *n.,* 4 *v.* —**brief′ness,** *n.*

Your letter was briefer than mine.
The lawyer had written several briefs.
The officers were briefing their men.

In the first sentence you could not replace *briefer* with the definition "using few words." To bring out the meaning of the sentence you would have to say "using fewer words":

Your letter was using (*or* used) fewer words than mine.

In the second sentence you could not say "several a formal statement." You would have to say "several formal statements":

The lawyer had written several formal statements.

In the third sentence you would have to change "give" in the definition to "were giving":

The officers were giving detailed information to their men.

In the above cases the definition has to be changed to suit the form of the word in the sentence. The same thing happens with most forms ending in *-ed*. For example:

> **a·vert** (ə vėrt′) **1** prevent; avoid: *The driver averted an accident by a quick turn of the steering wheel.* **2** turn away; turn aside: *She averted her eyes from the wreck. v.*

If you were replacing *averted* in the example sentence with its first meaning, you wouldn't say, "The driver prevent an accident. . . ." You would have to say, "The driver prevented an accident. . . ."

Examples

Many definitions are followed by one or more examples printed in italics. In the following entry, there is an example for every meaning except the last:

> **comb** (kōm) **1** a narrow, short piece of metal, rubber, plastic, etc. with teeth, used to arrange or clean the hair or to hold it in place: *Women sometimes wear combs in their hair as ornaments.* **2** anything shaped or used like a comb: *One kind of comb cleans and takes out the tangles in wool or flax.* **3** clean; take out tangles in; arrange with a comb: *I comb my hair before breakfast.* **4** search through: *We had to comb the whole city before we found our lost dog.* **5** the thick, red, fleshy piece on the top of the head of chickens and some other fowls: *A rooster has a larger comb than a hen has.* **6** honeycomb (def. 1). 1, 2, 5, 6 *n.*, 3, 4 *v.*

Such examples have several uses. They show the entry word in context, so that you can see how the word is used in sentences. They may suggest the kinds of situation in which a word is used. They often help to show the difference between one meaning of a word and another. They sometimes add to the information given in the definition.

Read the following, which is an entry printed without its examples:

> **chafe** (chāf) **1** rub: **2** make sore or become sore by rubbing: **3** make angry: **4** get angry: *v.*, **chafed, chaf·ing.**

Now look up the entry in the dictionary and see how much clearer it is when the examples are given.

Try writing your own examples for the following definitions:

1. **item 1** a separate thing or article: . . . .
2. **bottle 2** the amount that a bottle can hold: . . . .
3. **master 9** learn; become skilled at: . . . .
4. **interlock** join or fit tightly together; lock together: . . . .
5. **storm 4** a violent outburst or disturbance: . . . .

Working in groups of two, check your examples to make sure they fit the definitions and make good sense. Then compare them with the examples in the dictionary. In each case, decide whether your example, your partner's example, or the one in the dictionary is best. Be prepared to say why.

Examples in the dictionary are always printed in italics, and the definitions before them always end in a colon.

Pictures

The entry for *comb*, which is reproduced on the previous page, is accompanied in the dictionary by these two pictures:

A comb for hair

The comb of a rooster

These pictures help you to recognize what is being defined in definitions 1 and 5 of the entry. The pictures also help to show why these two kinds of comb are like each other.

Here are two more examples of pictures used in the dictionary:

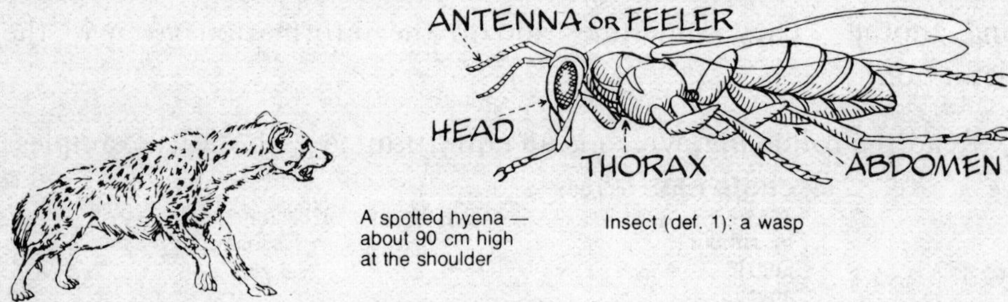

A spotted hyena — about 90 cm high at the shoulder

Insect (def. 1): a wasp

Note the important information given in the caption for the picture of a hyena. The caption for the right-hand drawing merely tells what kind of insect is pictured. In this case the more important information is given by the labels. What is another word for *antennae*?

In some of the pictures in the dictionary, the object is shown from two or more different points of view. For example:

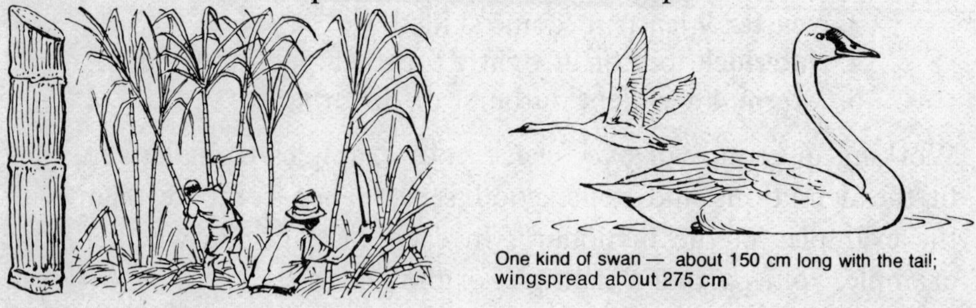

One kind of swan — about 150 cm long with the tail; wingspread about 275 cm

Sugar cane

The left-hand picture shows men cutting a field of sugar cane and also a close-up of part of a single cane. The right-hand picture shows two views of a swan, both swimming and flying.

Many of the pictures in the dictionary are actually diagrams. They are designed to show how something is made or how something works. Here is an example:

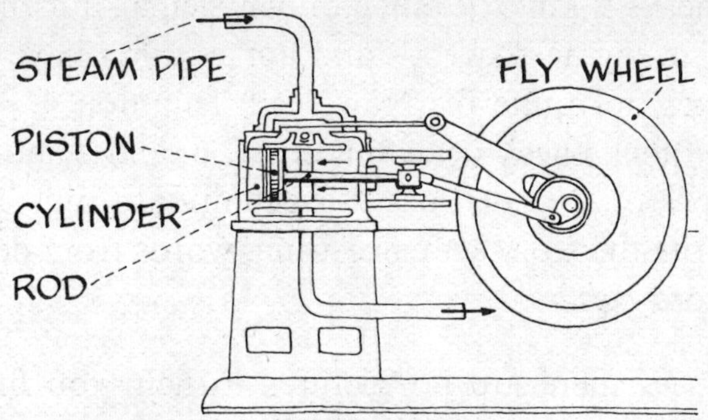

A steam engine. The pressure of the steam forced into the cylinder pushes the piston back and forth. This causes the rod to turn a shaft that passes on motion to wheels or other parts. The weight of the heavy flywheel attached to the shaft keeps the shaft turning evenly.

When looking at drawings like this, be sure to study the labels and the caption with the diagram. Together they give more details than could be said even in a long dictionary definition.

Finding a Meaning

When a word has more than one meaning, its different definitions are given different definition numbers. Usually the most common meaning is given first, but often that is not the meaning you want to look up. So you may have to look through several definitions before you find the right one. For example, suppose you read this sentence in a story:

> The engine roared, and Tina sat tight in the cutter as it bumped over the hard ridges of snow.

You can guess that it refers to some kind of vehicle that travels over snow, but you do not know what sort of vehicle. You want to know what *cutter* means in this sentence. You look up the word in the dictionary, and you find the following entry:

cut·ter (kut′ər) **1** a person who cuts, especially one whose work is cutting cloth to be made up into clothes. **2** a tool or machine for cutting: *a meat cutter, a bread cutter.* **3** a small horse-drawn sleigh. **4** a kind of sleigh pulled as a trailer by a snowmobile. **5** a small sailboat with one mast. **6** a boat belonging to a warship, used for carrying supplies and passengers to and from shore. **7** a small, armed ship used for patrolling coastal waters. *n.*

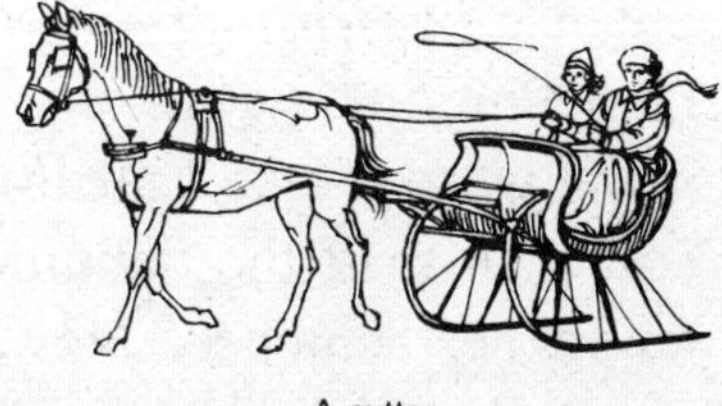

A cutter

Definition 1 refers to a person and definition 2 refers to a tool. Neither of these meanings fits the context of our story sentence. The picture might have led you straight to definition 3. This refers to a snow vehicle – a kind of horse-drawn sleigh. But the story sentence says, "The engine roared," and horses don't have engines – so definition 3 does not quite fit. Now read definition 4. This does fit the context. A quick check of definitions 5, 6, and 7 shows that they all refer to types of ship or boat. So definition 4 must be the right meaning. Rewrite the story sentence using words from definition 4 in place of the word *cutter*.

In some entries there are no pictures to help you find the right meaning, but there are example phrases and sentences. Suppose you read the following sentence in a newspaper article:

> He had a row with the hardware manager and took his custom to another store.

You know the word *custom*, but this use of the word does not fit with any meaning that you can think of. You look the word up in the dictionary and find the following entry:

> **cus·tom** (kus'təm) **1** any usual action: *It was his custom to rise early.* **2** a long-established habit that has almost the force of law: *He found it hard to adjust to the customs of his new country.* **3** for a special order: *Custom clothes are made specially, according to the order of one individual.* **4 customs,** *pl.* **a** taxes paid to the government on things brought in from a foreign country. **b** the office at a seaport, airport, or border-crossing point where imported goods are checked. **5** the regular business given by a customer: *That store would like to have your custom.* 1, 2, 4, 5 *n.*, 3 *adj.*
> ☛ See note at **habit.**

The easiest thing to do in this case is to read the examples to see if you can find the word used the way it is in the newspaper sentence. The example for definition 1 gives a use of the word you already know. The examples for definitions 2 and 3 show quite different uses of the word from that in the newspaper sentence. There is no example for definition 4, but this refers only to *customs*, and the newspaper sentence has *custom* – in the singular. Finally, you find the example for definition 5: *That store would like to have your custom.* This use of the word is like that in ". . . took his custom to another store." You then read the definition and find that it fits the context of the newspaper sentence. Now rewrite that sentence using one or two words from definition 5 in place of the word *custom*.

Which meaning of each of the following words is represented by the picture beside it? For each picture write down the word followed by the correct definition number.

coach (kōch) **1** a large, closed carriage with seats inside and, often, on top: *Coaches carried passengers along a regular run, stopping for meals and fresh horses.* **2** a passenger car of a railway train. **3** bus. **4** a type of automobile having four doors. **5** a person who teaches or trains athletes: *a football coach.* **6** a private teacher who helps a student prepare for a special test. **7** train or teach: *He asked his mother to coach him in arithmetic.* 1–6 *n.*, 7 *v.*

crane (krān) **1** a machine with a long, swinging arm, for lifting and moving heavy weights. **2** a large grey or white wading bird having long legs and neck and quite a long bill: *The sandhill crane is the most common kind in Canada.* **3** stretch the neck as a crane does: *He craned his neck to see over the crowd.* 1, 2 *n.*, 3 *v.*, **craned, cran·ing.**

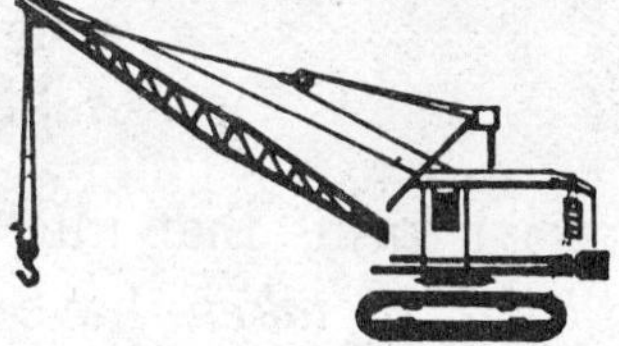

Remember

The dictionary gives you three aids to meaning: definitions, examples, and pictures. Get used to using all three of these aids. When you are trying to find a particular meaning in an entry, use examples and pictures to help you find the definition you want.

WHAT TO LOOK UP

On page xiv you discovered that you often have to change the form of words in a definition so that they fit the context in which you find the entry word. An example was:

> **a·vert** (ə vėrt′) **1** prevent; avoid: *The driver averted an accident by a quick turn of the steering wheel.* **2** turn away; turn aside: *She averted her eyes from the wreck.* *v.*

You found that you could not replace *averted* in the example sentence just with "prevent." The rewritten sentence would have to begin, "The driver prevented an accident. . . ."

Forms like *averted* are not given as separate entries in the dictionary, nor are forms like *averting*. If you want to look up *averted* or *averting*, you have to look at the entry for the root word *avert*.

Write down the entry word you would have to look up to find the meaning of the italicized word in each of the following sentences:

1. Mary had trouble *restraining* her anger.
2. We *anticipated* a cold winter.
3. Four hours *elapsed* before they heard the news.
4. The child was *terrified* by the movie.

Note that such forms as *apologized* and *apologizing*, *anticipated* and *anticipating* are shown at the end of the definitions for the root word. This is because a spelling change is necessary before endings can be added to the root word. (The final *-e* of *apologize* and *anticipate* is dropped before adding *-ed* or *-ing*.) Such forms are not given for words like *restrain* and *discuss*, in which *-ed* or *-ing* is added to the root word without any spelling change.

Some words do not add *-ed* but use special forms instead. For example:

sing **sang** **sung**
take **took** **taken**

Special forms that might be hard to recognize, such as *sang* or *sung*, *took* or *taken*, have separate entries in the dictionary. If you look them up, you will find a *cross reference*, a note that refers you to another entry, to the root word:

sang (sang) See **sing.** *He sang a solo.* *v.*

took (tůk) See **take.** *She took the car an hour ago.* *v.*

Such forms as *sang* and *took* are shown also at the end of the entries for their root words.

Write down the root words for the italicized forms in the following sentences. If you are not sure of an answer, look up the italicized form in the dictionary.

1. She *knew* the answer all along.
2. They *drove* a long way into the country.
3. The house had been *struck* by lightning.
4. The guilty child *slunk* away.
5. Several jokes were *woven* into the story.

Verb forms made by adding *-s*, such as *apologizes* and *restrains*, are not usually entered in the dictionary. Either an *-s* is added without any other change, or there is a spelling change like that made in adding *-ed*. For example:

carry **carries** **carried**

A few special verb forms ending in *-s* are entered as cross references to their root words. For example:

goes **has**

Words like *briefer* and *briefest* are not entered in the dictionary, because there is no spelling change before the endings *-er* and *-est* are added. However, if a spelling change is required when adding *-er* or *-est*, such forms are shown at the end of the entry for their root word. For example:

> **hap·py** (hap′ē) **1** feeling or showing pleasure and joy; glad; pleased; contented: *a happy smile.* **2** lucky; fortunate: *By a happy chance we found the watch just where I left it.* **3** clever and fitting; apt; successful and suitable: *a happy way of expressing an idea. adj.,* **hap·pi·er, hap·pi·est.**

The forms *happier* and *happiest* are shown after the definitions because the final *-y* of *happy* has to be changed to *-i* before adding *-er* and *-est*.

Suppose you want to find the meaning of the italicized word in each of the following sentences. Write down the root word you would have to look up in each case.

1. The cook baked the *largest* cake we'd ever seen.
2. We saw the *funniest* clown!
3. The visitors couldn't have been *friendlier*.
4. His answers were *glibber* than they should have been.
5. The weather is much *milder* now.

A few words use special forms instead of adding *-er* and *-est*. For example:

good	**better**	**best**
bad	**worse**	**worst**

Forms like *better*, *best* and *worse*, *worst* are entered separately as full entries in the dictionary. They are also shown in bold type at the end of the entries for their root words, *good* and *bad*.

Plural forms made simply by adding *-s* to a root word are not entered in the dictionary. But if a spelling change is required, the *-s* form is shown after the definitions for the root word:

> **hob·by** (hob′ē) something a person especially likes to work at or to study but which is not his main business: *Growing roses is our doctor's hobby. n., pl.* **hob·bies.**

Some words do not add *-s* but use special forms instead. For example:

man	**men**	**foot**	**feet**
child	**children**	**louse**	**lice**

Forms such as *men*, *children*, *feet*, and *lice* are shown at the end of the entries for their root words. These words are also entered separately as cross references to their root words. For example:

men (men) **1** plural of **man. 2** human beings; people in general: *Men and animals have some things in common. n. pl.*

lice (līs) plural of **louse.** *n.*

In each of the following sentences, replace the italicized word with its correct plural form. If you are not sure of any answer, look up the italicized word in the dictionary and find the plural form at the end of the entry.

1. I've been to three *party* this week.
2. There were several *child* in the driveway.
3. Three *goose* were blocking the road.
4. Everybody said the boys were *hero*.
5. The farmer had twelve cows and three *calf*.

OTHER KINDS OF ENTRY

Prefixes and Suffixes

Prefixes are word parts that do not occur by themselves but are added to roots to form beginnings of words. Some examples are:

dis- as in *disappear* **re-** as in *rebuild*
mis- as in *misfortune* **un-** as in *unable*

Simple prefixes like these are shown as separate entries in the dictionary. Look up *dis-*, *mis-*, *re-*, and *un-*, and write down what each means in the example word used above. Set up your answers like this:

1. **Dis-** in *disappear* means . . . .

In each of the following sentences, use a prefix in place of the dash to complete the word in brackets so that the sentence makes sense. In each case choose one of the following prefixes: *co-*, *de-*, *in-*[1], *in-*[2], *sub-*.

1. It is time to (____frost) the refrigerator.
2. We can get the job done if we all (____operate).
3. The land here will be (____divided) for new houses.
4. She is working on an (____laid) design for the table top.
5. The clumsy child seemed (____capable) of doing the job properly.

Then look up the entry for each prefix you have used, and write down what it means in the word in which you used it.

Suffixes are word parts that do not occur by themselves but are added to roots to form endings of words. Some examples are:

-able as in *comfortable* **-ment** as in *enjoyment*
-ful as in *cheerful* **-ous** as in *joyous*

Simple suffixes like these are shown as separate entries in the dictionary. Look up *-able*, *-ful*, *-ment*, and *-ous*, and write down what each means in the example word used above.

In each of the following sentences use a suffix in place of the dash to complete the word in brackets so that the sentence makes sense. In each case choose one of the following suffixes: *-ing*[1], *-ize*, *-ly*[2], *-ness*, *-ous*.

1. We thanked our helpers for their (kind____).
2. My mother has a great (long____) to see her birthplace.
3. We are not as (zeal____) as they are about this project.
4. The mixture will (vapor____) quickly.
5. We were lucky to have such (friend____) neighbors.

If you are not sure of an answer, make a guess and then look in the dictionary for the word you have guessed. Then look up the entry for each suffix you have used, and write down what it means in the word in which you used it.

Some words made by adding a suffix to a root are shown in the dictionary as separate entries. But, if their meaning is obvious, words with suffixes are shown as "run-ons" in bold type at the end of the entries for their root words. For example:

cas·u·al (kazh′ü əl) **1** happening by chance; not planned or expected: *Our long friendship began with a casual meeting at a party.* **2** careless; without plan or method: *I gave a casual glance at the newspaper. adj.* **—cas′u·al·ly,** *adv.* **—cas′u·al·ness,** *n.*

Casually and *casualness* are entered in this way because it is easy to tell what they mean if you know both the meaning of *casual* and the meanings of the suffixes *-ly* and *-ness*. Write down the meaning of *casually* and *casualness* in your own words, and then use each word in a sentence. Look up the suffixes *-ly*[1] and *-ness* if you are not sure what they mean.

Look up the following words to see which is a separate entry and which is a run-on. Use each one in a sentence, and then write down what the word means in the sentence in which you have used it.

6. careful
7. positively
8. searching
9. violinist
10. abductor

Compounds

Compounds are words in which two or more separate words have come together to make one. Examples are:

blackboard (*black* + *board*) **playground** (*play* + *ground*)
football (*foot* + *ball*) **windshield** (*wind* + *shield*)

Many compounds are usually written with a hyphen between the two parts. For example:

black-fly **high-sticking**
half-hearted **make-believe**
head-dress **tape-record**

Like most writers, you will often have to look in the dictionary to see if a compound is hyphenated or not.

Some pairs of words seem like compounds though they are actually written as two separate words. For example:

disc jockey **post office**
home run **white elephant**

Such two-word compounds are entered in the dictionary if their meaning is not obvious from the meanings of the two separate words. For example, a *white elephant* is not an elephant that is white. If you do not know the meaning of *white elephant*, look it up and then write it in an example sentence. On the other hand, a simple two-word compound like *hockey rink* (a rink for playing hockey) is not entered. A simple compound that is not entered in the dictionary is probably written as two words.

Some compounds actually consist of three words. These are also entered in the dictionary if their meaning is not obvious. Examples are:

fish and chips **horn of plenty** **chile con carne**

Look up the entries for the following combinations and write down for each a 1, H, or 2, to show if it is entered as one word (1), as a hyphenated word (H), or as two words (2):

1. bad + lands
2. watch + dog
3. first + aid
4. first + rate
5. booby + trap
6. deer + skin
7. fish + hook
8. water + polo
9. team + work
10. shooting + star

Write an example sentence for each of these ten compounds.

Idioms

She asked him to lend her a pencil.
He was holding a pencil in his hand.
The boy shovelling snow asked his brother to lend a hand.

You know the meaning of *lend* in the first sentence, and you know the meaning of *hand* in the second sentence. But do you know the meaning of *lend a hand* in the third sentence? If not, you will find the phrase explained at the entry for *lend*:

> **lend a hand,** help: *She lent a hand with the dishes.*
> **lend itself to,** be suitable for: *The old engine lent itself to our purposes.*
> **lend oneself to,** make oneself available for: *Don't lend yourself to foolish schemes.*

Lend a hand, *lend itself to*, and *lend oneself to* are all phrases that have special meanings beyond what you might guess from the meanings of their individual words. Such phrases are called *idioms*. They are entered in the dictionary after the definitions, part-of-speech labels, and run-on entries for the main entry word.

Lend a hand is entered also under *hand*, together with a number of other idioms, including such phrases as *hand in*, *hand on*, *hand out*, and *hand over*. Look up *hand* and find the meanings of these four idioms. Then write each one in a sentence. Do the same with the four idioms under *catch* and any two of the idioms under *make*.

Some idioms, like *lend a hand*, appear under two entry words in the dictionary. However, most idioms are entered once — under the entry for the most important word.

Rewrite each of the following sentences, using an idiom in place of the italicized words. The key word of the correct idiom is in brackets after each sentence. You can find the idiom by looking in the dictionary at the end of the entry for this key word.

1. The job won't take long if we all *work hard*. **(pitch)**
2. She is a sensible person, and her ideas are always *practical*. **(earth)**
3. After he has heard a song once, he can *play it without using written music*. **(ear)**
4. My mother gave me a *scolding* for being late for supper. **(piece)**
5. The lawyer had to *disagree* with the witness's statement. **(issue)**

Hidden Entries

> **rib·bon** (rib′ən) **1** a strip or band of silk, satin, velvet, etc.: *Bows for the hair, belts, and badges are often made of ribbon.* **2** anything like such a strip: *a typewriter ribbon.* **3 ribbons,** *pl.* torn pieces; shreds: *Her dress was torn to ribbons by the thorns she had come through. n.*

> **magnetic pole** **1** one of the two poles of a magnet. **2 Magnetic Pole,** one of the two positions on the earth's surface toward which a compass needle points: *The North Magnetic Pole is considerably south of the geographic North Pole.*

> **dead** (ded) **1** no longer living; that has died: *The flowers in my garden are dead.* **2 the dead,** all who no longer have life: *We remember the dead of our wars on Remembrance Day.*

Some words have special meanings in the plural (*ribbons*), when capitalized (*Magnetic Pole*), or when they come after *the* (*the dead*). In such cases the form with the special meaning is given in bold face after the definition number. Such forms are called *hidden entries*.

Find the hidden entry under each of the following entries. Then write an example sentence for each hidden entry.

1. glass
2. heart
3. prairie
4. president
5. red

Kinds of Entry - Summary

Words or phrases that you wish to look up may be shown in the dictionary in the following ways. Roman numerals in brackets after an item refer to the page on which that item is discussed.

as main entries: **one-word entries**
hyphenated words (*xxiv*)
two-word compounds (*xxiv*)
three-word compounds (*xxiv*)
homographs (*xii*)
prefixes (*xxii*)
suffixes (*xxiii*)

as hidden entries (*xxvi*)
as special forms (*xx*)
as run-ons (*xxiii*)
as idioms (*xxv*)

When you are looking up a word, try to think ahead about the way in which you will find it entered.

Sounds and Spellings

When you look up a word in the dictionary to check its spelling or meaning, you often need to find out its pronunciation to make sure you have found the right entry. Also, you often need to use the dictionary to find out how to pronounce a new word that you have seen in reading.

PRONUNCIATION SYMBOLS

The pronunciation of each one-word entry in the dictionary is shown in brackets immediately after the entry word. Each sound in a word has its own symbol, and that sound is shown always by the same pronunciation symbol.

Sometimes the pronunciation looks the same as the spelling of the word, as in the following examples:

bend (bend) **mask** (mask) **wisp** (wisp)
jam (jam) **nut** (nut) **yak** (yak)
lip (lip) **plan** (plan) **zip** (zip)

But in many cases English words are not pronounced exactly as they are spelled. So the pronunciations in the dictionary make use of a few special symbols. Pronounce each of the following words, and look carefully at the pronunciation symbols used.

game (gām) **mark** (märk) **toy** (toi) **war** (wôr)
leap (lēp) **murk** (mėrk) **town** (toun) **yolk** (yōk)
line (līn) **put** (pu̇t) **view** (vyü) **zoom** (züm)

The above words use special vowel symbols. In the following words it is the consonant symbols that are most important. Pronounce each word and note the pronunciation symbols used for the consonants.

sin (sin) **thin** (thin) **chick** (chik)
sing (sing) **then** (ŦHen) **witch** (wich)
sink (singk) **rose** (rōz) **judge** (juj)
shin (shin) **rouge** (rüzh) **yacht** (yot)

After each of the following sentences are the pronunciations of two words. Say these words aloud or to yourself and decide which one fits the blank in the sentence. Then rewrite the sentence with the normal spelling for the pronunciation you have chosen.

1. Ann is Dan's________sister. (tin) (twin)
2. She visited her aunt________. (twis) (twīs)
3. He chopped the wood with an________. (ask) (aks)
4. That bird has a long________. (nek) (nekst)
5. She decided to________a pie. (bak) (bāk)
6. A duck is supposed to say________. (krak) (kwak)
7. Mr. Hall drives a________. (truk) (tru̇k)
8. We didn't think his plan would________. (wėrk) (wôrk)
9. I broke the________on my skate. (strap) (skrap)
10. Everybody laughed at Terry's________. (jôk) (jōk)

What Is It?

Below each of the following pictures is the pronunciation for the word that the picture represents. Say each word aloud to yourself, and then write it down in its normal spelling.

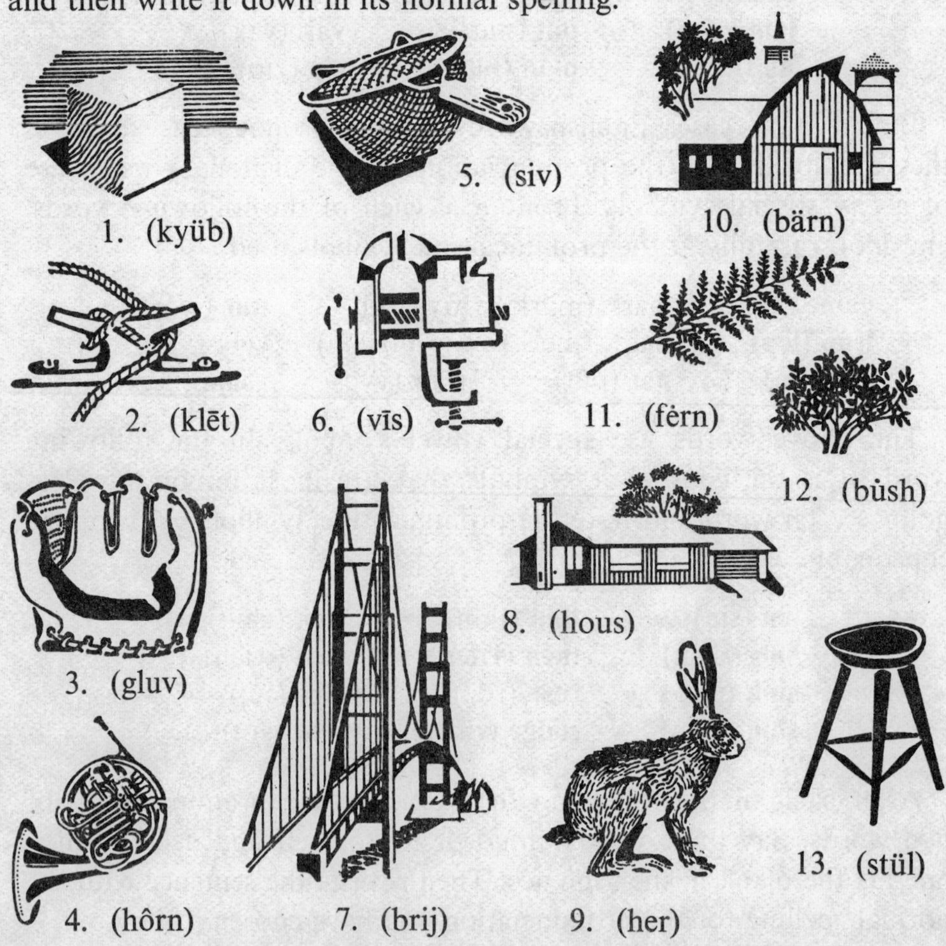

1. (kyüb)
2. (klēt)
3. (gluv)
4. (hôrn)
5. (siv)
6. (vīs)
7. (brij)
8. (hous)
9. (hėr)
10. (bärn)
11. (fėrn)
12. (bu̇sh)
13. (stül)

Schwa (ə)

The symbol (ə) stands for the vowel sound that is heard in the first syllable of *above* and the second syllable of *taken*, *pencil*, *lemon*, and *circus*. It is called the *schwa*, or neutral vowel. Say each of the following sentences aloud and listen for the schwa sound in the italicized words:

> The book was on a shelf *above* her bed.
> Someone has *taken* it in the past two hours.
> She thinks they took her *pencil*, too.
> They left a *lemon* there instead.
> Our house must be like a *circus*.

Say each of the following words aloud. Then write them down, underlining the syllables that are pronounced with schwa.

bottom	**buffalo**	**coral**
button	**gorilla**	**corral**
candle	**telephone**	**correct**

When you have finished, look up these entries, check your answers, and copy the pronunciations given in the dictionary.

PRONUNCIATION KEYS

Each pronunciation symbol used in the dictionary stands for one sound, and each symbol always stands for the same sound. A complete pronunciation key, showing all the symbols used, is given on the endpapers inside the front and back covers of the dictionary. A short pronunciation key, which shows all the special symbols that are used, is given at the top of every right-hand page. The short key looks like this:

> hat, āge, fär; let, ēqual, tėrm; it, īce
> hot, ōpen, ôrder; oil, out; cup, pu̇t, rüle
> əbove, takən, pencəl, lemən, circəs
> ch, child; ng, long; sh, ship
> th, thin; ᴛʜ, then; zh, measure

If you are not sure what sound a pronunciation symbol stands for, you can easily find out by looking at this key. For example, the key tells you:

> the symbol (a) stands for the sound of *a* as in *hat*.
> the symbol (ā) stands for the sound of *a* as in *age*.
> the symbol (ä) stands for the sound of *a* as in *barn*.

Using the pronunciation symbols, write down the pronunciation for each of the following words. Say each word aloud to yourself, then put down one symbol for each sound that you hear. Put brackets around the pronunciations.

1. **climb**
2. **creep**
3. **forge**
4. **great**
5. **learn**
6. **leave**
7. **love**
8. **pale**
9. **stone**
10. **thick**

When you have finished, look up these words in the dictionary and check the pronunciations you have written.

Under each of the following pictures are three pronunciations. Decide which one is the correct pronunciation for the word represented by the picture. Then write down the word and its pronunciation. Put the pronunciation in brackets.

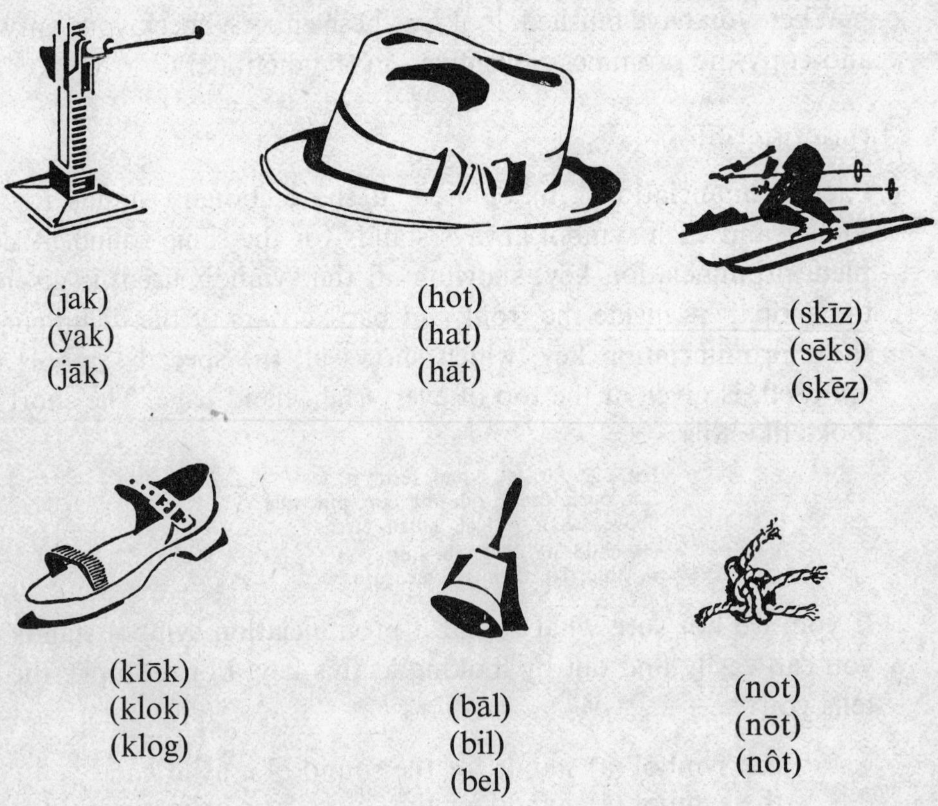

In most words of two or more syllables, one syllable is spoken with more force, or stress, than any of the others. In the dictionary pronunciations the stressed syllable is shown by a heavy raised mark (′) placed after it. For example, in the following words the stress is always on the first syllable:

bulbous (bul′bəs)
cocoa (kō′kō)
cotton (kot′ən)
deluge (del′yüj)
little (lit′əl)
lively (līv′lē)
massive (mas′iv)
nephew (nef′yü)
paper (pā′pər)
recent (rē′sənt)
token (tō′kən)
village (vil′ij)

In the following words the stress is always on the second syllable:

delight (di līt′)
delude (di lüd′)
excite (ek sīt′)
fatigue (fə tēg′)
insure (in shür′)
invent (in vent′)
neglect (ni glekt′)
perform (pər fôrm′)
prefer (pri fėr′)
reply (ri plī′)
request (ri kwest′)
sustain (səs tān′)

Say or listen to each of the following and decide which is the stressed syllable in each word. (Note that in the pronunciations the words are divided into syllables for you.) Then write the pronunciation of each word and add the stress mark after the stressed syllable.

basement (bās mənt)
certainty (sėr tən tē)
connect (kə nekt)
decide (di sīd)
historical (his tôr ə kəl)
microbe (mī krōb)
pattern (pat ərn)
pursue (pər sü)
ravine (rə vēn)
survivor (sər vī vər)
terrible (ter ə bəl)
turmoil (tėr moil)

When you have finished, discuss your answers with your group or with a partner. If you do not agree on where the stress goes in any particular word, look up that word in the dictionary and check your answer against the pronunciation given there.

In addition to the main stress, many words have one or two syllables that are spoken with more stress than the others, but with less stress than the main syllable. This lighter stress is shown by means of a lighter mark (′) placed after the syllable. Say or listen to the following examples:

demonstrate (dem′ən strāt′) **hippopotamus** (hip′ə pot′ə məs)
fascination (fas′ə nā′shən) **secretary** (sek′rə ter′ē)
handlebars (han′dəl bärz′) **terrify** (ter′ə fī′)

We call the main stress *primary stress* and the lighter stress *secondary stress.*

Syllables that do not have primary or secondary stress are called *unstressed syllables.* The vowel sound in unstressed syllables is often pronounced as schwa (ə). Reread the six examples above. Say them aloud or to yourself, and see how the schwa sound (ə) comes only in unstressed syllables.

Say or listen to the following words, and then write their pronunciations in parentheses. Mark the primary and secondary stresses, and remember to use schwa (ə) when it is the sound you hear in unstressed syllables.

civilize	**immigration**	**signify**
dragonfly	**indigestible**	**skyscraper**
drawbridge	**recognize**	**tangerine**
dromedary	**reverberate**	**tape-recorder**

When you have finished, check the pronunciations you have written against those in the dictionary.

Note that single-word or hyphenated compounds (*dragonfly*, *drawbridge*, *skyscraper*, *tape-recorder*) usually have a primary stress on the first part and a secondary stress on the second part.

Some types of hyphenated compounds have almost the same amount of stress on both parts. These words are marked with two primary stresses in the dictionary, although when they are pronounced by themselves the second stressed syllable usually has slightly more stress than the first. Some examples are:

far-reaching (fär′rēch′ing) **high-sticking** (hī′stik′ing)
hard-hearted (härd′här′tid) **skin-tight** (skin′tīt′)

Some words can be pronounced in more than one way. For example:

dew	Do you say (dyü) or (dü)?
missile	Do you say (mis′īl) or (mis′əl)?
whirl	Do you say (wėrl) or (hwėrl)?

In such cases both pronunciations are correct and both forms are given in the dictionary. The form given first in the questions above is the more common one across Canada as a whole, so it is given first in the dictionary. In spite of this, the second form may be more common in a certain area or with certain people. Usually, however, a person pronounces a word the same way all the time. You may say (skej′ül) or (shej′ül) for *schedule*, but you will confuse yourself if you use one pronunciation one moment and the other the next.

Sometimes, however, you do pronounce certain words in two ways. These words change their stress pattern when they change their use in a sentence. For example, which syllable of *record* is stressed in each of the following sentences?

The group is going to *record* a new song.
My brother bought a *record* of their weird music.

Below is the dictionary entry for *record*. The pronunciation shows that (ri kôrd′), with the stress on the second syllable, is used for definitions 1, 2, 6, and 7. Read these definitions, and read aloud the examples for definitions 1, 2, and 7.

re·cord (ri kôrd′ for 1, 2, 6, and 7, rek′ərd for 3–5 and 8–10) **1** set down in writing so as to keep for future use: *Listen to the speaker and record what he says.* **2** put in some permanent form; keep for remembrance: *History is recorded in books.* **3** the thing written or kept. **4** an official written account: *The secretary kept a record of what was done at the meeting.* **5** a thin, flat disk with narrow spiral grooves on its surface that reproduces sounds when played on a record player. **6** put music, words, or sounds on such a disk or on specially treated wire or tape. **7** tell; indicate: *The thermometer records temperature.* **8** the known facts about what a person, animal, ship, etc. has done: *He has a fine record at school.* **9** a remarkable performance or event, going beyond others of the same kind, especially the best achievement in a sport: *Who holds the record for the high jump?* **10** unequalled; better than before: *a record wheat crop.* 1, 2, 6, 7 *v.*, 3–5, 8, 9 *n.*, 10 *adj.*

The pronunciation (rek′ərd), with the stress on the first syllable, is given for definitions 3, 4, 5, 8, 9, 10. Read these definitions, and read aloud the examples for definitions 4, 8, 9, and 10.

Write the pronunciation for the italicized words in the following sentences. Make sure that you put in the stress marks after the right syllables. Put your pronunciations in brackets.

1. The principal will never *permit* us to go.
2. We will need a *permit* to enter the building.
3. There were several *objects* scattered on the desk.
4. Our teacher didn't *object* to our lateness.
5. Their laughter was an *insult* to the speaker.
6. We were careful not to *insult* the visitors.

Check the pronunciations you have written against those in the dictionary.

Now write the pronunciation for the italicized words as they would sound in the following sentences. If you need to know the meaning of the italicized word in any sentence, look it up in the dictionary.

7. There were piles of *refuse* rotting in the streets.
8. He could hardly *refuse* to help.
9. We took care to *close* the door quietly.
10. She was cold and stayed *close* to the fire.
11. A wooden arch formed the *entrance* to the campground.
12. Thc magician continued to *entrance* the children with his tricks.

If you have not already done so, look up *refuse*, *close*, and *entrance* in the dictionary. You will find that there are two entries for each of these spellings. Write down the pronunciations to complete the sentences below. Put the pronunciations in brackets.

Refuse[1] is pronounced (ri fyüz′), but *refuse*[2] is pronounced ____.
Close[1] is pronounced (klōz), but *close*[2] is pronounced ________.
Entrance[1] is pronounced (en′trəns), but *entrance*[2] is ________.

In these cases, the changes in pronunciation are used to distinguish *homographs* (words with the same spelling but different origins and meanings). Words with the same spelling do not necessarily have the same pronunciation.

Here are some other examples of homographs with different pronunciations. Look up each pair of entries, and then write an example sentence for each homograph. After each sentence, write in brackets the pronunciation of the homograph used.

buffet[1]/ buffet[2]	**lead[1]/ lead[2]**	**sow[1]/ sow[2]**
console[1]/ console[2]	**live[1]/ live[2]**	**wound[1]/ wound[2]**

VARIETIES OF SPELLING

Some words can be spelled in two different ways. Which spelling do you use for the following words?

centre/ center	**program/ programme**
labor/ labour	**traveller/ traveler**

Either of the forms given for each of these pairs is correct, and both forms are given in the dictionary. The form given first is the more common one across Canada as a whole, but you should use the one that is accepted in your school or area. In addition, use the same form all the time. Don't change from one to the other. Such words are entered in the dictionary in the following way:

> **cen·tre** or **cen·ter** (sen′tər) **1** a point within a circle or sphere equally distant from all points of the circumference or surface. **2** the middle point, place, or

Some words have a spelling that is much less common than the usual one. Such variations are shown at the ends of entries, like this:

> **di·a·logue** (dī′ə log′) **1** a conversation: *They had a long dialogue about plans for the camp program.* **2** the conversation written for a story, play, motion picture, etc.: *That book has a good plot and clever dialogue.* *n.* Also spelled **dialog.**

This means that you may meet the spelling *dialog* in some of your reading, but you should not use it yourself.

The less common forms, such as *center* and *dialog*, are also entered separately, and are cross-referred to their main entries, unless the two entries come next, or nearly next, to each other in alphabetical order.

> **cen·ter** (sen′tər) See **centre.**

Some spelling variations are entered as cross references, but the variations are not given at the main entries. For example:

> **kerb** (kėrb) See **curb.**

> **curb** (kėrb) **1** a raised border of concrete or stone along the edge of a street, driveway, etc. **2** a chain or a strap fastened to a horse's bit and passing under its lower jaw: *When the reins are pulled tight, the curb checks the horse.* **3** anything that checks or restrains. **4** hold in check; restrain: *You must curb your appetite if you want to lose weight.* 1–3 *n.,* 4 *v.*

In such cases the variation, *kerb*, is not used by Canadians at all. [illegible] entered in case you come across it in older writing or [illegible] other countries.

How do you look a word up in the dictionary if you don't know how to spell it? How, for example, would you find the spelling of the following words?

(sī)	(sīʹkik)
(sīʹəns)	(sī kolʹə jist)
(sīʹfər)	(sīʹklist)

Say each of the above words aloud to yourself. How many of them do you know how to spell?

Now let's put each of the words in a context. The blank in each of the following sentences is to be filled by the word shown in pronunciation symbols at the right. Write down as many of these words as you can in their correct spellings. Try to think of related words that may help you.

1. She gave a big________and looked very sad. (sī)
2. We read about atoms in our________book. (sīʹəns)
3. The message was in_______and couldn't be decoded. (sīʹfər)
4. She claimed to be a witch with_________powers. (sīʹkik)
5. A__________came to give us a reading test. (sī kolʹə jist)
6. The_________had to pedal hard against the wind. (sīʹklist)

Are there still some of the six words that you can't spell? If so, you will have to start guessing. If you can guess the first few letters correctly, then you can probably look up the word in the dictionary without any trouble.

To help yourself make good guesses, use the spelling chart on the next two pages. The words shown in pronunciation symbols at the top of this page all start with the sound (s), and the chart says that this sound at the beginning of words can be spelled as in: *cent*, *psalm*, *say*, or *science*.

Now look at the second sound, which is (ī). The chart shows that in the middle of words this sound can be spelled as in: *height*, *line*, *night*, *buying*, *skylark*. How can it be spelled at the end of words?

[illegible] the chart to test the possible spellings of each of the six words [illegible] not correctly guessed. Look up any words that you may [illegible] not yet sure of. Remember to use your knowledge [illegible] gives you the possibilities, and you have to [illegible]ledge to see which of the possibilities

Common Spellings of English Sounds

SOUND	BEGINNINGS OF WORDS	MIDDLES OF WORDS	ENDS OF WORDS
a	*a*nd, *au*nt	h*a*t, pl*ai*d, h*a*lf, l*au*gh	——
ā	*a*ge, *ai*d, *ei*ght, *eh*	f*a*ce, f*ai*l, str*aigh*t, p*ay*ment, g*ao*l, g*au*ge, br*ea*k, v*ei*n, r*ei*gn n*ei*ghbor	s*ay*, w*eigh*, bouqu*et*, th*ey*, matin*ée*, *eh*
ä	*ah*, *a*lmond, *a*rt	c*a*lm, b*a*rn, baz*aa*r, serg*ea*nt, h*ea*rt	b*aa*, hurr*ah*
b	*b*ad	ta*b*le, ra*bb*it	ru*b*, e*bb*
ch	*c*ello, *ch*ild	ri*ch*ness, wa*tch*ing, righ*te*ous, ques*ti*on, na*t*ure	mu*ch*, ca*tch*
d	*d*o	do*d*o, do*dd*er	re*d*
e	*a*ny, *ae*rial, *ai*r, *e*nd	m*a*ny, s*ai*d, s*ay*s, l*e*t, br*ea*d, h*ei*fer, l*eo*pard, fr*ie*nd, b*u*ry	——
ē	*ae*on, *e*qual, *ea*t, *ei*ther	C*ae*sar, m*e*tre, t*ea*m, n*ee*d, rec*ei*ve, p*eo*ple, k*ey*hole, mach*i*ne, bel*ie*ve, ph*oe*be	alg*ae*, qu*ay*, b*e*, fl*ea*, b*ee*, k*ey*, pit*y*
ėr	*er*mine, *ear*ly, *ir*k, *ur*ge	t*er*m, l*ear*n, f*ir*st, w*or*d, j*our*ney, t*ur*n, m*yr*tle	det*er*, voyag*eur*, f*ir*, c*ur*, b*urr*
f	*f*at, *ph*one	hei*f*er, co*ff*ee, lau*gh*ter, go*ph*er	roo*f*, bu*ff*, cou*gh*, lym*ph*
g	*g*o, *gh*ost, *gu*ess	bo*g*us, bo*gg*le, ro*gu*ish, e*x*act	ba*g*, e*gg*, ro*gue*
h	*h*e, *wh*o (hü), *wh*y (hwī)	block*h*ead	——
i	*e*namel, *i*n	mess*a*ge, b*ee*n, p*i*n, s*ie*ve, w*o*men, b*u*sy, b*ui*ld, h*y*mn	——
ī	*ai*sle, *aye*, *ei*ther, *eye*, *i*ce	h*ei*ght, l*i*ne, al*ig*n, m*igh*t, b*uy*ing, sk*y*lark	*aye*, *eye*, l*ie*, h*igh*, b*uy*, sk*y*, r*ye*
j	*g*em, *j*am	ba*dg*er, sol*di*er, e*d*ucate, tra*g*ic, exa*gg*erate, en*j*oy	bri*dge*, ra*ge*
k	*c*oat, *ch*emist, *k*ind, *q*uick, *qu*ay	re*c*ord, a*cc*ount, e*ch*o, lu*ck*y, a*cq*uire, ree*k*ing, li*qu*or, e*x*tra	ba*ck*, see*k*
l	*l*and, *ll*ama	on*l*y, fo*ll*ow	coa*l*, fi*ll*
m	*m*e	co*m*ing, cli*mb*ing, su*mm*er	ru*m*, co*mb*, sole*mn*
n	*gn*aw, *kn*ife, *n*ut, *pn*eumonia	jack-*kn*ife, mi*n*er, ma*nn*er	ma*n*, i*nn*
ng	——	i*n*k, fi*n*ger, si*ng*er	ri*ng*, to*ngue*

Common Spellings of English Sounds (continued)

SOUND	BEGINNINGS OF WORDS	MIDDLES OF WORDS	ENDS OF WORDS
o	*a*ll, *a*lmond, *au*to, *aw*ful, encore, *o*dd, *augh*t, *ough*t	w*a*tch, app*a*l, w*a*lk, f*a*ll, t*au*t, t*augh*t, c*au*lk, c*aw*ed, h*o*t, b*ough*t, c*a*lm	p*aw*
ō	*o*pen, *oa*ts, *oh*, *ow*n	y*eo*man, s*ew*n, b*o*gus, b*oa*t, f*o*lk, br*oo*ch, s*ou*l, fl*ow*n	b*eau*, s*ew*, potat*o*, t*oe*, *oh*, th*ough*, bl*ow*
ô	*a*ll, *au*to, *aw*ful, *oa*r, *o*rder	app*a*l, w*a*lk, t*a*ll, t*au*t, t*augh*t, c*au*lk, c*aw*ed, b*oa*rd, b*o*rn, fl*oo*ring, b*ough*t, m*ou*rn	p*aw*
oi	*oi*l, *oy*ster	b*oi*l, b*oy*hood	b*oy*
ou	*ou*t, *ow*l	b*ou*nd, dr*ough*t, h*ow*l	th*ou*, b*ough*, n*ow*
p	*p*en	ta*p*er, su*pp*er	u*p*
r	*r*un, *rh*ythm, *wr*ong	pa*r*ent, hu*rr*y	bea*r*, bu*rr*
s	*c*ent, *ps*alm, *s*ay, *sc*ience, *sw*ord	de*c*ent, ma*s*on, resu*sc*itate, ma*ss*ive, e*x*tra	ni*c*e, bogu*s*, mi*ss*, la*x*
sh	*ch*auffeur, *sch*wa, *sh*e, *s*ure	o*c*ean, ma*ch*ine, spe*ci*al, in*s*urance, con*sc*ience, nau*se*a, ten*si*on, i*ss*ue, mi*ss*ion, na*ti*on	wi*sh*, ca*che*
t	*pt*omaine, *t*ell, *Th*omas	la*t*er, la*tt*er, de*bt*or	bi*t*, mi*tt*, dou*bt*
th	*th*in	too*th*paste	ba*th*
ᴛʜ	*th*en	fa*th*er	smoo*th*, ba*the*
u	*o*ven, *u*p	c*o*me, d*oe*s, fl*oo*d, tr*ou*ble, c*u*p	——
u̇	——	w*o*lf, g*oo*d, sh*ou*ld, f*u*ll	——
ü	*oo*ze	n*eu*tral, m*o*ve, man*oeu*vre, f*oo*d, cr*ou*p, r*u*le, fr*ui*t	thr*ew*, sh*oe*, carib*ou*, thr*ough*, bl*ue*
yü	*eu*chre, *ewe*, *u*se, *you*, *Yu*le	b*eau*ty, f*eu*d, d*u*ty	qu*eue*, f*ew*, *ewe*, ad*ieu*, *you*, c*ue*
v	*v*ery	Ste*ph*en, o*v*er	o*f*, lo*v*e
w	*w*ill, *wh*eat	ch*o*ir, qu*i*ck, t*w*in	——
y	*y*oung	opin*i*on, hallelu*j*ah, can*y*on	——
z	*x*ylophone, *z*ero	rai*s*in, di*s*cern, sci*ss*ors, e*x*act, si*z*ing, da*zz*le	ha*s*, ma*z*e, bu*zz*
zh	——	gara*g*ed, divi*si*on, mea*s*ure, a*z*ure	rou*ge*
ə	*a*lone, *e*ssential, *o*blige, *u*pon	parti*c*ul*a*r, fount*ai*n, mom*e*nt, penc*i*l, bott*l*e, pris*m*, butt*o*n, cauti*ou*s, circ*u*s, zeph*y*r	sof*a*

Special Features

PART-OF-SPEECH LABELS

He liked the browns in that painting.
Her hair is browner than mine.
The cake was browning in the oven.

In the first sentence *browns* has an *-s* to show plural (more than one). It comes after the word *the*. It is the object of the word *liked* (it tells what he liked). Therefore *browns* in this sentence is called a noun.

In the second sentence *browner* has an *-er* ending to make it mean "more brown." It describes the noun *hair*. It is linked to *hair* by the word *is*. Therefore *browner* in this sentence is called an adjective.

In the third sentence *browning* has an *-ing* ending. It goes with the word *was*. It shows what the cake (the subject of the sentence) was doing. Therefore *browning* in this sentence is called a verb.

At the end of the dictionary entry for *brown* the abbreviations *n.*, *adj.*, and *v.* are used after the definitions numbers to show that def. 1 is a noun, def. 2 is an adjective, and def. 3 is a verb.

brown (broun) **1** a dark color like that of toast, potato skins, or coffee. **2** of or having this color: *Many Canadians have brown hair.* **3** make or become brown: *The cook browned the onions in hot butter.* 1 *n.*, 2 *adj.*, 3 *v.*

In cases where an entry word is only a noun, for example, the abbreviation *n.* is given at the end of the definitions without any number before it. For example:

fas·ci·na·tion (fas′ə nā′shən) **1** fascinating or being fascinated. **2** a very strong attraction; charm: *Stamp collecting has a fascination for some people.* *n.*

Words like *noun*, *adjective*, and *verb* are names for *parts of speech*. The eight parts of speech used in the dictionary, together with their abbreviations, are listed below. They are also shown in the Grammar Key inside the back cover.

noun	*n.*	pronoun	*pron.*
verb	*v.*	preposition	*prep.*
adjective	*adj.*	conjunction	*conj.*
adverb	*adv.*	interjection	*interj.*

Look up the dictionary entry for each part of speech and study what is said in the definitions.

You do not always need to know the part of speech of a word, but looking at the part-of-speech label can help you understand the definition. For example, you may not be sure from the entry for *fascination* on the previous page whether in the meaning of definition 1 it should be used as a noun or as an adjective. However, by looking at the part-of-speech label you can see that the word is a noun.

Part-of-speech labels can also help you to find the right meaning of a word. For instance, suppose you want to look up the meaning of *run* in the following sentence:

> The young page was given the run of the palace.

When you look up the entry for *run*, you find that it has forty meanings. However, you can tell that *run* is a noun in the sentence, so you look at the part-of-speech labels at the end of the entry. There you find that the definitions for noun uses of the word are: 23–25, 27–33, 35, 36, 38. In other words, you have to look at only thirteen out of the forty definitions, and you don't have to look at the first twenty-two definitions at all.

Now look up *run*, and write down the definition number and the definition for the meaning of the word in the sentence above. Then rewrite the sentence to give the same meaning without using the word *run*.

USAGE LABELS

> That guy's just a slob.
> He badly needs a bath.

The words *guy* and *slob* are good English words, but they are used in the first sentence in a way that would not be suitable in all situations. The word *badly* is used in the second sentence in a way that is different and less careful than its basic meaning of "in a bad manner." Words and meanings that are suitable only for certain kinds of speech or writing are given usage labels in the dictionary. For example:

guy[2] (gī) *Slang.* a man; fellow: *Most of the guys were at the party. n.*

slob (slob) **1** *Slang.* a stupid, untidy, or clumsy person. **2** *Cdn.* slob ice. *n.*

bad·ly (bad′lē) **1** in a bad manner: *She sings badly.* **2** *Informal.* very much: *He wants to go badly. adv.*

The label *Slang* refers to a word or to a word use that is not yet considered part of the general language. Slang terms are often colorful and expressive, and some slang may be especially popular at a particular time or with a particular group of people. Slang terms are used more in speech than in writing, and some teachers object to slang being used in any written work.

The label *Informal* means "not suitable for use in formal speech or writing." In other words, *badly*, as used in the example sentence on the previous page, may be all right in ordinary speech, in written conversation, or in a letter to a close friend, but it should not otherwise be used in written work.

Which words should be labelled *Informal* or *Slang* according to their uses in the following sentences? Write down each word you choose and the label you give to it. Then look up the words in the dictionary to check your answers.

1. If our dog is not better tomorrow, we'll take him to the vet.
2. We shouldn't have let her talk such tripe about our school.
3. He is lousy with ideas, but none of them are any good.
4. My brother made an awful to-do when I wore one of his shirts.
5. Our family clicked with the new neighbors from the beginning.

You can see from the entry on the previous page that definition 2 of *slob* is labelled *Cdn.* This label means that the word or meaning is used mainly in Canada and that it first came into the English language in Canada. Such words are called Canadianisms. Do you know the meaning of the following Canadianisms? If not, look them up in the dictionary. Then write an example sentence for each one.

bateau **muskeg**
break-up **oomiak**
lobstick **snye**

The dictionary also uses the labels *British* or *Esp. British* and *U.S.* or *Esp. U.S.* to show that a word or meaning is used mainly or especially in Great Britain or the United States, as the case may be. For example:

lor·ry (lôr′ē) *British.* a motor truck. *n., pl.* **lor·ries.**

pole·cat (pōl′kat′) **1** a small, dark-brown European animal related to the weasel. **2** *Esp. U.S.* the North American skunk. *n.*

What do you do if you see a fist in front of you? If you see a fist in the dictionary, don't run away, but follow where it points.

> **as·ter** (as′tər) a plant having daisy-like flowers with yellow centres. *n.*
> ☛ **Aster, asterisk,** and **asteroid** all come from the Greek word *aster,* meaning 'star,' related to Greek *astron,* from which **astronaut, astronomy,** etc. are formed.

The symbol is called a "printer's fist." It is used in the dictionary to point to special notes that appear at the end of certain entries and give extra information about the entry words. There are four kinds of fistnote in the *Canadian Junior Dictionary*, covering word histories, usage, homonyms, and synonyms.

Word histories

Many of the fistnotes, like the one above, tell about the history of words. The following explanations will help you to understand some of the terms used in the word histories:

> Old English—the English language before about 1100 A.D.
> Middle English—English from 1100 to about 1500 A.D.
> Old French—the French language before about 1400 A.D.
> Old Norse—the language of Scandinavia before about 1300 A.D.

Look up the fistnotes for the following entries, read them, and then write answers to the six questions below.

biscuit	**diesel**	**mesmerize**
bungalow	**equinox**	**mukluk**
calculate	**khaki**	**nostril**
daisy	**lieutenant**	**saskatoon**

1. Which of these twelve words came from French?
2. Which of the words came direct from Latin?
3. Which of the words existed in Old English?
4. Which came from a language of Asia?
5. Which were formed from the names of people?
6. Which are Canadianisms, and from what language did each of these come?

Usage

A number of fistnotes add to the definitions by giving advice on how words are used in sentences. Some refer to problems of spelling or pronunciation, some to matters of grammar, and others to the selection of appropriate language for a particular context or situation.

Look up the fistnotes for the following entries, read them, and then write an example sentence for each entry word, using the word as suggested in the fistnote.

between	**each**	**informal**
café	**habit**	**maybe**
can	**hardly**	**news**
childish	**illusion**	**numeral**

Homonyms

mane (mān) the long, heavy hair growing on the back of or around the neck of a horse, a lion, etc. *n.*
☛ **Mane** and **main** are pronounced the same.

Homonyms are words that sound the same but have different meanings and often different spellings. They are shown in the dictionary, as in the example above, in case you look up one word when you really want to look up a homonym for it. For instance, suppose you have just heard the following sentence, which is printed in phonetic symbols:

ᴛʜə ship wəz angʹkərd at hər bėrth.

You don't know what (bėrth) means in this sentence, but you look up the word you know has this pronunciation, which is *birth*. You don't find any meaning that fits the context, but you find the following fistnote:

birth (bėrth) **1** coming into life; being born: *the birth of a baby.* **2** a beginning: *the birth of a nation.* **3** bringing forth: *the birth of a plan.* **4** descent; family: *a person of Spanish birth. He was a man of humble birth.* *n.*
☛ **Birth** and **berth** are pronounced the same.

So you look up the entry *berth* and quickly find the meaning you want.

Sometimes it is useful to look up the fistnote for a word you know just to see what words are pronounced in the same way. For instance, you may not be sure how to spell the word that is put in phonetic symbols and within brackets in the following sentence:

There was a (kyü) of the people waiting to get into the concert.

You think the word begins with *qu*, so you could look through all the words in the dictionary that start with these two letters. But you also know that the word *cue* is pronounced in the same way. So you look up this word, find the entry for *cue*[1], and read its fistnote, which says:

☛ **Cue** and **queue** are pronounced the same.

You immediately know that *queue* is the spelling you are looking for.

Fill the blank in each of the following sentences with the correct spelling of the pronunciation shown in brackets to the right. If you are not sure which word to write in, use the homonym notes to help you find the right entry.

1. The boy was sitting on a ______ of straw. (bāl)
2. You can tell a ______ tree by its smooth bark. (bēch)
3. They were attacked by a ______ of blackflies. (hôrd)
4. The top card was the ______ of clubs. (nāv)
5. The eagle is a bird of ______. (prā)

Synonyms

☛ **Mad, crazy, insane** have similar meanings. **Insane** is the proper word to describe someone suffering from severe mental illness: *The man was so worried that he became insane.* **Mad** is used in the same way but often just means very reckless, or foolish: *Crossing the Pacific on a raft seems a mad thing to do.* **Crazy** suggests a more wild or disturbed state: *She is nearly crazy with fear.*

A few fistnotes help you to understand the differences between synonyms, words that have almost the same meaning. Read the example above, and decide whether you would use *mad*, *crazy*, or *insane* to fill the blank in the following sentence:

You would be _________ to dive from that bridge.

The following chart shows all the possible parts of entries in the *Canadian Junior Dictionary*. As you practise the use of the dictionary, get to know each of these entry parts. Learn whereabouts in an entry to find each piece of information, and try to see the different ways in which each part of an entry can help you.

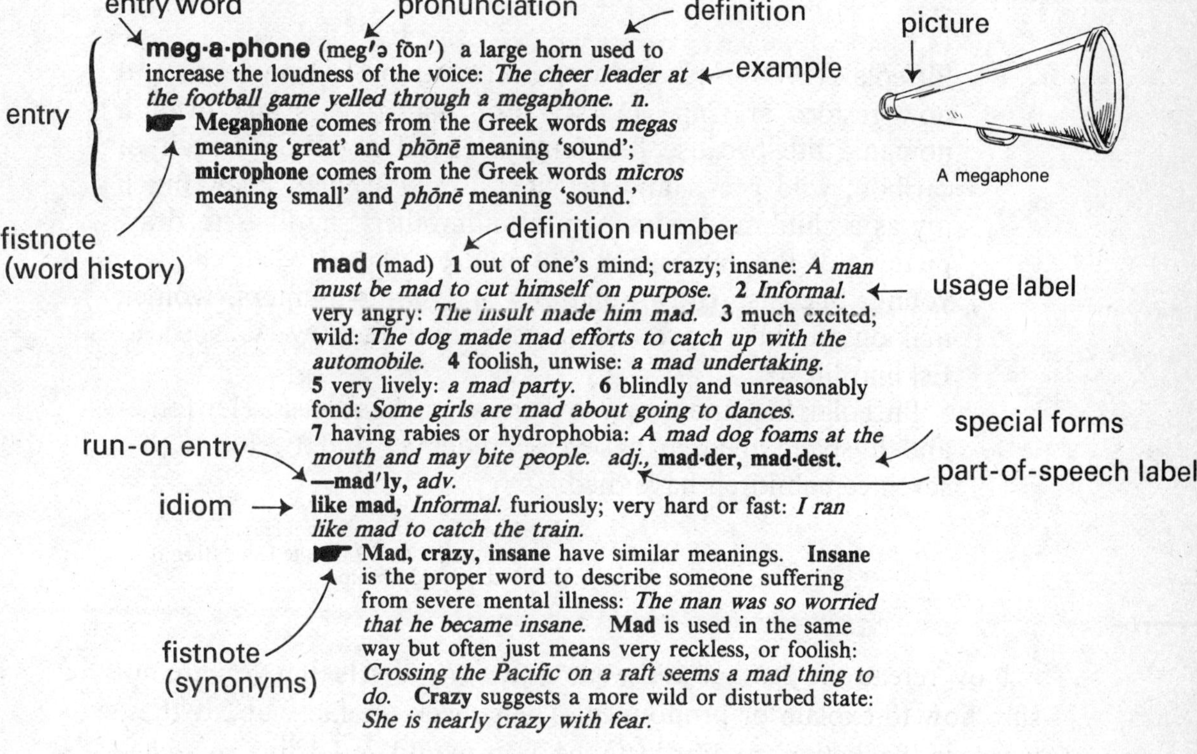

meg·a·phone (meg′ə fōn′) a large horn used to increase the loudness of the voice: *The cheer leader at the football game yelled through a megaphone. n.*

☛ **Megaphone** comes from the Greek words *megas* meaning 'great' and *phōnē* meaning 'sound'; **microphone** comes from the Greek words *mīcros* meaning 'small' and *phōnē* meaning 'sound.'

mad (mad) **1** out of one's mind; crazy; insane: *A man must be mad to cut himself on purpose.* **2** *Informal.* very angry: *The insult made him mad.* **3** much excited; wild: *The dog made mad efforts to catch up with the automobile.* **4** foolish, unwise: *a mad undertaking.* **5** very lively: *a mad party.* **6** blindly and unreasonably fond: *Some girls are mad about going to dances.* **7** having rabies or hydrophobia: *A mad dog foams at the mouth and may bite people. adj.,* **mad·der, mad·dest.**
—mad′ly, *adv.*
like mad, *Informal.* furiously; very hard or fast: *I ran like mad to catch the train.*

☛ **Mad, crazy, insane** have similar meanings. **Insane** is the proper word to describe someone suffering from severe mental illness: *The man was so worried that he became insane.* **Mad** is used in the same way but often just means very reckless, or foolish: *Crossing the Pacific on a raft seems a mad thing to do.* **Crazy** suggests a more wild or disturbed state: *She is nearly crazy with fear.*

man·ner (man′ər) **1** the way something happens or is done: *The trouble arose in a curious manner.* **2** a person's way of acting or behaving; a style or fashion: *She has a kind manner. He dresses in a strange manner.* **3** kind or kinds: *He saw all manner of birds in the forest.* **4 manners,** *pl.* **a** ways or customs: *Books and movies show us the manners of other times and places.* **b** ways of behaving towards others: *bad manners.* **c** polite behavior: *It is nice to see a child with manners. n.* ← hidden entry (def. 4)

☛ **Manner** and **manor** are pronounced the same.

↑ fistnote (homonyms)

may·be (mā′bē) possibly or perhaps; it may be so. *adv.*

☛ **Maybe** as an adverb is one word: *Maybe it will rain tomorrow.* **May be** as a verb phrase is two words: *He may be home soon.*

fistnote (usage)

Making the Most of It

USING THE DICTIONARY FOR READING

Read the following passage about Pitseolak (pit′sē ō′lak), an Eskimo artist. Try to guess from the context the meanings of any words you don't know.

> Pitseolak (1900–) was born on an island in Hudson Strait and now resides at Cape Dorset. For many years she lived a nomadic life because her family moved about in search of caribou, wild geese, and sea creatures. Pitseolak knew much joy as a child, and now, as a grandmother, she likes to draw pictures of the games Eskimo children played when she was young. She also draws pictures of Eskimo hunters, women making mukluks or sewing tents, and, in fact, every aspect of Eskimo life.
>
> Pitseolak has known sorrow as well as happiness. Her father and husband died in a severe epidemic, and twelve of her seventeen children have died.
>
> from *Something to Remember*, copyright © 1973 Gage Educational Publishing Limited.

Now reread the passage and write down any words that you are not sure how to explain or pronounce. Then check the facts about these words in the dictionary. For instance, how would you define *nomadic*? How do you think *nomadic* is pronounced? If you are not sure of the meaning or the pronunciation, check your answers against those in the dictionary. You might do the same with the word *epidemic*.

Perhaps you had to pause over the word *aspect*. If so, try to think of a synonym for this word, and then check your answer against the meanings given in the dictionary.

You may also have noted some words that you have met before but would like to know more about. For example, you may think you know what *caribou* and *mukluk* mean, but could you explain their meanings to another student? Do you know what language these two words come from? Use your dictionary to check your answers to both these questions.

The following paragraph is from a story about a storm at sea. It was written by a boy in Grade 4 called Craig, but it is his first draft only. You are going to proofread it for him. Read through the paragraph and make a note of any words or phrases that you think might need correcting.

The side of the ship had sprung a hole, and all of the sudden it bust apart. Water pored into the hul. We got the pumpers going, but they were hardly no use. Then it started to rain and thunder. All the guys on deck were panicing and screaming for help. It was like been in a hurr-icane. Then lightning struck the ship. The decks and cabin was on fire.

Use your dictionary if you are not sure how to correct some of Craig's mistakes, or if you are not sure whether some words are mistakes or not. For instance, is *bust* the correct past tense for *burst*? Where in the dictionary entry for *burst* would you find the answer? Where would you look in the dictionary to see if *panicing* is spelled correctly? If you need to, use the dictionary to see if Craig should have used *lightning* or *lightening*.

There are other words you may need to look up for different reasons. Is the word *hardly* used correctly? Should *guys* be used here, or is it slang? Is the word *hurricane* hyphenated in a proper place?

There are also idioms that you may need to check. Should Craig have written *sprung a hole*, or would the ship have *sprung* something else? Where would you look in the dictionary to find the right idiom? Is there another idiom that has been incorrectly written?

There are other errors in the paragraph, and there may well be other words that you want to check while you are making corrections.

When you have made all your corrections, write out the paragraph as if you were doing Craig's final copy.

This puzzle will help you review some of the things you have learned in this "Inside the Dictionary" section of the *Canadian Junior Dictionary*. Copy the puzzle form onto a sheet of squared paper, or use a machine copy of the page. Use the dictionary to help you solve the clues, then write the answers in the correct spaces.

1	2		3		4		5
6							
7							
					8		
9		10		11			
12			13		14	15	
			16	17			
18			19				

ACROSS

1. Dictionary entries are printed in the order of the_______. (8)
6. The prefix in *rebuild.* (2)
7. The run-on entry at *keep.* (6)
8. Second pronunciation of *been.* (3)
11. Prefix entered on page 143. (2)
12. Pronounced (üz). (4)
14. Drop the last letter of the entry after *cuirass.* (3)
16. The root word of *lice.* (5)
18. Homonym of *know.* (2)
19. Pronounced (nē). (4)

DOWN

1. The entry after *arithmetic.* (3)
2. The first guideword on page 326. (4)
3. The root word of *hopeful.* (4)
4. This entry has the first fistnote on page 38. (8)
5. The third entry word on page 618. (7)
9. Its abbreviation is *n.* (4)
10. The pronunciation of *is.* (2)
13. Another name for the *wapiti.* (3)
15. Pronounced (yüs). (3)
17. Entry word for the idiom *on and on.* (2)

Note: The figure in brackets at the end of each clue shows the total number of letters that are in the answer.

hat, āge, fär; let, ēqual, tėrm; it, īce
hot, ōpen, ôrder; oil, out; cup, pu̇t, rüle
əbove, takən, pencəl, lemən, circəs
ch, child; ng, long; sh, ship
th, thin; ᴛʜ, then; zh, measure

a or **A** (ā) the first letter of the alphabet: *There are two* a's *in* afraid. *n., pl.* **a's** or **A's.**

A ampere; amperes.

a (ə; *stressed,* ā or a) **1** any: *He didn't expect to catch a fish.* **2** one: *I want a litre of milk.* **3** each; every: *Christmas comes once a year.* **4** for each: *one dollar a metre. adj.,* or *indefinite article.*

a·back (ə bak′) **take aback,** take by surprise: *I was taken aback by his question. adv.*

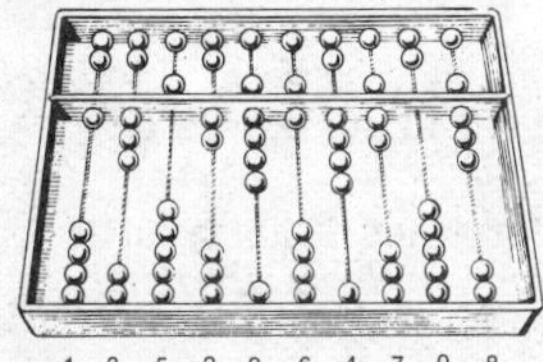

An abacus. The beads above the bar count 5 each when lowered to the bar. The beads below the bar count 1 each when raised to the bar. In the picture, the beads are set for 1 352 964 708.

ab·a·cus (ab′ə kəs) a frame with rows of counters or beads that slide back and forth: *Abacuses are used in China, Japan, Korea, etc. for counting. n., pl.* **ab·a·cus·es** or **ab·a·ci** (ab′ə sī′ or ab′ə sē′).

ab·a·lo·ne (ab′ə lō′nē) a sea animal of the snail family, found on the Pacific coast: *The lining of the abalone's large, flat shell is made into buttons and ornaments. n.*

a·ban·don (ə ban′dən) **1** give up entirely: *She abandoned the idea of being a nurse.* **2** desert, forsake, or leave any place, person, or thing without intending to return: *A good mother would never willingly abandon her baby. v.*

a·ban·doned (ə ban′dənd) deserted; forsaken: *an abandoned house. adj.*

a·bashed (ə basht′) made shy and slightly ashamed: *The boy was abashed when the teacher pointed out all his mistakes. v.*

a·bate (ə bāt′) **1** become less: *The storm has abated.* **2** make less: *The medicine abated his pain. v.,* **a·bat·ed, a·bat·ing.**

ab·at·toir (ab′ə twär′ or ab′ə twär′) a slaughterhouse, where cattle, pigs, sheep, etc. are killed and prepared for marketing. *n.*

ab·bess (ab′is or ab′es) the woman in charge of an abbey of nuns. *n.*

ab·bey (ab′ē) **1** the building or buildings where monks or nuns live a religious life. **2** a church or residence that was once an abbey: *Westminster Abbey. n., pl.* **ab·beys.**

ab·bot (ab′ət) the man in charge of an abbey of monks. *n.*

ab·bre·vi·ate (ə brē′vē āt′) make a word or phrase shorter so that a part stands for the whole: *We can abbreviate 'Saskatchewan' to 'Sask.' v.,* **ab·bre·vi·at·ed, ab·bre·vi·at·ing.**

ab·bre·vi·a·tion (ə brē′vē ā′shən) a shortened form, such as *Ont.* for *Ontario* or *M.P.* for *Member of Parliament. n.*

ab·di·cate (ab′də kāt′) give up a position of authority or responsibility; resign: *When the king abdicated his throne, his brother became king. v.,* **ab·di·cat·ed, ab·di·cat·ing.**

ab·di·ca·tion (ab′də kā′shən) giving up a position of authority or responsibility; resigning: *The abdication of King Edward VIII took place in 1936. n.*

ab·do·men (ab′də mən or ab dō′mən) **1** the part of the body that contains the stomach, the intestines, and certain other important organs; the belly. **2** the last of the three parts of an insect's body. See **insect** for picture. *n.*

ab·dom·i·nal (ab dom′ə nəl) of the abdomen; in the abdomen; for the abdomen: *Bending the body exercises the abdominal muscles. adj.*

ab·duct (ab dukt′) take a person away by force or by trickery; kidnap: *The police caught the man who tried to abduct the boy for ransom. v.* **—ab·duc′tor,** *n.*

ab·hor (ab hôr′) shrink from in horror; feel disgust for; hate strongly: *Some people abhor snakes. v.,* **ab·horred, ab·hor·ring.**

a·bide (ə bīd′) **1** put up with; endure: *A good housekeeper cannot abide dirt.* **2** stay; remain: *Abide with me for a time.* **3** dwell; reside. *v.,* **a·bode** or **a·bid·ed, a·bid·ing.**

abide by, a accept and follow out: *We shall abide by the umpire's decision.* **b** remain faithful to: *He will abide by his promise.*

a·bid·ing (ə bīd′ing) unending; lasting: *We hope for an abiding peace. adj.*

a·bil·i·ty (ə bil′ə tē) **1** power to do or act: *A horse has the ability to pull heavy loads.* **2** skill: *He has great ability as a hockey player.* **3** the power to do some special thing; talent: *She showed great musical ability in the way she played that difficult piece on the violin. n., pl.* **a·bil·i·ties.**

ab·ject (ab′jekt) **1** wretched; miserable: *The people in that remote village were living in abject poverty.* **2** deserving contempt: *Abject fear showed on the coward's face. adj.* **—ab·ject′ly,** *adv.*

a·blaze (ə blāz′) **1** on fire: *The forests were set ablaze by lightning.* **2** shining brightly; brightly lit: *The fair midway was ablaze with lights. adv., adj.*

a·ble (ā′bəl) **1** having power or skill: *Little children are able to walk, but they are not able to earn a living.* **2** skilful; competent: *She is an able teacher. adj.,* **a·bler, a·blest.**

-able a suffix meaning: **1** *(added to verbs)* that can be ____ed: *Enjoyable means that can be enjoyed.* **2** *(added to nouns)* suitable for____: *Comfortable means suitable for comfort.* **3** *(added to nouns)* inclined toward____: *Peaceable means inclined toward peace.*

a·bly (ā′blē) in an able manner; with skill; well: *She does her work ably. adv.*

ab·nor·mal (ab nôr′məl) not as it should be; very different from the ordinary; unusual: *It is abnormal for a man to have six fingers on each hand. adj.* **—ab·nor′mal·ly,** *adv.*

a·board (ə bôrd′) on board; in or on a ship, train, bus, airplane, etc. *adv.*

a·bode (ə bōd′) **1** a place to live in; a dwelling; a house. **2** See **abide.** 1 *n.,* 2 *v.*

a·bol·ish (ə bol′ish) do away with; put an end to: *Many people wish that nations would abolish war.* *v.*

ab·o·li·tion (ab′ə lish′ən) putting an end to: *the abolition of slavery.* *n.*

A–bomb (ā′bom′) atomic bomb. *n.*

a·bom·i·na·ble (ə bom′ə nə bəl) **1** disgusting; hateful: *Kidnapping is an abominable act.* **2** very unpleasant: *The weather for the picnic was abominable—rainy, windy, and cold.* *adj.*

abominable snowman a manlike monster supposed to live in the Himalaya mountains.

ab·o·rig·i·ne (ab′ə rij′ə nē′) one of the earliest known inhabitants of a country. *n.*

a·bound (ə bound′) **1** be plentiful: *Fish abound in the ocean.* **2** be well supplied; be filled: *The ocean abounds with fish.* *v.*

a·bout (ə bout′) **1** of or having to do with: *This is a story about horses.* **2** nearly; almost: *He has about finished his work.* **3** around: *A collar goes about the neck. Look about and tell me what you see.* 1, 3 *prep.*, 2, 3 *adv.*

about to, on the point of; going to; ready to: *The plane is about to take off.*

about turn, a command to face the opposite direction.

a·bove (ə buv′) **1** overhead; in a higher place: *The sky is above.* **2** over: *Look above the tall building to see the sun. Can you hear above the noise?* **3** more than: *Our club has above thirty members—thirty-five to be exact.* **4** above zero on the Fahrenheit scale: *The temperature is five above.* **5** beyond: *Go to the first house above the school.* **6** too high; superior to: *The spoiled child felt above washing dishes.* 1 *adv.*, 2, 3, 5, 6 *prep.*, 4 *adj.*

a·breast (ə brest′) side by side: *The soldiers marched three abreast.* *adv., adj.*

abreast of, keeping up with; not behind: *Read the newspapers to keep abreast of what is going on.*

a·bridge (ə brij′) make shorter, especially something written or printed: *This long story must be abridged.* *v.*, **a·bridged, a·bridg·ing.**

a·bridg·ment or **a·bridge·ment** (ə brij′mənt) a shortened form, especially of a book or a long magazine article: *This book is an abridgment of a three-volume history.* *n.*

a·broad (ə brod′ or ə brôd′) **1** outside one's country, especially overseas: *He is going abroad this summer to travel in England.* **2** widely: *The news of his coming spread abroad.* **3** outside the house: *Grandfather walks abroad only on warm days.* *adv.*

a·brupt (ə brupt′) **1** sudden: *He made an abrupt turn to avoid another car.* **2** very steep: *The road made an abrupt rise up the hill.* **3** short or sudden in speech or manner; blunt: *He was very gruff and had an abrupt way of speaking.* *adj.* **—a·brupt′ly,** *adv.* **—a·brupt′ness,** *n.*

ab·scess (ab′ses) a collection of pus in some part of the body: *An abscess results from an infection and usually makes a painful sore.* *n.*

ab·sence (ab′səns) **1** being away: *His absence from school was caused by illness.* **2** the time of being away: *He returned after an absence of two years.* **3** being without; a lack: *Darkness is the absence of light.* *n.*

ab·sent (ab′sənt for 1, ab sent′ for 2) **1** away; not present: *Three members of the class were absent.* **2** keep oneself away: *Do not absent yourself from school without reason.* 1 *adj.*, 2 *v.*

ab·sen·tee (ab′sən tē′) a person who is away. *n.*

ab·sent–mind·ed (ab′sənt mīn′did) not noticing what is happening around one, especially because the mind is thinking about other things. *adj.* **—ab′sent-mind′ed·ly,** *adv.*

ab·so·lute (ab′sə lüt′) **1** complete; perfect: *Try to tell the absolute truth.* **2** not limited in any way: *The dictator has absolute power.* *adj.*

ab·so·lute·ly (ab′sə lüt′lē for 1 and 2, ab′sə lüt′lē for 3) **1** completely: *His frostbitten hand was absolutely useless.* **2** certainly: *He spoke only when it was absolutely necessary.* **3** yes: *'Are you going to the game?' 'Absolutely!'* *adv.*

ab·solve (ab zolv′ or ab solv′) **1** declare free from sin. **2** clear of blame or guilt: *The principal absolved the pupil of any wrongdoing.* **3** set free from a promise or duty. *v.*, **ab·solved, ab·solv·ing.**

ab·sorb (ab zôrb′ or ab sôrb′) **1** take in or suck up liquids: *A sponge absorbs water. A blotter absorbs ink.* **2** take in and hold: *Anything black absorbs light that falls on it.* **3** take up all the attention of; interest very much: *The boy was absorbed in building a dam in the brook.* *v.*

ab·sorb·ent (ab zôr′bənt or ab sôr′bənt) able or ready to take in moisture, light, or heat: *Absorbent paper is used to dry the hands.* *adj.*

ab·sorb·ing (ab zôr′bing or ab sôr′bing) extremely interesting: *an absorbing story.* *adj.*

ab·sorp·tion (ab zôrp′shən or ab sôrp′shən) **1** taking in or sucking up, especially liquids: *the absorption of water by a sponge.* **2** having all one's interest taken up: *Everybody noticed the absorption of the children in their game.* *n.*

ab·stain (ab stān′) do without something; hold back; refrain: *If you abstain from eating rich foods, you will not get fat. She abstained from voting.* *v.*

ab·sti·nence (ab′stə nəns) deliberately not doing something; avoiding certain things, especially drugs, alcoholic drinks, or certain foods: *Abstinence sometimes requires effort.* *n.*

ab·stract (ab′strakt for 1–3, ab strakt′ for 4) **1** thought of apart from any particular object or real thing: *A lump of sugar is a real thing; the idea of sweetness is abstract.* **2** hard to understand; difficult: *Atomic theory is so abstract that it can be fully understood only by advanced students.* **3** a brief statement of the main ideas in an article, book, etc.; summary. **4** take away; remove: *We can abstract gold from ore.* 1, 2 *adj.*, 3 *n.*, 4 *v.* **—ab′stract·ly,** *adv.* **—ab′stract·ness,** *n.*

ab·surd (ab zėrd′ or ab sėrd′) plainly not true or sensible; foolish; ridiculous. *adj.* **—ab·surd′ly,** *adv.*

ab·surd·i·ty (ab zėr′də tē or ab sėr′də tē) **1** foolishness; lack of sense: *You can see the absurdity of wearing shoes on your head and hats on your feet.* **2** something absurd: *To say that every father has a daughter is an absurdity.* *n., pl.* **ab·surd·i·ties.**

a·bun·dance (ə bun′dəns) great plenty; a quantity

that is more than enough: *There was such an abundance of apples last year that many were fed to the pigs.* *n.*

a·bun·dant (ə bun′dənt) more than enough; very plentiful: *There are abundant oil reserves in Alberta.* *adj.* —**a·bun′dant·ly,** *adv.*

a·buse (ə byüz′ for 1, 3, and 6, ə byüs′ for 2, 4, 5, and 7) **1** make bad or wrong use of: *The policeman abused his authority by arresting a harmless onlooker.* **2** a bad or wrong use: *the abuse of a privilege.* **3** treat badly: *to abuse a child.* **4** bad treatment: *abuse of a helpless prisoner.* **5** a bad practice or custom: *the abuses of evil dictators.* **6** use harsh, insulting language to: *The angry captain abused the crew at the top of his voice.* **7** harsh, insulting language. 1, 3, 6 *v.,* **a·bused, a·bus·ing;** 2, 4, 5, 7 *n.*

a·byss (ə bis′) a very deep crack in the earth; a seemingly bottomless hole. *n.*

A.C. or **a.c.** alternating current.

a·cad·e·my (ə kad′ə mē) **1** a place for instruction. **2** a private high school. **3** a school where some special subject can be studied: *There are academies of medicine and painting.* *n., pl.* **a·cad·e·mies.**

A·ca·di·a (ə kā′dē ə) that part of old French Canada which included present-day Nova Scotia and New Brunswick: *Acadia was a French colony from 1604 to 1713.* *n.*

A·ca·di·an (ə kā′dē ən) **1** of or relating to Acadia or, sometimes, Nova Scotia. **2** a native of Acadia or one of his descendants. 1 *adj.,* 2 *n.*

ac·cel·er·ate (ak sel′ər āt′) **1** go or cause to go faster; speed up: *The engineer accelerates a train by turning on more power.* **2** cause to happen sooner; hasten: *Rest often accelerates a person's recovery.* *v.*

ac·cel·er·a·tion (ak sel′ər ā′shən) speeding up; an increase in speed. *n.*

ac·cel·er·a·tor (ak sel′ər ā′tər) **1** a means of increasing speed. **2** the pedal or lever that controls the flow of gasoline to an automobile engine. *n.*

ac·cent (ak′sent; sometimes, ak sent′ for 3 and 4) **1** the greater force with which a certain syllable in a word is pronounced as compared with other syllables in the same word; stress: *In 'abundant' the accent is on the second syllable.* **2** a mark (′) written or printed to show the spoken force of a syllable, as in *yes′ter day, to day′, to mor′row.* Some words have two accents, a heavy accent (′) and a light accent (′), as in *accelerator* (ak sel′ər ā′ter). **3** mark with an accent. **4** pronounce with an accent: *Is 'acceptable' accented on the first or second syllable?* **5** a distinctive manner of pronunciation heard in different parts of the same country, or in the speech of a person speaking a language not his own: *Hans still speaks English with a German accent.* **6** tone: *The little girl spoke to her doll in tender accents.* 1, 2, 5, 6 *n.,* 3, 4 *v.*

ac·cept (ak sept′) **1** take what is offered or given to one: *He accepted our gift.* **2** agree to; say yes to: *She accepted his proposal.* **3** take as satisfactory: *We accepted her excuse.* **4** receive with liking and approval; approve: *The children on the street soon accepted the girls in the new house.* *v.*

☛ See note at **except.**

ac·cept·a·ble (ak sep′tə bəl) **1** worth accepting; agreeable: *Flowers are an acceptable gift for a sick person.* **2** satisfactory: *The singer gave an acceptable performance, but it was not outstanding.* *adj.*

hat, āge, fär; let, ēqual, tėrm; it, īce
hot, ōpen, ôrder; oil, out; cup, pu̇t, rüle
əbove, takən, pencəl, lemən, circəs
ch, child; ng, long; sh, ship
th, thin; ᴛʜ, then; zh, measure

ac·cept·ance (ak sep′təns) **1** taking what is offered or given: *Her acceptance of their gift delighted the children.* **2** approval; taking as right, true, and sufficient: *Our plans for the school play have the acceptance of the principal.* *n.*

ac·cess (ak′ses) **1** the right to approach, enter, or use: *All children have access to the library during the afternoon.* **2** a way or means of approach: *Access to mountain towns is often difficult. Has he access to anyone who can help him?* *n.*

ac·ces·si·ble (ak ses′ə bəl) easy to get at; easy to reach: *A public library makes good books accessible. A telephone is put where it will be accessible.* *adj.*

ac·ces·so·ry (ak ses′ə rē) **1** something added that is useful in some way but not absolutely necessary: *He bought a mirror and some other accessories for his bicycle.* **2** something extra that is worn or carried with one's basic clothing: *All the accessories to her costume—gloves, stockings, and purse—were beautifully matched.* **3** added; helping the general effect: *His tie supplied an accessory touch of color.* **4** a person who helps another commit a crime, without actually being present: *A person who hides a criminal is an accessory.* 1, 2, 4 *n., pl.* **ac·ces·so·ries;** 3 *adj.*

access road a road built to reach a place or an area that is otherwise sealed off, as by dense bush, muskeg, etc.

ac·ci·dent (ak′sə dənt) **1** something harmful or unlucky that happens by chance: *an automobile accident.* **2** something that happens without being planned, intended, wanted or known in advance: *Their meeting was an accident.* *n.*

by accident, by chance; not on purpose: *I cut my foot by accident.*

ac·ci·den·tal (ak′sə den′təl) happening by chance; not planned or intended: *The injury to the player was accidental. The finding of the treasure was accidental.* *adj.* —**ac′ci·den′tal·ly,** *adv.*

ac·claim (ə klām′) **1** applaud; shout welcome to; show approval of: *The crowd acclaimed the fireman for rescuing a baby from the burning house.* **2** applause; approval: *The actor was received with great acclaim.* **3** elect to an office without opposition: *The voters acclaimed him mayor.* 1, 3 *v.,* 2 *n.*

ac·cla·ma·tion (ak′lə mā′shən) **1** a show of approval by a crowd: *The newly crowned queen received the acclamation of the people.* **2** an oral vote: *The club elected him president by acclamation.* *n.*

by acclamation, *Cdn.* without opposition in an election: *Since no candidate opposed him, Mr. Smith was elected by acclamation.*

ac·com·mo·date (ə kom′ə dāt′) **1** hold; have room for; lodge: *This big bedroom will easily accommodate both girls. Can you accommodate a party of five for two weeks?* **2** oblige; help out: *He wanted change for five dollars, but I could not accommodate him.* *v.,* **ac·com·mo·dat·ed, ac·com·mo·dat·ing.**

ac·com·mo·dat·ing (ə kom′ə dāt′ing) helpful; obliging: *The man was accommodating enough to lend me a quarter.* *adj.* —**ac·com′mo·dat′ing·ly,** *adv.*

ac·com·mo·da·tion (ə kom′ə dā′shən) **1** room; lodging for a time: *This hotel has accommodations for one hundred people.* **2** a help; favor: *It will be an accommodation to me if you will meet me tomorrow instead of today.* *n.*

ac·com·pa·ni·ment (ə kum′pə nē mənt) something added, especially to an action or to a melody in music: *She danced to the accompaniment of applause. He sang the song to a piano accompaniment.* *n.*

ac·com·pa·ny (ə kum′pə nē) **1** go along with: *He will accompany you on your walk.* **2** be or happen along with: *A high wind accompanied the rain.* **3** make music or sing along with other music. *v.,* **ac·com·pa·nied, ac·com·pa·ny·ing.**

ac·com·plice (ə kom′plis) a person who aids another in committing a crime: *Without an accomplice to open the door the thief could not have got into the building so easily.* *n.*

ac·com·plish (ə kom′plish) **1** do; carry out: *Did you accomplish your purpose?* **2** finish; complete: *He can accomplish more in a day than any other boy in the class.* *v.*

ac·com·plished (ə kom′plisht) expert; skilled: *an accomplished dancer.* *adj.*

ac·com·plish·ment (ə kom′plish mənt) **1** doing or carrying out; successful completion: *The accomplishment of his purpose took two months.* **2** something that has been done with knowledge, skill, and ability: *The teacher was proud of her pupils' accomplishments.* **3** a special skill: *She was a girl of many accomplishments, for she could sew, cook, play the piano, and sing.* *n.*

ac·cord (ə kôrd′) **1** agree: *His account of the accident accords with yours.* **2** agreement: *His opinion of war was in accord with hers.* 1 *v.,* 2 *n.*
of one's own accord, without being asked or without suggestion from anyone else: *A boy who goes to bed early of his own accord is indeed unusual.*

ac·cord·ance (ə kôr′dəns) agreement; harmony: *What he did was in accordance with what he said.* *n.*

ac·cord·ing·ly (ə kôr′ding lē) **1** in agreement with something that has been stated: *These are the rules. You can act accordingly or leave the club.* **2** therefore: *He was too sick to stay. Accordingly, we sent him home.* *adv.*

according to **1** in agreement with: *He came according to his promise.* **2** in proportion to: *You will be ranked according to the work you do.* **3** on the authority of: *According to this book, a tiger is really a big cat.*

ac·cor·di·on (ə kôr′dē ən) a musical instrument, made up of a bellows, metal reeds, and a set of keys at each end, which is played by forcing air through the reeds by means of the bellows: *In a piano accordion, one set of keys is like a piano keyboard and the other keys are buttons.* *n.*

ac·count (ə kount′) **1** telling in detail about an event or thing; an explanation; a story: *The boy gave his father an account of the ball game.* **2** a reason: *He was brought up not to lie on any account.* **3** sake: *Don't wait on my account.* **4** a statement of money received and spent; a record of business: *All stores, banks, and factories keep accounts.* **5** consider: *Solomon was accounted wise.* 1–4 *n.,* 5 *v.*
account for, a tell what has been done with; answer for: *The treasurer of the club had to account for the money paid to him and spent by him.* **b** explain: *Late frosts accounted for the poor fruit crop.*
on account, as part payment: *I bought my new camera by paying a dollar a week on account.*
on account of, because of; for the reason of: *The game was put off on account of rain.*
on no account, in no circumstances; for no reason: *On no account should you lie.*
on one's own account, for one's own sake or benefit: *He helps his father but repairs and sells used cars on his own account.*
take into account, allow for; consider: *When planning a vacation, you must take travelling time into account.*

ac·count·ant (ə koun′tənt) a person who looks after or checks business accounts. *n.*

ac·count·ing (ə koun′ting) the business of looking after or checking accounts. *n.*

ac·cu·mu·late (ə kyü′myə lāt′) **1** collect: *He accumulated a fortune by hard work.* **2** grow in amount or number; increase: *Dust had accumulated during the weeks she was gone.* *v.,* **ac·cu·mu·lat·ed, ac·cu·mu·lat·ing.**

ac·cu·mu·la·tion (ə kyü′myə lā′shən) **1** a mass of material collected: *His accumulation of old papers filled two closets.* **2** bringing together; collecting: *The accumulation of useful knowledge is one result of reading.* *n.*

ac·cu·ra·cy (ak′yə rə sē) exactness or correctness; freedom from errors or mistakes: *Arithmetic problems must be solved with accuracy.* *n.*

ac·cu·rate (ak′yə rit) exactly right; correct: *You can only be right in arithmetic if your answers are accurate.* *adj.* —**ac′cu·rate·ly,** *adv.*

ac·cu·sa·tion (ak′yə zā′shən) a charge of being or doing something bad: *The accusation against him was that he had stolen ten dollars.* *n.*

ac·cuse (ə kyüz′) charge with being or doing something bad: *The boys accused her of being a tattletale. The man was accused of speeding.* *v.,* **ac·cused, ac·cus·ing.**

ac·cus·tom (ə kus′təm) make familiar with by use or habit; get used to: *You can accustom yourself to almost any kind of food.* *v.*

ac·cus·tomed (ə kus′təmd) usual: *By Monday he was back in his accustomed place.* *adj.*
accustomed to, used to; in the habit of: *He was accustomed to hard work.*

A piano accordion

hat, āge, fär; let, ēqual, tėrm; it, īce
hot, ōpen, ôrder; oil, out; cup, pu̇t, rüle
əbove, takən, pencəl, lemən, circəs
ch, child; ng, long; sh, ship
th, thin; ᴛʜ, then; zh, measure

ace (ās) 1 a playing card having one spot: *In most card games, the ace is the highest card in a deck.* 2 a person expert at anything: *Peter is an ace at basketball.* 3 a combat pilot who has shot down a large number of enemy planes. *n.*

ache (āk) 1 a continuous pain, such as an earache, headache, or toothache. 2 suffer continuous pain; be in pain: *My back aches.* 3 *Informal.* wish very much: *During the hot days we ached to go swimming.* 1 *n.*, 2, 3 *v.*, **ached, ach·ing.**

a·chieve (ə chēv′) 1 do; carry out: *Did you achieve all that you expected to today?* 2 reach a certain end by one's own efforts: *He achieved fame as a swimmer.* *v.*, **a·chieved, a·chiev·ing.**

a·chieve·ment (ə chēv′mənt) 1 some plan or action carried out with courage or with unusual ability: *Sailing a submarine under the North Pole was a great achievement.* 2 the carrying out or reaching of an aim or purpose: *the achievement of our goal for the UNICEF collection.* *n.*

ac·id (as′id) 1 sour; sharp or biting to the taste: *Lemons are an acid fruit. Rhubarb has an acid taste.* 2 sharp in manner or temper: *The bitter, disappointed old man had an acid disposition.* 3 a chemical substance that unites with a base (def. 6) to form a salt: *The water solution for an acid tastes sour and turns blue litmus paper red.* 1, 2 *adj.*, 3 *n.*

ac·knowl·edge (ak nol′ij) 1 admit to be true: *He acknowledges his faults.* 2 recognize the merit, authority, or claims of: *The boys acknowledged him the best player on the baseball team.* 3 make known that one has received a favor, gift, message, etc.: *She acknowledged the gift with a pleasant letter.* *v.*, **ac·knowl·edged, ac·knowl·edg·ing.**

ac·knowl·edg·ment or **ac·knowl·edge·ment** (ak nol′ij mənt) 1 something given or done in return for a service or favor: *The receipt was the grocer's acknowledgment that my mother's bill had been paid. He waved in acknowledgment of the crowd's cheers.* 2 admitting something to be true: *The accused man made acknowledgment of his guilt.* *n.*

ac·me (ak′mē) the highest point: *A baseball player usually reaches the acme of his skill before he is thirty.* *n.*

Acorns

a·corn (ā′kôrn) the nut of an oak tree. *n.*

ac·quaint (ə kwānt′) make familiar: *'Let me acquaint you with the facts' means 'Let me make the facts known to you.'* *v.*

be acquainted with, have personal knowledge of persons or things: *I have heard about your friend, but I am not acquainted with him.*

ac·quaint·ance (ə kwān′təns) 1 a person known to you but not a close friend: *The actress had many acquaintances but few friends.* 2 a knowledge of persons or things gained from experience with them: *I have some acquaintance with French, but I do not know it well.* *n.*

ac·qui·esce (ak′wē es′) accept or agree to by keeping quiet or by not making objections: *Jim's parents acquiesced in the principal's decision that he should not be promoted.* *v.*, **ac·qui·esced, ac·qui·esc·ing.**

ac·quire (ə kwīr′) gain or get as one's own; get: *In a few years he acquired a store of his own.* *v.*, **ac·quired, ac·quir·ing.**

ac·qui·si·tion (ak′wə zish′ən) 1 acquiring or getting as one's own: *He spent many years in the acquisition of knowledge.* 2 something acquired or gained: *Her new acquisitions were two dresses, a hat, and a pair of shoes.* *n.*

ac·quit (ə kwit′) declare not guilty: *The jury acquitted the man who had been accused of stealing.* *v.*, **ac·quit·ted, ac·quit·ting.**

acquit oneself, do one's part; behave: *The soldiers acquitted themselves bravely in battle.*

a·cre (ā′kər) a measure of land, 160 square rods or 43 560 square feet (4047 square metres). *n.*

a·cre·age (ā′kər ij) the number of acres: *The acreage of this park is over 800.* *n.*

ac·rid (ak′rid) 1 sharp, bitter, or stinging: *Smoke feels acrid in your mouth and nose.* 2 sharp in manner or temper: *The bitter old woman had an acrid disposition.* *adj.*

ac·ro·bat (ak′rə bat′) a person who can dance on a rope or wire, swing on trapezes, turn handsprings, or do other such feats of bodily skill and strength. *n.*

ac·ro·bat·ics (ak′rə bat′iks) 1 tricks or performances of an acrobat; gymnastic feats. 2 tricks like those of an acrobat: *a monkey's acrobatics.* *n. pl.*

a·crop·o·lis (ə krop′ə lis) 1 the fortified hill in the centre of an ancient Greek city. 2 **the Acropolis,** the fortified hill of Athens, on which the Parthenon was built. *n.*

a·cross (ə kros′) 1 from one side to the other of; over: *The cat walked across the street.* 2 from one side to the other: *What is the distance across?* 3 on the other side of; beyond: *The woods are across the river.* 1, 3 *prep.*, 2 *adv.*

come across, find: *We come across hard words in some books.*

act (akt) 1 something done; a deed: *Slapping his face was a childish act.* 2 do something: *The firemen acted promptly and saved the burning house.* 3 have effect: *Yeast acted on the dough and made it rise.* 4 behave: *The boy acted badly in school.* 5 behave like: *Most people act the fool now and then.* 6 perform in a theatre, in motion pictures, on television, or over the radio; play a part: *My brother acts the part of the hero in the school play. He acts very well.* 7 a main division in a play or opera: *This play has three acts.* 8 one of several performances on a program: *the trained*

dog's act. **9** a law or decree: *the acts of Parliament.* 1, 7–9 *n.,* 2–6 *v.*
act as, serve as or do the work of: *John acted as class secretary last week.*
act for, take the place of: *While the principal was gone, the assistant principal acted for him.*
act on, follow; obey: *I shall certainly act on your suggestion.*
in the act of, in the doing of: *The farmer caught the boys in the act of stealing his apples.*

act·ing (ak′ting) taking another's place for a short time and doing his work: *Mr. Stone was the acting principal during the principal's absence. adj.*

ac·tion (ak′shən) **1** the process of doing something; acting: *The quick action of the firemen saved the building from complete destruction.* **2** something done; an act: *Giving the dog food was a kind action.* **3** a way of working: *This motor has a very easy action.* **4** battle; a part of a battle: *My grandfather was wounded in action in the Second World War.* **5 actions,** *pl.* conduct or behavior: *Mother punished me for my selfish actions. n.*
take action, start to do something: *The government took action to prevent forest fires.*

ac·tive (ak′tiv) **1** acting; working: *an active volcano, an active force.* **2** showing much action; lively; moving rather quickly: *Most children are more active than grown people. adj.* **—ac′tive·ly,** *adv.*

ac·tiv·i·ty (ak tiv′ə tē) **1** the state of being active; movement; the use of power: *mental activity, physical activity, activity in club work.* **2** an action: *The Mounted Police try to discover the activities of enemy spies.* **3** a certain action; something done under certain conditions: *outdoor activities, classroom activities. n., pl.* **ac·tiv·i·ties.**

ac·tor (ak′tər) a person who acts on a stage, in motion pictures, or on television or radio. *n.*
bad actor, a person, animal, or thing that is always misbehaving: *That horse is a bad actor; it kicks and bites at anyone who goes near.*

ac·tress (ak′tris) a female actor. *n.*

ac·tu·al (ak′chü əl) real; existing as a fact: *What he told us was not a dream but an actual happening. adj.*

ac·tu·al·ly (ak′chü əl ē) really; in fact: *Are you actually going to camp this summer or just wishing to go? adv.*

a·cute (ə kyüt′) **1** sharp and severe: *A toothache can cause acute pain.* **2** keen: *Dogs have an acute sense of smell. An acute thinker is clever and shrewd. adj.* **—a·cute′ly,** *adv.* **—a·cute′ness,** *n.*

acute angle an angle less than a right angle. See **angle**[1] for picture.

ad (ad) *Informal.* advertisement. *n.*

A.D. an abbreviation for the Latin words **anno Domini,** meaning in the year of our Lord, that is, after the birth of Christ: *From 200 B.C. to A.D. 500 is 700 years.*

Ad·am (ad′əm) in the Bible, the first man. *n.*

ad·a·mant (ad′ə mənt) firm; unyielding: *Columbus was adamant in refusing the requests of his sailors to turn back. adj.*

Adam's apple the lump in the front of the neck, formed by the larynx.

a·dapt (ə dapt′) **1** make fit or suitable: *A good writer adapts his words to the age and interests of his readers.* **2** change one's behavior so as to fit in with a new situation: *He has adapted well to his new school.* **3** alter so as to make suitable for a different use: *The farmer can adapt his barn for use as a garage. v.* **—a·dapt′er,** *n.*

a·dapt·a·ble (ə dap′tə bəl) changed or changing easily to fit different conditions: *Mother has an adaptable schedule. She is an adaptable person. adj.*

ad·ap·ta·tion (ad′ap tā′shən) **1** adapting or fitting: *He made a good adaptation to his new school.* **2** something made by adapting: *A film is often an adaptation of a novel.* **3** a change in form or habits to fit different conditions: *Wings are adaptations of the upper limbs for flight. n.*

add (ad) **1** put together: *When you add 4 and 2 and 3, you have 9.* **2** go on to say; say further: *She said good-bye and added that she had had a pleasant visit. v.*
add to, a put with: *She added sugar to her tea.* **b** make greater: *The fine day added to our pleasure.* **c** make an increase of: *He has added several stamps to his collection.*

ad·dend (ad′end or ə dend′) a number to be added to another number. See **addition** for picture. *n.*

ad·der (ad′ər) **1** a small, poisonous snake of Europe. **2** any of several small, harmless snakes of North America. *n.*

ad·dict (ad′ikt) a person who slavishly follows a habit and cannot break it. *n.*

ad·dict·ed (ə dik′tid) slavishly following a habit or practice: *He was so addicted to the use of tobacco that he smoked ten cigars a day. adj.*

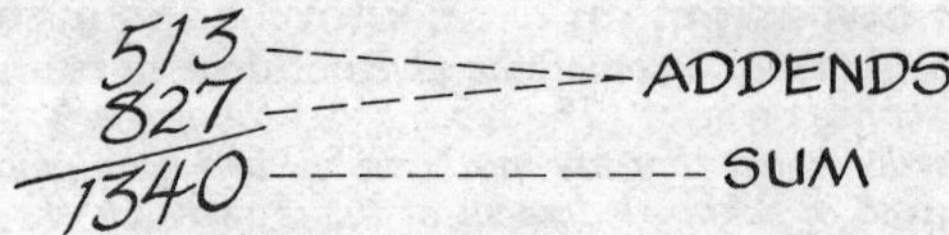

The parts of an addition problem

ad·di·tion (ə dish′ən) **1** the adding of one number or quantity to another: *2 + 2 = 4 is a simple addition.* **2** the adding of one thing to another: *The addition of flour will thicken gravy.* **3** something added: *Workmen are building an addition to this house. n.*
in addition or **in addition to,** besides: *In addition to the money for their work, the girls received free lunches.*

ad·di·tion·al (ə dish′ən əl) added; extra; more: *Mother will need additional help while there is so much company. adj.* **—ad·di′tion·al·ly,** *adv.*

ad·dress (ə dres′; also ad′res for 3, 4, and 5) **1** a speech, either spoken or written: *The Prime Minister gave an address over radio and television.* **2** speak to or write to: *He will address you on the subject of war and peace. The king was addressed as 'Your Majesty.'* **3** the place to which mail is directed: *Send the letter to her business address.* **4** the writing on an envelope or package that shows where it is to be sent: *The address was hard to read.* **5** write on an envelope or package the information that shows where it is to be sent: *Please address this letter for me.* 1, 3, 4 *n.,* 2, 5 *v.*
address oneself to, apply oneself to: *He addressed himself to the task of learning his lessons.*

hat, āge, fär; let, ēqual, tėrm; it, īce
hot, ōpen, ôrder; oil, out; cup, pu̇t, rüle
əbove, takən, pencəl, lemən, circəs
ch, child; ng, long; sh, ship
th, thin; ᴛʜ, then; zh, measure

ad·dress·ee (ə dres ē′ or ad′res ē′) the person to whom a letter, package, etc. is addressed. *n.*

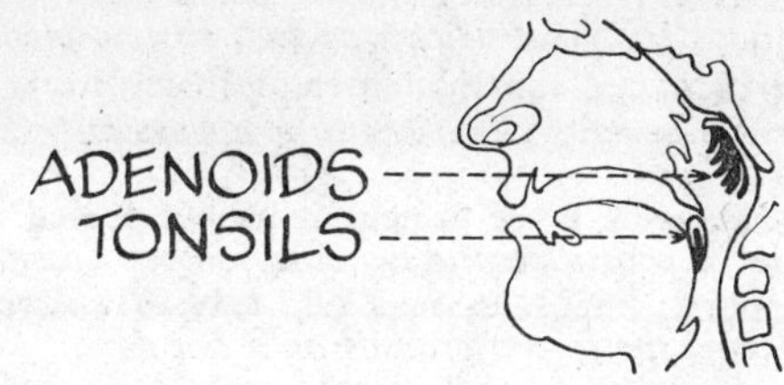

ad·e·noids (ad′ə noidz′) tissue in the upper part of the throat, just behind the nose, that usually shrinks and disappears in childhood, but can swell up and get in the way of natural breathing and speaking. *n. pl.*

a·dept (ə dept′) very skilful; expert: *She is adept in the use of a needle. adj.* **—a·dept′ly,** *adv.* **—a·dept′ness,** *n.*

ad·e·quate (ad′ə kwit) sufficient; enough; as much as is needed: *His wages are adequate to support three people. adj.* **—ad′e·quate·ly,** *adv.* **—ad′e·quate·ness,** *n.*

ad·here (ad hēr′) **1** stick fast, remain attached: *Mud adheres to shoes.* **2** hold closely or firmly: *He adhered to his plan. Most people adhere to the church of their parents. v.,* **ad·hered, ad·her·ing.**

ad·he·sive (ad hē′siv) **1** sticking fast; sticky: *adhesive tape.* **2** any substance, such as paste or glue, used to stick things together: *An adhesive is used to put a patch on an inner tube.* 1 *adj.,* 2 *n.*

ad·ja·cent (ə jā′sənt) next; adjoining: *The house adjacent to ours has just been sold. adj.* **—ad·ja′cent·ly,** *adv.*

ad·jec·ti·val (aj′ik tī′vəl) of or having to do with an adjective: *The ending* -like *in* childlike *is an adjectival suffix. adj.*

ad·jec·tive (aj′ik tiv) the name given to a class of words that limit or add to the meaning of words *(nouns)* naming persons, places, or things; any word in this class: *In 'a tiny creek' and 'The day is warm,' both* tiny *and* warm *are adjectives. Words like* green, old, short, sweet, *and* sour *are adjectives. n.*

ad·join (ə join′) be next to; be close to; be side by side: *His yard adjoins ours. Saskatchewan adjoins Alberta. We have adjoining desks. v.*

ad·journ (ə jėrn′) **1** put off until a later time: *The president adjourned the meeting until all the members of the club could be present.* **2** stop business for a time: *Court will adjourn until Monday morning at 10 o'clock. v.*

ad·just (ə just′) **1** arrange; change to make fit: *These desks and seats can be adjusted to the right height for any child.* **2** arrange or set machinery or controls to work as required: *to adjust a radio dial. He adjusted the brakes on his bicycle.* **3** fit oneself; adapt: *The boy from the country soon adjusted to city life. v.* **—ad·just′a·ble,** *adj.*

ad·just·ment (ə just′mənt) **1** changing to make fit; setting right to fit some standard or purpose: *The adjustment of seats to the right height for children is necessary for their comfort.* **2** an agreement to end a quarrel; settlement: *Try to make some adjustment of your differences so that you can work together without an argument. n.*

ad·min·is·ter (ad min′is tər) **1** manage the affairs of; direct: *The Minister of Defence administers a department of the government. A housekeeper administers a household.* **2** give to; apply: *A doctor administers medicine to sick people. Judges administer justice. v.*

ad·min·is·tra·tion (ad min′is trā′shən) **1** the managing of a business, office, etc.; management: *The administration of a big business requires skill in dealing with people.* **2** the group of persons in charge: *The principal and teachers are a part of the administration of a school.* **3** the government in office. **4** the term that a government is in office: *The Liberal administration lasted many years.* **5** a giving out or applying: *The Red Cross handled the administration of aid to the refugees. n.*

ad·mi·ra·ble (ad′mə rə bəl) **1** worth admiring: *Sir Wilfred Grenfell had an admirable character.* **2** excellent; very good: *Our family doctor is taking admirable care of the sick man. adj.* **—ad′mi·ra·bly,** *adv.*

ad·mi·ral (ad′mə rəl) an officer having the highest rank in a navy. *n.*

ad·mi·ra·tion (ad′mə rā′shən) **1** a feeling of wonder, pleasure, and approval: *Everyone has admiration for bravery.* **2** a person or thing that is admired: *Her talent in painting was the admiration of all her friends. n.*

ad·mire (ad mīr′) **1** regard with wonder, pleasure, and satisfaction: *We all admire a beautiful picture or a fine piece of work.* **2** think highly of: *Everyone admired his brave deed. v.,* **ad·mired, ad·mir·ing. —ad·mir′er,** *n.*

ad·mis·sion (ad mish′ən) **1** allowing to enter: *admission of aliens into a country.* **2** the right of entering or using a place, an office, etc.; permission to enter: *Every elementary school graduate has admission to high school.* **3** the price of being allowed to enter: *Admission to the show is one dollar.* **4** admitting something to be true; confessing: *His admission that he was to blame kept the other boys from being punished. n.*

ad·mit (ad mit′) **1** say something is real or true; confess: *He admits now that he was wrong.* **2** allow to enter: *This ticket will admit you to the circus. He was admitted to school this year. v.,* **ad·mit·ted, ad·mit·ting.**
admit of, leave room for; make allowance for: *The plans for our trip admit of no delays.*

ad·mit·tance (ad mit′əns) the right to enter; permission to enter: *She gained admittance to the television studio. n.*

ad·mon·ish (ad mon′ish) warn or advise a person about his faults in order that he may set them right: *The policeman admonished him for driving so fast. v.*

ad·mo·ni·tion (ad′mə nish′ən) advice to a person about his faults; a warning: *The teacher's admonitions to the student for her careless work were ignored. n.*

a·do (ə dü′) action; stir; fuss; trouble: *The family made much ado about the party. n.*

a·dopt (ə dopt′) 1 take or choose as one's own: *I liked your idea and adopted it.* 2 take a child of other parents to bring up as one's own: *The Browns have adopted a baby girl.* *v.*

a·dop·tion (ə dop′shən) 1 taking as one's own by choice: *Our club voted for the adoption of some new rules.* 2 of a child, being taken and treated as their own by adults other than his or her original parents: *Tim's adoption by his aunt changed his whole life.* *n.*

a·dor·a·ble (ə dôr′ə bəl) 1 worthy of being adored. 2 *Informal.* attractive; delightful: *an adorable child.* *adj.* **—a·dor′a·bly,** *adv.*

ad·o·ra·tion (ad′ə rā′shən) 1 the highest respect and love. 2 worship. *n.*

a·dore (ə dôr′) 1 respect and love deeply: *She adores her mother.* 2 worship: *'O! Come, let us adore Him,' sang the choir at Christmas.* 3 *Informal.* like very much: *I just adore that dress.* *v.,* **a·dored, a·dor·ing.**

a·dorn (ə dôrn′) add beauty to; decorate: *She adorned her hair with flowers.* *v.*

a·dorn·ment (ə dôrn′mənt) 1 something that adds beauty; an ornament: *Plants and flowers are an adornment to our balcony.* 2 making something attractive: *She was busy with the adornment of the room for the party.* *n.*

a·drift (ə drift′) drifting; floating without being guided: *They were adrift in a lifeboat for three days. The lost children were adrift in the fairground.* *adj., adv.*

a·droit (ə droit′) skilful: *Monkeys are adroit climbers. A good teacher is adroit in asking questions.* *adj.* **—a·droit′ly,** *adv.* **—a·droit′ness,** *n.*

a·dult (ə dult′ or ad′ult) 1 full-grown; grown-up; mature; having full size and strength. 2 a grown-up person. 3 any plant or animal grown to full size and strength. 1 *adj.,* 2, 3 *n.*

a·dul·ter·ate (ə dul′tər āt′) make weak or impure by adding another substance: *That store was fined for selling milk that had been adulterated with water.* *v.*

ad·vance (ad vans′) 1 move forward: *The angry crowd advanced toward the building.* 2 put forward: *The plan he advanced was not good.* 3 a forward movement; progress: *The army's advance was very slow.* 4 help forward: *to advance the cause of peace.* 5 promote: *He was advanced from lieutenant to captain.* 6 go up in price or value: *Sugar had advanced ten cents a kilogram.* 7 put up; raise: *The grocer advanced his prices on food when he had to pay more in the market.* 8 a rise in price or value: *an advance of one cent a litre.* 9 a personal approach; an approach made to gain something: *Bob made the first advances toward making up his quarrel with his sister.* 1, 2, 4–7 *v.,* **ad·vanced, ad·vanc·ing;** 3, 8, 9 *n.*

in advance, a in front. **b** ahead of time: *He paid his rent in advance.*

ad·vanced (ad vanst′) 1 in front of others: *Our army is in an advanced position.* 2 ahead of most others; at a high level: *The advanced class has studied history for three years.* 3 far along in life; very old: *His grandfather lived to the advanced age of ninety years.* *adj.*

ad·vance·ment (ad vans′mənt) 1 an advance; improvement: *Father says that loyalty and hard work are what usually bring an advancement in pay.* 2 promotion: *His good work won him advancement.* *n.*

ad·van·tage (ad van′tij) anything that is to the good, or is a benefit: *Good health is always an advantage.* *n.*

take advantage of, a use to help or benefit oneself: *Take advantage of your illness to catch up on your reading.* **b** use unfairly; impose upon: *Don't take advantage of me by asking me to run errands on a hot day.*

to one's advantage, to one's benefit or help: *It will be to your advantage to study hard if you wish to be a scientist.*

ad·van·ta·geous (ad′vən tā′jəs) favorable; helpful; profitable: *The enemy held an advantageous position on a hill.* *adj.* **—ad′van·ta′geous·ly,** *adv.*

ad·ven·ture (ad ven′chər) 1 a bold and difficuilt undertaking, usually exciting and somewhat dangerous: *A hunter of tigers has many adventures.* 2 an unusual experience: *The trip to Quebec City was an adventure for us.* *n.*

ad·ven·tur·er (ad ven′chər ər) a person who has or seeks adventures. *n.*

ad·ven·tur·ous (ad ven′chər əs) 1 fond of adventures; ready to take risks: *Simon Fraser was a bold, adventurous explorer.* 2 full of danger: *The discovery of the North Pole was an adventurous undertaking.* *adj.*

ad·verb (ad′vėrb) the name given to a class of words expressing time, place, manner, degree, or circumstance; any word in this class: *In 'He walked rapidly,' 'He came late,' and 'She is rather slow,'* rapidly, late, *and* rather *are adverbs. Words like* soon, never, here, very, *and* gladly *are adverbs.* *n.*

ad·ver·bi·al (ad vėr′bē əl) of or having to do with an adverb: *'He drove fast' shows an adverbial use of fast.* *adj.*

ad·ver·sar·y (ad′vər ser′ē) 1 an enemy: *The aim in war is to conquer one's adversaries.* 2 a person or group on the other side in a contest: *The boxer defeated his adversary.* *n., pl.* **ad·ver·sar·ies.**

ad·verse (ad′vėrs or ad vėrs′) 1 unfavorable: *His adverse comments discouraged me.* 2 harmful: *Dirt and disease have an adverse effect on the healthy development of children.* 3 acting in a contrary direction; opposing: *Adverse winds hinder planes.* *adj.*

ad·ver·si·ty (ad vėr′sə tē) distress; misfortune; hardship. *n., pl.* **ad·ver·si·ties.**

ad·ver·tise (ad′vər tīz′) give public notice of or announce, especially by emphasizing the desirable features of a product or service in order to make people want to buy it: *People who wish to sell things advertise them in newspapers, over the radio, on television, and in other ways.* *v.,* **ad·ver·tised, ad·ver·tis·ing.**

advertise for, ask for by a public notice: *He advertised for a job.*

ad·ver·tise·ment (ad′vər tīz′mənt or ad vėr′tis mənt) a public announcement or printed notice, especially one trying to persuade people to buy a product or service: *The store has an advertisement in the newspaper.* *n.*

ad·ver·tis·ing (ad′vər tīz′ing) 1 the business of preparing, publishing, or circulating advertisements. 2 advertisements. *n.*

ad·vice (ad vīs′) an opinion about what should be done: *Follow the doctor's advice.* *n.*

ad·vis·a·ble (ad vīz′ə bəl) wise; sensible; suitable: *It is not advisable for him to go while he is still sick. A hot-air furnace is not advisable for a large building.* *adj.*

ad·vise (ad vīz′) **1** give advice to: *He advised me to keep my money in the bank.* **2** inform: *We were advised of the dangers before we began our trip.* *v.,* **ad·vised, ad·vis·ing.**

ad·vis·er or **ad·vi·sor** (ad vīz′ər) a person who gives advice; a person whose job is to give advice: *a student adviser.* *n.*

ad·vo·cate (ad′və kāt′ for 1 or 2, ad′və kit for 2) **1** speak in favor of; recommend publicly: *He advocates building more good roads.* **2** a person who speaks in favor; a supporter: *Mr. Smith is an advocate of better school buildings.* 1 *v.,* **ad·vo·cat·ed, ad·vo·cat·ing;** 2 *n.*

A man using an adze to shape and smooth a log

adze (adz) a tool resembling an axe, but with a longer blade which is set across the end of the handle and curves inward: *An adze is used for shaping wood.* *n.* Sometimes spelled **adz.**

ae·on (ē′ən or ē′on) See **eon.**

aer·i·al (er′ē əl) **1** antenna (def. 2). **2** having to do with the air, taking place in the air, made for use in the air: *aerial warfare, an aerial camera.* 1 *n.,* 2 *adj.*

aer·o·nau·tics (er′ə no′tiks or er′ə nô′tiks) the design, manufacture, and operation of aircraft. *n.*

aer·o·plane (er′ə plān′) an airplane. *n.*

aer·o·sol (er′ə sol′) **1** a substance made up of very fine particles of a liquid or solid in a gas: *Smoke and fog are common aerosols.* **2** a container that uses liquid gas under pressure to release a substance as a spray or foam: *Hair spray, shaving soap, and many other products are available in aerosol cans.* *n.*

aer·o·space (er′ə spās′) **1** the earth's atmosphere and the space beyond it. **2** the planning, building, and operating of rockets, missiles, and other spacecraft. *n.*

a·far (ə fär′) far; far away; far off: *I saw him from afar.* *adv.*

af·fa·ble (af′ə bəl) easy to talk to; courteous and pleasant: *Our principal is a very friendly and affable man.* *adj.*

af·fair (ə fer′) **1** anything to be done; a matter of business: *The Prime Minister has many affairs to look after.* **2** any thing, matter, or happening: *The party on Saturday was a jolly affair.* *n.*

af·fect[1] (ə fekt′) **1** make something happen to; influence: *The amount of rain affects the growth of crops.* **2** act on in a harmful way: *The disease so affected his mind that he could not remember what he had done.* **3** stir the feelings of; touch the heart of: *The stories of starving children so affected him that he sent all his spare money for relief.* *v.*
☛ See note at **effect.**

af·fect[2] (ə fekt′) **1** pretend to have or feel: *He affected ignorance of the fight, but we knew that he had seen it all.* **2** like to wear or use: *She affects large hats.* *v.*

hat, āge, fär; let, ēqual, tėrm; it, īce
hot, ōpen, ôrder; oil, out; cup, pu̇t, rüle
əbove, takən, pencəl, lemən, circəs
ch, child; ng, long; sh, ship
th, thin; ᴛʜ, then; zh, measure

af·fec·ta·tion (af′ek tā′shən) an artificial or unnatural way of behaving or talking: *His English accent is an affectation, for he has never lived outside Alberta.* *n.*

af·fect·ed[1] (ə fek′tid) **1** acted on; influenced. **2** touched in the heart; stirred in feeling: *She was sad and much affected by her sister's illness.* *adj.*

af·fect·ed[2] (ə fek′tid) not natural; pretended; artificial: *His affected manner changed as soon as the guests had gone.* *adj.*

af·fec·tion (ə fek′shən) a friendly feeling; fondness; love: *The mother's affection for her baby was easy to see.* *n.*

af·fec·tion·ate (ə fek′shən it) loving; fond; showing affection: *He received an affectionate letter from his sister.* *adj.* **—af·fec′tion·ate·ly,** *adv.*

af·firm (ə fėrm′) say firmly; declare to be true; assert: *The Bible affirms that God is love.* *v.*

af·firm·a·tive (ə fėr′mə tiv) **1** saying yes; affirming: *His answer was affirmative.* **2** the side arguing in favor of a question being debated: *The affirmative is opposed by the negative.* 1 *adj.,* 2 *n.*
in the affirmative, expressing agreement by saying yes: *The principal replied in the affirmative when we requested that we have a class picnic.*

af·flict (ə flikt′) cause pain to; trouble very much; distress greatly: *Mother is afflicted with a bad headache.* *v.*

af·flic·tion (ə flik′shən) **1** pain; trouble; distress: *the affliction of war.* **2** a cause of pain, trouble, or distress; misfortune: *His blindness is an affliction.* *n.*

af·flu·ence (af′lü əns) wealth; riches: *Canada is a country of great affluence.* *n.*

af·flu·ent (af′lü ənt) very wealthy. *adj.* **—af′flu·ent·ly,** *adv.*

af·ford (ə fôrd′) **1** have the means; have the money, time, or strength: *Can we afford to buy a new car? He cannot afford to waste so much time.* **2** provide; give: *His own garden affords fresh vegetables for the family. Reading this story will afford real pleasure.* *v.*

af·front (ə frunt′) **1** insult openly and purposely: *The boy affronted the teacher by making a face at her.* **2** an open insult: *To be called a coward is an affront.* 1 *v.,* 2 *n.*

a·field (ə fēld′) away; away from home: *He wandered far afield in foreign lands.* *adv.*

a·fire (ə fīr′) on fire. *adj.*

a·flame (ə flām′) **1** in flames; on fire. **2** as if on fire; excited: *His mind was aflame with curiosity.* *adj.*

a·float (ə flōt′) **1** floating on the water or in the air: *The baby has four toy boats afloat in the bathtub.* **2** on a ship: *On our trip around the world, we were afloat 60 days and ashore 30 days.* *adv., adj.*

a·foot (ə fu̇t′) 1 on foot; walking: *Did you come all the way afoot?* 2 going on; in progress: *Great preparations for the dinner were afoot in the kitchen. adv., adj.*

a·fraid (ə frād′) 1 frightened; feeling fear: *She is afraid of snakes.* 2 sorry: *I'm afraid I must ask you to leave now. adj.*

a·fresh (ə fresh′) again: *If you spoil your drawing, start afresh. adv.*

Af·ri·can (af′rə kən) 1 of Africa; having something to do with Africa; from Africa. 2 a person born in or living in Africa. 1 *adj.,* 2 *n.*

African violet a tropical plant having violet, pink, or white flowers: *In Canada, African violets are grown indoors.*

aft (aft) to or at the back of a ship, boat, aircraft, or spacecraft. *adv.*

af·ter (af′tər) 1 behind: *You come after me in the line (prep.). 'Jill came running after' (adv.).* 2 later than: *After dinner we can go.* 3 later; following: *three hours after (adv.). In after years he did not get home very often (adj.).* 4 considering; because of: *After the way she acted, how can you like her?* 5 in search of; in pursuit of: *The dog ran after the rabbit.* 6 in spite of: *After all her sufferings, she is still cheerful.* 1, 2, 4–6 *prep.,* 1, 3 *adv.,* 3 *adj.*

af·ter·math (af′tər math′) a result; consequence: *The aftermath of war is hunger and disease. n.*

af·ter·noon (af′tər nün′) the time from noon to evening. *n.*

af·ter·thought (af′tər thot′ or af′tər thôt′) a thought that comes after the time when it might have been used. *n.*

af·ter·ward (af′tər wərd) afterwards. *adv.*

af·ter·wards (af′tər wərdz) later: *The bud was small at first, but afterwards it became a large flower. adv.*

a·gain (ə gen′ or ə gān′) another time; once more: *Come again to play. Say that again. adv.*

a·gainst (ə genst′ or ə gānst′) 1 in opposition to: *He spoke against the suggestion.* 2 upon: *Rain beats against the window.* 3 in preparation for: *Squirrels store up nuts against the winter.* 4 in defence from: *A fire is a protection against cold. prep.*

ag·ate (ag′it) 1 a stone with colored stripes or cloudy colors; a kind of quartz. 2 a marble resembling an agate, used in games. *n.*

age (āj) 1 a time of life: *the age of ten.* 2 a length of life: *Turtles live to a great age.* 3 a particular period of life: *old age.* 4 a certain period in history: *the atomic age.* 5 *Informal.* a long time: *I haven't seen you for an age.* 6 grow old: *He is aging fast.* 7 make old: *Worry ages a person.* 1–5 *n.,* 6, 7 *v.,* **aged, ag·ing** or **age·ing.**
of age, old enough to have full legal rights and responsibilities.

a·ged (ā′jid for 1, ājd for 2) 1 old; having lived a long time: *The aged woman was wrinkled and bent.* 2 of the age of: *She was aged six when she first went to school. adj.*

a·gen·cy (ā′jən sē) 1 a business that acts for a person or for another company: *An agency rented my house for me. Employment agencies help workers to get jobs, and find workers for people who need them.* 2 the means or action: *Through the agency of friends he was set free. n., pl.* **a·gen·cies.**

a·gen·da (ə jen′də) a list of things to be done or discussed: *the agenda for a meeting. n.*

a·gent (ā′jənt) 1 a person or company that acts for another: *The lady made her brother her agent while she was out of the city.* 2 any power or cause that produces an effect: *Yeast is an important agent in the making of beer. n.*

ag·gra·vate (ag′rə vāt′) 1 make worse; make more severe: *His bad temper was aggravated by his headache.* 2 annoy; irritate; provoke. *v.,* **ag·gra·vat·ed, ag·gra·vat·ing.**

ag·gra·va·tion (ag′rə vā′shən) 1 making worse or more severe: *We were alarmed by the aggravation of the crisis.* 2 something that aggravates: *Noise can be an aggravation to a headache. n.*

ag·gre·gate (ag′rə git or ag′rə gāt′ for 1, ag′rə gāt′ for 2) 1 total: *The aggregate value of the gifts was a hundred dollars.* 2 amount to: *The money collected will aggregate $1000.* 1 *n.,* 2 *v.,* **ag·gre·gat·ed, ag·gre·gat·ing.**

ag·gres·sion (ə gresh′ən) 1 the making by one nation of an attack without good cause on the rights or territories of another: *Russia was guilty of aggression against Czechoslovakia.* 2 any attack without good cause; the first step in a quarrel: *an aggression against a person's rights.* 3 the practice of making such attacks: *the aggression of a bully. n.*

ag·gres·sive (ə gres′iv) 1 taking the first step in an attack or quarrel; attacking: *An aggressive country is always ready to start a war.* 2 active; energetic; forceful: *The police began an aggressive campaign against speeding. adj.* **—ag·gres′sive·ly,** *adv.* **—ag·gres′sive·ness,** *n.*

ag·gres·sor (ə gres′ər) 1 one that begins an attack or quarrel. 2 a nation that starts a war: *Germany was the aggressor in September, 1939. n.*

ag·grieved (ə grēvd′) 1 upset or troubled by grief: *We were much aggrieved on learning of our grandfather's death.* 2 wronged; unjustly treated: *The boy felt aggrieved when he was punished for something he didn't do. adj.*

a·ghast (ə gast′) struck with surprise or horror: *The children were aghast at the visitor's bad manners. adj.*

ag·ile (aj′il or aj′əl) 1 moving quickly and easily; lively; nimble: *An acrobat has to be agile.* 2 able to think quickly: *You need an agile mind to solve puzzles. adj.* **—ag′ile·ly,** *adv.*

a·gil·i·ty (ə jil′ə tē) the ability to move quickly and easily: *The agility of the wrestler was quite amazing. n.*

hat, āge, fär; let, ēqual, tėrm; it, īce
hot, ōpen, ôrder; oil, out; cup, pu̇t, rüle
əbove, takən, pencəl, lemən, circəs
ch, child; ng, long; sh, ship
th, thin; ᴛʜ, then; zh, measure

ag·i·tate (aj′ə tāt′) 1 move or shake: *The slightest wind will agitate the leaves of some trees.* 2 disturb; excite: *She was much agitated by the news of her brother's accident.* *v.*, **ag·i·tat·ed, ag·i·tat·ing.**

ag·i·ta·tion (aj′ə tā′shən) 1 moving or shaking: *The agitation of the waves was a thrilling sight.* 2 a disturbance of body or mind; excitement: *His agitation would not let him sleep.* *n.*

a·go (ə gō′) 1 gone by; past: *I met her two years ago.* 2 in the past: *The first Europeans came to Canada long ago.* 1 *adj.*, 2 *adv.*

a·gog (ə gog′) eager; curious; excited. *adj.*

ag·o·niz·ing (ag′ə nīz′ing) causing great pain or suffering: *A toothache can be agonizing.* *adj.*

ag·o·ny (ag′ə nē) very great suffering of body or mind: *the agony of acute appendicitis.* *n., pl.* **ag·o·nies.**

a·gree (ə grē′) 1 have the same opinion: *We all agree in liking the teacher.* *I agree with you that arithmetic is hard.* 2 be alike or similar to; be in harmony: *Your story agrees with mine.* 3 get along well together: *Brothers and sisters don't always agree as well as they should.* 4 consent: *He agreed to go with us.* *v.*, **a·greed, a·gree·ing.**
agree with, have a good effect on; suit: *This food does not agree with me; it makes me sick.*

a·gree·a·ble (ə grē′ə bəl) 1 pleasant; pleasing: *The boy had an agreeable manner.* 2 willing: *If Mother is agreeable, we could go to the show this afternoon.* *adj.* —**a·gree′a·bly,** *adv.*

a·gree·ment (ə grē′mənt) 1 an understanding reached by two or more nations, persons, or groups of persons: *Nations make treaties and individuals make contracts; both are agreements.* 2 harmony: *There was perfect agreement between the two friends.* 3 coming to an understanding, especially in settling a dispute: *Every obstacle to agreement has been removed.* *n.*

ag·ri·cul·tur·al (ag′rə kul′chər əl) of or having to do with farming: *A hoe is an agricultural implement.* *adj.*

ag·ri·cul·ture (ag′rə kul′chər) farming; the process of cultivating the soil to make crops grow; the raising of crops and farm animals. *n.*

a·ground (ə ground′) on the shore; on the bottom in shallow water: *The ship ran aground and stuck in the sand.* *adv., adj.*

ah (ä) an exclamation of pain, sorrow, regret, pity, surprise, joy, admiration, dislike, or contempt. *interj.*

a·ha (ä hä′) an exclamation of triumph, satisfaction, surprise, joy, etc. *interj.*

a·head (ə hed′) 1 in front; before: *He told me to walk ahead.* 2 forward; onward: *Go ahead with this work.* 3 in advance: *Jim was ahead of his class in reading.* 4 in front, as in a race or game: *The Maple Leafs were ahead 3 to 1.* *adv.*
get ahead, succeed: *One needs a good education to get ahead today.*
get ahead of, a pass: *The runner tried hard to get ahead of his rival.* **b** do better than: *He studied hard to get ahead of the rest of the class.*

a·hoy (ə hoi′) a call used by sailors to attract attention: *Sailors say 'Ship, ahoy!' when they call to a ship.* *interj.*

aid (ād) 1 give support to; help: *The Red Cross aids flood victims.* 2 support; help: *When my arm was broken, I could not dress without aid.* 3 a helper or assistant: *Ann was a nurse's aid for a time.* 1 *v.*, 2, 3 *n.*

ail (āl) 1 to trouble; be the matter with: *What ails the child?* 2 be ill; feel sick: *She had been ailing for a week.* *v.*
☛ **Ail** and **ale** are pronounced the same.

ai·ler·on (ā′lər on′) the movable part of a wing of an airplane: *Ailerons help to keep an airplane balanced while flying.* See **airplane** for picture. *n.*

ail·ment (āl′mənt) an illness or sickness. *n.*

aim (ām) 1 point or direct a gun, a blow, etc. in order to hit: *He aimed at the lion but missed.* 2 the act of pointing or directing at something: *His aim was so poor that he missed the lion.* 3 to direct acts or words so as to influence a certain person or action: *His remarks were aimed at the boys who had not played fair.* 4 try; intend; direct one's efforts: *She aimed to please her teachers.* 5 a purpose or intention: *Her aim was to do two years' work in one.* 1, 3, 4 *v.*, 2, 5 *n.*

aim·less (ām′lis) without aim or purpose: *He had gone on an aimless walk but happened to meet some friends.* *adj.*

ain't (ānt) 1 am not; are not; is not. 2 have not; has not.
☛ **Ain't** has long been used in English, though it is unacceptable to most educated speakers. It should not be used in formal English.

air (er) 1 the mixture of gases that surrounds the earth: *Air consists of nitrogen, oxygen, hydrogen, and other gases.* 2 the space overhead; the sky: *Birds fly in the air.* 3 put out in the air; let air through: *It is good to air clothes often.* 4 make known: *Don't air your troubles too often.* 5 a melody or tune: *In music, the air is the leading part.* 6 a way; a look or manner: *He had the air of a child who was afraid.* 1, 2, 5, 6 *n.*, 3, 4 *v.*
airs, unnatural or showy manners: *Your friends will laugh if you put on airs.*
in the air, going around: *Wild rumors were in the air.*
on the air, broadcasting or being broadcast.
up in the air, *Informal.* uncertain; undecided: *Our plans for the party are still up in the air.*
☛ **Air, ere,** and **heir** are pronounced the same. **Air** and **err** are sometimes pronounced the same.

air base a military headquarters and airfield for air operations and training: *There is a large air base at Trenton, Ontario.*

air–con·di·tion (er′kən dish′ən) 1 supply with the equipment for air conditioning. 2 treat air by means of air conditioning. *v.*

air–con·di·tioned (er′kən dish′ənd) having air conditioning. *adj.*

air conditioner an apparatus used to air-condition a room, building, train, etc.

air conditioning a means of treating the air in buildings, rooms, trains, etc. to regulate its temperature and amount of moisture and to free it from dust.

air·craft (er′kraft′) 1 airplanes, airships, helicopters, or balloons. 2 any airplane, airship, helicopter, or balloon. *n., pl.* **air·craft.**

air·drome (er′drōm′) airport. *n.*

air element the branch of the Canadian Forces having to do with land-based aircraft, formerly known as the Royal Canadian Air Force.

air·field (er′fēld′) the landing field of an airport. *n.*

air gun a gun worked by compressed air.

air·line (er′līn′) or **air line** 1 a company operating a system of transportation by means of aircraft. 2 the system itself. 3 a route for aircraft; airway. *n.*

air liner a large airplane for carrying many passengers.

air mail 1 mail sent by aircraft. 2 the system of sending mail by aircraft.

air–mail (er′māl′) send or transport letters or packages by air mail. *v.*

air·man (er′mən) 1 the pilot of an airplane, airship, or balloon. 2 one of the crew of an aircraft. *n., pl.* **air′men** (er′mən).

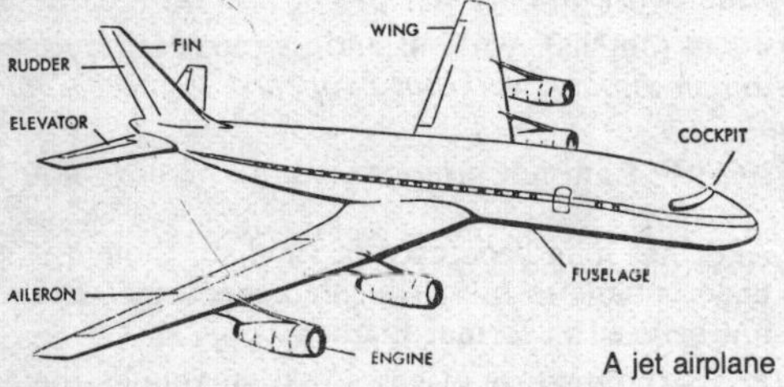

A jet airplane

air·plane (er′plān′) a self-propelled flying machine having one or more wings. *n.*

air·port (er′pôrt′) a place where aircraft carrying passengers or freight may land and take off and may load and unload: *An airport usually has several runways, a passenger building, and sheds for keeping and repairing aircraft.* *n.*

air pressure the force produced by air in a completely enclosed space: *The air pressure in a bicycle tire must not be allowed to get too low.*

air rifle a rifle that is worked by compressed air and shoots a single pellet or dart.

air·ship (er′ship′) a dirigible; a balloon that can be steered. See **dirigible** for picture. *n.*

air·strip (er′strip′) a temporary airfield. *n.*

air·tight (er′tīt′) 1 so tight that no air can get in or out. 2 leaving no opening: *The team had an airtight defence.* *adj.*

air·way (er′wā′) a route for airplanes. *n.*

air·ways (er′wāz′) airline (def. 1). *n.*

air·y (er′ē) 1 light as air; graceful; delicate: *She sang an airy tune.* 2 gay; light-hearted: *airy laughter.* 3 breezy; with air moving through it: *a large, airy room.* 4 of air; in the air: *birds and other airy creatures.* *adj.,* **air·i·er, air·i·est.**

aisle (īl) 1 a passage between rows of seats in a church, theatre, etc. 2 a long, narrow passage. *n.*

☞ **Aisle, I'll,** and **isle** are pronounced the same.

a·jar (ə jär′) slightly open: *Leave the door ajar.* *adv., adj.*

A·ke·la (ə kā′lə) cubmaster. *n.*

☞ This name comes from *Akela,* the Lone Wolf, the leader of the wolf pack in Rudyard Kipling's *The Jungle Book.*

a·kim·bo (ə kim′bō) with the hands on the hips and the elbows bent outward. *adv., adj.*

a·kin (ə kin′) 1 belonging to the same family; related: *They are akin to me; in fact, they are my cousins.* 2 alike: *The friends are akin in their love of sports.* *adj.*

al·a·bas·ter (al′ə bas′tər) 1 a smooth, white, translucent stone: *Alabaster is often carved into ornaments and vases.* 2 smooth, white, and translucent like alabaster. 1 *n.,* 2 *adj.*

a·larm (ə lärm′) 1 sudden fear; excitement caused by fear of danger: *The deer darted off in alarm.* 2 make uneasy; frighten: *The breaking of a branch under my foot alarmed the deer.* 3 a warning of approaching danger. 4 a bell or other device that makes a noise to warn or waken people. An **alarm clock** is a clock that can be set to ring at a certain time: *As a rule, alarm clocks are used to waken people in the morning.* 5 a call to arms or action: *The sentry sounded the alarm when the attack began.* 1, 3–5 *n.,* 2 *v.*

a·larm·ist (ə lär′mist) a person who is easily alarmed or who alarms others needlessly or on very slight grounds. *n.*

a·las (ə las′) oh dear!; an exclamation of sorrow, grief, regret, pity, or dread. *interj.*

Al·ber·tan (al bėr′tən) 1 a person born in or living in Alberta. 2 of or associated with Alberta. 1 *n.,* 2 *adj.*

al·bum (al′bəm) 1 a book with blank pages for holding things like photographs, pictures, and stamps. 2 a case for phonograph records. *n.*

al·co·hol (al′kə hol′ or al′kə hôl′) a colorless liquid that acts as a drug and is a part of beer, wine, whisky, gin, and other strong drinks: *Alcohol is used in medicines, in manufacturing, and as a fuel.* *n.*

al·co·hol·ic (al′kə hol′ik) 1 of alcohol: *alcoholic fumes.* 2 containing alcohol: *alcoholic drinks.* 3 a person who cannot help drinking too much alcohol. 1, 2 *adj.,* 3 *n.*

An alcove

al·cove (al′kōv) a small room or space opening into a larger room. *n.*

al·der (ol′dər or ôl′dər) a tree or shrub resembling a birch: *Alders usually grow in wet land.* *n.*

al·der·man (ol′dər mən or ôl′dər mən) a person elected to represent the people of a ward on the governing council of a city: *Our city council consists of the mayor and ten aldermen.* *n., pl.* **al·der·men** (ol′dər mən or ôl′dər mən).

hat, āge, fär; let, ēqual, tėrm; it, īce
hot, ōpen, ôrder; oil, out; cup, pu̇t, rüle
əbove, takən, pencəl, lemən, circəs
ch, child; ng, long; sh, ship
th, thin; ᴛʜ, then; zh, measure

ale (āl) a strong, light-colored beer made from malt and hops. *n.*

☛ **Ale** and **ail** are pronounced the same.

a·lert (ə lėrt′) 1 watchful; wide-awake: *The dog was alert to every sound.* 2 lively; nimble: *A sparrow is very alert in its movements.* 3 a signal warning of an attack by an enemy. 4 warn of an attack: *As the enemy bombers approached, a siren alerted the citizens.* 1, 2 *adj.*, 3 *n.*, 4 *v.* **—a·lert′ness,** *n.*

on the alert, watchful; ready at any instant for what is coming: *A sentry must be on the alert.*

al·fal·fa (al fal′fə) a plant with deep roots, leaves like clover, and bluish-purple flowers: *Alfalfa is used as a food for horses and cattle.* *n.*

al·gae (al′jē) a general name for seaweeds and certain fresh-water plants like them: *Some algae form a scum on the top of ponds.* *n. pl.*

Al·ger·i·an (al jēr′ē ən) 1 of or having to do with Algeria, a country in North Africa. 2 a person born in or living in Algeria. 1 *adj.*, 2 *n.*

a·li·as (ā′lē əs) 1 an assumed name; other name: *The spy's real name was Harrison, but he sometimes went by the alias of Johnson.* 2 otherwise called; with the assumed named of: *The thief's name was Jones, alias Williams.* 1 *n.*, *pl.* **a·li·as·es;** 2 *adv.*

al·i·bi (al′ə bī′) 1 a claim that an accused person was somewhere else when an offence was committed. 2 *Informal.* an excuse. 3 *Informal.* make an excuse. 1, 2 *n.*, *pl.* **al·i·bis;** 3 *v.*, **al·i·bied, al·i·bi·ing.**

al·ien (ā′lē ən) 1 a foreigner; a person who is not a citizen of the country he is living in. 2 of another country; foreign: *Arabic is an alien language to most Canadians.* 3 entirely different; strange: *Unkindness is alien to her nature.* 1 *n.*, 2, 3 *adj.*

a·light[1] (ə līt′) 1 get down; get off: *to alight from a horse, to alight from a train.* 2 come down from the air; come down from flight: *The bird alighted on our window sill.* *v.*

a·light[2] (ə līt′) on fire; lighted up: *The candle was still alight. Her face was alight with happiness.* *adv., adj.*

a·lign (ə līn′) bring into line; adjust to a line: *to align the sights of a gun.* *v.*

a·like (ə līk′) 1 similar; like one another: *These twins are very much alike.* 2 in the same way: *Robert and his father walk alike.* 1 *adj.*, 2 *adv.*

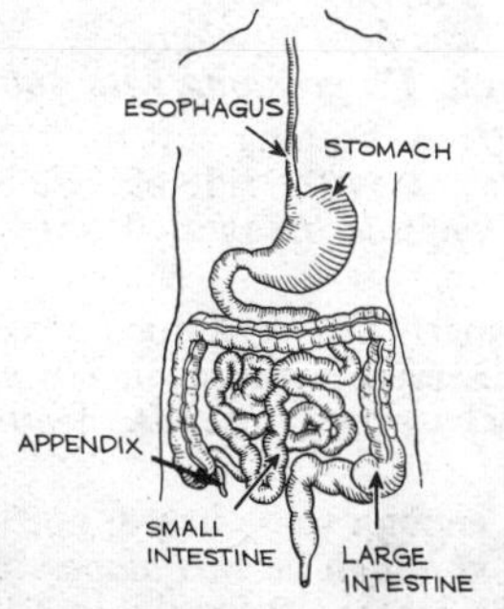

The alimentary canal of a human being

al·i·men·ta·ry canal (al′ə men′tə rē) the parts of the body through which food passes while it is being digested.

a·live (ə līv′) 1 living: *Was the snake alive or dead?* 2 active; lively; brisk. *adj.*

alive to, noticing; awake to; sensitive to: *Are you alive to what is going on?*

alive with, full of; swarming with: *The streets were alive with people.*

look alive!, hurry up!; be quick!

al·ka·li (al′kə lī′) 1 in science, a substance that is soluble in water and that neutralizes acids and forms salts with them; a base (def. 6): *Lye and ammonia are alkalis.* 2 a salt or mixture of salts found in some soils. *n.*

al·ka·line (al′kə līn′ or al′kə lin) 1 of or like an alkali. 2 containing an alkali: *The soil around the slough was alkaline.* *adj.*

all (ol or ôl) 1 the whole of: *The mice ate all the cheese.* 2 every one of: *all men, all those present.* **We all** means all of us; every one of us: *We all know him.* 3 everyone: *All of us are going.* 4 everything: *All is well.* 5 completely; entirely: *He was all tired out.* 1, 2 *adj.*, 3, 4 *pron.*, 5 *adv.*

all at once, suddenly: *All at once, the dog sprang at the cat.*

all but, almost; nearly: *He was all but dead from hunger, but he struggled on.*

at all, in any way or under any condition: *He refused to work at all.*

in all, counting every person or thing; altogether: *There were 100 men in all.*

☛ **All** and **awl** are pronounced the same.

Al·lah (al′ə or ä′lə) the Moslem name for God. *n.*

all–a·round (ol′ə round′ or ôl′ə round′) all-round. *adj.*

al·lege (ə lej′) 1 assert or declare: *This man alleges that his watch has been stolen.* 2 assert without proof: *The alleged theft really never happened.* *v.*, **al·leged, al·leg·ing.**

al·le·giance (ə lē′jəns) 1 the loyalty owed by a citizen to his government or by a subject to his ruler: *I pledge allegiance to the flag.* 2 loyalty; faithfulness; devotion: *His allegiance to his brother lasted all his life.* *n.*

al·le·lu·ia (al′ə lü′yə) hallelujah. *interj., n.*

al·ler·gic (ə lėr′jik) 1 having an allergy: *Some people who are allergic to eggs cannot eat them without breaking out in a rash.* 2 of or caused by allergy: *Hay fever is an allergic reaction.* *adj.*

al·ler·gy (al′ər jē) a condition of sickness or discomfort caused by something that is harmless to most people: *He has an allergy to strawberries and gets hives when he eats them.* *n.*

al·ley[1] (al′ē) 1 a narrow back street in a city or town. 2 a long, enclosed space for bowling. 3 a building having a number of alleys for bowling. *n.*, *pl.* **al·leys.**

al·ley[2] (al′ē) 1 a glass marble used in games. 2 **alleys,** any game played with such marbles: *The boys played alleys every day after school.* *n.*, *pl.* **al·leys.**

al·li·ance (ə lī′əns) **1** a formal bond between nations, families, etc. that agree to help each other in certain ways; joining of interests: *A joining by treaty of the interests of separate nations is an alliance.* **2** the nations or persons that belong to such a union. *n.*

al·lied (ə līd′ or al′īd) **1** united by agreement: *allied nations, allied armies.* **2** connected; related: *Reading and listening are allied activities. adj.*

An American alligator — about 3 m long with the tail

al·li·ga·tor (al′ə gā′tər) a large crawling animal with a long body, four short legs, a thick skin, and a long tail: *Alligators live mainly in the rivers and marshes of warm parts of America. n.*

al·lot (ə lot′) **1** divide and distribute in parts or shares: *The profits from the sale are allotted equally to the Boy Scouts and the Girl Guides.* **2** give to a person as his share; assign: *The principal allotted each class a part in the Dominion Day program. v.,* **al·lot·ted, al·lot·ting.**

al·low (ə lou′) **1** let; permit: *Mrs. Smith allows her children to go swimming alone. Dogs are not allowed on buses.* **2** give; let have: *She is allowed 50 cents a day for lunch at school. He allowed us $400 trade-in on our old car.* **3** set aside or set apart for a particular purpose: *The trip will cost you only $20; but you ought to allow $5 more for additional expenses. v.*
allow for, take into consideration: *She made the dress a little large to allow for shrinking when it was washed.*

al·low·ance (ə lou′əns) **1** a limited amount permitted; a definite portion or amount given out: *She has an allowance of 50 cents a week. The salesman offered us an allowance of $400 on our old car.* **2** an amount set aside for a particular purpose: *His estimate of the cost of the trip included an allowance of $100 for spending money. n.*
make allowance for, take into consideration; to allow for: *You must make allowance for the wishes of others.*

al·loy (al′oi) **1** a mixture of two or more metals: *Alloys are often harder, lighter, and stronger than the pure metals. Brass is an alloy of copper and zinc.* **2** an inferior metal mixed with a more valuable one: *This is not pure gold; there is some alloy in it. n.*

all right **1** all correct: *The answers were all right.* **2** satisfactory: *The work was not well done; but it was all right.* **3** yes: *'Will you come with me?' 'All right.'* **4** in good health; well: *He said he was feeling all right.* **5** in a satisfactory way: *The engine seemed to be working all right.*

all–round (ol′round′ or ôl′round′) able to do many things; useful in many ways: *an all-round athlete. adj.*

al·lude (ə lüd′) refer to indirectly; mention in passing: *Do not ask him about his failure; do not even allude to it. v.,* **al·lud·ed, al·lud·ing.**

al·lure (ə lür′) **1** fascinate; attract or charm: *Circus life allured him with its action and excitement.* **2** charm; fascination: *the allure of the sea.* 1 *v.,* **al·lured, al·lur·ing;** 2 *n.*

al·lu·sion (ə lü′zhən) an indirect or passing reference: *He was hurt by any allusion to his failure. n.*
☞ See note at **illusion.**

al·ly (ə lī′ for 1, al′ī or ə lī′ for 2) **1** combine or unite for some special purpose: *One country will ally itself with another to protect its people or its interests.* **2** a person or state united with another for some special purpose: *England and France were allies in World War II.* 1 *v.,* **al·lied, al·ly·ing;** 2 *n., pl.* **al·lies.**

al·ma·nac (ol′mə nak′ or ôl′mə nak′) a calendar of days, weeks, and months, often including information about the weather, the sun, moon, stars, tides, church days, and other facts. *n.*

al·might·y (ol mīt′ē or ôl mīt′ē) **1** possessing all power. **2 the Almighty,** God. 1 *adj.,* 2 *n.*

An almond, shown with and without its shell

al·mond (o′mənd or ä′mənd) **1** the nut or seed of a fruit growing in warm regions. **2** the tree the fruit grows on. **3** shaped like an almond. 1, 2 *n.,* 3 *adj.*

al·most (ol′mōst or ôl′mōst) nearly: *Nine is almost ten. adv.*

alms (omz or ämz) money or gifts to help the poor. *n. sing. or pl.*

a·loft (ə loft′) **1** far above the earth; high up: *Some birds fly thousands of feet aloft.* **2** high up among the sails and masts of a ship: *He went aloft to get a better view of the distant shore. adv., adj.*

a·lone (ə lōn′) **1** apart from other persons or things: *One tree stood alone on the hill.* **2** without anyone else: *One boy alone can do this work.* **3** without anything more: *Meat alone is not the best food for children.* 1–3 *adj.,* 1 *adv.*
leave alone or **let alone,** not bother; not meddle with: *Please let my doll alone.*

a·long (ə long′) **1** from one end of something to the other: *Trees are planted along the street.* **2** further; onward: *March along quickly.* **3** with oneself: *He took his dog along.* 1 *prep.,* 2, 3 *adv.*
all along, all the time: *He was here all along.*
along with, in company with: *I'll go along with you.*

a·long·side (ə long′sīd′ for 1, ə long′sīd′ for 2) **1** at the side: *Anchor alongside.* **2** by the side of; side by side with: *The boat was alongside the pier.* 1 *adv.,* 2 *prep.*

a·loof (ə lüf′) **1** away; apart: *One boy stood aloof from the other boys.* **2** reserved; withdrawn: *His aloof manner kept him from making many friends.* 1 *adv.,* 2 *adj.* **—a·loof′ness,** *n.*

a·loud (ə loud′) **1** loud enough to be heard; not in a whisper: *He spoke aloud, although he was alone. She read the story aloud to the others.* **2** loudly; in a loud voice: *He groaned aloud with pain. adv.*

al·pac·a (al pak′ə) **1** a South American sheeplike animal with long, soft, silky hair or wool: *The alpaca is a kind of llama.* **2** its wool. **3** cloth made from this wool. *n.*

hat, āge, fär; let, ēqual, tėrm; it, īce
hot, ōpen, ôrder; oil, out; cup, pu̇t, rüle
əbove, takən, pencəl, lemən, circəs
ch, child; ng, long; sh, ship
th, thin; ᴛʜ, then; zh, measure

al·pha·bet (al′fə bet′) 1 the set of letters used in writing a language: *The English alphabet has twenty-six letters.* 2 these letters arranged in a certain order, not as they are in words: *'D' is the fourth letter of the alphabet.* *n.*

al·pha·bet·i·cal (al′fə bet′ə kəl) arranged by letters in the order of the alphabet: *Dictionary entries are arranged in alphabetical order.* *adj.* —**al′pha·bet′i·cal·ly,** *adv.*

al·pha·bet·ize (al′fə bə tīz′) arrange in the order of the letters of the alphabet. *v.,* **al·pha·bet·ized, al·pha·bet·iz·ing.**

al·read·y (ol red′ē or ôl red′ē) before this time; by this time; even now: *You are half an hour late already. The baby has already broken his new toy.* *adv.*

al·so (ol′sō or ôl′sō) too; in addition: *That dress is pretty; it is also cheap.* *adv.*

Alta. Alberta.

al·tar (ol′tər or ôl′tər) 1 a table or stand in the most sacred part of a church or chapel. 2 a raised place built of earth or stone on which to make sacrifices or burn offerings to gods. *n.*

☞ **Altar** and **alter** are pronounced the same.

al·ter (ol′tər or ôl′tər) 1 make different; change: *If this coat is too large, a tailor can alter it to fit you.* 2 become different: *Since her summer on the farm, her whole outlook has altered.* *v.*

☞ See note at **altar.**

al·ter·a·tion (ol′tər ā′shən or ôl′tər ā′shən) a change: *Mother made some alterations in her new dress.* *n.*

al·ter·nate (ol′tər nāt′ or ôl′tər nāt′ for 1 and 2; ol tėr′nit or ôl tėr′nit, ol′tər nit or ôl′tər nit for 3, 4, and 5) 1 occur by turns, first one and then the other; be arranged by turns: *Squares and circles alternate in this row:* ○□○□○□○□○□○□○□○□. 2 take turns: *Lucy and her sister will alternate in setting the table.* 3 first one and then the other by turns: *The row has alternate squares and circles.* 4 every other: *I clean my room on alternate days because I don't have time every day.* 5 a person appointed to take the place of another if necessary; a substitute: *We had ten alternates on our hockey team.* 1, 2 *v.,* **al·ter·nat·ed, al·ter·nat·ing;** 3, 4 *adj.,* 5 *n.*

al·ter·nate·ly (ol′tər nit lē or ôl′tər nit lē, ol tėr′nit lē or ôl tėr′nit lē) by turns; first one and then the other. *adv.*

alternating current an electric current that reverses its direction at regular intervals.

al·ter·na·tive (ol tėr′nə tiv or ôl tėr′nə tiv) 1 giving or requiring a choice between two things: *Father offered the alternative plans of having a picnic or taking a trip on a steamboat.* 2 a choice between two things: *We have the alternative of going to a play or to a movie.* 3 one of the things to be chosen: *John chose the first alternative and stayed in school.* 1 *adj.,* 2, 3 *n.*

al·though (ol ᴛʜō′ or ôl ᴛʜō′) even if; in spite of the fact that; though: *Although it had rained all morning, they went on the hike.* *conj.*

al·tim·e·ter (al tim′ə tər or al′tə mē′tər) any instrument for measuring altitude: *Altimeters are used in aircraft to indicate height above the earth's surface.* *n.*

al·ti·tude (al′tə tyüd′ or al′tə tüd′) 1 height: *What altitude did the airplane reach?* 2 the height above sea level: *The altitude of Banff, Alberta, is 1380 metres.* 3 a high place: *At some altitudes the snow never melts.* *n.*

al·to (al′tō) 1 the lowest woman's voice; contralto. 2 a part in music to be sung by such a voice. 3 a person who sings this part. *n., pl.* **al·tos.**

al·to·geth·er (ol′tə geᴛʜ′ər or ôl′tə geᴛʜ′ər) 1 completely; entirely: *The house was altogether destroyed by fire.* 2 on the whole; considering everything: *Altogether, he was well pleased.* 3 all included: *Altogether there were ten books on the shelf.* *adv.*

al·um (al′əm) a white mineral salt used in medicine and in dyeing: *Alum is sometimes used to stop the bleeding of a small cut.* *n.*

al·u·min·i·um (al′ü min′ē əm) aluminum. *n.*

a·lu·mi·num (ə lü′mə nəm) a silver-white, very light and strong metal that does not tarnish easily: *Aluminum is used in aircraft and automobiles, for making pots and pans, and in many other products.* *n.*

al·ways (ol′wiz or ôl′wiz, ol′wāz or ôl′wāz) at all times; all the time: *Night always follows day. Mother is always cheerful.* *adv.*

am (am) a part of the present tense of the verb **be,** used with the pronoun *I: I am a student. I am going to the picnic today.* *v.*

a.m. or **A.M.** the time from midnight to noon: *Classes begin at 9 a.m.*

☞ **a.m.** is an abbreviation of the Latin words *ante meridiem* (an′tē mə rid′ē əm) meaning 'before noon.'

AM or **A.M.** amplitude modulation.

a·mal·gam·ate (ə mal′gə māt′) unite; combine; mix: *The two stores amalgamated to form one big store. The company amalgamated its three sales offices.* *v.,* **a·mal·gam·at·ed, a·mal·gam·at·ing.**

a·mass (ə mas′) heap together; pile up; accumulate: *The miser amassed a fortune.* *v.*

am·a·teur (am′ə chər or am′ə chür′) 1 a person who does something for pleasure, not for money or as a job: *Only amateurs can take part in the Olympics.* 2 a person who does something without showing the proper skills: *He plays the piano well, but on the violin he is an amateur, completely without training.* 3 of amateurs; made or done by amateurs: *an amateur play.* 1, 2 *n.,* 3 *adj.*

a·maze (ə māz′) surprise greatly; strike with sudden wonder: *She was so amazed by the surprise party that she could not think of anything to say.* *v.,* **a·mazed, a·maz·ing.**

a·maze·ment (ə māz′mənt) great surprise; sudden wonder: *The little girl was filled with amazement when she first saw the ocean.* *n.*

am·bas·sa·dor (am bas′ə dər) 1 a representative of highest rank sent by one government or ruler to another: *An ambassador lives in a foreign country and speaks and* *acts on behalf of his ruler or his government.* **2** a representative of a group who reflects its typical qualities: *Visiting Boy Scouts can be ambassadors of good will for their country.* *n.*

am·ber (am′bər) **1** a yellow or yellowish-brown substance resembling glass, used for jewellery and in making stems of pipes: *Amber is the resin of pine trees that grew long ago.* **2** made of amber: *amber beads.* **3** yellow or yellowish-brown: *amber beer.* 1, 3 *n.*, 2, 3 *adj.*

am·bi·tion (am bish′ən) **1** a strong desire for fame or success; a seeking after great power or a high position: *Because he was filled with ambition, he worked after school and on Saturdays.* **2** the thing for which one has a strong desire: *Her ambition was to be a great actress.* *n.*

am·bi·tious (am bish′əs) **1** having a strong desire for or to do something; very keen to succeed: *Being ambitious to get to university, my sister works hard.* **2** showing such desire: *He had an ambitious plan of building a rocket.* *adj.*

am·ble (am′bəl) **1** the way a horse goes when it first lifts the two legs on one side and then lifts the two on the other side. **2** go in that manner: *My horse can amble and trot.* **3** an easy, slow pace in walking. **4** go with an easy, slow pace. 1, 3 *n.*, 2, 4 *v.*, **am·bled, am·bling.**

am·bu·lance (am′byə ləns) an automobile, boat, or aircraft equipped to carry sick or wounded persons. *n.*

am·bush (am′bůsh) **1** a surprise attack from some hiding place on an approaching enemy. **2** attackers so hidden. **3** the place where the attackers are hidden. **4** attack from an ambush. **5** lying in wait: *They trapped their enemies by ambush and so were never defeated.* 1–3, 5 *n.*, 4 *v.*

a·me·ba (ə mē′bə) See **amoeba.**

a·men (ā′men′ or ä′men′) a word said at the end of a prayer: *'Amen' is supposed to mean 'May it become so' or 'Be it so!'* *interj.*

a·mend (ə mend′) **1** change: *The book of hockey rules has been amended many times.* **2** change for the better; correct: *It is time you amended your poor table manners.* *v.*

a·mend·ment (ə mend′mənt) **1** a change: *There have been many amendments to the rule book.* **2** a change for the better; a correction. *n.*

a·mends (ə mendz′) something given or paid to make up for a wrong, a loss, or an injury. *n. sing. or pl.*
make amends, make up for: *She promised to make amends for not doing her homework.*

A·mer·i·can (ə mer′ə kən) **1** of the United States; belonging to the United States: *Einstein became an American citizen.* **2** of America; in America: *Tomatoes, corn, and tobacco were originally American plants.* **3** a person born or living in North or South America: *The citizens of Mexico, Canada, and Argentina are sometimes called Americans in the broad sense of the term.* 1, 2 *adj.*, 3 *n.*

am·e·thyst (am′ə thist) **1** a purple or violet type of quartz, used for jewellery. **2** purple; violet. 1, 2 *n.*, 2 *adj.*

a·mi·a·ble (ā′mē ə bəl) good-natured and friendly; pleasant and agreeable: *Joan is a sweet, gentle, amiable girl.* *adj.*

a·mid (ə mid′) in the middle of; among: *The little church stood unharmed amid the ruins of the bombed village.* *prep.*

a·mid·ships (ə mid′ships) in or toward the middle of a ship. *adv.*

a·midst (ə midst′) amid. *prep.*

a·miss (ə mis′) wrong; not the way it should be; out of order: *Something is amiss when a boy will not eat for days.* *adv., adj.*
take amiss, be offended at because of a misunderstanding: *John had not meant to be rude to his mother, but she took his answer amiss.*

am·mo·nia (ə mōn′yə) **1** a colorless gas with a strong smell. **2** water with this gas dissolved in it: *Ammonia is useful for cleaning.* *n.*

am·mu·ni·tion (am′yə nish′ən) **1** powder, shot, bullets, bombs, and shells; military supplies that can be used against an enemy. **2** anything that can be shot, hurled, or thrown. *n.*

a·moe·ba (ə mē′bə) a very small animal having only one cell (def. 3): *Amoebas are so small that they can be seen only with a microscope.* *n., pl.* **a·moe·bas** or **a·moe·bae** (ə mē′bē or ə mē′bī). Sometimes spelled **ameba.**

a·mong (ə mung′) **1** surrounded by: *a house among the trees.* **2** a part of; a member of; one of: *Canada is among the largest countries of the world. His brothers were among the crowd.* **3** in equal portions to each of: *Divide the fruit among the boys.* *prep.*
among ourselves, yourselves, or **themselves, a** some with others: *The children quarrelled among themselves.* **b** each with all the others; as a group: *They agreed among themselves to have a party.*
☛ See note at **between.**

a·mongst (ə mungst′) among. *prep.*

a·mount (ə mount′) **1** quantity: *No amount of coaxing would make the dog leave his master.* **2** the total sum; the full value: *What is the amount of the bill for the groceries?* **3** add up; be equal: *The loss from the flood amounts to a million dollars. Keeping what belongs to another amounts to stealing.* 1, 2 *n.*, 3 *v.*

am·pere (am′pēr) a unit for measuring the strength of an electric current: *Ordinary light bulbs take from ¼ to ½ an ampere.* *Symbol:* A *n.*

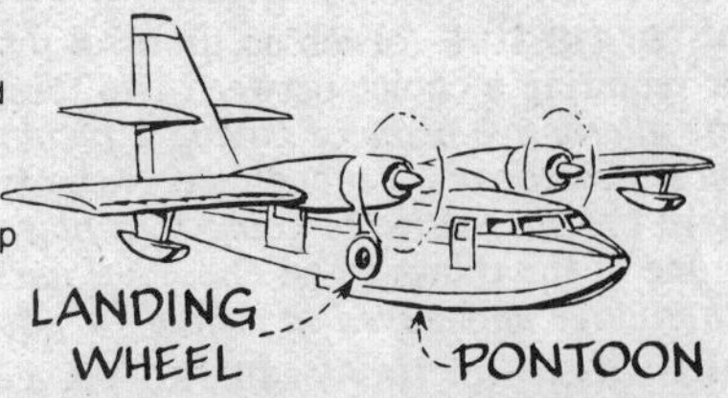

An amphibian (def. 3) The wheels are lowered for coming down on land. For coming down on water, the wheels are drawn up and the pontoon serves as a hull.

am·phib·i·an (am fib′ē ən) **1** an animal living both on land and in water: *Frogs are amphibians.* **2** a vehicle able to travel across land or water. **3** an aircraft so made that it can take off from or come down on either land or water. *n.*

am·phib·i·ous (am fib′ē əs) **1** able to live both on land and in water: *Frogs are amphibious.* **2** able to travel across land or water: *Some tanks are amphibious.* *adj.*

am·ple (am′pəl) 1 more than enough; abundant: *Take an ample supply of food, for we shall be gone all day.* 2 enough: *The money her mother gave her was ample for fares and lunches.* 3 large; big; roomy: *This house has ample closets.* *adj.* —**am′ply,** *adv.*

am·pli·fi·er (am′plə fī′ər) a device in or attached to a radio, phonograph, etc. for strengthening electrical impulses. *n.*

am·pli·fy (am′plə fī′) 1 make greater; make stronger: *When sound is amplified, it can be heard over a greater distance.* 2 make fuller; expand; enlarge: *The reporter had to amplify his description of the accident because the editor needed more details.* *v.,* **am·pli·fied, am·pli·fy·ing.**

am·pli·tude modulation (am′plə tyüd′ or am′plə tüd′) in broadcasting, the changing of the size of radio waves in order to transmit sound: *The abbreviation for amplitude modulation is AM.*

am·pu·tate (am′pyə tāt′) cut off, especially in a surgical operation: *The doctor amputated the soldier's wounded leg.* *v.,* **am·pu·tat·ed, am·pu·tat·ing.**

a·muse (ə myüz′) 1 cause to laugh or smile: *The playful puppy amused the baby.* 2 keep pleasantly interested; entertain: *The new toys amused the children.* *v.,* **a·mused, a·mus·ing.**

a·muse·ment (ə myüz′mənt) 1 enjoyment; pleasure; being amused: *The boy's amusement was so great that we all had to laugh with him.* 2 anything that amuses; entertainment; sport: *Most outdoor games are healthful amusements.* *n.*

an (ən; *stressed,* an) 1 any. 2 one: *Would you like an apple?* 3 each; every: *He earns one dollar an hour.* 4 for each: *fifty cents an apple.* *indefinite article.*

-an a suffix meaning: 1 of or having to do with ____: *Mohammedan means of or having to do with Mohammed.* 2 of or having to do with____or its people: *Asian means of or having to do with Asia or its people.* 3 a person born or living in ____: *Mexican means a person born in or living in Mexico.* Also **-ian.**

an·aes·the·tic (an′əs thet′ik) See **anesthetic.**

an·a·lyse or **an·a·lyze** (an′ə līz′) 1 separate into its parts: *A chemist can analyse water into two colorless gases, hydrogen and oxygen.* 2 examine the parts or elements of; find out the essential features of: *Many men have tried to analyse the causes of success. We analyse a sentence when we explain the form and use of every word in it.* *v.,* **an·a·lysed** or **an·a·lyzed, an·a·lys·ing** or **an·a·lyz·ing.**

a·nal·y·sis (ə nal′ə sis) 1 the separation of anything into its parts or elements: *The chemist made an analysis of the medicine to find out what it was made of.* 2 examining carefully and in detail: *Analysis of our plan showed that some changes should be made.* *n., pl.* **a·nal·y·ses** (ə nal′ə sēz′).

a·nat·o·my (ə nat′ə mē) 1 the structure of an animal or plant: *The anatomy of an earthworm is much simpler than that of a person.* 2 the science of the structure of animals or plants: *Anatomy is a part of biology.* *n.*

an·ces·tor (an′ses tər) a person from whom one is directly descended, such as one's father, mother, grandfather, or grandmother. *n.*

an·ces·tral (an ses′trəl) 1 of ancestors: *The ancestral*

hat, āge, fär; let, ēqual, tėrm; it, īce
hot, ōpen, ôrder; oil, out; cup, pu̇t, rüle
əbove, takən, pencəl, lemən, circəs
ch, child; ng, long; sh, ship
th, thin; ᴛʜ, then; zh, measure

home of the Acadians was France. 2 inherited from ancestors: *Curly hair is an ancestral trait in that family.* *adj.*

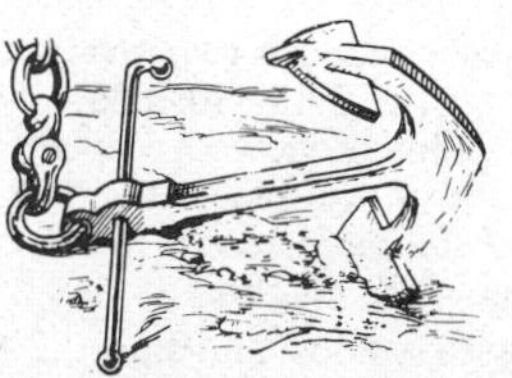
An anchor

an·chor (ang′kər) 1 a heavy piece of iron, usually having hooks, that is fastened to a ship or boat by a long chain or rope and dropped into the water: *A ship's anchor digs into the earth or catches onto the rocks at the bottom of a river, lake, etc. and so keeps the ship from drifting.* 2 hold in place with an anchor: *Can you anchor the ship?* 3 drop anchor: *The ship anchored in the bay.* 4 fix firmly: *We anchored the tent to the ground.* 5 anything that makes a person feel secure: *Her faith in God was her anchor during her great trouble.*
1, 5 *n.,* 2–4 *v.*

an·chor·age (ang′kər ij) a place to anchor. *n.*

an·cient (ān′shənt) 1 belonging to times long past: *In Egypt we saw the ruins of an ancient temple built six thousand years ago.* 2 very old: *An ancient house stood on the corner.* 3 **the ancients,** people who lived long ago, especially the Greeks and Romans. 1, 2 *adj.,* 3 *n.*

and (ənd; *stressed,* and) 1 as well as: *You can come and go in the car.* *Symbol:* & 2 added to; with: *4 and 2 make 6.* *conj.*

and·i·ron (and′ī′ərn) one of a pair of metal supports for wood in a fireplace; firedog. See **fireplace** for picture. *n.*

an·ec·dote (an′ik dōt′) a short account of some interesting incident or event: *Many anecdotes are told about Sir John A. Macdonald.* *n.*

a·nem·o·ne (ə nem′ə nē) a plant with slender stems and white flowers: *The anemone appears early in the spring.* *n.*

an·es·thet·ic (an′əs thet′ik) a substance that causes entire or partial loss of the feeling of pain, touch, etc.: *Anesthetics are used by doctors so that patients will feel no pain during operations.* *n.* Also spelled **anaesthetic.**

a·new (ə nyü′ or ə nü′) 1 again; once more: *He made so many mistakes that he had to begin his work anew.* 2 in a new way: *The architect planned the building anew.* *adv.*

an·gel (ān′jəl) 1 a messenger from God. 2 a person like an angel in goodness, innocence, and loveliness. *n.*

an·gel·ic (an jel′ik) 1 of angels; heavenly. 2 like that of an angel; pure; innocent; good and lovely: *an angelic face.* *adj.*

an·ger (ang′gər) 1 a feeling of wanting to get back at

a person, animal, or thing that hurts or wrongs one: *In a moment of anger, I hit my brother.* 2 make angry: *The boy's disobedience angered his father.* 1 *n.*, 2 *v.*

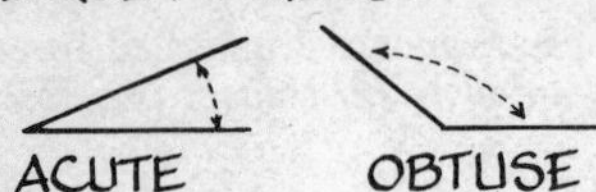

an·gle[1] (ang′gəl) **1** the space between two straight lines or surfaces that meet. **2** the figure formed by two such lines or surfaces. **3** a point of view: *From any angle the job was excellent.* **4** move, place, turn, or bend at an angle: *He angled the table across the corner of the room.* 1–3 *n.*, 4 *v.*, **an·gled, an·gling.**

an·gle[2] (ang′gəl) **1** fish with a hook and line. **2** try to get something by using tricks or schemes: *She angled for an invitation to his party by flattering him.* *v.*, **an·gled, an·gling.**

an·gler (ang′glər) a person who fishes with a hook and line. *n.*

an·gle·worm (ang′gəl wėrm′) earthworm. *n.*

An·gli·can (ang′glə kən) **1** of or having to do with the Anglican Church of Canada, or the Church of England or other associated churches. **2** a member of one of these churches. 1 *adj.*, 2 *n.*

Anglican Church of Canada a Christian church associated with the Church of England.

An·glo·phone or **an·glo·phone** (ang′glō fōn′) *Cdn.* an English-speaking person who lives in a bilingual or multilingual country. *n.*

An·glo–Sax·on (ang′glō sak′sən) **1** an Englishman of the period from about A.D. 450 to A.D. 1066: *King Alfred was an Anglo-Saxon.* **2** the kind of English spoken by these people; Old English. **3** a person of English descent. **4** of or having to do with the Anglo-Saxons or their speech. 1–3 *n.*, 4 *adj.*

an·gry (ang′grē) **1** feeling or showing anger: *I was very angry when he kicked my dog.* **2** moved by anger: *My friend's angry words hurt my feelings.* **3** stormy: *an angry sky.* *adj.*, **an·gri·er, an·gri·est. —an′gri·ly,** *adv.* **—an′gri·ness,** *n.*

an·guish (ang′gwish) very great pain or grief: *He was in anguish until the doctor set his broken leg.* *n.*

an·gu·lar (ang′gyə lər) **1** having angles; having sharp corners: *an angular piece of rock.* **2** somewhat thin and bony; not plump: *Many basketball players have tall, angular bodies.* *adj.*

an·i·mal (an′ə məl) **1** any living thing that is not a plant: *Most animals can move about while most plants cannot; most animals are unable to make their own food, but most plants can.* **2** any creature other than man. **3** any four-footed creature: *Cows, sheep, lions, and elephants are animals.* *n.*

an·i·mate (an′ə māt′) make lively and gay: *His funny stories animated the whole party.* *v.*, **an·i·mat·ed, an·i·mat·ing.**

an·i·mat·ed (an′ə māt′id) lively; vigorous: *The two boys had an animated discussion about yesterday's game.* *adj.*

animated cartoon a series of drawings arranged to be photographed and shown as a motion picture.

an·i·ma·tion (an′ə mā′shən) liveliness; spirit: *He acted his part with great animation.* *n.*

an·i·mos·i·ty (an′ə mos′ə tē) active or violent dislike; ill will: *The speaker's insults aroused the animosity of the crowd.* *n.*, *pl.* **an·i·mos·i·ties.**

an·kle (ang′kəl) **1** the joint that connects the foot with the leg. **2** the part of the leg between this joint and the calf. See **leg** for picture. *n.*

an·klet (ang′klit) **1** a short sock. **2** a band around the ankle: *An anklet may be an ornament, a brace, or a fetter.* *n.*

an·nex (ə neks′ for 1, an′eks for 2) **1** join or add a small thing to a larger thing: *Britain annexed Acadia in 1713.* **2** something added; an added part: *We are building an annex to the school.* 1 *v.*, 2 *n.*

an·nex·a·tion (an′ək sā′shən) annexing or being annexed: *the annexation of Acadia by Britain.* *n.*

an·ni·hi·late (ə nī′ə lāt′) destroy completely; wipe out of existence: *The flood annihilated more than thirty towns and villages.* *v.*, **an·ni·hi·lat·ed, an·ni·hi·lat·ing.**

an·ni·hi·la·tion (ə nī′ə lā′shən) complete destruction. *n.*

an·ni·ver·sa·ry (an′ə vėr′sə rē) **1** the yearly return of a special date: *Tomorrow is the anniversary of his birthday.* **2** a celebration of the yearly return of a special date: *a wedding anniversary.* *n.*, *pl.* **an·ni·ver·sa·ries.**

an·no Dom·i·ni (an′ō dom′ə nē′ or an′ō dom′ə nī′) A.D.; in the year of our Lord; after the birth of Christ.

an·nounce (ə nouns′) make known; give formal notice of: *Please announce to the children that there will be no school this afternoon.* *v.*, **an·nounced, an·nounc·ing.**

an·nounce·ment (ə nouns′mənt) **1** announcing; making known: *We waited for the announcement of the winner's name.* **2** what is announced or made known by private or public notice: *The preacher made several announcements.* *n.*

an·nounc·er (ə noun′sər) in radio or television, a person who introduces programs, reads news, etc. *n.*

an·noy (ə noi′) tease; bother; disturb; make angry: *The baby annoys his sister by pulling her hair.* *v.*

an·noy·ance (ə noi′əns) **1** a feeling of being bothered or irritated: *Her face showed her annoyance at the delay.* **2** anything that annoys: *The heavy traffic on our street is an annoyance.* *n.*

an·nu·al (an′yü əl) **1** coming once a year: *Your birthday is an annual event.* **2** in a year; for a year: *Mr. White's annual income is $7000.* **3** living one year or season: *Corn and beans are annual plants.* **4** a plant that lives just one year or season. 1–3 *adj.*, 4 *n.*

an·nu·al·ly (an′yü əl ē) yearly; each year; year by year. *adv.*

a·noint (ə noint′) **1** put oil on; rub with ointment: *Anoint sunburned skin with cold cream.* **2** apply ointment or oil to a person as a part of a ceremony: *The bishop anointed the new king.* *v.*

a·non (ə non′) **1** in a short time; soon. **2** again; at another time: *I won't say good-bye, for I shall see you anon.* *adv.*

anon. anonymous.

a·non·y·mous (ə non′ə məs) **1** by or from a person

whose name is not known or given: *An anonymous book is one published without the name of the author.* 2 of unknown name: *The author of this poem is anonymous.* *adj.*

an·oth·er (ə nuᴛʜ′ər) 1 one more: *Drink another glass of milk (adj.). He ate a bar of candy and then asked for another (pron.).* 2 a different: *Show me another kind of hat.* 3 a different one; someone or something else: *I don't like this book; give me another.* 1, 2 *adj.*, 1, 3 *pron.*

ans. answer.

an·swer (an′sər) 1 speak or write words in return to a question: *I asked him a question, but he would not answer.* 2 words spoken or written in return to a question: *The boy gave a quick answer.* 3 a gesture or act in return: *A nod was her only answer.* 4 act in return to a call, signal, etc.; respond: *He knocked on the door, but no one answered.* 5 a solution to a problem: *What is the correct answer?* 6 serve: *A sheet of paper answered for a tablecloth.* 1, 4, 6 *v.*, 2, 3, 5 *n.*

answer back, reply in a rude, saucy way.

answer for, be responsible for: *A father must answer for his child's acts.*

answer to, correspond to: *This boy answers to your description.*

ant (ant) a small insect that lives in tunnels in the ground or in wood: *Ants live together in large groups or communities called colonies.* *n.* **—ant′like′**, *adj.*

an·tag·o·nism (an tag′ə niz′əm) active opposition; conflict: *During the argument, John's antagonism showed plainly in his voice.* *n.*

an·tag·o·nist (an tag′ə nist) one who fights, struggles, or contends against another in a combat or contest of any kind; an opponent: *The knight defeated each antagonist who came against him.* *n.*

an·tag·o·nis·tic (an tag′ə nis′tik) acting against each other; opposing; conflicting: *Cats and dogs are antagonistic.* *adj.*

an·tag·o·nize (an tag′ə nīz′) 1 make an enemy of: *Her unkind remarks antagonized people who had been her friends.* 2 oppose. *v.*, **an·tag·o·nized, an·tag·o·niz·ing.**

ant·arc·tic (ant ärk′tik or ant är′tik) 1 at or near the South Pole; of the south polar region: *There is an antarctic continent.* 2 **the Antarctic, a** the south polar region. **b** the Antarctic Ocean. 1 *adj.*, 2 *n.*

Antarctic Circle an imaginary line around the earth 66½° south of the equator, marking off the south polar region.

Antarctic Ocean the ocean of the south polar region.

ante– a prefix meaning before, as in *antedate, anteroom.*

ant·eat·er (ant′ēt′ər) any of various animals that eat ants and termites, which they catch with their long, sticky tongues. *n.*

an·te·date (an′tē dāt′) come before in time; occur earlier than: *Shakespeare's 'Hamlet' antedates 'Macbeth' by about six years.* *v.*, **an·te·dat·ed, an·te·dat·ing.**

an·te·lope (an′tə lōp′) 1 one of a large group of four-legged animals found mainly in Africa, having hoofs, horns that are not shed, and, usually, long, slender legs: *Antelopes resemble deer, but belong to the same family as goats and cattle.* 2 a very swift, four-legged animal

hat, āge, fär; let, ēqual, tėrm; it, īce
hot, ōpen, ôrder; oil, out; cup, pu̇t, rüle
əbove, takən, pencəl, lemən, circəs
ch, child; ng, long; sh, ship
th, thin; ᴛʜ, then; zh, measure

A kind of African antelope, the gazelle — about 83 cm high at the shoulder

A pronghorn antelope — about 95 cm high at the shoulder

of the North American prairies; pronghorn. *n., pl.* **an·te·lope** or **an·te·lopes.**

an·ten·na (an ten′ə) 1 a feeler on the head of an insect, lobster, etc. See **insect** for picture. 2 in radio or television, a wire or set of wires for sending out or receiving electric waves. *n., pl.* **an·ten·nae** (an ten′ē) for 1, **an·ten·nas** for 2.

an·te·room (an′tē rüm′) a small room leading to a larger one; a waiting room. *n.*

an·them (an′thəm) 1 a song of praise, devotion, or patriotism: *'O Canada' is sung as the national anthem of Canada.* 2 a piece of sacred music, usually with words from some passage in the Bible. *n.*

an·ther (an′thər) the part of the stamen of a flower that bears the pollen. See **flower** for picture. *n.*

ant hill a heap of dirt piled up by ants around the entrance to their underground nest.

an·thra·cite (an′thrə sīt′) a type of hard, shiny coal that burns with very little smoke or flame. *n.*

anti– a prefix meaning: 1 against ____; opposed to ____: *Anti-aircraft means against aircraft. Antislavery means opposed to slavery.* 2 preventing or acting against ____: *Antiseptic means preventing or acting against infection.*

an·ti·bi·ot·ic (an′tē bī ot′ik) a drug produced by bacteria in fungi, etc. that destroys or weakens disease germs: *Penicillin is an antibiotic.* *n.*

an·ti·bod·y (an′tē bod′ē) a substance produced in the blood of animals or man, which destroys or weakens poisons found in bacteria, viruses, snake venom, etc. *n., pl.* **an·ti·bod·ies.**

an·tic·i·pate (an tis′ə pāt′) 1 expect; look forward to: *He had anticipated a good vacation in the mountains; but when the time came, he was sick.* 2 do before others do; be ahead of in doing: *The Chinese anticipated our discovery of gunpowder.* 3 understand ahead of time; consider in advance: *When Mother has a headache, Ruth anticipates all her wishes.* *v.*, **an·tic·i·pat·ed, an·tic·i·pat·ing.**

an·tic·i·pa·tion (an tis′ə pā′shən) anticipating or looking forward to; expectation: *The settler cut more wood than usual, in anticipation of a long winter.* *n.*

an·tics (an′tiks) funny gestures and actions; capers: *The clown amused us by his antics.* *n. pl.*

an·ti·dote (an′tē dōt′) any medicine that acts against a poison or a disease; a remedy: *Milk is an antidote for some poisons.* *n.*

an·ti·freeze (an′tē frēz′) a substance added to a liquid to lower its freezing point: *Alcohol is used as an antifreeze in automobile radiators because it prevents the water from freezing during cold weather.* *n.*

an·tip·a·thy (an tip′ə thē) strong dislike: *He felt an antipathy to snakes.* *n., pl.* **an·tip·a·thies.**

an·ti·quat·ed (an′tə kwāt′id) old fashioned; out-of-date: *Most science books written twenty years ago are now antiquated.* *adj.*

an·tique (an tēk′) **1** of times long ago; from times long ago: *This antique chair was made in 1750.* **2** something made long ago: *This carved chest is a real antique.* 1 *adj.,* 2 *n.*

an·tiq·ui·ty (an tik′wə tē) **1** oldness; great age: *That vase is of such great antiquity that nobody knows how old it is.* **2** times long ago, especially those before A.D. 476; the early ages of history: *Moses and Caesar were two great men of antiquity.* **3** the people of ancient times. *n., pl.* **an·tiq·ui·ties.**

an·ti·sep·tic (an′tə sep′tik) **1** a substance to kill disease germs and prevent infection: *Iodine is an antiseptic.* **2** preventing infection: *an antiseptic ointment.* 1 *n.,* 2 *adj.*

an·ti·tox·in (an′tē tok′sən) a substance formed in the body that makes a person safe from the poison of an infection or disease. *n.*

ant·ler (ant′lər) **1** a horn of a deer, elk, moose, etc. **2** a branch of such a horn. *n.*

an·to·nym (an′tə nim′) a word that means the opposite of another word: *'Hot' is the antonym of 'cold.'* *n.*

an·vil (an′vəl) an iron block on which metals such as iron are hammered and shaped while hot and soft. *n.*

anx·i·e·ty (ang zī′ə tē) **1** uneasy thoughts or fears about what may happen; a troubled, worried, or uneasy feeling: *Mothers feel anxiety when their children are sick.* **2** eager desire: *Her anxiety to succeed led her to work hard.* *n., pl.* **anx·i·e·ties.**

anx·ious (angk′shəs) **1** uneasy because of thoughts or fears about what may happen; troubled; worried: *Father felt anxious about the children, who had been gone an hour too long. The week of the flood was an anxious time for all of us.* **2** wishing very much; eager: *He was anxious for a bicycle. She was anxious to please her mother.* *adj.* **—anx′ious·ly,** *adv.* **—anx′ious·ness,** *n.*

an·y (en′ē) **1** one out of many: *Choose any book you like.* **2** some: *'Have you any fresh fruit?' (adj.). 'No, we haven't any' (pron.).* **3** at all: *Did she cry any?* **4** every: *Any child knows that.* 1, 2, 4 *adj.,* 2 *pron.,* 3 *adv.*

an·y·bod·y (en′ē bud′ē or en′ē bod′ē) any person; anyone: *Has anybody been here?* *pron.*

an·y·how (en′ē hou′) **1** in any way whatever: *It is wrong anyhow you look at it.* **2** in any case; at any rate; anyway: *I can see as well as you can, anyhow.* **3** carelessly; in ways that are not right and proper. *adv.*

an·y·one (en′ē wun′ or en′ē wən) anybody; any person: *Anyone in the school may come to the party.* *pron.*

an·y·thing (en′ē thing′) **1** any thing: *Have you anything to eat?* **2** at all: *Is your doll anything like mine?* 1 *pron.,* 2 *adv.*

an·y·way (en′ē wā′) in any case: *I am coming anyway, no matter what you say.* *adv.*

an·y·where (en′ē wer′ or en′ē hwer′) in, at, or to any place: *I will meet you anywhere you say.* *adv.*

a·or·ta (ā ôr′tə) the main artery that carries the blood from the left side of the heart to all parts of the body except the lungs. *n., pl.* **a·or·tas** or **a·or·tae** (ā ôr′tē or ā ôr′tī).

a·pace (ə pās′) swiftly; fast: *The summer flew by, and school days were coming on apace.* *adv.*

a·part (ə pärt′) **1** to pieces; in pieces; in separate parts: *The boy took the watch apart to see what made it tick.* **2** away from each other: *Keep the dogs apart.* **3** to one side; aside: *He stood apart from the others.* *adv.*

apart from, besides; except for: *Apart from that one mistake, it was a good plan.*

a·part·ment (ə pärt′mənt) a self-contained set of rooms to live in. *n.*

apartment block or **house** a building containing a number of apartments.

ap·a·thy (ap′ə thē) **1** a lack of feeling or interest; dullness of feeling; indifference: *The old miser heard the beggar's story with apathy.* **2** a lack of interest or desire for activity: *The apathy of the lazy boy was annoying.* *n.*

ape (āp) **1** a tail-less, long-armed animal resembling a monkey: *Apes are able to stand almost erect and to walk on two feet. Chimpanzees, gorillas, and gibbons are apes.* **2** a person who imitates or mimics. **3** imitate; mimic: *The girl aped the way the movie star fixed her hair.* 1, 2 *n.,* 3 *v.,* **aped, ap·ing. —ape′like′,** *adj.*

ap·er·ture (ap′ər chər) an opening; a gap or hole: *A window is an aperture for letting in light and air.* *n.*

a·pex (ā′peks) the highest point; peak; tip: *Every triangle has an apex.* *n., pl.* **a·pex·es** or **ap·i·ces** (ā′pə sēz′ or ap′ə sēz′).

a·phid (ā′fid or af′id) a very small insect that lives by sucking juices from plants. *n.*

a·piece (ə pēs′) each; for each one: *These apples are twelve cents apiece.* *adv.*

a·pol·o·get·ic (ə pol′ə jet′ik) **1** making an apology; expressing regret for a fault: *He sent me an apologetic note excusing his failure to come to my party.* **2** suggesting that one feels inferior or at a disadvantage: *He answered the principal in an apologetic voice.* *adj.*

hat, āge, fär; let, ēqual, tėrm; it, īce
hot, ōpen, ôrder; oil, out; cup, pủt, rüle
əbove, takən, pencəl, lemən, circəs
ch, child; ng, long; sh, ship
th, thin; ᴛʜ, then; zh, measure

a·pol·o·gize (ə pol′ə jīz′) say one is sorry; make an apology: *She apologized for hurting my feelings.* *v.*, **a·pol·o·gized, a·pol·o·giz·ing.**

a·pol·o·gy (ə pol′ə jē) **1** words saying one is sorry for an offence, fault, or accident; words asking pardon: *Make an apology to the lady for hitting her. We made our apologies for being late.* **2** a poor substitute: *One piece of toast is only an apology for breakfast.* *n., pl.* **a·pol·o·gies.**

a·pos·tle or **A·pos·tle** (ə pos′əl) **1** one of the twelve disciples chosen by Christ to go forth and preach the gospel to all the world. **2** any early Christian leader or missionary. *n.*

a·pos·tro·phe (ə pos′trə fē) a sign (') used: (1) to show the omission of one or more letters, as in *o'er* for *over, aren't* for *are not.* (2) to show the possessive forms of nouns, as in *John's book, the lion's den.* (3) to form certain plurals: *There are two* o's *in 'apology' and four* 9's in 959 990. *n.*

a·poth·e·car·y (ə poth′ə ker′ē) druggist. *n., pl.* **a·poth·e·car·ies.**

ap·pal or **ap·pall** (ə pol′ or ə pôl′) fill with horror; terrify; dismay: *She was appalled when she saw the river had risen to the doorstep. We were appalled at the thought of an atomic war.* *v.*, **ap·palled, ap·pal·ling.**

ap·pa·ra·tus (ap′ə rā′təs or ap′ə rat′əs) things necessary to carry out a purpose or for a particular use: *Tools, special instruments, and machines are apparatus. A chemical set is apparatus; so are a grocer's scales and the equipment in a gymnasium.* *n., pl.* **ap·pa·ra·tus** or **ap·pa·ra·tus·es.**

ap·par·el (ə par′əl or ə per′əl) **1** clothing or dress: *Does this store sell women's apparel?* **2** clothe; dress up: *Horseback riders, gaily apparelled, formed part of the circus parade.* 1 *n.*, 2 *v.*, **ap·par·elled** or **ap·par·eled, ap·par·el·ling** or **ap·par·el·ing.**

ap·par·ent (ə par′ənt or ə per′ənt) **1** plain to see; so plain as not to be missed: *The many beautiful tulips are apparent to all visitors in Ottawa during the spring.* **2** easily understood: *It is apparent that the days become shorter in November.* **3** seeming; that appears to be: *The apparent thief was innocent; we found the real thief later.* *adj.*

ap·par·ent·ly (ə par′ənt lē or ə per′ənt lē) **1** seemingly; as far as one can judge by appearances: *Apparently the baby had chicken pox.* **2** clearly; plainly: *He had quite apparently hurt his leg.* *adv.*

ap·pa·ri·tion (ap′ə rish′ən) **1** a ghost: *The apparition, clothed in white, glided through the wall.* **2** the appearance of something strange or unexpected. *n.*

ap·peal (ə pēl′) **1** ask earnestly for help, sympathy, etc.: *The children appealed to their mother when they were in trouble.* **2** an earnest request; a call to the feelings: *She made one last appeal to her father to forgive her.* **3** call on some person to decide some matter in your favor: *When Mother said 'No,' Steve would appeal to Father.* **4** a call on some person to decide some matter in your favor: *Sometimes his appeals were successful.* **5** be interesting, attractive, or enjoyable: *Blue and red appeal to me, but I don't like purple or yellow.* 1, 3, 5 *v.*, 2, 4 *n.*

ap·pear (ə pēr′) **1** be seen; come in sight: *One by one the stars appear.* **2** seem; look: *The apple appeared sound on the outside, but it was rotten inside.* **3** be published or otherwise presented to the public: *His latest book appeared a year ago. The movie will appear soon.* **4** show or present oneself in public: *The famous singer will appear on TV tonight.* *v.*

ap·pear·ance (ə pēr′əns) **1** appearing; coming in sight: *His appearance in the doorway was welcomed with shouts.* **2** a coming before the public: *The singer made her first appearance in a concert in Montreal.* **3** the outward look of anything: *The appearance of the old stone house made us think it was empty.* **4 appearances,** *pl.* outward show, especially when thought of in contrast to some underlying fault or misfortune: *After he lost his job, he found it hard to keep up appearances.* **5** something that appears; an object seen. *n.*

ap·pease (ə pēz′) **1** satisfy: *A good dinner will appease your hunger.* **2** make calm; quiet: *The mayor appeased the angry crowd by promising to build more houses.* *v.*, **ap·peased, ap·peas·ing.**

ap·pend (ə pend′) add to a larger thing; attach as a supplement: *A list of books for further reading is appended to the chapter.* *v.*

ap·pend·age (ə pen′dij) something attached to some larger thing; an addition: *The tail of a cat is an appendage.* *n.*

ap·pen·di·ci·tis (ə pen′də sī′tis) an inflammation of the appendix (def. 2.). *n.*

ap·pen·dix (ə pen′diks) **1** an addition at the end of a book or document. **2** a small growth attached to the large intestine. See **alimentary canal** for picture. *n., pl.* **ap·pen·dix·es** or **ap·pen·di·ces** (ə pen′də sēz′).

ap·pe·tite (ap′ə tīt′) **1** a desire for food: *Since she had no appetite, they had to coax her to eat.* **2** desire: *The lively boys had a great appetite for excitement and amusement.* *n.*

ap·pe·tiz·ing (ap′ə tīz′ing) arousing or exciting the appetite: *appetizing food.* *adj.*

ap·plaud (ə plod′ or ə plôd′) **1** express approval by clapping hands, shouting, etc.: *The audience at a concert or play applauds anything that is pleasing.* **2** approve; praise: *His parents applauded his decision to remain in school.* *v.*

ap·plause (ə ploz′ or ə plôz′) **1** approval expressed by clapping hands, shouting, etc.: *The applause for the singer's good performance was deafening.* **2** approval; praise. *n.*

ap·ple (ap′əl) **1** the firm, fleshy fruit of a tree widely grown in temperate regions: *Apples are usually red, yellow, or green, and are eaten either raw or cooked.* **2** the tree the fruit grows on. *n.*

ap·ple·sauce (ap′əl sos′ or ap′əl sôs′) apples cut in pieces and cooked with sugar and water until soft. *n.*

ap·pli·ance (ə plī′əns) a tool, a small machine, or some other device used in doing something: *Can openers, vacuum cleaners, washing machines, refrigerators, etc. are household appliances.* *n.*

ap·pli·cant (ap′lə kənt) a person who applies for a job, money, position, help, etc.: *Are you an applicant for this job?* *n.*

ap·pli·ca·tion (ap′lə kā′shən) **1** using; a use: *The application of what you know will help you solve new problems.* **2** applying or putting on: *the application of paint to a house.* **3** the thing applied: *This application is made of cold cream and ointment.* **4** a formal request: *I have put in my application to become a Boy Scout.* **5** continued effort; close attention: *By application to his work he got a better job.* *n.*

ap·ply (ə plī′) **1** put on: *He applied two coats of paint to the table.* **2** put into effect; use: *He knows the rule but does not know how to apply it.* **3** be useful or suitable; fit: *When does this rule apply?* **4** ask formally: *She applied for a job.* **5** set to work and stick to it: *She applied herself to her music.* *v.,* **ap·plied, ap·ply·ing.**

ap·point (ə point′) **1** name to an office or position; choose: *This man was appointed postmaster.* **2** decide on a time or place to see or meet someone: *He appointed the schoolhouse as the place for the meeting. We shall appoint 8 o'clock as the hour to begin.* *v.*

ap·point·ment (ə point′mənt) **1** naming to an office or position; choosing: *The appointment of Joan as secretary pleased her friends.* **2** an office or position. **3** an arrangement to see or meet someone at a certain place: *I have an appointment at 4 o'clock.* *n.*

ap·pre·ci·a·ble (ə prē′shē ə bəl) that can be appreciated; enough to be felt or estimated: *When he was ill, he suffered an appreciable loss of weight.* *adj.*

ap·pre·ci·ate (ə prē′shē āt′) **1** think highly of; recognize the worth or quality of; value; enjoy: *Almost everybody appreciates good food.* **2** be thankful for: *We appreciate your help.* **3** estimate; have an opinion of the value, worth, or quality of: *Everyone can appreciate the danger of war.* **4** be aware of: *A musician can appreciate small differences in sounds.* *v.,* **ap·pre·ci·at·ed, ap·pre·ci·at·ing.**

ap·pre·ci·a·tion (ə prē′shē ā′shən) **1** valuing highly; sympathetic understanding: *She has no appreciation of art and music.* **2** appreciating or valuing. *n.*

ap·pre·ci·a·tive (ə prē′shē ə tiv or ə prē′shē ā′tiv) having appreciation; showing appreciation; recognizing the value: *She was appreciative of the smallest kindness.* *adj.*

ap·pre·hend (ap′ri hend′) **1** understand; grasp with the mind: *I apprehended his meaning more from his gestures than from the queer sounds he made.* **2** look forward to with fear; fear and expect: *A guilty man apprehends danger in every sound.* **3** seize; arrest: *The thief was apprehended and put in jail.* *v.*

ap·pre·hen·sion (ap′ri hen′shən) **1** fearful expecting of danger or harm; fear; dread: *The roar of the hurricane filled us with apprehension.* **2** understanding; grasping by the mind: *He has a clear apprehension of the facts.* **3** seizing; an arrest: *the apprehension of a thief.* *n.*

ap·pre·hen·sive (ap′ri hen′siv) fearfully expecting danger or harm; afraid; anxious: *The captain was apprehensive for the safety of his passengers during the storm.* *adj.* **—ap′pre·hen′sive·ly,** *adv.* **—ap′pre·hen′·sive·ness,** *n.*

ap·pren·tice (ə pren′tis) **1** a person who is learning a trade or an art by working at it under skilled supervision. **2** set to work as an apprentice: *His father apprenticed him to a printer.* 1 *n.,* 2 *v.,* **ap·pren·ticed, ap·pren·tic·ing.**

ap·pren·tice·ship (ə pren′tis ship) **1** the condition of being an apprentice. **2** the time during which one is an apprentice. *n.*

ap·proach (ə prōch′) **1** come near or nearer in space or time: *Walk softly as you approach the bed. Winter is approaching.* **2** come near or nearer to in character, condition, or amount: *The wind was approaching a gale.* **3** coming near or nearer: *the approach of night.* **4** a way by which a place or a person can be reached: *The approach to the house was a narrow path. His best approach to the king lay through a friend.* **5** a way of dealing with something: *a new approach to mathematics.* 1, 2 *v.,* 3–5 *n.*

ap·proach·a·ble (ə prōch′ə bəl) **1** that can be approached: *The fishing camp was approachable from the south only.* **2** easy to approach: *He looks stern but is really very friendly and approachable.* *adj.*

ap·pro·pri·ate (ə prō′prē it for 1, ə prō′prē āt′ for 2 and 3) **1** suitable; proper: *Blue jeans and a sweater are appropriate clothes for the hike.* **2** set aside for some special use: *The town appropriates money for the care of its roads.* **3** take for oneself: *You should not appropriate other people's belongings without their permission.* 1 *adj.,* 2, 3 *v.,* **ap·pro·pri·at·ed, ap·pro·pri·at·ing. —ap·pro′pri·ate·ly,** *adv.*

ap·pro·pri·a·tion (ə prō′prē ā′shən) **1** a sum of money set aside for a special use: *The school received an appropriation of a thousand dollars for a new playground.* **2** taking for oneself: *His appropriation of the money was not right.* *n.*

ap·prov·al (ə prüv′əl) **1** approving; praise; favorable opinion: *We all like others to show approval of what we do.* **2** consent: *The principal gave approval to our plans.* *n.*

on approval, so that the customer can decide whether to buy or not; on trial: *Mother sent back the drapes that the store had sent on approval.*

ap·prove (ə prüv′) **1** think well of; be pleased with: *The teacher looked at the boy's work and approved it.* **2** agree; give approval: *I'm not sure I approve of what you want to do. I explained my plan to the rest of the class and they all approved.* **3** consent to: *Mother and Father approved our plans for the summer.* *v.,* **ap·proved, ap·prov·ing.**

ap·prox·i·mate (ə prok′sə mit for 1, ə prok′sə māt′ for 2) **1** nearly correct: *The approximate length of a nautical mile is 6080 feet; the exact length is 6080.20 feet.* **2** come near to; approach: *Your account of what happened approximated the truth, but there were several small errors. The crowd approximated a thousand people.* 1 *adj.,* 2 *v.,* **ap·prox·i·mat·ed, ap·prox·i·mat·ing. —ap·prox′i·mate·ly,** *adv.*

Apr. April.

ap·ri·cot (ap′rə kot′ or ā′prə kot′) **1** a pale orange-colored fruit, resembling a peach but smaller. **2** the tree the fruit grows on. **3** pale orange-yellow. 1–3 *n.,* 3 *adj.*

A·pril (ā′prəl) the fourth month of the year: *April has 30 days.* *n.*

☞ **April** came into English in the Middle Ages from the French name for this month.

hat, āge, fär; let, ēqual, tėrm; it, īce
hot, ōpen, ôrder; oil, out; cup, pu̇t, rüle
əbove, takən, pencəl, lemən, circəs
ch, child; ng, long; sh, ship
th, thin; ꟻH, then; zh, measure

April fool a person who gets fooled on April Fools' Day.

April Fools' Day April 1, a day observed by fooling people with tricks and practical jokes.

a·pron (ā′prən) 1 a garment worn over the front part of the body to protect one's clothes: *A carpenter's apron has pockets for nails.* 2 the front part of an area or surface: *The apron of a stage lies in front of the curtain. The apron of an airport is the paved area in front of the hangars or the main building.* *n.*

apt (apt) 1 fitted by nature; likely: *A careless person is apt to make mistakes.* 2 suitable or fitting: *His apt reply to the question showed that he had understood it very well.* 3 quick to learn: *Some pupils in our class are more apt than others.* *adj.* **—apt′ly,** *adv.* **—apt′ness,** *n.*

apt. apartment. *pl.* **apts.**

ap·ti·tude (ap′tə tyüd′ or ap′tə tüd′) 1 a natural tendency; ability; capacity: *Edison had a great aptitude for inventing things.* 2 readiness in learning; quickness to understand: *At school she shows great aptitude.* *n.*

a·quar·i·um (ə kwer′ē əm) 1 a pond, tank, or glass bowl in which living fish, water animals, and water plants are kept. 2 a building used for showing collections of living fish, water animals, and water plants: *The aquarium had many tanks with glass fronts.* *n., pl.* **a·quar·i·ums** or **a·quar·i·a** (ə kwer′ē ə).

a·quat·ic (ə kwat′ik or ə kwot′ik) 1 growing or living in water: *Water lilies are aquatic plants.* 2 taking place in or on water: *Swimming and sailing are aquatic sports.* *adj.*

An aqueduct

aq·ue·duct (ak′wə dukt′) 1 an artificial channel or large pipe for bringing water from a distance. 2 the structure that supports such a channel or pipe. *n.*

Ar·ab (ar′əb or er′əb) 1 a member of the native race of Arabia: *The Arabs are widely scattered over southwestern Asia and northern Africa.* 2 of or having to do with the Arabs or Abrabia. 1 *n.*, 2 *adj.*

A·ra·bi·an (ə rā′bē ən) 1 of or having to do with Arabia or the Arabs. 2 an Arab. 1 *adj.*, 2 *n.*

Ar·a·bic (ar′ə bik or er′ə bik) 1 of or having to do with the Arabs or their language. 2 the language of the Arabs. 1 *adj.*, 2 *n.*

Arabic numerals the figures 1, 2, 3, 4, 5, 6, 7, 8, 9, 0.

ar·a·ble (ar′ə bəl or er′ə bəl) fit for ploughing: *There is little arable land on the side of that mountain.* *adj.*

a·rach·nid (ə rak′nid) any of a large group of animals that includes spiders, scorpions, and mites: *An arachnid breathes air, has four pairs of walking legs, no antennae, and no wings; its body is usually divided into only two parts.* *n.*

ar·bi·trar·y (är′bə trer′ē) based on one's own wishes, notions, or will; not going by any rule or law: *A good judge tries to be fair and does not make arbitrary decisions.* *adj.*

ar·bi·trate (är′bə trāt′) 1 give a decision in a dispute. 2 settle a disagreement by agreeing to follow the decision of a judge, umpire, or committee: *When the two nations agreed to arbitrate their dispute, war was avoided.* *v.,* **ar·bi·trat·ed, ar·bi·trat·ing.**

ar·bi·tra·tion (är′bə trā′shən) the settlement of a disagreement by the decision of a judge, umpire, or committee: *The postmen's strike was settled by arbitration.* *n.*

ar·bor or **ar·bour** (är′bər) a shaded place formed by vines or other plants growing on frames or supports. *n.*

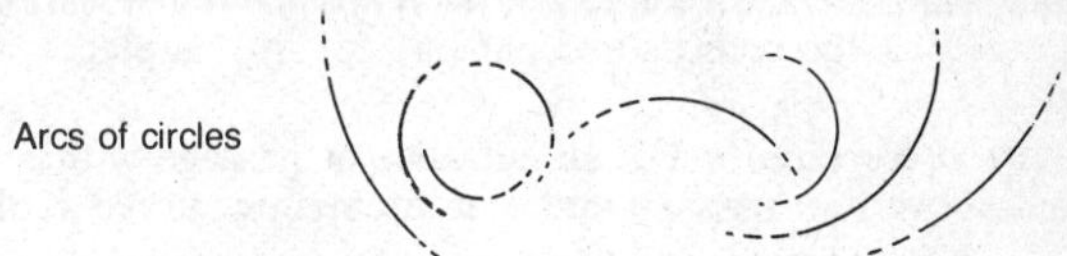

Arcs of circles

arc (ärk) 1 a part of a circle. 2 a curved line or path: *The football followed a graceful arc as it sailed between the goal posts.* 3 the stream of brilliant light or sparks formed as an electric current goes from one conductor to another. 4 form an arc: *The shooting star arced the heavens.* 1–3 *n.*, 4 *v.* **—arc′like′,** *adj.*

ar·cade (är kād′) 1 a passageway with an arched roof. 2 any covered passageway: *Some buildings have arcades with small stores along either side.* *n.*

arch[1] (ärch) 1 a curved structure that bears the weight of the material above it: *Arches often form the tops of doors, windows, and gateways.* See **keystone** for picture. 2 archway. 3 a monument forming an arch or arches. 4 bend into an arch; curve: *The wind arched the trees over the road.* 5 the part of the bottom of the foot between the ball and the heel: *Fallen arches cause flat feet.* See **leg** for picture. 1–3, 5 *n.*, 4 *v.*

arch[2] (ärch) 1 chief; principal: *When the arch rebel was caught the revolt died down.* 2 playfully mischievous: *The girl gave her mother an arch look and ran off.* *adj.*

ar·chae·ol·o·gist (är′kē ol′ə jist) a person skilled in archaeology or whose work is archaeology. *n.* Also spelled **archeologist.**

ar·chae·ol·o·gy (är′kē ol′ə jē) the study of the life and customs of ancient times by examination of the remains of cities, dwellings, monuments, etc.: *Students of archaeology excavate the sites of ancient towns and then study the traces or samples they find of tools, pottery, jewellery, etc.* *n.* Also spelled **archeology.**

arch·an·gel (ärk′ān′jel) an angel of high rank. *n.*

arch·bish·op (ärch′bish′əp) a bishop of the highest rank. *n.*

ar·che·ol·o·gist (är′kē ol′ə jist) See **archaeologist.**

ar·che·ol·o·gy (är′kē ol′ə jē) See **archaeology.**

arch·er (är′chər) a person who shoots with bow and arrows. See **arrow** for picture. *n.*

arch·er·y (är′chər ē) 1 the practice or art of shooting with bows and arrows. 2 a troop of archers: *The archery advanced, shooting steadily. n.*

ar·chi·pel·a·go (är′kə pel′ə gō′) 1 a sea having many islands in it. 2 a group of many islands: *The islands in the Arctic Ocean north of Canada are called the Canadian Archipelago. n., pl.* **ar·chi·pel·a·gos** or **ar·chi·pel·a·goes.**

ar·chi·tect (är′kə tekt′) a person who designs buildings and sees that his plans are followed by the people who actually put up the buildings. *n.*

ar·chi·tec·ture (är′kə tek′chər) 1 the science and art of building: *Architecture has to do with the planning of houses, churches, schools, and public and business buildings.* 2 a style or special manner of building: *Greek architecture made use of columns. n.*

ar·chives (är′kīvz) 1 a place where public records or historical papers are kept: *The Dominion Archives are in Ottawa.* 2 the records and papers kept in this place. *n. pl.*

arch·way (ärch′wā′) an entrance or passage with an arch above it; a passage under an arched or curved roof. *n.*

arc·tic (ärk′tik or är′tik) 1 at or near the North Pole; of the north polar region: *the arctic fox.* 2 **the Arctic,** a the north polar region. b the Arctic Ocean. 1 *adj.,* 2 *n.*

Arctic Circle an imaginary line around the earth 66½° north of the equator marking off the north polar region.

Arctic Ocean the ocean of the north polar region.

ar·dent (är′dənt) very enthusiastic; eager: *He became an ardent fisherman. adj.* **—ar′dent·ly,** *adv.*

ar·dor or **ar·dour** (är′dər) warmth of feeling; eagerness; great enthusiasm: *patriotic ardor. n.*

ar·du·ous (är′jü əs or är′dyü əs) hard to do; requiring much effort; difficult: *an arduous lesson. adj.*

are (är) a part of the present tense of the verb **be,** used with the singular *you* and the plurals *we, you,* and *they: John, are you coming? We are ready. You are next. They are waiting. v.*

ar·e·a (er′ē ə) 1 the amount of surface; the extent: *The area of this floor is 70 square metres.* 2 a region: *The Rocky Mountain area is the most mountainous in Canada.* 3 a level surface or space: *The playing area was marked off with white lines. n.*

a·re·na (ə rē′nə) 1 a space where contests or shows take place: *Roman gladiators fought with lions in the arena.* 2 any place of conflict: *The political arena demands men who can fight with words.* 3 a building in which indoor sports are played: *There is a basketball game at the arena tonight. n.*

aren't (ärnt) are not.

ar·gue (är′gyü) 1 discuss with someone who disagrees: *He argued with his sister about who should wash the dishes.* 2 give reasons for or against something: *One side argued for a larger army and the other argued against it.* 3 persuade by giving reasons: *He argued me into going.* 4 try to prove by reasoning: *Columbus argued that the world was round. v.,* **ar·gued, ar·gu·ing.**

ar·gu·ment (är′gyə mənt) 1 a discussion by persons who give reasons for and against different points of view; a debate: *He won the argument by producing figures to prove his point.* 2 an emotional disagreement; a dispute: *He had an argument with his brother about who won the card game.* 3 a reason or the reasons offered for or against something: *My argument for staying out late was not convincing to my mother. n.*

ar·id (ar′id or er′id) 1 having very little rainfall; dry: *Desert lands are arid.* 2 dull: *an arid, boring speech. adj.* **—ar′id·ly,** *adv.*

a·right (ə rīt′) correctly; rightly. *adv.*

a·rise (ə rīz′) 1 rise up; get up. 2 move upward: *Smoke arose from the chimney.* 3 come into being; come about: *Problems can arise in doing the simplest jobs. v.,* **a·rose, a·ris·en, a·ris·ing.**

a·ris·en (ə riz′ən) See **arise.** *John has not yet arisen from his bed. v.*

ar·is·toc·ra·cy (ar′is tok′rə sē or er′is tok′rə sē) 1 people of noble rank, title, or birth; the nobility: *Earls, dukes, and princes belong to the aristocracy.* 2 a class of persons superior because of intelligence, culture, or wealth. *n., pl.* **ar·is·toc·ra·cies.**

a·ris·to·crat (ə ris′tə krat′) 1 a person who belongs to the aristocracy; a noble. 2 anyone who has the tastes, opinions, manners, etc. of such a person. *n.*

a·ris·to·crat·ic (ə ris′tə krat′ik) belonging to or having to do with an aristocracy. *adj.*

a·rith·me·tic (ə rith′mə tik) the science and art of numbers: *When you study arithmetic, you learn to add, subtract, multiply, and divide. n.*

ark (ärk) 1 in the Bible, the large boat in which Noah saved himself, his family, and a pair of each kind of animal from the Flood. 2 a chest or box in which the Hebrews kept the two stone tablets containing the Ten Commandments (properly called the **Ark of the Covenant**). *n.*

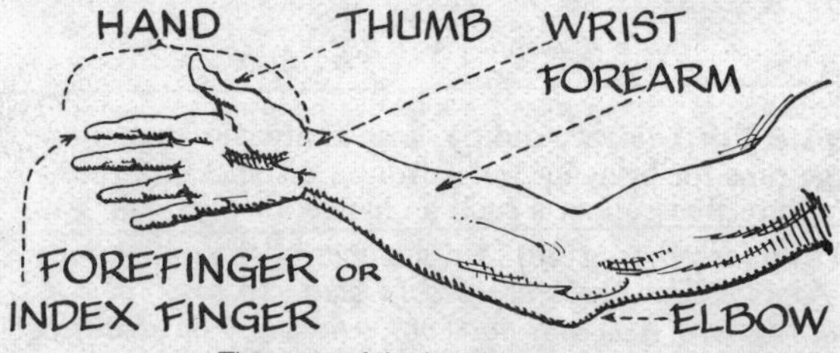

The parts of the human arm

arm¹ (ärm) 1 the part of a person's body between the shoulder and the hand. 2 something shaped or used like an arm: *the arm of a chair, an arm of the sea. n.*

arm² (ärm) 1 a weapon of any kind: *A gun, a sword, an axe, a stick—any of these might be arms for defence or attack.* See **arms.** 2 provide with weapons; supply with any means of defence or attack: *'Arm yourselves and be ready to fight,' said the leader. Each lawyer entered court armed with facts.* 3 take up arms: *The soldiers armed for battle.* 4 a branch of the armed forces: *The infantry, the artillery, and the armored corps are the principal arms of our land forces.* 1, 4 *n.,* 2, 3 *v.* **—arm′less,** *adj.*

ar·mad·a (är mad′ə or är mä′də) 1 a fleet of warships. 2 a fleet of airplanes. *n.*

hat, āge, fär; let, ēqual, tėrm; it, īce
hot, ōpen, ôrder; oil, out; cup, pu̇t, rüle
əbove, takən, pencəl, lemən, circəs
ch, child; ng, long; sh, ship
th, thin; ᴛʜ, then; zh, measure

An armadillo — about 45 cm long without the tail

ar·ma·dil·lo (är′mə dil′ō) a small burrowing animal that has a very hard shell: *Armadillos are found in South America and in some parts of southern North America.* *n., pl.* **ar·ma·dil·los.**

ar·ma·ment (är′mə mənt) **1** war equipment and supplies: *The two nations agreed to reduce their armaments.* **2** all the armed forces of a country. **3** the guns on a naval vessel, a tank, an airplane, etc. **4** the act or process of preparing for war. *n.*

arm·chair (ärm′cher′) a chair with sidepieces for the support of a person's arms or elbows. *n.*

armed forces the sea, land, and air elements of a country's defence organization, generally known as the navy, army, and air force.

arm·ful (ärm′fu̇l) as much as one arm can hold; as much as both arms can hold. *n., pl.* **arm·fuls.**

ar·mi·stice (är′mə stis) a stop in fighting; a temporary peace or truce. *n.*

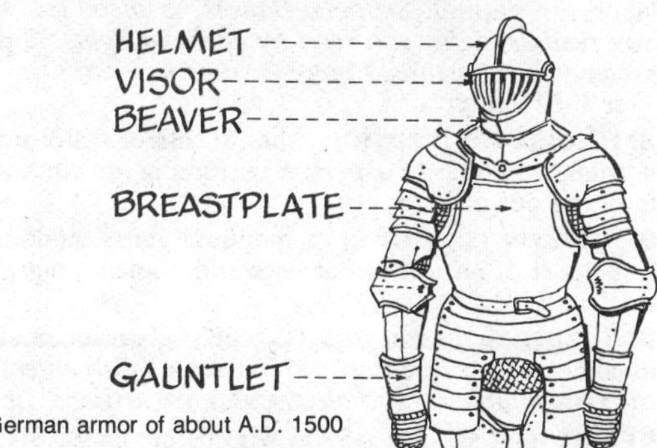

German armor of about A.D. 1500

ar·mor or **ar·mour** (är′mər) **1** a covering, often of metal, worn to protect the body in fighting. **2** any protective covering: *The steel plates of a warship and the scales of a fish are armor.* **3** the tanks and other armored vehicles of an army. *n.*

ar·mored or **ar·moured** (är′mərd) **1** covered or protected with armor: *an armored train or car.* **2** using tanks, armored cars, etc.: *an armored regiment.* *adj.*

ar·mor·ies or **ar·mour·ies** (är′mər ēz) armory (def. 3). *n. pl.*

ar·mor·y or **ar·mour·y** (är′mər ē) **1** a place where arms are kept. **2** a place where arms are made. **3** a building where militia or reserve army units do their training. *n., pl.* **ar·mor·ies** or **ar·mour·ies.**

arm·pit (ärm′pit′) the hollow under the arm at the shoulder. *n.*

arms (ärmz) **1** weapons: *We have the arms with which to fight.* **2** fighting; war: *A soldier is a man of arms.* **3** a design used as a symbol of a family, government, etc. See **coat of arms** for picture. *n. pl.*
take up arms, arm for attack or defence: *The settlers took up arms against the invaders.*
up in arms, very angry; in rebellion: *The students were up in arms when their holiday was cancelled.*

ar·my (är′mē) **1** an organized group of soldiers trained and armed for war: *British armies have fought in many lands.* **2** any group of people organized on military lines: *the Salvation Army.* **3** a very large number; a multitude: *an army of ants.* *n., pl.* **ar·mies.**

a·ro·ma (ə rō′mə) a pleasant, spicy smell; fragrance: *Just smell the aroma of the cake in the oven!* *n.*

ar·o·mat·ic (ar′ə mat′ik or er′ə mat′ik) sweet-smelling or fragrant; spicy: *The cinnamon tree has an aromatic bark.* *adj.*

a·rose (ə rōz′) See **arise.** *She arose from her chair.* *v.*

a·round (ə round′) **1** in a circle about: *He has travelled around the world.* **2** in a circle: *He spun around like a top.* **3** on all sides of: *The sun shines all around us.* **4** here and there; about: *We walked around to see the town.* **5** *Informal.* somewhere about; near: *Please wait around for an hour.* **6** *Informal.* approximately; about: *His hat cost around five dollars. I'll be home around six o'clock.* **7** along the edge or border of rather than straight through: *On our trip west we drove around Toronto.* 1, 3, 6, 7 *prep.,* 2, 4, 5 *adv.*

a·rouse (ə rouz′) **1** awaken. **2** excite; stir to action: *The attack aroused the whole country.* *v.,* **a·roused, a·rous·ing.**

ar·range (ə rānj′) **1** put in the proper order: *The table is arranged for dinner.* **2** plan; form plans: *Can you arrange to be at my house by six o'clock?* **3** adapt; fit: *This music for the violin is also arranged for the piano.* *v.,* **ar·ranged, ar·rang·ing.**

ar·range·ment (ə rānj′mənt) **1** putting or being put in proper order: *The arrangement of all our baggage in one car took some time.* **2** the way or order in which things or persons are put: *You can make six arrangements of the letters A, B, and C.*
3 arrangements, *pl.* plans or preparations: *All arrangements have been made for our trip.* **4** something arranged in a particular way: *a musical arrangement for the piano and violin.* *n.*

ar·ray (ə rā′) **1** order: *The troops were formed in battle array.* **2** put in order: *The general arrayed his troops for the battle.* **3** a display of persons or things: *The array of good players on the other team made our side look weak.* **4** clothes or dress: *bridal array, gorgeous array.* **5** to dress; dress in fine clothes; adorn: *She was arrayed like a queen.* 1, 3, 4 *n.,* 2, 5 *v.*

ar·rest (ə rest′) **1** seize by authority of the law; take to jail or court: *Policemen arrest thieves.* **2** stop; check: *Filling a tooth arrests decay.* **3** catch and hold: *Our attention was arrested by the sound of a shot.* **4** the seizing of a person by authority of law: *We saw the arrest of the burglar.* 1–3 *v.,* 4 *n.*

ar·riv·al (ə rīv′əl) **1** arriving; coming: *She is waiting for the arrival of the train.* **2** a person or thing that arrives: *The new arrivals were made welcome.* *n.*

ar·rive (ə rīv′) **1** come to a place: *We arrived in Kingston a week ago.* **2** come: *The time has arrived for you to study.* *v.,* **ar·rived, ar·riv·ing.**
arrive at, come to; reach: *You should arrive at school*

before nine o'clock. We have arrived at a decision.

ar·ro·gance (ar′ə gəns or er′ə gəns) too great pride; haughty behavior: *His arrogance showed that he felt himself superior to the others. n.*

ar·ro·gant (ar′ə gənt or er′ə gənt) boastfully proud; too proud; boasting too much; haughty: *I dislike arrogant people. adj.* —**ar′ro·gant·ly,** *adv.*

ar·row (ar′ō or er′ō) **1** a slender shaft or stick having a pointed tip, usually barbed, and feathers at the tail end: *An arrow is made to be shot from a bow.* **2** anything shaped like an arrow. **3** a sign (→) used to show direction or position in maps, on road signs, and in writing. *n.*

ar·row·head (ar′ō hed′ or er′ō hed′) the head or tip of an arrow, especially a separately made piece of stone or metal. See **barb** for picture. *n.*

ar·se·nal (är′sə nəl) a building for storing or making military weapons and ammunition. *n.*

ar·se·nic (är′sə nik) a greyish-white, tasteless powder that is a violent poison. *n.*

ar·son (är′sən) the crime of setting fire to a building or other property on purpose. *n.*

art[1] (ärt) **1** drawing, painting, or sculpture: *She is studying art and music.* **2** a branch of learning that depends more on special practice than on general principles: *Writing compositions is an art; grammar is a science.* **3** a set of principles or methods gained by experience: *the art of making friends, the art of war.* **4** some kind of skill or practical application of skill: *Cooking, sewing, and housekeeping are household arts.* **5** human skill or effort: *This well-kept garden owes more to art than to nature.* **6** a skilful act; cunning: *The witch deceived us by her arts. n.*

art[2] (ärt) an old form meaning **are:** *'Thou art' means 'You are.' v.*

ar·ter·y (är′tər ē) **1** any of the tubes that carry blood from the heart to all parts of the body. **2** a main road; an important channel: *Yonge Street is one of the main arteries of Toronto. n., pl.* **ar·ter·ies.**

artesian well (är tē′zhən) a deep well made by drilling, especially one from which water gushes up without pumping.

art·ful (ärt′fəl) **1** crafty; deceitful: *That cheat uses artful tricks to get people's money away from them.* **2** skilful; clever. *adj.* —**art′ful·ly,** *adv.* —**art′ful·ness,** *n.*

ar·ti·choke (är′tə chōk′) **1** a plant whose flowering head is cooked and eaten. **2** the Jerusalem artichoke. *n.*

Artichoke heads

ar·ti·cle (är′tə kəl) **1** a literary composition that is part of a magazine, newspaper, or book: *This newspaper has a good article on gardening.* **2** a separate part of anything written: *The third article of the club's constitution dealt with the privileges of members.* **3** a particular thing: *Bread is an important article of food.* **4** one of the words *a, an,* and *the,* which usually accompany nouns: *a book, an egg, the small boy. n.*

ar·ti·fice (är′tə fis) **1** a clever device; a trick: *She will use any artifice to get her own way.* **2** trickery; craft: *His conduct is free from artifice. n.*

ar·ti·fi·cial (är′tə fish′əl) **1** made by human skill or labor; not natural: *artificial flowers, artificial ice. When you read at night, you read by artificial light.* **2** put on; pretended: *an artificial voice or manner. adj.* —**ar′ti·fi′cial·ly,** *adv.*

artificial respiration the process of restoring normal breathing to a person by forcing air alternately into and out of his lungs.

ar·til·ler·y (är til′ər ē) **1** mounted guns; cannon. **2** the part of an army that uses and manages big guns. *n.*

ar·ti·san (är′tə zən or är′tə zan′) a workman skilled in some industry or trade; a craftsman: *Carpenters, masons, plumbers, and electricians are artisans. n.*

art·ist (är′tist) **1** a person who paints pictures. **2** a person who is skilled in any of the fine arts, such as sculpture, music, or literature. **3** a person who does work with skill and good taste. *n.*

ar·tis·tic (är tis′tik) **1** of art or artists. **2** done with skill and good taste. **3** having good color and design. *adj.*

art·less (ärt′lis) natural; simple; without any trickery: *Small children ask many artless questions. adj.* —**art′less·ly,** *adv.* —**art′less·ness,** *n.*

as (əz; stressed, az) **1** to the same degree; equally: *Beth is as tall as Ann.* **2** in the role or position: *Mary will act as teacher today.* **3** while: *As they were walking, the rain began.* **4** in the same way that: *Treat others as you wish them to treat you.* **5** for example: *Some animals, as dogs and cats, eat meat.* **Such as** also means for example. **6** because: *As he was a skilled worker, he received good wages.* 1, 5 *adv.,* 2 *prep.,* 3, 4, 6 *conj.*

as for, about; concerning; referring to: *We're leaving now; as for Sonia, she'll have to come on her own.*

as if, as it would be if: *The car looked as if it had been driven on rough roads.*

as of, beginning on: *As of April 30, we will be on daylight-saving time.*

as to, about; regarding; referring to: *We have no information as to the cause of the riot.*

☛ See note at **like**[1].

hat, āge, fär; let, ēqual, tėrm; it, īce
hot, ōpen, ôrder; oil, out; cup, pu̇t, rüle
 əbove, takən, pencəl, lemən, circəs
ch, child; ng, long; sh, ship
th, thin; ᴛʜ, then; zh, measure

as·bes·tos (as bes′təs or az bes′təs) a greyish-white fireproof mineral found in the form of fibres that can be made into a sort of cloth or felt: *Asbestos is used for mats to put under hot dishes.* *n.*

as·cend (ə send′) go up; rise; climb: *He watched the airplane ascend higher and higher. Few people ascend high mountains.* *v.*

as·cent (ə sent′) **1** going up; rising: *The sudden ascent of the elevator made me dizzy.* **2** climbing: *The ascent of Mount Everest was a difficult task.* **3** a place or way that slopes up: *The gradual ascent of the hill made it easy to climb.* *n.*

as·cer·tain (as′ər tān′) find out: *He telephoned home to ascertain if his father had arrived.* *v.*

as·cribe (əs krīb′) think of as caused by or belonging to: *The discovery of America is usually ascribed to Columbus. The police ascribed the automobile accident to fast driving.* *v.*, **as·cribed, as·crib·ing.**

ash[1] (ash) what remains of a thing after it has been thoroughly burned: *He flicked his cigarette ash into the fireplace. Ashes have to be regularly removed from fireplaces and furnaces.* *n.*

ash[2] (ash) **1** a kind of shade tree that is valuable for timber. **2** its springy, tough wood: *Ash is used in making hoe handles.* *n.*

a·shamed (ə shāmd′) **1** feeling shame; disturbed or uncomfortable because one has done something wrong, improper, or silly: *I was ashamed when I cried at the movies. She was ashamed of her foolishness.* **2** unwilling because of shame: *He was ashamed to tell his mother he had failed.* *adj.*

a·shore (ə shôr′) **1** on shore; on land: *The sailor had been ashore for months.* **2** to the shore: *The men rowed the captain ashore.* *adv.*

ash·tray (ash′trā′) a container for the ashes of cigarettes, cigars, and pipes. *n.*

A·sian (ā′zhən or ā′shən) **1** a person born in or living in Asia. **2** Asiatic (def. 1). 1 *n.*, 2 *adj.*

A·si·at·ic (ā′zhē at′ik or ā′shē at′ik) **1** of or having to do with Asia or its people. **2** Asian (def. 1). 1 *adj.*, 2 *n.*

a·side (ə sīd′) on one side; to one side: *Move the table aside. When Sam spoke aside to Paul, nobody else heard what he said.* *adv.*

ask (ask) **1** try to find out by words: *Why don't you ask the way?* **2** seek the answer to: *Ask any questions you wish.* **3** put a question to: *Ask him how old he is.* **4** try to get by words: *Ask her to sing. Ask for what you want.* **5** invite: *She asked ten guests to the party.* *v.*

a·skance (ə skans′) with suspicion or disapproval: *The students looked askance at the suggestion of having classes on Saturday.* *adv.*

a·skew (ə skyü′) to one side; out of the proper position; turned or twisted the wrong way: *Her hat is on askew. The bottom line of printing is askew.* *adv., adj.*

a·sleep (ə slēp′) **1** sleeping: *The cat is asleep.* **2** into a condition of sleep: *The tired boy fell asleep.* **3** without feeling; numb: *My foot is asleep.* 1, 3 *adj.*, 2 *adv.*

as·par·a·gus (əs par′ə gəs or əs per′ə gəs) **1** a plant whose tender, green shoots are used for food. **2** the shoots. *n.*

as·pect (as′pekt) **1** one side, part, or view of something: *We must consider this plan in its various aspects.* **2** a look or appearance: *The judge has a solemn aspect.* *n.*

as·pen (as′pən) any of several poplar trees whose leaves tremble and rustle in the slightest breeze. *n.*

as·phalt (as′folt or as′fôlt) **1** a dark-colored substance much like tar. **2** a smooth, hard mixture of this substance with crushed rock: *Asphalt is used to pave streets.* *n.*

as·pir·ant (əs pīr′ənt or as′pər ənt) a person who aspires; a person who seeks a position of honor: *There are many aspirants for the office of mayor.* *n.*

as·pir·a·tion (as′pə rā′shən) a longing; an earnest desire: *She had aspirations to be an actress.* *n.*

as·pire (əs pīr′) have an ambition for something; desire earnestly; seek: *He aspired to be captain of the team. Scholars aspire after knowledge.* *v.*, **as·pired, as·pir·ing.**

as·pi·rin (as′pə rin) a drug for headaches, colds, etc. *n.*

☛ In Canada, *Aspirin* is a trademark although the form *aspirin* is in general use.

ass (as) **1** a donkey. **2** a stupid, silly, or stubborn person; a fool. *n.*

as·sail (ə sāl′) set upon with violence; attack: *The enemy assailed our fort.* *v.*

as·sail·ant (ə sāl′ənt) a person who attacks: *The injured man did not know who his assailant was.* *n.*

as·sas·sin (ə sas′ən) a murderer, especially of a politically important person: *Assassins are often people hired to commit murder.* *n.*

as·sas·si·nate (ə sas′ə nāt′) murder a politically important person. *v.*, **as·sas·si·nat·ed, as·sas·si·nat·ing.**

as·sas·si·na·tion (ə sas′ə nā′shən) the murder of a politically important person. *n.*

as·sault (ə solt′ or ə sôlt′) **1** an attack; a sudden, vigorous attack. **2** to attack. 1 *n.*, 2 *v.*

as·sem·ble (ə sem′bəl) **1** gather together; bring together. **2** come together; meet. **3** put together; fit together: *Some boys like to assemble model airplanes.* *v.*, **as·sem·bled, as·sem·bling.**

as·sem·bly (ə sem′blē) **1** a group of people gathered together for some purpose; a meeting: *The principal called an assembly of the students for Monday morning.*

Leaves and shoots of asparagus

2 a meeting of lawmakers. 3 **legislative assembly,** a provincial parliament. 4 putting together; fitting together: *the assembly of the parts of a car.* 5 anything made up of parts fitted together: *the tail assembly of an aircraft.* *n., pl.* **as·sem·blies.**

assembly line a row of workers or machines along which work is passed until the final product is made: *Automobiles are produced on an assembly line.*

as·sem·bly·man (ə sem′blē mən) in Prince Edward Island, a member of the Legislative Assembly who is not a councillor. *n., pl.* **as·sem·bly·men** (ə sem′blē mən).

as·sent (ə sent′) 1 agree; express agreement: *Everyone assented to the plans for the party.* 2 an agreement; the acceptance of a proposal, statement, etc.: *She smiled her assent to the plan. Parliament gave assent to the bill.* 1 *v.,* 2 *n.*

as·sert (ə sėrt′) 1 declare; state positively: *He asserts that he will go whether we do or not.* 2 defend or insist on a right, a claim, etc.: *Assert your independence.* *v.*

assert oneself, a put oneself forward; make oneself noticed. **b** insist on one's rights.

as·ser·tion (ə sėr′shən) 1 a positive declaration; a very strong statement: *His assertion of innocence was believed by the jury.* 2 insisting on one's rights, a claim, etc. *n.*

as·set (as′et) 1 something having value: *The ability to get along with people is an asset.* 2 **assets,** *pl.* things of value; property: *His assets include a house, a car, bonds, and jewellery.* *n.*

as·sign (ə sīn′) 1 give as a share; allot: *The teacher assigned several problems for homework.* 2 appoint to a post or duty: *The captain assigned two soldiers to guard the gate.* 3 name definitely; fix or set: *The judge assigned a day for the trial.* *v.*

as·sign·ment (ə sīn′mənt) 1 something given as a task: *Today's assignment in arithmetic is ten problems.* 2 assigning; an appointment: *The soldier was informed of his assignment to a new base.* *n.*

as·sim·i·late (ə sim′ə lāt′) absorb; digest: *She does so much reading that she cannot assimilate it all. The human body will not assimilate sawdust.* *v.,* **as·sim·i·lat·ed, as·sim·i·lat·ing.**

as·sist (ə sist′) 1 give aid to; help: *She assisted her mother with the housework.* 2 take part or have a hand in: *He assisted in the scoring of the goal.* 3 in hockey, the credit given to a player who helps score a goal. 4 in baseball, the credit given to a player who helps to put an opposing player out. 5 an instance of giving help: *With an assist from me, he soon climbed the fence.* 1, 2 *v.,* 3–5 *n.*

as·sist·ance (ə sis′təns) help; aid. *n.*

as·sist·ant (ə sis′tənt) 1 a helper; an aid. 2 helping; assisting: *an assistant teacher.* 1 *n.,* 2 *adj.*

as·so·ci·ate (ə sō′shē āt′ for 1, 4, and 6, ə sō′shē it for 2, 3, and 5) 1 connect in thought: *We associate camping with summer.* 2 anything connected with something else. 3 joined in companionship, interest, etc.: *He is associate editor of the school paper.* 4 join as a companion, partner, or friend; keep company: *She associates only with people interested in sports.* 5 a companion; a partner; an ally: *I am one of his associates in this plan.* 6 join; combine; unite. 1, 4, 6 *v.,* **as·so·ci·at·ed, as·so·ci·at·ing;** 2, 5 *n.,* 3 *adj.*

as·so·ci·a·tion (ə sō′sē ā′shən) 1 associating or being associated: *I look forward to my association with the new students.* 2 a group of people joined together for some common purpose; a society: *Will you join the Young People's Association at our church?* 3 a connection or relationship; friendship: *They had enjoyed a close association over many years.* *n.*

as·sort·ed (ə sôr′tid) 1 selected so as to be of different kinds: *assorted cakes.* 2 arranged by kinds; classified: *socks assorted by size.* 3 suited to one another; matched: *They are a poorly assorted couple, always quarrelling.* *adj.*

as·sort·ment (ə sôrt′mənt) 1 a collection of various kinds: *an assortment of candies.* 2 arranging by kinds. *n.*

as·sume (ə süm′ or ə syüm′) 1 take for granted; suppose: *He assumed that the train would be on time.* 2 take upon oneself; undertake: *Tom assumed the leadership in planning the picnic.* 3 take on; put on: *He assumed an air of superiority.* 4 pretend: *He assumed ignorance of the fight.* *v.,* **as·sumed, as·sum·ing.**

as·sump·tion (ə sump′shən or ə sum′shən) 1 taking for granted; assuming: *She bustled about with an assumption of authority.* 2 something taken for granted: *His assumption that he would win the prize proved incorrect.* *n.*

as·sur·ance (ə shür′əns) 1 a statement intended to make a person more sure or certain: *Mother gave me her assurance that I could go to the circus.* 2 security; certainty; confidence: *We have the assurance of final victory.* 3 self-confidence: *His careful preparation gave him assurance in reciting.* 4 too much boldness; impudence. *n.*

as·sure (ə shür′) 1 make sure or certain: *The man assured himself that the bridge was safe before crossing it.* 2 tell positively: *The captain of the ship assured the passengers that there was no danger.* *v.,* **as·sured, as·sur·ing.**

as·sured (ə shürd′) 1 sure; certain: *You may be assured that he is safe.* 2 confident; bold. *adj.*

as·sur·ed·ly (ə shür′id lē) 1 surely; certainly. 2 confidently; boldly. *adv.*

as·ter (as′tər) a plant having daisy-like flowers with yellow centres. *n.*

☛ **Aster, asterisk,** and **asteroid** all come from the Greek word *aster,* meaning 'star,' related to Greek *astron,* from which **astronaut, astronomy,** etc. are formed.

as·ter·isk (as′tər isk) a star-shaped mark (*) used in printing and writing to call attention to a note at the bottom of the page, to show that something has been left out, etc. *n.*

☛ See note at **aster.**

a·stern (ə stėrn′) 1 at or toward the rear of a ship: *The captain went astern.* 2 backward: *The ship moved slowly astern.* 3 behind: *Some yachts tow small boats astern.* *adv.*

as·ter·oid (as′tər oid′) any of the many very small planets revolving about the sun, mainly between the orbits of Mars and Jupiter. *n.*

☛ See note at **aster.**

asth·ma (az′mə or as′mə) a chronic disease that causes coughing and difficulty in breathing. *n.*

a·stir (ə stėr′) in motion; up and about: *Even at midnight the whole town was astir.* *adv., adj.*

as·ton·ish (əs ton′ish) surprise greatly; amaze: *The gift of ten dollars astonished the little boy.* *v.*

as·ton·ish·ing (əs ton′ish ing) very surprising; amazing: *an astonishing sight.* *adj.* **—as·ton′ish·ing·ly,** *adv.*

as·ton·ish·ment (əs ton′ish mənt) great surprise; amazement; sudden wonder. *n.*

as·tound (əs tound′) surprise very greatly; amaze: *We were astounded by the beauty of Niagara Falls.* *v.*

a·stray (ə strā′) out of the right way; wandering: *Our dog has gone astray.* *adv., adj.*

a·stride (ə strīd′) with one leg on each side of: *He sits astride his horse.* *prep.*

as·tro·labe (as′trə lāb′ or as′trə lab′) an instrument used years ago in navigation for measuring the altitude of the sun or stars. *n.*

☞ **Astrolabe** comes from a Greek word *astrolabon,* meaning 'star-taking.'

as·trol·o·ger (əs trol′ə jər) a person skilled in astrology or whose work is astrology. *n.*

as·trol·o·gy (əs trol′ə jē) the study of the stars and planets to reveal their supposed influence on persons or events and to foretell the future. *n.*

☞ **Astrology** comes from Greek *astron,* meaning 'star,' and *-logos,* meaning 'treating of.'

as·tro·naut (as′trə not′ or as′trə nôt′) a pilot or member of the crew of a spacecraft. *n.*

☞ **Astronaut** comes from Greek *astron,* meaning 'star,' and *nautes,* meaning 'a sailor.'

as·tron·o·mer (əs tron′ə mər) a person skilled in astronomy or whose work is astronomy. *n.*

as·tron·o·my (əs tron′ə mē) the science that deals with the sun, moon, planets, stars, and other heavenly bodies. *n.*

☞ **Astronomy** comes from Greek *astron,* meaning 'star' and *nomos,* meaning 'distribution.'

as·tute (ə styüt′ or ə stüt′) shrewd; clever: *He was an astute businessman.* *adj.* **—as·tute′ly,** *adv.* **—as·tute′ness,** *n.*

a·sun·der (ə sun′dər) 1 in pieces; into separate parts: *Lightning split the tree asunder.* 2 apart; separate. 1 *adv.,* 2 *adj.*

a·sy·lum (ə sī′ləm) 1 an institution for the support and care of the mentally ill, the blind, orphans, or other unfortunate persons. 2 a refuge or shelter: *The author who had been accused of a political crime was given asylum in another country.* *n.*

at (at; unstressed, ət) 1 in; on; by or near: *He is at school. She is not at home.* 2 engaged in: *The children are at play.* 3 directly toward; in the direction of: *He shot the arrow at the deer.* 4 on or near the time of: *He goes to bed at nine o'clock.* 5 in a place or condition of: *England and France were at war.* 6 for: *We bought two books at a dollar each.* *Symbol:* @ 7 because of; as a result of: *They were delighted at the victory.* *prep.*

ate (āt) See **eat.** *John ate his dinner an hour ago.* *v.*

a·the·ist (ā′thē ist) a person who believes that there is no God. *n.*

ath·lete (ath′lēt) a person trained in exercises of strength, speed, and skill: *Baseball players and boxers are athletes.* *n.*

hat, āge, fär; let, ēqual, tėrm; it, īce
hot, ōpen, ôrder; oil, out; cup, pu̇t, rüle
əbove, takən, pencəl, lemən, circəs
ch, child; ng, long; sh, ship
th, thin; ᴛʜ, then; zh, measure

athlete's foot a contagious skin disease of the feet, caused by a fungus; ringworm of the feet.

ath·let·ic (ath let′ik) 1 strong and active. 2 of an athlete; like or suited to an athlete. 3 having to do with active games and sports: *He joined an athletic association.* *adj.*

ath·let·ics (ath let′iks) exercises of strength, speed, and skill; active games and sports. *n. pl.*

At·lan·tic (at lan′ tik) 1 the ocean lying east of North and South America and extending to Europe and Africa. 2 of the Atlantic Ocean. 3 on, in, over, or near the Atlantic Ocean: *Atlantic air routes.* 1 *n.,* 2, 3 *adj.*

Atlantic Provinces Newfoundland, Prince Edward Island, Nova Scotia, and New Brunswick.

at·las (at′ləs) a book of maps: *A big atlas includes maps of every country.* *n.*

at·mos·phere (at′məs fēr′) 1 the air that surrounds the earth; the air. 2 mental and moral surroundings; surrounding influence: *He lived in an atmosphere of poverty. Nuns live in a religious atmosphere.* 3 the air in any given place: *The atmosphere in the cave was damp.* *n.*

at·mos·pher·ic (at′məs fer′ik) 1 of or having to do with the atmosphere. 2 in the atmosphere: *Atmospheric conditions often prevent observations of the stars.* *adj.*

at·om (at′əm) 1 the smallest part of an element, that has all the properties of the element and can take part in a chemical reaction without being permanently changed: *Atoms are made up of protons, neutrons, and electrons.* 2 a very small particle; a tiny bit: *There is not an atom of truth in his whole story.* *n.*

atom bomb atomic bomb.

a·tom·ic (ə tom′ik) of atoms; having to do with atoms: *atomic research.* *adj.*

atomic bomb a bomb that uses the uncontrolled splitting of atoms to cause an explosion of tremendous force. Also, **A-bomb.**

atomic energy the energy that exists in atoms: *Some elements can be made to release atomic energy, either slowly in a reactor or very suddenly in a bomb.*

a·tone (ə tōn′) make up; make amends: *Allen atoned for his unkindness to Joan by taking her to the movies.* *v.,* **a·toned, a·ton·ing.**

a·tone·ment (ə tōn′mənt) 1 making up for something; giving satisfaction for a wrong, loss, or injury. 2 **the Atonement,** the sufferings and death of Christ. *n.*

a·top (ə top′) 1 on the top; at the top. 2 on the top of. 1 *adv.,* 2 *prep.*

a·tro·cious (ə trō′shəs) 1 very wicked or cruel; very savage or brutal: *The behavior of the barbarians was atrocious.* 2 *Informal.* very unpleasant: *The weather was simply atrocious.* *adj.* **—a·tro′cious·ly,** *adv.*

a·troc·i·ty (ə tros′ə tē) 1 very great wickedness or

cruelty: *Many acts of atrocity are committed in war.* 2 a very cruel or brutal act: *the atrocities of war.* *n., pl.* **a·troc·i·ties.**

at·tach (ə tach′) 1 fasten to: *The boy attached a rope to his sleigh.* 2 connect with for duty, etc.: *He was attached as mate to the ship 'Clio.'* 3 add at the end: *The signers attached their names to the petition.* 4 bind by affection: *She is much attached to her cousin.* 5 stick; belong; fasten itself: *The blame for this accident attaches to us all.* *v.*

at·tach·ment (ə tach′mənt) 1 attaching or being attached. 2 something that is attached or can be attached: *A vacuum cleaner has various attachments.* 3 a means of attaching or fastening. 4 affection: *Her attachment to the kitten was plain to see.* *n.*

at·tack (ə tak′) 1 set upon to hurt; go against as an enemy: *The dog attacked the cat.* 2 go at with vigor: *The hungry boy attacked his dinner as soon as it was served.* 3 an assault or attacking: *The attack of the enemy took us by surprise.* 4 make an attack; begin fighting: *The enemy attacked at dawn.* 5 a sudden illness: *an attack of flu.* 6 talk or write against: *The newspapers attacked the new prime minister.* 1, 2, 4, 6 *v.,* 3, 5 *n.*

at·tain (ə tān′) 1 arrive at; reach: *Grandfather has attained the age of eighty.* 2 gain; accomplish: *He attained his goal.* *v.*

at·tain·ment (ə tān′mənt) 1 attaining: *the attainment of our desires.* 2 something attained. 3 an accomplishment or ability: *Leonardo da Vinci was a man of varied attainments; he was an inventor, an artist, and an architect.* *n.*

at·tempt (ə tempt′) 1 try: *I will attempt to get better grades.* 2 trying; an effort: *He made an attempt to climb Mount Everest.* 1 *v.,* 2 *n.*

at·tend (ə tend′) 1 be present at: *Children must attend school.* 2 give care and thought; apply oneself: *Attend to your lessons.* 3 go with: *Noble ladies attend the queen.* 4 go with as a result: *Success often attends hard work.* 5 wait on; care for: *Nurses attend the sick.* *v.*

at·tend·ance (ə ten′dəns) 1 being present at a place; attending: *Attendance at all classes is compulsory.* 2 the persons attending; the number present: *The attendance at church was over 200 last Sunday.* *n.*

at·tend·ant (ə ten′dənt) 1 a person who waits on another, such as a servant or a follower. 2 waiting on another to help or serve: *an attendant nurse.* 3 accompanying; going with as a result: *attendant circumstances, weakness attendant on illness.* 1 *n.,* 2, 3 *adj.*

at·ten·tion (ə ten′shən) 1 care and thought; concentration: *The children paid attention to the teacher. Attention to one's lessons is important.* 2 the power of noticing: *He called my attention to the cat trying to catch the mouse.* 3 consideration: *The boy shows his mother much attention.* 4 **attentions,** *pl.* acts of courtesy or devotion: *My grandmother received many attentions, such as visits, books, candy, and flowers, when she was sick.* 5 a military attitude of readiness: *The soldier stood at attention during inspection.* *n.*

at·ten·tive (ə ten′tiv) 1 paying attention; observant: *Attentive pupils usually make the best grades.* 2 courteous; showing attention for or interest in: *The polite girl was attentive to her mother's guests.* *adj.* **—at·ten′tive·ly,** *adv.*

at·tic (at′ik) a room or space in a house just below the roof. *n.*

at·tire (ə tīr′) 1 clothes or dress, especially of a formal kind: *The queen was wearing evening attire.* 2 array; clothe; dress: *He was attired in a full military uniform.* 1 *n.,* 2 *v.,* **at·tired, at·tir·ing.**

at·ti·tude (at′ə tyüd′ or at′ə tüd′) 1 one's way of thinking, acting, or feeling: *His attitude toward school changed from dislike to enthusiasm.* 2 a position of the body suggesting an action, purpose, emotion, etc.: *the attitude of a boxer ready to fight.* *n.*

at·tor·ney (ə tėr′nē) 1 a person who has legal power to act for another. 2 a lawyer. *n., pl.* **at·tor·neys.**

attorney general a chief law officer. *n., pl.* **attorneys general** or **attorney generals.**

Attorney General 1 the chief law officer of Canada: *The Attorney General is a member of the Cabinet.* 2 the chief law officer of a province. *n., pl.* **Attorneys General** or **Attorney Generals.**

at·tract (ə trakt′) 1 draw to oneself: *A magnet attracts iron.* 2 be pleasing to; win the attention and liking of: *Bright colors attract children.* *v.*

at·trac·tion (ə trak′shən) 1 the act or power of drawing to oneself: *the attraction of a magnet for iron filings.* 2 anything that delights or attracts people: *The elephants were the chief attraction at the circus.* 3 charm; fascination. *n.*

at·trac·tive (ə trak′tiv) pleasing; winning attention and liking: *She wore an attractive hat.* *adj.*

at·trib·ute (ə trib′yüt for 1 and 2, at′rə byüt′ for 3 and 4) 1 consider as belonging to or appropriate to: *Most of us attribute the quality of courage to the early explorers.* 2 regard as an effect of; think of as caused by: *We attribute Edison's success to intelligence and hard work.* 3 a quality considered as belonging to a person or thing; a characteristic: *Patience is an attribute of a good teacher.* 4 a symbol: *The eagle is an attribute of Jupiter.* 1, 2 *v.,* **at·trib·ut·ed, at·trib·ut·ing;** 3, 4 *n.*

au·burn (o′bərn or ô′bərn) reddish brown. *n., adj.*

auc·tion (ok′shən or ôk′shən) 1 a public sale in which each thing is sold to the person who offers the most money for it. 2 sell at an auction. 1 *n.,* 2 *v.*

au·da·cious (o dā′shəs or ô dā′shəs) 1 bold; daring. 2 too bold; impudent: *The man was vexed by the boys' audacious behavior.* *adj.*

au·dac·i·ty (o das′ə tē or ô das′ə tē) 1 boldness. 2 rudeness or boldness; impudence: *He had the audacity to go to the party without being invited.* *n., pl.* **au·dac·i·ties.**

au·di·ble (o′də bəl or ô′də bəl) that can be heard; loud enough to be heard: *She spoke in such a low voice that her remarks were barely audible.* *adj.*

au·di·ence (o′dē əns or ô′dē əns) 1 the people gathered to hear or see a performance or presentation: *The audience cheered the principal's speech.* 2 the people reached by radio or television broadcasts, by books, etc. 3 a chance to be heard; a hearing: *He should have an audience with the committee, for his plan is good.* 4 an interview with a person of high

hat, āge, fär; let, ēqual, tėrm; it, īce
hot, ōpen, ôrder; oil, out; cup, pu̇t, rüle
əbove, takən, pencəl, lemən, circəs
ch, child; ng, long; sh, ship
th, thin; ᴛʜ, then; zh, measure

rank: *The king granted an audience to the famous general.* *n.*

au·di·o (o′dē ō or ô′dē ō) especially in television, of or having to do with sound: *The audio part of a script shows what is to be heard on a program; the video part describes what is to be seen.* *adj.*

au·di·tion (o dish′ən or ô dish′ən) a hearing to test the ability of a singer, actor, or other performer. *n.*

au·di·tor (o′də tər or ô′də tər) **1** a hearer; listener. **2** a person who examines and checks business accounts. *n.*

au·di·to·ri·um (o′də tô′rē əm or ô′də tô′rē əm) **1** a large room for an audience in a church, theatre, school, etc.; a large hall. **2** a building especially designed for giving lectures, concerts, etc. *n.*

Aug. August.

An auger. Each turn makes the spiral cutting edge bite further into the wood.

au·ger (o′gər or ô′gər) a tool for boring holes in wood. *n*

aught[1] (ot or ôt) anything: *You may go for aught I care.* *n.*

aught[2] (ot or ôt) a cipher; zero; nothing. *n.* Sometimes spelled **ought.**

aug·ment (og ment′ or ôg ment′) increase: *He bought some stamps to augment his collection.* *v.*

Au·gust (o′gəst or ô′gəst) the eighth month of the year: *August has 31 days.* *n.*

☛ **August** developed from an Old English word taken from the Latin name for this month. It was named after the first Roman emperor, Augustus Caesar.

au·gust (o gust′ or ô gust′) inspiring reverence and admiration; majestic: *The people were silent in the august presence of the king.* *adj.*

auk (ok or ôk) a diving sea bird having short wings that are used mainly as paddles: *Auks are found in arctic regions.* *n.*

aunt (ant) **1** a sister of one's father or mother. **2** the wife of one's uncle. *n.*

☛ The pronunciation (ant) is usual in Canada, but (änt) is common in New Brunswick and parts of Nova Scotia.

au·ro·ra bo·re·al·is (ô rô′rə bô′rē al′is or bô′rē ā′lis) streamers or bands of light appearing in the northern sky at night; northern lights.

aus·pic·es (os′pə siz or ôs′pə siz) **1** helpful influence or assistance; patronage: *The school fair was held under the auspices of the Home and School Association.* **2** omens; signs: *The ancient Romans used to observe the flight of birds for auspices to guide their actions.* *n. pl.*

aus·pi·cious (os pish′əs or ôs pish′əs) with signs of success; favorable; fortunate: *Our hockey team's easy win in its first game was an auspicious start to the season.* *adj.* **—aus·pi′cious·ly,** *adv.*

aus·tere (os tēr′ or ôs tēr′) **1** harsh; stern: *His father was a silent, austere man, very strict with his children.* **2** severely simple: *The tall, plain columns stood against the sky in austere beauty.* *adj.*

aus·ter·i·ty (os ter′ə tē or ôs ter′ə tē) restriction in spending; severe conditions owing to shortage of money: *The austerity of wartime was soon followed by prosperity in many countries.* *n., pl.* **aus·ter·i·ties.**

Aus·tral·ian (os trāl′yən or ôs trāl′yən) **1** of or having to do with Australia. **2** a person born in or living in Australia. 1 *adj.,* 2 *n.*

Aus·tri·an (os′trē ən or ôs′trē ən) **1** of or having to do with Austria, a country in central Europe. **2** a person born in or living in Austria. 1 *adj.,* 2 *n.*

au·then·tic (o then′tik or ô then′tik) **1** reliable: *We heard an authentic report of the wreck, given by one of the ship's officers.* **2** genuine; real: *We saw an authentic letter written by Sir Isaac Brock.* *adj.*

au·thor (o′thər or ô′thər) **1** a person who writes books, stories, or articles. **2** a person who creates or begins anything: *Are you the author of this scheme?* *n.*

au·thor·i·ta·tive (ə thôr′ə tā′tiv) **1** having authority; officially ordered: *Authoritative orders have arrived from headquarters.* **2** commanding: *In authoritative tones the policeman shouted, 'Keep back!'* **3** that ought to be believed or obeyed; having the authority of expert knowledge: *A doctor's statement concerning the cause of death is considered authoritative.* *adj.*

au·thor·i·ty (ə thôr′ə tē) **1** power; the right to command or act: *A father has authority over his children. A policeman has the authority to arrest careless drivers.* **2** a person who has power or right. **3 the authorities,** *pl.* the officials in control: *Who are the proper authorities to give permits to hunt or fish?* **4** a government body that runs some activity or business on behalf of the public: *the St. Lawrence Seaway Authority.* **5** a source of correct information or wise advice: *A good dictionary is an authority on the meaning of words.* *n., pl.* **au·thor·i·ties.**

au·thor·ize (o′thər īz′ or ô′thər īz′) **1** give someone the power or the right to: *The Prime Minister authorized him to attend the conference.* **2** give authority for; approve: *This dictionary authorizes the two spellings 'traveller' and 'traveler.' Parliament authorized the spending of money for a new post-office building.* *v.,* **au·thor·ized, au·thor·iz·ing.**

au·to (o′tō or ô′tō) automobile. *n., pl.* **au·tos.**

au·to·bi·og·ra·phy (o′tə bī og′rə fē or ô′tə bī og′rə fē) the story of a person's life written by himself. *n., pl.* **au·to·bi·og·ra·phies.**

au·to·crat (o′tə krat′ or ô′tə krat′) **1** an absolute ruler; a ruler having full power. **2** a person who uses his power in a harsh way: *My friend thinks her parents are autocrats.* *n.*

au·to·graph (o′tə graf′ or ô′tə graf′) **1** a person's name written by himself: *Many people collect the autographs of movie stars.* **2** write one's name on or in. 1 *n.,* 2 *v.*

au·to·mat·ic (o′tə mat′ik or ô′tə mat′ik) 1 made or set to move or act by itself: *an automatic lock, an automatic pump.* 2 done without thought or attention: *Breathing and swallowing are usually automatic.* 3 a gun that throws out the empty shell and reloads by itself: *Some automatics continue to fire until the pressure on the trigger is released.* 1, 2 *adj.*, 3 *n.*

au·to·mat·i·cal·ly (o′tə mat′ik lē or ô′tə mat′ik lē) in an automatic manner: *Electric refrigerators switch on and off automatically. The girl knitted automatically, chattering with her friend all the time. adv.*

au·to·ma·tion (o′tə mā′shən or ô′tə mā′shən) the use of automatic controls in the operation of machines: *In automation, electronic or mechanical devices do many of the tasks formerly performed by people. n.*

☛ **Automation** is made up of *automatic* and oper*ation.*

au·to·mo·bile (o′tə mə bēl′ or ô′tə mə bēl′) a passenger vehicle that carries its own engine and is driven on roads and streets; car. *n.*

☛ **Automobile** was originally a French word.

au·to·mo·tive (o′tə mō′tiv or ô′tə mō′tiv) of or having to do with cars, trucks, and other self-moving vehicles. *adj.*

au·tumn (o′təm or ô′təm) 1 the season of the year between summer and winter; the fall. 2 of autumn; coming in autumn: *autumn flowers, autumn rains. n.*

aux·il·ia·ry (og zil′yə rē or ôg zil′yə rē) 1 helping; assisting: *Some sailboats have auxiliary engines.* 2 a person or thing that helps; an aid: *A microscope is a useful auxiliary to the human eye.* 1 *adj.*, 2 *n.*, *pl.* **aux·il·ia·ries.**

a·vail (ə vāl′) 1 be of use or benefit to: *Money will not avail you after you are dead.* 2 help: *Talk will not avail without work. v.*

avail oneself of, take advantage of; profit by; make use of: *He availed himself of the opportunity to learn French.*

of no avail or **to no avail,** of no use or value: *Crying is of no avail now. I complained, but to no avail.*

a·vail·a·ble (ə vāl′ə bəl) 1 that can be used: *The saw is not available at the moment; Father is using it.* 2 that can be had: *All available tickets were sold. adj.*

av·a·lanche (av′ə lanch′) a large mass of snow and ice, or of dirt and rocks, sliding or falling down the side of a mountain. *n.*

av·a·rice (av′ə ris) greed; a greedy desire for money or property: *Avarice is a fault of misers. n.*

av·a·ri·cious (av′ə rish′əs) greedy for money or property: *He grabbed the money with avaricious fingers. adj.*

Ave. avenue.

a·venge (ə venj′) get revenge for: *The knight avenged the insult by defeating his enemy in a duel. v.*, **a·venged, a·veng·ing. —a·veng′er,** *n.*

avenge oneself, get revenge for a wrong done to oneself: *The brigand swore to avenge himself on those who betrayed him.*

av·e·nue (av′ə nyü′) 1 a wide street. 2 a road or walk bordered by trees. 3 a way of approach: *Hard work is a good avenue to success. n.*

av·er·age (av′ər ij) 1 in arithmetic, the quantity found by dividing the sum of several quantities by the number of those quantities: *The average of 3 and 10 and 5 is 6.* 2 find the average of: *Will you average those numbers for me?* 3 obtained by averaging: *The average temperature for the week was 22 degrees.* 4 have, make, or yield as an average: *The cost of their lunches averaged four dollars a week. He averages six hours of work a day.* 5 the usual sort or amount: *The amount of rain this year has been below average.* 6 usual; ordinary: *average intelligence.* 1, 5 *n.*, 2, 4 *v.*, **av·er·aged, av·er·ag·ing;** 3, 6 *adj.*

a·ver·sion (ə vėr′zhən) 1 a strong dislike: *Some people have an aversion to snakes.* 2 a thing or person that is disliked: *a pet aversion, a secret aversion. n.*

a·vert (ə vėrt′) 1 prevent; avoid: *The driver averted an accident by a quick turn of the steering wheel.* 2 turn away; turn aside: *She averted her eyes from the wreck. v.*

a·vi·ar·y (ā′vē er′ē) a place where many birds are kept. *n.*, *pl.* **a·vi·ar·ies.**

a·vi·a·tion (ā′vē ā′shən) the designing, making, and flying of aircraft. *n.*

a·vi·a·tor (ā′vē ā′tər) a person who flies an aircraft; pilot of an aircraft. *n.*

av·id (av′id) eager; greedy: *The miser was avid for gold. adj.*

av·o·ca·do (av′ə kä′dō) a tropical fruit shaped like a pear, with a dark-green skin and a very large seed. *n.*

av·o·ca·tion (av′ə kā′shən) something that a person does besides his regular business; a minor occupation; a hobby: *He is a lawyer, but writing stories in his avocation. n.*

a·void (ə void′) keep away from; keep out of the way of: *We avoided driving through large cities on our trip. v.* **—a·void′a·ble,** *adj.*

a·void·ance (ə void′əns) avoiding; keeping away from: *Her avoidance of her old friends caused her to be disliked. n.*

a·vow (ə vou′) declare frankly or openly; admit: *He avowed that he could not sing. v.*

a·vow·al (ə vou′əl) a frank or open declaration; an admission: *He made an avowal of his opinions even though they were unpopular. n.*

a·wait (ə wāt′) 1 wait for; look forward to: *He has awaited your coming for a week.* 2 be ready for; be in store for: *Many pleasures await you on your trip. v.*

a·wake (ə wāk′) 1 wake up; arouse: *We awoke from a sound sleep. The alarm clock awoke me.* 2 roused from sleep; not asleep: *He is always awake early.* 3 on the alert; watchful: *Our government is awake to that danger.* 1 *v.*, **a·woke** or **a·waked, a·wak·ing;** 2, 3 *adj.*

a·wak·en (ə wāk′ən) 1 wake up; rouse from sleep. 2 make alert or watchful. *v.*

a·wak·en·ing (ə wāk′ən ing) 1 waking up. 2 arousing: *awakening to danger. n.*

a·ward (ə wôrd′) 1 give after careful consideration; grant: *A medal was awarded to the woman who saved the child.* 2 something given after careful consideration; a prize: *His dog won the highest award.* 1 *v.*, 2 *n.*

a·ware (ə wer′) knowing; realizing; conscious: *I was too sleepy to be aware how cold it was. He is not aware of his danger. adj.* **—a·ware′ness,** *n.*

hat, āge, fär; let, ēqual, tėrm; it, īce
hot, ōpen, ôrder; oil, out; cup, pu̇t, rüle
əbove, takən, pencəl, lemən, circəs
ch, child; ng, long; sh, ship
th, thin; ᴛʜ, then; zh, measure

a·way (ə wā′) 1 from a place; to a distance: *Get away from the fire.* 2 at a distance; far: *The sailor was far away from home.* 3 absent; gone: *My mother is away today.* 4 in another direction; aside: *She looked sad and turned away.* 5 out of one's possession, notice, or use: *He gave his boat away.* 6 out of existence: *The sounds died away.* 7 without stopping: *He worked away at his writing.* 1, 2, 4–7 *adv.*, 2, 3 *adj.*

awe (o or ô) 1 great fear and wonder; fear and reverence: *We feel awe when we gaze up at vast mountains, or when we think of God's power and glory.* 2 cause to feel awe; fill with awe: *The majesty of the mountains awed us.* 1 *n.*, 2 *v.*, **awed, aw·ing.**

awe·some (o′səm or ô′səm) 1 causing awe: *The great fire was an awesome sight.* 2 showing awe; awed: *awesome admiration. adj.*

aw·ful (o′fəl or ô′fəl) 1 dreadful; causing fear: *an awful storm with thunder and lightning.* 2 impressive; deserving great respect: *the awful power of God.* 3 very bad, great, ugly, etc.: *His room was in an awful mess. adj.*

aw·ful·ly (o′fəl ē or ô′fəl ē) 1 terribly; dreadfully: *The broken leg hurt awfully.* 2 *Informal.* very; extremely: *I'm awfully sorry that I hurt your feelings. adv.*

a·while (ə wīl′ or ə hwīl′) for a short time: *He stayed awhile. adv.*

awk·ward (ok′wərd or ôk′wərd) 1 clumsy; not graceful in movement or shape: *Seals are very awkward on land, but are graceful in the water.* 2 not well suited to use: *The handle of this pitcher has an awkward shape.* 3 not easily managed: *This is an awkward corner to turn.* 4 embarrassing: *He asked me an awkward question. adj.* **—awk′ward·ly,** *adv.* **—awk′ward·ness,** *n.*

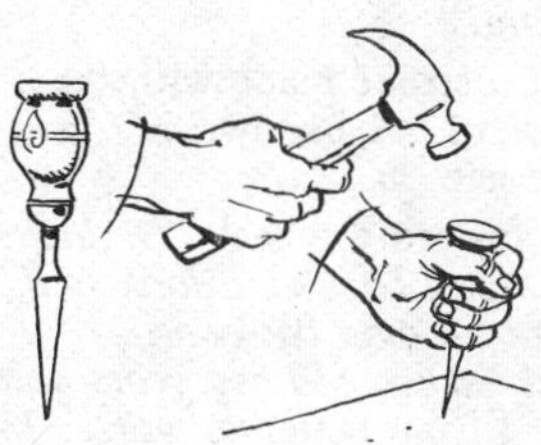
An awl being used to mark places for screws on a piece of wood

awl (ol or ôl) a pointed tool used for making small holes in leather or wood. *n.*
☛ **Awl** and **all** are pronounced the same.

Two awnings on a house

awn·ing (on′ing or ôn′ing) a piece of canvas, metal, wood, or plastic spread above a window, door, porch, deck, or patio for protection from the sun or rain. *n.*

a·woke (ə wōk′) See **awake.** *She awoke at seven. v.*

a·wry (ə rī′) 1 with a twist or turn to one side: *Her hat was blown awry by the wind.* 2 wrong: *Our plans have gone awry. adv.*

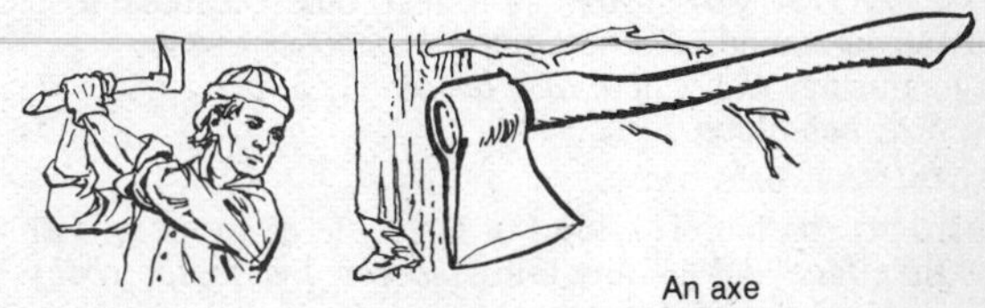
An axe

axe (aks) a tool for chopping wood: *The fireman used his axe to get through the roof of the burning house. n., pl.* **ax·es.** Sometimes spelled **ax.**

ax·is (ak′sis) an imaginary or real line that passes through an object and about which the object turns or seems to turn: *The earth's axis is an imaginary line through the North and South Poles. n., pl.* **ax·es** (ak′sēz).

ax·le (ak′səl) 1 a bar or shaft on which or with which a wheel turns. 2 a crossbar on the two ends of which wheels turn. *n.*

aye[1] or **ay** (ā) always; ever: *A mother's love lasts forever and aye. adv.*

aye[2] or **ay** (ī) 1 yes: *Aye, aye, sir.* 2 an affirmative answer, vote, or voter: *The ayes won when the vote was taken.* 1 *adv.*, 2 *n.*
☛ **Aye**[2], **eye,** and **I** are pronounced the same.

a·zal·ea (ə zāl′yə) a shrub bearing many flowers in a variety of colors. *n.*

az·ure (azh′ər or ā′zhər) blue: *On clear days there is an azure sky. n., adj.*

b or **B** (bē) the second letter of the alphabet: *There are two* b*'s in baby.* *n., pl.* **b's** or **B's.**

baa (bä or ba) **1** the sound a sheep makes. **2** make this sound. 1 *n.,* 2 *v.,* **baas, baaed, baa·ing.**

bab·ble (bab′əl) **1** make sounds like a baby: *My baby brother babbles and coos in his crib.* **2** talk that cannot be understood: *A confused babble filled the room.* **3** talk foolishly or too much: *She babbled on and on about her great adventure.* **4** foolish talk. **5** make a murmuring sound: *The little brook babbled away.* **6** murmuring: *the babble of a brook.* 1, 3, 5 *v.,* **bab·bled, bab·bling;** 2, 4, 6 *n.*

babe (bāb) baby. *n.*

ba·boon (ba bün′) a kind of large, fierce monkey with a doglike face and a short tail: *Baboons live in the rocky hills of Arabia and Africa.* *n.*

ba·by (bā′bē) **1** a very young child: *Some babies cry a good deal.* **2** the youngest of a family or group: *She may be the baby of the class, but she's as smart as any of us.* **3** young: *a baby lamb.* **4** small for its kind; small: *my baby finger.* **5** of or for a baby: *baby shoes.* **6** a person who acts like a baby: *Don't be a baby.* **7** treat as a baby: *to baby a sick child. It makes that boy very angry if he thinks he's being babied.* 1, 2, 5, 6 *n., pl.* **ba·bies;** 3, 4 *adj.,* 7 *v.,* **bab·ied, ba·by·ing.**

baby bonus *Informal.* the Family Allowance.

baby buggy baby carriage.

baby carriage a light carriage used for wheeling a baby about.

ba·by·ish (bā′bē ish) like a baby; childish. *adj.*

ba·by–sit (bā′bē sit′) take care of a child for a time while its parents are out or away from home. *v.,* **ba·by-sat, ba·by-sit·ting.**

ba·by–sit·ter (bā′bē sit′ər) a person who baby-sits. *n.*

bach·e·lor (bach′ə lər) a man who has not married. *n.*

back (bak) **1** the part of a person's body opposite to his face or to the front part of his body. **2** the upper part of an animal's body from the neck to the base of the backbone. **3** the side of anything away from you: *the back of the head, the back of the hand.* **4** opposite the front; behind the front: *the back seat of a car.* **5** the part of a chair or chesterfield that supports the back of a person sitting down. **6** support or help: *Many of his friends backed his plan.* **7** move in reverse; move away from the front: *He backed his car slowly. He backed away from the dog.* **8** behind in space or time: *Please walk back three steps. Have you read the back numbers of this paper? Some years back this land was all in farms.* **9** in return: *You should pay back what you borrow.* **10** in or to the place from which something or someone came: *Put the book back.* 1–3, 5 *n.,* 4, 8 *adj.,* 6, 7 *v.,* 8–10 *adv.*

back down, give up an attempt or claim; withdraw.

back of, behind: *The barn was back of the house.*

back out, *Informal.* withdraw; decide not to do something: *He was going to come on the trip, but he backed out.*

back·bone (bak′bōn′) **1** the series of small bones along the middle of the back in man and other mammals, birds, reptiles, amphibians, and fish: *The many separate bones of the backbone are held together by muscles and tendons that allow movement in different directions.* **2** the most important part; the chief strength or support. **3** strength of character: *A coward lacks the backbone to stand up for his beliefs.* *n.*

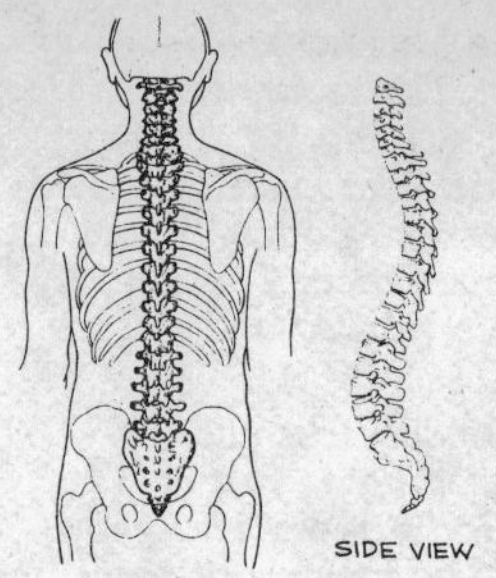

The backbone of a human being

back·fire (bak′fīr′) **1** an explosion of gas occurring too soon or in the wrong place in a gasoline engine. **2** explode in this way. **3** a fire set to check a prairie or forest fire by burning off the area in front of it. **4** have an unexpected bad result: *His plan backfired, and instead of getting rich he lost all his money.* **5** set an area of grass, brush, etc. on fire in order to check a prairie or forest fire. 1, 3 *n.,* 2, 4, 5 *v.*

back·ground (bak′ground′) **1** the part of a picture or scene toward the back: *The cottage stands in the foreground with the mountains in the background.* **2** a surface upon which things are made or placed: *Her dress had pink flowers on a white background.* **3** earlier conditions or events that help to explain some later condition or event: *We studied the background to the news.* **4** past experience, knowledge, and training: *He had the background of life on a farm.* *n.*

in the background, out of sight; not in clear view: *The shy boy kept in the background.*

back·hand (bak′hand′) **1** a stroke made with the back of the hand turned outward. **2** handwriting in which the letters slope to the left. *n.*

back·ward (bak′wərd) **1** toward the back: *He looked backward (adv.). She gave him a backward look (adj.).* **2** with the back first: *He tumbled over backward.* **3** toward the past: *He looked backward forty years and talked about his childhood.* **4** from better to worse: *In some towns living conditions improved; in some they went backward.* **5** slow in development: *Backward children need special help in school.* **6** late; behind time: *This is a backward season; spring is two weeks late.* **7** shy; bashful: *Shake hands with her; don't be backward.* 1–4 *adv.,* 1, 5–7 *adj.* **—back′ward·ness,** *n.*

☛ **Backward** and **backwards** are both used as adverbs: *He tumbled over backwards.*

back·wards (bak′wərdz) backward (defs. 1, 3–5). *adv.*

☛ See note at **backward.**

back·wa·ter (bak′wo′tər or bak′wô′tər) **1** a stretch of water that is held, thrown, or pushed back: *The beaver dam had caused a backwater to form above it at an angle to the main course of the stream.* **2** a backward place: *The town was often referred to as a backwater.* *n.*

back·woods (bak′wu̇dz′) uncleared forests or wild regions far away from towns. *n. pl.*

back·woods·man (bak′wu̇dz′mən) a man who lives

or works in the backwoods. *n., pl.* **back·woods·men** (-mən).

back·yard or **back yard** (bak′yärd′) a yard or garden behind a house: *He grows vegetables in his backyard.* *n.*

ba·con (bā′kən) salted and smoked meat from the back and sides of a pig. *n.*

bac·te·ri·a (bak tēr′ē ə) very tiny and simple plants, so small that they can usually be seen only through a microscope: *Certain bacteria cause diseases such as pneumonia and typhoid fever; others help with digestion in the intestines.* *n. pl.*

bac·te·ri·ol·o·gy (bak tēr′ē ol′ə jē) the science that deals with bacteria. *n.*

bad (bad) **1** not good; not as it ought to be: *It is bad for your eyes to read in a dim light.* **2** evil; wicked: *Only a very bad person would hurt someone who is helpless.* **3** not friendly; cross; disagreeable: *a bad temper.* **4** unfavorable: *He came at a bad time.* **5** severe: *A bad thunderstorm delayed the airplane.* **6** rotten; spoiled: *a bad egg.* **7** sorry: *I feel bad about losing your baseball.* **8** sick. *adj.,* **worse, worst.** —**bad′ness,** *n.*

not bad or **not half bad,** *Informal.* fairly good.

☞ **Bad** and **bade** are sometimes pronounced the same.

bade (bad or bād) See **bid** (defs. 1–3). *v.*

☞ **Bade** and **bad** are sometimes pronounced the same.

badge (baj) **1** something worn to show that a person belongs to a certain school, class, club, society, occupation, etc.: *Policemen wear badges. The Red Cross badge is a red cross on a white background.* **2** a symbol or sign: *A mayor's chain is his badge of office.* *n.*

badg·er (baj′ər) **1** a coarse-haired, grey, burrowing animal, related to the weasel but much larger and broader in the body: *Badgers hunt animals such as gophers by digging them out of their holes.* **2** its fur. **3** keep after someone; try again and again to convince: *A car salesman has been badgering my father for weeks.* 1, 2 *n.,* 3 *v.*

bad·lands (bad′landz′) a region of barren land such as that found in southwestern Saskatchewan and southeastern Alberta: *The skeletons of prehistoric animals have been found in the badlands.* *n.*

bad·ly (bad′lē) **1** in a bad manner: *She sings badly.* **2** *Informal.* very much: *He wants to go badly.* *adv.*

bad·min·ton (bad′min tən) a game in which either two or four players use light rackets to keep a shuttlecock moving back and forth over a high net. *n.*

baf·fle (baf′əl) **1** be too hard for a person to understand or solve: *This puzzle baffles me.* **2** a device for hindering or changing the flow of air, water, or sound waves: *a baffle for a jet engine.* 1 *v.,* **baf·fled, baf·fling;** 2 *n.*

bag (bag) **1** a container made of paper, cloth, leather, etc. that can be pulled together to close at the top: *Fresh vegetables are sometimes sold in plastic bags.* **2** something like a bag in its use or shape: *Mother calls her purse a bag.* **3** put into a bag or bags: *We bagged the cookies we had baked so we could sell them.* **4** swell; bulge: *His trousers bag at the knees.* **5** the game killed or caught at one time by a hunter. **6** kill or catch in hunting: *The hunter bagged many ducks.* 1, 2, 5 *n.,* 3, 4, 6 *v.,* **bagged, bag·ging.**

ba·gel (bā′gəl) a hard roll made of yeast dough shaped into a ring. *n.*

hat, āge, fär; let, ēqual, tėrm; it, īce
hot, ōpen, ôrder; oil, out; cup, pu̇t, rüle
əbove, takən, pencəl, lemən, circəs
ch, child; ng, long; sh, ship
th, thin; ᴛʜ, then; zh, measure

☞ **Bagel** comes from a Yiddish word meaning 'to twist.'

bag·gage (bag′ij) **1** the trunks, bags, suitcases, etc. that a person takes with him when he travels. **2** the equipment that an army takes with it, such as tents, blankets, dishes, etc. *n.*

bag·gy (bag′ē) hanging loosely; baglike: *The clown had baggy trousers.* *adj.,* **bag·gi·er, bag·gi·est.**

A bagpipe. The player blows air into the bag and, by pressing with his arm, controls the flow of air into the pipes that produce the sound.

bag·pipe (bag′pīp′) Often, **bagpipes,** *pl.* a musical instrument made of a tube, a bag for air, and pipes, associated chiefly with Scotland. *n.*

bail[1] (bāl) **1** the guarantee of money necessary to release an arrested person until he is to appear for trial: *The man gave bail for his son who was accused of setting fire to a barn.* **2** obtain the release of a person under arrest by making such a guarantee: *He bailed out his son.* 1 *n.,* 2 *v.*

☞ **Bail** and **bale** are pronounced the same.

bail[2] (bāl) the handle of a kettle or pail. See **pail** for picture. *n.*

☞ See note at **bail**[1].

bail[3] (bāl) dip and throw water out of a boat with a bucket, pail, dipper, etc. *v.*

bail out, drop from an airplane by parachute: *When the plane caught fire, the pilot bailed out.*

☞ See note at **bail**[1].

bairn (bern) *Scottish.* child. *n.*

bait (bāt) **1** anything, especially food, used to attract fish or other animals so that they may be caught: *Worms are often used as bait in fishing.* **2** put bait on a hook or in a trap. **3** anything used to tempt or attract a person to begin something he would not wish to do. **4** torment by unkind or annoying remarks: *Only a cruel person would bait a cripple.* 1, 3 *n.,* 2, 4 *v.*

bake (bāk) **1** cook food by dry heat without exposing it directly to the fire: *The cook bakes bread in an oven.* **2** dry or harden by heat: *to bake bricks or china.* **3** become baked: *Cookies bake quickly.* *v.,* **baked, bak·ing.**

bak·er (bāk′ər) a person who makes or sells bread, pies, cakes, etc. *n.*

baker's dozen thirteen.

bak·er·y (bāk′ər ē) a baker's shop; a place where bread, cakes, etc. are made or sold. *n., pl.* **bak·er·ies.**

baking powder a mixture including bicarbonate of soda and used to cause biscuits, cakes, etc. to rise.

baking soda bicarbonate of soda.

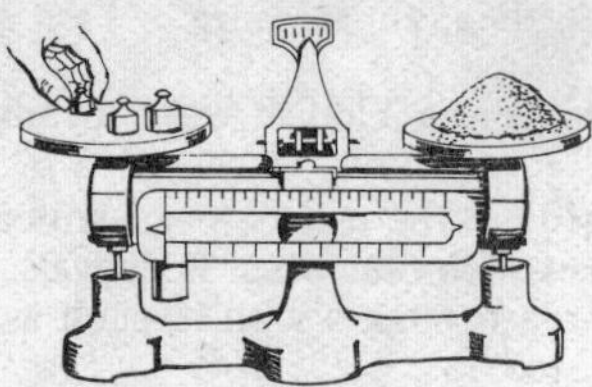

A balance. The thing to be weighed is put on one platform and metal weights of known value are added to the other until the two platforms balance.

bal·ance (bal′əns) **1** an instrument for weighing. **2** weigh two things against each other on scales or in one's hands to see which is heavier. **3** compare the value, importance, etc. of: *He balanced a trip to the Rockies against the chance of a summer job.* **4** equality in weight, amount, etc.: *He adjusted the balance between the two loudspeakers of his stereo set.* **5** a steady condition or position; steadiness: *He lost his balance and fell off the ladder.* **6** keep or put in a steady condition or position: *Can you balance a coin on its edge?* **7** steadiness of character: *His balance kept him from doing anything foolish during the game for the championship.* **8** the part that is left over; the remainder: *I will be away the balance of the week. I have a balance of $20 in the bank.* 1, 4, 5, 7, 8 *n.*, 2, 3, 6 *v.*, **bal·anced, bal·anc·ing.**

in the balance, undecided: *The outcome was in the balance until the last inning.*

bal·co·ny (bal′kə nē) **1** an outside projecting platform with an entrance from an upper floor of a building. **2** in a theatre or hall, a projecting upper floor with seats for an audience. *n., pl.* **bal·co·nies.**

bald (bold or bôld) **1** completely or partly without hair on the head. **2** without natural covering: *A mountain with no trees or grass on it is bald.* **3** bare; plain: *The bald truth is that he is a thief.* *adj.* **—bald′ly,** *adv.* **—bald′ness,** *n.*

bald eagle a large, powerful North American eagle, with white feathers on its head, neck, and tail.

bald prairie that part of the western prairie which is almost without trees.

bale (bāl) **1** a large bundle of merchandise or material securely wrapped or tied for shipping or storage: *a bale of paper.* **2** make into bales; tie in large bundles: *We saw a big machine bale hay.* 1 *n.*, 2 *v.*, **baled, bal·ing.**

☛ **Bale** and **bail** are pronounced the same.

bale·ful (bāl′fəl) evil; harmful: *The wicked witch gave the children a baleful glance.* *adj.* **—bale′ful·ly,** *adv.*

bal·er (bāl′ər) a machine that compresses and ties up into bundles such things as hay, straw, paper, and scrap metal. *n.*

balk (bok or bôk) **1** stop short and stubbornly refuse to go on: *My horse balked at the fence.* **2** prevent from going on; hinder: *The police balked the robber's plans.* *v.*

balk·y (bok′ē or bôk′ē) tending to stop short and stubbornly refuse to go on: *Mules are balky animals.* *adj.*, **balk·i·er, balk·i·est.**

ball[1] (bol or bôl) **1** a round or, sometimes, oval object that is thrown, kicked, knocked, bounced, or batted about in various games. **2** a game in which some kind of ball is thrown, hit, or kicked. **3** anything round or roundish; something that resembles a ball: *He bought a ball of string. He had a blister on the ball of his thumb.* **4** in baseball, a ball pitched too high, too low, or not over the plate, which the batter does not strike at. **5** a bullet for firearms; a round, solid object to be shot from a gun. *n.*

☛ **Ball** and **bawl** are pronounced the same.

ball[2] (bol or bôl) **1** a large, formal party with dancing. **2** *Slang.* a very good time; a lot of fun: *We had a ball at the party.* *n.*

☛ See note at **ball**[1].

bal·lad (bal′əd) **1** a simple song. **2** a poem that tells a story: *Ballads are often sung.* *n.*

bal·last (bal′əst) **1** something heavy carried in a ship to steady it. **2** something heavy carried in a balloon or dirigible to steady it: *The balloon used bags of sand for ballast.* **3** the gravel or crushed rock used in making the bed for a road or railway track. *n.*

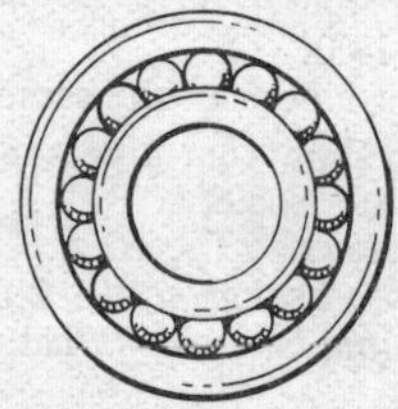

A ball bearing from the hub of a bicycle wheel

ball bearing **1** a grooved ring containing loose metal balls so that a shaft going through the ring can turn easily. **2** one of the metal balls so used.

bal·let (bal′ā or ba lā′) **1** an artistic dance that usually tells a story, performed in a theatre, concert hall, etc. **2** the art of creating or performing ballets: *She is studying ballet.* **3** a company of dancers that perform ballets. *n.*

bal·loon (bə lün′) **1** an air-tight bag filled with air or a gas lighter than air, so that it will rise and float: *Small balloons are used as toys and decorations; larger balloons can be used as signals, advertisements, etc.* **2** swell out like a balloon: *The sails of the boat ballooned in the wind.* 1 *n.*, 2 *v.*

bal·lot (bal′ət) **1** a piece of paper or other object used in voting: *He cast his ballot for the Liberal Party.* **2** the total number of votes cast. **3** vote or decide by using ballots. 1, 2 *n.*, 3 *v.*, **bal·lot·ed, bal·lot·ing.**

ball–point or **ball·point** (bol′point′ or bôl′point′) a pen having a small metal ball in place of a nib. *n.*

ball·room (bol′rüm′ or bôl′rüm′) a large room for dancing. *n.*

balm (bom or bäm) **1** a fragrant, oily, sticky substance obtained from certain kinds of trees, used to heal or to relieve pain. **2** anything that heals or soothes: *Mother's kind words were a balm to my wounded feelings.* *n.*

☛ **Balm** and **bomb** are sometimes pronounced the same.

balm of Gil·e·ad (gil′ē əd) **1** a kind of poplar tree; the balsam poplar. **2** the balsam fir.

balm·y (bom′ē or bäm′ē) mild; soft; gentle: *a balmy breeze.* *adj.*, **balm·i·er, balm·i·est.**

hat, āge, fär; let, ēqual, tėrm; it, īce
hot, ōpen, ôrder; oil, out; cup, pu̇t, rüle
ə̄bove, takən, pencəl, lemən, circəs
ch, child; ng, long; sh, ship
th, thin; ᴛʜ, then; zh, measure

bal·sa (bol′sə or bôl′sə) **1** a tropical American tree with wood that is light and strong. **2** the wood. *n.*

bal·sam (bol′səm or bôl′səm) **1** a sticky substance obtained from certain trees; balm. **2** a tree giving this substance; balsam fir. *n.*

balsam fir a kind of fir tree: *Balsam firs are much used as Christmas trees.*

balsam poplar a kind of poplar tree having oval or heart-shaped leaves.

bam·boo (bam bü′) a woody or treelike tropical grass with a stiff, hollow stem that has hard, thick joints: *He bought a fishing rod made of bamboo. n., pl.* **bam·boos.**

ban (ban) **1** make a rule against; forbid by law or authority: *Swimming is banned in this lake.* **2** the forbidding of an act or speech by authority: *There is a ban on parking cars in this narrow street.* 1 *v.,* **banned, ban·ning;** 2 *n.*

ba·nan·a (bə nan′ə) **1** a slightly curved, yellow tropical fruit with firm, creamy flesh: *Bananas grow in large bunches.* **2** the plant this fruit grows on: *The banana is like a tree with great, long leaves. n.*

band (band) **1** a number of persons or animals joined or acting together: *a band of robbers, a band of wild dogs.* **2** unite in a group: *The children banded together to buy a present for their teacher.* **3** a group of musicians playing various instruments together: *The band played several marches.* **4** *Cdn.* a group of reserve Indians recognized by the federal government as an official unit. **5** a thin, flat strip of material for binding, trimming, or some other purpose: *The oak box was strengthened with bands of iron. Put rubber bands around that package.* **6** put a band on: *People often band birds in order to identify them later.* **7** in radio broadcasting, a particular range of wave lengths or frequencies. **8** a stripe: *The white cup has a gold band.* 1, 3–5, 7, 8 *n.,* 2, 6 *v.*

band·age (ban′dij) **1** a strip of cloth or some other material used in dressing and binding up a wound or injury. **2** bind or dress with a bandage. 1 *n.,* 2 *v.,* **band·aged, band·ag·ing.**

Band–Aid (band′ād′) a trademark for a bandage made of a piece of cotton gauze attached to a strip of adhesive tape. *n.*

ban·dan·a or **ban·dan·na** (ban dan′ə) a large, colored handkerchief. *n.*

ban·dit (ban′dit) a highwayman; a robber. *n., pl.* **ban·dits** or **ban·dit·ti** (ban dit′ē).

ban·dy–leg·ged (ban′dē leg′id) having legs that curve outward like a bow; bowlegged. *adj.*

bang (bang) **1** a sudden, loud noise: *We heard the bang of a gun.* **2** make a sudden, loud noise: *The door banged as it blew shut.* **3** a violent, noisy blow: *He gave the drum a bang.* **4** hit with violent and noisy blows; strike noisily: *The baby was banging the pan with a spoon.* **5** shut with a noise; slam: *He banged the door.* 1, 3 *n.,* 2, 4, 5 *v.*

bangs (bangz) a fringe of hair cut short and worn over the forehead: *She has short hair and bangs. n. pl.*

ban·ish (ban′ish) **1** condemn to leave a country for a long time or forever: *The king banished some of his enemies.* **2** force to go away; drive away: *The children banished him from their game because he always cheated. v.*

ban·ish·ment (ban′ish mənt) **1** banishing: *The king ordered the banishment of his enemies.* **2** being banished; exile: *His banishment lasted for 20 years. n.*

ban·is·ter (ban′is tər) the handrail of a staircase together with its row of supports. *n.*

A banjo

ban·jo (ban′jō) a stringed musical instrument played with the fingers or a pick. *n., pl.* **ban·jos** or **ban·joes.**

bank¹ (bangk) **1** a long pile or heap: *There was a bank of snow over ten feet deep.* **2** pile up; heap up: *The tractors banked the snow by the side of the road.* **3** the ground bordering a river, lake, etc. **4** a shallow place in water; a shoal: *The famous Newfoundland fishing grounds called the Grand Banks are shallow places in the Atlantic caused by banks on the ocean floor.* **5** the tilting of an airplane to one side when making a turn. **6** tilt when making a turn: *The pilot banked the airplane steeply. The airplane banked as it turned south.* **7** turn down the draft or cover a fire with ashes so that it will burn slowly: *The janitor banked the fire for the night.* 1, 3–5 *n.,* 2, 6, 7 *v.*

bank² (bangk) **1** a place for keeping, lending, exchanging, and paying out money. **2** keep money in a bank: *My father banks at the branch near his office.* **3** put money in a bank: *I bank part of my allowance once a month.* **4** any place where reserve supplies are kept: *The place where blood is kept for transfusions is called a blood bank.* 1, 4 *n.,* 2, 3 *v.*
bank on, depend on: *I can bank on my teacher to help me.*

bank³ (bangk) a row or close arrangement of things: *a bank of switches, a bank of machines. n.*

bank·er¹ (bang′kər) a person or company that manages a bank. *n.*

bank·er² (bang′kər) *Cdn.* **1** a fisherman who fishes off the Grand Banks. **2** a fishing vessel that operates off the Grand Banks: *The banker came into port with its holds filled with cod. n.*

bank·ing (bang′king) the business of keeping, lending, exchanging, and issuing money. *n.*

bank·rupt (bang′krupt) **1** a person declared by a court to be unable to pay his debts: *The property of a bankrupt is divided among the people to whom he owes money.* **2** unable to pay one's debts. **3** make bankrupt: *His last business deal bankrupted him.* 1 *n.,* 2 *adj.,* 3 *v.*

ban·ner (ban′ər) **1** flag: *a school banner.* **2** leading or outstanding; foremost: *Ours was the banner class in* *relay and swimming races at school last week.* 1 *n.*, 2 *adj.*

ban·quet (bang′kwit) a formal dinner or a feast, often with speeches: *The teachers had a banquet for the principal when he retired.* *n.*

ban·tam (ban′təm) **1** a kind of small barnyard fowl: *We have a bantam rooster.* **2** a very small person, usually one fond of fighting. **3** in sports, a class for players under 15 years: *My brother plays hockey in a league for bantams.* *n.*

ban·ter (ban′tər) **1** playful teasing; joking: *She didn't mind her friends' banter about her freckles.* **2** tease playfully; make fun of. **3** talk in a joking way. 1 *n.*, 2, 3 *v.*

bap·tism (bap′tiz əm) the rite or ceremony of dipping a person into water or sprinkling water on him, as a sign of washing away sin and admission to the Christian church. *n.*

Bap·tist (bap′tist) **1** a member of a Christian church that believes in baptism by dipping the whole person under water. **2** of or having something to do with the Baptists. 1 *n.*, 2 *adj.*

bap·tize (bap tīz′) **1** dip into water or sprinkle with water as a sign of washing away sin and admission into the Christian church. **2** give a first name to a person at baptism; christen: *The baby was baptized Robert.* *v.*, **bap·tized, bap·tiz·ing.**

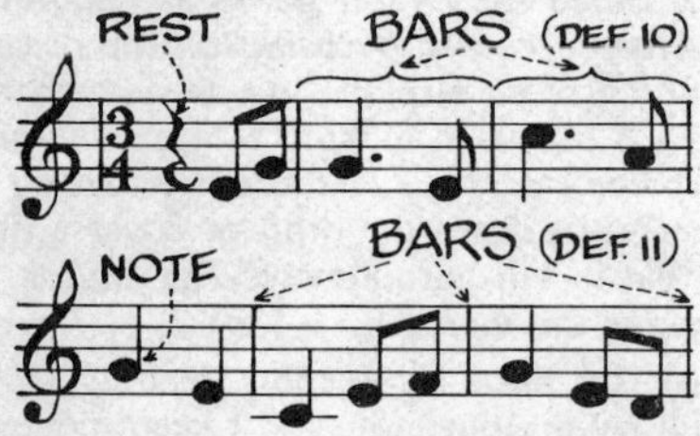

bar¹ (bär) **1** an evenly shaped piece of some solid, longer than it is wide or thick: *a bar of iron, a bar of soap, a bar of chocolate.* **2** a pole or rod put across a door, gate, window, etc. to fasten or shut off something: *Let down the pasture bars so that the cows may come in.* **3** put bars across; fasten or shut off: *He bars the doors every night.* **4** anything that blocks the way or prevents progress: *A bar of sand kept boats out of the harbor. His bad temper was a bar to making friends.* **5** block; obstruct: *The way out was barred by chairs.* **6** exclude; forbid: *All talking is barred during a study period.* **7** except; excluding: *He is the best student, bar none.* **8** a band of color; stripe. **9** mark with stripes or bands of color: *a chicken with barred feathers.* **10** a unit of rhythm in music: *The regular accent falls on the first note of each bar.* **11** the dividing line between two bars on the musical staff. **12** the whole group of practising lawyers: *After passing his law examinations, he was called to the bar.* **13** a counter or place where drinks and, sometimes, food are served. **14** a store counter over which certain articles are sold: *a snack bar, a record bar, a hat bar, a cosmetic bar.* 1, 2, 4, 8, 10–14 *n.*, 3, 5, 6, 9 *v.*, **barred, bar·ring;** 7 *prep.*

bar² (bär) a measure of air pressure: *The usual air pressure at sea level is one bar.* *n.*

barb (bärb) **1** a point sticking out and back from the main point. **2** equip with a barb. 1 *n.*, 2 *v.*

bar·bar·i·an (bär ber′ē ən) **1** a person belonging to a foreign tribe, thought to be uncivilized: *Rome was conquered by barbarian peoples.* **2** not civilized; considered to be rude, savage, or ignorant. 1 *n.*, 2 *adj.*

bar·bar·ic (bär bar′ik or bär ber′ik) **1** like barbarians; rough and rude; suited to an uncivilized people. **2** rich or splendid in a wild, foreign way: *The explorers were awed by the barbaric splendor of the ancient city.* *adj.*

bar·ba·rous (bär′bə rəs) **1** not civilized. **2** cruel: *Torture of prisoners is a barbarous custom.* *adj.* **—bar′ba·rous·ly,** *adv.*

bar·be·cue (bär′bə kyü′) **1** a grill or open fireplace for cooking meat, usually over charcoal. **2** an outdoor meal prepared on a barbecue. **3** meat roasted over an open fire. **4** roast meat over an open fire. **5** cook meat or fish in a highly flavored sauce. 1–3 *n.*, 4, 5 *v.*, **bar·be·cued, bar·be·cu·ing.**

☞ **Barbecue** is from a Spanish word that came from *barboka,* a word from Haiti meaning 'a framework of sticks.'

barbed (bärbd) having a barb or barbs: *a barbed fish-hook.* *adj.*

barbed wire twisted wire having sharp points on it every few inches, used for fences.

bar·ber (bär′bər) a person whose business is cutting hair and shaving or trimming beards. *n.*

bard (bärd) **1** a poet and singer of long ago: *The bard sang his own poems to the music of his harp.* **2** poet. *n.*

bare (ber) **1** without covering; not clothed; naked: *The sun burned his bare shoulders. Trees grew part way up the hill, but the top was bare.* **2** empty; not furnished: *The room was bare. The walls were bare of pictures.* **3** plain; not adorned: *He told us the bare facts.* **4** just enough and no more; mere: *He earns a bare living.* **5** make bare; uncover; reveal: *The dog bared his teeth.* 1–4 *adj.*, **bar·er, bar·est;** 5 *v.*, **bared, bar·ing. —bare′ness,** *n.*

☞ **Bare** and **bear** are pronounced the same.

bare·back (ber′bak′) without a saddle; on a horse's bare back: *to ride bareback, a bareback rider.* *adv., adj.*

bare·foot (ber′fu̇t′) without shoes and stockings on: *A barefoot child played in the puddles. If you go barefoot, watch out for broken glass.* *adj., adv.*

bare·head·ed (ber′hed′id) wearing nothing on the head. *adj.*

bare·ly (ber′lē) **1** only just; scarcely: *He has barely enough money to live on.* **2** poorly or scantily: *The room was furnished barely but neatly.* *adv.*

bar·gain (bär′gən) **1** an agreement to trade or exchange: *If you will take $5 for your book, it's a bargain.* **2** something offered for sale cheap or bought cheap: *This hat is a bargain.* **3** try to get good terms: *For ten minutes she stood bargaining with the farmer for his vegetables.* 1, 2 *n.*, 3 *v.*

bargain for, expect; be ready for: *We expected rain, but the hail was more than we bargained for.*

into the bargain, besides; also: *It is late, and I am tired into the bargain.*

barge (bärj) **1** a large, flat-bottomed boat for carrying freight. **2** a large boat used for excursions, pageants, and special occasions. **3** move clumsily like a barge: *He barged into the table and knocked the lamp over.* **4** *Informal.* push oneself rudely: *Don't barge in where you're not wanted.* 1, 2 *n.*, 3, 4 *v.*

bar·i·tone (bar′ə tōn′ or ber′ətōn′) **1** a male voice between tenor and bass. **2** a singer with such a voice. **3** a part sung by, or written for, such a voice. *n.*

bark[1] (bärk) **1** the tough outside covering of the trunk, branches, and roots of trees. **2** strip the bark from a tree. **3** scrape the skin from: *I fell down the steps and barked my shins.* 1 *n.*, 2, 3 *v.*

bark[2] (bärk) **1** the short, sharp sound a dog makes. **2** a sound like this: *the bark of a fox, a gun, or a cough.* **3** make this sound or one like it: *The dog barked.* **4** speak sharply or gruffly: *Some officers bark out their orders.* 1, 2 *n.*, 3, 4 *v.*

bark[3] (bärk) See **barque.**

bar·ley (bär′lē) the seed or grain of a grasslike plant, used for food and for making malt. *n.*

bar mitz·vah (bär′mits′və) **1** a ceremony that formally brings a boy into the Jewish religious community, usually held when the boy is thirteen years old. **2** a boy who has reached the age of thirteen, the age of religious responsibility.

☞ **Bar mitzvah** comes from the Hebrew words *bar misvah* meaning 'son of the divine law.'

barn (bärn) a building for storing hay, grain, and farm machinery and for sheltering farm animals. *n.*

bar·na·cle (bär′nə kəl) a small salt-water animal that has a shell and attaches itself to rocks, the bottoms of ships, the timbers of docks, etc. *n.*

barn·yard (bärn′yärd′) the yard around a barn for farm animals. *n.*

A barometer. A flexible box in this instrument expands or contracts with changes in air pressure and moves one of the pointers. The other pointer is set by hand and remains fixed, acting as a guide to how much the first pointer moves.

ba·rom·e·ter (bə rom′ə tər) **1** an instrument for measuring the pressure of the air and determining height above sea level: *A barometer shows probable changes in the weather.* **2** something that indicates changes: *Newspapers are often called barometers of public opinion.* *n.*

bar·on (bar′ən or ber′ən) **1** a nobleman of the lowest rank: *In the United Kingdom, a baron has 'Lord' before his name, instead of 'Baron' as in other European countries.* **2** during the Middle Ages, an English nobleman who held his lands directly from the king. *n.*

☞ **Baron** and **barren** are pronounced the same.

bar·on·ess (bar′ən is or ber′ən is) **1** the wife or widow of a baron. **2** a woman whose rank is equal to that of a baron. *n.*

hat, āge, fär; let, ēqual, tėrm; it, īce
hot, ōpen, ôrder; oil, out; cup, pu̇t, rüle
əbove, takən, pencəl, lemən, circəs
ch, child; ng, long; sh, ship
th, thin; ᴛʜ, then; zh, measure

bar·on·et (bar′ən it or ber′ən it, bar′ən et′ or ber′ən et′) in the United Kingdom, a man below a baron in rank and next above a knight. *n.*

barque (bärk) **1** a kind of sailing ship with three masts. **2** in poetry, any boat or ship. *n.* Also spelled **bark.**

bar·racks (bar′əks or ber′əks) **1** a building or group of buildings for soldiers to live in. **2** a building housing local detachments of the Royal Canadian Mounted Police. **3** *Informal.* a training centre of the Royal Canadian Mounted Police: *My brother is training at the RCMP barracks in Regina.* *n.*

☞ **Barracks** may be used with either a singular or a plural verb: *John wrote that his barracks was a lively place. The barracks were inspected daily.*

A barrel

bar·rel (bar′əl or ber′əl) **1** a container with round, flat ends and slightly curved sides: *Barrels are usually made of boards held together by hoops.* **2** the amount that a barrel can hold. **3** the metal tube of a gun, rifle, or pistol. *n.*

bar·ren (bar′ən or ber′ən) **1** not producing anything: *A desert is barren.* **2** not able to bear offspring. **3 barrens,** *pl. Cdn.* a barren stretch of land; wasteland: *The Barren Ground of northern Canada is often called the Barrens.* 1, 2 *adj.*, 3 *n.*

☞ **Barren** and **baron** are pronounced the same.

Barren Ground *Cdn.* the treeless, thinly populated region in northern Canada, lying between Hudson Bay on the east and Great Slave Lake and Great Bear Lake on the west: *Much of the Barren Ground is covered, in season, with short grass, moss, and small flowering plants.*

Barren Lands *Cdn.* the Barren Ground.

bar·rette (bə ret′) a pin with a clasp, used by women and girls for holding the hair in place. *n.*

bar·ri·cade (bar′ə kād′ or ber′ə kād′) **1** a rough, hastily made barrier for defence: *The soldiers cut down trees to make a barricade across the road.* **2** any barrier or obstruction. **3** block or obstruct with a barricade: *The soldiers barricaded the road with fallen trees.* 1, 2 *n.*, 3 *v.*, **bar·ri·cad·ed, bar·ri·cad·ing.**

bar·ri·er (bar′ē ər or ber′ē ər) **1** something that stands in the way: *A dam is a barrier holding back water.* **2** something stopping progress or preventing approach: *Lack of water was a barrier to the settlement of that region.* **3** something that separates or keeps apart: *The Atlantic Ocean is a barrier between the British Isles and Canada.* *n.*

bar·row (bar′ō or ber′ō) **1** a frame with two short

handles at each end, used for carrying a load. **2** wheelbarrow. *n.*

bar·ter (bär′tər) **1** trade by exchanging one kind of goods for another kind without using money: *The Indians bartered fur for beads and guns.* **2** trading in this way. 1 *v.,* 2 *n.*

base¹ (bās) **1** the part of a thing on which it rests; the bottom: *The machine rests on a wide base of steel.* See **column** for picture. **2** a starting place; headquarters: *Our army established a base to store supplies and from which to fight.* **3** establish; found: *His large business was based on good service.* **4** a basis or foundation: *This dog food has a meat base.* **5** a station or goal in certain games, such as baseball or hide-and-seek: *The player slid into third base.* **6** a chemical substance that unites with an acid to form a salt. 1, 2, 4–6 *n.,* 3 *v.,* **based, bas·ing. —base′ly,** *adv.* **—base′ness,** *n.*

☛ **Base** and **bass¹** are pronounced the same.

base² (bās) **1** mean and selfish; low; cowardly: *To betray a friend is a base action.* **2** having little value when compared with something else; inferior: *Iron and lead are base metals; gold and silver are precious metals.* *adj.,* **bas·er, bas·est.**

☛ See note at **base¹**.

base·ball (bās′bol′ or bās′bôl′) **1** a game played with bat and ball by two teams of nine players each, on a field with four bases. **2** the ball used in this game. *n.*

base·board (bās′bôrd′) **1** a line of boards around the walls of a room, next to the floor. **2** a board forming the base of anything: *He glued his model onto a wooden baseboard.* *n.*

base·ment (bās′mənt) the lowest storey of a building, partly or completely below ground; cellar. *n.*

ba·ses¹ (bā′sēz) plural of **basis.** *n.*

bas·es² (bā′siz) plural of **base¹**. *n.*

bash·ful (bash′fəl) uneasy and awkward in the company of strangers; shy: *The little girl was too bashful to greet us.* *adj.* **—bash′ful·ly,** *adv.* **—bash′ful·ness,** *n.*

ba·sic (bā′sik) forming the base; fundamental: *Addition, subtraction, multiplication, and division are the basic processes of arithmetic.* *adj.*

ba·sin (bā′sən) **1** a wide, shallow dish for holding liquids. **2** the amount that a basin can hold: *They have used up a basin of water already.* **3** a shallow area containing water: *Part of the harbor is a basin for sailboats.* **4** all the land drained by a river and the streams that flow into it: *the St. Lawrence basin.* *n.*

ba·sis (bā′sis) **1** the main part; base: *The basis of this medicine is an oil.* **2** foundation: *The basis of their friendship was their interest in baseball.* *n., pl.* **ba·ses** (bā′sēz).

bask (bask) warm oneself pleasantly: *The children enjoyed basking in the sun.* *v.*

bas·ket (bas′kit) **1** a container made of twigs, grasses, fibres, strips of wood, etc. woven together: *a clothes basket.* **2** the amount that a basket holds: *We bought a basket of peaches.* **3** anything that looks like or is shaped like a basket: *Some baskets for waste paper are made of metal.* **4** the ring and net used as a goal in basketball. **5** a score made in basketball by tossing the ball through the basket. *n.*

bas·ket·ball (bas′kit bol′ or bas′kit bôl′) **1** a game played with a large, round ball by two teams, usually of five players each. The players try to toss the ball through a ring into a net shaped like a basket but open at the bottom. **2** the ball used in this game. *n.*

Basque (bask) **1** a member of a people living in the mountains of southern France and northern Spain. **2** the language of this people. **3** of or having to do with the Basques or their language. 1, 2 *n.,* 3 *adj.*

bass¹ (bās) **1** having a deep, low sound. **2** the lowest adult male voice: *He sings bass in the choir.* **3** a singer with such a voice. **4** a part sung by, or written for, such a voice. *n., pl.* **bas·ses** (bās′iz).

☛ **Bass¹** and **base** are pronounced the same.

bass² (bas) a kind of fish found in both fresh and salt water, used for food. *n., pl.* **bass** or **bass·es.**

A bassoon

bas·soon (bə sün′) a deep-toned wind instrument with a double wooden tube and a curved metal mouthpiece. *n.*

bass vi·ol (bās′ vī′əl) double bass.

baste¹ (bāst) drip or pour melted fat or butter or a sauce on meat, fowl, etc. as it is roasting. *v.,* **bast·ed, bast·ing.**

baste² (bāst) sew temporarily with long, loose stitches: *Basted stitches are usually removed after the final sewing.* *v.,* **bast·ed, bast·ing.**

bat¹ (bat) **1** a specially shaped wooden stick or club, used to hit the ball in baseball, cricket, etc. **2** hit with a bat; hit: *He bats well. I batted the balloon over to him with my hand.* **3** a turn at batting: *Lynn, you are next at bat.* **4** a stroke; blow. 1, 3, 4 *n.,* 2 *v.,* **bat·ted, bat·ting.**

A little brown bat — about 9 cm long; wingspread about 35 cm

bat² (bat) a flying animal that resembles a mouse with skinlike wings: *Bats fly at night and most of them feed on insects.* *n.* **—bat′like′,** *adj.*

batch (bach) **1** a quantity of bread made at one baking. **2** a quantity of anything made as one lot or set: *Our second batch of candy was better than the first.* **3** a number of persons or things taken together: *He caught a fine batch of fish.* *n.*

ba·teau or **bat·teau** (ba tō′) *Cdn.* a light, flat-bottomed river boat: *Bateaux were used to carry freight and passengers between Montreal and Kingston.* *n., pl.* **ba·teaux** (ba tōz′).

hat, āge, fär; let, ēqual, tėrm; it, īce
hot, ōpen, ôrder; oil, out; cup, pu̇t, rüle
əbove, takən, pencəl, lemən, circəs
ch, child; ng, long; sh, ship
th, thin; ᴛʜ, then; zh, measure

bath (bath) **1** a washing of the body. **2** the water, towels, etc. for a bath: *Your bath is ready.* **3** a tub, a room, or other place for bathing: *The house had no bath, so we had one built.* **4** give a bath to: *Mother baths the baby every day.* **5** take a bath: *He always baths at night.* 1–3 *n., pl.* **baths** (baᴛʜz); 4, 5 *v.*

bathe (bāᴛʜ) **1** take a bath: *He bathes regularly.* **2** give a bath to: *He is bathing his dog.* **3** apply water to; wash or moisten with any liquid: *Bathe your feet if they are tired. The doctor told her to bathe her eyes with the lotion.* **4** go in swimming; go into a pool, river, lake, or ocean for pleasure. **5** cover or surround: *The valley was bathed in sunlight.* *v.,* **bathed, bath·ing.** **—bath′er,** *n.*

bathing suit (bā′ᴛʜ′ing) a garment worn for swimming.

bath·robe (bath′rōb′) a long, loose robe worn when going to and from a bath and when resting or lounging. *n.*

bath·room (bath′rüm′) **1** a room fitted up for taking baths and usually equipped with a washbasin and a toilet (def. 2). **2** a room containing a toilet (def. 2): *The boy said he wanted to go to the bathroom.* *n.*

bath·tub (bath′tub′) a tub to take a bath in. *n.*

ba·tik (bə tēk′) a method of making designs on cloth by dyeing only part at a time, protecting the remainder with a removable coating of melted wax. *n.*

ba·ton (ba ton′) **1** a staff or stick used as a mark of office or authority. **2** a stick passed from runner to runner in a relay race. **3** the stick used by the leader of an orchestra, band, etc. to indicate the beat and to direct the performance. **4** a light, hollow metal rod twirled for display: *She twirled a baton and walked ahead of the band in the parade.* *n.*

bat·tal·ion (bə tal′yən) **1** a formation of four companies within a regiment of infantry. **2** any large group organized to act together: *A battalion of volunteers helped to rescue the flood victims.* *n.*

bat·teau (ba tō′) See **bateau.** *n., pl.* **bat·teaux** (ba tōz′).

bat·ter[1] (bat′ər) strike with repeated blows so as to bruise, break, or get out of shape; pound: *The fireman battered down the door with a heavy axe.* *v.*

bat·ter[2] (bat′ər) a thick liquid mixture made by beating together flour, milk, eggs, etc.: *Cookies, pancakes, and muffins are made from batter.* *n.*

bat·ter[3] (bat′ər) the player whose turn it is to bat in baseball, cricket, etc. *n.*

battering ram a war machine consisting of a long thick pole carried by many soldiers, used in former times for breaking down the walls or gates of enemy castles and towns.

bat·ter·y (bat′ər ē or bat′rē) **1** a container holding materials that produce electricity by chemical action; a single electric cell: *Most flashlights work on two batteries.* **2** a set of two or more electric cells that produce electric current: *The car won't start because the battery is dead.* **3** any set of similar or connected things: *A battery of loudspeakers blared through the hall.* **4** a set of guns or other weapons for combined action in attack or defence: *Four batteries began firing on the enemy.* **5** a formation of several troops in an artillery regiment. *n., pl.* **bat·ter·ies.**

bat·tle (bat′əl) **1** a fight between opposing armed forces: *The battle for the island lasted six months.* **2** fighting; war: *His wounds were received in battle.* **3** any fight or contest: *a battle of words.* **4** fight; struggle; contend: *The swimmer had to battle a strong current. Our team is battling for first place in the hockey league.* 1–3 *n.,* 4 *v.,* **bat·tled, bat·tling.**

bat·tle–axe (bat′əl aks′) a kind of axe used as a weapon of war. *n., pl.* **bat·tle-ax·es.** Sometimes spelled **battle-ax.**

battle cry **1** the shout of soldiers in battle. **2** a slogan in any contest.

bat·tle·field (bat′əl fēld′) a place where a battle is fought or has been fought. *n.*

A battle-axe A battlement

bat·tle·ment (bat′əl mənt) a low wall for defence at the top of a tower or wall, with spaces through which men could shoot. *n.*

bat·tle·ship (bat′əl ship′) a very large warship having heavy armor and powerful guns. *n.*

bau·ble (bo′bəl or bô′bəl) a showy trifle having no real value: *Useless toys and trinkets are baubles.* *n.*

baux·ite (bok′sīt or bôk′sīt) a claylike mineral from which aluminum is obtained. *n.*

bawl (bol or bôl) **1** shout or cry out in a noisy way: *The peddler bawled his wares in the street.* **2** a shout at the top of one's voice. **3** weep loudly: *The small boy bawled whenever he hurt himself.* 1, 3 *v.,* 2 *n.*
bawl out, scold: *He bawled out his sister for denting his bicycle.*

☛ **Bawl** and **ball** are pronounced the same.

bay[1] (bā) a part of a sea or lake extending into the land. See **cove** for picture. *n.*

bay[2] (bā) **1** a space or division of a wall or building between columns, pillars, etc. **2** a part that sticks out from a wall and has a window or set of windows in it. **3** a compartment in an airplane, especially one for carrying bombs. **4** a recess, platform, etc. used for a special purpose: *The truck was backed up to the unloading bay of the warehouse.* *n.*

bay[3] (bā) **1** a long, deep howl or bark, especially of a large dog: *The hunters heard the distant bay of the hounds.* **2** howl; bark at: *Dogs sometimes bay at the* *moon.* **3** a stand made to face or keep off an enemy or pursuers when escape is impossible: *The stag stood at bay on the edge of the cliff.* **4** the position of the pursuers or enemies thus kept off: *The stag held the hounds at bay, but was killed by a hunter's arrow.* 1, 3, 4 *n.*, 2 *v.*

bay[4] (bā) a small evergreen tree with smooth, shiny leaves; a laurel tree: *Bay leaves are used for flavoring food. n.*

bay[5] (bā) **1** reddish brown: *a bay horse.* **2** a reddish-brown horse. 1, 2 *n.*, 1 *adj.*

bay·o·net (bā′ə nit) **1** a blade for piercing or stabbing, attached to the end of the barrel of a rifle. **2** pierce or stab with a bayonet. 1 *n.*, 2 *v.*, **bay·o·net·ed, bay·o·net·ing.**

☛ **Bayonet** comes from the French word for this blade, which was taken from *Bayonne,* the name of the town in France where bayonets were first made.

A bay window

bay window a window or set of windows projecting outward from a wall to form an alcove or small space in a room.

ba·zaar (bə zär′) **1** in Eastern countries, a street or streets full of shops. **2** a place for the sale of many kinds of goods. **3** a sale of things given by various people, held for some special purpose. *n.*

B.C.[1] before Christ. **B.C.** is used for times before Christ was born; **A.D.** is used for times after Christ was born: *From 20 B.C. to A.D. 50 is 69 years.*

B.C.[2] British Columbia.

be (bē) **1** have reality; exist: *The days of the pioneers are no more.* **2** take place; happen: *The circus was last month.* **3** have a particular place or position; remain; stay: *He will be here all year. The food is on the table.* **4** equal; represent: *A is excellent; B is good.* **5** belong to a particular group or class: *The new baby is a boy. My mother is a doctor. Elephants and mice are mammals.* **6** have or show a particular quality or condition: *I am sad. You are wrong. The book is red.* **7 Be** is also used with other verbs: *I am talking on the phone now. This house was built 50 years ago. They are going to visit their grandparents. v.*, **am, are, is; was, were; been, be·ing.**

☛ **Be** and **bee** are pronounced the same.

beach (bēch) **1** an almost flat shore of sand or little stones over which the water washes when high or at high tide. **2** run a boat ashore; draw up on the shore. 1 *n.*, 2 *v.*

☛ **Beach** and **beech** are pronounced the same.

beach·head (bēch′hed′) the first position established by an invading army on an enemy beach or shore. *n.*

bea·con (bē′kən) **1** a fire or light used as a signal to guide or warn: *The beacon in the window guided him through the blizzard to the house.* **2** a marker, signal light, or radio station that guides aircraft and ships through fogs, storms, etc. **3** a tall tower for a signal; lighthouse. *n.*

bead (bēd) **1** a small ball or bit of glass, metal, etc. with a hole through it, so that it can be strung on a thread with others like it. **2** put beads on; ornament with beads. **3 beads,** *pl.* **a** a string of beads: *She wore her new beads to the party.* **b** a rosary; a string of beads used in saying prayers. **4** any small, round body like a drop or bubble: *beads of sweat.* **5** a small, metal knob or ball at the front of a rifle or pistol barrel, used for taking aim. 1, 3–5 *n.*, 2 *v.* **—bead′like′,** *adj.*

draw a bead on, aim at.

bead·y (bē′dē) small, round, and shiny: *The parakeet has beady eyes. adj.*, **bead·i·er, bead·i·est.**

bea·gle (bē′gəl) a small hunting dog having smooth hair, short legs, and drooping ears. *n.*

beak (bēk) **1** a bird's bill, especially a strong, hooked bill that is useful in striking or tearing: *Eagles, hawks, and parrots have beaks.* **2** anything like a beak, such as the projecting prow of an ancient warship. *n.*

beak·er (bēk′ər) **1** a large glass container with a wide mouth and a pouring lip, used in laboratories. **2** a large cup or glass. *n.*

beam (bēm) **1** a large, long piece of timber, iron, or steel, for use in building. **2** the main horizontal support of a building or ship. **3** any long piece or bar: *The beam of a balance supports a pair of scales.* **4** a ray or rays of light: *The beam from the flashlight showed a kneeling man.* **5** send out rays of light; shine. **6** a bright look or smile. **7** look or smile brightly: *Her face beamed with delight.* **8** a radio signal directed in a straight line, used to guide aircraft, ships, etc. **9** direct a broadcast: *beam programs to the Yukon.* **10** the widest part of a ship. 1–4, 6, 8, 10 *n.*, 5, 7, 9 *v.*

bean (bēn) **1** a smooth, somewhat flat seed used as a vegetable: *pork and beans.* **2** the long pod containing such seeds: *When young and fresh, green or yellow beans are cooked as vegetables.* **3** any seed shaped like a bean: *Coffee beans are seeds of the coffee plant. n.* **—bean′like′,** *adj.*

☛ **Bean** and **been** are sometimes pronounced the same.

bean·bag (bēn′bag′) a small bag partly filled with dry beans, used to toss in play. *n.*

bear[1] (ber) **1** carry: *It takes two men to bear that stone.* **2** support: *That board is too thin to bear your weight.* **3** endure: *He cannot bear any more pain. She can't bear the noise.* **4** bring forth or produce: *This tree bore a fine lot of apples last year.* **5** give birth to: *Women bear children. That woman has borne four boys. He was born on June 4. v.*, **bore, borne** (or **born** for 5), **bear·ing. —bear′er,** *n.*

bear down, a press or push: *Don't bear down so hard.* **b** try hard; work seriously: *You'll have to bear down if you expect to pass the exam.*

bear on, have an effect on; have something to do with: *The answer did not bear on the question.*

☛ **Bear** and **bare** are pronounced the same.

bear[2] (ber) **1** a large, heavy animal with coarse, shaggy hair, a very short tail, and large, flat paws. **2** a gruff or surly person. *n.*

☛ See note at **bear**[1].

hat, āge, fär; let, ēqual, tėrm; it, īce
hot, ōpen, ôrder; oil, out; cup, pu̇t, rüle
əbove, takən, pencəl, lemən, circəs
ch, child; ng, long; sh, ship
th, thin; ᴛʜ, then; zh, measure

bear·a·ble (ber′ə bəl) that can be put up with or endured: *The pain was unpleasant but bearable.* *adj.*

beard (bērd) 1 the hair growing on a man's chin and cheeks. 2 something resembling or suggesting this: *The chin tuft of a goat and the stiff hairs around the beak of a bird are beards, as are the hairs on the heads of plants such as oats, barley, and wheat.* 3 face boldly; defy. 1, 2 *n.*, 3 *v.* **—beard′like′**, *adj.*

bear·ing (ber′ing) 1 a way of standing, sitting, walking, etc.; a manner: *A soldier should have a military bearing.* 2 connection in thought or meaning; relation: *His foolish question has no bearing on the problem.* 3 Usually, **bearings**, *pl.* a direction; a position in relation to other things: *I have lost my bearings.* 4 a part of a machine on which another part turns or slides. See **ball bearing** for picture. *n.*

beast (bēst) 1 any animal except man, especially a four-footed animal. 2 a coarse or brutal person. *n.* **—beast′like′**, *adj.*

beast·ly (bēst′lē) 1 like a beast; brutal; coarse; vile. 2 *Informal.* very bad or unpleasant: *beastly weather. I have a beastly headache.* *adj.*, **beast·li·er, beast·li·est.**

beat (bēt) 1 strike; strike again and again; whip: *The cruel rider beat his horse.* 2 a stroke or blow made again and again: *We heard the beat of a drum.* 3 defeat; overcome; get the better of: *Their team beat ours by a huge score.* 4 mix by stirring; mix by striking with a fork, spoon, or other utensil: *Mother is beating eggs for a cake.* 5 move up and down; flap: *The bird beat its wings.* 6 throb: *Her heart beat fast with joy.* 7 make a sound by being struck: *The drums beat loudly.* 8 a unit of time or accent in music: *three beats to a measure.* 9 mark time with drumsticks or by tapping with the hands, fingers, or feet. 10 a regular round or route, especially one taken by a policeman or watchman. 11 move against the wind by a zigzag course: *The sailboat beat along the coast.* 12 *Informal.* tired; worn out: *'I'm beat,' he said after swimming a mile.* 1, 3–7, 9, 11 *v.*, **beat, beat·en, beat·ing;** 2, 8, 10 *n.*, 12 *adj.*

☛ **Beat** and **beet** are pronounced the same.

beat·en (bēt′ən) 1 whipped; struck: *The beaten dog crawled to his master's feet.* 2 much walked on or travelled: *There was a wide beaten path across the lawn.* 3 discouraged by defeat; overcome: *After losing the game, they looked a beaten team.* 4 See **beat.** *We were beaten in football on Saturday.* 1–3 *adj.*, 4 *v.*

beat·ing (bēt′ing) 1 a whipping; punishment by blows. 2 a defeat. *n.*

beau (bō) 1 a young man who is courting a young woman. 2 a man who dresses with great care in the latest fashion. *n.*, *pl.* **beaus** or **beaux** (bōz).

☛ **Beau** and **bow**² are pronounced the same.

beau·te·ous (byü′tē əs) beautiful. *adj.*

beau·ti·ful (byü′tə fəl) very pleasing to see or hear; delighting the mind or senses: *a beautiful picture, beautiful music.* *adj.* **—beau′ti·ful·ly**, *adv.*

beau·ti·fy (byü′tə fī′) make beautiful; make more beautiful: *Flowers beautify a garden. We beautified the room with flowers.* *v.*, **beau·ti·fied, beau·ti·fy·ing.**

beau·ty (byü′tē) 1 the quality that pleases in a person, flowers, music, pictures, etc.: *She had beauty as well as intelligence. There is beauty in a fine thought or act.* 2 something beautiful: *the beauties of nature.* 3 a beautiful woman. *n.*, *pl.* **beau·ties.**

bea·ver¹ (bē′vər) 1 a soft-furred animal that has a broad, flat tail and feet adapted to swimming: *The beaver has been a Canadian emblem for over two hundred years. Beavers live both in water and on land.* 2 its soft, brown fur: *Father has a coat trimmed with beaver.* *n.*

A beaver — about 75 cm long without the tail; tail about 30 cm long and 16 cm wide

bea·ver² (bē′vər) the movable lower part of a helmet, protecting the mouth and chin. See **armor** for picture. *n.*

be·came (bi kām′) See **become.** *The seed became a plant.* *v.*

be·cause (bi koz′ or bi kôz′) for the reason that; since: *Most boys play ball because they enjoy the game. Because we were very late, we ran.* *conj.*

because of, by reason of; on account of: *We did not go because of the rain.*

beck (bek) a motion of the head or hand meant as a call or command: *An errand boy is at the beck and call of his boss.* *n.*

beck·on (bek′ən) signal by a motion of the hand or head: *He beckoned me to follow.* *v.*

be·come (bi kum′) 1 come to be; grow to be: *It is becoming colder. He became wiser as he grew older.* 2 seem proper for; suit; look well on: *That white dress becomes you.* *v.*, **be·came, be·come, be·com·ing.**

become of, happen to: *What has become of the box of candy?*

be·com·ing (bi kum′ing) fitting; suitable: *His conduct was becoming to a gentleman. Her dress is very becoming.* *adj.* **—be·com′ing·ly**, *adv.*

bed (bed) 1 anything to sleep or rest on. 2 any place where people or animals sleep or rest: *The cat made his bed by the fireplace.* 3 provide with a bed; put to bed: *the man bedded his horse down with straw.* 4 a flat base on which anything rests; foundation: *They set the pole in a bed of concrete.* 5 the ground under a body of water: *The bed of the river was muddy.* 6 a piece of ground in a garden in which plants are grown: *We have a large bed of roses.* 7 plant in a garden bed: *These tulips should be bedded in rich soil.* 8 a layer; stratum: *a bed of coal.* 1, 2, 4–6, 8 *n.*, 3, 7 *v.*, **bed·ded, bed·ding.**

bed·bug (bed′bug′) a small, reddish-brown, flat, blood-sucking insect found especially in beds: *A bedbug's bite is painful.* *n.*

bed·clothes (bed′klōz′ or bed′klōᴛʜz′) sheets, blankets, quilts, etc. *n. pl.*

bed·ding (bed′ing) 1 sheets, blankets, quilts, etc.; bedclothes. 2 material for beds: *Straw is used as bedding for cows and horses.* *n.*

bed·lam (bed′ləm) uproar; confusion: *When the home team won, there was bedlam in the arena.* *n.*

Bed·ou·in (bed′ü in) an Arab who lives in the deserts of Arabia or northern Africa. *n.*

☛ **Bedouin** comes from an Arabic word *badawin,* meaning 'desert dwellers.'

be·drag·gled (bi drag′əld) 1 wet and hanging limp: *She tried to comb her bedraggled hair.* 2 soiled by being dragged in the dirt: *The woman's long skirt was bedraggled from the wet streets.* *adj.*

bed·roll (bed′rōl′) a set of blankets or a sleeping bag that is rolled up and tied for carrying. *n.*

bed·room (bed′rüm′) a room to sleep in. *n.*

bed·side (bed′sīd′) the side of a bed: *The nurse sat by the sick woman's bedside.* *n.*

bed·spread (bed′spred′) a cover spread over other bedclothes during the day to keep them clean and neat. *n.*

bed·stead (bed′sted′) the wooden or metal framework of a bed. *n.*

bed·time (bed′tīm′) the usual time for going to bed: *His bedtime is nine o'clock.* *n.*

bee (bē) 1 a four-winged insect that lives in large groups and makes honey and wax: *Female bees can sting.* 2 a gathering for work or amusement: *a quilting bee, a spelling bee.* *n.*

☛ **Bee** and **be** are pronounced the same.

beech (bēch) 1 a tree with smooth, grey bark and glossy leaves: *The beech bears a sweet nut that is good to eat.* 2 the wood of this tree. *n.*

☛ **Beech** and **beach** are pronounced the same.

beef[1] (bēf) 1 the meat from a steer, cow, or bull, used for food. 2 a steer, cow, or bull when full grown and fattened for food. *n., pl.* (for def. 2) **beeves** (bēvz).

beef[2] (bēf) 1 *Slang.* complain: *Some people are always beefing.* 2 complaint. 1 *v.,* 2 *n.*

beef·steak (bēf′stāk′) a slice of beef for broiling or frying. *n.*

beef·y (bēf′ē) 1 like beef: *a beefy taste.* 2 strong; solid; heavy. *adj.,* **beef·i·er, beef·i·est.**

A honey bee   A beehive

bee·hive (bē′hīv′) 1 a hive or house for bees. 2 a busy, swarming place: *The shopping centre is a beehive on Friday nights.* *n.*

bee·line (bē′līn′) the straightest way between two places, like the flight of a bee to its hive. *n.*

been (bēn or bin) See **be.** *This boy has been present every day. The books have been read by every girl in the room. The two boys have been friends for many years.* *v.*

☛ **Been** and **bean** are sometimes pronounced the same. **Been** and **bin** are sometimes pronounced the same.

beer (bēr) 1 an alcoholic drink made from malt and, usually, hops. 2 a drink made from roots or plants, such as root beer, ginger beer. *n.*

☛ **Beer** and **bier** are pronounced the same.

beer parlor or **parlour** *Cdn.* a room in a hotel or tavern where beer is sold.

bees·wax (bēz′waks′) the wax produced by bees, from which they make their honeycomb. *n.*

beet (bēt) 1 a plant grown especially for its thick, fleshy root: *The leaves of beet are sometimes eaten as greens.* 2 its root: *Red beets are eaten as vegetables. Sugar is made from white beets.* *n.* —**beet′like′,** *adj.*

☛ **Beet** and **beat** are pronounced the same.

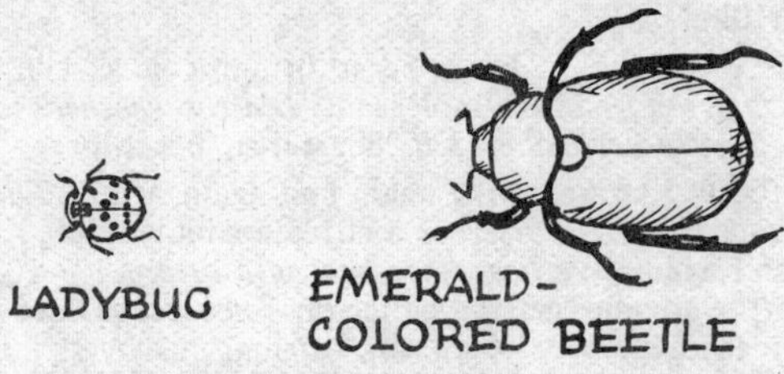

Two kinds of beetle

bee·tle (bē′təl) an insect whose front pair of wings are hard, shiny cases that cover the delicate rear pair of wings when at rest. *n.*

beeves (bēvz) plural of **beef**[1] (def. 2). *Beeves are shipped from the farm to the city.* *n.*

be·fall (bi fol′ or bi fôl′) happen; happen to: *Be careful that no harm befalls. An accident must have befallen them.* *v.,* **be·fell, be·fall·en, be·fall·ing.**

be·fell (bi fel′) See **befall.** *Evil befell the knight upon his lonely trip.* *v.*

be·fit (bi fit′) suit; be fit for; be proper for: *She always wears clothes that befit the occasion.* *v.,* **be·fit·ted, be·fit·ting.**

be·fore (bi fôr′) 1 earlier than: *We always play games before the bell rings.* 2 earlier: *Come at five o'clock, not before.* 3 before now; in time past: *He has never been late before.* 4 in front of; ahead of: *Walk before me.* 5 in front; ahead: *He went before to see if the road was safe.* 6 rather than; sooner than: *I'd starve before I'd surrender.* 1, 4, 6 *prep.,* 2, 3, 5 *adv.,* 6 *conj.*

be·fore·hand (bi fôr′hand′) ahead of time: *We got everything ready beforehand.* *adv., adj.*

be·friend (bi frend′) act as a friend to; help: *The policeman befriended the lost boy.* *v.*

beg (beg) 1 ask for food, clothes, or money as a charity: *The old man said that he had no way to live but by begging.* 2 ask as a favor; ask earnestly or humbly: *He begged his sister to forgive him.* 3 ask courteously: *I beg your pardon.* *v.,* **begged, beg·ging.**

beg off, free oneself from a promise, duty, etc. by asking: *Although he had promised to come to my party, he begged off because of a headache.*

be·gan (bi gan′) See **begin.** *Snow began to fall early in the evening.* *v.*

beg·gar (beg′ər) 1 a person who lives by begging.

2 a very poor person. 3 make poor; bring to poverty: *Your reckless spending will beggar your father.* 1, 2 *n.*, 3 *v.*

be·gin (bi gin′) 1 do the first part; make a start: *We will begin work soon. I began reading the book yesterday.* 2 come or bring into being: *The club began two years ago. Two brothers began the club.* *v.*, **be·gan, be·gun, be·gin·ning.**

be·gin·ner (bi gin′ər) a person who is doing something for the first time; a person who lacks skill and experience: *You skate well for a beginner.* *n.*

be·gin·ning (bi gin′ing) 1 a start: *Make a good beginning.* 1 the time when anything begins: *'In the beginning God created the heaven and the earth.'* 3 the first part: *I enjoyed this book from beginning to end.* 4 a first cause; a source; the origin: *One wrong decision was the beginning of all his misfortunes.* 5 that begins; first in order: *This is the beginning lesson of the spelling book.* 6 just starting: *a beginning student.* 1–4 *n.*, 5, 6 *adj.*

be·gone (bi gon′) go away: *'Begone!' said the prince. The prince bade him begone.* *interj.*, *v.*

be·go·ni·a (bi gō′nē ə or bi gōn′yə) a plant having waxy flowers with leaves that are often brightly colored. *n.*

be·gun (bi gun′) See **begin.** *The work was begun on Monday. It has begun to rain.* *v.*

be·half (bi haf′) interest; favor; support: *His friends will act in his behalf.* *n.*
in behalf of or **on behalf of,** in the interest of; for: *I am speaking in behalf of my friend.*

be·have (bi hāv′) 1 act: *The little boy behaves himself badly in school. The ship behaves well.* 2 act well; do what is right: *'Behave, or I'll take you home,' said her mother.* *v.*, **be·haved, be·hav·ing.**

be·hav·ior or **be·hav·iour** (bi hāv′yər) a way of acting; conduct; actions; acts: *His sullen behavior showed that he was angry.* *n.*

be·head (bi hed′) cut off the head of. *v.*

be·held (bi held′) See **behold.** *We beheld the strange creatures with fear. We had all beheld the effects of the disaster.* *v.*

be·hind (bi hīnd′) 1 at the back of: *Stand behind me.* 2 at the back; in the rear: *The dog's tail hung down behind.* 3 the fleshy part of the body where the legs join the back; buttocks; seat. 4 in support of; supporting: *His friends are behind him.* 5 later than: *The milkman is behind his usual time today.* 6 not on time; late: *The class is behind in its work.* 7 less advanced than: *He is behind the other boys in his class.* 1, 4, 5, 7 *prep.*, 2, 6 *adv.*, 3 *n.*

be·hold (bi hōld′) see; look; take notice: *They wanted to behold the sunrise. Behold! the king!* *v.*, **be·held, be·hold·ing;** *interj.*

be·hold·er (bi hōl′dər) an onlooker: *The man's strength amazed all the beholders.* *n.*

beige (bāzh) pale brown; light greyish brown. *n.*, *adj.*

be·ing (bē′ing) 1 See **be.** *The dog is being fed. Being hungry, he eats much.* 2 a person; a living creature: *Men, women, and children are human beings.* 3 life; existence: *This world came into being long ago.* 1 *v.*, 2, 3 *n.*

be·lat·ed (bi lāt′id) delayed; happening or coming late: *Your belated letter has arrived at last.* *adj.* —**be·lat′ed·ly,** *adv.*

hat, āge, fär; let, ēqual, tėrm; it, īce
hot, ōpen, ôrder; oil, out; cup, pu̇t, rüle
əbove, takən, pencəl, lemən, circəs
ch, child; ng, long; sh, ship
th, thin; ᴛʜ, then; zh, measure

belch (belch) 1 expel gas from the stomach through the mouth. 2 throw out with force: *The volcano belched fire and smoke.* 3 the act of belching. 1, 2 *v.*, 3 *n.*

bel·fry (bel′frē) 1 a tower for a bell or bells. 2 the space for the bell in a tower. *n.*, *pl.* **bel·fries.**

Bel·gian (bel′jən) 1 of or having to do with Belgium, a country in western Europe. 2 a person born in or living in Belgium. 1 *adj.*, 2 *n.*

be·lief (bi lēf′) 1 what is held to be true; something believed; opinion: *It was once common belief that the world was flat.* 2 acceptance as true or real; faith; trust: *He expressed his belief in the boy's honesty.* 3 religious faith; creed: *Most children follow the belief of their parents.* *n.*

be·liev·a·ble (bi lē′və bəl) that can be believed. *adj.*

be·lieve (bi lēv′) 1 think something is true or real: *We all believe that the earth is round.* 2 think somebody tells the truth: *His friends believe him.* 3 have faith; trust: *believe in God. A person has to believe in his friends.* 4 think; suppose: *I believe we are going to have a test.* *v.*, **be·lieved, be·liev·ing.** —**be·liev′er,** *n.*

be·lit·tle (bi lit′əl) cause to seem little or less important: *Jealous people belittled the explorer's great discoveries.* *v.*, **be·lit·tled, be·lit·tling.**

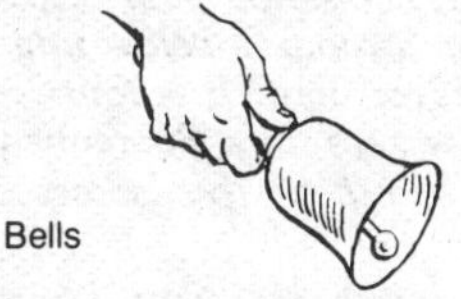
Bells

bell (bel) 1 a hollow metal cup that makes a musical sound when struck by a clapper or a hammer. 2 the stroke or sound of a bell: *Our teacher dismissed us before the bell.* 3 on shipboard, the stroke of a bell every half hour to tell time. *n.*

☛ **Bell** and **belle** are pronounced the same.

belle (bel) 1 a beautiful woman or girl. 2 the prettiest or most admired woman or girl: *She was the belle of the ball.* *n.*

☛ See note at **bell.**

bel·lig·er·ent (bə lij′ər ənt) 1 at war; engaged in war; fighting. 2 a nation or state at war: *The belligerents agreed on a truce.* 3 fond of fighting; warlike: *Some boys are belligerent.* 1, 3 *adj.*, 2 *n.* —**bel·lig′er·ent·ly,** *adv.*

bel·low (bel′ō) 1 roar as a bull does. 2 shout loudly: *The lifeguard bellowed to the boys to stay near the shore.* 3 shout angrily. 4 roar with pain. 5 a deep, roaring noise. 1–4 *v.*, 5 *n.*

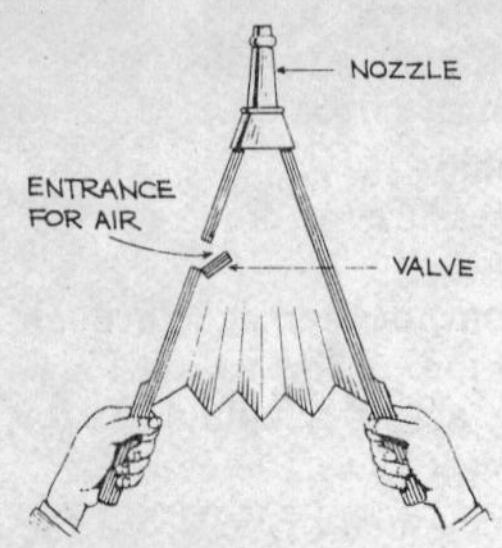

Bellows.
Air is sucked into the bellows as the sides are pulled apart. When the sides are pushed together, the valve closes and air is forced out through the nozzle.

bel·lows (bel′ōz) an instrument for producing a strong current of air, used for blowing a fire to make it burn or for sounding an organ, accordion, etc. *n. sing. or pl.*

bel·ly (bel′ē) **1** the lower part of the human body, which contains the stomach and intestines; abdomen. **2** the under part of an animal's body. **3** the stomach. **4** the bulging part of anything, or the hollow in it: *the belly of a sail.* **5** swell out; bulge: *The sails bellied in the wind.* 1–4 *n., pl.* **bel·lies;** 5 *v.,* **bel·lied, bel·ly·ing.**

belly button navel.

be·long (bi long′) have a proper place: *That book belongs on this shelf.* *v.*

belong to, a be the property of: *Does this cap belong to you?* **b** be a part of or be a member of: *She belongs to the Girl Guides.*

be·long·ings (bi long′ingz) things that belong to a person; possessions. *n. pl.*

be·lov·ed (bi luv′id or bi luvd′) **1** dearly loved; dear. **2** a person who is loved. 1 *adj.,* 2 *n.*

be·low (bi lō′) **1** in a lower place; to a lower place: *From the airplane we could see the fields below.* **2** to a lower floor or deck; downstairs: *The sailor went below.* **3** lower than; under: *My brother's room is below mine.* **4** less than; lower in rank or degree than: *It is four degrees below freezing.* **5** below zero on a Fahrenheit thermometer: *That morning it was thirty-five below.* 1, 2 *adv.,* 3, 4 *prep.,* 5 *adj.*

belt (belt) **1** a strip of leather, cloth, etc. worn around the body to support or hold in clothing, to hold tools or weapons, or as a decoration. **2** any broad strip or band: *a belt of trees.* **3** a region having distinctive characteristics: *The wheat belt is the region where wheat is grown.* **4** an endless band that transfers motion from one wheel or pulley to another: *A belt moves the fan in our automobile.* **5** put a belt around. **6** beat with a belt. **7** hit suddenly and hard: *The boxer belted his opponent across the ring.* 1–4 *n.,* 5–7 *v.*

bench (bench) **1** a long seat, usually of wood or stone. **2** a strong, heavy table used by a carpenter, or by any worker with tools and materials: *He worked at his bench in the basement.* **3** a judge or a group of judges sitting in a law court: *Bring the prisoner before the bench.* **4** a narrow stretch of high, flat land: *Apples are grown on the benches of the Okanagan Valley in British Columbia.* *n.*

bend (bend) **1** a part that is not straight; curve; turn: *There is a sharp bend in the road here.* **2** to curve; be crooked: *The branch began to bend as I climbed along it.* **3** make crooked; force out of a straight line: *The strong man bent the iron bar as if it had been made of rubber.* **4** move or turn in a certain direction; direct: *His steps were bent toward home now. She bent her mind to her homework.* **5** bow; stoop: *She bent down and picked up a stone.* **6** submit: *I bent to his will.* **7** force to submit: *The spirit of the rebels could not be bent.* 1 *n.,* 2–7 *v.,* **bent** or **bend·ed, bend·ing.**

be·neath (bi nēth′) **1** below; under; in a lower place: *What you drop will fall upon the spot beneath (adv.). The dog sat beneath the tree (prep.).* **2** unworthy of: *The proud girl thought washing dishes was beneath her.* 1 *adv.,* 1, 2 *prep.*

ben·e·dic·tion (ben′ə dik′shən) **1** the asking of God's blessing at the end of a service in church. **2** blessing. *n.*

ben·e·fac·tor (ben′ə fak′tər) a person who has helped others, either by gifts of money or by some kind act. *n.*

ben·e·fi·cial (ben′ə fish′əl) favorable; helpful; good for; productive of good: *Sunshine is beneficial to plants.* *adj.* **—ben′e·fi′cial·ly,** *adv.*

ben·e·fit (ben′ə fit) **1** an advantage; anything that is for the good of a person or thing: *Good roads are of great benefit to travellers.* **2** do good to: *Rest will benefit a sick person.* **3** to profit; receive good: *He benefited from the medicine. He will benefit from the new way of doing business.* 1 *n.,* 2, 3 *v.,* **ben·e·fit·ed, ben·e·fit·ing.**

be·nev·o·lence (bə nev′ə ləns) **1** goodwill; kindly feeling: *He always acted with benevolence.* **2** an act of kindness; something good that is done: *Her benevolences are well known.* *n.*

be·nev·o·lent (bə nev′ə lənt) charitable; kindly: *Contributing to a charity is a benevolent act.* *adj.* **—be·nev′o·lent·ly,** *adv.*

bent (bent) **1** See **bend.** *He bent the wire.* **2** not straight; curved; crooked: *The farmer's back was bent from years of toil.* **3** determined: *He is bent on being a sailor.* **4** an inclination or tendency: *He has a decided bent for drawing.* 1 *v.,* 2, 3 *adj.,* 4 *n.*

be·queath (bi kwēᴛʜ′ or bi kwēth′) **1** give or leave property, etc. by a will: *The father had bequeathed the farm to his son.* **2** hand down: *One age bequeaths its civilization to the next.* *v.*

be·reave (bi rēv′) deprive; leave desolate: *People are bereaved by the death of relatives and friends.* *v.,* **be·reaved** or **be·reft, be·reav·ing.**

be·reft (bi reft′) See **bereave.** *Bereft of hope and friends, the old man led a wretched life.* *v.*

be·ret (bə rā′ or ber′ā) a soft, round cap of wool, felt, etc. *n.*

ber·ry (ber′ē) **1** a small, juicy fruit, usually not having a stone: *Strawberries and currants are berries.* **2** gather berries: *We went berrying yesterday.* **3** the fruit of the coffee tree: *Coffee is made from the beans found inside ripe coffee berries.* **4** a dry seed or kernel: *a wheat berry.* 1, 3, 4 *n., pl.* **ber·ries;** 2 *v.,* **ber·ried, ber·ry·ing.**

☛ **Berry** and **bury** are pronounced the same.

berth (bėrth) **1** a place to sleep on a ship, train, or aircraft. **2** a place for a ship to stay when at anchor or at a wharf. **3** an appointment or position; job: *My brother has a berth as swimming instructor for the summer.* **4** a stand of timber. *n.*

☛ **Berth** and **birth** are pronounced the same.

be·seech (bi sēch′) ask earnestly; beg: *I beseech you*

hat, āge, fär; let, ēqual, tėrm; it, īce
hot, ōpen, ôrder; oil, out; cup, pu̇t, rüle
əbove, takən, pencəl, lemən, circəs
ch, child; ng, long; sh, ship
th, thin; ᴛʜ, then; zh, measure

to stop talking. *She besought the doctor to stop the pain. v.,* **be·sought, be·seech·ing.**

be·set (bi set′) **1** attack; attack on all sides: *In the swamp we were beset by mosquitoes.* **2** surround; hem in: *We may be beset by enemies or beset by fears. v.,* **be·set, be·set·ting.**

be·set·ting (bi set′ing) continually attacking: *Laziness is a loafer's besetting sin. adj.*

be·side (bi sīd′) **1** by the side of; near; close to: *Grass grows beside the brook.* **2** compared with: *She seems dull beside her sister.* **3** away from; not related to: *That question is beside the point and shows that you were not listening.* **4** besides. 1–3 *prep.,* 4 *adv.*

beside oneself, out of one's mind; crazy; upset: *He was beside himself with worry over his lost dog.*

be·sides (bi sīdz′) **1** also; more than that; moreover: *He didn't want to quarrel; besides he had come to enjoy himself.* **2** in addition to: *Others came to the picnic besides our own club members.* **3** other than; except: *Her mother spoke of no one besides her daughter.* 1 *adv.,* 2, 3 *prep.*

be·siege (bi sēj′) **1** try for a long time to capture by armed force; surround and try to capture: *The Greeks besieged the city of Troy for ten years.* **2** crowd around: *Hundreds of admirers besieged the famous astronaut.* **3** overwhelm with requests, questions, etc.: *During the flood, the Red Cross was besieged with calls for help. v.,* **be·sieged, be·sieg·ing.**

be·sought (bi sot′ or bi sôt′) See **beseech.** *v.*

best (best) **1** superior in relation to all or certain others; most excellent: *Who does the best work?* **2** in the most excellent way: *Who reads best?* **3** the best thing, condition, or person: *We want the best. He is the best in the class.* **4** largest; greatest: *He worked on his project for the best part of a day.* **5** outdo; defeat: *Our team was bested in the final game.* 1, 4 *adj.,* 2 *adv.,* 3 *n.,* 5 *v.*

at best, under the most favorable circumstances: *Summer is at best very short.*

get the best of, defeat.

make the best of, do as well as possible with: *Try to make the best of a bad job.*

bes·tial (bes′chəl) beastly; brutal. *adj.*

be·stow (bi stō′) give something as a gift; give: *The Governor General bestowed a medal on the boy who rescued the baby. v.*

bet (bet) **1** promise to give some money or a certain thing to someone if he is right and you are wrong: *I bet you a nickel I won't pass this test.* **2** a promise or pledge to give some money or a certain thing to someone if he is right and you are wrong: *I made a bet that I wouldn't pass.* **3** the money or thing promised: *I did pass; so I lost my bet (lost my nickel).* **4** be very sure: *I bet you are wrong about that.* 1, 4 *v.,* **bet** or **bet·ted, bet·ting;** 2, 3 *n.*

be·tide (bi tīd′) **1** happen to: *Woe betide you if you hurt my dog!* **2** happen: *No matter what betides, the family will hold together. v.,* **be·tid·ed, be·tid·ing.**

be·tray (bi trā′) **1** give away to the enemy: *The traitors betrayed their country.* **2** be unfaithful to: *She betrayed her friends by breaking her promise.* **3** show; reveal: *His wet shoes betrayed the fact that he had not worn his rubbers. v.*

be·troth (bi trōᴛʜ′) promise or engage to marry: *The prince and his true love were then betrothed. He betrothed his daughter to a rich man. v.*

be·troth·al (bi trō′ᴛʜəl) an engagement to be married. *n.*

bet·ter (bet′ər) **1** more good, useful, desirable, etc. than another: *He does better work than his brother.* **2** in a more excellent way: *Try to read better next time.* **3** improved in health: *I hope you are feeling better.* **4** improve; surpass: *He did his best to better his marks of last year. The other class cannot better our grades.* **5** a person or thing that is better: *Which is the better of the two dresses?* **6** greater; larger: *Four days is the better part of a week.* 1, 3, 6 *adj.,* 2 *adv.,* 4 *v.,* 5 *n.*

better off, in a better condition: *He is better off now that he has a new job.*

get the better of, defeat; be superior to: *The tortoise got the better of the hare.*

had better, should; ought to: *I had better go before it rains.*

bet·ter·ment (bet′ər mənt) improvement: *Doctors work for the betterment of their patients' health. n.*

be·tween (bi twēn′) **1** in the space or time separating two points, objects, places, etc.: *There is a distance of ten feet between the two trees. Come some time between three and four o'clock (prep.). We could not see the moon, for a cloud came between (adv.).* **2** in the range or part separating: *She earned between ten and twelve dollars.* **3** from one to the other of; joining; connecting: *There is a new highway between Toronto and Windsor.* **4** having to do with: *Will there be war between the two countries?* **5** in regard to one or the other of: *We must choose between the two books.* **6** by the joint action of: *They caught twelve fish between them.* 1–6 *prep.,* 1 *adv.*

between you and me, as a secret; confidentially: *This is between you and me; don't tell anyone else.*

☛ **Between** is used when the following reference is to two persons or things only: *My sister and I had less than a dollar between us.* **Among** is usually preferred when the following reference is to more than two persons or things: *The money was divided among the four of us.*

be·twixt (bi twikst′) between. *prep., adv.*

betwixt and between, in the middle; neither one nor the other.

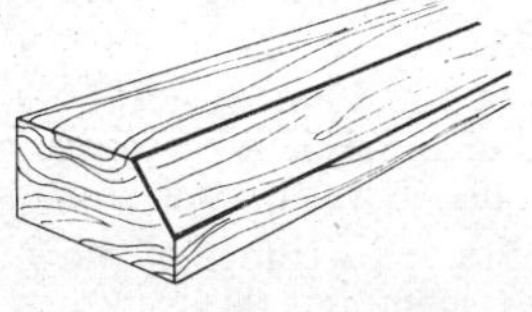

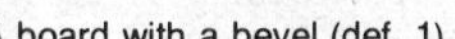

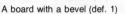

A board with a bevel (def. 1)

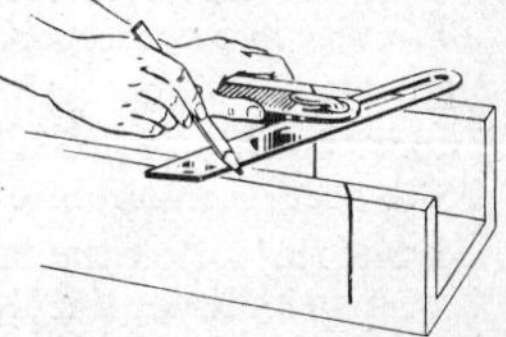

A bevel (def. 3) in use

bev·el (bev′əl) **1** a sloping edge: *The edge of the plate glass mirror has a bevel.* **2** cut a square edge to make a sloping edge; make slope: *The edges of the board have* *been bevelled with a plane.* **3** an instrument for drawing or measuring angles. 1, 3 *n.,* 2 *v.,* **bev·elled** or **bev·eled, bev·el·ling** or **bev·el·ing.**

bev·er·age (bev′ər ij) a liquid used or prepared for drinking: *Milk, tea, coffee, beer, and wine are beverages.* *n.*

bev·y (bev′ē) a small group: *He shot at a bevy of quail. He was talking to a bevy of girls.* *n., pl.* **bev·ies.**

be·wail (bi wāl′) mourn for; weep for; complain of: *The little girl was bewailing the loss of her doll.* *v.*

be·ware (bi wer′) be careful; be on your guard against: *Beware! danger is here. You must beware of swimming in a strong current.* *v.*

be·wil·der (bi wil′dər) confuse completely; puzzle; cause doubt and uncertainty: *The many decisions he had to make bewildered him. The little girl was bewildered by the crowds and noises. Some hard problems in arithmetic bewilder me.* *v.* **—be·wil′der·ment,** *n.*

be·witch (bi wich′) **1** put under a spell; use magic on: *The wicked fairy bewitched the princess, and made her fall into a long sleep.* **2** charm; delight very much: *We were all bewitched by our pretty little cousin.* *v.*

be·yond (bi yond′) **1** on or to the farther side of: *He lives beyond the sea.* **2** farther on than: *The road is beyond that hill.* **3** farther away: *Your ball did not fall here; look beyond for it.* **4** later than; past: *It is an hour beyond the time I should have gone.* **5** out of the reach or understanding of: *He was beyond the help of the doctor. The meaning of this story is beyond him.* **6** more than: *The price of the suit was beyond what he could pay. The picnic was beyond all we had hoped.* 1, 2, 4–6 *prep.,* 3 *adv.*

Cloth cut on the bias

bi·as (bī′əs) **1** a slanting line: *Cloth is cut on the bias when it is cut diagonally across the weave.* **2** an opinion formed before there is reason for it; a tendency to favor one side too much: *The speaker's bias was easy to recognize.* **3** to influence, usually unfairly. 1, 2 *n.,* 3 *v.,* **bi·assed** or **bi·ased, bi·as·sing** or **bi·as·ing.**

bi·assed or **bi·ased** (bī′əst) favoring one side too much; warped; prejudiced: *She was biassed where her children were concerned.* *adj.*

bib (bib) **1** a kind of napkin or small apron worn under the chin to protect clothing, especially at meals. **2** the part of an apron or overalls above the waist. *n.*

Bi·ble (bī′bəl) **1** the book of sacred writings of the Christian religion; the Old Testament and the New Testament. **2** a book of the sacred writings of any religion. *n.*

☛ **Bible** came into English through Old French and Latin from the Greek word *biblia,* meaning 'little books.'

bib·li·cal or **Bib·li·cal** (bib′lə kəl) **1** of the Bible: *biblical literature.* **2** according to the Bible: *biblical history.* **3** in the Bible: *a biblical reference to Solomon.* *adj.*

bi·car·bo·nate of soda (bī kär′bə nit) a white powder used in cooking, medicine, etc.; baking soda.

bick·er (bik′ər) **1** quarrel; squabble: *The children bickered all afternoon.* **2** a petty, noisy quarrel. 1 *v.,* 2 *n.*

bi·cus·pid (bī kus′pid) a double-pointed tooth: *A human adult has eight bicuspids.* See **teeth** for picture. *n.*

A bicycle

bi·cy·cle (bī′sə kəl) **1** a vehicle having two wheels, one behind the other, that support a light metal frame on which there are handles and a seat for the rider: *You ride a bicycle by pushing two pedals with your feet.* **2** ride a bicycle. 1 *n.,* 2 *v.,* **bi·cy·cled, bi·cy·cling.**

bid (bid) **1** command: *The captain bids his men go forward. Do as I bid you.* **2** say; tell: *His friends came to bid him goodbye.* **3** offer to pay a certain price: *First she bid $5 for the table. He then bid $6.* **4** an offer; the amount offered for a thing: *My bid was $7.* **5** invite: *The king bade the nobles stay for the feast.* 1–3, 5 *v.,* **bade** or **bid, bid·den** or **bid, bid·ding;** 4 *n.*

bid·den (bid′ən) See **bid.** *Twelve guests were bidden to the feast.* *v.*

bid·ding (bid′ing) **1** a command. **2** the offering of prices at an auction: *The bidding was slow at first but soon became lively.* **3** See **bid.** *His friends are bidding him good-bye.* 1, 2 *n.,* 3 *v.*

bide (bīd) continue; wait; abide. *v.,* **bode** or **bid·ed, bid·ed, bid·ing.**

bide one's time, wait for a good chance: *If you bide your time, you will probably get a better bargain.*

bi·en·ni·al (bī en′ē əl) **1** lasting two years. **2** a plant that lives two years: *Carrots and onions are biennials.* 1 *adj.,* 2 *n.*

bier (bēr) a movable stand on which a coffin or dead body is placed. *n.*

☛ **Bier** and **beer** are pronounced the same.

big (big) **1** great in amount or size; large: *a big room, a big book. An elephant is a big animal. Dogs are bigger than mice.* **2** grown up: *You are a big girl now.* **3** important: *This is big news.* *adj.,* **big·ger, big·gest.** **—big′ness,** *n.*

big·horn (big′hôrn′) a wild greyish-brown sheep of the Rocky Mountains. *n., pl.* **big·horn** or **big·horns.**

bike (bīk) *Informal.* bicycle. *n.*

bi·ki·ni (bi kē′nē) a brief two-piece bathing suit for women. *n.*

bile (bīl) a bitter, yellowish liquid secreted by the liver to aid digestion. *n.*

hat, āge, fär; let, ēqual, tėrm; it, īce
hot, ōpen, ôrder; oil, out; cup, pu̇t, rüle
əbove, takən, pencəl, lemən, circəs
ch, child; ng, long; sh, ship
th, thin; ᴛʜ, then; zh, measure

bil·ious (bil′yəs) 1 suffering from or caused by some trouble with the bile or liver: *a bilious condition, a bilious headache.* 2 peevish; cross. *adj.*

bill¹ (bil) 1 a statement of money owed for work done or things supplied: *The garage sent us a bill for repairing our car.* 2 send a statement of charges to: *The store will bill us on the first of the month.* 3 a piece of paper money: *a dollar bill.* 4 a written or printed public notice; advertisement; poster. 5 announce or advertise through such notices or posters: *Many interesting television programs are billed for next week.* 6 a written or printed statement; a list of items: *a bill of fare.* 7 a plan for a new law, suggested in Parliament and called an act if voted for by a majority: *The Prime Minister recommended several bills to Parliament.* 1, 3, 4, 6, 7 *n.*, 2, 5 *v.*
fill the bill, *Informal.* satisfy requirements.
foot the bill, *Informal.* pay or settle the bill.

bill² (bil) 1 the mouth of a bird; a beak. 2 a part of an animal shaped like a bird's bill: *the bill of a turtle.* 3 join beaks; touch bills. 1, 2 *n.*, 3 *v.*
bill and coo, show affection; kiss and talk as lovers do.

bill·board (bil′bôrd′) a large board, usually outdoors, on which to display advertisements or notices. *n.*

bill·fold (bil′fōld′) a folding case for carrying money, papers, etc.; wallet. *n.*

bil·liards (bil′yərdz) a game played with balls on a special table: *In billiards a long stick called a cue is used in hitting the balls.* *n.*

bil·lion (bil′yən) a thousand million (1 000 000 000) in Canada, the United States, and France; a million million (1 000 000 000 000) in the United Kingdom. *n., adj.*

bill of fare a list of the articles of food served at a meal or of those that can be ordered; menu.

bil·low (bil′ō) 1 a big wave: *The billows of the Atlantic dash on these islands. Billows of smoke rose from the chimney.* 2 rise or roll in great waves: *The wind made the lake's surface billow.* 3 swell out; bulge: *The sheets on the clothes line billowed in the wind.* 1 *n.*, 2, 3 *v.*

bil·ly goat (bil′ē) a male goat.

bin (bin) a box or enclosed place for holding grain, coal, etc. *n.*

☛ **Bin** and **been** are sometimes pronounced the same.

bind (bīnd) 1 tie together; hold together; fasten: *She bound up the package with bright ribbon.* 2 stick together: *Gravel or cinders can be bound by tar.* 3 fasten sheets of paper into a cover; put a cover on a book: *The pages were bound into a small book.* 4 hold by a promise, duty, law, etc.; oblige: *She is in duty bound to help us. Parents are bound to send their children to school.* 5 put a bandage on: *The nurse will bind your cut.* 6 put a border or edge on to strengthen or ornament: *They bound the frayed edge of the carpet.* *v.*, **bound, bind·ing.**

bind·er (bīn′dər) 1 a cover for holding loose sheets of paper together. 2 a machine that cuts stalks of grain and ties them into sheaves. *n.*

binder twine a strong, coarse string used for binding up grain into sheaves: *On a farm, binder twine has a thousand uses.*

bind·ing (bīn′ding) 1 the covering of a book. 2 a strip protecting or ornamenting an edge: *Binding is used on the seams of dresses.* 3 having force or power to hold to a promise, duty, law, etc.: *They signed their names so that the agreement would be binding.* 1, 2 *n.*, 3 *adj.*

bin·go (bing′gō) a game in which each player covers the numbers on his card as they are called out by a caller. *n.*

bi·noc·u·lars (bə nok′yə lərz) a double telescope joined as a unit for use with both eyes: *Field glasses and opera glasses are binoculars.* See **field glasses** for picture. *n. pl.*

bi·og·ra·phy (bī og′rə fē) the written story of a person's life. *n., pl.* **bi·og·ra·phies.**

bi·ol·o·gist (bī ol′ə jist) a person skilled in biology. *n.*

bi·ol·o·gy (bī ol′ə jē) the science of living things; the study of plant and animal life: *Botany and zoology are branches of biology.* *n.*

birch (bėrch) 1 a slender tree with smooth white bark. 2 its hard wood, used in making furniture. *n.*

bird (bėrd) an animal that lays eggs and has wings, two legs, and a body covered with feathers: *Most birds can fly.* *n.* —**bird′like′**, *adj.*
bird of prey, a bird that hunts animals: *Eagles, hawks, vultures, and owls are birds of prey.*

bird·seed (bėrd′sēd′) a mixture of small seeds used for feeding birds. *n.*

birth (bėrth) 1 coming into life; being born: *the birth of a baby.* 2 a beginning: *the birth of a nation.* 3 bringing forth: *the birth of a plan.* 4 descent; family: *a person of Spanish birth. He was a man of humble birth.* *n.*

☛ **Birth** and **berth** are pronounced the same.

birth·day (bėrth′dā′) 1 the day on which a person is born. 2 the day on which something began: *July 1, 1867, was the birthday of Canada.* 3 the yearly return of the day on which a person was born, or on which something began: *Tomorrow is my birthday; I will be ten years old then.* *n.*

birth·place (bėrth′plās′) 1 the place where a person was born. 2 the place of origin: *Kingston, Ontario, was the birthplace of hockey.* *n.*

birth·right (bėrth′rīt′) 1 the rights belonging to a person because he is the oldest son: *Esau sold his birthright to his brother.* 2 a right enjoyed by a person because he was born in a certain country, or because of any other fact about his birth: *'Freedom is our birthright!' he shouted.* *n.*

bis·cuit (bis′kit) 1 a kind of bread baked in small, soft cakes. 2 a thin, flat, dry bread or cake; cracker. *n., pl.* **bis·cuits** or **bis·cuit.**

☛ **Biscuit** comes from a French word that originally meant 'twice cooked.' See note at **zwieback.**

bish·op (bish′əp) 1 a clergyman of high rank, at the head of a church district. 2 one of the pieces in the game of chess. *n.*

bi·son (bī′sən) buffalo (def. 1). *n.*

bit[1] (bit) **1** a tool for boring or drilling. See **brace** for picture. **2** the part of a bridle that goes in the horse's mouth. See **bridle** and **harness** for pictures. *n.*

bit[2] (bit) **1** a small piece; a small amount: *bits of broken glass. A pebble is a bit of rock.* **2** somewhat; a little: *I am a bit tired.* **3** *Informal.* a short time: *People often say, 'Wait a bit.'* *n.*

bit[3] (bit) See **bite.** *He bit into the apple. A boy was bit by our dog.* *v.*

bitch (bich) a female dog, wolf, fox, etc. *n.*

bite (bīt) **1** seize, cut into, or cut off with the teeth: *She bit the apple. That nervous boy bites his fingernails.* **2** the act of biting: *The dog gave a bite or two at the bone.* **3** a piece bitten off; mouthful: *Eat the whole apple, not just a bite.* **4** a light meal; snack: *We usually have a bite before going to bed.* **5** wound with teeth, fangs, etc.; sting: *My dog never bites. A mosquito bit me.* **6** a wound made by biting or stinging: *The man soon recovered from the snake's bite.* **7** cause a smarting, sharp pain to: *His fingers are bitten by frost.* **8** take a strong hold of: *The jaws of a vise bite the wood they hold.* **9** take a bait; be caught: *The fish are biting well today.* 1, 5, 7–9 *v.,* **bit, bit·ten** or **bit, bit·ing;** 2–4, 6 *n.*

bit·ing (bīt′ing) **1** sharp; chilly; cutting: *Dress warmly before you go out in that biting wind.* **2** sarcastic; sneering: *Biting remarks hurt people's feelings.* *adj.* **—bit′ing·ly,** *adv.*

bit·ten (bit′ən) See **bite.** *The dog has bitten the little boy.* *v.*

bit·ter (bit′ər) **1** having a sharp, harsh, unpleasant taste: *bitter medicine.* **2** causing pain or grief; hard to admit or bear: *a bitter defeat. The death of his father was a bitter loss.* **3** showing pain or grief: *a bitter cry.* **4** of weather, very cold: *a bitter winter.* *adj.* **—bit′ter·ly,** *adv.* **—bit′ter·ness,** *n.*

bit·tern (bit′ərn) a wading bird that lives in marshes and has a peculiar booming cry: *A bittern is a small kind of heron.* *n.*

bi·tu·mi·nous coal (bə tyü′mə nəs or bə tü′mə nəs) a kind of coal that burns with much smoke and a yellow flame; soft coal.

biv·ou·ac (biv′ü ak′) **1** a camp outdoors without tents or with very small tents: *The soldiers made a bivouac for the night in a field.* **2** make camp outdoors in this way: *Boy Scouts often bivouac in summer.* 1 *n.,* 2 *v.,* **biv·ou·acked, biv·ou·ack·ing.**

blab (blab) tell secrets; talk too much. *v.,* **blabbed, blab·bing.**

black (blak) **1** the color of coal or soot; the opposite of white: *The black shows up against the white.* **2** of or having this color: *This print is black.* **3** make black; blacken: *I blacked my shoes before going to the party.* **4** without any light; very dark: *black clouds. The room was black as night.* **5** unhappy; gloomy: *This has been a black day.* **6** sullen; angry: *She gave me a black look.* **7** evil; wicked: *a black lie.* **8** having very dark skin. **9** a member of a dark-skinned race; Negro. 1, 9 *n.,* 2, 4, 5–8 *adj.,* 3 *v.* **—black′ly,** *adv.* **—black′ness,** *n.*

black-and-blue (blak′ənd blü′) bruised. *adj.*

black and white writing; print: *I asked him to put his promise down in black and white.*

black bear a large North American bear that has dense, black fur.

Blackberries

black·ber·ry (blak′ber′ē) the small, black or dark-purple fruit of certain bushes and vines: *Blackberries are sweet and juicy.* *n., pl.* **black·ber·ries.**

black·bird (blak′bėrd′) any of various North American birds so called because the male bird is mainly black: *The cowbird, grackle, and red-winged blackbird are blackbirds.* *n.*

black·board (blak′bôrd′) a dark, smooth surface for writing or drawing on with chalk. *n.*

black·en (blak′ən) **1** make black: *Soot blackened the snow.* **2** become black or very dark: *The sky blackened and soon it began to rain.* **3** damage; speak evil of: *Don't blacken my family's good name with false gossip.* *v.*

black-eyed Su·san (blak′īd′sü′zən) a yellow daisy having a black centre.

black-fly (blak′flī′) a small black fly whose bite is very painful. *n., pl.* **black-flies.**

black·guard (blag′ärd) a low, worthless person; scoundrel. *n.*

black·head (blak′hed′) a small black-tipped lump of dead cells and oil plugging a pore in the skin. *n.*

black·out (blak′out′) **1** turning out or concealing of all the lights of a city, district, etc. as a protection against an air raid. **2** a temporary blindness or unconsciousness resulting from lack of circulation of blood in the brain. *n.*

black·smith (blak′smith′) a man who works with and makes things out of iron: *Blacksmiths can mend tools and make horseshoes.* *n.*

black·top (blak′top′) **1** asphalt mixed with crushed rock, used as a pavement for highways, roads, and other surfaces. **2** a surface covered with this substance. *n.*

blad·der (blad′ər) **1** a soft, thin bag in the body that receives urine from the kidneys. **2** a strong bag, often made of rubber, that will hold liquids or air: *The rubber bag inside a football is a bladder.* *n.*

blade (blād) **1** the cutting part of certain things like a knife or sword: *My father's hunting knife has a very sharp blade.* **2** a sword. **3** a leaf of grass. **4** the flat, wide part of a leaf. **5** the flat, wide part of anything: *the blade of an oar or a paddle, the shoulder blade.* *n.* **—blade′like′,** *adj.*

blame (blām) **1** hold responsible for something bad or wrong: *We blamed the fog for our accident.* **2** the responsibility for something bad or wrong: *Carelessness deserves the blame for many mistakes.* **3** find fault with: *He will not blame us if we do our best.* **4** finding fault; reproof. 1, 3 *v.,* **blamed, blam·ing;** 2, 4 *n.*

be to blame, deserve to be blamed: *Each person said somebody else was to blame.*

blame on, attribute to: *The accident was blamed on the icy road.*

hat, āge, fär; let, ēqual, tėrm; it, īce
hot, ōpen, ôrder; oil, out; cup, pu̇t, rüle
əbove, takən, pencəl, lemən, circəs
ch, child; ng, long; sh, ship
th, thin; ᴛʜ, then; zh, measure

blame·less (blām′lis) not deserving blame; free from fault: *The saint led a blameless life.* *adj.* **—blame′less·ly,** *adv.* **—blame′less·ness,** *n.*

blanch (blanch) **1** turn white; become pale: *The boy blanched with fear when he saw the bear coming.* **2** loosen the skins of raw vegetables, nuts, etc. by plunging them first in boiling water and then in cold water. **3** make white; bleach. *v.*

bland (bland) **1** smooth; mild; soft; gentle: *a bland summer breeze. Baby food has a bland taste.* **2** agreeable; polite: *Our minister had a bland manner.* *adj.*

blank (blangk) **1** a space left empty or to be filled in: *Leave a blank after each word.* **2** not written or printed on: *blank paper.* **3** a paper with spaces to be filled in: *Fill out this application blank and return it to us.* **4** with spaces left for filling in: *Here is a blank form for you to fill in.* **5** an empty or vacant place: *When he read the hard questions his mind became a blank.* **6** without interest or meaning; empty: *There was a blank look on his face.* 1, 3, 5 *n.*, 2, 4, 6 *adj.* **—blank′ly,** *adv.* **—blank′ness,** *n.*

blan·ket (blang′kit) **1** a soft, heavy covering woven from wool, cotton, or other material: *Blankets are used to keep people or animals warm.* **2** anything like a blanket: *A blanket of snow covered the ground.* **3** cover with a blanket or anything like a blanket: *The snow blanketed the ground.* 1, 2 *n.*, 3 *v.*

blare (bler) **1** make a loud, harsh sound: *The trumpets blared, announcing the king's arrival.* **2** a loud, harsh sound: *The blare of the horn was startling.* 1 *v.*, **blared, blar·ing;** 2 *n.*

blast (blast) **1** a strong, sudden rush of wind or air: *the icy blasts of winter.* **2** the sound made by blowing a horn or trumpet. **3** blow up with dynamite or some other explosive: *The old building was blasted.* **4** an explosion: *The blast made our house shake.* **5** the explosive used to blow something up. **6** wither; shrivel; destroy: *The intense heat blasted the vines.* **7** *Slang.* a severe scolding: *His father gave him a blast for being late for dinner.* 1, 2, 4, 5, 7 *n.*, 3, 6 *v.*
blast off, of rockets and missiles, fire; take off: *Make ready to blast off.*

blast–off (blast′of′) of rockets and missiles, taking off: *All the parts of a rocket are checked carefully before blast-off.* *n.*

blaze¹ (blāz) **1** a bright flame or fire: *He could see the blaze of the campfire across the beach.* **2** burn with a bright flame: *A fire was blazing in the fireplace.* **3** a glow of brightness; glare: *the blaze of the noon sun.* **4** show bright colors or lights: *On New Year's Eve the big house blazed with lights.* **5** a bright display: *The tulips made a blaze of color in the garden.* **6** burst out in anger or excitement: *She blazed at the insult.* **7** violent outburst: *a blaze of temper.* 1, 3, 5, 7 *n.*, 2, 4, 6 *v.*, **blazed, blaz·ing.**

blaze² (blāz) **1** a mark made on a tree by cutting off some of its bark. **2** mark a tree in this way. **3** mark a path by blazing trees: *The hunters blazed a trail through the bush.* **4** a white mark on an animal's forehead. 1, 4 *n.*, 2, 3 *v.*, **blazed, blaz·ing.**

blaz·er (blāz′ər) a jacket, often dark blue, cut like a suit coat and usually worn as dressy but informal wear. *n.*

bleach (blēch) **1** whiten by exposing to sunlight: *Bleached bones lay on the desert.* **2** whiten by using chemicals: *The laundry bleached the stains out of the shirt.* **3** a chemical used to whiten. 1, 2 *v.*, 3 *n.*

bleach·ers (blēch′ərz) the roofless rows or tiers of seats at outdoor games such as baseball and football. *n. pl.*

bleak (blēk) **1** bare; swept by winds: *The rocky peaks of high mountains are bleak.* **2** chilly; cold: *a bleak wind.* **3** dreary; dismal: *A prisoner's life is bleak.* *adj.* **—bleak′ly,** *adv.* **—bleak′ness,** *n.*

blear·y (blēr′ē) dim; blurred: *Her eyes were bleary with weeping.* *adj.*, **blear·i·er, blear·i·est.**

bleat (blēt) **1** the cry made by a sheep, goat, or calf, or a sound like it. **2** make the cry of a sheep, goat, or calf, or a sound like it. 1 *n.*, 2 *v.*

bled (bled) See **bleed.** *The cut bled for ten minutes.* *v.*

bleed (blēd) **1** lose blood: *This cut is bleeding.* **2** take blood from: *Doctors used to bleed people when they were sick.* **3** lose sap, juice, etc. from a surface that has been cut or scratched: *The injured elm is bleeding.* **4** feel pity, sorrow, or grief: *My heart bleeds for the poor little orphan.* *v.*, **bled, bleed·ing.**

blem·ish (blem′ish) **1** a defect; flaw: *A scar or mole is a blemish on a person's skin.* **2** injure; mar: *One bad deed can blemish a good reputation.* 1 *n.*, 2 *v.*

blend (blend) **1** mix together; mix or become mixed so thoroughly that the things mixed cannot be distinguished or separated: *Even if you mix oil and water, they will not blend. Blend these ingredients for the cake.* **2** shade into each other: *The colors of the rainbow blend into one another.* **3** a thorough mixture made by blending: *This coffee is a blend of three varieties.* 1, 2 *v.*, **blend·ed, blend·ing;** 3 *n.*

bless (bles) **1** make holy: *to bless a church.* **2** ask God's favor for: *Bless these little children.* **3** wish good to; feel grateful to: *I bless him for his kindness.* **4** favor with prosperity, success, or happiness: *May this country always be blessed with prosperity.* **5** praise: *Bless the Lord, O my soul.* *v.*, **blessed** or **blest, bless·ing.**

bless·ed (bles′id or blest) **1** holy; sacred. **2** bringing happiness; joyful: *The birth of a baby is often called a blessed event.* **3** fortunate; happy: *We welcomed the blessed survivors of the shipwreck.* *adj.*

bless·ing (bles′ing) **1** a prayer asking God to show His favor; benediction: *At the end of the church service, the bishop gave the blessing. Before we began to eat, Father gave the blessing.* **2** a wish for happiness and success: *When he left home, he received his father's blessing.* **3** anything that makes people happy or contented: *A good temper is a great blessing.* *n.*

blest (blest) **1** See **bless.** *He was blest with good health.* **2** blessed. 1 *v.*, 2 *adj.*

blew (blü) See **blow.** *All night long the wind blew.* *v.*
☛ **Blew** and **blue** are pronounced the same.

blight (blīt) **1** any disease that causes plants or parts of plants to wither and die: *The apple crop was wiped out by blight.* **2** anything that causes destruction or ruin. **3** cause to wither and die; ruin; destroy: *Rain blighted our hopes for a picnic.* 1, 2 *n.*, 3 *v.*

blimp (blimp) a small dirigible. *n.*

blind (blīnd) **1** not able to see: *The man with the white cane is blind.* **2** make unable to see: *The bright lights blinded me for a moment.* **3** hard to see; hidden: *We were warned about the blind curve on the highway.* **4** make difficult to see; conceal: *Clouds blind the stars from my view.* **5** without the help of sight; by means of instruments instead of the eyes: *the blind flying of an aircraft at night (adj.), instruments that enable pilots to fly blind (adv.).* **6** without thought, judgment, or good sense: *blind fury, a blind guess.* **7** take away the power to understand or judge: *His prejudices blinded him.* **8** something that keeps out light or hinders sight; a window shade; shutter: *Most people pull down their blinds when they are going to bed.* **9** with only one opening: *The wild horses were driven into a blind canyon.* **10** a hiding place for a hunter: *When Father hunts ducks, he makes a blind so that he can keep out of sight.* 1, 3, 5, 6, 9 *adj.*, 2, 4, 7 *v.*, 5 *adv.*, 8, 10 *n.* **—blind′ness,** *n.*

blind alley **1** a passageway closed at one end. **2** anything that gives no chance for progress or improvement: *His last job proved to be a blind alley.*

blind·fold (blīnd′fōld′) **1** cover the eyes of to prevent seeing: *The robbers blindfolded and bound their victim.* **2** something covering the eyes to prevent seeing: *Putting a blindfold on the horse, the man led him from the burning barn.* **3** with the eyes covered: *He said he could walk the line blindfold.* 1 *v.*, 2 *n.*, 3 *adj.*

blind·ly (blīnd′lē) **1** in a blind way; as a blind person does; without vision. **2** without careful consideration; recklessly: *The besieged troops fought on blindly.* *adv.*

blind·man's buff (blīnd′mənz′) a game in which a blindfolded person tries to catch one of the several other players and tell who he is.

blink (blingk) **1** close the eyes and open them again quickly: *She blinked at the sudden light.* **2** move the eyelids; wink: *He blinked his eyes.* **3** shine with an unsteady light: *A little lantern blinked through the darkness.* *v.*

blip (blip) an image on a radar screen. *n.*

bliss (blis) very great happiness; perfect joy: *What bliss it is to plunge into the cool waves on a hot day!* *n.*

bliss·ful (blis′fəl) very happy; joyful. *adj.* **—bliss′ful·ly,** *adv.* **—bliss′ful·ness,** *n.*

blis·ter (blis′tər) **1** a little baglike swelling in the skin filled with watery matter, often caused by burns or rubbing: *My new shoes have made blisters on my heels.* **2** a swelling on the surface of a plant, on metal, on painted wood, or in glass. **3** raise a blister on: *Sunburn has blistered my back.* **4** become covered with blisters; have blisters: *People often blister when they get sunburned.* 1, 2 *n.*, 3, 4 *v.*

blithe (blīᴛʜ) happy and cheerful. *adj.*

bliz·zard (bliz′ərd) a blinding snowstorm with a very strong wind and very great cold. *n.*

bloat (blōt) swell; puff up: *His face was bruised and bloated after the fight.* *v.*

blob (blob) a small, soft drop or lump: *Blobs of wax covered the candlestick.* *n.*

block (blok) **1** a solid piece of wood, stone, metal, ice, etc.: *The Pyramids are made of blocks of stone.* **2** fill up so as to prevent passage or progress: *The country roads were blocked with snow.* **3** put things in the way of; obstruct; hinder: *Her sickness blocks my plans for the party.* **4** something that obstructs or hinders: *A block in traffic kept our car from moving on.* **5** a space in a city or town bounded by four streets: *one city block.* **6** the length of one side of a block in a city or town: *Walk one block east.* **7** a number of townships, usually surrounded by land that has not been surveyed: *the Peace River Block.* **8** a building containing a number of apartments: *an apartment block.* **9** a building having a number of offices in it, usually serving as an annex to another building: *the East Block of the Parliament Buildings in Ottawa, the Civic Block in Edmonton.* **10** a pulley on a hook: *a block and tackle.* 1, 4–10 *n.*, 2, 3 *v.*

block·ade (blok ād′) **1** the control of who and what goes into or out of a place by the use of an army or navy: *A complete blockade of all the harbors of Europe would require thousands of warships.* **2** put under such control. **3** anything that blocks up or obstructs. **4** block up; obstruct. 1, 3 *n.*, 2, 4 *v.*, **block·ad·ed, block·ad·ing.**

run the blockade, to sneak into or out of a port that is being blockaded.

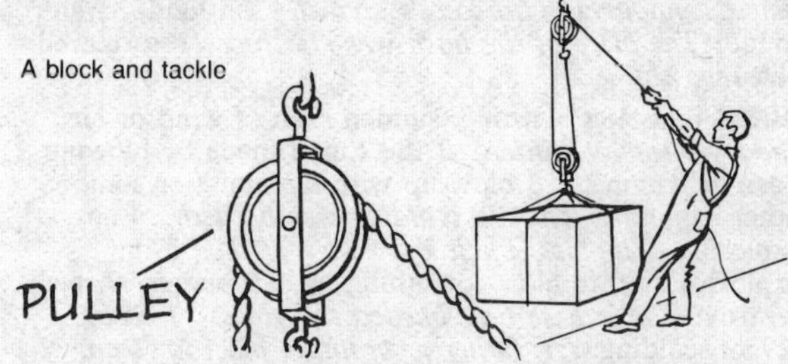

A block and tackle

block and tackle an arrangement of pulleys and ropes used in lifting or pulling heavy weights.

block·head (blok′hed′) a stupid person; fool. *n.*

block·house (blok′hous′) a fort or building with loopholes to shoot from. *n.*

blond (blond) **1** light in color: *blond hair, blond furniture.* **2** having yellow or light-brown hair, blue or grey eyes, and light skin: *blond people.* **3** a man or boy having such hair, eyes, and skin. 1, 2 *adj.*, 3 *n.* **—blond′ness,** *n.*

☛ As a noun, **blond** is used for men and boys and **blonde** is used for women and girls. The usual form for the adjective, however, is **blond** in all cases: *a blond young man, a blond actress.*

blonde (blond) a woman or girl having fair hair. *n.*
☛ See note at **blond.**

blood (blud) **1** the red liquid in the veins and the arteries; the red liquid that flows from a cut: *Blood is circulated by the heart, carrying oxygen and digested food to all parts of the body and taking away waste materials.* **2** the corresponding liquid in some animals: *The blood of most insects looks yellowish.* **3** family; parentage; descent: *Love of the sea runs in his blood.* **4** temper; state of mind: *There was bad blood between them.* *n.*

hat, āge, fär; let, ēqual, tėrm; it, īce
hot, ōpen, ôrder; oil, out; cup, pu̇t, rüle
əbove, takən, pencəl, lemən, circəs
ch, child; ng, long; sh, ship
th, thin; ᴛʜ, then; zh, measure

in cold blood, cruelly and on purpose; without emotion: *The bandits shot down three men in cold blood.*

blood bank 1 a supply of blood ready to be used in transfusions. 2 a place for storing a supply of blood.

blood·cur·dling (blud′kėr′dling) terrifying; horrible: *He told a bloodcurdling story about a haunted house.* *adj.*

blood donor a person who gives his blood to a blood bank: *The Red Cross always needs blood donors.*

blood·hound (blud′hound′) 1 a large, powerful dog with a keen sense of smell: *Bloodhounds are used to track criminals or people who have become lost.* *n.*

blood·shed (blud′shed′) the shedding of blood; slaughter: *War results in much bloodshed.* *n.*

blood·suck·er (blud′suk′ər) a leech or other animal that sucks blood. *n.*

blood·thirst·y (blud′thėrs′tē) eager to shed blood; cruel; murderous: *a bloodthirsty bandit.* *adj.*

blood vessel any tube in the body through which the blood circulates: *Arteries, veins, and capillaries are blood vessels.*

blood·y (blud′ē) 1 bleeding: *He came home with a bloody nose.* 2 covered or soaked with blood: *a bloody bandage.* 3 accompanied by much killing: *It was a bloody battle.* *adj.,* **blood·i·er, blood·i·est.**

bloom (blüm) 1 a flower; blossom. 2 have flowers; open into flowers; blossom: *Many plants bloom in spring.* 3 the condition or time of flowering: *The roses are in bloom now.* 4 the condition or time of greatest health, vigor, or beauty: *She was in the bloom of youth.* 5 be in the condition or time of greatest health, vigor, or beauty; flourish: *She was blooming with happiness.* 6 a glow of health and beauty. 7 the powdery coating on some fruits and leaves: *There is a bloom on grapes and plums.* 1, 3, 4, 6, 7 *n.,* 2, 5 *v.*

blos·som (blos′əm) 1 a flower, especially of a tree or other plant that produces fruit: *apple blossoms.* 2 the time of flowering; an early stage of growth: *a cherry tree in blossom.* 3 have flowers; open into flowers: *Pansies blossom throughout the summer.* 4 open out; develop: *She blossomed into a beautiful girl.* 1, 2 *n.,* 3, 4 *v.*

blot (blot) 1 a spot of ink or stain of any kind. 2 make blots on; stain; spot: *His pen slipped and blotted his paper in two places. This pen blots.* 3 dry with paper that soaks up ink: *Blot the page before you smear the ink.* 1 *n.,* 2, 3 *v.,* **blot·ted, blot·ting.**
blot out, a cover up entirely; hide: *He blotted out the mistake with ink.* **b** wipe out; destroy.

blotch (bloch) 1 a large, irregular spot or stain. 2 a place where the skin is red or broken out: *The poison ivy made her skin break out in blotches.* *n.*

blot·ter (blot′ər) a piece of blotting paper. *n.*

blotting paper a kind of soft paper used to dry writing by soaking up the ink: *Blotting paper is often needed when one is using a fountain pen.*

blouse (blouz) 1 a loose upper garment worn by women and children as a part of their outer clothing. 2 a loose-fitting garment for the upper part of the body: *Sailors wear blouses as a part of their uniforms.* *n.*

blow[1] (blō) 1 a hard hit; a knock; stroke: *He struck the man a blow that knocked him down.* 2 a sudden happening that causes misfortune or loss; a severe shock: *His mother's death was a great blow to him.* 3 a sudden attack: *The army struck a blow at the enemy.* *n.*
come to blows, start fighting.

blow[2] (blō) 1 send forth a strong current of air: *Blow on the fire or it will go out.* 2 move as a current of air: *The wind blew gently.* 3 drive or carry by a current of air: *The wind blew the curtain.* 4 force a current of air into, through, or against: *He blew his nose to clear it.* 5 break by an explosion: *The dynamite blew the wall to bits.* 6 make a sound by a current of air or steam: *The whistle blows at noon.* 7 pant; cause to pant: *The horse was blowing at the end of the race.* 8 puff up; swell with air: *to blow bubbles.* 9 a blowing. 10 a gale of wind: *Last night's big blow brought down several trees.* 1, 2–8 *v.,* **blew, blown, blow·ing;** 9, 10 *n.*
blow over, a pass by or over: *The storm has blown over.* **b** be forgotten: *In time the scandal blew over.*
blow up, a explode. **b** fill with air: *blow up a bicycle tire.* **c** *Informal.* become very angry: *Mother blew up at me for getting tar on the floor.* **d** arise; begin: *A storm suddenly blew up.* **e** enlarge a photograph.

blow·er (blō′ər) 1 a person or thing that blows: *a glass blower.* 2 a fan or other machine for forcing air into a building, furnace, mine, etc. *n.*

blow·gun (blō′gun′) 1 a tube through which a person blows arrows or darts. 2 peashooter. *n.*

blow·hole (blō′hōl′) 1 a hole for breathing in the top of the head of whales and some other animals. 2 a hole in the ice where whales, seals, etc. come to breathe. *n.*

blown (blōn) 1 out of breath; exhausted. 2 See **blow**[2]. *The wind has blown itself out.* 1 *adj.,* 2 *v.*

blow·out (blō′out′) 1 the bursting of an automobile tire. 2 a sudden or violent escape of air, steam, or the like. *n.*

blow·torch (blō′tôrch′) a small torch that shoots out a very hot flame: *A blowtorch is used to melt metal and burn off paint.* *n.*

blow·up (blō′up′) 1 an explosion. 2 *Informal.* a sudden explosion of anger; quarrel: *There was a big blowup in school when the theft was discovered.* 3 *Informal.* an enlargement of a photograph: *There's a blowup of our class picture on the wall.* *n.*

blub·ber (blub′ər) 1 the fat of whales and some other sea animals: *The oil obtained from whale blubber was formerly burned in lamps.* 2 weep noisily. 1 *n.,* 2 *v.*

bludg·eon (bluj′ən) 1 a short, heavy club. 2 strike with a heavy club. 1 *n.,* 2 *v.*

blue (blü) 1 the color of the clear sky in daylight. 2 having this color. 3 sad; discouraged: *I felt blue when I failed.* 4 **the blue, a** the sky: *A bolt of lightning struck from the blue.* **b** the sea: *Far out upon the blue sail many ships.* 5 **the blues,** *pl.* **a** *Informal.* a gloomy feeling; low spirits: *The poor guy has the blues again.* **b** a slow, sad song in a jazz rhythm. 1, 4, 5 *n.,* 2, 3 *adj.,* **blu·er, blu·est. —blue′ness,** *n.*
out of the blue, completely unexpected: *His visit came out of the blue.*
☛ **Blue** and **blew** are pronounced the same.

blue·bell (blü′bel′) a plant with blue flowers shaped

like bells: *The harebell and the wild hyacinth are two common bluebells.* *n.*

blue·ber·ry (blü′ber′ē) **1** a small, round, blue berry that is good to eat. **2** the shrub that this berry grows on. *n., pl.* **blue·ber·ries.**

blue·bird (blü′bėrd′) a small songbird of Canada and the northern United States: *The male bluebird is bright blue on the back and wings.* *n.*

blue·bot·tle (blü′bot′əl) a large fly having a blue abdomen and a hairy body. *n.*

blue·fish (blü′fish′) a blue-and-silver salt-water fish of the Atlantic coast, much valued as food. *n.*

A bluejay — about 30 cm long with the tail

blue·jay (blü′jā′) a noisy, chattering North American bird with a crest and a blue back. *n.*

blue·line (blü′līn′) either of the two blue lines drawn midway between the centre of a hockey rink and each goal. *n.*

Blue·nose (blü′nōz′) **1** a nickname for a Nova Scotian or, less often, a New Brunswicker: *Many Bluenoses are descended from Loyalists.* **2** a ship built in Nova Scotia and manned by Nova Scotians. *n.*

blue·print (blü′print′) **1** a photograph that shows white outlines on a blue background, used to copy drawings of building plans, maps, etc. **2** a detailed plan for doing anything. *n.*

bluff[1] (bluf) **1** a high, steep bank or cliff. **2** rising with a straight, broad front: *The ship anchored in the shelter of a bluff headland.* **3** *Cdn.* a clump of trees standing on the flat prairie; copse: *The farmhouse was screened from the wind by a bluff. A family of prairie chickens made its home in the bluff.* **4** abrupt, frank, and hearty in manner: *He had a bluff, hearty way about him.* 1, 3 *n.*, 2, 4 *adj.*

bluff[2] (bluf) **1** a show of pretended confidence put on to mislead others: *We say it is a bluff when a person lets others think he knows more than he really does.* **2** deceive by a show of pretended confidence: *He bluffed his way through the test.* **3** a threat that cannot be carried out. 1, 3 *n.*, 2 *v.* —**bluff′er,** *n.*

blu·ing (blü′ing) a blue liquid or powder put in water when rinsing clothes, in order to prevent white clothes from turning yellow. *n.*

blu·ish (blü′ish) somewhat blue. *adj.*

blun·der (blun′dər) **1** a stupid mistake. **2** make a stupid mistake. **3** stumble; move as if blind: *The injured boy blundered through the woods.* 1 *n.*, 2, 3 *v.* —**blun′der·er,** *n.*

A blunderbuss

blun·der·buss (blun′dər bus′) a short gun with a wide muzzle, formerly used to fire a quantity of shot a short distance. *n.*

blunt (blunt) **1** without a sharp edge or point; dull: *He sharpened the blunt knife.* **2** make less sharp; make less keen: *He blunted his knife on the stone.* **3** saying what one thinks very frankly, without trying to be tactful: *He thinks blunt speech proves he is honest.* 1, 3 *adj.*, 2 *v.* —**blunt′ly,** *adv.* —**blunt′ness,** *n.*

blur (blėr) **1** make confused in form or outline: *Mist blurred the hills.* **2** make dim: *Tears blurred my eyes.* **3** a blurred condition; dimness: *Everything was a blur because of the drops the doctor had put in my eyes.* **4** smear: *He blurred the picture by touching the page before the paint was dry.* **5** a blot; smear: *The letter had many blurs.* 1, 2, 4 *v.*, **blurred, blur·ring;** 3, 5 *n.*

blurt (blėrt) say suddenly or without thinking: *He blurted out the secret.* *v.*

blush (blush) **1** a reddening of the skin caused by shame, confusion, or excitement. **2** become red because of shame, confusion, or excitement: *She was so shy that she blushed every time she was spoken to.* **3** be ashamed: *I blushed at my brother's bad table manners.* **4** a rosy color: *The blush of dawn showed in the east.* 1, 4 *n.*, 2, 3 *v.*

blus·ter (blus′tər) **1** storm or blow noisily and violently: *The wind blustered around the house.* **2** a boisterous blowing. **3** talk with noise and violence: *When he was excited and angry, he blustered a great deal.* **4** noisy and violent talk: *We get tired of his angry bluster.* 1, 3 *v.*, 2, 4 *n.*

B.N.A. Act British North America Act.

bo·a (bō′ə) **1** a large tropical snake that is not poisonous but kills by coiling itself around its prey and squeezing it to death: *Anacondas, pythons, and boa constrictors are all boas.* **2** a long scarf made of fur or feathers, worn by women around the neck or shoulders. *n.*

boa con·stric·tor (kən strik′tər) a large boa of tropical North and South America.

boar (bôr) **1** a male pig, or hog. **2** a wild pig, or hog. *n.*

☞ **Boar** and **bore** are pronounced the same.

board (bôrd) **1** a broad, thin piece of wood for use in building, etc.: *We used boards 1 metre long for shelves in our new bookcase.* **2** cover with boards: *Father boards up the windows of our summer cottage in the fall.* **3** a flat piece of wood used for some special purpose: *an ironing board, a diving board.* **4** meals provided for pay: *Mrs. Adams gives good board.* **5** give food to for pay: *She boards three men in her house.* **6** get food for pay: *Mr. Jones boards at our house.* **7** a group of persons managing something; council: *a school board.* **8** a branch of a government department: *the National Film Board.* **9** get on a ship, train, aircraft, etc.: *We board the school bus at the corner every day.* 1, 3, 4, 7, 8 *n.*, 2, 5, 6, 9 *v.*

on board, on a train, aircraft, etc.: *When everybody was on board, the ship sailed.*

board·er (bôr′dər) a person who pays for meals, or for room and meals, at another's house. *n.*

hat, āge, fär; let, ēqual, tėrm; it, īce
hot, ōpen, ôrder; oil, out; cup, pu̇t, rüle
əbove, takən, pencəl, lemən, circəs
ch, child; ng, long; sh, ship
th, thin; ᴛʜ, then; zh, measure

☛ **Boarder** and **border** are pronounced the same.

board·ing (bôr′ding) **1** in hockey, checking an opposing player into the boards of the rink in a rough and illegal manner. **2** wooden boards considered together as building material. *n.*

boarding house a house where meals, or room and meals, are provided for pay.

boarding school a school with buildings where pupils live during the school year.

board of education a name sometimes given to a group of people, usually elected, who manage the schools in a certain area.

board of health the department of a local government in charge of public health.

boast (bōst) **1** speak too well of oneself or what one owns; brag: *He boasts about his new car.* **2** something said in praise of oneself; bragging words: *I don't believe his boast that he can win the race.* **3** something that one is proud of: *The medal he won at the swimming meet was his boast.* **4** have something to be proud of: *Our town boasts a new high school.* 1, 4 *v.*, 2, 3 *n.* —**boast′er,** *n.*

boast·ful (bōst′fəl) fond of bragging; boasting: *It is hard to listen very long to a boastful person. adj.* —**boast′ful·ly,** *adv.* —**boast′ful·ness,** *n.*

boat (bōt) **1** a small, open vessel for travelling on water, such as a motorboat or a rowboat. See **rowboat** and **sloop** for pictures. **2** a ship such as a steamboat or a freighter. **3** use a boat; go in a boat. **4** put or carry in a boat. 1, 2 *n.*, 3, 4 *v.*

boat·house (bōt′hous′) a house or shed for sheltering a boat or boats. *n.*

boatman (bōt′mən) **1** a man who rents out boats or takes care of them. **2** a man who rows or sails boats for pay. **3** a man who works on boats. *n., pl.* **boat·men** (bōt′mən).

boat·swain (bō′sən or bōt′swān′) an officer of a ship who has charge of the boats, anchors, ropes, and rigging: *The boatswain directs some of the work of the crew. n.*

bob[1] (bob) **1** move up and down, or to and fro, with short, quick motions: *The bird bobbed its head to pick up crumbs.* **2** a short, quick motion up and down, or to and fro. 1 *v.*, **bobbed, bob·bing;** 2 *n.*

bob[2] (bob) **1** a short haircut. **2** cut the hair short. **3** a float on a fishing line. 1, 3 *n.*, 2 *v.*, **bobbed, bob·bing.**

bob·by pin (bob′ē) a metal hairpin whose prongs close on and hold tightly to the hair.

bob·cat (bob′kat′) a kind of lynx found mostly in the United States, closely related to the Canada lynx but having a longer tail, shorter ears, and smaller paws. *n.*

bob·o·link (bob′ə lingk′) a common North American songbird that lives in fields and meadows. *n.*

bob·skate (bob′skāt′) a child's skate that consists of two sections of double runners and can be adjusted to the size of the wearer's foot. *n.*

bob·sled (bob′sled′) **1** a long sled with two sets of runners, having a steering wheel and brakes. **2** ride or coast on a bobsled. 1 *n.*, 2 *v.*

bob·white (bob′wīt′ or bob′hwīt′) a North American quail. *n.*

☛ The word **bobwhite** was originally an imitation of the sound this bird makes.

bode (bōd) be a sign of: *Dark clouds boded rain. v.,* **bod·ed, bod·ing.**
bode well, be a good sign.

bod·i·ly (bod′ə lē) **1** of the body; in the body: *bodily pain.* **2** in person: *The man whom we thought dead walked bodily into the room.* **3** as one group; entirely; as a whole: *The audience rose bodily to cheer the hero.* 1 *adj.*, 2, 3 *adv.*

bod·y (bod′ē) **1** the whole material part of a person, animal, or plant: *This boy has a strong, healthy body.* **2** the main part or trunk of an animal, not the head or limbs. **3** the main part of anything, such as the hull of a ship. **4** a group of persons or things: *A large body of children sang at the concert.* **5** a mass; portion of matter: *A lake is a body of water. The moon, the sun, and the stars are heavenly bodies.* **6** *Informal.* a person: *He is a good-natured body.* **7** substance: *Thick soup has more body than thin soup. n., pl.* **bod·ies.**

bod·y·check (bod′ē chek′) in hockey: **1** a defensive play in which a player throws the puck-carrier off stride by bumping him with his body. **2** throw the puck-carrier off stride by bumping him with one's body. 1 *n.*, 2 *v.*

bod·y·guard (bod′ē gärd′) a man or men who guard a person: *a bodyguard accompanies the Queen when she travels. n.*

bog (bog) **1** a piece of wet, soft, spongy ground; a marsh or swamp. **2** sink or get stuck in a bog. 1 *n.*, 2 *v.*, **bogged, bog·ging.**
bog down, get stuck as if in mud: *He bogged down in his science project and had to ask his teacher for help.*

bo·gey (bō′gē) **1** a goblin; an evil spirit. **2** a thing or person that is feared; bugbear: *Arithmetic was a bogey to that boy. n., pl.* **bo·geys.** Also spelled **bogy.**

bog·gy (bog′ē) soft and wet like a bog; marshy; swampy: *boggy ground. adj.,* **bog·gi·er, bog·gi·est.**

bo·gus (bō′gəs) not genuine; counterfeit; sham: *The cashier refused to accept the bogus twenty-dollar bill. adj.*

bo·gy (bō′gē) See **bogey.** *n., pl.* **bo·gies.**

boil[1] (boil) **1** bubble up and give off steam or vapor: *Water boils when heated to 100 degrees Celsius.* **2** bring a liquid to the heat at which it bubbles up: *Boil some water for tea.* **3** cook by boiling: *We boil the eggs four minutes.* **4** be excited; be stirred up: *He boiled*

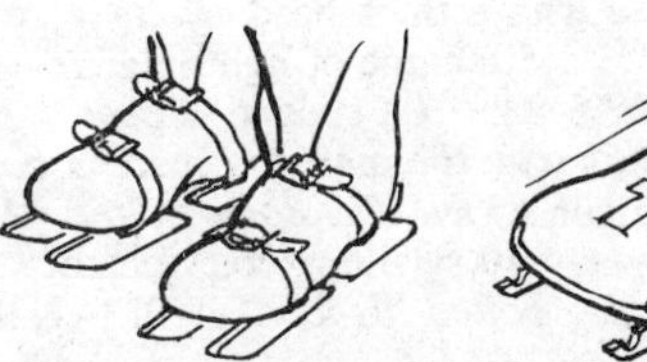
Bobskates

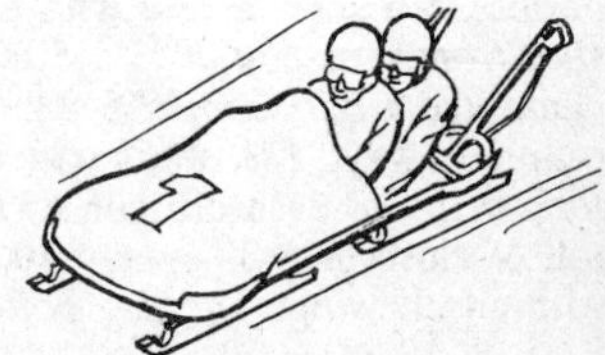
A bobsled

with anger. 5 a boiling condition: *Bring the mixture to a boil.* 1–4 *v.*, 5 *n.*

boil down, a make less by boiling: *Boil down the sauce to half the amount.* **b** shorten by getting rid of unimportant parts: *He boiled down his notes to a list of important facts.*

boil² (boil) a red, painful swelling on the skin, formed by pus around a hard core: *Boils are often caused by infection.* *n.*

boil·er (boil′ər) 1 a container for heating liquids. 2 a tank for making steam to heat buildings or drive engines. 3 a tank for holding hot water. *n.*

boiling point the temperature at which a liquid boils: *The boiling point of water at sea level is 100 degrees Celsius.*

bois·ter·ous (bois′tər əs or bois′trəs) 1 noisily cheerful: *a boisterous game.* 2 violent; rough: *a boisterous wind, a boisterous child.* *adj.* **—bois′ter·ous·ly,** *adv.* **—bois′ter·ous·ness,** *n.*

bold (bōld) 1 without fear; brave: *Lancelot was a bold knight.* 2 showing or requiring courage: *Climbing the steep mountain was a bold act.* 3 too free in manners; impudent: *The bold little boy made faces at us as we passed.* 4 striking; sharp and clear: *The mountains stood in bold outline against the sky.* *adj.* **—bold′ly,** *adv.* **—bold′ness,** *n.*

bo·le·ro (bə ler′ō) 1 a Spanish dance. 2 the music for it. 3 a very short, loose jacket worn open in front. *n., pl.* **bo·le·ros.**

boll (bōl) a rounded seed pod of a plant, especially that of cotton or flax. *n.*

☛ **Boll** and **bowl** are pronounced the same.

bol·ster (bōl′stər) 1 a long pillow for a bed. 2 a cushion or pad. 3 support, prop, or keep from falling: *The walls of the church are bolstered up with buttresses. Her sympathy bolstered his courage.* 1, 2 *n.*, 3 *v.*

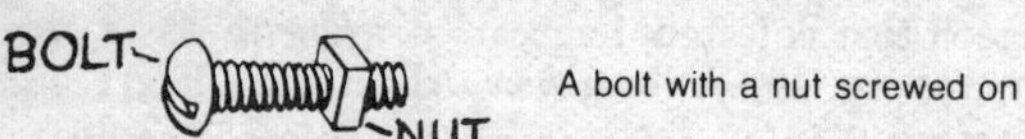

A bolt with a nut screwed on

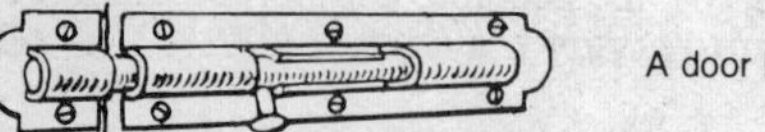
A door bolt

bolt (bōlt) 1 a rod with a head at one end and a place for a nut to be screwed on at the other: *Bolts are used to fasten things together or to hold something in place.* 2 a sliding fastener for a door, gate, etc. 3 the part of a lock moved by a key. 4 fasten with a bolt: *Bolt the doors.* 5 a short arrow with a thick head: *Bolts were shot from crossbows.* 6 a discharge of lightning: *It came like a bolt from the sky.* 7 a sudden start; running away: *The rabbit saw the man and made a bolt for safety.* 8 dash off; run away: *The horse bolted.* 9 a roll of cloth or wallpaper. 10 swallow food quickly without chewing: *The dog bolted his food.* 1–3, 5–7, 9 *n.*, 4, 8, 10 *v.*

bolt upright, stiff and straight: *Awakened by a noise, he sat bolt upright in bed.*

bomb (bom) 1 a container filled with gunpowder or some other explosive: *A bomb is set off by a fuse or by the force with which it hits something.* 2 a container filled with paint, an insect poison, or other liquid under pressure, that comes out as spray or foam: *Mother used a bomb to rid the house of moths.* 3 attack with bombs; hurl bombs at; drop bombs on. 1, 2 *n.*, 3 *v.*

☛ **Bomb** and **balm** are sometimes pronounced the same.

☛ **Bomb** came into English through French from a Latin word *bombus,* meaning 'booming' or 'humming.' Related English words such as **bombard** and **bombardier¹** came into English through separate French words from the same Latin word.

bom·bard (bom bärd′) 1 attack with bombs or heavy fire of shot and shell from big guns: *Our artillery bombarded the enemy all day.* 2 keep attacking vigorously: *She bombarded me with many questions.* *v.*

☛ See note at **bomb.**

bom·bar·dier¹ (bom′bər dēr′ or bom′ə dēr′) 1 a corporal in the artillery. 2 the man in a bomber who aims and releases the bombs. *n.*

☛ See note at **bomb.**

A bombardier

bom·bar·dier² (bom′bə dēr′) *Cdn.* a large vehicle for travelling over snow and ice, usually equipped with tracked wheels at the rear and a set of skis at the front. *n.*

☛ Named after Armand *Bombardier* (1908–1964), who invented and manufactured the machine.

bom·bard·ment (bom bärd′mənt) an attack with bombs or with heavy fire of shot and shell. *n.*

bomb·er (bom′ər) an airplane used to drop bombs on enemy troops, factories, cities, etc. *n.*

bomb·proof (bom′prüf′) strong or deep enough to be safe from bombs. *adj.*

bo·nan·za (bə nan′zə) 1 a rich mass of ore in a mine. 2 *Informal.* any source of great riches or profit: *My uncle said his store is turning out to be a bonanza.* *n.*

bond (bond) 1 anything that ties, binds, or unites: *a bond of affection between sisters.* 2 a certificate issued by a government or private company which promises to pay back with interest the money borrowed from the buyer of the certificate: *The city issued bonds to raise money for building a new playground.* 3 a written agreement by which a person says he will pay a certain sum of money if he does not perform certain duties properly. 4 **bonds,** *pl.* **a** chains; shackles: *the bonds of slavery.* **b** imprisonment. *n.*

bond·age (bon′dij) the condition of being held against one's will under the control or influence of some person or thing: *Slaves were kept in bondage.* *n.*

bone (bōn) 1 one of the pieces of the skeleton of an animal with a backbone: *a beef bone for soup. He broke two bones of the hand.* 2 take the bones out of: *We boned the fish before eating it.* 3 the hard substance of which bones are made. 1, 3 *n.*, 2 *v.*, **boned, bon·ing.** **—bone′less,** *adj.*

bon·fire (bon′fīr′) a fire built outdoors: *The young*

people sang songs around the bonfire. *n.*

bon·go (bong′gō) a small, tuned drum played in pairs with the hands. *n.*

bon·net (bon′it) **1** a head covering usually tied under the chin with strings or ribbons, worn by small children and formerly by older girls and women. **2** a cap worn by men and boys in Scotland. **3** a head-dress of feathers worn by North American Indians. *n.*

bon·nie or **bon·ny** (bon′ē) **1** fair to see; rosy and pretty: *What a bonnie baby!* **2** healthy-looking. *adj.,* **bon·ni·er, bon·ni·est.**

bon·spiel (bon′spēl′) in curling, a tournament among different clubs or among teams of the same club. *n.*

bo·nus (bō′nəs) something extra; something given in addition to what is due: *The company gave its workers a Christmas bonus.* *n.*

bon·y (bō′nē) **1** of bone. **2** like bone. **3** full of bones. **4** having big bones that stick out: *the bony hips of a thin horse.* **5** very thin. *adj.,* **bon·i·er, bon·i·est.**

boo (bü) **1** a sound made to show dislike or contempt or to frighten: *Boos were heard from those who didn't like the concert (n.).* *We were frightened when he jumped from behind the door and shouted, 'Boo!' (interj.).* **2** make such a sound. 1 *n., pl.* **boos;** 1 *interj.,* 2 *v.,* **booed, boo·ing.**

boo·by (bü′bē) **1** a fool; dunce. **2** a large sea bird of the tropics. *n., pl.* **boo·bies.**

booby trap a trick arranged to annoy some unsuspecting person.

book (bu̇k) **1** written or printed sheets of paper bound together: *She read the first ten pages in her book.* **2** blank sheets bound together: *You can keep your accounts in this book.* **3** a main division of a book: *The books of the Bible.* **4** something fastened together along one side like a book: *a book of matches, tickets, or cheques.* **5** make a reservation to get tickets or to engage service: *He had booked a passage from Montreal to England.* 1–4 *n.,* 5 *v.*

book·case (bu̇k′kās′) a piece of furniture with shelves for holding books. *n.*

book end a prop or support placed at the end of a row of books to hold them upright.

book·keep·er (bu̇k′kēp′ər) a person who keeps a record of business accounts. *n.*

book·keep·ing (bu̇k′kēp′ing) the work of keeping a record of business accounts. *n.*

book·let (bu̇k′lit) a little book; a thin book or pamphlet: *Booklets often have paper covers.* *n.*

book·mo·bile (bu̇k′mə bēl′) a large van that serves as a travelling branch of a library. *n.*

boom[1] (büm) **1** a deep, hollow sound like the roar of cannon or of big waves: *The big bell made a loud boom.* **2** make a deep hollow sound: *The big man's voice boomed out above the rest.* **3** a sudden activity and increase in business, prices, or values of property; rapid growth: *Our town is having such a boom that it is likely to double its size in two years.* **4** increase suddenly in activity; grow rapidly: *Business is booming.* 1, 3 *n.,* 2, 4 *v.*

boom[2] (büm) **1** a long pole or beam, used to extend the bottom of a sail. **2** the lifting and guiding pole of a derrick. See **crane** for picture. **3** a chain, cable, or line of timbers used to keep logs from floating away. **4** a large raft of logs being floated over water. *n.*

hat, āge, fär; let, ēqual, tėrm; it, īce
hot, ōpen, ôrder; oil, out; cup, pu̇t, rüle
əbove, takən, pencəl, lemən, circəs
ch, child; ng, long; sh, ship
th, thin; ᴛʜ, then; zh, measure

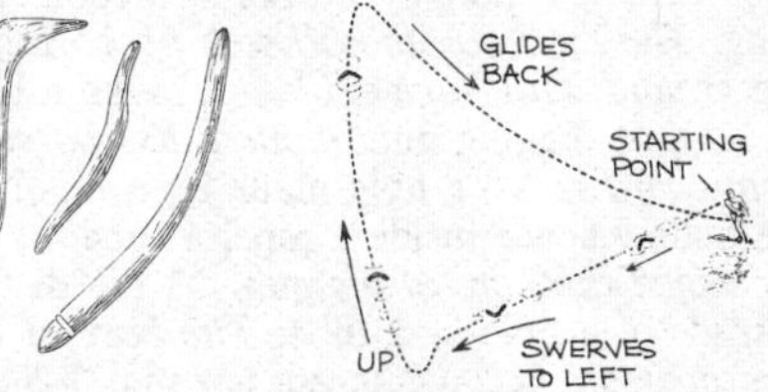

Three kinds of boomerang. The picture at the right shows how a boomerang returns to the thrower.

boom·er·ang (bü′mə rang′) a curved flat piece of wood used as a weapon by native peoples of Australia: *One kind of boomerang can be thrown so that it will return to the thrower if it misses its target.* *n.*

boon[1] (bün) **1** a blessing; a great benefit: *Those warm boots were a boon to me in the cold weather.* **2** something asked or granted as a favor. *n.*

boon[2] (bün) pleasant; jolly: *The two boys were boon companions.* *adj.*

boor (bür) a rude, bad-mannered person. *n.*

boost (büst) **1** a push or shove that helps a person in rising or advancing: *She gave her friend a boost over the wall.* **2** lift or push from below or behind. **3** raise; increase: *The store has boosted its prices.* **4** help by speaking well of: *The company is boosting its new product by ads in newspapers and on billboards.* 1 *n.,* 2–4 *v.*

boot (büt) **1** a covering, usually of leather or rubber, for the foot and part of the leg. **2** a kick: *He gave the ball a boot.* **3** give a kick to: *He booted the can off the sidewalk.* 1, 2 *n.,* 3 *v.*

boot·ee (bü′tē) a baby's soft shoe. *n.*

booth (büth) **1** a place where goods are sold or shown at a fair, market, etc. **2** a small, closed place for a telephone, motion-picture projector, etc. **3** a partly closed-off space in a restaurant or café, containing a table and seats for a few persons. *n., pl.* **booths** (büᴛʜz or büths).

boot·less (büt′lis) useless. *adj.*

boo·ty (bü′tē) **1** things taken from the enemy in war. **2** things seized by violence and robbery; plunder: *The pirates fought over the booty from the town they raided.* **3** any valuable thing or things obtained; prize. *n., pl.* **boo·ties.**

bor·der (bôr′dər) **1** the side, edge, or boundary of anything, or the part near it: *We pitched our tent on the border of the lake.* **2** form a boundary to; bound: *Manitoba borders part of Ontario.* **3** a boundary separating two provinces, states, countries, etc.: *We reached Detroit by crossing the border at Windsor.* **4** a strip on the edge of anything for strength or ornament: *The tablecloth had a lace border.* **5** put a border on:

We have bordered our garden with shrubs. 1, 3, 4 *n.*, 2, 5 *v.*
border on or **upon, a** touch at the border; be next to: *Canada borders on the United States.* **b** be close to; resemble: *His behavior bordered on absurdity.*
☛ **Border** and **boarder** are pronounced the same.

bore[1] (bôr) **1** make a hole by means of a tool that keeps turning: *The men dug the oil well by boring through the ground with huge drills.* **2** make a hole by pushing through or digging out: *A mole has bored its way under my garden.* **3** a hole made by a revolving tool. **4** the hollow space inside a pipe, a tube, or a gun barrel: *He cleaned the bore of his gun.* **5** the distance across the inside of a hole or a tube: *The bore of this pipe is 5 centimetres.* 1, 2 *v.*, **bored, bor·ing;** 3–5 *n.*
☛ **Bore** and **boar** are pronounced the same.

bore[2] (bôr) **1** make weary by tiresome talk or by being dull: *This book bores me so much that I cannot finish it.* **2** a tiresome or dull person or thing: *It is a bore to have to wash dishes three times a day.* 1 *v.*, **bored, bor·ing;** 2 *n.*
☛ See note at **bore**[1].

bore[3] (bôr) See **bear**[1]. *She bore her loss bravely.* *v.*
☛ See note at **bore**[1].

bo·ric ac·id (bôr′ik) a white, crystalline substance used as a mild antiseptic.

born (bôrn) **1** brought into life; brought forth: *A baby born on Sunday is supposed to be lucky.* **2** by birth; by nature: *a born athlete.* **3** See **bear**[1]. *He was born on May 17, 1900.* 1, 2 *adj.*, 3 *v.*

borne (bôrn) See **bear**[1]. *I have borne it as long as I can. I have borne the load for two kilometres. She has borne three children.* *v.*

bor·ough (bėr′ō) a town or township having its own local government: *North York is a borough of Metropolitan Toronto.* *n.*

bor·row (bôr′ō) **1** get something from another person with the understanding that it must be returned: *If you lend your book to him, he has borrowed the book from you.* **2** take and use as one's own; adopt; take: *The word 'wigwam' was borrowed from the Indians.* *v.* —**bor′row·er,** *n.*

bos·om (bu̇z′əm or bü′zəm) **1** the upper front part of the human body, especially the breasts of a woman. **2** the part of a garment worn over the upper front of the body: *She wore a flower on the bosom of her dress.* **3** the heart, thoughts, affections, etc.: *He kept the secret in his bosom.* **4** the centre or inmost part: *He did not mention it even in the bosom of his family.* **5** close; trusted: *Very dear friends are bosom friends.* 1–4 *n.*, 5 *adj.*

boss (bos) *Informal.* **1** a person who hires workers or watches over and directs them; foreman; manager. **2** give orders to: *He likes to boss people. Don't boss me around!* **3** direct; control: *Who is bossing this job?* 1 *n.*, 2, 3 *v.*

boss·y (bos′ē) *Informal.* fond of telling others what to do and how to do it: *That little boy is bossy.* *adj.*, **boss·i·er, boss·i·est.**

bo·tan·i·cal (bə tan′i kəl) **1** having to do with plants and plant life. **2** having to do with botany. *adj.*

bot·a·nist (bot′ə nist) a person skilled in botany. *n.*

bot·a·ny (bot′ə nē) the science of plants; the study of plants and plant life: *Botany is concerned with the structure, growth, classification, diseases, etc. of plants.* *n.*

botch (boch) **1** spoil by poor work; bungle: *The boy tried to make a model airplane, but he botched it.* **2** a poor piece of work. 1 *v.*, 2 *n.*

both (bōth) **1** two, when only two are considered; the one and the other: *Both houses are white.* **2** the two together: *Both belong to him.* **3** together; alike; equally: *He can both sing and dance (adv.). He was both strong and healthy (conj.).* 1 *adj.*, 2 *pron.*, 3 *adv.*, *conj.*

both·er (boTH′ər) **1** worry; fuss; trouble: *What a lot of bother about nothing.* **2** take trouble; concern oneself: *Don't bother about getting me a special breakfast; I'll eat what is here.* **3** a person or thing that causes worry, fuss, or trouble: *A door that will not shut is a bother.* **4** make uneasy, worried, or annoyed; irritate: *Hot weather bothers me.* 1, 3 *n.*, 2, 4 *v.*

bot·tle (bot′əl) **1** a container for holding liquids, usually made of glass, having a narrow neck and no handles. **2** the amount that a bottle can hold: *He could drink a whole bottle of milk.* **3** put into bottles. 1, 2 *n.*, 3 *v.*, **bot·tled, bot·tling.** —**bot′tle·like′,** *adj.*
bottle up, hold in; keep back; control: *He managed to bottle up his anger.*

bot·tle·neck (bot′əl nek′) **1** a narrow passageway or street: *Traffic moves slowly through that bottleneck.* **2** a person, thing, or condition that hinders progress: *Lack of co-operation was the bottleneck in our plan.* *n.*

bot·tom (bot′əm) **1** the lowest part: *The berries at the bottom of the basket were crushed.* **2** the part on which anything rests: *The bottom of that glass is wet.* **3** the ground under water: *the bottom of the sea.* **4** low land along a river. **5** the seat: *This chair needs a new bottom.* **6** the basis or foundation; the origin: *We must get to the bottom of the mystery.* **7** lowest; last: *I see a robin on the bottom branch of that tree. These are bottom prices.* 1–6 *n.*, 7 *adj.*

bot·tom·less (bot′əm lis) **1** without a bottom: *a bottomless chair.* **2** very, very deep: *He drowned in a bottomless lake.* *adj.*

bough (bou) one of the main branches on a tree: *The boys built a tree house in the boughs of an elm.* *n.*
☛ **Bough, bow**[1], and **bow**[3] are pronounced the same.

bought (bot or bôt) See **buy.** *We bought apples from the farmer. I have bought two new pencils.* *v.*

boul·der (bōl′dər) a large rock rounded or worn by the action of water and weather. *n.*

boul·e·vard (bu̇l′ə värd′) **1** a broad street. **2** the strip of grass between a sidewalk and a curb. **3** the centre strip dividing any road into two lanes for traffic going in opposite directions. *n.*

bounce (bouns) **1** spring into the air like a ball: *The baby likes to bounce up and down on the bed.* **2** cause to bounce: *Bounce the ball to me.* **3** a bound; spring; bouncing: *I caught the ball on the first bounce.* **4** come or go noisily, energetically, etc.: *She bounced out of the room.* 1, 2, 4 *v.*, **bounced, bounc·ing;** 3 *n.*

bound[1] (bound) **1** under some obligation; obliged: *I feel bound by my promise.* **2** certain; sure: *He is bound to come today.* **3** put in covers: *a bound book.* **4** See **bind.** *The men bound their prisoners with ropes.* 1–3 *adj.*, 4 *v.*

hat, āge, fär; let, ēqual, tėrm; it, īce
hot, ōpen, ôrder; oil, out; cup, pu̇t, rüle
əbove, takən, pencəl, lemən, circəs
ch, child; ng, long; sh, ship
th, thin; ᴛʜ, then; zh, measure

bound[2] (bound) **1** spring back; bounce: *The ball bounded from the wall.* **2** springing back; bounce: *I caught the ball on the first bound.* **3** leap or spring lightly along; jump: *The mountain goats bounded from rock to rock.* **4** a leap or jump: *With one bound the deer disappeared into the woods.* 1, 3 *v.*, 2, 4 *n.*

bound[3] (bound) **1** a boundary or limiting line; a limit: *the farthest bounds of the earth. Keep your hopes within bounds.* **2** form the boundary of; limit: *The country was bounded by the sea on two sides.* 1 *n.*, 2 *v.* **—bound′less,** *adj.*

out of bounds, outside the area allowed by rules, custom, or law: *He kicked the ball out of bounds. The town is out of bounds for the soldiers.*

bound[4] (bound) going; on the way: *Where are you bound? I am bound for home. v.*

bound·a·ry (boun′də rē) **1** a limiting line. **2** anything that serves as the dividing line between provinces, countries, etc.: *Lake Ontario forms part of the boundary between Canada and the United States. n., pl.* **bound·a·ries.**

boun·te·ous (boun′tē əs) **1** generous; given freely: *The rich man gave bounteous gifts to the poor.* **2** plentiful; abundant: *The farmer had a bounteous crop. adj.* **—boun′te·ous·ly, adv.**

boun·ti·ful (boun′tə fəl) **1** plentiful; abundant; more than enough: *We have a bountiful supply of tomatoes.* **2** generous; giving freely: *the help of bountiful friends. adj.* **—boun′ti·ful·ly,** *adv.* **—boun′ti·ful·ness,** *n.*

boun·ty (boun′tē) **1** whatever is given with generosity. **2** generosity. **3** a reward or premium: *Governments have sometimes offered bounties for killing animals considered a nuisance. n., pl.* **boun·ties.**

bou·quet (bü kā′ or bō kā′) **1** a bunch of flowers. **2** fragrance: *The perfume has a delicate bouquet. n.*

bout (bout) **1** a trial of strength; contest: *Those are the two boxers who will appear in the main bout.* **2** a spell; a period, especially one involving illness, effort, or endurance: *I have just had a long bout of the flu. n.*

bow[1] (bou) **1** bend the head or body in greeting, respect, etc.: *The people bowed before the king. Let us bow our heads in prayer.* **2** a bending of head or body in this way: *She answered his bow with a curtsy.* **3** express by a bow: *She bowed her thanks.* **4** cause to stoop; bend: *The old man was bowed by age.* **5** submit; yield: *The boy bowed to his parents' wishes.* 1, 3–5 *v.*, 2 *n.*

☛ **Bow**[1] and **bough** are pronounced the same.

bow[2] (bō) **1** a weapon for shooting arrows: *A bow usually consists of a length of springy wood bent by a string.* See **arrow** for picture. **2** a slender rod of springy wood with a flat band of horsehairs stretched between the two ends, for playing a violin, cello, etc.: *Violin bows used to be curved like the weapon.* **3** something curved; curved part: *A rainbow is a bow.* **4** a knot with a loop or loops: *a bow of ribbon. n.* **—bow′like,** *adj.*

☛ **Bow**[2] and **beau** are pronounced the same.

bow[3] (bou) the forward part of a ship, boat, or aircraft. See **aft** for picture. *n.*

☛ **Bow**[3] and **bough** are pronouncd the same.

bow·el (bou′əl) **1** the tube in the body into which food passes from the stomach; intestines. **2 bowels,** *pl.* the inner part of anything: *Miners dig for coal in the bowels of the earth. n.*

bow·er (bou′ər) **1** a shelter of leafy branches. **2** arbor. *n.*

bowl[1] (bōl) **1** a hollow, rounded dish, usually without handles. **2** the amount that a bowl can hold; bowlful. **3** a rounded part that is a receptacle: *the bowl of a spoon. The bowl of a pipe holds the tobacco. n.* **—bowl′-like′,** *adj.*

☛ **Bowl** and **boll** are pronounced the same.

bowl[2] (bōl) **1** a large, heavy ball used in certain games. **2** play the game of bowling. **3** roll or move along rapidly and smoothly: *Our car bowled merrily along.* 1 *n.*, 2, 3 *v.*

bowl over, a knock over: *The force of the wind nearly bowled him over.* **b** *Informal.* make helpless and confused: *I was bowled over by the bad news.*

☛ See note at **bowl**[1].

bow·leg·ged (bō′leg′id) having the legs curved outward. *adj.*

bowl·er[1] (bōl′ər) the player who throws the ball to the man at bat in cricket. *n.*

bowl·er[2] (bōl′ər) a man's hat having a small brim and a hard, round crown; derby. See **derby** for picture. *n.*

bowl·ful (bōl′fu̇l) as much as a bowl can hold. *n., pl.* **bowl·fuls.**

bowl·ing (bōl′ing) a game in which balls are rolled in such a way as to knock down bottle-shaped wooden pins: *There is bowling at the alley tonight. The ladies were bowling on the green. n.*

bowling alley 1 the lane or alley down which balls are rolled in the game of bowling. **2** an establishment having a number of lanes for bowling: *There is a snack bar at the bowling alley.*

bow·man (bō′mən) an archer; a soldier armed with bow and arrows. *n., pl.* **bow·men** (bō′mən).

bow·sprit (bou′sprit′) a pole or spar projecting forward from the bow of a ship: *Ropes attached to the bowsprit help to steady sails and masts.* See **schooner** for picture. *n.*

box[1] (boks) **1** a container, usually with a lid, made of wood, metal, cardboard, etc. to pack or put things in. **2** the amount that a box can hold: *We ate a whole box of cereal.* **3** pack in a box; put into a box. **4** an enclosed area for one or more persons: *a theatre box, a sentry box.* 1, 2, 4 *n.*, 3 *v.* **—box′like′,** *adj.*

box[2] (boks) **1** a blow with the open hand: *A box on the ear hurts.* **2** strike with such a blow. **3** fight with the fists as a sport: *He had not boxed since he left school.* 1 *n.*, 2, 3 *v.*

box[3] (boks) an ornamental shrub or small tree that stays green all winter. *n.*

box·car (boks′kär′) a railway freight car that is closed on all sides. *n.*

box·er (bok′sər) **1** a man who fights with his fists, usually in padded gloves and according to special rules.

2 a dog with a smooth, brown coat, related to the bulldog and terrier, but taller. *n.*

box·ing (bok′sing) the sport of fighting with fists. *n.*

boxing gloves padded gloves worn when boxing.

box office the place where tickets are sold in a theatre, hall, etc.

box spring a base for a bed, made up of coil springs set in a frame and covered with padded cloth: *A box spring is usually used with a mattress on top of it.*

boy (boi) **1** a male child from birth to about eighteen. **2** a fellow; chap: *He likes playing cards with the boys.* **3** *Informal.* an exclamation: *'Boy! It's hot!'* 1, 2 *n.*, 3 *interj.*

☛ **Boy** and **buoy** are sometimes pronounced the same.

boy·hood (boi′hůd) the time or condition of being a boy. *n.*

boy·ish (boi′ish) **1** of a boy: *boyish energy.* **2** like a boy: *a boyish young man.* **3** like that of a boy; suitable for a boy: *boyish behavior, boyish games. adj.* —**boy′ish·ly,** *adv.*

Boy Scout a member of the Boy Scouts.

Boy Scouts an organization for boys to develop manly behavior and usefulness to others.

boy·sen·ber·ry (boi′zən ber′ē) a purple berry, like a raspberry in flavor. *n., pl.* **boy·sen·ber·ries.**

A brace and bit. The user presses with one hand and turns with the other. A bit cuts in much the same way as an auger.

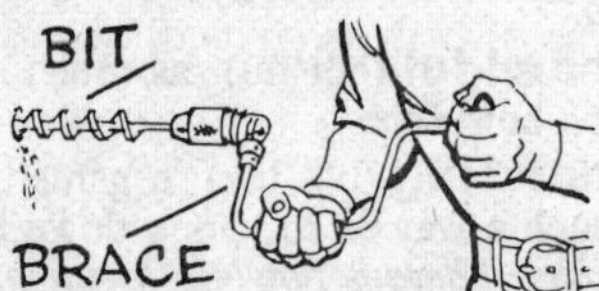

brace (brās) **1** something that holds parts together or in place; a support: *An iron rod or a piece of timber used to support a roof or a wall is called a brace. The dentist put a brace on the girl's teeth.* **2 braces,** *pl.* a pair of crossed straps that pass over the shoulders and are attached to the trousers at the back and front; suspenders. **3** give strength or firmness to; support: *He braced the roof with four poles.* **4** a pair; couple: *a brace of ducks.* **5** a handle for a tool used for boring: *a brace and bit.* 1, 2, 4, 5 *n.*, 3 *v.*, **braced, brac·ing.**

brace·let (brās′lit) a band or chain worn for ornament around the wrist or arm. *n.*

brack·en (brak′ən) **1** a large fern. **2** a field of such ferns. *n.*

brack·et (brak′it) **1** a support consisting of a flat piece of stone, wood, or metal projecting from a wall, used to hold up a shelf, an electric fixture, etc. See **shelf** for picture. **2** support with a bracket. **3** either of these signs, ( ), used to enclose words or figures; a parenthesis. **4** either of these signs, [ ], used to enclose words or figures. **5** enclose within brackets. 1, 3, 4 *n.*, 2, 5 *v.*

brag (brag) **1** boast: *He bragged about his new car.* **2** boasting talk. 1 *v.*, **bragged, brag·ging;** 2 *n.*

braid (brād) **1** a band formed by weaving together three or more strands of hair, ribbon, straw, etc.: *She wore her hair in braids.* **2** weave or twine three or more strands of hair, ribbon, straw, etc. together: *She can braid her own hair.* **3** a narrow band of fabric used to trim or bind clothing. 1, 3 *n.*, 2 *v.*

braille or **Braille** (brāl) a system of writing and printing for blind people: *The letters in braille are made of raised points and are read by touching them. n.*

☛ Named after Louis *Braille* (1809–1852), the Frenchman who invented this system. Louis Braille was blinded in an accident when he was three years old.

brain (brān) **1** the mass of nerve cells enclosed in the skull or head of persons and animals: *The brain is used in feeling and thinking.* **2** kill by smashing the skull of: *The trapper brained the injured wolf with a large stone.* **3** Often, **brains,** *pl.* intelligence: *A dog has more brains than a worm.* 1, 3 *n.*, 2 *v.*

brake[1] (brāk) **1** anything used to check speed by pressing, scraping, or rubbing against: *The brakes on a railway train press against the wheels.* **2** slow up or stop by using a brake: *to brake an automobile.* 1 *n.*, 2 *v.*, **braked, brak·ing.**

☛ **Brake** and **break** are pronounced the same.

brake[2] (brāk) a thick growth of bushes; a thicket. *n.*

☛ See note at **brake**[1].

brake[3] (brāk) any large fern. *n.*

☛ See note at **brake**[1].

brake·man (brāk′mən) a man who helps the conductor of a railway train: *Brakemen used to work the brakes on steam locomotives. n., pl.* **brake·men** (brāk′mən).

bram·ble (bram′bəl) a shrub with slender, drooping branches covered with prickly little thorns: *Blackberry and raspberry plants are brambles. n.*

bran (bran) the brown covering of wheat, rye, etc. separated from the main part of the kernel after it is ground. *n.*

branch (branch) **1** part of a tree that grows out from the trunk; any large, woody part of a tree above the ground except the trunk: *A very small branch is called a twig.* **2** a division; part: *a branch of a river, a branch of a family, a branch of a library. Arithmetic is a branch of learning.* **3** put out branches; spread in branches. **4** divide into branches: *The road branches at the bottom of the hill.* 1, 2 *n.*, 3, 4 *v.*

branch out, a put out branches. **b** extend one's interests, activities etc.

brand (brand) **1** a certain kind, grade, or make: *Do you like this brand of coffee?* **2** a name or mark that a company uses to distinguish its goods from the goods of others; trademark. **3** a mark made by burning the skin with a hot iron: *Cattle and horses on big ranches are marked with brands to show who owns them.* **4** an iron stamp for making such a mark. **5** mark by burning the skin with a hot iron: *In former times criminals were often branded.* **6** a mark of disgrace. **7** expose or mark as deserving disgrace: *He has been branded as a traitor.* **8** a piece of wood that is burning or partly burned. 1–4, 6, 8 *n.*, 5, 7 *v.*

bran·dish (bran′dish) shake or wave in a threatening manner: *The knight drew his sword and brandished it at his enemy. v.*

brand–new (brand′nyü′ or brand′nü′) very new; as new as if just made. *adj.*

bran·dy (bran′dē) a strong alcoholic liquor distilled from wine or fermented fruit juice. *n., pl.* **bran·dies.**

hat, āge, fär; let, ēqual, tėrm; it, īce
hot, ōpen, ôrder; oil, out; cup, pu̇t, rüle
əbove, takən, pencəl, lemən, circəs
ch, child; ng, long; sh, ship
th, thin; ᴛʜ, then; zh, measure

brant (brant) a small, dark, wild goose. *n., pl.* **brants** or **brant.**

brass (bras) **1** a yellow metal made of copper and zinc. **2** anything made of brass, such as door fittings and ornaments. **3** the metal wind instruments, usually made of brass, in a band or orchestra. *n.*

brave (brāv) **1** without fear; having courage; showing courage: *The brave girl went into the burning house to save a baby.* **2** meet without fear: *Soldiers brave much danger.* **3** a North American Indian warrior. 1 *adj.,* **brav·er, brav·est;** 2 *v.,* **braved, brav·ing;** 3 *n.* **—brave′ly,** *adv.* **—brave′ness,** *n.*

brav·er·y (brāv′ər ē) **1** courage: *The soldier's bravery won him a medal.* **2** fine appearance; finery: *She came to the party in all the bravery of her new dress and pink ribbons.* *n., pl.* **brav·er·ies.**

bra·vo (brä′vō) **1** well done! fine! excellent! **2** the cry of 'Bravo!': *The audience applauded the actors loudly and many bravos were heard.* 1 *interj.,* 2 *n., pl.* **bra·vos.**

brawl (brol or brôl) **1** a noisy or disorderly quarrel: *The hockey game turned into a brawl when the players began fighting.* **2** quarrel in a noisy and disorderly way. 1 *n.,* 2 *v.* **—brawl′er,** *n.*

brawn (bron or brôn) **1** muscle; firm, strong muscles. **2** muscular strength: *Football requires brains as well as brawn.* *n.*

brawn·y (bron′ē or brôn′ē) strong; muscular. *adj.,* **brawn·i·er, brawn·i·est. —brawn′i·ness,** *n.*

bray (brā) **1** the loud, harsh cry or noise made by a donkey. **2** a noise like it. **3** make a loud, harsh cry or noise: *The man brayed with laughter.* 1, 2 *n.,* 3 *v.*

bra·zen (brā′zən) **1** shameless; having no shame: *The brazen girl told lie after lie.* **2** loud or harsh: *the brazen bellow of a horn.* **3** made of brass. *adj.* **—bra′zen·ly,** *adv.*

brazen a thing out or **through,** act as if one did not feel ashamed of it.

Bra·zil·ian (brə zil′yən) **1** of or having to do with Brazil, a country in South America. **2** a person born in or living in Brazil. 1 *adj.,* 2 *n.*

breach (brēch) **1** an opening made by breaking down something solid; a gap: *There is a breach in the hedge where I ran into it with my bicycle.* **2** break through; make an opening in: *The enemy's fierce attack finally breached our lines.* **3** a breaking or neglect of a law, promise, friendship, etc.: *For me to leave now would be a breach of duty. There never was a breach between the two friends.* 1, 3 *n.,* 2 *v.*

bread (bred) **1** a food made of flour or meal mixed with milk or water and baked. **2** food; livelihood: *How will you earn your daily bread?* **3** cover with bread crumbs or meal before cooking: *She breaded the chicken before frying it.* 1, 2 *n.,* 3 *v.*

☛ **Bread** and **bred** are pronounced the same.

bread·fruit (bred′früt′) a large, round, starchy fruit grown in the islands of the Pacific Ocean: *When baked, breadfruit tastes somewhat like bread.* *n.*

breadth (bredth) how broad a thing is; the distance across; width: *He has travelled the length and the breadth of this land.* *n.*

break (brāk) **1** make come to pieces by a blow or pull: *Baby has broken her doll.* **2** come apart; crack; burst: *The plate broke into pieces when it fell on the floor.* **3** a broken place; crack: *a break in the wall.* **4** fail to keep; act against: *He never breaks a promise. People who break the law are punished.* **5** force one's way: *The man broke out of the locked room. A thief broke into the house.* **6** dig or plough land, especially for the first time: *In the forests of Upper Canada the pioneers had to work hard to break the ground.* **7** stop; put an end to: *to break a habit.* **8** decrease the force of; lessen: *Because the bushes broke his fall, he was not hurt.* **9** make known; reveal, especially something unpleasant: *Someone must break the news of the boy's accident to his mother.* **10** train to obey; tame: *to break a colt, to break a person's spirit.* **11** come suddenly: *The storm broke within ten minutes.* **12** change or stop suddenly: *The spell of rainy weather has broken. His voice broke with emotion.* **13** an abrupt or marked change: *a break in the weather.* **14** fail; become weak; give way: *The dog's heart broke when his master died.* **15** dawn; appear: *The day is breaking.* **16** go beyond: *The speed of the new train has broken all records.* **17** a breaking or shattering; fracture. **18** a short interruption in work, practice, etc.: *The coach told us to take a break for five minutes.* **19** *Slang.* chance; opportunity: *Finding the money was a lucky break.* 1, 2, 4–12, 14–16 *v.,* **broke, brok·en, break·ing;** 3, 13, 17–19 *n.*

break away, start before the signal: *The excited horse broke away at a fast gallop.*

break down, a go out of order; fail to work: *The car's engine broke down.* **b** collapse; become weak: *His health broke down.* **c** begin to cry: *She broke down when she heard the bad news.*

break even, *Informal.* finish with the same amount one started with; not win or lose: *He had hoped to sell his bicycle at a profit, but he could only break even.*

break in, a train; prepare for work or use: *He broke in the new office boy.* **b** enter by force: *The thieves broke in through the cellar.* **c** interrupt: *He broke in with a funny remark while the teacher was reading to us.*

break off, a stop suddenly: *He broke off in the middle of his speech.* **b** stop being friends: *She broke off with the old crowd.*

break out, a start suddenly; begin: *War broke out.* **b** have pimples, rashes, etc. on the skin: *The child broke out in measles.*

break up, a scatter: *The fog is breaking up.* **b** stop; put an end to: *The Boy Scouts broke up their meeting early.*

break with, stop being friends with: *He broke with me after our fight.*

☛ **Break** and **brake** are pronounced the same.

break·down (brāk′doun′) **1** a failure to work: *The machine had stopped because of a breakdown.* **2** a collapse; weakness; a loss of health: *If she keeps on worrying, she will have a nervous breakdown.* *n.*

break·er (brāk′ər) a wave that breaks into foam on the beach or on rocks. *n.*

break·fast (brek′fəst) **1** the first meal of the day. **2** eat breakfast: *They breakfasted at 7.30 a.m.* 1 *n.,* 2 *v.*

☛ **Breakfast** is a shortened form of an old phrase *to break one's fast.*

break–in (brāk′in′) burglary. *n.*

break·neck (brāk′nek′) likely to cause a broken neck; very dangerous: *The car travelled at breakneck speed. adj.*

break–up or **break·up** (brāk′up′) *Cdn.* **1** the breaking of the ice on a river or lake in spring: *We stood on the bridge and watched the break-up.* **2** especially in the North, the time when this happens; the spring: *They plan to start work on the new road after break-up. n.*

A breakwater

break·wa·ter (brāk′wo′tər or brāk′wô′tər) a wall or barrier built to break the force of waves. *n.*

breast (brest) **1** either of the milk-producing organs on the chest of the human female. **2** a similar organ in certain other female animals. **3** the upper front part of the human body between the shoulders and the stomach; the chest. **4** the heart or feelings: *Pity tore his breast.* **5** face or oppose; struggle with: *He breasted the waves with powerful strokes.* 1–4 *n.*, 5 *v.*

make a clean breast of, confess completely: *When he was shown proof that he had broken the window, he made a clean breast of it.*

breast·plate (brest′plāt′) a piece of armor for the chest. See **armor** for picture. *n.*

breath (breth) **1** air drawn into and forced out of the lungs: *Hold your breath a moment.* **2** a drawing in or forcing out of air: *She took a deep breath.* **3** moisture from breathing: *You can see your breath on a very cold day.* **4** the ability to breathe easily: *Running made him lose his breath.* **5** a slight movement in the air: *Not a breath was stirring. n.*

below one's breath, in a whisper.

catch one's breath, a gasp; pant. **b** stop for breath; rest: *The hikers sat down on a rock to catch their breath.*

under one's breath, in a whisper: *She was talking under her breath so we couldn't hear her.*

breathe (brēᴛʜ) **1** draw air into the lungs and force it out. **2** stop for breath; stop to rest after hard work or exercise: *At last there is time to breathe.* **3** whisper: *The mother breathed a word of encouragement in her son's ear.* **4** inspire; give: *His enthusiasm breathed new life into the team. v.*, **breathed, breath·ing.**

breath·er (brē′ᴛʜər) a short stop for breath; rest. *n.*

breath·less (breth′lis) **1** out of breath: *Running upstairs very fast made him breathless.* **2** holding one's breath because of fear, interest, excitement, etc.: *The beauty of the scenery left her breathless.* **3** without breath; lifeless. *adj.* **—breath′less·ly,** *adv.* **—breath′less·ness,** *n.*

breath·tak·ing (breth′tāk′ing) thrilling; exciting: *a breathtaking ride on a roller coaster. adj.*

bred (bred) See **breed.** *He bred cattle for market. v.*
☛ **Bred** and **bread** are pronounced the same.

breech (brēch) in a rifle or gun, the opening directly behind the barrel, into which the shells are put for firing. *n.*

breech·es (brich′iz) **1** short trousers fastened below the knees. **2** trousers. *n. pl.*

breed (brēd) **1** produce young: *Rabbits breed rapidly.* **2** raise or grow: *This farmer breeds cattle and pigs for market.* **3** produce; be the cause of: *Careless driving breeds accidents.* **4** bring up; train: *The captain bred his boy to be a sailor.* **5** race; stock: *Terriers and spaniels are breeds of dogs.* **6** kind; sort: *a strong, tough breed of men.* 1–4 *v.*, **bred, breed·ing;** 5, 6 *n.*

breed·ing (brēd′ing) **1** the producing of animals or plants, especially to get improved kinds: *The farmer kept cattle for breeding.* **2** bringing up; training; behavior; manners: *Politeness is a sign of good breeding. n.*

breeze (brēz) **1** a light, gentle wind. **2** *Informal.* move or proceed easily or briskly: *She breezed through her homework.* 1 *n.*, 2 *v.*, **breezed, breez·ing.**

breez·y (brēz′ē) **1** having many breezes; with light winds blowing: *It was a breezy day.* **2** lively and jolly: *We like his breezy, joking manner. adj.*, **breez·i·er, breez·i·est.**

breth·ren (breᴛʜ′rən) a plural of **brother** (defs. 2–4). *Many brethren of his church were at my cousin's funeral. n. pl.*

brev·i·ty (brev′ə tē) shortness; briefness: *The brevity of such an exciting story disappointed the boy. n.*

brew (brü) **1** make beer, ale, etc. by soaking, boiling, and fermenting malt, hops, etc. **2** make a drink by soaking something so as to draw out the flavor: *We brew tea by soaking tea leaves in very hot water.* **3** a drink that is brewed: *The last brew of beer tasted bad.* **4** bring about; plan; plot: *The boys whispering in the corner are brewing some mischief.* **5** begin to form; gather: *Dark clouds show that a storm is brewing.* 1, 2, 4, 5 *v.*, 3 *n.*

bri·ar or **bri·er**[1] (brī′ər) a thorny or prickly plant or bush, especially the wild rose. *n.*

bri·ar or **bri·er**[2] (brī′ər) **1** a hard wood much used for making tobacco pipes. **2** a pipe made of this wood: *He enjoyed puffing on his old briar. n.*

bribe (brīb) **1** anything given or offered to get someone to do something dishonest, unlawful, etc.: *The thief offered the policeman a bribe to let him go.* **2** a reward for doing something that a person does not want to do: *A child should not need a bribe to do well in school.* **3** offer a bribe to; give a bribe: *A gambler bribed one of the boxers to lose the fight.* 1, 2 *n.*, 3 *v.*, **bribed, brib·ing.**

brib·er·y (brīb′ər ē) **1** the giving or offering of a bribe. **2** the taking of a bribe. *n.*, *pl.* **brib·er·ies.**

brick (brik) **1** a block of clay baked by sun or fire: *Bricks are used to build houses and walls.* **2** such blocks considered together as building material: *Chimneys are usually built of brick.* **3** anything shaped like a brick: *Ice cream is often sold in bricks.* **4** cover or line with bricks: *They bricked the inside of the well.* **5** build with bricks: *It took him three weeks to brick the wall around his yard.* 1–3 *n.*, 4, 5 *v.*

hat, āge, fär; let, ēqual, tėrm; it, īce
hot, ōpen, ôrder; oil, out; cup, pu̇t, rüle
əbove, takən, pencəl, lemən, circəs
ch, child; ng, long; sh, ship
th, thin; ᴛʜ, then; zh, measure

brick in or **up,** close or fill up with bricks: *The old doorway was bricked up by the workmen.*

brid·al (brī′dəl) of a bride or a wedding. *adj.*
☞ **Bridal** and **bridle** are pronounced the same.

bride (brīd) a woman just married or about to be married. *n.*

bride·groom (brīd′grüm′) a man just married or about to be married. *n.*

brides·maid (brīdz′mād′) a young woman who attends the bride at a wedding. *n.*

A bridge

bridge[1] (brij) 1 something built over a river, road, etc. so that people, cars, trains, etc. can get across. See also **cantilever bridge** and **suspension bridge** for pictures. 2 make or form a bridge over: *A log bridged the brook. The engineers bridged the river.* 3 make a way over: *Politeness will bridge many difficulties.* 4 the platform above the deck of a ship for the officer in command. 5 the upper, bony part of the nose. 6 the curved part of a pair of eyeglasses that rests on the nose. 1, 4–6 *n.,* 2, 3 *v.,* **bridged, bridg·ing.**

bridge[2] (brij) a card game for two teams of two players each, played with 52 cards. *n.*

bridge·head (brij′hed′) 1 a position obtained and held by troops within enemy territory, used as a starting point for further attack. 2 any position that makes a good basis for further action or progress. *n.*

A bridle
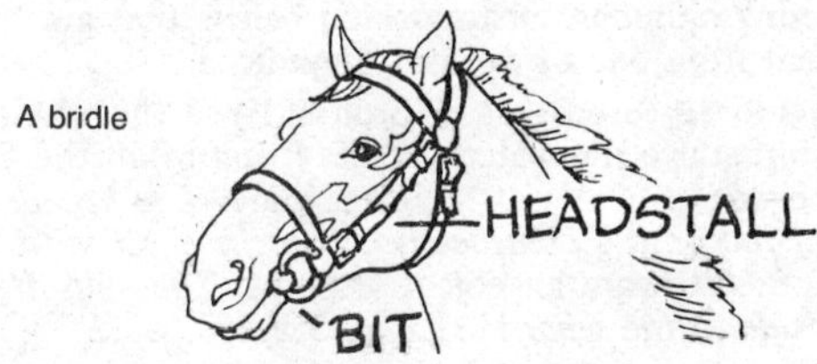

bri·dle (brī′dəl) 1 the part of a horse's harness that fits over the head: *The bridle holds the bit in the horse's mouth so that the rider or driver may guide and control the horse.* 2 put a bridle on. 3 anything that holds back or controls. 4 hold back; check; bring under control: *Bridle your temper.* 5 hold the head up high with the chin drawn back to show pride, scorn, or anger: *She bridled when we made fun of her new hat.* 1, 3 *n.,* 2, 4, 5 *v.,* **bri·dled, bri·dling.**
☞ **Bridle** and **bridal** are pronounced the same.

brief (brēf) 1 lasting only a short time: *a brief meeting.* 2 using few words: *a brief letter. Be as brief as you can.* 3 a formal statement or request: *Our community association presented a brief to the local council.* 4 give detailed information to: *The commanding officer briefed the pilots just before they took off.* 1, 2 *adj.,* 3 *n.,* 4 *v.* **—brief′ness,** *n.*

brief·ly (brēf′lē) 1 in a few words. 2 for a short time: *He bowed his head briefly during grace.* *adv.*

bri·er (brī′ər) See **briar.**

A brig

brig (brig) 1 a ship with two masts and square sails. 2 the prison on a warship. *n.*

bri·gade (bri gād′) 1 a part of an army, usually made up of two or more regiments. 2 any group of persons organized for some purpose: *A fire brigade puts out fires.* 3 *Cdn.* a fur brigade. *n.*

brig·and (brig′ənd) a robber, especially one who robs travellers on country roads. *n.*

brig·an·tine (brig′ən tēn′) a two-masted ship having the foremast square-rigged and the mainmast fore-and-aft-rigged. *n.*

bright (brīt) 1 giving much light; shining: *The stars are bright, but sunshine is brighter. A new copper pot is bright.* 2 very light or clear: *It is a bright day. Dandelions are bright yellow.* 3 clever: *A bright girl learns quickly.* 4 cheerful or lively: *Everybody was bright and gay at the party.* 5 likely to turn out well; favorable: *There is a bright outlook for the future.* 6 in a bright manner: *The fire shines bright.* 1–5 *adj.,* 6 *adv.* **—bright′ly,** *adv.* **—bright′ness,** *n.*

bright·en (brīt′ən) 1 become bright or brighter: *The sky brightened after the storm. Her face brightened as she read the good news.* 2 make bright or brighter: *Hope brightens our outlook on life.* *v.*

bril·liance (bril′yəns) 1 great brightness; sparkle. 2 splendor. 3 great ability: *His brilliance as a pianist was soon recognized all over the world.* *n.*

bril·liant (bril′yənt) 1 shining brightly; sparkling: *brilliant jewels, brilliant sunshine.* 2 splendid: *The royal banquet was a brilliant scene.* 3 showing or having great ability: *a brilliant performance. He is a brilliant musician.* 4 a diamond or other gem cut to sparkle brightly. 1–3 *adj.,* 4 *n.*

brim (brim) 1 the edge of a cup, glass, bowl, etc.: *You have filled my glass to the brim.* 2 fill to the brim; be full to the brim: *The pond is brimming with water after the heavy rain.* 3 the projecting edge of something: *The hat's wide brim shaded his eyes from the sun.* 1, 3 *n.,* 2 *v.,* **brimmed, brim·ming.**

brim·ful (brim′fu̇l′) full to the brim; full to the very top: *a basket brimful of raspberries.* *adj.*

brine (brīn) 1 very salty water: *Some pickles are kept in brine.* 2 a salt lake or sea; ocean. *n.*

bring (bring) 1 carry a thing or person from another

place; take along to a place or person: *Bring me a clean plate, please. The bus brought us home from school.* 2 cause to come: *What brings you into town today?* 3 influence; persuade; convince: *I can't bring myself to leave early.* *v.,* **brought, bring·ing.**

bring about, cause; cause to happen: *The flood was brought about by a heavy rain.*

bring around or **bring round, a** restore to consciousness: *When she fainted, they soon brought her around.* **b** win over to a belief or action; convince; persuade: *At first her parents refused to let her go to the party, but she brought them around eventually.*

bring forth, a give birth to; bear. **b** reveal; show.

bring off, carry out successfully: *He brought off a good business deal.*

bring on, cause; cause to happen: *I think my cold was brought on by lack of sleep.*

bring out, a reveal; show: *His paintings bring out the loneliness of the North.* **b** offer to the public: *She brought out a new book of poems recently.*

bring to, restore to consciousness: *She fainted when she heard the news, but they soon brought her to.*

bring up, a care for in childhood: *She brought up four children.* **b** educate or train, especially in behavior or manners: *His good manners showed he was well brought up.* **c** suggest for action or discussion: *Please bring your plan up at the meeting.* **d** stop suddenly: *The rider brought his horse up sharply at the high fence.* **e** vomit.

brink (bringk) **1** the edge at the top of a steep place: *the brink of the cliff.* **2** an edge: *His business is on the brink of ruin.* *n.*

brin·y (brīn'ē) salty. *adj.,* **brin·i·er, brin·i·est.**

brisk (brisk) **1** quick and active; lively: *a brisk walk.* **2** keen; sharp: *a brisk wind.* *adj.* **—brisk'ly,** *adv.* **—brisk'ness,** *n.*

bris·tle (bris'əl) **1** the short, stiff hair of some animals or plants: *Brushes are often made of the bristles of hogs.* **2** stand up straight: *The angry dog's hair bristled.* 1 *n.,* 2 *v.,* **bris·tled, bris·tling.**

bristle with, be thick with; be thickly set with: *The harbor bristled with boats and ships.*

Brit. **1** Britain. **2** British.

Brit·ish (brit'ish) **1** of Great Britain or its people. **2 the British,** the people of Great Britain. 1 *adj.,* 2 *n.*

Brit·ish Co·lum·bi·an (brit'ish kə lum'bē ən) **1** of or associated with British Columbia. **2** a person born in or living in British Columbia.

British North America Act the act of Parliament that in 1867 created the Government of Canada for the union of Ontario, Quebec, Nova Scotia, and New Brunswick. The other six provinces joined the federation as follows: Manitoba, 1870; British Columbia, 1871; Prince Edward Island, 1873; Alberta, 1905; Saskatchewan, 1905; and Newfoundland, 1949.

Brit·on (brit'ən) **1** a person born in or living in Great Britain. **2** one of the Celtic people who lived in southern Britain before the Roman conquest. *n.*

brit·tle (brit'əl) hard to the touch, but very easily broken; apt to break with a snap rather than bend: *Thin glass and dead twigs are brittle.* *adj.* **—brit'tle·ness,** *n.*

broach (brōch) **1** begin to talk about: *She broached the subject of a picnic to her parents.* **2** open by making a hole: *He broached a barrel of cider.* *v.*

☛ **Broach** and **brooch** are pronounced the same.

broad (brod or brôd) **1** wide; large across: *Many cars can go on that broad road.* **2** large; extensive: *He has broad experience in industry.* **3** not limited or narrow; of wide range: *Our minister has broad views and does not insist that everyone thinks as he does.* **4** not detailed; general: *Give the broad outlines of today's lesson.* **5** clear; full: *The theft was made in broad daylight.* *adj.* **—broad'ly,** *adv.*

broad·cast (brod'kast' or brôd'kast') **1** send out by radio or television: *Some stations broadcast twenty-four hours a day.* **2** something sent out by radio or television; a radio or television program: *The Prime Minister's broadcast from Ottawa lasted fifteen minutes.* **3** scatter or spread widely: *to broadcast seed.* **4** a scattering far and wide: *nature's broadcast of seed.* 1, 3 *v.,* **broad·cast** or **broad·cast·ed** for 1, **broad·cast** for 3, **broad·cast·ing;** 2, 4 *n.* **—broad'cast'er,** *n.*

broad·cloth (brod'kloth' or brôd'kloth') **1** a cotton or silk cloth with a plain weave and a smooth finish, used in making shirts, dresses, pyjamas, etc. **2** a woollen cloth with a smooth finish, used in making men's suits, coats, etc. *n.*

broad·en (brod'ən or brôd'ən) make or become broad or broader: *The river broadens at its mouth. Travel can broaden a person's sympathies for people from foreign lands.* *v.*

broad jump **1** an athletic event or contest in which contestants try to jump over as much ground as possible. **2** a jump of this kind.

broad·loom (brod'lüm' or brôd'lüm') **1** woven on a wide loom: *a broadloom carpet.* **2** material woven in this way: *grey broadloom.* 1 *adj.,* 2 *n.*

broad–mind·ed (brod'mīnd'id or brôd'mīnd'id) respecting opinions, customs, and beliefs that are different from one's own; not prejudiced. *adj.*

broad·side (brod'sīd' or brôd'sīd') **1** the whole side of a ship above the water. **2** the firing of all the guns on one side of a ship at the same time: *The broadside caught the pirates completely by surprise.* **3** with the side turned toward an object or point: *The ship drifted broadside to the wharf.* 1, 2 *n.,* 3 *adv.*

broad·sword (brod'sôrd' or brôd'sôrd') a sword with a broad, flat blade. *n.*

bro·cade (brō kād') a cloth woven with raised designs on it: *silk brocade.* *n.*

broc·co·li (brok'ə lē) a plant having green stems and flower heads, which are eaten as a vegetable. *n.*

☛ **Broccoli** came into English from the Italian name for this vegetable, *broccoli,* meaning 'little stalks.'

bro·chure (brō shür') a printed booklet or folder, usually having colorful pictures, that advertises or gives information about a certain thing: *I sent for a brochure on Quebec because we want to visit there this summer.* *n.*

broil (broil) **1** cook something by putting or holding it directly over the fire or heat on a rack, or under the heat in a pan. **2** be or make very hot: *We broiled in the hot sun.* *v.*

broil·er (broil'ər) **1** a pan or rack for broiling. **2** a young chicken for broiling. *n.*

broke (brōk) **1** See **break.** *She broke a toy.* **2** *Slang.*

without money: *He couldn't go to the movie because he was broke.* 1 *v.*, 2 *adj.*

bro·ken (brō′kən) 1 See **break.** *The window was broken by a ball.* *His sleep was broken by the noise of the party upstairs.* 2 in pieces; separated into parts by a break: *a broken cup.* 3 not even; rough: *broken ground.* 4 imperfectly spoken: *He speaks only broken French.* 5 weakened in strength, spirit, etc.; tamed; crushed: *He looked a broken man after his loss.* 1 *v.*, 2–5 *adj.*

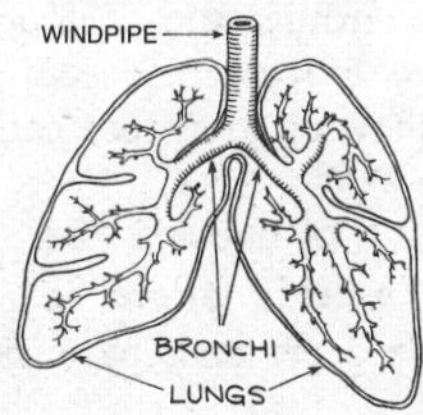

bron·chi (brong′kī) the two large, main branches of the windpipe, one going to each lung. *n. pl.*

bron·chi·al (brong′kē əl) having to do with the bronchial tubes. *adj.*

bronchial tubes the bronchi and their branching tubes.

bron·chi·tis (brong kī′tis) an inflammation of the lining of the bronchial tubes. *n.*

bron·co or **bron·cho** (brong′kō) a western pony: *Broncos are often wild or only partly tamed.* *n., pl.* **bron·cos** or **bron·chos.**

☛ **Bronco** came into English from the Spanish word *bronco,* meaning 'rough' or 'rude.'

bronze (bronz) 1 an alloy of copper and another metal, usually tin or zinc. 2 a statue, medal, etc. made of bronze: *A bronze was given to the boy who won the contest.* 3 yellowish brown; reddish brown. 4 make or become reddish brown: *The sailor was bronzed from the sun.* 1–3 *n.*, 3 *adj.*, 4 *v.*, **bron·zed, bronz·ing.**

brooch (brōch) an ornament for attaching to clothing, having a pin at the back with a clasp or catch to keep it closed: *Brooches are often made of gold or silver.* *n.*

☛ **Brooch** and **broach** are pronounced the same.

brood (brüd) 1 the young birds hatched at one time in the nest, or cared for together: *a brood of chicks.* 2 young animals or persons who share the same mother or are cared for by the same person: *That father and mother have a brood of ten children.* 3 sit on eggs in order to hatch them: *Don't disturb that hen; she's brooding.* 4 think a long time about some one unpleasant thing: *He brooded over his lost dog.* 1, 2 *n.*, 3, 4 *v.*

brook (brůk) a natural stream of water smaller than a river. *n.*

broom (brüm) 1 a brush with a long handle, used for sweeping. 2 a shrub with slender branches, small leaves, and yellow flowers. *n.*

broom·stick (brüm′stik′) the long handle of a broom. *n.*

broth (broth) a thin soup made from water in which meat or fish has been boiled. *n.*

broth·er (bruᴛʜ′ər) 1 a son of the same parents: *A boy is brother to the other children of his parents.* 2 a comrade; fellow, officer, etc. 3 a fellow member of a church. 4 a member of a religious order who is not a priest. *n., pl.* **broth·ers** for 1–4 or **breth·ren** for 2–4.

hat, āge, fär; let, ēqual, tėrm; it, īce
hot, ōpen, ôrder; oil, out; cup, půt, rüle
əbove, takən, pencəl, lemən, circəs
ch, child; ng, long; sh, ship
th, thin; ᴛʜ, then; zh, measure

broth·er·hood (bruᴛʜ′ər hůd′) 1 the bond between brothers; the feeling of brother for brother: *They had a strong feeling of brotherhood because they had worked together for many years.* 2 persons joined as brothers; an association of men with some common aim, characteristic, belief, or profession. *n.*

broth·er–in–law (bruᴛʜ′ər in lo′ or bruᴛʜ′ər in lô′) 1 the brother of one's husband or wife. 2 the husband of one's sister. *n., pl.* **broth·ers-in-law.**

broth·er·ly (bruᴛʜ′ər lē) 1 of a brother: *It is a brotherly trait to tease little sisters.* 2 like a brother; very friendly: *The scout gave the tenderfoot some brotherly advice.* *adj.*

brought (brot or brôt) See **bring.** *He brought his lunch yesterday.* *We were brought to school in a bus.* *v.*

brow (brou) 1 the forehead: *a wrinkled brow.* 2 the arch of hair over the eye; an eyebrow: *He has heavy, black brows over his eyes.* 3 the edge of a steep place; the top of a slope: *His house is on the brow of the hill.* *n.*

brown (broun) 1 a dark color like that of toast, potato skins, or coffee. 2 of or having this color: *Many Canadians have brown hair.* 3 make or become brown: *The cook browned the onions in hot butter.* 1 *n.*, 2 *adj.*, 3 *v.*

brown betty a baked pudding made of apples, sugar, and bread crumbs.

brown·ie (broun′ē) 1 in stories, a good-natured, helpful elf or fairy. 2 a small chocolate cake containing nuts: *Brownies are sweet and chewy.* *n.*

Brown·ie (broun′ē) a member of the junior division of the Girl Guides. *n.*

brown·ish (broun′ish) somewhat brown. *adj.*

browse (brouz) 1 feed on growing grass or the leaves and shoots of trees and bushes by nibbling and eating here and there; graze: *The sheep browsed in the meadow.* 2 read here and there in a book, library, etc.: *He spent the afternoon browsing in the library.* *v.*, **browsed, brows·ing.**

bru·in (brü′ən) a bear (def.1). *n.*

bruise (brüz) 1 an injury to the body, caused by a fall or a blow that breaks blood vessels without breaking the skin: *The bruise on my arm turned black and blue.* 2 an injury to the outside of a fruit, vegetable, plant, etc. 3 cause a bruise to: *I bruised my leg when I fell on the step.* 4 cause to be hurt: *His harsh words bruised her feelings.* 5 become bruised: *The flesh of a peach bruises easily.* 1, 2 *n.*, 3–5 *v.*, **bruised, bruis·ing.**

bru·net (brü net′) 1 dark-colored; having an olive color. 2 having dark-brown or black hair, usually brown or black eyes, and a dark skin. 3 a man or boy having dark hair. 1, 2 *adj.*, 3 *n.*

☛ As a noun, **brunet** is used for men and boys and **brunette** is used for women and girls. The usual form for the adjective, however, is **brunet** in all cases: *Henry and his sister are both brunet.*

bru·nette (brü net′) a woman or girl having dark hair. *n.*

☞ See note at **brunet.**

brunt (brunt) the main force or violence: *The island felt the brunt of the hurricane. Our regiment bore the brunt of the attack. n.*

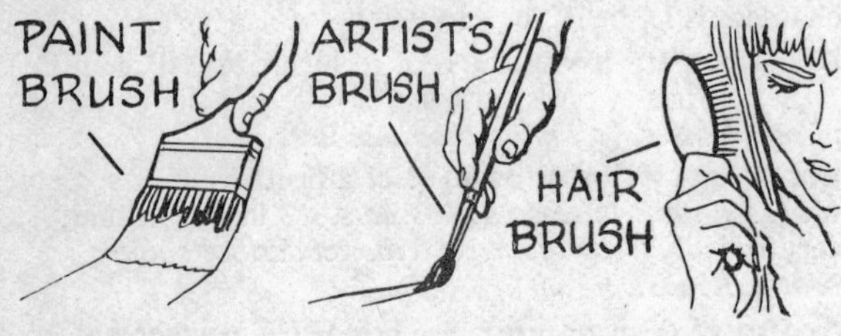

Three kinds of brush

brush¹ (brush) **1** a tool for cleaning, sweeping, scrubbing, and for putting on paint: *A brush is made of bristles, hair, or wires, set in a stiff back or fastened to a handle.* **2** clean, rub, paint, etc. with a brush; use a brush on: *She brushed her hair until it was shiny.* **3** brushing; a rub with a brush: *He gave his puppy a good brush.* **4** remove; wipe away: *The child brushed the tears from his eyes.* **5** touch lightly in passing: *No harm was done; the bumper of your car just brushed my fender.* **6** a light touch in passing: *Give the desk a brush with the cloth.* **7** a short, brisk fight or quarrel: *The strikers had a sharp brush with the police.* **8** the bushy tail of an animal, especially of a fox. 1, 3, 6–8 *n.*, 2, 4, 5 *v.*

brush up or **brush up on,** refresh the memory by study; review: *He brushed up on his arithmetic before writing the exam.*

brush² (brush) brushwood. *n.*

brush·wood (brush′wůd′) **1** branches broken or cut off. **2** small trees or bushes growing rather thickly together. *n.*

brusque (brusk) abrupt in manner or speech; blunt: *He was brusque in saying 'I don't like it' when he could have said 'No, thank you.' adj.*

Brus·sels sprouts (brus′əlz) **1** a variety of cabbage that has many small heads growing along a stalk. **2** the heads of this plant, used as a vegetable. Also spelled **brussels sprouts.**

bru·tal (brü′təl) coarse and savage; like a brute; cruel: *The Vikings were brutal in battle. adj.*

bru·tal·i·ty (brü tal′ə tē) **1** savageness; brutal conduct: *Torturing prisoners is an example of brutality.* **2** a brutal act. *n., pl.* **bru·tal·i·ties.**

brute (brüt) **1** an animal without power to reason. **2** not having power to reason: *brute creatures.* **3** a stupid, cruel, or coarse person. **4** without feeling: *Man has struggled long against the brute forces of nature.* 1, 3 *n.*, 2, 4 *adj.*

bu. bushel; bushels.

bub·ble (bub′əl) **1** a thin, round film of liquid enclosing air or gas: *soap bubbles. The surface of boiling water is covered with bubbles.* **2** a round space filled with air in a liquid or solid: *Sometimes there are bubbles in ice or in glass.* **3** have bubbles; make bubbles; send up or rise in bubbles: *Water bubbled up between the stones.* **4** make sounds like water boiling; gurgle: *The baby bubbled and cooed.* **5** something shaped like a bubble. 1, 2, 5 *n.*, 3, 4 *v.*, **bub·bled, bub·bling.**

bubble over, be very enthusiastic: *The boys bubbled over with ideas for the canoe trip.*

bubble gum a chewing gum that can be blown up so as to form a large bubble.

bub·bly (bub′lē) full of bubbles. *adj.*

buc·ca·neer (buk′ə nēr′) pirate. *n.*

buck¹ (buk) a male deer, goat, hare, rabbit, antelope, or sheep. *n.*

buck² (buk) **1** jump into the air with the back curved and come down with the front legs stiff: *His horse began to buck, but he stayed on.* **2** throw by bucking: *The cowboy was bucked off by the bronco.* **3** a throw or an attempt to throw by bucking. **4** charge against; work against: *The swimmer bucked the current with strong strokes. The football player bucked the opposing team's line.* 1, 2, 4 *v.*, 3 *n.*

buck up, *Informal.* cheer up; be brave or energetic: *Buck up; everything will be all right.*

buck³ (buk) *Slang.* dollar. *n.*

buck·et (buk′it) **1** a pail, especially one made of wood: *Buckets are used for carrying water, milk, etc.* **2** the amount that a bucket can hold: *Pour on about four buckets of water. n.*

bucket seat a small, low, single seat with a rounded back, used in sports cars, small airplanes, etc.

buck·le (buk′əl) **1** a catch or clasp to hold together two loose ends of a belt, strap, or ribbon. **2** fasten together with a buckle: *He buckled his belt.* **3** a metal ornament, especially one for a shoe. **4** bend out of shape; bulge, kink, or wrinkle under heavy strain or pressure: *The heavy snowfall caused the roof of the arena to buckle.* 1, 3 *n.*, 2, 4 *v.*, **buck·led, buck·ling.**

buckle down to, begin to work hard at: *He buckled down to his studies.*

buck·ler (buk′lər) a small, round shield. *n.*

buck·skin (buk′skin′) **1** a kind of strong, soft leather, yellowish or greyish in color, made from the skins of deer or sheep. **2 buckskins,** *pl.* clothing made of buckskin. *n.*

buck·wheat (buk′wēt′ or buk′hwēt′) **1** a plant having brown, triangular seeds and white flowers. **2** the seeds, used as food for animals or ground into flour. *n.*

bud (bud) **1** a small swelling on a plant that will grow into a flower, leaf, or branch. **2** a partly opened flower or leaf. **3** put forth buds: *The rosebush has budded.* 1, 2 *n.*, 3 *v.*, **bud·ded, bud·ding.**

in bud, in the time or condition of budding: *The pear tree will soon be in bud.*

Bud·dhism (bůd′iz əm, bü′diz əm, or bud′iz əm) a religion founded in northern India in the sixth century B.C. by Buddha, a great religious teacher: *Buddhism spread widely over central and eastern Asia and is today the main religion of Japan, Ceylon, and parts of Southeast Asia. n.*

hat, āge, fär; let, ēqual, tėrm; it, īce
hot, ōpen, ôrder; oil, out; cup, pu̇t, rüle
əbove, takən, pencəl, lemən, circəs
ch, child; ng, long; sh, ship
th, thin; ᴛʜ, then; zh, measure

Bud·dhist (bu̇d′ist, bü′dist, or bud′ist) 1 having to do with Buddha or Buddhism. 2 a believer in Buddhism. 1 *adj.*, 2 *n.*

bud·dy (bud′ē) *Informal.* a close friend; comrade; pal. *n., pl.* **bud·dies.**

budge (buj) move even a little: *The stone was so heavy that the child could not budge it.* *v.,* **budged, budg·ing.**

budg·er·i·gar (buj′ər i gär′) a small, brightly colored parakeet: *Budgerigars come originally from Australia.* *n.*

budg·et (buj′it) 1 an estimate of the amount of money that will probably be received and spent during a given time: *School expenses are an important part of our city budget.* 2 make a plan for spending: *He budgeted his allowance.* 1 *n.,* 2 *v.,* **budg·et·ed, budg·et·ing.**

budg·ie (buj′ē) *Informal.* budgerigar. *n.*

buff[1] (buf) 1 dull yellow. 2 a strong, soft, dull-yellow leather: *Buff was formerly made from buffalo skin and is now made from the skin of oxen.* 3 polish with a wheel or stick covered with leather. 1 *adj.,* 1, 2 *n.,* 3 *v.*

buff[2] (buf) *Informal.* a fan or enthusiast: *a hockey buff, a theatre buff.* *n.*

The buffalo of North America — about 175 cm high at the shoulder

A water buffalo of India — about 155 cm high at the shoulder

buf·fa·lo (buf′ə lō′) 1 a large North American wild animal closely related to cattle, having a big, shaggy head and very strong front legs; bison: *Great herds of buffalo used to graze on the plains.* 2 any of several kinds of large horned animals related to cattle: *The tame water buffalo is found in many parts of Asia; the wild buffalo of Africa is very fierce and dangerous.* *n., pl.* **buf·fa·loes, buf·fa·los,** or **buf·fa·lo.**

buf·fet[1] (buf′it) 1 a blow of the hand or fist. 2 strike with the hand or fist. 3 a knock, stroke, or hurt: *He withstood the buffets of the waves.* 4 knock about, strike, or hurt: *The waves buffeted him.* 5 fight or struggle against: *The boat buffeted heavy waves.* 1, 3 *n.,* 2, 4, 5 *v.,* **buf·fet·ed, buf·fet·ing.**

buf·fet[2] (bu̇ fā′ or bu fā′) 1 a low cabinet with a flat top, for holding dishes, silver, and table linen. 2 a counter where food and drinks are served. 3 a meal at which guests serve themselves from food laid out on a table or buffet. *n.*

bug (bug) 1 an insect without wings or with a front pair of wings thickened at the base, and having a pointed beak for piercing and sucking. 2 any insect or animal somewhat like an insect: *Ants, flies, and spiders are often called bugs.* 3 *Informal.* a disease germ: *the flu bug.* 4 *Informal.* a mechanical defect or difficulty: *a bug in the fire alarm system.* 5 *Informal.* a person who is very enthusiastic about something: *a camera bug.* 6 *Slang.* annoy; irritate: *His grumbling bugs me.* 7 *Informal.* a very small hidden microphone. 8 *Informal.* hide a small microphone in a room, telephone, etc. 1–5, 7 *n.,* 6, 8 *v.,* **bugged, bug·ging.**

bug·a·boo (bug′ə bü′) a cause of fear; something, usually imaginary, that frightens: *The foolish babysitter frightened the child with tales of witches, ghosts, and other bugaboos.* *n., pl.* **bug·a·boos.**

bug·bear (bug′ber′) 1 bugaboo. 2 a source of difficulty; snag: *Spelling has always been a bugbear for him.* *n.*

bug·gy (bug′ē) 1 a light carriage drawn by one horse and having a single large seat. 2 a wheeled cart used for shopping in a grocery store, etc. 3 a baby carriage. *n., pl.* **bug·gies.**

A buggy

A bugle

bu·gle (byü′gəl) a musical instrument like a small trumpet, made of brass or copper, and sometimes having keys or valves: *Bugles are sometimes used in the armed forces for sounding calls and orders.* *n.*

bu·gler (byü′glər) a person who blows a bugle. *n.*

build (bild) 1 make by putting materials together; construct: *Men build houses and ships. Birds build nests.* 2 the form, style, or manner in which something is put together: *An elephant has a heavy build.* 1 *v.,* **built, build·ing;** 2 *n.*

build·er (bil′dər) a person in the construction business. *n.*

build·ing (bil′ding) 1 something built: *Barns, houses, sheds, factories, and hotels are all buildings.* 2 the business, art, or process of making houses, stores, bridges, ships, etc. *n.*

built (bilt) See **build.** *The bird built a nest. It was built of twigs.* *v.*

bulb (bulb) 1 a round underground bud or stem from which certain plants grow: *Onions, tulips, and lilies grow from bulbs.* See **onion** for picture. 2 an electric light bulb. 3 any object with a rounded end or swelling part: *the bulb of a thermometer.* *n.* —**bulb′like′,** *adj.*

bulb·ous (bul′bəs) 1 shaped like a bulb; rounded and swelling: *The clown had a bulbous red nose.* 2 having bulbs; growing from bulbs: *Daffodils are bulbous plants.* *adj.*

bulge (bulj) 1 swell outward: *His pockets bulged with apples and candy.* 2 an outward swelling: *When the man leaned against the tent, he made a bulge in the canvas.* 1 *v.,* **bulged, bulg·ing;** 2 *n.*

bulk (bulk) 1 size, especially large size: *An elephant has bulk.* 2 the largest part: *The oceans form the bulk of the earth's surface.* 3 have size; be of importance. 1, 2 *n.,* 3 *v.*

bulk·head (bulk′hed′) 1 one of the upright partitions dividing a ship into watertight compartments. See the picture. 2 a wall or partition built to hold back water, earth, rocks, air, etc. *n.*

bulk·y (bul′kē) 1 large; taking up much space: *Bulky shipments are often sent in freight cars.* 2 hard to handle; clumsy: *She dropped the bulky package of curtain rods twice.* *adj.,* **bulk·i·er, bulk·i·est. —bulk′i·ly,** *adv.* **—bulk′i·ness,** *n.*

bull (bul) 1 the male of cattle, buffalo, etc. 2 the adult male of the moose, whale, elephant, seal, and other large animals. *n.*

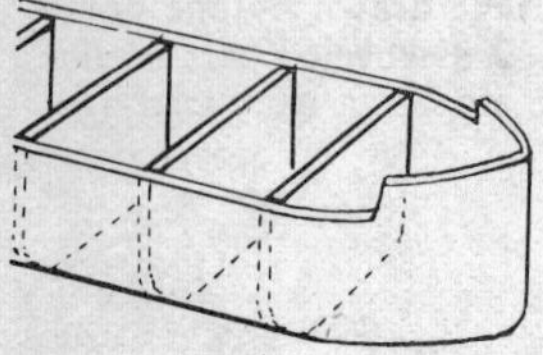
Bulkheads in a ship

A bulldog — about 33 cm high at the shoulder

bull·dog (bul′dog′) 1 a heavily built dog with a large head and short hair: *Bulldogs are not large, but they are very muscular and courageous.* 2 like that of a bulldog: *bulldog courage, a bulldog grip.* 1 *n.,* 2 *adj.*

bull·doz·er (bul′dōz′ər) a powerful tractor that moves dirt, rocks, etc. for grading, road building, etc. by means of a wide steel blade attached to the front. *n.*

bul·let (bul′it) a piece of lead, steel, or other metal shaped to be shot from a rifle, pistol, or other small gun. *n.*

bul·le·tin (bul′ə tən) 1 a short statement of news: *Newspapers print bulletins about sports, floods, election results, and other events of public importance.* 2 a magazine or newspaper appearing regularly, especially one published by a club or society for its members. *n.*

bulletin board a board on which notices are posted.

bull·fight (bul′fīt′) a fight between a man or men and a bull before spectators in an arena: *Bullfights are popular in Spain, Mexico, and parts of South America.* *n.*

bull·finch (bul′finch′) a European songbird with richly colored plumage and a short, stout bill. *n.*

bull·frog (bul′frog′) a large frog of North America that makes a loud, croaking noise. *n.*

bul·lion (bul′yən) bricks or bars of gold or silver. *n.*

bull·ock (bul′ək) 1 a young bull. 2 an ox or steer. *n.*

bull's–eye (bulz′ī) 1 the centre of a target: *Robin Hood's arrows always hit the bull's-eye.* 2 a shot that hits the centre: *He had three bull's-eyes in a row.* *n.*

bul·ly (bul′ē) 1 a person who teases, frightens, or hurts smaller or weaker people. 2 frighten into doing something by noisy talk or threats: *He was bullied into giving away his candy.* 1 *n., pl.* **bul·lies;** 2 *v.,* **bul·lied, bul·ly·ing.**

bul·rush (bul′rush′) a tall, slender plant that grows in wet places; cat-tail. *n.*

bul·wark (bul′wərk) 1 a defence; protection: *A free press and free speech are bulwarks of democracy.* 2 an earthwork or other wall for defence against the enemy. 3 a breakwater for protection against the force of the waves. 4 Usually, **bulwarks,** *pl.* the part of a ship's side that extends above the deck level. See **schooner** for picture. *n.*

bum[1] (bum) *Informal.* 1 an idle or good-for-nothing person; loafer; tramp. 2 get (food, money, etc.) by taking advantage of the kindness of other people; beg: *She tried to bum a ride.* 3 loaf around; idle about: *He spent his whole summer bumming around.* 1 *n.,* 2, 3 *v.,* **bummed, bum·ming.**

bum[2] (bum) *Informal.* the fleshy part of a person's body, where the legs join the back; seat; buttocks. *n.*

bum·ble·bee (bum′bəl bē′) a large bee with a thick, hairy body, usually banded with yellow. *n.*

bump (bump) 1 push, throw, or strike against something large or solid: *She bumped against the table in the dark.* 2 hit or come against with heavy blows: *That truck bumped our car.* 3 a heavy blow or knock: *The bump knocked our car across the road.* 4 move or proceed with bumps: *Our car bumped along the rough road.* 5 a swelling caused by a bump: *He has a bump on his head from getting hit by a baseball.* 6 any swelling or lump: *He tried to avoid the bump in the road.* 1, 2, 4 *v.,* 3, 5, 6 *n.*

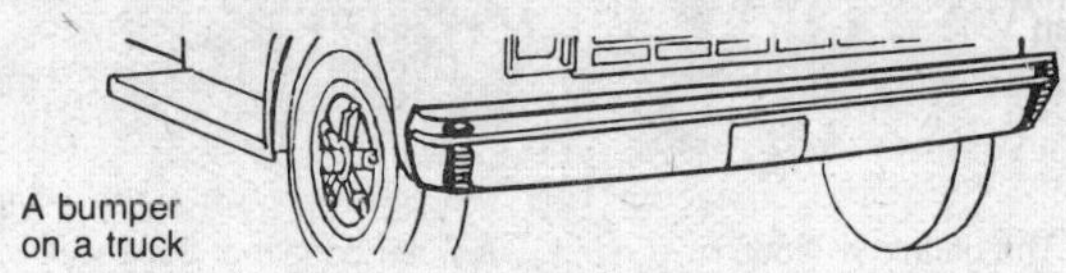
A bumper on a truck

bump·er (bum′pər) 1 the bar or bars of metal across the front and back of a car or truck. 2 unusually large: *The farmer raised a bumper crop of wheat last year.* 1 *n.,* 2 *adj.*

bump·y (bum′pē) 1 uneven; having bumps on the surface: *a bumpy road.* 2 causing bumps or jolts; rough: *a bumpy ride.* *adj.*

bun (bun) a small, round piece of dough that has been separately baked: *Buns are often slightly sweetened and may contain spice, raisins, or fruit.* *n.*

bunch (bunch) 1 a group of things of the same kind growing, fastened, placed, or thought of together: *a bunch of grapes, a bunch of flowers.* 2 *Informal.* a group of people, animals, etc.: *They're a friendly bunch.* 3 come together in one place: *The sheep were all bunched in one corner of the pen.* 4 bring together and make into a bunch: *We have bunched the flowers for you to carry home.* 1, 2 *n.,* 3, 4 *v.*

bun·dle (bun′dəl) 1 a number of things tied or wrapped together: *We gave away several bundles of old newspapers and magazines.* 2 a parcel or package. 3 wrap or tie together; make up into a bundle: *We bundled all our newspapers for the paper drive.* 4 send away in a hurry: *They bundled Roy off to the hospital in an ambulance.* 1, 2 *n.,* 3, 4 *v.,* **bun·dled, bun·dling.** **bundle up,** dress warmly.

bun·ga·low (bung′gə lō′) a one-storey house, often small; a house having no living space above the main floor. *n.*

☛ **Bungalow** came into English in the seventeenth century from a language of north-western India; the word came originally from a Hindi word *bangla,* meaning 'belonging to Bengal.' Part of old Bengal is now *Bangladesh,* which means 'Bengal nation.'

bun·gle (bung′gəl) spoil by doing or making in a clumsy way: *He tried to make a boat, but bungled the job.* *v.,* **bun·gled, bun·gling.** **—bun′gler,** *n.*

bun·ion (bun′yən) an enlargement of the first joint of the big toe, causing the toe to be permanently bent inwards: *Bunions are usually caused by pressure from wearing shoes that are too tight.* *n.*

bunk (bungk) 1 a narrow bed set against a wall like a shelf. 2 sleep in or occupy a bunk or makeshift bed: *We bunked in an old barn.* 1 *n.,* 2 *v.*

bunk·house (bungk′hous′) a building equipped with bunks for sleeping. *n.*

bun·ny (bun′ē) a pet name for a rabbit. *n., pl.* **bun·nies.**

bunt (bunt) 1 strike with the head or horns, as a goat does. 2 a push; shove. 3 in baseball, hit a ball lightly so that it goes to the ground and rolls only a short distance. 4 a hit made in this way. 1, 3 *v.,* 2, 4 *n.*

bun·ting[1] (bun′ting) 1 a thin cloth used for flags. 2 long pieces of cloth having the colors and designs of a flag, used to decorate buildings and streets on holidays and special occasions; flags. *n.*

bun·ting[2] (bun′ting) a small bird with a stout bill: *Buntings look very much like sparrows.* *n.*

buoy (boi or bü′ē) 1 a floating object anchored on the water to warn or guide: *Buoys mark hidden rocks or shallows, show the safe part of a channel, etc.* 2 a cork or plastic belt, ring, or jacket used in the water to keep a person from sinking; a life buoy or life preserver. 3 **buoy up, a** hold up; keep from sinking: *His life jacket buoyed him up until rescuers came.* **b** support or encourage: *Hope buoys him up, even when something goes wrong.* 1, 2 *n.,* 3 *v.*

☛ **Buoy** and **boy** are sometimes pronounced the same.

buoy·an·cy (boi′ən sē) 1 the power to float: *Wood has more buoyancy than iron.* 2 the power to keep things afloat: *Salt water has greater buoyancy than fresh water.* 3 a tendency to be cheerful and hopeful: *Her buoyancy kept us from being downhearted.* *n.*

buoy·ant (boi′ənt) 1 able to float: *Wood and cork are buoyant in water; iron and lead are not.* 2 able to keep things afloat: *Balloons can float because air is buoyant.* 3 light-hearted; cheerful and hopeful: *Children are usually more buoyant than old people.* *adj.*

bur (bėr) burr. *n.*

bur·den (bėr′dən) 1 something carried; a load of things, duty, work, etc. 2 anything difficult to carry or bear; a heavy load: *a burden of debts.* 3 put a burden on; load: *The mule was burdened with heavy bags of ore. She was burdened with worries.* 1, 2 *n.,* 3 *v.*

bur·den·some (bėr′dən səm) wearying; hard to bear; very heavy: *The Prime Minister's many duties are burdensome.* *adj.*

bur·dock (bėr′dok′) a coarse weed with prickly burrs and broad leaves. *n.*

bu·reau (byür′ō) 1 a certain kind of office or business: *We asked about the railway fares at a travel bureau.* 2 *Esp. U.S.* a branch of a government department. 3 dresser. *n., pl.* **bu·reaus.**

bur·glar (bėr′glər) a person who breaks into a house or other building to steal. *n.*

bur·glar·y (bėr′glər ē) breaking into a house or other building to steal. *n., pl.* **bur·glar·ies.**

hat, āge, fär; let, ēqual, tėrm; it, īce
hot, ōpen, ôrder; oil, out; cup, pu̇t, rüle
əbove, takən, pencəl, lemən, circəs
ch, child; ng, long; sh, ship
th, thin; ᴛʜ, then; zh, measure

bur·i·al (ber′ē əl) putting a dead body in a grave, in a tomb, or in the sea; burying. *n.*

bur·ied (ber′ēd) See **bury.** *The dog buried his bone. Many nuts were buried under the leaves.* *v.*

bur·lap (bėr′lap) 1 a coarse fabric often used to make bags and wrappings. 2 a fabric like this but having a tighter weave and lighter weight: *She made curtains of blue, beige, and yellow burlap.* *n.*

bur·ly (bėr′lē) strong; sturdy; big. *adj.,* **bur·li·er, bur·li·est. —bur′li·ness, n.**

burn (bėrn) 1 be on fire: *The campfire burned all night.* 2 set on fire; cause to burn: *They burn wood in the fireplace.* 3 destroy or be destroyed by fire: *Please burn those old papers.* 4 injure or be injured by fire, heat, or acid: *He burned his hand on the hot iron.* 5 an injury caused by fire, heat, or an acid; a burned place: *She got a burn on her arm where she touched it with a hot pan. Don't lie too long in the sun or you will get a painful burn.* 6 make by fire, heat, acid, etc.: *He burned designs on wood to make a picture. His cigar burned a hole in the rug.* 7 feel hot; give a feeling of heat to: *His forehead burns with fever.* 8 excite or be excited with anger, eagerness, etc.: *burn with fury, burning with enthusiasm.* 9 give light: *Lamps were burning in every room.* 1–4, 6–9 *v.,* **burned** or **burnt, burn·ing;** 5 *n.*
burn up, a consume: *This car burns up the gasoline.* **b** *Informal.* make angry: *His complaining burns me up.*

burn·er (bėr′nər) 1 the part of a lamp, stove, furnace, etc. where the flame is produced. 2 a thing or part that burns, or works by heat: *Some stoves are oil burners; others are gas burners.* *n.*

bur·nish (bėr′nish) 1 polish; shine: *The metal was burnished till it glistened.* 2 a polish or shine. 1 *v.,* 2 *n.*

bur·noose or **bur·nous** (bėr nüs′ or bėr′nüs) a long cloak with a hood, worn by Moors and Arabs. *n.*

burnt (bėrnt) See **burn.** *v.*

burp (bėrp) *Informal.* 1 a belch. 2 belch. 3 cause to belch: *The mother burped her baby.* 1 *n.,* 2, 3 *v.*

burr or **bur** (bėr) 1 a prickly, clinging seedcase or flower of some plants: *Burrs stick to cloth and fur.* 2 a plant or weed that has burrs. *n.*

bur·ro (bėr′ō or bu̇r′ō) a kind of small donkey. *n., pl.* **bur·ros.**

☛ **Burro** comes from Spanish *burro,* which developed from a Latin word *burricus,* meaning 'small horse.'

☛ **Burro** and **burrow** are sometimes pronounced the same.

bur·row (bėr′ō) 1 a hole dug in the ground: *Rabbits live in burrows.* 2 dig a hole in the ground: *The mole soon burrowed out of sight.* 3 dig: *Rabbits have burrowed the ground for miles around.* 4 search: *The woman burrowed through the pile of clothes looking for the lost ring.* 1 *n.,* 2–4 *v.*

☛ See note at **burro.**

burst (bėrst) **1** break open; break out suddenly; fly apart suddenly with force: *The bomb will burst.* **2** open or be opened suddenly or violently: *The trees had burst into bloom.* **3** go, come, do, etc. by force or suddenly: *Don't burst into the room without knocking.* **4** be very full: *bursting with enthusiasm. The barns were bursting with grain.* **5** act or change suddenly: *burst into tears.* **6** a bursting; outbreak: *There was a burst of laughter when the clown fell down.* **7** a sudden display of activity or energy: *He won the race with a burst of speed.* 1–5 *v.,* **burst, burst·ing;** 6, 7 *n.*

bur·y (ber′ē) **1** put a dead body in the earth, in a tomb, or in the sea: *The boys buried the dead bird.* **2** put away; cover up; hide: *The squirrels buried nuts under the dead leaves. v.,* **bur·ied, bur·y·ing.**

☛ **Bury** and **berry** are pronounced the same.

bus (bus) a large motor vehicle with seats inside: *Buses are used to carry passengers along a certain route. n., pl.* **bus·es** or **bus·ses.**

bush (bu̇sh) **1** a woody plant smaller than a tree, often with many separate branches starting from or near the ground. **2** open forest or wild land: *He disliked towns after living in the bush for many years.* **3** the tree-covered part of a farm; a bush lot or wood lot: *They went to the bush to get firewood. n.*

beat around the bush, avoid coming to the point of a matter: *Tell me the truth right away and don't beat around the bush.*

bushed (bu̇sht) *Informal.* **1** *Cdn.* acting strangely as a result of being isolated from people. **2** exhausted. *adj.*

bush·el (bu̇sh′əl) **1** a volume measure for grain, fruit, vegetables, and other dry things, equal to 4 pecks or 32 quarts (about 36 ℓ). **2** a container holding a bushel: *We bought a bushel of apples. n.*

bush line *Cdn.* an airline that transports freight and passengers over the northern bush country.

bush lot *Cdn.* that part of a farm where the trees have been left standing to provide firewood, fence posts, etc.; a wood lot.

bush pilot *Cdn.* an aviator who does most of his flying in the bush country of the far north.

bush·y (bu̇sh′ē) **1** spreading out like a bush; growing thickly: *a bushy beard.* **2** overgrown with bushes: *a bushy hill. adj.,* **bush·i·er, bush·i·est.**

bus·i·ly (biz′ə lē) in a busy manner; actively. *adv.*

busi·ness (biz′nis) **1** whatever one is busy at; work: *A carpenter's business is building with wood.* **2** a matter; affair: *That adventure was a bad business.* **3** trade; buying and selling: *This store does a big business.* **4** a commercial enterprise; an industrial establishment: *They sold their bakery business for $500 000.* **5** the right to act; responsibility: *Other people's business is not your business. n.*

mind your own business, avoid interfering in the affairs of others.

mean business, *Informal.* be in earnest; be serious: *When my mother's voice gets quiet like that, she means business!*

busi·ness·like (biz′nis līk′) having system and method; well managed: *She ran her store in a businesslike manner. adj.*

busi·ness·man (biz′nis man′ or biz′nis mən) **1** a man in business. **2** a man who is good at business: *He's no businessman. n., pl.* **busi·ness·men** (biz′nis men′ or biz′nis mən).

busi·ness·wom·an (biz′nis wu̇m′ən) **1** a woman in business. **2** a woman who is good at business: *The way she handled the project shows that she's a businesswoman. n., pl.* **busi·ness·wom·en** (biz′nis wim′ən).

bus·ses (bus′iz) a plural of **bus.** *n.*

bust (bust) **1** a statue of a person's head, shoulders, and chest. **2** the upper front part of the body, especially of a woman. *n.*

bus·tle (bus′əl) **1** be noisily busy and in a hurry: *The children bustled to get ready for the party.* **2** noisy or excited activity: *There was a great bustle as the children got ready for the party.* 1 *v.,* **bus·tled, bus·tling;** 2 *n.*

bus·y (biz′ē) **1** working; active; having plenty to do: *Mother is a busy person.* **2** full of work or activity: *Main Street is a busy place. Holidays are a busy time.* **3** make busy; keep busy: *The bees busied themselves at making honey.* **4** in use: *I tried to phone her, but her line was busy.* 1, 2, 4 *adj.,* **bus·i·er, bus·i·est;** 3 *v.,* **bus·ied, bus·y·ing.**

bus·y·bod·y (biz′ē bod′ē) a meddler; a person who interferes in the affairs of others. *n., pl.* **bus·y·bod·ies.**

but (but; *unstressed,* bət) **1** on the other hand: *You may go, but you must come home at six o'clock.* **2** except: *Father works every day in the week but Sunday.* **3** unless; except that: *It never rains but it pours.* **4** no more than; only: *We can but try. He is but a small boy.* **5** other than: *No one answered but me.* 1, 3 *conj.,* 2, 5 *prep.,* 4 *adv.*

butch·er (bu̇ch′ər) **1** a man whose work is killing animals to be sold for food. **2** a man who cuts up and sells meat. **3** kill animals for food: *Cattle, sheep, and pigs are butchered at the abattoir.* **4** kill people, wild animals, or birds needlessly or cruelly. **5** spoil by poor work; botch: *Don't butcher that song by singing too loudly.* 1, 2 *n.,* 3–5 *v.*

but·ler (but′lər) a man who is the head servant in a household. *n.*

butt[1] (but) **1** the thicker end of anything: *the butt of a gun.* **2** the end that is left; a stub or stump: *The butt of a cigarette. n.*

butt[2] (but) **1** an object of ridicule or scorn: *That strange boy was the butt of many jokes.* **2** target. *n.*

butt[3] (but) **1** strike or push by knocking hard with the head: *A goat butts.* **2** a push or blow with the head. 1 *v.,* 2 *n.*

butt in, *Slang.* meddle; interfere.

A butte

butte (byüt) a steep, flat-topped hill standing alone. *n.*

but·ter (but′ər) **1** the yellowish fat obtained by churning cream or whole milk. **2** put butter on: *Please butter my bread.* **3** something like butter in looks or use: *peanut butter, honey butter.* 1, 3 *n.,* 2 *v.*

hat, āge, fär; let, ēqual, tėrm; it, īce
hot, ōpen, ôrder; oil, out; cup, pu̇t, rüle
əbove, takən, pencəl, lemən, circəs
ch, child; ng, long; sh, ship
th, thin; ᴛʜ, then; zh, measure

but·ter·cup (but′ər kup′) a common plant with bright yellow flowers shaped like cups. *n.*

Butterfly: a kind of swallowtail — wingspread about 12 cm

but·ter·fly (but′ər flī′) an insect with a slender body and four large, often brightly colored wings. *n., pl.* **but·ter·flies.**

but·ter·milk (but′ər milk′) the fat-free liquid left after butter has been made from cream: *Milk can also be changed to buttermilk artificially. n.*

but·ter·nut (but′ər nut′) 1 an oily kind of walnut that is good to eat, grown in North America. 2 the tree it grows on. *n.*

but·ter·scotch (but′ər skoch′) a candy made from brown sugar and butter. *n.*

but·tocks (but′əks) the fleshy hind part of the body where the legs join the back; rump. *n. pl.*

but·ton (but′ən) 1 a knob or a flat piece of metal, plastic, etc. fixed on clothing and other things, to hold parts together or to decorate. 2 fasten the buttons of; close with buttons: *We buttoned our coats when the rain began.* 3 a knob or disk that is pushed, turned, etc. to cause something to work: *Push that button to start the machine.* 1, 3 *n.*, 2 *v.*

but·ton·hole (but′ən hōl′) 1 the hole or slit through which a button is passed. 2 make buttonholes in. 3 force someone to listen, as if holding him by the buttonhole of his coat: *He buttonholed me as I tried to sneak out of the room.* 1 *n.*, 2, 3 *v.*, **but·ton·holed, but·ton·hol·ing.**

but·tress (but′ris) 1 a support built against a wall or building to strengthen it. 2 any support like this; prop. 3 support and strengthen; bolster: *The pilot buttressed his report of the flight with photographs. The farmer buttressed the wall with large rocks.* 1, 2 *n.*, 3 *v.*

bux·om (buk′səm) plump and good to look at; healthy and cheerful: *The buxom waitress smiled at the customer. adj.*

buy (bī) 1 get by paying a price: *You can buy a pencil for five cents.* 2 *Informal.* a bargain: *That book was a real buy.* 1 *v.*, **bought, buy·ing;** 2 *n.*

☛ **Buy** and **by** are pronounced the same.

buzz (buz) 1 the humming sound made by flies, mosquitoes, or bees. 2 the low, confused sound of many people talking quietly: *The buzz of conversation stopped when the teacher entered the room.* 3 make a steady humming sound; hum loudly: *The radio should be fixed; it buzzes when you turn it on.* 4 approach quickly and closely with an airplane or a small boat: *A pilot buzzed our school yesterday.* 1, 2 *n.*, 3, 4 *v.*

buzz about, move about busily.

buz·zard (buz′ərd) 1 any of several kinds of hawk. 2 a kind of vulture: *Buzzards eat the flesh of dead animals. n.*

buzz·er (buz′ər) an electrical device that makes a buzzing sound as a signal: *a door buzzer. n.*

by (bī) 1 near; beside: *Stand by me. He lives close by.* 2 along; over; through: *They went by the main road.* 3 through the act of: *The thief was captured by a policeman.* 4 through the means or use of: *He travels by airplane.* 5 combined with in multiplication or dimensions: *a room three by five metres.* 6 in the measure of: *Eggs are sold by the dozen.* 7 as soon as; not later than: *Be here by six o'clock.* 8 during: *The sun shines by day.* 9 past: *days gone by. A car raced by.* 10 aside; away: *She puts money by every week to save for a new bicycle.* 11 according to: *They all work by the rules.* 12 in relation to: *She did well by her children.* 1–8, 11, 12 *prep.*, 1, 9, 10 *adv.*

by and by, after a while; soon: *Summer will come by and by.*

by and large, on the whole; in general: *By and large, it's a good book.*

by the way, incidentally: *By the way, what time is it?*

☛ **By** and **buy** are pronounced the same.

by–and–by (bi′ən bī′) the future. *n.*

by–e·lec·tion (bī′ə lek′shən) an election held in one riding because of the death or resignation of its Member of Parliament or of the Legislative Assembly. *n.*

by·gone (bī′gon′) 1 gone by; past; former: *The Romans lived in bygone days.* 2 something in the past. 1 *adj.*, 2 *n.*

let bygones be bygones, let the past be forgotten.

by–law (bī′lo′ or bī′lô′) a local law; a law made by a city, company, club, etc. for the control of its own affairs: *Our city has a by-law to control the height of buildings. n.*

by–pass (bī′pas′) 1 a road, channel, pipe, etc. providing a secondary route to be used instead of the main route: *Drivers use the by-pass when there is a lot of traffic.* 2 go around: *The new highway by-passes the city.* 1 *n.*, 2 *v.*

by–path (bī′path′) a side path or byway. *n.*

by–prod·uct (bī′prod′əkt) something of value produced in making or doing something else; not the main product: *Kerosene is a by-product of petroleum refining. n.*

by–road (bī′rōd′) a side road. *n.*

by·stand·er (bī′stan′dər) a person who stands near or looks on but does not take part: *Innocent bystanders are often hurt in street fights. n.*

by·way or **by–way** (bī′wā′) a side path or road; a way that is little used. *n.*

c or **C** 1 the third letter of the alphabet: *There are two* c's *in* bicycle. 2 the Roman numeral for 100. *n., pl.* **c's** or **C's.**

C Celsius.

cab (kab) 1 an automobile that can be hired with a driver, usually for short individual trips; taxi: *My mother telephoned for a cab to take her to the airport.* 2 a horse-drawn carriage that can be hired with a driver: *We rode through the park in a cab.* 3 the enclosed part of a truck or other vehicle where the driver or operator sits. *n.*

cab·bage (kab′ij) a vegetable whose thick leaves are closely folded into a round head. *n.*

cab·in (kab′ən) 1 a small, roughly built house; hut. 2 a room in a ship: *Our family had two cabins for the voyage to Europe.* 3 a place for passengers in an aircraft. *n.*

cab·i·net (kab′ə nit or kab′nit) 1 a piece of furniture having shelves or drawers to hold things, such as jewels, dishes, or letters. 2 the advisers of a prime minister or a premier: *The cabinet of a provincial government is called the Executive Council.* *n.*

cabinet minister the head of a department of the government; a member of the cabinet.

A cable

ca·ble (kā′bəl) 1 a strong, thick rope, usually made of wires twisted together: *The truck used a cable for towing the car.* 2 a bundle of electric wires protected from each other by insulation: *Telegraph messages are sent under the ocean by cable.* 3 a cablegram. 4 send a message across the ocean by underwater cable: *Susan cabled her sister in England.* 1–3 *n.,* 4 *v.,* **ca·bled, ca·bling.**

ca·ble·gram (kā′bəl gram′) a message sent across the ocean by underwater cable. *n.*

ca·boose (kə büs′) 1 a small car on a freight train in which the trainmen can work, rest, and sleep. 2 a kitchen on the deck of a ship. 3 *Cdn.* a movable bunkhouse used by lumberjacks, threshing crews, etc. 4 *Cdn.* a small cabin built on a sleigh and equipped with benches and a stove: *The farmer took his children to school in a caboose during winter.* *n.*

ca·ca·o (kə kā′ō) a tropical American tree that produces seeds from which cocoa and chocolate are made. *n., pl.* **ca·ca·os.**

cache (kash) 1 a hiding place: *The cache of stolen jewels was discovered by the police.* 2 *Cdn.* a storing place for food, furs, etc.: *The trapper made a cache to keep his food safe from wolves and other animals.* 3 the things hidden or stored in a cache. 4 hide or store in a cache. 1–3 *n.,* 4 *v.,* **cached, cach·ing.**

☛ **Cache** came into English from a French word *cache,* which was formed from *cacher,* meaning 'to hide.' Some of the Canadian meanings come from special Canadian French uses of *cache.*

cack·le (kak′əl) 1 the shrill, broken sound that a hen makes, especially after laying an egg. 2 make this sound. 3 a burst of shrill, harsh, or broken laughter: *Before the comedian finished the joke, there were a few cackles from the audience.* 4 laugh with shrill, harsh, or broken sounds: *After each joke the old man cackled his enjoyment.* 1, 3 *n.,* 2, 4 *v.,* **cack·led, cack·ling.**

A kind of low-growing cactus, the prickly pear

A giant cactus — up to 20 m high

cac·tus (kak′təs) a plant with a thick stem that is soft and spongy inside, usually having spines but no leaves: *Most cactuses grow in dry, hot regions.* *n., pl.* **cac·tus·es** or **cac·ti** (kak′tī).

cad·die or **cad·dy** (kad′ē) 1 a person who helps a golf player by carrying his clubs, finding lost balls, etc. 2 help a golf player in this way. 1 *n.,* 2 *v.,* **cad·died, cad·dy·ing.**

ca·dence (kā′dəns) 1 rhythm; beat: *The steady cadence of a march.* 2 a rising and falling sound: *She speaks with a pleasant cadence.* *n.*

ca·det (kə det′) a person who is training for service as an officer in the armed forces: *The cadets at the Royal Military College wear smart scarlet tunics.* *n.*

cad·mi·um (kad′mē əm) a soft, bluish-white metal resembling tin, used in alloys and in plating other metals to prevent rusting. *n.*

ca·fé (ka fā′) a place to buy and eat a meal. *n.*

☛ **Café** usually refers only to a small, informal place to eat. **Restaurant** may refer to any public eating place, from a very formal dining room to a small place with a counter and perhaps two or three tables.

caf·e·te·ri·a (kaf′ə tēr′ē ə) a café or restaurant where customers serve themselves. *n.*

caf·feine or **caf·fein** (kaf′ēn) a drug found in coffee and tea. *n.*

cage (kāj) 1 a frame or box closed in with wires or bars: *At the zoo there are many cages for wild animals and birds.* 2 put or keep in a cage: *After the lion was caught, it was caged.* 1 *n.,* 2 *v.,* **caged, cag·ing.**

cage·y (kāj′ē) *Informal.* 1 shrewd: *a cagey lawyer.* 2 cautious; wary: *He was too cagey to commit himself completely.* *adj.,* **cag·i·er, cag·i·est.**

cairn (kern) a pile of stones heaped up as a memorial, tomb, or landmark. *n.*

cake (kāk) 1 a baked mixture of flour, sugar, eggs, and other things: *a layer cake, a sponge cake, a fruit cake.* 2 any small, flat mass of food fried on both sides: *fish cake.* 3 a shaped mass: *a cake of soap, a cake of maple sugar.* 4 form into a solid mass; harden: *Mud cakes as it dries.* 1–3 *n.,* 4 *v.,* **caked, cak·ing.**

ca·lam·i·ty (kə lam′ə tē) 1 an event causing great misery or destruction: *The newspaper reported such calamities as fires and floods.* 2 serious trouble; misery: *Calamity may come to anyone.* *n., pl.* **ca·lam·i·ties.**

hat, āge, fär; let, ēqual, tėrm; it, īce
hot, ōpen, ôrder; oil, out; cup, pu̇t, rüle
əbove, takən, pencəl, lemən, circəs
ch, child; ng, long; sh, ship
th, thin; ᴛʜ, then; zh, measure

cal·ci·um (kal′sē əm) a substance that is part of lime, chalk, milk, bone, teeth, etc.: *For a healthy body, you need foods with calcium. n.*

cal·cu·late (kal′kyə lāt′) **1** add, subtract, multiply, divide, etc. in order to find out something: *Father calculated the cost of building a house.* **2** find out beforehand by any process of reasoning: *Can you calculate the day of the week on which New Year's Day will fall?* **3** *Informal.* plan; intend: *That remark was calculated to hurt my feelings. v.,* **cal·cu·lat·ed, cal·cu·lat·ing.**

☛ **Calculate** and **calculus** both come from the Latin word *calculus,* meaning 'stone' or 'a stone, pebble.' **Calculate** is from the verb *calculare,* meaning 'to count,' formed from *calculus,* because pebbles were used in counting. **Calculus** keeps the additional Latin meaning of the kind of stone formed in the body.

cal·cu·la·tion (kal′kyə lā′shən) **1** adding, subtracting, multiplying, or dividing to find a result: *The calculation of the total cost will take some time.* **2** a result found by calculating: *All my calculations are correct.* **3** careful thinking; deliberate planning: *The success of the program was the result of much calculation. n.*

cal·cu·la·tor (kal′kyə lā′tər) a machine that calculates, especially one that can multiply and divide as well as add and subtract. *n.*

cal·cu·lus (kal′kyə ləs) **1** a stone or hard mass formed in the body. **2** a hard substance that has collected on the teeth, formed by the action of bacteria on saliva and food particles; tartar. *n.*

☛ See note at **calculate.**

cal·dron (kol′drən or kôl′drən) See **cauldron.**

cal·en·dar (kal′ən dər) **1** a table showing the months and weeks of the year and the day of the week on which each date comes. **2** a list or schedule; record: *We have three winter carnivals on our calendar. n.*

calf¹ (kaf) **1** a young cow or bull. **2** a young elephant, whale, deer, etc.: *The children saw the new seal calves at the zoo.* **3** leather made of the skin of a calf. *n., pl.* **calves.**

calf² (kaf) the thick fleshy part of the back of the leg below the knee. See **leg** for picture. *n., pl.* **calves.**

cal·i·co (kal′ə kō′) **1** a cotton cloth that usually has colored patterns printed on one side. **2** spotted in colors: *a calico cat.* 1 *n., pl.* **cal·i·coes** or **cal·i·cos;** 2 *adj.*

ca·liph or **ca·lif** (kā′lif or kal′if) the former title of the head of certain Moslem states. *n.*

call (kol or kôl) **1** speak loudly; cry; shout: *He called from downstairs.* **2** a shout; cry: *I heard the swimmer's call for help.* **3** the special noise or cry an animal or bird makes: *The call of a moose came from the forest.* **4** make this noise or cry: *The crows called to each other from the trees around the meadow.* **5** give a signal to; arouse: *Call me at seven o'clock.* **6** command or ask to come: *He called his dog with a loud whistle.* **7** a command; invitation; summons: *Every farmer in the neighborhood answered the firemen's call for volunteers.* **8** give a name to; name: *His pals call him 'Shorty.' My sister is called Doria.* **9** read over aloud: *The teacher called the roll of the class.* **10** make a short visit or stop: *The minister called at our house yesterday.* **11** a short visit or stop: *a doctor's call.* **12** telephone: *Call me tomorrow morning.* **13** a calling by telephone: *I want to make a call to Montreal.* **14** end; stop: *The ball game was called because of rain.* 1, 4–6, 8–10, 12, 14 *v.,* 2, 3, 7, 11, 13 *n.*

call for, a go and get; stop and get. **b** need or require: *This recipe calls for two eggs.*

call off, a cancel: *We called off our trip.* **b** order back; order away: *Call off your dog.*

call on or **call upon, a** visit. **b** appeal to: *He called upon his friends for help.*

call up, a bring to mind: *The old friends called up childhood memories.* **b** telephone. **c** summon to the service of the country.

on call, ready or available: *There are doctors on call day and night.*

call·er (kol′ər or kôl′ər) **1** a person who makes a short visit: *The doctor said that the patient was now able to receive callers.* **2** a person who calls out names, dance steps, etc. at a square dance. *n.*

☛ **Caller** and **collar** are sometimes pronounced the same.

call·ing (kol′ing or kôl′ing) a profession, occupation, or trade: *The teacher took great pleasure in his calling. n.*

cal·lous (kal′əs) **1** hard; hardened: *Going barefoot makes the bottoms of the feet callous.* **2** unfeeling: *Only a callous person can see people suffering without trying to help them. adj.* **—cal·lous·ly,** *adv.*

☛ **Callous** and **callus** are pronounced the same.

cal·lus (kal′əs) a hard, thickened place on the skin. *n., pl.* **cal·lus·es.**

☛ See note at **callous.**

calm (kom or käm) **1** quiet; still; not stormy or windy; not stirred up: *a calm sea.* **2** peaceful; not excited: *a calm voice.* **3** quietness; stillness; absence of wind or motion. **4** the absence of excitement; peacefulness. **5** make calm; become calm: *Mother soon calmed the baby. The baby calmed down. The sea calmed.* 1, 2 adj., 3, 4 *n.,* 5 *v.* **—calm′ly,** *adv.* **—calm′ness,** *n.*

cal·o·rie or **cal·o·ry** (kal′ə rē) **1** unit for measuring the amount of heat. **2** a unit for showing the value of foods in producing heat and energy in the human body: *A medium-sized orange has about a hundred calories. n., pl.* **cal·o·ries.**

cal·u·met (kal′yə met′) a long decorated tobacco pipe smoked by the North American Indians on special occasions as a symbol of peace. *n.*

calve (kav) give birth to a calf. *v.,* **calved, calv·ing.**

calves (kavz) plural of **calf¹** and **calf².** *n.*

ca·lyx (kā′liks) the outer leaves that surround the unopened bud of a flower: *The calyx is made up of sepals. n.*

came (kām) See **come.** *He came to school too early this morning.* *v.*

cam·el (kam′əl) a large, four-legged desert animal having wide, cushioned feet and either one or two humps on its back: *Camels are used to carry riders and burdens in the deserts of Africa and Arabia because they can go a long time without drinking water.* See **dromedary** for picture. *n.*

A camera. When the shutter is opened, light rays reflected from the object pass through the lens and are focussed by it onto the film. Because the film is sensitive to light, it records the image.

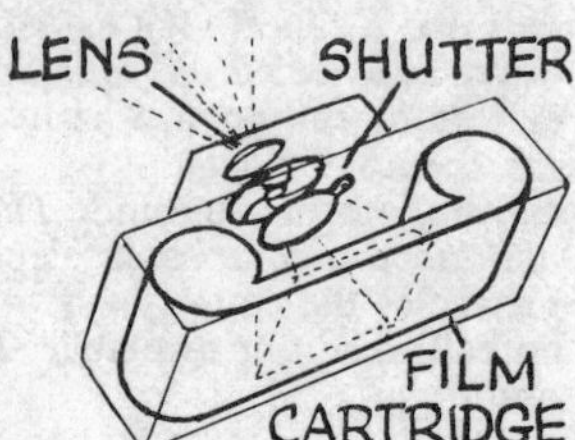

cam·er·a (kam′ər ə) **1** a machine for taking photographs or motion pictures. **2** in television, a device to convert pictures into electrical impulses for transmitting. *n.*

cam·ou·flage (kam′ə fläzh′) **1** an outward appearance that makes a person, animal, or thing seem to be part of its natural surroundings: *The white fur of a polar bear is a natural camouflage, for it prevents the bear from being easily seen against the snow.* **2** the practice of giving soldiers, weapons, etc. a false appearance to conceal them from the enemy. **3** give a false appearance to in order to conceal; disguise: *The hunters were camouflaged with shrubbery so that they blended with the green landscape. The boy camouflaged his embarrassment by laughing.* 1, 2 *n.*, 3 *v.*, **cam·ou·flaged, cam·ou·flag·ing.**

camp (kamp) **1** a group of tents, huts, or other shelter where people live for a time: *A marching army usually makes camp every night.* **2** make a camp; put up tents, huts, or other shelters and stay for a time: *We camped out for a week.* **3** a place where one lives in a tent or hut or outdoors: *There is a Boy Scout camp at the edge of the lake.* **4** the persons living in a camp: *The camp was awakened by the bugler.* 1, 3, 4 *n.*, 2 *v.* **—camp′er,** *n.*

break camp, pack up tents and equipment: *We broke camp early in the morning to return home.*

cam·paign (kam pān′) **1** in a war, a number of related military operations that are aimed at some special purpose: *The general planned a campaign to capture the enemy's most important city.* **2** a series of connected activities to do or get something: *Our town had a campaign to raise money for a new hospital.* **3** take part or serve in a campaign. 1, 2 *n.*, 3 *v.*

camp·fire (kamp′fīr′) **1** a fire in a camp for warmth or cooking. **2** a social gathering of campers, scouts, etc. *n.*

cam·phor (kam′fər) a white substance with a strong odor and a bitter taste: *Camphor is used to protect clothes from moths.* *n.*

cam·po·ree (kam′pə rē′) a gathering of boy scouts or girl guides for competitions in campcraft, etc. *n.*

camp robber Canada jay.

cam·pus (kam′pəs) the grounds and buildings of a college, university, or school. *n.*

can[1] (kan; *unstressed,* kən) a word used: **1** to mean that someone has the ability to do something: *I can swim quite well. I can't see because you're standing in my way.* **2** to mean that someone has a right to do something: *You can cross the street here. You can go at 4 o'clock.* **3** to mean that something has the power to do something: *My new model train can go very fast.* *v.*, **could.**

☞ In formal English we usually distinguish between **may,** meaning 'be allowed to' or 'have permission to,' and **can,** meaning 'know how to' or 'be able to': *You may go now. You may if you can. He can walk with crutches.* In informal English *can* is widely used to mean both 'be allowed to' and 'be able to': *Can I go now? You can if you want to. I can run faster than any of my friends.* In both formal and informal English, **may** is used also to indicate that something is possible: *It may be all right for her, but it is no good for me.*

can[2] (kan) **1** a container of metal, usually having a cover or lid: *an oil can, a milk can, a can of fruit.* **2** the contents of a can: *We ate a can of beans.* **3** preserve by putting in airtight cans or jars: *Mother cans fruit.* 1, 2 *n.*, 3 *v.*, **canned, can·ning.**

Can·a·da balsam (kan′ə də) a sticky, yellow resin obtained from the balsam fir tree.

Canada Day Dominion Day.

Canada goose a large wild goose of North America having a black head and neck, a white throat, and a brownish-grey body.

Canada jay a North American bird having black and grey feathers: *The Canada jay is also known as a lumberjack, a whisky-jack, a venison hawk, or a moosebird.*

Canada lynx a kind of lynx found in Canada and Alaska: *The large paws of the Canada lynx function like snowshoes in winter so it can run fast over the snow.* See **wildcat** for picture.

Ca·na·di·an (kə nā′dē ən) **1** of or having to do with Canada or its people. **2** a person born in or living in Canada. 1 *adj.*, 2 *n.*

Canadian English the kind of English spoken by English-speaking Canadians.

Canadian French the kind of French spoken by French-speaking Canadians.

Ca·na·di·an·ism (kə nā′dē ən iz′əm) **1** a word or expression originating in or peculiar to Canada: *The words 'muskeg' and 'caribou' are Canadianisms.* **2** a custom peculiar to Canada. **3** loyalty to Canada as an independent nation and devotion to her customs, traditions, and laws. *n.*

Canadian Shield a region of ancient rock encircling Hudson Bay and covering nearly half the mainland of Canada: *The Canadian Shield is rich in minerals, especially gold, copper, nickel, and iron ore.*

Ca·na·di·en (kə nā′ dē en′) a French Canadian. *n.*

ca·nal (kə nal′) **1** a waterway dug across land for ships or small boats to go through, or to carry water to places that need it: *A river is a natural waterway, but a canal is man-made.* **2** a tube in the body or in a plant for carrying food, liquid, or air: *The food that we eat goes through the alimentary canal.* *n.*

ca·nar·y (kə ner′ē) **1** a small, yellow songbird.

2 light yellow. 1, 2 *n., pl.* **ca·nar·ies;** 2 *adj.*

☞ The **canary** was named for the Canary Islands, where this bird was first seen. The name of the islands came through French and Spanish from the Latin name for one of these islands, *Canaria insula,* meaning 'Island of Dogs.'

can·cel (kan′səl) **1** cross out; mark, stamp, or punch something so that it cannot be used again: *The post office cancels the stamp on a letter that is mailed.* **2** put an end to or withdraw; do away with; stop: *He cancelled his order for the books. This payment will cancel your debt to me.* *v.,* **can·celled** or **can·celed, can·cel·ling** or **can·cel·ing.**

☞ **Cancel, chancel,** and **chancellor** came through different Old French words from forms of the Latin word *cancelli,* meaning the lattice or cross-bars at the gate of a monastery, court, etc. **Cancel** is from a Latin verb meaning 'to cross out,' formed from *cancelli,* because crossed lines resembling a lattice were used to cancel documents. **Chancel** is from a special meaning of *cancelli,* the part of a church behind the lattice. **Chancellor** is from the Latin word for the porter or secretary at the lattice of a court, etc.

can·cel·la·tion (kan′sə lā′shən) **1** cancelling or being cancelled: *We were sorry about the cancellation of the baseball game.* **2** marks made when something is cancelled or crossed out: *The small holes on the cheque are the cancellation marks.* *n.*

can·cer (kan′sər) **1** a very harmful growth in the body: *Cancer tends to spread and destroy the healthy tissues and organs of the body.* **2** an evil or harmful thing that tends to spread: *He says that the use of drugs is a cancer.* *n.*

can·did (kan′did) frank; sincere: *Please be candid and tell me just what you think.* *adj.* **—can′did·ly,** *adv.*

can·di·date (kan′də dāt′) a person who seeks or is proposed for some office or honor: *There are four candidates for the office of president of our club.* *n.*

can·dle (kan′dəl) a stick of tallow or wax with a wick in it, burned to give light: *He had eleven candles on his birthday cake. When the power went off during the storm, we had to use candles.* *n.*

not hold a candle to, not compare with: *The cake from the bakery could not hold a candle to the one John made.*

☞ **Candle** and **chandelier** came originally from the Latin word for candle, *candela,* formed from the verb *candere,* meaning 'to glisten, burn.' **Candle** developed from Old English *candel,* which came directly from Latin. **Chandelier** came into English much later from a French word formed from *chandelle,* meaning 'candle,' which had developed from *candela.*

can·dle·light (kan′dəl līt) the light from a candle. *n.*

can·dle·stick (kan′dəl stik′) a holder for a candle: *The candlestick makes the candle stand up straight.* *n.*

can·dor or **can·dour** (kan′dər) saying openly what one really thinks; honesty in giving one's view or opinion: *He expressed his views with great candor.* *n.*

can·dy (kan′dē) **1** a food made with sugar or syrup and flavoring: *We need sugar, milk, chocolate, and walnuts to make that kind of candy. Some children eat all the candy they can get.* **2** a piece of this: *Take a candy from the box.* **3** turn into sugar: *This honey has candied.* **4** cook in sugar; preserve by boiling in sugar: *She candied cherries and apricots.* 1, 2 *n., pl.* **can·dies;** 3, 4 *v.,* **can·died, can·dy·ing.**

hat, āge, fär; let, ēqual, tėrm; it, īce
hot, ōpen, ôrder; oil, out; cup, pu̇t, rüle
əbove, takən, pencəl, lemən, circəs
ch, child; ng, long; sh, ship
th, thin; ᴛʜ, then; zh, measure

cane (kān) **1** a slender stick used as an aid in walking: *On long walks, the old man took along his cane.* **2** a stick used to beat with: *A blow with a cane was an old form of punishment.* **3** beat with a cane. **4** a long, jointed stem, such as that of bamboo. **5** a plant having such stems: *Sugar cane, bamboo, and rattan are canes.* **6** make or repair with such stems: *He is caning a chair seat.* 1, 2, 4, 5 *n.,* 3, 6 *v.,* **caned, can·ing.**

ca·nine (kā′nin) **1** of or like a dog. **2** dog. **3** any animal belonging to a group of meat-eating animals including dogs, foxes, and wolves. **4** one of the four pointed teeth next to the incisors. See **teeth** for picture. 1 *adj.,* 2–4 *n.*

can·is·ter (kan′is tər) a small box or can, especially one used for flour, sugar, coffee, or tea. *n.*

can·ker (kang′kər) **1** a sore in the mouth. **2** anything that causes rot or decay or that destroys by a gradual eating away. *n.*

canned (kand) **1** put in a can; preserved by being put in airtight cans or jars. **2** *Slang.* preserved on a phonograph record or on tape; recorded: *canned music.* *adj.*

can·ner·y (kan′ər ē) a factory where food is canned. *n., pl.* **can·ner·ies.**

can·ni·bal (kan′ə bəl) **1** a person who eats human flesh: *Tribes of cannibals once lived on islands in the south Pacific Ocean.* **2** an animal that eats others of its own kind: *Many fish are cannibals.* *n.*

can·non (kan′ən) a big gun that is fixed to the ground or mounted on a carriage, especially the old-fashioned type of gun that fired cannon balls: *There are a number of fine cannon at Old Fort Henry in Kingston.* *n., pl.* **can·non** or **can·nons.**

☞ **Cannon** and **canon** are pronounced the same.

can·non·ade (kan′ən ād′) **1** a continued firing of cannon. **2** to attack with cannon. 1 *n.,* 2 *v.,* **can·non·ad·ed, can·non·ad·ing.**

cannon ball a large iron or steel ball, in former times fired from cannon.

can·not (kan′ot) can not.

can·ny (kan′ē) shrewd; cautious: *He was a canny investor and made a small fortune.* *adj.,* **can·ni·er, can·ni·est.**

Canoes

ca·noe (kə nü′) **1** a light, narrow boat having sharp ends, moved with a paddle. **2** paddle a canoe; go in a canoe. 1 *n., pl.* **ca·noes;** 2 *v.,* **ca·noed, ca·noe·ing.**

ca·noe·man (kə nü′mən) a man whose business is handling a canoe; voyageur: *The fur company employed many skilled canoemen.* *n., pl.* **ca·noe·men** (kə nü′mən).

can·on[1] (kan′ən) **1** a law of a church. **2** a rule by which a thing is judged; a standard: *the canons of good taste.* **3** the list of saints. **4** a list of books of the Bible accepted by the Christian church as being inspired by God. *n.*

☞ **Canon** and **cannon** are pronounced the same.

can·on[2] (kan′ən) a clergyman who has certain duties in a cathedral. *n.*

☞ See note at **canon**[1].

ca·ñon (kan′yən) See **canyon.**

can·o·py (kan′ə pē) **1** a covering fixed over a bed, throne, entrance, etc. or carried on poles over a person: *There is a striped canopy over the entrance to the hotel.* **2** a rooflike covering; a shelter or shade: *The trees formed a canopy over the old road.* *n., pl.* **can·o·pies.**

can't (kant) cannot.

can·ta·loupe or **can·ta·loup** (kan′tə lōp′) a kind of sweet, juicy melon; muskmelon. *n.*

can·tan·ker·ous (kan tang′kər əs) hard to get along with; quarrelsome: *The old man had a cantankerous way of speaking.* *adj.*

can·ta·ta (kən tä′tə or kən tat′ə) a musical composition having words and a story like an opera, but intended to be performed without scenery or action. *n.*

can·teen (kan tēn′) **1** a small container for carrying water or other drinks. **2** for members of the armed forces, a place for recreation and the sale of food and drinks. **3** a place in a factory, school, camp, etc. where food, drinks, and other articles are sold or given out. *n.*

can·ter (kan′tər) **1** a horse's gait faster than a trot but slower than a gallop. **2** move with this gait: *The horse cantered across the meadow.* 1 *n.*, 2 *v.*

can·ti·lev·er (kan′ti lē′vər or kan′te lev′ər) **1** a large, projecting bracket or beam that is fastened at one end only. **2** build with cantilevers: *Our balcony is cantilevered; theirs is supported by pillars.* 1 *n.*, 2 *v.*

The Quebec bridge — the longest cantilever span in the world

cantilever bridge a bridge made of two cantilevers, whose projecting ends meet in the middle but do not support each other.

Ca·nuck (kə nuk′) *Cdn. Informal.* **1** a Canadian. **2** a French Canadian. *n.*

can·vas (kan′vəs) **1** a strong cloth with a coarse weave, made of cotton, flax, or hemp, used to make tents, sails, certain articles of clothing, etc: *The tops of my sandals are made of canvas.* **2** a piece of canvas on which to paint a picture, especially in oils. **3** a picture painted on canvas: *The artist exhibited his best canvases at the fair.* *n.*

under canvas, a in tents. **b** with sails spread: *The boat left the harbor under canvas.*

☞ **Canvas** and **canvass** are pronounced the same.

can·vass (kan′vəs) **1** go about asking for subscriptions, votes, orders, etc.: *Each student canvassed his own block for contributions to the Red Cross.* **2** an attempt to get subscriptions, votes, orders, etc.: *We did a canvass of the district.* 1 *v.*, 2 *n.*

☞ See note at **canvas.**

can·yon (kan′yən) a narrow valley with high, steep sides, usually with a stream at the bottom. *n.*

☞ **Canyon** came into English from the Spanish word *cañon,* originally meaning 'large tube or pipe,' which the Spaniards of New Mexico used to describe canyons.

cap (kap) **1** a soft, close-fitting covering for the head, usually having little or no brim. **2** a special head covering worn to show rank, occupation, etc.: *a nurse's cap, a professor's cap and gown, a fool's cap.* **3** anything like a cap: *The stopper or top of a bottle is a cap. The top of a mushroom is called a cap.* **4** the highest part; the top. **5** put a cap on; cover the top of: *He capped the bottle. Whipped cream capped the dessert.* **6** match one thing with something as good or better: *The two clowns kept on capping each other's jokes.* **7** a small quantity of explosive in a wrapper or covering: *The boy bought some caps for his toy gun.* 1–4, 7 *n.*, 5, 6 *v.*, **capped, cap·ping.**

ca·pa·bil·i·ty (kā′pə bil′ə tē) ability to learn or do; power or fitness; capacity: *As a scientist, he has the capability of doing important research.* *n., pl.* **ca·pa·bil·i·ties.**

ca·pa·ble (kā′pə bəl) able; having fitness, power, or ability; efficient: *He did a very capable job and was rewarded with much praise.* *adj.* **—ca′pa·bly,** *adv.*

capable of, a having ability, power, or fitness for: *Some airplanes are capable of going 1500 kilometres per hour.* **b** open to; ready for: *a statement capable of being misunderstood.*

ca·pa·cious (kə pā′shəs) large and roomy; able to hold much: *a capacious closet.* *adj.*

ca·pac·i·ty (kə pas′ə tē) **1** the amount of room or space in a dish, a basket, a room, or a container of any kind: *This can has a capacity of four litres. This room has a seating capacity of 100 people.* **2** the ability to learn or do; the power or fitness: *A genius has a great capacity for learning.* **3** the position or relation: *He is here in the capacity of a teacher.* *n., pl.* **ca·pac·i·ties.**

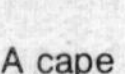

A cape

cape[1] (kāp) an outer garment, or a part of one, without sleeves, that falls loosely from the shoulders. *n.*

cape[2] (kāp) a point of land extending into the water. *n.*

hat, āge, fär; let, ēqual, tėrm; it, īce
hot, ōpen, ôrder; oil, out; cup, pu̇t, rüle
əbove, takən, pencəl, lemən, circəs
ch, child; ng, long; sh, ship
th, thin; ᴛʜ, then; zh, measure

ca·per (kā′pər) **1** leap or jump about in a playful way. **2** a playful leap or jump. **3** a prank; trick. 1 *v.*, 2, 3 *n.*

cap·il·lar·y (kap′ə ler′ē or kə pil′ə rē) **1** a blood vessel with a very slender, hairlike opening: *Capillaries join the end of an artery to the beginning of a vein.* **2** like a hair; very slender. 1 *n.*, *pl.* **cap·il·lar·ies;** 2 *adj.*

cap·i·tal[1] (kap′ə təl) **1** the city where the government of a country, province, or state is located: *Victoria is the capital of British Columbia.* **2** capital letter: *A capital is used at the beginning of a sentence or a proper name.* **3** important; leading: *The invention of the telephone was a capital advance in communication.* **4** of the best kind; excellent: *A maple tree gives capital shade.* **5** punishable by death: *Murder is a capital crime in many countries.* **6** the amount of money or property that a company or a person uses in carrying on a business: *A great deal of capital is needed to set up an aluminum plant.* 1, 2, 6 *n.*, 3, 4, 5 *adj.*
make capital of, use to one's own advantage: *He made capital of his father's fame to get the job.*

cap·i·tal[2] (kap′ə təl) the top part of a column or pillar. See **column** for picture. *n.*

cap·i·tal·ism (kap′ə tə liz′əm) an economic system in which private individuals own land, factories, and other means of production and use hired labor to produce goods and services for profit. *n.*

cap·i·tal·ist (kap′ə tə list) **1** a person whose money and property are used in carrying on business. **2** *Informal.* a wealthy person. *n.*

cap·i·tal·i·za·tion (kap′ə təl ə zā′shən) the act or practice of writing or printing with capital letters. *n.*

cap·it·al·ize (kap′ə təl īz′) write or print with capital letters: *He forgot to capitalize the first letter of the name.* *v.*, **cap·i·tal·ized, cap·i·tal·iz·ing.**
capitalize on, take advantage of: *We capitalized on the unexpected good weather by going on a picnic.*

capital letter the large form of a letter; A, B, C, D, etc., as distinguished from a, b, c, d, etc.

ca·price (kə prēs′) a sudden change of mind without reason; a notion or whim: *Her decision to wear only blue clothes was pure caprice.* *n.*

ca·pri·cious (kə prish′əs) likely to change suddenly without reason; changeable; fickle: *capricious weather. A spoiled child is often capricious.* *adj.*
—ca·pri′cious·ly, *adv.* **—ca·pri′cious·ness,** *n.*

cap·size (kap sīz′) upset; overturn; turn bottom side up: *Rough waves capsized the canoe.* *v.*, **cap·sized, cap·siz·ing.**

A capstan on a sailing ship. As it is turned, it winds or unwinds the rope that hoists the anchor.

cap·stan (kap′stən) a device that turns like a large, upright spool, used for winding in rope cables, anchor chains, etc.: *Capstans may be turned by manpower or by machinery.* *n.*

cap·sule (kap′səl or kap′syül) **1** a small case or covering: *Medicine is often given in capsules made of gelatin.* **2** the enclosed front section of a rocket, made to carry instruments, astronauts, etc. into space: *In flight the capsule can separate from the rest of the rocket and go into orbit or be directed back to earth.* **3** a dry seedcase that opens when ripe. *n.*

cap·tain (kap′tən) **1** a leader; chief: *Robin Hood was the captain of a merry band. John is the captain of the football team.* **2** an officer in the armed forces, ranking next above a lieutenant. **3** a commander of a ship. **4** lead or command as captain: *John will captain the team.* 1–3 *n.*, 4 *v.*

cap·tion (kap′shən) **1** a title or heading at the beginning of a page, article, chapter, etc. **2** an explanation or title accompanying a picture: *Pictures in newspapers and magazines usually have captions.* *n.*

cap·ti·vate (kap′tə vāt′) charm; fascinate: *The beautiful music captivated him. The children were captivated by the animal story.* *v.*, **cap·ti·vat·ed, cap·ti·vat·ing.**

cap·tive (kap′tiv) **1** a person or animal taken and held by force, skill, or trickery: *The army brought back many captives.* **2** taken and held; captured: *The captive soldiers were kept in a special prison.* 1 *n.*, 2 *adj.*

cap·tiv·i·ty (kap tiv′ə tē) the state of being held captive: *Some animals cannot bear captivity and die after a few weeks in a cage.* *n.*, *pl.* **cap·tiv·i·ties.**

cap·tor (kap′tər) a person who takes or holds a prisoner. *n.*

cap·ture (kap′chər) **1** take by force, skill, or trickery: *Three enemy soldiers were captured during the raid.* **2** anything taken in this way: *Captain Jones's first capture was a large ship.* **3** an act of capturing; the fact of capturing or being captured: *The capture of this ship took place on July 6.* **4** attract and hold: *The detective story captured the boy's attention.* 1, 4 *v.*, **cap·tured, cap·tur·ing;** 2, 3 *n.*

car (kär) **1** a passenger vehicle that carries its own engine and is used on roads and streets: *They made the trip by car.* **2** any vehicle that moves on wheels. **3** a wheeled vehicle running on rails, as a railway car or streetcar. **4** a part of a balloon, elevator, etc. for carrying passengers or cargo. *n.*

car·a·ga·na (kar′ə gan′ə or ker′ə gan′ə) **1** a shrub having small, light green leaves growing in pairs along a stem, much used on the prairies for hedges, windbreaks, etc.: *Caraganas grow well in dry climates.* *n.*

car·a·mel (kar′ə məl, ker′ə məl, or kär′məl) **1** sugar browned or burned over heat, used for coloring and flavoring. **2** a kind of candy flavored with this sugar. *n.*

car·at (kar′ət or ker′ət) **1** a unit of mass for precious stones, equal to 200 milligrams. **2** one of the 24 equal parts of a measure used in stating the quality of gold: *If a ring is 18 carats fine, it is 18 parts pure gold and 6 parts alloy.* *n.*
☛ **Carat** and **carrot** are pronounced the same.

car·a·van (kar′ə van′ or ker′ə van′) **1** a group of people travelling together for safety through difficult or dangerous country: *A caravan of Arab merchants and camels moved across the desert.* **2** the vehicles or beasts of burden used by such a group. **3** a truck or trailer with a small living unit. *n.*

car·a·way (kar′ə wā′) a plant that yields fragrant, spicy seeds which are used to flavor food. *n.*

car·bine (kär′bīn) a short light rifle. *n.*

car·bo·hy·drate (kär′bō hī′drāt) a substance composed of carbon, hydrogen, and oxygen: *Sugar and starch are carbohydrates. n.*

car·bol·ic acid (kär bol′ik) a poisonous acid obtained from coal tar, used in disinfectants and antiseptics.

car·bon (kär′bən) a common substance that is found along with other substances in all plants and animals: *Diamonds and graphite are pure carbon; coal is impure carbon. n.*

carbon di·ox·ide (dī ok′sīd) a gas that has no color or smell and is present in the atmosphere: *The air that comes from the lungs contains carbon dioxide. Plants absorb carbon dioxide from the air and use it to make plant tissue.*

carbon mon·ox·ide (mon ok′sīd) a poisonous gas that has no color or smell: *Carbon monoxide is present in the exhaust from an automobile engine.*

car·bu·re·tor (kär′bə rā′tər or kär′bə ret′ər) a device for mixing air with a liquid fuel: *There is a carburetor in an automobile engine. n.*

car·cass (kär′kəs) the body of a dead animal: *Steak is cut from a beef carcass. n.*

card[1] (kärd) **1** a flat piece of stiff paper or thin cardboard: *The store sells post cards and birthday cards, but not report cards.* **2** one of a deck of cards used in playing games. **3** See **cards.** *n.*

card[2] (kärd) **1** a wire brush or other tool with teeth. **2** clean or comb with such a tool: *Wool must be carded to smooth out the fibres before it is spun.* 1 *n.*, 2 *v.*

card·board (kärd′bôrd′) a fairly thick kind of stiff paper used for making cards, cartons, boxes, etc. *n.*

car·di·gan (kär′də gən) a sweater or knitted jacket that opens down the front and is usually collarless. *n.*

car·di·nal (kär′də nəl) **1** of first importance; chief; principal: *His idea was of cardinal importance to the plan.* The **cardinal numbers** are one, two, three, four, five, etc. The **cardinal points** of the compass are north, south, east, and west. **2** in the Roman Catholic Church, one of the high officials who are second to the Pope in rank: *Cardinals, who wear red robes and hats, are appointed by the Pope.* **3** bright, rich red. **4** a North American songbird. The male has bright-red feathers marked with grey and black. 1, 3 *adj.*, 2–4 *n.*

cards (kärdz) **1** a game or games played with a deck of cards. **2** the playing of such games: *All the guests were busy at cards. n. pl.*

in the cards, sure to happen: *It's in the cards that we'll have to cancel our trip again.*

put one's cards on the table, show what one has or can do; be open and frank.

care (ker) **1** a troubled state of mind because of fear of what may happen; worry: *Few people are completely free from care.* **2** serious attention: *A good cook does her work with care.* **3** an object of worry, concern, or attention: *He has always been a care to his mother.* **4** feel interest: *He cares about music.* **5** watchful keeping; charge: *Baby was left in her sister's care.* **6** food, shelter, and protection: *Your child will have the best of care.* **7** like; want; wish: *A cat does not care to be caged.* 1–3, 5, 6 *n.*, 4, 7 *v.*, **cared, car·ing.**

care for, a like: *I don't care for her.* **b** want or wish: *I don't care for any dessert, thanks.* **c** take charge of: *The nurse will care for him during the night.*

in care of, at the address or in the charge of: *Send it in care of the secretary. Symbol:* c/o

take care, be careful: *Take care on the icy path or you will slip.*

take care of, a take charge of; attend to: *A baby-sitter takes care of children. My father will take care of this bill.* **b** watch over; be careful with: *Take care of your money.*

ca·reen (kə rēn′) **1** tip to one side; tilt: *The ship careened in the strong wind.* **2** rush along with a bobbing, leaning movement: *The waitress careened among the tables, balancing a heavy tray on one hand. v.*

ca·reer (kə rēr′) **1** a general course of action or progress through life: *It is exciting to read about the careers of explorers.* **2** an occupation or profession: *He chose the armed forces for his career.* **3** rush along wildly: *The driverless truck careered down the hill.* 1, 2 *n.*, 3 *v.*

care·free (ker′frē′) without worry; light-hearted; happy. *adj.*

care·ful (ker′fəl) **1** thinking what one says; watching what one does; taking pains; watchful; cautious: *Be careful to tell the truth at all times.* **2** done with thought or effort; exact: *Arithmetic requires careful work.* **3** full of care or concern; attentive: *She was careful of the feelings of others. adj.* **—care′ful·ly,** *adv.* **—care′ful·ness,** *n.*

care·less (ker′lis) **1** not thinking or watching what one says or does: *One careless step may cost a life.* **2** done without enough thought or effort; not exact or thorough: *careless work, a careless worker.* **3** not caring or troubling. *adj.* **—care′less·ly,** *adv.* **—care′less·ness,** *n.*

ca·ress (kə res′) **1** touch or stroke tenderly; embrace or kiss. **2** a touch showing affection; a tender embrace or kiss. 1 *v.*, 2 *n.*

care·tak·er (ker′tāk′ər) a person, especially a janitor, who takes care of a building, estate, etc. *n.*

car·fare (kär′fer′) the money to pay for riding on a streetcar, bus, etc.: *He had enough money for carfare home. n.*

car·go (kär′gō) the freight carried by a ship or airplane; a load: *a cargo of wheat. n., pl.* **car·goes** or **car·gos.**

Car·ib·be·an (kar′ə bē′en or kə rib′ē ən) of or having to do with the Caribbean Sea or the islands in it. *adj.*

car·i·bou (kar′ə bü or ker′ə bü) any of several kinds of North American reindeer: *There are great herds of caribou in the Barren Lands. n., pl.* **car·i·bou** or **car·i·bous.** Also spelled **cariboo.**

☛ **Caribou** came into English through Canadian

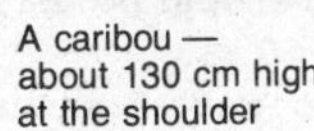
A caribou — about 130 cm high at the shoulder

French from a North American Indian word for this animal, meaning 'one that paws or scratches,' from the way it paws through snow to reach the grass underneath.

car·ies (ker′ēz or ker′ē ēz′) the process of decay in teeth or bones: *Caries of the teeth is caused by bacteria.* *n.*

car·il·lon (kar′ə lon′ or ker′ə lon′) a set of bells for playing melodies: *There is a carillon in the tower of the cathedral.* *n.*

car·i·ole[1] or **car·ri·ole**[1] (kar′ē ōl′ or ker′ē ōl′) **1** a small one-horse carriage. **2** a covered cart. *n.*

car·i·ole[2] or **car·ri·ole**[2] (kar′ē ōl′ or ker′ē ōl′) *Cdn.* **1** a one-horse sleigh resembling a cutter. **2** a dog sled, often richly decorated, equipped to carry one person lying down: *The sick trapper was brought to the post in a cariole.* **3** to ride in a cariole. 1, 2 *n.*, 3 *v.*, **car·i·oled** or **car·ri·olled, car·i·ol·ing** or **car·ri·ol·ling.**

car·load (kär′lōd′) **1** the number or amount that an automobile can carry: *We passed a carload of people bound for the party.* **2** the amount that a freight car can hold or carry: *a carload of grain.* *n.*

car·nage (kär′nij) the killing of a great number of people: *The carnage caused by the atomic bomb was shocking.* *n.*

car·na·tion (kär nā′shən) a red, white, or pink flower that has a spicy smell and is grown in gardens and greenhouses. *n.*

car·ni·val (kär′nə vəl) **1** a place of amusement or a travelling show having merry-go-rounds, games, etc. **2** feasting and merrymaking; a celebration. **3** a program of events involving a particular sport, institution, etc.: *There were many exhibitions of swimming and diving skill at the water carnival.* *n.*

☛ **Carnival** came into English in the sixteenth century through Italian from the Latin name for the period immediately before Lent, *carnelevamen,* meaning literally 'the putting aside of meat.'

car·niv·o·rous (kär niv′ə rəs) feeding chiefly on flesh: *Cats, dogs, lions, tigers, and bears are carnivorous animals.* *adj.*

car·ol (kar′əl or ker′əl) **1** a song of joy. **2** a hymn of joy: *Christmas carols.* **3** sing; sing joyously; praise with carols: *The birds carol in the early morning.* 1, 2 *n.*, 3 *v.*, **car·olled** or **car·oled, car·ol·ling** or **car·ol·ing.** —**car′ol·ler** or **car′ol·er,** *n.*

carp[1] (kärp) find fault; complain. *v.*

carp[2] (kärp) a bony fresh-water fish that lives in ponds and slow streams. *n.*

car·pen·ter (kär′pən tər) a worker who builds the wooden parts of houses, barns, ships, etc. *n.*

hat, āge, fär; let, ēqual, tėrm; it, īce
hot, ōpen, ôrder; oil, out; cup, pu̇t, rüle
əbove, takən, pencəl, lemən, circəs
ch, child; ng, long; sh, ship
th, thin; ᴛʜ, then; zh, measure

car·pen·try (kär′pən trē) the work of a carpenter. *n.*

car·pet (kär′pit) **1** a heavy, woven fabric used for covering floors and stairs. **2** a smooth, soft, or bright stretch of grass, flowers, etc.: *a carpet of leaves.* **3** to cover with a carpet: *In the spring the ground was carpeted with violets.* 1, 2 *n.*, 3 *v.*

car·riage (kar′ij or ker′ij) **1** a vehicle that moves on wheels: *Carriages are usually pulled by horses and are used to carry people.* **2** a wheeled frame which supports a gun and by which it is moved from place to place. **3** a moving part of a machine that supports another part: *a typewriter carriage.* **4** a manner of holding the head and body; bearing: *She has a queenly carriage.* **5** the taking of persons or goods from one place to another. **6** the cost of taking anything from one place to another: *Pay 50 cents for carriage.* *n.*

car·ri·er (kar′ē ər or ker′ē ər) **1** a person or thing that takes goods, packages, and messages from one place to another. **2** a person or thing that carries a disease: *Carriers are often healthy people that do not get the disease themselves but can pass its germs on to others.* *n.*

car·ri·ole (kar′ē ōl′ or ker′ē ōl′) See **cariole.**

car·ri·on (kar′ē ən or ker′ē ən) dead and decaying flesh: *Vultures live on carrion.* *n.*

car·rot (kar′ət or ker′ət) a plant having a long, tapering, yellowish-red or orange-colored root that is used as a vegetable. *n.*

☛ **Carrot** and **carat** are pronounced the same.

car·ry (kar′ē or ker′ē) **1** take from one place or time to another: *Buses carry passengers. This story will carry your thoughts back to the first of the year.* **2** bear the weight of; hold up; support: *Those columns carry the roof.* **3** hold one's body and head in a certain way: *This boy carries himself well.* **4** capture; win: *Our side carried the election for club president.* **5** cover the distance: *His voice will carry to the back of the room. This gun will carry one kilometre.* **6** keep in stock: *Our store carries men's clothing.* **7** transfer a number from one place or column in the sum to the next: *A 10 in the 1's column must be carried to the 10's column.* *v.*, **car·ried, car·ry·ing.**

carry away, arouse strong feeling in; to influence beyond reason: *The little girl was so carried away by the sad story that she began to cry.*

carry on, a do; manage or conduct: *He carried on a successful business.* **b** keep going; continue: *We must carry on in our effort to win the peace.* **c** *Informal.* behave wildly or foolishly: *The small boys really carried on at the party.*

carry out, do; get done; complete: *He carried out his job well.*

car·ry·all[1] (kar′ē ol′ or ker′ē ol′, kar′ē ôl′ or ker′ē ôl′) **1** a lightweight, covered one-horse carriage. **2** cariole. *n.*

☛ **Carryall**[1] is a variation of **cariole,** which comes from the Canadian French word for this sleigh. To

English speakers, *cariole* sounded like 'carry-all,' which described the sleigh.

car·ry·all² (kar′ē ol′ or ker′ē ol′, kar′ē ôl′ or ker′ē ôl′) 1 any of several vehicles so named because of their large capacity. 2 a large bag or basket. *n.*

☛ **Carryall²** is a noun use of the phrase 'carry all.'

car·sick (kär′sick′) feeling sick to the stomach as a result of the motion of a car, train, etc. *adj.* **—car′sick′ness,** *n.*

cart (kärt) 1 a vehicle with two wheels, used in farming and for carrying heavy loads: *Horses, donkeys, and oxen are often used to pull carts.* 2 a light wagon used for delivering goods or for general business. 3 a small, wheeled vehicle that is moved by hand: *a grocery cart.* 4 carry in a cart: *Cart away this rubbish.* 1–3 *n.,* 4 *v.*

put the cart before the horse, reverse the proper or natural order of things or ideas.

car·ti·lage (kär′tə lij) a tough, elastic substance forming parts of the skeleton of vertebrates; gristle: *The tip of the nose consists of cartilage and skin.* *n.*

car·ton (kär′tən) a box made of cardboard: *Pack the books in large cartons.* *n.*

car·toon (kär tün′) 1 a sketch or drawing showing persons, things, or events in an amusing way. 2 a comic strip. 3 a motion picture made from drawings rather than photographs: *Some of the old Mickey Mouse cartoons are on T.V. today.* *n.*

car·toon·ist (kär tün′ist) a person skilled in drawing cartoons. *n.*

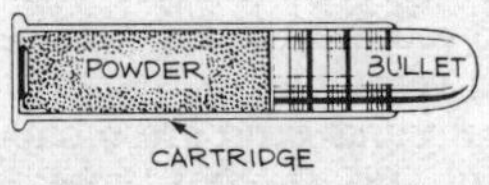

A cartridge

car·tridge (kär′trij) 1 a case made of metal, plastic, or cardboard for holding gunpowder. 2 a small container holding a refill of ink for a pen, a roll of film, etc.: *I bought several spare cartridges for my pen.* *n.*

cart·wheel (kärt′wēl′ or kärt′hwēl′) 1 the wheel of a cart. 2 a sideways handspring or somersault, made with the arms and legs stretched out stiffly like the spokes of a wheel. *n.*

carve (kärv) 1 cut into slices or pieces: *Father carves the meat at the table.* 2 cut; make by cutting: *Statues are often carved from marble, stone, or wood.* 3 decorate with figures or designs cut on the surface: *He carved the ivory box with great care.* *v.,* **carved, carv·ing. —carv′er,** *n.*

carv·ing (kär′ving) 1 carved work: *wood carving, stone carving, delicate carvings in ivory.* 2 See **carve.** *Father is carving the meat.* 1 *n.,* 2 *v.*

cas·cade (kas kād′) 1 a small waterfall. 2 anything like this: *Her dress had a cascade of ruffles down the front.* *n.*

case¹ (kās) 1 any special condition of a person or thing: *A case of measles kept me away from school.* 2 an instance or example: *The children agreed that every case of cheating should be punished. His accident was another case of reckless driving.* 3 a person who has a disease or injury; patient: *Hospitals had many cases of polio before a vaccine to prevent it was developed.* 4 a matter for a law court to decide: *The case will be brought before the court tomorrow.* *n.*

in any case, anyhow; no matter what happens: *In any case, you should prepare for the worst.*

in case of, in the event of; if there should be: *In case of fire walk quietly to the nearest door.*

case² (kās) 1 anything to hold or cover something: *Put the knife back in its case.* 2 a box: *There is a big case full of books in the hall.* *n.*

case·ment (kās′mənt) a window opening on vertical hinges. *n.*

cash (kash) 1 money in the form of coins and bills: *Mother didn't have enough cash with her to pay for the book, so she wrote a cheque.* 2 change into cash; give cash for: *The bank will cash your five-dollar cheque.* 3 get cash for: *I cashed three cheques for $10 each and got $30.* 1 *n.,* 2, 3 *v.*

cash·ew (kash′ü) 1 a small, kidney-shaped nut that is good to eat. 2 the tropical American tree that it grows on. *n.*

cash·ier¹ (kash ēr′) a person in charge of money in a bank, or in any business. *n.*

cash·ier² (kash ēr′) dismiss from the armed forces for some dishonorable act: *The dishonest officer was deprived of his rank and cashiered.* *v.*

cash·mere (kash′mēr) a fine, soft wool used in making sweaters, shawls, etc. *n.*

cash register a machine used in stores for holding the money paid for purchases and for totalling up the amount and number of the sales: *Some cash registers print the cost of each article and the total of the bill on a slip of paper, which is given to the customer as a receipt.*

cask (kask) barrel: *A cask may be large or small, and is usually made to hold liquids.* *n.*

cas·ket (kas′kit) 1 coffin. 2 a small box or chest, used to hold jewels, letters, etc. *n.*

cas·se·role (kas′ə rōl′) 1 a covered baking dish, in which food can be both cooked and served. 2 the food cooked and served in a casserole. *n.*

cast (kast) 1 throw; fling or hurl: *cast a stone. The thieves were cast into jail.* 2 throw one end of a fishing line out into the water. 3 throw off; let fall; shed: *The snake cast its skin.* 4 a throw; the distance a thing is thrown: *The fisherman made a long cast with his line.* 5 direct or turn: *He cast a glance of surprise at me.* 6 shape by pouring or squeezing into a mould to harden: *Metal is first melted and then cast.* 7 something made by casting: *A cast in the likeness of Laurier was set up as a monument.* 8 a mould used in casting. 9 a plaster support used to keep a broken bone in place while it is mending: *He had his arm in a cast for more than a month.* 10 select for a part in a play: *Our teacher has cast Robert as Long John Silver in the school play.* 11 the actors in a play: *The cast was listed in the program.* 12 the outward form or look; appearance: *His face had a gloomy cast.* 13 a slight amount of color; tinge: *a white dress with a pink cast.* 14 a squint. 1–3, 5, 6, 10 *v.,* **cast, cast·ing;** 4, 7–9, 11–14 *n.*

cast about, look around; search: *He cast about for an answer, but couldn't think of one.*

cast a ballot, vote.

hat, āge, fär; let, ēqual, tėrm; it, īce
hot, ōpen, ôrder; oil, out; cup, pu̇t, rüle
əbove, takən, pencəl, lemən, circəs
ch, child; ng, long; sh, ship
th, thin; ᴛʜ, then; zh, measure

cast down, a turn downward; lower: *His head was cast down in shame.* b make sad or discouraged: *He was cast down by the bad news.*
cast off, a let loose; set free: *cast off a boat from its moorings.* b make the last row of stitches in knitting.
☞ **Cast** and **caste** are pronounced the same.

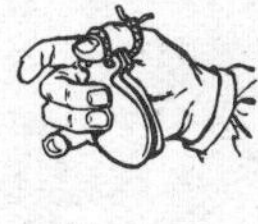
Castanets

cas·ta·net (kas′tə net′) a small instrument made of wood or ivory, consisting of two parts which are held in the hand and clicked together rhythmically, especially to accompany dancing. *n.*

caste (kast) 1 one of the social classes into which Hindus are divided: *By tradition a Hindu is born into the caste of his father and cannot depart from it.* 2 an exclusive social group; a distinct class. 3 a social system having distinct classes separated by differences of rank, wealth, or position. *n.*
☞ **Caste** and **cast** are pronounced the same.

cast·er or **cas·tor** (kas′tər) a small wheel on a swivel, set into the base of a piece of furniture or other heavy object to make it easier to move. *n.*

cast iron a hard, brittle form of iron made by melting iron and pouring it into a mould to harden.

A European castle
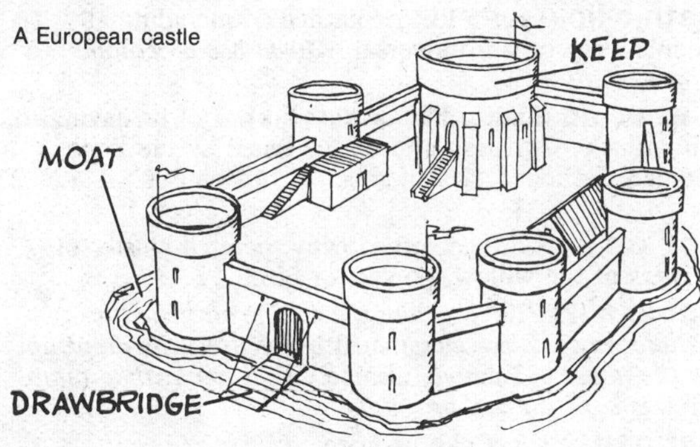

cas·tle (kas′əl) 1 a large building or group of buildings with thick walls, towers, and other defences against attack: *The knight rode over the drawbridge into the castle.* 2 a large and stately residence. 3 in chess, a piece shaped like a tower; rook. *n.*

cast·off (kast′of′) 1 something that has been thrown away or put aside as no longer useful: *You can use those gloves to work in the garden; they're castoffs. He always had to wear his older brother's castoffs.* 2 a person who has been abandoned or cast aside. *n.*

cas·tor (kas′tər) See **caster.**

castor oil a yellow oil obtained from the beans of a tropical plant, used as a strong laxative, a lubricant, etc.

cas·u·al (kazh′ü əl) 1 happening by chance; not planned or expected: *Our long friendship began with a casual meeting at a party.* 2 careless; without plan or method: *I gave a casual glance at the newspaper. adj.* —**cas′u·al·ly,** *adv.* —**cas′u·al·ness,** *n.*

cas·u·al·ty (kazh′ü əl tē or kazh′əl tē) 1 a member of the armed forces who has been wounded, killed, or captured: *The war produced many casualties.* 2 a person injured or killed in an accident: *The car was a wreck, but there were no casualties. n., pl.* **cas·u·al·ties.**

cat[1] (kat) 1 a small, tame, furry, meat-eating animal having short ears, long whiskers, and soft paws with claws that can be drawn in: *Cats can see better in dim light than people can.* 2 any animal of the group including cats, lions, tigers, and leopards. *n.*
let the cat out of the bag, tell a secret: *It was supposed to be a surprise party, but he let the cat out of the bag.*
rain cats and dogs, rain very hard.

cat[2] (kat) caterpillar tractor. *n.*

cat·a·logue (kat′ə log′) 1 a list of items in a collection, including comments or descriptions and sometimes pictures: *A library usually has a catalogue of its books, arranged in alphabetical order. Some business companies print catalogues showing pictures and prices of what they have to sell.* 2 make a list of; enter in the proper place in a list: *He catalogued all the insects in his collection.* 1 *n.,* 2 *v.,* **cat·a·logued, cat·a·logu·ing.** Also spelled **catalog.**

ca·tal·pa (kə tal′pə) a tree found mainly in the warm parts of eastern North America, having heart-shaped leaves, clusters of bell-shaped flowers, and long pods. *n.*

A catamaran
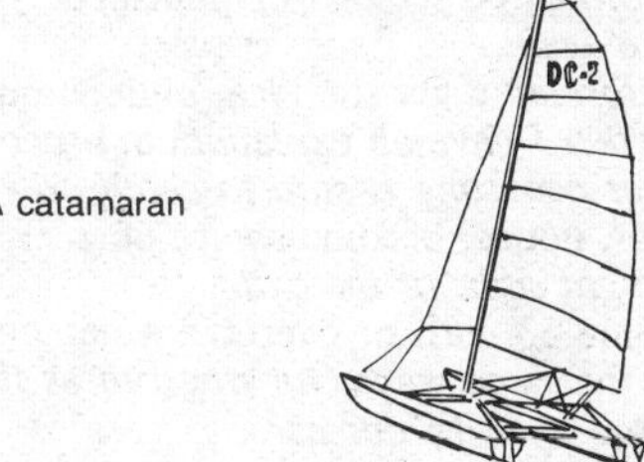

cat·a·ma·ran (kat′ə mə ran′) 1 a boat having two hulls or floats joined side by side by a frame. 2 *Cdn.* a type of sled consisting of a platform on two runners, used for hauling lumber, etc. 3 a raft made of two or more logs fastened beside each other but some distance apart, used in parts of India, South America, etc. *n.*

cat·a·pult (kat′ə pult′) 1 a weapon used in ancient times for shooting stones, arrows, etc. 2 slingshot. 3 a device for launching an airplane from the deck of a ship. 4 shoot from a catapult; throw; hurl: *He stopped his bicycle so suddenly that he was catapulted over the handle bars.* 1–3 *n.,* 4 *v.*

cat·a·ract (kat′ə rakt′) 1 a large, steep waterfall. 2 a violent rush or downpour of water. 3 a disease of the eye in which the lens develops a cloudy film causing faulty vision or blindness. *n.*

ca·tarrh (kə tär′) an inflamed condition, usually in the nose or throat, causing a discharge of mucus or phlegm. *n.*

ca·tas·tro·phe (kə tas′trə fē) a sudden, widespread,

or extraordinary disaster; a great calamity or misfortune: *A big earthquake or flood is a catastrophe. It was a catastrophe for the town when the mine closed and the men lost their jobs.* *n.*

cat·bird (kat′bėrd′) a North American songbird that can make a sound like a cat mewing. *n.*

cat·call (kat′kol′ or kat′kôl′) **1** a shrill cry or whistle to express scornful disapproval: *The speaker's promise of free money for everyone was met with catcalls.* **2** attack with or make catcalls: *They catcalled the speaker.* 1 *n.*, 2 *v.*

catch (kach) **1** take and hold something moving; seize; trap; capture: *Catch the ball with both hands. The cat catches mice. The policeman caught the thief. The rat was caught in the trap. We were caught in the storm.* **2** attract and hold the attention of: *Bright colors catch the baby's eye.* **3** take; get: *Paper catches fire easily. Put a warm coat on, or you will catch cold. He spoke so rapidly that I failed to catch the meaning of what he said. You have just five minutes to catch your train.* **4** come on suddenly; surprise: *Mother caught me with my hand in the cookie jar.* **5** take notice of; discover: *He thought I wouldn't catch his error.* **6** act as the catcher in baseball: *He catches for our school team.* **7** the act of catching: *He made a fine catch with one hand.* **8** anything that catches: *The catch on that door is broken.* **9** *Informal.* a hidden meaning; some difficulty that does not appear on the surface: *There is a catch to that question; be careful how you answer it.* **10** anything that is caught: *A dozen fish is a good catch.* **11** in music, a round (def. 23). 1–6 *v.*, **caught, catch·ing;** 7–11 *n.*

catch it, *Informal,* be scolded or punished: *We'll catch it if we are late again.*

catch on, *Informal.* **a** get the idea; understand: *She caught on when I gave an explanation.* **b** become popular: *That new song is sure to catch on.*

catch sight of, notice; become aware of; see: *The dog suddenly caught sight of the cat.*

catch up, come up with or overtake a person or thing going the same way: *Our dog ran as fast as he could to catch up with our car.*

catch–all (katch′ol′ or katch′ôl′) **1** a container for odds and ends: *That drawer is our kitchen catch-all.* **2** a term, question, explanation, etc. used to cover a number of possible examples: *'Etc.' in the definition is used as a catch-all.* *n.*

catch·er (kach′ər) a baseball player who stands behind the batter to catch the ball thrown by the pitcher. *n.*

catch·ing (kach′ing) causing infection; likely to spread from one person to another. *adj.*

catch·up (kach′əp) ketchup. *n.*

catch·y (kach′ē) attractive; easy to remember: *a catchy tune.* *adj.*, **catch·i·er, catch·i·est.**

cat·e·chism (kat′ə kiz′əm) **1** a book of questions and answers, especially one about religion. **2** any set of questions. *n.*

cat·e·go·ry (kat′ə gô′rē) a division in a scheme of classification; class: *Helen groups all people into two categories: those she likes and those she dislikes.* *n., pl.* **cat·e·go·ries.**

ca·ter (kā′tər) **1** provide food or supplies: *He runs a restaurant and also caters for weddings and parties.* **2** provide what is needed or wanted: *The new magazine caters to children who are interested in crafts.* *v.*

cat·er·pil·lar (kat′ər pil′ər) **1** the larva or wormlike form in which insects such as the butterfly and the moth hatch from the egg. **2** caterpillar tractor. *n.*

A caterpillar of one kind of moth — about 7 cm long

A caterpillar tractor

caterpillar tractor a tractor that can travel over rough land on wheels that run inside two endless belts of linked steel plates.

cat·fish (kat′fish′) any of several kinds of fish without scales and with long, slender feelers about the mouth that resemble a cat's whiskers. *n., pl.* **cat·fish** or **cat·fish·es.**

cat·gut (kat′gut′) the dried and twisted intestines of sheep or other animals, used for violin strings, racket strings, and surgical stitches. *n.*

ca·the·dral (kə thē′drəl) **1** the official church of a bishop: *The bishop has a throne in the cathedral.* **2** a large or important church. *n.*

cath·o·lic (kath′ə lik′ or kath′lik) including all people; very broad; universal: *Music has a catholic appeal.* *adj.*

Cath·o·lic (kath′ə lik′ or kath′lik) **1** of or having to do with the Christian church governed by the Pope; Roman Catholic. **2** a member of this church. 1 *adj.*, 2 *n.*

cat·kin (kat′kin) a soft, downy, pointed cluster of flowers of the willow, poplar, or birch. *n.*

cat·like (kat′līk′) **1** like a cat: *She stretched in a catlike way.* **2** noiseless; stealthy: *Catlike, he crept up to the house.* **3** active; nimble: *With one catlike jump, he was over the railing.* *adj.*

cat nap a short nap or doze. *n.*

cat·nip (kat′nip) a plant resembling mint, with scented leaves that cats like. *n.*

cat·skin·ner (kat′skin′ər) a person who operates a caterpillar tractor: *The catskinners worked long hours on the highway through the bush.* *n.*

cat·sup (kat′səp) ketchup. *n.*

cat–tail (kat′tāl′) a tall marsh plant with flowers in long, round, furry, brown spikes; bulrush. *n.*

cat·tle (kat′əl) **1** cows, bulls, and steers; oxen. **2** farm animals; livestock. *n.*

cat·tle·man (kat′əl mən) a man who raises or takes care of cattle. *n., pl.* **cat·tle·men** (kat′əl mən).

cat–train (kat′trān′) *Cdn.* a series of large sleds pulled by a caterpillar tractor: *Cat-trains are used in the North for hauling goods over the frozen muskeg in winter time.* *n.*

cat·walk (kat′wok′ or kat′wôk′) a narrow place to walk, as on a bridge. *n.*

hat, āge, fär; let, ēqual, tėrm; it, īce
hot, ōpen, ôrder; oil, out; cup, pu̇t, rüle
əbove, takən, pencəl, lemən, circəs
ch, child; ng, long; sh, ship
th, thin; ᴛʜ, then; zh, measure

caught (kot or kôt) See **catch.** *He caught the ball. The mouse was caught in a trap.* *v.*

☞ **Caught** and **cot** are sometimes pronounced the same.

caul·dron or **cal·dron** (kol′drən or kôl′drən) a large pot, kettle, or boiler: *Maple syrup may be boiled to sugar in a cauldron.* *n.*

A head of cauliflower

cau·li·flow·er (ko′lə flou′ər or kô′lə flou′ər) **1** a plant having a solid, white head with a few leaves around it. **2** the head itself, used as a vegetable. *n.*

caulk or **calk** (kok or kôk) fill up a seam, crack, or joint so that it will not leak; make watertight: *We had to caulk the seams of our boat again this spring.* *v.*

cause (koz or kôz) **1** a person, thing, or event that makes something happen: *The flood was the cause of much damage.* **2** make happen; make do; bring about: *The fire caused much damage. A loud noise caused me to jump back.* **3** a reason or occasion for action: *The hero's return was a cause for celebration. You have no cause to complain.* **4** a subject or movement in which many people take an interest: *World peace is the cause she works for.* 1, 3, 4 *n.*, 2 *v.*, **caused, caus·ing.**

☞ See note at **reason.**

cause·way (koz′wā′ or kôz′wā′) a raised road or path, usually built across wet ground or shallow water. *n.*

cau·tion (ko′shən or kô′shən) **1** the practice of taking care to be safe, or of never taking chances; being very careful: *Use caution in crossing streets.* **2** a warning: *A sign with 'Danger!' on it is a caution.* **3** warn; urge to be careful: *The policeman cautioned us against playing in the street.* 1, 2 *n.*, 3 *v.*

cau·tious (ko′shəs or kô′shəs) very careful; not taking chances: *My sister is a cautious driver.* *adj.* **—cau′tious·ly,** *adv.* **—cau′tious·ness,** *n.*

cav·al·cade (kav′əl kād′ or kav′əl kād′) **1** a procession of persons riding on horses, in carriages, or in automobiles. **2** a series of scenes or events: *a cavalcade of sports.* *n.*

cav·a·lier (kav′ə lēr′) **1** a horseman, mounted soldier, or knight. **2** a courteous gentleman. **3** careless in manner; free and easy; offhand: *He did not take us seriously, but just gave a cavalier reply.* **4** haughty: *People were often irritated by his cavalier attitude toward them.* 1, 2 *n.*, 3, 4 *adj.*

cav·al·ry (kav′əl rē) soldiers who fight on horseback. *n., pl.* **cav·al·ries.**

cave (kāv) **1** a hollow space underground: *He found four caves on the side of the hill.* **2 cave in,** fall in; sink: *The weight of the snow caused the roof of the arena to cave in.* 1 *n.*, 2 *v.*, **caved, cav·ing.**

cave–in (kāv′in′) **1** a caving in; collapse: *a cave-in of a tunnel.* **2** a place where something has caved in. *n.*

cave man a man who lived in caves in very early times.

cav·ern (kav′ərn) a large cave. *n.*

cav·ern·ous (kav′ər nəs) **1** like a cavern; large and hollow: *a cavernous cellar.* **2** full of caverns: *cavernous mountains.* *adj.*

cav·i·ty (kav′ə tē) a hole; a hollow place: *Cavities in teeth are caused by decay.* *n., pl.* **cav·i·ties.**

ca·vort (kə vôrt′) prance about: *A horse cavorts when he feels excited.* *v.*

caw (ko or kô) **1** the harsh cry made by a crow or raven. **2** make this cry. 1 *n.*, 2 *v.*

cay·use (kī yüs′) an Indian pony of the western parts of Canada and the United States. *n.*

CBC or **C.B.C.** the Canadian Broadcasting Corporation, a Crown corporation in the field of radio and television broadcasting.

cc or **c.c.** cubic centimetre; cubic centimetres. Also written cm^3.

Cdn. Canadian.

cease (sēs) stop: *The music ceased suddenly.* *v.*, **ceased, ceas·ing.**

cease·less (sēs′lis) never stopping; going on all the time. *adj.* **—cease′less·ly,** *adv.*

Ce·cro·pi·a moth (sə krō′pē ə) a large silkworm moth of eastern North America whose larvae feed on trees: *The Cecropia moth has a wing span of more than 15 centimetres.*

ce·dar (sē′dər) **1** an evergreen tree of the same family as the pine, having branches that spread widely, scale-like leaves, and fragrant, durable wood. **2** its light, soft, pale-brown wood: *Cedar is used for making posts, shingles, chests, etc.* *n.* See also **red cedar.**

cede (sēd) give up; surrender; hand over to another: *France ceded Canada to Britain after the defeat of Montcalm in 1759.* *v.*, **ced·ed, ced·ing.**

☞ **Cede** and **seed** are pronounced the same.

ce·dil·la (sə dil′ə) a mark like a comma that is put under the letter *c* in certain words to show that the *c* has the sound of *s: A cedilla is used in façade and similar words that come from French.* *n.*

ceil·ing (sēl′ing) **1** the inside top covering of a room. **2** the greatest height to which an aircraft can go under certain conditions: *That jet plane has a ceiling of over 18 kilometres.* **3** an upper limit: *A ceiling was placed on the amount of rent landlords could charge.* *n.*

cel·e·brate (sel′ə brāt′) **1** observe a special time or day with activities of a proper kind: *We celebrated Christmas with a tree and presents.* **2** have a joyful time; make merry: *The people celebrated when the war ended.* *v.*, **cel·e·brat·ed, cel·e·brat·ing.**

cel·e·brat·ed (sel′ə brāt′id) famous; well-known; much talked about: *Charles Dickens was a celebrated author.* *adj.*

cel·e·bra·tion (sel′ə brā′shən) **1** special services or activities in honor of a particular person, act, time, or day: *The university's centennial celebration was a big event.* **2** the act of celebrating. *n.*

ce·leb·ri·ty (sə leb′rə tē) **1** a famous person: *Some people collect autographs of celebrities.* **2** fame; being well known or much talked about. *n., pl.* **ce·leb·ri·ties.**

cel·er·y (sel′ər ē or sel′rē) a plant having long, crisp stalks which are eaten raw or cooked as a vegetable. *n.*

ce·les·tial (sə les′chəl) **1** of the sky; having something to do with the sky: *The sun, moon, planets, and stars are celestial bodies.* **2** heavenly; divine; very good or beautiful: *celestial music. adj.*

cell (sel) **1** a small room in a prison, convent, or monastery. **2** any small, hollow place: *Bees store honey in the cells of a honeycomb.* **3** a very small unit of living matter: *All animals and plants are made of cells, which are formed of a small amount of living matter, called protoplasm, surrounded by a very thin membrane. The body has blood cells, nerve cells, muscle cells, etc.* **4** a container holding materials that produce electricity by chemical action; a small battery: *He bought two cells for his flashlight. n.*

☛ **Cell** and **sell** are pronounced the same.

cel·lar (sel′ər) an underground room or rooms, usually under a building and often used for storing fuel and food; basement. *n.*

☛ **Cellar** and **seller** are pronounced the same.

cel·list (chel′ist) a person who is skilled in playing the cello. *n.*

A cello

cel·lo (chel′ō) a musical instrument shaped like a violin but much larger and having a lower, mellower tone: *When a cello is played, it rests upright on the floor and is held between the knees of the player, who is seated. n., pl.* **cel·los.** Also called **violoncello.**

cel·lo·phane (sel′ə fān′) a transparent substance somewhat like paper, made from cellulose: *Cellophane is used as a wrapping to keep food, candy, tobacco, etc. fresh and clean. n.*

cel·lu·lose (sel′yə lōs′) a substance that forms the walls of plant cells; the woody part of trees and plants: *Wood, cotton, flax, and hemp are largely cellulose. Cellulose is used to make paper, plastics, etc. n.*

Cel·si·us (sel′sē əs) of, based on, or according to the Celsius scale for measuring temperature, in which 0 degrees is the temperature at which water freezes and 100 degrees is the temperature at which water boils. *adj.*

☛ Named after Anders *Celsius* (1701-1744), a Swedish astronomer, who invented the Celsius scale.

Celsius thermometer a thermometer marked off according to the Celsius scale. See **thermometer** for picture.

Cel·tic (sel′tik or kel′tik) of or having to do with a people including the Irish, Highland Scots, Welsh, and ancient Britons. *adj.*

ce·ment (sə ment′) **1** a fine, grey powder made by burning clay and limestone, that becomes solid and hard when mixed with water: *Cement is mixed with water and sand, gravel, or crushed stone to make concrete.* **2** any soft substance that hardens to make things stick together: *rubber cement.* **3** fasten together or make firm with, or as if with, cement: *A broken plate can be cemented. The marriage of their daughter to their friends' son cemented their friendship.* **4** concrete: *Our basement has a cement floor.* **5** pour or spread concrete for: *The workmen were cementing the sidewalk.* 1, 2, 4 *n.,* 3, 5 *v.*

cem·e·ter·y (sem′ə ter′ē) a place for burying the dead; graveyard. *n., pl.* **cem·e·ter·ies.**

cen·ser (sen′sər) a container in which incense is burned. *n.*

☛ **Censer** and **censor** are pronounced the same.

cen·sor (sen′sər) **1** a person who examines and, if necessary, changes books, letters, motion pictures, etc. to see that they contain nothing offensive and are satisfactory to the government or to some other organization. **2** examine or change as a censor, often making changes or cutting out parts: *All letters from the battlefront were censored.* **3** take out a part or parts of news reports, letters, books, motion pictures, etc.: *Several scenes in the movie had been censored before it was shown in Manitoba.* 1 *n.,* 2, 3 *v.*

☛ See note at **censer.**

cen·sor·ship (sen′sər ship′) the act or practice of censoring: *Censorship of the news is common in time of war. n.*

cen·sure (sen′shər) **1** an expression of disapproval; unfavorable opinion; criticism: *Censure is sometimes harder to bear than punishment.* **2** find fault with; criticize: *His employer censured him for being late.* 1 *n.,* 2 *v.,* **cen·sured, cen·sur·ing.**

cen·sus (sen′səs) an official count of the people of a country or district: *A census is taken to find out the total number of people living there and the numbers in different age groups, occupations, etc. n.*

cent (sent) a coin of Canada and the United States: *There are 100 cents in one dollar. Symbol:* ¢ *n.*

A centaur

cen·taur (sen′tôr) in Greek myths, a monster that had the head, arms, and chest of a man, and the body and legs of a horse. *n.*

cen·ten·ni·al (sen ten′ē əl) **1** a hundredth anniversary: *Canada celebrated its centennial in 1967.* **2** of or having to do with 100 years or a hundredth anniversary: *a centennial project.* 1 *n.,* 2 *adj.*

cen·ter (sen′tər) See **centre.**

cen·ti·grade (sen′tə grād′) Celsius. *adj.*

hat, āge, fär; let, ēqual, tėrm; it, īce
hot, ōpen, ôrder; oil, out; cup, pu̇t, rüle
əbove, takən, pencəl, lemən, circəs
ch, child; ng, long; sh, ship
th, thin; ᴛʜ, then; zh, measure

cen·ti·me·tre (sen′tə mē′tər) a measure of length equal to 10 millimetres; one one-hundredth of a metre. *Symbol:* cm *n.* Also spelled **centimeter.**

cen·ti·pede (sen′tə pēd′) a small wormlike animal having a long, flat body and many pairs of legs. *n.*

☛ **Centipede** comes from French *centipède,* made up of Latin *centum,* meaning 'hundred,' and *pes, pedis,* meaning 'foot.'

cen·tral (sen′trəl) **1** of the centre; being or forming the centre: *The sun is central in the solar system.* **2** at, in, or near the centre: *The park is in the central part of the city. We shop at a central market.* **3** main; chief; principal: *What is the central idea in this story? adj.* **—cen′tral·ly,** *adv.*

Central American **1** of or having to do with Central America or its people. **2** a person born in or living in Central America.

cen·tre or **cen·ter** (sen′tər) **1** a point within a circle or sphere equally distant from all points of the circumference or surface. **2** the middle point, place, or part: *the centre of a room.* **3** the person, thing, or group in a middle position. **4** a point toward which people or things go, or from which they come; a main point: *Toronto is a centre of trade.* **5** place in or at a centre: *The table should be centred on the stage.* **6** collect or gather together at a centre: *A large number of soldiers are centred at Calgary.* **7** have a centre; be concentrated; focus: *All his hopes centred on being with the team.* 1–4 *n.,* 5–7 *v.,* **cen·tred** or **cen·tered, cen·tring** or **cen·ter·ing.**

cen·tu·ry (sen′chə rē) **1** each 100 years, counting from some special time, such as the birth of Christ: *The first century is 1 to 100; the nineteenth century is 1801 to 1900; the twentieth century is 1901 to 2000.* **2** a period of 100 years: *From 1824 to 1924 is a century. n., pl.* **cen·tu·ries.**

ce·ram·ics (sə ram′iks) **1** the art of making articles from baked clay. **2** articles of pottery, earthenware, porcelain, etc. *n.*

ce·re·al (sēr′ē əl) **1** any grass that produces a grain which is used as a food: *Wheat, rice, corn, oats, and barley are cereals.* **2** the grain. **3** food made from the grain: *Oatmeal and corn meal are cereals. n.*

☛ **Cereal** and **serial** are pronounced the same.

cer·e·mo·ni·al (ser′ə mō′nē əl) **1** of or having to do with ceremony: *The ceremonial costumes were beautiful.* **2** the formal actions suitable for an occasion: *Bowing the head and kneeling are ceremonials of religion.* **3** very formal: *The queen received her guests in a ceremonial way.* 1, 3 *adj.,* 2 *n.*

cer·e·mo·ni·ous (ser′ə mō′nē əs) very formal; extremely polite. *adj.*

cer·e·mo·ny (ser′ə mō′nē) **1** a special form or set of acts to be done on special occasions such as weddings, funerals, graduations, Christmas, or Easter: *The marriage ceremony was performed in the church.* **2** very polite conduct; a way of conducting oneself that follows all the rules of polite social behavior: *The old gentleman showed us to the door with a great deal of ceremony. n., pl.* **cer·e·mo·nies.**
stand on ceremony, be very formal; insist on formal behavior: *The premier does not stand on ceremony but always makes the people he meets feel comfortable and relaxed.*

ce·rise (sə rēz′ or sə rēs) bright, pinkish red. *n., adj.*

cer·tain (sėr′tən) **1** sure: *It is certain that 3 and 2 do not make 6.* **2** definite but not named; some: *Certain plants will not grow in this country. adj.*

cer·tain·ly (sėr′tən lē) **1** surely; without doubt. **2** yes; of course: *Certainly you may come to my party. adv.*

cer·tain·ty (sėr′tən tē) **1** freedom from doubt; being certain: *The man's certainty was amusing, for we knew that he was wrong.* **2** a fact that one is sure of: *Spring and summer are certainties. n., pl.* **cer·tain·ties.**

cer·tif·i·cate (sər tif′ə kit) a written or printed statement that may be used as proof of some fact: *Your birth certificate gives your full name and the date and place of your birth. n.*

cer·ti·fy (sėr′tə fī′) **1** declare something true or correct by a spoken, written, or printed statement: *The doctor certified that the woman was dead.* **2** guarantee the quality or value of: *The manufacturer has certified that this child's car seat is safe. v.,* **cer·ti·fied, cer·ti·fy·ing.**

ces·sa·tion (se sā′shən) ceasing; a pause; stop: *a cessation of fighting. n.*

chafe (chāf) **1** rub: *The mother chafed her child's cold hands to warm them.* **2** make sore or become sore by rubbing: *This stiff collar chafes my neck.* **3** make angry: *His big brother's teasing chafed him.* **4** get angry: *He chafed under his big brother's teasing. v.,* **chafed, chaf·ing.**

chaff[1] (chaf) **1** the stiff, strawlike bits around the grains of wheat, rye, or oats: *Chaff is separated from grain by threshing.* **2** hay or straw cut fine for feeding cattle. **3** worthless stuff; rubbish. *n.*

chaff[2] (chaf) **1** make fun of in a good-natured way before one's face: *The girls chaffed the French boy about his mistakes in speaking English.* **2** good-natured joking about a person to his face: *The French boy did not mind their chaff.* 1 *v.,* 2 *n.*

cha·grin (shə grin′) a feeling of disappointment, failure, or humiliation: *He felt chagrin because he did not get a prize. n.*

chain (chān) **1** a row of links joined together: *The dog is fastened to a post by a chain.* **2** a series of things joined or linked together: *a chain of mountains, a chain of happenings.* **3** fasten with a chain. **4** anything that binds or restrains. **5** bind; restrain. **6** keep in prison; make a slave of. **7 chains,** *pl.* imprisonment; bondage. 1, 2, 4, 7 *n.,* 3, 5, 6 *v.*

chain store one of a group of retail stores owned and operated by a single company.

chair (cher) **1** a single seat with a back and, sometimes, arms. **2** a position of dignity or authority: *Professor Smith occupies the chair of Astronomy at this college.* **3** the chairman of a meeting: *May we have a ruling on this point from the chair? n.*

chair·man (cher′mən) **1** the person in charge of a

meeting. 2 the head of a committee. 3 in New Brunswick, the elected head of a village council. *n., pl.* **chair·men** (cher′mən).

A chaise

chaise (shāz) a light carriage, usually with a folding top. *n.*

chal·ice (chal′is) a cup; goblet, especially one used in ceremonies. *n.*

chalk (chok or chôk) 1 a soft, white or grey limestone, made up mostly of very small sea shells: *Chalk is used for making lime.* 2 a material like chalk used to make white and colored crayons for writing or drawing on a blackboard. 3 mark, write, or draw with chalk. 1, 2 *n.*, 3 *v.*

chalk up, a write down or record. **b** score: *Our team chalked up twenty points.*

chalk·board (chok′bôrd′ or chôk′bôrd′) a board having a smooth, hard surface for writing or drawing on with chalk. *n.*

chalk·y (chok′ē or chôk′ē) 1 of chalk; containing chalk: *the chalky cliffs of Dover.* 2 like chalk; white as chalk: *The clown's face was chalky.* *adj.*, **chalk·i·er, chalk·i·est.**

chal·lenge (chal′ənj) 1 a sudden question demanding an answer: *'Who goes there?' was the challenge of the sentry.* 2 stop a person and question his right to do what he is doing or to be where he is: *When I tried to enter the building, the guard at the door challenged me.* 3 doubt; demand proof of before accepting as true: *The teacher challenged my statement that rice grows in Quebec.* 4 a demand for proof of the truth of a statement; a doubting or questioning of the truth of a statement: *Her challenge led me to read widely about Quebec.* 5 an invitation to a game or contest of any kind: *Giving a challenge often means that one undertakes to beat everybody else.* 6 invite to a contest: *The champion swimmer challenged anyone in the world to beat him.* 1, 4, 5 *n.*, 2, 3, 6 *v.*, **chal·lenged, chal·leng·ing. —chal′leng·er,** *n.*

cham·ber (chām′bər) 1 a room, especially a bedroom. 2 a group of lawmakers: *Parliament has two chambers, the Senate and the House of Commons.* 3 the hall where lawmakers meet: *The Senators meet in the Senate Chamber in Ottawa.* 4 any enclosed space in the body of animals or plants, or in some kinds of machinery: *The heart has four chambers. The part of a gun that holds the charge is called the chamber.* *n.*

cham·ber·lain (chām′bər lin) the person who manages the household of a king or of a great noble. *n.*

cha·me·le·on (kə mē′lē ən) 1 a lizard that can change the color of its skin. 2 a changeable or fickle person. *n.*

cham·ois (sham′ē) 1 a small, goatlike antelope that lives in the high mountains of Europe and southwestern Asia. 2 a soft leather made from the skin of sheep, goats, deer, etc. *n., pl.* **cham·ois.**

cham·pi·on (cham′pē ən) 1 a person, animal, or thing that wins first place in a game or contest: *the swimming champion of the world.* 2 first; ahead of all others: *a champion runner, a champion rose.* 3 a person who fights or speaks for another person; a person who defends a cause: *a great champion of peace.* 4 fight for; defend: *He championed his friend.* 1, 3 *n.*, 2 *adj.*, 4 *v.*

cham·pi·on·ship (cham′pē ən ship′) the position of champion; first place: *Our school won the championship in basketball.* *n.*

chance (chans) 1 an opportunity: *a chance to make some money.* 2 a possibility; probability: *There is a chance that the sick child will get well. The chances are against snow in May.* 3 fate; luck: *Chance led to the finding of the diamond mine.* 4 happen: *She chanced to notice a coin in the gutter.* 5 risk: *He took a chance when he swam the river.* 6 not expected; accidental: *We had a chance visit from Uncle Joe last week.* 1–3, 5 *n.*, 4 *v.*, **chanced, chanc·ing;** 6 *adj.*

by chance, a accidentally: *The meeting came about by chance.* **b** by some turn of events: *If by chance the weather clears, we can go for a swim.*

chance upon or **on,** happen to find or meet: *I chanced upon an old friend.*

chan·cel (chan′səl) the space around the altar of a church, used by the clergy and the choir: *The chancel is often separated from the rest of the church by a railing, lattice, or screen.* *n.*

☛ See note at **cancel.**

chan·cel·lor (chan′sə lər) 1 a high official in the government of certain countries. 2 the highest official in some universities. *n.*

☛ See note at **cancel.**

chan·de·lier (shan′də lēr′) a lighting fixture that hangs from a ceiling and has branches for individual lights. *n.*

☛ See note at **candle.**

change (chānj) 1 make different; become different: *She changed the room by painting the walls white. He had changed since they had seen him last.* 2 put something in place of another; take in place of: *change dirty clothes for clean ones. I changed seats with my brother.* 3 pass from one position or state to another: *The wind changed from east to south.* 4 passing from one position or state to another: *The change from flower to fruit is interesting to watch. A change from the city to the country in the summer is good for children.* 5 a thing to be used in place of another of the same kind: *a change of clothes.* 6 get or give small units of money that equal a larger unit: *Can you change a dollar bill for*

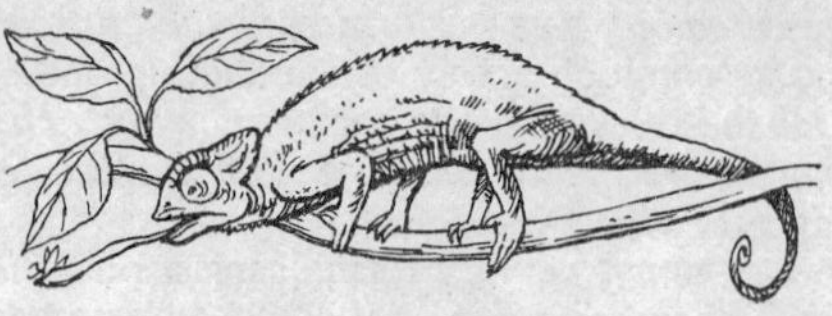

An African chameleon — about 20 cm long with the tail

ten dimes? **7** the money returned to a person when he has given an amount larger than the price of what he buys: *If you buy a fifty-cent loaf of bread and you give the baker a dollar, he will give you fifty cents in change.* **8** smaller units of money given in place of a large unit of money: *Please give me change for this dollar bill.* **9** coins: *I have a dollar bill and some change.* 1–3, 6 *v.*, **changed, chang·ing;** 4, 5, 7–9 *n.*

change·a·ble (chān′jə bəl) that can change; that does change; likely to change; variable; varying; fickle: *April weather is changeable.* *adj.* **—change′a·ble·ness,** *n.* **—change′a·bly,** *adv.*

chan·nel (chan′əl) **1** the bed of a stream, river, etc. **2** a body of water joining two larger bodies of water: *The English Channel lies between two seas.* **3** the deeper part of a waterway: *There is shallow water on both sides of the channel in this river.* **4** a passage for liquids; groove. **5** the means by which something is carried: *The information came through secret channels.* **6** a narrow band of electrical waves that carries the signals of a television or radio station. **7** form a channel in; cut out as one does a channel: *The river had channelled its way through the rocks.* 1–6 *n.*, 7 *v.*, **chan·nelled** or **chan·neled, chan·nel·ling** or **chan·nel·ing.**

chant (chant) **1** a song. **2** sing: *chant a melody.* **3** a song in which several syllables or words are sung on one tone: *Chants are often used in church services.* **4** sing in this way. **5** a psalm, prayer, or other song for chanting. **6** a monotonous way of talking. **7** keep talking about; say over and over again: *We chanted, 'Go team, go!'* 1, 3, 5, 6 *n.*, 2, 4, 7 *v.*

chant·ey (shan′tē or chan′tē) See **shanty**[2].

chan·ti·cleer (chan′tə klēr′) rooster. *n.*

cha·os (kā′os) very great confusion; complete disorder: *The tornado left chaos behind it.* *n.*

cha·ot·ic (kā ot′ik) very confused or disordered: *His room was a chaotic mess of clothes, books, and toys.* *adj.*

chap[1] (chap) **1** of skin, crack open; become rough: *Her lips become chapped in very cold weather.* **2** make rough: *Cold weather chapped his hands.* *v.*, **chapped, chap·ping.**

chap[2] (chap) *Informal.* a fellow; a man or boy: *Hello, old chap!* *n.*

chap·el (chap′əl) **1** a building for Christian worship, not so large as a church. **2** a small place for worship in a larger building. *n.*

chap·lain (chap′lən) a clergyman on duty with a family, court, regiment, warship, etc. *n.*

Chaps

chaps (shaps or chaps) backless leggings of tough leather, worn by cowboys to protect their pants when riding. *n. pl.*

hat, āge, fär; let, ēqual, tėrm; it, īce
hot, ōpen, ôrder; oil, out; cup, pu̇t, rüle
əbove, takən, pencəl, lemən, circəs
ch, child; ng, long; sh, ship
th, thin; ᴛʜ, then; zh, measure

chap·ter (chap′tər) **1** a main division of a book, written about a particular part of the subject or story. **2** a local division of an organization, which holds its own meetings; a branch of a club. *n.*

char[1] (chär) **1** burn to charcoal. **2** burn slightly; scorch: *The meat was charred.* *v.*, **charred, char·ring.**

char[2] (chär) a food and game fish, a kind of trout: *The char has a reddish underside, small scales, and colored spots.* *n.*

char·ac·ter (kar′ik tər or ker′ik tər) **1** nature; kind; sort: *What is the character of the plan you suggest? The trees on those islands are of a peculiar character.* **2** moral nature; moral strength or weakness: *The special ways in which any person feels, thinks, and acts, considered as good or bad, make up his character.* **3** a person in a play or book. **4** a person who attracts attention because he is different or odd: *The old captain was a character in the village.* **5** a letter, figure, or sign used in writing or printing: *There are 52 characters in our alphabet, consisting of 26 small letters and 26 capital letters.* *n.*

char·ac·ter·is·tic (kar′ik tər is′tik or ker′ik tər is′tik) **1** marking off or distinguishing a certain person or thing from others: *Bananas have their own characteristic smell.* **2** a special quality or feature: *The characteristic I like best in him is his cheerfulness. An elephant's trunk is its most noticeable characteristic.* 1 *adj.*, 2 *n.*

char·ac·ter·ize (kar′ik tər īz′ or ker′ik tər īz′) **1** describe the special qualities or features of: *I would characterize our teacher as a very friendly person.* **2** distinguish; mark out: *The camel is characterized by the humps on its back and an ability to go for a long time without water.* *v.*, **char·ac·ter·ized, char·ac·ter·iz·ing.**

char·coal (chär′kōl′) a black substance made by partly burning wood in a place from which the air is shut out: *Charcoal is used as fuel, in filters, and as a pencil for drawing.* *n.*

charge (chärj) **1** ask as a price; put a price on: *The grocer charged 75 cents a dozen for eggs.* **2** the price; the expense: *What is the charge for delivery?* **3** put down as a debt to be paid: *The store will charge things bought and send a bill at the end of the month.* **4** rush at; attack: *The soldiers charged the enemy.* **5** an attack: *The charge drove the enemy back.* **6** load, fill: *He charged the gun with powder and shot.* **7** restore the active materials of a storage battery: *The battery of a car charges automatically when the motor is running.* **8** the amount needed to load or fill something: *A gun is fired by exploding the charge of powder.* **9** an amount of electricity. **10** give a task or duty to; order: *Mother charged her to take good care of the baby.* **11** a duty or responsibility: *She accepted the charge to take good care of the baby.* **12** a person or thing under the care of someone: *Sick people are the charges of doctors and nurses.* **13** an order or direction: *the charge of a judge*

to a jury. **14** blame; accuse, especially in a court of law: *The driver was charged with speeding.* **15** an accusing: *He pleaded guilty to the charge and paid the fine.* 1, 3, 4, 6, 7, 10, 14 *v.,* **charged, charg·ing;** 2, 5, 8, 9, 11, 12, 13, 15 *n.*
in charge, in the position of responsibility: *The captain left the corporal in charge.*
in charge of, a having the care or management of: *My sister is in charge of the book department of the store.* **b** under the care or management of: *Furniture is in charge of another salesman.*
charg·er (chär′jər) a horse ridden in war. *n.*

A Roman chariot

char·i·ot (char′ē ət or cher′ē ət) a two-wheeled vehicle pulled by horses: *The chariot was used in ancient times for fighting, for racing, and for driving in processions.* *n.*
char·i·ta·ble (char′ə tə bəl or cher′ə tə bəl) **1** generous in helping poor or suffering people. **2** of or for charity: *The Salvation Army is a charitable organization.* **3** kindly in judging people and their actions: *Grandfathers are usually charitable towards the mistakes of their grandchildren.* *adj.* **—char′i·ta·ble·ness,** *n.* **—char′i·ta·bly,** *adv.*
char·i·ty (char′ə tē or cher′ə tē) **1** generous giving to the poor, or to institutions that look after the poor, the sick, and the helpless. **2** a fund or organization for helping the poor, the sick, and the helpless: *She gives money to the United Appeal and to other charities.* **3** kindness in judging the faults of other people. **4** love of one's fellow man. *n., pl.* **char·i·ties.**
char·ley horse (chär′lē) *Informal.* a stiffness or cramp in a muscle, especially of the leg or arm.
charm (chärm) **1** a quality or characteristic that delights or fascinates; the power of delighting: *We were impressed by the grace and charm of our hostess.* **2** please greatly; delight: *The boys were charmed by the sailor's tales of adventure.* **3** a small ornament or trinket worn on a watch chain, bracelet, etc. **4** a word, verse, act, or thing supposed to have magic power to help or harm people. **5** act on as if by magic: *His grandchildren's laughter charmed away the old man's troubles.* **6** give magic power to; protect as by a charm: *Sir Galahad seemed to have a charmed life.* 1, 3, 4 *n.,* 2, 5, 6 *v.*
charm·ing (chär′ming) very pleasing; delightful; fascinating: *a charming woman, a charming day.* *adj.* **—charm′ing·ly,** *adv.*
chart (chärt) **1** a map: *A sailor's chart shows the coasts, rocks, and shallow places of a sea.* **2** a sheet of information arranged in pictures, diagrams, etc. **3** make a chart of: *to chart the course of a ship.* 1, 2 *n.,* 3 *v.*
char·ter (chär′tər) **1** a written grant of certain rights by a ruler to his subjects, or by a legislature to citizens, or to companies formed to do special kinds of business: *All Canadian banks must have charters from the federal government.* **2** give a charter to. **3** hire a ship, aircraft, bus, etc. for private use: *He chartered a sailboat for a month.* 1 *n.,* 2, 3 *v.*
chase (chās) **1** follow after to catch or kill; hunt: *The cat chased the mouse.* **2** going after to catch or kill: *The thieves were caught after a thrilling automobile chase.* **3** hunting wild animals. **4** a hunted animal: *The chase escaped the hunter.* **5** drive; drive away: *English sparrows chase other birds from their nests.* **6** follow; pursue: *The catcher chased the ball.* 1, 5, 6 *v.,* **chased, chas·ing;** 2–4 *n.*
chasm (kaz′əm) a deep opening or crack in the earth. *n.*
chas·sis (shas′ē or chas′ē) **1** the frame that supports the body of an automobile, aircraft, etc. **2** the frame that encloses and supports the working parts of a radio, television set, etc. *n., pl.* **chas·sis** (shas′ēz or chas′ēz).
chaste (chāst) **1** pure; morally good. **2** decent; modest: *chaste behavior.* **3** simple in taste or style; simple; not too much ornamented. *adj.* **—chaste·ly,** *adv.*
chas·ten (chās′ən) **1** punish in order to improve: *God chastened Job.* **2** restrain from excess; subdue: *The father found it necessary to chasten his boisterous son.* *v.*
chas·tise (chas tīz′) **1** cause physical pain to a person or persons to make them improve; punish: *The children who broke the windows were chastised.* **2** criticize or tell off severely: *The coach chastised the players for being late.* *v.,* **chas·tised, chas·tis·ing.**
chat (chat) **1** easy, familiar talk: *We had a pleasant chat about old times.* **2** talk in an easy, familiar way: *We sat chatting by the fire after supper.* 1 *n.,* 2 *v.,* **chat·ted, chat·ting.**
châ·teau or **cha·teau** (sha tō′) **1** a French castle. **2** a large country house in France. **3** a building resembling such a house. *n., pl.* **châ·teaux** or **cha·teaux** (sha tōz′).
chat·ter (chat′ər) **1** talk constantly in a rapid, foolish way. **2** rapid, foolish talk. **3** make rapid, indistinct sounds: *Monkeys chatter.* **4** rapid, indistinct sounds: *The chatter of sparrows annoyed her.* **5** rattle together: *Cold makes your teeth chatter.* 1, 3, 5 *v.,* 2, 4 *n.* **—chat′ter·er,** *n.*
chat·ter·box (chat′ər boks′) a person who talks all the time. *n.*
chat·ty (chat′ē) fond of friendly, familiar talk. *adj.,* **chat·ti·er, chat·ti·est.**
chauf·feur (shō′fər or shō fər′) a person whose work is driving an automobile, usually as the employee of a private person or a company: *The president of the bank has a chauffeur.* *n.*
cheap (chēp) **1** low in price or cost; not expensive: *Fresh vegetables are cheap out in the country.* **2** charging low prices: *a cheap drugstore.* **3** easily obtained; costing little effort: *a cheap victory.* **4** of little merit or value: *cheap novels, cheap jewellery.* **5** cheaply: *I sold the car cheap to get rid of it.* 1–4 *adj.,* 5 *adv.* **—cheap′ness,** *n.*
feel cheap, feel inferior and ashamed: *He felt cheap about forgetting his sister's birthday.*
☞ **Cheap** and **cheep** are pronounced the same.
cheap·en (chēp′ən) **1** make or become cheap. **2** lower the reputation of; reduce the dignity of: *Rude actions cheapen one.* *v.*

hat, āge, fär; let, ēqual, tėrm; it, īce
hot, ōpen, ôrder; oil, out; cup, pu̇t, rüle
əbove, takən, pencəl, lemən, circəs
ch, child; ng, long; sh, ship
th, thin; ᴛʜ, then; zh, measure

cheap·ly (chēp′lē) **1** at a low price. **2** with little cost or effort. *adv.*

cheat (chēt) **1** deceive or trick; play or do business in a way that is not honest: *The peddler cheated the woman out of ten cents in change.* **2** a person who is not honest and does things to deceive and trick others. **3** a fraud or trick. 1 *v.*, 2, 3 *n.*

check (chek) **1** stop suddenly: *The boys checked their steps.* **2** a sudden stop: *The message gave a check to our plans.* **3** hold back; control: *to check one's anger.* **4** any person, thing, or event that controls or holds back action: *the check on a furnace, a hockey check.* **5** examine or compare to prove true or correct: *We ought to check her statement before we condemn her.* **6** find out; investigate: *When he checked, he found the money was gone.* **7** a test for correctness made by comparing: *My work will be a check on yours.* **8** a mark (✓) to show that something has been examined or compared, or that it is true or right: *The teacher put a check beside the correct answers.* **9** mark something examined or compared with a check: *How many answers did the teacher check as wrong?* **10** a ticket or metal piece given in return for a coat, hat, baggage, package, etc. to show ownership or the right to claim again later: *Show your baggage check when you want your trunk.* **11** leave or take for safekeeping: *check one's coat. The hotel checked our baggage.* **12** a written statement of the amount owed in a restaurant: *When we finished eating, Father asked the waitress for the check.* **13** a pattern made of squares: *Do you want a check or a stripe for your new dress?* **14** a single one of these squares: *The checks are small in this pattern.* **15** See **cheque.** 1, 3, 5, 6, 9, 11 *v.*, 2, 4, 7, 8, 10, 12–15 *n.*
check off, mark as checked and found true or right.
check on or **check up on,** find out about; seek more information on: *The police were checking up on her.*
check out, a leave and pay for a hotel or motel room, or leave a hospital: *We checked out of the hotel at noon.* **b** in a supermarket or other self-service store, check through and pay for one's purchases: *It took a long time to check out.*
☛ **Check** and **cheque** are pronounced the same.

check·book (chek′bu̇k′) See **cheque book.**

check·er·board (chek′ər bôrd′) a square board marked in a pattern of 64 squares of two alternating colors and used in playing checkers or chess. *n.*

check·ers (chek′ərz) a game played by two people, each with 12 flat, round pieces of wood, ivory, etc. on a board marked off into 64 squares of two alternating colors. *n.*

check–out (chek′out′) **1** in a supermarket or other self-service store, the process by which purchases are checked and paid for: *The check-out took only about a minute.* **2** the counter where this is done: *I went to the express check-out.* **3** in a hotel or motel, the time by which one must leave and pay for a room: *We missed the check-out and had to pay for another day.* *n.*

check·up (chek′up′) **1** a careful examination: *He took his car to the service station for a checkup.* **2** a thorough physical examination: *The doctor asked the patient to come to his office for a checkup.* *n.*

chee·cha·ko (chē cho′kō) *Cdn.* a newcomer; a tenderfoot or greenhorn: *It took the cheechako many months to learn the ways of the Yukon.* *n.*

cheek (chēk) **1** the side of the face below either eye. **2** saucy talk or behavior; impudence: *That's enough of your cheek!* *n.*

cheek·y (chēk′ē) *Informal.* saucy; impudent: *a cheeky child.* *adj.*, **cheek·i·er, cheek·i·est.** —**cheek′i·ly,** *adv.* —**cheek′i·ness,** *n.*

cheep (chēp) **1** make a noise like a young bird; chirp; peep. **2** a young bird's cry. 1 *v.*, 2 *n.*
☛ **Cheep** and **cheap** are pronounced the same.

cheer (chēr) **1** a shout of encouragement and support or praise: *Give three cheers for the boys who won the game.* **2** shout approval or praise: *The boys cheered loudly.* **3** urge on with cheers: *Everyone cheered our team.* **4** good spirits; hope; gladness: *The warmth of the fire and a good meal brought cheer to our hearts again.* **5** give joy to; make glad; comfort: *It cheered the old woman to have us visit her.* 1, 4 *n.*, 2, 3, 5 *v.*
cheer up, make or become happier; be glad: *Cheer up, perhaps we'll win the next game.*

cheer·ful (chēr′fəl) **1** full of cheer; joyful; glad: *She is a smiling, cheerful girl.* **2** pleasant; bringing cheer: *This is a cheerful, sunny room.* **3** willing: *a cheerful helper.* *adj.* —**cheer′ful·ly,** *adv.* —**cheer′ful·ness,** *n.*

cheer·i·ly (chēr′ə lē) in a cheerful or cheery manner; in a way suggesting or bringing cheer. *adv.*

cheer·lead·er (chēr′lē′dər) a person who leads a group in organized cheering, especially at high school or college athletic events: *The cheerleaders spent weeks practising the school yells.* *n.*

cheer·less (chēr′lis) gloomy; dreary. *adj.* —**cheer′less·ly,** *adv.* —**cheer′less·ness,** *n.*

cheer·y (chēr′ē) cheerful; pleasant; bright; gay: *Sunshine and the singing of birds are cheery.* *adj.*, **cheer·i·er, cheer·i·est.**

cheese (chēz) a solid food made from the curds of milk. *n.*

cheese·cloth (chēz′cloth′) a thin, very loosely woven cotton cloth, originally used for wrapping freshly made cheese. *n.*

chef (shef) **1** a head cook: *the chef of a large restaurant.* **2** any cook, especially one who is skilled in cooking. *n.*

chem·i·cal (kem′ə kəl) **1** of, having to do with, or in the science of chemistry: *Chemical research has made possible many new products.* **2** made by or used in the process of chemistry: *The burning of coal is a process of chemical change.* **3** any substance made by or used in a chemical process: *Chlorine and sodium bicarbonate are chemicals.* 1, 2 *adj.*, 3 *n.*

chemical element See **element** (def. 1).

chem·ist (kem′ist) **1** a person skilled in chemistry. **2** *Esp. British.* druggist. *n.*

chem·is·try (kem′is trē) the science that deals with simple substances (elements), the changes that take place when they combine to form compounds, and their behavior under various conditions. *n.*

cheque or **check** (chek) **1** a written order for a bank to take money from the account of the signer and pay it to the person or company named: *Father pays most of his bills by cheque.* 2 a blank form on which to write such an order: *He had two cheques left in his cheque book.* *n.*

☞ **Cheque** and **check** are pronounced the same.

cheque book or **check·book** (chek′bu̇k′) a book of blank cheques.

cher·ish (cher′ish) 1 hold dear; treat with tenderness; aid or protect: *A mother cherishes her baby.* 2 keep in mind; cling to: *The old woman cherished the hope of her son's return.* *v.*

cher·ry (cher′ē) 1 a small, round, juicy fruit having a pit in the centre: *Cherries are good to eat.* 2 the tree it grows on. 3 bright red: *cherry ribbons.* 1–3 *n., pl.* **cher·ries;** 3 *adj.*

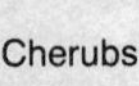

Cherubs

cher·ub (cher′əb) 1 an angel. 2 a picture or statue of a child with wings. 3 a beautiful or good child. *n., pl.* **cher·u·bim** for 1 and 2, **cher·ubs** for 3.

cher·u·bim (cher′ə bim′ or cher′yə bim′) a plural of **cherub.** *n.*

chess (ches) a game played by two persons, each with 16 pieces that can be moved in various ways on a board marked off into 64 squares of two alternating colors. *n.*

chest (chest) 1 the part of a person's or an animal's body enclosed by the ribs. 2 a large box with a lid, used for holding things: *a linen chest, a tool chest.* 3 a piece of furniture with drawers. *n.*

ches·ter·field (ches′tər fēld′) 1 a long, upholstered seat or couch having a back and arms; a sofa. 2 a kind of overcoat. *n.*

chest·nut (ches′nut) 1 a sweet, edible nut that has a prickly outer shell. 2 the tree it grows on. 3 a horse chestnut. 4 deep, reddish brown: *chestnut hair.* 5 a horse of this color. 1–5 *n.,* 4 *adj.*

chev·ron (shev′rən) 1 a V-shaped bar, usually of cloth, often worn on the sleeve of a uniform by members of the armed forces, a police force, etc. to show rank or years of service: *A sergeant wears three chevrons.* 2 any V-shaped design. *n.*

chew (chü) 1 crush or grind with or as if with teeth: *Some meat is hard to chew.* 2 chewing: *The puppy gave the rag a good chew.* 3 a piece for chewing; the thing chewed. 1 *v.,* 2, 3 *n.*

chewing gum gum for chewing: *Chewing gum is sweetened and flavored.*

chew·y (chü′ē) needing much chewing; becoming sticky when chewed: *a chewy caramel candy.* *adj.*

chick (chik) 1 a young chicken. 2 a young bird. 3 child. *n.*

chick·a·dee (chik′ə dē′) a small bird having black, white, and grey feathers. *n.*

☞ The word **chickadee** was originally an imitation of the sound this bird makes.

chick·en (chik′ən) 1 a young hen or rooster. 2 any hen or rooster. 3 the flesh of a chicken, used as food. *n.*

chick·en–heart·ed (chik′ən här′tid) cowardly; timid. *adj.*

chicken pox a mild contagious disease accompanied by a fever and by a rash on the skin: *Chicken pox is a common childhood disease.*

chick·weed (chik′wēd′) a common weed having small white flowers, whose leaves and seeds are eaten by birds. *n.*

chic·le (chik′əl) a tasteless, gumlike substance used in making chewing gum: *Chicle is the dried milky juice of a tree of tropical America.* *n.*

chid (chid) See **chide.** *Only yesterday the teacher chid him for being late.* *v.*

chide (chīd) reproach; blame; scold: *She chided her son for getting his new shirt dirty.* *v.,* **chid·ed** or **chid, chid·ing.**

chief (chēf) 1 the head of a group; leader; the person highest in rank or authority: *A fire chief is the head of a group of firefighters.* 2 the head of a tribe or clan. 3 leading; in authority; at the head: *the chief engineer of a building project.* 4 most important; main: *the chief thing to do.* 1, 2 *n.,* 3, 4 *adj.*

in chief, at the head or in the highest position.

chief·ly (chēf′lē) mainly; mostly: *We visited Ottawa chiefly to see the Parliament Buildings.* *adv.*

chief·tain (chēf′tən) 1 the chief of a tribe or clan. 2 a leader; the head of a group. *n.*

child (chīld) 1 baby. 2 a young boy or girl, especially one up to the early or mid teens. 3 a son or daughter: *There are three children in the Rico family.* *n., pl.* **chil·dren.**

child·birth (chīld′bėrth′) the act or process of giving birth to a child. *n.*

child·hood (chīld′hu̇d) 1 the state of being a child: *the carefree days of childhood.* 2 the time during which one is a child: *His childhood was very happy.* *n.*

child·ish (chīl′dish) 1 of a child. 2 like a child: *a childish person.* 3 not proper for a grown person; silly; weak: *It was childish of him to make such a fuss.* *adj.* —**child′ish·ly,** *adv.* —**child′ish·ness,** *n.*

☞ **Childish** and **childlike,** when applied to persons who are no longer children, are surprisingly different in meaning. **Childish** expresses a poor opinion by suggesting that the person lacks the self-control, good manners, or mature mind expected of an adult. **Childlike** expresses a favorable opinion by suggesting that the person still has certain good qualities associated with children, such as frankness, simplicity, and trust.

child·like (chīld′līk′) like a child; innocent; frank; simple: *The charming old lady had a childlike, honest manner.* *adj.*

☞ See note at **childish.**

chil·dren (chil′drən) plural of **child.** *n.*

chil·e con car·ne or **chil·i con car·ne** (chil′ē kon kär′nē) meat cooked with red peppers and, usually, beans.

chil·i (chil′ē) 1 a hot-tasting pod of red pepper, used for seasoning. 2 the tropical shrub it grows on. 3 chile con carne: *We had chili for supper last night.* *n., pl.* **chil·ies.**

chill (chil) 1 unpleasant coldness: *There was a distinct chill in the air.* 2 unpleasantly cold: *a chill, dreary day.* 3 make cold: *We chilled the pop in the refrigerator.* 4 become cold; feel cold. 5 a sudden coldness of the body with shivering: *She was very sick with chills and fever.* 1, 2, 5 *n.*, 3, 4 *v.*

chill·y (chil′ē) 1 cold; unpleasantly cool: *a chilly day.* 2 cold in manner; unfriendly: *She gave the uninvited guests a chilly greeting.* *adj.*, **chill·i·er, chill·i·est.**

chime (chīm) 1 a set of bells tuned to the musical scale, usually played by hammers or simple machinery. 2 the music made by a set of tuned bells. 3 ring out musically: *The bells chimed at midnight.* 4 agree; be in harmony: *His ideas chimed beautifully with mine.* 1, 2 *n.*, 3, 4 *v.*, **chimed, chim·ing.**

chime in, *Informal.* break into or join in a conversation: *As soon as he arrived, he chimed in with his views.*

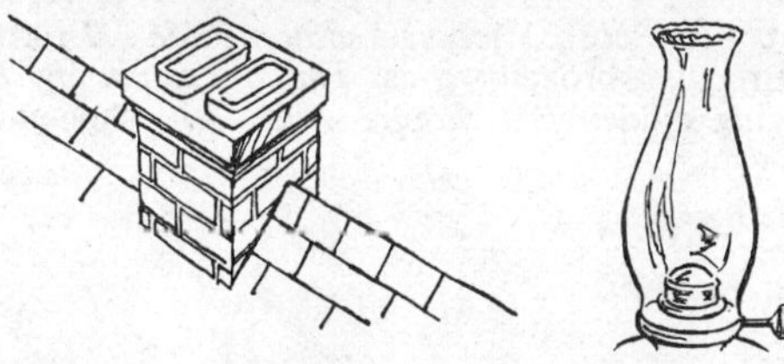

A chimney for a house

A chimney on a lamp

chim·ney (chim′nē) 1 an upright structure used to make a draft for a fire and carry away smoke: *Alice's house has two chimneys.* 2 a glass tube placed around the flame of a lamp. *n.*, *pl.* **chim·neys.**

chimney sweep one whose work is cleaning out chimneys.

chimp (chimp) *Informal.* chimpanzee. *n.*

A chimpanzee — about 140 cm tall

chim·pan·zee (chim′pan zē′ or chim pan′zē) a manlike ape of Africa: *Chimpanzees are very intelligent and easily trained.* *n.*

chin (chin) 1 the front of the lower jaw below the mouth. 2 **chin oneself,** hang by the hands from a bar and pull up until one's chin is even with the bar or above it. 1 *n.*, 2 *v.*, **chinned, chin·ning.**

chi·na (chī′nə) 1 a fine, white pottery made of clay baked by a special process, first used in China; porcelain: *Colored designs can be baked into china.* 2 dishes, vases, ornaments, etc. made of china. 3 pottery dishes of any kind. *n.*

Chi·nese (chī nēz′) 1 of China, a country in eastern Asia, its people, or their language. 2 a person born in or living in China: *There are many Chinese in Canada.* 3 any of the languages of China. 1 *adj.*, 2, 3 *n.*, *pl.* **Chi·nese.**

hat, āge, fär; let, ēqual, tėrm; it, īce
hot, ōpen, ôrder; oil, out; cup, pu̇t, rüle
əbove, takən, pencəl, lemən, circəs
ch, child; ng, long; sh, ship
th, thin; ᴛʜ, then; zh, measure

chink[1] (chingk) 1 a narrow opening; crack: *The chinks between the logs of the cabin let in wind and snow.* 2 fill in: *The cracks in the walls of the cabin were chinked with mud.* 1 *n.*, 2 *v.*

chink[2] (chingk) 1 a sound like glasses or coins striking against one another. 2 make such a sound. 1 *n.*, 2 *v.*

chi·nook (shi nu̇k′) *Cdn.* a warm winter wind that blows from the southwest across British Columbia and Alberta, and into Saskatchewan. *n.*

chinook arch *Cdn.* an arch of blue sky above the western horizon, often seen just before or during a chinook.

chip (chip) 1 a small, thin piece cut from wood or broken from stone or china. 2 a place in china or stone from which a small piece has been broken: *One of Mother's plates has a chip on the edge.* 3 cut or break small pieces from wood, stone, dishes, etc.: *He chipped off the old paint.* 4 become chipped easily: *These cups chip if they are not handled gently.* 5 a small, thin piece of food or candy: *chocolate chips.* 6 See **potato chip.** 1, 2, 5, 6 *n.*, 3, 4 *v.*, **chipped, chip·ping.**

chip·munk (chip′mungk) a small, striped North American ground squirrel. *n.*

☛ **Chipmunk** comes from a North American Indian word meaning 'headfirst.' The word was originally applied to the red squirrel from its way of going down a tree trunk.

chips (chips) potato chips. *n. pl.*

chirp (chėrp) 1 the short, sharp sound made by certain small birds and insects. 2 make a chirp: *Crickets and sparrows chirp.* 1 *n.*, 2 *v.*

A chisel

chis·el (chiz′əl) 1 a tool with a steel cutting edge at the end of a strong blade: *Chisels are used for shaping wood, stone, or metal.* 2 cut or shape with a chisel. 1 *n.*, 2 *v.*, **chis·elled** or **chis·eled, chis·el·ling** or **chis·el·ing.**

chiv·al·rous (shiv′əl rəs) having the qualities of an ideal knight; brave, courteous, helpful, and honorable. *adj.* **—chiv′al·rous·ly,** *adv.*

chiv·al·ry (shiv′əl rē) 1 the qualities of an ideal knight in the Middle Ages; bravery, honor, protection of the weak, devotion to women, and fairness to enemies. 2 the rules and customs of knights in the Middle Ages. *n.*

chlo·rin·ate (klô′rə nāt′) 1 combine or treat with

chlorine: *Paper pulp is chlorinated to bleach it.* **2** disinfect with chlorine: *The water in the city reservoirs is chlorinated.* *v.,* **chlo·rin·at·ed, chlo·rin·at·ing.**

chlo·rine (klô′rēn) a chemical element which at normal temperatures is a greenish-yellow, bad-smelling gas. *n.*

chlo·ro·form (klô′rə fôrm′) **1** a colorless liquid with a sweetish smell, used to dissolve rubber, resin, etc. and as an anesthetic. **2** put a person or animal to sleep with chloroform. **3** kill with chloroform. 1 *n.,* 2, 3 *v.*

chlo·ro·phyl or **chlo·ro·phyll** (klô′rə fil′) the green coloring matter of plants. *n.*

chock–full (chok′fu̇l′) as full as can be; completely full. *adj.* Also, **chuck-full.**

choc·o·late (chok′lit or chok′ə lit) **1** a dark brown substance used as a food or flavoring and made by roasting and grinding cacao seeds: *Chocolate has a strong, rich flavor.* **2** a drink made of chocolate with hot milk or water and sugar. **3** candy made of chocolate and sugar. **4** made of or flavored with chocolate. **5** dark brown. 1–3, 5 *n.,* 4, 5 *adj.*

choice (chois) **1** choosing; selection: *Be careful in your choice of friends.* **2** the person or thing chosen: *This hat is my choice.* **3** the power or chance to choose: *His father gave him his choice between a bicycle and a pony.* **4** a quantity and variety to choose from: *a wide choice of vegetables in the market.* **5** excellent; of fine quality: *The choicest fruit had the highest price.* 1–4 *n.,* 5 *adj.,* **choic·er, choic·est.**

choir (kwīr) **1** a group of singers, especially one that sings as part of a church service. **2** the part of the church set apart for the singers. *n.*

choke (chōk) **1** keep from breathing by squeezing or blocking up the windpipe: *The smoke almost choked the firemen.* **2** be unable to breathe: *He choked when some food stuck in his throat.* **3** the act of choking: *He gave a slight choke and then got his breath.* **4** the sound of choking: *We heard a choke behind us.* **5** check or put out by cutting off air; smother: *A bucket of sand will choke a fire.* **6** something that chokes, such as a valve that reduces the supply of air to an internal-combustion engine. **7** hold; control: *He choked down his anger and said nothing.* **8** fill up or block: *Sand is choking the river.* 1, 2, 5, 7, 8 *v.,* **choked, chok·ing;** 3, 4, 6 *n.*

choke back, hold back; keep in: *He choked back his angry words.*

choke off, put an end to; stop: *The rock slide choked off our water supply.*

choke up, fill with emotion; be or cause to be on the verge of tears: *People in the audience were choked up when the hero died.*

choke·cher·ry (chōk′cher′ē) a small wild cherry that grows in clusters on a tree: *Chokecherries cause the mouth to pucker when they are eaten.* *n., pl.* **choke·cher·ries.**

chol·er·a (kol′ər ə) **1** a painful disease of the stomach and intestines that is not infectious. **2** a more dangerous disease that is infectious: *Both kinds of cholera are marked by vomiting and cramps.* *n.*

choose (chüz) **1** pick out; select from a number: *Choose the cake you like best. He chose wisely.* **2** prefer and decide; think fit: *She chose to rest.* *v.,* **chose, cho·sen, choos·ing.**

chop[1] (chop) **1** cut by hitting with something sharp: *We chopped the wood with an axe. The boys chopped down five trees.* **2** cut into small pieces: *to chop up cabbage.* **3** a cutting blow. **4** a slice of meat, especially of lamb, veal, or pork, attached to a piece of rib. **5** move in small, jerky waves. 1, 2, 5 *v.,* **chopped, chop·ping;** 3, 4 *n.*

chop[2] (chop) **1** the jaw. **2 chops,** *pl.* the jaws, especially the fleshy covering of an animal's jaws: *The dog licked his chops.* *n.*

lick one's chops, *Slang.* enjoy the prospect of something good to come: *The children licked their chops over the coming holiday.*

chop·per (chop′ər) **1** a tool or machine for chopping: *A short axe and a heavy knife are kinds of choppers.* **2** *Slang.* helicopter. **3 choppers,** *pl. Slang.* teeth. *n.*

chop·py (chop′ē) **1** jerky: *a choppy ride.* **2** forming short, irregular, broken waves: *The lake is choppy today.* **3** changing suddenly: *a choppy wind.* *adj.,* **chop·pi·er, chop·pi·est.**

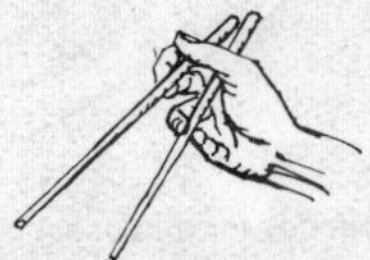
Chopsticks

chop·stick (chop′stik′) one of a pair of small, shaped sticks used, especially by the Chinese, Japanese, and Koreans, to raise food to the mouth. *n.*

chop su·ey (chop′ sü′ē) fried or stewed meat and vegetables cut up and cooked together in a sauce: *We had chop suey with rice at a Chinese restaurant.*

cho·ral (kô′rəl) **1** of a choir or chorus. **2** sung by a choir or chorus: *a choral hymn.* *adj.*

chord[1] (kôrd) a combination of three or more notes of music sounded at the same time in harmony. *n.*

☛ **Chord** and **cord** are pronounced the same.

chord[2] (kôrd) **1** a straight line connecting two points on a curve. **2** a feeling; emotion: *The song touched a sorrowful chord in him.* *n.*

☛ See note at **chord**[1].

chore (chôr) **1** an odd job; a minor task, especially one that must be done daily: *Feeding the chickens is one of the chores on a farm.* **2** a task that is disagreeable or irritating: *He found the work quite a chore.* *n.*

chor·tle (chôr′təl) **1** chuckle and snort at the same time: *'He chortled in his joy.'* **2** a combined chuckle and snort. 1 *v.,* 2 *n.*

☛ **Chortle** was made up by Lewis Carroll for *Through the Looking Glass* from the words *ch*uck*le* and sn*ort.*

cho·rus (kô′rəs) **1** a group of singers who sing together, such as a choir. **2** a song sung by many singers together: *The opera ended with a splendid chorus.* **3** the part of a song that is repeated after each stanza. **4** sing or speak all at the same time: *The birds were chorusing around me.* **5** saying by many at the same time: *My question was answered by a chorus of No's.* **6** a group of singers and dancers: *He was in the chorus of our school musical.* 1–3, 5, 6 *n.,* 4 *v.*

in chorus, all together at the same time: *The children sang 'O Canada' in chorus.*

chose (chōz) See **choose.** *She chose the red dress.* *v.*

hat, āge, fär; let, ēqual, tėrm; it, īce
hot, ōpen, ôrder; oil, out; cup, pu̇t, rüle
əbove, takən, pencəl, lemən, circəs
ch, child; ng, long; sh, ship
th, thin; ᴛʜ, then; zh, measure

cho·sen (chō′zən) 1 See **choose.** *Have you chosen a book from the library?* 2 picked out: *Six chosen scouts marched in front.* 1 *v.,* 2 *adj.*

chow·der (chou′dər) a thick soup or stew, often made of clams or fish with potatoes, onions, etc. *n.*

Christ (krīst) Jesus, the founder of the Christian religion. *n.*

chris·ten (kris′ən) **1** baptize a child as a Christian. **2** give a first name to a person at baptism: *The child was christened James.* **3** give a name to: *The new ship was christened before it was launched. v.*

Chris·ten·dom (kris′ən dəm) **1** Christian countries; the Christian part of the world. **2** all Christians. *n.*

chris·ten·ing (kris′ən ing) **1** baptism; the act or ceremony of baptizing and naming. *n.*

Chris·tian (kris′chən) **1** a person who believes in Christ. **2** a person whose life follows the teachings of Christ. **3** believing in or belonging to the religion of Christ: *the Christian church, Christian countries.* **4** showing a gentle, humble, helpful spirit: *Christian kindness.* **5** of Christ, His teachings, or His followers. 1, 2 *n.,* 3–5 *adj.*

Chris·ti·an·i·ty (kris′che an′ə tē) **1** the religion taught by Christ and His followers. **2** Christian beliefs or faith; Christian spirit or character. *n.*

Christian name one's first name; a given name used by one's friends and family: *'Victoria' is the Christian name of Victoria Peterson.*

Christ·mas (kris′məs) the yearly celebration of the birth of Christ on December 25. A **Christmas tree** is an evergreen tree hung with decorations at Christmas time. *n.*

chro·mi·um (krō′mē əm) a shiny, hard, brittle, metallic substance that does not rust or become dull easily: *Chromium is used in alloys and in plating. n.*

chro·mo·some (krō′mə sōm′) any of the tiny rod-shaped bodies that appear in the nucleus of a plant or animal cell when it divides: *Chromosomes carry the genes that pass on inherited characteristics. n.*

chron·ic (kron′ik) **1** of a disease, lasting a long time: *Rheumatism is often chronic.* **2** constant; habitual: *a chronic liar, a chronic smoker. adj.*

chron·i·cle (kron′ə kəl) **1** a record of happenings in the order in which they happened; a history or story. **2** write or tell the story of. 1 *n.,* 2 *v.,* **chron·i·cled, chron·i·cling. —chron′i·cler,** *n.*

chrys·a·lis (kris′ə lis) **1** the hard shell developed by a caterpillar that protects it while it changes into an adult butterfly. **2** the butterfly in this stage; pupa. *n.*

chry·san·the·mum (krə san′thə məm) a plant having ball-shaped flowers with many long, thin petals, that blooms in the fall. *n.*

chub·by (chub′ē) round and plump: *chubby cheeks. adj.,* **chub·bier, chub·bi·est.**

chuck (chuk) **1** a pat or tap: *a chuck under the chin.* **2** pat; tap. **3** a throw or toss. **4** throw; toss: *He chucked a stone into the river.* 1, 3 *n.,* 2, 4 *v.*

chuck–full (chuk′fu̇l′) chock-full. *adj.*

chuck·le (chuk′əl) **1** laugh to oneself: *Father chuckled as he watched the children trying to give the dog a bath.* **2** a soft laugh; quiet laughter. 1 *v.,* **chuck·led, chuck·ling;** 2 *n.*

chuck·wag·on (chuk′wag′en) in the West, a wagon that carries food and cooking equipment for cowboys, harvest hands, etc. *n.*

chuckwagon race *Cdn.* a race between chuckwagons drawn by horses, a thrilling and highly popular event at rodeos and stampedes in western Canada.

chug (chug) **1** a short, loud, explosive sound: *the chug of an engine.* **2** make such sounds. 1 *n.,* 2 *v.,* **chugged, chug·ging.**

chum (chum) *Informal.* **1** a very close friend. **2** be on very friendly terms: *Tom and Bill have chummed for years.* 1 *n.,* 2 *v.,* **chummed, chum·ming.**

chunk (chungk) a thick piece or lump: *a chunk of wood, bread, etc. n.*

church (chėrch) **1** a building for public, especially Christian, worship: *We walked past the church.* **2** the public worship of God in a church: *We went to church.* **3** Usually, **Church,** a group of persons with the same religious beliefs and under the same authority: *She is a member of the Presbyterian Church.* **4 the Church,** all Christians. **5** the profession of a clergyman: *He is going into the church as a career. n.*

Church of England the Christian church that is the national church of England.

church·yard (chėrch′yärd′) the ground around a church: *A churchyard is sometimes used for a burial ground. n.*

churl (chėrl) **1** a rude, surly person. **2** a peasant; a person of low birth. *n.*

churn (chėrn) **1** a container or machine in which butter is made from cream by beating and shaking. **2** beat and shake cream, etc. in a churn. **3** move as if beaten and shaken: *The water churns in the rapids.* 1 *n.,* 2, 3 *v.*

chute[1] (shüt) **1** an inclined passage, trough, etc. down which things are dropped or slid to a lower level: *There are chutes for carrying mail, dirty clothes, coal, etc. A toboggan slide is called a chute.* **2** rapids in a river; waterfall. *n.*

☛ **Chute** and **shoot** are pronounced the same.

chute[2] (shüt) *Informal.* parachute. *n.*

☛ See note at **chute**[1].

ci·ca·da (sə kā′də) a large insect with transparent wings: *The male cicada makes a shrill sound in hot, dry weather. n.*

ci·der (sī′dər) the juice pressed out of apples for use as a drink and in making vinegar. *n.*

ci·gar (sə gär′) a tight roll of dried tobacco leaves for smoking. *n.*

cig·a·rette (sig′ə ret′ or sig′ə ret′) a small roll of finely cut tobacco enclosed in a thin sheet of paper, for smoking. *n.* Also spelled **cigaret.**

cinch (sinch) **1** a strong band or belt, usually of leather, for fastening a saddle or pack on a horse. **2** fasten on with a cinch; bind firmly. **3** *Informal.*

something sure and easy: *We were a cinch to win the game.* 1, 3 *n.,* 2 *v.*

cin·der (sin′dər) 1 a piece of wood or coal partly burned and no longer flaming. 2 burned-up wood or coal; ash: *Cinders are made up of larger pieces than ashes are.* *n.*

cin·e·ma (sin′ə mə) 1 a motion picture. 2 a motion-picture theatre. 3 **the cinema,** motion pictures as an art form: *His interest in the cinema began in art and drama classes.* *n.*

cin·na·mon (sin′ə mən) 1 the inner bark of a tree that grows in the East Indies, used as a spice and in medicine. 2 a spice made from this bark. 3 light, reddish brown: *a cinnamon bear.* 1–3 *n.,* 3 *adj.*

ci·pher (sī′fər) 1 zero; 0. 2 a person or thing of no importance. 3 a method of secret writing; code: *He sent me a telegram in cipher.* 4 something in secret writing or code. 5 a key to a method of secret writing or code. 6 do arithmetic; use figures. 1–5 *n.,* 6 *v.*

☛ **Cipher** came into English from an Old French word *cifre,* which came from an Arabic word *sifr,* meaning 'zero' or 'empty.' See also note at **zero.**

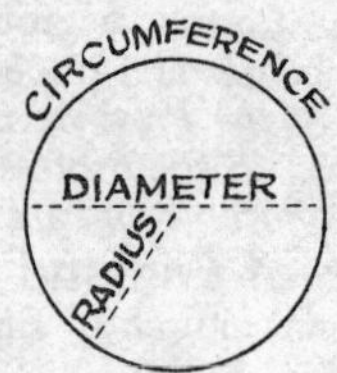

A circle

cir·cle (sėr′kəl) 1 a curved line of which every point is equally distant from a point called the centre. 2 the space bounded by such a line. 3 something resembling a circle or part of one: *a circle around the moon.* 4 a ring: *The girls danced in a circle.* 5 go round in a circle: *The airplane circled before it landed.* 6 form a circle around; surround: *A ring of forts circled the city.* 7 identify by drawing a circle around: *Circle the number of the answer you think is correct.* 8 a complete series or course of something that is repeated; cycle: *A year is a circle of 12 months.* 9 a group of people held together by the same interests: *the family circle, a circle of friends.* 1–4, 8, 9 *n.,* 5–7 *v.,* **cir·cled, cir·cling.**

cir·cuit (sėr′kit) 1 going around; moving around: *It takes a year for the earth to make its circuit of the sun.* 2 the complete path followed by an electric current. 3 a route followed repeatedly; a trip made regularly and having several stopovers: *a judge's circuit, a milkman's circuit.* 4 the area or region through which such circuits are made. 5 a line enclosing any space; boundary line. *n.*

cir·cu·i·tous (sər kyü′ə təs) roundabout: *To avoid unpaved roads, we took a circuitous route home.* *adj.*

cir·cu·lar (sėr′kyə lər) 1 round: *The full moon is circular.* 2 moving in a circle: *A merry-go-round makes a circular trip.* 3 a letter, notice, or advertisement sent to each of a number of people. 1, 2 *adj.,* 3 *n.*

cir·cu·late (sėr′kyə lāt′) 1 go around: *Water circulates in the pipes of a building. Money circulates as it goes from person to person.* 2 send around from person to person or place to place: *The children circulated the news of the holiday. This book has been widely circulated.* *v.,* **cir·cu·lat·ed, cir·cu·lat·ing.**

cir·cu·la·tion (sėr′kyə lā′shən) 1 going around; circulating: *Open windows increase the circulation of air in a room.* 2 the movement of the blood from the heart through the body and back to the heart. 3 the sending around of books, papers, news, etc. from person to person or place to place. 4 the number of copies of a newspaper, magazine, etc. that are sent out during a certain time. *n.*

cir·cu·la·to·ry (sėr′kyə lə tô′rē) having to do with circulation: *Arteries and veins are parts of the circulatory system of the human body.* *adj.*

cir·cum·fer·ence (sər kum′fər əns) 1 the boundary line of a circle: *Every point in the circumference of a circle is at the same distance from the centre.* See **circle** for picture. 2 the length of this line. 3 the distance around: *The big tree had a circumference of three metres.* *n.*

cir·cum·nav·i·gate (sėr′kəm nav′ə gāt′) sail completely around: *Magellan's ship circumnavigated the earth.* *v.,* **cir·cum·nav·i·gat·ed, cir·cum·nav·i·gat·ing.**

cir·cum·stance (sėr′kəm stans′) 1 one of a series of facts or events to be considered together: *The place, the weather, and other circumstances made the picnic a great success.* 2 a fact or event: *It was a lucky circumstance that she found her money.* 3 **circumstances,** *pl.* the condition of a person with regard to money: *A rich man is in good circumstances; a poor man is in bad circumstances.* 4 ceremony; display: *The procession advanced with pomp and circumstance.* *n.*

cir·cum·vent (sėr′kəm vent′) 1 get around or get the better of; outwit: *The police circumvented the strikers' plans to take over the factory.* 2 go around: *This route will circumvent the traffic on the main road.* *v.*

cir·cus (sėr′kəs) 1 a travelling show of acrobats, clowns, horses, riders, and wild animals. 2 the performers who give the show. 3 in ancient Rome, a round or oval space with rows of seats around it, each row higher than the one in front of it. *n.*

cir·rus (sir′əs) a thin, curling, wispy cloud very high in the air: *Cirrus clouds are so high that the water in them has frozen into ice crystals.* *n., pl.* **cir·ri** (sir′ī or sir′ē).

cis·tern (sis′tərn) a tank or reservoir, especially an underground tank for storing rainwater. *n.*

cit·a·del (sit′ə dəl) a fortress, especially one in a city: *Halifax has a famous citadel.* *n.*

ci·ta·tion (sī tā′shən) 1 a quotation or reference given as an authority for facts, opinions, etc. 2 an honorable mention for bravery in war: *My grandfather is proud of the citation he won in World War II.* 3 the commendation of a person for public service by some official or institution. *n.*

cite (sīt) 1 quote: *He cited the Bible and Shakespeare to prove his statement.* 2 refer to; mention; bring up as an example: *Can you cite another case like this one?* 3 mention publicly in praise of outstanding service to one's country, to humanity, etc. *v.,* **cit·ed, cit·ing.**

☛ **Cite, sight,** and **site** are pronounced the same.

cit·i·zen (sit′ə zən) 1 a person who by birth or by choice is a member of a state or nation that gives him certain rights and claims his loyalty: *Many immigrants*

hat, āge, fär; let, ēqual, tėrm; it, īce
hot, ōpen, ôrder; oil, out; cup, pu̇t, rüle
əbove, takən, pencəl, lemən, circəs
ch, child; ng, long; sh, ship
th, thin; ᴛʜ, then; zh, measure

have become citizens of Canada. 2 an inhabitant of a city or town. *n.*

cit·i·zen·ry (sit′ə zən rē) citizens as a group. *n.*

cit·i·zen·ship (sit′e zən ship′) the duties, rights, and privileges of a citizen. *n.*

cit·ric acid (sit′rik) a white, odorless, sour-tasting acid that occurs in lemons, limes, etc.: *Citric acid is used as a flavoring, as a medicine, and in making dyes.*

cit·ron (sit′rən) 1 a small, round melon having hard flesh that is used in making preserves and pickles. 2 a lemon-like fruit having a thick rind which is often preserved or candied for use in desserts and fruit cakes. *n.*

cit·rus (sit′rəs) any tree bearing lemons, limes, oranges, grapefruit, or similar fruit. *n.*

citrus fruit the fruit of a citrus tree.

cit·y (sit′ē) 1 a town of more than a certain size or level of importance: *Montreal and Toronto are the largest cities in Canada.* 2 the people living in a city: *The whole city was terrified by the great fire. n., pl.* **cit·ies.**

city hall the headquarters of the local government in a city: *The mayor's office is in the city hall.*

civ·ic (siv′ik) 1 of a city. 2 of citizenship: *Obeying the laws, voting, and paying taxes are civic duties.* 3 of citizens. *adj.*

civ·ics (siv′iks) the study of the duties, rights, and privileges of citizens. *n.*

civ·il (siv′əl) 1 of a citizen or citizens; having to do with citizens: *Civil war is war between two groups of citizens in the same country.* 2 not naval, military, or connected with the church: *civil defence, civil law.* 3 polite; courteous: *The boy answered our questions in a civil way. adj.*

ci·vil·ian (sə vil′yən) 1 a person who is not in the armed forces. 2 of civilians; not military or naval: *Soldiers often wear civilian clothes when on leave.* 1 *n.,* 2 *adj.*

ci·vil·i·ty (sə vil′ə tē) politeness; courtesy. *n., pl.* **ci·vil·i·ties.**

civ·i·li·za·tion (siv′ə lə zā′shən or siv′ə lī zā′shən) 1 a civilized condition. 2 a nation or people that have a complicated political and social system with knowledge of the arts and sciences: *The scientists found the remains of an ancient civilization.* 3 the ways of living of a race or nation: *There are differences between Chinese civilization and our own. n.*

civ·i·lize (siv′ə līz′) change a primitive social and political system to a much more complicated one that includes knowledge of the arts and sciences: *The church did much to civilize the Anglo-Saxons. v.,* **civ·i·lized, civ·i·liz·ing.**

civil servant a member of the civil service: *Post office workers are civil servants. A cabinet minister has a staff of civil servants.*

civil service the federal or provincial officials, clerks, etc. who do the day-to-day work of government departments: *The civil service handles public services such as issuing pensions, collecting taxes, and dealing with mail.*

clack (klak) 1 make a short, sharp sound: *The old lady's needles clacked as she knitted.* 2 a short, sharp sound: *We heard the clack of her heels on the sidewalk.* 1 *v.,* 2 *n.*

clad (klad) See **clothe.** *He was clad all in green. v.*

claim (klām) 1 demand as one's own or one's right: *Does anyone claim this pencil?* 2 such a demand: *She makes a claim to the pencil.* 3 a right or title to a thing; a right to demand something: *She has a claim on us because she is my mother's cousin.* 4 a piece of land that someone claims: *a miner's claim.* 5 deserve; require: *The care of the baby claims much of Mother's time.* 6 say strongly; maintain; declare as a fact: *She claimed that her answer was correct.* 1, 5, 6 *v.,* 2–4 *n.* **lay claim to,** demand or declare one's right to: *She laid claim to the records we were taking.*

clam (klam) 1 a shellfish resembling an oyster, having a soft body and a hinged double shell and living in sand along the seashore, or at the edges of lakes and rivers: *Some clams are good to eat.* 2 go out after clams; dig for clams. 1 *n.,* 2 *v.,* **clammed, clam·ming.**

clam·bake (klam′bāk′) a picnic where clams are baked or steamed. *n.*

clam·ber (klam′bər) climb, using both hands and feet; scramble: *The boys clambered up the steep hill. v.*

clam·my (klam′ē) cold and damp: *A frog is a clammy creature. adj.,* **clam·mi·er, clam·mi·est.**

clam·or or **clam·our** (klam′ər) 1 a loud noise, especially of voices; confused shouting. 2 make a loud noise. 3 a noisy demand. 4 demand or complain noisily: *The children were clamoring for candy.* 1, 3 *n.,* 2, 4 *v.*

clam·or·ous (klam′ər əs) loud and noisy. *adj.*

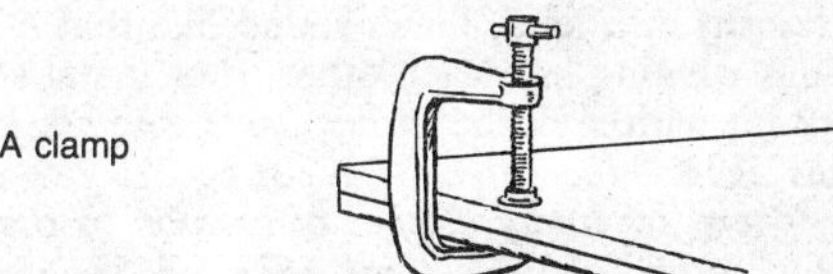
A clamp

clamp (klamp) 1 a device for holding things tightly together: *He used a clamp to hold the joint until the glue dried.* 2 fasten together with a clamp; fix in a clamp; strengthen with clamps: *A picture frame must be clamped together while the glue is drying.* 1 *n.,* 2 *v.*

clan (klan) 1 especially in Scotland, a group of related families that claim to be descended from a common ancestor. 2 a group of people closely joined together by some common interest. *n.*

clang (klang) 1 a loud, harsh sound such as that caused by metal striking metal: *The clang of the fire bell aroused the town.* 2 make such a sound: *The fire bells clanged.* 1 *n.,* 2 *v.*

clank (klangk) 1 a sound like the rattle of a heavy chain. 2 make such a sound: *The swords clashed and clanked as the men fought together.* 1 *n.,* 2 *v.*

clap (klap) 1 a sudden noise, such as a single burst of thunder, the sound of the hands struck together, or the sound of a loud slap. 2 make such a noise, especially

with the hands: *When the show was over, we all clapped.* **3** strike with a quick blow: *He clapped his friend on the back.* 1 *n.*, 2, 3 *v.*, **clapped, clap·ping.**
clap eyes on, *Informal.* look at; see.

clap·board (klap′bôrd or klab′ərd) **1** a thin board, thicker along one edge than the other, used to cover the outer walls of a wooden building. **2** cover with clapboards. 1 *n.*, 2 *v.*

clap·per (klap′ər) **1** the movable part inside a bell that strikes and rings the outer part. See **bell** for picture. **2** a device for making noise: *We had horns and clappers at the party.* *n.*

clar·i·fy (klar′ə fī′ or kler′ə fī′) **1** make clear by explaining: *His sister's explanation of the sentence clarified its meaning.* **2** make or become free of impurities; purify: *We clarified the cloudy liquid by using a filter.* *v.*, **clar·i·fied, clar·i·fy·ing.**

A clarinet

clar·i·net (klar′ə net′ or kler′ə net′) a wind instrument having a single reed and usually made of wood. *n.*

clar·i·on (klar′ē ən or kler′ē ən) **1** clear and shrill. **2** a trumpet with clear, shrill tones. 1 *adj.*, 2 *n.*

clar·i·ty (klar′ə tē or kler′ə tē) being clear; clearness. *n.*

clash (klash) **1** a loud, harsh sound like that of two hard things running into each other or of metal striking metal. **2** hit with a clash: *In her haste, she clashed the saucepans against the stove.* **3** a strong disagreement; a conflict: *There are many clashes of opinion in that family, for no two of them think alike.* **4** disagree strongly; be in conflict; go badly together: *His feelings and his judgment sometimes clash.* 1, 3 *n.*, 2, 4 *v.*

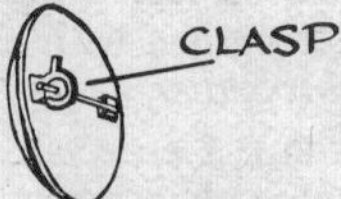

A clasp on a brooch

clasp (klasp) **1** a device, usually having a hook of some kind, used to fasten two parts or pieces together: *This suede belt has a gold clasp.* **2** fasten together with a clasp. **3** hold closely with the hand or the arms: *The mother clasped her baby to her breast. He clasped a knife in his hand.* **4** a firm grasp of the hand: *He gave my hand a warm clasp.* **5** a close hold: *The wrestler held his opponent in a firm clasp.* 1, 4, 5 *n.*, 2, 3 *v.*

class (klas) **1** a group of persons or things of the same kind. **2** a group of students taught together. **3** the meeting time for such a group: *The class was at nine o'clock.* **4** a group of students entering a school together and graduating in the same year: *The class of 1970 graduated in 1970.* **5** a rank of society: *Business people, teachers, and lawyers belong to the middle class.* **6** put in a class; classify. **7** grade; quality: *First class is the most costly way to travel.* 1–5, 7 *n.*, 6 *v.*

clas·sic (klas′ik) **1** an author or an artist of generally recognized excellence whose works serve as a standard, model, or guide: *Shakespeare is a classic.* **2** a book or artistic work of the highest rank or quality: *'Robinson Crusoe' is a classic.* **3** of the highest rank or quality; being used as an example of excellence of its kind: *a classic example of clear, attractive handwriting. The 1937 Ford car is classic.* **4** simple and fine in form: *the classic style of Bach's music.* **5** of the literature, art, and life of ancient Greece and Rome. **6 the classics,** the literature of ancient Greece and Rome. 1, 2, 6 *n.*, 3–5 *adj.*

clas·si·cal (klas′ə kəl) **1** of high artistic excellence: *She likes classical literature and music.* **2** of or having to do with the literature, art, and life of ancient Greece and Rome: *a classical scholar.* *adj.*

clas·si·fi·ca·tion (klas′ə fə kā′shən) **1** an arranging in classes or groups on the basis of similar qualities or features; grouping according to class or kind. **2** the arrangement or grouping so made: *This library has worked out a simple classification for its books.* *n.*

clas·si·fy (klas′ə fī′) arrange in groups or classes; group according to some system: *In the post office, mail is classified according to the places where it is to go.* *v.*, **clas·si·fied, clas·si·fy·ing.**

class·mate (klas′māt′) a member of the same class in school. *n.*

class·room (klas′rüm′) a room in which classes are held. *n.*

clat·ter (klat′ər) **1** a rattling noise: *the clatter of dishes.* **2** move or fall with a rattling noise; make a commotion: *The horses clattered over the stones.* **3** noisy talk. 1, 3 *n.*, 2 *v.*

clause (kloz or klôz) **1** a part of a sentence having a subject and a verb: *In 'He came before we left,' 'He came' is a main clause that could stand alone as a sentence and 'before we left' is a clause that modifies the main clause.* **2** a single provision of a law, treaty, or any other written agreement: *There is a clause in our contract that says we may not keep a dog in this building.* *n.*

claw (klo or klô) **1** a sharp, hooked nail on each toe of a bird: *The chicken scratched the earth with its claws.* **2** a similar nail on each toe of certain animals: *The cat's claws were very dangerous.* **3** a foot with such sharp, hooked nails: *The gopher was held tightly in the hawk's claws.* **4** anything like a claw in shape or use: *The pincers of lobsters or crabs are called claws. The part of a hammer used for pulling nails is the claw.* **5** scratch, tear, seize, or pull with claws or fingernails: *The kitten was clawing the screen door. The madman clawed at the walls.* 1–4 *n.*, 5 *v.*

clay (klā) a sticky kind of earth that can be easily shaped when wet and that hardens when dried or baked: *Bricks and dishes are made from various kinds of clay.* *n.*

clean (klēn) **1** free from dirt; not soiled or stained: *clean clothes. Soap and water make us clean.* **2** pure; innocent: *a clean heart.* **3** having clean habits: *Cats are clean animals.* **4** make clean: *clean a room. Washing cleans clothes.* **5** do cleaning: *I'm going to clean this*

hat, āge, fär; let, ēqual, tėrm; it, īce
hot, ōpen, ôrder; oil, out; cup, pu̇t, rüle
əbove, takən, pencəl, lemən, circəs
ch, child; ng, long; sh, ship
th, thin; ᴛʜ, then; zh, measure

morning. 6 clear; even; regular: *clean features.* 7 well-shaped; trim: *The clean lines of his new car.* 8 complete; entire; total: *The new owner of the newspaper made a clean sweep by dismissing all the workers and hiring new ones.* 9 completely; entirely; totally: *The horse jumped clean over the brook.* 1–3, 6–8 *adj.,* 4, 5 *v.,* 9 *adv.*

clean out, a make clean by emptying: *Clean out your desk.* **b** empty; use up: *The girls cleaned out a whole box of cookies.* **c** *Slang.* leave without money; take all a person's money.

clean up, a make clean by removing dirt, rubbish, etc.: *clean up the yard.* **b** put in order. **c** *Informal.* finish; complete: *I finally got my homework cleaned up.* **d** *Slang.* make money; profit: *He was expecting to clean up in a business deal, but he got cleaned out instead.*

clean·er (klēn′ər) 1 a person whose work is keeping buildings, windows, etc. clean. 2 anything that removes dirt, grease, or stains; cleanser. *n.*

clean·li·ness (klen′lē nis) being always, or nearly always, clean; cleanness: *Cleanliness is good for health.* *n.*

clean·ly[1] (klen′lē) clean; habitually clean: *A cat is a cleanly animal.* *adj.,* **clean·li·er, clean·li·est.**

clean·ly[2] (klēn′lē) in a clean manner: *The butcher's knife cut cleanly through the meat.* *adv.*

clean·ness (klēn′nis) being clean: *The cleanness of our rooms pleased Mother.* *n.*

cleanse (klenz) make clean. *v.,* **cleansed, cleans·ing.**

cleans·er (klenz′ər) a substance that cleans: *The housewife today can choose from many good cleansers.* *n.*

clear (klēr) 1 not cloudy, misty, or hazy; bright; light: *A clear sky is free from clouds.* 2 easy to see through; transparent: *clear glass.* 3 easily heard, seen, or understood; plain; distinct: *There is a clear view of the sea from that hill. He told a clear story.* 4 sure; certain: *It is clear that it is going to rain.* 5 make clean and free; get clear: *He will clear the land of trees.* 6 become clear: *It soon cleared after the thunder shower.* 7 in a clean manner; clearly; distinctly; entirely: *The bullet went clear through the door.* 8 get over or by without touching: *The jumper cleared the hurdle.* 1–4 *adj.,* 5, 6, 8 *v.,* 7 *adv.* —**clear′ly,** *adv.* —**clear′ness,** *n.*

clear out, a make clear by throwing out or emptying: *clear out a cupboard.* **b** *Informal.* go away; leave: *The audience cleared out of the burning theatre.*

clear up, a make or become clear: *The weather will clear up soon.* **b** clean up or straighten up. **c** explain: *He cleared up the question of his absence by saying he had been ill.*

in the clear, *Informal.* free of guilt or blame; innocent: *His report shows that the suspect is in the clear.*

clear–cut (klēr′kut′) 1 having clear, sharp outlines. 2 clear; definite; distinct: *He had clear-cut ideas about how to do his work.* *adj.*

clear·ing (klēr′ing) an open space of cleared land in a forest. *n.*

cleat (klēt) 1 one of several studs or bars of leather, plastic, etc. attached to the sole of a football boot, soccer boot, etc. to prevent slipping. 2 one of several bars of wood, metal, leather, etc. attached to a sloped gangplank or passageway to give better footing. 3 one of the raised bars placed at intervals across the track of a vehicle that travels over snow: *The cleats on a snowmobile track make possible a firmer grip on snow.* 4 a small, wedge-shaped block fastened to a spar, mast, etc. on a ship or boat as a support, check, etc. 5 a specially shaped piece of wood, metal, plastic, etc. fixed to a boat, ship, dock, etc. and used for securing ropes or lines. *n.*

cleav·age (klēv′ij) 1 the way in which a thing tends to split: *Slate shows a marked cleavage and can easily be separated into layers.* 2 a split or division. *n.*

cleave[1] (klēv) 1 cut, divide, or split open: *With one blow of the axe he cleft the log in two.* 2 pass through; pierce; penetrate: *The airplane swept across the sky cleaving the clouds.* 3 make by cutting: *cleave a path through the wilderness.* *v.,* **cleft** or **cleaved** or **clove, cleft** or **cleaved** or **clo·ven, cleav·ing.**

cleave[2] (klēv) hold fast to; cling: *He was so frightened that his tongue cleaved to the roof of his mouth.* *v.,* **cleaved, cleav·ing.**

A cleaver

cleav·er (klēv′ər) a butcher's chopper with a heavy blade and a short handle, used for cutting through meat or bone. *n.*

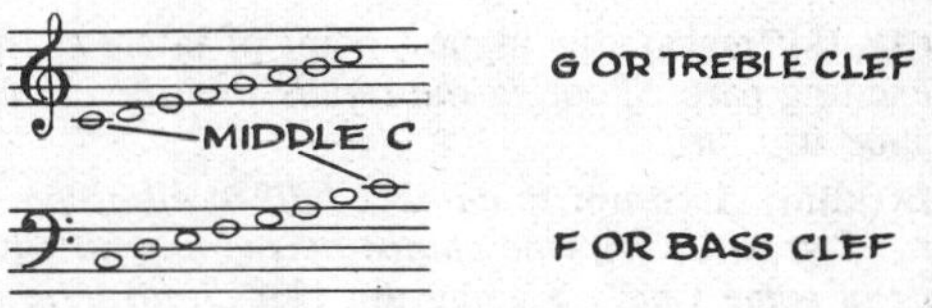

clef (klef) a symbol in music indicating the pitch of the notes on a staff. *n.*

cleft (kleft) 1 See **cleave**[1]. *His blow cleft the log in two.* 2 split; divided: *a cleft stick.* 3 a space or opening made by splitting; crack: *a cleft in the rock.* 1 *v.,* 2 *adj.,* 3 *n.*

clem·en·cy (klem′ən sē) 1 mercy: *The judge showed clemency to the prisoner.* 2 mildness of climate or weather. *n., pl.* **clem·en·cies.**

clench (klench) 1 close tightly together: *to clench one's teeth, to clench one's hand, a clenched fist.* 2 grasp firmly: *He clenched my arm.* 3 a tight grip: *I felt the clench of his hand on my arm.* 4 to clinch. 1, 2, 4 *v.,* 3 *n.*

cler·gy (klėr′jē) persons specially trained and officially appointed to carry out religious services: *Ministers, priests, and rabbis are members of the clergy.* *n., pl.* **cler·gies.**

cler·gy·man (klėr′jē mən) a minister, pastor, priest, or rabbi. *n., pl.* **cler·gy·men** (klėr′jē mən).

cler·ic (kler′ik) clergyman. *n.*

cler·i·cal (kler′ə kəl) **1** of a clerk; of clerks; for clerks: *This big bank employs many persons for clerical work.* **2** of a clergyman or the clergy: *The priest wore clerical robes in church.* *adj.*

clerk (klėrk) **1** a person employed to sell goods in a store or shop. **2** a person employed in an office to file records, copy letters, keep accounts, etc. **3** a public official in charge of files or records: *a township clerk.* **4** work as a clerk, especially in a store or shop: *He clerks in a drugstore.* 1–3 *n.*, 4 *v.*

clev·er (klev′ər) **1** bright; intelligent; having a ready mind: *She is the cleverest person in our class.* **2** skilful in doing some particular thing: *He is a clever carpenter.* **3** showing skill or intelligence: *a clever trick, a clever answer.* *adj.* **—clev′er·ly,** *adv.* **—clev′er·ness,** *n.*

clew (klü) a ball of thread or yarn. *n.*

☞ **Clew** and **clue** are pronounced the same.

click (klik) **1** a short, sharp sound: *We heard the click as he turned the key in the lock.* **2** make such a sound: *We heard a key click in the lock.* **3** *Slang.* get along well together: *We clicked from the start.* **4** *Slang.* succeed: *He's sure to click in that job.* 1 *n.*, 2–4 *v.*

cli·ent (klī′ənt) **1** a person for whom a lawyer acts. **2** customer. *n.*

cliff (klif) a steep, high face of rock or earth; precipice: *Great cliffs overhung the canyon.* *n.*

cli·mate (klī′mit) **1** the kind of weather a place has over a period of years: *Climate includes conditions of heat and cold, moisture and dryness, clearness and cloudiness, wind and calm.* **2** a region with certain conditions of heat and cold, rainfall, wind, sunlight, etc.: *The doctor ordered him to go to a drier climate.* *n.*

cli·max (klī′maks) the highest point of interest; the most exciting part: *Shooting the rapids was the climax of our canoe trip.* *n.*

climb (klīm) **1** go up: *to climb a hill, to climb a ladder.* **2** grow up: *A vine climbs by twining about a support of some kind.* **3** going up: *Our climb took two hours.* **4** go in any direction, especially with the help of the hands: *He climbed down the rope.* **5** increase: *The price of coffee has climbed during the past year.* 1, 2, 4, 5 *v.*, 3 *n.*

☞ **Climb** and **clime** are pronounced the same.

clime (klīm) **1** a country or region. **2** climate. *n.*

☞ See note at **climb.**

clinch (klinch) **1** fasten a driven nail by bending down the point. **2** fasten firmly; settle decisively: *A deposit of five dollars clinched the bargain.* **3** hold on tight, as in boxing or wrestling. **4** holding on tight: *The referee broke the boxers' clinch.* 1–3 *v.*, 4 *n.*

cling (kling) **1** attach oneself firmly; grasp; hold tightly: *The child clung to his mother.* **2** stick; be attached: *A vine clings to the wall.* **3** remain attached to an idea, belief, etc.: *He clings to the ways of his father.* *v.*, **clung, cling·ing.**

clin·ic (klin′ik) **1** a part of a hospital where people are treated for certain kinds of illness without having to stay overnight: *They have the latest equipment in the eye clinic.* **2** a place, separate from a hospital, where a group of doctors work together: *My uncle is the heart specialist in the new clinic near here.* **3** a session held to treat or prevent certain illnesses or injuries, or to provide a special service: *Our Red Cross clinic is open three evenings a week. There was a rabies clinic for pets in our community centre last week.* *n.*

clink (klingk) **1** a light, sharp, ringing sound, like that of glasses hitting together. **2** make a sharp, ringing sound: *The spoons and glasses clinked.* 1 *n.*, 2 *v.*

clink·er (kling′kər) a piece of the rough, hard mass left in a furnace or stove after coal has been burned; a large, rough cinder. *n.*

clip[1] (klip) **1** cut; cut out; cut short; trim with shears, scissors, or clippers: *clip the hair. Mother is going to clip this recipe and paste it in her cookbook.* **2** cut or trim the hair of a person or animal. **3** shear off the fleece of a sheep. **4** the act of clipping: *His hair needs a clip around the back of the neck.* **5** a fast pace: *Our bus passed through the village at quite a clip.* **6** *Informal.* hit or punch sharply: *The boxer clipped his opponent on the jaw.* **7** *Informal.* a sharp blow or punch. 1–3, 6 *v.*, **clipped, clip·ping;** 4, 5, 7 *n.*

a good clip, a fairly rapid pace: *She's coming at a good clip.*

clip[2] (klip) **1** hold tight; fasten: *to clip papers together.* **2** something used for clipping: *A clip for papers is often made of a piece of bent wire.* 1 *v.*, **clipped, clip·ping;** 2 *n.*

clip·board (klip′bôrd′) a small writing board having a heavy spring clip at one end for holding papers. *n.*

clip·per (klip′ər) **1** Often, **clippers,** *pl.* a tool for cutting: *hair clippers, a nail clipper.* **2** a sailing ship built for speed: *Clippers from Nova Scotia used to sail all over the world.* *n.*

clip·ping (klip′ing) a piece cut out of a newspaper, magazine, etc. *n.*

clique (klēk) a small, exclusive group of people within a larger group: *The club was run by a clique.* *n.*

cloak (klōk) **1** a loose outer garment with or without sleeves. **2** cover with a cloak. **3** anything that covers or hides: *He won my confidence, and then betrayed me under the cloak of friendship.* **4** hide: *He cloaked his evil purpose under friendly words.* 1, 3 *n.*, 2, 4 *v.*

cloak·room (klōk′rüm′) a room, especially in a school or other public building, where coats, hats, etc. can be left for a time. *n.*

clock (klok) **1** an instrument for measuring and showing time: *A clock is not made to be carried about as a watch is.* **2** measure or record the time of; time: *The coach clocked the three boys to see who was the fastest runner.* 1 *n.*, 2 *v.*

around the clock, all day and all night.

clock·wise (klok′wīz′) in the direction in which the hands of a clock move: *Turn the lid clockwise to tighten it.* *adv., adj.*

clock·work (klok′wėrk′) **1** the machinery of a clock. **2** machinery like that of a clock: *Toys that have to be wound up with a key are run by clockwork.* *n.*

like clockwork, with great regularity and smoothness: *The launching of the rocket went off like clockwork.*

clod (klod) **1** a lump of earth. **2** a stupid person. *n.*

hat, āge, fär; let, ēqual, tėrm; it, īce
hot, ōpen, ôrder; oil, out; cup, pu̇t, rüle
əbove, takən, pencəl, lemən, circəs
ch, child; ng, long; sh, ship
th, thin; ᴛʜ, then; zh, measure

clog (klog) **1** block by filling up; stop up: *leaves clogged the drain.* **2** become blocked or filled up: *The drain clogged with leaves.* **3** hinder the movement or operation of: *Sand clogged the reel of the fishing rod.* **4** any weight or other thing that hinders. **5** a shoe with a wooden sole. 1–3 *v.,* **clogged, clog·ging;** 4, 5 *n.*

A cloister (def. 1)

clois·ter (klois′tər) **1** a covered walk along the wall of a building, with a row of pillars on the open side: *A cloister is often built around the courtyard of a monastery, church, or college building.* **2** a convent or monastery. **3** a quiet place shut away from the world. **4** shut away in a quiet place. 1–3 *n.,* 4 *v.*

close[1] (klōz) **1** shut: *Close the door. The sleepy child's eyes are closing.* **2** bring together: *Close the ranks of the troops.* **3** come together. **4** come or bring to an end: *The meeting closed with a speech by the president.* **5** an end: *He spoke at the close of the meeting.* 1–4 *v.,* **closed, clos·ing;** 5 *n.*

close in, come near; approach from all sides: *The thief gave up when the police closed in. Night closed in.*

close in on, come near and surround or shut in on all sides: *The wolves closed in on the moose. I felt that the walls were closing in on me.*

☛ **Close** and **clothes** are often pronounced the same.

close[2] (klōs) **1** with little space between: *The buildings were huddled close.* **2** stifling; stuffy: *With the windows shut, the room was hot and close.* **3** near. **4** nearly equal: *The race was a close contest.* **5** stingy: *He was close with his money. adj.,* **clos·er, clos·est. —close′ly,** *adv.* **—close′ness,** *n.*

close quarters, a place or position with little space: *We are living in close quarters here.*

close–fit·ting (klōs′fit′ing) fitting tightly; tight: *a close-fitting jacket. adj.*

clos·et (kloz′it) **1** a small room or large cupboard used for storing things: *There is another coat in the closet.* **2** a small, private room for prayer or study. **3** shut up in a room for a private talk: *He was closeted with the lawyer for over an hour.* **4** toilet. 1, 2, 4 *n.,* 3 *v.*

close–up (klōs′up′) a picture taken at close range: *That is a good close-up of the flower. n.*

clot (klot) **1** a thickened mass: *A clot of blood formed in the cut.* **2** form into clots: *Bleeding stops when the blood clots.* 1 *n.,* 2 *v.,* **clot·ted, clot·ting.**

cloth (kloth) **1** material made from wool, silk, linen, cotton, or other fibre: *Cloth is used for clothing, curtains, bedding, etc.* **2** a piece of cloth used for a special purpose: *a cloth for the table. n.*

clothe (klōᴛʜ) **1** put clothes on; cover with clothes; dress. **2** provide with clothes: *It costs quite a bit to clothe a family of six.* **3** cover or wrap as if with clothes: *The trees are clothed in green leaves. He clothed his simple ideas in fancy words. v.,* **clothed** or **clad, cloth·ing.**

clothes (klōz or klōᴛʜz) coverings that people put on their bodies; garments: *They like stylish clothes. n. pl.*

☛ **Clothes** and **close** are often pronounced the same.

clothes peg **1** a peg for hanging clothes on. **2** clothes pin.

clothes pin a wooden or plastic clip to hold clothes on a line.

cloth·ing (klōᴛʜ′ing) clothes. *n.*

cloud (kloud) **1** a white, grey, or almost black mass in the sky, made up of tiny drops of water or ice particles: *Sometimes when it rains, the sky is completely covered with dark clouds.* **2** a mass of smoke or dust in the air. **3** cover with a cloud or clouds: *A mist clouded our view.* **4** become cloudy: *The sky clouded over.* **5** a great number of things moving close together: *a cloud of arrows, a cloud of birds in flight.* **6** anything that darkens or dims; a cause of gloom, trouble, suspicion, or disgrace: *A cloud hangs over his reputation.* **7** darken; dim; make or become gloomy: *His face clouded with anger.* 1, 2, 5, 6 *n.,* 3, 4, 7 *v.* **—cloud′less,** *adj.*

cloud·burst (kloud′bėrst′) a short, sudden, very heavy rainfall. *n.*

cloud·y (kloud′ē) **1** covered with clouds; having clouds in it: *The sky was cloudy.* **2** not clear: *a cloudy mixture.* **3** streaked; spotted: *cloudy marble.* **4** not carefully thought out; confused; indistinct: *cloudy ideas. His thinking was cloudy. adj.,* **cloud·i·er, cloud·i·est. —cloud′i·ly,** *adv.* **—cloud′i·ness,** *n.*

clout (klout) **1** a blow, hit, or knock: *He gave the boy a clout.* **2** strike, hit, or knock: *He clouted the ball over the fence.* **3** a cloth; rag. 1, 3 *n.,* 2 *v.*

clove[1] (klōv) a strong, fragrant spice made from the dried flower buds of a tree that grows in the tropics. *n.*

clove[2] (klōv) See **cleave**[1]. *He clove the log in two. v.*

clo·ven (klō′vən) **1** See **cleave**[1]. **2** divided into two parts: *Cows have cloven hoofs.* 1 *v.,* 2 *adj.*

clo·ver (klō′vər) a plant with leaves of three small leaflets and sweet-smelling rounded heads of red or white flowers: *Clover is grown as food for horses and cattle. n.*

in clover, *Informal.* enjoying a life of pleasure and luxury without work or effort.

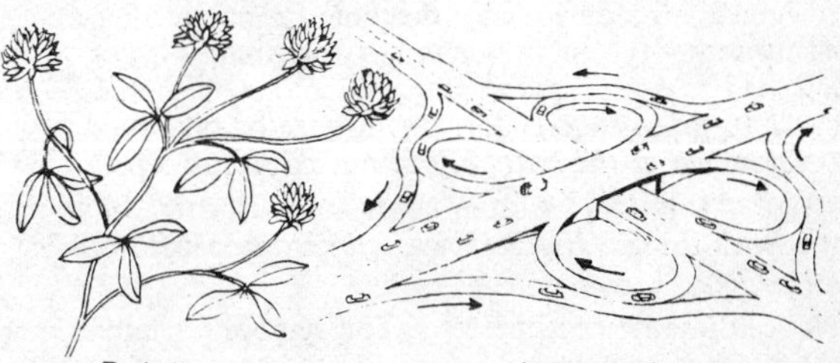

Red clover A cloverleaf

clo·ver·leaf (klō′vər lēf′) a series of roads at an intersection of two highways, so arranged that traffic may move from one highway to the other without crossing in front of other traffic. *n.*

clown (kloun) 1 a man whose business is making people laugh at his tricks and jokes: *The clowns in the circus were very funny.* 2 act like a clown; play tricks and jokes; act silly. 3 an awkward person with bad manners: *That clown does not know how to behave.* 1, 3 *n.,* 2 *v.*

cloy (kloi) make weary by too much, too sweet, or too rich food: *My appetite was cloyed by all the candy I had eaten.* *v.*

club (klub) 1 a heavy stick of wood, thick at one end, used as a weapon. 2 a stick or bat used in some games to hit a ball: *golf clubs.* 3 beat or hit with a club or something similar. 4 a group of people joined together for some special purpose: *a tennis club, a yacht club, a nature-study club.* 5 the building or rooms used by a club. 6 a playing card marked with one or more black designs on it shaped like this: ♣. 7 **clubs,** *pl.* the suit of such playing cards. 1, 2, 4, 5–7 *n.,* 3 *v.,* **clubbed, club·bing.**

club together, unite for some special purpose: *The children clubbed together to buy their mother a gift for her birthday.*

club·house (klub′hous′) a building used by a club. *n.*

cluck (kluk) 1 the sound a hen makes when calling to her chickens. 2 make such a sound. 1 *n.,* 2 *v.*

clue (klü) a guide to the solving of a mystery or problem: *The police could find no clues to help them in solving the crime.* *n.*

☛ **Clue** and **clew** are pronounced the same.

clump (klump) 1 a cluster: *a clump of trees.* 2 walk with a heavy, clumsy, noisy tread: *The lame man clumped along.* 1 *n.,* 2 *v.*

clum·sy (klum′zē) 1 awkward in moving: *The clumsy boy bumped into all the furniture.* 2 not well-shaped or well-made: *His rowboat was a clumsy affair made out of old boxes.* *adj.,* **clum·si·er, clum·si·est. —clum′si·ly,** *adv.*

clung (klung) See **cling.** *The child clung to her mother. The sticky mud had clung to my fingers.* *v.*

clus·ter (klus′tər) 1 a number of things of the same kind growing or grouped together: *a cluster of grapes, a little cluster of houses.* 2 be in a bunch; gather in a group: *The girls clustered around their teacher.* 1 *n.,* 2 *v.*

clutch (kluch) 1 a tight grasp; a firm hold by claw, paw, or hand: *The eagle flew away with a rabbit in its clutch.* 2 grasp tightly: *The girl clutched her doll to her breast.* 3 a device in a machine for connecting or disconnecting the engine or motor that makes it go. 1, 3 *n.,* 2 *v.*

clutch at, grasp eagerly for; try to seize or take hold of: *She clutched at the branch, but missed it and fell.*

clut·ter (klut′ər) 1 litter; confusion; disorder. 2 to litter with things: *His desk was all cluttered with books and papers.* 1 *n.,* 2 *v.*

cm centimetre; centimetres. The symbol for cubic centimetre is now cm^3.

co– a prefix meaning: 1 with; together: *Co-operate means to do something together or at the same time.* 2 fellow; joint: *A co-pilot is a fellow pilot, one who works with another pilot.*

Co. company: *Jones and Co. means Jones and Company.*

c.o. or **c/o** in care of.

coach (kōch) 1 a large, closed carriage with seats inside and, often, on top: *Coaches carried passengers along a regular run, stopping for meals and fresh horses.* 2 a passenger car of a railway train. 3 bus. 4 a type of automobile having four doors. 5 a person who teaches or trains athletes: *a football coach.* 6 a private teacher who helps a student prepare for a special test. 7 train or teach: *He asked his mother to coach him in arithmetic.* 1–6 *n.,* 7 *v.*

coach·man (kōch′mən) a man who drives a coach or carriage for a living. *n., pl.* **coach·men** (kōch′mən).

co·ag·u·late (kō ag′yə lāt′) change from a liquid to a thickened mass; thicken; clot: *Cooking coagulates the white of egg. Blood coagulates in contact with air.* *v.,* **co·ag·u·lat·ed, co·ag·u·lat·ing.**

coal (kōl) 1 a black mineral formed in the earth from partly decayed vegetable matter that has been under great pressure for a long time: *Coal is mined for use as a fuel.* 2 a piece or pieces of this mineral: *a bag of coal.* 3 supply or be supplied with coal: *The ship stopped just long enough to coal.* 4 a piece of wood, coal, etc. burning, partly burned, or all burned: *The big log had burned down to a few glowing coals.* 1, 2, 4 *n.,* 3 *v.*

co·a·li·tion (kō′ə lish′ən) a formal arrangement by which statesmen, political parties, etc. agree to work together for a certain period of time and for a special purpose: *If, after an election, no political party has a majority of seats in the House of Commons, one of the major parties may form a coalition with a smaller party in order to carry on government.* *n.*

coal oil a thin oil that is a by-product of petroleum, for use in stoves and lamps; kerosene: *Coal-oil lamps are still used in some places where electricity is not available.*

coal tar a black, sticky substance formed when gas is made from coal: *Coal tar, when distilled, yields certain medicines, dyes, flavorings, and perfumes.*

coarse (kôrs) 1 made up of fairly large parts: *coarse gravel.* 2 heavy or rough in looks or texture; not fine: *Burlap is a coarse material.* 3 common; poor; inferior: *coarse food.* 4 not delicate; crude; vulgar: *coarse language.* *adj.,* **coars·er, coars·est. —coarse′ly,** *adv.* **—coarse′ness,** *n.*

☛ **Coarse** and **course** are pronounced the same.

coars·en (kôr′sən) make coarse; become coarse. *v.*

coast (kōst) 1 the land along the sea; seashore: *Many ships were wrecked on the rocky coast.* 2 go along or near the shore of: *We coasted Newfoundland on our trip last winter.* 3 sail from harbor to harbor of a coast. 4 ride down a hill without using effort or power. 5 slide downhill on a sleigh. 1 *n.,* 2–5 *v.*

coast·al (kōs′təl) at the coast; along a coast; near a coast: *coastal defence, coastal shipping.* *adj.*

coast guard a government service whose work includes helping people in trouble at sea, ice-breaking in the North, and supplying and looking after lighthouses.

coat (kōt) 1 an outer garment of cloth, fur, etc. with sleeves. 2 any outer covering: *a dog's coat of hair, a coat of bark on a tree.* 3 a thin layer: *a coat of paint.* 4 cover or provide with a coat. 5 cover with a thin layer: *The floor is coated with varnish. This pill is coated with sugar.* 1–3 *n.,* 4, 5 *v.*

☛ **Coat** and **cote** are pronounced the same.

coat·ing (kōt′ing) a layer of any substance spread over a surface: *a coating of paint.* *n.*

coat of arms 1 a group of symbols or designs which show the marks of distinction of a noble family, a government, a city, etc.: *In the Middle Ages, each knight or lord had his own coat of arms.* 2 a shield, or drawing of a shield, so marked.

The coat of arms of Canada

A coat of mail

coat of mail a garment made of metal rings or plates, worn as armor.

coax (kōks) persuade by soft words; influence by pleasant ways: *She coaxed her father to let her go to the dance. I coaxed a smile from the baby. We coaxed the squirrel with peanuts.* *v.*

cob (kob) 1 the central part of an ear of corn, on which the grains grow. 2 a strong horse with short legs, often used for riding. *n.*

co·balt (kō′bolt or kō′bôlt) a silver-white metal used in making steel, paint, etc. *n.*

cob·bler (kob′lər) 1 a man whose work is mending shoes; shoemaker. 2 a fruit pie baked in a deep dish. *n.*

cob·ble·stone (kob′əl stōn′) a rounded stone that was formerly much used in paving: *The coach rattled over the cobblestones.* *n.*

co·bra (kō′brə) a very poisonous snake of Asia and Africa: *When excited, a cobra can flatten its neck so that the head takes on the appearance of a hood.* *n.*

cob·web (kob′web′) 1 a spider's web, or the stuff it is made of. 2 anything finespun or entangling like a spider's web: *The thief had to confess when he was caught in the cobweb of lies he had spun.* *n.*

cock[1] (kok) 1 a male chicken; rooster. 2 a male bird: *a turkey cock.* 3 a tap used to turn the flow of a liquid or gas on or off. 4 the hammer of a gun. 5 the position of the hammer of a gun when it is pulled back ready to fire. 6 pull back the hammer of a gun, ready to fire: *They heard a click as the pirate cocked his pistol.* 1–5 *n.,* 6 *v.*

cock of the walk, a person who has power over a group or situation.

cock[2] (kok) 1 turn or tilt upward to one side: *The little bird cocked his eye at me.* 2 an upward turn or bend of the nose, eye, or ear. 1 *v.,* 2 *n.*

cock[3] (kok) 1 a small pile of hay, rounded on top. 2 make such piles: *The farmer was cocking hay in the field.* 1 *n.,* 2 *v.*

cock·a·too (kok′ə tü′) a large, brightly colored parrot of Australia. *n., pl.* **cock·a·toos.**

hat, āge, fär; let, ēqual, tėrm; it, īce
hot, ōpen, ôrder; oil, out; cup, pu̇t, rüle
əbove, takən, pencəl, lemən, circəs
ch, child; ng, long; sh, ship
th, thin; ᴛʜ, then; zh, measure

cock·er spaniel (kok′ər) one of a breed of small dogs having long, silky hair and drooping ears.

cock·le (kok′əl) 1 a small shellfish that is good to eat. 2 its heart-shaped shell. 3 a small, light, shallow boat. *n.*

warm the cockles of one's heart, make one feel much pleased and encouraged: *His kind welcome warmed the cockles of my heart.*

cock·pit (kok′pit′) 1 a place where the pilot sits in an aircraft. 2 the open place in a boat where the pilot or passengers sit. 3 an enclosed space for fights between roosters or gamecocks. *n.*

cock·roach (kok′rōch) an insect often found in kitchens and around water pipes: *Cockroaches come out at night.* *n.*

cock·y (kok′ē) *Informal.* saucy and conceited: *He is a cocky little fellow.* *adj.,* **cock·i·er, cock·i·est.**

co·co (kō′kō) a tall palm tree on which coconuts grow. See **palm** for picture. *n., pl.* **co·cos.**

co·coa (kō′kō) 1 a reddish-brown powder made from chocolate (def.1) by pressing out most of the fat. 2 a drink made from this powder with sugar and milk or water. *n.*

co·co·nut or **co·coa·nut** (kō′kə nut′) the large, round, brown, hard-shelled fruit of the coco palm: *Coconuts have a thick white lining inside the shell that is good to eat and a white liquid in the centre called coconut milk.* *n.*

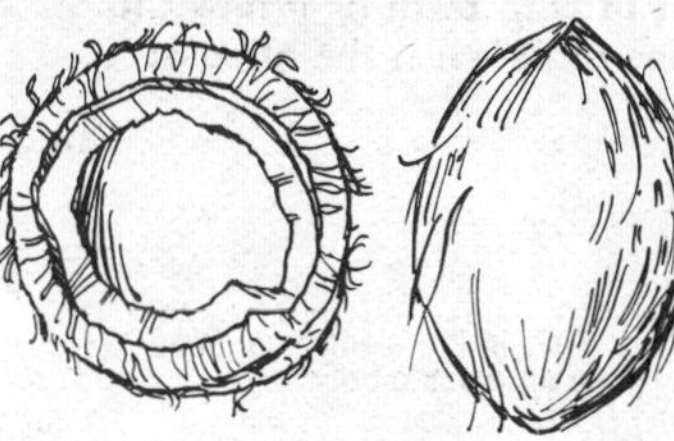
A coconut

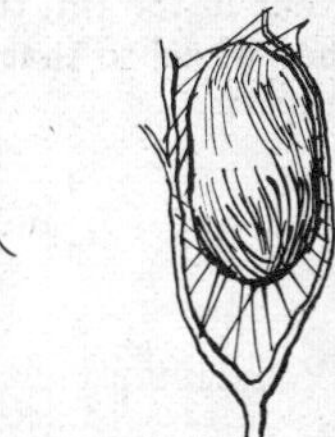
The cocoon of a silkworm

co·coon (kə kün′) a covering prepared by the larva of many kinds of insect, including the ant and the moth, to protect itself while it is changing into an adult: *Cocoons are usually of silk fibres produced by the insect, but some kinds include bits of leaves, twigs, etc.* *n.*

cod (kod) an important food fish found in the cold parts of the northern Atlantic Ocean. **Cod-liver oil** is a vitamin-rich oil extracted from the livers of cod. *n., pl.* **cod** or **cods.**

C.O.D or **c.o.d.** cash on delivery; collect on delivery.

cod·dle (kod′əl) 1 treat tenderly; pamper: *to coddle a sick child.* 2 cook in hot water without boiling: *Eggs are sometimes coddled.* *v.,* **cod·dled, cod·dling.**

code (kōd) 1 a collection of the laws of a country. 2 any set of rules: *A traffic code contains rules for driving.* 3 an arrangement of words or figures to keep a message short or secret; a system of secret writing. **4** a system of signals for sending messages by telegraph, flags, etc.: *Combinations of long and short sounds stand for letters in the code used in telegraphy.* **5** change or translate into a code; encode. 1–4 *n.*, 5 *v.*, **cod·ed, cod·ing.**

cod·fish (kod′fish′) cod. *n., pl.* **cod·fish** or **cod·fish·es.**

codg·er (koj′ər) *Informal.* a peculiar person. *n.*

co·erce (kō ėrs′) compel; force: *The prisoner was coerced into confessing to the crime.* *v.*, **co·erced, co·erc·ing.**

cof·fee (kof′ē) **1** dark-brown drink or flavoring made from the roasted and ground beans of a tall, tropical shrub. **2** coffee beans, especially when roasted and ground: *a bag of coffee.* *n.*

cof·fer (kof′ər) a box, chest, or trunk, especially one that is used to hold valuable things. *n.*

cof·fin (kof′ən) a box in which a dead body is buried; casket. *n.*

cog (kog) one of a series of teeth on the edge of a cogwheel. *n.*

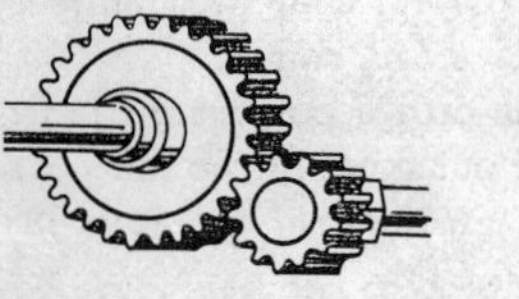

Cogwheels engaged. As one wheel turns, its teeth push against the teeth of the other wheel, causing it to turn.

Cogwheels disengaged

cog·wheel (kog′wēl′ or kog′hwēl′) a wheel with teeth cut in the rim that fit with teeth or grooves in another wheel so that one turns when the other is turned. *n.*

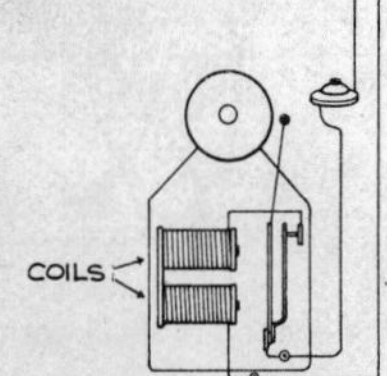

Coils in the electromagnet of an electric bell

coil (koil) **1** wind round and round in a series of circles to form a pile, a tube, or a curl: *The sailor coiled the rope so it would not take up much space.* **2** form a series of circles: *The snake coiled around a branch.* **3** one of a series of such circles: *One coil of the rope was smaller than the others.* **4** a series of such circles: *The coil of hose was hung on the wall.* **5** a wire wound round and round a core and used for carrying electric current. **6** a small pile of hay rounded on top; cock: *Cut hay is piled in coils for drying.* 1, 2 *v.*, 3–6 *n.*

coin (koin) **1** a piece of metal stamped by a government for use as money: *Nickels, dimes, and quarters are coins.* **2** metal money: *The Mint makes coin by stamping metals.* **3** make money by stamping metal; mint. **4** make up; invent: *to coin a new word or phrase.* 1, 2 *n.*, 3, 4 *v.*

coin money, *Informal.* become rich: *He is coining money in the oil business.*

coin·age (koin′ij) **1** the making of coins. **2** coins; metal money. **3** a system of coins: *Canada has a decimal coinage.* **4** making up; inventing: *the coinage of new words in connection with computers.* **5** the word, phrase, etc. invented. *n.*

co·in·cide (kō′in sīd′) **1** occupy the same place in space: *If these triangles △ △ were placed one on top of the other, they would coincide.* **2** occupy the same time: *The working hours of the two men coincided.* **3** be just alike; correspond exactly; agree: *Her opinion coincides with mine.* *v.*, **co·in·cid·ed, co·in·cid·ing.**

co·in·ci·dence (kō in′sə dəns) **1** exact correspondence; agreement; especially, the chance occurrence of two things together in such a way as to seem remarkable, fitting, etc.: *My cousin was born on the same day as I was. Isn't that a coincidence?* **2** coinciding; the occupying of the same time or place. *n.*

coke (kōk) the black substance that is left after coal has been heated in an oven from which most of the air has been shut out: *Coke is used as a fuel.* *n.*

col·an·der (kul′ən dər or kol′ən dər) a bowl or dish with many small holes in it, used to drain off liquids. *n.*

cold (kōld) **1** much less warm than the body: *Snow and ice are cold.* **2** less warm than it should be: *This coffee is cold.* **3** coldness; chilly weather: *Warm clothes protected us against the cold of winter.* **4** a common sickness that causes a stuffy or running nose and, sometimes, a cough or a sore throat. **5** not kind and sympathetic; unfriendly: *a cold greeting.* 1, 2, 5 *adj.*, 3, 4 *n.*

catch cold, become sick with a cold.

cold–blood·ed (kōld′blud′id) **1** having blood that is about as cold as the air or water around the animal: *Turtles are cold-blooded; dogs are warm-blooded.* **2** lacking in feeling; cruel: *The cold-blooded pirate sold all his captives into slavery.* *adj.*

cold cream a white, oily preparation put on the skin to soften, soothe, or cleanse it.

cold storage storage in a very cold place: *Many kinds of fruit and vegetables are kept in cold storage to keep them from spoiling.*

cole·slaw (kōl′slo′ or kōl′slô′) a salad made of sliced raw cabbage. *n.*

col·i·se·um (kol′ə sē′əm) a large building or stadium for games, contests, etc. *n.*

col·lage (kə läzh′) a picture made by pasting on a background an arrangement of items with different textures, colors, and shapes, such as parts of printed pictures, newspapers, fabrics, string, glass, etc. *n.*

☞ **Collage** came into modern English from the French word *collage,* meaning 'a gluing,' which came originally from a Greek word *kolla,* meaning *'glue.'*

col·lapse (kə laps′) **1** fall in; shrink together suddenly: *The little folding chair collapsed when my uncle sat down on it.* **2** falling in: *A heavy flood caused the collapse of the bridge.* **3** break down; fail suddenly: *Both his health and his business collapsed within a year.* **4** a breakdown; failure: *She is suffering from a nervous collapse.* **5** fold or push together: *collapse a telescope.* 1, 3, 5 *v.*, **col·lapsed, col·laps·ing;** 2, 4 *n.*

col·lar (kol′ər) **1** the part of a coat, a dress, or a shirt that forms a band around the neck. **2** a separate band of linen, lace, or other material worn around the neck. **3** a leather or metal band for a dog's neck. **4** a thick, padded oval that forms part of the harness of a draft animal, fitting around the neck and resting against the shoulders and chest: *The horse's collar is bearing the weight of the load he is pulling.* See **harness** for picture. **5** any of various rings or bands that fit around rods or pipes: *The mechanic put a collar on the shaft to keep it in place.* **6** put a collar on: *The owner collared the pup.* **7** seize by the collar; capture: *The policeman collared the thief.* 1–5 *n.*, 6, 7 *v.*

☛ **Collar** and **caller** are sometimes pronounced the same.

col·league (kol′ēg) an associate or fellow worker: *The doctor invited a colleague to examine the patient.* *n.*

col·lect (kə lekt′) **1** gather together; pick up: *The teacher collected the spelling exercises.* **2** come together in one place; assemble: *A crowd soon collects at the scene of an accident.* **3** pile up; form into a mass; accumulate: *Drifting snow collects behind snowfences. A great deal of dust has collected under the beds.* **4** bring together into one place as a hobby: *John collects stamps and coins.* **5** ask and receive pay for debts, bills, dues, or taxes: *A storekeeper collects money from people who owe him for goods.* *v.*

col·lect·ed (kə lek′tid) not confused or disturbed; in control of one's emotions: *She remained calm, cool, and collected.* *adj.*

col·lec·tion (kə lek′shən) **1** bringing together: *The collection of these stamps took ten years.* **2** coming together: *The collection of a crowd there was unexpected.* **3** a group of things gathered from many places and belonging together: *The library has a large collection of books.* **4** money gathered from people: *A church takes up a collection to help pay its expenses.* **5** a large quantity; a mass or heap: *There is a collection of dust in the unused room.* *n.*

col·lec·tive (kə lek′tiv) of a group; as a group; taken all together. *adj.*

col·lec·tor (kə lek′tər) **1** a person who collects things as a hobby: *There were a lot of coin collectors at the auction sale.* **2** something that collects or appears to collect: *All these ornaments are dust collectors.* **3** a person hired to collect money owed: *His father is a tax collector.* *n.*

col·lege (kol′ij) **1** an institution that gives degrees or diplomas, especially one that is not a university: *The Ontario College of Art. My cousin is at a community college.* **2** one of several institutions or divisions within a university. **3** *Informal.* university: *My older sister is going to college next fall.* *n.*

col·le·giate (kə lē′jit) **1** in Canada, a high school or secondary school. **2** in Canada, of or like a high school or high-school students. **3** of or like high-school or college students. 1 *n.*, 2, 3 *adj.*

col·lide (kə līd′) **1** rush against; hit or strike hard together: *In running around the corner, he collided with another boy.* **2** clash; conflict. *v.*, **col·lid·ed, col·lid·ing.**

col·lie (kol′ē or kō′lē) a large, long-haired breed of dog having a long pointed nose and a bushy tail: *Collies came originally from Scotland where they were trained to look after sheep.* *n.*

hat, āge, fär; let, ēqual, tėrm; it, īce
hot, ōpen, ôrder; oil, out; cup, pu̇t, rüle
əbove, takən, pencəl, lemən, circəs
ch, child; ng, long; sh, ship
th, thin; ᴛʜ, then; zh, measure

col·li·sion (kə lizh′ən) **1** a violent rushing against; hitting or striking hard together: *Eight people were killed in the automobile collision.* **2** a clash; conflict: *a collision of ideas.* *n.*

co·logne (kə lōn′) a sweet-smelling liquid, similar to perfume, but having a much weaker scent: *Cologne contains a small amount of perfume oil dissolved in alcohol and water.* *n.*

☛ **Cologne** is a short form of the French *eau de Cologne,* meaning 'water from Cologne.' Cologne, a city in West Germany, is where it was first made.

co·lon[1] (kō′lən) a mark (:) of punctuation used after an introductory sentence to show that an explanation, illustration, list, long quotation, etc. follows: *Every example sentence or phrase in this dictionary has a colon before it.* *n.*

co·lon[2] (kō′lən) the lower part of the large intestine. *n., pl.* **co·lons** or **co·la** (kō′lə).

colo·nel (kėr′nəl) in the armed forces, a commissioned officer ranking below a brigadier-general and above a lieutenant-colonel. *n.*

☛ **Colonel** and **kernel** are pronounced the same.

co·lo·ni·al (kə lō′nē əl) **1** of or having to do with a colony or colonies. **2** of the time when a nation was a colony: *colonial furniture.* **3** a person who lives in a colony. 1, 2 *adj.*, 3 *n.*

col·o·nist (kol′ə nist) **1** a person who helped to found a colony. **2** a person who lives in a colony during the period of settlement; a settler: *The first colonists in New France suffered from cold and hunger.* *n.*

col·o·ni·za·tion (kol′ə nə zā′shən) the establishment of a colony or colonies: *The English, French, Spanish, and Dutch took part in the colonization of North America.* *n.*

col·o·nize (kol′ə nīz′) establish a colony or colonies in: *The English colonized Newfoundland.* *v.*, **col·o·nized, col·o·niz·ing.**

col·on·nade (kol′ə nād′) a series of columns set the same distance apart. *n.*

col·o·ny (kol′ə nē) **1** a group of people who leave their own country and go to settle in another land, but who still remain citizens of their own country. **2** the settlement made by such a group of people. **3** a territory distant from the country that governs it: *During the nineteenth century, England added to its colonies in Africa and Asia.* **4** a number of people of one country, faith, or occupation living as a group: *There is a large Chinese colony in Vancouver. There are several Doukhobor colonies in Saskatchewan.* **5** a group of animals or plants of the same kind, living or growing together: *We found two colonies of ants under the steps.* *n., pl.* **col·o·nies.**

col·or or **col·our** (kul′ər) **1** red, yellow, blue, or any combination of them: *She never wears colors, but always dresses in black or white. The color that results from* *mixing yellow and blue is green.* **2** give color to; put color on; change the color of. **3** a paint, stain, or dye. **4** become or make red in the face; blush: *She colored when her mistake was mentioned.* **5** outward appearance; show: *His story has some color of truth.* **6** change to give a wrong idea: *The dishonest general colored his report of the battle.* **7 the colors** or **colours,** the flag of a nation, regiment, etc: *He carried the colors in the parade.* 1, 3, 5, 7 *n.,* 2, 4, 6 *v.*

show one's true colors or **colours,** show oneself as one really is: *In the fight, the bully showed his true colors and ran away.*

with flying colors or **colours,** successfully; triumphantly: *He passed the examination with flying colors.*

col·or–blind or **col·our–blind** (kul′ər blīnd′) unable to tell certain colors apart; unable to distinguish certain colors. *adj.*

col·or·cast or **col·our·cast** (kul′ər kast′) **1** a television program broadcast in color. **2** broadcast over television in color: *Some stations do not colorcast.* 1 *n.,* 2 *v.*

col·ored or **col·oured** (kul′ərd) **1** having color; not black or white: *I bought some colored construction paper.* **2** having a certain kind of color: *a green-colored leaf.* **3** of the black race or any race other than white. *adj.*

col·or·ful or **col·our·ful** (kul′ər fəl) picturesque; vivid: *a colorful scene. adj.*

col·or·ing or **col·our·ing** (kul′ər ing) **1** the pattern, kind, or degree of color or colors that a person or thing has: *His coloring is much better now since his health has improved.* **2** a substance used to give or add color: *There is coloring in margarine.* **3** a false appearance: *His lies have a coloring of truth. n.*

col·or·less or **col·our·less** (kul′ər lis) **1** without color. **2** not vivid; not interesting: *a colorless personality. adj.*

co·los·sal (kə los′əl) **1** huge; gigantic; vast: *a colossal statue, a colossal explosion.* **2** *Informal.* remarkable; outstanding. *adj.*

col·our (kul′ər) See **color.**

colt (kōlt) a young horse, donkey, etc., especially a male horse under four or five years old. *n.*

col·um·bine (kol′əm bīn′) a plant whose flowers have petals shaped like hollow spurs: *Wild columbines have red-and-yellow or blue-and-white flowers. n.*

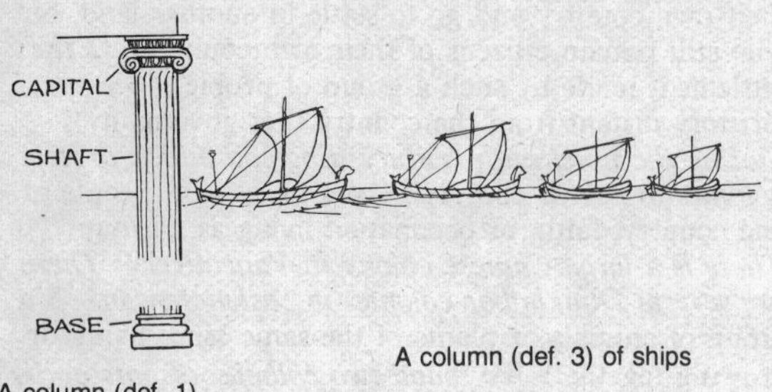

A column (def. 1)

A column (def. 3) of ships

col·umn (kol′əm) **1** a slender, upright structure; pillar: *Columns are usually made of stone, wood, or metal, and used as supports or ornaments to a building.* **2** anything that seems slender and upright like a column: *A column of smoke rose from the fire. She added a column of figures.* **3** a formation of soldiers or ships following one another. **4** a narrow division of a page reading from top to bottom, kept separate by lines or by blank spaces: *This page has two columns.* **5** a part of a newspaper used for a special subject or written by a special writer: *the sports column. n.*

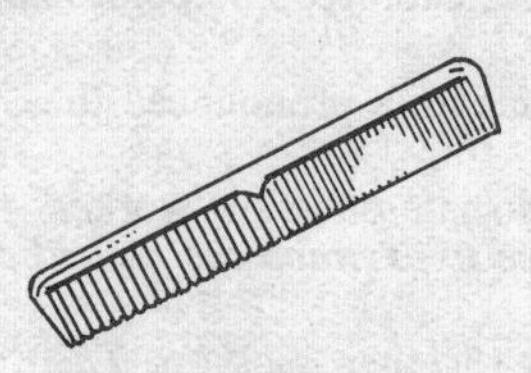
A comb for hair

The comb of a rooster

comb (kōm) **1** a narrow, short piece of metal, rubber, plastic, etc. with teeth, used to arrange or clean the hair or to hold it in place: *Women sometimes wear combs in their hair as ornaments.* **2** anything shaped or used like a comb: *One kind of comb cleans and takes out the tangles in wool or flax.* **3** clean; take out tangles in; arrange with a comb: *I comb my hair before breakfast.* **4** search through: *We had to comb the whole city before we found our lost dog.* **5** the thick, red, fleshy piece on the top of the head of chickens and some other fowls: *A rooster has a larger comb than a hen has.* **6** honeycomb (def. 1). 1, 2, 5, 6 *n.,* 3, 4 *v.*

com·bat (kom′bat) **1** fight against; struggle with: *Doctors combat disease.* **2** fighting between opposing armed forces; battle: *The soldier was wounded in combat.* **3** any fight or struggle. 1 *v.,* **com·bat·ted** or **com·bat·ed, com·bat·ting** or **com·bat·ing;** 2, 3 *n.*

com·ba·tant (kom′bə tənt or kəm bat′ənt) a fighter, especially a member of the armed forces who takes part in the actual fighting. *n.*

com·bi·na·tion (kom′bə nā′shən) **1** combining or being combined; union: *The combination of flour and water makes paste.* **2** one whole made by combining two or more different things: *The color purple is a combination of red and blue.* **3** a series of numbers or letters followed in opening a certain kind of lock: *He forgot the combination to his bicycle lock. n.*

com·bine (kəm bīn′ for 1, kom′bīn for 2, 3, and 4) **1** join two or more things together; unite: *All clubs combined in planning the hobby show. A wise man tries to combine work and play.* **2** a group of persons joined together for some common purpose: *The companies formed a combine to keep prices up.* **3** a machine used in harvesting: *A combine cuts and threshes grain in one operation.* **4** use a combine: *We combined the wheat last week.* 1, 4 *v.,* **com·bined, com·bin·ing;** 2, 3 *n.*

com·bus·ti·ble (kəm bus′tə bəl) capable of taking fire and burning: *Gasoline is highly combustible. adj.*

com·bus·tion (kəm bus′chən) the act or process of producing heat: *Many houses are heated by the rapid combustion of coal, oil, or gas. By slow combustion, the cells of the body transform food into energy and heat. n.*

hat, āge, fär; let, ēqual, tėrm; it, īce
hot, ōpen, ôrder; oil, out; cup, pu̇t, rüle
əbove, takən, pencəl, lemən, circəs
ch, child; ng, long; sh, ship
th, thin; ᴛʜ, then; zh, measure

come (kum) **1** move toward: *Come this way. One boy came toward me; the other boy went away.* **2** get near; arrive: *The train comes at noon.* **3** reach, extend: *The dress comes to her knees.* **4** take place; happen: *Snow comes in winter.* **5** get to be; turn out to be; become: *Her dream came true.* **6** be obtainable or sold: *This sweater comes in white and yellow.* *v.,* **came, come, com·ing.**

come about, take place; happen: *The smash-up came about by accident.*

come across, meet or find by chance: *He came across a dollar in the street.*

come along, improve; progress: *She is coming along well now.*

come back, a return. **b** be remembered: *The forgotten name came back to him next day.*

come down, a lose position, rank, etc. **b** be handed down: *Many fables have come down through the ages.*

come forward, offer oneself for work or duty; volunteer: *He came forward when a man was needed to do the job.*

come from, a be born in or to; be descended from; descend from: *That boy comes from a poor family.* **b** be a native or former resident of.

come in, a enter. **b** begin; be brought into use: *Steamboats came in after the invention of the steam engine.*

come into, a enter. **b** inherit: *His wife came into a lot of money.*

come off, a take place; happen: *When is the final game going to come off?* **b** turn out: *The concert came off well.*

come on, a improve; progress: *The sick man is coming on fine.* **b** meet by chance; find: *The hunters came on a herd of deer in the bush.* **c** make an entrance onto the stage: *The murderer comes on in the second act.*

come out, a be revealed or shown: *The sun came out from behind the clouds.* **b** result; finish an activity in a certain way: *How did the ball game come out?* **c** be offered to the public: *The new record is coming out next week.* **d** put in an appearance: *How many boys came out for baseball?* **e** turn out: *The snapshot did not come out very well.* **f** volunteer; offer one's services: *All the scouts came out to sell apples.*

come out with, a say frankly: *She thinks it was foolish for me to come out with my opinion.* **b** bring out: *The publisher has come out with a new edition.*

come to, a amount to; total; be equal to: *The bill comes to five dollars.* **b** return to consciousness: *The boxer came to in the dressing room.*

come up, arise; develop: *The question is sure to come up in class.*

come up with, provide; produce, especially in working on a problem: *He always came up with the right answer.*

come upon, meet or find by chance: *We came upon two friends at the plaza this morning.*

co·me·di·an (kə mē′dē ən) **1** an actor in comedies. **2** a person who amuses others with his funny talk and actions. *n.*

com·e·dy (kom′ə dē) **1** an amusing play or show having a happy ending. **2** an amusing happening. *n., pl.* **com·e·dies.**

come·ly (kum′lē) pleasant to look at; attractive. *adj.,* **come·li·er, come·li·est.**

com·er (kum′ər) *Informal.* a person who seems likely to succeed or who is showing promise: *Our hockey coach says Tom is a comer.* *n.*

com·et (kom′it) a bright heavenly body having a starlike centre and, often, a cloudy tail of light: *Comets move around the sun like planets, but in a long, oval course.* *n.*

com·fort (kum′fərt) **1** ease the grief or sorrow of: *Her mother's words comforted the sobbing child.* **2** anything that makes trouble or sorrow easier to bear: *to bring comfort to a suffering family.* **3** a person or thing that makes life easier or takes away hardships: *His sister is a great comfort to him.* **4** ease; freedom from hardships: *My father makes enough money for us to live in comfort.* 1 *v.,* 2–4 *n.*

com·fort·a·ble (kum′fər tə bəl) **1** giving a feeling of ease: *A soft, warm bed is comfortable.* **2** in comfort; at ease; free from pain or hardship: *The warm fire made him feel comfortable after a cold day outdoors.* *adj.* **—com′fort·a·bly,** *adv.*

com·fort·er (kum′fər tər) a padded or quilted covering for a bed. *n.*

com·ic (kom′ik) **1** amusing; funny: *A clown is a comic actor.* **2** of comedy; in comedies. **3** comedian. **4** comic strip. **5** comic book. **6 comics,** *pl.* the page or section of a newspaper or magazine containing comic strips. 1, 2 *adj.,* 3–6 *n.*

com·i·cal (kom′ə kəl) amusing; funny: *The clown's actions were comical.* *adj.*

comic book a book or magazine made up of one or more comic strips.

comic strip a series of drawings that tell a funny story, a series of happenings, or a story of adventure.

com·ing (kum′ing) now approaching; next: *this coming spring.* *adj.*

com·ma (kom′ə) a mark (,) of punctuation, usually used where a pause would be made in speaking a sentence aloud: *In the sentence under definition 1 of* **comfortable,** *notice the comma between 'soft' and 'warm.'* *n.*

com·mand (kə mand′) **1** give an order to; order; bid; direct: *The captain commanded the men to fire.* **2** an order; direction: *They obeyed the captain's command.* **3** be in authority over; have power over; be master of: *The captain commands his ship.* **4** the possession of authority; power; control: *The general is in command of the army.* **5** the soldiers, ships, district, etc. under a person who commands them: *The captain knew every man in his command.* **6** one of the main divisions of the Canadian Forces: *He is in Air Transport command at Trenton.* **7** control by position; overlook: *The fortress stands on a hill that commands the sea.* **8** be able to have and use: *He cannot command so large a sum of money.* **9** the ability to use; mastery: *A good storyteller must have a command of words.* **10** ask for and get: *Such sufferings command our sympathy. Food commands a higher price when it is scarce.* 1, 3, 7, 8, 10 *v.,* 2, 4–6, 9 *n.*

com·man·dant (kom′ən dant′) **1** the officer in command of a military base, camp, etc. **2** the officer in charge of a military college or training school. *n.*

com·mand·er (kə man′dər) 1 a person who commands: *Anyone who has people or supplies under his control is the commander of them.* 2 an officer in charge of an army or a part of an army. 3 an officer in the navy, ranking next below a captain and above a lieutenant commander. *n.*

com·mand·ment (kə mand′mənt) 1 an order; law. 2 one of the ten laws that, according to the Bible, God gave to Moses: *'Thou shalt not kill' is one of the Ten Commandments.* *n.*

com·man·do (kə man′dō) 1 a soldier who makes brief, daring raids on enemy territory and who does close-range fighting. 2 a group of such soldiers. *n., pl.* **com·man·dos** or **com·man·does.**

com·mem·o·rate (kə mem′ə rāt′) preserve or honor the memory of: *Christmas commemorates Christ's birth.* *v.,* **com·mem·o·rat·ed, com·mem·o·rat·ing.**

com·mence (kə mens′) begin; start: *The play will commence at ten o'clock.* *v.,* **com·menced, com·menc·ing.**

com·mence·ment (kə mens′mənt) 1 a beginning; start. 2 the day when a school or college gives diplomas, certificates, etc.; day of graduation. 3 the ceremonies held on this day. *n.*

com·mend (kə mend′) 1 praise: *Honesty is a virtue that everyone commends.* 2 hand over for safekeeping: *She commended the child to her aunt's care.* *v.*

com·men·da·tion (kom′ən dā′shən) 1 praise: *Good work deserves commendation.* 2 favorable mention; recommendation. *n.*

com·ment (kom′ent) 1 a note or remark that explains, praises, or finds fault with a book, a person, or a thing: *The teacher had written helpful comments on the last page of my composition.* 2 write notes or remarks that explain, praise, or find fault with a book, a play, a concert, etc. 3 make remarks about persons or things: *Everyone commented on her new hat.* 1 *n.,* 2, 3 *v.*

com·men·ta·tor (kom′ən tā′tər) 1 a person who describes sports or other events on radio and television as they are going on. 2 a person who comments on books, concerts, current events, etc., explaining or criticizing them. *n.*

com·merce (kom′ėrs) trade; buying and selling in large amounts between different places. *n.*

com·mer·cial (kə mėr′shəl) 1 having to do with trade or business. 2 supported by an advertiser: *a commercial radio program.* 3 an advertisement on radio or television, broadcast between programs or during a program: *The movie was interrupted by many commercials.* 1, 2 *adj.,* 3 *n.* —**com·mer′cial·ly,** *adv.*

com·mis·sion (kə mish′ən) 1 a written paper giving certain powers, privileges, and duties: *My brother has just received his commission as lieutenant in the infantry.* 2 give a person the right, the power, or the duty of doing something: *The club commissions one of its members to buy supplies.* 3 the thing a person is trusted to do; an errand: *The class gave me the commission of selecting a birthday present for our teacher.* 4 a group of people appointed or elected with authority to do certain things: *The Prime Minister should appoint a commission to find out why food costs so much.* 5 doing or committing; performance: *People are punished for the commission of crimes.* 6 pay based on a percentage of the amount of business done: *She gets a commission of 10 per cent on all the sales she makes.* 7 put into active service; make ready for use: *to commission a warship.* 1, 3–6 *n.,* 2, 7 *v.*

in commission, in service or use; ready for service or use; in working order: *I must get my broken bicycle in commission again.*

out of commission, not in service or use; not ready for use; not in working order: *Her bicycle was out of commission.*

com·mis·sion·aire (kə mish′ən er′) 1 a person whose job is to open doors, carry bags, etc. in front of a hotel or club. 2 a member of the Corps of Commissionaires: *Some Canadian cities employ commissionaires to check parking meters and to issue parking tickets.* *n.*

com·mis·sion·er (kə mish′ən ər) 1 a member of a commission. 2 an official in charge of some department of a government: *a police commissioner.* *n.*

com·mit (kə mit′) 1 hand over for safe keeping: *The sick man committed himself to the doctor's care. The judge committed the thief to prison.* 2 perform or do (usually something wrong): *A man who steals commits a crime.* 3 bind or involve oneself; pledge: *I have committed myself now and must keep my promise.* *v.,* **com·mit·ted, com·mit·ting.**

commit to memory, memorize or learn by heart.

commit to paper or **writing,** write down.

com·mit·tee (kə mit′ē) a group of persons appointed or elected to do some special thing: *The president of our club appointed a committee of five members to plan the picnic.* *n.*

com·mod·i·ty (kə mod′ə tē) anything that is bought and sold; an article of trade or commerce: *Groceries are commodities.* *n., pl.* **com·mod·i·ties.**

com·mo·dore (kom′ə dôr′) 1 the officer in charge of a convoy of ships. 2 a title given to the president of a yacht club. *n.*

com·mon (kom′ən) 1 belonging equally to all: *The house is the common property of the three brothers.* 2 general; of all; from all; by all: *By common consent of the class, he was chosen for president.* 3 generally known: *It is common knowledge that his parents won't let him go to parties.* 4 often met with; usual; familiar: *Snow is common in most of Canada.* 5 without rank; having no special position: *the common people. A common soldier is a private.* 6 below ordinary; having poor quality. 7 coarse and vulgar: *a common person.* 8 land owned or used by all the people of a village or town. 1–7 *adj.,* 8 *n.*

in common, equally with another or others; owned, used, done, etc. by both or all: *The two sisters have many interests in common.*

common denominator 1 a multiple that belongs to all the denominators of a group of fractions: *A common denominator of* $\frac{1}{2}$, $\frac{2}{3}$, *and* $\frac{3}{4}$ *is 12 because these three fractions can also be expressed as* $\frac{6}{12}$, $\frac{8}{12}$ *and* $\frac{9}{12}$. 2 a quality, opinion, etc. shared by all the persons or things in a group: *Interest in their community was the common denominator that brought the people of the neighborhood together.*

com·mon·ly (kom′ən lē) usually; generally: *Arithmetic is commonly taught in schools.* *adv.*

hat, āge, fär; let, ēqual, tėrm; it, īce
hot, ōpen, ôrder; oil, out; cup, pu̇t, rüle
əbove, takən, pencəl, lemən, circəs
ch, child; ng, long; sh, ship
th, thin; ᴛʜ, then; zh, measure

common multiple a number that can be divided by two or more other numbers without a remainder: *12 is a common multiple of 2, 3, 4, and 6; 6 is a common multiple of 2 and 3.*

com·mon·place (kom′ən plās′) 1 an ordinary or everyday thing: *Today television is a commonplace.* 2 an ordinary remark. 3 ordinary; not new or interesting: *The plot of the story was commonplace.* 1, 2 *n.*, 3 *adj.*

Com·mons (kom′ənz) 1 the House of Commons. 2 the members of the House of Commons: *This week the Commons voted on several important bills. n.*

common sense good sense in everyday affairs; practical intelligence: *Tom was not a very good student, but he had a lot of common sense.*

com·mon·wealth (kom′ən welth′) 1 the people who make up a nation; citizens of a state. 2 a nation in which the people have the right to make the laws, often a republic: *Brazil, Australia, and West Germany are commonwealths.* 3 a group of nations, persons, etc. united by some common bond or interest. 4 **the Commonwealth,** the Commonwealth of Nations: *Canada is a member of the Commonwealth. n.*

Commonwealth of Nations an association of a large number of countries, many of them now completely independent, that were once under British law and government: *All the independent members of the Commonwealth of Nations, including Canada and the United Kingdom, have equal status.*

com·mo·tion (kə mō′shən) confusion; noisy or violent movement; disturbance: *His voice could hardly be heard above the commotion. n.*

com·mune (kom′yün) 1 a community of people living together. 2 a unit of local government in China. *n.*

com·mu·ni·ca·ble (kə myü′nə kə bəl) that can be transferred or passed along to others: *Chicken pox is a communicable disease. adj.*

com·mu·ni·cate (kə myü′nə kāt′) 1 give information or news by talking, writing, etc.; send and receive messages: *He and his cousin communicate by letter. They asked his sister to communicate their wishes to him.* 2 pass along; transfer: *A stove communicates heat to a room.* 3 get in touch with; get through to: *It was impossible to communicate with my family during the storm. The teacher could not communicate with some of the pupils.* 4 be connected: *The dining room communicates with the kitchen. v.,* **com·mu·ni·cat·ed, com·mu·ni·cat·ing.**

com·mu·ni·ca·tion (kə myü′nə kā′shən) 1 the giving or exchanging of information or news by speaking, writing, etc.: *Noise on the telephone made communication impossible.* 2 the information or news given; a letter, message, etc. that gives information or news: *The communication came in time to allow her to change her plans.* 3 a means of going from one to the other; a passage: *There is no communication between these two rooms.* 4 **communications,** *pl.* a system of communicating by telephone, radio, etc.: *A network of communications links all parts of North America. n.*

com·mun·ion (kə myün′yən) 1 the exchange of thoughts and feelings; fellowship. 2 a quiet talk between persons who are dear to one another or are devoted to the same purpose; spiritual conversation. 3 **Communion,** the celebration of Jesus's last supper with his disciples before the Crucifixion. *n.*

com·mu·nism (kom′yə niz′əm) an economic and social system in which the state or community as a whole owns all property and controls the means of production and the distribution of goods. *n.*

com·mu·nist (kom′yə nist) 1 a person who favors or supports communism. 2 **Communist,** a member of the Communist Party. *n.*

Communist Party a political party that supports communism.

com·mu·ni·ty (kə myü′nə tē) 1 the people of any district or town: *This lake provides water for six communities.* 2 a group of people living together: *a community of monks.* 3 the public: *the approval of the community.* 4 ownership together; sharing together: *community of food supplies, community of ideas. n., pl.* **com·mu·ni·ties.**

community centre or **center** 1 a hall used for recreation, entertainment, public meetings, etc. in a community. 2 an arena run by the community as a centre for sporting events, skating, dancing, and other forms of entertainment: *The local hockey team plays its home games at the community centre.*

com·mute (kə myüt′) 1 exchange; substitute: *He commuted his foreign money into Canadian dollars.* 2 change an obligation, penalty, etc. for an easier one: *The prisoner's sentence of death was commuted to one of life imprisonment.* 3 travel regularly to and from work by train, bus, automobile, etc. *v.,* **com·mut·ed, com·mut·ing.**

com·mut·er (kə myüt′ər) a person who travels regularly to and from work by train, bus, automobile, etc. *n.*

com·pact[1] (kəm pakt′ or kom′pakt for 1 and 2, kom′pakt for 3 and 4) 1 closely and firmly packed together: *The leaves of a cabbage are folded into a compact head.* 2 using few words; brief and well organized: *He prepared a compact set of instructions for building a sailboat.* 3 a small case containing face powder or rouge. 4 an automobile that is smaller and cheaper than standard models. 1, 2 *adj.*, 3, 4 *n.* **—com·pact′ness,** *n.*

com·pact[2] (kom′pakt) an agreement: *We made a compact not to tell anyone our secret. n.*

com·pan·ion (kəm pan′yən) 1 a person who goes along with or accompanies another; one who shares in what another is doing; comrade: *The twins were companions in work and play.* 2 a person paid to live or travel with another as a friend and helper. 3 anything that matches or goes with another in kind, size, and color: *I can't find the companion to this mitt. n.*

com·pan·ion·a·ble (kəm pan′yən ə bəl) pleasant as a companion; agreeable; sociable. *adj.*

com·pan·ion·ship (kəm pan′yən ship) the state of being a companion; fellowship: *He enjoys the companionship of his dog. n.*

com·pan·ion·way (kəm pan′yən wā′) 1 a stairway leading from the deck of a ship to the rooms below. 2 the space where such a stairway is. *n.*

com·pa·ny (kum′pə nē) 1 a group of people joined together for some purpose, such as carrying on a business or acting plays. 2 companions: *You are known by the company you keep.* 3 companionship: *His dog provided the old man with company during the long winters.* 4 one or more guests or visitors: *They often have company in the evening.* 5 the part of an army commanded by a captain. 6 a troop of Girl Guides. *n., pl.* **com·pa·nies.**

keep company, go with; remain with for companionship: *My dog kept me company while you were away.*

part company, a go separate ways: *The hikers parted company at the gate.* **b** end companionship: *They parted company forever.*

company town a town built by a company for its workers, to whom it rents houses, provides services, etc.

com·pa·ra·ble (kom′pə rə bəl, kəm per′ə bəl, or kəm par′ə bəl) 1 able to be compared: *A fire is comparable with the sun; both give light and heat.* 2 fit to be compared: *A cave is not comparable to a house for comfort.* *adj.*

com·par·a·tive (kəm per′ə tiv or kəm par′ə tiv) 1 that compares: *He made a comparative study of bees and wasps.* 2 measured by comparison with something else: *Screens give us comparative freedom from flies.* 3 the second of three degrees of comparison, used when qualities are being compared: *'Taller' is the comparative of 'tall.' 'More quickly' is the comparative of 'quickly.'* 1, 2 *adj.,* 3 *n.* **—com·par′a·tive·ly,** *adv.*

com·pare (kəm per′) 1 find out or point out how persons or things are alike and how they are different: *She compared several samples of dress material before deciding which to buy.* 2 liken; say something is like something else: *The fins of a fish may be compared to the legs of a dog; both are used in getting from one place to another.* 3 be considered like or equal to: *Artificial light cannot compare with daylight.* *v.,* **com·pared, com·par·ing.**

beyond compare, without an equal; most excellent: *Her cakes are beyond compare.*

com·par·i·son (kəm per′ə sən or kəm par′ə sən) 1 the act or process of comparing; finding the likenesses and differences: *The teacher's comparison of the heart to a pump helped the children to understand its action.* 2 likeness; similarity: *There is no comparison between these two cameras; one is much better than the other.* *n.*

in comparison with, compared with: *Even a large lake is small in comparison with an ocean.*

com·part·ment (kəm pärt′mənt) 1 a separate division or section of anything; part of an enclosed space set off by walls or partitions: *That ship's hold is built in watertight compartments, so that if there is a leak in the compartment, the water will not get into the rest of the ship. Some pencil boxes have several compartments for holding different things.* 2 any part or division: *Those unhappy memories were locked away in a compartment of her mind.* *n.*

com·pass (kum′pəs) 1 an instrument for showing directions, consisting of a needle that points to the North Magnetic Pole, which is near the North Pole. 2 Also, **compasses,** *pl.* an instrument for drawing circles and curved lines and for measuring distances. 3 the space within limits; the area, extent, or range: *The old sailor had many adventures within the compass of his lifetime.* 4 in music, the range of a voice or an instrument. 5 go around; move around: *The astronaut compassed the earth many times in his space capsule.* 6 hem in; surround: *The lake is compassed by a ring of mountains.* 1–4 *n.,* 5, 6 *v.*

A compass (def. 1). The needle always points to the north, even when the instrument is turned.

A compass (def. 2). The pointed arm remains fixed as the drawing arm revolves.

com·pas·sion (kəm pash′ən) a feeling that leads one to help a person who is suffering; sympathy: *The doctor felt great compassion for his badly burned patient.* *n.*

com·pas·sion·ate (kəm pash′ən it) wishing to help those that suffer; merciful. *adj.*

com·pat·i·ble (kəm pat′ə bəl) able to exist together; that can get on well together; agreeing; in harmony: *My two sisters are always arguing; they are just not compatible.* *adj.*

com·pel (kəm pel′) 1 force: *The rain compelled us to stop our ball game.* 2 bring about by force: *to compel obedience.* *v.,* **com·pelled, com·pel·ling.**

com·pen·sate (kom′pən sāt′) 1 make an equal return to; give an equivalent to: *The hunter agreed to compensate the farmer for shooting his cow.* 2 balance by equal weight or power; make up for: *Skill sometimes compensates for lack of strength.* 3 pay: *The company compensated her for her extra work.* *v.,* **com·pen·sat·ed, com·pen·sat·ing.**

com·pen·sa·tion (kom′pən sā′shən) 1 something given to make up for something else; something that makes up for something else: *He lost my knife, but gave me a new one as compensation.* 2 pay: *He said that equal compensation should be given to men and women for equal work.* *n.*

com·pete (kəm pēt′) 1 try to do better than one or more other persons: *The two girls competed with each other right through school. John was competing against his friend for the public-speaking prize.* 2 take part in a contest: *My brother competed in the swimming meet.* *v.,* **com·pet·ed, com·pet·ing.**

com·pe·tent (kom′pə tənt) able; fitted: *A competent cook gets high wages. A doctor should be competent to treat many diseases.* *adj.*

com·pe·ti·tion (kom′pə tish′ən) 1 trying to do better than others; striving to excel: *Competition is a part of most games.* 2 rivalry: *The two boys enjoyed the spirit of competition that existed between them.* 3 a contest, especially one in which there is a prize for the winner: *She came first in the dancing competition.* *n.*

in competition with, competing against: *She was in*

hat, āge, fär; let, ēqual, tėrm; it, īce
hot, ōpen, ôrder; oil, out; cup, pu̇t, rüle
əbove, takən, pencəl, lemən, circəs
ch, child; ng, long; sh, ship
th, thin; ᴛʜ, then; zh, measure

competition with five other dancers.

com·pet·i·tive (kəm pet′ə tiv) 1 according to who is the best one taking part; determined by competition: *A competitive examination for the job of postal clerk will be held January 10.* 2 characterized by a desire to excel; concerned with trying to do better than others: *A first-rate athlete must possess a competitive spirit.* *adj.*

com·pet·i·tor (kəm pet′ə tər) 1 a person who tries to do better than others. 2 a rival: *Jackie will be Anne's main competitor in the high jump.* 3 a person who takes part in a contest: *There are many competitors for the golf championship.* *n.*

com·pile (kəm pīl′) 1 collect and bring together in one list or account: *He compiled the data for the report.* 2 make a book, report, etc. out of various materials: *It takes many experts to compile an encyclopedia.* *v.*, **com·piled, com·pil·ing.**

com·pla·cen·cy (kəm plā′sən sē) 1 satisfaction with oneself: *She solved the puzzle and smiled with complacency.* 2 contentment. *n.*

com·pla·cent (kəm plā′sənt) pleased or satisfied with oneself: *The winner's complacent smile annoyed some people.* *adj.* —**com·pla′cent·ly,** *adv.*

com·plain (kəm plān′) 1 say that something is wrong; find fault: *She complains that the room is cold.* 2 talk about one's pains, troubles, etc.: *He is always complaining that his health is poor.* *v.*

com·plaint (kəm plānt′) 1 a voicing of dissatisfaction; complaining; finding fault: *Her letter is filled with complaints about her new job.* 2 a formal accusation: *They filed a complaint with the police about their neighbors' 16 cats.* 3 a sickness or disease: *Influenza is a common complaint.* *n.*

com·ple·ment (kom′plə mənt for 1 and 2, kom′plə ment′ for 3) 1 something that completes or makes perfect: *She felt that the hat was necessary as a complement to her spring outfit.* 2 the number required to fill: *The ship now had its full complement of men.* 3 supply a lack of any kind; complete: *That hat was just what was needed to complement her outfit.* 1, 2 *n.*, 3 *v.*

☛ **Complement** and **compliment** are pronounced the same.

☛ Although **complement** and **compliment** have very different meanings, they are often confused in reading and writing because of their similar spelling. One can easily distinguish them by remembering that **complement** is related to *complete* and so has an 'e' after the 'l.' **Compliment** has to do with *praise* and has an 'i' in it.

com·plete (kəm plēt′) 1 with all the parts; whole; entire: *a complete set of garden tools.* 2 make whole or perfect; make up the full number or amount of: *She completed her set of dishes by buying a sugar bowl.* 3 thorough; total: *complete surprise, a complete mess.* 4 finish: *He completed his homework early in the evening.* 5 finished; done: *My homework is complete.* 1, 3, 5 *adj.*, 2, 4 *v.*, **com·plet·ed, com·plet·ing.** —**com·plete′ly,** *adv.*

com·ple·tion (kəm plē′shən) 1 finishing; the act of completing: *After the completion of the job, the workmen went home.* 2 a condition of being completed: *The work is near completion.* *n.*

comp·lex (kəm pleks′ or kom′pleks for 1 and 2, kom′pleks for 3) 1 made up of a number of parts. 2 complicated: *The directions for building the radio were so complex that we could not understand them.* 3 a group of related or connected buildings, structures, units, etc.: *The new complex includes a library, museum, and auditorium.* 1, 2 *adj.*, 3 *n.*

com·plex·ion (kəm plek′shən) 1 the color, quality, and general appearance of the skin, particularly of the face. 2 general appearance; nature; character: *The complexion of the war was changed by two great victories.* *n.*

com·plex·i·ty (kəm plek′sə tē) 1 the state or quality of being complicated; being complex: *The complexity of the road map puzzled him.* 2 something complex; a difficulty or complication: *This problem has many complexities.* *n.*, *pl.* **com·plex·i·ties.**

com·pli·cate (kom′plə kāt′) 1 make hard to understand or to settle; mix up; confuse: *Too many rules complicate a game.* 2 make worse or more mixed up: *Her headaches were complicated by eye trouble.* *v.*, **com·pli·cat·ed, com·pli·cat·ing.**

com·pli·cat·ed (kom′plə kāt′id) mixed up; hard to understand. *adj.*

com·pli·ca·tion (kom′plə kā′shən) 1 a complex or confused condition that is hard to understand or settle: *Such a complication of rules makes this game hard to learn.* 2 something that makes matters worse or harder to untangle or settle: *Pneumonia is sometimes a complication after serious operations.* *n.*

com·pli·ment (kom′plə mənt for 1 and 3, kom′plə ment′ for 2) 1 something good said about a person; something said in praise. 2 praise; pay a compliment to: *He complimented my mother on the way she had trained her children.* 3 **compliments,** *pl.* greetings: *In the box of flowers was a card saying 'With the compliments of a friend.'* 1, 3 *n.*, 2, *v.*

☛ **Compliment** and **complement** are pronounced the same. See second note at **complement.**

com·pli·men·ta·ry (kom′plə men′tə rē or kom′plə men′trē) 1 expressing a compliment; praising. 2 given free: *Father received two complimentary tickets to the circus.* *adj.*

com·ply (kəm plī′) act in agreement with a request or a command: *Father said, 'Please turn down the radio now,' and we complied.* *v.*, **com·plied, com·ply·ing.** **comply with,** obey or follow: *A patient should comply with his doctor's orders.*

com·pose (kəm pōz′) 1 make up: *The ocean is composed of salt water. The group was composed of three grown-ups and four children.* 2 put together; arrange into a system: *To compose a story or poem is to put it together with words. To compose a piece of music is to invent the tune and write down the notes.* 3 calm oneself; pull oneself together: *Try to stop crying and compose yourself before the doctor gets here.* *v.*, **com·posed, com·pos·ing.**

com·posed (kəm pōzd′) calm; quiet. *adj.*

com·pos·er (kəm pōz′ər) a writer of music. *n.*

com·pos·ite (kom′pə zit or kəm poz′it) 1 made up of various parts; compound: *The photographer made a* *composite picture by putting together parts of several others.* 2 something made up of various parts: *This picture is a composite.* 1 *adj.*, 2 *n.*

composite school *Cdn.* a secondary school in which a student may receive general, business, or technical instruction.

composite number a number that can be exactly divided by some number other than itself or 1; a number that has more than two factors: *8 is a composite number with four factors: 1, 2, 4, and 8. 5 is not a composite number; its only factors are 1 and 5.*

com·po·si·tion (kom′pə zish′ən) 1 the make-up of anything: *The composition of this candy includes sugar, chocolate, and milk.* 2 the putting together of a whole: *Writing sentences, making pictures, and setting type in printing are all forms of composition.* 3 something composed, such as a piece of music, writing, etc. 4 a short essay written as a school exercise: *I wrote a composition about my dog.* 5 a mixture of substances: *The dentist filled my tooth with a composition that has silver in it.* *n.*

com·po·sure (kəm pō′zhər) calmness; quietness; self-control: *During the funeral, the widow's composure was remarkable.* *n.*

com·pound (kom′pound for 1, 2 and 3, kəm pound′ for 4) 1 having more than one part: *'Steamship' is a compound word. A clover leaf is a compound leaf.* 2 mixture: *Many medicines are compounds.* 3 a substance formed by chemical combination of two or more substances: *Water is a compound of hydrogen and oxygen.* 4 mix; combine: *The druggist compounds the medicines that the doctor orders.* 1 *adj.*, 2, 3 *n.*, 4 *v.*

com·pre·hend (kom′pri hend′) 1 understand the meaning of: *If you can use a word correctly, you comprehend it.* 2 include; contain: *His report comprehended all the facts.* *v.*

com·pre·hen·sion (kom′pri hen′shən) the act or power of understanding: *Arithmetic is beyond the comprehension of a baby.* *n.*

com·pre·hen·sive (kom′pri hen′siv) 1 including much; covering everything or nearly everything: *a comprehensive test. The board of education made a comprehensive study of the need for new schools.* 2 able to understand many things: *a comprehensive mind.* *adj.*

comprehensive school a composite school.

com·press (kəm pres′ for 1, kom′pres for 2) 1 squeeze together; make smaller by pressure: *Paper is compressed into bales for recycling.* 2 a pad of cloth applied to a part of the body to stop bleeding or to provide medication, etc.: *Put this cold compress on your forehead.* 1 *v.*, 2 *n.*

compressed air air that has been put under extra pressure by being forced into a much smaller space than it usually occupies, so that it has a great deal of force when suddenly released: *Compressed air is used in automobile tires and to operate certain kinds of brakes and guns.*

com·pres·sor (kəm pres′ər) a machine for compressing air, gas, etc. *n.*

com·prise (kəm prīz′) consist of; include: *Canada comprises ten provinces and two territories.* *v.*, **com·prised, com·pris·ing.**

com·pro·mise (kom′prə mīz′) 1 settle a quarrel or difference of opinion by agreeing that each side will give up part of what it demands: *A good statesman knows how to compromise.* 2 a settlement of a quarrel or a difference of opinion by a partial yielding on both sides: *They both wanted the apple; their compromise was to share it.* 3 lay open to shame or suspicion: *You will compromise your good name if you go along with such a cheap trick.* 4 put in danger: *compromise national security.* 1, 3, 4 *v.*, **com·pro·mised, com·pro·mis·ing;** 2 *n.*

com·pul·sion (kəm pul′shən) the act of compelling; the use of force; force: *He can be made to take his medicine only by compulsion.* *n.*

com·pul·so·ry (kəm pul′sə rē) compelled; required: *Attendance at school is compulsory.* *adj.*

com·pu·ta·tion (kom′pyə tā′shən) reckoning; calculation: *Addition and subtraction are forms of computation.* *n.*

com·pute (kəm pyüt′) do by arithmetic; reckon; calculate: *It took some time to compute the cost of our trip.* *v.*, **com·put·ed, com·put·ing.**

com·put·er (kəm pyüt′ər) an electronic machine than can be set to perform mathematical calculations at very high speeds and can store vast amounts of information for later use: *All the technical information for building and flying this space rocket is stored in computers.* *n.*

com·rade (kom′rad or kom′rid) 1 a companion and friend; partner. 2 a fellow member of a union, political party, etc., especially of the Communist Party. *n.*

con[1] (kon) 1 against: *The two groups argued the question pro and con.* 2 a reason against: *The pros and cons of a question are the arguments for and against it.* 1 *adv.*, 2 *n.*

con[2] (kon) *Slang.* 1 trick; swindle: *He was conned into buying a used car that was worthless.* 2 a swindle: *The whole thing was just a con, but I fell for it.* 1 *v.*, **conned, con·ning;** 2 *n.*

con. concession road.

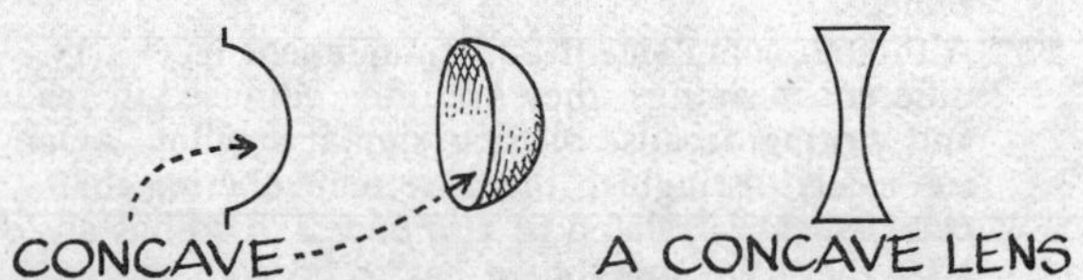

con·cave (kon kāv′ or kon′kāv) hollow and curved like the inside of a circle or sphere: *The palm of one's hand is slightly concave.* *adj.*

con·ceal (kən sēl′) hide: *He concealed the ball behind his back.* *v.*

con·ceal·ment (kən sēl′mənt) 1 concealing or keeping secret: *The witness's concealment of facts prevented a fair trial.* 2 the condition of being hidden or kept secret: *The documents were kept in concealment for fifty years.* 3 a means or place for hiding: *The soldiers could find no concealment in the open country.* *n.*

con·cede (kən sēd′) 1 admit; admit as true: *Everyone concedes that 2 and 2 make 4.* 2 allow a person to have; grant: *He conceded us the right to walk across his land.* *v.*, **conced·ed, con·ced·ing.**

con·ceit (kən sēt′) too much pride in oneself or one's

ability to do things: *In his conceit, the track star thought that no one could outrun him.* *n.*

con·ceit·ed (kən sēt′id) having too high an opinion of oneself; vain. *adj.*

con·ceiv·a·ble (kən sēv′ə bəl) imaginable: *We should take every conceivable precaution against fire.* *adj.*

con·ceive (kən sēv′) 1 form in the mind; think up: *The Wright brothers conceived the design of the first successful motor-powered plane.* 2 have or form an idea: *She couldn't conceive of his ever being keen on the project.* 3 become affected with; experience a feeling of: *He conceived a dislike for cats.* 4 become pregnant. 5 become pregnant with: *conceive a child.* *v.,* **con·ceived, con·ceiv·ing.**

con·cen·trate (kon′sən trāt′) 1 bring or come together to one place: *A magnifying glass can concentrate enough sunlight to scorch paper. The general concentrated his troops to attack the enemy's flank.* 2 pay close attention: *He concentrated on his reading so that he would understand the story.* 3 make stronger: *We concentrated this solution by boiling off some of the water.* 4 a substance that has been concentrated: *I bought a bottle of lemon juice concentrate.* 1–3 *v.,* **con·cen·trat·ed, con·cen·trat·ing;** 4 *n.*

con·cen·tra·tion (kon′sən trā′shən) 1 concentrating or being concentrated: *The concentration of all one's energy on a problem.* 2 close attention: *He gave the problem his full concentration.* *n.*

con·cept (kon′sept) a thought; a general notion or idea: *the concept of truth. Bravery, honor, and courtesy were three basic concepts of chivalry.* *n.*

con·cep·tion (kən sep′shən) 1 a thought or notion; idea; concept: *His conception of the problem was different from mine.* 2 forming an idea or thought. 3 becoming pregnant. *n.*

con·cern (kən sėrn′) 1 have to do with; be the business or affair of; interest: *The school play concerns every member of the class. This letter concerns nobody but me.* 2 anything that has to do with a person's work, business, or interests: *How I spend my money is my concern, not yours.* 3 troubled interest; anxiety: *The mother's concern over her sick child kept her awake all night.* 4 make anxious: *He didn't want to concern his friends with the details of the accident.* 5 a business company; firm. 1, 4 *v.,* 2, 3, 5 *n.*

concern oneself, a take an interest; be busy: *She will concern herself in the water sports program.* b be troubled or worried; be anxious: *Don't concern yourself; I have everything ready.*

of concern, of importance; of interest: *a matter of concern.*

con·cerned (kən sėrnd′) 1 interested; caring: *All concerned citizens are asked to attend the meeting on pollution.* 2 involved; having a connection: *All the students concerned in the school play were given time off for the dress rehearsal.* 3 troubled; worried; anxious: *His parents are quite concerned about his poor health.* *adj.*

con·cern·ing (kən sėr′ning) about; with regard to: *The policeman asked many questions concerning the accident.* *prep.*

con·cert (kon′sərt) a musical performance in which several musicians or singers take part. *n.*

in concert, all together; in agreement: *The rebel groups acted in concert to seize the building.*

hat, āge, fär; let, ēqual, tėrm; it, īce
hot, ōpen, ôrder; oil, out; cup, pu̇t, rüle
əbove, takən, pencəl, lemən, circəs
ch, child; ng, long; sh, ship
th, thin; ᴛʜ, then; zh, measure

con·cer·ti·na (kon′sər tē′nə) a roundish musical instrument made up of a bellows with a set of button keys at each end: *A concertina is like a small accordion.* *n.*

con·cer·to (kən cher′tō) a piece of music to be played by one or more principal instruments, such as a violin, piano, etc., with the accompaniment of an orchestra. *n., pl.* **con·cer·tos.**

con·ces·sion[1] (kən sesh′ən) 1 the act of conceding; yielding: *As a concession, Mother let me stay up an hour longer.* 2 anything conceded or yielded: *Lands or mines given by a government to a business company are usually called grants or concessions.* 3 the right to carry on business in a certain place: *a hotdog concession.* *n.*

con·ces·sion[2] (kən sesh′ən) 1 mainly in Ontario and Quebec, a subdivision of land within a township. 2 concession road: *My uncle lives on the third concession of Victoria township.* *n.*

concession road especially in Ontario, a rural road between concessions, running, as a rule, east and west: *Concession roads are usually 1¼ miles* (2 km) *apart.*

conch (kongk or konch) a large, spiral sea shell. *n.*

con·cil·i·ate (kən sil′ē āt′) win over; win the good will of; soothe: *She conciliated her angry little sister with a candy bar.* *v.,* **con·cil·i·at·ed, con·cil·i·at·ing.**

con·cise (kən sīs′) expressing much in few words; brief but full of meaning: *He gave a concise report of the meeting.* *adj.*

con·clude (kən klüd′) 1 finish; end: *She concluded her speech with a funny story.* 2 reach or arrive at a decision or opinion by reasoning: *From the clues we found, we concluded that the thief must have left in a hurry.* 3 settle; arrange: *The two countries concluded an agreement on trade.* *v.,* **con·clud·ed, con·clud·ing.**

con·clu·sion (kən klü′zhən) 1 an end: *the conclusion of the game.* 2 the last main division of a speech, essay, etc.: *A book or article often has a conclusion summing up all of the important points.* 3 a decision or opinion reached by reasoning: *He came to the conclusion that he must work harder to succeed.* 4 a settlement; arrangement: *Everyone was pleased by the conclusion of a peace between the two countries.* *n.*

con·clu·sive (kən klü′siv) decisive; definite: *a conclusive victory. The evidence against the burglar was conclusive.* *adj.*

con·coct (kən kokt′) 1 prepare: *The chef concocted a delicious dessert.* 2 make up; invent: *The prisoners concocted an impossible plan for escape.* *v.*

con·cord (kon′kôrd) agreement; peace; harmony: *concord between nations.* *n.*

con·course (kon′kôrs) 1 a running, flowing, or coming together: *The fort was built at the concourse of two rivers.* 2 a crowd. 3 a place where crowds gather or wait: *We met in the concourse of the railway station.* *n.*

con·crete (kon′krēt) **1** real; existing as an actual object, not merely as an idea or as a quality: *A painting is concrete; its beauty is abstract.* **2** a mixture of cement, water, and sand or gravel that hardens as it dries: *Concrete is used for foundations, whole buildings, sidewalks, roads, dams, and bridges.* **3** the hard substance resulting from the hardening of this mixture: *He fell and hurt his head on the concrete. That building has a concrete roof.* 1 *adj.*, 2, 3 *n.*

con·cur (kən kėr′) **1** agree; be of the same opinion: *The judges all concurred in the decision to give him the prize.* **2** work together: *The events of the week concurred to make it a great holiday.* *v.*, **con·curred, con·cur·ring.**

con·cus·sion (kən kush′ən) **1** a violent shaking; shock: *The concussion caused by the explosion broke many windows.* **2** an injury to the brain or spine from a blow or fall or other shock: *He suffered a severe concussion in the accident.* *n.*

con·demn (kən dem′) **1** express strong disapproval of: *We condemn cruelty and cruel people.* **2** pronounce guilty of crime or wrong: *The prisoner is sure to be condemned.* **3** sentence; doom: *The murderer was condemned to death.* **4** declare not sound or suitable for use: *This bridge has been condemned because it is no longer safe.* *v.*

con·dem·na·tion (kon′dem nā′shən) **1** strong disapproval: *He expressed his condemnation of the new plan.* **2** condemning or being condemned: *the prisoner's condemnation, the condemnation of an unsafe bridge.* *n.*

con·den·sa·tion (kon′den sā′shən) **1** condensing or being condensed: *the condensation of a story, the condensation of steam into water.* **2** something condensed; condensed mass: *A cloud is a condensation of water vapor in the atmosphere. There is a condensation of the book in that magazine.* *n.*

con·dense (kən dens′) **1** make or become denser or more compact; reduce the volume of: *Milk is condensed before it is canned.* **2** increase the strength of: *Light is condensed by means of lenses.* **3** change from a gas or a vapor to a liquid: *If steam touches cold surfaces, it condenses into water.* **4** say briefly; put into fewer words: *A long story can sometimes be condensed into a few sentences.* *v.*, **con·densed, con·dens·ing.**

condensed milk a thick, sweet, evaporated milk.

con·dens·er (kən den′sər) a device for receiving and holding a charge of electricity. *n.*

con·de·scend (kon′di send′) **1** come down willingly or graciously to the level of one's inferiors in rank: *The king condescended to eat with the beggars.* **2** grant a favor in a haughty or patronizing way: *The colonel's wife condescended to visit the corporal's family.* **3** stoop or lower oneself: *He would not condescend to taking a bribe.* *v.*

con·de·scend·ing (kon′di sen′ding) patronizing; acting in a way that shows scorn for others: *The women were annoyed by the haughty, condescending mannner of the colonel's wife.* *adj.*

con·di·tion (kən dish′ən) **1** the state in which a person or thing is; fitness: *The condition of his health kept him from doing heavy work. The victim of the accident was in poor condition.* **2** put in good condition: *Exercise conditions your muscles.* **3** social position; rank: *The premier's parents were people of humble condition.* **4** anything on which something else depends; something without which something else cannot exist: *Ability and effort are conditions of success.* **5** shape the behavior of; accustom: *This dog has been conditioned to expect food when he obeys a command.* 1, 3, 4 *n.*, 2, 5 *v.*

on condition that, if; provided that: *I'll go on condition that you will too.*

con·di·tion·al (kən dish′ən əl) depending on something else; subject to a condition or conditions: *'You may go if the sun shines' is a conditional promise.* *adj.*

con·dor (kon′dər) a large vulture having a neck and head bare of feathers: *Condors live on high mountains in South America and California.* *n.*

con·duct (kon′dukt for 1, kən dukt′ for 2–6) **1** a way of acting; behavior thought of as good or bad: *Her rude conduct was not excusable. He won a medal for good conduct.* **2** act or behave in a certain way: *At home he is disorderly, but in company he conducts himself well.* **3** manage; direct: *Mr Jones conducts a big business.* **4** direct an orchestra, choir, etc. as leader: *He conducts an orchestra of fifty instruments.* **5** go along with and show the way to; guide: *Conduct me to your leader. He conducted me through the museum.* **6** be a channel for; transmit: *Metals conduct heat and electricity.* 1 *n.*, 2–6 *v.*

safe conduct, guaranteed passage from one place to another without harm or danger: *The messenger was promised safe conduct through the enemy camp.*

con·duc·tion (kən duk′shən) in science, the passing along of heat, electricity, etc. by the transferring of energy from one particle to the next: *Radiators heat the air in a room by conduction.* *n.*

con·duc·tor (kən duk′tər) **1** a guide or leader; one who is conducting: *The conductor of an orchestra trains the musicians to work together, selects the music to be used, and directs the players during a performance.* **2** the person in charge of passengers on a train, a streetcar, or a bus. **3** anything that transmits heat, sound, or electricity: *Copper wire is widely used as a conductor of electricity.* *n.*

A cone (def. 1) The cone of a volcano A pine cone

cone (kōn) **1** a solid object that has a flat, round base and narrows evenly to a point at the top. **2** anything shaped like a cone: *an ice-cream cone, the cone of a volcano.* **3** the part that bears the seeds on pine, cedar, fir, and similar evergreen trees. *n.*

co·ney (kō′nē) **1** rabbit fur: *Her coat was trimmed with coney.* **2** rabbit. *n.*, *pl.* **co·neys.** Also spelled **cony.**

con·fec·tion·er·y (kən fek′shən er′ē) **1** candies, sweets, etc. **2** a place where sweets, ice cream, etc. are made or sold; candy store. *n.*, *pl.* **con·fec·tion·er·ies.**

hat, āge, fär; let, ēqual, tėrm; it, īce
hot, ōpen, ôrder; oil, out; cup, pu̇t, rüle
əbove, takən, pencəl, lemən, circəs
ch, child; ng, long; sh, ship
th, thin; ᴛʜ, then; zh, measure

con·fed·er·a·cy (kən fed′ər ə sē) 1 a union of countries or states. 2 a group of people joined together for a special purpose. *n., pl.* **con·fed·er·a·cies.**

con·fed·er·ate (kən fed′ər it for 1, 2, kən fed′ər āt′ for 3) 1 joined together for a special purpose; allied. 2 a person allied with others for a special purpose, often a bad one; accomplice: *The thief had three confederates.* 3 enter a union or alliance: *Newfoundland confederated with Canada in 1949. Four provinces of Canada confederated in 1867.* 1 *adj.,* 2 *n.,* 3 *v.*

con·fed·er·a·tion (kən fed′ər ā′shən) a confederacy: *The conference devised a plan for a confederation of the colonies. n.*

Con·fed·er·a·tion (kən fed′ər ā′shən) 1 the name given to the union of Ontario, Quebec, Nova Scotia, and New Brunswick in 1867: *Six other provinces have joined Confederation since 1867.* 2 **the Confederation,** the ten provinces of Canada. *n.*

con·fer (kən fėr′) 1 consult together; talk the matter over; exchange ideas: *The teacher conferred with the principal about the boy's promotion.* 2 give; award; bestow: *The Victoria Cross was conferred on the soldier by the Queen. v.,* **con·ferred, con·fer·ring.**

con·fer·ence (kon′fər əns) a meeting of interested persons to discuss a particular subject: *The teachers held a conference to discuss the new textbooks. n.*

con·fess (kən fes′) 1 acknowledge; admit; own up: *He confessed to eating all the cake. I confess you are right on one point.* 2 admit one's guilt: *The prisoner confessed.* 3 tell one's mistakes and sins, especially to a priest. *v.*

con·fes·sion (kən fesh′ən) 1 the act of confessing; owning up; telling one's mistakes or sins: *Confession is good for the soul.* 2 the thing confessed. *n.*

con·fide (kən fīd′) tell as a secret: *He confided his troubles to his brother. v.,* **con·fid·ed, con·fid·ing.**
confide in, a entrust a secret to: *She always confides in her sister.* **b** put trust in: *confide in God.*

con·fi·dence (kon′fə dəns) 1 firm belief or trust: *We have no confidence in a liar.* 2 firm belief in oneself and one's abilities: *He goes at his work with confidence.* 3 something told as a secret: *I listened to her confidences for half an hour. n.*

con·fi·dent (kon′fə dənt) 1 firmly believing; certain: *I feel confident that our team will win.* 2 sure of oneself and one's abilities: *She is a very confident person. adj.*

con·fi·den·tial (kon′fə den′shəl) 1 spoken or written as a secret: *The detective made a confidential report.* 2 trusted with secret matters: *A confidential secretary should not discuss his employer's business with other people. adj.*

con·fine (kən fīn′ for 1 and 2, kon′fīn for 3) 1 keep within limits; restrict: *I confine myself to two games a week.* 2 keep in; shut in: *He was confined in prison for two years. A cold confined him to the house.* 3 Usually, **confines,** *pl.* a boundary; border; limit: *These people have never been beyond the confines of their own valley.* 1, 2 *v.,* **con·fined, con·fin·ing;** 3 *n.*

con·fine·ment (kən fīn′mənt) 1 confining or being confined: *confinement indoors on account of a cold.* 2 the period for which a mother is confined to bed during and after childbirth. *n.*

con·firm (kən fėrm′) 1 make official by formal statement: *The treaty was confirmed by Parliament.* 2 make certain; put beyond doubt: *The witness confirmed the policeman's account of the accident. The travel agent confirmed her plane reservation.* 3 support; strengthen in an opinion, etc.: *He was confirmed in his purpose by all his friends.* 4 admit by a special ceremony to full membership in a church after required study and preparation. *v.*

con·fir·ma·tion (kon′fər mā′shən) 1 making sure by more information or evidence: *He phoned the arena for confirmation of the starting time for the game.* 2 something that confirms; proof: *Don't believe gossip that lacks confirmation.* 3 an assurance that one's plans have not been changed: *An airline requires confirmation of a ticket buyer's reservation.* 4 the ceremony of various churches, by which a person is admitted to full membership after completing the required study and preparation. *n.*

con·firmed (kən fėrmd′) settled; habitual: *a confirmed bachelor. adj.*

con·fis·cate (kon′fis kāt′) 1 seize for the public treasury: *The traitor's property was confiscated.* 2 seize by authority; take and keep: *The customs officer has confiscated the smuggled cigarettes. v.,* **con·fis·cat·ed, con·fis·cat·ing.**

con·fla·gra·tion (kon′flə grā′shən) a big fire that causes great destruction: *A conflagration destroyed most of the city. n.*

con·flict (kon′flikt for 1 and 2, kən flikt′ for 3) 1 a fight; struggle. 2 an active opposition of persons or ideas: *A conflict of opinion arose over what food was best for our rabbit.* 3 be opposed; clash; differ in thought and action. 1, 2 *n.,* 3 *v.*

con·form (kən fôrm′) 1 act according to law or rule; be in agreement with generally accepted standards: *Members must conform to the rules of our club.* 2 be like; correspond: *His ideas conform to those of his father. v.*

con·form·i·ty (kən fôr′mə tē) 1 likeness; similarity: *There was too much conformity among the houses in the new subdivision.* 2 action in agreement with generally accepted standards of business, law, conduct, or worship; fitting oneself and one's actions to the ideas of others. *n., pl.* **con·form·i·ties.**

con·found (kən found′) 1 mix up; confuse: *To confound two things means not to be able to tell them apart.* 2 surprise and puzzle: *The general was confounded by the violence of the enemy attack. v.*

con·front (kən frunt′) 1 meet face to face, especially as opponents; stand facing. 2 face boldly; oppose: *She whirled around and confronted the bully.* 3 bring face to face; place before: *We confronted the girl with the dish she had broken. v.*

con·fuse (kən fyüz′) 1 mix up; throw into disorder; bewilder: *So many people talking to me at once confused me.* 2 be unable to tell apart; mistake one thing for another: *People often confuse this girl with her twin sister. v.,* **con·fused, con·fus·ing.**

con·fu·sion (kən fyü′zhən) 1 a mixed-up condition of things or of the mind: *The confusion in the room showed that he had packed in a hurry.* 2 the mistaking of one thing for another: *Words like 'believe' and 'receive' sometimes cause confusion in spelling.* 3 tumult: *After the home team won, the arena was a scene of utter confusion.* *n.*

con·geal (kən jēl′) 1 harden or make solid by cold; freeze. 2 thicken; clot: *The blood around the wound had congealed.* *v.*

con·ge·ni·al (kən jē′nē əl) 1 having similar tastes and interests; getting on well together: *Congenial companions made the trip pleasant.* 2 agreeable; suitable; pleasing: *He is looking for more congenial work.* *adj.*

con·gest·ed (kən jes′tid) 1 overcrowded; filled too full: *The streets of this city are often congested with traffic.* 2 too full of blood or mucus: *His nose is congested as the result of a cold. The lungs are congested in pneumonia.* *adj.*

con·glom·er·a·tion (kən glom′ər ā′shən) a mixed-up mass of various things or persons: *There was such a conglomeration of things in the room that she didn't know what to clean up first.* *n.*

con·grat·u·late (kən grach′ə lāt′ or kən graj′ə lāt′) express pleasure at the happiness or good fortune of: *I congratulated my friend on her birthday.* *v.*, **con·grat·u·lat·ed, con·grat·u·lat·ing.**

con·grat·u·la·tion (kən grach′ə lā′shən or kən graj′ə lā′shən) 1 an expression of pleasure to someone because of his happiness or good fortune: *She wrote a letter of congratulation when her sister had a baby.* 2 **congratulations,** *pl.* expression of pleasure at another's happiness or good fortune: *Congratulations on your high marks at school.* *n.*

con·gre·gate (kong′grə gāt′) come together into a crowd or mass; assemble: *The people of Rome congregated in St. Peter's Square to see the Pope.* *v.*, **con·gre·gat·ed, con·gre·gat·ing.**

con·gre·ga·tion (kong′grə gā′shən) 1 coming together in a crowd or mass; assembling: *There was a congregation of bees around the hive.* 2 a gathering of people or things; assembly. 3 a group of people gathered together for religious worship or instruction. *n.*

con·gress (kong′gris) 1 meeting; coming together, especially a meeting of representatives to discuss some subject. 2 in some countries, an assembly of representatives of the people. 3 **Congress,** in the United States, the national lawmaking body consisting of the Senate and the House of Representatives, with members from each state. *n.*

con·i·cal (kon′ə kəl) cone-shaped; like a cone: *The wizard wore a conical hat.* *adj.*

co·ni·fer (kō′nə fər) a cone-bearing tree: *The pine, fir, spruce, hemlock, and larch are conifers.* *n.*

con·jec·ture (kən jek′chər) 1 a conclusion reached by guessing: *The detective's solution of the crime was mostly conjecture.* 2 reach a conclusion by guessing. 1 *n.*, 2 *v.*, **con·jec·tured, con·jec·tur·ing.**

con·junc·tion (kən jungk′shən) 1 a union; connection: *A severe illness in conjunction with the hot weather has left the baby very weak.* 2 a word that expresses a particular connection between clauses, phrases, or words: *'And,' 'or,' 'but,' 'though,' and 'if' are conjunctions.* *n.*

con·jure (kun′jər or kon′jər for 1 and 2, kən jür′ for 3) 1 compel to appear or disappear by a set form of words: *The wizard in the story conjured a dragon.* 2 perform tricks by very quick, deceiving movements of the hands. 3 make a solemn appeal to: *By all that is holy, I conjure you not to betray your country.* *v.*, **con·jured, con·jur·ing.**

conjure up, cause to appear as if by magic: *Grandma conjured up a bag of toys from the attic.*

con·nect (kə nekt′) 1 join one thing to another; fasten together; unite: *The plumber had to connect those pipes before the water could be turned on.* 2 think of one thing as being associated with or the cause of another: *We usually connect spring with sunshine and flowers.* 3 join with others in some business or interest; have any kind of practical relation with: *This store is connected with a chain of stores. He is connected with several clubs.* *v.*

con·nec·tion (kə nek′shən) 1 connecting or being connected: *The connection of our gas pipes took two days.* 2 something that connects; a connecting part; a bond or tie. 3 any kind of practical relation with another thing: *She has no connection with her brother's firm.* 4 the arranged meeting of trains, ships, airplanes, etc. so that passengers can change from one to the other without delay. 5 a relative: *She is a connection of ours by marriage.* *n.*

con·ning tower (kon′ing) a small tower on a submarine, used as an entrance and as a place for observation. See **submarine** for picture.

con·quer (kong′kər) 1 get by fighting; win in war: *to conquer a country.* 2 overcome by force; get the better of; defeat: *conquer an enemy, conquer a bad habit.* 3 be victorious; be the conqueror: *The general said he would conquer or die.* *v.*

con·quer·or (kong′kər ər) a person who conquers, especially in war. *n.*

con·quest (kon′kwest or kong′kwest) 1 the act of conquering: *the conquest of a country, the conquest of a bad habit.* 2 the thing conquered. *n.*

con·quis·ta·dor (kon kwis′tə dôr′ or kon kis′tə dôr′) one of the Spanish conquerors who came to South America and the southern parts of North America in the sixteenth century to look for gold: *The conquistadors conquered the Indian civilizations of Mexico and South America in their search for treasure.* *n.*

con·science (kon′shəns) a sense of right and wrong: *The boy's conscience prompted him to return the book he had stolen.* *n.*

con·sci·en·tious (kon′shē en′shəs) 1 careful to do what one knows is right; controlled by conscience. 2 done carefully and properly: *Conscientious work is careful and exact.* *adj.*

con·scious (kon′shəs) 1 knowing; having experience; aware: *She was not conscious of his presence in the room.* 2 awake; able to feel: *When he became conscious again, he asked what had happened.* 3 known to oneself: *Talking is more often conscious than breathing is.* *adj.*

con·scious·ness (kon′shəs nis) 1 the state of being conscious; awareness: *The injured man did not regain consciousness for two hours. People and animals have* *consciousness; plants and stones do not.* 2 all the thoughts and feelings of a person: *Everything of which you are conscious makes up your consciousness.* *n.*

con·se·crate (kon′sə krāt′) 1 set apart as sacred; make holy: *A church is consecrated to worship.* 2 set apart for a purpose; dedicate: *His life was consecrated to music.* *v.*, **con·se·crat·ed, con·se·crat·ing.**

con·sec·u·tive (kən sek′yə tiv) following one right after another: *Monday, Tuesday, and Wednesday are consecutive days. We went to the movies on three consecutive nights.* *adj.*

con·sent (kən sent′) 1 agree; give approval or permission: *His father would not consent to his leaving school.* 2 agreement; permission: *We have Mother's consent to go.* 1 *v.*, 2 *n.*

con·se·quence (kon′sə kwens′) 1 a result: *The consequence of his fall was a broken leg.* 2 importance: *The loss of that old hat is a matter of no consequence.* *n.*

take the consequences, accept what happens because of one's action: *If you do your work carelessly, you'll have to take the consequences.*

con·se·quent (kon′sə kwent′) resulting; following as an effect: *His illness and consequent absence put him behind in his work.* *adj.* —**con′se·quent·ly,** *adv.*

con·ser·va·tion (kon′sər vā′shən) preservation; the act of protecting from loss or being used up; the avoidance of waste: *The conservation of forests is very important.* *n.*

con·serv·a·tive (kən sėr′və tiv) 1 inclined to keep things as they are or were in the past; opposed to change: *Old people tend to be more conservative than young ones.* 2 not inclined to take risks; cautious; moderate: *This old, reliable company has conservative business methods.* 3 a person opposed to change. 4 often, **Conservative, a** a member of a conservative political party. **b** in Canada, a member of the Progressive-Conservative Party, one of the principal political groups; a person who supports the views and principles of this party. 1, 2 *adj.*, 3, 4 *n.*

Conservative Party in Canada, the Progressive Conservative Party.

con·serve (kən sėrv′ for 1, kon′sėrv for 2) 1 keep from harm or decay; keep from loss or from being used up; preserve: *Try to conserve your strength for the end of the race.* 2 fruit preserved in sugar; preserves; jam. 1 *v.*, **con·served, con·serv·ing;** 2 *n.*

con·sid·er (kən sid′ər) 1 think about in order to decide: *Take time to consider the problem.* 2 think to be; think of as: *E. J. Pratt is considered a great Canadian poet.* 3 allow for; take into account: *This watch runs very well, if you consider how old it is.* 4 be thoughtful of others and their feelings: *A kind person considers the feelings of others.* *v.*

con·sid·er·a·ble (kən sid′ər ə bəl) 1 worth thinking about; important: *Fifty dollars is a considerable sum of money.* 2 not a little; much: *A break in a water pipe may cause considerable trouble.* *adj.*

con·sid·er·a·bly (kən sid′ər ə blē) much; a good deal: *The boy was considerably older than he looked.* *adv.*

con·sid·er·ate (kən sid′ər it) thoughtful of others and their feelings: *A considerate person does not show impatience.* *adj.*

con·sid·er·a·tion (kən sid′ər ā′shən) 1 careful thought about something before making a decision: *Please give full consideration to my question.* 2 something thought of as a reason; something to be considered: *Price and quality are two considerations in buying anything.* 3 thoughtfulness for others and their feelings: *The girl's consideration for her mother was in sharp contrast with her brother's rudeness.* 4 money or other payment: *I'll cut your grass for a small consideration.* *n.*

in consideration of, a because of: *In consideration of his wife's poor health, he moved to a milder climate.* **b** in return for: *She gave him a present in consideration of his helpfulness.*

take into consideration, allow for; take into account; consider: *The judge took the boy's age into consideration.*

con·sid·er·ing (kən sid′ər ing) taking into account; making allowance for: *Considering his age, the little boy reads very well.* *prep.*

con·sign (kən sīn′) 1 hand over; deliver: *The man was consigned to prison.* 2 send; transmit: *The goods were consigned by rail.* *v.*

con·sist (kən sist′) be made up: *A week consists of seven days. A chair consists of a seat with a back, supported by four legs.* *v.*

con·sist·en·cy (kən sis′tən sē) 1 a degree of firmness or stiffness: *Icing for a cake must be of the right consistency to spread easily without dripping.* 2 keeping to the same principles, course of action, etc.: *He was much admired for his consistency of purpose.* 3 harmony; agreement: *There was little consistency between what he said and what he did.* *n., pl.* **con·sist·en·cies.**

con·sist·ent (kən sis′tənt) 1 thinking or acting today in agreement with what one thought yesterday; keeping to the same principles and habits: *He was always consistent in his attitude toward children.* 2 harmonious; in agreement: *Driving an automobile at very high speed is not consistent with safety.* *adj.*

con·so·la·tion (kon′sə lā′shən) 1 comfort. 2 a comforting person, thing, or event: *The widow found her children to be a great consolation.* *n.*

con·sole[1] (kən sōl′) offer comfort to. *v.*, **con·soled, con·sol·ing.**

con·sole[2] (kon′sōl) 1 the keyboard, stops, and pedals of an organ. 2 a cabinet made to stand on the floor and to contain a television set, radio, record player, etc. *n.*

con·sol·i·date (kən sol′ə dāt′) 1 unite; combine: *The three banks plan to consolidate and form a single large bank.* 2 make solid or firm; strengthen: *The army spent a day in consolidating its gains by digging trenches.* *v.*, **con·sol·i·dat·ed, con·sol·i·dat·ing.**

consolidated school a school built to replace two or more smaller ones, especially in country districts, so as to provide a greater range of facilities.

con·so·nant (kon′sə nənt) 1 a speech sound formed by completely or partially blocking the breath: *All languages include both consonants and vowels. The first and last sounds in 'tab' are consonants.* 2 any letter of the alphabet that is not a vowel: *Some consonants are the letters* b, c, d *and* f. *n.*

con·sort (kon′sôrt for 1, kən sôrt′ for 2) 1 a husband or wife, especially of a monarch. 2 keep company; associate: *They have consorted together for a long time. It is unwise to consort with criminals.* 1 *n.*, 2 *v.*

con·spic·u·ous (kən spik′yü əs) 1 easily seen: *A traffic sign should be placed where it is conspicuous.* 2 remarkable; worthy of notice: *Canada has played a conspicuous part in the work of the United Nations. adj.*

con·spir·a·cy (kən spir′ə sē) 1 a secret scheming or plotting with others to do something wrong: *A group of army officers were charged with conspiracy.* 2 the plot resulting from such planning: *All those in the conspiracy were punished. n., pl.* **con·spir·a·cies.**

con·spir·a·tor (kən spir′ə tər) a person who conspires; one who joins in a plot: *Conspirators planned to kill the king. n.*

con·spire (kən spīr′) 1 plan secretly with others to do something wrong; plot: *A group of thieves conspired to steal the jewels.* 2 act together: *All things conspired to make her birthday a happy one. v.*, **con·spired, con·spir·ing.**

con·sta·ble (kon′stə bəl) a police officer. *n.*

con·stan·cy (kon′stən sē) faithfulness; firmness in belief or feeling: *We admire the constancy of Columbus in looking for a way around the earth. n.*

con·stant (kon′stənt) 1 always the same; not changing: *If you walk due north, your direction is constant.* 2 never stopping: *We had three days of constant rain.* 3 continually happening: *A clock makes a constant ticking sound.* 4 faithful; loyal: *A constant friend helps you when you need help. adj.* **—con′stant·ly,** *adv.*

con·stel·la·tion (kon′stə lā′shən) a set or group of stars: *The Big Dipper is the easiest constellation to find. n.*

con·ster·na·tion (kon′stər nā′shən) dismay; paralysing terror: *To our consternation the train rushed on toward the burning bridge. n.*

con·sti·pat·ed (kon′stə pāt′id) suffering from constipation. *adj.*

con·sti·pa·tion (kon′stə pā′shən) a condition in which it is difficult or impossible to have a bowel movement. *n.*

con·stit·u·en·cy (kən stich′ü ən sē) 1 a district, or riding, represented by a Member of Parliament or a Member of the Legislative Assembly. 2 the voters in this district. *n., pl.* **con·stit·u·en·cies.**

con·stit·u·ent (kən stich′ü ənt) 1 forming a necessary part; making up: *Flour, liquid, salt, and yeast are constituent parts of bread.* 2 a part of a whole; a necessary part: *Sugar is the main constituent of candy.* 3 a voter in a constituency: *The Member of Parliament received many letters from his constituents.* 1 *adj.*, 2, 3 *n.*

con·sti·tute (kon′stə tyüt′ or kon′stə tüt′) 1 make up; form: *Seven days constitute a week.* 2 appoint; elect: *Mr. Jones was constituted President of the Home and School Association.* 3 set up; establish: *Some schools are especially constituted for teaching blind children. v.*, **con·sti·tut·ed, con·sti·tut·ing.**

con·sti·tu·tion (kon′stə tyü′shən or kon′stə tü′shən) 1 a person's physical or mental nature or make-up: *He has a very healthy constitution.* 2 the way in which anything is organized; the structure. 3 the fundamental principles according to which a country, a state, or a society is governed: *Many clubs have written constitutions. In Canada the British North America Act of 1867 is the basis of the written constitution. n.*

con·sti·tu·tion·al (kon′stə tyü′shən əl or kon′stə tü′shən əl) 1 of or in a person's constitution or nature: *A constitutional weakness makes him subject to colds.* 2 of the constitution of a country, state, or society: *Some lawyers are experts in constitutional law.* 3 a walk taken for the health. 1, 2 *adj.*, 3 *n.*

con·strain (kən strān′) force; compel: *He was constrained to accept his employer's decision or leave his job. v.*

con·straint (kən strānt′) 1 the holding back of natural feelings; embarrassed awkwardness: *We felt a little constraint with the new teacher for the first day or so.* 2 force; compulsion: *When he confessed the crime, he was acting under constraint. n.*

con·strict (kən strikt′) draw together; contract; compress: *The collar was too tight and constricted the dog's neck. v.*

con·struct (kən strukt′) put together; fit together; build: *Sentences are constructed of words. v.*

con·struc·tion (kən struk′shən) 1 the act of constructing, building, or putting together: *The construction of the bridge took nearly a month.* 2 the way in which a thing is constructed: *Cracks and leaks are signs of poor construction.* 3 something built or put together: *The doll's house was a construction of wood and cardboard.* 4 the arrangement of words in a sentence. 5 a meaning; interpretation: *She dislikes me and puts a bad construction upon everything I say or do. n.*

con·struc·tive (kən struk′tiv) building up so as to improve; helpful: *People appreciate constructive suggestions. adj.*

con·strue (kən strü′) show the meaning of; explain; interpret: *Different lawyers may construe the same law differently. v.*, **con·strued, con·stru·ing.**

con·sul (kon′səl) 1 an officer appointed by the government of a country to look after its business interests in a city of another country. 2 either of the two chief magistrates of the ancient Roman republic. *n.*

con·su·late (kon′sə lit) 1 the official residence and business offices of a consul: *He visited the Canadian consulate in New York.* 2 a consul's term of office. *n.*

con·sult (kən sult′) 1 seek information or advice from: *You can consult persons, books, or maps to find out what you wish to know.* 2 exchange ideas; talk things over: *He is consulting with his lawyer.* 3 take into consideration; have regard for: *A good teacher consults the interests of her class. v.*

con·sume (kən süm′ or kən syüm′) 1 eat or drink up: *We consumed a great deal of food at the birthday party.* 2 destroy; burn up: *A fire can consume a forest.*

3 use up; spend: *She consumes much of her time in reading.* 4 waste time, money, etc.: *Daydreaming consumes a lot of a child's time.* *v.,* **con·sumed, con·sum·ing.**

con·sum·er (kən süm′ər or kən syüm′ər) a person who uses food, clothing, or anything grown or made by producers: *A low price for wheat should reduce the price of flour to the consumer.* *n.*

con·sump·tion (kən sump′shən) 1 the act of using or using up: *This food is for our consumption on the trip.* 2 the amount used up: *The consumption of coal in that factory is five tonnes a day.* 3 a disease that destroys parts of the lungs; tuberculosis. *n.*

con·tact (kon′takt) 1 the condition of touching; touching together: *When two balls are in contact, one can be moved by touching the other.* 2 being in touch; connection; association: *The control tower lost contact with the pilot.* 3 a person with whom one can get in touch for business purposes: *He has a useful contact in an advertising agency.* 4 get in touch with; make a connection with: *There's been an accident! Contact the doctor immediately!* 1–3 *n.,* 4 *v.*

contact lens a thin, curved plastic lens to correct poor eyesight, worn on the front of the eyeball.

contacts (kon′takts) contact lenses: *He has worn contacts for years.* *n. pl.*

con·ta·gion (kən tā′jən) 1 the spreading of disease by touching. 2 a disease spread in this way. 3 the spreading or communication of any influence from one to another: *A contagion of fear swept through the audience and caused a panic.* *n.*

con·ta·gious (kən tā′jəs) 1 spread through contact; communicable: *Chicken pox is contagious.* 2 easily spread from one person to another: *Yawning and laughing are often contagious.* *adj.*

con·tain (kən tān′) 1 have within itself; hold as contents; include: *My purse contains money. Books contain information.* 2 be capable of holding: *That pitcher contains a litre.* 3 be equal to: *A metre contains 100 centimetres.* 4 control; hold back; restrain one's feelings: *He contained his anger. She could hardly contain herself when the boy kicked her dog.* 5 of numbers, be divisible by without a remainder: *12 will contain 1, 2, 3, 4, 6 and 12.* *v.*

con·tain·er (kən tān′ər) a box, can, jar, etc. used to hold or contain something: *A pitcher is a container.* *n.*

con·tam·i·nate (kən tam′ə nāt′) make impure; defile; pollute; corrupt: *Flies contaminate food.* *v.,* **con·tam·i·nat·ed, con·tam·i·nat·ing.**

con·tem·plate (kon′təm plāt′) 1 look at or think about for a long time: *He contemplated the puzzle for ten minutes before he tried to solve it.* 2 have in mind; consider; intend: *She is contemplating a trip to Europe.* 3 meditate: *All day he did nothing but contemplate.* *v.,* **con·tem·plat·ed,con·tem·plat·ing.**

con·tem·pla·tion (kon′təm plā′shən) 1 the act of looking at or thinking about something for a long time; deep thought: *He was sunk in contemplation.* 2 expectation; intention: *We are buying tents and other equipment in contemplation of a summer's camping.* *n.*

con·tem·po·rar·y (kən tem′pə rer′ē) 1 belonging to the same period of time. 2 a person who belongs to the same period of time: *Macdonald and Laurier were contemporaries.* 1 *adj.,* 2 *n., pl.* **con·tem·po·rar·ies.**

con·tempt (kən tempt′) 1 the feeling that a person

hat, āge, fär; let, ēqual, tėrm; it, īce
hot, ōpen, ôrder; oil, out; cup, pu̇t, rüle
əbove, takən, pencəl, lemən, circəs
ch, child; ng, long; sh, ship
th, thin; ᴛʜ, then; zh, measure

or act is mean and low; despising; scorn: *We feel contempt for a sneak.* 2 the condition of being despised; disgrace: *A cowardly traitor is held in contempt.* *n.*

con·tempt·i·ble (kən temp′tə bəl) deserving contempt or scorn: *Cowards and cheats are contemptible.* *adj.*

con·temp·tu·ous (kən temp′chü əs) showing contempt; scornful: *She was contemptuous of her little brother's efforts to look grown up.* *adj.*

con·tend (kən tend′) 1 fight; struggle: *The Arctic explorers had to contend with extreme cold, hunger, and loneliness.* 2 take part in a contest: *Five runners were contending in the first race.* 3 declare to be true; argue: *Columbus contended that the earth was round.* *v.*

con·tent[1] (kon′tent) 1 Usually, **contents,** *pl.* what is contained in anything; all things inside: *An old chair, a desk, and a bed were the only contents of the room.* 2 the facts or ideas stated; what is written in a book or said in a speech: *I could read her writing, but I couldn't understand the content of her essay.* 3 the amount contained: *Cream has a high fat content.* *n.*

☛ **Content**[1] refers mainly to the amount or quality of what is contained or included in something: *The content of a speech, argument, composition, etc.* **Contents** refers to the individual things contained in something: *the contents of a box.*

con·tent[2] (kən tent′) 1 satisfy; please: *Will it content you if I let you have the candy tomorrow?* 2 satisfied; contented: *They were content with just a short holiday. Then they were content to stay home.* 3 contentment; satisfaction: *The cat lay stretched out beside the fire in sleepy content.* 1 *v.,* 2 *adj.,* 3 *n.*

con·tent·ed (kən ten′tid) satisfied: *A contented person is happy with what he has.* *adj.* **—con·tent′ed·ly,** *adv.*

con·ten·tion (kən ten′shən) 1 arguing or disputing: *The main subject of contention was the proposed change in the school curriculum.* 2 a statement or point that one has argued for: *Columbus's contention that the earth was round proved to be true.* *n.*

con·tent·ment (kən tent′mənt) satisfaction; being pleased; quiet happiness. *n.*

con·test (kon′test for 1, kən test′ for 2) 1 a trial of skill to see who will win: *A game or race is a contest.* 2 to dispute; struggle against; fight: *He promised to contest the court's unfavorable decision.* 1 *n.,* 2 *v.*

con·test·ant (kən tes′tənt) a person who contests; a person who takes part in a contest: *My brother was a contestant in a quiz show.* *n.*

con·text (kon′tekst) the spoken or written text in which a particular word or group of words occurs: *It's unfair to judge his statement without knowing the context in which he made it.* *n.*

con·ti·nent (kon′tə nənt) 1 one of the seven great masses of land on the earth: *The continents are North*

America, South America, Europe, Africa, Asia, Australia, and Antarctica. 2 **the Continent,** the mainland of Europe. *n.*

con·ti·nen·tal (kon′tə nen′təl) 1 of a continent; like a continent. 2 usually, **Continental,** of or having to do with the mainland of Europe: *He likes Continental food. adj.*

Continental Divide the great ridge of the Rocky Mountains in North America: *The Continental Divide separates streams flowing toward the Pacific from those flowing toward the Atlantic.*

con·tin·u·al (kən tin′yü əl) 1 repeated many times; very frequent: *Dancing requires continual practice.* 2 never stopping: *the continual flow of the river. adj.* —**con·tin·′u·al·ly,** *adv.*

☛ **Continual** usually means 'repeated often with little rest between': *Because of the continual ringing of the doorbell all evening, she got very little rest.* **Continuous** usually means 'going on without interruption': *The continuous ringing of the doorbell finally woke him up.*

con·tin·u·ance (kən tin′yü əns) remaining; staying: *His continuance in school depends on his health. n.*

con·tin·u·a·tion (kən tin′yü ā′shən) 1 the going on with an activity or process: *He was looking forward to university as a continuation of his education.* 2 the act of going on with a thing after stopping; beginning again: *Continuation of the reading was difficult after so many interruptions.* 3 anything by which a thing is continued; an added part: *The continuation of the story will appear in next month's magazine. n.*

con·tin·ue (kən tin′yü) 1 keep up; keep on; go on; go on with: *We continued our work at the hospital. The road continues for miles.* 2 take up; carry on; go on after stopping: *The story will be continued next month. He ate lunch and then continued his work.* 3 last; endure: *The king's reign continued for 20 years.* 4 stay: *The children must continue at school until the end of June. He continues happy.* 5 maintain; cause to stay: *The mayor was continued in office for two terms. The club continued the president in office for another term. v.,* **con·tin·ued, con·tin·u·ing.**

con·ti·nu·i·ty (kon′tə nyü′ə tē or kon′tə nü′ə tē) being a connected whole or an unbroken series: *The story lacked continuity because there were too many unconnected happenings. n., pl.* **con·ti·nu·i·ties.**

con·tin·u·ous (kən tin′yü əs) connected; unbroken; without a stop: *a continuous line, a continuous sound, continuous work, a continuous line of cars. adj.* —**con·tin′u·ous·ly,** *adv.*

☛ See note at **continual.**

con·tort (kən tôrt′) twist; bend; draw out of shape: *The clown contorted his face. v.*

con·tor·tion (kən tôr′shən) 1 the act of twisting out of shape: *The little boy went through many contortions in trying to squeeze through the fence.* 2 a twisted condition: *The contortion of her face when she tasted the lemon was funny to see. n.*

con·tour (kon′tür) the outline of a figure; the outline of a country, a lake, a mountain, etc.: *The contour of the Atlantic coast of Canada is very irregular. A contour map shows outlines of hills, valleys, etc. n.*

con·tra·band (kon′trə band′) 1 against the law; prohibited: *The sale of stolen goods is contraband in Canada.* 2 smuggled goods: *Customs officials went through each bag looking for contraband.* 1 *adj.,* 2 *n.*

con·tract (kən trakt′ for 1–4, kon′trakt for 5, kon′trakt or kən trakt′ for 6) 1 draw together; make shorter: *Wrinkling the forehead contracts the brows.* 2 shrink; become shorter or smaller: *Wool fibres contract in hot water. An earthworm can contract.* 3 bring on oneself; form; start: *Try not to contract bad habits.* 4 get; catch a disease: *His hoarseness and coughing showed that he had contracted a cold.* 5 an agreement, especially a written agreement that can be enforced by law: *All professional hockey players sign contracts each year, agreeing to play for a certain salary.* 6 enter into a legal agreement; make a contract: *The builder contracted to build a new house for a certain price.* 1–4, 6 *v.,* 5 *n.*

con·trac·tion (kən trak′shən) 1 the process of contracting: *Cold causes the contraction of liquids, gases, and metals, whereas heat causes expansion.* 2 the state of being contracted. 3 something contracted; a shortened form: *'Can't' is a contraction of 'cannot.' n.*

con·trac·tor (kon′trak tər or kən trak′tər) a person who agrees to furnish materials or to do a piece of work for a certain price. *n.*

con·tra·dict (kon′trə dikt′) 1 say that a statement is not true; say the opposite of what another person has said: *She contradicted his version of the story. To contradict a guest is rude.* 2 be contrary to; go against: *Your story and your brother's story contradict each other. v.*

con·tra·dic·tion (kon′trə dik′shən) 1 the act of denying what has been said. 2 a statement or act that contradicts another; denial: *His reply was a clear contradiction of what his father had said. n.*

con·tra·dic·to·ry (kon′trə dik′tə rē) contradicting; saying the opposite: *Reports of the result of the battle were so contradictory that we did not know which side had won. adj.*

con·tral·to (kən tral′tō) 1 a woman's voice of low tone. 2 a part to be sung by a woman with such a voice. 3 a person who sings this part. *n., pl.* **con·tral·tos.**

con·trap·tion (kən trap′shən) device; gadget: *They invented a crazy contraption for removing the shells from boiled eggs. n.*

con·tra·ry (kon′trer ē for 1 and 2, kən trer′ē for 3) 1 opposed; opposite; completely different: *His reckless driving went contrary to the rules of the road.* 2 the opposite. 3 opposing others; stubborn: *The contrary boy refused to do as he was told.* 1, 3 *adj.,* 2 *n., pl.* **con·tra·ries.**

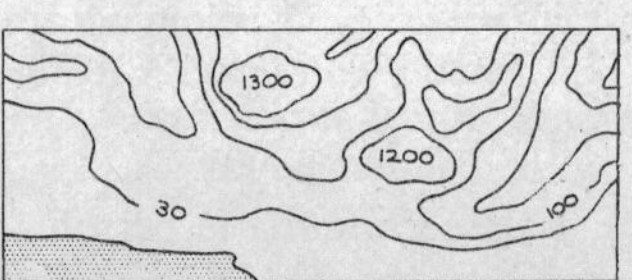

A contour map of the mountains shown in the sketch above

on the contrary, exactly the opposite of what has been said: *He didn't go straight home; on the contrary, he stopped at three different stores and even visited a friend.*

con·trast (kon′trast for 1 and 2, kən trast′ for 3 and 4) **1** a difference; a great difference: *Anybody can see the contrast between black and white.* **2** anything that shows differences when put side by side with something else: *Black hair is a sharp contrast to a light skin.* **3** place two things side by side so as to show their differences: *A fly and a bee were contrasted in our science class.* **4** show differences when compared or put side by side: *The black and gold contrast well in that design.* 1, 2 *n.*, 3, 4 *v.*

con·trib·ute (kən trib′yu̇t) **1** give money or help: *Will you contribute to the Red Cross? Everyone was asked to contribute suggestions for the party.* **2** write articles, stories, etc. for a newspaper or magazine. *v.*, **con·trib·ut·ed, con·trib·ut·ing.**

contribute to, help bring about: *Poor food contributed to the child's illness.*

con·tri·bu·tion (kon′trə byü′shən) **1** the act of giving money or help. **2** the money or help contributed; gift: *Her contribution to the picnic was a basket of apples.* **3** something written for a newspaper or magazine. *n.*

con·trib·u·tor (kən trib′yə tər) a person who writes articles, features, stories, etc. for a newspaper or magazine. *n.*

con·trite (kən trīt′ or kon′trīt) quiet and sad after doing something wrong; penitent: *The boy was contrite after he had hit his little sister. adj.*

con·triv·ance (kən trī′vəns) **1** something invented; a mechanical device: *A can opener is a handy contrivance.* **2** the act or manner of planning or designing: *By careful contrivance he managed to fit all his appointments into one afternoon.* **3** a plan or scheme. *n.*

con·trive (kən trīv′) **1** invent; design: *He contrived a new kind of engine.* **2** plan; scheme; plot: *to contrive a robbery.* **3** manage; arrange to have something happen: *I will contrive to be there by ten o'clock. v.*, **con·trived, con·triv·ing.**

con·trol (kən trōl′) **1** power; authority; direction: *A child is under its parents' control.* **2** have power or authority over; direct: *A captain controls his ship and its crew.* **3** hold back; keep down: *It is hard to control one's anger.* **4** the power or ability to restrain, check, or keep down: *He lost control of his temper.* **5** a device that regulates the working of a machine: *The control for our furnace is in the front hall.* **6 controls,** *pl.* the instruments and devices by which a car, aircraft, locomotive, etc. is operated: *The new pilot managed the controls better in taking off than in landing.* 1, 4–6 *n.*, 2, 3 *v.*, **con·trolled, con·trol·ling.**

control tower at an airfield, the building from which the taking off and landing of aircraft is controlled.

con·tro·ver·sial (kon′trə vėr′shəl) of, open to, or arousing controversy: *The controversial issues were finally settled. She is a controversial politician. adj.*

con·tro·ver·sy (kon′trə vėr′sē) a dispute; a long dispute; argument: *The controversy between the company and the union ended in a strike. n., pl.* **con·tro·ver·sies.**

co·nun·drum (kə nun′drəm) **1** a riddle; a puzzling question whose answer involves a play on words: *'When is a door not a door?' is a conundrum. The answer to this conundrum is 'When it's ajar.'* **2** any puzzling problem. *n.*

hat, āge, fär; let, ēqual, tėrm; it, īce
hot, ōpen, ôrder; oil, out; cup, pu̇t, rüle
əbove, takən, pencəl, lemən, circəs
ch, child; ng, long; sh, ship
th, thin; ᴛʜ, then; zh, measure

con·va·lesce (kon′və les′) recover health and strength after illness: *Mary will have to convalesce for three weeks after her operation. v.*, **con·va·lesced, con·va·lesc·ing.**

con·va·les·cence (kon′və les′əns) a gradual getting well after an illness: *Her convalescence is progressing well. n.*

con·va·les·cent (kon′və les′ənt) **1** recovering health and strength after illness. **2** a person recovering after illness: *There is a hospital for convalescents on our street.* 1 *adj.*, 2 *n.*

con·vec·tion (kən vek′shen) in science, the transfer of heat from one place to another by the movement of heated particles of a gas or liquid: *A forced-air furnace system heats a room by convection. n.*

con·vene (kən vēn′) **1** meet for some purpose; gather in one place; assemble: *Parliament convenes at least once a year.* **2** call together: *Any member may convene our club in an emergency. v.*, **con·vened, con·ven·ing.**

con·ven·er (kən vē′nər) See **convenor.**

con·ven·ience (kən vēn′yəns) **1** the fact or quality of being convenient: *He takes advantage of the convenience of packaged goods.* **2** comfort; advantage: *Many provincial parks have camping places for the convenience of tourists.* **3** anything handy or easy to use; something that saves trouble or work: *We find our folding table a great convenience. It will be a convenience if you can come to my house this time. n.*

at one's convenience, so as to suit one as to time, place, or other conditions: *come to pick me up at your convenience.*

con·ven·ient (kən vēn′yənt) **1** suitable; easy to use; saving trouble: *to use a convenient tool, take a convenient bus, live in a convenient house.* **2** easy to reach: *They arranged to meet at a convenient place.* **3** easily done; not troublesome: *Will it be convenient for you to bring your lunch to school? adj.* —**con·ven′ient·ly,** *adv.*

convenient to, *Informal.* near; easy to reach from: *The library is convenient to my apartment.*

con·ven·or or **con·ven·er** (kən vē′nər) a person who is responsible for calling together the members of a committee, club, etc. and who often acts as their chairman: *Mother is program convenor for the Home and School Association. n.*

con·vent (kon′vənt or kon′vent) **1** a group of women, called nuns, who live together and devote their lives to religion. **2** the building or buildings in which they live. *n.*

con·ven·tion (kən ven′shən) **1** a meeting arranged for some particular purpose: *A political party holds a convention to choose a new leader.* **2** general agreement or consent; custom: *Convention decides how people dress in public.* **3** a custom or practice approved by general agreement: *Using the right hand to shake hands is a convention.* *n.*

con·ven·tion·al (kən ven′shən əl) **1** depending on conventions; customary: *'Good morning' is a conventional greeting.* **2** ordinary; not interesting; not original: *His songs are really very conventional.* *adj.*

con·ver·sa·tion (kon′vər sā′shən) friendly talk; the exchange of thoughts by talking informally together: *There is much pleasure in good conversation.* *n.*

con·verse (kən vėrs′ for 1, kon′vėrs for 2) **1** talk with someone about something in an informal way: *The two old veterans liked conversing about their experiences in the war.* **2** conversation. 1 *v.*, **con·versed, con·vers·ing;** 2 *n.*

con·ver·sion (kən vėr′zhən or kən vėr′shən) **1** a turning; changing; change: *Heat causes the conversion of water into steam.* **2** a change from one belief or way of thinking to another: *His conversion to the Liberal Party was unexpected.* **3** in football, the act or fact of kicking a point after a touchdown. *n.*

con·vert (kən vėrt′ for 1, 2, and 6, kon′vėrt for 3, 4, and 5) **1** change; turn: *These machines convert pulp into paper. One last effort converted defeat into victory.* **2** cause to change from one belief or way of thinking to another: *This missionary converted many Indians to the Christian religion.* **3** a person who has been converted. **4** in football, a goal kicked after a touchdown. **5** the point made by successfully kicking a convert. **6** kick a goal after a touchdown: *Tom converted all three touchdowns last Saturday.* 1, 2, 6 *v.*, 3–5 *n.*

con·vert·i·ble (kən vėr′tə bəl) **1** capable of being converted: *A dollar bill is convertible into ten dimes.* **2** an automobile with a cloth roof that can be folded down behind the rear seat. 1 *adj.*, 2 *n.*

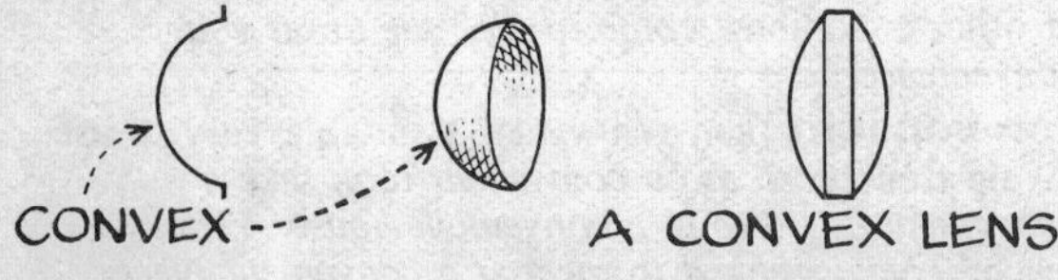

con·vex (kon veks′ or kon′veks) curved out, like the outside of a sphere or circle: *The crystal of a watch is slightly convex on the outside.* *adj.*

con·vey (kən vā′) **1** take from one place to another; carry: *A bus conveys passengers from the train to the boat.* **2** transmit; conduct: *A wire conveys an electric current.* **3** make known; communicate: *His words conveyed no meaning to his listeners.* *v.*

con·vey·ance (kən vā′əns) **1** a carrying or transmission; communication: *Books are for the conveyance of ideas.* **2** anything that conveys; a vehicle; carriage: *Trains and buses are public conveyances.* *n.*

con·vey·or (kən vā′ər) a mechanical device that carries things from one place to another: *Grain is carried from one floor of an elevator to another by means of a conveyor.* *n.*

con·vict (kən vikt′ for 1 and 2, kon′vikt for 3) **1** prove guilty: *The evidence convicted the guilty man.* **2** declare guilty: *The jury convicted the prisoner of murder.* **3** a person serving a prison sentence for some crime. 1, 2 *v.*, 3 *n.*

con·vic·tion (kən vik′shən) **1** the act of proving or declaring guilty: *The trial resulted in the conviction of John Doe.* **2** the state of being proved or declared guilty: *John Doe's conviction meant two years in prison for him.* **3** a firm belief: *It was Macdonald's conviction that Confederation must be achieved.* *n.*

con·vince (kən vins′) make a person feel sure; cause to believe; persuade firmly: *The mistakes she made convinced him that she had not studied her lesson.* *v.*, **con·vinced, con·vinc·ing.**

con·vinc·ing (kən vin′sing) that convinces: *a convincing argument.* *adj.* **—con·vinc′ing·ly,** *adv.*

con·voy (kon′voi) **1** go with in order to protect; escort: *Warships convoy merchant ships in time of war.* **2** an escort; protection: *The gold was moved from the truck to the bank under convoy of armed guards.* **3** the ship, fleet, supplies, etc. accompanied by a protecting escort: *The destroyers were responsible for the safety of the convoy.* 1 *v.*, 2, 3 *n.*

con·vulse (kən vuls′) **1** shake violently: *An earthquake convulsed the island.* **2** cause violent disturbance in: *Rage convulsed his face.* **3** throw into convulsions; shake with spasms of pain: *The sick child was convulsed before the doctor came.* **4** throw into fits of laughter; cause to shake with laughter: *The clown convulsed the audience with his funny acts.* *v.*, **con·vulsed, con·vuls·ing.**

con·vul·sion (kən vul′shən) **1** a violent contraction of the muscles: *The sick child's convulsions frightened its mother.* **2** a fit of laughter. **3** a violent disturbance: *An earthquake is a convulsion of the earth.* *n.*

con·vul·sive (kən vul′siv) **1** sudden, violent, etc., like a convulsion: *The dog made convulsive efforts to free itself from the chain.* **2** having convulsions. **3** producing convulsions. *adj.*

co·ny (kō′nē) See **coney.** *n.*, *pl.* **co·nies.**

coo (kü) **1** the soft, murmuring sound made by doves or pigeons. **2** make this sound. **3** murmur softly: *The mother cooed to her sick baby as she rocked it.* 1 *n.*, *pl.* **coos;** 2, 3 *v.*, **cooed, coo·ing.**

cook (ku̇k) **1** prepare food by using heat: *We use coal, wood, gas, oil, and electricity for cooking.* **2** undergo cooking; be cooked: *Let the meat cook slowly.* **3** a person who cooks. 1, 2 *v.*, 3 *n.*

cook·book (ku̇k′bu̇k′) a book containing recipes for cooking various kinds of food; a book of recipes. *n.*

cook·er·y (ku̇k′ər ē) **1** cooking: *the art of cookery.* **2** a cookhouse at a lumber camp or mine. *n.*, *pl.* **cook·er·ies.**

cook·house (ku̇k′hous′) a room or place for cooking, especially in a large camp. *n.*

cook·ie or **cook·y** (ku̇k′ē) a small, usually flat, sweet cake, made without baking soda or baking powder. *n.*, *pl.* **cook·ies.**

☛ **Cookie** comes from the Dutch word *koekje,* meaning 'little cake.'

cook–out (ku̇k′out′) cooking and eating a meal out-of-doors; a picnic, etc. where the food is cooked outside. *n.*

cool (kül) **1** somewhat cold; more cold than hot: *We sat in the shade where it was cool.* **2** allowing or giving

hat, āge, fär; let, ēqual, tėrm; it, īce
hot, ōpen, ôrder; oil, out; cup, pu̇t, rüle
əbove, takən, pencəl, lemən, circəs
ch, child; ng, long; sh, ship
th, thin; ᴛʜ, then; zh, measure

a cool feeling: *a cool dress.* **3** not excited; calm. **4** having little enthusiasm or interest; not cordial: *His former friend gave him a cool greeting.* **5** a cool part, place, or time: *the cool of the evening.* **6** become cool. **7** make cool: *We cooled the pop in the stream.* 1–4 *adj.,* 5 *n.,* 6, 7 *v.*

cool·er (kül′ər) an apparatus or container that cools food or drinks, or keeps them cool. *n.*

coo·lie (kü′lē) an unskilled laborer in parts of Asia. *n.*

☛ **Coolie** and **coulee** are pronounced the same.

coon (kün) raccoon. *n.*

coop (küp) **1** a small cage or pen for chickens, rabbits, etc. **2** keep or put in a coop. **3** confine, especially in a small place: *The children were cooped up indoors by the rain.* 1 *n.,* 2, 3 *v.*

☛ **Coop** and **coupe** are pronounced the same.

co–op (kō′op) co-operative: *She preferred to buy her groceries at the co-op. n.*

coop·er (küp′ər) a man who makes or repairs barrels, tubs, casks, etc. *n.*

co–op·er·ate (kō op′ər āt′) work together: *The children co-operated with their teachers in keeping their rooms neat. v.,* **co-op·er·at·ed, co-op·er·at·ing.**

co–op·er·a·tion (kō op′ər ā′shən) working together; united effort or labor: *Co-operation can accomplish many things that no individual could do alone. n.*

co–op·er·a·tive (kō op′ər ə tiv) **1** wanting or willing to work together with others: *He was the only child in the room who was not co-operative in keeping it neat.* **2** a union of consumers, growers, etc. for doing their own selling or buying: *Co-operatives may take the form of wheat-marketing agencies, general stores, gas stations, etc.* 1 *adj.,* 2 *n.*

co–or·di·nate (kō ôr′də nit for 1 and 2, kō ôr′də nāt′ for 3) **1** equal in importance; of equal rank. **2** an equal. **3** arrange in proper order; put in proper relation; adjust; harmonize: *A swimmer should co-ordinate the movements of his arms and legs.* 1 *adj.,* 2 *n.,* 3 *v.,* **co-or·di·nat·ed, co-or·di·nat·ing.**

co–or·di·na·tion (kō ôr′də nā′shən) **1** the condition of working together smoothly and easily, often used with reference to the muscles: *She became a better swimmer as her co-ordination improved.* **2** arrangement in the right order or relation: *She made an outline for her composition to help in the co-ordination of her ideas. n.*

coot (küt) **1** a dark-grey wading and swimming bird having short wings and large feet with lobes of skin on the toes that help in swimming: *Coots look like ducks.* **2** any of several kinds of wild duck. **3** *Informal.* a fool; simpleton. *n.*

cop (kop) *Informal.* policeman. *n.*

cope (kōp) struggle, keeping a chance of success; struggle and not fail; get on successfully: *Mother could not cope with all the housework and two sick children. v.,* **coped, cop·ing.**

co–pi·lot (kō′pī′lət) a pilot who works with another pilot. *n.*

co·pi·ous (kō′pē əs) plentiful; abundant: *There was a copious supply of wheat in the elevators. adj.*

cop·per (kop′ər) **1** a reddish metal that is easily shaped into wire or sheets and resists rust: *Copper is a good conductor of electricity.* **2** made of copper: *a copper kettle.* **3** reddish brown: *She had copper hair.* **4** a one-cent piece: *I found a copper on the sidewalk.* 1, 3, 4 *n.,* 2, 3 *adj.*

cop·per·head (kop′ər hed′) a poisonous North American snake, having a copper-colored head: *Adult copperheads are about 90 centimetres long. n.*

cop·ra (kop′rə) the dried meat of coconuts, from which coconut oil is obtained. *n.*

copse (kops) a number of small trees or bushes growing together; a thicket or grove of small trees; bluff (def. 3). *n.*

cop·y (kop′ē) **1** anything made to be just like another; anything made on the model of another: *One chair can be an exact copy of another.* **2** make a copy of: *Copy this page. She copied her friend's hat.* **3** be a copy of; be like; imitate: *The little boy copied his father's way of walking.* **4** one of a number of books, magazines, pictures, etc. made at the same printing: *Please get six copies of today's newspaper.* **5** written material ready to be set in print in newspapers, magazines, or books. 1, 4, 5 *n., pl.* **cop·ies;** 2, 3 *v.,* **cop·ied, cop·y·ing.**

cop·y·right (kop′ē rīt′) **1** a right to copy, given by law to an author, composer, artist, etc., making him or her for a certain number of years the only person who can sell, print, publish, or copy a particular work, or who can authorize others to do so: *Because Shakespeare's plays are not in copyright, anyone can produce them on stage without paying a fee.* **2** protect by getting a copyright: *Books, pieces of music, plays, etc. are usually copyrighted.* 1 *n.,* 2 *v.*

cor·al (kôr′əl) **1** a hard, red, pink, or white substance, formed by the accumulation of the skeletons of tiny sea animals: *Coral is often used in making jewellery.* **2** the sea animal whose skeleton forms coral. **3** deep pink; red: *a coral dress.* 1–3 *n.,* 3 *adj.*

cord (kôrd) **1** a thick, well-made string; a very thin rope. **2** a small insulated cable with fittings, used to connect a lamp or other electrical appliance to a socket. **3** anything resembling a cord, such as a cordlike part of an animal body: *spinal cord, vocal cords.* **4** a ridge or ridged pattern on cloth. **5** cloth with such ridges on it. **6 cords,** *pl.* trousers made of such cloth, especially corduroy. **7** a measure of cut wood. *n.*

☛ **Cord** and **chord** are pronounced the same.

cor·di·al (kôr′dē əl or kôr′jəl) **1** warm; friendly: *a cordial welcome.* **2** a warming drink, such as wine. 1 *adj.,* 2 *n.*

cor·di·al·i·ty (kôr′dē al′ə tē or kôr jal′ə tē) a cordial quality or feeling; warm friendliness: *The cordiality of his welcome made Tom feel at home. n., pl.* **cor·di·al·i·ties.**

cor·don (kôr′dən) a line of policemen, soldiers, etc. enclosing or guarding a place: *A cordon of police surrounded the thieves' hideout. n.*

cor·du·roy (kôr′də roi′) **1** thick cloth with close raised ridges. **2** having ridges like corduroy. **3 corduroys,** *pl.* corduroy trousers. 1, 3 *n.,* 2 *adj.*

corduroy road *Cdn.* a road made of logs laid crosswise, often across low, wet land.

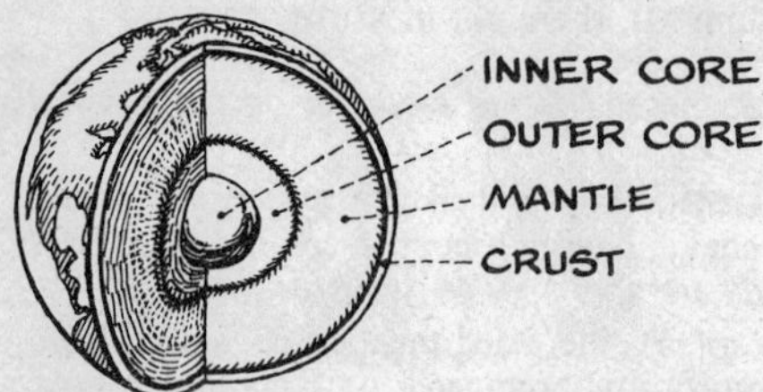

core (kôr) **1** the hard, central part containing the seeds of fruits like apples and pears. **2** take out the core of: *to core apples.* **3** the central or most important part: *the core of a speech.* **4** the central part of the earth, probably composed largely of molten iron and having a radius of about 3380 kilometres. 1, 3, 4 *n.*, 2 *v.*, **cored, cor·ing.**

☛ **Core** and **corps** are pronounced the same.

cork (kôrk) **1** the light, thick, outer bark of a tree called the cork oak: *Cork is used for bottle stoppers, floats for fishing lines, and floor and wall coverings.* **2** a shaped piece of cork: *the cork of a bottle.* **3** a stopper made of glass, rubber, etc. **4** stop up with a cork: *Fill these bottles and cork them carefully.* 1–3 *n.*, 4 *v.*

Corkscrews

cork·screw (kôrk′skrü′) **1** a tool used to pull corks out of bottles. **2** shaped like a corkscrew; spiral: *The plane did a corkscrew dive.* 1 *n.*, 2 *adj.*

cor·mo·rant (kôr′mə rənt) a large, black sea bird with a long neck and a pouch under its beak for holding captured fish. *n.*

A ripe ear of corn, shown in its husk

corn[1] (kôrn) **1** a grain with yellowish kernels that grow in rows along a thick core; maize; Indian corn: *Corn is cooked and eaten as a vegetable.* **2** the tall plant that it grows on. **3** any small, hard seed or grain: *a pepper corn.* *n.*

corn[2] (kôrn) a hardening of the skin with a tender sore spot: *Shoes that do not fit properly often cause corns on the toes.* *n.*

corn bread bread made of corn meal instead of flour.

corn·cob (kôrn′kob′) the central, woody part of an ear of corn, on which the kernels grow. *n.*

cor·ne·a (kôr′nē ə) the transparent outside coat on the front of the eyeball: *The cornea covers the iris and the pupil.* See **eye** for picture. *n.*

corned (kôrnd) preserved with strong salt water or dry salt: *corned beef or pork.* *adj.*

cor·ner (kôr′nər) **1** the place where two lines or surfaces meet: *the corner of a room.* **2** the place where two streets meet. **3** at a corner: *the corner drugstore.* **4** for a corner: *a corner shelf.* **5** put in a corner; drive into a corner: *I finally cornered our dog and got the leash on him.* **6** a piece to protect or decorate a corner of something: *The leather pocketbook has gold corners.* **7** a secret place; a place away from crowds: *The money was hidden in odd corners all over the house.* **8** a region or part; a place that is far away: *People have searched in all corners of the earth for gold.* **9** a difficult place: *His enemies had driven him into a corner.* **10** force into a difficult position: *The teacher cornered him with a direct question.* **11** gain control of: *He cornered the diamond market.* 1, 2, 6–9 *n.*, 3, 4 *adj.*, 5, 10, 11 *v.*

cor·net (kôr net′ or kôr′nit) a musical wind instrument resembling a trumpet and usually made of brass. *n.*

corn·field (kôrn′fēld′) a field in which corn is grown. *n.*

corn·flow·er (kôrn′flou′ər) a plant having blue, pink, or purple flowers. *n.*

corn·husk (kôrn′husk′) the husk of an ear of corn. *n.*

cor·nice (kôr′nis) **1** a moulded projecting part forming the top of a pillar, the wall of a building, etc. **2** any similar moulding or band around the walls of a room near the ceiling. *n.*

corn meal meal made by grinding up dried corn.

corn·stalk (kôrn′stok′ or kôrn′stôk′) a stalk, or stem, of a corn plant. *n.*

corn·starch (kôrn′stärch′) a kind of flour made from corn, used to thicken puddings, custard, etc. *n.*

A cornucopia, or horn of plenty

cor·nu·co·pi·a (kôr′nyə kō′pē ə) **1** a horn-shaped container or ornament: *Cornucopias are hung on Christmas trees.* **2** a decorated curved horn overflowing with fruits and flowers, used as a symbol of a good harvest or any time of prosperity. *n.*

corn·y (kôr′nē) *Slang.* too ordinary, simple, or unsophisticated for certain tastes: *corny jokes. That movie has some corny love scenes.* *adj.*, **corn·i·er, corn·i·est.**

co·rol·la (kə rol′ə) the petals of a flower. *n.*

cor·o·na·tion (kôr′ə nā′shən) the ceremony of crowning a monarch. *n.*

cor·o·ner (kôr′ə nər) an official appointed by a local government to investigate any death not clearly due to

hat, āge, fär; let, ēqual, tėrm; it, īce
hot, ōpen, ôrder; oil, out; cup, pu̇t, rüle
əbove, takən, pencəl, lemən, circəs
ch, child; ng, long; sh, ship
th, thin; ᴛʜ, then; zh, measure

natural causes: *A coroner is usually a medical doctor.* *n.*

cor·o·net (kôr′ə net′) 1 a small crown worn as a mark of high rank: *A king wears a crown; a prince, a coronet.* 2 a circle of gold, jewels, or flowers worn around the head as an ornament. *n.*

cor·po·ral[1] (kôr′pə rəl) of or having to do with the body; physical: *Spanking is a corporal punishment.* *adj.*

cor·po·ral[2] (kôr′pə rəl) the lowest-ranking non-commissioned officer in the armed forces: *A corporal is one rank below a sergeant.* *n.*

cor·po·ra·tion (kôr′pə rā′shən) a group of persons who obtain a charter giving them as a group certain rights and privileges: *A corporation can buy or sell as if its members were a single person.* *n.*

corps (kôr) 1 in the armed forces, a formation made up of more than one division. 2 one of the branches of an army that provides special services: *the Signal Corps.* 3 a group of people with special training, organized for working together: *A large hospital has a corps of nurses.* *n., pl.* **corps** (kôrz).

☛ **Corps** and **core** are pronounced the same.

corpse (kôrps) a dead body, usually that of a human being. *n.*

Corps of Commissionaires an organization of ex-servicemen who can be hired as gatekeepers, guards, night watchmen, etc.: *Members of the Corps of Commissionaires, who wear dark-blue uniforms, are often employed to protect property.*

cor·pu·lent (kôr′pyə lənt) fat; stout: *The corpulent man had some difficulty squeezing through the narrow door.* *adj.*

cor·pus·cle (kôr′pəs əl or kôr′pus əl) any of the cells that form a large part of the blood: *Red corpuscles carry oxygen from the lungs to various parts of the body; some white corpuscles destroy disease germs.* *n.*

cor·ral (kə ral′) 1 a pen for horses, cattle, etc. 2 drive into or keep in a corral. 3 hem in; surround; capture: *We corralled the enemy's advance guard.* 1 *n.,* 2, 3 *v.,* **cor·ralled, cor·ral·ling.**

cor·rect (kə rekt′) 1 free from mistakes; true; right: *the correct answer.* 2 agreeing with a good standard of taste; proper: *correct manners.* 3 change to what is right: *Correct any errors before you hand in your paragraphs.* 4 point out or mark the mistakes in: *The teacher corrects and returns the test papers.* 5 punish; set right by punishing; find fault with in order to improve: *The mother corrected the child.* 1, 2 *adj.,* 3–5 *v.* —**cor·rect′ly,** *adv.*

cor·rec·tion (kə rek′shən) 1 the act or process of correcting; setting right: *The correction of all my mistakes took nearly an hour.* 2 something put in place of an error or mistake: *Write in your corrections neatly.* 3 punishment: *A prison is sometimes called a house of correction.* *n.*

cor·re·spond (kôr′ə spond′) 1 agree; be in harmony: *His friendly manner corresponded with what they had been told of him.* 2 be similar; have the same function, value, effect, etc. in its own context: *The arms of a man correspond to the wings of a bird.* 3 exchange letters; write letters to one another: *They rarely saw each other but they corresponded for many years.* *v.*

cor·re·spond·ence (kôr′ə spon′dəns) 1 agreement: *Your account of the accident has little correspondence with the story he told.* 2 an exchange of letters; friendly letter-writing. 3 letters: *He read the correspondence concerning the order.* *n.*

cor·re·spond·ent (kôr′ə spon′dənt) 1 a person who exchanges letters with another: *They have been regular correspondents for over two years.* 2 a person employed to send news from a distant place: *Toronto newspapers have correspondents in London, Bonn, Paris, and elsewhere.* *n.*

cor·ri·dor (kôr′ə dər) a long hallway; a passage in a large building from which doors lead into rooms: *My mother's office is at the end of the corridor.* *n.*

cor·rode (kə rōd′) eat away gradually: *Rust corrodes iron.* *v.,* **cor·rod·ed, cor·rod·ing.**

cor·ro·sion (kə rō′zhən) 1 the act or process of corroding: *Corrosion had greatly weakened the body of the car.* 2 a corroded condition. 3 a product of corroding, such as rust. *n.*

cor·ru·gate (kôr′ə gāt′) give a wavelike surface to; make wrinkles in: *The shack had a roof of corrugated iron. Some cartons are made of corrugated paper or cardboard.* *v.,* **cor·ru·gat·ed, cor·ru·gat·ing.**

cor·rupt (kə rupt′) 1 evil; wicked: *a corrupt man.* 2 make evil or wicked: *His desire for wealth finally corrupted him.* 3 influenced by bribes; dishonest: *a corrupt judge.* 4 bribe; influence by bribes: *He failed in his attempt to corrupt the policeman.* 1, 3 *adj.,* 2, 4 *v.*

cor·rup·tion (kə rup′shən) 1 making or being made evil or wicked. 2 evil conduct. 3 bribery; dishonesty: *The police force must be kept free of corruption.* *n.*

cor·sage (kôr säzh′) a flower or small bouquet to be carried or to be worn on a woman's dress. *n.*

cor·set (kôr′sit) a close-fitting undergarment worn about the waist and hips to support or shape the body. *n.*

co·si·ly (kō′zə lē) in a cosy manner. *adv.* Also spelled **cozily.**

co·si·ness (kō′zi nəs) being cosy. *n.* Also spelled **coziness.**

cos·met·ic (koz met′ik) a preparation for beautifying the skin or hair: *Powder, rouge, and face creams are cosmetics.* *n.*

cos·mic (koz′mik) 1 having to do with the whole universe: *Cosmic forces produce stars and meteors.* 2 vast. *adj.*

cosmic rays extremely powerful streams of energy from outer space that enter the earth's atmosphere at very high speeds.

cos·mo·naut (koz′mə not′ or koz′mə nôt′) astronaut. *n.*

☛ **Cosmonaut** is made up of Greek *cosmos* meaning 'world' and *nautes,* meaning 'sailor.' It was first made up in Russian and is usually applied to Soviet spacemen.

cos·mos (koz′məs) 1 the whole universe thought of

as following a plan of organization. **2** a tall plant with white, pink, purple, or yellow flowers that bloom in the fall or late summer. *n.*

cost (kost) **1** the price paid: *The cost of this hat was $18.* **2** the loss or the sacrifice: *The poor fox escaped from the trap at the cost of a leg.* **3** be obtained at the price of: *This hat costs $18.* **4** require: *The school play had cost much time and effort.* 1, 2 *n.*, 3, 4 *v.*, **cost, cost·ing.**

at all costs or **at any cost,** regardless of expense; by all means; no matter what must be done: *They had to catch the next boat at all costs, or lose their last chance to escape.*

cost·ly (kost′lē) **1** of great value: *The queen had costly jewels.* **2** costing much: *costly mistakes. adj.*, **cost·li·er, cost·li·est.**

cos·tume (kos′tyüm or kos′chüm for 1, 2, and 3, kos tyüm′ or kos chüm′ for 4) **1** dress; outer clothing; a style of dress. **2** dress belonging to another time or place: *In our play the actors wore Indian costumes.* **3** a complete set of outer garments: *a hunting costume.* **4** provide a costume for; dress. 1–3 *n.*, 4 *v.*, **cos·tumed, cos·tum·ing.**

co·sy (kō′zē) **1** warm and comfortable; snug: *She liked to read in a cosy corner by the fire.* **2** a hatlike cloth covering for a teapot, used to keep the tea hot. 1 *adj.*, **co·si·er, co·si·est;** 2 *n., pl.* **co·sies.** Also spelled **cozy.**

cot (kot) a narrow bed: *A cot is sometimes made of canvas stretched on a frame that folds together. n.*

☛ **Cot** and **caught** are sometimes pronounced the same.

cote (kōt) a shelter for animals or birds. *n.*

☛ **Cote** and **coat** are pronounced the same.

cot·tage (kot′ij) **1** a house at a summer resort. **2** a small house. *n.*

cottage cheese a soft, white cheese made from the curds of sour milk.

cot·ton (kot′ən) **1** soft, white fibres in a fluffy mass around the seeds of a plant, used in making fabrics, thread, etc. **2** the plant that produces these fibres. See the picture. **3** thread made of cotton fibres. **4** cloth made of cotton thread. **5** made of cotton: *She bought two cotton dresses. n.*

cot·ton·tail (kot′ən tāl′) the common North American wild rabbit, having brownish or greyish fur and a fluffy tail with a white or light grey underside. *n.*

cot·ton·wood (kot′ən wu̇d′) **1** a kind of North American poplar tree with seeds having tufts that look like cotton. **2** the soft wood of this tree. *n.*

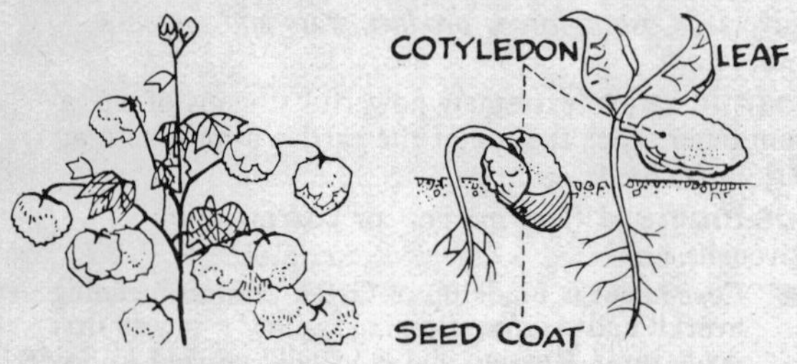

A cotton plant

The cotyledons of a bean seedling

cot·y·le·don (kot′ə lē′dən) a part of a seed containing the first leaf, or one of the first pair of leaves, and carrying food for the developing plant. *n.*

couch (kouch) **1** a bed or chesterfield for sleep or rest. **2** any place for sleep or rest: *The deer got up from its grassy couch.* **3** put in words; express: *His thoughts were couched in beautiful language.* 1, 2 *n.*, 3 *v.*

cou·gar (kü′gər) a large, usually sand-colored wildcat found in many parts of North and South America, having short, black ears and a very long, black-tipped tail; mountain lion: *Cougars usually hunt at night.* See **wildcat** for picture. *n.*

cough (kof) **1** force air from the lungs suddenly with a short, harsh noise or series of noises. **2** the act of coughing. **3** the sound of coughing: *He heard a cough outside the room.* **4** a condition or illness that is marked by coughing: *A cold is often accompanied by a cough.* 1 *v.*, 2–4 *n.*

cough up, a force out of the throat or lungs by coughing. **b** *Slang.* give; bring out; pay what is due: *The crook tried to keep more than his share of the stolen money, but the rest of the gang made him cough up.*

could (ku̇d; *unstressed,* kəd) See **can**[1]. *She would sing if she could. He could eat. v.*

could·n't (ku̇d′ənt) could not.

cou·lee (kü′lē) a deep ravine or gulch: *A coulee is usually dry in summer. n.*

☛ **Coulee** and **coolie** are pronounced the same.

coun·cil (koun′səl) **1** a group of people called together to give advice and discuss or settle questions: *a council of war.* **2** a small group of persons elected by the people to make laws for and manage a city, town, village, municipal district, or township. *n.*

☛ **Council** and **counsel** are pronounced the same.

☛ **Council** is used only as a noun, and it always refers to a group of people. **Counsel** can be used as a noun or a verb. As a noun it means 'adviser' or 'advice'; as a verb it means 'to advise.'

coun·cil·lor or **coun·ci·lor** (koun′sə lər) **1** an elected member of the council of a town, village, etc. **2** in Prince Edward Island, a member of the Legislative Assembly elected by the property owners. *n.*

coun·sel (koun′səl) **1 take counsel,** exchange ideas; talk things over; consult together: *He took counsel with his friends as to what he should do.* **2** advice: *A wise person gives good counsel.* **3** a person or group that gives advice about the law; a lawyer or group of lawyers: *He acted as counsel for the defence.* **4** give advice to; advise: *She counsels high school students.* **5** recommend: *He counselled immediate action.* 1–3 *n.*, 4, 5 *v.*, **coun·selled** or **coun·seled, coun·sel·ling** or **coun·sel·ing.**

☛ **Counsel** and **council** are pronounced the same. See second note at **council.**

coun·sel·lor or **coun·sel·or** (koun′sə lər) **1** a person who gives advice; adviser. **2** lawyer. **3** a person who supervises, especially at a summer camp. *n.*

count[1] (kount) **1** name numbers in order: *The child can count to ten.* **2** add up; find the number of: *He counted the books and found there were fifty.* **3** an adding up; a finding out how many: *A count showed that more than 5000 votes had been cast.* **4** the total number; amount: *The exact count was 5170.* **5** include in counting; take account of: *Let's not count that game.* **6** be included in counting or consideration: *Your first* *trial is only for practice; it won't count.* **7** have an influence; be of account or value: *All our tests and projects count toward our final grade.* **8** consider: *He counts himself fortunate in having good health.* 1, 2, 5–8 *v.*, 3, 4 *n.*

count for, be worth: *His argument counted for little against theirs.*

count in, *Informal.* include: *Count me in for the party!*

count off, divide into equal groups by counting: *Count off in fours from the left.*

count on, a depend on; rely on; trust: *Can I count on you to help?* **b** reckon on; plan on; expect: *Count on spending at least three dollars for dinner.*

count out, a *Informal.* fail to consider; fail to include: *If you go skiing, count me out.* **b** declare a fallen boxer the loser when he cannot get up after ten seconds have been counted: *He was counted out in the third round of the fight.*

count[2] (kount) a European nobleman having a rank about the same as that of a British earl. *n.*

count·down or **count–down** (kount′doun′) **1** the period of time leading up to the firing of a missile or rocket. **2** the calling out of the minutes and, in the last stage, the seconds of this period as they pass. *n.*

coun·te·nance (koun′tə nəns) **1** an expression of the face: *His angry countenance showed how he felt.* **2** a face or features: *The king had a noble countenance.* **3** approve or encourage: *The parents countenanced the boys' friendship.* **4** approval: *He gave countenance to their plan, but no active help.* 1, 2, 4 *n.*, 3 *v.*, **coun·te·nanced, coun·te·nanc·ing.**

count·er[1] (koun′tər) **1** an imitation coin. **2** something used for counting: *Round, flat disks, called chips, are often used as counters to keep score in card games.* **3** a long table in a store or bank on which money is counted out, and across which goods are given to customers. *n.*

coun·ter[2] (koun′tər) **1** contrary; opposed: *He acted counter to his solemn promise.* **2** oppose: *He countered my proposal with one of his own.* 1 *adv.*, 2 *v.*

counter– a word element meaning: **1** against: *To counteract means to act against.* **2** in return: *A counterattack is an attack in return for an earlier one.* **3** so as to correspond: *A counterpart is a part that corresponds.*

coun·ter·act (koun′tər akt′) act against; hinder: *She took a cold shower to counteract her sleepiness.* *v.*

coun·ter–clock·wise (koun′tər klok′wīz′) in the direction opposite to that in which the hands of a clock go. *adv., adj.*

coun·ter·feit (koun′tər fit) **1** copy money, pictures, handwriting, etc. in order to deceive: *He was sent to prison for counterfeiting twenty-dollar bills.* **2** something copied and passed as genuine: *This twenty-dollar bill is a counterfeit.* **3** not genuine: *a counterfeit stamp.* **4** pretend: *She counterfeited interest in order to be polite.* 1, 4 *v.*, 2 *n.*, 3 *adj.*

coun·ter·pane (koun′tər pān′) bedspread. *n.*

coun·ter·part (koun′tər pärt′) a person or thing closely resembling another: *This twin is her sister's counterpart. Our principal phoned his counterpart in another school.* *n.*

coun·ter·sign (koun′tər sīn′) **1** a secret signal; a watchword or password: *The soldier had to give the countersign before he could pass the sentry.* **2** a secret sign or signal given in answer to another. *n.*

hat, āge, fär; let, ēqual, tėrm; it, īce
hot, ōpen, ôrder; oil, out; cup, pu̇t, rüle
əbove, takən, pencəl, lemən, circəs
ch, child; ng, long; sh, ship
th, thin; ᴛʜ, then; zh, measure

count·ess (koun′tis) **1** the wife or widow of a count or an earl. **2** a lady equal in rank to a count or earl in her own right. *n.*

count·less (kount′lis) too many to count: *the countless stars.* *adj.*

coun·try (kun′trē) **1** the land; a region: *The hill country to the north was rough and mountainous.* **2** a nation; state: *the country of France.* **3** the land where a person was born or is living: *In my own country the customs are very different.* **4** the people of a country: *All the country loved the king.* **5** land without many houses, such as wild, open land or farmland: *He likes the country better than the city.* **6** of or in the country as opposed to the city: *He likes country food and country air.* 1–5 *n., pl.* **coun·tries;** 6 *adj.*

coun·try·man (kun′trē mən) **1** a man of one's own country: *We will protect our countrymen.* **2** a man who lives in the country. *n., pl.* **coun·try·men** (kun′trē mən).

coun·try·side (kun′trē sīd′) land outside cities and towns, especially with reference to its features such as trees, flowers, hills, and valleys, and its general appearance: *The countryside looked beautiful in the fall sun.* *n.*

coun·try·wom·an (kun′trē wu̇m′ən) **1** a woman of one's own country. **2** a woman who lives in the country. *n., pl.* **coun·try·wom·en.**

coun·ty (koun′tē) one of the geographical districts into which certain countries, states, and provinces are divided for purposes of government: *There are counties in Nova Scotia, New Brunswick, Quebec, Ontario, and Alberta. In Ontario some counties have been displaced by larger districts called regions.* *n., pl.* **coun·ties.**

coupe (küp) a closed, two-door automobile, usually seating two to five people. *n.*

☛ **Coupe** and **coop** are pronounced the same.

cou·pé (kü pā′ or küp) coupe. *n.*

cou·ple (kup′əl) **1** two things of the same kind that go together; a pair. **2** a man and woman who are married or engaged. **3** the partners in a dance. **4** join together: *to couple two freight cars.* 1–3 *n.*, 4 *v.*, **cou·pled, cou·pling.**

cou·plet (kup′lit) two lines of verse that rhyme and have the same rhythm. *n.*

Example: And then my heart with pleasure fills,
And dances with the daffodils.

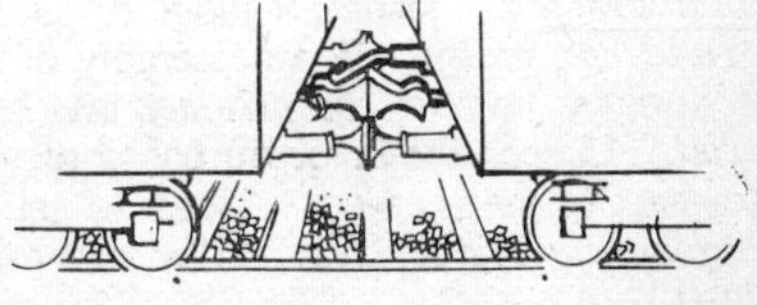
A coupling between two railway cars

cou·pling (kup′ling) **1** a device for joining together parts of machinery. **2** a device used to join together two railway cars. *n.*

cou·pon (küʹpon or kyüʹpon) **1** part of a ticket, advertisement, package, etc. that gives the person who holds it certain rights: *She saved the coupons that came with each cake of soap to get free cups and saucers.* **2** a printed statement of interest due on a bond, which can be cut from the bond and presented for payment. *n.*

cour·age (kėrʹij) bravery; the strength of mind to control fear and act firmly in the face of danger and difficulties. *n.*

cou·ra·geous (kə rāʹjəs) brave; full of courage. *adj.*

cou·reur de bois (kü rėrʹdə bwoʹ) *Cdn.* in the North and Northwest, a French or halfbreed woodsman, trapper, canoeman, etc.: *The coureurs de bois played an important part in the fur trade.* *pl.* **cou·reurs de bois.**

cour·i·er (kėrʹē ər or kürʹē ər) a person whose job is carrying messages, especially official government messages: *Government dispatches were sent by courier.* *n.*

course (kôrs) **1** an onward movement: *the course of events. She gets little rest in the course of her daily work.* **2** a direction taken: *Our course was straight to the north.* **3** a line of action: *The only sensible course was to go home.* **4** a way; a path or track; channel: *the course of a stream.* **5** a series of like things arranged in some regular order: *a course of lectures in history.* **6** a part of a meal served at one time: *The first course was chicken soup.* **7** the regular order; the ordinary way of proceeding: *the course of nature.* **8** an area marked out for a game or sport: *a golf course, a race course.* **9** a row of bricks or stones in a wall. **10** hunt with hounds. **11** run; move at a fast pace: *The blood courses through the arteries.* 1–9 *n.,* 10, 11 *v.,* **coursed, cours·ing.**
in due course, in reasonable time; after a while: *I know he will be here in due course.*
of course, a as might be expected; needless to say; naturally: *Of course it will rain on the weekend.* **b** certainly; without question: *Of course I'll do it.*
☛ **Course** and **coarse** are pronounced the same.

cours·er (kôrʹsər) a swift horse. *n.*

court (kôrt) **1** a space partly or wholly enclosed by walls or buildings; courtyard: *The apartment house is built around a court.* **2** a short street: *Our house is on York Court.* **3** a place marked off for a game: *a tennis court, a handball court.* **4** a place where a king, emperor, or other sovereign lives; a royal palace. **5** the family, household, or followers of a king, emperor, or other sovereign: *The court of King Solomon was noted for its splendor.* **6** a sovereign and his advisers as a ruling body or power: *By order of the Court of St. James is by order of the British government.* **7** an assembly held by a king, emperor, or other sovereign. **8** a place where justice is administered. **9** the persons who administer justice; a judge or judges: *The court found him guilty.* **10** an assembly of such persons to administer justice: *The prisoner was brought to court for trial.* **11** seek the favor of; try to please. **12** make love to; seek to marry; woo. **13** try to get; seek: *to court applause. The reckless soldier courted danger.* 1–10 *n.,* 11–13 *v.*

cour·te·ous (kėrʹtē əs) polite: *It is a courteous act to help an old lady to cross the street.* *adj.*

cour·te·sy (kėrʹtə sē) **1** polite behavior; thoughtfulness for others. **2** a considerate or polite act: *The girl's courtesies were much appreciated.* *n., pl.* **cour·te·sies.**
by courtesy of or **through the courtesy of,** with the consent of; with the permission or approval of: *The poem is included in that book by courtesy of the author.*

court·house (kôrtʹhousʹ) **1** a building in which courts of law are held. **2** a building used for the government of a county. *n.*

cour·ti·er (kôrʹtē ər) a person often present at the court of a prince, king, emperor, etc.; a court attendant. *n.*

court·ly (kôrtʹlē) having or showing manners fit for a king's court; polite; elegant. *adj.,* **court·li·er, court·li·est.**

court–mar·tial (kôrtʹmärʹshəl) **1** a court made up of officers and set up to try a person in the armed forces who has been accused of breaking military law. **2** a trial by such a court: *The captain's court-martial will be held next week.* **3** try by such a court. 1, 2 *n., pl.* **courts-mar·tial;** 3 *v.,* **court-mar·tialled** or **court-mar·tialed, court-mar·tial·ling** or **court-mar·tial·ing.**

court·room (kôrtʹrümʹ) a room where a law court is held. *n.*

court·ship (kôrtʹship) the condition or time of courting in order to marry; wooing: *Their courtship was a happy time.* *n.*

court·yard (kôrtʹyärdʹ) a space enclosed by walls, in or near a large building: *Two big buses stood in the courtyard of the hotel.* *n.*

cous·in (kuzʹən) the son or daughter of one's uncle or aunt: *First cousins have the same grandparents; second cousins have the same great-grandparents; and so on for third and fourth cousins.* *n.*

cove (kōv) a small, sheltered bay; the mouth of a creek; an inlet on the shore. *n.*

cov·e·nant (kuvʹə nənt) **1** a solemn agreement between two or more persons or groups: *The two countries entered into a covenant to fight as allies.* **2** agree solemnly to do certain things. 1 *n.,* 2 *v.*

cov·er (kuvʹər) **1** put something over or around so as to protect, keep warm, hide, etc.: *Pull the blind to cover the window. He covered the sleeping child with his coat.* **2** be over; occupy the surface of; spread over: *Snow covered the ground.* **3** anything that protects or hides: *She always puts covers on her school books.* **4** hide: *The burglar was careful to cover his tracks.* **5** protection; shelter: *We took cover in an old cabin during the storm. The soldiers attacked under cover of darkness.* **6** go or travel over: *We covered over 400 kilometres on the first day of our trip.* **7** include; take in: *This book covers the year's work in spelling.* **8** report or photograph events, meetings, etc.: *He covered the meetings of city council.* **9** be enough for; provide for: *I had enough money to cover the cost of an ice-cream cone for each of us.* **10** stand behind; support: *The shortstop covered the second baseman in*

hat, āge, fär; let, ēqual, tėrm; it, īce
hot, ōpen, ôrder; oil, out; cup, pu̇t, rüle
əbove, takən, pencəl, lemən, circəs
ch, child; ng, long; sh, ship
th, thin; ᴛʜ, then; zh, measure

case the ball got by him. **11** aim at in a threatening way: *One robber covered the cashier with a pistol while the other emptied the money drawer.* 1, 2, 4, 6–11 *v.,* 3, 5 *n.*

cover up, hide or conceal, especially something wrong: *He tried to cover up his guilt.*

under cover, a hidden; secret: *He kept his activities under cover.* **b** secretly: *Spies work under cover.*

cov·er·alls (kuv′ər olz′ or kuv′ər ôlz′) a strong outer garment that includes shirt and pants in a single unit, usually worn to protect other clothing: *Mechanics wear coveralls. n. pl.*

A covered wagon

covered wagon a large wagon having an arched canvas cover that can be taken off: *Covered wagons were pulled by horses or oxen.*

cov·er·ing (kuv′ər ing) anything that covers: *Our chesterfield has a new covering. n.*

cov·er·let (kuv′ər lit) an outer covering of a bed; a bedspread. *n.*

cov·ert (kuv′ərt) **1** secret; hidden; disguised: *During the long speech, he cast covert glances at his watch.* **2** a shelter; a hiding place. 1 *adj.,* 2 *n.*

cov·et (kuv′it) desire eagerly, especially something that belongs to another: *The boy coveted his cousin's new bat. v.*

cov·et·ous (kuv′ə təs) desiring things that belong to others. *adj.*

cov·ey (kuv′ē) a small flock, especially of partridges. *n., pl.* **cov·eys.**

cow[1] (kou) **1** the full-grown female of cattle: *Some kinds of cows are kept for milking.* **2** the female of various other large animals: *a buffalo cow, an elephant cow, a cow moose. n.*

cow[2] (kou) make afraid; frighten: *Don't let his threats cow you. v.*

cow·ard (kou′ərd) a person who lacks courage or gives in to fear; one who runs from danger. *n.*

cow·ard·ice (kou′ər dis) lack of courage; the state of being easily overcome by fear: *The deserter was guilty of cowardice. n.*

cow·ard·ly (kou′ərd lē) without courage; like a coward. *adj.*

cow·bell (kou′bel′) a bell hung around a cow's neck so that its sound will indicate where she is. *n.*

cow·bird (kou′bėrd′) a small North American blackbird that is often found with cattle. *n.*

cow·boy (kou′boi′) a man who looks after cattle on a ranch and on the range. *n.*

cow·catch·er (kou′kach′ər) a metal frame on the front of a locomotive, streetcar, etc., intended to clear the tracks of anything in the way. *n.*

cow·er (kou′ər) crouch in fear or shame: *The whipped dog whimpered and cowered under the table. v.*

cow·girl (kou′gėrl′) a woman or girl who looks after cattle. *n.*

cow hand a cowboy or cowgirl.

cow·hide (kou′hīd′) **1** the hide of a cow. **2** leather made from it: *cowhide boots. n.*

cowl (koul) **1** a monk's cloak with a hood. **2** the hood itself. See the picture. *n.*

cow·lick (kou′lik′) a small tuft of hair that will not lie flat. *n.*

cow·punch·er (kou′pun′chər) a cowboy or cowgirl. *n.*

cow·slip (kou′slip) a marsh plant having bright-yellow flowers that bloom in early spring. *n.*

cox·swain (kok′sən or kok′swān′) the man who steers a boat or ship and directs the crew. *n.*

coy (koi) **1** shy; modest; bashful. **2** seeming more shy than one really is: *The actress wore a coy smile. adj.*

A cowl

A coyote — about 45 cm high at the shoulder

coy·o·te (kī ō′tē, kī′ōt, or kī′üt) a North American wild animal related to the dog, having yellow or yellowish-grey fur and noted for the way it howls at night: *Coyotes are found mostly on the Prairies, and eat gophers, rats, rabbits, etc. n., pl.* **coy·o·tes** or **coy·o·te.**

co·zi·ly (kō′zə lē) See **cosily.**

co·zi·ness (kō′zi nəs) See **cosiness.**

co·zy (kō′zē) See **cosy.** *adj.,* **co·zi·er, co·zi·est;** *n., pl.* **co·zies.**

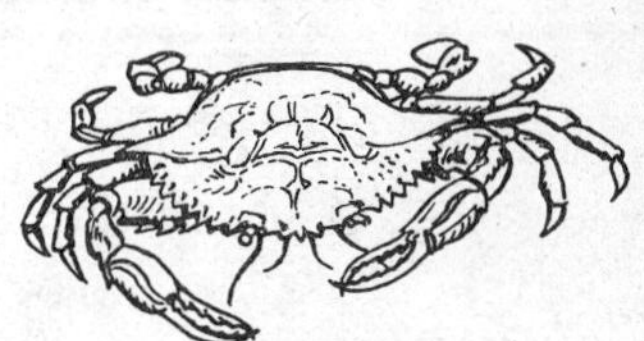
A blue crab — shell about 15 cm wide

crab[1] (krab) a shellfish with eight legs, two claws, and a broad, flat, shell covering. *n.*

crab[2] (krab) **1** a crab apple. **2** a bad-tempered person; one who is always complaining or finding fault. **3** be always complaining or finding fault: *Some people crab too much.* 1, 2 *n.,* 3 *v.,* **crabbed, crab·bing.**

crab apple **1** a small, sour apple used in making jelly. **2** the tree it grows on.

crab·bed (krab′id or krabd) **1** crabby. **2** hard to

make out or read: *The teacher objected to crabbed handwriting.* *adj.*

crab·by (krab′ē) *Informal.* cross, peevish, or ill-natured. *adj.,* **crab·bi·er, crab·bi·est.**

crab grass a coarse grass that spreads rapidly.

crack (krak) **1** a split or opening made by breaking without separating into parts: *There is a crack in this cup.* **2** break without separating into parts: *You have cracked the window.* **3** a sudden, sharp noise like that made by loud thunder, by a whip, or by something breaking. **4** make or cause to make a sudden, sharp noise: *The whip cracked. He cracked the whip.* **5** break with a sharp noise: *The tree cracked loudly and fell. We cracked the nuts.* **6** a hard, sharp blow. 1, 3, 6 *n.,* 2, 4, 5 *v.*

crack a joke, tell a joke or say something funny.

crack up, a crash or smash: *He cracked up two airplanes in one month.* **b** *Informal.* suffer a mental or physical collapse: *She was in danger of cracking up under the strain.*

cracked up, *Informal.* claimed: *That book is not what it is cracked up to be.*

crack·er (krak′ər) **1** a thin, crisp biscuit or wafer: *a soda cracker, a graham cracker.* **2** a small paper roll used as a party favor, containing a motto, a paper cap, etc. *n.*

crack·le (krak′əl) **1** make slight, sharp sounds: *A fire crackled on the hearth.* **2** a slight, sharp sound, such as paper makes when it is crushed. 1 *v.,* **crack·led, crack·ling;** 2 *n.*

crack–up (krak′up′) **1** a crash or smash: *That pilot has been in more than one crack-up.* **2** *Informal.* a mental or physical collapse. *n.*

cra·dle (krā′dəl) **1** a baby's little bed, usually on rockers or swinging on a frame. **2** hold as in a cradle: *She cradled the sleepy child in her arms.* **3** put or rock in a cradle. **4** the place where anything begins its growth: *The sea is thought to have been the cradle of life.* **5** a frame to support a ship, aircraft, or other large object while it is being built, repaired, lifted, etc. **6** the part of a telephone that supports the receiver. **7** a box on rockers designed to wash gold from earth. **8** a frame fastened to a scythe for laying grain evenly as it is cut. 1, 4–8 *n.,* 2, 3 *v.,* **cra·dled, cra·dling.**

A cradle on a scythe A cradle-board

cra·dle–board (krā′dəl bôrd′) a board and framework used by North American Indian mothers for carrying their babies: *When the cradle-board is tied to the mother's back, she is free to do work with her hands.* *n.*

craft (kraft) **1** skill: *These totem poles show the craft of the Indians who carved them.* **2** a trade or art requiring skilled work: *Carpentry is a craft.* **3** skill in deceiving others; sly tricks: *He got all their money from them by craft.* **4** boats, ships, or airplanes: *Craft of all kinds come into the Port of Montreal every day.* **5** a boat, ship, or aircraft: *There is a strange craft at the dock.* *n.*

crafts·man (krafts′mən) a skilled workman: *The maker of this beautiful table was obviously a craftsman.* *n., pl.* **crafts·men** (krafts′mən).

craft·y (kraf′tē) skilful in deceiving others: *The crafty thief escaped by disguising himself as a waiter.* *adj.,* **craft·i·er, craft·i·est.**

crag (krag) a steep, rugged rock rising above others. *n.*

crag·gy (krag′ē) **1** having many crags; rocky: *a craggy hillside.* **2** rugged; uneven: *a craggy face.* *adj.,* **crag·gi·er, crag·gi·est.**

cram (kram) **1** force into; force down; stuff: *He crammed all his clothes into the bag.* **2** fill too full: *The hall was crammed with many people.* **3** attempt to learn much in a short time; study hurriedly a short time before an examination: *He had to cram for two weeks to catch up on his work.* *v.,* **crammed, cram·ming.**

cramp (kramp) **1** shut into a small space: *The two of us were cramped in the telephone booth.* **2** a sudden, painful contracting or pulling together of muscles, often from chill or strain: *The swimmer was seized with a cramp.* **3 cramps,** *pl.* very sharp pains in the abdomen. **4** limit; restrict: *His work was cramped by the very short time he could spend on it.* 1, 4 *v.,* 2, 3 *n.*

cran·ber·ry (kran′ber′ē) a firm, sour, dark-red berry that grows on trailing vines in marshes: *Cranberries are used in making sauce and jelly.* *n., pl.* **cran·ber·ries.**

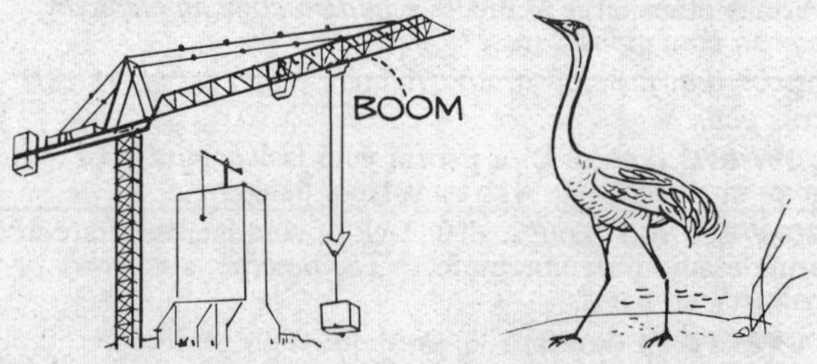

Crane (def. 1): a derrick

One kind of crane (def. 2) — about 95 cm long with the tail

crane (krān) **1** a machine with a long, swinging arm, for lifting and moving heavy weights. **2** a large grey or white wading bird having long legs and neck and quite a long bill: *The sandhill crane is the most common kind in Canada.* **3** stretch the neck as a crane does: *He craned his neck to see over the crowd.* 1, 2 *n.,* 3 *v.,* **craned, cran·ing.**

cra·ni·um (krā′nē əm) **1** the skull. **2** the part of the skull enclosing the brain. *n.*

crank (krangk) **1** a part or handle of a machine connected at right angles to another part to set it in motion: *the crank of a pencil sharpener.* **2** work or start by means of a crank: *He had to crank the old Model T car to start it.* **3** *Informal.* an odd person; a person who has strange ideas or habits. **4** *Informal.* a cross or ill-tempered person. 1, 3, 4 *n.*, 2 *v.*

crank·y (krang′kē) cross; irritable: *The baby has been cranky all morning.* *adj.*, **crank·i·er, crank·i·est.**

cran·ny (kran′ē) a small, narrow opening; a crack or crevice: *There were many nooks and crannies in the wall.* *n., pl.* **cran·nies.**

crape (krāp) See **crepe.**

crash (krash) **1** a sudden, loud noise like many dishes falling and breaking, or like sudden, loud band music. **2** make such a noise: *The thunder crashed.* **3** fall, hit, or break with force and a loud noise: *The dishes crashed to the floor.* **4** falling, hitting, or breaking with force and a loud noise. **5** the violent striking of one hard thing against another; collision: *No one was injured in the car crash.* **6** strike violently and shatter: *The bullet crashed through the window.* **7** fall to the earth in such a way as to be damaged or wrecked: *The airplane went out of control and crashed.* **8** such a fall or landing: *The skilful pilot brought down the damaged airplane without a crash.* **9** sudden ruin; a business failure. 1, 4, 5, 8, 9 *n.*, 2, 3, 6, 7 *v.*

A crate containing a bicycle

crate (krāt) **1** a large frame, box, or basket made of wicker or of strips of wood, used for shipping goods. **2** pack in a crate for shipping. 1 *n.*, 2 *v.*, **crat·ed, crat·ing.**

cra·ter (krā′tər) **1** the opening at the top of a volcano. **2** a big hole shaped like a bowl: *The battlefield was full of craters made by exploding shells.* *n.*

cra·vat (krə vat′) a necktie, especially a wide one. *n.*

crave (krāv) **1** long for; desire very strongly: *A starving man craves food.* **2** ask earnestly for; beg: *He craved a favor of the king.* *v.*, **craved, crav·ing.**

crav·ing (krāv′ing) a longing or yearning; a very strong desire: *A starving man has a craving for food.* *n.*

craw·fish (kro′fish′ or krô′fish′) crayfish. *n., pl.* **craw·fish** or **craw·fish·es.**

crawl (krol or krôl) **1** move slowly with the body on or close to the ground: *Worms, snakes, and insects crawl.* **2** move slowly on hands and knees; creep: *Babies usually crawl before they walk. The boys crawled through a hole in the wall.* **3** move slowly: *The traffic crawled on the icy roads.* **4** crawling; a slow movement: *The traffic was moving at a crawl.* **5** swarm with crawling things: *The ground was crawling with ants.* **6** feel creepy: *My flesh crawled at the thought of the huge snakes.* **7** a fast way of swimming by means of overarm strokes and a continuous kicking motion. 1–3, 5, 6 *v.*, 4, 7 *n.* **—crawl′er,** *n.*

crawl·y (krol′ē or krôl′ē) a feeling as if things are crawling over one's skin; creepy. *adj.*, **crawl·i·er, crawl·i·est.**

cray·fish (krā′fish′) a fresh-water animal resembling a small lobster. *n., pl.* **cray·fish** or **cray·fish·es.**

☞ **Crayfish** came into Middle English as *crevisse* from Old French *crevice,* which developed from an older German word *krebiz,* meaning 'a crab.' The form *crayfish* came about because the second syllable of *crevisse* was mistakenly associated with *fish.*

hat, āge, fär; let, ēqual, tėrm; it, īce
hot, ōpen, ôrder; oil, out; cup, pu̇t, rüle
əbove, takən, pencəl, lemən, circəs
ch, child; ng, long; sh, ship
th, thin; ᴛʜ, then; zh, measure

cray·on (krā′on or krā′ən) **1** a stick or pencil of chalk, charcoal, or a waxlike colored substance, for drawing or writing. **2** draw with a crayon. **3** a drawing made with crayons. 1, 3 *n.*, 2 *v.*

craze (krāz) **1** a short-lived, eager interest in doing some one thing: *One year he had a craze for collecting beetles; the next year he had a craze for making model ships.* **2** make diseased or injured in the mind; make crazy: *She was nearly crazed with pain.* 1 *n.*, 2 *v.*, **crazed, craz·ing.**

cra·zy (krā′zē) **1** having a diseased mind; insane: *That crazy man thought he was Napoleon.* **2** *Informal.* very eager or enthusiastic: *She is so crazy about cats that she brings home every stray she finds.* **3** not strong or sound; shaky: *That crazy bridge ought to be repaired.* *adj.*, **cra·zi·er, cra·zi·est.**

☞ See note at **mad.**

creak (krēk) **1** squeak loudly: *Hinges on doors creak when they need oiling. New shoes sometimes creak.* **2** a creaking noise. 1 *v.*, 2 *n.*

☞ **Creak** and **creek** are usually pronounced the same.

creak·y (krēk′ē) creaking; squeaky: *creaky floors, creaky hinges.* *adj.*, **creak·i·er, creak·i·est.**

cream (krēm) **1** the yellowish part of milk that contains fat: *Cream rises to the top when milk that is not homogenized is allowed to stand. Butter is made from cream.* **2** food made of cream; food like cream: *ice cream, chocolate creams.* **3** make into a smooth mixture like cream: *The cook creamed butter and sugar together for a cake.* **4** an oily preparation put on the skin to make it smooth and soft. **5** yellowish white. **6 the cream,** the best part of anything: *the cream of the crop. The cream of a class is made up of the best students.* 1, 2, 4–6 *n.*, 3 *v.*, 5 *adj.*

cream·er·y (krēm′ər ē) **1** a place where butter and cheese are made. **2** a place where cream, milk, and butter are bought and sold. *n., pl.* **cream·er·ies.**

cream·y (krēm′ē) **1** like cream. **2** having much cream in it. **3** having the color of cream: *creamy skin.* *adj.*, **cream·i·er, cream·i·est.**

crease (krēs) **1** a line or mark produced by folding; a fold; a ridge or wrinkle: *Men's pants are pressed with creases down the front.* **2** make creases in; fall into creases. **3** *Cdn.* in hockey and lacrosse, a small, rectangular area marked off in front of a goal. 1, 3 *n.*, 2 *v.*, **creased, creas·ing.**

cre·ate (krē āt′) **1** make a thing that has not existed before: *The Bible says that God created all things.* **2** make something original by intelligence and skill: *This garden was created from a gravel quarry. She has* *created an amazing painting.* 3 be the cause of: *Do not create a disturbance.* *v.,* **cre·at·ed, cre·at·ing.**

cre·a·tion (krē ā′shən) 1 the act of creating or of making a thing that has not been made before. 2 all things that have been created; the world; the universe: *Let all creation praise the Lord.* 3 a thing produced by intelligence and skill, usually something important or original. 4 **the Creation,** the creating of the universe by God. *n.*

cre·a·tive (krē ā′tiv) having the power to create; inventive; productive: *Sculptors are creative artists.* *adj.*

cre·a·tor (krē ā′tər) 1 a person who creates. 2 **the Creator,** God. *n.*

crea·ture (krē′chər) any living person or animal. *n.*

cred·i·ble (kred′ə bəl) believable or reliable; trustworthy: *He gave a credible imitation of the famous comic.* *adj.*

cred·it (kred′it) 1 belief in the truth of something; faith; trust: *One cannot be blamed for placing little credit in the words of a liar.* 2 believe in the truth of something; have faith in; trust: *It was difficult to credit the boy's strange explanation for his absence.* 3 confidence or trust in a person's ability and intention to pay later for something he wishes to buy or borrow now: *He had no trouble getting credit for his purchase.* 4 the amount of money a person has in an account: *He had a credit of $5000 in his savings account.* 5 add to an account as a deposit: *The bank credited his account with $100.00.* 6 reputation for paying debts: *If you pay your bills on time, your credit will be good.* 7 good reputation: *a man of credit.* 8 recognition; honor: *The person who does the work should get the credit.* 9 a person or thing that brings honor or praise: *The author's latest novel is a credit to her.* 1, 3, 4, 6–9 *n.,* 2, 5 *v.*

do credit to, bring honor or recognition to: *His quick action did credit to his courage.*

credit with, attribute to: *You will have to credit him with some sense for not panicking during the fire.*

give one credit for, think that one has: *Give him credit for some intelligence and let him try the job himself.*

on credit, on a promise to pay later: *He bought a new car on credit.*

cred·it·a·ble (kred′ə tə bəl) bringing praise or honor: *a creditable performance.* *adj.*

cred·i·tor (kred′ə tər) a person to whom money or goods are due; one to whom a debt is owed. *n.*

cred·u·lous (krej′ə ləs) too ready to believe; easily deceived: *She was so credulous that the other children could fool her easily.* *adj.*

creed (krēd) 1 a brief statement of the essential points of Christian belief. 2 a set of beliefs, principles, or opinions: *It was his creed that work should come before play.* *n.*

creek (krēk or krik) 1 *Cdn.* a small freshwater stream. 2 a narrow bay running inland for some distance from the sea. *n.*

☛ **Creek** and **creak** are usually pronounced the same, though *creek* is still pronounced (krik) by some older people.

creel (krēl) 1 a basket for holding fish that have been caught. 2 a basketlike trap placed underwater for catching fish, lobsters, etc. *n.*

creep (krēp) 1 move slowly with the body close to the ground or floor; crawl: *A baby learns to creep before it learns to walk.* 2 move in a slow and stealthy way: *The hunter crept silently through the woods.* 3 move timidly: *The dog crept into the living room.* 4 grow along the ground or over a wall by means of clinging stems: *Ivy creeps.* 5 feel as if things were creeping over the skin: *It made my flesh creep to hear her moan.* 6 creeping; a slow movement. 1–5 *v.,* **crept, creep·ing;** 6 *n.*

creep·y (krēp′ē) having or causing a feeling of horror, as if things were creeping over one's skin; frightened or frightening: *a creepy howl.* *The ghost stories made us creepy.* *adj.,* **creep·i·er, creep·i·est.**

crepe or **crêpe** (krāp) 1 a kind of cloth woven with a crinkled surface. 2 a piece of black crepe used as a sign of mourning: *The officers all wore crepe armbands to the funeral.* 3 crepe paper. 4 a raw or synthetic rubber made with a crinkled surface and often used for the soles of shoes. *n.* Also spelled **crape.**

crepe paper very thin crinkled paper used for making party decorations, etc.

crept (krept) See **creep.** *The baby crept over to its mother.* *We had crept up on the enemy without their seeing us.* *v.*

A crescent shape

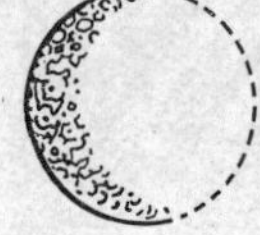

The moon as a crescent

cres·cent (kres′ənt) 1 the shape of the moon as seen from the earth in its first or last quarter. 2 anything that curves in a similar way, such as a street or a row of houses. 3 shaped like the moon when it is small and thin: *a crescent pin.* 1, 2 *n.,* 3 *adj.*

☛ **Crescent** comes from an Old French word *creissant,* which developed from a form of the Latin verb *crescere,* meaning 'grow' or 'increase.' The word was first used in English to describe the visible shape of the moon during the first quarter.

cress (kres) any of several plants whose leaves have a peppery taste and are used as a garnish or in salad: *The most familiar cress is water cress.* *n.*

crest (krest) 1 a tuft of feathers, or a growth of skin on the head of a bird or animal: *A rooster's comb is one kind of a crest.* 2 a decoration of plumes or feathers worn on a helmet. 3 a decoration at the top of a coat of arms: *A family crest is sometimes put on silver, dishes, letter paper, etc.* See **coat of arms** for picture. 4 an emblem, often of felt cloth, worn by members of various organizations, athletic teams, etc.: *a hockey crest.* *The soldier wore his regimental crest on the breast pocket of his blue blazer.* 5 the top part; top of a hill, wave, ridge, etc.; peak; summit. *n.*

crest·ed (kres′tid) having a crest: *a crested bird, a crested shield.* *adj.*

crest·fall·en (krest′fol′ən or krest′fôl′ən) dejected; discouraged: *She came home crestfallen because she had failed the examination.* *adj.*

hat, āge, fär; let, ēqual, tėrm; it, īce
hot, ōpen, ôrder; oil, out; cup, pu̇t, rüle
əbove, takən, pencəl, lemən, circəs
ch, child; ng, long; sh, ship
th, thin; ŦH, then; zh, measure

cre·vasse (krə vas′) a deep crack or crevice in the ice of a glacier. *n.*

crev·ice (krev′is) a narrow split or crack: *Tiny ferns grew in crevices in the stone wall.* *n.*

crew[1] (krü) 1 the people who operate a ship, rowboat, aircraft, etc.: *The entire crew of the destroyer was drowned.* 2 a group of people working or acting together: *a repair crew on the railway.* 3 a gang; mob: *The boys on that street are a rough crew.* *n.*

crew[2] (krü) See **crow**[1]. *The cock crew at dawn.* *v.*

crib (krib) 1 a small bed with high, barred sides: *The sides on a crib are intended to keep the baby from falling out.* 2 a rack or manger for feeding animals. 3 a building or box for storing grain, salt, etc.: *a corn crib.* 4 a framework of logs or timbers used in building. 5 *Informal.* use somebody's words or ideas, pretending that they are one's own: *His test was marked zero because he cribbed.* 1–4 *n.*, 5 *v.*, **cribbed, crib·bing.**

crick·et[1] (krik′it) a black insect related to the grasshopper: *On a summer evening crickets can often be heard chirping merrily.* *n.*

crick·et[2] (krik′it) an outdoor game played by two teams of eleven players each, with ball, bats, and wickets. *n.*

cried (krīd) See **cry.** *I cried when my turtle died. The baby had cried at first, but later she liked the water.* *v.*

cries (krīz) plural of **cry.** *n.*

crime (krīm) 1 a deed that is against the law; an illegal act: *Murder is a crime.* 2 an evil act; a sin. *n.*

crim·i·nal (krim′ə nəl) 1 a person who has committed a crime. 2 guilty of crime: *a criminal person.* 3 illegal; wrong; immoral: *a criminal offence. Murder is a criminal act.* 4 having to do with or related to crime; concerned with crime: *criminal law, a criminal lawyer.* 1 *n.*, 2–4 *adj.*

crim·son (krim′zən) 1 deep red. 2 turn deep red in color: *His face crimsoned with shame.* 1 *n.*, *adj.*, 2 *v.*

cringe (krinj) 1 shrink from danger or pain; crouch in fear: *The dog cringed at the sight of the whip.* 2 bow down timidly; try to get favor or attention by servile behavior: *The beggar cringed as he put out his hand for money.* *v.*, **cringed, cring·ing.**

crin·kle (kring′kəl) 1 become wrinkled; cause to wrinkle: *His suit was crinkled from lying on the floor.* 2 a wrinkle; a ripple. 3 rustle: *Paper crinkles when it is crushed.* 1, 3 *v.*, **crin·kled, crin·kling;** 2 *n.*

crip·ple (krip′əl) 1 a person who cannot use parts of his body, especially his feet or legs, properly because of being injured or deformed. 2 make a cripple of. 3 damage; weaken: *The ship was crippled by the storm.* 1 *n.*, 2, 3 *v.*, **crip·ple, crip·pling.**

cri·sis (krī′sis) 1 a turning point in a serious illness, after which it is known whether the patient is expected to live or die. 2 an important or deciding event; a point at which a change must come: *The Battle of Waterloo was a crisis in Napoleon's career.* 3 a time of danger or anxious waiting: *England faced a crisis during the Battle of Britain.* *n., pl.* **cri·ses** (krī′sēz).

crisp (krisp) 1 firm and stiff but breaking or snapping easily and sharply: *Dry toast is crisp. Fresh celery is crisp.* 2 fresh; sharp and clear; bracing: *The air was cool and crisp.* 3 short and decided; clear-cut: *a crisp manner.* 4 curly and wiry: *crisp hair.* 5 make crisp; become crisp. 1–4 *adj.*, 5 *v.*

criss·cross (kris′kros′) 1 marked or made with crossed lines; crossed; crossing: *Plaids have a crisscross pattern.* 2 crosswise: *He laid the sticks crisscross in the fireplace.* 3 mark or cover with crossed lines: *Little cracks crisscrossed the wall.* 4 come and go across: *Buses and cars crisscross the city.* 1 *adj.*, 2 *adv.*, 3, 4 *v.*

crit·ic (krit′ik) 1 a person who makes a judgment, especially one concerning books, music, pictures, plays, acting, etc. 2 a person who disapproves or finds fault: *She was such a constant critic that the other girls did not like her.* *n.*

crit·i·cal (krit′ə kəl) 1 inclined to find fault or disapprove: *A critical person often seems to look for things to complain about.* 2 coming from one who is skilled as a critic: *He knows enough to make a critical judgment.* 3 of a crisis; being important at a time of danger and difficulty: *The reinforcements arrived on the scene just at the critical moment.* *adj.*

crit·i·cism (krit′ə siz′əm) 1 unfavorable remarks or judgments; the act of finding fault. 2 the making of judgments; an approving or disapproving. 3 the work of a critic. *n.*

crit·i·cize (krit′ə sīz′) 1 blame; find fault with: *Do not criticize him until you know all the facts.* 2 judge or speak as a critic. *v.*, **crit·i·cized, crit·i·ciz·ing.**

crit·ter (krit′ər) *Informal.* 1 any living creature. 2 an animal, especially a cow, raised on a farm or ranch. *n.*

☛ **Critter** is a dialect form of the word **creature.**

croak (krōk) 1 a deep, hoarse sound, made by a frog, crow, or raven. 2 make croaks. 3 be always prophesying evil. 4 be dissatisfied; grumble. 5 *Slang.* die. 1 *n.*, 2–5 *v.*

Crocheting

cro·chet (krō shā′) 1 a kind of needlework made of thread by using one needle, with a hooked end, called a crochet hook: *Crochet is a popular craft this year and our friends are crocheting sweaters, caps, and shawls.* 2 make an article or fabric of thread by using a hooked needle. 1 *n.*, 2 *v.*, **cro·cheted** (krō shād′), **cro·chet·ing** (krō shā′ing). —**cro·chet′er** (krō shā′ər), *n.*

crock (krok) a pot or jar made of baked clay. *n.*

crock·er·y (krok′ər ē) dishes, jars, etc. made of baked clay; earthenware. *n.*

croc·o·dile (krok′ə dīl′) a large crawling animal, closely related to the alligator, but faster moving and having a narrower snout: *Crocodiles live mainly in the* *rivers and marshes of the warm parts of Africa, Asia, and America.* *n.*

The garden crocus

The prairie crocus

cro·cus (krō′kəs) **1** a small plant that blooms very early in the spring and has white, yellow, or purple flowers. **2** the flower of this plant. **3** a prairie wild flower having large purple or violet blossoms in early spring: *The prairie crocus is the floral emblem of Manitoba.* *n.*

crone (krōn) an old woman who is thin and withered. *n.*

cro·ny (krō′nē) a very close friend; chum. *n., pl.* **cro·nies.**

crook (krůk) **1** the curved or bent part of anything: *the crook of a hockey stick.* **2** to hook, bend, or curve: *He crooked his finger at me.* **3** a bend or curve. **4** a shepherd's hooked staff. **5** *Informal.* a person who is not honest; thief or swindler. 1, 3–5 *n.*, 2 *v.*, **crooked** (krůkt), **crook·ing.**

crook·ed (krůk′id) **1** not straight; bent; curved; twisted: *a crooked stick.* **2** dishonest: *a crooked lawyer.* *adj.*

croon (krün) murmur or hum; sing in a low tone: *The mother was crooning to her baby.* *v.*

crop (krop) **1** plants grown or gathered for use, especially for use as food: *Wheat is the main crop of the Prairie Provinces.* **2** the whole amount of the produce of any type of plant or tree that is yielded in one season: *The potato crop was very small this year.* **3** anything like a crop; group; collection: *a crop of new paperbacks in the bookstore.* **4** cut or bite off the top of: *Sheep had cropped the grass short.* **5** clip or cut short: *The horse's tail was cropped.* **6** the act or result of cropping: *A short haircut is a crop.* **7** the baglike swelling in a bird's food passage, where food is prepared for digestion. **8** a short whip having a loop instead of a lash: *a riding crop.* 1–3, 6–8 *n.*, 4, 5 *v.*, **cropped, crop·ping.**

crop out, appear or come to the surface: *Ridges of rock cropped out all over the hillside.*

crop up, appear or occur unexpectedly: *All sorts of difficulties cropped up.*

cro·quet (krō kā′) an outdoor game played by knocking balls through small wire arches by means of mallets. *n.*

cro·quette (krō ket′) a small patty or ball of ground meat or fish, chopped vegetables, etc. *n.*

cross (kros) **1** a stick or post with another across it like a T or an ×. **2 the Cross,** the cross on which Jesus died. **3** any thing, design, or mark shaped like a cross: *A cross is the symbol of the Christian religion. A person who cannot write his name makes a cross.*

Crosses (def. 3)

4 mark with a ×. **5** draw a line across: *In writing you cross the letter 't.' Cross off my name on your list. He crossed out the wrong word.* **6** set or lay across; put one thing across another: *He crossed his arms.* **7** move from one side to another; go across: *to cross a bridge.* **8** lie across; make the form of a cross: *Lansdowne Avenue crosses Main Street. The two streets cross.* **9** make the sign of a cross on or over: *The priest crossed himself.* **10** mix breeds of animals or plants: *A new plant is sometimes made by crossing two others.* **11** a mixing of kinds, breeds, or races. **12** the result of such mixing: *A mule is a cross between a horse and a donkey.* **13** hinder; oppose: *If anyone crosses him he gets very angry.* **14** in a bad temper. **15** a burden of duty or suffering: *A patient person bears his cross without complaining.* 1–3, 11, 12, 15 *n.*, 4–10, 13 *v.*, 14 *adj.* —**cross′ly,** *adv.* —**cross′ness,** *n.*

cross one's mind, occur to one; come to one's mind: *Telling a lie never crossed his mind.*

cross·bar (kros′bär′) a bar, line, or stripe going crosswise. *n.*

cross·bones (kros′bōnz′) two bones placed crosswise, usually below a skull, to mean death: *Poisonous products have to be marked with a skull and crossbones.* *n. pl.*

A crossbow

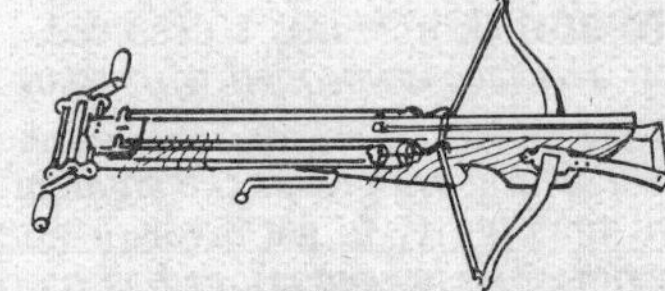

cross·bow (kros′bō′) an old-time weapon having a bow and a grooved wooden crosspiece to direct arrows, stones, etc. *n.*

cross·breed (kros′brēd′) **1** breed by mixing kinds, breeds, or races: *Canadian breeders are trying to produce new and very hardy livestock for northern climates by crossbreeding cattle with yaks.* **2** an individual or breed produced by crossbreeding: *A mule is a crossbreed produced by crossing a horse and a donkey.* 1 *v.*, **cross·bred, cross·breed·ing;** 2 *n.*

cross–coun·try (kros′kun′trē) **1** across fields or open country instead of by road or over a track: *a cross-country race.* **2** going or reaching across a country: *The folk singer made a cross-country tour.* *adj.*

cross·cut (kros′kut′) **1** a cut, course, or path going across: *Take a crosscut through the fields.* **2** used or made for cutting across: *a crosscut saw.* 1 *n.*, 2 *adj.*

cross–ex·am·ine (kros′eg zam′ən) **1** in law, question closely to test the truth of evidence: *The first witness for the prosecution was cross-examined by the defence for two hours.* **2** question closely or severely:

hat, āge, fär; let, ēqual, tėrm; it, īce
hot, ōpen, ôrder; oil, out; cup, pu̇t, rüle
əbove, takən, pencəl, lemən, circəs
ch, child; ng, long; sh, ship
th, thin; ᴛʜ, then; zh, measure

You don't have to cross-examine me, I'm just telling you what I heard. *v.*, **cross-ex·am·ined, cross-ex·am·in·ing.**

cross–eyed (kros′īd′) having one eye or both eyes turned in toward the nose. *adj.*

cross·ing (kros′ing) **1** a place where lines, tracks, etc. cross: *The red signal lights at the railway crossing were flashing.* **2** a place at which a street, river, etc. may be crossed: *White lines mark the crossing.* **3** the act of crossing, especially a voyage across water: *We had a rough crossing.* *n.*

cross·leg·ged (kros′leg′id or kros′legd′) **1** with the ankles crossed and the knees apart. **2** with one leg over the other and the knees together. *adj.*

cross·piece (kros′pēs′) a piece of wood, metal, etc. that is placed across something. *n.*

cross reference an instruction in one part of a book, index, etc. to look in another part for more information. At the entry **cried,** the cross reference 'See **cry**' means that you will find the meanings of the verb under this entry.

cross·road (kros′rōd′) **1** a road that crosses another. **2** a road that connects main roads. **3 crossroads,** *pl.* a place where roads cross: *At the crossroads we stopped and read the signboards.* *n.*

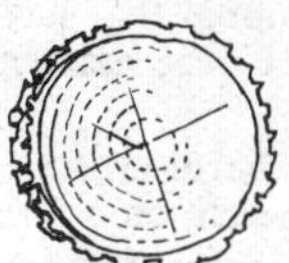

Cross sections

cross section **1** the act of cutting anything across: *Tomatoes can be sliced by making a series of cross sections.* **2** a piece cut in this way: *He cut the banana into cross sections to serve it.* **3** a sample; a small selection of people, things, etc. chosen to stand for an entire group: *They wanted to get the opinions of a cross section of the community.*

cross·walk (kros′wok′ or kros′wôk′) a street crossing marked with white lines: *In some cities all vehicles must stop when pedestrians are using a crosswalk.* *n.*

cross·ways (kros′wāz′) crosswise. *adv.*

cross·wise (kros′wīz′) **1** across. **2** in the form of a cross. *adv.*

cross·word puzzle (kros′wėrd′) a puzzle with numbered clues to certain words and with sets of blank squares to be filled in, one letter to a square, with the answers. Some of the words read across and some downwards, so that some letters belong to two words that cross each other.

crotch (kroch) **1** a forked piece or part: *The nest was in the crotch of a tree.* **2** the place where the human body divides into its two legs. *n.*

crouch (krouch) **1** stoop low with bent legs like an animal ready to spring, or like a person hiding. **2** shrink down in fear; cower. **3** a crouching position: *A baseball catcher's squatting position is called a crouch.* 1, 2 *v.*, 3 *n.*

croup (krüp) a disease of the throat and windpipe that causes a cough and difficult breathing. *n.*

crow^{1} (krō) **1** the loud cry of a rooster. **2** make this cry. **3** a happy sound made by a baby. **4** make this sound. **5** boast; show one's happiness and pride: *to crow over one's victory, to crow over one's defeated enemy.* 1, 3 *n.*, 2, 4, 5 *v.*, **crowed** or, for 2, **crew, crowed, crow·ing.**

crow^{2} (krō) a large, glossy, black bird with a harsh cry. *n.*

crow·bar (krō′bär′) a bar of iron used to lift things or pry them apart. *n.*

crowd (kroud) **1** a large number of people together: *A crowd gathered to hear the speaker.* **2** people in general; the masses: *Many newspapers appeal to the crowd.* **3** a large number of things or animals together. **4** *Informal.* a set; group: *He and his crowd went to the dance.* **5** collect in large numbers: *to crowd around the swimming pool.* **6** fill; fill too full: *Shoppers crowded the store.* **7** push; shove; press; cram: *to crowd into a building.* 1–4 *n.*, 5–7 *v.*

A crown

crown (kroun) **1** a head covering of precious metal and jewels, worn by a monarch. **2** the power and authority of a monarch; royal power. **3** of a crown; having to do with a crown: *crown jewels.* **4** a wreath for the head: *The winner of the race received a crown.* **5** to honor; reward: *His hard work was crowned with success.* **6** the head. **7** the top; the highest part: *the crown of a hat, the crown of a mountain, the crown of the head.* **8** be on top of; cover the highest part of: *A fort crowns the hill.* **9** the part of a tooth that appears above the gum, or an artificial substitute for it. **10** put a crown on: *to crown a king, to crown a tooth.* **11** a former British coin that was worth 5 shillings. 1, 2, 4, 6, 7, 9, 11 *n.*, 3 *adj.*, 5, 8, 10 *v.*

Crown corporation an agency or company through which the Government of Canada or one of the provincial governments carries on certain activities: *Air Canada, the C.B.C., and the St. Lawrence Seaway Authority are examples of Crown corporations.*

crow's–nest or **crows–nest** (krōz′nest′) on a ship, a platform for the lookout, near the top of a mast. *n.*

cru·cial (krü′shəl) very important; critical; decisive: *It is a crucial act for a nation to declare war.* *adj.*

cru·ci·fix (krü′sə fiks′) a cross with the figure of the crucified Christ on it. *n.*

cru·ci·fix·ion (krü′sə fik′shən) **1** the act of putting to death by nailing or binding the hands and feet to a cross. **2 Crucifixion, a** the putting to death of Christ on the cross. **b** a picture, statue, etc. of Christ's death. *n.*

cru·ci·fy (krü′sə fī′) **1** put to death by nailing or binding the hands and feet to a cross. **2** treat severely; torture. **3** blame and punish for the errors or crimes of someone else: *The newspapers crucified the mayor for a mistake made by his secretary. v.,* **cru·ci·fied, cru·ci·fy·ing.**

crude (krüd) **1** in a natural or raw state: *Crude oil is oil as it is pumped from the wells before it is refined and prepared for use.* **2** rough: *a crude log cabin, a crude chair made out of a box.* **3** lacking finish, grace, taste, or refinement: *the crude manners of a rude person. adj.,* **crud·er, crud·est.**

cru·el (krü′əl) **1** ready to give pain to others or to delight in their suffering; hardhearted: *a cruel master.* **2** showing a cruel nature: *cruel acts.* **3** causing pain or suffering: *a cruel war, a cruel disease. adj.*

cru·el·ty (krü′əl tē) **1** readiness to give pain to others or to delight in their suffering; having a cruel nature. **2** a cruel act or acts. *n., pl.* **cru·el·ties.**

Cruets

cru·et (krü′ət) a glass bottle to hold vinegar, oil, etc. for the table. *n.*

cruise (krüz) **1** sail about from place to place: *He bought a yacht so that he could cruise along the coast.* **2** a voyage from place to place with or without a special destination: *We went for a cruise on the Great Lakes last summer.* **3** travel or journey from place to place, especially without a particular destination: *The taxi cruised about in search of passengers. Many police cars are cruising the streets.* 1, 3 *v.,* **cruised, cruis·ing;** 2 *n.*

cruis·er (krüz′ər) **1** a warship with less armor and more speed than a battleship. **2** a police car used for patrolling streets and highways. *n.*

crul·ler (krul′ər) a kind of doughnut made by twisting together pieces of rich, sweet dough and frying them in fat. *n.*

crumb (krum) **1** a very small piece broken from bread, cake, etc.: *He left crumbs all over the floor.* **2** a little bit: *a crumb of comfort.* **3** break into crumbs. **4** *Slang.* a worthless person; a person of no importance. 1, 2, 4 *n.,* 3 *v.*

crum·ble (krum′bəl) **1** break into small pieces or crumbs: *Do not crumble your bread on the floor.* **2** fall to pieces; decay: *The old wall was crumbling away at the edges. v.,* **crum·bled, crum·bling.**

crum·ple (krum′pəl) **1** crush together: *He crumpled the letter into a ball.* **2** wrinkle: *'This is the cow with the crumpled horn.' v.,* **crum·pled, crum·pling.**

crunch (krunch) **1** crush noisily with the teeth: *He crunched the celery.* **2** make a sound of or like such crushing: *The hard snow crunched under our feet.* **3** the act or sound of crunching. 1, 2 *v.,* 3 *n.*

cru·sade (krü sād′) **1 Crusade,** any one of the Christian military expeditions between the years 1096 and 1272 to recover the Holy Land from the Moslems. **2** a vigorous movement against a public evil or in favor of some new idea: *Everyone was asked to join the crusade against cancer.* **3** take part in a crusade. 1, 2 *n.,* 3 *v.,* **cru·sad·ed, cru·sad·ing.**

cru·sad·er (krü sād′ər) a person who takes part in a crusade. *n.*

crush (krush) **1** squeeze together so violently as to break or bruise. **2** wrinkle or crease by wear or rough handling: *His hat was crushed when the girl sat on it.* **3** break into fine pieces by grinding, pounding, or pressing. **4** a violent pressure like grinding or pounding. **5** a mass of people crowded close together: *There was a terrific crush at the football game.* **6** subdue; conquer: *The enemy was crushed.* 1–3, 6 *v.,* 4, 5 *n.*

crust (krust) **1** the hard outside part of bread. **2** a piece of the crust; any hard, dry piece of bread. **3** rich dough rolled out thin and baked for pies. **4** any hard outside covering: *The snow had a crust that was thick enough to walk on.* **5** the solid outside part of the earth. See **core** for picture. **6** cover with a crust; form into a crust; become covered with a crust: *By the next day the snow had crusted over.* 1–5 *n.,* 6 *v.*

crus·ta·cean (krus tā′shən) an animal that has a hard shell and lives mostly in water: *Crabs, lobsters, and shrimps are crustaceans. n.*

crust·y (krus′tē) **1** having a crust; hard; crustlike: *crusty bread.* **2** harsh in manner, speech, etc.: *She was a crusty person but really very kind. adj.,* **crust·i·er, crust·i·est.**

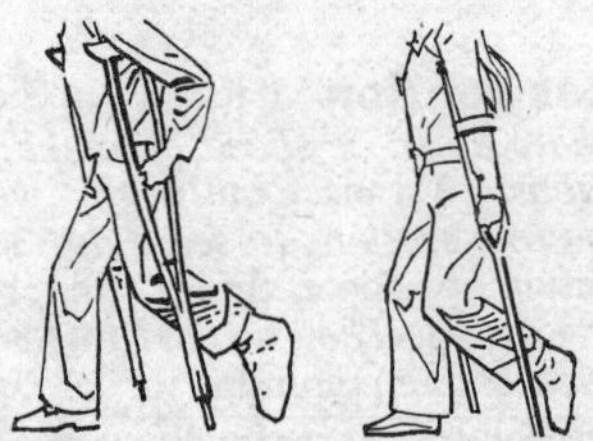

Crutches

crutch (kruch) **1** a support designed to help a lame person walk. **2** a support or prop; anything like a crutch in shape or use: *The lame soldier found that his rifle made a good crutch. n.*

cry (krī) **1** call loudly: *He cried, 'Help!'* **2** a loud call; a shout: *We heard the drowning man's cry for help.* **3** make a noise from grief or pain, usually with tears. **4** shed tears; weep. **5** a fit of weeping. **6** a noise made by a person in pain, grief, anger, etc. **7** offer for sale by shouting out the names of the things to be sold: *Peddlers cry their wares in the streets.* **8** announce in public: *The king ordered the news cried in the streets.* **9** a call that means things are for sale. **10** a call or noise made by an animal: *a gull's cry, the cry of a wolf.* **11** a call to action; slogan: *a war cry.* 1, 3, 4, 7, 8 *v.,* **cried, cry·ing;** 2, 5, 6, 9–11 *n., pl.* **cries.**

crys·tal (kris′təl) **1** a clear, transparent mineral that looks like ice. **2** a piece of glass cut to a form for use or ornament: *Crystals are used as beads, and hung around lights.* **3** transparent glass of good quality: *The wine glasses were made of crystal.* **4** clear and

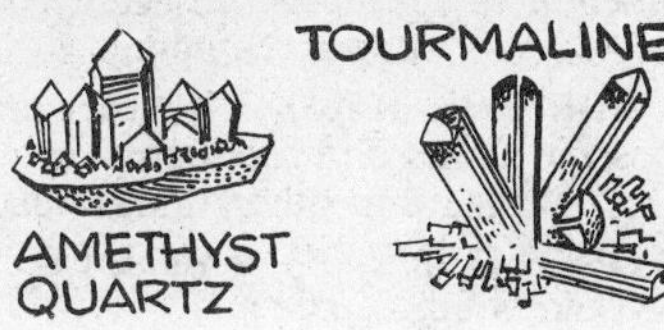

Crystals (def. 7)

hat, āge, fär; let, ēqual, tėrm; it, īce
hot, ōpen, ôrder; oil, out; cup, pu̇t, rüle
əbove, takən, pencəl, lemən, circəs
ch, child; ng, long; sh, ship
th, thin; ᴛʜ, then; zh, measure

transparent like crystal: *crystal water.* 5 made of crystal: *crystal ornaments.* 6 the glass over the face of a watch. 7 one of the regularly shaped pieces with angles and flat surfaces into which many substances solidify: *crystals of snow.* 1–3, 6, 7 *n.*, 4, 5 *adj.*

crys·tal·line (kris′tə līn′ or kris′təl in) 1 made of crystals: *Sugar and salt are crystalline.* 2 as brilliant and clear as crystal. *adj.*

crys·tal·lize (kris′təl īz′) 1 form into crystals: *Water crystallizes to form snow.* 2 form into definite shape: *His vague ideas crystallized into a clear plan.* *v.*, **crys·tal·lized, crys·tal·liz·ing.**

cub (kub) 1 a young bear, fox, wolf, lion, etc. 2 a boy who belongs to the Wolf Cubs. *n.*

Cu·ban (kyü′bən) 1 of or having to do with Cuba, an island country in the West Indies. 2 a person born in or living in Cuba. 1 *adj.*, 2 *n.*

cub·by·hole (kub′ē hol′) a small, enclosed space. *n.*

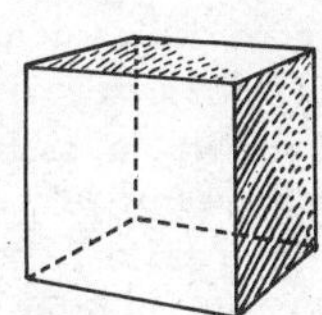
A cube (def. 1)

cube (kyüb) 1 a solid with six square faces or sides, all equal. 2 make or form into the shape of a cube: *The beets we had for dinner were cubed instead of sliced.* 3 ice cube. 4 the product when a number is used three times as a factor: *125 is the cube of 5, for 5×5×5=125.* 1, 3, 4 *n.*, 2 *v.*, **cubed, cub·ing.**

cu·bic (kyü′bik) 1 cube-shaped. 2 having length, breadth, and thickness: *A cubic metre is the volume of a cube whose edges are each one metre long.* *adj.*

cu·bi·cle (kyü′bə kəl) a small room or compartment, especially one of the divisions of a large dormitory. *n.*

cu·bit (kyü′bit) an ancient measure of length, about 50 centimetres: *Once a cubit meant the length of the forearm, from the elbow down.* *n.*

cub·mas·ter (kub′mas′tər) a man in charge of a pack of Wolf Cubs. *n.*

cub pack a group made up of several dens or sixes of Wolf Cubs.

cuck·oo (ku̇k′ü) 1 a bird whose call sounds much like its name: *The common European cuckoo lays its eggs in the nests of other birds instead of hatching them itself. The North American cuckoo builds its own nest and has a call less like the name.* 2 a bird call that sounds like the word *cuckoo.* *n., pl.* **cuck·oos.**

cuckoo clock a clock with a toy bird that pops suddenly out of a little door and makes a sound like that of a European cuckoo to mark the hours or quarter hours.

cu·cum·ber (kyü′kum bər) 1 a long, fleshy, green vegetable eaten raw, often in a salad, or used to make pickles. 2 the vine it grows on. *n.*

cud (kud) the food brought back from the first stomach of cattle or similar animals for a slow second chewing in the mouth. *n.*

cud·dle (kud′əl) 1 hold close and lovingly in one's arms or lap: *She was cuddling the little kittens.* 2 lie close and comfortably; curl up: *The two puppies cuddled together in front of the fire.* *v.*, **cud·dled, cud·dling.**

cudg·el (kuj′əl) 1 a short, thick stick used as a weapon; club. 2 beat with a cudgel. 1 *n.*, 2 *v.*, **cudg·elled** or **cudg·eled, cudg·el·ling** or **cudg·el·ing.** **cudgel one's brains,** try very hard to think.

cue[1] (kyü) 1 the last words of an actor's speech in a play, which serve as the signal for another actor to come on the stage or to speak. 2 a signal like this to a singer or musician. 3 a hint as to what should be done: *Take your cues from me at the party.* *n.*

☛ **Cue** and **queue** are pronounced the same.

cue[2] (kyü) a long stick used for striking the ball in the game of billiards or pool. *n.*

☛ See note at **cue**[1].

cuff[1] (kuf) 1 the part of the sleeve of a shirt, blouse, etc. that goes around the wrist. 2 the turned-up fold around the bottom of a sleeve or of a trouser leg. *n.*

cuff[2] (kuf) 1 hit with the hand; slap. 2 a slap, usually on the head or face. 1 *v.*, 2 *n.*

cuff link a device for linking together the open ends of a shirt cuff.

cui·rass (kwi ras′) 1 a piece of armor for the body, made of a breastplate and a plate for the back fastened together. See **armor** for picture. 2 the breastplate alone. *n.*

cull (kul) 1 pick out; select: *The weakest chicks were culled from the flock.* 2 something picked out as inferior or worthless: *Poor fruit and animals not up to standard are called culls.* 1 *v.*, 2 *n.*

cul·mi·nate (kul′mə nāt′) 1 reach its highest point: *The dramatic action of the play culminated in a murder.* 2 finish or result in: *The grandstand show culminated in a fireworks display.* *v.*, **cul·mi·nat·ed, cul·mi·nat·ing.**

cul·pa·ble (kul′pə bəl) deserving blame: *The policeman was dismissed for culpable neglect of duty.* *adj.*

cul·prit (kul′prit) 1 an offender; a person guilty of a fault or a crime. 2 a prisoner in court who has been accused of a crime. *n.*

cul·ti·vate (kul′tə vāt′) 1 prepare and use land to raise crops by ploughing it, planting seeds, and taking care of the growing plants. 2 help plants grow by labor and care: *Her grandmother cultivates roses.* 3 loosen the ground around growing plants to kill weeds, etc. 4 improve; develop by study or training: *It takes time, thought, and effort to cultivate the mind.* 5 give time, thought, and effort to mastering: *He cultivates good manners.* 6 seek to win the friendship of: *She cultivated* *people who could help her.* *v.,* **cul·ti·vat·ed, cul·ti·vat·ing.**

cul·ti·va·tion (kul′tə vā′shən) **1** the act of preparing land and growing crops by ploughing, planting, and necessary care: *Better cultivation of soil will result in better crops.* **2** the state of being prepared, ploughed, planted, etc.: *Only half the farm was under cultivation.* **3** the giving of time and thought to improving and developing the body, mind, or manners. **4** the result of improvement or growth through education and experience; culture. *n.*

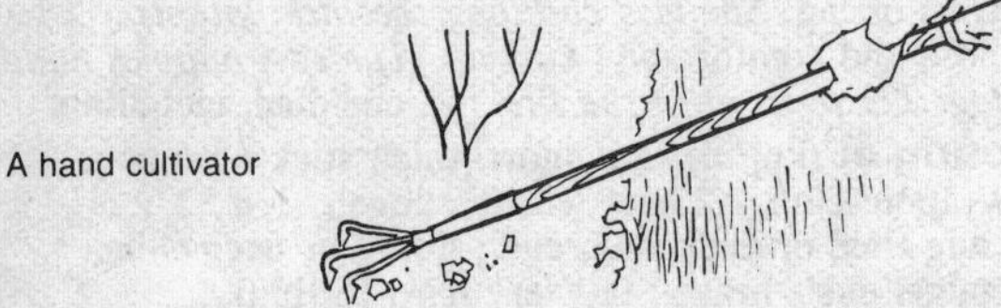

A hand cultivator

cul·ti·va·tor (kul′tə vā′tər) a tool or machine used to loosen the ground and destroy weeds: *A cultivator is pulled or pushed between rows of growing plants.* *n.*

cul·tur·al (kul′chər əl) of or having to do with culture: *Literature, art, and music are cultural studies.* *adj.*

cul·ture (kul′chər) **1** refinement of feelings, thoughts, manners, etc. **2** the customs and arts of a nation or people at a certain time: *She spoke on the culture of the ancient Vikings and that of the present-day Norwegians.* **3** the development of the mind or body by training, education, etc. **4** the preparation of land and production of crops. **5** proper care given to the production of bees, fish, silkworms, viruses, etc.: *An understanding of bee culture is necessary for the production of the best honey.* **6** a growth of viruses, bacteria, etc. in a special solution for scientific study or for use as a medicine. *n.*

cul·tured (kul′chərd) **1** having or showing culture; well-educated; refined. **2** produced or raised by culture (def. 5): *cultured pearls.* *adj.*

cul·vert (kul′vərt) a small channel or drain that allows water to run under a road or railway. *n.*

cum·ber·some (kum′bər səm) hard to manage; clumsy; burdensome; troublesome: *Long, awkward sentences are cumbersome.* *adj.*

cu·mu·lus (kyü′myə ləs) a piled-up, rounded mass of white cloud having a flat base. *n., pl.* **cu·mu·li** (kyü′myə lī′ or kyü′myə lē′).

cun·ning (kun′ing) **1** skilful or sly ways of getting what one needs or wants, or of escaping one's enemies: *The thief showed a great deal of cunning in the way he escaped.* **2** clever in deceit; sly: *a cunning spy.* **3** skilful; clever in doing: *With cunning hand he shaped the little statue.* **4** skill: *His hand has not lost its cunning.* **5** pretty and dear; attractive: *Kittens and babies are cunning.* 1, 4 *n.,* 2, 3, 5 *adj.*

cup (kup) **1** a small but rather deep dish to drink from: *Most cups have handles.* **2** as much as a cup holds: *She drank a cup of milk.* **3** anything shaped like a cup: *The petals of some flowers form a cup.* **4** shape like a cup: *He cupped his hands to catch the ball.* **5** an ornamental cup given to the winner of a contest; trophy. 1–3, 5 *n.,* 4 *v.,* **cupped, cup·ping.**

cup·board (kub′ərd) **1** a closet or cabinet with shelves for dishes and food supplies. **2** a closet for storing clothing and other things. *n.*

cup·cake (kup′kāk′) a small cake baked in a tin shaped like a cup. *n.*

cup·ful (kup′fu̇l) as much as a cup can hold. *n., pl.* **cup·fuls.**

Cu·pid (kyü′pid) **1** the Roman god of love, the son of Venus: *Cupid is usually represented as a winged boy with bow and arrows.* **2 cupid,** a figure of a winged boy used as a symbol of love: *Many valentines have cupids on them.* *n.*

A cupola (def. 2)

cu·po·la (kyü′pə lə) **1** a round dome forming the roof of a building or part of a building. **2** a small dome or tower on top of a roof. *n.*

cur (kėr) a worthless dog; mongrel. *n.*

cur·a·ble (kyür′ə bəl) that can be cured. *adj.*

cu·rate (kyür′it) an assistant clergyman; the helper of a pastor, rector, or vicar. *n.*

cu·ra·tor (kyü rā′tər) the person in charge of all or part of a museum, library, etc.: *The curator of an art museum knows a great deal about pictures.* *n.*

curb (kėrb) **1** a raised border of concrete or stone along the edge of a street, driveway, etc. **2** a chain or a strap fastened to a horse's bit and passing under its lower jaw: *When the reins are pulled tight, the curb checks the horse.* **3** anything that checks or restrains. **4** hold in check; restrain: *You must curb your appetite if you want to lose weight.* 1–3 *n.,* 4 *v.*

curd (kėrd) **1** the thick part of milk that separates from the watery part when the milk sours: *Cheese is made from curds.* **2** form into curds. 1 *n.,* 2 *v.*

cur·dle (kėr′dəl) form into curds: *Milk curdles when it is kept too long.* *v.,* **cur·dled, cur·dling.**

cure (kyür) **1** bring back to health; make well: *The sick child was soon cured.* **2** get rid of: *to cure a cold, to cure a bad habit.* **3** a remedy; something that removes or relieves disease or any undesirable condition: *a cure for sore eyes, a cure for laziness.* **4** preserve bacon or other meat by drying or salting. 1, 2, 4 *v.,* **cured, cur·ing;** 3 *n.*

cur·few (kėr′fyü) **1** the giving of a signal, such as a bell ringing, at a fixed time in the evening directing persons, usually children, to leave the streets. **2** the signal given. **3** the time when it is given: *Everybody had to be indoors by curfew.* **4** a regulation forbidding persons, usually children, to be on the streets after a certain hour. *n.*

cu·ri·os·i·ty (kyür′ē os′ə tē) **1** eager desire to know: *Curiosity got the better of her, and she opened the forbidden door.* **2** a strange, rare object: *One of his* curiosities was a drinking cup made of the horn of a deer. *n., pl.* **cu·ri·os·i·ties.**

cu·ri·ous (kyür′ē əs) **1** eager to know: *Small children are very curious, and they ask many questions.* **2** strange; odd; unusual: *a curious old book. adj.*

curl (kėrl) **1** twist or roll into coils: *Mother has to curl her hair, but mine curls naturally.* **2** take the form of coils or twists: *Paper curls when it burns.* **3** rise in coils: *Smoke curls slowly from the chimney.* **4** a curled lock of hair. **5** anything curled or bent into a curve: *A carpenter's shavings are curls.* **6** slide a curling stone down the ice. **7** engage in the game of curling: *My brother likes to curl.* 1–3, 6, 7 *v.,* 4, 5 *n.*

curl up, lie down or sit in a comfortable, relaxed position, with the legs tucked up: *curled up in a big chair. She curled up by the fire with a book.*

curl·er (kėr′lər) **1** a person who takes part in the game of curling. **2** a device on which hair is twisted to make it curl. *n.*

curl·ing (kėr′ling) a game played on ice, in which large, round stones are slid toward a target at the end of the rink: *Curling is a popular sport in Canada. n.*

A curling stone

A woman curling

curling stone or **rock** the object, usually made of granite, slid down the ice in the game of curling.

curl·y (kėr′lē) **1** having a tendency to curl; curling: *curly hair.* **2** having curls or curly hair: *a curly head. adj.,* **curl·i·er, curl·i·est.**

cur·rant (kėr′ənt) **1** a small, seedless raisin made from certain sorts of small, sweet grapes: *Currants are often used in puddings, cakes, and buns.* **2** a small, sour, red, white, or black berry, used for jelly, wine, preserves, etc. **3** the bush that this berry grows on. *n.*

☛ **Currant** and **current** are pronounced the same.

cur·ren·cy (kėr′ən sē) **1** the money in actual use in a country: *Canadian currency cannot be used in Mexico.* **2** circulation; a passing from person to person: *The people who spread a rumor give it currency.* **3** general use or acceptance; common occurrence: *Words such as 'couldst' and 'thou' have little currency nowadays. n., pl.* **cur·ren·cies.**

cur·rent (kėr′ənt) **1** a flow; stream: *Running water or moving air makes a current.* **2** the flow of electricity through a wire, etc. **3** the course or movement of events or of opinions: *Newspapers influence the current of public opinion.* **4** of the present time: *current fashions, the current month. The current issue of a magazine is the latest one issued.* **5** in general use; passing from person to person: *current money, current jokes.* 1–3 *n.,* 4, 5 *adj.*

☛ **Current** and **currant** are pronounced the same.

cur·ry[1] (kėr′ē) rub and clean a horse with a brush or scraper. *v.,* **cur·ried, cur·ry·ing.**

curry favor, seek favor by flattery, attention, etc.

cur·ry[2] (kėr′ē) **1** a peppery sauce or powder. **2** food flavored with curry: *Curry is a popular dish in India.* **3** prepare or flavor food with curry: *curried rice, curried lamb.* 1, 2 *n., pl.* **cur·ries;** 3 *v.,* **cur·ried, cur·ry·ing.**

hat, āge, fär; let, ēqual, tėrm; it, īce
hot, ōpen, ôrder; oil, out; cup, pu̇t, rüle
əbove, takən, pencəl, lemən, circəs
ch, child; ng, long; sh, ship
th, thin; ᴛʜ, then; zh, measure

cur·ry·comb (kėr′ē kōm′) a brush with metal teeth for rubbing and cleaning a horse. *n.*

curse (kėrs) **1** ask a god to bring evil or harm on: *He cursed his enemy solemnly.* **2** the words that a person says when he asks a god to curse someone or something. **3** bring evil or harm on; trouble greatly; torment: *cursed with misfortune. She is cursed with a bad temper.* **4** a source of trouble or friction: *His bad temper is a curse to him.* **5** swear; use bad language. **6** the words used in swearing: *His talk was full of curses.* 1, 3, 5 *v.,* **cursed, curs·ing;** 2, 4, 6 *n.*

curt (kėrt) short and rude; abrupt: *Her curt answer made him angry. adj.*

cur·tail (kėr tāl′) cut short; cut off part of: *His father curtailed his allowance. v.*

cur·tain (kėr′tən) **1** a piece of cloth or other similar material hung at windows or in doorways to protect from sun, wind, or rain, to separate, conceal, or darken, or to decorate. **2** a hanging screen that separates the stage of a theatre from the part where the audience is. **3** provide with a curtain; hide by means of a curtain: *We took two sheets and curtained off a space in the corner.* **4** anything that covers or hides: *A curtain of fog fell over the harbor.* 1, 2, 4 *n.,* 3 *v.*

curt·sey (kėrt′sē) See **curtsy.** *n., pl.* **curt·seys;** *v.,* **curt·seyed, curt·sey·ing.**

curt·sy (kėrt′sē) **1** a bow of respect or greeting by women, made by bending the knees and lowering the body slightly. **2** make a curtsy. 1 *n., pl.* **curt·sies;** 2 *v.,* **curt·sied, curt·sy·ing.**

cur·va·ture (kėr′və chər) **1** curving or bending: *We watched the gradual curvature of the plane's vapor trail.* **2** a curved condition, especially one that is not normal: *She had an operation to correct a curvature of the spine. n.*

curve (kėrv) **1** a line that has no straight part. **2** bend so as to form a line that has no straight part. **3** something having the shape of a curve; bend: *There have been many accidents on that curve in the road.* **4** in baseball, a ball thrown with a spin so that it swerves in flight. 1, 3, 4 *n.,* 2 *v.,* **curved, curv·ing.**

cush·ion (ku̇sh′ən) **1** a soft pillow or pad for a chesterfield, chair, etc., used to sit, lie, or kneel on. **2** anything that makes a soft place: *a cushion of moss.* **3** supply with a cushion. **4** *Cdn.* an enclosed ice surface, especially an outdoor one, on which hockey is played. 1, 2, 4 *n.,* 3 *v.*

cuss (kus) *Informal.* **1** curse: *He cussed me out for a whole half minute.* **2** an odd or troublesome person or animal: *Tell that cuss to get over here now!* **3** a curse. 1 *v.,* 2, 3 *n.*

cus·tard (kus′tərd) a baked, boiled, or frozen mixture of eggs, milk, and sugar: *Custard is a healthful dessert. n.*

cus·to·di·an (kus tō′dē ən) 1 a guardian or keeper: *the custodian of a museum.* 2 a caretaker; janitor. *n.*

cus·to·dy (kus′tə dē) the keeping; charge; care: *Parents have the custody of their young children.* *n., pl.* **cus·to·dies.**

in custody, in prison; in the charge of the police.

cus·tom (kus′təm) 1 any usual action: *It was his custom to rise early.* 2 a long-established habit that has almost the force of law: *He found it hard to adjust to the customs of his new country.* 3 for a special order: *Custom clothes are made specially, according to the order of one individual.* 4 **customs,** *pl.* **a** taxes paid to the government on things brought in from a foreign country. **b** the office at a seaport, airport, or border-crossing point where imported goods are checked. 5 the regular business given by a customer: *That store would like to have your custom.* 1, 2, 4, 5 *n.*, 3 *adj.*

☛ See note at **habit.**

cus·tom·ar·y (kus′təm er′ē) usual; according to custom: *It is customary for Canadians to stand up when 'O Canada' is played.* *adj.*

cus·tom·er (kus′təm ər) 1 a person who buys. 2 *Informal.* a person; fellow: *a rough customer.* *n.*

custom house or **customs house** a government building, usually at a seaport or a border-crossing point, where customs are collected.

customs officer a government official who examines goods being brought into a country and charges any tax that may be payable.

cut (kut) 1 open, remove, or separate with something sharp: *to cut meat, timber, one's nails, etc.* 2 make by cutting: *He cut a hole through the wall with an axe.* 3 an opening made by a knife or sharp-edged tool: *He has a bandage on the cut.* 4 pierce or wound with something sharp: *She cut her finger on the broken glass.* 5 hit or strike sharply: *The cold wind cut me to the bone.* 6 *Informal.* refuse to recognize socially: *The boys cut the new student at the party.* 7 hurt the feelings of: *His mean remark cut me.* 8 an action or speech that hurts the feelings. 9 a piece cut off or cut out: *a cut of meat.* 10 a way or place that has been made by cutting or digging: *The train went through a deep cut in the side of the mountain.* 11 reduce; decrease: *We cut expenses last month.* 12 a reduction; decrease: *a cut in prices.* 13 a way straight across or through; short cut. 14 go by a direct way; go: *Let's cut through the woods and get ahead of the others.* 15 cross; divide by crossing: *A brook cuts that field.* 16 an engraved block or plate used for printing; a picture made from such a block. 17 the way in which a thing is cut; a style or fashion: *the cut of a coat.* 1, 2, 4–7, 11, 14, 15 *v.*, **cut, cut·ting;** 3, 8–10, 12, 13, 16, 17 *n.*

cut down, a cause to fall by cutting: *cut down a tree.* **b** reduce; decrease: *cut down expenses.*

cut in, a go in suddenly: *The accident was caused by the truck cutting in to the line of traffic.* **b** break in; interrupt: *She cut in before the speaker had finished.*

cut it out, *Slang.* stop doing it.

cut off, a remove from the outside of something by cutting: *cut off the bark of a tree.* **b** shut off: *Our power was cut off for an hour yesterday.*

cut out, a remove from inside of by cutting: *He cut the core out of the apple.* **b** make or form by cutting: *Her mother showed her how to cut out paper dolls.* **c** move out of an assigned or expected position: *The reckless driver suddenly cut out from his own lane.* **d** *Slang.* stop: *He was told to cut out the teasing.*

cut teeth, have teeth grow through the gums: *Babies are sometimes cranky when cutting teeth.*

cut up, a cut into small pieces: *cut up straw.* **b** *Slang.* show off; play tricks; misbehave: *The father was annoyed because his son was cutting up.*

cute (kyüt) *Informal.* 1 pretty and lovable: *a cute baby.* 2 clever; shrewd; cunning: *That was a cute trick!* *adj.*, **cut·er, cut·est.**

cu·ti·cle (kyü′tə kəl) the skin around a fingernail or toenail. *n.*

cut·lass (kut′ləs) a short, heavy, slightly curved sword. See the picture. *n.*

cut·ler·y (kut′lər ē) 1 knives, scissors, and other cutting instruments. 2 knives, forks, and spoons for table use. *n.*

cut·let (kut′lit) 1 a slice of meat for broiling or frying: *a veal cutlet.* 2 a flat, fried cake of chopped meat or fish. *n.*

cut·out (kut′out′) a shape or design to be cut out: *Some books for children have cutouts.* *n.*

A cutlass A cutter

cut·ter (kut′ər) 1 a person who cuts, especially one whose work is cutting cloth to be made up into clothes. 2 a tool or machine for cutting: *a meat cutter, a bread cutter.* 3 a small horse-drawn sleigh. 4 a kind of sleigh pulled as a trailer by a snowmobile. 5 a small sailboat with one mast. 6 a boat belonging to a warship, used for carrying supplies and passengers to and from shore. 7 a small, armed ship used for patrolling coastal waters. *n.*

cut·ting (kut′ing) 1 a small shoot cut from a plant to grow a new plant. 2 a newspaper clipping. 3 for cutting: *Shears and scissors are cutting implements.* 4 that hurts the feelings: *a cutting remark.* 5 a way cut through a hill: *a railway cutting.* 1, 2, 5 *n.*, 3, 4 *adj.*

cut·up (kut′up′) *Slang.* a person who shows off or plays tricks. *n.*

cut·worm (kut′wėrm′) a moth caterpillar that feeds on the stalks of young plants, cutting them off near or below the surface of the ground: *Cutworms have smooth skin and are grey or black in color.* *n.*

cy·cle (sī′kəl) 1 any period of time or complete process of growth or action that repeats itself in the same order: *The seasons of the year—spring, summer, autumn, and winter—make a cycle.* 2 a complete set or series. 3 all the stories or legends told about a certain hero or event: *There is a cycle of stories about the adventures of King Arthur and his knights.* 4 a bicycle, tricycle, or motorcycle. 5 ride a cycle, especially a bicycle. 1–4 *n.*, 5 *v.*, **cy·cled, cy·cling.**

cy·clist (sī′klist) the rider of a cycle, such as a bicycle or motorcycle. *n.*

cy·clone (sī′klōn) **1** a severe windstorm resulting from a condition of low pressure, with winds moving in a spiral toward the centre, where the air pressure is lowest: *Hurricanes and typhoons are cyclones.* **2** a low-pressure condition or weather system that can produce such storms: *Cyclones may be thousands of kilometres across.* **3** any violent windstorm with spiralling winds, such as a tornado. *n.*

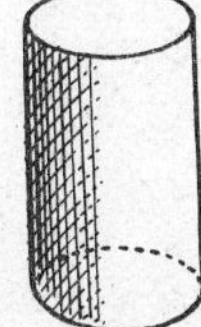
A cylinder (def. 1)

cyl·in·der (sil′ən dər) **1** a hollow or solid body shaped like a roller. **2** the piston chamber of an engine. *n.*

cy·lin·dri·cal (sə lin′drə kəl) shaped like a cylinder: *Candles, water pipes, and cans of fruit are usually cylindrical. adj.*

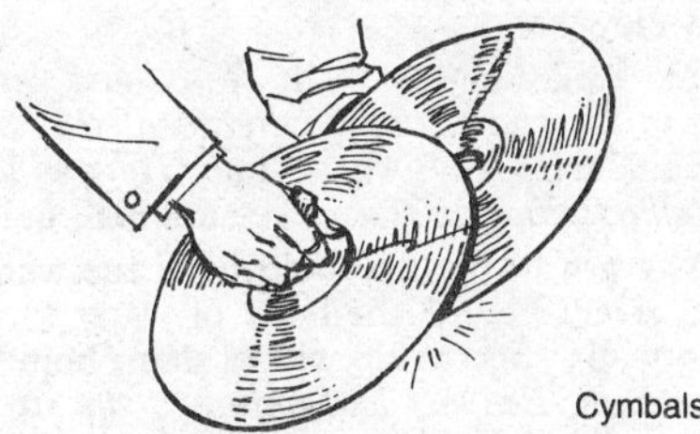
Cymbals

cym·bal (sim′bəl) one of a pair of brass plates that are struck together to make a ringing sound: *Cymbals are used in brass bands and symphony orchestras. n.*

cy·press (sī′prəs) one of a large group of evergreen trees and shrubs with hard wood and, usually, small, scalelike leaves: *Three kinds of cypress found in Canada are the white cedar, the western red cedar, and the red juniper. n.*

Cyp·ri·ot (sip′rē ət) **1** of or having to do with Cyprus, an island country south of Turkey. **2** a person born in or living in Cyprus. 1 *adj.,* 2 *n.*

cyst (sist) a baglike growth in animals or plants that usually contains fluid and has no outside opening: *Cysts often occur on a person's skin when an oil gland becomes blocked. n.*

czar or **tsar** (zär) **1** an emperor: *When Russia had an emperor, his title was Czar.* **2** a person with absolute power: *Al Capone was a czar of crime. n.*

cza·ri·na or **tsa·ri·na** (zä rē′nə) the wife of a Russian emperor. *n.*

Czech (chek) a person born in or living in Czechoslovakia, a country in central Europe. *n.*

Czech·o·slov·ak (chek′ə slō′vak) **1** of or having to do with Czechoslovakia. **2** Czech. **3** the language of Czechoslovakia. 1 *adj.,* 2, 3 *n.*

Czech·o·slo·va·ki·an (chek′ə slō vak′ē ən) Czechoslovak. *adj., n.*

d or **D** (dē) 1 the fourth letter of the alphabet: *There are two* d's *in* dead. 2 the Roman numeral for 500. *n., pl.* **d's** or **D's.**

dab (dab) 1 touch lightly; tap; peck: *The girl dabbed at her face with a powder puff.* 2 a light touch or blow; a tap or peck: *The cat made a dab at the butterfly.* 3 put on with light strokes. 4 a small, soft or moist mass: *dabs of butter.* 5 a little bit: *a dab of paint.* 1, 3 *v.,* **dabbed, dab·bing;** 2, 4, 5 *n.*

dab·ble (dab′əl) 1 put in and out of water; splash: *We dabbled our feet in the pool.* 2 work at a little; do in a half-hearted or superficial way: *dabble at painting. He likes to dabble in the stock market. v.,* **dab·bled, dab·bling.**

dachs·hund (dash′hůnd′ or daks′hůnd′) a small dog with a long body, short legs, and large, drooping ears. *n.*

dad (dad) father. *n.*

dad·dy (dad′ē) father. *n., pl.* **dad·dies.**

dad·dy–long·legs (dad′ē long′legz′) a small animal related to the spider, having a small body and six very long, thin, bent legs. *n., pl.* **dad·dy-long·legs.**

daf·fo·dil (daf′ə dil′) a plant having long, slender leaves and yellow or white trumpet-shaped flowers that bloom in spring: *Daffodils are a kind of narcissus and grow from bulbs.* See the picture. *n.*

daft (daft) 1 silly; foolish: *What a daft thing to do!* 2 crazy: *Go out in this rain? You must be daft. adj.*

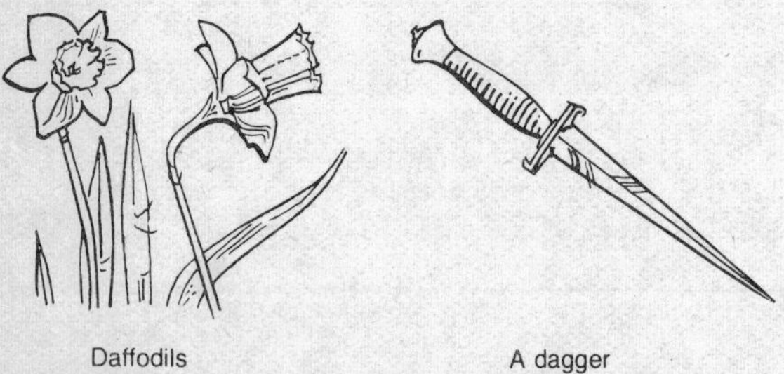

Daffodils A dagger

dag·ger (dag′ər) a small weapon with a short, pointed blade: *A dagger is used for stabbing. n.*

dahl·ia (dāl′yə or dal′yə) a tall plant with showy flowers of many colors and varieties. *n.*

dai·ly (dā′lē) 1 done, happening, or appearing every day: *a daily visit, a daily paper.* 2 a newspaper printed every day. 3 every day; day by day: *His strength is increasing daily.* 1 *adj.,* 2 *n., pl.* **dai·lies;** 3 *adv.*

dain·ty (dān′tē) 1 fresh, delicate, and pretty: *The violet is a dainty spring flower.* 2 delicate in tastes and feeling: *She is dainty about her eating.* 3 good to eat; delicious. 4 a choice bit of food; something very pleasing to eat: *Candy and nuts are dainties.* 1–3 *adj.,* **dain·ti·er, dain·ti·est;** 4 *n., pl.* **dain·ties. —dain′ti·ly,** *adv.*

dair·y (der′ē) 1 a room or building where milk and cream are kept and made into butter and cheese. 2 a farm where milk and cream are produced and butter and cheese made. 3 a store or company that sells milk, cream, butter, and cheese. *n., pl.* **dair·ies.**

dair·y·maid (der′ē mād′) a girl or woman who works in a dairy (def. 1). *n.*

dair·y·man (der′ē mən) 1 the owner or manager of a dairy. 2 a man who works in a dairy. *n., pl.* **dair·y·men** (der′ē mən).

da·is (dā′is) a raised platform at the end of a hall or large room: *The king's throne stood on a dais. n.*

Daisies

dai·sy (dā′zē) a plant of the same family as the aster, having flowers with a yellow centre and ray-like petals: *Some kinds of daisies have only white flowers; others have white or pink flowers. n., pl.* **dai·sies.**

☛ **Daisy** has developed from the Old English name for this flower, *daeges ēage,* meaning 'eye of day.' It was given this name because its petals close around the yellow centre in the evening and open out again in the morning.

dale (dāl) valley. *n.*

dal·ly (dal′ē) 1 play or toy with: *He dallied with the idea of going to the show, but finally decided to stay home.* 2 loiter; linger idly; waste time: *He was late because he dallied along the way. v.,* **dal·lied, dal·ly·ing.**

dam¹ (dam) 1 a wall built to hold back the water of a stream, creek, river, etc. 2 the body of water formed behind such a wall. 3 provide with a dam; hold back by means of a dam: *Beavers had dammed the stream.* 4 hold back; block: *He tried to dam back his tears.* 1, 2 *n.,* 3, 4 *v.,* **dammed, dam·ming.**

☛ **Dam** and **damn** are pronounced the same.

dam² (dam) a female parent among sheep, cattle, horses, and other four-footed creatures. *n.*

☛ See note at **dam¹**.

dam·age (dam′ij) 1 injury or harm that lessens value or usefulness: *The accident did very little damage to either car.* 2 injure or harm so as to lessen value or usefulness; hurt: *He damaged his thumb when he hit it with the hammer.* 3 **damages,** *pl.* money claimed by law or paid to make up for some harm done to a person or his property: *The man who was hit by the car asked for $5000 damages.* 1, 3 *n.,* 2 *v.,* **dam·aged, dam·ag·ing.**

dam·ask (dam′əsk) 1 silk woven into an elaborate pattern: *hangings of damask.* 2 linen with woven designs, used especially for tablecloths and serviettes. *n.*

dame (dām) 1 in the United Kingdom, a title given to a woman who has received an honorable rank equal to that of a knight: *Dame Edith Sitwell.* 2 the legal title of the wife or widow of a knight or baronet. 3 an elderly woman. 4 in former times, a lady. *n.*

damn (dam) 1 declare to be bad or inferior; condemn: *The critics damned the new book.* 2 doom to hell. 3 swear or swear at by saying 'damn'; curse. 4 a saying of 'damn'; a curse. 1–3 *v.,* 4 *n.*

☛ **Damn** and **dam** are pronounced the same.

damp (damp) 1 slightly wet; moist: *This house is*

damp in rainy weather. 2 moisture: *One could feel the damp in the morning air.* 3 dampen (def. 2). 4 check; stifle: *to damp a fire.* 5 a poisonous gas that gathers in mines: *The mine disaster was caused by exploding damp.* 1 *adj.*, 2, 5 *n.*, 3, 4 *v.*

hat, āge, fär; let, ēqual, tėrm; it, īce
hot, ōpen, ôrder; oil, out; cup, pu̇t, rüle
əbove, takən, pencəl, lemən, circəs
ch, child; ng, long; sh, ship
th, thin; ᴛʜ, then; zh, measure

damp·en (dam′pən) 1 make moist or slightly wet: *Mother dampens clothes before she irons them.* 2 cast a chill over; depress; discourage: *The bad news dampened our spirits.* *v.*

damp·er (dam′pər) 1 anything that discourages or checks: *The accident put a damper on the picnic.* 2 a movable plate to control the draft in a stove or furnace. *n.*

damp·ness (damp′nis) 1 the state of being damp or moist: *After the rain he was chilled by the dampness of his clothes.* 2 moisture: *One could feel the dampness in the air.* *n.*

dam·sel (dam′zəl) a maiden or young girl. *n.*

dance (dans) 1 move in time with music: *She can dance very well.* 2 a movement in time with music. 3 some special group of steps: *The waltz is a well-known dance.* 4 a party where people dance. 5 one round of dancing: *May I have the next dance?* 6 a piece of music for dancing. 7 jump up and down; move in a lively way: *See that boat dancing on the water.* 8 cause to dance; lead or conduct by dancing: *He danced his partner across the ballroom floor.* 1, 7, 8 *v.*, **danced, danc·ing;** 2–6 *n.* **—danc′er,** *n.*

dance hall a public hall or room in which dances are held.

dan·de·li·on (dan′də lī′ən) a weed having deeply notched leaves and bright-yellow flowers with many long, narrow petals. *n.*

dan·dle (dan′dəl) 1 move a child up and down on the knees or in the arms: *The old man liked to dandle his grandson on his knee.* 2 pet; pamper. *v.*, **dan·dled, dan·dling.**

dan·druff small, whitish flakes of skin that come off the scalp in large numbers. *n.*

dan·dy (dan′dē) 1 a man very careful of his dress and appearance. 2 *Informal.* anything that is excellent or pleasing: *That goal was a dandy!* 3 *Informal.* excellent; first-rate: *Everything is just dandy.* 1, 2 *n.*, *pl.* **dan·dies;** 3 *adj.*

Dane (dān) a person born in or living in Denmark, a small country in northern Europe. *n.*

dan·ger (dān′jər) 1 a chance of harm; nearness to harm; risk; peril: *A mountain climber's life is full of danger.* 2 anything that may cause harm: *Hidden rocks are a danger to ships.* *n.*
in danger of, liable to (with the accompanying threat of injury, harm, or death): *The old bridge is in danger of collapsing. The sick man is in danger of dying.*

dan·ger·ous (dān′jər əs) likely to cause harm; not safe; risky: *The road around the mountain is dangerous.* *adj.*

dan·gle (dang′gəl) 1 hang and swing loosely: *The curtain cord dangles.* 2 hold or carry something so that it sways loosely: *The nurse dangled the toys in front of the baby.* 3 hang about; follow: *The pretty girl had several boys dangling around her.* *v.*, **dan·gled, dan·gling.**

Dan·ish (dān′ish) 1 of or having to do with the Danes or Denmark. 2 the language of Denmark. 3 *Informal.* Danish pastry: *Let's have a Danish for dessert.* 1 *adj.*, 2, 3 *n.*

Danish pastry a rich, flaky pastry made with yeast.

dank (dangk) moist; wet; unpleasantly damp: *The cave was dark, dank, and chilly.* *adj.*

dap·per (dap′ər) 1 neat; trim. 2 small and active: *a dapper horse.* *adj.*

dap·ple (dap′əl) 1 spotted: *John has a dapple horse.* 2 mark or become marked with spots: *The lawn under the trees was dappled with spots of sunlight.* 1 *adj.*, 2 *v.*, **dap·pled, dap·pling.**

dap·pled (dap′əld) spotted: *a dappled horse.* *adj.*

dare (der) 1 be bold; be bold enough to: *He doesn't dare dive from the bridge.* 2 have courage to try; face or meet boldly; not be afraid of: *The explorer dared the perils of the Barren Ground.* 3 challenge: *I dare you to jump.* 4 a challenge: *I took his dare to jump.* 1–3 *v.*, **dared** or **durst, dared, dar·ing;** 4 *n.*
I dare say, probably; maybe; perhaps: *I dare say his success was due to his hard work.*

dare·dev·il (der′dev′əl) 1 a very reckless person, one who is ready to dare almost anything or anyone. 2 very reckless: *a daredevil racing driver.* 1 *n.*, 2 *adj.*

dar·ing (der′ing) 1 boldness; the courage to take risks. 2 bold; fearless. 1 *n.*, 2 *adj.*

dark (därk) 1 without light: *A night without a moon is dark.* 2 approaching black in color: *She has dark-brown eyes.* 3 nightfall: *He couldn't stay out after dark.* 4 gloomy: *Rain and clouds make a dark day.* 5 darkness: *Do not be afraid of the dark.* 6 hidden; secret: *He kept his past dark.* 1, 2, 4, 6 *adj.*, 3, 5 *n.* **—dark′ness,** *n.*
in the dark, without knowledge or information; in ignorance: *He left me in the dark about his plans.*

Dark Ages the early part of the Middle Ages in Europe, from the fifth to the eleventh century.

dark·en (där′kən) make dark or darker; become dark or darker. *v.*

dar·ling (där′ling) 1 a person very dear to another; a person much loved. 2 very dear; much loved. 1 *n.*, 2 *adj.*

darn¹ (därn) 1 mend by weaving rows of thread or yarn across a hole or torn place. 2 a place so mended. 1 *v.*, 2 *n.*

darn² (därn) damn: *'Darn' is used to express mild annoyance or irritation.* *v.*, *n.*

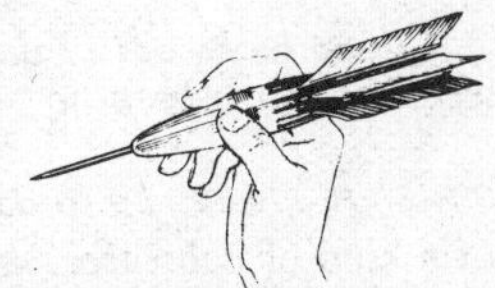

A dart

dart (därt) 1 a slender, pointed weapon, thrown by the

hand or shot from a device. **2 darts,** *pl.* a game in which players throw small darts at a round board that has two small rings in the centre, from which twenty numbered sections radiate. 3 throw or shoot suddenly and quickly: *The Eskimos darted spears at the seal.* 4 a sudden, swift movement. 5 move suddenly and swiftly: *The deer saw us and darted away.* 6 send suddenly: *The girl darted an angry glance at her younger sister.* 7 a tapered seam designed to make a garment fit better. 1, 2, 4, 7 *n.*, 3, 5, 6 *v.*

dash (dash) 1 throw: *We dashed water over him.* 2 splash: *The artist dashed some green paint on the canvas to represent a distant forest.* 3 rush: *They dashed by in a hurry.* 4 throw and break; smash: *He dashed the bowl to bits on a rock.* 5 ruin: *Our hopes were dashed.* 6 a small amount: *Put in just a dash of pepper.* 7 a short race: *the 50 metre dash.* 8 a mark (—) used in writing or printing to show a break in thought, the omission of letters or words, etc. 9 energy; spirit; liveliness: *He certainly has a lot of dash.* 1–5 *v.*, 6–9 *n.*

dash off, do, make, write, etc. quickly: *He dashed off a letter to his friend.*

dash·board (dash′bôrd′) 1 a panel beneath the front window in a car, truck, aircraft, etc. having instruments and gauges for the use of the operator. 2 a protection on the front of a wagon, boat, etc. that prevents mud or water from being splashed into it. *n.*

dash·ing (dash′ing) 1 full of energy and spirit; lively. 2 showy: *The soldiers wore dashing uniforms.* *adj.*

da·ta (dā′tə or dat′ə) facts; things known or accepted; information: *Names, ages and other data about the class are written in the teacher's book.* *n. pl.* of **datum.**

☛ In informal English **data** is often used with a singular verb when it refers to a group of facts considered together: *The data you have collected is not enough to convince me.* In formal English, however, **data** is always treated as a plural: *We will analyse the data that have been obtained.*

date[1] (dāt) 1 the time when something happens or happened: *The date of their wedding was September 30, 1960.* 2 a statement of time: *There is a date stamped on every piece of Canadian money.* 3 mark the time of; put a date on: *Please date your letter.* 4 find out the date of; give a date to: *The scientist was unable to date the fossil.* 5 a period of time: *At that date there were no airplanes.* 6 an appointment for a certain time. 7 have or make a social appointment with a person of the opposite sex: *She dates only on Saturday evenings.* 8 the person with whom such an appointment is made: *He asked her to be his date for the school dance.* 1, 2, 5, 6, 8 *n.*, 3, 4, 7 *v.*, **dat·ed, dat·ing.**

date from, belong to a certain period of time; have its origin in: *The oldest house in town dates from the 1780's.*

out of date, out of fashion: *That dress looks out of date.*

to date, up to the present time: *There have been no replies to date.*

up to date, in fashion: *His clothes are always up to date.*

date[2] (dāt) the sweet fruit of a kind of palm tree. *n.*

daub (dob or dôb) 1 cover with plaster, clay, mud, or any soft material that will stick. 2 paint badly: *She is no artist; she just daubs.* 3 a badly painted picture. 1, 2 *v.*, 3 *n.*

daugh·ter (do′tər or dô′tər) 1 a female child in relation to either or both of her parents. 2 a female descendant. 3 a girl or woman attached to a country, cause, etc. as a child is to its parents: *a daughter of France.* *n.*

daugh·ter–in–law (do′tər in lo′ or dô′tər in lô′) the wife of one's son. *n., pl.* **daugh·ters-in-law.**

daunt (dont or dônt) frighten; discourage: *Danger did not daunt the explorer.* *v.*

daunt·less (dont′lis or dônt′lis) brave; not to be frightened or discouraged: *He is a dauntless pilot.* *adj.*

dav·en·port (dav′ən pôrt′) a long couch having a back and arms; sofa; chesterfield: *Some davenports can be opened up to make a bed.* *n.*

daw·dle (do′dəl or dô′dəl) waste time; be idle; loiter: *Don't dawdle over your work.* *v.*, **daw·dled, daw·dling.**

dawn (don or dôn) 1 the beginning of day; the first light in the east. 2 the beginning: *before the dawn of history.* 3 grow light: *The day dawned bright and clear.* 4 grow clear to the eye or mind: *It dawned on me that she was expecting a present.* 5 begin; appear: *A new era of peace is dawning.* 1, 2 *n.*, 3–5 *v.*

day (dā) 1 the time of light between sunrise and sunset: *Days are longer in summer than in winter.* 2 the 24 hours of day and night; the time the earth takes to turn on its axis. 3 the hours for work; the working day: *She works an eight-hour day.* 4 a certain period of time: *the present day, in days of old.* *n.*

call it a day, *Informal.* stop work: *I'm tired; let's call it a day.*

win the day, be victorious; win a game, battle or contest: *The debate is over; our side has won the day.*

day·break (dā′brāk′) dawn; the time when it first begins to get light in the morning. *n.*

day–care centre (dā′ker′) a place where babies and small children are cared for during the day: *She takes her baby to a day-care centre each morning before she goes to work.*

day·dream (dā′drēm′) 1 a dreamy thinking about pleasant things. 2 think about pleasant things in a dreamy way: *She spent a whole hour just daydreaming.* 1, *n.*, 2 *v.*

day·light (dā′līt′) 1 the light of day: *Artificial light is not so good for the eyes as daylight.* 2 daytime. 3 dawn; daybreak: *He was up at daylight.* *n.*

daylight–saving time time that is one hour ahead of standard time, giving more daylight in summer evenings. Clocks are set ahead one hour in the spring and back one hour in the fall.

day nursery day-care centre.

day·time (dā′tīm′) the time when it is day and not night. *n.*

daze (dāz) 1 confuse; bewilder: *She was so dazed by her fall that she didn't know where she was. The child was dazed by the sudden noise and bright lights.* 2 a confused state of mind; bewilderment: *He was in a daze from the accident and he could not understand what was happening.* 1 *v.*, **dazed, daz·ing;** 2 *n.*

daz·zle (daz′əl) 1 hurt the eyes with too bright a light, or with quick-moving lights: *To look straight at the sun dazzles the eyes.* 2 overcome the sight or the mind with anything very bright or beautiful: *The*

hat, āge, fär; let, ēqual, tėrm; it, īce
hot, ōpen, ôrder; oil, out; cup, pu̇t, rüle
əbove, takən, pencəl, lemən, circəs
ch, child; ng, long; sh, ship
th, thin; ᴛʜ, then; zh, measure

pianist's fine performance dazzled the audience. 3 a dazzling, bewildering brightness: *the dazzle of powerful electric lights.* 1, 2 *v.*, **daz·zled, daz·zling;** 3 *n.*

d.c. direct current.

DDT or **D.D.T.** an odorless, powerful poison formerly used to kill insects: *DDT may no longer be used in Canada because of the harm it can do to people and animals other than insects.*

☛ **DDT** is an abbreviation for *dichloro-diphenyl-trichloroethane.*

de– a prefix meaning: **1** the opposite of: *Decipher means to do the opposite of writing in cipher. Defrost means do the opposite of producing frost.* **2** down: *Depress means press down.* **3** away, off: *Deport means send (carry) away. Derail means cause to go off the rails.*

dea·con (dē′kən) **1** an officer of a church who helps the minister in church duties not connected with preaching. **2** a member of the clergy immediately below a priest in rank. *n.*

dead (ded) **1** no longer living; that has died: *The flowers in my garden are dead.* **2 the dead,** all who no longer have life: *We remember the dead of our wars on Remembrance Day.* **3** without life: *Stone is dead matter.* **4** dull or quiet; not active: *a dead game, a dead party.* **5** without force, power, spirit, feeling, activity, etc.: *This old battery is dead.* **6** sure: *a dead shot, a dead certainty.* **7** complete: *dead silence, a dead loss.* **8** completely; fully: *He was dead wrong that time.* **9** directly; straight: *Walk dead ahead three kilometres.* **10** the time when there is the least life stirring: *the dead of night.* 1, 3, 4-7 *adj.*, 2, 10 *n.*, 8, 9 *adv.*

dead·en (ded′ən) make dull or weak; lessen the force of: *Some medicines are given to deaden pain. The force of the blow was deadened by his heavy clothing. v.*

dead end **1** a street or passage closed at one end so that there is only one entrance or exit. **2** a point in a discussion, plan, etc. beyond which progress is impossible: *When the committee reached a dead end, they decided to drop the plan.*

dead letter **1** a letter that no one has claimed or that cannot be delivered or returned to the sender because an address is wrong, impossible to read, or incomplete.

dead·line (ded′līn′) a time limit; the latest possible time to do something: *The newspaper reporter didn't have his story ready before the deadline, so it couldn't be published. n.*

dead·lock (ded′lok′) **1** a position in which it is impossible to act or continue because of disagreement: *The employers and strikers were at a deadlock.* **2** bring or come to such a position: *The talks were deadlocked for weeks.* 1 *n.*, 2 *v.*

dead·ly (ded′lē) **1** causing death; likely to cause death; fatal: *a deadly disease, the deadly berries of a poisonous bush.* **2** like that of death: *deadly paleness.* **3** filled with hatred that lasts till death: *The two warriors were deadly enemies.* **4** extremely: *'Washing dishes is deadly dull,' she said.* **5** dull: *The party was a deadly affair.* 1–3, 5 *adj.*, **dead·li·er, dead·li·est;** 4 *adv.*

deaf (def) **1** not able to hear. **2** not able to hear well. **3** not willing to hear: *A miser is deaf to all requests for money. adj.* **—deaf′ness,** *n.*

deaf·en (def′ən) **1** make deaf: *He was deafened by an accident in childhood.* **2** stun with noise: *The explosion deafened her. v.*

deal (dēl) **1** have to do: *Arithmetic deals with numbers.* **2** act or behave: *Teachers should deal fairly with their pupils.* **3** carry on business; buy and sell: *This garage deals in gasoline, oil, tires, etc.* **4** *Informal.* a bargain: *She got a good deal on her television set.* **5** give: *One fighter dealt the other a hard blow.* **6** give out among several; distribute: *In card games, one player deals the cards to the others.* **7** giving out; an arrangement or plan: *a new deal.* 1–3, 5, 6 *v.*, **dealt, deal·ing;** 4, 7 *n.*

deal out, give out or distribute.

a good deal or **great deal,** a large part or portion; a large amount: *A great deal of her money is spent on holiday trips.*

square deal, fair treatment; honest service: *You will get a square deal at that store.*

deal·er (dēl′ər) **1** a person who trades; any person who is in the business of buying and selling: *a car dealer, an art dealer.* **2** in card games, a person who gives the cards to each of the players. *n.*

deal·ing (dēl′ing) **1** a way of doing business: *He is respected for his honest dealing.* **2** behavior toward others: *He is honored for his fair dealing.* **3 dealings,** *pl.* **a** business activities: *The fur trader was honest in his dealings with the trappers.* **b** actions; behavior: *The teacher tried to be fair in all his dealings with students. n.*

dealt (delt) See **deal.** *The cards are dealt. v.*

dear (dēr) **1** much loved; precious: *His sister was very dear to him.* **2** a darling; a dear one: *'Come, my dear,' said Mother.* **3** much valued. *Dear* is used as a polite form of address at the beginning of letters: *Dear Sir, Dear Isabel.* **4** high in price; expensive: *Fresh fruit is not so dear these days.* **5** very much; much: *That mistake will cost you dear.* **6** an exclamation of surprise, trouble, etc.: *Oh, dear! My head aches.* 1, 3, 4 *adj.*, 2 *n.*, 5 *adv.*, 6 *interj.*

☛ **Dear** and **deer** are pronounced the same.

dear·ly (dēr′lē) **1** fondly: *Mother loves her baby dearly.* **2** at a high price: *He bought his new car dearly.* **3** very much: *You will regret your foolish behavior dearly. adv.*

dearth (dėrth) scarceness; lack; too small a supply: *There was a dearth of grain during the drought. n.*

death (deth) **1** the act of dying; the ending of life in human beings, animals, or plants: *He faced death with courage.* **2** any ending that is like dying: *the death of an empire.* **3** the state or condition of being dead: *In death his face looked peaceful.* **4** any condition like that of being dead. *n.*

at death's door, about to die; almost dead.

put to death, kill.

to death, beyond endurance; extremely: *She was bored to death.*

to the death, to the last resource; to the last extreme: *fight to the death.*

death·less (deth′lis) immortal; eternal. *adj.*

death·ly (deth′lē) 1 like that of death: *Her face was deathly pale.* 2 causing death: *a deathly famine. adj.*

de·base (di bās′) 1 lessen the value of: *debased coinage.* 2 dishonor; lessen the moral worth of: *You debase yourself by evil actions. v.,* **de·based, de·bas·ing.**

de·bate (di bāt′) 1 consider; discuss; talk about reasons for and against: *I am debating buying a car.* 2 a discussion of reasons for and against: *There has been much debate about which girl to choose for captain.* 3 a public argument for and against a question in a meeting: *We heard a debate over the radio.* 4 a discussion that takes place in Parliament: *The debate on defence costs lasted for two weeks.* 5 argue or discuss both sides of a subject in public. 1, 5 *v.,* **de·bat·ed, de·bat·ing;** 2–4 *n.*

de·bris (də brē′ or dā′brē) scattered fragments; ruins; rubbish: *The street was covered with debris from the explosion. n.*

debt (det) 1 something owed to another: *He paid off all his debts in a year.* 2 an obligation to pay; the condition of owing: *to get out of debt. He is in debt to the automobile dealer for his car. n.*

debt·or (det′ər) a person who owes something to another: *If I borrow a dollar from you, I am your debtor. n.*

Dec. December.

dec·ade (dek′ād) ten years: *From 1900 to 1910 was a decade. Two decades are 20 years. n.*

de·cay (di kā′) 1 become rotten: *Old fruits and vegetables decay. Your teeth decay if they are not cared for.* 2 a rotting condition: *The decay in the tree trunk had not proceeded very far.* 3 grow less in power, strength, wealth, or beauty: *Many nations have grown great and then decayed.* 4 growing less in power, strength, wealth, or beauty. 1, 3 *v.,* 2, 4 *n.*

de·cease (di sēs′) 1 death: *His decease was sudden.* 2 die. 1 *n.,* 2 *v.,* **de·ceased, de·ceas·ing.**

de·ceased (di sēst′) 1 dead: *The deceased man's belongings were sent to his wife.* **2 the deceased,** a particular dead person or persons: *The deceased had been a famous actor.* 1 *adj.,* 2 *n.*

de·ceit (di sēt′) 1 a deceiving, lying, or cheating; the act of making a person believe as true something that is false: *The girl was guilty of deceit.* 2 a dishonest trick; a lie spoken or acted. 3 the quality in a person that makes him tell lies or cheat. *n.*

de·ceit·ful (di sēt′fəl) 1 ready or willing to deceive or lie: *a deceitful person.* 2 deceiving; misleading: *a deceitful act. adj.*

de·ceive (di sēv′) 1 make someone believe as true something that is false; mislead: *The boy tried to deceive his mother, but she knew what he had done.* 2 lie; use deceit. *v.,* **de·ceived, de·ceiv·ing.**

De·cem·ber (di sem′bər) the twelfth and last month of the year: *December has 31 days. n.*

☛ **December** came into English through Old French from the Latin name for this month, *December,* from *decem,* meaning 'ten.' December was the tenth month of the ancient Roman calendar.

de·cen·cy (dē′sən sē) 1 the state of being decent; proper behavior: *Common decency requires that you pay for the window you broke.* **2 decencies,** *pl.* the things required for a proper standard of living. *n., pl.* **de·cen·cies.**

de·cent (dē′sənt) 1 respectable; proper and right: *It is not decent to make fun of a crippled person. All Father's stories were decent.* 2 good enough; fairly good; adequate: *I get decent marks at school.* 3 not severe; rather kind: *His boss was very decent about his being late for work. adj.*

de·cep·tion (di sep′shən) 1 the act of deceiving: *She used deception to get what she wanted.* 2 a trick meant to deceive; a fraud or sham: *Dishonest businessmen are often guilty of deception. n.*

de·cep·tive (di sep′tiv) 1 deceiving: *There was a deceptive silence before the attack began.* 2 meant to deceive: *The player scored on a deceptive shot. adj.*

DECIBELS	SOUNDS
1	faintest sound heard
10	whisper; rustling of leaves
30	quiet conversation
50	quiet radio; average home
70	typewriter; average factory
90	police whistle; heavy traffic
110	deafening factory noise
130	sound vibrations *felt*, as with thunder or a jet plane close by

dec·i·bel (des′ə bel′) a unit for measuring the loudness of a sound. *n.*

de·cide (di sīd′) 1 settle: *Let us decide the question by tossing a coin.* 2 give judgment: *Mother decided in favor of a small car.* 3 resolve; make up one's mind: *He decided to be a sailor. v.,* **de·cid·ed, de·cid·ing.**

de·cid·ed (di sīd′id) 1 definite; unquestionable: *The home team had a decided advantage.* 2 resolute; firm; determined: *Tom was a very decided person. adj.* —**de·cid′ed·ly,** *adv.*

☛ **Decided** and **decisive** should not be confused. **Decided** means 'definite': *His height gave him a decided advantage in the game.* **Decisive** means 'having or giving a definite or clear result': *The battle ended in a decisive victory.*

dec·i·mal (des′ə məl) 1 based on or having to do with the number 10: *The metric system is a decimal system of measurement.* 2 a numeral having a decimal point; decimal number: *The numerals 23.6, 3.09, and 0.728 are decimals.* 3 decimal point: *Put the decimal between the units and the tenths.* 1 *adj.,* 2, 3 *n.*

decimal fraction 1 a decimal number. 2 a decimal number less than one.

decimal number a number including a fraction whose denominator is 10, 100, 1000, etc., usually written in decimal form. *Examples:* 0.2, 9.93, 4.1.

decimal point the period between the units and the tenths of a decimal fraction: *The decimal point separates the whole number from the fractional part of a decimal number.*

dec·i·me·tre (des′i mē′tər) a measure of length equal to ten centimetres: *One cubic decimetre is equal to one litre. Symbol:* dm *n.* Also spelled **decimeter.**

de·ci·pher (di sī′fər) 1 make out the meaning of something that is not clear: *I can't decipher this poor handwriting. We will try to decipher the mystery.* 2 change something in cipher or code to ordinary

hat, āge, fär; let, ēqual, tėrm; it, īce
hot, ōpen, ôrder; oil, out; cup, pu̇t, rüle
ə bove, takən, pencəl, lemən, circəs
ch, child; ng, long; sh, ship
th, thin; ᴛʜ, then; zh, measure

language: *The spy deciphered the secret message.* *v.*

de·ci·sion (di sizh′ən) **1** the act of deciding; making up one's mind: *He had not yet come to a decision about which color to use.* **2** a judgment reached or given: *The judge gives a decision in a lawsuit.* **3** firmness; determination: *A man of decision makes up his mind what to do and then does it.* *n.*

de·ci·sive (di sī′siv) **1** having or giving a clear result; settling something beyond question: *a decisive victory.* **2** having or showing decision: *a decisive answer.* *adj.*
☛ See note at **decided.**

deck (dek) **1** one of the floors or platforms extending from side to side and often from end to end of a ship: *The upper, main, middle, and lower decks of a ship resemble the storeys of a house.* **2** a part or floor resembling the deck of a ship: *a sun deck, the deck of an airplane.* **3** a pack of playing cards. **4** adorn; cover; dress: *She was decked out in white linen.* 1–3 *n.*, 4 *v.*

dec·la·ra·tion (dek′lə rā′shən) **1** a public statement or formal announcement: *a declaration of war.* **2** a strong statement: *Nobody believed his declaration that he had never been there.* **3** a statement acknowledging possession of income, goods, etc. for purposes of taxation. *n.*

de·clare (di kler′) **1** announce publicly or formally; make known: *Parliament has the power to declare war.* **2** say openly or strongly: *The boy declared that he would never go back to school again.* **3** acknowledge being in possession of income, goods, etc.: *Travellers returning to Canada must declare to the customs officers what they have bought abroad.* *v.*, **de·clared, de·clar·ing.**

de·cline (di klīn′) **1** refuse politely: *The man declined my offer of help. They asked her to go along, but she declined.* **2** bend or slope down: *The hill declines to a fertile valley.* **3** grow less in strength and power; grow worse: *He is getting old and his strength has begun to decline.* **4** a losing of strength, wealth, beauty, etc.; growing worse: *the decline of a person's strength.* **5** falling to a lower level; sinking: *the decline of the sun to the horizon, a decline in prices.* 1–3 *v.*, **de·clined, de·clin·ing;** 4, 5 *n.*

de·com·pose (dē′kəm pōz′) **1** decay; rot or become rotten: *Fruit decomposes rapidly in the heat.* **2** separate a substance into what it is made of: *A prism decomposes sunlight into its many colors.* *v.*, **de·com·posed, de·com·pos·ing.**

de·com·po·si·tion (dē′kom pə zish′ ən) the act or process of decomposing: *fruit spoiled by decomposition, the decomposition of water into hydrogen and oxygen.* *n.*

dec·o·rate (dek′ə rāt′) **1** make beautiful; trim; adorn: *We decorated the Christmas tree with colored lights.* **2** paint or paper a room, house, etc. **3** give a badge, ribbon, or medal to: *The general decorated the soldier for his brave act.* *v.*, **dec·o·rat·ed, dec·o·rat·ing.**

dec·o·ra·tion (dek′ə rā′shən) **1** the act of decorating. **2** anything used to decorate; an ornament. **3** a badge, ribbon, or medal given as an honor: *The soldier wore many decorations.* *n.*

dec·o·ra·tive (dek′ə rə tiv or dek′ə rā′tiv) decorating; ornamental; helping to make beautiful: *The flowered curtains were highly decorative.* *adj.*

dec·o·ra·tor (dek′ə rā′ tər) a person who decorates. An **interior decorator** plans and arranges the furnishings of homes, clubs, and offices. *n.*

de·co·rum (di kô′rəm) propriety of action, speech, dress, etc.: *You behave with decorum when you do what is fit and proper.* *n.*

de·coy (di koi′ for 1, 4 and 5, dē′koi for 2, 3 and 6) **1** lead wild birds, animals, etc. into a trap or near the hunter. **2** an artificial bird used to lure real birds into a trap or within range of a hunter's gun. **3** a bird or other animal trained to lure others of its kind into a trap. **4** lead or tempt into danger; entice. **5** *Cdn.* deke. **6** any person or thing used to lead or tempt into danger; a lure. 1, 4, 5 *v.*, 2, 3, 6 *n.*

de·crease (di krēs′ for 1 and 2, dē′krēs for 3 and 4) **1** become less: *Hunger decreases as one eats.* **2** make less: *decrease prices.* **3** becoming less: *A decrease in humidity made the hot weather more comfortable.* **4** the amount by which a thing becomes less or is made less: *The decrease in temperature was at least ten degrees.* 1, 2 *v.*, **de·creased, de·creas·ing;** 3, 4 *n.*

de·cree (di krē′) **1** something ordered or settled by authority; an official decision; law: *A decree of the government set the date of Thanksgiving Day.* **2** order or settle by authority: *The government decreed that the election would take place July 8.* 1 *n.*, 2 *v.*, **de·creed, de·cree·ing.**

ded·i·cate (ded′ə kāt′) **1** set apart for a purpose: *The land on which the battle was fought was dedicated to the memory of the soldiers who had died there.* **2** give up wholly or earnestly to some person or purpose: *The minister dedicated his life to the service of God.* **3** address a book or other work to a friend or patron: *The author dedicated his book to his teacher as a mark of respect.* *v.*, **ded·i·cat·ed, ded·i·cat·ing.**

ded·i·ca·tion (ded′ə kā′shən) **1** setting apart or being set apart for a sacred or solemn purpose: *The dedication of the new church took place yesterday.* **2** very great and constant interest; close attachment; complete loyalty (to some person or purpose): *a dedication to music. Because of his dedication to his king, the baron refused to join the revolt.* **3** the words dedicating a book, poem, etc. to a friend or patron: *The dedication appears at the front of the book.* *n.*

de·duce (di dyüs′ or di düs′) reach a conclusion by reasoning; infer: *After looking at the evidence, the inspector deduced the cause of the fire.* *v.*, **de·duced, de·duc·ing.**

de·duct (di dukt′) take away; subtract. *v.*

de·duc·tion (di duk′shən) **1** the act of taking away; subtraction: *No deduction in salary is made for absence due to illness.* **2** the amount deducted. **3** the act of reaching a conclusion by reasoning; inference: *A person using deduction reasons from general laws to particular cases.* **4** a conclusion reached by reasoning: *The detective made the deduction after a careful study of the facts.* *n.*

deed (dēd) **1** something done; an act. **2** a brave, skilful, or unusual act: *The deeds of Joan of Arc.* **3** an action; doing; performance: *a good deed. Deeds, not words, are needed.* **4** a written or printed agreement: *The buyer of land receives a deed to the property from the former owner.* **5** transfer by deed: *He deeded his house to his daughter.* 1–4 *n.,* 5 *v.*

deem (dēm) think; believe; consider: *The lawyer deemed it unwise to take the case to court. v.*

deep (dēp) **1** going a long way down from the top or surface: *The ocean is deep here. The men dug a deep well to get pure water.* **2** far down; far on: *The men dug deep before they found water.* **3** going a long way back from the front: *The lot on which the house stands is 40 metres deep.* **4** low in pitch: *My father has a deep voice.* **5** requiring or showing much thought and study: *Such a deep book has to be read slowly.* **6** earnest; heartfelt: *Deep feeling is hard to put into words.* **7** strong; great; intense; extreme: *A person in a deep sleep is not easily wakened.* **8 the deep,** the sea. 1, 3–7 *adj.,* 2 *adv.,* 8 *n.* **—deep′ly,** *adv.*

deep·en (dēp′ən) make or become deeper: *It was necessary to deepen the ditch. His frown deepened as he became more worried. v.*

White-tailed deer — about 1 m high at the shoulder

deer (dēr) one of a group of cud-chewing animals with long legs and small, split hooves, including the elk, caribou, moose, mule deer, reindeer, and white-tailed deer: *Deer are distantly related to cattle, but have antlers instead of horns. n., pl.* **deer.**

☛ **Deer** and **dear** are pronounced the same.

deer·skin (dēr′skin′) **1** the hide of a deer. **2** leather made from deerskin: *deerskin moccasins.* **3 deerskins,** *pl.* clothing made from this leather. *n.*

def. definition.

de·face (di fās′) spoil the appearance of; mar: *Thoughtless children have defaced the desks by marking on them. v.,* **de·faced, de·fac·ing.**

de·feat (di fēt′) **1** overcome; win a victory over: *to defeat the enemy in battle, to defeat another school in basketball.* **2** make useless; undo: *defeat someone's plans.* **3** an overcoming or conquering: *Tom's defeat of Joe.* **4** being overcome or conquered: *Joe's defeat by Tom.* 1, 2 *v.,* 3, 4 *n.*

de·fect (dē′fekt or di fekt′) **1** a fault; a blemish or imperfection: *A piece of cloth sometimes shows defects in weaving.* **2** the lack of something needed for completeness; a falling short: *A bad temper was the one defect in his kind and generous nature. n.*

de·fec·tive (di fek′tiv) not complete; not perfect; faulty: *We returned the toaster because it was defective. adj.*

de·fence or **de·fense** (di fens′) **1** any thing, act, or word that defends, guards, or protects: *Years ago walls were built around cities as a defence against attack. A heavy, warm coat is a defence against a cold wind.* **2** the act of defending: *The armed forces are responsible for the defence of the country.* **3** in games, a team or player defending a goal: *Our hockey team has a good defence.* **4** a defendant and his lawyer: *a witness for the defence. n.* **—de·fence′less** or **de·fense′less,** *adj.*

de·fence·man or **de·fense·man** (di fens′mən) a player in hockey, football, etc. whose job is to prevent the opposing player from approaching the goal. *n., pl.* **de·fence·men** or **de·fense·men** (di fens′mən).

de·fend (di fend′) **1** keep safe; guard from attack or harm; protect. **2** act, speak, or write in favor of: *The newspapers defended the mayor's action.* **3** fight or contest a claim or lawsuit. *v.* **—de·fend′er,** *n.*

de·fend·ant (di fen′dənt) a person formally accused or sued in a court of law: *The defendant pleaded not guilty to the charge of theft. n.*

de·fense (di fens′) See **defence.**

de·fen·sive (di fen′siv) **1** defending; ready to defend; intended to defend: *France fought a defensive war.* **2** the position or attitude of defence: *After its attack failed, the army returned to the defensive.* 1 *adj.,* 2 *n.*
on the defensive, ready to defend, apologize, or explain: *She has been criticized so much that she is always on the defensive.*

de·fer[1] (di fėr′) put off; delay: *The examinations were deferred because so many children were sick. v.,* **de·ferred, de·fer·ring.**

de·fer[2] (di fėr′) yield; submit to another's judgment, opinion, or wishes: *He deferred to his sister's wishes. v.,* **de·ferred, de·fer·ring.**

def·er·ence (def′ər əns) **1** the act of yielding to the judgment, opinion, wishes, etc. of another: *The mayor showed no deference to public opinion.* **2** respect; regard: *The insolent children should have shown more deference to their principal. n.*
in deference to, out of respect or regard for: *In deference to his father's wishes, he worked hard at his studies.*

de·fi·ance (di fī′əns) **1** defying; the act of standing up against authority and refusing to recognize or obey it: *He shouted his defiance at the warden.* **2** open resistance to power; open refusal to obey: *The students showed defiance. n.*
in defiance of, in open opposition to; showing contempt or disregard for: *His rebellious behavior was in defiance of his father's wishes.*

de·fi·ant (di fī′ənt) showing defiance; openly resisting or offering a challenge; hostile: *The boy said, 'I won't!' in a defiant manner. The tiger gave a defiant roar when it was cornered. adj.*

de·fi·cien·cy (di fish′ən sē) **1** a lack or absence of something needed: *Some illnesses are caused by a deficiency of certain vitamins.* **2** the amount by which a thing falls short or is too small: *If something you want to buy costs $10 and you have only $6, the deficiency is $4. n., pl.* **de·fi·cien·cies.**

de·fi·cient (di fish′ənt) lacking; incomplete; not enough: *His diet was deficient in protein. adj.*

de·file[1] (di fīl′) **1** make dirty, bad-smelling, or in any way disgusting. **2** destroy the pureness or cleanness of anything sacred: *The rebels defiled the church by using it as an arms dump. v.,* **de·filed, de·fil·ing.**

hat, āge, fär; let, ēqual, tėrm; it, īce
hot, ōpen, ôrder; oil, out; cup, pu̇t, rüle
əbove, takən, pencəl, lemən, circəs
ch, child; ng, long; sh, ship
th, thin; ᴛʜ, then; zh, measure

de·file[2] (di fīl′ or dē′fīl) **1** to march in a line. **2** a narrow way through which troops can march only in narrow columns. **3** a steep and narrow valley. 1 *v.,* **de·filed, de·fil·ing;** 2, 3 *n.*

de·fine (di fīn′) **1** make clear the meaning of; explain the nature of: *A dictionary defines words.* **2** fix; settle; describe in detail: *The powers of the courts are defined by law.* **3** settle the limits of: *The boundary between Canada and the United States is defined by treaty.* **4** make distinct in outline; cause to stand out by contrast: *The city's skyline was clearly defined against the prairie sky.* *v.,* **de·fined, de·fin·ing.**

def·i·nite (def′ə nit) **1** clearly defined; precise; exact: *Ten is a definite number.* **2** clear; not vague: *Not being sure of his facts, he refused to give a definite answer.* *adj.*

definite article the word **the.**

de·fi·nite·ly (def′ə nit lē) **1** in a definite manner. **2** certainly: *Will you go? Definitely.* *adv.*

def·i·ni·tion (def′ə nish′ən) **1** the act of explaining the nature of a thing; a making clear of the meaning of a word or group of words: *Dictionaries are concerned with definition.* **2** a statement in which the nature of a thing is explained or the meaning of a word or group of words is made clear: *The definitions in this dictionary are numbered.* *n.*

de·form (di fôrm′) **1** spoil the form or shape of: *Shoes that are too tight deform the feet.* **2** make ugly: *Anger deforms the face.* *v.*

de·form·i·ty (di fôr′mə tē) **1** a part of the body that is not as it should be, such as a hump on the back, or a stump instead of a foot. **2** the state or fact of being deformed: *Many deformities of the body can now be corrected.* **3** an ugliness of mind or body. *n., pl.* **de·form·i·ties.**

de·fraud (di frod′ or di frôd′) to cheat; take money, rights, etc. away from by fraud: *The dishonest lawyer defrauded the widow of her savings.* *v.*

de·frost (dē frost′) remove frost or ice from: *to defrost a refrigerator.* *v.*

deft (deft) skilful; nimble; clever: *A violinist's fingers must be deft.* *adj.*

de·fy (di fī′) **1** set oneself openly against authority; resist boldly: *Now that the boy was earning his own living he could defy his father's strict rules. The thief defied the law and was arrested.* **2** withstand; resist: *This strong fort defies capture.* **3** challenge a person to do something: *She defied him to prove that she had made a mistake.* *v.,* **de·fied, de·fy·ing.**

de·grade (di grād′) **1** reduce to a lower rank, often as a punishment; take away a position or an honor from: *The captain was degraded for disobeying orders.* **2** make bad; lower in value; debase: *You degrade yourself when you tell a lie.* *v.,* **de·grad·ed, de·grad·ing.**

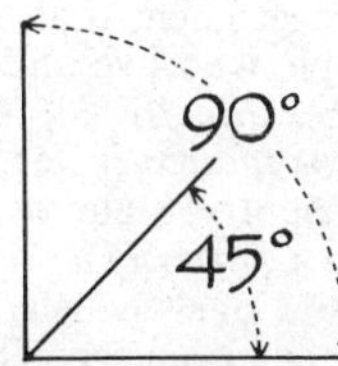

Two angles with the degrees marked

de·gree (di grē′) **1** a step in a scale; a stage in a process: *There are many degrees of rank in the armed forces.* **2** the amount or extent: *The degree of danger was great. To what degree are you interested in reading?* **3** a unit for measuring temperature: *The boiling point of water is 100 degrees Celsius. Symbol:* ° **4** a unit for measuring an angle or an arc of a circle: *In the diagram, one angle measures 45 degrees and the other 90 degrees.* **5** rank: *A princess is a lady of high degree.* **6** a title given to a student by a university or college for successfully completing a certain course of studies: *a Bachelor of Arts degree, a Master of Science degree.* *n.*

by degrees, gradually: *By degrees the lake became warm enough to swim in.*

de·hy·drate (dē hī′drāt) **1** take water or moisture from; dry: *Milk can be dehydrated to form a powder.* **2** lose water or moisture: *We get thirsty in hot weather because our bodies dehydrate when we sweat.* *v.*

deign (dān) condescend; think fit: *So conceited a man would never deign to notice us.* *v.*

de·i·ty (dē′ə tē) **1** a god or goddess: *Jupiter was the ruler of the ancient Roman deities.* **2 the Deity,** God. *n., pl.* **de·i·ties.**

de·ject·ed (di jek′tid) sad; discouraged: *The defeated boxer wore a dejected frown.* *adj.* **—de·ject′ed·ly,** *adv.*

deke (dēk) *Cdn. Slang.* in hockey: **1** draw a player out of position by faking a play in one direction or way and then making it in another. **2** a play made in this way. 1 *v.,* **deked, dek·ing;** 2 *n.*

de·lay (di lā′) **1** put off till a later time: *They had to delay the party for a week.* **2** the act of putting off till a later time: *The delay upset their plans.* **3** make late; keep waiting; hinder the progress of: *The accident delayed the train for two hours.* **4** be late; go slowly; stop along the way: *She asked him not to delay on his errand.* **5** stopping along the way; a wait: *They could afford no further delay.* 1, 3, 4 *v.,* 2, 5 *n.*

del·e·gate (del′ə git or del′ə gāt′ for 1, del′ə gāt′ for 2 and 3) **1** a person given power or authority to act for others; a representative: *Our club sent two delegates to the meeting.* **2** appoint or send a person as a representative: *The children delegated her to buy the flowers.* **3** give over the power or authority to act to some other person or institution: *The provinces have delegated some of their rights to the Federal Government.* 1 *n.,* 2, 3 *v.,* **del·e·gat·ed, del·e·gat·ing.**

del·e·ga·tion (del′ə gā′shən) **1** delegating or being delegated: *the delegation of authority.* **2** a group of chosen representatives: *Each club sent a delegation to the meeting.* *n.*

de·lete (di lēt′) strike out or take out anything written or printed; remove; cross out: *He deleted the last sentence from his composition.* *v.,* **de·let·ed, de·let·ing.**

de·lib·er·ate (di lib′ər it for 1, 2 and 3, di lib′ər āt′ for 4 and 5) **1** intended; done on purpose; thought over beforehand: *His excuse was a deliberate lie.* **2** slow and careful in deciding what to do: *A deliberate person takes* *a long time to make up his mind.* 3 slow but with firmness and purpose: *The old man walked with deliberate steps.* 4 think over carefully; consider: *She was deliberating on where to hang the new picture.* 5 talk over reasons for and against; debate: *Parliament was deliberating the question of raising taxes.* 1–3 *adj.,* 4, 5 *v.,* **de·lib·er·at·ed, de·lib·er·at·ing. —de·lib′er·ate·ly,** *adv.*

de·lib·er·a·tion (di lib′ər ā′shən) 1 careful thought: *After long deliberation, he decided not to go.* 2 a talking about reasons for or against something; debate: *the deliberations of the Legislative Assembly.* 3 slowness and care: *He aimed his gun with great deliberation.* *n.*

del·i·ca·cy (del′ə kə sē) 1 fineness of weave, quality, or make; slightness and grace: *delicacy of silks or colors, the delicacy of a baby's skin.* 2 fineness of feeling for small differences: *delicacy of hearing or touch.* 3 need of care, skill, or tact: *A matter of great delicacy is one that requires careful handling.* 4 thought for the feelings of others. 5 a shrinking from what one considers offensive or not modest. 6 weakness; the condition of being easily hurt or made ill: *The child's delicacy was a worry to his parents.* 7 a choice kind of food; dainty: *Nuts and candy are delicacies.* *n., pl.* **del·i·ca·cies.**

del·i·cate (del′ə kit) 1 gently pleasing the senses; mild; soft: *delicate foods, delicate colors, delicate fragrance.* 2 of fine weave, quality, or make; thin; easily broken: *A spider's web is very delicate.* 3 requiring care, skill, or tact: *a delicate situation, a delicate question.* 4 very quickly responding to slight changes of condition; finely sensitive: *delicate instruments, a delicate sense of touch.* 5 easily hurt or made ill: *She is a very delicate child.* *adj.*

de·li·cious (di lish′əs) very pleasing or satisfying; delightful, especially to taste or smell: *a delicious cake.* *adj.* **—de·li′cious·ly,** *adv.*

de·light (di līt′) 1 great pleasure; joy: *She took great delight in her dolls.* 2 something that gives great pleasure: *Dancing is her delight.* 3 please greatly: *The circus delighted the audience.* 4 have great pleasure: *Children delight in surprises.* 1, 2 *n.,* 3, 4 *v.*

de·light·ed (di līt′id) greatly pleased; joyful; glad. *adj.* **—de·light′ed·ly,** *adv.*

de·light·ful (di līt′fəl) giving joy; very pleasing: *a delightful ride, a delightful person.* *adj.*

de·lin·quent (di ling′kwənt) 1 failing to do what is required by law or duty; guilty of a fault or an offence. 2 a delinquent person; offender; criminal. 1 *adj.,* 2 *n.*

de·lir·i·ous (di lir′ē əs) 1 out of one's senses for a short time; wandering in mind; raving: *The fever had made him delirious.* 2 wildly excited: *When the good news came, she was delirious with excitement.* *adj.*

de·lir·i·um (di lir′ ē əm) 1 a disorder of the mind that occurs during fevers, insanity, drunkenness, etc.: *Delirium is characterized by restlessness, excitement, strange ideas, and wild talk.* 2 wild excitement. *n.*

de·liv·er (di liv′ər) 1 carry and give out; distribute: *The mailman delivers letters.* 2 give up; hand over: *He delivered his mother's message to Mrs. Brown.* 3 give forth in words: *The traveller delivered an interesting talk about his journey. The jury delivered its verdict.* 4 strike; throw: *The fighter delivered a blow.* 5 set free; save from evil or trouble: *'Deliver us from evil.'* 6 help in the birth of: *The doctor delivered the baby at noon.* *v.* **—de·liv′er·er,** *n.*

de·liv·er·ance (di liv′ər əns) a rescue; release; freedom: *The soldiers rejoiced in their deliverance from prison.* *n.*

de·liv·er·y (di liv′ər ē) 1 the act of carrying and handing over letters, goods, etc.: *Milk deliveries are made by most dairies.* 2 giving up; handing over: *The captive was released upon the delivery of his ransom.* 3 a manner of speaking; a way of giving a speech or lecture: *Our minister has an excellent delivery.* 4 the act of giving birth. 5 any act of delivering: *the delivery of a hard blow.* *n., pl.* **de·liv·er·ies.**

dell (del) a small, sheltered glen or valley, usually with trees in it. *n.*

del·ta (del′tə) the deposit of earth and sand, usually three-sided, that collects at the mouth of some rivers: *Part of Vancouver is in the delta of the Fraser River.* *n.*

de·lude (di lüd′) mislead; deceive: *He deluded himself into believing he would pass his examination without studying.* *v.,* **de·lud·ed, de·lud·ing.**

del·uge (del′yüj) 1 a great flood: *After the dam broke, the deluge washed away the bridge.* 2 a heavy fall of rain. 3 to flood; overflow: *Water deluged our cellar when the big pipe broke.* 4 overwhelm as if by a flood: *The movie star was deluged with requests for her autograph.* 5 any overwhelming rush: *Most stores have a deluge of orders just before Christmas.* 1, 2, 5 *n.,* 3, 4 *v.,* **del·uged, del·ug·ing.**

de·lu·sion (di lü′zhən) a false belief or opinion: *The insane man had a delusion that he was a king.* *n.*

de luxe or **de·luxe** (də lůks′ or də luks′) of especially good quality; splendid; costly. *adj.*

delve (delv) 1 search carefully for information: *The scholar delved in many libraries for facts.* 2 dig. *v.,* **delved, delv·ing.**

de·mand (di mand′) 1 ask for as a right: *The prisoner demanded a trial.* 2 ask for with authority: *The policeman demanded the boys' names.* 3 call for; require; need: *Training a puppy demands patience.* 4 a claim: *Their mother had many demands upon her time.* 5 a call; request: *Taxicabs are in great demand on rainy days. The supply of apples was greater than the demand.* 1–3 *v.,* 4, 5 *n.*

de·mean·or or **de·mean·our** (di mēn′ər) behavior; manner; the way a person acts and looks: *She has a quiet, modest demeanor.* *n.*

de·mer·it (dē mer′it) 1 a fault; defect. 2 a mark against a person's record for unsatisfactory behavior or performance: *She already has three demerits on her driver's licence.* *n.*

de·moc·ra·cy (di mok′rə sē) 1 a government that is elected and thus controlled by the people who live under it: *In a democracy the people rule either directly through meetings that all may attend or indirectly through elected representatives.* 2 a country, state, or community having such a government: *Canada is a democracy.* 3 the treatment of others as one's equals: *The teacher's democracy made him popular among his pupils.* *n., pl.* **de·moc·ra·cies.**

dem·o·crat (dem′ə krat′) 1 a person who believes

hat, āge, fär; let, ēqual, tėrm; it, īce
hot, ōpen, ôrder; oil, out; cup, pu̇t, rüle
əbove, takən, pencəl, lemən, circəs
ch, child; ng, long; sh, ship
th, thin; ᴛʜ, then; zh, measure

that a government should be run by the people who live under it. **2** a person who treats other people as his equals. *n.*

dem·o·crat·ic (dem′ə krat′ik) **1** of or like a democracy. **2** treating other people as one's equals: *The queen's democratic ways made her dear to her people. adj.* **—dem′o·crat′i·cal·ly,** *adv.*

de·mol·ish (di mol′ish) pull or tear down; destroy: *Shells and bombs demolished the fortress. v.*

de·mon (dē′mən) **1** an evil spirit; devil; fiend. **2** a very wicked or cruel person. *n.*

a demon for, a person having an unusual capacity, desire, or appetite for: *a demon for work, a demon for punishment, a demon for practising.*

dem·on·strate (dem′ən strāt′) **1** show clearly; prove: *Can you demonstrate that the earth is round?* **2** teach by carrying out experiments, or by showing and explaining samples or specimens: *If you will come with me to the laboratory, I will demonstrate the process to you.* **3** advertise a product or process by showing its use and explaining its operation: *The salesman demonstrated the electric drill by boring holes in a piece of steel plate.* **4** show openly: *He demonstrated his love for his niece by giving her a big hug.* **5** take part in a parade, meeting, etc. to show feelings, usually of protest or demand: *An angry crowd demanding more police protection demonstrated in front of the city hall. v.,* **dem·on·strat·ed, dem·on·strat·ing.**

dem·on·stra·tion (dem′ən strā′shən) **1** a clear proof: *a demonstration that the earth is round.* **2** the act of teaching by carrying out experiments or by showing and explaining samples or specimens. **3** an advertising display in which the use of a product or process is shown and its operation explained: *The saleswoman promised to give the teacher a demonstration of the new overhead projector.* **4** an open show or expression of feeling: *He greeted them with every demonstration of joy.* **5** a showing of feeling by a meeting, a parade, or the like: *The happy students put on a big victory demonstration after the game. n.*

de·mon·stra·tive (di mon′strə tiv) **1** expressing one's affections freely and openly: *The girl's demonstrative greeting embarrassed her shy brother.* **2** in grammar, pointing out: This *and* that *are demonstrative pronouns and also demonstrative adjectives.* **3** in grammar, a pronoun or adjective that points out: This *and* that *are demonstratives.* 1, 2 *adj.,* 3 *n.*

de·mote (di mōt′) put back to a lower grade; reduce in rank: *She was demoted from Grade 4 to Grade 3 when the teacher found she could not do the work. v.,* **de·mot·ed, de·mot·ing.**

de·mure (di myür′) **1** quiet and modest in behavior: *a demure young lady.* **2** seeming more modest and proper than one really is: *The tomboy wore a demure expression during the interview. adj.* **—de·mure′ly,** *adv.* **—de·mure′ness,** *n.*

den (den) **1** a wild animal's home; lair: *The bear's den was in a cave.* **2** a room, usually small and cosy, where a person can read, work or think in privacy: *He often retired to his den after dinner.* **3** a small, dirty, unattractive room, house, etc.: *The beggars lived in dens along the waterfront.* **4** a group of eight to ten Wolf Cubs. *n.*

den of thieves, a a place where thieves or criminals gather or live. **b** a group or band of thieves or criminals.

de·ni·al (di nī′əl) **1** saying that something is not so: *We listened to his denial of the existence of ghosts.* **2** saying that one does not hold to or believe in: *Galileo made a public denial of his statement that the earth went around the sun.* **3** refusing: *The principal's denial of our request seemed unfair. n.*

den·im (den′əm) **1** a heavy, coarse cotton cloth, used for overalls, work, and casual clothes, etc. **2 denims,** *pl.* overalls or pants made of this cloth. *n.*

de·nom·i·na·tion (di nom′ə nā′shən) **1** a name, especially a name for a class of things. **2** a religious group, usually represented by a number of local churches: *The Presbyterians and the Baptists are two Protestant denominations.* **3** a class or kind of units: *Reducing* $\frac{5}{12}$, $\frac{1}{3}$, *and* $\frac{1}{6}$ *to the same denomination gives* $\frac{5}{12}$, $\frac{4}{12}$, *and* $\frac{2}{12}$. *n.*

de·nom·i·na·tor (di nom′ə nā′tər) the number below the line in a fraction, which states the number of parts into which the whole has been divided: *In* $\frac{3}{4}$, *4 is the denominator, and 3 is the numerator. n.*

de·note (di nōt′) indicate; be the sign of; mean: *A fever usually denotes sickness. If a teacher writes 'Excellent' on a pupil's exercise, it denotes very good work. v.,* **de·not·ed, de·not·ing.**

de·nounce (di nouns′) **1** speak against; express strong disapproval of: *The judge denounced people who drive carelessly.* **2** give information against; accuse: *He denounced his own brother as a thief. v.,* **de·nounced, de·nounc·ing.**

dense (dens) **1** closely packed together; thick: *a dense forest, a dense fog.* **2** stupid; dull; slow-thinking: *His dense look showed he did not understand the problem. adj.,* **dens·er, dens·est.**

den·si·ty (den′sə tē) **1** closeness; compactness; thickness: *The density of the forest prevented us from seeing more than a little way ahead.* **2** the amount of matter in a particular unit of volume: *A cubic metre of lead has more mass than a cubic metre of wood, so we say lead has a greater density than wood. n., pl.* **den·si·ties.**

dent (dent) **1** a hollow made by a blow or pressure; a dint: *Bullets had made dents in the soldier's steel helmet.* **2** make a dent in; dint: *The blow from the hammer dented the table.* **3** become dented: *Soft wood dents easily.* 1 *n.,* 2, 3 *v.*

☛ **Dent** and **dint** are two forms that developed from the Old English word *dynt,* meaning 'a stroke or blow.' Because they were so similar in sound to the verb *indent,* originally meaning 'make a toothlike cut,' they came to mean the hollow or mark made by a blow. The modern phrase **by dint of** comes from the old expression *by dint of sword,* in which *dint* had its original meaning of 'a blow.' See also note at **indent.**

den·tal (den′təl) **1** of or for the teeth: *Proper dental care is important for healthy teeth.* **2** of, by, or for a dentist or his work: *dental bills, dental work. adj.*

den·ti·frice (den′tə fris) a paste, powder, or liquid for cleaning the teeth. *n.*

den·tin (den′tin) dentine. *n.*

den·tine (den′tēn) the hard, bony material beneath the enamel of teeth: *Dentine forms the main part of a tooth. n.*

den·tist (den′tist) a doctor whose work is the care of teeth: *A dentist fills cavities in teeth and cleans and extracts them. n.*

de·nun·ci·a·tion (di nun′sē ā′shən) public condemnation; an expression of strong disapproval: *The speaker began with a denunciation of everything. n.*

de·ny (di nī′) **1** say that something is not true: *The prisoner denied the charge made against him. The city officials deny that there is a flu epidemic.* **2** say that one does not hold to or believe in: *He denied the principles of communism.* **3** refuse: *I could not deny her the favor.* **4** disown; refuse to acknowledge: *He denied his signature. v.,* **de·nied, de·ny·ing.**

de·o·dor·ant (dē ō′dər ənt) a preparation that destroys odors. *n.*

de·part (di pärt′) **1** go away; leave: *The train departs at 6:15 p.m.* **2** turn away from; change: *He departed from his usual way of working. v.*

de·part·ment (di pärt′mənt) a separate part of some whole; special branch; division: *the toy department of a store, the fire department of a municipal government. n.*

department store a store that sells many different kinds of articles arranged in separate departments.

de·par·ture (di pär′chər) **1** the act of going away; leaving: *His departure was very sudden.* **2** turning away; a change: *a departure from their old custom.* **3** starting on a new course of action or thought: *Learning to ski will be a new departure for me, for I have never done anything like it. n.*

de·pend (di pend′) **1** be a result of; be controlled or influenced by: *The success of our picnic depends partly on the weather. Health depends on good food.* **2** get support; rely for help: *Children depend on their parents for food, clothing, and shelter.* **3** rely; trust: *You can depend on this timetable from the depot. v.*
that depends or **it depends,** the answer will be determined by certain conditions or actions which are not yet definitely known or understood: *'Can we go to the movies tomorrow?' 'That depends,' answered Mother.*

de·pend·a·ble (di pen′də bəl) reliable; trustworthy: *People like a dependable newspaper. adj.*

de·pend·ant (di pen′dənt) a person who depends on someone else for food, clothing, and shelter: *A man's children are usually his dependants. n.*

☛ Many people take care to use **dependent** for the adjective and **dependant** for the noun: *He has no dependent children. They have three dependants.* However, **dependent** may be used for both adjective and noun.

de·pend·ence (di pen′dəns) **1** the fact or condition of being dependent: *the dependence of crops on the weather.* **2** trust; reliance: *Do not put your dependence in him, for he may fail you.* **3** reliance on another for support or help: *The boy wished to go to work so that he could end his dependence on his uncle. n.*

de·pend·ent (di pen′dənt) **1** trusting to another person or thing for support; relying on another for help: *A child is dependent on its parents.* **2** a person who is supported by another; dependant. **3** depending; possible if something else takes place: *Good crops are dependent on the right kind of weather.* 1, 3 *adj.,* 2 *n.*
☛ See note at **dependant.**

de·pict (di pikt′) represent by drawing, painting, or describing; portray: *The artist and the writer both tried to depict the splendor of the sunset. v.*

de·plore (di plôr′) be very sorry about; express great sorrow for: *We deplore the accident. v.,* **de·plored, de·plor·ing.**

de·port (di pôrt′) **1** banish; expel; remove: *When an alien is deported, he is sent out of the country, usually back to his native land.* **2** behave or conduct oneself in a particular manner: *The boys were trained to deport themselves like gentlemen. v.*

de·port·ment (di pôrt′mənt) behavior; conduct; the way a person acts: *A gentleman is known by his deportment. n.*

de·pose (di pōz′) put out of office or a position of authority; remove from a throne: *The king was deposed by the revolution. v.*

de·pos·it (di poz′it) **1** put down; lay down; leave lying: *He deposited his bundles on the table. The flood deposited a layer of mud in the streets.* **2** the material laid down or left lying by natural means: *There is often a deposit of sand and mud at the mouth of a river.* **3** put in a place to be kept safe: *Deposit your money in the bank.* **4** something put in a certain place to be kept safe: *She made two deposits to her account.* **5** pay as a pledge to do something or to pay more later: *If you will deposit $5, the store will reserve the coat for you until you pay the rest.* **6** the money paid as a pledge of this sort: *a $5 deposit.* **7** a mass of some mineral in rock or in the ground: *deposits of coal.* 1, 3, 5 *v.,* 2, 4, 6, 7 *n.*

de·pos·i·tor (di poz′ə tər) a person who deposits, especially one who deposits money in an account: *As a new depositor he received a book of cheques and deposit slips. n.*

dep·ot (dep′ō or dē′pō) **1** a bus or railway station. **2** a storehouse, especially for military supplies. **3** a military recruiting and distribution centre: *After his release from hospital, the soldier was sent to a depot before being returned to his regiment. n.*

de·press (di pres′) **1** make sad or gloomy: *Rainy weather always depresses me. She was depressed by the bad news.* **2** press down; lower: *When you play the piano, you depress the keys.* **3** make less active; weaken: *Some medicines depress the action of the heart. v.*

de·pres·sion (di presh′ən) **1** a pressing down; lowering or sinking: *The heavy weight of snow caused a depression of the shed's roof.* **2** a low place; hollow: *Water filled the depressions in the ground.* **3** low spirits; sadness: *Three sunny days cured the boy's depression.* **4** a lowering of activity; dullness of trade: *Many people lost their jobs during the business depression.* **5** the economic depression that began in 1929 and lasted about 10 years. *n.*

de·prive (di prīv′) **1** take away from by force: *The people deprived the king of his power.* **2** keep from having or doing: *The children were deprived of supper. Worrying deprived him of sleep. v.,* **de·prived, de·priv·ing.**

hat, āge, fär; let, ēqual, tėrm; it, īce
hot, ōpen, ôrder; oil, out; cup, pu̇t, rüle
əbove, takən, pencəl, lemən, circəs
ch, child; ng, long; sh, ship
th, thin; ᴛʜ, then; zh, measure

dept. department.

depth (depth) **1** the distance from the top to the bottom: *the depth of a hole, the depth of a lake.* **2** the distance from front to back: *The depth of our playground is 90 metres.* **3** the deepest or most central part of anything: *in the depth of the forest, in the depths of despair, in the depth of winter.* **4** a deep quality; deepness: *It was a hole of considerable depth.* **5** the quality of being full of thought or meaning: *The philosopher was noted for the depth of his ideas.* *n.*
out of one's depth, a in water so deep that one cannot touch the bottom. **b** in a situation too difficult to understand or cope with: *He was out of his depth in the arithmetic class.*

dep·u·ty (dep′yə tē) a person appointed to do the work or take the place of another: *A deputy minister is an assistant to a minister of the cabinet.* *n., pl.* **dep·u·ties.**

Dep·u·ty (dep′yə tē) in Quebec, a member of the National Assembly. *n., pl.* **Dep·u·ties.**

de·rail (dē rāl′) cause a train, etc. to run off the rails. *v.*

A derby

der·by (dėr′bē) **1** a stiff hat that has a rounded crown and a narrow brim; a bowler hat. **2** a contest or race: *a fishing derby, a dog derby.* *n., pl.* **der·bies.**
☛ **Derby** comes originally from the title of the Earls of *Derby* in England. In 1780, the twelfth Earl of Derby founded an annual horse-race, which came to be called the Derby and gave its name to many other kinds of races and also, in North America, to the bowler hat often worn by spectators at horse races.

de·ride (di rīd′) make fun of; laugh at in scorn: *The boys derided him because he wore old-fashioned clothes.* *v.,* **de·rid·ed, de·rid·ing.**

de·ri·sion (di rizh′ən) scornful laughter; jeering; ridicule: *Children dread the derision of their playmates.* *n.*

de·ri·sive (di rī′siv) mocking; ridiculing: *a derisive smile.* *adj.*

de·rive (di rīv′) **1** get; receive; obtain: *He derives much pleasure from his books.* **2** make or create new words by adding suffixes or prefixes: *From* kind *may be derived* kinder, kindness, *and* unkind *by adding* -er, -ness, *and* un-. **3** trace back to: *We derive the word* table *from a French word.* *v.,* **de·rived, de·riv·ing.**

de·rog·a·to·ry (di rog′ə tô′rē) lessening the value of; belittling; unfavorable: *The stranger's derogatory remarks about the town and its people made him unpopular.* *adj.*

der·rick (der′ik) **1** a machine for lifting and moving heavy objects: *A derrick has a long arm that swings at an angle from the base of an upright post or frame.* See **crane** for picture. **2** a towerlike framework over an oil well, gas well, etc., which holds the drilling and hoisting machinery. *n.*

de·scend (di send′) **1** go or come down from a higher to a lower place: *They slowly descended the stairs. The river descends from the mountains to the sea.* **2** go or come down from an earlier to a later time: *That is a superstition descended from the Middle Ages.* **3** go from greater to smaller numbers; go from higher to lower on any scale: *75-50-25 form a series that descends.* *v.*
descend from, have as ancestors; derive from: *He is descended from Scottish pioneers in Nova Scotia.*
descend on or **upon, a** make a sudden attack on: *The wolves descended on the sheep and killed them.* **b** arrive suddenly in numbers: *Many tourists descended upon the town during the exhibition.*

de·scend·ant (di sen′dənt) **1** a person born of a certain family or group: *He is a descendant of the United Empire Loyalists.* **2** an offspring; a child, grandchild, great-grandchild, etc.: *You are a direct descendant of your parents, grandparents, great-grandparents, etc.* *n.*

de·scent (di sent′) **1** coming or going down from a higher to a lower place: *the descent of a balloon.* **2** a downward slope: *We climbed down a steep descent.* **3** coming down from parent to child: *We can trace the descent of red hair in this family through five generations.* **4** a family line; ancestors: *I can trace my descent back to a family in Poland.* *n.*
☛ **Descent** and **dissent** are pronounced the same.

de·scribe (di skrīb′) **1** tell in words how a person looks, feels, or acts, or how a place, a thing, or an event looks; tell or write about. **2** draw the outline of; trace: *The spinning top described a figure 8.* *v.,* **de·scribed, de·scrib·ing.**

de·scrip·tion (di skrip′shən) **1** a spoken or written account that gives a picture in words: *The traveller's description of the Rockies was thrilling to read.* **2** a kind or sort: *I have seen no dog of any description today.* *n.*

de·scrip·tive (di skrip′tiv) describing; that tells about by using description: *Write a descriptive paragraph about a flower garden.* *adj.*

des·ert[1] (dez′ərt) **1** a region with very little water and plant or animal life; barren, desolate land: *The Sahara Desert is a great, sandy region in the northern part of Africa.* **2** barren and desolate: *Saudi Arabia is largely desert land.* **3** not inhabited or cultivated: *Robinson Crusoe was shipwrecked on a desert island.* 1 *n.,* 2, 3 *adj.*

de·sert[2] (di zėrt′) **1** go away, and leave; abandon; forsake; run away from duty: *The evil parents in the story deserted their children. The guard deserted his post.* **2** leave military service without permission and with no intention of returning: *The soldier who had deserted was caught and brought back for trial.* **3** fail; leave: *The boy's courage deserted him when he met the snarling dog.* *v.* —**de·sert′er,** *n.*
☛ **Desert**[2], **desert**[3], and **dessert** are pronounced the same.

de·sert[3] (di zėrt′) Usually, **deserts,** *pl.* what is deserved; a suitable reward or punishment: *When the* *dog bit him, he got his just deserts for throwing stones at it.* *n.*

☛ See note at **desert**[2].

de·serve (di zėrv′) have a right to; have a claim to; be worthy of: *Because of his hard work, he deserves a promotion. Good work deserves good pay.* *v.,* **de·served, de·serv·ing.**

de·sign (di zīn′) **1** a drawing, plan, or sketch made to serve as a pattern from which to work: *a design for a machine, a dress design.* **2** an arrangement of details, form, and color in painting, weaving, building, etc.; pattern: *a wallpaper design in tan and brown.* **3** make a first sketch of; arrange the form and color of; draw in outline: *to design a dress.* **4** the art of making designs, patterns, or sketches: *Architects are skilled in design.* **5** plan out; form in the mind: *The author designed an exciting plot.* **6** a plan in mind to be carried out; a purpose: *The enemy's design was to capture the fortress.* **7** set apart; intend: *The nursery was designed for the baby's use.* 1, 2, 4, 6 *n.,* 3, 5, 7 *v.*

des·ig·nate (dez′ig nāt′) **1** mark out; point out; show: *Red lines designate main roads on this map.* **2** name: *The ruler of a kingdom is designated king or queen.* *v.,* **des·ig·nat·ed, des·ig·nat·ing.**

de·sign·ing (di zīn′ing) **1** scheming; plotting: *a designing woman.* **2** the art of making designs, patterns, sketches, etc.: *She studies dress designing at school.* 1 *adj.,* 2 *n.*

de·sir·a·bil·i·ty (di zīr′ə bil′ə tē) the state or quality of being desirable: *Nobody doubts the desirability of good health.* *n.*

de·sir·a·ble (di zīr′ə bəl) worth wishing for; worth having; pleasing; satisfying: *They are looking for a desirable place to live.* *adj.*

de·sire (di zīr′) **1** wish earnestly for; long for: *A miser desires money more than anything else.* **2** an earnest wish; a longing: *His desire for success kept him working hard.* **3** ask for or request, especially in a formal manner: *The Governor General desires your presence in his office.* **4** something wished for: *His greatest desire was a bicycle.* 1, 3 *v.,* **de·sired, de·sir·ing;** 2, 4 *n.*

de·sir·ous (di zīr′əs) desiring; wishing. *adj.*
desirous of, eagerly wishing for; longing for: *He was desirous of going to Europe.*

de·sist (di sist′ or di zist′) stop; cease; discontinue: *He continued fighting although he had been asked several times to desist.* *v.*
desist from, cease; discontinue: *The judge ordered him to desist from fighting.*

desk (desk) a piece of furniture with one or more drawers and a flat or sloping top on which to write or rest books, papers, etc. *n.*

des·o·late (des′ə lit for 1, 2, and 4, des′ə lāt′ for 3 and 5) **1** not producing anything; barren: *desolate land.* **2** not lived in; deserted: *a desolate house.* **3** make unfit to live in: *The Vikings desolated the lands they attacked.* **4** unhappy; forlorn: *The hungry child looked desolate.* **5** make unhappy: *They were desolated to hear that their friends were going away.* 1, 2, 4 *adj.,* 3, 5 *v.,* **des·o·lat·ed, des·o·lat·ing.**

des·o·la·tion (des′ə lā′shən) **1** the act of making desolate: *the desolation of a country by an invading army.* **2** a ruined or devastated condition: *After the fire the forest land was in complete desolation.* **3** lonely or deserted condition: *the desolation of the Barren Ground.* **4** sadness; lonely sorrow: *There was desolation in the eyes of the condemned man.* *n.*

de·spair (di sper′) **1** a loss of hope; being without hope; a dreadful feeling that nothing good can happen: *Despair seized them as they felt the boat sinking.* **2** a person or thing that causes loss of hope: *The naughty girl was the despair of her parents.* **3** lose hope; be without hope: *The doctors despaired of saving the child's life.* 1, 2 *n.,* 3 *v.*

des·patch (dis pach′) See **dispatch.**

des·patch·er (dis pach′ ər) See **dispatcher.**

des·per·ate (des′pər it) **1** no longer caring what happens because hope is gone: *A person who commits suicide is usually desperate.* **2** ready to run any risk: *a desperate robber.* **3** having little chance for hope or cure; very dangerous: *a desperate illness.* *adj.*

des·per·a·tion (des′pər ā′shən) a hopeless and reckless feeling; a readiness to try anything: *When he saw that the stairs were on fire, he jumped out of the window in desperation.* *n.*

de·spise (di spīz′) look down upon; scorn; think of as being unworthy of attention: *Most people despise a traitor.* *v.,* **de·spised, de·spis·ing.**

de·spite (di spīt′) in spite of: *The boys went for a walk despite the rain.* *prep.*

de·spoil (di spoil′) rob; plunder: *The invaders despoiled the palace.* *v.*

de·spond·ent (di spon′dənt) having lost heart, courage, or hope; depressed; dejected: *The losers were despondent.* *adj.*

des·pot (des′pot or des′pət) **1** an absolute ruler; tyrant: *In ancient times many rulers were despots.* **2** any person who uses his power to get his own way: *Their father was a despot at home.* *n.*

des·sert (di zėrt′) a course served at the end of a meal: *Pie, cake, puddings, and ice cream are common desserts.* *n.*

☛ **Dessert, desert**[2], and **desert**[3] are pronounced the same.

des·ti·na·tion (des′tə nā′shən) the place to which a person or thing is going: *The traveller's destination was Ottawa.* *n.*

des·tine (des′tən) **1** intend; set apart for a purpose or use: *The prince was destined from his birth to be a king.* **2** cause by fate: *The letter was destined never to reach him.* *v.,* **des·tined, des·tin·ing.**
destined for, a intended to go to; bound for: *ships destined for England.* **b** intended for: *Her brother was destined for the ministry.*

des·ti·ny (des′tə nē) **1** one's lot or fortune; what becomes of a person or thing in the end: *It was his destiny to become a national hero.* **2** what will happen; believed to be determined beforehand to happen in spite of efforts to change or prevent it: *He struggled in vain against his destiny.* *n., pl.* **des·ti·nies.**

des·ti·tute (des′tə tyüt′ or des′tə tüt′) being without necessities such as food, clothing, and shelter: *A destitute family needs help.* *adj.*
destitute of, having no; without: *The tyrant was destitute of pity.*

hat, āge, fär; let, ēqual, tėrm; it, īce
hot, ōpen, ôrder; oil, out; cup, pu̇t, rüle
əbove, takən, pencəl, lemən, circəs
ch, child; ng, long; sh, ship
th, thin; ᴛʜ, then; zh, measure

de·stroy (di stroi′) 1 break to pieces; spoil; ruin; make useless: *Some children destroy all their toys.* 2 put an end to; do away with: *A heavy rain destroyed all hope of a picnic.* 3 kill: *Forest fires destroy many trees every year.* *v.*

de·stroy·er (di stroi′ər) a small, fast warship equipped with guns, torpedoes, etc. *n.*

de·struc·tion (di struk′shən) 1 the act of destroying: *A crowd watched the destruction of the old building.* 2 ruin: *The storm left destruction behind it.* *n.*

de·struc·tive (di struk′tiv) 1 destroying; causing destruction: *Fires and earthquakes are destructive.* 2 guilty of destroying; in the habit of causing destruction: *She was a very destructive child.* 3 not helpful; not constructive: *Destructive criticism shows things to be wrong without showing how to correct them.* *adj.*

de·tach (di tach′) 1 unfasten; loosen and remove; separate: *She detached a charm from her bracelet.* 2 separate a number of soldiers, ships, tanks, etc. from the main body for some special duty: *One squad of soldiers was detached to guard the road.* *v.*

de·tached (di tacht′) 1 separate from others; isolated: *A detached house is not in a solid row with others.* 2 not influenced by one's interests or prejudices, or those of others: *They asked her to settle the argument because she would remain calm and detached.* *adj.*

de·tach·ment (di tach′mənt) 1 separation. 2 lack of interest: *He watched the motion picture with detachment.* 3 troops or ships sent away on or assigned to some special duty: *He belonged to the machine-gun detachment.* 4 the smallest unit in the organization of the Royal Canadian Mounted Police or other police force: *Some rural detachments of the RCMP have only one or two officers.* *n.*

de·tail (dē′tāl or di tāl′) 1 a small or particular part; item: *All the details of getting ready for the birthday party were left to the children.* 2 the process of dealing with particular things one by one: *She does not enjoy the detail of keeping accounts.* 3 tell fully; tell even the small and unimportant parts: *The new boy detailed to us all the wonders he had seen in his travels.* 4 a small group of men chosen for some special duty: *The captain sent a detail of ten men to guard the bridge.* 5 choose for special duty: *Police were detailed to hold back the crowd watching the parade.* 1, 2, 4 *n.*, 3, 5 *v.*

go into detail, describe or discuss each small part or particular of something: *His description was very general: he did not go into detail.*

in detail, part by part; with all the details: *She described the inside of the airplane in detail.*

de·tain (di tān′) 1 keep from going ahead; hold back; delay: *I was detained by the heavy snowstorm.* 2 keep from going away; hold as a prisoner: *The police detained the suspected thief for questioning.* *v.*

de·tect (di tekt′) find out; make out; discover; catch: *Could you detect any odor in the room? He was detected stealing cookies.* *v.*

de·tec·tive (di tek′tiv) 1 a police officer whose work is investigating crime. 2 a person who works for a company or organization as an investigator. *n.*

de·ten·tion (di ten′shən) 1 keeping in custody; confinement: *A jail is used for the detention of persons who have been arrested.* 2 the act of detaining or holding back. 3 being detained; a delay: *The problem with the airplane resulted in a three-hour detention for the passengers at the airport.* *n.*

de·ter (di tėr′) discourage; keep back; hinder: *The extreme heat deterred us from going downtown.* *v.*, **de·terred, de·ter·ring.**

de·ter·gent (di tėr′jənt) 1 cleansing. 2 a substance other than soap, used for cleansing: *Many people use detergent for washing dishes.* 1 *adj.*, 2 *n.*

de·ter·mi·na·tion (di tėr′mə nā′shən) 1 a deciding; settling beforehand: *The determination of what presents to buy took a long time.* 2 the act of finding out the exact amount or kind by weighing, measuring, calculating, etc.: *the determination of the amount of gold in a sample of ore.* 3 a fixed purpose; great firmness in carrying out a purpose: *The boy's determination was not weakened by the difficulties he met.* *n.*

de·ter·mine (di tėr′mən) 1 make up one's mind very firmly; decide: *He determined to become the best scout in his troop.* 2 find out exactly; get definite knowledge of: *A diver was hired to determine the location of the sunken wreck.* 3 be the deciding fact in reaching a certain result; bring about a certain result: *The number of questions correctly answered determines the mark received on the examination.* *v.*, **de·ter·mined, de·ter·min·ing.**

de·ter·mined (di tėr′mənd) 1 with one's mind firmly made up; resolved: *The determined explorer kept on his way in spite of the storm.* 2 firm; resolute: *His determined look showed that he had made up his mind.* *adj.*

de·ter·min·er (di tėr′mə nər) in grammar, a specifying word such as *the, a, her,* or *this,* that comes before a noun or before an adjective followed by a noun. *n.*

de·test (di test′) dislike very much; hate: *Many people detest snakes.* *v.*

de·test·a·ble (di tes′tə bəl) deserving to be detested; hateful: *a detestable crime.* *adj.*

de·throne (di thrōn′) put off a throne; remove from ruling power. *v.*, **de·throned, de·thron·ing.**

de·tour (dē′tür) 1 a road or way that is used when the main or direct road cannot be travelled. 2 a roundabout way: *We took a detour through the park on our way home.* 3 use a roundabout way; make a detour: *We detoured around the flooded part of the highway.* 1, 2 *n.*, 3 *v.*

dev·as·tate (dev′əs tāt′) destroy; ravage; lay waste; make unfit to live in: *The long war devastated much of Europe.* *v.*, **dev·as·tat·ed, dev·as·tat·ing.**

dev·as·ta·tion (dev′əs tā′shən) 1 the act of laying waste or of destroying; destruction. 2 the condition or state of being laid waste; desolation: *The people were shocked at the devastation resulting from the forest fire.* *n.*

de·vel·op (di vel′əp) 1 grow; mature: *Plants develop from seeds.* 2 cause to grow and mature: *Exercise and* *wholesome food develop healthy bodies.* 3 bring into being; come to have: *A boy may develop an interest in collecting stamps.* 4 work out in greater and greater detail: *Gradually we developed our plans for the Boys' Club.* 5 change, especially by means of construction work, from a natural or near natural state to one that serves another purpose: *The plan to develop the park was strongly opposed by the public. The government is developing the water power of the northern rivers for industry.* 6 make more urban, more up-to-date, or more industrialized: *They have developed the old downtown area.* 7 treat a photographic plate or film with chemicals so that the picture shows: *I took the film in to be developed. v.*

de·vel·op·ment (di vel′əp mənt) 1 the act of working out in greater detail: *The development of an airplane that would fly took many years of experimenting.* 2 the process of developing; growth: *The parents followed their child's development with pride.* 3 a happening; an outcome or result; news: *Newspapers give information about the latest development in world affairs.* 4 bringing into being: *the development of a new kind of motor.* 5 changing something from a natural or older state for a particular purpose: *the development of the waterfront for industry.* 6 the product or result of developing in this way: *The old farm is now a large housing development.* 7 a group of buildings constructed by the same person or company: *The new development will have business offices and stores.* 8 the developing of a film. *n.*

de·vice (di vīs′) 1 a mechanical invention used for a special purpose; machine; apparatus: *A can opener is a device for opening cans.* 2 a plan; scheme; sometimes, a trick: *By some device the thief got the boy to let him into the house.* 3 a drawing or figure used in a pattern or as an ornament. *n.*

leave to one's own devices, leave to do as one thinks best: *The teacher left us to our own devices in choosing the books for our reports.*

dev·il (dev′əl) 1 **the Devil,** the evil spirit, the enemy of goodness, or Satan. 2 any evil spirit. 3 a person who is especially wicked, reckless, clever, active, etc. 4 prepare food with hot seasoning: *devilled ham, devilled eggs.* 1–3 *n.,* 4 *v.,* **dev·illed** or **dev·iled, dev·il·ling** or **dev·il·ing. —dev′il·ish,** *adj.*

de·vise (di vīz′) think out; plan; contrive; invent: *The boys are trying to devise some scheme for earning the money for their trip. v.,* **de·vised, de·vis·ing.**

de·void (di void′) **devoid of,** entirely without; empty; lacking: *devoid of sense. A well devoid of water is useless. adj.*

de·vote (di vōt′) 1 give up oneself, one's money, time, or efforts to some person, purpose, or service: *He devoted himself to his children.* 2 set apart for any particular purpose: *The museum devotes two floors to animal exhibits. v.,* **de·vot·ed, de·vot·ing.**

de·vot·ed (di vō′tid) very loyal; faithful: *a devoted friend. adj.*

de·vo·tion (di vō′shən) 1 a deep, steady affection; a feeling of loyalty: *the devotion of a mother to her child.* 2 a giving up or being given up to some person, purpose, or service: *the devotion of much time to study. Her devotion to the Girl Guides made her attend every meeting.* 3 **devotions,** *pl.* worship, prayers, or praying. *n.*

de·vour (di vour′) 1 eat: *The wolves devoured the caribou.* 2 eat like an animal; eat very hungrily: *The hungry boy was devouring his dinner.* 3 consume; destroy: *The fire devoured the forest.* 4 take in with eyes or ears in a hungry, greedy way: *to devour a new book. v.*

de·vout (di vout′) 1 religious; active in worship and prayer. 2 earnest; sincere; hearty: *devout thanks, a devout follower. adj.*

dew (dyü or dü) 1 moisture that condenses from the air and collects in small drops on cool surfaces during the night: *In the morning there are drops of dew on the grass and flowers.* 2 to wet with dew; moisten. 1 *n.,* 2 *v.*

☞ **Dew** and **due** are pronounced the same. **Dew** and **do**[1] are sometimes pronounced the same.

dew·drop (dyü′drop′ or dü′drop′) a drop of dew. *n.*

dew point the air temperature at which moisture in the air begins to condense to form dew.

dew–worm (dyü′wėrm′ or dü′wėrm′) a large earthworm that comes to the surface at night when there is dew on the grass: *Dew-worms make excellent fish bait. n.*

dew·y (dyü′ē or dü′ē) 1 wet with dew: *dewy grass.* 2 looking as if wet with dew: *dewy eyes. adj.,* **dew·i·er, dew·i·est.**

dex·ter·i·ty (deks ter′ə tē) 1 skill in using the hands: *A good surgeon works with dexterity.* 2 skill in using the mind; cleverness: *Dexterity in questioning witnesses helped the lawyer win many cases. n.*

di·a·bol·ic (dī′ə bol′ik) devilish; very cruel or wicked; fiendish: *The police discovered a diabolic plot to poison the drinking water. adj.* **—di′a·bol′i·cal·ly,** *adv.*

di·a·bol·i·cal (dīə bol′ə kəl) diabolic. *adj.*

di·a·crit·i·cal mark (dī′ə krit′ə kəl) a small mark like ′ or ′ accompanying a letter to indicate pronunciation, accent, etc.

di·a·dem (dī′ə dem′) 1 crown. 2 an ornamental band of cloth formerly worn as a crown. *n.*

di·ag·nose (dī′əg nōs′) find out the nature of by an examination: *The doctor diagnosed the child's disease as measles. v.,* **di·ag·nosed, di·ag·nos·ing.**

di·ag·no·sis (dī′əg nō′sis) 1 finding out what disease a person or animal has by examination and careful study of the symptoms. 2 a careful study of the facts about something to find out its essential features, faults, etc.: *a diagnosis of a plane crash.* 3 a decision reached after careful study of symptoms or facts: *The doctor will give me his diagnosis today. The diagnosis showed that defective parts caused the plane crash. n., pl.* **di·ag·no·ses** (dī′əg nō′sēz).

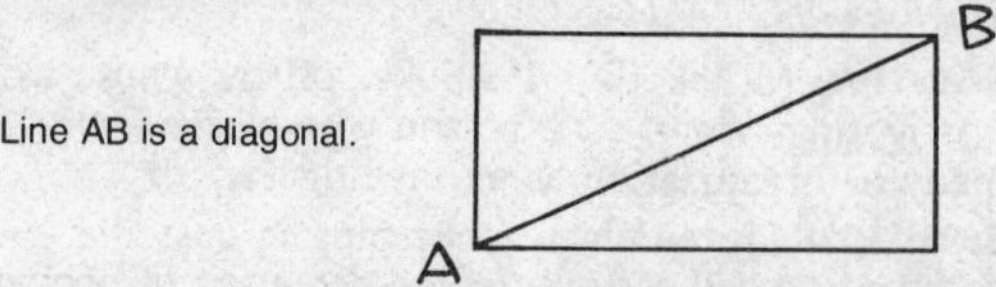

Line AB is a diagonal.

di·ag·o·nal (dī ag′ə nəl) 1 a straight line joining any two corners that are not next to each other of a figure having four or more sides. **2** taking the direction of a diagonal; slanting: *a ship sailing on a diagonal course, a diagonal stripe in cloth.* 1 *n.*, 2 *adj.* **—di·ag'o·nal·ly,** *adv.*

di·a·gram (dī'ə gram') **1** a drawing or sketch showing important parts of a thing: *A diagram may be an outline, a plan, a drawing, a figure, a chart, or a combination of any of these, made to show clearly what a thing is or how it works. A plan of a house or a steamship is a diagram.* **2** put on paper, a blackboard, etc. in the form of a drawing or sketch; make a diagram of. 1 *n.*, 2 *v.*

The dials on an electric meter, showing how many kilowatt hours of electric power have been used

di·al (dī'əl or dīl) **1** a marked surface on which a moving pointer indicates a measurement of some kind: *The face of a clock or of a compass is a dial. A dial may show the amount of water in a tank or the amount of steam pressure in a boiler.* **2** the plate, disk, etc. of a radio or television set with numbers, letters, etc. on it for tuning in to a station. **3** the circular device on many telephones that is rotated for signalling the required telephone number when making a call. **4** make a call by means of a telephone dial: *She dialled her father's office.* **5** sundial. 1–3, 5 *n.*, 4 *v.*, **di·alled** or **di·aled, di·al·ling** or **di·al·ing.**

di·a·lect (dī'ə lekt') a form of speech peculiar to a district or class: *the Scottish dialect, the dialect of Lunenburg, Nova Scotia.* *n.*

di·a·logue (dī'ə log') **1** a conversation: *They had a long dialogue about plans for the camp program.* **2** the conversation written for a story, play, motion picture, etc.: *That book has a good plot and clever dialogue.* *n.* Also spelled **dialog.**

di·am·e·ter (dī am'ə tər) **1** a straight line passing through the centre from one side of a circle or sphere to the other side. See **circle** for picture. **2** the length of such a line; the measurement through the centre: *The diameter of the earth is about 13 000 kilometres. The tree trunk was almost 80 centimetres in diameter.* *n.*

dia·mond (dī'mənd or dī'ə mənd) **1** a colorless or tinted precious stone, formed of pure carbon in crystals: *Diamond is the hardest substance known.* **2** a figure shaped like this ◇. **3** the space inside the lines that connect the bases in baseball. **4** a playing card marked with one or more red, diamond-shaped designs on it. **5 diamonds,** *pl.* the suit of such playing cards. *n.*

di·a·per (dī'ə pər or dī'pər) **1** a piece of cloth folded up, or a pad of other absorbent material, used as underpants for a baby; napkin. **2** put a diaper on. 1 *n.*, 2 *v.*

di·a·phragm (dī'ə fram') **1** a partition of muscles and tendons separating the cavity of the chest from the cavity of the abdomen. See **kidney** for another picture. **2** a thin disk or cone that moves rapidly to and fro when sounds are directed at it, used in telephone receivers, loudspeakers, earphones, and other instruments. *n.*

hat, āge, fär; let, ēqual, tėrm; it, īce
hot, ōpen, ôrder; oil, out; cup, pu̇t, rüle
əbove, takən, pencəl, lemən, circəs
ch, child; ng, long; sh, ship
th, thin; ᴛʜ, then; zh, measure

di·a·ry (dī'ə rē) **1** an account, written down each day, of what has happened to one, or what one has done or thought, during that day. **2** a book for keeping such an account with a blank space for each day: *She kept a daily record of her activities in a large diary.* *n.*, *pl.* **di·a·ries.**

☛ **Diary** and **journal** are related words. **Diary** comes from the Latin word *diarium* with the same meaning, formed from *diarius* meaning 'daily.' **Journal** comes from French *journal* with the same meaning. **Journalism** and **journalist** come from French words formed from *journal.* *Journal* developed from Latin *diurnalis,* meaning 'a daily portion.' *Diurnalis* and *diarius* were both formed from Latin *dies,* meaning 'day.' See also note at **journey.**

di·a·tom (dī'ə təm) any one of many tiny, one-celled algae that have hard shells made up mostly of silica. *n.*

di·a·ton·ic scale (dī'ə ton'ik) in music, a standard major or minor scale of eight tones: *The scales of C major and A minor are diatonic scales.*

dib (dib) **1** a small marble, usually made of clay. **2 dibs,** *pl.* the game played with such marbles. *n.*

dice (dīs) **1** small cubes with a different number of spots (one to six) on each side: *Dice are used in playing certain games. One of these cubes is often referred to as a dice.* **2** use dice in gambling. **3** cut into small cubes: *Carrots are sometimes diced before being cooked.* 1 *n. pl.* of **die**[3]; 2, 3 *v.*, **diced, dic·ing.**

dick·er (dik'ər) trade by barter or by bargaining: *Father dickered with the salesman in an attempt to get a reduction in price.* *v.*

dic·tate (dik'tāt or dik tāt' for 1 and 2, dik'tāt for 3) **1** say or read something aloud for another person or other persons to write or type: *The teacher dictated a spelling list. He dictates many letters to his secretary.* **2** speak with authority; make others do what one says: *Big nations often dictate to little ones. No one is going to dictate to me.* **3** a direction or order that is to be carried out or obeyed: *the dictates of a ruler, the dictates of one's conscience.* 1, 2 *v.*, **dic·tat·ed, dic·tat·ing;** 3 *n.*

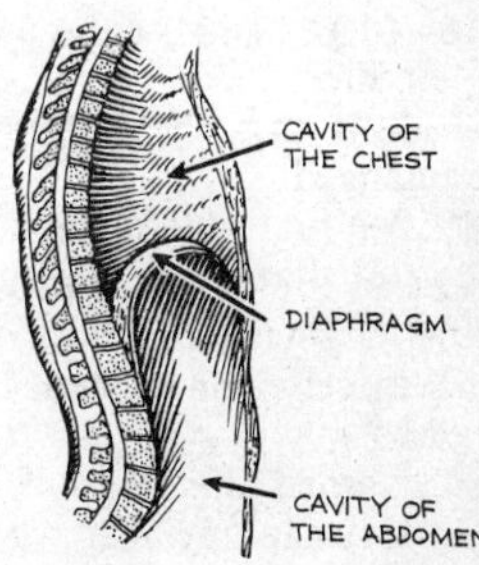

The diaphragm of a human being

dic·ta·tion (dik tā′shən) **1** the act of saying or reading something aloud for another person or persons to write down: *The pupils wrote to the teacher's dictation.* **2** the words dictated: *The secretary took the dictation and typed it out later.* *n.*

dic·ta·tor (dik′tā tər or dik tā′tər) **1** a person exercising absolute authority: *The dictator of a country has complete power over its people.* **2** a person whose authority is widely accepted in some special field: *a dictator of men's fashions.* *n.*

dic·tion (dik′shən) one's manner of expressing ideas in words; a style of speaking or writing: *Good diction includes skill in the choice and arrangement of words.* *n.*

dic·tion·ar·y (dik′shən er′ē) a book that explains the meanings and uses of words and expressions, and shows how they are spelled and, usually, how they are pronounced: *The entries in a dictionary are arranged alphabetically. The dictionary also gives the histories of some words.* *n., pl.* **dic·tion·ar·ies.**

did (did) See **do.** *Did he go to school yesterday? Yes, he did.* *v.*

did·n't (did′ənt) did not.

die[1] (dī) **1** stop living; become dead. **2** lose force or strength; come to an end; stop: *The music died away. The motor sputtered and died.* **3 dying,** *Informal.* wanting very much: *I'm just dying to go with you on your trip. We're dying for a meal.* *v.,* **died, dy·ing.**

☛ **Die** and **dye** are pronounced the same.

☛ **Die** is generally followed by *of* when illness is the cause of death: *He died of cancer.* However *from* is sometimes used when injury is the cause: *He died from a wound.*

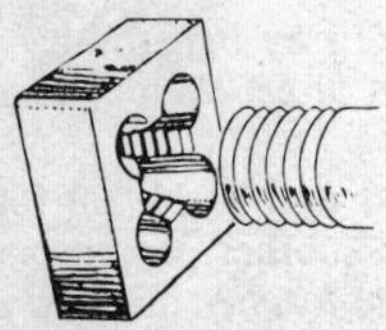

A die for cutting the threads of bolts. As the die is turned, it screws onto the bolt and cuts a thread on it.

die[2] (dī) **1** any tool or apparatus for shaping, cutting, or stamping things, usually under pressure: *A die is usually a metal block or plate cut in a special way.* **2** a tool for cutting threads on pipes, bolts, etc. *n., pl.* **dies.**

☛ See first note at **die**[1].

die[3] (dī) a small cube used in certain games. See **dice.** *n., pl.* **dice.**

the die is cast, the decision has been made and cannot be changed.

☛ See first note at **die**[1].

die·sel (dē′zəl) **1** diesel engine. **2** powered by a diesel engine: *a diesel locomotive.* **3** of or having to do with diesel engines: *diesel fuel, a diesel mechanic.* 1 *n.,* 2, 3 *adj.*

☛ Named after Rudolf *Diesel* (1858-1913), the German engineer who developed this engine.

diesel engine an engine that burns oil with heat caused by the compression of air.

di·et (dī′ət) **1** the usual food and drink for a person or animal: *The diet of the giraffe consists of young leaves and shoots.* **2** any special selection of food eaten during an illness, in an attempt to lose or gain weight, etc.: *The doctor ordered a diet of liquids for the sick child.* **3** eat special food or drink, especially in order to lose or gain weight: *He can't eat sweets because he's dieting.* 1, 2 *n.,* 3 *v.,* **di·et·ed, di·et·ing.**

di·e·ti·tian (dī′ə tish′ən) a person trained to plan meals with a proper proportion of various kinds of food: *Many hospitals and schools employ dietitians.* *n.*

dif·fer (dif′ər) **1** be unlike; be different: *My answers differed from hers. Cars and trucks differ greatly in use.* **2** have or express a different opinion; disagree: *They differed about how they should spend the money. He is a stubborn boy, determined to differ with his teacher.* *v.*

dif·fer·ence (dif′rəns or dif′ər əns) **1** the state or condition of being unlike: *the difference of night and day.* **2** the way of being different; the point in which people or things are different: *The only difference between the twins is that Bob's hair is wavy.* **3** what is left after subtracting one number from another: *The difference between 6 and 15 is 9.* See **subtraction** for picture. **4** the amount or extent by which one thing differs from another: *The difference in size between Nova Scotia and Ontario is great.* **5** a dispute; disagreement: *The children had a difference over a name for the new puppy.* *n.*

dif·fer·ent (dif′rənt or dif′ər ənt) **1** not alike; not like: *People have different names. An automobile is different from a cart.* **2** not the same; separate; distinct: *We called three different times but never found her at home.* **3** not like others or most others; unusual: *He insists on being different in the way he dresses.* *adj.* **—dif′fer·ent·ly,** *adv.*

dif·fi·cult (dif′ə kult′) **1** hard to do or understand: *Cutting down the tree was difficult. Arithmetic is difficult for some people.* **2** hard to deal with, get along with, or please: *The boy was often difficult.* *adj.*

dif·fi·cul·ty (dif′ə kul′tē) **1** something that is hard to do or understand: *The problem presented many difficulties.* **2** something that stands in the way of getting things done, such as lack of money, lack of people to help, lack of understanding, or objections to plans. **3** the degree to which a thing is difficult: *The difficulty of the job was greater than we thought it would be.* **4** hard work: *Some children have a great deal of difficulty in learning how to spell.* **5** trouble: *What is your difficulty?* *n., pl.* **dif·fi·cul·ties.**

make difficulties, cause trouble; hinder by raising objections.

dif·fi·dent (dif′ə dənt) shy; lacking in self-confidence: *He was too diffident to ask the teacher directly.* *adj.*

dig (dig) **1** use a shovel, spade, hands, claws or snout to make a hole or to turn over ground: *Dogs bury bones and dig them up later.* **2** make by digging: *They dug a cellar.* **3** make a way by digging: *They dug through the mountain to make a road.* **4** get by digging: *to dig potatoes, to dig clams.* **5** a thrust or poke: *The boy gave his friend a dig in the ribs.* **6** make a thrust or stab into; prod: *The rider dug his spurs into the horse.* 1–4, 6 *v.,* **dug, dig·ging;** 5 *n.*

dig in, a *Informal.* work hard: *We dug in and finished the job quickly.* **b** make a protective trench: *The soldiers dug in during the shelling.*

hat, āge, fär; let, ēqual, tėrm; it, īce
hot, ōpen, ôrder; oil, out; cup, pu̇t, rüle
əbove, takən, pencəl, lemən, circəs
ch, child; ng, long; sh, ship
th, thin; ᴛʜ, then; zh, measure

di·gest (dī jest′ or di jest′ for 1 and 2, dī′jest for 3) **1** change food in the stomach so that it can be taken into the blood and used as nourishment. **2** think over something until one understands it clearly: *It often takes a long time to digest new ideas.* **3** a brief statement of the contents of a longer book or article. 1, 2 *v.,* 3 *n.*

di·gest·i·ble (dī jes′tə bəl or di jes′tə bəl) capable of being digested; easily digested: *Raw onions are not very digestible. adj.*

di·ges·tion (dī jes′chən or di jes′chən) **1** the digesting of food. **2** the ability to digest: *She is often sick because her digestion is poor. n.*

di·ges·tive (dī jes′tiv or di jes′tiv) having to do with digestion: *Saliva is one of the digestive juices. adj.*

dig·ger (dig′ər) **1** a machine for digging. **2** *Informal.* a nickname for an Australian. *n.*

dig·it (dij′it) **1** a finger or toe. **2** any of the figures 0, 1, 2, 3, 4, 5, 6, 7, 8, 9: *Sometimes 0 is not called a digit but is known as a cipher. n.*

dig·ni·fied (dig′nə fīd′) having or showing dignity; noble; stately; of great worth: *The Premier has a dignified manner. adj.*

dig·ni·fy (dig′nə fī′) give dignity to; make noble, worthwhile, or worthy: *Their little farmhouse was dignified by the great elms around it. v.,* **dig·ni·fied, dig·ni·fy·ing.**

dig·ni·tar·y (dig′nə ter′ē) a person who has a position of honor: *A bishop is a church dignitary. n., pl.* **dig·ni·tar·ies.**

dig·ni·ty (dig′nə tē) **1** a quality of character or ability that wins the respect and high opinion of others; the state or condition of being noble, worthy, or stately: *A judge should maintain the dignity of his position.* **2** a high office, rank, or title; a position of honor: *He may attain the dignity of the presidency.* **3** a proud and self-respecting character or manner: *She spoke with dignity.* **4** a stately appearance: *the dignity of a cathedral. n., pl.* **dig·ni·ties.**

dike (dīk) **1** a bank of earth or a dam built as a defence against flooding: *The dikes in Holland hold back the sea.* **2** provide with dikes. **3** ditch. 1, 3 *n.,* 2 *v.,* **diked, dik·ing.** Also spelled **dyke.**

di·lap·i·dat·ed (di lap′ə dāt′id) falling to pieces; partly ruined or decayed through neglect: *The abandoned town was full of dilapidated houses. adj.*

di·late (dī lāt′ or di lāt′) **1** make or become larger or wider: *The pupil of the eye dilates when the light gets dim.* **2** speak or write at length: *The mayor did not have time to dilate on the subject. v.,* **di·lat·ed, di·lat·ing.**

di·lem·ma (di lem′ə) a situation in which a person has to choose between two things when either choice seems unpleasant or undesirable: *Her dilemma was that she had to give up her holiday or miss playing in the softball finals. n.*

dil·i·gence (dil′ə jəns) being diligent; careful effort; the ability to work hard and steadily: *The student's diligence was rewarded with high marks. n.*

dil·i·gent (dil′ə jənt) hard-working; industrious: *Employers prefer diligent employees. adj.*

dill (dil) **1** a plant whose spicy seeds or leaves are used to flavor foods, especially pickles. **2** its seeds or leaves. **3** a dill pickle. *n.*

dill pickle a cucumber pickle flavored with dill.

dil·ly–dal·ly (dil′ē dal′ē) loiter; waste time; trifle. *v.,* **dil·ly-dal·lied, dil·ly-dal·ly·ing.**

di·lute (di lüt′ or dī lüt′) **1** make weaker or thinner by adding water or some other liquid. **2** weakened or thinned by water or some other liquid. 1 *v.,* **di·lut·ed, di·lut·ing;** 2 *adj.*

dim (dim) **1** not bright; not clear; not distinct: *dim light.* **2** not clearly or completely perceived or distinguished: *He had a dim memory of the event.* **3** not perceiving or distinguishing clearly or completely: *Her eyesight is getting dimmer.* **4** make or become dim: *We dimmed our lights when we reached the city streets.* 1–3 *adj.,* **dim·mer, dim·mest;** 4 *v.,* **dimmed, dim·ming.** **—dim′ly,** *adv.* **—dim′ness,** *n.*

dime (dīm) a coin of Canada and the United States, worth 10 cents: *Ten dimes make one dollar. n.*

di·men·sion (di men′shən or dī men′shən) **1** the measurement of length, breadth, or thickness: *The dimensions of my room are 4.2 metres by 3.1 metres.* **2** the size; extent: *It was a building of considerable dimensions. n.*

di·min·ish (di min′ish) make or become smaller in size, amount, or importance: *The heat diminished as the sun went down. v.*

di·min·u·tive (di min′yə tiv) small; tiny: *A midget is a diminutive person. adj.*

dim·mer (dim′ər) a device that dims an electric light. *n.*

dim·ple (dim′pəl) **1** a small hollow, usually in the cheek or chin. **2** make or show dimples in. **3** form dimples: *Her cheeks dimple whenever she smiles.* 1, *n.,* 2, 3 *v.,* **dim·pled, dim·pling.**

din (din) **1** a loud, confused noise that lasts for some time. **2** make a din. **3** say one thing over and over: *He was always dinning into our ears the importance of hard work.* 1 *n.,* 2, 3 *v.,* **dinned, din·ning.**

dine (dīn) **1** eat dinner. **2** give dinner to; give a dinner for: *The Chamber of Commerce dined the famous traveller. v.,* **dined, din·ing.**

din·er (dīn′ər) **1** a person who is eating dinner. **2** a railway car in which meals are served. **3** a small eating place, usually near a main highway. *n.*

ding–dong (ding′dong′) the sound made by a bell or anything like a bell; continuous ringing. *n.*

din·ghy (ding′gē) **1** a small rowboat. **2** a small boat used as a tender or lifeboat by a large boat. **3** a small sailboat. *n., pl.* **din·ghies.**

din·gy (din′jē) dirty-looking; lacking brightness or freshness; dull: *The old curtains were dingy. adj.,* **din·gi·er, din·gi·est.**

dining room a room in which dinner and other meals are served.

din·ner (din′ər) **1** the main meal of the day: *Some people have their dinner in the evening; others have it at noon.* **2** a formal meal in honor of some person or occasion: *The city officials gave the team a dinner to celebrate their victory.* *n.*

A dinosaur — about 22 m long

di·no·saur (dī′nə sôr′ or din′ə sôr′) any of a group of extinct reptiles: *Some dinosaurs were bigger than elephants; others were smaller than cats.* *n.*

dint (dint) 1 a hollow made by the force of a blow or by pressure; dent. 2 make a dent in. 3 become dented. 1 *n.*, 2, 3 *v.*

by dint of, by the force of or by means of: *By dint of hard work the job was completed on schedule.*

☞ See note at **dent.**

di·o·cese (dī′ə sis′) the district over which a bishop has authority. *n.*

dip (dip) 1 put under water or any liquid and lift quickly out again: *She dipped her hand into the pool.* 2 go under water and come quickly out again. 3 a dipping of any kind, especially a plunge into and out of a tub of water, the ocean, etc. 4 take up in the hollow of the hand or with a pail, pan, or other container: *dip up water from a well, dip up a sample of wheat.* 5 put one's hand, a spoon, etc. into to take out something: *He dipped into the jar and snatched a handful of cookies.* 6 a creamy mixture of foods eaten by dipping into it with a cracker, piece of bread, etc.: *a cheese dip.* 7 a liquid in which to dip something: *The sheep were driven through a dip to disinfect their coats.* 8 make a candle by putting a wick into hot tallow or wax. 9 lower and raise again quickly: *The ship's flag was dipped as a salute.* 10 slope downward: *The road dips into the valley.* 11 a sudden drop: *a dip in prices, a dip in the road.* 1, 2, 4, 5, 8–10 *v.*, **dipped** or **dipt, dip·ping;** 3, 6, 7, 11 *n.*

diph·the·ri·a (dif thēr′ē ə or dip thēr′ē ə) a dangerous infectious disease of the throat: *Years ago many children died of diphtheria.* *n.*

diph·thong (dif′thong′ or dip′thong′) 1 a vowel sound made up of two vowels run together and pronounced in one syllable, such as *oi* in *noise* or *ou* in *out.* 2 two vowel letters representing a single vowel sound, as *ea* in *eat.* *n.*

di·plo·ma (di plō′mə) a written or printed paper given by a school or college, which says that a person has completed a certain course of study, or has been graduated after a certain amount of work. *n.*

di·plo·ma·cy (də plō′mə sē) 1 the management of relations between nations: *The making of international agreements is an important part of diplomacy.* 2 skill in managing such relations: *The new trade agreement between Canada and China required great diplomacy on the part of both governments.* 3 skill in dealing with others; tact: *It was his diplomacy that kept the quarrelsome members from breaking up the club.* *n.*

dip·lo·mat (dip′lə mat′) 1 a person whose work is to handle the relations of his country with other nations. 2 a person skilful in dealing with people. *n.*

dip·lo·mat·ic (dip′lə mat′ik) 1 of or having to do with the management of relations between nations: *Ambassadors and consuls to foreign countries are in the diplomatic service.* 2 skilful in dealing with people; tactful: *a diplomatic policeman. He gave a diplomatic answer to avoid hurting his friend's feelings.* *adj.*

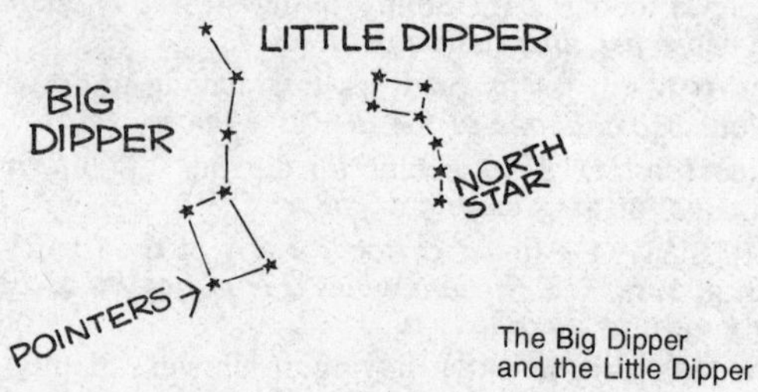

The Big Dipper and the Little Dipper

dip·per (dip′ər) 1 a long-handled cup or larger container for lifting water or other liquids. 2 **Dipper,** either of two groups of stars in the northern sky resembling dippers in shape; the Big Dipper or the Little Dipper. *n.*

dire (dīr) causing great fear or suffering; dreadful: *the dire results of a flood.* *adj.*

in dire need, in desperate or extreme need: *During the flood, many people were in dire need of food.*

di·rect (di rekt′ or dī rekt′) 1 manage; control; guide: *The teacher directs the work of the pupils.* 2 order; command: *The policeman directed the traffic to stop.* 3 tell or show the way: *Can you direct me to the airport? Signposts direct travellers.* 4 point; aim: *The fireman directed his hose at the flames. We should direct our efforts to a useful end.* 5 put the address on a letter, package, etc. 6 without a stop or turn; straight: *Our house is in direct line with the school. A bee makes a direct flight home to the hive.* 7 in an unbroken line of descent: *Queen Elizabeth II is a direct descendant of Queen Victoria.* 8 frank; truthful; plain: *The boy gave direct answers. She made a direct denial of the charge of cheating.* 9 directly: *This airplane goes to Winnipeg direct, without stopping on the way.* 1–5 *v.*, 6–8 *adj.*, 9 *adv.*

direct current an electric current that flows in one direction: *The current from all batteries is direct current.*

di·rec·tion (di rek′shən or dī rek′shən) 1 guidance; management; control: *The school is under the direction of a good principal.* 2 an order or command. 3 knowing or telling what to do, how to do, where to go, etc.; an instruction: *Can you give me directions on how to get to the lake?* 4 the address on a letter or package. 5 the course taken by a moving body, such as a ball or a bullet. 6 any way in which one may face or point: *North, south, east, and west are directions. Our school is in one direction and the post office is in another.* 7 a line of action; a tendency, etc.: *His interests have taken a new direction.* *n.*

di·rect·ly (di rekt′lē or dī rekt′lē) 1 in a direct line or manner; straight: *This road runs directly north.* 2 exactly; absolutely: *directly opposite.* 3 immediately; at once: *Come home directly.* *adv.*

di·rec·tor (di rek′tər or dī rek′tər) a manager; a person who directs: *A person who directs the production* *of a play, a motion picture, or a show on television or radio is called a director. n.*

di·rec·to·ry (di rek′tə rē or dī rek′tə rē) a list of names and addresses: *A telephone book is a directory. n., pl.* **di·rec·to·ries.**

dirge (dėrj) a song or tune of grief for a person's death. *n.*

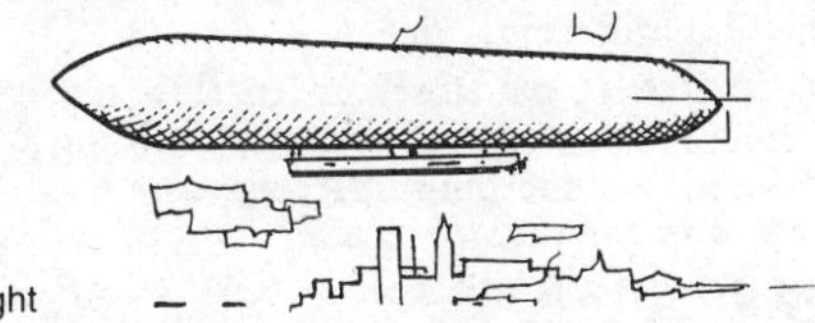

A dirigible in flight

dir·i·gi·ble (dir′ə jə bəl) a large cigar-shaped balloon that can be steered and is equipped to carry passengers; an airship: *A dirigible is filled with a gas that is lighter than air. n.*

dirk (dėrk) dagger. *n.*

dirt (dėrt) **1** mud, dust, earth, or anything like them: *Dirt soils skin, clothing, houses, or furniture.* **2** loose earth or soil. **3** uncleanness in action, thought or speech: *Some people object to dirt in movies. n.*

dirt·i·ness (dėr′tē nis) a dirty condition. *n.*

dirt·y (dėr′tē) **1** not clean; soiled by mud, dust, earth, or anything like them: *Children playing in the mud get dirty.* **2** not clear or pure in color: *a dirty red.* **3** low; mean; unfair: *a dirty trick.* **4** not decent; obscene: *a dirty joke.* **5** stormy; rough: *It was the dirtiest weather I ever saw.* **6** make dirty; soil: *Don't dirty your new dress by playing outside in this wet weather. The burglar dirtied his face to make himself hard to see in the dark.* 1–5 *adj.,* **dirt·i·er, dirt·i·est;** 6 *v.,* **dirt·ied, dirt·y·ing.**

dis– a prefix meaning: **1** the opposite of a condition: *Discontent is the opposite of content.* **2** the reverse of an action: *Disentangle is the reverse of entangle.*

dis·a·bil·i·ty (dis′ə bil′ə tē) **1** a lack of ability or power: *His disability was due to illness.* **2** something that disables: *Deafness is a disability for a musician. n., pl.* **dis·a·bil·i·ties.**

dis·a·ble (dis ā′bəl) deprive of ability or power; make useless; cripple: *His father was severely disabled in the accident. v.,* **dis·a·bled, dis·a·bling.**

dis·ad·van·tage (dis′əd van′tij) **1** a lack of advantage; an unfavorable condition: *Her shyness was a disadvantage in company.* **2** harm; loss: *The candidate's enemies spread rumors to his disadvantage. n.*

dis·a·gree (dis′ə grē′) **1** fail to agree; be different: *Your story disagrees with his.* **2** have unlike opinions; differ: *Doctors sometimes disagree.* **3** quarrel. **4** have a bad effect; be harmful: *Some foods disagree with him. v.,* **dis·a·greed, dis·a·gree·ing.**

dis·a·gree·a·ble (dis′ə grē′ə bəl) **1** not to one's liking; not pleasant: *A headache is disagreeable.* **2** not friendly; bad-tempered; cross: *She is sometimes disagreeable until she has her breakfast. adj.*

dis·a·gree·ment (dis′ə grē′mənt) **1** failure to agree; difference of opinion. **2** a quarrel; dispute: *After long discussion they settled their disagreement. n.*

dis·ap·pear (dis′ə pēr′) **1** pass from sight: *The little dog disappeared down the road.* **2** pass from existence; be lost: *When spring comes, the snow disappears. v.*

hat, āge, fär; let, ēqual, tėrm; it, īce
hot, ōpen, ôrder; oil, out; cup, pu̇t, rüle
əbove, takən, pencəl, lemən, circəs
ch, child; ng, long; sh, ship
th, thin; ᴛʜ, then; zh, measure

dis·ap·pear·ance (dis′ə pēr′əns) the act of disappearing: *The disappearance of the general brought about a search of the area. n.*

dis·ap·point (dis′ə point′) fail to satisfy one's desire, wish, or hope: *The circus disappointed him, for there was no elephant. We were disappointed that our cousin could not come. v.*

dis·ap·point·ment (dis′ə point′mənt) **1** the state of being disappointed; the feeling one has when one does not get what was expected or hoped for: *When she did not get a new bicycle, the disappointment seemed too great to bear.* **2** a person or thing that causes disappointment: *The dull clown was a disappointment to the audience.* **3** the act or fact of disappointing: *Ben's disappointment of their wishes showed that they could not rely on him. n.*

dis·ap·prov·al (dis′ə prüv′əl) an expression of opinion or feeling against; opinion against; dislike: *Father's disapproval showed in his frown. n.*

dis·ap·prove (dis′ə prüv′) consider not good or not suitable; have or express an opinion against: *Some parents disapprove of dancing. v.,* **dis·ap·proved, dis·ap·prov·ing.**

dis·arm (dis ärm′) **1** take weapons away from: *The police captured the bandits and disarmed them.* **2** stop having armed forces; reduce the size of armed forces. **3** remove anger, dislike, or suspicion: *The little boy's smile could usually disarm those who were about to scold or punish him.* **4** make harmless: *The soldiers disarmed the big bomb. v.*

dis·ar·ma·ment (dis är′mə mənt) **1** the act of disarming. **2** the reduction or limitation of armed forces and their equipment: *An international meeting was held to discuss plans for disarmament. n.*

dis·ar·range (dis′ə rānj′) disturb the arrangement of; put out of order: *The whole house was disarranged in the search for her pet snake. v.*

dis·as·ter (də zas′tər) an event that causes much suffering or loss; a great misfortune: *A flood, fire, shipwreck, earthquake, or great loss of money is a disaster. n.*

dis·as·trous (də zas′trəs) bringing disaster; causing danger, suffering, loss, pain, or sorrow to many people: *The train wreck was disastrous. adj.*

dis·band (dis band′) break up; dismiss: *When peace was declared, many regiments were disbanded. v.*

dis·be·lief (dis′bi lēf′) a lack of belief; refusal to believe: *When he heard the news, he stared in disbelief at the messenger. n.*

dis·be·lieve (dis′bi lēv′) have no belief in: *His mother disbelieved his story. v.,* **dis·be·lieved, dis·be·liev·ing.**

disc (disk) See **disk.**

dis·card (dis kärd′ for 1, dis′kärd for 2) **1** throw aside; give up as useless or worn out: *You can discard* *clothes, ways of doing things, or beliefs.* 2 something thrown aside: *That old book is a discard from the school library.* 1 *v.,* 2 *n.*

into the discard, among things thrown aside: *That old book can go into the discard now; I don't want it.*

dis·cern (di sėrn′ or di zėrn′) see clearly; distinguish; recognize; perceive: *She looked where he pointed, but could discern nothing. When there is so much propaganda, it is hard to discern the truth. v.*

dis·charge (dis chärj′ for 1, 3, 5, 7, 10, and 11, dis chärj′ or dis′chärj for 2, 4, 6, 8, 9, and 12) 1 unload cargo or passengers from a ship, airplane, train, bus, etc.: *The airplane's passengers were discharged at the new terminal.* 2 an unloading: *The discharge of this cargo will not take long.* 3 fire off; shoot: *to discharge a gun.* 4 the firing off of a gun, a blast, etc.: *The discharge of dynamite could be heard from here.* 5 release; let go; dismiss: *to discharge a patient from a hospital, to discharge a committee.* 6 the act of letting go; a release: *The convict expects his discharge from prison next month.* 7 give off; let out: *The wound was still discharging pus.* 8 giving off; letting out: *In a thunderstorm there is a discharge of electricity from the clouds.* 9 something given off or let out: *the watery discharge from a sore.* 10 pay; settle: *discharge a debt.* 11 perform; carry out: *He discharged all the errands he had been given.* 12 carrying out; performance: *A public official should be honest in the discharge of his duties.* 1, 3, 5, 7, 10, 11 *v.,* **dis·charged, dis·charg·ing;** 2, 4, 6, 8, 9, 12 *n.*

dis·ci·ple (də sī′pəl) 1 a believer in the thought and teaching of any leader; a follower. 2 one of the twelve original followers of Jesus. *n.*

dis·ci·pline (dis′ə plin) 1 training, especially of the mind or character. 2 a trained condition of order and obedience; order kept among school pupils, soldiers, or members of any group: *When the fire broke out, the pupils showed good discipline.* 3 train; bring to a condition of order and obedience; bring under control: *A good officer must know how to discipline men.* 4 punishment: *A little discipline would do him a world of good.* 5 punish: *The rebellious convicts were severely disciplined.* 1, 2, 4 *n.,* 3, 5 *v.,* **dis·ci·plined, dis·ci·plin·ing.**

dis·claim (dis klām′) refuse to recognize as one's own; deny connection with: *The motorist disclaimed responsibility for the accident. v.*

dis·close (dis klōz′) 1 open to view; uncover: *The lifting of the curtain disclosed a beautiful Christmas tree.* 2 make known: *The letter discloses a secret. v.,* **dis·closed, dis·clos·ing.**

dis·col·or or **dis·col·our** (dis kul′ər) 1 change or spoil the color of; stain: *Smoke had discolored the building.* 2 become changed in color: *Many materials discolor if exposed to bright sunshine. v.*

dis·com·fort (dis kum′fərt) 1 lack of comfort: *He felt considerable discomfort after the operation.* 2 a feeling of embarrassment, confusion, etc.: *Her discomfort increased as her guilt became more and more evident.* 3 something that causes discomfort: *Life in the Barrens has many discomforts. n.*

dis·con·nect (dis′kə nekt′) separate; unfasten; undo or break the connection of: *He disconnected the electric fan by pulling out the plug. v.*

dis·con·nect·ed (dis′kə nek′tid) without order or connection; broken; confused: *The injured man's account of the accident was so disconnected that it was hard to tell what had happened. adj.*

dis·con·tent (dis′kən tent′) an uneasy feeling of dissatisfaction; a dislike of what one has and a desire for something different. *n.*

dis·con·tent·ed (dis′kən ten′tid) not contented; not satisfied; displeased and restless; disliking what one has and wanting something different: *She was discontented with life in the country. adj.*

dis·con·tin·ue (dis′kən tin′yü) stop; give up; put an end or stop to: *The morning train has been discontinued. The doctor discontinued his visits. v.,* **dis·con·tin·ued, dis·con·tin·u·ing.**

dis·cord (dis′kôrd) 1 harsh, clashing sounds. 2 in music, a lack of harmony in notes sounded at the same time. 3 a difference of opinion; disagreement; unfriendly relations: *There was discord among the players on the losing team. Angry discord spoiled the meeting. n.*

dis·cord·ant (dis kôr′dənt) 1 harsh; clashing: *The sound of some automobile horns is discordant.* 2 not in harmony: *a discordant note in music.* 3 not in agreement; not fitting together: *Many discordant views were expressed. adj.*

dis·count (dis′kount, sometimes dis kount′ for 1 and 3) 1 take off a certain amount from a price: *The store discounts 3 per cent on all bills paid when due.* 2 the amount taken off a price: *During the sale the dealer allowed a 10 per cent discount on all cash purchases.* 3 take off from a statement; allow for exaggeration in: *You must discount what Jack tells you, for he is too fond of a good story.* 1, 3 *v.,* 2 *n.*

discount store, a store that sells its goods for less than the regular price.

dis·cour·age (dis kėr′ij) 1 take away the courage of; destroy the hopes of: *Repeated failure discourages anyone.* 2 try to prevent by disapproving; frown upon: *All her friends discouraged her from such a dangerous swim.* 3 make unattractive; make seem not worthwhile: *The chill of autumn soon discouraged their picnics. v.,* **dis·cour·aged, dis·cour·ag·ing.**

dis·cour·age·ment (dis kėr′ij mənt) 1 the state of being or feeling discouraged: *Failure is often followed by discouragement.* 2 something that discourages: *The defeat was a great discouragement for the troops.* 3 the act of discouraging. *n.*

dis·course (dis′kôrs for 1 and 2, dis kôrs′ for 3) 1 a long written or spoken discussion of some subject: *Sermons and lectures are discourses.* 2 talk; conversation: *The friendly discourse lasted all evening.* 3 to talk; converse. 1, 2 *n.,* 3 *v.,* **dis·coursed, dis·cours·ing.**

dis·cour·te·ous (dis kėr′tē əs) not courteous; not polite; rude: *a discourteous act. adj.*

dis·cour·te·sy (dis kėr′tə sē) 1 impoliteness; rudeness. 2 a rude or impolite act: *He was scolded for his discourtesies to the neighbors. n., pl.* **dis·cour·te·sies.**

dis·cov·er (dis kuv′ər) find out; see or learn of for the first time: *No one has discovered a way to turn copper into gold. v.* **—dis·cov′er·er,** *n.*

dis·cov·er·y (dis kuv′ər ē) 1 finding out; the seeing

hat, āge, fär; let, ēqual, tėrm; it, īce
hot, ōpen, ôrder; oil, out; cup, pu̇t, rüle
əbove, takən, pencəl, lemən, circəs
ch, child; ng, long; sh, ship
th, thin; ᴛʜ, then; zh, measure

or learning of something for the first time. 2 the thing found out: *One of Benjamin Franklin's discoveries was that lightning was caused by electricity.* *n., pl.* **dis·cov·er·ies.**

dis·cred·it (dis kred′it) 1 cast doubt on; destroy belief or trust in a person, a story, or something thought to be true: *The lawyer discredited the witness by showing that he had lied. His story discredits her account of the trip.* 2 refuse to believe: *We discredit her because she has lied so often.* 3 do harm to the reputation of; give a bad reputation to: *Losing five battles discredited the general among his troops.* 4 the loss of good name or standing; disgrace: *The young thief brought discredit to his family.* 5 a person or thing that causes loss of good name or standing: *The traitor was a discredit to his country.* 1–3 *v.*, 4, 5 *n.*

dis·creet (dis krēt′) 1 careful and sensible in speech and action: *a discreet lawyer.* 2 showing good sense; showing good judgment: *a discreet remark.* *adj.*

dis·cre·tion (dis kresh′ən) 1 the freedom to judge or choose: *It is within the principal's discretion to punish a pupil.* 2 good judgment; carefulness in speech and action; caution: *You will need discretion to criticize him without hurting his feelings.* *n.*

dis·crim·i·nate (dis krim′ə nāt′) 1 make or see a difference between; distinguish: *He is partly color-blind and cannot discriminate between red and green.* 2 make a distinction: *The law ought not to discriminate against any race, creed, or color.* *v.*, **dis·crim·i·nat·ed, dis·crim·i·nat·ing.**

dis·crim·i·na·tion (dis krim′ə nā′shən) 1 the act of making or recognizing differences and distinctions: *Do not buy clothes without discrimination.* 2 the ability to make fine distinctions: *She is a person of discrimination.* 3 the act of making or showing a difference in treatment: *Discrimination in race or creed when hiring people is against the law.* *n.*

dis·cuss (dis kus′) talk over; consider from various points of view: *The class discussed several problems. His mother discussed his failure with his teacher.* *v.*

dis·cus·sion (dis kush′ən) talk; talk about the reasons for and against; the act of discussing things: *His arrival caused much discussion in the village. After two hours' discussion we seemed no nearer a decision.* *n.*

dis·dain (dis dān′) 1 scorn; look down on; consider beneath oneself: *The honest official disdained the offer of a bribe.* 2 scorn; looking down on a person or an act as beneath one: *He treated his younger brothers and sisters with disdain.* 1 *v.*, 2 *n.* **—dis·dain′ful,** *adj.*

dis·ease (də zēz′) 1 sickness; illness: *People, animals, and plants are all liable to suffer from disease.* 2 any particular illness: *Chicken pox is an infectious disease.* *n.*

dis·eased (də zēzd′) having a disease; being diseased: *a diseased hand, a diseased elm.* *adj.*

dis·em·bark (dis′em bärk′) land from a ship or an airplane: *We disembarked from the ocean liner at Montreal. The passengers were disembarked at the Regina airport.* *v.*

dis·fa·vor or **dis·fa·vour** (dis fā′vər) 1 dislike; disapproval: *The employees looked with disfavor on any attempt to change their cafeteria.* 2 being regarded with dislike or disapproval: *The ambassador was in disfavor with the government at home.* *n.*

dis·fig·ure (dis fig′ər or dis fig′yər) spoil the appearance of; hurt the beauty of: *Huge advertising signs disfigure the countryside. A scar disfigured his face.* *v.*, **dis·fig·ured, dis·fig·ur·ing.**

dis·grace (dis grās′) 1 a loss of respect or honor: *The boy's disgrace was deeply felt by his mother.* 2 cause to lose honor; dishonor; bring shame upon: *He disgraced his family by his behavior.* 3 anything that causes dishonor or shame: *Their unfriendly treatment of the new neighbors was a disgrace.* 1, 3 *n.*, 2 *v.*, **dis·graced, dis·grac·ing.**
in disgrace, in a state of dishonor or shame: *The girl was in disgrace for cheating on an exam.*

dis·grace·ful (dis grās′fəl) shameful; causing dishonor or loss of respect; deserving disgrace: *Her behavior was disgraceful.* *adj.* **—dis·grace′ful·ly,** *adv.*

dis·guise (dis gīz′) 1 make changes in clothes or appearance to hide who one really is or to look like someone else: *In his Santa Claus costume, my uncle was well disguised.* 2 the use of a changed or unusual dress and appearance in order not to be recognized: *Detectives sometimes depend on disguise.* 3 the clothes or actions used to hide or deceive: *Women's clothes and a wig formed his disguise.* 4 hide what something really is; make something seem like something else: *The pirates disguised their ship. He disguised his hatred by a show of friendly interest.* 1, 4 *v.*, **dis·guised, dis·guis·ing;** 2, 3 *n.*

dis·gust (dis gust′) 1 strong dislike; sickening dislike: *We feel disgust for bad odors or tastes.* 2 arouse sickening dislike in: *The smell of the carcass beside the road disgusted them.* 3 displease by offensive conduct: *Their cursing disgusted him.* 1 *n.*, 2, 3 *v.*

dis·gust·ed (dis gus′tid) 1 filled with disgust. 2 *Informal.* fed up; tired: *She said she was disgusted with their constant quarrelling.* *adj.* **—dis·gust′ed·ly,** *adv.*

dish (dish) 1 anything to serve food in, such as a plate, platter, bowl, cup, or saucer. 2 the amount of food served in a dish: *I ate two dishes of ice cream.* 3 the food served: *Sliced peaches with cream is the dish I like best.* 4 put into a dish for serving at the table: *You may dish the dinner now.* 1–3 *n.*, 4 *v.*
dish up, put in a dish to serve: *She asked Mary to dish up the potatoes.*

dis·heart·en (dis här′tən) discourage; depress: *Long illness is disheartening.* *v.*

di·shev·elled or **di·shev·eled** (də shev′əld) 1 rumpled; disordered; untidy: *a dishevelled appearance.* 2 hanging loosely or in disorder: *dishevelled hair.* *adj.*

dish·ful (dish′fu̇l) as much as a dish can hold. *n., pl.* **dish·fuls.**

dis·hon·est (dis on′ist) 1 unfair; not fair: *Lying, cheating, and stealing are dishonest.* 2 not honest; ready to cheat; not upright: *A person who lies or steals is dishonest.* 3 arranged to work in an unfair way: *a dishonest card game, dishonest scales.* *adj.*

dis·hon·es·ty (dis on′is tē) 1 lying, cheating, or stealing; a lack of honesty. 2 something done or said that is dishonest: *He was guilty of many dishonesties.* *n., pl.* **dis·hon·es·ties.**

dis·hon·or or **dis·hon·our** (dis on′ər) 1 disgrace; shame; loss of reputation or standing. 2 a person or thing that causes dishonor: *A thief is a dishonor to his family.* 3 bring reproach or shame to: *A crooked police officer dishonors the entire force.* 1, 2 *n.*, 3 *v.*

dis·hon·or·a·ble or **dis·hon·our·a·ble** (dis on′ər ə bəl) without honor; disgraceful; shameful. *adj.*

dish·pan (dish′pan′) a pan in which to wash dishes. *n.*

dish·wash·er (dish′wosh′ər) 1 a person who washes dishes. 2 a machine for washing dishes, glasses, etc. *n.*

dis·in·fect (dis′in fekt′) destroy the harmful bacteria, etc. in or on: *A doctor's instruments are disinfected before they are used.* *v.*

dis·in·fect·ant (dis′in fek′tənt) a means for destroying harmful bacteria, etc.: *Alcohol and chlorine are disinfectants.* *n.*

dis·in·te·grate (dis in′tə grāt′) break up; separate into small parts or bits: *The explosion completely disintegrated the building. The old papers had disintegrated into a pile of fragments and dust.* *v.*, **dis·in·te·grat·ed, dis·in·te·grat·ing.**

dis·in·ter·est·ed (dis in′tris tid or dis in′tər es′tid) not having or showing selfish motives; not concerned with one's own interests: *The mayor's support of the building program was completely disinterested.* *adj.* ☞ See note at **interested.**

disk or **disc** (disk) 1 a flat, thin, round object shaped like a coin. 2 a round, flat surface, or a surface that seems so. 3 a record for a record player, phonograph, gramophone, etc. *n.*

disk jockey or **disc jockey** *Informal.* a person who makes a living playing records for a radio station.

dis·like (dis līk′) 1 a feeling of not liking; a feeling against: *I have a dislike of rain and fog.* 2 not like; object to; have a feeling against: *He dislikes studying and would rather play football.* 1 *n.*, 2 *v.*, **dis·liked, dis·lik·ing.**

dis·lo·cate (dis′lō kāt′) 1 cause one or more of the bones of a joint to be shifted out of place: *He dislocated his shoulder when he fell.* 2 disturb; put out of order; upset: *Our plans for a picnic were dislocated by the bad weather.* *v.*, **dis·lo·cat·ed, dis·lo·cat·ing.**

dis·lodge (dis loj′) drive or force out of a place, position, etc.: *The workman used a crowbar to dislodge a heavy stone from the wall. Heavy fire dislodged the enemy from the fort.* *v.*, **dis·lodged, dis·lodg·ing.**

dis·loy·al (dis loi′əl) not loyal; faithless: *A disloyal servant let thieves into the house.* *adj.*

dis·loy·al·ty (dis loi′əl tē) unfaithfulness: *The traitor was shot for disloyalty to his country.* *n., pl.* **dis·loy·al·ties.**

dis·mal (diz′məl) 1 dark; gloomy: *Damp caves and rainy days are dismal.* 2 dreary; miserable: *Sickness often makes a person feel dismal.* *adj.*

dis·man·tle (dis man′təl) 1 remove furniture, equipment, etc. from: *to dismantle a house, a fort, or a ship.* 2 pull down; take down; take apart: *We had to dismantle the bookcases to move them.* *v.*, **dis·man·tled, dis·man·tling.**

dis·may (dis mā′) 1 a loss of courage because of dislike or fear of what is about to happen or what has happened: *The mother was filled with dismay when her son confessed he had robbed a store.* 2 trouble greatly; make afraid: *The thought that she might fail the history test dismayed her.* 1 *n.*, 2 *v.*

dis·miss (dis mis′) 1 send away; allow to go: *The teacher dismissed the class at noon.* 2 remove from office or service; not allow to keep a job: *She dismissed the cook because his cooking was so poor.* 3 put away; stop thinking about: *They decided it was time to dismiss their troubles.* *v.*

dis·miss·al (dis mis′əl) 1 the act of dismissing: *The school board's dismissal of the teacher was the cause of a demonstration by the students.* 2 the state or fact of being dismissed. 3 a written or spoken order dismissing someone: *He received his dismissal in silence.* *n.*

dis·mount (dis mount′) 1 get off a horse, bicycle, etc.: *The cavalry dismounted near the woods.* 2 knock, throw, or otherwise remove another person from a horse: *The first knight dismounted the second.* 3 take a thing from its setting or support: *The cannon were dismounted for shipping to another fort.* *v.*

dis·o·be·di·ence (dis′ə bē′dē əns) refusal to obey; failure to obey: *Disobedience cannot be allowed in the army.* *n.*

dis·o·be·di·ent (dis′ə bē′dē ənt) failing to follow orders or rules; refusing to obey. *adj.*

dis·o·bey (dis′ə bā′) fail to follow orders or rules; refuse to obey: *The child was spanked when he disobeyed his father.* *v.*

dis·or·der (dis ôr′dər) 1 lack of order; confusion: *The disorder of the children's room was shocking.* 2 disturb the regular order or working of; throw into confusion: *A series of accidents disordered the shop.* 3 a tumult; riot. 4 a sickness or disease: *a disorder of the stomach.* 1, 3, 4 *n.*, 2 *v.*

dis·or·der·ly (dis ôr′dər lē) 1 not orderly; untidy; confused: *The troops fled in a disorderly rout.* 2 causing disorder; making a disturbance; breaking rules; unruly: *a disorderly mob.* *adj.*

dis·or·gan·ize (dis ôr′gən īz′) throw into confusion or disorder: *Heavy snowstorms disorganized the train service.* *v.*, **dis·or·gan·ized, dis·or·gan·iz·ing.**

dis·own (dis ōn′) refuse to recognize as one's own; cast off: *He disowned his disobedient son. The politician disowned his former views.* *v.*

dis·patch or **des·patch** (dis pach′) 1 send off to some place for some purpose: *He dispatched a messenger to tell the king what had happened.* 2 the act of sending off a letter, a messenger, etc.: *Please hurry the dispatch of this telegram.* 3 a written message, such as a news report or a report to a government by an ambassador or other official: *This dispatch has been two days on the way.* 4 get something done promptly: *The job was quickly dispatched.* 5 promptness in doing anything; speed: *This boy works with neatness and dispatch.* 6 kill: *He dispatched the deer with his first shot.* 7 *Informal.* finish off; eat up: *The hungry girl quickly dispatched the meal.* 1, 4, 6, 7 *v.*, 2, 3, 5 *n.*

dis·patch·er or **des·patch·er** (dis pach′ər) a

person who dispatches: *He has a part-time job as a dispatcher for a taxi company.* *n.*

dis·pel (dis pel′) disperse; drive away and scatter: *The captain's cheerful laugh dispelled their fears.* *v.,* **dis·pelled, dis·pel·ling.**

dis·pense (dis pens′) **1** give out; distribute: *The Red Cross dispensed food and clothing to the homeless refugees.* **2** apply; carry out; cause to operate: *Judges and law courts dispense justice.* **3** prepare and give out: *A druggist dispenses medicines.* *v.,* **dis·pensed, dis·pens·ing.**

dispense with, a get rid of; do away with: *He dispensed with the old papers by burning them. The dictator dispensed with his enemies by killing them.* **b** get along without; do without: *To lose weight, one should dispense with eating rich, sugary food.*

dispense with someone's services, dismiss someone from a job or post; fire someone: *The store keeper decided to dispense with the lazy clerk's services.*

dis·pens·er (dis pens′ər) a container, often automatic, which is so made that it releases its contents one at a time: *There are dispensers for gum, chocolate bars, sandwiches, cigarettes, etc.* *n.*

dis·perse (dis pėrs′) **1** scatter; send in different directions: *The mounted police dispersed the rioters.* **2** go in different directions: *The crowd dispersed when the game was over.* *v.,* **dis·persed, dis·pers·ing.**

dis·place (dis plās′) **1** take the place of; put something else in the place of: *The automobile has displaced the horse and buggy.* **2** remove from a position of authority: *The police chief was displaced by a younger man.* **3** put out of place; move from its usual place or position: *When he returned, he saw that several of his tools had been displaced.* *v.,* **dis·placed, dis·plac·ing.**

dis·play (dis plā′) **1** show; reveal: *He displayed his good nature by answering all our questions.* **2** showing; exhibition: *He did not like the boy's display of bad temper.* **3** show in a special way, so as to attract attention: *The boys' suits were displayed in the big window of the store.* **4** a planned showing of a thing, for some special purpose; exhibit: *Grade 4 had two displays of children's drawings.* 1, 3 *v.,* 2, 4 *n.*

dis·please (dis plēz′) offend; annoy; not please: *By failing to obey your mother you displeased her.* *v.,* **dis·pleased, dis·pleas·ing.**

dis·pleas·ure (dis plezh′ər) annoyance; disapproval; slight anger: *We feel displeasure at something we dislike. His displeasure could be heard in his angry tones.* *n.*

dis·pos·al (dis pōz′əl) **1** the act of getting rid of something: *the disposal of garbage.* **2** dealing with; a settling: *His disposal of the difficulty pleased everybody.* **3** placing in a certain order or position; arrangement: *The disposal of the chairs along the sides of the hall left plenty of space for dancing.* *n.*

at one's disposal, ready for one's use or service at any time: *She put all her books at her guests' disposal.*

dis·pose (dis pōz′) put in a certain order or position; arrange: *The ships were disposed in a straight line.* *v.,* **dis·posed, dis·pos·ing.**

dispose of, a get rid of: *Dispose of that rubbish.* **b** give away or sell: *The Salvation Army will dispose of this clothing. The agent disposed of all their property for $5000.* **c** arrange; settle: *The club disposed of all its business in an hour.*

hat, āge, fär; let, ēqual, tėrm; it, īce
hot, ōpen, ôrder; oil, out; cup, pu̇t, rüle
əbove, takən, pencəl, lemən, circəs
ch, child; ng, long; sh, ship
th, thin; ᴛʜ, then; zh, measure

dis·posed (dis pōzd′) having a particular disposition or attitude: *a well-disposed young man. How were they disposed toward the plan?* *adj.*

disposed to, inclined; tending: *He is always disposed to get mad at the least little thing.*

dis·po·si·tion (dis′pə zish′ən) **1** one's usual way of acting toward others or of thinking about things: *a cheerful disposition, a selfish disposition.* **2** a tendency; an inclination or natural bent: *a disposition to argue.* **3** putting in order; an arrangement: *Before the battle the general carefully checked the disposition of his troops.* *n.*

dis·prove (dis prüv′) prove false or incorrect: *Sam disproved Bill's statement that he had less candy by weighing both boxes.* *v.,* **dis·proved, dis·prov·ing.**

dis·pute (dis pyüt′) **1** argue; debate: *She refused to dispute the matter.* **2** an argument; debate. **3** a quarrel because of a difference of opinion: *The dispute between the two countries threatened to break out into war.* **4** disagree with a statement; say that a statement is false or doubtful: *The insurance company disputed his claim for damages to his car.* **5** fight for; fight over: *The soldiers disputed every inch of ground when the enemy attacked.* 1, 4, 5 *v.,* **dis·put·ed, dis·put·ing;** 2, 3 *n.*

dis·qual·i·fy (dis kwol′ə fī′) **1** make unfit; make unable to do something: *His lame foot disqualified him for active work.* **2** declare unfit or unable to do something: *He was disqualified from voting because he was in jail.* **3** in sports, withhold the right to play or the right to win a competition: *The hockey team was disqualified by the referee for refusing to come out on the ice.* *v.,* **dis·qual·i·fied, dis·qual·i·fy·ing.**

dis·re·gard (dis′ri gärd′) **1** pay no attention to; take no notice of: *Disregarding his clothing, he jumped into the lake to save the child.* **2** neglect; lack of attention: *The reckless driver was arrested for his disregard of traffic laws.* 1 *v.,* 2 *n.*

dis·re·pair (dis′ri per′) a bad condition; a need of repairs: *A car in a state of disrepair may be too unsafe to drive.* *n.*

dis·rep·u·ta·ble (dis rep′yə tə bəl) **1** having a bad reputation; shady: *Some dance halls are disreputable places.* **2** shabby; much worn: *a disreputable old hat.* *adj.*

dis·re·spect (dis′ri spekt′) rudeness; lack of respect: *I am sure he meant no disrespect by his remark.* *n.*

dis·re·spect·ful (dis′ri spekt′fəl) rude; showing no respect; lacking in courtesy to elders or superiors: *The disrespectful boy laughed at his father.* *adj.*

dis·rupt (dis rupt′) break up; split: *A violent quarrel disrupted the meeting.* *v.*

dis·sat·is·fac·tion (dis′sat is fak′shən) discontent; displeasure: *Poor food caused dissatisfaction among the soldiers.* *n.*

dis·sat·is·fied (dis sat′is fīd′) discontented; displeased: *When we do not get what we want, we are dissatisfied.* *adj.*

dis·sect (di sekt′ or dī sekt′) **1** cut up or apart, especially an animal or plant so as to examine it or study how it is made. **2** examine part by part; analyse: *The committee dissected the applicants' qualifications for the job.* *v.*

dis·sen·sion (di sen′shən) a disputing or quarrelling; hard feelings caused by a difference in opinion: *There was dissension at the party when some children got prizes and others didn't.* *n.*

dis·sent (di sent′) **1** disagree; think differently; express a different opinion from others: *Most of the class wanted to have a picnic, but three boys dissented.* **2** disagreement; difference of opinion: *Dissent among the members broke up the club meeting.* 1 *v.*, 2 *n.*

☛ **Dissent** and **descent** are pronounced the same.

dis·sim·i·lar (di sim′ə lər) unlike; different; not similar: *dissimilar opinions.* *adj.*

dis·si·pate (dis′ə pāt′) **1** scatter; spread in different directions. **2** disappear: *The fog had dissipated by 9 a.m.* **3** cause to disappear; dispel: *The sun dissipated the clouds.* **4** spend foolishly; waste on things of little value: *The extravagant son soon dissipated his father's fortune.* *v.*, **dis·si·pat·ed, dis·si·pat·ing.**

dis·solve (di zolv′) **1** make liquid; become liquid, especially by putting or being put into a liquid: *You can dissolve sugar in water. Sugar dissolves in water.* **2** put an end to: *to dissolve an agreement or a partnership.* **3** fade away: *My dream dissolved when I woke up.* *v.*, **dis·solved, dis·solv·ing.**

dis·so·nant (dis′ə nənt) **1** clashing; not in harmony: *the dissonant sounds of an orchestra tuning up.* **2** out of harmony with other views or persons; disagreeing: *Her dissonant views always made the meetings unpleasant and long.* *adj.*

dis·suade (di swād′) persuade not to do something: *The father finally dissuaded his son from leaving school.* *v.*, **dis·suad·ed, dis·suad·ing.**

dis·tance (dis′təns) **1** the space in between: *The distance from the farm to the town is five kilometres.* **2** a long way; far away: *The farm is situated quite a distance from the highway.* *n.*

in the distance, a long way off: *The sailors saw a light in the distance.*

dis·tant (dis′tənt) **1** far away in space: *Vancouver is distant from Quebec City. The earth is distant from the moon.* **2** away: *The town is five kilometres distant.* **3** far apart in time, relationship, likeness, etc.; not close: *A third cousin is a distant relative.* **4** not friendly: *She gave him only a distant nod.* *adj.*

dis·taste (dis tāst′) dislike: *His distaste for carrots showed clearly on his face.* *n.*

dis·taste·ful (dis tāst′fəl) unpleasant; disagreeable; offensive: *a distasteful medicine, a distasteful task.* *adj.*

dis·tem·per (dis tem′pər) **1** an infectious disease of dogs and other animals: *An animal with distemper has a short, dry cough and becomes very weak.* **2** any sickness of the mind or body; disorder; disease. *n.*

dis·tend (dis tend′) stretch out; expand; swell out: *His cheeks distended when he blew his bugle. The balloon was distended almost to bursting point.* *v.*

dis·til or **dis·till** (dis til′) **1** treat a liquid such as water by boiling it to make a vapor and then cooling the vapor to condense it: *Distilled water is pure because the impurities in the original water do not vaporize when the water does.* **2** obtain by distilling: *Gasoline is distilled from crude oil.* **3** give off in drops: *These flowers distil a sweet nectar.* *v.*, **dis·tilled, dis·til·ling.**

dis·til·la·tion (dis′tə lā′shən) **1** a distilling. **2** something distilled: *Kerosene is a distillation of petroleum.* *n.*

dis·tinct (dis tingkt′) **1** separate; not the same: *two distinct sounds.* **2** different in quality or kind: *Mice are distinct from rats.* **3** clear; easily seen, heard, or understood: *Your speech and writing should be distinct.* **4** unmistakable; definite: *She had a distinct lisp.* *adj.* —**dis·tinct′ly,** *adv.*

dis·tinc·tion (dis tingk′shən) **1** making a difference; distinguishing from others: *He treated all alike, without distinction.* **2** a difference: *What is the distinction between ducks and geese?* **3** a mark or sign of honor: *He won many distinctions for bravery.* **4** excellence; superiority: *The Governor General is a man of character and distinction.* *n.*

dis·tinc·tive (dis tingk′tiv) clearly distinguishing from others; special; characteristic: *Boy Scouts wear a distinctive uniform.* *adj.*

dis·tin·guish (dis ting′gwish) **1** see the differences between; tell apart: *Can you distinguish cotton cloth from linen?* **2** see or hear clearly; make out plainly: *It was too dark for her to distinguish the outline of the house.* **3** make different; be a special quality or feature of: *A trunk distinguishes the elephant.* **4** make famous or well-known: *He distinguished himself by winning three prizes.* *v.*

dis·tin·guished (dis ting′gwisht) **1** famous; well-known: *a distinguished artist.* **2** showing excellence; bringing honor or distinction: *He received a medal for distinguished conduct.* *adj.*

dis·tort (dis tôrt′) **1** pull or twist out of shape; make crooked or ugly: *His face was distorted with rage.* **2** change from the truth: *The man distorted the facts of the accident to escape blame.* *v.*

dis·tract (dis trakt′) **1** draw away the mind or attention: *Noise distracts me from my studying.* **2** confuse; disturb: *Several people talking at once distract a listener.* **3** put out of one's mind; make almost insane: *The mother was distracted while her child was lost. The wounded dog was almost distracted with fear.* *v.*

dis·trac·tion (dis trak′shən) **1** the act of drawing away the mind or the attention. **2** anything that draws away the mind or the attention: *Noise is a distraction when someone is trying to study.* **3** confusion of mind: *The mother of the lost child scarcely knew what she was doing in her distraction.* **4** an amusement; a source of relief from thought, grief, or work: *Movies are a convenient distraction when one needs to relax.* *n.*

dis·tress (dis tres′) **1** great pain or sorrow; anxiety; trouble: *The loss of her job caused her great distress.* **2** cause pain or sorrow to; make unhappy. **3** misery; misfortune: *The forest fire caused great distress in the mining town.* **4** a dangerous condition; a difficult situation: *A sinking ship is in distress.* 1, 3, 4 *n.*, 2 *v.*

dis·trib·ute (dis trib′yət) **1** give some to each; deal out: *She distributed the candy among the children.* **2** spread; scatter: *Distribute the paint evenly over the wall.* **3** divide into parts: *The children were distributed* *into three groups for the tour.* 4 arrange; sort out: *A post-office clerk distributes mail when he puts each letter into the proper bag. v.,* **dis·trib·ut·ed, dis·trib·ut·ing.**

dis·tri·bu·tion (dis′trə byü′shən) 1 the act of distributing: *After the contest the distribution of prizes to the winners took place.* 2 a way of being distributed: *If some children get more candy than others, there is an uneven distribution.* 3 anything distributed. *n.*

dis·trict (dis′trikt) 1 a part of a larger area; a region: *Northern Ontario is the leading gold-mining district in Canada. They lived in a fashionable district of the city.* 2 a part of a country, a province, or a city marked off for a special purpose, such as providing schools, electing officials, etc.: *a school district, a local improvement district. The Northwest Territories are divided into three districts: Mackenzie, Keewatin, and Franklin. n.*

dis·trust (dis trust′) 1 have no confidence in; not trust; not depend on: *A fat man learns to distrust wobbly chairs.* 2 lack of trust; lack of belief in the goodness of: *She could not overcome her distrust of the stranger.* 1 *v.,* 2 *n.*

dis·turb (dis tėrb′) 1 destroy the peace, quiet, or rest of: *Heavy truck traffic disturbed the neighborhood all day long.* 2 break in upon with noise or change: *Do not disturb the baby; he is asleep.* 3 put out of order: *Someone has disturbed all my papers.* 4 make uneasy; trouble: *He was disturbed to hear of her illness. v.*

dis·turb·ance (dis tėr′bəns) 1 a disturbing or being disturbed. 2 anything that disturbs: *The roar of the traffic was a disturbance.* 3 confusion; disorder: *The police were called to quell the disturbance.* 4 uneasiness; trouble; worry: *mental disturbance. n.*

ditch (dich) 1 a long, narrow trench dug in the earth: *Ditches are usually used to carry off water.* 2 dig a ditch in. 3 run into or cause to run into a ditch: *The drunken driver ditched his car.* 4 abandon, especially an airplane in flight: *The pilot had to ditch the airplane because one of the engines was on fire.* 1 *n.,* 2–4 *v.*

dit·to (dit′ō) 1 the same; exactly the same as appeared before. 2 a mark (〃) that stands for ditto. *Example:*

6 kg beans at 90¢ $5.40
4 〃 〃 〃 〃 .....$3.60 *n., pl.* **dit·tos.**

dit·ty (dit′ē) a short, simple song or poem. *n., pl.* **dit·ties.**

di·van (dī′van or di van′) a long, low, soft couch. *n.*

dive (dīv) 1 plunge headfirst into the water. 2 the act of diving. 3 a downward plunge of an airplane. 4 to plunge the body, the hand, or the mind suddenly into anything: *He dived into his pocket and fished out a dollar.* 1, 4 *v.,* **dived** or **dove, dived, div·ing;** 2, 3 *n.*

☛ **Dived** and **dove** are both used for the past tense of **dive,** though **dived** seems to be more widely preferred in writing and in formal English.

A diver in a diving suit

div·er (dīv′ər) 1 a person whose occupation is to work under water. 2 a diving bird: *The loon is a well-known Canadian diver. n.*

hat, āge, fär; let, ēqual, tėrm; it, īce
hot, ōpen, ôrder; oil, out; cup, pu̇t, rüle
əbove, takən, pencəl, lemən, circəs
ch, child; ng, long; sh, ship
th, thin; ᴛʜ, then; zh, measure

di·verge (di vėrj′ or dī vėrj′) extend or lie in different directions from a given point or from each other; branch off: *Their paths diverged at the corner and each went his own way. v.*

di·vers (dī′vərz) various; several different: *She leafed through divers books in the library. adj.*

di·verse (di vėrs′, dī vėrs′, or dī′vėrs) different; completely unlike: *A great many diverse opinions were expressed at the meeting. adj.*

di·ver·sion (di vėr′zhən or dī vėr′zhən) 1 a turning aside: *A magician's talk creates a diversion of attention so that people do not see how he does his tricks.* 2 a source of relief from work, care, etc.; amusement; pastime: *Watching television is a popular diversion. n.*

di·ver·si·ty (di vėr′sə tē or dī vėr′sə tē) 1 complete difference; unlikeness: *Their diversity did not prevent them from being friends.* 2 variety: *The diversity of food on the table made it hard for him to choose. n., pl.* **di·ver·si·ties.**

di·vert (di vėrt′ or dī vėrt′) 1 turn aside: *A ditch diverted water from the stream into the fields. The rattle diverted the baby's attention from the knife.* 2 amuse; entertain: *We were diverted by the clown's tricks. v.*

di·vide (di vīd′) 1 separate into parts: *A brook divides the field. The river divides and forms two streams.* 2 separate into equal parts: *When you divide 8 by 2, you get 4. Symbol:* ÷ 3 give some of to each; share: *The children divided the candy.* 4 to separate in feeling, opinion, etc.; disagree: *The school divided on the choice of a motto.* 5 a ridge of land separating the regions drained by two different river systems. The Rocky Mountains are called the **Great Divide.** 1–4 *v.,* **di·vid·ed, di·vid·ing;** 5 *n.*

div·i·dend (div′ə dend) 1 a number or quantity to be divided. See **division** for picture. 2 money earned by a company and divided among the owners of the company. *n.*

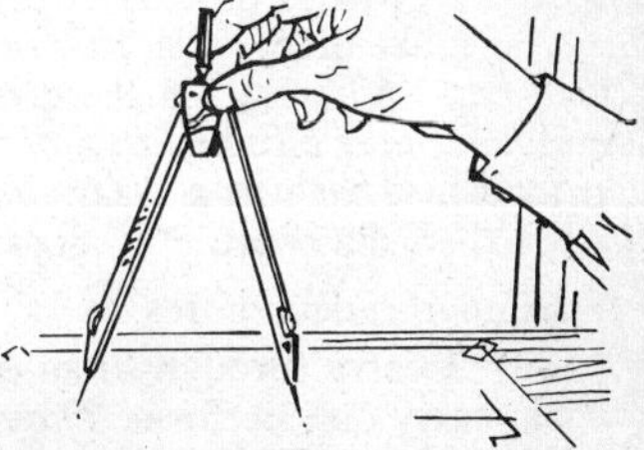

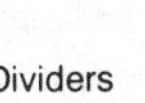

Dividers

di·vid·ers (di vīd′ers) an instrument having two movable legs ending in metal points, used for dividing lines, measuring distances, etc. *n. pl.*

di·vine (di vīn′) 1 of God or a god. 2 by or from God. 3 to or for God; sacred; holy. 4 like God or a god; heavenly. 5 *Informal.* excellent; unusually good or great: *'What a divine hat!' cried Sue.* 6 a clergyman who knows much about theology; a minister or priest. 7 find out or foretell by inspiration, by magic, or by guessing; predict. 1–5 *adj.,* 6 *n.,* 7 *v.,* **di·vined, di·vin·ing.**

diving suit a waterproof suit with a helmet into which air can be pumped through a tube: *Diving suits are worn by people working underwater.*

di·vin·i·ty (di vin′ə tē) 1 a divine being; god. 2 a divine nature or quality: *The divinity of Christ is accepted by Christians.* *n., pl.* **di·vin·i·ties.**

di·vis·i·ble (di viz′ə bəl) capable of being divided: *In arithmetic 12 is divisible by 4.* *adj.*

5 QUOTIENT
DIVISOR 15)78 DIVIDEND
75
3 REMAINDER

The parts of a division problem

di·vi·sion (di vizh′ən) 1 dividing; being divided. 2 the act of giving some to each; sharing: *division of labor.* 3 the process of dividing one number by another: *26 ÷ 2 = 13 is a simple division.* 4 something that divides, such as a boundary or partition. 5 one of the parts into which a thing is divided; group; section: *a division of the animal kingdom. Some divisions of the army fought in Italy.* 6 a difference of opinion, thought, or feeling; disagreement. *n.*

di·vi·sor (di vī′zər) a number or quantity by which another is divided. *n.*

di·vorce (di vôrs′) 1 the legal ending of a marriage. 2 end legally a marriage between: *The judge divorced Mr. and Mrs. Jones.* 3 release from marriage by getting a divorce: *She divorced her husband.* 4 a separation: *In this country there is a complete divorce of government and church.* 5 separate: *In sports, exercise and play are not divorced.* 1, 4 *n.,* 2, 3, 5 *v.,* **di·vorced, di·vorc·ing.**

di·vulge (di vulj′) tell; reveal; make known: *The traitor divulged secret plans to the enemy.* *v.,* **di·vulged, di·vulg·ing.**

diz·zi·ness (diz′ē nis) a dizzy condition. *n.*

diz·zy (diz′ē) 1 likely to fall, stagger, or spin around; not steady: *When you spin round and round and stop suddenly, you feel dizzy.* 2 confused; bewildered: *The noise and crowds of the city streets made the little boy dizzy.* 3 make dizzy: *The ride on the merry-go-round dizzied her.* 4 likely to make dizzy; causing dizziness: *The mountaineer climbed to a dizzy height.* 5 *Informal.* silly; foolish: *That was a dizzy thing to do.* 1, 2, 4, 5 *adj.,* **diz·zi·er, diz·zi·est;** 3 *v.,* **diz·zied, diz·zy·ing.**

dm decimetre; decimetres.

do¹ (dü) 1 carry through to an end any action or piece of work; carry out; perform: *Do your work well.* 2 make; produce: *Walt Disney did a movie about Snow White and the seven dwarfs.* 3 be the cause of; bring about: *Your work does you credit.* 4 act; behave: *You have done wisely.* 5 deal with; take care of: *do the dishes, do one's hair.* 6 be satisfactory: *This hat will do.* 7 **Do** is also used: **a** in asking questions: *Do you like milk?* **b** to make what one says stronger: *I do want to go. Do come, please.* **c** to stand for another verb already used: *My dog goes where I do. Her brother walks just as she does.* **d** in expressions that contain **not:** *People talk; animals do not.* *v.,* **does, did, done, do·ing.**
do away with, a put an end to; abolish: *do away with a rule.* **b** kill.
do up, wrap up; tie up: *do up a package.*
How do you do? How are you? (a greeting).
☛ **Do¹** is sometimes pronounced the same as **dew** and **due.**

The eight-tone musical scale

do² (dō) the first or last tone of the standard musical scale. *Do, re, mi, fa, sol, la, ti, do* are the names of the tones of the scale. *n.*
☛ **Do², doe,** and **dough** are pronounced the same.

do·cile (dō′sīl, dos′īl, or dos′əl) 1 easily managed; obedient: *a docile dog.* 2 easily taught; willing to learn: *a docile pupil.* *adj.*

Docks (defs. 1 and 2) with a ship loading

dock¹ (dok) 1 a platform built on the shore or out from the shore; a wharf or pier. 2 the water between two piers, permitting the entrance of ships. 3 bring a ship alongside a dock: *The sailors docked the liner with hardly a bump.* 4 come into a dock: *The ship will dock at ten o'clock.* 1, 2 *n.,* 3, 4 *v.*

dock² (dok) 1 the solid, fleshy part of an animal's tail. 2 cut short; cut off the end of: *Dogs' tails are sometimes docked.* 3 cut down; take away part of: *The company docked the men's wages if they came late to work.* 1 *n.,* 2, 3 *v.*

dock³ (dok) the place where an accused person stands in a law court. *n.*

doc·tor (dok′tər) 1 a person having a licence to practise medicine or perform surgery: *a medical doctor.* 2 any of certain other professional persons who treat unhealthy persons or animals: *Dentists, chiropracters, and veterinarians are doctors.* 3 give medical treatment to: *Mother doctors us for ordinary colds.* 4 a person who has taken the highest degree possible in a university: *Doctor of Philosophy.* 5 alter, weaken, or interfere with something: *The dishonest cashier doctored the accounts.* 1, 2, 4 *n.,* 3, 5 *v.*

doc·trine (dok′trən) 1 what is taught as the belief of a church, a nation, or a group of persons; a belief: *Christian doctrine.* 2 what is taught; teachings: *the doctrines of mathematics.* *n.*

hat, āge, fär; let, ēqual, tėrm; it, īce
hot, ōpen, ôrder; oil, out; cup, pu̇t, rüle
əbove, takən, pencəl, lemən, circəs
ch, child; ng, long; sh, ship
th, thin; ᴛʜ, then; zh, measure

doc·u·ment (dok′yə mənt) something written or printed that gives information and can be used as proof of some fact; any object used as evidence: *Letters, maps, and pictures are documents.* *n.*

doc·u·men·ta·ry (dok′yə men′tə rē or dok′yə men′trē) **1** consisting of documents; in writing, print, etc.: *The man's own letters were documentary evidence of his guilt.* **2** presenting or recording factual information in an artistic way: *a documentary film.* **3** a motion picture, radio or television program, book, etc. that presents factual information in an artistic way. 1, 2 *adj.,* 3 *n., pl.* **doc·u·men·ta·ries.**

dodge (doj) **1** move quickly to one side: *As I watched, he dodged into the shadow of the house.* **2** move quickly in order to get away from a person, a blow, or something thrown: *He dodged the ball as it came flying toward his head.* **3** a sudden movement to one side: *A dodge saved his head.* **4** get away from or avoid by some trick: *He has dodged washing dishes again.* **5** *Informal.* a trick or scheme: *a clever dodge.* 1, 2, 4 *v.,* **dodged, dodg·ing;** 3, 5 *n.* **—dodg·er,** *n.*

dodge·ball (doj′bol′ or doj′bôl′) a game in which players forming a circle or two opposite lines try to hit opponents in the centre with a large ball. *n.*

do·do (dō′dō) a large, clumsy bird not able to fly: *Dodos are now extinct.* *n., pl.* **do·dos** or **do·does.**

doe (dō) the female of deer, antelope, rabbits, hare, and most other animals whose male is called a buck. *n.*

☞ **Doe, do**[2] and **dough** are pronounced the same.

does (duz) See **do.** *Does she sing well?* *v.*

does·n't (duz′ənt) does not.

doff (dof) take off: *He doffed his hat as the women went by.* *v.*

☞ **Doff** developed from a contraction of *do off,* meaning 'take or put off; remove.'

A dog on a lumberjack's tool

dog (dog) **1** a tame, four-legged, meat-eating animal kept as a household pet or used for such purposes as guarding people or property, hunting, or leading the blind: *The different breeds of dog vary in size from the tiny chihuahua, which can fit into a teacup, to the Irish wolfhound, which is about 85 centimetres high at the shoulder.* **2** hunt or follow like a dog: *The police dogged the suspected thief.* **3** something made to hold or grip like a dog's teeth. 1, 3 *n.,* 2 *v.,* **dogged, dog·ging.**

dog·catch·er (dog′kach′ər) a person whose job is to pick up stray dogs and take them to the pound. *n.*

dog days a period of very hot and uncomfortable weather during July or August.

dog–eared (dog′ērd′) **1** of a page in a book, having a corner folded down. **2** of a book, having many pages folded down at the corners; looking much used: *She found a dog-eared old copy of her favorite novel in a second-hand bookstore.* *adj.*

dog·ged (dog′id) obstinate; persistent: *His dogged effort helped him to win the race.* *adj.*

dog·house (dog′hous′) a small house or shelter for a dog. *n.*

in the doghouse, *Slang.* in trouble with somebody; in disfavor: *She's in the doghouse with her brother because she borrowed his sweater and got it dirty.*

dog·trot (dog′trot′) a gentle, easy trot. *n.*

dog·wood (dog′wu̇d′) one of several kinds of tree having large white or pinkish flowers in the spring, which develop into red or blue berries by the fall: *The dogwood flower is the floral emblem of British Columbia.* *n.*

doi·ly (doi′lē) a small piece of linen, lace, paper, etc. used under plates, vases, etc. *n., pl.* **doi·lies.**

do·ings (dü′ingz) things done; actions: *Mrs. Brown was deeply interested in the doings of her neighbors.* *n. pl.*

dol·drums (dol′drəmz) **1** certain regions of the ocean near the equator where the wind is very light or constantly shifting: *Sailing ships caught in the doldrums were often unable to move for days.* **2** dullness; a gloomy feeling; low spirits: *The whole family was in the doldrums because of the rainy weather.* *n. pl.*

dole (dōl) **1** a portion of money, food, etc. given in charity. **2** a small portion. **3** give in small quantities: *Mother doled out one piece of candy a day to each child.* **4** the relief money given by a government to unemployed people. 1, 2, 4 *n.,* 3 *v.,* **doled, dol·ing.**

dole·ful (dōl′fəl) sad; mournful; dreary; dismal: *The hound gave a doleful howl.* *adj.*

doll (dol) **1** a toy made to resemble a human being: *Mary got a lovely doll for Christmas.* **2** a pretty child, girl, or woman. *n.*

dol·lar (dol′ər) **1** the unit of money in Canada, the United States, and some other countries: *One hundred cents make one dollar, which is usually written $1.00. Symbol:* $ **2** a paper note or a coin worth 100 cents: *He gave me four quarters for a dollar. His father gave him a silver dollar.* *n.*

☞ **Dollar** came into English through Low German from an early German word *thaler,* short for *Joachimsthaler,* a kind of silver coin. *Joachimsthal* was the name of a valley in Germany where the silver for this coin was found.

dol·lop (dol′əp) *Informal.* **1** a portion or serving, large or small: *a dollop of ice cream.* **2** apply or spread on heavily. 1 *n.,* 2 *v.*

doll·y (dol′ē) **1** a child's name for a doll. **2** a small, low frame on wheels, used to move heavy things: *The fridge was moved on a dolly.* *n., pl.* **doll·ies.**

dol·or·ous (dol′ər əs) **1** mournful; sorrowful: *She uttered a heart-broken, dolorous cry.* **2** grievous; painful: *The dolorous day was ending.* *adj.*

dol·phin (dol′fən) a sea mammal related to the whale

and porpoise, having a snout shaped like a beak: *Dolphins are often trained to perform in aquariums.* *n.*

dolt (dōlt) a dull, stupid person. *n.*

do·main (dō mān′) **1** the territory under the control of one ruler or government. **2** the land owned by one person; an estate. **3** a field of thought and action: *Sir John A. Macdonald was a leader in the domain of politics.* *n.*

The dome of the Alberta legislature

dome (dōm) **1** a large, rounded roof on a circular or many-sided base. **2** anything that is or appears high and rounded: *the dome of a hill, the dome of the sky.* *n.*

do·mes·tic (də mes′tik) **1** of the home, household, or family affairs: *domestic cares, a domestic scene.* **2** fond of home. **3** a household servant: *Butlers, cooks, and maids are domestics.* **4** not wild; tame: *Horses, dogs, cats, cows, and pigs are domestic animals.* **5** of or made in one's own country; not foreign: *domestic news. Canadians eat a lot of domestic cheese.* 1, 2, 4, 5 *adj.*, 3 *n.*

do·mes·ti·cate (də mes′tə kāt′) tame; change animals and plants from a wild to a tame state: *The dog was one of the first animals to be domesticated.* *v.*, **do·mes·ti·cat·ed, do·mes·ti·cat·ing.**

dom·i·nant (dom′ə nənt) **1** ruling; governing; controlling; most influential: *The Prime Minister was the dominant figure at the meeting. Hockey is Canada's dominant sport in winter.* **2** rising high above its surroundings; towering: *Dominant hills sheltered the bay.* *adj.*

dom·i·nate (dom′ə nāt′) **1** control or rule by strength or power: *The boy dominates his smaller friend. Dandelions will dominate over grass if they are not kept out.* **2** rise high above; tower over: *The mountain dominates the city and its harbor.* *v.*, **dom·i·nat·ed, dom·i·nat·ing.**

dom·i·na·tion (dom′ə nā′shən) control; rule; dominating: *The island became free after years of domination by foreign countries.* *n.*

dom·i·neer·ing (dom′ə nēr′ing) tending to force one's will on others; overbearing: *She was unpopular as club president because she was too domineering.* *adj.*

do·min·ion (də min′yən) **1** rule; control: *The British had dominion over a large part of the world.* **2** a territory under the control of one ruler or government: *British dominions.* **3** **Dominion,** a name used for some self-governing countries in the Commonwealth of Nations: *For many years Canada was officially called the Dominion of Canada.* **4** Often, **Dominion,** in Canada: **a** under the control or authority of the federal government. **b** relating to the country as a whole; national in scope. *n.*

Dominion Day a national holiday commemorating the creation of the Dominion of Canada on July 1, 1867. Also called **Canada Day.**

Two dominoes

dom·i·no (dom′ə nō′) **1** **dominoes,** *pl.* a game played with small pieces of bone, wood, etc. that are either blank or marked with dots. **2** one of the pieces used in playing this game. **3** a loose cloak and a small mask worn as a disguise, especially at masquerade parties. *n., pl.* **dom·i·noes** or **dom·i·nos.**

☛ **Dominoes,** meaning the game, is plural in form and singular in use: *Dominoes is played with 28 flat, oblong pieces of bone or wood.*

don¹ (don) **1** **Don,** a Spanish title meaning Mr. or Sir: *Don Felipe.* **2** *Informal.* in England, a teacher at a college or a university. **3** in some Canadian universities and colleges, an official in charge of a residence. *n.*

don² (don) put on: *The knight donned his armor.* *v.*, **donned, don·ning.**

☛ **Don²** is a contraction of *do on,* meaning 'put on.'

do·nate (dō′nāt or dō nāt′) give; contribute: *He donated ten dollars.* *v.*, **do·nat·ed, do·nat·ing.**

do·na·tion (dō nā′shən) **1** the act of giving. **2** a gift or contribution: *Everyone was called upon to make donations to the Red Cross.* *n.*

done (dun) **1** finished; completed; ended. **2** cooked; cooked enough: *The steak was done just right.* **3** *Informal.* worn out; exhausted. **4** See **do¹**. *Have you done all your homework?* 1–3 *adj.*, 4 *v.*

☛ **Done** and **dun** are pronounced the same.

A donkey — usually about 1 m high at the shoulder

don·key (dong′kē) **1** one of several kinds of tame or wild four-footed animal related to the horse, but smaller, and having larger ears, a shorter neck and mane, and smaller hooves than a horse. **2** a stubborn person; a silly or stupid person: *Don't be such a donkey!* *n., pl.* **don·keys.**

do·nor (dō′nər) a person who gives; a giver: *Hospitals welcome blood donors.* *n.*

don't (dōnt) do not.

doo·dle (dü′dəl) **1** make drawings or marks of any kind while thinking of something else; draw absent-mindedly: *He doodled while he was talking on the telephone.* **2** a drawing or mark made absent-mindedly. 1 *v.*, **doo·dled, doo·dling;** 2 *n.*

doom (düm) **1** fate. **2** a terrible fate; ruin; death: *The soldiers marched to their doom.* **3** judgment; sentence: *The judge pronounced the guilty man's doom.* **4** condemn to some punishment: *The prisoner was*

hat, āge, fär; let, ēqual, tėrm; it, īce
hot, ōpen, ôrder; oil, out; cup, pu̇t, rüle
əbove, takən, pencəl, lemən, circəs
ch, child; ng, long; sh, ship
th, thin; ᴛʜ, then; zh, measure

doomed to death. **5** cause to come to an unhappy end: *Her plan seemed doomed to failure because everything had gone wrong from the beginning.* 1–3 *n.*, 4, 5 *v.*

door (dôr) **1** a movable slab of wood, stone, or metal, intended for closing an opening in a wall of a building: *A door may turn on hinges or slide open and shut. Most rooms have doors.* **2** any movable part resembling a door: *the door of a cupboard.* **3** doorway: *I saw him just as he came through the door.* *n.*
out of doors, not in a house or building; outside.

door·bell (dôr′bel′) a bell to be rung as a signal that someone wishes to have the door opened. *n.*

door·knob (dôr′nob′) a round handle on a door. *n.*

door·man (dôr′mən or dôr′man′) **1** a person whose work is opening the door of a hotel, store, apartment building, etc. for people going in or out. **2** a person who guards a door. *n., pl.* **door·men** (dôr′mən or dôr′men′).

door·nail (dôr′nāl′) a nail with a large head. *n.*
dead as a doornail, entirely dead.

door·step (dôr′step′) a step leading from an outside door to the ground. *n.*

door·way (dôr′wā′) an opening to be closed by a door. *n.*

dope (dōp) **1** *Slang.* a habit-forming narcotic drug, such as heroin or opium. **2** *Slang.* give such a drug to, often as an anesthetic: *The doctor doped her before setting her broken leg.* **3** *Slang.* information: *What's the latest dope on the strike?* **4** *Slang.* a very stupid person. **5** a thick varnish or similar liquid applied to a fabric to strengthen or waterproof it: *He bought some dope for the model airplane he was building.* 1, 3–5 *n.*, 2 *v.*, **doped, doping.**

dope·y or **dop·y** (dōp′ē) *Slang.* very stupid. *adj.*

dor·mant (dôr′mənt) asleep; quiet as if asleep; inactive: *Bears and tulip bulbs are dormant during the winter.* *adj.*

A dormer

A double bass

dor·mer (dôr′mər) **1** an upright window that projects from a sloping roof. **2** the projecting part of a roof that contains such a window. *n.*

dor·mi·to·ry (dôr′mə tô′rē) **1** a sleeping room large enough for a number of beds. **2** a building containing a large number of sleeping rooms: *Many colleges have dormitories for students.* *n., pl.* **dor·mi·to·ries.**

dor·mouse (dôr′mous′) a tiny animal found in Africa, Asia, and Europe, related to the rat and mouse, having fine, soft fur, large black eyes, and a tail as long as its body: *Dormice sleep during the day and hunt for food at night.* *n., pl.* **dor·mice** (dôr′mīs′).

do·ry (dô′rē) a rowboat with a narrow, flat bottom and high sides: *Dories are often used by ocean fishermen.* *n., pl.* **do·ries.**

dose (dōs) **1** the amount of a medicine to be taken at one time. **2** give medicine to: *The doctor dosed him with penicillin.* **3** the amount of anything given as a remedy: *A good dose of praise made her feel happier.* 1, 3 *n.*, 2 *v.*, **dosed, dos·ing.**

dot (dot) **1** a small spot or point; a tiny, round mark: *There is a dot over each 'i' in this line.* **2** mark with a dot or dots. **3** be here and there in: *Boats of many kinds dotted the lake.* 1 *n.*, 2, 3 *v.*, **dot·ted, dot·ting.**
on the dot, at exactly the right time: *The meeting is at 5 o'clock and you must be there on the dot.*

dot·age (dōt′ij) a weak-minded, childish condition that sometimes comes with old age. *n.*

dote (dōt) be weak-minded and childish because of old age. *v.*, **dot·ed, dot·ing.**
dote on or **upon,** be foolishly fond of; be too fond of: *The old lady dotes on her grandson.*

dou·ble (dub′əl) **1** twice as much, as large, as strong, etc.: *The man was given double pay for working on Sunday.* **2** twice: *She earns double his salary.* **3** a number or amount twice as large: *Four is the double of two.* **4** make twice as much; make twice as many: *He doubled his money in ten years by investing it wisely.* **5** become twice as much: *Money left in a savings account will double in about ten years.* **6** made of two like parts; in a pair: *double doors, double windows.* **7** having two meanings, characters, etc.: *The word* bear *has a double meaning: 'carry' and 'a certain animal.'* **8** a person or thing just like another: *I saw your double yesterday.* **9** fold over: *Jack doubled his slice of bread to make a sandwich. The boy doubled his fists.* **10** turn suddenly and sharply; turn back on one's own trail: *The fox doubled on its track and escaped the dogs.* **11** a turn made like this. **12** go around: *The ship doubled Cape Horn.* **13** having more than one set of petals: *Some roses are double, others single.* **14** take another's place: *Tom doubled for me when I couldn't get to the meeting.* **15** in baseball, a two-base hit: *He hit a double in the last inning.* **16** make a two-base hit. 1, 6, 7, 13 *adj.*, 2 *adv.*, 3, 8, 11, 15 *n.*, 4, 5, 9, 10, 12, 14, 16 *v.*, **dou·bled, dou·bling.**
double back, a fold over: *She doubled back the cloth to make a hem.* **b** go back the same way that one came: *He decided he must have passed the house, so he doubled back and tried again.*
double up, a fold up; fold back: *He doubled up the dollar bill and put it in his pocket.* **b** draw the knees up toward the chest; bend the upper part of the body toward the lower part: *He doubled up in pain.* **c** share a room, a bed, etc. with another: *When guests came, the two brothers had to double up.*

double bass a large stringed instrument with a deep bass tone, the largest member of the modern violin family: *When a double bass is played, it rests upright on the floor and the player stands behind it.* See the picture.

dou·ble–head·er (dub′əl hed′ər) two baseball games between the same teams on the same day, one right after the other. *n.*

dou·ble–joint·ed (dub′əl join′tid) having very

flexible joints that allow fingers, arms, legs, etc. to bend in unusual ways. *adj.*

A doublet

dou·blet (dub′lit) a man's close-fitting jacket: *Men wore doublets in Europe from about 1400 to about 1600.* *n.*

double window a window together with a storm window, made either in one piece or as separate structures.

dou·bloon (dub lün′) a former Spanish gold coin. *n.*

dou·bly (dub′lē) in a double manner, amount, or degree: *Doubly careful means twice as careful.* *adv.*

doubt (dout) **1** not believe; not be sure; feel uncertain: *The captain doubted that the damaged ship would reach land.* **2** difficulty in believing: *Faith casts out doubt.* **3** an uncertain state of mind: *We were in doubt as to which road to take.* 1 *v.,* 2, 3 *n.*

no doubt, surely; certainly: *No doubt we will win in the end.*

without doubt, without question; certainly: *He will pass the test without doubt.*

doubt·ful (dout′fəl) **1** unclear; not distinct; not certain: *a doubtful advantage. It is doubtful whether he ever saw his friend again.* **2** full of doubt; feeling uncertain: *They were doubtful about their chances of winning the game.* **3** suspicious; questionable: *a person with a doubtful past.* *adj.*

doubt·less (dout′lis) without doubt; surely: *He will doubtless arrive on time.* *adv.*

dough (dō) **1** the mixture of flour, milk, fat, and other materials from which bread, biscuits, pies, etc. are made. **2** *Slang.* money. *n.*

☛ **Dough, do**[2], and **doe** are pronounced the same.

dough·nut (dō′nut′) a small cake of sweetened dough cooked in deep fat: *A doughnut is often made in the shape of a ring.* *n.*

Douk·ho·bor or **Duk·ho·bor** (dü′kə bôr′) a member of a Christian sect that had its origin in Russia about 200 years ago: *Several thousand Doukhobors left Russia in 1898 and settled in western Canada.* *n.*

douse (dous) **1** plunge into water or any other liquid: *The blacksmith doused the red-hot horseshoe to cool it.* **2** throw water over; drench: *He doused his brother with a pail of water.* **3** put out a light. *v.,* **doused, dous·ing.**

dove[1] (duv) a bird with a thick body, short legs, and a beak enlarged at the tip; a kind of pigeon: *The dove is often a symbol of peace.* *n.*

dove[2] (dōv) See **dive.** *The diver dove deep into the water after the sunken treasure.* *v.*

☛ See note at **dive.**

dow·dy (dou′dē) **1** dressed in a dull or unimaginative way: *a dowdy person.* **2** not stylish; shabby: *The old lady wore a dowdy coat and a shapeless hat.* *adj.,* **dow·di·er, dow·di·est.**

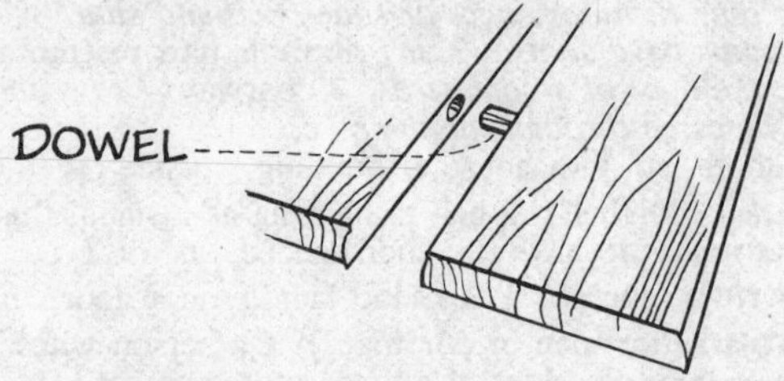

dow·el (dou′əl) a peg on a piece of wood, metal, etc., made to fit into a corresponding hole on another piece and so form a joint fastening the two pieces together. *n.*

down[1] (doun) **1** to a lower place: *They ran down from the top of the hill.* **2** in a low place: *They lived down in the valley.* **3** from an earlier time to a later time: *The story has come down through many years.* **4** from a larger to a smaller amount, degree, etc.: *everyone from the hotel manager down to the shoeshine boy. The temperature has gone down.* **5** *Informal.* a period of bad luck or unhappiness: *Her life is full of ups and downs.* **6** down along: *You can ride down a hill, sail down a river, or walk down a street.* **7** put down: *He downed Fred and sat on top of him.* **8** on paper; in writing: *Put his name down in the book.* **9** as a down payment: *He paid $10 down when he bought his bicycle.* **10** a chance to move a football forward: *In Canadian football, a team is allowed three downs in which to move the ball forward ten yards (about nine metres).* 1-4, 8, 9 *adv.,* 6 *prep.,* 7 *v.,* 5, 10 *n.*

down[2] (doun) **1** soft feathers: *the down on a duck.* **2** soft hair or fluff; fuzz: *The down on a boy's chin develops into a beard.* *n.*

down[3] (doun) *Esp. British.* Usually, **downs,** *pl.* a stretch of rolling, grassy land: *Epsom Downs.* *n.*

down·cast (doun′kast′) **1** turned downward: *She stood before us with downcast eyes.* **2** dejected; sad; discouraged: *He was downcast because of his failure.* *adj.*

down·fall (doun′fol′ or doun′fôl′) a bringing to ruin; a sudden overthrow of a great person, institution, or nation through a change in fortune: *the downfall of a hero, the downfall of an empire.* *n.*

down·heart·ed (doun′här′tid) discouraged; dejected; depressed. *adj.*

down·hill (doun′hil′) **1** down the slope of a hill; downward. **2** going or sloping downward: *a downhill run.* 1 *adv.,* 2 *adj.*

down·pour (doun′pôr′) a heavy rainfall. *n.*

down·right (doun′rīt′) **1** thorough; complete: *a downright thief, a downright lie.* **2** thoroughly; completely: *He was downright rude to me.* **3** plain; positive: *His downright answer made his opinion clear.* 1, 3 *adj.,* 2 *adv.*

down·stairs (doun′sterz′) **1** down the stairs: *Bill slipped and tumbled downstairs.* **2** on or to a lower floor: *I went downstairs for breakfast. The downstairs rooms are dark.* **3** the lower floor or floors: *He lived in the downstairs of the house.* 1, 2 *adv.,* 2 *adj.,* 3 *n.*

hat, āge, fär; let, ēqual, tėrm; it, īce
hot, ōpen, ôrder; oil, out; cup, pu̇t, rüle
əbove, takən, pencəl, lemən, circəs
ch, child; ng, long; sh, ship
th, thin; ᴛʜ, then; zh, measure

down·stream (doun′strēm′) **1** in the direction of the current of a stream or river: *It is easy to swim or row downstream.* **2** farther along in the direction of the current of a stream or river: *The sawmill was downstream from the town.* 1 *adv.,* 2 *adj.*

down·town (doun′toun′) **1** to or in the lower part of a town. **2** to or in the main part or business part of a town: *Mother has gone downtown shopping.* **3** the business section or main part of a town. 1, 2 *adv., adj.,* 3 *n.*

down·ward (doun′wərd) **1** toward a lower place: *He hurried downward toward the bottom of the hill.* **2** toward a later time. *adv., adj.*

down·wards (doun′wərdz) downward. *adv.*

down·y (dou′nē) **1** of soft feathers, hair, or fluff. **2** covered with down. **3** soft as down; fluffy: *A kitten's fur is downy. adj.,* **down·i·er, down·i·est.**

dow·ry (dou′rē) the money or property that a bride brings to her husband. *n., pl.* **dow·ries.**

doz. dozen.

doze (dōz) **1** sleep lightly; be half asleep: *We found him dozing in the armchair.* **2** a light sleep; nap. 1 *v.,* **dozed, doz·ing;** 2 *n.*

doz·en (duz′ən) 12; a group of 12. *n., pl.* **doz·ens** or *(after a number)* **doz·en.**

Dr. or **Dr** **1** Doctor: *Dr. M. H. Smith.* **2** Drive: *220 Rideau Dr., Ottawa.*

drab (drab) **1** dull; not attractive: *We saw the drab houses of the coal-mining town.* **2** dull brownish-grey. 1, 2 *adj.,* 2 *n.*

draft (draft) **1** a current of air. **2** a device for controlling a current of air: *He opened the draft of the furnace to make the fire burn faster.* **3** a plan; sketch. **4** make a plan or sketch of. **5** a rough copy: *He made three different drafts of his speech before he had it in final form.* **6** write out a rough copy of. **7** a selection of persons for some special purpose: *During the war, the United States used the draft to build up its army and navy.* **8** the persons chosen for special service. **9** select for some special purpose: *Ten men from the battalion were drafted for guard duty.* **10** the act of pulling loads. **11** for pulling loads: *A draft horse is used for pulling wagons and ploughs.* **12** all the fish caught in one drawing of a net. **13** the depth of water a ship needs for floating, or the depth it sinks into the water, especially when loaded. **14** the amount taken in one drink. **15** drawn from a keg or other container: *draft beer.* **16** a note from one bank to another, ordering that a certain sum of money be paid to the person named. 1–3, 5, 7, 8, 10, 12–14, 16 *n.,* 4, 6, 9 *v.,* 11, 15 *adj.* Also spelled **draught. —draft·y,** *adj.*

drag (drag) **1** pull or move along heavily or slowly; pull or draw along the ground: *A team of horses dragged the big log out of the forest.* **2** go too slowly: *A piece of music drags if played too slowly. Time drags when you have nothing to do.* **3** pull a net, hook, harrow, etc. over or along for some purpose: *People drag a lake for fish or for a drowned person's body.* **4** trail along the ground: *Her skirt was dragging in the dust of the street.* **5** anything that holds back; an obstruction or hindrance: *A lazy player is a drag on a hockey team.* 1–4 *v.,* **dragged, drag·ging;** 5 *n.*

drag·net (drag′net′) **1** a net pulled over the bottom of a river, pond, etc. or along the ground: *Dragnets are used to catch fish and small birds.* **2** an extensive search or hunt to catch or round up criminals, etc.: *Twenty of the gang were arrested in the police dragnet. n.*

drag·on (drag′ən) in old stories, a fierce creature like a huge snake having wings and claws: *Some dragons were said to breathe fire. n.*

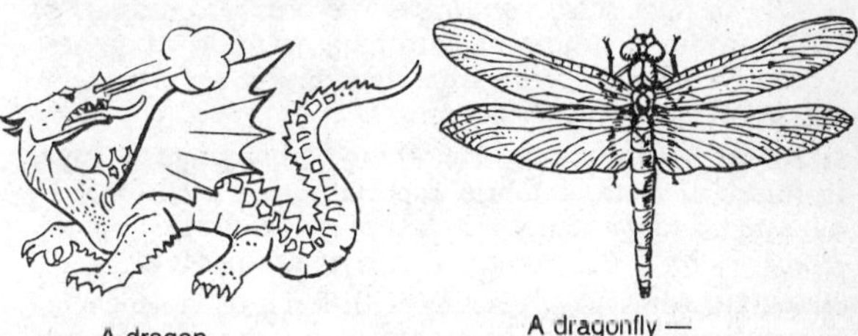
A dragon
A dragonfly — wingspread about 7 cm

drag·on·fly (drag′ən flī′) a large, harmless insect with a long, slender body and two pairs of gauzy wings: *Dragonflies dart rapidly about catching flies, mosquitoes, and other insects. n., pl.* **drag·on·flies.**

dra·goon (drə gün′) **1** in former times, a soldier who was mounted on a horse and was armed with a heavy musket. **2** a soldier in any of several cavalry regiments: *Most dragoon regiments are now equipped with tanks or other armored vehicles.* **3** force by violence; bully or oppress: *She cannot be dragooned into doing something she does not want to do.* 1, 2 *n.,* 3 *v.*

drain (drān) **1** draw off water or any liquid; draw liquid from; empty of liquid: *to drain a cup. Farmers sometimes drain swamps to get more land for crops.* **2** dry by the flowing off of water: *Set the dishes here to drain.* **3** a channel or pipe for carrying off water or waste of any kind: *a cellar drain.* **4** take away from slowly; use up little by little: *War drains a country of its people and money.* **5** a slow taking away; using up little by little: *Working or playing too hard is a drain on your strength.* 1, 2, 4 *v.,* 3, 5 *n.*

drain·age (drān′ij) **1** the drawing off or draining of water: *The drainage of the swamps cleared the area of mosquitoes.* **2** a system of channels or pipes for carrying off water or waste of any kind. **3** what is drained off. *n.*

drake (drāk) a male duck. *n.*

dra·ma (dram′ə or drä′mə) **1** a play such as one sees in a theatre; a story written to be acted out by actors on a stage. **2** the art of writing and producing plays: *He wants to study drama.* **3** a part of real life that has the excitement of a story: *The history of Arctic exploration is a great and thrilling drama. n.*

dra·mat·ic (drə mat′ik) **1** of drama; having to do with plays. **2** sudden; exciting; full of action or feeling: *There was a dramatic pause and then the lion leaped. adj.*

dra·mat·i·cal·ly (drə mat′ə klē) in a dramatic manner. *adv.*

dram·a·tist (dram′ə tist) a writer of plays. *n.*

dram·a·tize (dram′ə tīz′) **1** arrange or present in the form of a play: *The children dramatized the story of Rip Van Winkle.* **2** make exciting and thrilling: *He had a way of dramatizing the stories he told the children.* *v.,* **dram·a·tized, dram·a·tiz·ing.**

drank (drangk) See **drink.** *She drank her milk an hour ago.* *v.*

drape (drāp) **1** cover or hang with cloth falling loosely in folds, especially as a decoration: *The stage was draped with velvet.* **2** arrange clothes, hangings, etc. to hang loosely in folds: *Can you drape this skirt?* **3 drapes,** *pl.* large curtains that are made to hang in folds; draperies: *There are drapes on the large windows in the living room.* 1, 2 *v.,* **draped, drap·ing;** 3 *n.*

drap·er·y (drā′pər ē) **1** clothing or hangings arranged in folds. **2** cloth or fabric, especially that used for hangings and garments. **3 draperies,** *pl.* drapes: *draperies for a large window.* *n., pl.* **dra·per·ies.**

dras·tic (dras′tik) **1** acting with force or violence; forceful and violent: *The general was a drastic man who showed no mercy.* **2** extreme; extraordinary: *The police undertook drastic measures to put a stop to the bank robberies.* *adj.*

draught (draft) See **draft.**

draw (dro or drô) **1** pull; drag; haul: *The horses draw the wagon.* **2** pull out; pull up; take out: *Draw a pail of water from this well. She drew ten dollars from the bank.* **3** get; receive: *He draws his pay each Friday.* **4** attract; cause to come: *A parade always draws crowds.* **5** make a picture or likeness of anything with pen, pencil, crayon, etc.: *Draw a circle. He draws very well.* **6** in certain games, an equal score for both sides. **7** breathe in; inhale: *to draw a breath.* **8** make long or longer; stretch: *to draw out a rubber band. The men drew the rope taut.* **9** of a ship or boat, sink to a certain depth in floating: *A ship draws more water when it is loaded than when it is empty. The big ship draws 8.5 metres of water.* **10** move: *The car drew near.* **11** make a draft of air to carry off smoke: *The chimney does not draw well.* **12** reach; come to: *draw the wrong conclusions.* **13** a narrow valley: *The rancher found his strayed cattle grazing in a draw.* **14** a lottery: *Jack won a bicycle in a draw.* 1–5, 7–12 *v.,* **drew, drawn, draw·ing;** 6, 13, 14 *n.*

draw out, a make or become longer; stretch: *Rain draws out a summer day. The movie was long and drawn out.* **b** persuade to talk: *When mother saw the new boy was shy and quiet, she tried to draw him out.*

draw up, a write out in proper form: *The lawyer drew up my father's will.* **b** stop: *The taxi drew up at the entrance.*

draw·back (dro′bak′ or drô′bak′) a disadvantage; anything that makes a situation or experience less complete or satisfying: *Our trip was interesting, but the rainy weather was a drawback.* *n.*

draw·bridge (dro′brij′ or drô′brij′) a bridge that can be entirely or partly lifted, lowered, or moved to one side: *In old castles drawbridges were lifted to keep out enemies. A drawbridge over a river is lifted to let boats pass.* See **castle** for picture. *n.*

draw·er[1] (dro′ər or drô′ər) a person or thing that draws: *a drawer of water, a drawer of pictures.* *n.*

draw·er[2] (drôr) a box equipped with handles and built to slide in and out of a table, dresser, desk, etc.: *He kept his shirts in the dresser drawer.* *n.*

draw·ers (drôrz) underwear fitting over the legs and around the waist: *Drawers are worn in cold weather.* *n. pl.*

draw·ing (dro′ing or drô′ing) **1** a picture, sketch, plan, or design done with pen, pencil, crayon, etc. **2** the making of such a sketch, plan, etc.: *Drawing is taught in art classes.* *n.*

drawing room a room for receiving or entertaining guests; a parlor.

drawl (drol or drôl) **1** talk in a slow way, making the vowels of words very long: *He drawled a lazy answer.* **2** a way of talking in which the vowels of words are made long: *English speakers in some regions have a drawl.* 1 *v.,* 2 *n.*

drawn (dron or drôn) See **draw.** *That old horse has drawn many loads.* *v.*

dread (dred) **1** look forward to with fear: *He dreaded his visits to the dentist.* **2** great fear: *She had a sincere dread of ghosts. The old man lived in dread of winter.* **3** causing terror, fear, or awe; dreaded: *That dread tyrant rules without mercy.* 1 *v.,* 2 *n.,* 3 *adj.*

dread·ful (dred′fəl) **1** causing dread; terrible; fearful: *The dragon was a dreadful creature.* **2** *Informal.* very bad; very unpleasant: *I have a dreadful cold.* *adj.* **—dread′ful·ly,** *adv.*

dream (drēm) **1** something thought, felt, seen, or heard during sleep. **2** something unreal, like a dream: *The boy had dreams of being a hero.* **3** think, feel, see, or hear during sleep; have dreams: *He dreamed he was a Mountie.* **4** have daydreams; form fancies: *The girl dreamed of being a famous scientist.* **5** think of something as possible; imagine: *The day seemed so bright I never dreamed there would be rain.* **6** something having great beauty or charm. 1, 2, 6 *n.,* 3–5 *v.,* **dreamed** or **dreamt, dream·ing.**

dream·er (drēm′ər) a person whose ideas do not fit real conditions: *People say he failed because he was nothing but a dreamer.* *n.*

dream·land (drēm′land′) **1** a wonderful land that exists only in dreams or the imagination: *The little girl said she had had a wonderful adventure in dreamland the night before.* **2** a beautiful and desirable place: *Their new property was a dreamland.* *n.*

in dreamland, asleep.

dreamt (dremt) See **dream.** *v.*

dream·y (drēm′ē) **1** full of dreams: *a dreamy sleep.* **2** like a dream; vague; dim: *a dreamy recollection.* **3** fond of daydreaming; fanciful; not practical: *a dreamy person.* **4** causing dreams; soothing: *dreamy songs.* *adj.,* **dream·i·er, dream·i·est.**

drear·y (drēr′ē) dull; without cheer; gloomy: *Cloudy days are often very dreary.* *adj.,* **drear·i·er, drear·i·est.**

dredge (drej) **1** a machine with a scoop or series of buckets for cleaning out or deepening a harbor or channel. **2** clean out or deepen with a dredge. **3** an apparatus with a net, used for gathering oysters, etc. from the bottom of a river or the sea. **4** bring up or gather with a dredge. 1, 3 *n.,* 2, 4 *v.,* **dredged, dredg·ing.**

dregs (dregz) **1** the solid bits of matter that settle to the bottom of a liquid: *There are often dregs in the* *bottom of a wine barrel.* **2** the most worthless part: *the dregs of society.* *n. pl.*

drench (drench) wet thoroughly; soak: *We were drenched by the cloudburst.* *v.*

dress (dres) **1** an outer garment worn by women, girls, and babies. **2** clothing, especially outer clothing: *The children care very little about dress.* **3** put clothes on. **4** wear clothes properly and attractively: *Her friends thought she didn't know how to dress.* **5** make ready for use, cooking, etc.: *The butcher will dress the chickens for you.* **6** care for; arrange: *Mother has her hair dressed each week.* **7** put medicine, bandages, etc. on a wound or sore: *The nurse dressed the wound every day.* **8** form in a straight line: *The captain ordered the soldiers to dress their ranks.* 1, 2 *n.*, 3–8 *v.*, **dressed, dress·ing.**

dress·er[1] (dres′ər) **1** a person whose work is to help another person with dressing: *The movie star had a dresser.* **2** a person who dresses a store window, a display counter, etc. **3** a person who dresses properly and attractively: *She is a smart dresser.* *n.*

dress·er[2] (dres′ər) **1** a piece of furniture with drawers for clothes and, usually, a mirror. **2** a piece of furniture with shelves for dishes. *n.*

dress·ing (dres′ing) **1** a sauce for salad, meat, fish, etc. **2** a mixture of bread crumbs, seasoning, etc., used to stuff chickens, turkeys, etc. before cooking. **3** the medicine, bandage, etc. put on a wound or sore. *n.*

dressing gown a loose robe worn while dressing or resting.

dress·mak·er (dres′māk′ər) a person, usually a woman, whose work is making women's or children's dresses, etc. *n.*

dress·y (dres′ē) *Informal.* stylish and formal; not casual: *That outfit is too dressy for a wiener roast.* *adj.*, **dress·i·er, dress·i·est.**

drew (drü) See **draw.** *He drew a picture of his mother.* *v.*

drib·ble (drib′əl) **1** flow or let flow in drops or small amounts; trickle: *He allowed the water to dribble from the bottle.* **2** drip from the mouth: *The baby dribbles on his bib.* **3** dropping; dripping: *All we could get out of the hose was a dribble.* **4** move a ball along by bouncing it or giving it short kicks. 1, 2, 4 *v.*, **drib·bled, drib·bling;** 3 *n.*

dried (drīd) See **dry.** *I dried my hands. This bread has been dried in the oven.* *v.*

dri·er (drī′ər) **1** more dry: *This towel is drier than that one.* **2** See **dryer.** 1 *adj.*, 2 *n.*

drift (drift) **1** be carried along by currents of air or water: *A raft drifts if it is not steered.* **2** carry along: *The current was drifting us along.* **3** go along or live without a goal or without knowing where one will come out: *Some people have a purpose in life; others just drift.* **4** the motion of being carried along by wind or water: *the drift of an iceberg.* **5** the direction of drifting: *The drift of the current is to the south.* **6** the meaning; the direction of thought: *I caught the drift of his speech, but I couldn't understand all the details.* **7** heap or be heaped up by the wind: *The wind is so strong that the snow is drifting on the highways.* **8** snow, sand, etc. heaped up by the wind: *After the heavy snow there were deep drifts in the yard.* 1–3, 7 *v.*, 4–6, 8 *n.*

drift·wood (drift′wůd′) wood carried along by water or washed ashore from the water. *n.*

hat, āge, fär; let, ēqual, tėrm; it, īce
hot, ōpen, ôrder; oil, out; cup, pu̇t, rüle
əbove, takən, pencəl, lemən, circəs
ch, child; ng, long; sh, ship
th, thin; ᴛʜ, then; zh, measure

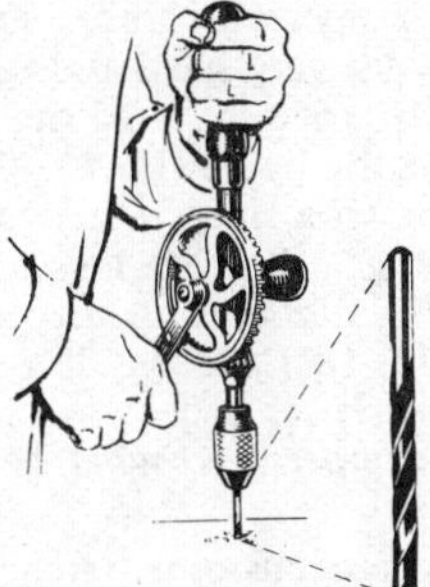

A drill. It has two handles so that it may be used vertically or horizontally. The cutting part, called the bit, works like an auger.

drill[1] (dril) **1** a tool or machine for boring holes. **2** bore with a drill; use a drill. **3** teach by having a person or persons do a thing over and over: *The teacher drilled the class in arithmetic.* **4** the process of doing a thing over and over for practice: *The teacher gave the class plenty of drill in arithmetic.* **5** group instruction and training in physical exercises or in marching, handling a gun, and other duties of soldiers. **6** do physical or military exercises. **7** cause to do such exercises: *The sergeant was drilling the recruits.* 1, 4, 5 *n.*, 2, 3, 6, 7 *v.*

drill[2] (dril) a machine for planting seeds in rows: *This kind of drill makes a small furrow, drops the seed, and then covers the furrow.* *n.*

drink (dringk) **1** swallow anything liquid, such as water or milk: *The boys drink milk for breakfast.* **2** anything liquid swallowed to make one less thirsty. **3** suck up; absorb: *The dry soil drank up the rain.* **4** alcoholic liquor. **5** drink liquor. 1, 3, 5 *v.*, **drank, drunk, drink·ing;** 2, 4 *n.*

drink in, take in eagerly with the senses: *We sat there quietly, drinking in the beautiful scene.*

drink·er (dringk′ər) a person who drinks, especially one who drinks liquor as a habit or to excess. *n.*

drip (drip) **1** fall or let fall in drops: *Rain drips from an umbrella.* **2** falling in drops. **3** be so wet that drops fall: *His forehead was dripping with perspiration.* 1, 3 *v.*, **dripped, drip·ping;** 2 *n.*

drip·ping (drip′ing) the fat that drips from roasting meat: *Some people like beef dripping spread on bread.* *n.*

drive (drīv) **1** make go; cause to move: *Drive the dog away. He drove the cow out of the barn.* **2** make go in or through by force: *to drive a nail.* **3** manage; operate; guide by steering: *to drive a car, to drive a motorboat.* **4** bring about or obtain by being clever, shrewd, forceful, etc.: *He drove a good bargain when he bought his bicycle.* **5** go or travel in a car or other vehicle: *We drove out into the country for the afternoon.* **6** carry or transport in a car or other vehicle: *The truck driver drove the boys all the way to Toronto.* **7** a trip, usually short, taken in a car or other vehicle: *a Sunday drive.* **8** a road, usually in street names: *Winona Drive.* **9** driveway (def. 1): *He left his car in the drive all night.*

10 capacity for hard work; forceful action; energy: *His success was largely due to his great drive.* **11** force to work hard: *The men said their boss drove them too harshly.* **12** a special effort; a campaign to raise money: *a bottle drive. Our church had a drive to get money for a new building.* **13** dash or rush with force: *The ship drove onto the rocks.* **14** hit very hard and fast: *to drive a golf ball.* **15** a very hard, fast hit. **16** the moving overland of a herd of cattle by cowboys. **17** the floating of a great many logs down a river: *Drives are held when the ice melts in spring.* **18** move logs in large numbers down a river: *The lumberjacks drove the logs to the mill.* 1–6, 11, 13, 14, 18 *v.,* **drove, driv·en, driv·ing;** 7–10 , 12, 15–17 *n.* **—driv·er,** *n.*

drive at, intend; mean: *I didn't understand what he was driving at.*

drive–in (drīv′in′) a place where customers may make purchases, eat, attend movies, etc. while seated in their cars. *n.*

driv·el (driv′əl) **1** let saliva run from the mouth. **2** saliva running from the mouth. **3** stupid, foolish talk; silly nonsense. 1 *v.,* **driv·elled** or **driv·eled, driv·el·ling** or **driv·el·ing;** 2, 3 *n.*

driv·en (driv′ən) See **drive.** *Mr. Jones has just driven past. v.*

drive·way (drīv′wā′) **1** a private road, usually leading from the street to a house or garage. **2** *Cdn.* a road, usually one that is lined with trees and lawns. *n.*

driz·zle (driz′əl) **1** rain gently, in very small drops like mist. **2** very small drops of rain resembling mist. 1 *v.,* **driz·zled, driz·zling;** 2 *n.*

droll (drōl) odd and amusing; quaint and laughable: *We smiled at the monkey's droll tricks. adj.*

A dromedary — about 180 cm high at the shoulder

drom·e·dar·y (drom′ə der′ē) a swift Arabian camel raised for riding and racing, usually having one hump. *n., pl.* **drom·e·dar·ies.**

drone[1] (drōn) **1** a male bee: *Drones do no work in the hive.* **2** a person not willing to work; idler. *n.*

drone[2] (drōn) **1** make a deep, continuous, humming sound: *Bees droned among the flowers.* **2** such a sound: *Soldiers listened for the drone of the airplane motors.* **3** talk or say in a monotonous voice: *to drone a prayer.* 1, 3 *v.,* **droned, dron·ing;** 2 *n.*

drool (drül) **1** let saliva run from the mouth as a teething baby does. **2** saliva running from the mouth. 1 *v.,* 2 *n.*

droop (drüp) **1** hang down; bend down: *These flowers will soon droop if they are not put in water. Flags droop when there is no breeze.* **2** the act or condition of hanging down; a bending position: *The droop of the branches brought them within our reach.* **3** become weak; lose strength and energy: *The boy's spirit drooped when he failed to make the team. The patient drooped as his illness got worse.* **4** become discouraged; be sad and gloomy: *She's been drooping around the house all day.* 1, 3, 4 *v.,* 2 *n.*

drop (drop) **1** a small, roundish mass of liquid, usually formed in falling: *a drop of rain, a drop of blood.* **2** an object that is small and roundish, resembling such a mass: *a cough drop, a lemon drop.* **3** fall or let fall in such small masses of liquid: *Rain drops from the sky. He had to drop some medicine into his sore eye.* **4** a very small amount of liquid: *She takes just a drop of milk in her coffee.* **5** **drops,** *pl.* liquid medicine given in drops: *The doctor gave her some drops for her ear.* **6** the distance down; the length of a fall: *a drop of ten metres.* **7** a sudden fall: *a drop in prices. The temperature took a big drop last night.* **8** take a sudden fall: *The price of tomatoes always drops in August.* **9** let fall: *He dropped the package.* **10** cause to fall: *The boxer dropped his opponent with one hard punch.* **11** fall dead or wounded: *The soldier dropped when the bullet hit him.* **12** fall from tiredness: *I'm so tired, I could drop.* **13** cause to fall dead or wounded; kill: *The hunter dropped the deer with one shot.* **14** go lower; sink: *The sun dropped below the horizon.* **15** make lower; cause to become lower: *He dropped his voice to a whisper.* **16** let go; dismiss: *He was dropped from the football team.* **17** leave out; omit: *Drop the* e *in* drive *before adding* -ing. **18** stop; end; close: *They agreed to let the quarrel drop.* **19** go with the current or tide: *The raft dropped down the river.* **20** set down from a ship, automobile, etc.: *The taxi driver dropped his passengers at the corner.* 1, 2, 4–7 *n.,* 3, 8–20 *v.,* **dropped, drop·ping.**

a drop in the bucket, a very small amount compared with the rest.

drop behind or **back,** lose ground, fall behind: *When the runner became tired he dropped behind.*

drop by, in, or **over,** come to visit: *Drop over to our house tonight.*

drop off, a go to sleep: *He dropped off in his armchair.* **b** become less; fall: *Sales of chewing gum have dropped off this year.* **c** stop: *I think I'll drop off at the grocery store.*

drought (drout) **1** a long period of dry weather; continued lack of rain. **2** a lack of water; dryness: *Drought damages crops. n.*

drove[1] (drōv) See **drive.** *We drove twenty miles yesterday. v.*

drove[2] (drōv) **1** a group of cattle, sheep, pigs, etc. moving or driven along together; a herd or flock: *We sent a drove of cattle to market.* **2** many people moving along together; a crowd. *n.*

drown (droun) **1** die under water or some other liquid because of lack of air to breathe: *The fisherman almost drowned when his boat overturned.* **2** kill by keeping under water or some other liquid. **3** be stronger or louder than; keep from being heard: *The boat's whistle drowned what the girl was trying to tell us.* **4** get rid of: *He tried to drown his sorrow in excitement. v.*

drowse (drouz) be half asleep: *She drowsed, but she did not quite fall asleep. v.,* **drowsed, drows·ing.**

drow·si·ly (drou′zə lē) in a drowsy manner. *adv.*

drow·sy (drou′zē) **1** sleepy; half asleep. **2** making one sleepy: *It was a warm, quiet, drowsy afternoon. adj.,* **drow·si·er, drow·si·est.**

hat, āge, fär; let, ēqual, tėrm; it, īce
hot, ōpen, ôrder; oil, out; cup, pu̇t, rüle
əbove, takən, pencəl, lemən, circəs
ch, child; ng, long; sh, ship
th, thin; ᴛʜ, then; zh, measure

drub (drub) 1 beat with something; thrash. 2 defeat thoroughly: *Our team was drubbed at soccer.* *v.,* **drubbed, drub·bing.**

drudge (druj) 1 a person who does hard, tiresome, or disagreeable work; a slave; an overworked servant. 2 do tiresome or disagreeable work. 1 *n.,* 2 *v.,* **drudged, drudg·ing.**

drudg·er·y (druj′ər ē) work that is hard, without interest, or disagreeable: *She thinks that washing dishes every day is drudgery.* *n., pl.* **drudg·er·ies.**

drug (drug) 1 a substance (other than food) that, when taken into the body, produces a change in functions of the body; a substance used as a medicine: *Aspirin is a drug.* 2 a substance that brings drowsiness or sleep, or lessens pain by dulling the nerves: *Opium is a drug.* 3 give drugs to, particularly drugs that are harmful or cause sleep: *The witch drugged the princess.* 4 mix harmful drugs with food or drink: *The spy drugged the soldier's drink.* 5 affect or overcome the body or the senses in a way not natural: *The wine had drugged him.* 1, 2 *n.,* 3–5 *v.,* **drugged, drug·ging.**
drug on the market, an article that is too abundant, is no longer in demand, or has too slow a sale.

drug·gist (drug′ist) a person licensed to sell drugs, medicines, etc. *n.*

drug·store (drug′stôr′) a store where drugs and other medicines are sold: *A drugstore usually sells soft drinks, cosmetics, magazines, etc. as well as drugs.* *n.*

drum (drum) 1 a musical instrument that makes a sound when it is beaten, tapped, or brushed: *A drum is usually a hollow cylinder, having a parchment cover stretched tight over each end.* 2 play the drum; make a sound by beating a drum. 3 beat, tap, or strike again and again: *He drummed on the table with his fingers.* 4 teach or drive into one's head by repeating over and over: *Her mother finally drummed it into her that she should take her wet boots off at the door.* 5 a drum-shaped container to hold oil, food, etc.: *an oil drum.* 6 anything shaped like a drum: *a brake drum.* 7 eardrum. 1, 5–7 *n.,* 2–4 *v.,* **drummed, drum·ming.**

drum·mer (drum′ər) a person skilled in playing a drum. *n.*

drum·stick (drum′stik′) 1 a stick for beating a drum. 2 the lower, meaty part of the leg of a cooked chicken, turkey, etc. *n.*

drunk (drungk) 1 overcome by alcoholic liquor: *He was so drunk he could not stand up.* 2 a person who is often in such a state; drunkard. 3 very much excited or affected: *He was drunk with success.* 4 See **drink.** *The child has not yet drunk his milk.* 1, 3 *adj.,* 2 *n.,* 4 *v.*
☛ As an adjective, **drunk** is generally used after a noun but **drunken** before a noun.

drunk·ard (drungk′ərd) a person who is often drunk; a person who frequently drinks too much liquor. *n.*

drunk·en (drungk′ən) 1 drunk. 2 caused by or resulting from being drunk: *a drunken quarrel.* *adj.*
☛ See note at **drunk.**

dry (drī) 1 not wet; not moist: *Dust is dry. This bread is dry.* 2 make or become dry: *She was drying dishes. The towels soon dried in the breeze.* 3 having little or no rain: *a dry climate.* 4 not giving milk: *The cow is dry.* 5 empty of water: *The kettle is dry.* 6 thirsty; wanting a drink. 7 solid; not liquid: *dry measure, on dry land.* 8 not interesting; dull: *a dry speech.* 9 quiet and intelligent: *dry humor.* 10 without butter: *dry toast.* 11 not permitted by law to sell liquor: *a dry township.* 12 *Informal.* a person who believes it should be illegal to sell liquor. 1, 3–11 *adj.,* **dri·er, dri·est;** 2 *v.,* **dried, dry·ing;** 12 *n.* **—dry′ness,** *n.*
dry up, a become or cause to become completely without water or some other liquid: *The creek dried up last summer. The intense heat dried up the grass.* **b** *Slang.* stop talking: *Why don't you dry up?*

dry cell an electric cell in which the chemical producing the current is made into paste with gelatin, sawdust, etc., so that its contents cannot spill.

dry–clean (drī′klēn′) clean clothes, fabrics, etc. by dry cleaning. *v.*

dry cleaning the cleaning of fabrics without water, by the use of such liquids as naphtha and gasoline.

dry·dock (drī′dok′) an area where a ship may be repaired, set between two piers and built watertight. *n.*

dry·er or **dri·er** (drī′ər) 1 a person who dries. 2 a machine that removes water by heat, air, etc.: *a clothes dryer, a hair dryer, a grain dryer.* 3 a substance mixed with paint or varnish to make it dry more quickly. *n.*

dry goods cloth, ribbons, laces, etc.

dry·ly (drī′lē) with quiet and intelligent humor: *He spoke dryly of the many characters he had known.* *adv.*

dry measure a set of units for measuring such things as grain or fruit:
2 pints = 1 quart
8 quarts = 1 peck
4 pecks = 1 bushel

du·al (dyü′əl or dü′əl) consisting of two parts; double; twofold: *The automobile had dual controls, one set for the learner and one for the teacher.* *adj.*

dub (dub) 1 make a man a knight by striking his shoulder lightly with a sword. 2 give a title to; name or call: *Because of his very blond hair, the boys dubbed him 'Whitey.'* *v.,* **dubbed, dub·bing.**

du·bi·ous (dyü′bē əs or dü′bē əs) 1 doubtful; uncertain: *She looked this way and that in a dubious manner.* 2 of questionable character; probably bad: *He called it a dubious scheme for making money.* *adj.*

duch·ess (duch′is) 1 the wife or widow of a duke. 2 a woman with a rank equal to that of a duke. *n.*

duch·y (duch′ē) the lands ruled by a duke or a duchess. *n., pl.* **duch·ies.**

A mallard duck — about 60 cm long with the tail

duck¹ (duk) a wild or tame swimming bird having a thick body, a short neck and legs, a flat bill, and webbed feet: *Ducks are very often raised for food and for their eggs. n.*

duck² (duk) 1 plunge or dip the head or the whole body under water and come up quickly, as a duck does; put under water for a short time. 2 a quick plunge below the water. 3 lower the head or bend the body quickly to keep off a blow: *She ducked to avoid a low branch.* 4 a sudden lowering of the head or bending of the body. 1, 3 *v.*, 2, 4 *n.*

duck³ (duk) a strong cotton or linen cloth, lighter and finer in weave than canvas: *Duck is used for small sails, and for outer clothing by sailors and by people living in hot climates. n.*

duck·bill (duk′bil′) a small water animal of Australia that lays eggs like a bird, but nurses its young with milk like other mammals: *The duckbill has webbed feet and a beak like a duck's. n.*

duck·ling (duk′ling) a young duck. *n.*

due (dyü or dü) 1 owed as a debt; owing; to be paid as a right: *The money due him for his work was paid today. Respect is due to older people.* 2 a person's right; what is owed or due to a person: *Courtesy is his due while he is your guest.* 3 proper; rightful; fitting: *He has his due reward for good work.* 4 **dues,** *pl.* a fee or regular charge, especially for membership in an organization: *Club dues have to be paid before the end of each year.* 5 looked for; expected; set by agreement; promised to come or to do: *The train is due at noon. He is due to speak twice tomorrow.* 6 straight; exactly; directly: *due west.* 1, 3, 5 *adj.*, 2, 4 *n.*, 6 *adv.*

due to, caused by: *The accident was due to his careless use of the gun.*

☛ **Due** and **dew** are pronounced the same. **Due** and **do**¹ are sometimes pronounced the same.

du·el (dyü′əl or dü′əl) 1 a formal fight to settle a quarrel: *Duels were fought (with guns, swords, etc.) between two persons in the presence of two others called seconds.* 2 any fight or contest between two opponents: *The two opposing lawyers fought a duel of wits in the law court.* 3 fight a duel. 1, 2 *n.*, 3 *v.*, **du·elled** or **du·eled, du·el·ling** or **du·el·ing.**

du·et (dyü et′ or dü et′) 1 a piece of music for two voices or instruments. 2 two singers or players performing together. *n.*

dug (dug) See **dig.** *The dog dug a hole in the ground. The potatoes have all been dug. v.*

dug·out (dug′out′) 1 a rough shelter or dwelling formed by digging into the side of a hill, trench, etc.: *During war, soldiers use dugouts for protection against bullets and bombs.* 2 a boat made by hollowing out a large log. 3 a large excavation used to hold water: *Some dugouts are used for watering cattle; others are used for irrigating land.* 4 a small shelter at the side of a baseball field, used by players not on the field. *n.*

duke (dyük or dük) a nobleman ranking next below a prince: *In Great Britain, most men of this rank are members of the royal family. n.*

duke·dom (dyük′dəm or dük′dəm) the territory ruled by a duke. *n.*

Duk·ho·bor (dü′kə bôr′) See **Doukhobor.**

dull (dul) 1 not sharp or pointed: *a dull knife, a dull pain.* 2 not bright or clear: *dull eyes, a dull color, a dull day, a dull sound.* 3 slow in understanding; stupid: *a dull mind, a dull boy.* 4 not interesting or pleasant; boring: *a dull book, a dull joke.* 5 not active: *The furnace business is usually dull in summer.* 6 make or become dull. 1–5 *adj.*, 6 *v.* **—dull′ness** or **dul′ness,** *n.* **—dul′ly,** *adv.*

du·ly (dyü′lē or dü′lē) as due; according to what is due; rightly; suitably: *The debt was duly paid. adv.*

dumb (dum) 1 not able to speak: *Even intelligent animals are dumb.* 2 silent; not speaking: *He would not answer, but remained dumb.* 3 *Informal.* stupid; dull: *She's pretty dumb; she doesn't understand any of the games we play. adj.*

A dumb-bell

dumb–bell (dum′bel′) 1 a short bar of wood or iron with large, heavy, round ends: *A dumb-bell is lifted or swung around to exercise the muscles of the arms, back, etc.* 2 *Slang.* a stupid person. *n.*

dumb·found (dum′found′) See **dumfound.**

dum·found (dum′found′) amaze to the point of making unable to speak; bewilder; confuse. *v.*

dum·my (dum′ē) 1 a figure of a person, used to display clothing in store windows, to shoot at in rifle practice, to tackle in football, etc. 2 *Informal.* a stupid person with no more sense than such a figure. 3 made to resemble the real thing; make-believe: *dummy swords.* 1, 2 *n.*, *pl.* **dum·mies;** 3 *adj.*

dump (dump) 1 empty out; throw down: *The truck backed up to the curb and dumped the coal on the sidewalk.* 2 a place for throwing rubbish. 3 a heap of rubbish. 4 a place for storing military supplies: *an ammunition dump.* 1 *v.*, 2–4 *n.*

dump·ling (dump′ling) 1 a rounded piece of dough, boiled or steamed and served with meat. 2 a small pudding made by enclosing fruit in a piece of dough and boiling or steaming it. *n.*

dumps (dumps) *Informal.* low spirits. *n. pl.*

in the dumps, feeling gloomy or sad: *He was in the dumps because his bike was broken.*

dun¹ (dun) 1 a demand for payment, especially of a debt. 2 demand payment from again and again: *The landlord dunned the tenant until the tenant paid the overdue rent.* 1 *n.*, 2 *v.*, **dunned, dun·ning.**

☛ **Dun** and **done** are pronounced the same.

dun² (dun) dull, greyish brown. *n., adj.*

☛ See note at **dun**¹.

dunce (duns) 1 a child slow at learning his lessons in school. 2 a stupid person. *n.*

dune (dyün or dün) a mound or ridge of loose sand heaped up by the wind. *n.*

dung (dung) waste matter from the bowels of animals; manure: *Dung is much used as fertilizer. n.*

hat, āge, fär; let, ēqual, tėrm; it, īce
hot, ōpen, ôrder; oil, out; cup, pu̇t, rüle
əbove, takən, pencəl, lemən, circəs
ch, child; ng, long; sh, ship
th, thin; ᴛʜ, then; zh, measure

dun·ga·ree (dung′gə rē′) **1** a coarse cotton cloth, used for work clothes, sails, etc. **2** **dungarees,** *pl.* trousers or clothing made of this cloth. *n.*

☛ **Dungaree** comes from a Hindi word *dungrī,* the name for a kind of coarse Indian calico cloth.

dun·geon (dun′jən) a strong underground room to keep prisoners in. *n.*

dunk (dungk) **1** dip something to eat into a liquid: *dunk doughnuts in coffee.* **2** *Informal.* push somebody into water. *v.*

dupe (dyüp or düp) **1** a person easily deceived or tricked. **2** deceive; trick: *The dishonest peddler duped his customers.* 1 *n.,* 2 *v.,* **duped, dup·ing.**

du·pli·cate (dyü′plə kit or dü′plə kit for 1 and 2, dyü′plə kāt′ or dü′plə kāt′ for 3) **1** exactly alike: *We have duplicate keys for the front door.* **2** one of two things exactly alike; an exact copy: *He mailed the letter, but kept a duplicate.* **3** make an exact copy of; repeat exactly. 1 *adj.,* 2 *n.,* 3 *v.,* **du·pli·cat·ed, du·pli·cat·ing.**
in duplicate, in two copies: *This application must be made out in duplicate.*

du·ra·ble (dyür′ə bəl or dür′ə bəl) lasting a long time; not soon injured or worn out. *adj.*

du·ra·tion (dyü rā′shən or dü rā′shən) the time during which something lasts: *The strike was expected to be of short duration. They lived in the country for the duration of the war.* *n.*

dur·ing (dyür′ing or dür′ing) **1** at some time in; in the course of: *Come to see us sometime during the day.* **2** throughout: *The boys played during the storm.* *prep.*

dusk (dusk) **1** the time just before dark; twilight. **2** shade; gloom: *He sat quietly in the dusk of the pine woods.* *n.*

dusk·y (dus′kē) **1** somewhat dark or gloomy: *The dusky part of the evening.* **2** dark-colored; dark-skinned: *a dusky complexion.* *adj.,* **dusk·i·er, dusk·i·est.**

dust (dust) **1** fine, dry earth; any fine powder: *Dust lay thick in the street. The old papers had turned to dust. The bee is covered with yellow dust from the flowers.* **2** get dust off; brush or wipe the dust from: *Mother dusts the furniture after sweeping.* **3** sprinkle with dust or powder: *The nurse dusted powder over the baby.* **4** ground; earth. 1, 4 *n.,* 2, 3 *v.*
bite the dust, *Slang.* fall dead or wounded: *A shot rang out and one of the outlaws bit the dust.*
throw dust in someone's eyes, deceive or mislead a person: *The escape plan depended on his success in throwing dust in the eyes of the police.*

dust·er (dus′tər) **1** a cloth, brush, etc. used to take the dust off things. **2** a light dress or robe that opens down the front, usually without a belt and worn especially when doing light household chores. *n.*

dust·pan (dust′pan′) a flat pan, shaped like a broad shovel, for sweeping dust into from the floor. *n.*

dust·y (dus′tē) **1** covered with dust. **2** like dust; dry and powdery. **3** having the color of dust. *adj.,* **dust·i·er, dust·i·est.**

Dutch (duch) **1** of or having to do with the Netherlands, a small country in western Europe. **2** the people of the Netherlands. **3** their language. 1 *adj.,* 2, 3 *n.*

du·ti·ful (dyü′tə fəl or dü′tə fəl) doing the duties required of one; obedient: *a dutiful daughter.* *adj.*

du·ty (dyü′tē or dü′tē) **1** the thing that is right to do; what a person ought to do: *It is your duty to obey the laws.* **2** obligation: *A sense of duty makes a person do what he thinks is right.* **3** the things a person has to do in his work: *The mailman's first duties were to sort and deliver the mail.* **4** proper behavior owed to an older or superior person; obedience; respect. **5** a tax on taking articles out of, or bringing them into, a country. *n., pl.* **du·ties.**

dwarf (dwôrf) **1** a person, an animal, or a plant much smaller than the usual size for its kind. **2** in fairy tales, a tiny, often ugly, person who has magic powers. **3** below the usual size for its kind; stopped in growth: *a dwarf maple.* **4** keep from growing large. **5** cause to seem small by contrast or by distance: *That tall building dwarfs all those around it.* 1, 2 *n., pl.* **dwarfs** or **dwarves** (dwôrvz); 3 *adj.,* 4, 5 *v.*

dwell (dwel) live; make one's home: *The princess dwelt in a beautiful castle.* *v.,* **dwelt** or **dwelled, dwell·ing. —dwell′er,** *n.*
dwell on, think, speak, or write about for a long time.

dwell·ing (dwel′ing) a house; a place in which people live: *a two-family dwelling.* *n.*

dwelling place dwelling.

dwelt (dwelt) See **dwell.** *v.*

dwin·dle (dwin′dəl) become smaller and smaller; shrink a little at a time: *During the war the supply of food dwindled rapidly.* *v.,* **dwin·dled, dwin·dling.**

dye (dī) **1** a substance used to color cloth, hair, etc.: *Some dyes are vegetable, others chemical. We bought some blue dye.* **2** a color produced by treatment with a liquid containing dye: *A good dye will not fade.* **3** color by dipping into or treating with a liquid containing coloring matter: *to have a dress dyed.* **4** to color or stain: *The wounded soldier's blood dyed the ground red.* 1, 2 *n.,* 3, 4 *v.,* **dyed, dye·ing.**

☛ **Dye** and **die** are pronounced the same.

dy·ing (dī′ing) See **die.** *the dying year. The woman was dying.* *adj.*

dyke (dīk) See **dike.** *n., v.,* **dyked, dyk·ing.**

dy·nam·ic (dī nam′ik) **1** having to do with energy or force in motion. **2** active; forceful: *The teacher has a dynamic way of talking.* *adj.*

dy·na·mite (dī′nə mīt′) **1** a powerful explosive often used in blasting rocks. **2** blow up with dynamite: *They planned to dynamite the bridge.* 1 *n.,* 2 *v.,* **dy·na·mit·ed, dy·na·mit·ing.**

dy·na·mo (dī′nə mō′) a machine that changes mechanical energy into electric energy; generator: *They make their own electricity with a small dynamo run by a gasoline engine.* *n., pl.* **dy·na·mos.**

dy·nas·ty (dī′nəs tē or din′əs tē) a succession of rulers who belong to the same family. *n., pl.* **dy·nas·ties.**

dys·en·ter·y (dis′ən ter′ē or dis′ən trē) a painful disease of the intestines, with discharges of blood and mucus. *n.*

e or **E** (ē) the fifth letter of the alphabet: *There are two* e's *in* see. *n., pl.* **e's** or **E's.**

E. or **E** 1 east. 2 eastern.

each (ēch) **1** every one of two or more persons or things considered separately or one by one: *Each boy has a name.* **2** every single one: *Each of the girls has a doll. He gave a pencil to each.* **3** all of a group, thought of as individuals: *We each have our work to do.* **4** apiece; for every single one: *These pencils cost ten cents each.* 1 *adj.,* 2, 3 *pron.,* 4 *adv.*

☞ As a pronoun, **each** is singular: *Each of these students has a different teacher.* When **each** is an adjective modifying a noun, however, it is the noun that decides whether the verb is singular or plural: *Each child is getting a balloon. The three children each have a new toy.*

each other each the other: *'The two boys struck each other' means 'Each of the two boys struck the other one.'*

ea·ger (ē′gər) filled with keen desire for; wanting very much; impatient to do or get something: *The child is eager to eat the candy. The team was eager for victory. adj.* **—ea′ger·ly,** *adv.* **—ea′ger·ness,** *n.*

A bald eagle — about 88 cm long with the tail

ea·gle (ē′gəl) a large bird of prey having a hooked bill, strong feet with sharp, curved claws, and keen eyesight: *Eagles eat small animals and other birds. n.*

eagle eye, the ability to see far and clearly; sharp eye.

ear[1] (ēr) **1** the part of the body by which people and animals hear. **2** the sense of hearing. **3** the ability to distinguish small differences in sounds: *She has a good ear for music.* **4** something shaped like the external part of an ear. *n.*

be all ears, eager to hear something.

give ear, listen or attend.

go in one ear and out the other, make no impression.

play by ear, play an instrument or a composition without using written music.

wet behind the ears, *Informal.* inexperienced; not yet able to cope; quite immature.

ear[2] (ēr) **1** the part of certain plants that contains the grains: *The grains of corn, wheat, oats, barley, and rye are formed on ears.* **2** develop into ears; form ears: *Soon the corn will ear.* 1 *n.,* 2 *v.*

ear·ache (ēr′āk′) a pain in the ear. *n.*

ear·drum (ēr′drum′) the thin membrane that stretches across the middle ear and vibrates when sound waves strike it. *n.*

earl (ėrl) a British noble ranking below a marquis but above a viscount: *The wife of an earl is called a countess. n.*

ear·ly (ėr′lē) **1** near the beginning: *his early years, (adj.). The heroine appears early in the book (adv.).* **2** that happens or arrives before the usual, normal, or expected time: *an early dinner, an early spring.* **3** before the usual or expected time: *Please come early.* 1, 2 *adj.,* **ear·li·er, ear·li·est;** 1, 3 *adv.*

ear·mark (ēr′märk′) **1** a mark made on the ear of an animal to show who owns it. **2** a special mark, quality, or feature that identifies or gives information about a person or thing; sign. **3** make an earmark on. **4** identify or give information about: *Careful work earmarks a good student.* **5** set aside for some special purpose: *Fifty dollars of the profit from the game were earmarked to buy new team sweaters.* 1, 2 *n.,* 3–5 *v.*

ear·muffs (ēr′mufs′) a pair of coverings to put over the ears to keep them warm. *n. pl.*

earn (ėrn) **1** get in return for work or service; be paid: *She earns fifty dollars a day.* **2** do enough work for: *He is paid more than he really earns.* **3** deserve and get; win: *For his brave act the soldier earned a medal. v.*

☞ **Earn** and **urn** are pronounced the same.

ear·nest (ėr′nist) **1** strong and firm in purpose; eager and serious: *an earnest worker.* **2** firm in beliefs: *an earnest Christian. adj.* **—ear′nest·ly,** *adv.* **—ear′nest·ness,** *n.*

in earnest, a determined or sincere: *We could see she was in earnest about the project.* **b** determinedly or sincerely.

earn·ings (ėr′ningz) money earned; wages; profits: *Most of his earnings went for food and rent. n. pl.*

ear·phone (ēr′fōn′) a receiver for a telephone, telegraph, radio, or hearing aid, that is fastened over the ear. *n.*

ear·ring (ēr′ring′) an ornament for the ear. *n.*

ear·shot (ēr′shot′) the distance a sound can be heard; the range of hearing: *We shouted, but he was out of earshot. n.*

earth (ėrth) **1** the planet on which we live, a great sphere that moves around the sun; the globe: *The earth is round. China is on the other side of the earth.* **2** soil; ground: *The earth in his garden is good for growing vegetables.* **3** the ground: *The arrow fell to earth 100 metres away. n.*

down to earth, seeing things as they really are; practical.

earth·en (ėr′thən) **1** made of earth. **2** made of baked clay: *an earthen jug. adj.*

earth·en·ware (ėr′thən wer′) dishes or containers made of baked clay: *Pottery or crockery is earthenware. n.*

earth·ly (ėrth′lē) **1** having to do with the earth, man's world, and not with heaven: *He thinks only of earthly things.* **2** possible, conceivable: *That rubbish is no earthly use. adj.*

earth·quake (ėrth′kwāk′) a shaking or sliding of the ground, caused by changes far beneath the earth's surface. *n.*

earth·worm (ėrth′wėrm′) the commonest worm that lives in the earth: *Earthworms are helpful in loosening the soil.* See **worm** for picture. *n.*

ease (ēz) **1** freedom from pain or trouble; comfort: *When school is out, I am going to live a life of ease for a whole week.* **2** make free from pain or trouble. **3** freedom from trying hard: *He enjoyed the ease of his part-time job.* **4** make less; lighten: *Some medicines*

ease pain. 5 make easy; loosen: *The belt is too tight; ease it a little.* 6 move slowly and carefully: *He eased the big box through the door.* 1, 3 *n.*, 2, 4–6 *v.*, **eased, eas·ing.**
at ease, a free from pain or trouble; comfortable. **b** with the hands behind the back, the feet apart, and the body somewhat relaxed: *The soldiers were ordered to stand at ease.*
ease off or **up, a** lessen; lighten. **b** loosen.
with ease, without having to try hard: *He learned to spell with ease.*

ea·sel (ē′zəl) a stand for supporting a picture, blackboard, etc. *n.*

eas·i·er (ēz′ē ər) not so hard; less difficult; more easy. *adj.*

eas·i·ly (ēz′ə lē) 1 in an easy manner; without difficulty or great effort: *He solved the puzzle easily.* 2 without pain or trouble; comfortably: *A few hours after the operation, the patient was resting easily.* 3 by far; without question: *He is easily the best player on the field.* *adv.*

east (ēst) 1 the direction of the sunrise. See **compass** for picture. 2 toward the east: *They travelled east for two days.* 3 from the east: *an east wind.* 4 the part of any country toward the east. 5 Also, **East,** the part of the world, country, or continent toward the east. 6 **the East, a** in Canada, the eastern part of Canada or the United States: *Nova Scotia is in the East.* **b** the Orient; the countries in Asia: *China and Japan are in the East.* **c** Russia and the countries allied with her. 1, 4–6 *n.*, 2 *adv.*, 3 *adj.*
down East, in Canada: **a** any point to the east of Winnipeg, especially that part east of Quebec. **b** in or toward any place east of Winnipeg, especially that part east of Quebec.

East·er (ēs′tər) 1 the day for celebrating Christ's rising from the dead; a yearly church festival that comes on a Sunday between March 21 and April 26. 2 of Easter; for Easter: *Easter music.* 1 *n.*, 2 *adj.*

Easter egg a colored egg, either real or made of chocolate, glass, etc. used as a gift or ornament at Easter.

east·er·ly (ēs′tər lē) 1 toward the east. 2 from the east: *an easterly wind.* *adj., adv.*

east·ern (ēs′tərn) 1 toward the east: *an eastern trip.* 2 from the east: *eastern tourists.* 3 of or in the east; of or in the eastern part of the country: *Halifax is an eastern port.* 4 of or in the Orient or Asia: *eastern countries, eastern customs.* *adj.*

East·ern·er (ēs′tər nər) a person born in or living in the eastern part of the country: *In the West, Ontario people are referred to as Easterners. In Ontario, Maritimers are referred to as Easterners.* *n.*

Eastern Townships most of that part of Quebec lying south of the St. Lawrence River and west of a line drawn southeast from Quebec City to the United States border: *The Eastern Townships were settled by United Empire Loyalists.*

East Indian 1 of or having to do with India or the East Indies. 2 a person born in or living in India or the East Indies.

East Indies (in′dēz) 1 a name used to refer to the region now shown on maps as Indonesia: *Indonesia was once called the Dutch East Indies.* 2 a name applied at one time to India, Indochina, the Malay Archipelago, and nearby islands.

hat, āge, fär; let, ēqual, tėrm; it, īce
hot, ōpen, ôrder; oil, out; cup, pu̇t, rüle
əbove, takən, pencəl, lemən, circəs
ch, child; ng, long; sh, ship
th, thin; ᴛʜ, then; zh, measure

east·ward (ēst′wərd) toward the east; east: *He walked eastward. The orchard is on the eastward slope of the hill.* *adv., adj.*

eas·y (ēz′ē) 1 not hard to do or get: *an easy lesson.* 2 free from pain, discomfort, trouble, or worry: *an easy life.* 3 giving comfort or rest: *an easy chair.* 4 not strict or harsh: *easy terms. That teacher is an easy marker.* 5 smooth and pleasant; not awkward: *easy manners, an easy way of speaking.* *adj.*, **eas·i·er, eas·i·est.**

eas·y·go·ing (ēz′ē gō′ing) usually taking matters easily; tending not to worry: *He's an easygoing person: I've never seen him angry.* *adj.*

eat (ēt) 1 chew and swallow: *Cows eat grass and grain.* 2 have a meal: *Where shall we eat?* 3 destroy as if by eating; wear away: *The flames ate up the wood. The acid has eaten through the metal.* *v.*, **ate, eat·en, eat·ing.** **—eat′er,** *n.*

eat·a·ble (ēt′ə bəl) 1 fit to eat; edible. 2 Usually, **eatables,** *pl.* food. 1 *adj.*, 2 *n.*

eat·en (ēt′ən) See **eat.** *Have you eaten your dinner?* *v.*

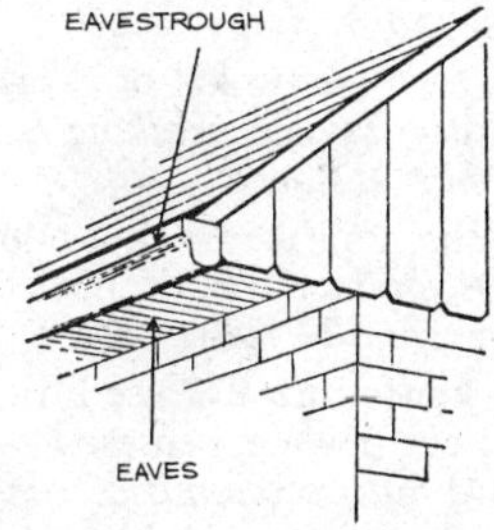

eaves (ēvz) the lower edge of a roof that stands out a little from the building. *n. pl.*

eaves·drop (ēvz′drop′) listen to what one is not supposed to hear; listen secretly to private conversation. *v.*, **eaves·dropped, eaves·drop·ping. —eaves′drop·per,** *n.*

eaves·trough (ēvz′trof′) a gutter placed under the eaves of a roof to catch rain water and carry it away. See **eaves** for picture. *n.*

ebb (eb) 1 a flowing of the tide away from the shore; the fall of the tide. 2 flow out; fall: *We waded farther out as the tide ebbed.* 3 a growing less or weaker; decline; a low point: *His fortunes were at their lowest ebb.* 4 grow less or weaker; decline: *His courage began to ebb as he neared the haunted house.* 1, 3 *n.*, 2, 4 *v.*

eb·on·y (eb′ən ē) a hard, usually black wood that is easy to carve: *Ebony is used especially for such ornamental objects as statues and inlays on wooden furniture.* *n.*, *pl.* **eb·on·ies.**

ec·cen·tric (ek sen′trik) 1 out of the ordinary; not usual; peculiar; odd: *eccentric clothes, eccentric habits.*

2 a person who behaves in an unusual manner. 1 *adj.*, 2 *n.*

ech·o (ek′ō) 1 sounding again: *An echo is heard when sound waves are bounced back from a cliff or hill.* 2 send back or repeat sound: *The hills echoed the sound of the explosion.* 3 repeat or be repeated in sound; resound: *The boom echoed through the valley.* 4 say or do what another says or does: *That girl is always echoing her mother.* 1 *n., pl.* **ech·oes;** 2–4 *v.,* **ech·oed, ech·o·ing.**

é·clair (ē kler′ or ā kler′) an oblong piece of pastry filled with whipped cream or custard and covered with chocolate or other icing. *n.*

e·clipse (ē klips′) 1 a complete or partial darkening of the sun or the moon: *An eclipse of the sun occurs when the moon passes between the earth and the sun. An eclipse of the moon occurs when the earth passes between the sun and the moon, thus leaving the moon in shadow.* 2 cut off the light from, and so make invisible; darken. 3 a loss of importance or reputation; failure for a time: *The boxer has suffered an eclipse.* 4 shine much more brightly than; cast into the shade; surpass: *In sports he quite eclipsed his older brother.* 1, 3 *n.*, 2, 4 *v.,* **e·clipsed, e·clips·ing.**

e·col·o·gy (ē kol′ə jē) the study of the relation of living things to their surroundings and to each other: *The way in which human beings change the natural world around them is part of ecology. n.*

e·co·nom·ic (ē′kə nom′ik or ek′ə nom′ik) having to do with economics. *adj.*

e·co·nom·i·cal (ē′kə nom′ə kəl or ek′ə nom′ə kəl) avoiding waste; thrifty; saving: *Walking is an economical way of travelling short distances. adj.*

e·co·nom·ics (ē′kə nom′iks or ek′ə nom′iks) the science of how men produce wealth, how they distribute it among themselves, and how they use it. *n.*

e·con·o·mize (i kon′ə mīz′) 1 use little of; use to the best advantage. 2 cut down expenses: *Prices have gone up so much that we must economize. v.,* **e·con·o·mized, e·con·o·miz·ing.**

e·con·o·my (i kon′ə mē) 1 making the most of what one has; thrift; freedom from waste in the use of anything. 2 saving: *Many little economies were necessary.* 3 the managing of affairs and resources to the best advantage; management. *n., pl.* **e·con·o·mies.**

ec·sta·sy (ek′stə sē) a state of very great joy; strong feeling that delights or thrills; rapture: *The little girl was in ecstasies over her first Christmas tree. n., pl.* **ec·sta·sies.**

–ed a suffix meaning: 1 that the action referred to has already taken place: *He worked all day yesterday.* 2 having or supplied with, as in *bearded, pale-faced, tender-hearted.* 3 having the characteristics of, as in *honeyed.*

ed·dy (ed′ē) 1 a small whirlpool or whirlwind; water, air, or smoke whirling around. 2 whirl: *The water eddied down the drain.* 1 *n., pl.* **ed·dies;** 2 *v.,* **ed·died, ed·dy·ing.**

edge (ej) 1 the line or place where something ends; the part that is farthest from the middle; the side: *the edge of the paper.* 2 the thin side that cuts: *The knife had a very sharp edge.* 3 move sideways: *She edged her way through the crowd.* 4 move little by little: *He edged his chair nearer to the fire.* 5 win a narrow victory over: *Our hockey team edged the visitors 3-2.* 1, 2 *n.*, 3–5 *v.,* **edged, edg·ing.**
on edge, disturbed; nervous; tense: *Everyone was on edge during the air raid. When he quit smoking, his nerves were on edge for days.*

edge·ways (ej′wāz′) with the edge forward; in the direction of the edge. *adv.*

ed·i·ble (ed′ə bəl) fit to eat; eatable: *Not all mushrooms are edible. adj.*

e·dict (ē′dikt) a decree; a public order by some authority. *n.*

ed·i·fice (ed′ə fis) a building, especially a large or imposing one. *n.*

ed·it (ed′it) 1 prepare for publication, correcting errors, checking facts, etc.: *The teacher is editing famous speeches for use in schoolbooks.* 2 have charge of a newspaper, magazine, dictionary, etc. and decide what shall be printed in it: *Two girls were chosen to edit the class bulletin. v.*

e·di·tion (i dish′ən) 1 all the copies of a book, newspaper, etc. printed just alike and at or near the same time: *The first edition of 'Robinson Crusoe' was printed in 1719.* 2 the form in which a book is printed: *The new edition of 'Mother Goose' has better pictures than the older editions. Some books appear in pocket editions. n.*

ed·i·tor (ed′ə tər) a person who edits or whose work is editing. *n.*

ed·i·to·ri·al (ed′ə tô′rē əl) 1 an article in a newspaper or magazine, or a comment in a broadcast, giving the opinion or attitude of the publisher, editor, speaker, etc. on some subject. 2 of an editor: *editorial work.* 1 *n.*, 2 *adj.*

ed·u·cate (ej′ü kāt′) 1 teach or train. 2 send to school. *v.,* **ed·u·cat·ed, ed·u·cat·ing.**

ed·u·ca·tion (ej′ü kā′shən) 1 schooling; teaching: *In Canada, public schools offer an education to all children.* 2 the knowledge and abilities gained through training: *A person with education knows how to speak, write, and read well. n.*

ed·u·ca·tion·al (ej′ü kā′shən əl) 1 having to do with education: *an educational association.* 2 giving education: *an educational motion picture. adj.*

–ee a suffix meaning: 1 a person who is ____: *An absentee is a person who is absent.* 2 a person who is ____ed: *An appointee is a person who is appointed.*

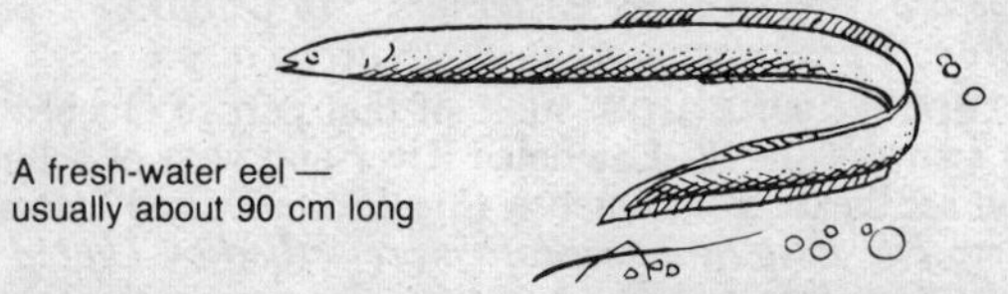

A fresh-water eel — usually about 90 cm long

eel (ēl) a long, slippery fish shaped like a snake: *Because an eel is hard to hold, we say 'as slippery as an eel.' n.*

ee·rie or **ee·ry** (ēr′ē) strange; weird; causing fear: *an eerie scream. adj.,* **ee·ri·er, ee·ri·est.**

ee·ri·ly (ēr′ə lē) in an eerie way; in a way that causes fear: *The shutters of the old, deserted house creaked eerily. adv.*

hat, āge, fär; let, ēqual, tėrm; it, īce
hot, ōpen, ôrder; oil, out; cup, pu̇t, rüle
əbove, takən, pencəl, lemən, circəs
ch, child; ng, long; sh, ship
th, thin; ᴛʜ, then; zh, measure

ef·face (ə fās′) 1 rub out; blot out; do away with; destroy; wipe out: *It takes many years to efface the terrible memories of a war.* 2 keep oneself from being noticed: *The shy boy effaced himself by staying in the background.* *v.,* **ef·faced, ef·fac·ing.**

ef·fect (i fekt′) 1 a result; what is caused: *The overturned boats were the effect of the gale.* 2 bring about; make happen: *The war effected changes all over the world.* 3 the impression produced: *This painting of the mountains gives a fine effect of space and distance.* **4 effects,** *pl.* goods; belongings: *He lost all of his personal effects in the fire.* 1, 3, 4 *n.,* 2 *v.*
for effect, for show; to impress others.
give effect to, put in operation; make active.
in effect, a in result; in fact; really. **b** in operation: *The new rules are now in effect.*
take effect, begin to operate; become active: *The new prices will take effect on January 1st.*

☛ Because the pronunciations of **effect** and **affect** are very similar, they are often confused in writing. Most commonly, **effect** is a noun, meaning 'result,' and **affect** is a verb, meaning 'to influence': *We still don't know what effect the new rule will have. The new rule will affect everybody.* However, **effect** is also used as a verb in formal English, with the meaning 'bring about': *He effected an improvement in the working conditions at his factory.*

ef·fec·tive (i fek′tiv) 1 able to cause something. 2 able to cause some desired result: *These new drugs are very effective.* 3 in operation; active: *These laws will become effective on New Year's Day.* *adj.*

ef·fec·tu·al (i fek′chü əl) producing the effect desired; capable of producing the effect desired: *Penicillin is an effectual medicine for many diseases.* *adj.* **—ef·fec′tu·al·ly,** *adv.*

ef·fi·cien·cy (ə fish′ən sē) the ability to do things without waste; activity that counts toward a purpose: *The carpenter worked with great efficiency.* *n.*

ef·fi·cient (ə fish′ənt) able to do a job without waste of time, energy, etc.; capable: *An efficient cook receives good pay.* *adj.*

ef·fort (ef′ərt) 1 the use of energy and strength to do something; trying hard: *Climbing a steep hill takes effort.* 2 a hard try; a strong attempt: *The loser was congratulated for his fine effort.* 3 the result of effort; anything done with effort: *Works of art are artistic efforts.* *n.*

egg[1] (eg) 1 the round or oval body that is laid by the female of birds and most reptiles and fish, from which the young come. 2 the contents of an egg, especially a hen's egg, used as food: *Father likes two boiled eggs for breakfast.* *n.*

egg[2] (eg) urge by taunts, dares, etc.: *Other boys egged him on to fight.* *v.*

egg cell a cell of a female plant or animal that produces offspring when fertilized by a male sperm cell.

egg·plant (eg′plant′) 1 a large, egg-shaped fruit, used as a vegetable and having a glossy, purple skin when ripe. 2 the plant bearing such fruit. *n.*

egg·shell (eg′shel′) 1 the shell covering an egg. 2 very thin and delicate; fragile like an eggshell: *eggshell china.* 1 *n.,* 2 *adj.*

e·go (ē′gō) 1 the individual as a whole in his capacity to think, feel, and act; self. 2 *Informal.* conceit: *The bright boy's ego annoyed many people.* *n., pl.* **e′gos.**

e·gret (ē′gret or eg′ret) a large bird, a kind of heron found mostly in the southern United States, that grows long plumes on its back during the nesting season: *Most egrets are pure white.* *n.*

E·gyp·tian (i jip′shən) 1 of or having to do with Egypt. 2 a person born in or living in Egypt. 3 the language of the ancient Egyptians. 1 *adj.,* 2, 3 *n.*

ei·der or **eider duck** (ī′dər) a large sea duck, usually black and white. *n.*

ei·der–down (ī′dər doun′) 1 the soft feathers from the breasts of eiders, used as trimming and to fill bed coverings. 2 a quilt stuffed with these feathers. *n.*

eight (āt) one more than seven; 8: *Four and four make eight.* *n., adj.*

eight·een (ā′tēn′) eight more than ten; 18. *n., adj.*

eight·eenth (ā′tēnth′) 1 next after the 17th; last in a series of eighteen; 18th: *If you stand eighteenth in your class, there are seventeen ahead of you.* 2 one of 18 equal parts. *adj., n.*

eighth (ātth) 1 next after the seventh; last in a series of eight; 8th: *August is the eighth month of the year.* 2 one of 8 equal parts. *adj., n.*

eight·i·eth (ā′tē ith) 1 next after the 79th; last in a series of 80; 80th. 2 one of 80 equal parts. *adj., n.*

eight·y (ā′tē) eight times ten; 80. *n., pl.* **eight·ies;** *adj.*

ei·ther (ē′ᴛʜər or ī′ᴛʜər) 1 one or the other of two: *You may read either book (adj.). Choose either of the candy bars (pron.). Either come in or go out (conj.).* 2 each of two: *On either side of the river lie fields of corn.* 3 any more than another; also: *If you do not go, I shall not go either.* 1, 2 *adj.,* 1 *pron., conj.,* 3 *adv.*

e·ject (i jekt′) throw out; turn out; drive out: *The volcano ejected smoke, ashes, and lava.* *v.*

eke out (ēk) 1 add to; increase; help: *She eked out her income by working in the evenings.* 2 barely make a living by various schemes or makeshifts: *He eked out a bare living by doing odd jobs.* *v.,* **eked out, ek·ing out.**

e·lab·o·rate (i lab′ə rit for 1, i lab′ə rāt′ for 2) 1 worked out with great care; having many details; complicated: *Her mother wore an elaborate evening gown.* 2 work out with great care; add details to: *The inventor spent months in elaborating his plans for a new engine.* 1 *adj.,* 2 *v.,* **e·lab·o·rat·ed, e·lab·o·rat·ing.**

e·lapse (i laps′) pass; slip away; glide by: *Many hours elapsed while the boy slept.* *v.,* **e·lapsed, e·laps·ing.**

e·las·tic (i las′tik) 1 having the power of returning to a certain shape after being stretched or pressed out of that shape: *Toy balloons, sponges, and steel springs are elastic.* 2 being able to recover easily or quickly: *His elastic spirits never let him be discouraged for long.* 3 tape or fabric woven partly of rubber threads: *She put new elastic in the sleeves of her blouse.* 4 a rubber band. 1, 2 *adj.,* 3, 4 *n.*

e·las·tic·i·ty (i las′tis′ə tē or ē′las tis′ə tē) an elastic quality: *Rubber has great elasticity.* *n.*

e·lat·ed (i lāt′id) in high spirits; joyful: *They were elated when their team won.* *adj.*

e·la·tion (i lā′shən) high spirits, joy. *n.*

el·bow (el′bō) **1** the joint between the upper arm and forearm. See **arm** for picture. **2** the outer part of this joint, especially the point formed when the arm is bent: *He felt a sharp pain as an elbow dug into his ribs.* **3** something bent or curved so that it resembles a bent arm: *A sharp turn in a road or a river may be called an elbow. An elbow is often used to change the direction of a pipe line.* **4** push, thrust, or nudge with the elbow: *The bully elbowed the little boy.* **5** make one's way by pushing or thrusting with the elbows: *He elbowed his way to the front of the crowd.* 1–3 *n.,* 4, 5 *v.*
at one's elbow, near at hand; close by: *When John did his homework, his dictionary was always at his elbow.*

eld·er (el′dər) **1** older: *my elder brother.* **2** an older person: *The children showed respect for their elders.* **3** an officer of a church. 1 *adj.,* 2, 3 *n.*

el·der·ber·ry (el′dər ber′ē) **1** a shrub or tree having flat clusters of white flowers and black or red berries that are sometimes used in making wine. 2 the berry of such a plant. *n., pl.* **el·der·ber·ries.**

eld·er·ly (el′dər lē′) somewhat old. *adj.*

☛ **Elderly,** used only for describing people, means past middle age and getting old: *He is an elderly man, about sixty or sixty-five.* **Old,** describing people, animals, or things, means not young or new. For people and animals, **old** suggests being near the end of life; for things, it means having existed or been in use for a long time: *They are old friends.*

eld·est (el′dist) oldest. *adj.*

e·lect (i lekt′) **1** choose by voting: *The club elected a new president.* **2** choose; pick out: *A student must take some subjects; he can elect others.* *v.*

e·lec·tion (i lek′shən) **1** the act or process of choosing by vote: *In our city we have an election every two years.* **2** choice. **3** See **general election.** *n.*

e·lec·tric (i lek′trik) **1** of electricity; having to do with electricity. **2** charged with electricity: *an electric battery.* **3** run by electricity: *an electric train.* **4** making use of electricity to increase loudness through an amplifier and loudspeaker system: *His older brother had an electric guitar.* **5** exciting; thrilling. *adj.*

e·lec·tri·cal (i lek′trə kəl) electric. *adj.*

electric eye a photo-electric cell: *An electric eye can operate a device that will make a door open when the light reaching the cell is interrrupted or changed by a person, car, etc. that passes in front of it.*

electric field the space surrounding an electrically charged body within which it produces electric force.

e·lec·tri·cian (i lek′trish′ən) a person who repairs or installs electric wiring, electric appliances, electric motors, etc. *n.*

e·lec·tric·i·ty (i lek′tris′ə tē) **1** a form of energy that can produce light and heat, etc.: *Lightning is caused by electricity.* **2** an electric current: *Our refrigerator is run by electricity.* *n.*

e·lec·tri·fy (i lek′trə fī′) **1** charge with electricity. **2** equip for the use of electric power; provide with electric-power service. **3** excite; thrill: *The speaker electrified his audience with a description of his experiences in the jungle.* *v.,* **e·lec·tri·fied, e·lec·tri·fy·ing.**

e·lec·trode (i lek′trōd) either of the two terminals of a battery or any other source of electricity. *n.*

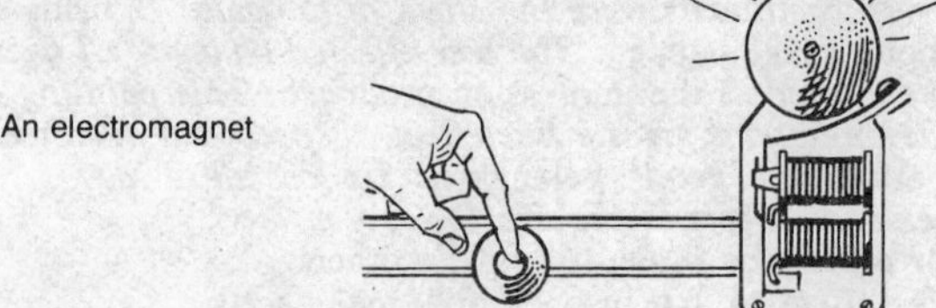
An electromagnet

e·lec·tro·mag·net (i lek′trō mag′nit) a powerful magnet made by coiling wire around an iron core and applying an electrical current to the coil. *n.*

e·lec·tron (i lek′tron) in science, an elementary particle carrying one unit of negative electric charge, found outside the nucleus of every kind of atom. *n.*

e·lec·tron·ic (i lek′tron′ik or ē′lek tron′ik) of or having to do with electrons or electronics. *adj.*

e·lec·tron·ics (i lek′tron′iks or ē′lek tron′iks) the branch of science that deals with the study of electrons in motion: *Radar, radio, television, etc. are based on the principles of electronics.* *n.*

el·e·gance (el′ə gəns) refined grace and richness; luxury free from coarseness: *We admired the elegance of the lady's clothes.* *n.*

el·e·gant (el′ə gənt) showing good taste; refined; superior: *elegant furnishings.* *adj.*

el·e·ment (el′ə mənt) **1** a simple substance, one of over 100 that cannot be separated into simpler parts by chemical means: *Gold, iron, oxygen, carbon, and tin are elements. In ancient times, people thought that there were four elements earth, water, air, and fire.* **2** one of the parts of which anything is made up: *Honesty, industry, and kindness are elements of a good life.* **3** a simple or necessary part; first principle: *He learned the elements of swimming in a few weeks.* **4** in Canada, one of the three branches of the armed forces: Sea (S), Land (L), and Air (A). **5 the elements,** *pl.* the forces of the atmosphere, especially in bad weather: *The raging storm seemed to be a war of the elements.* *n.*

el·e·men·ta·ry (el′ə men′tə rē or el′ə men′trē) introductory; dealing with the simpler parts: *We learned addition and subtraction in elementary arithmetic.* *adj.*

elementary school **1** a school of six grades for pupils from about six to twelve years of age, followed by junior high school. **2** a school of eight (or seven) grades for pupils from about six to fourteen years, followed by high school.

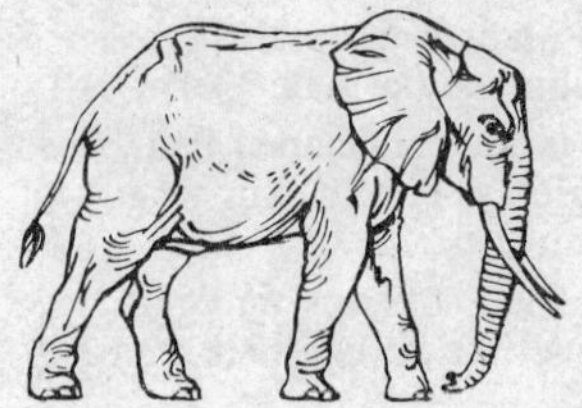
An African elephant — about 3.5 m high at the shoulder

el·e·phant (el′ə fənt) a huge, strong animal of Africa and Asia having thick, grey skin, large, floppy ears, thick legs, long tusks, and a long flexible snout called a trunk: *The elephant is the largest land animal now living. Ivory comes from elephant tusks.* *n.*

el·e·vate (el′ə vāt′) raise; lift up: *He spoke from an elevated platform. The winning players elevated the captain to their shoulders.* *v.,* **el·e·vat·ed, el·e·vat·ing.**

el·e·va·tion (el′ə vā′shən) **1** a raised place; a high place. **2** the height above the earth's surface: *The airplane fell from an elevation of 500 metres.* **3** the height above sea level: *The elevation of that city is 1200 metres.* **4** an elevating or being elevated. *n.*

A prairie elevator

el·e·va·tor (el′ə vā′tər) **1** anything that raises or lifts up. **2** a machine for carrying people or freight up and down in a building. **3** a building for storing grain: *Elevators are a familiar sight on the prairies.* **4** a hinged piece on the tail of an aircraft that is raised or lowered to make the machine go upward or downward. See **airplane** for picture. *n.*

e·lev·en (i lev′ən) **1** one more than ten; 11. **2** a team of eleven football or cricket players. 1, 2 *n.,* 1 *adj.*

e·lev·enth (i lev′ənth) **1** next after the 10th; last in a series of eleven; 11th. **2** one of 11 equal parts. *adj., n.*

elf (elf) in stories, a tiny being that is full of mischief; fairy. *n., pl.* **elves.**

el·i·gi·ble (el′ə jə bəl) **1** fit or proper to be chosen; desirable: *an eligible bachelor.* **2** qualified; meeting all requirements set by law or rule: *Pupils must pass in all subjects to be eligible for the team.* *adj.*

e·lim·i·nate (i lim′ə nāt′) **1** remove; get rid of: *Bridges over railway tracks eliminate the danger in crossing.* **2** put out of a championship competition by reason of defeat: *Our school was eliminated in the first round of the hockey playoffs.* *v.,* **e·lim·i·nat·ed, e·lim·i·nat·ing.**

e·lim·i·na·tion (i lim′ə nā′shən) **1** a removing or getting rid of: *The committee discussed the elimination of Christmas examinations.* **2** being put out of a championship competition by reason of defeat. **3** the passing off or expelling of waste matter, as from the body: *Constipation is a matter of faulty elimination.* *n.*

elk (elk) **1** a large deer of Europe and Asia, having broad antlers resembling those of a moose. **2** a large, red deer of North America; the wapiti. *n., pl.* **elks** or **elk.**

el·lipse (i lips′) an oval having both ends alike. See **oval** for picture. *n.*

el·lip·tic (i lip′tik) elliptical. *adj.*

el·lip·ti·cal (i lip′tə kəl) of or like an ellipse: *The coffee table had an elliptical glass top.* *adj.*

elm (elm) **1** a tall, graceful shade tree. **2** its hard, heavy wood. *n.*

e·lon·gate (i long′gāt′) **1** lengthen; extend; stretch:

hat, āge, fär; let, ēqual, tėrm; it, īce
hot, ōpen, ôrder; oil, out; cup, pu̇t, rüle
əbove, takən, pencəl, lemən, circəs
ch, child; ng, long; sh, ship
th, thin; ᴛʜ, then; zh, measure

He elongated the elastic band to fit it around his papers. **2** long and thin: *the elongate leaf of a willow.* 1 *v.,* **e·lon·gat·ed, e·lon·gat·ing;** 2 *adj.*

e·lope (i lōp′) run away to get married. *v.,* **e·loped, e·lop·ing.**

el·o·quence (el′ə kwəns) **1** a flow of speech that has grace and force: *The eloquence of the speaker moved all hearts.* **2** the power to win by speaking; the art of speaking so as to stir the feelings. *n.*

el·o·quent (el′ə kwənt) **1** having eloquence. **2** very expressive: *His frown was eloquent of his displeasure.* *adj.*

else (els) **1** other; different; instead: *Will somebody else speak? What else could I say?* **2** differently: *How else can he act?* **3** (usually following *or*) otherwise; if not: *You must hurry, or else you'll miss the bus.* 1 *adj.,* 2, 3 *adv.*

or else, *Informal.* or suffer for it; or pay a penalty: *You'd better return my bike, or else.*

else·where (els′wer′ or els′hwer′) in or to some other place; somewhere else. *adv.*

e·lude (i lüd′) avoid or escape by quickness or cleverness; slip away from: *The fox eluded the dogs.* *v.,* **e·lud·ed, e·lud·ing.**

e·lu·sive (i lü′siv) **1** hard to describe or understand: *I had an idea that was too elusive to be put into words.* **2** tending to elude or escape: *The elusive fox got away from the hunters.* *adj.*

elves (elvz) plural of **elf.** *n.*

e·ma·ci·at·ed (i mā′she āt′id or i mā′sē āt′id) thin from losing flesh: *The invalid was pale and emaciated.* *adj.*

e·man·ci·pate (i man′sə pāt′) set free from slavery of any kind; release: *Women have been emancipated from many old restrictions.* *v.,* **e·man·ci·pat·ed, e·man·ci·pat·ing.**

em·balm (em bom′ or em bäm′) treat a dead body with spices or drugs to keep it from decaying. *v.*

em·bank·ment (em bangk′mənt) a raised bank of earth, stone, etc. used to hold back water, support a roadway, etc. *n.*

em·bark (em bärk′) **1** go on board a ship or an aircraft: *The troops embarked for France.* **2** put on board a ship or an aircraft: *The general embarked his troops.* **3** set out; start. *v.*

embark on, begin or enter upon: *After leaving university, the young man embarked on a business career.*

em·bar·rass (em bar′əs or em ber′əs) 1 disturb; make self-conscious: *She embarrassed me by asking if I really liked her.* 2 hinder: *A lack of trucks embarrassed the army's movements.* *v.*

em·bar·rass·ment (em bar′əs mənt or em ber′əs mənt) 1 uneasiness; shame: *Blushes showed her embarrassment at the guest's rudeness to her friends.* 2 something that embarrasses: *The bad-mannered boy was an embarrassment to his parents.* *n.*

em·bas·sy (em′bə sē) 1 the headquarters of an ambassador: *Canada has an embassy in Paris.* 2 one or more persons sent, usually to the ruler or government of a country, with authority to make some arrangement. *n., pl.* **em·bas·sies.**

em·bat·tled (em bat′əld) drawn up ready for battle; prepared for battle. *adj.*

em·bed (em bed′) 1 plant in a bed: *He embedded the bulbs in a box of sand.* 2 fix or enclose in a surrounding mass: *Precious stones are found embedded in rock.* *v.,* **em·bed·ded, em·bed·ding.**

em·ber (em′bər) 1 a piece of wood or coal still glowing in the ashes of a fire. 2 **embers,** *pl.* ashes in which there is still some fire: *He stirred the embers to make them blaze up again.* *n.*

em·bez·zle (em bez′əl) steal by putting to one's own use money that one is keeping for some other person or group of persons: *The treasurer embezzled $2000 from the club's funds.* *v.,* **em·bez·zled, em·bez·zling.**

em·bit·ter (em bit′ər) make bitter: *The unhappy old man was embittered by the loss of all his money.* *v.*

em·blem (em′bləm) a symbol; the sign of an idea; token: *The beaver and the maple leaf are both emblems of Canada. The dove is an emblem of peace.* *n.*

em·bod·y (em bod′ē) 1 give body to; give reality to: *A building embodies the idea of the architect.* 2 form into a body; include: *A dictionary embodies a great deal of information about words.* *v.,* **em·bod·ied, em·bod·y·ing.**

em·boss (em bos′) decorate with a design that stands out from the surface, made by pressing or moulding: *Canadian coins are embossed with letters and figures.* *v.*

em·brace (em brās′) 1 fold in the arms to show love; hold in the arms; hug: *A mother embraces her baby.* 2 take up; accept: *He eagerly embraced the offer of a trip to Mexico.* 3 include; contain: *The cat family embraces lions and tigers.* 4 surround; enclose: *Vines embraced the hut.* 5 a hug. 1–4 *v.,* **em·braced, em·brac·ing;** 5 *n.*

em·broi·der (em broi′dər) 1 ornament cloth with a design or pattern of stitches; sew at embroidery. 2 add imaginary details to; exaggerate: *He didn't exactly tell lies, but he did embroider his stories.* *v.*

em·broi·der·y (em broi′dər ē) ornamental designs sewn with a needle; embroidered work or material. *n., pl.* **em·broi·der·ies.**

em·bry·o (em′brē ō′) 1 an animal in the earlier stages of its development, before birth or hatching: *A chicken within an egg is an embryo.* 2 an undeveloped plant within a seed. *n., pl.* **em·bry·os.**

e·mend (i mend′) free from faults or errors; correct. *v.*

em·er·ald (em′ər əld) 1 a clear, bright-green precious stone. 2 bright green. 1, 2 *n.,* 2 *adj.*

e·merge (i mėrj′) come out; come up; come into view: *The sun emerged from behind a cloud. Many facts emerged as a result of the investigation.* *v.,* **e·merged, e·merg·ing.**

e·mer·gen·cy (i mėr′jən sē) 1 an unexpected or sudden event or situation that calls for immediate action: *He keeps a box of tools in his car for emergencies.* 2 for use in case of such a situation: *an emergency door, an emergency brake.* 3 carried out or performed in such a situation: *The surgeon performed an emergency operation on the badly injured man.* 1 *n., pl.* **e·mer·gen·cies;** 2, 3 *adj.*

em·er·y (em′ər ē) a hard, dark mineral that is used for grinding, smoothing, and polishing metals, stones, etc. *n.*

em·i·grant (em′ə grənt) a person who leaves his own country to settle in another. *n.*

☛ See note at **emigrate.**

em·i·grate (em′ə grāt′) leave one's own country to settle in another: *Many Italians have emigrated to Canada.* *v.,* **em·i·grat·ed, em·i·grat·ing.**

☛ **Emigrate** means move out of a country or region; **immigrate** means move into a country or region. An *emigrant* from Norway might be an *immigrant* to Canada.

em·i·gra·tion (em′ə grā′shən) 1 leaving one's own country to settle in another: *In recent years there has been much emigration from Europe to Canada.* 2 a movement of emigrants. *n.*

em·i·nence (em′ə nəns) 1 a high position in affairs; greatness; fame: *Edison won eminence as an inventor.* 2 a high place; a mountain, hill, or other high point of land. *n.*

em·i·nent (em′ə nənt) high; above all others; distinguished: *The Governor General is an eminent man.* *adj.*

em·is·sar·y (em′ə ser′ē) a person sent on a mission or errand, especially one sent secretly. *n., pl.* **em·is·sar·ies.**

e·mit (i mit′) send out; give off: *A volcano emits smoke. The lion emitted a roar of rage.* *v.,* **e·mit·ted, e·mit·ting.**

e·mo·tion (i mō′shən) a strong feeling of any kind: *Joy, grief, fear, hate, love, anger, and excitement are emotions.* *n.*

e·mo·tion·al (i mō′shən əl) 1 of the emotions. 2 appealing to the emotions: *The next speaker made an emotional plea for money to help crippled children.* 3 easily excited: *Emotional people are likely to cry if they hear sad music or read sad stories.* *adj.* —**e·mo′tion·al·ly,** *adv.*

A human embryo, about 6 weeks old

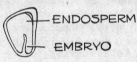

ENDOSPERM

EMBRYO

The embryo of a corn plant inside a seed

hat, āge, fär; let, ēqual, tėrm; it, īce
hot, ōpen, ôrder; oil, out; cup, pu̇t, rüle
əbove, takən, pencəl, lemən, circəs
ch, child; ng, long; sh, ship
th, thin; ᴛʜ, then; zh, measure

em·per·or a man who is the ruler of an empire. *n.*

em·pha·sis (em′fə sis) **1** stress; importance: *That school puts emphasis on arithmetic and reading.* **2** the special force of voice put on particular syllables, words, or phrases; stress: *In reading, our teacher puts emphasis upon the most important words.* *n., pl.* **em·pha·ses** (em′fə sēz′).

em·pha·size (em′fə sīz′) **1** give special force to; stress; make important: *He emphasized his point by banging his fist on the table.* **2** call attention to: *The great number of automobile accidents emphasizes the need for careful driving.* *v.,* **em·pha·sized, em·pha·siz·ing.**

em·phat·ic (em fat′ik) said or done with force; meant to stand out; clear; positive; emphasized: *Her answer was an emphatic 'No!'* *adj.*

em·phat·i·cal·ly (em fat′ik lē) in an emphatic manner; to an emphatic degree. *adv.*

em·pire (em′pīr) **1** a group of countries or states under one ruler or government: *the British Empire.* **2** a country ruled by an emperor or empress: *the Japanese Empire.* **3** power; rule. *n.*

em·ploy (em ploi′) **1** give work and pay to: *The hotel employs a cook.* **2** use: *You employ a knife, fork, and spoon in eating.* **3** keep busy: *She often employed herself in reading.* *v.*

em·ploy·ee (em ploi′ē) a person who works for some person or firm for pay. *n.*

em·ploy·er (em ploi′ər) a person or firm that employs one or more persons. *n.*

em·ploy·ment (em ploi′mənt) **1** what a person does for a living; work: *He was not satisfied with his employment. He had great difficulty finding employment.* **2** an employing or being employed: *A large office requires the employment of many people.* **3** use: *There is a clever employment of color in that painting.* *n.*

em·pow·er (em pou′ər) give power or authority to: *The treasurer was empowered to pay certain bills.* *v.*

em·press (em′pris) **1** the wife of an emperor. **2** a woman who rules over an empire. *n.*

emp·ti·ness (emp′tē nis) the state or condition of being empty; lack of contents. *n.*

emp·ty (emp′tē) **1** with nothing in it: *The birds had gone and their nest was left empty.* **2** pour out or take out all that is in a thing: *He emptied his glass quickly.* **3** become empty: *The hall emptied as soon as the concert was over.* **4** flow out: *The St. Lawrence River empties into the Gulf of St. Lawrence.* **5** not real; meaningless: *An empty promise is insincere.* 1, 5 *adj.,* **emp·ti·er, emp·ti·est;** 2–4 *v.,* **emp·tied, emp·ty·ing.**

em·u·late (em′yə lāt′) try to equal or excel: *The proverb tells us to emulate the industry of the ant.* *v.,* **em·u·lat·ed, em·u·lat·ing.**

e·mul·sion (i mul′shən) **1** a mixture of two liquids that do not dissolve in each other: *In an emulsion very fine drops of one of the liquids are scattered evenly through the other.* **2** a milky liquid containing very tiny drops of fat or of some other substance. *n.*

en·a·ble (en ā′bəl) make able; give ability, power, or means to: *Airplanes enable people to travel through the air.* *v.,* **en·a·bled, en·a·bling.**

en·act (en akt′) make into law: *Parliament enacted a bill to raise money for national defence.* *v.*

e·nam·el (i nam′əl) **1** a glasslike substance melted and then cooled to make a smooth, hard surface: *Different colors of enamel are used to cover or decorate metal, pottery, etc.* **2** a paint or varnish used to make a smooth, hard, glossy surface. **3** the smooth, hard, glossy, outer layer that covers and protects the crown of a tooth. **4** cover or decorate with enamel. 1–3 *n.,* 4 *v.,* **e·nam·elled** or **e·nam·eled, e·nam·el·ling** or **e·nam·el·ing.**

en·camp (en kamp′) **1** make camp: *It took the soldiers only an hour to encamp.* **2** live in a camp for a time: *They encamped there for three weeks.* *v.*

en·camp·ment (en kamp′mənt) **1** the act of forming a camp. **2** camp. *n.*

–ence a suffix meaning: **1** the act or fact of ___ing: *Dependence is the act or fact of depending on someone or something.* **2** the condition of being ___: *Absence is the condition of being absent. Confidence is the condition of being confident.*

en·chant (en chant′) **1** use magic on; put under a spell: *The witch had enchanted the princess.* **2** delight greatly; charm: *The dance music enchanted them.* *v.*

en·chant·ing (en chan′ting) charming; very delightful. *adj.*

en·chant·ment (en chant′mənt) **1** the use of magic spells; a spell or charm: *In 'The Wizard of Oz' Dorothy finds herself at home again by the enchantments of the Good Witch.* **2** something that delights or charms: *We felt the enchantment of the moonlight on the lake.* *n.*

en·chan·tress (en chan′tris) **1** a woman who makes magic spells; a witch. **2** a delightful, charming woman. *n.*

en·cir·cle (en sėr′kəl) **1** form a circle around; surround: *Trees encircled the pond.* **2** go in a circle around: *The moon encircles the earth.* *v.,* **en·cir·cled, en·cir·cling.**

en·close (en klōz′) **1** shut in on all sides; surround. **2** put a wall or fence around. **3** put in an envelope along with something else: *A cheque was enclosed with the letter.* *v.,* **en·closed, en·clos·ing.** Also spelled **inclose.**

en·clo·sure (en klō′zhər) **1** an enclosing or being enclosed. **2** an enclosed place: *An enclosure for animals is sometimes called a pen.* **3** something that encloses: *A wall or fence is an enclosure.* **4** anything enclosed with something else, especially in an envelope: *He sent several newspaper clippings as enclosures with his letter.* *n.* Also spelled **inclosure.**

en·com·pass (en kum′pəs) go or reach all the way around; encircle: *The atmosphere encompasses the earth.* *v.*

en·core (ong′kôr or on′kôr) **1** a demand by the audience for the repetition of a song, for another appearance by a performer, etc. **2** the repetition of a song, etc. in response to such a demand: *The pianist played two encores.* *n.*

en·coun·ter (en koun′tər) **1** meet unexpectedly: *What if we should encounter a bear?* **2** an unexpected meeting. 3 be faced with: *He encountered many difficulties before the job was done.* 4 meet as an enemy. 5 a battle; a meeting of two opposed forces, teams, etc. 1, 3, 4 *v.*, 2, 5 *n.*

en·cour·age (en kėr′ij) 1 give hope, courage, or confidence to; urge on: *The cheers of the crowd encouraged him.* 2 give help to; be favorable to: *High prices for grain encourage farming.* *v.*, **en·cour·aged, en·cour·ag·ing.**

en·cour·age·ment (en kėr′ij mənt) 1 an urging on toward success. 2 something that gives hope, courage, or confidence: *The new equipment was a great encouragement to our team.* *n.*

en·croach (en krōch′) 1 go beyond proper or usual limits: *The sea encroached upon the shore and covered the beach.* 2 trespass upon the property or rights of another; intrude: *A good salesman will not encroach upon his customer's time.* *v.*

en·cum·ber (en kum′bər) 1 hold back; hinder: *Heavy shoes encumber anyone in the water.* 2 fill; block up: *His yard was encumbered with old carts and other rubbish.* 3 burden with weight, difficulties, cares, debt, etc.: *Mother is encumbered with household cares.* *v.* Also spelled **incumber.**

en·cum·brance (en kum′brəns) a burden; something that is useless or in the way; hindrance: *Shoes would be an encumbrance to a swimmer.* *n.* Also spelled **incumbrance.**

en·cy·clo·pe·di·a or **en·cy·clo·pae·di·a** (en sī′klə pē′dē ə) 1 a book or set of books giving information arranged alphabetically on all branches of knowledge. 2 a book treating one subject very thoroughly, with its articles arranged alphabetically: *a medical encyclopedia.* *n.*

end (end) 1 the last part: *He read through to the end of the book.* 2 the edge or outside limit of an object or area; boundary: *Those trees mark the end of their property. Drive to the end of the road.* 3 the point where something that has length stops or ceases to be: *Every stick has two ends. She sat at the end of the table.* 4 have a boundary: *Their property ends here.* 5 bring or come to its last part; finish: *Let us end this fight.* 6 form the end of; be the end of: *This chapter ends the book.* 7 a purpose; what is aimed at in doing any piece of work: *He had this end in mind—to do his work without a mistake.* 8 in curling, one of the divisions of a game: *My father's team was beaten in the last end.* 9 in rugby football, the player at either end of the line. 1–3, 7–9 *n.*, 4–6 *v.*

end to end, with the end of one object set next to the end of another; endways: *The dominoes were arranged end to end on the table.*

end up, finish: *He'll end up at the top of his class. He ended up as a wealthy man.*

hold or **keep one's end up,** do one's part or carry one's share fully in an undertaking or performance: *He was less experienced than the others, but he kept his end up very well.*

in the end, finally; at last: *Everything will turn out all right in the end.*

on end, a upright in position: *He stood the dominoes on end.* **b** one after another: *It snowed for days on end.*

no end, *Informal.* very much; very many: *That car causes no end of trouble.*

en·dan·ger (en dān′jər) cause danger to: *A war endangers millions of lives.* *v.*

en·dear (en dēr′) make dear: *Her kindness endeared her to all of us.* *v.*

en·deav·or or **en·deav·our** (en dev′ər) 1 try hard; make an effort; strive: *A runner endeavors to win a race.* 2 an effort; attempt. 1 *v.*, 2 *n.*

end·ing (en′ding) an end; the last part: *The story had a sad ending.* *n.*

end·less (end′lis) 1 having no end; never stopping; lasting or going on forever: *the endless motion of the stars.* 2 appearing to have no end; seeming never to stop: *an endless task.* 3 joined in a circle; without ends: *The chain that turns the back wheel of a bicycle is an endless chain.* *adj.*

end of steel *Cdn.* 1 the limit to which tracks have been laid for a railway. 2 a town at the end of a railway line; the terminus of a northern railway.

en·dorse (en dôrs′) 1 approve; support: *Parents heartily endorsed the plan for a school playground.* 2 write one's name or instructions on the back of a cheque, money order, or other document: *He had to endorse the cheque before the bank would cash it.* *v.*, **en·dorsed, en·dors·ing.** **—en·dorse′ment,** *n.*

en·do·sperm (en′dō spėrm′) the nourishment for the embryo enclosed in the seed of a plant. See **embryo** for picture. *n.*

en·dow (en dou′) 1 give money or property to provide an income for: *The rich man endowed a college.* 2 give at birth; provide with some ability, quality, or talent: *Nature endowed her with musical talent.* *v.*

en·dow·ment (en dou′mənt) 1 the money or property given to a person or institution to provide an income. 2 a gift from birth; talent: *A good sense of rhythm is a natural endowment.* 3 the act of endowing. *n.*

en·dur·ance (en dyür′əns or en dür′əns) 1 the ability to last and to withstand hard wear: *A man must have great endurance to run 40 kilometres in a day.* 2 the power to stand something without giving out; holding out; bearing up: *His endurance of the pain was remarkable.* *n.*

en·dure (en dyür′ or en dür′) 1 last; keep on: *These statues have endured a thousand years.* 2 undergo; bear; stand: *Those brave people endured much pain.* *v.*, **en·dured, en·dur·ing.**

end·ways (end′wāz′) 1 on end. 2 with the end forward; lengthways. 3 end to end: *He placed all the boards endways in a line.* *adv.*

end·wise (end′wīz′) endways. *adv.*

en·e·my (en′ə mē) 1 a person or group that hates and tries to harm another: *Two countries fighting against each other are enemies.* 2 a hostile force, nation, army, fleet, or air force; person, ship, etc. of a hostile nation. 3 of an enemy: *an enemy ship.* 4 anything harmful: *Frost is an enemy of flowers.* 1, 2, 4 *n.*, *pl.* **en·e·mies;** 3 *adj.*

en·er·get·ic (en′ər jet′ik) full of energy; active; eager to work; full of force: *Cool autumn days make some people feel energetic.* *adj.*

en·er·get·i·cal·ly (en′ər jet′ik lē) with energy; vigorously. *adv.*

hat, āge, fär; let, ēqual, tėrm; it, īce
hot, ōpen, ôrder; oil, out; cup, pu̇t, rüle
əbove, takən, pencəl, lemən, circəs
ch, child; ng, long; sh, ship
th, thin; ᴛʜ, then; zh, measure

en·er·gy (en′ər jē) 1 vigor; the will to work or act: *The boy is so full of energy that he cannot keep still.* 2 the power to work or act; force: *All our energies were used in keeping the fire from spreading.* *n., pl.* **en·er·gies.**

en·fold (en fōld′) 1 fold in; wrap up: *The old lady was enfolded in a shawl.* 2 embrace; clasp: *The mother enfolded her baby in her arms.* *v.*

en·force (en fôrs′) 1 force obedience to; cause to be carried out: *Policemen enforce the traffic laws.* 2 force; compel: *We have laws to enforce the payment of income taxes.* *v.,* **en·forced, en·forc·ing.**

en·force·ment (en fôrs′mənt) an enforcing: *Strict enforcement of the laws against speeding will reduce automobile accidents.* *n.*

en·gage (en gāj′) 1 take up, or occupy the attention or time of: *TV engages the attention of many people.* 2 hire; employ: *They engaged a cook for the summer.* 3 arrange to secure for occupation or use; reserve: *We engaged a room in the hotel.* 4 bind by a promise or contract; pledge: *He engaged to pay for his bicycle at the end of the month.* 5 promise or pledge to marry: *John is engaged to Anne.* 6 attract; catch and hold; capture: *Bright objects engage a baby's attention.* 7 come into contact with in battle; attack: *Canadian troops have engaged the enemy on many battlefields.* 8 fit into; lock together; interlock: *The teeth of one gear engage with those of another.* See **cogwheel** for picture. *v.,* **en·gaged, en·gag·ing.**

engage in, a keep busy with; take part in; be active in: *He engages in many sports.* **b** take up the attention of: *Mother engaged the milkman in conversation.*

en·gaged (en gājd′) 1 pledged to marry: *The engaged girl has a diamond ring.* 2 busy; occupied: *Engaged in conversation, they did not see us.* *adj.*

en·gage·ment (en gāj′mənt) 1 a promise; pledge: *An honest person fulfils all his engagements.* 2 the time between becoming pledged to marry and the actual wedding: *They got married after an engagement of six months.* 3 a meeting with someone at a certain time; an appointment. 4 battle. *n.*

en·gag·ing (en gāj′ing) attractive; pleasing: *She has an engaging smile.* *adj.*

en·gine (en′jən) 1 a machine for applying power to some work, especially a machine that can start others moving. 2 the machine that pulls a railway train; locomotive. 3 anything that is used to bring about a result; machine; instrument: *Those big guns are engines of war.* *n.*

en·gi·neer (en′jə nēr′) 1 a man who makes, takes care of, or runs engines: *The driver of a locomotive is an engineer.* 2 a person skilled in a branch of engineering. 3 do the work of an engineer. 4 guide; manage: *She engineered the whole job from start to finish.* 1, 2 *n.,* 3, 4 *v.*

en·gi·neer·ing (en′jə nēr′ing) the application of science to such practical uses as the design and building of structures and machines, and the making of many products of modern technology: *Knowledge of engineering is needed in building railways, bridges, and dams.* *n.*

Eng·lish (ing′glish) 1 of or having to do with England, its people, or their language. 2 the people of England. 3 the language of England and many other countries: *The English spoken in Canada is called Canadian English.* 1 *adj.,* 2, 3 *n.*

English horn a wooden musical instrument resembling an oboe, but larger and having a lower tone.

Eng·lish·man (ing′glish mən) a man born in or living in England. *n., pl.* **Eng·lish·men** (ing′glish mən).

Eng·lish·wom·an (ing′glish wu̇m′ən) a woman born in or living in England. *n., pl.* **Eng·lish·wom·en** (ing′glish wim′ən).

en·grave (en grāv′) 1 carve in; carve in an artistic way: *The jeweller engraved the boy's initials on the back of the watch.* 2 cut in lines on wood, stone, metal, or glass plates for printing. 3 fix firmly: *His mother's face was engraved on his memory.* *v.,* **en·graved, en·grav·ing.**

en·grav·ing (en grāv′ing) 1 the art or act of a person who engraves. 2 a copy of a picture made from an engraved plate; print. *n.*

en·gross (en grōs′) occupy wholly; fill the mind of: *She was engrossed in an interesting story.* *v.*

en·gulf (en gulf′) swallow up; overwhelm: *The waves engulfed the boat.* *v.*

en·hance (en hans′) add to; make greater: *The gardens enhanced the beauty of the house.* *v.,* **en·hanced, en·hanc·ing.**

e·nig·ma (i nig′mə) something difficult to understand; a riddle; anything puzzling: *He was an enigma to his neighbors; he never went out, and yet his house was always dark.* *n.*

en·joy (en joi′) 1 have or use with joy; be happy with; take pleasure in: *We enjoyed our visit to the museum.* 2 have as an advantage or benefit: *He enjoys good health.* *v.*

enjoy oneself, be happy; have a good time: *Enjoy yourself at the party.*

en·joy·a·ble (en joi′ə bəl) pleasant; giving joy: *an enjoyable evening.* *adj.*

en·joy·ment (en joi′mənt) 1 pleasure; joy; delight. 2 the condition of having as an advantage or benefit; possession or use: *The son now has the enjoyment of his father's car.* *n.*

en·large (en lärj′) 1 make larger: *We are planning to enlarge our house.* 2 grow larger. *v.,* **en·larged, en·larg·ing.**

enlarge on, talk or write more about: *The chairman of the school board enlarged on his earlier statement about the plan for a new school.*

en·large·ment (en lärj′mənt) 1 the act of making larger. 2 anything that enlarges something else; addition. 3 a photograph or other thing that has been made larger. *n.*

en·light·en (en līt′ən) make clear; give the light of truth and knowledge to; inform; instruct: *His travels enlightened him about many things he had not known before.* *v.*

en·list (en list′) 1 join. 2 join the armed forces. 3 get the support of: *The mayor enlisted the churches of our city to work for more parks.* *v.*

en·liv·en (en līv′ən) make lively, active, gay, or cheerful: *Spring enlivens all nature. Bright curtains enliven a room.* *v.*

en·mi·ty (en′mə tē) the feeling that enemies have for each other; hatred. *n., pl.* **en·mi·ties.**

e·nor·mous (i nôr′məs) extremely large; huge: *Long ago there were enormous animals in the world.* *adj.*

e·nough (i nuf′) **1** as many as needed: *Are there enough seats for all?* **2** as much as is wanted or needed: *Has he had enough to eat?* **3** sufficiently; until no more is needed or wanted: *Have you played enough?* 1 *adj.*, 2 *n.*, 3 *adv.*

en·quire (en kwīr′) inquire. *v.,* **en·quired, en·quir·ing.**

en·quir·y (en kwīr′ē) inquiry. *n., pl.* **en·quir·ies.**

en·rage (en rāj′) make very angry; make furious; madden: *The dog was enraged by the teasing.* *v.,* **en·raged, en·rag·ing.**

en·rich (en rich′) make rich or richer: *An education enriches your mind. You can enrich a food by adding cream or butter. Fertilizer enriches the soil.* *v.*

en·rol or **en·roll** (en rōl′) **1** write in a list: *The secretary enrolled our names.* **2** have one's name written in a list. **3** make a member. **4** become a member. **5** enlist: *He enrolled in the armed forces.* *v.,* **en·rolled, en·rol·ling.**

en·rol·ment or **en·roll·ment** (en rōl′mənt) **1** enrolling. **2** the number enrolled: *The school has an enrolment of 200 students.* *n.*

en route (on rüt′) on the way: *We shall stop at Toronto en route from Montreal to Winnipeg.*

en·shrine (en shrīn′) **1** enclose in a shrine: *A fragment of the Cross is enshrined in the cathedral.* **2** keep sacred: *Memories of happier days were enshrined in the old beggar's heart.* *v.,* **en·shrined, en·shrin·ing.**

en·sign (en′sīn) **1** a flag or banner: *the Red Ensign.* **2** the sign of a person's rank, position, or power. *n.*

en·slave (en slāv) make a slave or slaves of; take away freedom from. *v.,* **en·slaved, en·slav·ing.**

en·sue (en sü′ or en syü′) **1** come after; follow: *The ensuing year means the year following.* **2** happen as a result: *In his anger he hit the man, and a fight ensued.* *v.,* **en·sued, en·su·ing.**

en·sure (en shür′) **1** make sure or certain: *Careful planning and hard work ensured the success of the party.* **2** make sure of getting; secure: *A letter of introduction will ensure you an interview.* **3** make safe; protect: *Proper clothing ensured us against the cold.* *v.,* **en·sured, en·sur·ing.**

☛ **Ensure** is the usual spelling for 'make sure or certain'; **insure** is the usual spelling for 'arrange for money payment in case of loss, accident, or death': *Check your work to ensure its accuracy. They insured their house against fire.*

en·tan·gle (en tang′gəl) **1** get twisted up and caught: *Threads are easily entangled.* **2** involve; get into difficulty: *Do not entangle my brother in your schemes.* *v.,* **en·tan·gled, en·tan·gling.**

en·tan·gle·ment (en tang′gəl mənt) **1** an entangling or being entangled. **2** anything that entangles; snare; something difficult to get out of or through: *The trench was protected by a barbed-wire entanglement.* *n.*

en·ter (en′tər) **1** go into; come into: *He entered the house.* **2** go in; come in: *Let them enter.* **3** join; become a part or member of: *The men entered the armed forces.* **4** cause to join; enrol: *Parents enter their children in school.* **5** begin; start: *After years of training, the doctor entered the practice of medicine.* **6** write or print in a book, list, etc.: *A dictionary enters words in alphabetical order.* **7** make a record of: *The teller entered the deposit in my bank book.* *v.*

enter into, a begin to take part in: *He entered into conversation with the woman next to him on the bus.* **b** form part of: *That question doesn't enter into the problem.*

enter on or **upon,** begin; start: *He entered on his professional duties as soon as he finished law school.*

en·ter·prise (en′tər prīz′) **1** an important, difficult, or dangerous undertaking. **2** any undertaking; project: *He had two enterprises—raising chickens and collecting butterflies.* **3** a readiness to start projects; energy in starting projects: *The successful businessman showed great enterprise.* *n.*

en·ter·pris·ing (en′tər prīz′ing) likely to start projects; ready to face difficulties: *Employers like enterprising young people.* *adj.*

en·ter·tain (en′tər tān′) **1** make fun for; please; amuse: *A circus entertains children.* **2** have as a guest or guests: *She entertained ten people at dinner.* **3** have guests; invite people to one's home: *She entertains a great deal.* **4** take into the mind; consider: *They refused to entertain such a foolish idea.* *v.* **—en′ter·tain′er,** *n.*

en·ter·tain·ment (en′tər tān′mənt) **1** something that interests, pleases, or amuses, such as a show or a circus. **2** an entertaining or being entertained. **3** the act or practice of paying attention to the comfort and desires of guests: *The host devoted himself to the entertainment of his guests.* *n.*

en·thral or **en·thrall** (en throl′ or en thrôl′) **1** captivate; fascinate; charm: *'Treasure Island' is an enthralling story.* **2** make a slave of. *v.,* **en·thralled, en·thrall·ing.**

en·throne (en thrōn′) **1** set on a throne. **2** place highest of all; exalt: *Sir Wilfrid Laurier is enthroned in the hearts of his countrymen.* *v.,* **en·throned, en·thron·ing.**

en·thu·si·asm (en thü′zē az′əm) eager interest; zeal: *Hunting and fishing arouse enthusiasm in many boys.* *n.*

en·thu·si·ast (en thü′zē ast′ or en thü′zē əst) a person who is filled with eager interest or zeal: *a baseball enthusiast.* *n.*

en·thu·si·as·tic (en thü′zē as′tik) full of enthusiasm; eagerly interested. *adj.*

en·thu·si·as·ti·cal·ly (en thü′zē as′tik lē) with enthusiasm; in an enthusiastic way. *adv.*

en·tice (en tīs′) attract; lead into something by raising hopes or desires; tempt: *The smell of food enticed the hungry children into the house.* *v.,* **en·ticed, en·tic·ing.**

en·tire (en tīr′) whole; complete; having all the parts: *The entire platoon was wiped out.* *adj.* **—en·tire′ly,** *adv.*

en·tire·ty (en tīr′tē or en tīr′ə tē) completeness; the whole: *He enjoyed the concert in its entirety.* *n., pl.* **en·tire·ties.**

en·ti·tle (en tī′təl) **1** give a claim or right: *The one who guesses the answer is entitled to ask the next question.* **2** give the title of; name: *The author entitled his book 'Treasure Island.' The Queen is also entitled 'Defender of the Faith.'* *v.,* **en·ti·tled, en·ti·tling.**

hat, āge, fär; let, ēqual, tėrm; it, īce
hot, ōpen, ôrder; oil, out; cup, pu̇t, rüle
əbove, takən, pencəl, lemən, circəs
ch, child; ng, long; sh, ship
th, thin; ᴛʜ, then; zh, measure

en·trance[1] (en′trəns) 1 the act of entering: *The actor's entrance was greeted with applause.* 2 a place by which to enter. 3 the right to enter; permission to enter: *The prince had entrance to the best society. The knight gained entrance to the castle.* *n.*

en·trance[2] (en trans′) 1 put into a trance. 2 delight; carry away with joy: *The girl was entranced by her new doll.* *v.,* **en·tranced, en·tranc·ing.**

en·treat (en trēt′) keep asking earnestly; beg and pray: *She entreated her father not to send her away to school.* *v.*

en·treat·y (en trēt′ē) earnest request: *Her father gave in to her entreaties.* *n., pl.* **en·treat·ies.**

en·trench (en trench′) 1 surround with a trench; fortify with trenches: *The soldiers were entrenched opposite the enemy.* 2 establish firmly: *Exchanging gifts at Christmas is a custom entrenched by long tradition.* *v.*

en·trust (en trust′) 1 trust; charge with a trust: *We entrusted him with the money to pay the fares.* 2 give the care of; hand over for safekeeping: *While travelling, they entrusted their son to his grandparents. He entrusted his life to his doctor.* *v.*

en·try (en′trē) 1 the act of entering. 2 a place by which to enter; the way to enter: *An entrance hall is an entry.* 3 something written or printed in a book, list, etc.: *Each word explained in a dictionary is an entry.* 4 a person or thing that takes part in a contest: *The dog race had nine entries.* *n., pl.* **en·tries.**

entry word in a dictionary, a word listed in alphabetical order and followed by information concerning its pronunciation, meaning, etc.: *Entry words are usually printed in heavy black type.*

en·twine (en twīn′) 1 twine together. 2 twine around: *Roses and honeysuckle entwine the little cottage.* *v.,* **en·twined, en·twin·ing.**

e·nu·mer·ate (i nyü′mər āt′ or i nü′mər āt′) 1 name one by one; give a list of: *He enumerated the days of the week.* 2 *Cdn.* make up or enter in a list of voters in an area. *v.,* **e·nu·mer·at·ed, e·nu·mer·at·ing.**

e·nu·mer·a·tor (i nyü′mər ā′tər or i nü′mər ā′tər) *Cdn.* a person who makes up a list of voters in an area. *n.*

e·nun·ci·ate (i nun′sē āt′) 1 speak or pronounce words: *The trained actor enunciates very distinctly.* 2 announce; state definitely: *The scientist has enunciated a new theory.* *v.,* **e·nun·ci·at·ed, e·nun·ci·at·ing.**

e·nun·ci·a·tion (i nun′sē ā′shən) 1 one's manner of pronouncing words. 2 an announcement; statement: *the enunciation of a set of rules.* *n.*

en·vel·op (en vel′əp) wrap, cover, or hide: *The baby was so enveloped in blankets that we could hardly see her face. Fog enveloped the village.* *v.,* **en·vel·oped, en·vel·op·ing.**

en·ve·lope (en′və lōp′ or on′və lōp′) 1 a folded and gummed paper cover in which a letter or anything flat may be mailed. 2 a wrapper; covering. *n.*

en·vi·a·ble (en′vē ə bəl) to be envied; desirable: *She has an enviable school record.* *adj.*

en·vi·ous (en′vē əs) 1 wishing to have something that someone else has: *She was envious of her friend's new bicycle.* 2 disliking someone who has more than oneself: *The weak are often envious of the strong.* *adj.*

en·vi·ron·ment (en vī′rən mənt) 1 all the surrounding things, conditions, or influences that affect the growth and development of living things: *A child's character is greatly influenced by his home environment.* 2 surroundings: *an environment of poverty. Banff has a beautiful environment.* *n.*

en·voy (en′voi) 1 a messenger. 2 a diplomat next below an ambassador in rank. *n.*

en·vy (en′vē) 1 discontent or ill will at another's good fortune because one wishes it had been his; dislike for a person who has what one wants: *The boys were filled with envy when they saw her new bicycle.* 2 feel envy toward: *Some people envy the rich.* 3 feel envy because of: *He envied his friend's success.* 4 the object of such feeling; the person or thing envied: *She was the envy of the younger girls in the school.* 1, 4 *n., pl.* **en·vies;** 2, 3 *v.,* **en·vied, en·vy·ing.**

en·zyme (en′zīm or en′zim) in plants and animals, a substance produced by living cells that speeds up chemical changes without being changed itself: *Without enzymes to speed them up, body processes would be so slow that life as we know it would be impossible.* *n.*

e·on (ē′ən or ē′on) a very long time; many thousands of years: *Eons passed before life existed on earth.* *n.*

e·phem·er·al (i fem′er əl) lasting only a day or only a very short time. *adj.*

ep·ic (ep′ik) 1 a long and noble poem that tells of the adventures of one or more great heroes: *Homer's 'Odyssey' is an epic.* 2 grand in style: *Flying over the Atlantic for the first time was an epic deed.* 1 *n.,* 2 *adj.*

ep·i·dem·ic (ep′ə dem′ik) 1 a rapid spreading of a disease so that many people have it at the same time: *All the schools in the city were closed during the epidemic of measles.* 2 affecting many people at the same time; widespread: *An outbreak of flu became epidemic last winter. The wild rumors had reached epidemic proportions.* 1 *n.,* 2 *adj.*

ep·i·lep·sy (ep′ə lep′sē) a disorder of certain parts of the brain that causes sudden convulsions and total or partial loss of consciousness. *n.*

ep·i·lep·tic (ep′ə lep′tik) 1 of or having to do with epilepsy: *Most epileptic seizures can be controlled with drugs.* 2 suffering from epilepsy. *adj.*

ep·i·sode (ep′ə sōd′) a single happening or group of happenings in real life or in a story: *The year he spent in France was an important episode in the artist's life.* *n.*

e·pis·tle (i pis′əl) 1 a letter, especially an instructive or a formal one. 2 **Epistle,** in the Bible, any of the letters written by the Apostles to various churches and individuals: *A number of Epistles are included in the New Testament.* *n.*

ep·i·taph (ep′ə taf′) a short statement in memory of a dead person, usually put on a tombstone. *n.*

e·poch (ē′pok or ep′ək) 1 a period of time; era. 2 a period of time in which striking things happened: *The years leading to Confederation were an epoch in*

Canada's history. **3** the starting point of such a period: *The invention of the steam engine marked an epoch in the evolution of industry.* *n.*

e·qual (ē′kwəl) **1** the same (in amount, size, number, or value): *These two roasts are equal in weight.* **2** be the same as (in amount, size, etc.): *Four times five equals twenty.* *Symbol:* = **3** a person or thing similar in rank or excellence: *In spelling she had no equal.* **4** make or do something equal to; match: *He tried hard to equal the scoring record.* 1 *adj.*, 2, 4 *v.*, **e·qualled** or **e·qualed, e·qual·ling** or **e·qual·ing;** 3 *n.* **—e′qual·ly,** *adv.*

equal to, **a** the same as: *Ten dimes are equal to one dollar.* **b** strong enough for; capable of: *One horse is not equal to pulling a load of five tonnes.*

e·qual·i·ty (i kwol′ə tē) exact likeness in size, number, value, rank, etc.: *The rebels demanded equality for all citizens.* *n., pl.* **e·qual·i·ties.**

e·qual·ize (ē′kwəl īz′) make the same: *The last goal equalized the score.* *v.*, **e·qual·ized, e·qual·iz·ing.**

e·qual–sign (ē′kwəl sīn′) the sign =, used in equations. *n.* Also, **equals sign.**

e·qua·tion (i kwā′zhən) a mathematical statement that two quantities are equal. *Example:* 4 + 5 = 9. *n.*

e·qua·tor (i kwā′tər) an imaginary circle around the middle of the earth, halfway between the North Pole and the South Pole: *Canada is north of the equator.* See **latitude** for picture. *n.*

e·qua·to·ri·al (ek′wə tô′rē əl or ē′kwə tô′rē əl) **1** of or near the equator: *equatorial countries.* **2** like conditions at or near the equator: *The heat this week was almost equatorial.* *adj.*

e·qui·lat·er·al (ē′kwə lat′ər əl) having all sides equal: *In an equilateral triangle all three sides are the same length and all three angles are the same.* *adj.*

e·qui·lib·ri·um (ē′kwə lib′rē əm or ek′wə lib′rē əm) balance; a state of balance: *The acrobat in the circus maintained his equilibrium on a tightrope.* *Scales are in equilibrium when the weights on each side are equal.* *n.*

e·qui·nox (ē′kwə noks′ or ek′wə noks′) either of the times in the year when the sun crosses the equator and day and night are of equal length: *There is an equinox about March 21 and another about September 22.* *n.*

☛ **Equinox** comes from a Latin word *aequinoctium,* formed from *aequus,* meaning 'equal,' and *nox, noctis,* meaning 'night.'

e·quip (i kwip′) fit out; provide; furnish with all that is needed: *The school equips each player with a complete hockey outfit.* *Is the ship fully equipped?* *v.*, **e·quipped, e·quip·ping.**

e·quip·ment (i kwip′mənt) **1** a fitting out or providing. **2** what one is equipped with; an outfit: *A soldier must keep his equipment in order.* *n.*

e·quiv·a·lent (i kwiv′ə lənt) **1** the same in amount, number, value, meaning, etc.; equal: *Nodding one's head is equivalent to saying yes.* **2** something equivalent: *He accepted the equivalent of his wages in groceries.* 1 *adj.*, 2 *n.*

–er[1] a suffix meaning: **1** a person or thing that ____s: *An admirer is a person who admires somebody or something.* *A burner is something that burns fuel.* **2** a person born in or living in ____: *A Newfoundlander is a person born in or living in Newfoundland.* *A villager is a person who lives in a village.*

–er[2] a suffix used with certain adjectives and adverbs to mean 'more': *Softer means more soft.* *Slower means more slow.*

☛ Normally, **-er** ('more') and **-est** ('most') are used with all adjectives and adverbs of one syllable and with some of two syllables: *sweet—sweeter, soon—sooner, narrow—narrowest.* **More** and **most** are used with most adjectives and adverbs of two syllables and with all of more than two syllables: *most famous, more quickly, most beautiful.*

e·ra (ēr′ə) **1** an age in history; a historical period: *The decade from 1929 to 1939 is often called the Depression Era.* **2** a system of reckoning time from some important or significant happening, date, etc.: *We live in the 20th century of the Christian era.* *n.*

e·rad·i·cate (i rad′ə kāt′) **1** get entirely rid of; destroy completely: *Yellow fever has been eradicated in some countries.* **2** pull out by the roots: *to eradicate weeds from a garden.* *v.*, **e·rad·i·cat·ed, e·rad·i·cat·ing.**

e·rase (i rās′) **1** rub out; scrape out: *He erased the wrong answer and wrote in the right one.* **2** remove all trace of; blot out: *The blow on his head erased from his memory the details of the accident.* *v.*, **e·rased, e·ras·ing.**

e·ras·er (i rās′ər) something used for erasing marks made with pencil, ink, chalk, etc.: *Some pencils are equipped with erasers.* *n.*

ere (er) before: *He will come ere long.* *prep.*

☛ **Ere, air,** and **heir** are pronounced the same. **Ere** and **err** are sometimes pronounced the same.

e·rect (i rekt′) **1** straight up; not tipping; not bending: *A telegraph pole stands erect.* **2** set up; build: *That building was erected forty years ago.* 1 *adj.*, 2 *v.*

e·rec·tion (i rek′shən) **1** a setting up; raising: *The erection of the tent took only a few minutes.* **2** anything erected; a building or other structure. *n.*

er·mine (ėr′mən) **1** a weasel that is brown in summer but white in winter, except for a black tip on its tail. **2** its soft, white winter fur, used for women's coats, as trim for robes, etc.: *The official robes of English judges are trimmed with ermine as a symbol of purity and fairness.* *n., pl.* **er·mines** or **er·mine.**

e·rode (i rōd′) eat out; eat away; wear away: *Water erodes soil and rock.* *v.*, **e·rod·ed, e·rod·ing.**

e·ro·sion (i rō′zhən) an eating away; the process of being worn away gradually: *In geography we study the erosion of the earth by wind and water.* *n.*

err (ėr or er) **1** go wrong; make a mistake: *Everyone errs at some time or other.* **2** be wrong. **3** do wrong; sin: *'To err is human; to forgive divine.'* *v.*

☛ **Err** is sometimes pronounced the same as **air, ere,** and **heir.**

er·rand (er′ənd) **1** a trip to do something: *She has gone on an errand to the store.* **2** what one is sent to do: *She did ten errands in one trip.* *n.*

er·rat·ic (ə rat′ik) **1** uncertain; irregular: *an erratic clock.* **2** odd; unusual: *His erratic manner puzzled many people.* *adj.*

er·ro·ne·ous (ə rō′nē əs) mistaken; incorrect; wrong: *Years ago many people held the erroneous belief that the earth was flat.* *adj.*

er·ror (er′ər) a mistake; something done that is wrong;

something that is not the way it ought to be: *I failed my test because of errors in spelling.* *The accident was caused by an error in judgment.* *n.*
in error, a wrong or mistaken: *The teacher was in error.* **b** by mistake: *He got on the westbound bus in error.*

e·rupt (i rupt′) **1** burst forth: *Hot water erupted from the geyser.* **2** throw forth: *The volcano erupted lava and ashes.* **3** break out in a rash: *Her skin erupted when she had measles.* *v.*

e·rup·tion (i rup′shən) **1** the act of bursting forth. **2** a throwing forth of lava, etc. from a volcano or of hot water from a geyser. **3** a rash; red spots on the skin: *When a person has measles, his skin is in a state of eruption.* **4** an outbreak; outburst: *an eruption of violence.* *n.*

–es a form of the suffix *s* used after such letters as *s, z, sh,* and *ch: masses, buzzes, rushes, churches.*

es·ca·late (es′kə lāt′) increase or expand by stages: *Small battles can easily escalate into major wars.* *v.,* **es·ca·lat·ed, es·ca·lat·ing.**

es·ca·la·tor (es′kə lā′tər) a moving stairway: *The big department store had escalators going up and down from each floor.* *n.*

es·cape (es kāp′) **1** get free; get out and away: *The soldier escaped from the enemy's prison.* **2** keep free or safe from: *We all escaped the measles.* **3** the act of escaping. **4** a way of escaping: *There was no escape from the trap.* 1, 2 *v.,* **es·caped, es·cap·ing;** 3, 4 *n.*

es·cort (es′kôrt for 1–5, es kôrt′ for 6) **1** a person or group accompanying one or more other persons to protect them: *The royal party was provided with an escort of Mounties.* **2** one or more ships, aircraft, etc. serving as a guard: *During World War II Canada's destroyers served as escorts to many convoys.* **3** a person or group accompanying one or more other persons to do them honor or to show them courtesy. **4** an armed guard placed in charge of a prisoner to prevent his escape. **5** a man or boy who accompanies a woman or girl on a walk, to a dance, etc.: *a charming escort.* **6** accompany as an escort: *Warships escorted the royal yacht.* *Four policemen escorted the dangerous criminal to prison.* *The Prime Minister escorted the hostess in to dinner.* *John escorted Mary to the movies.* 1–5 *n.,* 6 *v.*

–ese a suffix meaning: **1** of, belonging to, or having to do with: *Japanese art is art of Japan.* **2** a person born in or living in: *A Portuguese is a person born in or living in Portugal.* **3** the language of: *Chinese is the language of China.*

Es·ki·mo (es′kə mō′) **1** a member of a race that lives on the arctic shores of North America and Asia. **2** the language of the Eskimos. *n., pl.* **Es·ki·mos** or **Es·ki·mo.**

☛ **Eskimo** came into English through French and Danish from a North American Indian word meaning 'eaters of raw flesh'. The Eskimos have always called themselves **Inuit**. See also note at **Inuit**.

Eskimo dog a strong dog used by the Eskimos to pull sleds.

e·soph·a·gus (ē sof′ə gəs or i sof′ə gəs) the passage for food from the mouth to the stomach; the gullet. See **alimentary canal** for picture. *n., pl.* **e·soph·a·gi** (-jī′ or -gē′).

es·pe·cial (es pesh′əl) special; chief; more than others: *Your birthday is an especial day for you.* *adj.*

hat, āge, fär; let, ēqual, tėrm; it, īce
hot, ōpen, ôrder; oil, out; cup, pu̇t, rüle
əbove, takən, pencəl, lemən, circəs
ch, child; ng, long; sh, ship
th, thin; ᴛʜ, then; zh, measure

es·pe·cial·ly (es pesh′əl ē) particularly; principally; chiefly: *This paint is especially designed for use outdoors.* *adv.*

es·pi·o·nage (es′pē ə nij or es′pē ə näzh′) spying; the use of spies: *Nations practise espionage to find out other countries' secrets.* *n.*

es·say (es′ā for 1, e sā′ for 2, es′ā or e sā′ for 3) **1** a short written work with a particular subject or theme, usually showing the author's personal viewpoint: *An essay may contain two or three pages or be almost as long as a book.* **2** try; attempt: *He essayed a very difficult jump.* **3** a try or attempt. 1, 3 *n.,* 2 *v.*

es·sence (es′əns) **1** that which makes a thing what it is; the necessary part or parts: *Kindness of heart is the essence of politeness.* **2** a concentrated substance that has the flavor, fragrance, or effect of the plant or fruit from which it is taken: *essence of peppermint.* *n.*

es·sen·tial (ə sen′shəl) **1** needed to make a thing what it is; basic; necessary; very important: *Good food and enough rest are essential to good health.* **2** an absolutely necessary element or quality; a basic part: *Learn the essentials first; then learn the details.* 1 *adj.,* 2 *n.* **—es·sen′tial·ly,** *adv.*

–est a suffix used with some adjectives and adverbs to mean 'most': *Warmest means the most warm.* *Slowest means the most slow.*

☛ See note at **-er**[2].

es·tab·lish (es tab′lish) **1** set up and keep going for some time: *to establish a government or a business.* *The English established colonies in America.* **2** settle in a position; set up in business: *A new doctor has established himself on this street.* **3** cause to be accepted and used for a long time: *to establish a custom.* **4** show beyond dispute; prove: *to establish a fact.* *v.*

es·tab·lish·ment (es tab′lish mənt) **1** setting up; establishing: *The establishment of the business took several years.* **2** being established. **3** something established: *A household, a large store, a church, or an army may be called an establishment.* *n.*

es·tate (es tāt′) **1** that which a person owns: *When the rich man died, he left an estate of two million dollars.* *Land and buildings are called real estate.* **2** a large piece of land belonging to a person: *He has a beautiful estate 40* km *from Toronto, with a country house and a swimming pool on it.* **3** a condition or stage in life: *He will receive his inheritance when he reaches man's estate.* *n.*

es·teem (es tēm′) **1** think highly of: *We esteem people of good character.* **2** a very favorable opinion; respect; high regard: *Courage is held in esteem.* **3** think; consider: *I esteem it my duty to fight.* 1, 3 *v.,* 2 *n.*

es·ti·mate (es′tə mit for 1 and 3, es′tə māt′ for 2 and 4) **1** a judgment or opinion as to how much, how many, how good, etc.: *His estimate of the length of the fish was 40 centimetres.* **2** form a judgment or an opinion: *She* *estimated it would take four hours to weed the garden.* **3** a statement of what certain work will cost, made by one willing to do the work: *The painter's estimate for painting the house was $600.* **4** fix the worth, size, amount, etc., especially in a rough way; calculate approximately. 1, 3 *n.*, 2, 4 *v.*, **es·ti·mat·ed, es·ti·mat·ing.**

es·ti·ma·tion (es′tə mā′shən) **1** opinion; judgment: *In my estimation, your plan will not work.* **2** esteem; respect; regard: *hold in high estimation.* **3** the act or process of estimating: *His job included the estimation of the cost of painting houses.* *n.*

es·tu·ar·y (es′chü er′ē) **1** the wide mouth of a river flowing into the sea, where its current meets the tide and is influenced by it: *The estuary of the St. Lawrence River is over 320 kilometres long.* **2** an inlet of the sea. *n., pl.* **es·tu·ar·ies.**

etc. et cetera.

☛ **Etc.** is usually read 'and so forth.' For example, the definition of *equality* reads 'exact likeness in size, number, value, rank, etc.' **Etc.** in such definitions shows that the meaning applies to many items similar to the ones mentioned.

et cet·er·a (et set′ər ə) and so forth; and others; and the rest; and so on; and the like.

☛ **Et cetera** is a Latin phrase meaning 'and others.' Since the *et* itself means 'and,' there is no need to put *and* before it. It is wrong to write *and et cetera* or *and etc.*

etch (ech) **1** engrave by using acid to eat a drawing or design into a metal plate, glass, etc. **2** make drawings or designs by this method. *v.*

etch·ing (ech′ing) **1** a picture or design printed from an etched plate. **2** the process of engraving a drawing or design on a metal plate, glass, etc. by means of acid. *n.*

e·ter·nal (i tėr′nəl) **1** without beginning or ending; lasting throughout all time: *eternal life.* **2** always and forever the same. **3** seeming to go on forever: *The baby's eternal crying worried the mother.* *adj.*

e·ter·ni·ty (i tėr′nə tē) **1** all time; all the past and all the future. **2** a period of time that seems endless: *The injured man waited an eternity for the ambulance to arrive.* **3** the endless period after death. *n., pl.* **e·ter·ni·ties.**

e·ther (ē′thər) **1** a colorless, strong-smelling liquid that evaporates rapidly and produces unconsciousness when it is breathed in. **2** the regions high above us; clear sky. *n.*

e·the·re·al (i thēr′ē əl) **1** light; airy; delicate. **2** not of the earth; heavenly. *adj.*

eth·nic (eth′nik) **1** of or having to do with various groups of people and their characteristics, customs, and languages. **2** *Cdn., Informal.* an immigrant who is not a native speaker of English or French; a person of foreign birth or descent: *There are ethnics in Toronto from many parts of Europe.* **3** *Cdn.* of or having to do with such persons: *ethnic newspapers, ethnic dances.* 1, 3 *adj.*, 2 *n.*

☛ The use of **ethnic** in definitions 2 and 3 has become common in Canada though many people consider it unacceptable and others find it insulting and inaccurate.

et·i·quette (et′ə ket′) the customary rules for behavior in society: *Etiquette requires a man to rise when a woman enters the room.* *n.*

-ette a suffix meaning: **1** small: *A kitchenette is a small kitchen.* **2** substitute; imitation: *Leatherette is imitation leather.*

et·y·mol·o·gy (et′ə mol′ə jē) **1** an explanation of where a word comes from and a description of the changes it has gone through in its history: *An etymology is given in this dictionary for the word* Eskimo. **2** the study of the origins of words: *She is interested in etymology.* *n., pl.* **et·y·mol·o·gies.**

eu·ca·lyp·tus (yü′kə lip′təs) a very tall tree that is common in Australia: *The eucalyptus is valued for its timber and for the oil from its leaves, used as medicine.* *n., pl.* **eu·ca·lyp·tus·es, eu·ca·lyp·ti** (-tī or -tē).

eu·chre (yü′kər) **1** a simple card game played by two, three, or four persons using the thirty-two highest cards in the deck. **2** a social gathering during which people play euchre. *n.*

Eu·ro·pe·an (yür′ə pē′ən) **1** of or having to do with Europe or its people. **2** a person who was born in or lives in Europe: *Frenchmen, Germans, and Spaniards are Europeans.* 1 *adj.*, 2 *n.*

e·vac·u·ate (i vak′yü āt′) **1** leave empty; withdraw from: *The soldiers will evacuate the town later today.* **2** make empty: *to evacuate the bowels..* *v.*, **e·vac·u·at·ed, e·vac·u·at·ing.**

e·vade (i vād′) get away from by trickery; avoid by cleverness: *Criminals evade the law. When Father asked who broke the window, I tried to evade the question by changing the subject.* *v.*, **e·vad·ed, e·vad·ing.**

e·val·u·ate (i val′yü āt′) **1** judge the worth, quality, or importance of: *Our compositions are being evaluated by the new teacher.* **2** find or decide the value of: *This old clock has been evaluated by an expert. It was evaluated at $900.* *v.*, **e·val·u·at·ed, e·val·u·at·ing.**

e·val·u·a·tion (i val′yu a′shən) **1** evaluating: *The evaluation of all this antique furniture will take some time.* **2** an estimate of worth or quality: *The coach made too high an evaluation of the centre's ability to score.* *n.*

e·vap·o·rate (i vap′ə rāt′) **1** turn into vapor: *Boiling water evaporates rapidly.* **2** remove moisture, especially water, from: *Heat is used to evaporate milk.* **3** vanish; disappear; fade away: *His good resolutions evaporated soon after New Year's Day.* *v.*, **e·vap·o·rat·ed, e·vap·o·rat·ing.**

e·vap·o·ra·tion (i vap′ə rā′shən) **1** a changing of a liquid or solid into vapor. **2** being changed into vapor: *Wet clothes on a line become dry by evaporaton of the water in them.* **3** the removal of water or other liquid. *n.*

e·va·sive (i vā′siv or i vā′ziv) tending or trying to evade. *adj.*

eve (ēv) **1** the evening or day before some holiday or special day: *Christmas Eve.* **2** the time just before: *on the eve of battle.* **3** evening. *n.*

Eve (ēv) in the Bible, the first woman. *n.*

e·ven (ē′vən) **1** level; flat; smooth: *The country is even, with no high hills.* **2** at the same level: *The snow is even with the window.* **3** keeping about the same; regular; uniform: *The car goes with an even motion. This boy has an even temper.* **4** equal; no more or less

hat, āge, fär; let, ēqual, tėrm; it, īce
hot, ōpen, ôrder; oil, out; cup, pu̇t, rüle
əbove, takən, pencəl, lemən, circəs
ch, child; ng, long; sh, ship
th, thin; ᴛʜ, then; zh, measure

than: *They divided the money in even shares.* **5** make equal; tie: *even the score.* **6** make level or of similar length: *She evened the edges by trimming them.* **7** See **even number. 8** without a remainder: *Twelve apples make an even dozen.* **9** just: *He went away even as you came.* **10** indeed: *He is ready, even eager, to fight.* **11** though one would not expect it; as one would not expect: *Even young children can understand it. Even the last man arrived on time. I will come even if I am tired.* **12** still; yet: *You can read even better if you try.* 1–4, 8 *adj.*, 5, 6 *v.*, 9–12 *adv.*, 7 *n.* **—e′ven·ly,** *adv.*

eve·ning (ēv′ning) **1** the last part of day and early part of night; the time between day and night. **2** the time between sunset and bedtime: *We spent the evening watching television. n.*

e·ven·ly (ē′vən lē) **1** smoothly; at the same level, speed, etc.: *Spread the frosting evenly on the cake.* **2** equally: *Divide the money evenly. adv.*

even number a number that has no remainder when divided by 2: *The even numbers are 4, 6, 8, etc.*

e·vent (i vent′) **1** a happening: *current events.* **2** an important happening: *The discovery of oil in Alberta was certainly an event.* **3** the result or outcome: *We made careful plans and awaited the event.* **4** a contest in a sports program: *The broad jump was the last event. n.*

at all events or **in any event,** in any case; whatever happens.

in the event of, in the case of: *In the event of rain the party will be held indoors.*

in the event that, if it should happen that; supposing: *In the event that the roads are icy, we will not come.*

e·vent·ful (i vent′fəl) **1** full of events; having many unusual happenings: *Our day at the fall fair was highly eventful.* **2** having important results; important: *July 1, 1867, Dominion Day, was an eventful day for Canadians. adj.*

e·ven·tide (ē′vən tīd′) evening. *n.*

e·ven·tu·al (i ven′chü əl) coming in the end: *His eventual success after several failures surprised them. adj.* **—e·ven′tu·al·ly,** *adv.*

ev·er (ev′ər) **1** at any time: *Is he ever at home?* **2** at all times; always: *A mother is ever ready to help her children.* **3** by any chance; at all: *What did you ever do to make him so angry? adv.*

ever so, *Informal.* very: *The ocean is ever so deep.*

ev·er·green (ev′ər grēn′) **1** remaining green all year: *evergreen leaves.* **2** having leaves or needles all year: *evergreen trees.* **3** a tree, shrub, or plant that keeps its leaves or needles all year: *Pine, spruce, cedar, tamarack, and ivy are evergreens.* **4 evergreens,** *pl.* evergreen twigs or branches used for decoration. 1, 2 *adj.*, 3, 4 *n.*

ev·er·last·ing (ev′ər las′ting) **1** lasting forever; never stopping. **2** lasting a long time. **3** lasting too long; tiresome: *his everlasting complaints. adj.*

ev·er·more (ev′ər môr′) always; forever. *adv., n.*

eve·ry (ev′rē) **1** each one of the entire number of: *Read every word on the page. Every boy must have his own book.* **2** all possible; complete: *I have every reason to trust her. adj.*

every now and then, from time to time: *Every now and then, we have a frost that ruins the crop.*

every other, every second: *If you write on every other line, you can get only half as much on a page.*

every which way, *Informal.* in all directions; helter-skelter: *He tripped and his books and papers flew every which way.*

eve·ry·bod·y (ev′re bud′ē or ev′rē bod′ē) every person: *Everybody likes our minister. pron.*

eve·ry·day (ev′rē dā′) **1** of every day; daily: *Accidents are everyday occurrences.* **2** for every ordinary day; not for Sundays or holidays: *A person wears everyday clothes to work.* **3** usual; ordinary; not exciting: *She had only an everyday story to tell. adj.*

eve·ry·one or **every one** (ev′rē wun′ or ev′rē wən) each one; everybody: *Everyone took his books home. pron.*

eve·ry·thing (ev′rē thing′) every thing; all things: *She does everything she can to help her mother. pron.*

eve·ry·where (ev′rē wer′ or ev′rē hwer′) in every place; in all places or lands: *A smile is understood everywhere. adv.*

e·vict (i vict′) **1** expel a tenant from a building or from land by lawful means: *When he failed to pay his rent, he was evicted from the house.* **2** expel or put out by force. *v.*

ev·i·dence (ev′ə dəns) **1** facts; proof; anything that shows or makes clear: *The jam on his face was evidence that he had been in the kitchen. His first day's work gave evidence of his speed.* **2** make easy to see or understand; show clearly: *His smiles evidenced his pleasure.* 1 *n.*, 2 *v.*, **ev·i·denced, ev·i·denc·ing.**

in evidence, easily seen or noticed: *A crying baby is much in evidence.*

ev·i·dent (ev′ə dənt) easy to see or understand; clear; plain: *It is evident that children grow up. adj.*

e·vil (ē′vəl) **1** bad; wrong; that does harm: *an evil deed.* **2** something bad; an evil quality or act. **3** something causing harm; something that takes away happiness and prosperity: *War is a great evil.* 1 *adj.*, 2, 3 *n.*

e·voke (i vōk′) call forth; bring out: *A good joke evokes a laugh. v.*, **e·voked, e·vok·ing.**

ev·o·lu·tion (ev′ə lü′shən or ē′və lü′shən) **1** a gradual development: *the evolution of the flower from the bud, the evolution of one kind of animal or plant from a simpler kind.* **2** the theory that all living things developed from a few simple forms of life, or from a single form. *n.*

e·volve (i volv′) unfold; develop gradually: *The boys evolved a plan for earning money during their summer vacation. v.*, **e·volved, e·volv·ing.**

ewe (yü) a female sheep. *n.*

☛ **Ewe** and **yew** are pronounced the same. **Ewe** and **you** are sometimes pronounced the same.

ex– a prefix meaning: **1** out of; from; out: *Express means press out.* **2** completely; thoroughly: *Exterminate means terminate (finish or destroy) thoroughly.* **3** former; formerly: *An ex-member is a former member.*

ex·act (eg zakt′) **1** not having or making mistakes;

correct; accurate: *an exact measurement, the exact amount, an exact thinker.* 2 demand and get: *If he does the work, he can exact payment for it.* 1 *adj.*, 2 *v.*

ex·act·ing (eg zak′ting) 1 requiring much; hard to please: *an exacting boss.* 2 requiring effort, care, or attention: *Flying an airplane is exacting work.* *adj.*

ex·act·ly (eg zakt′lē) 1 without error; precisely. 2 just so; quite right: *'Exactly,' exclaimed the teacher when the girl gave the right answer.* *adv.*

ex·ag·ger·ate (eg zaj′ər āt′) make too large; say or think something is greater than it is; go beyond the truth: *The little boy exaggerated when he said there were a million cats in the back yard.* *v.*, **ex·ag·ger·at·ed, ex·ag·ger·at·ing.**

ex·ag·ger·a·tion (eg zaj′ər ā′shən) 1 a statement that goes beyond the truth: *It is an exaggeration to say you would rather die than touch a snake.* 2 going beyond the truth: *His constant exaggeration made people distrust him.* *n.*

ex·alt (eg zolt′ or eg zôlt′) 1 place or make high in rank, honor, power, character, or quality: *We exalt a man when we elect him to high office.* 2 praise; glorify; honor: *God shall be exalted.* *v.*

ex·am (eg zam′) *Informal.* examination. *n.*

ex·am·i·na·tion (eg zam′ə nā′shən) 1 a careful check; inspection: *The doctor made a careful examination of my eyes.* 2 a set of questions to test knowledge or skill; a formal test: *The teacher gave us an examination in arithmetic.* *n.*

ex·am·ine (eg zam′ən) 1 look at closely and carefully: *The doctor examined the wound.* 2 test; test the knowledge or ability of; ask questions. *v.*, **ex·am·ined, ex·am·in·ing.**

ex·am·ple (eg zam′pəl) 1 a sample; one thing taken to show what the others are like: *Vancouver is an example of a busy city.* 2 a model; pattern of something to be imitated or avoided: *A father should try to be a good example to his sons. I hope that his failure through lack of effort will be an example to you all.* 3 an instance or sample that serves to illustrate a way of doing or making something: *The problems in the arithmetic textbook were accompanied by examples.* 4 an instance or case, especially of punishment intended as a warning to others: *As an example to others, the captain had the insolent sailor whipped.* *n.*

for example, as an illustration or illustrations; for instance: *Children play many games; baseball, for example.*

make an example of, treat sternly, or punish, as a sample of the result of misbehavior: *The teacher made an example of John by making him write 'I won't talk in class' one hundred times.*

set an example, give, show, or be a model of behavior for others: *The cubmaster set a good example for his pack.*

ex·as·per·ate (eg zas′pər āt′) irritate very much; annoy greatly; make angry: *The little boy's noise exasperated his father.* *v.*, **ex·as·per·at·ed, ex·as·per·at·ing.**

ex·as·per·a·tion (eg zas′pər ā′shən) extreme annoyance, anger, or irritation: *The girl wept from exasperation.* *n.*

ex·ca·vate (eks′kə vāt′) 1 make a hole by removing dirt, sand, rock, etc.: *The construction company will begin to excavate tomorrow.* 2 make by digging; dig: *The workmen excavated a tunnel through solid rock.* 3 dig out; scoop out: *Big machines excavated the dirt and loaded it into trucks.* 4 uncover by digging: *They excavated the ancient buried city.* *v.*, **ex·ca·vat·ed, ex·ca·vat·ing.**

ex·ca·va·tion (eks′kə vā′shən) 1 a digging out; a digging. 2 a hole made by digging. *n.*

ex·ceed (ek sēd′) go beyond; be more or greater than: *The sum of 5 and 7 exceeds 10. The motorist was fined for exceeding the speed limit.* *v.*

ex·ceed·ing (ek sēd′ing) very great; unusual: *She is a girl of exceeding beauty.* *adj.* —**ex·ceed′ing·ly,** *adv.*

ex·cel (ek sel′) 1 be better than; do better than: *He excelled his classmates in spelling.* 2 be better than others; do better than others: *Solomon excelled in wisdom.* *v.*, **ex·celled, ex·cel·ling.**

ex·cel·lence (ek′sə ləns) a very high quality; the state of being better than others: *This province boasts of the excellence of its climate.* *n.*

Ex·cel·len·cy (ek′sə lən sē) a title of honor used in speaking to or of the Governor General, an ambassador, a bishop, etc. *n.*, *pl.* **Ex·cel·len·cies.**

ex·cel·lent (ek′sə lənt) exceptionally good; better than others: *Excellent work deserves high praise.* *adj.*

ex·cept (ek sept′) 1 leaving out; other than: *He works every day except Sunday.* 2 leave out: *The teacher excepted him from the examination list.* 1 *prep.*, 2 *v.*

☛ Because the pronunciation of **except** and **accept** are similar, they are often confused in writing. **Accept** is always a verb, with the basic meaning of 'take to oneself': *He accepted the gift.* **Except** is usually a preposition meaning 'but' or 'besides': *Everyone except John went home.* However, **except** is sometimes used as a verb with the meaning 'exclude': *It is a very good composition if we except the last paragraph.*

ex·cept·ing (ek sep′ting) leaving out; except: *All the boys were ready, excepting Bob.* *prep.*

ex·cep·tion (ek sep′shən) 1 a leaving out: *She likes all her studies with the exception of arithmetic.* 2 something left out: *She praised them all, with two exceptions.* 3 anything that is different from the rule: *He comes on time every day; today is an exception.* 4 an objection. *n.*

take exception, a object: *take exception to the plan.* **b** be offended: *She took exception to the remark that her sister was stupid.*

ex·cep·tion·al (ek sep′shən əl) unusual; out of the ordinary: *This warm weather is exceptional for January. She is an exceptional student.* *adj.* —**ex·cep′tion·al·ly,** *adv.*

ex·cess (ek ses′, also ek′ses for 3) 1 the part that is too much: *Pour off the excess.* 2 the amount by which one thing is greater than another: *The excess of 7 over 5 is 2.* 3 extra; more than the desirable amount: *She went on a diet to get rid of her excess weight.* 1, 2 *n.*, 3 *adj.*

in excess of, more than: *The contributions were in excess of $5000.*

to excess, too much: *He eats candy to excess.*

ex·ces·sive (ek ses′iv) too much; too great; extreme: *An hour is an excessive amount of time for dressing.* *adj.* —**ex·ces′sive·ly,** *adv.*

hat, āge, fär; let, ēqual, tėrm; it, īce
hot, ōpen, ôrder; oil, out; cup, pu̇t, rüle
əbove, takən, pencəl, lemən, circəs
ch, child; ng, long; sh, ship
th, thin; ꟻH, then; zh, measure

ex·change (eks chānj′) **1** give for something else: *She would not exchange her house for a palace.* **2** give in trade for something regarded as of equal value: *I will exchange ten dimes for a dollar.* **3** replace a purchase or have it replaced: *We cannot exchange swim suits.* **4** what is traded. **5** a place where things are traded: *Stocks are bought, sold, and traded in a stock exchange.* **6** a central telephone office. 1–3 *v.*, **ex·changed, ex·chang·ing;** 4–6 *n.*

ex·cit·a·ble (ek sīt′ə bəl) easily stirred up or aroused: *an excitable dog. adj.*

ex·cite (ek sīt′) **1** stir up the feelings of: *The news of war excited everybody.* **2** arouse: *His new jacket excited envy among the other boys.* **3** stir to action: *If you do not excite the dog, he will stay quiet. v.*, **ex·cit·ed, ex·cit·ing.**

ex·cit·ed (ek sīt′id) stirred up; aroused: *The crowd became excited during the close race. adj.* **—ex·cit′ed·ly,** *adv.*

ex·cite·ment (ek sīt′mənt) **1** an excited state or condition: *The baby's first step caused great excitement in the family.* **2** something that excites: *The hockey game provided first rate excitement.* **3** noisy activity; commotion; ado: *What's all the excitement? n.*

ex·claim (eks klām′) cry out; speak suddenly in surprise, strong feeling, etc.: *'Here you are at last!' exclaimed his mother. v.*

ex·cla·ma·tion (eks′klə mā′shən) something said suddenly as the result of surprise or strong feeling. *Examples: Oh! Hurray! Well! Help! Look! Listen! n.*

exclamation mark or **point** a mark (!) after a word or sentence to show that it was an exclamation. *Example: Hurray! We are going to the circus.*

ex·clam·a·to·ry (eks klam′ə tô′rē) using, containing, or expressing exclamation: *an exclamatory sentence. adj.*

ex·clude (eks klüd′) **1** shut out; keep out: *Blinds exclude light. The government excludes immigrants who have certain diseases.* **2** drive out and keep out: *Perfect faith excludes doubt. v.*, **ex·clud·ed, ex·clud·ing.**

ex·clud·ing (eks klü′ding) except for; with the exception of; not counting: *All of the neighbors, excluding those away on holidays, will be at the picnic. prep.*

ex·clu·sion (eks klü′zhən) shutting out or being shut out: *Her exclusion from the club hurt her feelings. n.*

ex·clu·sive (eks klü′siv) **1** each shutting out the other: *'Baby' and 'adult' are exclusive terms since a person cannot be both.* **2** shutting out all or most: *This school is exclusive; only very bright children can go to it.* **3** single; sole; not divided or shared with others: *An inventor has an exclusive right for a certain number of years to make what he has invented.* **4** very particular about choosing friends, members, patrons, etc.: *It is hard to get admitted to an exclusive club. adj.*
exclusive of, leaving out; not counting: *There are 26 days in that month, exclusive of Sundays.*

ex·clu·sive·ly (eks klü′siv lē) with the exclusion of all others: *That selfish girl looks out for herself exclusively. adv.*

ex·cur·sion (eks kėr′zhən) **1** a trip taken for interest or pleasure, often by a number of people together: *Our club went on an excursion to the mountains.* **2** a short journey. *n.*

ex·cus·a·ble (eks kyü′zə bəl) that can or ought to be excused: *Her anger was excusable since they had been so rude. adj.*

ex·cuse (eks kyüz′ for 1–4, eks kyüs′ for 5) **1** offer an apology for; try to remove the blame of: *She excused her own faults by blaming others.* **2** be a reason or explanation for: *Sickness excuses absence from school.* **3** pardon; forgive: *Excuse me; I have to go now. He excused her carelessness in upsetting his paint.* **4** free from duty; let off: *You are excused from washing the dishes today.* **5** a reason, real or pretended, that is given; an explanation: *He had many excuses for coming late.* 1–4 *v.*, **ex·cused, ex·cus·ing;** 5 *n.*
excuse oneself, a ask to be pardoned: *He excused himself for bumping into me by saying that he was in a hurry.* **b** ask permission to leave: *I excused myself from the table.*

ex·e·cute (ek′sə kyüt′) **1** carry out; do: *The nurse executed the doctor's orders.* **2** put into effect; enforce: *The will was executed by the lawyer.* **3** put to death according to law: *The murderer was executed.* **4** make according to a plan or design: *An artist executes a painting. v.*, **ex·e·cut·ed, ex·e·cut·ing.**

ex·e·cu·tion (ek′sə kyü′shən) **1** carrying out; doing: *the execution of duties.* **2** putting into effect: *the execution of a law.* **3** a way of carrying out or doing; skill: *The pianist's execution of his program was excellent.* **4** putting to death according to law: *The execution took place at dawn.* **5** making according to a plan or design. *n.*

ex·e·cu·tion·er (ek′sə kyü′shən ər) a person who puts criminals to death according to law. *n.*

ex·ec·u·tive (eg zek′yə tiv) **1** having to do with management: *An executive job has to do with the managing of a business, a company, etc.* **2** a manager; person who carries out what he or another has decided should be done: *The president of a business is an executive.* **3** a person, group, or branch of government that has the duty and power of putting laws into effect. 1 *adj.*, 2, 3 *n.*

Executive Council the cabinet of a provincial government, consisting of the Premier and his ministers.

ex·em·pli·fy (eg zem′plə fī′) show by example; be an example of: *Knights exemplified courage and courtesy. v.*, **ex·em·pli·fied, ex·em·pli·fy·ing.**

ex·empt (eg zempt′) **1** make free from: *She was exempted from the test because she had been away from school.* **2** freed from: *School property is exempt from all taxes.* 1 *v.*, 2 *adj.*

ex·er·cise (ek′sər sīz′) **1** activity to train the body or keep it healthy: *Running and playing volleyball are forms of exercise.* **2** take part or cause to take part in such activity: *A person should exercise daily. The man on the sidewalk was exercising his dog.* **3** something that gives practice or training: *Open your math books and do the exercises on page 50.* **4** active use or practice: *Keeping one's temper requires the exercise of* *self-control.* 5 put into use; use actively: *Please exercise care in crossing the road.* 6 a formal activity; performance: *The opening exercises in our Sunday school are a song and a prayer.* 1, 3, 4, 6 *n.*, 2, 5 *v.*, **ex·er·cised, ex·er·cis·ing.**

ex·ert (eg zėrt′) use; put into use; use fully: *A clever fighter exerts both strength and skill. A ruler exerts authority. v.*
exert oneself, make an effort; try hard; strive: *We had to exert ourselves to get there on time.*

ex·er·tion (eg zėr′shən) 1 effort: *The exertions of the firemen kept the fire from spreading.* 2 use; active use; a putting into action: *Unwise exertion of authority may cause rebellion. n.*

ex·hale (eks hāl′) 1 breathe out: *We exhale air from our lungs.* 2 give off as vapor. *v.*, **ex·haled, ex·hal·ing.**

ex·haust (eg zost′ or eg zôst′) 1 empty completely: *to exhaust a well.* 2 use up: *to exhaust the supply of water, to exhaust one's strength or money.* 3 tire out: *The climb up the hill exhausted us.* 4 the escape of used steam, gasoline, etc. from a machine. 5 a means or way for used steam, gasoline, etc. to escape from an engine. 6 the used steam, gasoline, etc. that escapes: *The exhaust from an automobile engine is poisonous.* 1–3 *v.*, 4–6 *n.*

ex·haust·ed (eg zos′tid or eg zôs′tid) 1 used up: *During the famine, food supplies soon became exhausted.* 2 worn out; very tired. *adj.*

ex·haus·tion (eg zos′chən or eg zôs′chən) 1 emptying; using up. 2 extreme fatigue: *At the end of the race, some runners dropped from exhaustion. n.*

ex·hib·it (eg zib′it) 1 show: *The child exhibited a bad temper at an early age. He exhibits interest whenever you talk about dogs.* 2 show publicly: *You should exhibit your roses in the flower show.* 3 something shown to the public: *Their exhibit of tomatoes won the prize at the fall fair.* 1, 2 *v.*, 3 *n.*

ex·hi·bi·tion (ek′sə bish′ən) 1 the act of showing: *He said he had never seen such an exhibition of bad manners.* 2 a public show: *The art school held an exhibition of paintings.* 3 a thing or things shown publicly; exhibit. 4 a public showing of farm animals, produce, manufactured goods, etc., accompanied by amusements such as side shows, rides, games, and other forms of entertainment; a big fair: *the Canadian National Exhibition. n.*

ex·hil·a·rate (eg zil′ə rāt′) 1 refresh; invigorate; enliven: *The girls were exhilarated by their early-morning swim.* 2 make cheerful or merry; gladden: *The children were exhilarated by the fun and games at the birthday party. v.*, **ex·hil·a·rat·ed, ex·hil·a·rat·ing.**

ex·hort (eg zôrt′) urge strongly; advise earnestly: *The preacher exhorted his hearers to live a better life. v.*

ex·ile (eg′zīl or ek′sīl) 1 make a person go from home or country, often by law as a punishment; banish: *The prince was exiled from his country for life.* 2 a person who is banished from his native land: *He has been an exile for ten years.* 3 such banishment: *Exile on a lonely island was his fate.* 1 *v.*, **ex·iled, ex·il·ing;** 2, 3 *n.*

ex·ist (eg zist′) 1 be: *The world has existed a long time.* 2 be real: *Do fairies exist or not?* 3 live: *A man cannot exist without air.* 4 occur; be recorded; be known as a matter of record: *Cases exist of persons who cannot smell anything. v.*

ex·ist·ence (eg zis′təns) 1 being: *to come into existence.* 2 being real; reality: *Not many people believe in the existence of ghosts.* 3 way of life; life: *Many bush pilots lead a dangerous existence. n.*

ex·it (eg′zit or ek′sit) 1 a way out: *The theatre had six exits.* 2 the departure of a player from the stage: *The actor made a graceful exit.* 3 the act of going out: *When the cat came in, the mice made a hasty exit. n.*

ex·o·dus (ek′sə dəs) going out; a departure, especially of a large number of people: *Every summer there is an exodus from the city. n.*

ex·or·bi·tant (eg zôr′bə tənt) very excessive; much too high: *Four dollars is an exorbitant price to pay for a dozen eggs. adj.*

ex·ot·ic (eg zot′ik) foreign; strange: *When we travelled in Asia, we ate many exotic foods. adj.*

ex·pand (eks pand′) 1 increase in size; enlarge; swell: *The balloon expanded as it was filled with air. Heat expanded the metal.* 2 spread out; open out; unfold; extend: *As the plant grew, its leaves and flowers gradually expanded. A bird expands its wings before flying.* 3 express in fuller form or greater detail: *The writer expanded one sentence into a paragraph. v.*

ex·panse (eks pans′) an open or unbroken stretch; a widespread area or surface: *The Pacific Ocean is a vast expanse of water. n.*

ex·pan·sion (eks pan′shən) 1 spreading out so as to occupy more space: *Heat caused the expansion of the gas in the balloon.* 2 growing larger; swelling: *The expanding gas caused the expansion of the balloon.* 3 being expanded; increase in size, volume, capacity, etc.: *The expansion of the factory doubled the amount of goods it produced. n.*

ex·pect (eks pekt′) 1 look forward to; think likely to come or happen: *We expect hot days in summer.* 2 look forward to with reason or confidence; desire and feel sure of getting: *They expect to be married in June.* 3 count on as necessary or right: *A soldier is expected to be properly dressed.* 4 *Informal.* think; suppose; guess: *I expect we'll have to go to bed early on Christmas Eve. v.*

ex·pect·ant (eks pek′tənt) expecting; that anticipates pleasure: *She opened her Christmas present with an expectant smile. adj.* —**ex·pect′ant·ly,** *adv.*
expectant mother, a woman who is expecting a baby.

ex·pec·ta·tion (eks′pek tā′shən) 1 expecting something to come or happen; anticipation. 2 something expected. 3 a good reason for expecting something; a prospect: *He has expectations of inheriting money from a rich uncle. n.*

ex·pec·to·rate (eks pek′tə rāt′) cough up and spit out phlegm, etc.; spit. *v.*, **ex·pec·to·rat·ed, ex·pec·to·rat·ing.**

ex·pe·di·ent (eks pē′dē ənt) 1 useful; helping to bring about some result: *She decided it would be expedient to take an umbrella.* 2 a way of getting something: *If you wish a fire and have no matches, you can try such expedients as using flint, steel, and tinder.* 1 *adj.*, 2 *n.*

ex·pe·di·tion (eks′pə dish′ən) 1 a journey for a special purpose, such as war, discovery, or collecting new plants. 2 the people, ships, etc. that make such a

hat, āge, fär; let, ēqual, tėrm; it, īce
hot, ōpen, ôrder; oil, out; cup, pu̇t, rüle
əbove, takən, pencəl, lemən, circəs
ch, child; ng, long; sh, ship
th, thin; ᴛʜ, then; zh, measure

journey: *a well-equipped expedition.* 3 promptness; speed: *He completed his work with expedition. n.*

ex·pel (eks pel′) 1 drive out with much force: *A bullet is expelled from the barrel of a gun.* 2 put out: *A troublesome pupil may be expelled from school. v.,* **ex·pelled, ex·pel·ling.**

ex·pend (eks pend′) spend; use up. *v.*

ex·pen·di·ture (eks pen′də chür′ or eks pen′də chər) 1 a spending; using up: *A large piece of work requires the expenditure of much money, time, and effort.* 2 the amount of money, time, energy, etc. spent or used up: *Her expenditures for Christmas presents totalled fifty dollars. n.*

ex·pense (eks pens′) 1 the cost; the charge: *The expense of the trip was very slight. He travelled at his uncle's expense. They had many a laugh at his expense.* 2 a cause of spending: *Running an automobile is an expense.* 3 a paying out of money; outlay: *Her time at university put her father to considerable expense. n.*

ex·pen·sive (eks pen′siv) costly; high-priced: *He had a very expensive knife that cost $10. adj.*

ex·pe·ri·ence (eks pēr′ē əns) 1 what happens to a person: *We had several pleasant experiences on our trip. People learn by experience.* 2 practice; knowledge gained by doing or seeing things: *Have you had any experience in this kind of work?* 3 feel; have happen to one: *to experience very great pain.* 1, 2 *n.*, 3 *v.,* **ex·pe·ri·enced, ex·pe·ri·enc·ing.**

ex·pe·ri·enced (eks pēr′ē ənst) skilful or wise because of experience (def. 2); expert; practised: *an experienced teacher, an experienced nurse. adj.*

ex·per·i·ment (eks per′ə ment′ for 1, eks per′ə mənt for 2) 1 try in order to find out; make trials or tests: *A baby experiments with his hands. That man is experimenting with dyes to get the color he wants.* 2 a trial or test to find out something: *a cooking experiment. Scientists test theories by experiment.* 1 *v.*, 2 *n.*

ex·per·i·men·tal (eks per′ə men′təl) 1 based on experiments: *Chemistry is an experimental science.* 2 used for experiments: *We worked in the experimental room.* 3 for testing or trying out: *They are growing an experimental variety of wheat. adj.*

ex·pert (eks′pėrt) 1 a person who has much skill or who knows a great deal about some special thing: *She is an expert at figure skating.* 2 having much skill; knowing a great deal about some special thing: *an expert painter.* 1 *n.*, 2 *adj.*

ex·pi·ra·tion (ek′spə rā′shən) 1 coming to an end: *the expiration of a contract.* 2 breathing out. *n.*

ex·pire (ek spīr′) 1 come to an end: *You must obtain a new automobile licence when your old one expires.* 2 die. 3 breathe out: *Used air is expired from the lungs. v.,* **ex·pired, ex·pir·ing.**

ex·plain (eks plān′) 1 make plain or clear; tell the meaning of; tell how to do: *The teacher explained long division to the class.* 2 state the cause of; give reasons for: *Can somebody explain her absence? v.*

ex·pla·na·tion (eks′plə nā′shən) 1 the act of explaining; a clearing up of a difficulty or mistake: *He did not understand the teacher's explanation of long division.* 2 something that explains: *This diagram is a good explanation of how an automobile engine works. n.*

ex·plan·a·to·ry (eks plan′ə tô′rē) helping to explain or make clear: *Read the explanatory part of a lesson before you try to do the problems. adj.*

ex·plic·it (eks plis′it) clearly expressed; distinctly stated; definite: *He gave such explicit directions that everyone understood them. adj.*

ex·plode (eks plōd′) 1 blow up; burst with a loud noise: *The building was destroyed when the old boiler exploded.* 2 cause to explode; set off: *Many boys explode firecrackers on the 24th of May.* 3 burst forth noisily: *The speaker's mistake was so funny the audience exploded with laughter.* 4 cause to be rejected; destroy belief in: *Columbus helped to explode the theory that the earth is flat. v.,* **ex·plod·ed, ex·plod·ing.**

ex·ploit (eks′ploit for 1, eks ploit′ for 2 and 3) 1 a bold, unusual act; a daring deed: *Old stories tell about the exploits of famous heroes.* 2 make use of; turn to practical account: *A mine is exploited for its minerals.* 3 make unfair or selfish use of: *Nations used to exploit their colonies, taking as much wealth out of them as they could.* 1 *n.*, 2, 3 *v.*

ex·plo·ra·tion (eks′plə rā′shən) 1 a travelling in little-known lands or seas for the purpose of discovery. 2 going over carefully; looking into closely; examining: *An exploration of all the possibilities for escape was necessary before he could make his plan. n.*

ex·plore (eks plôr′) 1 travel over little-known lands or seas for the purpose of discovery: *Champlain explored the Ottawa River and Georgian Bay.* 2 go over carefully; examine: *The children explored the new house from attic to cellar. v.,* **ex·plored, ex·plor·ing.** —**ex·plor′er,** *n.*

ex·plo·sion (eks plō′zhən) 1 a blowing up; a bursting with a loud noise: *The explosion of the bomb shook the whole neighborhood.* 2 a loud noise caused by something blowing up: *People quite far away heard the explosion.* 3 a noisy bursting forth; outbreak: *explosions of anger, an explosion of laughter. n.*

ex·plo·sive (eks plō′siv) 1 capable of exploding; likely to explode: *Gunpowder is explosive.* 2 a substance that is capable of exploding: *Explosives are used in making fireworks.* 3 tending to burst forth noisily: *The irritable old man had an explosive temper.* 1, 3 *adj.*, 2 *n.*

ex·port (eks′pôrt, also eks pôrt′ for 1) 1 send articles, or goods, out of one country for sale and use in another: *Canada exports millions of tonnes of wheat each year.* 2 the act of selling or shipping articles or goods to another country. 3 the goods, or articles, so sold and shipped: *Asbestos is an important export of Quebec.* 1 *v.*, 2, 3 *n.*

ex·pose (eks pōz′) 1 lay open; uncover; leave without protection: *While crossing the open field, the soldiers were exposed to enemy fire. Foolish actions expose a person to ridicule.* 2 put in plain sight; display: *Goods are exposed for sale in a store.* 3 make known; reveal: *He exposed the plot to the police.* 4 allow light to reach and act on a photographic film or plate. *v.*, **ex·posed, ex·pos·ing.**

ex·po·si·tion (eks′pə zish′ən) 1 a public show or exhibition: *The Canadian National Exhibition is an exposition.* 2 an explanation: *The exposition of a scientific theory. n.*

ex·po·sure (eks pō′zhər) 1 the act of exposing; laying open or making known: *The exposure of the real criminal cleared the innocent man. Anyone would dread public exposure of all his faults.* 2 being left without protection: *Exposure to the rain has spoiled this chair.* 3 a position in relation to the sun and wind: *A house with a southern exposure is open to sun and wind from the south.* 4 abandoning; putting out without shelter. 5 the part of a photographic film used for one picture. 6 the time taken to get an image on a photographic film or plate. *n.*

ex·pound (eks pound′) 1 make clear; explain: *The teacher expounds each new rule or principle in arithmetic to the class.* 2 set forth or state in detail. *v.*

ex·press (eks pres′) 1 put into words: *Try to express your ideas clearly.* 2 show by look, voice, or action: *A smile expresses joy.* 3 clear and definite: *It was his express wish that we should go without him.* 4 a quick or direct means of sending: *Packages and money can be sent by express in trains or airplanes.* 5 send by some quick means: *to express a package.* 6 by express; directly: *Send your trunk express to Saskatoon.* 7 fast; that goes direct from one point to another: *an express train.* 8 a train, bus, elevator, etc. that goes direct from one point to another without making intermediate stops: *The express is expected at five o'clock.* 9 press out: *to express juice from grapes.* 1, 2, 5, 9 *v.*, 3, 7 *adj.*, 4, 8 *n.*, 6 *adv.*

express oneself, say what one thinks: *A good speaker expresses himself clearly.*

ex·pres·sion (eks presh′ən) 1 putting into words: *the expression of an idea.* 2 a word or group of words used as a unit: *'Wise guy' is a slang expression.* 3 showing by look, voice, or action: *Her sigh was an expression of sadness.* 4 a look that shows feeling: *A grin is a happy expression.* 5 the bringing out of the meaning or beauty of something read, spoken, sung, or played: *Try to read with more expression. n.*

ex·pres·sive (eks pres′iv) 1 serving to indicate or express: *Alas! is a word expressive of sadness.* 2 having or showing much feeling: *'His skin hung on his bones' is a more expressive sentence than 'He was very thin.' adj.*

ex·press·ly (eks pres′lē) 1 plainly; definitely: *You are expressly forbidden to touch it.* 2 specially; on purpose: *I came expressly to bring it to you. adv.*

ex·press·way (eks pres′wā′) a highway for fast driving; a highway that stretches for long distances with few intersections: *A modern expressway runs between Toronto and Hamilton. n.*

ex·pul·sion (eks pul′shən) 1 the act of driving out or forcing out: *expulsion of air from the lungs.* 2 being forced out: *Expulsion from school is a punishment for bad behavior. n.*

ex·qui·site (eks′kwi zit) 1 very lovely; delicate; beautifully made: *The violet is an exquisite flower.* 2 sharp; intense: *exquisite pain, exquisite joy.* 3 of highest excellence; most admirable: *She has exquisite manners. adj.*

ex·tend (eks tend′) 1 stretch out: *to extend your hand, an extended visit, a road that extends from Halifax to Truro.* 2 give; grant: *Several organizations extend help to poor people. v.*

ex·ten·sion (eks ten′shən) 1 stretching out: *The extension of one's right hand is a sign of friendship.* 2 addition: *A new extension was built onto the old school. n.*

ex·ten·sive (eks ten′siv) far-reaching; large: *extensive changes, an extensive park. adj.*

ex·tent (eks tent′) 1 the size, space, length, amount, or degree to which a thing extends: *Railways carry people and goods through the whole extent of the country. The extent of a judge's power is limited by law.* 2 something extended; an extended space: *a vast extent of prairie. n.*

ex·te·ri·or (eks tēr′ē ər) 1 the outside; the outward appearance: *I saw only the exterior of the house, not the interior. The man has a harsh exterior, but a kind heart.* 2 outer: *Skin is the exterior covering of our bodies.* 3 coming from without; happening outside: *exterior influences.* 1 *n.*, 2, 3 *adj.*

ex·ter·mi·nate (eks tėr′mə nāt′) destroy completely: *This poison will exterminate rats. v.*, **ex·ter·mi·nat·ed, ex·ter·mi·nat·ing.**

ex·ter·nal (eks tėr′nəl) 1 outer; outside: *the external wall of a house.* 2 outside ourselves: *External influences affect our lives.* 3 **externals,** *pl.* outward appearances as opposed to real character: *Do not judge people by such externals as clothing or length of hair.* 1, 2 *adj.*, 3 *n.* **—ex·ter′nal·ly,** *adv.*

ex·tinct (eks tingkt′) 1 no longer existing: *The dinosaur is an extinct animal.* 2 no longer burning; inactive: *an extinct volcano. adj.*

ex·tinc·tion (eks tingk′shən) 1 an extinguishing: *The extinction of the lights left us in total darkness.* 2 being extinguished; extinct condition: *The caribou was once threatened with extinction. n.*

ex·tin·guish (eks ting′gwish) 1 put out: *Water extinguished the fire.* 2 wipe out; destroy; bring to an end: *One failure after another extinguished her hope. v.*

ex·tol or **ex·toll** (eks tōl′) praise highly: *The newspapers extolled the courage of the astronauts. v.*, **ex·tolled, ex·tol·ling.**

ex·tra (eks′trə) 1 beyond what is usual, expected, or needed: *extra pay, extra fare.* 2 anything that is extra: *Her bill for extras was $30.* 3 a special edition of a newspaper: *An extra announced the end of the war.* 4 more than usually; especially: *extra fine quality, an extra fast race.* 1 *adj.*, 2, 3 *n.*, 4 *adv.*

ex·tract (eks trakt′ for 1, eks′trakt for 2) 1 draw out, usually with some effort; take out: *to extract oil from olives or iron from the earth, to extract a tooth.* 2 something drawn out or taken out: *He read several extracts from the poem. Vanilla extract is made from vanilla beans.* 1 *v.*, 2 *n.*

ex·traor·di·nar·y (eks trôr′də ner′ē or eks′trə ôr′də ner′ē) beyond what is ordinary; very unusual; remarkable; special: *Two and a half metres is an extraordinary height for a man. adj.* **—ex·traor′di·nar′i·ly,** *adv.*

ex·trav·a·gance (eks trav′ə gəns) 1 careless and

hat, āge, fär; let, ēqual, tėrm; it, īce
hot, ōpen, ôrder; oil, out; cup, pu̇t, rüle
əbove, takən, pencəl, lemən, circəs
ch, child; ng, long; sh, ship
th, thin; ᴛʜ, then; zh, measure

lavish spending; waste: *His extravagance kept him in debt most of the time.* **2** a going beyond the bounds of reason: *The extravagance of his story made us doubt him.* **3** an extravagant action, idea, purchase, etc.: *Her extravagances were few.* *n.*

ex·trav·a·gant (eks trav′ə gənt) **1** spending much and spending it carelessly; wasteful: *an extravagant person.* **2** costing more than is fit and proper: *They spent a whole day's pay on an extravagant dinner.* **3** beyond the bounds of reason: *extravagant praise.* *adj.*

ex·treme (eks trēm′) **1** much more than usual; very great; very strong: *extreme love for one's country.* **2** at the very end; the farthest possible; last: *I know the boy on the extreme right of that group.* **3** something extreme; one of two things as far or as different as possible from each other: *Love and hate are two extremes of feeling.* *1, 2 adj.,* 3 *n.* —**ex·treme′ly,** *adv.*
go to extremes, do or say too much.

ex·trem·i·ty (eks trem′ə tē) **1** the very end; the tip. **2 extremities,** *pl.* the hands and feet. **3** the highest degree; the ultimate: *To be allowed to eat whatever one wishes would be the extremity of happiness.* **4** an extreme action: *The soldiers were forced to the extremity of shooting into the mob to stop its advance.* **5** a very great danger or need: *People on a sinking ship are in extremity.* *n., pl.* **ex·trem·i·ties.**

ex·tri·cate (eks′trə kāt′) release; set free from entanglements, difficulties, embarrassing situations, etc.: *The dog got caught in the briars and had trouble extricating itself.* *v.,* **ex·tri·cat·ed, ex·tri·cat·ing.**

ex·ult (eg zult′) be very glad; rejoice greatly: *The winners exulted in their victory.* *v.*

ex·ult·ant (eg zul′tənt) exulting; rejoicing greatly; triumphant: *an exultant shout.* *adj.*

ex·ul·ta·tion (eg′zul tā′shən) great joy; triumph: *There was exultation over the army's victory.* *n.*

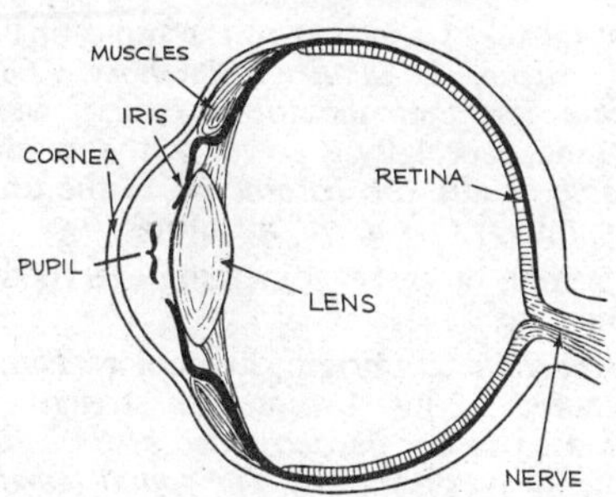

A diagram of the human eye, shown from the side

eye (ī) **1** either of the two organs of the body by which men and animals see. **2** the colored part of this organ; iris: *She has brown eyes.* **3** something like or suggesting an eye: *the eye of a needle, the eye of a potato.* **4** a look or glance: *He cast an eye in her direction.* **5** look at; observe; gaze at: *The children eyed the stranger curiously.* 1–4 *n.,* 5 *v.,* **eyed, ey·ing** or **eye·ing.**
catch one's eye, attract one's attention: *The bright red hat caught my eye.*
have an eye for, have the power of seeing with special appreciation or understanding: *A successful artist has an eye for color.*
in the eye(s) of, in the judgment, opinion, or view of: *In the eyes of most doctors, smoking is dangerous to health.*
keep an eye on, watch; take care of: *Keep an eye on my bike while I go into the store.*
see eye to eye, agree; be in agreement: *Mother and Father usually see eye to eye in matters affecting the children.*
☛ **Eye, aye,** and **I** are pronounced the same.

eye·ball (ī′bol′ or ī′bôl′) the eye without the surrounding lids and bony socket. See **eye** for picture. *n.*

eye·brow (ī′brou′) **1** the arch or strip of hair above the eye. **2** the bony ridge that the hair above the eye grows on. *n.*

eye·glass (ī′glas′) **1** a lens to aid poor vision. **2 eyeglasses,** *pl.* a pair of glass or plastic lenses to help vision: *Eyeglasses are often called spectacles.* See **spectacles** for picture. *n.*

eye·lash (ī′lash′) **1** one of the hairs on the edge of the eyelid. **2** one row or fringe of such hairs. *n.*

eye·let (ī′lit) **1** a small, round hole for a lace or cord to go through. **2** the metal ring that is set around such a hole to strengthen it. *n.*
☛ **Eyelet** and **islet** are pronounced the same.

eye·lid (ī′lid′) the cover of skin, upper or lower, by means of which the eyes can be opened and shut. *n.*

eye·piece (ī′pēs′) the lens or lenses in a telescope, microscope, etc. that are nearest the eye of the user. See **microscope** for picture. *n.*

eye·sight (ī′sīt′) sight; the power to see: *Driving at night requires good eyesight.* *n.*

eye·tooth (ī′tüth′) an upper canine tooth. See **teeth** for picture. *n., pl.* **eye·teeth.**

f or **F** (ef) the sixth letter of the alphabet: *There are two* f's *in offer.* *n., pl.* **f's** or **F's.**

fa·ble (fā′bəl) **1** a story that is made up to teach a lesson: *Fables are often about animals who can talk, such as 'The Hare and the Tortoise.'* **2** a story that is not true. *n.*

fab·ric (fab′rik) any woven or knitted material; cloth. *n.*

fab·u·lous (fab′yə ləs) **1** too extraordinary to seem possible; beyond belief; amazing: *That antique shop charges fabulous prices.* **2** of or belonging to a fable; imaginary: *The centaur is a fabulous monster.* *adj.*

fa·çade (fə sod′) **1** the front of a building. **2** a front or outward part of anything, especially when thought of as concealing something, such as an error, weakness, or scheme: *a façade of honesty.* *n.*

face (fās) **1** the front part of the head: *The eyes, nose, and mouth are parts of the face.* **2** a look or expression: *His face was sad.* **3** an ugly or peculiar look made by twisting or distorting one's face: *The boy made a face at his sister.* **4** the front part; the surface: *the face of the earth.* **5** the side of a watch, clock, card, etc. that shows the numbers or signs: *He turned one of the cards face upwards.* **6** outward appearance: *This action, on the face of it, looks bad.* **7** to front toward: *The house faces the street. The picture faces page 60 in my book.* **8** meet; confront; stand up to: *He had the courage to face his problems.* **9** turn in the direction of; take a position opposite to: *He was told to face the wall. One dancer faced the other.* **10** cover with something, especially a different material: *That wooden house is being faced with brick.* 1–6 *n.,* 7–10 *v.,* **faced, fac·ing.**
face off, in hockey, lacrosse, etc., put a puck, ball, etc. into play by dropping or placing it between the sticks of two players facing each other: *The referee starts a hockey game by facing off the puck at centre ice.*
face to face, with faces toward each other: *The two boxers stood face to face.*
face to face with, in the presence of: *The wounded soldier stood face to face with death.*
face up to, meet bravely or boldly: *face up to an enemy.*
in the face of, in the presence of: *The man showed no fear in the face of danger.*
lose face, lose dignity or prestige.
to one's face, in one's presence; in front of one: *She repeated the gossip to the teacher's face.*

face·cloth (fās′kloŧħ′) a cloth, like a small towel, used for washing the face or body. *n.*

face–off (fās′of′) in hockey, the act of putting the puck into play; the act of facing off: *The last goal was scored from the face-off.* *n.*

Facets of a diamond

fac·et (fas′it) **1** one of the small, polished surfaces of a cut gem. **2** any one of several sides or views, as of a character or personality: *Selfishness was a facet of his character that we seldom saw.* *n.*

fa·cial (fā′shəl) **1** of the face: *facial expression.* **2** for the face: *facial tissue.* **3** a massage or treatment for the face. 1, 2 *adj.,* 3 *n.*

fa·cil·i·tate (fə sil′ə tāt′) make easy; lessen the labor of; help forward; assist: *Mother's vacuum cleaner facilitates her housework.* *v.,* **fa·cil·i·tat·ed, fa·cil·i·tat·ing.**

fa·cil·i·ty (fə sil′ə tē) **1** ease; absence of difficulty: *The boy ran and dodged with such facility that no one could catch him.* **2** the ability to do anything easily, quickly, or smoothly: *He has great facility in telling lies.* **3** Usually, **facilities,** *pl.* something that makes an action easy; aid; convenience: *Ropes, swings, and sand piles are facilities for play.* *n., pl.* **fa·cil·i·ties.**

fact (fakt) **1** anything known to be true or to have happened; a true statement: *It is a fact that the world is round.* **2** what is real; truth: *The fact is, I did not want to go to the dance.* **3** something said or supposed to be true or to have really happened; assertion. **4** an actual deed, act, or event: *The War of 1812 is a historic fact. We doubted his facts.* *n.*

fac·tion (fak′shən) a group of people in a political party, church, club, etc. acting together to support a particular point of view: *There was a large faction in the club in favor of changing the membership rules.* *n.*

fac·tor (fak′tər) **1** any one of the causes that helps bring about a result; one element in a situation: *Ability, industry, and health are factors of his success in school.* **2** any of the numbers or expressions that produce a given number or quantity when multiplied together: *2 and 5 are factors of 10.* **3** separate into factors. 1, 2 *n.,* 3 *v.*

fac·to·ry (fak′tə rē or fak′trē) **1** a building or group of buildings where things are manufactured: *A factory usually has machines in it.* **2** in former times, a trading post: *Moose Factory, Ontario.* *n., pl.* **fac·to·ries.**

fac·tu·al (fak′chü əl) concerned with fact; consisting of facts: *a factual account.* *adj.*

fac·ul·ty (fak′əl tē) **1** a power of the mind or body: *the faculty of hearing, the faculty of memory. Old people sometimes lose their faculties.* **2** the power to do some special thing, especially a power of the mind: *She has a remarkable faculty for arithmetic.* **3** the teachers of a college or university. *n., pl.* **fac·ul·ties.**

fad (fad) a fashion or craze; something everybody is doing for a time. *n.*

fade (fād) **1** become less bright; lose color: *Those curtains have faded.* **2** lose freshness or strength; wither: *The flowers in her garden faded at the end of the summer.* **3** die away; disappear: *The sound faded after the train went by.* **4** cause to fade: *Sunlight will fade the colors in some fabrics.* *v.,* **fad·ed, fad·ing.**

fag (fag) work or cause to work hard until wearied: *The horse was fagged by the heavy loads he pulled in the mine all day.* *v.,* **fagged, fag·ging.**

fag·got (fag′ət) a bundle of sticks or twigs tied together for fuel. *n.*

Fahr·en·heit (far′ən hīt′ or fer′ən hīt′) of, based on, or according to the Fahrenheit scale for measuring temperature: *32 degrees Fahrenheit is the temperature at which water freezes; 212 degrees Fahrenheit is the temperature at which water boils.* *adj.*

fail (fāl) **1** fall short of success; not succeed: *He tried hard to win the race, but he failed to do so.* **2** fall short of a passing mark in a test, examination, or course in school: *She failed history last year.* **3** fall short of what is wanted or expected: *After a long drought, the crops*

hat, āge, fär; let, ēqual, tėrm; it, īce
hot, ōpen, ôrder; oil, out; cup, put, rüle
əbove, takən, pencəl, lemən, circəs
ch, child; ng, long; sh, ship
th, thin; ᴛʜ, then; zh, measure

failed. **4** become too little; decrease so as to be no longer enough: *When the supplies failed, the explorers died of hunger. The light failed before the game was over.* **5** neglect; not do: *He rarely fails to follow his father's advice.* **6** be of no use to when needed: *When I was in trouble, my friends failed me.* **7** stop performing or operating: *During the storm, the boat's motor failed.* **8** lose strength; grow weak; die or wither away: *The sick man's heart was failing.* **9** not make enough profit to stay in business; go bankrupt: *He opened a fruit store, but he failed before twelve months had passed.* *v.*
without fail, surely; for certain: *He promised to report regularly without fail.*

fail·ing (fāl′ing) **1** failure. **2** a fault or weakness; defect: *He is a charming person in spite of his failings.* **3** in the absence of; lacking; without: *Failing good weather, the game will be played indoors.* 1, 2 *n.*, 3 *prep.*

fail·ure (fāl′yər) **1** a falling short of success; lack of success: *failure in one's work.* **2** the fact of not getting a passing mark in a test, examination, or course in school. **3** a falling short of what is wanted or expected: *failure of crops.* **4** a loss of strength; becoming weak: *failure of eyesight.* **5** not making enough profit to stay in business; becoming bankrupt: *the failure of a company.* **6** a person or thing that has failed: *The picnic was a failure because it rained.* *n.*

faint (fānt) **1** not clear or plain; dim: *a faint picture, a faint idea, faint colors.* **2** weak; exhausted; feeble: *The drowning girl cried 'Help!' in a faint voice.* **3** a temporary condition in which a person lies as if asleep and does not know what is going on around him. **4** fall into this condition: *He fainted at the sight of his bleeding finger.* 1, 2 *adj.*, 3 *n.*, 4 *v.*
feel faint, feel ready to faint.
☛ **Faint** and **feint** are pronounced the same.

faint–heart·ed (fānt′här′tid) lacking courage; cowardly; timid. *adj.*

fair¹ (fer) **1** not favoring one more than the other or others; just; honest: *Everyone admires a fair judge. He is fair even to the people he dislikes.* **2** according to the rules: *fair play.* **3** pretty good; not good and not bad; average: *There is a fair crop of wheat this year.* **4** light; not dark: *She had fair hair and skin.* **5** clear; sunny; not cloudy or stormy: *The weather will be fair today.* **6** beautiful; pleasant to look at: *a fair maiden.* **7** in an honest, straightforward manner; honestly: *to play fair.* 1–6 *adj.*, 7 *adv.* **—fair′ness,** *n.*
☛ **Fair** and **fare** are pronounced the same.

fair² (fer) **1** a gathering of people, especially in country areas in the fall, for the purpose of showing farm animals, products, machinery, preserved fruit, baked goods, etc.: *Mr. Gibson's bull won first prize in the competition at the fair. We enjoyed the horse show at the Royal Winter Fair.* **2** a gathering of people for the buying and selling of goods, often held at regular times during the year: *a trade fair.* **3** an entertainment and sale of articles; bazaar: *Our church held a fair to raise money.* *n.*
☛ See note at **fair¹**.

fair game **1** animals or birds that it is lawful to hunt. **2** a person or thing considered suitable or reasonable to pursue or attack: *She was fair game for political cartoonists because of her odd way of dressing.*

fair·ground (fer′ground′) an outdoor space where fairs are held. *n.*

fair·ly (fer′lē) **1** in a fair manner; justly. **2** not extremely; to a moderate degree; rather; somewhat: *She is a fairly good pupil, neither bad nor very good.* *adv.*

fair·y (fer′ē) **1** in stories, a tiny being, usually very lovely and delicate, who could help or harm human beings. **2** of fairies: *fairy tales.* **3** like a fairy; lovely; delicate: *wings of fairy gossamer.* 1 *n.*, *pl.* **fair·ies;** 2, 3 *adj.*
☛ **Fairy** and **ferry** are pronounced the same.

fair·y·land (fer′ē land′) **1** the place where the fairies are supposed to live. **2** a charming and pleasant place. *n.*

fairy tale **1** a story about fairies or other beings with magical powers: *Many fairy tales are very old.* **2** an untrue story; falsehood; lie: *I'm tired of her fairy tales about all the things she did on her trip.*

faith (fāth) **1** believing without proof; trust; confidence: *We have faith in our friends.* **2** belief in God or in God's promises. **3** religion: *He is of the Protestant faith.* **4** being faithful; loyalty: *Good faith is honesty of intention; bad faith is intent to deceive.* **5** a promise to remain loyal: *The captured soldiers refused to break faith even under torture.* *n.*
in bad faith, dishonestly or insincerely.
in good faith, honestly or sincerely: *Although the boys had done the wrong thing, they had acted in good faith.*

faith·ful (fāth′fəl) **1** worthy of trust; loyal: *a faithful friend, a faithful servant.* **2** true to fact; accurate: *The witness gave a faithful account of what happened.* *adj.*

faith·less (fāth′lis) not true to duty or to one's promises; not loyal: *A traitor is a person who is faithless to his country.* *adj.*

fake (fāk) **1** make up to seem satisfactory; hide defects: *He faked an answer.* **2** a fraud: *The beggar's limp was a fake.* **3** false: *The kidnapper sent a fake telegram.* 1 *v.*, **faked, fak·ing;** 2 *n.*, 3 *adj.*

fal·con (fol′kən, fal′kən, or fôl′kən) **1** a bird of prey, related to the hawk and eagle, having a hooked bill and long, strong, pointed wings for swift flight. **2** a falcon or a hawk trained to hunt and kill birds and small game: *In the Middle Ages, hunting with falcons was a popular sport.* *n.*

fall (fol or fôl) **1** drop or come down from a higher place: *Snow is falling fast. His hat fell off. Leaves fall from the trees.* **2** a dropping from a higher place: *The fall from his horse hurt him.* **3** the amount that comes down: *We measured the fall of rain for a year.* **4** the distance anything drops or comes down: *The fall of the river here is two metres.* **5** waterfall. **6** come down suddenly from a standing position: *He fell on his knees.* **7** coming down suddenly from a standing position: *The child had a bad fall when he tripped on the step.* **8** become bad or worse: *He was tempted and fell.* **9** becoming bad or worse; ruin or destruction: *Adam's fall, the fall of Rome.* **10** be taken by any evil: *The city has fallen into the power of its enemies.* **11** pass into some condition, position, etc.: *He fell sick. The baby* *fell asleep. The boy and girl fell in love.* **12** happen: *Night falls early in winter.* **13** come by lot or chance: *Our choice fell on him.* **14** become lower or less: *Prices are falling. The water in the river has fallen one metre.* **15** becoming lower or less: *a fall in prices, the fall of the tide.* **16** be divided: *His story falls into five parts.* **17** the season of the year between summer and winter; autumn. 1, 6, 8, 10–14, 16 *v.,* **fell, fall·en, fall·ing;** 2–5, 7, 9, 15, 17 *n.*

fall back, retreat; go toward the rear: *The soldiers fell back to a stronger position.*

fall back on, a go back to for safety. **b** turn to for help or support: *In time of trouble, he knew he could fall back on his father.*

fall behind, fail or be unable to keep up; drop back: *Before the race was half over, the slow runners had fallen a lap behind.*

fall in, a take a place in line: *'Fall in!' said the officer to the soldiers.* **b** meet: *On our trip we fell in with some interesting people.* **c** agree: *They fell in with our plans.*

fall off, drop; become less: *Attendance at baseball games falls off late in the season.*

fall on, attack: *The thieves fell on the man and stole his money.*

fall out, a leave a place in line: *'Fall out!' said the officer to the soldiers.* **b** quarrel; stop being friends.

falls, a waterfall: *Niagara Falls.*

fall through, fail: *His plans fell through.*

fall to, a begin to fight or attack: *The swordsman fell to with great enthusiasm.* **b** begin to eat: *The boys fell to as soon as they sat down.*

fall upon, attack: *The pirates fell upon the city.*

fall·en (fol′ən or fôl′ən) **1** dropped: *They picked up some fallen apples.* **2** overthrown; ruined: *a fallen emperor.* **3 the fallen,** the dead: *The battlefield was covered with the fallen.* **4** See **fall.** *Much rain has fallen.* 1, 2 *adj.,* 3 *n.,* 4 *v.*

fall fair *Cdn.* a fair held in the fall in a community for the exhibiting and judging of livestock, produce, and crafts, often with horse races, dances, and other forms of entertainment.

fall–out (fol′out′ or fôl′out′) the radio-active substance that falls to earth after the explosion of an atomic or hydrogen bomb. *n.*

fal·low (fal′ō) **1** ploughed but not seeded for a season or more; uncultivated: *fallow land.* **2** of land, the state of being ploughed and left unseeded for a season, in order to destroy weeds, improve the soil, etc.: *Half the farm was in summer fallow.* **3** land ploughed and left unseeded in this way: *The ground was wet, so they walked around the fallow.* 1 *adj.,* 2, 3 *n.*

false (fols or fôls) **1** not true; not correct; wrong: *false statements. The singer was so nervous that she sang two false notes.* **2** disloyal; deceitful: *a false friend, a man false to his promise.* **3** used in order to deceive: *false weights, false signals. A ship sails under false colors when she raises the flag of a country other than her own.* **4** not real; artificial: *false teeth, false diamonds. adj.,* **fals·er, fals·est. —false′ness,** *n.*

false step, a a wrong step; a stumble: *One false step and the climber would fall to his death.* **b** a mistake or blunder: *The police were waiting for the suspect to make a false step.*

false·hood (fols′hu̇d or fôls′hu̇d) **1** a false statement; lie. **2** an attempt to deceive; pretence: *They exposed the falsehood of his earlier life. n.*

fal·si·ty (fol′sə tē or fôl′sə tē) **1** the condition or quality of being false: *the falsity of his smile. The falsity of the statement was obvious from the start.* **2** something false; lie. *n., pl.* **fal·si·ties.**

fal·ter (fol′tər or fôl′tər) **1** not go straight on; hesitate; waver; lose courage: *The soldiers faltered for a moment as their captain fell.* **2** become unsteady in movement; stumble; stagger. **3** speak in hesitating and broken words: *Greatly embarrassed, he faltered out his thanks. v.*

fame (fām) the fact, state, or condition of being well known; having a good deal said or written about one: *Fame comes to people who do great things. n.*

famed (fāmd) famous; well-known. *adj.*

fa·mil·iar (fə mil′yər) **1** known to all; common: *A knife is a familiar tool.* **2** well-known: *a familiar tune, a familiar face.* **3** well acquainted: *Mary is familiar with French.* **4** close; personal; intimate: *Those familiar friends know each other very well.* **5** too friendly; forward: *His manner is too familiar. adj.*

fa·mil·iar·i·ty (fə mil′yar′ə tē or fə mil′yer′ə tē) **1** close acquaintance: *His skill as a mechanic showed his familiarity with motors.* **2** freedom of behavior suitable only to friends; lack of formality or ceremony. **3** an instance of such behavior: *She dislikes such familiarities as the use of her first name by people she has just met. n., pl.* **fa·mil·iar·i·ties.**

fam·i·ly (fam′ə lē or fam′lē) **1** a father, a mother, and their children: *Our town has about a thousand families.* **2** the children of a father and mother; offspring: *She brought up a family.* **3** a group of people living in the same house. **4** all of a person's relatives. **5** a group of related people; tribe; race. **6** a group of related animals or plants: *Lions, tigers, and leopards belong to the cat family.* **7** any group of related or similar things: *a family of languages. n., pl.* **fam·i·lies.**

Family Allowance an allowance paid to mothers by the Federal Government for each child under 16 years of age.

fam·ine (fam′ən) **1** an extreme lack of food in a place; a time of starving: *Many people died during the famine in India.* **2** a very great shortage of anything: *a coal famine.* **3** starvation: *Many people died of famine. n.*

fam·ish (fam′ish) be very hungry; starve: *'Let's eat!' cried Tom; 'I'm famished.' v.*

fa·mous (fā′məs) very well-known; noted: *A great crowd of people greeted the famous hero. adj.*

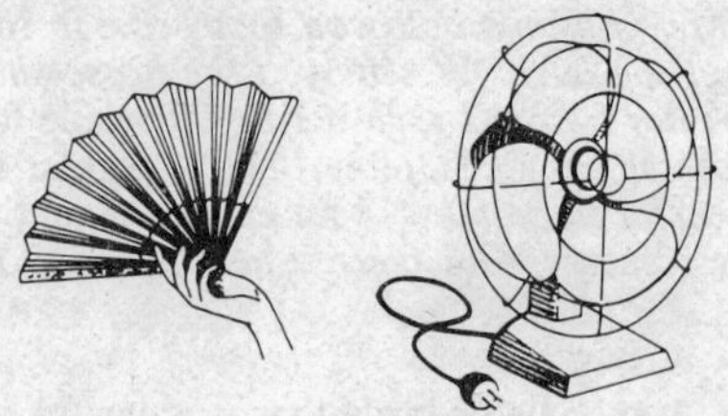

Two kinds of fan

fan[1] (fan) **1** an instrument or device with which to stir the air in order to cool or ventilate a room, or to cool one's face, or to blow dust away. **2** stir the air; blow on; stir up: *Fan the fire to make it burn faster.* 3 use a fan on: *She fanned herself.* 4 anything that is flat and spread out like an open fan. 5 in baseball, strike out: *He fanned three times in one game. The pitcher fanned five batters.* 1, 4 *n.*, 2, 3, 5 *v.* **fanned, fan·ning.**

fan² (fan) 1 a person extremely interested in hockey, movies, radio, etc.; buff: *He's a baseball fan and has many books of stories about games and players.* 2 an admirer of an actor, writer, etc. *n.*

fa·nat·ic (fə nat′ik) a person who is carried away beyond reason by his feelings or beliefs: *My friend was such a fanatic about fresh air that he would not stay in any room with the windows closed.* *n.*

fan·ci·ful (fan′sē fəl) 1 showing fancy; quaint; odd; fantastic: *a fanciful decoration.* 2 led by fancy; using fancies: *Hans Christian Andersen was a fanciful writer.* 3 suggested by fancy; imaginary; unreal: *A story about fairyland is fanciful.* *adj.*

fan·cy (fan′sē) 1 picture to oneself; imagine: *Can you fancy yourself in fairyland?* 2 one's power to imagine: *Dragons, fairies, and giants are creatures of fancy.* 3 something imagined or supposed: *Is it a fancy, or do I hear a sound?* 4 like; be fond of: *She fancies the idea of having a picnic.* 5 a liking: *a fancy for bright ties. They took a great fancy to each other and became close friends.* 6 showy: *a fancy dancer.* 7 of high quality: *fancy pears.* 8 extravagant: *fancy prices.* 1, 4 *v.*, **fan·cied, fan·cy·ing;** 2, 3, 5 *n.*, *pl.* **fan·cies;** 6–8 *adj.*, **fan·ci·er, fan·ci·est.**

fancy dress, clothes worn by people dressed as pirates, clowns, etc. at parties.

fancy oneself, think highly of oneself: *That girl really fancies herself.*

fan·fare (fan′fer) 1 a short tune or call sounded by trumpets, bugles, hunting horns, etc. 2 a loud show of activity, talk, etc.; a showy flourish. *n.*

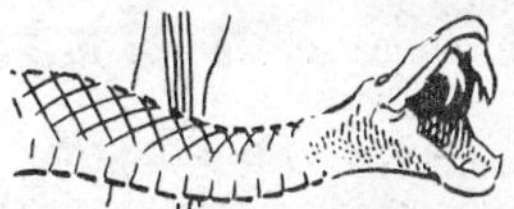

The fangs of a rattlesnake

fang (fang) 1 a long, sharp tooth by which certain animals, such as dogs, wolves, etc., seize and hold prey; canine tooth: *The hungry wolf buried its fangs in the caribou's neck.* 2 a hollow or grooved tooth by which a poisonous snake injects poison into its prey. 3 a long, slender, tapering part of anything, such as the root of a tooth or the prong of a fork. *n.*

fan·tas·tic (fan tas′tik) 1 very fanciful; unreal; existing only in the imagination: *The idea that a house can float in the air is fantastic.* 2 strange and wild in shape or manner: *The firelight cast weird, fantastic shadows on the walls.* 3 *Informal.* unbelievably good, quick, high, etc.: *That store charges fantastic prices.* *adj.*

fan·ta·sy (fan′tə sē) 1 the imagination; the play of the mind: *Fantasy accounts for many dreams.* 2 a picture in the mind. 3 wild imagining; fanciful thinking: *Spaceships were once thought to be pure fantasy.* 4 a wild, strange fancy; a fanciful idea: *The boy lived with many fantasies.* *n.*, *pl.* **fan·ta·sies.**

far (fär) 1 a long way; a long way off: *The moon is far from the earth.* 2 more distant: *He lives on the far side of the hill.* 3 very much: *It is far better to go by train.* 1, 3 *adv.*, 2 *adj.*, **far·ther, far·thest.**

by far, very much: *He was by far the better swimmer.*

hat, āge, fär; let, ēqual, tėrm; it, īce
hot, ōpen, ôrder; oil, out; cup, pu̇t, rüle
əbove, takən, pencəl, lemən, circəs
ch, child; ng, long; sh, ship
th, thin; ᴛʜ, then; zh, measure

far and away, very much: *He was far and away the best student.*

so far, a to this point; to that point. **b** until now or then: *Our team has won every game so far this season.*

far·a·way (fär′ə wā′) 1 distant; far away: *faraway countries.* 2 dreamy: *A faraway look in her eyes showed that she was thinking of something else.* *adj.*

fare (fer) 1 the money that a person pays to ride in a train, car, bus, etc. 2 food provided or eaten: *dainty fare.* 3 be fed: *We fared very well at Grandmother's.* 4 do; get on: *He is faring well in school.* 5 go: *to fare forth on a journey.* 1, 2 *n.*, 3–5 *v.*, **fared, far·ing.**

☞ **Fare** and **fair** are pronounced the same.

Far East China, Japan, and other parts of eastern Asia.

fare·well (fer′wel′) 1 good luck; goodbye. 2 good wishes at parting: *They said their farewells on the station platform.* 3 parting; last: *a farewell kiss, an actress's farewell performance.* 1, 2 *n.*, *interj.*, 3 *adj.*

far–fetched (fär′fecht′) not likely; hard to believe; forced or strained: *a far-fetched excuse. Her ideas for parties were always a bit far-fetched.* *adj.*

farm (färm) 1 the land and buildings that a person uses to raise crops or animals. 2 raise crops or animals either to eat or to sell: *Her father farms for a living.* 3 cultivate land: *He farms forty hectares.* 1 *n.*, 2, 3 *v.* **—farm′er,** *n.*

farm out, a let for hire: *He farms out the right to pick berries on his land.* **b** send a professional athlete to a less advanced league so that he can gain experience.

farm·house (färm′hous′) the dwelling house on a farm. *n.*

farm·ing (fär′ming) the business of raising crops or animals on a farm; agriculture. *n.*

farm·land (färm′land′ or färm′lənd) land suitable for or used for raising crops or grazing. *n.*

farm·yard (färm′yärd′) the yard connected with the buildings of a farm or enclosed by them. *n.*

far–off (fär′of′) distant; far away: *far-off lands.* *adj.*

far–reach·ing (fär′rēch′ing) having a wide influence or effect; extending far: *The effects of World War II were far-reaching.* *adj.*

far–see·ing (fär′sē′ing) 1 able to see far. 2 looking ahead; planning wisely for the future. *adj.*

far–sight·ed (fär′sīt′id) 1 not being able to see near things as clearly as distant things. 2 looking ahead; planning wisely for the future. *adj.*

far·ther (fär′ᴛʜər) more distant; a greater distance: *Three kilometres is farther than two. We walked farther than we meant to.* *adj., adv.*

far·thest (fär′ᴛʜist) 1 most distant: *Ours is the house farthest down the road.* 2 to or at the greatest distance. 1 *adj.*, 2 *adv.*

far·thing (fär′ᴛʜing) a former British coin, worth a fourth of a penny. *n.*

fas·ci·nate (fas′ə nāt′) 1 delight; enchant: *She fascinates everyone by her beauty and charm.* 2 hold motionless by strange power or by terror: *Snakes are said to fascinate small birds.* *v.*, **fas·ci·nat·ed, fas·ci·nat·ing.**

fas·ci·na·tion (fas′ə nā′shən) 1 fascinating or being fascinated. 2 a very strong attraction; charm: *Stamp collecting has a fascination for some people.* *n.*

fash·ion (fash′ən) 1 the way a thing is shaped or made or done: *He walks in a peculiar fashion.* 2 the current custom in dress, manners, speech, etc.; style: *She likes to read about the latest fashions.* 3 make, shape, or form: *He fashioned a whistle out of a piece of wood.* 1, 2 *n.*, 3 *v.*

fash·ion·a·ble (fash′ən ə bəl) following the fashion; stylish: *fashionable clothes.* *adj.*

fast[1] (fast) 1 quick; rapid; swift: *A fast runner can beat a slow one.* 2 quickly; rapidly; swiftly: *Airplanes go fast.* 3 showing a time ahead of the real time: *That clock is fast.* 4 too free or wild: *He led a fast life, drinking and gambling.* 5 firmly fixed: *This color is fast and will not wash out. The boat was made fast to the dock.* 6 firmly: *He held fast to the bar as the roller-coaster car started to hurtle downhill.* 7 firm: *They were fast friends.* 1, 3–5, 7 *adj.*, 2, 6 *adv.*

fast asleep, completely or fully asleep: *The baby is fast asleep.*

fast[2] (fast) 1 go without food; eat little or nothing; go without certain kinds of food: *Members of that church fast on certain days.* 2 the act or fact of going without food. 3 a day or period of fasting: *The fast lasted over the religious holiday.* 1 *v.*, 2, 3 *n.*

fas·ten (fas′ən) 1 tie, lock, or make hold together in any way: *to fasten a dress, to fasten a door, to fasten two railway cars together.* 2 fix; direct: *The baby fastened her eyes on the Christmas tree. He tried to fasten the blame on me.* *v.*

fas·ten·er (fas′ən ər) a device for fastening things together: *Zippers and buttons are fasteners.* *n.*

fas·ten·ing (fas′ən ing) a device used to fasten things together: *Locks, bolts, clasps, hooks, and buttons are all fastenings.* *n.*

fas·tid·i·ous (fas tid′ē əs or fas tid′yəs) hard to please; very careful and fussy: *a fastidious eater, fastidious about clothes.* *adj.*

fast·ness (fast′nis) 1 the quality of being fast. 2 a strong, safe place; stronghold: *The bandits hid in their mountain fastness.* *n.*

fat (fat) 1 a white or yellow, oily substance formed in the bodies of animals and also in some seeds. 2 having much of this oily substance: *fat meat.* 3 having much flesh; round and well fed: *a fat little puppy. His father is a big, fat man.* 4 large; filled with good things: *His mother sent him a fat parcel of food.* 5 make or become fat. 1 *n.*, 2–4 *adj.*, **fat·ter, fat·test;** 5 *v.*, **fat·ted fat·ting. —fat′ness,** *n.*

live off the fat of the land, have the best of everything.

fa·tal (fā′təl) 1 causing death: *fatal accidents.* 2 causing destruction or ruin: *The loss of all their money was fatal to their plans.* 3 fateful: *At last the fatal day for the contest arrived.* *adj.*

fa·tal·i·ty (fə tal′ə tē or fā tal′ə tē) a fatal accident or happening; a death: *There were several fatalities on the highways last weekend.* *n.*, *pl.* **fa·tal·i·ties.**

fate (fāt) 1 a power that is believed to fix what is to happen: *Fate is beyond any person's control. He does not believe in fate.* 2 what is fixed to happen. 3 one's lot or fortune; what happens to a person, group, etc.: *In every race it was her fate to be beaten. History shows the fate of many nations.* 4 **Fates,** *pl.* in Greek and Roman myths, the three goddesses who controlled human life: *One of the Fates spun the thread of life, one decided how long it should be, and one cut it off.* *n.*

☛ **Fate** and **fete** are pronounced the same.

fate·ful (fāt′fəl) 1 controlled by fate. 2 determining what is to happen; decisive: *a fateful battle.* 3 causing death, destruction, or ruin; disastrous: *a fateful flood.* *adj.*

fa·ther (fo′ᴛʜər) 1 a male parent: *Her father died when she was quite young.* 2 be the father of. 3 take care of as a father does: *That generous old man fathers all the boys in the neighborhood.* 4 a man who acted as leader, founder, inventor, etc.: *Fathers of Confederation. Alexander Graham Bell was the father of the telephone.* 5 be the cause of; originate: *The inventor of the light bulb fathered many other inventions.* 6 a title of respect used in addressing a priest. 7 **the Father,** God. 1, 4, 6, 7 *n.*, 2, 3, 5 *v.*

fa·ther–in–law (fo′ᴛʜər in lo′ or fo′ᴛʜər in lô′) the father of one's husband or wife. *n.*, *pl.* **fa·thers-in-law.**

fa·ther·land (fo′ᴛʜər land′) one's native country; the land of one's ancestors. *n.*

fa·ther·ly (fo′ᴛʜər lē) 1 of a father. 2 like a father; like a father's: *The old gentleman gave the little boy a fatherly smile.* *adj.*

Fathers of Confederation the men, led by Sir John A. Macdonald, who brought about the confederation of the original provinces of Canada in 1867.

fath·om (faᴛʜ′əm) 1 a measure of six feet, a little under two metres, used mainly in speaking of the depth of water: *The ship sank in 10 fathoms.* 2 find the depth of. 3 get to the bottom of; understand: *I can't fathom what you're driving at.* 1 *n.*, 2, 3 *v.*

fa·tigue (fə tēg′) 1 weariness: *He was pale from fatigue.* 2 make weary or tired. *1 n.*, 2 *v.*, **fa·tigued, fa·ti·guing.**

fat·ten (fat′ən) 1 make fat: *Pigs are fattened for market.* 2 become fat. *v.*

fat·ty (fat′ē) 1 of fat; containing fat. 2 like fat; oily or greasy: *a fatty substance.* *adj.*, **fat·ti·er, fat·ti·est.**

fau·cet (fo′sit or fô′sit) a device for turning on or off a flow of liquid; a tap. See **tap** for picture. *n.*

fault (folt or fôlt) 1 something that is not as it should be; a flaw or defect: *Her dog has two faults: it eats too much, and it howls at night.* 2 mistake. 3 a cause for blame; responsibility: *Whose fault was it?* *n.*

find fault, find mistakes or complain: *The boy said that his father was always finding fault.*

find fault with, object to or criticize: *The teacher was always finding fault with badly done homework.*

fault·less (folt′lis or fôlt′lis) without a single fault or defect; perfect. *adj.*

fault·y (fol′tē or fôl′tē) having faults; imperfect; defective: *a faulty flashlight.* *adj.*, **fault·i·er, fault·i·est.**

hat, āge, fär; let, ēqual, tėrm; it, īce
hot, ōpen, ôrder; oil, out; cup, pu̇t, rüle
əbove, takən, pencəl, lemən, circəs
ch, child; ng, long; sh, ship
th, thin; ᴛʜ, then; zh, measure

A faun

faun (fon or fôn) in Roman legends and myths, a minor god that helped farmers and shepherds: *A faun was thought to look like a man, but to have the ears, horns, tail, and legs of a goat.* *n.*

☛ **Faun** and **fawn** are pronounced the same.

fau·na (fo′nə or fô′nə) all the animals of a particular region or time: *the fauna of Australia.* *n.*

☛ **Fauna** comes from the Latin word *Fauna,* the name of a Roman rural goddess.

fa·vor or **fa·vour** (fā′vər) **1** an act of kindness: *Will you do me a favor?* **2** show kindness to; oblige: *Favor us with a song.* **3** liking; approval: *They will look with favor on your plan.* **4** like; approve: *We favor his plan.* **5** give more than is fair to: *He thought the teacher favored his twin brother.* **6** a small gift, especially one given as a souvenir at a party: *Paper hats were handed out as favors to guests at the New Year's Ball.* **7** look like: *She favors her mother.* 1, 3, 6 *n.,* 2, 4, 5, 7 *v.*

in favor of, a on the side of. **b** to the advantage of: *The referee's decision was in favor of the other team.*

in his favor, for him; to his benefit.

fa·vor·a·ble or **fa·vour·a·ble** (fā′vər ə bəl or fāv′rə bəl) **1** favoring; approving: *a favorable answer.* **2** being to one's advantage; helping: *a favorable wind.* *adj.* **—fa′vor·a·bly** or **fa′vour·a·bly,** *adv.*

fa·vor·ite or **fa·vour·ite** (fā′vər it or fāv′rit) **1** most liked: *What is your favorite flower?* **2** a person or thing liked better than others; one liked very much: *He is a favorite with everybody.* **3** a person, horse, etc. expected to win a contest. 1 *adj.,* 2, 3 *n.*

fa·vour (fā′vər) See **favor.**

A fawn of a white-tailed deer

fawn[1] (fon or fôn) **1** a deer less than a year old. **2** light, yellowish brown: *She was wearing a fawn coat.* 1, 2 *n.,* 2 *adj.*

☛ **Fawn** and **faun** are pronounced the same.

fawn[2] (fon or fôn) **1** try to win favor or attention by flattery or slavish acts: *Many flattering relatives fawned on the rich old man.* **2** of dogs, etc., show fondness by crouching, wagging the tail, licking the hand, etc. *v.*

☛ See note at **fawn**[1].

faze (fāz) *Informal.* disturb; worry; bother: *A scolding doesn't faze her at all.* *v.,* **fazed, faz·ing.**

☛ **Faze** and **phase** are pronounced the same.

fear (fēr) **1** a feeling that danger or evil is near; terror; dread: *His fear made him move through the jungle very carefully.* **2** feel fear in the presence of; be afraid of: *Our cat fears the big dog next door. Babies fear loud noises.* **3** have an uneasy feeling; feel anxious or concerned: *I fear that I am going to miss the train.* **4** an uneasy feeling; concern; anxiety: *Many people expressed fear about the safety of the astronauts.* 1, 4 *n.,* 2, 3 *v.*

fear·ful (fēr′fəl) **1** causing fear; terrible; dreadful: *The great fire was a fearful sight.* **2** feeling fear; frightened. **3** showing fear: *a fearful child.* **4** *Informal.* very bad or unpleasant: *I have a fearful cold.* *adj.*

fear·less (fēr′lis) afraid of nothing; brave. *adj.* **—fear′less·ly,** *adv.*

fear·some (fēr′səm) **1** causing fear; frightful: *The fire was a fearsome sight.* **2** timid; afraid: *She always was a fearsome child.* *adj.*

fea·si·ble (fē′zə bəl) capable of being carried out; possible without difficulty or damage: *The committee selected the plan that seemed most feasible.* *adj.*

feast (fēst) **1** a rich meal prepared for some special occasion and for a number of guests: *We went to the wedding feast.* **2** eat many good things; have a feast. **3** provide a rich meal for: *The king feasted his friends.* **4** give pleasure or joy to; delight: *We feasted our eyes on the sunset.* **5** celebration: *Christmas and Easter are the most important Christian feasts.* 1, 5 *n.,* 2–4 *v.*

feat (fēt) a great achievement; an act showing great skill, strength, or daring: *Landing on the moon was a remarkable feat.* *n.*

☛ **Feat** and **feet** are pronounced the same.

feath·er (feᴛʜ′ər) **1** one of the light, thin growths that cover a bird's skin: *Because feathers are soft and light, they are often used to fill pillows.* **2** supply or cover with feathers. 1 *n.,* 2 *v.*

feather in one's cap, something to be proud of.

feather one's nest, take advantage of chances to get rich.

feath·er·y (feᴛʜ′ə rē) **1** having feathers; covered with feathers. **2** like feathers: *feathery snow.* *adj.*

fea·ture (fē′chər) **1** a part of the face: *The eyes, nose, mouth, chin, and forehead are features.* **2** a distinct part or quality; some thing or part that stands out and attracts attention: *The plan had many good features. An outstanding feature of British Columbia is the Rocky Mountain range.* **3** a main attraction, especially a long movie: *They are showing a good feature this week.* **4** a special article, column, etc. in a newspaper or magazine. **5** give special prominence or emphasis to: *A great actor was featured in the movie. The store was featuring radios in its fall sale.* 1–4 *n.,* 5 *v.,* **fea·tured, fea·tur·ing.**

Feb. February.

Feb·ru·ar·y (feb′rü er′ē or feb′yü er′ē) the second month of the year: *February has 28 days except in leap years, when it has 29.* *n., pl.* **Feb·ru·ar·ies.**

☛ **February** came into English through Old French

from the Latin name for this month. The Romans named the month after a festival that was held at this time.

fed (fed) See **feed.** *We fed the birds yesterday. Have they been fed today?* v.

fed·er·al (fed′ər əl) 1 of the central government of Canada, not of any province or city alone: *Delivering mail is a federal responsibility.* 2 formed by an agreement between groups, provinces, states, etc.: *Canada and the United States both became nations by federal union.* adj.

Federal Government the elected government of Canada, which sits in Ottawa and controls defence, foreign affairs, criminal law, etc.

fed·er·a·tion (fed′ər ā′shən) a league; a union by agreement, often a union of provinces, states, or nations: *Canada was formed as a federation.* n.

fee (fē) a charge; money paid for some service or privilege: *Dentists charge a fee for fixing teeth.* n.

fee·ble (fē′bəl) weak: *a feeble old man, a feeble mind, a feeble cry, a feeble attempt.* adj., **fee·bler, fee·blest.** **—fee′ble·ness,** n.

feed (fēd) 1 give food to: *We feed a baby because he cannot feed himself.* 2 give as food to: *Feed this grain to the chickens.* 3 eat: *We put cows to feed in the pasture.* 4 food for animals: *Give the chickens their feed.* 5 supply with material: *The stokers fed coal to the furnaces.* 1–3, 5 *v.*, **fed, feed·ing;** 4 *n.*

feed·back (fēd′bak′) 1 in computers, etc., the returning to a system of part of what it produces in order to change or control what it will produce from then on. 2 *Informal.* news; information on the results of one's actions that will influence one's future decisions or actions: *Since there was no feedback from the usual sources, he wasn't sure whether he ought to continue his investigation.* n.

feed·er (fēd′ər) 1 a device that supplies food to a person or animal: *We have a feeder for birds in our back yard.* 2 anything that supplies something else with material: *A brook is a feeder for a river. A branch road that brings traffic to a main highway is a feeder.* n.

feel (fēl) 1 touch: *Feel the cloth.* 2 try to touch; try to find by touching: *He felt in his pocket for a match.* 3 find out by touching: *Feel how cold my hands are.* 4 be aware of: *He felt the cool breeze. She felt the heat.* 5 be; have the feeling of being: *She feels glad. He feels angry. We felt hot. She felt sure.* 6 give the feeling of being; seem: *The air feels cold. Your dress feels wet.* 7 have in one's mind; experience: *They feel pity. I felt pain. He felt fear of the thunder.* 8 have a feeling: *I felt for the poor, lonesome dog. Try to feel more kindly toward her. I feel that he will come.* 9 the way in which something feels to the touch: *Wet soap has a greasy feel.* 1–8 *v.*, **felt, feel·ing;** 9 *n.*

feel like, *Informal.* **a** have a desire for; want: *I feel like an ice-cream cone.* **b** seem as if it is going to: *It feels like rain.* **c** seem like to the sense of touch: *The cat's fur felt like silk.*

feel·er (fēl′ər) 1 something that feels: *The long feelers on the heads of insects help them find their way.* See **insect** for picture. 2 a suggestion, remark, hint, or question meant to bring out the plans, opinions, or purposes of others: *The mayor put out a feeler to learn what the council thought of his plan.* n.

feel·ing (fēl′ing) 1 the sense of touch: *By feeling we tell what is hard from what is soft.* 2 a sensation; the condition of being aware: *She had no feeling of heat, cold, or pain.* 3 emotion: *Joy, sorrow, fear, and anger are feelings. The loss of the ball game stirred up much feeling.* 4 **feelings,** *pl.,* **a** the sensitive areas of a person's being that may be hurt or offended: *His feelings are easily hurt.* **b** sympathy: *His feelings were touched by the child's cry of pain.* 5 opinion; impression: *What is your feeling about this idea?* 6 that feels; sensitive: *a feeling heart.* 7 pity; sympathy. 1–5, 7 *n.*, 6 *adj.*

feet (fēt) plural of **foot.** *A dog has four feet.* n.

☛ **Feet** and **feat** are pronounced the same.

feign (fān) 1 pretend: *Some animals feign death when in danger.* 2 make up with intent to deceive: *to feign an excuse.* v.

feint (fānt) 1 a movement made with the purpose of deceiving; a sham attack or blow: *The fighter made a feint at his opponent with his right hand and struck with his left.* 2 make a movement with the purpose of deceiving: *The fighter feinted with his right hand and struck his opponent with his left.* 3 pretence: *He made a feint of studying while actually listening to the radio.* 1, 3 *n.*, 2 *v.*

☛ **Feint** and **faint** are pronounced the same.

feld·spar (feld′spär′) a crystalline mineral, white or red in color: *Feldspar is used for making glass and pottery.* n.

fe·line (fē′līn) 1 of or having to do with cats and other animals of the cat family. 2 any animal belonging to this group: *House cats, tigers, leopards, and panthers are felines.* 3 like a cat; stealthy: *With noiseless, feline movements the hunter stalked the deer.* 1, 3 *adj.*, 2 *n.*

fell[1] (fel) See **fall.** *Snow fell last night.* v.

fell[2] (fel) 1 cause to fall; knock down: *One blow felled him to the ground.* 2 cut down a tree: *Loggers will fell these trees.* v.

fell[3] (fel) 1 cruel; fierce; terrible: *a fell blow.* 2 deadly; destructive: *a fell disease.* adj.

fel·low (fel′ō) 1 a man, boy, dog, etc.: *Never mind, old fellow. Poor fellow!* 2 a companion; one of the same class; an equal: *He was cut off from his fellows.* 3 the other one of a pair; a mate: *I have the fellow of your glove.* 4 being in the same or a like condition: *fellow citizens, fellow sufferers.* 1–3 *n.*, 4 *adj.*

☛ **Fellow** developed from an Old English word *fēolaga,* meaning 'partner, associate,' which in turn came from Old Norse *félagi,* meaning literally 'fee-layer, one who lays down a fee (for a partnership).'

fel·low·ship (fel′ō ship′) 1 companionship; friendliness. 2 being one of a group; membership; sharing: *I have enjoyed my fellowship with you in this club.* 3 a group of people having the same tastes or interests. n.

fel·on (fel′ən) a person who has committed a serious crime; a criminal: *Thieves and murderers are felons.* n.

fel·o·ny (fel′ə nē) a serious crime, such as burglary or murder. *n., pl.* **fel·o·nies.**

felt[1] (felt) See **feel.** *He felt the cat's soft fur. Things are felt with the hands.* v.

hat, āge, fär; let, ēqual, tėrm; it, īce
hot, ōpen, ôrder; oil, out; cup, pu̇t, rüle
əbove, takən, pencəl, lemən, circəs
ch, child; ng, long; sh, ship
th, thin; ᴛʜ, then; zh, measure

felt[2] (felt) 1 a kind of cloth that is not woven but made by rolling and pressing wool, hair, or fur together. 2 made of felt: *a felt hat.* 1 *n.,* 2 *adj.*

fe·male (fē′māl) 1 a woman or girl. 2 of women or girls: *Sewing is usually a female occupation.* 3 belonging to the sex that gives birth to young or produces eggs: *Mares, cows, and hens are female animals.* 4 an animal belonging to this sex. 1, 4 *n.,* 2, 3 *adj.*

fem·i·nine (fem′ə nin) 1 of women or girls: *Jewellery and lace are usually feminine belongings.* 2 like a woman; womanly. *adj.*

fen (fen) a marsh or swamp; bog. *n.*

fence (fens) 1 something put around a yard, garden, field, farm, etc. to show where it ends or to keep people or animals out or in: *Most fences are made of wood, wire, or metal. A stone fence is a wall. A fence of growing bushes is a hedge.* 2 put a fence around. 3 fight, now only in sport, with long, slender swords called foils; compete in fencing (def. 1). 1 *n.,* 2, 3 *v.,* **fenced, fenc·ing.** —**fenc′er,** *n.*
on the fence, not having made up one's mind which side to take.

Fencing with foils

fenc·ing (fen′sing) 1 the art of fighting, now only as a sport, with swords or foils. 2 material for a fence (def. 1). *n.*

fend·er (fen′dər) 1 a curved protective covering over the wheels of an automobile, truck, etc.; mudguard: *The fenders prevent mud from splashing when the vehicle is moving.* 2 a guard, made of plastic, rubber, rope, etc., used to protect the sides of a boat: *Fenders may be attached to the side of the boat or to the dock.* 3 a metal guard, frame, or screen in front of a fireplace to keep hot coals and sparks from the room. *n.*

fer·ment (fər ment′ for 1, 2, and 5, fėr′ment for 3 and 4) 1 undergo a gradual chemical change, becoming sour or alcoholic and giving off bubbles of gas: *Vinegar is formed when cider ferments.* 2 cause such a change in. 3 a substance that causes other substances to ferment: *Yeast is used as a ferment in brewing beer.* 4 tumult; excitement: *The school was in a ferment.* 5 excite; be excited. 1, 2, 5 *v.,* 3, 4 *n.*

fer·men·ta·tion (fėr′mən tā′shən) 1 the act or process of fermenting: *Fermentation causes milk to sour and bread to rise.* 2 excitement; unrest: *There was a long period of fermentation before the outbreak of revolution.* *n.*

fern (fėrn) a kind of plant that has roots, stems, and leaves, but no flowers: *The tiny seeds (called spores) of the fern grow in the little brown dots on the backs of the feathery leaves.* *n.*

fe·ro·cious (fə rō′shəs) fierce; savage: *a ferocious tiger.* *adj.*

fe·roc·i·ty (fə ros′ə tē) fierceness; savage behavior: *The Vikings were noted for their ferocity in battle.* *n., pl.* **fe·roc·i·ties.**

fer·ret (fer′it) 1 a kind of weasel used for killing rats, driving rabbits from their holes, etc. 2 hunt with ferrets. 3 hunt; search: *The detectives ferreted out the criminal.* 1 *n.,* 2, 3 *v.*

Fer·ris wheel (fer′is wēl′ or fer′is hwēl′) a large, revolving, wheel-like framework of steel equipped with swinging seats that hang from its rim: *Ferris wheels are found in the amusement areas of fairs, exhibitions, and carnivals.*

fer·ry (fer′ē) 1 a boat that carries people and goods back and forth across a river or narrow stretch of water. 2 carry back and forth by boat: *Hundreds of cars are ferried to Prince Edward Island every day.* 3 a place where a ferryboat operates. 4 go across in a ferryboat: *They ferried to Wolfe Island last Sunday.* 1, 3 *n., pl.* **fer·ries;** 2, 4 *v.,* **fer·ried, fer·ry·ing.**
☞ **Ferry** and **fairy** are pronounced the same.

fer·ry·boat (fer′ē bōt′) a ferry (def. 1). *You can travel from Nova Scotia to Prince Edward Island by ferryboat.* *n.*

fer·tile (fėr′tīl or fėr′təl) 1 capable of bearing seeds, fruit, or young: *The apple tree was remarkably fertile. Having a baby proves that a woman is fertile.* 2 of soil, capable of producing plants, crops, etc.: *Sand is not very fertile.* 3 of animals, capable of giving birth to many young: *Rabbits are fertile creatures, for they have litters of young more often than many other animals.* 4 productive of many ideas; inventive: *a fertile mind.* *adj.*

fer·til·i·ty (fėr til′ə tē) the condition of being fertile: *Fertility of the mind means power to produce many ideas.* *n.*

fer·ti·li·za·tion (fėr′tə lə zā′shən) 1 fertilizing or being fertilized. 2 the joining of male and female reproductive cells to form a cell that will develop into a new individual. *n.*

fer·ti·lize (fėr′tə līz′) 1 make fertile. 2 cause something to start growing. 3 make soil richer by adding manure or some other fertilizer: *Many farmers fertilize their land every year.* *v.,* **fer·ti·lized, fer·ti·liz·ing.**

fer·ti·liz·er (fėr′tə līz′ər) manure or any substance that makes soil richer in plant foods when it is spread over or put into the soil. *n.*

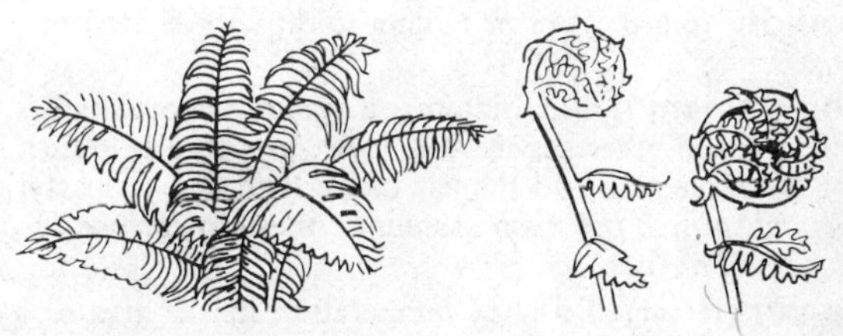
A kind of fern common in New Brunswick

Fiddleheads of this fern

fer·vent (fėr′vənt) showing warmth of feeling; very earnest; intense: *a fervent plea. adj.*

fer·vid (fėr′vid) showing great warmth of feeling; intensely emotional: *a fervid public speaker. adj.*

fer·vor or **fer·vour** (fėr′vər) great warmth of feeling; enthusiasm; earnestness: *The patriot's voice trembled from the fervor of his emotion. n.*

fes·ti·val (fes′tə vəl) **1** a day or special time of rejoicing or feasting, often in memory of some great happening: *Christmas and Easter are two festivals of the Christian church.* **2** a celebration; entertainment: *Every year the city has a music festival during the first week in May.* **3** a competition among drama groups, orchestras, etc. for recognition as the best in a region: *the Dominion Drama Festival. n.*

fes·tive (fes′tiv) of or suitable for a feast or holiday; gay; merry: *Her birthday was a festive occasion. adj.*

fes·tiv·i·ty (fes tiv′ə tē) a festive activity; something done to celebrate: *The wedding festivities were very exciting. n., pl.* **fes·tiv·i·ties.**

fes·toon (fes tün′) **1** flowers, leaves, ribbons, etc. hanging in a curve: *The flags were hung on the wall in colorful festoons.* **2** decorate with festoons: *The house was festooned with Christmas decorations.* 1 *n.,* 2 *v.*

fetch (fech) **1** go and get; bring: *Please fetch me my glasses.* **2** be sold for: *These eggs will fetch a good price. v.*

fetch·ing (fech′ing) *Informal.* charming; attractive: *She wore a fetching hat. adj.*

fete or **fête** (fāt) **1** a gala entertainment or celebration, usually held outdoors; festival: *She is holding a fete for the benefit of the hospital.* **2** give parties for; entertain: *The engaged couple were feted by their friends.* 1 *n.,* 2 *v.,* **fet·ed** or **fêt·ed, fet·ing** or **fêt·ing.**

☛ **Fete** and **fate** are pronounced the same.

fet·ter (fet′ər) **1** a chain or shackle for the feet: *Fetters prevented a prisoner's escape.* **2** bind with fetters; chain the feet of. **3** anything that shackles or binds; restraint. **4** bind; restrain: *The boy had to learn to fetter his temper.* 1, 3 *n.,* 2, 4 *v.*

fe·tus or **foe·tus** (fē′təs) an embryo of human beings, animals, or birds, during the later stages of its development in the womb or in the egg. *n.*

feud (fyüd) **1** a long and deadly quarrel between families, often passed on from one generation to another. **2** bitter hatred between two persons or groups. **3** engage in a deadly quarrel, especially one between families: *They have been feuding with their neighbors for years.* 1, 2 *n.,* 3 *v.*

feu·dal (fyü′dəl) of or having to do with feudalism. *adj.*

feu·dal·ism (fyü′dəl iz′əm) a system under which military and other service was given to a lord in return for his protection and the use of his land and property: *Feudalism was the main system of Western Europe in the Middle Ages. n.*

fe·ver (fē′vər) **1** a body temperature that is greater than usual: *A sick person usually has a fever.* **2** any sickness that heats the body and makes the heart beat fast: *scarlet fever.* **3** an excited, restless condition: *a fever of excitement. n.*

fe·vered (fē′vərd) **1** having fever; hot with fever: *a fevered brow.* **2** excited; restless: *Fevered excitement swept the crowd watching the first moon landing on the large TV screen. adj.*

fe·ver·ish (fē′vər ish) **1** having fever: *A feverish child is usually ill.* **2** having some fever but not much. **3** caused by fever: *feverish thirst, feverish dreams.* **4** excited; restless: *He packed his bags in feverish haste. adj.*

few (fyü) **1** not many: *There are few women more than* 185 cm *tall.* **2** a small number: *Only a few of the boys had bicycles.* 1 *adj.,* 2 *n.*

A fez

fez (fez) a felt cap, usually red and ornamented with a long, black tassel. *n.*

fi·an·cé (fē′än sā′ or fē′än sā′) a man to whom a woman is engaged to be married: *She introduced her fiancé to her friends. n.*

fi·an·cée (fē′än sā′ or fē′än sā′) a woman to whom a man is engaged to be married: *He had known his fiancée since childhood. n.*

fi·as·co (fē as′kō) a failure; breakdown: *The wiener roast was a complete fiasco because they forgot to bring the wieners. n., pl.* **fi·as·cos** or **fi·as·coes.**

fib (fib) *Informal.* **1** a lie about some small matter. **2** tell such a lie: *He fibbed when he said he had not eaten the last cookie in the box.* 1 *n.,* 2 *v.,* **fibbed, fib·bing.**

fi·bre or **fi·ber** (fī′bər) **1** one of the threadlike parts or strands that form certain plant and animal substances: *muscle fibres.* **2** a substance made up of such threadlike parts: *Hemp fibre can be spun into rope or woven into a coarse cloth.* **3** texture: *cloth of coarse fibre.* **4** character; nature: *A person of strong moral fibre can resist temptation. n.*

fick·le (fik′əl) changing; not constant; likely to change without reason: *fickle fortune, a fickle friend. adj.*

fic·tion (fik′shən) **1** stories telling mainly of imaginary happenings to imaginary people: *Short stories and novels are fiction.* **2** imaginary happenings; make-believe: *Her account of the adventure was pure fiction. The newspaper article was so imaginative that it was hard to tell fact from fiction.* **3** a made-up story: *The report of the school burning down turned out to be a fiction. n.* —**fic′tion·al,** *adj.*

fic·ti·tious (fik tish′əs) **1** not real; imaginary; made-up: *Characters in stories are usually fictitious.* **2** used in order to deceive; false: *The criminal used a fictitious name. adj.*

fid·dle (fid′əl) **1** *Informal.* violin. **2** *Informal.* play on a violin. **3** make aimless movements; play restlessly: *The nervous boy fiddled with his hat.* 1 *n.,* 2, 3 *v.,* **fid·dled, fid·dling.** —**fid′dler,** *n.*

fid·dle·head (fid′əl hed′) the young leaves, or fronds, of certain ferns, eaten as a delicacy: *Fiddleheads are*

hat, āge, fär; let, ēqual, tėrm; it, īce
hot, ōpen, ôrder; oil, out; cup, put, rüle
əbove, takən, pencəl, lemən, circəs
ch, child; ng, long; sh, ship
th, thin; ᴛʜ, then; zh, measure

found especially in Nova Scotia and New Brunswick. See **fern** for picture. *n.*

fid·dle·neck (fid′əl nek′) fiddlehead. *n.*

fi·del·i·ty (fə del′ə tē or fī del′ə tē) **1** loyalty; being faithful. **2** accuracy; exactness: *He told of his adventures with clarity and fidelity.* *n., pl.* **fi·del·i·ties.**

fidg·et (fij′it) **1** move about restlessly; be uneasy: *My little brother fidgets if he has to sit still a long time.* **2 the fidgets,** a state of being restless or uneasy: *The long tiresome speech gave us the fidgets.* 1 *v.,* 2 *n.* **—fidg′et·y,** *adj.*

fie (fī) for shame; shame: *Fie upon you!* *interj.*

field (fēld) **1** a piece of land used for crops or for pasture: *a wheat field.* **2** land with few or no trees: *They rode through forest and field.* **3** a piece of land used for some special purpose: *a playing field.* **4** land yielding some product: *the coal fields of Alberta, the gold fields of South Africa.* **5** the place where military activities are engaged in, especially a battlefield. **6** a large, flat space; broad surface: *A field of ice surrounds the North Pole.* **7** a range of opportunity or interest; sphere of special activity: *the field of politics, the field of art, the field of science.* **8** the whole group of competitors in a race or other contest: *At the halfway mark in the marathon, a Canadian was leading the field.* **9** in baseball, stop a batted ball and throw it in. 1–8 *n.,* 9 *v.*

in the field, a an area where military activity is taking place, especially fighting. **b** in baseball, in the playing area beyond the infield or diamond.

field day a day set aside for athletic contests and outdoor sports.

field·er (fēl′dər) **1** in baseball, a player who is stationed outside the diamond to stop the ball and throw it in. **2** in cricket, a person playing a similar position. *n.*

Field glasses

field glasses a pair of small, portable telescopes made for use with both eyes together: *Field glasses are often used by bird watchers.*

field goal in football, a goal counting three points scored by kicking the ball between the uprights and above the bar of the goal post.

field hockey a game played on a grass field by two teams whose players, except the goalie, use curved sticks and try to drive a ball into the opposing team's goal.

field trip a trip to give students special opportunities for observing facts relating to a particular field of study: *The teacher took her class on a field trip to teach them about different kinds of trees.*

fiend (fēnd) **1** a devil; an evil spirit. **2** a very wicked or cruel person. **3** *Informal.* a person who indulges excessively in some habit, practice, game, etc.: *He is a fiend for work.* *n.*

fiend·ish (fēn′dish) very cruel or wicked; devilish: *fiendish torture.* *adj.*

fierce (fērs) **1** savage; wild: *a fierce lion.* **2** raging; violent: *fierce anger, a fierce wind.* **3** *Informal.* intense; extreme: *The heat was fierce.* *adj.,* **fierc·er, fierc·est.** **—fierce′ly,** *adv.* **—fierce′ness,** *n.*

fier·y (fīr′ē) **1** containing fire; burning; flaming. **2** like fire; very hot; brilliant; glowing: *She wore a fiery red dress.* **3** full of feeling or spirit: *a fiery speech.* **4** easily aroused or excited: *a fiery temper.* *adj.,* **fier·i·er, fier·i·est.**

fi·es·ta (fē es′tə) **1** a religious festival; a saint's day. **2** a holiday or festivity. *n.*

fife (fīf) **1** a small, shrill musical instrument like a flute, played by blowing: *Fifes are used with drums to make music for marching.* **2** play on a fife. 1 *n.,* 2 *v.,* **fifed, fif·ing.**

fif·teen (fif′tēn′) five more than ten; 15. *n., adj.*

fif·teenth (fif′tēnth′) **1** next after the 14th; last in a series of fifteen; 15th. **2** one of 15 equal parts. *adj., n.*

fifth (fifth) **1** next after the 4th; last in a series of five; 5th. **2** one of 5 equal parts: *Twenty cents is a fifth of a dollar.* *adj., n.*

fif·ti·eth (fif′tē ith) **1** next after the 49th; last in a series of fifty; 50th. **2** one of 50 equal parts. *adj., n.*

fif·ty (fif′tē) five times ten; 50. *n., pl.* **fif·ties;** *adj.*

fig (fig) **1** a small, soft, sweet fruit that grows in warm regions: *Figs are usually dried like dates and raisins.* **2** the tree figs grow on. *n.*

fight (fīt) **1** take part in a violent struggle: *When boys fight, they try to hit one another. Countries fight with armies.* **2** a combat or contest: *A fight ends when one side gives up.* **3** a quarrel. **4** take part in a fight against; struggle against: *to fight disease. We may fight against our own feelings and desires.* **5** disagree angrily; quarrel: *The girls were always fighting about one thing or another.* **6** the power or will to fight: *There is fight in the old dog yet.* 1, 4, 5 *v.,* **fought, fight·ing;** 2, 3, 6 *n.*

fight back, offer resistance; show fight: *They had no heart to fight back.*

fight it out, fight until one side wins.

fight off, a turn back; repel: *Fight off an enemy attack.* **b** overcome; stop the progress of: *He took some pills in order to fight off a cold.*

fight on, continue struggling.

fight shy of, keep away from.

show fight, resist; be ready to fight: *The hunted animal was too weary to show fight.*

fight·er (fīt′ər) **1** one that fights. **2** an airplane equipped for combat: *During World War II many Canadians flew fighters in battle.* *n.*

fig·ure (fig′ər or fig′yər) **1** a symbol for a number: *The symbols 1, 2, 3, etc. are called figures.* **2** use numbers to find out the answer to some problem. **3 figures,** *pl.* calculations using figures; arithmetic: *She was never very good at figures.* **4** price: *His figure for that house is very high.* **5** a shape in geometry: *Squares, triangles, cubes, and other such shapes are* *called figures.* **6** a form or shape: *I could see the figure of a woman against the window.* **7** a person considered from the point of view of appearance, manner, etc.: *The poor old woman was a figure of distress. He cut a poor figure.* **8** a person; character: *Samuel de Champlain was a great figure in Canadian history.* **9** be conspicuous; appear: *The names of great leaders figure in the story of human progress.* **10** a picture; drawing; diagram; illustration: *This dictionary makes use of many figures to help explain the meanings of words.* **11** a design or pattern: *They disliked the figures on the wallpaper.* **12** decorate with a design or pattern. **13** think; consider. 1, 3–8, 10, 11 *n.*, 2, 9, 12, 13 *v.*, **fig·ured, fig·ur·ing.**

figure of speech, an expression in which words are used out of their literal meaning or in unusual combinations to add beauty or force: *'He is as strong as a horse' is a figure of speech.*

figure on, *Informal.* depend on; rely on: *We are figuring on your help in painting the house.*

figure out, a find out by using figures: *She soon figured out how much it would cost.* **b** think out; understand: *He couldn't figure out what was meant.*

fig·ured (fig′ərd or fig′yərd) **1** decorated with a design or pattern; not plain. **2** formed; shaped. *adj.*

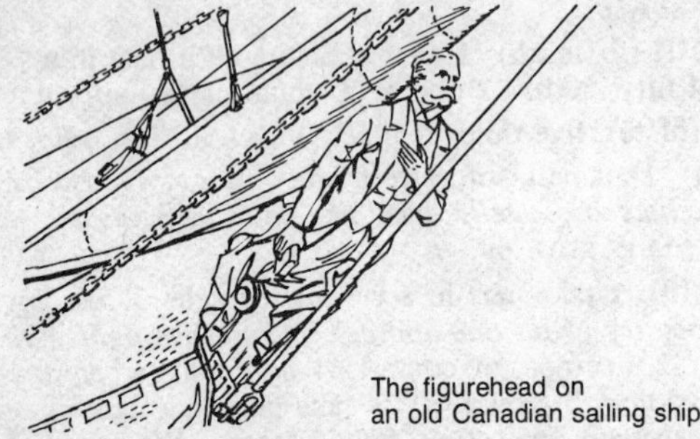

The figurehead on an old Canadian sailing ship

fig·ure·head (fig′ər hed′ or fig′yər hed′) **1** a person who is the head in name only, having no real authority or responsibility. **2** a statue or carving decorating the bow of a ship. *n.*

fig·ure–skate (fig′ər skāt′ or fig′yər skāt′) engage in figure skating. *v.*, **fig·ure-skat·ed, fig·ure-skat·ing.**

fig·ure–skat·er (fig′ər skā′tər or fig′yər skā′tər) a person who figure-skates. *n.*

figure skating the art or practice of performing figures and balletic programs on ice skates, often to music.

fil·a·ment (fil′ə mənt) **1** a very fine thread. **2** a very slender part that is like a thread: *The wire that gives off light in an electric light bulb is a filament. n.*

fil·bert (fil′bərt) **1** a hazelnut, the thick-shelled, sweet nut of any kind of hazel: *Filberts are good to eat.* **2** the tree or shrub it grows on. *n.*

filch (filch) steal in small quantities: *He filched apples from the basket. v.*

file[1] (fīl) **1** a place for keeping papers in order. **2** a set of papers kept in order. **3** put away papers or letters in order. **4** a row of persons or things one behind another: *a file of soldiers, six ships sailing in file.* **5** march or move in a such a row. 1, 2, 4 *n.*, 3, 5 *v.*, **filed, fil·ing.**

on file, in a file; put away and kept in order: *The principal keeps all our school reports on file.*

Files

file[2] (fīl) **1** a steel tool with many small ridges or teeth on it: *The rough surface of a file is used to wear away hard substances or to smooth rough materials.* **2** smooth or wear away with a file. 1 *n.*, 2 *v.*, **filed, fil·ing.**

fi·let (fi lā′) a slice of fish or meat without bones or fat; fillet. *n.*

fil·i·al (fil′ē əl) of a son or daughter; due from a son or daughter toward a mother or father: *The children treated their parents with filial respect. adj.*

filing cabinet a set of steel or wooden drawers for storing files of letters or other papers.

fil·ings (fīl′ingz) the small pieces of iron, wood, etc. that have been removed by a file. *n. pl.*

fill (fil) **1** make full; put into until there is room for nothing more: *Fill this bottle with water. Fill this hole with something.* **2** become full: *The well filled with water.* **3** take up all the space in: *Children filled the room.* **4** something that fills: *Earth or rock used to make uneven land level is called fill.* **5** all that is needed or wanted: *He ate his fill.* **6** supply what is needed for: *The druggist filled the doctor's prescription.* **7** stop up or close by putting something in: *After the dentist had taken out the decayed part, he filled my tooth.* 1–3, 6, 7 *v.*, 4, 5 *n.*

fill out, complete a question form, an application etc.; enter requested information on a form.

fil·let (fil′ət) **1** a slice of meat or fish without bones or fat. **2** cut into fillets: *John filleted the fish.* 1 *n.*, 2 *v.*

fill·ing (fil′ing) anything put in to fill something: *a filling in a tooth. n.*

fil·ly (fil′ē) a young female horse; a mare that is less than four or five years old. *n.*

film (film) **1** a very thin layer, surface, or coating, often of liquid: *a film of dew. Oil poured on water will spread and make a film.* **2** cover or become covered with a film: *Tears filmed his eyes.* **3** a roll or sheet of thin material covered with a special coating and used to take photographs: *He bought two rolls of film for the camera.* **4** motion picture: *We saw a film about animals.* **5** make a motion picture of: *Walt Disney filmed the story of Pinocchio.* **6** photograph for motion pictures: *They filmed the scene three times.* 1, 3, 4 *n.*, 2, 5, 6 *v.*

film·y (fil′mē) **1** like film; very thin. **2** covered with a film. *adj.*, **film·i·er, film·i·est.**

fil·ter (fil′tər) **1** a device for passing water or other liquids, or air, through felt, paper, sand, or charcoal, in order to remove impurities. **2** the material a filter is made of. **3** pass or flow slowly through a filter: *The*

hat, āge, fär; let, ēqual, tėrm; it, īce
hot, ōpen, ôrder; oil, out; cup, pu̇t, rüle
ə bove, takən, pencəl, lemən, circəs
ch, child; ng, long; sh, ship
th, thin; ᴛʜ, then; zh, measure

water filters through the sand. 4 put through a filter: *We filter this water for drinking.* 5 act as a filter for: *The charcoal filtered the water.* 6 remove by a filter. 1, 2 *n.,* 3–6 *v.*

filter tip a cigarette having a filter at one end, for filtering impurities from the smoke.

filth (filth) 1 foul, disgusting dirt: *Filth clogged the drain from the sink.* 2 foul, disgusting speech or thought. *n.*

☛ **Filth** developed from an Old English word, *fȳlth,* meaning 'the condition of being foul, or decomposed.'

filth·y (fil′thē) very dirty; foul. *adj.,* **filth·i·er, filth·i·est.**

fin (fin) 1 one of the movable, winglike parts of a fish's body, with which it moves the water in swimming and in balancing itself. See **fish** for picture. 2 anything shaped or used like a fin: *the tail fin of an airplane.* 3 flipper (def. 2). *n.*

☛ **Fin** and **Finn** are pronounced the same.

fi·nal (fī′nəl) 1 at the end; coming last: *The book was interesting from the first to the final chapter.* 2 deciding; settling. 3 something final: *The last examination of a school term is a final.* 4 **finals,** *pl.* the last or deciding set in a series of games, examinations, etc. 1, 2 *adj.,* 3, 4 *n.*

fi·na·le (fə nal′ē or fə nä′lē) 1 the last part of a piece of music or a play. 2 the last part; the end. *n.*

fi·nal·ize (fī′nəl īz′) bring to a conclusion; complete or finish in such a manner as to be final: *The committee hopes to finalize its report next week. v.*

☛ The word **finalize** is widely used, though many people object to its use in formal English.

fi·nal·ly (fī′nəl ē) at the end; at last: *The lost dog finally came home. adv.*

fi·nance (fī′nans or fə nans′) 1 money matters: *The millionaire had proved his skill in finance.* 2 provide money for: *Mrs. Jones financed her son's way through university.* 3 **finances,** *pl.* money; funds; revenues. 1, 3 *n.,* 2 *v.,* **fi·nanced, fi·nanc·ing.**

fi·nan·cial (fə nan′shəl or fī nan′shəl) having to do with money matters: *His financial affairs are in bad condition. adj.*

fin·an·cier (fin′ən sēr′ or fī′nən sēr′) a person occupied or skilled in money matters: *Bankers are financiers. n.*

finch (finch) a small songbird: *Sparrows, buntings, and canaries are finches. n.*

find (fīnd) 1 meet with; come upon: *He found a dollar in the road. People who look for trouble often find it.* 2 look for and get: *Please find my hat for me.* 3 get; get the use of: *Can you find time to do this?* 4 reach; arrive at: *Water finds its level.* 5 learn; discover: *We found that he could not swim.* 6 decide and declare: *The jury found the thief guilty.* 7 provide; supply: *He tried to find food and lodging for his friend.* 8 something found. 1–7 *v.,* **found, find·ing;** 8 *n.* **—find′er,** *n.*

find oneself, learn one's abilities and make good use of them.

find out, learn about; come to know; discover.

fine[1] (fīn) 1 very small or thin: *Thread is finer than rope. Sand is finer than gravel. A spider web is fine.* 2 excellent; of high quality: *Everybody praised her fine singing. Montcalm was a fine general.* 3 delicate: *fine linen.* 4 refined: *fine manners.* 5 clear; pleasant: *fine weather. adj.,* **fin·er, fin·est. —fine′ly,** *adv.* **—fine′ness,** *n.*

fine[2] (fīn) 1 a sum of money paid as a punishment for not doing the right thing. 2 make pay such a sum: *The judge fined him ten dollars for speeding.* 1 *n.,* 2 *v.,* **fined, fin·ing.**

fin·er·y (fīn′ər ē) showy clothes or ornaments. *n., pl.* **fin·er·ies.**

fin·ger (fing′gər) 1 one of the five end parts of the hand, especially the four besides the thumb. See **arm** for picture. 2 anything shaped or used like a finger. 3 touch or handle with the fingers; use the fingers on: *to finger the keyboard of a piano.* 1, 2 *n.,* 3 *v.*

fin·ger·ling (fing′ger ling) a small fish no longer than a finger. *n.*

fin·ger·nail (fing′gər nal′) the hard layer of horn at the end of a finger. *n.*

finger paint any kind of thickened water colors for use in finger painting.

finger painting 1 a way of applying paint by using fingers, palms, or the whole hands instead of brushes. 2 a design or picture painted in this way: *She put her best finger painting up on the wall.*

fin·ger·print (fing′gər print′) 1 an imprint of the markings on the inner surface of the last joint of a thumb or finger: *The murderer was identified by the fingerprints he left on the gun.* 2 take the fingerprints of. 1 *n.,* 2 *v.*

fin·i·cal (fin′ə kəl) too dainty or particular; too exact; fussy: *He's terribly finical about his food. adj.*

fin·ick·y (fin′ə kē) finical. *adj.*

fin·ish (fin′ish) 1 complete; bring to an end; reach the end of: *to finish a dress, to finish one's dinner, to finish a race.* 2 the end: *a fight to the finish.* 3 the way in which the surface is prepared: *a smooth finish on furniture.* 4 prepare the surface of in some way. 5 perfection; polish: *There is an expert finish to this photographer's work.* 1, 4 *v.,* 2, 3, 5 *n.*

☛ **Finish** and **Finnish** are pronounced the same.

Finn (fin) a person born in or living in Finland, a country in northern Europe. *n.*

☛ **Finn** and **fin** are pronounced the same.

Finn·ish (fin′ish) 1 of or having to do with Finland. 2 the language of Finland. 1 *adj.,* 2 *n.*

☛ **Finnish** and **finish** are pronounced the same.

fiord (fyôrd) a long, narrow bay bordered by steep cliffs: *Norway has many fiords. n.* Also spelled **fjord.**

A branch of fir with cones

fir (fėr) an evergreen tree resembling a pine: *Small firs* *are often used for Christmas trees. n.*

☛ **Fir** and **fur** are pronounced the same.

fire (fīr) **1** the flame, heat, and light caused by something burning: *Fire destroys many acres of forest each summer in Canada. Fire has many valuable uses.* **2** a burning mass of fuel: *Put more wood on the fire.* **3** fuel arranged for burning: *He built a fire in the fireplace ready for lighting later.* **4** a destructive burning: *A great fire destroyed the furniture factory.* **5** cause to burn; set on fire: *The gardener fired the pile of dead leaves.* **6** dry with heat; bake: *Clay bricks are fired to make them hard.* **7** supply fuel to; tend: *The men fired the steamship's huge furnaces.* **8** arouse; excite; inflame: *Stories of adventure fire the imagination.* **9** heat of feeling; readiness to act; excitement: *Their hearts were filled with patriotic fire.* **10** discharge a rifle, cannon, etc.: *The hunter fired four times at the fleeing deer.* **11** the discharging of guns: *The enemy's fire continued all night.* **12** *Informal.* dismiss from a job. 1–4, 9, 11 *n.*, 5–8, 10, 12 *v.*, **fired, fir·ing.**

catch fire, begin to burn: *Be careful that the curtains don't catch fire from the lamp.*

on fire, a burning. **b** excited: *The troops were on fire with the desire for victory.*

play with fire, meddle with something dangerous.

under fire, a exposed to shooting from the enemy's guns: *Soldiers are under fire in a battle.* **b** attacked; blamed.

fire·arm (fīr′ärm′) a rifle, pistol, or other gun such as a person can carry. *n.*

fire·boat (fīr′bōt′) a boat having equipment for putting out fires on a ship, dock, etc. *n.*

fire·brand (fīr′brand′) **1** a piece of burning wood. **2** a person who stirs up angry feelings in others. *n.*

fire·break (fīr′brāk′) a strip of land that has been cleared of trees or on which the sod has been turned over so as to prevent the spreading of a forest fire or a prairie fire. *n.*

fire·crack·er (fīr′krak′ər) a paper roll containing gunpowder and a fuse: *Firecrackers explode with a loud noise. n.*

fire department a municipal department in charge of the fighting and preventing of fires.

fire·dogs (fīr′dogz′) a pair of metal supports for wood in a fireplace. See **fireplace** for picture. *n. pl.*

A fire engine

fire engine a truck equipped with a pump, hoses, ladders, and other equipment for fighting fires.

fire escape a stairway or ladder used when a building is on fire.

fire extinguisher a container filled with chemicals that can be sprayed on a fire to extinguish it.

fire·fight·er (fīr′fīt′ər) **1** a member of a fire department; fireman. **2** a person who fights forest fires. *n.*

Fireflies. The line between them shows their actual length.

fire·fly (fīr′flī′) a small insect that gives off flashes of light that can be seen in the dark. *n., pl.* **fire·flies.**

fire hall **1** a building in which fire-fighting equipment is kept. **2** the headquarters of a fire department: *Permits for burning rubbish may be obtained at the fire hall.*

fire·light (fīr′līt′) the light from a fire. *n.*

fire·man (fīr′mən) **1** a man whose work is putting out fires. **2** a man who looks after fires in engines, furnaces, etc. *n., pl.* **fire·men** (fīr′mən).

A fireplace

fire·place (fīr′plās′) a place built to hold a fire: *There was a cheery blaze in the fireplace. n.*

fire·proof (fīr′prüf′) **1** that will not burn, or will not burn easily: *A building made entirely of steel and concrete is fireproof.* **2** make so that it will not burn, or not burn easily: *to fireproof a roof, to fireproof a theatre curtain.* 1 *adj.*, 2 *v.*

fire–reels (fīr′rēlz′) *Cdn.* fire engine. *n.*

fire·side (fīr′sīd′) **1** the space around the fireplace. **2** the hearth. **3** the home. **4** beside the fire: *fireside comfort.* 1–3 *n.*, 4 *adj.*

fire station fire hall.

fire–truck (fīr′truk′) fire engine. *n.*

fire·wood (fīr′wu̇d′) wood for burning in a stove, fireplace, etc. *n.*

fire·works (fīr′wėrks′) firecrackers, sky rockets, and other things that make a loud noise or a beautiful, fiery display, especially at night. *n. pl.*

firm¹ (fėrm) **1** not yielding when pressed: *firm flesh, firm ground.* **2** solid; fixed in place; not easily shaken or moved: *a tree firm in the earth.* **3** not easily changed; determined; resolute; positive: *a firm purpose, voice, character, or belief.* **4** not changing; staying the same; steady: *a firm price. adj.* **—firm′ness,** *n.*

firm² (fėrm) two or more persons in business together; a company: *an old and trusted firm. n.*

fir·ma·ment (fėr′mə mənt) the sky; the arch of the heavens. *n.*

first (fėrst) **1** coming before all others; lst: *He is first in his class.* **2** before all others; before anything else: *Ladies first. Before crossing the street, first look both ways.* **3** what is first; the beginning. **4** for the first time: *When I first met her, she was a child.* **5** rather; sooner: *The soldiers said they would never give up their*

flag, but would die first. 1 *adj.*, 2, 4, 5 *adv.*, 3 *n.*
at first, in the beginning: *At first, he did not like school.*

first aid the emergency treatment given to an injured person before a doctor comes.

first-class (fėrst′klas′) 1 of the highest class or best quality; excellent. 2 having the most comfortable accommodations on a ship, train, or aircraft: *First-class travel is expensive.* *adj.*

first-hand (fėrst′hand′) direct; from the original source: *first-hand information.* *adj., adv.*

first-rate (fėrst′rāt′) 1 of the highest class. 2 *Informal.* excellent; very good: *The meals are first-rate at that hotel.* *adj.*

firth (fėrth) especially in Scotland, a narrow arm of the sea, often the mouth of a river. *n.*

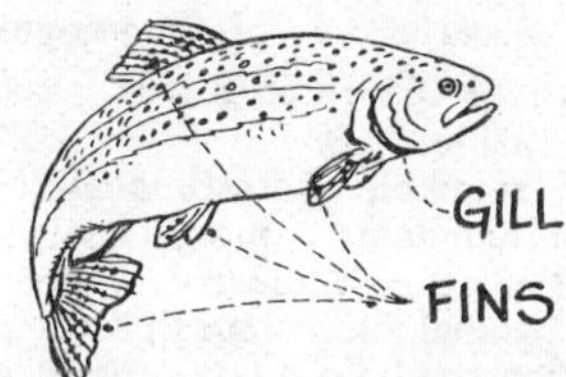

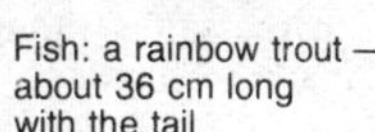
Fish: a rainbow trout — about 36 cm long with the tail

fish (fish) 1 a cold-blooded animal that lives in the water, has gills instead of lungs for breathing, and has a long backbone for support: *Fish are usually covered with scales and have fins for swimming.* 2 the flesh of fish used for food. 3 catch fish; try to catch fish: *The boys have been away fishing all day.* 4 search by groping about inside something: *He fished in his pockets for a match.* 5 try to get back or pick up something, as if with a hook: *He fished with a stick for his watch, which had fallen through a grating.* 6 find and take out: *He fished the map from the drawer.* 1, 2 *n., pl.* **fish** or **fish·es;** 3–6 *v.*

☛ The plural of **fish** is usually *fish* except when speaking definitely of different kinds of fish: *She had a string of eight fish. Most of the income of the island is from three fishes: cod, halibut, and salmon.*

fish and chips a dish consisting of fried fish and French fried potatoes.

fish·er (fish′ər) 1 an animal or bird that catches fish to eat. 2 an animal resembling a weasel, but larger; marten: *Fishers are trapped for their valuable fur.* 3 the fur of the fisher. *n.*

☛ **Fisher** and **fissure** are pronounced the same.

fish·er·man (fish′ər mən) a man who fishes, especially one who makes a living by doing so. *n., pl.* **fish·er·men** (fish′ər mən).

fish·er·y (fish′ər ē) 1 the occupation of catching fish. 2 a place for catching fish: *Salmon is the main catch in the Pacific fisheries.* *n., pl.* **fish·er·ies.**

fish flake a slatted platform used for drying fish: *Fish flakes are a familiar sight in Newfoundland fishing villages.*

fish-hook (fish′hůk′) a hook used to catch fish. See **barb** for picture. *n.*

fish·pond (fish′pond′) a pond in which there are fish, especially an ornamental pool where fish, such as goldfish, are kept in captivity. *n.*

fish stick 1 a frozen fish fillet packaged in the form of a short, oblong stick for ease in shipping and handling: *Each year, thousands of fish sticks are shipped from the Maritimes to markets in central Canada.* 2 a portion of fish, often breaded and pre-cooked, frozen and packaged for retail sale.

hat, āge, fär; let, ēqual, tėrm; it, īce
hot, ōpen, ôrder; oil, out; cup, půt, rüle
əbove, takən, pencəl, lemən, circəs
ch, child; ng, long; sh, ship
th, thin; ᴛʜ, then; zh, measure

fis·sion (fish′ən) a splitting apart, as of atoms to produce tremendous amounts of energy: *Atomic bombs are exploded by fission.* *n.*

fis·sure (fish′ər) a split; crack; long, narrow opening: *Water dripped from a fissure in the rock.* *n.*

☛ **Fissure** and **fisher** are pronounced the same.

fist (fist) the hand closed tightly: *He shook his fist at me.* *n.*

fit[1] (fit) 1 having the necessary qualities; right; suitable: *Grass is a fit food for cows; it is not fit for human beings. A lace dress is fit for parties.* 2 healthy and strong: *He is now well and fit for work.* 3 be right, proper, or suitable to: *Let the punishment fit the crime.* 4 make right, proper, or suitable: *to fit the action to the word.* 5 try to make fit; adjust: *He had trouble fitting the new part to the old machine.* 6 install; attach: *It took two hours to fit the new radio in the car.* 7 try to make fit; adjust: *Father was fitting new seat covers on our car.* 8 be of the proper shape and size: *The last piece of the puzzle didn't fit. The dress fitted her.* 9 the way something fits: *The coat was not a very good fit.* 1, 2 *adj.*, **fit·ter, fit·test;** 3–8 *v.*, **fit·ted, fit·ting;** 9 *n.* **—fit′ness,** *n.*
fit out, supply with everything needed.

fit[2] (fit) 1 a sudden, sharp attack of sickness: *a fit of colic.* 2 any sudden, sharp attack: *a fit of anger.* 3 a short period of doing some one thing: *a fit of laughing.* *n.*
by fits and starts, starting, stopping, beginning again, and so on; irregularly.

fit·ful (fit′fəl) irregular; going on and then stopping for a while: *a fitful sleep, a fitful conversation.* *adj.*

fit·ting (fit′ing) 1 right; proper; suitable; fit: *The happy ending was quite fitting.* 2 a trying on of unfinished clothes to see if they will fit. 3 **fittings,** *pl.* furnishings; fixtures: *Desks, chairs, and files are office fittings.* 1 *adj.*, 2, 3 *n.*

five (fīv) one more than four; 5. *n., adj.*

five pins a bowling game in which a large ball is rolled down a long, indoor alley with the aim of knocking down all of the five pins arranged upright at the other end: *Five pins is a popular Canadian game.*

fix (fiks) 1 make firm; become firm: *The man fixed the post in the ground. The boy fixed the spelling lesson in his mind.* 2 settle; set: *to fix a price, to fix an amount to be raised, to fix on a day for a picnic.* 3 direct or hold steady the eyes, attention, etc.; be directed. 4 put or place definitely: *She fixed blame on the leader.* 5 make or become stiff or rigid: *eyes fixed in death.* 6 *Informal.* set right; put in order; arrange: *to fix one's hair.* 7 mend or repair: *to fix a watch.* 8 *Informal.* a position hard to get out of: *The boy who cried 'Wolf' got himself into a bad fix.* 1–7 *v.*, **fixed, fix·ing;** 8 *n.*

fixed (fikst) 1 not movable; firm. 2 settled; set;

definite: *fixed charges for taxis.* **3** steady; not moving. *adj.*

fix·ture (fiks′chər) something put in place to stay: *A chandelier is a lighting fixture.* *n.*

fizz (fiz) **1** make a hissing sound. **2** a hissing sound; bubbling: *the fizz of soda water.* 1 *v.*, 2 *n.*

fiz·zle (fiz′əl) **1** hiss or sputter weakly: *The firecracker fizzled instead of exploding with a bang.* **2** a hissing; sputtering. 1 *v.*, **fiz·zled, fiz·zling;** 2 *n.*

fjord (fyôrd) See **fiord.**

fl. fluid.

flab·by (flab′ē) lacking firmness or force; soft or weak: *flabby flesh, a flabby will.* *adj.*, **flab·bi·er, flab·bi·est.**

flag[1] (flag) **1** a piece of cloth, often rectangular, that shows the emblem of a country, of a unit of the armed forces, or of some other organization: *The Canadian flag has a red maple leaf on a white background flanked by two red bars.* **2** a piece of cloth, often rectangular and of bright color, used as a decoration: *The hall was decorated with many flags.* **3** a piece of cloth of a certain shape, color, or design that has a special meaning: *A red flag is often a sign of danger, a white flag of surrender, a black flag of disaster.* **4** wave a flag or the arms with the intention of bringing something to a stop: *He flagged the train before it reached the broken bridge.* **5** communicate by means of flags: *The destroyer flagged a message to the freighter.* **6** place a flag or flags on; decorate with flags. 1–3 *n.*, 4–6 *v.*, **flagged, flag·ging.**

flag[2] (flag) the iris plant or flower: *We have lovely purple flags in our garden.* *n.*

flag[3] (flag) get tired; grow weak; droop: *Her horse was flagging, but she urged him on.* *v.*, **flagged, flag·ging.**

flag·on (flag′ən) **1** a container for liquids, having a handle, a spout, and a cover. **2** a large bottle holding about two litres. *n.*

flag·pole (flag′pōl′) a pole from which a flag is flown. *n.*

flag·stone (flag′stōn′) a large, flat stone, used for paving walks, patios, etc. *n.*

flail (flāl) **1** an instrument for threshing grain by hand: *A flail consists of a wooden handle with a short, heavy stick fastened at one end by a thong.* **2** strike with a flail. **3** beat; thrash. 1 *n.*, 2, 3 *v.*

flair (fler) a natural talent: *The poet had a flair for making rhymes. My sister has a flair for bargains.* *n.*

☛ **Flair** and **flare** are pronounced the same.

flake (flāk) **1** a flat, thin piece, usually not very large and often rather loosely held together: *a flake of snow, flakes of rust, corn flakes.* **2** come off in flakes; separate into flakes. **3** a slatted platform used for drying fish; fish flake. 1, 3 *n.*, 2 *v.*, **flaked, flak·ing.**

flam·boy·ant (flam boi′ənt) flaming; gorgeous; striking in a showy way: *flamboyant colors, flamboyant designs.* *adj.*

flame (flām) **1** one of the glowing tongues of light, usually red or yellow, that are seen when a fire blazes up: *Flames are caused when gas or vapor is burning. The house burst into flames.* **2** blaze; rise up in flames: *The dying fire suddenly flamed brightly.* **3** a blaze; burning with flames. **4** something like flame. 1, 3, 4 *n.*, 2 *v.*, **flamed, flam·ing.**

A red flamingo — about 150 cm high when standing

fla·min·go (flə ming′gō) a tropical wading bird with very long legs and neck, and feathers that vary from pink to scarlet. *n.*, *pl.* **fla·min·gos** or **fla·min·goes.**

flam·ma·ble (flam′ə bəl) easily set on fire; inflammable. *adj.*

☛ **Flammable** and **inflammable** mean the same, though **inflammable** is more usual in Canada (except in science and industry, where care is taken to use **flammable**). Note that the opposite is **non-flammable,** not **non-inflammable.**

flank (flangk) **1** the part of the side of the body between the hip and the ribs of animals or people. **2** the side of a mountain, building, etc. **3** be at the side of: *A garage flanked the house.* **4** the far right or the far left side of an army, fort, or fleet. **5** get around the side of an enemy's army in order to attack. 1, 2, 4 *n.*, 3, 5 *v.*

flan·nel (flan′əl) **1** a soft, warm material made of wool. **2** facecloth. *n.*

flap (flap) **1** swing or sway about loosely: *The sail flapped in the breeze.* **2** strike noisily with something broad and loose. **3** a blow from something broad and loose: *a flap from a beaver's tail.* **4** move wings up and down; fly by flapping the wings: *The goose flapped its wings but could not rise from the ground. At last it did rise and flapped heavily away through the air.* **5** a flapping motion; a flapping noise: *We heard the flap of a bird's wings.* **6** a piece hanging or fastened at one edge only: *He straightened the flap over the opening to his jacket pocket.* 1, 2, 4 *v.*, **flapped, flap·ping;** 3, 5, 6 *n.*

flap·jack (flap′jak′) pancake. *n.*

flare (fler) **1** flame up briefly or unsteadily, sometimes with smoke: *The lamp flared when it was turned too high.* **2** a blaze; a bright, brief, unsteady flame: *The burning match gave a last flare.* **3** burst into sudden action or feeling. **4** spread out in the shape of a bell: *This skirt flares at the bottom.* **5** spreading out into a bell shape. **6** a part that spreads out: *the flare of a skirt.* 1, 3, 4 *v.*, **flared, flar·ing;** 2, 5, 6 *n.*

flare up, a burst into sudden flame: *The dying fire flared up briefly.* **b** break out in a sudden outburst of emotion, such as anger or hatred: *His temper flared up and he struck out with his fist.*

☛ **Flare** and **flair** are pronounced the same.

flash (flash) **1** a sudden, brief light or flame: *a flash of lightning.* **2** give out such a light or flame: *The lighthouse flashes signals twice a minute.* **3** come suddenly; pass quickly: *A bird flashed across the road.* **4** a sudden, short feeling, outburst, or display: *a flash of hope, a flash of temper, a flash of wit.* **5** give out or send out like a flash. **6** a brief news report: *a news flash.* 1, 4, 6 *n.*, 2, 3, 5 *v.*

hat, āge, fär; let, ēqual, tėrm; it, īce
hot, ōpen, ôrder; oil, out; cup, pu̇t, rüle
əbove, takən, pencəl, lemən, circəs
ch, child; ng, long; sh, ship
th, thin; ᴛʜ, then; zh, measure

flash in the pan, a sudden, showy attempt or effort that often fails or is not followed by further efforts.
in a flash, in a very short time: *It all happened in a flash.*

flash bulb a bulb that gives a very bright light for an instant, used for taking photographs indoors, in shadow, or at night.

flash card one of a set of cards showing letters, words, figures, pictures, etc., intended mainly to be shown for a few moments for drills in reading, arithmetic, or some other subject.

flash cube a cube-shaped device containing four flash bulbs, that can be attached to certain kinds of camera so that four flash pictures can be taken without having to change bulbs.

flash·light (flash′līt′) a portable electric light: *Flashlights are operated by batteries.* *n.*

flash·y (flash′ē) 1 flashing; brilliant for a short time. 2 showy; gaudy: *He tries to impress the girls by wearing flashy clothes.* *adj.*, **flash·i·er, flash·i·est.**

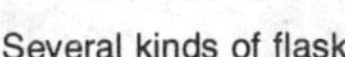

Several kinds of flask

flask (flask) 1 any bottle-shaped container, especially one having a narrow neck: *Flasks of thin glass are used in chemical laboratories for heating liquids.* 2 a small glass or metal bottle with flat sides, made to be carried in the pocket. *n.*

flat¹ (flat) 1 smooth and level; even: *flat land. This floor is flat.* 2 horizontal; at full length: *lying flat on the ground.* 3 the flat part: *He struck his enemy with the flat of his sword.* 4 land that is smooth and level. 5 not very deep or thick: *a flat dish, a flat bone.* 6 positive; not to be changed: *A flat refusal is complete. We paid a flat rate with no extra charges.* 7 without much interest or flavor; dull: *a flat voice, flat food. This is the flattest lemonade I have ever tasted.* 8 below the true pitch: *to sing flat.* 9 a tone one half step below natural pitch: *music written in B flat.* 10 the sign in music (♭) that shows this. 11 flatly: *He fell flat on the floor.* 12 make flat; become flat. 13 a flat tire. 1, 2, 5–7 *adj.*, **flat·ter, flat·test;** 3, 4, 9, 10, 13 *n.*, 8, 11 *adv.*, 12 *v.*, **flat·ted, flat·ting.** —**flat′ly,** *adv.* —**flat′ness,** *n.*

flat² (flat) an apartment or set of rooms on one floor. *n.*

flat–bot·tomed (flat′bot′əmd) having a flat bottom: *a flat-bottomed boat.* *adj.*

flat·car (flat′kär′) a railway freight car without roof or sides. *n.*

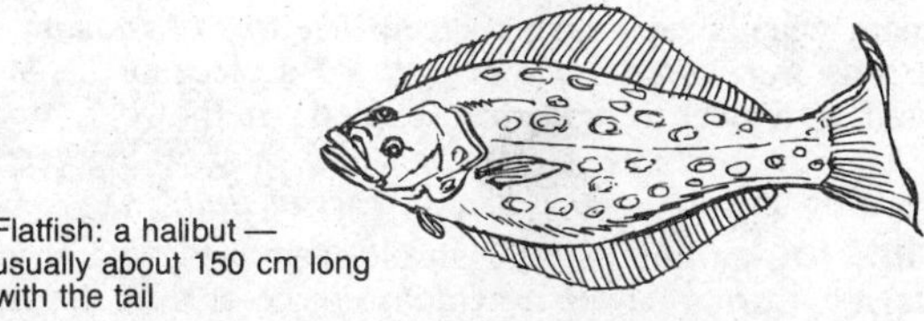
Flatfish: a halibut — usually about 150 cm long with the tail

flat·fish (flat′fish′) a flat-bodied fish: *Halibut, flounder, and sole are flatfish.* *n., pl.* **flat·fish** or **flat·fish·es.**

flat·i·ron (flat′ī′ərn) an iron with a flat surface for smoothing cloth. *n.*

flat·ten (flat′ən) make flat; become flat: *The silk has been wrinkled, but it will flatten out again if you iron it.* *v.*

flat·ter (flat′ər) 1 praise too much; praise beyond the truth. 2 show as more beautiful or better looking than is actually the case: *This picture flatters him.* 3 try to win over or please by praise, often not true. *v.* —**flat′ter·er,** *n.*

flat·ter·y (flat′ər ē) 1 the act of flattering. 2 words of praise, usually untrue or exaggerated: *Some people use flattery to get favors.* *n., pl.* **flat·ter·ies.**

flaunt (flont or flônt) 1 show off: *She flaunts her riches before her friends.* 2 wave proudly: *banners flaunting in the breeze.* *v.*

fla·vor or **fla·vour** (flā′vər) 1 a taste, especially a characteristic taste: *Chocolate and vanilla have different flavors.* 2 give added taste to; season: *We use salt, pepper, and spices to flavor food.* 3 a characteristic quality: *Stories about ships and sailors have a flavor of the sea.* 1, 3 *n.*, 2 *v.*

fla·vor·ing or **fla·vour·ing** (flā′vər ing) something used to give a particular taste to food or drink: *chocolate flavoring.* *n.*

fla·vour (flā′vər) See **flavor.**

flaw (flo or flô) a slight defect or fault; crack: *a flaw in a glass. His nasty temper is the only flaw in his character.* *n.*

flaw·less (flo′lis or flô′lis) perfect; without defect: *a flawless diamond.* *adj.*

flax (flaks) 1 a slender, upright plant having small, narrow leaves and blue flowers: *Linseed oil is made from flax seeds.* 2 the fibres from the stems of this plant prepared for spinning: *Flax is spun into linen thread for making linen cloth.* *n.*

flax·en (flak′sən) 1 made of flax. 2 like flax; pale-yellow: *flaxen hair.* *adj.*

flay (flā) 1 remove the skin from by whipping or lashing: *The tyrant had his enemies flayed alive.* 2 scold severely: *The angry man flayed his servant with his tongue.* *v.*

A flea. The line beside it shows its actual length.

flea (flē) a small jumping insect without wings: *Fleas feed on blood.* *n.*
☛ **Flea** and **flee** are pronounced the same.

fleck (flek) 1 a spot or patch of color, light, etc.: *Freckles are brown flecks on the skin.* 2 mark with spots of color, light, etc.: *The bird's breast is flecked with brown.* 1 *n.*, 2 *v.*

fled (fled) See **flee.** *The enemy fled when the cavalry attacked.* v.

fledg·ling or **fledge·ling** (flej′ling) **1** a young bird just able to fly. **2** a young, inexperienced person. *n.*

flee (flē) **1** run away: *The robbers tried to flee, but they were caught.* **2** go quickly: *The clouds are fleeing before the wind.* *v.,* **fled, flee·ing.**

☛ **Flee** and **flea** are pronounced the same.

fleece (flēs) **1** the wool that covers a sheep: *The coat of wool cut off or shorn from one sheep is called a fleece.* **2** cut the wool coat from a sheep. **3** strip of money or belongings; rob; cheat: *The gamblers fleeced him of a large sum.* 1 *n.,* 2, 3 *v.,* **fleeced, fleec·ing.**

fleec·y (flēs′ē) like a fleece; soft and white: *Fleecy clouds floated in the blue sky.* *adj.,* **fleec·i·er, fleec·i·est.**

fleet[1] (flēt) **1** a group of ships under one command: *the Canadian fleet.* **2** a group of boats, aircraft, automobiles, etc. moving or working together: *a fleet of fishing boats. A fleet of trucks carried the soldiers.* *n.*

fleet[2] (flēt) fast moving; rapid: *a fleet horse.* *adj.*

fleet·ing (flēt′ing) passing swiftly; soon gone. *adj.*

flesh (flesh) **1** of a human or animal body, the softer substance that covers the bones and is covered by skin: *Flesh consists mostly of muscles and fat.* **2** meat, especially of a sort not usually eaten by human beings: *horse flesh.* **3** the human body as opposed to the mind and soul: *'The spirit is willing, but the flesh is weak.'* **4** the soft part or the edible part of fruits and vegetables: *The McIntosh apple has crisp, juicy, white flesh.* *n.*

flesh and blood, one's family or relatives by birth; a child or relative by birth.

in the flesh, **a** alive. **b** actually present, not merely thought of; in person: *There stood John in the flesh.*

flesh·y (flesh′ē) **1** having much flesh: *The calf is the fleshy part of the lower leg.* **2** plump; fat. *adj.,* **flesh·i·er, flesh·i·est.**

fleur–de–lis (flėr′də lē′ or flėr′də lēs′) **1** the iris plant or flower. **2** the royal coat of arms of France. **3** the floral emblem of the province of Quebec. *n., pl.* **fleurs-de-lis** (flėr′də lē′ or flėr′də lēz′).

flew (flü) See **fly**[2]. *The bird flew away.* *v.*

☛ **Flew, flu,** and **flue** are pronounced the same.

flex (fleks) bend: *He slowly flexed his stiff arm.* *v.*

flex·i·ble (flek′sə bəl) **1** bending without breaking; not stiff; easily bent: *Leather, rubber, and wire are flexible materials.* **2** easily adapted to fit various uses, conditions, etc.: *His plans are flexible and he can come any day.* *adj.*

flick (flik) **1** a sudden, light blow or stroke: *The farmer drove the fly from his horse's head by a flick of his whip.* **2** strike lightly with a whip, finger, etc.: *He flicked the dust from his shoes with a handkerchief.* **3** move with a jerk: *The boys flicked wet towels at each other.* **4** a sudden jerk; a short, quick movement: *The fisherman made a short cast with a flick of his wrist.* 1, 4 *n.,* 2, 3 *v.*

flick·er[1] (flik′ər) **1** shine with a wavering, unsteady light: *The firelight flickered on the walls.* **2** a wavering, unsteady light or flame. **3** move lightly and quickly in and out, or back and forth: *The tongue of the snake flickered at us.* **4** a flickering movement: *the flicker of an eyelash.* 1, 3 *v.,* 2, 4, *n.*

flick·er[2] (flik′ər) a type of woodpecker that is common in North America. *n.*

fli·er (flī′ər) See **flyer.**

flies[1] (flīz) plural of **fly.** *n.*

flies[2] (flīz) See **fly**[2]. *A bird flies.* *v.*

A flight of stairs

flight[1] (flīt) **1** the act or manner of flying: *the flight of a bird through the air.* **2** the distance a bird, bullet, aircraft, etc. flies. **3** a group of things flying through the air together: *a flight of six airplanes.* **4** a trip in an aircraft. **5** a soaring above or beyond the ordinary: *a flight of fancy.* **6** a set of stairs or steps from one landing or one storey of a building to the next. *n.*

flight[2] (flīt) **1** the act of running away: *The soldiers were relieved to see the enemy in flight.* **2** an escape: *The flight of the prisoners was soon discovered.* *n.*

flight·y (flīt′ē) likely to have sudden fancies; full of whims; giddy: *She was too flighty to be reliable.* *adj.,* **flight·i·er, flight·i·est.**

flim·sy (flim′zē) **1** light and thin; slight; frail; without strength; easily broken: *The tissue paper she used to wrap my present was flimsy and tore off.* **2** not serious or convincing: *Her excuse was so flimsy that everybody laughed at her.* *adj.,* **flim·si·er, flim·si·est.**

flinch (flinch) **1** draw back or shrink from difficulty, danger, or pain: *The baby flinched when he touched the hot radiator.* **2** the act of drawing back: *He took his punishment without a flinch.* 1 *v.,* 2 *n.*

fling (fling) **1** throw forcefully; hurl violently: *The angry man flung his hat on the floor.* **2** a violent throw. **3** move rapidly; rush; flounce: *She flung angrily out of the room.* **4** move a part of the body in an impulsive, unrestrained way: *The girl happily flung her arms around her mother's neck.* **5** a time of doing as one pleases: *She had her fling when she was young.* **6** a lively Scottish dance: *the Highland fling.* 1, 3, 4 *v.,* **flung, fling·ing;** 2, 5, 6 *n.*

have a fling at, *Informal.* have a try at; attempt: *He had a fling at swimming across the river.*

flint (flint) **1** a very hard kind of stone that makes a spark when struck against steel: *The tips of Indian arrows were often made of flint.* **2** a piece of this stone, used with steel to light fires, explode gunpowder, etc.: *Flints are used in cigarette lighters.* **3** anything very hard or unyielding: *He had a heart of flint.* *n.*

flint·lock (flint′lok′) **1** an old-fashioned type of gun having a firing device in which a piece of flint striking against steel makes sparks to set off gunpowder. **2** the firing device in such a gun. *n.*

hat, āge, fär; let, ēqual, tėrm; it, īce
hot, ōpen, ôrder; oil, out; cup, pu̇t, rüle
əbove, takən, pencəl, lemən, circəs
ch, child; ng, long; sh, ship
th, thin; ᴛʜ, then; zh, measure

flint·y (flin′tē) 1 containing flint: *a flinty rock formation.* 2 hard like flint: *The boys were tired after walking over the flinty asphalt.* 3 hard; unyielding: *The sergeant had flinty eyes.* *adj.,* **flint·i·er, flint·i·est.**

flip (flip) 1 toss or move by the snap of a finger and thumb: *The man flipped a coin on the counter.* 2 move with a jerk or toss; flick: *The driver flipped his whip at a fly. The twig flipped back and scratched his face.* 3 a snap; a smart tap; a sudden jerk: *The cat gave the kitten a flip on the ear.* 4 turn over quickly: *He flipped the pages of the magazine. She flipped the eggs before serving them.* 5 a quick overturning: *The airplane took a flip just before it crashed.* 1, 2, 4 *v.,* **flipped, flip·ping;** 3, 5 *n.*

flip·pant (flip′ənt) smart or pert in speech or manner; not respectful: *The boy gave a flippant answer.* *adj.*

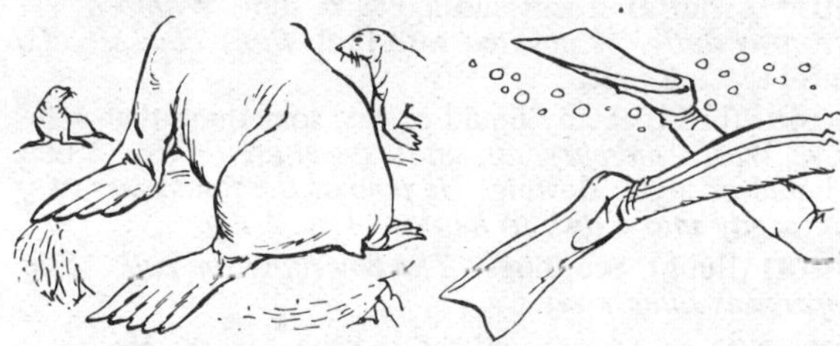

The flippers of a seal — Rubber flippers for the feet

flip·per (flip′ər) 1 a broad, flat fin especially adapted for swimming: *Seal flippers are a popular food in Newfoundland.* 2 a piece of rubber or plastic that fits onto the foot and has a broad, flat blade extending from the toe, used by swimmers to give extra power, especially when swimming under water: *A pair of flippers is part of every skindiver's equipment.* *n.*

flirt (flėrt) 1 play at being in love with someone; try frivolously or playfully to win a person's attention and affection: *The girl's father advised her not to flirt with boys.* 2 a person who flirts. 3 move quickly to and fro: *She flirted her fan to attract attention.* 1, 3 *v.,* 2 *n.*

flit (flit) 1 fly lightly and quickly; flutter: *A hummingbird flitted by.* 2 pass lightly and quickly: *Many idle thoughts flitted through his mind as he lay in the sun.* *v.,* **flit·ted, flit·ting.**

float (flōt) 1 stay on top of or be held up by air, water, or other liquid: *A cork floats but a stone sinks.* 2 anything that stays up or holds up something else in water: *A raft is a float. A cork on a fish line is a float.* 3 move along without trying; be moved along by the movement of what one is in or on: *The boat floated out to sea.* 4 a low, flat car that carries something to be shown in a parade. 5 a drink with ice cream in it: *an orange float.* 1, 3 *v.,* 2, 4, 5 *n.*

flock (flok) 1 animals of one kind that feed and move about in a group: *a flock of sheep, a flock of geese, a flock of birds.* 2 people of the same church group. 3 a large number; a crowd. 4 go in a flock; keep in groups: *Sheep usually flock together.* 5 come crowding; crowd: *The children flocked around the Christmas tree.* 1–3 *n.,* 4, 5 *v.*

floe (flō) a field or sheet of floating ice: *Seals are often found on floes.* *n.*

flog (flog) beat or whip hard. *v.,* **flogged, flog·ging.**

flood (flud) 1 fill to overflowing: *A wave flooded the holes I had dug in the sand.* 2 flow over or into: *When the heavy snow melted last spring, the river rose and flooded our fields.* 3 become covered or filled with water: *During the thunderstorm, our cellar flooded.* 4 cover the surface of something with water: *The attendants flooded the ice before every hockey game.* 5 a flow of water over what is usually dry land: *The heavy rains caused a serious flood in the district near the river.* 6 **the Flood,** the water that, according to the Bible, covered the earth in the time of Noah. 7 a large amount of water. 8 a great outpouring of anything: *a flood of words, a flood of light.* 9 fill, cover, or overcome, as with a flood: *The room was flooded with moonlight.* 1–4, 9 *v.,* 5–8 *n.*
in flood, filled to overflowing with an unusual amount of water: *The river was in flood.*

flood·light (flud′līt′) 1 a lamp that gives a broad beam of light: *Several floodlights were used to illuminate the stage.* 2 the broad beam of light from such a lamp. 3 illuminate with floodlights: *The baseball field was brightly floodlit for the night game.* 1, 2 *n.,* 3 *v.,* **flood·lit, flood·light·ing.**

floor (flôr) 1 the surface or part of a room that one walks or stands on: *The floor of this room is made of wood.* 2 put a floor in or on: *We will floor this room with oak.* 3 the flat surface at the bottom of anything: *They dropped their net to the floor of the ocean.* 4 a storey of a building: *Five families live on the fourth floor.* 5 knock down: *Steve floored him with one blow.* 6 *Informal.* confuse or puzzle completely: *The last question on the examination floored us all.* 7 the part of an assembly hall where the members sit: *the floor of the House of Commons.* 8 the right to speak in an assembly or at a meeting: *He began his speech as soon as he got the floor.* 1, 3, 4, 7, 8 *n.,* 2, 5, 6 *v.*

floor·ing (flôr′ing) material for making floors: *Tile is often used as flooring for bathrooms.* *n.*

flop (flop) 1 move loosely or heavily; flap around clumsily: *The fish flopped helplessly on the deck.* 2 fall, drop, throw, or move heavily or clumsily: *He flopped down into a chair.* 3 the act of flopping. 4 the sound made by flopping. 5 change or turn suddenly. 6 *Informal.* failure: *The new play was a flop.* 7 *Informal.* fail. 1, 2, 5, 7 *v.,* **flopped, flop·ping;** 3, 4, 6 *n.*

flop·py (flop′ē) *Informal.* flopping; tending to flop: *She bought a sun hat with a big floppy brim.* *adj.,* **flop·pi·er, flop·pi·est.**

flo·ral (flô′rəl) 1 of or having to do with flowers: *a floral exhibit, floral decorations.* 2 resembling flowers: *a floral design.* *adj.*

flor·in (flôr′ən) a gold or silver coin in use at various times in different countries of Europe. *n.*

flo·rist (flô′rist) a person who raises or sells flowers. *n.*

floss (flos) 1 short, loose silk fibres. 2 a shiny, untwisted silk thread made from such fibres: *Floss is* *used for cleaning between the teeth.* **3** soft, silky fluff or fibres: *Milkweed pods contain white floss.* *n.*

flounce[1] (flouns) **1** go with an angry or impatient movement of the body: *With an angry comment she flounced out of the room.* **2** an angry or impatient fling or turn of the body. 1 *v.,* **flounced, flounc·ing;** 2 *n.*

flounce[2] (flouns) **1** a wide strip of cloth gathered at the top edge and sewn to a dress, skirt, chesterfield cover, etc. as trimming; ruffle. **2** trim with a flounce or flounces. 1 *n.,* 2 *v.,* **flounced, flounc·ing.**

floun·der[1] (floun′dər) **1** struggle without making much progress; plunge about: *Men and horses were floundering in the deep snow beside the road.* **2** be clumsy or confused and make mistakes: *The girl was frightened by the audience and floundered through her song.* *v.*

floun·der[2] (floun′dər) a flatfish that has a large mouth. *n., pl.* **floun·der** or **floun·ders.**

flour (flour) **1** the fine meal made by grinding grain, especially wheat. **2** cover with flour. 1 *n.,* 2 *v.*

flour·ish (flėr′ish) **1** grow or develop with vigor; do well; thrive: *Your radishes are flourishing. His newspaper business grew and flourished.* **2** wave in the air: *He flourished the letter when he saw us.* **3** waving about: *The pianist gave a flourish of his hands and began to play.* **4** a showy decoration in handwriting. **5** a showy trill or passage in music: *a flourish of trumpets.* **6** a display or show of enthusiasm, heartiness, etc.: *The agent showed us about the house with much flourish.* 1, 2 *v.,* 3–6 *n.*

flout (flout) treat with disdain or contempt; mock; scoff at: *The disobedient boy flouted his mother's advice.* *v.*

flow (flō) **1** run like water: *A stream flows past the house.* **2** a current; stream: *There is a constant flow of water from the spring.* **3** glide; move easily: *a flowing movement in a dance, flowing verse.* **4** hang loosely: *flowing robes, a flowing tie.* **5** any smooth, steady movement: *a flow of words.* **6** pouring out: *a flow of blood.* 1, 3, 4 *v.,* 2, 5, 6 *n.*

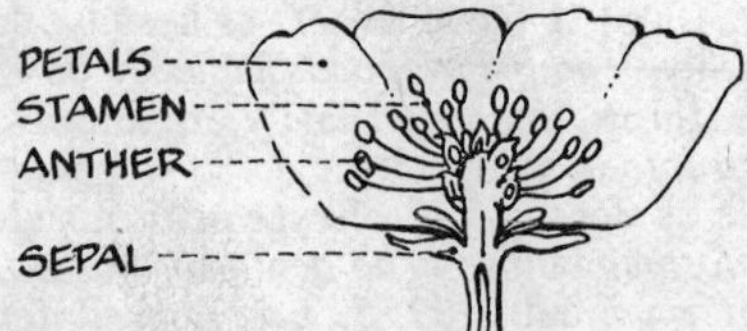

The parts of a flower

flow·er (flou′ər) **1** a blossom; the part of a plant or tree that produces the seed: *Bees gather nectar from flowers.* **2** a plant grown for its blossoms: *He sent his mother a bouquet of beautiful flowers.* **3** produce flowers; bloom; cover with flowers. **4** the finest part of a thing: *The flower of the country's youth was killed in the war.* 1, 2, 4 *n.,* 3 *v.*

flow·er·pot (flou′ər pot′) a pot to hold soil for a plant to grow in. *n.*

flow·er·y (flou′ər ē) **1** having many flowers. **2** full of fine words and fanciful expressions: *a flowery speech.* *adj.,* **flow·er·i·er, flow·er·i·est.**

flown (flōn) See **fly**[2]. *The bird has flown. The flag is flown on all government buildings.* *v.*

flu (flü) influenza. *n.*

☞ **Flu, flew,** and **flue** are pronounced the same.

flue (flü) a tube, pipe, or other enclosed passage for smoke or hot air: *A chimney often has several flues.* *n.*

☞ See note at **flu.**

flu·ent (flü′ənt) **1** flowing smoothly and easily: *Long practice enabled him to speak fluent French.* **2** speaking or writing easily and rapidly: *He was a fluent speaker.* *adj.*

fluff (fluf) **1** soft, light, downy particles: *Woollen blankets often have fluff on them.* **2** a soft, light, downy mass: *The little kitten looked like a fluff of fur.* **3** shake up into a soft, light mass: *Mother fluffs the pillows when she makes the bed.* 1, 2 *n.,* 3 *v.*

fluff·y (fluf′ē) **1** soft and light like fluff: *Whipped cream is fluffy.* **2** covered with fluff: *fluffy chicks.* *adj.,* **fluff·i·er, fluff·i·est.**

flu·id (flü′id) **1** any liquid or gas; something that will flow: *Water, mercury, air, and oxygen are fluids.* **2** like a liquid or a gas; flowing: *He poured the fluid mass of hot candy into a dish to harden.* 1 *n.,* 2 *adj.*

flung (flung) See **fling.** *The boy flung the ball. The paper was flung away.* *v.*

flunk (flungk) *Informal.* fail in school work: *He flunked his chemistry examination but passed all the others.* *v.*

flu·o·res·cent (flü′ə res′ənt or flůr es′ənt) that gives off light when it absorbs energy: *A fluorescent lamp gives off light when the coating on the inside of its tube absorbs energy from electrons produced by an electric current.* *adj.*

fluor·i·date (flůr′ə dāt′) add a fluoride to: *The water supply of many cities has been fluoridated to try to prevent tooth decay in children.* *v.,* **fluor·i·dat·ed, fluor·i·dat·ing.**

fluor·i·da·tion (flůr′ə dā′shən) the act or process of adding a fluoride. *n.*

flu·o·ride (flü′ə rīd′ or flůr′īd) a compound of fluorine and another element or compound. *n.*

flu·o·rine (flü′ə rēn′ or flůr′ēn) a poisonous, greenish-yellow chemical element normally occurring as a flammable gas: *Fluorine is similar to chlorine.* *n.*

flur·ry (flėr′ē) **1** a sudden gust of wind: *The flurry lifted off his hat and carried it away.* **2** a light fall of snow or, less usually, rain: *snow flurries.* **3** a sudden commotion; state of excitement: *a flurry of alarm.* **4** cause to be confused; excite or agitate: *The sight of the audience so flurried the young actor that he forgot his lines.* 1–3 *n., pl.* **flur·ries;** 4 *v.,* **flur·ried, flur·ry·ing.**

flush[1] (flush) **1** blush; glow: *The girl flushed when they laughed at her.* **2** cause to blush or glow: *Exercise flushed his face.* **3** a rosy glow or blush: *The flush of sunrise was on the clouds.* **4** a sudden rush; a rapid flow. **5** wash or cleanse with a sudden rush of water over or through: *The city streets were flushed every night.* 1, 2, 5 *v.,* 3, 4 *n.*

flush[2] (flush) **1** even; level: *Make that shelf just flush with this one. Their edges should be flush.* **2** having plenty; well supplied: *He received his summer wage, so is flush just now.* *adj.*

flush with money, having plenty of money; being well supplied with cash: *After a winter in the woods, loggers are usually flush with money.*

hat, āge, fär; let, ēqual, tėrm; it, īce
hot, ōpen, ôrder; oil, out; cup, pu̇t, rüle
əbove, takən, pencəl, lemən, circəs
ch, child; ng, long; sh, ship
th, thin; ᴛʜ, then; zh, measure

flush[3] (flush) start up suddenly; cause to start up suddenly: *Our dog flushed a partridge in the woods.* *v.*

flus·ter (flus′tər) **1** excite; confuse: *She was flustered by her surprise party.* **2** confusion. 1 *v.*, 2 *n.*

A flute

flute (flüt) **1** a long, slender wind instrument, played by blowing across a hole near one end: *Different tones are made on a flute by opening and closing holes along the tube with the fingers or with keys.* **2** play on a flute. 1 *n.*, 2 *v.*, **flut·ed, flut·ing.**

flut·ist (flüt′ist) a person who is skilled in playing a flute. *n.*

flut·ter (flut′ər) **1** wave back and forth quickly and lightly: *The flag fluttered in the breeze.* **2** flap the wings; flap: *The chickens fluttered excitedly when they saw the dog.* **3** come or go with a trembling or wavy motion: *The young bird fluttered to the ground.* **4** move restlessly. **5** tremble: *Her heart fluttered.* **6** a fluttering. **7** a state of excitement: *The appearance of the Queen caused a great flutter in the crowd.* 1–5 *v.*, 6, 7 *n.*

fly[1] (flī) **1** one of several kinds of insect with two wings: *The common housefly is a great nuisance.* See **maggot** for picture. **2** a fish-hook with feathers, silk, tinsel, etc. on it to make it look like a fly. *n., pl.* **flies.**

fly[2] (flī) **1** move through the air with wings: *Some birds fly long distances.* **2** float or wave in the air: *Our flag flies every day.* **3** cause to fly: *The boys are flying kites.* **4** travel through the air in an aircraft. **5** move swiftly; go rapidly: *The ship flies before the wind.* **6** run away. **7** a piece of canvas that serves as an extra, outer flap for a tent. **8** an opening in a garment, especially in the front of trousers. **9** a baseball hit high into the air with a bat: *She enjoys catching flies.* **10** hit a baseball high into the air: *The batter flied into left field.* 1–6, 10 *v.*, **flew, flown, fly·ing** for 1–6, **flied, fly·ing** for 10; 7–9 *n., pl.* **flies.**

fly·catch·er (flī′kach′ər) a bird that catches insects while flying. *n.*

fly·er or **fli·er** (flī′ər) **1** something that flies, such as a bird or an insect. **2** pilot. **3** a handbill, used for advertising. **4** a very fast train, bus, etc. *n.*

fly·ing (flī′ing) **1** See **fly**[2]. **2** short and quick: *She paid us a flying visit last week.* 1 *v.*, 2 *adj.*
with flying colors or **colours,** successfully; triumphantly: *He passed the examination with flying colors.*

flying boat a type of seaplane having a boatlike hull.

flying buttress a support for a wall, joined to the wall at an angle from a pier that stands a short distance away: *Flying buttresses, developed in the Middle Ages, allowed architects to make taller buildings with thinner walls than were possible before.*

flying fish a tropical sea fish having fins like wings that enable it to leap through the air.

flying saucer a disklike object that some people claim to have seen flying at great speed over various parts of the world.

fly swat·ter (swot′ər) a device for killing flies, usually consisting of a long handle to which is attached a broad, flat piece of perforated rubber, plastic, etc. *n.*

fly·wheel (flī′wēl′ or flī′hwēl′) a heavy wheel attached to machinery to keep the speed even. See **steam engine** for picture. *n.*

FM, F.M., or **f.m.** frequency modulation.

foal (fōl) **1** a young horse or donkey; colt or filly. **2** give birth to a foal. 1 *n.*, 2 *v.*

foam (fōm) **1** a mass of very small bubbles. **2** form foam: *Ginger ale foams when shaken up.* **3** break into foam: *The stream foams on the rocks.* **4** a spongy material made from plastics, rubber, etc. 1, 4 *n.*, 2, 3 *v.* **—foam′y,** *adj.*

foam rubber a firm, spongy foam of natural or synthetic rubber.

fo·ci (fō′sī or fō′kī) a plural of **focus.** *n.*

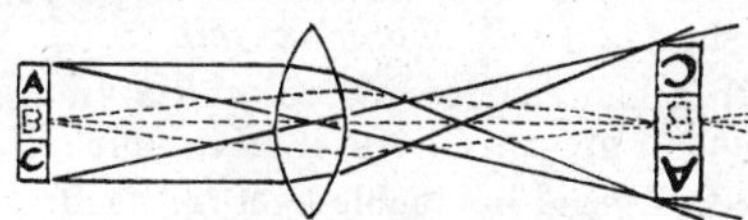

Rays of light brought to a focus by a lens

fo·cus (fō′kəs) **1** a point at which rays of light, heat, etc. meet after being reflected from a mirror or bent by a lens. **2** bring rays of light, heat, etc. together at such a point: *The lens focussed the sun's rays on a piece of paper so that they burned a hole in it.* **3** adjust a lens, the eye, etc. so that it brings rays of light together to give a clear image: *A near-sighted person cannot focus accurately on distant objects.* **4** the proper adjustment of a lens, the eye, etc. to give a clear image. **5** bring an image, etc. into focus. **6** a central point of attraction, attention, activity, etc.: *The new baby was the focus of attention.* **7** concentrate: *When studying, he focussed his mind on his lessons.* 1, 4, 6 *n., pl.* **fo·cus·es** or **fo·ci** (fō′sī or fō′kī); 2, 3, 5, 7 *v.*, **fo·cus·ses** or **fo·cus·es, fo·cussed** or **fo·cused, fo·cuss·ing** or **fo·cus·ing.**

A California flying fish — about 46 cm long

fod·der (fod′ər) coarse food for horses, cattle, etc.: *Hay and cornstalks are fodder.* *n.*

foe (fō) enemy. *n.*

foe·tus (fē′təs) See **fetus.**

fog (fog) **1** a cloud of fine drops of water that forms just above the earth's surface; thick mist. **2** cover with fog. **3** make misty or cloudy: *Something fogged six of our photographs.* **4** a confused or puzzled condition: *His mind was in a fog during most of the examination.* 1, 4 *n.,* 2, 3 *v.,* **fogged, fog·ging.**

fo·gey or **fo·gy** (fō′gē) a person who is behind the times; a person having old-fashioned ideas. *n., pl.* **fo·geys** or **fo·gies.**

fog·gy (fog′ē) **1** having much fog; misty. **2** not clear; dim; blurred: *His understanding of geography was rather foggy.* *adj.,* **fog·gi·er, fog·gi·est.**

fog·horn (fog′hôrn′) a horn or siren used in foggy weather to warn ships of danger from rocks, collision, etc.: *The destroyer sounded her foghorn so that other ships would be aware of her presence.* *n.*

fo·gy (fō′gē) See **fogey.**

foi·ble (foi′bəl) a weak point; a weakness in character: *People like him in spite of his foibles.* *n.*

foil[1] (foil) outwit; prevent from carrying out plans: *The hero foiled the villain.* *v.*

foil[2] (foil) metal beaten, hammered, or rolled into a very thin sheet: *tin foil, aluminum foil.* *n.*

foil[3] (foil) a long, narrow sword with a knob or button on the point to prevent injury, used in fencing. *n.*

fold[1] (fōld) **1** bend or double over on itself: *He folded the letter and put it in an envelope.* **2** a layer of something folded: *He hid the money between the folds of his blanket.* **3** bend till close to the body: *He folded his arms across his chest.* **4** put the arms around and hold tenderly: *A mother folds her child to her breast.* **5** wrap: *He folded the pills in a piece of blue paper.* 1, 3–5 *v.,* 2 *n.*

fold[2] (fōld) **1** a pen for sheep. **2** sheep kept in a pen. **3** a church group; congregation; church. *n.*

–fold a suffix meaning: **1** times as many; times as great: *'A fourfold increase' is an increase to four times as great.* **2** having or divided into ____parts: *Manifold means having many parts.*

fold·er (fōl′dər) **1** a holder for papers, made of cardboard doubled once. **2** a small book made up of one or more folded sheets. *n.*

fo·li·age (fō′lē ij) the leaves of a plant, especially of a tree. *n.*

folk (fōk) **1** people as a group: *Most city folk know very little about farming.* **2** a tribe; nation. **3 folks, a** people. **b** *Informal.* relatives: *How are all your folks?* **4** having to do with the common people. **5** having to do with folk songs or folk music: *a folk festival.* 1–3 *n., pl.* **folk** or **folks;** 4, 5 *adj.*

folk dance **1** an old dance popular among the common people of a country. **2** the music for such a dance.

folk·lore (fōk′lôr′) the beliefs, legends, customs, etc. of a people or tribe, as passed on from generation to generation. *n.*

folk music **1** music of the common people, handed down from generation to generation: *Much very old folk music has been written down only within the last two hundred years.* **2** any of many kinds of modern popular music, usually similar in style to traditional folk music.

folk song **1** a song originating, as a rule, among the common people and handed down from generation to generation. **2** a modern song imitating or similar to a traditional folk song.

folk·sy (fōk′sē) *Informal.* **1** friendly; social: *It was just a nice, folksy evening.* **2** plain and unpretentious: *folksy furniture.* *adj.,* **folk·si·er, folk·si·est.**

folk tale a story or legend originating, as a rule, among the common people and handed down from generation to generation.

fol·low (fol′ō) **1** go or come after: *Sheep follow a leader. Night follows day. He leads; we follow.* **2** result from; result: *Misery follows war. If you eat too much candy, a stomach ache will follow.* **3** go along: *Follow this road to the corner.* **4** use; obey; act according to; take as a guide: *Follow her advice.* **5** keep the eyes on: *I could not follow that bird's flight.* **6** keep the mind on: *He found it hard to follow the conversation.* **7** take as one's work or profession: *He expects to follow the law.* *v.*

follow suit, a play a card of the same suit as that first played. **b** follow the example of another.

follow through, a continue a movement or swing to the full extent of the stroke: *Most golfers follow through after hitting the ball.* **b** carry out fully; complete: *When one begins a job, one should try to follow it through.*

follow up, a follow closely and steadily. **b** carry out to the end. **c** increase the effect of by repeating an action: *He followed up his first request by asking again a week later.*

fol·low·er (fol′ō ər) **1** a person who follows the ideas or beliefs of another: *Christians are followers of Christ.* **2** a member of the household of a king or nobleman. *n.*

fol·low·ing (fol′ō ing) **1** a group of followers. **2** that follows; next after: *If that was Sunday, then the following day must have been Monday.* 1 *n.,* 2 *adj.*

fol·ly (fol′ē) **1** the state of being foolish or showing lack of sense: *It was folly to eat so much candy.* **2** a foolish act, practice, or idea; something silly. *n., pl.* **fol·lies.**

fond (fond) **1** loving; liking: *a fond look.* **2** loving foolishly or too much. *adj.* **—fond′ly,** *adv.* **—fond′ness,** *n.*

be fond of, a have a liking for: *My uncle is fond of children.* **b** like to eat: *Most cats are fond of fish.*

fon·dle (fon′dəl) pet; caress lovingly: *Mothers like to fondle their babies.* *v.,* **fon·dled, fon·dling.**

font (font) **1** a basin holding water for baptism. **2** a basin for holy water. **3** fountain. **4** source: *the font of truth.* *n.*

food (füd) **1** anything that plants, animals, or people eat or drink to keep them alive and make them grow: *Milk and green vegetables are valuable foods for human beings.* **2** what is eaten: *Give him food and drink.* **3** anything that causes growth: *Books are food for the mind.* *n.*

fool (fül) **1** a person without sense; a person who acts in a senseless and unreasonable way. **2** a clown formerly kept by a king or lord to amuse people; jester. **3** act like a fool for fun; play; joke: *The teacher told him*

hat, āge, fär; let, ēqual, tėrm; it, īce
hot, ōpen, ôrder; oil, out; cup, pu̇t, rüle
ənbove, takən, pencəl, lemən, circəs
ch, child; ng, long; sh, ship
th, thin; ᴛʜ, then; zh, measure

not to fool during class. **4** make a fool of; deceive; trick. 1, 2 *n.,* 3, 4 *v.*

fool·har·dy (fül′här′dē) foolishly bold; rash: *The man made a foolhardy attempt to go over Niagara Falls in a barrel. adj.,* **fool·har·di·er, fool·har·di·est.**

fool·ish (fül′ish) without sense; silly; unwise: *Her foolish talk annoyed her father. adj.* **—fool′ish·ness,** *n.*

fool·proof (fül′prüf′) so safe or simple that even a fool can use or do it: *a foolproof device, a foolproof plan. adj.*

foot (fu̇t) **1** the end part of a leg; the part that a person or animal stands on. **2** the lowest part; the bottom or base: *the foot of a column, the foot of a hill, the foot of a page.* **3** walk: *The boys footed the whole twenty kilometres.* **4** *Informal.* pay: *Father foots the bill.* **5** a measure of length (30.48 centimetres) equalling 12 inches: *Three feet equal one yard. My father is six feet tall. Symbol:* ′ **6** one of the parts into which a line of poetry is divided: *The following line has four feet: 'The boy/ stood on/ the burn/ ing deck.'/* 1, 2, 5, 6 *n., pl.* **feet;** 3, 4 *v.*

put one's foot down, *Informal.* make up one's mind and act firmly.

put one's foot in it, *Informal.* get into trouble by meddling; blunder.

foot·ball (fu̇t′bol′ or fu̇t′bôl′) **1** an air-filled, leather-covered ball used in kicking-games: *Footballs of different shapes are used in soccer and football.* **2** a game in which a football is kicked, passed, or carried toward the opposing goal: *Canadian football is somewhat different from American football with regard to rules, size of field, number of players, number of downs, etc.* **3** a game in which the ball must be driven toward the opposing goal without the use of the hands: *This kind of football is usually called soccer in Canada. n.*

foot·fall (fu̇t′fol′ or fu̇t′fôl′) the sound of a footstep coming or going. *n.*

foot·hill (fu̇t′hil′) a low hill at the base of a mountain or mountain range: *We visited a cattle ranch in the foothills of the Rockies. n.*

foot·hold (fu̇t′hōld′) **1** a place to put a foot; a support for the feet: *There was scarcely a foothold to be seen on the face of the cliff.* **2** a firm and secure position: *It is hard to break a habit that has gained a foothold. n.*

foot·ing (fu̇t′ing) **1** a firm placing or position of the feet: *He lost his footing and fell down on the ice.* **2** a place to put a foot; a support for the feet: *The steep cliff gave us no footing.* **3** a firm and secure position: *He worked hard to gain a footing in his new job.* **4** a basis of understanding; relationship: *His friendship with his neighbors was on a good footing.* **5 footings,** *pl.* the concrete foundations of a building, wall, etc. *n.*

foot·man (fu̇t′mən) a male servant who answers the bell, waits on table, goes with an automobile or carriage to open the door, etc.: *Footmen, who usually wear special uniforms, are now found mainly in royal palaces. n., pl.* **foot·men** (fu̇t′mən).

foot·path (fu̇t′path′) a path for people on foot. *n.*

foot·print (fu̇t′print′) the mark made by a foot. *n.*

foot·sore (fu̇t′sôr′) having sore feet from much walking: *The hike left us footsore and hungry. adj.*

foot·step (fu̇t′step′) **1** a person's step. **2** the sound of steps coming or going: *We heard footsteps in the hall. n.*

follow in someone's footsteps, do as another has done.

foot·stool (fu̇t′stül′) a low stool on which to rest the feet when one is sitting in a chair. *n.*

foot·wear (fu̇t′wer′) shoes, slippers, stockings, etc. *n.*

for (fôr) **1** in place of: *He gave me a new book for the old one.* **2** in support of; in favor of: *He stands for honest government.* **3** in return; in consideration of: *These grapefruit are eight for a dollar. We thanked him for his kindness.* **4** with the object or purpose of taking, achieving, or obtaining: *He went for a walk. He is looking for a job.* **5** in order to become, have, keep, get to, etc.: *He ran for his life. She is hunting for her cat. He has just left for Halifax.* **6** meant to belong to or with, or to be used by or with; suited to: *a box for gloves, books for children.* **7** with a feeling toward: *She has an eye for beauty. We longed for home.* **8** with regard or respect to: *Isn't it warm for April? Too little sleep is bad for the health.* **9** because of; by reason of: *shout for joy. He was punished for stealing.* **10** as far as: *We walked for a kilometre.* **11** as long as: *We worked for an hour.* **12** as being: *They know it for a fact.* **13** because: *We can't go, for it is raining.* 1–12 *prep.,* 13 *conj.*

☞ **For, fore,** and **four** are pronounced the same.

for·age (fôr′ij) **1** hay, grain, or other food for horses, cattle, etc. **2** hunt or search for anything, especially food: *The boys foraged in the kitchen till they found some cookies. The man made a living by foraging for old metal.* **3** a hunt or search for food: *to go on a forage.* **4** get by hunting or searching about: *The campers foraged some dry wood for a fire.* **5** collect or take food from, sometimes by force; plunder: *The invading army foraged the countryside.* 1, 3 *n.,* 2, 4, 5 *v.,* **for·aged, for·ag·ing.**

for·ay (fôr′ā) a raid for plunder: *Armed bandits made forays on the villages and took away cattle. n.*

for·bade or **for·bad** (fər bad′ or fər bād′) See **forbid.** *The doctor forbade the sick boy to leave his bed. v.*

for·bear (fôr ber′) **1** hold back; keep from doing, saying, using, etc.: *The boy forbore to hit back because the other boy was smaller. It was all she could do to forbear from crying.* **2** be patient; control oneself. *v.,* **for·bore, for·borne, for·bear·ing.**

for·bear·ance (fôr ber′əns) patience; control; not acting against someone when you have a right to do so: *His forbearance under abuse was admirable. n.*

for·bid (fər bid′) not allow; say one must not do; make a rule against: *The teacher forbids whispering during class. If my father had known that I was going, he would have forbidden it. v.,* **for·bade** or **for·bad, for·bid·den** or **for·bid, for·bid·ding.**

for·bid·den (fər bid′ən) **1** not allowed; against the law or the rules: *He was fined for parking in a forbidden area.* **2** See **forbid.** *My father has forbidden me to go swimming in that river.* 1 *adj.,* 2 *v.*

for·bid·ding (fər bid′ing) 1 causing fear or dislike; hostile; grim: *The enemy soldier's look was forbidding.* 2 looking dangerous or unpleasant; threatening: *The coast was rocky and forbidding.* 3 See **forbid.** 1, 2 *adj.*, 3 *v.*

for·bore (fôr bôr′) See **forbear.** *He forbore from showing his anger. v.*

for·borne (fôr bôrn′) See **forbear.** *We have forborne from vengeance. v.*

force (fôrs) 1 power or strength: *The force of the wind broke the ship's mast.* 2 strength used against a person or thing; violence: *The rebels captured the village by force.* 3 make a person act against his will; make do by force: *Give it to me at once, or I will force you to.* 4 get or take by force: *He forced the key out of her hand.* 5 break through: *to force a door.* 6 press or urge to violent effort: *She forced herself to one last burst of speed and won the race.* 7 hurry the growth of anything: *The rhubarb was forced by growing it in a dark, warm place.* 8 a group of people who work together: *the police force, our office force.* 9 **the forces,** the armed forces; armed services. 10 any cause that produces, changes, or stops motion in a body: *the force of gravitation, magnetic force.* 1, 2, 8–10 *n.*, 3–7 *v.*, **forced, forc·ing.**
in force, a in use: *The old rules are still in force.* **b** in large numbers; with full strength: *The enemy attacked us in force.*

force·ful (fôrs′fəl) having much force; forcible; effective; vigorous; strong: *a forceful manner. adj.*

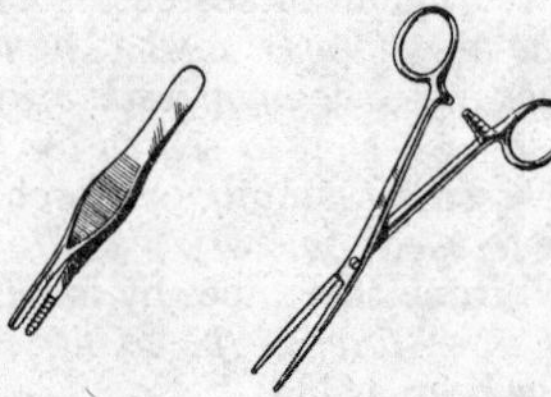
Two kinds of forceps used in surgery

for·ceps (fôr′seps or fôr′səps) a pair of small pincers or tongs used by surgeons, dentists, etc. for seizing and holding: *Dentists use forceps for pulling teeth. n., pl.* **for·ceps.**

for·ci·ble (fôr′sə bəl) 1 made or done by force; using force: *The thieves were charged with forcible entry into the house.* 2 having or showing force; strong; powerful: *a forcible speaker. adj.*

ford (fôrd) 1 a place where a river or stream is shallow enough to cross by walking or driving through the water. 2 cross a river or stream by walking or driving through the water: *They spent an hour looking for a place to ford the river.* 1 *n.*, 2 *v.*

fore (fôr) 1 at the front; toward the beginning or front; forward. 2 the front part, especially of a ship or boat. See **aft** for picture. 3 in golf, a shout of warning to persons ahead who are liable to be struck by the ball. 1 *adj., adv.*, 2 *n.*, 3 *interj.*
☞ **Fore, for,** and **four** are pronounced the same.

fore– a prefix meaning: 1 front: *Forefoot means the front foot.* 2 before; beforehand: *Foresee means see beforehand.*

fore–and–aft (fôr′ənd aft′) lengthwise on a ship; from bow to stern: *Fore-and-aft sails are set lengthwise.* See **schooner** for picture. *adj.*

fore·arm¹ (fôr′ärm′) the part of the arm between the elbow and the wrist. See **arm** for picture. *n.*

fore·arm² (fôr ärm′) prepare for trouble ahead of time; arm beforehand: *To be forewarned is to be forearmed. v.*

fore·bear (fôr′ber) an ancestor; forefather: *He is proud of his pioneer forebears. n.*

fore·bod·ing (fôr bōd′ing) a feeling that something bad is going to happen: *As the storm grew worse, the travellers were filled with foreboding. n.*

fore·cast (fôr′kast′) 1 prophesy; tell what is coming: *Cooler weather is forecast for tomorrow.* 2 a prophecy; a statement of what is coming: *What is the weather forecast for today?* 1 *v.*, **fore·cast** or **fore·cast·ed, fore·cast·ing;** 2 *n.*

fore·cas·tle (fōk′səl or fôr′kas′əl) 1 the upper deck in front of the foremast of a ship or boat. 2 the sailors' rooms in a merchant ship, formerly in the forward part of the ship. *n.*

fore·fa·ther (fôr′fo′ᴛʜər) ancestor. *n.*

fore·fin·ger (fôr′fing′gər) the finger next to the thumb; the first finger. See **arm** for picture. *n.*

fore·foot (fôr′fůt′) one of the front feet of an animal. *n., pl.* **fore·feet.**

fore·front (fôr′frunt′) 1 the place of greatest importance, activity, etc. 2 the foremost part. *n.*

fore·go (fôr gō′) do without; give up: *She decided to forego the movies and do her lessons. v.*, **fore·went, fore·gone, fore·go·ing.** Also spelled **forgo.**

fore·go·ing (fôr′gō′ing) preceding; going before: *There are many pictures in the foregoing pages. adj.*

fore·gone (fôr′gon′) 1 See **forego.** 2 previous; that has gone before. 1 *v.*, 2 *adj.*
foregone conclusion, a fact that was almost surely known beforehand: *It was a foregone conclusion that there would be traffic jams while the road was being repaired.*

fore·ground (fôr′ground′) the part of a picture or scene nearest the observer; the part toward the front: *The cottage is in the foreground and the mountains are in the background. n.*

fore·head (fôr′hed′ or fôr′id) the part of the face above the eyes. *n.*

for·eign (fôr′ən) 1 outside one's own country: *She has travelled much in foreign countries.* 2 coming from outside one's own country: *a foreign ship, a foreign language, foreign money.* 3 having to do with other countries: *foreign trade.* 4 not belonging: *Sitting still all day is foreign to that healthy boy's nature. adj.*

for·eign·er (fôr′ən ər) a person from another country; outsider. *n.*

fore·leg (fôr′leg′) one of the front legs of an animal. *n.*

fore·man (fôr′mən) 1 the person in charge of a group of workers; the person in charge of the work in some part of a factory. 2 the chairman of a jury. *n., pl.* **fore·men** (fôr′mən).

fore·mast (fôr′mast′ or fôr′məst) the mast nearest the bow of a ship. See **schooner** for picture. *n.*

fore·most (fôr′mōst′) 1 first: *I am foremost in line (adj.). He stumbled and fell head foremost (adv.).* 2 chief; leading: *the foremost scientist.* 1, 2 *adj.*, 1 *adv.*

hat, āge, fär; let, ēqual, tėrm; it, īce
hot, ōpen, ôrder; oil, out; cup, pu̇t, rüle
əbove, takən, pencəl, lemən, circəs
ch, child; ng, long; sh, ship
th, thin; ᴛʜ, then; zh, measure

fore·noon (fôr′nün′) the time between early morning and noon. *n.*

fore·paw (fôr′po′ or fôr′pô′) a front paw. *n.*

fore·saw (fôr so′ or fôr sô′) See **foresee.** *Mother put up a big picnic lunch, because she foresaw how hungry we would be.* *v.*

fore·see (fôr ′sē′) see or know beforehand: *We didn't take our bathing suits, because we could not foresee that the water would be warm.* *v.*, **fore·saw, fore·seen, fore·see·ing.**

fore·seen (fôr sēn′) See **foresee.** *Nobody could have foreseen how cold it would be.* *v.*

fore·sight (fôr′sīt′) **1** the power to see or know beforehand what is likely to happen. **2** careful thought for the future; prudence: *To be successful, a man must have foresight.* *n.*

for·est (fôr′ist) **1** thick woods; woodland, often covering many miles. **2** plant with trees; cover with trees. 1 *n.*, 2 *v.*

for·est·er (fôr′is tər) **1** a government official whose job is to guard against fires and to protect timber in a forest. **2** a person skilled in forestry. *n.*

for·est·ry (fôr′is trē) the science and art of planting and taking care of forests. *n.*

fore·tell (fôr tel′) tell beforehand; predict; prophesy: *Who can foretell what a baby will do next?* *v.*, **fore·told, fore·tell·ing.**

fore·thought (fôr′thot′ or fôr′thôt′) **1** previous thought or consideration; planning. **2** careful thought for the future; prudence; foresight: *A little forethought will often prevent mistakes.* *n.*

fore·told (fôr tōld′) See **foretell.** *The Weather Office had foretold the cold wave.* *v.*

for·ev·er (fər ev′ər) **1** without ever coming to an end; for ever. **2** always; all the time: *That woman is forever talking.* *adv.*

for·ev·er·more (fər ev′ər môr′) forever. *adv.*

fore·warn (fôr wôrn′) warn beforehand: *The dark clouds forewarned us of a thunderstorm.* *v.*

fore·went (fôr went′) See **forego.** *She forewent dessert.* *v.*

for·feit (fôr′fit) **1** lose or have to give up by one's own act, neglect, or fault: *He forfeited his life by his careless driving.* **2** something lost or given up because of some act, neglect, or fault: *A headache was the forfeit he paid for staying up late.* **3** lost or given up: *His lands were forfeit.* 1 *v.*, 2 *n.*, 3 *adj.*

for·gave (fər gāv′) See **forgive.** *She forgave my mistake.* *v.*

forge[1] (fôrj) **1** a furnace or open fireplace where metal is heated to a high temperature before being hammered into shape: *The blacksmith took the white-hot horseshoes out of the forge.* See **anvil** for picture. **2** a blacksmith's shop. **3** heat metal to a high temperature and then hammer it into shape: *The blacksmith forged the bar of iron into a big strong hook.* **4** a place where iron or some other metal is melted and refined. **5** make; shape or form: *They forged a strong and lasting friendship.* **6** make or write something false or counterfeit: *The supposed will of the dead man had been forged.* **7** sign a name other than one's own in order to obtain something under false pretences: *He was sent to jail for forging cheques.* 1, 2, 4 *n.*, 3, 5–7 *v.*, **forged, forg·ing. —forg′er,** *n.*

forge[2] (fôrj) move forward slowly but steadily: *One runner forged ahead of the others and won the race.* *v.*, **forged, forg·ing.**

for·get (fər get′) **1** let go out of the mind; fail to remember: *I couldn't introduce her because I had forgotten her name.* **2** fail to think of; fail to do, take notice, etc.: *She said she would not forget to send him a postcard.* **3** leave behind unintentionally: *She had to return home because she forgot her purse.* *v.*, **for·got, for·got·ten** or **for·got, for·get·ting.**

for·get·ful (fər get′fəl) **1** apt to forget; having a poor memory. **2** heedless: *forgetful of danger.* *adj.* **—for·get′ful·ness,** *n.*

for·get–me–not (fər get′mē not′) **1** a small blue flower. **2** the plant the flower grows on. *n.*

for·give (fər giv′) pardon; give up the wish to punish; not have hard feelings about or toward: *She forgave her brother for breaking her doll. Please forgive my mistake.* *v.*, **for·gave, for·giv·en, for·giv·ing.**

for·giv·en (fər giv′ən) See **forgive.** *Your mistakes have been forgiven.* *v.*

for·give·ness (fər giv′nis) the act of forgiving; pardon. *n.*

for·go (fôr gō′) See **forego.** *v.*, **for·went, for·gone, for·go·ing.**

for·gone (fôr gon′) See **forgo.** *v.*

for·got (fər got′) See **forget.** *He was so busy that he forgot to eat his lunch.* *v.*

for·got·ten (fər got′ən) See **forget.** *He has forgotten much of what he learned.* *v.*

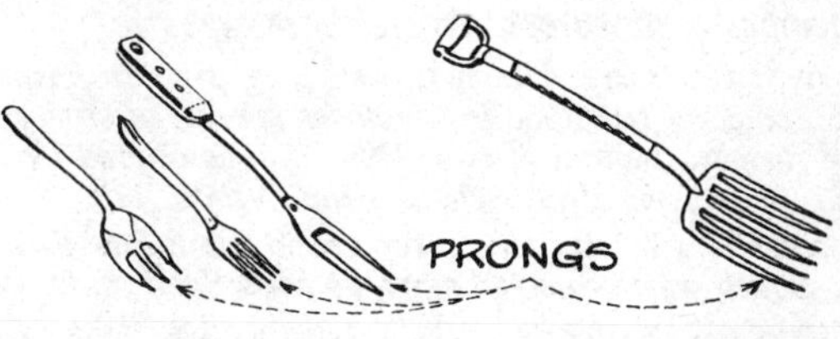

Forks (def. 1) A fork (def. 2)

fork (fôrk) **1** an implement having a handle and two or more long, pointed prongs with which to lift food. **2** a much larger implement with which to lift hay; pitchfork. **3** lift, throw, or dig with a fork. **4** the part of a tree, road, or stream where it divides into two parts: *the fork of a road. She sat in the fork of the tree.* **5** one of the branches into which anything is divided. **6** have forks; divide into forks: *There is a garage where the road forks.* 1, 2, 4, 5 *n.*, 3, 6 *v.*

for·lorn (fôr lôrn′) **1** left alone; neglected; deserted: *The lost kitten, a forlorn little animal, was wet and dirty.* **2** wretched in feeling or looks; unhappy: *The weeping child looked very forlorn.* *adj.*

form (fôrm) **1** shape: *Circles and triangles are forms.*

The form of a tree appeared out of the fog. **2** to shape; make: *The cook formed the dough into loaves.* **3** take shape: *Ice formed in the pail.* **4** a mould or pattern: *Ice cream is often made in forms.* **5** become: *Water forms ice when it freezes.* **6** make up; compose: *Parents and children form a family.* **7** organize; establish: *We formed a club.* **8** develop: *Form good habits while you are young.* **9** a kind; sort: *Ice, snow, and steam are forms of water.* **10** manner; method: *Her form in swimming is excellent.* **11** formality; ceremony: *He said 'Good morning' as a matter of form, although he hardly noticed me.* **12** arrangement: *In what form did he put the list of words?* **13** a document with printing or writing on it and blank spaces to be filled in: *To get a licence, you must fill out a form.* 1, 4, 9–13 *n.,* 2, 3, 5–8 *v.*

for·mal (fôr′məl) **1** stiff; not familiar and homelike: *a formal bow.* **2** according to set customs or rules. **3** done with the proper forms; clear and definite: *A written contract is formal agreement to do something.* **4** having to do with the form, not the content, of a thing. **5** a social gathering at which formal dress is worn: *Are you going to the formal on Saturday evening?* **6** a gown worn to formal social gatherings: *She was dressed in her first formal.* 1–4 *adj.,* 5, 6 *n.*
—**for′mal·ly,** *adv.*
☛ See note at **informal.**

for·mal·i·ty (fôr mal′ə tē) **1** an outward form; ceremony; something required by custom: *the formalities of a wedding or a funeral.* **2** attention to forms and customs: *Visitors at the court of the king are received with formality.* *n., pl.* **for·mal·i·ties.**

for·ma·tion (fôr mā′shən) **1** the forming, making, or shaping of something: *We can observe the formation of water from steam. The formation of words is a fascinating study.* **2** the way in which something is arranged; arrangement; order: *troops in battle formation. There was an interesting formation of ice crystals on the window.* **3** the thing formed: *Those clouds are formations of tiny drops of water in the sky.* *n.*

for·mer (fôr′mər) **1** earlier; past; long past: *In former times, cooking was done in fireplaces instead of stoves.* **2 the former,** the first of two: *When Sue is offered ice cream or pie, she always chooses the former.* *adj.*

for·mer·ly (fôr′mər lē) in time past; some time ago: *Mrs. Smith was formerly known as Miss Snell.* *adv.*

for·mi·da·ble (fôr′mə də bəl) hard to overcome; hard to deal with; to be dreaded: *A long examination is more formidable than a short test.* *adj.*

for·mu·la (fôr′myə lə) **1** a recipe; prescription: *a formula for making soap.* **2** a mixture, especially one for feeding a baby, made according to a recipe or prescription. *n.*

for·mu·late (fôr′myə lāt′) state definitely or systematically: *Our ideas of fair treatment for all Canadians are formulated in a Bill of Rights.* *v.* **for·mu·lat·ed, for·mu·lat·ing.**

for·sake (fôr sāk′) give up; leave; leave alone: *He ran away, forsaking his home and friends.* *v.,* **for·sook, for·sak·en, for·sak·ing.**

for·sak·en (fôr sāk′ən) **1** deserted; abandoned; forlorn: *a forsaken house.* **2** See **forsake.** *She has forsaken her friends.* 1 *adj.,* 2 *v.*

for·sook (fôr sůk′) See **forsake.** *He forsook his family.* *v.*

for·sooth (fôr süth′) in truth; indeed. *adv.*

for·syth·i·a (fôr sith′ē ə or fôr sī′thē ə) a shrub having many bell-shaped, yellow flowers in early spring before its leaves come out. *n.*

fort (fôrt) a strong building or place that can be defended against an enemy. *n.*

forth (fôrth) **1** forward: *From that day forth he lived alone.* **2** out; into view: *The sun came forth from behind the clouds.* **3** away: *Go forth and seek your fortune.* *adv.*
and so forth, and so on; and the like: *We ate cake, candy, nuts, and so forth.*

forth·com·ing (fôrth′kum′ing or fôrth kum′ing) **1** about to appear; approaching: *The forthcoming week will be busy.* **2** coming forth; ready when wanted: *'If you need help, it will be forthcoming,' Father promised.* *adj.*

forth·right (fôrth′rīt′) frank and outspoken; straightforward; direct: *Mr. Jones made forthright objections to the proposal.* *adj.*

forth·with (fôrth′with′) at once; immediately: *She said she would be there forthwith.* *adv.*

for·ti·eth (fôr′tē ith) **1** next after the 39th; last in a series of forty; 40th. **2** one of 40 equal parts. *adj., n.*

for·ti·fi·ca·tion (fôr′tə fə kā′shən) **1** the act of making strong or adding strength: *The general was responsible for the fortification of the town.* **2** a wall or a fort built to make a place strong. **3** a place made strong by building walls and forts. *n.*

for·ti·fy (fôr′tə fī′) **1** build forts, walls, etc.; strengthen against attack: *The general ordered the troops to fortify their position.* **2** make strong; add strength to: *Vitamins fortify the body against illness.* *v.,* **for·ti·fied, for·ti·fy·ing.**

for·ti·tude (fôr′tə tyüd′ or fôr′tə tüd′) courage in facing pain, danger, or trouble; firmness of spirit: *His fortitude during the crisis was praiseworthy.* *n.*

fort·night (fôrt′nīt′) two weeks. *n.*

for·tress (fôr′tris) a place built with walls and defences; a large and well-protected fort. *n.*

for·tu·nate (fôr′chə nit) **1** having good luck; lucky. **2** bringing good luck; having favorable results: *a fortunate event.* *adj.*

for·tune (fôr′chən) **1** a great deal of money or property; riches; wealth: *One of the gold-seekers made a fortune.* **2** what is going to happen to a person; fate: *Gypsies often claim that they can tell people's fortunes.* **3** luck; chance; what happens: *Fortune was against us; we lost.* **4** good luck; success; prosperity. *n.*

for·ty (fôr′tē) four times ten; 40. *n., pl.* **for·ties;** *adj.*

forty winks a short nap.

fo·rum (fô′rəm) **1** the public square of an ancient Roman city, where business was done and courts and public assemblies were held. **2** an assembly for the discussion of questions of public interest: *An open forum is held in the community centre every Tuesday evening.* *n.*

for·ward (fôr′wərd) **1** onward; ahead: *Forward, march!* **2** to the front: *come forward (adv.), the forward part of a ship (adj.).* **3** advanced: *a child forward for his years.* **4** help on: *He did all he could to forward his* friend's plans. 5 send on farther: *to forward a letter.* 6 ready; eager: *He knew his lesson and was forward with his answers.* 7 pert; bold: *It is rude to be so forward.* 1, 2 *adv.*, 2, 3, 6, 7 *adj.*, 4, 5 *v.*

for·wards (fôr′wərdz) forward: *Most animals move forwards more often than backwards.* *adv.*

for·went (fôr went′) See **forgo.** *v.*

fos·sil (fos′əl) 1 the remains of prehistoric animals or plants preserved in rocks where they have become petrified: *Fossils of ferns are sometimes found in coal. Bone fossils of dinosaurs have been discovered in Alberta.* 2 traces of animal life preserved in ancient rocks: *fossil footprints.* 3 a person or thing that is out-of-date or old-fashioned. *n.*

fos·ter (fos′tər) 1 help the growth or development of; encourage: *Our city fosters libraries, parks, and playgrounds.* 2 bring up; help to grow; make grow. 3 care for as one's own child. 4 in the same family, but not related by birth: *A foster child is a child brought up by a person not his parent. Foster parents, that is a foster mother and a foster father, are persons who bring up someone else's child.* 1–3 *v.*, 4 *adj.*

fought (fot or fôt) See **fight.** *He fought bravely yesterday. A battle was fought there.* *v.*

foul (foul) 1 very dirty; impure; nasty: *We opened the windows to let out the foul air.* 2 make dirty or impure; pollute: *Exhaust fumes foul the air.* 3 become dirty or impure: *Spark plugs foul if not cared for properly.* 4 unfair; against the rules. 5 See **foul play** (def. 1). 6 See **foul ball.** 7 hit against: *Their boat fouled ours.* 8 hitting against: *One boat went foul of the other.* 9 get tangled up with: *The rope they threw fouled our anchor chain.* 10 clog up: *Grease has fouled this drain.* 11 unfavorable; stormy: *foul weather.* 1, 4, 8, 11 *adj.*, 2, 3, 7, 9, 10 *v.*, 5, 6 *n.*

foul up, a make a mess of; bungle. **b** put out of order: *A piece of loose rope fouled up the boat's propeller.* **c** make dirty or impure. **d** become dirty or impure.

☛ **Foul** and **fowl** are pronounced the same.

foul ball in baseball, a ball hit so that it falls outside the base lines.

foul play 1 in football, basketball, etc., an unfair play. 2 treachery; violence: *The man seemed to have died in his sleep, but the police suspected foul play.*

found¹ (found) See **find.** *We found the treasure. The lost child was found.* *v.*

found² (found) establish: *The English founded a colony in the new country.* *v.*

foun·da·tion (foun dā′shən) 1 the part of a building that serves as a basis for the walls: *The foundation of the house was entirely underground.* 2 the basis of a belief, idea, argument, etc.: *This report has no foundation in fact.* 3 the act of founding or establishing: *The foundation of King's College took place in 1788.* *n.*

found·er¹ (foun′dər) a person who founds or establishes. *n.*

foun·der² (foun′dər) 1 fall down; stumble; break down: *The cattle foundered in the swamp.* 2 fill with water and sink: *The ship foundered in the storm.* *v.*

found·ling (found′ling) a baby or little child found deserted. *n.*

found·ry (foun′drē) a place where metal is melted and moulded; a place where things are made of melted metal. *n.*, *pl.* **found·ries.**

hat, āge, fär; let, ēqual, tėrm; it, īce
hot, ōpen, ôrder; oil, out; cup, pu̇t, rüle
əbove, takən, pencəl, lemən, circəs
ch, child; ng, long; sh, ship
th, thin; ᴛʜ, then; zh, measure

fount (fount) 1 fountain. 2 source: *He is a fount of knowledge.* *n.*

A fountain

foun·tain (foun′tən) 1 a stream or spray of water rising into the air. 2 a decorative structure through which water is forced into the air in a stream or spray. 3 a spring of water. 4 a device by which a jet of water is forced upward so that people may get a drink: *a drinking fountain.* 5 soda fountain. 6 source: *He found that his father was a fountain of information.* *n.*

fountain pen a pen that automatically supplies liquid ink to the nib from a rubber or plastic tube inside.

four (fôr) one more than three; 4: *A dog has four legs.* *n.*, *adj.*

☛ **Four, for,** and **fore** are pronounced the same.

four·fold (fôr′fōld′) 1 four times as much or as many. 2 having four parts. 1, 2 *adj.*, 1 *adv.*

four·score (fôr′skôr′) four times twenty; 80. *adj.*, *n.*

four·teen (fôr′tēn′) four more than ten; 14. *n.*, *adj.*

four·teenth (fôr′tēnth′) 1 next after the 13th; last in a series of fourteen; 14th. 2 one of 14 equal parts. *adj.*, *n.*

fourth (fôrth) 1 next after the 3rd; last in a series of four; 4th. 2 a quarter; one of four equal parts: *Twenty-five cents is one fourth of a dollar.* *adj.*, *n.*

fowl (foul) 1 any bird: *a water fowl.* 2 any of several kinds of large birds raised for meat and eggs: *Chickens, ducks, geese, etc. are fowls.* 3 the flesh of such a bird used for food. *n.*, *pl.* **fowls** or **fowl.**

☛ **Fowl** and **foul** are pronounced the same.

A red fox — about 65 cm long without the tail

fox (foks) 1 a small wild animal related to the dog, having pointed ears and nose, and a long bushy tail: *In many stories the fox gets the better of other animals by his cunning.* 2 the fur of this animal. 3 a cunning or crafty person; a person noted for his ability to get the better of other people. *n.*

fox terrier one of a breed of small, active dogs, originally used to drive foxes from their holes: *Fox* *terriers are white with brown or black spots and may have smooth or rough hair.* See **terrier** for picture.

fox·y (fok′sē) crafty; like a fox. *adj.*, **fox·i·er, fox·i·est.**

foy·er (foi′ər) 1 an entrance hall used as a lounging room in a theatre or hotel; lobby. 2 any entrance hall. *n.*

fra·cas (frā′kəs or frak′əs) a noisy quarrel or fight; disturbance; uproar; brawl. *n.*

frac·tion (frak′shən) 1 one or more of the equal parts of a whole: *½, ¼, and ¾ are fractions.* 2 a very small part, amount, etc.; not all of a thing; fragment: *He has done only a fraction of his homework. n.*

frac·ture (frak′chər) 1 a break or crack: *A fracture of the thigh bone takes a long time to mend.* 2 break or crack: *The boy fell from a tree and fractured his arm.* 3 breaking or being broken. 4 the breaking of a bone or cartilage. 1, 3, 4 *n.*, 2 *v.*, **frac·tured, frac·tur·ing.**

frag·ile (fraj′īl or fraj′əl) easily broken; delicate; frail: *Be careful; that thin glass is fragile. adj.*

frag·ment (frag′mənt) a part broken off; a piece of something broken: *When she broke the dish, she tried to put the fragments back together. n.*

fra·grance (frā′grəns) a sweet and pleasing smell: *the fragrance of roses. n.*

fra·grant (frā′grənt) sweet-smelling. *adj.*

frail (frāl) 1 not strong; weak; physically delicate: *John is a frail child.* 2 easily broken or damaged; fragile: *Fine china is frail. Be careful; those branches are a very frail support. adj.* —**frail′ness,** *n.*

frail·ty (frāl′tē) 1 the quality of being frail. 2 a fault or weakness in character: *the frailties of mankind. n., pl.* **frail·ties.**

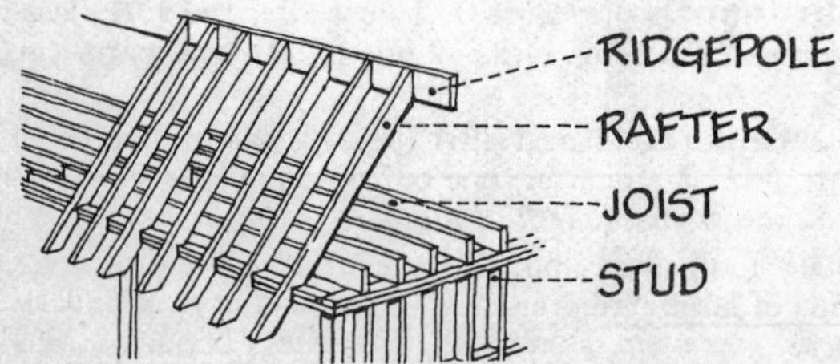

Part of the frame of a house

frame (frām) 1 a supporting structure over which something is stretched or built: *the frame of a house.* 2 bodily structure: *The wrestler had a heavy frame.* 3 make or put together; plan: *Laws are framed in Parliament.* 4 the border in which a thing is set: *a window frame, a picture frame.* 5 put a border around; enclose with a frame: *It costs money to get a picture framed.* 1, 2, 4 *n.*, 3, 5 *v.*, **framed, fram·ing.**

frame of mind, the way a person is thinking or feeling at a certain time; mood: *He woke up in an irritable frame of mind.*

frame house a house made of a wooden framework covered with boards.

frame·work (frām′wėrk′) a support or skeleton; the stiff part that gives shape: *The bridge had a steel framework. n.*

franc (frangk) the unit of money in France, Belgium, and Switzerland: *The French franc is worth about 20 cents. n.*

☛ **Franc** and **frank** are pronounced the same.

Fran·co·phone or **fran·co·phone** (frangk′ə fōn′) *Cdn.* a French-speaking person who lives in a bilingual country. *n.*

frank (frangk) free in expressing one's real thoughts and feelings; not hiding what is in one's mind; not afraid to say what one thinks: *She had a frank way of talking. adj.* —**frank′ly,** *adv.* —**frank′ness,** *n.*

☛ **Frank** and **franc** are pronounced the same.

frank·furt·er (frangk′fėr tər) wiener. *n.*

frank·in·cense (frangk′in sens′) a fragrant resin from certain Asiatic or African trees that gives off a sweet, spicy odor when burned. *n.*

fran·tic (fran′tik) 1 very much excited: *He made frantic motions to stop the approaching car.* 2 beside oneself with fear or grief; wild with rage or pain: *The mother was frantic when her baby was stolen. adj.*

fran·ti·cal·ly (fran′tik lē) in a frantic manner; with wild excitement: *He signalled frantically for the train to stop. adv.*

fra·ter·nal (frə tėr′nəl) brotherly. *adj.*

fra·ter·ni·ty (frə tėr′nə tē) a group of men or boys joined together for fellowship or for some other purposes: *There are student fraternities in some Canadian universities. n., pl.* **fra·ter·ni·ties.**

fraud (frod or frôd) 1 dishonest dealing; cheating; trickery: *A person who passes counterfeit money is guilty of fraud.* 2 something that is not what it seems to be. 3 *Informal.* a person who is not what he pretends to be. *n.*

fraught (frot or frôt) loaded; filled: *A battlefield is fraught with horror. adj.*

fray[1] (frā) a fight; a noisy quarrel. *n.*

fray[2] (frā) 1 separate into threads; make or become ragged or worn along the edge: *Long wear had frayed the collar and cuffs of his old shirt.* 2 wear away; rub *v.*

freak (frēk) 1 something very queer or unusual: *A green leaf growing in the middle of a rose would be called a freak of nature.* 2 a sudden change of mind without reason; an odd notion or fancy. *n.*

freck·le (frek′əl) 1 a small, light-brown spot on the skin. 2 make freckles on: *The sun freckles the skin of some people.* 3 become marked with freckles. 1 *n.*, 2, 3 *v.*, **freck·led, freck·ling.** —**freck·ly,** *adj.*

free (frē) 1 loose; not fastened or shut up: *The hens were allowed to run free in the yard.* 2 not under another's control; not being a slave. 3 not held back from acting or thinking as one pleases: *free speech, free nations.* 4 without anything to pay: *Children under 12 attend free (adv.). These tickets are free (adj.).* 5 giving or using without restriction; generous: *He is always free with money.* 6 make free; let go; let loose: *They had trouble freeing the boat from the weeds. The prisoner was freed early for good behavior.* 7 to clear: *He will have to free himself of this charge of stealing.* 1–5 *adj.*, **fre·er, fre·est;** 4 *adv.* 6, 7 *v.*, **freed, free·ing.**

free and easy, paying little attention to rules and customs: *His free and easy manner was not typical of the diplomatic service.*

free from or **of,** without: *free from fear, air free of dust.*

hat, āge, fär; let, ēqual, tėrm; it, īce
hot, ōpen, ôrder; oil, out; cup, pu̇t, rüle
əbove, takən, pencəl, lemən, circəs
ch, child; ng, long; sh, ship
th, thin; ᴛʜ, then; zh, measure

free·boot·er (frē′büt′ər) a pirate; buccaneer. *n.*

free·dom (frē′dəm) **1** the condition of being free. **2** the power to do, say, or think as one pleases; liberty. **3** free use: *We gave our guest the freedom of the house.* **4** too great liberty: *We did not like the freedom of his manner.* **5** ease of movement or action. *n.*

Free·dom·ite (frē′dəm īt′) a member of the Sons of Freedom, a Doukhobor sect. *n.*

free·hand (frē′hand′) done by hand without using instruments, measurements, etc.: *freehand drawing. adj.*

free·ly (frē′lē) **1** in a free manner. **2** generously; willingly: *He gave freely of his time. adv.*

free·man (frē′mən) a person not a slave or a serf; a man who could own land. *n., pl.* **free·men** (frē′mən).

free·way (frē′wā′) a high-speed highway on which no tolls are charged. *n.*

freeze (frēz) **1** turn into ice: *The water in the pond has frozen.* **2** cause something to become hard and stiff by lowering the temperature to below 0 degrees Celsius: *By freezing meat we can keep it from spoiling.* **3** become very cold: *The boys in the tent will freeze in this weather.* **4** kill or damage by frost: *This cold weather will freeze the flowers. The tomato plants froze last night but some of them may survive.* **5** freeze over. **6** become clogged by pieces of ice: *The car stalled because the gas line froze. When the pipes froze, we couldn't get water from the tap.* **7** a state of extreme coldness; frost; freezing: *The freeze last night damaged the apple trees.* **8** become motionless, usually because of fear: *The mouse froze as the snake moved toward it.* **9** make a part of the body numb by injecting or applying drugs, usually to reduce or eliminate pain: *The dentist froze the patient's gums before taking out the tooth.* 1–6, 8, 9 *v.,* **froze, fro·zen, freez·ing;** 7 *n.*

☞ **Freeze** and **frieze** are pronounced the same.

freez·er (frēz′ər) **1** a refrigerator cabinet in which the temperature is kept below freezing: *Food put in a freezer may be kept for a long time.* **2** a machine to freeze ice cream. *n.*

freeze–up (frēz′up′) *Cdn.* the time of year when the rivers and lakes freeze over; the onset of winter: *Freeze-up came late last year. n.*

freez·ing (frēz′ing) **1** See **freeze.** *The water in the puddles is freezing.* **2** freezing point, especially that of water: *It's below freezing outside.* **3** *Informal.* very cold: *It's freezing in here!* 1 *v.,* 2 *n.,* 3 *adj.*

freezing point the temperature at which a liquid freezes: *The freezing point of water at sea level is 0 degrees Celsius.*

freight (frāt) **1** the goods that a ship or a train carries: *It took a whole day to unload the freight.* **2** the carrying of goods on a train, ship, or aircraft: *He sent the box by freight.* **3** the price paid for carrying. **4** a freight train: *The freight was early last night. n.*

freight car a railway car for carrying freight.

freight·er (frāt′ər) a ship or aircraft that carries mainly freight. *n.*

French (french) **1** of or having to do with France, its people, or their language. **2** the people of France. **3** the French language: *The kind of French spoken in Canada is called Canadian French.* **4** French Canadian; of or having to do with French Canada, French Canadians, or their language. 1, 4 *adj,* 2, 3 *n.*

French Canada **1** French Canadians as a group; all French Canadians. **2** the province of Quebec, where most French Canadians live.

French Canadian **1** a Canadian whose ancestors came from France. **2** of or having to do with French Canada or French Canadians: *French-Canadian customs.* **3** the language of the French Canadians; Canadian French.

French fries (french′ frīz′) potatoes that have been **French fried,** that is, cut into long, square-sided strips and cooked in boiling fat until crisp on the outside.

A French horn

French horn a brass wind instrument that has a mellow tone.

French·man (french′mən) **1** a man born in or living in France. **2** French Canadian (def. 1). *n., pl.* **French·men** (french′mən).

French Shore *Cdn.* **1** the west coast of Newfoundland. **2** an area originally settled by the Acadian French, located on the southwest coast of Nova Scotia.

fren·zied (fren′zēd) frantic; wild; very much excited: *frenzied shouts. adj.*

fren·zy (fren′zē) **1** a state of near madness: *She was in a frenzy of grief when she heard of her son's death.* **2** a state of very great excitement: *The spectators were in a frenzy after the home team finally scored. n.*

fre·quen·cy (frē′kwən sē) **1** the rate of occurrence: *The flashes of light came with a frequency of three per minute.* **2** a frequent occurrence: *The doctors were worried about the frequency of his heart attacks.* **3** the number of times that an electric wave is sent through the air each second: *Different radio and television stations broadcast at different frequencies so that their signals can be received distinctly. n., pl.* **fre·quen·cies.**

frequency mod·u·la·tion (moj′ə lā′shən) in broadcasting, the changing of the frequency of radio waves in order to transmit sound: *Frequency modulation reduces static. The abbreviation for frequency modulation is FM.*

fre·quent (frē′kwənt for 1, fri kwent′ for 2) **1** happening often, near together, or every little while: *Storms are frequent in March.* **2** be often in; go to often: *Frogs frequent ponds, streams, and marshes.* 1 *adj.,* 2 *v.*

fre·quent·ly (frē′kwənt lē) often. *adv.*

fresh (fresh) **1** newly made, grown, or gathered: *These* are fresh vegetables. Is this milk fresh? 2 new; recent: *Is there any fresh news from home?* 3 not salty: *There is fresh water in the Great Lakes.* 4 not artificially preserved: *Fresh foods usually have more flavor than canned ones.* 5 not tired out: *Put in fresh horses.* 6 healthy-looking. 7 pure; cool: *a fresh breeze.* 8 another; additional: *He deserves a fresh start.* 9 *Slang.* too bold; impudent: *fresh talk. adj.* **—fresh′ness,** *n.*

fresh·en (fresh′ən) 1 make new, pure, or bright: *He thought it would be a good idea to freshen the paint on the house.* 2 become stronger: *The runner freshened after the first five laps. v.*
freshen up, do something to make, or feel, fresh: *He freshened up by taking a bath and changing his clothes.*

fresh·et (fresh′it) a rush of water caused by heavy rains or melted snow. *n.*

fresh·man (fresh′mən) a student in the first year of a university course. *n., pl.* **fresh·men** (fresh′mən).

fresh–wa·ter (fresh′wo′tər or fresh′wô′tər) of or living in water that is not salty: *The catfish is a fresh-water fish. adj.*

fret[1] (fret) 1 worry; be peevish; be discontented: *Don't fret over your mistakes. Babies sometimes fret in hot weather.* 2 make peevish; make discontented: *Her failures fretted her.* 3 a condition of worry or discontent: *She is in a fret about her test.* 1, 2 *v.,* **fret·ted, fret·ting;** 3 *n.*

fret[2] (fret) one of a series of ridges of wood, ivory, or metal on a guitar, banjo, etc. to show where to put the fingers to produce particular tones. *n.*

fret·ful (fret′fəl) peevish; unhappy; discontented; inclined to fret: *My baby brother is fretful because he is cutting a tooth. adj.*

Fri. Friday.

fri·ar (frī′ər) a man who belongs to one of certain religious brotherhoods of the Roman Catholic Church. *n.*

fric·tion (frik′shən) 1 a rubbing of one thing against another, such as skates on ice, hand against hand, a brush on shoes: *Matches are lighted by friction.* 2 the resistance to motion of surfaces that touch: *Oil reduces friction in engines. With five people aboard, there was too much friction between the toboggan and the snow.* 3 conflict of differing ideas, opinions, etc.; disagreement: *Political differences continued to cause friction between the two countries. n.*

Fri·day (frī′dē or frī′dā) the sixth day of the week, following Thursday. *n.*
☛ **Friday** developed from Old English *Frīgedæg,* meaning 'day of Frīg'; Frīg was the Germanic goddess of love.

fridge (frij) *Informal.* refrigerator. *n.*

fried (frīd) 1 cooked in hot fat. 2 See **fry.** *I fried the ham. Are the potatoes fried?* 1 *adj.,* 2 *v.*

friend (frend) 1 a person who knows and likes another. 2 a person who favors and supports: *She was a generous friend to the poor.* 3 a person who belongs to the same side or group: *'Are you friend or foe?' n.* **—friend′less,** *adj.*

friend·ly (frend′lē) 1 of a friend: *a friendly greeting.* 2 like a friend; like a friend's. 3 on good terms: *friendly relations between countries.* 4 wanting to be a friend: *a friendly dog.* 5 favoring; favorable: *a friendly breeze. adj.,* **friend·li·er, friend·li·est. —friend′li·ness,** *n.*

friend·ship (frend′ship) 1 the state of being friends. 2 a liking between friends. 3 a friendly feeling; friendly behavior: *His smile radiated friendship. n.*

fries (frīz) 1 See **fry.** *She fries eggs with the bacon.* 2 French fries. 1 *v.,* 2 *n. pl.*

A frieze

frieze (frēz) a band of decoration around a room, building, or mantel: *A frieze may be painted or carved. n.*
☛ **Frieze** and **freeze** are pronounced the same.

frig·ate (frig′it) 1 a modern warship smaller than a destroyer. 2 in former times, a three-masted sailing warship of medium size. *n.*

fright (frīt) 1 sudden fear; sudden terror: *The boy was pale with fright when he was rescued from the top of the cliff.* 2 *Informal.* a person or thing that is ugly, shocking, or ridiculous: *She looked a fright in that hat. n.*

fright·en (frīt′ən) make afraid. *v.*

fright·en·ing (frīt′ning or frīt′ən ing) 1 capable of causing fright or fear: *a frightening experience.* 2 See **frighten.** *He seemed to take pleasure in frightening children.* 1 *adj.,* 2 *v.*

fright·ful (frīt′fəl) 1 causing fright or horror; dreadful: *There was a frightful thunderstorm last night.* 2 unattractive; unpleasant; uncomfortable: *a frightful person, a frightful trip, a frightful mess. adj.*

frig·id (frij′id) 1 very cold: *a frigid climate.* 2 cold in feeling or manner; stiff; chilling: *a frigid stare, frigid conversation. adj.*

Frigid Zone a region within the Arctic or the Arctic Circle. See **zone** for picture.

frill (fril) 1 ruffle. 2 anything added merely for show; a useless ornament: *It was a plain house with few frills. n.* **—frill′y,** *adj.*

Two styles of fringe

fringe (frinj) 1 a border or trimming made of threads, cords, etc., either loose or tied together in small bunches: *The chesterfield had a fringe along the bottom edge.* 2 anything like this; border: *A fringe of hair hung over her forehead.* 3 make a border for. 4 be a border for; border: *Bushes fringed the road.* 1, 2 *n.,* 3, 4 *v.* **fringed, fring·ing.**

frisk (frisk) 1 run and jump about playfully; dance and skip in play: *Our lively puppy frisks all over the house.* 2 *Slang.* search a person for hidden weapons, stolen goods, etc. by running a hand quickly over his or her clothes. *v.*

frisk·y (fris′kē) playful; lively. *adj.,* **frisk·i·er, frisk·i·est.**

frit·ter[1] (frit′ər) waste little by little: *He frittered away the afternoon trying to decide what to do.* *v.*

frit·ter[2] (frit′ər) a small cake of batter, sometimes containing fruit or other food, that is fried in deep fat: *apple fritters.* *n.*

friv·o·lous (friv′ə ləs) **1** lacking in seriousness or sense; silly: *Her frivolous behavior was out of place in church.* **2** of little worth or importance: *He wasted his time on frivolous matters.* *adj.* **—friv′o·lous·ly,** *adv.*

fro (frō) **to and fro,** first one way and then back again; back and forth: *A rocking chair goes to and fro.*

frock (frok) **1** a gown or dress: *What a pretty frock!* **2** a robe worn by a clergyman. *n.*

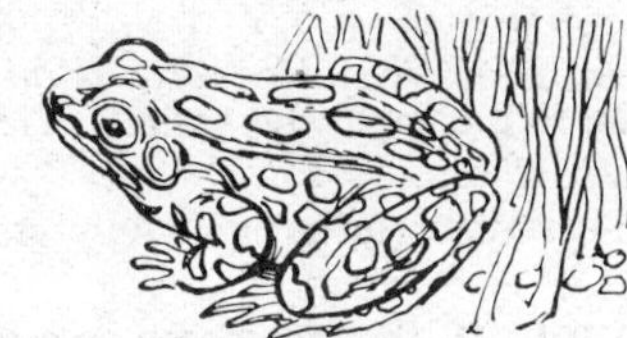

One kind of frog—about 7 cm long

frog (frog) a small, leaping animal with webbed feet that lives in or near water: *Frogs hatch from eggs as tadpoles, which live in the water until they grow legs.* *n.*

frog in the throat, *Informal.* a slight hoarseness caused by soreness or swelling in the throat.

frog·man (frog′man′ or frog′mən) a skindiver, especially one in or working for the armed forces: *He was a frogman in the navy.* See **skindiver** for picture. *n., pl.* **frog·men** (frog′men′ or frog′mən).

frol·ic (frol′ik) **1** a joyous game or party; play; fun. **2** play about joyously; have fun together: *The children frolicked with the puppy.* 1 *n.,* 2 *v.,* **frol·icked, frol·ick·ing.**

frol·ic·some (frol′ik səm) playful; merry. *adj.*

from (frəm; when stressed, frum or from) **1** out of; of: *Bricks are made from clay. Steel is made from iron.* **2** beginning with; starting out from: *Study the lesson from page 10 to page 15. The train from Montreal will arrive at noon.* **3** originated in; having as a source: *The river flows from the mountain. Much of our asbestos is from Quebec.* **4** because of: *He is suffering from a cold. The slave was weak from hunger.* **5** as being unlike; as distinguished from: *Anyone can tell apples from oranges.* **6** off: *He took some books from the table.* **7** out of the possession of: *He took the knife from the baby.* *prep.*

frond (frond) the leaf of a fern or of a palm tree. *n.*

front (frunt) **1** the first part: *the front of a car.* **2** the part that faces forward: *She spilled milk down the front of her dress.* **3** in war, the place where fighting is going on: *He spent many weeks at the front.* **4** the land facing a lake, an ocean, a street, etc. **5** something worn on or fastened onto the front. **6** on or in the front; at the front: *a front room.* **7** have the front toward; face: *Her house fronts the river.* **8** the dividing surface between two different air masses: *The weather report says there is a cold front approaching from the northwest.* 1–5, 8 *n.,* 6 *adj.,* 7 *v.*

eyes front! look forward! direct the eyes ahead!

in front of, in a place or position before a person or thing: *He stood in front of me.*

hat, āge, fär; let, ēqual, tėrm; it, īce
hot, ōpen, ôrder; oil, out; cup, pu̇t, rüle
əbove, takən, pencəl, lemən, circəs
ch, child; ng, long; sh, ship
th, thin; ᴛʜ, then; zh, measure

fron·tier (fron tēr′, frun tēr′, or fron′tēr) **1** the last edge of settled country, where the wilds begin: *The Yukon is part of Canada's present-day frontier. Frontier life is often harsh.* **2** a part of one country that touches on the border of another; a boundary line or border between two countries. *n.*

frost (frost) **1** a condition of freezing: *There was frost in the air last night. The plants were killed by a heavy frost.* **2** cold weather. **3** moisture frozen on or in a solid surface; feathery crystals of ice formed when water vapor in the air condenses at a temperature below freezing: *frost on the grass, frost on windows.* **4** cover with frost. **5** cover with anything that suggests frost, such as icing: *Mother frosted a cake with sugar and white of egg mixed together.* 1–3 *n.,* 4, 5 *v.*

frost·bite (frost′bīt′) the freezing of some part of the body; the result of such freezing. *n.*

frost·bit·ten (frost′bit′ən) injured by severe cold: *My ears were frostbitten.* *adj.*

frost·ing (fros′ting) **1** a mixture of sugar and some liquid, with flavoring, to cover cake; icing. **2** a dull finish on glass or metal. *n.*

frost·y (fros′tē) **1** cold enough for frost: *a frosty morning.* **2** covered with frost: *The glass is frosty.* **3** cold and unfriendly; with no warmth of feeling: *a frosty manner.* *adj.,* **frost·i·er, frost·i·est.**

froth (froth) **1** a mass of very small bubbles; foam: *There was froth on the mad dog's lips.* **2** to foam: *The mad dog frothed at the mouth.* **3** cause to foam by beating, pouring, etc. **4** something light and trifling; unimportant talk: *His conversation was mostly froth.* 1, 4 *n.,* 2, 3 *v.*

frown (froun) **1** a drawing together of the brows, usually in deep thought or in strong feeling. **2** draw the brows together, as in deep thought or anger: *He frowned with annoyance.* **3** look displeased or angry. 1 *n.,* 2, 3 *v.*

frown on, disapprove of: *Many people frown on gambling.*

froze (frōz) See **freeze.** *The water in the pond froze last week.* *v.*

fro·zen (frō′zən) **1** hardened with cold; turned into ice: *a river frozen over, frozen pudding.* **2** kept at a temperature below freezing to prevent spoiling: *frozen foods, frozen meat.* **3** killed or injured by frost: *frozen flowers.* **4** cold and unfeeling: *a frozen heart.* **5** too frightened or stiff to move: *frozen to the spot in horror.* **6** See **freeze.** *The water has frozen to ice.* 1–5 *adj.,* 6 *v.*

fru·gal (frü′gəl) **1** without waste; not wasteful; saving; using things well: *My aunt, who is a frugal housekeeper, buys and uses food carefully.* **2** costing little; barely enough: *He ate a frugal supper of bread and milk.* *adj.*

fruit (früt) **1** the product of a tree, bush, shrub, or vine that is good to eat: *Apples, pears, oranges, bananas, peaches, and plums are fruit.* **2** the part of a plant that contains the seeds: *Pea pods, acorns, and grains of wheat are fruits.* **3** a useful product of plant growth: *fruits of* *the earth.* 4 the result of anything: *His invention was the fruit of much effort.* 5 produce fruit. 1–4 *n.*, 5 *v.*

fruit·cake (früt′kāk′) a rich cake containing raisins, currants, spices, etc. *n.*

fruit·ful (früt′fəl) 1 producing much fruit. 2 producing much of anything. 3 having good results; bringing benefit or profit: *A successful plan is fruitful.* *adj.*

fruit·less (früt′lis) 1 having no results; useless; unsuccessful: *fruitless efforts.* 2 producing no fruit. *adj.*

fruit nappie or **fruit nappy** a small dish in which dessert such as fruit may be served.

fruit·y (früt′ē) tasting or smelling like fruit. *adj.*, **fruit·i·er, fruit·i·est.**

frus·trate (frus′trāt) foil; bring to nothing; defeat; baffle: *Heavy rains frustrated our plans for a picnic.* *v.*, **frus·trat·ed, frus·trat·ing.**

fry[1] (frī) 1 cook in hot fat, in a deep or shallow pan: *She is frying potatoes.* 2 a social gathering where some special fried food is served: *a fish fry.* 1 *v.*, **fried, fry·ing;** 2 *n.*, *pl.* **fries.**

fry[2] (frī) 1 young fish. 2 small, adult fish that move about together in large groups or schools: *Sardines are classed as fry.* *n.*

small fry, a children: *This movie is not for small fry.* **b** people or things having little importance.

frying pan a shallow pan with a long handle, used for frying food.

out of the frying pan into the fire, straight from one danger or difficulty into a worse one: *It was a case of out of the frying pan into the fire when he escaped from the kidnappers' cabin and found himself faced with a bear.*

ft. 1 foot; feet. 2 fort.

fu·el (fyü′əl) 1 something burned to provide heat or power: *Have we enough fuel? Coal, wood, gas, and oil are fuels.* 2 anything that keeps up or increases a feeling: *Her insults were fuel to his hatred.* 3 supply with fuel. 1, 2 *n.*, 3 *v.*, **fu·elled** or **fu·eled, fu·el·ling** or **fu·el·ing.**

fu·gi·tive (fyü′jə tiv) 1 a person who is running away or has run away: *The murderer became a fugitive from justice.* 2 running away; having run away: *a fugitive slave.* 3 lasting a very short time; passing swiftly: *the fugitive hours.* 1 *n.*, 2, 3 *adj.*

–ful a suffix meaning: 1 full of ___: *Cheerful means full of cheer.* 2 showing ___: *Careful means showing care.* 3 enough to fill a ___: *A cupful means enough to fill a cup.*

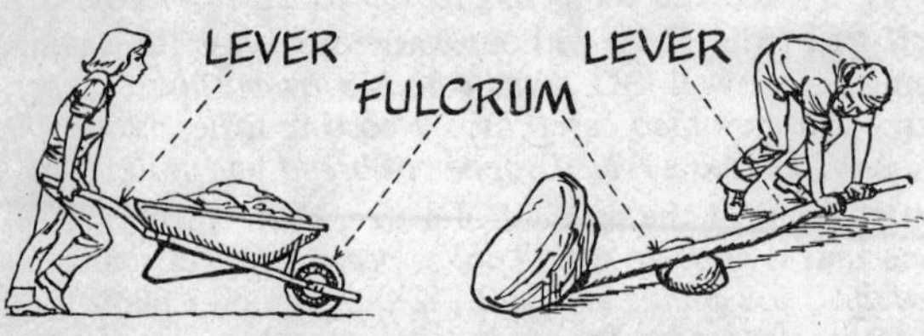

ful·crum (fůl′krəm or ful′krəm) the support on which a lever turns or is supported in moving or lifting something. *n.*, *pl.* **ful·crums** or **ful·cra** (ful′krə).

ful·fil or **ful·fill** (fůl fil′) 1 carry out a promise, prophecy, etc. 2 perform or do a duty, command, etc.: *She fulfilled all the teacher's requests.* 3 satisfy a requirement, etc.; answer a purpose: *The house was small, but it fulfilled their needs.* *v.*, **ful·filled, ful·fill·ing.**

ful·fil·ment or **ful·fill·ment** (fůl fil′mənt) the act of fulfilling; completion; accomplishment: *Winning the race brought him a feeling of fulfilment.* *n.*

full (fůl) 1 that can hold no more: *a full cup.* 2 complete; entire: *a full supply of clothes.* 3 completely: *Fill the pail full.* 4 plump; round; well filled out: *a full face.* 5 having wide folds or much cloth: *a full skirt.* 6 squarely; directly: *The ball hit him full in the face.* 1, 2, 4, 5 *adj.*, 3, 6 *adv.*

full of, filled with: *Her room is full of toys.*

to the full, completely; entirely: *He satisfied his ambition to the full.*

full–grown (fůl′grōn′) fully grown: *a full-grown dog.* *adj.*

full moon the moon seen as a whole circle.

full·ness (fůl′nis) being full: *The bag bulged because of its fullness.* *n.*

ful·ly (fůl′ē) 1 completely; entirely: *Was he fully satisfied?* 2 quite: *He could not fully describe what he had seen.* *adv.*

fum·ble (fum′bəl) 1 feel or grope about clumsily; search awkwardly: *He fumbled in the darkness for the doorknob. She fumbled for words to express her thanks.* 2 handle awkwardly; let drop instead of catching and holding: *The first baseman fumbled the ball, and two runs were scored.* 3 an awkward attempt to find or handle something. 1, 2 *v.*, **fum·bled, fum·bling;** 3 *n.*

fume (fyüm) 1 vapor, gas, or smoke, especially if harmful or strong: *The strong fumes of the acid nearly choked him.* 2 give off vapor, gas, or smoke: *The candle fumed, sputtered, and went out.* 3 let off one's rage in angry complaints: *He fumed about the slowness of the train.* 1 *n.*, 2, 3 *v.*, **fumed, fum·ing.**

fu·mi·gate (fyü′mə gāt′) disinfect with fumes; expose to fumes: *They fumigated the building to kill the vermin.* *v.*, **fu·mi·gat·ed, fu·mi·gat·ing.**

fun (fun) playfulness; merry play; amusement; joking: *They had a lot of fun at the party.* *n.*

for fun or **in fun,** as a joke; playfully.

make fun of, laugh at; ridicule.

func·tion (fungk′shən) 1 proper work; purpose; use: *The function of the stomach is to help digest food.* 2 work; be used; act: *This table functions as my desk. This old fountain pen does not function very well.* 3 a formal public or social gathering for some purpose: *She attended five different functions last week.* 1, 3 *n.*, 2 *v.*

fund (fund) 1 a sum of money set aside for a special purpose: *Our school has a fund of $2000 to buy books with.* 2 a stock or supply ready for use: *There is a fund of knowledge in a dictionary.* 3 **funds,** *pl.* **a** money ready to use: *We took $10 from the club's funds to buy a flag.* **b** money: *He used up his allowance and is low in funds.* *n.*

fun·da·men·tal (fun′də men′təl) 1 forming a basis; essential. 2 something that forms a basis; an essential part: *the fundamentals of grammar.* 1 *adj.*, 2 *n.*

hat, āge, fär; let, ēqual, tėrm; it, īce
hot, ōpen, ôrder; oil, out; cup, pu̇t, rüle
əbove, takən, pencəl, lemən, circəs
ch, child; ng, long; sh, ship
th, thin; ᴛʜ, then; zh, measure

fu·ner·al (fyü′nər əl) 1 the ceremonies that accompany the burial or burning of the dead, usually including holding a religious service and taking the body to the place of burial. 2 of a funeral; suitable for a funeral: *A funeral march is very slow.* 1 *n.,* 2 *adj.*

fun·gi (fung′gī or fung′gē, fun′jī or fun′jē) a plural of **fungus.** *n.*

Fungi growing on a tree

fun·gus (fung′gəs) 1 a plant without flowers, leaves, or green coloring matter: *Mushrooms, toadstools, moulds, and mildews are fungi.* 2 a diseased spongy growth on the skin. *n., pl.* **fun·gi** or **fun·gus·es.**

A funnel for pouring

fun·nel (fun′əl) 1 a tapering, open vessel ending at the bottom in a tube: *He used a funnel to pour the gas into the tank.* 2 the smoke-stack or chimney on a steamship or steam engine. *n.*

fun·ny (fun′ē) 1 causing laughter; amusing; comical: *a funny clown, a funny story.* 2 *Informal.* strange; peculiar; odd: *funny behavior. adj.,* **fun·ni·er, fun·ni·est.**

fur (fėr) 1 the soft coat of hair that covers many animals. 2 skin with such hair on it: *Fur is used to make, cover, trim, or line clothing.* 3 Usually, **furs,** *pl.* a garment made of fur: *Mother's furs keep her warm. n.*
☛ **Fur** and **fir** are pronounced the same.

fur brigade *Cdn.* formerly, a convoy of freight canoes or dog sleds that carried furs and other goods from remote trading posts.

fu·ri·ous (fyür′ē əs) 1 raging; violent: *a furious storm.* 2 full of wild, fierce anger: *Father was furious when he learned of the broken window. adj.*

furl (fėrl) roll up; fold up: *to furl a sail, to furl a flag. The seagulls furled their wings. v.*

fur·long (fėr′long) a measure of distance equal to ⅛ of a mile, or about 200 metres. *n.*

fur·lough (fėr′lō) leave of absence: *The soldier has two weeks' furlough. n.*

fur·nace (fėr′nis) 1 a device for providing heat for buildings by warming water or air that circulates through pipes and radiators, hot-air registers, etc.: *We have an oil furnace in our house.* 2 a device for providing intense heat for use in separating metal from ore, in treating metal, in producing coke, etc. *n.*

fur·nish (fėr′nish) 1 supply; provide: *to furnish an army with blankets. The sun furnishes heat.* 2 supply with beds, chairs, tables, etc.: *to furnish a bedroom. v.*

fur·nish·ings (fėr′nish ingz) 1 the furniture or equipment for a room, house, etc. 2 accessories of dress; articles of clothing: *That store sells men's furnishings. n. pl.*

fur·ni·ture (fėr′nə chər) the articles needed in a house or room, such as chairs, tables, beds, desks, etc. *n.*

fu·ror (fyür′ôr) an outburst of wild enthusiasm or excitement: *When the favorite won the race, there was a great furor among the spectators. n.*

fur·ri·er (fėr′ē ər) 1 a dealer in furs. 2 a person whose work is preparing furs or making or repairing fur garments. *n.*

Furrows
cut by ploughshares

fur·row (fėr′ō) 1 the long, narrow track in the earth cut by a plough. 2 cut furrows in. 3 wrinkle: *a furrow in one's brow.* 4 make wrinkles in: *The old man's face was furrowed with age.* 1, 3 *n.,* 2, 4 *v.*

fur·ry (fėr′ē) 1 covered with fur. 2 soft like fur: *a furry woollen glove. adj.,* **fur·ri·er, fur·ri·est.**

fur·ther (fėr′ᴛʜər) 1 farther: *on the further side.* 2 more: *Do you need further help?* 3 help forward: *Mother furthered our plans.* 4 furthermore. 1, 2 *adj.,* 3 *v.,* 4 *adv.*

fur·ther·more (fėr′ᴛʜər môr′) moreover; also; besides. *adv.*

fur·ther·most (fėr′ᴛʜər mōst′) farthest. *adj.*

fur·thest (fėr′ᴛʜist) farthest in space or time: *Cut down the furthest tree in the first row. Of all his family, Grandfather could remember furthest into the past. adj., adv.*

fur·tive (fėr′tiv) 1 done by stealth; secret: *He made a furtive attempt to read his sister's letter.* 2 sly; stealthy; shifty: *The thief had a furtive manner. adj.* **—fur′tive·ly,** *adv.*

fu·ry (fyür′ē) 1 a rage; a storm of anger. 2 violence; fierceness: *the fury of a hurricane. n., pl.* **fu·ries.**

fuse[1] (fyüz) 1 the part of an electric circuit that melts and breaks the circuit if the current becomes dangerously strong. 2 a slow-burning wick or other device used to set off a bomb or a blast of gunpowder, so that one may have time to move to a safe distance after lighting it: *Firecrackers have fuses. n.*

fuse[2] (fyüz) 1 melt; join together by melting: *Copper and zinc are fused to make brass.* 2 blend; unite. *v.,* **fused, fus·ing.**

fu·se·lage (fyü′zə läzh′ or fyü′zə lij) the body of an airplane: *The fuselage holds the passengers and the cargo.* See **airplane** for picture. *n.*

fu·sion (fyü′zhən) **1** the act or process of fusing or melting; melting together. **2** a blending or union: *A new party was formed by the fusion of two political groups.* *n.*

fuss (fus) **1** much bother about small matters; useless talk and worry; attention given to something not worth it: *There was a great deal of fuss about the lost nickel.* **2** make a fuss: *She fussed about with her work in a nervous manner.* 1 *n.,* 2 *v.*

fuss·y (fus′ē) **1** hard to please; never satisfied: *A sick person is sometimes so fussy that he can't be pleased.* **2** elaborately made: *It was a very fussy dress, with bows, ruffles, and lace.* *adj.,* **fuss·i·er, fuss·i·est.**

fu·tile (fyü′tīl or fyü′təl) not successful; useless: *His attempts to solve the puzzle were futile.* *adj.*

fu·ture (fyü′chər) **1** time to come; what is to come: *You cannot change the past, but you can do better in the future.* **2** coming; that will be: *She wished them happiness in their future years.* 1 *n.,* 2 *adj.*

fuzz (fuz) **1** light, loose fibres or hairs; down: *Caterpillars and peaches are covered with fuzz.* **2** *Slang.* Usually, **the fuzz,** the police. *n.*

fuzz·y (fuz′ē) **1** covered with light, soft hair or with a soft, fluffy substance: *a fuzzy little kitten. Some peaches are fuzzy.* **2** of or like fuzz. **3** not clear in outline; blurred; hazy: *His eyes were so weak that everything appeared fuzzy.* *adj.,* **fuzz·i·er, fuzz·i·est.** **—fuzz′i·ly,** *adv.* **—fuzz′i·ness,** *n.*

hat, āge, fär; let, ēqual, tėrm; it, īce
hot, ōpen, ôrder; oil, out; cup, pu̇t, rüle
əbove, takən, pencəl, lemən, circəs
ch, child; ng, long; sh, ship
th, thin; ᴛʜ, then; zh, measure

g or **G** (jē) the seventh letter of the alphabet: *There are two* g's *in* gag. *n., pl.* **g's** or **G's.**

g gram; grams.

gab (gab) *Informal.* **1** chatter; gabble; idle talk. **2** talk too much; chatter; gabble. 1 *n.,* 2 *v.,* **gabbed, gab·bing. —gab′by,** *adj.*

gab·ble (gab′əl) **1** talk rapidly while making little or no sense. **2** rapid talk that makes little or no sense. 1 *v.,* **gab·bled, gab·bling;** 2 *n.*

ga·ble (gā′bəl) the end of a ridged roof, with the three-cornered piece of wall that it covers. *n.*

gad (gad) go about looking for pleasure or excitement: *She was always gadding about town. v.,* **gad·ded, gad·ding.**

gad·a·bout (gad′ə bout′) *Informal.* a person who goes about looking for pleasure or excitement; a person fond of going from place to place. *n.*

gad·fly (gad′flī′) **1** a fly that stings cattle, horses, and other animals; a horsefly. **2** a person who irritates others, especially by calling attention to their faults. *n.*

gadg·et (gaj′it) a small mechanical, electrical, or electronic device or contrivance: *My older brother is always buying gadgets for his car. n.*

Gael·ic (gā′lik) **1** of or having to do with the Celtic people of Scotland or Ireland, or their language. **2** the language of these people: *Many people born on the islands of Scotland still speak Gaelic.* 1 *adj.,* 2 *n.*

gag (gag) **1** something put in a person's mouth to keep him from talking or crying out. **2** stop up the mouth of with a gag: *The bandits tied the watchman's arms and gagged him.* **3** strain in an effort to vomit. **4** *Informal.* something said to cause a laugh; a joke: *Everyone thought the comedian's gags were funny.* 1, 4 *n.,* 2, 3 *v.,* **gagged, gag·ging.**

gage (gāj) See **gauge.** *n., v.,* **gaged, gag·ing.**

gai·e·ty (gā′ə tē) **1** the state or condition of being gay: *Her gaiety helped the party.* **2** bright appearance: *gaiety of dress. n., pl.* **gai·e·ties.** Also spelled **gayety.**

gai·ly (gā′lē) **1** as if gay; merrily; happily. **2** brightly: *She was gaily dressed. adv.* Also spelled **gayly.**

gain (gān) **1** get; obtain; secure: *The king gained possession of more lands.* **2** profit: *How much did I gain by that?* **3** an increase, addition or advantage; what is gained: *a gain in speed, a gain of ten per cent.* **4 gains,** *pl.* profits; earnings; winnings. **5** make progress: *The sick child is gaining.* **6** win: *He was sure he would gain the prize.* **7** get to; arrive at; reach: *The swimmer gained the shore.* **8** of a timepiece, run fast: *My watch gains about 10 minutes each week.* 1, 2, 5–8 *v.,* 3, 4 *n.*

gain on, catch up to; overtake: *One boat is gaining on another.*

gain·say (gān′sā′) deny; contradict; dispute: *We could not gainsay his opinion. v.,* **gain·said** or **gain·sayed** (gān′sed′), **gain·say·ing.**

gait (gāt) the kind of steps used in going along; a manner of walking or running: *He has a lame gait because of an injured foot. A gallop is one of the gaits of a horse. n.*

☛ **Gait** and **gate** are pronounced the same.

gai·ter (gā′tər) an outer covering of cloth or leather for the leg below the knee or for the ankle, for outdoor wear. *n.*

gal. gallon; gallons.

ga·la (gā′lə or gal′ə) **1** a festive occasion; festival. **2** festive: *In our family, Thanksgiving and Christmas are gala days.* 1 *n.,* 2 *adj.*

gal·ax·y (gal′ək sē) **1** a large number of stars forming one system. **2** a brilliant or splendid group: *The queen was followed by a galaxy of brave knights and fair ladies. n., pl.* **gal·ax·ies.**

gale (gāl) **1** a very strong wind. **2** a noisy outburst: *gales of laughter. n.*

gall[1] (gol or gôl) **1** a bitter liquid made in the liver. **2** bitterness; hate: *His heart was filled with gall.* **3** *Slang.* audacity; rude boldness; nerve: *He had a lot of gall talking to the teacher in such a nasty way. n.*

gall[2] (gol or gôl) annoy; irritate: *The child was galled by being scolded so much. v.*

gall[3] (gol or gôl) a lump or ball on the leaves, stems, or roots of plants caused by insects, fungi, bacteria, etc.: *Ink is made from the galls of oak trees. n.*

gal·lant (gal′ənt for 1 and 2; gə lant′ or gal′ənt for 3) **1** noble in spirit or in looks; brave: *King Arthur was a gallant knight.* **2** showing respect and courtesy to women. **3** a man who is very polite and attentive to women. 1, 2 *adj.,* 3 *n.*

gal·lant·ry (gal′ən trē) **1** bravery; dashing courage: *The colonel had won a medal for gallantry.* **2** respect and courtesy to women. **3** a gallant act or speech. *n., pl.* **gal·lant·ries.**

gal·le·on (gal′ē ən) a large sailing ship of former times, usually having several decks: *There were many galleons in the Spanish Armada.* See the picture. *n.*

gal·ler·y (gal′ər ē) **1** a hall or long, narrow passage. **2** a balcony looking down into a large hall or room. **3** the highest balcony of a theatre: *Seats in the gallery usually cost less than seats elsewhere.* **4** the people who sit in the highest balcony of a theatre. **5** a building or room used to show collections of paintings, sculptures, and other works of art: *an art gallery. n., pl.* **gal·ler·ies.**

A galleon   A galley

gal·ley (gal′ē) **1** a long, narrow ship of former times, having oars and sails: *Galleys were often rowed by slaves or convicts.* 2 the kitchen of a ship. *n., pl.* **gal·leys.**

gal·li·vant (gal′ə vant′) go about seeking pleasure; gad about. *v.*

gal·lon (gal′ən) a measure for liquids equal to four quarts and about the same as 4.5 litres. *n.*

gal·lop (gal′əp) **1** a fast gait of a horse or other four-footed animal: *In a gallop, all four feet are off the ground together at each leap.* **2** ride at a gallop: *The cowboy galloped across the field.* **3** a ride taken at this gait: *We went for a gallop across the prairie.* **4** go at a gallop: *The pony galloped up to the fence.* **5** cause to go at a gallop: *He galloped his horse down the road.* **6** go very fast; hurry: *The excited little girl galloped down the street as fast as her legs would carry her.* 1, 3 *n.,* 2, 4–6 *v.*

gal·lows (gal′ōz) **1** a wooden frame made of a crossbar on two upright posts, used for hanging criminals. **2 the gallows,** punishment by hanging: *Many people are against the gallows.* *n., pl.* **gal·lows** or **gal·lows·es.**

ga·losh (gə losh′) usually, **galoshes,** *pl.* a rubber or plastic-soled overshoe often having a rubber or plastic top as well, worn in wet or snowy weather. *n.*

gal·va·nize (gal′və nīz′) **1** apply an electric current to. **2** arouse suddenly; startle: *The whole country was galvanized by the threat of war.* **3** cover iron or steel with a thin coating of zinc to prevent rust. *v.,* **gal·va·nized, gal·va·niz·ing.**

gam·ble (gam′bəl) **1** play games of chance for money or other prize. **2** take great risks in business; take a risk. **3** a bet or wager. **4** a risky act or undertaking: *Investing money in newly discovered mines is a gamble.* 1, 2 *v.,* **gam·bled, gam·bling;** 3, 4 *n.*

gam·bler (gam′blər) **1** a person who gambles. **2** a person who gambles a great deal, especially one who makes his living by gambling. *n.*

gam·bol (gam′bəl) **1** a frolic; a running and jumping about in play. **2** frolic; run and jump about; play: *The lambs were gambolling in the meadow.* 1 *n.,* 2 *v.,* **gam·bolled** or **gam·boled, gam·bol·ling** or **gam·bol·ing.**

game (gām) **1** a way of playing; amusement: *a game with bat and ball, a game of tag.* **2** the things needed for a game: *This store sells games.* **3** a contest with certain rules: *Our team did their best to win the game.* **4** any one of a number of contests making up an organized series: *Our hockey team plays 40 games a year. The tennis champion won four games out of six.* **5** the score in a game: *At the end of the first period the game was 6 to 3 in our favor.* **6** a scheme or plan: *He tried to trick us, but we saw through his game.* **7** animals and birds that are hunted or caught. **8** the flesh of wild animals and birds when used for food. **9** brave; plucky; daring to do a thing: *Are you game to swim across the river?* **10** gamble. 1–8 *n.,* 9 *adj.,* **gam·er, gam·est;** 10 *v.,* **gamed, gam·ing.**
make game of, make fun of; laugh at.

game law a law made for the protection of game (def. 7) in certain seasons and areas.

game warden an official whose duty it is to enforce the game laws in a certain district.

gamma rays (gam′ə) powerful rays of very high frequency, given off by radium, etc.: *Gamma rays are similar to X rays but of shorter length.*

gan·der (gan′dər) an adult male goose. *n.*

gang (gang) **1** a group of people acting or going around together: *Criminals often form gangs.* **2** a group of people working together under one foreman: *Two gangs of workmen were mending the road.* *n.*
gang up, come together into a group for some purpose: *We ganged up to give a party for our coach.*
gang up on, oppose as a group: *Let's gang up on that bully.*

gan·gling (gang′gling) awkwardly tall and thin; lank. *adj.*

A gangplank

gang·plank (gang′plangk′) a movable bridge used by persons and animals in passing on and off a ship. *n.*

gan·grene (gang′grēn) the decay of a part of a living person or animal when the blood supply is interfered with by injury, infection, freezing, etc. *n.*

gang·ster (gang′stər) a member of a gang of criminals. *n.*

gang·way (gang′wā′) **1** passageway. **2** a passageway on a ship: *This ship has a gangway between the rail and the cabins.* **3** gangplank. **4** *Informal.* get out of the way, please! stand aside and make room! 1–3 *n.,* 4 *interj.*

gant·let (gont′lit or gônt′lit) See **gauntlet**[2].

gaol (jāl) *British.* jail. *n.*

gap (gap) **1** a broken place; opening: *a gap in a fence or wall.* **2** an unfilled space; blank: *My diary is not complete; there are gaps in it.* **3** a pass through mountains. *n.*

gape (gāp) **1** open wide: *A deep hole in the earth gaped before us.* **2** open the mouth wide; yawn. **3** opening the mouth wide; yawning. **4** stare with the mouth open: *The children gaped when they saw the huge birthday cake.* 1, 2, 4 *v.,* **gaped, gap·ing;** 3 *n.*

ga·rage (gə räzh′, gə raj′ or gə razh′) **1** a place for keeping automobiles. **2** a shop for repairing automobiles. *n.*

garb (gärb) **1** the way one is dressed. **2** clothing. **3** clothe: *The doctor was garbed in white from head to toe.* 1, 2 *n.,* 3 *v.*

gar·bage (gär′bij) **1** waste from the kitchen or dining room; scraps of food to be thrown away: *The garbage was wrapped in old newspapers.* **2** trash; rubbish. **3** *Informal.* anything of no value. *n.*

gar·den (gär′dən) **1** a piece of ground used for growing vegetables, flowers, or fruits. **2** take care of a garden: *He liked to garden, for it kept him out of doors.* **3** a park or other place where plants or animals may be viewed by the public. 1, 3 *n.,* 2 *v.*

gar·den·er (gärd′nər or gär′də nər) **1** a person hired to take care of a garden. **2** a person who makes a garden or works in a garden: *Father is a keen gardener.* *n.*

hat, āge, fär; let, ēqual, tėrm; it, īce
hot, ōpen, ôrder; oil, out; cup, pu̇t, rüle
ə above, takən, pencəl, lemən, circəs
ch, child; ng, long; sh, ship
th, thin; ᴛʜ, then; zh, measure

gar·de·nia (gär dēn′yə or gär dē′nē ə) a shrub having a sweet-smelling, roselike, white or yellow flower with waxy petals. *n.*

gar·den·ing (gärd′ning or gär′dən ing) the preparation and care of gardens: *Some people find great pleasure in gardening.* *n.*

gar·gle (gär′gəl) **1** wash the inside of the throat with liquid kept in motion by the outgoing breath: *He treated his sore throat by gargling with salt water.* **2** a liquid used for gargling. 1 *v.*, **gar·gled, gar·gling;** 2 *n.*

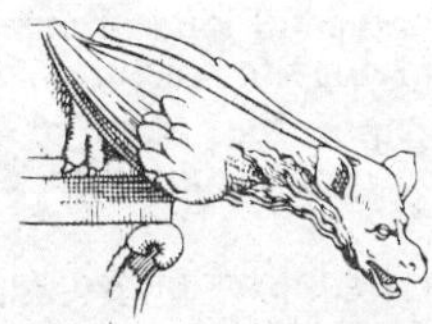

A gargoyle

gar·goyle (gär′goil) **1** a spout ending in a grotesque head, usually for carrying off rain water. **2** a projection or ornament on a building resembling a gargoyle. *n.*

gar·ish (ger′ish or gar′ish) unpleasantly bright; glaring; showy; gaudy: *Many people objected to the garish neon signs along the main street.* *adj.*

gar·land (gär′lənd) **1** a wreath of flowers, leaves, etc. **2** decorate with garlands. 1 *n.*, 2 *v.*

gar·lic (gär′lik) **1** a plant resembling an onion whose strong-smelling bulb is composed of small sections called cloves. **2** a bulb or clove of this plant, used to season meats, salads, etc: *The flavor of garlic is much stronger than that of onion.* *n.*

gar·ment (gär′mənt) any article of clothing. *n.*

gar·ner (gär′nər) gather and store away: *Wheat is cut and garnered at harvest time. Squirrels garner nuts in the fall.* *v.*

gar·net (gär′nit) **1** a deep-red semiprecious stone. **2** deep red. 1, 2 *n.*, 2 *adj.*

gar·nish (gär′nish) **1** something laid on or around food as a decoration: *a garnish of parsley.* **2** decorate food. 1 *n.*, 2 *v.*

gar·ret (gar′it or ger′it) a space in a house just below a sloping roof; attic. *n.*

gar·ri·son (gar′ə sən or ger′ə sən) **1** the troops stationed in a fort or town, usually for purposes of defending it. **2** a place where such troops are stationed. **3** station troops in a fort or town to defend it. **4** take over or occupy as a garrison. 1, 2 *n.*, 3, 4 *v.*

gar·ter (gär′tər) a band or strap, usually of elastic, used to hold up a sock or a stocking. *n.*

garter snake a harmless snake, brown or green with long, yellow stripes.

gas[1] (gas) **1** vapor; a substance that is not a solid or a liquid; any substance when it is like air in form: *Oxygen and hydrogen are gases at ordinary temperatures.* **2** any mixture of gases that can be burned, obtained from coal and other substances: *Gas was once much used for lighting and is now used for cooking and heating.* **3** chemical vapors used for specific effects on men, animals, insects, etc.: *Laughing gas is sometimes used as an anesthetic. Poison gas has been used in warfare. Tear gas is often used to subdue rioters.* **4** use such vapors on; treat with such vapors: *The police were forced to gas the violent criminals who refused to leave the building.* **5** vapors accumulated in or released from the stomach, usually as a result of indigestion or some other stomach disorder: *He suffers from gas pains.* 1–3, 5 *n.*, *pl.* **gas·es;** 4 *v.*, **gassed, gas·sing.**

gas[2] (gas) Informal. **1** gasoline: *The price of gas has gone up.* **2** supply with gasoline. 1 *n.*, 2 *v.*, **gassed, gas·sing.**

gas up, fill the tank of a motor vehicle with gasoline: *Be sure to gas up before going on a long trip.*

gas·e·ous (gas′ē əs or gā′sē əs) in the form of gas; of or like gas: *Steam is water in a gaseous condition.* *adj.*

gash (gash) **1** a long, deep cut or wound. **2** make a long, deep cut or wound in. 1 *n.*, 2 *v.*

gas·o·line (gas′ə lēn′ or gas′ə lēn′) a colorless liquid made from petroleum: *Gasoline, which evaporates and burns very easily, is used as fuel for automobiles, airplanes, tractors, etc.* *n.* Also spelled **gasolene.**

gasp (gasp) **1** a sudden, short intaking of breath through the mouth: *A gasp often indicates suspense, shock, or fear.* **2** one of a series of short breaths caused by having difficulty in breathing: *After her hard run, her breath came in gasps.* **3** breathe with a series of short difficult breaths: *The exhausted runner gasped for air.* **4** utter with gasps: *'Help! Help!' gasped the drowning man.* 1, 2 *n.*, 3, 4 *v.*

gas station a place for supplying automobiles with gasoline, motor oil, water, etc.

gas·tric (gas′trik) of or having to do with the stomach. *adj.*

gate (gāt) **1** a door or some other barrier used to close off an opening in a wall, fence, etc.: *The children liked to swing on the garden gate.* **2** an opening in a wall, fence, etc., usually fitted with a door, turnstile, or some other barrier. **3** a barrier intended to prevent entrance, stop traffic, etc.: *Level crossings are often equipped with gates to stop cars when a train is passing.* **4** the number of people who attend a ball game, theatre performance, etc.: *The rink manager was expecting a good gate at the play-off game.* *n.*

give the gate to, *Informal.* **a** dismiss or turn away. **b** in hockey, give a player a penalty, thus putting him off the ice.

☛ **Gate** and **gait** are pronounced the same.

gate·post (gāt′pōst′) one of the posts on either side of a gate: *A swinging gate is fastened to one gatepost and closes against the other.* *n.*

gate·way (gāt′wā′) **1** an opening in a wall, fence, etc., fitted with a gate or some other barrier. **2** a way to go in or out; a way to get to something: *A college education is one gateway to success. Winnipeg is known as the 'Gateway to the West.'* *n.*

gath·er (gaᴛʜ′ər) **1** collect; bring into one place: *He gathered his books and papers and started off to school.* **2** come together: *A crowd gathered at the scene of the* accident. 3 pick; glean or pluck: *The farmers gathered their crops.* 4 put together in the mind: *I gathered from his words that he was very upset.* 5 pull together in folds: *The dressmaker gathered the skirt at the top. She gathered her brows in a frown.* 6 one of the little folds between the stitches when cloth is pulled together in this way. 1–5 *v.*, 6 *n.*

gath·er·ing (gaᴛʜ′ər ing) an assembly; meeting: *The preacher was asked to speak to the gathering.* *n.*

gau·cho (gou′chō) a cowboy or herdsman in the southern plains of South America. *n.*

gaud·y (god′ē or gôd′ē) too bright and gay to be in good taste; cheap and showy: *She would be attractive if she did not wear such gaudy jewellery.* *adj.*, **gaud·i·er, gaud·i·est.**

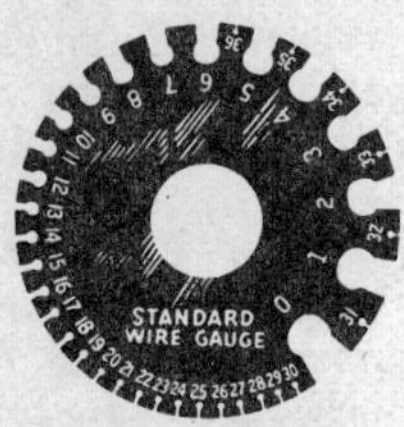

A gauge for measuring wire. Size nine wire fits the hole marked 9.

gauge (gāj) 1 a standard measure; a measure: *There are gauges of the capacity of a barrel, the thickness of sheet iron, the diameter of a shot-gun bore, wire, etc.* 2 an instrument for measuring: *A steam gauge measures the pressure of steam.* 3 measure exactly with a measuring device: *He had a special instrument to gauge the width of the metal strips.* 4 estimate; judge: *It was difficult to gauge the character of the stranger.* 1, 2 *n.*, 3, 4 *v.*, **gauged, gaug·ing.** Also spelled **gage.**

gaunt (gont or gônt) 1 very thin and bony; having hollow eyes and a starved look: *Hunger and suffering make people gaunt.* 2 looking bare and gloomy; desolate; grim: *The ancient castle stood gaunt on the hilltop.* *adj.*

gaunt·let[1] (gont′lit or gônt′lit) 1 an iron glove that was part of a knight's armor. See **armor** for picture. 2 a stout, heavy glove with a deep, flaring cuff, used by some workmen. *n.*

throw down the gauntlet, offer a challenge.

gaunt·let[2] (gont′lit or gônt′lit) formerly, a military punishment. *n.* Also spelled **gantlet.**

run the gauntlet, a carry out an action in spite of danger threatening on all sides: *During the war, convoys ran the gauntlet of enemy submarines.* **b** run between two rows of men, each of whom strikes the runner as he passes. **c** be exposed to unfriendly attacks or criticism.

gauze (goz or gôz) a thin, light cloth that is easy to see through: *Gauze is often used for bandages.* *n.* —**gauz′y,** *adj.*

gave (gāv) See **give.** *He gave me some of his candy.* *v.*

gav·el (gav′əl) a small mallet used by a presiding officer to signal for attention or order: *The chairman rapped on the table twice with his gavel.* *n.*

gawk (gok or gôk) 1 an awkward person; clumsy fool. 2 *Informal.* stare rudely or stupidly: *The tourist stood gawking at the strange sights.* 1 *n.*, 2 *v.*

gawk·y (gok′ē or gôk′ē) awkward; clumsy: *a gawky fourteen-year-old lad.* *adj.*, **gawk·i·er, gawk·i·est.**

gay (gā) 1 happy and full of fun; merry: *The young people were gay as they decorated the gym for the dance.* 2 bright-colored: *a gay dress.* *adj.*, **gay·er, gay·est.**

gay·e·ty (gā′ə tē) See **gaiety.** *n., pl.* **gay·e·ties.**

gay·ly (gā′lē) See **gaily.**

gaze (gāz) 1 look long and steadily: *For hours he sat gazing at the stars.* 2 a long, steady look. 1 *v.*, **gazed, gaz·ing;** 2 *n.*

ga·zelle (gə zel′) a small, graceful kind of antelope with large, soft eyes. See **antelope** for picture. *n.*

ga·zette (gə zet′) 1 newspaper: *the 'Weekly Gazette.'* 2 an official government journal containing lists of appointments, promotions, etc. *n.*

gaz·et·teer (gaz′ə tēr′) a dictionary of geographical names. *n.*

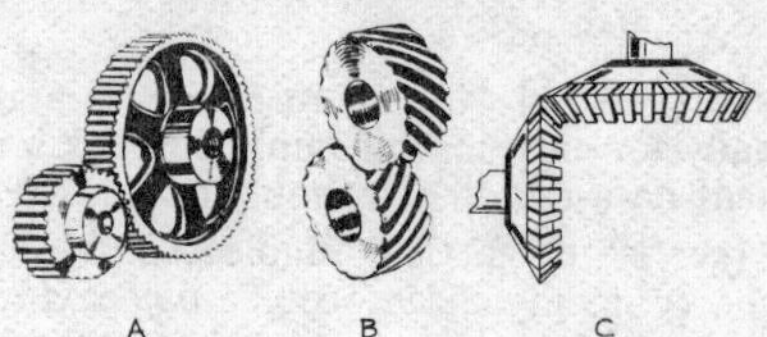

Gears:
A, to change the speed of axle rotation
B, with angled teeth to run more quietly
C, to change the direction of rotation

gear (gēr) 1 a wheel having teeth that fit into teeth in another wheel; wheels turning one another by teeth. 2 one of several sets of gears to which a motor may be connected: *top gear, reverse gear. An automobile in low gear moves slowly, but strongly.* 3 any arrangement of gears or moving parts; machinery: *the steering gear of a car.* 4 equipment needed for some purpose, such as harness, tools, clothing, or household goods: *He took his fishing gear on the holiday trip.* 5 adjust; adapt: *The steel industry was geared to the needs of war.* 1–4 *n.*, 5 *v.*

in gear, connected to the motor.

out of gear, not connected to the motor.

gear·shift (gēr′shift′) a device for connecting a motor, etc. to any of several sets of gears. *n.*

geck·o (gek′ō) a small, insect-eating lizard found in the tropics, having suction pads on its toes for climbing: *Geckos sleep during the day and feed at night.* *n.*

gee (jē) 1 a command to horses, oxen, etc. directing them to turn to the right. 2 turn to the right. 3 an exclamation or mild oath. 1, 3 *interj.*, 2 *v.*, **geed, gee·ing.**

geese (gēs) plural of **goose.** *n.*

Gei·ger counter (gī′gər) a device that detects and measures radioactivity.

gel·a·tin or **gel·a·tine** (jel′ə tən) an odorless, tasteless substance obtained by boiling the bones, hoofs, and other waste parts of animals: *Gelatin is used in making glue, jellied desserts, camera film, etc.* *n.*

geld·ing (gel′ding) a male animal, especially a horse, that has had its sex glands removed. *n.*

gem (jem) 1 a precious stone; jewel: *Diamonds and*

hat, āge, fär; let, ēqual, tėrm; it, īce
hot, ōpen, ôrder; oil, out; cup, pu̇t, rüle
ə above, takən, pencəl, lemən, circəs
ch, child; ng, long; sh, ship
th, thin; ᴛʜ, then; zh, measure

rubies are gems. 2 a person or thing that is very beautiful. 3 the most precious thing: *The gem of his collection was a rare Persian stamp.* *n.*

gen·der (jen′dər) 1 in grammar, a system of grouping words such as nouns, pronouns, and adjectives into two or more classes according to features of structure or meaning: *English shows gender in distinguishing* he, she, *and* it. 2 one of these classes: *The feminine gender in French includes the words for table, moon, city, and girl.* *n.*

gene (jēn) in a plant or animal cell, a tiny part of a chromosome that determines what an inherited characteristic will be and how it will develop: *Some of the genes inherited from one's parents determine the color of one's hair, eyes, and skin.* *n.*

☞ **Gene** and **jean** are pronounced the same.

gen·er·al (jen′ər əl or jen′rəl) 1 of all; for all; from all: *A government takes care of the general welfare.* 2 widespread; not limited to a few; for many; from many: *There is a general interest in television.* 3 not detailed; lacking detail: *He made only a general plan.* 4 not specialized: *a general magazine.* *A general reader reads different kinds of books.* 5 chief: *The Postmaster General is the head of the Post-Office Department.* 6 a high officer in command of many men in an army. 1–5 *adj.,* 6 *n.*

in general, commonly; usually; as a rule: *In general, people get along fairly well together.*

general election in Canada, an election in which citizens have the right to vote for Members of Parliament or, within a province, for Members of the Legislative Assembly.

gen·er·al·i·za·tion (jen′ər əl ə zā′shən or jen′rəl ə zā′shən) 1 the act or process of generalizing. 2 a general idea, statement, principle, or rule: *Her argument was weakened by too many generalizations.* *n.*

gen·er·al·ize (jen′ər əl īz′ or jen′rəl īz′) 1 make into one general statement; bring under a common heading, class, or law: *All men, women, and children can be generalized under the term 'human being.'* 2 draw a general conclusion from particular facts: *If you have seen cats, tigers, and leopards eat meat, you can generalize and say, 'Animals of the cat family eat meat.'* 3 talk idefinitely or vaguely; use general statements: *The commentators generalized about the incident because they did not know any details.* *v.*

gen·er·al·ly (jen′ər əl ē or jen′rə lē) 1 in most cases; usually: *He is generally on time.* 2 for the most part; widely: *It was once generally believed that the earth is flat.* 3 in a general way; not specially: *Speaking generally, our coldest weather comes in January.* *adv.*

general store a store that carries a wide variety of goods for sale: *Most villages and small towns have a general store.*

A Geiger counter. The probe detects the amount of radiation, which is shown on the dial.

gen·er·ate (jen′ər āt′) produce; cause to be: *Boiling water generates steam. The steam can generate electricity by turning an electric generator.* *v.,* **gen·er·at·ed, gen·er·at·ing.**

gen·er·a·tion (jen′ər ā′shən) 1 the people born in the same period: *Your parents belong to one generation; you belong to the following generation.* 2 about thirty years, or the time from the birth of one generation to the birth of the next generation. 3 one step, or stage, in the history of a family: *The picture showed four generations—great-grandmother, grandmother, mother, and baby.* 4 the act or process of producing: *Steam and water power are used for the generation of electricity.* *n.*

gen·er·a·tor (jen′ər ā′tər) a piece of apparatus for generating or producing electricity, gas, or steam. *n.*

gen·er·os·i·ty (jen′ər os′ə tē) 1 the act or condition of being generous; unselfishness; willingness to share with others: *The millionaire was renowned for his generosity.* 2 nobleness of mind; freedom from meanness: *By forgiving his enemy, he showed generosity.* 3 a generous act; generous behavior. *n., pl.* **gen·er·os·i·ties.**

gen·er·ous (jen′ər əs or jen′rəs) 1 willing to share with others; unselfish: *a generous boy.* 2 noble and forgiving; not mean: *a generous mind.* 3 large; plentiful: *A quarter of a pie is a generous helping.* *adj.*

gen·e·sis (jen′ə sis) origin; creation; coming into being. *n., pl.* **gen·e·ses** (jen′ə sēz′)

ge·ni·al (jē′nē əl or jēn′yəl) 1 smiling and pleasant; cheerful and friendly; kindly: *a genial welcome, the genial policeman.* 2 helping growth; pleasantly warming; comforting: *genial sunshine.* *adj.*

ge·nie (jē′nē) a powerful spirit: *When Aladdin rubbed his lamp, the genie came and did what Aladdin asked.* *n.*

gen·i·tal (jen′ə təl) having to do with sexual reproduction; of the sex organs. *adj.*

gen·i·tals (jen′ə təlz) the external sex organs. *n. pl.*

ge·ni·us (jē′nē əs or jēn′yəs) 1 very great natural power of mind: *Genius is shown by an extraordinary ability to think, invent, or create.* 2 a person having such power: *Einstein was a genius.* 3 a great natural ability: *A great actor has a genius for acting.* *n., pl.* **ge·ni·us·es.**

gen·tian (jen′shən) a plant with usually blue flowers, growing mostly in hilly regions. *n.*

gen·tile or **Gen·tile** (jen′tīl) 1 a person who is not a Jew. 2 not Jewish. 1 *n.,* 2 *adj.*

gen·til·i·ty (jen til′ə tē) good manners; refinement: *The lady had an air of gentility.* *n., pl.* **gen·til·i·ties.**

gen·tle (jen′təl) 1 mild; not severe, rough, or violent: *a gentle tap.* 2 soft; low: *The cat was purring with a gentle sound.* 3 moderate: *gentle heat, a gentle slope.* 4 kindly; friendly: *a gentle disposition.* 5 easy to manage: *a gentle horse.* 6 of good family and social position; well-born: *The princess was of gentle origin.* 7 refined; polite. **8** treat in a soothing way: *The rider gentled his excited horse.* 1–7 *adj.,* **gen·tler, gen·tlest;** 8 *v.,* **gen·tled, gen·tling. —gen′tle·ness,** *n.*

gen·tle·man (jen′təl mən) **1** a man of good family and social position. **2** a man who is honorable, polite, and considerate of others. **3** a polite term for any man. *n., pl.* **gen·tle·men** (jen′təl mən). **—gen′tle·man·ly,** *adj.*

gen·tle·wom·an (jen′təl wům′ən) **1** a woman of good family and social position. **2** a woman attendant of a lady of rank. *n., pl.* **gen·tle·wom·en** (jen′təl wim′ən).

gen·tly (jen′tlē) **1** in a gentle way; tenderly; softly. **2** gradually: *a gentle sloping hillside. adv.*

gen·u·ine (jen′yü ən or jen′yü īn′) **1** real; true: *genuine leather, a genuine diamond.* **2** frank; free from pretence; sincere: *genuine sorrow. adj.*

ge·o·graph·ic (jē′ə graf′ik) geographical. *adj.*

ge·o·graph·i·cal (jē′ə graf′ə kəl) of or having to do with geography. *adj.*

ge·og·ra·phy (jē og′rə fē) **1** the study of the earth's surface, climate, continents, countries, peoples, industries, and products. **2** the surface features of a place, region, or country. **3** a book about geography. *n., pl.* **ge·og·ra·phies.**

ge·o·log·i·cal (jē′ə loj′ə kəl) of or having to do with geology. *adj.*

ge·ol·o·gist (jē ol′ə jist) a person skilled in geology. *n.*

ge·ol·o·gy (jē ol′ə jē) the science that deals with the earth's crust, the layers of which it is composed, and their history. *n.*

ge·om·e·try (jē om′ə trē) the branch of mathematics that measures and compares lines, angles, surfaces, and solids. *n.*

George Cross (jôrj′ kros′) a medal awarded for acts of valor other than those performed in battle: *The George Cross may be won by civilians.*

ge·ra·ni·um (jə rā′nē əm or jə rān′yəm) **1** a house or garden plant with showy flowers of scarlet, pink, or white. **2** a wild plant with pink or purple flowers. *n.*

ger·bil (jėr′bəl) one of a group of small animals closely related to the mouse and rat and having long hind legs: *Gerbils are often kept as pets. n.*

germ (jėrm) **1** a simple animal or plant, especially one that causes diseases: *Germs are too small to be seen without a microscope.* **2** the earliest form of a living thing; a seed or bud. **3** the beginning of anything: *Counting was the germ of arithmetic. n.*

Ger·man (jėr′mən) **1** of Germany, its people, or their language. **2** a person born in or living in Germany. **3** the language of Germany. 1 *adj.,* 2, 3 *n.*

Ger·man·ic (jėr man′ik) **1** a group of languages, including English, German, Dutch, Norwegian, Swedish, Danish, and Icelandic, that have developed from a single common language that was spoken in Europe about 2500 years ago. **2** of or having to do with this group of languages. 1 *n.,* 2 *adj.*

German measles a contagious disease resembling measles but less severe.

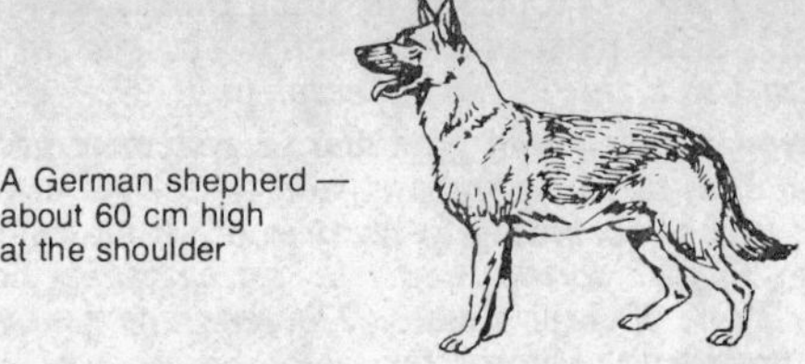

A German shepherd — about 60 cm high at the shoulder

German shepherd one of a breed of large, intelligent, short-haired dogs, usually greyish or brown and black in color: *German shepherds are often trained to work with soldiers or police, to guide the blind, etc.*

ger·mi·cide (jėr′mə sīd′) any substance that kills germs, especially disease germs: *Carbolic acid is a part of many germicides. n.*

ger·mi·nate (jėr′mə nāt′) **1** begin to grow; develop; sprout: *In the spring, seeds germinate in the warm, moist soil.* **2** cause to grow. *v.,* **ger·mi·nat·ed, ger·mi·nat·ing.**

ges·ture (jes′chər) **1** a movement of the hands, arms, or any part of the body, used instead of words to help express an idea or a feeling: *A speaker often makes gestures with his hands or arms to stress something that he is saying.* **2** any action for effect or to impress others: *Her refusal of a peppermint was merely a gesture; she really wanted one.* **3** make gestures; use gestures. 1, 2 *n.,* 3 *v.,* **ges·tured, ges·tur·ing.**

get (get) **1** obtain; receive; gain: *I got a new coat yesterday.* **2** reach; arrive: *I got home early last night. Your letter got here yesterday.* **3** cause to be or do: *Get the windows open. She got her work done.* **4** become: *It is getting colder.* **5** persuade; influence: *Try to get him to come.* **6** begin; start: *We soon got talking about our days at camp.* **7** possess; have (used with some form of **have**): *She has got black hair.* **8** understand; comprehend: *I don't get the point.* **9** must (used with some form of **have**): *You've got to come to the party.* **10** go; come: *His boat got in yesterday.* **11** prepare: *Jane helped her mother get dinner. v.,* **got, got** or **got·ten, get·ting.**

get across, make something clearly understood: *The teacher used slides to get the idea across.*

get along, a be on good terms: *He doesn't get along with his neighbors.* **b** do well enough; manage: *We don't have a lot of money but we get along.* **c** move along.

get around, a overcome opposition by charm, flattery, etc.; win over: *Her winning smile often helped her to get around her father.* **b** spread from one person to another: *It doesn't take long for bad news to get around.*

get at, a reach: *We could not get at the cat in the tree without a ladder.* **b** find out: *Try to get at the truth.* **c** *Informal.* tamper with; influence with money or threats.

get away, a go away; leave: *We hope to get away early tomorrow.* **b** escape: *The dog broke his leash and got away.*

get away with, take or do something and escape safely: *He thought he could get away with being late, but he was caught.*

get by, do well enough; manage all right: *They got by on his small salary.*

get down, make downhearted; discourage; depress: *The hot weather was getting him down.*

get down to, a begin: *It took him a long time to get down to work.* **b** reach by removing what stands in the way: *After much questioning of the witness, the lawyer got down to the truth.*

hat, āge, fär; let, ēqual, tėrm; it, īce
hot, ōpen, ôrder; oil, out; cup, pu̇t, rüle
əbove, takən, pencəl, lemən, circəs
ch, child; ng, long; sh, ship
th, thin; ᴛʜ, then; zh, measure

get even, a pay back for a wrong done; obtain revenge: *He promised to get even with his sister for twisting his arm.* **b** win back what was lost: *After he had lost 25 marbles, he played all afternoon trying to get even.*
get in, a go in; enter: *She got in the canoe very carefully.* **b** put in: *He got everything in one suitcase.* **c** arrive; arrive home: *What time did you get in last night?*
get off, a come down from or out of: *He got off the bus at North Bay.* **b** take off: *She couldn't get her ring off.* **c** escape the full punishment deserved: *The naughty boy got off with a scolding.*
get on, a go up on or into: *She fell as she was getting on her bicycle.* **b** put on: *He had grown so fat, he couldn't get his pants on.* **c** succeed: *He worked hard in hopes of getting on.* **d** agree; be on good terms: *Fred and his sister couldn't get on.* **e** advance; move ahead: *The driver urged his horses to get on. It was getting on toward noon when they left.*
get out, a go out; leave: *The boy was told to get out of the house.* **b** become known: *It didn't take long for the news to get out.* **c** escape: *Ten convicts got out of the prison last night.* **d** take out: *He couldn't get the candies out of the jar.*
get over, recover from: *He was a long time getting over his illness.*
get through, a get to the end of; finish: *She always gets through her homework quickly.* **b** complete or cause to complete successfully: *He got through the test. His friends' help got him through.* **c** make or get a telephone connection: *I tried to phone you, but I couldn't get through.* **d** make oneself understood; succeed in communicating: *No one can get through to her when she's angry.*
get together, a bring together; meet: *They arranged to get together at our house.* **b** come to an agreement: *The workers and their employer couldn't get together about wages.*
get up, a arise: *He got up at six o'clock.* **b** stand up; rise up: *She got up from the chair.* **c** prepare: *He spent all evening getting up the next day's lesson.*

get·a·way (get′ə wā′) *Informal.* **1** the act of getting away; escape: *The bank robbers made their getaway in a laundry truck.* **2** the start of a race. *n.*

gey·ser (gī′zər, gī′sər, or gā′zər) a spring that sends up fountains or jets of hot water and steam at intervals: *There are geysers in Yellowstone National Park. n.*

ghast·ly (gast′lē) **1** horrible: *Murder is a ghastly crime.* **2** like a dead person or ghost; deathly pale: *The sick man's face was ghastly. adj.,* **ghast·li·er, ghast·li·est.**

gher·kin (gėr′kən) **1** a small, prickly kind of cucumber often used for pickles. **2** any small, young cucumber used for pickles. *n.*

ghost (gōst) **1** the spirit of a dead person: *A ghost is supposed to live in another world and appear to living people as a pale, dim, shadowy form.* **2** anything pale, dim, or shadowy like a ghost; a faint image; slightest suggestion: *a ghost of a smile, not a ghost of a chance. n.*

ghost·ly (gōst′lē) like a ghost: *A ghostly form walked across the stage. adj.,* **ghost·li·er, ghost·li·est.**

ghost town a town that has become empty and lifeless; a town that has been deserted by all its inhabitants: *When the gold rush was over, the once-flourishing community became a ghost town.*

ghoul (gül) **1** in Oriental stories, a horrible demon, believed to feed on corpses. **2** a person who robs graves or corpses. *n.*

gi·ant (jī′ənt) **1** a man of great size or very great power. **2** an imaginary being like a huge man. **3** huge: *a giant potato.* 1, 2 *n.*, 3 *adj.*

gib·bon (gib′ən) a small, long-armed ape of southeastern Asia and the East Indies: *Gibbons live in trees. n.*

gibe (jīb) **1** a jeer; sneer: *The gibes of the fans didn't bother the referee.* **2** scoff; sneer; jeer. 1 *n.*, 2 *v.*, **gibe, gib·ing.**

gib·lets (jib′lits) the heart, liver, and gizzard of a fowl. *n. pl.*

gid·dy (gid′ē) **1** dizzy; having a whirling in one's head: *It makes me giddy to go on a merry-go-round.* **2** causing dizziness; likely to make dizzy: *The couples whirled and whirled in their giddy dance.* **3** never serious; living for the pleasure of the moment; in a whirl: *That giddy girl thinks only of having a good time. adj.,* **gid·di·er, gid·di·est.**

gift (gift) **1** something given; present: *the gift of a thousand dollars to a church, a Christmas gift.* **2** a natural talent; a special ability: *a gift for painting. n.*

gift·ed (gif′tid) very able; having special ability: *She is a gifted musician and will probably become a concert pianist. adj.*

A gig (def. 1)

gig (gig) **1** a light, two-wheeled carriage drawn by one horse. **2** a small boat used by a ship's captain for going to and from shore. *n.*

gi·gan·tic (jī gan′tik) **1** like a giant: *Paul Bunyan was a gigantic lumberjack.* **2** huge; enormous: *a gigantic building project. adj.*

gig·gle (gig′əl) **1** laugh in a silly or nervous way: *The girls giggled in their embarrassment.* **2** a silly or nervous laugh. 1 *v.*, **gig·gled, gig·gling;** 2 *n.*

gild (gild) **1** cover with a thin layer of gold. **2** make a thing look bright and pleasing: *The rays from the full moon gilded the lake. v.*
☞ **Gild** and **guild** are pronounced the same.

gill[1] (gil) one of the breathing organs of certain animals that live under water: *Fish, tadpoles, and crabs have gills.* See **fish** for picture. *n.*

gill[2] (jil) a small liquid measure, equal to one fourth of a pint and about the same as 142 millilitres. *n.*

gilt (gilt) **1** gilded. **2** the material with which a thing is gilded: *The gilt is coming off this frame.* 1 *adj.*, 2 *n.*
☞ **Gilt** and **guilt** are pronounced the same.

gim·let (gim′lit) a small tool with a screw point, for boring holes. *n.*

gin¹ (jin) a strong, colorless alcoholic drink, usually made from grain and usually flavored with juniper berries. *n.*

gin² (jin) **1** a machine for separating cotton from its seeds. **2** separate cotton from its seeds. 1 *n.*, 2 *v.*, **ginned, gin·ning.**

gin·ger (jin′jər) **1** a spice made from the root of a tropical plant: *Ginger is used for flavoring and in medicine.* **2** the root: *Ginger is sometimes preserved in syrup and sometimes candied.* **3** *Informal.* liveliness; energy: *That horse has plenty of ginger. n.*

ginger ale a bubbling drink flavored with ginger: *Ginger ale is a popular soft drink.*

gin·ger·bread (jin′jər bred′) a kind of cake flavored with ginger. *n.*

gin·ger·snap (jin′jər snap′) a thin, crisp, cookie flavored with ginger. *n.*

ging·ham (ging′əm) a kind of cloth, usually cotton or part cotton: *The patterns of gingham are usually in stripes, plaids, or checks. n.*

gip·sy (jip′sē) See **gypsy.** *n., pl.* **gip·sies.**

gi·raffe (jə raf′) a large African animal with a very long neck and legs and a spotted skin: *Giraffes are the tallest living animals. n.*

gird (gėrd) **1** put a belt or girdle around. **2** fasten with a belt or girdle: *to gird up one's clothes.* **3** get ready: *Soldiers gird themselves for battle. v.*, **girt** or **gird·ed, gird·ing.**

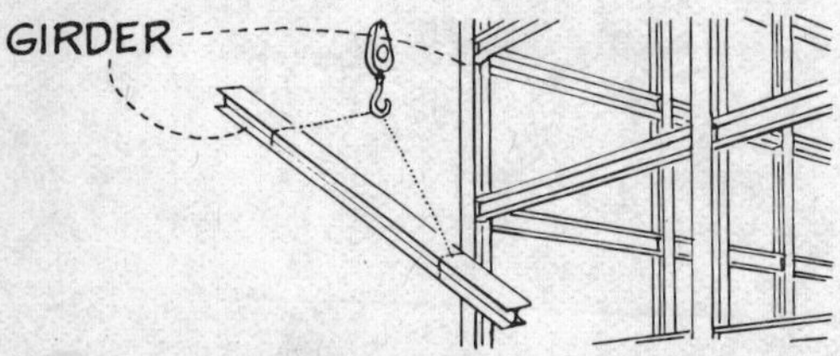

gird·er (gėr′dər) a main supporting beam: *Steel girders are often used to make the framework of bridges and tall buildings. n.*

gir·dle (gėr′dəl) **1** a belt, sash, cord, etc. worn around the waist. **2** anything that surrounds: *a girdle of trees around a pond.* **3** a kind of elastic corset. **4** put a girdle on or around. **5** surround, as with a girdle: *The house was girdled by tall elms.* 1–3 *n.*, 4, 5 *v.*, **gir·dled, gir·dling.**

girl (gėrl) **1** a female child. **2** a young, unmarried woman. **3** a female servant. **4** sweetheart: *He took his girl to the movies. n.*

Girl Guide a member of the Girl Guides.

Girl Guides an organization for girls that seeks to develop health and character as well as a knowledge of homemaking.

girl·hood (gėrl′hůd) the time of being a girl: *The old woman recalled her girlhood with pleasure. n.*

girl·ish (gėr′lish) **1** of a girl. **2** like that of a girl. **3** proper for girls: *She thought she was too old now for such girlish games. adj.*

girt (gėrt) See **gird.** *The knight girt himself for battle. v.*

girth (gėrth) **1** the measure around anything: *a man of large girth, the girth of a tree.* **2** the strap or band that keeps the saddle or harness in place on a horse. See **harness** and **saddle** for pictures. *n.*

gist (jist) the real point; the main idea: *The gist of his argument was clear. n.*

give (giv) **1** hand over as a present; make a present of: *He likes to give books to his friends.* **2** hand over: *Give me that pencil.* **3** pay: *He can't give that much for a football.* **4** let have; cause to have: *Don't give the teacher any trouble. Give me permission to leave.* **5** deal; cause by some action of the body: *Some boys give hard blows even in play. He gave the ball a kick.* **6** present or offer: *This newspaper gives a full story of the game.* **7** produce; yield; supply: *This farm gives large crops. His reading gives him knowledge.* **8** put forth; utter: *He gave a cry of pain.* **9** yield to force: *The lock gave when he pushed hard against the door.* **10** a yielding to force. 1–9 *v.*, **gave, giv·en, giv·ing;** 10 *n.* **—giv′er,** *n.*

give away, a give as a present. **b** give as a bride: *She asked her older brother to give her away at the wedding.* **c** cause to become known; reveal; betray: *The spy gave away secrets to the enemy.*

give back, return: *Give back the book you borrowed.*

give in, a stop fighting and admit defeat: *After many defeats, the enemy decided to give in.* **b** hand in: *He gave in his history project when it was due.*

give out, a send out; put forth: *The roses gave out a sweet smell.* **b** distribute: *The boys gave out the handbills.* **c** make known: *The news was given out at midnight.* **d** become used up: *The food gave out during the famine.* **e** become worn out or exhausted: *The old man's strength gave out during the long walk.*

give up, a hand over; surrender: *The commander decided to give up the fort.* **b** stop having or doing: *He was wise to give up smoking.* **c** stop trying: *He tried hard to learn Russian but he finally gave up.* **d** devote entirely: *He gave himself up to his studies.*

giv·en (giv′ən) **1** stated: *You must finish the test in a given time.* **2** See **give.** *That book was given to me.* 1 *adj.*, 2 *v.*

given to, inclined or disposed towards: *The old soldier was given to boasting.*

given name a name given to a person in addition to his or her family name: *'Gordon' and 'Charles' are the given names of Gordon Charles McRae.*

giz·zard (giz′ərd) a bird's second stomach, where the food from the first stomach is ground up fine. *n.*

gla·cial (glā′shəl) **1** of ice or glaciers; having much ice or many glaciers: *the glacial age.* **2** made by the pressure and movement of glaciers or great masses of ice: *There are many glacial rivers in western Canada.* **3** like ice; very cold; icy: *She gave him a glacial stare. adj.*

gla·cier (glā′shər or glās′yər) a large mass of ice formed from the snow on high ground and moving very slowly down a mountain side or along a valley. *n.*

glad (glad) **1** happy; pleased: *She is glad to be well again.* **2** bringing joy; pleasant: *The glad news made her happy.* **3** bright; gay: *The glad sunshine cheered us. adj.*, **glad·der, glad·dest. —glad′ly,** *adv.* **—glad′ness,** *n.*

hat, āge, fär; let, ēqual, tėrm; it, īce
hot, ōpen, ôrder; oil, out; cup, put, rüle
əbove, takən, pencəl, lemən, circəs
ch, child; ng, long; sh, ship
th, thin; ᴛʜ, then; zh, measure

glad·den (glad′ən) make glad; become glad: *His heart was gladdened by the news.* v.

glade (glād) a little open space in a wood or forest. *n.*

glad·i·a·tor (glad′ē ā′tər) a slave, captive, or paid fighter who fought at the public shows in ancient Rome. *n.*

glad·i·o·lus (glad′ē ō′ləs) a plant with spikes of large, handsome flowers in various colors. *n., pl.* **glad·i·o·li** (glad′ē ō′lī) or **glad·i·o·lus·es.**

glam·or or **glam·our** (glam′ər) 1 charm; mysterious fascination: *The glamor of Hollywood is felt by many young people. She uses perfume to increase her glamor.* 2 a magic spell or charm; a magic enchantment. *n.*

glam·or·ous (glam′ər əs) fascinating; charming. *adj.*

glam·our (glam′ər) See **glamor.**

glance (glans) 1 a quick look: *I gave him only a glance.* 2 look quickly. 3 hit and go off at a slant: *The spear glanced off the wall and missed him by a few centimetres.* 1 *n.*, 2, 3 *v.*, **glanced, glanc·ing.**

gland (gland) an organ in the body that makes and gives out some substance: *Glands make the liquid that moistens the mouth. A cow has glands that make milk.* *n.*

glare (gler) 1 a strong, unpleasant light; a light that shines so brightly that it hurts the eyes: *The glare from the ice made his eyes sore.* 2 shine strongly or unpleasantly; shine so as to hurt the eyes. 3 a fierce, angry stare. 4 stare fiercely and with anger: *The angry man glared at his disobedient son.* 1, 3 *n.*, 2, 4 *v.*, **glared, glar·ing.**

glare ice ice that has a smooth, glossy surface.

glar·ing (gler′ing) 1 See **glare.** *She was dazzled by the glaring headlights.* 2 too bright and showy: *She wore a blouse of a glaring red.* 3 very easily seen: *The student made a glaring error in spelling.* 1 *v.*, 2, 3 *adj.*

glass (glas) 1 a hard substance that breaks easily and can usually be seen through: *Windows are made of glass.* 2 a tumbler or similar drinking vessel made of glass, plastic, etc.: *a drinking glass. He filled a glass with water.* 3 the amount a glass can hold: *Drink a glass of water.* 4 mirror: *Look at yourself in the glass.* 5 **glasses,** *pl.* eyeglasses; spectacles. See **spectacles** for picture. 6 a lens, telescope, windowpane, or other thing made of glass. 7 made of glass: *a glass dish.* 8 cover or protect with glass. 1–6 *n.*, 7 *adj.*, 8 *v.*

glass·ful (glas′fu̇l) as much as a drinking glass will hold. *n., pl.* **glass·fuls.**

glass·ware (glas′wer′) articles made of glass. *n.*

glass·y (glas′ē) 1 like glass; smooth; easily seen through: *glassy water.* 2 having a fixed, stupid stare: *The dazed man's eyes were glassy.* *adj.*, **glass·i·er, glass·i·est.**

glaze (glāz) 1 put glass in; cover with glass: *Pieces of glass cut to the right size are used to glaze windows and picture frames.* 2 a smooth, glassy surface or glossy coating: *the glaze on a china cup, a glaze of ice on the walk.* 3 make a glossy or glassy surface on vases, dishes, foods, etc. 4 become glossy or glassy: *The man's eyes were glazed with pain.* 1, 3, 4 *v.*, **glazed, glaz·ing;** 2 *n.*

gleam (glēm) 1 a flash or beam of light: *We saw the gleam of headlights through the rain.* 2 send forth a gleam; shine. 3 a short appearance: *a gleam of hope.* 1, 3 *n.*, 2 *v.*

glean (glēn) 1 gather grain left on the field by reapers. 2 gather little by little: *The spy gleaned information from the soldier's talk.* *v.*

glee (glē) 1 joy; delight; mirth: *The children laughed with glee.* 2 a song for three or more voices carrying different parts. *n.*

glee·ful (glē′fəl) filled with glee; merry; joyous: *a gleeful laugh.* *adj.*

glen (glen) a small, narrow valley. *n.*

glib (glib) speaking or spoken too smoothly and easily to be sincere: *He was full of glib excuses.* *adj.*, **glib·ber, glib·best.**

glide (glīd) 1 move along smoothly, evenly, and easily: *Birds, ships, dancers, and skaters glide.* 2 a smooth, even, easy movement. 1 *v.*, **glid·ed, glid·ing;** 2 *n.*

A glider

glid·er (glī′dər) an airplane without a motor: *Rising air currents keep a glider up in the air.* *n.*

glim·mer (glim′ər) 1 a faint, unsteady light. 2 shine with a faint, unsteady light: *The candle glimmered and went out.* 3 a vague idea or feeling; a faint glimpse: *The doctor's report gave only a glimmer of hope that the patient would recover.* 1, 3 *n.*, 2 *v.*

glimpse (glimps) 1 a very brief view; a short look: *I got a glimpse of the falls as our train went by.* 2 catch a brief view of: *I glimpsed her dress as she went by.* 1 *n.*, 2 *v.*, **glimpsed, glimps·ing.**

glint (glint) 1 a gleam or flash: *There was a glint of steel as the man swung his axe.* 2 gleam or flash: *His eyes glinted fiercely in the light.* 1 *n.*, 2 *v.*

glis·ten (glis′ən) 1 a sparkle or glitter. 2 shine; sparkle; glitter: *The sweat glistened on his brow.* 1 *n.*, 2 *v.*

glit·ter (glit′ər) 1 glisten; sparkle; shine with a bright, sparkling light: *The jewels glittered in the sunlight.* 2 a bright, sparkling light: *There was a cold glitter in the man's eyes.* 3 the bright, sparkling ice that forms on everything outdoors after a rain that freezes. 1 *v.*, 2, 3 *n.*

gloat (glōt) gaze at or think about intently and with satisfaction: *The miser gloated over his gold.* *v.*

glob·al (glō′bəl) world-wide: *the threat of global war.* *adj.*

globe (glōb) 1 anything that is round like a ball. 2 the earth; world. 3 a sphere with a map of the earth or the sky on it. *n.*

glob·ule (glob′yül) a very small ball; a tiny drop: *Globules of sweat stood out on his forehead.* *n.*

gloom (glüm) **1** darkness; deep shadow; dim light: *He could hardly see in the gloom.* **2** dark thoughts and feelings; low spirits; sadness: *He sat there, lost in gloom.* *n.*

gloom·y (glü′mē) **1** dark; dim: *a gloomy day.* **2** in low spirits; sad; melancholy: *Her thoughts were gloomy during the thunderstorm.* **3** dismal; causing gloom: *a gloomy book.* *adj.,* **gloom·i·er, gloom·i·est. —gloom′i·ly,** *adv.*

glo·ri·fy (glô′rə fī′) **1** give glory to; make glorious. **2** to worship or praise: *We sing hymns to glorify God.* **3** make more beautiful or splendid: *Sunset glorified the valley.* *v.,* **glo·ri·fied, glo·ri·fy·ing.**

glo·ri·ous (glô′rē əs) **1** having or deserving praise and honor. **2** giving honor; worthy of high praise: *Our army won a glorious victory.* **3** magnificent or splendid: *It was a glorious pageant.* *adj.*

glo·ry (glô′rē) **1** great praise and honor; fame: *His victories brought him glory.* **2** something that brings praise and honor: *Her real glory was not her beauty but her success as a doctor.* **3** be proud; rejoice: *The mother gloried in the success of her son.* **4** brightness; splendor; beauty: *We were amazed by the glory of the northern lights.* **5** heaven: *the saints in glory.* 1, 2, 4, 5 *n., pl.* **glo·ries;** 3 *v.,* **glo·ried, glo·ry·ing.**

glory in, take great pride or delight in: *John's mother gloried in his success as a pianist.*

gloss (glos) **1** a smooth, shiny surface on anything: *That varnished furniture has a gloss.* **2** put a smooth, shiny surface on. 1 *n.,* 2 *v.*

gloss over, smooth over something or make something seem right even though it is wrong: *He tried to gloss over his mistakes.*

glos·sa·ry (glos′ə rē) a list of unusual or difficult words with explanations: *Some schoolbooks have glossaries at the end.* *n., pl.* **glos·sa·ries.**

gloss·y (glos′ē) smooth and shiny: *glossy paint.* *adj.,* **gloss·i·er, gloss·i·est.**

glove (gluv) **1** a covering for the hand, usually having separate places for each of the four fingers and the thumb. **2** a padded covering to protect the hand: *a hockey glove, a baseball glove.* *n.*

glow (glō) **1** the shine from something that is red-hot or white-hot: *The glow from the burning coals gave a little light to the room.* **2** a similar shine without heat: *The firefly's glow was fascinating.* **3** shine as if red-hot or white-hot. **4** a bright, warm color: *the glow of a sunset.* **5** the warm feeling or color of the body: *the glow of health on his cheeks.* **6** show a warm color; look warm: *Her cheeks glowed as she danced.* **7** an eager look on the face: *a glow of interest.* **8** look eager or pleased: *His face glowed at the idea.* 1, 2, 4, 5, 7 *n.,* 3, 6, 8 *v.*

glow·er (glou′ər) stare; scowl: *The sullen boy glowered at his father.* *v.*

glow–worm (glō′wėrm′) any insect larva or wormlike insect that glows in the dark: *Fireflies develop from some glow-worms.* *n.*

glue (glü) **1** a substance used to stick things together. **2** stick together with glue. **3** fasten tightly: *During the ride down the mountain, his hands were glued to the steering wheel.* 1 *n.,* 2, 3 *v.,* **glued, glu·ing. —glue′y,** *adj.*

glum (glum) gloomy; dismal; sullen: *a glum look.* *adj.,* **glum·mer, glum·mest.**

glut·ton (glut′ən) **1** a greedy eater; a person who eats too much. **2** a person who never seems to have enough of something: *That boxer is a glutton for punishment.* *n.*

glyc·er·in (glis′ər in) a colorless, syrupy, sweet liquid obtained from fats and oils, used in ointments, lotions, explosives, etc. *n.*

gnarl (närl) a knot in wood; a hard, rough lump. *n.*

gnarled (närld) containing gnarls; knotted; twisted; rugged: *The farmer's gnarled hands grasped the plough.* *adj.*

gnash (nash) strike or grind the teeth together; grind together: *The pirates gnashed their teeth in rage.* *v.*

gnat (nat) a small, two-winged insect or fly: *Most gnats can sting.* *n.*

gnaw (no or nô) wear away by biting: *A mouse has gnawed right through the oatmeal box.* *v.*

gnome (nōm) a dwarf supposed to live in the earth and to guard treasures of precious metals and stones. *n.*

go (gō) **1** move along: *Cars go on the road.* **2** move away; leave: *Don't go yet.* **3** be in motion; act; work; run: *Does your watch go well?* **4** make a certain sound: *The cork went 'Pop!'* **5** get to be; become: *to go mad.* **6** be habitually; be: *to go hungry for a week.* **7** proceed; advance: *to go to Edmonton. The wheels go round.* **8** extend; reach: *His memory does not go back that far.* **9** pass: *The summer holidays go quickly.* **10** be given: *First prize goes to the winner.* **11** turn out; have a certain result: *How did the game go?* **12** have its place; belong: *This book goes on the top shelf.* *v.,* **went, gone, go·ing.**

go ahead, *Informal.* continue; proceed: *You can go ahead with the game now.*

go at, a attack: *With a snarl, the dog went at the intruder.* **b** *Informal.* begin on: *The boys went at the dinner as if they were starving.*

go back on, *Informal.* **a** be unfaithful or disloyal to: *He went back on his friends.* **b** fail to live up to: *He went back on his word.*

go by, a pass: *The hours went by slowly.* **b** be guided by; follow: *He promised to go by the rules.* **c** be known by: *She goes by the nickname of 'Slim.'*

go in for, *Informal.* take part in; spend time and energy at: *She used to go in for basketball.*

go into, in arithmetic, be contained in: *3 goes into 9 three times.*

go off, a leave; depart: *They went off to Toronto last night.* **b** explode; be fired: *The gun went off accidentally.* **c** stop functioning; cease working: *The hydro went off during the storm.*

go on, a proceed; move forward: *After a short rest, we decided to go on.* **b** start functioning: *The radio goes on when you turn this switch.* **c** behave: *If you go on that way, you'll get into trouble.* **d** happen; take place: *Nobody seemed to know what was going on.*

go out, a go to parties, movies, about town, etc. **b** stop burning: *Don't let the fire go out.* **c** go dark: *The lights went out during the storm.*

go through, a go to the end of; do all of; finish: *I went through two books over the weekend.* **b** undergo;

hat, āge, fär; let, ēqual, tėrm; it, īce
hot, ōpen, ôrder; oil, out; cup, pu̇t, rüle
əbove, takən, pencəl, lemən, circəs
ch, child; ng, long; sh, ship
th, thin; ꞩH, then; zh, measure

experience: *She went through some hard times.* **c** search: *He went through his pockets to find a nickel.* **d** use up; spend; exhaust: *She went through all her money.*
go through with, complete; carry out to the end: *He disliked the job so much that he refused to go through with it.*
go up, a ascend; rise: *This elevator is going up.* **b** increase: *The price of gasoline went up last week.*
go with, a keep company with: *He's been going with Jean for a long time.* **b** agree with in color or style: *That doesn't go with your suit.*
on the go, *Informal.* always moving or doing something: *A busy person is on the go from morning till night.*

goad (gōd) **1** a pointed stick for driving cattle. **2** anything that drives or urges one on. **3** drive or urge on; act as a goad to: *Hunger goaded him to steal a loaf of bread.* 1, 2 *n.,* 3 *v.*

goal (gōl) **1** the space between two posts into which, in certain games, a player tries to shoot a puck, kick a ball, etc. in order to score. **2** the act of scoring in such a manner. **3** the point or points counted for scoring a goal; a score: *Our team won, four goals to three.* **4** the finish line of a race. **5** something for which an effort is made; something wanted; one's aim or object in doing something: *His goal was to pass his examinations with high marks. My brother's goal is to be a great doctor.* *n.*

goal·er (gōl′ər) goalie. *n.*

goal·ie (gōl′ē) the player who guards the goal to prevent scoring in such games as hockey, lacrosse, etc. *n.*

goal·keep·er (gōl′kēp′ər) goalie. *n.*

goal tender goalie.

A domestic goat — about 90 cm high at the shoulder

goat (gōt) **1** a cud-chewing animal having hollow horns and, usually, long hair: *Goats are closely related to sheep but are stronger, less timid, and more active.* **2** *Slang.* a person made to take the blame or suffer for the mistakes of others; scapegoat. *n.*
get one's goat, *Informal.* make a person angry or annoyed; get any reaction from a person by teasing.

goat·herd (gōt′hėrd′) a person who takes care of goats. *n.*

goat·skin (gōt′skin′) **1** the hide of a goat. **2** leather made from the hide of goats: *a goatskin bag.* *n.*

gob·ble[1] (gob′əl) eat fast and greedily. *v.,* **gob·bled, gob·bling.**

gob·ble[2] (gob′əl) **1** the noise a turkey makes. **2** make this noise or one like it. 1 *n.,* 2 *v.,* **gob·bled, gob·bling.**

gob·bler (gob′lər) a male turkey. *n.*

go–be·tween (gō′bi twēn′) a person who goes back and forth between others with messages, proposals, suggestions, etc.: *He acted as a go-between in the settlement of the strike.* *n.*

Goblets

gob·let (gob′lit) a drinking glass with a base and stem. *n.*

gob·lin (gob′lən) a mischievous elf in the form of an ugly dwarf. *n.*

God (god) in certain religions, the maker and ruler of the universe; the Supreme Being. *n.*

god (god) **1** a being thought to have greater powers than any man has. **2** an image or likeness of a god. **3** some person or thing thought to be more important than anything else: *His father was a god to him.* *n.*

god·child (god′chīld′) a child for whom a grown-up person takes vows at baptism. *n., pl.* **god·chil·dren.**

god·dess (god′is) **1** a female god. **2** a very beautiful or charming woman. *n.*

god·fa·ther (god′fo′ꞩHər) a man who takes vows for a child when it is baptized: *The godfather promises to help the child to be a good Christian.* *n.*

god·like (god′līk′) **1** like God or a god; divine. **2** suitable for God or a god. *adj.*

god·ly (god′lē) obeying, loving, and fearing God; religious; pious. *adj.,* **god·li·er, god·li·est.**

god·moth·er (god′muꞩH′ər) a woman who takes vows for a child when it is baptized. *n.*

god·par·ent (god′per′ənt) a godfather or godmother. *n.*

goes (gōz) See **go.** *He goes to school.* *v.*

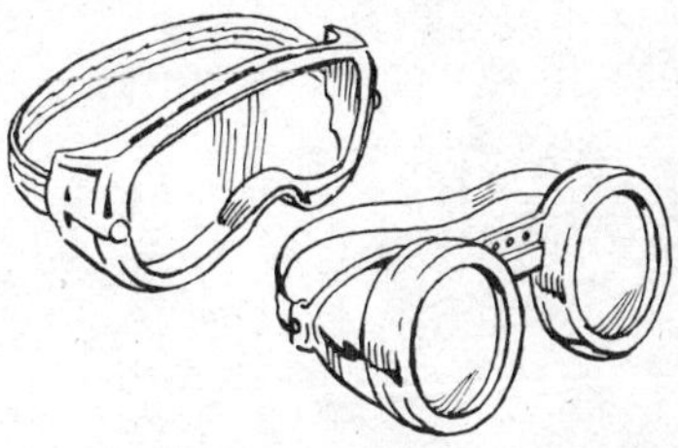

Two kinds of goggles

gog·gles (gog′əlz) a pair of large, close-fitting spectacles for protecting the eyes from light or dust: *He wore goggles while he was welding the broken steel rod.* *n. pl.*

go·ing (gō′ing) **1** going away; leaving: *His going was very sudden.* **2** moving; in action; working; running: *Set the clock going.* **3** the condition of the ground or road for walking or riding: *The going is bad through this muddy road.* **4** that goes; that can or will go. 1, 3 *n.*, 2, 4 *adj.*

be going to, will; be about to: *It is going to rain soon.*

goings on (gō′ingz) actions; behavior; conduct: *Her parents were unhappy about the goings on at the party.*

goi·tre or **goi·ter** (goi′tər) **1** a disease of a gland in the throat, which often produces a large swelling: *Goitre is usually caused by a lack of iodine in the body.* **2** the swelling itself. *n.*

gold (gōld) **1** a heavy, soft, yellow precious metal: *Wedding rings are made of gold.* **2** money in large sums; wealth; riches. **3** made of gold: *His father bought him a gold watch.* **4** a bright, beautiful, or precious thing or material: *Wheat is prairie gold.* **5** bright yellow: *gold hair.* 1, 2, 4, 5 *n.*, 3, 5 *adj.*

gold·en (gōl′dən) **1** made of gold: *golden dishes.* **2** containing gold. **3** shining like gold; bright yellow: *golden hair.* **4** very good; extremely favorable, valuable, or important: *golden deeds, a golden opportunity.* **5** very happy; flourishing: *a golden age. adj.*

gold·en·rod (gōl′dən rod′) a plant with tall stalks of small, yellow flowers that bloom in the fall. *n.*

gold·eye (gōld′ī′) *Cdn.* an edible fresh-water fish that is native to rivers and lakes from Ontario to the Northwest Territories: *Goldeye is smoked and dyed before being sold for food. n., pl.* **gold·eye** or **gold·eyes.**

gold·finch (gōld′finch′) a small, yellow songbird marked with black. *n.*

gold·fish (gōld′fish′) a small fish of a golden color kept in garden pools or in glass bowls indoors. *n., pl.* **gold·fish** or **gold·fish·es.**

gold rush a sudden movement of people to a place where gold has just been found: *The Klondike gold rush began after gold was discovered there in 1896.*

gold·smith (gōld′smith′) a man who makes articles of gold. *n.*

golf (golf) **1** an outdoor game played by hitting a small, hard ball with certain kinds of clubs: *A golf player tries to drive his ball into each of a number of holes with as few strokes as possible.* **2** play the game of golf: *He golfs every Saturday.* 1 *n.*, 2 *v.* **—golf′er,** *n.*

A gondola

gon·do·la (gon′də lə) **1** a long, narrow boat with a high peak at each end, used on the canals of Venice. **2** a freight car that has low sides and no top. **3** a car that hangs under a dirigible and holds the motors, passengers, etc. **4** *Cdn.* a broadcasting booth near the roof of a hockey arena: *There is a gondola in Maple Leaf Gardens. n.*

gone (gon) **1** moved away; left. **2** lost. **3** dead. **4** used up; consumed. **5** See **go.** *He has gone far away.* 1–4 *adj.*, 5 *v.*

gon·er (gon′ər) *Informal.* a person or thing that is dead, ruined, past help, etc. *n.*

gong (gong) a piece of metal shaped like a bowl or saucer and making a loud noise when struck: *A gong is a kind of bell. n.*

good (gu̇d) **1** having high quality; well-done: *a good piece of work.* **2** behaving well; that does what is right: *a good boy.* **3** right; as it ought to be: *Do what seems good to you.* **4** desirable: *a good book for children.* **5** satisfying; sufficient in size and quality: *a good meal.* **6** pleasant: *Have a good time.* **5** kind; friendly: *Say a good word for me.* **8** real; genuine: *It is not always easy to tell counterfeit money from good money.* **9** not spoiled; sound: *a good apple.* **10** well suited to its purpose: *A craftsman insists on good tools.* **11** thorough; complete: *do a good job.* **12** that which is good: *He always looked for the good in people.* **13** benefit; advantage; use: *What good will it do?* 1–11 *adj.*, **bet·ter, best;** 12, 13 *n.*

as good as, almost; practically: *The day is as good as over.*

for good, forever; finally; permanently: *He has left Canada for good.*

make good, a make up for; pay for: *He said he'd make good the damage done by his car.* **b** fulfil; carry out: *make good a promise.* **c** succeed; prosper: *His parents expected him to make good.*

good–bye or **good–by** (gu̇d′bī′) farewell: *'Good-bye,' shouted John as he ran off. n.*

good–for–noth·ing (gu̇d′fər nuth′ing) **1** worthless; useless. **2** a person who is worthless or useless. 1 *adj.*, 2 *n.*

Good Friday the Friday before Easter.

good–look·ing (gu̇d′lu̇k′ing) handsome; attractive: *a good-looking woman. adj.*

good·ly (gu̇d′lē) **1** pleasant; excellent; fine: *a goodly land.* **2** good-looking: *a goodly youth.* **3** considerable: *a goodly quantity. adj.*, **good·li·er, good·li·est.**

good–na·tured (gu̇d′nā′chərd) pleasant; kindly; obliging; cheerful. *adj.*

good·ness (gu̇d′nis) the state or quality of being good. *n.*

goods (gu̇dz) **1** belongings; personal property: *He gave half of his goods to the poor.* **2** things for sale; wares. *n. pl.*

good–sized (gu̇d′sīzd′) somewhat large: *a good-sized helping. adj.*

good–tem·pered (gu̇d′tem′pərd) easy to get along with; cheerful; agreeable. *adj.*

good will **1** kindly feeling; a friendly attitude. **2** the reputation and steady trade that a business has with its customers.

good·y (gu̇d′ē) *Informal.* **1** something very good to eat; a piece of candy or cake: *There were lots of goodies at the party.* **2** an exclamation of pleasure: *Are we going today? Oh, goody!* 1 *n., pl.* **good·ies;** 2 *interj.*

goose (güs) **1** a tame or wild water bird resembling a duck, but larger and having a longer neck: *A male goose is called a gander.* See the picture. **2** the female of this bird. **3** the flesh of this bird used as food. **4** a silly person: *'What a goose you are!' n., pl.* **geese.**

goose·ber·ry (güs′ber′ē or güz′bər ē) **1** a small, sour berry, used to make pies, tarts, jam, etc.: *Some kinds of gooseberry have prickly skins.* 2 the thorny bush that this berry grows on. *n., pl.* **goose·ber·ries.**

hat, āge, fär; let, ēqual, tėrm; it, īce
hot, ōpen, ôrder; oil, out; cup, pu̇t, rüle
 əbove, takən, pencəl, lemən, circəs
ch, child; ng, long; sh, ship
th, thin; ᴛʜ, then; zh, measure

A Canada goose — about 85 cm long with the tail

A gopher — about 20 cm long without the tail

go·pher (gō′fər) a small gnawing animal of the prairies, related to the chipmunk: *Gophers dig holes in the ground.* *n.*

☛ **Gopher** comes from a French word *gaufre,* meaning 'honeycomb.' The name was probably given because of the gopher's habit of burrowing in the ground and honeycombing it, and because of the similarity of this French word to a North American Indian word *magofer,* the name for a burrowing land tortoise.

gore[1] (gôr) blood that is spilled; thick blood: *The battlefield was covered with gore.* *n.*

gore[2] (gôr) wound with a horn or tusk: *The savage bull gored the farmer to death.* *v.,* **gored, gor·ing.**

gore[3] (gôr) a long tapering piece of cloth put or made in a skirt, sail, etc. to give greater width or to change the shape. *n.*

gorge (gôrj) 1 a deep, narrow valley, usually steep and rocky. 2 eat greedily until full: *Don't gorge yourself.* 1 *n.,* 2 *v.,* **gorged, gorg·ing.**

gor·geous (gôr′jəs) richly colored; splendid: *The peacock has spread his gorgeous tail. The gorgeous sunset thrilled us all.* *adj.*

go·ril·la (gə ril′ə) the largest and most powerful ape: *The gorilla is found in the forests of central Africa.* *n.*

gor·y (gôr′ē) bloody. *adj.,* **gor·i·er, gor·i·est.**

gos·ling (goz′ling) a young goose. *n.*

gos·pel (gos′pəl) 1 the teachings of Jesus and the Apostles. 2 **Gospel,** any one of the first four books of the New Testament, those by Matthew, Mark, Luke, and John. 3 anything earnestly believed: *Drink plenty of water; that is my gospel.* 4 absolute truth. *n.*

☛ **Gospel** developed from Old English *gōdspel,* meaning 'good news.'

gos·sa·mer (gos′ə mər) 1 a film or thread of cobweb. 2 any very thin, light cloth or substance: *a dress of gossamer.* 3 thin and light: *gossamer wings.* 1, 2 *n.,* 3 *adj.*

gos·sip (gos′ip) 1 idle talk, not always true, about other people and their affairs. 2 repeat what one knows or hears about other people and their affairs. 3 a person who talks in this way. 1, 3 *n.,* 2 *v.,* **gos·siped, gos·sip·ing.**

got (got) See **get.** *We got the letter yesterday. We had got tired of waiting for it.* *v.*

☛ Both **got** and **gotten** are accepted as the past participle of the verb **get.** Some people use only one or the other, but some use either one, depending on the rhythm of the sentence.

got·ten (got′ən) See **get.** *He has gotten himself into trouble twice this week.* *v.*

☛ See note at **got.**

gouge (gouj) 1 a chisel with a curved blade: *Gouges are used for cutting round grooves or holes in wood.* 2 cut with a gouge; dig out. 3 a groove or hole made by gouging: *There was a long gouge in the desk top.* 1, 3 *n.,* 2 *v.,* **gouged, goug·ing.**

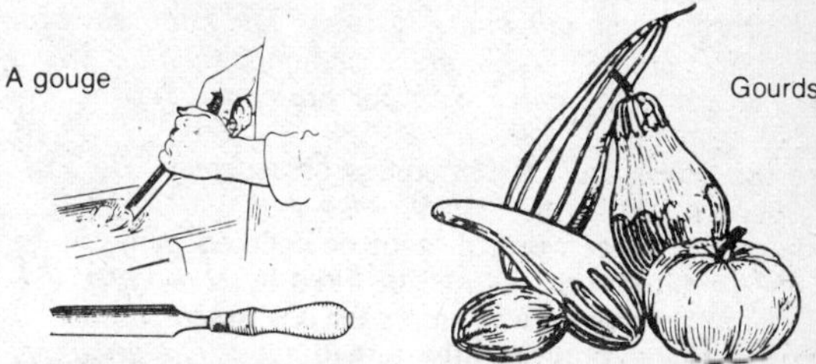

A gouge

Gourds

gourd (gôrd or gürd) 1 the fruit of a plant whose hard, dried shell is used for cups, bottles, bowls, etc. 2 the plant itself. 3 a cup, bottle, bowl, etc. made from such a dried shell. *n.*

gov·ern (guv′ərn) rule; control; manage: *govern a country, govern one's temper.* *v.*

☛ **Govern, governess, government,** and **governor** all came into English from separate Old French words which developed from forms of the Latin verb *gubernare,* meaning 'to steer, direct, or rule.' The Latin verb came from a Greek verb *kubernân,* meaning 'steer.'

gov·ern·ess (guv′ər nis) a woman who teaches children in a private home. *n.*

☛ See note at **govern.**

gov·ern·ment (guv′ərn mənt) 1 the ruling of a country. 2 the person or persons ruling a country at any time. 3 a system of ruling: *Canada has a democratic government.* 4 rule; control. *n.*

☛ See note at **govern.**

Government House 1 the official residence of the Governor General in Ottawa, also known as Rideau Hall. 2 the official residence of the Lieutenant-Governor of a province.

gov·er·nor (guv′ər nər) 1 a man who rules or governs. 2 an official elected as the executive head of a state: *Each state in the United States of America has a governor.* 3 the appointed ruler of a colony; the representative of a monarch in a colony. 4 a device arranged to keep a machine or motor going at an even speed. *n.*

☛ See note at **govern.**

Governor General in Canada, the representative of the Queen (or King), appointed on the advice of the Prime Minister for a term of five years.

gown (goun) 1 a woman's dress. 2 a loose outer garment: *Judges, clergymen, members of a university, and students graduating from university wear gowns to show their position, profession, etc.* 3 a nightgown or dressing gown. *n.*

grab (grab) **1** seize suddenly; snatch: *The dog grabbed the meat and ran.* **2** a snatching; a sudden seizing: *She made a grab for the apple.* 1 *v.,* **grabbed, grab·bing;** 2 *n.*

grace (grās) **1** a pleasing or agreeable quality; beauty of form or movement. **2** the favor and love of God. **3** a short prayer of thanks given before or after a meal. **4** behavior put on to seem attractive: *Their daughter came home from boarding school full of little airs and graces.* **5** Usually, **Grace,** a title used in speaking to or of a duke, duchess, or archbishop: *May I assist Your Grace? He spoke a few words to his Grace the Duke of Bedford.* **6** an allowance of time: *The bank gave him three days' grace.* **7** give grace or honor to: *She was asked to grace the party with her presence.* 1–6 *n.,* 7 *v.,* **graced, grac·ing.**

have the grace, have the goodness or courtesy: *He had the grace to say he was sorry.*

in one's bad graces, out of favor or disliked by.

in one's good graces, favored or liked by: *I wonder if I am in the teacher's good graces or bad graces.*

with bad grace, unpleasantly; unwillingly: *The apology was made with bad grace.*

with good grace, pleasantly; willingly: *He obeyed the order with good grace.*

grace·ful (grās′fəl) beautiful in form or movement; pleasing; agreeable: *a graceful birch tree, a graceful dance, a graceful speech of thanks. adj.* —**grace′ful·ly,** *adv.*

gra·cious (grā′shəs) **1** pleasant and kindly; courteous: *She received her guests in a gracious manner that made them feel at ease.* **2** pleasant and kindly to people of lower social position: *The Queen greeted her with a gracious smile. adj.*

grack·le (grak′əl) a kind of blackbird whose black feathers have a bronze lustre: *Grackles are often mistaken for starlings. n.*

grade (grād) **1** one of the divisions of a school course: *the sixth grade.* **2** a degree in rank, quality, or value: *Grade A butter is the best in quality.* **3** arrange in classes; arrange according to size, value, etc.; sort: *These apples are graded by size.* **4** a number or letter that shows how well one has done: *Her grade in English is B.* **5** give a grade to: *The teacher graded the papers.* **6** the slope of a road or railway track: *The car had trouble getting up the steep grade.* **7** make more nearly level; even out: *The workmen graded the land around the new house.* 1, 2, 4, 6 *n.,* 3, 5, 7 *v.,* **grad·ed, grad·ing.**

grade crossing a place where a railway track crosses a road or another railway track on the same level; a level crossing.

grade school an elementary school; a grammar school.

grad·u·al (graj′ü əl) by degrees too small to be separately noticed; little by little: *a gradual increase in sound. The hill had a gradual slope. adj.* —**grad′u·al·ly,** *adv.*

grad·u·and (graj′ü and′) a student who is about to graduate. *n.*

grad·u·ate (graj′ü āt′ for 1 and 3, graj′ü it or graj′ü āt′ for 2) **1** finish the course of a school or college and be given a diploma or paper saying one has done so: *Mary's brother graduated from university last year.* **2** a person who has graduated and has a diploma. **3** mark out in equal spaces: *My ruler is graduated in centimetres.* 1, 3 *v.,* **grad·u·at·ed, grad·u·at·ing;** 2 *n.*

☛ The pronunciation (graj′ü āt′) for the noun is most commonly heard among Westerners.

grad·u·a·tion (graj′ü ā′shən) **1** a graduating from a school or college: *He was looking forward to graduation.* **2** the ceremony of graduating; graduating exercises. *n.*

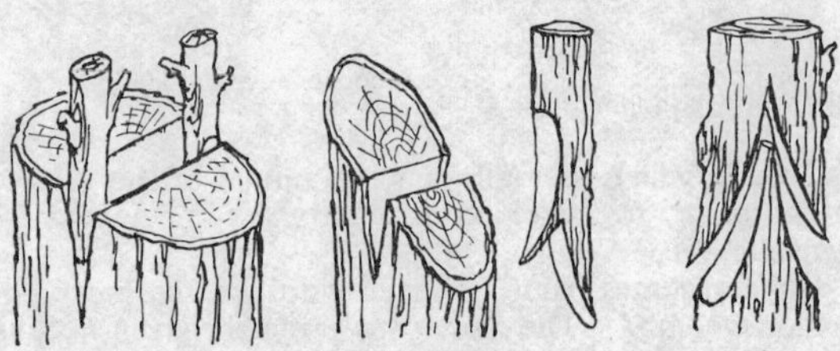

Three kinds of plant graft. The pieces are tied or taped together and kept moist until the graft begins to grow.

graft[1] (graft) **1** a shoot from one tree or plant fixed in a slit in another tree or plant, to grow there as a part of it: *A graft from a fine apple tree may be put on a worthless one to improve it.* **2** make a graft; put a shoot from one plant into another. 1 *n.,* 2 *v.*

graft[2] (graft) **1** the taking of money dishonestly, especially by government officials in positions of trust. **2** obtain money by graft. 1 *n.,* 2 *v.*

gra·ham (grā′əm) made from whole wheat flour: *graham wafers. adj.*

☛ Named after an American, Sylvester *Graham* (1794–1851), who supported reforms in nutrition.

grain (grān) **1** the seed of plants like wheat, oats, and corn. **2** the plants that these seeds or seedlike fruits grow on: *The farmer was busy cutting his grain.* **3** one of the tiny bits of which sand, sugar, salt, etc. are made up: *A few grains of sugar lay on the table.* **4** a very small weight about the same as 0.06 grams: *A pound equals 7000 grains.* **5** the smallest possible amount; tiniest bit: *a grain of truth.* **6** the little lines and markings in wood, marble, etc.; the arrangement of the particles of anything: *Mahogany has a fine grain.* **7** natural character; disposition: *Laziness was against the grain for her. n.*

grain elevator a building for storing grain. See **elevator** for picture.

gram (gram) a measure of mass: *There are 1000 grams in a kilogram. Symbol:* g *n.* Also spelled **gramme.**

gram·mar (gram′ər) **1** the study of the forms of words and the ways in which they are arranged to form sentences. **2** the system of the forms and uses of words in a particular language: *Grammar is often thought of as a set of rules.* **3** the use of words according to this system: *Good grammar is important in formal writing. n.*

gram·mat·i·cal (grə mat′ə kəl) **1** according to the grammar (def. 2) of a particular language: *Our French teacher speaks grammatical English but has a French accent.* **2** of grammar: *'Between you and I' is a grammatical mistake. adj.*

gramme (gram) See **gram.**

hat, āge, fär; let, ēqual, tėrm; it, īce
hot, ōpen, ôrder; oil, out; cup, pu̇t, rüle
əbove, takən, pencəl, lemən, circəs
ch, child; ng, long; sh, ship
th, thin; ᴛʜ, then; zh, measure

gram·o·phone (gram′ə fōn′) a record player; phonograph. *n.*

gran·a·ry (gran′ə rē or grān′ə rē) a place or building where grain is stored. *n., pl.* **gran·a·ries.**

☛ The pronunciation (grān′ə rē) shows the influence of the word **grain** and is very common in grain-growing areas.

grand (grand) **1** large and of fine appearance: *grand mountains.* **2** fine; noble; dignified; stately; splendid: *a very grand palace, grand music, a grand old man.* **3** highest or very high in rank; chief: *a grand duke.* **4** great; important; main: *the grand staircase.* **5** complete; comprehensive: *the grand total.* **6** very pleasing: *a grand time. adj.*

gran·dad or **grand·dad** (gran′dad′ or grand′dad′) *Informal.* grandfather (def. 1). *n.*

Grand Banks or **Grand Bank** a shallow region, or shoal, of the ocean lying southeast of Newfoundland: *The Grand Banks are famous as a fishing ground for cod.*

grand·child (gran′chīld′ or grand′chīld′) a child of one's son or daughter. *n., pl.* **grand·chil·dren.**

grand·daugh·ter (gran′do′tər or grand′do′tər, gran′dô′tər or grand′dô′tər) a daughter of one's son or daughter. *n.*

gran·deur (gran′jər or gran′jür) greatness; majesty; nobility; dignity; splendor: *The grandeur of Niagara Falls is famous. n.*

grand·fa·ther (gran′fo′ᴛʜər or grand′fo′ᴛʜər) **1** the father of one's father or mother. **2** any forefather. *n.*

grand·ma (gran′mä′, gram′mä′, or grand′mä′) *Informal.* grandmother. *n.*

grand·moth·er (gran′muᴛʜ′ər or grand′muᴛʜ′ər) the mother of one's mother or father. *n.*

grand·pa (gran′pä′, gram′pä′, or grand′pä′) *Informal.* grandfather. *n.*

grand·par·ent (gran′per′ənt or grand′per′ənt) a grandfather or grandmother. *n.*

grand piano a large harp-shaped piano with horizontal strings.

grand·son (gran′sun′ or grand′sun′) a son of one's son or daughter. *n.*

grand·stand (gran′stand′ or grand′stand′) the main seating place for people at an athletic field, race track, parade, etc.: *Grandstands are usually covered. n.*

grange (grānj) a farm with its buildings; farmstead. *n.*

gran·ite (gran′it) a kind of very hard rock, much used for buildings, monuments, etc.: *Granite is usually grey. n.*

gran·nie or **gran·ny** (gran′ē) *Informal.* **1** grandmother. **2** an old woman. *n., pl.* **gran·nies.**

grant (grant) **1** allow; give what is asked: *to grant a request.* **2** admit: *I grant that you are right so far.* **3** give. **4** a gift, especially land or rights given by the government: *The companies that built the railways received large grants of land from the government.* 1–3 *v.,* 4 *n.*

take for granted, assume to be true; accept as proved or as agreed to: *It is taken for granted that one must eat to live. We took it for granted that John would do well.*

grape (grāp) a small, round fruit, red, purple, or pale-green, that grows in bunches on a vine: *Grapes are eaten, or made into raisins or wine. n.*

grape·fruit (grāp′früt′) a large, pale-yellow, mildly sour fruit of the same family as oranges and lemons: *Grapefruit are popular as a breakfast fruit. n., pl.* **grape·fruit** or **grape·fruits.**

grape·vine (grāp′vīn′) **1** the vine that bears grapes. **2** *Informal.* a way by which reports are mysteriously spread: *He learned through the grapevine that he had passed the examination. n.*

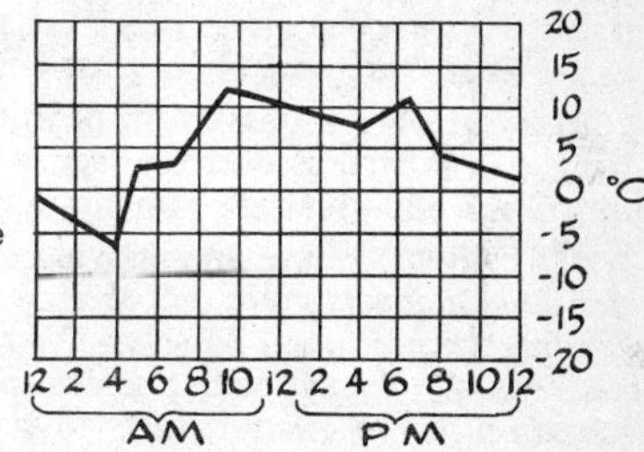

A graph of the temperatures on a fall day. At noon the temperature was 10°C.

graph (graf) a line or diagram showing how one quantity depends on or changes with another: *You could draw a graph to show how your weight has changed each year with your change in age. n.*

graph·ic (graf′ik) **1** producing by words the effects of a picture; lifelike; vivid: *The returned soldier gave a graphic account of the battle.* **2** of or shown by a diagram: *a graphic record of school attendance for a month.* **3** of or about drawing, painting, engraving, etc.: *He is studying the graphic arts. adj.*

graph·ite (graf′īt) a soft, black form of carbon used for lead in pencils and for greasing machinery. *n.*

grap·ple (grap′əl) **1** seize and hold fast; grip or hold firmly. **2** seizing and holding fast; a firm grip or hold. **3** struggle; fight: *The wrestlers grappled in the centre of the ring. He grappled with the problem for an hour before he solved it.* **4** a grappling iron. 1, 3 *v.,* **grap·pled, grap·pling;** 2, 4 *n.*

grappling iron an iron bar with hooks at one end for seizing and holding something.

grasp (grasp) **1** seize; hold fast by closing the fingers around: *He grasped the railing to keep from falling.* **2** a seizing and holding tightly; a clasp of the hand. **3** the power of seizing and holding; reach: *Success is within his grasp.* **4** control; possession. **5** understand: *to grasp the meaning of the word.* **6** understanding: *She has a good grasp of arithmetic.* 1, 5 *v.,* 2–4, 6 *n.*

grasp at, a try to take hold of: *The drowning man grasped at the lifebuoy.* **b** accept eagerly: *He grasped at the chance to become president.*

grasp·ing (grasp′ing) eager to get all that one can; greedy. *adj.*

grass (gras) **1** the green plants having long slender leaves and stems, that cover fields, lawns, and pastures: *Horses, cows, and sheep eat grass.* **2** a plant that has jointed stems and long, narrow leaves: *Wheat, corn, and sugar cane are grasses. n.*

grass hockey the game of field hockey.

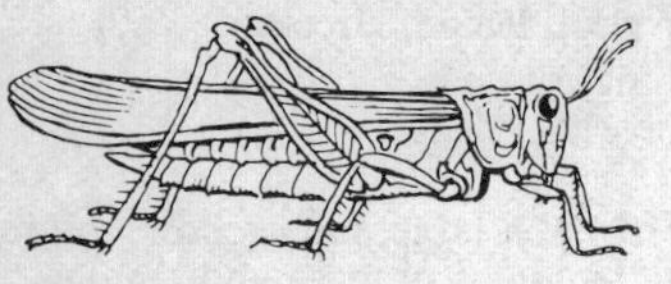
A grasshopper — about 3 cm long

grass·hop·per (gras′hop′ər) a winged insect having strong legs for jumping. *n.*

grass·land (gras′land′) land with grass on it, used for pasture. *n.*

grass·y (gras′ē) 1 covered with grass; having much grass: *a grassy slope.* 2 of grass: *a grassy bed.* 3 like grass: *We shredded green paper for a grassy setting for Easter eggs.* *adj.,* **grass·i·er, grass·i·est.**

grate[1] (grāt) 1 a framework of iron bars to hold a fire. 2 iron bars, as over a prison window. *n.*

☛ **Grate** and **great** are pronounced the same.

grate[2] (grāt) 1 have an annoying or unpleasant effect: *Her rude manners grate on other people.* 2 make a grinding sound; sound harshly: *The chalk grated on the blackboard.* 3 move with a harsh sound: *The door grated on its old, rusty hinges.* 4 wear down or grind off in small pieces: *to grate cheese.* *v.,* **grat·ed, grat·ing.**

☛ See note at **grate**[1].

grate·ful (grāt′fəl) feeling gratitude; thankful: *They were grateful for our help.* *adj.* —**grate′ful·ly,** *adv.*

grat·i·fi·ca·tion (grat′ə fə kā′shən) 1 gratifying: *The gratification of every wish of every person is not possible.* 2 something that pleases or satisfies: *His success was a great gratification to his parents.* *n.*

grat·i·fy (grat′ə fī′) 1 please; give pleasure or satisfaction to: *Praise gratifies most people.* 2 satisfy; indulge: *A drunkard gratifies his craving for liquor.* *v.,* **grat·i·fied, grat·i·fy·ing.**

grat·ing[1] (grāt′ing) a grate; a framework of parallel or crossed bars: *Windows in a prison, bank, or ticket office have gratings over them.* *n.*

grat·ing[2] (grāt′ing) 1 irritating; unpleasant: *a grating voice.* 2 harsh or jarring in sound. *adj.*

grat·i·tude (grat′ə tyüd′ or grat′ə tüd′) a kindly feeling because of a favor received; a desire to do a favor in return; thankfulness. *n.*

grave[1] (grāv) 1 a hole dug in the ground where a dead body is to be buried. 2 any place of burial: *a watery grave.* 3 death: *an early grave.* *n.*

grave[2] (grāv) 1 earnest; thoughtful; serious: *grave words.* 2 important; demanding serious thought: *The judge had to make a grave decision.* *adj.,* **grav·er, grav·est.** —**grave′ly,** *adv.*

grav·el (grav′əl) 1 pebbles and pieces of rock coarser than sand: *Gravel is much used for roads and walks.* 2 lay or cover with gravel. 1 *n.,* 2 *v.,* **grav·elled** or **grav·eled, grav·el·ling** or **grav·el·ing.**

grave·yard (grāv′yärd′) a place for burying the dead; cemetery; burial ground. *n.*

grav·i·tate (grav′ə tāt′) 1 move or tend to move by gravitation. 2 settle down; sink; fall: *The sand and dirt in the water gravitated to the bottom of the bottle.* 3 tend to go; be strongly attracted: *The attention of the crowd gravitated to the new jet plane.* *v.,* **grav·i·tat·ed, grav·i·tat·ing.**

grav·i·ta·tion (grav′ə tā′shən) the fact that the earth pulls any object toward it and that the sun, moon, stars, and other such bodies in the universe do the same; the force or pull that makes bodies in the universe tend to move toward one another. *n.*

grav·i·ty (grav′ə tē) 1 the natural force that causes objects to move or tend to move toward the centre of the earth: *Gravity causes objects to have weight.* 2 the natural force that makes objects move or tend to move toward each other; gravitation. 3 heaviness; weight: *He balanced the long pole at its centre of gravity.* 4 a serious manner; serious behavior: *The look of gravity on the child's face was rather amusing.* 5 serious nature; importance: *The gravity of the situation was greatly increased by threats of war.* *n., pl.* **grav·i·ties.**

gra·vy (grā′vē) 1 the juice that comes out of meat in cooking. 2 a sauce for meat, potatoes, etc. made from this juice. *n., pl.* **gra·vies.**

gray (grā) See **grey.**

gray·ish (grā′ish) See **greyish.**

gray jay Canada jay.

gray·ling (grā′ling) a fresh-water fish resembling a trout, but having a longer and higher dorsal fin. *n.*

graze[1] (grāz) 1 feed on growing grass: *Cattle were grazing in the field.* 2 put cattle, sheep, etc. to feed on growing grass or a pasture. *v.,* **grazed, graz·ing.**

graze[2] (grāz) 1 touch lightly in passing; rub lightly against: *The car grazed the garage door.* 2 scrape the skin from: *The bullet grazed his shoulder.* 3 a light rub or scrape. 1, 2 *v.,* **grazed, graz·ing;** 3 *n.*

grease (grēs) 1 soft animal fat. 2 any thick, oily substance. 3 rub grease on: *Indians greased their bodies.* 4 put grease or oil in or on: *He had his car greased at the gas station.* 1, 2 *n.,* 3, 4 *v.,* **greased, greas·ing.**

greas·y (grēs′ē) 1 having grease on it. 2 containing much grease; oily: *greasy food.* 3 like grease; smooth; slippery: *The roads were greasy after the snowfall.* *adj.,* **greas·i·er, greas·i·est.**

great (grāt) 1 big; large: *a great house, a great crowd.* 2 much; more than is usual: *great pain, great kindness.* 3 important; high in rank; remarkable: *a great singer, a great event, a great picture.* *adj.* —**great′ly,** *adv.* —**great′ness,** *n.*

☛ **Great** and **grate** are pronounced the same.

great·coat (grāt′kōt′) a heavy overcoat. *n.*

Great Divide in Canada, the height or crest of land extending northwest along the Rocky Mountain range, from which rivers flow west to the Pacific Ocean or east and north to Hudson Bay and the Arctic Ocean; the Continental Divide.

great–grand·child (grāt′gran′chīld′ or grāt′grand′chīld′) a grandchild of one's son or daughter. *n., pl.* **great-grand·chil·dren.**

great–grand·fa·ther (grāt′gran′fo′ᴛʜər or grāt′grand′fo′ᴛʜər) the father of a grandparent. *n.*

great–grand·moth·er (grāt′gran′muᴛʜ′ər or grāt′grand′muᴛʜ′ər) the mother of a grandparent. *n.*

great horned owl a large, powerful bird of prey, the largest Canadian owl, mostly brown and white and having large ear tufts: *The great horned owl hunts many different birds and small animals.*

Great Lakes the five large bodies of fresh water that

are included in the St. Lawrence waterway; Lakes Superior, Michigan, Huron, Erie, and Ontario.

grebe (grēb) a tail-less water bird resembling a loon and having partly webbed feet and a pointed bill: *Most grebes have crests or ruffs during the nesting season.* *n.*

greed (grēd) the state or practice of wanting more than one's share; greedy behavior; greedy desire: *a miser's greed for money.* *n.*

greed·y (grēd′ē) **1** wanting to get more than one's share. **2** wanting to get a great deal. **3** wanting to eat a great deal in a hurry. *adj.,* **greed·i·er, greed·i·est.** **—greed′i·ly,** *adv.* **—greed′i·ness,** *n.*

Greek (grēk) **1** of Greece, its people, or their language. **2** a person born in or living in Greece. **3** the language of Greece. 1 *adj.,* 2, 3 *n.*

Greek Orthodox of or having to do with a group of Christian churches, especially the main Christian churches in eastern Europe and western Asia, which are united by common beliefs and traditions.

green (grēn) **1** the color of most growing plants, of grass, and of the leaves of trees in summer. **2** having this color; of this color. **3** not ripe; not fully grown: *Most green fruit is not good to eat.* **4** not dried, cured, seasoned, or otherwise prepared to use: *green tobacco.* **5** not trained: *He is certainly green in business.* **6** a piece of ground covered with grass. **7** the patch of smooth lawn or sand around each hole on a golf course. **8 greens,** *pl.* **a** green leaves and branches used for decoration, wreathes, garlands, etc. **b** leaves and stems of plants used as food: *salad greens.* 1, 6–8 *n.,* 2–5 *adj.*

green·horn (grēn′hôrn′) *Informal.* **1** a person without experience. **2** a person easy to trick or cheat. *n.*

green·house (grēn′hous′) a building with a glass roof and glass sides, kept warm for growing plants; a hothouse. *n.*

green·ish (grēn′ish) somewhat green. *adj.*

greet (grēt) **1** say 'Hello,' 'How do you do,' 'Welcome,' etc. to; address in welcome; hail. **2** receive: *His speech was greeted with cheers.* **3** meet; present itself to: *When she opened the door, the strangest sight greeted her eyes.* *v.*

greet·ing (grēt′ing) **1** the act or words of a person who greets somebody; a welcome. **2 greetings,** *pl.* friendly wishes on a special occasion: *Christmas greetings.* *n.*

gre·nade (grə nād′) a small bomb: *The soldiers threw grenades into the enemy's trenches.* *n.*

gren·a·dier (gren′ə dēr′) **1** in former times, a soldier who threw grenades. **2** today, a soldier in any one of several infantry regiments. *n.*

grew (grü) See **grow.** *It grew cold last night.* *v.*

grey (grā) **1** any shade obtained by mixing black and white. **2** having a shade between black and white: *Ashes, lead, and hair getting white with age are grey.* **3** dark; gloomy; dismal: *a grey day.* **4** make or become grey. 1 *n.,* 2, 3 *adj.,* 4 *v.* Also spelled **gray.**

grey·hound (grā′hound′) a tall, slender hunting dog with a long nose: *Greyhounds can run very fast.* *n.*

grey·ish (grā′ish) somewhat grey. *adj.* Also spelled **grayish.**

grid (grid) **1** a framework of parallel iron bars; grating; grill. **2** a system of survey lines running parallel to the lines of latitude and longitude, used in the division of an

hat, āge, fär; let, ēqual, tėrm; it, īce
hot, ōpen, ôrder; oil, out; cup, pu̇t, rüle
əbove, takən, pencəl, lemən, circəs
ch, child; ng, long; sh, ship
th, thin; ᴛʜ, then; zh, measure

area into counties, sections, etc. **3** one of these lines: *Country roads are often built along a grid.* *n.*

grid·dle (grid′əl) a heavy, flat plate, usually of metal, on which to cook bacon, pancakes, etc. *n.*

grid·i·ron (grid′ī′ərn) **1** grill (def. 1). **2** a football field. *n.*

grief (grēf) **1** heavy sorrow; great sadness. **2** a cause of sadness or sorrow: *Her son's incurable illness was a great grief to her.* *n.*

come to grief, have trouble; fail: *Although he worked hard, his plan came to grief.*

griev·ance (grēv′əns) a real or imagined wrong; a reason for being annoyed or angry: *The captain told his men to report any grievances to him.* *n.*

grieve (grēv) **1** feel grief; be very sad: *She grieved over her kitten's death.* **2** cause to feel grief; make sad: *His mother's death grieved him greatly.* *v.,* **grieved, griev·ing.**

griev·ous (grēv′əs) **1** hard to bear; causing great pain or suffering; severe: *grievous cruelty.* **2** very evil or offensive; outrageous: *Wasting food when people are starving is a grievous wrong.* **3** causing grief: *a grievous loss.* **4** full of grief; showing grief: *a grievous cry.* *adj.*

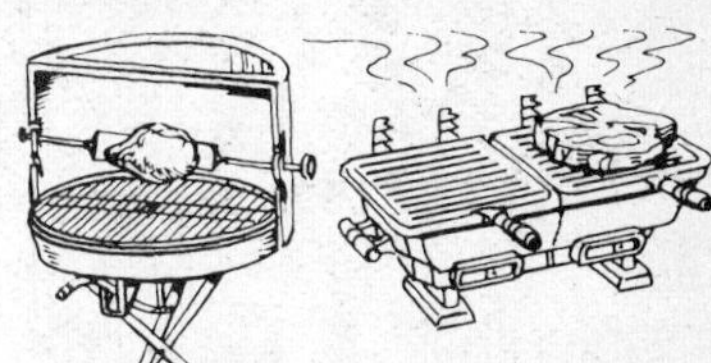
Two kinds of grill

grill (gril) **1** a framework of metal bars used for broiling meat, fish, etc. **2** broil; cook by holding near the fire. **3** a dish of broiled meat, fish, etc. **4** a dining room in a hotel or restaurant that specializes in serving broiled meat, fish, etc. **5** torture with heat. **6** question severely and persistently: *The detectives grilled the prisoner until he finally confessed.* 1, 3, 4 *n.,* 2, 5, 6 *v.*

grim (grim) **1** stern; harsh; fierce; without mercy: *grim, stormy weather.* **2** not yielding; not relenting: *The losing team fought on with grim resolve.* **3** looking stern, fierce, or harsh: *Father was grim when he heard about the six broken windows.* **4** horrible; frightful; ghastly: *He made grim jokes about death and ghosts.* *adj.,* **grim·mer, grim·mest.**

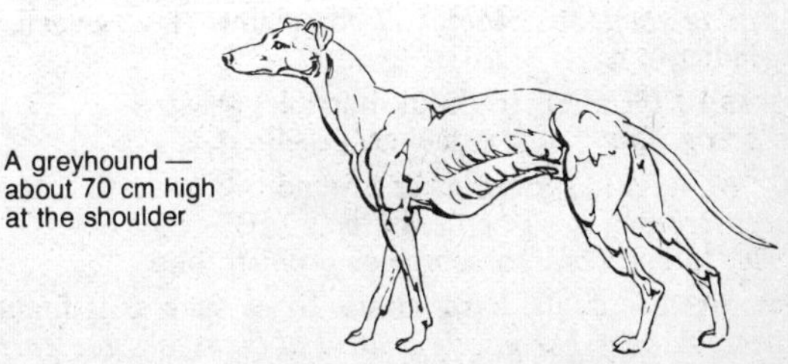
A greyhound — about 70 cm high at the shoulder

gri·mace (grə mās′ or grim′is) **1** a twisting of the face; an ugly or funny smile: *a grimace caused by pain.* **2** make faces: *The clown grimaced at the children.* 1 *n.,* 2 *v.,* **gri·maced, gri·mac·ing.**

grime (grīm) **1** dirt rubbed deeply and firmly into a surface: *the grime on a coal miner's hands.* **2** make very dirty. 1 *n.,* 2 *v.,* **grimed, grim·ing.**

grim·y (grīm′ē) covered with grime; very dirty. *adj.,* **grim·i·er, grim·i·est.**

grin (grin) **1** smile broadly. **2** a broad smile. **3** draw back the lips and show the teeth: *The wolf grinned in an ugly way.* 1, 3 *v.,* **grinned, grin·ning;** 2 *n.*

grind (grīnd) **1** crush into bits, into meal, or into powder: *That mill grinds corn. His teeth ground the meat.* **2** produce or make by grinding: *grind flour.* **3** crush by harsh rule: *The slaves were ground down by their masters.* **4** sharpen, smooth, or wear by rubbing on something rough: *He ground the axe on the grindstone.* **5** rub harshly together: *to grind one's heel into the earth, to grind one's teeth.* **6** work by turning a handle; produce by turning a crank: *He grinds out music from a street organ.* **7** *Informal.* long, hard work or study: *To some of us, arithmetic is a grind.* 1–6 *v.,* **ground, grind·ing;** 7 *n.* **—grind′er,** *n.*

A grindstone

grind·stone (grīn′stōn′ or grīnd′stōn′) a flat, round stone set in a frame and turned by hand, foot, or a motor: *A grindstone is used to sharpen tools, such as axes and knives, or to smooth and polish things.* *n.*

grip (grip) **1** seizing and holding tight; a tight grasp; a firm hold. **2** seize and hold tight; take a firm hold on: *The dog gripped the stick.* **3** handle: *the grip of a suitcase.* **4** a certain way of gripping the hand as a sign of belonging to some secret society. **5** a small suitcase or handbag. **6** firm control: *The country is in the grip of winter.* **7** get and keep the interest and attention of: *An exciting story grips the reader.* 1, 3–6 *n.,* 2, 7 *v.,* **gripped, grip·ping.**

gripe (grīp) *Informal.* **1** complain: *He was always griping about something.* **2** complaint. 1 *v.,* **griped, grip·ing;** 2 *n.*

gris·ly (griz′lē) frightful; horrible; ghastly: *a grisly sight.* *adj.,* **gris·li·er, gris·li·est.**

grist (grist) **1** grain to be ground. **2** grain that has been ground; meal or flour. *n.*
grist to one's mill, a source of profit to one.

gris·tle (gris′əl) hard, elastic tissue such as is found in meat: *A baby has gristle instead of bone in some parts of the skull.* *n.*

grit (grit) **1** very fine bits of gravel or sand: *There was grit in the spinach.* **2** pluck; endurance; courage: *The fighter showed lots of grit.* **3** grind; make a grating sound by holding closed and rubbing: *He gritted his teeth and then plunged into the cold water.* 1, 2 *n.,* 3 *v.,* **grit·ted, grit·ting. —grit′ty,** *adj.*

Grit (grit) *Informal.* **1** a member of the Liberal party in Canada. **2** of or associated with the Liberals. 1 *n.,* 2 *adj.*

griz·zled (griz′əld) grey; greyish. *adj.*

griz·zly (griz′lē) **1** greyish. **2** grizzly bear. 1 *adj.,* **griz·zli·er, griz·zli·est;** 2 *n., pl.* **griz·zlies.**
☛ **Grizzly** and **grisly** are pronounced the same.

grizzly bear a large, fierce, grey or brownish-grey bear of western North America.

groan (grōn) **1** a sound made down in the throat to express grief, pain, or disapproval; a deep, short moan: *We heard the groans of the wounded men.* **2** give a groan or groans. **3** be loaded or burdened: *The table groaned with food.* 1 *n.,* 2, 3 *v.*
☛ **Groan** and **grown** are pronounced the same.

gro·cer (grō′sər) a merchant who sells food and household supplies. *n.*

gro·cer·y (grō′sər ē or grōs′rē) **1** a store that sells food and household supplies. **2 groceries,** *pl.* food and household supplies sold by a grocer. *n., pl.* **gro·cer·ies.**

gro·ce·te·ri·a (grō′sə tēr′ē ə) a grocery store in which the customers wait on themselves, paying for their purchases at a cashier's counter. *n.*

groom (grüm) **1** a man who is a servant; a man or boy who has charge of horses. **2** feed and take care of horses; rub down and brush. **3** take care of the appearance of; make neat and tidy: *She was brought up to groom herself carefully.* **4** bridegroom. 1, 4 *n.,* 2, 3 *v.*

groove (grüv) **1** a long, narrow channel or furrow, especially one cut by a tool: *My desk has a groove for pencils. The plate rests in a groove on the rack.* **2** any similar channel; rut: *Wheels leave grooves in a dirt road.* **3** make a groove in: *The sink shelf is grooved so that the water will run off.* **4** a fixed way of doing things: *It is hard for him to get out of a groove.* 1, 2, 4 *n.,* 3 *v.,* **grooved, groov·ing.**

grope (grōp) **1** feel about with the hands: *He groped for a flashlight when the lights went out.* **2** search here and there rather blindly: *The detectives groped for some clue to the murder.* **3** find by feeling about with the hands; feel one's way slowly: *The blind man groped his way to the door.* *v.,* **groped, grop·ing.**

gros·beak (grōs′bēk′) a bird of the finch family having a large, stout bill. *n.*

gross (grōs) **1** with nothing taken out; total; whole; entire: *The gross receipts are all the money taken in.* **2** the total amount. **3** twelve dozen; 144. **4** obviously bad; glaring: *gross misconduct. She makes gross errors in pronunciation.* **5** coarse; vulgar: *Her manners are too gross for a lady.* **6** too big and fat; overfed: *a gross man.* **7** thick; heavy; dense: *the gross growth of a jungle.* 1, 4–7 *adj.,* 2, 3 *n.*

gro·tesque (grō tesk′) **1** odd or unnatural in shape, appearance, manner, etc.; fantastic; queer: *The book had pictures of hideous dragons and other grotesque monsters.* **2** ridiculous; absurd: *The monkey's grotesque antics made the children laugh.* *adj.*

hat, āge, fär; let, ēqual, tėrm; it, īce
hot, ōpen, ôrder; oil, out; cup, pu̇t, rüle
əbove, takən, pencəl, lemən, circəs
ch, child; ng, long; sh, ship
th, thin; ꟻH, then; zh, measure

grot·to (grot'ō) 1 cave. 2 an artificial cave made for coolness or pleasure. *n., pl.* **grot·toes** or **grot·tos.**

grouch (grouch) *Informal.* 1 be sulky or ill-tempered; complain. 2 a sulky person: *Why must she be such a grouch?* 1 *v.,* 2 *n.*

grouch·y (grouch'ē) sulky; sullen; discontented. *adj.,* **grouch·i·er, grouch·i·est.**

ground[1] (ground) 1 the surface of the earth: *Snow covered the ground.* 2 earth; soil: *The ground was hard.* 3 any piece of land or region used for some purpose: *The West was his favorite hunting ground.* 4 **grounds,** *pl.* the land, lawns, and gardens around a house, college, etc. 5 **grounds,** *pl.* the small bits that sink to the bottom of a drink such as coffee or tea; dregs; sediment. 6 of, on, at, or near the ground: *the ground floor of a building.* 7 put on the ground; cause to touch the ground. 8 run aground; hit the bottom or shore: *The boat grounded in shallow water.* 9 the foundation for what is said, thought, or done; a basis or reason: *There is no ground for complaining of his conduct. On what grounds do you say that is true?* 10 fix firmly; establish: *This class is well grounded in arithmetic.* 11 background: *The cloth has a blue pattern on a white ground.* 12 connect an electric wire with the ground. 1–5, 9, 11 *n.,* 6 *adj.,* 7, 8, 10, 12 *v.*

from the ground up, completely; entirely; thoroughly: *He learned his father's business from the ground up.*

gain ground, go forward, advance, progress: *During the second day of fighting, the army began to gain ground.*

give ground, retreat; yield: *Under our attack the enemy was forced to give ground.*

lose ground, a retreat. **b** fall back; give up what has been gained: *As soon as the runner became tired, he began to lose ground.*

stand one's ground, keep one's position; refuse to retreat or yield: *Even though the boxer was hurt, he stood his ground.*

ground[2] (ground) See **grind.** *The wheat was ground to make flour. v.*

A groundhog — about 50 cm long without the tail

ground·hog (ground'hog') a North American burrowing animal of the marmot family; woodchuck: *Groundhogs grow fat in summer and sleep in their burrows all winter. n.*

Groundhog Day February 2, when the groundhog is supposed to come out of his hole to see whether the sun is shining; if the sun is shining and he sees his shadow, he returns to his hole for six more weeks of winter.

group (grüp) 1 a number of persons or things together: *A group of children were playing tag.* 2 form into a group: *The children grouped themselves in front of the monkey's cage.* 3 bring together; arrange in a group: *She grouped the tulips in one vase, the roses in another.* 1 *n.,* 2, 3 *v.*

grouse[1] (grous) a game bird with feathered legs. *n., pl.* **grouse.**

grouse[2] (grous) *Informal.* 1 grumble; complain. 2 complaint. 3 a person who complains; grumbler. 1 *v.,* **groused, grous·ing;** 2, 3 *n.*

grove (grōv) a group of trees standing together: *An orange grove is an orchard of orange trees. n.*

grov·el (grov'əl) lie face downward; crawl at someone's feet; humble oneself: *The dog grovelled before its master when he raised his whip. v.,* **grov·elled** or **grov·eled, grov·el·ling** or **grov·el·ing.**

grow (grō) 1 become bigger; increase: *His business has grown fast.* 2 live and become big: *Few trees grow in the desert.* 3 cause to grow; raise: *We grow wheat in many parts of Canada.* 4 become: *It grew cold. v.,* **grew, grown, grow·ing.**

grow on or **upon,** have an increasing effect or influence on: *The habit grew on me.*

grow out of, a get too big for; outgrow: *When I grew out of my jacket, I gave it to my little brother.* **b** result from; develop from: *The riot grew out of the bad conditions in the factory.*

grow up, become full-grown; become an adult: *What will you be when you grow up?*

growl (groul) 1 a sound like that made by a fierce dog; a deep, warning snarl. 2 make such a sound: *The dog growled at the tramp.* 3 grumble; complain about things: *The soldiers growled about the poor food.* 1 *n.,* 2, 3 *v.*

grown (grōn) 1 arrived at full growth: *A grown man is an adult.* 2 See **grow.** *The corn has grown very tall.* 1 *adj.,* 2 *v.*

☛ **Grown** and **groan** are pronounced the same.

grown–up (grōn'up') 1 arrived at full growth. 2 an adult: *The boy went to church with the grown-ups.* 3 of or suitable for an adult: *grown-up clothes.* 1, 3 *adj.,* 2 *n.*

growth (grōth) 1 the process of growing; development. 2 the amount grown; increase; progress: *one year's growth.* 3 what has grown or is growing: *A thick growth of bushes covered the ground. n.*

grub (grub) 1 a smooth, thick, wormlike larva of an insect, especially that of a beetle. 2 dig; dig up; root out of the ground: *Pigs grub for roots.* 3 to toil. 4 *Slang.* food. 1, 4 *n.,* 2, 3 *v.,* **grubbed, grub·bing.**

grub·by (grub'ē) 1 dirty; grimy: *grubby hands.* 2 infested with grubs: *grubby apples. adj.,* **grub·bi·er, grub·bi·est.**

grudge (gruj) 1 ill will; a sullen feeling against; a dislike of long standing: *He carried a grudge because he*

A ruffed grouse — about 45 cm long with the tail

lost the fight. 2 feel anger or dislike toward a person because of something; envy the possession of: *He grudged me my little prize even though he had won a bigger one.* 3 give or let have unwillingly: *The mean man grudged his horse the food that it ate.* 1 *n.*, 2, 3 *v.*, **grudged, grudg·ing.**

grudg·ing·ly (gruj′ing lē) unwillingly. *adv.*

gru·el (grü′əl) a thin, almost liquid food made by boiling oatmeal, etc. in water or milk. *n.*

grue·some (grü′səm) causing fear or horror; horrible; frightful: *a gruesome sight. adj.*

gruff (gruff) 1 deep and harsh; hoarse: *He is a kind man with a gruff voice.* 2 rough; rude; unfriendly; bad-tempered: *a gruff manner. adj.* —**gruff′ly,** *adv.*

grum·ble (grum′bəl) 1 complain in a rather sullen way; mutter in discontent; find fault. 2 a mutter of discontent; a bad-tempered complaint. 3 make a low, heavy sound like distant thunder: *His stomach was grumbling from hunger.* 1, 3 *v.*, **grum·bled, grum·bling;** 2 *n.*

grump·y (grum′pē) surly; ill-humored; gruff: *The grumpy old man used to find fault with everything. adj.*, **grump·i·er, grump·i·est.**

grunt (grunt) 1 the deep, hoarse sound that a pig makes. 2 a sound like this: *The old man got out of his chair with a grunt.* 3 make this sound. 4 say with this sound: *The sullen boy grunted his apology.* 1, 2 *n.*, 3, 4 *v.*

guar·an·tee (gar′ən tē′ or ger′ən tē′) 1 a promise to pay or do something if another fails to do it; a pledge to replace or repair goods if they are not satisfactory. 2 make such a promise; give a guarantee for: *This company guarantees its clocks for a year.* 3 undertake to secure for another: *He will guarantee us possession of the house by May.* 4 secure against or from: *His insurance guaranteed him against money loss in case of fire.* 5 promise to do something; pledge that something has been or will be: *I guarantee that I'll be on time.* 6 make sure or certain: *Wealth does not guarantee happiness.* 7 an assurance; promise: *Wealth is not a guarantee of happiness.* 1, 7 *n.*, 2–6 *v.*, **guar·an·teed, guar·an·tee·ing.**

guard (gärd) 1 watch over; take care of; keep safe: *The dog guards the house.* 2 defend: *The goalie guards the goal.* 3 keep from escaping: *The soldiers guarded the prisoners day and night.* 4 check; hold back; keep under control: *Guard your tongue.* 5 something that guards; any safety device: *A guard was placed in front of the fire.* 6 a person or group that guards. 7 a position of defence in boxing or fencing. 8 a careful watch: *A soldier kept guard over the prisoners.* 9 a player on either side of the centre in rugby football. 10 either of the two players serving as defencemen in basketball. 1–4 *v.*, 5–10 *n.*

guard against, avoid or prevent by being careful: *His mother told him to guard against getting his feet wet.*

off guard, unready; unprepared: *The pitcher was off guard when the ball was hit to him.*

on guard, watchful; ready to defend or protect: *A dog stood on guard.*

stand guard, do sentry duty: *The soldier stood guard at the gate of the fort.*

☛ See note at **warden.**

guard·i·an (gär′dē ən or gärd′yən) 1 a person who takes care of another or of some special thing. 2 a person appointed by law to take care of the affairs of someone who is young or cannot take care of them himself. 3 protecting: *My guardian angel must have looked after me.* 1, 2 *n.*, 3 *adj.*

☛ See note at **warden.**

guard·rail (gärd′rāl′) a rail or railing used for protection. *n.*

guess (ges) 1 form an opinion of something when one does not know exactly: *Let us guess at the height of the tree.* 2 an opinion formed without really knowing: *My guess is that it will rain tomorrow.* 3 get right or find out by guessing: *Can you guess the answer to that riddle?* 4 think; believe; suppose: *I guess he is really sick after all.* 1, 3, 4 *v.*, 2 *n.*

guess·work (ges′wėrk′) work, action, or results based on guessing; guessing: *There is a lot of guesswork involved in buying a used car. n.*

guest (gest) 1 a person who is received and entertained by another; visitor. 2 a person who is staying at a hotel, motel, etc. *n.*

guid·ance (gīd′əns) guiding; direction; leadership: *Under her mother's guidance, she learned how to cook. n.*

guide (gīd) 1 show the way; lead; direct: *The Indian guided the hunters.* 2 a person or thing that shows the way: *Tourists and hunters sometimes hire guides. Your feelings are often a poor guide for actions and beliefs.* 3 guidebook. 4 Girl Guide. 1 *v.*, **guid·ed, guid·ing;** 2–4 *n.*

guide·book (gīd′buk′) a book of directions and information, especially one for travellers. *n.*

guided missile an object that is thrown or shot and can be accurately guided, usually by means of electronic impulses that it receives from a controlling device on the ground.

Guid·er (gīd′ər) an adult who is associated in some way with the Girl Guides or Brownies. *n.*

guide word in a dictionary, either of the two words appearing at the top of a page: *The guide word at the left is the same as the first entry word on the page; the one at the right is the same as the last entry word on the page.*

guild (gild) 1 a society for mutual aid or for some common purpose: *the Canadian Guild of Potters.* 2 in the Middle Ages, a union of the men in one trade, formed to keep standards high and to look out for their common interests. *n.*

☛ **Guild** and **gild** are pronounced the same.

guile (gīl) crafty deceit; cunning; crafty behavior; sly tricks: *By guile the fox got the cheese from the crow. n.*

guil·lo·tine (gil′ə tēn′) 1 a machine for cutting off people's heads with a heavy blade that slides up and down in grooves made in two posts. 2 a machine for cutting paper. *n.*

☛ **Guillotine** comes from a French word with the same spelling. This machine was named after Joseph-Ignace *Guillotin,* a French doctor who was a member of the Revolutionary Assembly and suggested the use of this machine as a quick and merciful way of executing persons condemned to death.

guilt (gilt) the fact or state of having done wrong;

hat, āge, fär; let, ēqual, tėrm; it, īce
hot, ōpen, ôrder; oil, out; cup, pu̇t, rüle
əbove, takən, pencəl, lemən, circəs
ch, child; ng, long; sh, ship
th, thin; ᴛʜ, then; zh, measure

being guilty; being to blame: *The evidence proved his guilt.* *n.*

☞ **Guilt** and **gilt** are pronounced the same.

guilt·less (gilt′lis) not guilty; free from guilt; innocent. *adj.*

guilt·y (gil′tē) **1** having done wrong; deserving to be blamed and punished: *The jury pronounced the prisoner guilty of murder.* **2** knowing or showing that one has done wrong: *The boy who hit the cat had a guilty look.* *adj.,* **guilt·i·er, guilt·i·est.** **—guilt′i·ly,** *adv.*

guin·ea fowl (gin′ē) a bird resembling a pheasant, having dark-grey feathers with small white spots: *A guinea fowl can fly better than an ordinary fowl.*

☞ The **guinea fowl** was named for the part of Africa from which it originally came. *Guinea* was the name given by the Portuguese in the sixteenth century to a region on the west coast of Africa. The name *guinea* was also applied loosely to other things or animals that came from a distant country, as in **guinea pig,** which originally came from South America.

A guinea fowl — about 60 cm long with the tail

A guinea pig — about 25 cm long

guinea pig **1** a short-eared, short-tailed animal kept as a pet and for experiments: *A guinea pig is like a big, fat, harmless rat.* **2** any person or thing used for experiment or for testing something: *The school used our class as guinea pigs to test the new timetable.*

☞ See note at **guinea fowl.**

guise (gīz) **1** a style of dress: *The spy went in the guise of a monk so that he would not be recognized.* **2** appearance: *an old theory under a new guise.* **3** a pretended appearance; pretence: *He deceived the enemy by his guise of ignorance and dullness.* *n.*

Two kinds of guitar

gui·tar (gə tär′) **1** a musical instrument, which, as a rule, has six strings played with the fingers or with a pick. **2** an electric guitar. *n.*

☞ **Guitar** and **zither** have come into English from different languages (**guitar** from Spanish and **zither** from German), but they both originally came from one ancient Greek word, *kithara,* the name of a stringed instrument similar to a lyre.

gulch (gulch) a very deep, narrow valley with steep sides. *n.*

gulf (gulf) **1** a large bay; an arm of an ocean or sea extending into the land: *The Gulf of St. Lawrence lies at the mouth of the St. Lawrence River, on the east coast of Canada.* **2** a very deep break or cut in the earth. **3** a wide separation: *The quarrel left a gulf between the old friends.* *n.*

Sea gulls — about 60 cm long with the tail

gull (gul) a graceful grey-and-white bird living on or near large bodies of water: *A gull has long wings, webbed feet, and a thick, strong beak.* *n.*

gul·li·ble (gul′ə bəl) easily deceived or cheated: *The gullible woman believed everything the glib salesman said.* *adj.*

gul·ly (gul′ē) **1** a narrow gorge; a small valley with steep sides. **2** a ditch made by heavy rains or running water: *After the storm, the newly seeded lawn was covered with gullies.* *n., pl.* **gul·lies.**

gulp (gulp) **1** swallow eagerly or greedily: *Don't gulp your milk.* **2** the act of swallowing. **3** the amount swallowed at one time; a mouthful. **4** keep in; choke back; repress: *The disappointed boy gulped down a sob.* **5** gasp; choke. 1, 4, 5 *v.,* 2, 3 *n.*

gum¹ (gum) **1** a sticky juice of certain trees and plants that hardens in the air and dissolves in water: *Gum is used to make glue, drugs, candy, etc.* **2** a tree that yields gum. **3** gum prepared for chewing. **4** stick or stick together with gum: *The stamp was gummed onto the letter.* 1–3 *n.,* 4 *v.,* **gummed, gum·ming.**

gum² (gum) Often, **gums,** *pl.* the flesh around the teeth. *n.*

gum·bo (gum′bō) **1** the okra plant, including its pods. **2** soup thickened with okra pods: *chicken-gumbo soup.* **3** soil that becomes sticky and heavy when wet, especially that found on the western prairies: *It took him an hour to clean the gumbo off his boots.* *n., pl.* **gum·bos.**

☞ **Gumbo** comes from an African word *kingombo,* which was the original name for the okra plant in Africa.

gum·drop (gum′drop′) a stiff, jelly-like piece of candy. *n.*

gum tree a tree that yields gum: *The sweet gum, sour gum, and eucalyptus are gum trees.*

gun (gun) **1** a weapon with a long metal tube for shooting bullets, shot, etc.: *An artillery piece or a cannon is correctly called a gun; rifles, pistols, and* *revolvers are commonly called guns.* **2** anything resembling a gun in use or shape: *a spray gun.* **3** the shooting of a gun as a signal or salute: *The Governor General gets twenty-one guns as a salute.* **4** shoot with a gun; hunt with a gun: *He went gunning for rabbits.* 1–3 *n.,* 4 *v.,* **gunned, gun·ning.**

stick to one's guns, refuse to retreat, yield, or give up.

gun·boat (gun′bōt′) a small warship that can be used in shallow water. *n.*

gun·fire (gun′fīr′) the shooting of a gun or guns. *n.*

gun·lock (gun′lok′) the part of a gun that controls the hammer and fires the charge. *n.*

gun·ner (gun′ər) **1** a man trained to fire artillery pieces; a soldier who handles and fires big guns. **2** a naval officer in charge of a ship's guns. **3** a person, especially a private soldier, serving in the artillery. **4** a person who hunts with a shotgun, rifle, etc. *n.*

gun·pow·der (gun′pou′dər) a powder that explodes with force when touched with fire: *Gunpowder is used in guns, blasting, and fireworks. n.*

gun·shot (gun′shot′) **1** a shot fired from a gun. **2** the shooting of a gun: *We heard gunshots.* **3** the distance that a gun will shoot: *within gunshot. n.*

gun·wale (gun′əl) the upper edge of a ship's or boat's side. See **rowboat** for picture. *n.*

gup·py (gup′ē) a very small, brightly colored fish of tropical fresh water, often kept in aquariums: *The female guppy bears live young instead of producing eggs. n., pl.* **gup·pies.**

gur·gle (gėr′gəl) **1** flow or run with a bubbling sound: *Water gurgles when it is poured out of a bottle or flows among stones.* **2** a bubbling sound. **3** make a bubbling sound: *The baby gurgled happily.* 1, 3 *v.,* **gur·gled, gur·gling;** 2 *n.*

gush (gush) **1** a rush of water or other liquid from an enclosed space: *If you get a deep cut, there usually is a gush of blood.* **2** rush out suddenly; pour out. **3** give out a rush of emotional or silly talk. 1 *n.,* 2, 3 *v.*

gush·er (gush′ər) an oil well that gives oil in great quantities without pumping. *n.*

gus·set (gus′it) **1** a triangle-shaped piece of material inserted in a dress, the upper part of a shoe, etc. to give greater strength or more freedom of movement. **2** a bracket or plate used to reinforce the joints of a structure such as a building or bridge. *n.*

gust (gust) **1** a sudden violent rush of wind, often whirling: *A gust upset the small sailboat.* **2** an outburst of anger or other feeling: *Gusts of laughter greeted the clown. n.* **—gust′y,** *adj.*

gus·to (gus′tō) keen relish; hearty enjoyment: *The hungry boy ate his dinner with gusto. n., pl.* **gus·tos.**

gut (gut) **1** the intestine. **2** a tough string made from the twisted and dried intestines of sheep or other animals: *Gut is used for violin strings and for the strings in tennis rackets.* **3** a narrow channel or gully. **4** remove the insides of: *They gutted the fish.* **5** destroy the inside of: *The building was gutted by fire.* **6 guts,** *pl. Slang.* courage, pluck, or the ability to endure pain, discomfort, etc. 1–3, 6 *n.,* 4, 5 *v.,* **gut·ted, gut·ting.**

gut·ter (gut′ər) **1** a channel or ditch along the side of a street or road to carry off water; the low part of a street beside the sidewalk. **2** a channel or trough along the lower edge of a roof to carry off rain water. See **eaves** for picture. **3** flow or melt in streams: *The candle guttered when the melted wax ran down its sides.* 1, 2 *n.,* 3 *v.*

guy[1] (gī) **1** a rope, chain, or wire attached to something to steady it. **2** guide, steady, or secure with a guy or guys: *The mast was guyed by four ropes.* 1 *n.,* 2 *v.,* **guyed, guy·ing.**

☛ **Guy**[1] probably came through French or Dutch from an old Low German word meaning a small rope for trussing up sails.

guy[2] (gī) *Slang.* a man; fellow: *Most of the guys were at the party. n.*

☛ **Guy**[2] is considered slang, although it is widely used in informal speech. **Guy**[2] comes from *Guy* Fawkes, an Englishman who was hanged for leading an unsuccessful plot to blow up the British king and parliament in 1605. A custom then developed in England of publicly burning a dummy 'guy' at an annual celebration. 'Guy' came to refer to a strange-looking person, and later became a slang term meaning simply 'man.'

guy rope one of several ropes attached to a tent for pegging it to the ground so as to hold it in position.

gym (jim) gymnasium. *n.*

gym·na·si·um (jim nā′zē əm) a room, building, etc. fitted up for physical exercise or training and for indoor athletic sports. *n.*

gym·nas·tics (jim nas′tiks) exercises for developing the muscles, such as are done in a gymnasium. *n. pl.*

gyp·sy or **gip·sy** (jip′sē) **1** a person belonging to a wandering race of dark-skinned, dark-eyed people who probably came from India long ago. **2** a person who looks or lives like a gypsy. **3** of the gypsies: *a gypsy girl.* 1, 2 *n., pl.* **gyp·sies;** 3 *adj.*

☛ **Gypsy** was formed from the word *Egyptian,* because in the sixteenth century, when the gypsies first came to Great Britain, they were thought to have come from Egypt.

gy·rate (jī′rāt or jī rāt′) move in a circle or spiral; whirl; rotate: *A top gyrates. v.,* **gy·rat·ed, gy·rat·ing.**

gy·ro·scope (jī′rə skōp′) an instrument consisting of a wheel with a heavy rim, so mounted that the axle can be pointed in any direction, the wheel still being able to turn freely. Once the wheel is spinning, the axle will remain pointing in the same direction even if the support or outside frame is turned or tilted. *n.*

hat, āge, fär; let, ēqual, tėrm; it, īce
hot, ōpen, ôrder; oil, out; cup, pu̇t, rüle
əbove, takən, pencəl, lemən, circəs
ch, child; ng, long; sh, ship
th, thin; ᴛʜ, then; zh, measure

h or **H** (āch) the eighth letter of the alphabet: *There are two* h's *in hothouse.* *n., pl.* **h's** or **H's.**

h hour; hours.

ha[1] (ho, hä, or ha) 1 an exclamation of surprise, joy, or triumph: *'Ha! I've caught you!' cried the giant to Jack.* 2 in writing, a way of indicating laughter: *'Ha! ha! ha!' laughed the boys.* *interj.*

ha[2] hectare.

hab·it (hab′it) 1 a custom or practice; usual way of acting: *Everyone should form the habit of brushing his teeth after every meal. Doing a thing over and over again makes it a habit.* 2 the dress of persons belonging to a religious order: *a nun's habit.* 3 a woman's riding dress: *The lady on the white horse wore a black habit.* *n.*

☛ **Habit** and **custom** have very similar meanings, but they are used somewhat differently. **Habit** refers to a settled practice or tendency of an individual person, something the person does without thinking: *Brushing one's teeth becomes a habit.* **Custom** refers especially to a usage adopted by a group of people or an individual and continued over a long period of time: *It is a custom among some people to eat fish on Fridays.*

hab·it·a·ble (hab′ə tə bəl) fit to live in. *adj.*

hab·it·ant (hab′ə tont′ or ab′ə ton′) *Cdn.* 1 a French-Canadian farmer. 2 having to do with French Canadians or French Canada, especially with regard to country life. 1 *n.*, 2 *adj.*

hab·i·tat (hab′ə tat′) the place where an animal or plant naturally lives or grows: *The jungle is the habitat of tigers.* *n.*

hab·i·ta·tion (hab′ə tā′shən) 1 a place or building to live in; home; dwelling. 2 inhabiting; living in: *Is the house fit for habitation? Habitation of this house is not allowed.* *n.*

ha·bit·u·al (hə bich′ü əl) 1 done by habit: *a habitual smile, habitual courtesy.* 2 regular; steady: *A habitual reader reads a great deal.* 3 usual; customary: *Ice and snow are a habitual sight in arctic regions.* *adj.* **—ha·bit′u·al·ly,** *adv.*

hack[1] (hak) 1 cut roughly: *He hacked the box apart with a dull axe.* 2 a rough cut. 3 a notch cut in the ice at one end of a curling rink, used as a foothold when a player throws his rock. 4 give short, dry coughs: *The boy hacked all night.* 5 a short dry cough. 1, 4 *v.*, 2, 3, 5 *n.*

hack[2] (hak) 1 a carriage for hire. 2 *Informal.* taxi. 3 an old or worn-out horse. 4 a horse for ordinary riding: *They rented hacks at the riding stable.* 5 a person hired to do routine writing; drudge. 6 working or done merely for money; hired: *a hack writer, a piece of hack writing.* 1–5 *n.*, 6 *adj.*

hack·saw (hak′so′ or hak′sô′) a saw for cutting metal, consisting of a narrow, fine-toothed blade fixed in a frame. *n.*

had (had) See **have.** *She had a party. A fine time was had by all who came.* *v.*

had·dock (had′ək) a food fish of the northern Atlantic, resembling a cod but smaller. *n., pl.* **had·dock** or **had·docks.**

had·n't (had′ənt) had not.

haft (haft) the handle of a knife, sword, etc. *n.*

hag (hag) 1 a very ugly old woman. 2 witch. *n.*

hag·gard (hag′ərd) looking worn out from pain, fatigue, worry, hunger, etc.; worn by care: *The haggard faces of the rescued miners showed how they had suffered.* *adj.*

hail[1] (hāl) 1 small, roundish pieces of ice coming down from the clouds in a shower; frozen rain: *Hail fell with such violence that it broke windows.* 2 fall in hail: *Sometimes it hails during a summer thundershower.* 3 a shower resembling hail: *A hail of bullets met the soldiers.* 4 pour down in a shower like hail: *The angry mob hailed blows on the thief.* 1, 3 *n.*, 2, 4 *v.*

☛ **Hail** and **hale** are pronounced the same.

hail[2] (hāl) 1 greet; cheer; shout in welcome to: *The crowd hailed the winner.* 2 Greetings! Welcome! a greeting: *Hail to the chief!* 3 call loudly to; shout to: *The boys hailed passing cars to beg a ride.* 4 a loud call; shout: *The ship sailed on, paying no attention to our hails.* 1, 3 *v.*, 2 *interj.*, 4 *n.*

hail from, come from: *both these ships hail from Montreal.*

☛ See note at **hail**[1].

hail·stone (hāl′stōn′) a frozen drop of rain: *Hailstones are usually very small, but sometimes they are as big as marbles or even golf balls.* *n.*

hair (her) 1 a fine, threadlike outgrowth from the skin of human beings and animals. 2 a mass of such growths: *The little girl's hair was fine and silky.* *n.* **—hair′less,** *adj.*

not turn a hair, not show any sign of being disturbed or embarrassed.

split hairs, make too fine distinctions.

☛ **Hair** and **hare** are pronounced the same.

hair·brush (her′brush′) a brush for taking care of the hair. *n., pl.* **hair·brush·es.**

hair·cut (her′kut′) a cutting of the hair. *n.*

hair·do (her′dü′) a way of arranging the hair. *n., pl.* **hair·dos.**

hair·dress·er (her′dres′ər) a person who takes care of or cuts people's hair. *n.*

hair·pin (her′pin′) 1 a pin, usually a U-shaped piece of wire, shell, etc., used by women to keep the hair in place. 2 shaped like a hairpin; U-shaped: *a hairpin bend.* 1 *n.*, 2 *adj.*

hair–rais·ing (her′rāz′ing) *Informal.* making the hair seem to stand on end; terrifying: *Uncle John tells hair-raising stories.* *adj.*

hair·y (her′ē) 1 covered with hair; having much hair: *hairy hands, a hairy ape.* 2 like hair. *adj.*, **hair·i·er, hair·i·est.**

hale[1] (hāl) strong and well; healthy. *adj.*, **hal·er, hal·est.**

☛ **Hale** and **hail** are pronounced the same.

hale[2] (hāl) 1 compel to go: *The man was haled into court.* 2 drag by force. *v.*, **haled, hal·ing.**

☛ See note at **hale**[1].

half (haf) 1 one of two equal parts: *A half of 4 is 2. Two halves make a whole.* 2 making a half of; needing as much more to make a whole: *a half litre, a half barrel.* 3 to a half of the full amount or degree: *a glass half full of milk.* 4 partly: *She spoke half aloud. The meat was only half cooked.* 1 *n., pl.* **halves;** 2, 3 *adj.,* 4 *adv.*
not half bad, fairly good.

half·back (haf′bak′) in football, soccer, etc., a player whose position is behind the forward line. *n.*

half–breed (haf′brēd′) 1 a person whose parents are of different races, especially a person of mixed white and North American Indian blood. 2 a person whose parents are half-breeds: *There are many half-breeds in the Canadian North. n.*

half brother a brother related through one parent only.

half dollar a coin of Canada and the United States, worth 50 cents.

half–heart·ed (haf′här′tid) lacking enthusiasm or interest; not earnest: *a half-hearted attempt. adj.*

half–mast (haf′mast′) a position halfway or part way down from the top of a mast or staff: *When the King died, flags were lowered to half-mast as a mark of respect. n.*

half sister a sister related through one parent only.

half·way (haf′wā′) 1 half the way; half the required distance: *The rope reached only halfway to the boat.* 2 one half: *The lesson is halfway finished.* 3 midway: *The inn served as a halfway house between the two towns.* 4 incomplete; not going far enough; inadequate: *Halfway measures are never satisfactory.* 1, 2 *adv.,* 3, 4 *adj.*
go or **meet halfway,** do one's share toward reaching an agreement or toward patching up a quarrel.

half–wit (haf′wit′) 1 a feeble-minded person. 2 a stupid, foolish person: *Only a half-wit would try to ski on that icy slope. n.*

hal·i·but (hal′ə bət) a very large flatfish, much used as food. *n., pl.* **hal·i·but** or **hal·i·buts.**

hall (hol or hôl) 1 a way to go through a building: *A hall ran the length of the upper floor of the house.* 2 a passage or room at the entrance of a building: *Leave your umbrella in the hall.* 3 a large room for holding meetings, parties, banquets, etc.: *Our town needs a larger hall for community concerts.* 4 a building for public business, assemblies, etc.: *The mayor's office is in the town hall.* 5 a building of a school or college. *n.*
☛ **Hall** and **haul** are pronounced the same.

hal·le·lu·jah or **hal·le·lu·iah** (hal′ə lü′yə) 1 Praise ye the Lord! 2 a song of praise. 1 *interj.,* 2 *n.*

hal·loo (hə lü′) 1 a call or shout to attract attention. 2 give such a call or shout: *The stranded seamen hallooed to the passing ship.* 1 *n., pl.* **hal·loos;** 2 *v.,* **hal·looed, hal·loo·ing.**

hal·low (hal′ō) make holy or sacred: *'Hallowed be Thy name.' v.*

Hal·low·een or **Hal·low·e'en** (hal′ō ēn′, hal′ə wēn′, or hol′ə wēn′) the evening of October 31; the eve of All Saints' Day. *n.*

hall·way (hol′wā′ or hôl′wā′) a hall or corridor; a passage in a building. *n.*

ha·lo (hā′lō) 1 a ring of light around a shining body such as the sun, the moon, or a star. 2 a golden circle or disk of light shown about the head of a holy person, as in pictures of saints and angels. 3 a kind of splendor, glory, or glamor: *A halo of romance surrounds King Arthur and his knights. n., pl.* **ha·los** or **ha·loes.**

halt[1] (holt or hôlt) 1 stop: *The soldiers halted for a short rest.* 2 a stop: *All work came to a halt.* 1 *v.,* 2 *n.*

halt[2] (holt or hôlt) 1 be in doubt; hesitate: *Shyness made the boy halt as he talked.* 2 lame; crippled; limping. 3 **the halt,** persons who halt, limp, or hesitate. 1 *v.,* 2 *adj.,* 3 *n.*

hal·ter (hol′tər or hôl′tər) 1 a rope or strap for leading or tying an animal. 2 a rope for hanging a person. 3 a backless and sleeveless blouse that usually fastens behind the neck and across the back: *She wore shorts and halter to the picnic. n.*

halve (hav) 1 divide into two equal parts; share equally: *The two girls agreed to halve expenses on their trip.* 2 reduce to half: *The new machine will halve the time and cost of doing the work by hand. v.,* **halved, halv·ing.**
☛ **Halve** and **have** are pronounced the same.

halves (havz) plural of **half:** *Two halves make one whole. n.*
go halves, share equally.

hal·yard (hal′yərd) a rope used to raise or lower a sail, yard, or flag. *n.*

ham (ham) 1 salted and smoked meat from the upper part of a hog's hind leg. 2 an amateur radio operator. *n.*

ham·burg·er (ham′bėr gər) 1 ground beef. 2 this meat shaped into flat cakes and fried or broiled, especially when served in a split bun. *n.*

ham·let (ham′lit) a small group of houses situated in the country and having no fixed boundaries: *A hamlet is usually smaller than a village and has no local government of its own. n.*

A hammer (def. 1)

ham·mer (ham′ər) 1 a tool with a metal head and a handle, used to drive nails and to beat metal into shape. 2 something shaped or used like a hammer: *the hammer of a gun explodes the charge.* 3 drive, hit, or work with a hammer: *to hammer nails.* 4 beat into shape with a hammer: *The metal was hammered into ornaments.* 5 pound; hit again and again: *The angry man hammered on the door with his fist.* 6 fasten by using a hammer. 7 force by repeated efforts: *She hammered the formulas into her head until she had memorized them.* 1, 2 *n.,* 3–7 *v.*
hammer and tongs, with all one's force and strength: *The two boys fought hammer and tongs.*
hammer at, work hard at; keep working hard at: *He hammered at his homework till it was finished.*
hammer away, a work hard at; keep working at: *She hammered away at her homework till it was finished.*

hat, āge, fär; let, ēqual, tėrm; it, īce
hot, ōpen, ôrder; oil, out; cup, pu̇t, rüle
əbove, takən, pencəl, lemən, circəs
ch, child; ng, long; sh, ship
th, thin; ᴛʜ, then; zh, measure

He hammered away till the job was done. **b** keep nagging; badger: *He hammered away at his mother till he got what he wanted.*

hammer out, a beat into shape with a hammer. **b** make clear by much thinking or talking: *The boys finally hammered out the plans for their clubhouse.*

A hammock

ham·mock (ham′ək) a swinging bed or couch made of canvas, netted cord, etc. that is suspended at both ends. *n.*

ham·per¹ (ham′pər) get in the way of; hold back; hinder: *A lame leg and a heavy bundle hampered the old farmer. v.*

ham·per² (ham′pər) a large container, often a wicker basket, usually having a cover: *a picnic hamper, a clothes hamper. n.*

ham·ster (ham′stər) a small, short-tailed animal of the rat family, having large pouches in its cheeks: *Hamsters, which resemble guinea pigs, are often kept as pets. n.*

hand (hand) **1** the end part of the arm, which takes and holds objects: *Each hand has four fingers and a thumb.* See **arm** for picture. **2** anything like a hand: *The hands of a clock or watch show the time.* **3** a hired worker who uses his hands: *a farm hand, a factory hand.* **4** give with the hand; pass: *Please hand me a spoon.* **5** help with the hand: *The hotel doorman handed the lady into her car.* **6** a part or share in doing something: *He had no hand in the matter.* **7** side: *At her left hand stood two men.* **8** one's style of handwriting: *He writes in a clear hand.* **9** skill; ability: *This painting shows the hand of a master.* **10** a person skilled or practiced at doing something: *He is an old hand at camping.* **11** a promise of marriage. **12** a measure used in giving the height of horses, etc.; the breadth of a hand, about 10 centimetres: *This horse is 18 hands high.* **13** the cards held by a player in one round of a card game. **14** a single round in a card game. 1–3, 6–14 *n.*, 4, 5 *v.*

at second hand, from a source other than the original source: *The story he had heard at second hand proved to be an exaggeration.*

change hands, pass from one person to another: *During the big sale, a lot of money changed hands.*

from hand to mouth, without being able to put something aside for the future: *During the long strike, many men with families lived from hand to mouth.*

hand down, pass along: *His old clothes were handed down to his younger brother.*

hand in, give or pass to a person in authority: *The tests were handed in to the teacher.*

hand on, pass along: *He read the note and handed it on to the person next to him.*

hand out, give out; distribute: *The storekeeper handed out free suckers.*

hand over, give; give back: *When John asked for his book, I handed it over.*

hand to hand, close together; at close quarters: *to fight hand to hand.*

have one's hands full, have as much to do as one can manage.

in one's hands, a in one's possession or control: *The property is no longer in my hands.* **b** in one's care or charge: *George left his bicycle in John's hands.*

lend a hand, help or assist: *He asked his brother to lend a hand with the chores.*

off one's hands, out of one's care or charge: *The babysitter was glad when the sick child was taken off her hands.*

on hand, a within reach; close by: *There were enough tools on hand to fix the engine.* **b** in stock: *The supermarket had lots of oranges on hand.*

on the other hand, considering the other side of the question or argument: *I want the bicycle very much; on the other hand, I can't afford to buy it.*

out of hand, a out of control: *The angry crowd soon got out of hand.* **b** at once; without hesitation: *The boy was expelled out of hand.*

out of one's hands, off one's hands: *When he got sick, the job was taken out of his hands.*

take in hand, a bring under control: *The father promised to take his badly behaved son in hand.* **b** consider; deal with: *The principal promised to take the matter in hand.*

try one's hand, try to do; test one's ability: *After trying his hand at politics, he soon went back into business.*

hand·bag (han′bag′ or hand′bag′) **1** a woman's small bag for money, keys, cosmetics, etc.; purse. **2** a small travelling bag to hold clothes, etc. *n.*

hand·ball (han′bol′ or han′bôl′, hand′bol′ or hand′bôl′) **1** a game played by hitting a small ball against a wall with the hand. **2** the ball used in this game. *n.*

hand·bill (han′bil′ or hand′bil′) a printed announcement, advertisement, etc. to be handed out to people. *n.*

hand·book (han′bu̇k′ or hand′bu̇k′) a small book of directions or reference. *n.*

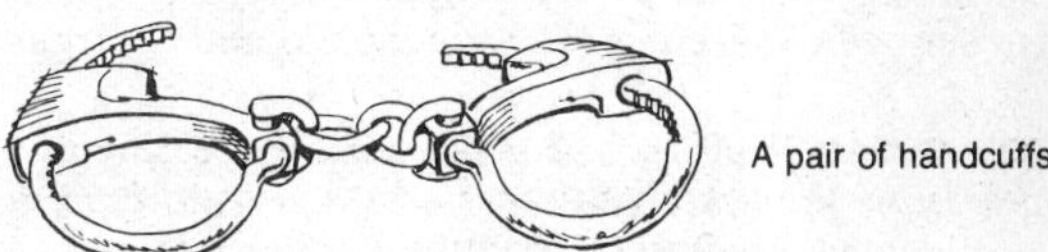

A pair of handcuffs

hand·cuff (han′kuf′ or hand′kuf′) **1** a device to keep a person from using his hands, usually consisting of two steel bracelets joined by a short chain that are fastened around the wrists. **2** put handcuffs on: *He was handcuffed to the post.* 1 *n.*, 2 *v.*

hand·ful (han′fu̇l′ or hand′fu̇l′) **1** as much or as many as the hand can hold: *a handful of candy.* **2** a small number or quantity: *A handful of men could defend this mountain pass against hundreds.* **3** *Informal.* a person or thing that is difficult to handle or control: *That boy is quite a handful.* *n., pl.* **hand·fuls.**

hand·grip (han′grip′ or hand′grip′) 1 handshake. 2 anything used as a gripping place for the hand; handle: *the handgrips on the handlebars of a bicycle.* *n.*

hand·i·cap (han′di kap′) 1 something that puts a person at a disadvantage; hindrance; mental or physical defect: *A sore throat is a handicap to a singer.* 2 put at a disadvantage as by a mental or physical defect; hinder: *The little girl's blindness handicapped her greatly.* 3 a contest in which rules are applied to ensure that nobody has an unfair advantage or is at an unfair disadvantage. 4 the advantage or disadvantage given in such a contest or game: *If a runner has a handicap of 5 metres in a 100 metre dash, it means that he has to run either 95 metres or 105 metres.* 5 give such a handicap to: *The Sports Committe handicapped me 5 metres.* 1, 3, 4 *n.,* 2, 5 *v.,* **hand·i·capped, hand·i·cap·ping.**

hand·i·craft (han′di kraft′) 1 skilful use of the hands: *The design on the leather purse showed fine handicraft.* 2 a trade or art requiring skill with the hands: *Basket weaving is a handicraft.* 3 something made by hand: *Our display of handicrafts includes sewing and woodworking.* *n.*

hand·ker·chief (hang′kər chif or hang′kər chēf′) a soft square of cloth used for wiping the nose, face, hands, etc.: *Large handkerchiefs are sometimes worn over the head or around the neck.* *n.*

han·dle (han′dəl) 1 a part of a thing made to be held or grasped by the hand: *Spoons, pitchers, hammers, and pails have handles.* 2 touch, feel, or use with the hand: *Don't handle that until you wash your hands.* 3 manage; direct: *The captain handles his soldiers well.* 4 behave or perform in a certain way when driven, managed, directed, etc.: *This car handles easily.* 5 treat: *The poor cat had been roughly handled by the cruel children.* 6 deal in; trade in: *This shop handles meat and groceries.* 1 *n.,* 2–6 *v.,* **han·dled, han·dling.**

han·dle·bars (han′dəl bärz′) the part of a bicycle, motorcycle, etc. that the rider holds and steers by. *n. pl.*

hand·maid (han′mād′ or hand′mād′) a female servant or attendant. *n.*

hand·rail (hand′rāl′) a railing used as a guard or support on a stairway, platform, etc. *n.*

hand·shake (han′shāk′ or hand′shāk′) the clasping and shaking of hands by two people as a sign of friendship when meeting or parting, or to seal a bargain. *n.*

hand·some (han′səm) 1 good-looking; pleasing in appearance: *We usually say that a man is handsome, but that a woman is pretty or beautiful.* 2 fairly large; considerable: *Ten thousand dollars is a handsome sum of money.* 3 generous: *a handsome gift.* *adj.,* **hand·som·er, hand·som·est.**

hand·spring (han′spring′ or hand′spring′) a kind of somersault in which a person turns his heels over his head while balancing on one or both hands so that he lands on his feet: *A cartwheel is one kind of handspring.* *n.*

hand–to–hand (han′tə hand′ or hand′tə hand′) close together; at close quarters: *a hand-to-hand fight.* *adj., adv.*

hand·writ·ing (hand′rīt′ing) 1 writing by hand; writing with pen, pencil, etc. 2 one's manner or style of writing: *He recognized his mother's handwriting on the envelope.* *n.*

hand·y (han′dē) 1 easy to reach or use; saving work; useful: *a handy tool. There were handy shelves near the kitchen sink.* 2 skilful with the hands: *He is handy with tools.* *adj.,* **hand·i·er, hand·i·est.**

hand·y·man (han′dē man′) a man who does odd jobs. *n., pl.* **hand·y·men** (han′dē men′).

hang (hang) 1 fasten or be fastened to something above: *Hang your cap on the hook. The swing hangs from a tree.* 2 fasten or be fastened so as to swing or turn freely: *hang a door on its hinges.* 3 put or be put to death by hanging with a rope around the neck: *He was hanged several weeks after being sentenced to death.* 4 droop; bend down: *She hung her head in shame.* 5 cover or decorate with things that are fastened to something above: *All the walls were hung with pictures.* 6 the way a thing hangs: *She didn't like the hang of her new skirt.* 7 *Informal.* the way of using or doing something: *Riding a bicycle is easy after you get the hang of it.* 8 *Informal.* the idea; meaning: *After studying an hour, he finally got the hang of the lesson.* 1–5 *v.,* **hung** (or, usually, **hanged** for 3), **hang·ing;** 6–8 *n.*

hang on, a hold tight. **b** be unwilling to let go, stop or leave: *The dying man hung on to life for several days.* **c** depend on: *My decision hangs on your answer.*

hang over, be likely to happen to; threaten: *The possibility of being punished hung over him for days.*

☛ In formal English, the preferred form of the past tense of **hang** (def. 3) is **hanged:** *The murderer was hanged.* In informal English, however, this meaning of **hang** is treated like others: *We hung a picture. They hung him for his crimes.*

hang·ar (hang′ər) a shed for aircraft. *n.*

☛ **Hangar** and **hanger** are pronounced the same.

hang·er (hang′ər) anything on which something else is hung: *a coat hanger.* *n.*

☛ See note at **hangar.**

hang·ing (hang′ing) 1 death by hanging with a rope around the neck. 2 something that hangs from a wall, bed, doorway, etc.: *Curtains and draperies are hangings.* 3 that hangs: *She bought a hanging fixture for the living room.* 1, 2 *n.,* 3 *adj.*

hang·man (hang′mən) a man who hangs criminals who have been sentenced to death by hanging. *n., pl.* **hang·men** (hang′mən).

hang·nail (hang′nāl′) a bit of skin that hangs partly loose near a finger nail. *n.*

hank (hangk) 1 a coil or loop: *a hank of hair.* 2 a bundle of yarn, especially one containing a definite length. *n.*

hank·y (hang′kē) *Informal.* handkerchief. *n., pl.* **hank·ies.**

Ha·nuk·kah or **Ha·nuk·ka** (hä′nü kä′) an eight-day Jewish festival that falls in December: *Hanukkah is a feast of dedication.* *n.*

hap·haz·ard (hap′haz′ərd) 1 random; casual; not planned: *Haphazard answers are usually wrong.* 2 by chance; at random; casually: *He took a card haphazard from the deck.* 1 *adj.,* 2 *adv.*

hap·pen (hap′ən) 1 take place; occur: *Nothing interesting happens here.* 2 be or take place by chance: *Accidents will happen.* 3 have the fortune to; chance: *I*

hat, āge, fär; let, ēqual, tėrm; it, īce
hot, ōpen, ôrder; oil, out; cup, pu̇t, rüle
ə above, takən, pencəl, lemən, circəs
ch, child; ng, long; sh, ship
th, thin; ꟻH, then; zh, measure

happened to sit next to a famous hockey player. 4 be done to; go wrong with: *Something has happened to this lock; the key won't turn.* *v.*

as it happens, by chance; as it turns out: *As it happens, I have no money with me.*

happen on or **upon,** a meet by chance. b find by chance: *She happened on a dime while looking for her ball.*

happen to, be the fate of; because of: *Nobody knew what happened to the last explorer.*

hap·pen·ing (hap′ən ing) an event; occurrence; anything that happens. *n.*

hap·pi·ly (hap′ə lē) 1 in a happy manner; with pleasure, joy, and gladness: *She lives happily.* 2 by luck; with good fortune: *Happily he saved her from falling.* *adv.*

hap·pi·ness (hap′ē nis) 1 the state of being happy; gladness. 2 good luck; good fortune. *n.*

hap·py (hap′ē) 1 feeling or showing pleasure and joy; glad; pleased; contented: *a happy smile.* 2 lucky; fortunate: *By a happy chance we found the watch just where I left it.* 3 clever and fitting; apt; successful and suitable: *a happy way of expressing an idea.* *adj.,* **hap·pi·er, hap·pi·est.**

hap·py–go–luck·y (hap′ē gō luk′ē) taking things easily; trusting to luck: *Those people are certainly happy-go-lucky.* *adj.*

har·ass (har′əs or hə ras′) 1 trouble by repeated attacks: *The pirates harassed the villages along the coast.* 2 annoy; disturb; worry: *The old lady was harassed by the noisy children.* *v.*

har·bor or **har·bour** (här′bər) 1 a place of shelter for ships: *Many yachts are in the harbor.* 2 any place of shelter. 3 give shelter to: *The dog's shaggy hair harbors fleas.* 4 keep in the mind: *Don't harbor grudges.* 1, 2 *n.,* 3, 4 *v.*

hard (härd) 1 not soft; not yielding to the touch: *Rocks are hard.* 2 firm; solid: *His muscles were hard.* 3 firmly; solidly: *to hold hard.* 4 not yielding to influence; stern: *He was a hard father.* 5 needing much ability, effort, or time; difficult: *a hard job, a hard lesson, a hard man to get on with.* 6 with steady effort or much energy: *Try hard to lift this log.* 7 with vigor or violence: *It is raining hard.* 8 vigorous or violent: *a hard storm, a hard run.* 9 severe; causing much pain, trouble, care, etc.: *Last winter was a hard winter. When our father was out of work, we had a hard time.* 10 severely; badly: *It will go hard with the murderer if he is caught.* 11 not pleasant; harsh: *a hard laugh. That man has a hard face.* 12 See **hard water.** 1, 2, 4, 5, 8, 9, 11, 12 *adj.,* 3, 6, 7, 10 *adv.* **—hard′ness,** *n.*

hard by, near: *The house stands hard by the bridge.*

hard of hearing, somewhat deaf.

hard up, *Informal.* needing money or anything very badly: *He is always hard up the day before he is paid. It rained throughout our holiday, and we were hard up for things to do.*

hard–boiled (härd′boild′) 1 boiled until hard: *hard-boiled eggs.* 2 *Informal.* not easily moved by the feelings; tough; rough. *adj.*

hard coal coal that burns with very little smoke or flame; anthracite.

hard·en (här′dən) make hard; become hard. *v.*

hard–head·ed (härd′hed′id) not easily excited or deceived; practical; shrewd. *adj.*

hard–heart·ed (härd′här′tid) without pity; cruel; unfeeling: *a hard-hearted tyrant.* *adj.*

har·di·hood (här′dē hu̇d′) boldness; daring: *The boy's hardihood was amazing.* *n.*

har·di·ly (här′də lē) boldly. *adv.*

hard·ly (härd′lē) 1 only just; barely: *We hardly had time to eat breakfast.* 2 not quite; not altogether: *He may have exaggerated, but it is hardly fair to call him a liar.* 3 most probably not: *They will hardly come in all this rain.* *adv.*

☛ **Hardly** and **scarcely** are treated as negatives and so should not have another negative with them. *The film showed hardly nothing that was new to us* should be *The film showed hardly anything that was new to us. I didn't scarcely have enough money* should be *I scarcely had enough money.*

hard·ship (härd′ship) something hard to bear; a hard condition of living: *Hunger, cold, and sickness were among the hardships of pioneer life.* *n.*

hard·ware (härd′wer′) articles made from metal: *Locks, hinges, nails, screws, utensils, and tools are hardware.* *n.*

hard water water containing minerals that hinder the action of soap.

hard·wood (härd′wu̇d′) any hard, heavy wood: *Oak, cherry, maple, ebony, and mahogany are hardwoods.* *n.*

har·dy (här′dē) 1 able to bear hard treatment; strong; robust: *Cold weather does not kill hardy plants.* 2 bold; daring. *adj.,* **har·di·er, har·di·est.**

hare (her) an animal with long ears, a divided upper lip, a short tail, and long hind legs: *A hare is very much like a rabbit, but larger.* *n.*

☛ **Hare** and **hair** are pronounced the same.

hare·bell (her′bel′) a slender plant with blue, bell-shaped flowers; bluebell. *n.*

hark (härk) listen. *v.*

hark back, a go back; turn back: *His ideas hark back twenty years.* b return to a previous point or subject: *He is always harking back to his time at camp.*

hark·en (här′kən) hearken; listen. *v.*

harm (härm) 1 hurt; damage: *The accident did a lot of harm to the car.* 2 evil; wrong: *What harm is there in borrowing a friend's bicycle?* 3 hurt or damage: *The driver was not harmed in the accident.* 1, 2 *n.,* 3 *v.* **—harm′ful,** *adj.* **—harm′less,** *adj.*

A harmonica

har·mon·i·ca (här mon′ə kə) a small musical instrument having several reeds that are caused to vibrate by air from the mouth controlled by the tongue and lips; mouth organ. *n.*

har·mo·ni·ous (här mō′nē əs) 1 agreeing in feelings, ideas, or actions; getting on well together; not disturbed by disagreement: *The children played together in a* *harmonious group.* **2** arranged so that parts are orderly or pleasing; going well together: *A beautiful picture has harmonious colors.* **3** sweet-sounding; musical: *the harmonious sounds of a choir singing Christmas carols. adj.*

har·mo·nize (här′mə nīz′) **1** bring into harmony or agreement; make harmonious: *The chairman had to harmonize several different points of view.* **2** go or put together in a pleasing way: *The colors used in the room harmonized. v.,* **har·mo·nized, har·mo·niz·ing.**

har·mo·ny (här′mə nē) **1** an agreement of feelings, ideas, or actions; getting on well together: *There was perfect harmony between the two brothers. His plans are in harmony with mine.* **2** an orderly or pleasing arrangement of parts; going well together: *a harmony of design and color.* **3** the sounding together of musical notes in a chord. **4** a sweet or musical sound; music. *n., pl.* **har·mo·nies.**

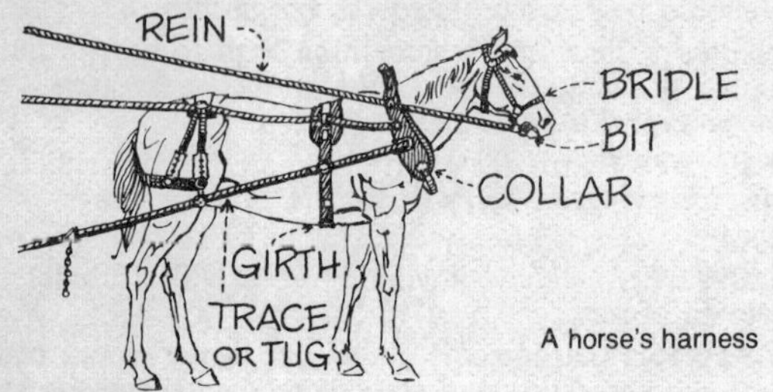

A horse's harness

har·ness (här′nis) **1** leather fittings for a horse or other animal, which connect it to a carriage, plough, etc. or are used in riding: *Reins, collar, and bridle are parts of a horse's harness.* **2** an arrangement of straps to fasten or hold: *a parachute harness, a shoulder harness. We need a harness for the baby's crib.* **3** put harness on: *Harness the horse.* **4** control and put to work: *We have harnessed these streams by dams and machinery.* 1, 2 *n.,* 3, 4 *v.*

in harness, at one's regular work: *She was glad to get back in harness again after her long vacation.*

A harp

harp (härp) **1** a triangular stringed musical instrument played with the fingers: *Most modern harps are large instruments with many strings.* **2** play on the harp. 1 *n.,* 2 *v.*

harp on, talk about a subject very much or too much.

harp·ist (här′pist) a person skilled in playing a harp. *n.*

har·poon (här pün′) **1** a spear with a rope tied to it used for catching whales and other sea animals: *Harpoons are thrown by hand or shot from a gun.* **2** strike, catch, or kill with a harpoon. 1 *n.,* 2 *v.* —**har·poon′er,** *n.*

A disk harrow

har·row (har′ō or her′ō) **1** a heavy frame with iron teeth or upright disks: *Harrows are used by farmers to break up ploughed ground into smaller pieces or to cover seed with earth.* **2** draw a harrow over. **3** hurt; wound. **4** arouse uncomfortable feelings in; distress: *He harrowed us with a tale of ghosts.* 1 *n.,* 2–4 *v.*

har·ry (har′ē or her′ē) **1** raid and rob with violence: *The pirates harried the towns along the coast.* **2** worry; torment: *Fear of losing his job harried the clerk. v.,* **har·ried, har·ry·ing.**

harsh (härsh) **1** rough to the touch, taste, eye, or ear; sharp and unpleasant: *a harsh voice, a harsh climate.* **2** cruel; unfeeling; severe: *a harsh man. adj.* —**harsh′ness,** *n.*

hart (härt) a male deer, especially the red deer after its fifth year: *The hart is also known as a stag. n.*
☞ **Hart** and **heart** are pronounced the same.

har·um-scar·um (her′əm sker′əm) **1** reckless; rash; thoughtless: *What a harum-scarum child you are!* **2** recklessly; wildly: *He rushed harum-scarum down the main street.* **3** a reckless person. 1 *adj.,* 2 *adv.,* 3 *n.*

har·vest (här′vist) **1** the reaping and gathering in of grain and other food crops, usually in late summer or early autumn. **2** the time or season of the harvest. **3** gather in for use: *harvest wheat.* **4** one season's yield of any natural product; crop: *The oyster harvest was small this year.* **5** the result or consequences: *He is reaping the harvest of his mistakes.* 1, 2, 4, 5 *n.,* 3 *v.*

har·vest·er (här′vis tər) a machine for harvesting crops, especially grain. *n.*

harvest moon the full moon at harvest time, or about September 23.

has (haz) See **have.** *Who has my book? He has been sick. v.*

hash (hash) **1** a mixture of cooked meat, potatoes, etc. chopped into small pieces and fried or baked. **2** chop into small pieces. **3** mixture. **4** a mess or muddle. 1, 3, 4 *n.,* 2 *v.*

make a hash of, make a mess of: *She made a hash of mounting stamps in her album.*

settle one's hash, *Informal.* subdue or silence someone completely; put an end to someone.

has·n't (haz′ənt) has not.

hasp (hasp) a clasp or fastening for a door, window, trunk, box, etc., especially a hinged metal clasp that fits over a staple or into a hole and is fastened by a peg, padlock, etc. *n.*

has·sle (has′əl) *Informal.* **1** a struggle; argument: *There was a hassle about who was going to ride in the front seat of the car.* **2** trouble; annoyance; bother: *Driving in city traffic is too much of a hassle. Traffic jams create a lot of hassle.* **3** struggle; argue. **4** worry; annoy; bother: *The film star was being hassled by* *newspaper reporters.* 1, 2 *n.*, 3, 4 *v.*, **has·sled, has·sling.**

has·sock (has′ək) a padded footstool or thick cushion to rest the feet on, sit on, or kneel on. *n.*

haste (hāst) 1 trying to be quick; a hurry: *All his haste was of no use.* 2 hasten. 1 *n.*, 2 *v.*, **hast·ed, hast·ing.**
in haste, in a hurry; quickly: *Bring the doctor in haste.*
make haste, hurry; to be quick.

has·ten (hās′ən) 1 hurry; cause to be quick; speed: *Do not hasten everyone off to bed.* 2 be quick; go fast: *She hastened to explain.* *v.*

hast·i·ly (hās′tə lē) in a hasty way. *adv.*

hast·y (hās′tē) 1 quick; hurried: *a hasty glance, a hasty trip to town.* 2 rash; not well thought out: *His hasty decisions caused many mistakes.* 3 easily angered; quick-tempered: *a hasty old gentleman.* *adj.*, **hast·i·er, hast·i·est.**

hat (hat) 1 a covering for the head: *A hat usually has a crown and a brim.* 2 provide with a hat; put a hat on: *The lady was beautifully gowned and hatted.* 1 *n.*, 2 *v.*, **hat·ted, hat·ting.**

hatch[1] (hach) 1 produce young from an egg or eggs: *Our hen just hatched some chicks.* 2 keep eggs warm until the young come out: *It took three weeks to hatch those hens' eggs.* 3 come out from the egg: *Three of the chickens hatched today.* 4 produce living young: *Not all eggs hatch properly.* 5 arrange; plan, especially in secret; plot: *The robbers were hatching an evil scheme.* *v.*

hatch[2] (hach) 1 an opening in a ship's deck through which cargo is loaded. 2 the trap door covering this opening: *The hatches were closed tightly during the storm.* 3 an opening in the roof or floor of a building; a trap door. *n.*

hatch·er·y (hach′ər ē) a place for hatching eggs of fish, hens, etc. *n.*, *pl.* **hatch·er·ies.**

hatch·et (hach′it) a small axe with a short handle for use with one hand. *n.*
bury the hatchet, make peace.

hate (hāt) 1 dislike very much: *The rebel hated the dictator.* 2 a very strong dislike: *She felt a hate of snakes. Her hate for lies would not let her be friends with any girl who lied.* 1 *v.*, **hat·ed, hat·ing;** 2 *n.* **—hat′er,** *n.*

hate·ful (hāt′fəl) 1 causing hate: *hateful behavior.* 2 feeling hate; showing hate: *She was always making hateful remarks.* *adj.*

ha·tred (hā′trid) a very strong dislike; hate. *n.*

haugh·ty (ho′tē or hô′tē) 1 too proud of oneself and too scornful of others: *A haughty girl is always unpopular.* 2 showing too great a pride of oneself and scorn for others: *haughty words.* *adj.*, **haugh·ti·er, haugh·ti·est.**

haul (hol or hôl) 1 pull or drag with force: *The logs were hauled to the mill by horses.* 2 the act of hauling; a hard pull. 3 the load hauled: *Powerful trucks are used for these heavy hauls.* 4 the distance that a load is hauled: *It is a long haul across the Rockies.* 5 an amount won, taken, etc. at one time; a catch: *The fishing boats made a good haul today.* 6 change the course of a ship. 1, 6 *v.*, 2–5 *n.*

☛ **Haul** and **hall** are pronounced the [illegible]

haunch (h[illegible]h) 1 the pa[illegible] around t[illegible] and loin c[illegible] for foo[illegible]

hat, āge, fär; let, ēqual, tėrm; it, īce
hot, ōpen, ôrder; oil, out; cup, pu̇t, rüle
əbove, takən, pencəl, lemən, circəs
ch, child; ng, long; sh, ship
th, thin; TH, then; zh, measure

haunt (hont or hônt) 1 of a ghost, appear frequently to a person or in a place; be continually present at a place: *People say ghosts haunt that old house.* 2 go often to; visit frequently: *They haunt the new bowling alley.* 3 a place visited often: *The swimming pool was a favorite haunt of the boys in the summer.* 4 be often with: *Memories of his youth haunted the old man.* 5 ghost. 1, 2, 4 *v.*, 3, 5 *n.*

haunt·ed (hon′tid or hôn′tid) visited by ghosts: *a haunted house.* *adj.*

have (hav) 1 hold: *I have a book in my hand.* 2 possess; own: *He has a big house and farm. A house has windows. She has no news of her brother.* 3 know; understand: *She has your idea.* 4 cause somebody to do something or cause something to be done: *Please have the boy bring my mail. She will have the car washed for me.* 5 get; take: *You need to have a rest.* 6 experience: *Have a pleasant time. They had trouble with this engine.* 7 allow; permit: *She won't have any noise while she is reading.* 8 become the father or mother of: *My married sister wants to have children.* 9 *Have* is also used with words like asked, *been, broken, done,* or *called* to express completed action: *They have eaten. She had gone before. I have called her. They will have seen her by Sunday.* *v.*, **has, had, hav·ing.**
have to, must: *All animals have to sleep. He will have to go now because it is very late.*

☛ **Have** and **halve** are pronounced the same.

ha·ven (hā′vən) 1 a harbor, especially one providing shelter from a storm. 2 a place of shelter and safety: *The hunters found the deserted cabin a welcome haven from the storm.* *n.*

have·n't (hav′ənt) have not.

hav·er·sack (hav′ər sak′) a bag used by soldiers and hikers for carrying food, utensils, etc., when on a march or hike. *n.*

hav·oc (hav′ək) very great destruction or injury: *Tornadoes, severe earthquakes, and plagues create widespread havoc.* *n.*
play havoc with, injure severely; ruin.

haw[1] (ho or hô) 1 the red berry of the hawthorn. 2 the hawthorn. *n.*

haw[2] (ho or hô) 1 a word of command to horses, oxen, etc., directing them to turn to the left. 2 turn to the left. 1 *interj.*, *n.*, 2 *v.*

A red-tailed hawk — about 55 cm long with the tail

hawk[1] (hok or hôk) 1 a bird of prey with a strong,

hooked beak, and large, curved claws: *Long ago hawks were trained to hunt and kill other birds.* **2** hunt with trained hawks. 1 *n.,* 2 *v.*

hawk² (hok or hôk) **1** carry goods about for sale, as a street peddler does. **2** advertise by shouting that goods are for sale. *v.*

hawk³ (hok or hôk) clear the throat in a noisy manner. *v.*

haw·ser (ho′zər or hô′zər) a large, stout rope or a thin, steel cable, used for mooring or towing ships. *n.*

haw·thorn (ho′thôrn′ or hô′thôrn′) a shrub or small tree with many thorns and clusters of fragrant white, red, or pink flowers and red berries. *n.*

hay (hā) **1** grass cut and dried as food for cattle and horses. **2** cut and dry grass for hay: *The men are haying in the east field.* 1 *n.,* 2 *v.*

☛ **Hay** and **hey** are pronounced the same.

hay·cock (hā′kok′) a small pile of hay in a field. *n.*

hay fever an allergy with effects like those of a cold, caused by the pollen of ragweed and other plants.

hay·loft (hā′loft′) a place above a stable or barn where hay is stored. *n.*

hay·mow (hā′mou′ or hā′mō′) **1** a place in a barn for storing hay. **2** the hay stored in a barn. *n.*

hay·rack (hā′rak′) **1** a rack or frame used for holding hay to be eaten by cattle, horses, etc. **2** a framework on a wagon used in hauling hay, straw, etc. **3** the wagon and framework together. *n.*

hay·rick (hā′rik′) haystack. *n.*

hay·stack (hā′stak′) a large pile of hay outdoors. *n.*

haz·ard (haz′ərd) **1** a risk; danger: *The life of an explorer is full of hazards.* **2** chance. **3** take a chance with; risk: *I would hazard my life on his honesty.* 1, 2 *n.,* 3 *v.*

haz·ard·ous (haz′ər dəs) dangerous; risky; perilous. *adj.*

haze¹ (hāz) **1** a small amount of mist or smoke in the air: *A thin haze veiled the distant hills.* **2** a vague condition of the mind; slight confusion: *After he was hit on the head, everything was in a haze for him.* *n.*

haze² (hāz) force to do unnecessary or ridiculous tasks; torment. *v.,* **hazed, haz·ing.**

ha·zel (hā′zəl) **1** a shrub or small tree whose light-brown nuts are good to eat. **2** greenish brown: *hazel eyes.* 1, 2 *n.,* 2 *adj.*

ha·zel·nut (hā′zəl nut′) the nut of a hazel. *n.*

ha·zy (hā′zē) **1** misty; smoky: *a hazy sky.* **2** not distinct; obscure: *a hazy idea.* *adj.,* **ha·zi·er, ha·zi·est.**

H.B.C. Hudson's Bay Company.

H–bomb (āch′bom′) hydrogen bomb. *n.*

he (hē) **1** a boy, man, or male animal already referred to and identified: *John has to work hard, but he likes his job and it pays him well.* **2** a male: *There were three he's and two she's in the litter of kittens.* **3** anyone: *He who hesitates is lost.* 1, 3 *pron., pl.* **they;** 2 *n., pl.* **he's.**

head (hed) **1** the top part of the human body, where the eye, ears, and mouth are. **2** the front of an animal, where the eyes, ears, and mouth are. **3** the top part of anything: *the head of a pin, a cabbage, a crane, a drum, or a barrel.* **4** the front part or face of anything: *the head of a procession, the head of a street.* **5** a likeness of a head, especially as a work of art: *A marble head of the emperor was in the museum.* **6** the side of a coin bearing the likeness of a head, especially that of a king, queen, president, etc.: *The head of a Canadian coin carries a portrait of Queen Elizabeth II.* **7** at the front or top. **8** be at the front or top of: *to head a parade.* **9** coming from in front: *a head wind, a head sea.* **10** move toward; face toward: *Our ship headed south.* **11** the chief person; leader. **12** chief; leading: *a head clerk.* **13** be the chief or captain of; lead: *Who will head the team?* **14** a person; individual: *The dinner will cost nine dollars a head.* **15** a unit, used in counting animals: *He sold fifty head of cattle and ten head of horses.* **16** the striking part of a tool or implement: *the head of a hammer, the head of a golf club.* **17** mind; understanding; intelligence: *He has a good head for figures.* **18** topic: *He arranged his speech under four heads.* **19** a crisis; conclusion: *His sudden refusal brought matters to a head.* **20** pressure: *a head of steam.* **21** the source: *the head of a brook.* 1–6, 11, 14–21 *n.,* 7, 9, 12 *adj.,* 8, 10, 13 *v.*

give one his head, let him go as he pleases.

go to one's head, a affect one's mind. **b** make one dizzy. **c** make one conceited.

head off, get in front of; check: *The cowboys tried to head off the stampeding herd.*

head on, with the head or front first: *The car crashed head on into the wall.*

head over heels, a in a somersault. **b** hastily; rashly. **c** completely; thoroughly.

heads up, be careful; watch out: *Heads up! The Principal's coming.*

out of one's head, *Informal.* crazy.

over one's head, too hard for one to understand.

head·ache (hed′āk′) a pain in the head. *n.*

head·board (hed′bôrd′) a board or frame that forms the head of a bed. *n.*

head·cheese (hed′chēz′) a jellied loaf formed of parts of the head and feet of pigs cut up, cooked, and seasoned. *n.*

head–dress (hed′dres′) a covering or decoration for the head. *n.*

head·er (hed′ər) a fall, dive, or plunge headfirst: *He took a header into the water.* *n.*

head·first (hed′fėrst′) with the head first: *She slid headfirst down the hill.* *adv.*

head·ing (hed′ing) **1** the part forming the head, top, or front. **2** something written or printed at the top of a page. **3** the title of a page, chapter, etc.; topic. *n.*

head·land (hed′lənd or hed′land′) a cape; a point of land jutting out into water. *n.*

head·light (hed′līt′) a light at the front of a vehicle, such as an automobile, a streetcar, or a train. *n.*

head·line (hed′līn′) a title line over an article in a newspaper or at the top of a page in a book or magazine. *n.*

head·long (hed′long′) **1** headfirst: *to plunge headlong into the sea.* **2** with great haste and force: *to rush headlong into the crowd.* **3** in too great a rush; without stopping to thin[illegible]: *The boy was always rushing headlong into trouble.* a[illegible] *adj.*

head·man ([illegible]an′ or hed[illegible]eader. *n., pl.* **head·me**[illegible]′me[illegible]

hat, āge, fär; let, ēqual, tėrm; it, īce
hot, ōpen, ôrder; oil, out; cup, pu̇t, rüle
əbove, takən, pencəl, lemən, circəs
ch, child; ng, long; sh, ship
th, thin; ᴛʜ, then; zh, measure

head–on (hed′on′) with the head or front first: *The two cars were involved in a head-on collision. The two mountain goats clashed head-on. adj., adv.*

head·phone (hed′fōn′) a telephone or radio receiver held on the head, against the ears. *n.*

head·quar·ters (hed′kwôr′tərz) **1** in the armed forces, the place where the commander in chief or the officer in charge lives or has his office; the place from which orders are sent out. **2** the main office; the centre of operations or of authority: *The headquarters of the Canadian Red Cross Society are in Toronto. n. pl. or sing.*

head·stall (hed′stol′ or hed′stôl′) the part of a bridle or halter that fits over a horse's head. See **bridle** for picture. *n.*

head start **1** an advantage or lead allowed someone at the beginning of a race: *The smaller boy was given a head start.* **2** an advantage gained by beginning something before somebody else: *That team is playing better hockey than we are because they had a head start in practising.*

head·strong (hed′strong′) rashly or foolishly determined to have one's own way; hard to control or manage; obstinate. *adj.*

head·wa·ters (hed′wo′tərz or hed′wô′tərz) the sources or upper parts of a river. *n. pl.*

head·way (hed′wā′) **1** forward motion: *The ship could make no headway against the strong wind and tide.* **2** progress with work, etc. **3** clear space, such as in a doorway or under an arch. *n.*

heal (hēl) **1** make well; bring back to health; cure. **2** grow well; become well: *His cut finger healed in a few days. v.*

☛ **Heal, heel,** and **he'll** are pronounced the same.

health (helth) **1** the state of being well or not sick; freedom from illness of any kind. **2** the condition of the body: *good health, poor health.* **3** a toast drunk in honor of a person with a wish that he may be healthy and happy: *We all drank a health to the bride. n.*

health·ful (helth′fəl) giving health; good for the health: *a healthful diet, healthful exercise. adj.*

☛ In formal English, a distinction is usually made between **healthful,** meaning 'giving health,' and **healthy,** meaning 'having good health.' Places and food are **healthful;** people and animals are **healthy.**

health·y (hel′thē) **1** having good health: *a healthy baby.* **2** giving health; good for the health. *adj.,* **health·i·er, health·i·est.**

☛ See note at **healthful.**

heap (hēp) **1** a pile of many things thrown or lying together: *a heap of stones, a sand heap.* **2** form into a heap; gather in heaps: *She heaped the dirty clothes beside the washing machine.* **3** give generously or in large amounts: *The man heaped insults on his enemy.* **4** fill to the point of overflowing; load: *His mother heaped potatoes on his plate. His friends heaped praise on him.* 1 *n.,* 2–4 *v.*

hear (hēr) **1** perceive or be able to receive sounds through the ear: *The old man could not hear well enough to know what I was saying.* **2** receive some sound through the ear: *Can you hear my watch tick?* **3** listen: *The town crier shouted, 'Hear ye! Hear ye!'* **4** listen to: *You must hear what he has to say.* **5** listen to and favor: *Lord, hear my prayer.* **6** receive information: *Have you heard from your brother in St. John's? v.,* **heard, hear·ing. —hear′er,** *n.*

☛ **Hear** and **here** are pronounced the same.

heard (hėrd) See **hear.** *I heard the noise. The gun was heard two kilometres away. v.*

☛ **Heard** and **herd** are pronounced the same.

hear·ing (hēr′ing) **1** the power to hear; the sense by which sound is perceived: *The old man's hearing was so poor that he did not know the telephone had rung.* **2** the act or process of perceiving sound: *Hearing the good news made him happy.* **3** a chance to be heard: *The judge gave both sides a hearing.* **4** the distance that a sound can be heard: *to talk freely in the hearing of others. Mother stays within hearing of the baby. n.*

heark·en (här′kən) listen. *v.*

hear·say (hēr′sā′) common talk; gossip. *n.*

hearse (hėrs) a vehicle, usually an automobile, used in funerals to carry the coffin. *n.*

heart (härt) **1** the part of the body that pumps the blood. **2** the feelings; the mind or the soul: *She has a kind heart.* **3** the centre or seat of human feelings and ideals: *Her heart was filled with pride when her son won the medal.* **4** love; deep affection: *She gave her heart to Daddy.* **5** courage; enthusiasm: *The losing team showed plenty of heart.* **6** the middle or centre: *the heart of the forest.* **7** the main or most important part: *the very heart of the matter.* **8** a figure shaped like a heart: *There was a big, red heart on the front of the valentine card.* **9** a playing card marked with one or more red heart-shaped designs on it. **10 hearts,** *pl.* **a** the suit of such playing cards. **b** a game in which players try to get rid of cards of this suit. *n.*

after one's own heart, just as one likes it; pleasing one perfectly.

at heart, in one's deepest thoughts or feelings: *He is kind at heart, though he appears to be gruff.*

break the heart of, crush with sorrow or grief.

by heart, a by memory. **b** from memory.

learn by heart, memorize: *She learned the poem by heart.*

take heart, be encouraged.

take to heart, think seriously about: *He took his father's advice to heart.*

with all one's heart, a sincerely. **b** gladly.

☛ **Heart** and **hart** are pronounced the same.

heart attack a sudden failure of the heart to beat.

heart·break (härt′brāk′) a crushing sorrow or grief. *n.*

heart·break·ing (härt′brāk′ing) crushing with sorrow or grief. *adj.*

heart·bro·ken (härt′brō′kən) crushed by sorrow or grief. *adj.*

heart·en (här′tən) cheer; cheer up; encourage: *This good news will hearten you. v.*

heart·felt (härt′felt′) sincere; genuine: *heartfelt sympathy. adj.*

hearth (härth) **1** the floor, usually stone, of a fireplace: *A hearth extends some distance in front of the* *actual fireplace.* 2 the fireside; the home: *The soldier longed for his own hearth.* *n.*

hearth·stone (härth′stōn′) 1 a stone forming a hearth. 2 the fireside; home. *n.*

heart·i·ly (här′tə lē) 1 with sincere feeling; warmly: *She welcomed her cousins heartily.* 2 with a good will; in good spirits for what one is doing: *to set to work heartily.* 3 with a good appetite: *to eat heartily.* 4 very; completely: *My mother was heartily tired of housework.* *adv.*

heart·i·ness (här′tē nis) 1 sincerity. 2 warmth: *The heartiness of his laugh was pleasant.* *n.*

heart·less (härt′lis) without kindness or sympathy; unfeeling; cruel. *adj.*

heart·y (här′tē) 1 cheerful; warm and friendly; eager; full of feeling; sincere: *a hearty laugh, hearty wishes for a happy birthday.* 2 strong and well; vigorous: *to be hale and hearty at sixty.* 3 providing plenty to eat; substantial: *A hearty meal satisfied his hunger.* *adj.,* **heart·i·er, heart·i·est.**

heat (hēt) 1 the condition of being hot; hotness; warmth: *the heat of a fire.* 2 make warm or hot: *The stove heats the room.* 3 become warm or hot: *The room is heating slowly. The soup is heating up.* 4 the hot weather: *the heat of summer.* 5 violence; excitement: *In the heat of the argument he said things he was sorry for later.* 6 one trial in a race: *He won the first heat, but lost the final race.* 1, 4–6 *n.,* 2, 3 *v.*

heat·er (hēt′ər) a device that gives heat or warmth, such as a stove, furnace, or radiator. *n.*

heath (hēth) 1 open wasteland with heather or low bushes growing on it; moor: *A heath has few or no trees.* 2 a low bush growing on such land: *Heather is one kind of heath.* *n.*

hea·then (hē′ᴛʜən) 1 a person who does not believe in the God of the Bible; a person who is not a Christian, a Jew, or a Moslem. 2 people who are heathen. 3 of or having to do with heathens: *heathen temples.* 4 a person who is thought to have no religion or culture. 1, 2, 4 *n., pl.* **hea·thens** or **hea·then;** 3 *adj.*

heath·er (heᴛʜ′ər) a low shrub having small light-purple flowers: *Heather is common on the heaths of Scotland and England.* *n.*

heat shield a coating or covering of special material on the nose cone of a missile or spacecraft to protect it from the heat produced when it re-enters the earth's atmosphere.

heave (hēv) 1 lift with force or effort: *He heaved the heavy box into the wagon.* 2 lift and throw: *The sailors heaved the anchor overboard.* 3 pull with force or effort; haul: *They heaved on the rope.* 4 give a sigh, groan, etc. with a deep, heavy breath. 5 rise and fall alternately: *The waves heaved in the storm.* 6 breathe hard; pant. 7 rise; swell; bulge: *The ground heaved during the earthquake.* 8 a heaving; throw: *With a mighty heave he pushed the boat into the water.* 1–7 *v.,* **heaved** or **hove, heav·ing;** 8 *n.*

heave ho!, a sailors' cry when pulling up the anchor, or pulling on any rope or cable.

heave in sight, come into view.

heave to, stop a ship; stop.

heav·en (hev′ən) 1 in religious use, the place where God and His angels live and where the blessed go after death. 2 **Heaven,** God; Providence: *It was the will of Heaven.* 3 a place or condition of greatest happiness. 4 Usually, **heavens,** *pl.* the upper air; the sky: *Millions of stars were shining in the heavens.* *n.*

heav·en·ly (hev′ən lē) 1 of or in heaven: *God is our heavenly Father.* 2 like heaven; suitable for heaven; very happy, beautiful, or excellent: *a heavenly spot, heavenly peace.* 3 of or in the heavens: *The sun, the moon, and the stars are heavenly bodies.* *adj.*

heav·i·ly (hev′ə lē) in a heavy way or manner: *He fell heavily to the floor.* *adv.*

heav·i·ness (hev′ē nis) 1 the state or condition of being heavy; great mass. 2 sadness: *A great heaviness lay on her heart.* *n.*

heav·y (hev′ē) 1 hard to lift or carry; having much mass: *Iron is heavy and feathers are light.* 2 of more than usual mass for its kind: *heavy silk, heavy bread.* 3 large; greater than usual: *a heavy rain, a heavy crop, a heavy meal, a heavy vote, a heavy sea, a heavy sleep.* 4 weighted down; laden: *air heavy with moisture. Her eyes were heavy with sleep. His heavy heart was full of sorrow.* 5 cloudy: *a heavy sky.* 6 hard to bear or endure: *Her troubles grew heavier.* 7 hard to deal with: *A heavy road is muddy or sandy. A heavy slope is a steep one.* *adj.,* **heav·i·er, heav·i·est.**

He·brew (hē′brü) 1 a Jew; a descendant of one of the desert tribes led by Moses that settled in Palestine. 2 Jewish. 3 the ancient language of the Jews, in which the Old Testament was recorded. 4 a modern language used in present-day Israel: *Hebrew and Arabic are the official languages of Israel.* 1, 3, 4 *n.,* 2 *adj.*

heck·le (hek′əl) harass and annoy a speaker by asking bothersome questions, etc. *v.,* **heck·led, heck·ling.**

hec·tare (hek′ter or hek′tär) a unit of measurement for area, equal to 10 000 square metres: *Two football fields side by side make a square area that is equal to almost exactly 1 hectare. Symbol:* ha *n.*

hec·tic (hek′tik) 1 very exciting; wild: *He leads a hectic life.* 2 feverish; hot and flushed. *adj.*

he'd (hēd) 1 he had. 2 he would.

☞ **He'd** and **heed** are pronounced the same.

hedge (hej) 1 a thick row of bushes or small trees planted as a fence. 2 put a hedge around: *to hedge a garden.* 3 avoid giving a direct answer; evade questions. 1 *n.,* 2, 3 *v.,* **hedged, hedg·ing.**

hedge in, hem in; surround on all sides: *The town was hedged in by mountains and a forest.*

A hedgehog—about 23 cm long

hedge·hog (hej′hog′) 1 a small animal of Europe with spines on its back: *When attacked, hedgehogs roll up into a bristling ball.* 2 the porcupine of North America. *n.*

heed (hēd) 1 give careful attention to; take notice: *Heed what I say.* 2 careful attention; notice: *She pays heed to her clothes.* 1 *v.,* 2 *n.*

☛ **Heed** and **he'd** are pronounced the same.

heed·less (hēd′lis) careless; thoughtless. *adj.*

heel¹ (hēl) **1** the back part of a person's foot, below the ankle. **2** the part of a stocking or shoe that covers the heel. **3** the part of a shoe or boot that is under the heel or raises the heel. **4** put a heel or heels on. **5** anything shaped, used, or placed at an end like a heel: *The end crust of a loaf of bread is sometimes called a heel.* 1–3, 5 *n.*, 4 *v.*

☛ **Heel, heal,** and **he'll** are pronounced the same.

heel² (hēl) **1** lean over to one side; tilt; tip: *The ship heeled as it turned.* **2** the act of heeling. 1 *v.*, 2 *n.*

☛ See note at **heel¹**.

hef·ty (hef′tē) *Informal.* **1** weighty; heavy: *That's a hefty load.* **2** large; considerable: *They got a hefty bill for repairs. adj.*

heif·er (hef′ər) a young cow that has not had a calf. *n.*

height (hīt) **1** the tallness of anyone or anything; the point to which anything rises above the ground: *My father's height is 187 centimetres.* **2** the distance above sea level. **3** Usually, **heights**, *pl.* **a** a place high above level ground; hill; mountain; escarpment: *The climbers scaled the heights with great difficulty.* **b** the highest part; top; pinnacle: *As a hockey player, he reached the heights of success.* **4** the highest point; the greatest degree: *Fast driving on icy roads is the height of folly. n.*

☛ The form *heighth* (hītth) is sometimes heard, but the standard form is *height* (hīt).

height·en (hīt′ən) **1** make or become higher. **2** make or become stronger or greater; increase: *She put rouge on her cheeks to heighten their color. v.*

height of land **1** a region higher than its surroundings. **2** *Cdn.* a watershed; divide (def. 5): *A height of land marks the boundary between Labrador and Quebec. n.*

heir (er) a person who has the right to somebody's property or title after the death of its owner: *The rich man adopted the boy and made him his heir. n.*

☛ **Heir, air,** and **ere** are pronounced the same. **Heir** and **err** are sometimes pronounced the same.

heir·ess (er′is) **1** an heir who is a woman or girl. **2** a woman or girl inheriting great wealth: *The singer married an heiress. n.*

heir·loom (er′lüm′) a possession handed down from generation to generation: *This clock is a family heirloom. n.*

held (held) See **hold¹**. *Mother held the new baby. The swing is held by strong ropes. v.*

Helicopters

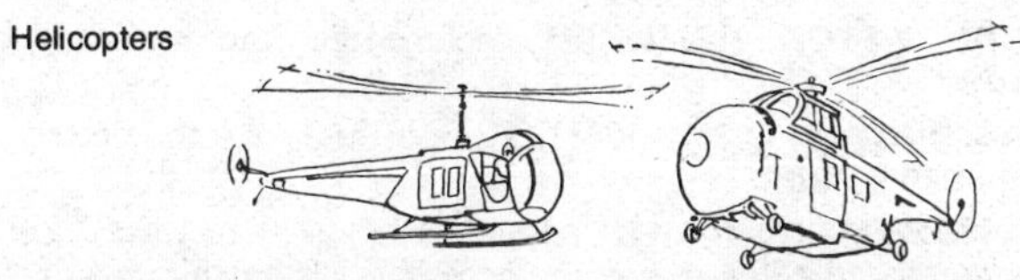

hel·i·cop·ter (hel′ə kop′tər) an aircraft that is lifted from the ground and kept in the air by horizontal propellers. *n.*

☛ **Helicopter** comes from a French word *hélicoptère*, which was formed from Greek *heliko*, meaning 'spiral' and *ptéron*, meaning 'wing.'

hat, āge, fär; let, ēqual, tėrm; it, īce
hot, ōpen, ôrder; oil, out; cup, pu̇t, rüle
əbove, takən, pencəl, lemən, circəs
ch, child; ng, long; sh, ship
th, thin; ᴛʜ, then; zh, measure

hel·i·port (hel′ə pôrt′) an airport for helicopters: *Heliports may be built on the tops of buildings. n.*

he·li·um (hē′lē əm) a very light gas that will not burn, much used in balloons and dirigibles. *n.*

hell (hel) **1** in religious use, the place where wicked persons are punished after death. **2** any place or state of wickedness, torment, or misery: *War is hell. n.*

he'll (hēl) he will.

☛ **He'll, heal,** and **heel** are pronounced the same.

hel·lo (he lō′ or hə lō′) **1** a call or exclamation to attract attention, express a greeting or surprise, etc.: *He said, 'Hello, Bill!'* **2** a call or shout: *The girl gave a loud hello to tell us where she was.* 1 *interj.*, 2 *n.*, *pl.* **hel·los.**

helm (helm) **1** the handle or wheel by which a ship is steered. **2** a position of control or guidance: *The Prime Minister is at the country's helm. n.*

Helmets worn by a knight, a football player, and an astronaut

hel·met (hel′mit) a covering to protect the head: *Knights wore helmets as part of their armor. Soldiers wear steel helmets; firemen often wear leather helmets.* See also **armor** for picture. *n.*

helms·man (helmz′mən) the man who steers a ship. *n., pl.* **helms·men** (helmz′mən).

help (help) **1** aid: *I need some help with my work.* **2** assist or aid: *Father sometimes helps with the housework.* **3** a means of making better: *The medicine was a help.* **4** make better: *The doctor helped my sore throat.* **5** give food to; serve with food: *Help your aunt to milk and sugar, please.* **6** avoid; keep from: *He cannot help going to sleep.* **7** being helped: *The dying woman was beyond help.* **8** one or more employees: *The storekeeper treats his help well.* 1, 3, 7, 8 *n.*, 2, 4–6 *v.* —**help′er**, *n.*

help yourself, do what you wish, take what you wish, etc.: *Help yourself until I am ready to go.*

help·ful (help′fəl) giving help; useful. *adj.*

help·ing (hel′ping) a portion of food. *n.*

help·less (help′lis) **1** not able to help oneself: *A little baby is helpless.* **2** without help or protection. *adj.* —**help′less·ly**, *adv.* —**help′less·ness**, *n.*

hel·ter–skel·ter (hel′tər skel′tər) **1** with headlong, disorderly haste: *The children ran helter-skelter when the big dog came bounding toward them.* **2** disorderly; confused: *There was a helter-skelter collection of books and papers on her desk.* 1 *adv.*, 2 *adj.*

Hems on a serviette and a skirt

hem[1] (hem) **1** a border or edge on a garment; the edge made by folding over the cloth and sewing it down. **2** fold over and sew down the edge of: *She hemmed six serviettes.* 1 *n.,* 2 *v.,* **hemmed, hem·ming.**
hem in, around or **about, a** surround on all sides. **b** keep from getting away or moving freely.

hem[2] (hem) **1** a clearing of the throat, used to attract attention or show doubt or hesitation. **2** make this sound. 1 *n.,* 2 *v.,* **hemmed, hem·ming.**
hem and haw, hesitate in speaking, especially to put off answering a question, making up one's mind, etc.: *He hemmed and hawed because he didn't know what to say.*

hem·i·sphere (hem′ə sfēr′) **1** half of a sphere or globe. **2** half of the earth's surface: *North and South America are in the Western Hemisphere; Europe, Asia, and Africa are in the Eastern Hemisphere. All the countries north of the equator are in the Northerm Hemisphere. n.*

hem·lock (hem′lok) **1** a poisonous plant having spotted stems, finely divided leaves, and small, white flowers. **2** an evergreen tree of the same family as the pine: *Hemlock bark is used in tanning.* **3** the wood of this tree. *n.*

hemp (hemp) a tall plant of Asia whose tough fibres are made into heavy string, rope, and coarse cloth. *n.*

hen (hen) **1** a female domestic fowl: *a hen and her chickens.* **2** the female of other birds: *a hen sparrow. n.*

hence (hens) **1** therefore: *It is very late, hence you must go to bed.* **2** from now: *Come back a week hence.* **3** from here: *Go hence, I pray thee.* **4 Hence!** Go away! *Hence! foul fiend.* 1–3 *adv.,* 4 *interj.*

hence·forth (hens′fôrth′) from now on. *adv.*

her (hėr) **1** a girl, woman, or female animal already referred to and identical: *Ida is not here and I have not seen her.* **2** of her; belonging to her; done by her: *She has left her book. The cat won't let you touch her kittens. She has finished her work.* 1 *pron.,* 2 *adj.*
☛ **Her** (def. 2) and **hers** are the possessive forms of **she. Her** (def. 2) is always followed by a noun: *This is her doll.* **Hers** stands alone: *This doll is hers.*

her·ald (her′əld) **1** a person who carries messages and makes announcements: *The king sent two heralds to the duke.* **2** bring news of; announce: *The robins heralded the arrival of spring.* **3** a person or thing that goes or is sent before and shows that something more is coming: *Dawn is the herald of the day.* 1, 3 *n.,* 2 *v.*

herb (ėrb or hėrb) **1** a plant whose leaves and stems are used for medicine, seasoning, or food: *Sage, mint, and lavender are herbs.* **2** a flowering plant whose stems live only one season. *n.*

her·biv·o·rous (hėr biv′ə rəs) feeding on grass or other plants: *Cattle are herbivorous animals. adj.*

Her·cu·les (hėr′kyə lēz′ or hėr′kyů lēz′) a hero of Greek and Roman mythology, famous for his great strength and for twelve tasks he performed. *n.*

herd (hėrd) **1** a number of animals together: *a herd of cows, a herd of horses, a herd of elephants. The animals in a herd are usually large and all of one kind.* **2** a large number of people. **3** the common people; people as a mass or mob. **4** join together; flock together: *Many animals herd for protection.* **5** form into a flock, herd, or group. **6** drive; tend, or take care of cattle or sheep. 1–3 *n.,* 4–6 *v.*
☛ **Herd** and **heard** are pronounced the same.

herd·er (hėr′dər) herdsman. *n.*

herds·man (hėrdz′mən) a man who tends a herd. *n., pl.* **herds·men** (hėrdz′mən).

here (hēr) **1** in this place; at this place: *We live here in the summer. We shall stop here.* **2** to this place: *Bring the children here for their lesson.* **3** this place: *Where do we go from here?* **4** now; at this time: *Here the speaker paused.* **5** an answer showing that one is present at a roll call. 1, 2, 4 *adv.,* 3, 5 *n.*
☛ **Here** and **hear** are pronounced the same.

here·a·bout (hēr′ə bout′) around here; about this place; near here. *adv.*

here·a·bouts (hēr′ə bouts′) hereabout. *adv.*

here·af·ter (hēr af′tər) **1** after this; in the future. **2** the life or time after death. 1 *adv.,* 2 *n.*

here·by (hēr bī′) by this; by this means: *The licence read, 'You are hereby given the right to hunt in Ontario.' adv.*

he·red·i·tar·y (hə red′ə ter′ē) **1** coming by inheritance: *'Prince' is a hereditary title.* **2** holding a position by inheritance: *The Queen of England is a hereditary ruler.* **3** passed down or caused by heredity: *Color blindness is hereditary.* **4** taken from one's parents or ancestors: *a hereditary belief. adj.*

he·red·i·ty (hə red′ə tē) **1** the passing down of physical and mental qualities from parents to children: *His blue eyes are a result of heredity.* **2** the qualities that have been passed down to a child from its parents. *n.*

here·in (hēr in′) in this; in here. *adv.*

here's (hērz) here is.

her·e·sy (her′ə sē) **1** a belief different from the accepted belief of a church, school, or profession. **2** the holding of such a belief. *n., pl.* **her·e·sies.**

her·e·tic (her′ə tik) a person who holds a belief that is different from the accepted belief of his church, school, or profession. *n.*

here·to·fore (hēr′tə fôr′) before this time; until now. *adv.*

here·up·on (hēr′ə pon′) **1** upon this. **2** immediately after this. *adv.*

here·with (hēr wiTH′ or hēr with′) **1** with this: *I am sending ten cents in stamps herewith.* **2** by this means. *adv.*

her·it·age (her′ə tij) what is or may be handed on to a person from his ancestors; inheritance. *n.*

her·mit (hėr′mit) a person who goes away from other people and lives by himself: *A hermit often lives a religious life. n.*

he·ro (hēr′ō) **1** a man who does great and brave deeds and is admired for them. 2 the most important male person in a story, play, motion picture, etc. 3 a man who is outstanding in sports, etc.: *a football hero.* *n., pl.* **he·roes.**

he·ro·ic (hi rō′ik) 1 like a hero or heroine in deeds or in qualities; brave; noble: *the heroic deeds of our firemen.* 2 of or about heroes and their deeds: *The 'Odyssey' is a heroic poem.* 3 unusually bold or daring: *Only heroic measures could save the town from the flood.* *adj.*

her·o·in (her′ō ən) a very harmful, habit-forming drug. *n.*

her·o·ine (her′ō in) 1 a woman or girl admired for her bravery or great deeds. 2 the most important female person in a story, play, motion picture, etc. *n.*

her·o·ism (her′ō iz′əm) 1 great courage: *an act of heroism.* 2 a very brave act; doing something noble at great cost to oneself. *n.*

Great blue herons — about 120 cm long with the tail

her·on (her′ən) a wading bird having a long neck, a long bill, and long legs. *n.*

her·ring (her′ing) a small food fish of the northern Atlantic Ocean: *Herring come near the shore to lay their eggs.* *n., pl.* **her·ring** or **her·rings.**

hers (hėrz) 1 of her; belonging to her: *This money is hers.* 2 the one or ones belonging to her: *Your answers are wrong; hers are right.* *pron.*
☛ See note at **her.**

her·self (hėr self′) 1 a form used instead of **she** or **her** when referring back to the subject of the sentence: *She hurt herself. She did it by herself. The cat saw herself in the glass.* 2 a form of **she** or **her** used to make a statement stronger: *She brought the book herself. She herself did it.* 3 her usual self: *In those fits she is not herself.* *pron.*

he's (hēz) 1 he is. 2 he has: *He's broken his hockey stick.*

hes·i·tate (hez′ə tāt′) 1 hold back; feel doubtful; be undecided; show that one has not yet made up one's mind: *I hesitated about taking his side until I knew the whole story.* 2 feel that perhaps one shouldn't; be unwilling; not want: *I hesitated to ask you because you were so busy.* 3 stop an instant; pause: *He hesitated before asking the question.* *v.,* **hes·i·tat·ed, hes·i·tat·ing.**

hes·i·ta·tion (hez′ə tā′shən) 1 the act of hesitating; doubt; unwillingness; delay. 2 speaking with short stops or pauses: *a hesitation in one's speech.* *n.*

hew (hyü) 1 cut; chop: *He hewed down the tree.* 2 cut into shape; form by cutting with an axe, adze, etc.: *They hewed the logs into beams.* *v.,* **hewed, hewed** or **hewn, hew·ing.**
☛ **Hew** and **hue** are pronounced the same.

hewn (hyün) See **hew.** *v.*

hey (hā) a sound made to attract attention, express

hat, āge, fär; let, ēqual, tėrm; it, īce
hot, ōpen, ôrder; oil, out; cup, pu̇t, rüle
əbove, takən, pencəl, lemən, circəs
ch, child; ng, long; sh, ship
th, thin; ᴛʜ, then; zh, measure

surprise or other feeling, or ask a question: *Hey! stop! Hey, there!* *interj.*
☛ **Hey** and **hay** are pronounced the same.

hi (hī) a call of greeting; hello. *interj.*
☛ **Hi** and **high** are pronounced the same.

hi·ber·nate (hī′bər nāt′) spend the winter in sleep, as bears, groundhogs, and some other wild animals do. *v.,* **hi·ber·nat·ed, hi·ber·nat·ing.**

hi·ber·na·tion (hī′bər nā′shən) a hibernating. *n.*

hic·cough (hik′up) See **hiccup.**

hic·cup (hik′up) 1 an involuntary catching of the breath. 2 catch the breath in this way; have the hiccups. 3 **hiccups,** *pl.* the state of having one hiccup after another. 1, 3 *n.,* 2 *v.,* **hic·cupped, hic·cup·ping.**

hick·o·ry (hik′ə rē) 1 a North American tree having nuts that can be eaten. 2 the tough, hard wood of this tree. *n., pl.* **hick·o·ries.**

hid (hid) See **hide**[1]. *The dog hid his bone.* *v.*

hid·den (hid′ən) 1 put or kept out of sight; secret; not clear: *Her speech was full of hidden meanings.* 2 See **hide**[1]. *The moon was hidden behind a dark cloud.* 1 *adj.,* 2 *v.*

hide[1] (hīd) 1 put or keep out of sight: *Hide it where no one else will know of it or know where it is.* 2 shut off from sight; cover up: *Clouds hide the sun.* 3 keep secret: *She hid her disappointment.* 4 hide oneself: *I'll hide, and you find me.* *v.,* **hid, hid·den** or **hid, hid·ing.**

hide[2] (hīd) an animal's skin, either raw or tanned. *n.*

hide–and–seek (hīd′ən sēk′) a children's game in which some of the players hide and others try to find them. *n.* Also **hide-and-go-seek.**

hide·a·way (hīd′ə wā′) 1 a place of hiding. 2 a quiet, restful place, especially one in an isolated area, for a person or small group of people to be alone: *He had a little hideaway by a lake where he went to escape from the noise and confusion of the city.* *n.*

hid·e·ous (hid′ē əs) ugly; frightful; horrible: *a hideous monster.* *adj.* —**hid′e·ous·ly,** *adv.*

hide–out (hīd′out′) a place for hiding or being alone. *n.*

A KINGLY
GIFT OF AN
OFFERING TABLE
TO
RA-HORUS
THE GREAT
GOD
LORD OF
HEAVEN
Egyptian hieroglyphics

hi·er·o·glyph·ic (hī′ər ə glif′ik) 1 a picture of an object standing for a word, idea, or sound; a character or symbol standing for a word, idea, or sound: *The ancient Egyptians used hieroglyphics instead of an alphabet like ours.* 2 a system of writing that uses hieroglyphics. *n.*

☛ **Hieroglyphic** came into English through either French or late Latin from a Greek word *hieroglyphikos,* meaning 'sacred writing,' which was formed from *hieros,* meaning 'sacred' and *gluphē,* meaning 'carving.'

hi–fi (hī′fī′ for 1, hī′fī′ for 2 and 3) *Informal.* 1 high-fidelity. 2 the high-fidelity reproduction of music. 3 the equipment for such reproduction. 1 *adj.,* 2, 3 *n.*

high (hī) 1 tall: *high mountains.* 2 up above the ground: *a high jump, an airplane high in the air.* 3 a senior to others in rank or position; up above others: *A general has high rank.* b superior; above others in personal qualities: *Sir William Laurier was a person of high character.* 4 greater, stronger, or better than others; great: *a high price, a high wind.* 5 most important; chief; main: *the high altar.* 6 at or to a high point, place, rank, amount, degree, price, etc.: *The eagle flies high. Strawberries come high in winter. Gamblers play high.* 7 above the normal pitch; shrill; sharp: *a high voice.* 1–5, 7 *adj.,* 6 *adv.*

high and dry, a up out of the water: *The fish was high and dry on the beach.* b alone; without help: *He has left me high and dry with all this work to do.*

high seas, the open ocean: *The high seas are outside the authority of any country.*

high spirits, cheerfulness; gaiety.

high tide, the time when the ocean comes up highest on the shore.

high time, a the time just before it is too late: *It was high time that he began to study.* b *Informal.* a lively, jolly time at a party, etc.

☛ **High** and **hi** are pronounced the same.

High Commissioner the chief representative of one Commonwealth country in another.

high–fi·del·i·ty (hī′fī del′ə tē or hī′fə del′ə tē) indicating reproduction by a radio or phonograph of the full range of sound or something approaching it, with a minimum of distortion. *adj.*

high jump an athletic contest or event in which the contestants try to jump over a bar as high as possible.

high·land (hī′lənd) 1 a country or region that is higher and hillier than the neighboring country. 2 **the Highlands,** a hilly region in northern and western Scotland. *n.*

Highland fling a lively dance of the Highlands of Scotland.

high·light (hī′līt′) 1 the most interesting or most striking part, event, scene, etc.: *The highlight of our trip was the drive along the Cabot Trail.* 2 make prominent: *The new product was highlighted in all the company's brochures.* 3 the effect or representation of bright light. 1, 3 *n.,* 2 *v.*

high·ly (hī′lē) 1 in a high degree; very; very much: *highly amusing, highly recommended.* 2 very favorably; with great praise or honor: *to speak highly of your best friend.* 3 at a high price: *highly paid. adv.*

high·ness (hī′nis) 1 the state or condition of being high; height. 2 **Highness,** a title of honor given to members of royal families: *The Prince of Wales is addressed as 'Your Highness' and spoken of as 'His Royal Highness.'* *n.*

high–rise (hī′rīz′) 1 having many storeys: *high-rise office buildings.* 2 a tall building having many storeys: *They live on the 23rd floor of a high-rise downtown.* 1 *adj.,* 2 *n.*

high·road (hī′rōd′) 1 a main road; highway. 2 a direct and easy way: *There is no highroad to success. n.*

high school a school attended after elementary or public school; a secondary school: *Some provinces have junior high schools, intermediate between elementary and high school.*

high–stick·ing (hī′stik′ing) in hockey, an illegal check made by striking or hindering an opposing player with one's stick carried above shoulder level: *He received a penalty for high-sticking. n.*

high–strung (hī′strung′) very sensitive; very nervous. *adj.*

high·way (hī′wā′) 1 a main road or route: *We took the highway to Hamilton.* 2 a public road. *n.*

high·way·man (hī′wā′mən) a man who robs travellers on a public road. *n., pl.* **high·way·men** (hī′wā′mən).

hike (hīk) 1 take a long walk; tramp; march: *The scouts hiked in to the hills.* 2 a tramp or march. 1 *v.,* **hiked, hik·ing;** 2 *n.*

hi·lar·i·ous (hə ler′ē əs) 1 very merry; noisily cheerful: *It was a hilarious party.* 2 very funny: *The joke was hilarious. adj.*

hi·lar·i·ty (hə lar′ə tē or hə ler′ə tē) noisy gaiety. *n.*

hill (hil) 1 a raised part of the earth's surface, smaller than a mountain. 2 a little heap or pile: *Ants and moles make hills. The soil put over and around the roots of a plant is a hill.* 3 a plant with a little heap of soil over and around its roots: *a hill of corn. n.* —**hill′y,** *adj.*

hill·bil·ly (hil′bil′ē) a person who lives in the backwoods or in a mountainous region, especially in the southern United States. *n., pl.* **hill·bil·lies.**

hill·side (hil′sīd′) the side of a hill. *n.*

hill·top (hil′top′) the top of a hill. *n.*

hilt (hilt) the handle of a sword or dagger. See **sword** for picture. *n.*

him (him) the boy, man, or male animal already referred to and identified: *Jim is smaller than you are, so treat him gently. pron.*

☛ **Him** and **hymn** are pronounced the same.

him·self (him self′) 1 a form used instead of **he** or **him** when referring back to the subject of the sentence: *He cut himself. He asked himself what he really wanted. He kept the toy for himself.* 2 a form of **he** or **him** used to make a statement stronger: *Did you see Roy himself?* 3 his usual self: *He feels himself again. pron.*

hind[1] (hīnd) back; rear: *The mule kicked up its hind legs. adj.*

hind[2] (hīnd) a female deer, especially after its third year. *n., pl.* **hind** or **hinds.**

hin·der (hin′dər) keep back; hold back; get in the way of; make hard to do: *Deep mud hindered travel. v.*

Hin·di (hin′dē) the official language of India: *Hindi is*

hat, āge, fär; let, ēqual, tėrm; it, īce
hot, ōpen, ôrder; oil, out; cup, pu̇t, rüle
əbove, takən, pencəl, lemən, circəs
ch, child; ng, long; sh, ship
th, thin; ᴛʜ, then; zh, measure

the most widely spoken of the many languages of India. *n.*

hind·quar·ter (hīnd′kwôr′tər) the hind leg and loin of a carcass of beef, lamb, etc. *n.*

hin·drance (hin′drəns) **1** a person or thing that hinders; obstacle: *If you won't help, don't be a hindrance. The noise was a hindrance to our studying.* **2** hindering. *n.*

A hinge on a gate

hinge (hinj) **1** a joint on which a door, gate, cover, lid, etc. moves back and forth. **2** furnish with hinges; attach by hinges. **3** hang or turn on a hinge. **4** depend: *The success of the picnic will hinge on the weather.* 1 *n.*, 2–4 *v.*, **hinged, hing·ing.**

hint (hint) **1** a slight sign; an indirect suggestion: *A small black cloud gave a hint of the coming storm.* **2** give a slight sign of; suggest in an indirect way: *She hinted that she wanted to go to bed by saying, 'Do you often stay up this late?'* 1 *n.*, 2 *v.*

hip (hip) **1** the part of the human body that projects on each side below the waist. **2** a similar part in animals, where the hind leg joins the body. *n.*

A hippopotamus — about 140 cm high at the shoulder

hip·po·pot·a·mus (hip′ə pot′ə məs) a huge, thick-skinned, hairless animal found in and near the rivers of Africa: *Hippopotamuses, which often weigh as much as four tonnes, live on plants.* *n.*, *pl.* **hip·po·pot·a·mus·es** or **hip·po·pot·a·mi** (hip′ə pot′ə mī).

☛ **Hippopotamus** came into English through Latin from the Greek word *hippopotamos,* meaning 'the horse of the river.'

hire (hīr) **1** pay for the use of a thing: *hire a car.* **2** pay for the work or services of a person: *The storekeeper hired ten clerks for the Christmas rush.* **3** payment for the use of a thing or the work or services of a person: *Some men fight for glory; some fight for hire.* 1, 2 *v.*, **hired, hir·ing;** 3 *n.*
for hire, for use or work in return for payment.
hire out, give one's work in return for payment: *He hired out as a carpenter.*

his (hiz) **1** of him; belonging to him: *His name is Bill. This is his book.* **2** the one or ones belonging to him: *My books are new; his are old.* 1, 2 *pron.*, 1 *adj.*

hiss (his) **1** make a sound like that of the *s* in *see: The snake hissed as we approached.* **2** such a sound: *There was a loud hiss as the water boiled over onto the hot stove.* **3** make this sound as a sign of disapproval: *The audience hissed at the poor play.* **4** show disapproval of by hissing: *The audience hissed the actors.* **5** the sound of hissing to express disapproval: *The actor was upset by the hisses of the crowd.* 1, 3, 4 *v.*, 2, 5 *n.*

his·to·ri·an (his tô′rē ən) a person who has much knowledge of history, especially one who writes about or teaches history. *n.*

his·tor·ic (his tôr′ik) famous or important in history: *Halifax and Kingston are historic cities. July 1, 1867, is a historic day for Canada.* *adj.*

his·tor·i·cal (his tôr′ə kəl) **1** of or having to do with history: *a historical town.* **2** according to history; based on history: *a historical novel.* **3** known to be real or true; in history, not in legend: *It is a historical fact that Sir John A. Macdonald was the first Prime Minister of Canada.* *adj.*

his·to·ry (his′tə rē or his′trē) **1** a statement of what has happened. **2** the story of a person or a nation: *the history of Canada.* **3** a known past: *This ship has an interesting history.* *n.*, *pl.* **his·to·ries.**

hit (hit) **1** come against with force; give a blow to; strike: *When children fight, they hit each other. She hit the ball with a bat. He hit his head against the shelf. The man hit out at the thieves who attacked him.* **2** get to what is aimed at: *His second arrow hit the bull's-eye.* **3** come upon; meet with; find: *We hit the right road in the dark. The girls hit upon a plan for making money.* **4** distress; cause distress to: *As he lifted the heavy box, a sharp pain hit him in the back.* **5** a blow; stroke. **6** a successful attempt, performance or production: *The new play is the hit of the season.* 1–4 *v.*, **hit, hit·ting;** 5, 6 *n.* **—hit′ter,** *n.*
be hard hit, be affected deeply or painfully: *She was hard hit by the news of her mother's death.*
hit it off, *Informal.* agree or get along well with someone: *Tom hit it off well with his new friend.*

hitch (hich) **1** fasten with a hook, ring, rope, strap, etc.: *He hitched his horse to a post.* **2** fasten; catch; become fastened or caught: *A knot made the rope hitch.* **3** move or pull with a jerk: *He hitched his chair nearer to the fire.* **4** a short, sudden pull or jerk: *The sailor gave his pants a hitch.* **5** an obstacle; a going wrong: *A hitch in their plans made them miss the train.* **6** a kind of knot used for temporary fastening: *He put a hitch in the rope.* **7** tie such a knot: *She hitched the rope around the spar.* 1–3, 7 *v.*, 4–6 *n.*

hitch·hike (hich′hīk′) travel by walking and begging free rides: *The boys hitchhiked from Calgary to Edmonton.* *v.*, **hitch·hiked, hitch·hik·ing. —hitch′hik′er,** *n.*

hith·er (hiᴛʜ′ər) **1** here; to this place. **2** on this side; nearer. 1 *adv.*, 2 *adj.*
hither and thither, here and there.

hith·er·to (hiᴛʜ′ər tü′) up to this time; until now. *adv.*

hive (hīv) **1** a house or box for bees to live in. See **beehive** for picture. **2** a large number of bees living together: *The whole hive was busy.* **3** a busy place full of people: *On Saturdays the department store is a hive.* **4** live close together as bees do. 1–3 *n.*, 4 *v.*, **hived, hiv·ing.**

hives (hīvz) a condition in which the skin itches and shows patches of red: *Some people are allergic to strawberries and get hives when they eat them. n.*

H.M. 1 His Majesty. 2 Her Majesty.

H.M.C.S. 1 His Majesty's Canadian Ship. 2 Her Majesty's Canadian Ship: *H.M.C.S. St. Laurent.*

H.M.S. 1 His Majesty's Ship. 2 Her Majesty's Ship.

ho (hō) **1** an exclamation of surprise, joy, or scornful laughter. **2** an exclamation to get attention: *The captain said, 'Ho, men! Listen to me.' interj.*
☞ **Ho** and **hoe** are pronounced the same.

hoard (hôrd) **1** save and store up: *The squirrel hoarded nuts for the winter. The miser hoarded his money.* **2** the things stored: *The squirrel kept his hoard in a tree.* 1 *v.*, 2 *n.*
☞ **Hoard** and **horde** are pronounced the same.

hoar·frost (hôr′frost′) white frost: *The leaves were covered with hoarfrost. n.*

hoarse (hôrs) **1** sounding rough and deep: *the hoarse sound of the bullfrog.* **2** having a rough voice: *A bad cold has made him hoarse. adj.*, **hoars·er, hoars·est.** —**hoarse′ness,** *n.*
☞ **Hoarse** and **horse** are pronounced the same.

hoar·y (hôr′ē) **1** white or grey. **2** white or grey with age: *They saw a hoary old woman coming toward them.* **3** old: *the hoary ruins of a castle. adj.*, **hoar·i·er, hoar·i·est.**

hoax (hōks) **1** a mischievous trick; especially, a made-up story: *The report of an attack on earth from Mars was a hoax.* **2** play a mischievous trick on; deceive. 1 *n.*, 2 *v.*

hob·ble (hob′əl) **1** walk awkwardly; limp: *The wounded man hobbled away.* **2** a limping walk. **3** put a strap, rope, etc. around the legs of an animal, especially a horse, so that it can move a little but not run away. **4** a rope or strap used to hobble an animal. 1, 3 *v.*, **hob·bled, hob·bling;** 2, 4 *n.*

hob·by (hob′ē) something a person especially likes to work at or to study but which is not his main business: *Growing roses is our doctor's hobby. n., pl.* **hob·bies.**

hob·by·horse (hob′ē hôrs′) **1** a stick with a horse's head, used as a child's plaything. **2** rocking horse. **3** *Informal.* a favorite topic: *Father is on his hobbyhorse of cutting costs. n.*

hob·gob·lin (hob′gob′lin) **1** a mischievous elf; goblin. **2** something imaginary that gives rise to fear. *n.*

hob·nail (hob′nāl′) a short nail with a large head: *Hobnails are used to protect the soles of heavy shoes. n.*

ho·bo (hō′bō) tramp. *n., pl.* **ho·bos** or **ho·boes.**

hock (hok) the second joint above the hoof on the hind leg of a horse, cow, etc. *n.*

hock·ey (hok′ē) **1** a game played on ice by two teams of six players wearing skates and carrying hooked sticks, with which they try to shoot a black rubber disk, the puck, into the opposing team's goal. **2** a field game played with curved sticks and a small ball: *Field hockey is not as well known to Canadians as ice hockey. n.*

hod (hod) **1** a trough or tray with a long straight handle, used by builders for carrying bricks, mortar, etc. on the shoulder. See the picture. **2** a pail for carrying coal. See **scuttle** for picture. *n.*

hodge·podge (hoj′poj′) a disorderly mixture; a mess or jumble. *n.*

A hod used to carry mortar

A hoe

hoe (hō) **1** an implement with a small blade set across the end of a long handle, used for loosening soil, cutting small weeds, etc. **2** loosen, dig, or cut with a hoe. **3** use a hoe. 1 *n., pl.* **hoes;** 2, 3 *v.*, **hoed, hoe·ing.**
☞ **Hoe** and **ho** are pronounced the same.

hog (hog) **1** pig. **2** a full-grown pig raised for food. **3** a selfish, greedy, or dirty person. **4** *Slang.* take more than one's share of: *Don't hog the ice cream.* 1–3 *n.*, 4 *v.*, **hogged, hog·ging.**

hog·gish (hog′ish) **1** like a hog (def. 3); greedy; very selfish. **2** dirty; filthy. *adj.*

hogs·head (hogz′hed′) **1** a large barrel or cask containing from 100 to 140 gallons, about 455 to 635 litres. **2** a liquid measure equal to 54 gallons, about 245 litres. *n.*

hoist (hoist) **1** raise on high; lift up, often with ropes and pulleys: *to hoist a flag, to hoist sails, to hoist blocks of stone in building.* **2** a hoisting; lift: *He gave me a hoist up the wall.* **3** an elevator or other apparatus for lifting heavy loads. 1 *v.*, 2, 3 *n.*

hold[1] (hōld) **1** grasp and keep: *Hold my watch while I play this game.* **2** a grasp or grip: *Take a good hold of this rope.* **3** something to hold by: *She looked for a hold on the smooth rock but couldn't find any.* **4** keep in some place or position: *Hold the dish level. He will hold the paper steady while you draw.* **5** keep from acting; keep back: *to hold one's tongue. Hold your breath.* **6** keep: *The soldiers held the fort against the enemy.* **7** keep in; contain: *This cup will hold water. How much will it hold? This theatre holds five hundred people.* **8** have: *Shall we hold a meeting of the club? She holds much property in the city. That man holds two jobs in our town. He holds a high opinion of you.* **9** consider; think: *People once held that the world was flat.* **10** be faithful: *He held to his promise.* **11** be true: *Will this rule hold in all cases?* 1, 4–11 *v.*, **held, hold·ing;** 2, 3 *n.*

hold in, a keep in; keep back. **b** control; restrain: *He was so angry he couldn't hold in his temper.*

hold on, a keep one's hold: *He held on to the overturned boat till help came.* **b** keep on; continue. **c** stop!

hold out, a continue; last: *The water would not hold out much longer.* **b** keep resisting; not give in: *The company of soldiers held out for six days until help arrived.*

hold over, a keep longer than originally scheduled: *The movie was so popular that it was held over for another*

hat, āge, fär; let, ēqual, tėrm; it, īce
hot, ōpen, ôrder; oil, out; cup, pu̇t, rüle
əbove, takən, pencəl, lemən, circəs
ch, child; ng, long; sh, ship
th, thin; ᴛʜ, then; zh, measure

week. **b** postpone: *The game has been held over until next week.*
hold up, a keep from falling. **b** display; show: *He held up the prize for everyone to see.* **c** continue; last; endure. **d** stop: *The policeman held up the traffic.* **e** stop by force and rob.
lay hold of, seize; grasp.

hold² (hōld) the lowest part of a ship's interior: *A ship's cargo is carried in its hold.* *n.*

hold·er (hōl′dər) **1** a person who holds something: *An owner or possessor of property is a holder.* **2** anything to hold something else with: *Pads of cloth are used as holders for lifting hot dishes.* *n.*

hold·ing (hōl′ding) land; a piece of land. *n.*

hold·up (hōld′up′) **1** *Informal.* the act of stopping by force and robbing. **2** stopping; delay: *She got out of her car to see what the holdup was.* *n.*

hole (hōl) **1** an open place: *a hole in a stocking.* **2** a hollow place in something solid: *Rabbits dig holes in the ground to live in.* **3** a place that is lower than the parts around it: *a hole in the road.* **4** a small, dark, dirty place. **5** make a hole or holes in: *The side of the ship was holed by the iceberg.* 1–4 *n.*, 5 *v.*, **holed, hol·ing.**
hole up, a of animals, go into a hole: *Bears hole themselves up during the winter.* **b** *Slang.* go into hiding for a time: *The robbers holed up in an old cabin.*
☛ **Hole** and **whole** are pronounced the same.

hol·i·day (hol′ə dā′) **1** a day when one does not work; a day for pleasure and enjoyment: *July 1st is a holiday for all Canadians.* **2** vacation. **3 holidays,** *pl.* the time spent away from work or school: *She always goes to the Girl Guide camp during the summer holidays.* *n.*
☛ **Holiday** developed from an Old English word, *hāligdaeg,* meaning 'holy day.'

ho·li·ness (hō′lē nis) **1** being holy or sacred. **2 Holiness,** a title used in speaking to or of the Pope. *n.*

hol·ler (hol′ər) *Informal.* **1** shout. **2** a loud cry or shout. 1 *v.*, 2 *n.*

hol·low (hol′ō) **1** having nothing, or only air, inside; empty; with a hole inside; not solid: *A tube or pipe is hollow. Most rubber balls are hollow.* **2** shaped like a bowl or cup: *a hollow dish for vegetables.* **3** a hollow place; hole: *a hollow in the road.* **4** dig or cut out to a hollow shape; form by making hollow: *He hollowed a whistle out of a piece of wood.* **5** valley: *Sleepy Hollow.* **6** as if coming from something hollow; dull: *a hollow voice, a hollow groan, the hollow boom of a foghorn.* **7** deep and sunken: *A starving person has hollow eyes and cheeks.* **8** not real or sincere; false: *hollow promises, hollow joys.* **9** hungry: *By twelve o'clock we feel rather hollow.* 1, 2, 6–9 *adj.*, 3, 5 *n.*, 4 *v.*
—hol′low·ness, *n.*
hollow out, form by hollowing.

Holly

hol·ly (hol′ē) an evergreen tree or shrub with shiny, sharp-pointed green leaves and bright-red berries, used especially as Christmas decorations. *n., pl.* **hol·lies.**

hol·ly·hock (hol′ē hok′) a tall plant with clusters of large flowers of various colors. *n.*

hol·ster (hōl′stər) a leather case for a pistol, usually attached to a belt. *n.*

ho·ly (hō′lē) **1** belonging to God; set apart for God's service; coming from God; sacred: *the Holy Bible, Holy Communion.* **2** like a saint; spiritually perfect; very good; pure in heart: *a holy man.* *adj.*, **ho·li·er, ho·li·est.**
holy of holies, the most sacred place.
☛ **Holy** and **wholly** are pronounced the same.

hom·age (hom′ij) **1** respect; reverence; honor: *Everyone paid homage to the great leader.* **2** in former times, a formal acknowledgment by a vassal that he owed loyalty and service to his lord. **3** a formal statement, or oath, of loyalty and service owed to one's sovereign. *n.*

home (hōm) **1** the place where a person or family lives; one's own house: *Her home is at 25 South Street.* **2** the place where a person was born or brought up; one's own town or country: *His home is Ottawa.* **3** a private house; a house, especially a new house built for occupation by one family: *There are some lovely homes for sale in the new subdivision.* **4** any place where a person or animal lives or is able to rest and be safe: *A beaver makes his home at the water's edge.* **5** a place where a thing is especially common: *The Canadian tundra is the home of the musk-ox.* **6** a place where people who are homeless, poor, old, sick, blind, etc. may live: *a home for orphans.* **7** having something to do with one's home or country: *Write me all the home events.* **8** at or to one's own home or country: *I want to go home.* **9** the goal in many games. **10** to the place where it belongs; to the thing aimed at: *drive a nail home. The spear struck home to the tiger's heart.* 1–6, 9 *n.*, 7 *adj.*, 8, 10 *adv.*
☛ In general usage, **home** refers to any place that is the centre of one's family life; **house** refers only to a building. In the advertising of real estate, etc. **home** is usually used in place of **house** because it suggests the comfort and happiness of family life.

Home and School Association an association of parents and teachers who meet from time to time in the interests of school children.

home·brew (hōm′brü′) **1** beer brewed at home. **2** *Cdn.* in sports, a professional athlete who is a native of the country he is playing in. *n.*

home·land (hōm′land′) the country that is one's home; one's native land. *n.*

home·less (hōm′lis) without a home. *adj.*

home·like (hōm′līk′) like home; friendly; familiar; comfortable: *a homelike atmosphere.* *adj.*

home·ly (hōm′lē) **1** plain; not good-looking: *She was rather a homely girl.* **2** suited to home life; simple: *homely food, homely pleasures.* *adj.*, **home·li·er, home·li·est.**

home·made (hōm′mād′) made at home: *homemade bread. adj.*

home·mak·er (hōm′māk′ər) a woman who manages a home and its affairs; housewife. *n.*

home plate in baseball, the block or slab beside which a player stands to bat the ball, and to which he must return, after hitting the ball and rounding the bases, in order to score.

hom·er (hōm′ər) in baseball, home run. *n.*

home run in baseball, a run scored on a hit that makes it possible for the batter to run round all the bases without a stop.

home·sick (hōm′sik′) overcome by sadness because home is far away; ill with longing for home. *adj.* **—home′sick′ness,** *n.*

home·spun (hōm′spun′) **1** spun or made at home. **2** cloth made of yarn spun at home. **3** a loose, but strong, cloth that looks like homespun. **4** plain; simple: *homespun manners.* 1, 4 *adj.,* 2, 3 *n.*

home·stead (hōm′sted′) **1** a house with its land and other buildings; a farm with its buildings. **2** in the West, public land granted to a settler under certain conditions by the federal government. **3** settle on such land: *His grandfather homesteaded in Saskatchewan.* 1, 2 *n.,* 3 *v.*

home·ward (hōm′wərd) toward home: *We turned homeward. The ship is on her homeward course. adv., adj.*

home·wards (hōm′wərdz) homeward. *adv.*

home·work (hōm′wėrk′) **1** a lesson or lessons to be studied or prepared outside the classroom. **2** any work done at home. *n.*

home·y (hōm′ē) like home; cosy and comfortable: *The old inn had a very homey atmosphere. adj.,* **hom·i·er, hom·i·est.**

hom·i·cide (hom′ə sīd′ or hō′mə sīd′) the killing of one human being by another: *Intentional homicide is murder. n.*

ho·mog·e·nize (hə moj′ə nīz′) make similar throughout; distribute parts or ingredients evenly: *The milk we buy from dairies has usually been homogenized so that the cream will not rise to the top (but remains evenly mixed throughout the milk). v.,* **ho·mog·e·nized, ho·mog·e·niz·ing.**

hom·o·graph (hom′ə graf′) a word having the same spelling as another but a different origin and a different meaning: Mail, *meaning 'letters,' and* mail, *meaning 'armor,' are homographs. In this dictionary homographs are separate entries, each one identified by a small number after it. n.*

hom·o·nym (hom′ə nim′) a word having the same pronunciation as another, but a different meaning: Meat *and* meet *are homonyms. n.*

Hon. Honourable.

hon·est (on′ist) **1** fair and upright; truthful; not lying, cheating or stealing: *He was an honest man.* **2** obtained by fair means; without lying, cheating, or stealing: *honest profits. He lived an honest life.* **3** not hiding one's real nature; frank; open: *She has an honest face.* **4** not mixed with something of less value; genuine; pure: *Stores should sell honest goods. adj.* **—hon′est·ly,** *adv.*

hon·es·ty (on′is tē) **1** fairness and uprightness. **2** truthfulness. *n.*

hon·ey (hun′ē) **1** a thick, sweet liquid that bees make out of the nectar they collect from flowers. **2** the drop of sweet liquid found in many flowers; nectar: *Honey attracts bees to flowers.* **3** sweetness. **4** darling; dear. *n., pl.* **hon·eys.**

hon·ey·bee (hun′ē bē′) a bee of a kind that makes honey and wax that can be used by people. See **bee** for picture. *n.*

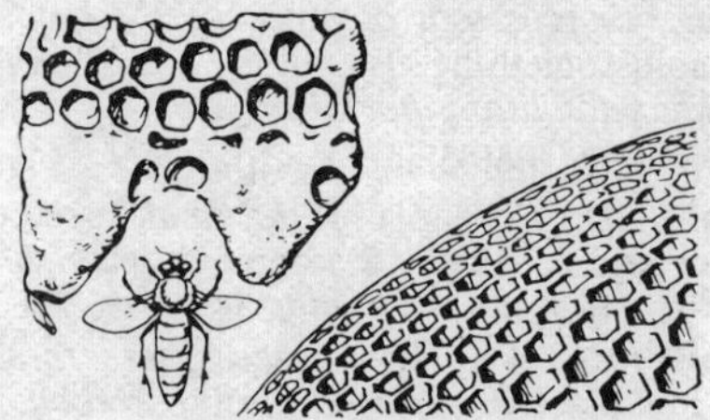
Honeycombs

hon·ey·comb (hun′ē kōm′) **1** a structure of wax containing rows of six-sided cells, made by bees to store honey, pollen, and their eggs. **2** anything like this. **3** like a honeycomb: *a honeycomb weave of cloth, a honeycomb pattern in knitting.* **4** pierce with many holes or tunnels: *The rock was honeycombed with underground passages.* 1, 2 *n.,* 3 *adj.,* 4 *v.*

hon·ey·dew (hun′ē dyü′ or hun′ē dü′) **1** a sweet substance that oozes from the leaves of certain plants in hot weather. **2** a kind of melon having sweet, green flesh and a smooth, whitish skin. *n.*

hon·ey·moon (hun′ē mün′) **1** the holiday spent together by a newly married couple. **2** spend or have a honeymoon. 1 *n.,* 2 *v.*

hon·ey·suck·le (hun′ē suk′əl) a climbing shrub with fragrant white, yellow, or red flowers. *n.*

honk (hongk) **1** the cry of a wild goose. **2** any similar sound: *the honk of an automobile horn.* **3** make or cause to make such a sound: *We honked as we drove past our friends' house.* 1, 2 *n.,* 3 *v.*

hon·or or **hon·our** (on′ər) **1** credit for acting well; glory, fame, or reputation; good name: *It was greatly to his honor that he refused the reward.* **2 honors,** *pl.* a special mention or grade given to a student for having done work much above the average. **3** a source of credit; a person or thing that reflects honor: *She is an honor to her family and school.* **4** a nice sense of what is right or proper; nobility of mind: *A man of honor always keeps his promises.* **5** great respect; high regard: *Our Queen is held in honor.* **6** an act that shows respect or high regard: *funeral honors, military honors.* **7** respect highly; think highly of. **8** show respect to: *We honor our country's dead soldiers on Remembrance Day.* **9 Honor,** a title of respect used in speaking to or of a judge, mayor, etc.: *'Yes, Your Honor.' Her Honor will make a short speech.* 1–6, 9 *n.,* 7, 8 *v.*

hon·or·a·ble or **hon·our·a·ble** (on′ər ə bəl) **1** having or showing a sense of what is right and proper; honest; upright: *It was not honorable for him to cheat.* **2** bringing or deserving honor or honors: *honorable wounds.* **3** accompanied by honor or honors: *an honorable burial, an honorable discharge.* **4** noble; worthy of honor: *an honorable name, to perform honorable deeds.* **5 Honorable,** Honourable. *adj.* **—hon′or·a·bly** or **hon′our·a·bly,** *adv.*

hon·or·ar·y (on′ər er′ē) **1** given or done as an honor: *an honorary membership.* **2** as an honor only; without pay or regular duties: *That association has an honorary secretary as well as a regular paid secretary who does the actual work. adj.*

hon·our (on′ər) See **honor.**

Hon·our·a·ble or **Hon·or·a·ble** (on′ər ə bəl) a title given to members of the Privy Council (which includes the Federal Cabinet), to the Speakers of the House of Commons and the provincial legislative assemblies, and to certain senior judges. *adj.*

☛ The spelling **Honourable,** rather than **Honorable,** is usually kept in Canada for the official title of Cabinet ministers, etc.

hood[1] (hůd) **1** a soft covering for the head and neck, either separate or as part of a cloak: *My raincoat has a hood.* **2** anything like a hood in shape or use. **3** a covering over the engine of an automobile. **4** cover with a hood. 1–3 *n.,* 4 *v.*

hood[2] (hůd) *Slang.* hoodlum. *n.*

-hood a suffix that means: **1** the state or condition of being ____: *Boyhood means the state or condition of being a boy. Likelihood means the state or condition of being likely.* **2** the character or nature of ____: *Manhood means the character or nature of a man.*

hood·lum (hüd′ləm) *Informal.* **1** a young rowdy; street ruffian: *He was a bit of a hoodlum when he was young.* **2** a criminal, especially one who uses force; gangster. *n.*

hoof (hüf or hůf) **1** a hard, horny covering on the feet of horses, cattle, sheep, pigs, and some other animals. **2** the whole foot of such animals. *n., pl.* **hoofs** or **hooves.**

on the hoof, alive; not killed and butchered.

hoofed (hüft or hůft) having hoofs. *adj.*

hook (hůk) **1** a piece of metal, wood, or other stiff material, curved or having a sharp angle for catching, holding, or fastening something or for hanging things on: *a fish hook, a clothes hook.* **2** catch or take hold of with a hook: *hook a fish.* **3** fasten with a hook or hooks: *Please hook the gate. Will you hook my dress for me?* **4** make something by using a hook: *Grandma used canvas and strips of cloth to hook the rug in my bedroom.* **5** anything curved or bent like a hook: *A reaping hook is a large, curved knife for cutting down grass or grain.* **6** a sharp bend: *a hook in a river.* 1, 5, 6 *n.,* 2–4 *v.*

by hook or by crook, in any way at all; by fair means or foul.

hook up, connect an electric light or appliance; arrange and connect the parts of a radio set, telephone, etc.

hook·worm (hůk′wėrm′) **1** a kind of worm that enters the body of a person or animal through the skin and fastens itself to the wall of the small intestine, causing a disease that makes the victim weak and drowsy. **2** the disease itself. *n.*

hook·y (hůk′ē) **play hooky,** *Informal.* stay away from school without permission; play truant. *n.*

hoop (hüp) **1** a ring or a flat band in the form of a circle: *a hoop for holding together the staves of a barrel.* **2** bind or fasten together with a hoop or hoops. **3** a large wooden, iron, or plastic circle used as a toy by children: *The boy rolled his hoop along the sidewalk.* **4** a circular frame used to hold out a woman's skirt. **5** in croquet, one of the metal arches through which players try to hit the balls. 1, 3–5 *n.,* 2 *v.*

hat, āge, fär; let, ēqual, tėrm; it, īce
hot, ōpen, ôrder; oil, out; cup, půt, rüle
əbove, takən, pencəl, lemən, circəs
ch, child; ng, long; sh, ship
th, thin; ᴛʜ, then; zh, measure

☛ **Hoop** and **whoop** are sometimes pronounced the same.

hoo·ray (hů rā′) hurrah. *interj., n., v.*

hoot (hüt) **1** the sound that an owl makes. **2** make this sound or one like it. **3** a shout to show disapproval or scorn. **4** make such a shout. **5** show disapproval of, or scorn for, by hooting: *The audience hooted the speaker's plan.* **6** force or drive by hooting: *They hooted the speaker off the platform.* **7** *Informal.* a tiny amount; a bit: *He doesn't give a hoot what happens.* 1, 3, 7 *n.,* 2, 4–6 *v.*

hooves (hüvz or hůvz) a plural of **hoof.** *n.*

hop[1] (hop) **1** spring, or move by springing, on one foot: *How far can you hop on your right foot?* **2** spring, or move by springing, with both or all feet at once: *Many birds hop.* **3** jump over: *to hop a ditch.* **4** a hopping; spring. 1–3 *v.,* **hopped, hop·ping;** 4 *n.*

hop off, get off or out of quickly or with a jump: *He hopped off the ladder.*

hop on, get on or into quickly or with a jump: *He hopped on the bus.*

hop[2] (hop) **1** a vine having flower clusters that look like small pine cones. **2 hops,** *pl.* the dried, ripe flower clusters of the hop vine, used to flavor beer and other malt drinks. *n.*

hope (hōp) **1** a feeling that what one desires will happen: *Her promise to help gave me hope that we could finish the job on time.* **2** wish and expect: *I hope to do well in school this year.* **3** something hoped for. **4** a cause of hope; a person or thing that others have hope in: *He is the hope of the family.* 1, 3, 4 *n.,* 2 *v.,* **hoped, hop·ing.**

hope·ful (hōp′fəl) **1** feeling or showing hope; expecting to receive what one wants: *a hopeful attitude.* **2** giving hope; likely to succeed. *adj.*

hope·less (hōp′lis) **1** feeling no hope: *He was disappointed so often that he became hopeless.* **2** giving no hope: *a hopeless illness. adj.*

hop·per (hop′ər) **1** a person or thing that hops such as a grasshopper or other hopping insect. **2** a container into which things are put before being fed or emptied into a machine, storage bin, etc.; the receiver in various machines: *Some cement mixers are equipped with hoppers. There is a hopper at the top of a coffee grinder. n.*

hop·scotch (hop′skoch′) a children's game in which the players hop over the lines of a figure drawn on the ground and pick up an object thrown or kicked into one of the numbered squares of the figure. *n.*

horde (hôrd) **1** a multitude; crowd; swarm: *hordes of grasshoppers.* **2** a wandering tribe or troop: *a horde of gypsies. n.*

☛ **Horde** and **hoard** are pronounced the same.

ho·ri·zon (hə rī′zən) **1** the line where the earth and sky seem to meet: *You cannot see beyond the horizon.* **2** the limit of one's thinking, experience, interest, or outlook. *n.*

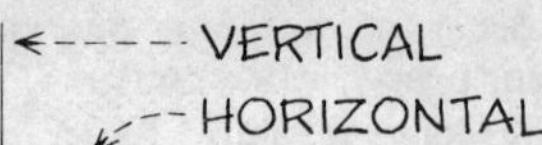

hor·i·zon·tal (hôr′ə zon′təl) 1 parallel to the horizon; at right angles to a vertical line. 2 flat; level. 3 something such as a line, direction, or position, that is horizontal: *Measure the length of the horizontal.* 1, 2 *adj.*, 3 *n.*

A powder horn A hunting horn

horn (hôrn) 1 a hard growth, usually curved and pointed, on the heads of cattle, sheep, goats, and some other animals. 2 anything that sticks up on the head of an animal: *a snail's horns, an insect's horns.* 3 the substance or material of horns or of something like horn: *A person's fingernails, the beaks of birds, the hoofs of horses, and tortoise shells are all made of horn.* 4 a container made by hollowing out a horn: *a drinking horn, a powder horn.* 5 a musical instrument shaped like a horn and formerly made of horn, sounded by blowing into the smaller end: *The brass section of an orchestra includes several kinds of horn.* See **French horn** for picture. 6 a device sounded as a warning signal: *an automobile horn. n.*
horn in, *Slang.* meddle or intrude: *He kept trying to horn in on our conversation.*

horned toad a small lizard having a broad, flat body, short tail, and many spines.

hor·net (hôr′nit) a large wasp that can give a very painful sting. *n.*

horn of plenty cornucopia (def. 2).

horn·y (hôr′nē) 1 made of horn or of a substance like it. 2 hard like horn: *The farmer's hands were horny from work. adj.,* **horn·i·er, horn·i·est.**

hor·ri·ble (hôr′ə bəl) 1 causing horror; frightful; shocking; terrible: *a horrible crime, a horrible disease.* 2 *Informal.* extremely unpleasant: *a horrible noise. adj.* —**hor′ri·bly,** *adv.*

hor·rid (hôr′id) 1 terrible; frightful. 2 *Informal.* very unpleasant: *a horrid little boy, a horrid day. adj.*

hor·ri·fy (hôr′ē fī′) 1 cause to feel horror. 2 shock very much: *We were horrified by the wreck. v.,* **hor·ri·fied, hor·ri·fy·ing.**

hor·ror (hôr′ər) 1 terror and disgust caused by something frightful or shocking. 2 a very strong dislike: *That little girl has a horror of snakes and spiders.* 3 something that causes great fear or disgust. *n.*

horse (hôrs) 1 a large four-legged animal with solid hoofs and a mane and tail of long, coarse hair: *Horses have been used from very early times for riding and carrying and pulling loads.* 2 soldiers on horses; cavalry: *a troop of horse.* 3 a supporting frame with legs; a trestle: *Five boards laid on two horses made our picnic table. n.*

Horses: a draft horse and a racing horse

horse around, *Slang.* fool around; get into mischief.
the horse's mouth, the original source; the person who knows: *news straight from the horse's mouth.*
☛ **Horse** and **hoarse** are pronounced the same.

horse·back (hôrs′bak′) 1 the back of a horse. 2 on the back of a horse: *to ride horseback.* 1 *n.*, 2 *adv.*

horse chestnut 1 a shade tree with spreading branches, large leaves, clusters of showy, white flowers, and glossy, brown nuts. 2 its nut: *Horse chestnuts are not good to eat. n.*

horse·fly (hôrs′flī′) a large fly that bites animals, especially horses. *n., pl.* **horse·flies.**

horse·hair (hôrs′her′) the hair from the mane or tail of a horse: *a horsehair sofa. n.*

horse·man (hôrs′mən) 1 a man who rides on horseback. 2 a man who is skilled in riding or managing horses. *n., pl.* **horse·men** (hôrs′mən).

horse·man·ship (hôrs′mən ship′) skill in riding or managing horses. *n.*

horse·play (hôrs′plā′) rough, boisterous fun. *n.*

horse·pow·er (hôrs′pou′ər) a unit of power equal to 746 watts, used for measuring the power of engines, motors, etc.: *One horsepower is about three-quarters of a kilowatt; therefore, a 40* hp *outboard motor would be about equal to a 30* kW *outboard motor. Symbol:* hp *n.*

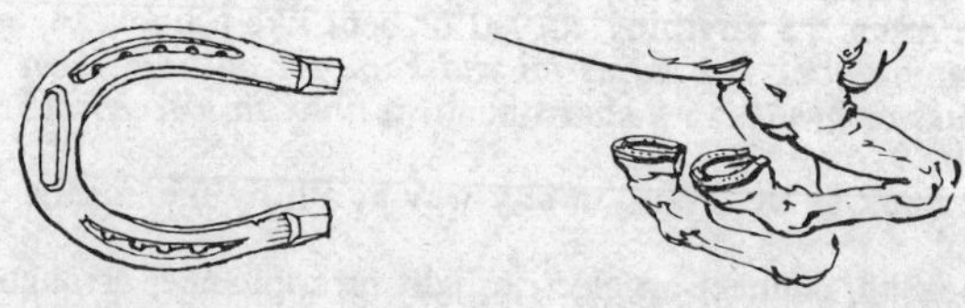

Horseshoes

horse·shoe (hôrs′shü′) 1 a U-shaped metal plate nailed to a horse's hoof to protect it. 2 anything shaped like a horseshoe: *a horseshoe of flowers.* 3 **horseshoes,** *pl.* a game in which the players try to throw horseshoes over or near a stake 40 feet (about 12 metres) away. *n.*
☛ **Horseshoes** (def. 3) is plural in form and singular in use: *Horseshoes is played outdoors.*

horse·wom·an (hôrs′wům′ən) 1 a woman who rides on horseback. 2 a woman skilled in riding or managing horses. *n., pl.* **horse·wom·en** (hôrs′wim′ən).

hose (hōz) 1 stockings. 2 a tube of rubber or something else that will bend, for carrying any liquid for short distances: *A hose is used in pumping gasoline into automobiles.* See **nozzle** for picture. 3 put water on

hat, āge, fär; let, ēqual, tėrm; it, īce
hot, ōpen, ôrder; oil, out; cup, pu̇t, rüle
əbove, takən, pencəl, lemən, circəs
ch, child; ng, long; sh, ship
th, thin; ᴛʜ, then; zh, measure

with a hose. 1 *n. pl.*, 2 *n., pl.* **hos·es,** 3 *v.*, **hosed, hos·ing.**

ho·sier·y (hō′zhər ē) hose; stockings. *n.*

hos·pi·ta·ble (hos′pi tə bəl or hos pit′ə bəl) **1** giving or liking to give a welcome, food and shelter, and friendly treatment to guests or strangers: *a hospitable family, a hospitable reception.* **2** willing and ready to consider; receptive: *a person hospitable to new ideas.* *adj.* **—hos′pi·ta·bly,** *adv.*

☛ See note at **hospital.**

hos·pi·tal (hos′pi təl) a place for the care of the sick or injured. *n.*

☛ **Hospital, hospitable, hospitality,** and **hostel** all came into English through Old French from forms of the Latin word *hospes,* meaning 'guest' or 'host.' **Hotel** came into English much later from a modern French development of the Old French word *hostel.* **Hostel** and **hotel** are, therefore, different forms of the same Old French word.

hos·pi·tal·i·ty (hos′pə tal′ə tē) friendly reception; generous treatment of guests or strangers: *He was renowned for his hospitality.* *n., pl.* **hos·pi·tal·i·ties.**

☛ See note at **hospital.**

hoss (hos) *Informal.* horse. *n.*

host¹ (hōst) **1** a person who receives another person at his house as his guest. **2** the keeper of an inn or hotel. **3** to act as host. 1, 2 *n.*, 3 *v.*

host² (hōst) a large number: *A host of stars glittered in the sky.* *n.*

hos·tage (hos′tij) a person given up to another or held by an enemy as a pledge: *They said the hostage would be kept safe and would be returned when their enemies' promises had been carried out.* *n.*

hos·tel (hos′təl) **1** a lodging place, especially a supervised lodging place for young travellers. **2** an inn; hotel. *n.*

☛ See note at **hospital.**

host·ess (hōs′tis) **1** a woman who receives another person as her guest. **2** a woman who greets customers in a restaurant and, usually, shows them to a table. *n.*

hos·tile (hos′tīl or hos′təl) **1** of an enemy or enemies: *the hostile army.* **2** opposed; unfriendly; unfavorable: *a hostile look.* *adj.*

hos·til·i·ty (hos til′ə tē) **1** the feeling that an enemy has; being an enemy; unfriendliness: *He showed signs of hostility toward our plan.* **2** the state of being at war. **3 hostilities,** *pl.* acts of war; warfare; fighting. *n., pl.* **hos·til·i·ties.**

hos·tler (os′lər or hos′lər) a person who takes care of horses at an inn or stable. *n.*

hot (hot) **1** having much heat; very warm: *That fire is hot. The sun is hot today. The long race made the runners hot.* **2** having a sharp, burning taste: *Pepper and mustard are hot.* **3** fiery: *a hot temper, hot with rage.* **4** with much heat: *The sun beats hot upon the sand.* **5** full of great interest or enthusiasm; very eager: *The boys were hot after the treasure.* **6** new; fresh: *a hot scent, a hot trail.* **7** following closely: *The sheriff was hot on the heels of the bandits.* **8** in games, very near or approaching what one is searching for. 1–3, 5–8 *adj.*, **hot·ter, hot·test;** 4 *adv.* **—hot′ly,** *adv.*

hot·bed (hot′bed′) **1** a bed of earth surrounded by a low frame and covered with glass or plastic to protect new plants so that they can begin growing early in spring: *Mother starts her tomatoes in a hotbed every year.* **2** any place where something is encouraged to grow and develop rapidly: *These slums are a hotbed of crime.* *n.*

hot cake a flapjack or pancake.
go or **sell like hot cakes,** be sold quickly: *The candy we made for the fall fair sold like hot cakes.*

hot dog **1** a sandwich made of a hot wiener enclosed in a long bun and usually served with mustard, relish, etc. **2** wiener.

ho·tel (hō tel′) **1** a place where rooms and meals are supplied to the public, especially to travellers, for pay. **2** *Cdn. Informal.* a place where beer and wine are sold for drinking on the premises; beer parlor. *n.*

☛ See note at **hospital.**

hot·house (hot′hous′) a building with a glass roof and sides kept warm for growing plants; greenhouse. *n.*

hot rod *Slang.* an automobile with a motor that has been rebuilt to give it extra speed and power.

hot water *Informal.* trouble: *I'll be in hot water with my parents if I don't get home soon.*

hound (hound) **1** a dog of any of various breeds, most of which hunt by scent and have large, drooping ears and short hair. **2** any dog. **3** keep on chasing or driving: *The police hounded the thief until they caught him.* **4** urge on continually or repeatedly; keep urging or pestering: *She hounded me until I finally gave her the book.* 1, 2 *n.*, 3, 4 *v.*

hour (our) **1** sixty minutes: *Twenty-four hours make a day.* *Symbol:* h **2** one of the 12 points that measure time from noon to midnight and from midnight to noon: *Some clocks strike the hours and the half hours.* **3** the time of day: *The hour is 7.30.* **4** a particular or fixed time: *Our breakfast hour is seven o'clock.* **5 hours,** *pl.* the time for work, study, etc.: *Our school hours are 9 to 12 and 1 to 4.* *n.*

☛ **Hour** and **our** are pronounced the same.

An hourglass

hour·glass (our′glas′) a device for measuring time, requiring just an hour for its contents, usually sand, to go from a glass bulb or container on top to one on the bottom. *n.*

hour·ly (our′lē) **1** every hour: *Give two doses of the medicine hourly.* **2** done, happening, or counted every hour: *There are hourly reports of the news on this radio station. His hourly wage is now $3.90.* 1 *adv.*, 2 *adj.*

house (hous for 1–3, 5–8, houz for 4) **1** a building in which people live. **2** a building for any purpose: *a hen house, an engine house.* **3** a family, especially a noble

family: *He was a prince of the house of David.* 4 take or put into a house; put under cover: *Where can we house all these children? The campers housed their provisions in a shack.* 5 a business firm. 6 an assembly for making laws: *In Canada, the House of Commons is the Lower House; the Senate is the Upper House.* 7 an audience; attendance: *The singer sang to a large house.* 8 in curling, the goal or target. 1–3, 5–8 *n., pl.* **hous·es** (hou′ziz); 4 *v.,* **housed, hous·ing.**
on the house, paid for by the owner of the business; free: *After visiting the candy factory, we were each given a box of chocolates on the house.*
☞ See note at **home.**

house·boat (hous′bōt′) a boat that can be used as a place to live in. *n.*

house·bro·ken (hous′brō′kən) of a pet, such as a cat, dog, etc., trained to live cleanly indoors. *adj.*

house·fly (hous′flī′) a fly that lives around and in houses, feeding on food and garbage. *n., pl.* **house·flies.**

house·hold (hous′hōld′) 1 all the people living in a house; family; a family and servants. 2 of a household; having to do with a household; domestic: *household expenses, household cares.* 1 *n.,* 2 *adj.*

house·keep·er (hous′kēp′ər) 1 a person, usually a woman, who manages a home and its affairs and does the housework. 2 a woman who is hired to direct the servants that do the housework in a home, hotel, etc. *n.*

house·keep·ing (hous′kēp′ing) the management of a home and its affairs; doing the housework. *n.*

House of Assembly in Newfoundland, the provincial legislature.

House of Commons 1 in Canada, the body of elected representatives who meet in Ottawa to make laws and debate questions of government: *There are 264 members of the House of Commons.* 2 the chamber in which the representatives, or members, meet.

house·top (hous′top′) the top of a house; the roof. *n.*

house·wife (hous′wīf′) a woman who manages a home and its affairs for her family. *n.*

house·work (hous′wėrk′) the work to be done in housekeeping, such as washing, ironing, cleaning, and cooking. *n.*

hous·ing (hou′zing) 1 sheltering; providing houses as homes. 2 houses; dwellings: *That city does not have enough housing.* 3 a frame or plate for holding together and protecting the parts of a machine. *n.*

hove (hōv) See **heave.** *The sailors hove at the ropes.* *v.*

hov·el (hov′əl or huv′əl) a house that is small, crude, and unpleasant to live in. *n.*

hov·er (hov′ər or huv′ər) 1 stay in or near one place in the air: *The hummingbird hovered in front of the flower.* 2 stay in or near one place; wait nearby: *The dogs hovered around the kitchen door at mealtime.* 3 be in an uncertain condition; waver: *The sick man hovered between life and death.* *v.*

how (hou) 1 in what way; by what means: *I wonder how you go there? How can it be done? Tell me how it happened.* 2 to what degree or amount: *How tall are you? How hot is it? How much shall I bring you? How long will it take you to do this?* 3 in what state or condition: *How is your health? Tell me how she is. How do I look?* 4 for what reason; why: *How is it you are late?* *adv.*
☞ **How come** is an informal shortening of 'How does it come that ...' or 'How did it come that ...': *How come you didn't call me last night?*

how·ev·er (hou ev′ər) 1 nevertheless; yet; in spite of that: *We were very late for dinner; however, there was plenty left for us.* 2 to whatever extent, degree, or amount; no matter how: *I'll come however busy I am.* 3 in whatever way; by whatever means: *However did you get so dirty?* 1 *conj.,* 2, 3 *adv.*

howl (houl) 1 give a long, loud, mournful cry: *Our dog sometimes howls at night. The winter winds howled around our cabin.* 2 a long, loud, mournful cry: *the howl of a wolf.* 3 give a long, loud cry of pain, rage, distress, etc. 4 a loud cry of pain, rage, etc. 5 yell; shout: *It was so funny that we howled with laughter.* 6 a yell or shout: *We heard howls of laughter.* 7 *Informal.* something causing laughter: *The skit by the teachers was a howl.* 8 force or drive by howling: *The angry mob howled the speaker off the platform.* 1, 3, 5, 8 *v.,* 2, 4, 6, 7 *n.*

hr. hour; hours.

H.R.H. 1 Her Royal Highness. 2 His Royal Highness.

hrs. hours.

hub (hub) 1 the central part of a wheel. See **wheel** for picture. 2 a centre of interest, importance, activity, etc.: *London is the hub of the Commonwealth.* *n.*

hub·bub (hub′ub) a loud, confused noise; an uproar: *There was a hubbub when the crowd was told to move.* *n.*

huck·le·ber·ry (huk′əl ber′ē) 1 a small berry similar to a blueberry, but having 10 hard seeds. 2 the shrub it grows on. *n., pl.* **huck·le·ber·ries.**

hud·dle (hud′əl) 1 crowd close: *The sheep huddled in a corner of the pen.* 2 crowd or put close together: *She huddled all four boys into one bed.* 3 curl oneself up: *The cat huddled on the cushion. The rescued swimmer sat huddled in a blanket by the fire.* 4 a confused heap or mass of people or things crowded together: *Her books and papers were in a huddle in the corner of the room.* 5 in football, a grouping of players behind the line of scrimmage to receive signals, plan the next play, etc. 6 form such a group. 7 *Informal.* a secret conference. 1–3, 6 *v.,* **hud·dled, hud·dling;** 4, 5, 7 *n.*
go into a huddle, *Informal.* talk things over secretly: *After the meeting, the lawyer went into a huddle with his partner.*

Hudson's Bay Company a British trading company founded in 1670 to carry on the fur trade with the Indians of North America: *The Hudson's Bay Company has played a great part in the exploration and development of Canada's Northwest.*
☞ **Hudson's Bay Company** is the popular and traditional name of The Company of Adventurers of England Trading into Hudson's Bay.

hue (hyü) a color, shade, or tint: *The girls' dresses showed almost all the hues of the rainbow.* *n.*
☞ **Hue** and **hew** are pronounced the same.

huff (huf) a fit of anger or peevishness: *He walked out in a huff when he was told his dog wasn't allowed in the store.* *n.*

huff·y (huf′ē) 1 offended: *She's still huffy because of the argument you had.* 2 tending to be easily offended; touchy. *adj.,* **huff·i·er, huff·i·est.**

hug (hug) 1 put the arms around and hold close; embrace: *The girl hugs her big doll.* 2 a tight clasp with the arms; an embrace: *Give Mother a hug.* 3 cling firmly or fondly to: *They still hug their belief in his story.* 4 keep close to: *The boat hugged the shore.* 1, 3, 4 *v.,* **hugged, hug·ging;** 2 *n.*

huge (hyüj) extremely large or great: *a huge sum of money. A whale or an elephant is a huge animal. adj.,* **hug·er, hug·est. —huge′ly,** *adv.*

huh (hu) a sound made to express surprise, contempt, or to ask a question. *interj.*

hu·la (hü′lə) 1 a native Hawaiian dance that tells a story through movement, especially movement of the hands. 2 the music for such a dance. *n.*

hulk (hulk) 1 the body of an old or worn-out ship. 2 a big, clumsy ship. 3 a big, clumsy person or thing. *n.*

☛ **Hulk** developed from an Old English word *hulc,* meaning 'ship.'

hulk·ing (hul′king) big and clumsy. *adj.*

hull (hul) 1 the body or frame of a ship: *Masts, sails, and rigging are not part of the hull.* 2 the main body or frame of a seaplane, airship, etc. 3 the outer covering of a seed. 4 a calyx of some fruits: *We call the green leaves at the stem of a strawberry its hull.* 5 remove the hull or hulls from. 1–4 *n.,* 5 *v.*

hul·la·ba·loo (hul′ə bə lü′) a loud noise or disturbance; uproar. *n.*

hum (hum) 1 make a continuous murmuring sound like that of a bee or of a spinning top: *The sewing machine hums busily. The downtown streets hum all day.* 2 a continuous murmuring sound: *the hum of bees, the hum of the city streets.* 3 sing with closed lips, not sounding words: *She was humming a tune.* 4 put or bring by humming: *The mother hummed her baby to sleep.* 5 *Informal.* be busy and active: *The new president made things hum.* 1, 3–5 *v.,* **hummed, hum·ming;** 2 *n.*

hu·man (hyü′mən) 1 of or belonging to mankind; that people have: *Selfishness is a human weakness. The history of Canada has great human interest.* 2 being a person or persons; having the form or qualities of people: *Men, women, and children are human beings. Those monkeys look almost human.* 3 a human being; person. 1, 2 *adj.,* 3 *n.* **—hu′man·ly,** *adv.*

human being a man, woman, or child; any person: *Human beings are the only animals able to reason.*

hu·mane (hyü mān′) kind; not cruel or brutal: *We believe in the humane treatment of prisoners. adj.* **—hu·mane′ly,** *adv.*

hu·man·i·ty (hyü man′ə tē) 1 people; mankind: *All humanity will be helped by advances in medical sciences.* 2 the nature of man: *Humanity is a mixture of good and bad qualities.* 3 humane treatment; kindness: *Treat animals with humanity. n., pl.* **hu·man·i·ties.**

hum·ble (hum′bəl) 1 low in position or condition; not important or grand: *He has a humble position at the factory. They live in a humble two-room cottage.* 2 modest; not proud: *a humble opinion. Defeat and failure make people humble.* 3 make humble; make lower in position, condition, or pride. 1, 2 *adj.,*

hat, āge, fär; let, ēqual, tėrm; it, īce
hot, ōpen, ôrder; oil, out; cup, pu̇t, rüle
əbove, takən, pencəl, lemən, circəs
ch, child; ng, long; sh, ship
th, thin; ᴛʜ, then; zh, measure

hum·bler, hum·blest; 3 *v.,* **hum·bled, hum·bling. —hum′ble·ness,** *n.* **—hum′bly,** *adv.*

hum·bug (hum′bug′) 1 a person who pretends to be what he is not; a cheat; sham. 2 cheat; deceive with a sham. 3 nonsense; foolishness: *Dad says our argument is humbug.* 4 a hard candy, usually brown with light stripes. 1, 3, 4 *n.,* 2 *v.*

hum·drum (hum′drum′) without variety; commonplace; dull: *a humdrum movie. adj.*

hu·mid (hyü′mid) moist; damp: *The air is very humid near the sea. adj.*

hu·mid·i·fy (hyü mid′ə fī′) make moist or damp: *This air conditioner will also humidify the air. v.,* **hu·mid·i·fied, hu·mid·i·fy·ing. —hu·mid′i·fi′er,** *n.*

hu·mid·i·ty (hyü mid′ə tē) 1 moistness; dampness: *The humidity today is worse than the heat.* 2 the amount of moisture in the air: *The humidity is high today. n.*

hu·mil·i·ate (hyü mil′ē āt′) lower the pride, dignity, or self-respect of; make ashamed: *We felt humiliated by our failure. The boys humiliated their parents by behaving badly in front of the guests. v.,* **hu·mil·i·at·ed, hu·mil·i·at·ing.**

hu·mil·i·a·tion (hyü mil′ē ā′shən) a lowering of pride, dignity, or self-respect; making or being made ashamed. *n.*

hu·mil·i·ty (hyü mil′ə tē) humbleness of mind; lack of pride; meekness. *n.*

Ruby-throated hummingbirds — about 10 cm long with the tail

hum·ming·bird (hum′ing bėrd′) a very small, brightly colored North American bird with a long, narrow bill and narrow wings that move so rapidly they make a humming sound. *n.*

hum·mock (hum′ək) 1 a very small, rounded hill. 2 a bump or ridge in a field of ice. *n.*

hu·mor or **hu·mour** (hyü′mər) 1 a funny or amusing quality: *The speech was full of humor and so made everybody laugh.* 2 the ability to see or show the funny or amusing side of things: *Stephen Leacock was famous for his humor.* 3 a state of mind; a mood or temper: *Is the teacher in a good humor this morning? I feel in the humor for working.* 4 give in to the fancies and whims of a person; agree with: *Sick children often have to be humored.* 1–3 *n.,* 4 *v.*

out of humor or **humour,** angry; cross; in a bad mood.
sense of humor or **humour,** the ability to see the amusing side of things.

hu·mor·ist (hyü′mər ist) a humorous talker or writer; a person who tells or writes jokes and funny stories. *n.*

hu·mor·ous (hyü′mər əs) full of humor; funny; amusing: *a humorous story. adj.*

hu·mour (hyü′mər) See **humor.**

hump (hump) **1** a rounded lump that sticks out: *Some camels have two humps on their backs.* **2** raise or bend up into a hump: *The cat humped its back when it saw the dog.* 1 *n.,* 2 *v.*
over the hump, past a difficult time or test.

hump·back (hump′bak′) **1** hunchback. **2** a large whale that has a humplike fin on its back. **3** a kind of Pacific salmon. *n.*

hump·backed (hump′bakt′) hunchbacked. *adj.*

hu·mus (hyü′məs) a dark-brown or black part of soil formed from dead leaves and other vegetable matter: *Humus contains valuable plant foods. n.*

hunch (hunch) **1** a hump. **2** draw, bend, or form into a hump: *He sat hunched up with his chin on his knees.* **3** move, push, or shove by jerks. **4** *Informal.* a feeling or suspicion that cannot be explained: *I had a hunch we would win the game.* 1, 4 *n.,* 2, 3 *v.*

hunch·back (hunch′bak′) **1** a person with a crooked back that forms a hump at the level of the shoulders. **2** a crooked back that has a hump at the shoulders. *n.*

hunch·backed (hunch′bakt′) having a hunchback. *adj.*

hun·dred (hun′drəd) ten times ten; 100: *There are one hundred cents in a dollar. n., adj.*

hun·dred·fold (hun′drəd fōld′) a hundred times as much or as many. *adj., adv., n.*

hun·dredth (hun′drədth) **1** next after the 99th; last in a series of 100; 100th. **2** one of 100 equal parts. *adj., n.*

hung (hung) See **hang.** *He hung up his cap. Your dress has hung here all day. v.*

Hun·gar·i·an (hung ger′ē ən) **1** of or having to do with Hungary, a country in central Europe. **2** a person born in or living in Hungary. **3** the language of Hungary. 1 *adj.,* 2, 3 *n.*

hun·ger (hung′gər) **1** an uncomfortable or painful feeling or a weak condition caused by lack of food: *After being two days without food, the caged lion roared with hunger.* **2** a desire or need for food: *The little boy who ran away from home soon felt hunger.* **3** feel hunger; be hungry. **4** strong desire; longing: *a hunger for books.* **5** have a strong desire: *The lonely girl hungered for friends.* 1, 2, 4 *n.,* 3, 5 *v.*

hun·gry (hung′grē) **1** feeling a desire or need for food: *Mother says the boys in our family always seem to be hungry.* **2** showing hunger: *The cook saw a hungry look on the beggar's face.* **3** having a strong desire; eager: *hungry for knowledge. adj.,* **hun·gri·er, hun·gri·est.** **—hun′gri·ly,** *adv.*

hunk (hungk) *Informal.* a big lump, piece, or slice: *a hunk of cheese. n.*

hunt (hunt) **1** go after game and other wild animals to catch or kill them for food or sport. **2** the act of hunting: *Our gear for the duck hunt is all ready.* **3** search; seek; look: *to hunt for a lost book.* **4** a search; an attempt to find something. 1, 3 *v.,* 2, 4 *n.*
hunt out, seek and find.

hunt·er (hun′tər) **1** a person who hunts. **2** a horse or dog trained for hunting. *n.*

hunt·ress (hun′tris) a woman who hunts: *The Roman goddess Diana was a huntress. n.*

hunts·man (hunts′mən) hunter. *n., pl.* **hunts·men** (hunts′mən).

Hurdles for racing

hur·dle (hėr′dəl) **1** in a race, a barrier for people or horses to jump over. **2 hurdles,** *pl.* a race in which the runners jump over hurdles. **3** jump over: *The horse hurdled both the fence and the ditch.* **4** an obstacle or difficulty. **5** overcome an obstacle or difficulty. **6** a frame made of sticks and used as a temporary fence. 1, 2, 4, 6 *n.,* 3, 5 *v.,* **hur·dled, hur·dling.**

hurl (hėrl) **1** throw with much force: *The man hurled his spear at one bear, and the dogs hurled themselves at the other.* **2** speak with strong feeling; utter violently: *He hurled insults at me. v.*

hur·rah (hə rä′) **1** a shout of joy, approval, etc.: *'Hurrah!' they shouted as the team scored again (interj.). Give a hurrah for the hero! (n.).* **2** shout hurrahs; cheer: *They hurrahed when they saw the soldiers go by.* 1 *interj., n.,* 2 *v.*

hur·ray (hə rā′) hurrah. *interj., n., v.*

hur·ri·cane (hėr′ə kān′) **1** a storm with a violent wind and, usually, very heavy rain: *The wind in a hurricane blows over 120 kilometres per hour. Hurricanes are common in the tropics.* **2** a sudden, violent outburst: *a hurricane of cheers. n.*

hur·ried (hėr′ēd) done or made in a hurry; hasty: *a hurried reply. The burglar made a hurried departure before the police arrived. adj.* **—hur′ried·ly,** *adv.*

hur·ry (hėr′ē) **1** drive, carry, send, or move quickly: *They hurried the sick child to the doctor.* **2** move or act with more than an easy or natural speed: *If you hurry, your work may be poor. He hurried to get the doctor.* **3** a hurried movement or action: *In her hurry she dropped the eggs.* **4** an eagerness to have quickly or do quickly: *She was in a hurry to see her father.* **5** urge to act or move quickly; hasten; urge to great speed: *Don't hurry the driver.* **6** hasten; make go on or occur more quickly: *Please hurry dinner.* 1, 2, 5, 6 *v.,* **hur·ried, hur·ry·ing;** 3, 4 *n., pl.* **hur·ries.**

hurt (hėrt) **1** cause pain to; wound; injure: *The stone hurt his foot badly.* **2** a cut, bruise, or fracture; any wound or injury. **3** suffer pain; be the source of pain: *My hand hurts.* **4** have a bad effect on; do damage or harm to: *Will it hurt this hat if it gets wet?* **5** a bad effect; harm, damage or injury: *His failure was a great*

hat, āge, fär; let, ēqual, tėrm; it, īce
hot, ōpen, ôrder; oil, out; cup, pu̇t, rüle
əbove, takən, pencəl, lemən, circəs
ch, child; ng, long; sh, ship
th, thin; ᴛʜ, then; zh, measure

hurt to his pride. *It would do no hurt to get the house painted this summer.* 1, 3, 4 *v.,* **hurt, hurt·ing;** 2, 5 *n.*

hurt·ful (hėrt′fəl) causing pain, harm, or damage: *a mean and hurtful remark. adj.*

hur·tle (hėr′təl) dash or drive violently; rush violently: *The train hurtled past. The driver was hurtled against the windshield when the car crashed. v.,* **hur·tled, hur·tling.**

hus·band (huz′bənd) **1** a married man, especially when thought of in connection with his wife. **2** manage carefully; be saving of: *A sick man must husband his strength.* 1 *n.,* 2 *v.*

☛ **Husband** developed from Old English *hūsbonda,* which came from an Old Norse word *húsbóndi,* meaning 'master of a house,' made up of *hús,* meaning 'house,' and *bóndi,* meaning 'residing, having a household.'

hus·band·man (huz′bənd mən) farmer. *n., pl.* **hus·band·men** (huz′bənd mən).

hus·band·ry (huz′bənd rē) **1** farming. **2** the management of one's affairs: *To let a roof leak would be bad husbandry.* **3** careful management; thrift. *n.*

hush (hush) **1** stop making a noise; make or become silent or quiet: *The wind has hushed. Hush your dog.* **2** a stopping of noise; silence; quiet; stillness. 1 *v.,* 2 *n.*

husk (husk) **1** the dry outer covering of certain seeds or fruits: *An ear of corn has a husk.* **2** the dry or worthless outer covering of anything. **3** remove the husk from: *Husk the corn.* 1, 2 *n.,* 3 *v.*

husk·y[1] (hus′kē) **1** dry in the throat; hoarse; rough of voice: *A cold sometimes causes a husky cough.* **2** of, like, or having husks: *a husky covering.* **3** big and strong: *a husky young man. adj.,* **husk·i·er, husk·i·est. —husk′i·ness,** *n.*

husk·y[2] or **Husk·y** (hus′kē) **1** a strong dog, used in the North for pulling sleds. **2** Eskimo dog. *n., pl.* **husk·ies** or **Husk·ies.**

☛ **Husky**[2] comes from an early form of the word *Eskimo.*

hus·tle (hus′əl) **1** hurry: *Mother hustled the boys to bed.* **2** push or shove roughly: *hustle along through the crowd. The other boys hustled him along the street.* **3** *Informal.* go or work quickly or with energy: *He had to hustle to earn enough money to support his family.* **4** a hustling: *It was done with much hustle and bustle. It was a hustle to get the dishes washed by seven o'clock.* 1–3 *v.,* **hus·tled, hus·tling;** 4 *n.* **—hus′tler,** *n.*

hut (hut) a small, roughly made house; a small cabin: *The boys built a hut in the woods. n.*

hutch (huch) **1** a pen for rabbits, etc. **2** a box; chest; bin. **3** a cupboard, open or with glass doors, having shelves for dishes, etc. and set on a buffet. **4** a high cupboard with usually open shelves on the upper part; china cabinet. *n.*

Hut·ter·ite (hut′ ər īt′) **1** a member of a religious group that came originally from Austria, now living mainly in Alberta and Manitoba: *Hutterites live in agricultural communities and keep to their own customs and traditions.* **2** of or having to do with this group. 1 *n.,* 2 *adj.*

hy·a·cinth (hī′ə sinth′) a spring plant that grows from a bulb and has a spike of small, fragrant, bell-shaped flowers. See the picture. *n.*

hy·brid (hī′brid) **1** the offspring of two animals or plants of different species, varieties, etc.: *Most garden roses are hybrids.* **2** anything of mixed origin: *A word formed of parts from different languages is a hybrid.* **3** bred from two different species, varieties, etc.: *A mule is a hybrid animal.* 1, 2 *n.,* 3 *adj.*

Hyacinths

A hydrant

hy·drant (hī′drənt) a large, upright pipe with a valve for drawing water directly from a water main; hose connection on a street, road, etc.: *Hydrants are used to get water to put out fires and to wash the streets. n.*

☛ Words beginning with *hydro-* or *hydr-,* all of which have something to do with water, came originally from a form of the Greek word *hudōr,* meaning 'water,' combined with another word or a suffix.

hy·drau·lic (hī dro′lik or hī drô′lik) **1** having to do with water or other liquids in motion. **2** operated by the pressure of water or other liquid: *a hydraulic press, hydraulic brakes. adj.*

☛ See note at **hydrant.**

hy·dro (hī′drō) **1** hydro-electric power: *Niagara Falls provides hydro for many factories.* **2** electricity: *The hydro was off for two hours during the storm. n.*

hy·dro–e·lec·tric (hī′drō i lek′trik) developing electricity from water power: *There is a large hydro-electric power plant on the St. Lawrence Seaway. adj.*

☛ See note at **hydrant.**

hy·dro·foil (hī′drə foil′) **1** one of a set of blades or fins attached to the hull of a boat at an angle so that the boat, when moving, is lifted just clear of the water: *Hydrofoils reduce friction and thus increase speed.* **2** a boat equipped with hydrofoils. *n.*

☛ See note at **hydrant.**

hy·dro·gen (hī′drə jən) a colorless, odorless gas that burns easily: *Hydrogen, which weighs less than any other known element, combines with oxygen to form water. n.*

☛ See note at **hydrant.**

hydrogen bomb a bomb that uses the fusion of atoms to cause an explosion of tremendous force: *A hydrogen bomb, which is many times more powerful than an atomic bomb, is also called an H-bomb.*

hy·dro·pho·bi·a (hī′drə fō′bē ə) the disease of rabies, especially in human beings: *Rabies in people is called hydrophobia because one of the symptoms is a dislike and fear of water and other liquids. n.*

☛ See note at **hydrant.**

hy·dro·plane (hī′drə plān′) **1** a motorboat that glides on the surface of water. **2** an aircraft that can take off from and land on water; seaplane. See **seaplane** for picture. *n.*

☛ See note at **hydrant.**

A spotted hyena — about 90 cm high at the shoulder

hy·e·na (hī ē′nə) a wild, wolflike animal of Africa and Asia: *Hyenas, which avoid contact with other animals, are noted for their terrifying yells. n.*

hy·giene (hī′jēn) the rules of health; the science of keeping well. *n.*

hy·ing (hī′ing) See **hie.** *v.*

hymn (him) **1** a song in praise or honor of God. **2** any song of praise. *n.*

☛ **Hymn** and **him** are pronounced the same.

hym·nal (him′nəl) a book of hymns. *n.*

hy·phen (hī′fən) a mark (-) used to join the parts of a compound word, or the parts of a word divided at the end of a line of printing or writing. *n.*

hy·phen·ate (hī′fən āt′) join by a hyphen; write or print with a hyphen. *v.,* **hy·phen·at·ed, hy·phen·at·ing.**

hyp·no·tism (hip′nə tiz′əm) putting into a sleeplike state; hypnotizing. *n.*

hyp·no·tist (hip′nə tist′) a person skilled in hypnotizing. *n.*

hyp·no·tize (hip′nə tīz′) put into a state somewhat like sleep, but more active, in which a person has little will of his own and little feeling. A hypnotized person acts out the suggestions of the person who has hypnotized him. *v.,* **hyp·no·tized, hyp·no·tiz·ing.**

hy·poc·ri·sy (hi pok′rə sē) pretending to be what one is not; pretence, especially of goodness or religion. *n., pl.* **hy·poc·ri·sies.**

hyp·o·crite (hip′ə krit′) a person who pretends to be what he is not, especially one who puts on an appearance of goodness or religion; pretender. *n.*

hys·te·ri·a (his tēr′ē ə or his ter′ē ə) **1** a nervous disorder that causes fits of laughing and crying, imaginary or real illnesses, lack of self-control, etc. **2** senseless excitement. *n.*

hys·ter·i·cal (his ter′ə kəl) **1** unnaturally excited. **2** showing extreme lack of control; unable to stop laughing or crying; suffering from hysteria: *hysterical with grief. adj.* —**hys·ter′i·cal·ly,** *adv.*

hat, āge, fär; let, ēqual, tėrm; it, īce
hot, ōpen, ôrder; oil, out; cup, pu̇t, rüle
əbove, takən, pencəl, lemən, circəs
ch, child; ng, long; sh, ship
th, thin; ᴛʜ, then; zh, measure

i or **I** (ī) **1** the ninth letter of the alphabet: *There are two* i's *in* Indian. **2** **I,** the Roman numeral for 1. *n., pl.* **i's** or **I's.**

I (ī) the person who is speaking or writing: *John said, 'I am ten years old.' I like my dog, and he likes me. pron., pl.* **we.**

☛ **I, aye**², and **eye** are pronounced the same.

–ian a form of the suffix **-an** used in certain words, such as **Canadian.**

ice (īs) **1** water made solid by cold; frozen water. **2** of or having to do with ice. **3** make cool with ice; put ice in or around: *an iced drink.* **4** a frozen dessert, usually one made of sweetened fruit juice. **5** cover with icing. **6** a frozen surface for skating, hockey, curling, etc. **7** in hockey, shoot a puck from one end of the rink to the other: *When a puck is iced by a team, it is taken back to that team's end and faced off.* **8** put a hockey team into play: *Our town iced a good hockey team.* **9** **the ice,** especially in Newfoundland, the edge of the Arctic ice fields, where seal-hunting takes place. 1, 4, 6, 9 *n.,* 2 *adj.,* 3, 5, 7, 8 *v.,* **iced, ic·ing.**

ice age **1** any of the times when much of the earth was covered with glaciers. **2** Often, **Ice Age,** the most recent such time, when much of the northern hemisphere was covered with glaciers.

ice·berg (īs'bėrg') a large mass of ice floating in the sea: *About 90 per cent of an iceberg is below the surface of the water. n.*

☛ **Iceberg** comes from a Dutch word *ijsberg,* meaning 'mountain of ice.'

ice–box (īs'boks') **1** an insulated box in which food is kept cool by ice. **2** refrigerator. *n.*

ice·break·er (īs'brāk'ər) a strong boat or ship with a reinforced bow and powerful motors, used to break a channel through ice. *n.*

ice cube a piece of ice, usually having six sides, used for chilling drinks or food.

ice field **1** a large sheet of ice floating in the sea, larger than a floe. **2** a large sheet of ice on land.

Ice·land·er (īs'lan'dər or īs'lən dər) a person born in or living in Iceland, an island country in the North Atlantic Ocean. *n.*

Ice·lan·dic (īs lan'dik) **1** of or having to do with Iceland. **2** the language of Iceland. 1 *adj.,* 2 *n.*

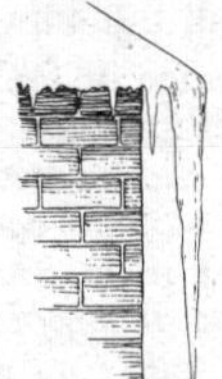
An icicle

i·ci·cle (ī'si kəl) a pointed, hanging stick of ice formed by the freezing of dripping water. *n.*

ic·ing (ī'sing) a mixture of sugar and some liquid, often with the beaten whites of eggs, flavoring, etc.; frosting: *Icing is used to cover cakes. n.*

i·cy (ī'sē) **1** like ice; very cold: *an icy blast of wind.* **2** having much ice; covered with ice: *icy roads.* **3** of ice. **4** without warm feeling; cold and unfriendly: *He gave her an icy stare. adj.,* **i·ci·er, i·ci·est. —i'ci·ly,** *adv.* **—i'ci·ness,** *n.*

I'd (īd) **1** I would. **2** I had.

i·de·a (ī dē'ə) **1** a plan, picture, or belief in the mind: *Eating candy and playing with toys are that little child's idea of happiness.* **2** a thought, fancy, or opinion: *She is always ready to express her ideas. I had an idea that everything would turn out well.* **3** the point or purpose: *The idea of a vacation is to get a rest. n.*

i·de·al (ī dē'əl) **1** a perfect type; a model to be imitated; what one would wish to be: *Her mother is her ideal. Religion holds up high ideals for us to follow.* **2** perfect; just as one would wish: *The fine day was ideal for our picnic.* 1 *n.,* 2 *adj.*

i·de·al·ist (ī dē'əl ist) **1** a person who acts according to high ideals; a person who has high ideals. **2** a person who neglects practical matters in following ideals. *n.*

i·den·ti·cal (ī den'tə kəl) **1** the same: *That is the identical pen I lost.* **2** exactly alike: *The two new pennies were identical. adj.*

i·den·ti·fi·ca·tion (ī den'tə fə kā'shən) **1** an identifying or being identified. **2** something used to identify a person or thing: *She showed her driver's license as identification. n.*

i·den·ti·fy (ī den'tə fī') **1** recognize as being, or show to be, a particular person or thing; prove to be the same: *He identified the bag as his by telling what it contained.* **2** make the same; treat as the same: *The good king identified his people's welfare with his own. v.,* **i·den·ti·fied, i·den·ti·fy·ing.**

i·den·ti·ty (ī den'tə tē) **1** being oneself or itself, and not another; who or what one is: *The writer concealed his identity by signing his stories with a pen name.* **2** exact likeness; sameness: *The identity of the two crimes led the police to think that the same person committed them. n., pl.* **i·den·ti·ties.**

id·i·om (id'ē əm) **1** a phrase or expression whose meaning cannot be understood from the ordinary meanings of its individual words: *'How do you do?' and 'I've caught cold' are English idioms.* **2** dialect: *He spoke in the idiom of the Ottawa Valley.* **3** a people's way of expressing themselves: *It is often hard to put Eskimo ideas into the English idiom. n.*

id·i·ot (id'ē ət) **1** a person born with little ability to learn; a person who does not develop mentally. **2** a very stupid or foolish person: *He was an idiot to behave like that. n.*

id·i·ot·ic (id'ē ot'ik) very stupid or foolish: *We couldn't understand her idiotic behavior. adj.*

i·dle (ī'dəl) **1** doing nothing; not busy; not working: *idle hands, the idle hours of a holiday.* **2** lazy; not willing to work: *The idle boy would not study.* **3** useless; worthless: *idle talk.* **4** without any good reason or cause: *idle fears, idle rumors.* **5** be idle; waste time; do nothing: *Are you going to spend your whole vacation just idling?* **6** run slowly without transmitting power: *The motor of a car idles when it is out of gear and running slowly.* 1–4 *adj.,* **i·dler, i·dlest;** 5, 6 *v.,* **i·dled, i·dling. —i'dle·ness,** *n.*

idle away, spend wastefully: *She idled away many hours lying in the hammock.*

☞ **Idle** and **idol** are pronounced the same.

i·dler (ī′dlər) a lazy person. *n.*

i·dly (ī′dlē) in an idle manner; doing nothing. *adv.*

i·dol (ī′dəl) **1** an image or other object worshipped as a god. **2** a person or thing that is loved or admired very much: *The baby girl was the idol of her family. n.*

☞ **Idol** and **idle** are pronounced the same.

i·dol·ize (ī′dəl īz′) **1** love or admire very much: *The boy idolizes his older sister.* **2** worship as an idol; make an idol of: *The boys idolized the hockey star. v.,* **i·dol·ized, i·dol·iz·ing.**

if (if) **1** supposing that; on condition that; in case: *Come if you can. If it rains tomorrow, we shall stay at home.* **2** whether: *I wonder if he called.* **3** although; even though: *He is strong, if little. conj.*

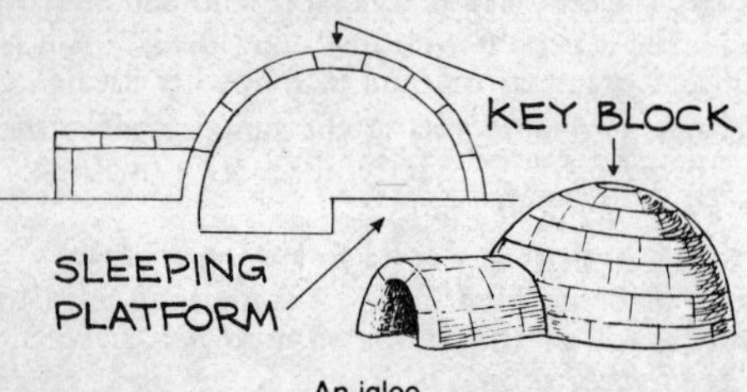

An igloo

ig·loo (ig′lü) an Eskimo house or hut, especially one shaped like a dome and built of blocks of hard snow. *n., pl.* **ig·loos.**

☞ **Igloo** comes from an eastern Eskimo word *iglu,* meaning 'a dwelling.'

ig·ne·ous (ig′nē əs) **1** of or having to do with fire. **2** produced by fire, great heat, or the action of a volcano: *Granite is an igneous rock. adj.*

ig·nite (ig nīt′) **1** set on fire: *The match was ignited by scraping it against the sidewalk.* **2** take fire; begin to burn: *Gasoline ignites easily. v.,* **ig·nit·ed, ig·nit·ing.**

ig·ni·tion (ig nish′ən) **1** setting on fire. **2** catching on fire. **3** in a gasoline engine, the apparatus for controlling the sparks that fire the mixture of air and gasoline in the cylinders. *n.*

ig·no·ble (ig nō′bəl) **1** mean; base; without honor: *To betray a friend is ignoble.* **2** not of noble birth or position; humble: *Thomas Beckett came from an ignoble family. adj*

ig·no·rance (ig′nə rəns) a lack of knowledge; being ignorant. *n.*

ig·no·rant (ig′nə rənt) **1** knowing little or nothing; without knowledge: *People who live in the city are often ignorant of farm life.* **2** caused by or showing lack of knowledge: *an ignorant remark.* **3** unaware; uninformed: *He was ignorant of the fact that his house had been burned. adj.*

ig·nore (ig nôr′) pay no attention to; disregard: *The teacher ignored the noise her pupils were making. v.,* **ig·nored, ig·nor·ing.**

i·gua·na (i gwä′nə) a large climbing lizard found in tropical America. *n.*

ill (il) **1** sick; having some disease; not well: *ill with a fever.* **2** sickness; disease: *She told us about all the ills she had had.* **3** bad; evil; harmful: *an ill wind, to do a person an ill turn.* **4** badly; harmfully: *work ill done. His strength is ill used in bullying other children.* **5** an evil; harm: *Poverty is an ill.* 1, 3 *adj.,* **worse, worst;** 2, 5 *n.,* 4 *adv.*

☞ **Ill** is a more formal word than **sick.** Both words mean the same, however, except that in informal use **sick** is often given the special meaning 'nauseated.'

I'll (īl) I will.

☞ **I'll, aisle,** and **isle** are pronounced the same.

ill–bred (il′bred′) badly brought up; impolite; rude. *adj.*

il·le·gal (i lē′gəl) not lawful; against the law; forbidden by law: *illegal parking. adj.* **—il·le′gal·ly,** *adv.*

il·leg·i·ble (i lej′ə bəl) very hard or impossible to read: *The ink had faded so that many words were illegible. adj.*

ill feeling dislike; mistrust: *There has been ill feeling between them ever since they quarrelled.*

il·lit·er·ate (i lit′ər it) **1** unable to read or write: *He did not go to school and is illiterate.* **2** a person who is unable to read or write. **3** showing a lack of education: *He writes in a very illiterate way.* 1, 3 *adj.,* 2 *n.*

ill–na·tured (il′nā′chərd) cross; disagreeable. *adj.*

ill·ness (il′nis) **1** a sickness or disease: *Scarlet fever is a serious illness.* **2** poor health; a sickly condition: *She suffered from long periods of illness. n.*

il·log·i·cal (i loj′ə kəl) **1** not logical. **2** not reasonable; foolish: *an illogical fear of the dark. adj.*

ill–tem·pered (il′tem′pərd) having or showing a bad temper; cross. *adj.*

ill–treat (il′trēt′) treat cruelly; treat badly; do harm to; abuse. *v.*

il·lu·mi·nate (i lü′mə nāt′) **1** light up; make bright: *The room was illuminated by four large lamps. The big searchlight illuminates the top of the tower.* **2** make clear; explain: *Our teacher could illuminate almost any subject we studied. v.,* **il·lu·mi·nat·ed, il·lu·mi·nat·ing.**

il·lu·mi·na·tion (i lü′mə nā′shən) **1** a lighting up; making bright: *Illumination in this room is by four lamps.* **2** the light supplied: *The illumination from four lamps is enough.* **3** making clear; an explanation. *n.*

il·lu·mine (i lü′mən) light up; make bright: *A smile often illumines a face. v.,* **il·lu·mined, il·lu·min·ing**

il·lu·sion (i lü′zhən) **1** an appearance or feeling that misleads because it is not real; something that deceives by giving a false idea: *That slender, snow-covered bush at the gate gave me an illusion of a woman waiting there.* **2** a false idea or belief: *Many people have the illusion that wealth is the chief cause of happiness. n.*

☞ **Illusion** and **allusion** are sometimes confused. An **illusion** is a misleading appearance: *The large car she drives gives an illusion of wealth.* An **allusion** is an indirect reference or slight mention: *He made several allusions to Spain so we gathered that he had been there recently.*

il·lus·trate (il′əs trāt′) **1** make clear or explain by stories, examples, comparisons, etc.: *The way that a pump works was used to illustrate how the heart sends blood around the body.* **2** provide with pictures, diagrams, maps, etc. that explain or decorate: *This book is well illustrated. v.,* **il·lus·trat·ed, il·lus·trat·ing.**

il·lus·tra·tion (il′əs trā′shən) **1** a picture, diagram,

hat, āge, fär; let, ēqual, tėrm; it, īce
hot, ōpen, ôrder; oil, out; cup, pu̇t, rüle
əbove, takən, pencəl, lemən, circəs
ch, child; ng, long; sh, ship
th, thin; ᴛʜ, then; zh, measure

map, etc. used to explain or decorate something. 2 a story, example, comparison, etc. used to make clear or explain something: *The teacher cut an apple into four equal parts as an illustration of what ¼ means.* 3 the act or process of illustrating: *Illustration is used in teaching.* *n.*

il·lus·tra·tor (il′əs trā′tər) an artist who makes pictures to be used as illustrations for books, stories, etc. *n.*

il·lus·tri·ous (i lus′trē əs) very famous; great; outstanding: *Canada's Governor General is an illustrious man.* *adj.*

ill will unkind or unfriendly feeling; dislike; hate: *I bear you no ill will.*

im– a form of **in-** used before the letters *p, m,* and *b,* as in *impatient, immigrate, immobile.*

I'm (īm) I am.

im·age (im′ij) 1 a likeness or copy: *You will see your image in this mirror. She is almost the exact image of her mother.* 2 a likeness made of stone, wood, or some other material; idol; statue: *The shelf was full of little images of all sorts of animals. The ancient Greeks and Romans worshipped images of their gods.* 3 a picture in the mind: *I can shut my eyes and see images of things and persons.* 4 make or form an image of. 5 reflect as a mirror does: *The clouds were imaged in the still waters of the lake.* 1–3 *n.*, 4, 5 *v.*, **im·aged, im·ag·ing.**

i·mag·i·na·ble (i maj′ə nə bəl) that can be imagined; possible: *Cinderella was dressed in the loveliest gown imaginable.* *adj.*

i·mag·i·nar·y (i maj′ə ner′ē) existing only in the imagination; not real: *Fairies are imaginary. The equator is an imaginary line around the earth midway between the North and South Poles.* *adj.*

i·mag·i·na·tion (i maj′ə nā′shən) 1 imagining; the power of forming in the mind pictures of things not present to the senses: *The child's imagination filled the woods with strange animals and fairies.* 2 the ability to create new things or ideas or to combine old ones in new forms: *Poets, artists, and inventors make use of their imagination.* 3 a creation in the mind; a fancy. *n.*

i·mag·i·na·tive (i maj′ə nə tiv) 1 showing imagination: *Fairy tales are imaginative. This child's poem is imaginative.* 2 having a good imagination; able to imagine well: *The imaginative child made up stories about life on other planets.* 3 of imagination: *the imaginative part of the mind.* *adj.*

i·mag·ine (i maj′ən) 1 picture in one's mind; form an image or idea of: *The girl likes to imagine herself an actress.* 2 suppose; guess: *I cannot imagine what you mean.* *v.*, **i·mag·ined, i·mag·in·ing.**

im·be·cile (im′bə səl) 1 a person who has a weak mind and can learn to do only very simple tasks. 2 weak in mind; very stupid: *an imbecile question.* 3 a very stupid or foolish person: *Don't be an imbecile.* 1, 3 *n.*, 2 *adj.*

im·i·tate (im′ə tāt′) 1 try to be like or act like; follow the example of: *The boy imitates his older brother.* 2 make or do something like; copy: *A parrot imitates the sounds it hears.* 3 act like, especially for amusement: *He made us laugh by imitating a baby, an old man, and a bear.* 4 be like; look like: *Plastic is often made to imitate wood.* *v.*, **im·i·tat·ed, im·i·tat·ing.**

im·i·ta·tion (im′ə tā′shən) 1 an imitating: *We learn many things by imitation.* 2 copy: *Give as good an imitation as you can of a rooster crowing.* 3 not real: *The imitation diamonds were made of glass.* 1, 2 *n.*, 3 *adj.*

im·mac·u·late (i mak′yə lit) 1 without spot or stain; absolutely clean: *The newly washed shirts were immaculate.* 2 without fault; in perfect order: *His appearance was immaculate.* 3 pure; without sin. *adj.* **—im·mac′u·late·ly,** *adv.*

im·ma·ter·i·al (im′ə tēr′ē əl) not important, not significant: *This error is immaterial.* *adj.*

im·ma·ture (im′ə chür′ or im′ə tyür′) not mature; not ripe; not full-grown or developed. *adj.*

im·meas·ur·a·ble (i mezh′ər ə bəl) too vast to be measured; very great. *adj.* **—im·meas′ur·a·bly,** *adv.*

im·me·di·ate (i mē′dē it) 1 coming at once; without delay: *Please send an immediate reply.* 2 with nothing in between; direct: *the immediate result.* 3 closest; nearest; next: *Our immediate neighbor is Mrs. Jones.* 4 close; near: *the immediate neighborhood.* 5 having to do with the present: *What are your immediate plans?* *adj.*

im·me·di·ate·ly (i mē′dē it lē) 1 at once; without delay: *The alarm sounded, and the firemen left immediately.* 2 next; with nothing between; directly. *adv.*

im·me·mo·ri·al (im′ə mô′rē əl) extending back beyond the bounds of memory; very old: *time immemorial.* *adj.*

im·mense (i mens′) very big; huge; vast: *An ocean is an immense body of water.* *adj.* **—im·mense′ly,** *adv.*

im·men·si·ty (i men′sə tē) vastness; boundless or vast extent: *the ocean's immensity.* *n., pl.* **im·men·si·ties.**

im·merse (i mėrs′) 1 dip or lower into a liquid until covered by it. 2 involve deeply; absorb: *immersed in thought.* *v.*, **im·mersed, im·mers·ing.**

im·mi·grant (im′ə grənt) a person who comes into a country or region to live: *Canada has many immigrants from Europe.* *n.*

☛ See note at **emigrate.**

im·mi·grate (im′ə grāt′) come into a country or region to live. *v.*, **im·mi·grat·ed, im·mi·grat·ing.**

☛ See note at **emigrate.**

im·mi·gra·tion (im′ə grā′shən) 1 coming into a country or region to live: *There has been immigration to Canada from most of the countries of Europe.* 2 the persons who immigrate; immigrants: *The immigration of 1956 included many people from Hungary.* *n.*

im·mi·nent (im′ə nənt) likely to happen soon; about to occur: *The black clouds, thunder, and lightning show that a storm is imminent.* *adj.* **—im′mi·nent·ly,** *adv.*

im·mo·bile (i mō′bīl or i mō′bəl) 1 not movable; firmly fixed. 2 not moving; not changing; motionless: *The cat lay immobile for some minutes, watching the bird.* *adj.*

im·mo·bi·lize (i mō′bə līz′) make immobile or almost

immobile: *an immobilized truck. She has been immobilized by a severe back injury.* *v.,* **im·mo·bi·lized, im·mo·bi·liz·ing.**

im·mor·al (i môr′əl) wrong; wicked: *Lying and stealing are immoral.* *adj.* **—im·mor′al·ly,** *adv.*

im·mor·tal (i môr′təl) **1** living forever; never dying; everlasting: *A man's body dies, but his soul may be immortal. The fame of Shakespeare should be immortal.* **2** a person living forever. **3 immortals,** *pl.* the gods of ancient Greece and Rome. **4** a person remembered or famous forever: *Shakespeare is one of the immortals.* 1 *adj.,* 2–4 *n.*

im·mor·tal·i·ty (im′ôr tal′ə tē) **1** endless life; living forever. **2** fame that is likely to last forever. *n.*

im·mov·a·ble (i müv′ə bəl) **1** that cannot be moved; firmly fixed: *immovable mountains.* **2** firm; steadfast: *an immovable purpose.* *adj.* **—im·mov′a·bly,** *adv.*

im·mune (i myün′) **1** not susceptible; protected from disease, poison, etc.; having immunity: *Some people are immune to poison ivy; they can touch it without getting a rash.* **2** exempt; being free from some duty or obligation, or from something unpleasant: *immune from taxes. Nobody is immune from criticism.* *adj.*

im·mu·ni·ty (i myü′nə tē) **1** resistance to disease, poison, etc.: *One attack of measles usually gives a person immunity to that disease.* **2** freedom: *The law gives immunity from taxation to schools and churches.* *n., pl.* **im·mu·ni·ties.**

im·mu·ni·za·tion (im′yə nī zā′shən) immunizing or being immunized: *Immunization against disease is a standard practice. Immunization against smallpox lasts about three years.* *n.*

im·mu·nize (im′yə nīz′) protect from disease; make immune: *Vaccination immunizes people against smallpox.* *v.*

imp (imp) **1** a young or small devil or demon. **2** a mischievous child. *n.*

im·pact (im′pakt) a striking of one thing against another; collision: *The impact of the stone against the window shattered the glass.* *n.*

im·pair (im per′) make worse; damage; harm; weaken: *Poor food impaired his health.* *v.*

im·pale (im pāl′) **1** pierce through with something pointed; fasten with something pointed: *The butterflies were impaled on small pins stuck in a sheet of cork.* **2** make helpless as if by piercing: *The teacher impaled the cheeky student with a look of ice.* *v.,* **im·paled, im·pal·ing.**

im·part (im pärt′) **1** give a part or share of; give: *The new furniture imparted an air of newness to the old house.* **2** communicate; tell: *The interviewer asked her to impart the secret of her success.* *v.*

im·par·tial (im pär′shəl) showing no more favor to one side than to the other; fair; just: *A judge should be impartial.* *adj.* **—im·par′tial·ly,** *adv.*

im·pass·a·ble (im pas′ə bəl) not passable; so that one cannot go through or across: *Snow and ice made the road impassable.* *adj.*

im·pas·sioned (im pash′ənd) full of strong feeling; rousing; ardent: *The general made an impassioned speech to his soldiers.* *adj.*

im·pas·sive (im pas′iv) not showing any feeling or emotion; unmoved: *He listened with an impassive face.* *adj.* **—im·pas′sive·ly,** *adv.*

im·pa·tience (im pā′shəns) **1** a lack of patience; being impatient. **2** uneasiness and eagerness; restlessness. *n.*

im·pa·tient (im pā′shənt) **1** not patient; not willing to bear delay, opposition, pain, bother, etc.: *He is impatient with his little sister.* **2** restless: *The horses were impatient to start the race.* **3** showing lack of patience: *an impatient answer.* *adj.* **—im·pa′tient·ly,** *adv.*

im·peach (im pēch′) **1** call in question: *to impeach a person's honor.* **2** accuse; charge with wrongdoing. **3** bring a public official to trial before a special court for wrong conduct during office: *The judge was impeached for taking a bribe.* *v.*

im·pede (im pēd′) hinder; obstruct: *The deep snow impeded travel.* *v.,* **im·ped·ed, im·ped·ing.**

im·ped·i·ment (im ped′ə mənt) **1** a hindrance or obstacle. **2** a defect in speech: *Stuttering is an impediment.* *n.*

im·pel (im pel′) **1** drive; force; cause: *Hunger impelled the lazy man to work.* **2** cause to move; drive forward; push along: *The wind impelled the boat to shore.* *v.,* **im·pelled, im·pel·ling.**

im·pend·ing (im pen′ding) likely to happen soon; about to occur (used especially of something unpleasant): *She dreaded the impending exams.* *adj.*

im·pen·e·tra·ble (im pen′ə trə bəl) **1** that cannot be entered, pierced, or passed through: *The thorny branches made a thick, impenetrable hedge.* **2** that cannot be seen into or understood; impossible to explain or understand: *an impenetrable mystery.* *adj.*

im·per·a·tive (im per′ə tiv) **1** not to be avoided; urgent; necessary: *It is imperative that this very sick child should stay in bed.* **2** a command: *The great imperative is 'Love thy neighbor as thyself.'* 1 *adj.,* 2 *n.*

im·per·cep·ti·ble (im′pər sep′tə bəl) that cannot be perceived or felt; very slight; gradual: *The differences between the original painting and the copy were almost imperceptible.* *adj.* **—im·per·cep′ti·bly,** *adv.*

im·per·fect (im pėr′fikt) **1** not perfect; having some defect or fault: *A crack in the cup made it imperfect.* **2** not complete; lacking some part. *adj.* **—im·per′fect·ly,** *adv.*

im·per·fec·tion (im′pər fek′shən) **1** a lack of perfection; imperfect condition or character. **2** a fault; defect: *The imperfections in the picture showed that it had been painted in a hurry.* *n.*

im·pe·ri·al (im pēr′ē əl) **1** of or having to do with an empire or its ruler. **2** supreme; majestic; magnificent. *adj.*

im·pe·ri·al·ism (im pēr′ē əl iz′əm) **1** the policy of extending the rule or authority of one country over other countries and territories. **2** an imperial system of government. *n.*

im·per·il (im per′əl) put in danger: *He imperilled their lives by standing up and rocking the rowboat.* *v.,* **im·per·illed** or **im·per·iled, im·per·il·ling** or **im·per·il·ing.**

im·pe·ri·ous (im pēr′ē əs) haughty; arrogant; domineering; overbearing. *adj.*

im·per·son·al (im pėr′sən əl) **1** referring to all or any persons, not to any special one: *'First come, first served' is an impersonal remark. In the expression 'One* *must do his best,' the word 'one' is impersonal.* 2 having no existence as a person: *Electricity is an impersonal force.* *adj.* —**im·per'son·al·ly,** *adv.*

impersonal pronoun any of the words *it, one, they* or *you* when used to refer to a person or thing not named or identified: *It is cold today. One must do his best. They say that life begins at forty. You should be careful in crossing the street.*

im·per·son·ate (im pėr'sən āt') 1 pretend to be; mimic the voice, appearance, and manners of, especially in trying to deceive: *The thief impersonated a policeman.* 2 represent in personal form; be a typical example of: *To many people, Henry Hudson impersonates the spirit of adventure.* *v.,* **im·per·son·at·ed, im·per·son·at·ing.**

im·per·ti·nence (im pėr'tə nəns) 1 an impertinent quality; impudence; insolence. 2 an impertinent act or impertinent speech: *The remark was an impertinence and they were angry at the speaker.* *n.*

im·per·ti·nent (im pėr'tə nənt) saucy; impudent; insolent; rude: *Talking back to older people is impertinent.* *adj.*

im·pet·u·ous (im pech'ü əs) 1 acting hastily, rashly, or with sudden feeling: *Children are usually more impetuous than adults.* 2 moving with great force or speed: *the impetuous rush of water over Niagara Falls.* *adj.* —**im·pet'u·ous·ly,** *adv.*

im·pe·tus (im'pə təs) 1 the force with which an object moves: *the impetus of a moving automobile. Anything that you can stop easily has little impetus.* 2 a driving force; incentive: *His ambition was an impetus to work for success.* *n.*

im·pi·ous (im'pē əs or im pī'əs) not pious; not having or not showing reverence for God; wicked. *adj.*

im·ple·ment (im'plə mənt for 1; im'plə ment' for 2) 1 a useful piece of equipment; tool; instrument; utensil: *Brooms, shovels, can openers, rakes, axes, and ploughs are all implements.* 2 carry out; get done: *Do not undertake a project unless you can implement it.* 1 *n.,* 2 *v.*

im·plore (im plôr') 1 beg earnestly for: *The prisoner implored pardon.* 2 beg a person to do something: *She implored her mother to give permission for her to go on the trip.* *v.,* **im·plored, im·plor·ing.**

im·ply (im plī') mean something without saying it outright; express in an indirect way; suggest: *Silence often implies consent. The teacher's smile implied that she had forgiven us.* *v.,* **im·plied, im·ply·ing.**

☛ **Imply** and **infer** do not mean the same thing. A writer or speaker **implies** something in his words or manner: *She implied by the look in her eyes that she did not intend to keep the appointment.* A reader or listener **infers** something from what he reads, sees, or hears: *They inferred from the principal's announcement that she already knew who had broken the window.*

im·po·lite (im'pə līt') not polite; rude. *adj.* —**im'po·lite'ly,** *adv.*

im·port (im pôrt' for 1 and 3, im'pôrt for 2, 4, and 5) 1 bring in from a foreign country for sale or use: *Canada imports sugar from Cuba.* 2 an article brought into a country: *Rubber is a useful import.* 3 mean; have as meaning: *What does this message import?* 4 meaning; significance: *Explain your remark; I do not understand its import.* 5 importance: *It is a matter of great import.* 1, 3 *v.,* 2, 4, 5 *n.*

hat, āge, fär; let, ēqual, tėrm; it, īce
hot, ōpen, ôrder; oil, out; cup, pu̇t, rüle
əbove, takən, pencəl, lemən, circəs
ch, child; ng, long; sh, ship
th, thin; ᴛʜ, then; zh, measure

im·por·tance (im pôr'təns) being important; significance, consequence, or value: *Anybody can see the importance of good health.* *n.*

im·por·tant (im pôr'tənt) 1 meaning much; having value or influence: *important business, an important occasion.* 2 having social position or influence: *The mayor is an important man in our town.* 3 acting as if important; self-important; seeming to have influence: *He ran around giving orders in an important manner.* *adj.* —**im·por'tant·ly,** *adv.*

im·por·ta·tion (im'pôr tā'shən) 1 the bringing in of merchandise from foreign countries. 2 something brought in; import: *Her shawl is a recent importation from Mexico.* *n.*

im·pose (im pōz') put a burden, tax, punishment, etc. on: *The judge imposed a fine of $500 on the guilty man.* 2 force or thrust one's authority or influence on another or others. 3 force or thrust oneself or one's company on another or others. *v.,* **im·posed, im·pos·ing.**
impose on or **upon, a** take advantage of; use in a selfish way: *to impose on the good nature of others.* **b** deceive; cheat; trick.

im·pos·ing (im pōz'ing) impressive because of size, appearance, or dignity; commanding attention: *The Peace Tower of the Parliament Buildings is an imposing structure.* *adj.*

im·pos·si·bil·i·ty (im pos'ə bil'ə tē) 1 being impossible: *We all realize the impossibility of living long without food.* 2 something impossible. *n., pl.* **im·pos·si·bil·i·ties.**

im·pos·si·ble (im pos'ə bəl) 1 that cannot be done or used: *an impossible task, an impossible plan.* 2 that cannot be or happen: *It is impossible for two and two to be six.* 3 that cannot be true: *an impossible story.* 4 that cannot be put up with; not able to be tolerated: *an impossible person.* *adj.* —**im·pos'si·bly,** *adv.*

im·pos·tor (im pos'tər) 1 a person who assumes a false name or character. 2 a deceiver; cheat. *n.*

im·pov·er·ish (im pov'ər ish) 1 make very poor. 2 exhaust the strength, richness, or resources of: *Careless farming impoverishes the soil.* *v.*

im·prac·ti·ca·ble (im prak'tə kə bəl) 1 that cannot be done without greater difficulty, expense, etc. than is wise or sensible; impossible to put into practice: *His suggestion was impracticable.* 2 that cannot be used: *an impracticable road.* *adj.*

im·prac·ti·cal (im prak'tə kəl) not practical; not useful: *To build a bridge across the Atlantic Ocean would be an impractical scheme.* *adj.*

im·preg·na·ble (im preg'nə bəl) able to resist attack; not yielding to force, persuasion, etc.: *an impregnable fortress, an impregnable argument.* *adj.*

im·press (im pres' for 1–4, im'pres for 5) 1 have a strong effect on the mind or feelings of: *A hero impresses us with his courage.* 2 fix in the mind: *She repeated the words to impress them on her memory.*

3 make marks on by pressing or stamping: *We can impress wax with a seal.* 4 imprint or stamp. 5 an impression; a special mark or quality; stamp: *An author leaves the impress of his personality on what he writes.* 1–4 *v.*, 5 *n.*

im·pres·sion (im presh′ən) 1 an effect produced on a person: *Punishment seemed to make little impression on the child.* 2 an idea or notion: *I have a vague impression that I left the house unlocked.* 3 a mark made by pressing or stamping: *The thief had left an impression of his feet in the garden.* *n.*

im·pres·sive (im pres′iv) making an impression on the mind, feelings, conscience, etc.: *an impressive sermon, an impressive storm, an impressive ceremony.* *adj.* —**im·pres′sive·ly,** *adv.*

im·print (im′print for 1 and 2, im print′ for 3, 4, and 5) 1 a mark made by pressure; print: *the imprint of a foot in the sand.* 2 an impression; mark: *Suffering left its imprint on her face.* 3 mark by pressing or stamping: *to imprint a postmark on an envelope.* 4 put by pressing: *He imprinted a kiss on his mother's cheek.* 5 fix in the mind: *The dramatic scene was imprinted in her memory.* 1, 2 *n.*, 3–5 *v.*

im·pris·on (im priz′ən) 1 put in prison; keep in prison. 2 confine closely; restrain. *v.*

im·pris·on·ment (im priz′ən mənt) 1 putting or keeping in prison. 2 being put or kept in prison. *n.*

im·prob·a·ble (im prob′ə bəl) not probable; not likely to happen; not likely to be true: *an improbable story.* *adj.*

im·promp·tu (im promp′tyü or im promp′tü) without thought or preparation beforehand: *Her speech was very good even though it was an impromptu one.* *adj., adv.*

im·prop·er (im prop′ər) 1 wrong; not correct: *Among most Canadians 'ain't' is considered improper.* 2 not suitable: *That bright dress is improper for a funeral.* 3 not decent: *They were shocked by the boys' improper language.* *adj.* —**im·prop′er·ly,** *adv.*

improper fraction a fraction equal to or greater than 1: *Examples of improper fractions are* $\frac{3}{2}$, $\frac{27}{4}$, $\frac{8}{5}$, $\frac{12}{12}$.

im·prove (im prüv′) 1 make better: *You could improve your handwriting if you tried.* 2 become better: *His health is improving.* *v.*, **im·proved, im·prov·ing.**

im·prove·ment (im prüv′mənt) 1 making or becoming better: *His schoolwork shows much improvement since last term.* 2 a change or addition that adds value: *The improvements in his house cost over $1000.* 3 a better condition; anything that is better than another; advance: *Travelling by automobile is an improvement over travelling by Red River cart.* *n.*

im·pro·vise (im′prə vīz′) 1 compose or sing, speak, recite, etc. without preparation: *He improvised a new verse for the school song at the football game.* 2 make or provide offhand, using whatever materials, etc. happen to be available: *The girls improvised a tent out of two blankets and some long poles.* *v.*, **im·pro·vised, im·pro·vis·ing.**

im·pru·dent (im prü′dənt) not prudent; rash; unwise: *Not bothering to think ahead, he made an imprudent decision.* *adj.*

im·pu·dence (im′pyə dəns) being impudent; insolence; great rudeness. *n.*

im·pu·dent (im′pyə dənt) rudely bold; insolent; forward: *The impudent boy made faces at the teacher.* *adj.* —**im′pu·dent·ly,** *adv.*

im·pulse (im′puls) 1 a sudden, driving force of influence; thrust; push: *the impulse of a wave, the impulse of pity.* 2 a sudden inclination or tendency to act: *A mob is influenced more by impulse than by reason.* *n.*

im·pul·sive (im pul′siv) 1 acting upon impulse; easily moved: *The impulsive child gave all his money to the beggar.* 2 coming from a sudden impulse: *an impulsive sneer.* 3 driving with sudden force; able to impel: *an impulsive force.* *adj.* —**im·pul′sive·ly,** *adv.*

im·pu·ni·ty (im pyü′nə tē) freedom from punishment, injury, or other unpleasant consequences: *If laws are not enforced, crimes are committed with impunity.* *n.*

im·pure (im pyür′) 1 not pure; dirty; unclean: *The air in cities is often impure.* 2 mixed with something, especially a substance of lower value: *The salt we use is slightly impure.* 3 bad; corrupt: *impure thoughts.* *adj.*

im·pu·ri·ty (im pyür′ə tē) 1 a lack of purity; being impure. 2 an impure thing or element; anything that makes something else impure: *Filtering the water removed some of its impurities.* *n., pl.* **im·pu·ri·ties.**

in (in) **In** shows position with reference to space, time, state, circumstances, etc. 1 within; inside: *in the box. We live in the country in the summer.* 2 at; during; after: *You can easily do this in an hour. I will be back in an hour.* 3 into: *Go in the house.* 4 from among; out of: *one in a hundred.* 5 because of; for: *The party is in honor of Maria's birthday.* 6 in or into some place, position, condition, etc.: *Come in. Lock the dog in. Mrs. Smith is in. A sheepskin coat has the woolly side in.* 1–5 *prep.*, 6 *adv.*

in for, unable to avoid; sure to get or have: *We are in for a storm.*

ins and outs, a the turns and twists; nooks and corners: *the ins and outs of the road.* **b** the different parts; details: *The manager knows the ins and outs of the business better than the owner.*

in that, because.

☛ **In** and **inn** are pronounced the same.

☛ **In** generally shows location; **into** generally shows direction: *He was in the house. He came into the house. He was in a stupor. He fell into a deep sleep.* Informally, **in** is often used with certain words instead of **into:** *She fell in the creek.*

in. inch; inches.

in–[1] a prefix meaning: not; the opposite of; the absence of: *inexpensive means not expensive. Inattention means the opposite of attention.*

☛ **In-** occurs as **il-** before *l*, as **im-** before *b, m,* and *p*, and as **ir-** before *r*.

in–[2] a prefix meaning: in; into; on; upon: *Inhale means to breath in. Inscribe means to write on.*

☛ See note at **in-**[1].

in·a·bil·i·ty (in′ə bil′ə tē) a lack of ability, means, or power; being unable. *n.*

in·ac·ces·si·ble (in′ək ses′ə bəl) 1 hard to get at; hard to reach or enter: *A fort on top of a steep hill is inaccessible.* 2 that cannot be reached at all. *adj.*

hat, āge, fär; let, ēqual, tėrm; it, īce
hot, ōpen, ôrder; oil, out; cup, pu̇t, rüle
 əbove, takən, pencəl, lemən, circəs
ch, child; ng, long; sh, ship
th, thin; ᴛʜ, then; zh, measure

in·ac·cu·ra·cy (in ak′yə rə sē) 1 a lack of accuracy; being inaccurate: *The inaccuracy of the report was not hard to prove.* 2 mistake. *n., pl.* **in·ac·cu·ra·cies.**

in·ac·cu·rate (in ak′yə rit) not accurate; not exact; containing mistakes: *an inaccurate report. adj.* —**in·ac′cu·rate·ly,** *adv.*

in·ac·tive (in ak′tiv) not active; idle; slow: *Bears are inactive during the winter. adj.*

in·ad·e·quate (in ad′ə kwit) not adequate; not enough; not as much as is needed: *inadequate preparation for a test. adj.* —**in·ad′e·quate·ly,** *adv.*

in·ad·vis·a·ble (in′əd vīz′ə bəl) not advisable; unwise; not prudent. *adj.*

in·ane (in ān′) silly or foolish; senseless: *That was an inane thing to do. We soon tired of his inane remarks. adj.* —**in·ane′ly,** *adv.*

in·ap·pro·pri·ate (in′ə prō′prē it) not appropriate; not suitable; not fitting: *Jokes are inappropriate at a funeral. adj.*

in·as·much as (in′əz much′) because; since; in view of the fact that: *Inasmuch as he was smaller than the other boys, he was given a head start in the race.*

in·at·ten·tive (in′ə ten′tiv) not attentive; negligent; careless. *adj.*

in·au·di·ble (in o′də bəl or in ô′də bəl) that cannot be heard: *The street noises were almost inaudible at the back of the house. adj.*

in·au·gu·rate (in o′gyə rāt′ or in ô′gyə rāt′) 1 install in office with a ceremony: *The new mayor was inaugurated last week.* 2 make a formal beginning of; begin: *The invention of the airplane inaugurated a new era in transportation.* 3 open for public use with a ceremony or celebration: *The new playground was inaugurated with a parade and ball game. v.,* **in·au·gu·rat·ed, in·au·gu·rat·ing.**

in·au·gu·ra·tion (in o′gyə rā′shən or in ô′gyə rā′shən) 1 the act or ceremony of installing a person in office. 2 a beginning, especially a formal one. 3 the opening or bringing into use of a public building, etc. with a ceremony or celebration: *We were present at the inauguration of the new City Hall. n.*

in·born (in′bôrn′) born in a person; natural: *an inborn sense of rhythm. adj.*

In·ca (ing′kə) 1 a member of a highly civilized Indian people who ruled a large empire in western South America before the Spanish conquest in the 1500′s. 2 a ruler of the Incas. *n., pl.* **In·cas** or **In·ca.** —**In′can,** *n., adj.*

in·can·des·cent (in′kən des′ənt) 1 glowing with heat; red-hot or white-hot. 2 intensely bright; brilliant: *The snow was incandescent in the sunlight. adj.*

incandescent lamp light bulb.

in·ca·pa·ble (in kā′pə bəl) having very little ability; not capable; not efficient: *He was fired because he was an incapable mechanic. adj.*

incapable of, a without the power, ability, or fitness for: *A blind man is incapable of driving a car.* b not susceptible to; not open or ready for: *incapable of exact measurement. Gold is incapable of rusting.*

in·cense¹ (in′sens) 1 a substance giving off a sweet smell when burned. 2 the perfume or smoke from it. 3 something sweet like incense: *the incense of flowers, the incense of success. n.*

in·cense² (in sens′) make very angry; fill with rage: *Cruelty incenses kind people. v.,* **in·censed, in·cens·ing.**

in·cen·tive (in sen′tiv) something that urges a person on; the cause of action or effort; motive; stimulus: *The fun of playing the game was a greater incentive than the prize. n.*

in·ces·sant (in ses′ənt) never stopping; continual: *The roar of Niagara Falls is incessant. The incessant noise from the factory kept her awake all night. adj.* —**in·ces′sant·ly,** *adv.*

inch (inch) 1 a measure of length; 1/12 of a foot (2.54 cm). *Symbol:* ″ 2 move slowly or little by little: *The worm inched along.* 1 *n., pl.* **inch·es;** 2 *v.*

by inches, by degrees; gradually.
within an inch of, very near; very close to: *The man was within an inch of death.*

in·ci·dent (in′sə dənt) 1 a happening; event. 2 a happening thought of as forming part of a main story or series of events: *The battle was just one incident in the general's exciting life.* 3 liable to happen; belonging: *Hardships are incident to the life of an explorer.* 1, 2 *n.,* 3 *adj.*

in·ci·den·tal (in′sə den′təl) 1 happening or likely to happen along with something else more important: *Certain discomforts are incidental to camping out.* 2 occurring by chance: *an incidental meeting of an old friend on the street.* 3 something incidental: *On our trip we spent $89 for meals, room, and bus fare, and $6.50 for incidentals, such as candy, magazines, and stamps.* 1, 2 *adj.,* 3 *n.*

in·ci·den·tal·ly (in′sə dent′lē or in′sə den′təl ē) in an incidental manner; as an incident along with something else: *She mentioned incidentally that she had had no dinner. adv.*

in·cin·er·a·tor (in sin′ər ā′tər) a furnace or other apparatus for burning garbage, etc. *n.*

in·cip·i·ent (in sip′ē ənt) just beginning; in an early stage: *The medicine stopped the boy's incipient cold. adj.*

in·ci·sion (in sizh′ən) a cut made in something: *The doctor made a small incision to remove all the glass from her foot. n.*

in·ci·sor (in sī′zər) a tooth having a sharp edge for cutting; one of the front teeth: *We have eight incisors in all.* See **teeth** for picture. *n.*

in·cite (in sīt′) urge on; stir up; rouse: *Their captain's example incited the men to bravery. v.,* **in·cit·ed, in·cit·ing.**

in·clem·ent (in klem′ənt) 1 rough and stormy: *We had inclement weather throughout our vacation.* 2 severe; harsh: *an inclement ruler. adj.*

in·cli·na·tion (in′klə nā′shən) 1 a preference or liking: *Our family has an inclination for sports.* 2 tendency: *Many middle-aged people have an inclination to become fat.* 3 a leaning; a bending or bowing: *A nod is an inclination of the head.* 4 a slope or slant: *That high roof has a sharp inclination. n.*

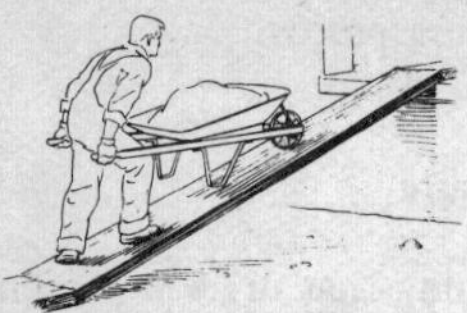
A man pushing a wheelbarrow up an incline

in·cline (in klīn′ for 1, 2, 3, and 6, in′klīn or in klīn′ for 4 and 5) **1** be favorable; be willing; tend: *Dogs incline to eat meat as a food. The men in our family incline to be fat.* **2** make favorable; make willing; influence: *Incline your hearts to obey God's laws.* **3** to slope; to slant. **4** a slope; slant: *That roof has a very steep incline.* **5** a sloping surface: *The side of a hill is an incline.* **6** lean; bend or bow: *He inclined his head in prayer.* 1–3, 6 *v.,* **in·clined, in·clin·ing;** 4, 5 *n.*

in·clined (in klīnd′) **1** favorable; willing; tending: *I am inclined to agree with you. adj.*

in·close (in klōz′) enclose. *v.,* **in·closed, in·clos·ing.**

in·clo·sure (in klō′zhər) enclosure. *n.*

in·clude (in klüd′) **1** put in a total, a class, or the like; reckon in a count: *The price includes the land, house, and furniture. All on board the ship were lost, including the captain.* **2** contain; comprise: *Their farm includes about 65 hectares. v.,* **in·clud·ed, in·clud·ing.**

in·clu·sion (in klü′zhən) **1** including or being included. **2** the thing included. *n.*

in·clu·sive (in klü′siv) including: *'Read pages 10 to 20 inclusive' means begin with page 10 and read through to the very end of page 20. adj.*

in·cog·ni·to (in kog′nə tō′ or in′kog nē′tō) **1** with one's name, character, rank, etc. concealed; in disguise: *The prince travelled incognito to avoid crowds and ceremonies.* **2** a disguised condition: *His incognito was not successful and he was recognized almost immediately.* 1 *adv., adj.,* 2 *n., pl.* **in·cog·ni·tos.**

in·come (in′kum) what comes in from property, business, work, etc.; money that comes in; receipts: returns: *A person's yearly income is all the money that he gets in a year. n.*

income tax a government tax on a person's income.

im·com·pa·ra·ble (in kom′pə rə bəl or in′kəm per′ə bəl) without an equal; matchless: *Helen of Troy had incomparable beauty. adj.*

in·com·pe·tent (in kom′pə tənt) **1** not competent; without ability, power, or fitness. **2** an incompetent person: *There were so many incompetents in the group that the whole project failed.* 1 *adj.,* 2 *n.*

in·com·plete (in′kəm plēt′) not complete; lacking some part; unfinished. *adj.*

in·com·pre·hen·si·ble (in′kom pri hen′sə bəl) impossible to understand. *adj.*

in·con·ceiv·a·ble (in′kən sēv′ə bəl) **1** impossible to imagine: *A circle without a centre is inconceivable.* **2** hard to believe; incredible: *The new jet can travel at an inconceivable speed. adj.*

in·con·sid·er·ate (in′kən sid′ər it) not thoughtful of others; thoughtless. *adj.*

in·con·sist·ent (in′kən sis′tənt) **1** not in agreement; not consistent: *The policeman's failure to arrest the thief was inconsistent with his duty.* **2** not keeping to the same principles or habits; changeable: *An inconsistent person is always changing his opinions. adj.* **—in′con·sist′ent·ly,** *adv.*

in·con·spic·u·ous (in′kən spik′yü əs) not conspicuous; attracting little or no attention: *The woman's dress was an inconspicuous grey. adj.* **—in′con·spic′u·ous·ly,** *adv.*

in·con·stant (in kon′stənt) not constant; changeable; fickle. *adj.*

in·con·ven·ience (in′kən vēn′yəns) **1** trouble; bother; a lack of convenience or ease. **2** a cause of trouble, difficulty, or bother. **3** cause trouble, difficulty, or bother to: *Will it inconvenience you to carry this package to your mother?* 1, 2 *n.,* 3 *v.,* **in·con·ven·ienced, in·con·ven·ienc·ing.**

in·con·ven·ient (in′kən vēn′yənt) not convenient; causing trouble, difficulty, or bother; troublesome: *Shelves that are too high to reach easily are inconvenient. adj.* **—in′con·ven′ient·ly,** *adv.*

in·cor·po·rate (in kôr′pə rāt′) **1** make something a part of something else; join or combine something with something else: *We will incorporate your suggestion in this new plan.* **2** form into a corporation: *When the business became large, the owners incorporated it. v.,* **in·cor·po·rat·ed, in·cor·po·rat·ing.**

in·cor·rect (in′kə rekt′) **1** containing errors or mistakes; not correct; wrong. **2** not proper. *adj.* **—in′cor·rect′ly,** *adv.*

in·crease (in krēs′ for 1, in′krēs for 2 and 3) **1** make or become greater, more numerous, more powerful, etc.: *The driver increased the speed of the car. His mass has increased by six kilograms. These flowers will increase every year.* **2** a gain in size, numbers, etc.; growth: *There was a great increase in student enrolment last year.* **3** an addition; the amount added; the result of increasing: *an increase of six cents a litre.* 1 *v.,* **in·creased, in·creas·ing;** 2, 3 *n.*

on the increase, increasing: *The movement of people to the cities is on the increase.*

in·creas·ing·ly (in krēs′ing lē) more and more: *As we travelled south, the weather became increasingly warmer. adv.*

in·cred·i·ble (in kred′ə bəl) hard to believe; seeming too extraordinary to be possible: *It seems incredible that anyone could be so stupid. The hero fought with incredible bravery. adj.* **—in·cred′i·bly,** *adv.*

☞ **Incredible** and **incredulous** have different meanings. **Incredible** means unbelievable: *His story of having seen a ghost seemed incredible to his family.* **Incredulous** means not ready to believe; showing a lack of belief: *He told his incredulous father that he would show the evidence that night.*

in·cred·u·lous (in krej′ə ləs) **1** not willing or likely to believe; doubting: *Most people are incredulous about ghosts and witches.* **2** showing a lack of belief: *Father listened to our story with an incredulous smile. adj.* **—in·cred′u·lous·ly,** *adv.*

☞ See note at **incredible.**

in·cu·bate (in′kyə bāt′ or ing′kyə bāt′) **1** sit on eggs in order to hatch them; brood. **2** keep eggs, bacteria, etc. warm so that they will hatch or grow. *v.,* **in·cu·bat·ed, in·cu·bat·ing.**

in·cu·ba·tor (in′kyə bā′tər or ing′kyə bā′tər) **1** an apparatus for keeping eggs, bacteria, etc. warm so that

hat, āge, fär; let, ēqual, tėrm; it, īce
hot, ōpen, ôrder; oil, out; cup, pu̇t, rüle
 əbove, takən, pencəl, lemən, circəs
ch, child; ng, long; sh, ship
th, thin; ᴛʜ, then; zh, measure

they will hatch or grow. **2** a similar apparatus for protecting babies born very small or very early. *n.*

in·cum·ber (in kum′bər) encumber. *v.*

in·cum·brance (in kum′brəns) encumbrance. *n.*

in·cur (in kėr′) run into or meet with something unpleasant; bring on oneself: *incur many expenses. The explorers incurred great danger when they tried to cross the rapids. v.,* **in·curred, in·cur·ring.**

in·cur·a·ble (in kyür′ə bəl) **1** not capable of being cured; that cannot be healed or remedied: *an incurable invalid, an incurable disease.* **2** a person having an incurable disease. 1 *adj.*, 2 *n.*

in·debt·ed (in det′id) owing money or gratitude; in debt; obliged: *We are indebted to scientists for many of our comforts. adj.*

in·de·cent (in dē′sənt) **1** not decent; in very bad taste; improper: *He showed an indecent lack of gratitude for the man who had saved his life.* **2** not modest; morally bad; obscene. *adj.*

in·de·ci·sion (in′di sizh′ən) lack of decision; a tendency to delay or to hesitate; a tendency to change one's mind or to put off deciding. *n.*

in·deed (in dēd′) **1** in fact; in truth; really; surely: *She is hungry; indeed, she is almost starving. War is indeed terrible.* **2** an expression of surprise, doubt, contempt, etc.: *Indeed! I never would have thought it.* 1 *adv.*, 2 *interj.*

in·de·fat·i·ga·ble (in′di fat′ə gə bəl) never getting tired or giving up; tireless: *an indefatigable worker. adj.*

in·def·i·nite (in def′ə nit) **1** not clearly defined; not exact; vague: *'Maybe' is a very indefinite answer.* **2** not limited: *We have an indefinite time to finish this work. adj.* **—in·def′i·nite·ly,** *adv.*

indefinite article either of the articles **a** and **an.** 'A dog' or 'an animal' means 'any dog' or 'any animal'; 'the dog' means 'a certain or particular dog.'

in·del·i·ble (in del′ə bəl) **1** that cannot be erased or removed; permanent: *indelible ink. Three years as a soldier left an indelible impression on his memory.* **2** capable of making an indelible mark: *an indelible pencil. adj.*

Indented moulding

in·dent (in dent′) **1** make or form notches or jags in an edge, line, border, etc.: *an indented coastline. The rim of the plate was indented.* **2** begin a line of writing, typing, or printing farther from the left margin than other lines: *The first line of a paragraph is usually indented. v.*

☛ **Indent** comes from a Norman French word *endenter,* meaning 'make a toothlike cut in.' Indenting was used for contracts or deeds that were made up in two or more copies, with each copy having an identical cut on the margin.

in·de·pend·ence (in′di pen′dəns) freedom from the control, support, influence, or help of others: *The American colonies won independence from England. n.*

in·de·pend·ent (in′di pen′dənt) **1** not needing, wanting, or getting help from others; not connected with others: *independent work, independent thinking.* **2** not influenced by others; thinking or acting for oneself: *An independent person votes as he pleases.* **3** guiding, ruling, or governing oneself; not under another's rule: *Canada is an independent member of the Commonwealth of Nations.* **4** a person who is independent in thought or behavior. 1–3 *adj.*, 4 *n.* **—in′de·pend′ent·ly,** *adv.*

in·de·scrib·a·ble (in′di skrīb′ə bəl) that cannot be described; beyond description: *a scene of indescribable beauty. adj.*

in·de·struct·i·ble (in′di struk′tə bəl) that cannot be destroyed. *adj.*

in·dex (in′deks) **1** a list of what is in a book, telling on what pages to find names, topics, etc.: *An index is usually put at the end of the book and arranged in alphabetical order.* **2** provide with an index; make an index of. **3** something that points out or shows; a sign: *A man's face is often an index of his mood.* **4** pointer: *A dial or scale usually has an index.* 1, 3, 4 *n., pl.* **in·dex·es** or **in·di·ces;** 2 *v.*

index finger the finger next to the thumb; forefinger.

In·di·an (in′dē ən) **1** a member of the race of people that was living in North and South America before the Europeans came; an American Indian. **2** of or having to do with American Indians: *an Indian camp, Indian blankets, an Indian language.* **3** of, living in, or belonging to India or the East Indies: *Indian elephants, Indian temples, Indian costumes.* **4** a person born in or living in India or the East Indies. 1, 4 *n.*, 2, 3 *adj.*

Indian club a bottle-shaped wooden club that is swung for exercise.

Indian corn a variety of cereal grass first raised by American Indians; maize: *Various forms of Indian corn have been developed, such as sweetcorn and popcorn.* See **corn** for picture.

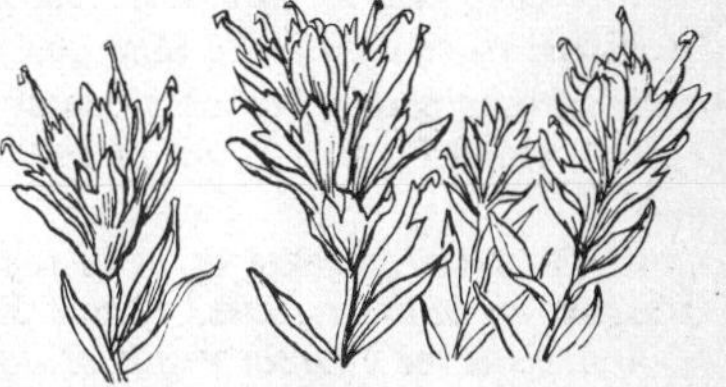
A kind of Indian paintbrush found on the slopes of the Rockies

Indian paintbrush any of various wild plants having spikes of flowers and showy, bright scarlet or orange leaves just below the flowers.

Indian summer a time of mild, dry, hazy weather in late autumn.

in·di·cate (in′də kāt′) **1** point out; show; make known: *The arrow on the sign indicates the way to go. A thermometer indicates the temperature.* **2** be a sign or hint of: *Fever indicates illness.* **3** give a sign or hint of: *A dog indicates its feelings by growling, whining, barking or wagging its tail. v.,* **in·di·cat·ed, in·di·cat·ing.**

in·di·ca·tion (in′də kā′shən) something that indicates;

a sign: *There was no indication that the house was occupied.* *n.*

in·di·ca·tor (in′də kā′tər) **1** a person or thing that indicates. **2** a pointer on the dial of an instrument that shows the amount of heat, pressure, speed, etc. See **dial** for picture. *n.*

in·di·ces (in′də sēz′) a plural of **index.** *n.*

in·dict (in dīt′) **1** formally charge with an offence or crime; accuse: *She has been indicted for leaving the scene of the accident.* **2** of a grand jury, find enough evidence against an accused person to justify a trial. *v.*

in·dif·fer·ence (in dif′rəns or in dif′ər əns) **1** a lack of interest or attention; not caring: *The boy's indifference to his homework worried his parents.* **2** little or no importance: *It was a matter of indifference to him whether his hands were clean or dirty.* *n.*

in·dif·fer·ent (in dif′rənt or in dif′ər ənt) **1** not caring one way or the other; having or showing no interest: *Rose enjoyed the trip, but Sue was indifferent. She was indifferent to every suggestion.* **2** unimportant; not mattering much: *The time for starting is indifferent to me.* **3** not bad, but less than good; just fair: *an indifferent player.* *adj.* **—in·dif′fer·ent·ly,** *adv.*

in·dig·e·nous (in dij′ə nəs) native; originating or produced in a particular country; growing or living naturally in a certain region, soil, climate, etc.: *Musk-ox are indigenous to Canada.* *adj.*

in·di·gest·i·ble (in′də jes′tə bəl) that cannot be properly digested; hard to digest. *adj.*

in·di·ges·tion (in′də jes′chən) inability to digest food properly; difficulty in digesting food: *I ate too quickly and have been suffering from indigestion as a result.* *n.*

in·dig·nant (in dig′nənt) angry at something unworthy, unfair, or mean: *She was indignant at the man who kicked her dog.* *adj.* **—in·dig′nant·ly,** *adv.*

in·dig·na·tion (in′dig nā′shən) anger at something unworthy, unfair, or mean; anger mixed with scorn: *Cruelty to animals arouses his indignation.* *n.*

in·dig·ni·ty (in dig′nə tē) an injury to dignity; lack of respect or proper treatment: *Bill felt that being called 'Willie, dear' was an indignity.* *n., pl.* **in·dig·ni·ties.**

in·di·go (in′də gō′) **1** a blue dye formerly obtained from various plants, but now usually made artificially. **2** deep, violet blue. 1, 2 *n., pl.* **in·di·goes** or **in·di·goes;** 2 *adj.*

in·di·rect (in′də rekt′ or in′dī rekt′) **1** not direct; not straight: *an indirect route.* **2** not directly connected: *Happiness is an indirect result of doing one's work well.* **3** not straightforward and to the point: *She would not say yes or no, but gave an indirect answer.* *adj.* **—in′dir·ect′ly,** *adv.*

in·dis·creet (in′dis krēt′) not discreet; not wise and judicious: *The boy's indiscreet remark made the stranger feel insulted.* *adj.* **—in·dis·creet′ly,** *adv.*

in·dis·cre·tion (in′dis kresh′ən) **1** being indiscreet; lack of good judgment: *His indiscretion in insulting the stranger embarrassed us.* **2** an indiscreet act. *n.*

in·dis·pen·sa·ble (in′dis pen′sə bəl) absolutely necessary: *Air is indispensable to life.* *adj.*

in·dis·posed (in′dis pōzd′) **1** slightly ill. **2** not inclined; unwilling: *The men were indisposed to work nights.* *adj.*

in·dis·tinct (in′dis tingkt′) not distinct; not clear to eye, ear, or mind; confused: *an indistinct picture. We could hear an indistinct roar from the distant ocean.* *adj.* **—in′dis·tinct′ly,** *adv.*

in·di·vid·u·al (in′də vij′ü əl) **1** person: *He is a tall individual.* **2** a single person, animal, or thing: *We saw a herd of giraffes containing 30 individuals.* **3** single; separate; for one only: *Benches are for several people; chairs are individual seats. Washbowls are for general use; toothbrushes are for individual use.* **4** belonging to or marking off one person or thing specially: *She has an individual style of handwriting.* 1, 2 *n.,* 3, 4 *adj.*

in·di·vid·u·al·i·ty (in′də vij′ü al′ə tē) **1** individual character; the sum of the qualities that make one person or thing different from another. **2** the condition of being individual; existence as an individual. *n., pl.* **in·di·vid·u·al·i·ties.**

in·di·vid·u·al·ly (in′də vij′ü əl ē) **1** personally; one at a time; as individuals: *Sometimes our teacher helps us individually.* **2** each from the others: *People differ individually.* *adv.*

in·di·vis·i·ble (in′də viz′ə bəl) that cannot be divided. *adj.*

in·do·lence (in′də ləns) laziness; dislike of work; idleness. *n.*

in·do·lent (in′də lənt) lazy; disliking work. *adj.* **—in′dol·ent·ly,** *adv.*

in·dom·i·ta·ble (in dom′ə tə bəl) that cannot be conquered; unyielding: *indomitable courage.* *adj.*

in·door (in′dôr′) **1** done, played, used, etc. in a house or building: *indoor skating.* **2** that is indoors: *an indoor rink.* *adj.*

in·doors (in′dôrz′) in or into a house or building: *Go indoors.* *adv.*

in·dorse (in dôrs′) endorse. *v.,* **in·dorsed, in·dors·ing.**

in·duce (in dyüs′ or in düs′) **1** lead on; influence; persuade: *Advertisements induce people to buy.* **2** cause; bring about: *The doctor says that this medicine will induce sleep.* *v.,* **in·duced, in·duc·ing.**

in·duce·ment (in dyüs′mənt or in düs′mənt) something that influences or persuades; incentive: *The prize was an inducement to try hard to win the contest.* *n.*

in·duct (in dukt′) put formally into a position, office, etc.: *They will induct him as secretary.* *v.*

in·dulge (in dulj′) **1** yield to the wishes of; humor: *We often indulge a sick person.* **2** give in to one's pleasure; let oneself have, use, or do what one wants: *He indulges in tobacco.* **3** give in to; let oneself have, use, or do: *She indulged her fondness for candy by eating a whole box.* *v.,* **in·dulged, in·dulg·ing.**

in·dul·gence (in dul′jəns) **1** yielding to the wishes of another or allowing oneself one's own desires. **2** something indulged in: *Luxuries are indulgencies.* **3** a favor or privilege: *He was forever seeking indulgences.* *n.*

in·dul·gent (in dul′jənt) **1** giving in to another's wishes or whims; too kind or agreeable: *The indulgent mother brought her boy everything he wanted.* **2** making allowances; lenient; not critical: *Our indulgent teacher praised every poem we wrote.* *adj.* **—in·dul′gent·ly,** *adv.*

hat, āge, fär; let, ēqual, tėrm; it, īce
hot, ōpen, ôrder; oil, out; cup, pu̇t, rüle
əbove, takən, pencəl, lemən, circəs
ch, child; ng, long; sh, ship
th, thin; ᴛʜ, then; zh, measure

in·dus·tri·al (in dus′trē əl) of or having to do with industry: *Industrial workers work at trades or in factories. adj.*

in·dus·tri·ous (in dus′trē əs) working hard and steadily: *An industrious student usually has good marks. adj.*

in·dus·try (in′dəs trē) 1 any branch of business, trade, or manufacture: *the automobile industry. Industries dealing with steel, copper, coal, and oil employ thousands of people.* 2 the production of goods; manufacturing in general: *He would rather be a teacher than work in industry.* 3 steady effort; close attention to work: *Industry and thrift favor success. n., pl.* **in·dus·tries.**

in·ed·i·ble (in ed′ə bəl) not fit to eat: *Some toadstools are inedible. adj.*

in·ef·fec·tive (in′ə fek′tiv) not producing the desired effect; of little use: *An ineffective medicine fails to cure a disease or relieve pain. adj.*

in·ef·fec·tu·al (in′ə fek′chü əl) failing to have the effect wanted; useless: *The searchlights were ineffectual in the fog. adj.*

in·ef·fi·cien·cy (in′ə fish′ən sē) a lack of efficiency; an inability to get things done. *n.*

in·ef·fi·cient (in′ə fish′ənt) 1 not efficient; not able to produce an effect without waste of time or energy; wasteful: *A machine that uses too much power is inefficient.* 2 not able to get things done; incapable: *an inefficient housekeeper. adj.* **—in′ef·fi′cient·ly,** *adv.*

in·ept (in ept′) 1 inappropriate; not suitable: *He would be an inept choice as captain.* 2 awkward; clumsy; incompetent: *That was an inept performance.* 3 foolish; absurd: *inept ideas. adj.* **—in·ept′ly,** *adv.* **—in·ept′ness,** *n.*

in·e·qual·i·ty (in′ē kwol′ə tē) 1 a lack of equality; being unequal in amount, size, value, rank, etc.: *There is a great inequality between the salaries of a bank president and an office clerk.* 2 a lack of evenness, regularity, or uniformity: *There are many inequalities in a circle that is drawn freehand. n., pl.* **in·e·qual·i·ties.**

in·ert (in ėrt′) 1 lifeless; having no power to move or act: *A stone is an inert mass of matter.* 2 inactive; slow; sluggish. *adj.*

in·er·tia (in ėr′shə) a tendency to remain in the state one is in and not start changes: *The family talked about leaving Canada, but their inertia prevented them from actually moving. n.*

in·es·ti·ma·ble (in es′tə mə bəl) too good, great, valuable, etc. to be measured or estimated: *Freedom is an inestimable privilege. adj.*

in·ev·i·ta·ble (in ev′ə tə bəl) not to be avoided; sure to happen; certain to come: *Death is inevitable. adj.* **—in·ev′i·ta·bly,** *adv.*

in·ex·act (in′ig zakt′) not exact; with errors or mistakes; not just right. *adj.*

in·ex·cus·a·ble (in′iks kyüz′ə bəl) that ought not to be excused; that cannot be justified: *Bad manners are inexcusable. adj.* **—in′ex·cus′a·bly,** *adv.*

in·ex·haust·i·ble (in′ig zos′tə bəl or in′ig zôs′tə bəl) 1 that cannot be exhausted; very abundant: *The wealth of our country seems inexhaustible to many people.* 2 tireless: *an inexhaustible swimmer. adj.*

in·ex·o·ra·ble (in ek′sə rə bəl) relentless; unyielding; not influenced by prayers or entreaties: *The forces of nature are inexorable. adj.* **—in·ex′or·a·bly,** *adv.*

in·ex·pen·sive (in′iks pen′siv) not expensive; cheap; low-priced. *adj.*

in·ex·pe·ri·ence (in′iks pēr′ē əns) a lack of experience or practice; a lack of skill or wisdom gained by experience. *n.*

in·ex·pe·ri·enced (in′iks pēr′ē ənst) not experienced; without practice; lacking the skill and wisdom gained by experience. *adj.*

in·ex·plic·a·ble (in′iks plik′ə bəl or in eks′plə kə bəl) mysterious; that cannot be explained: *an inexplicable fire. adj.*

in·fal·li·ble (in fal′ə bəl) 1 free from error; that cannot be mistaken: *an infallible rule.* 2 absolutely reliable; sure: *infallible obedience. adj.*

in·fa·mous (in′fə məs) 1 deserving or causing a very bad reputation; very wicked: *an infamous act.* 2 having a very bad reputation; in public disgrace: *an infamous traitor. adj.*

in·fa·my (in′fə mē) 1 a very bad reputation; public disgrace: *His acts brought infamy to his family and himself.* 2 extreme wickedness: *Treason is an act of infamy. n., pl.* **in·fa·mies.**

in·fan·cy (in′fən sē) 1 babyhood; early childhood. 2 an early stage of anything: *Space travel is still in its infancy. n., pl.* **in·fan·cies.**

in·fant (in′fənt) 1 a baby; a very young child. 2 of or for an infant: *an infant dress, infant food.* 3 in an early stage; just beginning to develop: *an infant industry.* 1 *n.,* 2, 3 *adj.*

in·fan·tile (in′fən tīl′) 1 of an infant or infants: *infantile diseases.* 2 like an infant; babyish; childish: *Her father was annoyed at her infantile behavior. adj.*

infantile paralysis poliomyelitis.

in·fan·try (in′fən trē) 1 soldiers trained, equipped, and organized to fight on foot. 2 the branch of an army made up of such soldiers. *n., pl.* **in·fan·tries.**

☛ **Infantry** came into English through French from an Italian word *infanteria,* formed from *infante,* meaning 'young man' or 'foot soldier.' It is, therefore, related to the word *infant.*

in·fect (in fekt′) 1 cause disease in by introducing germs: *Dirt infects an open cut. Anyone with a bad cold may infect the people around him.* 2 influence, especially in feeling or mood, by spreading from one person to another: *The captain's courage infected his soldiers. v.*

in·fec·tion (in fek′shən) 1 a causing of disease in people, animals, and plants by the introduction of germs or viruses: *Air, water, clothing, and insects may all be means of infection.* 2 a disease caused by the introduction of germs or viruses: *Measles is an infection that spreads from one person to another.* 3 an influence, feeling, or idea spreading from one to another. *n.*

in·fec·tious (in fek′shəs) 1 spread by infection:

Measles is an infectious disease. 2 apt to spread from one to another: *He has a jolly, infectious laugh.* *adj.*

in·fer (in fėr′) find out by reasoning; conclude: *Seeing the frown on his mother's face, the boy inferred that she was displeased.* *v.,* **in·ferred, in·fer·ring.**

☛ See note at **imply.**

in·fer·ence (in′fər əns) 1 the process of inferring; finding out by reasoning: *What happened is only a matter of inference; no one saw the accident.* 2 that which is inferred; conclusion: *What inference do you draw from smelling smoke?* *n.*

in·fe·ri·or (in fēr′ē ər) 1 low in quality; below the average: *an inferior mind, an inferior grade of coffee.* 2 lower in quality; not so good; worse: *Her grades are inferior to her sister's. This cloth is inferior to real silk.* 3 lower in position, rank, or importance: *A lieutenant is inferior to a captain.* 4 a person who is lower in rank or station: *A good leader gets on well with his inferiors.* 1–3 *adj.,* 4 *n.*

in·fe·ri·or·i·ty (in fēr′ē ôr′ə tē) an inferior condition or quality. *n.*

in·fer·nal (in fėr′nəl) 1 of hell. 2 fit to have come from hell; diabolic: *infernal heat. The heartless conqueror showed infernal cruelty.* *adj.*

in·fer·no (in fėr′nō) 1 hell. 2 a place or thing that seems to be like hell: *Within half an hour of the start of the fire, the whole building was a raging inferno.* *n., pl.* **in·fer·nos.**

in·fest (in fest′) trouble or disturb frequently or in large numbers: *Mosquitoes infest swamps. The mountains were infested by robbers.* *v.*

in·fi·del (in′fə dəl) 1 a person who does not believe in religion. 2 a person who does not accept a particular faith: *Moslems call Christians infidels.* *n.*

in·field (in′fēld′) 1 the part of a baseball field within the base lines; diamond (def. 3). 2 the first, second, and third basemen and shortstop of a baseball team: *That team has a good infield.* *n.*

in·fi·nite (in′fə nit) 1 without limits or bounds; endless: *the infinite extent of space.* 2 very great: *Teaching little children takes infinite patience.* *adj.* —**in′fi·nite·ly,** *adv.*

in·fin·i·ty (in fin′ə tē) 1 the state of being infinite: *the infinity of space.* 2 an infinite amount, number, or extent. *n., pl.* **in·fin·i·ties.**

in·firm (in fėrm′) weak; feeble: *The woman was old and infirm.* *adj.*

in·firm·a·ry (in fėr′mə rē) 1 a place for the care of the sick or injured in a school or institution. 2 any small hospital. *n., pl.* **in·fir·ma·ries.**

in·fir·mi·ty (in fėr′mə tē) 1 weakness; feebleness. 2 a sickness; illness: *the infirmities of age.* *n., pl.* **in·fir·mi·ties.**

in·flame (in flām′) 1 excite; make more violent: *Her stirring speech inflamed the crowd.* 2 make or become unnaturally hot, red, sore, or swollen: *The smoke had inflamed the fireman's eyes.* *v.,* **in·flamed, in·flam·ing.**

in·flam·ma·ble (in flam′ə bəl) 1 easily set on fire: *Paper and gasoline are inflammable.* 2 easily excited or aroused; excitable: *an inflammable temper.* *adj.*

☛ See note at **flammable.**

in·flam·ma·tion (in′flə mā′shən) 1 a diseased condition of some part of the body, marked by heat, redness, swelling, and pain. 2 an imflaming or being inflamed. *n.*

in·flate (in flāt′) 1 blow out or swell with air or gas: *to inflate a balloon.* 2 swell or puff out: *After his success, he was inflated with pride.* 3 increase prices or currency beyond a reasonable or normal amount. *v.,* **in·flat·ed, in·flat·ing.**

in·fla·tion (in flā′shən) 1 a swelling with air, gas, pride, etc. 2 a swollen state; too great expansion. 3 an increase of the currency of a country by issuing much paper money. 4 a sharp and sudden rise of prices resulting from too great an increase in the supply of paper money or bank credit. *n.*

in·flec·tion (in flek′shən) a change in the tone or pitch of the voice: *Questions often end with a rising inflection.* *n.*

in·flex·i·ble (in flek′sə bəl) 1 firm; not yielding: *Neither threats nor promises could change the captain's inflexible determination.* 2 not easily bent; stiff; rigid: *an inflexible rod.* *adj.*

in·flict (in flikt′) 1 cause to have or suffer; give a stroke, blow, or wound: *A knife can inflict a bad wound on a person.* 2 impose suffering, punishment, something unwelcome, etc.: *Only cruel people like to inflict pain. Mrs. Jones inflicted herself upon her relatives for a long visit.* *v.*

in·flu·ence (in′flü əns) 1 the power of persons or things to act on others; the power to affect the behavior of others without using force: *Use your influence to persuade your friends to join our club.* 2 a person or thing that has such power: *Jane was a good influence in our club.* 3 have an effect on; have power over: *The moon influences the tides. What we read influences our thinking.* 1, 2 *n.,* 3 *v.,* **in·flu·enced, in·flu·enc·ing.**

in·flu·en·tial (in′flü en′shəl) 1 having influence: *Influential friends helped him to get a good job.* 2 using influence; producing results. *adj.*

in·flu·en·za (in′flü en′zə) an infectious disease resembling a very bad cold, but much more dangerous and exhausting; flu. *n.*

in·form (in fôrm′) 1 tell; give knowledge, facts, or news to: *Report cards inform parents about a child's progress at school.* 2 give information to the police or some other authority: *The thief who was caught informed against the others who had escaped.* *v.*

in·for·mal (in fôr′məl) not formal; without ceremony or strict rules: *an informal party.* *adj.* —**in·for′mal·ly,** *adv.*

☛ **Informal English** is the kind of English used by educated people in everyday speaking or writing; **formal English** is used in lectures, speeches, learned articles, legal documents, etc.

in·form·ant (in′fôr′mənt) a person who gives information to another: *She believed her informant because he had seen the accident happen.* *n.*

in·for·ma·tion (in′fər mā′shən) 1 knowledge; facts; news: *A dictionary gives information about words. The general sent the people information of his victory.* 2 an informing: *This guidebook is for the information of travellers.* *n.*

in·fra–red (in′frə red′) of or having to do with the long, invisible light waves just beyond the red end of the color spectrum: *Most of the heat from sunlight,*

hat, āge, fär; let, ēqual, tėrm; it, īce
hot, ōpen, ôrder; oil, out; cup, pu̇t, rüle
əbove, takən, pencəl, lemən, circəs
ch, child; ng, long; sh, ship
th, thin; ᴛʜ, then; zh, measure

incandescent lamps, resistance wires, etc. is from infrared rays. adj.

in·fre·quent (in frē′kwənt) not frequent; occurring seldom or far apart; scarce. *adj.* —**in·fre′quent·ly,** *adv.*

in·fringe (in frinj′) **1** act contrary to or violate a law, obligation, right, etc.: *A false label infringes the food and drug laws.* **2** trespass; encroach: *Do not infringe upon the rights of others.* *v.,* **in·fringed, in·fring·ing.**

in·fu·ri·ate (in fyür′ē āt′) fill with anger; make furious; enrage: *The man was infuriated when the dog snapped at him.* *v.,* **in·fu·ri·at·ed, in·fu·ri·at·ing.**

in·fuse (in fyüz′) **1** put in; pour: *The captain infused his own courage into his soldiers.* **2** inspire: *He infused the soldiers with his courage.* **3** steep or soak in a liquid to draw out flavor, minerals, etc. or to make a drink, drug, or other preparation: *Tea leaves are infused in hot water to make tea.* *v.,* **in·fused, in·fus·ing.**

–ing[1] a suffix meaning: **1** an action or the result, product, material, etc. of an action: *Walking is the action of one who walks. A drawing is the result of the act of drawing.* **2** of one or more that ____: *The smoking habit is the habit of one who smokes.*

–ing[2] **1** a suffix that forms the present participle of a verb: *She's been fishing all morning.* **2** a suffix meaning: that ____s: *Lasting happiness is happiness that lasts. A growing child is a child that grows.*

in·ge·ni·ous (in jē′nē əs) **1** clever; skilful in planning or making: *The ingenious boy made a radio set.* **2** cleverly planned or made: *This trap is an ingenious device.* *adj.* —**in·gen′ious·ly,** *adv.*

☛ **Ingenious** and **ingenuous** are quite different in meaning. **Ingenious** means clever; skilful: *Fay is so ingenious that she is sure to think of some way of doing this work more easily.* **Ingenuous** means frank; sincere; simple: *The ingenuous child had never thought of being suspicious of what other people told him.*

in·ge·nu·i·ty (in′jə nyü′ə tē or in′jə nü′ə tē) skill in planning or inventing; cleverness: *ingenuity in making toys.* *n., pl.* **in·ge·nu·i·ties.**

in·gen·u·ous (in jen′yü əs) **1** frank; open; sincere: *The honest boy gave an ingenuous account of his acts, concealing nothing.* **2** simple; natural: *Little children are ingenuous.* *adj.* —**in·gen′u·ous·ly,** *adv.* —**in·gen′u·ous·ness,** *n.*

☛ See note at **ingenious.**

in·got (ing′gət) a mass of metal, such as gold, silver, or steel, cast into a block or bar. *n.*

in·gra·ti·ate (in grā′shē āt′) bring oneself into favor: *He tried to ingratiate himself with the teacher by giving him presents.* *v.,* **in·gra·ti·at·ed, in·gra·ti·at·ing.**

in·grat·i·tude (in grat′ə tyüd′ or in grat′ə tüd′) a lack of gratitude or thankfulness; being ungrateful. *n.*

in·gre·di·ent (in grē′dē ənt) one of the parts of a mixture: *The ingredients of a cake usually include eggs, sugar, flour, and flavoring.* *n.*

in·hab·it (in hab′it) live in: *fish inhabit the sea.* *v.*

in·hab·it·ant (in hab′ə tənt) a person or animal that lives in a place: *Our town has almost 5000 inhabitants.* *n.*

in·hale (in hāl′) draw into the lungs; breathe in air, gas, fragrance, tobacco smoke, etc. *v.,* **in·haled, in·hal·ing.**

in·her·ent (in hēr′ənt or in her′ənt) existing as a natural or basic quality of a person or thing: *Her inherent curiosity about nature led her to study botany.* *adj.*

in·her·it (in her′it) **1** get or have after another person dies; receive as an heir: *Mrs. Chan's nephew inherited the farm after she died.* **2** get or possess from one's ancestors through heredity: *She inherits her blue eyes from her father.* *v.*

in·her·it·ance (in her′ə təns) **1** the act of inheriting: *She received her house by inheritance from an aunt.* **2** anything inherited: *The house was her inheritance. Good health is a fine inheritance from one's parents.* *n.*

in·hib·it (in hib′it) check; stop or hold back by obstructing or restricting: *The soldier's sense of duty inhibited his impulse to run away.* *v.*

in·hos·pi·ta·ble (in hos′pi tə bəl or in′hos pit′ə bəl) not hospitable; not making visitors comfortable: *The inhospitable people would not give us food or water.* *adj.*

in·hu·man (in hyü′mən) without kindness; brutal; cruel: *It was an inhuman act to kidnap the child and terrorize the parents.* *adj.*

in·iq·ui·ty (in ik′wə tē) **1** very great injustice; wickedness. **2** a wicked and unjust act. *n., pl.* **in·iq·ui·ties.**

i·ni·tial (i nish′əl) **1** occurring at the beginning; first; earliest: *His initial effort at skating was a failure.* **2** the first letter of a word: *The initials P.E.I. stand for Prince Edward Island.* **3** to mark or sign with initials: *Mr. Conrad A. Smith initialled the note C.A.S.* 1 *adj.,* 2 *n.,* 3 *v.,* **i·ni·tialled** or **i·ni·tialed, i·ni·tial·ling** or **i·ni·tial·ing.**

i·ni·ti·ate (i nish′ē āt′ for 1–3, i nish′ē it for 4) **1** be the one to start; set going; begin: *this year the school will initiate a series of free concerts.* **2** admit a person by special forms or ceremonies into a group or society: *The old members initiated the new members.* **3** help to get a first understanding; introduce into the knowledge of some art or subject: *to initiate a person into business methods.* **4** a person who is initiated. 1–3 *v.,* **i·ni·ti·at·ed, i·ni·ti·at·ing;** 4 *n.*

i·ni·ti·a·tion (i nish′ē ā′shən) **1** the act or process of being initiated; starting something; beginning: *the initiation of the free concerts.* **2** a formal admission into a group or society. **3** the ceremonies by which one is admitted into a group or society: *Many members of the club showed up for the initiation.* *n.*

i·ni·ti·a·tive (i nish′ē ə tiv or i nish′ə tiv) **1** the active part in taking the first steps in any undertaking; the lead: *She is shy and does not take the initiative in making acquaintances.* **2** the readiness and ability to get things started: *A good leader must have initiative.* *n.*

in·ject (in jekt′) **1** force liquid, medicine, etc. into a cavity, passage, or tissue: *Drugs are often injected into the body.* **2** throw in; introduce: *The stranger injected a remark into their conversation.* *v.*

in·jec·tion (in jek′shən) **1** the act or process of

injecting: *Those drugs are given by injection as well as through the mouth. They enjoyed the injection of the stranger's jokes into the dull discussion.* **2** something injected. *n.*

in·junc·tion (in jungk′shən) a command; order: *He obeyed his mother's injunction to hurry straight home. n.*

in·jure (in′jər) **1** do damage to; harm; hurt: *Do not break or injure the bushes in the park.* **2** be unfair to; do wrong to. *v.,* **in·jured, in·jur·ing.**

in·ju·ri·ous (in jür′ē əs) causing injury; harmful: *Hail is injurious to crops. adj.*

in·ju·ry (in′jər ē) **1** a hurt or loss caused to or endured by a person or thing; harm; damage: *She escaped from the train wreck without injury.* **2** a wound; hurt; an act that harms or damages: *He received a serious injury in the accident. The accident will certainly be an injury to the reputation of the airline.* **3** unfairness; injustice; wrong: *You did me an injury when you said I lied. n., pl.* **in·ju·ries.**

in·jus·tice (in jus′tis) **1** lack of justice. **2** an unjust act: *To send an innocent man to jail is an injustice. n.*

ink (ingk) **1** a liquid used for writing, printing, or drawing. **2** put ink on; mark or stain with ink. 1 *n.,* 2 *v.*

ink·ling (ingk′ling) a hint; a slight suggestion; a vague notion: *We had no inkling that the party was for us. n.*

ink·well (ingk′wel′) a container used to hold ink on a desk or table. *n.*

ink·y (ingk′ē) **1** dark like ink; black: *inky shadows.* **2** covered with ink; stained with ink. *adj.,* **ink·i·er, ink·i·est.**

in·laid (in′lād′) **1** set in the surface as a decoration or design: *The desk had an inlaid design of light wood in dark.* **2** decorated with a design or material set in the surface: *The box had an inlaid cover. adj.*

in·land (in′lənd for 1 and 4, in′land′ or in′lənd for 2 and 3) **1** away from the coast or the border; having to do with or situated in the interior: *an inland sea.* **2** the interior of a country; land away from the border or the coast. **3** in or toward the interior. **4** not foreign; domestic: *inland trade.* 1, 4 *adj.,* 2 *n.,* 3 *adv.*

in–law (in′lo′ or in′lô′) *Informal.* a relative by marriage: *They had his in-laws visiting last week. n.*

in·lay (in′lā′) **1** set as a decoration or design into a shallow recess in a surface: *inlay narrow strips of gold into the enamel.* **2** decorate with something set into the surface: *Inlay a wooden box with silver.* **3** an inlaid decoration, design, or material: *an enamel ring with gold inlays.* 1, 2 *v.,* **in·laid, in·lay·ing;** 3 *n.*

in·let (in′let′ or in′lət) **1** a narrow strip of water running from a larger body of water into the land or between islands: *The fishing village was on a small inlet of the sea.* **2** entrance. *n.*

in·mate (in′māt′) a person who lives with others in the same building, especially one in a prison, hospital, asylum, etc. *n.*

in·most (in′mōst′) **1** farthest in; deepest within: *We went to the inmost depths of the mine.* **2** most private or personal: *Her inmost desire was to be an astronaut. adj.*

inn (in) a place where travellers and others can get a room to sleep in and meals: *Hotels have largely taken the place of the old inns. n.*

☛ **Inn** and **in** are pronounced the same.

in·ner (in′ər) **1** farther in; inside: *an inner room.* **2** private; secret: *She kept her inner thoughts to herself. adj.*

inner ear the space behind the three bones of the middle ear: *In human beings, the inner ear contains the organs that control balance and that change sound into nerve impulses.*

in·ner·most (in′ər mōst′) farthest in; inmost: *the innermost parts. adj.*

inner tube a separate rubber tube that fits inside some tires and is inflated with air.

in·ning (in′ing) **1** in baseball, the time when each team is at bat. **2** **innings,** *pl.* in cricket, the period of a game when one team is batting: *This is our second innings.* **3** Often, **innings,** *pl.* the time a person or party is in power; a chance or opportunity for action: *The younger children had their innings when the teenagers were away at camp. n.*

inn·keep·er (in′kēp′ər) a person who owns, manages, or keeps an inn. *n.*

in·no·cence (in′ə səns) **1** freedom from sin, wrong, or guilt; being innocent: *The accused man proved his innocence of the crime.* **2** simplicity; lack of cunning: *The saint had the innocence of a little child. n.*

in·no·cent (in′ə sənt) **1** doing no wrong; free from sin or wrong; not guilty: *The policeman shot at the murderer but hit an innocent bystander.* **2** without knowledge of evil, and so free from sin or wrong: *as innocent as a baby.* **3** doing no harm: *innocent amusements.* **4** an innocent person. 1–3 *adj.,* 4 *n.* **—in′no·cent·ly,** *adv.*

in·noc·u·ous (i nok′yü əs) harmless; not damaging: *innocuous medicine, innocuous remarks. adj.* **—in·noc′u·ous·ly,** *adv.*

in·no·vate (in′ə vāt′) make changes; bring in something new or do something in a new way: *It is difficult to innovate when people feel that the old way of doing something is better. v.,* **in·no·vat·ed, in·no·vat·ing.**

in·no·va·tion (in′ə vā′shən) **1** a change made in the established way of doing things: *The new principal made many innovations.* **2** the making of changes; bringing in new things or new ways of doing things: *The use of postal codes is an innovation. n.*

In·nu·it (in′ü it, in′yü it, or in′yə wit) *Cdn.* See **Inuit.**

in·nu·mer·a·ble (i nyü′mər ə bəl or i nü′mər ə bəl) too many to count; very many: *innumerable stars. adj.*

in·oc·u·late (in ok′yə lāt′) **1** give to a person or animal a preparation made from killed or weakened disease bacteria or viruses so that the individual will not get a disease or will suffer only a very mild form of the disease: *The doctor will inoculate the baby against smallpox.* **2** use disease bacteria or viruses to prevent diseases. *v.,* **in·oc·u·lat·ed, in·oc·u·lat·ing.**

in·oc·u·la·tion (in ok′yə lā′shən) the act or process of inoculating: *Inoculation has greatly reduced the number of deaths from diphtheria and typhoid fever. n.*

in·of·fen·sive (in′ə fen′siv) not offensive; harmless: not arousing objections: *He made an inoffensive comment. adj.*

hat, āge, fär; let, ēqual, tėrm; it, īce
hot, ōpen, ôrder; oil, out; cup, pu̇t, rüle
əbove, takən, pencəl, lemən, circəs
ch, child; ng, long; sh, ship
th, thin; ᴛʜ, then; zh, measure

in·or·gan·ic (in′ôr gan′ik) 1 not having the structure of animals and plants: *Minerals are inorganic.* 2 not having to do with the processes or activities of living animals and plants. *adj.*

in·quest (in′kwest) 1 a legal inquiry led by a coroner, usually with a jury, held to find out the cause of a sudden death: *An inquest is held when there is a possibility that death was the result of a crime or of a situation that could be dangerous to other people.* 2 a jury appointed to hold such an inquiry: *The inquest was told that a witness had been delayed.* 3 any other investigation into the causes of an event, situation, etc. *n.*

in·quire (in kwīr′) 1 try to find out by questions; ask: *He telephoned the hotel to inquire about a room.* 2 make a search for information, knowledge, or truth: *The man read many old books and documents while inquiring into the history of the town.* *v.,* **in·quired, in·quir·ing.** Also **enquire.**

in·quir·y (in kwīr′ē or in′kwə rē) 1 a question: *The guide answered all our inquiries.* 2 a search for truth, information, or knowledge. 3 inquiring; asking. *n., pl.* **in·quir·ies.** Also **enquiry.**

in·quis·i·tive (in kwiz′ə tiv) 1 curious; asking many questions: *Children are usually inquisitive.* 2 too curious; prying into other people's affairs: *The old man is inquisitive about what his neighbors do.* *adj.* **—in·quis′i·tive·ly,** *adv.* **—in·quis′i·tive·ness,** *n.*

in·road (in′rōd′) 1 a raid or attack; entry by force. 2 an advance or attack that lessens or destroys something: *Her illness made inroads on her strength.* *n.*

in·sane (in sān′) 1 not sane; suffering from severe mental illness: *Insane people are kept in asylums.* 2 extremely foolish: *'What an insane plan!'* *adj.* **—in·sane′ly,** *adv.*

☛ See note at **mad.**

in·san·i·ty (in san′ə tē) 1 the condition of being insane; madness; mental illness. 2 extreme folly: *It is insanity to drive a car without any brakes.* *n., pl.* **in·san·i·ties.**

in·sa·tia·ble (in sā′shə bəl) that cannot be satisfied: *The boy had an insatiable appetite for candy.* *adj.*

in·scribe (in skrīb′) 1 write or engrave on; mark: *The ring was inscribed with her name. How shall we inscribe the bracelet? Please inscribe my initials on it.* 2 impress deeply: *His father's words are inscribed on his memory.* *v.,* **in·scribed, in·scrib·ing.**

in·scrip·tion (in skrip′shən) something inscribed: *the inscription on a monument, on a coin, or on an old temple.* *n.*

in·scru·ta·ble (in skrü′tə bəl) that cannot be understood; so mysterious or obscure that one cannot make out its meaning: *an inscrutable look.* *adj.*

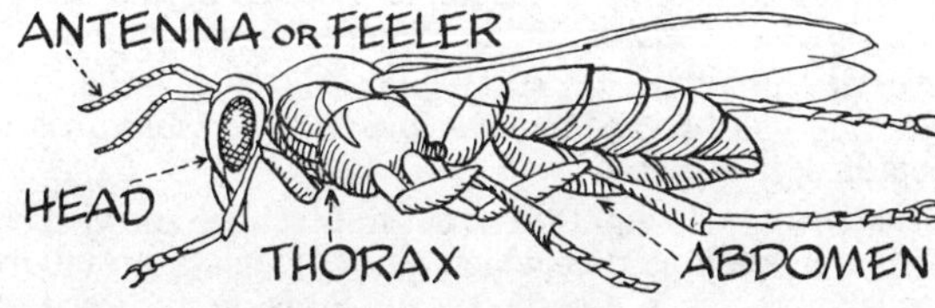

Insect (def. 1): a wasp

in·sect (in′sekt) 1 any of a group of small animals with no backbone and with the body divided into three parts, having three pairs of legs and, usually, two pairs of wings: *Flies, mosquitoes, gnats, and bees are insects.* 2 any similar small animal with its body divided into several parts, having several pairs of legs: *Spiders and centipedes are often called insects.* *n.*

☛ **Insect** comes from Latin *insectum,* formed from the verb *insecare,* meaning to 'cut into' or 'cut up.' An insect's body is divided into segments which make it look as if it had been cut.

in·sec·ti·cide (in sek′tə sīd′) a substance for killing insects. *n.*

in·sen·si·ble (in sen′sə bəl) 1 not sensitive; not able to feel or notice: *We were thrilled by the lovely view, but Tom was insensible to it. A blind man is insensible to colors.* 2 not aware: *The boys in the boat were insensible of the danger.* 3 not able to feel anything; unconscious: *The man hit by a truck was insensible for four hours.* 4 not easily felt or realized: *The room grew cold by insensible degrees.* *adj.*

in·sen·si·tive (in sen′sə tiv) 1 not sensitive; not responsive to beauty, the feelings of others, etc.: *an insensitive nature.* 2 numb; not able to feel anything: *An injection made the gum insensitive so that the dentist's drilling did not hurt.* *adj.*

in·sen·si·tiv·i·ty (in sen′sə tiv′ə tē) lack of sensitivity. *n.*

in·sep·a·ra·ble (in sep′ə rə bəl) that cannot be separated or parted: *inseparable friends. Heat is inseparable from fire.* *adj.*

in·sert (in sėrt′ for 1, in′sėrt for 2) 1 put in; set in: *to insert a key into a lock, to insert a letter into a word.* 2 something put in or set in: *The book contained an insert of several pages of pictures.* 1 *v.,* 2 *n.*

in·ser·tion (in sėr′shən) 1 the act of inserting: *The insertion of one word can change the meaning of a whole sentence.* 2 something inserted: *Insertions of lace trimmed the sleeves from shoulder to cuff.* *n.*

in·side (in′sīd′ for 1, 2, 3, 6, in′sīd′ for 4, 5) 1 the part within; the inner surface: *The inside of the box was lined with colored paper.* 2 the contents: *The inside of the book was more interesting than the cover.* 3 being on the inside: *an inside seat, the inside pages of a magazine.* 4 within; in or into the inner part: *Please go inside.* 5 inside of; in: *The nut is inside the shell.* 6 secret; done or known by those inside: *The police needed inside information and questioned the maid.* 1, 2 *n.,* 3, 6 *adj.,* 4 *adv.,* 5 *prep.*

inside out, a so that what should be inside is outside; with the inside showing: *He turned his pockets inside out.* **b** completely: *He learned his lessons inside out.*

in·sid·i·ous (in sid′ē əs) 1 crafty; sly; tricky. 2 working secretly or subtly; developing gradually without attracting attention: *insidious disease.* *adj.* **—in·sid′i·ous·ly,** *adv.*

in·sight (in′sīt′) 1 an understanding or awareness

based on a seeing of the inside or inner nature of something: *Take the machine apart and get an insight into how it works.* 2 wisdom and understanding in dealing with people or with facts: *We study science to gain insight into the world we live in.* *n.*

in·sig·ni·a (in sig′nē ə) 1 the emblems, badges, or other distinguishing marks of a high position or honor: *The crown, orb, and sceptre are the insignia of kings.* 2 the distinguishing badges, crests, etc. of a unit or branch of the armed forces. *n. pl.*

☛ **Insignia** is always a plural noun. It came from the plural of a Latin word *insigne,* meaning 'badge.'

in·sig·nif·i·cant (in′sig nif′ə kənt) 1 having little use or importance: *A cent is an insignificant amount of money.* 2 having little or no meaning: *insignificant chatter.* *adj.* —**in′sig·nif′i·cant·ly,** *adv.*

in·sin·cere (in′sin sēr′) not sincere; not honest or candid. *adj.* —**in′sin·cere′ly,** *adv.*

in·sin·u·ate (in′sin′yü āt′) 1 hint; suggest in an indirect way: *Without making any direct charges, he insinuated that the mayor had accepted bribes.* 2 push in or get in by an indirect, subtle way: *The stray cat insinuated itself into the kitchen. The spy insinuated himself into the confidence of important army officers.* *v.,* **in·sin·u·at·ed, in·sin·u·at·ing.**

in·sist (in sist′) keep firmly to some demand, statement, or position; take a stand and refuse to give in: *He insists that he had a right to use his brother's tools. Mother insists that we wash our hands before eating.* *v.*

in·sist·ence (in sis′təns) 1 the act of insisting: *Remember Mother's insistence that we comb our hair.* 2 being insistent. *n.*

in·sist·ent (in sis′tənt) 1 insisting; continuing to make a strong, firm demand or statement: *Although it was raining, he was insistent about going for a walk.* 2 compelling attention or notice; pressing; urgent: *An insistent knocking on the door woke us up.* *adj.* —**in·sist′ent·ly,** *adv.*

in·so·lence (in′sə ləns) bold rudeness; insulting behavior or speech: *The man was irritated by his son's insolence.* *n.*

in·so·lent (in′sə lənt) boldly rude; insulting: *the insolent boy was punished for shouting at his father.* *adj.* —**in′so·lent·ly,** *adv.*

in·som·ni·a (in som′nē ə) not being able to sleep; sleeplessness: *He suffers from insomnia.* *n.*

in·spect (in spekt′) 1 look over carefully; examine: *A dentist inspects the children's teeth twice a year.* 2 examine formally; look over officially: *Government officials inspect factories and mines to make sure that they are safe for workers.* *v.*

in·spec·tion (in spek′shən) 1 an inspecting: *An inspection of the roof showed no leaks.* 2 a formal or official examination: *The soldiers lined up for their daily inspection by their officers.* *n.*

in·spec·tor (in spek′tər) 1 an officer or official appointed to inspect: *a milk inspector.* 2 a police officer, usually ranking next below a superintendent. *n.*

in·spi·ra·tion (in′spə rā′shən) 1 influence of thought and strong feelings on actions, especially on good or creative actions: *Some people get inspiration from sermons, some from poetry.* 2 a person or thing that arouses effort to do well: *The captain is an inspiration to his men.* 3 an idea that is inspired; a sudden, brilliant idea: *Many inventions are the result of inspiration.* 4 the drawing of air into the lungs; breathing in. *n.*

in·spire (in spīr′) 1 put thought, feeling, life, force, etc. into: *The coach inspired the girls with a desire to win.* 2 cause thought or feeling: *The leader's courage inspired confidence in others.* 3 fill with a thought or feeling; influence: *A chance to try again inspired him with hope.* 4 suggest; cause to be told or written: *His enemies inspired false stories about him.* 5 breathe in; draw air into the lungs. *v.,* **in·spired, in·spir·ing.**

in·stall (in stol′ or in stôl′) 1 place in office with ceremonies: *The new judge was installed without delay.* 2 put in a place or position; settle: *The cat installed itself in the easy chair.* 3 put in position for use: *The owner of the house had new plumbing installed.* *v.*

in·stal·ment or **in·stall·ment** (in stol′mənt or in stôl′mənt) 1 a part of a sum of money or a debt to be paid at stated times: *She has to pay an instalment of $15 each month on her coat till she has paid $135.* 2 one of several parts issued at different times as part of a series: *This magazine has a serial story in six instalments.* *n.*

in·stance (in′stəns) 1 a person or thing serving as an example; a case: *Her rude question was an instance of bad manners.* 2 a stage or step in an action; occasion: *In this instance he decided not to go with them to the drive-in.* *n.*

for instance, as an example: *Her many hobbies include, for instance, skating and stamp collecting.*

in·stant (in′stənt) 1 a particular moment: *Stop talking this instant!* 2 a moment of time: *He paused for an instant.* 3 immediate: *The medicine gave instant relief from pain.* 4 pressing; urgent: *When there is a fire there is an instant need for action.* 5 prepared beforehand and requiring little or no cooking, mixing, or additional ingredients: *instant pudding, instant potatoes.* 1, 2 *n.,* 3–5 *adj.*

in·stan·ta·ne·ous (in′stən tā′nē əs) coming or done in an instant; happening or made in an instant: *A flash of lightning is instantaneous. When the speaker finished talking the applause was instantaneous.* *adj.* —**in′stan·ta′ne·ous·ly,** *adv.*

in·stant·ly (in′stənt lē) in an instant; at once; immediately. *adv.*

in·stead (in sted′) in place of someone or something; as a substitute: *She stayed home, and her sister went riding instead.* *adv.*

instead of, rather than; in place of; as a substitute for: *Instead of studying, she read a story.*

in·step (in′step) 1 the upper surface of the human foot between the toes and the ankle. See **leg** for picture. 2 the part of a shoe, stocking, etc. over the instep. *n.*

in·sti·gate (in′stə gāt′) stir up; set in motion, especially something undesirable: *Foreign agents instigated a rebellion.* *v.,* **in·sti·gat·ed, in·sti·gat·ing.**

in·stil or **in·still** (in stil′) put in little by little: *Reading good books instils a love for fine literature.* *v.,* **in·stilled, in·still·ing.**

in·stinct (in′stingkt) 1 a natural feeling, knowledge, or power, such as that which guides animals; an inborn tendency to act in a certain way: *Birds do not learn to fly but fly by instinct.* 2 a natural tendency or ability; talent: *Even as a child, the artist had an instinct for color.* *n.*

hat, āge, fär; let, ēqual, tėrm; it, īce
hot, ōpen, ôrder; oil, out; cup, pu̇t, rüle
əbove, takən, pencəl, lemən, circəs
ch, child; ng, long; sh, ship
th, thin; ᴛʜ, then; zh, measure

in·stinc·tive (in stingk′tiv) of or having to do with instinct; caused or done by instinct; born in an animal or person, not learned: *Climbing is instinctive in monkeys.* *adj.* **—in·stinc′tive·ly,** *adv.*

in·sti·tute (in′stə tyüt′ or in′stə tüt′) **1** an organization or society for some special purpose: *the Institute for the Blind. An art institute teaches and displays art.* **2** the building used by such an organization or society: *We spent the afternoon in the Art Institute.* **3** set up; establish; begin; start: *The police instituted an inquiry into the causes of the accident.* 1, 2 *n.*, 3 *v.*, **in·sti·tut·ed, in·sti·tut·ing.**

in·sti·tu·tion (in′stə tyü′shən or in′stə tü′shən) **1** an organization or society established for some public or social purpose: *A church, school, college, hospital, asylum, or prison is an institution.* **2** a building used for the work of an institution. **3** an established law or custom: *Giving presents on Christmas is an institution. Marriage is an institution among most peoples of the earth.* **4** a beginning; starting; establishing: *The school has planned the institution of a hockey team this winter.* *n.*

in·struct (in strukt′) **1** teach; train; educate. **2** give directions to; order: *The doctor instructed him to go to bed and rest. The owner of the house instructed his agent to sell it.* **3** inform; tell: *Her lawyer instructed her that the contract would be signed on March 1st.* *v.*

in·struc·tion (in struk′shən) **1** teaching or educating. **2** the knowledge or teaching given: *In this geography class, instruction includes town planning.* **3 instructions,** *pl.* directions, orders. *n.*

in·struc·tive (in struk′tiv) useful for instruction; giving knowledge or information; instructing: *A trip around the world is an instructive experience.* *adj.* **—in·struc′tive·ly,** *adv.*

in·struc·tor (in struk′tər) teacher. *n.*

in·stru·ment (in′strə mənt) **1** a tool or mechanical device: *a dentist's instruments.* **2** a device for producing musical sounds: *wind instruments, stringed instruments. A violin, a cello, and a piano were the instruments in the trio.* **3** a device for measuring, recording, or controlling: *A thermometer is an instrument for measuring temperature.* **4** anything with or by which something is done; a person made use of by another; means: *The master criminal used many men and women as instruments in his crimes.* *n.*

in·stru·men·tal (in′strə men′təl) **1** acting or serving as a means; useful; helpful: *His uncle was instrumental in getting him a job.* **2** played on or written for musical instruments: *The singer was accompanied by instrumental music.* *adj.*

in·sub·or·di·nate (in′sə bôr′də nit) resisting authority; not obedient; unruly. *adj.*

in·suf·fer·a·ble (in suf′ər ə bəl) unbearable: *His insufferable insolence cost him many friends.* *adj.*

in·suf·fi·cient (in′sə fish′ənt) not enough; less than is needed: *He was tired because he had had insufficient sleep.* *adj.* **—in′suf·fi′cient·ly,** *adv.*

in·su·late (in′sə lāt′) **1** keep from losing or transferring electricity, heat, sound, etc., especially by covering, packing, or surrounding with a material that does not conduct electricity, heat, etc.: *Telephone wires are often insulated by a covering of rubber.* **2** pack with material that will not burn, so as to prevent the spread of fire: *The builder insulated the wall between the garage and the house.* **3** set apart; separate from others; isolate. *v.*, **in·su·lat·ed, in·su·lat·ing.**

in·su·la·tion (in′sə lā′shən) **1** insulating or being insulated: *The electrician checked the insulation of the wiring.* **2** the material used in insulating: *Asbestos is often used as insulation against fire.* *n.*

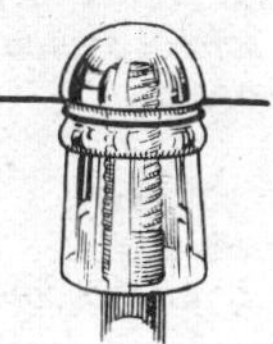

A glass insulator for electric wires. With such insulators, wires can be fastened to poles without any loss of current.

in·su·la·tor (in′sə lā′tər) that which insulates; something that prevents the passage of electricity, heat, or sound: *Glass is an effective insulator.* *n.*

in·sult (in sult′ for 1, in′sult for 2) **1** treat with scorn, abuse, or great rudeness: *The rebels insulted the flag by throwing mud on it.* **2** an insulting speech or action: *To be called a coward is an insult.* 1 *v.*, 2 *n.*

in·su·per·a·ble (in sü′pər ə bəl) that cannot be passed over or overcome: *The mountain ridge proved to be an insuperable barrier so the explorers had to turn back.* *adj.* **—in·su′per·a·bly,** *adv.*

in·sur·ance (in shür′əns) **1** an insuring of property, person, or life: *fire insurance, burglary insurance, accident insurance, life insurance, health insurance.* **2** the business of insuring property, life, etc.: *My uncle works in insurance.* **3** the amount of money for which a person or thing is insured: *He has $20 000 insurance, which his wife will receive if he dies first.* **4** the amount of money paid for insurance; premium: *His fire insurance is $100 a year.* *n.*

in·sure (in shür′) **1** make safe; protect: *More care will insure you against making so many mistakes.* **2** make sure or certain; ensure: *Check your work to insure its accuracy.* **3** make safe against loss by making small regular payments to an insurance company that agrees to pay a certain sum of money in case of loss, accident, or death: *He insured his car against accident, theft, and fire.* **4** arrange for money payment in case of loss, accident, or death: *An insurance company will insure your house against fire.* *v.*, **in·sured, in·sur·ing.**
☛ See note at **ensure.**

in·sur·gent (in sėr′jənt) **1** a person who rises in revolt; rebel: *The insurgents captured the town.* **2** rising in revolt; rebellious: *The insurgent slaves burned their masters' houses.* 1 *n.*, 2 *adj.*

in·sur·rec·tion (in′sə rek′shən) a revolt or rebellion. *n.*

in·tact (in takt′) untouched; uninjured; whole; with no part missing: *The money was returned intact by the boy who found it.* *adj.*

in·take (in′tāk′) 1 a place where water, air, gas, etc. enters a channel, pipe, or other narrow opening. 2 the act or process of taking in. 3 the amount or thing taken in: *The intake through the pipe was 20 000 litres a day.* *n.*

in·tan·gi·ble (in tan′jə bəl) 1 not capable of being touched or felt: *Sound and light are intangible.* 2 not easily grasped by the mind; vague: *She had that intangible quality called charm.* 3 something intangible. 1, 2 *adj.*, 3 *n.*

in·te·ger (in′tə jər) any member of the set of positive and negative whole numbers and zero. *n.*

in·te·grate (in′tə grāt′) bring separate units or parts together into a whole; unite: *The two school systems were integrated to cut costs.* *v.*, **in·te·grat·ed, in·te·grat·ing.**

in·teg·ri·ty (in teg′rə tē) 1 honesty; sincerity; uprightness: *A man of integrity is respected.* 2 completeness; wholeness: *The integrity of the country was guaranteed by treaty.* *n.*

in·tel·lect (in′tə lekt′) 1 the power of knowing; understanding: *Our actions are influenced by our intellect, will, and feelings.* 2 intelligence; high mental ability: *a woman of intellect.* 3 a person of high mental ability: *He was one of the great intellects of his time.* *n.*

in·tel·lec·tu·al (in′tə lek′chü əl) 1 of the intellect: *Thinking is an intellectual process.* 2 needing or using intelligence: *Teaching is an intellectual occupation.* 3 having or showing intelligence: *an intellectual person, an intellectual face.* 4 a person who is well informed and intelligent. 1–3 *adj.*, 4 *n.*

in·tel·li·gence (in tel′ə jəns) 1 the ability to learn and know; understanding; mind: *A dog has more intelligence than a worm.* 2 knowledge; news; information: *The spy gave the government secret intelligence of the plans of the enemy.* *n.*

in·tel·li·gent (in tel′ə jənt) having or showing intelligence; able to learn and know; quick to understand: *Elephants and horses are intelligent animals.* *adj.* **—in·tel′li·gent·ly,** *adv.*

in·tel·li·gi·ble (in tel′ə jə bəl) capable of being understood; clear. *adj.*

in·tem·per·ance (in tem′pər əns) 1 a lack of moderation or self-control; excess: *His intemperance in gambling cost him his job.* 2 too much drinking of intoxicating liquor. *n.*

in·tem·per·ate (in tem′pər it) 1 not moderate; lacking in self-control; excessive: *an intemperate appetite, an intemperate anger.* 2 drinking too much intoxicating liquor. 3 not temperate; extreme in temperature; severe: *an intemperate winter.* *adj.* **—in·tem′per·ate·ly,** *adv.*

in·tend (in tend′) 1 have in mind as a purpose; plan: *We intend to go home soon. He intends that his sons shall go to university.* 2 mean for a particular purpose or use: *That gift was intended for you.* *v.*

in·tense (in tens′) 1 very much; very great; very strong; extreme: *intense happiness. A bad burn causes intense pain. Intense heat melts iron.* 2 having or showing strong feeling: *An intense person is one who feels things very deeply.* *adj.* **—in·tense′ly,** *adv.*

in·ten·si·fy (in ten′sə fī′) make or become intense or more intense: *Blowing on a fire intensifies the heat. Her first failure only intensified her desire to succeed.* *v.*, **in·ten·si·fied, in·ten·si·fy·ing.**

in·ten·si·ty (in ten′sə tē) 1 being intense; great strength; extreme degree: *the intensity of sunlight, intensity of thought, intensity of feeling.* 2 the amount or degree of strength of electricity, heat, light, sound, etc. per unit of area, volume, etc. *n.*, *pl.* **in·ten·si·ties.**

in·ten·sive (in ten′siv) very deep and thorough: *An intensive study of a few books is more valuable than much careless reading.* *adj.* **—in·ten′sive·ly,** *adv.*

in·tent (in tent′) 1 the purpose; intention: *The thief shot with intent to kill.* 2 the meaning; significance: *What is the intent of that remark?* 3 very attentive; having the eyes or thoughts earnestly fixed on something; earnest: *an intent look, intent on a task.* 4 much interested; determined: *He was intent on succeeding. She is intent on doing her best.* 1, 2 *n.*, 3, 4 *adj.* **—in·tent′ly,** *adv.*

to all intents and purposes, in almost every way; almost; practically.

in·ten·tion (in ten′shən) intending; a purpose; design; plan: *The boy hurt his sister's feelings without intention. Their intention is to travel next summer.* *n.*

in·ten·tion·al (in ten′shən əl) done on purpose; meant; planned; intended: *His insult was intentional; he wanted to hurt your feelings.* *adj.* **—in·ten′tion·al·ly,** *adv.*

in·ter (in tėr′) put a dead body into a grave or tomb; bury. *v.*, **in·terred, in·ter·ring.**

inter– a prefix that means: 1 together; one with the other: *Intercommunicate means communicate together.* 2 among members of a group: *Interschool means between or among schools.*

in·ter·cede (in′tər sēd′) ask a favor on behalf of another; plead for another: *Jack did not dare ask the teacher himself; so Ned interceded with her for Jack.* *v.*, **in·ter·ced·ed, in·ter·ced·ing.**

in·ter·cept (in′tər sept′) 1 take or seize on the way from one place to another: *to intercept a letter or a messenger.* 2 check; stop: *to intercept the flight of a criminal.* *v.*

in·ter·ces·sion (in′tər sesh′ən) the act of interceding or of pleading for another: *Mother's intercession prevented a quarrel between the sisters.* *n.*

in·ter·change (in′tər chānj′ for 1, in′tər chānj′ for 2 and 3) 1 put each of two or more persons or things in the other's place: *The two girls interchanged hats.* 2 putting each of two or more persons or things in the other's place: *The word 'team' may be turned into 'meat' by the interchange of the end letters.* 3 a road that permits traffic from one highway to change to another without crossing in front of other traffic; cloverleaf. 1 *v.*, **in·ter·changed, in·ter·chang·ing;** 2, 3 *n.*

in·ter·change·a·ble (in′tər chān′jə bəl) capable of being used in place of each other: *This saw has several interchangeable blades.* *adj.* **—in′ter·change′a·bly,** *adv.*

in·ter·course (in′tər kôrs′) communication; dealings between people; the exchange of thoughts, services, and feelings: *Airplanes, good roads, and telephones make intercourse with different parts of the country far easier than it was fifty years ago.* *n.*

in·ter·est (in′trist or in′tər ist) 1 a feeling of wanting to know, see, do, own, share in, or take part: *He has an interest in reading and in collecting stamps.* 2 arouse

hat, āge, fär; let, ēqual, tėrm; it, īce
hot, ōpen, ôrder; oil, out; cup, put, rüle
əbove, takən, pencəl, lemən, circəs
ch, child; ng, long; sh, ship
th, thin; ᴛʜ, then; zh, measure

such a feeling in; make curious and hold the attention of: *A good story interests us.* 3 the power of arousing such feelings: *A dull book lacks interest.* 4 a share or part in property and actions: *Father has a half interest in that farm.* 5 cause a person to take a share or part in; arouse the concern, curiosity, or attention of: *The agent tried to interest us in buying a car. We were interested in the results of the election.* 6 a thing in which a person has a share or part: *Any activity, pastime, or hobby can be an interest.* 7 a group of people having the same activity, business, etc.: *the farming interests, mining interests.* 8 advantage; profit; benefit: *Father and Mother look after the interests of the family.* 9 money paid for the use of money, usually a percentage of the amount invested, borrowed, or loaned: *The interest on the loan was 10 per cent a year.* 1, 3, 4, 6–9 *n.*, 2, 5 *v.*

in·ter·est·ed (in′tris təd, in′tər is təd, or in′tər es′təd) 1 feeling or showing interest: *an interested spectator.* 2 having an interest or share. *adj.*

☛ The adjective **interested** has two opposites. **Uninterested** is just its negative and means 'having no feeling about a matter': *He was uninterested in the outcome of the game.* **Disinterested** means 'free from selfish motives; impartial; fair': *A disinterested onlooker offered to referee the game.*

in·ter·est·ing (in′tris ting, in′tər is ting, or in′tər es′ting) arousing interest; holding one's attention: *Stories about travel and adventures are interesting. adj.* **—in′ter·est·ing·ly,** *adv.*

in·ter·fere (in′tər fēr′) 1 clash; come into opposition with: *Because the two plans interfere with each other, one must be changed. I will come on Saturday if nothing interferes.* 2 disturb the affairs of others; meddle: *That woman is always interfering in other people's affairs. v.,* **in·ter·fered, in·ter·fer·ing.**
interfere with, hinder: *The weather interfered with our plans.*

in·ter·fer·ence (in′tər fēr′əns) 1 the act or fact of interfering: *Her interference spoiled our game.* 2 something that interferes: *His interruption of the meeting was an unnecessary interference.* 3 in radio or television, the interruption of a desired signal by other signals. 4 in football, hockey, and other sports, the obstruction of an opposing player in a way not allowed by the rules. *n.*

in·ter·im (in′tər im) 1 meantime; the time between: *They couldn't leave till the rain stopped, so they played cards in the interim.* 2 for the meantime; temporary: *an interim report.* 1 *n.*, 2 *adj.*

in·te·ri·or (in tēr′ē ər) 1 the inner surface or part; inside: *The interior of the house was beautifully decorated.* 2 on the inside; inner. 3 the part of a region or country away from the coast or border: *There are deserts in the interior of Asia.* 4 away from the coast or border. 1, 3 *n.*, 2, 4 *adj.*

in·ter·ject (in′tər jekt′) throw in between other things; insert: *Every now and then the speaker interjected a joke or story to keep us interested. v.*

in·ter·jec·tion (in′tər jek′shən) 1 an exclamation of surprise, sorrow, delight, or some other feeling: *Some common interjections are: oh! ah! and hurrah!* 2 something interjected; a remark thrown in; exclamation. *n.*

in·ter·lace (in′tər lās′) 1 arrange or cross threads, strips, branches, etc. so that they go over and under each other; weave together: *Baskets are made by interlacing reeds or fibres.* 2 cross each other over and under; mingle together: *The branches of the trees interlaced above the path. The pilot looked down on interlacing roads and streams. v.,* **in·ter·laced, in·ter·lac·ing.**

in·ter·lock (in′tər lok′) join or fit tightly together; lock together: *The two stags were fighting with their horns interlocked. The different pieces of a jigsaw puzzle interlock. v.*

in·ter·lop·er (in′tər lōp′ər) a person who forces himself in where he is not wanted or has no right to be; intruder. *n.*

in·ter·lude (in′tər lüd′) 1 anything thought of as filling the time between two things: *There was an interlude of sunshine between two showers.* 2 a piece of music played between the parts of a song, church service, etc. *n.*

in·ter·me·di·ar·y (in′tər mē′dē er′ē) 1 a person who acts for one person with another; go-between: *The teacher acted as intermediary between the students and the principal.* 2 going or being between; intermediate: *A chrysalis is an intermediary stage between a caterpillar and a butterfly.* 1 *n.*, 2 *adj.*

in·ter·me·di·ate (in′tər mē′dē it) 1 being or occurring between; middle: *The intermediate department of the Sunday School is between the primary and the senior departments. Grey is intermediate between black and white.* 2 something in between. 1 *adj.*, 2 *n.* **—in′ter·me′di·ate·ly,** *adv.*

in·ter·mi·na·ble (in tėr′mə nə bəl) endless; so long as to seem endless; very long and tiring. *adj.* **—in·ter′mi·na·bly,** *adv.*

in·ter·min·gle (in′tər ming′gəl) mix together; mingle: *The hostess encouraged guests with different interests to intermingle at her parties. v.,* **in·ter·min·gled, in·ter·min·gling.**

in·ter·mis·sion (in′tər mish′ən) 1 a time between periods of activity; pause: *The band played from eight to twelve with a short intermission at ten.* 2 a stopping for a time; interruption: *The rain continued all day without intermission. n.*

in·ter·mit·tent (in′tər mit′ənt) stopping and beginning again; pausing at intervals: *The intermittent noise of the railway trains kept her awake. adj.* **—in′ter·mit′tent·ly,** *adv.*

in·tern[1] (in tėrn′ for 1, in′tėrn for 2) 1 force to stay in a certain place: *The captured soldiers were interned in a camp for prisoners of war.* 2 a person who is interned. 1 *v.*, 2 *n.*

in·tern[2] (in′tėrn) a medical doctor receiving practical training in a hospital: *Doctors have to serve as interns, usually for one year, before they can practise medicine on their own. n.*

in·ter·nal (in tėr′nəl) 1 inner; on the inside: *An accident often causes internal injuries as well as cuts and* *bruises.* 2 having to do with affairs within a country; domestic: *internal politics.* *adj.* **—in·ter′nal·ly,** *adv.*

in·ter·na·tion·al (in′tər nash′ən əl or in′tər nash′nəl) 1 between or among nations: *A treaty is an international agreement.* 2 having to do with the relations between nations: *international law.* *adj.* **—in′ter·na′tion·al·ly,** *adv.*

in·ter·plan·e·tar·y (in′tər plan′ə ter′ē) situated or taking place between the planets; in the region of the planets: *interplanetary gases, interplanetary travel.* *adj.*

in·ter·pose (in′tər pōz′) 1 put between; insert. 2 come or be between other things. 3 put forward; break in with; interrupt: *He interposed an objection at this point.* *v.,* **in·ter·posed, in·ter·pos·ing.**

in·ter·pret (in tėr′prit) 1 explain the meaning of: *to interpret a hard piece in a book, to interpret a dream.* 2 bring out the meaning of a dramatic part, a character, music, etc.: *The actor interpreted the part of the soldier with wonderful skill.* 3 understand according to one's own judgment: *We interpreted your silence as consent.* 4 serve as an interpreter; change conversation, speeches, etc. from one language to another: *He interprets for our Spanish visitors.* *v.*

in·ter·pre·ta·tion (in tėr′prə tā′shən) 1 an interpreting; explanation: *What is your interpretation of his queer behavior?* 2 a bringing out of the meaning of a dramatic part, music, etc.: *The actor's interpretations were praised by the newspapers. A musician usually has his own interpretation of a piece of music.* *n.*

in·ter·pret·er (in tėr′prə tər) a person whose work is translating speech from one language into another. *n.*

in·ter·ro·gate (in ter′ə gāt′) ask questions of; examine or get information from by asking questions: *The principal interrogated the boy about the work he had done in his former school.* *v.,* **in·ter·ro·gat·ed, in·ter·ro·gat·ing.**

in·ter·ro·ga·tion (in ter′ə gā′shən) 1 questioning. 2 question. *n.*

interrogation mark or **point** question mark (?).

in·ter·rog·a·tive (in′tə rog′ə tiv) 1 asking a question; having the form of a question: *an interrogative sentence, an interrogative tone of voice.* 2 a word used in asking a question: Who, why, *and* what *are interrogatives.* 1 *adj.,* 2 *n.*

in·ter·rupt (in′tə rupt′) 1 break in upon talk, work, rest, a person speaking, etc.; hinder; stop: *A fire drill interrupted the lesson.* 2 cause a break; break in: *It is not polite to interrupt when someone is talking.* 3 make a break in: *A building interrupts the view from that window.* *v.*

in·ter·rup·tion (in′tə rup′shən) 1 an interrupting; breaking in on. 2 being interrupted; a break; stopping: *The rain continued without interruption all day.* 3 something that interrupts. *n.*

in·ter·sect (in′tər sekt′) 1 cut or divide by passing through or crossing: *A path intersects the field.* 2 cross each other: *Streets usually intersect at right angles.* *v.*

in·ter·sec·tion (in′tər sek′shən) 1 an intersecting: *the intersection of a railway with a highway.* 2 a point or place where one thing crosses another: *In the diagram X and Y are intersections.* *n.*

in·ter·sperse (in′tər spėrs′) 1 vary with something put here and there: *The grass is interspersed with beds of flowers.* 2 scatter or place here and there among other things: *Bushes were interspersed among trees.* *v.,* **in·ter·spersed, in·ter·spers·ing.**

in·ter·stel·lar (in′tər stel′ər) among or between the stars: *the vastness of interstellar space. Man dreams of interstellar travel.* *adj.*

in·ter·twine (in′tər twīn′) twist around each other: *Two vines intertwined on the wall.* *v.,* **in·ter·twined, in·ter·twin·ing.**

in·ter·val (in′tər vəl) 1 the time or space between: *There is an interval of a week between Christmas and New Year's Day. She has intervals of freedom from pain. There are trees at intervals of 10 metres.* 2 in music, the difference in pitch between two tones. *n.*
at intervals, a now and then: *Stir the pudding at intervals.* **b** here and there: *We saw many lakes at intervals along the way.*

in·ter·vene (in′tər vēn′) 1 come between; be between: *A week intervenes between Christmas and New Year's Day.* 2 come in or come between to stop or change something or to help settle a dispute: *The Prime Minister was asked to intervene in the coal strike.* *v.,* **in·ter·vened, in·ter·ven·ing.**

in·ter·ven·tion (in′tər ven′shən) 1 an intervening: *The strike was settled by the intervention of the federal government.* 2 interference, especially by one nation in the affairs of another. *n.*

in·ter·view (in′tər vyü′) 1 meeting in person to talk over something special: *Father had an interview with the teacher about my work.* 2 a meeting between a reporter and a person from whom information is sought for publication or broadcast. 3 a printed report or broadcast giving the exact words of such a meeting. 4 meet and talk with, especially to obtain information: *Reporters from the newspaper interviewed the returning explorers.* 1–3 *n.,* 4 *v.* **—in′ter·view′er,** *n.*

in·ter·weave (in′tər wēv′) 1 weave together: *She interwove the different colored threads in a beautiful design.* 2 mix together; connect closely: *In his book he has interwoven the stories of two families.* *v.,* **in·ter·wove** or **in·ter·weaved, in·ter·wov·en** or **in·ter·wove** or **in·ter·weaved, in·ter·weav·ing.**

in·ter·wove (in′tər wōv′) See **interweave.** *v.*

in·ter·wo·ven (in′tər wō′vən) See **interweave.** *v.*

in·tes·tine (in tes′tən) either of two parts of the alimentary canal extending from the stomach: *Partially digested food passes from the stomach into the small intestine for further digestion and absorption of nutrients by the blood, and into the large intestine for elimination of wastes.* In grown people, the **small intestine** is about 640 centimetres long; the **large intestine** is about 165 centimetres long. See **alimentary canal** for picture. *n.*

in·ti·ma·cy (in′tə mə sē) deep friendship; close association; being intimate. *n., pl.* **in·ti·ma·cies.**

in·ti·mate[1] (in′tə mit) 1 very familiar; known very

B
Y
X
A

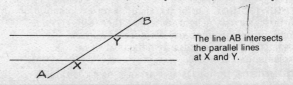

The line AB intersects the parallel lines at X and Y.

hat, āge, fär; let, ēqual, tėrm; it, īce
hot, ōpen, ôrder; oil, out; cup, pu̇t, rüle
əbove, takən, pencəl, lemən, circəs
ch, child; ng, long; sh, ship
th, thin; ᴛʜ, then; zh, measure

well: *intimate friend.* **2** resulting from close familiarity; close: *an intimate knowledge.* **3** personal; private: *A diary is a very intimate book.* **4** a close friend: *He invited his intimates to a special dinner.* 1–3 *adj.*, 4 *n.* **—in′ti·mate·ly,** *adv.*

in·ti·mate[2] (in′tə māt′) hint or suggest: *She intimated with a smile that she was pleased.* *v.*, **in·ti·mat·ed, in·ti·mat·ing.**

in·ti·ma·tion (in′tə mā′shən) an indirect suggestion; hint: *A frown may be an intimation of disapproval.* *n.*

in·tim·i·date (in tim′ə dāt′) frighten; make afraid; influence by fear: *The robbers intimidated the banker by threatening him with a pistol.* *v.*, **in·tim·i·dat·ed, in·tim·i·dat·ing.**

in·to (in′tü) **1** to the inside of; toward and inside: *Come into the house. We drove into the city. I will look into the matter.* **2** to the condition of; to the form of: *Don't get into mischief. Divide the apple into three parts. Cold weather turns water into ice.* **3** to a further time in: *He worked on into the night.* **4** against: *He wasn't watching and ran into the wall.* **5** in arithmetic, going into; dividing into: *3 into 9 is 3.* *prep.*
☛ See note at **in.**

in·tol·er·a·ble (in tol′ər ə bəl) unbearable; too much to be endured: *The pain from the toothache was intolerable.* *adj.*

in·tol·er·ance (in tol′ər əns) **1** lack of tolerance; unwillingness to let others do and think as they choose, especially in matters of religion. **2** being unable or unwilling to endure: *She doesn't listen to the radio, because of her intolerance of popular music.* *n.*

in·tol·er·ant (in tol′ər ənt) not tolerant; not willing to let others do and think as they choose, especially in matters of religion. *adj.*
intolerant of, not able to endure; unwilling to endure: *intolerant of hot, humid weather.*

in·tox·i·cate (in tok′sə kāt′) **1** make drunk: *Too much wine intoxicates people.* **2** excite greatly; exhilarate: *The victory so intoxicated the team that they jumped for joy.* *v.*, **in·tox·i·cat·ed, in·tox·i·cat·ing.**

in·tox·i·ca·tion (in tok′sə kā′shən) **1** an intoxicated condition; drunkenness. **2** great excitement. **3** in medicine, poisoning. *n.*

in·trench (in trench′) entrench. *v.*

in·trep·id (in trep′id) fearless; dauntless; very brave: *A policeman or soldier must be intrepid.* *adj.* **—in·trep′id·ly,** *adv.*

in·tri·cate (in′trə kit) with many twists and turns; perplexing; entangled; complicated: *an intricate knot, an intricate plot, an intricate design, an intricate piece of machinery, intricate directions.* *adj.* **—in′tri·cate·ly,** *adv.*

in·trigue (in trēg′ or in′trēg for 1 and 2, in trēg′ for 3 and 4) **1** secret plotting; crafty dealings: *The royal palace was filled with intrigue.* **2** a craft plot; a secret scheme: *The king's younger brother took part in the intrigue to make himself king.* **3** form and carry out plots; plan in a secret or sly way: *He will fight openly, but he is too honorable to intrigue against you.* **4** excite the curiosity and interest of: *The book's unusual title intrigued me.* 1, 2 *n.*, 3, 4 *v.*, **in·trigued, in·tri·guing.**

in·tro·duce (in′trə dyüs′ or in′trə düs′) **1** bring in: *He introduced a new subject into the conversation.* **2** put in; insert: *The doctor introduced a long tube into the man's throat.* **3** bring into use, notice, knowledge, etc.: *to introduce a new fashion, to introduce a reform.* **4** make known; bring into acquaintance with: *Mrs. Miller, may I introduce Mr. Goodman? The principal introduced the speaker to us.* **5** bring forward: *to introduce a question for debate.* **6** begin; start: *He introduced his speech with a joke.* *v.*, **in·tro·duced, in·tro·duc·ing.**

in·tro·duc·tion (in′trə duk′shən) **1** an introducing: *The introduction of steel made skyscrapers easy to build.* **2** something that introduces; the first part of a book, speech, piece of music, etc. leading up to the main part. **3** being introduced: *We were waiting for an introduction to him.* **4** something introduced; a thing brought into use: *Television is a later introduction than radio.* *n.*

in·tro·duc·to·ry (in′trə duk′tə rē or in′trə duk′trē) used to introduce; serving as an introduction; preliminary: *introductory remarks.* *adj.*

in·trude (in trüd′) **1** thrust oneself in; come where one isn't wanted: *Do not intrude upon the privacy of your neighbors.* **2** give when not wanted; force in: *Do not intrude your opinions on others.* *v.*, **in·trud·ed, in·trud·ing. —in·trud′er,** *n.*

in·tru·sion (in trü′zhən) the act of intruding; coming unasked and unwanted: *The stranger's intrusion into the discussion was unwelome.* *n.*

in·trust (in trust′) entrust. *v.*

in·tu·i·tion (in′tyü ish′ən or in′tü ish′ən) **1** the power of knowing or understanding something directly without reasoning: *Intuition told him that the stranger was honest.* **2** something known in this way; hunch. *n.*

I·nu·it (in′ü it, in′yü it, or in′yə wit) **1** a people living mainly in the arctic regions of the world; the Eskimo: *The Inuit are the original inhabitants of the Arctic.* **2** of or having to do with these people or their language: *Inuit games, an Inuit word.* 1 *n. pl.*, 2 *adj.*
☛ **Inuit** is the name these people have for themselves; it means 'the people' or 'men'. In Canada, **Inuit** is now used in preference to **Eskimo.**

in·un·date (in′ən dāt′) overflow; flood: *Heavy rains caused the river to rise and inundate the valley.* *v.*, **in·un·dat·ed, in·un·dat·ing.**

in·un·da·tion (in′ən dā′shən) an overflowing; flood. *n.*

in·vade (in vād′) **1** enter with force or as an enemy; attack: *Soldiers invaded the country to conquer it. Grasshoppers invade the fields and eat the crops. Disease invades the body.* **2** enter as if to take possession: *Tourists invaded the city. Night invades the sky.* **3** interfere with; break in on; violate: *The law punishes people who invade the rights of others.* *v.*, **in·vad·ed, in·vad·ing. —in·vad′er,** *n.*

in·va·lid[1] (in′və lid) **1** a person who is weak because of sickness or injury: *An invalid cannot get about and do things.* **2** not well; disabled. **3** for the use of invalids: *an invalid chair.* **4** remove from active service because of sickness or injury: *The wounded soldier was invalided home.* 1 *n.*, 2, 3 *adj.*, 4 *v.*

in·val·id² (in val′id) not valid; without force or effect; without value: *Unless a cheque is signed, it is invalid.* *adj.*

in·val·u·a·ble (in val′yə bəl or in val′yü ə bəl) priceless; very precious; valuable beyond measure: *Good health is an invaluable blessing.* *adj.*

in·var·i·a·ble (in ver′ē ə bəl) always the same; not changing: *After dinner it was his invariable habit to take a walk.* *adj.* —**in·var′i·a·bly,** *adv.*

in·va·sion (in vā′zhən) **1** the act or fact of invading; entering by force: *There has been no invasion of England since 1066.* **2** an interference or intrusion: *She objected to the invasion of her privacy.* *n.*

in·vei·gle (in vā′gəl or in vē′gəl) mislead by trickery; trick by flattery or persuasion: *The saleswoman inveigled the poor girl into buying four hats.* *v.,* **in·vei·gled, in·vei·gling.**

in·vent (in vent′) **1** make for the first time; think out something new: *Alexander Graham Bell invented the telephone.* **2** make up; think up: *to invent an excuse.* *v.*

in·ven·tion (in ven′shən) **1** making something new: *The Chinese are credited with the invention of gunpowder.* **2** the thing invented: *Radio was a wonderful invention.* **3** the power of inventing: *To be a good writer of stories a person needs invention.* **4** a made-up story; a false statement: *His excuse for being late was pure invention.* *n.*

in·ven·tive (in ven′tiv) good at inventing; quick to invent things: *an inventive mind. An inventive person thinks up ways to save time, money, and work.* *adj.*

in·ven·tor (in ven′tər) a person who invents: *Alexander Graham Bell was a great inventor.* *n.*

in·ven·to·ry (in′vən tô′rē) **1** a detailed list of articles. **2** a collection of articles that are or may be listed in detail; stock: *The storekeeper had a sale to reduce his inventory.* **3** make a detailed list of; enter in a list: *Some stores inventory their stock once a month.* 1, 2 *n., pl.* **in·ven·to·ries;** 3 *v.,* **in·ven·to·ried, in·ven·to·ry·ing.**

in·vert (in vėrt′) **1** turn upside down: *He inverted the glass and the water ran out.* **2** turn the other way; reverse in position, direction, order, etc.: *If you invert 'I can,' you have 'Can I?'* *v.*

in·ver·te·brate (in vėr′tə brāt′ or in vėr′tə brit) **1** without a backbone. **2** an animal without a backbone: *Worms and insects are invertebrates; fish, amphibians, reptiles, birds, and mammals are vertebrates.* 1 *adj.,* 2 *n.*

in·vest (in vest′) **1** use money to buy something that is expected to produce a profit, or income, or both: *If I had any money to spare I would invest it in land.* **2** spend or put in time, energy, etc. for later benefit: *The volunteer group invested its energies in developing new playgrounds.* **3** clothe; cover; surround: *Darkness invests the earth by night.* **4** give power, authority, or right to: *He invested his lawyer with complete power to act for him.* **5** put in office with a ceremony: *A king is invested by being crowned.* *v.*

in·ves·ti·gate (in ves′tə gāt′) search into carefully; examine closely: *Detectives investigate crimes. Scientists investigate nature to learn more about it.* *v.,* **in·ves·ti·gat·ed, in·ves·ti·gat·ing.**

in·ves·ti·ga·tion (in ves′tə gā′shən) a careful search; a detailed or careful examination: *The police officer carried out an investigation of the accident.* *n.*

in·ves·ti·ga·tor (in ves′tə gā′tər) a person who investigates. *n.*

in·vest·ment (in vest′mənt) **1** investing; a laying out of money: *Getting an education is a wise investment of time and money.* **2** something bought that is expected to yield money as interest, or profit, or both: *Mr. Smith has a good income from wise investments. He considers Canada Savings Bonds a safe investment.* *n.*

in·ves·tor (in ves′tər) a person who invests money. *n.*

in·vig·or·ate (in vig′ər āt′) give vigor to; fill with life and energy: *The brisk weather was invigorating. He felt invigorated after his swim.* *v.,* **in·vig·or·at·ed, in·vig·or·at·ing.**

in·vin·ci·ble (in vin′sə bəl) impossible to overcome; unconquerable: *The champion wrestler seemed invincible.* *adj.* —**in·vin′ci·bly,** *adv.*

in·vis·i·ble (in viz′ə bəl) **1** not visible; not capable of being seen: *Thought is invisible. Germs are invisible to the naked eye.* **2** not in sight; hidden: *The queen kept herself invisible in the palace.* *adj.*

in·vi·ta·tion (in′və tā′shən) **1** a request to come to some place or to do something: *Formal invitations are written or printed. The children received invitations to the party.* **2** the act of inviting. *n.*

in·vite (in vīt′) **1** ask someone politely to come to some place or to do something: *He invited his friends to the party. We invited her to join our club.* **2** make a polite request for: *She invited our opinion of her story.* **3** give a chance for; tend to cause: *The letter invites some questions. Carelessness invites trouble.* **4** attract; tempt: *The calm water invited us to swim.* *v.,* **in·vit·ed, in·vit·ing.**

in·vit·ing (in vīt′ing) attractive; tempting: *The soft bed was most inviting to the tired man.* *adj.*

in·vo·ca·tion (in′və kā′shən) the act of calling upon God or another divine being in prayer; an appealing for help or protection: *A church service often begins with an invocation.* *n.*

in·voice (in′vois) **1** a list of goods bought, showing prices, amounts, shipping charges, etc.; a bill. **2** the form used for such a list. **3** make an invoice of; enter on an invoice: *Has that order been invoiced?* 1, 2 *n.,* 3 *v.,* **in·voiced, in·voic·ing.**

in·voke (in vōk′) **1** call on God or another divine being in prayer; appeal to for help or protection. **2** ask earnestly for; beg for: *The condemned criminal invoked the judge's mercy.* **3** call forth by magic: *Aladdin invoked the genie of the magic lamp.* *v.,* **in·voked, in·vok·ing.**

in·vol·un·tar·y (in vol′ən ter′ē) **1** not voluntary; not done of one's own free will; unwilling: *He was threatened until he gave involuntary consent to the plan.* **2** not controlled by the will: *Breathing is mainly involuntary.* **3** not intended; not done on purpose: *An accident is involuntary.* *adj.* —**in·vol′un·tar·i·ly,** *adv.*

in·volve (in volv′) **1** having as a necessary part; take in; include: *Housework involves cooking, washing dishes, sweeping, and cleaning.* **2** bring into difficulty, danger, etc.: *One foolish mistake can involve you in a good deal of trouble.* **3** entangle; complicate: *Long, involved*

hat, āge, fär; let, ēqual, tėrm; it, īce
hot, ōpen, ôrder; oil, out; cup, pu̇t, rüle
əbove, takən, pencəl, lemən, circəs
ch, child; ng, long; sh, ship
th, thin; ᴛʜ, then; zh, measure

sentences are hard to understand. 4 take up the attention of; occupy: *She was involved in working out a puzzle.* *v.,* **in·volved, in·volv·ing.**

in·vul·ner·a·ble (in vul′nər ə bəl) 1 that cannot be wounded or injured: *The knight was invulnerable in his armor.* 2 strong enough to resist attack; not easily overcome: *an invulnerable argument.* *adj.* **—in·vul′ner·a·bly,** *adv.*

in·ward (in′wərd) 1 toward the inside or centre: *a passage leading inward. Try to turn your toes inward.* 2 placed within; internal: *the inward parts of the body.* 3 into the mind or soul: *Turn your thoughts inward.* 4 in the mind or soul: *inward peace, inward happiness.* 1, 3 *adv.,* 2, 4 *adj.*

in·ward·ly (in′wərd lē) 1 on the inside; within. 2 toward the inside or centre. 3 in the mind or soul. 4 not openly; secretly: *He was inwardly pleased, but he said nothing.* *adv.*

in·wards (in′wərdz) inward. *adv.*

i·o·dine (ī′ə dīn′) 1 a substance in the form of greyish-black crystals that occur naturally in combination with other substances: *Iodine is used in medicine, in photography, and in making dyes.* 2 a brown liquid containing iodine, used as an antiseptic. *n.*

i·on (ī′ən or ī′on) an atom or group of atoms having a negative or positive electric charge as a result of having lost or gained one or more electrons: *Positive ions are formed by the loss of electrons; negative ions are formed by the gain of electrons.* *n.*

i·on·o·sphere (ī on′ə sfēr′) a region of the earth's atmosphere above the stratosphere: *The ionosphere has many ions and free electrons produced by radiation from the sun and cosmic rays.* *n.*

i·rate (ī′rāt or ī rāt′) angry. *adj.* **—i′rate·ly,** *adv.*

ire (īr) anger. *n.*

An iris

i·ris (ī′ris) 1 a plant with sword-shaped leaves and large flowers. 2 its flower: *The iris is the unofficial floral emblem of Quebec.* 3 the colored part around the pupil of the eye. See **eye** for picture. *n.*

I·rish (ī′rish) 1 of or having to do with Ireland, a large island west of England, its people, or their language. 2 the people of Ireland. 3 their language. 1 *adj.,* 2, 3 *n.*

irk (ėrk) annoy; disgust; bore: *It irks us to wait for people who are always late.* *v.*

irk·some (ėrk′səm) tiresome; tedious: *Washing dishes all day would be an irksome task.* *adj.*

i·ron (ī′ərn) 1 a useful metal, from which tools, machinery, etc. are made: *Steel is made from iron.* 2 made of iron: *an iron fence.* 3 something made of iron or steel: *a branding iron, a waffle iron.* 4 a golf club with an iron or steel head. 5 firm; hard; strong: *an iron constitution, an iron will.* 6 **irons,** *pl.* chains or bands of iron; handcuffs; shackles. 7 an implement with a flat surface to press clothing. 8 smooth or press with an iron: *Mother ironed the sheets.* 1, 3, 4, 6, 7 *n.,* 2, 5 *adj.,* 8 *v.*

i·ron·ic (ī ron′ik) 1 expressing one thing and meaning the opposite: *'Speedy' would be an ironic name for a snail.* 2 opposite to what would naturally be expected: *It was ironic that the man was run over by his own car.* *adj.*

i·ron·i·cal (ī ron′i kəl) ironic. *adj.* **—i·ron′i·cal·ly,** *adv.*

i·ro·ny (ī′rə nē) 1 a way of speaking or writing in which the meaning intended is the opposite of that expressed: *It is irony to call the thin boy 'Fatty.'* 2 an event or outcome which is the opposite of what would naturally be expected: *It was an amusing irony when a fake diamond was stolen instead of the real one. By the irony of fate the farmers had rain when they needed sun, and sun when they needed rain.* *n., pl.* **i·ro·nies.**

ir·reg·ular (i reg′yə lər) 1 not regular; not according to rule; out of the usual order or natural way: *irregular breathing.* 2 not even; not smooth, not straight: *Newfoundland has a very irregular coastline.* 3 not according to law or morals: *irregular behavior.* *adj.*

ir·reg·u·lar·i·ty (i reg′yə lar′ə tē or i reg′yə ler′ə tē) 1 a lack of regularity, being irregular: *the irregularity of the coastline.* 2 something irregular: *There were a number of irregularities in the evidence.* *n., pl.* **ir·reg·u·lar·i·ties.**

ir·rel·e·vant (i rel′ə vənt) not to the point; off the subject: *He interrupted the discussion several times with irrelevant remarks about the weather.* *adj.* **—ir·rel′e·vant·ly,** *adv.*

ir·re·sist·i·ble (ir′i zis′tə bəl) that cannot be resisted; too great to be withstood; overwhelming: *an irresistible desire to laugh.* *adj.*

ir·res·o·lute (i rez′ə lüt′) not resolute; unable to make up one's mind; not sure of what one wants; hesitating: *Irresolute persons make poor leaders.* *adj.* **—ir·res′o·lute·ly,** *adv.* **—ir·res′o·lute·ness,** *n.*

ir·re·spon·si·ble (ir′i spon′sə bəl) not having or not showing a sense of responsibility: *It was irresponsible to leave the broken glass on the sidewalk.* *adj.* **—ir·re·spon′si·bly,** *adv.*

ir·rev·er·ent (i rev′ər ənt) not reverent; disrespectful. *adj.* **—ir·rev′er·ent·ly,** *adv.*

ir·ri·gate (ir′ə gāt′) 1 supply land with water by means of ditches, sprinklers, etc.: *Farmers irrigate dry land to make crops grow better.* 2 supply or wash a wound, cavity in the body, etc. with a continuous flow of some liquid: *Irrigate the nose and throat with hot water.* *v.,* **ir·ri·gat·ed, ir·ri·gat·ing.**

ir·ri·ga·tion (ir′ə gā′shən) supplying land with water from ditches, sprinklers, etc.; irrigating: *Irrigation is needed to make crops grow in dry regions.* *n.*

ir·ri·ta·ble (ir′ə tə bəl) 1 easily made angry; impatient: *When the rain spoiled her plans, she was* *irritable for the rest of the day.* 2 more sensitive than is natural or normal: *A baby's skin is often quite irritable.* *adj.*

ir·ri·tate (ir′ə tāt′) 1 make impatient or angry; annoy; vex: *The boy's foolish questions irritated his mother. Flies irritate horses.* 2 make unnaturally sensitive or sore: *Too much sun irritates the skin.* *v.,* **ir·ri·tat·ed, ir·ri·tat·ing.**

ir·ri·ta·tion (ir′ə tā′shən) 1 the act or process of irritating; annoyance; vexation. 2 an irritated condition: *An irritation in his nose made him sneeze.* *n.*

is (iz) a form of **be** used with *he, she, it* or the name of a person, thing, etc.: *The earth is round. He is at school. He is working late tonight.* *v.*
as is, as it is now; in its present condition.

Is·lam (is′ləm or is läm′) 1 the Moslem religion. 2 Moslems as a group. 3 Moslem countries; the Moslem part of the world. *n.*

is·land (ī′lənd) 1 a body of land smaller than a continent and completely surrounded by water: *Cuba is a large island. To reach the island, you go on a boat.* 2 something that suggests a piece of land surrounded by water: *The city built a safety island at the busy intersection.* *n.*

is·land·er (ī′lən dər) a person born or living on an island: *Newfoundlanders are islanders; so are Prince Edward Islanders.* *n.*

isle (īl) 1 a small island. 2 island. *n.*
☛ **Isle, aisle,** and **I'll** are pronounced the same.

is·let (ī′lit) a little island. *n.*
☛ **Islet** and **eyelet** are pronounced the same.

is·n't (iz′ənt) is not.

i·so·bar (ī′sə bär′) a line on a weather map connecting places having the same average air pressure. *n.*

i·so·late (ī′sə lāt′) place apart; separate from others; keep alone: *People with contagious diseases should be isolated.* *v.,* **i·so·lat·ed, i·so·lat·ing.**

i·so·la·tion (ī′sə lā′shən) 1 setting apart or being set apart: *The warden's isolation of the most troublesome prisoners reduced unrest in the jail. The isolation of infectious persons is essential.* 2 the state of being separated from other persons or things: *Robinson Crusoe lived for many years in isolation.* *n.*

Is·rae·li (iz rā′lē) 1 a person born in or living in modern Israel, a country in southwestern Asia. 2 of or having to do with modern Israel. 1 *n., pl.* **Is·rael·is;** 2 *adj.*

is·sue (ish′ü) 1 send out; put forth: *This magazine is issued every week.* 2 something sent out: *Did you read the last issue of our weekly paper?* 3 a sending out; putting forth: *The next issue of new stamps will be on June 11.* 4 come or go out; proceed: *Smoke was issuing from the chimney.* 5 a coming forth; a flowing out or discharge: *A nosebleed is an issue of blood from the nose.* 6 the result; outcome: *The issue of the game remained uncertain until the last moment.* 7 distribute; give out to a person or persons: *Heavy boots were issued to all enlisted men.* 8 a point to be debated or discussed. 9 problem: *The voters had four issues to decide.* 1, 4, 7 *v.,* **is·sued, is·su·ing;** 2, 3, 5, 6, 8, 9 *n.*
at issue, in question; to be considered or decided.
take issue, disagree: *I take issue with you on that point.*

-ist a suffix meaning: 1 a person who does or makes: *A tourist is a person who makes tours.* 2 one who knows about or is skilled: *A biologist is a person who knows about biology. A pianist is a person who is skilled with a piano.* 3 one who believes in: *An idealist is a person who believes in ideals.*

The Isthmus of Panama

isth·mus (is′məs) a narrow strip of land, with water on both sides, connecting two larger bodies of land: *The Isthmus of Panama connects North America and South America.* *n.*

it (it) 1 a thing, part, animal, or person already spoken about: *Here is your paper; read it. The cat is beautiful, isn't it? Is it a boy or a girl?* 2 something impersonal or indefinite that is being referred to: *What is it you want? It snows in winter. Now it is my turn.* 3 in certain games, the player who must do a certain thing, such as touch, find, or guess: *The boy who was it chased the other children.* 1, 2 *pron., pl.* **they;** 3 *n.*

I·tal·ian (i tal′yən) 1 of Italy, a country in southern Europe, its people or their language. 2 a person born in or living in Italy. 3 the language of Italy. 1 *adj.,* 2, 3 *n.*

i·tal·ic (i tal′ik) 1 of or in type whose letters slant to the right: *These words are in italic type.* 2 **italics,** *pl.* type whose letters slant to the right. 1 *adj.,* 2 *n.*
☛ **Italic** type was introduced by an Italian printer in Venice in the seventeenth century and was named *italic* to distinguish it from the upright letters of roman type.

i·tal·i·cize (i tal′ə sīz′) 1 print in type in which the letters slant to the right: *The letters in these words have been italicized.* 2 underline words with a single line to indicate italics: *We italicize words that are to be emphasized or distinguished.* *v.,* **i·tal·i·cized, i·tal·i·ciz·ing.**

itch (ich) 1 a ticklish, prickling feeling in the skin that makes one want to scratch. 2 a disease causing this feeling. 3 cause this feeling: *Mosquito bites itch.* 4 feel this way in the skin: *My finger itches.* 5 a restless, uneasy feeling, longing, or desire for anything: *She always had an itch to get away and explore.* 6 have such a desire: *He itched to find out their secret.* 1, 2, 5 *n.,* 3, 4, 6 *v.*

i·tem (ī′təm) 1 a separate thing or article: *The list had twelve items on it.* 2 a piece of news; a bit of information: *There were several interesting items in today's paper.* *n.*

i·tem·ize (ī′təm īz′) give each item of; list by items: *The storekeeper itemized the bill to show each article and its cost.* *v.,* **i·tem·ized, i·tem·iz·ing.**

it'll (it′əl) it will.

its (its) of it; belonging to it: *The cat chased its tail. This chair has lost one of its legs.* *pron., adj.*

it's (its) **1** it is: *It's my turn.* **2** it has: *It's been a beautiful day.*

it·self (it self′) **1** a form used instead of **it** when referring back to the subject of the sentence: *The horse tripped and hurt itself. The dog saw itself in the mirror.* **2** a form of **it** used to make a statement stronger: *The land itself is worth more than they paid for the house. pron.*

I've (īv) I have.

i·vo·ry (īv′rē or ī′və rē) **1** a hard, white substance composing the tusks of elephants, walrus, etc.: *Ivory is easy to carve and is used in many kinds of ornament.* **2** creamy white: *ivory paint.* 1, 2 *n.,* 2 *adj.*

i·vy (ī′vē) **1** a climbing plant with smooth, shiny evergreen leaves. **2** any of various other climbing plants, such as poison ivy. *n., pl.* **i·vies.**

–ize a suffix meaning: **1** make ___: *Legalize means to make legal. Centralize means to make central.* **2** become ___: *Crystallize means to become crystal.* **3** engage in or make use of: *To apologize is to engage in making an apology.* **4** treat or combine with: *To macadamize is to treat with macadam.* **5** subject or affect with: *Criticize means to subject to criticism.*

j or **J** (jā) the tenth letter of the alphabet: *Few English words have two* j's. *n., pl.* **j's** or **J's.**

jab (jab) **1** thrust with something pointed; poke: *He jabbed his fork into the potato.* **2** a thrust with something pointed; poke: *She gave him a jab with her elbow.* 1 *v.,* **jabbed, jab·bing;** 2 *n.*

jab·ber (jab′ər) **1** talk very fast in a confused, senseless way; chatter. **2** very fast, confused, or senseless talk; chatter. 1 *v.,* 2 *n.*

Two types of jack (def. 1) for automobiles

jack (jak) **1** a device for lifting or pushing up heavy weights a short distance: *Jacks are sometimes used to raise a house so that a cellar may be added.* **2** lift or push up with a jack: *jack up a car.* **3** a small flag, especially one used on a ship to show nationality or as a signal. **4** a playing card with a picture of a court page on it; knave. **5** in a child's game, a pebble or piece of metal tossed up and caught. **6** a man or fellow. **7** an electrical device to receive a plug. 1, 3–7 *n.,* 2 *v.*
jack up, *Informal.* raise prices, wages, etc.: *Stores jacked up many prices this month.*

jack·al (jak′əl, jak′ol, or jak′ôl) a wild animal of Asia, Africa, and southeastern Europe, closely related to the dog, having a bushy tail, a pointed nose, and, usually, greyish-yellow or brown hair: *Jackals feed mostly on animals they find dead.* *n.*

jack·ass (jak′as′) **1** a male donkey. **2** a very stupid person; fool. *n.*

jack·daw (jak′do′ or jak′dô′) a small bird of the crow family: *Jackdaws are very common in Europe and North Africa.* *n.*

jack·et (jak′it) **1** a short coat. **2** an outer covering: *a book jacket.* *n.*

jack·fish (jak′fish′) pike. *n., pl.* **jack·fish** or **jack·fish·es.**

jack–in–the–pul·pit (jak′ in ᴛʜə pu̇l′pit) a plant having a greenish, petal-like sheath arched up over a spike of tiny flowers. *n.*

jack–knife (jak′nīf′) **1** a large, strong pocketknife. **2** double up like a jack-knife: *The truck and trailer jack-knifed at a turn on the highway.* 1 *n., pl.* **jack-knives;** 2 *v.,* **jack-knifed, jack-knif·ing.**

jack of all trades a person who can do many different kinds of work fairly well.

jack–o'–lan·tern (jak′ə lan′tərn) a pumpkin hollowed out and cut to look like a face, used as a lantern at Halloween. *n.*

jack pine any of several kinds of North American pine.

jack–rab·bit (jak′rab′it) a large hare of western North America, having very long ears and long back legs. *n.*

jacks (jaks) a child's game in which pebbles or pieces of metal are tossed up and caught or picked up in various ways. *n. pl.*

jade (jād) a hard stone, usually green or white, used for jewellery and ornaments. *n.*

jad·ed (jā′did) worn out; tired; weary: *a jaded horse, a jaded appearance.* *adj.*

jag·ged (jag′id) with sharp points sticking out; unevenly cut or torn: *We cut our bare feet on the jagged rocks.* *adj.*

jag·uar (jag′wär or jag′yü är′) a fierce animal much like a leopard, but more heavily built: *Jaguars live in forests in tropical America.* *n.*

jail (jāl) **1** a prison, especially one for persons awaiting trial or being punished for a minor offence. **2** put in jail; keep in jail. 1 *n.,* 2 *v.*

jail·er or **jail·or** (jāl′ər) a keeper of a jail. *n.*

ja·lop·y (jə lop′ē) *Informal.* an old automobile or airplane in a poor state of repair: *Is she still driving that old jalopy?* *n., pl.* **ja·lop·ies.**

jam¹ (jam) **1** press or squeeze tightly between surfaces: *The ship was jammed between two rocks.* **2** crush by squeezing; bruise: *I jammed my fingers in the door.* **3** press or squeeze tightly together: *They jammed us all into one bus.* **4** push or shove: *He jammed his fist into the other fellow's face.* **5** fill or block up by crowding: *The river was jammed with logs.* **6** stick or catch so as not to work properly: *The window has jammed.* **7** make unworkable: *The key broke off and jammed the lock.* **8** a mass of people or things crowded together so that they cannot move freely: *There was an awful jam at the football game.* **9** *Informal.* a difficulty or tight spot: *She got into a jam because of the lost key.* **10** a jamming or being jammed. 1–7 *v.,* **jammed, jam·ming;** 8–10 *n.*

jam² (jam) a preserve made by boiling fruit with sugar until thick: *raspberry jam.* *n.*

jan·gle (jang′gəl) **1** sound harshly; make a loud, clashing noise: *The pots and pans jangled in the kitchen.* **2** cause to make a hard, clashing sound: *He jangled a bell.* **3** a harsh sound; clashing noise or ring: *the jangle of the telephone.* **4** make tense or strained; upset: *Their continual complaints jangled her nerves.* 1, 2, 4 *v.,* **jan·gled, jan·gling;** 3 *n.*

jan·i·tor (jan′ə tər) a person hired to take care of a building or offices; caretaker. *n.*

Jan·u·ar·y (jan′yə wer′ē or jan′yü er′ē) the first month of the year: *January has 31 days.* *n.*

☛ **January** came into English through Old French from the Latin name for this month, which was based on the name of an ancient god, *Janus,* who had two faces, one looking forwards and one looking backwards.

Jap·a·nese (jap′ə nēz′) **1** of Japan, a country east of Asia, its people, or their language: *Japanese art.* **2** a person born in or living in Japan. **3** the language of Japan. 1 *adj.,* 2, 3 *n., pl.* **Jap·a·nese.**

jar¹ (jär) **1** a deep container made of earthenware, stone, or glass, with a wide mouth. **2** the amount such a container holds: *George will eat a whole jar of jam at breakfast.* *n.*

jar² (jär) **1** cause to shake or rattle; vibrate: *The heavy footsteps jarred my desk so that I had trouble writing.* **2** a shake; rattle. **3** make a harsh, grating noise: *When*

hat, āge, fär; let, ēqual, tėrm; it, īce
hot, ōpen, ôrder; oil, out; cup, pu̇t, rüle
əbove, takən, pencəl, lemən, circəs
ch, child; ng, long; sh, ship
th, thin; ᴛʜ, then; zh, measure

he opened the car door, its bottom corner jarred against the sidewalk. **4** a harsh, grating noise. **5** have a harsh, unpleasant effect on; send a shock through the ears, nerves, feelings, etc.: *The children's playful screams jarred his nerves.* **6** a slight shock to the ears, nerves, feelings, etc. **7** clash; quarrel: *We did not get on well together; our opinions always jarred.* 1, 3, 5, 7 *v.,* **jarred, jar·ring;** 2, 4, 6 *n.*

jas·per (jas′pər) a colored quartz, usually red, yellow, or brown. *n.*

jaunt (jont or jônt) **1** a short journey or excursion, especially for pleasure. **2** take a short pleasure trip or excursion. 1 *n.,* 2 *v.*

jaun·ty (jon′tē or jôn′tē) easy and lively; carefree: *When you are well and happy, you usually feel jaunty. He walks with a jaunty step. adj.,* **jaun·ti·er, jaun·ti·est.**

jave·lin (jav′lin) **1** a light spear thrown by hand. **2** a wooden or metal spear, thrown for distance in track and field contests. *n.*

jaw (jo or jô) **1** either of the upper and lower bones, or sets of bones, that together form the framework of the mouth: *The lower jaw is movable.* **2** the lower part of the face. **3 jaws,** *pl.* **a** a narrow entrance to a valley, pass, channel, etc. **b** the parts in a tool or machine that grip and hold: *A vise has jaws. n.*

jay (jā) one of several kinds of bird found in North America and Europe and related to the crow, often brightly colored and often having a crest and a long tail: *Jays are noisy birds that can make many different sounds. Two kinds of jay found in Canada are the Canada jay and the bluejay. n.*

jay·walk (jā′wok′ or jā′wôk′) *Informal.* walk across a street at a place other than a regular crossing or without paying attention to traffic. *v.* **—jay′walk′er,** *n.*

jazz (jaz) **1** a popular, lively music with a strong but varied rhythm, wavering and wailing sounds, etc.: *Jazz is native to the United States.* **2** of or like jazz: *jazz records.* 1 *n.,* 2 *adj.*

jeal·ous (jel′əs) **1** fearful that a person one loves may love or prefer someone else: *When my brother sees Mother holding the new baby, he becomes jealous.* **2** envious; full of envy: *Jill's sister is jealous of her good grades.* **3** watchful in keeping or guarding something; careful: *Each province is jealous of its rights within Confederation.* **4** close; watchful; suspicious: *The dog was such a jealous guardian of the little girl that he would not let her cross the street. adj.* **—jeal′ous·ly,** *adv.*

jeal·ous·y (jel′əs ē) dislike or fear of rivals; a jealous condition or feeling. *n., pl.* **jeal·ous·ies.**

jean (jēn) **1** a strong cotton cloth. **2 jeans,** *pl.* **a** pants made of a strong cotton cloth: *The cowboy was wearing blue jeans under his chaps.* **b** overalls. *n.*
☛ **Jean** and **gene** are pronounced the same.

jeep (jēp) a small but powerful automobile in which power is transmitted to all four wheels: *Jeeps are used by soldiers, builders, farmers, etc. n.*

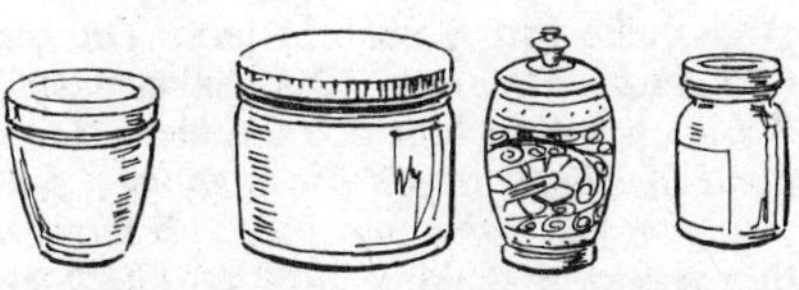
Jars

jeer (jēr) **1** make fun in a rude or unkind way; scoff: *Do not jeer at the mistakes or misfortunes of others.* **2** a mocking or insulting remark. 1 *v.,* 2 *n.*

Je·ho·vah (ji hō′və) in the Old Testament, one of the names of God. *n.*

jel·ly (jel′ē) **1** a food that is liquid when hot but rather firm when cold: *Jelly can be made by boiling fruit juice and sugar together, or by cooking bones and meat in water, or by using some stiffening preparation like gelatin.* **2** a substance that resembles jelly: *petroleum jelly.* **3** become jelly; turn into jelly: *The chicken soup jellied when it was chilled in the refrigerator.* 1, 2 *n., pl.* **jel·lies;** 3 *v.,* **jel·lied, jel·ly·ing.**

jel·ly·bean (jel′ē bēn′) a small, bean-shaped jellied candy, coated in different colors. *n.*

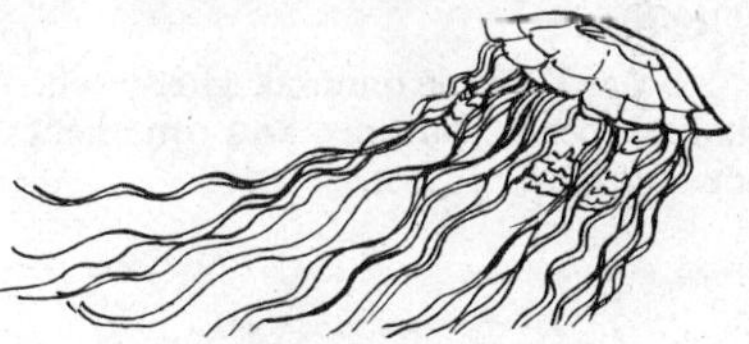
A jellyfish. It moves through the water by opening and closing like an umbrella. The tentacles carry food into the mouth.

jel·ly·fish (jel′ē fish′) a boneless sea animal with a body formed of a mass of jelly-like tissue that is almost transparent: *Most jellyfish have long, trailing tentacles that may have stinging hairs or feelers. n., pl.* **jel·ly·fish** or **jel·ly·fish·es.**

jeop·ard·ize (jep′ər dīz′) put in danger; risk; endanger: *Soldiers jeopardize their lives in war. v.,* **jeop·ard·ized, jeop·ard·iz·ing.**

jeop·ard·y (jep′ər dē) danger; risk: *The firefighters put their lives in jeopardy when they entered the burning building. n.*

jerk[1] (jėrk) **1** a sudden, sharp pull, twist, or start: *His old car started with a jerk.* **2** pull or twist suddenly: *If the water is unexpectedly hot, you jerk your hand out.* **3** move with a jerk: *The old wagon jerked along.* **4** *Slang.* a stupid or simple person. 1, 4 *n.,* 2, 3 *v.*

jerk[2] (jėrk) preserve meat by cutting it in long, thin slices and drying it in the sun: *The Indians taught the early explorers and settlers in North America how to jerk beef. v.*

jer·kin (jėr′kən) a short, close-fitting coat or jacket without sleeves: *Men used to wear leather jerkins in the 16th and 17th centuries. n.*

jerk·y (jėr′kē) with sudden starts and stops; with jerks. *adj.,* **jerk·i·er, jerk·i·est.**

jer·sey (jėr′zē) **1** a close-fitting sweater that is pulled on over the head. **2** a stretchy knitted cloth made by a machine. *n., pl.* **jer·seys.**

Jer·sey (jėr′zē) one of a breed of small, usually fawn-colored cattle that give very rich milk. *n., pl.* **Jer·seys.**
☛ Named for the island of *Jersey* in the English Channel, from where these cattle originally came.

Jerusalem artichoke (jə rü′sə ləm) 1 a kind of sunflower whose root is edible. 2 the root of this plant. *n.*

jest (jest) 1 joke. 2 to joke; make a joke. 3 make fun of; laugh at: *They all jested at the stranger's ideas.* 4 the act of making fun of; mockery. 5 something intended to be mocked or laughed at. 1, 4, 5 *n.*, 2, 3 *v.* **in jest,** in fun; not seriously: *His words were spoken in jest.*

jest·er (jes′tər) a person who jests: *In the Middle Ages, kings often had jesters to amuse them with tricks, antics, and jokes. n.*

Je·sus (jē′zəs) Jesus Christ, the founder of the Christian religion: *'Jesus' means 'God is salvation.' n.*

jet[1] (jet) 1 a stream of gas or liquid sent with force, especially from a small opening: *A fountain sends up a jet of water.* 2 a spout or nozzle for sending out a jet. 3 shoot forth in a jet or forceful stream; gush out: *Water jets from the broken pipe.* 4 a jet plane. 1, 2, 4 *n.*, 3 *v.*, **jet·ted, jet·ting.**

jet[2] (jet) 1 a hard, black mineral, glossy when polished, used for making beads, buttons, and ornaments. 2 deep, glossy black: *jet hair.* 1, 2 *n.*, 2 *adj.*

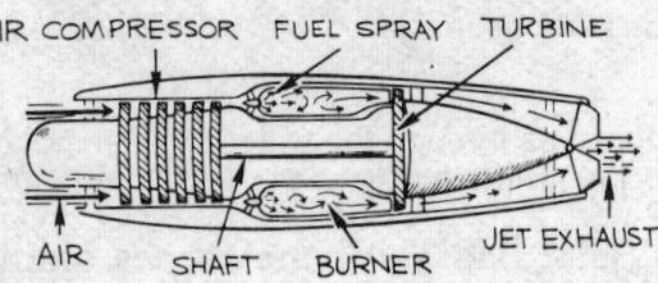

A jet engine. The air is sucked in through the front of the engine, compressed, and mixed with fuel. This mixture is burned in the burners, giving off gas that passes out in a powerful jet through the rear of the engine, pushing the airplane forward.

jet engine an engine using jet propulsion.

jet plane an airplane that is driven by one or more jet engines.

jet–pro·pelled (jet′prə peld′) drive by jet propulsion. *adj.*

jet propulsion propulsion in one direction by means of a jet of air, gas, etc. forced in the opposite direction.

jet·ty (jet′ē) 1 a structure of stones, timbers, etc. projecting out from the shore to break the force of the current or waves; breakwater. See **breakwater** for picture. 2 a landing place; a pier or dock. *n., pl.* **jet·ties.**

Jew (jü) 1 a person descended from the people led by Moses, who settled in Palestine and now live in Israel and many other countries; Hebrew. 2 a person whose religion is Judaism. *n.*

jew·el (jü′əl) 1 a precious stone; gem: *Jewels are worn in pins and other ornaments.* 2 a valuable ornament to be worn, set with precious stones. 3 a person or thing that is very precious. 4 a gem or other piece of hard material used as a bearing in a watch. 5 set or adorn with jewels or with things like jewels: *a jewelled comb, a sky jewelled with stars.* 1–4 *n.*, 5 *v.*, **jew·elled** or **jew·eled, jew·el·ling** or **jew·el·ing.**

jew·el·ler or **jew·el·er** (jü′əl ər or jü′lər) a person who makes, sells, or repairs jewels, watches, silverware, rings, etc.: *He took his watch to the jeweller's to have it repaired. n.*

jew·el·ler·y or **jew·el·ry** (jü′əl rē or jül′rē) jewels and ornaments set with gems: *She keeps her jewellery in a small, locked box. n.*

Jew·ish (jü′ish) of the Jews; belonging to the Jews; characteristic of the Jews: *Jewish beliefs. adj.*

jib (jib) a triangular sail set in front of the foremast of a boat or ship. See **schooner** for picture. *n.*

jibe (jīb) *Informal.* be in harmony; agree: *There were no problems in forming the club, because they found that their ideas jibed very well. v.*, **jibed, jib·ing.**

jif·fy (jif′ē) *Informal.* a very short time; moment: *I'll be there in a jiffy. n., pl.* **jif·fies.**

jig[1] (jig) 1 a lively dance. 2 the music for such a dance. 3 dance a jig. 1, 2 *n.*, 3 *v.*, **jigged, jig·ging.** **the jig is up,** it's all over; there is no more chance.

jig[2] (jig) 1 a fishing lure made of one or more fish-hooks weighted with pieces of bright bone or metal: *Jigs are usually pulled through the water from a moving boat.* 2 fish with a jig. 1 *n.*, 2 *v.*, **jigged, jig·ging.**

jig·gle (jig′əl) 1 shake or jerk slightly: *Please don't jiggle the desk when I'm trying to write.* 2 a slight shake; a light jerk. 1 *v.*, **jig·gled, jig·gling;** 2 *n.*

jig·saw (jig′so′ or jig′sô′) a saw with a narrow blade mounted in a frame and worked with an up-and-down motion, used to cut curves or irregular lines. *n.*

jigsaw puzzle a picture cut into irregular pieces that can be fitted together again.

jin·gle (jing′gəl) 1 a sound like that of little bells, or of coins or keys striking together. 2 make such a sound: *The sleigh bells jingled.* 3 cause to jingle: *He jingled the coins in his pocket.* 4 a verse or song that repeats sounds or has a catchy rhythm: *Mother Goose rhymes are jingles.* 1, 4 *n.*, 2, 3 *v.*, **jin·gled, jin·gling.**

jinx (jingks) *Slang.* 1 a person or thing that is believed to bring bad luck: *He must be a jinx; we've lost every game since he joined the team.* 2 bring bad luck to. 1 *n.*, 2 *v.*

jit·ters (jit′ərz) *Slang.* a state of great nervousness: *I've got the jitters about my tennis match tomorrow. n. pl.*

job (job) 1 a piece of work: *He had the job of painting the boat.* 2 work done for pay; employment: *Her brother is hunting for a job.* 3 anything a person has to do: *I'm not going to wash the supper dishes; that's your job. n.*

jock·ey (jok′ē) 1 a person whose occupation is riding horses in races. 2 manoeuvre so as to get an advantage: *The crews were jockeying their boats to get into the best position for the race.* 1 *n., pl.* **jock·eys;** 2 *v.*, **jock·eyed, jock·ey·ing.**

joc·u·lar (jok′yə lər) funny; joking: *He spoke in a jocular way about his experiences as a policeman. adj.*

joc·und (jok′ənd) cheerful; merry; gay: *a jocund manner. adj.*

jog[1] (jog) 1 shake with a push or jerk: *You may jog his elbow to get his attention.* 2 a shake, push, or nudge. 3 stir up with a hint or reminder: *He tied a string around his finger to jog his memory.* 4 a hint or reminder: *to give your memory a jog.* 5 move up or down with a jerk or a shaking motion: *The horse jogged along, and jogged me on his back.* 6 go forward heavily and slowly: *The tired boys jogged home.* 7 run at a slow, steady rate: *My father goes jogging every day for exercise.* **8** a walk or slow trot. 1, 3, 5–7 *v.,* **jogged, jog·ging;** 2, 4, 8 *n.*

jog[2] (jog) a part that sticks out or in; the unevenness in a line or surface: *We hid behind a jog in the wall.* *n.*

jog·gle (jog′əl) **1** shake slightly. **2** a slight shake. 1 *v.,* **jog·gled, jog·gling;** 2 *n.*

john (jon) *Slang.* toilet. *n.*

John Bull (jon′bůl′) a character used to represent England and its people: *John Bull is often pictured as a stout, red-faced man in top hat and high black boots.*

John·ny Ca·nuck (jon′ē kə nuk′) *Cdn.* **1** a Canadian, especially a Canadian soldier. **2** a character representing Canada and Canadians: *Johnny Canuck can do a lot more than just play hockey.*

join (join) **1** bring or put together; connect, fasten, or clasp together: *to join hands, to join an island to the mainland by a bridge, to join two points.* **2** come together; meet: *The two roads join here. The stream joins the river just below the mill.* **3** unite; make or become one: *to join in marriage.* **4** take part with others: *to join in a song.* **5** become a member of: *He joined a boys' club. My uncle has joined the army.* **6** take or return to one's place in: *After a few days on shore the sailor joined his ship.* *v.*

joint (joint) **1** the place at which two things or parts are joined together. **2** the way parts are joined: *The carpenter made a neat joint.* **3** connect by a joint or joints. **4** in an animal, the joining of two bones in such a way as to allow movement. **5** one of the parts of which a jointed thing is made up: *the middle joint of the finger.* **6** a large piece of meat for roasting. **7** shared or done by two or more persons: *By our joint efforts we managed to push the car back on the road.* **8** joined together; sharing: *My brother and I are joint owners of this dog.* **9** *Slang.* a place or building, especially a cheap, low place for eating, drinking, or entertainment. 1, 2, 4–6, 9 *n.,* 3 *v.,* 7, 8 *adj.*
out of joint, a out of place at the joint. **b** out of order; in bad condition.

joint·ly (joint′lē) together; as partners: *The two girls owned the boat jointly.* *adv.*

joist (joist) one of the parallel beams of timber or steel which support the boards of a floor or of a ceiling. See **frame** for picture. *n.*

joke (jōk) **1** something said or done to make somebody laugh; something funny; jest. **2** make jokes; say or do something as a joke; jest. **3** a person or thing laughed at. 1, 3 *n.,* 2 *v.,* **joked, jok·ing.**

jok·er (jō′kər) **1** a person who tells funny stories or plays tricks on others. **2** *Slang.* any person; a fellow: *Who does that joker think he is?* **3** in some games, an extra playing card. *n.*

jol·li·ty (jol′ə tē) fun; gaiety. *n., pl.* **jol·li·ties.**

jol·ly (jol′ē) **1** merry; very cheerful; full of fun. **2** *Informal.* pleasant; delightful. *adj.,* **jol·li·er, jol·li·est.**

jolt (jōlt) **1** jar; shake up: *The wagon jolted us when it went over the rocks.* **2** move with a shock or jerk: *The car jolted across the rough ground.* **3** a jar; jerk: *He put his brakes on suddenly, and the car stopped with a jolt.* **4** a sudden surprise or shock: *The loss of the money was a severe jolt.* 1, 2 *v.,* 3, 4 *n.*

jon·quil (jong′kwəl) a yellow or white flower much like a daffodil. *n.*

hat, āge, fär; let, ēqual, tėrm; it, īce
hot, ōpen, ôrder; oil, out; cup, půt, rüle
əbove, takən, pencəl, lemən, circəs
ch, child; ng, long; sh, ship
th, thin; ᴛʜ, then; zh, measure

jos·tle (jos′əl) shove, push, or crowd against; elbow roughly: *We were jostled by the big crowd at the entrance to the circus.* *v.,* **jos·tled, jos·tling.**

jot (jot) **1** a little bit; very small amount: *I do not care a jot.* **2** write briefly or in haste: *The clerk jotted down the order.* 1 *n.,* 2 *v.,* **jot·ted, jot·ting.**

jounce (jouns) **1** shake up and down; bounce; bump; jolt: *The old car jounced along the rough road.* **2** a bump or jolt: *She sat down with a jounce.* 1 *v.,* **jounced, jounc·ing;** 2 *n.*

jour·nal (jėr′nəl) **1** a daily record: *A diary, a ship's log, and a written account of what happens at each meeting of a society are all journals.* **2** a book for keeping such a record. **3** a newspaper or magazine. *n.*
☛ See note at **diary.**

jour·nal·ism (jėr′nəl iz′əm) the work of writing for, editing, managing, or publishing a newspaper or magazine. *n.*

jour·nal·ist (jėr′nəl ist) a person engaged in journalism: *Editors and reporters are journalists.* *n.*

jour·ney (jėr′nē) **1** a trip, especially a fairly long one: *a journey around the world.* **2** travel; take a trip: *to journey to New Brunswick.* 1 *n., pl.* **jour·neys;** 2 *v.,* **jour·neyed, jour·ney·ing.**
☛ **Journey** comes from an old French word *journee,* meaning 'what is done or accomplished in a day,' for example, a day's travel, a day's work. **Journeyman** comes from this meaning of *journey,* referring to a day's wages. A journeyman was one who had finished his apprenticeship in his trade and so was qualified to be paid for his daily work. *Journee* developed from Latin *diurnus,* meaning 'of one day,' from *dies,* meaning 'day.' See also note at **diary.**

jour·ney·man (jėr′nē mən) a workman who has completed an apprenticeship or is otherwise qualified to practise his trade: *Originally, journeymen were hired and paid by the day.* *n., pl.* **jour·ney·men** (jėr′nē mən).
☛ See note at **journey.**

A joust

joust (joust or just) **1** a combat between two knights on horseback, armed with lances. **2** fight with lances on horseback: *Knights used to joust with each other for sport.* 1 *n.,* 2 *v.* **—joust′er,** *n.*

Jove (jōv) the Roman god Jupiter, king of gods and men. *n.*

jo·vi·al (jō′vē əl) kindly and full of fun; good-natured and merry: *Santa Claus is pictured as a jovial old fellow.* *adj.*

jowl (joul) 1 the part under the jaw; jaw. 2 the cheek. *n.*

joy (joi) 1 a strong feeling of pleasure; gladness; happiness: *He jumped for joy when he saw the notice announcing the circus.* 2 something that causes gladness or happiness: *On a hot day, a cool swim is a joy.* *n.*

joy·ful (joi′fəl) 1 glad; happy: *a joyful heart.* 2 causing joy: *joyful news.* 3 showing joy: *a joyful look.* *adj.* **—joy′ful·ly,** *adv.*

joy·ous (joi′əs) joyful; glad; gay: *a joyous song.* *adj.* **—joy′ous·ly,** *adv.*

joy ride a ride in an automobile for pleasure, especially when the car is driven recklessly or is used without the owner's permission.

joy–ride (joi′rīd′) *Informal.* take a joy ride. *v.,* **joy-rode, joy-rid·den, joy-rid·ing.**

Jr. Junior.

ju·bi·lant (jü′bə lənt) expressing or showing joy; rejoicing: *The people were jubilant when the war was over.* *adj.* **—ju′bi·lant·ly,** *adv.*

ju·bi·lee (jü′bə lē′) 1 an anniversary thought of as a time of rejoicing: *a fiftieth wedding jubilee.* 2 a time of rejoicing or great joy: *to have a jubilee in celebration of a victory.* *n.*

☛ **Jubilee** comes originally from a Hebrew word *yōbēl,* meaning 'ram,' so named because in the Old Testament a special year was proclaimed by the Jews every fifty years by blowing a ram's horn.

Ju·da·ism (jü′dā iz′əm) 1 the religion of the Jews, based on the teaching of Moses and the prophets as found in the Old Testament. 2 the following of Jewish rules and customs. *n.*

judge (juj) 1 a government official appointed to hear and decide cases in a law court. 2 hear and decide cases as a judge in a law court. 3 a person chosen to settle a dispute or to decide who wins a race, contest, etc. 4 settle a dispute; decide on the winner in a race, a debate, etc. 5 a person who can decide on how good a thing is: *a good judge of dogs, a poor judge of poetry, a judge of character.* 6 form an opinion or estimate about: *to judge the merits of a book.* 7 think; suppose: *I judged that you had forgotten to come.* 8 consider and blame; criticize: *You had little cause to judge him so harshly.* 1, 3, 5 *n.,* 2, 4, 6–8 *v.,* **judged, judg·ing.**

judg·ment or **judge·ment** (juj′mənt) 1 an opinion or estimate: *In my judgment Beth is prettier than Louise.* 2 the ability to form opinions; good sense: *Since she has judgment in such matters, we will ask her.* 3 the act of judging. 4 a decision made by anybody who judges. 5 criticism; condemnation: *Do not pass judgment on your neighbors.* *n.*

ju·di·cial (jü dish′əl) 1 of or having to do with courts of law, judges, or the administration of justice. 2 of or suitable for a judge; impartial: *a judicial mind.* *adj.* **—ju·di′cial·ly,** *adv.*

ju·di·cious (jü dish′əs) wise; sensible; having, using, or showing good judgment: *Judicious parents encourage their children to make their own decisions.* *adj.* **—ju·di′cious·ly,** *adv.*

ju·do (jü′dō) a modern form of jujitsu. *n.*

jug (jug) a container for holding liquids: *A jug usually has a handle and either a spout or a narrow neck.* *n.*

jug·gle (jug′əl) 1 do tricks that require skill of hand or eye: *He juggled with knives by balancing them on his nose.* 2 do such tricks with: *He can juggle three balls, keeping them all in the air at once.* 3 change so as to deceive or cheat: *The dishonest cashier juggled the accounts to hide his theft.* *v.,* **jug·gled, jug·gling.**

jug·gler (jug′lər) a person who can do juggling tricks. *n.*

jug·u·lar (jug′yə lər) 1 of the neck or throat. 2 one of the two large veins in each side of the neck and head. 1 *adj.,* 2 *n.*

juice (jüs) 1 the liquid part of fruits, vegetables, and meats: *the juice of a lemon, meat juice.* 2 a fluid in the body: *The juices of the stomach help to digest food.* *n.*

juic·y (jüs′ē) full of juice; having much juice: *a juicy orange.* *adj.,* **juic·i·er, juic·i·est.**

ju·jit·su (jü jit′sü) a Japanese method of wrestling or fighting without weapons that uses the strength and weight of an opponent to his or her disadvantage. *n.*

☛ **Jujitsu** comes from a Japanese word *jūjutsu* (pronounced 'jujitsu') from *jū,* meaning 'soft, yielding,' and *jutsu,* meaning 'art.'

Ju·ly (jù lī′ or jə lī′) the seventh month of the year: *July has 31 days.* *n., pl.* **Ju·lies.**

☛ **July** came into English through Old French from the Latin name for this month. The month was named after Julius Caesar because he was born at this time of the year.

jum·ble (jum′bəl) 1 mix or confuse: *She jumbled up everything in the drawer when she was hunting for her gloves.* 2 a mixed-up mess; state of confusion. 1 *v.,* **jum·bled, jum·bling;** 2 *n.*

jum·bo (jum′bō) *Informal.* 1 a big, clumsy person, animal, or thing; something unusually large of its kind. 2 very big: *a jumbo ice-cream cone.* 1 *n., pl.* **jum·bos;** 2 *adj.*

jump (jump) 1 spring from the ground; leap; bound: *The frisky cat quickly jumped off the table and across the porch.* 2 a spring from the ground; leap; bound. 3 cause to jump: *to jump a horse over a fence.* 4 give a sudden start or jerk: *We often jump when a sudden noise startles us.* 5 a sudden, nervous start or jerk: *He gave a jump at the noise of the gun.* 6 rise suddenly: *prices jumped.* 7 a sudden rise: *a jump in costs.* 1, 3, 4, 6 *v.,* 2, 5, 7 *n.*

jump at, accept eagerly and quickly: *jump at a chance, jump at an offer.*

jump·er[1] (jump′ər) a person or thing that jumps. *n.*

jump·er[2] (jump′ər) 1 a sleeveless dress, usually worn over a blouse. 2 a loose jacket: *Workmen and sailors often wear jumpers to protect their clothes.* *n.*

jump·y (jum′pē) 1 moving by jumps; making sudden, sharp jerks: *The car made a jumpy start from the stop light.* 2 easily excited or frightened; nervous: *He's jumpy because he's sure we're going to be late.* *adj.,* **jump·i·er, jump·i·est. —jump′i·ly,** *adv.*

junc·tion (jungk′shən) 1 joining or being joined: *the junction of two rivers.* 2 a place of joining or meeting: *A railway junction is a place where railway lines meet or cross.* *n.*

hat, āge, fär; let, ēqual, tėrm; it, īce
hot, ōpen, ôrder; oil, out; cup, pu̇t, rüle
əbove, takən, pencəl, lemən, circəs
ch, child; ng, long; sh, ship
th, thin; ᴛʜ, then; zh, measure

junc·ture (jungk′chər) **1** a point or line where two things join; joint. **2** joining or being joined. *n.*
at this juncture, when affairs are in this state at this moment: *At this juncture the doctor decided to operate.*

June (jün) the sixth month of the year: *June has 30 days. n.*

☛ **June** came into English through Old French from the Latin name for this month, *Junonius,* meaning the month of the goddess Juno.

jun·gle (jung′gəl) wild land thickly overgrown with bushes, vines, trees, etc.: *Jungles are hot and humid regions with many kinds of plants and wild animals. n.*

jun·ior (jün′yər) **1** the younger, used of a son having the same name as his father: *John Parker, Junior, is the son of John Parker, Senior.* **2** a younger person: *He is his brother's junior by two years.* **3** of or for young people: *a junior bed.* **4** of lower rank or shorter service; of less standing than some others: *the junior partner, a junior officer.* **5** a person of lower rank or shorter service. 1, 3, 4 *adj.,* 2, 5 *n.*

junior high school a school consisting of grades 7, 8, and 9; any school intermediate between elementary school and high school.

ju·ni·per (jü′nə pər) an evergreen shrub or tree having small berry-like cones: *The red cedar is a kind of juniper. n.*

junk[1] (jungk) **1** old newspapers, metal, and other rubbish; trash. **2** *Informal.* throw away or discard as junk: *We junked the old garden chairs last fall.* 1 *n.,* 2 *v.*

A junk

junk[2] (jungk) a Chinese sailing ship. *n.*

Ju·pi·ter (jü′pə tər) **1** in Roman myths, the chief god, ruler of gods and men. **2** the largest planet. *n.*

ju·ror (jür′ər) a member of a jury. *n.*

ju·ry (jür′ē) **1** a group of persons chosen to hear evidence in a court of law and sworn to give a decision according to the evidence presented to them: *The question put before a jury is, 'Is the prisoner guilty or not?'* **2** any group of persons chosen to give a judgment or to decide who is the winner in a contest: *The jury gave her poem the first prize. n., pl.* **ju·ries.**

just (just) **1** right; fair: *a just reward, a just price.* **2** righteous: *a just life.* **3** true; correct; exact: *just weights.* **4** exactly: *That is just a metre.* **5** very close; immediately: *There was a picture just above the fireplace.* **6** a very short while ago: *He just left.* **7** barely: *I just managed to catch the train.* **8** no more than; only; merely: *He is just an ordinary man.* **9** *Informal.* quite; truly; positively: *The weather is just glorious.* 1–3 *adj.,* 4–9 *adv.*
just now, only a very short time ago: *I saw him just now.*

jus·tice (jus′tis) **1** just conduct; fair dealing: *Judges should have a sense of justice.* **2** fairness; rightness; being just: *the justice of a claim. n.*
do justice to, a treat fairly. **b** see the good points of; show the proper appreciation for: *The crowd's applause did not do justice to his performance.*
do oneself justice, do as well as one really can do: *He did not do himself justice on the test.*

jus·ti·fi·a·ble (jus′tə fī′ə bəl) capable of being justified; proper: *An act is justifiable if it can be shown to be just or right. adj.* **—jus′ti·fi′a·bly,** *adv.*

jus·ti·fi·ca·tion (jus′tə fə kā′shən) **1** justifying or being justified. **2** the fact or circumstance that justifies; a good reason or excuse: *What is your justification for being so late? n.*

jus·ti·fy (jus′tə fī′) **1** give a good reason for: *The fine quality of the cloth justifies its high cost.* **2** show to be just or right: *Can you justify your act?* **3** clear of blame or guilt: *One is justified in shooting a man in self-defence. v.,* **jus·ti·fied, jus·ti·fy·ing.**

jut (jut) **1** stick out; project; stand out: *The pier jutted out from the shore into the water.* **2** a part that sticks out; projection. 1 *v.,* **jut·ted, jut·ting;** 2 *n.*

jute (jüt) a strong fibre used for making coarse fabrics, rope, etc.: *Jute is obtained from two tropical plants. n.*

ju·ve·nile (jü′və nīl′ or jü′və nəl) **1** young; youthful; immature: *juvenile behavior.* **2** a young person. **3** of or for boys and girls: *juvenile books, a juvenile court.* **4** a book for boys and girls. 1, 3 *adj.,* 2, 4 *n.*

k or **K** (kā) the 11th letter of the alphabet: *There are two* k's *in* kick. *n., pl.* **k's** or **K's.**

kale (kāl) any of several kinds of cabbage that have loose leaves instead of a firm head: *Kale looks like spinach. n.*

ka·lei·do·scope (kə lī′də skōp′) **1** a tube containing bits of colored glass and two or more mirrors: *As a kaleidoscope is turned, it reflects continually changing patterns.* **2** anything that changes continually; a continually changing pattern: *A circus is a kaleidoscope of activity. n.*

☛ **Kaleidoscope** comes from a combination of the Greek words *kalos,* meaning 'beautiful,' and *eidos,* meaning 'shape,' together with the English *-scope,* meaning an instrument with which to see or observe.

kan·ga·roo (kang′gə rü′) an animal of Australia having small forelegs and very strong hind legs, which give it great leaping power: *The female kangaroo has a pouch in front in which she carries her young. n., pl.* **kan·ga·roos** or **kan·ga·roo.**

ka·o·lin (kā′ə lin) a fine, white clay, used in making porcelain. *n.*

ka·pok (kā′pok or kap′ək) the silky fibres around the seeds of a tropical tree, used for stuffing pillows, mattresses, etc. *n.*

kar·at (kar′ət or ker′ət) See **carat.**

ka·ra·te (kə rä′tē) a Japanese system of self-defence without weapons, based on the use of certain kinds of hand or foot blows that can cripple or kill. *n.*

ka·ty·did (kā′tē did′) a large, green insect resembling a grasshopper. *n.*

☛ The word **katydid** was originally an imitation of the sound the male of this insect makes.

A kayak

kay·ak (kī′ak) **1** an Eskimo canoe made of skins stretched over a light frame of wood or bone with an opening in the middle for a person. **2** a similar craft made of other material. *n.*

ka·zoo (kə zü′) a toy musical instrument made of a tube partly sealed off at one end so that it produces a buzzing when one hums into the tube. *n.*

keel (kēl) **1** the main timber or steel piece that extends the whole length of the bottom of a ship or boat: *The whole ship is built up on the keel.* **2** a part, as on an aircraft, that is like a ship's keel. **3** turn upside down; upset. 1, 2 *n.,* 3 *v.*

keel over, a turn upside down; upset: *The sailboat keeled over in the storm.* **b** fall over suddenly: *He keeled over in a faint.*

keen (kēn) **1** sharp enough to cut well: *a keen blade.* **2** sharp; cutting: *a keen wind.* **3** able to do its work quickly and accurately: *a keen mind, a keen sense of smell.* **4** *Informal.* full of enthusiasm; eager: *a keen player. adj.* **—keen′ly,** *adv.*

keen·ness (kēn′nis) **1** a keen or cutting quality; sharpness: *the keenness of an axe, the keenness of the cold wind, the keenness of a man's appetite.* **2** interest in; enthusiasm for: *His keenness for outdoor sports was easy to see. n.*

keep (kēp) **1** have for a long time or forever: *You may keep this book.* **2** have and not let go; hold; detain: *They were kept in prison. He was kept in hospital for ten days.* **3** not tell or reveal: *Will you promise to keep my secret?* **4** have and take care of: *My uncle keeps chickens.* **5** take care of and protect: *The bank keeps money for people.* **6** have; hold: *Keep this in mind.* **7** hold back; prevent: *Keep the baby from crying.* **8** stay the same; continue to be: *Keep awake. Keep going along this road.* **9** cause to continue; cause to stay the same: *Keep the baby warm. He kept the fire burning.* **10** maintain in good condition: *keep a garden. Mother keeps house.* **11** stay in good condition; be preserved: *Butter will keep in a refrigerator.* **12** do the right thing with; observe; celebrate: *Scrooge learned how to keep Christmas.* **13** be faithful to: *keep a promise.* **14** food and a place to sleep: *He earns his keep.* **15** the strongest part of a fortress or castle. See **castle** for picture. 1–13 *v.,* **kept, keep·ing;** 14, 15 *n.* **—keep′er,** *n.*

for keeps, a for the winner to keep his winnings. **b** *Informal.* forever.

keep on, go on; continue: *The boys kept on swimming in spite of the rain.*

keep up, a continue; prevent from ending: *We kept up a small fire.* **b** maintain in good condition. **c** remain close or alongside; not fall behind.

keep up with, not fall behind; go or move as fast as: *You walk so fast that I can't keep up with you.*

keep·ing (kēp′ing) **1** care; charge: *Their uncle paid for the keeping of the orphaned children.* **2** observance; celebration: *the keeping of Thanksgiving Day.* **3** agreement; harmony: *Don't trust him; his actions are not in keeping with his promises. n.*

keep·sake (kēp′sāk′) something kept in memory of the giver: *My friend gave me his picture as a keepsake. n.*

keg (keg) a small barrel. *n.*

kelp (kelp) **1** a large, tough, brown seaweed. **2** ashes of seaweed, used as a source of iodine. *n.*

kel·vin (kel′vin) **1 Kelvin,** of, based on, or according to a scale of temperature used in science, on which 0 represents the coldest possible state, equal to −273.16 degrees Celsius. **2** a unit of temperature on this scale: *One kelvin is equal to one degree Celsius. Symbol: K* 1 *adj.,* 2 *n.*

☛ Named after William Thomson, Lord *Kelvin* (1824–1907), the British scientist who developed this scale.

ken (ken) **1** the range of sight. **2** the range of knowledge: *What happens on Mars is beyond our ken.* **3** in Scotland, know. 1, 2 *n.,* 3 *v.,* **kenned, ken·ning.**

ken·nel (ken′əl) **1** a house for a dog or dogs. **2** Often, **kennels,** *pl.* **a** a place where dogs are bred. **b** a place where dogs may be lodged and cared for. *n.*

kept (kept) See **keep.** *He kept the book I gave him. The milk was kept in bottles. v.*

kerb (kėrb) See **curb.**

hat, āge, fär; let, ēqual, tėrm; it, īce
hot, ōpen, ôrder; oil, out; cup, pu̇t, rüle
əbove, takən, pencəl, lemən, circəs
ch, child; ng, long; sh, ship
th, thin; ŦH, then; zh, measure

A kerchief

ker·chief (kėr′chif) **1** a piece of cloth worn over the head or around the neck. **2** handkerchief. *n.*

ker·nel (kėr′nəl) **1** the softer part inside the hard shell of a nut or inside the stone of a fruit. **2** a grain or seed like that of wheat or corn. **3** the central or important part of anything, around which it is formed or built up: *the kernel of an argument. n.*

☛ **Kernel** and **colonel** are pronounced the same.

ker·o·sene (ker′ə sēn′) a thin oil made from petroleum, used as a fuel; coal oil. *n.*

ketch (kech) a small sailing ship with a large mainmast toward the bow and a smaller mast toward the stern. *n., pl.* **ketch·es.**

ketch·up (kech′əp) a sauce used with meat, fish, etc.: *Tomato ketchup is made of tomatoes, onions, salt, sugar, and spices. n.* Also, **catchup, catsup.**

ket·tle (ket′əl) **1** any metal container for boiling liquids, cooking fruit, etc. **2** a metal container with a handle and a spout, for heating water; teakettle. *n.*

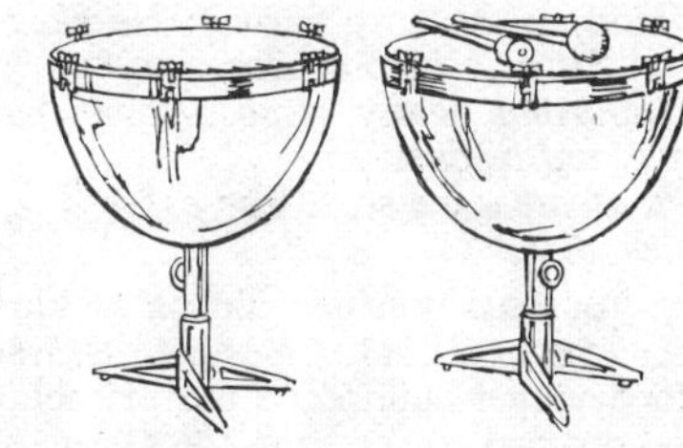
Kettledrums

ket·tle·drum (ket′əl drum′) a drum consisting of a large, hollow bowl of brass or copper and a top of parchment. *n.*

Keys for locks

key[1] (kē) **1** an instrument, usually metal, that locks and unlocks; something that turns the bolt in a lock: *I lost the key to the padlock on my bicycle.* **2** anything like this in shape or use: *a key to wind a clock, a key to open a tin.* **3** the answer to a puzzle or problem: *The key to this puzzle will be published next week.* **4** a sheet or book of answers: *a key to a test.* **5** a systematic explanation of abbreviations or symbols used in a dictionary, map, etc.: *There is a pronunciation key at the beginning of this dictionary.* **6** a place that commands or gives control of a sea, a district, etc. because of its position: *Gibraltar is the key to the Mediterranean.* **7** controlling; very important: *the key industries of a country.* **8** one of a set of parts pressed down by the fingers in playing a piano, and in operating a typewriter or other instruments: *Don't hit the keys so hard.* **9** a scale or system of related tones in music based on a particular tone: *a song written in the key of B flat.* **10** a tone of voice; a style of thought or expression: *The widow wrote in a sorrowful key.*
11 regulate the pitch of; tune: *to key a piano in preparation for a concert.* 1–6, 8–10 *n., pl.* **keys;** 7 *adj.,* 11 *v.,* **keyed, key·ing.**

key up, raise the courage or nerve of: *She keyed herself up to ask for a higher salary. The coach keyed up the team for the big game.*

☛ Key and quay are pronounced the same.

☛ Key[1] developed from an Old English word *cǣg,* having the same meaning.

key[2] (kē) a low island; reef: *There are keys south of Florida. n., pl.* **keys.**

☛ See first note at **key**[1].

☛ Key[2] comes from an older form of the word **quay.**

key·board (kē′bôrd′) the set of keys in a piano, typewriter, calculator, etc. *n.*

key·note (kē′nōt′) **1** in music, the note on which a scale or system of tones is based. **2** the main idea or guiding principle: *World peace was the keynote of his speech. n.*

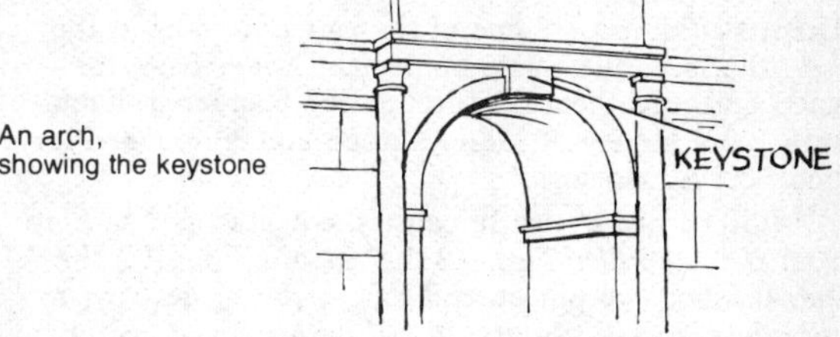

An arch, showing the keystone

key·stone (kē′stōn′) **1** the middle stone at the top of an arch, holding the other stones or pieces in place.
2 anything on which other related parts depend: *Freedom is the keystone of our policy. n.*

kg kilogram; kilograms.

khak·i (kär′kē, kä′kē, kak′ē) **1** a dull, yellowish brown. **2** a heavy cloth of this color, often used for soldiers' uniforms. 1 *adj.,* 1, 2 *n., pl.* **khak·is.**

☛ **Khaki** came into English from Urdu, a language of India and now Pakistan. The Urdu word *khākī,* meaning 'dusty,' came originally from a Persian word *khāk,* meaning 'dust.'

kick (kik) **1** strike out with the foot: *This horse kicks.* **2** strike with the foot: *My brother kicked me.* **3** drive, force, or move by kicking: *to kick a ball along the ground, to kick off one's shoes, to kick up dust.* **4** a blow with the foot: *The horse's kick knocked the boy* *down.* **5** the recoil or backward motion of a gun when it is fired. **6** spring back when fired; recoil: *This shotgun kicks.* **7** *Informal.* grumble; find fault. **8** *Slang.* thrill; excitement: *He gets a kick out of gambling.* 1–3, 6, 7 *v.*, 4, 5, 8 *n.*

kick out, *Informal.* expel or turn out in a humiliating or disgraceful way: *She should be kicked out of our club.*

kick up, *Slang.* start; cause: *She kicks up a lot of trouble.*

kick·off (kik′of′) **1** the start of a football game: *The kickoff is scheduled for 2:00 p.m.* **2** the start of any activity. *n.*

kid¹ (kid) **1** a young goat. **2** the leather made from the skin of a young goat, used for gloves, shoes, etc. **3** *Informal.* child: *The kids went to the circus.* *n.*

kid² (kid) *Slang.* tease playfully; talk in a joking way: *He's always kidding.* *v.*, **kid·ded, kid·ding.**

kid·nap (kid′nap) carry off and hold a person by force: *The banker's son was kidnapped and held for ransom. The gang planned to kidnap the movie star.* *v.*, **kid·napped** or **kid·naped, kid·nap·ping** or **kid·nap·ing.**

kid·nap·per or **kid·nap·er** (kid′nap ər) a person who carries off and holds another by force: *The kidnappers demanded a ransom.* *n.*

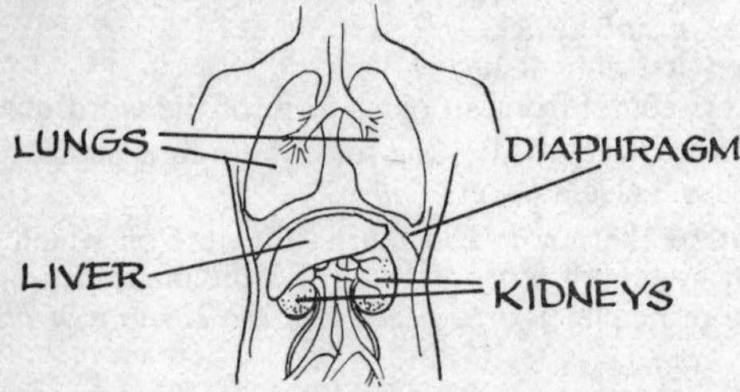

kid·ney (kid′nē) **1** one of the pair of organs in the body that separate waste matter and water from the blood and pass them off through the bladder in liquid form. **2** a kidney or kidneys of an animal, cooked for food. *n., pl.* **kid·neys.**

kill (kil) **1** put to death; cause the death of: *The blow from the axe killed him.* **2** the act of killing. **3** the animal killed. **4** put an end to; get rid of; destroy: *to kill odors, to kill rumors, to kill faith.* **5** use up time: *We killed an hour at the zoo.* **6** *Informal.* overcome completely: *My sore foot is killing me. His jokes really kill me.* 1, 4–6 *v.*, 2, 3 *n.* —**kill′er,** *n.*

kill·deer (kil′dēr′) a small wading bird that has a loud, shrill cry; the commonest plover of North America. *n., pl.* **kill·deers** or **kill·deer.**

kiln (kiln or kil) a furnace or oven for burning, baking, or drying something: *Limestone is burned in a kiln to make lime. Bricks are baked in a kiln.* *n.*

ki·lo (kē′lō or kil′ō) **1** kilogram. **2** kilometre. *n., pl.* **ki·los.**

kil·o·gram (kil′ə gram′) a measure of mass equal to 1000 grams: *A litre of water weighs one kilogram.* *Symbol:* kg *n.* Also spelled **kilogramme.**

kil·o·me·tre (kil′ə mē′tər or kə lom′ə tər) a measure of length equal to 1000 metres: *It takes about 10 minutes to walk a kilometre.* *Symbol:* km *n.* Also spelled **kilometer.**

kil·o·watt (kil′ə wot′) a unit of electric power equal to 1000 watts. *Symbol:* kW *n.*

kilt (kilt) **1** a pleated, knee-length skirt worn especially by men in the Scottish Highlands and by soldiers in Scottish and Irish regiments, including those in Canada. **2** a similar garment worn by women and girls. *n.*

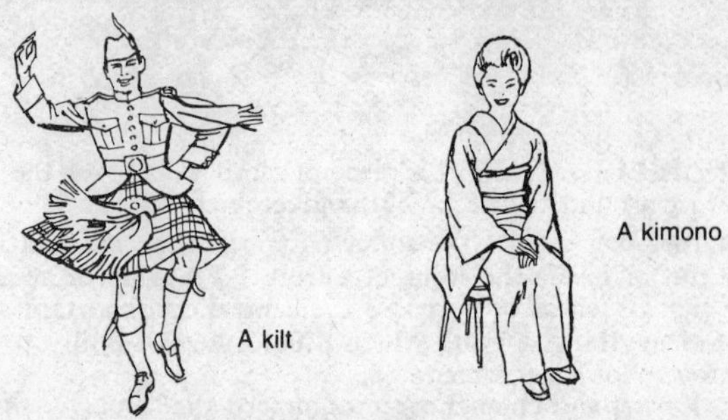
A kilt

A kimono

ki·mo·no (kə mō′nə) **1** a loose outer garment held in place by a sash, worn by men and women in Japan. **2** a loose dressing gown. *n., pl.* **ki·mo·nos.**

kin (kin) **1** a person's family or relatives; kindred: *All our kin came to the family reunion.* **2** related: *My cousins are kin to me.* **3** family relationship: *What kin is she to you?* 1, 3 *n.*, 2 *adj.*

next of kin, nearest living relative: *His next of kin is his father.*

kind¹ (kīnd) friendly; doing good rather than harm: *The kind girl tried to help people and make them happy.* *adj.*

kind² (kīnd) class; sort; variety: *He likes most kinds of candy. A kilt is a kind of skirt.* *n.*

kind of, *Informal.* nearly; almost; somewhat; rather: *The room was kind of dark.*

of a kind, of the same sort: *The cakes were all of a kind—chocolate.*

kin·der·gar·ten (kin′dər gär′tən or kin′də gär′tən) **1** the year of school that comes before Grade 1. **2** a school for younger children; a nursery school. *n.*

☛ **Kindergarten** comes from the German *Kindergarten,* meaning 'a children's garden or yard.'

kind–heart·ed (kīnd′här′tid) having or showing a kind heart; kindly; sympathetic. *adj.*

kin·dle (kin′dəl) **1** set on fire; light: *Light the paper with a match to kindle the bonfire.* **2** catch fire; begin to burn: *This damp wood will never kindle.* **3** stir up; arouse: *His cruelty kindled our anger.* *v.*, **kin·dled, kin·dling.**

kind·li·ness (kīnd′lē nis) **1** a kindly feeling or quality. **2** a kindly act. *n.*

kin·dling (kin′dling) material, such as small pieces of wood, for starting a fire. *n.*

kind·ly (kīnd′lē) **1** kind; friendly: *kindly faces, kindly people.* **2** in a kind or friendly way: *The children liked the old woman because she always treated them kindly.* **3** pleasantly; agreeably: *He does not take kindly to criticism.* 1 *adj.*, **kind·li·er, kind·li·est;** 2, 3 *adv.*

kind·ness (kīnd′nis) **1** a kind nature; being kind: *We admire his kindness.* **2** kind treatment: *Thank you for your kindness.* **3** a kind act: *He showed me many kindnesses.* *n., pl.* **kind·ness·es.**

kin·dred (kin′drid) **1** like; similar; connected: *She learned about dew, frost, and kindred facts of nature.*

hat, āge, fär; let, ēqual, tėrm; it, īce
hot, ōpen, ôrder; oil, out; cup, pu̇t, rüle
əbove, takən, pencəl, lemən, circəs
ch, child; ng, long; sh, ship
th, thin; ᴛʜ, then; zh, measure

2 related: *kindred tribes.* **3** a person's family or relatives. **4** family relationship: *Does he claim kindred with you?* **5** being alike; resemblance: *There is kindred among the words 'receive,' 'receipt,' and 'reception.'* 1, 2 *adj.,* 3–5 *n.*

kin·folk (kin′fōk′) kinsfolk. *n.*

king (king) **1** the male ruler of a nation; male sovereign: *Richard the Lion-Hearted was a king of England.* **2** a person, animal, or thing that is best or most important in a certain sphere or class: *The lion is called the king of the beasts. Babe Ruth was a king of baseball.* **3** in chess, the chief piece. **4** in checkers, a piece that has moved entirely across the board. **5** a playing card bearing a picture of a king. *n.*

king·bird (king′bėrd′) a quarrelsome bird of the flycatcher family. *n.*

king·dom (king′dəm) **1** a country that is governed by a king or a queen. **2** a realm or province: *The mind is the kingdom of thought.* **3** one of the three divisions of the natural world: *We speak of the animal kingdom, the vegetable kingdom, and the mineral kingdom.* *n.*

One kind of kingfisher — about 33 cm long with the tail

king·fish·er (king′fish′ər) a bright-colored bird having a large head and a strong beak: *North American kingfishers eat fish; some of the European kinds eat insects.* *n.*

king·ly (king′lē) **1** of a king or kings; of royal rank. **2** fit for a king: *a kingly crown.* **3** like a king; royal; noble: *kingly pride.* **4** as a king does. 1–3 *adj.,* **king·li·er, king·li·est;** 4 *adv.*

king–size (king′sīz′) *Informal.* unusually large or long for its kind: *a king-size bed.* *adj.*

kink (kingk) **1** a twist or curl in thread, rope, hair, etc. **2** form a kink or kinks; make kinks in: *The rope kinked as he rolled it up. Don't kink the clothes line.* **3** pain or stiffness in the muscles of the neck, back, etc. **4** a mental twist; a queer idea: *The old man had many kinks.* 1, 3, 4 *n.,* 2 *v.*

kins·folk (kinz′fōk′) a person's family or relatives; kin. *n. pl.* Also, **kinfolk.**

kin·ship (kin′ship) **1** being kin; family relationship: *His kinship with the owner of the factory helped him to get a job.* **2** relationship. **3** resemblance: *Tennis and badminton have a kinship.* *n.*

kins·man (kinz′mən) a male relative: *Uncles are kinsmen.* *n., pl.* **kins·men** (kinz′mən).

kins·wom·an (kinz′wu̇m′ən) a female relative. *n., pl.* **kins·wom·en** (kinz′wim′ən).

kirk (kėrk) a Scottish word for church. *n.*

kiss (kis) **1** touch with the lips as a sign of love, greeting, or respect. **2** a touch with the lips as a sign of love, greeting, or respect. **3** touch gently: *A soft wind kissed the tree tops.* **4** a gentle touch. **5** a kind of candy wrapped in a twist of paper. 1, 3 *v.,* 2, 4, 5 *n.*

kit (kit) **1** a set of materials, supplies, or tools required for a particular job or purpose: *a first-aid kit, a sewing kit, a shaving kit.* **2** a set of parts intended to be put together to make a particular thing: *a radio kit, a model airplane kit.* **3** a set of printed materials issued for instruction and information: *a selling kit, a visitor's kit.* **4** the uniform or other clothing and personal equipment required for a certain activity: *a soldier's kit, skiing kit.* **5** *Informal.* any lot, set, or collection of persons or things. *n.*

kit–bag (kit′bag′) a cylindrical bag, usually made of canvas, for carrying personal belongings. *n.*

kitch·en (kich′ən) a room where food is cooked or prepared. *n.*

Kites flying

kite (kīt) **1** a light frame covered with paper, cloth, or plastic: *Kites are flown in the air on the end of a long string.* **2** a hawk with long, pointed wings. *n.*

kith (kith) friends. *n.*
kith and kin, friends and relatives.

kit·ten (kit′ən) a young cat. *n.*

kit·ty (kit′ē) kitten. *n., pl.* **kit·ties.**

kit·ty–cor·ner (kit′ē kôr′nər) **1** on the diagonal; diagonally opposite: *The barn is kitty-corner from the house.* **2** diagonally: *They walked kitty-corner across the intersection.* 1 *adj.,* 2 *adv.*

ki·wi (kē′wē) a bird of New Zealand that cannot fly, having shaggy feathers, a long, slender bill and tiny, useless wings: *The kiwi is about the size of a chicken.* *n.*

km kilometre; kilometres.

knack (nak) a special skill; the power to do something easily: *That clown has the knack of making very funny faces.* *n.*

A knapsack

knap·sack (nap′sak′) a leather or canvas bag for carrying clothes, equipment, etc. on the back. *n.*

knave (nāv) **1** a tricky or dishonest fellow; rogue.

2 a playing card, usually called a jack. *n.*

☞ **Knave** and **nave** are pronounced the same.

knav·er·y (nāv′ər ē) 1 trickery; dishonesty; the behavior of a knave or rascal. 2 a tricky, dishonest act. *n., pl.* **knav·er·ies.**

knav·ish (nāv′ish) tricky; dishonest: *a knavish fellow. adj.* **—knav′ish·ly,** *adv.*

knead (nēd) 1 mix flour, clay, etc. into a dough or paste by pressing and stretching, usually with the hands: *Machines have been invented to knead bread dough.* 2 make or shape by kneading. 3 press and squeeze with the hands; massage: *The trainer kneaded the muscles of the runner. v.*

☞ **Knead** and **need** are pronounced the same.

knee (nē) 1 the joint between the thigh and the lower leg. See **leg** for picture. 2 anything like a bent knee in shape or position. 3 strike with the knee. 4 the part of pants, stockings, etc. covering the knee. 1, 2, 4 *n.,* 3 *v.,* **kneed, knee·ing.**

knee·cap (nē′kap′) the flat, movable bone at the front of the knee. *n.*

kneel (nēl) 1 go down on one's knee or knees: *She knelt down to pull a weed from the flower bed.* 2 remain in this position: *They knelt in prayer for several minutes. v.,* **knelt** or **kneeled, kneel·ing.**

knell (nel) 1 the sound of a bell rung slowly after a death or at a funeral. 2 ring slowly; toll. 3 something regarded as a sign or warning of death, failure, etc.: *Their refusal rang the knell of our hopes.* 1, 3 *n.,* 2 *v.*

knelt (nelt) See **kneel.** *She knelt and prayed. v.*

knew (nyü or nü) See **know.** *She knew the right answer. v.*

☞ **Knew** and **new** are pronounced the same.

knick·er·bock·ers (nik′ər bok′ərz) knickers. *n. pl.*

knick·ers (nik′ərz) short, loose-fitting trousers gathered in at, or just below, the knee. *n. pl.*

knick–knack (nik′nak′) a pleasing trifle; an ornament or trinket. *n.*

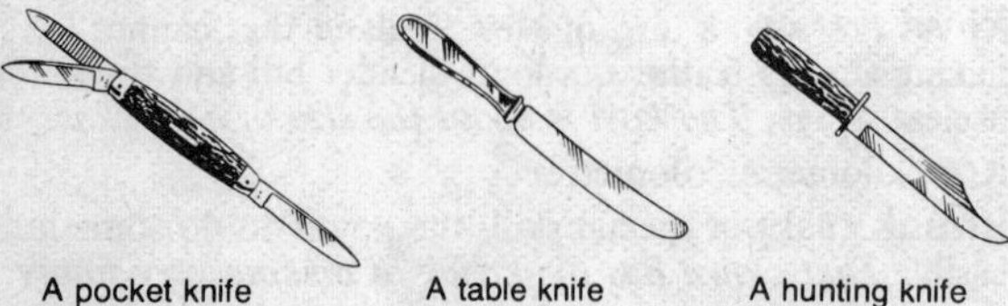

A pocket knife A table knife A hunting knife

knife (nīf) 1 a thin, flat, metal blade fastened in a handle so that it can be used to cut or spread. 2 a sharp blade forming part of a tool or machine: *The knives of a lawn mower cut the grass.* 3 cut or stab with a knife. 4 pierce or cut as with a knife: *The wind knifed through his coat.* 1, 2 *n., pl.* **knives** (nīvz); 3, 4 *v.,* **knifed, knif·ing.**

knight (nīt) 1 in the Middle Ages, a man raised to an honorable military rank and pledged to do good deeds: *After serving as a page and squire, a man was made a knight by the king or a lord.* 2 in modern times, a man raised to an honorable rank because of great achievement or service: *A knight has the title* Sir *before his name.* 3 raise to the rank of knight: *He was knighted by the Queen.* 4 one of the pieces in the game of chess. 1, 2, 4 *n.,* 3 *v.*

☞ **Knight** and **night** are pronounced the same.

knight–er·rant (nīt′er′ənt) a knight travelling in search of adventure. *n., pl.* **knights-er·rant.**

knight·hood (nīt′hu̇d) 1 the rank of a knight. 2 the character or qualities of a knight. 3 knights as a group: *all the knighthood of France. n.*

knight·ly (nīt′lē) 1 of a knight; brave; generous; courteous. 2 as a knight should do; bravely; generously; courteously. 1 *adj.,* 2 *adv.*

☞ **Knightly** and **nightly** are pronounced the same.

Knitting

knit (nit) 1 make cloth or an article of clothing by looping yarn or thread together with long needles, or by machinery which forms similar interlocking loops: *She is knitting a sweater. Jersey is knitted cloth.* 2 join closely and firmly together: *David and Jonathan were knit in friendship.* 3 grow together: *A broken bone knits.* 4 draw the brows together in wrinkles: *She knits her brows when she frowns. v.,* **knit·ted or knit, knit·ting. —knit′ter,** *n.*

knives (nīvz) plural of **knife.** *n.*

knob (nob) 1 a rounded lump. 2 the handle on a door, drawer, etc.: *the knob on the dial of a television set. n.*

knock (nok) 1 give a hard blow or blows to with the fist, knuckles, or anything hard; hit: *She knocked him on the head.* 2 a hit: *The hard knock made her cry.* 3 hit and cause to fall: *Mark ran against another boy and knocked him down.* 4 make a noise by hitting: *She knocked on the door.* 5 the sound of knocking: *The knock on the door made us all jump with surprise.* 6 a thumping or rattling sound in an engine: *We learned that the knock was caused by loose parts.* 7 make a noise, especially a rattling or pounding noise: *That engine knocks.* 1, 3, 4, 7 *v.,* 2, 5, 6 *n.*

knock about, *Informal.* **a** wander from place to place. **b** hit repeatedly.

knock down, take apart: *We knocked down the bookcase and packed it in the car.*

knock off, *Informal.* **a** take off; deduct: *knock off 50 cents from the price.* **b** stop work: *We knock off at noon for lunch.*

knock out, hit so hard as to make helpless or unconscious.

knock together, make or put together hastily: *The boys knocked together a sort of raft out of old boards.*

A knocker on a door

knock·er (nok′ər) a hinged knob, ring, or the like, fastened on a door for use in knocking. *n.*

hat, āge, fär; let, ēqual, tėrm; it, īce
hot, ōpen, ôrder; oil, out; cup, pu̇t, rüle
əbove, takən, pencəl, lemən, circəs
ch, child; ng, long; sh, ship
th, thin; ᴛʜ, then; zh, measure

knock·out (nok′out′) 1 the act of rendering unconscious or helpless by a punch: *The boxer won the fight by a knockout.* 2 *Slang.* a person or thing considered outstanding; a success: *The party was a knockout.* *n.*

knoll (nōl) a small, rounded hill; mound. *n.*

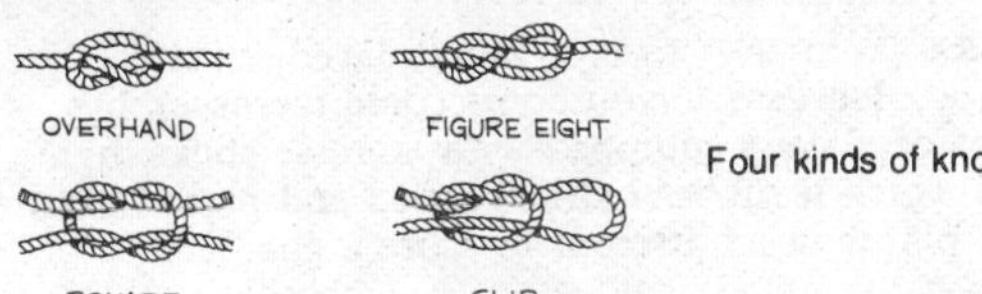

Four kinds of knot

knot (not) 1 a fastening made by tying or twining together pieces of cord, rope, string, etc.: *a square knot, a slip knot.* 2 tie or twine together in a knot. 3 tangle in knots: *My thread has knotted.* 4 ribbon made up into an ornament to be put on a dress, etc.; a bow of ribbon: *a shoulder knot.* 5 a group; cluster: *There was a knot of children around each sailor.* 6 the hard mass formed in a tree where a branch grows out, which shows as a roundish, cross-grained piece in a board. 7 lump: *A knot sometimes forms in a tired muscle.* 8 the measure of speed used on ships; one nautical mile (1852 metres) per hour: *This ship's usual speed is about 18 knots.* 9 unite closely in a way that is hard to undo; bind. 1, 4–8 *n.*, 2, 3, 9 *v.*, **knot·ted, knot·ting.**

☛ **Knot** and **not** are pronounced the same. **Naught** and **nought** are sometimes pronounced the same as **knot** and **not.**

knot·hole (not′hōl′) a hole in a board where a knot has fallen out. *n.*

knot·ty (not′ē) 1 full of knots: *knotty wood.* 2 difficult; puzzling: *a knotty problem.* *adj.*, **knot·ti·er, knot·ti·est.**

know (nō) 1 have the facts of; be skilled in: *He knows arithmetic. An artist must know his art.* 2 have the facts and be sure that they are true: *We know that 2 and 2 are 4. Dr. Jones does not guess; he knows.* 3 have knowledge or skill: *Mother knows from experience how to cook.* 4 tell apart from others: *How many kinds of birds do you know?* 5 be acquainted with: *I know her very well, but I don't know her sister.* *v.*, **knew, known, know·ing.**

☛ **Know** and **no** are pronounced the same.

know·ing (nō′ing) 1 having knowledge. 2 clever; shrewd. 3 suggesting shrewd or secret understanding: *a knowing look.* *adj.*

know·ing·ly (nō′ing lē) 1 in a knowing way. 2 on purpose: *David would not knowingly hurt anyone.* *adv.*

knowl·edge (nol′ij) 1 what one knows: *a hunter's knowledge of guns.* 2 all that is known or can be learned: *Science is a part of knowledge.* 3 the act or fact of knowing: *The knowledge of our victory caused great joy.* *n.*

known (nōn) 1 in the knowledge of everyone; widely recognized: *a known fact, a known artist.* 2 See **know.** *Champlain is known as an explorer.* 1 *adj.*, 2 *v.*

knuck·le (nuk′əl) 1 a joint in a finger, especially the joint between a finger and the rest of the hand. 2 the knee or hock joint of an animal used as food: *boiled pigs' knuckles.* 3 press or rub with the knuckles. 1, 2 *n.*, 3 *v.*

knuckle down, a *Informal.* work hard. **b** submit; yield: *He would not knuckle down under their attacks.*

knuckle under, submit; give in: *He refused to knuckle under to his enemies.*

ko·a·la (kō ä′lə) a grey, furry animal of Australia that carries its young in a pouch: *Koalas live in trees.* *n.*

Ko·ran (kô rän′ or kô ran′) the sacred book of the Moslems, made up of reports of the revelations made by Allah to the prophet Mohammed: *The Koran is the basis of the laws and customs by which Moslems regulate their lives.* *n.*

Ko·re·an (kə rē′ən or kô rē′ən) 1 of or having to do with Korea, a small country in eastern Asia, its people, or their language. 2 a person born in or living in Korea. 3 the language of Korea. 1 *adj.*, 2, 3 *n.*

ko·sher (kō′shər) 1 fit to eat according to Jewish religious law: *Kosher meat is from an animal killed by a rabbi in a certain way.* 2 dealing in products that meet the requirements of Jewish law: *a kosher butcher.* 3 *Slang.* all right; proper: *It's not kosher to change the rules once the game has started.* *adj.*

☛ **Kosher** comes from a Hebrew word *kāshēr,* meaning 'proper.'

kW kilowatt; kilowatts.

l or **L** (el) **1** the 12th letter of the alphabet: *There are two* l's *in* label. **2 L,** the Roman numeral for 50. *n., pl.* **l's** or **L's.**

l litre; litres. Also written ℓ.

la (lä) the sixth tone of the musical scale. See **do**[2] for picture. *n.*

la·bel (lā′bəl) **1** a slip of paper or other material attached to anything and marked to show what or whose it is, or where it is to go: *Can you read the label on the box?* **2** put or write a label on: *The bottle is labelled 'Poison.'* **3** describe as; call; name: *He labelled the boastful man a liar.* 1 *n.*, 2, 3 *v.*, **la·belled** or **la·beled, la·bel·ling** or **la·bel·ing.**

la·bor or **la·bour** (lā′bər) **1** the effort in doing or making something; work; toil: *He was well paid for his labor.* **2** a piece of work to be done; task: *The king gave Hercules twelve labors to perform.* **3** do work; work hard; toil: *He labored all day in the mill.* **4** workers as a group: *Labor favors safe working conditions.* **5** move slowly and heavily: *The ship labored in the heavy seas. The old car labored as it climbed the steep hill.* 1, 2, 4 *n.*, 3, 5 *v.*

lab·o·ra·to·ry (lab′rə tô′rē or lə bô′rə trē) a place where scientific work is done: *a chemical laboratory. n., pl.* **lab·o·ra·to·ries.**

Labor Day or **Labour Day** the first Monday in September, a holiday in honor of labor and laborers.

la·bor·er or **la·bour·er** (lā′bər ər) **1** worker. **2** a person who does work that requires strength rather than skill or training. *n.*

la·bo·ri·ous (lə bô′rē əs) **1** requiring much work; requiring hard work: *Climbing a mountain is laborious.* **2** willing to work hard; hard-working: *Ants and bees are laborious insects.* **3** showing signs of effort; not easy: *laborious breathing. adj.* —**la·bo′ri·ous·ly,** *adv.*

labor union or **labour union** an association of workers to protect and promote their interests.

lab·y·rinth (lab′ə rinth′) a place through which it is hard to find one's way; maze. *n.*

lace (lās) **1** an open weaving or net of fine thread in an ornamental pattern. **2** trim with lace: *a velvet cloak laced with gold.* **3** a cord, string, or leather strip for pulling or holding together: *These shoes need new laces.* **4** put laces through; pull or hold together with a lace or laces: *Lace up your shoes.* 1, 3 *n.*, 2, 4 *v.*, **laced, lac·ing.**

lac·er·ate (las′ər āt′) **1** tear roughly; mangle: *The bear's claws lacerated the hunter's arm.* **2** cause pain or suffering to; distress: *The coach's sharp words lacerated his feelings. v.*, **lac·er·at·ed, lac·er·at·ing.**

lack (lak) **1** be without: *Some guinea pigs lack tails.* **2** the fact or condition of being without: *Lack of food made him hungry; lack of fire made him cold.* **3** have not enough: *This book lacks excitement.* **4** shortage; not having enough: *Lack of rest made her tired.* 1, 3 *v.*, 2, 4 *n.*

lack·ey (lak′ē) **1** a male servant; footman. **2** a follower who obeys as if he were a servant. *n., pl.* **lack·eys.**

lack·ing (lak′ing) **1** without; not having: *Lacking butter, we ate jam on our bread.* **2** not having enough; deficient: *A weak person is lacking in strength.* **3** absent; not present: *Water is lacking in a desert.* 1 *prep.*, 2, 3 *adj.*

lac·quer (lak′ər) **1** a varnish used to give a protective coating or a shiny appearance to metals, wood, paper, etc. **2** coat with lacquer. **3** articles coated with lacquer. 1, 3 *n.*, 2 *v.*

la·crosse (lə kros′) *Cdn.* a game played, either indoors (**box lacrosse**) or outdoors (**field lacrosse**), by two teams of players equipped with lacrosse sticks, by means of which a rubber ball is carried and passed from player to player in an attempt to score a goal. *n.*

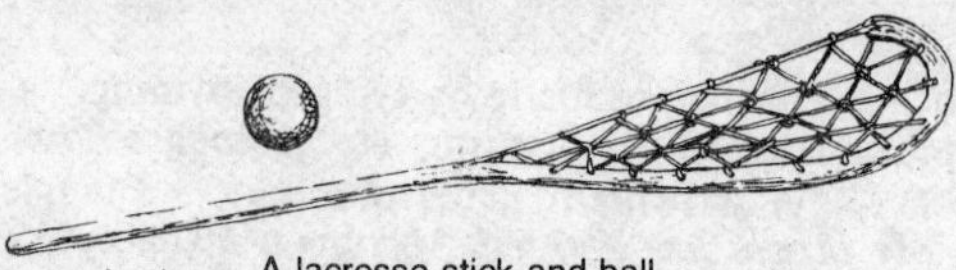
A lacrosse stick and ball

lacrosse stick an L-shaped stick strung with leather thongs that form a kind of pouch for carrying the ball in the game of lacrosse.

lac·y (lās′ē) **1** of lace. **2** like lace: *the lacy leaves of a fern. adj.*, **lac·i·er, lac·i·est.**

lad (lad) a boy; a young man. *n.*

lad·der (lad′ər) **1** a set of rungs or steps fastened into two long sidepieces, for use in climbing up or down. See the picture. **2** a means of climbing higher: *Hard work is a ladder to success.* **3** a run in a knitted fabric, especially in a stocking. *n.*

la·den (lā′dən) loaded; burdened: *The camels were laden with bundles of silk and rice. adj.*

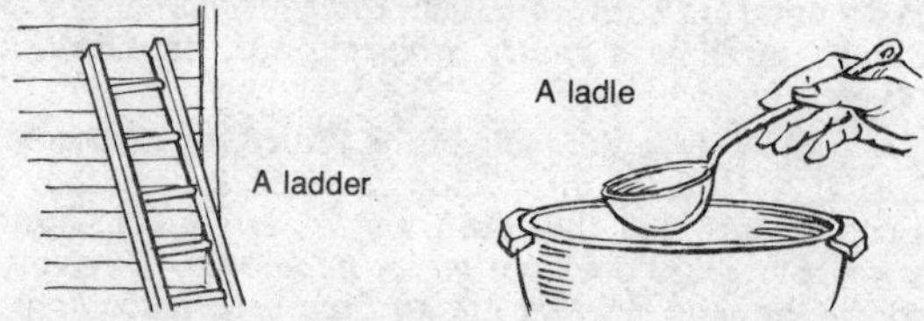
A ladle

A ladder

la·dle (lā′dəl) **1** a large, cup-shaped spoon with a long handle, for dipping out liquids. **2** use such a spoon to dip and carry or serve: *The cook is ladling the soup.* 1 *n.*, 2 *v.*, **la·dled, la·dling.**

la·dy (lā′dē) **1** a woman of refinement and courtesy. **2** a woman of high social position. **3** any woman: *Our teacher is a nice lady.* **4** a woman who has the rights and authority of a lord. **5 Lady,** a title used in speaking to or of women of certain ranks in the United Kingdom. *n., pl.* **la·dies.**

Our Lady, the Virgin Mary.

☛ In formal English, **lady** is used to mean a woman of high social position. Though **lady** is often used in everyday speech to refer to any woman (*lady cab driver, lady clerk*), the word is now usually considered rather affected. Many people would consider **woman** the better word in all such cases.

☛ **Lady** developed from an Old English word *hlǣfdīge,* meaning 'servant or dairy woman,' made up of *hlāf,* meaning 'loaf,' and *-dīg-*, meaning 'to knead.' Compare the note at **lord.**

la·dy·bird (lā′dē bėrd′) ladybug. *n.*

la·dy·bug (lā′dē bug′) a small beetle having a rounded back, usually red or orange with black spots: *Ladybugs eat harmful insects. n.*

la·dy–in–wait·ing (lā′dē in wāt′ing) a lady who is an attendant of a queen or princess. *n., pl.* **la·dies-in-wait·ing.**

la·dy's–slip·per (lā′dēz slip′ər) one of several kinds of wild orchid found in many parts of the world, whose flower looks something like a slipper or moccasin: *The pink lady's-slipper is the provincial flower of Prince Edward Island.* *n.*

lag (lag) **1** move too slowly; fall behind: *The child lagged because he was tired.* **2** falling behind: *There is a long lag in forwarding mail to us.* 1 *v.,* **lagged, lag·ging;** 2 *n.*

la·goon (lə gün′) **1** a pond or small lake connected with a larger body of water. **2** shallow water separated from the sea by low ridges of sand. *n.*

laid (lād) See **lay**[1]. *He laid down the heavy bundle. Those eggs were laid this morning.* *v.*

laid up, *Informal.* forced by illness or injury to stay indoors or in bed.

lain (lān) See **lie**[2]. *The snow has lain on the ground a week.* *v.*

☛ **Lain** and **lane** are pronounced the same.

lair (ler) the den or resting place of a wild animal. *n.*

laird (lerd) *Scottish.* an owner of land. *n.*

☛ **Laird** is another form of **lord.** See the note at **lord.**

lake (lāk) a large body of water usually surrounded by land: *There are hundreds of lakes in the Northwest Territories.* *n.*

lamb (lam) **1** a young sheep. **2** the meat from a lamb: *roast lamb.* **3** give birth to a lamb or lambs. **4** a young, innocent, or dear person. 1, 2, 4 *n.,* 3 *v.*

lame (lām) **1** not able to walk properly; having a hurt leg or foot; crippled. **2** stiff and sore: *His arm is lame from playing ball.* **3** make lame; cripple: *The accident lamed him for life.* **4** poor; not very good: *Stopping to play is a lame excuse for being late to school.* 1, 2, 4 *adj.,* **lam·er, lam·est;** 3 *v.,* **lamed, lam·ing. —lame′ly,** *adv.* **—lame′ness,** *n.*

la·ment (lə ment′) **1** feel or show grief for; mourn for: *lament the dead.* **2** feel or show grief; weep: *Why does she lament so?* **3** an expression of grief or sorrow; wail. **4** a poem, song, or tune that expresses grief. **5** feel sorry about; regret: *We lamented his absence.* 1, 2, 5 *v.,* 3, 4 *n.*

lam·en·ta·ble (lam′ən tə bəl) **1** to be regretted or pitied; giving cause for sorrow: *a lamentable accident. It was a lamentable day when our dog was run over.* **2** not so good; inferior: *The singer gave a lamentable performance.* *adj.*

lam·en·ta·tion (lam′ən tā′shən) loud grief; mourning; wailing; cries of sorrow. *n.*

Lamps from ancient and modern times

lamp (lamp) **1** a device that provides artificial light: *a gas lamp, a street lamp, a floor lamp. An oil lamp holds oil and a wick by which the oil is burned.* **2** a similar device that gives heat: *a spirit lamp.* **3** a device for providing healthful rays: *a sun lamp.* *n.*

hat, āge, fär; let, ēqual, tėrm; it, īce
hot, ōpen, ôrder; oil, out; cup, pu̇t, rüle
əbove, takən, pencəl, lemən, circəs
ch, child; ng, long; sh, ship
th, thin; ᴛʜ, then; zh, measure

lam·prey (lam′prē) a water animal having a body like an eel, gill slits like a fish, and a large, round mouth: *Lampreys attach themselves by their mouths to fish from which they suck body fluids.* *n., pl.* **lam·preys.**

lance (lans) **1** a long wooden spear with a sharp iron or steel head: *The knights carried lances.* See **joust** for picture. **2** pierce with a lance. **3** cut open with a surgeon's knife: *The dentist lanced the gum where a new tooth had difficulty coming through.* 1 *n.,* 2, 3 *v.,* **lanced, lanc·ing.**

lance–cor·por·al (lans′kôr′pə rəl) a non-commissioned officer of the lowest rank in the armed forces of some countries. *n.*

land (land) **1** the solid part of the earth's surface: *dry land.* **2** ground; soil: *This is good land for a garden.* **3** ground used as property: *The farmer invested in land and machinery.* **4** a country; region: *Switzerland is a mountainous land.* **5** the people of a country; nation: *She collected folk songs from all the land.* **6** come to land; bring to land: *The ship landed at the pier. The pilot landed the airplane in a field.* **7** put on land; set ashore: *The ship landed its passengers.* **8** go on shore from a ship or boat: *The passengers landed.* **9** come to a stop; arrive: *The burglar landed in jail. The car landed in the ditch.* **10** cause to arrive: *This boat will land you in London.* **11** *Informal.* catch; get: *to land a job, to land a fish.* 1–5 *n.,* 6–11 *v.*

land·fall (land′fol′ or land′fôl′) **1** a sighting of land. **2** the land sighted or reached after a voyage or flight: *The explorer's landfall was near the mouth of the St. Lawrence.* *n.*

land·ing (lan′ding) **1** a coming to land; coming ashore: *There are thousands of take-offs and landings at this airport each year. The army made a landing in France.* **2** a place where persons or goods are landed from a ship, helicopter, etc.: *A wharf, dock, or pier is a landing for boats.* **3** a platform between flights of stairs. See **flight** for picture. *n.*

landing field a field large enough and smooth enough for aircraft to land on and take off from safely.

landing gear the wheels, pontoons, etc. under an aircraft: *When on land or water, an aircraft rests on its landing gear.*

landing strip a runway, often unpaved or temporary, for aircraft to take off from and land on.

land·la·dy (land′lā′dē) **1** a woman who owns buildings or land that she rents to others. **2** a woman who keeps a boarding house, lodging house, or inn. *n., pl.* **land·la·dies.**

land·lord (land′lôrd′) **1** a person who owns buildings or land that he rents to others. **2** the keeper of a boarding house, lodging house, or inn. *n.*

land·mark (land′märk′) **1** something familiar or easily seen, used as a guide: *That tall tower makes a good landmark.* **2** any important fact or event; any happening that stands out above others: *The inventions* *of the printing press, telegraph, telephone, and radio are landmarks in the history of communication. n.*

Land of the Little Sticks a region of stunted trees at the southern end of the Barren Ground in northern Canada.

land·own·er (land′ōn′ər) a person who owns land. *n.*

land·scape (land′skāp′) 1 a view of scenery on land: *The two hills and the valley between them formed a beautiful landscape.* 2 a painting, etching, etc. showing such a view. 3 make land more pleasant to look at by arranging trees, shrubs, flowers, etc.: *The builder agreed to landscape the lot around the new house.* 1, 2 *n.*, 3 *v.*, **land·scaped, land·scap·ing.**

lane (lān) 1 a narrow road or path, especially one between hedges, walls, or fences. 2 any narrow way: *The bride and groom walked down a lane formed by two lines of wedding guests.* 3 an alley between buildings. 4 a course or route used by cars, ships, or aircraft going in the same direction. *n.*

☞ **Lane** and **lain** are pronounced the same.

lan·guage (lang′gwij) 1 human speech, spoken or written: *Without language, men would be like animals.* 2 the speech used by one nation, tribe, or other similar group of people: *the French language.* 3 a form, style, or kind of speech or writing: *bad language, Shakespeare's language.* 4 the wording or words: *The lawyer explained the language of the contract to us.* 5 the expression of thoughts or feelings otherwise than by words: *sign language. A dog's language is made up of barks, looks, and actions. n.*

lan·guid (lang′gwid) feeling weak; without energy; drooping: *A hot, sticky day makes a person feel languid. adj.* **—lan′guid·ly,** *adv.*

lan·guish (lang′gwish) 1 grow weak; droop: *The flowers languished from lack of water.* 2 suffer for a long period under unfavorable conditions: *languish in poverty. Wild animals often languish in captivity.* 3 droop with longing; pine with love or grief: *She languished for home. v.*

lank (langk) 1 long and thin; slender: *a lank boy, lank grasses.* 2 straight and flat; not curly or wavy: *lank locks of hair. adj.*

lank·y (lang′kē) awkwardly long and thin; tall and ungainly: *He folded his lanky body into the low armchair. adj.,* **lank·i·er, lank·i·est.**

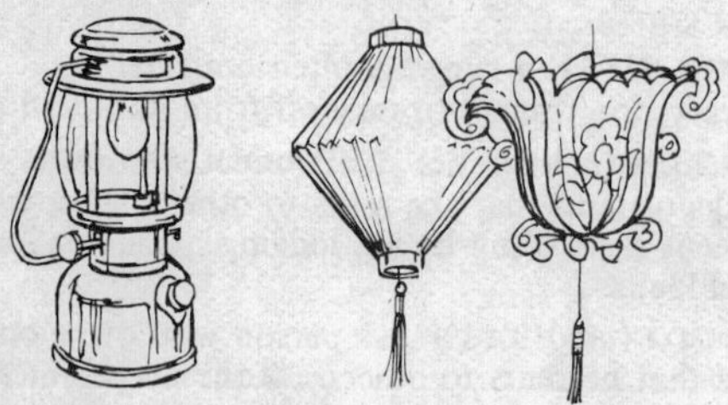

A kerosene lantern

Paper lanterns

lan·tern (lan′tərn) a case to protect a light from wind, rain, etc.: *A lantern has sides of glass, paper, or some other material through which the light can shine. n.*

lap¹ (lap) 1 the front part from the waist to the knees of a person sitting down, with the clothing that covers it: *Mother holds the baby on her lap.* 2 the place where anything rests or is cared for: *the lap of the gods. n.* **in the lap of luxury,** in luxurious circumstances.

☞ **Lap** and **Lapp** are pronounced the same.

lap² (lap) 1 lay or lie together, one partly over or beside another; overlap: *We lapped shingles on the roof.* 2 the part that laps over. 3 wind or wrap around; fold over or about something: *Lap this edge over that.* 4 one time around a race track: *Who won the first lap of the race?* 5 a part of any course travelled: *The last lap of our hike was the toughest.* 1, 3 *v.*, **lapped, lap·ping;** 2, 4, 5 *n.*

☞ See note at **lap¹**.

lap³ (lap) 1 drink by lifting up with the tongue; lick: *Cats and dogs lap up water.* 2 move or beat gently with a lapping sound; splash gently: *Little waves lapped against the boat.* 3 the act of lapping: *The cat took one lap at the sour milk and turned away.* 4 the sound of lapping: *The lap of the waves against the boat put me to sleep.* 1, 2 *v.*, **lapped, lap·ping;** 3, 4 *n.*

☞ See note at **lap¹**.

la·pel (lə pel′) the front part of a coat that is folded back just below the collar. *n.*

Lapp (lap) 1 a member of a people living in Lapland, a region of northern Scandinavia and the north-western Soviet Union. 2 the language of the Lapps, related to Finnish. *n.*

☞ **Lapp** and **lap** are pronounced the same.

lapse (laps) 1 a slight mistake or error; slip: *a lapse of memory, a lapse of speech.* 2 slip back; sink down: *The house lapsed into ruin. He sometimes lapses from good behavior.* 3 a slipping by; passing away: *A minute is a short lapse of time.* 4 slip by; pass away: *The boy's interest in the story soon lapsed.* 5 the ending of a right, privilege, etc. because not renewed, not used, etc.: *the lapse of a lease.* 6 end in this way: *She allowed her driver's licence to lapse.* 1, 3, 5 *n.*, 2, 4, 6 *v.*, **lapsed, laps·ing.**

lar·board (lär′bərd) 1 the side of a ship to the left of a person looking from the stern toward the bow; port. 2 on the left side of a ship. 1 *n.*, 2 *adj.*

lar·ce·ny (lär′sə nē) theft. *n., pl.* **lar·ce·nies.**

larch (lärch) a tree with small cones and needles that fall off in the autumn. *n.*

lard (lärd) 1 the fat of pigs or hogs, melted down and made clear: *Lard is used for cooking.* 2 put lard on; grease: *Lard the pan well.* 3 put strips of bacon or pork in meat or poultry before cooking. 4 give variety to; enrich: *The mayor larded his speech with jokes and stories.* 1 *n.*, 2–4 *v.*

lar·der (lär′dər) 1 pantry; a place where food is kept. 2 a supply of food: *The hunters' larder included deer meat, flour, bacon, and salt. n.*

large (lärj) 1 of more than the usual size, amount, or

hat, āge, fär; let, ēqual, tėrm; it, īce
hot, ōpen, ôrder; oil, out; cup, pu̇t, rüle
əbove, takən, pencəl, lemən, circəs
ch, child; ng, long; sh, ship
th, thin; ᴛʜ, then; zh, measure

number; big: *Canada is a large country. Large crowds come to see our team play.* 2 of great scope or range; extensive; broad: *a man of large experience. adj.,* **larg·er, larg·est.**

at large, a free: *Is the escaped prisoner still at large?* **b** as a whole; altogether: *The people at large want peace.*

large·ly (lärj′lē) to a great extent; for the most part: *This region consists largely of desert. adv.*

lar·i·at (lar′ē ət or ler′ē ət) **1** a long rope with a noose at one end; lasso. **2** a rope for fastening horses, mules, etc. to a stake while they are grazing. *n.*

lark¹ (lärk) **1** a small songbird of Europe, Asia, and northern Africa: *Larks often sing while soaring in the air.* **2** any of several similar songbirds in America. See **meadow lark** for picture. *n.*

lark² (lärk) **1** something that is good fun; a merry or gay time: *What a lark we had at the picnic.* **2** have fun; play: *The boy was always larking.* 1 *n.,* 2 *v.*

lark·spur (lärk′spėr) a plant with tall stalks and clusters of blue, pink, or white flowers. *n.*

lar·ri·gan (lar′ə gən or ler′ə gən) *Cdn.* an oiled leather moccasin. *n.*

lar·va (lär′və) **1** the early form of an insect from the time it leaves the egg until it becomes a pupa: *A caterpillar is the larva of a butterfly or moth. Maggots are the larvae of flies. The silkworm is a larva.* See **pupa** for picture. **2** a young form of certain animals that is different in structure from the adult form: *A tadpole is the larva of a frog or toad. n., pl.* **lar·vae** (lär′vē).

la·ryn·gi·tis (lar′ən jī′tis or ler′ən jī′tis) a sore and swollen condition of the larynx: *A person with laryngitis finds it difficult and even painful to talk. n.*

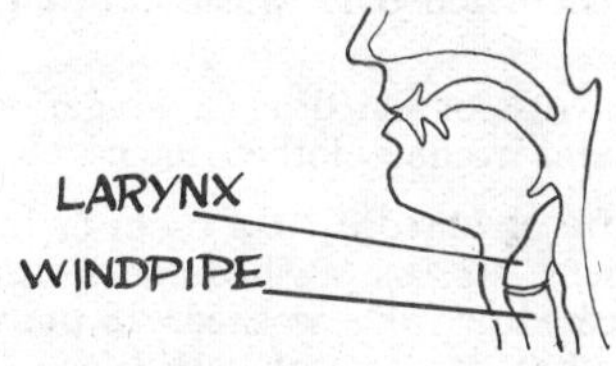

lar·ynx (lar′ingks or ler′ingks) the cavity at the upper end of the windpipe containing the vocal cords. *n., pl.* **la·ryn·ges** (lə rin′jēz) or **lar·ynx·es.**

la·ser (lā′zər) a device that produces a very narrow, intense beam of light of only one wavelength and going in only one direction: *Laser beams can cut through metal and are used in surgery, communications, etc. n.*

lash¹ (lash) **1** a whip, especially the part that is attached to the handle: *The leather lash cut the horse's side.* **2** a stroke or blow with a whip: *The driver gave his horse a lash.* **3** strike with a whip: *The driver of the team lashed her horses on.* **4** beat back and forth: *A lion lashes its tail. The wind is lashing the sails.* **5** attack severely with words; scold sharply: *The captain lashed the crew with his tongue.* **6** strike violently; hit: *The horse lashed at him with its hoofs.* **7** one of the hairs on the edge of the eyelid; eyelash. 1, 2, 7 *n.,* 3–6 *v.*

lash² (lash) tie or fasten with a rope or cord: *We lashed logs together to make a raft. v.*

lass (las) a girl or young woman. *n.*

las·sie (las′ē) a young girl; lass. *n.*

las·so (la sü′) **1** a long rope with a noose at the end, used for catching horses and cattle; lariat: *The cowboy threw a lasso over the steer's head and pulled the animal to the ground.* **2** catch with a lasso. 1 *n., pl.* **las·sos** or **las·soes;** 2 *v.,* **las·soed, las·so·ing.**

last¹ (last) **1** coming after all others; final: *the last page of a book. Z is the last letter of the alphabet.* **2** after all others; at the end: *Ned came last in the line.* **3** latest; most recently: *When did you see him last?* **4** most unlikely: *Fighting is the last thing she would do.* **5** a person or thing that comes after all others: *She was the last in the line.* **6** the end: *You have not heard the last of this.* **7** previous; the one before this one: *The last movie we saw was much better than this western.* **8** next before a specified point of time: *last night, last week, last year.* 1, 4, 7, 8 *adj.,* 2, 3 *adv.,* 5, 6 *n.*

at last, at the end; after a long time; finally: *So you have come home at last.*

last² (last) **1** go on; hold out; continue to be; endure: *How long will our money last? The storm lasted three days.* **2** continue in good condition, force, etc.: *I hope these shoes last a year. v.*

last³ (last) a block shaped like a person's foot, on which shoes and boots are formed or repaired. *n.*

last·ing (las′ting) that lasts; that will last; that will last a long time: *The experience had a lasting effect on him. adj.*

last·ly (last′lē) finally; in the last place: *Lastly, I want to thank all of you for your help. adv.*

A latch on a door

latch (lach) **1** a catch for fastening a door, gate, or window, often one not needing a key: *A latch consists of a movable piece of metal or wood that fits into a notch or opening.* **2** fasten with a latch: *Latch the door.* 1 *n.,* 2 *v.*

late (lāt) **1** after the usual or proper time: *We had a late supper (adj). He worked late (adv).* **2** near the end; at an advanced time: *It rained late in the evening (adv.). He came home in the late evening (adj.).* **3** recent: *The late storm did much harm.* **4** recently dead: *The late Harvey Todd was a fine man.* **5** gone out of or retired from office: *The late Prime Minister is still working actively.* 1–5 *adj.,* **lat·er** or **lat·ter, lat·est** or **last;** 1, 2 *adv.,* **lat·er, lat·est** or **last. —late′ness,** *n.*

of late, lately; recently: *I haven't seen him of late.*

late·ly (lāt′lē) a little while ago; not long ago; recently: *He has not been looking well lately. adv.*

la·tent (lā′tənt) present or available but not used or brought to light; undeveloped: *a latent talent. The power of a seed to grow into a plant remains latent if it is not planted. adj.*

lat·er·al (lat′ər əl) of the side; at the side; from the side; toward the side: *a lateral pass. A lateral fin of a fish grows from its side. adj.*

la·tex (lā′teks) 1 a milky liquid found in certain plants, such as milkweeds, poppies, and plants yielding rubber. 2 a mixture of rubber or a plastic and water, used in paint, adhesives, etc. *n.*

lath (lath) 1 a thin, narrow strip of wood, used with others like it to form a support for the plaster of a wall, ceiling, etc., or to make a lattice. 2 a wire cloth or sheet of metal with holes in it, used in place of laths. 3 cover or line with laths. 1, 2 *n., pl.* **laths** (laᴛʜz or laths); 3 *v.*

lathe (lāᴛʜ) a machine for holding pieces of wood, metal, etc. and turning them rapidly against a cutting tool that shapes them. *n.*

lath·er (laᴛʜ′ər) 1 the foam made from soap or detergent mixed in water. 2 put lather on: *He lathers his face before shaving.* 3 form a lather: *This soap lathers well.* 4 foam formed in sweating: *the lather on a horse after a race.* 5 become covered with such foam: *The horse lathered from his hard gallop.* 1, 4 *n.*, 2, 3, 5 *v.*

Lat·in (lat′ən) 1 the language of the ancient Romans. 2 of Latin; in Latin: *Latin poetry, Latin grammar, a Latin scholar.* 3 a member of any of the peoples whose languages come from Latin: *The Italians, French, Spanish, Portuguese, and Romanians are Latins.* 4 of these peoples or their languages. *1, 3 n.*, 2, 4 *adj.*

Latin America South America, Central America, Mexico, and most of the West Indies.

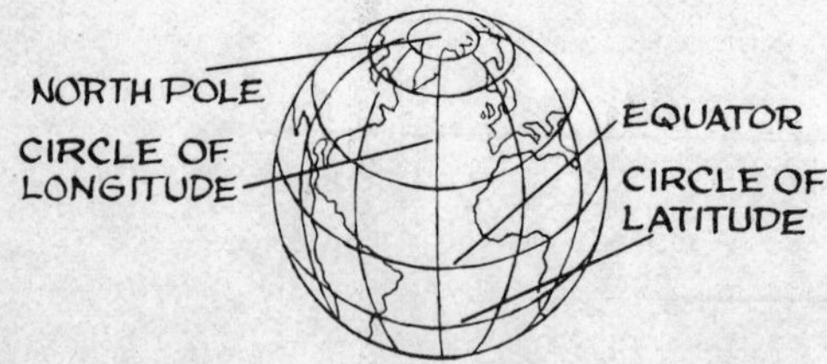

lat·i·tude (lat′ə tyüd′ or lat′ə tüd′) 1 the distance north or south of the equator, measured in degrees: *On maps, lines parallel to the equator represent latitudes.* 2 a place or region having a certain latitude: *Polar bears live in the cold latitudes.* 3 room to act or think; freedom from narrow rules: *Their parents gave them a great deal of latitude in choosing their clothes. n.*

lat·ter (lat′ər) 1 more recent; later; toward the end: *the latter part of the week, the old man's latter days.* 2 **the latter,** the second of two: *Canada and the United States are in North America; the former lies north of the latter. adj.*

lat·tice (lat′is) 1 a structure of crossed wooden or metal strips with open spaces between them. 2 form into a lattice: *The cook latticed strips of dough across the pie.* 3 furnish with a lattice: *The windows are latticed with iron bars.* 1 *n.*, 2, 3 *v.*, **lat·ticed, lat·tic·ing.**

laud (lod or lôd) praise: *We lauded his efforts. v.*

laugh (laf) 1 make the sounds and the movements of the face and body that show amusement or pleasure at humor or nonsense, etc.: *We all laughed at the joke.* 2 the act or sound of laughing: *a hearty laugh.* 3 drive, put, bring, etc. by or with laughing: *The little girl laughed her tears away.* 1, 3 *v.*, 2 *n.*

laugh at, a make fun of; ridicule: *They laughed at me for believing in ghosts.* **b** disregard or make light of: *He laughed at danger.*

laugh off, pass off or dismiss with a laugh: *She laughed off my warning that the ice was not safe and walked out to the middle of the pond.*

laugh·a·ble (laf′ə bəl) causing laughter; amusing; funny: *a laughable mistake. adj.*

laugh·ter (laf′tər) 1 the action of laughing: *The clown's antics brought forth laughter from the children.* 2 the sound of laughing: *Laughter filled the room. n.*

launch[1] (lonch or lônch) 1 cause to slide into the water; set afloat: *The new ship was launched from the supports on which it was built.* 2 start; set going; set out: *His friends launched him in business by lending him money. He used the money to launch a new business. The traveller launched into a long description of her voyage.* 3 throw; hurl; send out: *launch a rocket or missile. The bow launched arrows into the air. The angry man launched wild threats against his enemies.* 4 the act of launching a rocket, ship, aircraft, etc.: *We watched the space launch on television.* 1–3 *v.*, 4 *n.*

launch[2] (lonch or lônch) 1 the largest boat carried by a warship. 2 an open motorboat used for pleasure. *n.*

launching pad a surface or platform on which a rocket or missile is prepared for launching and from which it is shot into the air.

laun·der (lon′dər or lôn′dər) wash and iron clothes, linens, etc. *v.*

laun·dress (lon′dris or lôn′dris) a woman whose work is washing and ironing clothes, linens, etc. *n.*

laun·dry (lon′drē or lôn′drē) 1 a room or building where clothes, linens, etc. are washed and ironed. 2 clothes, etc. washed or to be washed. 3 the washing and ironing of clothes, etc. *n., pl.* **laun·dries.**

lau·rel (lô′rəl) 1 a small evergreen tree with smooth, shiny leaves: *The ancient Greeks and Romans made wreaths of laurel to put on the heads of persons they wished to honor.* 2 any tree or shrub like this: *The mountain laurel has beautiful clusters of pale-pink blossoms.* 3 **laurels,** *pl.* **a** high honor; fame. **b** victory. *n.*

Lau·ren·tian (lô ren′shən) of or having to do with the St. Lawrence River or the region on either side of it. *adj.*

Laurentian Shield the Canadian Shield.

lav·a (lav′ə or lä′və) 1 hot melted rock flowing from a volcano. 2 rock formed by the cooling of this melted rock: *Some lavas are hard and glassy; others are light and porous. n.*

lav·a·to·ry (lav′ə trē or lav′ə tô′rē) 1 a room where a person can wash his hands and face. 2 a toilet or washroom. *n., pl.* **lav·a·to·ries.**

lav·en·der (lav′ən dər) 1 pale purple. 2 a small shrub with spikes of fragrant, pale-purple flowers, yielding an oil much used in perfumes. 3 the dried flowers, leaves, and stalks of the lavender plant, used to perfume linens or clothes. 1–3 *n.*, 1 *adj.*

lav·ish (lav′ish) **1** very free or too free in giving or spending: *The man was lavish with his money.* **2** more than enough; given or spent too freely: *a lavish helping of pudding.* **3** give or speak very freely or too freely: *It is a mistake to lavish kindness on ungrateful people.* 1, 2 *adj.*, 3 *v.* —**lav′ish·ly,** *adv.*

law (lo or lô) **1** a rule or regulation made by a country, province, state, etc. for all the people who live there: *Good citizens obey the laws.* **2** a system of such rules formed to protect society: *English law, international law.* **3** the study of such a system of rules; the profession of a lawyer: *He is studying law.* **4** any rule that must be obeyed: *The laws of a game are the rules by which it is played.* **5** a statement of what always occurs under certain conditions: *Scientists study the laws of nature.* *n.*

law·ful (lo′fəl or lô′fəl) **1** according to law; done as the law directs: *lawful arrest.* **2** allowed by law; rightful: *lawful demands.* *adj.* —**law′ful·ly,** *adv.*

law·less (lo′lis or lô′lis) **1** paying no attention to the law; breaking the law: *A thief leads a lawless life.* **2** hard to control; unruly: *a lawless mob.* **3** having no laws: *a lawless frontier town.* *adj.* —**law′less·ly,** *adv.* —**law′less·ness,** *n.*

law·mak·er (lo′māk′ər or lô′māk′ər) a person who helps make the laws of a country, province, etc.; legislator. *n.*

law·mak·ing (lo′māk′ing or lô′māk′ing) **1** having the duty and power of making laws; legislative. **2** the making of laws; legislation. 1 *adj.*, 2 *n.*

lawn[1] (lon or lôn) land covered with grass kept closely cut, especially near or around a house. *n.*

lawn[2] (lon or lôn) a kind of fine linen or cotton cloth. *n.*

lawn mower a machine with revolving blades for cutting the grass on a lawn.

law·suit (lo′süt′ or lô′süt′) a case in a law court; an application to a court for justice: *Injustices are often remedied by lawsuits.* *n.*

law·yer (loi′yər, lo′yər, or lô′yər) a person whose work is giving advice about the laws or acting for others in a law court. *n.*

lax (laks) **1** not tight or firm; slack: *The package was tied so loosely that the cord was lax.* **2** not strict; careless: *lax behavior. Don't let yourself become lax about doing your homework.* **3** not exact; vague. *adj.* —**lax′ly,** *adv.* —**lax′ness,** *n.*

lax·i·ty (lak′sə tē) a lax condition or quality; slackness. *n.*

lay[1] (lā) **1** place in a certain position; put down: *Lay your hat on the table.* **2** bring down; beat down: *The crops were laid low by a storm.* **3** place in a lying-down position: *Lay the baby down gently.* **4** place or set: *Lay your hand on your heart. The scene of the story is laid in Montreal.* **5** put: *Lay aside that book for me. The horse laid his ears back.* **6** put in place: *to lay bricks. The men came to lay our new carpet.* **7** put into a certain state or condition: *to lay a wound open.* **8** put down as a bet; offer as a bet: *I lay $5 he will not come.* **9** give forth; produce an egg or eggs from the body: *Birds, fish, and reptiles lay eggs. All the hens were laying well.* **10** See **lay of the land.** 1–9 *v.*, **laid, lay·ing;** 10 *n.*

lay about, hit on all sides.

hat, āge, fär; let, ēqual, tėrm; it, īce
hot, ōpen, ôrder; oil, out; cup, pu̇t, rüle
əbove, takən, pencəl, lemən, circəs
ch, child; ng, long; sh, ship
th, thin; ᴛʜ, then; zh, measure

lay aside, lay away, or **lay by,** put away for future use; save: *I laid away a dollar a week toward buying a bicycle.*

lay down, a declare; state: *The umpire laid down the conditions for settling the dispute.* **b** give; sacrifice: *lay down one's life for the cause of freedom.*

lay in, put aside for the future; provide: *The trapper laid in enough supplies for the winter.*

lay into, a *Informal.* beat; thrash: *She laid into the vicious dog with a stick.* **b** *Slang.* scold: *My parents laid into me for not doing my homework.*

lay off, a put out of work for a time: *During the slack season many workers were laid off.* **b** mark off: *He laid off the boundaries of the tennis court.* **c** *Informal.* stop teasing or interfering with: *Let's lay off the new boy and give him a chance.*

lay oneself out, make a big effort; take great pains: *He laid himself out to be agreeable.*

lay out, a arrange; plan; mark off: *The road was laid out but not yet paved.* **b** spread out: *Supper was laid out on the table.* **c** *Slang.* spend: *I had to lay out a lot of money for my new bicycle.*

lay up, a put away for future use; save: *After the sailing season was over we laid our boat up for the winter.* **b** cause to stay in bed or indoors because of illness or injury: *The flu laid him up for a week.*

☛ Although **lay** is often used for both **lay**[1] and **lie**[2], in standard English the two verbs are always kept distinct: **lie, lay, lain** and **lay, laid, laid. Lie** does not take an object: *He lay down for a rest. The village lies in a valley.* **Lay** always takes an object: *We laid a new floor in the kitchen. Lay the book on the table.*

lay[2] (lā) See **lie**[2]. *After a long walk I lay down for a rest.* *v.*

lay·er (lā′ər) **1** one thickness or fold: *the layer of clothing next to the skin, a layer of clay between two layers of sand. A layer cake is one made of two or more layers put together.* **2** one that lays: *That hen is a champion layer.* *n.*

lay·man (lā′mən) **1** a member of a church who is not a clergyman: *The priest and several laymen planned the church budget.* **2** a person who is not a member of a particular profession: *It is hard for most laymen to understand doctors' prescriptions.* *n.*, *pl.* **lay·men** (lā′mən).

lay·off (lā′of′) **1** a temporary dismissal of workers: *Because of a shortage of steel, there was a layoff at the plant.* **2** the time during which such a dismissal lasts. *n.*

lay of the land **1** the nature of the place; the position of hills, water, woods, etc.: *Spies were sent out to find out the lay of the land.* **2** the existing situation; condition of things.

la·zi·ness (lā′zē nis) dislike of work; unwillingness to work or be active; being lazy. *n.*

la·zy (lā′zē) **1** not willing to work or be active: *She was too lazy to get up to turn off the TV.* **2** moving slowly; not very active: *A lazy stream winds through the* *meadows.* *adj.*, **la·zi·er, la·zi·est.**

lb. pound; pounds.

lbs. pounds.

lea (lē) a grassy field; a meadow or pasture. *n.*
☛ **Lea** and **lee** are pronounced the same.

lead¹ (lēd) **1** show the way by going along with or in front of: *He led the horses to water.* **2** be first among: *She leads the class in spelling.* **3** guidance or direction; example: *Many scientists followed the lead of his research.* **4** guide or direct in action, policy, opinion, etc.; influence; persuade: *Such actions lead us to distrust them.* **5** be a way or road: *Hard work leads to success.* **6** pass or spend time in some special way: *He leads a quiet life in the country.* **7** go first; begin a game or other activity: *You may lead this time.* **8** be chief of; command; direct: *A general leads an army. A woman led the singing.* **9** the place of leader; the place in front: *He always takes the lead when we plan to do anything.* **10** the right to go or play first: *It is your lead this time.* **11** the principal part in a play, film, etc. **12** the amount that one is ahead: *He had a lead of three metres at the halfway mark.* **13** a guiding indication; clue: *He was not sure where to look for the information, but the librarian gave him some good leads.* 1, 2, 4–8 *v.*, **led, lead·ing;** 3, 9–13 *n.*

lead² (led) **1** a soft, heavy, bluish-grey metal: *Lead is used to make sinkers for fishing lines.* **2** made of lead: *lead pipe.* **3** something made of lead. **4** bullets; shot: *a hail of lead.* **5** a long, thin piece of graphite or other substance in or for a pencil. **6** a weight on a line used to find out the depth of water; plumb. 1, 3–6 *n.*, 2 *adj.*
☛ **Lead²** and **led** are pronounced the same.

lead dog (lēd′) the dog that leads a team of huskies; leader.

lead·en (led′ən) **1** made of lead: *a leaden casket.* **2** heavy; hard to lift or move: *The tired runner could hardly lift his leaden legs.* **3** dull; gloomy: *We had become a bit leaden by the time our team scored.* **4** bluish-grey: *Do you suppose those leaden clouds mean snow?* *adj.*

lead·er (lēd′ər) **1** a person who leads, or who is well fitted to lead: *a patrol leader, an orchestra leader.* **2** a short piece of nylon, wire, etc. used to attach a hook or a lure to a fishing line. **3** the dog that leads a dog-sled team: *The leader was a powerful husky.* *n.*

lead·er·ship (lēd′ər ship′) **1** the state or position of being a leader. **2** the ability to lead: *Leadership is a great asset to a politician.* *n.*

leaf (lēf) **1** one of the thin, usually flat, green parts of a tree or other plant that grow on the stem or grow up from the roots. **2** put forth leaves: *The trees along the river leaf earlier than those on the hill.* **3** a petal of a flower: *a rose leaf.* **4** a sheet of paper: *Each side of the leaf of a book is a page.* **5** turn the pages: *leaf through a book.* **6** a very thin piece or sheet of metal: *gold leaf.* **7** the flat, movable piece of a table top: *We put two extra leaves in the table to make it larger for the party.* 1, 3, 4, 6, 7 *n., pl.* **leaves;** 2, 5 *v.*
turn over a new leaf, start all over again, try to do or be better in the future: *I promised to turn over a new leaf and study harder.*

leaf·less (lēf′lis) having no leaves. *adj.*

leaf·let (lēf′lit) **1** a small, flat or folded sheet of printed matter: *advertising leaflets.* **2** a small or young leaf. *n.*

leaf·y (lēf′ē) **1** having many leaves; covered with leaves. **2** resembling a leaf: *We chose a fabric with a leafy design.* *adj.*, **leaf·i·er, leaf·i·est.**

league¹ (lēg) **1** a union of persons, parties, or nations formed to help one another. **2** a group of teams that play a schedule of games against each other: *a hockey league.* **3** associate in a league; form a league. 1, 2 *n.*, 3 *v.*, **leagued, lea·guing.**
in league, united; in association: *They were in league against us. The suspected spies were thought to be in league with the enemy.*

league² (lēg) an old measure of distance equal to 3 miles, or almost 5 kilometres. *n.*

leak (lēk) **1** a hole or crack, caused either by accident or by wear and tear, that lets something in or out: *a leak in a boat, a roof, a tire, etc.* **2** let something in or out that is meant to stay where it is: *My boat leaks and lets water in. That pipe leaks gas.* **3** go in or out through a hole or crack, or in ways suggesting a hole or crack: *The gas leaked out. Spies somehow leaked into the city.* **4** a leakage: *a leak of water, a news leak.* **5** make or become known: *The secret leaked out. We think he leaked the story to some friends.* 1, 4 *n.*, 2, 3, 5 *v.*
☛ **Leak** and **leek** are pronounced the same.

leak·age (lēk′ij) **1** a leaking; an entering or escaping through a leak. **2** that which leaks in or out. **3** the amount of leaking: *The leakage was estimated at 40 litres an hour.* *n.*

lean¹ (lēn) **1** stand slanting, not upright; bend: *The small tree leans over in the wind.* **2** rest in a sloping or slanting position: *Lean against me.* **3** set or put in a leaning position: *Lean the ladder against the wall.* **4** the act of leaning; inclination: *The old barn has more of a lean this year.* **5** depend: *to lean on a friend's advice.* **6** tend or incline; show a preference: *to lean toward mercy. Her favorite sport was tennis, but now she leans more to swimming.* 1–3, 5, 6 *v.*, **leaned** or **leant, lean·ing;** 4 *n.*

lean² (lēn) **1** not fat; thin: *a lean horse.* **2** meat having little fat. **3** producing little; scant: *a lean harvest, a lean year for business.* 1, 3 *adj.*, 2 *n.*

leant (lent) See **lean¹**. *v.*

Lean-tos on a barn in Quebec

lean–to (lēn′tü′) **1** a small building attached to another, with a roof sloping downward from the side of the larger building. **2** a crude shelter built or leaning against posts, trees, rock, etc.: *Hunters have a supply of wood in a lean-to here.* *n., pl.* **lean-tos.**

leap (lēp) **1** a jump or spring. **2** jump: *That frog leaps very high.* **3** pass, come, rise, etc. as if with a leap or bound: *An idea leaped to her mind. A sudden breeze made the flames leap.* **4** jump over: *He leaped the wall.* 1 *n.*, 2–4 *v.*, **leaped** or **leapt, leap·ing.**

hat, āge, fär; let, ēqual, tėrm; it, īce
hot, ōpen, ôrder; oil, out; cup, pu̇t, rüle
 əbove, takən, pencəl, lemən, circəs
ch, child; ng, long; sh, ship
th, thin; ᴛʜ, then; zh, measure

Girls playing leapfrog

leap·frog (lēp′frog′) a game in which one player leaps over the bent back of another. *n.*

leapt (lept or lēpt) See **leap.** *v.*

leap year a year having 366 days, the extra day being February 29: *A year is a leap year if its number can be divided exactly by four, except years at the end of a century, which must be exactly divisible by 400; thus 1960 and 2000 are leap years, whereas 1900 and 1961 are not.*

learn (lėrn) **1** gain knowledge or skill: *Some children learn slowly.* **2** memorize: *She will learn the poem for a recitation at the concert.* **3** find out; come to know: *He learned that ¼ + ¼ = ½.* **4** find out about; gain knowledge of: *She is learning history and geography.* **5** become able by study or practice: *In school we learn to read.* *v.,* **learned** or **learnt, learn·ing.**

☛ **Learn** should not be confused with **teach.** Standard English keeps these two verbs completely distinct: *I learned how to play chess. He taught me how to play chess.*

learn·ed (lėr′nid) showing, having, or requiring much knowledge; scholarly: *a learned man, a learned book.* *adj.*

learn·ing (lėr′ning) **1** the gaining of knowledge or skill. **2** knowledge gained by study; scholarship: *a woman of great learning.* *n.*

learnt (lėrnt) See **learn.** *v.*

lease (lēs) **1** a written agreement giving the right to use property for a certain length of time, usually by paying rent. **2** the length of time for which such an agreement is made: *They have a long lease on the property.* **3** rent: *We have leased an apartment for one year. The landlord has already leased all the apartments.* 1, 2 *n.,* 3 *v.,* **leased, leas·ing.**

leash (lēsh) **1** a strap, chain, etc. for holding or leading an animal: *The girl leads the dog on a leash.* **2** fasten or hold with a leash; control. 1 *n.,* 2 *v.*
hold in leash, control.

least (lēst) **1** less than any other; smallest: *Ten cents is a little money; five cents is less; one cent is least.* **2** the smallest amount; the smallest thing: *The least you can do is to thank him.* **3** to the smallest extent, amount, or degree: *He liked that book least of all.* 1 *adj.,* 2 *n.,* 3 *adv.*
at least, a at the lowest estimate: *The temperature was at least 35° C.* **b** at any rate; in any case: *He may have been late, but at least he came.*

leath·er (leᴛʜ′ər) a material made from the skins of animals by removing the hair and then tanning them: *Her new gloves are made of leather.* *n.*

leath·ern (leᴛʜ′ərn) made of leather. *adj.*

leath·er·y (leᴛʜ′ər ē) like leather; tough: *Exposure to harsh weather had made his face leathery.* *adj.*

leave[1] (lēv) **1** go away: *We leave tonight.* **2** go away from: *They left the room. He has left his home and friends and gone to sea.* **3** stop living in, belonging to, or working at or for: *to leave the country, to leave the Boy Scouts, to leave one's job.* **4** go without taking; let stay behind: *I left a book on the table.* **5** let stay in a certain condition: *to leave unsaid or undone. I was left alone as before. The story left him unmoved.* **6** let alone: *Then the potatoes must be left to boil for half an hour.* **7** give to family, friends, charity, etc. when one dies: *He left a fortune to his two sons.* **8** give or hand over to someone else to do: *I left the driving to my sister.* **9** not attend to: *I will leave my homework till tomorrow.* *v.,* **left, leav·ing.**
leave off, stop: *Continue the story from where I left off.*
leave out, not say, do, or put in; omit: *She left out two words when she read the sentence.*

leave[2] (lēv) **1** consent; permission: *They gave him leave to go.* **2** permission to stay away or be absent from work, school, etc.: *The crew will have leave in this port.* **3** the length of time that such permission lasts: *Their annual leave is thirty days.* *n.*
take leave of, say good-bye to.

leave[3] (lēv) put forth leaves: *Trees leave in the spring.* *v.,* **leaved, leav·ing.**

leav·en (lev′ən) **1** any substance, such as yeast, that will cause fermentation and make dough rise. **2** a small amount of fermenting dough kept for this purpose. **3** raise with leaven; make dough light or lighter. 1, 2 *n.,* 3 *v.*

leaves (lēvz) **1** plural of **leaf. 2** plural of **leave**[2]**:** *The soldier had two leaves in one year.* *n.*

lec·ture (lek′chər) **1** a speech or planned talk on a chosen subject; such a talk written down or printed. **2** give a lecture. **3** a scolding: *My mother gives me a lecture when I come home late.* **4** scold. 1, 3 *n.,* 2, 4 *v.,* **lec·tured, lec·tur·ing.**

lec·tur·er (lek′chər ər) **1** a person who gives a lecture or lectures. **2** a teacher of junior rank at some universities. *n.*

led (led) See **lead**[1]. *The policeman led the children across the street. That blind man is led by his dog.* *v.*

☛ **Led** and **lead**[2] are pronounced the same.

ledge (lej) **1** a narrow shelf: *a window ledge.* **2** a shelf or ridge of rock. *n.*

lee (lē) **1** shelter. **2** the side or part sheltered or away from the wind: *The wind was so fierce that we ran to the lee of the house.* **3** sheltered or away from the wind: *the lee side of a ship.* 1, 2 *n.,* 3 *adj.*

☛ **Lee** and **lea** are pronounced the same.

leech (lēch) **1** a worm living in ponds and streams that sucks the blood of animals: *Doctors used to use leeches to suck blood from sick people.* **2** a person who persistently tries to get what he can out of others, without doing anything to earn it. *n.*

leek (lēk) a vegetable resembling a long onion, but

having a milder flavor: *The leek is the emblem of Wales.* *n.*

☛ **Leek** and **leak** are pronounced the same.

leer (lēr) **1** a sly, nasty look to the side; an evil glance. **2** give a sly, evil glance. 1 *n.,* 2 *v.*

leer·y (lēr′ē) *Informal.* wary; suspicious: *He was leery of snakes. We are leery of his advice. adj.*

lee·ward (lē′wərd or lü′ərd) **1** on the side away from the wind. **2** the side away from the wind; lee. **3** in the direction toward which the wind is blowing. 1, 3 *adj., adv.,* 2 *n.*

left[1] (left) **1** of the side that is toward the west when the main side faces north: *A soldier never salutes with his left hand, only with his right.* See **right** for picture. **2** on this side when one is looking to the front: *Take a left turn at the next light.* **3** on or to the left side: *Turn left.* **4** the left side or hand: *He sat at my left.* 1, 2 *adj.,* 3 *adv.,* 4 *n.*

left[2] (left) See **leave**[1]. *He left his hat in the hall. The newspaper is left at our door. She left at four o'clock. v.*

left–hand (left′hand′) **1** on or to the left. **2** of, for, or with the left hand. *adj.*

left–hand·ed (left′han′did) **1** using the left hand more easily and readily than the right. **2** done with the left hand. **3** made to be used with the left hand. *adj.*

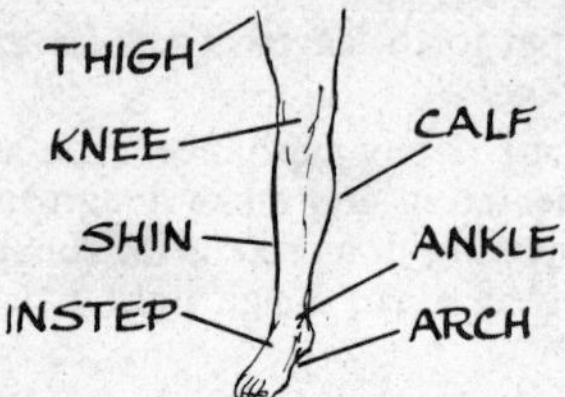

The parts of the human leg

leg (leg) **1** one of the limbs on which people and animals stand and walk: *Dogs have four legs and human beings have two.* **2** a part of a garment that covers a leg: *I fell and tore the right leg of my pants.* **3** anything shaped or used like a leg; any support that is much longer than it is wide: *a table leg.* **4** one of the parts or stages of any course: *They were happy to be on the last leg of their long trip. n.*

on one's last legs, about to fail, collapse, or die: *I feel as if I am on my last legs but a swim will revive me.*

pull one's leg, *Informal.* fool, trick, or make fun of one: *I didn't know he was pulling my leg until I heard you laugh.*

leg·a·cy (leg′ə sē) the money or other property left to a person by the will of someone who has died. *n., pl.* **leg·a·cies.**

le·gal (lē′gəl) **1** of law: *legal knowledge.* **2** of lawyers: *legal advice.* **3** according to law; lawful: *Hunting is legal only during certain seasons. adj.*

leg·end (lej′ənd) **1** a story coming down from the past, which many people have believed: *The stories about Robin Hood are legends, not history.* **2** such stories as a group. **3** what is written on a coin or medal: *Read the legend on a five-cent piece.* **4** words accompanying a picture, map, or diagram. *n.*

leg·end·ar·y (lej′ən der′ē) of a legend or legends: *Robin Hood is a legendary person. adj.*

Leggings

leg·gings (leg′ingz) extra outer coverings of cloth or leather for the legs, for use out of doors; gaiters. *n. pl.*

leg·i·ble (lej′ə bəl) **1** that can be read. **2** easy to read; plain and clear: *Her handwriting is quite large and legible. adj.*

le·gion (lē′jən) **1** a division in the ancient Roman army, containing several thousand foot soldiers and several hundred horsemen. **2** a large body of soldiers; army. **3** a great many; a very large number: *Legions of grasshoppers destroyed the crops. n.*

leg·is·late (lej′is lāt′) make laws: *Parliament legislates for Canada. v.,* **leg·is·lat·ed, leg·is·lat·ing.**

leg·is·la·tion (lej′is lā′shən) **1** the making of laws: *Parliament has the power of legislation.* **2** the laws made: *Important legislation is reported in today's newspaper. n.*

leg·is·la·tive (lej′is lā′tiv) **1** having to do with making laws: *legislative reforms.* **2** having the duty and power of making laws: *Parliament is a legislative body.* **3** ordered by law; made to be as it is by law: *a legislative decree. adj.* **—leg′is·la′tive·ly,** *adv.*

Legislative Assembly in Canada, the group of representatives elected to the legislature of a province.

leg·is·la·tor (lej′is lā′tər) a person who makes laws; a member of a group that makes laws: *M.P.'s and M.L.A.'s are legislators. n.*

leg·is·la·ture (lej′is lā′chər) **1** a group of persons that has the duty and the power to make laws for a country, province, or state: *Each Canadian province has a legislature.* **2** the place where the legislators meet. *n.*

le·git·i·mate (lə jit′ə mit) **1** rightful; lawful: *The Prince of Wales is the legitimate heir to the throne of England.* **2** allowed; acceptable: *Sickness is a legitimate reason for absence from school. adj.* **—le·git′i·mate·ly,** *adv.*

leis·ure (lezh′ər or lē′zhər) **1** the time free from required work, in which a person may rest, amuse himself, and do the things he likes to do: *He hasn't much leisure for reading.* **2** free; not busy: *leisure hours.* 1 *n.,* 2 *adj.*

leis·ure·ly (lezh′ər lē or lē′zhər lē) without hurry; taking plenty of time: *He was a man of leisurely habits. He walked leisurely through the park. adj., adv.*

lem·ming (lem′ing) a small arctic animal related to the mouse, having greyish or brownish fur, a short tail, and furry feet. *n.*

lem·on (lem′ən) **1** an acid-tasting, light-yellow fruit that grows in warm climates: *The drink was flavored with lemon.* **2** the tree this fruit grows on. **3** pale

hat, āge, fär; let, ēqual, tėrm; it, īce
hot, ōpen, ôrder; oil, out; cup, pu̇t, rüle
əbove, takən, pencəl, lemən, circəs
ch, child; ng, long; sh, ship
th, thin; ᴛʜ, then; zh, measure

yellow. **4** a soft drink flavored with lemon juice. **5** *Slang.* a thing or person that is considered inferior or disagreeable: *The last car he bought was a lemon.* 1–5 *n.*, 3 *adj.*

lem·on·ade (lem′ən ād′) a drink made of lemon juice, sugar, and water. *n.*

lend (lend) **1** let another have or use for a time: *Will you lend me your bicycle for an hour?* **2** make a loan or loans: *Banks lend money to persons they can trust. A person who borrows should be willing to lend.* **3** give; contribute; add: *A lace curtain lends charm to a window. The Red Cross is quick to lend aid in time of disaster.* *v.*, **lent, lend·ing. —lend′er,** *n.*

lend a hand, help: *She lent a hand with the dishes.*

lend itself to, be suitable for: *The old engine lent itself to our purposes.*

lend oneself to, make oneself available for: *Don't lend yourself to foolish schemes.*

length (length) **1** how long a thing is; what a thing measures from end to end: *the length of your arm, the length of a room, eight centimetres in length.* **2** the distance covered by something: *The length of a race is the distance run. He swam three lengths of the pool.* **3** how long something lasts or goes on: *the length of a visit, a speech, or a book.* **4** a long stretch or extent: *Quite a length of hair hung down in a braid.* **5** a piece of cloth, pipe, lumber, etc. of a given length, often either cut from a larger piece, or meant to be joined to another piece: *a length of rope, three lengths of pipe.* *n.*

at length, a at last; finally: *At length, after many delays, the meeting started.* **b** with all the details; fully: *He told of his adventures at length.*

keep at arm's length, discourage from becoming friendly.

length·en (leng′thən) **1** make longer: *A tailor can lengthen your trousers.* **2** become or grow longer: *Your legs have lengthened a great deal since you were five years old.* *v.*

length·ways (length′wāz′) in the direction of the length: *She cut the cloth lengthways. The tailor made a lengthways cut.* *adv., adj.*

length·wise (length′wīz′) lengthways. *adv., adj.*

length·y (leng′thē) long; too long: *His directions were so lengthy that everybody got confused.* *adj.*, **length·i·er, length·i·est.**

len·ient (lē′nē ənt or lēn′yənt) mild or gentle; merciful: *a lenient judge, a lenient punishment.* *adj.* **—len′ient·ly,** *adv.*

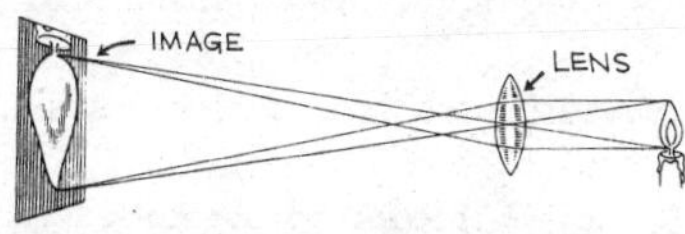

A lens. The kind of lens shown above bends light rays to produce a magnified image.

lens (lenz) **1** a piece of glass, or something like glass, that will bring closer together or send wider apart the rays of light passing through it: *The lenses of a telescope make things look larger and nearer.* **2** the part of the eye that directs light rays upon the retina. See **eye** for picture. *n., pl.* **lens·es.**

lent (lent) See **lend.** *I lent you my pencils. He had lent me his knife.* *v.*

Lent (lent) the forty weekdays before Easter, observed in many Christian churches as a time for fasting and the repenting of sins. *n.*

len·til (len′təl) a vegetable much like a bean: *Dried lentils are used in soup.* *n.*

leop·ard (lep′ərd) **1** a large, fierce animal of Africa and Asia, having dull-yellowish fur spotted with black. **2** the jaguar or American leopard. *n.*

lep·er (lep′ər) a person who has leprosy. *n.*

lep·ro·sy (lep′rə sē) an infectious disease which causes sores on the skin and injury to the nerves, and which may result in paralysis and deformity. *n.*

less (les) **1** smaller: *of less width, less importance.* **2** not so much; not so much of: *to have less rain, to put on less butter, to eat less meat.* **3** fewer: *Five is two less than seven.* **4** a smaller amount or quantity: *He could do no less. I weigh less than before. We refuse to take less than $5.* **5** to a smaller extent or degree; not so; not so well: *less bright, less important, less known, less talked of.* **6** with something taken away; without; minus: *five less two, a coat less one sleeve.* 1–3 *adj.*, 4 *n.*, 5 *adv.*, 6 *prep.*

more or less, a somewhat: *We are all more or less impatient.* **b** about; approximately: *The cost is $50, more or less.*

less·en (les′ən) **1** grow less: *The fever lessened during the night.* **2** make less. *v.*

☛ **Lessen** and **lesson** are pronounced the same.

less·er (les′ər) **1** less; smaller. **2** the less important of two. 1 *adj.*, 2 *n.*

les·son (les′ən) **1** something to be learned or taught; something that has been learned or taught. **2** a unit of teaching or learning; what is to be studied or taught at one time: *Our math text is divided into 20 lessons.* **3** a meeting of a student or class with a teacher to study a given subject: *She has gone for a piano lesson. There will be no lesson today.* **4** an instructive experience, serving to encourage or warn: *The accident was a lesson to me.* **5** a selection from the Bible, read as part of a church service. *n.*

☛ **Lesson** and **lessen** are pronounced the same.

lest (lest) **1** for fear that: *Be careful lest you fall from that tree.* **2** that (after words meaning fear, danger, etc.): *They were afraid lest he should come too late to save them.* *conj.*

let (let) **1** allow; permit: *Let the dog have a bone.* **2** allow to run out: *Doctors used to let some of the blood of patients suffering from fever.* **3** rent; hire out: *Mrs. Bacon lets rooms to students.* **4** be rented: *The house lets for $200 a month.* **5 Let** is used in giving suggestions or giving commands: *'Let's go fishing' means 'I suggest that we go fishing.' Let everyone do his duty.* **6** suppose; assume: *Let the two lines be parallel.* *v.*, **let, let·ting.**

let down, a lower: *He let the box down from the roof.* **b** slow up: *As her interest in the work wore off, she began*

to let down. **c** disappoint: *Don't let us down today; we're counting on you to help us.*
let in, admit; permit to enter: *Let in some fresh air.*
let off, a allow to go free; release: *let off steam. I was let off with a warning to do better in the future.* **c** fire; explode: *let off a firecracker.*
let on, *Informal.* **a** allow to be known; reveal one's knowledge of: *He didn't let on his surprise at the news.* **b** make believe; pretend: *She let on that she didn't see me.*
let out, a permit to go out. **b** make a garment larger: *This skirt can be let out.* **c** rent: *Has the room been let out yet?*
let up, *Informal.* stop, pause: *They refused to let up in the fight.*

let's (lets) let us.

let·ter (let′ər) **1** a symbol or sign, used alone or combined, that represents speech sounds; a character of an alphabet: *Both* mast *and* mash *have four letters. There are twenty-six letters in the English alphabet.* **2** mark with letters: *Please letter a new sign.* **3** a written or printed message: *She told me about her vacation in a letter.* 1, 3 *n.,* 2 *v.*
to the letter, very exactly; just as one has been told: *I carried out your order to the letter.*
☞ Sometimes a single sound is represented by a combination of letters, as in *ba***th** and *ma***tch.** Also, the same combination can stand for different sounds, as in *b***ough** and *r***ough.**

let·ter–per·fect (let′ər pėr′fikt) **1** knowing one's part or lesson perfectly: *He worked hard to learn his part in the play and was soon letter-perfect.* **2** correct in every detail: *The secretary's typing was letter-perfect. adj.*

let·tuce (let′is) a garden plant having large, crisp, green leaves that are much used in salads. *n.*

let–up (let′up′) *Informal.* a stop or pause. *n.*

lev·ee[1] (lev′ē) **1** a bank built to keep a river from overflowing: *Many citizens manned the levees during the flood.* **2** a landing place for boats. *n.*
☞ **Levee** and **levy** are pronounced the same.

lev·ee[2] (lev′ē) a formal reception: *He received an invitation to the Governor General's levee. n.*
☞ See note at **levee**[1].

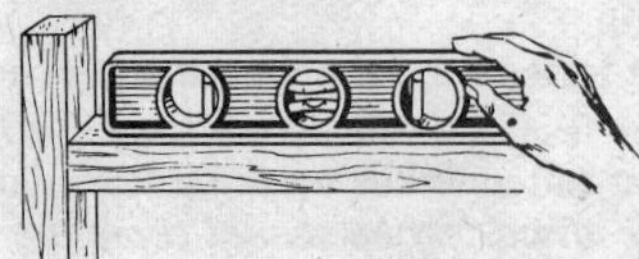

A level (def. 4). It has a glass tube containing a liquid with an air bubble in it. The air bubble stays in the centre if the surface is level; if not, it moves to one side.

lev·el (lev′əl) **1** flat; even; having the same height everywhere: *a level floor.* **2** of equal height, importance, etc.: *The table is level with the edge of the window. The two runners remained level for most of the race.* **3** something that is level. **4** an instrument for showing whether a surface is level. **5** make level; put on the same level: *The contractor levelled the ground with a bulldozer.* **6** lay low; bring to the level of the ground: *The tornado levelled every house in the valley.* **7** raise and hold level for shooting; aim: *The soldier levelled his rifle.* **8** height: *The flood rose to a level of ten metres.* **9** a grade or standard: *She reached a high level of skill.* **10** *Informal.* steady; sensible: *a level head.* 1, 2, 10 *adj.,* 3, 4, 8, 9 *n.,* 5–7 *v.,* **lev·elled** or **lev·eled, lev·el·ling** or **lev·el·ing.**
on the level, *Informal.* fair and straightforward; honest.

level crossing a place where a railway track crosses a road or another railway track at the same level.

le·ver (lē′vər or lev′ər) **1** a bar for raising or moving something: *A crowbar is used as a lever.* See **fulcrum** for picture. **2** any bar working on an axis or support: *the gearshift lever of an automobile. n.*

lev·y (lev′ē) **1** order to be paid: *The government levies taxes to pay its expenses.* **2** money collected by authority or force. **3** draft or enlist men for an army: *Troops are levied in time of war.* **4** the men drafted or enlisted for an army. 1, 3 *v.,* **lev·ied, lev·y·ing;** 2, 4 *n., pl.* **lev·ies.**
levy war on, make war on.
☞ **Levy** and **levee** are pronounced the same.

li·a·ble (lī′ə bəl) **1** likely; unpleasantly likely: *Glass is liable to break. You are liable to slip on ice.* **2** in danger of having, doing, etc.: *We are all liable to diseases.* **3** responsible; bound by law to pay: *The Post Office Department is not liable for damage to a parcel sent by mail unless the parcel is insured.* **4** under obligation; subject: *Citizens are liable to jury duty. adj.*

li·ar (lī′ər) a person who tells lies; a person who says what is not true. *n.*

lib·er·al (lib′ər əl or lib′rəl) **1** generous: *a liberal giver, a liberal donation.* **2** plentiful; abundant: *a liberal supply.* **3** broad-minded; not narrow in one's ideas: *a liberal thinker.* **4** not limited; broad: *A liberal education develops the mind broadly.* **5** a person favorable to progress and reforms. **6** Often, **Liberal, a** a member of a liberal political party. **b** in Canada, a member of the Liberal Party, one of the principal political groups; a person who supports the views and principles of this party. 1–4 *adj.,* 5, 6 *n.*

lib·er·al·i·ty (lib′ər al′ə tē) **1** generosity; generous behavior: *We were allowed to use the pool because of the liberality of the club members.* **2** a tolerant and progressive nature: *The community showed liberality in welcoming immigrants of different beliefs and customs. n., pl.* **lib·er·al·i·ties.**

Liberal Party one of the principal political parties of Canada.

lib·er·ate (lib′ər āt′) set free. *v.,* **lib·er·at·ed, lib·er·at·ing.**

lib·er·ty (lib′ər tē) **1** freedom; independence: *The prisoner yearned for liberty. The colony finally won its liberty.* **2** the right or power to do as one pleases; the power or opportunity to do something: *liberty of speech.* **3** the permission granted to a sailor to go ashore. **4** too great freedom: *The author took liberties with the facts to make the story more interesting. n., pl.* **lib·er·ties.**
at liberty, a free: *The escaped lion is still at liberty.* **b** allowed; permitted: *You are at liberty to make any choice you please.* **c** not busy: *The principal will see you as soon as he is at liberty.*

li·brar·i·an (lī brer′ē ən) **1** a person in charge of a library or part of a library. **2** a person trained for work in a library. *n.*

hat, āge, fär; let, ēqual, tėrm; it, īce
hot, ōpen, ôrder; oil, out; cup, pu̇t, rüle
əbove, takən, pencəl, lemən, circəs
ch, child; ng, long; sh, ship
th, thin; ᴛʜ, then; zh, measure

li·brar·y (lī′brer′ē) 1 a collection of books: *He borrowed a book from the teacher's library.* 2 a room or building where a collection of books, magazines, phonograph records, etc. is kept to be used, rented, or borrowed: *He goes to the library every Saturday.* *n., pl.* **li·brar·ies.**

li·bret·to (lə bret′ō) 1 the words of an opera or other long musical composition. 2 a book containing these words. *n., pl.* **li·bret·tos.**

lice (līs) plural of **louse.** *n.*

li·cence or **li·cense** (lī′səns) 1 permission given by law to do something: *He has a licence to drive a car.* 2 the paper, card, plate, etc. showing such permission: *The barber hung his licence on the wall.* 3 the fact or condition of being allowed to do something. 4 too much liberty of action; a lack of proper control; the abuse of freedom: *The children were given licence to invade their neighbors' gardens.* *n.*

li·cense or **li·cence** (lī′səns) 1 permit by law; give a licence to: *A doctor is licensed to practise medicine.* 2 give authority to do something: *Who licensed you to wear my tie?* *v.,* **li·censed** or **li·cenced, li·cens·ing** or **li·cenc·ing.**

li·chen (lī′kən) a flowerless plant that looks somewhat like moss and grows in patches on rocks, trees, and other hard surfaces: *Lichens are grey, yellow, brown, black, or green.* *n.*

lick (lik) 1 pass the tongue over: *to lick a stamp.* 2 lap up with the tongue: *The cat licked the milk.* 3 a stroke of the tongue over something: *He gave the ice-cream cone a big lick.* 4 pass about or play over like a tongue: *The flames were licking the roof.* 5 a place where natural salt is found and where animals go to lick it up. 6 a small quantity: *She didn't do a lick of work.* 7 *Informal.* blow: *I lost the fight, but I got in a few good licks.* 8 *Informal.* beat or thrash. 9 *Informal.* defeat in a fight, etc.; conquer. 1, 2, 4, 8, 9 *v.,* 3, 5–7 *n.*

lic·o·rice (lik′ə rish, lik′rish, or lik′ə ris) 1 the sweet-tasting, dried root of a European plant. 2 a black substance obtained from this root, used in medicine and candy. 3 candy flavored with licorice. *n.* Also spelled **liquorice.**

☛ **Licorice** came into English through Old French from a Greek word *glukurrhiza,* from *glukus,* meaning 'sweet,' and *rhizā,* meaning 'root.'

lid (lid) 1 a movable cover; top: *the lid of a box.* 2 the cover of skin that is moved in opening and shutting the eye; the eyelid. *n.*

lie[1] (lī) 1 something said that is not true; something that is not true said to deceive: *Saying his friend stole it was a lie.* 2 speak falsely; tell a lie: *He says that he has never lied, but I think he is lying when he says it.* 1 *n.,* 2 *v.,* **lied, ly·ing.**

☛ Lie and lye are pronounced the same.

lie[2] (lī) 1 have one's body in a flat position along the ground or other surface: *to lie on the grass, to lie in bed.* 2 rest on a surface: *The book was lying on the table.* 3 be kept or stay in a given state: *to lie idle, to lie hidden, to lie unused.* 4 be; be placed: *land that lies high, a road that lies among trees, a ship lying offshore at anchor. The lake lies to the south of us.* 5 exist; be found to be: *The cure for ignorance lies in education.* *v.,* **lay, lain, ly·ing.**

lie to, of a ship, etc., come almost to a stop, facing the wind: *During the storm, the sailing ship lay to.*

☛ See note at **lie**[1]. See note at **lay**[1].

liege (lēj) in the Middle Ages: 1 a lord who gave protection to his vassals in return for their loyal service. 2 a vassal obliged to serve a lord in return for his protection. *n.*

lieu (lü) **in lieu of,** in place of; instead of. *n.*

lieu·ten·ant (lef ten′ənt or lü ten′ənt) 1 a person who acts for someone senior to him in authority: *The coach used the two boys as his lieutenants.* 2 a junior officer in the armed forces. *n.*

☛ **Lieutenant** comes from a French word *lieutenant,* made up of *lieu,* meaning 'place,' and *tenant,* meaning 'holding.' A lieutenant held the place of (or acted for) a captain who was absent.

lieu·ten·ant–colo·nel (lef ten′ənt kėr′nəl or lü ten′ənt kėr′nəl) an officer in the armed forces senior to a major and junior to a colonel. *n.*

lieutenant commander a naval officer senior to a lieutenant and junior to a commander, having the same rank as a major.

lieu·ten·ant–gen·er·al (lef ten′ənt jen′ər əl or jen′rəl, or lü ten′ənt jen′ər əl or jen′rəl) an officer in the armed forces senior to a major-general and junior to a general. *n.*

lieu·ten·ant–gov·er·nor (lef ten′ənt guv′ər nər) the official head of a provincial government, appointed by the Governor General in Council, for a term of five years. *n.*

life (līf) 1 living or being alive: *People, animals, and plants, all of which grow and reproduce, have life; rocks and minerals do not.* 2 the time of being alive: *He enjoyed a long life.* 3 the time of existence or action; a period of being in power, able to operate, etc.: *the short life of that government, a machine's life.* 4 a living being; person: *Five lives were lost in the fire.* 5 living things: *The desert island had almost no animal or vegetable life.* 6 a way of living: *a dull life, country life.* 7 an account of a person's life: *Several lives of Mackenzie King have been written.* 8 spirit; vigor: *Put more life into your work.* *n., pl.* **lives** (līvz).

as large or **as big as life, a** as big as the living person or thing. **b** in person.

life and limb, keeping alive and unhurt; survival: *fearful for life and limb.*

life belt a life preserver in the shape of a thick ring, worn around the chest and under the arms.

life·boat (līf′bōt′) a strong boat specially built for saving lives at sea or along the coast. *n.*

life buoy a life preserver.

life·guard (līf′gärd′) a person who is trained in lifesaving and whose job is to guard the safety of swimmers and bathers at a public pool or beach. *n.*

life·less (līf′lis) 1 not alive; without life: *a lifeless statue. Stones are lifeless.* 2 dead: *The lifeless body floated ashore.* 3 having no living things: *a lifeless planet.* 4 dull: *It was a lifeless party.* *adj.*

life·like (līf′līk′) like life; looking as if alive; like the real thing: *a lifelike portrait. adj.*

life·long (līf′long′) lasting all one's life: *a lifelong friendship. adj.*

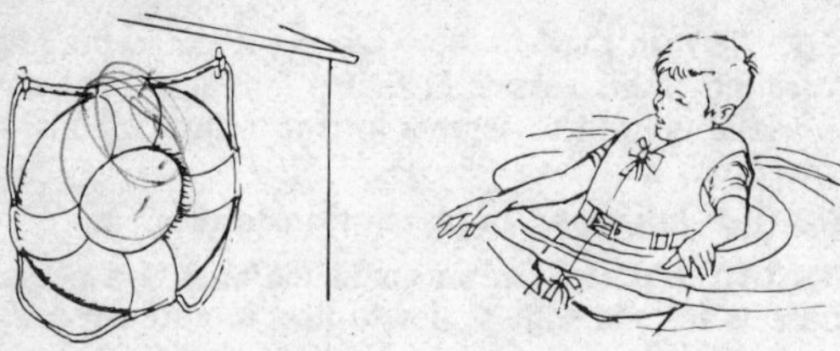

Two kinds of life preserver

life preserver a wide belt, jacket, circular tube, etc. designed to keep a person afloat in the water until rescued.

life raft a raft for saving lives in a shipwreck or the wreck of an aircraft at sea.

life·sav·ing (līf′sāv′ing) **1** a saving of people's lives, especially keeping people from drowning. **2** designed or used to save people's lives: *lifesaving classes, lifesaving equipment.* 1 *n.,* 2 *adj.*

life–size (līf′sīz′) as big as the living person, animal, etc.: *a life-size statue. adj.*

life·time (līf′tīm′) the time of being alive; the period during which a life lasts: *Grandfather has seen many changes during his lifetime. n.*

lift (lift) **1** raise; raise up higher; raise into the air; take up; pick up: *Father lifted the baby from the bed.* **2** rise and go; go away: *The fog lifted at dawn.* **3** go up; be raised: *This window will not lift.* **4** the act of lifting. **5** the distance through which a thing is lifted. **6** a helping hand: *I gave him a lift with the heavy box.* **7** a ride in a vehicle given to a pedestrian or hiker; free ride: *He often gave the neighbor's boy a lift to school.* **8** an improvement in spirits: *The promotion gave him a lift.* **9** *Esp. British.* elevator. 1–3 *v.,* 4–9 *n.*

lift·off (lift′of′) the firing or launching of a rocket: *The liftoff took place at 3 o'clock yesterday. n.*

lig·a·ment (lig′ə mənt) a band of strong tissue that connects bones or holds parts of the body in place. *n.*

light¹ (līt) **1** that by which we see; the form of radiant energy that acts on the retina of the eye: *The sun gives light to the earth.* **2** having light or much light: *a light room.* **3** anything that gives light: *The sun, a lamp, or a lighthouse is called a light.* **4** bright or clear: *It is light as day.* **5** brightness or clearness; illumination: *a strong light, a dim light.* **6** daytime; daylight: *The workman got up before light.* **7** knowledge or information: *We need more light on this subject.* **8** the aspect in which a thing is viewed: *The principal put the matter in the right light.* **9** a means of letting in light; a window or division of a window. **10** a bright part: *light and shade in a painting.* **11** pale in color; approaching white: *light hair, light blue.* **12** give light to; provide with light: *The room is lighted by six windows.* **13** show the way by giving light: *His flashlight lighted us through the tunnel.* **14** make bright or clear: *a face lighted by a smile.* **15** become light: *The sky lights up at sunset.* **16** set fire to: *She lighted the candles.* **17** take fire: *Matches light when you strike them.* **18** a model or example: *The actor was a leading light in the theatre.* 1, 3, 5–10, 18 *n.,* 2, 4, 11 *adj.,* 12–17 *v.,* **light·ed** or **lit, light·ing.**

bring to light, reveal; expose: *Many facts were brought to light.*

in the light of, because of; considering: *In the light of all these facts, what you did was right.*

shed or **throw light on,** make clear; explain.

light² (līt) **1** easy to carry; not heavy: *a light load.* **2** not looking heavy; graceful; delicate: *a light bridge, light carving.* **3** having little mass for its size: *Feathers are light.* **4** having less than usual mass: *light clothing.* **5** easy to bear or do: *light punishment, a light task.* **6** moving easily: *a light step.* **7** lightly armed or equipped: *light infantry.* **8** less than usual in amount, force, or strength: *a light rain, a light sleep, a light wine, a light meal.* **9** not important: *light losses.* **10** happy; cheerful: *a light laugh.* **11** not serious enough: *a light mind, light of purpose.* **12** aiming to entertain; not serious: *light reading.* **13** porous; sandy: *light soil. adj.* **—light·ly,** *adv.*

light in the head, a dizzy. **b** silly; foolish.

make light of, treat as of little importance.

light³ (līt) **1** come down to the ground; alight: *He lighted from his horse.* **2** come down from flight: *A bird lighted on the branch.* **3** come by chance: *His eye lighted upon a coin in the road.* **4** fall suddenly: *The blow lit on his head. v.,* **light·ed** or **lit, light·ing.**

light bulb a glass bulb containing a filament of very fine wire that becomes white-hot and gives off light when an electric current flows through it.

light·en¹ (līt′ən) **1** brighten; become brighter: *Dawn lightens the sky. Her face lightened.* **2** flash with lightning: *It thundered and lightened outside. v.*

light·en² (līt′ən) **1** reduce the load of; make or become lighter: *to lighten taxes.* **2** make or become more cheerful: *The good news lightened their hearts. v.*

light–head·ed (līt′hed′id) **1** dizzy; giddy; out of one's head: *The sick man was light-headed from fever.* **2** silly; thoughtless: *That frivolous, light-headed girl thinks of nothing but parties and clothes. adj.*

light–heart·ed (līt′här′tid) carefree; cheerful; gay. *adj.* **—light′-heart′ed·ly,** *adv.*

A lighthouse

light·house (līt′hous′) a tower or framework with a bright light that shines far over the water: *Lighthouses are usually located at dangerous places to warn and guide ships. n.*

light·ness¹ (līt′nis) **1** brightness; clearness. **2** paleness; light color. **3** the amount of light: *The lightness of the sky showed that the rain was over. n.*

light·ness² (līt′nis) **1** being light; the state of not being heavy: *The lightness of this load is a relief after the heavy one I was carrying.* 2 being cheerful or happy: *lightness of spirits.* 3 a lack of proper seriousness: *Such lightness of conduct is not permitted in a courtroom.* *n.*

light·ning (līt′ning) a flash of light in the sky caused by a discharge of electricity between clouds, or between a cloud and the earth's surface: *The sound that lightning makes is called thunder.* *n.*

lightning bug firefly.

lightning rod a metal rod fixed on a building or ship to conduct lightning into the earth or water to prevent fire.

light·weight (līt′wāt′) 1 a person or thing of less than average mass. 2 light in mass. 3 a boxer who weighs over 57.2 kg (126 lbs.) and not more than 61.2 kg (135 lbs.). 1, 3 *n.*, 2 *adj.*

light-year (līt′yēr′) the distance that light travels in one year; almost 10 million million kilometres: *The light-year is used to measure the distance between stars.* *n.*

lik·a·ble (līk′ə bəl) having qualities that win good will or friendship; pleasing; popular: *a likable person.* *adj.*

like[1] (līk) 1 much the same as; similar to: *Mary is like her sister. I never saw anything like it.* 2 in the same way as; as well as: *She can sing like a bird.* 3 of the same form, kind, amount, etc.; the same or almost the same: *John's uncle promised him $10 if he could earn a like sum.* 4 such as one would expect of; typical of: *Isn't that just like a boy!* 5 in the right condition for: *I feel like working.* 6 giving promise of: *It looks like rain.* 7 a person or thing like another: *We shall not see his like again.* 1, 2, 4–6 *prep.*, 3 *adj.*, 7 *n.*

and the like, and similar things; and other things of the same class: *At the zoo we saw tigers, lions, leopards, and the like.*

☛ In standard written English, a distinction is made between the use of **like** and **as.** **As** and **as if** are used to introduce clauses of comparison: *He still writes as he used to when he was a child. Act as if you were familiar with the place.* **Like** is used in phrases of comparison: *She swims like a fish. He writes like a child.* In informal English, however, **like** is often used in place of **as** to introduce clauses: *He writes like he used to when he was a child.*

like[2] (līk) 1 be pleased with; be satisfied with: *My cat likes milk.* 2 have a kindly or friendly feeling for: *The children like their new teacher.* 3 wish for; wish: *I'd like more time to finish this. Come whenever you like.* **4 likes,** *pl.* likings; preferences: *Mother knows all my likes and dislikes.* 1–3 *v.*, **liked, lik·ing;** 4 *n.*

-like a suffix meaning: 1 like; similar to: *Wolflike means like a wolf.* 2 like that of; characteristic of: *Childlike means like that of a child.* 3 suited to; fit or proper for: *Businesslike means suited to business.*

like·li·hood (līk′lē hu̇d′) probability: *Is there any likelihood of rain this afternoon?* *n.*

like·ly (līk′lē) 1 probable: *One likely result of this heavy rain is the rising of the river.* 2 probably: *I shall very likely be at home all day.* 3 to be expected: *It is likely to be hot in August.* 4 suitable: *Is this a likely place to fish?* 5 promising: *a likely boy.* 1, 3–5 *adj.*, **like·li·er, like·li·est;** 2 *adv.*

lik·en (līk′ən) compare; represent as like. *v.*

like·ness (līk′nis) 1 a resemblance; being alike: *The boy's likeness to his father was striking.* 2 something

hat, āge, fär; let, ēqual, tėrm; it, īce
hot, ōpen, ôrder; oil, out; cup, pu̇t, rüle
əbove, takən, pencəl, lemən, circəs
ch, child; ng, long; sh, ship
th, thin; ᴛʜ, then; zh, measure

that is like; a picture or snapshot: *The great artist painted a likeness of the Queen.* 3 the appearance or shape: *His fairy godmother came to him in the likeness of a bird.* *n.*

like·wise (līk′wīz′) 1 the same: *See what I do; now you do likewise.* 2 also; moreover; too: *Ruth must go home now, and Jane likewise.* *adv.*

lik·ing (līk′ing) 1 a preference or taste: *He had a liking for apples.* 2 a fondness or kindly feeling: *She had a liking for children.* 3 See **like**[2]. 1, 2 *n.*, 3 *v.*

li·lac (lī′lək or lī′lok) 1 a shrub with clusters of tiny, fragrant, pale, pinkish-purple or white blossoms. 2 pale, pinkish purple. 1, 2 *n.*, 2 *adj.*

lilt (lilt) 1 sing or play a tune in a light, tripping manner. 2 a lively song or tune with a swing. 3 a way of speaking in which the pitch of the voice varies in a pleasing manner: *He talks with an Irish lilt.* 4 a lively, springing movement. 1 *v.*, 2–4 *n.*

A tiger lily

lil·y (lil′ē) 1 a plant that grows from a bulb: *Lilies have beautiful bell-shaped flowers.* 2 the bell-shaped flower of any lily plant: *The tiger, or prairie, lily is the floral emblem of Saskatchewan.* 3 like a white lily; pure and lovely. 1, 2 *n.*, *pl.* **lil·ies;** 3 *adj.*

lily of the valley a plant having tiny, sweet-smelling, bell-shaped white flowers arranged up and down a single flower stem. *pl.* **lilies of the valley.**

li·ma bean (lī′mə) 1 a broad, flat, light-green bean used for food. 2 the plant that it grows on.

limb (lim) 1 a leg, arm, or wing. 2 a large branch; bough: *They sawed the dead limb off the tree.* *n.*

life and limb. See **life.** *The old bridge is a danger to life and limb.*

lim·ber (lim′bər) 1 bending easily; flexible: *Willow is a limber wood. She has limber fingers.* 2 make or become supple or easily flexed: *He is stiff when he begins to skate, but limbers up quickly.* 1 *adj.*, 2 *v.*

lime[1] (līm) 1 a white substance obtained by burning limestone, shells, bones, etc.: *Lime is used to make mortar and to improve soil.* 2 put lime on: *He drained the land and limed it.* 1 *n.*, 2 *v.*, **limed, lim·ing.**

lime[2] (līm) 1 a greenish-yellow fruit that resembles a lemon but is smaller and sourer. 2 the tree this fruit grows on. 3 a soft drink flavored with lime juice. *n.*

lime[3] (līm) the linden tree. *n.*

lime·stone (līm′stōn′) a kind of rock used for building and for making lime: *Marble is a kind of limestone.* *n.*

lim·it (lim′it) 1 the farthest point or edge; where something ends or must end: *the limit of one's vision. I have reached the limit of my patience.* 2 **limits,** *pl.* boundary; bounds: *Keep within the limits of the school grounds.* 3 set a limit to; restrict: *We must limit the expense to $10.* 1, 2 *n.,* 3 *v.*

lim·it·ed (lim′ə tid) 1 kept within limits; restricted: *a limited space, a limited number of seats.* 2 travelling fast and making only a few stops: *a limited train or bus. adj.*

limp[1] (limp) 1 a lame step or walk. 2 walk with a limp: *After falling down the stairs, he limped for several days.* 1 *n.,* 2 *v.*

limp[2] (limp) not stiff or firm; tending to bend or droop: *The lettuce had lost its crispness and was quite limp. I am so tired I feel as limp as a rag. adj.* **—limp′ly,** *adv.* **—limp′ness,** *n.*

lim·pid (lim′pid) clear; transparent: *a spring of limpid water, limpid eyes. adj.*

lin·age (līn′ij) See **lineage**[2].

lin·den (lin′dən) a tree having heart-shaped leaves and clusters of small, sweet-smelling, yellowish flowers: *A linden is often used for shade and ornament. n.*

line[1] (līn) 1 a piece of rope, cord, or wire: *a clothes line, a fish line, a telegraph line.* 2 a cord for measuring, making level, etc. 3 a long, narrow mark: *Draw two lines here.* 4 mark with lines: *Please line your paper with a pencil and ruler.* 5 cover with lines: *a face lined with age.* 6 a wrinkle or crease: *the lines in his face. The fortune teller studied the lines on the palm of my hand.* 7 an edge or boundary: *That hedge marks our property line.* 8 a straight line: *The lower edges of the two pictures are about on a line.* 9 a row of persons or things: *a line of cars.* 10 form a line along; arrange a line along: *Cars lined the road for a kilometre.* 11 a row of words on a page or in a newspaper column: *a column of 40 lines.* 12 a single row of words in poetry. 13 a connected series of persons or things following one another in time: *one's family line.* 14 a certain way of doing: *Please proceed on these lines till further notice. He followed the same line as last time.* 15 a course, track, or direction: *the line of march of an army, a railway line.* 16 a branch of business; a kind of activity: *the dry-goods line. This is not my line.* 17 a kind or brand of goods: *He carries the best line of shoes in town.* 18 in warfare, the front: *The reserves moved up to the line.* 19 in Ontario, a concession road: *He lives on the second line.* 20 **the line,** a the border between two countries, especially that between Canada and the United States: *We often go across the line for a vacation.* b the equator. 1–3, 6–9, 11–20 *n.,* 4, 5, 10 *v.,* **lined, lin·ing.**

all along the line, at every point; everywhere: *This car has given trouble all along the line.*

bring into line, cause to agree or conform: *She will bring the other members into line and the club will accept her plan.*

in line, a in a line: *The children are all in line.* b in agreement: *This plan is in line with their ideas.*

line up, form a line; form into a line: *Cars were lined up along the road.*

out of line, not in agreement; not suitable or proper: *Her last remark was out of line. He's always out of line with the rest of the club members.*

read between the lines, get more from the words than they say; find a hidden meaning.

line[2] (līn) 1 put a layer of material such as paper, cloth, or felt inside a dress, hat, box, bag, etc. 2 serve the purpose of a lining: *This piece of satin would line the coat very nicely. v.,* **lined, lin·ing.**

lin·e·age[1] (lin′ē ij) descent in a direct line from an ancestor: *He is proud of his lineage. n.*

line·age[2] (līn′ij) 1 the number of lines on a printed page. 2 the orderly arrangement of lines. *n.* Also spelled **linage.**

lin·e·ar (lin′ē ər) 1 of a line or lines. 2 made of lines; making use of lines: *a linear drawing.* 3 in a line or lines: *a linear arrangement of trees.* 4 of length. *adj.*

lin·en (lin′ən) 1 cloth or thread made from flax. 2 articles made of linen or some substitute: *Tablecloths, serviettes, sheets, towels, and shirts are all called linen. n.*

lin·er[1] (līn′ər) a ship or airplane belonging to a transportation system. *n.*

lin·er[2] (līn′ər) something that serves as a lining: *a diaper liner, a hat liner. n.*

lin·ger (ling′gər) stay on; go slowly, as if unwilling to leave: *Daylight lingers long in summer. She lingered after the others left. v.*

lin·ge·rie (lan′zhə rē′) women's undergarments, nightgowns, etc. *n.*

lin·ing (līn′ing) a layer of material covering the inner surface of something: *the lining of a coat. n.*

link (lingk) 1 one ring or loop of a chain. 2 anything that joins as a link joins: *a cuff link.* 3 join as a link does; unite or connect: *Your story links up with what John told us.* 1, 2 *n.,* 3 *v.*

links (lingks) a golf course. *n. sing.* or *pl.*

lin·net (lin′it) a small songbird of Europe, Asia, and Africa. *n.*

li·no·le·um (lə nō′lē əm) 1 a floor covering made by putting a hard surface of ground cork mixed with linseed oil on a canvas or burlap back. 2 any similar floor covering. *n.*

lin·seed (lin′sēd′) the seed of flax. *n.*

linseed oil a yellowish oil pressed from linseed, used in making paints, printing inks, and linoleum.

lint (lint) 1 the soft down or fleecy material obtained by scraping linen. 2 tiny bits of thread or shreds of fabric: *We can see lots of lint on the carpet. n.*

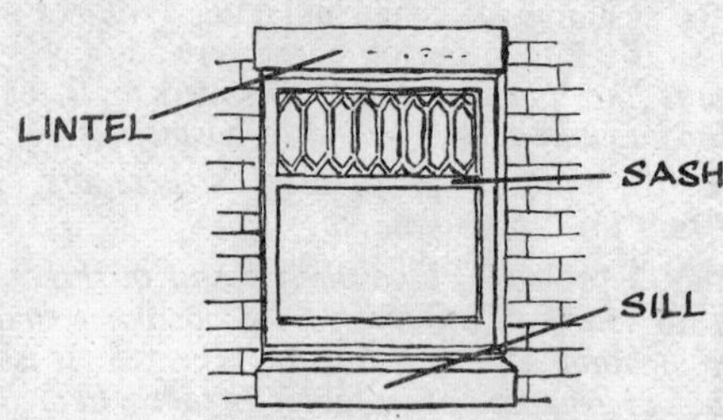

lin·tel (lin′təl) a horizontal beam or stone above a door or window to carry the weight of the wall above it. *n.*

li·on (lī′ən) 1 a large, strong animal of the cat family, having a dull-yellow coat, found in Africa and southern Asia: *The male lion has a full, flowing mane.* 2 a person who is very brave and strong. 3 a famous person. *n.*

li·on·ess (lī′ən is) a female lion. *n.*

lion's share the biggest or best part: *She managed to get the lion's share of the cake before the rest of us got there.*

lip (lip) 1 either one of the two fleshy, movable edges of the mouth. 2 the folding or bent-out edge of any opening: *the lip of a pitcher.* 3 expressed in words, but not heartfelt or deep; only on the surface: *The hypocrite gave lip service to the church.* 1, 2 *n.*, 3 *adj.*
keep a stiff upper lip, be brave or firm; show no fear or discouragement.

lip reading the process of understanding speech by watching the movements of a speaker's lips: *He is so good at lip reading that many people don't realize he's deaf.*

lip·stick (lip′stik′) 1 a small stick of a cosmetic, used for coloring the lips. 2 the rouge itself: *There was some lipstick on the rim of the cup.* *n.*

liq·ue·fy (lik′wə fī′) change into a liquid; make or become liquid: *Liquefied air is extremely cold.* *v.*, **liq·ue·fied, liq·ue·fy·ing.**

li·queur (li kyür′) a sweet, highly-flavored alcoholic drink. *n.*

liq·uid (lik′wid) 1 a substance that is not a solid or a gas; a substance that flows freely like water. 2 in the form of a liquid; melted: *liquid soap, butter heated until it is liquid.* 3 clear and bright like water. 4 clear and smooth-flowing in sound: *the liquid notes of a bird.* 5 easily turned into cash: *Canada Savings Bonds are a liquid investment.* 1 *n.*, 2–5 *adj.*

liq·uor (lik′ər) 1 an alcoholic drink, such as brandy, whisky, or rum. 2 any liquid, especially a liquid in which food is packaged, canned, or cooked: *Pickles are put up in a salty liquor.* *n.*

liq·uo·rice (lik′ə rish, lik′ rish, or lik′ə ris) See **licorice.**

lisp (lisp) 1 use a sound of *th* instead of the sound of *s* or *z* in speaking: *A person who lisps might say 'Thing a thong' for 'Sing a song.'* 2 the act, habit, or sound of speaking in this way: *He speaks with a lisp.* 3 speak imperfectly: *Babies are said to lisp.* 1, 3 *v.*, 2 *n.*

list[1] (list) 1 a series of names, numbers, words, or phrases: *a shopping list.* 2 make a list of; enter in a list: *A dictionary lists words in alphabetic order.* 1 *n.*, 2 *v.*

list[2] (list) 1 a tipping to one side; tilt: *the list of a ship.* 2 tip to one side; tilt: *The sinking ship was listing so that water lapped her decks.* 1 *n.*, 2 *v.*

lis·ten (lis′ən) 1 try to hear; attend so as to hear: *She listened for the sound of a car. I like to listen to music.* 2 give heed to advice, temptation, etc.; pay attention: *I don't know how to repair it because I did not listen.* *v.* **—lis′ten·er,** *n.*
listen in, a listen to others talking on a telephone: *I listened in on the extension.* **b** listen to the radio: *Listen in next week for another drama.*

list·less (list′lis) seeming too tired to care about anything; not interested in things; not caring to be active: *a dull and listless mood.* *adj.* **—list′less·ly,** *adv.*

lists (lists) in the Middle Ages, a place where knights fought in tournaments. *n. pl.*

lit[1] (lit) See **light**[1]. *Have you lit the candles?* *v.*

hat, āge, fär; let, ēqual, tėrm; it, īce
hot, ōpen, ôrder; oil, out; cup, pu̇t, rüle
əbove, takən, pencəl, lemən, circəs
ch, child; ng, long; sh, ship
th, thin; ᴛʜ, then; zh, measure

lit[2] (lit) See **light**[3]. *Two birds lit on my window sill.* *v.*

li·ter (lē′tər) See **litre.**

lit·er·al (lit′ər əl or lit′rel) 1 following the exact words of the original: *A literal translation of a story is not always the best one.* 2 taking words in their usual meaning, without exaggeration or imagination; matter of fact: *the literal meaning of a word, a literal type of mind.* *adj.*

lit·er·al·ly (lit′ər əl ē or lit′rə lē) word for word; without exaggeration or imagination: *Write the story literally as it happened.* *adv.*

lit·er·ar·y (lit′ər er′ē) 1 having to do with literature. 2 knowing much about literature. *adj.*

lit·er·ate (lit′ər it) 1 able to read and write. 2 a person who can read and write. 1 *adj.*, 2 *n.*

lit·er·a·ture (lit′ər ə chər, lit′rə chər, or lit′ər ə chür′) 1 the writings of a period or of a country, especially those kept alive by the excellence of their style or thought: *Stephen Leacock is a famous name in Canadian literature.* 2 all the books and articles on a subject: *the literature of stamp collecting.* 3 the study of literature: *I am going to take literature and mathematics this spring.* 4 *Informal.* printed matter of any kind: *Election campaign literature informs people about the candidates.* *n.*

lithe (līᴛʜ) bending easily; supple: *lithe of body, a lithe willow.* *adj.* **—lithe′ly,** *adv.*

lit·mus (lit′məs) a blue coloring matter. *n.*

litmus paper paper treated with litmus: *Litmus paper will turn red when put into acid and back to blue when put into alkali.*

li·tre (lē′tər) a measure of capacity: *I drink a litre of milk a day.* *Symbol:* l or ℓ *n.* Also spelled **liter.**

A litter (def. 6)

lit·ter (lit′ər) 1 little bits left about in disorder; things scattered about: *He should pick up his own litter.* 2 scatter things about; leave odds and ends lying around; make untidy: *You have littered the room with your papers.* 3 the young animals born at the same time from one mother: *a litter of puppies.* 4 straw, hay, etc. used as bedding for animals. 5 a stretcher for carrying a sick or wounded person. 6 a framework to be carried on men's shoulders, or by beasts of burden, with a couch usually enclosed by curtains: *Litters usually carry one passenger.* 1, 3–6 *n.*, 2 *v.*

lit·tle (lit′əl) 1 not big or large; small: *A grain of sand* *is little.* 2 short; not long in time or distance: *Wait a little while and I'll go a little way with you.* 3 not much; small in number, amount, degree, or importance: *A sick child eats little food.* 4 small in mind, feeling, nature, or power: *Only a little man would punch a child.* 5 a small amount: *He managed to save a little while he was working.* 6 a short time or distance: *After a little he felt much better. Move a little to the left.* 7 to a small extent; not much: *He travels little. The book was little known to us.* 8 hardly at all: *A coward is little liked.* 1–4 *adj.,* **less** or **less·er, least;** or **lit·tler, lit·tlest;** 5, 6 *n.,* 7, 8 *adv.,* **less, least. —lit'tle·ness,** *n.*

little by little, by a small amount at a time; slowly; gradually.

make little of, treat or represent as of little importance: *She made little of her troubles.*

not a little, much; very: *He was not a little upset by the accident.*

think little of, not value much; consider as unimportant or worthless.

live[1] (liv) 1 have life; be alive; exist: *All creatures have an equal right to live.* 2 remain alive: *He managed to live through the war.* 3 last or endure: *Her good name will live forever.* 4 keep up life: *Most men live by working.* 5 feed: *Lions live upon other animals.* 6 pass life: *to live well, to live a life of ease.* 7 dwell: *My aunt lives in Victoria. Who lives in this house?* 8 carry out or show in life: *to live one's ideals.* 9 have a rich and full life: *Those people know how to live! v.,* **lived, liv·ing.**

live down, live so worthily that some fault or sin of the past is overlooked or forgotten: *He is determined to live down that disgrace.*

live up to, act according to; do what is expected or promised: *The car has not lived up to the salesman's description.*

live[2] (līv) 1 having life; alive: *a live dog.* 2 burning or glowing: *live coals.* 3 full of energy or activity: *She's a very live girl, always on the go.* 4 carrying an electric current: *a live wire.* 5 charged with explosive: *a live cartridge.* 6 in radio or television, broadcast as performed and not from a tape or film made beforehand: *a live television show.* 7 of recordings or broadcasts, made as performed: *The concert was recorded live.* 1–6 *adj.,* 7 *adv.*

live·li·hood (līv'lē hůd') a means of living, that is, of obtaining the money necessary to buy food, clothing, and shelter; a means of supporting oneself: *He writes for a livelihood. He earns his livelihood as a farmer. n.*

live·li·ness (līv'lē nis) a lively quality or condition; vigor; gaiety. *n.*

live·long (liv'long') for the whole length of; whole; entire: *She is busy the livelong day. adj.*

live·ly (līv'lē) 1 full of life and spirit; active: *A good night's sleep made us all lively again.* 2 exciting: *We had a lively time during the hurricane.* 3 bright; vivid: *lively colors.* 4 cheerful; gay: *a lively conversation.* 5 bouncing well and quickly: *a lively tennis ball.* 6 in a lively manner. 1–5 *adj.,* **live·li·er, live·li·est;** 6 *adv.*

liv·en (līv'ən) make or become more lively; brighten: *As he grew well, his spirits began to liven again. v.*

liv·er (liv'ər) 1 the large, reddish-brown organ in people and some animals that makes bile and aids in the absorption of food: *The liver frees the blood of its waste matter and changes some of its substances.* See **kidney** for picture. 2 the liver of an animal used as food. *n.*

liv·er·y (liv'ər ē or liv'rē) 1 any uniform provided for servants, or adopted by any group or profession. 2 the feeding, stabling, and care of horses for pay. 3 a stable where horses are cared for or hired out. *n., pl.* **liv·er·ies.**

lives (līvz) plural of **life.** *n.*

live·stock (līv'stok') farm animals: *Cows, horses, sheep, and pigs are livestock. n.*

live wire 1 a wire through which an electric current is flowing: *It is dangerous to touch an unprotected live wire.* 2 *Informal.* an energetic, wide-awake person: *He is such a live wire that he's always busy and active.*

liv·id (liv'id) 1 having a dull-bluish or greyish color, as from a bruise: *livid marks on an arm.* 2 very pale: *livid with shock.* 3 flushed; reddish: *livid with anger.* 4 *Informal.* very angry: *Their insults made him livid. adj.*

liv·ing (liv'ing) 1 having life; being alive: *a living plant.* 2 being alive: *The old woman was filled with the joy of living.* 3 **the living,** all people who are alive. 4 a means of keeping alive; livelihood: *He earned his living as a grocer.* 5 a manner of life: *healthful living.* 6 full of life; vigorous; strong; active: *a living faith.* 7 in actual existence; still in use; alive: *a living language.* 8 true to life; vivid; lifelike: *a picture that is the living image of a person.* 9 of life; for living in: *poor living conditions.* 10 sufficient to live on: *a living wage.* 1, 6–10 *adj.,* 2–5 *n.*

living room a room for general family use.

liz·ard (liz'ərd) a reptile with a long body, long tail, movable eyelids, and usually four legs: *The iguana, chameleon, and horned toad are lizards. n.*

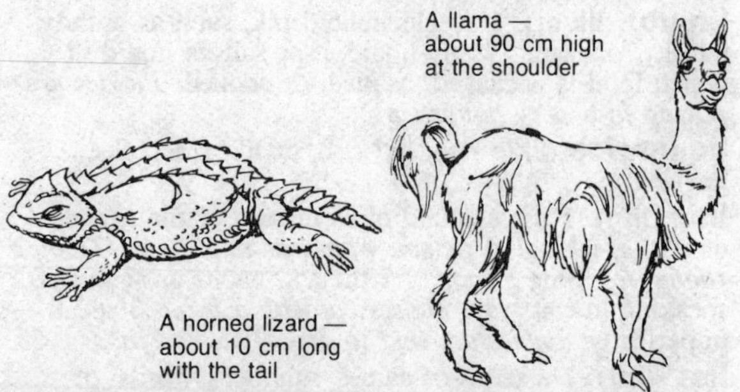
A llama — about 90 cm high at the shoulder

A horned lizard — about 10 cm long with the tail

lla·ma (lä'mə or lam'ə) a woolly-haired South American animal resembling a camel, but smaller and without a hump: *Llamas are used as beasts of burden. n., pl.* **lla·mas** or **lla·ma.**

lo (lō) look! see! behold! *interj.*

☛ **Lo** and **low** are pronounced the same.

load (lōd) 1 what one is carrying; a burden: *The cart has a load of hay. That's a load off my mind!* 2 the amount that usually is carried: *Send us four loads of sand.* 3 place on or in a carrier of some kind: *The longshoremen are loading grain.* 4 put whatever is to be carried in or on: *to load a ship.* 5 burden; oppress: *load the mind with worries.* 6 **loads,** *pl. Informal.* a great quantity or number: *We have loads of marshmallows for the campfire.* 7 one charge of powder and shot for a gun. 8 put a charge in a gun. 1, 2, 6, 7 *n.,* 3–5, 8 *v.*

☛ **Load** and **lode** are pronounced the same.

hat, āge, fär; let, ēqual, tėrm; it, īce
hot, ōpen, ôrder; oil, out; cup, pu̇t, rüle
əbove, takən, pencəl, lemən, circəs
ch, child; ng, long; sh, ship
th, thin; ᴛʜ, then; zh, measure

load·ed (lōd′id) *Informal.* full of half-hidden and unexpected meanings and suggestions: *Loaded questions are often intended to trap a person into saying more than he wants to say.* *adj.*

load·stone (lōd′stōn′) **1** a magnetic stone that attracts iron and steel. **2** something that attracts: *Gold was the loadstone that drew men to the Yukon.* *n.* Also spelled **lodestone.**

loaf[1] (lōf) **1** bread that is shaped and baked as one piece. **2** anything like a loaf in shape: *a meat loaf.* *n., pl.* **loaves.**

loaf[2] (lōf) spend time idly; do nothing: *I can loaf all day Saturday.* *v.*

loam (lōm) rich, fertile earth in which decaying and decayed plant matter is mixed with clay and sand. *n.*

loan (lōn) **1** a lending: *She asked for the loan of his pen.* **2** anything that is lent, especially money: *He asked his brother for a loan.* **3** make a loan; lend: *His brother loaned him the money.* 1, 2 *n.*, 3 *v.*

☛ **Loan** and **lone** are pronounced the same.

loath (lōth) unwilling: *The little girl was loath to leave her mother.* *adj.* Also spelled **loth.**

loathe (lōᴛʜ) feel strong dislike and disgust for; abhor; hate: *We loathe rotten food or a nasty smell.* *v.,* **loathed, loath·ing.**

loath·ing (lōᴛʜ′ing) strong dislike and disgust; intense aversion. *n.*

loath·some (lōᴛʜ′səm) disgusting; making one feel sick: *a loathsome odor.* *adj.* **—loath′some·ly,** *adv.*

loaves (lōvz) plural of **loaf**[1]. *n.*

lob·by (lob′ē) **1** an entrance hall; a vestibule or waiting room: *a hotel lobby, a theatre lobby.* **2** a room or hall outside a legislative chamber: *the lobby of the House of Commons.* **3** a person or group that tries to influence legislators. **4** try to influence legislators: *The textile manufacturers are lobbying for a tax on imported fabrics.* 1–3 *n., pl.* **lob·bies;** 4 *v.,* **lob·bied, lob·by·ing.**

lobe (lōb) a rounded projecting part of something: *The lobe of the ear is the rounded lower end.* *n.*

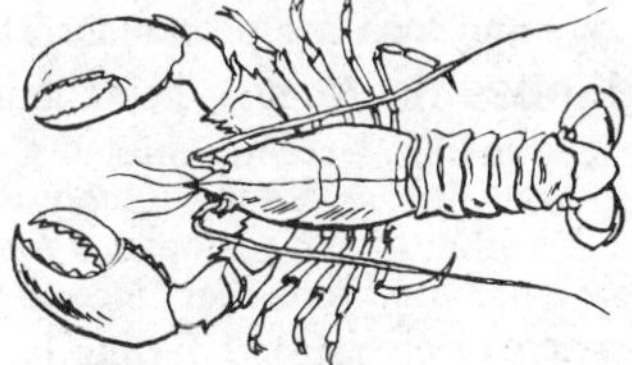
A lobster — about 30 to 60 cm long with the claws

lob·ster (lob′stər) **1** a sea animal having two big claws in front and eight legs. **2** its flesh, used as food. *n.*

lob·stick (lob′stik′) *Cdn.* in the North, a spruce or pine tree trimmed of all but the top branches: *Travellers often use lobsticks as landmarks.* *n.* Also, **lopstick.**

lo·cal (lō′kəl) **1** of or having to do with a certain place or places; limited to a certain place or places: *the local doctor, local news.* **2** of just one part of the body: *a local pain, local disease, local application of a remedy.* **3** making all, or almost all, stops: *a local train.* **4** a train, bus, etc. that stops at all of the stations on its route. 1–3 *adj.,* 4 *n.* **—lo′cal·ly,** *adv.*

local government district local improvement district.

local improvement district *Cdn.* in some provinces, a district administered by provincial officials because it is too thinly populated to have a municipal government of its own.

lo·cal·i·ty (lō kal′ə tē) one place and the places near it; region, district, or neighborhood. *n., pl.* **lo·cal·i·ties.**

lo·cate (lō′kāt or lō kāt′) **1** establish in a place: *He located his new store in Yellowknife.* **2** establish oneself in a place: *Early settlers located where there was water.* **3** find out the exact position of: *The general tried to locate the enemy's camp.* **4** state or show the position of: *Locate Regina on the map.* *v.,* **lo·cat·ed, lo·cat·ing.**
be located, be situated: *Ottawa is located on a river.*

lo·ca·tion (lō kā′shən) **1** locating or being located: *The Scouts argued about the location of the camp.* **2** a position or place: *The cottage was in a sheltered location.* **3** a plot of ground marked out by boundaries: *a mining location.* *n.*
on location, at a place outside the studio for the purpose of filming a motion picture: *All the outdoor scenes were shot on location.*

loch (lok) *Scottish.* **1** lake. **2** an arm of the sea partly shut in by land. *n.*

☛ **Loch** and **lock** are pronounced the same, though **loch** has a special pronunciation in Scotland.

Locks in a canal. They enable ships to go where there were formerly waterfalls, or to go around a dam. If the ship enters from below, the gates are closed, the water level is raised (by means of pipes) to equal the level above the lock, then the upper gates are opened. If the ship enters from above, the process is reversed.

lock[1] (lok) **1** a means of fastening doors, boxes, etc. usually needing a key of special shape to open it. **2** fasten with a lock: *I forgot to lock the door.* **3** shut something in or out or up: *We lock up jewels in a safe.* **4** an enclosed section of a canal, dock, etc. in which the level of the water can be changed by letting water in or out, to raise or lower ships. **5** the part of a gun by means of which it is fired. **6** join, fit, jam, or link together: *The girls locked arms and walked down the street together.* 1, 4, 5 *n.,* 2, 3, 6 *v.*

☛ See note at **loch.**

lock[2] (lok) **1** a curl of hair. **2 locks,** *pl.* the hair of the head: *The child has curly locks.* *n.*

☛ See note at **loch.**

lock·er (lok′ər) **1** a chest, drawer, closet, or cupboard that can be locked. **2** a refrigerated compartment for storing frozen foods. *n.*

lock·et (lok′it) a little ornamental case of gold, silver, etc. for holding a picture of someone or a lock of hair: *A locket is usually worn around the neck on a chain.* *n.*

lock·jaw (lok′jo′ or lok′jô′) a form of tetanus in which the jaws become firmly closed. *n.*

lock·smith (lok′smith′) a person who makes or repairs locks and keys. *n.*

lo·co·mo·tion (lō′kə mō′shən) the act or power of moving from place to place: *Walking, swimming, and flying are common forms of locomotion.* *n.*

lo·co·mo·tive (lō′kə mō′tiv) **1** a railway engine. **2** any engine that goes from place to place on its own power. *n.*

lo·cust (lō′kəst) **1** any of various kinds of grasshopper: *Certain kinds of locusts come in great swarms, destroying the crops.* **2** cicada. **3** a tree having small, rounded leaflets and clusters of sweet-smelling, white flowers. *n.*

lode (lōd) a vein of metal ore: *The miners struck a rich lode of copper.* *n.*

☛ **Lode** and **load** are pronounced the same.

lode·stone (lōd′stōn′) See **loadstone.**

lodge (loj) **1** live in a place for a time. **2** supply with a place to sleep or live in for a time: *Can you lodge us for the weekend?* **3** a place to live in; a house, especially a small or temporary house: *My uncle rents a lodge in the mountains every summer.* **4** live in a rented room or rooms: *We are merely lodging at present.* **5** get caught or stay in a place without falling or going farther: *My kite lodged in the branches of a big tree.* **6** put or send into a particular place: *The hunter lodged a bullet in the lion's heart.* **7** put before some authority: *We lodged a complaint with the police.* **8** a branch of a club or society. **9** the place where such a group meets. **10** an Indian dwelling. **11** the den of an animal such as a beaver or otter. 1, 2, 4–7 *v.,* **lodged, lodg·ing;** 3, 8–11 *n.*

lodg·er (loj′ər) a person who lives in a rented room or rooms. *n.*

lodg·ing (loj′ing) **1** a place to live in for a time: *a lodging for the night.* **2 lodgings,** *pl.* a rented room or rooms in a house, not in a hotel. *n.*

loft (loft) **1** attic. **2** a room under the roof of a barn: *This loft is full of hay.* **3** a gallery in a church or hall: *a choir loft.* **4** the upper floor of a business building or warehouse. *n.*

loft·y (lof′tē) **1** very high: *lofty mountains.* **2** exalted; dignified; grand: *lofty aims.* **3** proud; haughty: *He had a lofty contempt for others.* *adj.,* **loft·i·er, loft·i·est.**

log (log) **1** a length of wood just as it comes from the tree. **2** cut down trees, cut them into logs, and get them out of the forest. **3** the daily record of a ship's voyage. **4** enter in a ship's log. **5** the record of an airplane trip, performance of an engine, etc. **6** a float for measuring the speed of a ship. 1, 3, 5, 6 *n.,* 2, 4 *v.,* **logged, log·ging.**

lo·gan (lō′gən) *Cdn.* a backwater or pocket in a stream. *n.*

lo·gan·ber·ry (lō′gən ber′ē) a large, purplish-red berry, a variety of blackberry, that grows mainly along the Pacific coast of North America. *n., pl.* **lo·gan·ber·ries.**

☛ Named after Judge J. H. *Logan* of California who first grew the berry in 1881.

log·ger (log′ər) a person whose work is felling trees and getting them to the mill; a lumberjack. *n.*

log·ging (log′ing) the work of cutting down trees, sawing them into logs, and removing them from the forest. *n.*

log·ic (loj′ik) **1** the science of getting new and valid information by reasoning from facts that one already knows. **2** reasoning; the use of argument: *The lawyer won his case because his logic was sound.* **3** reason; sound sense: *There is much logic in what you say.* *n.*

log·i·cal (loj′ə kəl) **1** having to do with logic; according to the principles of logic: *logical reasoning.* **2** reasonable: *Fatigue is a logical result of poor nutrition.* **3** reasoning correctly: *a clear and logical mind.* *adj.* **—log′i·cal·ly,** *adv.*

loin (loin) **1** Usually, **loins,** *pl.* the part of the body between the ribs and the hips: *The loins are on both sides of the backbone and nearer to it than the flanks.* **2** a piece of meat from this part of an animal: *a loin of pork.* *n.*

gird up one's loins, get ready for action.

loi·ter (loi′tər) **1** linger idly; stop and play along the way: *She loitered along the street, looking into all the store windows.* **2** spend time idly: *to loiter the hours away.* *v.*

loll (lol) **1** recline or lean in a lazy manner: *to loll on a chesterfield.* **2** hang loosely or droop: *A dog's tongue lolls out in hot weather.* **3** allow to hang or droop: *A dog lolls out his tongue.* *v.*

lol·li·pop (lol′ē pop′) a piece of hard candy on the end of a small stick; sucker. *n.*

lone (lōn) **1** alone; single: *The lone traveller was glad to reach home.* **2** lonesome; lonely: *They lived a lone life.* *adj.*

☛ **Lone** and **loan** are pronounced the same.

lone·li·ness (lōn′lē nis) being lonely; solitude. *n.*

lone·ly (lōn′lē) **1** feeling oneself alone and longing for company or friends: *He was lonely while his brother was away.* **2** without many people: *a lonely road.* **3** alone: *a lonely tree.* *adj.,* **lone·li·er, lone·li·est.**

lone·some (lōn′səm) **1** feeling lonely. **2** making one feel lonely: *a lonesome journey.* *adj.,* **lone·som·er, lone·som·est.**

long[1] (long) **1** that measures much from end to end: *A centimetre is short; a kilometre is long. A year is a long time. He told a long story.* **2** in length: *My table is one metre long.* **3** having a long, narrow shape: *a long board.* **4** a long time: *Summer will come before long.* **5** for a long time: *I can't stay long.* **6** for its whole length: *all summer long, all day long.* 1–3 *adj.,* **long·er** (long′gər), **long·est** (long′gist); 4 *n.,* 5, 6 *adv.*

as long as or **so long as,** provided that.

a long face, a sad expression.

in the long run, over a long period of time; eventually: *The system will work out well in the long run.*

the long and short of it, the sum total of something; substance: *He told us the long and short of it when we arrived.*

hat, āge, fär; let, ēqual, tėrm; it, īce
hot, ōpen, ôrder; oil, out; cup, pu̇t, rüle
əbove, takən, pencəl, lemən, circəs
ch, child; ng, long; sh, ship
th, thin; ᴛʜ, then; zh, measure

long² (long) wish very much; desire greatly: *He longed for his mother. She longed to see him.* *v.*

long·hand (long′hand′) ordinary writing, not shorthand or typewriting. *n.*

long·horn (long′hôrn′) one of a breed of cattle having very long horns. *n.*

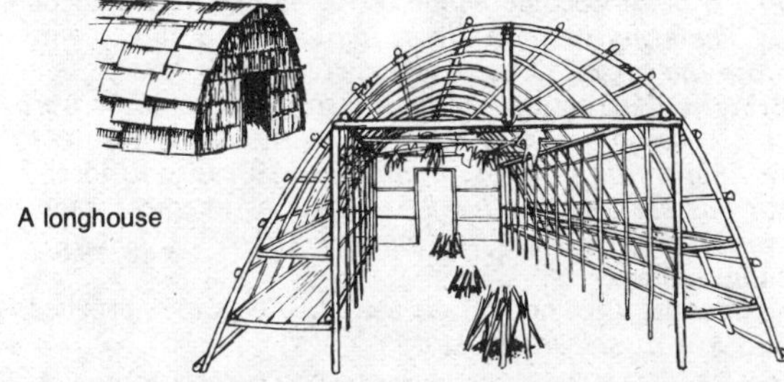

A longhouse

long·house (long′hous′) a large dwelling of certain North American Indian tribes, especially the Iroquois, in which several families of a community lived together. *n.*

long·ing (long′ing) **1** an earnest desire: *a longing for home.* **2** having or showing earnest desire: *a longing look.* 1 *n.,* 2 *adj.* **—long′ing·ly,** *adv.*

long·ish (long′ish) somewhat long. *adj.*

lon·gi·tude (lon′jə tyüd′ or lon′jə tüd′, long′gə tyüd′ or long′gə tüd′) a distance east or west on the earth's surface, measured in degrees: *On maps, lines running between the North and South Poles represent longitudes.* See **latitude** for picture. *n.*

lon·gi·tu·di·nal (lon′jə tyü′də nəl or lon′jə tü′də nəl, long′gə tyü′də nəl or long′gə tü′də nəl) **1** of length; in length: *longitudinal measurements.* **2** running lengthwise: *Our living room drapes have longitudinal stripes.* **3** of longitude: *a longitudinal difference.* *adj.*

long·shore·man (long′shôr′mən) a man whose work is loading and unloading ships. *n., pl.* **long·shore·men** (-mən).

look (lu̇k) **1** see; try to see; turn the eyes: *Look at the pictures.* **2** search: *I looked through the drawer to see if I could find my keys.* **3** a glance; seeing: *He took a quick look at the magazine.* **4** examine; pay attention: *You must look at all the facts.* **5** have a view; face: *The house looks to the south.* **6** seem; appear: *She looks pale.* **7** show how one feels by one's appearance: *He said nothing but looked his disappointment.* **8** appearance: *A deserted house has a desolate look.* **9 looks,** *pl.* personal appearance: *Good looks means a good appearance.* 1, 2, 4–7 *v.,* 3, 8, 9 *n.*

look after, attend to; take care of: *She looked after her little brother.*

look down on, despise; scorn.

look for, expect: *We'll look for you tonight.*

look forward to, expect: *We look forward to seeing you. When the crops failed, they knew they had to look forward to a bad winter.*

look in, make a short visit: *She said she'd look in on her way back.*

look into, examine; investigate.

look on, a watch without taking part: *The teacher conducted the experiment while we looked on.* **b** regard; consider: *I look on her as a very able person.*

look oneself, seem like oneself; look well: *She has been quite ill and still doesn't look herself.*

look out, be careful; watch out: *Look out for cars as you cross the street.*

look over, examine; inspect: *The police officer looked over his driver's licence.*

look to, a attend to; take care of. **b** turn to for help.

look up, a find; refer to: *She looked up the word in the dictionary.* **b** *Informal.* call on; visit: *Look me up when you come to town.*

look up to, respect; admire.

looking glass mirror.

look·out (lu̇k′out′) **1** a careful watch for someone to come or for something to happen: *Keep a lookout for Mother. Be on the lookout for trouble.* **2** a place from which to watch, as for forest fires: *A crow's-nest is a lookout.* **3** a person or group of persons having the duty of watching: *The lookout cried, 'Land ho!'* *n.*

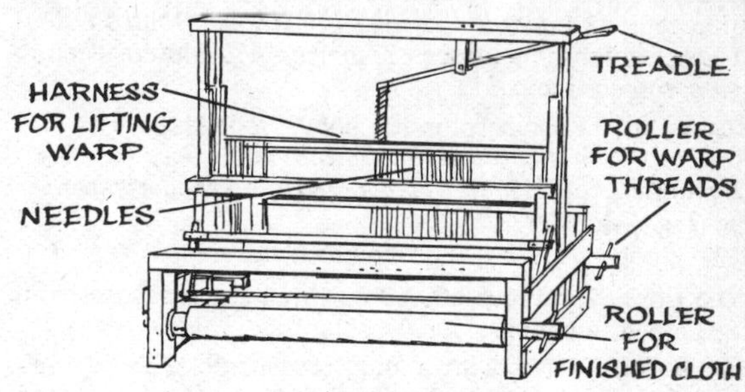

A hand loom for use on a table

loom¹ (lüm) a frame or machine for weaving cloth. *n.*

loom² (lüm) appear dimly or vaguely as a large, often threatening, shape: *A large iceberg loomed through the thick, grey fog.* *v.*

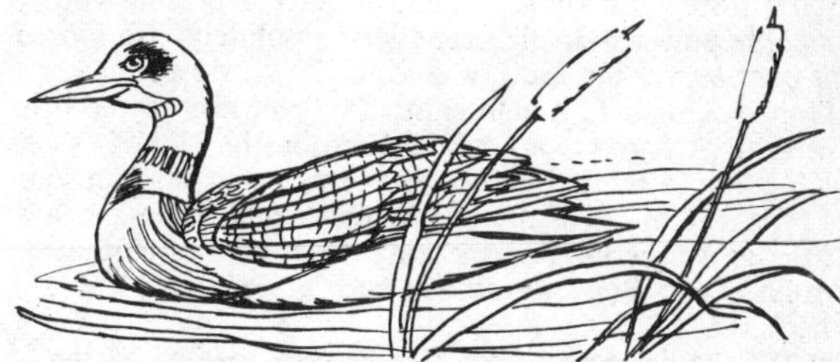

A common loon — about 80 cm long with the tail

loon¹ (lün) a large diving bird: *Loons have a loud, wild cry.* *n.*

loon² (lün) a worthless or stupid person. *n.*

loop (lüp) **1** the shape of a curved string, ribbon, bent wire, etc. that crosses itself. **2** a thing, bend, course, or motion shaped somewhat like this: *In handwriting, 'b,' 'g,' 'h,' and 'l' often have loops. The road makes a wide loop around the lake.* **3** a fastening or ornament formed of cord, etc. bent and crossed. **4** make a loop or loops in. **5** a turn like the letter *ℓ*, especially one made by an airplane. 1–3, 5 *n.,* 4 *v.*

loop·hole (lüp′hōl′) **1** a small opening in a wall for looking through, for letting in air, or for firing through at an enemy outside. **2** a means of escape: *The clever lawyer found a loophole in the law to save the prisoner, even though he was guilty. n.*

loose (lüs) **1** not firmly set or fastened: *a loose tooth, a loose thread.* **2** not tight: *loose clothing.* **3** not bound together: *loose papers.* **4** not put up in a box, can, etc.: *loose coffee.* **5** free; not shut in or up: *We leave the dog loose at night.* **6** not close or solid; having spaces: *cloth with a loose weave.* **7** not strict or exact: *a loose account of the accident.* **8** with little control or restraint: *loose conduct, a loose character.* **9** set free; let go: *They loosed the prisoners.* **10** make loose; untie; unfasten: *to loose a knot.* 1–8 *adj.,* **loos·er, loos·est;** 9, 10 *v.,* **loosed, loos·ing. —loose′ly,** *adv.*

loose–leaf (lüs′lēf′) having pages or sheets of paper that can be taken out and replaced: *a loose-leaf notebook. adj.*

loos·en (lüs′ən) **1** make loose or looser; untie; unfasten: *The doctor loosened the stricken man's collar.* **2** become loose or looser: *Your ring will loosen when your fingers are cold. v.*

loot (lüt) **1** spoils; plunder; booty: *loot taken by soldiers from a captured town, burglar's loot.* **2** plunder; rob: *The burglar looted the jewellery store.* 1 *n.,* 2 *v.* **—loot′er,** *n.*

☛ **Loot** and **lute** are pronounced the same.

lop (lop) **1** cut; cut off. **2** cut branches or twigs from. *v.,* **lopped, lop·ping.**

lope (lōp) **1** run with a long, easy stride: *The coyote loped along the trail.* **2** a long, easy stride. 1 *v.,* **loped, lop·ing;** 2 *n.*

lop·sid·ed (lop′sīd′id) larger or heavier on one side than the other; unevenly balanced; leaning to one side. *adj.* **—lop′sid′ed·ly,** *adv.* **—lop′sid′ed·ness,** *n.*

lop·stick (lop′stik′) lobstick. *n.*

lord (lôrd) **1** a ruler, master, or chief; a person who has the power. **2** rule proudly or absolutely: *He lorded it over us.* **3 the Lord, a** God. **b** Christ. **4** in the United Kingdom, a man entitled by courtesy to the title of lord: *A baron is a lord.* **5 Lord,** in the United Kingdom, **a** a titled nobleman belonging to the House of Lords, the upper of the two branches of Parliament. **b** a title used in writing or speaking about men of certain ranks: *Lord Beaverbrook was born in Ontario.* 1, 3–5 *n.,* 2 *v.*

☛ **Lord** developed from Old English *hlāford,* earlier *hlāfweard,* made up of *hlāf,* meaning 'loaf,' and *weard,* meaning 'keeper.' Compare the note at **lady.**

lord·ly (lôrd′lē) **1** like a lord; suitable for a lord; grand; magnificent. **2** haughty; insolent; scornful: *His lordly airs annoyed many people. adj.,* **lord·li·er, lord·li·est.**

Lord·ship (lôrd′ship) *British.* a title used in speaking to or of a lord: *your Lordship, his Lordship. n.*

Lord's Supper Jesus' last supper with His disciples.

lore (lôr) **1** the facts and stories about a certain subject: *fairy lore, bird lore, Greek lore.* **2** learning; knowledge. *n.*

lor·ry (lôr′ē) *British.* a motor truck. *n., pl.* **lor·ries.**

lose (lüz) **1** not have any longer; have taken away from one by accident, carelessness, parting, death, etc.: *to lose one's life, to lose a limb, a father, or a friend.* **2** be unable to find: *to lose one's way, to lose a book.* **3** fail to keep or maintain; cease to have: *lose patience, lose all fear.* **4** miss; fail to get, catch, see, hear, or understand: *lose a train, to lose a few words of what was said.* **5** be or become worse off in money, in numbers, etc.: *The army lost heavily in the battle.* **6** fail to win: *to lose the prize.* **7** be defeated: *Our team lost.* **8** bring to destruction; ruin: *The ship and its crew were lost.* **9** waste; spend or let go by without any result: *to lose time waiting, to lose a chance.* **10** cause to lose: *That one act lost him his job.* **11** of a timepiece, run slow: *That clock loses five minutes a day. v.,* **lost, los·ing. —los′er,** *n.*

lose oneself, a let oneself go astray. **b** become absorbed: *I had lost myself in the story.*

loss (los) **1** a losing or being lost: *The loss of one's health is serious, but the loss of a pencil is not.* **2** the person or thing lost: *The fire was finally put out, but her house was a complete loss.* **3** the harm or disadvantage caused by losing something; the value of the thing lost: *The loss from the fire was $10 000.* **4** a defeat: *Our team had two losses and one tie out of ten games played. n.*

at a loss, puzzled; not sure; uncertain; in difficulty: *He was at a loss for words.*

lost (lost) **1** See **lose.** *I lost my new pencil. My ruler is lost, too.* **2** no longer had or kept: *lost friends.* **3** missing; no longer to be found: *lost books.* **4** not won: *a lost battle, a lost prize.* **5** hopeless: *a lost cause.* **6** not used to good purpose; wasted: *lost time.* **7** destroyed; ruined: *a lost soul.* 1 *v.,* 2–7 *adj.*

lost in, completely absorbed or interested in: *He was lost in dreams.*

lost to, no longer concerned about: *She was enjoying herself so much, she was lost to all sense of responsibility.*

lot (lot) **1** a number of persons or things considered as a group; a collection: *This lot of oranges is not so good as the last.* **2** Often, **lots,** *pl. Informal.* a great many; a great deal: *a lot of books. I have a lot of marbles. You have lots of time.* **3** a plot of ground: *His house is between two empty lots.* **4** a portion or part: *He divided the shipment of fruit into ten lots.* **5** one of a set of objects, such as bits of paper, wood, etc., used to decide something by chance: *We drew lots to see who should be captain.* **6** such a method of deciding: *It was settled by lot.* **7** a choice made in this way: *The lot fell to me.* **8** what one gets by lot; one's share. **9** one's fate or fortune: *It was his lot to die in battle. n.*

☛ **Lot** (def.2) is informal, and is generally avoided in formal English. In informal English, one would say, 'He tried lots of different shots, but he lost the game.' In formal English, one would say, 'He tried a variety of shots' or 'He tried many different shots.'

loth (lōth) See **loath.**

lo·tion (lō′shən) a liquid medicine or cosmetic which is applied to the skin: *Lotions are used to relieve pain, to heal, to cleanse, or to beautify the skin. n.*

lot·ter·y (lot′ər ē) a scheme for distributing prizes by lot or chance: *In a lottery a large number of tickets are sold, only some of which win prizes. n., pl.* **lot·ter·ies.**

loud (loud) **1** not quiet or soft; making a great sound: *a loud voice. A gun goes off with a loud noise.* **2** in a loud manner: *The hunter called long and loud.* 3 *Informal.* showy in dress or manner: *loud clothes.* 1, 3 *adj.*, 2 *adv.* **—loud′ly,** *adv.* **—loud′ness,** *n.*

loud·speak·er (loud′spēk′ər) a device for making sounds louder, especially in a radio or phonograph. *n.*

lounge (lounj) 1 stand, stroll, sit, or lie at ease in a lazy way: *He lounged in an old chair.* 2 a comfortable and informal room in which one can lounge and be at ease: *a theatre lounge.* 3 a couch or chesterfield. 1 *v.*, **lounged, loung·ing;** 2, 3 *n.*

louse (lous) 1 a small, wingless insect that infests the hair or skin of people, causing irritation. 2 any of various similar insects that infest animals or plants: *We spray plants to kill the lice.* *n., pl.* **lice.**

lous·y (lou′zē) 1 *Informal.* bad; poor; miserable: *I don't like the job because the pay is lousy.* 2 *Slang.* dirty; nasty; mean: *a lousy swindler.* 3 *Slang.* well supplied with: *lousy with money.* 4 infested with lice. *adj.*, **lous·i·er, lous·i·est. —lous′i·ly,** *adv.*

lout (lout) an awkward, stupid fellow; boor: *The lout didn't even wipe his muddy boots when he came in.* *n.*

lov·a·ble (luv′ə bəl) deserving love; endearing: *She was a very lovable person, always most kind and thoughtful.* *adj.*

love (luv) 1 a deep feeling of fondness and friendship; great affection or devotion: *love of one's family, love for a sweetheart.* 2 have such a feeling for: *She loves her mother. I love my country.* 3 a person who is loved; sweetheart. 4 a strong liking: *a love of books.* 5 like very much; take great pleasure in: *He loves music. Most people love ice cream.* 1, 3, 4 *n.*, 2, 5 *v.*, **loved, lov·ing.**
fall in love, begin to love; come to feel love.
in love, feeling love.

love·li·ness (luv′lē nis) beauty. *n.*

love·ly (luv′lē) 1 beautiful in appearance or character; lovable: *She is one of the loveliest girls we know.* 2 *Informal.* very pleasing; delightful: *We had a lovely holiday.* *adj.*, **love·li·er, love·li·est.**

lov·er (luv′ər) 1 a person who is in love with another. 2 a person having a strong liking: *a lover of books.* *n.*

lov·ing (luv′ing) affectionate; fond. *adj.* **—lov′ing·ly,** *adv.*

low¹ (lō) 1 not high or tall: *a low bridge. This stool is very low.* 2 near the ground, floor, or base: *a low shelf, a low jump.* 3 of humble rank: *She rose from a low position to president of the company.* 4 mean; coarse; vulgar: *low talk, a low person.* 5 feeble; weak: *The sick man is very low today.* 6 unfavorable; poor: *The boys had a low opinion of cowards.* 7 small; less than usual in amount, degree, price, pitch, etc.: *Twelve cents a litre is rather low for gasoline.* 8 nearly used up: *Our furnace oil is low.* 9 in music, not high in the scale; deep in pitch: *a low note.* 10 not loud: *a low whisper.* 11 at or to a low point, place, rank, amount, degree, price, pitch, etc.: *Speak low. The sun sank low. Supplies are running low.* 12 with little energy or joy; sad: *low spirits.* 1–10, 12 *adj.*, 11 *adv.*
lie low, *Informal.* stay hidden; keep still: *The robbers will lie low for a time.*
low tide, the time when the ocean is lowest on the shore.
☛ **Low** and **lo** are pronounced the same.

low² (lō) 1 make the sound of a cow mooing; moo. 2 the sound a cow makes; mooing. 1 *v.*, 2 *n.*
☛ See note at **low¹**.

hat, āge, fär; let, ēqual, tėrm; it, īce
hot, ōpen, ôrder; oil, out; cup, pu̇t, rüle
əbove, takən, pencəl, lemən, circəs
ch, child; ng, long; sh, ship
th, thin; ᴛʜ, then; zh, measure

low·down (lō′doun′) *Slang.* the actual facts or truth: *Can you give me the lowdown on what happened at the meeting?* *n.*

low–down (lō′doun′) *Informal.* low; mean; nasty: *a low-down trick.* *adj.*

low·er (lō′ər) 1 let down or haul down: *We lower the flag at night.* 2 make lower: *to lower the volume of the radio.* 3 sink; become lower: *The sun lowered slowly.* 4 more low: *lower grades. Prices were lower last year than this.* 1–3 *v.*, 4 *adj.*, *adv.*

Lower Canada an older name for the province of Quebec: *Lower Canada was lower down the St. Lawrence River than Upper Canada.*

Lower Lakes the most southerly of the Great Lakes, Lakes Erie and Ontario.

low·land (lō′lənd) land that is lower and flatter than the neighboring country. *n.*

low·ly (lō′lē) 1 low in rank, station, position, or development: *a lowly servant, a lowly occupation.* 2 humble or meek; modest in feeling, behavior, or condition: *He had a lowly opinion of himself.* 3 humbly or meekly. 1, 2 *adj.*, **low·li·er, low·li·est;** 3 *adv.*

loy·al (loi′əl) 1 true and faithful to love, promise, or duty. 2 faithful to one's king, government, or country: *a loyal citizen.* *adj.* **—loy′al·ly,** *adv.*

loy·al·ist (loi′əl ist) 1 a person who supports the existing government, king, etc. especially in time of revolt. 2 **Loyalist,** a United Empire Loyalist. *n.*

loy·al·ty (loi′əl tē) loyal feeling or behavior; faithfulness. *n., pl.* **loy·al·ties.**

loz·enge (loz′inj) 1 a small tablet of medicine or a piece of candy: *Cough drops are sometimes called lozenges.* 2 a design or figure shaped like this: ◇; diamond. *n.*

lu·bri·cant (lü′brə kənt) oil, grease, etc. for putting on parts of machines that move against one another, to make them work smoothly and easily. *n.*

lu·bri·cate (lü′brə kāt′) 1 put oil, grease, etc. on parts of machines; put a lubricant on. 2 make slippery or smooth. *v.*, **lu·bri·cat·ed, lu·bri·cat·ing.**

lu·bri·ca·tion (lü′brə kā′shən) 1 a lubricating or being lubricated. 2 oil, grease, etc. used for lubricating. *n.*

lu·cid (lü′sid) 1 easy to follow or understand; clear: *A good explanation is lucid.* 2 sane: *Insane persons sometimes have lucid intervals.* *adj.* **—lu′cid·ly,** *adv.*

luck (luk) 1 that which seems to happen or come to one by chance; fortune; chance: *Luck was against the losers. Luck favored me and I won.* 2 good fortune: *Lots of luck to you. He thinks a horseshoe brings luck.* *n.*
in luck, having good luck; lucky: *I am in luck today; I found a quarter.*
out of luck, having bad luck; unlucky.
try one's luck, see what one can do: *Try your luck with*

this puzzle.

luck·i·ly (luk′ə lē) by good luck; fortunately. *adv.*

luck·less (luk′lis) having bad luck; bringing bad luck *That Friday was a luckless day for me.* *adj.*

luck·y (luk′ē) 1 having good luck: *He was lucky to win the card game yesterday.* 2 bringing good luck: *a lucky day, a lucky charm.* *adj.,* **luck·i·er, luck·i·est.**

lu·di·crous (lü′də krəs) absurd but amusing; ridiculous: *the ludicrous acts of a clown.* *adj.* —**lu′di·crous·ly,** *adv.*

lug[1] (lug) pull along or carry with effort; drag: *The children lugged home a big Christmas tree.* *v.,* **lugged, lug·ging.**

lug[2] (lug) a projecting part used to hold or grip something: *Some tractors have lugs on their wheels.* *n.*

lug·gage (lug′ij) baggage. *n.*

luke·warm (lük′wôrm′) 1 neither hot nor cold; fairly warm. 2 showing little enthusiasm; half-hearted: *a lukewarm greeting.* *adj.*

lull (lul) 1 hush to sleep: *The mother lulled the crying baby.* 2 make or become calm or more nearly calm; quiet: *The captain lulled our fears.* *The wind lulled.* 3 a period of less noise or activity; brief calm: *We ran home during a lull in the storm.* 1, 2 *v.,* 3 *n.*

lul·la·by (lul′ə bī′) a song to lull a baby to sleep. *n., pl.* **lul·la·bies.**

lum·ba·go (lum bā′gō) a sickness causing pain in the muscles of the small of the back and in the loins. *n.*

lum·ber[1] (lum′bər) 1 timber, logs, beams, boards, etc. roughly cut and prepared for use. 2 cut and prepare lumber. 3 household articles no longer in use; old furniture and other useless things that take up room. 1, 3 *n.,* 2 *v.*

lum·ber[2] (lum′bər) move along heavily and noisily: *The old stagecoach lumbered down the road.* *v.*

lum·ber·jack (lum′bər jak′) 1 a man whose work is cutting down trees and getting the logs out to the mills; logger. 2 *Cdn.* a Canada jay. *n.*

lum·ber·man (lum′bər mən) 1 lumberjack. 2 a man whose work is buying and selling timber or lumber. *n., pl.* **lum·ber·men** (lum′bər mən).

lu·min·ous (lü′mə nəs) 1 shining by its own light: *The sun and stars are luminous.* 2 full of light; bright: *a luminous sunset.* 3 treated with some substance that glows in the dark: *The numbers on some watches are luminous.* 4 clear; easily understood: *He explained the method in a luminous way.* *adj.*

lump[1] (lump) 1 a solid mass of no particular shape: *a lump of coal.* 2 a swelling; a bump: *There is a lump on my head where I bumped it.* 3 put together; deal with in a mass or as a whole: *We will lump all our expenses.* 4 form into a lump or lumps: *The pudding lumped because it was not stirred.* 5 a small cube or oblong piece of sugar. 1, 2, 5 *n.,* 3, 4 *v.*

lump sum, a an amount of money that covers the entire cost of something when given in payment: *He paid for the car in a lump sum rather than by instalments.* **b** an amount of money that covers the cost of a number of items: *I was given a lump sum for all my expenses.*

in a lump, as a whole or in one amount.

lump[2] (lump) *Informal.* put up with; endure: *If you don't like it, you can lump it.* *v.*

lump·y (lump′ē) 1 full of lumps: *The gravy is lumpy.* 2 covered with lumps: *This is lumpy ground.* *adj.,* **lump·i·er, lump·i·est.**

lu·nar (lü′nər) 1 of the moon: *a lunar eclipse.* 2 like the moon. *adj.*

lunar month the period of one complete revolution of the moon around the earth; the interval between one new moon and the next, about 29½ days.

lu·na·tic (lü′nə tik) 1 an insane person. 2 insane. 3 extremely foolish; idiotic: *a lunatic search for buried treasure.* 1 *n.,* 2, 3 *adj.*

lunch (lunch) 1 a light meal between breakfast and dinner: *We usually have lunch at noon.* 2 a light meal eaten at any time: *We had a lunch at bedtime.* 3 food for a lunch: *Leave your lunch in the locker.* 4 eat a light meal. 1–3 *n.,* 4 *v.*

lunch·eon (lun′chən) 1 a lunch. 2 a formal lunch. *n.*

lung (lung) either one of the pair of breathing organs found in the chest of man and of other animals with backbones: *The lungs absorb oxygen from the air, give the blood the oxygen it needs, and relieve it of carbon dioxide.* See **kidney** for picture. *n.*

lunge[1] (lunj) 1 any sudden forward movement; a thrust: *The catcher made a lunge toward the ball.* 2 move suddenly forward; thrust: *The dog lunged at the stranger.* 1 *n.,* 2 *v.,* **lunged, lung·ing.**

lunge[2] or **'lunge** (lunj) *Informal.* muskellunge. *n.*

lurch[1] (lėrch) 1 a sudden leaning or roll to one side: *The car gave a lurch and overturned.* 2 make a lurch; stagger: *The wounded deer lurched forward.* 1 *n.,* 2 *v.*

lurch[2] (lėrch) in certain games, a condition in which one player scores nothing or is badly beaten. *n.*

leave in the lurch, leave in a helpless condition or in a difficult situation: *He was counting on them to help him set up the gym for the party, but they left him in the lurch.*

lure (lür) 1 attraction: *Many people feel the lure of the sea.* 2 lead away or into something by awakening desire; attract; tempt: *Bees are lured by the scent of flowers.* 3 a decoy; a bait. 4 attract with a bait: *We lured the fox into a trap.* 1, 3 *n.,* 2, 4 *v.,* **lured, lur·ing.**

lu·rid (lür′id) 1 lighted up with a red or fiery glare: *The sky was lurid with the flames of the burning city.* 2 glaring in brightness or color: *Her dress was a lurid yellow.* 3 terrible; sensational; startling: *The detective told some lurid stories.* *adj.*

lurk (lėrk) stay about without arousing attention; wait out of sight: *A tiger was lurking in the jungle outside the village.* *v.*

lus·cious (lush′əs) 1 delicious; richly sweet: *a luscious peach.* 2 very pleasing to the senses, especially those of taste and smell. *adj.*

lush (lush) 1 tender and juicy; growing thick and green: *Lush grass grew along the river bank.* 2 characterized by abundant growth: *We passed many lush fields.* *adj.*

lus·tre or **lus·ter** (lus′tər) 1 a bright shine on the surface: *the lustre of pearls.* 2 brightness: *Her eyes lost their lustre.* 3 fame; glory; brilliance: *Heroic deeds add lustre to a nation's history.* *n.*

lus·trous (lus′trəs) having lustre; shining; glossy: *lustrous satin.* *adj.*

hat, āge, fär; let, ēqual, tėrm; it, īce
hot, ōpen, ôrder; oil, out; cup, pu̇t, rüle
əbove, takən, pencəl, lemən, circəs
ch, child; ng, long; sh, ship
th, thin; ᴛʜ, then; zh, measure

lus·ty (lus′tē) strong and healthy; full of vigor: *a lusty boy.* *adj.,* **lust·i·er, lust·i·est.**

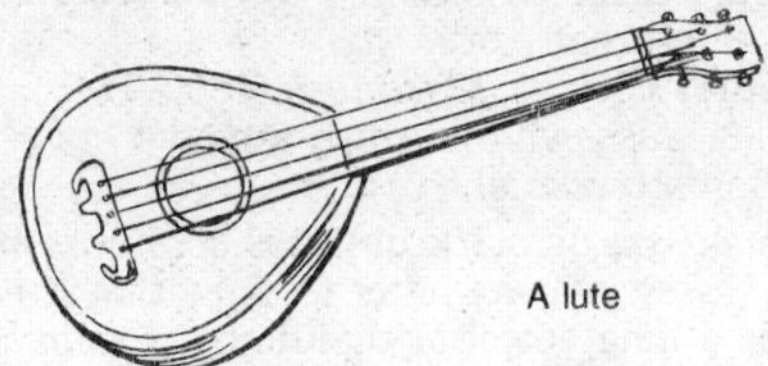

A lute

lute (lüt) a stringed musical instrument, much used in the 1500's and 1600's: *A lute is like a large mandolin and is played by plucking the strings.* *n.*

☛ **Lute** and **loot** are pronounced the same.

lux·u·ri·ant (lug zhür′ē ənt) **1** growing in a vigorous and healthy way; thick and lush: *In spring the grass on our lawn is luxuriant. She has a luxuriant head of hair.* **2** rich in ornament. *adj.* **—lux·u′ri·ant·ly,** *adv.*

☛ **Luxuriant** and **luxurious** are related words with very different meanings.

lux·u·ri·ous (lug zhür′ē əs) **1** fond of luxury; tending toward luxury; self-indulgent. **2** giving luxury; very comfortable and beautiful: *Some theatres are luxurious.* *adj.* **—lux·u′ri·ous·ly,** *adv.*

☛ See note at **luxuriant.**

lux·u·ry (luk′shə rē) **1** the comforts and beauties of life beyond what are really necessary: *After two weeks of being stranded in the wilderness, he thought of his home as luxury.* **2** the use of the best and most costly food, clothes, houses, furniture, and amusements: *The movie star soon became accustomed to luxury.* **3** anything that one enjoys, usually something choice and costly: *He saves some money for luxuries such as fine paintings.* **4** something pleasant but not necessary: *Candy is a luxury.* *n., pl.* **lux·u·ries.**

-ly¹ a suffix meaning in a ____way or manner: *Cheerfully means in a cheerful way. Slightly means in a slight manner.*

-ly² a suffix meaning: **1** like a ____: *Ghostly means like a ghost.* **2** like that of a ____: *Brotherly means like that of a brother.* **3** of each or every____: *Daily means of every day.*

lye (lī) a strong solution used in making soap and in cleaning. *n.*

☛ **Lye** and **lie** are pronounced the same.

ly·ing¹ (lī′ing) **1** the telling of a lie; the habit of telling lies. **2** false; not truthful: *a lying report.* **3** See **lie¹**. 1 *n.,* 2 *adj.,* 3 *v.*

ly·ing² (lī′ing) See **lie²**. *I'm lying down.* *v.*

lymph (limf) a nearly colorless liquid from the tissues of the body, resembling blood without the red corpuscles: *Lymph bathes and nourishes the tissues.* *n.*

lynch (linch) kill or put to death, usually by hanging, without a proper trial: *The angry mob lynched an innocent man.* *v.*

☛ **Lynch** comes from *Lynch's law,* which was named after an American (Virginian) magistrate of the 1700's.

lynx (lingks) **1** a kind of wildcat found in North America, Europe, and Asia, having a short tail, pointed ears with long tufts of hair on them, and large paws: *The two kinds of lynx found in North America are the Canada lynx and the bobcat.* **2** the Canada lynx. See **wildcat** for picture. *n., pl.* **lynx·es** or **lynx.**

A lyre

lyre (līr) an ancient stringed instrument resembling a small harp. *n.*

lyr·ic (lir′ik) **1** a short poem expressing personal emotion: *A love poem, a lament, and a hymn might all be lyrics.* **2** having to do with such poems: *a lyric poet.* **3** of, expressed in, or suitable for song. **4 lyrics,** *pl.* the words for a song. 1, 4 *n.,* 2, 3 *adj.*

lyr·i·cal (lir′ə kəl) **1** emotional; poetic: *She became almost lyrical when she described the scenery.* **2** lyric (defs. 2 and 3). *adj.* **—lyr′i·cal·ly,** *adv.*

m or **M** (em) 1 the 13th letter of the alphabet: *There are two* m's *in* madam. 2 the Roman numeral for 1000. *n., pl.* **m's** or **M's.**

m metre; metres.

ma (mo, mä, or ma) *Informal.* mamma; mother. *n.*

ma'am (mam) *Informal.* madam. *n.*

ma·cad·am (mə kad′əm) a road or pavement made by rolling layers of broken stones until they are smooth and solid. Oil or tar is usually added to bind the stones together. *n.*

☞ Named after John L. *McAdam* (1756–1836), a Scottish engineer, who invented this process of road making.

mac·a·ro·ni (mak′ə rō′nē) a flour paste that has been dried, usually in the form of hollow tubes, to be cooked for food. *n.*

mac·a·roon (mak′ə rün′) a small, very sweet cookie, made of ground almonds or coconut, white of egg, and sugar. *n.*

ma·caw (mə kô′) a large parrot of South and Central America, with a long tail, brilliant feathers, and a harsh voice. *n.*

ma·chet·e (mə shet′ē or mə shet′) a large, heavy knife, used as a tool and weapon in South America, Central America, and the West Indies. *n.*

ma·chine (mə shēn′) 1 an arrangement of fixed and moving parts for doing work, each part having some special job to do: *Sewing machines and washing machines make housework easier.* 2 a device for applying force or changing its direction: *Levers and pulleys are simple machines.* 3 an automobile. 4 make or finish with a machine. 1–3 *n.,* 4 *v.,* **ma·chined, ma·chin·ing.**

machine gun a gun that can keep up a rapid fire of bullets, the firing of one shell starting the machinery that fires the next.

ma·chin·er·y (mə shēn′ ər ē) 1 machines: *There is a lot of machinery in a shoe factory.* 2 the parts or works of a machine: *He examined the machinery of his watch.* 3 any combination of persons or things by which something is kept going or something is done: *Policemen, judges, courts, and prisons are the machinery of the law.* *n., pl.* **ma·chin·er·ies.**

machine shop a workshop where machines or parts of machines are made or repaired.

machine tool a tool or machine worked by power, used to form metal into desired shapes by cutting, hammering, squeezing, etc.

ma·chin·ist (mə shēn′ist) 1 a person who runs a machine. 2 a man who makes and repairs machinery. *n.*

mack·er·el (mak′ər əl) a salt-water fish of the North Atlantic, much used for food. *n., pl.* **mack·er·el** or **mack·er·els.**

mack·i·naw (mak′ə no′ or mak′ə nô′) 1 a kind of short coat made of heavy woollen cloth. 2 a kind of thick woollen blanket that often has bars of color, used in the North and West by Indians, trappers, etc. *n.*

☞ **Mackinaw** comes from the original name for *Mackinac Island* in Lake Huron: *Michilimackinac,* which is from a North American Indian word meaning 'a large turtle.'

mack·in·tosh (mak′ən tosh′) 1 a waterproof coat; a raincoat. 2 waterproof cloth. *n.*

☞ Named after Charles *Macintosh* (1766–1843), a Scottish chemist, who invented a method of waterproofing material.

ma·cron (mak′ron or mā′kron) a short horizontal line (-) placed over a vowel letter to show that it is pronounced as a long vowel or diphthong. *Examples:* cāme, bē. *n.*

mad (mad) 1 out of one's mind; crazy; insane: *A man must be mad to cut himself on purpose.* 2 *Informal.* very angry: *The insult made him mad.* 3 much excited; wild: *The dog made mad efforts to catch up with the automobile.* 4 foolish, unwise: *a mad undertaking.* 5 very lively: *a mad party.* 6 blindly and unreasonably fond: *Some girls are mad about going to dances.* 7 having rabies or hydrophobia: *A mad dog foams at the mouth and may bite people.* *adj.,* **mad·der, mad·dest.** —**mad′ly,** *adv.*

like mad, *Informal.* furiously; very hard or fast: *I ran like mad to catch the train.*

☞ **Mad, crazy, insane** have similar meanings. **Insane** is the proper word to describe someone suffering from severe mental illness: *The man was so worried that he became insane.* **Mad** is used in the same way but often just means very reckless, or foolish: *Crossing the Pacific on a raft seems a mad thing to do.* **Crazy** suggests a more wild or disturbed state: *She is nearly crazy with fear.*

mad·am (mad′əm) a polite title used in speaking to a lady or of a lady: *Madam, would you like a chair?* *n.*

mad·ame (mad′əm or mä däm′) a French title for a married woman. *n., pl.* **mes·dames** (me däm′).

mad·cap (mad′kap′) 1 a person who does wild things without stopping to think first. 2 wild or hasty. 1 *n.,* 2 *adj.*

mad·den (mad′ən) 1 make crazy. 2 make very angry or excited; irritate greatly. *v.*

made (mād) See **make.** *The cook made the cake. It was made of flour, milk, butter, eggs, and sugar.* *v.*

☞ **Made** and **maid** are pronounced the same.

mad·e·moi·selle (mad′ə mə zel′) a French word meaning Miss. *n.*

made-up (mād′up′) 1 invented; not real: *a made-up story.* 2 painted, powdered, etc.: *made-up lips.* *adj.*

mad·house (mad′hous′) 1 an asylum for the insane. 2 a place of uproar and confusion: *The arena was a madhouse after the home team won the championship game.* *n.*

mad·man (mad′man′ or mad′mən) an insane man; a crazy person. *n., pl.* **mad·men** (mad′men′ or mad′mən).

mad·ness (mad′nis) 1 the state or condition of being crazy; the loss of one's mind. 2 a great rage or fury: *In his madness he struck his best friend.* 3 folly: *It was madness to take a sailboat out in that storm.* *n.*

Ma·don·na (mə don′ə) 1 Mary, the mother of Jesus. 2 a picture or statue of her. *n.*

mag·a·zine (mag′ə zēn′ or mag′ə zēn′) 1 a publication issued regularly, containing stories, pictures, etc.: *Most magazines are published either weekly or monthly.* 2 a room in a fort or warship for keeping

hat, āge, fär; let, ēqual, tėrm; it, īce
hot, ōpen, ôrder; oil, out; cup, pu̇t, rüle
əbove, takən, pencəl, lemən, circəs
ch, child; ng, long; sh, ship
th, thin; ᴛʜ, then; zh, measure

The magazine of a rifle

gunpowder and other explosives. **3** a building for storing explosives, guns, food, or other military supplies. **4** a place for holding cartridges in a repeating or automatic gun. **5** a place for holding the roll of film in a camera. *n.*

ma·gen·ta (mə jen′tə) purplish red. *n., adj.*

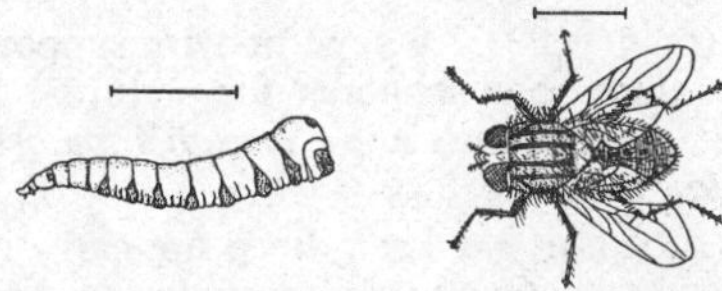
A maggot (at left) and an adult fly (at right). The lines above them show their actual length.

mag·got (mag′ət) a fly in the earliest, legless stage, just after leaving the egg: *Maggots often live in decaying matter. n.*

mag·ic (maj′ik) **1** the pretended art of using secret charms, spirits, etc. to make unnatural things happen: *The fairy's magic changed the brothers into swans.* **2** done by magic or as if by magic: *A magic palace stood in place of their hut.* **3** something that produces results as if by magic: *The magic of her voice charmed the audience.* **4** the art or skill of producing magical effects by tricks or juggling: *The magician pulled flags from his pocket by magic.* 1, 3, 4 *n.,* 2 *adj.*

mag·i·cal (maj′ə kəl) done by magic or as if by magic: *The waving of the magician's wand produced a magical effect. adj.* —**mag′i·cal·ly,** *adv.*

ma·gi·cian (mə jish′ən) **1** a person who uses magic (def. 1): *The wicked magician cast a spell over the princess.* **2** a person who uses magic (def. 4) to entertain: *The magician pulled three rabbits out of his hat. n.*

mag·is·trate (maj′is trāt′) a judge in a county court. *n.*

magistrates' court a court that deals with minor offences.

mag·ma (mag′mə) the very hot, fluid substance that is found below the earth's crust and from which lava and certain rocks are formed. *n.*

mag·nate (mag′nāt) an important or powerful person, especially in business or industry: *a railroad magnate. n.*

mag·ne·sia (mag nē′zhə or mag nē′zē ə) a white, tasteless powder used in medicine as a laxative, and in making fertilizers and some building materials. *n.*
☛ See note at **magnet.**

mag·ne·si·um (mag nē′zē əm or mag nē′zhē əm) a light, silver-white metal that burns with a dazzling white light. *n.*
☛ See note at **magnet.**

mag·net (mag′nit) **1** a stone or piece of metal that attracts iron or steel to it. **2** anything that attracts: *Our rabbits were a magnet that attracted all the children in the neighborhood. n.*
☛ The words **magnet** and **magnesia** both come from a Greek phrase meaning 'stone of *Magnesia,*' an ancient city in Asia Minor. **Magnesium** came later from **magnesia.**

mag·net·ic (mag net′ik) **1** having the properties of a magnet: *the magnetic needle of a compass.* **2** having something to do with magnetism. **3** very attractive: *a magnetic personality. adj.*

magnetic field the space around a magnet or electric current in which its magnetic force is effective.

magnetic pole **1** one of the two poles of a magnet. **2 Magnetic Pole,** one of the two positions on the earth's surface toward which a compass needle points: *The North Magnetic Pole is considerably south of the geographic North Pole.*

mag·net·ism (mag′nə tiz′əm) **1** the properties or qualities of a magnet; the showing of magnetic properties or force. **2** the power to attract or charm: *The boy's magnetism makes him a leader among his schoolmates. n.*

mag·net·ize (mag′nə tīz′) **1** give the properties or qualities of a magnet to: *You can magnetize a needle by rubbing it with a magnet.* **2** attract or influence a person: *Her beautiful voice magnetized the audience. v.,* **mag·net·ized, mag·net·iz·ing.**

mag·ne·to (mag nē′tō) a small machine which uses a magnetic field to produce an electric current: *In some engines, a magneto supplies an electric spark to explode the gasoline vapor. n., pl.* **mag·ne·tos.**

mag·nif·i·cence (mag nif′ə səns) richness of material, color, and ornament; grand beauty; splendor: *We were dazzled by the magnificence of the royal jewels. n.*

mag·nif·i·cent (mag nif′ə sənt) richly colored or decorated; grand; stately; splendid: *the magnificent palace of a king, a magnificent view of the mountains. adj.* —**mag·nif′i·cent·ly,** *adv.*

mag·ni·fy (mag′nə fī′) **1** cause to look larger than the real size: *A microscope magnifies bacteria so that they can be seen and studied.* **2** make too much of; go beyond the truth in telling: *She not only tells tales, but she magnifies them. v.,* **mag·ni·fied, mag·ni·fy·ing.**

magnifying glass a lens or combination of lenses that causes things to look larger.

mag·ni·tude (mag′nə tyüd′ or mag′nə tüd′) **1** greatness of size. **2** great importance or effect: *The war brought problems of very great magnitude to many nations.* **3** a measure of the brightness of a star: *Stars of the first magnitude are the brightest. n.*

A magnolia blossom

mag·no·lia (mag nō′lē ə) a North American tree

having large white, pink, or purplish flowers. *n.*

☛ Named after Pierre *Magnol* (1638–1715), a French scientist.

mag·pie (mag′pī′) **1** a noisy, black-and-white bird having a long tail and short wings. **2** a person who chatters. *n.*

ma·hog·a·ny (mə hog′ə nē) **1** a tree that grows in tropical America. **2** the hard, dark, reddish-brown wood of this tree: *Because mahogany takes a very high polish, it is much used in making furniture.* **3** dark, reddish brown. 1–3 *n., pl.* **ma·hog·a·nies;** 3 *adj.*

maid (mād) **1** a young, unmarried woman; a girl. **2** a woman servant: *a kitchen maid.* **3** See **maid of honor.** *n.*

☛ **Maid** and **made** are pronounced the same.

maid·en (mād′ən) **1** a young, unmarried woman; a girl or maid. **2** of a girl or maid: *maiden grace.* **3** new; untried; unused. **4** first: *A ship's maiden voyage is its first voyage.* **5** unmarried: *a maiden aunt.* 1 *n.,* 2–5 *adj.*

maiden name the family name a woman had before she was married: *Mrs. Brown's maiden name was Fraser.*

maid of honor **1** an unmarried woman who is the chief attendant of the bride at a wedding. **2** an unmarried lady who attends a queen or a princess.

mail[1] (māl) **1** letters, post cards, papers, parcels, etc. sent or to be sent by post. **2** the system by which such mail is sent, managed by the Post Office Department: *You can pay most bills by mail.* **3** all that comes by one post or delivery: *He opened the box to look for the mail.* **4** a train, boat, etc. that carries mail. **5** post; send by mail; put in a mailbox: *He mailed the letter for his mother.* 1–4 *n.,* 5 *v.*

☛ **Mail** and **male** are pronounced the same.

mail[2] (māl) armor made of metal rings, small loops of chain linked together, or plates, for protecting the body against the enemy's arrows, spears, etc. See **coat of mail** for picture. *n.*

☛ See note at **mail**[1].

mail·box (māl′boks′) **1** a public box from which mail is collected; a post box. **2** a private box to which mail is delivered. *n.*

mail·man (māl′man′ or māl′mən) a postman; a man who carries or delivers mail. *n., pl.* **mail·men** (māl′men′ or māl′mən).

maim (mām) cause permanent damage to or loss of a part of the body; cripple or disable: *He lost two toes in the accident, but we were glad that he was not more seriously maimed.* *v.*

main (mān) **1** most important; largest: *the main dish at dinner, the main street of a town.* **2** a large pipe for water, gas, etc.: *When the water main broke, our cellar was flooded.* **3** the open sea; the ocean: *Our daring fleet shall sail the main.* 1 *adj.,* 2, 3 *n.*

in the main, for the most part; chiefly; mostly: *Her grades were excellent in the main.*

with might and main, with all one's force: *They argued with might and main.*

☛ **Main** and **mane** are pronounced the same.

main·land (mān′land′ or mān′lənd) the main part of a continent or land mass; land that is not a small island or peninsula. *n.*

main·land·er (mān′land′ər or mān′lənd ər) a person who lives on the mainland. *n.*

main·ly (mān′lē) for the most part; mostly; chiefly: *He is interested mainly in sports and he neglects his schoolwork.* *adv.*

main·mast (mān′mast′ or mān′məst) the principal mast of a ship. See **schooner** for picture. *n.*

main·sail (mān′sāl′ or mān′səl) the largest sail on the mainmast of a ship. See **schooner** for picture. *n.*

main·spring (mān′spring′) **1** the principal spring in a clock, watch, etc. **2** the chief cause or influence. *n.*

main·stay (mān′stā′) **1** a rope or wire supporting the mainmast of a ship. See **schooner** for picture. **2** the main support: *Loyal friends are a person's mainstay in time of trouble.* *n.*

main·tain (mān tān′) **1** keep; keep up; carry on: *maintain a business. One must maintain one's balance when riding a bicycle.* **2** keep in good repair: *He employs a mechanic to maintain his fleet of trucks.* **3** pay the expenses of; provide for: *He maintains his family.* **4** uphold; argue for; keep to in argument or discussion: *to maintain an opinion; she maintains her innocence.* **5** declare to be true: *She maintained that she was innocent.* *v.*

☛ **Maintain** comes from French but goes back to a Latin phrase meaning 'hold by the hand.'

main·te·nance (mān′tə nəns) **1** maintaining: *Maintenance of quiet is necessary in a hospital.* **2** being maintained; support: *A government collects taxes to pay for its maintenance.* **3** keeping in good repair: *The army devotes much time to the maintenance of its equipment.* **4** enough to support life; a means of living: *His small farm provides a maintenance, but not much more.* *n.*

maize (māz) **1** a plant whose grain grows on large ears; corn. See **corn** for picture. **2** yellow. 1, 2 *n.,* 2 *adj.*

☛ **Maize** and **maze** are pronounced the same.

ma·jes·tic (mə jes′tik) grand; noble; dignified; stately. *adj.* —**ma·jes′ti·cal·ly,** *adv.*

maj·es·ty (maj′is tē) **1** a stately appearance; dignity; nobility: *We were much impressed by the majesty of the coronation ceremony.* **2** supreme power or authority: *Policemen and judges uphold the majesty of the law.* **3 Majesty,** a title used in speaking to or of a king, queen, emperor, empress, etc.: *Your Majesty, His Majesty, Her Majesty.* *n., pl.* **maj·es·ties.**

ma·jor (mā′jər) **1** larger; greater; more important: *The major part of a little baby's life is spent in sleeping.* **2** an officer in the armed forces, ranking next above a captain. 1 *adj.,* 2 *n.*

ma·jor–gen·er·al (mā′jər jen′ə rəl or mā′jər jen′rəl) an officer in the armed forces, senior to a brigadier-general and junior to a lieutenant-general. *n.*

ma·jor·i·ty (mə jôr′ə tē) **1** the larger number or greater part; more than half: *A majority of the students passed the test.* **2** the number by which the votes on one side are more than those on the other: *Since James had 18 votes to John's 12, James had a majority of 6.* **3** the legal age of responsibility: *A person who has reached his majority may manage his own affairs.* *n., pl.* **ma·jor·i·ties.**

hat, āge, fär; let, ēqual, tėrm; it, īce
hot, ōpen, ôrder; oil, out; cup, pu̇t, rüle
əbove, takən, pencəl, lemən, circəs
ch, child; ng, long; sh, ship
th, thin; ᴛʜ, then; zh, measure

make (māk) **1** bring into being; put together; build; form; shape: *to make a rag rug, to make a poem, to make a boat, to make a medicine.* **2** the way in which a thing is made; a style, build, or character: *Do you like the make of that coat?* **3** a kind; a brand: *What make of car is this?* **4** have the qualities needed: *Wood makes a good fire.* **5** cause; bring about: *to make a noise, to make peace.* **6** force to: *Make him stop hitting me.* **7** cause to be or become something: *to make a room warm, to make a fool of oneself.* **8** become; turn out to be: *She will make a good teacher.* **9** get ready for use; arrange: *to make the beds.* **10** earn; gain: *to make good marks, to make one's living.* **11** do; perform: *to make a journey, to make an attempt, to make a mistake.* **12** amount to; add up to; count as: *2 and 3 make 5. That makes 40 cents you owe me.* **13** think of as; figure to be: *I make the distance across the room 3 metres.* **14** reach; arrive at: *Will the ship make harbor?* **15** *Informal.* get on; get a place on: *He made the football team.* **16** go; travel: *Some airplanes make 1000 kilometres per hour.* **17** cause the success of: *One big business deal made the young man.* 1, 4–17 *v.*, **made, mak·ing;** 2, 3 *n.* **—mak′er,** *n.*

make away with, a get rid of. **b** kill. **c** steal: *The treasurer made away with the club's funds.*

make believe, pretend: *The girl liked to make believe she was a queen.*

make fast, attach firmly.

make for, a go toward: *Make for the hills!* **b** help bring about: *Careful driving makes for fewer accidents.*

make off with, steal; take without permission: *He made off with some apples.*

make out, a write out: *He made out his application for camp.* **b** show to be; try to prove: *That makes me out most selfish.* **c** understand: *The boy had a hard time making out the problem.* **d** see with difficulty; distinguish: *I can barely make out what these letters are.* **e** *Informal.* get along; manage: *We must try to make out with what we have.*

make over, a alter; make different: *to make over a dress.* **b** hand over; transfer ownership of: *Grandfather made over his farm to my father.*

make up, a put together: *to make up cloth into a dress.* **b** invent: *to make up a story.* **c** give or do in place of: *to make up for lost time.* **d** become friends again after a quarrel. **e** put paint, powder, or other cosmetics on the face. **f** arrange; set up: *to make up a page of type, to make up an edition of a newspaper.* **g** decide: *Make up your mind.* **h** complete; fill out: *We need two more eggs to make up a dozen.*

make–be·lieve (māk′bi lēv′) **1** pretence: *Fairies live in the land of make-believe.* **2** pretended: *Children often have make-believe playmates.* 1 *n.*, 2 *adj.*

make·shift (māk′shift′) **1** something used for a time in the place of the proper thing: *When the electric lights went out, we used candles as a makeshift.* **2** used for a time instead of the proper thing: *The boys made a makeshift tent out of a blanket.* 1 *n.*, 2 *adj.*

make–up (māk′up′) **1** the way in which a thing is made up or put together; composition: *The make-up of a magazine is either the arrangement of type, illustrations, etc. or the kind of articles, stories, etc. used.* **2** nature; constitution: *People of a nervous make-up are excitable.* **3** the powder, paint, wigs, etc. used by actors taking part in a play: *His make-up was so effective that we didn't recognize him.* **4** powder, rouge, lipstick, etc. put on the face; cosmetics. *n.*

mal·a·dy (mal′ə dē) a sickness, illness, or disease. *n., pl.* **mal·a·dies.**

ma·lar·i·a (mə ler′ē ə) a disease that causes chills, fever, and sweating: *Malaria is transmitted by the bite of certain mosquitoes that have bitten infected persons.* *n.*

☛ **Malaria** comes from an Italian word, a shortening of *mala aria* meaning 'bad air,' for the disease was once thought to be caused by foul air coming from swamps.

male (māl) **1** a man, boy, or he-animal: *All fathers are males.* **2** of or having to do with men or boys: *male love of fighting.* **3** belonging to the sex that can father young: *Bulls and stallions are male animals.* **4** composed of men or boys: *a male choir.* 1 *n.*, 2–4 *adj.*

☛ **Male** and **mail** are pronounced the same.

Mal·e·mute (mal′ə myüt′ or mal′ə müt′) **1** a hardy, strong breed of dog, used for pulling sleds. **2** a member of a group of Eskimos. *n.*

mal·func·tion (mal′fungk′shən) **1** an improper functioning; failure to work or perform: *a malfunction of the body or in a machine.* **2** function badly; work or perform improperly. 1 *n.*, 2 *v.*

mal·ice (mal′is) active ill will; a wish to hurt or make suffer; spite: *She spoke frankly but without malice.* *n.*

ma·li·cious (mə lish′əs) showing ill will; wishing to hurt or make suffer; spiteful: *I think that story is malicious gossip.* *adj.*

ma·lign (mə līn′) **1** speak evil of, often falsely; slander: *You malign him unjustly when you call him stingy, for he gives all he can afford to give.* **2** evil or injurious: *Gambling often has a malign influence.* **3** hateful; malicious. 1 *v.*, 2, 3 *adj.*

ma·lig·nant (mə lig′nənt) **1** extremely evil, hateful, or malicious. **2** extremely harmful; capable of causing death: *Cancer is a malignant growth.* *adj.*

mal·lard (mal′ərd) a kind of wild duck: *The male mallard has a greenish-black head and a white band around his neck.* See **duck** for picture. *n., pl.* **mal·lards** or **mal·lard.**

mal·le·a·ble (mal′ē ə bəl) **1** that can be hammered or pressed into various shapes without being broken: *Gold, silver, copper, and tin are malleable and can be beaten into thin sheets.* **2** adaptable; yielding: *A malleable person is easily persuaded to change his plans.* *adj.*

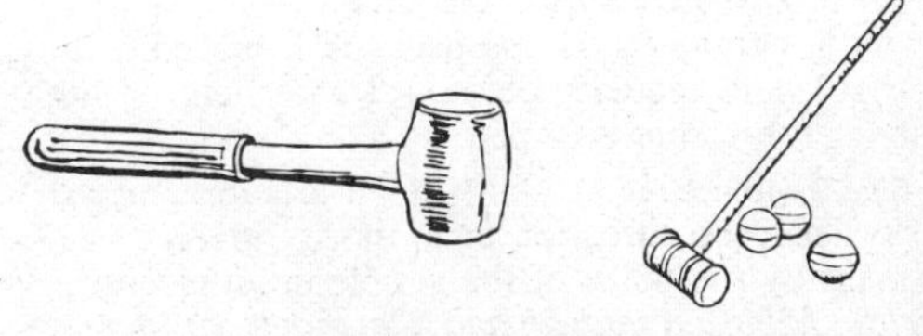

Two kinds of mallet

mal·let (mal′it) **1** a hammer having a head of wood,

rubber, or other fairly soft material. **2** a long-handled wooden mallet used to play croquet or polo. *n.*

mal·nu·tri·tion (mal′nyü trish′ən or mal′nü trish′ən) a poorly nourished condition: *Malnutrition may come from eating the wrong kinds of food as well as from eating too little.* *n.*

malt (molt or môlt) **1** grain, usually barley, that is soaked in water until it sprouts and is then dried and aged: *Malt has a sweet taste and is used in making beer and ale.* **2** prepare with malt: *Malted milk is a food.* 1 *n.*, 2 *v.*

mal·treat (mal trēt′) treat roughly or cruelly; abuse: *Only mean persons maltreat animals.* *v.*

ma·ma or **mam·ma** (mo′mə or mä′mə) mother. *n.*

mam·mal (mam′əl) any of a class of warm-blooded animals that have a backbone, and the females of which have glands that produce milk for feeding their young: *Human beings, cattle, dogs, cats, and whales are all mammals.* *n.*

mam·moth (mam′əth) **1** a large kind of elephant, now extinct, having a hairy skin and long, curved tusks. **2** huge; gigantic: *Digging the St. Lawrence Seaway was certainly a mammoth undertaking.* 1 *n.*, 2 *adj.*

man (man) **1** an adult male human being: *A man is a boy who has grown up.* **2** a human being; a person: *Death comes to all men.* **3** the human race: *Man has existed for thousands of years.* **4** men as a group; the average man: *the man of today.* **5** a male follower, servant, or employee: *Robin Hood and his merry men.* **6** husband: *man and wife.* **7** one of the pieces used in playing such games as chess and checkers. **8** supply with men: *We can man ten ships.* **9** operate or get ready to operate: *She is manning the controls. Man the guns.* 1-7 *n.*, *pl.* **men** (men); 8, 9 *v.*, **manned, mann·ing.**

to a man, every one of them; all: *We accepted his idea to a man.*

Man. Manitoba.

man·age (man′ij) **1** control; conduct; handle; direct: *A good rider manages his horse well. They hired a man to manage the business.* **2** succeed in doing something: *I managed to get the job done.* **3** get along: *We managed on very little money.* *v.*, **man·aged, man·ag·ing.**

man·age·ment (man′ij mənt) **1** control; handling; direction: *The new store failed because of bad management.* **2** the persons that manage a business or an institution: *The management of the store decided to keep it open every evening.* *n.*

man·ag·er (man′ij ər) a person who manages, especially one who manages a business: *a store manager.* *n.*

man·da·rin (man′də rin) **1** a small, sweet, spicy orange with a thin, very loose peel. **2 Mandarin,** the main language of modern China. **3** an official of high rank under the Chinese emperor. *n.*

man·date (man′dāt or man′dit) **1** a command or official order. **2** a direction or authority given to a government by the votes of the people in an election: *The Prime Minister said he had a mandate to increase taxes.* *n.*

man·di·ble (man′də bəl) **1** an organ in insects for seizing and biting: *The ant seized the dead fly with its mandibles.* **2** either part of a bird's beak. **3** a jaw, especially the lower jaw. *n.*

man·do·lin (man′də lin′) a stringed musical instrument. *n.*

mane (mān) the long, heavy hair growing on the back of or around the neck of a horse, a lion, etc. *n.*
☛ **Mane** and **main** are pronounced the same.

ma·neu·ver (mə nü′vər) See **manoeuvre.**

man·ful (man′fəl) manly; brave. *adj.* **—man′ful·ly,** *adv.*

man·ga·nese (mang′gə nēz′ or mang′gə nēs′) a hard, brittle, greyish-white metal: *Manganese is used in making steel, glass, paints, and medicines.* *n.*

mange (mānj) a skin disease of animals, accompanied by scabs and loss of hair. *n.*

man·ger (mān′jər) a box or trough in a barn or stable built against the wall for horses and cows to eat from. See **stall** for picture. *n.*

man·gle (mang′gəl) **1** cut or tear roughly: *His arm was badly mangled in the accident.* **2** do or play badly; ruin: *The child mangled the music because it was too difficult for her to play.* *v.*, **man·gled, man·gling.**

man·go (mang′gō) **1** a tart, juicy fruit with a thick, yellowish-red rind: *Ripe mangoes are delicious.* **2** the tropical tree this fruit grows on. *n.*, *pl.* **man·goes** or **man·gos.**

man·grove (mang′grōv) a tree having branches that send down many roots which look like new trunks or stems but twine together to make dense thickets: *Mangroves grow in the tropics in swamps and along the banks of rivers.* *n.*

man·gy (mān′jē) **1** having the mange; with the hair falling out: *a mangy dog.* **2** shabby and dirty: *a mangy house.* *adj.*

man·hole (man′hōl′) a hole through which a workman may enter a sewer, a steam boiler, etc. to carry out inspection and repairs. *n.*

man·hood (man′hu̇d) **1** the condition or time of being a man. **2** courage; manliness. **3** men as a group: *the manhood of Canada.* *n.*

ma·ni·a (mā′nē ə) **1** a kind of insanity characterized by great excitement. **2** an unusual fondness; a craze: *She has a mania for dancing and going to parties.* *n.*

ma·ni·ac (mā′nē ak′) an insane person; raving lunatic. *n.*

man·i·cure (man′ə kyür′) **1** to care for the hands and fingernails. **2** the care of the hands and fingernails. 1 *v.*, 2 *n.*

man·i·fest (man′ə fest′) **1** clear to the eye or to the mind; plain: *The thief left so many clues that his guilt was manifest.* **2** show plainly; prove. **3** a list of the cargo of a ship or aircraft. 1 *adj.*, 2 *v.*, 3 *n.*

man·i·fes·ta·tion (man′ə fəs tā′shən) showing; making manifest; an act that shows or proves: *Entering the burning building was a manifestation of her courage.* *n.*

man·i·fold (man′ə fōld′) **1** of many kinds; many and various: *manifold duties.* **2** having many parts or forms: *The hero was praised for his manifold goodness.* *adj.*

ma·nip·u·late (mə nip′yə lāt′) **1** handle or operate, especially with skill: *He taught her how to manipulate the gears of the car.* **2** manage by clever use of influence, especially unfair influence: *He so manipulated*

hat, āge, fär; let, ēqual, tėrm; it, īce
hot, ōpen, ôrder; oil, out; cup, pu̇t, rüle
əbove, takən, pencəl, lemən, circəs
ch, child; ng, long; sh, ship
th, thin; ᴛʜ, then; zh, measure

the ball team that he was elected captain. **3** treat unfairly; change for one's own purpose or advantage: *The clerk manipulated the company's accounts to cover up his theft.* *v.,* **ma·nip·u·lat·ed, ma·nip·u·lat·ing.**

man·i·to (man′ə tō′) manitou. *n.*

A compound leaf of the Manitoba maple

Man·i·to·ba maple (man′ə tō′bə) a variety of maple tree common in western Canada.

Man·i·to·ban (man′ə tō′bən) **1** a person born in or living in Manitoba. **2** of or associated with Manitoba. 1 *n.,* 2 *adj.*

man·i·tou (man′ə tü′) the spirit worshipped by some North American Indians as a force of nature. *n.*

man·kind (man′kīnd′ for 1, man′kīnd′ for 2) **1** the human race; all human beings. **2** men; the male sex: *Mankind and womankind both like praise.* *n.*

man·li·ness (man′lē nis) a manly quality; manly behavior. *n.*

man·ly (man′lē) **1** like a man; as a man should be; strong, frank, brave, noble, independent, and honorable: *On his father's death, the boy set to work in a very manly way.* **2** suitable for a man: *Boxing is a manly sport.* *adj.,* **man·li·er, man·li·est.**

man–made (man′mād′) made by man; not natural; artificial: *a man-made lake.* *adj.*

man·na (man′ə) **1** in the Bible, the food miraculously supplied to the people of Israel in the wilderness. **2** a much-needed thing that is unexpectedly supplied: *The gift of $5000 was manna to the poor family.* *n.*

man·ner (man′ər) **1** the way something happens or is done: *The trouble arose in a curious manner.* **2** a person's way of acting or behaving; a style or fashion: *She has a kind manner. He dresses in a strange manner.* **3** kind or kinds: *He saw all manner of birds in the forest.* **4 manners,** *pl.* **a** ways or customs: *Books and movies show us the manners of other times and places.* **b** ways of behaving towards others: *bad manners.* **c** polite behavior: *It is nice to see a child with manners.* *n.*

☞ **Manner** and **manor** are pronounced the same.

ma·noeu·vre or **ma·neu·ver** (mə nü′vər) **1** a planned movement of troops or warships: *The army practises warfare by holding manoeuvres.* **2** perform manoeuvres; cause troops to perform manoeuvres. **3** a skilful plan or movement; clever trick: *His superior manoeuvres won the game.* **4** plan skilfully; use clever tricks; scheme: *He is always manoeuvring to gain some advantage over others.* **5** force by some scheme; get by clever tricks: *She manoeuvred her mother into letting her have a party.* **6** move or manipulate skilfully: *He manoeuvred his car with ease through the heavy traffic.* 1, 3 *n.,* 2, 4–6 *v.,* **ma·noeu·vred** or **ma·neu·vered, ma·noeu·vring** or **ma·neu·ver·ing.**

man–of–war (man′əv wôr′) a warship of a type used in former times. *n., pl.* **men-of-war.**

man·or (man′ər) **1** a large estate, part of which was set aside for the lord, and the rest divided among his peasants: *In the Middle Ages, if the lord sold his manor, the peasants or serfs were sold with it.* **2** a large holding of land. *n.*

☞ **Manor** and **manner** are pronounced the same.

man·sion (man′shən) a large house; a stately residence. *n.*

man·slaugh·ter (man′slo′tər or man′slô′tər) **1** the killing of a human being. **2** in law, the accidental killing of a human being: *The charge against the prisoner was changed from murder to manslaughter.* *n.*

man·tel (man′təl) **1** a shelf above a fireplace. **2** a decorative framework around a fireplace: *a mantel of tile.* See **fireplace** for picture. *n.*

☞ **Mantel** is pronounced like **mantle** but is spelled differently and has a different meaning. Although both go back to the same word in Latin, they came into English at different times and developed in separate ways.

man·tel·piece (man′təl pēs′) a shelf above a fireplace. *n.*

man·tis (man′tis) an insect that holds its forelegs doubled up as if praying. *n.*

man·tle (man′təl) **1** a loose cloak without sleeves. **2** anything that covers like a mantle: *The ground had a mantle of snow.* **3** cover with a mantle. **4** the part of the earth beneath the crust and above the outer core. See **core** for picture. 1, 2, 4 *n.,* 3 *v.,* **man·tled, man·tling.**

☞ See note at **mantel.**

man·u·al (man′yü əl) **1** a book that is easy to understand and use; a handbook: *A cookbook is a manual.* **2** of the hands; done with the hands: *manual labor.* 1 *n.,* 2 *adj.*

manual training training in work done with the hands, especially in making things out of wood, plastic, or metal; practice in various arts and crafts.

man·u·fac·ture (man′yə fak′chər) **1** to make by hand or machine: *A big factory manufactures goods in large quantities by using machines and dividing the work up among many people.* **2** the making of something by hand or by machine, especially in large quantities. **3** invent; make up: *The dishonest lawyer manufactured evidence.* 1, 3 *v.,* **man·u·fac·tured, man·u·fac·tur·ing;** 2 *n.*

man·u·fac·tur·er (man′yə fak′chər ər) a person whose business is manufacturing; the owner of a factory. *n.*

ma·nure (mə nyür′ or mə nür′) **1** a substance, especially animal waste, put on or in the soil to make it productive: *The dirt from a stable is a kind of manure.* **2** put manure in or on. 1 *n.,* 2 *v.,* **ma·nured, ma·nur·ing.**

man·u·script (man′yə skript′) a book or paper written by hand or with a typewriter. *n.*

man·y (men′ē) **1** in great number: *There are many children in the city.* **2** a large number of people or things: *There were many at the fair.* 1 *adj.,* **more, most;** 2 *n., pron.*

a good many, a fairly large number.

map (map) 1 a flat drawing of the earth's surface or of part of it, usually showing countries, towns, rivers, seas, mountains, etc. 2 a drawing of the sky or of part of it, showing the positions of the stars, etc. 3 make a map of; show on a map. 4 plan; arrange in detail: *Each Monday we mapped out the week's work.* 1, 2 *n.,* 3, 4 *v.,* **mapped, map·ping.**

☛ **Map** may refer especially to a plan of roads or other routes on land, while **chart** is used especially for plans showing air or sea routes. An **atlas** is a book of maps covering a large area or the whole world.

ma·ple (mā′pəl) 1 a tree grown for shade, ornament, its wood, or its sap: *There are many kinds of maples.* 2 a flavoring made from maple sugar or maple syrup: *She liked maple ice cream.* *n.*

A maple leaf

maple leaf 1 a leaf of the maple tree. 2 this leaf as a popular Canadian emblem: *'The Maple Leaf Forever' was written in 1867 by Alexander Muir.*

maple sugar sugar made from the sap of one kind of maple.

maple syrup syrup made from the sap of one kind of maple.

mar (mär) spoil the beauty of; damage; injure: *Weeds mar a garden. The nails in the workmen's shoes have marred all our newly finished floors.* *v.,* **marred, mar·ring.**

Mar. March.

ma·ra·ca (mə rä′kə) an instrument consisting of seeds, pebbles, etc. enclosed in a dry gourd and shaken like a rattle: *Maracas are usually played in pairs.* *n.*

mar·a·thon (mar′ə thon′ or mer′ə thon′) 1 a foot race of 26 miles, 385 yards (about 42 kilometres). 2 any long race or contest: *a marathon swim, a marathon dance.* *n.*

☛ Named after *Marathon,* the place in Greece where the ancient Greeks won a victory over the Persians in 490 B.C. A Greek messenger ran 26 miles from Marathon to Athens to bring the news of victory.

mar·ble (mär′bəl) 1 a hard limestone, white or colored, that can take a beautiful polish: *Marble is much used for statues and in buildings.* 2 made of marble. 3 like marble; hard; unfeeling: *a marble heart.* 4 to color in imitation of the patterns in marble: *The kitchen counter top had a marbled pattern.* 5 a small ball of marble, clay, glass, etc. used in games. 6 **marbles,** any game played with marbles. 1, 5, 6 *n.,* 2, 3 *adj.,* 4 *v.,* **mar·bled, mar·bling.**

march (märch) 1 to walk as soldiers do, in time and with steps of the same length. 2 the act or fact of marching: *The students' march was a great success and earned hundreds of dollars for charity.* 3 music meant for marching: *We enjoy listening to marches.* 4 the distance marched. 5 a long, hard walk. 6 to walk or go steadily: *The spy marched to his death.* 7 progress: *History records the march of events.* 8 to cause to march or go: *His mother marched him right off home with her.* 1, 6, 8 *v.,* 2–5, 7 *n.*

steal a march, gain an advantage without being noticed.

March (märch) the third month of the year: *March has 31 days.* *n.*

☛ **March** came into English through Old French from the Latin name for this month, *Martius,* meaning the month of the god Mars.

Mar·di gras (mär′dē grä′) the last day before Lent. It is celebrated in some places with parades and festivities.

☛ **Mardi gras** comes from French and means 'fat Tuesday,' that is, meat-eating Tuesday.

mare (mer) a female horse, donkey, etc. *n.*

mar·ga·rine (mär′jə rin or mär′jə rēn′) a substitute for butter, formerly made from beef fat but now made from vegetable oils: *We like margarine on bread.* *n.*

mar·gin (mär′jən) 1 an edge or border: *There were some lovely willows on the margin of the lake.* 2 the blank space around the writing or printing on a page: *Do not write in the margin.* 3 the space left at the left-hand side, or sometimes on both sides, by a person writing or typing. 4 an extra amount; the amount beyond what is necessary; difference: *We always allow a margin of fifteen minutes in catching a train.* *n.*

mar·i·gold (mar′ə gōld′ or mer′ə gōld′) a plant with yellow, orange, or red flowers. *n.*

ma·ri·na (mə rē′nə) a place along a water front where boats may be moored and where fuel and equipment may be bought. *n.*

☛ See note at **marine.**

ma·rine (mə rēn′) 1 of the sea; found in the sea; produced by the sea: *Seals and whales are marine animals.* 2 of shipping: *marine law.* 3 of a navy: *marine power.* 4 for use at sea: *marine supplies.* 5 shipping; a fleet: *our merchant marine.* 6 a soldier formerly serving only at sea, now also on land and in the air. 1–4 *adj.,* 5, 6 *n.*

☛ **Marine, marina, mariner,** and **maritime** come from Italian, French, and Latin words, but all come originally from Latin *mare* (mä′re) meaning 'sea.'

mar·i·ner (mar′ə nər or mer′ə nər) a sailor; seaman. *n.*

☛ See note at **marine.**

A marionette. One set of strings moves the legs and another moves the arms, head, and body.

mar·i·o·nette (mar′ē ə net′ or mer′ē ə net′) a doll or puppet moved by strings or by the hands. *n.*

hat, āge, fär; let, ēqual, tėrm; it, īce
hot, ōpen, ôrder; oil, out; cup, pu̇t, rüle
əbove, takən, pencəl, lemən, circəs
ch, child; ng, long; sh, ship
th, thin; ᴛʜ, then; zh, measure

mar·i·time (mar′ə tīm′ or mer′ə tīm′) **1** on or near the sea: *Halifax is a maritime city.* **2** living near the sea: *Many maritime peoples live from fishing.* **3** of the sea; having to do with shipping and sailing: *Ships and sailors are governed by maritime law. adj.*

☛ See note at **marine.**

Maritime Provinces the provinces along the east coast of Canada, especially New Brunswick, Nova Scotia, and Prince Edward Island.

☛ The **Maritime Provinces** and **Maritimes** do not usually include Newfoundland; the **Atlantic Provinces** include the Maritime Provinces and Newfoundland.

Mar·i·tim·er (mar′ə tīm′ər or mer′ə tīm′ər) a person born in or living in the Maritime Provinces. *n.*

Mar·i·times (mar′ə tīmz′ or mer′ə tīmz′) the Maritime Provinces. *n. pl.*

mark[1] (märk) **1** a trace or impression made by some object on another: *A line, dot, spot, stain, or scar is a mark.* **2** make a mark on by stamping, cutting, writing, etc.: *Be careful not to mark the table.* **3** an object, arrow, line, dot, etc. put as a guide or sign: *a mark for pilots, the starting mark in a race, a question mark.* **4** show by means of a sign: *Mark all the large cities on this map. This post marks the city limits.* **5** something that indicates quality or character; label: *Remove the price mark from your new suit. Courtesy is a mark of good breeding.* **6** put a sign on an article, as a tag, label, brand, or seal, to show the price, quality, maker, or owner. **7** show clearly; make plain: *A tall pine marks the beginning of the trail. A frown marked her displeasure.* **8** set off; give interest or importance to: *Many important inventions mark the last 150 years.* **9** a cross or other sign made by a person who cannot write, instead of signing his name: *Make your mark here.* **10** a letter or number to show how well one has done; grade or rating: *My mark in arithmetic was B.* **11** give grades to; rate: *The teacher marked our examination papers.* **12** something to be aimed at; target; goal: *Standing there, the lion was an easy mark.* **13** what is usual, proper, or expected; standard: *A tired person does not feel up to the mark.* **14** give attention to; notice; observe; see: *Mark how carefully he moves. Mark well my words.* 1, 3, 5, 9, 10, 12, 13 *n.*, 2, 4, 6–8, 11, 14 *v.* —**mark′er,** *n.*

beside the mark, a not hitting the thing aimed at. **b** having nothing to do with the subject; not appropriate.

make one's mark, succeed; become well known.

mark off or **mark out,** make lines, etc. to show the position of or to separate: *We marked out a tennis court. The hedge marks off one yard from another.*

mark out for, set aside for; select for: *He seemed marked out for trouble.*

mark time, move the feet as in marching, but without going forward.

mark up, a spoil the look of by making marks on: *Don't mark up the desks.* **b** increase the price of.

of mark, important or famous: *That doctor is a man of mark.*

mark[2] (märk) the unit of money in Germany. The mark of West Germany *(Deutsche Mark)* is worth about 30 cents. The mark of East Germany *(Ostmark)* is worth about 45 cents. *n.*

marked (märkt) **1** having a mark or marks on it. **2** very noticeable; very plain: *There are marked differences between an apple and an orange. adj.*

marked man a person, such as a suspected criminal, who is picked out as someone to watch or take action against: *After he was seen near the scene of the murder, John was a marked man.*

mar·ket (mär′kit) **1** a meeting of people for the purpose of buying and selling: *There is a fruit and vegetable market here every Saturday.* **2** an open space or covered building where food, cattle, etc. are shown for sale. **3** buy or sell in a market. **4** sell: *The farmer cannot market all of his wheat.* **5** a store for the sale of food: *a meat market.* **6** the chance to buy or sell: *There is always a market for gold.* **7** the demand for goods: *There was not enough cheese to supply the market.* **8** a region in which goods may be sold: *Great Britain is a market for Canadian cheese.* 1, 2, 5–8 *n.*, 3, 4 *v.*

be in the market for, be a possible buyer of: *Tom is in the market for a new bike.*

mar·ket·place (mär′kət plās′) a place where a market is held. *n.*

mark·ing (mär′king) **1** a mark or marks. **2** the arrangement of marks: *I like the marking on your cat's coat. n.*

marks·man (märks′mən) a person who shoots, especially one who shoots well: *He is noted as a marksman. A good marksman always hits the target. n., pl.* **marks·men** (märks′mən).

mar·lin (mär′lən) a large sea fish related to the swordfish. *n.*

mar·ma·lade (mär′mə lād′) a preserve similar to jam, made of oranges or similar fruit: *In making marmalade, the peel is usually sliced and boiled with the fruit. n.*

mar·mo·set (mär′mə set′ or mär′mə zet′) a very small monkey having soft, thick fur: *Marmosets live in Central and South America. n.*

mar·mot (mär′mət) one of several kinds of animal related to the squirrel, found in North America, Europe, and Asia, having a thick body and a bushy tail: *Groundhogs, or woodchucks, and prairie dogs are marmots. n.*

ma·roon[1] (mə rün′) dark brownish-red. *adj., n.*

ma·roon[2] (mə rün′) **1** put a person ashore and leave him on a desert island or in a desolate place: *Pirates used to maroon people on desert islands.* **2** leave in a lonely, helpless position: *During the storm we were marooned in a cabin miles from town. v.*

mar·quess (mär′kwis) *Esp. Brit.* marquis. *n.*

mar·quis (mär′kwis or mär kē′) a nobleman ranking below a duke and above an earl or count. *n.*

mar·riage (mar′ij or mer′ij) **1** married life; living together as husband and wife: *We wished the bride and groom a happy marriage.* **2** the ceremony of being married; a wedding. **3** a close union: *The marriage of words and melody in that song was unusually effective. n.*

mar·ried (mar′ēd or mer′ēd) 1 living together as husband and wife. 2 having a husband or wife. 3 of husband and wife: *Married life has many duties.* 4 See **marry.** 1–3 *adj.,* 4 *v.*

mar·row[1] (mar′ō or mer′ō) 1 a soft substance that fills the hollow, central part of most bones. 2 the inmost or important part: *The icy wind chilled me to the marrow.* *n.*

mar·row[2] (mar′ō or mer′ō) a kind of oblong squash; a vegetable marrow: *Some ripe marrows have a light-yellow skin.* *n.*

mar·ry (mar′ē or mer′ē) 1 join as husband and wife: *The minister married them.* 2 take as husband or wife: *James planned to marry Ida.* 3 become married: *She married late in life.* *v.,* **mar·ried, mar·ry·ing.**

Mars (märz) 1 the Roman god of war. 2 the planet next beyond the earth: *Mars is the fourth planet in order from the sun.* *n.*

marsh (märsh) low land covered at times by water; soft, wet land; a swamp. *n.*

mar·shal (mär′shəl) 1 an officer of various kinds: *a fire marshal.* 2 a high officer in an army: *a field marshal.* 3 a person who arranges the order of march in a parade: *a parade marshal.* 4 arrange in proper order: *He took great care in marshalling his facts for the debate.* 5 a person in charge of events or ceremonies. 6 conduct with ceremony: *The foreign visitor was marshalled into the presence of the king.* 1–3, 5 *n.,* 4, 6 *v.,* **mar·shalled** or **mar·shaled, mar·shal·ling** or **mar·shal·ing.**

☛ **Marshal** and **martial** are pronounced the same.

marsh·mal·low (märsh′mal′ō or märsh′mel′ō) a soft, usually white, spongy candy, covered with powdered sugar. *n.*

marsh·y (mär′shē) soft and wet like a marsh: *a marshy field.* *adj.,* **marsh·i·er, marsh·i·est.**

mar·su·pi·al (mär sü′pē əl) an animal that carries its young in a pouch: *Kangaroos and opossums are marsupials.* *n.*

mart (märt) a market; a centre of trade: *Toronto and Montreal are the great marts of Canada.* *n.*

mar·ten (mär′tən) 1 a slender animal like a weasel, but larger, valued for its fur. 2 its fur. *n.*

☛ **Marten** and **martin** are pronounced the same.

mar·tial (mär′shəl) 1 of war; suitable for war: *martial music.* 2 fond of fighting; warlike; brave: *a man of martial spirit.* *adj.*

☛ **Martial** and **marshal** are pronounced the same.

Mar·tian (mär′shən) 1 of the planet Mars. 2 a supposed inhabitant of the planet Mars. 1 *adj.,* 2 *n.*

mar·tin (mär′tən) a large swallow with a short beak and a forked tail. *n.*

☛ **Martin** and **marten** are pronounced the same.

mar·tyr (mär′tər) 1 a person who is put to death or is made to suffer greatly because of his religion or other beliefs. 2 put a person to death or torture because of his religion or other beliefs. 1 *n.,* 2 *v.*

mar·vel (mär′vəl) 1 something wonderful; an astonishing thing: *Television and the airplane are among the marvels of invention.* 2 be filled with wonder; be astonished: *She marvelled at the beautiful sunset.* 1 *n.,* 2 *v.,* **mar·velled** or **mar·veled, mar·vel·ling** or **mar·vel·ing.**

mar·vel·lous or **mar·vel·ous** (mär′vəl əs) 1 causing wonder; extraordinary. 2 improbable; imaginative: *Children like hearing of marvellous events, such as those in the tale of Aladdin and his lamp.* 3 *Informal.* excellent; splendid; fine: *a marvellous time.* *adj.*

mas·cot (mas′kot) an animal, person, or thing supposed to bring good luck: *The boys kept the stray dog as a mascot.* *n.*

mas·cu·line (mas′kyə lin) 1 of men; male. 2 like a man; manly; strong; vigorous: *masculine courage.* *adj.*

mash (mash) 1 a soft mixture; a soft mass. 2 beat into a soft mass; crush to a uniform mass: *I'll mash the potatoes.* 3 a warm mixture of bran or meal and water for horses and other animals. 1, 3 *n.,* 2 *v.*

mask (mask) 1 a covering for the face, worn for disguise, for protection, or in fun: *a Halloween mask. The burglar wore a mask.* 2 cover the face with a mask. 3 a clay, wax, or plaster likeness of a person's face. 4 a disguise: *He hid his evil plans under a mask of friendship.* 5 to hide or disguise: *A smile masked his disappointment.* 1, 3, 4 *n.,* 2, 5 *v.*

☛ **Mask** and **masque** are pronounced the same.

ma·son (mā′sən) a man whose work is building with stone, brick, or similar materials. *n.*

Masonry

ma·son·ry (mā′sən rē) 1 the work done by a mason; walls, chimneys, etc. made of stone, brick, or similar materials. 2 the trade or skill of a mason. *n., pl.* **ma·son·ries.**

masque (mask) 1 an amateur dramatic entertainment, with fine costumes and scenery: *Masques were often given in England in the 16th and 17th centuries at court and at the homes of nobles.* 2 a masquerade. *n.*

☛ **Masque** and **mask** are pronounced the same.

mas·quer·ade (mas′kər ād′) 1 a party or dance at which masks and fancy costumes are worn. 2 take part in a masquerade. 3 a disguise; a false pretence. 4 disguise oneself; go about under false pretences: *The king masqueraded as a beggar to find out if his people really liked him.* 1, 3 *n.,* 2, 4 *v.,* **mas·quer·ad·ed, mas·quer·ad·ing.**

mass[1] (mas) 1 a lump: *a mass of dough.* 2 a large quantity together: *a mass of flowers.* 3 form or collect into a mass: *It would be better to mass the peonies behind the roses than to mix them.* 4 the majority; the greater part: *the great mass of men.* 5 on a large scale: *mass buying.* 6 bulk; size: *the huge mass of an iceberg.* 7 the quantity of matter anything contains: *The mass of a piece of lead is not changed by melting it.* 8 **the masses,** *pl.* the common people; the general population: *Most television programs are entertainment for the masses.* 1, 2, 4, 6–8 *n.,* 3 *v.,* 5 *adj.*

hat, āge, fär; let, ēqual, tėrm; it, īce
hot, ōpen, ôrder; oil, out; cup, pu̇t, rüle
əbove, takən, pencəl, lemən, circəs
ch, child; ng, long; sh, ship
th, thin; ᴛʜ, then; zh, measure

Mass or **mass²** (mas) 1 the central service of worship in the Roman Catholic Church and in some other churches: *The family went to Mass.* 2 a piece of music written for certain parts of the Mass. *n.*

mas·sa·cre (mas′ə kər) 1 a wholesale, pitiless slaughter of people or animals. 2 kill many people or animals needlessly or cruelly. 1 *n.*, 2 *v.*, **mas·sa·cred, mas·sa·cring.**

mas·sage (mə säzh′) 1 a rubbing and kneading of the muscles and joints to make them work better and to increase the circulation of the blood: *One feels good after a thorough massage.* 2 give a massage to: *Let me massage your back for you.* 1 *n.*, 2 *v.*, **mas·saged, mas·sag·ing.**

mas·sive (mas′iv) 1 big and heavy; large and solid: *a massive wrestler.* 2 giving the impression of being large and broad: *a massive forehead. adj.*

mass media the various modern means of communication that reach a vast audience, such as television, radio, motion pictures, newspapers, and magazines.

mast (mast) 1 a long pole of wood or steel set upright on a ship to support the sails and rigging. See **schooner** for picture. 2 any tall, upright pole: *a flag mast, a tall TV mast. n.*
before the mast, serving as an ordinary sailor, because sailors (not officers) used to sleep in the forward part of the ship.

mas·ter (mas′tər) 1 a person who rules or commands people or things; an employer; an owner; the one in control; the head of a household, ship, etc. 2 a male teacher, especially in private schools. 3 a title of respect for a boy: *First prize goes to Master Henry Butler.* 4 an expert, such as a great artist or a skilled workman. 5 a picture by a great artist: *an old master.* 6 of a master; by a master. 7 main; controlling: *a master plan.* 8 become the master of; conquer or control: *She learned to master her temper.* 9 learn; become skilful at: *He has mastered riding his bicycle.* 10 See **master key.** 1–5, 10 *n.*, 6, 7 *adj.*, 8, 9 *v.*

mas·ter·ful (mas′tər fəl) 1 fond of power or authority; domineering. 2 expert; skilful; masterly: *The actor gave a masterful performance. adj.*
—mas′ter·ful·ly, *adv.*

master key a key that opens all the locks in a building, apartment block, etc.

mas·ter·ly (mas′tər lē) expert; skilful: *Emily Carr was a masterly painter. adj.*

mas·ter·piece (mas′tər pēs′) 1 anything done or made with wonderful skill; a perfect piece of art or workmanship. 2 a person's greatest piece of work. *n.*

mas·ter·y (mas′tər ē) 1 power such as a master has; rule; control. 2 the upper hand; victory: *Two teams competed for mastery.* 3 very great skill or knowledge: *Our teacher has a mastery of many subjects. n., pl.* **mas·ter·ies.**

mast·head (mast′hed′) the top of a ship's mast. *n.*

mas·tiff (mas′tif) a large, strong dog with drooping ears and hanging jowls. *n.*

mat (mat) 1 a piece of fabric made of woven rushes, straw, rope, fibre, etc. and used for covering a floor, wiping mud from the shoes, etc.: *A mat is like a small rug.* 2 a piece of material to put under a dish, vase, lamp, etc.: *A mat is often put under a hot dish to protect the table.* 3 anything growing thickly packed or tangled together: *a mat of weeds, a mat of hair.* 4 pack or tangle together like a mat: *The swimmer's wet hair was matted. The fur collar mats when it gets wet.* 1–3 *n.*, 4 *v.*, **mat·ted, mat·ting.**

mat·a·dor (mat′ə dôr′) the chief performer in a bullfight: *The matador kills the bull with his sword. n.*

match¹ (mach) a short, slender piece of wood or pasteboard, tipped with a mixture that takes fire when rubbed on a rough or specially prepared surface. *n.*

match² (mach) 1 a person or thing equal to another or much like another; an equal; a mate: *A boy is not a match for a man.* 2 be equal to in a contest: *No one could match the skill of the unknown archer.* 3 two persons or things that are alike or go well together: *Those two horses make a good match.* 4 be alike; go well together: *The rugs and the wallpaper match.* 5 find the equal of or one exactly like: *to match a vase so as to have a pair.* 6 a game or contest: *a boxing match, a tennis match.* 7 try one's skill, strength, etc. against; oppose: *Harry matched his strength against Ray's.* 8 a marriage: *David and Linda made a match of it.* 9 marry: *The duke matched his daughter with the king's son.* 10 a person considered as a possible husband or wife: *That young man was considered a good match.* 1, 3, 6, 8, 10 *n.*, 2, 4, 5, 7, 9 *v.*

match·less (mach′lis) so great or wonderful that it cannot be equalled. *adj.*

match·lock (mach′lok′) an old form of gun fired by lighting the charge of powder with a wick or cord. *n.*

mate (māt) 1 one of a pair: *Where is the mate to this glove?* 2 either of two animals or birds (male and female) who have come together as a pair: *The eagle mourned his dead mate.* 3 put, bring, or come together as a pair: *Birds mate in the spring.* 4 a husband or wife. 5 marry. 6 the officer of a ship who is one rank below the captain: *On large ships there is usually more than one mate: a first mate, a second mate, and, sometimes, a third mate.* 7 an assistant. 8 a companion or fellow worker: *John and Bill were mates in the army.* 1, 2, 4, 6–8 *n.*, 3, 5 *v.*, **mat·ed, mat·ing.**

ma·te·ri·al (mə tēr′ē əl) 1 what is used to make or do something: *dress material, building materials, writing materials, the material of which history is made.* 2 of matter or things; physical: *the material world.* 3 of the body: *Food and shelter are material comforts.* 4 that matters; important: *Hard work was a material factor in his success.* 1 *n.*, 2–4 *adj.*

ma·te·ri·al·ize (mə tēr′ē əl īz′) 1 become an actual fact; be realized: *Our plan for the party did not materialize.* 2 appear or cause to appear in material or bodily form: *A spirit materialized from the smoke of the magician's fire. v.*

ma·te·ri·al·ly (mə tēr′ē əl ē) 1 physically: *He improved materially and morally.* 2 considerably; greatly: *The tide helped the progress of the boat materially. adv.*

ma·ter·nal (mə tėr′nəl) 1 of or like a mother; motherly. 2 related on the mother's side of the family: *Everyone has two paternal grandparents and two maternal grandparents. adj.*

☛ **Maternal, matrimony,** and **matron** all come originally from the Latin word *mater,* meaning 'mother.'

math (math) *Informal.* mathematics. *n.*

math·e·mat·i·cal (math′ə mat′ə kəl) 1 of mathematics; having something to do with mathematics: *Mathematical problems are not always easy.* 2 exact; accurate: *She drew the diagram with mathematical correctness. adj.* —**math′e·mat′i·cal·ly,** *adv.*

math·e·ma·ti·cian (math′ə mə tish′ən) a person skilled in mathematics or whose work is mathematics. *n.*

math·e·mat·ics (math′ə mat′iks) the study of number, measurement, and space: *Arithmetic is one branch of mathematics. n.*

mat·i·née or **mat·i·nee** (mat′ə nā′ or mat′ə nā′) a dramatic or musical performance held in the afternoon. *n.*

mat·ri·mo·ny (mat′rə mō′nē) marriage. *n.*

☛ See note at **maternal.**

ma·tron (mā′trən) 1 an older married woman or widow. 2 a woman who manages the household matters of a hospital, school, or other institution. *n.*

☛ See note at **maternal.**

mat·ter (mat′ər) 1 what things are made of; material; substance: *Matter occupies space.* 2 an affair: *business matters, a matter of life and death.* 3 what is said or written, thought of apart from the way in which it is said or written; content: *There was very little matter of interest in his speech.* 4 grounds or cause; basis: *If a man is robbed, he has matter for complaint to the police.* 5 an instance or case; a thing: *a matter of fact, a matter of record, a matter of business.* 6 things written or printed: *reading matter.* 7 an amount or quantity: *a matter of two days, a matter of ten dollars.* 8 importance: *Let it go since it is of no matter.* 9 be important: *Nothing seems to matter when you are very sick.* 1–8 *n.,* 9 *v.*

as a matter of fact, in truth; in reality.

for that matter, so far as that is concerned.

matter of course, something that is to be expected.

no matter, a it is not important. **b** regardless of: *He wants a bicycle, no matter what it costs.*

What is the matter? What is wrong?

mat·ter–of–fact (mat′ər əv fakt′) sticking to facts; not imaginative or fanciful: *a matter-of-fact report. adj.*

mat·ting (mat′ing) fabric of grass, straw, hemp, or other fibre, used for covering floors, for mats, for wrapping material, etc. *n.*

mat·tress (mat′ris) a thick pad made of cotton, foam rubber, hair, straw, or other material encased in a covering of strong cloth, and used on a bed or as a bed: *Many mattresses have springs inside. n.*

ma·ture (mə chür′ or mə tyür′) 1 ripe or full-grown: *Grain is harvested when it is mature.* 2 indicating that full development has been reached: *a mature face, mature thinking.* 3 ripen; come or bring to full growth: *These apples are maturing fast.* 4 fully worked out; carefully thought out; fully developed: *By next year we will have mature plans for the subway.* 5 develop fully: *He matured his plans.* 1, 2, 4 *adj.,* 3, 5 *v.,* **ma·tured, ma·tur·ing.**

ma·tu·ri·ty (mə chür′ə tē or mə tyür′ə tē) 1 a state of ripeness; full development: *She had reached maturity by the time she was twenty.* 2 the condition of being completed or ready: *When their plans reached maturity, they were able to begin. n.*

maul (mol or môl) 1 beat and pull about; handle roughly: *Don't maul the cat.* 2 a very heavy hammer or mallet. 1 *v.,* 2 *n.*

mau·so·le·um (mo′sə lē′əm or mô′sə lē′əm) a large, magnificent tomb. *n.*

mauve (mōv, mov, or môv) delicate, pale purple. *n., adj.*

maw (mo or mô) 1 the mouth and throat of an animal, especially a meat-eating animal. 2 the stomach of an animal or bird. *n.*

max·im (mak′səm) a rule of conduct; a proverb: *'A stitch in time saves nine' and 'Look before you leap' are maxims. n.*

max·i·mum (mak′sə məm) 1 the largest or highest amount; the greatest possible amount: *25 kilometres in one day was the maximum that any of our club walked last summer.* 2 largest; highest; greatest possible: *The maximum score on this test is 100.* 1 *n., pl.* **max·i·mums** or **max·i·ma** (mak′sə mə); 2 *adj.*

may (mā) 1 be permitted or allowed to: *You may go now. May I have an apple?* 2 be possible that it will: *It may rain tomorrow. The train may be late.* 3 it is hoped that: *May you have a pleasant trip. v.,* **might.**

☛ See note at **can.**

May (mā) the fifth month of the year: *May has 31 days. n.*

☛ **May** came into English through Old French from the Latin name for this month, *Maius,* meaning the month of the goddess Maia.

Ma·ya (mä′yə) one of an ancient Indian people who lived in Central America and Mexico: *The Mayas had a high degree of civilization from about A.D. 350 to about A.D. 800, long before they were discovered by the Spaniards. n., pl.* **Ma·yas.** —**Ma′yan,** *adj., n.*

may·be (mā′bē) possibly or perhaps; it may be so. *adv.*

☛ **Maybe** as an adverb is one word: *Maybe it will rain tomorrow.* **May be** as a verb phrase is two words: *He may be home soon.*

May·day (mā′dā′) an international signal of distress used in emergencies by ships and aircraft. *n.*

May Day the first day of May, celebrated by hanging May baskets, crowning the queen of the May, dancing around a pole decorated with flowers or ribbons, etc.: *May Day is the day chosen by the workers of many countries as a day for celebrating the dignity of labor.*

may·on·naise (mā′ə nāz′) a thick dressing for salads, made of egg yolk, oil, vinegar or lemon juice, and seasoning. *n.*

may·or (mā′ər) the person at the head of the government of a city, town, or village. *n.*

maze (māz) 1 a network of paths through which it is hard to find one's way: *A guide led us through the maze of caves.* 2 a state of confusion; a muddled condition: *He was in such a maze that he couldn't speak. n.*

hat, āge, fär; let, ēqual, tėrm; it, īce
hot, ōpen, ôrder; oil, out; cup, pu̇t, rüle
əbove, takən, pencəl, lemən, circəs
ch, child; ng, long; sh, ship
th, thin; ᴛʜ, then; zh, measure

☛ **Maze** and **maize** are pronounced the same.

mbar millibar; millibars.

Mc·In·tosh (mak′ən tosh′) a bright-red winter apple having crisp, white flesh. *n.*

☛ Named after John *McIntosh,* an Ontario farmer, who found an apple tree of this kind while clearing his farm in 1811.

McIntosh Red the McIntosh apple.

M.D. Doctor of Medicine.

me (mē) I and **me** refer to the person speaking: *She said, 'Give the dog to me. I like it and it likes me.' pron.*

☛ It is good English to say *It is me* (or *It's me)* in speech, though some people consider *It is I* to be correct in writing. Except in writing conversation, *It's me* can usually be avoided in written work.

mead[1] (mēd) *Poetic.* meadow. *n.*

mead[2] (mēd) an alcoholic drink made from honey and water. *n.*

mead·ow (med′ō) **1** a piece of grassy land, especially one used for growing hay. **2** low, grassy land near a stream. *n.*

A western meadow lark — about 25 cm long with the tail

meadow lark a bird of North America about as big as a robin, having a yellow breast marked with black.

mea·gre or **mea·ger** (mē′gər) **1** poor or scanty: *a meagre meal.* **2** thin or lean: *a meagre face. adj.*

meal[1] (mēl) **1** breakfast, lunch, dinner, supper, or tea. **2** the food eaten or served at any one time. *n.*

meal[2] (mēl) **1** grain ground up: *corn meal.* **2** anything ground to a powder. *n.*

meal·y (mēl′ē) like meal; dry and powdery: *mealy potatoes. adj.,* **meal·i·er, meal·i·est.**

mean[1] (mēn) **1** refer to; denote: *The word 'meat' means 'animal flesh used for food.' We use dictionaries to learn what words mean.* **2** have as its thought or message: *Can you make out what this sentence means?* **3** be a sign of; indicate: *What is that look supposed to mean?* **4** intend; have as a purpose; have in mind: *Do you think they mean to fight us? v.,* **meant, mean·ing.**

mean well by, have kindly feelings toward.

☛ **Mean** and **mien** are pronounced the same.

mean[2] (mēn) **1** not noble; petty; unkind: *It is mean to spread gossip.* **2** of low quality or grade; poor: *'He is no mean scholar' means 'He is a good scholar.'* **3** low in social position or rank; humble: *A peasant is of mean birth; a king is of noble birth.* **4** of poor appearance; shabby: *The poor widow lived in a mean hut.* **5** stingy or selfish: *A miser is mean about money.* **6** *Informal.* hard to manage; troublesome; bad-tempered: *a mean horse. adj.*

☛ See note at **mean**[1].

mean[3] (mēn) **1** average; halfway between two extremes: *The mean number between 3 and 9 is 6.* **2** a condition, quality, or course of action halfway between two extremes: *For an adult, eight hours is a happy mean between too much sleep and too little.* **3** in mathematics, the average: *The mean of 3 and 9 is 6.* **4** See **means.** 1 *adj.,* 2–4 *n.*

☛ See note at **mean**[1].

me·an·der (mē an′dər) **1** follow a winding course: *A brook meanders through the meadow.* **2** to wander aimlessly: *We were meandering through the park. v.*

mean·ing (mēn′ing) **1** that which is meant or intended: *The meaning of that sentence is clear.* **2** that means something; expressive: *a meaning look.* 1 *n.,* 2 *adj.*

mean·ness (mēn′nis) **1** being selfish in small things; stinginess. **2** being mean in grade or quality; poorness. **3** a mean act. *n.*

means (mēnz) **1** the method or methods by which something is made to happen or brought about: *The airplane is a fast means of travel. We won the game by fair means.* **2** riches; wealth: *He is a man of means. n.*

by all means, without fail; certainly: *By all means visit me one day.*

by any means, in any possible way; at any cost.

by means of, by the use of; through; with: *I found my dog by means of a notice in the paper.*

by no means, certainly not; not at all; in no way: *This work is by no means easy.*

☛ **Means** (def. 1) can be singular or plural. **Means** (def. 2) is always plural.

meant (ment) See **mean**[1]. *He explained what he meant. That sign was meant as a warning. v.*

mean·time (mēn′tīm′) **1** the time between: *The carnival opens Friday, and in the meantime we will make our costumes.* **2** in the time between: *Classes finish at 12 noon and begin again at 2 p.m.; meantime we can swim and have lunch.* 1 *n.,* 2 *adv.*

mean·while (mēn′wīl′ or mēn′hwīl′) meantime. *n., adv.*

mea·sles (mē′zəlz) **1** an infectious disease characterized by a bad cold, fever, and a breaking out of small, red spots on the skin: *Measles is a disease that is much more common in children than in grown-ups.* **2** a disease resembling measles but less severe; German measles. *n.*

mea·sly (mē′zlē) *Slang.* scanty; meagre: *My son thinks he gets a measly allowance. adj.,* **mea·sli·er, mea·sli·est.**

meas·ure (mezh′ər) **1** find out the size, amount, length, width, height, depth, etc. of anything, usually by means of some kind of gauge: *When we measured the room, we found that it was 6 metres long, 4.5 metres wide, and 2.2 metres high. We measured the capacity of the pail by finding out how many litres of water it would hold.* **2** mark off or out in metres, grams, litres, etc.: *Measure off 2 metres of this silk. Measure out 5 kilograms of potatoes.* **3** compare with a standard or with some other person or thing by estimating, judging, or acting: *The soldier measured his strength with that of his enemy in a hand-to-hand fight.* **4** be of a certain size or amount: *Buy some paper that measures 330 by 203 millimetres.* **5** size or amount: *His waist measure is 70 centimetres.* **Short measure** means less than it should be; **full measure** means all it should be. **6** serve as a means of measuring: *A clock measures time.* **7** something with which to measure: *A teaspoon, a metre-stick, and a litre jug are useful measures.* **8** a unit or standard of measure, such as a metre, hectare, kilogram, or litre. **9** a system of measurement: *liquid measure, dry measure, square measure.* **10** a limit or bound: *Her joy knew no measure. His delight was beyond measure.* **11** quantity, extent, degree, or proportion: *Accidents can in great measure be prevented. The measure of his courage was remarkable.* **12** a bar of music. See **bar** for picture. **13** an action meant as the means to an end: *What measures shall we take to find out who the thief was?* **14** a proposed law; a law: *This measure has passed the Senate.* 1–4, 6 *v.,* **meas·ured, meas·ur·ing;** 5, 7–14 *n.*

measure up, have the necessary features; meet a required standard: *The party did not measure up to her expectations.*

meas·ure·ment (mezh′ər mənt) **1** measuring or finding the size, quantity, or amount: *The measurement of length by a metre-stick is easy.* **2** the size found by measuring: *The measurements of the room are 6 by 4.5 metres. n.*

meat (mēt) **1** animal flesh used for food: *Fish and poultry are usually not called meat.* **2** food: *meat and drink.* **3** the part of anything that can be eaten: *The meat of the walnut is tasty.* **4** the essential part or parts: *the meat of an argument, the meat of a book. n.*

☛ **Meat, meet,** and **mete** are pronounced the same.

Mec·ca (mek′ə) **1** one of the two capitals of Saudi Arabia, in the western part: *Because Mohammed was born there, Moslems turn toward Mecca when praying and go there on pilgrimages.* **2** any place that pilgrims, tourists, and others long to visit. *n.*

me·chan·ic (mə kan′ik) a person skilled with tools, especially one who makes, repairs, or uses machines: *an automobile mechanic. n.*

me·chan·i·cal (mə kan′ə kəl) **1** having to do with machinery or mechanisms: *Mechanical problems are usually more interesting to boys than to girls.* **2** made or worked by machinery. **3** like a machine; without expression: *Her reading is very mechanical. adj.* **—me·chan′i·cal·ly,** *adv.*

me·chan·ics (mə kan′iks) **1** the science dealing with force and motion. **2** knowledge about machinery. *n.*

mech·a·nism (mek′ə niz′əm) **1** a machine or its working parts: *Something must be wrong with the mechanism of our refrigerator.* **2** a system of parts working together as the parts of a machine do: *the mechanism of the body.* **3** the means or way by which something is done: *Committees are a useful mechanism for getting things done. n.*

mech·a·nize (mek′ə nīz′) **1** do by machinery, rather than by hand: *Much housework can be mechanized.* **2** replace men or animals by machinery in a business, etc. *v.,* **mech·a·nized, mech·a·niz·ing.**

med·al (med′əl) a small piece of metal, often resembling a coin, stamped with a design and words: *The captain won a medal for bravery. She won the gold medal for having the highest marks in the school. A medal was struck to commemorate the moon landing. n.*

☛ **Medal** and **meddle** are pronounced the same.

me·dal·lion (mə dal′yən) **1** a large medal. **2** a round or oval design or ornament: *A design on a book or a pattern in lace may be called a medallion. n.*

med·dle (med′əl) busy oneself with or in other people's things or affairs without being asked or needed: *Don't meddle with my toys. That busybody has been meddling in my business. v.,* **med·dled, med·dling. —med′dler,** *n.*

☛ **Meddle** and **medal** are pronounced the same.

med·dle·some (med′əl səm) meddling; interfering; likely to meddle in other people's affairs. *adj.*

me·di·a (mē′dē ə) a plural of **medium** (defs. 3 and 4): *Newspapers, magazines, and billboards are important media for advertising. n.*

me·di·ae·val (mē′dē ē′vəl or med′ē ē′vəl) See **medieval.**

me·di·ate (mē′dē āt′) **1** come in to help settle a dispute; act in order to bring about an agreement between persons or sides: *Mother mediated in the quarrel between the two boys.* **2** bring about by acting as a go-between: *The judge mediated a settlement of the strike. v.,* **me·di·at·ed, me·di·at·ing.**

med·i·cal (med′ə kəl) having to do with healing or with the science and art of medicine: *medical advice, medical schools, medical supplies. adj.*

med·i·care (med′ə ker′) a government program of insurance for paying hospital and other medical expenses. *n.*

me·dic·i·nal (mə dis′ə nəl) having value as medicine; healing; relieving. *adj.*

med·i·cine (med′ə sən or med′sən) **1** any substance, such as a drug, used to cure disease or improve health. **2** the study or science of curing disease or improving health; the treatment of diseases or sickness: *The young man decided to study medicine. n.*

medicine man a man supposed by North American Indians and other primitive peoples to have magic power over disease, evil spirits, and other things.

me·di·e·val or **me·di·ae·val** (mē′dē ē′vəl or med′ē ē′vəl) belonging to the Middle Ages, the period from about A.D. 500 to about A.D. 1450: *medieval customs. adj.*

me·di·o·cre (mē′dē ō′kər or mē′dē ō′kər) of average quality; ordinary, but less than satisfactory: *a mediocre cake, a mediocre student. adj.*

med·i·tate (med′ə tāt′) **1** think quietly; reflect: *You should meditate on the lesson taught by the fable of the hare and tortoise.* **2** think about; consider; plan: *Our general was meditating an attack. v.,* **med·i·tat·ed, med·i·tat·ing.**

med·i·ta·tion (med′ə tā′shən) continued thought; quiet thought. *n.*

me·di·um (mē′dē əm) **1** having a middle position, quality, or condition: *Eggs can be cooked hard, soft, or medium. A medium height for a man is 170 centimetres.* **2** that which is in the middle; neither one extreme nor the other; a middle condition: *Life in a*

hat, āge, fär; let, ēqual, tėrm; it, īce
hot, ōpen, ôrder; oil, out; cup, pu̇t, rüle
əbove, takən, pencəl, lemən, circəs
ch, child; ng, long; sh, ship
th, thin; ᴛʜ, then; zh, measure

small town is a happy medium between city and country life. 3 a substance or agent through which anything acts; a means: *Radio is a medium of communication.* 4 a substance in which something can live: *Water is the medium in which most fish live.* 5 a person through whom messages from the spirits of the dead are supposedly sent to the living. 1 *adj.,* 2–5 *n., pl.* **me·di·ums** or, for 3, 4, **me·di·a** (mē′dē ə).

med·ley (med′lē) 1 a mixture of things that ordinarily do not belong together. 2 a piece of music made up of parts from other pieces. *n., pl.* **med·leys.**

meek (mēk) 1 not easily angered; mild; patient. 2 submitting tamely when ordered about or injured by others: *The boy was as meek as a lamb after he was punished. adj.* **—meek′ness,** *n.*

meet¹ (mēt) 1 come face to face with something or someone coming from the other direction: *Our car met another car on a narrow road.* 2 come together; join: *Two roads met near the church.* 3 keep an appointment with: *Meet me at one o'clock.* 4 come to know; be introduced to: *Have you met my sister?* 5 receive and welcome on arrival: *I must go to the station to meet my mother.* 6 pay when due: *He was unable to meet his debts.* 7 satisfy; comply with: *He was unable to meet her demands. Father did his best to meet the family's needs.* 8 assemble: *Parliament will meet next month.* 9 a meeting or gathering; a competition: *a racing meet, an athletic meet.* 1–8 *v.,* **met, meet·ing;** 9 *n.*

meet with, a come across: *We met with rough weather.* **b** have or get: *The plan met with approval.*

☛ **Meet, meat,** and **mete** are pronounced the same.

meet² (mēt) suitable; proper; fitting: *It is meet that you should help your friends. adj.*

☛ See note at **meet¹**.

meet·ing (mēt′ing) 1 coming together: *He looked forward to the meeting with his uncle.* 2 an assembly of persons for worship: *a prayer meeting.* 3 any assembly: *Our club held a meeting.* 4 the place where things meet: *a meeting of roads. n.*

meeting house 1 a building used for worship. 2 a building used for meetings.

meg·a·lith (meg′ə lith′) a stone of great size, especially in monuments left by people of prehistoric times. *n.*

☛ **Megalith** comes from the Greek words *megas* meaning 'great' and *lithos* meaning 'stone.'

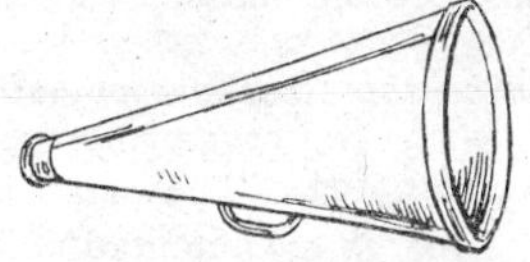

A megaphone

meg·a·phone (meg′ə fōn′) a large horn used to increase the loudness of the voice: *The cheer leader at the football game yelled through a megaphone. n.*

☛ **Megaphone** comes from the Greek words *megas* meaning 'great' and *phōnē* meaning 'sound'; **microphone** comes from the Greek words *mīcros* meaning 'small' and *phōnē* meaning 'sound.'

mel·an·chol·y (mel′ən kol′ē) 1 sadness; low spirits; a tendency to be sad. 2 sad or gloomy: *A melancholy man is not very good company.* 3 causing sadness: *a melancholy scene.* 1 *n.,* 2, 3 *adj.*

mel·low (mel′ō) 1 ripe, soft, and with a good flavor; sweet and juicy: *a mellow apple.* 2 soft and rich: *a violin with a mellow tone, velvet with a mellow color.* 3 softened and made gentle by age and experience. 4 make mellow; become mellow: *The apples mellowed after we picked them. Time had mellowed his youthful temper.* 1–3 *adj.,* 4 *v.*

me·lo·di·ous (mə lō′dē əs) sweet-sounding; pleasing to the ear; musical: *a melodious voice. adj.*

mel·o·dy (mel′ə dē) 1 sweet music; any sweet sound. 2 a succession of single tones in music; a tune: *She sang some sweet old melodies. Music has melody, harmony, and rhythm.* 3 the main tune in music having harmony; the air. *n., pl.* **mel·o·dies.**

mel·on (mel′ən) a large, juicy fruit that grows on a vine: *Watermelons and cantaloupes or muskmelons are common kinds of melon. n.*

melt (melt) 1 change from solid to liquid by the action of heat: *Ice becomes water when it melts. Great heat melts iron.* 2 dissolve: *Sugar melts in water.* 3 disappear gradually: *As the sun came out, the clouds melted away.* 4 blend or merge gradually: *In the rainbow the green melts into blue, the blue into violet. Dusk melted the colors of the hills into a soft grey.* 5 soften; cause to become sympathetic: *Pity for his wounded enemy melted his heart. v.*

melting point the temperature at which a solid substance melts.

mem·ber (mem′bər) 1 one who belongs to a group: *Every member of the family came home for Christmas. Our church has over five hundred members.* 2 a limb; a part of a human or animal body or of a plant, especially a leg, arm, wing, or branch. *n.*

Member of Parliament in Canada, a title given to each of the representatives elected to the Federal Parliament in Ottawa.

Member of Provincial Parliament in Ontario, a Member of the Legislative Assembly.

Member of the Legislative Assembly a title given to each of the representatives elected to the legislatures of most Canadian provinces.

mem·ber·ship (mem′bər ship′) 1 the state or fact of being a member: *Do you enjoy your membership in the Boy Scouts?* 2 the members: *The whole membership of the club was present.* 3 the number of members: *The membership of our club is over 30. n.*

mem·brane (mem′brān) 1 a thin, soft skin, sheet, or layer of animal tissue, lining or covering some part of the body: *One kind of membrane lines the stomach and another covers the front of the eyeball.* 2 a similar layer of vegetable tissue. *n.*

mem·o (mem′ō) memorandum. *n.*

mem·o·ra·ble (mem′ə rə bəl) worth remembering; not to be forgotten; notable: *The play 'Peter Pan' has many memorable scenes. adj.*

mem·o·ran·dum (mem′ə ran′dəm) 1 a short written statement for future use; a note to aid the memory: *He* *made a memorandum of his appointment with the dentist.* 2 an informal letter, note, or report. *n., pl.* **mem·o·ran·dums** or **mem·o·ran·da** (mem′ə ran′də).

me·mo·ri·al (mə mô′rē əl) 1 something that is a reminder of some event or person, such as a statue, an arch or column, a book, or a holiday. 2 helping people to remember some person, thing, or event: *We have memorial services on Remembrance Day.* 1 *n.,* 2 *adj.*

mem·o·rize (mem′ə rīz′) commit to memory; learn by heart: *We have all memorized the alphabet.* *v.,* **mem·o·rized, mem·o·riz·ing.**

mem·o·ry (mem′ə rē) 1 the ability to remember or keep in the mind: *She has a better memory than her sister has.* 2 a person, thing, or event that is remembered: *His mother died when he was small; she is only a memory to him now.* 3 all that a person remembers. 4 the length of past time that is remembered: *This is the hottest summer within my memory.* *n., pl.* **mem·o·ries.**

in memory of, as a help in remembering; as a remembrance of: *On November 11 we observe a two-minute silence in memory of those who died fighting for our country.*

men (men) 1 plural of **man.** 2 human beings; people in general: *Men and animals have some things in common.* *n. pl.*

men·ace (men′is) 1 a threat: *In dry weather forest fires are a great menace.* 2 threaten: *Floods menaced the valley towns with destruction.* 1 *n.,* 2 *v.,* **men·aced, men·ac·ing.**

me·nag·er·ie (mə naj′ər ē) 1 a collection of wild animals kept in cages for exhibition. 2 the place where such animals are kept. *n.*

mend (mend) 1 put in good condition again; repair: *to mend a road, to mend a broken doll, to mend stockings.* 2 set right; improve: *He should mend his manners.* 3 a place that has been mended: *The mend in your dress hardly shows.* 4 get back one's health: *The child will soon mend if she drinks plenty of milk.* 1, 2, 4 *v.,* 3 *n.*

on the mend, getting better.

men·folk (men′fōk′) 1 men. 2 the men of a family or other group. *n. pl.*

me·ni·al (mē′nē əl) 1 belonging to or suited to a servant; low; mean: *Cinderella had to do menial tasks.* 2 a servant who does the humblest and most unpleasant tasks. 1 *adj.,* 2 *n.*

Men·non·ite (men′ən īt′) a member of a Christian group that believes that the church should be separate from the government, that babies and young children do not need to be baptized, and that it is always wrong to go to war: *Some Mennonites wear very plain clothes and live simply. Mennonites have fine farms in western Canada and in Ontario.* *n.*

☞ Named after *Menno* Simons (1492–1559), the Dutch leader of the group.

-ment a suffix meaning: 1 the act of ____ing: *Enjoyment means the act of enjoying.* 2 the state of being ____ed: *Amazement means the state of being amazed.* 3 the product or result of ____ing: *Pavement means the result of paving.* 4 the thing that ____s: *Inducement means the thing that induces.*

men·tal (men′təl) 1 of the mind: *a mental test, mental illness.* 2 for the mind; done by the mind: *mental arithmetic.* 3 having a mental disease or weakness. 4 for people having mental illness: *a mental hospital.* *adj.* —**men′tal·ly,** *adv.*

men·tion (men′shən) 1 speak about: *Do not mention the accident before the children.* 2 a short statement about; reference to: *There was mention of our school party in the newspaper.* 1 *v.,* 2 *n.*

men·u (men′yü) 1 a list of the food served at a meal. 2 the food served: *Everybody enjoyed the fine menu.* *n.*

me·ow (mē ou′) 1 the sound made by a cat or kitten. 2 make this sound or one like it. 1 *n.,* 2 *v.*

mer·ce·nar·y (mėr′sə ner′ē) 1 working for money only; acting with money as the motive. 2 a soldier serving for pay in a foreign army. 1 *adj.,* 2 *n., pl.* **mer·ce·nar·ies.**

mer·chan·dise (mėr′chən dīz′ or mėr′chən dīs′) goods for sale; articles bought and sold. *n.*

mer·chant (mėr′chənt) 1 a person who buys and sells. 2 storekeeper. 3 trading; having something to do with trade: *merchant ships.* 1, 2 *n.,* 3 *adj.*

mer·ci·ful (mėr′si fəl) having mercy; showing or feeling mercy; full of mercy. *adj.*

mer·ci·less (mėr′si lis) without pity; having no mercy; showing no mercy: *The invaders' attack on the town was merciless.* *adj.*

mer·cu·ry (mėr′kyə rē) 1 a heavy, silver-white metal that is liquid at ordinary temperatures. 2 the column of mercury in a thermometer or barometer. *n.*

Mer·cu·ry (mėr′kyə rē) 1 in Roman myths, the messenger of the gods. 2 the planet nearest the sun. *n.*

mer·cy (mėr′sē) 1 more kindness than justice requires; kindness beyond what can be claimed or expected: *The judge showed mercy to the young offender.* 2 something to be thankful for; a blessing: *We thank the Lord for all his mercies. It's a mercy that they arrived safely through the storm.* *n., pl.* **mer·cies.**

at the mercy of, in the power of: *Without shelter we were at the mercy of the storm.*

mere (mēr) nothing else than; only: *The cut was a mere scratch. The mere sight of a dog makes him afraid.* *adj.,* **mer·est.**

mere·ly (mēr′lē) simply; only; and nothing more; and that is all. *adv.*

merge (mėrj) 1 swallow up; absorb; combine: *The brothers decided to merge their two businesses.* 2 combine or blend: *Traffic from this road merges with eastbound traffic on the highway. The walker merged into the darkness.* *v.,* **merged, merg·ing.**

mer·ger (mėr′jər) the act of merging; combination: *One big company was formed by the merger of four small ones.* *n.*

me·rid·i·an (mə rid′ē ən) 1 an imaginary circle passing through any place on the earth's surface and through the North and South Poles. 2 the half of such a circle from pole to pole: *All the places on the same meridian have the same longitude.* 3 the highest point that the sun or any star reaches in the sky. 4 the highest point; the time of greatest success and happiness: *The meridian of life is the prime of life.* *n.*

me·ringue (mə rang′) 1 a mixture of white of egg and sugar, beaten stiff: *Meringue is often spread on pies, puddings, etc. and lightly browned in the oven.* 2 a

hat, āge, fär; let, ēqual, tėrm; it, īce
hot, ōpen, ôrder; oil, out; cup, pu̇t, rüle
 əbove, takən, pencəl, lemən, circəs
ch, child; ng, long; sh, ship
th, thin; ᴛʜ, then; zh, measure

small cake or shell made of this mixture. *n.*

me·ri·no (mə rē′nō) 1 a kind of sheep having long, fine wool. 2 a soft yarn made from the wool of this sheep. *n., pl.* **me·ri·nos.**

mer·it (mer′it) 1 goodness; worth or value: *Each child will get a mark according to the merit of his work.* 2 something that deserves reward or praise. 3 deserve: *A hard-working boy merits praise.* 4 Usually, **merits,** *pl.* actual facts or qualities, whether good or bad: *The judge will consider the case on its merits.* 1, 2, 4 *n.,* 3 *v.*

mer·maid (mėr′mād′) an imaginary sea maiden having the form of a fish from the waist down. *n.*

mer·man (mėr′man′ or mėr′mən) an imaginary man of the sea having the form of a fish from the waist down. *n., pl.* **mer·men** (mėr′men′ or mėr′mən).

mer·ry (mer′ē) 1 full of fun; loving fun; laughing and gay: *a merry laugh.* 2 happy; joyful: *a merry party.* *adj.,* **mer·ri·er, mer·ri·est. —mer′ri·ly,** *adv.* **—mer′ri·ment,** *n.*

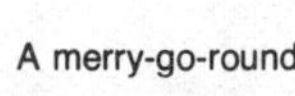

A merry-go-round

mer·ry–go–round (mer′ē gō round′) 1 a set of animal figures and seats on a platform that is driven round and round by machinery and that people ride for fun. 2 any whirl or rapid round: *The holidays were a merry-go-round of parties.* *n.*

mer·ry·mak·er (mer′ē māk′ər) a person who is being merry or who is engaged in merrymaking. *n.*

mer·ry·mak·ing (mer′ē māk′ing) laughter and gaiety; fun. *n.*

mesh (mesh) 1 one of the open spaces of a net, sieve, or screen: *This net has small meshes.* 2 cord, wire, etc. used in a net or screen: *He found an old fly swatter made of wire mesh.* 3 **meshes,** *pl.* web, network: *Seaweed was caught in the meshes of the net.* 4 catch or be caught in a net. 5 engage or become engaged: *The teeth of the small gear mesh with the teeth of a larger one.* See **cogwheel** for picture. 1–3 *n.,* 4, 5 *v.*
in mesh, in gear; fitted together.

mes·mer·ize (mes′mər īz′) hypnotize. *v.,* **mes·mer·ized, mes·mer·iz·ing.**
☛ Named after Franz *Mesmer* (1734–1815), an Austrian doctor, who made hypnotism popular.

mess (mes) 1 a dirty or untidy mass or group of things; a dirty or untidy condition: *Look what a mess you have made of your dress, playing in that dirt.* 2 make dirty or untidy: *He messed up his book by scribbling on the pages.* 3 confusion or difficulty: *His affairs are in a mess.* 4 make a failure of; spoil: *He messed up his chances of winning the race.* 5 an unpleasant or unsuccessful affair or state of affairs: *He made a mess of his final examinations.* 6 an organization for social purposes of persons in the armed services: *He was secretary of the sergeants' mess.* 7 the dining room, lounge, etc. used by members of such an organization: *He spent every Saturday evening at the mess.* 8 a portion of food, especially of soft food: *a mess of porridge, a mess of fish.* 1, 3, 5–8 *n.,* 2, 4 *v.*
mess about or **mess around,** busy oneself without seeming to accomplish anything.

mes·sage (mes′ij) information or instructions sent from one person to another: *a message of welcome, a radio message.* *n.*

mes·sen·ger (mes′ən jər) 1 a person who carries a message or goes on an errand. 2 a sign that something is coming; a herald: *Dawn is the messenger of the day.* *n.*

Mes·si·ah (mə sī′ə) 1 the expected savior of the Jewish people. 2 in Christian use, Jesus. *n.*

Messrs. messieurs, used before names as the plural of **Mr.:** *Messrs. Smith and Jones.*

mess·y (mes′ē) in a mess; untidy; dirty. *adj.,* **mess·i·er, mess·i·est.**

met (met) See **meet**[1]. *My father met us this morning at ten o'clock. We were met at the gate by our three dogs.* *v.*

met·al (met′əl) 1 a substance that is usually shiny, a good conductor of heat and electricity, and can be made into wire, or hammered into sheets. Gold, silver, copper, iron, lead, tin, and aluminum are metals. 2 an alloy or mixture of these, such as steel and brass. 3 made of metal, or of a mixture of metals: *a metal container, a metal coin.* 4 material; substance: *Cowards are not made of the same metal as heroes.* *n.*
☛ **Metal** and **mettle** are pronounced the same.

me·tal·lic (mə tal′ik) 1 of or containing metal: *a metallic substance.* 2 like metal in lustre, hardness, etc.: *a metallic cloth, a metallic voice.* *adj.*

met·a·phor (met′ə fər or met′ə fôr′) the use of a word to describe something different from its normal meaning, thus suggesting that the two things are alike. *Examples: a blanket of snow, tongues of flame, a heart of stone, a man of iron. Metaphors are used for lively and vivid descriptions in speech and writing.* *n.*

mete (mēt) give to each his share or what is due him; distribute: *The contest judge will mete out praise and blame.* *v.,* **met·ed, met·ing.**
☛ **Mete, meat,** and **meet** are pronounced the same.

me·te·or (mē′tē ər) a mass of stone or metal that comes toward the earth from outer space at enormous speed: *Meteors become so hot from hurtling through the air that they glow and usually burn up.* *n.*

me·te·or·ic (mē′tē ôr′ik) 1 of meteors: *a meteoric shower.* 2 flashing like a meteor; swift; brilliant and soon ended: *a singer's meteoric rise to fame.* *adj.*

me·te·or·ite (mē′tē ər īt′) a mass of stone or metal that has fallen to the earth from outer space; a fallen meteor. *n.*

me·te·or·ol·o·gy (mē′tē ər ol′ə jē) the science of the atmosphere and weather: *Weather forecasting is a part of meteorology.* *n.*

me·ter[1] (mē′tər) See **metre**[1] and **metre**[2].
☛ **Meter** and **metre** are pronounced the same.

me·ter[2] (mē′tər) a device that measures, or measures

and records: *a parking meter, a water meter.* *n.*

meth·od (meth′əd) 1 a way of doing something: *a method of teaching music. Roasting is one method of cooking meat.* 2 order or system in getting things done or in thinking: *If you used more method, you wouldn't waste so much time.* *n.*

me·thod·i·cal (mə thod′ə kəl) 1 done according to a method; orderly: *The student made a methodical check of his work.* 2 arranged or acting according to a method: *A scientist is usually a methodical thinker.* *adj.*

Meth·od·ist (meth′ə dist) a member of a Christian church that had its origin in England in the eighteenth century: *In Canada, most Methodists now belong to the United Church of Canada.* *n.*

Mé·tis or **Me·tis** (mā tēs′ or mā tē′) a person of mixed European (especially French) and North American Indian descent; a half-breed. *n., pl.* **Mé·tis** or **Me·tis.**

me·tre[1] (mē′tər) 1 any kind of poetic rhythm; the arrangement of beats or accents in a line of poetry: *The metre of 'Jack and Jill went up the hill' is different from that of 'One, two, buckle my shoe.'* 2 musical rhythm; the arrangement of beats in music: *Three-fourths metre is waltz time.* *n.* Also spelled **meter.**

☛ Metre and **meter** are pronounced the same.

me·tre[2] (mē′tər) a unit of length: *A door is about two metres high. Symbol:* m *n.* Also spelled **meter.**

☛ See note at **metre**[1].

me·tre–stick (mē′tər stik′) a measuring stick that is one metre long and is marked off in centimetres and millimetres. *n.*

met·ric system (met′rik) a decimal system of weights and measures, or one which counts by tens. It is based on the metre for length, the gram for mass, and the litre for volume.

met·ro·nome (met′rə nōm′) a clocklike device that can be adjusted to tick at different speeds: *Children practising music sometimes use a metronome to help them keep time.* *n.*

me·trop·o·lis (mə trop′ə lis) 1 the most important city of a country or region: *London is the metropolis of England.* 2 a large city; an important centre: *Montreal is a busy metropolis.* *n.*

met·ro·pol·i·tan (met′rə pol′ə tən) of a large city; belonging to large cities: *metropolitan newspapers.* *adj.*

metropolitan area the area or region including a large city and its suburbs.

met·tle (met′əl) disposition; spirit; courage. *n.* **on one's mettle,** ready to do one's best.

☛ Mettle and **metal** are pronounced the same.

mew (myü) 1 the sound made by a cat or kitten. 2 make this sound: *Our kitten mews when it gets hungry.* 1 *n.*, 2 *v.*

mewl (myül) cry like a baby; whimper. *v.*

☛ Mewl and **mule** are pronounced the same.

Mex·i·can (mek′sə kən) 1 of Mexico or its people. 2 a person born in or living in Mexico. 1 *adj.*, 2 *n.*

mez·za·nine (mez′ə nēn′) 1 a partial storey between two main floors of a building: *Many hotels have a mezzanine between the ground floor and the next main floor up.* 2 in a theatre, the lowest balcony, or its front section: *Tickets are $5.00 for seats in the mezzanine and $3.00 for the second balcony.* *n.*

mg milligram; milligrams.

mi (mē) the third note of a musical scale. See **do**[2] for picture. *n.*

mi. mile; miles.

mi·ca (mī′kə) a mineral that divides into thin, partly transparent layers: *Mica withstands heat and is used for insulation.* *n.*

mice (mīs) plural of **mouse.** *n.*

mi·crobe (mī′krōb) a living organism of very small size; a germ: *Some microbes cause diseases.* *n.*

mi·cro·film (mī′krō film′) a film for making very small photographs of pages of a book, newspapers, records, etc., to preserve them in a very small space. *n.*

mi·cro·phone (mī′krə fōn′) an instrument for increasing the loudness of sounds or for transmitting sounds. Microphones change sounds into variations of an electric current and are used in recording and in radio and television broadcasting. *n.*

☛ See note at **megaphone.**

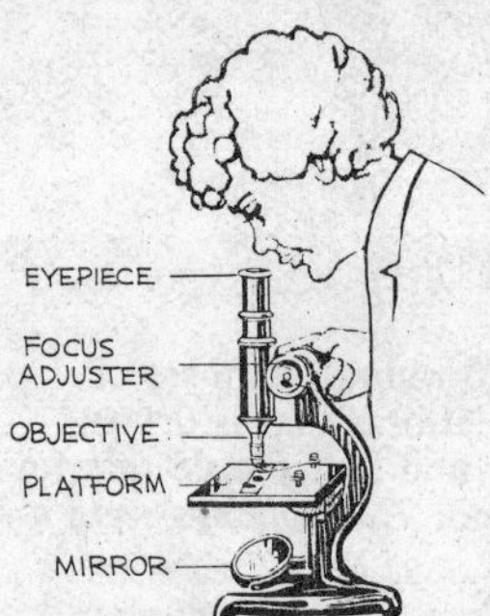

A microscope. There are magnifying lenses in the eyepiece and objective. The mirror reflects light up through the platform, which has an opening in it or is made of glass.

mi·cro·scope (mī′krə skōp′) an instrument with a lens or combination of lenses for making small objects look larger so that one can see things not visible to the naked eye. *n.*

mi·cro·scop·ic (mī′krə skop′ik) 1 that cannot be seen without using a microscope; tiny: *microscopic germs.* 2 like a microscope; suggesting a microscope: *a microscopic eye for mistakes.* 3 of a microscope; with a microscope: *She made a microscopic examination of a fly's wing.* *adj.*

mid[1] (mid) middle. *adj.*

mid[2] or **'mid** (mid) amid. *prep.*

mid·day (mid′dā′) 1 the middle of the day; noon. 2 of or like midday: *the midday meal.* 1 *n.*, 2 *adj.*

mid·dle (mid′əl) 1 halfway between; in the centre; at the same distance from either end or side: *the middle house in the row.* 2 the point or part that is the same distance from each end or side; the centre: *the middle of the road.* 3 in between; medium: *a man of middle size.* 1, 3 *adj.*, 2 *n.*

mid·dle–aged (mid′əl ājd′) between youth and old age; from about 40 to about 60 years of age. *adj.*

Middle Ages the period in European history between ancient and modern times, from about A.D. 500 to about 1450.

middle ear a hollow space between the eardrum and the inner ear: *In humans the middle ear contains three small bones that pass on sound waves from the eardrum to the inner ear.*

hat, āge, fär; let, ēqual, tėrm; it, īce
hot, ōpen, ôrder; oil, out; cup, pu̇t, rüle
əbove, takən, pencəl, lemən, circəs
ch, child; ng, long; sh, ship
th, thin; ᴛʜ, then; zh, measure

Middle East the region between the eastern Mediterranean and India: *Egypt, Israel, and Saudi Arabia are countries of the Middle East.*

Middle English the language spoken in Great Britain from about 1100 to about 1450.

mid·dy (mid′ē) a loose blouse like a sailor's, having a collar with a broad flap at the back. *n., pl.* **mid·dies.**

midge (mij) a kind of very small insect. *n.*

midg·et (mij′it) **1** a person very much smaller than normal: *We saw midgets in the circus.* **2** anything much smaller than the usual size for its kind. **3** very small: *a midget submarine.* 1, 2 *n.,* 3 *adj.*

mid·land (mid′lənd) **1** the middle part of a country; the interior. **2** in or of the midland. 1 *n.,* 2 *adj.*

mid·night (mid′nīt′) twelve o'clock at night; the middle of the night. *n.*

mid·ship·man (mid′ship′mən) **1** a junior officer training for a commission in a navy. **2** in former times, a boy who assisted the officers of a ship. *n., pl.* **mid·ship·men** (mid′ship′mən).

midst[1] (midst) middle. *adj., n.*
in our midst, among us: *a traitor in our midst.*
in the midst of, a in the middle of; among: *The bomb fell in the midst of the crowd.* **b** during: *The announcement was made in the midst of the program.*

midst[2] or **′midst** (midst) amidst. *prep.*

mid·sum·mer (mid′sum′ər) **1** the middle of summer. **2** the time around June 21. *n.*

mid·way (mid′wā′) **1** halfway; in the middle: *midway between the two towns (adv.), a midway point on the chart (adj.).* **2** at a fair or exhibition, the place for games, rides, and other amusements. 1 *adv., adj.,* 2 *n.*

mid·win·ter (mid′win′tər) **1** the middle of winter. **2** the time around December 21. *n.*

mien (mēn) one's manner of holding the head and body; a way of acting and looking: *The colonel had the mien of a soldier.* *n.*
☛ **Mien** and **mean** are pronounced the same.

might[1] (mīt) See **may**[1]. *Mother said that we might play in the barn. He might have done it when you were not looking.* *v.*
☛ **Might** and **mite** are pronounced the same.

might[2] (mīt) great power; strength: *Work with all your might.* *n.*
with might and main, with all one's strength.
☛ See note at **might**[1].

might·i·ly (mīt′ə lē) **1** in a mighty manner; powerfully; vigorously: *Samson strove mightily and pulled the pillars down.* **2** very much; greatly: *We were mightily pleased at winning.* *adv.*

might·y (mīt′ē) **1** showing strength or power; strong; powerful: *a mighty ruler, a mighty force.* **2** very great: *a mighty famine.* **3** *Informal.* very or extremely: *a mighty cold day.* *adj.,* **might·i·er, might·i·est.**

mi·grant (mī′grənt) **1** migrating; roving: *Crops of apples are picked by migrant workers.* **2** a person, animal, bird, or plant that migrates. 1 *adj.,* 2 *n.*

mi·grate (mī′grāt or mī grāt′) **1** move from one place to settle in another: *Pioneers from Ontario migrated to all parts of what are now the Prairie Provinces.* **2** go from one region to another with the change in the seasons: *Most birds migrate to warmer countries in the winter.* *v.,* **mi·grat·ed, mi·grat·ing.**

mi·gra·tion (mī grā′shən) **1** a moving from one place to another. **2** a number of people or animals migrating together. *n.*

mil·age (mīl′ij) See **mileage.**

milch (milch) giving milk; kept for the milk it gives: *a milch cow.* *adj.*

mild (mīld) **1** gentle; kind: *a mild old gentleman.* **2** calm; warm; temperate; not harsh or severe: *a mild climate, a mild winter.* **3** soft or sweet to the senses; not sharp, sour, bitter, or strong in taste: *mild cheese.* *adj.*

mil·dew (mil′dyü or mil′dü) **1** a coating or discoloring caused by fungi that appears on clothes, leather, etc. during damp weather: *Damp clothes left in a pile will show mildew in a few days.* **2** a plant disease in which a fungus grows on the plant: *Mildew killed the rosebuds in our garden.* **3** cover or become covered with mildew: *A pile of damp clothes in his closet mildewed.* 1, 2 *n.,* 3 *v.*

mile (mīl) **1** a measure of distance on land equal to 5280 feet (about 1609 metres), called a **statute mile.** **2** a measure of about 6080 feet (1852 metres) used in air and sea navigation, called a **nautical mile.** *n.*

mile·age (mīl′ij) the number of miles covered or travelled: *The mileage on our speedometer last year was 10 000 miles.* *n.* Sometimes spelled **milage.**

mile·stone (mīl′stōn′) **1** a stone set up to show the distance in miles to a certain place. **2** an important event: *The invention of printing was a milestone in the progress of education.* *n.*

mil·i·tant (mil′ə tənt) **1** warlike; aggressive; fighting. **2** aggressively active in serving a cause or in spreading a belief: *a militant churchman.* **3** a person aggressively active in serving a cause or in spreading a belief. 1, 2 *adj.,* 3 *n.*

mil·i·tar·y (mil′ə ter′ē) **1** of soldiers or war: *military training, military history.* **2** done by soldiers: *military manoeuvres.* **3** fit for soldiers: *military discipline.* **4** suitable for war; warlike: *military valor.* **5** belonging to the armed forces. *adj.*
the military, the armed forces; soldiers: *The military did rescue work during the flood.*

mi·li·tia (mə lish′ə) a part of the army made up of citizens who are not regular soldiers but who undergo training for emergency duty or national defence. *n.*

milk (milk) **1** the white liquid produced by female mammals as food for their young, especially that from cows, which we drink and use in cooking. **2** a liquid resembling this, such as the white juice of a plant, tree, or nut: *coconut milk.* **3** draw milk from; strip of milk: *He used to milk twenty cows a day.* 1, 2 *n.,* 3 *v.*
—milk′er, n.

milk·maid (milk′mād′) a woman whose job is to milk cows. *n.*

milk·man (milk′man′ or milk′mən) a man who sells milk or delivers it to customers. *n., pl.* **milk·men** (milk′men′ or milk′mən).

milk shake a drink consisting of milk, flavoring, and often ice cream, shaken or beaten until frothy.

milk·weed (milk′wēd′) a weed whose stem contains a white juice that looks like milk. *n.*

milk·y (mil′kē) 1 like milk; white as milk. 2 of milk; containing milk. *adj.,* **milk·i·er, milk·i·est.**

Milky Way 1 a broad band of faint light that stretches across the sky at night: *The Milky Way is made up of countless stars, too far away to be seen separately without a telescope.* 2 the galaxy in which these countless stars are found: *The earth, sun, and all the planets around the sun are part of the Milky Way.*

A mill (def. 2)

mill (mil) 1 a machine for grinding or crushing: *A flour mill grinds wheat into flour. A coffee mill grinds coffee seeds.* 2 a building containing a machine for grinding grain. 3 grind: *Some wheat will be milled before it is exported.* 4 a building where manufacturing is done: *A paper mill makes paper from wood pulp.* 5 move around in a confused way: *There were many people milling around after the parade.* 1, 2, 4 *n.,* 3, 5 *v.*

mill·er (mil′ər) 1 a person who owns or runs a mill, especially a flour mill. 2 a moth whose wings look as if they were powdered with flour. *n.*

mil·let (mil′it) 1 a grain used for food in Europe, Asia, and Africa. 2 the plant that it grows on: *In North America millet is grown chiefly for hay. n.*

mil·li·bar (mil′ə bär′) a measure of pressure; one one-thousandth of a bar: *Air pressure readings are sometimes given in millibars. Symbol:* mbar *n.*

mil·li·gram (mil′ə gram′) one one-thousandth of a gram. *Symbol:* mg *n.* Also spelled **milligramme.**

mil·li·li·tre (mil′ə lē′tər) one one-thousandth of a litre. *Symbol:* ml *n.* Also spelled **milliliter.**

mil·li·metre (mil′ə mē′tər) one one-thousandth of a metre. *Symbol:* mm *n.* Also spelled **millimeter.**

mil·li·ner (mil′ə nər) a person who makes, trims, or sells women's hats. *n.*

mil·li·ner·y (mil′ə ner′ē) 1 women's hats. 2 the business of making, trimming, or selling women's hats. *n.*

mil·lion (mil′yən) 1 one thousand thousand (1 000 000). 2 a very large number; very many: *She can always think of a million reasons for not helping with the dishes. n., adj.*

mil·lion·aire (mil′yən er′) 1 a person who has a million or more dollars or owns property worth that amount. 2 a very wealthy person. *n.*

mil·lionth (mil′yənth) 1 last in a series of a million. 2 one of a million equal parts. *adj., n.*

mill·stone (mil′stōn′) 1 one of a pair of round, flat stones used for grinding corn, wheat, etc. 2 a heavy burden. *n.*

mill wheel a wheel that is turned by water and supplies power for a mill. See **mill** for picture.

mime (mīm) 1 a form of drama in which the actors use movement and gestures but no words; pantomime. 2 communicating through gestures but without the use of words: *He told his story in mime.* 3 communicate in this way: *The Eskimo boy mimed his story of the seal hunt.* 4 an actor, especially in a pantomime. 1, 2, 4 *n.,* 3 *v.,* **mimed, mim·ing.**

mim·e·o·graph (mim′ē ə graf′) 1 a machine for making copies of written or typewritten material, or of drawings. 2 make copies on a mimeograph. 1 *n.,* 2 *v.*

mim·ic (mim′ik) 1 make fun of by imitating: *We like to get him to mimic our old music teacher.* 2 a person or thing that imitates. 3 copy closely; imitate: *A parrot can mimic a person's voice.* 4 resemble closely: *Some insects mimic leaves.* 5 not real, but imitated or pretended for some purpose: *The soldiers staged a mimic battle for the visiting general.* 1, 3, 4 *v.,* **mim·icked, mim·ick·ing;** 2 *n.,* 5 *adj.*

min minute; minutes.

min·a·ret (min′ə ret′) a slender high tower attached to a Moslem mosque, having one or more projecting balconies from which a crier calls the people to prayer. *n.*

mince (mins) 1 chop up into very small pieces. 2 made with mincemeat: *mince pie.* 3 speak or move in a prim, affected way. 1, 3 *v.,* **minced, minc·ing;** 2 *adj.*

mince·meat (mins′mēt′) a mixture of chopped suet, apples, raisins, currants, spices, etc., and sometimes meat, used as a filling for pies. *n.*

mind (mīnd) 1 the part of a person that knows, thinks, remembers, wishes, chooses, feels emotion, etc.: *The old man's mind remained active.* 2 intelligence or mental ability; the intellect: *Mastering arithmetic requires a good mind.* 3 what one thinks or feels: *Speak your mind freely.* 4 notice; observe. 5 be careful concerning: *Mind the step.* 6 take care: *Mind that you come on time.* 7 attend to; take care of: *Please mind the baby.* 8 obey: *Mind your father and mother.* 9 the memory: *Keep the rules in mind.* 10 feel bad about; object to: *I minded parting from my friends. Some people don't mind cold weather.* 1–3, 9 *n.,* 4–8, 10 *v.*

bear in mind, keep one's attention on; remember.

be of one mind, have the same opinion; agree: *They were both of one mind.*

have a mind to, intend to; think of doing: *I have a mind to watch hockey tonight.*

make up one's mind, decide: *I made up my mind to study harder and get better grades.*

on one's mind, in one's mind; in one's thoughts.

set one's mind on, want very much.

to one's mind, to one's way of thinking; in one's opinion.

mind·ful (mīnd′fəl) being aware or careful: *Mindful of your advice, I went slowly. adj.*

mine[1] (mīn) the one or ones belonging to me: *This book is mine. Your shoes are black; mine are brown. pron.*

hat, āge, fär; let, ēqual, tėrm; it, īce
hot, ōpen, ôrder; oil, out; cup, pu̇t, rüle
əbove, takən, pencəl, lemən, circəs
ch, child; ng, long; sh, ship
th, thin; ŦH, then; zh, measure

mine[2] (mīn) **1** a large hole or space dug in the earth in order to get out valuable minerals: *a coal mine, a gold mine.* **2** dig a mine; make a hole or space underground. **3** dig into for coal, gold, etc.: *to mine the earth.* **4** get from a mine: *to mine coal, to mine gold, etc.* **5** a rich or plentiful source: *The book proved to be a mine of information about spaceships.* **6** an underground passage in which gunpowder is placed to blow up an enemy's forts, etc. **7** make underground passages below. **8** a bomb placed under the surface of water, on the ground, or buried just below the ground, to blow up an enemy's ships, troops, or equipment. **9** lay mines under: *to mine the mouth of a harbor.* 1, 5, 6, 8 *n.,* 2–4, 7, 9 *v.,* **mined, min·ing.**

min·er (mī′nər) a man who works in a mine: *a coal miner. n.*

☛ **Miner** and **minor** are pronounced the same.

min·er·al (min′ər əl) **1** a substance obtained by mining or digging in the earth: *Coal is a mineral.* **2** any natural substance that is neither plant nor animal: *Salt and sand are minerals.* **3** of minerals: *There are mineral deposits at the mouth of the river.* **4** containing minerals: *mineral water.* 1, 2 *n.,* 3, 4 *adj.*

min·er·al·o·gy (min′ər ol′ə jē) the science that deals with minerals. *n.*

min·gle (ming′gəl) **1** mix; blend: *The two rivers that join mingle their waters.* **2** associate: *He is very shy and does not mingle much with the children at school. v.,* **min·gled, min·gling.**

min·i·a·ture (min′ə chər or min′ē ə chər) **1** a small model or copy: *In the museum there is a miniature of the ship 'Victory.'* **2** done or made on a very small scale; tiny: *She had miniature furniture for her doll's house.* **3** a very small painting, usually a portrait. 1, 3 *n.,* 2 *adj.*

min·i·mum (min′ə məm) **1** the least amount or smallest quantity possible or permitted: *Everyone agreed that seven holidays was a satisfactory minimum for the year.* **2** the least possible; lowest: *Eighteen is the minimum age for voting in some provinces. The workers wanted a minimum wage of two dollars an hour.* 1 *n., pl.* **min·i·mums** or **min·i·ma** (min′ə mə); 2 *adj.*

min·ing (mī′ning) **1** the working of mines for ore, coal, etc. **2** the laying of explosive mines. *n.*

min·ion (min′yən) a servant or follower willing to do anything he is ordered to do by his master. *n.*

min·is·ter (min′is tər) **1** a clergyman serving a church; a spiritual guide; a pastor. **2** act as a servant or nurse; be of service or aid; be helpful: *to minister to a sick man's wants.* **3** a person who is given charge of a department of the government: *the Minister of Finance.* **4** a person sent to a foreign country to represent his own government: *the British minister to France.* 1, 3, 4 *n.,* 2 *v.*

min·is·try (min′is trē) **1** the office, duties, or time of service of a minister. **2** the ministers of a church. **3** the ministers of a government. **4** a government department under a minister. **5** the act of ministering or serving. *n., pl.* **min·is·tries.**

mink (mingk) **1** a small animal, related to the weasel, that lives in water part of the time. **2** its valuable brown fur. *n.*

min·now (min′ō) **1** any of various small fresh-water fish belonging to the carp family. **2** any very small fish. *n.*

mi·nor (mī′nər) **1** smaller; lesser; less important: *minor details, minor errors.* **2** a person who is legally considered not an adult. In various provinces, minors are under 18, 19, and 21 years of age: *While you are still a minor, you need the consent of a parent or guardian to marry and you cannot make legal contracts.* 1 *adj.,* 2 *n.*

☛ **Minor** and **miner** are pronounced the same.

mi·nor·i·ty (mə nôr′ə tē) the smaller number or part; less than half: *A minority of the children wanted a party, but the majority chose a picnic. n., pl.* **mi·nor·i·ties.**

min·strel (min′strəl) **1** in the Middle Ages, a singer or musician who went about and sang or recited poems, often of his own making. **2** formerly, a singer or musician in the household of a lord. **3** a member of a company of performers, either Negro or with blackened faces and hands, who entertain with songs, music, and jokes: *Minstrel shows were very popular until the end of the 1800's. n.*

mint[1] (mint) **1** a sweet-smelling plant used for flavoring: *Chopped mint leaves are used in a sauce to serve with roast lamb.* **2** a piece of candy flavored with mint. *n.*

mint[2] (mint) **1** a place where money is made by government authority. **2** to make coins. **3** *Informal.* a large amount: *A million dollars is a mint of money.* 1, 3 *n.,* 2 *v.*

min·u·end (min′yü end′) a number or quantity from which another is to be subtracted: *In 100–23 = 77, the minuend is 100.* See **subtraction** for picture. *n.*

min·u·et (min′yü et′) **1** a slow, stately dance, popular in the 1700's. **2** the music for it. *n.*

mi·nus (mī′nəs) **1** less; decreased by: *12 minus 3 leaves 9. Symbol:* – **2** *Informal.* lacking: *a book minus its cover. prep.*

min·ute[1] (min′it) **1** one of the 60 equal periods of time that make up an hour; 60 seconds. *Symbol:* min **2** a short time; an instant: *I'll be there in a minute.* **3** an exact point of time: *The minute you see him coming, please tell me.* **4 minutes,** *pl.* an official account of what happened at a meeting. *n.*

mi·nute[2] (mī nyüt′ or mī nüt′) **1** very small; tiny: *a minute speck of dust.* **2** going into or concerned with small details: *He gave me minute instructions about how to do my work. adj.*

mir·a·cle (mir′ə kəl) **1** a wonderful happening that is beyond the known laws of nature: *It would be a miracle if the sun stood still in the heavens for an hour.* **2** something marvellous; a wonder: *It was a miracle you weren't hurt in that accident. n.*

mi·rac·u·lous (mə rak′yə ləs) **1** going against the known laws of nature: *In the Bible story, Christ's raising of Lazarus from the dead was miraculous.* **2** wonderful; marvellous: *Meeting you here is miraculous good fortune. adj.* **—mi·rac′u·lous·ly,** *adv.*

mi·rage (mə räzh′) a misleading appearance in which

some distant scene is viewed as being close and, often, upside down. In a mirage, the actual scene is reflected by layers of air of different temperatures. *n.*

mire (mīr) 1 soft, deep mud; slush. 2 get stuck in mire: *He mired his car and had to go for help.* 1 *n.*, 2 *v.*, **mired, mir·ing.**

mir·ror (mir′ər) 1 a glass in which you can see yourself; a looking glass; a surface that reflects light. 2 reflect as a mirror does: *The water was so still that it mirrored the trees along the bank.* 3 whatever reflects or gives a true description: *This book is a mirror of the life of the pioneers.* 4 give a true description or picture of: *The book mirrored colonial life in Canada.* 1, 3 *n.*, 2, 4 *v.*

mirth (mėrth) merry fun; laughter: *His sides shook with mirth.* *n.*

mirth·ful (mėrth′fəl) merry; jolly. *adj.*

mis– a prefix meaning: 1 bad; wrong, as in *misdeed, misconduct.* 2 badly; wrongly, as in *misbehave, misjudge.*

mis·ad·ven·ture (mis′əd ven′chər) 1 bad luck. 2 an instance of bad luck; an unfortunate accident: *By some misadventure the letter got lost.* *n.*

mis·be·have (mis′bi hāv′) behave badly. *v.*, **mis·be·haved, mis·be·hav·ing.**

mis·cel·la·ne·ous (mis′ə lā′nē əs) not all of one kind or nature: *He had a miscellaneous collection of stones, butterflies, marbles, stamps, and many other things.* *adj.*

mis·chance (mis chans′) misfortune; bad luck: *By some mischance he didn't receive my telegram.* *n.*

mis·chief (mis′chif) 1 conduct that causes harm or trouble, often without meaning it: *A child's mischief may cause a serious fire.* 2 harm; injury, usually done by some person: *Go away, or I'll do you a mischief.* 3 a person who does harm or causes annoyance, often just in fun: *The boy was a little mischief.* 4 merry teasing: *Her eyes were full of mischief.* *n.*

mis·chie·vous (mis′chə vəs) 1 causing mischief; naughty: *mischievous behavior.* 2 harmful: *mischievous gossip.* 3 full of pranks and teasing fun: *mischievous children.* *adj.*

mis·con·duct (mis kon′dukt) 1 bad behavior. 2 bad management: *The misconduct of that business nearly ruined it.* *n.*

mis·deed (mis dēd′) a bad act; wicked deed. *n.*

mis·de·mean·or or **mis·de·mean·our** (mis′di mēn′ər) 1 a minor offence against a law: *Breaking a traffic law is a misdemeanor.* 2 a wrong deed. *n.*

mi·ser (mī′zər) a person who loves money for its own sake; one who lives poorly in order to save money and keep it. *n.*

mis·er·a·ble (miz′rə bəl or miz′ər ə bəl) 1 unhappy; wretched: *A sick child is often miserable.* 2 causing trouble or unhappiness: *I have a miserable cold.* 3 poor; pitiful: *They live in a miserable, cold house.* *adj.* **—mis′er·a·bly,** *adv.*

mi·ser·ly (mī′zər lē) of or like a miser; stingy. *adj.*

mis·er·y (miz′ər ē or miz′rē) 1 a miserable, unhappy state of mind: *Think of the misery of having no home or friends.* 2 poor, mean, miserable conditions: *Some very poor people live in misery, without beauty or comfort around them.* *n.*, *pl.* **mis·er·ies.**

mis·fire (mis fīr′) 1 fail to fire or explode properly: *The pistol misfired.* 2 a failure to discharge or explode properly. 3 go wrong; fail: *The robber's scheme misfired.* 1, 3 *v.*, **mis·fired, mis·fir·ing;** 2 *n.*

mis·fit (mis′fit′) 1 a bad fit: *Do not buy shoes that are misfits.* 2 a person who is not suited to his job or does not get along well with other people. *n.*

mis·for·tune (mis fôr′chən) 1 bad luck: *She had the misfortune to break her arm.* 2 a piece of bad luck; unlucky accident. *n.*

mis·giv·ing (mis giv′ing) a feeling of doubt, suspicion, or anxiety: *We started off through the storm with some misgivings.* *n.*

mis·judge (mis juj′) judge wrongly or unjustly: *The archer misjudged the distance to the target, and his arrow fell short. The teacher soon discovered that she had misjudged the girl's character.* *v.*, **mis·judged, mis·judg·ing.**

mis·lay (mis lā′) put in a place and then forget the place: *Mother is always mislaying her glasses.* *v.*, **mis·laid, mis·lay·ing.**

mis·lead (mis lēd′) 1 cause to go in the wrong direction: *Our guide misled us in the woods, and we got lost.* 2 cause to do wrong: *Bad companions often mislead young people.* 3 lead to think what is not so; deceive: *His lies misled me.* *v.*, **mis·led, mis·lead·ing.**

mis·lead·ing (mis lēd′ing) 1 causing wrong conclusions: *The detectives lost time following up the misleading information.* 2 causing mistakes or wrongdoing: *Bad advice can be misleading.* *adj.*

mis·led (mis led′) See **mislead.** *The boy was misled by bad companions.* *v.*

mis·pro·nounce (mis′prə nouns′) pronounce incorrectly: *Many people mispronounce the word 'mischievous.'* *v.*, **mis·pro·nounced, mis·pro·nounc·ing.**

mis·read (mis rēd′) 1 read wrongly. 2 misunderstand; interpret wrongly: *She misread my reply and expected me to be early instead of late.* *v.*, **mis·read** (mis red′), **mis·read·ing.**

miss[1] (mis) 1 fail to hit: *He fired twice, but both shots missed.* 2 a failure to hit or reach: *to make more misses than hits.* 3 fail to find, get, or meet: *I set out to meet my father, but in the dark I missed him.* 4 let slip by: *I missed the chance of a ride to town.* 5 escape or avoid: *I just missed being hit.* 6 fail to catch: *to miss a train.* 7 leave out: *to miss a word in reading.* 8 fail to hear or understand: *What did you say? I missed a word or two.* 9 fail to keep, do, or be present at: *I missed my music lesson today.* 10 notice the absence of: *I did not miss my purse till I got home.* 11 feel keenly the absence of: *He missed his mother when she went away.* 12 fail to work properly; misfire: *The car was missing on two cylinders.* 1, 3–12 *v.*, 2 *n.*

miss[2] (mis) a young unmarried woman or girl. *n.*

Miss (mis) a title put before the name of a girl or an unmarried woman: *Miss Brown, the Misses Brown, the Miss Browns.* *n.*

mis·shap·en (mis shāp′ən) badly shaped; deformed. *adj.*

mis·sile (mis′īl or mis′əl) 1 an object that is thrown, hurled, or shot, such as a stone, bullet, arrow, or lance.

hat, āge, fär; let, ēqual, tėrm; it, īce
hot, ōpen, ôrder; oil, out; cup, pu̇t, rüle
ǝbove, takǝn, pencǝl, lemǝn, circǝs
ch, child; ng, long; sh, ship
th, thin; ᴛʜ, then; zh, measure

2 a self-propelled rocket containing explosives: *Missiles can be launched from land, air, or water.* *n.*

mis·sing (mis′ing) **1** out of its usual place: *The missing ring was found under the dresser. One of the books was missing.* **2** absent: *Four children were missing from class today.* *adj.*

mis·sion (mish′ǝn) **1** sending or being sent on some special work; an errand: *He was sent on a mission to a foreign government.* **2** a group of persons sent out on some special business: *He was one of a mission sent by our government to France. A mission was sent to the Arctic by the Anglican Church.* **3** the business on which a person or group is sent: *Their mission was to blow up the bridge.* **4** the station or headquarters of a religious mission. **5** one's business or purpose in life; one's calling: *It is her mission to care for her brother's children.* *n.*

mis·sion·ar·y (mish′ǝn er′ē) **1** a person who goes on the work of a religious mission: *Missionaries tried to get the Indians to become Christians.* **2** of religious missions or missionaries. 1 *n., pl.* **mis·sion·ar·ies;** 2 *adj.*

mis·spell (mis spel′) spell incorrectly. *v.,* **mis·spelled** or **mis·spelt, mis·spell·ing.**

mist (mist) **1** a cloud of very fine drops of water in the air; fog. **2** come down in mist; rain in very fine drops: *It is misting.* **3** anything that dims, blurs, or obscures: *The ideas were lost in a mist of long words.* **4** cover with a mist; put a mist before; make dim: *Tears misted her eyes.* **5** become covered with a mist: *The windows are misting.* 1, 3 *n.,* 2, 4, 5 *v.*

mist over or **mist up,** become covered with mist.

mis·take (mis tāk′) **1** an error; blunder; misunderstanding of the meaning or use of something: *I used your towel by mistake.* **2** make a mistake; misunderstand what is seen or heard: *I was mistaken when I said she would not come.* **3** take wrongly; take to be some other person or thing: *I mistook that stick for a snake.* 1 *n.,* 2, 3 *v.,* **mis·took, mis·tak·en, mis·tak·ing.**

mis·tak·en (mis tāk′ǝn) **1** wrong in opinion; having made a mistake: *A mistaken person should admit that he was wrong.* **2** wrong; wrongly judged; misplaced: *It was a mistaken kindness to give that boy more candy, for it will make him sick.* **3** See **mistake.** 1, 2 *adj.,* 3 *v.* **—mis·tak′en·ly,** *adv.*

Mis·ter (mis′tǝr) Mr., a title put before a man's name or the name of his office: *Mr. Smith, Mr. Speaker. Dr. Jones did not like to be called 'Mister Jones.'* *n.*

Mistletoe growing on the branch of a tree

mis·tle·toe (mis′ǝl tō′) a plant having small white berries, which grows as a parasite on trees: *Mistletoe is used as a Christmas decoration.* *n.*

mis·took (mis tu̇k′) See **mistake.** *I mistook you for your sister yesterday.* *v.*

mis·tress (mis′tris) **1** the woman who is at the head of a household. **2** a woman or country who is in control or can rule: *England was sometimes called mistress of the seas.* **3** a woman or girl who owns an animal, especially a dog or a horse. **4** a woman who has a thorough knowledge or mastery: *She is complete mistress of the art of cookery.* **5** a woman teaching in a school, or at the head of a school, or giving lessons in a special subject: *the dancing mistress.* *n.*

mis·trust (mis trust′) **1** feel no confidence in; doubt: *She mistrusted her ability to learn to swim.* **2** a lack of trust or confidence: *Because of his mistrust of banks, he kept his money at home.* 1 *v.,* 2 *n.*

mist·y (mis′tē) **1** full of or covered with mist: *misty hills, misty air.* **2** not clearly seen or outlined: *The boys saw a misty shape in the graveyard.* **3** as if seen through a mist; vague; indistinct: *a misty idea.* *adj.,* **mist·i·er, mist·i·est.**

mis·un·der·stand (mis′un dǝr stand′) understand wrongly; give the wrong meaning to: *She misunderstood what the teacher said, and so did the wrong thing.* *v.,* **mis·un·der·stood, mis·un·der·stand·ing.**

mis·un·der·stand·ing (mis′un dǝr stan′ding) **1** a failure to understand; a mistake as to meaning; a wrong understanding. **2** a disagreement: *After their misunderstanding they scarcely spoke to each other for months.* *n.*

mis·un·der·stood (mis′un dǝr stu̇d′) See **misunderstand.** *v.*

mis·use (mis yüz′ for 1 and 2, mis yüs′ for 3) **1** to use for the wrong purpose: *He misuses his knife at the table by lifting food with it.* **2** to treat badly: *He misuses his sled dogs by driving them too hard.* **3** a wrong use: *I notice a misuse of the word 'who' in your letter.* 1, 2 *v.,* **mis·used, mis·us·ing;** 3 *n.*

mite (mīt) **1** anything very small; little bit: *I can't eat a mite of breakfast.* **2** a coin of little value: *Though poor, she gave her mite to charity.* **3** a very tiny animal that lives in foods, on plants, or on other animals. *n.*
☛ **Mite** and **might** are pronounced the same.

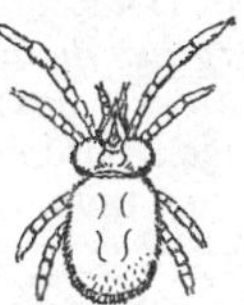

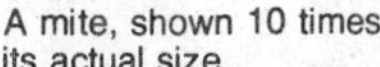

A mite, shown 10 times its actual size

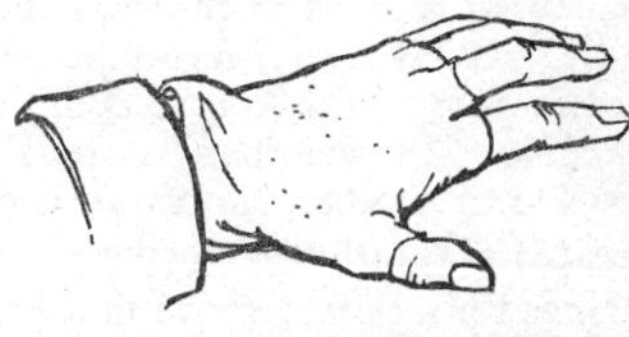

A mitt (def. 1)

mitt (mit) **1** a hand covering that resembles a glove but does not cover the fingers. **2** a glove with a pad on the palm and fingers, used by baseball players. **3** mitten. *n.*

mit·ten (mit′ǝn) a kind of winter glove, covering the four fingers together and the thumb separately. *n.*

mix (miks) **1** put together; stir well together: *We mix butter, sugar, milk, and flour for a cake.* **2** prepare by blending different things: *to mix a cake.* **3** an already-mixed preparation: *a cake mix.* **4** join; be mixed: *Oil and water will not mix.* **5** get along together; make friends easily: *She found it difficult to mix with strangers. He doesn't mix very well.* 1, 2, 4, 5 *v.*, 3 *n.*
mix up, a confuse: *I was so mixed up that I lost my way.* **b** involve; concern: *He was mixed up in a plot to overthrow the king.*

mixed (mikst) **1** formed of different kinds: *mixed candy, mixed tea.* **2** of or for persons of both sexes: *A mixed chorus will sing at our concert. adj.*

mixed number a number made up of a whole number and a fraction, such as 1½.

mix·er (mik′sər) **1** a person or thing that mixes: *a bread mixer.* **2** a person who gets along well with others, making friends easily: *Father and Mother are good mixers. n.*

mix·ture (miks′chər) **1** mixing: *The mixture of the paints took two hours.* **2** something that has been mixed; a product of mixing: *Orange is a mixture of yellow and red. n.*

ml millilitre; millilitres.

M.L.A. Member of the Legislative Assembly.

mo. month; months.

moan (mōn) **1** a long, low sound of suffering. **2** any similar sound: *the moan of the wind.* **3** make moans. **4** complain: *He was always moaning about his luck.* 1, 2 *n.*, 3, 4 *v.*
☛ **Moan** and **mown** are pronounced the same.

moat (mōt) **1** a deep, wide ditch dug around a castle or town as a protection against enemies: *Moats were usually kept filled with water.* See **castle** for picture. **2** a similar ditch used to separate areas in a zoo. *n.*
☛ **Moat** and **mote** are pronounced the same.

mob (mob) **1** a large number of people; crowd. **2** a lawless crowd, easily moved to act without thinking. **3** to crowd around in eagerness, curiosity, anger, etc.: *The eager children mobbed the popcorn man.* **4** attack with violence as a mob does. **5** *Slang.* a group of criminals who work together; gang. 1, 2, 5 *n.*, 3, 4 *v.*, **mobbed, mob·bing.**
☛ **Mob** comes from a Latin phrase *mobile vulgus* meaning 'mobile (or fickle) crowd.'

mo·bile[1] (mō′bīl or mō′bəl) **1** capable of being moved easily; moving easily; movable: *The artillery has many mobile guns. The tongue is mobile. A car is a mobile machine.* **2** easily changed; quick to change from one position to another: *mobile features, a mobile mind. adj.*

mo·bile[2] (mō′bīl or mō′bēl) a decoration of hung and balanced pieces that move in a breeze: *The children used heavy paper and string to make a mobile like our plastic one. n.*

moc·ca·sin (mok′ə sən) a style of shoe having the sides and sole formed from one piece of leather: *North American Indians made moccasins from the skins of deer. n.*

mock (mok) **1** laugh at; make fun of. **2** make fun of by copying or imitating: *The thoughtless children mocked the limp of the crippled boy.* **3** not real; being an imitation: *a mock king, a mock battle, mock modesty.* **4** an action or speech that mocks; mockery. 1, 2 *v.*, 3 *adj.*, 4 *n.*

mock·er·y (mok′ər ē) **1** making fun; ridicule: *Their mockery of her hat hurt her feelings.* **2** a person or thing to be made fun of: *Through his foolishness he became a mockery of the village.* **3** a poor copy or imitation: *Joan's pie was a mockery of her mother's cooking. n., pl.* **mock·er·ies.**

mock·ing·bird (mok′ing bėrd′) a songbird that imitates the songs of other birds. *n.*

mode (mōd) **1** the manner or way in which a thing is done: *Riding on a donkey is a slow mode of travel.* **2** the style, fashion, or custom that is current; the way most people are behaving, talking, dressing, etc. *n.*

mod·el (mod′əl) **1** a small copy: *a model of a ship or an engine, a model of an island.* **2** a figure in clay or wax that is to be copied in marble, bronze, etc.: *a model for a statue.* **3** make, shape, or fashion; design or plan: *Model a bird's nest in clay.* **4** a particular style or design of a thing: *Some car makers produce a new model every year.* **5** a thing or person to be imitated: *The boy wrote so well that the teacher used his composition as a model for the class.* **6** follow as a model: *He modelled himself on his father.* **7** just right or perfect, especially in conduct: *She was a model child.* **8** a person who poses for artists, photographers, etc. **9** a person employed to help sell clothing by wearing it for customers to see. **10** be a model: *She models for advertisements on TV.* 1, 2, 4, 5, 8, 9 *n.*, 3, 6, 10 *v.*, **mod·elled** or **mod·eled, mod·el·ling** or **mod·el·ing;** 7 *adj.*

mod·er·ate (mod′ər it for 1 and 2, mod′ər āt′ for 3 and 4) **1** kept or keeping within proper bounds; not extreme: *moderate expenses, moderate styles.* **2** fair; medium; not very large or good: *to make a moderate profit.* **3** make less violent; become less extreme or violent: *The wind is moderating.* **4** act as chairman; preside over: *Our hockey coach will moderate a panel discussion on the plans for a sports program.* 1, 2 *adj.*, 3, 4 *v.*, **mod·er·at·ed, mod·er·at·ing.**

mod·er·a·tion (mod′ər ā′shen) **1** freedom from excess; proper restraint: *Some people never learn the value of moderation. It is all right to eat candy in moderation.* **2** the act of moderating or of moving away from an extreme: *We all welcomed the moderation of the uncomfortably hot weather. n.*

mod·ern (mod′ərn) of the present time; of times not long past: *Color television is a modern invention. adj.*

mod·est (mod′ist) **1** not thinking too highly of oneself; not vain; humble: *In spite of the honors he received, the scientist remained a modest man.* **2** bashful; not bold; shy. **3** having or showing a sense of what is fit and proper: *People liked the modest behavior of the children.* **4** not too great; not asking too much: *a modest request. adj.*

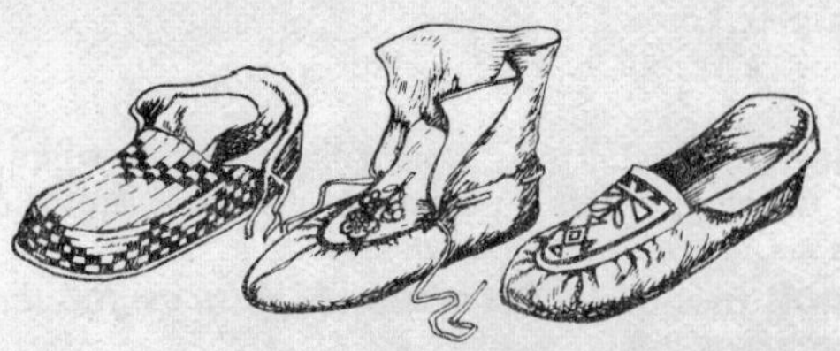

Moccasins

hat, āge, fär; let, ēqual, tėrm; it, īce
hot, ōpen, ôrder; oil, out; cup, pu̇t, rüle
ə̇bove, takən, pencəl, lemən, circəs
ch, child; ng, long; sh, ship
th, thin; ᴛʜ, then; zh, measure

mod·es·ty (mod′is tē) 1 freedom from vanity; being modest or humble. 2 being shy or bashful. 3 decency of actions, thoughts, clothing, etc. *n., pl.* **mod·es·ties.**

mod·i·fi·ca·tion (mod′ə fə kā′shən) 1 a partial alteration or change: *With these modifications your composition will do for the school paper.* 2 modifying or being modified; toning down: *With the modification of his anger he could think clearly again.* 3 a modified form or variety: *The most recent modification of the long-range missile performs flawlessly.* *n.*

mod·i·fy (mod′ə fī′) 1 change somewhat: *to modify the terms of a lease.* 2 make less; tone down; make less severe or strong: *He has modified his demands.* 3 limit the meaning of; qualify: *Adverbs modify verbs and adjectives.* *v.,* **mod·i·fied, mod·i·fy·ing.**

Mo·ham·med (mō ham′id) the founder of a great religion of Asia and Africa. *n.*

Mo·ham·med·an (mō ham′ə dən) See **Moslem.**

Mo·ham·med·an·ism (mō ham′ə dən iz′əm) the religion founded by Mohammed, usually called Islam. *n.*

moist (moist) slightly wet; damp. *adj.* **—moist′ness,** *n.*

moist·en (moi′sən) make moist; become moist: *to moisten the lips. Her eyes moistened with tears.* *v.*

mois·ture (mois′chər) a slight wetness; water or other liquid spread in very small drops in the air or on a surface: *Dew is moisture that collects at night on the grass.* *n.*

mo·lar (mō′lər) a tooth with a broad surface for grinding: *A person's back teeth are molars.* See **teeth** for picture. *n.*

mo·las·ses (mə las′iz) a sweet syrup: *Molasses is obtained in the process of making sugar from sugar cane.* *n.*

mold (mōld) See **mould.**

mold·er (mōl′dər) See **moulder.**

mold·ing (mōl′ding) See **moulding.**

mold·y (mōl′dē) See **mouldy.**

mole[1] (mōl) a spot on the skin, present from birth, and usually brown. *n.*

One kind of mole — about 13 cm long without the tail

mole[2] (mōl) a small animal that lives underground most of the time: *Moles have velvety fur and small, weak eyes.* *n.*

mol·e·cule (mol′ə kyül′) 1 the smallest particle into which a substance can be divided without chemical change. 2 a very small particle. *n.*

mole·hill (mōl′hil′) 1 a small mound or ridge of earth raised up by moles burrowing under the ground. 2 something insignificant. *n.*
make a mountain out of a molehill, give great importance to something which is really insignificant.

mo·lest (mə lest′) meddle with and injure; interfere with and trouble: *It is cruel to molest animals.* *v.*

mol·lusc or **mol·lusk** (mol′əsk) an animal having a soft body that is usually protected by a shell: *Snails, oysters, and clams are molluscs.* *n.*

molt (mōlt) See **moult.**

molt·en (mōl′tən) 1 made liquid by heat; melted: *molten steel.* 2 made by melting and casting: *a molten statue.* *adj.*

mo·ment (mō′mənt) 1 a very short space of time; an instant: *In a moment, all was changed.* 2 a particular point of time: *I started home the very moment I received your message.* 3 importance or significance: *The Premier was busy on a matter of moment.* *n.*

mo·men·tar·i·ly (mō′mən ter′ə lē) 1 for a moment: *He hesitated momentarily.* 2 at every moment; from moment to moment: *The danger was increasing momentarily.* 3 at any moment: *We are expecting the postman momentarily.* *adv.*

mo·men·tar·y (mō′mən ter′ē) lasting for only a moment: *momentary hesitation.* *adj.*

mo·men·tous (mō men′təs) very important: *Choosing between peace and war is a momentous decision.* *adj.*

mo·men·tum (mō men′təm) 1 the force with which a body moves: *A falling object gains momentum as it falls.* 2 the force resulting from movement: *The runner's momentum carried him far beyond the finish line.* *n.*

Mon. Monday.

mon·arch (mon′ərk) 1 a king, queen, emperor, etc.; a ruler. 2 a very large, orange-and-black butterfly. *n.*

mon·arch·ist (mon′ər kist) a person who supports or favors government by a monarch. *n.*

mon·ar·chy (mon′ər kē) 1 government by a monarch. 2 a nation governed by a monarch. *n., pl.* **mon·ar·chies.**

mon·as·ter·y (mon′əs ter′ē) a building or buildings where monks or nuns live and work according to religious rules. *n., pl.* **mon·as·ter·ies.**

Mon·day (mun′dē or mun′dā′) the second day of the week, the day after Sunday. *n.*
☛ **Monday** developed from Old English *monandæg,* meaning 'day of the moon.'

mon·ey (mun′ē) 1 coins and paper notes for use in buying and selling: *He has five dollars in Canadian money.* 2 wealth: *He is a man of money.* *n., pl.* **mon·eys** or **mon·ies.**
make money, a earn or receive money. **b** become rich.

money order an order for the payment of money: *You can buy a money order at the post office or a bank and mail it so as to avoid sending cash through the mail.*

mon·goose (mong′güs) a slender animal of Africa and Asia, like a ferret: *The mongoose is used for destroying rats and is noted for its ability to kill poisonous snakes.* *n., pl.* **mon·goos·es.**

mon·grel (mong′grəl or mung′grəl) 1 an animal or plant of mixed breed, especially a dog. 2 of mixed breed, race, origin, or nature: *a mongrel speech that is half Spanish and half Indian.* 1 *n.*, 2 *adj.*

mon·ies (mun′ēz) a plural of **money.** *n.*

mon·i·tor (mon′ə tər) **1** a pupil in school with special duties, such as helping to keep order and taking attendance. **2** a person who gives advice or warning. **3** a device used for checking and listening to radio and television transmissions, telephone messages, etc., as they are being recorded or broadcast. **4** check and listen to by using such a device. 1–3 *n.*, 4 *v.*

monk (mungk) a man who makes religious vows and, usually, lives in a monastery. *n.*

One kind of South American monkey — body without the tail about 33 cm long; tail about 43 cm long

mon·key (mung′kē) **1** an animal of the group most like man: *Monkeys are very intelligent animals.* **2** one of the smaller animals in this group, not a chimpanzee, gorilla, or other large ape. **3** a person, especially a child, who is full of mischief. **4** *Informal.* play; fool; trifle: *Don't monkey with the television set.* 1–3 *n.*, *pl.* **mon·keys;** 4 *v.*, **mon·keyed, mon·key·ing.**

mon·o·cle (mon′ə kəl) an eyeglass for one eye. *n.*

mon·o·gram (mon′ə gram′) a design made by combining letters, usually of a person's initials: *Monograms are often used on notepaper, table linen, jewellery, etc.* *n.*

mon·o·logue (mon′ə log′) **1** a long speech by one person. **2** a scene or short play for one actor, often written to tell a story, to show character, or to describe a humorous or dramatic situation. *n.* Also spelled **monolog.**

mon·o·plane (mon′ə plān′) an airplane having one set of wings: *Most modern airplanes are monoplanes.* *n.*

mo·nop·o·ly (mə nop′ə lē) **1** the exclusive control of a commodity or service: *The only milk company in our town has a monopoly on milk sales.* **2** the exclusive possession or control of something: *No one person has a monopoly on virtue.* **3** a product or service that is exclusively controlled or nearly so: *In some provinces, the telephone service is a government monopoly.* **4** a person or company having such control. *n.*, *pl.* **mo·nop·o·lies.**

mon·o·syl·la·ble (mon′ə sil′ə bəl) a word of one syllable: *'Yes' and 'grand' are monosyllables.* *n.*

mon·o·tone (mon′ə tōn′) sameness of tone, style of writing, color, etc.: *Don't read in a monotone; use more expression.* *n.*

mo·not·o·nous (mə not′ə nəs) **1** continuing in the same tone: *She spoke in a monotonous voice.* **2** not varying; without change: *monotonous food.* **3** wearying because of its sameness: *monotonous work.* *adj.*

mo·not·o·ny (mə not′ə nē) **1** sameness of tone or pitch: *The monotony of the man's voice was irritating.* **2** a lack of variety. **3** wearisome sameness. *n.*

mon·soon (mon sün′) **1** a seasonal wind of the Indian Ocean and southern Asia: *The monsoon blows from the southwest from April to October and from the northeast during the rest of the year.* **2** the rainy season during which this wind blows from the southwest. *n.*

mon·ster (mon′stər) **1** any animal or plant that is unlike those usually found in nature: *A two-headed cow is a monster.* **2** an imaginary creature of strange appearance: *The story was about monsters from Mars. Mermaids and centaurs are monsters.* **3** a huge creature or thing. **4** a person who is evil or cruel. *n.*

mon·strous (mon′strəs) **1** huge; enormous. **2** unnaturally formed or shaped; like a monster. **3** shocking; horrible; dreadful. *adj.*

month (munth) one of the twelve periods of time into which a year is divided. *n.*

month·ly (munth′lē) **1** of a month; for a month; lasting a month: *a monthly supply.* **2** done, happening, or paid once a month: *a monthly meeting, a monthly examination.* **3** once a month; every month: *Some magazines come monthly.* **4** a magazine published once a month. 1, 2 *adj.*, 3 *adv.*, 4 *n.*, *pl.* **month·lies.**

mon·u·ment (mon′yə mənt) **1** something set up to keep a person or an event from being forgotten; anything that keeps alive the memory of a person or an event: *A monument may be a building, pillar, arch, statue, tomb, or stone.* **2** a permanent or prominent instance or example: *The St. Lawrence Seaway is a monument of engineering.* *n.*

mon·u·men·tal (mon′yə men′təl) **1** of a monument. **2** serving as a monument. **3** like a monument. **4** weighty and lasting; important: *The British North America Act is a monumental document.* **5** very great: *monumental ignorance.* *adj.*

moo (mü) **1** the sound made by a cow. **2** make this sound. 1 *n.*, *pl.* **moos;** 2 *v.*, **mooed, moo·ing.**

mood (müd) a state of mind or feeling: *I am in the mood to play just now; I don't want to study.* *n.*

mood·y (müd′ē) **1** likely to have changes of mood. **2** often having gloomy moods: *She has been moody ever since she lost her job.* **3** sunk in sadness; gloomy; sullen: *The little girl sat in moody silence.* *adj.*, **mood·i·er, mood·i·est. —mood′i·ly,** *adv.* **—mood′i·ness,** *n.*

Phases of the moon

moon (mün) **1** a heavenly body that revolves around the earth once in about 29½ days: *The moon shines in the sky at night and looks bright because it reflects the sun's light.* **2** about a month or 29½ days: *The Indians counted time by moons.* **3** a natural or artificial satellite: *the moons of Jupiter.* **4** something shaped like the moon. **5** wander about idly; gaze in a dreamy way: *Don't moon when you have work to do.* 1–4 *n.*, 5 *v.*

moon·beam (mün′bēm′) a ray of moonlight. *n.*

moon·light (mün′līt′) **1** the light of the moon. **2** having the light of the moon: *a moonlight night.* *n.*

hat, āge, fär; let, ēqual, tėrm; it, īce
hot, ōpen, ôrder; oil, out; cup, pu̇t, rüle
əbove, takən, pencəl, lemən, circəs
ch, child; ng, long; sh, ship
th, thin; ᴛʜ, then; zh, measure

moon·lit (mün′lit′) lighted by the moon. *adj.*

moor[1] (mür) put or keep a ship or boat in place by means of ropes or chains fastened to the shore or to anchors. *v.*

moor[2] (mür) in the British Isles, open waste land, usually hilly or high up and having low plant growth. *n.*

moor·ing (mür′ing) **1** a place where a ship is anchored or tied up. **2 moorings,** *pl.* the ropes, cables, or anchors by which a ship is made fast. *n.*

moor·land (mür′land′ or mür′lənd) an area of moors. *n.*

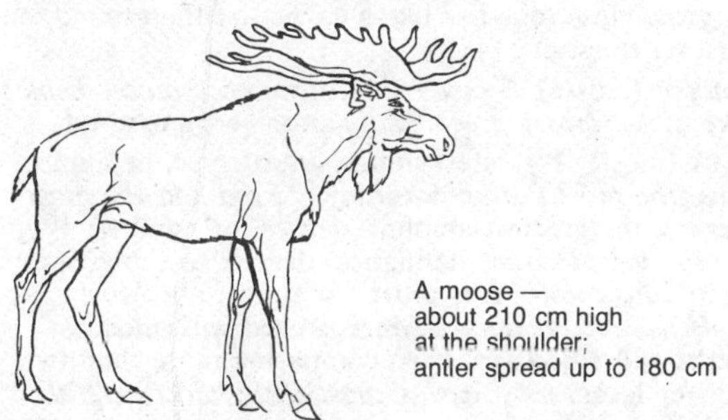

A moose — about 210 cm high at the shoulder; antler spread up to 180 cm

moose (müs) a large deerlike animal that lives in Canada and the northern part of the United States. *n., pl.* **moose.**

moose·bird (müs′bėrd′) *Cdn.* the Canada jay. *n.*

mop (mop) **1** a bundle of coarse yarn, rags, or cloth fastened at the end of a stick, for cleaning floors, dishes, etc. **2** wash or wipe up; clean with a mop: *to mop the floor.* **3** wipe tears or sweat from: *He mopped his brow with his handkerchief.* **4** something like a mop: *The barber will cut his mop of hair before he goes to his new job.* 1, 4 *n.,* 2, 3 *v.,* **mopped, mop·ping.**

mope (mōp) be dull, silent, and sad. *v.,* **moped, mop·ing.**

mo·raine (mə rān′) a mass or ridge of rocks, dirt, etc. deposited at the sides or end of a glacier after being carried down or pushed aside by the pressure of ice. *n.*

mor·al (môr′əl) **1** good in character or conduct; virtuous according to civilized standards of right and wrong; right; just: *a moral act, a moral man.* **2** capable of understanding right and wrong: *A little baby is not a moral being.* **3** having to do with character, or with the difference between right and wrong: *Whether finders should be keepers is a moral question.* **4 morals,** *pl.* character or behavior in matters of right and wrong: *The boy's morals were excellent.* **5** the lesson, inner meaning, or teaching of a fable, a story, or an event: *The moral of the story was 'Look before you leap.'* **6** teaching a good lesson; having a good influence: *a moral book.* **7** that encourages and gives confidence: *We gave moral support to the team by cheering loudly.* 1–3, 6, 7 *adj.,* 4, 5 *n.*

☛ A common error is to use **moral** (concerning right conduct) instead of **morale** (mental condition as regards courage, confidence, enthusiasm, etc.).

mo·rale (mə ral′ or mə räl′) mental condition or attitude as regards courage, confidence, enthusiasm, etc.: *The morale of the team was low after its defeat.* *n.*

☛ See note at **moral.**

mo·ral·i·ty (mə ral′ə tē) **1** the right or wrong of an action: *They argued about the morality of using animals for medical research.* **2** the doing of right; virtue: *He ranks very high in both intelligence and morality.* *n., pl.* **mo·ral·i·ties.**

mor·al·ly (môr′əl ē) **1** in a moral manner: *She tried to behave morally.* **2** from a moral point of view: *What he did was morally wrong.* *adv.*

mo·rass (mə ras′) a piece of low, soft, wet ground; a swamp. *n.*

mor·bid (môr′bid) **1** unhealthy; not wholesome; sickly: *His mother thinks his liking of horror movies is morbid.* **2** caused by disease; characteristic of disease; diseased: *Cancer is a morbid growth.* **3** horrible; frightful: *the morbid details of a murder.* *adj.*

more (môr) **1** greater in amount, degree, or number: *more heat, more men. A dozen is more than ten.* **2** a greater or additional amount, degree, or number: *Tell me more about your camping trip. We need more than four men for a lacrosse team.* **3** in a higher degree; to a greater extent: *A burn hurts more than a scratch does.* **4** in addition; further; again: *Take one step more. Sing once more.* **5** further; additional: *This plant needs more sun.* **6 More** is used with most adverbs and adjectives when comparing two things or ideas: *more easily, more truly, more careful. 'More common' means 'commoner.'* 1, 5 *adj.,* 2 *n.,* 3, 4, 6 *adv.*
more or less, a somewhat: *Most people are more or less selfish.* **b** about; approximately: *The distance is fifty kilometres, more or less.*

more·o·ver (môr ō′vər) also; besides; furthermore: *I don't want to go skating and, moreover, the ice is too thin.* *adv.*

morgue (môrg) a place, usually in a police station or hospital, in which unclaimed bodies of dead persons are kept until they can be identified and taken away by their family or friends. *n.*

Mor·mon (môr′mən) a member of the Church of Jesus Christ of Latter-day Saints, founded in the United States in 1830 by Joseph Smith. *n.*

morn (môrn) in poetry, morning; dawn. *n.*

☛ **Morn** and **mourn** are pronounced the same.

morn·ing (môr′ning) the early part of the day, ending at noon. *n.*

morn·ing–glo·ry (môr′ning glô′rē) a climbing vine that has heart-shaped leaves and funnel-shaped flowers of blue, lavender, pink, or white. *n., pl.* **morn·ing-glo·ries.**

mo·ron (môr′on) a person not able to develop mentally beyond the usual level of a child of twelve years. *n.*

mo·rose (mə rōs′) gloomy; sullen: *The unfriendly boy wore a morose expression.* *adj.*

mor·row (môr′ō) the following day or time: *We expect her on the morrow.* *n.*
good morrow, an old way of saying 'Good morning.'

Morse code (môrs) a signalling system by which letters, numbers, etc. are represented by dots, dashes, and spaces or by long and short sounds or flashes of light.

☛ Named after Samuel F. B. *Morse* (1791–1872), American inventor of the telegraph.

mor·sel (môr′səl) **1** a small bite; a mouthful. **2** a piece or fragment. *n.*

mor·tal (môr′təl) **1** sure to die sometime. **2** a being that is sure to die sometime: *All living creatures are mortals.* **3** of man; of mortals: *Mortal flesh has many pains and diseases.* **4** a man; a human being: *No mortal should strive against God.* **5** causing death: *a mortal wound, a mortal illness.* **6** lasting until death: *a mortal enemy, a mortal battle.* **7** very great; deadly: *mortal terror.* **8** in the Roman Catholic Church, causing death of the soul: *Killing your brother would be a mortal sin.* 1, 3, 5–8 *adj.*, 2, 4 *n.*

mor·tal·ly (môr′təl ē) **1** so as to cause death: *mortally wounded by a bullet.* **2** very greatly; bitterly: *mortally offended. adv.*

mor·tar¹ (môr′tər) a mixture of lime, cement, sand, and water, used for holding bricks or stones together. *n.*

A mortar and pestle

mor·tar² (môr′tər) **1** a very short artillery piece for shooting shells or fireworks high into the air. **2** a bowl of very hard material, in which substances may be pounded to a powder. *n.*

mort·gage (môr′gij) a claim on property, given to a person, bank, or firm that has loaned money in case the money is not repaid when due. *n.*

mor·ti·fi·ca·tion (môr′tə fə kā′shən) extreme embarrassment, shame, or humiliation: *The boy was overcome with mortification when he spilled milk on his host's suit. n.*

mor·ti·fy (môr′tə fī′) wound a person's feelings; make a person feel humbled or ashamed: *A mother is mortified when her child behaves badly. v.,* **mor·ti·fied, mor·ti·fy·ing.**

mos. months.

A mosaic

mo·sa·ic (mō zā′ik) a picture or design made of small pieces of stone, glass, wood, etc. of different colors, set together or inlaid: *Mosaics are used in the floors, walls, or ceilings of some fine buildings. n.*

Mos·lem (moz′ləm) **1** a follower of Mohammed; a believer in the religion founded by him. **2** of Mohammed or the religion founded by him. 1 *n., pl.* **Mos·lems** or **Mos·lem;** 2 *adj.*

mosque (mosk) a Moslem place of worship. *n.*

mos·qui·to (məs kē′tō) a small, slender insect: *The female mosquito can pierce the skin of people and animals and draw blood, causing a sting that itches. n., pl.* **mos·qui·toes** or **mos·qui·tos.**

moss (mos) very small, soft, green or brown plants that grow close together like a carpet on the ground, on rocks, on trees, etc. *n.*

moss·y (mos′ē) **1** covered with moss: *a mossy bank.* **2** like moss: *mossy green. adj.,* **moss·i·er, moss·i·est.**

most (mōst) **1** greatest in amount, degree, or number: *I have the most fun on Saturday. Fred had the most votes.* **2** the greatest amount, degree, or number: *Who gave the most?* **3** in the highest degree; to the greatest extent: *This tooth hurts most.* **4** almost all: *Most people like ice cream.* **5 Most** is used with most adverbs and adjectives when comparing more than two things or ideas: *most easily, most truly, most careful.* 1, 4 *adj.*, 2 *n.*, 3, 5 *adv.*

at most, not more than.

for the most part, mainly; usually.

☛ **Most** is often used in informal speech in place of **almost:** *A drop in prices will appeal to most everybody.* This usage may sometimes be followed in writing conversation, but is ordinarily out of place in written English.

-most a suffix meaning: greatest in amount, degree, or number as in *foremost, uppermost, topmost.*

most·ly (mōst′lē) almost all; for the most part; mainly; chiefly. *adv.*

mote (mōt) a speck of dust. *n.*

☛ **Mote** and **moat** are pronounced the same.

mo·tel (mō tel′) a roadside hotel or a group of furnished cottages or cabins providing overnight lodging for motorists. *n.*

☛ **Motel** is from *mo*tor and ho*tel.*

One kind of moth — wingspread about 11 cm

moth (moth) **1** a winged insect very much like a butterfly, but flying mostly at night. **2** a small winged insect that lays eggs in wool, fur, etc.: *The larvae of the moth eats holes in clothes. n.*

moth·er (muᴛʜ′ər) **1** a female parent. **2** take care of: *She mothers her baby sister.* **3** the cause or source of anything. **4** the head of a community of nuns. **5** belonging to one because of birth; native: *Scotland is my mother country, and English is my mother tongue.* 1, 3, 4 *n.*, 2 *v.*, 5 *adj.*

moth·er·hood (muᴛʜ′ər hůd′) the state of being a

hat, āge, fär; let, ēqual, tėrm; it, īce
hot, ōpen, ôrder; oil, out; cup, pu̇t, rüle
əbove, takən, pencəl, lemən, circəs
ch, child; ng, long; sh, ship
th, thin; ᴛʜ, then; zh, measure

mother: *The young wife was proud of her motherhood.* *n.*

moth·er–in–law (muᴛʜ′ər in lo′ or muᴛʜ′ər in lô′) the mother of one's husband or wife. *n., pl.* **mothers-in-law.**

moth·er·ly (muᴛʜ′ər lē) like a mother; like a mother's; kindly: *a motherly person, a motherly action, motherly love.* *adj.*

moth·er–of–pearl (muᴛʜ′ər əv pėrl′) the hard, smooth, glossy lining of the shell of the pearl oyster and certain other shells: *Mother-of-pearl is used to make buttons and ornaments.* *n.*

mo·tion (mō′shən) **1** the condition or state of moving; a movement or a change of position or place: *He swayed with the motion of the moving train. Every object is either in motion or at rest.* **2** make a movement, as of the hand or head, to show one's meaning: *She motioned to show us the way.* **3** show a person what to do by such a motion: *He motioned me out.* **4** a formal suggestion made in a meeting or court of law, to be voted on: *The motion to adjourn was carried.* 1, 4 *n.*, 2, 3 *v.*

mo·tion·less (mō′shən lis) not moving. *adj.*

motion picture a series of pictures on a continuous strip of film, projected on a screen in such rapid succession that the viewer gets the impression that the persons and things pictured are moving; a moving picture or movie.

mo·ti·vate (mō′tə vāt′) make someone want to act; provide with a motive: *Pride in his home motivated the boy to cut the grass on the lawn.* *v.*

mo·tive (mō′tiv) **1** the thought or feeling that makes one act: *His motive in going was a wish to travel.* **2** that makes something move: *Steam and electricity supply motive power.* 1 *n.*, 2 *adj.*

mot·ley (mot′lē) **1** made up of different colors and of different things; varied: *a motley collection of old books and toys.* **2** a suit of more than one color worn by clowns: *At the party he wore motley.* 1 *adj.*, 2 *n., pl.* **mot·leys.**

mo·tor (mō′tər) **1** an engine that makes a machine go: *an electric motor, a gasoline motor.* **2** run by a motor: *a motor bicycle.* **3** an automobile. **4** travel by automobile. **5** causing or having to do with motion: *Motor nerves arouse muscles to action.* 1, 3 *n.*, 4 *v.*, 2, 5 *adj.*

mo·tor·boat (mō′tər bōt′) a boat that is propelled by a motor. *n.*

motor car an automobile.

mo·tor·cy·cle (mō′tər sī′kəl) **1** a two-wheeled vehicle run by a motor. **2** travel by motorcycle. 1 *n.*, 2 *v.*, **mo·tor·cy·cled, mo·tor·cy·cling.**

mo·tor·ist (mō′tər ist) a person who drives or travels in an automobile. *n.*

mo·tor·ize (mō′tər īz′) **1** furnish with a motor. **2** supply with motor-driven vehicles: *We don't see horse-drawn vehicles now that store delivery is motorized.* *v.*, **mo·tor·ized, mo·tor·iz·ing.**

mo·tor·man (mō′tər mən) **1** a man who runs a streetcar or subway train. **2** a man who runs a motor. *n., pl.* **mo·tor·men** (mō′tər mən).

mot·tled (mot′əld) spotted or streaked with different colors. *adj.*

mot·to (mot′ō) **1** a brief sentence adopted as a rule of conduct: *'Think before you speak' is a good motto.* **2** a sentence, word, or phrase written or engraved on some object. *n., pl.* **mot·toes** or **mot·tos.**

mould[1] or **mold** (mōld) **1** a hollow shape in which anything is formed or cast: *a jelly mould, a metal mould. When poured into a mould, many liquids will harden into the shape of the mould.* **2** the shape or form which is given by a mould: *The moulds of ice cream were bells and bows.* **3** the model according to which anything is shaped: *The son is formed in his father's mould.* **4** make or form into shape: *We are moulding clay to make model animals. Her character was moulded by suffering.* 1–3 *n.*, 4 *v.*

mould[2] or **mold** (mōld) **1** a woolly or furry growth of fungus that appears on food and other animal or vegetable substances when they are left too long in a warm, moist place. **2** become covered with this woolly growth: *The boots moulded in the damp cellar.* 1 *n.*, 2 *v.*

mould[3] or **mold** (mōld) soft, rich, crumbly soil; earth mixed with decaying leaves, manure, etc.: *Many wild flowers grow in the forest mould.* *n.*

mould·er[1] or **mold·er** (mōl′dər) crumble away; break up gradually into dust. *v.*

mould·er[2] or **mold·er** (mōl′dər) a person or thing that moulds; a person who shapes something. *n.*

mould·ing or **mold·ing** (mōl′ding) **1** something moulded. **2** a shaped strip of wood or plaster, such as that often used around the upper walls of a room: *Mouldings may be simply ornamental, or they may be used to support pictures, to cover electric wires, etc.* *n.*

mould·y or **mold·y** (mōl′dē) **1** covered with a fuzzy growth of mould: *a mouldy crust of bread.* **2** musty or stale: *There was a mouldy smell in the deserted house.* *adj.*, **mould·i·er** or **mold·i·er, mould·i·est** or **mold·i·est.**

moult or **molt** (mōlt) shed the feathers, skin, etc. before a new growth: *Birds and snakes moult.* *v.*

mound (mound) **1** a bank or heap of earth or stones. **2** the slightly elevated ground from which a baseball pitcher pitches. *n.*

mount[1] (mount) **1** go up: *to mount a hill or a ladder.* **2** get up on: *to mount a horse, to mount a platform.* **3** get on a horse: *He mounted in haste.* **4** put on a horse; furnish with a horse: *The police who patrol this park are mounted.* **5** a horse for riding: *The general had an excellent mount.* **6** rise; increase; rise in amount: *The cost of living mounts steadily.* **7** put in proper position or order for use: *The scientist mounted the sample on a slide for his microscope.* **8** fix in a proper setting: *We mount photographs on cards.* **9** that on which anything is mounted, fixed, supported, or placed: *the mount for a picture.* 1–4, 6–8 *v.*, 5, 9 *n.*

mount[2] (mount) a mountain or high hill. **Mount** is often used before the names of mountains: *Mount Royal.* *n.*

moun·tain (moun′tən) **1** a very high hill: *the Rocky*

Mountains. **2** of or having something to do with mountains: *mountain air, mountain plants.* **3** a large heap or pile of anything: *a mountain of rubbish.* **4** a huge amount: *He overcame a mountain of difficulties.* *n.*

make a mountain out of a molehill, give great importance to something which is really insignificant.

moun·tain·eer (moun′tə nēr′) **1** a person who lives in the mountains. **2** a person skilled in mountain climbing. *n.*

mountain goat the white antelope of the Rocky Mountains.

mountain lion cougar.

moun·tain·ous (moun′tə nəs) **1** covered with mountain ranges: *mountainous country.* **2** huge: *a mountainous wave. adj.*

mountain range a row of connected mountains; a large group of mountains.

moun·tain·side (moun′tən sīd′) the slope of a mountain below the summit. *n.*

Mount·ie or **mount·ie** (moun′tē) *Informal.* a member of the Royal Canadian Mounted Police, a force maintained by the Government of Canada. *n., pl.* **Mount·ies** or **mount·ies.**

mourn (môrn) **1** grieve. **2** feel or show sorrow over: *She mourned her lost doll. v.* **—mourn′er,** *n.*

☛ **Mourn** and **morn** are pronounced the same.

mourn·ful (môrn′fəl) full of grief; sad; sorrowful: *a mournful voice. adj.*

mourn·ing (môr′ning) **1** the wearing of black or some other color to show sorrow for a person's death. **2** the draping of buildings or the flying of flags at half-mast as an outward sign of sorrow for death. **3** clothes or decorations worn to show sorrow for death: *The widow was dressed in mourning. n.*

A house mouse — about 10 cm long without the tail

mouse (mous; sometimes, mouz for 2) **1** any of many kinds of small, usually greyish or brownish gnawing animal, especially the common house mouse: *White mice are a variety of house mouse.* **2** hunt for mice; catch mice for food: *Cats and owls often go mousing at night.* 1 *n., pl.* **mice;** 2 *v.,* **moused, mous·ing.**

mous·ey or **mous·y** (mous′ē) resembling or suggesting a mouse in color, appearance, behavior, etc.: *She had mousey hair. adj.*

mous·tache (mus′tash or mə stash′) See **mustache.**

mouth (mouth for 1–4, mouᴛʜ for 5 and 6) **1** the opening through which a person or animal takes in food; the space in the head containing the tongue and teeth. **2** the part of the face around the mouth; the lips: *Use your serviette to wipe your mouth.* **3** an opening suggesting a mouth: *the mouth of a cave, the mouth of a bottle.* **4** a part of a river, creek, etc. where its waters empty into some other body of water: *the mouth of the St. Lawrence River.* **5** utter words in an affected, pompous way: *I dislike actors who mouth their speeches.* **6** a grimace; pout: *The foolish boy made mouths at us.* 1–4, 6 *n.,* 5 *v.*

down in the mouth, *Informal.* in low spirits; discouraged.

the horse's mouth, the original source; the person who knows: *The news came straight from the horse's mouth.*

mouth·ful (mouth′fu̇l) **1** the amount the mouth can easily hold. **2** what is taken into the mouth at one time. **3** a small amount. *n., pl.* **mouth·fuls.**

mouth organ harmonica.

mouth·piece (mouth′pēs′) **1** the part of a pipe, horn, etc. that is placed in or against a person's mouth. **2** a person, newspaper, etc. that speaks for others. *n.*

mov·a·ble (müv′ə bəl) **1** that can be moved: *Our fingers are movable.* **2** that can be carried from place to place as personal belongings can. **3** anything that can be carried from place to place: *The house was bare; all the furniture and other movables had been taken away.* **4** changing from one date to another in different years: *Easter is a movable holiday.* 1, 2, 4 *adj.,* 3 *n.*

move (müv) **1** change the place or position of: *Do not move your hand. I'm going to move that chair nearer the window.* **2** change place or position: *The child moved in his sleep.* **3** the act of moving; movement: *If you make a move, the dog will bark. We had nice weather for our move to the country.* **4** change one's place of living or working: *We move to the country next week.* **5** put or keep in motion; shake; stir: *The wind moves the leaves.* **6** make progress; go: *The train moves out slowly.* **7** impel; arouse a person to laughter, anger, pity, etc.: *What moved you to do this? The sad story moved her.* **8** do something about; act: *God moves in a mysterious way.* **9** an action taken to bring about some result: *His next move was to earn some money.* **10** the moving of a piece in chess and other games: *That was a good move.* **11** a player's turn to move: *It is your move now.* **12** in a meeting, bring forward or propose: *Mr. Chairman, I move that the report of the treasurer be adopted.* 1, 2, 4–8, 12 *v.,* **moved, mov·ing;** 3, 9–11 *n.* **—mov·er,** *n.*

move in, move oneself, one's family, one's belongings, etc. into a new place to live or work.

move out, move oneself, one's family, belongings, etc. out of a place where one has lived or worked.

on the move, moving about: *They are restless and always on the move.*

move·a·ble (müv′ə bəl) See **movable.**

move·ment (müv′mənt) **1** the act of moving: *We run by movements of the legs.* **2** the moving parts of a machine; a special group of parts that move on each other: *The movement of a watch consists of many little wheels.* **3** in music, the kind of rhythm and speed a piece has: *The movement of a waltz is very different from that of a march.* **4** one section of a long piece of music: *The program included only the first movement of the symphony.* **5** a program by a group of people to bring about some one thing: *the movement for peace.* **6** an emptying of the bowels. *n.*

mov·ie (müv′ē) motion picture. *n.*

mow[1] (mō) **1** cut down with a machine or a scythe: *to mow grass. The men are mowing today.* **2** cut down the grass or grain from: *to mow a field.* **3** destroy at a sweep or in large numbers, as if by mowing: *The firing of the enemy mowed down our men like grass.* *v.,* **mowed, mowed** or **mown, mow·ing. —mow′er,** *n.*

mow[2] (mou or mō) **1** the place in the barn where hay, alfalfa, grain, or straw is piled or stored. **2** a pile of hay, grain, etc. in a barn. *n.*

mown (mōn) See **mow.** *New-mown hay is hay that has just been cut. adj.*

☛ **Mown** and **moan** are pronounced the same.

MP or **M.P.** Member of Parliament.

mph or **m.p.h.** miles per hour.

MPP or **M.P.P.** Member of Provincial Parliament.

Mr. or **Mr** (mis′tər) Mister, a title put in front of a man's name or the name of his official position: *Mr. Jackson, Mr. Speaker.*

Mrs. or **Mrs** (mis′iz) a title put in front of a married woman's name: *Mrs. Jackson.*

Ms. or **Ms** (miz) a title used in front of the name of a married or unmarried woman or girl: *Ms. Jackson.*

Mt. mount; mountain: *Mt. Edith Cavell.*

much (much) **1** in great amount or degree: *much rain, much pleasure, not much money.* **2** nearly; about: *This is much the same as the others.* **3** a great amount: *I did not hear much of the talk. Eating too much of this cake will make you sick.* **4** to a high degree; greatly: *I was much pleased with the toy.* 1 *adj.,* **more, most;** 2, 4 *adv.,* **more, most;** 3 *n.*

make much of, pay much attention to or do much for.

not much of a, not a very good: *Six dollars a day is not much of a wage.*

too much for, more than a match for; more than one can cope with, stand, or bear: *The examination was too much for him. Their team was too much for ours.*

mu·ci·lage (myü′sə lij) a sticky, gummy substance used to make things stick together. *n.*

muck (muk) dirt; filth. *n.*

mu·cous mem·brane (myü′kəs mem′brān) the lining of the nose, throat, and other cavities of the body that open to the air.

mu·cus (myü′kəs) a slimy substance that is secreted by and moistens the mucous membranes: *A cold in the head causes a discharge of mucus. n.*

mud (mud) earth so wet that it is soft and sticky: *The earth turned to mud when it rained. Mud covered the bottom of the pond. n.*

mud·dle (mud′əl) **1** mix up; cause confusion or disorder in: *to muddle a piece of work.* **2** think or act in a confused, blundering way: *to muddle over a problem, to muddle through a difficulty.* **3** make confused or stupid: *The more you talk, the more you muddle me.* **4** a mess; disorder or confusion: *When Mother came home, she found the house in a muddle.* 1–3 *v.,* **mud·dled, mud·dling;** 4 *n.*

mud·dy (mud′ē) **1** of or like mud: *muddy footprints on the floor.* **2** having much mud; covered with mud: *a muddy road, muddy shoes.* **3** clouded with mud; dull; not pure: *muddy water, a muddy color.* **4** confused; not clear: *muddy thinking.* **5** make muddy; become muddy. 1–4 *adj.,* **mud·di·er, mud·di·est;** 5 *v.,* **mud·died, mud·dy·ing.**

mud·guard (mud′gärd′) a guard or shield so placed as to protect riders from the mud thrown back by the moving wheels of a vehicle: *My bicycle has two mudguards. n.*

hat, āge, fär; let, ēqual, tėrm; it, īce
hot, ōpen, ôrder; oil, out; cup, pu̇t, rüle
əbove, takən, pencəl, lemən, circəs
ch, child; ng, long; sh, ship
th, thin; ᴛʜ, then; zh, measure

muff (muf) **1** a covering, usually of fur, for keeping both hands warm. One hand is put in at each end. **2** fail to catch and hold a ball when it comes into one's hands. **3** a clumsy failure to catch and hold a ball that comes into one's hands: *The catcher's muff allowed the runner to score.* **4** handle awkwardly; bungle: *My brother muffed his chance to get that job.* 1, 3 *n.,* 2, 4 *v.*

muf·fin (muf′ən) a small, round cake made of wheat flour, corn meal, or the like, often without sugar: *Muffins are eaten with butter, and usually served hot. n.*

muf·fle (muf′əl) **1** wrap or cover up in order to keep warm and dry: *She muffled her throat in a warm scarf.* **2** wrap or cover in order to soften or stop the sound: *A bell can be muffled with cloth.* **3** dull or deaden a sound. *v.,* **muf·fled, muf·fling.**

muf·fler (muf′lər) **1** a wrap or scarf worn around the neck for warmth. **2** anything used to deaden sound: *An automobile engine has a muffler attached to the exhaust pipe. n.*

mug (mug) **1** a china or metal drinking cup with a handle, usually heavy, used without a saucer. **2** the amount a mug holds: *to drink a mug of milk. n.*

mug·gy (mug′ē) warm, damp, and close: *The weather was muggy. adj.,* **mug·gi·er, mug·gi·est.**

muk·luk (muk′luk) *Cdn.* a high, waterproof boot, often made of sealskin, worn by Eskimos and others in the North. *n.*

☛ **Mukluk** comes from an Eskimo word for a kind of seal.

mu·lat·to (mə lat′ō or myü lat′ō) a person having one white and one Negro parent. *n., pl.* **mu·lat·toes.**

mul·ber·ry (mul′ber′ē) **1** any of various trees with small, berrylike fruit that can be eaten. The leaves of one kind are used for feeding silkworms. **2** its sweet fruit. **3** dark, purplish red. 1–3 *n., pl.* **mul·ber·ries;** 3 *adj.*

mulch (mulch) **1** straw, leaves, loose earth, etc. spread on the ground around trees or plants: *Mulch is used to protect roots from cold or heat, to prevent evaporation of moisture from the soil, or to keep fruit clean.* **2** to cover with straw, leaves, etc. 1 *n.,* 2 *v.*

mule[1] (myül) **1** an animal that is part donkey and part horse: *The mule has the form and size of a horse, but the large ears, small hoofs, and tufted tail of a donkey.* **2** *Informal.* a stupid or stubborn person. **3** a kind of spinning machine. *n.*

☛ **Mule** and **mewl** are pronounced the same.

mule[2] (myül) a kind of slipper worn by women. *n.*

☛ See note at **mule**[1].

mu·le·teer (myü′lə tēr′) a driver of mules. *n.*

mul·ish (myül′ish) like a mule; stubborn; obstinate. *adj.*

mul·ti·ple (mul′tə pəl) **1** of, having, or involving

many parts, elements, relations, etc.: *a man of multiple interests.* **2** a number that contains another number a certain number of times without a remainder: *12 is a multiple of 3.* 1 *adj.*, 2 *n.*

mul·ti·pli·cand (mul′tə plə kand′) the number to be multiplied by another: *In 5 times 497, the multiplicand is 497.* *n.*

27 — MULTIPLICAND } FACTORS
3 — MULTIPLIER }
81 — PRODUCT

The parts of a multiplication question

mul·ti·pli·ca·tion (mul′tə plə kā′shən) **1** multiplying or being multiplied. **2** the operation of multiplying one number by another. *n.*

mul·ti·pli·er (mul′tə plī′ər) **1** a person or thing that multiplies. **2** the number by which another number is to be multiplied: *In 5 times 8, 5 is the multiplier.* *n.*

mul·ti·ply (mul′tə plī′) **1** take a number or quantity a given number of times: *To multiply 6 by 3 means to take 6 three times, making 18.* *Symbol:* x **2** increase in number or amount: *The dangers and difficulties multiplied as we went on.* *v.*, **mul·ti·plied, mul·ti·ply·ing.**

mul·ti·tude (mul′tə tyüd′ or mul′tə tüd′) a great many; a crowd: *a multitude of difficulties, a multitude of enemies.* *n.*

mum¹ (mum) silent; saying nothing: *Keep mum about this; tell no one.* *adj.*

mum² (mum) *Informal.* mother. *n.*

mum·ble (mum′bəl) **1** speak indistinctly, as a person does when his lips are partly closed. **2** the act or fact of talking indistinctly; indistinct speech: *There was a mumble of protest from the team against the umpire's decision.* 1 *v.*, **mum·bled, mum·bling;** 2 *n.*

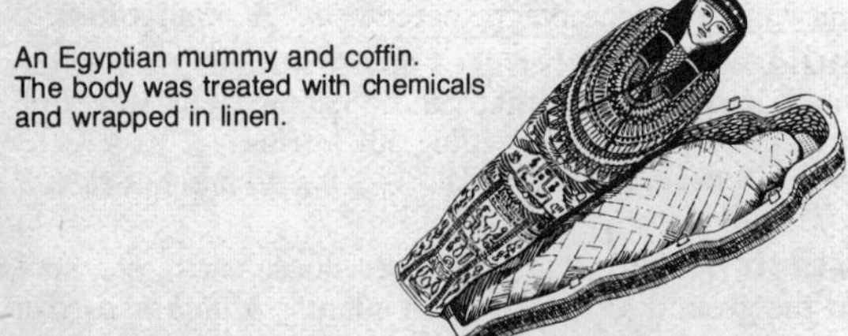
An Egyptian mummy and coffin. The body was treated with chemicals and wrapped in linen.

mum·my¹ (mum′ē) a dead body preserved from decay: *Egyptian mummies have lasted more than 3000 years.* *n., pl.* **mum·mies.**

☛ **Mummy** came through French and Latin from an Arabic word *mūmiyā,* which came from a Persian word *mūm,* meaning 'wax.' Wax was used in preserving dead bodies.

mum·my² (mum′ē) *Informal.* mother. *n.*

mumps (mumps) a contagious disease that causes swelling of the neck and face and difficulty in swallowing. *n.*

munch (munch) chew vigorously and steadily; chew noisily: *The horse munched its oats.* *v.*

mu·nic·i·pal (myü nis′ə pəl) **1** of or having something to do with the affairs of a city, town, or other municipality: *The provincial police assisted the municipal police.* **2** run by a municipality: *municipal affairs.* *adj.*

mu·nic·i·pal·i·ty (myü nis′ə pal′ə tē) a city, town, county, district, township, or other area having local self-government. *n., pl.* **mu·nic·i·pal·i·ties.**

mu·ni·tion (myü nish′ən) Usually, **munitions,** *pl.* material used in war: *Munitions are military supplies such as guns, powder, or bombs.* *n.*

mu·ral (myür′əl) **1** on a wall: *A mural painting is painted on the wall of a building.* **2** a picture painted on a wall. 1 *adj.*, 2 *n.*

mur·der (mėr′dər) **1** the intentional and unlawful killing of a human being: *He was convicted of murder.* **2** an instance of such a crime: *There has never been a murder in this town.* **3** kill a human being intentionally: *Cain murdered his brother.* **4** do something very badly; spoil or ruin: *She murdered the song every time she tried to sing it.* 1, 2 *n.*, 3, 4 *v.*

mur·der·er (mėr′dər ər) a person who murders somebody. *n.*

mur·der·ous (mėr′dər əs) **1** able or likely to kill: *The villain aimed a murderous blow at the hero's back.* **2** ready or intending to murder: *a murderous villain.* *adj.*

murk (mėrk) darkness; gloom: *A light flashed through the murk of the night.* *n.*

murk·y (mėr′kē) dark; gloomy: *a murky prison, a wet, murky day.* *adj.*, **murk·i·er, murk·i·est.**

mur·mur (mėr′mər) **1** a soft, low, indistinct sound that rises and falls a little but goes on without breaks: *the murmur of a stream or of voices in another room.* **2** make a soft, low, indistinct sound. **3** a softly spoken word or speech. **4** say in a murmur: *The shy girl murmured her thanks.* 1, 3 *n.*, 2, 4 *v.*

mus·cle (mus′əl) **1** the tissue in the bodies of people and animals that can be tightened or loosened so as to make the body move. **2** a special bundle of such tissue that moves some particular bone or part: *You can feel the muscles in your arm.* **3** strength. *n.*

☛ **Muscle** comes from a Latin word *musculus,* meaning 'a little mouse,' because some muscles were thought to look like a running mouse when flexed and then relaxed.

☛ **Muscle** and **mussel** are pronounced the same.

mus·cu·lar (mus′kyə lər) **1** of the muscles: *a muscular strain, muscular activity.* **2** having well-developed muscles; strong: *a muscular arm.* *adj.*

muse (myüz) think in a dreamy way; think: *The boy spent the whole afternoon in musing about being an astronaut.* *v.*, **mused, mus·ing.**

Muse (myüz) in Greek myths, one of the nine goddesses of the fine arts and sciences. *n.*

mu·se·um (myü zē′əm) the building or rooms in which a collection of objects illustrating science, history, art, or other subjects is kept and displayed. *n.*

☛ **Museum** is from a Latin word meaning 'a place or seat of the Muses.'

mush¹ (mush) **1** corn meal boiled in water. **2** any soft, thick mass: *The heavy rain made mush of the old dirt road.* *n.*

mush² (mush) **1** a command to advance, given to sled dogs. **2** urge sled dogs onward by shouting commands:

He mushed his dog team through the blinding storm. **3** follow a dog sled on foot: *For six days he mushed across the Barren Ground.* **4** a journey made by dog sled, especially while driving the team from behind the sled. 1, 4 *n.*, 2, 3 *v.*

Three mushrooms — stalks 5 to 12 cm high

mush·room (mush′rüm) **1** a small fungus, shaped like an umbrella, that grows very fast: *Some mushrooms are good to eat; some are poisonous.* **2** of or like a mushroom. **3** of very rapid growth: *a mushroom town.* **4** grow rapidly: *His business mushroomed when he opened the new store.* 1–3 *n.*, 4 *v.*

mush·y (mush′ē) **1** like mush; pulpy. **2** *Informal.* weakly sentimental: *The children thought it a mushy story.* *adj.*

mu·sic (myü′zik) **1** the art of putting sounds together in beautiful, pleasing, or interesting arrangements. **2** such arrangements of sounds: *I like listening to music.* **3** written or printed signs for tones: *This book prints the words and music for the song.* **4** any pleasant sound: *the music of a bubbling brook. We were made drowsy by the music of the wind blowing through the trees.* *n.*
face the music, *Informal.* meet trouble boldly or bravely.
set to music, provide the words of a song with music.

mu·si·cal (myü′zə kəl) **1** of or having to do with music: *musical knowledge, musical instruments.* **2** like music; melodious and pleasant: *a musical voice.* **3** set to music or accompanied by music: *a musical comedy, the musical ride of the R.C.M.P.* **4** fond of music. **5** skilled in music; talented as a musician. **6** a stage entertainment or motion picture in which a story is told mainly through music, singing, and dancing. 1–5 *adj.*, 6 *n.* **—mu′si·cal·ly,** *adv.*

musical instrument a piano, violin, or other instrument for producing music.

music box a box or case containing apparatus for producing music mechanically.

mu·si·cian (myü zish′ən) a person skilled in music, especially one who earns a living by singing, playing, composing, or conducting music: *An orchestra is made up of many musicians.* *n.*

musk (musk) a substance with a strong and lasting odor, used in making perfumes: *Musk is found in a special gland in one kind of deer.* *n.*

mus·keg (mus′keg) *Cdn.* **1** a swamp or marsh. **2** an area of bog composed of decaying plant life, especially moss: *There are vast regions of muskeg in northern Alberta.* *n.*

mus·kel·lunge (mus′kə lunj′) a very large fresh-water fish of the pike family: *The muskellunge is valued as a food and game fish.* *n.*, *pl.* **mus·kel·lunge.**

mus·ket (mus′kit) a kind of old gun: *Soldiers used muskets before rifles were invented.* *n.*

mus·ket·eer (mus′kə tēr′) a soldier armed with a musket. *n.*

musk·mel·on (musk′mel′ən) a kind of sweet, juicy melon; cantaloupe. *n.*

hat, āge, fär; let, ēqual, tėrm; it, īce
hot, ōpen, ôrder; oil, out; cup, pu̇t, rüle
əbove, takən, pencəl, lemən, circəs
ch, child; ng, long; sh, ship
th, thin; ᴛʜ, then; zh, measure

A musk-ox — about 150 cm high at the shoulder

musk–ox (musk′oks′) *Cdn.* an arctic animal having a shaggy coat and a musky smell: *The musk-ox looks like a sheep in some ways and like an ox in others.* *n.*, *pl.* **musk-ox** or **musk-ox·en.**

musk·rat (musk′rat′) **1** a water animal of North America, like a rat but larger and with webbed hind feet. **2** its dark-brown fur: *Muskrat is valuable for garments.* *n.*

☞ **Muskrat** comes from *musk* and *rat* because it looks like a rat and has a smell like musk.

mus·lin (muz′lən) a cotton cloth in a plain weave, used for dresses, curtains, sheets, etc. *n.*

mus·quash (mus′kwosh) *Cdn.* muskrat. *n.*

muss (mus) *Informal.* **1** put into disorder; rumple: *The child's dress was mussed.* **2** disorder; a mess: *Straighten up your room; it's in a dreadful muss.* 1 *v.*, 2 *n.*

mus·sel (mus′əl) a mollusc having two hinged parts to its shell: *Sea mussels have dark-blue shells and can be eaten. The shells of fresh-water mussels are used to make buttons.* *n.*

☞ **Mussel** and **muscle** are pronounced the same.

must (must) **1** be obliged to; be forced to: *All men must eat to live.* **2** ought to; should: *I must keep my promise. You must read this story.* **3** be certain to be, do, etc.: *The man must be crazy to talk so. I must seem very rude.* **4** something necessary; obligation: *This rule is a must.* 1–3 *v.*, 4 *n.*

mus·tache (mus′tash or mə stash′) **1** the hair that grows on a man's upper lip, especially when groomed and not shaved smooth: *The captain had a bristling, black mustache.* **2** the hairs or bristles growing near the mouth of an animal. *n.* Sometimes spelled **moustache.**

mus·tang (mus′tang) a small, wild or half-wild horse of the North American plains. *n.*

mus·tard (mus′tərd) **1** a yellow powder or paste used as a seasoning to give food a pungent taste. **2** the plant from whose seeds it is made. *n.*

mus·ter (mus′tər) **1** assemble; gather together; collect. **2** an assembly or collection. **3** summon: *to muster up courage.* 1, 3 *v.*, 2 *n.*

must·n't (mus′ənt) must not: *Father says we mustn't skate here.* *v.*

mus·ty (mus′tē) **1** having a smell or taste suggesting mould or damp; mouldy: *a musty room, musty crackers.*

2 stale; out-of-date: *musty laws about witches.* *adj.*, **mus·ti·er, mus·ti·est.**

mu·ta·tion (myü tā′shən) 1 a change; alteration. 2 a sudden change in the genetic structure of an animal or plant that produces a new feature or characteristic. 3 a new variety of animal or plant resulting from such a change. *n.*

mute (myüt) 1 silent; not making any sound: *The little girl stood mute with embarrassment.* 2 dumb; unable to speak. 3 a person who cannot speak. 4 a clip or some other device put on a musical instrument to soften the sound. 5 soften or deaden the sound of a musical instrument: *He muted the strings of his violin.* 1, 2 *adj.*, 3, 4 *n.*, 5 *v.*, **mut·ed, mut·ing.**

mu·ti·late (myü′tə lāt′) cut, tear, or break off a part of; injure badly by cutting, tearing, or breaking off some part: *The book was badly mutilated by someone who had torn some pages and written on others.* *v.*, **mu·ti·lat·ed, mu·ti·lat·ing.**

mu·ti·neer (myü′tə nēr′) a person who takes part in a mutiny. *n.*

mu·ti·nous (myü′tə nəs) rebellious: *a mutinous look.* *adj.*

mu·ti·ny (myü′tə nē) 1 an open rebellion against lawful authority, especially by sailors or soldiers against their officers. 2 take part in a mutiny; to rebel. 1 *n.*, *pl.* **mu·ti·nies;** 2 *v.*, **mu·ti·nied, mu·ti·ny·ing.**

mut·ter (mut′ər) 1 speak or utter low and indistinctly, with lips partly closed. 2 complain; grumble. 3 muttered words: *We heard a mutter of discontent.* 1, 2 *v.*, 3 *n.*

mut·ton (mut′ən) the meat from a sheep: *We had roast mutton for dinner.* *n.*

mu·tu·al (myü′chü əl) 1 done, said, felt, etc. by each toward the other; given and received: *mutual promises, mutual dislike.* 2 each to the other: *mutual enemies.* 3 belonging to each of several: *We are happy to have him as our mutual friend.* *adj.* **—mu′tu·al·ly,** *adv.*

A muzzle on a dog

muz·zle (muz′əl) 1 the nose, mouth, and jaws of a four-footed animal. 2 a cover or cage of straps or wires for putting over an animal's head and mouth to keep it from biting or eating. 3 attach or put on such a covering. 4 compel to keep silent about something; prevent from expressing views: *The government muzzled the newspapers during the rebellion.* 5 the open front end of a gun, pistol, rifle, etc. 1, 2, 5 *n.*, 3, 4 *v.*, **muz·zled, muz·zling.**

my (mī) 1 of me; belonging to me: *I learned my lesson. My house is just around the next corner.* 2 *Informal.* exclamation of surprise: *My! What a big cat.* 1 *adj.*, 2 *interj.*

☛ **My** and **mine** are the possessive forms of *I.* **My** is always followed by a noun: *This is my hat.* **Mine** stands alone: *This hat is mine.*

my·na or **my·nah** (mī′nə) any of various Asiatic starlings that can imitate human speech sounds: *We have trained our pet myna to say many words.* *n.*

myr·i·ad (mir′ē əd) 1 a very great number: *There are myriads of stars.* 2 countless: *We saw myriad stars that summer night.* 1 *n.*, 2 *adj.*

my·self (mī self′) 1 a form used instead of **me** when referring back to the subject of the sentence: *I hurt myself. I can do it by myself.* 2 a form of **I** or **me** used to make a statement stronger: *I will go myself. I can cook for myself. I hurt myself.* 3 my real or true self: *I hope to be myself again soon.* *pron.*, *pl.* **our·selves.**

mys·te·ri·ous (mis tēr′ē əs) 1 full of mystery; hard to explain or understand; secret; hidden: *Electricity is mysterious.* 2 suggesting mystery: *a mysterious look.* *adj.*

mys·ter·y (mis′tər ē) 1 a secret; something that is hidden or unknown. 2 secrecy; obscurity. 3 something that is not explained or understood: *the mystery of the migration of birds.* 4 a story, play, etc. about strange or secret events: *My sister likes reading mysteries.* *n.*, *pl.* **mys·ter·ies.**

mys·ti·fy (mis′tə fī′) 1 bewilder purposely; puzzle; perplex: *The magician's tricks mystified the audience.* 2 make mysterious. *v.*, **mys·ti·fied, mys·ti·fy·ing.**

myth (mith) 1 a legend or story, usually one that attempts to account for something in nature: *The myth of Proserpina is the ancient Roman explanation of summer and winter.* 2 any invented story. 3 an imaginary person or thing: *That girl's wealthy uncle was a myth invented to impress the other girls.* *n.*

myth·i·cal (mith′ə kəl) 1 of a myth; like a myth; in myths: *mythical monsters, mythical places.* 2 not real; made-up: *Their wealth is merely mythical.* *adj.*

my·thol·o·gy (mi thol′ə jē) 1 a group of myths related to a particular people or person: *Greek mythology.* 2 the study of myths. *n.*, *pl.* **my·thol·o·gies.**

hat, āge, fär; let, ēqual, tėrm; it, īce
hot, ōpen, ôrder; oil, out; cup, pu̇t, rüle
əbove, takən, pencəl, lemən, circəs
ch, child; ng, long; sh, ship
th, thin; ᴛʜ, then; zh, measure

n or **N** (en) the 14th letter of the alphabet: *There are two* n's *in* none. *n., pl.* **n's** or **N's.**

N. or **N** 1 North. 2 Northern.

n. 1 north. 2 northern. 3 noun.

nab (nab) *Informal.* 1 catch or seize suddenly; grab. 2 arrest: *The police soon nabbed the thief.* *v.*

nag[1] (nag) find fault with all the time; irritate or annoy by peevish complaints; scold: *A tired mother sometimes nags her children. When Kay was sick, she nagged at everybody.* *v.,* **nagged, nag·ging.**

nag[2] (nag) a horse, especially one that is old and worn out. *n.*

nai·ad or **Nai·ad** (nī′ad or nā′ad) in Greek and Roman myths, a nymph guarding a stream. *n.*

nail (nāl) 1 a small, slender piece of metal to be hammered into or through pieces of wood or other material to hold them together. 2 fasten with a nail or nails. 3 hold or keep fixed; make secure: *We should nail him to his promise.* 4 *Informal.* catch; seize. 5 the hard, horny layer at the end of a finger or toe. 1, 5 *n.,* 2–4 *v.*
hit the nail on the head, *Informal.* guess or understand correctly; say or do something just right.
nail down, a fix with nails: *The shingles were nailed down with a hammer.* **b** *Informal.* win, settle, or get with certainty: *He nailed down first place in the singing competition.*

na·ïve or **na·ive** (nī ēv′ or nä ēv′) simple in nature; like a child; artless: *The young woman was naïve and believed his tall story.* *adj.*

na·ked (nā′kid) 1 with no clothes on: *The boys enjoyed swimming naked.* 2 bare; not covered; stripped of usual cover: *The trees stood naked in the snow.* 3 not protected; exposed: *a naked sword.* 4 without addition of anything else; plain: *the naked truth.* *adj.* **—na′ked·ness,** *n.*
naked eye, the bare eye, not helped by any glass, telescope, or microscope.

name (nām) 1 the word or words by which a person, animal, place, or thing is spoken of or to: *Our dog's name is Jack. The name of our country is Canada.* 2 give a name to: *They named the baby Mary.* 3 call by name; mention by name: *Three persons were named in the report.* 4 give the right name for: *Can you name these flowers?* 5 reputation: *He made a name for himself as a writer.* 6 having a reputation that is known by a name: *The candy in this store is not a name brand.* 7 mention or speak of; state: *She named several reasons for her decision.* 8 nominate; appoint: *Jim was named captain of the team.* 9 choose; settle on: *They named the day for their wedding.* 1, 5 *n.,* 2–4, 7–9 *v.,* **named, nam·ing;** 6 *adj.*
call names, insult by using bad names; swear at.
in the name of, a on the authority of; acting for: *He bought the car in the name of his father.* **b** for the sake of: *We did it in the name of charity.*

name·less (nām′lis) 1 having no name: *a nameless baby.* 2 not marked with a name: *a nameless grave.* 3 not named; unknown: *a book by a nameless writer.* 4 that cannot be named or described: *a strange, nameless longing.* *adj.*

name·ly (nām′lē) that is to say: *Only two pupils got 100 in the test—namely, Fred and Jean.* *adv.*

name·sake (nām′sāk′) a person having the same name as another, especially one named after another: *Wilfrid was proud to be the namesake of Sir Wilfrid Laurier.* *n.*

nan·ny goat (nan′ē) a female goat.

nap[1] (nap) 1 a short sleep: *Most babies have a nap in the afternoon.* 2 take a short sleep: *Grandfather naps in his armchair.* 1 *n.,* 2 *v.,* **napped, nap·ping.**

nap[2] (nap) the soft, short, woolly threads or hairs on the surface of cloth: *the nap on velvet.* *n.*

nape (nāp) the back of the neck. *n.*

naph·tha (nap′thə or naf′thə) a liquid made from petroleum, coal tar, etc., used as fuel, to dissolve some substances, to thin paint, etc. *n.*

nap·kin (nap′kin) 1 a piece of cloth or paper used at meals for protecting the clothing or for wiping the lips or fingers; a serviette. 2 a baby's diaper. *n.*

nap·pie or **nap·py** (nap′ē) a small dish used for serving fruit; a fruit dish. *n.*

nar·cis·sus (när sis′əs) a spring plant having yellow or white flowers and growing from a bulb: *Jonquils and daffodils are varieties of narcissus.* *n., pl.* **nar·cis·sus·es** or **nar·cis·si** (när sis′ī).

nar·rate (na rāt′) tell the story of. *v.,* **nar·rat·ed, nar·rat·ing.**

nar·ra·tion (na rā′shən) 1 the act of telling. 2 the form of composition that relates an event or a story: *Novels, short stories, histories, and biographies are types of narration.* *n.*

nar·ra·tive (nar′ə tiv or ner′ə tiv) 1 a story: *His trip through the Far East made an interesting narrative.* 2 the telling of stories. 3 that narrates: *'Hiawatha' is a narrative poem.* 1, 2 *n.,* 3 *adj.*

nar·ra·tor (nar ā′tər) a person who tells a story. *n.*

nar·row (nar′ō or ner′ō) 1 not wide; having little width; less wide than usual for its kind: *narrow ribbon. A path 30 centimetres wide is narrow.* 2 limited; small: *He had only a narrow circle of friends.* 3 make narrow; become narrow; decrease in width: *The road narrows here.* 4 close; with a small margin: *a narrow escape.* 5 lacking sympathy; not tolerant; prejudiced: *That man has a narrow mind and says that all modern art is rubbish.* 1, 2, 4, 5 *adj.,* 3 *v.*
the narrows, narrow part of a river, strait, sound, valley, pass, etc.

nar·row–mind·ed (nar′ō mīn′did or ner′ō mīn′did) lacking understanding; blind to other points of view; prejudiced. *adj.*

nar·whal (när′wəl or när′hwəl) a toothed whale of the arctic seas. The male has a long tusk extending forward from a tooth in the upper jaw. *n.*

na·sal (nā′zəl) 1 of, in, or from the nose: *nasal bones, a nasal discharge.* 2 speaking or spoken through the nose: *His voice had a nasal quality.* 3 a speech sound that is made by speaking through the nose: *The final sounds in 'ram,' 'ran,' and 'rang' are nasals.* 1, 2 *adj.,* 3 *n.*

na·stur·tium (nə stėr′shəm) a plant having yellow, orange, and red flowers. *n.*

☛ **Nasturtium** comes from the Latin name for this flower, which developed from Latin *nāsus,* meaning 'nose,' and *tortium,* meaning 'twisted,' from *torquere,* 'to twist, torture,' because of the sharpness of the flower's odor.

nas·ty (nas′tē) **1** disgustingly dirty; filthy: *a nasty room, a nasty word or story, a nasty mind.* **2** very unpleasant: *nasty weather, nasty medicines, a nasty cut, a nasty temper, a nasty person. adj.,* **nas·ti·er, nas·ti·est.**

na·tion (nā′shən) **1** a group of people occupying the same country, united under the same independent government, and, usually, speaking the same language: *The Prime Minister appealed to the nation for support of his plan.* **2** a people, race, or tribe; those having the same descent, history, and, as a rule, language: *the Scottish nation.* **3** such a group considered as a political unity: *the French-Canadian nation.* **4 the nation,** the country: *There was cold weather throughout the nation over the weekend.* **5** a North American Indian tribe, especially one belonging to a confederacy: *the Sioux nation. n.*

na·tion·al (nash′nəl or nash′ə nəl) **1** of a nation; affecting or belonging to a whole nation: *national laws, a national disaster.* **2** a citizen of a nation: *Each year many nationals of Canada visit the United States.* 1 *adj.,* 2 *n.*

National Assembly in Quebec, the group of representatives elected to the legislature; legislative assembly.

na·tion·al·ism (nash′nel iz′əm or nash′ən əl iz′əm) **1** patriotic feelings or efforts. **2** the desire and plans for national independence. *n.*

na·tion·al·ist (nash′nəl ist or nash′ən əl ist) a person who believes in nationalism. *n.*

na·tion·al·i·ty (nash′nal′ə tē or nash′ə nal′ə tē) **1** the fact of belonging to a nation: *His passport showed that his nationality was Canadian.* **2** the condition of being an independent nation; nationhood. *n., pl.* **na·tion·al·i·ties.**

na·tion·al·ly (nash′nəl ē or nash′ən əl ē) **1** as a nation. **2** throughout the nation: *The opposition leader's speech was broadcast nationally. adv.*

national park land kept by the federal government for people to enjoy because of its beautiful scenery, historical interest, etc.: *Jasper National Park is in Alberta.*

na·tion·hood (nā′shən hu̇d′) the condition or state of being a nation; the fact of having national existence: *A colony achieves nationhood when it becomes an independent country. n.*

na·tive (nā′tiv) **1** a person born in a certain place or country: *He is a native of Montreal.* **2** born in a certain place or country: *He is a native son of Canada.* **3** belonging to one because of his birth: *Canada is my native land.* **4** belonging to a person because of his country or the nation to which he belongs: *French is his native language.* **5** born in a person; natural: *native ability, native courtesy.* **6** an animal or plant that originated in a place. **7** originating, grown, or produced in a certain place: *The Manitoba maple is native to Canada.* 1, 6 *n.,* 2, 3–5, 7 *adj.*

na·tiv·i·ty (nə tiv′ə tē) **1** birth. **2 the Nativity, a** the birth of Christ. **b** Christmas. *n., pl.* **na·tiv·i·ties.**

nat·u·ral (nach′rəl or nach′ə rəl) **1** produced by nature; coming or occurring in the ordinary course of events: *natural feelings, natural curls, a natural complexion, a natural death, a natural result.* **2** belonging to the nature one is born with: *natural ability. It is natural for ducks to swim.* **3** in accordance with the facts of some special case: *a natural response.* **4** like nature; true to life: *The picture looked natural.* **5** of or about nature: *natural history, the natural sciences.* **6** in the state produced by nature; not artificial: *Coal and oil are natural products.* **7** free from affectation or restraint: *a natural manner.* **8** in music, not changed in pitch by a sharp or flat: *C natural. adj.*

nat·u·ral·ist (nach′rəl ist or nach′ə rəl ist) a person who makes a study of animals or plants. *n.*

nat·u·ral·ize (nach′rəl īz′ or nach′ə rəl īz′) grant the rights of citizenship to persons native to other countries; admit to citizenship: *The government naturalizes many New Canadians every year. He is a naturalized Canadian. v.,* **nat·u·ral·ized, nat·u·ral·iz·ing.**

nat·u·ral·ly (nach′rəl ē or nach′ə rəl ē) **1** in a natural way: *Speak naturally; don't try to imitate some actress.* **2** by nature: *a naturally obedient child.* **3** as might be expected; of course: *She offered me some candy; naturally, I took it. adv.*

natural number a whole number.

natural resource a kind of material that is supplied by nature and is useful or necessary to man: *Minerals and forests are natural resources.*

na·ture (nā′chər) **1** the way things are and grow in the world without the aid or interference of man: *It is a law of nature.* **2** the outdoor world of plant and animal life as contrasted with the man-made world of cities, houses, and industry: *He is a lover of nature.* **3** the qualities or abilities with which a person or animal is born: *It is the nature of birds to build nests and of men to talk.* **4** character: *Cruelty is not in her nature.* **5** sort; kind: *books of a scientific nature. n.*

nature study the study of animals, plants, and other things and events in nature.

naught (not or nôt) nothing: *All his work went for naught. n.*

☛ **Naught, knot, not,** and **naught** are pronounced the same (to rhyme with *got*) by most Canadians.

naugh·ti·ness (no′tē nis or nô′tē nis) bad behavior; disobedience; mischief. *n.*

naugh·ty (no′tē or nô′tē) bad; not obedient: *The naughty child hit his baby sister. adj.,* **naugh·ti·er, naugh·ti·est.**

nau·se·a (no′zē ə or nô′zē ə, no′shə or nô′shə) **1** the feeling that one is about to vomit. **2** extreme disgust; loathing. *n.*

☛ **Nausea** originally meant 'seasickness'; like **nautical,** it came through Latin from the Greek word *naus,* meaning 'ship.' See note at **noise.**

nau·ti·cal (no′tə kəl or nô′tə kəl) having something to do with ships, sailors, or navigation. *adj.*

☛ See note at **nausea.**

na·val (nā′vəl) **1** of or for warships or the navy: *naval supplies, a naval officer.* **2** having a navy: *the naval powers. adj.*

hat, āge, fär; let, ēqual, tėrm; it, īce
hot, ōpen, ôrder; oil, out; cup, pu̇t, rüle
ə̇bove, takən, pencəl, lemən, circəs
ch, child; ng, long; sh, ship
th, thin; ᴛʜ, then; zh, measure

☛ **Naval** and **navel** are pronounced the same.

nave (nāv) the main part of a church or cathedral between the side aisles. *n.*

☛ **Nave** and **knave** are pronounced the same.

na·vel (nā′vəl) the mark or hollow in the middle of the surface of the abdomen. *n.*

☛ See note at **naval.**

nav·i·ga·ble (nav′ə gə bəl) that ships can travel on: *The St. Lawrence River is deep enough to be navigable. adj.*

nav·i·gate (nav′ə gāt′) **1** sail, steer, or manage a ship, aircraft, etc.: *Much skill is needed to navigate an airplane.* **2** sail on or over a river, sea, etc.: *Many ships navigate the St. Lawrence Seaway each year.* **3** travel by water; sail. **4** plot the position and course of a ship, aircraft, etc. *v.,* **nav·i·gat·ed, nav·i·gat·ing.**

nav·i·ga·tion (nav′ə gā′shən) **1** the act of navigating. **2** the art or science of figuring out the position and course of a ship, aircraft, etc. *n.*

nav·i·ga·tor (nav′ə gā′tər) **1** a person skilled in the science of navigating ships or aircraft: *The ship took on a special navigator to guide her through the dangerous waters. He served as a navigator in the air force.* **2** a person who sails the seas, especially an explorer. *n.*

na·vy (nā′vē) Often, **Navy.** all the ships of war of a country, with their officers and men. *n., pl.* **na·vies.**

navy blue a dark blue.

nay (nā) **1** formerly, no. **2** not only that, but also: *We are willing—nay, eager—to go.* **3** a vote or voter against something. 1, 2 *adv.,* 3 *n.*

☛ **Nay** and **neigh** are pronounced the same.

N.B. **1** New Brunswick. **2** an abbreviation of the Latin words *nota bene,* meaning 'note well.'

N.C.O. a non-commissioned officer.

NDP or **N.D.P.** New Democratic Party.

N.E. or **NE** **1** northeast. **2** northeastern.

near (nēr) **1** close; not far; not distant: *They searched far and near. Christmas is drawing near.* **2** close to; not far from: *We live near Regina. My birthday is near Dominion Day.* **3** come or draw near to; approach: *The vacation was nearing its end.* **4** closely: *It was five o'clock as near as he could guess.* **5** close in feeling: *a near friend.* **6** close in family relationship: *a near cousin.* **7** short; direct: *They took the nearest route to town.* **8** by a close margin: *a near escape.* **9** *Informal.* almost; nearly: *She was near crazy with fright.* **10** stingy. 1, 5–8, 10 *adj.,* 1, 4, 9 *adv.,* 2 *prep.,* 3 *v.* **—near′ness,** *n.*
come near doing, almost do: *I came near losing my glasses.*
near at hand, a within easy reach. **b** not far in the future.

near·by (nēr′bī′) near; close at hand: *They live in a nearby house* (*adj.*). *They live nearby* (*adv.*). *adj., adv.*

Near East the countries of southwestern Asia, sometimes including other nearby countries.

near·ly (nēr′lē) **1** almost: *It is nearly bedtime.* **2** closely: *It will cost more than we can afford, as nearly as I can figure it. adv.*

near–sight·ed (nēr′sīt′id) not able to see far; seeing distinctly at a short distance only: *Near-sighted people usually wear glasses. adj.*

neat (nēt) **1** clean and in order: *a neat desk, a neat room, a neat dress.* **2** able and willing to keep things in order: *a neat child.* **3** well-formed; in proportion: *a neat design.* **4** skilful; clever: *a neat trick. adj.* **—neat′ness,** *n.*

neb·u·la (neb′yə lə) a cloudlike cluster of stars or a mass of dust particles visible in the sky at night. *n.*

nec·es·sar·i·ly (nes′ə ser′ə lē) **1** because of necessity: *Leaves are not necessarily green.* **2** as a necessary result: *War necessarily causes misery and waste. adv.*

nec·es·sar·y (nes′ə ser′ē) **1** that must be, be had, or be done; required: *Death is a necessary end.* **2** something essential; something that cannot be done without: *Food, clothing, and shelter are necessaries of life.* 1 *adj.,* 2 *n., pl.* **nec·es·sar·ies.**

ne·ces·si·tate (nə ses′ə tāt′) make necessary: *His broken leg necessitated an operation. v.,* **ne·ces·si·tat·ed, ne·ces·si·tat·ing.**

ne·ces·si·ty (nə ses′ə tē) **1** extreme need; something that has to be: *We understand the necessity of eating.* **2** anything that cannot be done without; an essential thing: *Food and water are necessities.* **3** that which forces one to act in a certain way: *Necessity often drives people to do disagreeable things. n., pl.* **ne·ces·si·ties.**
of necessity, because it must be: *We left early of necessity; there is no bus service at night.*

neck (nek) **1** the part of the body that connects the head with the shoulders. **2** the part of a garment that fits around the neck: *the neck of a shirt.* **3** a narrow part like a neck: *a neck of land, the neck of a vase. n.*
neck and neck, being equal or even in a race or contest: *The two horses ran neck and neck for a kilometre.*
risk one's neck, put oneself in a dangerous position: *You risk your neck when you don't use your seat belt.*

neck·er·chief (nek′ər chif) a cloth worn around the neck. *n.*

neck·lace (nek′lis) a string of jewels, gold, silver, beads, etc. worn around the neck as an ornament. *n.*

neck·tie (nek′tī′) a narrow band of cloth worn around the neck and tied in front. *n.*

nec·tar (nek′tər) **1** in ancient Greek legends, the drink of the gods. **2** any delicious drink. **3** a sweet liquid found in many flowers: *Bees gather nectar and make it into honey. n.*

nec·tar·ine (nek′tər ēn′ or nek′tə rēn′) a kind of peach having no down on its skin. *n.*

need (nēd) **1** be in want of; ought to have; be unable to do without: *I need a new hat. Plants need water.* **2** anything wanted or lacking; that for which a want is felt: *In the desert their need was fresh water.* **3** want; lack of a useful or desired thing: *The loss by our team showed the need of practice.* **4** a time or condition of difficulty: *He was a friend in need. He did not fail us in our need.* **5** a lack of money; the state or condition of being poor: *This family's need was so great the children did not have shoes.* **6** must; should; have to; ought to: *I have need to go to town. You need not bother. Why need you go today? Do not stay longer* *than you need.* **7** something that has to be; requirement: *There is no need to hurry.* 1, 6 *v.*, 2–5, 7 *n.*

if need be, if it has to be.

☛ **Need** and **kneed** are pronounced the same.

need·ful (nēd′fəl) needed; necessary: *a needful change. adj.*

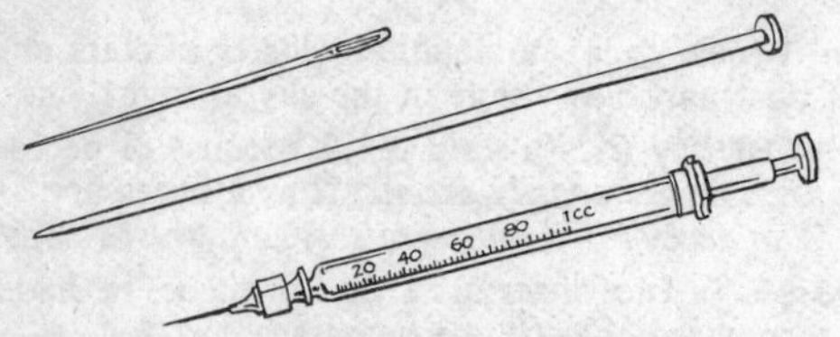

A sewing needle, a knitting needle, and a hypodermic needle

nee·dle (nē′dəl) **1** a slender tool, pointed at one end with a hole, or eye, at the other to pass a thread through, used in sewing. **2** a slender rod used in knitting. **3** a rod with a hook at one end, used in crocheting. **4** a thin steel pointer on a compass or on electrical machinery. **5** a slender tube with a sharp point, used for injecting or extracting something: *The doctor stuck the needle into my arm.* **6** the needle-shaped leaf of the fir, pine, spruce, or larch. **7** *Informal.* tease; goad or incite: *The boys needled him into losing his temper.* 1–6 *n.*, 7 *v.*, **nee·dled, nee·dling.**

need·less (nēd′lis) not needed; unnecessary: *It is silly to take a needless risk. adj.*

nee·dle·work (nē′dəl wėrk′) work done with a needle; sewing; embroidery. *n.*

need·n't (nēd′ənt) need not. *v.*

need·y (nē′dē) very poor; not having enough to live on: *a needy family. adj.*, **need·i·er, need·i·est.**

ne'er (ner) in poetry, never. *adv.*

negative (neg′ə tiv) **1** saying no: *His answer was negative.* **2** a word or statement that says no or denies: *'I won't' is a negative.* **3** the side that says no or argues against a question being debated; side opposing the affirmative. **4** not positive or helpful: *His negative suggestions are not encouraging.* **5** having more electrons than protons: *a negative particle.* **6** of or having something to do with the kind of electricity produced on resin when it is rubbed on silk. **7** minus; counting down from zero: *Three below zero is a negative quantity.* **8** showing an absence of the germs, signs, etc. of an illness. **9** showing the light parts dark and the dark parts light: *the negative image on a photographic plate.* **10** a photographic image in which the lights and shadows are reversed: *Prints are made from negatives.* 1, 4–9 *adj.*, 2, 3, 10 *n.*

in the negative, expressing disagreement by saying no; denying: *Most of the replies were in the negative.*

neg·lect (ni glekt′) **1** give too little care or attention to: *neglect one's health.* **2** leave undone; not attend to: *The maid neglected her work.* **3** omit; fail: *Don't neglect to water the plants.* **4** the act or fact of neglecting: *His neglect of the truth was astonishing.* **5** a want of attention to what should be done: *That car has been ruined by neglect.* **6** being neglected: *The children suffered from neglect.* 1–3 *v.*, 4–6 *n.*

neg·li·gence (neg′lə jəns) **1** neglect; lack of proper care or attention: *Because of the owner's negligence, the house was in great need of repair.* **2** careless conduct; indifference. *n.*

neg·li·gent (neg′lə jənt) **1** showing neglect. **2** careless; indifferent: *His negligent behavior resulted in an accident. adj.*

ne·go·ti·ate (ni gō′shē āt′) **1** talk over and arrange terms: *The rebels negotiated for peace with the government.* **2** arrange for: *They finally negotiated a peace treaty. We negotiated the sale of our house.* **3** *Informal.* get past or over: *The car negotiated the sharp curve by slowing down. v.*, **ne·go·ti·at·ed, ne·go·ti·at·ing.**

ne·go·ti·a·tion (ni gō′shē ā′shən) talking over and arranging; arrangement: *Negotiations for the new school are finished. n.*

Ne·gro (nē′grō) **1** a person belonging to any of the black races of Africa. **2** any person having black ancestors: *Millions of Negroes live in America.* **3** of, having to do with, or resembling Negroes. 1, 2 *n.*, 3 *adj.*

neigh (nā) **1** the sound that a horse makes. **2** make such a sound. 1 *n.*, 2 *v.*

☛ **Neigh** and **nay** are pronounced the same.

neigh·bor or **neigh·bour** (nā′bər) **1** someone who lives in the next house or nearby. **2** a person or thing that is near or next to another: *The big tree brought down several of its smaller neighbors as it fell.* **3** be near or next to; adjoin. **4** a fellow human being: *One should be kind to one's neighbor.* 1, 2, 4 *n.*, 3 *v.*

neigh·bor·hood or **neigh·bour·hood** (nā′bər hu̇d′) **1** the region near some place or thing: *She lives in the neighborhood of the mill.* **2** a place; a district: *Is your new house in an attractive neighborhood?* **3** the people of a place or district: *The whole neighborhood came to the big party.* **4** neighborly feeling or conduct. *n.*

in the neighborhood of, *Informal.* somewhere near; about: *The car cost in the neighborhood of $2500.*

neigh·bor·ing or **neigh·bour·ing** (nā′bər ing) living or being near; bordering: *We heard the bird calls from the neighboring woods. adj.*

neigh·bor·ly or **neigh·bour·ly** (nā′bər lē) kindly; friendly. *adj.*

neither (nē′ᴛʜər or nī′ᴛʜər) **1** not either: *Neither you nor I will go (conj.). Neither statement is true (adj.). Neither of the statements is true (pron.).* **2** nor yet; nor: *'They toil not, neither do they spin.'* 1, 2 *conj.*, 1 *adj.*, 1 *pron.*

ne·on (nē′on) an element that is a colorless, odorless gas: *Tubes containing neon are used in electric signs and television sets. n.*

neph·ew (nef′yü) the son of one's brother or sister; the son of one's brother-in-law or sister-in-law. *n.*

Nep·tune (nep′tyün or nep′tün) **1** the Roman god of the sea. **2** a large planet so far from the earth and the sun that it cannot be seen with the naked eye. *n.*

nerve (nėrv) **1** a fibre or bundle of fibres connecting the brain or spinal cord with the eyes, ears, muscles, glands, etc. **2** mental strength; courage: *The diver lost his nerve and wouldn't go off the high board.* **3** put strength and courage in: *The soldiers nerved themselves for the battle.* **4** *Informal.* rude boldness; impudence. 1, 2, 4 *n.*, 3 *v.*, **nerved, nerv·ing.**

get on one's nerves, *Informal.* annoy or irritate one.

hat, āge, fär; let, ēqual, tėrm; it, īce
hot, ōpen, ôrder; oil, out; cup, pu̇t, rüle
əbove, takən, pencəl, lemən, circəs
ch, child; ng, long; sh, ship
th, thin; ᴛʜ, then; zh, measure

nerv·ous (nėr′vəs) **1** of the nerves: *The brain is a part of the nervous system of the human body.* **2** easily excited or upset: *A person who has been overworking is likely to become nervous.* **3** restless or uneasy; timid: *She is nervous about staying alone at night.* **4** strong; vigorous: *The artist painted with quick, nervous strokes.* *adj.* **—nerv′ous·ness,** *n.*

-ness a suffix meaning: being____: *Blackness means being black. Carefulness means being careful.*

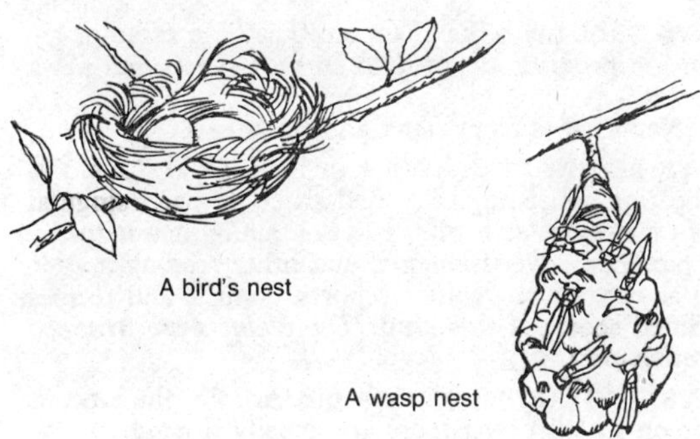
A bird's nest

A wasp nest

nest (nest) **1** a structure shaped something like a bowl, built by birds out of twigs, straw, etc. as a place in which to lay their eggs and protect their young: *a robin's nest.* **2** a structure or place used by animals or insects for a similar purpose: *a squirrel's nest, a wasp nest.* **3** the birds, animals, or insects living in a nest. **4** a warm, cosy place; a place to sleep: *The little girl made a nest among the cushions and snuggled down in it.* **5** something suggesting a nest: *a nest of boxes, baskets, or bowls, the smaller fitting within the larger.* **6** a place where evil or harmful persons gather; a den: *a nest of thieves.* **7** make and use a nest: *The bluebirds are nesting here now.* **8** to hunt for nests. **9** to place or fit together in a nest: *The chairs were nested and placed along the wall.* 1–6 *n.,* 7–9 *v.*

nest egg **1** a natural or artificial egg left in a nest so that a hen will continue to lay eggs there. **2** something, usually a sum of money, put aside for future use: *When he got married, he had already saved quite a nest egg.*

nes·tle (nes′əl) **1** settle oneself or be settled comfortably and cosily: *nestle down in a big chair, a house nestling among trees.* **2** press close in love or for comfort: *A mother nestles her baby in her arms.* *v.,* **nes·tled, nes·tling.**

nest·ling (nest′ling) a bird too young to leave the nest. *n.*

net[1] (net) **1** an open fabric made of string, cord, thread, or wire, knotted together in such a way as to leave large or small holes regularly arranged: *Veils are made of very fine net.* **2** a piece of netting used for some special purpose: *a fish net, a hair net, a tennis net.* **3** a lacelike cloth. **4** a trap or snare: *The guilty boy was caught in a net of his own lies.* **5** catch in a net: *The boy was thrilled when he netted his first fish.* 1–4 *n.,* 5 *v.,* **net·ted, net·ting.**

net[2] (net) **1** real or actual; clear and free of deductions or additions: *A net gain or profit is the actual gain after all working expenses have been paid. The net weight of a glass jar of candy is the weight of the candy itself.* **2** to gain: *The sale netted me a good profit.* 1 *adj.,* 2 *v.,* **net·ted, net·ting.**

net·ting (net′ing) a netted or meshed material: *mosquito netting, wire netting for window screens.* *n.*

net·tle (net′əl) **1** a kind of plant having sharp hairs on the leaves and stems that sting the skin when touched. **2** sting the mind; irritate; make angry: *Father was nettled by the boy's frequent interruptions.* 1 *n.,* 2 *v.,* **net·tled, net·tling.**

net·work (net′wėrk′) **1** a net. **2** any system of lines that cross: *a network of vines, a network of highways.* **3** a group of radio or television stations, so connected that the same program may be broadcast by all: *the French network of C.B.C. radio.* *n.*

neu·ter (nyü′tər or nü′tər) neither masculine nor feminine; neither male nor female: *'It' is a neuter pronoun. Worker bees are neuter.* *adj.*

neu·tral (nyü′trəl or nü′trəl) **1** not taking part in a quarrel, contest, or war: *Switzerland was neutral during the last two wars in Europe.* **2** a neutral person or country; one not taking part in a war. **3** being neither one thing nor the other; indefinite. **4** having little or no color; greyish. **5** neither acid nor alkaline. **6** of electricity, neither positive nor negative. 1, 3–6 *adj.,* 2 *n.*

neu·tral·i·ty (nyü tral′ə tē or nü tral′ə tē) the condition of being neutral; the policy of not taking part in a quarrel, contest, or war. *n.*

neu·tral·ize (nyü′trəl īz′ or nü′trəl īz′) **1** make neutral; keep from taking part in war: *There was talk of neutralizing Belgium.* **2** take away the power or effect of something by using an opposite power or force: *Bases neutralize acids. The dim light neutralizes the bright colors in this room.* *v.,* **neu·tral·ized, neu·tral·iz·ing.**

neu·tron (nyü′tron or nü′tron) in science, an elementary particle having no electrical charge, found in the nucleus of every kind of atom except that of hydrogen. *n.*

nev·er (nev′ər) **1** not ever; at no time: *He never had to work for a living.* **2** in no case; not at all; to no extent or degree: *He will be never the wiser.* *adv.*
never mind, a pay no attention to; forget about: *Never*

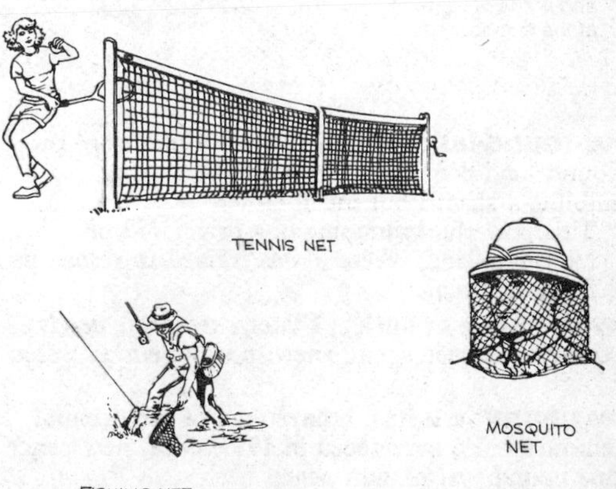
TENNIS NET

MOSQUITO NET

FISHING NET

mind the noise. Never mind your coats. **b** it doesn't matter; forget it.

nev·er·more (nev′ər môr′) never again. *adv.*

nev·er·the·less (nev′ər ᴛʜə les′) however; none the less; for all that; in spite of it: *She was very tired; nevertheless, she kept on working. adv.*

new (nyü or nü) **1** not existing before; having been made, grown, thought of, or produced only a short time ago: *a new invention, a new idea, a new house.* **2** having been known only a short time, though existing before: *a new galaxy. The detective uncovered several new facts.* **3** recently gained or bought: *a new dress, a new car.* **4** recently come or arrived: *Our class has a new teacher.* **5** up-to-date; recent; modern: *the new styles.* **6** as if made new; fresh: *to go on with new courage. After taking a shower, he felt a new man.* **7** not yet used or accustomed to: *She is still new to the work.* **8** not yet familiar; strange: *The work is still new to her.* **9** beginning a stage in a series; beginning a repeating of something: *a new year. The new moon is seen as a thin crescent.* **10** (used in compounds) newly; recently or lately: *new-mown hay, a new-found friend.* 1–9 *adj.,* 10 *adv.*

☛ New and **knew** are pronounced the same.

new·born (nyü′bôrn′ or nü′bôrn′) **1** recently or only just born: *a newborn baby.* **2** ready to start a new life; born again. *adj.*

New Bruns·wick·er (nyü′brunz′wik′ər or nü′brunz′wik′ər) a person born in or living in New Brunswick.

New Canadian **1** a person who has recently arrived in Canada from another country and plans to become a Canadian citizen. **2** a person who has recently become a Canadian citizen.

new·com·er (nyü′kum′ər or nü′kum′ər) a person who has just come or who came not long ago. *n.*

New Democratic Party a Canadian political party founded in 1961.

New·found·land·er (nyü′fənd land′ər or nü′fənd land′ər) a person born in or living in Newfoundland. *n.*

A Newfoundland dog — about 70 cm high at the shoulder

New·found·land dog (nyü′found′lənd dog′ or nü′found′lənd dog′) a shaggy, intelligent dog resembling a spaniel but much larger.

☛ This powerful swimming dog originated in Newfoundland, where it was trained to rescue people from drowning.

new·ly (nyü′lē or nü′lē) **1** lately; recently: *newly discovered.* **2** once again; anew: *newly painted walls. adv.*

new penny a British bronze coin of the decimal system of money, introduced in 1971. 100 new pence = one pound. *n., pl.* **new pence.**

news (nyüz or nüz) **1** something told as having just happened; information about something that has just happened or will soon happen: *The news that our teacher was leaving made us sad.* **2** a report of a happening or happenings in a newspaper, on television, radio, etc.: *We listened to the news on the radio. n.*

break the news, make something known; tell something.

☛ Though plural in form, **news** is used as a singular: *The news from the various districts is sent to a central office.*

news·cast (nyüz′kast′ or nüz′kast′) a radio or television program devoted to current events and news bulletins. *n.*

☛ **Newscast** is from *news* and broad*cast.*

news·pa·per (nyüz′pā′pər or nüz′pā′pər) **1** a publication consisting of folded sheets of paper printed daily or weekly, as a rule, and containing news stories and pictures, advertisements, and other reading matter, such as editorials, weather reports, comics, and recipes. **2** printed sheets of this kind: *The plants were wrapped in newspaper. n.*

news·print (nyüz′print′ or nüz′print′) the kind of paper on which newspapers are usually printed. *n.*

news·reel (nyüz′rēl′ or nüz′rēl′) a motion picture showing current events. *n.*

news·stand (nyüz′stand′ or nüz′stand′) a place where newspapers and magazines are sold. *n.*

newt (nyüt or nüt) a small salamander that lives in water part of the time. *n.*

New Testament the part of the Bible that contains the life and teachings of Christ recorded by His followers, together with their own experiences and teachings.

New World North America and South America.

New Year or **New Year's** the first day or days of the year.

New Year's Day January 1.

New Zea·land·er (zē′lən dər) a person born in or living in New Zealand, a country of islands in the south Pacific Ocean.

next (nekst) **1** following at once; nearest: *We'll catch the next train.* **2** the first time after this: *When you next come, bring it.* **3** nearest to: *We live in the house next the church.* **4** in the place or time or position that is nearest: *I am going to do my arithmetic problems next.* 1, 3 *adj.,* 2, 4 *adv.*

next to, a nearest to: *Who is the girl next to you?* **b** almost; nearly: *His savings are next to nothing.*

N.F. Newfoundland.

Nfld. Newfoundland.

nib (nib) **1** the point of a pen. **2** the point or tip of anything. *n.*

nib·ble (nib′əl) **1** eat away with quick, small bites, as a rabbit or a mouse does. **2** bite gently or lightly: *A fish nibbles at the bait.* **3** a nibbling; a small bite. 1, 2 *v.,* **nib·bled, nib·bling;** 3 *n.*

nice (nīs) **1** pleasing; agreeable; satisfactory: *a nice day, a nice ride, a nice child.* **2** thoughtful or kind: *He was nice to us.* **3** very fine; subtle; precise: *a nice distinction, a nice shade of meaning. adj.,* **nic·er, nic·est.**

niche (nich) **1** a recess or hollow in a wall for a statue, vase, etc. **2** a suitable place or position; a place for which a person is suited: *John will find his niche in the world. n.*

hat, āge, fär; let, ēqual, tėrm; it, īce
hot, ōpen, ôrder; oil, out; cup, pu̇t, rüle
əbove, takən, pencəl, lemən, circəs
ch, child; ng, long; sh, ship
th, thin; ᴛʜ, then; zh, measure

nick (nik) **1** a place where a small bit has been cut or broken out: *She hit a saucer and made a nick in the edge of it.* **2** make a nick or nicks in. 1 *n.*, 2 *v.*
in the nick of time, just at the right moment.

nick·el (nik′əl) **1** a hard, silvery white metallic element: *Nickel is much used in mixtures with other metals.* **2** a coin containing nickel; a five-cent piece. *n.*

nick·name (nik′nām′) **1** a short or familiar form of a proper name: *'The Alex' is a nickname for 'Royal Alexandra Theatre.' Elizabeth's nickname is 'Betty.'* **2** a name used instead of a proper name: *Roy's nickname was 'Buzz.'* **3** give a nickname to: *They nicknamed the tall boy 'Shorty.'* 1, 2 *n.*, 3 *v.*, **nick·named, nick·nam·ing.**

nic·o·tine (nik′ə tēn′) a poison contained in tobacco. *n.*

☛ Named after Jacques *Nicot* (1530–1600), a French ambassador to Portugal, who introduced tobacco into France about 1560.

niece (nēs) the daughter of one's brother or sister; the daughter of one's brother-in-law or sister-in-law. *n.*

nig·gard·ly **1** stingy: *a niggardly man.* **2** stingily. **3** meanly small or scanty: *a niggardly gift.* 1, 3 *adj.*, 2 *adv.*

nigh (nī) **1** near. **2** nearly. 1, 2 *adv.*, 1 *adj.*, **nigh·er, nigh·est** or **next;** 1 *prep.*

night (nīt) **1** the time between evening and morning; the time from sunset to sunrise, especially when it is dark. **2** the darkness of night; the dark. **3** evening; nightfall. *n.*

☛ **Night** and **knight** are pronounced the same.

night·fall (nīt′fol′ or nīt′fôl′) the coming of night. *n.*

night·gown (nīt′goun′) **1** a loose garment worn in bed by girls and women. **2** nightshirt. *n.*

night·in·gale (nīt′ən gāl′ or nīt′ing gāl′) a small, reddish-brown bird of Europe noted for the sweet song of the male: *The nightingale sings at night as well as in the daytime.* *n.*

night·ly (nīt′lē) **1** happening every night. **2** every night: *Performances are given nightly except on Sunday.* **3** happening at night: *nightly dew.* **4** at night; by night: *Many animals come out only nightly.* 1, 3 *adj.*, 2, 4 *adv.*

☛ **Nightly** and **knightly** are pronounced the same.

night·mare (nīt′mer′) **1** a frightening dream. **2** a very unpleasant or frightening experience: *The dust storm was a nightmare.* *n.*

night·shirt (nīt′shėrt′) a loose garment worn in bed by boys and men. *n.*

night·time (nīt′tīm′) the time between evening and morning. *n.*

night watch **1** a watch or guard kept during the night. **2** a person or persons keeping such a watch.

nil (nil) nothing. *n.*

nim·ble (nim′bəl) **1** quick-moving; active and sure-footed; light and quick: *The goats were nimble in climbing among the rocks.* **2** quick to understand and to reply; clever: *The boy's nimble mind solved the problem quickly.* *adj.*, **nim·bler, nim·blest.** —**nim′bly,** *adv.*

nine (nīn) **1** one more than eight; 9: *Six and three make nine.* **2** a set of nine persons or things. 1, 2 *n.*, 1 *adj.*

nine·teen (nīn′tēn′) nine more than ten; 19. *n., adj.*

nine·teenth (nīn′tēnth′) **1** next after the 18th; last in a series of nineteen; 19th. **2** one of 19 equal parts. 1 *adj.*, 1, 2 *n.*

nine·ti·eth (nīn′tē ith) **1** next after the 89th; last in a series of ninety; 90th. **2** one of 90 equal parts. 1 *adj.*, 1, 2 *n.*

nine·ty (nīn′tē) nine times ten; 90. *n., pl.* **nine·ties;** *adj.*

ninth (nīnth) **1** next after the 8th; last in a series of nine; 9th. **2** one of 9 equal parts. 1 *adj.*, 1, 2 *n.*

nip[1] (nip) **1** squeeze tight and suddenly; pinch; bite: *The crab nipped my toe.* **2** a tight squeeze or pinch; a sudden bite. **3** injure or spoil, as by frost or wind: *Some of our tomato plants were nipped by frost.* **4** an injury caused by frost. **5** a sharp cold; a chill: *There is a nip in the air this morning.* **6** have a sharp, biting effect on: *The cold wind nipped our ears.* 1, 3, 6 *v.*, **nipped, nip·ping;** 2, 4, 5 *n.*
nip and tuck, *Informal.* even in a race or contest.

nip[2] (nip) a small drink: *a nip of brandy.* *n.*

nip·ple (nip′əl) **1** the small projection through which a baby or young animal gets its mother's milk. **2** the mouthpiece of a baby's bottle. *n.*

ni·tro·gen (nī′trə jən) a gas without color, taste, or odor that forms about four fifths of the air: *Nitrogen is needed for the growth of all plants.* *n.*

nit·wit (nit′wit′) *Slang.* a very stupid person. *n.*

no (nō) **1** a word used to deny, refuse, or disagree; the opposite of **yes:** *Will you come with us? No. Can a cow fly? No.* **2** not in any degree; not at all: *He is no better. Dogs have no wings.* **3** not any; not a: *He has no friends.* **4** a vote against; a person voting against: *The noes won.* 1, 4 *n.*, *pl.* **noes;** 1, 2 *adv.*, 3 *adj.*

☛ **No** and **know** are pronounced the same.

No. number.

no·bil·i·ty (nō bil′ə tē) **1** people of noble rank, title, or birth: *Earls, counts, and marquises belong to the nobility.* **2** noble birth; noble rank. **3** noble character. *n., pl.* **no·bil·i·ties.**

no·ble (nō′bəl) **1** high and great by birth, rank, or title: *a noble family.* **2** a person high and great by birth, rank, or title: *A duke is a noble.* **3** high and great in character; showing greatness of mind; good: *a noble person, a noble deed.* **4** excellent; fine; splendid; magnificent: *Niagara Falls is a noble sight.* 1, 3, 4 *adj.*, **no·bler, no·blest;** 2 *n.*

no·ble·man (nō′bəl mən) a man of noble rank, title, or birth. *n., pl.* **no·ble·men** (nō′bəl mən).

no·bly (nō′blē) in a noble manner; in a splendid way; as a noble person would do. *adv.*

no·bod·y (nō′bud′ē or nō′bod′ē) **1** no one; no person. **2** a person of no importance. 1 *pron.*, 2 *n.*, *pl.* **no·bod·ies.**

noc·tur·nal (nok tėr′nəl) **1** of the night: *Stars are a* *nocturnal sight.* **2** in the night: *a nocturnal visitor.* **3** active in the night: *The owl is a nocturnal bird. The bat is a nocturnal animal.* **4** closed by day, open by night: *a nocturnal flower. adj.*

nod (nod) **1** bow the head slightly and raise it again quickly. **2** show agreement by nodding. **3** a nodding of the head: *He gave us a nod as he passed.* **4** let the head fall forward and bob about when sleepy or falling asleep. **5** be sleepy; become careless and dull. **6** droop, bend, or sway back and forth: *Trees nod in the wind.* 1, 2, 4–6 *v.,* **nod·ded, nod·ding;** 3 *n.*

no·ël (nō el′) **1** a Christmas song; carol. **2 Noël,** Christmas. *n.*

noise (noiz) **1** a sound that is not musical or pleasant; loud or harsh sound: *The noise kept me awake.* **2** any sound: *the noise of rain on the roof.* **3** tell; spread the news of: *It was noised abroad that the king was dying.* 1, 2 *n.,* 3 *v.,* **noised, nois·ing.**

☛ **Noise,** which originally meant a 'din' or 'loud disturbance,' comes through French from Latin *nausea,* meaning 'seasickness,' from the unpleasant din made by a shipful of seasick passengers. See note at **nausea.**

noise·less (noiz′lis) making no noise; making little noise: *She owned a noiseless typewriter. adj.*

nois·i·ly (noiz′ə lē) in a noisy manner. *adv.*

nois·y (noiz′ē) **1** making much noise: *a noisy boy, a noisy crowd, a noisy little clock.* **2** full of noise: *a noisy street, a noisy house, the noisy city.* **3** having much noise with it: *a noisy quarrel, a noisy game. adj.,* **nois·i·er, nois·i·est.**

no·mad (nō′mad) **1** a member of a tribe that moves from place to place in order to have pasture for its cattle or to be near its own food supply: *Some Arabs and Eskimos are nomads.* **2** a person who is always on the move. *n.*

no·mad·ic (nō mad′ik) of nomads or their life; wandering; roving: *The Sioux were one of many nomadic tribes of North American Indians. adj.*

nom·i·nate (nom′ə nāt′) **1** to name as candidate for an office: *Mrs. Smith was nominated for Member of Parliament.* **2** appoint to an office or duty: *The Prime Minister nominated him Secretary of State. v.,* **nom·i·nated, nom·i·nat·ing.**

nom·i·na·tion (nom′ə nā′shən) **1** the naming of someone as a candidate for an office: *The nominations for president of the club were written on the blackboard.* **2** a selection for office; an appointment to office. **3** being nominated: *Her friends were pleased by her nomination. n.*

nom·i·nee (nom′ə nē′) a person nominated to or for an office. *n.*

non– a prefix meaning: not____; opposite of____; lack of____: *Non-breakable means not breakable. Non-living means not living. Non-completion means lack of completion.*

non·cha·lant (non′shə lont′ or non′shə lənt) without enthusiasm; coolly unconcerned; indifferent: *She remained quite nonchalant during all the excitement. adj.*

non–com·mis·sioned (non′kə mish′ənd) without a commission; not commissioned: *Sergeants and corporals are non-commissioned officers. adj.*

non–con·duc·tor (non′kən duk′tər) a substance that does not readily allow heat, electricity, or sound to pass through it: *Rubber is a non-conductor of electricity. n.*

none (nun) **1** not any: *We have none of that paper left.* **2** no one; not one: *None of these is a special case.* **3** no persons or things: *None have arrived.* **4** to no extent; not at all: *Our supply is none too great.* 1–3 *pron.,* 4 *adv.* **—none the less,** nevertheless.

☛ **None** and **nun** are pronounced the same.

non·sense (non′sens) **1** words, ideas, or acts without meaning: *The magician talks nonsense as he is doing the tricks.* **2** foolish talk or doings; a plan or suggestion that is foolish: *It is nonsense to say that we can walk that far in an hour. n.*

non–stop (non′stop′) without stopping: *We took a non-stop flight from Toronto to Rome. We flew non-stop from Regina to Montreal. adj., adv.*

noo·dles (nü′dəlz) a food made of flour and water, or flour and eggs, resembling macaroni but made in flat strips. *n. pl.*

nook (nůk) **1** a cosy little corner. **2** a hidden spot; a sheltered place: *There is a wonderful nook in the woods behind our house. n.*

noon (nün) 12 o'clock in the daytime; the middle of the day. *n.*

noon·day (nün′dā′) noon: *Lunch is our noonday meal. n.*

no one or **no–one** (nō′wun′) no person; nobody: *No one was hurt in the car accident. pron.*

A noose

noose (nüs) **1** a loop with a slip knot that tightens as the string or rope is pulled: *Nooses are used especially in lassos and snares.* **2** catch with a noose; snare. 1 *n.,* 2 *v.,* **noosed, noos·ing.**

nor (nôr) **1** and no: *There was neither river nor stream in that desert.* **2** and not: *I have not been there, nor am I going. conj.*

nor·mal (nôr′məl) **1** of the usual standard or type; regular; usual: *The normal temperature of the human body is 37 degrees Celsius. It's normal for children to be energetic.* **2** the usual state or level: *He is fifteen centimetres above normal for his age.* 1 *adj.,* 2 *n.*

nor·mal·ly (nôr′məl ē) in the normal way; regularly; if things are normal: *A child normally begins to lose his first teeth at six years. adv.*

Norse (nôrs) **1** of or having to do with ancient Scandinavia, its people, or their language. **2** the people of ancient Scandinavia; Norsemen. 1 *adj.,* 2 *n.*

Norse·man (nôrs′mən) a member of a tall, blond people that lived in ancient Scandinavia: *The Vikings were Norsemen. n., pl.* **Norse·men** (nôrs′mən).

north (nôrth) **1** the direction to which a compass needle points; the direction to the right as one faces the setting sun. See **compass** for picture. **2** toward the north; farther toward the north: *Drive north for the next block.* **3** coming from the north: *a north wind.* **4** in the north; living in the north. **5** Also, **North,** the part of the world, country, or continent toward the north. **6 the North,** in Canada, the northern parts of the provinces from Quebec westward and the territory lying north of these provinces: *A great deal is being done to develop the natural resources of the North.* 1, 5, 6 *n.*, 2 *adv.*, 3, 4 *adj.*

North American 1 of or having to do with North America or its people. 2 a person born in or living in North America.

north·east (nôrth′ēst′) 1 the direction halfway between north and east. 2 a place that is in the northeast part or direction. 3 of, at, in, to, toward, or from the northeast: *a northeast wind* (*adj.*). *They travelled northeast* (*adv.*). 1, 2 *n.*, 3 *adj.*, *adv.*

north·east·ern (nôrth′ēs′tərn) of, at, in, to, toward, or from the northeast. *adj.*

north·er·ly (nôr′ᴛʜər lē) 1 toward the north: *The windows face northerly.* 2 from the north: *a northerly wind.* *adv.*, *adj.*

north·ern (nôr′ᴛʜərn) 1 toward the north: *the northern side of a building.* 2 coming from the north: *a northern breeze.* 3 of or in the north: *northern countries.* 4 of or in the North of Canada: *Churchill is a northern port.* *adj.*

North·ern·er (nôr′ᴛʜər nər) a person born in or living in the North. *n.*

northern lights the streamers and bands of light that appear in the northern sky at night; aurora borealis.

north·ern·most (nôr′ᴛʜərn mōst′) farthest north. *adj.*

North·land (nôrth′land′) the northern regions of Canada: *The Yukon is a fast-growing part of Canada's Northland.* *n.* Also, **northland.**

North Pole the northern end of the earth's axis. See **latitude** for picture.

North Star the bright star almost directly above the North Pole.

north·ward (nôrth′wərd) toward the north; north: *He walked northward. The orchard is on the northward slope of the hill. Rocks lay northward of the ship's course.* *adv.*, *adj.*

north·wards (nôrth′wərdz) northward. *adv.*

north·west (nôrth′west′) 1 the direction halfway between north and west. 2 a place that is in the northwest part or direction. 3 of, at, in, to, toward, or from the northwest: *a northwest wind* (*adj.*). *They travelled northwest* (*adv.*). 1, 2 *n.*, 3 *adj.*, *adv.*

Northwest the general region of Canada north and west of the Great Lakes. *n.*

North West Company a group of fur traders formed in Canada during the late 1700's.

north·west·ern (nôrth′wes′tərn) of, at, in, to, toward, or from the northwest. *adj.*

North West Mounted Police a former name of the Royal Canadian Mounted Police.

Nor·we·gian (nôr wē′jən) 1 of or having to do with Norway, a country in northern Europe. 2 a person born in or living in Norway. 3 the language of Norway. 1 *adj.*, 2, 3 *n.*

nose (nōz) 1 the part of the face or head that stands out just above the mouth: *The nose has openings for breathing and smelling.* 2 the sense of smell: *Most dogs have a good nose. A mouse has a good nose for cheese.* 3 discover by smell; smell out. 4 smell; sniff at. 5 rub with the nose: *The cat nosed its kittens.* 6 a part that stands out, especially the bow of a ship, boat, or aircraft:

hat, āge, fär; let, ēqual, tėrm; it, īce
hot, ōpen, ôrder; oil, out; cup, put, rüle
əbove, takən, pencəl, lemən, circəs
ch, child; ng, long; sh, ship
th, thin; ᴛʜ, then; zh, measure

We saw the steamer's nose poking around the cliff. 7 push with the nose or forward end: *The bulldozer nosed the great rock off the road.* 8 push one's way carefully: *The boat nosed along between the rocks.* 9 search for; pry into. 1, 2, 6 *n.*, 3–5, 7–9 *v.*, **nosed, nos·ing.**

look down one's nose at, treat with contempt or scorn.

pay through the nose, *Informal.* pay a great deal too much.

poke one's nose into, *Informal.* pry into; meddle in: *The old gossip was always poking her nose into people's business.*

turn up one's nose at, treat with contempt or scorn.

nose·bleed (nōz′blēd′) a flow of blood from the nose. *n.*

nose–dive (nōz′dīv′) 1 a swift plunge downward by an aircraft. 2 a sharp, sudden drop: *The thermometer took a nose-dive during the night.* 3 of an aircraft, plunge swiftly downward. 4 take a sharp, sudden drop: *The price of gasoline nose-dived overnight.* 1, 2 *n.*, 3, 4 *v.*, **nose-dived, nose-div·ing.**

nos·ey (nōz′ē) too curious about other people's business; prying; inquisitive: *Adults are often annoyed by nosey children.* *adj.*, **nos·i·er, nos·i·est.** Also spelled **nosy.**

nos·tril (nos′trəl) either of the two openings in the nose: *Air is breathed into the lungs through the nostrils.* *n.*

☛ **Nostril** comes from the combining of two Old English words (*nosu* + *thyrel*), meaning 'nose hole.'

nos·y (nōz′ē) See **nosey.**

not (not) a word used to make a negative statement: *Six and two do not make ten. He has not been here. She has come but he has not.* *adv.*

☛ **Not** and **knot** are pronounced the same. **Naught** and **nought** are sometimes pronounced the same as **not** and **knot.**

no·ta·ble (nō′tə bəl) 1 worthy of notice; striking; remarkable; important: *a notable event, a notable man.* 2 an important or famous person: *Many notables attended the Governor General's levee.* 1 *adj.*, 2 *n.* **—no′ta·bly,** *adv.*

Notches on a stick

notch (noch) 1 a V-shaped nick or cut made in an edge or on a curving surface: *The Indians cut notches on a stick to keep count of numbers.* 2 make a notch or notches in. 3 a deep, narrow pass or gap between mountains. 4 *Informal.* a grade; step; degree: *In this hot weather many people set their air conditioners several notches higher.* 1, 3, 4 *n.*, 2 *v.*

note (nōt) 1 a short sentence, phrase, or single word, written down to remind one of what was in a book, a speech, an agreement, etc.; memorandum: *Sometimes our* *teacher has us take notes on what we read. I must make a note of that.* **2** write down as a thing to be remembered. **3** a comment or piece of information in a book, often added to help students. **4** a very short letter: *a note of thanks.* **5** a formal letter from one government to another: *Italy sent a note of protest to France.* **6** a written promise to pay a certain amount of money at a certain time. **7** greatness; fame: *Sir Wilfrid Laurier was a person of note.* **8** observe; notice; give attention to: *Now note what I do next.* **9** in music, the written sign to show the pitch and the length of a sound. See **bar** for picture. **10** a single musical sound: *Sing this note for me.* **11** any one of the keys of a piano: *strike the wrong note.* **12** a song or call of a bird. **13** a tone of voice or way of expression: *There was a note of anxiety in her voice.* 1, 3–7, 9–13 *n.*, 2, 8 *v.*, **not·ed, not·ing.**

take note of, give attention to or notice: *Take note of the time, please; we must not be late.*

note·book (nōt′bu̇k′) a book in which to write notes of things to be learned or remembered. *n.*

not·ed (nōt′id) well-known; famous; specially noticed: *Samson was noted for his strength. adj.*

note·pa·per (nōt′pā′pər) paper used for writing letters. *n.*

note·wor·thy (nōt′wėr′ᴛʜē) worthy of notice; remarkable: *The first flight across the Atlantic was a noteworthy achievement. adj.*

noth·ing (nuth′ing) **1** not anything: *Nothing arrived by mail.* **2** a thing of no value or importance; a person of no importance: *People regard him as a nothing.* **3** zero. **4** not at all: *She is nothing like her sister in looks.* 1–3 *n.*, 4 *adv.*

no·tice (nō′tis) **1** heed; attention: *Take no notice of her. A sudden movement caught his notice.* **2** see; take note of; give attention to: *I noticed a hole in my stocking.* **3** advance information; warning: *The driver sounded his horn to give notice that he wanted to pass.* **4** a written or printed sign; a paper posted in a public place; a large sheet of paper giving information or directions: *We saw a notice of this week's movie outside the theatre.* **5** a warning or announcement that one is leaving or must leave rented quarters or a job: *A month's notice is required from anyone wishing to end this agreement.* 1, 3–5 *n.*, 2 *v.*, **no·ticed, no·tic·ing.**

no·tice·a·ble (nō′tis ə bəl) easily seen or noticed: *Our kitten is very noticeable because its fur is yellow. adj.*

no·ti·fy (nō′tə fī′) let know; give notice to; announce to; inform: *Our teacher notified us that there would be a test on Monday. We have a letter notifying us that Uncle John will visit us soon. v.*, **no·ti·fied, no·ti·fy·ing.**

no·tion (nō′shən) **1** an idea; understanding: *He has no notion of what I mean.* **2** an opinion; view; belief: *One common notion is that red hair goes with a quick temper.* **3** an inclination; whim: *She had a notion to visit her grandmother.* **4 notions,** *pl.* small, useful articles, such as pins, needles, thread, tape, etc. *n.*

no·to·ri·ous (nō tô′rē əs) well-known or commonly known because of something unfavorable or unpleasant: *That notorious criminal has been sent to prison. adj.*

not·with·stand·ing (not′with stan′ding or not′wiᴛʜ stan′ding) **1** in spite of: *He bought it notwithstanding the price.* **2** in spite of the fact that: *Notwithstanding there was need for haste, he still delayed.* **3** nevertheless: *It is raining; but I shall go, notwithstanding.* 1 *prep.*, 2 *conj.*, 3 *adv.*

nought (not or nôt) **1** zero; 0: *Put two noughts after a six to make six hundred.* **2** nothing; naught. *n.*

☛ **Nought, knot, naught,** and **not** are pronounced the same (to rhyme with *got*) by most Canadians.

noun (noun) a word used as the name of a person, place, thing, quality, or event: *Words like* John, table, school, kindness, skill, *and* party *are nouns. n.*

nour·ish (nėr′ish) **1** make grow, or keep alive and well, with food; feed: *Milk is all that is needed to nourish a newborn baby.* **2** maintain; foster; support; encourage: *to nourish a hope. v.*

nour·ish·ment (nėr′ish mənt) food. *n.*

Nov. November.

No·va Sco·tian (nō′və skō′shən) **1** a person born in or living in Nova Scotia. **2** of or concerning Nova Scotia.

nov·el (nov′əl) **1** of a new kind or nature; strange; new: *Flying gives people a novel sensation. Novel decorations added to the success of the party.* **2** a story with characters and a plot, long enough to fill one or more volumes: *Novels are usually about people and events such as might be met with in real life.* 1 *adj.*, 2 *n.*

nov·el·ist (nov′ə list) a writer of novels. *n.*

nov·el·ty (nov′əl tē) **1** newness: *After the novelty of washing dishes wore off, Mary lost interest.* **2** a new or unusual thing: *Staying up late was a novelty to the children, and they enjoyed it.* **3 novelties,** *pl.* small, unusual articles, such as toys, cheap jewellery, etc. *n., pl.* **nov·el·ties.**

No·vem·ber (nō vem′bər) the eleventh month of the year; the month before December: *November has 30 days. n.*

☛ **November** came into English through Old French from the Latin name for this month, *November,* from *novem,* meaning 'nine.' November was the ninth month of the ancient Roman calendar.

nov·ice (nov′is) **1** one who is new to what he is doing; a beginner: *Novices are likely to make some mistakes.* **2** a person who is training to become a monk or nun but who has not yet taken final vows. *n.*

now (nou) **1** at this time: *He is here now. We do not believe in ghosts now.* **2** by this time: *She must have reached the city now.* **3** the present; this time: *by now, until now, from now on.* **4** since; now that: *Now I am older, I have changed my mind. Now you mention it, I do remember.* **5** as things are; as it is: *Now I can never believe you again.* **6** then; next: *Now you see it; now you don't. We have signed the petition and it now goes to the school principal.* **7 Now** is used in many sentences where it makes very little difference in the meaning: *Now what do you mean? Oh, come now! Now you knew that was wrong.* 1, 2, 5–7 *adv.*, 3 *n.*, 4 *conj.*

just now, only a few moments ago.

now and again, from time to time; once in a while.

now and then, from time to time; once in a while.

now·a·days (nou′ə dāz′) at the present day; in these times: *Nowadays people travel in automobiles rather than carriages. adv.*

hat, āge, fär; let, ēqual, tėrm; it, īce
hot, ōpen, ôrder; oil, out; cup, pu̇t, rüle
əbove, takən, pencəl, lemən, circəs
ch, child; ng, long; sh, ship
th, thin; ᴛʜ, then; zh, measure

no·where (nō′wer′ or nō′hwer′) in no place; at no place; to no place. *adv.*

nox·ious (nok′shəs) extremely harmful; poisonous: *Poison ivy is a noxious plant; avoid touching its leaves. adj.*

A hose with a nozzle attached

noz·zle (noz′əl) a tip or spout put on a hose, pipe, can, etc. to allow one to control the outward flow of liquid or gas: *He adjusted the nozzle so that the water came out in a fine spray. n.*

N.S. Nova Scotia.

nu·cle·ar (nyü′klē ər or nü′klē ər) **1** of or having to do with nuclei or a nucleus. **2** of or having to do with atoms or atomic energy; atomic: *a nuclear reactor, the nuclear age. adj.*

nu·cle·us (nyü′klē əs or nü′klē əs) **1** a central part or thing around which other parts or things are collected: *The family is the nucleus of our society.* **2** a beginning, to which additions are to be made: *His five-dollar bill became the nucleus of a flourishing bank account.* **3** in science, a group of particles forming the central part of an atom and carrying a positive charge: *Almost all nuclei consist of protons and neutrons.* **4** in science, a mass of protoplasm found in most plant and animal cells, without which a cell cannot grow and divide. *n., pl.* **nu·cle·i** (nyü′klē ī or nü′klē ī) or **nu·cle·us·es.**

nude (nyüd or nüd) **1** with one's clothing removed; naked. **2** a naked figure in painting, sculpture, or photography. 1 *adj.,* 2 *n.*

in the nude, without clothes on; naked: *The boys went swimming in the nude.*

nudge (nuj) **1** push slightly; jog with the elbow to attract attention, etc. **2** a slight push or jog: *When he gave me a nudge, I spilled the milk.* 1 *v.,* **nudged, nudg·ing;** 2 *n.*

nug·get (nug′it) **1** a lump, especially a lump of gold in its natural state. **2** anything valuable: *nuggets of wisdom. n.*

nui·sance (nyü′səns or nü′səns) any thing or person that annoys, troubles, offends, or is disagreeable: *Flies are a nuisance. n.*

nuisance ground *Cdn.* a garbage dump; a place where worn-out and useless junk is thrown.

null (nul) **1** not binding; of no effect; as if not existing: *A promise obtained by force is legally null.* **2** not any; zero. *adj.*

null and void, without legal force or effect; worthless.

numb (num) **1** having lost the power of feeling or moving: *My fingers are numb with cold.* **2** make numb. **3** dull the feelings of: *The old lady was numbed with grief when her grandchild died.* 1 *adj.,* 2, 3 *v.*

num·ber (num′bər) **1** a word that tells exactly how many: *Two, thirteen, twenty-one, fifty, and one hundred are numbers.* **2** the count or sum of a group of things or persons: *The number of boys in our class is twenty.* **3** find out the number of; count. **4** a figure or mark that stands for a number; a numeral: *2, 7, and 9 are numbers.* **5** give a number to: *The pages of this book are numbered.* **6** be or amount to a certain number: *The provinces of Canada number ten. Montreal numbers over a million people.* **7** a quantity, especially a rather large quantity: *We saw a number of birds. There were numbers who stayed out of school that day.* **8** include as one of a class or collection: *I number you among my best friends.* **9** one of a numbered series, often a particular numeral or set of numerals identifying a person or thing: *a telephone number, a house number. Symbol:* # **10** a single part of a program, etc.: *The program consisted of four musical numbers.* **11** an issue of a magazine: *The May number has an unusually good story.* **12** limit; fix the number of: *The old man's years are numbered.* **13** in grammar, a word form or ending that shows whether one or more than one is meant: *'Boy' and 'ox' are in the singular number; 'boys' and 'oxen' are in the plural number.* 1, 2, 4, 7, 9–11, 13 *n.,* 3, 5, 6, 8, 12 *v.*

without number, too many to be counted: *stars without number.*

☛ See note at **numeral.**

num·ber·less (num′bər lis) very numerous; too many to count: *There are numberless fish in the sea. adj.*

nu·mer·al (nyü′mər əl or nü′mər əl) a word, figure, or a group of figures standing for a number. 2, 15, and 100 are Arabic numerals. II, XV, and C are Roman numerals for 2, 15, and 100. *n.*

☛ A **numeral** is a figure that stands for a number. A **number** is the idea of a quantity or amount. The numerals 15 and XV stand for the same number.

nu·mer·a·tor (nyü′mər ā′tər or nü′mər ā′tər) the number above the line in a fraction: *In ⅜, 3 is the numerator, and 8 is the denominator. n.*

nu·mer·i·cal (nyü mer′ə kəl or nü mer′ə kəl) having something to do with number or numbers; in numbers; by numbers. *adj.*

nu·mer·ous (nyü′mər əs or nü′mər əs) **1** very many: *The child asked numerous questions.* **2** in great numbers: *He has a numerous acquaintance among politicians. adj.*

nun (nun) a woman who is a member of a religious order and lives a life of service, prayer, and worship: *Some nuns teach; some care for the sick. n.*

☛ **Nun** and **none** are pronounced the same.

nup·tial (nup′shəl or nup′chəl) **1** of marriage or weddings. **2 nuptials,** *pl.* a wedding or the wedding ceremony. 1 *adj.,* 2 *n.*

nurse (nėrs) **1** a person who takes care of the sick, the injured, or the old, or is trained to do this: *Hospitals employ many nurses.* **2** be or act as a nurse for sick people; wait on or take care of the sick. **3** a woman who cares for and brings up the young children or babies of other persons: *Mrs. Jones has hired a new nurse.* **4** make grow; nourish and protect: *nurse a plant, nurse a hatred in the heart.* **5** use or treat with special care: *He nursed his sore arm by using it very little.*

6 feed milk to a baby at the breast. 7 suck milk from a mother's breast. 1, 3 *n.,* 2, 4–7 *v.,* **nursed, nurs·ing.**

nurse·maid (nėrs′mād′) a girl or woman employed to care for children. *n.*

nurs·er·y (nėr′sər ē) 1 a room set apart for the use of babies and children. 2 See **day-care centre.** 3 See **nursery school.** 4 a place where young plants are grown for transplanting or sale. *n., pl.* **nurs·er·ies.**

nursery rhyme a short poem for young children: *'Humpty Dumpty sat on a wall' is the beginning of a famous nursery rhyme.*

nursery school a school for children over three years and, usually, under five.

nur·ture (nėr′chər) 1 bring up; care for; rear: *She nurtured the child as if he had been her own.* 2 the act or process of raising or rearing; bringing up; training; education. 3 nourish: *Minerals in the soil nurture the plants.* 4 food; nourishment. 1, 3 *v.,* **nur·tured, nur·tur·ing;** 2, 4 *n.*

nut (nut) 1 a dry fruit or seed with a hard, woody or leathery shell and a kernel inside: *Some nuts, including walnuts, almonds, and pecans, are good to eat.* 2 the kernel of a nut. 3 a small block, usually of metal, that screws on to a bolt to hold the bolt in place. See **bolt** for picture. *n.*

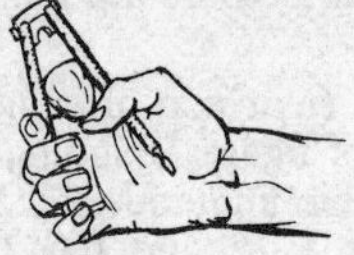
A nutcracker

nut·crack·er (nut′krak′ər) an instrument for cracking the shells of nuts. *n.*

nut·meg (nut′meg′) a hard spicy seed about as big as a marble, obtained from the fruit of a tree growing in the East Indies: *Nutmeg is grated and used for flavoring food.* *n.*

nu·tri·tion (nyü trish′ən or nü trish′ən) food; nourishment: *A balanced diet gives good nutrition.* *n.*

nu·tri·tious (nyü trish′əs or nü trish′əs) nourishing; valuable as food: *Oranges and cheese are nutritious.* *adj.*

nut·shell (nut′shel′) the shell of a nut. *n.*
in a nutshell, in a very brief form; in a few words.

nuz·zle (nuz′əl) poke or rub with the nose; press the nose against: *The calf nuzzles its mother.* *v.,* **nuz·zled, nuz·zling.**

N.W. or **NW** 1 northwest. 2 northwestern.

N.W.M.P. North West Mounted Police.

N.W.T. Northwest Territories.

ny·lon (nī′lon) 1 an extremely strong and durable plastic substance, used to make clothing, utensils, bristles, etc. 2 **nylons,** *pl.* stockings made of nylon. *n.*

nymph (nimf) 1 in Greek and Roman myths, a lesser goddess of nature, who lived in seas, rivers, springs, hills, woods, or trees. 2 any of certain insects in the stage of development between larva and adult. It resembles the adult but has no wings. *n.*

hat, āge, fär; let, ēqual, tėrm; it, īce
hot, ōpen, ôrder; oil, out; cup, pu̇t, rüle
əbove, takən, pencəl, lemən, circəs
ch, child; ng, long; sh, ship
th, thin; ᴛʜ, then; zh, measure

o or **O¹** (ō) 1 the 15th letter of the alphabet: *There are two* o's *in* polo. 2 zero. *n., pl.* **o's** or **O's.**

☛ **O, Oh,** and **owe** are pronounced the same.

O² or **Oh** (ō) 1 a word used before a person's name to show respect, to gain attention, etc.: *O King, hear my plea!* 2 a word used to express surprise, joy, pain, and other feelings: *O, dear me! interj.*

☛ **O** is usually used only before a name or something treated as a name: *O Canada. O Happy Day!* In other cases, **Oh** is generally used. See note at **O¹**.

Leaves of the North American oak

oak (ōk) 1 any of several kinds of trees or shrubs found in most parts of the world, having nuts that are called acorns: *A great oak stood in front of the house.* 2 the hard wood of the oak tree: *The ship had timbers of oak. n.*

oak·en (ōk′ən) made of oak wood: *an oaken bucket. adj.*

oar (ôr) 1 a long pole with a broad, flat blade at one end, used for rowing or steering a boat. See **rowboat** for picture. 2 a person who rows: *He is the best oar in the crew. n.*

☛ **Oar, or,** and **ore** are pronounced the same.

oar·lock (ôr′lok′) a notch or U-shaped support for holding the oar in place while rowing. *n.*

oars·man (ôrz′mən) 1 a man who rows. 2 a man who rows well. *n., pl.* **oars·men** (ôrz′mən).

o·a·sis (ō ā′sis) 1 a fertile spot in the desert: *Water is always available at an oasis.* 2 any fertile spot in a barren land; any pleasant place in a desolate region. *n., pl.* **o·a·ses** (ō ā′sēz).

oat (ōt) 1 a plant whose seed is used in making oatmeal and as a food for horses. 2 **oats,** *pl.* the seeds of the oat plant. *n.*

oath (ōth) 1 a solemn promise or statement that something is true, especially such a promise made to a judge, coroner, etc.: *If a person tells lies after taking an oath, he can be punished by the law.* 2 a curse; a word used in swearing: *The pirate cursed us with fearful oaths. n., pl.* **oaths** (ōᴛʜz or ōths).

under oath, bound by an oath: *He gave his evidence under oath.*

oat·meal (ōt′mēl′) 1 oats made into meal; ground oats; rolled oats. 2 porridge made from rolled oats or oatmeal: *We often have oatmeal with milk for breakfast. n.*

o·be·di·ence (ō bē′dē əns) the act or habit of doing what one is told; a submitting to authority or law: *Our puppy is learning obedience. Soldiers act in obedience to orders. n.*

o·be·di·ent (ō bē′dē ənt) doing what one is told; willing to obey: *The obedient dog came at his master's whistle. adj.* —**o·be′di·ent·ly,** *adv.*

ob·e·lisk (ob′ə lisk) a tapering, four-sided shaft of stone with a top shaped like a pyramid. See the picture. *n.*

o·bey (ō bā′) 1 do what one is told to do: *The dog obeyed and went home.* 2 follow the orders of: *We obey our father.* 3 act in accordance with; comply with: *A good citizen obeys the laws.* 4 yield to the control of: *A car obeys the driver. A horse obeys the rein. v.*

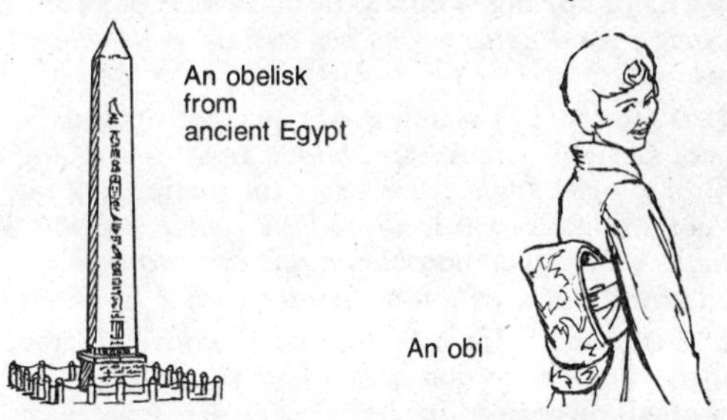

An obelisk from ancient Egypt

An obi

ob·i (ō′bē) a long, broad sash worn around the waist of a kimono by Japanese women and children. *n.*

object (ob′jikt for 1, 2, and 3, əb jekt′ for 4 and 5) 1 anything that can be seen or touched: *What is that object by the fence? A dark object moved between me and the door.* 2 a person or thing toward which feeling, thought, or action is directed: *an object of study. The blind cripple was an object of charity. Bob was the object of his dog's affection.* 3 something aimed at; an end or purpose; a goal: *My object in coming here was to get her address.* 4 make objections; be opposed; feel dislike: *I made my suggestion, but John objected. Many people object to loud noise.* 5 give as a reason against something: *Mother objected that the weather was too wet to play outdoors.* 1–3 *n.,* 4, 5 *v.*

ob·jec·tion (əb jek′shən) 1 something said in objecting; a reason or argument against something: *One of the objections to the new plan was that it would cost too much.* 2 a feeling of disapproval or dislike: *A lazy person has strong objections to working. n.*

ob·jec·tion·a·ble (əb jek′shən ə bəl) 1 likely to be objected to. 2 unpleasant: *objectionable manners. adj.*

ob·jec·tive (əb jek′tiv) 1 something aimed at: *My objective this summer will be to learn to play tennis better.* 2 existing outside the mind as an actual object, and not merely in the mind as an idea; real: *Buildings are objective; ideas are subjective.* 3 dealing with facts or objects, not with the thoughts and feelings of the speaker, writer, painter, etc.; impersonal: *A scientist must be objective in his experiments. Instead of the usual prejudiced report, we had a truly objective one this year.* 1 *n.,* 2, 3 *adj.*

ob·li·gate (ob′lə gāt′) bind morally or legally; pledge: *A witness in court is obligated to tell the truth. v.,* **ob·li·gat·ed, ob·li·gat·ing.**

ob·li·ga·tion (ob′lə gā′shən) 1 a duty under the law; a duty due to a promise or contract; a duty on account of social relationship or kindness received: *Taxes are an obligation that may fall on everybody. The man is under obligation to paint our house first. A person's first obligation is to the people he loves.* 2 a binding legal agreement; bond; contract: *The firm was not able to meet its obligations.* *n.*

o·blige (ə blīj′) **1** bind by a promise, contract, or duty; compel; force: *The law obliges parents to send their children to school. I am obliged to leave early to catch my train.* **2** put under a debt of thanks for a favor or service: *She obliged us with a song.* **3** do a favor to: *Kindly oblige me by closing the door.* *v.,* **o·bliged, o·blig·ing.**

o·blig·ing (ə blīj′ing) willing to do favors; helpful: *Her obliging good nature wins her friends everywhere she goes.* *adj.*

ob·lique (əb lēk′) **1** slanting; not straight up and down; not straight across: *An oblique angle is any angle that is not a right angle.* See **angle** for picture. **2** not direct; not straightforward: *an oblique glance, an oblique movement. She made an oblique reference to her illness, but did not mention it directly.* *adj.*

ob·lit·er·ate (əb lit′ər āt′) blot out; remove all traces of; destroy: *The heavy rain obliterated all footprints.* *v.,* **ob·lit·er·at·ed, ob·lit·er·at·ing.**

ob·liv·i·on (əb liv′ē ən) **1** the condition of being entirely forgotten: *Many ancient cities have long since passed into oblivion.* **2** the condition of being unaware of what is going on; forgetfulness: *Grandfather sat by the fire in peaceful oblivion.* *n.*

ob·liv·i·ous (əb liv′ē əs) forgetful; not mindful; unaware: *The book was so interesting that she was oblivious of her surroundings.* *adj.*

ob·long (ob′long) **1** longer than broad: *an oblong loaf of bread.* **2** a rectangle that is not a square. See **rectangle** for picture. 1 *adj.,* 2 *n.*

ob·nox·ious (əb nok′shəs) offensive; very disagreeable; hateful: *His disgusting manners made him obnoxious.* *adj.*

o·boe (ō′bō) a wooden wind instrument in which the tone is produced by a double reed. *n.*

☞ **Oboe** comes from a French word *hautbois* meaning 'high wood,' but the present spelling and pronunciation come from Italian.

ob·scene (əb sēn′ or ob sēn′) offending decency; impure; filthy: *We were annoyed by the man's obscene swearing at the hockey players.* *adj.*

ob·scen·i·ty (əb sen′ə tē or əb sēn′ə tē) **1** obscene quality. **2** obscene language or behavior; an obscene word or act. *n., pl.* **ob·scen·i·ties.**

ob·scure (əb skyür′) **1** not distinct; not clear: *an obscure shape, obscure sounds, an obscure view.* **2** hidden; not easily discovered: *an obscure path.* **3** hard to understand; not clearly expressed: *An obscure sentence in her letter puzzled us.* **4** not well-known; attracting no notice: *an obscure little village, an obscure poet, an obscure job in the government.* **5** dark; dim: *an obscure corner.* **6** make obscure; dim; darken; hide from view: *Clouds obscure the sun.* 1–5 *adj.,* **ob·scur·er, ob·scur·est;** 6 *v.,* **ob·scured, ob·scur·ing.**

ob·scu·ri·ty (əb skyür′ə tē) **1** a lack of clearness; difficulty in being understood: *The obscurity of the paragraph makes several meanings possible.* **2** something obscure; thing hard to understand; doubtful or vague meaning: *The movie had so many obscurities that we didn't enjoy it.* **3** the state or condition of being unknown: *The Premier rose from obscurity to fame.* **4** dimness; lack of light: *The dog hid in the obscurity of the thick bushes.* *n., pl.* **ob·scu·ri·ties.**

ob·serv·ance (əb zėr′vəns) **1** observing or keeping laws or customs: *the observance of the Sabbath.* **2** an act performed as a sign of worship or respect; a religious ceremony. *n.*

ob·serv·ant (əb zėr′vənt) observing; quick to notice; watchful: *If you are observant in the fields and woods, you will find many flowers that others fail to notice.* *adj.*

ob·ser·va·tion (ob′zər vā′shən) **1** the act, habit, or power of seeing and noting: *His keen observation helped him to become a good scientist.* **2** the fact of being seen; notice; being seen: *The tramp escaped observation.* **3** something seen and noted: *The student of bird life kept a record of his observations.* **4** a remark; comment: *'Haste makes waste,' was Father's observation when Bill spilled the ice cream.* *n.*

ob·serv·a·to·ry (əb zėr′və tô′rē) **1** a place or building equipped with a telescope, etc. for observing the stars and other heavenly bodies. **2** a high place or building for observing facts or happenings of nature. *n., pl.* **ob·serv·a·to·ries.**

ob·serve (əb zėrv′) **1** see and note; notice: *Did you observe anything strange in his behavior?* **2** examine for some special purpose; study: *An astronomer observes the stars.* **3** remark; comment: *'Bad weather,' the captain observed.* **4** keep; follow in practice: *All hockey players must observe the rules.* **5** show regard for; celebrate: *to observe Christmas.* *v.,* **ob·served, ob·serv·ing.** —**ob·serv′er,** *n.*

ob·serv·ing (əb zėr′ving) observant; quick to notice. *adj.*

ob·so·lete (ob′sə lēt′) **1** no longer in use: *Wooden warships are obsolete.* **2** out of date; old-fashioned: *We still use this machine though it is obsolete.* *adj.*

ob·sta·cle (ob′stə kəl) something that stands in the way or stops progress; a hindrance: *A tree fallen across the road was an obstacle to traffic. Blindness is an obstacle in some kinds of work.* *n.*

ob·sti·na·cy (ob′stə nə sē) **1** a stubborn nature; stubborn behavior: *Obstinacy drove the boy to repeat his statement even after he knew it was wrong.* **2** an obstinate act. *n., pl.* **ob·sti·na·cies.**

ob·sti·nate (ob′stə nit) **1** stubborn; not giving in: *In spite of her father's advice, the obstinate girl went her own way.* **2** hard to control or treat: *an obstinate cough.* *adj.*

☞ **Obstinate** (def. 1) and **stubborn** both mean fixed in purpose or opinion. **Obstinate** suggests being unreasonable in refusing to give in. **Stubborn** suggests being firm enough not to give in.

ob·struct (əb strukt′) **1** block up; make hard to pass through: *Fallen trees obstruct the road.* **2** be in the way of; hinder: *Trees obstruct our view of the ocean. A strike obstructed the work of the factory.* *v.*

ob·struc·tion (əb struk′shən) **1** anything that obstructs; something in the way; an obstacle: *The soldiers had to get over such obstructions as ditches and barbed wire. Anger is an obstruction to clear thinking.* **2** blocking or hindering: *the obstruction of progress by prejudices.* *n.*

ob·tain (əb tān′) **1** get through effort; come to have:

hat, āge, fär; let, ēqual, tėrm; it, īce
hot, ōpen, ôrder; oil, out; cup, pu̇t, rüle
əbove, takən, pencəl, lemən, circəs
ch, child; ng, long; sh, ship
th, thin; ᴛʜ, then; zh, measure

He worked hard to obtain the prize. We study to obtain knowledge. 2 be in use; be customary; prevail: *Different rules obtain in different schools.* *v.*

ob·tain·able (əb tān′ə bəl) that can be obtained. *adj.*

ob·tuse (əb tyüs′ or əb tüs′) 1 not sharp; blunt. 2 slow in understanding; dull or stupid: *The boy was too obtuse to take the hint.* *adj.*

obtuse angle an angle greater than 90 degrees but less than 180 degrees; an angle greater than a right angle. See **angle** for picture.

obvious (ob′vē əs) easily seen or understood; not to be doubted; plain: *It is obvious that two and two make four. It is obvious that a blind man ought not to drive an automobile.* *adj.*

oc·ca·sion (ə kā′zhən or ō kā′zhən) 1 a particular time: *We have met Mr. Smith on several occasions.* 2 a special event: *The jewels were worn only on great occasions.* 3 a good chance; an opportunity: *The trip gave us an occasion to get better acquainted.* 4 a cause; a reason: *The dog that was the occasion of the quarrel had run away.* 5 to cause; bring about: *Her queer behavior occasioned a good deal of talk.* 1–4 *n.*, 5 *v.*
on occasion, now and then; once in a while.

oc·ca·sion·al (ə kā′zhən əl) 1 happening or coming now and then, or once in a while: *We had fine weather except for an occasional thunderstorm.* 2 caused by or used for some special time or event: *He composed a piece of occasional music to be played at the opening concert in the new auditorium.* *adj.*

oc·ca·sion·al·ly (ə kā′zhən əl ē) now and then; once in a while; at times. *adv.*

Oc·ci·dent (ok′sə dənt) 1 the countries in Europe and America; the West: *The Occident and the Orient have many different ideals and customs.* 2 **occident,** the west. *n.*

Oc·ci·den·tal (ok′sə den′təl) 1 Western; of the Occident. 2 a native of the West: *Europeans are Occidentals.* 3 **occidental,** western. 1, 3 *adj.*, 2 *n.*

oc·cult (ə kult′ or ok′ult) 1 beyond the bounds of ordinary knowledge; mysterious. 2 outside the laws of the natural world; magical: *Astrology is an occult science.* *adj.*

oc·cu·pant (ok′yə pənt) a person who occupies: *the occupant of the chair. The occupant of the shack stepped out as I approached.* *n.*

oc·cu·pa·tion (ok′yə pā′shən) 1 one's business or employment; a trade: *Teaching is a teacher's occupation.* 2 possession; occupying or being occupied: *the occupation of a town by the enemy, the occupation of a house by a family.* *n.*

oc·cu·py (ok′yə pī′) 1 take up; fill: *The building occupies an entire block. The lessons occupy the morning.* 2 keep busy; engage; employ: *Sports often occupy a boy's attention.* 3 take possession of: *The enemy occupied our fort.* 4 keep possession of; have; hold: *A judge occupies an important position.* 5 live in: *The owner occupies the house.* *v.*, **oc·cu·pied, oc·cu·py·ing.**

oc·cur (ə kėr′) 1 happen; take place: *Storms often occur in winter.* 2 be found; exist: *'E' occurs in print more often than any other letter.* 3 come to mind; suggest itself: *Has it occurred to you to close the windows?* *v.*, **oc·curred, oc·cur·ring.**

oc·cur·rence (ə kėr′əns) 1 an occurring: *The occurrence of storms delayed our trip.* 2 a happening; an event: *an unexpected occurrence.* *n.*

o·cean (ō′shən) 1 the body of salt water that covers almost three fourths of the earth's surface; the sea. 2 any of its five main divisions—the Atlantic, Pacific, Indian, Arctic, and Antarctic oceans. *n.*

o·ce·lot (ō′sə lot′ or os′ə lot′) a spotted wildcat resembling a leopard, found from Texas through South America. *n.*

o'clock (ə klok′) according to a time shown on the clock: *It is one o'clock.*

☞ **O'clock** is a shortening of the older expression *of the clock.*

Oct. October.

oc·ta·gon (ok′tə gon′) a plane figure having eight angles and eight sides. See the picture. *n.*

oc·tag·o·nal (ok tag′ə nəl) having eight angles and eight sides. *adj.*

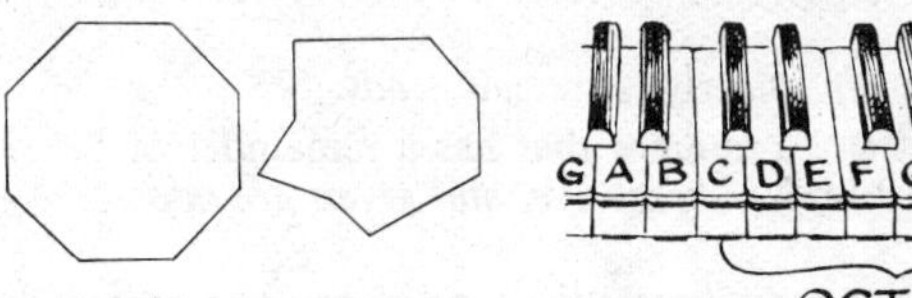

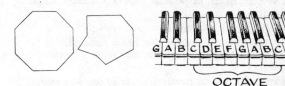

Two kinds of octagon An octave on the piano

oc·tave (ok′tiv) 1 in music, the interval between a tone and another tone having twice or half as many vibrations: *From middle C to the C above is an octave.* 2 the eighth tone above (or below) and including a given tone, having twice (or half) as many vibrations per second. 3 the series of tones or of keys of an instrument filling the interval between a tone and its octave. 4 the sounding together of a tone and its octave. *n.*

Oc·to·ber (ok tō′bər) the tenth month of the year: *October has 31 days.* *n.*

☞ **October** developed from an Old English word taken from the Latin name for this month, *October,* from *octo,* meaning 'eight.' October was the eighth month of the ancient Roman calendar.

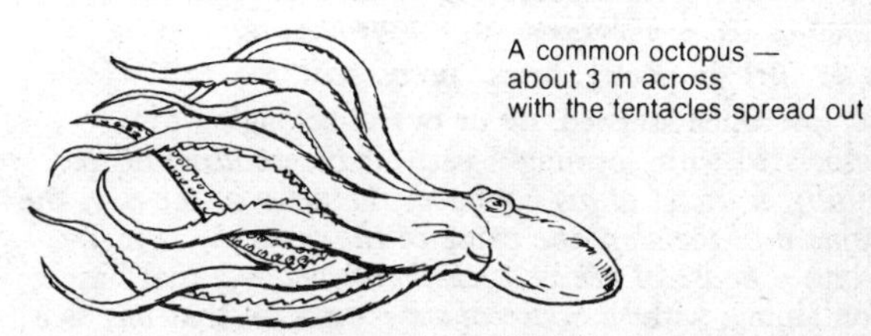

A common octopus — about 3 m across with the tentacles spread out

oc·to·pus (ok′tə pəs) 1 a sea animal having a soft

body and eight arms with suckers on them: *The octopus is a mollusc.* 2 anything that reaches out or grasps as an octopus does: *The octopus of organized crime threatens the business life of every major city.* *n.*

oc·u·list (ok′yə list) a doctor who examines eyes and treats diseases of the eyes. *n.*

☛ An **oculist,** an **optometrist,** and an **optician** all have to do with the health of the eyes. An **oculist** is a doctor who can treat diseases of the eye as well as recommending eyeglasses. An **optometrist** is not a doctor but is trained to examine eyes and recommend eyeglasses. An **optician** supplies the lenses for eyeglasses and fits them into frames.

odd (od) 1 left over: *Here are seven plums for three of you; John may have the odd one. Pay the bill with this money and keep the odd change.* 2 being one of a pair or set of which the rest is missing: *There seems to be an odd stocking in the wash.* 3 extra; occasional: *odd jobs, odd moments, odd players.* 4 with some extra: *six hundred odd children in school, thirty odd dollars.* 5 See **odd number.** 6 strange; peculiar; queer: *It is odd that I cannot remember his name, because his face is familiar.* *adj.*

odd·i·ty (od′ə tē) 1 strangeness; queerness; peculiarity: *the oddity of wearing a fur coat over a bathing suit.* 2 a strange, queer, or peculiar person or thing. *n., pl.* **odd·i·ties.**

odd·ly (od′lē) queerly; strangely. *adv.*

odd number a number that has a remainder of 1 when divided by 2: *Three, five, and seven are odd numbers.*

odds (odz) 1 a difference in favor of one and against another; an advantage: *The odds are in our favor and we should win. In betting, odds of 3 to 1 means that 3 will be paid if the bet is lost for every 1 that will be received if it is won.* 2 in games, an extra allowance given to the weaker side. *n. pl.*

at odds, quarrelling or disagreeing: *The two boys had been at odds for months.*

odds and ends, things left over; odd pieces; scraps; remnants.

the odds are, the chances are; the probability is: *Since we are a better team, the odds are we will win.*

ode (ōd) a poem full of noble feeling expressed with dignity and, often, addressed to some person or thing: *Ode to a Nightingale.* *n.*

o·di·ous (ō′dē əs) very displeasing; hateful; offensive: *odious behavior.* *adj.*

o·dor or **o·dour** (ō′dər) 1 a smell or scent: *the odor of roses, the odor of garbage.* 2 reputation: *Those boys were in bad odor because they were suspected of stealing.* *n.* **—o′dor·less** or **o′dour·less,** *adj.*

o'er (ôr) in poetry, over. *prep., adv.*

of (əv; when stressed, uv or ov) 1 belonging to; associated with; forming a part of: *the children of the family, a friend of his boyhood, the news of the day, the captain of the ship, the cause of the quarrel.* 2 made from: *a house of bricks, a castle of sand.* 3 that has; containing; with: *a house of six rooms.* 4 that has as a quality: *a look of pity, a woman of good judgment.* 5 that is; named: *the city of Vancouver.* 6 away from; from: *north of Brandon, to take leave of a friend.* 7 in regard to; concerning; about: *think well of someone, be fond of, be hard of heart. She is sixteen years of age.* 8 as a result of; through: *die of grief.* 9 out of: *She came of a noble family. Her family expected much of her.* *prep.*

off (of) 1 from the usual or correct position, condition, etc.: *He took off his hat.* 2 away; at a distance; to a distance: *He went off in his car.* 3 from; away from; far from: *He pushed me off my seat. You are off the road.* 4 not on; not connected: *The electricity is off.* 5 supported by; using the resources of: *He lived off his relatives.* 6 without work: *an afternoon off. He often goes swimming during off hours.* 7 so as to stop: *Turn the water off. The game was called off.* 8 wholly; in full: *She cleared off her desk.* 9 in a specified condition in regard to money, property, etc.: *The Smiths are very well off.* 10 of ships at sea, just away from: *The boat anchored off the fort.* 11 on the right-hand side; right: *The near horse and the off horse make a team.* 12 not very good; not up to average: *Bad weather made last summer an off season for fruit.* 13 possible; not very likely: *I came on the off chance that I would find you.* 14 on one's way: *It's late and we must be off.* 15 no longer due to take place: *Our trip to Europe is off.* 16 in error; wrong: *Your figures are way off.* 1, 2, 6–8, 14 *adv.,* 3, 5, 10 *prep.,* 4, 9, 11–13, 15, 16 *adj.*

be off, go away; leave quickly.

off and on, now and then: *He has lived in Europe off and on for ten years.*

of·fence or **of·fense** (ə fens′ or ō fens′) 1 a breaking of the law; a sin: *The punishment for that offence is two years in prison. Murder is an offence against God and man.* 2 the condition of being offended; hurt feelings; anger: *He tried not to cause offence.* 3 offending or hurting someone's feelings: *No offence was intended.* 4 something that offends or causes displeasure: *Rudeness is always an offence.* 5 the act of attacking: *The army proved weak in offence.* 6 an attacking team or force: *Our football team has a good offence.* *n.*

give offence, offend.

take offence, be offended.

of·fend (ə fend′ or ō fend′) 1 pain; displease; hurt the feelings of; make angry: *My friend was offended by my laughter.* 2 sin; do wrong: *In what way have I offended?* *v.*

of·fend·er (ə fen′dər) 1 a person who offends. 2 a person who does wrong or breaks a law: *No parking here; offenders will be fined $5.* *n.*

of·fense (ə fens′ or ō fens′) See **offence.**

of·fen·sive (ə fen′siv) 1 giving offence; irritating; annoying: *'Shut up' is an offensive remark.* 2 unpleasant; disagreeable; disgusting: *The bad eggs had an offensive odor.* 3 used for attack; having something to do with attack: *offensive weapons, an offensive war for conquest.* 4 a position or attitude of attack: *The army took the offensive.* 5 an attack: *An offensive against polio was begun when the proper vaccine was developed.* 1–3 *adj.,* 4, 5 *n.*

of·fer (of′ər) 1 hold out to be taken or refused; present: *to offer one's hand, to offer a gift. He offered us his help.* 2 be willing; volunteer: *He offered to help us.* 3 propose; suggest: *She offered a few ideas to improve the plan.* 4 present in worship: *offer prayers.* 5 try; attempt: *The thieves offered no resistance to the* policemen. He did not offer to hit back. 6 present itself; occur: *I will come if opportunity offers.* 7 the act of offering: *an offer of money, an offer to sing, an offer of marriage, an offer of $30 000 for a house.* 1–6 *v.*, 7 *n.*

of·fer·ing (of′ər ing) a contribution or gift. *n.*

off·hand (of′hand′) 1 at once; without previous thought or preparation: *The carpenter could not tell offhand how much the work would cost.* 2 done or made on the spur of the moment, without previous thought or planning: *His offhand remarks were often very funny.* 1 *adv.*, 2 *adj.*

of·fice (of′is) 1 the place in which the work of a business or profession is done; a room or rooms in which to do such work: *The executive offices were on the second floor.* 2 a position, especially a public position: *The M.P. was appointed to the office of Minister of Defence.* 3 the duty of one's position; one's job or work: *It is his office to open the mail.* 4 the staff of persons carrying on work in an office: *Half the office is on vacation.* 5 an attention; an act of kindness or unkindness; a service or an injury: *Through the good offices of a friend, I was able to get a ticket to the game.* *n.*

of·fi·cer (of′ə sər) 1 a person who commands others in the armed forces such as a colonel, a lieutenant, or a captain. 2 a person who holds an office in the government, the church, the public service, etc.: *a police officer, a health officer.* 3 the president, vice-president, secretary, treasurer, etc. of a company, club, society, etc. *n.*

of·fi·cial (ə fish′əl or ō fish′əl) 1 a person who holds a public position or who is in charge of some public work or duty: *Postmasters are government officials.* 2 a person holding office; an officer: *bank officials.* 3 of or having to do with an office or officers: *The policeman was on official business. Policemen wear an official uniform.* 4 having authority: *An official record is kept of the proceedings of Parliament.* 5 suitable for a person in office: *the official dignity of a judge.* 1, 2 *n.*, 3–5 *adj.* **—of·fi′cial·ly,** *adv.*

off·set (of′set′ for 1, of′set′ for 2) 1 make up for; compensate for: *The better roads offset the greater distance.* 2 something that makes up for something else; a compensation: *In football, his weight and strength were an offset to his slowness.* 1 *v.*, **off·set, off·set·ting;** 2 *n.*

off·shoot (of′shüt′) 1 a shoot from a main stem; a branch: *an offshoot of a plant.* 2 anything coming, or thought of as coming, from a main part, stock, race, etc.: *an offshoot of a mountain range.* *n.*

off·shore (of′shôr′) 1 toward the water; from the shore: *The wind was blowing offshore.* 2 off or away from the shore: *an offshore wind, offshore fisheries.* 1 *adv.*, 2 *adj.*

off·spring (of′spring′) the young of a person, animal, or plant; descendant: *Every one of his offspring had red hair just like his own.* *n.*

oft (oft) often. *adv.*

of·ten (of′ən or of′tən) many times; frequently: *He comes here often.* *adv.*

of·ten·times (of′ən tīmz′ or of′tən tīmz′) often. *adv.*

o·gre (o′gər) 1 in stories, a giant or monster that eats people. 2 a dreaded or cruel person. *n.*

hat, āge, fär; let, ēqual, tėrm; it, īce
hot, ōpen, ôrder; oil, out; cup, pu̇t, rüle
əbove, takən, pencəl, lemən, circəs
ch, child; ng, long; sh, ship
th, thin; ᴛʜ, then; zh, measure

Oh or **oh** (ō) 1 a word used before a person's name in beginning to speak: *Oh, Mary, look!* 2 a word used to express surprise, joy, pain, and other feelings: *Oh, dear me! Oh! joy! Oh, what a pity!* *interj.* Also spelled **O.**

☛ **Oh, O,** and **owe** are pronounced the same. **Oh** is preferred to **O,** except before names. See note at **O**[2].

oil (oil) 1 any of several kinds of thick, fatty or greasy liquids that are lighter than water, that burn easily, and that will not mix or dissolve in water but will dissolve in alcohol: *Mineral oils, such as kerosene, are used for fuel; animal and vegetable oils, such as olive oil, are used in cooking and medicine.* 2 petroleum. 3 put oil on or in. 4 paint made by grinding coloring matter in oil: *The art class is now painting with oils.* 5 a painting in oils: *We like the oils of that artist better than her water colors.* 1, 2, 4, 5 *n.*, 3 *v.*

strike oil, a find oil by boring a hole in the earth. **b** find something very profitable.

oil·cloth (oil′kloth′) a cloth made waterproof and glossy on one side by coating it with a mixture of oil, clay, and coloring: *Oilcloth is used to cover shelves, tables, etc.* *n.*

oil drum a drum-shaped metal container for holding oil.

Oilskins

oil·skin (oil′skin′) 1 cloth treated with oil to make it waterproof. 2 **oilskins,** *pl.* a coat and trousers made of such cloth. *n.*

oil well a well drilled in the earth to get oil.

oil·y (oil′ē) 1 of oil: *an oily smell.* 2 containing oil: *oily salad dressing.* 3 covered or soaked with oil: *oily rags.* 4 like oil; smooth; slippery. *adj.*, **oil·i·er, oil·i·est.**

oint·ment (oint′mənt) a substance made from oil or fat, often containing medicine, used on the skin to heal or to make it soft: *Cold cream and salve are ointments.* *n.*

O.K. or **OK** (ō′kā′) *Informal.* 1 all right; correct; approved: *The new schedule was O.K.* 2 approve. 3 approval: *The principal gave us his O.K.* 1 *adj., adv.*, 2 *v.*, **O.K.'d** or **OK'd, O.K.'ing** or **OK'ing;** 3 *n., pl.* **O.K.'s** or **OK's.** Also spelled **okay.**

o·ka·pi (ō kā′pē) an African mammal like the giraffe, but smaller and with a much shorter neck. *n., pl.* **o·ka·pis** or **o·ka·pi.**

o·kay (ō′kā′) See **O.K.**

o·kra (ō′krə) 1 a plant with sticky pods. 2 its pods, used as a vegetable and in soups. *n.*

old (ōld) 1 not young; having been or existed for some time; aged: *An old wall surrounds the castle. We are old friends.* 2 of age; in age: *The baby is ten months old.* 3 not new; not recent: *an old debt, an old family, an old excuse.* 4 belonging to the past; dating far back; ancient: *old civilizations.* 5 much worn by age or use; worn: *an old coat, old clothes.* 6 former: *An old pupil came back to visit his teacher.* 7 that seems old; like an old person in some way: *That child is old for her years.* 8 having much experience: *He is an old hand at swimming.* 9 the time of long ago; the past: *the heroes of old.* 10 **the old,** old people: *a home for the old.* 1–8 *adj.,* **old·er** or **eld·er, old·est** or **eld·est;** 9, 10 *n.*
old age, the last part of life when a person is very old; the years of life from about 65 on.
Old Country, the native land of persons living elsewhere: *To many New Canadians Great Britain is the Old Country.*

old·en (ōl′dən) old; of old; ancient: *King Arthur lived in olden times. adj.*

Old English the language used by the English people before 1100: *Old English developed from the Germanic dialects spoken by the Angles and Saxons, who invaded Britain in the fifth and sixth centuries A.D.*

old–fash·ioned (ōld′fash′ənd) 1 of an old fashion; out of date in style, construction, etc.: *an old-fashioned dress.* 2 keeping to old ways, ideas, etc.: *an old-fashioned housekeeper. adj.*

Old French the language spoken in France from about A.D. 800 to about 1300: *Old French developed from Latin.*

old maid 1 a woman who has not married and seems unlikely to do so. 2 a prim, fussy person: *What an old maid he is!* 3 a simple card game.

Old Norse the language spoken by the people of Scandinavia from about A.D. 700 to about 1300.

Old Testament the earlier part of the Bible, which contains the religious and social laws of the Hebrews, a record of their history, their important literature, and writings of their prophets.

old–tim·er (ōld′tī′mər) *Informal.* a person who has long been a resident, member, or worker in a place, group, or community. *n.*

Old World Europe, Asia, and Africa.

o·le·o·mar·ga·rine (ō′lē ō mär′jə rin or ō′lē ō mär′jə rēn′) margarine. *n.*

ol·ive (ol′iv) 1 a kind of evergreen tree with grey-green leaves: *The olive tree grows in warm regions.* 2 the fruit of this tree: *Olives are eaten green or ripe.* 3 yellowish green: *The uniform was made of olive cloth.* 4 yellowish brown: *The man had an olive complexion.* 1–4 *n.,* 3, 4 *adj.*

olive branch a branch of the olive tree, long used as an emblem of peace.

olive oil oil pressed from olives, used in cooking, in medicine, etc.

O·lym·pic games (ō lim′pik gāmz′) 1 contests in athletics, poetry, and music, held every four years by the ancient Greeks. 2 modern athletic contests imitating the athletic contests of these games, held every four years in a different country: *Athletes from many nations compete in the Olympic games.*

om·e·lette or **om·e·let** (om′ə lit or om′lit) a food dish of eggs beaten with milk or water, cooked, and folded over: *Omelettes are sometimes filled with chopped meat, mushrooms, or some other filling. n.*

o·men (ō′mən) a sign of what is to happen; an object or event that is believed to mean good or bad fortune: *Spilling salt is said to be an omen of misfortune. n.*

om·i·nous (om′ə nəs) unfavorable; threatening: *The watchdog gave an ominous growl. adj.*

o·mis·sion (ō mish′ən) 1 omitting or leaving out: *The printer was blamed for the omission of a paragraph in copying the story.* 2 anything omitted: *His song was the only omission from the program. n.*

o·mit (ō mit′) 1 leave out: *He made many mistakes in spelling by omitting letters.* 2 fail to do; neglect: *She omitted making her bed. v.,* **o·mit·ted, o·mit·ting.**

om·nip·o·tent (om nip′ə tənt) having all power; almighty: *an omnipotent ruler. adj.*

on (on) 1 above and supported by: *This book is on the table.* 2 touching so as to cover, be around, etc.: *There's new paint on the ceiling. Put the ring on her finger.* 3 close to; along the edge of: *a house on the shore. He lives on the next street.* 4 in the direction of; toward: *The soldiers marched on the capital.* 5 against; upon: *The picture is on the wall.* 6 toward something: *Some played; the others looked on.* 7 farther: *March on.* 8 by means of; by the use of: *This news is on good authority.* 9 in the condition of; in the process of: *on purpose, on duty.* 10 not early or late in: *on time, on schedule.* 11 in or into a condition, process, manner, or action: *Turn the gas on.* 12 taking place: *The race is on.* 13 at the time of; during: *They greeted us on our arrival.* 14 from a given time; forward: *later on, from that day on.* 15 concerning: *a book on animals.* 16 for the purpose of: *He went on an errand.* 17 among: *I am on the committee.* 1–5, 8–10, 13, 15–17 *prep.,* 6, 7, 11, 14 *adv.,* 12 *adj.*
and so on, and more of the same.
on and off, at some times and not others; now and then.
on and on, without stopping: *The woman talked on and on.*

once (wuns) 1 one time: *Read it once more.* 2 at some one time in the past; formerly: *That big man was once a little baby.* 3 if ever; after: *Most boys like to swim, once they have learned how.* 4 even a single time; ever: *If the facts once became known everyone would laugh at her.* 1, 2, 4 *adv.,* 3 *conj.*
at once or **all at once, a** immediately: *You must come at once.* **b** at the same time: *All three boys spoke at once.*
once and for all or **once for all,** finally.
once in a while, at one time or another; now and then: *We see our neighbors on the next farm once in a while.*
once upon a time, long ago.

one (wun) 1 the first and lowest number; the number 1. 2 a single: *A man has one head and one neck.* 3 a

An olive branch

The emblem of the United Nations, showing olive branches as a symbol of peace

single person or thing: *I like the ones in that box.* **4** some: *One day he will be sorry.* **5** some person or thing: *One of Bliss Carman's poems was chosen for our new reader.* **6** any person, standing for people in general: *One does not like to be left out.* **7** the same: *All face one way.* **8** joined together; united: *The class was one in its approval.* **9** a certain: *A short speech was made by one John Smith.* 1, 3 *n.*, 2, 4, 7–9 *adj.*, 5, 6 *pron.*

all one, a exactly the same: *They are all one in their love of hockey.* **b** making no difference: *It is all one to me whether you stay or go.*

at one, in agreement: *The two judges were at one about the winner.*

one by one, one after another: *They came out the door one by one.*

one or two, a few.

☛ **One** and **won** are pronounced the same.

one·self (wun self′) **1** a form used instead of **one** when referring back to the subject of the sentence: *At the age of seven one ought to dress oneself.* **2** a form of **one** used to make a statement stronger: *One can go oneself.* **3** one's real or true self: *It's nice to be oneself again after an illness.* *pron.*

one–sid·ed (wun′sīd′id) **1** seeing only one side of a question; partial; unfair; prejudiced: *The umpire seemed one-sided in his decisions.* **2** uneven; unequal: *If one team is much better than the other, a game is one-sided.* **3** having one side larger or more developed than the other. **4** having but one side. *adj.*

one–track (wun′trak′) *Informal.* understanding or dealing with one thing at a time: *a one-track mind.* *adj.*

An onion bulb

on·ion (un′yən) a plant with a root shaped like a bulb which is used as a vegetable and as a seasoning: *Onions have a sharp, strong smell and taste.* *n.*

on·look·er (on′lu̇k′ər) a spectator; a person who watches without taking part. *n.*

on·ly (ōn′lē) **1** by itself or themselves; one and no more: *Muriel and John are their only children. This was their one and only hope. This is the only road home.* **2** just; merely: *He sold only two. She was in Europe only last week.* **3** and no one else; and nothing more; and that is all: *Only he remained. I did it only through friendship.* **4** except that; but: *I could do it, only it would be wrong. He would have started, only it rained.* **5** best; finest: *He is the only boy for me!* **6** but then; it must be added that: *We had camped right beside a stream, only the water was not fit to drink.* 1, 5 *adj.*, 2, 3 *adv.*, 4, 6 *conj.*

if only, I wish: *If only the sun would shine!*

only too, very: *She was only too glad to help us.*

on·rush (on′rush′) a violent forward movement: *He was knocked down by the onrush of water.* *n.*

on·set (on′set′) **1** an attack: *The onset of the enemy took us by surprise.* **2** the beginning: *The onset of this disease is gradual.* *n.*

hat, āge, fär; let, ēqual, tėrm; it, īce
hot, ōpen, ôrder; oil, out; cup, pu̇t, rüle
əbove, takən, pencəl, lemən, circəs
ch, child; ng, long; sh, ship
th, thin; ᴛʜ, then; zh, measure

on·slaught (on′slot′ or on′slôt′) a vigorous attack: *The pirates made an onslaught on the ship.* *n.*

Ont. Ontario.

On·tar·i·an (on ter′ē ən) **1** a person born in or living in Ontario. **2** of or concerning Ontario. 1 *n.*, 2 *adj.*

on·to (on′tü) on to; to a position on: *to throw a ball onto the roof, to get onto a horse, a boat driven onto the rocks.* *prep.*

on·ward (on′wərd) on; further on; toward the front; forward: *The army marched onward. An onward movement began.* *adv., adj.*

on·wards (on′wərdz) onward. *adv.*

oo·loo (ü′lü) *Cdn.* a crescent-shaped, bone-handled knife used by Eskimo women. *n.* Also spelled **ulu.**

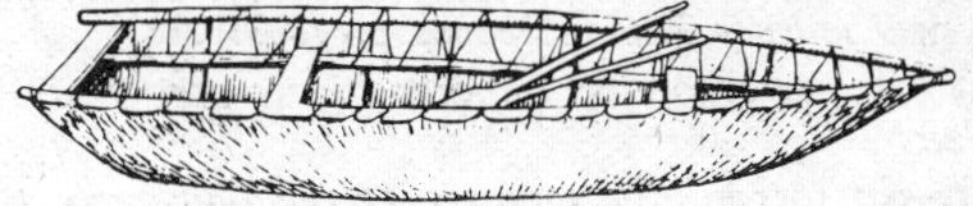

An oomiak

oo·mi·ak (ü′mē ak′) *Cdn.* an open Eskimo boat made of skins covering a wooden frame and propelled by paddles: *Oomiaks are used for freight and are usually worked by women.* *n.* Also spelled **umiak.**

ooze[1] (üz) **1** pass slowly through one or more small openings; leak little by little: *Blood oozed from his scraped knee. The mud oozed into his boots.* **2** disappear or drain away: *His courage oozed away as he waited.* *v.*, **oozed, ooz·ing.**

ooze[2] (üz) soft mud or slime, especially that at the bottom of a pond, river, lake, or ocean. *n.*

o·pal (ō′pəl) a kind of stone that shows beautiful changes in color: *The ring was set with a milky-white opal.* *n.*

o·paque (ō pāk′) not letting light through; not transparent: *Muddy water is opaque.* *adj.*

opaque projector an apparatus for projecting material that is written, drawn, or printed: *An opaque projector projects images directly from paper or books rather than from transparencies.*

o·pen (ō′pən) **1** not shut; not closed; letting anything or anyone in or out: *The open windows let in the fresh air.* **2** not having its door, gate, lid, etc. closed; not shut up: *an open box, an open drawer, an open house.* **3** not closed in: *the open sea, an open field, an open car.* **4 the open,** open or clear space; open country; the open air: *City people like to get out in the open.* **5** that may be entered, used, shared, etc. by all, or by a person or persons mentioned: *an open meeting, an open market. The race is open to boys under 15.* **6** make or become open: *to open a path through the woods.* **7** not covered or protected; exposed: *an open fire, an open jar, open to* *temptation.* 8 unfilled; not taken: *There is an hour open before the last meeting. The job in the bank is still open.* 9 not hidden or secret: *open war, open disregard of rules.* 10 frank and sincere: *an open heart. Please be open with me.* 11 generous: *Please give with an open hand.* 12 spread out or unfold: *to open a fan, a book, or a letter.* 13 unfolded; spread out: *an open flower, letter, or book.* 14 start or set up; establish: *to open a new store, an office, an account.* 15 begin: *to open a debate. School opens in September.* 16 free from frost: *an open winter.* 17 free from hindrance, especially from ice: *open water on the lake, a river or harbor now open.* 18 have or make entrance; allow entry: *The door opens into the dining room.* 19 come apart or burst open: *a crack where the earth had opened. The clouds opened, and the sun shone through.* 1–3, 5, 7–11, 13, 16, 17 *adj.*, 4 *n.*, 6, 12, 14, 15, 18, 19 *v.* **—o′pen·ly,** *adv.*

open a person's eyes, make a person see what is really going on.

open to, ready to take; willing to consider: *open to suggestions.*

open up, a make or become open. **b** open a way to and develop: *The early settlers opened up the West.*

open air the outdoors: *Children like to play in the open air.*

o·pen–air (ō′pən er′) outdoor: *an open-air concert. adj.*

open house 1 an occasion when a school, university, factory, etc. is opened for inspection by the public: *We saw a computer at the open house.* 2 a party or other social event that is open to all who wish to come.

o·pen·ing (ō′pən ing) 1 an open or clear space; a gap or hole: *an opening in a wall, an opening in the forest.* 2 the first part; the beginning: *the opening of his lecture.* 3 first; beginning: *the opening words of his speech.* 4 a formal beginning: *The opening of the new theatre will be at three o'clock tomorrow afternoon.* 5 a job, place, or position that is open or vacant: *an opening for a teller in a bank, an opening for a teacher in a school.* 6 a favorable chance or opportunity: *In talking with your mother, I made an opening to ask her about sending you to camp. As soon as I saw an opening, I got up quickly and left the room.* 1, 2, 4–6 *n.*, 3 *adj.*

open mind a mind ready to consider new ideas.

o·pen–mind·ed (ō′pən mīn′did) having or showing a mind open to new ideas. *adj.*

op·er·a (op′ər ə) a play that is mostly sung, usually with costumes, scenery, and an orchestra: *'Carmen' is a popular opera. n.*

op·er·ate (op′ər āt′) 1 be at work; run: *The machinery operates night and day.* 2 keep at work; manage: *The boy operates the elevator. The company operates three factories.* 3 take effect; produce an effect; work: *Several causes operated to bring on the war. The medicine operated quickly.* 4 treat the body, especially using instruments, to remedy an injury, disease, etc.: *The doctor operated on the injured man. v.*, **op·er·at·ed, op·er·at·ing.**

op·er·a·tion (op′ər ā′shən) 1 working: *The operation of a railway needs many men.* 2 the way a thing works: *The operation of this machine is simple.* 3 doing; activity: *the operation of brushing one's teeth.* 4 a treatment, especially one using instruments, to remove or heal a diseased or injured part of the body: *Taking out the tonsils is a common operation.* 5 a movement of soldiers, ships, supplies, etc.: *naval and military operations.* 6 something done to a number or quantity in mathematics: *Addition, subtraction, multiplication, and division are the four commonest operations in arithmetic. n.*

in operation, in action or in use.

op·er·a·tor (op′ər ā′tər) 1 a person who operates. 2 a skilled worker who runs a machine, telephone switchboard, telegraph, etc. *n.*

op·er·et·ta (op′ər et′ə) a short, amusing opera with some words spoken rather than sung. *n.*

o·pin·ion (ə pin′yən or ō pin′yən) 1 what one thinks; a view or belief based on judgment rather than knowledge: *I try to learn the facts and form my own opinions. Everyone has a poor opinion of a coward.* 2 a formal judgment made by an expert; professional advice: *Mother asked the doctor for an opinion about the cause of my headache. n.*

o·pi·um (ō′pē əm) a powerful drug that causes sleep and eases pain: *Opium is made from a kind of poppy. n.*

o·pos·sum (ə pos′əm) a small animal that lives most of the time in trees and carries its young in a pouch; possum: *When an opossum is caught or frightened, it becomes unconscious and appears to be dead. n.*

op·po·nent (ə pō′nənt) a person who is on the other side in a fight, game, or argument; a person fighting, struggling, or speaking against another: *He defeated his opponent in the election. n.*

op·por·tu·ni·ty (op′ər tyü′nə tē or op′ər tü′nə tē) a good chance; favorable time or convenient occasion: *I had an opportunity to earn some money picking blueberries. I have had no opportunity to give him your message, because I have not seen him. n., pl.* **op·por·tu·ni·ties.**

op·pose (ə pōz′) 1 be against; be in the way of; act, fight, or struggle against; try to hinder; resist: *The enemy opposed the advance of our army. Many people oppose the death penalty.* 2 put against as a defence or reply: *Let us oppose good nature to anger.* 3 put in contrast: *Night is opposed to day. Love is opposed to hate. We talked about bus travel as opposed to train travel. v.*, **op·posed, op·pos·ing.**

op·po·site (op′ə zit) 1 placed against; face to face; back to back: *Look at the opposite page.* 2 as different as can be; just contrary: *North and south are opposite directions. Sour is opposite to sweet.* 3 a thing or person as different as can be: *Black is the opposite of white. A brave boy is the opposite of a coward.* 4 directly across from: *opposite the church.* 1, 2 *adj.*, 3 *n.*, 4 *prep.*

op·po·si·tion (op′ə zish′ən) 1 action against; resistance: *The mob offered opposition to the police.* 2 contrast: *His views were in opposition to mine.* 3 the political party or parties not in power: *In Parliament the party having the second largest number of elected members is called the official opposition.* 4 any opponent or group of opponents: *Our team easily defeated the opposition. n.*

op·press (ə pres′ or ō pres′) 1 govern harshly; keep down unjustly or by cruelty: *A good government will*

hat, āge, fär; let, ēqual, tėrm; it, īce
hot, ōpen, ôrder; oil, out; cup, pu̇t, rüle
əbove, takən, pencəl, lemən, circəs
ch, child; ng, long; sh, ship
th, thin; ᴛʜ, then; zh, measure

not oppress the poor. 2 weigh down; lie heavily on; burden: *A fear of trouble ahead oppressed my spirits.* *v.*

op·pres·sion (ə presh′ən or ō presh′ən) 1 cruel or harsh treatment: *The oppression of the people by the dictator caused the war. They fought against oppression.* 2 a heavy, weary feeling. *n.*

op·pres·sive (ə opres′iv or ō pres′iv) 1 hard to bear; burdensome: *The great heat was oppressive.* 2 harsh; severe; unjust: *Oppressive measures were taken to crush the rebellion.* *adj.*

op·pres·sor (ə pres′ər or ō pres′ər) a person who is cruel or unjust to people under him. *n.*

opt (opt) choose or decide: *The class opted for a field trip.* *v.*

op·ti·cal (op′tə kəl) 1 visual; of the eye or the sense of sight: *an optical illusion. Being short-sighted is an optical defect.* 2 made to assist sight: *Telescopes and microscopes are optical instruments.* *adj.*

op·ti·cian (op tish′ən) a maker or seller of eyeglasses. *n.*

☛ See note at **oculist.**

op·ti·mism (op′tə miz′əm) a tendency to look on the bright side of things. *n.*

op·ti·mist (op′tə mist) a person who looks on the bright side of things. *n.*

op·ti·mis·tic (op′tə mis′tik) 1 inclined to look on the bright side of things. 2 hoping for the best: *I am optimistic about the chance of good weather this weekend.* *adj.*

op·tion (op′shən) 1 the right or freedom to choose. 2 a choosing; choice: *Our option was to play volleyball instead of basketball.* *n.*

op·tom·e·trist (op tom′ə trist) a person who examines eyes and recommends the kind of eyeglasses needed. *n.*

☛ See note at **oculist.**

or (ôr) 1 word used to express a choice, or a difference, or to connect words or groups of words of equal importance in a sentence: *Is it sweet or sour? Shall we walk or ride?* 2 and if not; otherwise: *Either eat this or go hungry. Hurry, or you will be late.* 3 that is; being the same as: *The Eskimo built an igloo, or a dome-shaped snow house.* *conj.*

☛ **Or, oar,** and **ore** are pronounced the same.

–or a suffix meaning a person or thing that ____s: *Actor means a person that acts. Generator means a thing that generates.*

or·a·cle (ôr′ə kəl) 1 in ancient times, an answer to a question, given by a god through a priest. 2 the place where the god gave answers. 3 the priest, or other means by which the god's answer was given. 4 a person who gives wise advice. *n.*

o·ral (ô′rəl) 1 spoken; using speech: *An oral agreement is not enough; we must have a written promise.* 2 of the mouth: *The oral opening in an earthworm is small.* *adj.*

o·ral·ly (ô′rəl ē) 1 by spoken words: *The speech was delivered orally.* 2 by or through the mouth: *The medicine was taken orally.* *adv.*

or·ange (ôr′inj) 1 a round, reddish-yellow, juicy fruit that is good to eat: *Oranges grow in warm climates.* 2 the tree it grows on. 3 the color made by mixing red and yellow. 4 of or having this color: *She wore an orange dress.* 1–3 *n.,* 4 *adj.*

o·rang–ou·tang (ô rang′ü tang′) orang-utan. *n.*

o·rang–u·tan (ô rang′ü tan′) a large ape of the forests of the East Indies, having very long arms and long, reddish-brown hair: *Orang-utans live in trees much of the time and eat fruits and leaves.* *n.*

☛ **Orang-utan** comes from the Malay words *orang* meaning 'man' and *utan* meaning 'wild.'

o·ra·tion (ô rā′shən) a formal public speech delivered on a special occasion. *n.*

or·a·tor (ôr′ə tər) 1 a person who makes an oration. 2 a person who can speak very well in public. *n.*

or·a·to·ry[1] (ôr′ə tô′rē) skill in public speaking; fine speaking. *n.*

or·a·to·ry[2] (ôr′ə tô′rē) a small chapel; a room set apart for prayer. *n., pl.* **or·a·to·ries.**

orb (ôrb) 1 a sphere or globe. 2 the sun or the moon, a planet or a star. *n.*

☛ **Orb** and **orbit** both come originally from Latin *orbis,* meaning 'circle.'

or·bit (ôr′bit) 1 the path of a heavenly body, planet, or satellite around another body in space: *the earth's orbit around the sun, the moon's orbit about the earth, the orbit of a weather satellite around the earth.* See the picture. 2 travel in an orbit: *The announcer said the satellite began to orbit at 8:04 a.m.* 3 put into an orbit: *We plan to orbit a new weather satellite.* 1 *n.,* 2, 3 *v.*

☛ See note at **orb.**

or·chard (ôr′chərd) 1 a piece of ground on which fruit trees are grown. 2 the trees in an orchard: *The orchard should bear a good crop this year.* *n.*

or·ches·tra (ôr′kis trə) 1 a group of musicians who play together on various instruments, usually including stringed instruments. 2 the violins, cellos, horns, and other instruments played together by such a group. 3 the part of a theatre just in front of the stage, where the musicians sit to play. 4 the main floor of a theatre, especially the part near the front: *Buy two seats in the orchestra.* *n.*

or·ches·tral (ôr kes′trəl) of an orchestra; composed for or performed by an orchestra. *adj.*

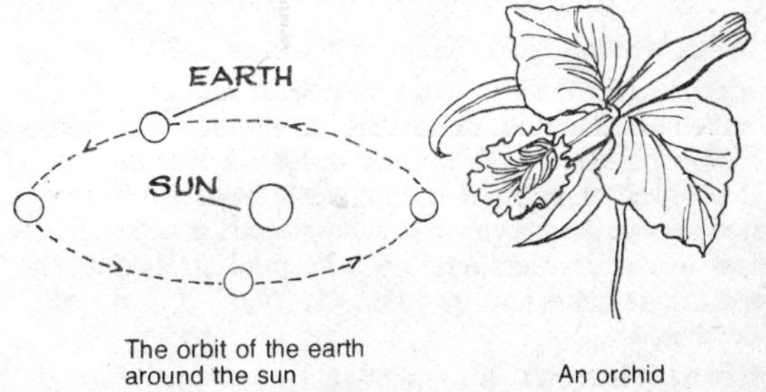

The orbit of the earth around the sun

An orchid

or·chid (ôr′kid) 1 any of a group of plants with beautiful flowers that often have strange shapes and colors. 2 the flower of one of these plants. 3 light purple. 1–3 *n.,* 3 *adj.*

or·dain (ôr dān′) 1 order; decide; pass as a law: *The law ordains that the murderers shall go to prison.* 2 officially appoint or consecrate as a clergyman. *v.*

or·deal (ôr dēl′) a severe test or experience: *the ordeal of being lost in the snowstorm. n.*

or·der (ôr′dər) 1 the way one thing follows another: *in order of size, in alphabetical order, to copy them in order.* 2 a condition in which every part or piece is in its right place: *to put a room in order.* 3 put in proper condition; arrange: *to order one's affairs.* 4 a condition or state: *My affairs are in good order.* 5 the way the world works; the way things happen: *the order of nature.* 6 the state or condition of things in which the law is obeyed and there is no trouble: *The police officer tried hard to keep order. Order was established.* 7 a command; telling what to do: *The orders of the captain must be obeyed.* 8 tell what to do; command; bid: *The judge ordered the people in the courtroom to be quiet.* 9 give a request or directions for: *Please order dinner for me. You order for both of us.* 10 a spoken or written request for goods that one wants to buy or receive: *Mother gave the grocer an order for two dozen eggs.* 11 the goods so requested: *Mother asked when they would deliver our order.* 12 a paper saying that money is to be given or paid, or something handed over: *a money order.* 13 a kind or sort: *to have ability of a high order.* 14 a group of people banded together for some purpose or united by something they share in common: *the Franciscan order, the Imperial Order Daughters of the Empire, the lower orders of society.* 15 a title of distinction: *the Order of Merit, the Order of the British Empire.* 16 a portion or serving of food: *'I'd like one order of fish and chips, please.'* 1, 2, 4–7, 10–16 *n.,* 3, 8, 9 *v.*

by order, according to an order given by the proper person: *by order of the Premier.*

in order, a in the right arrangement or condition. b working properly. c allowed by the rules of a meeting, etc.

in order that, so that; with the aim that.

in order to, as a means to; with a view to; for the purpose of: *She worked hard in order to win the prize.*

in short order, quickly: *They got the broken window replaced in short order.*

on order, having been ordered but not yet received.

out of order, a in the wrong arrangement or condition. b not working properly. c against the rules of a meeting, etc.

to order, according to the buyer's wishes.

or·der·ly (ôr′dər lē) 1 in order; with regular arrangement, method, or system: *an orderly arrangement of dishes on shelves, an orderly mind.* 2 keeping order; well behaved or regulated: *an orderly class.* 3 in the armed services, a serviceman who attends a superior officer to carry orders, etc. 4 a hospital attendant who keeps things clean and in order. 1, 2 *adj.,* 3, 4 *n., pl.* **or·der·lies.**

ordinal number a number that shows order or position in a series. *First, second, third,* etc. are ordinal numbers; *one, two, three,* etc. are cardinal numbers.

or·di·nance (ôr′də nəns) a rule or law made by authority; a decree: *Some cities have ordinances forbidding Sunday amusements. n.*

or·di·nar·i·ly (ôr′də ner′ə lē) commonly; usually; normally: *We ordinarily go to the movies on Saturday. adv.*

or·di·nar·y (ôr′də ner′ē) 1 usual; common; normal: *His ordinary lunch consists of soup, a sandwich, and milk.* 2 somewhat below the average: *The speech was ordinary and tiresome. adj.*

out of the ordinary, unusual; not regular.

ord·nance (ôrd′nəns) 1 military weapons and equipment of all kinds. 2 artillery; big guns or cannon. *n.*

ore (ôr) mineral or rock containing enough metal to make mining profitable. *n.*

☛ **Ore, oar,** and **or** are pronounced the same.

or·gan (ôr′gən) 1 a musical instrument played by means of keys and pedals and sounded by air being blown through pipes of different lengths: *Organs are used especially in church.* 2 a similar instrument in which the sound is pronounced by electronic means. 3 any part of an animal or plant fitted to perform a certain task: *The eyes, stomach, heart, and lungs are organs of the body. Stamens and pistils are organs of flowers.* 4 a means of action; an instrument: *A court is an organ of government. n.*

or·gan·die or **or·gan·dy** (ôr′gən dē) a fine, thin, cotton cloth with a crisp finish, used for dresses, curtains, etc. *n.*

or·gan·ic (ôr gan′ik) 1 of the bodily organs; affecting the structure of an organ: *an organic disease.* 2 of, having to do with, or obtained from plants or animals: *organic fertilizer.* 3 made up of related parts, but being a unit: *Canada is an organic whole made up of ten provinces and two territories. adj.*

or·gan·ism (ôr′gən iz′əm) 1 a living body having organs or an organized structure; an individual animal or plant. 2 a whole made up of related parts that work together: *A community may be spoken of as a social organism. n.*

or·gan·ist (ôr′gən ist) a person who plays an organ: *a church organist. n.*

or·gan·i·za·tion (ôr′gən ə zā′shən) 1 a group of persons united for some purpose: *Churches, clubs, and political parties are organizations.* 2 the grouping and arranging of parts to form a whole; the act of organizing: *The organization of a big picnic takes time and thought.* 3 the way in which a thing's parts are arranged to work together: *The organization of the human body is very complicated. n.*

or·gan·ize (ôr′gən īz′) 1 arrange to work or come together as a whole: *The general organized his soldiers into a powerful fighting force.* 2 plan and lead, get started, or carry out: *The explorer organized an expedition to the North Pole.* 3 arrange in a system: *She organized her thoughts. He organized his stamp collection. v.,* **or·gan·ized, or·gan·iz·ing.**

O·ri·ent (ô′rē ənt) the East; the countries in Asia: *China and Japan are important nations of the Orient. n.*

o·ri·ent (ô′rē ent′ for 1 and 2, ô′rē ənt for 3) 1 get in the right relationship with the surrounding things or persons; adjust to a situation: *She found it hard to orient herself to living in a big city. He is trying to orient himself to becoming blind.* 2 place in a certain position or to face in a certain direction: *The building is oriented north and south.* 3 in poetry, the east. 1, 2 *v.,* 3 *n.*

hat, āge, fär; let, ēqual, tėrm; it, īce
hot, ōpen, ôrder; oil, out; cup, pu̇t, rüle
əbove, takən, pencəl, lemən, circəs
ch, child; ng, long; sh, ship
th, thin; ᴛʜ, then; zh, measure

O·ri·en·tal (ô′rē en′təl) 1 Eastern; of the Orient. 2 a native of the East: *Chinese are Orientals.* 3 **oriental,** eastern: *oriental music.* 1, 3 *adj.,* 2 *n.*

o·ri·en·tate (ô′rē en tāt′) orient (defs. 1 and 2). *v.,* **o·ri·en·tat·ed, o·ri·en·tat·ing.**

or·i·fice (ôr′ə fis) a mouth; an opening or hole: *the orifice of a tube or pipe.* *n.*

or·i·ga·mi (ôr′i gä′mē) the Japanese art of folding paper to make flower and animal forms, without using paste, scissors, etc. *n.*

or·i·gin (ôr′ə jin) 1 the beginning; the starting point; the thing from which anything comes: *Nobody remembered the origin of the quarrel.* 2 parentage; birth: *The general was a man of humble origin.* *n.*

o·rig·i·nal (ə rij′ə nəl) 1 belonging to the beginning; first; earliest: *The hat has been marked down from its original price. The French were the original settlers of Quebec.* 2 fresh; novel; not done before or copied: *It is hard to plan original games for a party. She wrote an original poem.* 3 inventive; able to do, make, or think something new: *The inventor had an original mind.* 4 anything from which something else is copied, imitated, or translated: *The original of this picture is in Rome.* 5 the language in which a book was first written: *Our minister can read the New Testament in the original.* 6 an unusual person. 1–3 *adj.,* 4–6 *n.*

o·rig·i·nal·i·ty (ə rij′ə nal′ə tē) 1 the ability to do, make, or think up something new: *The painter was praised for his originality.* 2 freshness; novelty: *the originality of his ideas.* *n.*

o·rig·i·nal·ly (ə rij′ə nəl ē) 1 by origin: *His family was originally Irish.* 2 at first; in the first place: *a house originally small.* 3 in an original manner: *The room is decorated very originally.* *adv.*

o·rig·i·nate (ə rij′ə nāt′) 1 cause to be; invent: *to originate a new style of painting.* 2 come into being; begin; arise: *Where did that story originate?* *v.,* **o·rig·i·nat·ed, o·rig·i·nat·ing.**

o·ri·ole (ô′rē əl or ô′rē ōl′) any of several birds having yellow-and-black or orange-and-black feathers. *n.*

or·na·ment (ôr′nə mənt for 1 and 2, ôr′nə ment′ for 3) 1 something pretty; something to add beauty: *Lace, jewels, vases, and statues are ornaments. We bought more ornaments for our Christmas tree.* 2 a person or act that adds beauty, grace, or honor: *She is so charming she would be an ornament to any society.* 3 add beauty to; make more pleasing or attractive; decorate: *A single brooch ornamented her dress.* 1, 2 *n.,* 3 *v.*

or·na·men·tal (ôr′nə men′təl) used for ornament, decorative: *ornamental plants, an ornamental staircase.* *adj.*

or·nate (ôr nāt′) much adorned; much ornamented: *She liked ornate furniture.* *adj.*

or·ner·y (ôr′nər ē) *Informal.* mean and stubborn: *an ornery person.* *adj.*

or·phan (ôr′fən) 1 a child whose parents are dead. 2 make an orphan of: *The war orphaned me when I was five years old.* 1 *n.,* 2 *v.*

or·phan·age (ôr′fən ij) a home for orphans. *n.*

or·tho·don·tist (ôr′thə don′tist) a dentist who specializes in straightening and adjusting teeth. *n.*

or·tho·dox (ôr′thə doks′) 1 having generally accepted views or opinions, especially in religion. 2 approved by convention; usual; customary: *The orthodox Christmas dinner is turkey and plum pudding.* *adj.*

Orthodox Church a group of Christian churches in eastern Europe and western Asia that do not recognize the Pope as the supreme head of the Church.

os·prey (os′prē or os′prā) a large bird having a strong hooked bill and a head without feathers, related to the vulture and the hawk: *Ospreys feed on fish.* *n., pl.* **os·preys.**

os·ten·ta·tion (os′tən tā′shən) a display or showing off intended to impress others or to attract attention: *the ostentation of a rich, vain man.* *n.*

os·ten·ta·tious (os′tən tā′shəs) 1 done for display; intended to attract notice: *She rode her new bicycle up and down in front of our house in an ostentatious way.* 2 showing off; liking to attract notice: *He was always an ostentatious boy.* *adj.*

An ostrich — about 2 m high to the top of the head

os·trich (os′trich) a large bird of Africa and Arabia that can run fast but cannot fly: *Ostriches are the largest of existing birds.* *n.*

oth·er (uᴛʜ′ər) 1 remaining: *Don is here, but the other boys are at school.* 2 additional or further: *I have no other books with me.* 3 not the same as one or more already mentioned: *Come some other day.* 4 different: *I would not have him other than he is.* 5 some other person or thing: *She helps others.* 6 in any different way; otherwise: *I could not do other than I did.* 1–4 *adj.,* 5 *pron.,* 6 *adv.*

every other, every second; alternate: *We have spelling every other day.*

none other than, no one else but: *The presentation was made by none other than the Prime Minister.*

the other day, night, etc., recently.

oth·er·wise (uᴛʜ′ər wīz′) 1 in a different way; differently: *I could not act otherwise.* 2 different: *It might have been otherwise.* 3 in other ways: *He is noisy, but otherwise a nice boy.* 4 under other circumstances; in a different condition: *He reminded me of what I should otherwise have forgotten.* 5 or else; if not: *Come at once; otherwise you will be too late.* 1, 3, 4 *adv.,* 2 *adj.,* 5 *conj.*

ot·ter (ot′ər) 1 a water animal that eats fish: *The otter is a good swimmer and has webbed toes with claws.* 2 its short, thick, glossy fur: *Some winter coats are made of otter.* *n., pl.* **ot·ters** or **ot·ter.**

ouch (ouch) an exclamation expressing sudden pain. *interj.*

ought[1] (ot or ôt) 1 have a duty; be obliged: *You ought to obey your parents.* 2 be right or suitable: *The theatre ought to allow children in free.* 3 be wise: *I ought to go before it rains.* 4 be expected: *At your age you ought to know better.* 5 be very likely: *It ought to be a fine day tomorrow.* *v.*

☛ *Had ought* and *hadn't ought* are not used in careful English. Avoid: *He had ought to win the race.* Use: *He ought to win the race.*

☛ **Ought** and **aught** are pronounced the same.

ought[2] (ot or ôt) aught; anything. *n., adv.*

☛ See second note at **ought**[1].

ought[3] (ot or ôt) the cipher 0; zero. *n.*

☛ See second note at **ought**[1].

ounce (ouns) 1 a measure of weight, 1/16 of a pound in ordinary weight (about 28 grams) and 1/12 of a pound in troy weight (about 31 grams). 2 a measure of volume for liquids (about 28 cubic centimetres): *There are twenty fluid ounces in an imperial pint.* 3 a little bit; a very small amount: *He hadn't an ounce of strength left after moving all the furniture.* *n.*

our (our or är) of us; belonging to us: *We need our coats now.* *adj.*

☛ **Our, ours** are the possessive forms of *we*. **Our** is always followed by a noun: *This is our car.* **Ours** stands alone: *This car is ours.*

☛ **Our** and **hour** are often pronounced the same.

ours (ourz or ärz) the one or ones belonging to us: *This garden is ours. Ours is a large house. I like ours better than yours.* *pron.*

☛ See first note at **our.**

our·self (our self′ or är self′) myself. **Ourself** is used by an author, king, judge, etc.: *'We shall ourself reward the victor,' said the queen.* *pron.*

our·selves (our selvz′ or är selvz′) 1 a form used instead of **us** when referring back to the subject of the sentence: *We cook for ourselves. We cannot see ourselves as others see us.* 2 a form of **we** or **us** used to make a statement stronger: *We will do the work ourselves.* 3 our real or true selves: *We weren't ourselves when we did that.* *pron. pl.*

–ous a suffix meaning: 1 having; having much; full of, as in *joyous.* 2 characterized by, as in *scandalous.*

oust (oust) force out; drive out: *The sparrows have ousted the bluebirds from their nest.* *v.*

out (out) 1 away; forth: *The water will rush out.* 2 not in or at a place, position, or state: *That dress is out of fashion. The miners are going out on strike.* 3 into the open air: *He went out at noon.* 4 not at home; away from one's office, work, etc.: *My mother is out just now.* 5 not having power; not in possession: *The Liberals are out; the Conservatives are in.* 6 not burning: *The fire is out. The lights were out.* 7 not in use, action, fashion, etc.: *Full skirts are out this season.* 8 not correct: *He was out in his figuring.* 9 into the open; made public; made known; into being; so as to be seen: *The secret is out now. His new book is out. Many flowers were coming out. A rash broke out on his chest.* 10 aloud; plainly: *Speak out so that all can hear.* 11 go or come out: *Murder will out.* 12 to or at an end: *Let them work it out.* 13 completely: *to fit out a boat.* 14 to others: *to let out rooms. Give out the books.* 15 from among others; from a stock or set: *Pick out an apple for me. She picked out a new coat.* 16 in baseball, in such a way as to lose one's turn at bat: *He struck out. He flied out.* 17 not at bat; in the field: *We were soon out and the other team was at bat.* 1–4, 10, 12–16 *adv.,* 5–9, 17 *adj.,* 11 *v.*

out of, a from within: *He came out of the house.* b not within: *He is out of town.* c away from: *forty kilometres out of Calgary.* d beyond the reach of: *The sun faded out of sight.* e without: *He is out of work. We are out of coffee.* f from: *It is made out of tin.* g from among: *We picked our puppy out of that litter.* h because of: *I went only out of curiosity.*

out of hand, out of control: *The excited crowd soon got out of hand.*

out– a prefix meaning: 1 outward; forth; away, as in *outburst, outgoing.* 2 outside; at a distance, as in *outfield, outlying.* 3 more than; longer than, as in *outlive, outnumber.* 4 better than, as in *outdo, outrun.*

out–and–out (out′ən out′) thorough; complete: *an out-and-out defeat.* *adj.*

out·board (out′bôrd′) 1 a boat equipped with an outboard motor. 2 the motor itself. *n.*

outboard motor a small motor attached to the outside of the stern of a boat.

out·break (out′brāk′) 1 breaking out: *outbreaks of anger.* 2 a riot; a public disturbance. *n.*

out·build·ing (out′bil′ding) a shed or building built against or near a main building: *Barns are outbuildings on a farm.* *n.*

out·burst (out′bėrst′) bursting forth: *an outburst of laughter, an outburst of anger.* *n.*

out·cast (out′kast′) 1 a person or animal cast out from home and friends: *Criminals are outcasts of society. That kitten was just a little outcast when Jim found it.* 2 being an outcast; homeless; friendless. 1 *n.,* 2 *adj.*

out·come (out′kum′) a result; a consequence: *the outcome of a race.* *n.*

out·cry (out′krī′) 1 crying out; a sudden cry or scream. 2 a great noise or clamor. *n., pl.* **out·cries.**

out·dat·ed (out dāt′id) out-of-date; old-fashioned; obsolete: *The coal-oil lamp is outdated.* *adj.*

out·did (out did′) See **outdo.** *The girls outdid the boys in neatness.* *v.*

out·dis·tance (out dis′təns) leave behind; outstrip: *She outdistanced all the other runners and won the race.* *v.,* **out·dis·tanced, out·dis·tanc·ing.**

out·do (out dü′) do more or better than; surpass: *Men will outdo boys in most things.* *v.,* **out·did, out·done, out·do·ing.**

out·done (out dun′) See **outdo.** *The girls were outdone by the boys in baseball.* *v.*

out·door (out′dôr′) done, used, or living outdoors: *outdoor games.* *adj.*

out·doors (out′dôrz′) 1 out in the open air; not indoors: *Mother won't let us go outdoors until it stops raining.* 2 the world outside of buildings; the open air. 1 *adv.,* 2 *n.*

out·er (out′ər) 1 of or on the outside: *The outer door is locked.* 2 farther out; farther from the centre: *the outer suburbs of the city.* *adj.*

hat, āge, fär; let, ēqual, tėrm; it, īce
hot, ōpen, ôrder; oil, out; cup, pu̇t, rüle
əbove, takən, pencəl, lemən, circəs
ch, child; ng, long; sh, ship
th, thin; ᴛʜ, then; zh, measure

out·er·most (out′ər mōst′) farthest out. *adj.*

outer space 1 space immediately beyond the atmosphere: *The moon is in outer space.* 2 space between the planets or between the stars. *n.*

out·field (out′fēld′) 1 in baseball, the part of the field beyond the diamond or infield. 2 the three players in the outfield. *n.*

out·fit (out′fit) 1 all the articles necessary for any undertaking or purpose: *a sailor's outfit, the outfit for a camping trip, a bride's outfit.* 2 furnish with everything necessary for any purpose; equip: *He outfitted himself for camp.* 3 a group working together, such as a military unit: *His father and mine were in the same outfit during the war.* 1, 3 *n.*, 2 *v.*, **out·fit·ted, out·fit·ting.**

out·go·ing (out′gō′ing) 1 going out; departing: *outgoing steamships. He will replace the outgoing premier.* 2 friendly; sociable: *She is a very outgoing person. adj.*

out·grew (out grü′) See **outgrow.** *He used to stutter, but he outgrew it. v.*

out·grow (out grō′) 1 grow too large for: *to outgrow one's clothes.* 2 grow beyond or away from; get rid of by growing older: *to outgrow a babyish habit.* 3 grow faster or taller than: *He has outgrown his older brother.* *v.*, **out·grew, out·grown, out·grow·ing.**

out·grown (out grōn′) See **outgrow.** *Some of my last year's clothes are now outgrown. v.*

out·growth (out′grōth′) a natural development, product, or result: *This big store is an outgrowth of the little shop he started ten years ago. n.*

out·house (out′hous′) 1 a building or shed outside the main house. 2 an outside toilet. *n.*

out·ing (out′ing) a short pleasure trip; a walk or drive; a holiday spent outdoors away from home: *On Sunday the family went on an outing to the beach. n.*

out·last (out last′) last longer than. *v.*

out·law (out′lo′ or out′lô′) 1 a person outside the protection of the law; exile; outcast. 2 a lawless person; criminal. 3 make or declare a person an outlaw. 4 make or declare unlawful: *A group of nations agreed to outlaw war.* 1, 2 *n.*, 3, 4 *v.*

out·lay (out′lā′) 1 an expense; a laying out of money; spending: *a large outlay for clothing.* 2 the amount spent: *an outlay of eleven dollars. n.*

out·let (out′let′ or out′lət) 1 a means or place of letting out or getting out; a way out; an opening or exit: *the outlet of a lake, an outlet for one's energies.* 2 a place in a wall, etc. for inserting an electric plug to make connection with an electric circuit. See **plug** for picture. *n.*

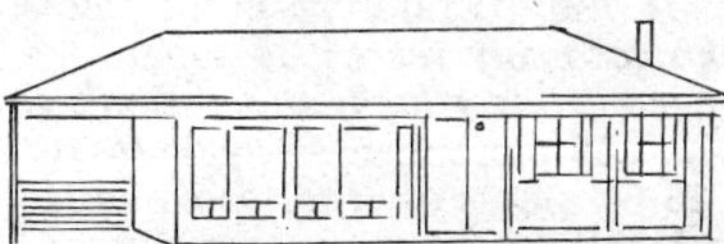

An outline of a house

out·line (out′līn′) 1 the line that shows the shape of an object: *The outline of Italy suggests a boot. We saw the outlines of the mountains against the evening sky.* 2 a drawing or style of drawing that gives only outer lines: *Make an outline of the scene before you paint it.* 3 draw the outer line of anything: *to outline a map of Italy.* 4 a brief plan; a rough draft: *Make an outline before trying to write a composition. The teacher gave a brief outline of the work planned for the term.* 5 give a plan of; sketch: *She outlined their trip abroad.* 1, 2, 4 *n.*, 3, 5 *v.*, **out·lined, out·lin·ing.**

in outline, a with only the outline shown. **b** with only the main features.

out·live (out liv′) live longer than; last longer than: *She outlived her older sister. The idea was good once, but it has outlived its usefulness. v.*, **out·lived, out·liv·ing.**

out·look (out′lu̇k′) 1 what one sees on looking out; a view: *The room has a pleasant outlook.* 2 what seems likely to happen; a prospect: *Because of the black clouds, the outlook for our picnic is not very good.* 3 a way of thinking about things; an attitude of mind; a point of view: *He had a gloomy outlook on life. n.*

out·ly·ing (out′lī′ing) lying outside the boundary; far from the centre; remote: *the outlying houses in the settlement. adj.*

out·num·ber (out num′bər) be more than; exceed in number: *They outnumbered us three to one. v.*

out–of–date (out′əv dāt′) old-fashioned; not in present use: *A horse and buggy is an out-of-date means of travelling. adj.*

out–of–door (out′əv dôr′) outdoor. *adj.*

out–of–doors (out′əv dôrz′) 1 outdoor. 2 outdoors. 1 *adj.*, 2 *n.*, *adv.*

out·port (out′pôrt′) *Cdn.* a small harbor, especially one of the isolated fishing villages along the coasts of Newfoundland. *n.*

out·post (out′pōst′) 1 a guard, or small number of soldiers, placed at some distance from an army or camp, to prevent surprise attack. 2 the place where they are stationed. 3 a settlement or village in an outlying place: *an outpost in the North. n.*

out·put (out′pu̇t′) 1 the amount produced; the product or yield: *the daily output of automobiles.* 2 putting forth: *With a sudden output of effort he moved the rock. n.*

out·rage (out′rāj′; sometimes, out rāj′ for 2 and 3) 1 an act showing no regard for the rights or feelings of others; a very offensive act; a shameful act of violence; an offence or insult: *Setting Mr. Brown's house on fire was an outrage.* 2 insult; offend greatly or arouse great anger in. 3 break the law, a rule of morality, etc. openly; treat as nothing at all: *She outraged all rules of behavior.* 1 *n.*, 2, 3 *v.*, **out·raged, out·rag·ing.**

out·ra·geous (out rā′jəs) shocking; very bad or insulting: *outrageous language. adj.*

out·ran (out ran′) See **outrun.** *He outran me easily. v.*

out·rig·ger (out′rig′ər) a framework ending in a float, extending outward from the side of a light boat or canoe to keep it from turning over. *n.*

out·right (out′rīt′) 1 altogether; entirely; not

gradually: *We paid for our car over two years, but I wish we had bought it outright.* 2 openly; without restraint: *We laughed outright.* 3 complete; thorough: *He would have to be an outright thief to do that.* 4 downright; straightforward; direct: *an outright refusal.* 1, 2 *adv.*, 3, 4 *adj.*

out·run (out run′) 1 run faster than: *He can outrun his older sister.* 2 leave behind; go beyond; pass the limits of: *His story was interesting but it had outrun the facts, and we could not believe it all.* *v.*, **out·ran, out·run, out·run·ning.**

out·set (out′set′) setting out; a start; a beginning: *At the outset, it looked like a nice day.* *n.*

out·side (out′sīd′) 1 the side or surface that is out; the outer part: *the outside of a house.* 2 on the outside; of or nearer the outside: *the outside leaves.* 3 on or to the outside; outdoors: *Run outside and play.* 4 the space that is beyond or not inside. 5 out of; beyond the limits of: *Stay outside the house. That is outside my plans.* 6 *Informal.* highest; largest: *an outside estimate of the cost.* 7 *Informal.* slight; small: *He had only an outside chance of winning the race.* 8 *Cdn.* the settled parts of Canada: *In the North, people refer to the rest of Canada as the outside.* 1, 4, 8 *n.*, 2, 6, 7 *adj.*, 3 *adv.*, 5 *prep.*

at the outside, at the most; at the limit: *I can do it in a week, at the outside.*

out·sid·er (out′sīd′ər) 1 a person not belonging to a particular group, set, company, party, district, etc. 2 *Cdn.* a person who does not live in the North: *The people of Whitehorse, Y.T., call the people of Edmonton outsiders.* *n.*

out·skirts (out′skėrts′) the outer parts or edges of a town, district, etc.; the outlying parts: *He has a farm on the outskirts of town.* *n. pl.*

out·spo·ken (out′spō′kən) frank; not reserved: *an outspoken person, an outspoken criticism.* *adj.*

out·spread (out′spred′) 1 spread out; extended: *an eagle with outspread wings.* 2 spread out; extend. 1 *adj.*, 2 *v.*, **out·spread, out·spread·ing.**

out·stand·ing (out stan′ding) 1 standing out from others; well-known; important: *She is an outstanding basketball player.* 2 unpaid: *outstanding debts.* 3 needing attention: *outstanding letters.* *adj.*

out·stretched (out′strecht′) stretched out; extended: *He welcomed his old friend with outstretched arms.* *adj.*

out·strip (out strip′) 1 go faster than; leave behind in a race: *A horse can outstrip a man.* 2 do better than; excel: *He can outstrip most boys both in sports and in studies.* *v.*, **out·stripped, out·strip·ping.**

out·ward (out′wərd) 1 going toward the outside; turned toward the outside: *an outward motion. She gave one outward glance.* 2 toward the outside; away: *Porches extend outward from both houses.* 3 outer: *He walked to the outward limits of the field.* 4 on the outside: *He turned the coat with the lining outward.* 5 that can be seen; plain to see; on the surface: *outward behavior.* 1, 3, 5 *adj.*, 2, 4 *adv.*

out·ward·ly (out′wərd lē) 1 on the outside or outer surface. 2 in appearance: *Though frightened, the boy remained outwardly calm.* *adv.*

out·wards (out′wərdz) outward. *adv.*

out·weigh (out wā′) 1 weigh more than. 2 exceed in value, importance, influence, etc.: *The advantages of the plan outweigh its disadvantages.* *v.*

out·wit (out wit′) get the better of; be too clever for: *The prisoner outwitted his guards and escaped.* *v.*, **out·wit·ted, out·wit·ting.**

out·worn (out′wôrn′) 1 worn out: *outworn clothes.* 2 out-of-date; outgrown: *outworn opinions, outworn habits.* *adj.*

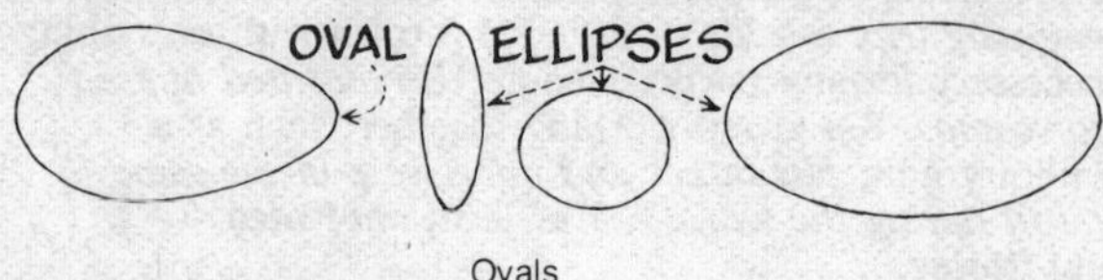

Ovals

o·val (ō′vəl) 1 shaped like an egg. 2 shaped like an ellipse. 3 something having an oval shape. 1, 2 *adj.*, 3 *n.*

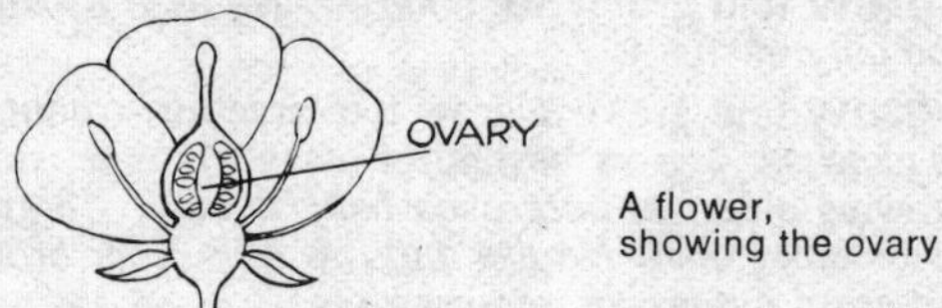

A flower, showing the ovary

o·va·ry (ō′və rē) 1 the part of an animal in which eggs are produced. 2 the part of a plant enclosing the young seeds. *n.*, *pl.* **o·va·ries.**

o·va·tion (ō vā′shən) an enthusiastic burst of applause: *The Premier received a great ovation.* *n.*

ov·en (uv′ən) 1 a space in a stove or near a fireplace for baking food. 2 a small furnace for heating or drying. *n.*

o·ver (ō′vər) 1 above in place or position: *the sky over our heads.* 2 above in authority, power, etc.: *We have a captain over us.* 3 above and to the other side of; across: *leap over a wall. Can you climb over that hill?* 4 across a space or distance: *Go over to the store for me.* 5 out and down from an edge or from an upright position: *The ball went too near the edge and rolled over. When he lost his balance, he fell over.* 6 out and down from; down from the edge of: *He fell over the edge of the cliff.* 7 about or upon, so as to cover: *Cover the tar over with sand until it has hardened.* 8 at all or various places on; on: *A smile came over her face. Farms were scattered over the valley.* 9 here and there on or in; round about; all through: *to travel over the province. He went over everything in his pocket, looking for the letter.* 10 from end to end of; along: *We drove over the new highway.* 11 again: *Do that three times over. I will have to do my homework over.* 12 at an end: *The play is over.* 13 during; in the course of: *He wrote this book over many years.* 14 about; concerning; at: *He is troubled over his health. Don't go to sleep over your work.* 15 more than; beyond: *It cost over twenty dollars.* 16 by means of: *They spoke over the telephone.* 17 more; besides; in excess or addition: *He spent twenty cents and had five cents over.* 18 the other side up; upside down: *Turn over a page. Roll over and over.* 1–3, 6, 8–10, 13–16 *prep.*, 4, 5, 7, 11, 12, 17, 18 *adv.*

over again, once more: *Let's do that over again.*

over and over, again and again: *He keeps telling the same story over and over.*

over– a prefix meaning: **1** too; too much; too long, etc., as in *overcrowded, oversleep.* **2** extra, as in *overtime.* **3** over, as in *overflow, overlord.*

Overalls

o·ver·alls (ō′vər olz′ or ō′vər ôlz′) loose trousers worn over clothes to keep them clean: *Overalls usually have a part that covers the chest.* *n. pl.*

o·ver·arm (ō′vər ärm′) with the arm raised above the shoulder; overhand: *an overarm stroke, to throw overarm.* *adj., adv.*

o·ver·ate (ō′vər āt′) See **overeat.** *I have a stomach ache because I overate.* *v.*

o·ver·bear·ing (ō′vər ber′ing) inclined to dictate; forcing others to one's own will; masterful; domineering: *That old man is a very overbearing person.* *adj.*

o·ver·board (ō′vər bôrd′) from a ship or boat into the water: *Throw that heavy box overboard.* *adv.*
go overboard, go too far in an effort because of extreme enthusiasm: *She went overboard and bought more than she needed.*
throw overboard, a throw into the water. **b** *Informal.* get rid of; give up; abandon; discard: *We threw those plans overboard; we will have our party later.*

o·ver·came (ō′vər kām′) See **overcome.** *She overcame her shyness.* *v.*

o·ver·cast (ō′vər kast′) **1** cloudy; dark; gloomy: *The sky was overcast before the storm.* **2** cover or be covered with clouds or darkness. **3** sew over and through the edges of a seam with long stitches to prevent ravelling. 1 *adj.,* 2, 3 *v.,* **o·ver·cast, o·ver·cast·ing.**

o·ver·coat (ō′vər kōt′) a coat worn for warmth over regular clothing. *n.*

o·ver·come (ō′vər kum′) **1** get the better of; win the victory over; conquer; defeat: *We can overcome difficulties, enemies, and our own faults.* **2** make weak or helpless: *The child was overcome by weariness and slept.* **3** confuse: *The girl was so overcome by the noise and the lights of the city that she couldn't speak.* *v.,* **o·ver·came, o·ver·come, o·ver·com·ing.**

o·ver·crowd (ō′vər kroud′) crowd too much; put in too much or too many. *v.*

o·ver·did (ō′vər did′) See **overdo.** *v.*

o·ver·do (ō′vər dü′) **1** do or attempt too much: *She overdoes exercise. She overdid and became tired.* **2** exaggerate: *The funny scenes in the play were overdone.* **3** cook too much: *overdone vegetables.* *v.,* **o·ver·did, o·ver·done, o·ver·do·ing.**

o·ver·done (ō′vər dun′) See **overdo.** *v.*

o·ver·due (ō′vər dyü′ or ō′vər dü′) more than due; due some time ago but not yet arrived, paid, etc.: *The train is overdue. This bill is overdue.* *adj.*

o·ver·eat (ō′vər ēt′) eat too much. *v.,* **o·ver·ate, o·ver·eat·en, o·ver·eat·ing.**

hat, āge, fär; let, ēqual, tėrm; it, īce
hot, ōpen, ôrder; oil, out; cup, pu̇t, rüle
əbove, takən, pencəl, lemən, circəs
ch, child; ng, long; sh, ship
th, thin; ŦH, then; zh, measure

o·ver·eat·en (ō′vər ēt′ən) See **overeat.** *v.*

o·ver·flow (ō′vər flō′ for 1–6, ō′vər flō′ for 7) **1** flow over the top: *Stop! The milk is overflowing the cup.* **2** have the contents flowing over: *My cup is overflowing.* **3** flow over the bounds: *Rivers often overflow in the spring.* **4** cover; flood: *The river overflowed my garden.* **5** extend out beyond; be too many for: *The crowd overflowed the little room and filled the hall.* **6** be very abundant: *an overflowing harvest, overflowing kindness.* **7** an overflowing; an excess: *The overflow from the glass ran into the sink.* 1–6 *v.,* **o·ver·flowed, o·ver·flown, o·ver·flow·ing;** 7 *n.*

o·ver·grew (ō′vər grü′) See **overgrow.** *v.*

o·ver·grow (ō′vər grō′) grow over: *The wall is overgrown with vines.* *v.,* **o·ver·grew, o·ver·grown, o·ver·grow·ing.**

o·ver·grown (ō′vər grōn′) grown too big: *an overgrown tree.* *adj.*

o·ver·hand (ō′vər hand′) with the hand raised above the shoulder: *an overhand throw, to pitch overhand.* *adj., adv.*

o·ver·hang (ō′vər hang′ for 1, ō′vər hang′ for 2) **1** hang over; project over: *Trees overhang the street to form an arch of branches.* **2** something that projects: *The overhang of the roof shaded the flower bed beneath.* 1 *v.,* **o·ver·hung, o·ver·hang·ing;** 2 *n.*

o·ver·haul (ō′vər hol′ or ō′vər hôl′ for 1 and 2, ō′vər hol′ or ō′vər hôl′ for 3) **1** examine completely and make repairs or changes that are needed: *Once a year we overhaul our boat.* **2** gain upon; overtake: *The pirate's ship was overhauling ours.* **3** an overhauling. 1, 2 *v.,* 3 *n.*

o·ver·head (ō′vər hed′ for 1, ō′vər hed′ for 2 and 3) **1** over the head; above: *the stars overhead, the family overhead, the flag overhead.* **2** placed above; placed high up: *overhead wires.* **3** general expenses of running a business, such as rent, lighting, heating, taxes, repairs, etc. 1 *adv.,* 2 *adj.,* 3 *n.*

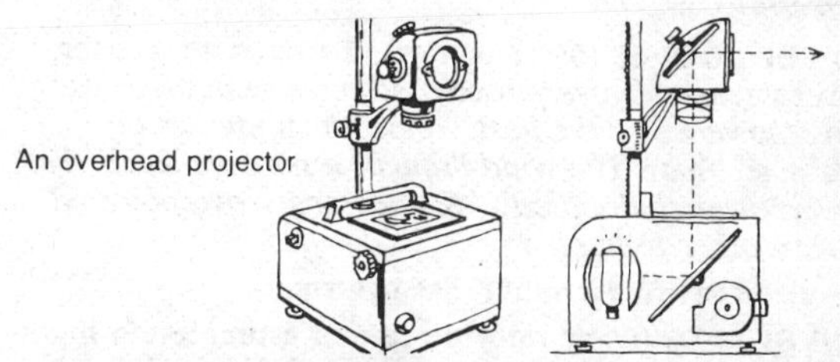
An overhead projector

overhead projector a projecting device in which transparencies are placed on a glass surface that is lit from below, the image being focussed and reflected onto a wall or screen by means of an overhead lens and mirror.

o·ver·hear (ō′vər hēr′) hear when one is not meant to hear: *They spoke so loudly that I could not help* *overhearing what they said.* *v.,* **o·ver·heard, o·ver·hear·ing.**

o·ver·heard (ō′vər hėrd′) See **overhear.** *I overheard what you told him.* *v.*

o·ver·heat (ō′vər hēt′) heat too much. *v.*

o·ver·hung (ō′vər hung′ for 1, ō′vər hung′ for 2) 1 hung from above: *an overhung door.* 2 See **overhang.** *A big awning overhung the sidewalk.* 1 *adj.,* 2 *v.*

o·ver·joyed (ō′vər joid′) very joyful; filled with joy; delighted. *adj.*

o·ver·laid (ō′vər lād′) See **overlay.** *The workmen overlaid the dome with gold.* *v.*

o·ver·land (ō′vər land′) on land; by land: *an overland route. We travelled overland from Winnipeg to Vancouver.* *adj., adv.*

o·ver·lap (ō′vər lap′) 1 lap over; place or be placed so that one piece covers part of the next: *Shingles on a roof are laid to overlap each other.* 2 the part or amount that overlaps: *Allow for an overlap of several inches.* 1 *v.,* **o·ver·lapped, o·ver·lap·ping;** 2 *n.*

o·ver·lay (ō′vər lā′ for 1 and 2, ō′vər lā′ for 3) 1 something laid over something else; a covering. 2 an ornamental layer: *The lid of the box had a gold overlay.* 3 cover the surface of: *The dome is overlaid with gold.* 1, 2 *n.,* 3 *v.,* **o·ver·laid, o·ver·lay·ing.**

o·ver·load (ō′vər lōd′ for 1, ō′vər lōd′ for 2) 1 load too heavily: *to overload a boat.* 2 too great a load: *The overload of electric current broke the circuit.* 1 *v.,* 2 *n.*

o·ver·look (ō′vər lu̇k′) 1 fail to see: *Here are some letters that you overlooked.* 2 pay no attention to; excuse: *I will overlook your bad behavior this time.* 3 have a view of from above; be higher than: *This high window overlooks half the city.* *v.*

o·ver·lord (ō′vər lôrd′) a person who is lord over another lord or other lords: *The duke was the overlord of the barons and knights who held land from him.* *n.*

o·ver·night (ō′vər nīt′) 1 for one night: *to stay overnight with a friend.* 2 done, occurring, etc. from one day to the next: *an overnight stop.* 3 for use for one night: *An overnight bag contains articles needed for one night's stay.* 1 *adv.,* 2, 3 *adj.*

o·ver·pass (ō′vər pas′) a bridge over a road, railroad, canal, etc.: *An overpass was built to replace the level crossing.* *n.*

o·ver·pow·er (ō′vər pou′ər) 1 overcome; master; overwhelm: *He overpowered all his enemies. I was overpowered by the heat.* 2 be much greater or stronger than: *The wind brought a horrible smell that overpowered all others. Sudden anger overpowered every other feeling.* *v.*

o·ver·ran (ō′vər ran′) See **overrun.** *v.*

o·ver·rate (ō′vər rāt′) to rate or estimate too highly: *He overrated his strength and soon had to ask for help.* *v.,* **o·ver·rat·ed, o·ver·rat·ing.**

o·ver·rule (ō′vər rül′) 1 decide against an argument, objection, etc.; reject: *The president overruled my plan.* 2 prevail over; be stronger than: *The majority overruled me.* *v.,* **o·ver·ruled, o·ver·rul·ing.**

o·ver·run (ō′vər run′) 1 spread over rapidly or in great numbers: *Weeds had overrun the old garden. The barn was overrun with rats.* 2 invade and conquer, occupy, or destroy: *The enemy troops overran most of our country.* 3 run or go beyond; exceed: *The speaker overran the time set for him.* *v.,* **o·ver·ran, o·ver·run, o·ver·run·ning.**

o·ver·saw (ō′vər so′ or ō′vər sô′) See **oversee.** *v.*

o·ver·sea (ō′vər sē′ or ō′vər sē′) overseas. *adv., adj.*

o·ver·seas (ō′vər sēz′ for 1 and 4, ō′vər sēz′ for 2 and 3) 1 across the sea; beyond the sea; abroad: *travel overseas.* 2 done, used, or serving overseas: *overseas service.* 3 of countries across the sea; foreign: *overseas trade.* 4 of the armed forces, serving across the sea, especially in Europe: *My father was overseas during the war.* 1, 4 *adv.,* 2, 3 *adj.*

o·ver·see (ō′vər sē′) look after and direct work or workers; superintend; manage: *to oversee a factory.* *v.,* **o·ver·saw, o·ver·seen, o·ver·see·ing.**

o·ver·seen (ō′vər sēn′) See **oversee.** *v.*

o·ver·se·er (ō′vər sē′ər) a person who oversees the work of others. *n.*

o·ver·shad·ow (ō′vər shad′ō) 1 be or appear more important than: *The boy overshadowed his older brother as a hockey player.* 2 cast a shadow over. *v.*

o·ver·shoe (ō′vər shü′) a waterproof shoe or boot, often made of rubber, worn over another shoe to keep the foot dry and warm. *n.*

o·ver·sight (ō′vər sīt′) 1 a failure to notice or think of something: *Through an oversight, the kitten got no supper last night.* 2 watchful care: *While children are at school, they are under their teacher's oversight and direction.* *n.*

o·ver·sleep (ō′vər slēp′) sleep beyond a certain hour; sleep in; sleep too long. *v.,* **o·ver·slept, o·ver·sleep·ing.**

o·ver·slept (ō′vər slept′) See **oversleep.** *I overslept and missed the bus.* *v.*

o·ver·spread (ō′vər spred′) spread over: *A smile overspread his broad face.* *v.,* **o·ver·spread, o·ver·spread·ing.**

o·ver·step (ō′vər step′) go beyond; exceed: *He overstepped the limits of politeness by that answer.* *v.,* **o·ver·stepped, o·ver·step·ping.**

o·ver·take (ō′vər tāk′) 1 come up with; catch up to: *The blue car overtook our truck.* 2 come upon suddenly: *A storm had overtaken the children.* *v.,* **o·ver·took, o·ver·tak·en, o·ver·tak·ing.**

o·ver·tak·en (ō′vər tāk′ən) See **overtake.** *v.*

o·ver·threw (ō′vər thrü′) See **overthrow.** *v.*

o·ver·throw (ō′vər thrō′ for 1 and 2, ō′vər thrō′ for 3) 1 take away the power of; defeat: *The nobles overthrew the king.* 2 overturn; upset; knock down. 3 a defeat; an upset: *The overthrow of his plans left him much discouraged.* 1, 2 *v.,* **o·ver·threw, o·ver·thrown, o·ver·throw·ing;** 3 *n.*

o·ver·thrown (ō′vər thrōn′) See **overthrow.** *v.*

o·ver·time (ō′vər tīm′) 1 extra time; time beyond the regular hours: *He was paid extra for overtime.* 2 wages for this period. 3 beyond the regular hours: *He worked overtime.* 4 of or for overtime: *overtime work.* 5 in games, a period or periods beyond the normal game time. 1, 2, 5 *n.,* 3 *adv.,* 4 *adj.*

o·ver·took (ō′vər tu̇k′) See **overtake.** *v.*

o·ver·ture (ō′vər chər) 1 a proposal; an offer: *The enemy is making overtures for peace.* 2 a musical

hat, āge, fär; let, ēqual, tėrm; it, īce
hot, ōpen, ôrder; oil, out; cup, pu̇t, rüle
əbove, takən, pencəl, lemən, circəs
ch, child; ng, long; sh, ship
th, thin; ᴛʜ, then; zh, measure

composition played by the orchestra as an introduction to an opera, or to some other long musical composition. *n.*

o·ver·turn (ō′vər tėrn′ for 1, 2, and 3, ō′vər tėrn′ for 4) **1** turn upside down. **2** upset; fall down; fall over: *The boat overturned.* **3** make fall down; overthrow; defeat; destroy the power of: *The rebels overturned the government.* **4** an overturning. 1–3 *v.,* 4 *n.*

o·ver·weight (ō′vər wāt′) having too much weight: *That boy is overweight. We had to pay extra for our overweight baggage. adj.*

o·ver·whelm (ō′vər welm′ or ō′vər hwelm′) **1** crush; overcome completely: *She was overwhelmed with grief.* **2** cover completely as a flood would: *A wave overwhelmed the boat. v.*

o·ver·work (ō′vər wėrk′ for 1 and 2, sometimes ō′vər wėrk′ for 1) **1** too much or too hard work. **2** to work too hard or too long. 1 *n.,* 2 *v.*

owe (ō) **1** have to pay: *I owe the grocer a dollar.* **2** be in debt: *He is always owing for something.* **3** be obliged or indebted for: *We owe a great deal to our parents.* **4** be obliged to give or offer: *We owe friends our trust. v.,* **owed, ow·ing.**

☛ **Owe, o,** and **oh** are pronounced the same.

ow·ing (ō′ing) due; owed: *to pay what is owing. adj.*

owing to, on account of; because of: *Owing to a serious illness, she was absent from school for more than a month.*

One kind of owl — about 75 cm long with the tail

owl (oul) a bird having a big head, big eyes, and a short, hooked beak: *Owls hunt mice and small birds at night. Some kinds of owls have tufts of feathers on their heads called 'horns' or 'ears.' n.*

own (ōn) **1** have; possess: *I own many books.* **2** of oneself; belonging to oneself or itself: *This is my own book. She makes her own dresses.* **3** admit that one owns: *His father will not own him.* **4** admit; confess: *I own you are right. I own to being afraid.* 1, 3, 4 *v.,* 2 *adj.*

come into one's own, a get what belongs to one. **b** get the success or credit that one deserves.

hold one's own, keep one's position; not be forced back.

of one's own, belonging to oneself.

on one's own, not ruled or directed by someone else.

own up, confess: *The prisoner owned up to the crime.*

own·er (ōn′ər) one who owns: *The owner of the dog bought him a collar. n.*

own·er·ship (ōn′ər ship) being an owner; the possessing of something; the right of possession: *He claimed ownership of a boat that he found drifting down the river. n.*

ox (oks) **1** a domestic bull with the male glands removed, used for farm work and for beef: *An ox is slow but very strong.* **2** any of the group of animals, with horns and cloven hoofs, to which cattle, buffaloes, and bison belong. *n., pl.* **ox·en.**

ox·bow (oks′bō′) **1** a U-shaped piece of wood placed under and around the neck of an ox, with the upper ends inserted in the bar of the yoke. See **yoke** for picture. **2** a U-shaped bend in a river. *n.*

ox·cart (oks′kärt′) a cart drawn by oxen. *n.*

ox·en (ok′sən) plural of **ox.** *n.*

ox·ford (oks′fərd) a kind of low shoe, laced over the instep. See **shoe** for picture. *n.*

ox·i·dize (ok′sə dīz′) combine with oxygen: *When a substance burns or rusts, it is oxidized. Water oxidizes some metals. v.,* **ox·i·dized, ox·i·diz·ing.**

ox·y·gen (ok′sə jən) a gas without color or odor that forms about one fifth of the air: *Animals and plants cannot live without oxygen. Fire will not burn without oxygen. n.*

Oysters — usually about 12 cm long

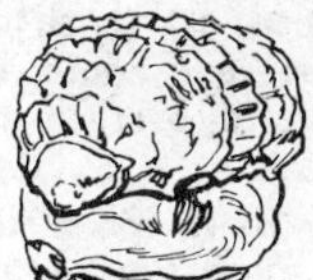

oys·ter (ois′tər) a kind of shellfish or mollusc much used as food, having a rough, irregular shell in two halves: *Oysters are found in shallow water along seacoasts. Some kinds of oysters yield pearls. n.*

oz. ounce; ounces.

o·zone (ō′zōn) **1** a form of oxygen with a sharp odor. **2** *Informal.* pure air that is refreshing. *n.*

p or **P** (pē) the 16th letter of the alphabet: *There are two* p's *in* paper. *n., pl.* **p's** or **P's.**
mind one's p's and q's, be careful about what one says or does.

p. page.

pa (po, pä, or pa) *Informal.* papa; father. *n.*

P.A. public address system.

pace (pās) **1** a step. **2** walk with regular steps: *The tiger paced up and down his cage.* **3** the length of a step in walking; about 80 cm: *There were perhaps ten paces between me and the bear.* **4** to measure by paces: *We paced off the distance and found it to be 69 paces.* **5** a way of stepping: *The walk, trot, and gallop are some of the paces of a horse.* **6** a rate of speed; speed: *He sets a fast pace in walking.* **7** set the pace for: *A motorboat will pace the boys training for the rowing match.* 1, 3, 5, 6 *n.*, 2, 4, 7 *v.*, **paced, pac·ing.**
keep pace with, keep up with or go as fast as.
set the pace, a set a rate of speed that others are expected to keep up with. **b** be an example or model for others to follow.

Pa·cif·ic (pə sif′ik) **1** the ocean between Asia and North and South America. **2** of the Pacific Ocean. **3** on, in, over, or near the Pacific Ocean: *Pacific air routes.* 1 *n.*, 2, 3 *adj.*

pa·cif·ic (pə sif′ik) **1** loving peace; not warlike: *a pacific nation.* **2** peaceful; calm; quiet: *pacific weather. adj.*

pac·i·fy (pas′ə fī′) **1** make calm; quiet down; give peace to: *Can't you pacify that screaming baby? We tried to pacify the man we bumped into.* **2** bring order to: *Soldiers were sent to pacify the country. v.*, **pac·i·fied, pac·i·fy·ing.**

pack (pak) **1** a bundle of things wrapped up or tied together for carrying: *The soldier carried a pack on his back.* **2** put together in a bundle, box, bale, etc.: *Pack your books in this box. We pack onions in bags.* **3** fill with things; put one's things into: *Pack your trunk.* **4** press or crowd closely together: *A hundred men were packed into one small room.* **5** a set; lot; a number together: *a pack of thieves, a pack of nonsense, a pack of lies.* **6** a number of animals hunting together: *Wolves hunt in packs; lions hunt alone.* **7** a company or troop of Wolf Cubs or Brownies. **8** a complete set of playing cards (usually 52). **9** a large area of floating pieces of ice pushed together: *The ship forced its way through the pack.* **10** carry in a pack: *He packed his supplies into the bush.* **11** make tight with something that water, steam, air, etc. cannot leak through: *The plumber packed the joint between two sections of pipe.* 1, 5–9 *n.*, 2–4, 10, 11 *v.*
pack off, send away: *The child was packed off to bed.*
send packing, send away abruptly.

pack·age (pak′ij) **1** a bundle of things packed or wrapped together; a box with things packed in it; a parcel. **2** put in a package. 1 *n.*, 2 *v.*

pack animal an animal used for carrying loads or packs.

pack·et (pak′it) **1** a small package; a parcel: *a packet of letters.* **2** packet boat. *n.*

packet boat a boat that carries mail, passengers, and goods regularly on a fixed route.

packing house a place where meat, fruit, vegetables, etc. are prepared and packed to be sold.

pact (pakt) an agreement: *The three nations signed a peace pact. n.*

pad[1] (pad) **1** something soft used for comfort, protection, or stuffing; a cushion: *Mother had a pad made for the baby's carriage.* **2** fill with something soft; stuff: *to pad a chair, a padded suit for football.* **3** a number of sheets of paper fastened tightly together; a tablet. **4** the launching platform for a rocket or missile: *The man-made satellite rose from the pad at midnight.* **5** a cushionlike part on the bottom side of the feet of dogs, foxes, and some other animals. **6** the foot of such animals. **7** the large floating leaf of a water lily. **8** a cloth soaked in ink for use with a rubber stamp. **9** use words just to fill space; make a written paper or speech longer by using unnecessary words: *Don't pad your compositions.* 1, 3–8 *n.*, 2, 9 *v.*, **pad·ded, pad·ding.**

pad[2] (pad) walk or trot softly: *A wolf padded through the forest. v.*

pad·ding (pad′ing) **1** material used to pad with, such as foam rubber, cotton, or straw. **2** unnecessary words used to make a written paper or speech longer. *n.*

pad·dle[1] (pad′əl) **1** a short oar with a broad blade at one end or both ends, usually held with both hands in rowing a boat or canoe. See **canoe** for picture. **2** move a boat or canoe with a paddle or paddles. **3** the act of paddling; a turn at the paddle. **4** one of the broad boards fixed around a water wheel or a paddle wheel to push, or be pushed by, the water. **5** a paddle-shaped piece of wood used for stirring, for mixing, for beating clothes, etc. **6** *Informal.* beat with a paddle or something similar; spank. 1, 3–5 *n.*, 2, 6 *v.*, **pad·dled, pad·dling.**

pad·dle[2] (pad′əl) **1** move the hands or feet about in water. **2** wade in water without shoes and stockings: *Children love to paddle at the beach. v.*, **pad·dled, pad·dling.**

paddle wheel a wheel that propels a boat through the water by means of an arrangement of paddles.

pad·dock (pad′ək) **1** a small field near a stable or house, used for exercising animals or as a pasture. **2** a pen for horses at a race track. *n.*

pad·dy (pad′ē) a field of rice. *n.*

A padlock

pad·lock (pad′lok′) **1** a lock that can be put on and removed: *A padlock hangs by a curved bar, hinged at one end and, when locked, snapped shut at the other.* **2** fasten with such a lock. 1 *n.*, 2 *v.*

pa·gan (pā′gən) **1** a person who is not a Christian, a Jew, or a Moslem; one who worships more than one god; a heathen: *The ancient Greeks and Romans were pagans.* **2** of or having to do with pagans; heathen: *pagan customs.* **3** a person who has no religion. 1, 3 *n.*, 2 *adj.*

page[1] (pāj) **1** one side of a leaf or sheet of paper: *a page in this book.* **2** a record: *the pages of history.* **3** a happening or time considered as part of history: *The* *settling of the West is an exciting page in our history.* *n.*

page² (pāj) **1** a servant, often a boy, who runs errands, carries hand luggage, etc. for guests at hotels, etc.: *The pages at hotels usually wear uniforms.* **2** try to get a message to a person by means of an announcement, either by a page or on a public address: *The store manager paged the lost boy's mother on the P.A.* **3** a messenger in the House of Commons, the Senate, or the Legislative Assembly. **4** in former times, a young man who was preparing to be a knight. 1, 3, 4 *n.*, 2 *v.*, **paged, pag·ing.**

pag·eant (paj′ənt) **1** a show; an elaborate spectacle; a procession in costume; a display: *The coronation of the new king was a splendid pageant.* **2** a public entertainment that represents scenes from history, legend, or the like: *Our school gave a pageant of the coming of Jacques Cartier to Canada.* *n.*

pa·go·da (pə gō′də) a temple having many storeys with a roof curving upward from each storey: *There are pagodas in India, Japan, and China.* See the picture. *n.*

paid (pād) See **pay.** *I have paid my bills. These bills are all paid.* *v.*

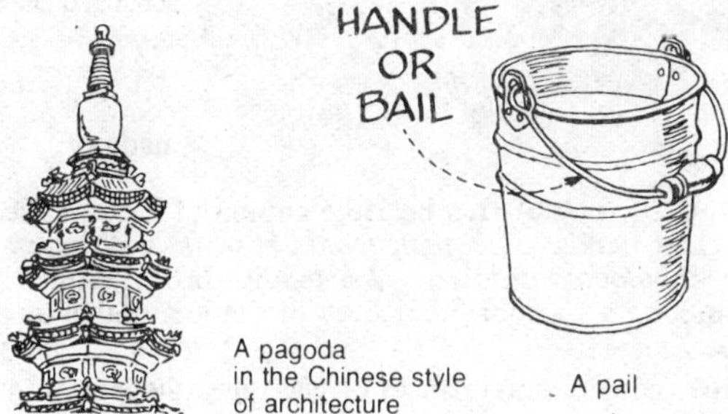

A pagoda in the Chinese style of architecture

A pail

pail (pāl) **1** a container, usually round, for carrying liquids that has a wide top and a single handle that is attached at each side. **2** the amount a pail holds. *n.*

☛ **Pail** and **pale** are pronounced the same.

pail·ful (pāl′fu̇l) the amount that fills a pail. *n., pl.* **pail·fuls.**

pain (pān) **1** a feeling of being hurt; suffering in body or mind: *A cut causes pain. He had a pain in his back. The death of her father caused her great pain.* **2** cause to suffer; give pain: *Her father's death still pains her. Does your tooth pain you?* 1 *n.*, 2 *v.* **—pain′less,** *adj.*

on or **under pain of,** as a way of avoiding the punishment or penalty of: *The traitor was ordered to leave the country on pain of death.*

take pains, be careful: *She took pains to be neat with her paper.*

☛ **Pain** and **pane** are pronounced the same.

pain·ful (pān′fəl) causing pain; unpleasant; hurting: *a painful injury, a painful duty.* *adj.*

pains·tak·ing (pānz′tāk′ing) very careful; particular: *a painstaking painter.* *adj.*

paint (pānt) **1** a mixture of a solid coloring matter and liquid that can be put on a surface to dry as a colored coating. **2** the solid coloring matter alone: *a box of paints.* **3** use paint; cover or decorate with paint: *to paint a house.* **4** make a picture or pictures with paints: *The artist painted the lights of the city. He draws well but he prefers to paint.* **5** picture vividly in words. 1, 2 *n.*, 3–5 *v.* **—paint′er,** *n.*

hat, āge, fär; let, ēqual, tėrm; it, īce
hot, ōpen, ôrder; oil, out; cup, pu̇t, rüle
əbove, takən, pencəl, lemən, circəs
ch, child; ng, long; sh, ship
th, thin; ᴛʜ, then; zh, measure

paint·brush (pānt′brush′) a brush for putting on paint. *n.*

paint·ing (pān′ting) **1** a picture; something painted. **2** the act of one who paints. *n.*

pair (per) **1** a set of two; two that go together: *a pair of shoes, a pair of horses.* **2** arrange or be arranged in sets of two: *Her gloves were neatly paired in a drawer.* **3** a single thing consisting of two parts that cannot be used separately: *a pair of scissors, a pair of trousers.* **4** two people who are married or are engaged to be married. **5** join in love and marriage. **6** two animals that are mated. **7** to mate. 1, 3, 4, 6 *n.*, 2, 5, 7 *v.*

pair off, arrange in pairs; form into pairs: *The boys and girls paired off to learn the new dance.*

☛ **Pair, pare,** and **pear** are pronounced the same.

pa·ja·mas (pə jam′əz or pə jä′məz) See **pyjamas.**

Pa·ki·stan·i (pak′ə stan′ē) **1** of or having to do with Pakistan, a country in southern Asia. **2** a person born in or living in Pakistan. 1 *adj.*, 2 *n.*

pal (pal) a chum, playmate, or comrade. *n.*

pal·ace (pal′is) **1** the official home of king, queen, bishop or some other important person. **2** a very fine house or building. *n.*

pal·at·a·ble (pal′ə tə bəl) agreeable to the taste; pleasing: *The lunch was not very palatable. I find your suggestion quite palatable.* *adj.*

pal·ate (pal′it) **1** the roof of the mouth: *The bony part in front is the hard palate; the fleshy part at the back is the soft palate.* **2** the sense of taste: *The new flavor pleased his palate.* *n.*

☛ **Palate, palette,** and **pallet** are pronounced the same.

pa·la·tial (pə lā′shəl) like a palace; fit for a palace; magnificent: *a palatial apartment.* *adj.*

pale¹ (pāl) **1** without much color; whitish: *When you have been ill, your face is often pale.* **2** not bright; dim: *pale blue. The street lamp gave a pale light in the fog.* **3** turn pale: *Her face paled at the bad news.* 1, 2 *adj.*, **pal·er, pal·est;** 3 *v.*, **paled, pal·ing.**

☛ **Pale** and **pail** are pronounced the same.

pale² (pāl) **1** a long, narrow board, pointed at the top, used for fences. See the picture. **2** a boundary: *Murderers are outside the pale of civilized society.* *n.*

☛ See note at **pale¹.**

pale·face (pāl′fās′) a white person: *The North American Indians are said to have called white people palefaces.* *n.*

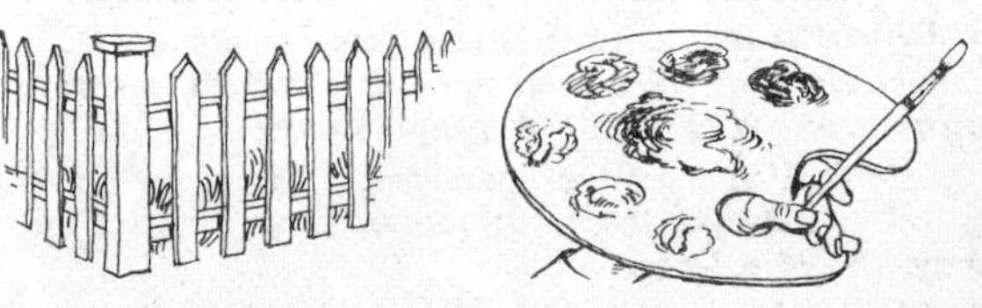

A fence made of pales

A palette

pal·ette (pal′it) **1** a thin board, usually oval or oblong, with a thumb hole at one end, used by painters to lay and mix colors on. **2** a set of colors on this board. *n.*

☞ **Palette, palate,** and **pallet** are pronounced the same.

pal·frey (pol′frē or pôl′frē) a gentle riding horse, especially one used by ladies. *n., pl.* **pal·freys.**

pal·i·sade (pal′ə sād′) **1** a fence of stakes set firmly in the ground to enclose or defend. **2** Usually, **palisades,** *pl.* a line of high, steep cliffs. *n.*

pall[1] (pol or pôl) **1** a heavy cloth, often made of velvet, spread over a coffin, a hearse, or a tomb. **2** a dark, gloomy covering: *A thick pall of smoke shut out the sun from the city. n.*

☞ **Pall**[1] comes from the Latin word *pallium* meaning 'cloak.'

pall[2] (pol or pôl) become distasteful or very tiresome because there has been too much: *Even the most tasty food palls if it is served day after day. v.*

☞ **Pall**[2] is a shortening of *appal.*

pall·bear·er (pol′ber′ər or pôl′ber′ər) one of the men who walk with or carry the coffin at a funeral. *n.*

pal·let (pal′it) a bed of straw; a poor bed. *n.*

☞ **Pallet, palate,** and **palette** are pronounced the same.

pal·lid (pal′id) lacking color; pale: *a pallid face. adj.*

pal·lor (pal′ər) lack of color from fear, illness, death, etc.; paleness. *n.*

palm[1] (pom or päm) **1** the inside of the hand between the wrist and the fingers. **2** conceal in the hand: *The magician palmed the nickel.* 1 *n.,* 2 *v.*

palm off, pass off or get accepted by tricks, fraud, or false representation.

Coco palms

palm[2] (pom or päm) **1** any of many kinds of trees growing in warm climates: *Most palms are tall and have leaves at the top.* **2** a leaf or stalk of leaves of a palm tree used as a symbol of victory or triumph. **3** a victory; triumph: *He bore off the palm both in tennis and in track. n.*

Palm Sunday the Sunday before Easter Sunday.

pal·pi·tate (pal′pə tāt′) **1** beat very rapidly: *a palpitating heart.* **2** quiver; tremble: *His body palpitated with terror. v.,* **pal·pi·tat·ed, pal·pi·tat·ing.**

pal·sy (pol′zē or pôl′zē) paralysis; a loss of the power to feel, to move, or to control motion in any part of the body. *n., pl.* **pal·sies.**

pal·try (pol′trē or pôl′trē) almost worthless; petty; trifling: *a paltry sum of money. Pay no attention to paltry gossip. adj.,* **pal·tri·er, pal·tri·est.**

pam·pas (pam′pəz or pam′pəs) the vast, treeless, grassy plains of South America. *n. pl.*

pam·per (pam′pər) indulge too much; allow too many privileges: *to pamper a child. v.*

pam·phlet (pam′flit) a short printed work, usually with no binding or having a stapled paper cover. *n.*

pan (pan) **1** a dish for cooking and other household uses, usually broad, shallow, and with no cover. **2** anything like this: *Gold and other metals are sometimes obtained by washing ore in pans.* **3** wash gravel, sand, etc. in a pan to separate the gold. **4** a flat cake of drifting ice, often having upturned edges. 1, 2, 4 *n.,* 3 *v.,* **panned, pan·ning.**

pan out, turn out or work out: *His latest scheme panned out well.*

pan·cake (pan′kāk′) a thin, flat cake made of batter and fried in a pan or on a griddle. *n.*

pan·cre·as (pan′krē əs) a gland near the stomach that helps digestion: *The pancreas of animals when used for food is called the sweetbread. n.*

Giant pandas — about 120 cm long

pan·da (pan′də) **1** a bearlike animal of Tibet, called the giant panda: *The giant panda is white with black legs, shoulders, and ears.* **2** a reddish-brown animal resembling a raccoon, that lives in the mountains of India. *n.*

pane (pān) a single sheet of glass in a division of a window, a door, or a sash. *n.*

☞ **Pane** and **pain** are pronounced the same.

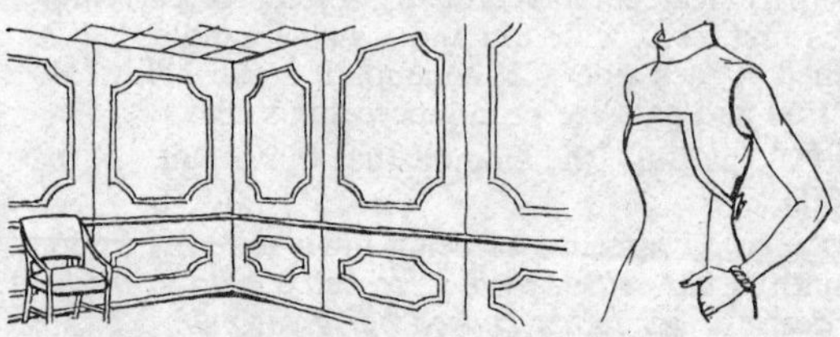

Panels in a wall A panel in a dress

pan·el (pan′əl) **1** a separate strip or surface that is usually set off in some way from what is around it: *Panels may be in a door or other woodwork, on large pieces of furniture, or made as parts of a dress.* **2** arrange in panels; furnish or decorate with panels: *The room was panelled with oak.* **3** a long, narrow picture, hanging, or design. **4** a list of persons called as jurors; the members of a jury. **5** a group of selected persons brought together to discuss a question or topic: *The panel gave its opinion on the recent election.* **6** a group of persons who ask questions in certain guessing games and other entertainments on radio and TV shows. **7** a board containing the instruments, controls, or indicators used in operating an automobile, aircraft, computer, or other mechanism. 1, 3–7 *n.,* 2 *v.,* **pan·elled** or **pan·eled, pan·el·ling** or **pan·el·ing.**

panel discussion a discussion of a particular question or topic by a group of people, usually experts: *We listened to a panel discussion on the radio.*

hat, āge, fär; let, ēqual, tėrm; it, īce
hot, ōpen, ôrder; oil, out; cup, pu̇t, rüle
əbove, takən, pencəl, lemən, circəs
ch, child; ng, long; sh, ship
th, thin; ᴛʜ, then; zh, measure

pan·el·ist or **pan·el·list** (pan′əl ist) one of a group of persons making up a panel (defs. 5 and 6). *n.*

pang (pang) a sudden, short, sharp pain or feeling: *the pangs of a toothache. A pang of pity moved her heart. n.*

pan·han·dle[1] (pan′han′dəl) a narrow strip of land that projects like the handle of a pan. *n.*

pan·han·dle[2] (pan′han′dəl) beg, especially in the streets. *v.,* **pan·han·dled, pan·han·dling.**

pan·ic (pan′ik) **1** a sudden fear that causes one to lose self-control; unreasoning fear: *There was panic when the theatre caught fire.* **2** affect or be affected with panic: *The driver panicked when his brakes failed.* 1 *n.*, 2 *v.*, **pan·icked, pan·ick·ing.**

☞ **Panic** is from a Latin word that came from the Greek word *panikos* meaning 'of Pan.' Pan, a Greek god of woods and fields, was once thought to cause fear.

pan·o·ram·a (pan′ə ram′ə) **1** a wide, unbroken view of a surrounding region: *a panorama of beach and sea.* **2** a picture of a landscape or other scene often shown as if seen from a central point; a picture unrolled a part at a time and made to pass continuously before the spectators. **3** a complete survey of some subject: *a panorama of the development of the snowmobile.* **4** a continuously passing or changing scene: *the panorama of city life. n.*

A pansy

pan·sy (pan′zē) a garden flower resembling a violet but much larger and having flat, velvety petals: *Pansies usually have petals of several colors. n., pl.* **pan·sies.**

pant (pant) **1** breathe hard and quickly: *He is panting from playing tennis.* **2** a short, quick breath. **3** speak with short, quick breaths: *'Come quick. Come quick,' panted Alec.* **4** be eager; long very much: *I am just panting for my turn.* 1, 3, 4 *v.*, 2 *n.*

pan·ther (pan′thər) **1** cougar. **2** leopard. **3** jaguar. *n.*

pan·ties (pan′tēz) **1** short pants worn as underwear by girls and women. **2** pants worn by babies. *n. pl.*

pan·to·mime (pan′tə mīm′) **1** a play without words, in which the actors express themselves by gestures. **2** gestures without words. *n.*

pan·try (pan′trē) a small room in which food, dishes, silver, table linen, etc. are kept. *n., pl.* **pan·tries.**

pants (pants) *Informal.* **1** the common name for trousers. **2** panties. *n. pl.*

pap (pap) soft food for infants or invalids. *n.*

pa·pa (po′pə or pä′pə) father; daddy. *n.*

pa·per (pā′pər) **1** a material in the form of thin sheets, made from wood pulp, rags, etc. and used for writing, printing, wrapping packages, and many other purposes: *This book is made of paper.* **2** a piece or sheet of paper. **3** a piece or sheet of paper with writing or printing on it; a document: *Important papers were stolen.* **4 papers,** *pl.* documents telling who or what one is. **5** newspaper. **6** an article; an essay: *Professor Smith read a paper on the teaching of English.* **7** made of paper: *paper dolls, paper money.* **8** like paper; thin: *almonds with paper shells.* **9** wallpaper. **10** to cover with wallpaper: *to paper a room.* 1–6, 9 *n.*, 7, 8 *adj.*, 10 *v.*

on paper, a in writing or in print. **b** in theory: *His idea is all right on paper but it won't work in practice.*

☞ **Paper** came into English through Old French from Latin *papyrus,* meaning 'paper,' which came from Greek *papyros,* meaning 'papyrus.'

pa·per·back (pā′pər bak′) a book with a paper binding or cover, usually sold at a low price. *n.*

pa·per·boy (pā′pər boi′) a boy who delivers or sells newspapers. *n.*

pa·per·girl (pā′pər gėrl′) a girl who delivers or sells newspapers. *n.*

pa·pier–mâché (pā′pər mə shā′) paper pulp mixed with some stiffener and used for modelling: *Papier-mâché becomes hard and strong when dry. n.*

☞ **Papier-mâché** is from French *papier mâché,* meaning 'chewed paper.'

pa·poose (pa püs′) a North American Indian baby. *n.*

☞ **Papoose** comes from a North American Indian word meaning 'child.'

pap·ri·ka (pap rē′kə) the ground, dried fruit of certain mild peppers used as a seasoning in food. *n.*

pa·py·rus (pə pī′rəs) **1** a tall water plant from which the ancient Egyptians, Greeks, and Romans made a kind of paper to write on. **2** a writing material made from the pith of papyrus plants. **3** an ancient record written on papyrus. *n., pl.* **pa·py·ri** (pə pī′rī or pə pī′rē)

☞ See note at **paper.**

par (pär) **1** equality; an equal level: *The gains and losses are about on a par. He is quite on a par with his brother in intelligence.* **2** an average or normal amount, degree, or condition: *A sick person feels below par.* **3** in golf, the number of strokes set as an expert score for any one hole: *The sum of the par scores for each hole is par for the course. n.*

par·a·ble (par′ə bəl or per′ə bəl) a short, simple story used to teach some truth or moral lesson: *Jesus taught in parables. n.*

A parachute. It is fastened on by means of a harness and can be folded into a pack that is usually worn on the back or the chest.

par·a·chute (par′ə shüt′ or per′ə shüt′) **1** an

apparatus made to give a slow, gradual fall to a person or thing that jumps or is dropped from an aircraft: *The top of a parachute resembles that of an umbrella and is made from nylon or silk.* **2** come or send down by a parachute: *The pilot of the burning plane parachuted safely to the ground.* 1 *n.*, 2 *v.*, **par·a·chut·ed, par·a·chut·ing.**

pa·rade (pə rād′) **1** a march for display; a procession: *The circus had a parade.* **2** to march in a procession; to walk proudly as if in a parade. **3** a group of people walking for display or pleasure. **4** a great show or display: *The modest man did not make a parade of his wealth.* **5** make a great show of. **6** a military display or review of troops. **7** come together in military order for review or inspection. 1, 3, 4, 6 *n.*, 2, 5, 7 *v.*

par·a·dise (par′ə dīs′ or per′ə dīs′) **1** heaven. **2** a place or condition of great happiness: *The summer camp was a paradise for him.* *n.*

par·a·dox (par′ə doks′ or per′ə doks′) **1** a statement that may be true but seems to say two opposite things: *'More haste, less speed' and 'The child is father to the man' are paradoxes.* **2** a person or thing that seems to be full of contradictions. *n.*

par·af·fin (par′ə fin or per′ə fin) a white, tasteless, waxy substance, used for making candles and for sealing jars of jelly or jam. *n.*

par·a·graph (par′ə graf′ or per′ə graf′) **1** a group of sentences relating to the same idea or topic and forming a distinct part of a chapter, letter, or other piece of writing: *Paragraphs usually begin on a new line and are indented.* **2** divide into paragraphs. **3** separate note or item of news in a newspaper. 1, 3 *n.*, 2 *v.*

par·a·keet (par′ə kēt or per′ə kēt) any of various small parrots, most of which have slender bodies and long tails. *n.*

par·al·lel (par′ə lel′ or per′ə lel′) **1** at or being the same distance apart everywhere, like the two rails of a railway track. **2** be at the same distance from throughout the length: *The street parallels the railway.* **3** a parallel line or surface. **4** any of the imaginary parallel circles around the earth, marking degrees of latitude: *The 49th parallel marks much of the boundary between Canada and the United States.* **5** a comparison to show likeness: *to draw a parallel between this winter and last winter.* **6** find a case that is similar or parallel to: *Can you parallel that for friendliness?* **7** similar; corresponding: *It is interesting to observe parallel customs in different countries.* **8** be like; be similar to: *Your story closely parallels what he told me.* 1, 7 *adj.*, 2, 6, 8 *v.*, **par·al·leled, par·al·lel·ing;** 3–5 *n.*

par·a·lyse or **par·a·lyze** (par′ə līz′ or per′ə līz′) **1** affect with a lessening or loss of the power of motion or feeling: *His left arm was paralysed.* **2** make powerless or helplessly inactive; cripple: *Fear paralysed my mind.* *v.*, **par·a·lysed** or **par·a·lyzed, par·a·lys·ing** or **par·a·lyz·ing.**

pa·ral·y·sis (pə ral′ə sis) **1** a lessening or loss of the power of motion or sensation in any part of the body: *The accident left him with paralysis of the legs.* **2** a condition of helpless lack of activity; a crippling: *The war caused a paralysis of trade.* *n.*, *pl.* **pa·ral·y·ses** (pə ral′ə sēz).

par·a·mount (par′ə mount or per′ə mount′) above others; chief in importance; supreme: *Truth is of paramount importance.* *adj.*

par·a·pet (par′ə pət or per′ə pət, par′ə pet′ or per′ə pet′) **1** a low wall or bank of stones, earth, etc. to protect soldiers. See **rampart** for picture. **2** a low wall at the edge of a balcony, roof, bridge, etc. *n.*

par·a·pher·nal·ia (par′ə fər nā′lē ə or per′ə fər nā′lē-ə, par′ə fər nāl′yə or per′ə fər nāl′yə) personal belongings or equipment: *He leaves his hockey paraphernalia all over the house.* *n. pl.*

par·a·site (par′ə sīt or per′ə sīt) **1** an animal or plant that lives on or in another from which it gets its food: *Lice are parasites on animals. Mistletoe is a parasite on oak trees.* **2** a person who lives on others without making any useful and fitting return: *The lazy man was a parasite on his family.* *n.*

par·a·sol (par′ə sol′ or per′ə sol′, par′ə sôl′ or per′ə sôl′) a light umbrella used as a sunshade. *n.*

☛ **Parasol** comes from a French variation of an Italian word *parasole,* a combining of a form of the verb *parare,* meaning 'to defend or shelter from,' and *sole,* meaning 'sun.' Compare **umbrella.**

par·a·troop·er (par′ə trüp′ər or per′ə trüp′ər) a soldier trained to use a parachute for descent from an aircraft into a battle area. *n.*

par·cel (pär′səl) **1** a bundle of things wrapped or packed together; a package: *The lady had her arms filled with parcels and gifts.* **2** a container with things packed in it: *Put your shirts in this parcel.* **3** a piece: *a parcel of land.* **4** a group; lot; collection: *He agreed to buy the whole parcel of books.* **5** make into a parcel. 1–4 *n.*, 5 *v.*, **par·celled** or **par·celed, par·cel·ling** or **par·cel·ing.**
parcel out, divide into portions or distribute in portions.

parch (pärch) make or become dry or thirsty: *He was parched with the heat.* *v.*

parch·ment (pärch′mənt) **1** the skin of sheep or goats, prepared for use as writing material. **2** a manuscript or document written on parchment. **3** a kind of paper that looks like parchment. *n.*

par·don (pär′dən) **1** forgiveness: *I beg your pardon but I'm afraid I am late.* **2** forgive: *Grandmother pardons us when we make mischief.* **3** set free from punishment: *The Governor General pardoned the offender.* **4** setting free from punishment. 1, 4 *n.*, 2, 3 *v.*

pare (per) **1** cut, trim, or shave off the outer part of; peel: *to pare an apple.* **2** cut away little by little: *to pare down expenses.* *v.*, **pared, par·ing.**

☛ **Pare, pair,** and **pear** are pronounced the same.

par·ent (per′ənt) **1** a father or mother. **2** any animal or plant that produces offspring or seed. **3** a source; cause: *Danger is the parent of fear.* *n.*

par·ent·age (per′ən tij) descent from parents; family line; ancestors. *n.*

pa·ren·tal (pə ren′təl) of or having to do with a parent or parents; like a parent's: *parental advice.* *adj.*

pa·ren·the·ses (pə ren′thə sēz′) plural of **parenthesis:** *The pronunciations on this page are enclosed in parentheses.* *n.*

pa·ren·the·sis (pə ren′thə sis) **1** a word, phrase, sentence, etc. inserted within a sentence to explain or qualify something. **2** either or both of two curved lines ( ) used to set off such an expression. *n.*, *pl.* **pa·ren·the·ses.**

hat, āge, fär; let, ēqual, tėrm; it, īce
hot, ōpen, ôrder; oil, out; cup, pu̇t, rüle
əbove, takən, pencəl, lemən, circəs
ch, child; ng, long; sh, ship
th, thin; ᴛʜ, then; zh, measure

Parent–Teacher Association an organization made up of parents and teachers who meet from time to time in the interests of school children.

pa·ri·ah (pə rī′ə) an outcast. *n.*

par·ish (par′ish or per′ish) **1** a district that has its own church and clergyman. **2** the people of a parish. **3** in New Brunswick, a political unit similar to a township. **4** in Quebec, a municipality similar to a township and related to a religious parish. *n.*

pa·rish·ion·er (pə rish′ə nər) a member of a parish. *n.*

park (pärk) **1** a piece of land in or near a city, town, etc. set apart for public recreation: *Let's have a picnic in the park.* **2** a large area of land kept as a recreation area (for camping, picnicking, hiking, canoeing, etc.) and as a refuge for wildlife: *Canada has fine national and provincial parks.* **3** leave an automobile, etc. for a time in a certain place: *Park your car here.* **4** a place to leave an automobile, etc. for a time. **5** *Informal.* place, put, or leave: *Just park your books on the table.* 1, 2, 4 *n.*, 3, 5 *v.*

Parkas

par·ka (pär′kə) **1** a fur jacket with a hood, worn in the North. **2** a long woollen shirt or jacket with a hood: *Parkas are popular as winter wear in many parts of Canada.* *n.*

park·land (pärk′land′) **1** the region between the foothills of the Rockies and the prairie. **2** the wooded region between the Barren Ground and the prairie. **3** land kept free from buildings, factories, etc. and maintained as a public park: *Parklands are intended to preserve the scenic beauty of the countryside.* *n.*

park·way (pärk′wā′) a broad road through an area kept up as a park, made attractive by grass, trees, flowers, etc.: *There is a beautiful parkway running through Ottawa.* *n.*

par·ley (pär′lē) **1** a conference or informal talk, especially one with an enemy to discuss terms: *The general held a parley with the enemy about exchanging prisoners.* **2** discuss matters, especially with an enemy. 1 *n.*, *pl.* **par·leys;** 2 *v.*, **par·leyed, par·ley·ing.**

par·lia·ment (pär′lə mənt) an assembly of elected members who make up the highest lawmaking body in certain countries, including Canada and Great Britain: *The Canadian Parliament is composed of the Senate and the House of Commons.* *n.*

par·lia·men·ta·ry (pär′lə men′tə rē) **1** of a parliament: *parliamentary authority.* **2** according to the rules and customs of a parliament or other lawmaking body: *A club is run by the rules of parliamentary procedure.* *adj.*

par·lor or **par·lour** (pär′lər) **1** a room for receiving or entertaining guests; a sitting room or living room. **2** a room or rooms specially furnished or equipped for a certain kind of business: *a beauty parlor, a funeral parlor.* **3** a place where refreshments of various kinds are sold: *an ice-cream parlor, a beer parlor.* *n.*

pa·role (pə rōl′) **1** a conditional release from prison or jail before the full term is served. **2** give a conditional release from jail or prison before the full term is served: *The prisoner was paroled after serving two years of his three-year sentence.* 1 *n.*, 2 *v.*

A grey parrot — about 30 cm long with the tail

par·rot (par′ət or per′ət) **1** a bird having a stout, hooked bill and, often, bright-colored feathers: *Some parrots can imitate sounds and repeat words and sentences.* **2** a person who repeats words or acts without understanding them. **3** repeat without understanding: *The small child parroted the words of the song.* 1, 2 *n.*, 3 *v.*

par·ry (par′ē or per′ē) **1** ward off; turn aside a thrust or weapon: *He parried the sword with his dagger.* **2** avoid; dodge: *She parried our question by asking us one.* *v.*, **par·ried, par·ry·ing, par·ries.**

pars·ley (pärs′lē) a garden plant having finely divided, fragrant leaves: *Parsley is used to flavor food and to garnish meat or fish.* *n.*

pars·nip (pärs′nip) a vegetable that is the long, tapering, whitish root of a plant belonging to the same family as the carrot. *n.*

par·son (pär′sən) **1** a minister in charge of a parish. **2** any clergyman or minister. *n.*

par·son·age (pär′sən ij) the house provided for a minister by a church. *n.*

part (pärt) **1** something less than the whole: *He ate part of an apple.* **2** each of several equal quantities into which a whole may be divided; a fraction: *A dime is a tenth part of a dollar.* **3** a thing that helps to make up a whole: *A radio has many parts.* **4** a share: *He had no part in the mischief.* **5** a side in a dispute or contest: *He always takes his brother's part.* **6** a character in a play; the words spoken by a character: *Anne took the part of the heroine in our play.* **7** divide into two or more pieces. **8** force apart; divide: *The mounted policeman parted the crowd.* **9** go apart; separate: *The friends parted in anger.* **10** a dividing line left in combing one's hair. **11** comb the hair away from a dividing line. **12** one of the voices or instruments in music: *The four parts in singing are soprano, alto, tenor, and bass.* **13** the music for one voice or instrument. **14** partly; in some measure or degree. 1–6, 10, 12, 13 *n.*, 7–9, 11 *v.*, 14 *adv.*

for the most part, mostly: *The attempts were for the most part unsuccessful.*
in good part, in a friendly or gracious way: *He took the teasing in good part.*
in part, in some measure or degree; to some extent; partly.
part and parcel, a necessary part: *Practising is part and parcel of learning to play the piano.*
part with, give up; let go.
take part, take or have a share.

par·take (pär tāk′) take or have a share or part: *We are having lunch. Will you partake? Will you partake of this cake?* *v.,* **par·took, par·tak·en, par·tak·ing.**

par·tak·en (pär tāk′ən) See **partake.** *v.*

Par·the·non (pär′thə non′ or pär′thə nən) in Athens, the temple of the goddess Athena on the Acropolis: *The Parthenon is considered one of the finest examples of ancient Greek architecture.* *n.*

par·tial (pär′shəl) **1** not complete; not total: *Father has made a partial payment on our new car.* **2** inclined to favor one side more than another; favoring unfairly: *A father should not be partial to any one of his children.* *adj.* —**par′tial·ly,** *adv.*
partial to, having a liking for; favorably inclined: *He is partial to sports.*

par·tic·i·pant (pär tis′ə pənt) one who shares or participates. *n.*

par·tic·i·pate (pär tis′ə pāt′) have a share; take part: *The teacher participated in the children's games.* *v.,* **par·tic·i·pat·ed, par·tic·i·pat·ing.**

par·tic·i·pa·tion (pär tis′ə pā′shən) participating; taking part. *n.*

par·ti·cle (pär′tə kəl) a very little bit: *I got a particle of dust in my eye.* *n.*

par·tic·u·lar (pər tik′yə lər) **1** apart from others; considered separately; single: *That particular chair is already sold.* **2** belonging to some one person, thing, group, occasion, etc.: *His particular task is to care for the dog. A particular characteristic of a skunk is its smell.* **3** different from others; unusual; special: *This vacation was of particular importance to her, for she was going to Brazil. Harry is a particular friend of Dick.* **4** hard to please; wanting everything to be just right; very careful: *She is very particular; nothing but the best will do.* **5** an individual part; an item or point: *The work is complete in every particular.* 1–4 *adj.,* 5 *n.*
in particular, especially: *We drove around, not going anywhere in particular.*

par·tic·u·lar·ly (pər tik′yə lər lē) **1** in a high degree; especially: *The teacher praised Peggy particularly. I am particularly fond of Jim. She mentioned that point particularly.* **2** in a particular manner; in detail; in all its parts: *The inspector examined the machine particularly.* *adv.*

part·ing (pär′ting) **1** a departure; going away or taking leave: *The friends were sad at parting.* **2** given, taken, spoken, done, etc. on going away: *a parting gift, a parting request, a parting shot.* **3** a division; a separation. **4** a place of division or separation: *Her hair is arranged with a side parting.* 1, 3, 4 *n.,* 2 *adj.*

par·ti·san (pär′tə zən or par′tə zan′) **1** a strong supporter of a person, party, or cause; one whose support is based on feeling rather than on reasoning. **2** of a partisan; like a partisan: *partisan politics.* 1 *n.,* 2 *adj.*

par·ti·tion (pär tish′ən) **1** a division into parts: *the partition of a man's wealth when he dies.* **2** divide into parts: *to partition an empire among three brothers, to partition a house into rooms.* **3** something that divides and separates, such as a removable wall between rooms. 1, 3 *n.,* 2 *v.*

par·ti·zan (pär′tə zən or pär′tə zan′) See **partisan.**

part·ly (pärt′lē) in part; in some measure or degree: *He is partly to blame.* *adv.*

part·ner (pärt′nər) **1** one who shares: *My sister was the partner of my walks.* **2** a member of a company or firm who shares the risks and profits of the business. **3** a wife or husband. **4** a companion in a dance. **5** a player on the same team or side during a game. *n.*

part·ner·ship (pärt′nər ship′) **1** being a partner; an association; a joint interest: *a business partnership, the partnership of marriage.* **2** a company or firm with two or more partners (def. 2). *n.*

part of speech any of the classes into which words are grouped according to their use or function in sentences: *Nouns, verbs, adjectives, and adverbs are four of the parts of speech.*
☛ Many words in English can function as more than one part of speech. In *I can run fast* the word *run* is a verb; in *I am going for a run* the same word is a noun.

par·took (pär tu̇k′) See **partake.** *v.*

A Hungarian partridge — about 30 cm long with the tail

par·tridge (pär′trij) any of several game birds belonging to the same family as the quail and pheasant. *n., pl.* **par·tridg·es** or **par·tridge.**

part–time (pärt′tīm′) for part of the usual time: *a part-time job.* *adj.*

par·ty (pär′tē) **1** a gathering of a group of people to have a good time together: *She had a party on her birthday.* **2** a group of people doing something together: *a sewing party, a dinner party, a scouting party.* **3** a group of people wanting the same kind of government or action: *the Liberal Party, the Conservative Party.* **4** of or having to do with a party: *party feeling.* **5** one who takes part in, aids, or knows about: *He was a party to our secret.* **6** *Informal.* a person: *He lent the book to a third party.* **7** any one of two or more persons or families using the same telephone line. 1–3, 5–7 n., pl. **par·ties;** 4 *adj.*

party line a telephone line having more than one person or family making use of it.

pass (pas) **1** go by; move past: *The parade passed. We passed the big truck. Many people pass our house every day.* **2** move on: *The days pass quickly. The salesman passed from house to house.* **3** go from one to

hat, āge, fär; let, ēqual, tėrm; it, īce
hot, ōpen, ôrder; oil, out; cup, pu̇t, rüle
əbove, takən, pencəl, lemən, circəs
ch, child; ng, long; sh, ship
th, thin; ᴛʜ, then; zh, measure

another: *The property passed from father to son. Hot words passed when the men quarrelled.* **4** hand around: *Please pass the butter.* **5** get through or by: *The ship passed the channel. The bill passed Parliament.* **6** be successful in an examination: *He passed arithmetic.* **7** success in an examination. **8** the act of passing: *The invading army made a swift pass through the country.* **9** come to an end; die: *King Arthur passed in peace.* **10** go beyond; exceed; surpass: *Your story passes belief.* **11** use or spend: *We passed the days happily.* **12** go away; depart: *The pain will soon pass.* **13** change: *Water passes to a solid state when it freezes.* **14** take place; happen: *She can tell you all that has passed.* **15** be accepted: *That rayon material can pass as silk. She could pass for twenty.* **16** give approval to: *The inspector passed the item after examining it.* **17** in card playing, to give up a chance to bid or to play a hand. **18** go without notice: *He was rude, but let that pass.* **19** move: *Pass your hand over the velvet and feel how soft it is.* **20** a note, licence, etc. allowing one to do something: *He needed a pass to enter the fort.* **21** a free ticket: *a pass to the circus.* **22** a state or condition: *Things have reached a strange pass when children give orders to their parents.* **23** a narrow road, path, channel, etc.: *A pass crosses the mountains.* **24** throw or direct something from one person to another: *He passed the puck too far ahead.* **25** a throw of the ball to another player in basketball, football, etc. 1–6, 9–19, 24 *v.*, **passed, pass·ing;** 7, 8, 20–23, 25 *n.* **—pas′ser,** *n.*

bring to pass, cause to be; accomplish.

come to pass, take place; happen.

pass out, a give out; distribute. **b** *Slang.* faint, lose consciousness.

pass over, fail to notice; overlook; disregard: *The teacher passed over my mistake.*

pass up, give up; renounce: *pass up a chance to go to college.*

pas·sage (pas′ij) **1** a hall or way through a building; passageway. **2** a means of passing; a way through: *He asked for passage through the crowd.* **3** passing: *the passage of time.* **4** a piece from a speech, writing, or musical composition: *a passage from the Bible.* **5** a trip or journey, especially by sea: *We had a stormy passage across the Atlantic.* **6** making into law by vote of a legislature: *the passage of a bill.* *n.*

pas·sage·way (pas′ij wā′) a way along which one can pass; a passage: *Halls and alleys are passageways.* *n.*

pas·sen·ger (pas′ən jər) a traveller in a train, bus, boat, airplane, etc., usually one who pays a fare. *n.*

passenger pigeon a wild pigeon of North America, no longer in existence: *Passenger pigeons flew great distances in large flocks.*

pass·er–by (pas′ər bī′) a person who passes by. *n., pl.* **pass·ers-by.**

pass·ing (pas′ing) **1** going by; a departure: *the passing of summer.* **2** done or given in passing: *a passing smile.* **3** allowing one to pass an examination or test: *I scored a passing mark.* **4** not lasting; fleeting: *a passing idea; a passing fashion.* 1 *n.*, 2–4 *adj.*

in passing, by the way; incidentally: *In passing, I'd like to compliment you on your excellent work.*

pas·sion (pash′ən) **1** very strong feeling: *Love and hate are passions.* **2** a rage; violent anger: *He flew into a passion.* **3** a very strong liking: *She has a passion for music.* **4** anything for which a strong liking is felt: *Music is her passion.* **5 the Passion,** the sufferings of Jesus on the Cross or after the Last Supper. *n.*

pas·sion·ate (pash′ən it) **1** having or showing strong feelings: *The pioneers of our country were passionate believers in freedom.* **2** easily moved to strong feeling. **3** resulting from strong feeling: *He made a passionate speech against surrender.* *adj.*

pas·sive (pas′iv) **1** not acting in return; being acted on without itself acting: *a passive mind or disposition.* **2** not resisting; yielding or submitting to the will of another: *The slaves gave passive obedience to their master.* *adj.*

Pass·o·ver (pas′ō′vər) an annual Jewish holiday in memory of the escape of the Hebrews from Egypt. It is so called because according to the Bible a destroying angel 'passed over' the houses of the Hebrews when it killed the first-born child in every Egyptian home. *n.*

pass·port (pas′pôrt) a paper or book giving official permission to travel in a foreign country, under the protection of one's own government. **2** anything that gives one admission or acceptance: *An interest in gardening was a passport to my aunt's favor.* *n.*

pass·word (pas′wėrd′) a secret word or phrase that identifies a person speaking it and allows him to pass. *n.*

past (past) **1** gone by; ended: *Summer is past. Our troubles are past.* **2** just gone by: *The past year was full of trouble. For some time past she has been ill.* **3** time gone by; time before: *Life began far back in the past.* **4** a past life or history; what has happened: *He cannot change his past.* **5** the verb form that refers to past time: *The past of 'do' is 'did.'* **6** beyond; farther on than: *The arrow went past the mark.* **7** after; later than: *half past two. It is past noon.* **8** so as to pass by or beyond: *In the morning the bus goes past our house once every ten minutes.* 1, 2 *adj.*, 3–5 *n.*, 6–8 *prep.*

☛ **Past** is never used as a verb. The past tense of the word **pass** is **passed.**

paste (pāst) **1** a mixture, such as flour and water, that will stick things together. **2** to stick with paste. **3** dough for pastry. **4** a soft mixture: *Clay and water is mixed into a paste for making the pottery.* **5** a hard, glassy material used in making imitations of precious stones. 1, 3–5 *n.*, 2 *v.*, **past·ed, past·ing.**

pas·tel (pas tel′) **1** a kind of crayon used in drawing. **2** a drawing made with such crayons. **3** a soft, pale shade of some color. **4** soft and pale: *pastel pink, pastel shades.* 1–3 *n.*, 4 *adj.*

pas·teur·ize (pas′chər īz′) heat milk, beer, etc. to a high temperature and chill it quickly to destroy harmful bacteria. *v.*

☛ **Pasteurize** is named after Louis *Pasteur* (1822–1895), a French chemist who discovered this way of destroying bacteria.

pas·time (pas′tīm′) a pleasant way of passing time; a form of amusement or recreation: *Games and sports are pastimes.* *n.*

pas·tor (pas′tər) a minister in charge of a church; a spiritual guide. *n.*

pas·tor·al (pas′tər əl) 1 of shepherds or country life: *a pastoral poem.* 2 simple or naturally beautiful like the country: *a pastoral scene.* 3 of a pastor or his duties: *a pastoral letter. adj.*

pas·try (pās′trē) 1 food made of baked flour paste, made rich with lard or butter. 2 pies, tarts, and other foods wholly or partly made of rich flour paste. 3 a pie, tart, etc. of this kind. *n., pl.* **pas·tries.**

pas·tur·age (pas′chər ij) 1 the growing grass and other plants that cattle, sheep, or horses feed on. 2 pasture land. *n.*

pas·ture (pas′chər) 1 a grassy field or hillside; grassy land on which cattle, sheep, or horses can feed. 2 grass and other growing plants: *These fields afford excellent pasture.* 3 put cattle, sheep, etc. out to pasture. 4 feed on growing grass, etc. 1, 2 *n.,* 3, 4 *v.,* **pas·tured, pas·tur·ing.**

pat (pat) 1 strike or tap lightly with something flat: *The baker patted the dough into a flat cake.* 2 tap lightly with the hand as a sign of sympathy, approval, or affection: *to pat a dog.* 3 a light stroke or tap with the hand or something flat. 4 the sound made by patting. 5 a small mass, especially of butter. 6 apt; suitable; to the point: *a pat reply.* 1, 2 *v.,* **pat·ted, pat·ting;** 3–5 *n.,* 6 *adj.*

have pat or **know pat,** *Informal.* have perfectly; know thoroughly: *John has the history lesson pat.*

stand pat, *Informal.* keep the same position; hold to things as they are and refuse to change: *Many people were angry with the government but the Prime Minister stood pat.*

patch (pach) 1 a piece of some material put on to mend a hole or a tear. 2 a protective pad for placing over an injured eye: *The doctor ordered him to wear a patch over his right eye.* 3 a small piece of cloth. 4 put patches on; mend; protect or decorate with a patch or patches. 5 a small area different from that around it: *a patch of brown on the skin.* 6 a piece of ground: *a garden patch.* 1–3, 5, 6 *n.,* 4 *v.*

patch up, a put an end to; settle: *He did his best to patch up the quarrel.* **b** put right hastily or for a time: *patch up a leaking tap.* **c** put together hastily or poorly: *Mother patched up a costume for Halloween.*

patch·work (pach′wėrk′) 1 pieces of cloth of various colors or shapes sewn together: *She made a cover of patchwork for the cushion.* 2 anything like this: *From the airplane, we saw a patchwork of fields and woods.* 3 made in this way: *a patchwork quilt.* 4 sewing things in this way: *Mother enjoys patchwork.* 1, 2, 4 *n.,* 3 *adj.*

pate (pāt) the top of the head; the head: *a bald pate. n.*

pa·tel·la (pə tel′ə) kneecap. *n.*

pat·ent (pat′ənt or pā′tənt for 1–4, pā′tənt for 5) 1 a right given by a government to a person by which he is the only one allowed to make, use, or sell a new invention for a certain number of years. 2 protected by a patent. 3 get a patent for: *The inventor patented many inventions.* 4 an official documentation from a government giving a right or privilege. 5 evident; plain: *It is patent that cats dislike dogs.* 1, 4 *n.,* 2, 5 *adj.,* 3 *v.*

patent leather leather with a very glossy, smooth surface, usually black: *Some shoes are made of patent leather.*

pa·ter·nal (pə tėr′nəl) 1 of or like a father; fatherly. 2 related on the father's side of the family: *Every person has two paternal grandparents and two maternal grandparents. adj.*

path (path) 1 a track made by people or animals walking: *A path is usually too narrow for cars or wagons.* 2 a way made to walk upon: *He laid stone for a garden path.* 3 a line or route along which a person or thing moves; a track: *The moon has a regular path through the sky.* 4 a way of acting or behaving; a way of life: *Some choose paths of glory; some choose paths of ease. n., pl.* **paths** (paᴛʜz).

pa·thet·ic (pə thet′ik) pitiful; arousing pity: *A lost child is a pathetic sight. adj.*

pa·thos (pā′thos) the quality in speech, writing, music, events, or a scene that arouses a feeling of pity or sadness. *n.*

path·way (path′wā′) path. *n.*

pa·tience (pā′shəns) 1 the ability to accept calmly things that trouble or annoy, or that require long waiting or effort: *When watching the mouse hole, the cat showed patience.* 2 long, hard work; steady effort: *This carving shows the skill and patience of the artist. n.*

pa·tient (pā′shənt) 1 having patience; showing patience. 2 a person who is being treated by a doctor, dentist, etc. 1 *adj.,* 2 *n.*

pat·i·o (pat′ē ō) 1 an inner court or yard open to the sky: *Houses in Spanish countries are often built around patios.* 2 a terrace for outdoor meals, lounging, etc. *n., pl.* **pat·i·os.**

pa·tri·arch (pā′trē ärk′) 1 the father and ruler of a family or tribe: *In the Bible, Abraham, Isaac, and Jacob were patriarchs.* 2 a venerable old man. *n.*

pa·tri·ot (pā′trē ət or pat′rē ət) a person who loves his country and gives it loyal support. *n.*

pa·tri·ot·ic (pā′trē ot′ik or pat′rē ot′ik) 1 loving one's country. 2 showing love and loyal support of one's country. *adj.*

pa·tri·ot·ism (pā′trē ət iz′əm or pat′rē ət iz′əm) love and loyal support of one's country. *n.*

pa·trol (pə trōl′) 1 go the rounds as a watchman or a policeman does: *The sentries patrolled the camp.* 2 the persons who patrol: *The patrol was changed at midnight.* 3 the act or process of going the rounds to watch or guard: *He was on patrol last night.* 4 a group of soldiers, ships, or airplanes sent out to find out all they can about the enemy. 5 one of the subdivisions of a troop of Boy scouts or Girl Guides: *There are eight people in a patrol, including a patrol leader and a second.* 1 *v.,* **pa·trolled, pa·trol·ling;** 2–5 *n.*

pa·tron (pā′trən) 1 a person who buys regularly at a given store or goes regularly to a certain hotel, restaurant, etc. 2 a person who gives his approval and support to some person, art, cause, or undertaking: *a patron of artists.* 3 guarding; protecting: *a patron saint.* 1, 2 *n.,* 3 *adj.*

pa·tron·age (pā′trən ij or pat′rən ij) 1 the regular business given to a hotel, store, etc. by customers. 2 the favor, encouragement, or support given by a patron. 3 the power to give jobs or favors: *the patronage of a mayor or reeve. n.*

pa·tron·ize (pā′trən īz′ or pat′rən īz′) 1 be a regular customer of; give regular business to: *We patronize our neighborhood stores.* 2 act as a patron toward; support or protect: *to patronize the ballet.* **3** treat in a haughty, condescending way: *Children do not like being patronized by adults.* *v.,* **pa·tron·ized, pa·tron·iz·ing.**

pat·ter[1] (pat′ər) **1** make rapid taps: *The rain pattered on the windowpane. Bare feet pattered along the hard floor.* **2** a series of quick taps, or the sound they make: *the patter of rain, the patter of little feet.* 1 *v.,* 2 *n.*

pat·ter[2] (pat′ər) **1** talk or say rapidly and easily, without much thought: *patter a prayer.* **2** rapid and easy talk: *a magician's patter.* 1 *v.,* 2 *n.*

pat·tern (pat′ərn) **1** an arrangement of forms and colors; a design: *the patterns of wallpaper, rugs, cloth, or jewellery.* **2** a model or guide for something to be made: *She used a paper pattern in cutting out her new dress.* **3** a fine example; a model to be followed: *The captain was a pattern of manliness.* **4** make according to a pattern: *She patterned herself after her mother.* **5** any arrangement: *behavior pattern, speech pattern.* 1–3, 5 *n.,* 4 *v.*

pat·ty (pat′ē) **1** a hollow shell of pastry filled with chicken, oysters, etc. **2** a small, round, flat piece of food or candy: *chicken patties, peppermint patties.* *n., pl.* **pat·ties.**

paunch (ponch or pônch) **1** the belly or stomach. **2** a large, protruding belly. *n.*

pau·per (po′pər or pô′pər) a very poor person; a person supported by charity. *n.*

pause (poz or pôz) **1** a moment of silence; a brief stop; a rest: *He made a short pause and then went on reading.* **2** stop for a time; wait: *The dog paused when he heard me.* **3** in music, a sign (𝄑 or 𝄐) above or below a note or rest, meaning that it is to be held for a longer time. 1, 3 *n.,* 2 *v.,* **paused, paus·ing.**

pave (pāv) cover a street, sidewalk, etc. with a pavement: *pave a road with concrete.* *v.,* **paved, pav·ing.**
pave the way, make preparation; make something smooth or easy: *He paved the way for me by doing careful work.*

pave·ment (pāv′mənt) **1** a covering or surface for streets, sidewalks, etc., made of stones, gravel, concrete, asphalt, etc. **2** a paved road. *n.*

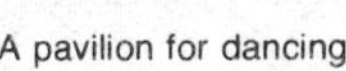

A pavilion for dancing

pa·vil·ion (pə vil′yən) **1** a light building, usually one somewhat open, used for shelter, pleasure, etc. **2** a large tent, often luxurious, for entertainment or shelter. **3** any building that houses an exhibition at a fair. *n.*

pav·ing (pāv′ing) **1** the material for pavement. **2** pavement. *n.*

paw (po or pô) **1** the foot of a four-footed animal having claws: *Cats and dogs have paws.* **2** strike or scrape with the paws, hoofs, or feet: *The cat pawed the mouse she had caught. The horse pawed the ground, eager to be going.* **3** *Informal.* handle awkwardly or rudely: *The women pawed the dresses on the bargain counter.* 1 *n.,* 2, 3 *v.*

pawn[1] (pon or pôn) **1** leave something with another person as security that borrowed money will be returned; pledge: *He pawned his watch to buy food until he could get work.* **2** something left as security. 1 *v.,* 2 *n.*
in pawn, in another's possession as security: *His watch is in pawn to the man who lent him money.*

hat, āge, fär; let, ēqual, tėrm; it, īce
hot, ōpen, ôrder; oil, out; cup, pu̇t, rüle
əbove, takən, pencəl, lemən, circəs
ch, child; ng, long; sh, ship
th, thin; ᴛʜ, then; zh, measure

pawn[2] (pon or pôn) **1** in the game of chess, one of the 16 pieces that are of lowest value and are often given up to gain some advantage. **2** an unimportant person or thing used by somebody to gain some advantage for himself: *The rebel general used his friends as pawns in his race for power.* *n.*

pawn·bro·ker (pon′brō′kər or pôn′brō′kər) a person who lends money on articles that are left with him as security for the loan. *n.*

pawn·shop (pon′shop′ or pôn′shop′) a pawnbroker's shop. *n.*

pay (pā) **1** give money for goods, services, or work: *Father paid the plumber by cheque.* **2** money given for goods, services, or work; wages or salary: *He gets his pay every Saturday.* **3** give money for: *Pay your fare.* **4** give what is due: *He owes it and must pay.* **5** give; offer; make: *to pay attention, to pay a compliment, pay a visit.* **6** be worth while: *It paid her to be patient.* **7** a return for favors or hurts: *Dislike is the pay for being mean.* **8** reward or punish: *He paid them for their insults by causing them trouble.* **9** requiring a cash payment or the putting in of coins or tokens: *a pay telephone.* 1, 3–6, 8 *v.,* **paid, pay·ing;** 2, 7, 9 *n.*
pay back, a return borrowed money. **b** give the same treatment as received: *I'll pay her back for her hospitality by inviting her to dinner.*
pay off, a give all the money that is owed; pay in full. **b** get even with; get revenge on.
pay up, pay; pay in full.

pay·ment (pā′mənt) **1** the act or fact of paying. **2** the amount paid: *a monthly payment of $10.* **3** pay; reward or punishment: *The family's happiness was the only payment Mother wanted.* *n.*

pea (pē) **1** a round seed in the pod of a plant, used as a vegetable. See **pod** for picture. **2** the plant itself. **3 sweet pea,** a climbing plant with delicate flowers of many colors. *n., pl.* **peas.**

peace (pēs) **1** freedom from war or strife of any kind; public quiet, order, and security: *We are working for world peace.* **2** an agreement between enemies to end war. **3** quiet; calm; stillness: *peace of mind. We enjoy the peace of the country.* *n.*
at peace, a not in a state of war. **b** not quarrelling. **c** in a state of quietness; quiet; peaceful.
hold one's peace, be silent; keep still.
☛ **Peace** and **piece** are pronounced the same.

peace·a·ble (pēs′ə bəl) liking peace; keeping peace: *Peaceable people keep out of quarrels.* *adj.*

peace·ful (pēs′fəl) **1** quiet; calm; full of peace: *It was peaceful in the mountains.* **2** keeping peace: *peaceful neighbors.* *adj.*

peace pipe a pipe smoked by North American Indians as a token or pledge of peace; a calumet.

peach (pēch) **1** a juicy, roundish fruit having a soft, pinkish-yellow, fuzzy skin and a rough stone or pit: *Peaches grow on trees that blossom in the spring.* **2** the tree it grows on. **3** yellowish pink. 1–3 *n.*, 3 *adj.*

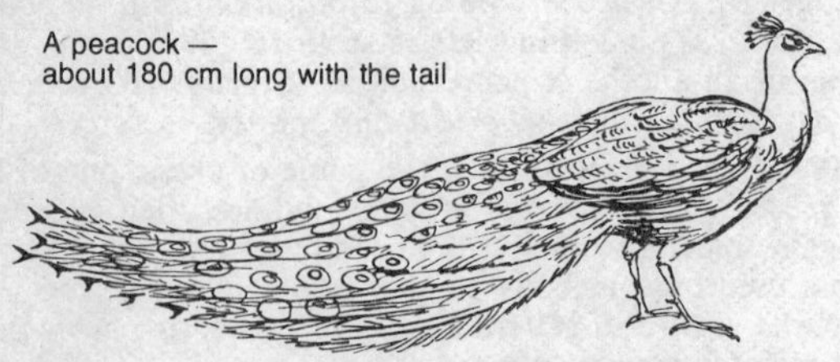
A peacock — about 180 cm long with the tail

pea·cock (pē′kok′) **1** a large male bird having beautiful green, blue, and gold feathers, and a splendid tail: *The peacock's tail feathers have spots resembling eyes and can be spread out and held upright like a fan.* **2** a person who is vain and fond of showing off. *n., pl.* **pea·cocks** or **pea·cock.**

pea·hen (pē′hen′) the female of the peacock. *n.*

peak (pēk) **1** the pointed top of a mountain or hill: *snowy peaks.* **2** a mountain that stands alone. **3** any pointed end or top: *the peak of a beard, the peak of a roof.* **4** the highest point: *to reach the peak of one's profession.* **5** the front part or the brim of a cap. *n.*
☛ **Peak** and **peek** are pronounced the same.

peaked (pēkt or pēk′id) having a peak; pointed: *a peaked hat. adj.*

peal (pēl) **1** a loud, long sound: *a peal of thunder, peals of laughter.* **2** the loud ringing of bells. **3** a chime; a set of bells. **4** ring out; ring: *The bells pealed forth their message of Christmas joy.* 1–3 *n.*, 4 *v.*

pea·nut (pē′nut′) a seed like a nut, growing in pods that ripen underground: *Peanuts are used for food when roasted and their oil is used in cooking. n.*

peanut butter a food made of peanuts ground until soft and smooth: *Peanut butter is spread on bread, crackers, etc.*

A pear

pear (per) **1** a sweet, juicy fruit rounded at one end and smaller toward the stem end. **2** the tree it grows on. *n.*
☛ **Pear, pair,** and **pare** are pronounced the same.

pearl (pėrl) **1** a white or blue-grey gem that has a soft shine like satin: *Pearls are formed inside the shell of a kind of oyster, or in other similar shellfish.* **2** anything that looks like a pearl, such as a dewdrop, or a tear. **3** a very fine one of its kind: *She is a pearl among women.* **4** very pale, clear, bluish grey. **5** mother-of-pearl: *pearl buttons.* 1–5 *n.*, 4 *adj.*

peas·ant (pez′ənt) **1** a farmer of the working class in Europe. **2** of peasants: *peasant labor. n.*

peas·ant·ry (pez′ənt rē) peasants. *n.*

pea·shoot·er (pē′shü′tər) a toy blowgun through which to blow dried peas and other small objects. *n.*

peat (pēt) a mass of partly rotted moss, grass, or other plants dug, cut, and dried for use as fuel. *n.*

peat moss a kind of moss from which peat has formed or may form. It is dried and used as fertilizer.

peb·ble (peb′əl) a small stone, usually worn smooth and round by being rolled about by water. *n.*

peb·bly (peb′lē) having many pebbles; covered with pebbles: *The pebbly beach hurt our bare feet. adj.*

pe·can (pē′kan or pi kan′) **1** an edible nut that is shaped like an olive and has a smooth, thin shell. **2** the tree it grows on: *Pecans grow in the southern United States. n.*

peck[1] (pek) **1** strike at and pick up with the beak: *The hen pecked corn.* **2** a stroke made with the beak: *The hen gave me a peck.* **3** make by striking with the beak: *The woodpeckers pecked holes in the trees.* **4** a hole or mark made by pecking: *We saw the pecks in the wood.* **5** make a pecking motion. **6** *Informal.* eat only a little, bit by bit: *Because she is not feeling well, she just pecks at her food.* **7** *Informal.* a light or hurried kiss. 1, 3, 5, 6 *v.*, 2, 4, 7 *n.*

peck[2] (pek) **1** a unit of dry measure, eight quarts or one fourth of a bushel (about 9.1 litres): *a peck of beans, a peck of potatoes.* **2** a container for measuring, holding just a peck. **3** a great deal: *a peck of trouble. n.*

pe·cul·iar (pi kyül′yər) **1** strange; odd; unusual: *It is peculiar that he has not come, for he promised he would. It was peculiar that the fish market had no fish last Friday.* **2** special; belonging to one person or thing and not to another; particular: *This book has a peculiar value. Some minerals are peculiar to the Canadian Shield. adj.*

pe·cu·li·ar·i·ty (pi kyü′lē ar′ə tē) **1** being peculiar; strangeness; oddness: *We noticed the peculiarity of his manner at once.* **2** some little thing that is strange or odd: *One of his peculiarities is that his two eyes are not the same color. n., pl.* **pe·cu·li·ar·i·ties.**

ped·al (ped′əl) **1** a lever worked by the foot; the part on which the foot is placed to move any kind of machinery: *Organs and pianos have pedals for changing the tone of the music.* **2** work or use the pedals of; move by pedals: *He pedalled his bicycle slowly up the hill.* 1 *n.*, 2 *v.*, **ped·alled** or **ped·aled, ped·al·ling** or **ped·al·ing.**
☛ **Pedal** and **peddle** are pronounced the same.

ped·dle (ped′əl) **1** carry from place to place and sell: *to peddle fruit.* **2** sell or deal out in small quantities: *to peddle newspapers, to peddle gossip.* **3** travel about with things to sell. *v.*, **ped·dled, ped·dling.**
☛ See note at **pedal.**

ped·dler (ped′lər) a person who travels about selling things that he carries in a pack, in a cart, or on a truck. *n.* Also spelled **pedlar.**

ped·es·tal (ped′is təl) **1** the base on which a column or a statue stands. **2** the base of a tall vase, lamp, etc. *n.*

hat, āge, fär; let, ēqual, tėrm; it, īce
hot, ōpen, ôrder; oil, out; cup, pu̇t, rüle
əbove, takən, pencəl, lemən, circəs
ch, child; ng, long; sh, ship
th, thin; ᴛʜ, then; zh, measure

on a pedestal, in an important position or place of honor: *He put his wife on a pedestal and said she could do no wrong.*

pe·des·tri·an (pə des′trē ən) 1 a person who goes on foot; a walker: *Pedestrians have to watch for cars turning corners.* 2 going on foot; walking. 3 without imagination; dull; slow: *a pedestrian style in writing.* 1 *n.*, 2, 3 *adj.*

ped·i·gree (ped′ə grē′) 1 the list of the ancestors of a person or animal; a family tree. 2 ancestors; line of descent. *n.*

ped·lar (ped′lər) See **peddler.**

pe·dom·e·ter (pə dom′ə tər) an instrument for recording the number of steps taken and thus measuring the distance travelled. *n.*

peek (pēk) 1 look quickly and slyly; peep: *You must not peek while you are counting in such games as hide-and-seek.* 2 a quick, sly look. 1 *v.*, 2 *n.*

☞ **Peek** and **peak** are pronounced the same.

peel (pēl) 1 the rind or outer covering of fruit or vegetables. 2 strip the skin, rind, or bark from: *to peel an orange, to peel a potato.* 3 strip: *The Indians peeled the bark from trees to make canoes.* 4 come off: *When I was sunburned, my skin peeled. The paint on the shed is peeling.* 1 *n.*, 2–4 *v.*

keep one's eyes peeled, *Informal.* be on the alert: *Keep your eyes peeled for cars turning off the highway here.*

peep¹ (pēp) 1 look through a small or narrow hole or crack. 2 a look through a hole or crack; a little look: *to take a peep into the pantry.* 3 look secretly. 4 a secret look: *Take a peep at the presents.* 5 look out, as if peeping; come partly out: *Violets peeped among the leaves. Her toe peeped through the hole in her stocking.* 1, 3, 5 *v.*, 2, 4 *n.*

peep² (pēp) 1 the cry of a young bird or chicken; a sound like a chirp or a squeak. 2 make such a sound; chirp. 1 *n.*, 2 *v.*

peep·hole (pēp′hōl′) a hole through which one may peep. *n.*

peer¹ (pēr) 1 a person of the same rank, ability, etc. as another; an equal: *He is so fine a man that it would be hard to find his peer.* 2 a man who has a title or who is high and great by birth: *Dukes, marquises, earls, counts, viscounts, and barons are peers.* *n.*

☞ **Peer** and **pier** are pronounced the same.

peer² (pēr) 1 look closely to see clearly, as a near-sighted person does: *She peered at the tag to read the price.* 2 come out slightly; peep out: *The sun was peering from behind a cloud.* *v.*

☞ See note at **peer¹**.

peer·less (pēr′lis) without an equal; matchless: *His peerless performance won him a prize.* *adj.*

peeve (pēv) *Informal.* 1 make cross; annoy. 2 an annoyance. 1 *v.*, 2 *n.*

pee·vish (pē′vish) cross; fretful; complaining: *A peevish child is unhappy and makes others unhappy.* *adj.*

pee·wee (pē′wē) 1 a very small person or thing. 2 in boys' sports, a player aged between 8 and 12. *n.*

☞ **Peewee** and **pewee** are pronounced the same.

peg (peg) 1 a pin or small bolt of wood or metal used to fasten parts together, to hang things on, to stop a hole, to make fast a rope or string on, to mark the score in a game, etc. 2 fasten or hold with pegs: *We must peg down our tent.* 3 mark with pegs: *The boys pegged out the spaces for parking bicycles.* 1 *n.*, 2, 3 *v.*, **pegged, peg·ging.**

peg away, work hard and steadily: *He pegged away at his studies so that he would get high marks.*

take down a peg, lower the pride of; humble.

peg·board (peg′bôrd′) a board with evenly spaced holes in which pegs, or hooks, are inserted to hold tools, displays, etc. *n.*

P.E.I. Prince Edward Island.

Pe·king·ese (pē′kin ēz′ or pē′king ēz′) a small dog with long hair and a broad, flat face. *n.*, *pl.* **Pe·king·ese.** Sometimes spelled **Pekinese.**

White pelicans — about 160 cm long with the tail; wingspread usually about 265 cm

pel·i·can (pel′ə kən) a very large fish-eating water bird having a huge bill and a pouch on the bottom side of the bill for scooping up and holding food. *n.*

pel·let (pel′it) 1 a little ball of mud, paper, hail, snow, food, medicine, etc.; a pill. 2 a bullet. *n.*

pell–mell (pel′mel′) 1 in a rushing, tumbling mass or crowd: *The children dashed pell-mell down the beach and into the waves.* 2 in headlong haste. *adv.*

pelt¹ (pelt) 1 throw things at; attack; assail: *The boys were pelting the dog with stones.* 2 beat heavily: *The rain came pelting down.* 3 speed: *The horse is coming at full pelt.* *v.*

pelt² (pelt) the skin of a sheep, goat, or small fur-bearing animal before it is tanned. *n.*

pem·mi·can (pem′i kən) *Cdn.* lean meat that has been dried, pounded, and mixed with fat: *Pemmican was the usual food of the voyageurs.* *n.*

☞ **Pemmican** comes from Cree *pimii,* meaning 'fat,' + *-kan,* meaning 'prepared.'

pen¹ (pen) 1 a tool used in writing with ink. 2 write: *I penned a few words to Father today.* 1 *n.*, 2 *v.*, **penned, pen·ning.**

pen² (pen) 1 a small, closed yard for cows, sheep, pigs, chickens, etc. 2 a small enclosure, such as a playpen for a baby. 3 shut in a pen. 4 shut in; confine closely: *He had me penned in a corner where I could not escape.* 1, 2 *n.*, 3, 4 *v.*, **penned** or **pent, pen·ning.**

pe·nal·ize (pē′nəl īz′ or pen′əl īz′) 1 declare punishable by law or by rule; set a penalty for: *Fouls are penalized in many games.* 2 inflict a penalty on; punish: *Our football team was penalized five yards.* *v.*, **pe·nal·ized, pe·nal·iz·ing.**

pen·al·ty (pen′əl tē) 1 a punishment for breaking a

law or rule: *His penalty for speeding was a fine of twenty dollars.* 2 a disadvantage placed on a side or player for breaking the rules of some game or contest. 3 a disadvantage attached to some act or condition: *the penalties of being rich.* *n., pl.* **pen·al·ties.**

penalty box in hockey, a special bench where players awarded penalties spend their time off the ice.

pen·ance (pen′əns) punishment borne to show sorrow for sin, to make up for a wrong done, and to obtain pardon for sin. *n.*

do penance, do something to show that one is sorry or repents: *She did penance for hurting her sister by staying home from the circus.*

pence (pens) a plural of **penny.** *n.*

pen·cil (pen′səl) 1 a pointed tool to write or draw with, usually made of wood and having a long thin piece of black or colored material in the centre. 2 mark, write, or draw with a pencil. 1 *n.,* 2 *v.,* **pen·cilled** or **pen·ciled, pen·cil·ling** or **pen·cil·ing.**

pend·ant (pen′dənt) a hanging ornament, such as a locket, worn around the neck. *n.*

pend·ing (pend′ing) 1 waiting to be decided or settled: *while the agreement was pending.* 2 while waiting for; until: *Pending his return, let us get ready.* 3 during: *pending the investigation.* 1 *adj.,* 2, 3 *prep.*

pen·du·lum (pen′jə ləm or pen′dyə ləm) a weight so hung from a fixed point that it is free to swing to and fro: *The movement of the works of a tall clock is often timed by a pendulum.* See the picture. *n.*

pen·e·trate (pen′ə trāt′) 1 pass into or through: *The bullet penetrated two centimetres into the wall.* 2 pierce through; make a way: *Our eyes could not penetrate the darkness. Even where the trees were thickest, the sunshine penetrated.* 3 soak through; spread through: *The rain penetrated our clothes. The smell penetrated the whole house.* 4 see into; understand: *I could not penetrate the mystery.* *v.,* **pen·e·trat·ed, pen·e·trat·ing.**

pen·e·trat·ing (pen′ə trā′ting) 1 sharp; piercing: *The judge gave the criminal a penetrating look.* 2 having an acute mind; understanding thoroughly. *adj.*

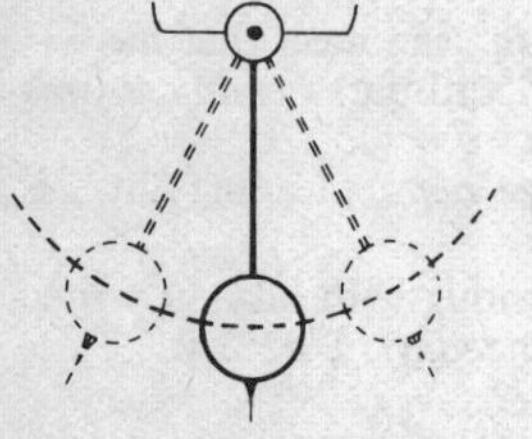
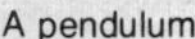
A pendulum

Emperor penguins — about 120 cm high

pen·guin (peng′gwin) a black and white sea bird having wings like flippers, which it uses for diving and swimming, not for flying: *Penguins live in Antarctica and other cold areas of the Southern Hemisphere.* *n.*

pen·i·cil·lin (pen′ə sil′ən) a very powerful drug for destroying bacteria: *Penicillin, which is made from fungus mould, is used in treating certain diseases.* *n.*

pen·in·su·la (pən in′sə lə or pən in′syə lə) a piece of land almost surrounded by water, or extending far out into the water: *Nova Scotia is a large peninsula.* *n.*

pe·nis (pē′nis) the sex organ of a male animal. *n.*

pen·i·tence (pen′ə təns) sorrow for doing wrong; repentance. *n.*

pen·i·tent (pen′ə tənt) 1 sorry for doing wrong; repentant: *The penitent child promised never to cheat again.* 2 one who is sorry for sin, especially one who is doing penance under the direction of a church. 1 *adj.,* 2 *n.*

pen·i·ten·tia·ry (pen′ə ten′shə rē) a prison, especially a federal prison for persons convicted of serious crimes. *n., pl.* **pen·i·ten·tia·ries.**

pen·knife (pen′nīf′) a small pocketknife. *n., pl.* **pen·knives.**

pen·man (pen′mən) a person who has good handwriting. *n., pl.* **pen·men** (pen′mən)

pen·man·ship (pen′mən ship′) skill in writing with pen, pencil, etc.: *The pupils admired the teacher's penmanship.* *n.*

pen name a name used by a writer instead of his real name.

pen·nant (pen′ənt) 1 a flag, usually long and narrow, used on ships, for signalling, as a school banner, etc. 2 a flag or other trophy competed for in an athletic contest: *Our team won the baseball pennant.* *n.*

pen·ni·less (pen′i lis) without a cent; very poor: *a penniless family. The thief snatched my purse and left me penniless in the big city.* *adj.*

pen·ny (pen′ē) 1 a cent; a copper coin of Canada and the United States. 2 See **new penny.** 3 a former British bronze coin equal to one twelfth of a shilling, or about one cent. 4 a sum of money. *n., pl.* **pennies** or (for defs. 2 and 3) **pence.**

a pretty penny, a large sum of money.

pen·sion (pen′shən) 1 a regular payment to a person that is not wages: *Pensions are often paid because of old age, long service, special merit, or injuries received.* 2 give a pension to: *Most companies pension a worker when he retires.* 1 *n.,* 2 *v.*

pen·sion·er (pen′shən ər) a person who receives a pension. *n.*

pen·sive (pen′siv) thoughtful in a serious or sad way: *She was in a pensive mood and sat staring out the window.* *adj.*

pent (pent) closely confined; penned; shut: *The crippled child was pent up in the house all winter.* See **pent-up.** *adj.*

pent·house (pent′hous′) an apartment or house built on the top of a building. *n.*

pent–up (pent′up′) shut up; closely confined: *Her pent-up feelings could no longer be restrained, and she burst into tears.* *adj.*

pe·o·ny (pē′ə nē) a garden plant having large, showy red, pink, or white flowers. *n., pl.* **pe·o·nies.**

peo·ple (pē′pəl) 1 men, women, and children; persons: *There were ten people present.* 2 a race or nation: *the Canadian people, the peoples of Asia.* 3 persons in general; the public: *People are funny.* 4 persons of a place, class, or group: *city people, Prairie people, the people here.* 5 persons in relation to a superior: *the king and his people, a pastor and his people.* 6 the common people; the lower classes: *The French nobles oppressed the people.* 7 fill or provide with people: *Canada was very largely peopled by Europeans.* 8 *Informal.* family; relatives: *He spends his*

hat, āge, fär; let, ēqual, tėrm; it, īce
hot, ōpen, ôrder; oil, out; cup, pu̇t, rüle
ə above, takən, pencəl, lemən, circəs
ch, child; ng, long; sh, ship
th, thin; ᴛʜ, then; zh, measure

holidays with his people. 1–6, 8 *n.*, 7 *v.*, **peo·pled, peo·pling.**

pep (pep) *Informal.* **1** spirit; energy; vim. **2 pep up,** fill with energy or enthusiasm; put new life into: *She did her best to pep up the party.* 1 *n.*, 2 *v.*, **pepped, pep·ping.**

pep·per (pep′ər) **1** a seasoning with a hot taste, used for soups, meats, and vegetables: *Pepper is made by grinding the berries of the pepper plant.* **2** a hollow red or green vegetable that is often baked, fried, or used in pickles. **3** season or sprinkle with pepper. **4** sprinkle thickly: *His face is peppered with freckles.* **5** hit with small objects sent thick and fast: *They peppered the enemy with bullets.* 1, 2 *n.*, 3–5 *v.*

pep·per·corn (pep′ər kôrn′) one of the dried berries of the pepper plant that are ground up to make pepper. *n.*

pep·per·mint (pep′ər mint′) **1** an herb grown for its oil, used in medicine and in candy. **2** this oil. **3** candy flavored with this oil. *n.*

pep·py (pep′ē) *Slang.* full of pep; lively: *Scotch terriers are peppy dogs. adj.*

per (pėr) **1** for each: *a litre of milk per child, ten cents per gram.* **2** by; through; by means of: *I sent this per my son. prep.*

per·cale (pər kāl′) a closely woven cotton cloth with a smooth finish: *Many bed sheets are made of percale. n.*

per·ceive (pər sēv′) **1** be aware of through the senses; see, hear, taste, smell, or feel: *Did you perceive the colors of that bird?* **2** take in with the mind; observe: *I soon perceived that I could not make him change his mind. v.*, **per·ceiv·ed, per·ceiv·ing.**

per cent or **per·cent** (pər sent′) **1** hundredths; parts in each hundred: *5 per cent is 5 out of each 100, or 5/100 of the whole. Five per cent (5%) of 40 is 2. Symbol: %* **2** for each hundred; in each hundred: *Seven per cent of all the children failed. n.*

per·cent·age (pər sen′tij) **1** the rate or proportion of each hundred; a part of each hundred: *What percentage of children were absent?* **2** a part or proportion: *A large percentage of schoolbooks now have colored pictures. n.*

per·cep·ti·ble (pər sep′tə bəl) that can be perceived: *The other ship was barely perceptible in the fog. adj.*

per·cep·ti·bly (pər sep′tə blē) in a perceptible way or amount. *adv.*

per·cep·tion (pər sep′shən) **1** perceiving: *His perception of the change came in a flash.* **2** the power of perceiving: *a keen perception.* **3** the understanding that is the result of perceiving: *Having a clear perception of what was wrong, he soon corrected it. n.*

perch[1] (pėrch) **1** a bar, branch, or anything else on which a bird can come to rest. **2** alight and rest: *A robin perched on our porch railing.* **3** a rather high seat or position. **4** sit, especially on something high: *He perched on a stool.* **5** to place high up: *The village was perched on a high hill.* 1, 3 *n.*, 2, 4, 5 *v.*

perch[2] (pėrch) **1** a small fresh-water fish, used for food. **2** a similar salt-water fish. *n., pl.* **perch** or **perch·es.**

per·co·late (pėr′kə lāt′) **1** drip or drain through small holes or spaces: *Let the coffee percolate for seven minutes.* **2** filter through; permeate: *Water percolates sand. v.*, **per·co·lat·ed, per·co·lat·ing.**

per·co·la·tor (pėr′kə lā′tər) a kind of coffee pot in which boiling water continually bubbles up through a tube and drips down through ground coffee. *n.*

per·cus·sion (pər kush′ən) **1** the striking of one body against another with force; a blow: *Caps are exploded by percussion.* **2** the sound made by the striking of one body against another with force. *n.*

percussion instrument a musical instrument played by striking it, such as a drum or cymbal.

per·en·ni·al (pər en′ē əl) **1** lasting through the whole year: *a perennial stream.* **2** lasting for a very long time: *the perennial beauty of the hills.* **3** living more than two years: *perennial garden plants.* **4** a perennial plant: *Roses are perennials.* 1–3 *adj.*, 4 *n.*

per·fect (pėr′fikt for 1, 3, 5 and 6, pər fekt′ for 2 and 4) **1** having no faults; not spoiled at any point: *a perfect spelling paper, a perfect apple, a perfect life. Perfect work shows great care.* **2** remove all faults from; make perfect; add the finishing touches to: *perfect an invention. The artist was perfecting his picture.* **3** having all its parts; complete: *The set was perfect; nothing was missing or broken.* **4** carry through; complete: *to perfect a plan.* **5** exact: *a perfect copy, a perfect circle.* **6** entire; utter: *a perfect stranger to us.* 1, 3, 5, 6 *adj.*, 2, 4 *v.* **—per′fect·ly,** *adv.*

per·fec·tion (pər fek′shən) **1** a perfect or faultless condition; the highest excellence. **2** a perfect person or thing: *His work is always perfection.* **3** making complete or perfect: *The perfection of our plans will take another week. n.*

to perfection, perfectly: *He played the violin concerto to perfection.*

per·fo·rate (pėr′fə rāt′) **1** make a hole or holes through: *The target was perforated by bullets.* **2** make a row or rows of holes through: *Sheets of postage stamps are perforated. v.*, **per·fo·rat·ed, per·fo·rat·ing.**

per·fo·ra·tion (pėr′fə rā′shən) a hole or series of holes bored or punched through something: *He removed the coupon by tearing along the perforation. n.*

per·form (pər fôrm′) **1** do or carry out: *Perform your duties well. The surgeon performed an operation.* **2** put into effect; fulfil: *Perform your promise.* **3** act, play, sing, or do tricks in public. *v.*

per·form·ance (pər fôr′məns) **1** carrying out or doing: *in the performance of one's regular duties.* **2** the thing performed; act; deed: *The child's kicks and screams made a disgraceful performance.* **3** the giving of a play, circus, or other show: *The evening performance is at 8 o'clock. n.*

per·form·er (pər fôr′mər) a person who performs for the entertainment of others; a player. *n.*

per·fume (pėr′fyüm or pər fyüm′ for 1 and 3, pər fyüm′ for 2) **1** a liquid having a sweet smell. **2** fill with a sweet odor: *Flowers perfumed the air.* **3** a sweet smell: *We enjoyed the perfume of the flowers.* 1, 3 *n.*, 2 *v.*, **per·fumed, per·fum·ing.**

per·haps (pər haps′) maybe; it may be; possibly: *Perhaps a letter will come today.* *adv.*

per·il (per′əl) a chance of harm; danger: *This bridge is not safe; cross it at your peril.* *n.*

per·il·ous (per′ə ləs) dangerous; full of peril: *a perilous journey.* *adj.*

pe·rim·e·ter (pə rim′ə tər) **1** the outer boundary of a figure or area: *the perimeter of a circle. A fence marks the perimeter of the field.* **2** the distance around such a boundary. *n.*

pe·ri·od (pēr′ē əd) **1** a portion of time: *He visited us for a short period.* **2** a portion of time marked off by events that happen again and again; a time after which the same things begin to happen again: *A month, from new moon to new moon, is a period.* **3** a certain series of years: *the period of the depression.* **4** one of the portions of time into which a school day is divided. **5** the dot (.) marking the end of most sentences or showing an abbreviation, as in Mr. or Dec. **6** one of the three twenty-minute divisions of a hockey game. *n.*

pe·ri·od·ic (pēr′ē od′ik) occurring, appearing, or done again and again at regular intervals: *periodic attacks of malaria.* *adj.*

pe·ri·od·i·cal (pēr′ē od′ə kəl) **1** a magazine that appears regularly. **2** published at regular intervals, less often than daily. **3** periodic. 1 *n.*, 2, 3 *adj.*

pe·ri·od·i·cal·ly (pēr′ē od′ik lē) **1** at regular intervals. **2** every now and then: *My aunt visits us periodically.* *adv.*

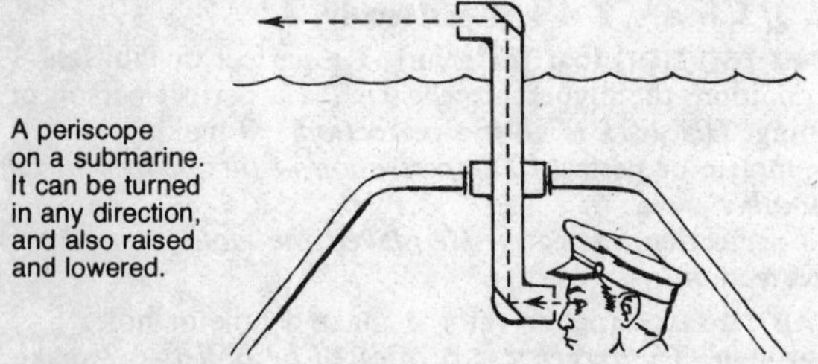
A periscope on a submarine. It can be turned in any direction, and also raised and lowered.

per·i·scope (per′ə skōp′) **1** an instrument that allows those in a submarine or trench to get a view of the surface: *A periscope is a tube with an arrangement of mirrors that reflect light rays down the tube.* **2** an arrangement of mirrors used for seeing round corners, looking over the heads of people in a crowd, etc. *n.*

per·ish (per′ish) **1** be destroyed; die: *Buildings perish in flames. Flowers perish when frost comes.* **2** decay; become spoiled: *Fruit will perish quickly in hot weather.* *v.*

per·ish·a·ble (per′ish ə bəl) liable to spoil or decay: *Fresh fruit is perishable.* *adj.*

per·ju·ry (pėr′jər ē) the act of telling a lie in a court of law after swearing to tell the truth. *n.*

perk (pėrk) raise smartly or briskly: *The sparrow perked up his tail.* *v.*
perk up, brighten up; become lively and vigorous: *We all perked up after a good lunch.*

perk·y (pėr′kē) smart; brisk; saucy; pert: *a perky squirrel.* *adj.*

per·ma·frost (pėr′mə frost′) ground that is permanently frozen: *There is a great deal of permafrost in the Canadian North.* *n.*

per·ma·nence (pėr′mə nəns) the state or condition of being permanent; a lasting quality or condition: *the permanence of the sun.* *n.*

per·ma·nent (pėr′mə nənt) **1** lasting; intended to last; not for a short time only: *a permanent filling in a tooth.* **2** *Informal.* permanent wave. 1 *adj.*, 2 *n.*

permanent wave a wave put in the hair by a special process so as to last for a long time.

per·me·ate (pėr′mē āt′) **1** spread through the whole of; pass through; soak through: *The smoke permeated the house.* **2** penetrate: *Water will easily permeate a cotton dress.* *v.*, **per·me·at·ed, per·me·at·ing.**

per·mis·si·ble (pər mis′ə bəl) that can be permitted; allowable. *adj.*

per·mis·sion (pər mish′ən) consent; leave; the act of permitting or allowing: *He asked the teacher's permission to go early. Father gave me his permission to use his camera.* *n.*

per·mit (pər mit′ for 1, pėr′mit for 2) **1** let; allow: *I will go on Monday if the weather permits. Mr. Nash permitted us to swim in his pond.* **2** a formal written order giving permission to do something: *Have you a permit to fish in this lake?* 1 *v.*, **per·mit·ted, per·mit·ting;** 2 *n.*

per·ni·cious (pər nish′əs) that will destroy or ruin; causing great harm or damage: *pernicious habits, pernicious insects.* *adj.*

per·pen·dic·u·lar (pėr′pən dik′yə lər) **1** upright; standing straight up: *a perpendicular cliff.* **2** at right angles: *One line is perpendicular to another when it makes a square corner with another. The floor of a room is perpendicular to the side walls and parallel to the ceiling.* **3** a perpendicular line, plane, or position. 1, 2 *adj.*, 3 *n.*

per·pe·trate (pėr′pə trāt′) do or commit a crime, fraud, trick, or anything bad or foolish: *The two thieves perpetrated the robbery of the jewellery store.* *v.*, **per·pe·trat·ed, per·pe·trat·ing.**

per·pet·u·al (pər pech′ü əl) **1** eternal; lasting forever: *the perpetual hills.* **2** lasting throughout life: *a perpetual income.* **3** continuous; never ceasing: *a perpetual stream of visitors, perpetual motion.* *adj.* —**per·pet′u·al·ly,** *adv.*

per·pet·u·ate (pər pech′ü āt′) make perpetual; keep from being forgotton: *The Brock Monument was built to perpetuate the memory of a great man.* *v.*, **per·pet·u·at·ed, per·pet·u·at·ing.**

per·plex (pər pleks′) trouble with doubt; puzzle; bewilder: *This problem is hard enough to perplex even the teacher.* *v.*

per·plex·i·ty (pər plek′sə tē) **1** a perplexed condition; the state of being puzzled or of not knowing what to do or how to act: *His perplexity was so great that he had to ask for advice.* **2** something that perplexes: *There are many perplexities in such a job.* *n., pl.* **per·plex·i·ties.**

per·se·cute (pėr′sə kyüt′) **1** pursue to injure; treat badly; do harm to again and again; oppress: *The cruel boy persecuted the kitten by throwing stones at it.* **2** treat badly because of one's principles or beliefs: *Christians were persecuted in ancient Rome.* *v.*, **per·se·cut·ed, per·se·cut·ing.**

per·se·cu·tion (pėr′sə kyü′shən) **1** treating badly;

hat, āge, fär; let, ēqual, tėrm; it, īce
hot, ōpen, ôrder; oil, out; cup, pu̇t, rüle
əbove, takən, pencəl, lemən, circəs
ch, child; ng, long; sh, ship
th, thin; ᴛʜ, then; zh, measure

oppressing: *The boy's persecution of the kitten was cruel.* 2 being treated badly or harmed again and again: *The boy's brother didn't take part in the kitten's persecution.* *n.*

per·se·ver·ance (pėr′sə vēr′əns) sticking to a purpose or an aim; never giving up what one has set out to do: *By perseverance the lame boy learned to swim.* *n.*

per·se·vere (pėr′sə vēr′) continue steadily in doing something hard; persist: *To try, try, try again is to persevere.* *v.,* **per·se·vered, per·se·ver·ing.**

per·sim·mon (pər sim′ən) a North American plumlike fruit that is very bitter when green, but sweet and tasty when ripe. *n.*

per·sist (pər sist′) 1 continue firmly; refuse to stop or be changed: *He persists in eating with his spoon. She persisted till she had solved the difficult problem.* 2 last; stay; endure: *On some very high mountains snow persists throughout the year.* *v.*

per·sist·ence (pər sis′təns) 1 being persistent: *the persistence of a fly buzzing around one's head.* 2 the continuing existence: *the persistence of a cough.* *n.*

per·sist·ent (pər sis′tənt) 1 persisting; not giving up, especially in the face of dislike, disapproval, or difficulties: *a persistent worker.* 2 lasting; going on; continuing: *a persistent headache that lasted for three days.* *adj.*

per·son (pėr′sən) 1 a man, woman, or child; a human being: *Any person who wishes may come to the fair.* 2 the human body; the bodily appearance: *The person of the king was well guarded. He kept his person neat and trim.* *n.*
in person, with or by one's own action or presence; personally: *Come in person; do not write or phone.*

per·son·age (pėr′sən ij) 1 a person of importance. 2 a character in a book or a play. *n.*

per·son·al (pėr′sən əl) 1 belonging to a person; private: *a personal letter.* 2 done in person; directly by oneself, not through others or by letter: *a personal visit.* 3 of the body or bodily appearance: *personal beauty or charms.* 4 about or against a person or persons: *personal remarks, personal abuse.* *adj.*
☛ Do not confuse **personal** and **personnel. Personal** is usually an adjective and is stressed on the first syllable. **Personnel** is a noun and is stressed on the last syllable.

per·son·al·i·ty (pėr′sə nal′ə tē) 1 the personal or individual quality that makes one person be different or act differently from another: *A baby two weeks old does not have much personality.* 2 the pleasing or attractive qualities of a person: *The boy is developing a fine personality.* 3 a remark made about or against one particular person: *Tactful people avoid personalities.* 4 a person; personage: *personalities of TV and theatre.* *n., pl.* **per·son·al·i·ties.**

per·son·al·ly (pėr′sən əl ē) 1 in person; not by the aid of others: *The hostess personally saw to the comfort of her guests.* 2 as far as oneself is concerned: *Personally, I like apples better than oranges.* 3 as a person: *We like him personally, but we dislike his way of life.* 4 as being meant for oneself: *He intended no insult to you; do not take what he said personally.* *adv.*

per·son·i·fi·ca·tion (pər son′ə fə kā′shən) 1 a striking example; type: *A miser is the personification of greed.* 2 a person or creature imagined as representing a thing or idea: *Satan is the personification of evil.* 3 a figure of speech in which a lifeless thing or quality is spoken of as if alive. *Examples: The music sobbed. Duty calls us.* *n.*

per·son·i·fy (pər son′ə fī′) 1 be a type of: *Satan personifies evil.* 2 regard or represent as a person. We often personify the sun and moon, referring to the sun as *he* and the moon as *she.* *v.*

per·son·nel (pėr′sə nel′) persons employed in any work, business, or service: *All personnel are invited to the office party.* *n.*
☛ See note at **personal.**

per·spec·tive (pər spek′tiv) 1 the art of picturing objects on a flat surface so as to give the appearance of distance. 2 the effect of distance on the appearance of objects: *Railway tracks seem to meet at the horizon because of perspective.* 3 the effect that the distance of events in time has on the mind: *Perspective makes many happenings of last year seem less important.* *n.*

per·spi·ra·tion (pėr′spə rā′shən) 1 sweat: *Her forehead was damp with perspiration.* 2 sweating or perspiring. *n.*

per·spire (pər spīr′) sweat: *We perspire when we work hard in the hot weather.* *v.,* **per·spired, per·spir·ing.**

per·suade (pər swād′) win over to do or believe; make willing by urging or arguing: *I knew I should study, but he persuaded me to go to the movies. We persuaded Harry that he should leave.* *v.,* **per·suad·ed, per·suad·ing.**

per·sua·sion (pər swā′zhən) 1 the act of persuading: *All our persuasion was of no use; she would not come.* 2 the power of persuading. 3 a firm belief; a conviction: *He and his brother were of different political persuasions.* 4 religious belief; a religious denomination: *All Christians are not of the same persuasion.* *n.*

per·sua·sive (pər swā′siv) able to persuade; effective in persuading: *The salesman had a very persuasive way of talking.* *adj.*

pert (pėrt) saucy; bold; too forward or free in speech or action: *a pert girl, a pert reply.* *adj.*

per·tain (pər tān′) 1 belong or be connected as a part or possession: *We own the house and the land pertaining to it.* 2 refer; be related: *'Pertaining to school' means 'having something to do with school.'* 3 be appropriate: *We had turkey and everything else that pertains to Thanksgiving Day.* *v.*

per·ti·nent (pėr′tə nənt) having something to do with what is being considered; relating to the matter in hand; to the point: *If your question is pertinent, I will answer it.* *adj.*

per·turb (pər tėrb′) disturb greatly; make uneasy or troubled: *Mother was much perturbed by my illness.* *v.*

pe·ruse (pə rüz′) read, especially thoroughly and carefully: *I always peruse the newspaper at breakfast.* *v.,* **pe·rused, pe·rus·ing.**

Pe·ru·vi·an (pə rü′vē ən) 1 of or having to do with Peru, a country in South America. 2 a person born in or living in Peru. 1 *adj.*, 2 *n.*

per·vade (pər vād′) go or spread throughout; be throughout: *The odor of pines pervades the air. Weariness pervaded his whole body. v.,* **per·vad·ed, per·vad·ing.**

per·verse (pər vėrs′) 1 contrary and willful; stubborn: *The perverse child did just what we told him not to do.* 2 wicked; persistent in wrongdoing. *adj.*

per·vert (pər vėrt′ for 1 and 2, pėr′vėrt for 3) 1 give a wrong meaning to: *His enemies perverted his friendly remark and made it into an insult.* 2 use for wrong purposes or in a wrong way: *A clever criminal perverts his talents.* 3 a perverted person. 1, 2 *v.*, 3 *n.*

pes·ky (pes′kē) *Informal.* troublesome; annoying: *a pesky cold, pesky mosquitoes. adj.*

pe·so (pā′sō) the unit of money in countries of Latin America and the Philippines. *n., pl.* **pe·sos.**

pes·si·mist (pes′ə mist) a person inclined to look on the dark side of things or to see all the difficulties and disadvantages. *n.*

pes·si·mis·tic (pes′ə mis′tik) having a tendency to look on the dark side of things: *He was pessimistic about his chances of passing the examination. adj.*

pest (pest) any animal or person that causes trouble, injury, or destruction; a nuisance: *Flies and mosquitoes are pests. Insect pests destroyed our crop. n.*

pes·ter (pes′tər) annoy; trouble; vex: *Flies pester us. Don't pester me with foolish questions. v.*

pes·ti·lence (pes′tə ləns) a disease that spreads rapidly, causing many deaths: *Smallpox, yellow fever, and the plague are pestilences. n.*

pes·tle (pes′əl) a tool for pounding or crushing something to a powder in a mortar. See **mortar** for picture. *n.*

pet[1] (pet) 1 an animal kept as a favorite and treated with affection. 2 a darling or favorite: *teacher's pet.* 3 treated as a pet: *That girl has a pet rabbit.* 4 treat as a pet; stroke or pat; touch lovingly and gently: *She is petting the kitten.* 5 favorite: *a pet chair, a pet theory.* 1, 2 *n.*, 3, 5 *adj.*, 4 *v.*, **pet·ted, pet·ting.**

pet[2] (pet) a fit of being cross or peevish: *When he didn't get his way, he jumped on his bicycle and rode off in a pet. n.*

pet·al (pet′əl) one of the parts of a flower that are usually colored: *A rose has many petals.* See **flower** for picture. *n.*

pe·tite (pə tēt′) little; small and dainty: *a petite woman or girl. adj.*

pe·ti·tion (pə tish′ən) 1 a formal request to someone in authority for some privilege, right, or benefit: *The people on our street signed a petition asking the city council for a new sidewalk.* 2 ask earnestly; make a formal request to: *They petitioned the mayor to use his influence with the city council.* 1 *n.*, 2 *v.*

pet·rel (pet′rəl) a small black-and-white sea bird with long, pointed wings. *n.*

☛ **Petrel** and **petrol** are pronounced the same.

pet·ri·fy (pet′rə fī′) 1 replace animal or vegetable cells with mineral deposits; turn into stone: *There is a petrified forest in Arizona.* 2 paralyse with fear, horror, or surprise: *The hiker was petrified as the snake came near. v.,* **pet·ri·fied, pet·ri·fy·ing.**

pet·rol (pet′rəl) *Esp. British.* gasoline. *n.*

☛ **Petrol** and **petrel** are pronounced the same.

pe·tro·le·um (pə trō′lē əm) an oily, dark-colored liquid that is found in the earth: *Gasoline, kerosene, and paraffin are made from petroleum. n.*

pet·ti·coat (pet′ē kōt′) a skirt worn beneath a dress or outer skirt by women and girls. *n.*

pet·ty (pet′ē) 1 small; having little importance or value: *She insisted on telling me all her petty troubles.* 2 mean: *A gossip has a petty mind.* 3 lower in rank or importance; subordinate: *My brother is a petty official in that big company. adj.,* **pet·ti·er, pet·ti·est.**

pet·u·lant (pech′ů lənt) peevish; likely to have little fits of bad temper; irritable over trifles: *The spoiled girl was often petulant. adj.*

pe·tu·ni·a (pə tyü′nē ə or pə tü′nē ə) a common garden plant that has flowers shaped like funnels. *n.*

pew (pyü) a bench in church for people to sit on, having a back and often fastened to the floor. *n.*

pe·wee (pē′wē) a small North American bird with an olive-colored or grey back. *n.*

☛ **Pewee** and **peewee** are pronounced the same.

pew·ter (pyü′tər) 1 an alloy of tin with lead, copper, or other metals. 2 dishes or other utensils made of this alloy: *She cleans the pewter. n.*

phan·ta·sy (fan′tə sē) See **fantasy.**

phan·tom (fan′təm) 1 an image in the mind which seems to be real: *His fevered brain filled the room with phantoms from the past.* 2 a vague, dim, or shadowy appearance; a ghost. *n.*

Phar·aoh (fer′ō) a title given to the kings of ancient Egypt. *n.*

phar·ma·cist (fär′mə sist) a person who prepares drugs, medicine, etc.; a druggist. *n.*

phar·ma·cy (fär′mə sē) 1 the preparation and dispensing of drugs and medicines. 2 a drugstore. 3 the department of a hospital where drugs, medicine, etc. are prepared. *n., pl.* **phar·ma·cies.**

phase (fāz) 1 one of the changing states or stages of development of a person or thing: *At present his voice is changing; that is a phase all boys go through.* 2 one side, part, or view of a subject: *What phase of arithmetic are you studying now?* 3 the shape of the moon or of a planet as it is seen at a given time. See **moon** for picture. *n.*

☛ **Phase** and **faze** are pronounced the same.

A ring-necked pheasant — about 84 cm long with the tail

pheas·ant (fez′ənt) a game bird related to the domestic fowl and the peacock, having a long tail and brilliant feathers: *Wild pheasants live in many parts of Europe and America. n., pl.* **pheas·ants** or **pheas·ant.**

hat, āge, fär; let, ēqual, tėrm; it, īce
hot, ōpen, ôrder; oil, out; cup, pu̇t, rüle
əbove, takən, pencəl, lemən, circəs
ch, child; ng, long; sh, ship
th, thin; ᴛʜ, then; zh, measure

phe·nom·e·na (fə nom′ə nə) a plural of **phenomenon.** *n.*

phe·nom·e·nal (fə nom′ə nəl) extraordinary: *a phenomenal memory. adj.*

phe·nom·e·non (fə nom′ə non′) **1** a fact, event, or circumstance that can be observed: *Lightning is an electrical phenomenon. Fever and inflammation are phenomena of disease.* **2** something or someone extraordinary or remarkable: *An eclipse is an interesting phenomenon. The fond parents think their child is a phenomenon. n., pl.* **phe·nom·e·na** or (especially for def. 2) **phe·nom·e·nons.**

phi·al (fī′əl) a small bottle; vial. *n.*

phil·an·throp·ic (fil′ən throp′ik) charitable; benevolent; kindly. *adj.*

phi·lan·thro·pist (fə lan′thrə pist) a person who gives money for or works for the welfare of mankind. *n.*

phi·lat·e·list (fə lat′ə list) a collector of postage stamps, postmarks, etc. *n.*

phi·lat·e·ly (fə lat′ə lē) the collecting, arranging, and study of postage stamps, stamped envelopes, postcards, etc. *n.*

phi·los·o·pher (fə los′ə fər) **1** a person who studies philosophy. **2** a person who has a system of philosophy. **3** a person who is calm and reasonable under hard conditions, accepting life and making the best of it. *n.*

phil·o·soph·ic (fil′ə sof′ik) **1** of philosophy. **2** wise, calm, and reasonable. *adj.*

phil·o·soph·i·cal (fil′ə sof′ə kəl) philosophic. *adj.*

phi·los·o·phy (fə los′ə fē) **1** the study of the truth or principles of all real knowledge; the study of the most general causes and principles of the universe. **2** a set of principles about the nature of the universe and man's place in it. *n., pl.* **phi·los·o·phies.**

phlegm (flem) the thick discharge from the throat and nose that accompanies a cold. *n.*

phlox (floks) a common garden plant that has showy flower clusters of various colors. *n.*

phoe·be (fē′bē) a small North American bird with a greyish-brown back, a yellowish-white breast, and a low crest on the head. *n.*

phone (fōn) *Informal.* telephone. *n., v.,* **phoned, phon·ing.**

pho·net·ic (fə net′ik) **1** of or having to do with sounds made with the voice. **2** representing the sounds of speech: *In this dictionary, the phonetic symbol* (ə) *stands for the vowel sound in the second syllable of* taken, pencil, lemon, circus. *adj.*

pho·net·ics (fə net′iks) the science dealing with sounds made in speech. *n.*

phon·ics (fon′iks or fō′niks) the study of speech sounds as they are represented by letters; the use of relationships between sound and meaning in learning to read. *n.*

pho·no·graph (fō′nə graf′) record player. *n.*

pho·ny (fō′nē) *Slang.* **1** not genuine; fake. **2** a fake; pretender. 1 *adj.,* 2 *n.*

phos·pho·rus (fos′fə rəs) a solid, waxlike chemical element that burns slowly at ordinary temperatures and glows in the dark. *n.*

pho·to (fō′tō) *Informal.* photograph. *n., pl.* **pho·tos.**

pho·to–e·lec·tric cell (fō′tō i lek′trik) a vacuum tube that varies the flow of current according to the amount of light reaching its sensitive element; electric eye. Changes of current operate machines that open doors, set off alarms, etc.

pho·to·graph (fō′tə graf′) **1** a picture made with a camera: *A photograph is made by the action of light rays from the thing pictured, coming through the lens of the camera onto a piece of film.* See **camera** for picture. **2** take a photograph of. 1 *n.,* 2 *v.*

pho·tog·ra·pher (fə tog′rə fər) **1** a person who takes photographs. **2** a person whose business is taking photographs. *n.*

pho·tog·ra·phy (fə tog′rə fē) the taking of photographs. *n.*

phrase (frāz) **1** a short, simple, or striking group of words: *He spoke in simple phrases, so that the children understood him. 'Call up' is the common phrase for 'make a telephone call to.'* **2** express in a particular way: *She phrased her excuse in polite words.* **3** a group of words used as a unit in a clause or sentence: *In 'He went to the house' the words 'to the house' are a prepositional phrase.* 1, 3 *n.,* 2 *v.,* **phrased, phras·ing.**

phys·i·cal (fiz′ə kəl) **1** of the body: *physical exercise, physical strength, physical education.* **2** of matter; material: *His physical strength was weak, but his mental and moral strength was very great. The tide is a physical force.* **3** according to the laws of nature: *It is a physical impossibility to stop the earth's movement around the sun.* **4** of the science of physics. *adj.* **—phys′i·cal·ly,** *adv.*

physical education instruction in how to exercise and take care of the body, especially as a course at school or college.

phy·si·cian (fə zish′ən) a doctor of medicine. *n.*

phys·i·cist (fiz′ə sist) a person skilled in physics or whose work is physics. *n.*

phys·ics (fiz′iks) the science that deals with matter and energy, and the relationships between them: *Physics includes the study of force, motion, heat, light, sound, and electricity. n.*

phys·i·ol·o·gy (fiz′ē ol′ə jē) the science dealing with the normal working of living things or their parts: *animal physiology, human physiology, vegetable physiology, the physiology of the blood. n.*

phy·sique (fə zēk′) the body; bodily structure, organization, or development: *Samson was a man of strong physique. n.*

pi·an·ist (pē an′ist or pē′ə nist) a person who plays the piano. *n.*

A grand piano

pi·an·o (pē an′ō) a large musical instrument having

strings that sound when struck by hammers operated by the keys on a keyboard. *n., pl.* **pi·an·os.**

pi·az·za (pē at′sə for 1, pē az′ə for 2) **1** in Italy, an open public square in a town. **2** a large porch or veranda along one or more sides of a house. *n.*

pic·co·lo (pik′ə lō′) a small flute, sounding an octave higher than an ordinary flute. *n., pl.* **pic·co·los.**

pick¹ (pik) **1** choose; select: *I picked a winning horse at the races.* **2** a choice or selection: *This red rose is my pick.* **3** the best one or the best part: *We got a high price for the pick of our peaches.* **4** pull away with the fingers; gather: *We pick fruit or flowers.* **5** the amount of a crop picked at one time. **6** pierce, dig into, or break up with some pointed tool: *to pick ground, to pick rocks.* **7** use something pointed to remove things from: *to pick one's teeth, to pick a bone.* **8** pull apart: *The woollen stuffing in the pillow has matted and needs to be picked.* **9** play with a plucking motion: *The boy picked the banjo.* **10** something held in the fingers and used to pluck the strings of a musical instrument. **11** seek and find an excuse for; seek and find: *He picked a quarrel with her.* 1, 4, 6–9, 11 *v.*, 2, 3, 5, 10 *n.* **—pick′er,** *n.*

pick a lock, open a lock with a pointed instrument, wire, etc.

pick a pocket, steal from a person's pocket.

pick at, a pull on with the fingers: *The sick man picked at the blankets.* **b** eat a bit at a time: *She just picked at her food because she did not like it.*

pick off, shoot one at a time.

pick on, *Informal.* **a** find fault with: *The teacher picked on him for always being late.* **b** annoy; tease: *The bigger boys picked on the new boy during recess.*

pick out, a choose; select: *Pick out a dress you will like to wear.* **b** distinguish a thing from its surroundings: *Can you pick me out in this group picture?*

pick over, look over carefully: *pick over vegetables before buying.*

pick up, a take up: *The boy picked up a stone. She picked up the chance to make some money by baby-sitting.* **b** get by chance: *The woman picked up a bargain at the dress sale.* **c** learn without being taught: *He picks up games easily.* **d** take up into a vehicle or ship: *The bus picked up passengers at every other corner.* **e** *Informal.* recover; improve: *He seemed to pick up quickly after his fever.* **f** go faster; increase in speed.

pick² (pik) **1** pickaxe. **2** a sharp-pointed tool: *Ice is broken into pieces with a pick. n.*

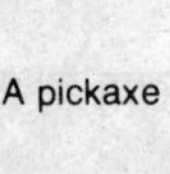
A pickaxe

pick·axe or **pick·ax** (pik′aks′) a heavy metal tool that is pointed at one or both ends and has a long wooden handle, used for breaking up dirt, rocks, etc. *n.*

pick·er·el (pik′ər əl) a kind of large fresh-water fish with a long, narrow, pointed head, used for food. *n., pl.* **pick·er·el** or **pick·er·els.**

pick·et (pik′it) **1** a pointed stake or peg placed upright to make a fence, to tie a horse to, etc. **2** enclose with pickets; fence. **3** tie to a picket: *Picket your horse here.* **4** a small body of troops, or a single man, posted at some place to watch for the enemy and guard against surprise attacks. **5** a person stationed by a labor union near a place of work where there is a strike: *Pickets try to keep workers from working or customers from buying.* **6** station as pickets. **7** station pickets at or near: *to picket a factory during a strike.* 1, 4, 5 *n.*, 2, 3, 6, 7 *v.*

pick·le (pik′əl) **1** a cucumber or other vegetable preserved in salt water, vinegar, or some other liquid. **2** preserve in pickle: *Grandmother pickled several quarts of beets.* **3** the liquid in which vegetables and meat can be preserved. **4** *Informal.* trouble; difficulty: *I got in a bad pickle today.* 1, 3, 4 *n.*, 2 *v.*, **pick·led, pick·ling.**

pick·pock·et (pik′pok′it) a person who steals from people's pockets. *n.*

pick–up (pik′up′) **1** a picking up: *the daily pick-up of mail.* **2** a device that transforms into electrical current the vibrations set up in a phonograph needle by variations in the grooves in a record. **3** a small, light truck with an open back, for collecting and delivering light loads. *n.*

pic·nic (pik′nik) **1** a pleasure trip with a meal in the open air. **2** go on such a trip: *Our family often picnics at the beach.* **3** eat in picnic style. 1 *n.*, 2, 3 *v.*, **pic·nicked, pic·nick·ing. —pic′nick·er,** *n.*

pic·to·ri·al (pik tô′rē əl) **1** having to do with pictures; expressed in pictures: *A photograph album is a pictorial record.* **2** making a picture for the mind; vivid: *a pictorial way of writing.* **3** illustrated by pictures: *a pictorial history, a pictorial magazine. adj.*

pic·ture (pik′chər) **1** a drawing, painting, portrait, or photograph; a printed copy of any of these: *That book contains a good picture of him.* **2** a scene: *The trees and brook make a lovely picture.* **3** something beautiful: *She was a picture in her new dress.* **4** draw, paint, etc.; make into a picture: *The artist pictured the saints.* **5** likeness; image: *She is the picture of her mother. He was the picture of despair.* **6** form a picture of in the mind; imagine: *It is hard to picture life a hundred years ago.* **7** a mental image; idea: *I have a clear picture of the problem.* **8** a vivid description. **9** show by words; describe vividly: *The soldier pictured the battle. The speaker pictured the suffering of the poor.* **10** a motion picture. **11** an image on a television screen. 1–3, 5, 7, 8, 10, 11 *n.*, 4, 6, 9 *v.*, **pic·tured, pic·tur·ing.**

pic·tur·esque (pik′chər esk′) **1** quaint or interesting enough to be used as the subject of a picture: *a picturesque old mill.* **2** making a picture for the mind; vivid: *picturesque language. adj.*

pie (pī) fruit, meat, etc. enclosed in pastry and baked: *apple pie, chicken pie. n.*

pie·bald (pī′bold′ or pī′bôld′) **1** spotted in two colors, especially black and white. **2** a piebald animal, especially a horse. 1 *adj.*, 2 *n.*

piece (pēs) **1** one of the parts into which a thing is divided or broken; a bit: *The cup broke in pieces.* **2** a portion; limited part; small quantity: *a piece of land containing one hectare, a piece of bread.* **3** a single thing of a set or class: *This set of china has 144 pieces.* **4** a single work of art: *a piece of music, a piece of poetry.* **5** an example or instance: *Sleeping with a light on in the room is a piece of nonsense.* **6** the quantity in which goods are made: *She bought the whole piece of muslin.* **7** make or repair by adding or joining pieces: *Mother pieced a quilt last week.* **8** join the pieces of. **9** a coin: *A nickel is a five-cent piece.* 1–6, 9 *n.*, 7, 8 *v.*, **pieced, piec·ing.**

a piece of one's mind, a scolding: *He gave the boy a piece of his mind for coming late again.*

☞ **Piece** and **peace** are pronounced the same.

piece·meal (pēs′mēl′) **1** piece by piece; a little at a time: *work done piecemeal.* **2** piece from piece; to pieces; into fragments: *The lamb was torn piecemeal by the wolves. n.*

pied (pīd) having patches of two or more colors; many-colored. *adj.*

pier (pēr) **1** a structure built out over the water, and used as a walk or a landing place for ships. See **dock** and **quay** for pictures. **2** a breakwater. **3** one of the solid supports on which the arches of a bridge rest; a pillar. See **bridge** for picture. **4** the solid part of a wall between windows, doors, etc. *n.*

☞ **Pier** and **peer** are pronounced the same.

pierce (pērs) **1** make a hole in; bore into or through: *A nail pierced the tire of our car.* **2** go into; go through: *A tunnel pierces the mountain.* **3** force a way through or into: *The cold wind pierced our clothes. A sharp cry pierced the air.* **4** make a way through with the eye or mind: *to pierce a disguise, to pierce a mystery.* **5** affect sharply with some feeling: *Her heart was pierced with grief. v.*, **pierced, pierc·ing.**

pierc·ing (pēr′sing) that pierces; penetrating; sharp; keen: *piercing cold, a piercing look. adj.*

pi·e·ty (pī′ə tē) **1** being pious or having reverence for God; holiness: *The priest was well known for his piety.* **2** a pious act, remark, or belief. *n., pl.* **pi·e·ties.**

pig (pig) **1** a mammal, especially one that is raised for its meat, having a long snout with a flat end, a heavy body, and a short thin tail. **2** *Informal.* a person who seems or acts like a pig; one who is greedy, dirty, dull, sullen, or stubborn. *n.*

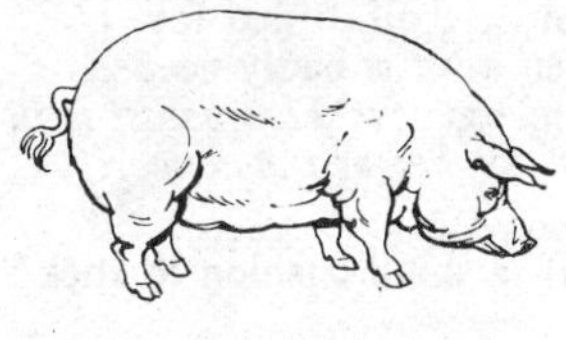

A pig

One kind of pigeon — about 38 cm long with the tail

pi·geon (pij′ən) any of a group of birds, often bluish-grey, with plump bodies and short legs. *n.*

pi·geon·hole (pij′ən hōl′) **1** a small place built, usually as one of a series, for a pigeon to nest in. **2** one of a set of boxlike compartments for holding papers and other articles in a desk, cabinet, etc. **3** put in a pigeonhole; put away. **4** classify and lay aside in memory where one can refer to it. **5** put aside with the idea of dismissing, forgetting, or neglecting. 1, 2 *n.*, 3–5 *v.*

pi·geon–toed (pij′ən tōd′) having the toes turned inward. *adj.*

pig·gy·back (pig′ē bak′) **1** a carrying or being carried on the back or shoulders: *He gave the child a piggyback.* **2** on the back or shoulders. **3** transporting loaded truck trailers on freight trains: *We sent the shipment piggyback to Winnipeg.* **4** carry by piggyback. 1 *n.*, 2, 3 *adv.*, 4 *v.*

hat, āge, fär; let, ēqual, tėrm; it, īce
hot, ōpen, ôrder; oil, out; cup, pu̇t, rüle
əbove, takən, pencəl, lemən, circəs
ch, child; ng, long; sh, ship
th, thin; ᴛʜ, then; zh, measure

piggy bank (pig′ē) **1** a small container in the shape of a pig, with a slot in the top for coins. **2** any coin bank.

pig–head·ed (pig′hed′id) stupidly obstinate or stubborn. *adj.*

pig·ment (pig′mənt) **1** a coloring matter: *Paint and dyes are made by mixing pigments with liquid.* **2** a substance that colors animal and plant tissue: *The color of a person's hair, skin, and eyes is due to pigment in the cells of the body. n.*

pig·my (pig′mē) See **pygmy.**

pig·pen (pig′pen′) **1** a pen where pigs are kept. **2** a filthy place. *n.*

pig·sty (pig′stī′) pigpen. *n., pl.* **pig·sties.**

pig·tail (pig′tāl′) a braid of hair hanging from the back of the head. *n.*

pike[1] (pīk) a weapon having a long wooden handle and a pointed metal head, once carried by foot soldiers; a spear. *n.*

pike[2] (pīk) a sharp point; a spike. *n.*

pike[3] (pīk) a large slender fresh-water fish with a pointed head. *n.*

pile[1] (pīl) **1** many things lying one upon another in a more or less orderly way: *a pile of wood.* **2** a heap; a mass like a hill or mound: *a pile of dirt.* **3** make into a pile; heap evenly; heap up: *The boys piled the blankets in a corner.* **4** gather or rise in piles: *Snow piled against the fences.* **5** *Informal.* a large amount: *a pile of work, a pile of dishes.* **6** a heap of wood on which a dead body or sacrifice is burned. **7** a reactor. 1, 2, 5–7 *n.*, 3, 4 *v.*

pile in or **out,** go in or out in a confused rush: *pile out into the street.*

pile up, heap up, collect together: *We will pile up all the money earned by class projects and give it to the playground fund.*

pile[2] (pīl) a heavy beam driven upright into the ground or the bed of a river to help support a bridge, wharf, building, etc. *n.*

pile[3] (pīl) **1** a soft, thick nap on velvet, plush, and many carpets: *The pile of that Chinese rug is almost two centimetres long.* **2** soft, fine hair or down; wool. *n.*

pil·fer (pil′fər) steal in small quantities: *The tramp pilfered some apples from the barrel. v.*

pil·grim (pil′grəm) **1** a person who goes on a journey to a sacred or holy place as an act of religious devotion: *In the Middle Ages, many people used to go as pilgrims to Jerusalem and to holy places in Europe.* **2** a traveller; wanderer. **3 Pilgrim,** one of the English settlers who founded Plymouth, Massachusetts, in 1620. *n.*

pil·grim·age (pil′grə mij) **1** a pilgrim's journey; a journey to some sacred place. **2** a long journey, especially one to see or visit a special place, etc. *n.*

pill (pil) **1** medicine made up into a tiny tablet or capsule to be swallowed whole. **2** a very small ball of anything. **3** something unpleasant that has to be endured: *Our defeat was a bitter pill.* *n.*

pil·lage (pil′ij) **1** to plunder; rob with violence: *Pirates pillaged the towns along the coast.* **2** plunder; robbery. 1 *v.,* **pil·laged, pil·lag·ing;** 2 *n.*

Pillars used as supports for a building

pil·lar (pil′ər) **1** a slender, upright structure; column: *Pillars are usually made of stone, wood, or metal and used as supports or ornaments for a building.* **2** anything slender and upright like a pillar: *a pillar of smoke.* **3** an important support or supporter: *He is known to be a pillar of the church.* *n.*

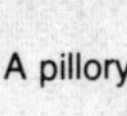

A pillory

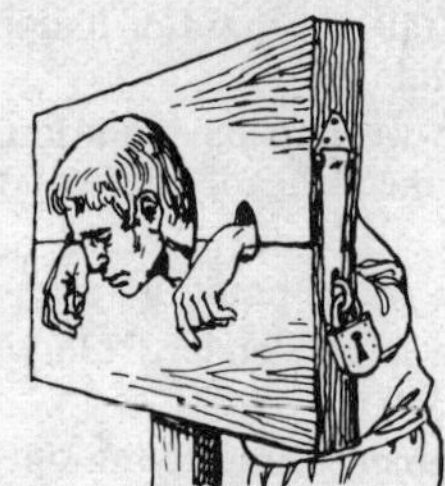

pil·lo·ry (pil′ə rē) **1** a frame of wood with holes through which a person's head and hands were put: *In former times, the pillory was used as a punishment, being set up in a public place where the crowd could make fun of the offender.* **2** expose to public ridicule, contempt, or abuse: *The newspapers pilloried the cruel father.* 1 *n., pl.* **pil·lo·ries;** 2 *v.,* **pil·lo·ried, pil·lo·ry·ing.**

pil·low (pil′ō) **1** a bag or case filled with feathers, down, or some other soft material, usually to support the head when resting or sleeping. **2** rest as on a pillow: *He pillowed his head on a pile of leaves.* 1 *n.,* 2 *v.*

pil·low·case (pil′ō kās′) a removable cloth cover for a pillow. *n.*

pi·lot (pī′lət) **1** a person who operates the controls of an aircraft in flight. **2** a man whose business is to steer ships in or out of a harbor or through dangerous waters: *A ship takes on a pilot before coming into a strange harbor.* **3** the man who steers a ship. **4** act as a pilot of; steer: *This businessman pilots his own airplane.* **5** a guide or leader. **6** guide or lead: *The manager piloted us through the big factory.* 1–3, 5 *n.,* 4, 6 *v.*

pi·men·to (pə men′tō) a kind of sweet red pepper, used as a vegetable, relish, and stuffing for green olives. *n.*

pim·ple (pim′pəl) a small, inflamed swelling of the skin. *n.*

pin (pin) **1** a short, slender piece of wire with a point at one end and a head at the other, used for fastening things together. **2** a kind of badge with a pin or clasp to fasten it to the clothing: *She wore her class pin.* **3** a brooch. **4** a peg made of wood, metal, or plastic used to fasten things together, hold something, or hang things on: *a clothes pin.* **5** anything that fastens: *a bobby pin.* **6** fasten with a pin or pins; put a pin through. **7** hold fast in one position: *When the tree fell, it pinned his shoulder to the ground.* **8** a bottle-shaped piece of wood used in the game of ninepins, tenpins, etc. 1–5, 8 *n.,* 6, 7 *v.,* **pinned, pin·ning.**

on pins and needles, very anxious or uneasy.

pin down, hold or bind to an undertaking or pledge.

pin on, *Informal.* fix blame, responsibility, etc. on: *The police could not pin the crime on him.*

pin·a·fore (pin′ə fôr′) **1** an apron that covers most of the dress. **2** a light dress without sleeves. *n.*

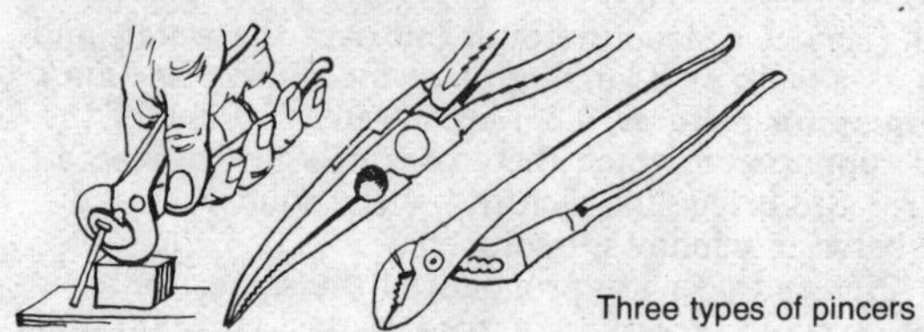

Three types of pincers

pin·cer (pin′sər) **1 pincers,** *pl.* a tool with hinged handles and jaws for gripping and holding. **2** a claw of a crab, lobster, etc., used to grip or pinch. *n.*

pinch (pinch) **1** squeeze with thumb and forefinger: *He pinched his little sister's arm.* **2** squeeze or press so as to hurt; get squeezed: *He pinched his finger in the door.* **3** a sharp pressure that hurts; a squeeze: *the pinch of tight shoes.* **4** sharp discomfort or distress: *the pinch of hunger.* **5** cause to shrink or become thin: *a face pinched by hunger.* **6** a time of special need; emergency: *We will ask for help in a pinch.* **7** as much as can be taken up with the tips of finger and thumb: *a pinch of salt.* **8** be stingy. **9** be stingy with: *The miser knew how to pinch pennies.* **10** *Slang.* steal; pilfer: *His father caught him pinching apples.* 1, 2, 5, 8–10 *v.,* 3, 4, 6, 7 *n.*

pinch–hit (pinch′hit′) **1** in baseball, to bat for another player, especially when a hit is badly needed. **2** take another's place in an emergency: *The pianist is ill and our teacher will pinch-hit for her at the concert tonight.* *v.*

pin·cush·ion (pin′kůsh′ən) a small cushion to stick pins in until needed. *n.*

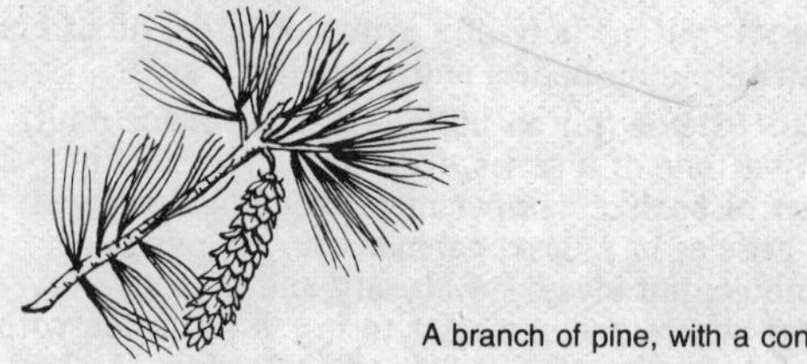

A branch of pine, with a cone

pine[1] (pīn) **1** any of several evergreen trees that have cones and needle-shaped leaves: *Many pines are of value for lumber, tar, turpentine, etc.* **2** the wood of the pine: *The walls were panelled with pine.* *n.*

hat, āge, fär; let, ēqual, tėrm; it, īce
hot, ōpen, ôrder; oil, out; cup, pu̇t, rüle
əbove, takən, pencəl, lemən, circəs
ch, child; ng, long; sh, ship
th, thin; ᴛʜ, then; zh, measure

pine[2] (pīn) **1** long eagerly; yearn: *The mother was pining to see her son.* **2** waste away with pain, hunger, grief, or desire. *v.,* **pined, pin·ing.**

A pineapple

pine·ap·ple (pīn′ap′əl) a large, juicy, tropical fruit resembling a large pine cone. *n.*

ping–pong (ping′pong′) table tennis. *n.*

pin·ion (pin′yən) **1** the outermost joint of a bird's wing. **2** a wing. **3** any one of the stiff flying feathers of the wing. **4** bind; bind the arms of; bind to something: *The thieves pinioned the man's arms.* 1–3 *n.,* 4 *v.*

pink (pingk) **1** the color made by mixing red and white; light or pale red. **2** of or having this color. **3** a garden plant with spicy-smelling flowers of various colors, mostly white, pink, and red: *A carnation is one kind of pink.* **4** the highest degree or condition: *By exercising every day he kept himself in the pink of health.* 1, 3, 4 *n.,* 2 *adj.*

pink·eye (pingk′ī′) a contagious disease that causes soreness of the membrane that lines the eyelids and covers the eyeball. *n.*

pink·ish (pingk′ish) somewhat pink. *adj.*

pin money a small amount of money used to buy extra things for one's own use.

pin·nace (pin′is) **1** a ship's boat. **2** a very small schooner. *n.*

pin·na·cle (pin′ə kəl) **1** a high peak or point of rock. **2** the highest point: *at the pinnacle of his fame.* **3** a slender turret or spire. *n.*

pint (pīnt) a unit of capacity equal to half a quart. *n.*

pin·to (pin′tō) **1** spotted in two or more colors. **2** a pinto horse. 1 *adj.,* 2 *n., pl.* **pin·tos.**

pin·wheel (pin′wēl′ or pin′hwēl′) **1** a toy made of a wheel fastened to a stick by a pin so that it revolves in the wind. **2** a kind of firework that revolves when lighted. *n.*

pi·o·neer (pī′ə nēr′) **1** a person who settles in a region that has not been settled before. **2** a person who goes first or does something first, and so prepares a way for others. **3** prepare or open up for others; take the lead: *Astronauts are pioneering in exploring outer space.* 1, 2 *n.,* 3 *v.*

pi·ous (pī′əs) **1** religious; devoted to a religious life. **2** appearing or pretending to be religious: *a pious fraud. adj.*

pip[1] (pip) the seed of an apple, orange, grape, etc. *n.*

pip[2] (pip) a disease of birds. *n.*

give one the pip, *Informal.* make one sick; disgust one; irritate one: *That man's nasty way of talking gives me the pip.*

pipe (pīp) **1** a tube through which a liquid or gas flows. **2** carry by means of a pipe or pipes. **3** supply with pipes: *Our street is being piped for gas.* **4** a tube of clay, wood, etc. with a bowl at one end, for smoking. **5** a musical instrument with a single tube into which the player blows. **6 pipes,** *pl.* a bagpipe. **7** play music on a pipe. **8** any one of the tubes in an organ. **9** make a shrill noise; sing in a shrill voice. **10** a high-pitched song or note: *the pipe of a lark in the morning.* 1, 4–6, 8, 10 *n.,* 2, 3, 7, 9 *v.,* **piped, pip·ing. —pip′er,** *n.*

pipe down, *Slang.* be quiet; shut up.

pipe·line (pīp′līn′) a line of pipes for carrying gas, oil, or other liquids: *Some pipelines are several hundred kilometres long.* *n.*

pip·ing (pīp′ing) **1** a shrill sound: *the piping of frogs in the spring.* **2** shrill. **3** pipes: *copper piping.* 1, 3 *n.,* 2 *adj.*

piping hot, very hot.

pi·ra·cy (pī′rə sē) robbery on the sea. *n., pl.* **pi·ra·cies.**

pi·rate (pī′rit) **1** one who attacks and robs ships; a robber on the sea. **2** be a pirate. **3** publish or use without the author's, inventor's, or owner's permission. 1 *n.,* 2, 3 *v.,* **pi·rat·ed, pi·rat·ing.**

pis·til (pis′təl) the seed-bearing part of a flower. See **flower** for picture. *n.*

☛ **Pistil** and **pistol** are pronounced the same.

pis·tol (pis′təl) a small, short gun held and fired with one hand: *A revolver is a kind of pistol.* *n.*

☛ See note at **pistil.**

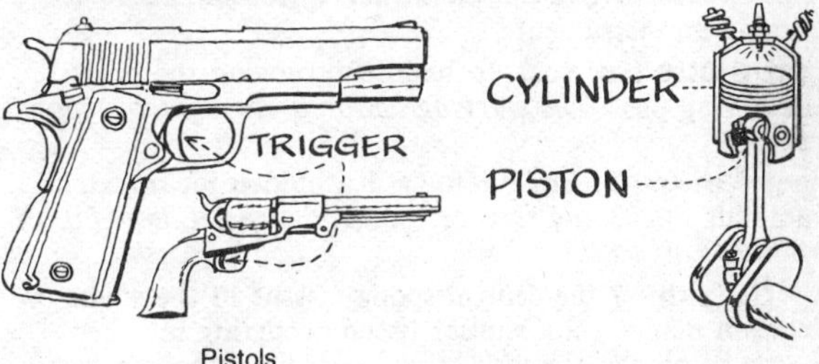

Pistols

pis·ton (pis′tən) in an engine, a short cylinder, or a flat, round piece of wood or metal, fitting closely inside a tube or hollow cylinder in which it is moved back and forth by the force of exploding vapor or steam: *A piston receives or transmits motion by means of a rod that is attached to it.* *n.*

pit[1] (pit) **1** a natural hole in the ground. **2** a hole dug deep in the earth: *A lion was trapped in the pit.* *A mine or the shaft of a mine is a pit.* **3** a hollow on the surface of anything; a hole. **4** a little hole or scar such as is left by smallpox. **5** to mark with small pits or scars. **6** set to fight or compete; match: *The man pitted his brains against the strength of the bear.* 1–4 *n.,* 5, 6 *v.,* **pit·ted, pit·ting.**

pit[2] (pit) **1** the hard seed of a cherry, peach, plum, date, etc. **2** remove the pits from fruit. 1 *n.,* 2 *v.,* **pit·ted, pit·ting.**

pitch[1] (pich) 1 throw; fling; hurl; toss: *The men were pitching horseshoes. He pitched a penny in the pail.* 2 in baseball, to throw a ball to the man batting. 3 fix firmly in the ground; set up: *to pitch a tent.* 4 fall or plunge forward: *The man lost his balance and pitched down the cliff.* 5 plunge with the bow rising and then falling: *The ship pitched about in the storm.* 6 a point or position; a degree: *The poor man has reached the lowest pitch of bad fortune.* 7 the degree of highness or lowness of a sound. 8 the act or manner of pitching. 9 the amount of slope: *Some roads in the Rocky Mountains have a very steep pitch.* 1–5 *v.*, 6–9 *n.*
pitch in, work hard: *All the boys pitched in to get the job done.*
pitch into, *Informal.* attack.

pitch[2] (pich) 1 a black, sticky substance made from tar or turpentine, used to fill the seams of wooden ships, to cover roofs, to make pavements, etc. 2 to cover with pitch. 3 resin from certain evergreen trees. 1, 3 *n.*, 2 *v.*

pitch·blende (pich′blend′) a mineral occurring in black, pitchlike masses: *Pitchblende is a source of radium and uranium. n.*

pitch·er[1] (pich′ər) 1 a container with a lip at one side and a handle at the other: *Pitchers are used for holding and pouring out water, milk, etc.* 2 the amount that a pitcher holds. *n.*

pitch·er[2] (pich′ər) the player on a baseball team who throws the ball to the batter. *n.*

pitch·fork (pich′fôrk′) a large fork with a long handle for lifting and throwing hay or straw. See **fork** for picture. *n.*

pitch pipe a small musical pipe having one or more notes, used to give the pitch (def. 7) for singing or for tuning an instrument.

pit·e·ous (pit′ē əs) to be pitied; moving the heart; deserving pity: *The starving children are a piteous sight. adj.*

pit·fall (pit′fol′ or pit′fôl′) 1 a hidden pit to catch animals in. 2 any trap or hidden danger: *Life is full of pitfalls. n.*

pith (pith) 1 the central spongy tissue in the stems of certain plants. 2 a similar tissue occurring in other parts of plants: *the pith of an orange.* 3 the important or essential part: *the pith of a speech. n.*

pit·i·a·ble (pit′ē ə bəl) 1 to be pitied; moving the heart; deserving pity. 2 deserving contempt; mean; to be scorned: *His half-hearted attempts to help with the work were pitiable. adj.*

pit·i·ful (pit′ē fəl) 1 to be pitied; arousing pity: *The deserted children were a very pitiful sight.* 2 deserving contempt; mean; to be scorned: *Driving away after hitting a dog is a pitiful act. adj.*

pit·i·less (pit′ē lis) without pity or mercy. *adj.*

pi·tu·i·tar·y gland (pə tyü′ə ter′ē or pə tü′ə ter′ē) a small oval gland at the base of the brain that produces hormones that stimulate growth and regulate many bodily functions.

pit·y (pit′ē) 1 sympathy; sorrow for another's suffering or distress; a feeling for the sorrows of others. 2 feel pity for: *She pitied any child who was hurt.* 3 a cause for pity or regret; something to be sorry for: *It is a pity to be kept in the house in fine weather.* 1, 3 *n.*, *pl.* **pit·ies;** 2 *v.*, **pit·ied, pit·y·ing.**
have or **take pity on,** show pity for.

piv·ot (piv′ət) 1 a shaft, pin, or point on which something turns. 2 mount on, attach by, or provide with a pivot. 3 turn on a pivot or something like a pivot: *pivot on one's heel.* 4 that on which something turns, hinges, or depends; a central point: *His ability to lead made him the pivot of the team.* 1, 4 *n.*, 2, 3 *v.*

pix·ie or **pix·y** (pik′sē) a fairy or elf. *n.*, *pl.* **pix·ies.**

piz·za (pēt′sa) an Italian dish, usually made of a layer of bread dough covered with a tasty mixture of tomatoes, cheese, olives, etc. and baked. *n.*

pkg. package.

pl. plural.

plac·ard (plak′ärd) 1 a notice to be posted in a public place; a poster. 2 put placards on or in: *The circus placarded the city with advertisements.* 1 *n.*, 2 *v.*

pla·cate (plak′āt, plā′kāt, or plə kāt′) soothe or satisfy the anger of; make peaceful: *He did his best to placate the angry woman. v.*, **pla·cated, pla·cat·ing.**

place (plās) 1 a particular part of space: *This is a good place for a picnic.* 2 a city, town, village, district, island, etc.: *What place do you come from?* 3 a building or spot used for some particular purpose: *A church is a place of worship. A store or office is a place of business.* 4 a house or dwelling: *The Smiths have a beautiful place in the country.* 5 a part or spot in something: *a sore place on one's foot. The dentist filled the decayed place in the tooth.* 6 the proper or natural position: *There is a time and place for everything. Each book is in its place on the shelf.* 7 a rank or position: *He won first place in the contest. The servant filled his place well.* 8 a position in time; the part of time occupied by an event: *The performance went too slowly in several places.* 9 in arithmetic, the position of a figure in a number or series: *in the third decimal place.* 10 a space or seat for a person: *We took our places at the table.* 11 put in a particular spot, position, or condition: *Place the books on the table. The child was placed in a home. We placed an order for hats with this store. The people placed confidence in their leader.* 12 give the place, position, or condition of; identify: *I remember his name, but I cannot place him.* 13 finish among the leaders in a race or competition: *He failed to place in the first race and was eliminated.* 14 work or employment; a job: *He tried to get a place in a store on Saturdays.* 15 duty; business: *It is not my place to find fault.* 1–10, 14, 15 *n.*, 11–13 *v.*, **placed, plac·ing.**
give place, a make room. **b** yield; give in: *His anger gave place to remorse.*
in place of, instead of: *Use water in place of milk in that recipe.*
out of place, a not in the proper or usual place. **b** inappropriate or coming at a bad time: *Party clothes would be out of place on the playground. Chatter is out of place at a concert.*
take place, happen; occur.

plac·er (plas′ər) a deposit of sand, gravel, or earth in the bed of a stream, containing particles of gold or other valuable minerals. *n.*

placer mining the process of washing loose gravel or sand for gold or other minerals: *Placer mining was a common practice in the Klondike.*

hat, āge, fär; let, ēqual, tėrm; it, īce
hot, ōpen, ôrder; oil, out; cup, pu̇t, rüle
əbove, takən, pencəl, lemən, circəs
ch, child; ng, long; sh, ship
th, thin; ᴛʜ, then; zh, measure

plac·id (plas′id) calm; peaceful; quiet: *a placid lake, a placid temper.* *adj.*

plague (plāg) **1** a very dangerous disease that spreads rapidly and often causes death. **2** any epidemic disease; pestilence. **3** a punishment thought to be sent by God. **4** cause to suffer from disease or calamity. **5** anything or anyone that torments, vexes, annoys, troubles, offends, or is disagreeable: *My hay fever is a plague this year.* **6** vex; annoy; bother: *Stop plaguing me for money.* 1–3, 5 *n.*, 4, 6 *v.*, **plagued, pla·guing.**

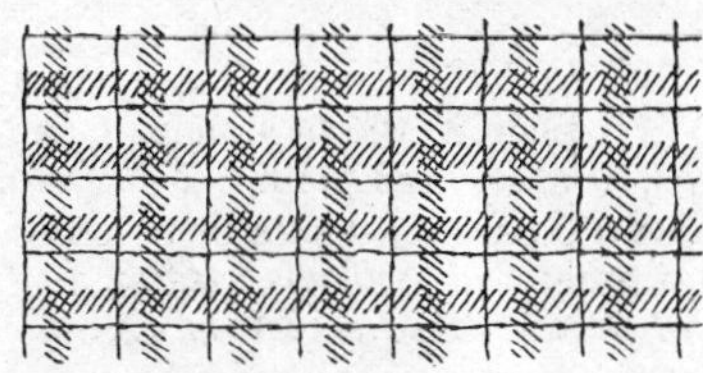
Plaid cloth

plaid (plad) **1** any cloth with a pattern of checks or crisscross stripes. **2** a pattern of this kind. **3** a long piece of woollen cloth, usually having a pattern of checks or stripes in many colors, worn over one shoulder by the Scottish Highlanders. **4** crisscross stripes. *n.*
☞ **Plaid** comes from a Scots Gaelic word *plaide,* meaning 'blanket.'

plain (plān) **1** clear; easy to understand; easily seen or heard: *The meaning is plain.* **2** clearly; in a plain manner: *Speak it plain.* **3** without ornament or decoration: *a plain dress.* **4** all of one color; without a printed or woven pattern: *a plain blue dress.* **5** not rich or highly seasoned: *plain food.* **6** common; ordinary; simple in manner: *a plain man of the people.* **7** not pretty: *a plain girl.* **8** frank; honest; sincere: *plain speech.* **9** a flat stretch of land; prairie: *the western plains. Cattle wandered over the plain.* 1, 3–8 *adj.*, 2 *adv.*, 9 *n.*
☞ **Plain** and **plane** are pronounced the same.

plain·tive (plān′tiv) mournful; sad: *a plaintive song.* *adj.*

plait (plāt or plat for 1 and 2, plāt or plēt for 3) **1** a braid: *She wore her hair in a plait.* **2** to braid: *She plaits her hair.* **3** pleat (defs. 1 and 2). 1, 3 *n.*, 2, 3 *v.*
☞ **Plait** and **plate** are sometimes pronounced the same.

plan (plan) **1** a way of making or doing something that has been worked out beforehand: *Our summer plans were upset by Mother's illness.* **2** think out beforehand how something is to be made or done; design or scheme: *The police planned a new attempt to find the criminals.* **3** have in mind as a purpose; intend: *We are planning to take a long vacation this year.* **4** a drawing or diagram to show how a garden, a floor of a house, a park, etc. is arranged. See the picture. **5** make a drawing or diagram of. 1, 4 *n.*, 2, 3, 5 *v.*, **planned, plan·ning.**

plane¹ (plān) **1** a flat or level surface. **2** flat; level. **3** a standard of conduct, thought, or achievement; a level: *Try to keep your work on a high plane.* **4** a thin, flat or curved surface that helps to support an airplane. **5** an airplane. 1, 3–5 *n.*, 2 *adj.*
☞ **Plane** and **plain** are pronounced the same.

plane² (plān) **1** a carpenter's tool with a blade for smoothing or shaping wood. **2** to smooth wood with a plane. 1 *n.*, 2 *v.*, **planed, plan·ing.**
☞ See note at **plane¹**.

plan·et (plan′it) one of the heavenly bodies that move around the sun in regular paths: *Mercury, Venus, Earth, Mars, Jupiter, Saturn, Uranus, Neptune, and Pluto are planets.* *n.*

plan·e·tar·i·um (plan′ə ter′ē əm) a place with an apparatus that shows the movements of the sun, moon, planets, and stars by projecting lights on the inside of a dome. *n.*

plan·e·tar·y (plan′ə ter′ē) of a planet; having to do with planets. *adj.*

plank (plangk) **1** a long, flat piece of sawed timber thicker than a board. **2** to cover or furnish with planks. 1 *n.*, 2 *v.*
walk the plank, be put to death by being forced to walk off a plank extending from a ship's side over the water: *Pirates used to make their prisoners walk the plank.*

plank·ton (plangk′tən) the small animal and plant organisms that float or drift in water, especially at or near the surface. *n.*

plan·ner (plan′ər) a person who plans. *n.*

plant (plant) **1** any living thing that is not an animal: *Trees, bushes, vines, grass, vegetables, and seaweed are all plants.* **2** a living thing that has leaves, roots, and a soft stem, and is small in contrast with a tree or shrub: *a tomato plant, a house plant.* **3** a young growth ready to be set out in another place: *The farmer set out 100 cabbage plants.* **4** put in the ground to grow: *Farmers plant seeds.* **5** provide with seed or plants; put seed in: *He planted his garden with beans.* **6** set firmly; put; place: *Columbus planted the flag of Spain in the ground. The boy planted his feet far apart.* **7** establish a colony, city, etc.; settle. **8** put in or instil ideas, feelings, etc.: *Parents try to plant ideals in their children.* **9** the building, machinery, tools, etc. used in a business or institution: *There is an aluminum plant in Kingston.* 1–3, 9 *n.*, 4–8 *v.*

plan·tain¹ (plan′tān) **1** a kind of large banana. **2** the plant that it grows on. *n.*

plan·tain² (plan′tān) a common weed having large, spreading leaves close to the ground and long, slender spikes carrying flowers and seeds. *n.*

plan·ta·tion (plan tā′shən) **1** a large farm or estate on which such crops as cotton, tobacco, or sugar are

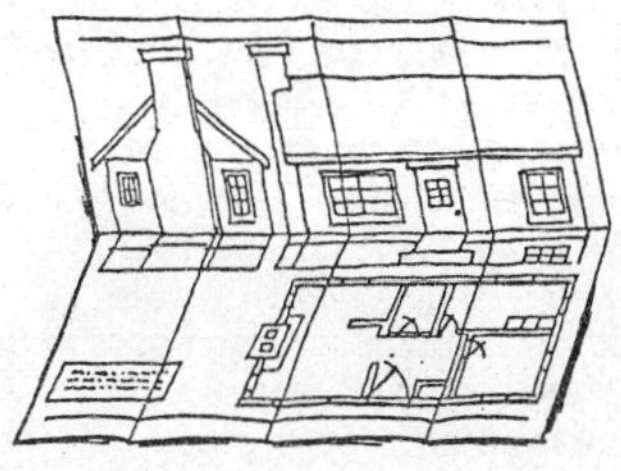
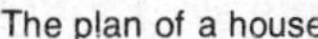
The plan of a house

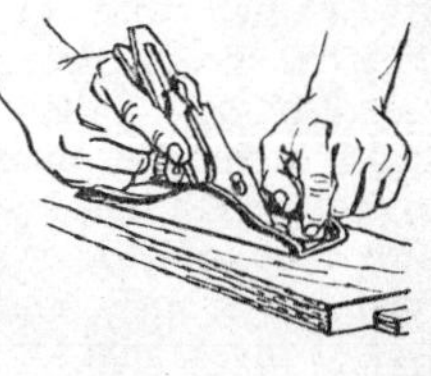
A plane. The blade is fastened at a slant between the two handles. It is raised or lowered to shave more or less wood at each stroke.

grown: *The work on a plantation is done by laborers who live there.* 2 a large group of trees or other plants that have been planted. 3 a colony; settlement: *Plantations were established in Newfoundland in the early 1600's.* *n.*

plant·er (plan′tər) 1 a person who owns or runs a plantation: *a cotton planter.* 2 a machine for planting: *a corn planter.* 3 an early settler; colonist. 4 a box, stand, or other holder used for growing plants indoors, on a patio or balcony, etc. *n.*

plas·ma (plaz′mə) the clear, almost colorless, liquid part of blood or lymph, in which the corpuscles or blood cells float. *n.*

plas·ter (plas′tər) 1 a soft mixture of lime, sand, and water that hardens in drying, used for covering walls or ceilings. 2 cover walls, ceilings, etc. with plaster. 3 spread with anything thickly: *His shoes were plastered with mud.* 4 a substance spread on cloth, which will stick to the body and protect cuts, relieve pain, etc. 1, 4 *n.*, 2, 3 *v.*

plas·ter·board (plas′tər bôrd′) a thin board made of a layer of plaster between layers of pressed felt, covered with paper: *Plasterboard is much used in building walls and partitions.* *n.*

plaster of Paris a mixture of powdered gypsum and water, which hardens quickly. It is used for making moulds, casts, etc.

plas·tic (plas′tik) 1 any of various man-made materials that are made from chemicals and are shaped or moulded when hot: *Some plastics are very strong and tough. Nylon is a plastic.* 2 made of such a material: *plastic cups.* 3 easily moulded or shaped: *Clay, wax, and plaster are plastic substances.* 4 moulding or giving shape to materials: *Sculpture is a plastic art.* 1 *n.*, 2–4 *adj.*

Plas·ti·cine (plas′ti sēn′) the trademark for a substance used for modelling, especially by children. *n.*

plas·tics (plas′tiks) 1 the range of man-made materials and products that are made from chemicals and are shaped or moulded when hot: *Plastics are often used in place of glass, leather, wood, metal, wool, etc.* 2 the branch of chemistry that deals with the study and use of such materials. *n.*

plastic surgery surgery that restores or improves the outer appearance of the body: *He underwent plastic surgery to straighten his broken nose.*

plate (plāt) 1 a dish, usually round, that is almost flat: *Our food is served on plates.* 2 the contents of such a dish: *a small plate of stew.* 3 something having a similar shape: *A plate is passed in our church to receive the collection.* 4 the food served to one person at a meal. 5 dishes or utensils made of silver or gold or covered with a thin layer of silver or gold: *The family plate included a silver pitcher, candelsticks, and the usual knives, forks, and spoons.* 6 cover with a thin layer of silver, gold, or some other metal. 7 a thin, flat sheet or piece of metal: *The warship was covered with steel plates.* 8 cover with metal plates for protection. 9 a platelike part, organ, or structure: *Some reptiles and fish have a covering of horny or bony plates.* 10 a thin, flat piece of metal, plastic, etc., on which something is engraved: *Plates are used for printing pictures.* 11 a thin sheet of glass coated with chemicals that are sensitive to light: *Plates are sometimes used in taking photographs.* 12 a piece of firm material with false teeth set into it. 13 in baseball, the home base. 1–5, 7, 9–13 *n.*, 6, 8 *v.*, **plat·ed, plat·ing.**

☛ **Plate** and **plait** are sometimes pronounced the same.

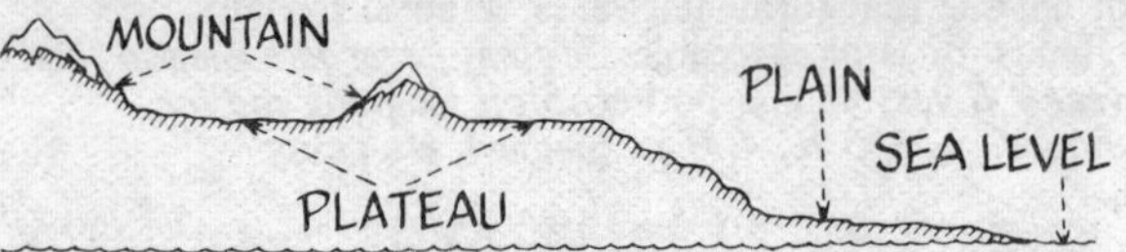

pla·teau (pla tō′) 1 a plain in the mountains or at a height above sea level; a large, high plain. 2 a level of progress or achievement, especially where there is no further progress for a time: *Our volleyball team improved rapidly and then reached a plateau.* *n., pl.* **pla·teaus.**

plat·form (plat′fôrm) 1 a raised, level surface: *There is a platform beside the track at the railway station. The hall has a platform for speakers.* 2 a plan of action or statement of beliefs of a group: *The platform of the new political party demands lower taxes.* *n.*

plat·i·num (plat′ə nəm) a heavy, precious metal that looks like silver: *Platinum does not tarnish or melt easily and is used in jewellery.* *n.*

pla·toon (plə tün′) 1 a group of soldiers acting as a unit: *A platoon is smaller than a company and larger than a section.* 2 a small group of people. *n.*

plat·ter (plat′ər) a large flat dish for serving food, especially meat. *n.*

plat·y·pus (plat′ə pəs) the duckbill. *n., pl.* **plat·y·pus·es** or **plat·y·pi** (plat′ə pī).

plau·si·ble (plo′zə bəl or plô′zə bəl) 1 appearing true, reasonable, or fair: *His story sounded plausible to us.* 2 apparently worthy of confidence but often not really so: *a plausible liar.* *adj.*

play (plā) 1 fun; sport; something done to amuse oneself: *All work and no play makes Jack a dull boy. The children are happy at play.* 2 have fun; do something in sport; perform: *The kitten plays with its tail. Jack played a joke on his sister.* 3 take part in a game: *Children play tag and ball.* 4 take part in a game against: *Our team played the sixth-grade team.* 5 put in the game; cause to play or be played: *Each coach played his best goalie. Play your ten of hearts.* 6 a turn, move, or act in a game: *It is your play next. He made a good play at checkers.* 7 the act of carrying on a game: *Play was slow in the first half of the game.* 8 a story acted on the stage: *'Peter Pan' is a charming play.* 9 act a part; act the part of: *Mary Martin played Peter Pan.* 10 act in a certain way: *to play the fool, to play fair.* 11 action: *fair play, foul play. He brought all his strength into play to move the rock.* 12 make believe; pretend in fun: *Let's play that the hammock is a boat.* 13 make music; produce music on an instrument: *play a tune.* 14 perform on a musical instrument: *play a piano.* 15 move lightly or quickly: *A breeze played on the water. The poet's fancy played over the old legend and gave it new form.* 16 a light, quick movement: *the play of sunlight on leaves.* 17 freedom for action, motion, etc.: *The boy gave his fancy full play in telling what he could do with a million dollars.* 18 cause to act or to move; direct in a constant manner over an area: *to play a hose on a burning building. The ship*

hat, āge, fär; let, ēqual, tėrm; it, īce
hot, ōpen, ôrder; oil, out; cup, pu̇t, rüle
əbove, takən, pencəl, lemən, circəs
ch, child; ng, long; sh, ship
th, thin; ᴛʜ, then; zh, measure

played its light along the coast. **19** do something foolishly or pointlessly; trifle: *Do not play with your food. Don't play with matches.* 1, 6–8, 11, 16, 17 *n.*, 2–5, 9, 10, 12–15, 18, 19 *v.*

play into the hands of, act so as to give the advantage to.

play off, hold a competition in which players or teams are pitted against each other to decide the champion.

play on, take advantage of; make use of: *She played on her mother's good nature.*

play up, make the most of; exploit.

play up to, *Slang.* try to get the favor of; flatter: *play up to a famous person.*

play·er (plā′ər) **1** a person who plays: *a baseball player, a card player.* **2** an actor in a theatre. **4** a person who plays a musical instrument. **4** a device that plays: *a record player. n.*

play·fel·low (plā′fel′ō) a playmate. *n.*

play·ful (plā′fəl) **1** full of fun; fond of playing. **2** joking; not serious: *a playful remark. adj.*

play·ground (plā′ground′) a place for outdoor play. *n.*

play·house (plā′hous′) **1** a small house for a child to play in. **2** a theatre. *n.*

playing card a card used in playing games, usually one of a set of 52 cards including four suits (def. 9) of 13 cards each.

play·mate (plā′māt′) a person who plays with another. *n.*

play·off (plā′of′) **1** an extra game or round played off to settle a tie. **2** one of a series of games played by the top teams in a league to determine the winner of a championship. *n.*

play·pen (plā′pen′) a small enclosure for very young children to play in. *n.*

play·thing (plā′thing′) a thing to play with; a toy. *n.*

play·wright (plā′rīt′) a writer of plays; a dramatist. *n.*

☛ *Wright* in **playwright** is not related to **write,** but is an old English word meaning 'maker' or 'builder,' which is still found in a few compound words and family names.

pla·za (plaz′ə or plä′zə) **1** a shopping centre. **2** a public square in a city or town. *n.*

plea (plē) **1** a request or appeal; asking: *The giant laughed at Jack's plea for mercy.* **2** an excuse: *The plea of the man who drove past the red light was that he did not see it. n.*

plead (plēd) **1** offer reasons for or against something; argue: *He pleaded the cause of the Indians.* **2** ask earnestly; make an earnest appeal: *When the rent was due, the poor man pleaded for more time.* **3** offer as an excuse: *The woman who stole pleaded poverty.* **4** speak for in a law court: *He had a good lawyer to plead his case.* **5** answer to a charge in a law court: *The prisoner pleaded guilty to the charge of theft. v.*, **plead·ed** or **pled, plead·ing.**

pleas·ant (plez′ənt) **1** that pleases; giving pleasure: *a pleasant swim on a hot day.* **2** easy to get along with; friendly. **3** fair; not stormy: *pleasant weather. adj.*

pleas·ant·ry (plez′ənt rē) **1** a good-natured joke; a witty remark. **2** lively, good-humored talk: *The air was filled with pleasantries after the wedding. n.*

please (plēz) **1** give enjoyment to; be agreeable to: *Toys please children. Sunshine and flowers please most people.* **2** be agreeable; satisfy: *Such a fine meal cannot fail to please.* **3** wish; think fit: *Do what you please.* **4 Please** is a polite way of asking: *Come here, please. v.*, **pleased, pleas·ing.**

be pleased, a be moved to pleasure: *He was pleased at the good news.* **b** like; choose: *I will be pleased to go.*

pleas·ing (plēz′ing) giving pleasure; pleasant: *a very well-mannered and pleasing young man, a pleasing smile. adj.*

pleas·ure (plezh′ər) **1** the feeling of being pleased; delight; joy: *The boy's pleasure in the gift was good to see.* **2** something that pleases; a cause of joy or delight: *It would be a pleasure to see you again.* **3** anything that amuses; sport; play: *He takes his pleasure in riding and hunting.* **4** one's will, desire, or choice: *Is it your pleasure to go now? n.*

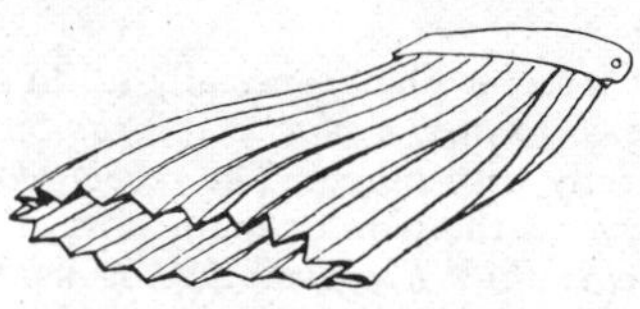

A skirt with pleats

pleat (plēt) **1** a flat, usually narrow, fold made by doubling material on itself. **2** fold or arrange in pleats: *a pleated skirt.* 1 *n.*, 2 *v.*

pled (pled) See **plead.** *The man pled for mercy. v.*

pledge (plej) **1** a solemn promise: *Mr. Jones signed a pledge to give money to charity.* **2** to promise solemnly: *We pledge loyalty to our country.* **3** cause to promise solemnly; bind by a promise: *They pledged the hearers to secrecy.* **4** something that secures or makes safe; security: *I left my watch as pledge for the money I borrowed.* **5** give as security. **6** drink in honor of someone and wish him well: *The knights rose from the banquet table to pledge the king.* **7** something given to show favor or love or as a promise of something to come: *He gave her a brooch as a pledge of his friendship.* 1, 4, 7 *n.*, 2, 3, 5, 6 *v.*, **pledged, pledg·ing.**

plen·te·ous (plen′tē əs) plentiful. *adj.*

plen·ti·ful (plen′tə fəl) more than enough; ample; abundant: *Thirty litres of gasoline is a plentiful supply for a ninety kilometre trip. Apples are cheap now because they are plentiful. adj.*

plen·ty (plen′tē) a full supply; all that one needs; a large enough number or amount: *You have plenty of time to catch the train. n.*

pli·a·ble (plī′ə bəl) **1** easily bent; flexible; supple: *Willow twigs are pliable.* **2** easily influenced; yielding: *He is too pliable to be a good leader. adj.*

pli·ant (plī′ənt) **1** bending easily; pliable: *pliant leather.* **2** easily influenced; yielding: *a pliant nature. adj.*

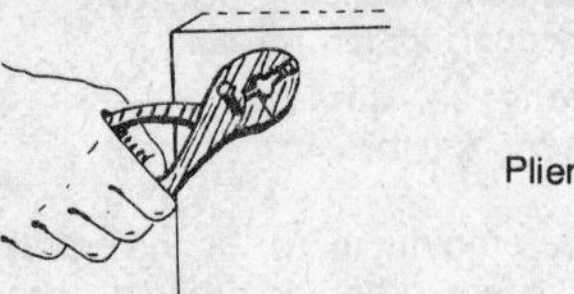
Pliers

pli·ers (plī′ərz) a hinged tool used for bending or cutting wire, for holding small objects, etc. *n. pl. or sing.*

plight[1] (plīt) a condition or state, usually bad: *He was in a sad plight when he became ill and had no money. n.*

plight[2] (plīt) pledge; promise solemnly: *to plight one's loyalty. v.*

plod (plod) **1** walk heavily; trudge: *The old man plods wearily along the road.* **2** proceed in a slow or dull way; work patiently with effort: *That boy plods away at his arithmetic lessons until he learns them. v.,* **plod·ded, plod·ding.**

plop (plop) **1** a sound like that of a flat object striking water without a splash. **2** make such a sound. 1 *n.,* 2 *v.*

plot (plot) **1** a secret plan, especially to do something wrong: *Two men formed a plot to rob the bank.* **2** to plan; plan secretly with others: *The rebels plotted against the government.* **3** the plan or main story of a play, novel, poem, etc.: *Boys like plots dealing with adventure and mystery.* **4** a small piece of ground: *a garden plot.* **5** divide land into plots: *The farm was plotted out into house lots.* **6** a map or diagram. **7** make a map or diagram of; mark something on a map or diagram: *The nurse plotted the patient's temperature over several days.* 1, 3, 4, 6 *n.,* 2, 5, 7 *v.,* **plot·ted, plot·ting.**

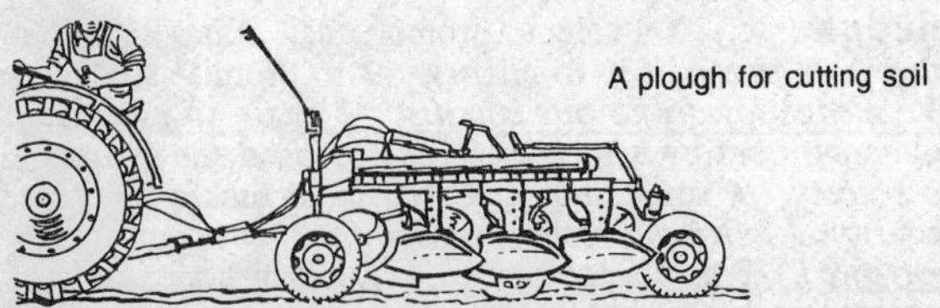
A plough for cutting soil

plough or **plow** (plou) **1** a farm implement used for cutting the soil and turning it over. **2** turn over the soil with a plough; use a plough: *plough a field. He was ploughing yesterday.* **3** a machine for removing snow, usually called a snowplough. **4** move through anything as a plough does; advance slowly and with effort: *The ship ploughed through the heavy waves.* 1, 3 *n.,* 2, 4 *v.*

plough·man or **plow·man** (plou′mən) **1** a man who guides a plough. **2** a farm worker. *n., pl.* **plough·men** or **plow·men** (plou′mən).

plough·share or **plow·share** (plou′sher′) the part of a plough that cuts the soil. See **plough** for picture. *n.*

plov·er (pluv′ər) a shore bird having a short tail and bill and long pointed wings. *n.*

plow (plou) See **plough.**

pluck (pluk) **1** pick; pull off: *She plucked flowers in the garden.* **2** pull; pull at; tug; jerk: *She plucked at the loose threads of her coat. He plucked the strings of his guitar.* **3** pull the feathers out of: *The farmer's wife was busy plucking chickens.* **4** courage: *The cat showed pluck in fighting the dog.* 1–3 *v.,* 4 *n.*

pluck·y (pluk′ē) having or showing courage: *a plucky dog. adj.,* **pluck·i·er, pluck·i·est.**

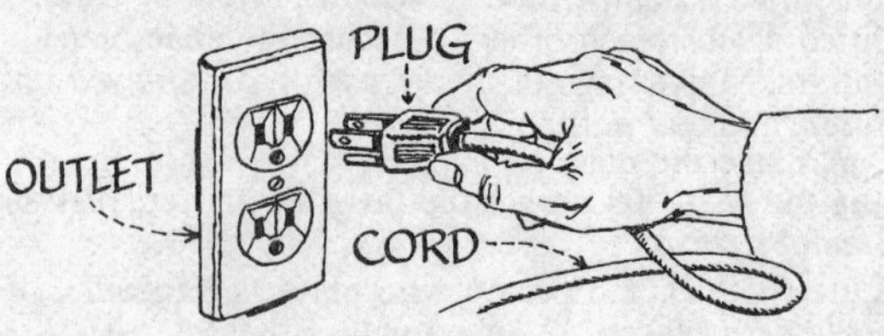

plug (plug) **1** a piece of wood or some other substance used to stop up a hole. **2** a disc of rubber or metal for stopping the drain of a sink, basin, bathtub, etc. **3** stop up or fill with a plug. **4** a device to make an electrical connection: *Some plugs screw into sockets; others have prongs.* **5** a cake of pressed tobacco; a piece of this cut off for chewing. **6** *Informal.* work steadily; plod: *She plugged away at the typewriter.* **7** *Informal.* recommend or advertise, especially on a radio or television program: *plug a new product.* **8** *Informal.* an advertisement or recommendation, especially on a radio or television program. **9** a lure for catching fish. 1, 2, 4, 5, 8, 9 *n.,* 3, 6, 7 *v.,* **plugged, plug·ging.**

plug in, make an electrical connection by inserting a plug.

plum (plum) **1** a round, juicy fruit having a smooth skin and a stone or pit: *Plums are red, green, purple, or yellow.* **2** the tree that it grows on. **3** a raisin in a pudding or cake. **4** something very good or desirable: *This new job is a fine plum for him.* **5** dark bluish-purple. 1–5 *n.,* 5 *adj.*

☛ **Plum** and **plumb** are pronounced the same.

plum·age (plü′mij) the feathers of a bird: *A parrot has bright plumage. n.*

plumb (plum) **1** a small weight used on the end of a line to find the depth of water or to see if a wall is vertical. **2** test or adjust by a plumb line; sound: *Our line was not long enough to plumb the depths of the lake.* **3** get to the bottom of: *No one could plumb the deep mystery.* 1 *n.,* 2, 3 *v.*

☛ **Plumb** and **plum** are pronounced the same.

plumb·er (plum′ər) a man whose work is putting in and repairing water pipes and fixtures in buildings: *When the water pipe froze, we sent for a plumber. n.*

plumb·ing (plum′ing) **1** the work or trade of a plumber. **2** the water pipes and fixtures in a building: *the bathroom plumbing. n.*

plume (plüm) **1** a large, long feather; a feather. **2** a feather ornament. **3** furnish with plumes. **4** smooth or arrange the feathers of: *The eagle plumed its wing.* **5** show pride in oneself: *She plumed herself on her skill in dancing.* 1, 2 *n.,* 3–5 *v.,* **plumed, plum·ing.**

plum·met (plum′it) **1** plunge; drop: *plummet into the sea.* **2** plumb. 1 *v.,* 2 *n.*

plump[1] (plump) rounded out; fat in an attractive way: *A healthy baby has plump cheeks. adj.*

plump[2] (plump) **1** fall or drop heavily or suddenly: *All out of breath, she plumped down on a chair.* **2** *Informal.* a sudden plunge; a heavy fall. **3** *Informal.* the sound made by a plunge or fall. **4** heavily or suddenly: *The lunch basket fell plump into the pond.*

He ran plump into me. 1 *v.,* 2, 3 *n.,* 4 *adv.*

plum pudding a rich, cooked pudding containing raisins, currants, spices, etc.

plun·der (plun′dər) 1 rob by force; rob: *The pirates entered the harbor and began to plunder the town.* 2 things stolen; booty; loot: *The pirates buried their plunder in a secret place.* 3 robbing by force: *In olden times soldiers often gained great wealth by the plunder of a conquered city.* 1 *v.,* 2, 3 *n.*

plunge (plunj) 1 throw or thrust with force into something, especially a liquid: *plunge one's hand into water.* 2 throw suddenly or violently into a certain condition: *plunge the world into war, plunge the room into darkness.* 3 throw oneself into water, danger, a fight, etc.: *He plunged into the river and saved the boy.* 4 a sudden rush or jump. 5 rush or dash: *The runner plunged ahead to win the race.* 6 pitch or lurch suddenly and violently: *The ship plunged about in the storm.* 1–3, 5, 6 *v.,* **plunged, plung·ing;** 4 *n.*

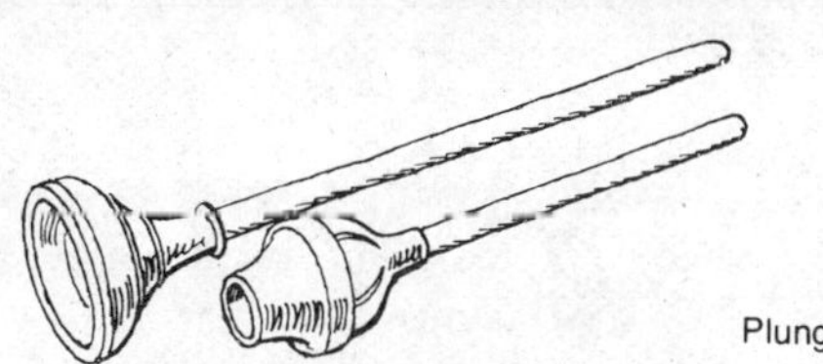

Plungers

plung·er (plun′jər) a rubber suction cup on a long stick, used for unplugging stopped-up drains, toilets, etc. *n.*

plu·ral (plür′əl) 1 referring to more than one: *Scissors is a plural noun. The plural form of 'boy' is 'boys.'* 2 the form of a word used to show that more than one are meant: *The plural of 'book' is 'books,' of 'man' 'men,' and of 'this' 'these.' 'Books,' 'men,' and 'these' are all plurals.* 1 *adj.,* 2 *n.*

plus (plus) 1 added to: *Three plus two equals five.* 2 and also: *The work of an engineer requires intelligence plus experience.* 3 and more: *His mark was B plus.* 4 the sign (+) meaning that the quantity following it is to be added. 1, 2 *prep.,* 3 *adj.,* 4 *n.*

plush (plush) a fabric like velvet but thicker and softer. *n.*

Plu·to (plü′tō) 1 in Greek and Roman myths, the god of the region of the dead. 2 the planet that is farthest from the sun. *n.*

plu·to·ni·um (plü tō′nē əm) a radio-active, metallic element used to produce atomic energy. *n.*

ply[1] (plī) 1 work with; use: *The dressmaker plies her needle.* 2 keep up work on; work steadily at or on: *The rowers plied their oars. The enemy plied our messenger with questions to make him tell his errand.* 3 supply with in a pressing manner: *ply a person with food and drink.* 4 go back and forth regularly between certain places: *The bus plies between the station and the hotel.* *v.,* **plied, ply·ing.**

☞ **Ply**[1] is a different form of *apply.*

ply[2] (plī) a thickness, fold, or twist: *Three-ply rope is made up of three twists.* *n., pl.* **plies.**

☞ **Ply**[2] comes from an early French word which came from Latin *plicare,* meaning 'to fold.'

ply·wood (plī′wu̇d′) a board or boards made of several thin layers of wood glued together. *n.*

p.m. the time from noon to midnight: *His birthday party lasted till 8 p.m.*

hat, āge, fär; let, ēqual, tėrm; it, īce
hot, ōpen, ôrder; oil, out; cup, pu̇t, rüle
əbove, takən, pencəl, lemən, circəs
ch, child; ng, long; sh, ship
th, thin; ᴛʜ, then; zh, measure

☞ **p.m.** is an abbreviation of Latin *post meridiem,* meaning 'after noon.'

P.M. 1 Prime Minister. 2 p.m.

pneu·mat·ic (nyü mat′ik or nü mat′ik) 1 filled with air; containing air: *a pneumatic tire.* 2 worked by air pressure: *a pneumatic drill.* 3 having to do with air and other gases. *adj.*

pneu·mo·nia (nyü mōn′yə or nü mōn′yə) a disease in which the lungs are inflamed. *n.*

P.O. Post Office.

poach[1] (pōch) 1 trespass on another's land, especially to hunt or fish. 2 take game or fish without any right. *v.*

poach[2] (pōch) 1 cook an egg by breaking it into boiling water and leaving it there three or four minutes. 2 cook an egg in a very small pan over boiling water. *v.*

pock (pok) a pimple, mark, or pit on the skin, caused by smallpox and certain other diseases. *n.*

pock·et (pok′it) 1 a small pouch or bag sewn into clothing for carrying money, or small articles. 2 put in one's pocket. 3 small enough to go in a pocket: *a pocket camera.* 4 a hollow place: *He hid in a pocket in the side of the hill.* 5 a small bag or pouch: *the pockets in a billiard table.* 6 a hole in the earth containing gold or other ore: *The miner struck a pocket of silver.* 7 shut in; hem in. 8 hold back; suppress; hide: *He pocketed his pride and said nothing.* 9 take and endure, without doing anything about it: *He pocketed the insult.* 10 take secretly or dishonestly: *One partner pocketed all the profits.* 11 any current or condition in the air that causes an airplane to drop suddenly. 1, 3–6, 11 *n.,* 2, 7–10 *v.*

be out of pocket, spend or lose money.

in pocket, having or gaining money.

pock·et·book (pok′it bu̇k′) 1 *Esp. U.S.* a woman's purse. 2 a case or folder for carrying money, papers, etc. in a pocket. *n.*

pock·et·knife (pok′it nīf′) a small knife having one or more blades that fold into the handle. *n., pl.* **pock·et·knives.**

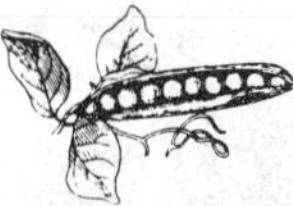

A pod opened to show the peas inside

pod (pod) the shell or case in which plants like beans and peas grow their seeds. *n.*

po·em (pō′əm) 1 a piece of writing in which the words are arranged in lines having a regularly repeated accent. 2 composition showing great beauty of language or thought. *n.*

po·et (pō′it) a person who writes poems: *Wordsworth and Tennyson were poets.* *n.*

po·et·ic (pō et′ik) 1 having to do with poems or poets. 2 suitable for poems or poets: *'Alas,' 'o'er,' and 'blithe' are poetic words.* 3 showing imaginative language or thought: *She has such poetic fancies as calling the clouds sheep and the new moon a boat.* *adj.*

po·et·i·cal (pō et′ə kəl) poetic. *adj.*

po·et·ry (pō′it rē) **1** poems: *Have you read much poetry?* **2** the art of writing poems: *Shakespeare and Milton are considered masters of English poetry. n.*

poin·set·ti·a (poin set′ē ə) a plant having a small flower surrounded by large, scarlet leaves that look like petals: *Poinsettias are much used as Christmas decorations. n.*

☞ Named after Joel R. *Poinsett* (1779–1851), an American, who discovered the plant in Mexico.

point (point) **1** a sharp end: *the point of a needle.* **2** a dot; a punctuation mark: *A period is a point.* **3** a position without length or width: *Two lines meet or cross at a point.* **4** a particular place or spot: *He drew a circle around a certain point on the map.* **5** any particular or definite position, condition, or time; degree; stage: *freezing point, boiling point. At that point he lost interest in the game.* **6** an item; detail: *The speaker replied to the argument point by point.* **7** a special quality or feature: *Courage and endurance were his good points.* **8** the main idea or purpose: *Your answer is not to the point. I did not get the point of his argument.* **9** give force to speech or action: *The preacher told a story to point his advice.* **10** direct a finger, weapon, etc.; aim: *Don't point your gun at me.* **11** show position or direction with the finger: *He pointed the way to the village over the hills.* **12** have or face a specified direction: *The sign points north.* **13** any of the 32 positions indicating direction on the card of a compass: *North, northeast, south, southwest, etc. are called points of the compass.* **14** a piece of land with a sharp end sticking out into the water; a cape. **15** a unit of scoring or measuring: *Four points make a game in tennis. He now has five points of the fifteen he needs for a diploma.* **16** See **point of view.** 1–8, 13–16 *n.*, 9–12 *v.*

beside the point, having nothing to do with the subject; not appropriate.

make a point, state an idea or opinion clearly and logically.

make a point of, insist on: *He always made a point of being on time.*

on the point of, just about to; on the verge of: *She was on the point of going out when a neighbor came in.*

point out, show or call attention to: *Please point out my mistakes.*

to the point, on the subject; relevant to the subject at hand: *His speech was brief and to the point.*

point–blank (point′blangk′) **1** aimed straight at the mark; direct; plain and blunt: *a point-blank question.* **2** directly; straight: *He refused point-blank to do the work.* **3** at very close range: *He fired point-blank at the target.* 1 *adj.*, 2, 3 *adv.*

point·ed (poin′tid) **1** having a point or points: *a pointed roof.* **2** sharp; piercing: *a pointed wit.* **3** directed; aimed: *a pointed remark.* **4** emphatic: *He showed her pointed attention. adj.*

point·er (poin′tər) **1** a long, tapering stick used in pointing things out on a map, blackboard, etc. **2** a hand of a clock, meter, etc. **3** a short-haired hunting dog: *A pointer is trained to show where game is by standing still with his head and body pointing towards the game and with his tail straight.* **4** *Informal.* hint; suggestion: *She gave him some pointers on improving his tennis. n.*

point of view **1** a position from which one looks at something. **2** an attitude of mind: *Farmers and campers have different points of view about rain.*

poise (poiz) **1** the way in which the body, head, etc. are held: *We admired the major's poise.* **2** mental balance; self-control: *She has perfect poise both of mind and body.* **3** keep balanced; balance: *The athlete poised the weight in the air before throwing it. Poise yourself on your toes.* 1, 2 *n.*, 3 *v.*, **poised, pois·ing.**

poi·son (poi′zən) **1** a drug or other substance very dangerous to health and capable of causing death: *Gas, arsenic, and opium are poisons.* **2** kill or harm by poison: *He poisoned the heroine of the story.* **3** put poison in or on: *He did it by poisoning her porridge.* **4** anything deadly or harmful: *Hate becomes a poison in the mind.* **5** have a very harmful effect on: *Lies poison the mind. He poisoned his friend's mind against the girl.* 1, 4 *n.*, 2, 3, 5 *v.*

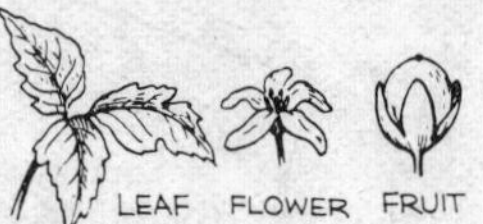

Poison ivy

poison ivy a plant that looks like ivy and causes a painful rash on most people if they touch it.

poison oak a kind of poison ivy that grows as a shrub.

poi·son·ous (poi′zən əs) **1** containing poison; very harmful to life and health: *The rattlesnake's bite is poisonous.* **2** having a harmful effect: *a poisonous lie. adj.*

poke (pōk) **1** push against with something pointed; thrust into; jab: *to poke a person in the ribs, to poke a fire.* **2** thrust; push: *He poked his head in the kitchen window.* **3** a poking; a thrust; a push. **4** *Informal.* punch: *He threatened to poke his brother in the nose.* **5** *Informal.* a punch. **6** go in a lazy way; loiter: *He poked along the street.* 1, 2, 4, 6 *v.*, **poked, pok·ing;** 3, 5 *n.*

pok·er[1] (pōk′ər) a metal rod for stirring a fire. *n.*

pok·er[2] (pōk′ər) a card game. *n.*

pok·ey or **pok·y** (pōk′ē) **1** moving or acting slowly; slow; dull: *a pokey old man.* **2** small and cramped; confined; mean: *a pokey little room. adj.*, **pok·i·er, pok·i·est.**

po·lar (pō′lər) **1** of or near the North or South Pole: *It is very cold in the polar regions.* **2** of the poles of a magnet, electric battery, etc. *adj.*

A polar bear — about 2.5 m long without the tail

polar bear a large, white bear living in the arctic regions.

hat, āge, fär; let, ēqual, tėrm; it, īce
hot, ōpen, ôrder; oil, out; cup, pu̇t, rüle
əbove, takən, pencəl, lemən, circəs
ch, child; ng, long; sh, ship
th, thin; ᴛʜ, then; zh, measure

pole[1] (pōl) **1** a long, slender piece of wood, metal, etc.: *a telephone pole, a flagpole, a ski pole.* **2** push or make something go with a pole. 1 *n.*, 2 *v.*, **poled, pol·ing.**

☛ **Pole** and **poll** are pronounced the same.

pole[2] (pōl) **1** either end of the earth's axis: *The North Pole and the South Pole are opposite each other.* **2** either of two parts where opposite forces are strongest: *A magnet or a battery has both a positive pole and a negative pole.* *n.*

poles apart, very much different; in strong disagreement: *Their viewpoints on the subject were poles apart.*

☛ See note at **pole**[1].

Pole (pōl) a person born in or living in Poland, a country in central Europe. *n.*

☛ See note at **pole**[1].

pole·cat (pōl′kat′) **1** a small, dark-brown European animal related to the weasel. **2** *Esp. U.S.* the North American skunk. *n.*

pole·star (pōl′stär′) the North Star, a star that is almost directly above the North Pole and was formerly much used as a guide by sailors. *n.*

pole vault a jump or leap over a high bar by using a long pole.

pole–vault (pōl′volt′ or pōl′vôlt′) vault over a high, horizontal bar by using a long pole. *v.*

po·lice (pə lēs′) **1** the department of government whose duty is to guard people's lives and property, to preserve peace and order, and to arrest those who commit crimes. **2** the people who carry out this duty for a community. **3** to guard or keep order in: *to police the streets.* 1, 2 *n.*, 3 *v.*, **po·liced, po·lic·ing.**

police dog **1** a kind of large, strong dog that looks like a wolf; German shepherd dog. See **German shepherd** for picture. **2** any dog trained to work with policemen.

po·lice·man (pə lēs′mən) a member of the police; a police officer. *n., pl.* **po·lice·men** (pə lēs′mən).

pol·i·cy[1] (pol′ə sē) a plan of action; a way of management: *It is poor policy to promise more than you can give. The candidate explained his party's policy.* *n., pl.* **pol·i·cies.**

pol·i·cy[2] (pol′ə sē) a written agreement about insurance: *My fire insurance policy states that I shall receive $15 000 if my house burns down.* *n., pl.* **pol·i·cies.**

po·li·o (pō′lē ō) poliomyelitis. *n.*

po·li·o·my·e·li·tis (pō′lē ō mī′ə lī′tis) a serious infectious disease that causes paralysis of various muscles and often results in death; infantile paralysis. *n.*

pol·ish (pol′ish) **1** make smooth and shiny: *to polish shoes.* **2** become smooth and shiny; take on a polish: *This leather polishes well.* **3** a substance used to give smoothness or shine: *silver polish.* **4** put into a better condition; improve; refine: *She wants to polish her French this year.* **5** shininess; smoothness: *The polish of the furniture reflected our faces like a mirror.* **6** refinement; elegance: *Her excellent manners were evidence of her polish.* 1, 2, 4 *v.*, 3, 5, 6 *n.*

Pol·ish (pō′lish) **1** of or having to do with Poland, a country in central Europe. **2** the language of Poland. 1 *adj.*, 2 *n.*

po·lite (pə līt′) **1** behaving properly; having or showing good manners: *The polite boy gave the lady his seat on the bus.* **2** refined; elegant: *She wished to learn all the customs of polite society.* *adj.*

po·lite·ness (pə līt′nis) a polite nature; good manners; proper behavior. *n.*

pol·i·tic (pol′ə tik) wise in looking out for one's own interests; prudent: *He thought it politic to put some money in the bank.* *adj.*

po·lit·i·cal (pə lit′ə kəl) having something to do with public affairs or the government: *Treason is a political offence. Who shall vote is a political question.* *adj.*

pol·i·ti·cian (pol′ə tish′ən) a person who gives much time to political affairs; a person who is active in politics: *Politicians are busy near election time.* *n.*

pol·i·tics (pol′ə tiks′) **1** the management of public affairs; the science and art of government: *Mackenzie King was engaged in politics for many years.* **2** political ideas or opinions: *My father's politics were strongly against rule by one man.* *n. sing. or pl.*

pol·ka (pōl′kə) **1** a kind of lively dance. **2** the music for this dance. *n.*

poll (pōl) **1** a voting; a collection of votes: *The class had a poll to decide where it would have its picnic.* **2** the number of votes cast: *If it rains on election day, there is usually a light poll.* **3** the place where votes are cast and counted: *The polls will be open all day.* **4** receive as votes: *The mayor polled a record vote.* **5** take or register the votes of. **6** a survey of public opinion concerning a particular subject. 1–3, 6 *n.*, 4, 5 *v.*

☛ **Poll** and **pole** are pronounced the same.

pol·len (pol′ən) the fine, yellowish powder made up of the male cells of flowers: *The pollen of a flower is carried on the anthers.* *n.*

pol·li·wog (pol′ē wog′) tadpole. *n.*

pol·lute (pə lüt′) make dirty; defile: *The water at the bathing beach was polluted by waste from the factory.* *v.*, **pol·lut·ed, pol·lut·ing.**

A man playing polo

po·lo (pō′lō) a game played by men on horseback with long-handled mallets and a wooden ball. *n.*

pol·y·gon (pol′i gon′) a figure having three or more angles and straight sides. *n.*

Pol·y·ne·sian (pol′ə nē′zhən) **1** of or having to do with Polynesia, a large group of islands in the Pacific

Ocean. **2** a dark-skinned person born in or living in Polynesia. **3** the languages of Polynesia, including Maori and Hawaiian. 1 *adj.,* 2, 3 *n.*

pol·yp (pol′ip) a small water animal with a tubelike body and fingerlike tentacles around its mouth to gather in food: *Polyps often grow in colonies, with their bases connected. Corals are polyps. n.*

pome·gran·ate (pom′gran′it) a reddish-yellow fruit having a thick skin, red pulp, and many seeds: *The pulp and seeds of the pomegranate have a pleasant, slightly sour taste. n.*

pom·mel (pom′əl or pum′əl for 1 and 2, pum′əl for 3) **1** the raised front part of a saddle. See **saddle** for picture. **2** a rounded knob on the hilt of a sword. **3** See **pummel.** 1, 2 *n.,* 3 *v.,* **pom·melled,** or **pom·meled, pom·mel·ling** or **pom·mel·ing.**

pomp (pomp) a splendid show or display; magnificence: *The king was crowned with great pomp. n.*

pom·pom (pom′pom) an ornamental tuft or ball of feathers, silk, or the like, worn on a hat or dress, on the shoes, etc. *n.*

pom·pon (pom′pon) pompom. *n.*

pom·pous (pom′pəs) fond of display; acting proudly; trying to seem magnificent: *The leader of the band bowed in a pompous manner. adj.*

pon·cho (pon′chō) a large piece of cloth with a slit in the middle for the head to go through: *Ponchos are worn in South America as cloaks. Waterproof ponchos are used by hikers and campers. n.*

pond (pond) a body of still water, smaller than a lake: *a duck pond, a mill pond. n.*

pon·der (pon′dər) think over; consider carefully: *to ponder a problem. v.*

pon·der·ous (pon′dər əs) **1** very heavy. **2** heavy and clumsy: *A hippopotamus is ponderous.* **3** dull; tiresome: *The speaker talked in a ponderous way. adj.*

pon·iard (pon′yərd) dagger. *n.*

pon·tiff (pon′tif) the Pope, the head of the Roman Catholic Church. *n.*

Pontoons supporting a bridge

pon·toon (pon tün′) **1** a low, flat-bottomed boat. **2** such a boat, or some other floating structure, used as one of the supports of a temporary bridge. **3** a boat-shaped part of an aircraft, used for coming down on or taking off from water. See **amphibian** and **seaplane** for pictures. *n.*

po·ny (pō′nē) a kind of small horse: *Ponies are usually less than 130 centimetres tall at the shoulder. n., pl.* **po·nies.**

A standard poodle — about 48 cm high at the shoulder

poo·dle (pü′dəl) one of a breed of intelligent pet dogs with thick, curly, wool-like hair that does not shed. *n.*

☞ **Poodle** is from German *pudeln,* meaning 'splash.' In German, the dog was called a *Pudelhund,* 'a splash dog,' because it was used by hunters to bring game from water.

pool[1] (pül) **1** a small body of water; a small pond. **2** a tank of water to swim or bathe in: *Our school has a fine pool.* **3** a deep, still part in a stream: *Trout are often found in the pools of a brook.* **4** a puddle of any spilled liquid: *a pool of grease under a car. n.*

pool[2] (pül) **1** a game like billiards, played with balls on a special table. **2** put things or money together for common advantage: *The boys pooled their savings to buy a boat.* **3** the things or money put together by different persons for common advantage. 1, 3 *n.,* 2 *v.*

poor (pür) **1** having few things or nothing. **2 the poor,** persons who have barely enough to keep themselves alive. **3** not good in quality; lacking something needed: *poor soil, a poor crop, poor milk, a poor cook, poor health.* **4** needing pity; unfortunate: *This poor little boy has hurt himself.* 1, 3, 4 *adj.,* 2 *n.*

poor·ly (pür′lē) **1** in a poor manner; not enough; badly: *A desert is poorly supplied with water. He did poorly in the test.* **2** in bad health: *She had been feeling poorly for several days.* 1 *adv.,* 2 *adj.*

pop (pop) **1** make a short, quick, explosive sound: *The firecrackers popped in bunches.* **2** a short, quick, explosive sound: *We heard the pop of a cork.* **3** burst open with such a sound: *When you pop corn, the heat makes the kernels burst open.* **4** move, go, or come suddenly or unexpectedly: *Our neighbor popped in for a short call.* **5** thrust or put suddenly: *She popped her head out through the window.* **6** *Informal.* shoot; fire a gun or pistol. **7** a fizzy soft drink: *strawberry pop.* 1, 3–6 *v.,* **popped, pop·ping;** 2, 7 *n.*

pop·corn (pop′kôrn′) **1** a kind of corn, the kernels of which burst open and puff out when heated. **2** the white, puffed-out kernels. *n.*

Pope or **pope** (pōp) the head of the Roman Catholic Church: *the Pope, the last three popes. n.*

pop·gun (pop′gun′) a toy gun that shoots with a popping sound. *n.*

pop·lar (pop′lər) **1** a tree that grows rapidly: *The cottonwood is one kind of poplar.* **2** the soft wood of this tree: *Boxes are very often made of poplar. n.*

poplar bluff a grove of poplar trees: *The farmhouse nestled in the shady poplar bluff.*

pop·py (pop′ē) a plant with showy red, yellow, or white flowers: *Opium is made from the seed of one kind of poppy. n., pl.* **pop·pies.**

pop·u·lace (pop′yə ləs) the people in general; the masses. *n.*

☞ **Populace** and **populous** are pronounced the same.

pop·u·lar (pop′yə lər) **1** liked by many people: *He is* *the most popular boy in the school. We have a popular prime minister.* **2** suited to or intended for many people: *popular prices, popular education.* **3** widespread among many people; of people in general: *It is a popular belief that black cats bring bad luck. adj.*

pop·u·lar·i·ty (pop′yə lar′ə tē or pop′yə ler′ə tē) being liked by most people. *n.*

pop·u·late (pop′yə lāt′) **1** inhabit: *Toronto is thickly populated.* **2** furnish with inhabitants: *Europeans populated much of the Canadian West. v.,* **pop·u·lat·ed, pop·u·lat·ing.**

pop·u·la·tion (pop′yə lā′shən) **1** the people of a city, country, or district. **2** the number of people: *The population of this town is over 55 000. n.*

pop·u·lous (pop′yə ləs) full of people; having many people per square mile: *Montreal is Canada's most populous city. adj.*

☛ **Populous** and **populace** are pronounced the same.

por·ce·lain (pôr′sə lin) very fine earthenware; china: *Teacups are often made of porcelain. n.*

porch (pôrch) **1** a covered entrance to a building; a veranda: *Our house has a big porch.* **2** a stoop; a platform at the entrance to a house. *n.*

A porch

A North American porcupine — about 90 cm long with the tail

por·cu·pine (pôr′kyə pīn′) a gnawing animal related to the guinea pig, having sharp spines or quills on its back and tail. *n.*

☛ **Porcupine** is from Old French *porc espin,* which came from Latin *porcus,* meaning 'pig' + *spinus,* meaning 'spine.'

pore¹ (pôr) study long and steadily: *He would rather pore over a book than play with friends. v.,* **pored, por·ing.**

☛ **Pore** and **pour** are pronounced the same.

pore² (pôr) a very small opening: *Sweat comes through the pores in the skin. n.*

☛ See note at **pore¹**.

pork (pôrk) the meat of a pig or hog used for food. *n.*

po·rous (pô′rəs) full of pores or tiny holes; able to soak in water, air, etc.: *Cloth and blotting paper are both porous. adj.*

por·poise (pôr′pəs) **1** a sea mammal from about 1.5 metres to 2.5 metres long that looks like a small whale: *Porpoises eat fish.* **2** dolphin. *n., pl.* **por·pois·es** or **por·poise.**

por·ridge (pôr′ij) a food made of oatmeal or other cereal boiled in water or milk until it thickens. *n.*

port¹ (pôrt) **1** a harbor; a place where ships and boats can take shelter from storms. **2** a place where ships and boats can load and unload; a town or city with a harbor: *Halifax and Vancouver are important Canadian ports. n.*

hat, āge, fär; let, ēqual, tėrm; it, īce
hot, ōpen, ôrder; oil, out; cup, pu̇t, rüle
əbove, takən, pencəl, lemən, circəs
ch, child; ng, long; sh, ship
th, thin; ᴛʜ, then; zh, measure

port² (pôrt) an opening in the side of a ship for letting in light and air; a porthole. *n.*

port³ (pôrt) **1** the left side of a ship or aircraft when facing the front. See **aft** for picture. **2** on the left side of a ship. **3** turn or shift to the left side: *'Port your helm,' ordered the captain.* 1, 2 *n.,* 3 *v.*

port⁴ (pôrt) a strong, sweet, dark-red wine. *n.*

port·a·ble (pôr′tə bəl) **1** capable of being carried or moved easily: *a portable typewriter.* **2** a temporary building on the grounds of an overcrowded school, used as an extra classroom. 1 *adj.,* 2 *n.*

por·tage (pôr′tij or pôr täzh′) **1** the act of carrying canoes, boats, provisions, etc. overland from one stretch of water to another: *We found the last portage the most difficult.* **2** carry canoes, etc. from one stretch of water to another: *We had to portage five times during the trip.* **3** a place where such carrying takes place: *The hunters pitched camp at the portage.* 1, 3 *n.,* 2 *v.,* **por·taged, por·tag·ing.**

por·tal (pôr′təl) a door, gate, or entrance, usually an imposing one. *n.*

port·cul·lis (pôrt kul′is) a strong gate or grating of iron that can be raised or lowered, used to close the gateway of an ancient castle or fortress. See the picture. *n.*

por·tend (pôr tend′) indicate beforehand; give warning of: *Black clouds portend a storm. v.*

por·tent (pôr′tent) a warning of coming evil; a sign or omen: *The black clouds were a portent of bad weather. n.*

por·ter¹ (pôr′tər) **1** a man employed to carry loads or baggage. **2** an attendant in a sleeper or a parlor car of a railway train. *n.*

por·ter² (pôr′tər) a person who guards a door or entrance: *The porter let them in. n.*

port·hole (pôrt′hōl′) an opening in a ship's side to let in light and air. *n.*

A portcullis

A portico

por·ti·co (pôr′tə kō′) a roof supported by columns, forming a porch or a covered walk. *n., pl.* **por·ti·coes** or **por·ti·cos.**

por·tion (pôr′shən) **1** a part or share: *A portion of each school day is devoted to arithmetic.* **2** a quantity of food served for one portion: *The restaurant serves large portions.* **3** divide into parts or shares: *When he* *died, his money was portioned out among his children.* 1, 2 *n.*, 3 *v.*

port·ly (pôrt′lē) **1** stout; having a large body: *a portly man.* **2** stately; dignified. *adj.,* **port·li·er, port·li·est.**

por·trait (pôr′trit or pôr′trāt) **1** a picture of a person, especially of the face. **2** a picture in words; description. *n.*

por·tray (pôr trā′) **1** describe or picture in words: *The book 'Black Beauty' portrays the life of a horse.* **2** make a likeness of in a drawing or painting; make a picture of. **3** represent in a play or movie; act. *v.*

Por·tu·guese (pôr′chù gēz′ or pôr′chù gēz′) **1** of or having to do with Portugal, a country in southwestern Europe. **2** a person born in or living in Portugal. **3** the language of Portugal: *Portuguese is also the chief language of Brazil.* 1 *adj.*, 2, 3 *n.*

pose (pōz) **1** a position of the body; a way of holding the body: *That snapshot shows her in an attractive pose.* **2** hold a position: *He posed for an hour for his portrait.* **3** put in a certain position; put: *The photographer posed him before taking his picture.* **4** an attitude assumed for affect; a pretence; an affectation: *She takes the pose of being an invalid when really she is well and strong.* **5** pretend; make a pretence, especially for effect: *He posed as a rich man though he owed more than he owned.* **6** put forward; state: *pose a question.* 1, 4 *n.*, 2, 3, 5, 6 *v.*, **posed, pos·ing.**

po·si·tion (pə zish′ən) **1** a place where a thing or person is: *Mother didn't like the position of the chesterfield. Your careless remark put me in an awkward position.* **2** a way of being placed: *Put the baby in a comfortable position.* **3** the proper place: *Each soldier got into position to defend the fort.* **4** a job: *He has a position in a bank.* **5** a rank; a standing, especially high standing: *He was raised to the position of captain.* **6** the place held by a player on a team: *My position on the hockey team was defence.* **7** a way of thinking; set of opinions: *What is your position on this question? n.*

pos·i·tive (poz′ə tiv) **1** permitting no question; without doubt; sure: *We have positive knowledge that the earth moves around the sun.* **2** too sure: *Her positive manner annoys people.* **3** definite; emphatic: *'No, I will not' was his positive refusal.* **4** that may be thought of as real and present: *Light is a positive thing; darkness is only the absence of light.* **5** that surely does something or adds something; practical: *Don't just make a negative criticism; give us some positive help.* **6** of the kind of electrical charge produced by rubbing glass with silk. **7** a photographic print: *She kept the positives and sent back the negatives.* **8** greater than zero; plus: *Positive numbers are used to count things.* 1–6, 8 *adj.*, 7 *n.* **—pos′i·tive·ly,** *adv.*

pos·se (pos′ē) a group of men summoned by a law officer to help him: *Posses were often formed to capture criminals during frontier days in the American West. n.*

pos·sess (pə zes′) **1** own; have: *The old general possessed great force and wisdom.* **2** hold as property; hold; occupy. **3** control; influence strongly: *She was possessed by the desire to be rich.* **4** control by an evil spirit: *He fought like one possessed. v.*

pos·ses·sion (pə zesh′ən) **1** possessing; holding: *Our soldiers fought hard for possession of the hilltop.* **2** ownership: *At his father's death he came into possession of a million dollars.* **3** something possessed; property: *Please move your possessions from my room.* **4** a territory under the rule of a country: *Greenland is a possession of Denmark.* **5** self-control. *n.*

pos·ses·sive (pə zes′iv) **1** showing possession, ownership, etc.: *'My' and 'your' are two of the possessive pronouns.* **2** the possessive form of a word. **3** a word showing possession: *In 'the boy's book,' the word 'boy's' is a possessive.* **4** having a strong desire to own things: *That boy has a possessive nature.* 1, 4 *adj.*, 2, 3 *n.*

pos·ses·sor (pə zes′ər) owner; a person who possesses; holder. *n.*

pos·si·bil·i·ty (pos′ə bil′ə tē) **1** being possible: *There is a possibility that the train will be late.* **2** any thing or event that is possible; a person considered as a possible choice: *He would be a good possibility for captain. There are many possibilities. A whole week of rain is a possibility. n., pl.* **pos·si·bil·i·ties.**

pos·si·ble (pos′ə bəl) **1** that can be; that can be done; that can happen: *Come if possible. It is possible to cure tuberculosis.* **2** that can be true or a fact: *It is possible that he went. adj.*

pos·si·bly (pos′ə blē) **1** by any possibility; no matter what happens: *I cannot possibly go.* **2** perhaps: *Possibly you are right. adv.*

pos·sum (pos′əm) opossum. *n.*
play possum, pretend to be dead or asleep.

post[1] (pōst) **1** a length of timber, iron, etc. firmly set up, usually to support something else: *a signpost, a gatepost, the posts of a bed.* **2** fasten a notice up in a place where it can easily be seen: *The list of winners will be posted soon.* **3** make known by means of a posted notice; offer publicly: *to post a reward.* **4** announce in a notice: *Her train is posted as on time.* **5** put up notices warning people to keep out of: *That farmer posts his land.* **6** the post, line, etc. where a race starts or ends. 1, 6 *n.*, 2–5 *v.*

post[2] (pōst) **1** a place where a soldier, policeman, etc. is stationed; a place where one is supposed to be when one is on duty: *When the fire alarm sounds, each man rushes to his post.* **2** a place where soldiers are stationed. **3** send to a station or post: *The captain posted guards at the door.* **4** a job or position. **5** a trading station, especially in unsettled country. 1, 2, 4, 5 *n.*, 3 *v.*

post[3] (pōst) **1** a system for carrying letters, packages, etc.; the mail: *I shall send the package by post.* **2** a single delivery of mail: *The post has just come.* **3** send by mail; put into the mailbox; mail: *to post a letter.* **4** travel with haste; hurry. 1, 2 *n.*, 3, 4 *v.*

post·age (pōs′tij) the amount paid on anything sent by mail. *n.*

post·al (pōs′təl) having something to do with mail and post offices: *postal regulations. adj.*

postal card post card.

post box a box into which letters, parcels, etc. are put for delivery by the Post Office.

post card a card for sending a message by mail: *Some post cards have pictures on one side.*

post·er (pōs′tər) **1** a large printed advertisement or notice, often illustrated, put up in some public place.

2 a large printed picture or message, used for room decoration. *n.*

pos·ter·i·ty (pos ter′ə tē) the generations of the future: *Posterity may travel to distant planets. n.*

pos·tern (pōs′tərn or pos′tərn) a back door or gate. *n.*

post·haste (pōst′hāst′) very speedily; in great haste. *adv.*

post·man (pōst′mən) a man who carries and delivers mail for the government; a mailman. *n., pl.* **post·men** (pōst′mən).

post·mark (post′mark′) **1** an official mark stamped on mail to cancel the postage stamp and record the place and date of mailing. **2** stamp with a postmark. 1 *n.*, 2 *v.*

post·mas·ter (pōst′mas′tər) a person in charge of a post office. *n.*

post office **1** a place where mail is handled and postage stamps are sold. **2** Often, **Post Office,** the government department in charge of mail.

post·pone (pōs pōn′ or pōst pōn′) put off till later; put off to a later time; delay: *The ball game was postponed because of rain. v.,* **post·poned, post·pon·ing.**

post·script (pōst′skript) **1** an addition to a letter, written after the writer's name has been signed. **2** an additional part added to any composition, book, article, etc. *n.*

pos·ture (pos′chər) **1** the position of the body; the way of holding the body: *Good posture is important to health.* **2** take a position: *The dancer postured before the mirror, bending and twisting her body.* 1 *n.*, 2 *v.*, **pos·tured, pos·tur·ing.**

po·sy (pō′zē) **1** a flower. **2** a bunch of flowers; a bouquet. *n., pl.* **po·sies.**

pot (pot) **1** any one of many kinds of deep containers made of iron, tin, aluminum, glass, clay, etc.: *a cooking pot, a flower pot, a coffee pot.* **2** the amount a pot will hold: *He had a pot of beans.* **3** put into a pot: *We potted young tomato plants.* 1, 2 *n.*, 3 *v.*, **pot·ted, pot·ting.**

pot·ash (pot′ash′) **1** any of several substances made from wood ashes, etc., and used in making soap, fertilizers, etc. **2** any of several minerals used in agriculture and industry. *n.*

po·ta·to (pə tā′tō) **1** a round, hard, starchy tuber with a very thin skin, used as a vegetable: *white potato.* **2** sweet potato. *n., pl.* **po·ta·toes.**

potato chip **1** a crisp, thin, dry slice of potato that has been fried in deep fat: *We each took a soft drink and a bag of potato chips.* **2** a slice of potato, usually oblong, fried in deep fat and eaten while hot: *Potato chips are often eaten with fried fish.*

po·tent (pō′tənt) powerful; having great power; strong: *a potent remedy for a disease. adj.*

po·ten·tate (pō′tən tāt′) a ruler having great power: *the potentates of ancient India. The Roman emperors were potentates. n.*

po·ten·tial (pə ten′shəl) **1** possible as opposed to actual; capable of coming into being or action: *a potential danger.* **2** something potential; possibility. 1 *adj.*, 2 *n.*

pot·hole (pot′hōl′) **1** a deep, round hole, especially one made in the rocky bed of a river by stones and gravel being spun around in the current. **2** a hole in the surface of a road. *n.*

hat, āge, fär; let, ēqual, tėrm; it, īce
hot, ōpen, ôrder; oil, out; cup, pu̇t, rüle
əbove, takən, pencəl, lemən, circəs
ch, child; ng, long; sh, ship
th, thin; ᴛʜ, then; zh, measure

po·tion (pō′shən) a drink, especially one that is used as a medicine or poison, or in magic. *n.*

pot·latch (pot′lach) a West-Coast Indian gift-giving ceremony and festival. *n.*

pot·ter¹ (pot′ər) a person who makes pottery. *n.*

pot·ter² (pot′ər) keep busy in a rather useless way; putter: *She potters about the house all day, but she gets very little done. v.*

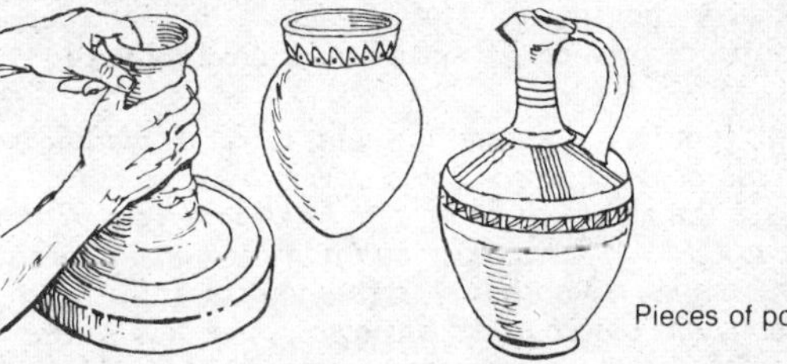

Pieces of pottery

pot·ter·y (pot′ər ē) **1** pots, dishes, vases, etc. made from clay and hardened by heat. **2** the art or business of making such things. **3** a place where such pots, dishes, vases, etc. are made. *n., pl.* **pot·ter·ies.**

pouch (pouch) **1** a bag or sack: *a postman's pouch.* **2** a fold of skin that is like a bag: *A kangaroo carries its young in a pouch. n.*

poul·try (pōl′trē) birds raised for their meat or eggs, such as chickens, turkeys, ducks, and geese. *n.*

pounce (pouns) **1** come down with a rush and seize something: *The cat pounced upon the mouse.* **2** dash, come, or jump suddenly: *The actor pounced onto the stage.* **3** a sudden swoop or pouncing. 1, 2 *v.*, **pounced, pounc·ing;** 3 *n.*

pound¹ (pound) **1** a measure of weight; 16 ounces (about 0.45 kilograms). **2** a unit of troy weight; 12 ounces (about 0.37 kilograms). **3** a unit of money of Great Britain, worth about $2.00 in Canadian money: *One pound is equal to 100 new pence. Symbol* (for def. 3): £ *n., pl.* **pounds** or **pound.**

pound² (pound) **1** hit hard again and again; hit heavily: *He pounded the door with his fist.* **2** beat hard; throb: *After a hard run your heart pounds.* **3** crush to powder or pulp by beating. **4** move heavily: *He pounded down the hill to catch the bus. v.*

pound³ (pound) an enclosed place in which to keep stray animals: *The dogcatcher took the collie to the city pound. n.*

pour (pôr) **1** cause to flow in a steady stream: *I poured the milk from the bottle into the cups.* **2** flow in a steady stream: *The crowd poured out of the church. The rain poured down for over an hour.* **3** a heavy rain. 1, 2 *v.*, 3 *n.*

☛ **Pour** and **pore** are pronounced the same.

pout (pout) **1** thrust or push out the lips, as a displeased or sulky child does. **2** a pushing out of the lips when displeased or sulky. 1 *v.*, 2 *n.*

pov·er·ty (pov′ər tē) 1 the condition of being poor or needy: *Being out of work causes poverty.* 2 a lack of what is needed; poor quality: *The poverty of the soil makes the crops small.* *n.*

pow·der (pou′dər) 1 a solid reduced to dust by pounding, crushing, drying, etc. 2 make into powder; become powder: *The soil powdered in the heat.* 3 something made or prepared as a powder: *face powder, talcum powder, powders taken as medicine.* 4 sprinkle or cover with powder. 5 put powder on the face. 6 sprinkle: *The ground was lightly powdered with snow.* 7 gunpowder. 1, 3, 7 *n.,* 2, 4–6 *v.*

powder horn the horn of an animal made into a container for gunpowder. See **horn** for picture.

pow·der·y (pou′dər ē) 1 of powder. 2 like powder; in the form of powder. 3 sprinkled or covered with powder. *adj.*

pow·er (pou′ər) 1 strength; might; force: *Penicillin is a medicine of great power. Bulldozers have great power.* 2 the ability to do or act: *I will give you all the help in my power. The fairy had power to change into different shapes.* 3 authority; right; control; influence: *Parliament has power to declare war. Jack was in the power of the giant.* 4 a person, nation, or thing who has authority or influence: *Five powers held a peace conference.* 5 energy or force that can do work: *Running water can be used to operate a turbine and produce electric power.* 6 provide with power or energy: *a boat powered by an outboard motor.* 7 operated by a motor; equipped with its own motor: *a power drill.* 8 the capacity of an instrument to magnify: *An object seen through a microscope with a power of ten looks ten times its actual size.* 1–5, 7, 8 *n.,* 6 *v.*
in power, having control or authority: *the government in power.*

pow·er·ful (pou′ər fəl) having great power or force; mighty; strong: *a powerful man, a powerful medicine, a powerful sermon, a powerful nation.* *adj.*

pow·er·house (pou′ər hous′) a building containing boilers, engines, dynamos, etc., for producing electric power. *n.*

pow·er·less (pou′ər lis) without power; helpless: *The mouse was powerless in the cat's claws.* *adj.*

pow·wow (pou′wou′) 1 a North American Indian ceremony, usually accompanied by magic, feasting, and dancing, performed for the cure of disease, success in hunting, etc. 2 a council or conference of or with North American Indians. 3 *Informal.* any conference or meeting. 4 hold a powwow; confer. 1–3 *n.,* 4 *v.*

☛ **Powwow** comes from a North American Indian word *pauwaw,* meaning 'he dreams.' A medicine man was called a *powwow* because it was thought he had learned his craft from dreams.

pp. pages.

P.Q. Province of Quebec.

pr. pair.

prac·ti·ca·ble (prak′tə kə bəl) 1 that can be done; capable of being put into practice: *a practicable idea.* 2 that can be used: *a practicable road.* *adj.*

prac·ti·cal (prak′tə kəl) 1 having to do with action or practice rather than thought or theory: *Earning a living is a practical matter.* 2 able to be put into practice; useful in practice: *a practical plan. His legal knowledge was not very practical when he became a chemist.* 3 having good sense: *A practical person does not spend his time and money foolishly.* *adj.*

prac·ti·cal·ly (prak′tik lē) 1 really; in effect: *He practically runs the team.* 2 *Informal.* almost; nearly: *We are practically home.* *adv.*

prac·tice (prak′tis) 1 the doing of something many times over in order to gain skill: *Practice makes perfect.* 2 the skill gained by experience or exercise: *He was out of practice at batting.* 3 the process of being or doing something: *His plan is good in theory, but not in actual practice.* 4 the usual way; the custom: *It is the practice at the factory to blow a whistle at noon.* 5 the business of a doctor or a lawyer: *Dr. Adams has sold his practice to a younger doctor.* 6 a period set aside for practising: *He went to hockey practice last night.* *n.*

prac·tise or **prac·tice** (prak′tis) 1 do something again and again so as to learn to do it well: *She practised her piano lesson.* 2 follow, observe, or use day after day: *You must learn to practise moderation. Practise what you preach.* 3 work at or follow as a profession: *to practise law or medicine.* 4 do something as a profession: *My uncle practises as a lawyer.* *v.,* **prac·tised** or **prac·ticed, prac·tis·ing** or **prac·tic·ing.**

prac·tised or **prac·ticed** (prak′tist) skilled, expert; experienced: *He is a practised musician.* *adj.*

prai·rie (prer′ē) 1 a large tract of level or rolling land with grass but few or no trees. 2 **the Prairies,** *pl.* the great, almost treeless plain that covers much of central and southern Manitoba, Saskatchewan, and Alberta. *n.*

prairie chicken any of several grouse that live on the prairies of North America.

prairie dog an animal like a groundhog but smaller: *Prairie dogs bark.*

Prairie Provinces Manitoba, Saskatchewan, and Alberta.

prairie schooner a large covered wagon formerly used on the plains of North America, especially by American settlers.

praise (prāz) 1 saying that a thing or person is good; words that tell the worth or value of a thing or person: *When he won the race, his friends heaped praise upon him.* 2 express approval or admiration of: *Everyone praised the winning team for its fine play.* 3 worship in words or song. 1 *n.,* 2, 3 *v.,* **praised, prais·ing.**

praise·wor·thy (prāz′wėr′ᴛʜē) deserving praise or approval: *a praiseworthy act.* *adj.*

prance (prans) 1 spring about on the hind legs: *Horses prance when they feel lively.* 2 move gaily or proudly: *The children pranced about in their new Halloween costumes.* *v.,* **pranced, pranc·ing.**

prank (prangk) a playful trick; a piece of mischief: *On April Fool's Day people play pranks on each other.* *n.*

prate (prāt) talk a great deal in a foolish way; prattle. *v.,* **prat·ed, prat·ing.**

prat·tle (prat′əl) 1 talk in a foolish way; babble. 2 foolish or childish talk. 1 *v.,* **prat·tled, prat·tling;** 2 *n.*

prawn (pron or prôn) any of several shellfish resembling a large shrimp. *n.*

pray (prā) 1 ask from God; speak to God in worship: *They prayed for peace.* 2 ask earnestly: *They prayed the kidnappers to let them go.* 3 please: *Pray come.* *v.*

☛ **Pray** and **prey** are pronounced the same.

hat, āge, fär; let, ēqual, tėrm; it, īce
hot, ōpen, ôrder; oil, out; cup, pu̇t, rüle
əbove, takən, pencəl, lemən, circəs
ch, child; ng, long; sh, ship
th, thin; ᴛʜ, then; zh, measure

prayer (prer) 1 an earnest request, especially one made to God: *Their prayers were answered.* 2 the act of praying: *They stood a moment in prayer.* 3 a form of worship: *We always have morning prayers.* 4 an arrangement of words to be used in praying: *a book of prayers.* *n.*

pre– a prefix meaning: before in place, time, order, or rank, as in *prehistoric, premeditate, prepay.*

preach (prēch) 1 speak on a religious subject; deliver a sermon. 2 urge; recommend strongly: *He was always preaching exercise and fresh air.* 3 give earnest advice: *Grandmother is forever preaching about good table manners.* *v.*

preach·er (prēch′ər) a person who preaches; a clergyman or minister. *n.*

pre·car·i·ous (pri ker′ē əs or pri kar′ē əs) uncertain; not safe; not secure; dangerous: *A soldier leads a precarious life. His hold on the branch was precarious.* *adj.*

pre·cau·tion (pri ko′shən or pri kô′shən) 1 care taken beforehand: *Locking doors is a precaution against thieves.* 2 taking care beforehand: *Proper precaution is wise when handling sharp knives.* *n.*

pre·cede (prē sēd′) 1 go before; come before: *A band preceded the first float in the parade.* 2 be higher than in rank or importance: *A major precedes a captain.* *v.,* **pre·ced·ed, pre·ced·ing.**

prec·e·dent (pres′ə dənt or prē′sə dənt) an action that may serve as an example or reason for later action: *Since last year's school picnic set a precedent, we can have another one this year.* *n.*

pre·ced·ing (prē sēd′ing) going before; coming before; previous: *Look at the preceding page.* *adj.*

pre·cept (prē′sept) a rule of action or behavior: *'If at first you don't succeed, try, try again' is a familiar precept.* *n.*

pre·cinct (prē′singkt) the space within a boundary: *Do not leave the school precincts during school hours.* *n.*

pre·cious (presh′əs) 1 having great value: *Gold and silver are often called the precious metals. Diamonds and rubies are precious stones.* 2 much loved; dear: *a precious child.* *adj.*

prec·i·pice (pres′ə pis) a very steep cliff or slope; the face of a cliff. *n.*

pre·cip·i·tate (pri sip′ə tāt′, also pri sip′ə tit for 2) 1 hasten the beginning of; bring about suddenly: *to precipitate a war.* 2 with great haste and force; plunging or rushing; hasty; rash: *precipitate actions.* 3 throw down, fling, hurl, send, or plunge in a violent, sudden, or headlong manner: *to precipitate a rock down a cliff, to precipitate oneself into a struggle.* 4 condense moisture from vapor in the form of rain, dew, etc. 1, 3, 4 *v.,* **pre·cip·i·tat·ed, pre·cip·i·tat·ing;** 2 *adj.*

pre·cip·i·ta·tion (pri sip′ə tā′shən) 1 throwing down or falling headlong. 2 sudden haste; unwise or rash speed. 3 a sudden bringing on: *the precipitation of a quarrel.* 4 the depositing of moisture in the form of rain, dew, snow, etc. 5 something that is precipitated, such as rain or snow. *n.*

pre·cip·i·tous (pri sip′ə təs) 1 like a precipice; very steep: *precipitous cliffs.* 2 hasty; rash: *Running away was a precipitous action.* *adj.*

pre·cise (pri sīs′) 1 exact; accurate; definite: *The precise distance was 1.73 kilometres.* 2 careful: *precise handwriting. She is precise in her manners.* 3 strict: *We had precise orders to come home by nine o'clock.* *adj.* **—pre·cise′ly,** *adv.*

pre·ci·sion (pri sizh′ən) accuracy; exactness: *the precision of a machine.* *n.*

pre·clude (pri klüd′) shut out; make impossible; prevent: *The heavy thunderstorm precluded our going to the beach.* *v.,* **pre·clud·ed, pre·clud·ing.**

pre·co·cious (pri kō′shəs) developed earlier than usual in knowledge, skill, etc.: *This very precocious child could read well at the age of four.* *adj.*

pred·a·tor (pred′ə tər) an animal that lives by preying upon other animals. *n.*

pred·a·to·ry (pred′ə tô′rē) living by preying upon other animals: *Lions and tigers are predatory animals; hawks and owls are predatory birds.* *adj.*

pred·e·ces·sor (pred′ə ses′ər or prē′də ses′ər) a person holding a position or office before another: *Edward VII was the predecessor of George V.* *n.*

pre·dic·a·ment (pri dik′ə mənt) an unpleasant, difficult, or dangerous situation: *She was in a predicament when she missed the last train home.* *n.*

pred·i·cate (pred′ə kit) the word or words in a sentence that tell what is said about the subject. In 'Men work,' 'The men dug wells,' and 'The men are soldiers,' *work, dug wells,* and *are soldiers* are all predicates. *n.*

pre·dict (pri dikt′) tell beforehand; prophesy: *The weather bureau predicts rain for tomorrow.* *v.*

pre·dic·tion (pri dik′shən) a prophecy: *The official predictions about the weather often come true.* *n.*

pre·dom·i·nant (pri dom′ə nənt) 1 having more power, authority, or influence than others; superior: *Will Russia be the predominant nation in Europe in 50 years?* 2 most extensive; most noticeable: *Green was the predominant color in the forest.* *adj.*

pre·dom·i·nate (pri dom′ə nāt′) be greater in power, strength, influence, or numbers: *Sedans predominate over hardtops.* *v.,* **pre·dom·i·nat·ed, pre·dom·i·nat·ing.**

preen (prēn) 1 smooth or arrange the feathers with the beak, as a bird does. 2 dress oneself carefully. *v.*

pre·fab·ri·cate (prē fab′rə kāt′) put together parts in advance; especially, make sections of a house or other building so that they can be quickly put together on the site. *v.*

pref·ace (pref′is) a short note at the beginning of a book, writing, or speech: *A preface sometimes explains how a book came to be written.* *n.*

pre·fer (pri fėr′) 1 like better; choose rather: *I will come later, if you prefer. She prefers reading to sewing. I would prefer to go home.* 2 put forward; present: *In a few words he preferred his claim to the position of manager. The constable preferred charges of speeding against the driver.* *v.,* **pre·ferred, pre·fer·ring.**

pref·er·a·ble (pref′ər ə bəl) to be preferred; more desirable. *adj.*

pref·er·a·bly (pref′ər ə blē) by choice: *She wants a new secretary, preferably one who is a college graduate. adv.*

pref·er·ence (pref′ər əns) liking better; the favoring of one above another: *A teacher should not show preference for any one of her pupils. n.*

pre·fix (prē′fiks for 1 and 2, prē fiks′ for 2) **1** a syllable, syllables, or word put at the beginning of a word to change its meaning or make another word, as in *pre*historic, *un*like. **2** put before: *We prefix 'Mr.' to a man's name.* 1 *n.,* 2 *v.*

preg·nant (preg′nənt) **1** soon to become a mother; soon to give birth. **2** filled with meaning: *A pregnant silence warned of the attack. adj.*

pre·his·tor·ic (prē′his tôr′ik) of or belonging to times before histories were written: *We find stone tools made by prehistoric men. adj.*

prej·u·dice (prej′ə dis) **1** an opinion formed without taking time and care to judge fairly: *The old man had a prejudice against doctors.* **2** cause a prejudice in; fill with prejudice: *That one happening has prejudiced me against all lawyers.* **3** harm or injury: *I will do nothing to the prejudice of my cousin in this matter.* **4** to harm or injure. 1, 3 *n.,* 2, 4 *v.,* **prej·u·diced, prej·u·dic·ing.**

prel·ate (prel′it) a clergyman of high rank, such as a bishop. *n.*

pre·lim·i·nar·y (pri lim′ə ner′ē) **1** coming before the main business; leading to something more important: *After preliminary remarks by the principal, the school play began.* **2** a preliminary step; something preparatory: *A physical examination is a preliminary to joining the armed forces.* 1 *adj.,* 2 *n., pl.* **pre·lim·i·nar·ies.**

prel·ude (prel′yüd or prē′lüd) **1** anything serving as an introduction: *The German invasion of Poland was a prelude to World War II.* **2** in music, a composition, or part of it, that introduces another composition or part: *We heard the organist play a prelude to the church service. n.*

pre·ma·ture (prē′mə chür′ or prem′ə chür′) before the proper time; too soon: *His premature arrival spoiled our plan to surprise him. adj.*

pre·med·i·tate (prē med′ə tāt′) consider or plan beforehand: *a premeditated murder. The general premeditated his plan before giving the order to attack. v.,* **pre·med·i·tat·ed, pre·med·i·tat·ing.**

pre·mier (prē′mēr) **1** in Canada, a prime minister of a province: *The ten premiers attended a conference with the Prime Minister in Ottawa.* **2** the chief officer of a government. **3** first in rank or quality. 1, 2 *n.,* 3 *adj.*

prem·is·es (prem′ə siz) a house or building with its grounds: *The woman asked the boys to keep their dogs off her premises. Our office needs larger premises now. n. pl.*

pre·mi·um (prē′mē əm) **1** a reward, especially one given to encourage a person to buy; prize: *Some magazines give premiums in return for new subscriptions.* **2** something more than the ordinary price or wage: *We bought the car with special seats, but we had to pay a premium of $100.* **3** money paid regularly for an insurance policy: *Father pays premiums on his life insurance four times a year. n.*

pre·oc·cu·pied (prē ok′yə pīd′) **1** absorbed; completely occupied: *The boy was preoccupied with his homework.* **2** too concerned with one thing to concentrate on another; distracted: *He was too preoccupied with his holiday plans to do his homework. adj.*

pre·paid (prē pād′) See **prepay.** *Please send this shipment prepaid. v.*

prep·a·ra·tion (prep′ə rā′shən) **1** preparing or making ready: *He sharpened the knife in preparation for carving.* **2** a state of being ready. **3** anything done to get ready: *He made careful preparations for his holidays.* **4** a specially made medicine, food, or mixture of any kind: *The preparation included camphor. n.*

pre·par·a·to·ry (pri par′ə tô′rē or pri per′ə tô′rē) **1** preparing or making ready: *Some jobs require one to take preparatory courses.* **2** as an introduction; preliminary: *preparatory remarks. adj.*

pre·pare (pri per′) **1** make ready; get ready: *He does his homework while his mother prepares supper.* **2** make by a special process: *The witch prepared a magic brew. v.,* **pre·pared, pre·par·ing.**

pre·pay (prē pā′) pay or pay for in advance. *v.*

prep·o·si·tion (prep′ə zish′ən) a word that shows relationships of time, direction, position, etc. between other words: With, for, by *and* in *are prepositions in the sentence 'A man with rugs for sale walked by our house in the morning.' n.*

prep·o·si·tion·al (prep′ə zish′ən əl) having to do with a preposition or prepositions: *A prepositional phrase is a phrase that begins with a preposition. adj.*

pre·pos·ter·ous (pri pos′tər əs) against nature, reason, or common sense; absurd; senseless; foolish: *It would be preposterous to shovel snow with a teaspoon. That the moon is made of green cheese is surely a preposterous notion. adj.*

Pres·by·te·ri·an (prez′bə tēr′ē ən or pres′ bə tēr′ē ən) **1** of or having to do with a Protestant church that is governed by elders who are all of equal rank: *The Presbyterian Church is the most important church in Scotland.* **2** a member of this church. 1 *adj.,* 2 *n.*

pre·scribe (pri skrīb′) **1** order; direct: *Good citizens do what the laws prescribe.* **2** order as medicine or treatment: *The doctor prescribed a complete rest for her.* **3** give medical advice. *v.,* **pre·scribed, pre·scrib·ing.**

pre·scrip·tion (pri skrip′shən) **1** a written direction or order for preparing and using a medicine: *a prescription for a cough. Symbol:* ℞ **2** the medicine. *n.*

pres·ence (prez′əns) **1** being present in a place: *I knew of his presence in the other room.* **2** a place where a person is: *The messenger was admitted to my presence.* **3** appearance; bearing: *a man of noble presence. n.*

in the presence of, in the sight or company of: *He signed his name in the presence of two witnesses.*

presence of mind ability to think calmly and quickly when taken by surprise.

pres·ent[1] (prez′ənt) **1** being in a proper or expected place; at hand; not absent: *Every member of the class was present.* **2** at this time; being or occurring now: *the*

hat, āge, fär; let, ēqual, tėrm; it, īce
hot, ōpen, ôrder; oil, out; cup, pu̇t, rüle
əbove, takən, pencəl, lemən, circəs
ch, child; ng, long; sh, ship
th, thin; ᴛʜ, then; zh, measure

present ruler, present prices. **3** now; this time; the time being: *That is enough for the present. At present people need courage.* **4** the present tense or a verb form in that tense. 1, 2 *adj.*, 3, 4 *n.*

pre·sent[2] (pri zent′ for 1, and 3–7, prez′ənt for 2) **1** give: *They presented flowers to their teacher.* **2** a gift; something given: *a birthday present.* **3** introduce; make acquainted; bring a person before somebody: *Miss Smith, may I present Mr. Brown? She was presented at court.* **4** offer; set forth in words: *The speaker presented arguments for his side.* **5** offer to view or notice: *The new post office presents a fine appearance.* **6** bring before the public: *Our class presented a play.* **7** hand in; send in: *The grocer presented his bill.* 1, 3–7 *v.*, 2 *n.*
present with, give to: *Our class presented the school with a picture.*

pre·sent·a·ble (pri zen′tə bəl) **1** suitable in appearance, dress, manners, etc. for being introduced into society or company: *After cleaning the cellar, he had to make himself presentable.* **2** suitable to be offered or given: *Make the work presentable before you hand it in.* *adj.*

pres·en·ta·tion (prez′ən tā′shən) **1** giving or delivering: *the presentation of a gift or a speech.* **2** the gift that is presented. **3** an offering to be seen; an exhibition or showing: *the presentation of a play or motion picture.* **4** a formal introduction: *the presentation of a lady to the Queen.* *n.*

pres·ent·ly (prez′ənt lē) **1** before long; soon: *The clock will strike presently.* **2** at present; now: *The Prime Minister is presently in Ottawa.* *adv.*

present participle a participle that indicates time that is now. In 'Singing merrily, we turn our steps toward home,' *singing* is a present partciple.

pres·er·va·tion (prez′ər vā′shən) **1** preserving or keeping safe: *Doctors work for the preservation of our health.* **2** being preserved or being kept safe: *an excellent state of preservation.* *n.*

pre·serve (pri zėrv′) **1** keep from harm or change; keep safe; protect. **2** keep up; maintain: *It is sometimes hard to preserve one's sense of humor.* **3** prepare food to keep it from spoiling: *Boiling with sugar, salting, smoking, and pickling are different ways of preserving food.* **4** Usually, **preserves,** *pl.* fruit cooked with sugar and sealed from the air: *Mother made some plum preserves.* **5** a place where wild animals, fish, or trees and plants are protected: *People are not allowed to hunt on the preserves.* 1–3 *v.*, **pre·served, pre·serv·ing;** 4, 5 *n.* **—pre·ser′ver,** *n.*

pre·side (pri zīd′) **1** hold the place of authority; have charge of a meeting: *Our principal will preside at our election of school officers.* **2** have authority; have control: *The manager presides over the business of this store.* *v.*, **pre·sid·ed, pre·sid·ing.**

pres·i·den·cy (prez′ə dən sē) **1** the office of president: *She was elected to the presidency of the Junior Club.* **2** the time during which a president is in office: *Her presidency lasted two years.* *n., pl.* **pres·i·den·cies.**

pres·i·dent (prez′ə dənt) **1** the chief officer of a company, college, society, club, etc. **2** Often, **President,** the highest officer of a modern republic. *n.*

pres·i·den·tial (prez′ə den′shəl) of or belonging to a president or presidency; having to do with a president or presidency: *a presidential election, a presidential candidate.* *adj.*

press[1] (pres) **1** use force or weight against; push with steady force; force: *Press the button to ring the bell.* **2** squeeze; squeeze out: *Press all the juice from the oranges.* **3** clasp; hug: *Mother pressed the baby to her.* **4** make smooth; flatten: *You press clothes with an iron.* **5** force; pressure: *The press of many duties keeps Mother busy.* **6** a machine for pressing: *a printing press, an ironing press.* **7** newspapers, magazines, and the people who work for them: *Our school picnic was reported by the press.* **8** keep on pushing one's way; push forward: *The boys pressed on in spite of the wind.* **9** a crowd: *The little boy was lost in the press.* **10** urge; keep asking somebody earnestly: *Because it was so stormy, we pressed our guest to stay all night.* 1–4, 8, 10 *v.*, 5–7, 9 *n.*

press[2] (pres) force into service, usually naval or military: *Naval officers used to visit towns and ships to press men for the fleet.* *v.*

press gang in former times, a group of men whose job it was to obtain men, often by force, for service in the navy or army.

press·ing (pres′ing) requiring immediate action or attention; urgent: *pressing business.* *adj.*

pres·sure (presh′ər) **1** the continued action of a weight or force: *The small box was flattened by the pressure of the heavy book on it. The pressure of the wind filled the sails of the boat.* **2** the force per unit of area: *The pressure in this bicycle tire is too low.* **3** a state of trouble or strain: *the pressure of poverty, working under pressure.* **4** a compelling influence: *Pressure was brought to bear to make him work.* *n.*

pres·sur·ize (presh′ə rīz′) keep the atmospheric pressure inside the cabin of an aircraft at a normal level in spite of the altitude. *v.*

pres·tige (pres tēzh′ or pres tēj′) reputation, influence, or distinction, based on what is known about one's abilities, achievements, associations, etc.: *His prestige rose when the boys learned that his father was a hockey star.* *n.*

pres·to (pres′tō) **1** quickly. **2** quick. **3** a quick part in a piece of music. 1 *adv.*, 2 *adj.*, 3 *n., pl.* **pres·tos.**

pre·sum·a·ble (pri züm′ə bəl or pri zyüm′əbəl) that can be presumed or taken for granted; probable; likely: *Noon is the presumable time of their arrival unless they are delayed.* *adj.* **—pre·sum′a·bly,** *adv.*

pre·sume (pri züm′ or pri zyüm′) **1** suppose; take for granted without proving: *You'll play out of doors, I presume, if there is sunshine.* **2** take upon oneself; venture; dare: *May I presume to tell you what to do?* **3** take an unfair advantage: *Don't presume on his good nature by borrowing from him every week.* *v.*, **pre·sumed, pre·sum·ing.**

pre·sump·tion (pri zump′shən) **1** something taken for granted; a conclusion based on good evidence: *Since he had the stolen jewels in his pocket, the presumption was that he was the thief.* **2** unpleasant boldness: *It is* *presumption to go to a party when one has not been invited. n.*

pre·sump·tu·ous (pri zump′chü əs) acting without permission or right; forward; too bold. *adj.*

pre·tence or **pre·tense** (pri tens′ or prē′tens) **1** a false appearance: *Under pretence of picking up the handkerchief, she took the money.* **2** a false claim: *The girl made a pretence of knowing the answer.* **3** pretending; make-believe: *His anger was all pretence.* **4** a display or showing off: *Her manner is modest and free from pretence. n.*

pre·tend (pri tend′) **1** make believe: *Let's pretend that we are soldiers.* **2** claim: *I don't pretend to be a musician.* **3** claim falsely: *She pretends to like you, but talks about you behind your back.* **4** lay claim: *James Stuart pretended to the English throne. v.*

pre·tense (pri tens′ or prē′tens) See **pretence.**

pre·ten·sion (pri ten′shən) **1** a claim: *The young prince has pretensions to the throne.* **2** the practice of doing things for show or to make a fine impression; a showy display: *The other girls were annoyed by her pretensions. n.*

pre·ten·tious (pri ten′shəs) **1** making claims to excellence or importance: *a pretentious person.* **2** doing things for show or to make a fine appearance; showy: *She had a pretentious style of entertaining guests. adj.*

pre·text (prē′tekst) a false reason concealing the real reason; a misleading excuse; a pretence: *He used his sore finger as a pretext for not going to school. n.*

pret·ty (prit′ē) **1** attractive or pleasing: *a pretty face, a pretty dress, a pretty tune, pretty manners.* **2** fairly; rather: *It is pretty late.* 1 *adj.,* **pret·ti·er, pret·ti·est;** 2 *adv.*

pret·zel (pret′səl) a hard biscuit, usually made in the shape of a knot and salted on the outside. *n.*

☛ **Pretzel** is from German *Brezel,* meaning 'a bracelet.'

pre·vail (pri vāl′) **1** exist in many places; be in general use: *The custom of hanging up stockings on Christmas Eve still prevails.* **2** be the most usual or strongest: *Yellow is the prevailing color in her room.* **3** be the stronger; win the victory; succeed: *The knights prevailed against their foe. v.*

prevail on or **prevail upon,** persuade: *Can't I prevail upon you to stay for dinner?*

prev·a·lence (prev′ə ləns) widespread occurrence; general use: *the prevalence of complaints about the weather, the prevalence of automobiles. n.*

prev·a·lent (prev′ə lənt) widespread; in general use; common: *Colds are prevalent in the winter. adj.*

pre·vent (pri vent′) **1** keep from: *Illness prevented him from doing his work.* **2** keep from happening: *Rain prevented the game.* **3** hinder: *I'll meet you at six if nothing prevents. v.*

pre·ven·tion (pri ven′shən) **1** the act of preventing or hindering: *the prevention of fire.* **2** something that prevents. *n.*

pre·ven·tive (pri ven′tiv) **1** that prevents or hinders: *preventive measures against disease.* **2** something that prevents: *Vaccination is a preventive against smallpox.* 1 *adj.,* 2 *n.*

pre·view (prē′vyü′) **1** an advance view, inspection, survey, etc.: *a preview of things to come.* **2** an advance showing of scenes from a motion picture, play, television program, etc. *n.*

pre·vi·ous (prē′vē əs) coming before; that came before; earlier: *She did better in the previous lesson. adj.* **—pre′vi·ous·ly,** *adv.*

prey (prā) **1** an animal hunted or seized for food: *Mice and birds are the prey of cats.* **2** a person or thing injured; a victim: *to be a prey to fear, to be a prey to disease. n.*

birds of prey and **beasts of prey,** birds and animals, such as hawks and lions, that hunt and kill other animals for food.

prey on or **upon, a** hunt and kill for food: *Cats prey on mice.* **b** be a strain upon; injure; irritate: *Worry about her debts preys upon her mind.*

☛ **Prey** and **pray** are pronounced the same.

price (prīs) **1** the amount for which a thing is sold or can be bought; the cost to the buyer: *The price of this hat is $9.00.* **2** put a price on; set the price of: *The hat was priced at $9.00.* **3** *Informal.* ask the price of; find out the price of: *Mother is pricing rugs.* **4** what must be given or done to obtain a thing; the amount paid for any result: *We paid a heavy price for the victory, for we lost ten thousand soldiers.* **5** a reward offered for the capture of a person alive or dead: *Every member of the gang has a price on his head.* 1, 4, 5 *n.,* 2, 3 *v.,* **priced, pric·ing.**

at any price, at any cost, no matter how great: *He wanted to win at any price.*

price·less (prīs′lis) beyond price; very valuable: *The Art Gallery has a collection of priceless paintings by famous artists. adj.*

prick (prik) **1** a sharp point. **2** a little hole or mark made by a sharp point. **3** make a little hole or mark on with a sharp point: *I pricked the map with a pin to show our route.* **4** a pain like that made by a sharp point. **5** cause sharp pain to: *Thorns prick. The cat pricked me with its claws.* 1, 2, 4 *n.,* 3, 5 *v.*

prick up the ears, a point the ears upward: *The dog pricked up its ears.* **b** listen carefully; give sudden attention: *The boy pricked up his ears when the teacher started talking about a trip.*

prick·le (prik′əl) **1** a small, sharp point; a thorn. **2** feel a prickly or smarting sensation: *Her skin prickled when she saw the big snake.* 1 *n.,* 2 *v.,* **prick·led, prick·ling.**

prick·ly (prik′lē) **1** having many sharp points or thorns: *a prickly rosebush, a prickly porcupine.* **2** sharp and stinging; smarting: *a prickly feeling. Heat sometimes causes a prickly redness of the skin. adj.,* **prick·li·er, prick·li·est.**

prickly pear a pear-shaped, edible fruit of a certain kind of cactus.

pride (prīd) **1** a high opinion of one's own worth or possessions: *Pride in our city should make us help to keep it clean.* **2** pleasure or satisfaction in something concerned with oneself: *take pride in a hard job well done.* **3** something that one is proud of: *Her youngest child is her great pride.* **4** too high an opinion of oneself; scorn of others: *Pride goes before a fall.* **5** pride oneself on, be proud of: *We pride ourselves on our clean streets.* 1–4 *n.,* 5 *v.,* **prid·ed, prid·ing.**

☛ **Pride** and **pried** are pronounced the same.

pried (prīd) See **pry.** *v.*
☛ See note at **pride.**

pries (prīz) plural of **pry**[2]. *n.*
☛ **Pries** and **prize** are pronounced the same.

priest (prēst) **1** a clergyman or minister; a person authorized to perform religious ceremonies. **2** a special servant of a god: *the priests of Apollo. n.*

priest·ess (prēs′tis) a woman who serves at an altar or in sacred rites: *a priestess of the goddess Diana. n., pl.* **priest·ess·es.**

prig (prig) someone who is smug and thinks he is a better person than others. *n.*

prim (prim) precise, neat, proper, or formal: *a prim appearance, a prim garden. adj.* **prim·mer, prim·mest.**

pri·ma·ry (prī′mer′ē or prī′mər ē) **1** first in time; first in order. **2** first in importance; chief: *The primary reason for the party is to celebrate his birthday. adj.*

primary accent primary stress.

primary color one of three colors that can be mixed together to make any other color: *In painting, the primary colors are red, yellow, and blue; in light, they are red, green, and blue.*

primary school the first three or four grades of elementary school.

primary stress **1** the strongest stress in the pronunciation of a word. **2** the mark (′) used to show where this stress falls.

pri·mate (prī′māt or prī′mit) **1** any of the highest order of mammals, including human beings, apes, and monkeys. **2** an archbishop or bishop ranking above all other bishops in a country or church province. *n.*

prime[1] (prīm) **1** first in rank or order; chief: *His prime object was to get enough to eat.* **2** first in quality; first-rate; excellent: *prime ribs of beef.* **3** the best part; the best time; the best condition: *A man of forty is in the prime of life.* **4** prime number. 1, 2 *adj.,* 3, 4 *n.*

prime[2] (prīm) **1** cover a surface with a first coat of paint or oil so that the finishing coat of paint will not soak in. **2** pour water into a pump to start action. **3** supply a gun with powder. *v.,* **primed, prim·ing.**

prime minister the chief minister in certain governments; the head of the cabinet: *The Prime Minister of Canada is the first minister of the Federal Government at Ottawa.*

prime number a number not exactly divisible by any whole number other than itself and 1; prime: *2, 3, 5, 7, and 11 are prime numbers; 4, 6, and 9 are composite numbers.*

prim·er[1] (prim′ər) **1** a first book in reading. **2** a beginner's book: *a primer of chemistry. n.*

prim·er[2] (prī′mər) **1** a cap or cylinder of gunpowder used for firing a charge of dynamite, etc. **2** a first coat of paint, etc. *n.*

pri·me·val (prī mē′vəl) **1** of or having to do with the earliest time: *In its primeval state the earth was without any form of life.* **2** ancient: *primeval forests untouched by the axe. adj.*

prim·i·tive (prim′ə tiv) **1** of early times; of long ago: *Primitive people often lived in caves.* **2** first of the kind: *primitive Christians.* **3** very simple; such as people had early in human history: *A primitive way of making fire is by rubbing two sticks together. adj.*

hat, āge, fär; let, ēqual, tėrm; it, īce
hot, ōpen, ôrder; oil, out; cup, pu̇t, rüle
əbove, takən, pencəl, lemən, circəs
ch, child; ng, long; sh, ship
th, thin; ᴛʜ, then; zh, measure

primp (primp) dress carefully or fussily. *v.*

prim·rose (prim′rōz′) **1** any of a large group of plants with flowers of various colors: *The common primrose of Europe is pale yellow.* **2** pale yellow. 1, 2 *n.,* 2 *adj.*

prince (prins) **1** a son of a king or queen or of a king's or queen's son. **2** a ruler or monarch. **3** a man of highest rank; the best; the chief: *a merchant prince, a prince of artists. n.*

Prince Edward Islander a person born in or living in Prince Edward Island.

prince·ly (prins′lē) **1** of a prince or his rank; royal. **2** like a prince; noble. **3** fit for a prince; magnificent: *He earns a princely salary. adj.,* **prince·li·er, prince·li·est.**

Prince of Wales a title given regularly since 1343 to the eldest son of the monarch of England.

prin·cess (prin′sis or prin′ses) **1** a daughter of a king or queen or of a king's or queen's son. **2** the wife or widow of a prince. *n.*

prin·ci·pal (prin′sə pəl) **1** most important; chief; main: *St. John's is the principal city of Newfoundland.* **2** the chief person, such as the head of a school. **3** a sum of money on which interest is paid. 1 *adj.,* 2, 3 *n.*
☛ **Principal** and **principle** are pronounced the same.

prin·ci·pal·i·ty (prin′sə pal′ə tē) a small state or country ruled by a prince. *n., pl.* **prin·ci·pal·i·ties.**

prin·ci·pal·ly (prin′sə plē or prin′sə pəl ē) for the most part; above all; chiefly. *adv.*

prin·ci·ple (prin′sə pəl) **1** a fact or belief on which other ideas are based: *Science is based on the principle that things can be explained.* **2** a rule of action or conduct: *I make it a principle to save some money each week.* **3** uprightness; honor: *Joseph Howe was a man of principle.* **4** a rule of science explaining how things act: *the principle by which a machine works. n.*
☛ **Principle** and **principal** are pronounced the same.

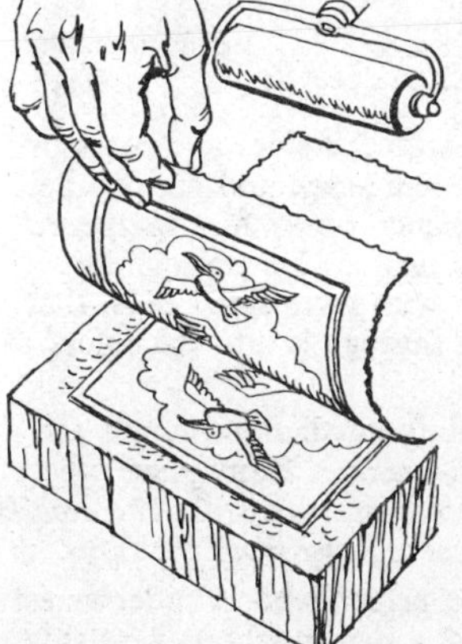

A print (def. 8) being pulled off a wooden block into which a design has been cut. For this kind of print, the background of the design is cut away and the raised parts that are left are covered with ink. A sheet of paper is then pressed onto the inked block. When the paper is pulled off, it shows the block design in reverse.

print (print) **1** use type, plates, etc. and ink or dye to

reproduce words, pictures, or designs on paper or some other surface: *This cloth is printed.* 2 reproduce letters, words, etc. on with type, etc. and ink or dye: *This photograph was printed in several newspapers.* 3 cause to be printed; publish: *Who prints this newspaper?* 4 words, letters, etc. reproduced in ink by type: *This book has clear print.* 5 make letters the way they look in print instead of in writing: *Print your name clearly.* 6 mark cloth, paper, etc. with patterns or designs: *This machine prints wallpaper.* 7 cloth with a pattern pressed on it: *Amy has two dresses made of cotton print.* 8 a picture or design printed from an engraved plate, block, etc. 9 produce marks or figures by pressure; stamp; impress. 10 a mark made by pressing or stamping: *He saw prints of a man's feet on the ground.* 11 a photograph produced from a negative. 12 produce a photograph by transmission of light through a negative. 1–3, 5, 6, 9, 12, *v.*, 4, 7, 8, 10, 11 *n.*
in print, of books, etc., still available from the publisher.
out of print, no longer sold by the publisher.

print·er (prin′tər) a person whose business or work is printing or setting type. *n.*

print·ing (prin′ting) 1 the producing of books, newspapers, etc. by stamping in ink or dye from movable type, plates, etc. 2 printed words, letters, etc. 3 letters made like those in print. *n.*

printing press a machine for printing from type, plate, etc.

pri·or[1] (prī′ər) coming before; earlier: *I can't go with you because I have a prior engagement. adj.*
prior to, earlier than; before.

pri·or[2] (prī′ər) the head of a priory or monastery for men: *Monks obey their prior. n.*

pri·or·ess (prī′ər is) the woman at the head of a convent or priory for women. *n.*

pri·or·i·ty (prī ôr′ə tē) 1 the fact of being earlier in time: *The priority of the invention of the telephone to that of television is a known fact.* 2 coming before in order or importance: *Fire engines have priority over other traffic. n., pl.* **pri·or·i·ties.**

pri·o·ry (prī′ə rē) a religious house governed by a prior or prioress. *n., pl.* **pri·o·ries.**

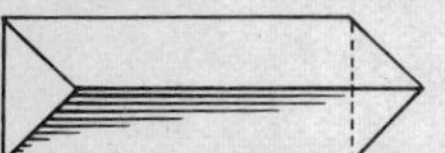
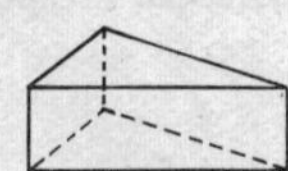

Prisms (def. 2)

prism (priz′əm) 1 a solid with flat sides and bases or ends that have the same size and shape and are parallel to one another: *A six-sided pencil before it is sharpened has the shape of one kind of prism.* 2 a transparent prism, often of glass, usually with three-sided ends, that separates white light passing through it into the colors of the spectrum. *n.*

pris·on (priz′ən) 1 a building in which criminals are confined: *Burglars are put in prison.* 2 any place where a person or animal is shut up against his will: *The small apartment was a prison to the big dog from the farm. n.*

pris·on·er (priz′ən ər) 1 a person who is under arrest or held in a jail or prison. 2 a person who is kept shut up against his will, or who is not free to move. *n.*
prisoner of war, a person taken by the enemy in war.

pri·va·cy (prī′və sē) 1 being private; the state of being away from others: *in the privacy of one's home.* 2 secrecy: *He told me his reasons in strict privacy. n., pl.* **pri·va·cies.**

pri·vate (prī′vit) 1 not for the public; for just a few special people or for one: *a private road, a private house, a private letter.* 2 not public; personal: *the private life of a king, my private opinion.* 3 secret: *a private drawer.* 4 having no public office: *a private citizen.* 5 a soldier of the lowest rank: *John's brother was promoted from private to corporal last week.* 1–4 *adj.*, 5 *n.* —**pri′vate·ly,** *adv.*
in private, a not publicly: *My father spoke to the principal in private.* **b** secretly: *We met in private to plan his surprise birthday party.*

pri·va·teer (prī′və tēr′) 1 an armed ship owned by private persons and holding a government commission to attack and capture enemy ships. 2 the commander or one of the crew of a privateer. 3 to cruise as a privateer. 1, 2 *n.*, 3 *v.*

pri·va·tion (prī vā′shən) the lack of the comforts or necessities of life: *Many children were hungry or homeless because of privation during the war. n.*

priv·et (priv′it) any of several shrubs much used for hedges. *n.*

priv·i·lege (priv′ə lij or priv′lij) a special right, advantage, or favor: *He has given us the privilege of using his television set. n.*

priv·i·leged (priv′ə lijd or priv′lijd) having a special advantage or advantages: *In former times the nobility in Europe was a privileged class. adj.*

priv·y (priv′ē) 1 private. A **privy council** is a body of personal advisers to a ruler. 2 secret. 3 a toilet, usually an outhouse. 1, 2 *adj.*, 3 *n.*
privy to, having secret or private knowledge of.

Privy Council in Canada, the body of advisers to the Governor General, made up of the ministers of the Federal Cabinet and all former cabinet ministers.

Privy Councillor a member of the Privy Council: *Privy Councillors hold office for life, but can advise the Governor General only while they are cabinet ministers.*

prize[1] (prīz) 1 a reward won or offered in a contest or competition: *Prizes will be given for the three best stories.* 2 given as a prize. 3 worthy of a prize: *prize vegetables.* 4 a reward worth working for. 1, 4 *n.*, 2, 3 *adj.*
☛ **Prize** and **pries** are pronounced the same.

prize[2] (prīz) a thing or person captured from the enemy in war. *n.*
☛ See note at **prize**[1]

prize[3] (prīz) value highly: *Mother prizes her best china. v.,* **prized, priz·ing.**
☛ See note at **prize**[1].

prize[4] (prīz) pry[2]. *v.,* **prized, priz·ing.**
☛ See note at **prize**[1].

pro[1] (prō) 1 in favor of; for. 2 a reason in favor of: *The pros and cons of a question are the arguments for and against it.* 1 *adv.*, 2 *n., pl.* **pros.**

pro[2] (prō) *Informal.* a professional, especially a professional athlete. *n., pl.* **pros.**

prob·a·bil·i·ty (prob′ə bil′ə tē) 1 being likely or probable; a good chance: *There is a probability of rain.* 2 something likely to happen: *A storm is a probability for tomorrow. n., pl.* **prob·a·bil·i·ties.**
in all probability, probably.

hat, āge, fär; let, ēqual, tėrm; it, īce
hot, ōpen, ôrder; oil, out; cup, pu̇t, rüle
əbove, takən, pencəl, lemən, circəs
ch, child; ng, long; sh, ship
th, thin; ꟛH, then; zh, measure

prob·a·ble (prob′ə bəl) 1 likely to happen: *Cooler weather is probable after this shower.* 2 likely to be true: *Something he ate is the probable cause of his pain.* *adj.*

prob·a·bly (prob′ə blē) more likely than not. *adv.*

pro·ba·tion (prō bā′shən) 1 a trial or testing of conduct, qualifications, etc.: *Bill was admitted to the sixth grade on probation.* 2 the system of letting young offenders against the law, or first offenders, go free under the supervision of a probation officer. *n.*

probation officer an officer appointed by a court of law to supervise offenders who have been placed on probation.

probe (prōb) 1 search into; examine thoroughly; investigate: *to probe into the causes of a crime, to probe one's thoughts or feelings to find out why one acted as one did.* 2 a thorough examination; an investigation. 3 an investigation, usually by a lawmaking body, in an effort to discover evidences of law violation. 4 a slender instrument for exploring something: *A doctor or dentist uses a probe to explore the depth or direction of a wound or cavity. A Geiger counter uses a probe to detect the amount of radiation in radioactive matter, such as a rock.* 5 a spacecraft carrying scientific instruments to record or report back information about planets, etc.: *a lunar probe.* 6 examine with a probe. 1, 6 *v.*, **probed, prob·ing;** 2–5 *n.*

prob·lem (prob′ləm) 1 a question, especially a difficult question. 2 a matter or cause of doubt or difficulty: *a problem child.* 3 something to be worked out: *a problem in arithmetic.* *n.*

pro·ce·dure (prə sē′jər) a way of proceeding; a method for doing things: *What is the procedure for nominating a candidate?* *n.*

pro·ceed (prə sēd′) 1 go on after having stopped; move forward: *Please proceed with your story. The train proceeded at the same speed as before.* 2 begin to carry on any activity: *He proceeded to light his pipe.* 3 come forth; issue; go out: *Heat proceeds from fire.* *v.*

pro·ceeds (prō′sēdz) the money obtained from a sale, etc.: *The proceeds from the school play will be used to buy a new curtain for the stage.* *n. pl.*

pro·cess (prō′ses or pros′es) 1 a set of actions or changes in a special order: *By what process is cloth made from wool?* 2 treat or prepare by some special method: *This cloth has been processed to make it waterproof.* 1 *n.*, 2 *v.*
in process, a in the course or condition: *In process of time the house will be finished.* b in the course or condition of being done: *The author has just finished one book and has another in process.*

pro·ces·sion (prə sesh′ən) 1 something that moves forward; persons marching or riding: *A funeral procession filled the street.* 2 an orderly moving forward: *We formed lines to march in procession onto the platform.* *n.*

pro·claim (prə klām′) make known publicly and officially; declare publicly: *War was proclaimed. The people proclaimed him king.* *v.*

proc·la·ma·tion (prok′lə mā′shən) an official announcement; a public declaration: *When a general election is to be held, a proclamation is issued by the government.* *n.*

pro·cure (prə kyür′) 1 obtain by care or effort; get: *A friend procured a position in the bank for my big brother. It is hard to procure water in a desert.* 2 bring about; cause: *The traitors procured the death of the prince.* *v.*, **pro·cured, pro·cur·ing.**

prod (prod) 1 poke or jab with something pointed: *to prod an animal with a stick.* 2 stir up; urge on; goad: *to prod a lazy boy to action by threats and entreaties.* 3 a poke; a thrust: *That prod in the ribs hurt.* 4 a stick with a sharp point; a goad. 1, 2 *v.*, **prod·ded, prod·ding;** 3, 4 *n.*

prod·i·gal (prod′ə gəl) 1 spending too much; wasting money or other things; wasteful: *Canada has been prodigal of its forests.* 2 a person who is wasteful or extravagant: *The father welcomed the prodigal back home.* 1 *adj.*, 2 *n.*

pro·di·gious (prə dij′əs) 1 very great; huge; vast: *The ocean contains a prodigious amount of water.* 2 wonderful; marvellous: *It was a prodigious achievement.* *adj.*

prod·i·gy (prod′ə jē) a marvel; a wonder: *An infant prodigy is a child remarkably brilliant in some respect.* *n., pl.* **prod·i·gies.**

pro·duce (prə dyüs′ or prə düs′ for 1, 2, 3, and 6, prod′yüs or prō′düs for 4 and 5) 1 make; bring into existence: *This factory produces stoves.* 2 bring about; cause: *Hard work produces success.* 3 bring forth; supply or yield: *Hens produce eggs. The tree produced only 100 litres of apples this year.* 4 what is produced; the yield: *Vegetables are a garden's produce.* 5 fruit and vegetables: *He owns a produce market.* 6 bring forward; show; present: *Produce your proof. Our class produced a play.* 1–3, 6 *v.*, **pro·duced, pro·duc·ing;** 4, 5 *n.*

pro·duc·er (prə dyüs′ər or prə düz′ər) 1 a person who grows or manufactures things that are used by others. 2 a person in charge of presenting a play, a motion picture, a television program, etc. *n.*

prod·uct (prod′əkt) 1 that which is produced; a result of work or of growth: *factory products, farm products.* 2 a number or quantity resulting from multiplying two or more numbers together: *The product of 5 and 8 is 40.* See **multiplication** for picture. *n.*

pro·duc·tion (prə duk′shən) 1 the act of producing; manufacture: *His business is the production of automobiles.* 2 something that is produced: *The school play was a fine production.* 3 the total amount produced: *The company's production has increased this year.* *n.*

pro·duc·tive (prə duk′tiv) 1 producing; bringing forth: *That field is productive only of weeds. Hasty words are productive of quarrels.* 2 producing food or other useful articles: *Farming is productive labor.* 3 producing much; fertile: *a productive farm, a productive writer.* *adj.*

pro·fane (prə fān′ or prō fān′) 1 with contempt or disregard for God or holy things: *profane language, a profane man.* 2 treat holy things with contempt or disregard: *The soldiers profaned the church by stabling horses there.* 3 not sacred; worldly: *Mozart wrote both religious and profane music.* 1, 3 *adj.,* 2 *v.,* **pro·faned, pro·fan·ing.**

pro·fan·i·ty (prə fan′ə tē) 1 swearing; the use of profane language. 2 being profane; lack of reverence. *n., pl.* **pro·fan·i·ties.**

pro·fess (prə fes′) 1 claim to have; claim: *He professed the greatest respect for the law. I don't profess to be an expert.* 2 declare openly: *He professed his loyalty to his country.* *v.*

pro·fes·sion (prə fesh′ən) 1 an occupation requiring special education, such as law, medicine, teaching, or the ministry. 2 the people engaged in such an occupation: *The medical profession favors this law.* 3 an open declaration: *I welcomed her profession of friendship for us.* 4 a declaration of belief in a religion. *n.*

pro·fes·sion·al (prə fesh′ən əl) 1 of or having to do with a profession: *professional skill, a professional manner.* 2 engaged in a profession: *A lawyer or a doctor is a professional person.* 3 making a business or trade of something that others do for pleasure: *a professional baseball player, professional musicians.* 4 a person who does this. 5 done or engaged in by professionals: *a professional ball game.* 1–3, 5 *adj.,* 4 *n.*

pro·fes·sor (prə fes′ər) 1 a teacher of the highest rank in a college or university. 2 *Informal.* any teacher at a college or university. *n.*

prof·fer (prof′ər) 1 offer for acceptance; present: *We proffered regrets at having to leave so early.* 2 an offer made: *His proffer of advice was accepted.* 1 *v.,* 2 *n.*

pro·fi·cient (prə fish′ənt) advanced in any art, science, or subject; skilled; expert: *She was very proficient in music.* *adj.*

Profile of the Indian leader Crowfoot

pro·file (prō′fīl) 1 a side view, especially of the human face. 2 an outline. 3 a concise description of a person's abilities, character, or career: *The magazine carried an interesting profile of the Lieutenant-Governor.* *n.*

prof·it (prof′it) 1 the gain from a business; what is left when the cost of goods and of carrying on the business is subtracted from the amount of money taken in: *The profits in this business are not large.* 2 make a gain from business; make a profit. 3 advantage; benefit: *What profit is there in worrying?* 4 get advantage; gain; benefit: *A wise person profits from his mistakes.* 1, 3 *n.,* 2, 4 *v.*

☛ **Profit** and **prophet** are pronounced the same.

prof·it·a·ble (prof′ə tə bəl) 1 providing a profit in money: *The sale held by the Girl Guides was very profitable.* 2 giving a gain or benefit; useful: *We spent a profitable afternoon in the library.* *adj.* **—prof′it·a·bly,** *adv.*

pro·found (prə found′) 1 very deep: *a profound sigh, a profound sleep.* 2 strongly felt; very great: *profound despair, profound sympathy.* 3 having or showing great depth of knowledge or understanding: *a profound book, a profound thinker.* *adj.* **—pro·found′ly,** *adv.*

pro·fuse (prə fyüs′) 1 very abundant: *profuse thanks.* 2 spending or giving much; lavish; extravagant: *He was so profuse with his money that he is now poor.* *adj.*

pro·fu·sion (prə fyü′zhən) 1 a great abundance: *There was a profusion of gulls on the breakwater.* 2 extravagance; lavishness. *n.*

prog·e·ny (proj′ə nē) children; offspring; descendants: *Kittens are a cat's progeny.* *n., pl.* **prog·e·nies.**

pro·gram or **pro·gramme** (prō′gram) 1 a list of items or events; a list of performers, players, etc.: *a concert program, a theatre program, a hockey program.* 2 the items making up an entertainment: *The entire program was delightful.* 3 a plan of what is to be done: *a school program, a business program, a government program.* 4 a set of instructions for an electronic computer or other automatic machine, outlining the steps to be performed by the machine in a specific operation. 5 arrange or enter in a program. 6 draw up a program or plan for. 1–4 *n.,* 5, 6 *v.*

pro·gress (prō′gres or prog′res for 1 and 3, prə gres′ for 2 and 4) 1 advance; growth; development; improvement: *the progress of science.* 2 get better; advance; develop: *We progress in learning step by step.* 3 moving forward; going ahead: *to make rapid progress on a journey.* 4 move forward; go ahead: *The building of the city hall has progressed a great deal this week.* 1, 3 *n.,* 2, 4 *v.*

pro·gres·sive (prə gres′iv) 1 making progress; advancing to something better; improving: *a progressive nation.* 2 favoring progress; wanting improvement or reform. 3 a person who favors improvement and reform in government, religion, or business: *Our doctor is a progressive in his beliefs.* 4 moving forward; developing: *a progressive disease.* 1, 2, 4 *adj.,* 3 *n.*

Progressive Conservative 1 a member of the Progressive-Conservative Party. 2 a person who supports the policies of this party. 3 of or having to do with this party: *the Progressive-Conservative policy.*

Progressive–Conservative Party one of the principal political parties of Canada.

pro·hib·it (prō hib′it) 1 forbid by law or authority: *Picking flowers in the park is prohibited.* 2 prevent: *The high price prohibits my buying the bicycle.* *v.*

pro·hi·bi·tion (prō′ə bish′ən) 1 prohibiting or forbidding: *The prohibition of swimming in the city's reservoirs is sensible.* 2 a law or laws against making or selling alcoholic liquors. *n.*

pro·ject (prō′jekt or proj′ekt for 1 and 3, prə jekt′ for 2, 4, 5, and 6) 1 a plan or scheme: *Flying in a heavy machine was once thought an impossible project.* 2 to plan; scheme. 3 an undertaking; enterprise: *He is busy with several projects.* 4 throw or cast forward: *A catapult projects stones.* 5 cause to fall on a surface: *Motion pictures are projected on the screen. The tree projects a shadow on the grass.* 6 stick out: *The rocky point projects far into the water.* 1, 3 *n.,* 2, 4–6 *v.*

pro·jec·tile (prə jek′tīl or prə jek′təl) any object that is thrown, hurled, or shot, such as a rocket, stone, or bullet. *n.*

hat, āge, fär; let, ēqual, tėrm; it, īce
hot, ōpen, ôrder; oil, out; cup, pu̇t, rüle
əbove, takən, pencəl, lemən, circəs
ch, child; ng, long; sh, ship
th, thin; ᴛʜ, then; zh, measure

pro·jec·tion (prə jek′shən) 1 a part that projects or sticks out: *rocky projections on the face of a cliff.* 2 sticking out: *The projection of these nails is dangerous.* 3 throwing or casting forward: *the projection of a shell from a gun, the projection of pictures on a screen.* *n.*

pro·jec·tor (prə jek′tər) an apparatus for projecting a picture on a screen. *n.*

pro·lif·ic (prə lif′ik) 1 producing many offspring: *Rabbits are prolific.* 2 producing much: *a prolific garden, a prolific writer.* *adj.*

pro·long (prə long′) make longer; draw out; stretch: *Good care may prolong a sick person's life. The dog uttered prolonged howls whenever the family left the house.* *v.*

prom·e·nade (prom′ə nād′ or prom′ə näd′) 1 a walk for pleasure or for show: *The Easter promenade is well known as a fashion show.* 2 walk about or up and down for pleasure or display: *He promenaded back and forth on the ship's deck.* 3 a public place for such a walk: *Toronto had a famous promenade called the 'Boardwalk.'* 1, 3 *n.*, 2 *v.*, **prom·e·nad·ed, prom·e·nad·ing.**

prom·i·nence (prom′ə nəns) 1 the state or condition of being prominent, distinguished, or conspicuous: *the prominence of Winston Churchill as a leader, the prominence of football as a sport.* 2 something that juts out or projects, especially upward: *A hill is a prominence.* *n.*

prom·i·nent (prom′ə nənt) 1 well-known; important: *a prominent citizen.* 2 easy to see: *A single tree in a field is prominent.* 3 standing out; projecting: *Some insects have prominent eyes.* *adj.*

prom·ise (prom′is) 1 the words that bind a person to do or not to do something: *A man of honor always keeps his promise.* 2 give one's word; make a promise: *He promised to stay till we came.* 3 make a promise of: *to promise help.* 4 an indication of what may be expected: *The clouds give promise of rain.* 5 that which gives hope of success: *This pupil shows promise in music.* 6 give hope of; give indication of: *The rainbow promises fair weather. The dark clouds promise rain.* 1, 4, 5 *n.*, 2, 3, 6 *v.*, **prom·ised, prom·is·ing.**

prom·is·ing (prom′is ing) likely to turn out well: *a promising student.* *adj.*

A promontory

prom·on·to·ry (prom′ən tô′rē) a high point of land extending from the coast into the water; a headland. *n.*, *pl.* **prom·on·to·ries.**

pro·mote (prə mōt′) 1 raise in rank or importance: *Pupils who pass this test will be promoted to the next higher grade.* 2 help to grow or develop; help to success: *A kindly feeling toward other countries will promote peace. The company needs publicity to promote its new product.* 3 help to organize; start: *Several bankers promoted the new company.* *v.*, **pro·mot·ed, pro·mot·ing.**

pro·mo·tion (prə mō′shən) 1 an advance in rank or importance: *The clerk was given a promotion and an increase in salary.* 2 helping to grow or develop; helping along to success: *The doctors were busy in the promotion of a health campaign.* *n.*

prompt (prompt) 1 quick; on time: *Be prompt to obey.* 2 done at once; made without delay: *I expect a prompt answer.* 3 cause someone to do something: *His curiosity prompted him to ask questions.* 4 suggest; inspire: *A kind thought prompted the gift.* 5 remind a speaker, actor, etc. of the words or actions needed: *Bill will prompt you if you forget your lines in the play.* 1, 2 *adj.*, 3–5 *v.*

prompt·er (promp′tər) a person who tells actors, speakers, etc. what to say when they forget. *n.*

prone (prōn) 1 inclined; liable: *We are prone to think evil of people we don't like.* 2 lying face down: *He is prone on his bed.* *adj.*

prong (prong) one of the pointed ends of a fork, antler, etc. See **fork** for picture. *n.*

prong·horn (prong′hôrn′) an animal resembling an antelope, found in western North America: *The pronghorn is not closely related to any other animal.* *n.*

pro·noun (prō′noun) a word used to indicate without naming, such as *you, it, they, him, we, your, whose, this,* or *whoever;* a word used instead of a noun: *In 'John did not like to go because he was sick,' 'he' is a pronoun used in the second part of the sentence to avoid repeating 'John.'* *n.*

pro·nounce (prə nouns′) 1 make the sounds of; speak: *Pronounce your words clearly.* 2 declare a person or thing to be: *The doctor pronounced her cured.* 3 declare solemnly or positively: *The judge pronounced sentence on the prisoner.* *v.*, **pro·nounced, pro·nounc·ing.**

pro·nounced (prə nounst′) strongly marked; emphatic; decided: *She has very pronounced likes and dislikes.* *adj.*

pro·nun·ci·a·tion (prə nun′sē ā′shən) 1 the way of sounding words: *Most dictionaries give the pronunciation of each entry word.* 2 speaking; the act of making the sounds of words. *n.*

proof (prüf) 1 a way or means of showing beyond doubt the truth of something: *Is what you say a guess or have you proof?* 2 establishment of the truth of anything. 3 testing; a trial: *That box looks big enough; but let us put it to the proof.* *n.*
proof against, able to resist; not able to be harmed by: *Now we know that we are proof against being taken by surprise.*

prop (prop) 1 hold up by placing a support under or against: *Prop the clothes line with a stick.* 2 support; sustain: *prop a failing cause.* 3 a support: *Many branches are heavy with apples and need a prop.* 1, 2 *v.*, **propped; prop·ping;** 3 *n.*

prop·a·gan·da (prop′ə gan′də) 1 systematic efforts to spread opinions or beliefs, especially by twisting or slanting facts: *The insurance companies engaged in health propaganda.* 2 the opinions or beliefs thus spread: *The enemy spread false propaganda about us.* *n.*

prop·a·gate (prop′ə gāt′) 1 produce offspring; reproduce: *Trees propagate themselves by seeds.* 2 cause to increase in number by the production of young: *Cows and sheep are propagated on farms.* 3 spread news, knowledge, etc.: *Don't propagate unkind reports.* *v.,* **prop·a·gat·ed, prop·a·gat·ing.**

pro·pane (prō′pān) a heavy, colorless, flammable gas: *We have a propane stove in our summer cottage.* *n.*

pro·pel (prə pel′) drive forward; force ahead: *to propel a boat by oars, a person propelled by ambition.* *v.,* **pro·pelled, pro·pel·ling.**

A ship's propeller

An airplane propeller

pro·pel·ler (prə pel′ər) a device with revolving blades, for propelling boats and aircraft. *n.*

pro·pen·si·ty (prə pen′sə tē) a natural inclination or bent; leaning: *Most boys have a propensity for playing with machinery.* *n., pl.* **pro·pen·si·ties.**

prop·er (prop′ər) 1 correct; right; fitting: *Night is the proper time to sleep, and bed is the proper place.* 2 in the strict sense of the word: *The population of Vancouver proper does not include that of the suburbs.* 3 decent; respectable: *proper conduct.* 4 referring to a particular person, place, institution, etc.: *'John Smith,' 'Canada,' and 'The Royal Military College' are all proper names.* *adj.*

prop·er·ly (prop′ər lē) 1 in a proper, correct, or suitable manner: *This job must be done properly.* 2 rightly; justly: *An honest man is properly indignant at the offer of a bribe.* 3 strictly: *Properly speaking, a whale is not a fish.* *adv.*

proper noun a noun naming a particular person, place, or thing. *John, Winnipeg,* and *Monday* are proper nouns. *Boy, city,* and *day* are common nouns.

prop·er·ty (prop′ər tē) 1 any thing or things owned; a possession or possessions: *This house is the property of Mr. Jones. Ask for your purse at the lost-property office.* 2 land; buildings, houses, etc.: *He owns some property out West.* 3 ownership; the people who own land, etc.: *the demands of property for lower taxes.* 4 a quality or power belonging specially to something: *Soap has the property of removing dirt. Copper has several important properties.* 5 **properties,** *pl.* the furniture, weapons, etc. used in staging a play, motion-picture, or television scene. *n., pl.* **prop·er·ties.**

proph·e·cy (prof′ə sē) 1 a telling of what will happen; foretelling future events: *the gift of prophecy.* 2 something told about the future. *n., pl.* **proph·e·cies.**

proph·e·sy (prof′ə sī′) tell what will happen; foretell; predict: *The sailor prophesied a severe storm.* *v.,* **proph·e·sied, proph·e·sy·ing.**

proph·et (prof′it) 1 a person who tells what will happen: *Don't be a bad-luck prophet.* 2 a person who believes his preaching to be inspired by God: *Every religion has its prophets.* *n.*

☛ **Prophet** and **profit** are pronounced the same.

pro·phet·ic (prə fet′ik) 1 belonging to a prophet; such as a prophet has: *prophetic power.* 2 containing prophecy: *a prophetic saying.* 3 giving warning of what is to happen: *Thunder is prophetic of showers.* *adj.*

pro·pi·tious (prə pish′əs) favorable: *It seemed propitious weather for our trip.* *adj.*

pro·por·tion (prə pôr′shən) 1 the relation of one thing to another in size, number, amount, or degree: *Each girl's pay will be in proportion to the work she does. Mix water and orange juice in the proportions of three to one by adding three measures of water to each measure of orange juice.* 2 a proper relation between parts: *His short legs were not in proportion to his long body.* 3 fit one thing to another so that they go together: *The designs in that rug are well proportioned.* 4 a part or share: *A large proportion of British Columbia is mountainous.* 5 **proportions,** *pl.* **a** size or extent: *Canada has forests of huge proportions.* **b** dimensions: *The proportions of the furniture are wrong for this small room.* 1, 2, 4, 5 *n.,* 3 *v.*

pro·pos·al (prə pōz′əl) 1 a plan or scheme; suggestion: *The club will now hear this member's proposal.* 2 an offer of marriage. 3 the act of proposing: *Proposal is easier than performance.* *n.*

pro·pose (prə pōz′) 1 put forward; suggest: *I propose that we take turns at the swing.* 2 present the name of someone for an office: *I am proposing Jack for president.* 3 intend; plan: *She proposes to save half of all she earns.* 4 make an offer of marriage. *v.,* **pro·posed, pro·pos·ing.**

prop·o·si·tion (prop′ə zish′ən) 1 what is offered to be considered; proposal: *The tailor made a proposition to buy out his rival's business.* 2 a statement; an assertion: *The speaker discussed the proposition that women should get the same pay as men.* 3 a statement that is to be proved true, as in a debate. 4 a problem to be solved: *a proposition in arithmetic.* *n.*

pro·pri·e·tor (prə prī′ə tər) an owner, especially of a business. *n.*

pro·pri·e·ty (prə prī′ə tē) 1 the quality of being proper; fitness. 2 proper behavior: *She acted with propriety.* 3 **proprieties,** *pl.* the customs and rules of proper behavior: *The proprieties require that a boy stand up when he is introduced to a lady.* *n., pl.* **pro·pri·e·ties.**

pro·pul·sion (prə pul′shən) 1 a driving forward or onward. 2 a propelling force or impulse: *Most large aircraft are powered by the propulsion of jet engines.* *n.*

pro·sa·ic (prō zā′ik) like prose; ordinary; not exciting: *The new play was long and rather prosaic.* *adj.*

prose (prōz) the ordinary form of spoken or written language; language not arranged in verse: *Stories can be told in poetry or prose.* *n.*

pros·e·cute (pros′ə kyüt′) 1 bring before a court of law: *Reckless drivers will be prosecuted.* 2 carry out; follow up: *He started an inquiry into the cause of the fire, and prosecuted it for several weeks.* *v.,* **pros·e·cut·ed, pros·e·cut·ing.**

pros·e·cu·tion (pros′ə kyü′shən) 1 the carrying on of a lawsuit: *The prosecution will be stopped if the*

hat, āge, fär; let, ēqual, tėrm; it, īce
hot, ōpen, ôrder; oil, out; cup, pu̇t, rüle
əbove, takən, pencəl, lemən, circəs
ch, child; ng, long; sh, ship
th, thin; ᴛʜ, then; zh, measure

stolen money is returned. 2 the side that starts action against another in a court of law: *The prosecution makes certain charges against the defence.* 3 carrying out or following up: *In prosecution of his plan, he stored away a supply of food. n.*

pros·e·cu·tor (pros′ə kyü′tər) 1 Usually, **Crown prosecutor,** a lawyer who presents the case against a person accused of a crime. 2 a person who starts legal proceedings against another person in civil court: *Who is the prosecutor in this case? n.*

pros·pect (pros′pekt) 1 anything expected or looked forward to: *The prospects for our gardens are good this year.* 2 looking forward; an expectation: *The prospect of a vacation is pleasant.* 3 a view or scene: *The prospect from the mountain was grand.* 4 to search or look: *to prospect for gold, to prospect a region for silver.* 5 a person who may be a customer, candidate, etc.: *The salesman had several prospects in mind.* 1–3, 5 *n.,* 4 *v.*
in prospect, expected; looked forward to.

pro·spec·tive (prə spek′tiv) 1 probable; expected: *a prospective client.* 2 looking forward in time; future: *her prospective husband. adj.* **—pro·spec′tive·ly,** *adv.*

pros·pec·tor (pros′pek′tər) a person who explores or examines a region, searching for gold, silver, oil, uranium, etc. or estimating the value of some product of the region. *n.*

pros·per (pros′pər) 1 be successful; have good fortune; flourish: *His business prospered.* 2 make successful. *v.*

pros·per·i·ty (pros per′ə tē) success; good fortune; a prosperous condition: *We wished him prosperity in his new career. n.*

pros·per·ous (pros′pər əs) successful; thriving; doing well; fortunate: *A prosperous person is one who is happy, healthy, paying his way, and getting on well in his work. adj.*

pros·trate (pros′trāt) 1 lay down flat; cast down: *The captives prostrated themselves before the conqueror.* 2 lying flat with face downward: *He stumbled and fell prostrate on the floor.* 3 make very weak or helpless; exhaust: *Sickness often prostrates people.* 4 helpless; overcome: *She is prostrate with her great grief.* 1, 3 *v.,* **pros·trat·ed, pros·trat·ing;** 2, 4 *adj.*

pro·tect (prə tekt′) shield from harm or danger; shelter; defend; guard: *Protect yourself from danger. Protect the baby's eyes from the sun. v.*

pro·tec·tion (prə tek′shən) 1 protecting; being kept from harm; defence: *The police force is for our protection.* 2 a thing or person that prevents damage: *This apron is my protection against paint splatters. n.*

pro·tec·tive (prə tek′tiv) 1 protecting; being a defence: *the hard protective covering of a turtle.* 2 preventing injury to those around: *a protective device on a machine. adj.*

pro·tec·tor (prə tek′tər) a person or thing that protects; a defender. *n.*

pro·tein (prō′tēn) one of the substances that contain nitrogen and are a necessary part of the cells of animals and plants: *Meat, milk, cheese, eggs, and beans contain protein. n.*

pro·test (prō′test for 1, prə test′ for 2, 3, and 4) 1 a statement that denies or objects strongly: *They yielded only after protest.* 2 make objections; object: *The boys protested against having girls in the game.* 3 object to: *She protested the umpire's decision.* 4 declare solemnly; assert: *The accused man protested his innocence.* 1 *n.,* 2–4 *v.*
under protest, unwillingly; objecting.

Prot·es·tant (prot′is tənt) 1 a member of certain Christian churches other than the Roman Catholic or Eastern Orthodox: *Baptists, Presbyterians, Anglicans, United Church members and many others are all Protestants.* 2 of Protestants or their religion. 1 *n.,* 2 *adj.*

pro·ton (prō′ton) in science, an elementary particle carrying one unit of positive electric charge, found in the nucleus of every kind of atom: *Each kind of atom has a different number of protons; for instance, the nucleus of a hydrogen atom has one proton; that of an oxygen atom has eight. n.*

pro·to·plasm (prō′tə plaz′əm) a colorless substance somewhat like soft jelly or white of egg that is the living substance of all plant and animal cells. *n.*

pro·to·type (prō′tə tīp′) the first or primary type of anything; the original or model: *A modern ship has its prototype in the hollowed log used by primitive peoples. n.*

pro·tract (prō trakt′) draw out; lengthen in time: *a protracted illness. v.*

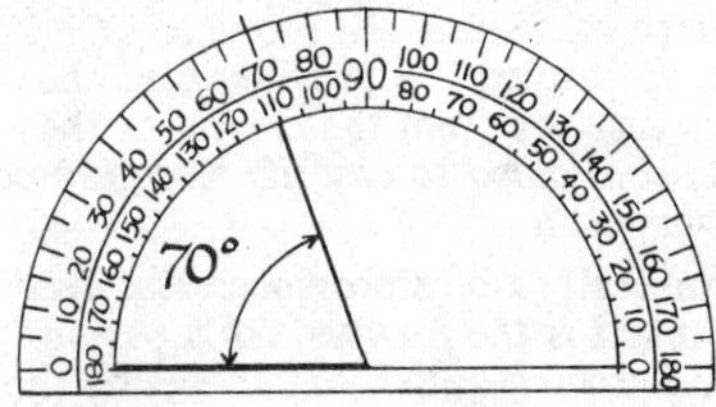

A protractor

pro·trac·tor (prō trak′tər) an instrument for drawing or measuring angles. *n.*

pro·trude (prō trüd′ or prə trüd′) 1 thrust forth; stick out: *The saucy child protruded her tongue.* 2 be thrust forth; project: *His teeth protrude too far. v.,* **pro·trud·ed, pro·trud·ing.**

proud (proud) 1 thinking well of oneself: *He was too proud to cry when he cut himself.* 2 thinking too well of oneself; haughty: *He was too proud to share a taxi with a stranger.* 3 feeling or showing pleasure or satisfaction: *I am proud to call him my friend.* 4 very pleasing to one's feelings or one's pride: *It was a proud moment for him when he shook hands with the Premier.* 5 grand; magnificent: *The big ship was a proud sight. adj.* **—proud′ly,** *adv.*
proud of, thinking well of; being well satisfied with: *be proud of oneself, be proud of one's family.*

prove (prüv) 1 show to be true or certain: *Please prove the answer you gave.* 2 turn out; be found to be: *The book proved interesting. The boy proved to be our friend after all.* 3 show oneself to be: *He proved himself honest.* 4 try out; test: *The test pilot spent* *months proving the new plane.* *v.*, **proved, proved** or **prov·en, prov·ing.**

prov·en (prüv′ən) proved. See **prove.** *v.*

prov·en·der (prov′ən dər) 1 dry food for animals, such as hay or corn. 2 *Informal.* food. *n.*

prov·erb (prov′ėrb) a short, wise saying used for a long time by many people: *'Haste makes waste' is a proverb.* *n.*

pro·vide (prə vīd′) 1 supply; furnish: *Sheep provide us with wool.* 2 supply what is needed: *Parents provide for their children.* 3 take care for the future: *to provide against accident, to provide for old age.* 4 arrange in advance; state as a condition beforehand: *Our club's rules provide that dues must be paid monthly.* *v.*, **pro·vid·ed, pro·vid·ing.**

pro·vid·ed (prə vīd′id) on the condition that; if: *She will go provided her friends can go also.* *conj.*

prov·i·dence (prov′ə dəns) 1 God's care and help: *Trusting in providence, the Pilgrims sailed for the unknown world.* 2 care for the future: *Greater providence on the father's part would have kept the children from poverty.* *n.*

prov·i·dent (prov′ə dənt) careful in providing for the future; having or showing foresight: *Provident men save money for their families.* *adj.*

prov·ince (prov′əns) 1 one of the ten divisions of Canada established by the British North America Act: *Newfoundland became the tenth province on April 1, 1949.* 2 proper work or activity: *Astronomy is not within the province of biology.* 3 a division; a department: *the province of science, the province of literature, the province of history.* 4 **provinces,** *pl.* the parts of a country at a distance from the capital or the largest cities: *He was accustomed to city life and did not like living in the provinces.* *n.*

pro·vin·cial (prə vin′shəl) 1 of a province: *The head of a provincial government is the premier.* 2 a person born in or living in the provinces (def. 4). 3 having the manners, speech, dress, point of view, etc. of people living in the provinces (def. 4). 1, 3 *adj.*, 2 *n.*

provincial park *Cdn.* a tract of land established as a preserve for wild life and as a holiday area by a provincial government: *Algonquin Park in Ontario is a well-known provincial park.*

Provincial Parliament in Ontario, the Legislative Assembly.

pro·vi·sion (prə vizh′ən) 1 a statement making a condition: *A provision of the lease is that the rent must be paid promptly.* 2 providing; preparation: *Mr. Archer invested money to make provision for his children's future.* 3 care taken for the future; an arrangement made beforehand: *There is a provision for making the building larger if necessary.* 4 that which is made ready; a supply; a stock, especially of food; food. 5 **provisions,** *pl.* a supply of food and drink: *They took plenty of provisions on their trip.* 6 to supply with provisions. 1–5 *n.*, 6 *v.*

pro·vi·sion·al (prə vizh′ən əl) for the time being; temporary: *a provisional agreement, a provisional government.* *adj.* —**pro·vi′sion·al·ly,** *adv.*

prov·o·ca·tion (prov′ə kā′shən) 1 something that stirs one up; a cause of anger: *Though the other boys' remarks were a provocation, he kept his temper.* 2 the act of provoking. *n.*

pro·voke (prə vōk′) 1 make angry; vex: *She provoked him by her teasing.* 2 stir up; excite: *An insult provokes a person to anger.* 3 call forth; bring about; cause; start into action: *The Prime Minister's speech provoked much discussion.* *v.*, **pro·voked, pro·vok·ing.**

prow (prou) 1 the front part of a ship or boat; the bow. See **schooner** for picture. 2 the projecting front part of anything: *the prow of an aircraft.* *n.*

prow·ess (prou′is) 1 bravery; daring. 2 brave or daring acts. 3 unusual skill or ability: *Her prowess as a skater was widely recognized.* *n.*

prowl (proul) 1 go about slowly and secretly, hunting for something to eat or steal: *Many wild animals prowl at night.* 2 wander: *He got up and prowled about his room.* 3 prowling: *It was only a wild animal on its nightly prowl.* 1, 2 *v.*, 3 *n.*

prox·y (prok′sē) 1 a person authorized to act for another: *John acted as proxy for the child's godfather at the christening.* 2 the authority given to someone to act on behalf of another: *He could not come to the meeting but arranged to vote by proxy.* *n.*, *pl.* **prox·ies.**

prude (prüd) a person who appears to be too proper or too modest. *n.*

pru·dence (prü′dəns) careful thought before taking action; good judgment: *The general's prudence was much admired.* *n.*

pru·dent (prü′dənt) planning carefully ahead of time; taking no chances: *A prudent man saves part of his wages.* *adj.*

prune[1] (prün) a dried sweet plum: *We had stewed prunes for breakfast.* *n.*

prune[2] (prün) 1 cut out useless parts from: *Prune that tree. The editor pruned the needless words from the writer's manuscript.* 2 cut off; cut out: *Prune all the dead branches.* *v.*, **pruned, prun·ing.**

pry[1] (prī) look with curiosity; peep: *She is always prying into other people's affairs.* *v.*, **pried, pry·ing.**

pry[2] (prī) 1 raise or move by force: *Pry up that stone with your pickaxe.* 2 a lever for prying. 3 get with much effort: *We finally pried the secret out of him.* 1, 3 *v.*, **pried, pry·ing;** 2 *n.*, *pl.* **pries.**

P.S. 1 postscript. 2 Public School.

psalm (som or säm) 1 a sacred song or poem. 2 **Psalm,** one of the sacred songs that together form a book of the Old Testament. *n.*

pshaw (sho or shô) an exclamation expressing impatience, contempt, or dislike. *interj.*

psy·chi·a·try (sī kī′ə trē) the study and treatment of mental disorders. *n.*

psy·chic (sī′kik) 1 of the soul or mind; mental: *illness due to psychic causes.* 2 outside the known laws of physics; supernatural: *Some people believe ghosts are psychic forms.* *adj.*

psy·chol·o·gy (sī kol′ə jē) the study of the mind and the ways of thought: *Psychology tries to explain why people act and think and feel as they do.* *n.*, *pl.* **psy·chol·o·gies.**

pt. pint; pints.

P.T. physical training.

P.T.A. Parent-Teacher Association.

hat, āge, fär; let, ēqual, tėrm; it, īce
hot, ōpen, ôrder; oil, out; cup, pu̇t, rüle
əbove, takən, pencəl, lemən, circəs
ch, child; ng, long; sh, ship
th, thin; ᴛʜ, then; zh, measure

pto·maine (tō′mān) any of several chemical compounds produced in decaying food. Food poisoning is caused not by ptomaines, as formerly believed, but by bacteria or other sources of infection. *n.*

pu·ber·ty (pyü′bər tē) the stage of life at which a person is first able to produce offspring; the physical beginning of manhood and womanhood: *Puberty usually comes at about 14 in boys and about 12 in girls.* *n.*

pub·lic (pub′lik) 1 of, belonging to, or concerning the people as a whole: *public affairs, public buildings.* 2 all the people: *inform the public.* 3 for all the people; serving all the people: *public meetings, public libraries, public schools.* 4 known to many or all; not private: *a matter of public knowledge.* 1, 3, 4 *adj.,* 2 *n.*
in public, publicly; openly; not in private or secret: *to stand up in public for what you believe.*

public address system an arrangement of loudspeakers used to carry speeches, messages, music, etc. to an audience in a large room, in different rooms of one building, or in the open air.

pub·li·ca·tion (pub′lə kā′shən) 1 a book, newspaper, or magazine; anything that is published: *This magazine is a weekly publication.* 2 the printing and selling of books, newspapers, magazines, etc. *n.*

pub·lic·i·ty (pub lis′ə tē) 1 public notice: *the publicity that actors desire.* 2 the measures used for getting, or the process of getting, public notice: *a campaign of publicity for a new automobile.* *n.*

pub·lic·ly (pub′lik lē) 1 in a public manner; openly. 2 by the public. *adv.*

public opinion the opinion of the people in a country, community, etc.: *make a survey of public opinion.*

public school 1 in Canada and the United States, a free school maintained by taxes. 2 in England, a private school.

pub·lish (pub′lish) 1 prepare and offer a book, paper, map, piece of music, etc. for sale or distribution. 2 make publicly or generally known: *Don't publish the faults of your friends.* *v.*

pub·lish·er (pub′lish ər) a person or company whose business is to produce and sell books, newspapers, magazines, etc. *n.*

puck[1] (puk) a hard, black, rubber disk used in the game of hockey: *He shot the puck into the net.* *n.*

puck[2] (puk) a mischievous spirit; a goblin. *n.*

puck·er (puk′ər) 1 draw into wrinkles or irregular folds: *to pucker one's brow, to pucker cloth in sewing. The baby's lips puckered just before he began to cry.* 2 a wrinkle; an irregular fold: *This coat does not fit; there are puckers at the shoulders.* 1 *v.,* 2 *n.*

pud·ding (pu̇d′ing) a soft cooked food, usually sweet, such as rice pudding. *n.*

pud·dle (pud′əl) 1 a small pool of water, especially dirty water: *a puddle of rain water.* 2 a small pool of any liquid: *a puddle of ink.* *n.*

pudg·y (puj′ē) short and fat or thick: *a child's pudgy hand, a pudgy little man.* *adj.*

puff (puf) 1 blow with short, quick blasts: *The bellows puffed on the fire.* 2 a short, quick blast: *A puff of wind blew away the letter.* 3 breathe fast and hard: *She puffed as she climbed the stairs.* 4 smoke: *puff a cigar.* 5 swell with air: *He puffed out his cheeks.* 6 swell with pride: *He puffed out his chest when the teacher praised his work.* 7 the act or process of swelling. 8 a small pad for putting powder on the skin, etc. 9 a light pastry filled with whipped cream, jam, etc.: *a cream puff.* 1, 3–6 *v.,* 2, 7–9 *n.*

A common puffin — about 30 cm long with the tail

puf·fin (puf′ən) a sea bird of the northern Atlantic and Pacific coasts that has a high, narrow, furrowed bill of several colors. *n.*

puff·y (puf′ē) 1 puffed out; swollen: *Her eyes are puffy from crying.* 2 blowing or breathing in puffs. *adj.,* **puff·i·er, puff·i·est.**

pug·na·cious (pug nā′shəs) having the habit of fighting; fond of fighting: *a pugnacious young man.* *adj.*

pug nose (pug′) a short, turned-up nose.

pull (pu̇l) 1 move something by grasping it and drawing toward oneself: *pull the trigger of a gun. Pull the door open; don't push it.* 2 move, usually with effort or force: *pull a sleigh uphill.* 3 take hold of and tug: *The boy pulled his sister's hair. He pulled at his tie.* 4 take hold of and draw out: *to pull weeds. Father uses the claw of his hammer to pull nails. My father had to have a tooth pulled.* 5 move; go: *The policeman had the speeding driver pull over to the side of the road and stop.* 6 tear: *to pull a flower apart, to pull down a building.* 7 row: *Pull for the shore as fast as you can!* 8 stretch too far; strain: *The football player pulled a ligament in his leg.* 9 the act of pulling; a tug: *The boy gave a pull on the rope.* 10 the effort of pulling; effort: *It was a hard pull to get up the hill.* 11 a handle, rope, ring, or other thing to pull by: *a bell pull, a curtain pull.* 12 a force that attracts: *magnetic pull.* 13 *Informal.* perform; carry through: *Don't pull any tricks.* 1–8, 13 *v.,* 9–12 *n.*
pull oneself together, get control of one's mind, energies, etc.
pull out, leave: *The train pulled out of the station.*
pull through, get through a difficult or dangerous situation.
pull up, bring or come to a halt; stop.

pul·let (pu̇l′it) a young hen, usually less than a year old. *n.*

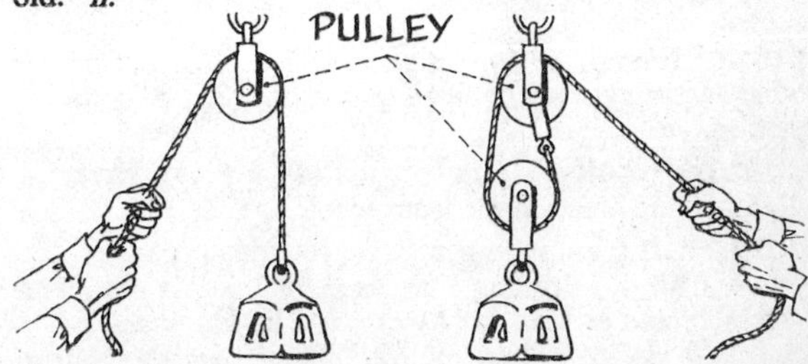

pul·ley (pu̇l′ē) a wheel with a grooved rim in which a

rope, belt, or wire can run, making it possible to raise weights or change the direction of the pull: *The fan belt of a car runs on pulleys.* *n., pl.* **pul·leys.**

pull·o·ver (půl′ō′vər) a sweater put on by pulling it over the head. *n.*

pulp (pulp) 1 the soft, fleshy part of any fruit or vegetable. 2 the soft inner part of a tooth, containing blood vessels and nerves. 3 any soft, wet mass: *Paper is made from wood ground to a pulp.* *n.*

pul·pit (půl′pit) 1 a platform or raised structure in a church from which the minister preaches. 2 clergymen or their sermons: *The pulpit is against horse racing on Sunday.* *n.*

pulp·wood (pulp′wůd′) any soft wood suitable for reducing to pulp to make paper: *Canada's forests produce large quantities of pulpwood.* *n.*

pul·sate (pul′sāt) 1 beat; throb: *The patient's heart was pulsating rapidly.* 2 vibrate; quiver. *v.,* **pul·sat·ed, pul·sat·ing.**

pulse (puls) 1 the beating of the arteries caused by the rush of blood into them after each contraction of the heart. 2 the rate of this beating: *The nurse took the man's pulse by holding his wrist and counting the beats.* 3 any regular, measured beat: *the pulse in music, the pulse of an engine.* *n.*

pul·ver·ize (pul′vər īz′) 1 grind to powder or dust. 2 become dust. *v.,* **pul·ver·ized, pul·ver·iz·ing.**

pu·ma (pyü′mə) cougar. *n.*

pum·ice (pum′is) a light, spongy stone thrown up from volcanoes, used for cleaning, smoothing, and polishing. *n.*

pum·mel (pum′əl) strike or beat; beat with the fists; pommel. *v.,* **pum·melled** or **pum·meled, pum·mel·ling** or **pum·mel·ing.** Also spelled **pommel.**

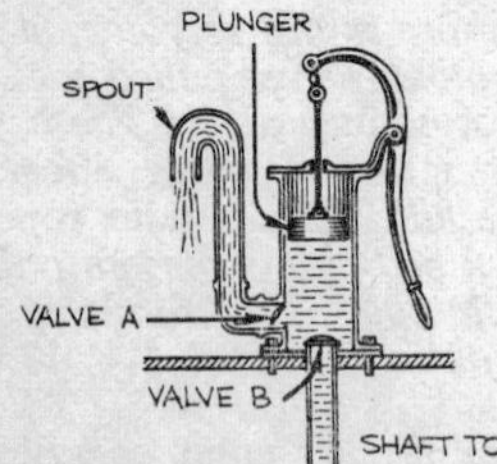

A water pump.
As the handle is pushed down, the plunger is raised, pulling water upward through valve B from the shaft.
As the handle is raised, the plunger moves downward, forcing water through valve A and out of the spout.

pump¹ (pump) 1 a machine for forcing liquids or gases into or out of things: *a water pump, an oil pump.* 2 move liquids, air, etc. by a pump: *to pump water from the well into a pail.* 3 blow air into: *Pump up the car's tires.* 4 *Informal.* get information out of; try to get information out of: *Don't let him pump you.* 1 *n.,* 2–4 *v.*

pump² (pump) a low-cut shoe with no laces, straps, or other fastenings: *white dancing pumps.* See **shoe** for picture. *n.*

pum·per·nick·el (pum′pər nik′əl) a heavy, dark, slightly sour bread made from whole, coarse rye. *n.*

pump·kin (pump′kin) a large, roundish, orange-yellow fruit of a trailing vine, used for making pies, as a vegetable and as food for livestock: *The boy made a pumpkin jack-o'-lantern for Halloween.* See the picture. *n.*

pun (pun) 1 the humorous use of a word where it can have different meanings; a play on words: *'We must all hang together or we shall all hang separately' is a famous pun.* 2 make puns. 1 *n.,* 2 *v.,* **punned, pun·ning.**

punch¹ (punch) 1 hit with the fist: *They punched each other like boxers. Boys punch; girls usually slap.* 2 a quick thrust or blow. 3 herd or drive cattle: *He punched cows for a living.* 1, 3 *v.,* 2 *n.*

A pumpkin

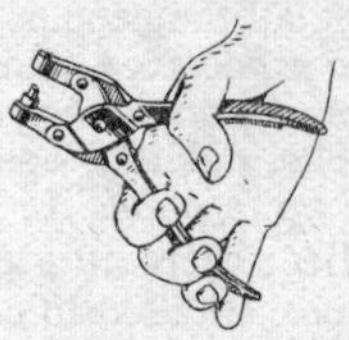

A punch

punch² (punch) 1 a tool for making holes. 2 pierce a hole in: *The train conductor punches the tickets.* 1 *n.,* 2 *v.*

punch³ (punch) a drink made of different liquids mixed together. *n.*

punc·tu·al (pungk′chü əl) prompt; on time: *He is punctual to the minute.* *adj.*

punc·tu·ate (pungk′chü āt′) 1 use periods, commas, and other marks in writing or printing to help make the meaning clear. 2 put punctuation marks in. 3 interrupt now and then: *a speech punctuated with cheers.* 4 give point or emphasis to: *He punctuated his remarks with gestures.* *v.,* **punc·tu·at·ed, punc·tu·at·ing.**

punc·tu·a·tion (pungk′chü ā′shən) 1 the use of periods, commas, and other marks to help make the meaning of a sentence clear: *Punctuation does for writing or printing what pauses and changes in the pitch of the voice do for speech.* 2 punctuation marks. *n.*

punctuation mark a mark used in writing or printing to help make the meaning of a sentence clear: *Periods, commas, colons, question marks, and exclamation marks are punctuation marks.*

punc·ture (pungk′chər) 1 a hole made by something pointed. 2 make such a hole in. 3 have or get a puncture. 4 the act or process of puncturing. 1, 4 *n.,* 2, 3 *v.,* **punc·tured, punc·tur·ing.**

pun·gent (pun′jənt) 1 sharply affecting taste and smell: *a pungent pickle, the pungent smell of burning leaves.* 2 sharp; biting: *pungent criticism.* *adj.*

pun·ish (pun′ish) 1 cause a person pain, loss, or discomfort for some fault or offence: *Father sometimes punishes us when we do wrong.* 2 cause pain, loss, or discomfort for: *The law punishes crime.* *v.*

pun·ish·a·ble (pun′ish ə bəl) 1 liable to punishment: *Murder is sometimes punishable by hanging.* 2 deserving punishment: *a punishable offence.* *adj.*

pun·ish·ment (pun′ish mənt) 1 punishing or being punished. 2 pain, suffering, or loss: *Her punishment for stealing was a year in prison.* *n.*

punk¹ (pungk) 1 a preparation that burns very slowly, often used to light fireworks. 2 decayed wood used as tinder. *n.*

punk² (pungk) *Slang.* 1 poor or bad in quality. 2 a young, inexperienced, or worthless person. 1 *adj.,* 2 *n.*

punt[1] (punt) 1 kick a football before it touches the ground after being dropped from the hands. 2 such a kick: *The punt went over the goal line.* 1 *v.*, 2 *n.*

punt[2] (punt) 1 a shallow boat with a flat bottom, propelled by oars or with a pole. 2 propel a boat by pushing with a pole against the bottom of a river, pond, etc. 3 use a punt; travel by punt: *We loved to punt on the river.* 1 *n.*, 2, 3 *v.*

pu·ny (pyü′nē) 1 weak; of less than usual size and strength. 2 not important; petty. *adj.*, **pu·ni·er, pu·ni·est.**

pup (pup) 1 a young dog; a puppy. 2 a young fox, wolf, coyote, etc. *n.*

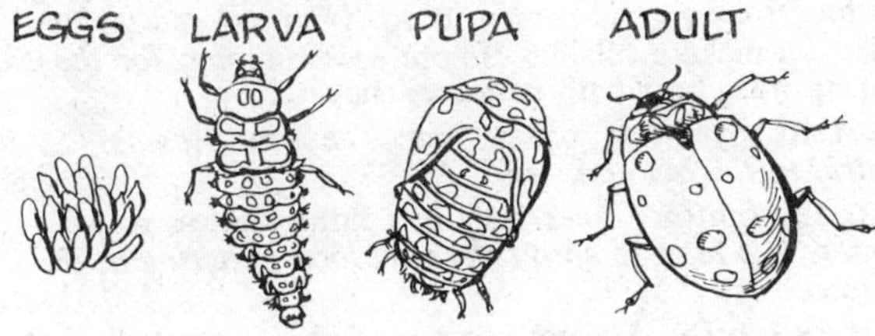

Four stages in the life of a ladybug

pu·pa (pyü′pə) 1 a stage between the larva and the adult in the development of many insects: *In the pupa stage the insect is enclosed in a case.* 2 an insect in this stage: *A chrysalis is a pupa.* *n., pl.* **pu·pae** (pyü′pē) or **pu·pas.**

pu·pil[1] (pyü′pəl) a person who is learning in school or is being taught by someone: *The music teacher takes private pupils.* *n.*

pu·pil[2] (pyü′pəl) the opening in the centre of the iris of the eye which looks like a black spot: *The pupil is the only place where light can enter the eye.* See **eye** for picture. *n.*

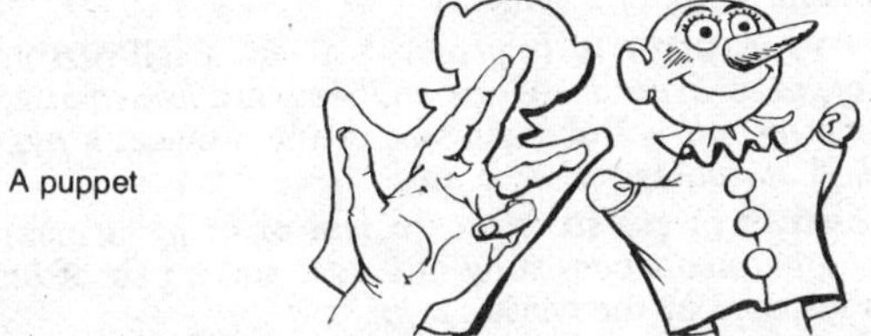
A puppet

pup·pet (pup′it) 1 a figure made to look like a person or animal and moved by wires, strings, or the hands. See **marionette** for another picture. 2 anybody who is not independent, who waits to be told how to act, or who does what somebody else says. *n.*

pup·py (pup′ē) a young dog. *n., pl.* **pup·pies.**

pur·chase (pėr′chəs) 1 get by paying a price; buy: *We purchased a new car.* 2 the act of buying: *the purchase of a new car.* 3 the thing bought: *That hat was a good purchase.* 4 get in return for something: *to purchase safety at the cost of happiness.* 5 a firm hold to help move something, or to keep from slipping: *Wind the rope twice around the tree to get a better purchase.* 1, 4 *v.*, **pur·chased, pur·chas·ing;** 2, 3, 5 *n.* **—pur′chas·er,** *n.*

pure (pyür) 1 perfect; not mixed with anything else; spotless: *pure gold, pure truth.* 2 nothing else than; mere: *They won by pure luck.* 3 with no evil; without sin: *a pure mind.* *adj.*, **pur·er, pur·est. —pure·ly,** *adv.*

pure·bred (pyür′bred′) 1 of pure breed or stock; having ancestors known to have all belonged to one

hat, āge, fär; let, ēqual, tėrm; it, īce
hot, ōpen, ôrder; oil, out; cup, pu̇t, rüle
əbove, takən, pencəl, lemən, circəs
ch, child; ng, long; sh, ship
th, thin; ᴛʜ, then; zh, measure

breed: *purebred Holstein cows.* 2 an animal or plant of this kind. 1 *adj.*, 2 *n.*

pu·rée (pyü rā′ or pyür′ā) 1 food boiled soft and put through a sieve or a blender. 2 a thick soup. 3 make into purée. 1, 2 *n.*, 3 *v.*

purge (pėrj) 1 make clean; clear of anything unclean or undesirable: *The king tried to purge his land of treachery.* 2 the act of purging. 1 *v.*, **purged, purg·ing;** 2 *n.*

pu·ri·fi·ca·tion (pyür′ə fə kā′shən) purifying or being purified. *n.*

pu·ri·fy (pyür′ə fī′) make pure: *Filters are used to purify water.* *v.*, **pu·ri·fied, pu·ri·fy·ing.**

pu·ri·tan (pyür′ə tən) 1 a person who is very strict in morals and religion. 2 of or having to do with such people. 3 **Puritan,** a member of a group in the Church of England during the 1500's and 1600's who wanted simpler forms of worship and stricter morals. 4 **Puritan,** of or having to do with this group. 1, 3 *n.*, 2, 4 *adj.*

pu·ri·ty (pyür′ə tē) 1 freedom from dirt or mixture; clearness; cleanness: *the purity of drinking water.* 2 freedom from evil; innocence: *No one doubts the purity of Joan of Arc's motives.* *n.*

pur·loin (pėr loin′) steal. *v.*

pur·ple (pėr′pəl) 1 a dark color made by mixing red and blue. 2 of or having this color. 3 purple cloth or clothing, especially as worn by emperors, kings, etc. to indicate high rank. 1, 3 *n.*, 2 *adj.*
born to the purple, born in a royal or imperial family: *The prince was born to the purple.*

pur·plish (pėr′plish) somewhat purple. *adj.*

pur·port (pər pôrt′) claim or appear, often falsely: *The letter purported to be from the governor but in fact his aide wrote it.* *v.*

pur·pose (pėr′pəs) 1 a plan; an aim or intention; something one intends to get or do: *His purpose was to pass his exams.* 2 the object or end for which a thing is made, done, used, etc.: *What is the purpose of this machine?* 3 to plan; aim; intend. 1, 2 *n.*, 3 *v.*, **pur·posed, pur·pos·ing.**
on purpose, with a purpose; not by accident: *He tripped me on purpose.*

pur·pose·ful (pėr′pəs fəl) having a purpose: *He worked with purposeful movements.* *adj.*

pur·pose·ly (pėr′pəs lē) on purpose: *Did you leave the door open purposely?* *adv.*

purr (pėr) 1 a low, murmuring sound such as a cat makes when pleased. 2 make this sound. 1 *n.*, 2 *v.*

A purse (def. 1)

purse (pėrs) 1 a little bag or case for carrying money,

usually carried in a handbag or pocket. 2 a handbag: *She put her keys and gloves in her purse.* 3 money; funds: *The family purse cannot afford a vacation.* 4 a sum of money offered as a prize or gift: *A purse was made up for the victims of the fire.* 5 draw together; press into folds or wrinkles: *She pursed her lips and frowned.* 1–4 *n.*, 5 *v.*, **pursed, purs·ing.**

pur·sue (pər sü′) 1 follow to catch or kill; chase: *The dogs pursued the rabbit.* 2 strive for; try to get; seek: *to pursue pleasure.* 3 carry on; keep on with: *She pursued the study of music for four years.* 4 continue to annoy or trouble: *The boy pursued his father with questions.* *v.*, **pur·sued, pur·su·ing. —pur·su′er,** *n.*

pur·suit (pər süt′) 1 the act of pursuing; a chase: *The dog was in hot pursuit of the cat. The pursuit of the escaped convict continued all night.* 2 an occupation or pastime: *Fishing is one of his favorite pursuits.* *n.*

pus (pus) a thick, yellowish-white fluid formed in infected sores. *n.*

push (pu̇sh) 1 move something away by pressing against it: *Push the door; don't pull it.* 2 press hard: *We pushed with all our strength.* 3 thrust: *Trees push their roots down into the ground.* 4 go forward by force: *We pushed through the crowd.* 5 urge; make go forward: *He pushed his plans strongly. Please push this job and get it done this week.* 6 *Informal.* urge the use, sale, etc. of: *The supermarkets are pushing beef this week.* 7 a pushing: *Give the door a push.* 8 *Informal.* force; the power to succeed: *She has plenty of push.* 1–6 *v.*, 7, 8 *n.*

push around, *Informal.* treat roughly or with contempt; bully.

push off, move from shore: *We pushed off in the boat.*

push button a small button or knob pushed to switch an electric current on or off.

push·cart (pu̇sh′kärt′) a light cart that is pushed by hand: *The peddler's pushcart was filled with melons.* *n.*

puss (pu̇s) cat. *n.*

puss·y (pu̇s′ē) 1 a cat: *The pussy was curled up near the fire.* 2 a catkin. *n., pl.* **puss·ies.**

pussy willow a small willow with silky catkins.

put (pu̇t) 1 place; lay; set; cause to be in some place or position: *I put sugar in my tea. Put away your toys. She is putting on her hat.* 2 cause to be in some state, condition, position, or relation: *Put your room in order. Put the question in writing. The murderer was put to death.* 3 express: *The teacher puts things clearly.* 4 set a particular place, point, amount, etc.: *He puts the distance at five kilometres.* 5 apply: *A doctor puts his skill to good use.* *v.*, **put, put·ting.**

put about, change direction.

put aside, away or **by,** save for future use.

put down, a put an end to: *The rebellion was quickly put down.* **b** write down.

put forth, a grow; sprout; issue: *put forth buds.* **b** use fully; exert: *put forth effort.*

put in, a do; spend time doing: *He always puts in a good day's work.* **b** enter a place for safety, supplies, etc.: *The ship put in at Vancouver.* **c** make a claim, plea, or offer: *She put in for a loan.*

put off, a lay aside; make wait: *Don't put off going to the dentist.* **b** go away; start out: *The ship put off for England.*

put on, a clothe or adorn oneself with; don: *She put on her new hat.* **b** assume or take on, especially as a pretence: *She put on an air of innocence.* **c** add to; increase: *The driver put on speed.* **d** apply or exert: *put on pressure.* **e** present on a stage; produce: *The class put on a play.*

put out, a extinguish; make an end to; destroy: *to put out a fire.* **b** go; turn; proceed: *The ship put out to sea.* **c** provoke; offend. **d** dislocate: *I put out my knee when I fell.* **e** cause to be out in a game. **f** publish.

put through, carry out with success.

put up, a offer: *put a house up for sale.* **b** build: *put up a monument.* **c** lay aside work. **d** prepare or pack food for later use. **e** preserve fruit, vegetables, etc. **f** give lodging or food to. **g** get a person to do: *Who put you up to this?* **h** make available: *He put up the money for the car.*

put up with, bear with patience; endure.

pu·trid (pyü′trid) rotten; foul: *The meat became putrid in the hot sun.* *adj.*

put·ter (put′ər) keep busy in a rather useless way; potter: *She likes to spend the afternoon puttering in the garden.* *v.*

put·ty (put′ē) 1 a soft mixture of powdered chalk and linseed oil, used mainly for fastening panes of glass into window frames. 2 stop up, fill up, or cover with putty: *He puttied up the holes in the woodwork before painting it.* 1 *n., pl.* **put·ties;** 2 *v.*, **put·tied, put·ty·ing.**

puz·zle (puz′əl) 1 a hard problem: *How to get all my things into one trunk is a puzzle.* 2 a problem or task to be done for fun: *This puzzle has seven pieces of wood to fit together.* 3 make unable to understand something; perplex: *How the cat got out puzzled us.* 4 be perplexed. 5 exercise one's mind on something hard: *He puzzled over his arithmetic problems all evening.* 1, 2 *n.*, 3–5 *v.*, **puz·zled, puz·zling.**

puzzle out, find out by thinking or trying hard: *puzzle out the meaning of a sentence.*

pyg·my or **pig·my** (pig′mē) 1 a very small person: *The pygmies living in Africa and Asia are less than 150 centimetres tall.* 2 of small size or importance: *a pygmy mind.* 1 *n., pl.* **pyg·mies;** 2 *adj.*

py·ja·mas or **pa·ja·mas** (pə jam′əz or pə jä′məz) sleeping garments consisting of a coat and a pair of loose pants fastened at the waist. *n. pl.*

☛ **Pyjamas** comes from Persian *paejamah,* from *pae,* meaning 'leg' + *jamah,* meaning 'garment.'

py·lon (pī′lon) 1 a post or tower for guiding aircraft pilots. 2 a tall steel framework used to carry high-tension wires across country. 3 either of a pair of high supporting structures marking an entrance at either end of a bridge. *n.*

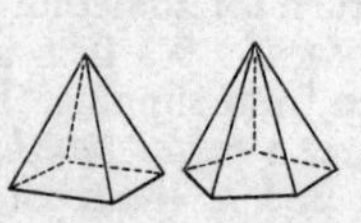

Two types of pyramid (def. 1)

One of the huge stone pyramids of Egypt

pyr·a·mid (pir′ə mid′) 1 a solid form having triangular sides that meet at a point. 2 anything having a form like that of a pyramid: *a pyramid of stones.* **3 the Pyramids,** *pl.* the huge, massive stone pyramids, serving as royal tombs, built by the ancient Egyptians. *n.*

pyre (pīr) a pile of wood for burning a dead body. *n.*

py·ro·ma·ni·ac (pī′rə mā′nē ak′) a person with an uncontrollable desire to set things on fire. *n.*

py·thon (pī′thon) any of several large snakes of Asia, Africa, and Australia that kill their prey by squeezing: *Pythons usually live in trees near water.* *n.*

hat, āge, fär; let, ēqual, tėrm; it, īce
hot, ōpen, ôrder; oil, out; cup, pu̇t, rüle
əbove, takən, pencəl, lemən, circəs
ch, child; ng, long; sh, ship
th, thin; ᴛʜ, then; zh, measure

q or **Q** (kyü) the 17th letter of the alphabet: *In most English words,* q *occurs in the combination* qu. *n., pl.* **q's** or **Q's.**

qt. quart; quarts.

quack¹ (kwak) **1** the sound a duck makes. **2** make this sound or one like it. 1 *n.,* 2 *v.*

quack² (kwak) **1** a dishonest person who pretends to be a doctor. **2** an ignorant pretender to knowledge or skill: *Don't pay a quack to tell your fortune. n.*

quad·ri·lat·er·al (kwod′rə lat′ər əl) **1** having four sides and four angles. **2** a plane figure having four sides and four angles. 1 *adj.,* 2 *n.*

quad·ru·ped (kwod′rə ped′) an animal that has four feet. *n.*

quad·ru·plet (kwod rü′plit or kwod′rə plit) **1** one of four children born at the same time from the same mother. **2** a group of four. *n.*

quaff (kwof or kwaf) drink in large swallows; drink deeply. *v.*

quag·mire (kwag′mīr′) soft, muddy ground; a boggy place. *n.*

quail¹ (kwāl) any of various plump game birds belonging to the same family as the partridge: *The bobwhite is a kind of quail. n., pl.* **quails** or **quail.**

quail² (kwāl) be afraid; lose courage; shrink back with fear: *The slave quailed at his master's look. v.*

quaint (kwānt) strange or odd in an interesting, pleasing, or amusing way: *Old photographs seem quaint to us today. adj.*

quake (kwāk) **1** shake; tremble: *She quaked with fear.* **2** shaking; trembling. **3** an earthquake. 1 *v.,* **quaked, quak·ing;** 2, 3 *n.*

Quak·er (kwāk′ər) a member of a Christian group called the Society of Friends: *Quakers favor simple religious services and refuse to fight in a war or to take oaths. n.*

qual·i·fi·ca·tion (kwol′ə fə kā′shən) **1** that which makes a person fit for a job, task, office, etc.: *Good eyesight is a necessary qualification for a marksman.* **2** something that limits or restricts: *His enjoyment of the trip had one qualification: his friends could not enjoy it too. n.*

qual·i·fied (kwol′ə fīd′) **1** fitted; competent: *He is fully qualified for his job.* **2** limited; modified: *His qualified answer was, 'I will go, but only if you will come with me.' adj.*

qual·i·fy (kwol′ə fī′) **1** make fit or competent: *Can you qualify yourself for the job?* **2** become fit; show oneself fit: *Can you qualify for the Boy Scouts? He qualified for the tennis tournament.* **3** limit; make less strong; change somewhat: *Qualify your statement that dogs are loyal by adding 'usually.' v.,* **qual·i·fied, qual·i·fy·ing.**

qual·i·ty (kwol′ə tē) **1** something special about a person or object that makes it what it is: *One quality of iron is hardness; one quality of sugar is sweetness. She had many good qualities.* **2** grade of excellence; degree of worth: *That is a poor quality of cloth.* **3** merit; excellence: *Look for quality rather than quantity. n., pl.* **qual·i·ties.**

qualm (kwom or kwäm) **1** a sudden disturbing feeling in the mind; uneasiness; a misgiving or doubt: *I tried the test with some qualms.* **2** a disturbance or scruple of conscience: *She felt some qualms at staying away from church.* **3** a momentary feeling of faintness or sickness. *n.*

quan·ti·ty (kwon′tə tē) **1** an amount: *Equal quantities of nuts and raisins were used in the cake.* **2** a large amount; large number: *The baker buys flour in quantity. She owns quantities of books. n., pl.* **quan·ti·ties.**

quar·an·tine (kwôr′ən tēn′) **1** isolate from others to prevent the spread of an infectious disease: *My brother was quarantined for three weeks when he had scarlet fever.* **2** detention, isolation, and other measures taken to prevent the spread of an infectious disease: *Our house was in quarantine for three weeks.* 1 *v.,* **quar·an·tined, quar·an·tin·ing;** 2 *n.*

quar·rel (kwôr′əl) **1** an angry dispute; a fight with words: *The children had a quarrel over the division of the candy.* **2** fight with words; dispute or disagree angrily: *The children were quarrelling when Mother came home.* **3** a cause for a dispute or disagreement: *A bully likes to pick quarrels. He said he had no quarrel with the government.* **4** find fault: *It is useless to quarrel with fate.* 1, 3 *n.,* 2, 4 *v.,* **quar·relled** or **quar·reled, quar·rel·ling** or **quar·rel·ing.**

quar·rel·some (kwôr′əl səm) too ready to quarrel; fond of fighting and disputing: *A quarrelsome child has few friends. adj.*

quar·ry¹ (kwôr′ē) **1** a place where stone is dug, cut, or blasted out for use in building. **2** obtain from a quarry: *He watched the workmen quarry a huge block of stone.* 1 *n., pl.* **quar·ries;** 2 *v.,* **quar·ried, quar·ry·ing.**

quar·ry² (kwôr′ē) an animal chased in a hunt; game; prey. *n., pl.* **quar·ries.**

quart (kwôrt) **1** a measure of capacity for liquids, equal to one fourth of a gallon (about 1.14 litres): *a quart of milk.* **2** a measure of capacity for dry things, equal to one eighth of a peck (about 1100 cubic centimetres): *a quart of berries. n.*

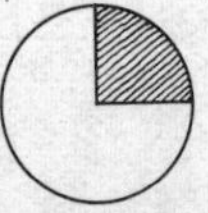

One quarter of this circle is shaded.

quar·ter (kwôr′tər) **1** one of four equal parts; half of a half; one fourth: *a quarter of an apple, a quarter of lamb. A quarter of an hour is 15 minutes.* **2** divide into fourths: *She quartered the apple.* **3** one fourth of a dollar; 25 cents. **4** a coin of Canada and the United States worth 25 cents: *Have you change for a quarter?* **5** a point of the compass; direction: *We learned that each of the four points of the compass is called a quarter. From what quarter did the wind blow?* **6** a region or section; a place: *They live in a new quarter of town.* **7 quarters,** *pl.* a place to live or stay in: *officers' quarters. The baseball team has winter quarters in Florida.* **8** give a place to live: *Troops were quartered in the town.* **9** mercy to an enemy: *The pirates gave no quarter.* **10** one of the four phases of the moon: *The quarters of the moon are four periods of about seven days each.* **11** one of four equal periods of play in football, basketball, etc. **12** being one of four equal

hat, āge, fär; let, ēqual, tėrm; it, īce
hot, ōpen, ôrder; oil, out; cup, pu̇t, rüle
əbove, takən, pencəl, lemən, circəs
ch, child; ng, long; sh, ship
th, thin; ᴛʜ, then; zh, measure

parts; being equal to only about one fourth of full measure. 1, 3–7, 9–12 *n.*, 2, 8 *v.*

at close quarters, at close range; close together: *The two armies were at close quarters for several days.*

quar·ter·back (kwôr′tər bak′) in football, the player whose position is immediately behind the centre of the line of scrimmage: *The quarterback usually directs his team's play on the field.* *n.*

quarter horse a strong horse originally bred for racing on quarter-mile tracks.

quar·ter·ly (kwôr′tər lē) **1** happening, done, etc. four times a year: *to make quarterly payments on one's insurance.* **2** once each quarter of a year: *Father pays his income tax quarterly.* **3** a magazine that is published four times a year. 1 *adj.*, 2 *adv.*, 3 *n.*, *pl.* **quar·ter·lies.**

quar·ter·mas·ter (kwôr′tər mas′tər) in the armed forces, the officer who has charge of providing quarters, clothing, etc. for troops. *n.*

quar·ter·staff (kwôr′tər staf′) an old weapon consisting of a stout pole 1.8 to 2.5 metres long, tipped with iron. *n.*, *pl.* **quar·ter·staves** (kwôr′tər stāvz′).

quar·tet or **quar·tette** (kwôr tet′) **1** a group of four singers or players performing together. **2** a piece of music for four voices or instruments. **3** any group of four. *n.*

quartz (kwôrts) a very hard mineral found in many kinds of rock: *Common quartz crystals are colorless and transparent. Amethyst, jasper, and many other colored stones are kinds of quartz.* *n.*

qua·sar (kwā′sär) a distant, starlike object in the universe: *Quasars emit light as well as strong radio waves.* *n.*

qua·ver (kwā′vər) **1** shake; tremble: *The old man's voice quavered.* **2** sing or say in trembling tones. **3** a shaking or trembling, especially of the voice. 1, 2 *v.*, 3 *n.*

quay (kē) a solid landing place where ships load and unload, often built of stone. See the picture. *n.*

☛ **Quay** and **key** are pronounced the same.

Que. Quebec.

A quay

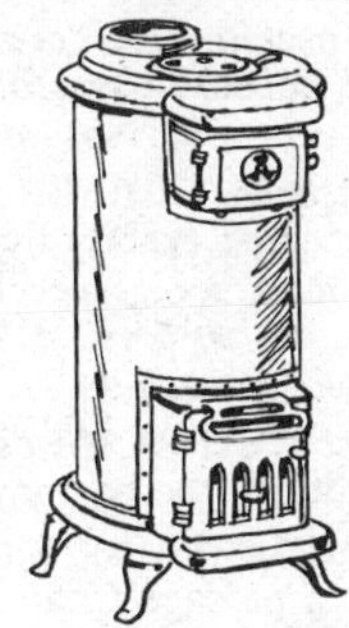
A Quebec heater

Quebec heater a kind of stove for heating rooms.

Que·beck·er (kwi bek′ər or kā bek′ər) a person born in or living in the province of Quebec. *n.*

Que·bec·ois (kā bek wä′) *French.* a person from Quebec. *n.*

queen (kwēn) **1** the wife of a king. **2** a female ruler of a nation: *Queen Elizabeth II.* **3** a woman judged to be first in importance or best in beauty or some other quality: *the queen of society, the queen of the May.* **4** in a colony of bees, ants, etc., a female that lays eggs: *There is usually only one queen in a hive of bees.* **5** in chess, a piece that can move in any straight or diagonal row. *n.*

queen mother the widow of a former king and mother of a reigning king or queen.

queer (kwēr) **1** strange; odd; peculiar: *a queer remark.* **2** not well; faint; giddy: *a queer feeling.* *adj.*

quell (kwel) put down; overcome: *The police quelled the riot.* *v.*

quench (kwench) **1** put an end to; stop: *to quench a thirst.* **2** drown out; put out: *Water will quench a fire.* *v.*

que·ry (kwēr′ē) **1** a question. **2** ask; ask about; inquire into. **3** express doubt about. **4** the sign (?) put after a question. 1, 4 *n.*, *pl.* **que·ries;** 2, 3 *v.*, **que·ried, que·ry·ing.**

quest (kwest) **1** a hunt; search: *She went to the library in quest of something to read.* **2** search or seek for; hunt. **3** an expedition or journey in search of something noble, ideal, or holy: *There are many stories about the quest for the Holy Grail.* 1, 3 *n.*, 2 *v.*

ques·tion (kwes′chən) **1** something asked in order to get information. **2** ask in order to get information: *The police questioned the witness of the accident.* **3** a matter to be talked over or considered; problem: *They were discussing an important question.* **4** a matter to be voted upon: *The president asked if the club members were ready for the question.* **5** to doubt; dispute: *I question the truth of many fish stories.* 1, 3, 4 *n.*, 2, 5 *v.*

beside the question, off the subject.

beyond question, without a doubt; not to be disputed: *The statements in that book are true beyond question.*

out of the question, not to be considered; impossible.

without question, without a doubt; not to be disputed: *He is without question the brightest student in the school.*

ques·tion·a·ble (kwes′chən ə bəl) **1** open to question; doubtful; uncertain: *Whether your statement is true is questionable.* **2** of doubtful honesty or morality: *questionable behavior.* *adj.*

question mark the mark (?) put after a question in writing or printing.

queue (kyü) **1** a line of people, automobiles, etc.: *There was a long queue in front of the theatre.* **2** form or stand in a long line: *We had to queue to get tickets.* **3** a braid of hair hanging down the back. 1, 3 *n.*, 2 *v.*

☛ **Queue** and **cue** are pronounced the same.

☛ **Queue** came into English through French from Latin *cauda,* meaning *'tail.'*

quick (kwik) **1** fast and sudden; swift: *The cat made a quick jump. Many weeds have a quick growth.*

2 coming soon; prompt: *a quick reply.* 3 not patient; hasty: *a quick temper.* 4 acting quickly; lively; ready: *a quick wit, a quick ear.* 5 quickly: *Come quick!* 6 tender, sensitive flesh, especially the flesh under a fingernail or toenail: *The child bit his nails down to the quick.* 7 the tender, sensitive part of one's feelings: *The boy's pride was cut to the quick by the words of blame.* 8 living persons: *the quick and the dead.* 1–4 *adj.*, 5 *adv.*, 6–8 *n.* —**quick′ly,** *adv.* —**quick′ness,** *n.*

quick·en (kwik′ən) 1 hasten; move more quickly: *Quicken your pace.* 2 stir up; make alive: *He quickened the hot ashes into flames. Reading adventure stories quickened his imagination.* 3 become more active or alive: *His pulse quickened.* *v.*

quick·sand (kwik′sand′) 1 soft, wet sand that will not hold heavy weight: *The horse was swallowed by the quicksand.* 2 an expanse of such sand: *There are dangerous quicksands in Scotland.* *n.*

quick·sil·ver (kwik′sil′vər) mercury. *n.*

qui·et (kwī′ət) 1 making no sound; with little or no noise: *quiet footsteps, a quiet room.* 2 still; moving very little: *a quiet river.* 3 at rest; not busy: *a quiet evening at home.* 4 peaceful; gentle: *a quiet girl, quiet manners.* 5 stillness; peace; freedom from disturbance: *to read in quiet.* 6 make quiet: *The mother quieted her frightened child.* 7 become quiet: *The wind quieted down.* 8 not showy or bright: *Grey is a quiet color.* 1–4, 8 *adj.*, 5 *n.*, 6, 7 *v.* —**qui′et·ness,** *n.*

qui·et·en (kwī′ət ən) cause to become still or peaceful; make quiet: *The mother quietened her frightened child.* *v.*

quieten down, become quiet: *The wind quietened down.*

A man using a quill

quill (kwil) 1 a large, stiff feather. 2 the hollow stem of a feather. 3 anything made from the hollow stem of a feather, such as a pen or toothpick. 4 a stiff, sharp hair or spine: *A porcupine has quills on its back.* *n.*

quilt (kwilt) 1 a cover for a bed, usually made of two pieces of cloth with a soft pad between, held in place by lines of stitching. 2 to make quilts. 3 to stitch together with a soft lining: *quilt a bathrobe.* 1 *n.*, 2, 3 *v.*

quince (kwins) a hard, yellowish, sour fruit, used for preserves and jelly. *n.*

quin·tet or **quin·tette** (kwin tet′) 1 a group of five singers or players performing together. 2 a piece of music for five voices or instruments. 3 any group of five. *n.*

quin·tu·plet (kwin tyü′plit, kwin tü′plit, or kwin′tə plit) one of five children born at the same time from the same mother. *n.*

quirk (kwėrk) 1 a peculiar way of acting: *The old man has many quirks.* 2 a sudden twist or turn: *a quirk in a road, a mental quirk.* *n.*

quit (kwit) 1 stop: *The men quit work at five. It will soon be time to quit.* 2 leave: *His big brother is quitting school this June.* 3 rid; free; clear: *I gave him money to be quit of him.* 1, 2 *v.*, **quit** or **quit·ted, quit·ting;** 3 *adj.*

quite (kwīt) 1 completely; entirely: *a hat quite out of fashion. I am quite alone.* 2 really; truly: *Her illness was quite a shock.* 3 very; rather; somewhat: *It is quite hot.* *adv.*

quits (kwits) even or on equal terms by having given or paid back something: *After the dime was returned, the boys were quits.* *adj.*

call it quits, abandon an attempt to do something: *Since we could not manage to set up camp in the rain, we finally called it quits and hiked home.*

quit·ter (kwit′ər) *Informal.* a person who shirks or gives up easily. *n.*

quiv·er¹ (kwiv′ər) 1 shake; shiver; tremble: *The dog quivered with excitement.* 2 shaking or trembling: *A quiver of his mouth showed that he was about to cry.* 1 *v.*, 2 *n.*

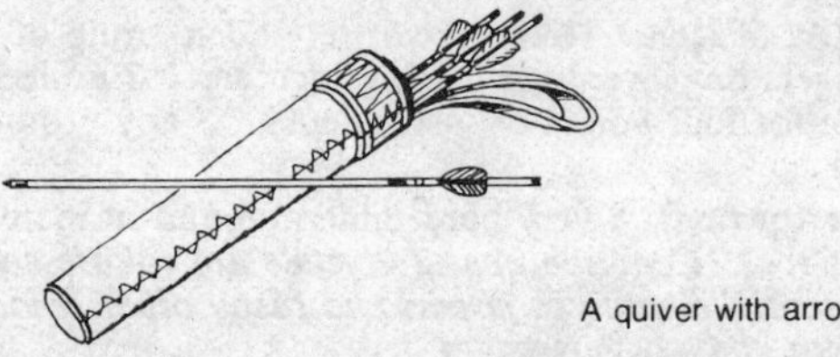
A quiver with arrows

quiv·er² (kwiv′ər) a case to hold arrows. *n.*

quiz (kwiz) 1 a short or informal test: *Each week the teacher gives us a quiz in geography.* 2 give such a test to: *quiz a class in history.* 3 question; interrogate: *The lawyer quizzed the witness.* 1 *n.*, 2, 3 *v.*, **quizzed, quiz·zing.**

quoit (kwoit) 1 a heavy, flattish iron or rope ring thrown to encircle a peg stuck in the ground or to come as close to it as possible. 2 **quoits,** the game so played. *n.*

quo·ta (kwō′tə) a share that is allowed, required, or expected: *Each member of the club was given his quota of tickets to sell for the party. The grain elevators accept a certain quota of wheat from each farmer.* *n.*

quo·ta·tion (kwō tā′shən) 1 somebody's words repeated exactly by another person; a passage quoted from a book, speech, etc.: *From what author does this quotation come?* 2 quoting: *Quotation is a habit of some preachers.* *n.*

quotation mark one of a pair of marks (' ') used to indicate the beginning and end of a quotation.

quote (kwōt) 1 repeat the exact words of; give words or a passage from: *She often quotes her husband. The minister quoted from the Bible.* 2 a quotation. 1 *v.*, **quot·ed, quot·ing;** 2 *n.*

quoth (kwōth) an old word meaning **said:** *'Come hither,' quoth the prince.* *v.*

quo·tient (kwō′shənt) a number obtained by dividing one number by another: *If you divide 26 by 2, the quotient is 13.* See **division** for picture. *n.*

hat, āge, fär; let, ēqual, tėrm; it, īce
hot, ōpen, ôrder; oil, out; cup, pu̇t, rüle
əbove, takən, pencəl, lemən, circəs
ch, child; ng, long; sh, ship
th, thin; ᴛʜ, then; zh, measure

r or **R** (är) the 18th letter of the alphabet: *There are two r's in carry.* *n., pl.* **r's** or **R's.**
the three R's, reading, writing, and arithmetic.

rab·bi (rab'ī) a teacher of the Jewish law and religion; a leader of a Jewish congregation. *n., pl.* **rab·bis.**
☛ **Rabbi** came into English through Old French and Latin from Hebrew *rabbī,* meaning 'my master.'

rab·bit (rab'it) a burrowing mammal with soft fur, long ears, and long hind legs: *A rabbit can make long jumps. Rabbits are related to hares and are smaller.* See the picture. *n.*

rab·ble (rab'əl) a disorderly crowd; a mob. *n.*

rab·id (rab'id) **1** having rabies; mad: *a rabid dog.* **2** unreasonably extreme; fanatical; violent: *The rebels are rabid idealists.* *adj.*

ra·bies (rā'bēz) a disease of dogs and certain other animals; hydrophobia: *If bitten by an infected dog, a person may get rabies.* *n.*

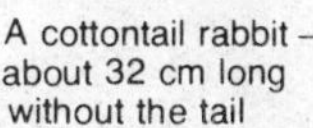

A cottontail rabbit — about 32 cm long without the tail

A raccoon — about 60 cm long without the tail

rac·coon (ra kün') **1** a small, greyish-brown animal having a bushy, ringed tail and a dark patch around the eyes: *Most of the time raccoons live in trees and are active at night.* **2** the fur of this animal: *a raccoon coat.* *n.* Also spelled **racoon.**

race[1] (rās) **1** a contest of speed, as in running, driving, sailing, etc.: *a horse race, a boat race.* **2** take part in a contest for speed: *Our horse will race tomorrow.* **3** run a race with; try to beat in a contest of speed: *I'll race you to the corner.* **4** any contest that suggests a race: *a political race.* **5** run; move fast: *Race to the doctor for help.* **6** make go fast: *Don't race the motor.* **7** a strong or rapid current of water: *a mill race.* 1, 4, 7 *n.,* 2, 3, 5, 6 *v.,* **raced, rac·ing.**

race[2] (rās) **1** a group of living things having similar characteristics or ancestry: *the human race, the race of birds.* **2** a group, class, or kind, especially of people: *the brave race of seamen.* *n.*

race course **1** a route or track for racing. **2** a place or area where races are held.

rac·er (rās'ər) **1** a person, animal, ship, or machine that takes part in races. **2** a North American snake that can move very fast: *Racers live on frogs, mice, and insects.* *n.*

race track a piece of ground laid out for racing, usually circular or oval.

ra·cial (rā'shəl) **1** having something to do with a race of persons, animals, or plants; characteristic of a race: *racial features.* **2** concerning two or more races: *racial problems, racial wars.* *adj.*

rack (rak) **1** a frame with bars, shelves, or pegs to hold, arrange, or keep things on: *a towel rack, a hat rack, a baggage rack.* **2** an instrument once used for torturing people by stretching them. **3** hurt very much: *racked with grief. A toothache racked his jaw.* **4** to stretch; strain. 1, 2 *n.,* 3, 4 *v.*
rack one's brains, think as hard as one can.

rack·et[1] (rak'it) **1** a loud noise; a din; loud talk. **2** *Informal.* a dishonest scheme for getting money from people. *n.*

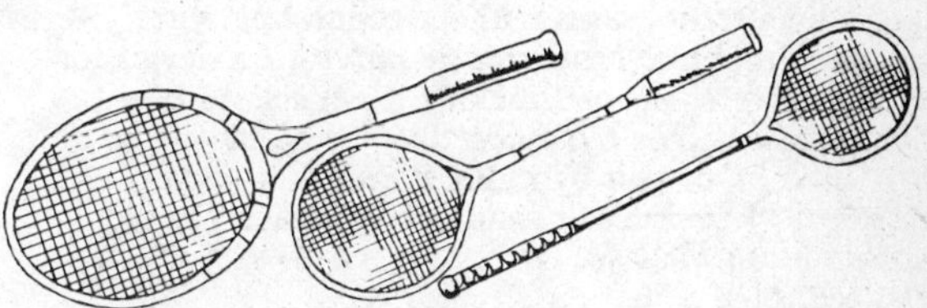

Rackets for tennis, badminton, and squash

rack·et[2] (rak'it) a light, wide bat made of network stretched on a frame. *Rackets are used in tennis, badminton, and other games.* *n.*

ra·coon (ra kün') See **raccoon.**

ra·dar (rā'där) an instrument for determining the distance, direction, speed, etc. of unseen objects by the reflection of radio waves. *n.*
☛ **Radar** is formed from *ra*dio *d*etecting *a*nd *r*anging.

ra·di·ance (rā'dē əns) brightness: *the radiance of the sun, the radiance of a smile.* *n.*

ra·di·ant (rā'dē ənt) **1** shining; bright; beaming: *radiant sunshine, a radiant smile.* **2** sent off in rays from some source; radiated: *We get radiant heat from the sun.* *adj.*

radiant energy energy in the form of rays or waves, especially electromagnetic waves: *X rays, radio waves, and visible light are forms of radiant energy.*

ra·di·ate (rā'dē āt') **1** give out rays of: *The sun radiates light and heat.* **2** issue in rays: *Heat radiates from hot steam pipes.* **3** give out; send forth: *His face radiates joy.* **4** spread out from or as from a centre: *Roads radiate from the city in every direction.* *v.,* **ra·di·at·ed, ra·di·at·ing.**

ra·di·a·tion (rā'dē ā'shən) **1** the act or process of giving out light, heat, or other radiant energy. **2** the energy radiated: *The radiation from an atomic bomb is dangerous to life.* **3** a radio-active ray or rays: *Radiation is harmful to living tissue.* *n.*

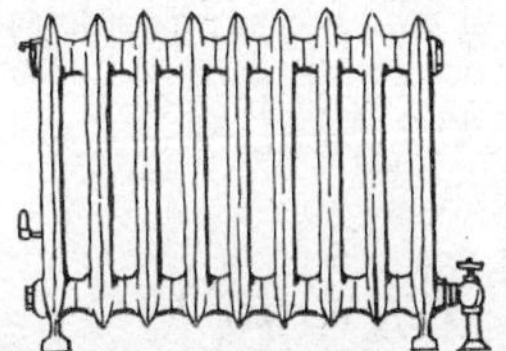

A radiator

ra·di·a·tor (rā'dē ā'tər) **1** a device for heating a room, hall, etc., consisting of pipes through which hot water or steam passes. **2** a device for circulating water: *The radiator of an automobile gives off heat very fast and so cools the water inside it.* *n.*

rad·i·cal (rad′ə kəl) 1 going to the root; fundamental: *Cruelty is a radical fault. If she wants to lose weight, she must make a radical change in her diet.* 2 extreme; favoring extreme changes or reforms. 3 a person who favors extreme changes or reforms, especially in politics; a person with extreme opinions. 1, 2 *adj.,* 3 *n.*

ra·di·i (rā′dē ī′) a plural of **radius.** *n.*

ra·di·o (rā′dē ō′) 1 the sending and receiving of sound signals by electric waves without connecting wires: *We can listen to music broadcast by radio.* 2 a device for sending or receiving and making it possible to hear sounds so sent: *His radio cost $30.* 3 of, having to do with, used in, or sent by radio: *a radio set, radio speeches.* 4 transmit or send out by radio: *The ship radioed a call for help.* 1, 2 *n., pl.* **ra·di·os;** 3 *adj.,* 4 *v.,* **ra·di·oed, ra·di·o·ing.**

ra·di·o–ac·tive (rā′dē ō ak′tiv) giving off radiant energy as a result of the breaking up of atoms: *Radium and uranium are radio-active. adj.*

ra·di·o–ac·tiv·i·ty (rā′dē ō ak tiv′ə tē) 1 the property of being radio-active. 2 the radiation given off. *n.*

A radio telescope

radio telescope a device consisting of a radio receiver and a large, bowl-shaped antenna for detecting and recording radio waves coming from stars and other objects that are beyond the range of ordinary telescopes.

rad·ish (rad′ish) a small, crisp root with a red or white skin, used as a relish and in salads. *n.*

ra·di·um (rā′dē əm) a metallic element that gives off powerful rays: *Radium is used in treating cancer and in making luminous paint. n.*

ra·di·us (rā′dē əs) 1 any line going straight from the centre to the outside of a circle or a sphere: *Any spoke of a wheel is a radius.* See **circle** for picture. 2 a circular area measured by the length of its radius: *The explosion could be heard within a radius of ten kilometres. n., pl.* **ra·di·i** (rā′dē ī) or **ra·di·us·es.**

raf·fle (raf′əl) 1 a sale in which many people each pay a small sum for a chance to win a prize. 2 sell an article by a raffle. 1 *n.,* 2 *v.*

A raft

raft (raft) 1 logs or boards fastened together to make a floating platform: *We floated down the stream on a log raft.* 2 send by raft; carry on a raft. 1 *n.,* 2 *v.*

raft·er (raf′tər) a slanting beam of a roof. See **frame** for picture. *n.*

rag (rag) 1 a torn or waste piece of cloth: *Use clean rags to rub this mirror bright. Her mother made her a rag doll.* 2 a small piece of cloth: *a polishing rag.* 3 **rags,** *pl.* tattered or worn-out clothes: *The beggar was dressed in rags. n.*

in rags, torn or worn out: *Her clothes were in rags.*

rage (rāj) 1 a state of violent anger: *Mad with rage, he dashed into the fight. He flew into a rage.* 2 talk or act violently: *Keep your temper; don't rage. A storm is raging.* 3 what everybody wants for a short time; the fashion: *Red ties are all the rage this season.* 1, 3 *n.,* 2 *v.,* **raged, rag·ing.**

rag·ged (rag′id) 1 worn or torn into rags: *ragged clothing.* 2 wearing torn or badly worn-out clothing: *a ragged beggar.* 3 not smooth and tidy; rough; uneven: *an old dog's ragged coat, a ragged garden. adj.*

raid (rād) 1 a sudden attack: *The pirates planned a raid on the harbor.* 2 attack suddenly: *The enemy raided our camp.* 3 an entering and seizing what is inside: *The hungry boys made a raid on the pantry.* 4 force a way into; enter and seize what is in: *The police raided the house where the thieves had hidden the jewels.* 1, 3 *n.,* 2, 4 *v.*

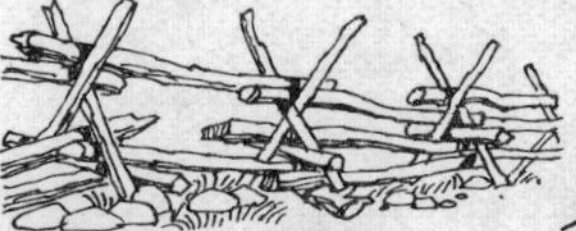

A fence of wooden rails Steel rails of a train track

rail[1] (rāl) 1 a long bar of wood or of metal: *fence rails, stair rails. Bars laid along the ground for a railway track are called rails.* 2 a railway: *We travel by rail and by boat. n.*

rail off, shut off or separate with bars or with a fence: *They railed off a space for the horses.*

rail[2] (rāl) complain bitterly; use violent and reproachful language: *He railed at his hard luck. v.*

rail·ing[1] (rāl′ing) 1 a fence of rails. 2 a rail to hold, on a staircase, balcony, etc. *n.*

rail·ing[2] (rāl′ing) violent complaints or reproaches; jeers. *n.*

rail·road (rāl′rōd′) 1 a railway. 2 to work on a railway: *He has been railroading all his life.* 3 *Informal.* send along or get done quickly or too quickly to be fair: *His enemies tried to railroad him to prison without a fair trial.* 1 *n.,* 2, 3 *v.*

rail·way (rāl′wā′) 1 a road or track with parallel steel rails on which the wheels of engines, cars, etc. go: *Engines pull trains on the railway.* See **rail**[1] for picture. 2 tracks, stations, trains, and other property of a system of transportation that uses rails, together with the people who manage them: *One of Canada's railways is owned by the government. n.*

rai·ment (rā′mənt) clothing; garments. *n.*

rain (rān) 1 water falling in drops from the clouds: *Rain is formed from moisture condensed from water vapor in the atmosphere. The rain wet the windows.* 2 the fall of such drops: *There was a light rain this morning.* 3 to fall in drops of water: *It rained all day.* 4 a thick, fast fall of anything: *a rain of bullets.* 5 to fall like rain: *Sparks rained down from the burning building.* 6 send like rain: *The children rained flowers*

hat, āge, fär; let, ēqual, tėrm; it, īce
hot, ōpen, ôrder; oil, out; cup, pu̇t, rüle
əbove, takən, pencəl, lemən, circəs
ch, child; ng, long; sh, ship
th, thin; ᴛʜ, then; zh, measure

on the May queen. 1, 2, 4 *n.*, 3, 5, 6 *v.*

☛ **Rain, reign,** and **rein** are pronounced the same.

rain·bow (rān′bō′) an arch of colored light, showing the different colors of the spectrum, that is seen in the sky when the sun's rays are seen through rain, mist, or spray: *The seven colors of the rainbow are violet, indigo, blue, green, yellow, orange, and red.* *n.*

rain·coat (rān′kōt′) a waterproof coat worn for protection from rain. *n.*

rain·drop (rān′drop′) a drop of rain. *n.*

rain·fall (rān′fol′ or rān′fôl′) **1** a shower of rain. **2** the amount of water in the form of rain, sleet, or snow that falls within a given time and area: *The yearly rainfall in Vancouver is much greater than that in Regina.* *n.*

rain·y (rān′ē) **1** having rain; having much rain: *April is a rainy month.* **2** bringing rain: *The sky is filled with dark, rainy clouds.* **3** wet with rain: *rainy streets.* *adj.*, **rain·i·er, rain·i·est.**

rainy day a possible time of greater need in the future: *save money for a rainy day.*

raise (rāz) **1** lift up; put up: *Children in school raise their hands to answer. The soldiers raised a white flag.* **2** cause to rise: *The automobiles raised a cloud of dust.* **3** lift up in mind, rank, or position: *The boy raised himself by hard study to be a great lawyer.* **4** increase in degree, amount, price, pay, etc.: *to raise prices, to raise the rent, to raise one's courage.* **5** an increase in amount: *a raise in pay.* **6** bring together; get together; gather: *The leader raised an army.* **7** grow; breed: *The farmer raises chickens and corn.* **8** bring up; rear: *Parents raise their children.* **9** cause; bring about: *A funny remark raises a laugh.* **10** bring forward; mention: *The speaker raised an interesting point.* **11** build; build up; set up: *People raise monuments to soldiers who have died for their country.* **12** rouse; stir up: *The dogs had raised a rabbit and were chasing it.* **13** put an end to: *Our soldiers raised the siege of the fort by driving away the enemy.* **14** bring back to life: *to raise the dead.* 1–4, 6–14 *v.*, **raised, rais·ing;** 5 *n.*

raise the roof, *Slang.* make a disturbance; create an uproar or confusion.

rai·sin (rā′zən) a sweet, dried grape. *n.*

ra·jah (rä′jə) a ruler or chief in India, and in some other eastern countries. *n.*

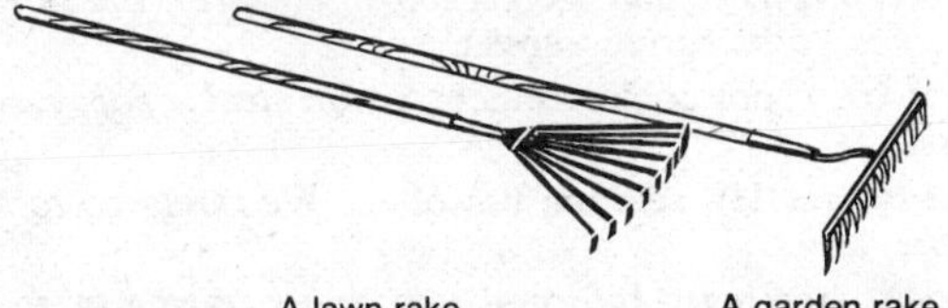

A lawn rake A garden rake

rake (rāk) **1** a long-handled tool having a bar at one end with teeth in it: *A rake is used for smoothing the soil or gathering together loose leaves, hay, or straw.* **2** move with a rake: *Rake the leaves off the grass.* **3** make clear, clean, or smooth with a rake: *Rake the yard.* **4** use a rake: *I like to rake.* **5** gather; gather together: *He raked up money to rent a canoe.* **6** search carefully: *He raked the newspapers for descriptions of the accident.* **7** fire guns along the length of a ship or a line of soldiers. 1 *n.*, 2–7 *v.*, **raked, rak·ing.**

ral·ly (ral′ē) **1** bring together; bring together again; get in order again: *The commander was able to rally the fleeing troops.* **2** come together for a common purpose or action: *The children rallied to help clean up the school after the fun fair.* **3** come to help: *He rallied to the side of his frightened sister.* **4** recover health and strength: *The sick man may rally now.* **5** the act of rallying; recovery. **6** a meeting or assembly of many people for a common purpose or action: *a political rally, a sports-car rally.* 1–4 *v.*, **ral·lied, ral·ly·ing;** 5, 6 *n.*, *pl.* **ral·lies.**

ram (ram) **1** a male sheep. **2** butt against; strike head on; strike violently: *One ship rammed the other ship. In the dark, I rammed my head against the steel door.* **3** push hard; drive down or in by strong force or effort: *He rammed the bolt into the wall.* **4** a device for striking heavy blows: *A battering ram knocks walls down.* 1, 4 *n.*, 2, 3 *v.*, **rammed, ram·ming.**

ram·ble (ram′bəl) **1** wander about: *We rambled here and there through the woods.* **2** a walk for pleasure, not to go to any special place. **3** talk or write about first one thing and then another with no clear connections. 1, 3 *v.*, **ram·bled, ram·bling;** 2 *n.*

ram·bling (ram′bling) **1** going from one thing to another without clear connection; moving from one subject to another: *a rambling speech.* **2** extending in irregular ways in various directions; not planned in an orderly way: *a rambling old farmhouse.* *adj.*

A ramp onto an expressway

ramp (ramp) a sloping walk or roadway connecting two different levels of a building, road, etc.; a slope: *We entered the plane by means of a ramp. There is a steep ramp in front of our garage.* *n.*

ram·page (ram′pāj for 1; ram pāj′ or ram′pāj for 2) **1** a spell of violent behavior; fit of rushing wildly about; wild outbreak: *The mad elephant went on a rampage and killed its keeper.* **2** rush wildly about; behave violently; rage. 1 *n.*, 2 *v.*

ram·pant (ram′pənt) **1** growing without any check: *The vines ran rampant over the fence.* **2** passing beyond restraint or usual limits; unchecked: *Anarchy was rampant after the dictator died.* *adj.*

ram·part (ram′pärt) a wide bank of earth, often with

a wall on top, built around a fort to help defend it. *n.*

ram·pike (ram′pīk′) the bleached skeleton of a dead tree, especially one killed by fire. *n.*

ram·rod (ram′rod′) **1** a rod for ramming down the charge in a gun that is loaded from the muzzle. **2** a rod for cleaning the barrel of a gun. *n.*

ram·shack·le (ram′shak′əl) loose and shaky; likely to come apart: *the ramshackle old buildings. adj.*

ran (ran) See **run.** *The dog ran after the cat. v.*

ranch (ranch) **1** a large farm with grazing land, used for raising cattle, sheep, or horses. **2** any farm, especially one used to raise one kind of animal or crop: *a fruit ranch, a chicken ranch.* **3** to work on a ranch; operate a ranch. 1, 2 *n.,* 3 *v.*

ranch·er (ran′chər) a person who owns, manages, or works on a ranch. *n.*

ran·cid (ran′sid) **1** stale; spoiled: *rancid butter.* **2** tasting or smelling like stale fat or butter: *a rancid odor. adj.*

ran·dom (ran′dəm) by chance; with no plan: *Because he was not listening, he had to give a random answer to the teacher's question. adj.*

at random, by chance; with no plan: *She took a book at random from the shelf.*

rang (rang) See **ring**[2]. *The telephone rang. v.*

range (rānj) **1** the distance between certain limits; an extent: *a range of colors to choose from, a range of prices from 5 cents to 25 dollars, the range of hearing.* **2** vary within certain limits: *The prices in this store range from 5 cents to 25 dollars.* **3** the distance a gun can shoot. **4** a place to practise shooting: *a rifle range.* **5** land for grazing. **6** wander over; rove; roam: *Buffaloes once ranged the plains. Our talk ranged over all that had happened on our holidays.* **7** a row or line of mountains. **8** a row or line. **9** put in a row or rows: *Range the books by size.* **10** put in groups or classes. **11** a district in which certain plants or animals live. **12** run in a line; extend: *a boundary ranging east and west.* **13** be found; occur: *a plant ranging from Canada to Mexico.* **14** a stove for cooking. 1, 3–5, 7, 8, 11, 14 *n.,* 2, 6, 9, 10, 12, 13 *v.,* **ranged, rang·ing.**

rang·er (rān′jər) **1** a person employed to guard a tract of forest. **2** a soldier of certain regiments originally organized for fighting in the North American forests: *Butler's Rangers, the Queen's Rangers.* **3** Also, **Ranger,** a member of the senior branch of the Girl Guides, for girls over 16 years. *n.*

rank[1] (rangk) **1** a row or line of people or things, especially soldiers. **2 the ranks,** *pl.* private soldiers and junior non-commissioned officers. **3** arrange in a row or line. **4** a position; a grade or class: *He retired with the rank of colonel.* **5** a high position: *A duke is a man of rank.* **6** have a certain place or position in relation to other persons or things: *Bill ranked low in the test.* **7** put in some special order in a list: *Rank the continents in order of size.* 1, 2, 4, 5 *n.,* 3, 6, 7 *v.*

rank[2] (rangk) **1** large and coarse: *rank grass.* **2** growing thickly. **3** having an unpleasant, strong smell or taste: *rank meat, rank tobacco.* **4** strongly marked; extreme: *rank ingratitude, rank nonsense. adj.*

ran·kle (rang′kəl) be sore; cause soreness; continue to give pain: *The memory of the insult rankled in his mind. v.,* **ran·kled, ran·kling.**

ran·sack (ran′sak) search thoroughly through, especially to rob or plunder: *The thief ransacked the house for jewellery. v.*

ran·som (ran′səm) **1** the price paid or demanded before a captive is set free: *The robbers held the travellers as prisoners in hope of getting a ransom.* **2** obtain the release of a captive by paying a price: *They ransomed the kidnapped child with a large sum of money.* 1 *n.,* 2 *v.*

rant (rant) speak wildly, extravagantly, violently, or noisily. *v.*

rap (rap) **1** a quick, light blow; a light, sharp knock: *a rap on the door.* **2** knock sharply; tap: *The chairman rapped on the table for order.* 1 *n.,* 2 *v.,* **rapped, rap·ping.**

☛ **Rap** and **wrap** are pronounced the same.

rape[1] (rāp) **1** seizing and carrying off by force. **2** seize and carry off. 1 *n.,* 2 *v.,* **raped, rap·ing.**

rape[2] (rāp) a plant whose leaves are used as food for sheep or pigs and whose seeds produce an oil of commercial value: *A great deal of rape is grown on the Prairies. n.*

rap·id (rap′id) **1** very quick; swift: *a rapid walk; a rapid worker.* **2 rapids,** *pl.* a part of a river where the water rushes very swiftly, often over rocks near the surface: *The boat overturned in the rapids.* 1 *adj.,* 2 *n.* —**rap′id·ly,** *adv.*

ra·pid·i·ty (rə pid′ə tē) quickness; swiftness; speed. *n.*

ra·pi·er (rā′pē ər) a long, light sword used for thrusting. *n.*

rapt (rapt) lost in delight; completely entranced or absorbed: *The girls listened to the story with rapt attention. adj.*

rap·ture (rap′chər) strong feeling that absorbs the mind; very great joy: *The mother gazed with rapture at her newborn baby. n.*

rap·tur·ous (rap′chər əs) full of rapture; feeling rapture; expressing rapture. *adj.*

rare[1] (rer) **1** not usually found or seen: *Pelicans are rare birds in Canada.* **2** not happening often: *Earthquakes are rare in Alberta.* **3** unusually good or great: *Edison had rare powers as an inventor.* **4** thin; not dense: *The higher we go above the earth, the rarer the air is. adj.,* **rar·er, rar·est.**

rare[2] (rer) not cooked much: *a rare steak. adj.,* **rar·er, rar·est.**

rare·ly (rer′lē) seldom; not often: *We rarely go to a movie. adv.*

rar·ing (rer′ing) *Informal.* very eager: *raring to go, raring for a fight. adj.*

rar·i·ty (rer′ə tē) **1** something rare: *A man over a hundred years old is a rarity.* **2** the quality of being rare or scarce; scarcity: *The rarity of diamonds makes them valuable.* **3** a lack of density; thin condition: *the rarity of the air on high mountains. n., pl.* **rar·i·ties.**

ras·cal (ras′kəl) **1** a dishonest person; a rogue. **2** a mischievous child: *My dad says your brothers are rascals. n.*

ras·cal·ly (ras′kəl ē) mean; dishonest; bad: *To steal the poor boy's lunch was a rascally trick. adj.*

rash[1] (rash) too hasty; careless; reckless; taking too much risk: *It is rash to cross the street without looking both ways.* *adj.*

rash[2] (rash) a breaking out with many small red spots on the skin. *n.*

rasp (rasp) **1** make a harsh, grating sound: *The file rasped on the scythe blade.* **2** a harsh, grating sound: *the rasp of crickets, a rasp in a person's voice.* **3** grate on; irritate: *Her feelings were rasped.* **4** scrape with a rough instrument. **5** a coarse file with pointed teeth. 1, 3, 4 *v.*, 2, 5 *n.*

Raspberries

rasp·ber·ry (raz′ber′e) **1** a small fruit that grows on bushes: *Raspberries are usually red or black, but some kinds are white or yellow.* **2** the bush this fruit grows on. **3** *Slang.* a sound of disapproval or derision made with the tongue and lips. *n., pl.* **rasp·ber·ries.**

rat (rat) **1** a long-tailed, gnawing animal resembling a mouse, but larger: *Rats are grey, black, brown, or white.* **2** *Slang.* a low, mean, disloyal person. *n.*
smell a rat, suspect a trick or scheme: *I smelled a rat when none of the boys came.*

rate (rāt) **1** a quantity, amount, or degree measured in proportion to something else: *The rate of interest is 6 cents on the dollar. The car was going at the rate of 80 kilometres per hour.* **2** a price: *We pay the regular rate.* **3** put a value on: *We rated the house as worth $20 000.* **4** rank; estimate; consider; regard: *He was rated as one of the richest men in town.* **5** a class; grade: *first rate, second rate.* **6** be regarded; be classed; rank: *She rates high as a musician.* **7** *Informal.* have value; be worthy of: *He doesn't rate. She rates the best seat in the house.* 1, 2, 5 *n.*, 3, 4, 6, 7 *v.*, **rat·ed, rat·ing.**
at any rate, anyway; in any case.

rate·pay·er (rāt′pā′ər) a person who pays municipal taxes. *n.*

rath·er (raᴛʜ′ər or rä′ᴛʜər) **1** more willingly: *I would rather go today than tomorrow.* **2** more properly; with better reason: *This is rather for your father to decide than for you.* **3** more precisely; more truly: *We sat up till one o'clock Monday night, or, rather, Tuesday morning.* **4** to some extent; somewhat; more than a little: *After working so long he was rather tired.* **5** *Informal.* yes, indeed! certainly! very much so! 1–4 *adv.*, 5 *interj.*

rat·i·fi·ca·tion (rat′ə fə kā′shən) confirmation; approval: *the ratification of a treaty by Parliament.* *n.*

rat·i·fy (rat′ə fī′) confirm; approve: *Parliament ratified the treaty.* *v.*, **rat·i·fied, rat·i·fy·ing.**

rat·ing (rāt′ing) **1** a class or grade. **2** a non-commissioned sailor in the navy: *Ten officers and ratings were lost in the battle.* *n.*

ra·ti·o (rā′shē ō′ or rā′shō) the relation of one number or quantity to another: *'He has sheep and cows in the ratio of 10 to 3' means that he has ten sheep for every three cows. The ratio of 10 to 3 is written as 10:3;*

hat, āge, fär; let, ēqual, tėrm; it, īce
hot, ōpen, ôrder; oil, out; cup, pu̇t, rüle
əbove, takən, pencəl, lemən, circəs
ch, child; ng, long; sh, ship
th, thin; ᴛʜ, then; zh, measure

10/3, 10 ÷ 3, or 10/3. The ratios of 3 to 5 and 6 to 10 are the same. *n., pl.* **ra·ti·os.**

ra·tion (rash′ən or rā′shən) **1** a fixed allowance of food; the daily allowance of food for a person or animal. **2** a portion of anything dealt out; share: *rations of sugar, rations of coal.* **3** allow only certain amounts to: *to ration citizens when supplies are scarce.* **4** distribute in limited amounts: *Food was rationed to the public in wartime.* 1, 2 *n.*, 3, 4 *v.*

ra·tion·al (rash′ən əl) **1** sensible; reasonable; reasoned out: *When very angry, people seldom act in a rational way.* **2** able to think and reason clearly: *As children grow older, they become more rational.* **3** of reason; based on reasoning: *There is a rational explanation for thunder and lightning.* *adj.*

rational number in mathematics, any number that can be expressed as an integer or as a ratio between two integers, excluding zero as a denominator. 2, 5, and ½ are rational numbers.

rat·tan (ra tan′) the stems of a kind of palm tree, used for wickerwork, canes, etc. *n.*

rat·tle (rat′əl) **1** make or cause to make a number of short, sharp sounds: *The window rattled in the wind. She rattled the dishes.* **2** a number of short, sharp sounds: *We hear the rattle of the milk bottles in the morning.* **3** move with short, sharp sounds: *The old car rattled down the street.* **4** a toy or instrument that makes a noise when it is shaken: *The baby shakes his rattle.* **5** talk or say quickly: *He rattled on with his story. She rattled off the names of her friends.* **6** *Informal.* disturb; confuse; upset: *She was so rattled that she forgot her speech.* 1, 3, 5, 6 *v.*, **rat·tled, rat·tling;** 2, 4 *n.*

rat·tler (rat′lər) *Informal.* rattlesnake. *n.*

rat·tle·snake (rat′əl snāk′) a poisonous snake with a thick body and a broad head, that makes a rattling noise with its tail. See **snake** for picture. *n.*

rau·cous (ro′kəs or rô′kəs) hoarse; harsh-sounding: *We heard the raucous caw of a crow in the field of corn.* *adj.*

rav·age (rav′ij) **1** lay waste; damage greatly; destroy: *The forest fire ravaged many square kilometres of country.* **2** violence; destruction; great damage: *War causes ravage.* 1 *v.*, **rav·aged, rav·ag·ing;** 2 *n.*

rave (rāv) **1** talk wildly: *An excited, angry person raves; so does a madman.* **2** talk with too much enthusiasm: *She raved about her food.* *v.*, **raved, rav·ing.**

rav·el (rav′əl) fray out; separate into threads: *The sweater has ravelled at the wrist.* *v.*, **rav·elled** or **rav·eled, rav·el·ling** or **rav·el·ing.**

ra·ven (rā′vən) **1** a large, black bird, resembling a crow but larger. **2** deep, glossy black: *She has raven hair.* 1–2 *n.*, 2 *adj.*

rav·en·ous (rav′ən əs) **1** very hungry: *a ravenous boy.* **2** greedy. *adj.*

ra·vine (rə vēn′) a long, deep, narrow valley: *The river had worn a ravine between the two hills.* *n.*

rav·i·o·li (rav′ē ō′lē) small, thin pieces of dough filled with chopped meat, cheese, etc: *Ravioli is cooked by boiling in water, and is usually served with a highly seasoned tomato sauce.* *n.*

rav·ish (rav′ish) **1** fill with delight: *The prince was ravished by Cinderella's beauty.* **2** carry off by force: *The wolf ravished the lamb from the flock.* *v.*

rav·ish·ing (rav′ish ing) very delightful; enchanting: *jewels of ravishing beauty.* *adj.*

raw (ro or rô) **1** not cooked: *raw meat.* **2** in the natural state; not manufactured, treated or prepared: *raw materials. Raw milk has not been pasteurized.* **3** not experienced; not trained: *a raw soldier in the army.* **4** damp and cold: *raw weather.* **5** with the skin off; sore: *a raw spot on a horse where the harness rubbed.* **6** *Slang.* harsh; unfair: *a raw deal.* *adj.*

raw–boned (ro′bōnd′ or rô′bōnd′) having little flesh on the bones; gaunt. *adj.*

raw·hide (ro′hīd′ or rô′hīd′) the untanned skin of cattle: *Rawhide is used to make ropes, thongs, whips, etc.* *n.*

raw material a substance in its natural state, before being manufactured, treated, or prepared: *Iron ore, coffee beans, and hides are raw materials.*

ray[1] (rā) **1** a line or beam of light: *the rays of the sun.* **2** a line or stream of radiant energy in the form of heat, electricity, light, etc.: *X rays.* **3** a thin line like a ray, coming out from a centre. **4** any part like a ray: *The petals of a daisy and the arms of a starfish are rays.* **5** a slight trace; faint gleam: *a ray of hope, a ray of intelligence.* *n.*

ray[2] (rā) any of various fish, related to the shark, that have broad, flat bodies with very broad fins. *n.*

ray·on (rā′on) a fibre or fabric made from cellulose. *n.*

raze (rāz) tear down; destroy completely: *The old school was razed to the ground, and a new, larger one was built.* *v.,* **razed, raz·ing.**

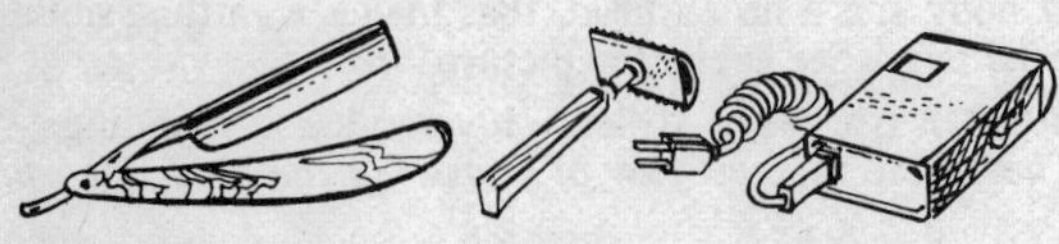

A straight razor used by barbers   A safety razor   An electric razor

ra·zor (rā′zər) a device or instrument used for shaving: *an electric razor, a safety razor.* *n.*

razz (raz) *Slang.* **1** laugh at; make fun of. **2** strong disapproval; derision. **3** express disapproval of; boo: *The angry crowd razzed the umpire.* 1, 3 *v.,* 2 *n.*

R.C.M.P. Royal Canadian Mounted Police.

rd. or **Rd.** road.

re (rā) the second tone of the musical scale. See **do**[2] for picture. *n.*

re– a prefix meaning: **1** again; anew; once more, as in *reappear, rebuild, reopen, re-enter.* **2** back, as in *recall, repay, replace.*

reach (rēch) **1** get to; arrive at; come to: *Your letter reached me yesterday.* **2** stretch out; hold out: *A hand reached from the dark and seized him.* **3** stretch; extend in space, time, influence, etc.: *Canada reaches from sea to sea. The radio reaches millions.* **4** touch: *I cannot reach the top of the wall. The anchor reached bottom.* **5** move to touch or seize something; try to get: *The man reached for his gun.* **6** amount to; be equal to: *The cost of the war reached billions.* **7** *Informal.* take or pass with the hand: *Please reach me the sugar.* **8** get to; communicate with: *I could not reach him by telephone. Men are reached by flattery.* **9** reaching or stretching out: *By a long reach the drowning man grasped the rope.* **10** the extent or distance of reaching: *Food and water were left within reach of the sick dog.* **11** range; power; capacity: *Philosophy is beyond a child's reach; he cannot understand it.* **12** a long stretch or extent: *a reach of water.* 1–8 *v.,* 9–12 *n.*

re·act (rē akt′) **1** act back; have an effect on the one that is acting: *Unkindness often reacts on the unkind person and makes him unhappy.* **2** act in response: *Dogs react to kindness by showing affection. Some people react against fads.* **3** act by chemical process: *Acids react on metals.* *v.*

re·ac·tion (rē ak′shən) **1** action in response to some influence or force: *Our reaction to a joke is to laugh. The doctor carefully observed his patient's reactions to the tests.* **2** in science, the process by which two substances act on each other to form one or more different substances: *The reaction between nitrogen and hydrogen produces ammonia.* *n.*

re·ac·tor (rē ak′tər) an apparatus that produces controlled atomic energy, instead of an explosion as in a bomb. *n.*

read[1] (rēd) **1** get the meaning of symbols such as those used in writing or printing: *We read books. The blind girl reads special raised print by touching it with her fingers.* **2** learn from writing or printing: *We read of heroes of other days.* **3** speak out loud the words of writing or print: *Please read it to me.* **4** show by figures, letters, signs, etc.: *The thermometer reads 20 degrees. The ticket reads 'From Regina to Calgary.'* **5** study: *He is reading law.* **6** get the meaning of; understand: *He could read distrust on my face.* **7** give the meaning of; interpret: *to read the future.* *v.,* **read** (red), **read·ing.**

☛ **Read**[1] and **reed** are pronounced the same.

read[2] (red) **1** having knowledge gained by reading; informed: *a well-read man. He is widely read in history.* **2** See **read**[1]. *I read that book last year.* 1 *adj.,* 2 *v.*

☛ **Read**[2] and **red** are pronounced the same.

read·er (rēd′ər) a book for learning and practising reading. *n.*

read·i·ly (red′ə lē) **1** quickly; without delay: *A bright boy answers readily when called on.* **2** easily; without difficulty: *The parts fit together readily.* **3** willingly. *adv.*

read·i·ness (red′ē nis) **1** the state of being ready: *Everything is in readiness for the party.* **2** quickness; promptness. **3** ease. **4** willingness. *n.*

read·ing (rēd′ing) **1** in school, the study of how to get the meaning of written or printed words. **2** speaking out loud written or printed words; a public recital. **3** written or printed matter read or to be read: *There's good reading in this magazine.* **4** the

hat, āge, fär; let, ēqual, tėrm; it, īce
hot, ōpen, ôrder; oil, out; cup, pu̇t, rüle
əbove, takən, pencəl, lemən, circəs
ch, child; ng, long; sh, ship
th, thin; ᴛʜ, then; zh, measure

information shown on a gauge or the scale of an instrument: *The reading of the thermometer was 16 degrees.* 5 interpretation: *Each actor gave the lines a different reading.* *n.*

read·y (red′ē) **1** prepared for immediate action or use; prepared: *The soldiers are ready for battle. Dinner is ready. We were ready to start at nine.* **2** willing: *The soldiers were ready to die for their country. She is ready to forgive.* **3** likely; liable: *He is too ready to find fault.* **4** quick; prompt: *a ready wit, ready help.* **5** easy to get at; immediately available: *ready money.* *adj.,* **read·i·er, read·i·est.**

read·y-made (red′ē mād′) ready for immediate use; made for anybody who will buy: *This store sells ready-made clothes.* *adj.*

re·al (rē′əl or rēl) **1** existing as a fact; not imagined; not made up; actual; true: *real pleasure, the real reason.* **2** genuine: *the real thing, real diamonds.* *adj.*

real estate land, together with the buildings, fences, trees, water, minerals, etc. that belong with it.

re·al·ise (rē′əl īz′) See **realize.** *v.,* **re·al·ised, re·al·is·ing.**

re·al·i·ty (rē al′ə tē) **1** actual existence; the true state of affairs: *I doubted the reality of what he had seen; I thought he must have dreamed it.* **2** a real thing; an actual fact: *Slaughter and destruction are the terrible realities of war.* *n., pl.* **re·al·i·ties.**

in reality, really; in fact: *We thought he was joking, but in reality he was serious.*

re·al·i·za·tion (rē′əl ə zā′shən) **1** the making real or being made real of something imagined or planned: *The realization of her hope to be an actress made her happy.* **2** clear understanding; full awareness: *The explorers had a full realization of the dangers they would face.* *n.*

re·al·ize (rē′əl īz′) **1** understand clearly; be fully aware of: *The teacher realizes now how hard you worked.* **2** make real: *Her uncle's present made it possible for her to realize her dream of going to Europe.* *v.,* **re·al·ized, re·al·iz·ing.** Also, **realise.**

re·al·ly (rē′əl ē or rē′lē) **1** actually; truly; in fact: *We should learn to accept things as they really are.* **2** an expression of surprise, disbelief, or disapproval: *Really, Tom? You must be kidding!* *adv.*

realm (relm) **1** a kingdom. **2** a region; range; extent: *The Prime Minister's realm of influence is very wide.* **3** a particular field of something: *the realm of biology, the realm of poetry.* *n.*

re·al·tor (rē′əl tər) a person who is a member of an organization of persons engaged in the business of buying and selling real estate. *n.*

ream (rēm) **1** 500, sometimes 480, sheets of paper of the same size and quality. **2** *Informal.* a very large quantity: *He took reams of notes.* *n.*

☛ **Ream** is from Old French *raime,* which came originally from Arabic *raimah,* meaning 'bundle.'

reap (rēp) **1** cut grain. **2** gather a crop. **3** cut grain or gather a crop from: *The farmer reaps his field.* **4** get as a return or reward: *Kind acts often reap happy smiles.* *v.*

reap·er (rēp′ər) a person or machine that cuts grain or gathers a crop. *n.*

re·ap·pear (rē′ə pēr′) come into sight again. *v.*

rear¹ (rēr) **1** the back part; the back: *The kitchen is in the rear of the house.* **2** in the back; at the back: *Leave by the rear door of the bus.* **3** the last part of an army, fleet, etc.: *The Service Corps brought up the rear.* 1, 3 *n.,* 2 *adj.*

rear² (rēr) **1** make grow; help to grow; bring up: *The mother was very careful in rearing her children.* **2** set up; build: *The men of old reared altars to their gods. The pioneers soon reared churches in their settlements.* **3** raise; lift up: *The snake reared its head.* **4** of an animal, rise on the hind legs: *The horse reared as the fire engine dashed past.* *v.*

re·ar·range (rē′ə rānj′) **1** arrange in a new or different way: *Mother rearranged the furniture in the living room.* **2** arrange again; put back in position: *When John dropped his airplane kit, he had to rearrange all the pieces.* *v.,* **re·ar·ranged, re·ar·rang·ing.**

rea·son (rē′zən) **1** a cause or motive for an action, feeling, etc.: *Tell me your reasons for not liking him.* **2** an explanation: *Sickness is the reason for her absence.* **3** think things out; solve new problems: *Man can reason.* **4** the ability or power to think: *That poor old man has lost his reason.* **5** good sense; common sense: *The stubborn child was at last brought to reason.* **6** consider; discuss; argue: *Reason with her and try to make her change her mind.* 1, 2, 4, 5 *n.,* 3, 6 *v.*

stand to reason, be reasonable and sensible: *It stands to reason that he would resent your insults.*

☛ **Reason** and **cause** often mean nearly the same, but they must not be confused. A **reason** explains why or how something happens: *His reason for being late was that his car would not start.* A **cause** is what makes something happen: *The extreme cold was the cause of his car not starting.*

rea·son·a·ble (rē′zən ə bəl) **1** according to reason; sensible; not foolish. **2** moderate; fair: *a reasonable price.* *adj.* **—rea′son·a·bly,** *adv.*

rea·son·ing (rē′zən ing) **1** the process of drawing conclusions from facts. **2** reasons; arguments. *n.*

re·as·sure (rē′ə shür′) restore to confidence: *The captain's confidence during the storm reassured the passengers.* *v.,* **re·as·sured, re·as·sur·ing.**

reb·el (reb′əl for 1 and 2, ri bel′ for 3 and 4) **1** a person who resists or fights against authority instead of obeying: *The rebels armed themselves against the government.* **2** defying law or authority: *a rebel army.* **3** resist or fight against law or authority: *The soldiers decided to rebel.* **4** feel or express a great dislike or opposition: *We rebelled at having to stay in on so fine a day.* 1 *n.,* 2 *adj.,* 3, 4 *v.,* **re·belled, re·bel·ling.**

re·bel·lion (ri bel′yən) **1** organized resistance against the authority of a government; a revolt: *the Riel Rebellion.* **2** an act of resistance against any authority; a revolt or fight against any restriction: *The slaves plotted rebellion against their master.* *n.*

re·bel·lious (ri bel′yəs) **1** defying authority; acting like a rebel: *a rebellious army.* **2** hard to manage; disobedient: *The rebellious boy would not obey the school rules.* *adj.*

re·birth (rē′bėrth′ or rē bėrth′) new birth; being born again: *a rebirth of confidence, a rebirth of interest in bicycling.* *n.*

re·born (rē bôrn′) born again: *Our hopes were reborn after the team's victory.* *adj.*

re·bound (ri bound′ for 1, rē′bound′ for 2) **1** spring back. **2** springing back: *You hit the ball on the rebound in handball.* 1 *v.*, 2 *n.*

re·buff (ri buf′) **1** a blunt or sudden check to a person or animal that makes advances, offers help, makes a request, etc.: *We tried to be friendly, but his rebuff made us think he wanted to be left alone.* **2** give a rebuff to: *The friendly dog was rebuffed by a kick.* 1 *n.*, 2 *v.*

re·build (rē′ bild′) build again: *The snowman fell down and the children are trying to rebuild it.* *v.*, **re·built, re·build·ing.**

re·built (rē′ bilt′) See **rebuild.** *v.*

re·buke (ri byük′) **1** express disapproval of; reprove: *The teacher rebuked the child for throwing paper on the floor.* **2** an expression of disapproval; a scolding: *The child feared the teacher's rebuke.* 1 *v.*, **re·buked, re·buk·ing;** 2 *n.*

re·call (ri kol′ or ri kôl′) **1** call back to mind; remember: *I can recall stories that my mother told me years ago.* **2** call back; order back: *The captain was recalled from the front line.* **3** take back; withdraw: *I shall recall my order for a new coat because I have had one given me.* **4** calling back; ordering back. 1–3 *v.*, 4 *n.*

re·cap·ture (rē kap′chər) **1** capture again; have again. **2** bring back; recall: *The picture album recaptured the days of the horse and buggy.* *v.*, **re·cap·tured, re·cap·tur·ing.**

re·cede (ri sēd′) **1** go backward; move backward: *Houses and trees seem to recede as you ride past in a train.* **2** slope backward: *He has a chin that recedes.* *v.*, **re·ced·ed, re·ced·ing.**

re·ceipt (ri sēt′) **1** a written statement that money, a package, a letter, etc. has been received: *Sign the receipt for this parcel.* **2** write on a bill, etc. that something has been received or paid for: *Pay the bill and ask the grocer to receipt it.* **3 receipts,** *pl.* money received: *Our expenses were less than our receipts.* **4** a receiving or being received: *On receipt of the news of his father's death he went home.* 1, 3, 4 *n.*, 2 *v.*

re·ceive (ri sēv′) **1** take something sent or offered: *We receive many presents at Christmas.* **2** be given; get: *The soldier received a letter from home.* **3** experience; suffer; endure: *to receive blows, to receive punishment.* **4** take; support; bear; hold: *The boat received a heavy load. A basin receives the water from the fountain.* **5** take or let into the mind; accept: *to receive new ideas, to receive news, to receive an education.* **6** let into one's house, society, etc.: *The people of the neighborhood were glad to receive the new couple.* **7** be at home to friends and visitors: *She receives on Tuesdays.* **8** in radio or television, change electromagnetic waves into sound or picture signals: *Our radio receives well since we put in new batteries.* *v.*, **re·ceived, re·ceiv·ing.**

re·ceiv·er (ri sēv′ər) **1** a person who receives: *The receiver of a gift should thank the giver.* **2** anything that receives: *Public telephones have coin receivers for nickels, dimes, and quarters.* **3** the part of a telephone that is held to the ear. **4** a device that changes electromagnetic waves into sound signals: *a radio or television receiver.* *n.*

re·cent (rē′sənt) **1** done, made, or happening not long ago: *recent events.* **2** not long past; modern: *a recent period of history.* *adj.* **—re′cent·ly,** *adv.*

re·cep·ta·cle (ri sep′tə kəl) any container or place used to put things in: *Bags, baskets, and vaults are all receptacles.* *n.*

re·cep·tion (ri sep′shən) **1** the act of receiving: *Her calm reception of the bad news surprised us.* **2** being received: *Her reception as a club member pleased her.* **3** a manner of receiving: *We were given a warm reception on returning home.* **4** a gathering to receive and welcome people: *Our school gave a reception for our new principal.* **5** the quality of the sound in a radio or of the sound and picture signals in a television set. *n.*

re·cep·tion·ist (ri sep′shə nist) a person employed in an office to welcome visitors, direct them where to go, give out information, etc. *n.*

re·cep·tive (ri sep′tiv) able, quick, or ready to receive ideas, suggestions, or impressions: *a receptive mind.* *adj.*

re·cess (ri ses′, also rē′ses for 1, 3, and 5) **1** a time during which work stops: *Our school has an hour's recess at noon.* **2** take a recess: *The committee recessed for lunch.* **3** a part in a wall or other surface, set back from the rest: *This long seat will fit nicely in that recess.* **4** put in a recess; set back. **5** an inner place or part: *the recesses of a cave, the recesses of one's thoughts.* 1, 3, 5 *n.*, 2, 4 *v.*

rec·i·pe (res′ə pē) **1** a set of directions for preparing something to eat: *Please give me your recipe for cookies.* **2** a set of directions for preparing anything or reaching some result: *Hard work is a good recipe for success.* *n.*

re·cip·i·ent (ri sip′ē ənt) a person who receives something: *All the recipients of the prizes had their names printed in the paper.* *n.*

re·cit·al (ri sīt′əl) **1** a telling of facts in detail: *Her recital of her experiences in the hospital bored her hearers.* **2** a public performance given by a group of pupils of piano, dance, etc. **3** a musical entertainment, usually given by a single performer: *A famous pianist is going to give a recital Tuesday afternoon.* *n.*

rec·i·ta·tion (res′ə tā′shən) **1** reciting; a telling of facts in detail. **2** reciting a prepared lesson by pupils before a teacher. **3** the repeating of something from memory before an audience. **4** a piece repeated from memory. *n.*

re·cite (ri sīt′) **1** say over; repeat: *The pupils recited their lessons. He can recite that poem from memory.* **2** tell in detail: *He recited the day's adventures.* *v.*, **re·cit·ed, re·cit·ing.**

reck·less (rek′lis) rash; heedless; careless: *Reckless of danger, the boy played with a loaded gun. Reckless driving causes many automobile accidents.* *adj.*

reck·on (rek′ən) **1** find the number or value of; count: *Reckon the cost before you decide.* **2** consider; judge: *He is reckoned a fine speller.* **3** *Informal.* think; suppose. *v.*

reckon on, a count on; take into account: *He didn't*

hat, āge, fär; let, ēqual, tėrm; it, īce
hot, ōpen, ôrder; oil, out; cup, pu̇t, rüle
əbove, takən, pencəl, lemən, circəs
ch, child; ng, long; sh, ship
th, thin; ᴛʜ, then; zh, measure

reckon on breaking his leg when he decided to try skiing. **b** depend on; rely on: *Can we reckon on your help?*

reckon with, take into account; face: *We are going to have to reckon with higher prices for food.*

reck·on·ing (rek′ən ing) **1** a count or calculation: *By my reckoning we are ten kilometres from home.* **2** the settling of an account: *a day of reckoning. n.*

re·claim (ri klām′) **1** bring back to a useful, good condition: *The farmer reclaimed the swamp by draining it.* **2** get from discarded things: *to reclaim rubber from old tires.* **3** get back: *He had difficulty reclaiming the money he had lent. v.*

rec·la·ma·tion (rek′lə mā′shən) restoration to a useful, good condition: *the reclamation of deserts by irrigation. n.*

re·cline (ri klīn′) lean back; lie down: *The tired woman reclined on the couch. v.,* **re·clined, re·clin·ing.**

rec·luse (rek′lüs or ri klüs′) a person who lives shut up or withdrawn from the world. *n.*

rec·og·ni·tion (rek′əg nish′ən) **1** knowing again; recognizing; being recognized: *By a good disguise he escaped recognition.* **2** an acknowledgment: *We all insisted on complete recognition of our rights.* **3** favorable notice: *The actor soon won recognition from the public. n.*

rec·og·nize (rek′əg nīz′) **1** know again: *You have grown so much that I scarcely recognized you.* **2** acknowledge; accept; admit: *He recognized his duty to defend his country. v.,* **rec·og·nized, rec·og·niz·ing.**

re·coil (ri koil′, also rē′koil for 3) **1** draw back; shrink back: *Most people would recoil at seeing a snake in the path.* **2** spring back: *The gun recoiled after I fired it.* **3** drawing or springing back. 1, 2 *v.,* 3 *n.*

rec·ol·lect (rek′ə lekt′) remember. *v.*

rec·ol·lec·tion (rek′ə lek′shən) **1** the act or power of calling back to mind. **2** remembrance; memory: *This had been the hottest summer within my recollection.* **3** something remembered. *n.*

rec·om·mend (rek′ə mend′) **1** speak in favor of; suggest favorably: *The teacher recommended Jim for the job. Can you recommend a good adventure story?* **2** advise: *The doctor recommended that she stay in bed.* **3** make pleasing or attractive: *The location of the camp recommends it as a summer home. v.*

rec·om·men·da·tion (rek′ə men dā′shən) **1** recommending. **2** anything that recommends a person or thing. **3** words of advice or praise. *n.*

rec·om·pense (rek′əm pens′) **1** pay back; pay a person; reward: *The fishermen recompensed their guide generously.* **2** make a fair return for anything lost, damaged, etc.: *The insurance company recompensed him for the loss of his car.* **3** a return for anything lost, damaged, etc.: *He demanded recompense for the broken window.* **4** a payment or reward: *He asked for fair recompense for the work he had done.* 1, 2 *v.,* **rec·om·pensed, rec·om·pens·ing;** 3, 4 *n.*

rec·on·cile (rek′ən sīl′) **1** make friends again: *The children had quarrelled but were soon reconciled.* **2** settle a quarrel or difference: *The teacher had to reconcile disputes among her pupils.* **3** make agree; bring into harmony: *It is impossible to reconcile his story with the facts.* **4** make satisfied or content with: *It is hard to reconcile oneself to being sick a long time. v.,* **rec·on·ciled, rec·on·cil·ing.**

rec·on·cil·i·a·tion (rek′ən sil′ē ā′shən) settlement or adjustment of disagreements or differences: *a reconciliation of opposite points of view. n.*

rec·on·noi·tre or **rec·on·noi·ter** (rek′ə noi′tər or rē′kə noi′tər) **1** approach and examine or observe in order to learn something: *Our scouts will reconnoitre the enemy's position before we attack.* **2** approach a place and make a first survey of it: *It seemed wise to reconnoitre before entering the town. v.,* **rec·on·noi·tred** or **rec·on·noi·tered, rec·on·noi·tring** or **rec·on·noi·ter·ing.**

re·con·sid·er (rē′kən sid′ər) consider again: *The assembly voted to reconsider the bill. v.*

re·con·struct (rē′kən strukt′) construct again; rebuild; make over: *Much of the city had to be reconstructed after the fire. v.*

re·cord (ri kôrd′ for 1, 2, 6, and 7, rek′ərd for 3–5 and 8–10) **1** set down in writing so as to keep for future use: *Listen to the speaker and record what he says.* **2** put in some permanent form; keep for remembrance: *History is recorded in books.* **3** the thing written or kept. **4** an official written account: *The secretary kept a record of what was done at the meeting.* **5** a thin, flat disk with narrow spiral grooves on its surface that reproduces sounds when played on a record player. **6** put music, words, or sounds on such a disk or on specially treated wire or tape. **7** tell; indicate: *The thermometer records temperature.* **8** the known facts about what a person, animal, ship, etc. has done: *He has a fine record at school.* **9** a remarkable performance or event, going beyond others of the same kind, especially the best achievement in a sport: *Who holds the record for the high jump?* **10** unequalled; better than before: *a record wheat crop.* 1, 2, 6, 7 *v.,* 3–5, 8, 9 *n.,* 10 *adj.*

off the record, not to be recorded or quoted: *The Prime Minister was speaking off the record.*

on record, written down, printed, or otherwise made available: *The facts of the murder case are now on record.*

☛ **Record** originally meant 'to learn by heart' or 'to remember' and came through Old French from Latin *recordare,* made up of *re-,* meaning 'back' and *cordis,* meaning 'heart' or 'mind.'

A recorder

re·cord·er (ri kôr′dər) **1** a person whose business is to make and keep records. **2** a machine, or part of a machine, that records: *The recorder of a cash register adds up and prints the amount of sales made.* **3** tape-recorder. **4** a wooden musical instrument having a tone like that of a flute. *n.*

re·cord·ing (ri kôr′ding) a sound record made on a disk or tape. *n.*

record player an instrument that plays back sounds that have been recorded on disks; phonograph.

re–count (rē′kount′) count again. *v.*

re·count[1] (ri kount′) tell in detail; give an account of: *He recounted the events of the day.* *v.*

re·count[2] (rē′kount′) a second count: *A recount of the votes was made.* *n.*

re·course (rē′kôrs) 1 turning for help or protection; appealing: *Our recourse in illness is to a doctor.* 2 a person or thing appealed to or turned to for help or protection: *A child's great recourse in trouble is its mother.* *n.*

have recourse to, appeal to; turn to for help: *When we do not know what a word means, we have recourse to a dictionary.*

re–cov·er (rē′kuv′ər) put a new cover on: *We had our chesterfield re-covered.* *v.*

re·cov·er (ri kuv′ər) 1 get back something lost, taken away, or stolen: *recover one's temper or health, recover a lost purse.* 2 make up for something lost or damaged: *recover lost time.* 3 get well; get back to a normal condition: *She is recovering from a cold.* *v.*

re·cov·er·y (ri kuv′ər ē) 1 coming back to health or normal condition: *We heard of your recovery from fever.* 2 a getting back of something that was lost, taken away, stolen, or sent out: *the recovery of a space capsule.* 3 getting back to a proper position or condition: *He started to fall, but made a quick recovery.* *n., pl.* **re·cov·er·ies.**

rec·re·a·tion (rek′rē ā′shən) play or amusement: *Walking, gardening, and reading are quiet forms of recreation.* *n.*

rec·re·a·tion·al (rek′rē ā′shən əl) of or having to do with recreation. *adj.*

recreation room a room for recreation such as playing games, lounging, dancing, and other informal activities: *Many families have a recreation room in their basement.*

re·cruit (ri krüt′) 1 a newly enlisted member of the armed forces. 2 get people to join one of the armed forces. 3 a new member of any group or class: *The Nature Club needs recruits.* 4 get new members; get people to join: *recruit volunteers, recruit teachers.* 1, 3 *n.*, 2, 4 *v.*

Rectangles

rec·tan·gle (rek′tang′gəl) a four-sided figure with four right angles. *n.*

rec·tan·gu·lar (rek tang′gyə lər) shaped like a rectangle. *adj.*

rec·ti·fy (rek′tə fī′) 1 make right; put right; adjust; remedy: *The storekeeper admitted his mistake and was willing to rectify it.* 2 in electronics, change an alternating current into a direct current. *v.,* **rec·ti·fied, rec·ti·fy·ing.**

rec·tor (rek′tər) 1 in the Anglican Church, a clergyman who has charge of a parish. 2 in the Roman Catholic Church, a priest who has charge of a congregation or religious house. 3 in some schools, colleges, or universities, the head or principal. *n.*

rec·to·ry (rek′tə rē) a rector's house. *n.*

re·cu·per·ate (ri kü′pər āt′) 1 regain health; get well: *After his illness he took a month's holiday to recuperate.* 2 get back; regain: *He worked hard to recuperate the money that was stolen from him.* *v.,* **re·cu·per·at·ed, re·cu·per·at·ing.**

re·cur (ri kėr′) 1 come up again; occur again; be repeated: *Leap year recurs every four years.* 2 return in thought or speech: *Old memories often recurred to him. He recurred to the matter of cost.* *v.,* **re·curred, re·cur·ring.**

re·cur·rent (ri kėr′ənt) occurring again; repeated; recurring: *recurrent attacks of hay fever.* *adj.*

red (red) 1 the color of blood or of the lips. 2 of or having the color of blood or of the lips: *red paint, red ink.* 3 favoring revolution. 4 **Red,** a person who favors revolution, especially a communist. 1, 4 *n.*, 2, 3 *adj.,* **red·der, red·dest.**

in the red, *Informal.* in debt; losing money.

see red, *Informal.* become very angry.

☛ **Red** and **read**[2] are pronounced the same.

red·cap (red′kap′) a man whose work is carrying luggage at a railway station, bus station, etc. *n.*

red cedar a kind of juniper with fragrant rose-brown wood used for chests, pencils, etc.

red·coat (red′kōt′) 1 in former times a British soldier. 2 a member of the R.C.M.P. *n.*

Red Cross a group of societies in over 100 nations, that work to relieve human suffering in time of war or peace. Major projects of the Canadian Red Cross are the free blood transfusion service and the water safety program. The badge of most societies is a red cross on a white background, but societies in Moslem countries have a red crescent, and are called Red Crescent societies.

red·den (red′ən) 1 make or become red. 2 blush: *Her face reddened with shame.* *v.*

red·dish (red′ish) somewhat red. *adj.*

re·deem (ri dēm′) 1 buy back: *The property on which money was lent was redeemed when the loan was paid back.* 2 pay off: *He redeemed the debt.* 3 make up for: *A very good feature will sometimes redeem several bad ones.* 4 fulfil; carry out; make good: *We redeem a promise by doing what we said we would.* 5 set free; rescue; save; deliver: *redeemed from sin.* *v.*

re·demp·tion (ri demp′shən) 1 the act of buying back or paying off. 2 a ransom. 3 a deliverance or rescue. 4 deliverance from sin; salvation. *n.*

Red Ensign until 1965, the distinctive flag of Canada.

red–hand·ed (red′han′did) in the very act of crime, mischief, etc.: *The robber was caught red-handed.* *adj.*

red·head (red′hed′) a person having red hair. *n.*

red hot *Informal.* hot dog.

red–hot (red′hot′) 1 very hot: *a red-hot iron.* 2 very enthusiastic; excited; violent: *a red-hot fanatic.* 3 fresh from the source: *red-hot rumors.* *adj.*

hat, āge, fär; let, ēqual, tėrm; it, īce
hot, ōpen, ôrder; oil, out; cup, pu̇t, rüle
ə above, takən, pencəl, lemən, circəs
ch, child; ng, long; sh, ship
th, thin; ᴛʜ, then; zh, measure

re·dis·cov·er (rē′dis kuv′ər) discover again or anew. *v.*

red–let·ter (red′let′ər) memorable; especially happy: *Graduation is a red-letter day in one's life.* *adj.*

re·do (rē′ dü′) do again; do over: *He lost his homework and had to redo it.* *v.*

re·dou·ble (rē dub′əl) **1** double again. **2** double; increase greatly: *When he saw land ahead, the swimmer redoubled his speed.* **3** double back: *The fox redoubled on his trail to escape the hunters.* *v.,* **re·dou·bled, re·dou·bling.**

re·doubt·a·ble (ri dout′ə bəl) deserving to be feared or dreaded: *a redoubtable opponent.* *adj.*

re·dress (ri dres′, also rē′dres for 2) **1** set right; repair; remedy: *King Arthur tried to redress wrongs in his kingdom.* **2** setting right; relief. 1 *v.,* 2 *n.*

Red River a river flowing northward through southern Manitoba and emptying into Lake Winnipeg.

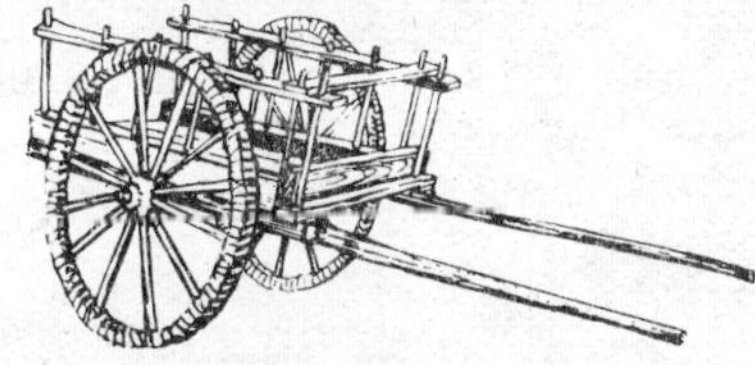

A Red River cart

Red River cart *Cdn.* a strong two-wheeled cart pulled by oxen or horses: *Red River carts were used by pioneers in the West.*

red·skin (red′skin′) a North American Indian. *n.*

re·duce (ri dyüs′ or ri düs′) **1** make less; make smaller; decrease: *We have reduced expenses this year. She is trying to reduce her weight.* **2** become less in weight: *His doctor advised him to reduce.* **3** bring down; lower: *Misfortune reduced that poor woman to begging.* **4** change to another form: *The chalk was reduced to powder. If you reduce the fraction $^{15}/_{35}$ to its lowest terms, you have $^{3}/_{7}$.* **5** bring to a certain state, form, or condition: *The teacher soon reduced the noisy class to order. I was reduced to tears by the cruel words.* *v.,* **re·duced, re·duc·ing.**

re·duc·tion (ri duk′shən) **1** reducing or being reduced: *a reduction of ten kilograms in weight.* **2** the amount by which a thing is reduced: *The reduction in cost was $5.* **3** a copy of something on a smaller scale. *n.*

re·dun·dant (ri dun′dənt) not needed; extra: *a redundant word.* *adj.*

red·wing (red′wing′) a blackbird of North America. The male has a scarlet patch on each wing. *n.*

red–winged blackbird (red′wingd′) redwing.

red·wood (red′wu̇d′) **1** an evergreen tree, sometimes growing to a height of 90 metres. **2** the brownish-red wood of this tree. *n.*

reed (rēd) **1** a kind of tall grass with a hollow stalk that grows in wet places. **2** anything made from the stalk of a reed, such as a pipe to blow on or an arrow. **3** a thin piece of wood, metal, or plastic in a musical instrument that produces sound when a current of air moves it. *n.*

☞ **Reed** and **read**[1] are pronounced the same.

reed instrument a musical instrument that produces sound by means of a vibrating reed or reeds: *Oboes, clarinets, and saxophones are reed instruments.*

reef[1] (rēf) a narrow ridge of rocks or sand at or near the surface of the water: *The ship was wrecked on the hidden reef.* *n.*

reef[2] (rēf) **1** the part of a sail that can be rolled or folded up to reduce its size. **2** reduce the size of a sail by rolling or folding up a part of it. 1 *n.,* 2 *v.*

reek (rēk) **1** a strong, unpleasant smell: *We noticed the reek of rotting vegetables as we entered the cottage.* **2** send out a strong, unpleasant smell: *She reeked cheap perfume.* 1 *n.,* 2 *v.*

☞ **Reek** and **wreak** are pronounced the same.

reel[1] (rēl) **1** a frame like a spool, for winding thread, rope, wire, a line for fishing, etc. **2** a spool; a roller. **3** something wound on a reel: *two reels of motion-picture film.* **4** to wind on a reel. **5** draw with a reel or by winding: *He reels in fish.* 1–3 *n.,* 4, 5 *v.*
reel off, say, write, or make in a quick, easy way: *My grandfather can reel off stories by the hour.*

reel[2] (rēl) **1** sway, swing, or rock under a blow or shock: *The boy reeled when the ball struck him.* **2** sway in standing or walking: *The dazed boy reeled down the street.* **3** be in a whirl; be dizzy: *His head was reeling after the fast dance.* *v.*

reel[3] (rēl) **1** a lively dance: *the Highland reel, the Virginia reel.* **2** the music for this dance. *n.*

re–en·ter (rē en′tər) enter again; go in again. *v.*

re–en·try (rē en′trē) entering again or returning, especially of a rocket or spacecraft into the earth's atmosphere after flight in outer space. *n.*

reeve (rēv) in Ontario and the western provinces, the elected head of a rural municipal council; in Ontario, also the head of a village or township council: *The reeve was elected by acclamation.* *n.*

re·fer (ri fėr′) **1** direct attention to or speak about: *Our pastor often referred to the Bible.* **2** relate; apply: *The rule refers only to special cases.* **3** send or direct for information, help, or action: *Our teacher is referring us to many good books.* **4** hand over; submit: *Let's refer our disputes to Mother.* **5** turn for information or help: *A person refers to a dictionary to find the meanings of words.* **6** think of as belonging or due; assign: *Some people refer all their troubles to bad luck instead of to poor work.* *v.,* **re·ferred, re·fer·ring.**

ref·er·ee (ref′ər ē′) **1** a judge of play in certain games or sports, including hockey, football, and boxing. **2** a person to whom something is referred for decision or settlement. **3** to act as a referee. 1, 2 *n.,* 3 *v.,* **ref·er·eed, ref·er·ee·ing.**

ref·er·ence (ref′ər əns) **1** the act of directing the attention: *This history contains many references to larger histories.* **2** a statement referred to: *You will find that reference on page 16.* **3** something used for information or help: *A dictionary is a book of reference. Look in* *the reference library.* **4** a person who can give information about another person's character or ability: *He gave his principal as a reference.* **5** a statement about someone's character or ability: *The boy had excellent references from men for whom he had worked.* **6** relation; respect; regard: *The test is to be taken by all pupils without reference to age or grade.* *n.*

re·fill (rē′ fil′ for 1, rē′fil′ for 2) **1** fill again. **2** something to refill with: *Refills can be bought for some kinds of pens and pencils.* 1 *v.,* 2 *n.*

re·fine (ri fīn′) **1** make pure; become pure: *Sugar, oil, and metals are refined before they are used.* **2** make or become fine, polished, or cultivated: *Reading good books helped to refine her speech.* *v.,* **re·fined, re·fin·ing.**

re·fined (ri fīnd′) **1** free from impurities: *refined sugar.* **2** free from coarseness or vulgarity; polished; cultivated: *refined tastes, refined manners, a refined voice.* *adj.*

re·fine·ment (ri fīn′mənt) **1** a refined quality of feeling, taste, manners, or language: *Good manners and correct speech are marks of refinement.* **2** the act or result of refining: *Gasoline is produced by the refinement of petroleum.* *n.*

re·fin·er·y (ri fīn′ər ē) a building and machinery for purifying metal, sugar, petroleum, or other things. *n., pl.* **re·fin·er·ies.**

re·fit (rē′ fit′ for 1, rē′fit for 2) **1** fit, prepare, or equip for use again: *The old ship was refitted for the voyage.* **2** fitting, preparing, or equipping for use again: *The ship went to the drydock for a refit.* 1 *v.,* **re·fit·ted, re·fit·ting;** 2 *n.*

re·flect (ri flekt′) **1** turn back or throw back light, heat, sound, etc.: *The sidewalks reflect heat on a hot day.* **2** give back an image of: *The mirror reflects my face.* **3** reproduce or show like a mirror: *The newspaper reflected the owner's opinions.* **4** think; think carefully: *Take time to reflect before doing important things.* **5** cast blame, reproach, or discredit: *That child's bad behavior reflects on his home training.* **6** serve to cast or bring: *A brave act reflects credit on the person who does it.* *v.*

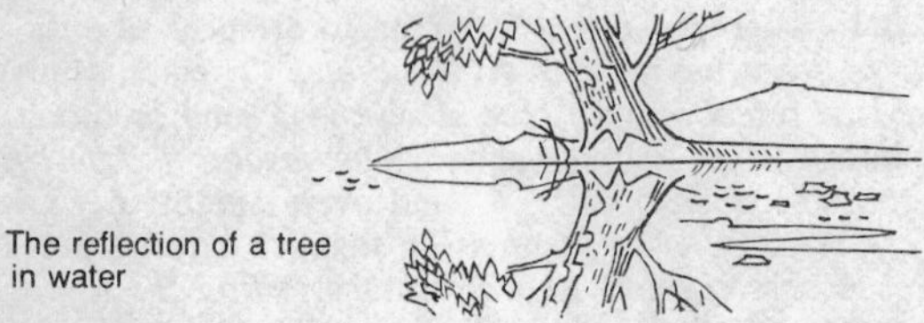

The reflection of a tree in water

re·flec·tion (ri flek′shən) **1** the act of reflecting. **2** something reflected. **3** a likeness; an image: *We saw the reflection of the tree in the still water.* **4** thinking; careful thinking: *On reflection, the plan seemed too dangerous.* **5** an idea or remark resulting from careful thinking; idea; remark. **6** a remark or action that casts blame or discredit. *n.*

re·flec·tor (ri flek′tər) any thing, surface, or device that reflects light, heat, etc., especially a piece of glass or metal for reflecting light in a particular direction. *n.*

re·flex (rē′fleks) an automatic action in direct response to a stimulation of certain nerve cells: *Sneezing and shivering are reflexes.* *n.*

re·for·est (rē′ fôr′ist) plant again with trees. *v.*

re·for·est·a·tion (rē′fôr is tā′shən) replanting or being replanted with trees. *n.*

re·form (ri fôrm′) **1** make better; improve by removing faults: *Prisons should try to reform wrongdoers instead of just punishing them.* **2** correct one's own faults; improve one's behavior: *The boy promised to reform if given another chance.* **3** an improvement; a change to improve conditions: *The new government made many reforms.* 1, 2 *v.,* 3 *n.*

ref·or·ma·tion (ref′ər mā′shən) a change for the better; an improvement. *n.*

re·form·a·to·ry (ri fôr′mə tô′rē) an institution for reforming young offenders against the law; a prison for juveniles. *n., pl.* **re·form·a·to·ries.**

re·form·er (ri fôr′mer) a person who reforms, or tries to reform, some state of affairs, custom, etc.; supporter of reforms. *n.*

re·fract (ri frakt′) bend a ray of light, etc. from a straight course: *Water refracts light.* *v.*

The refraction of light rays entering the water makes the straw appear to be broken at the water line.

re·frac·tion (ri frak′shən) the turning or bending of a ray of light, sound waves, a stream of electrons, etc. when passing from one medium into another of different density. *n.*

re·frain[1] (ri frān′) hold oneself back: *Refrain from wrongdoing.* *v.*

re·frain[2] (ri frān′) a phrase or verse repeated regularly in a song or poem; a chorus. *n.*

re·fresh (ri fresh′) make fresh again; renew: *His bath refreshed him. Cool drinks are refreshing on a warm day. He refreshed his memory by a glance at the book.* *v.*

re·fresh·ing (ri fresh′ing) **1** that refreshes: *a cool, refreshing drink.* **2** welcome as a pleasing change. *adj.*

re·fresh·ment (ri fresh′mənt) **1** refreshing or being refreshed. **2** anything that refreshes. **3 refreshments,** *pl.* food or drink: *Cake and lemonade were the refreshments at our party.* *n.*

re·frig·er·ate (re frij′ər āt) make or keep cool or cold: *Milk, meat, and ice cream must be refrigerated to prevent spoiling.* *v.,* **re·frig·er·at·ed, re·frig·er·at·ing.**

re·frig·er·a·tor (ri frij′ər ā′tər) an appliance, closet, or room equipped for keeping things, especially food and drink, cool. *n.*

ref·uge (ref′yüj) **1** protection or shelter from danger or trouble: *The bear found a refuge in the cave. The cat took refuge in a tree.* **2** any person or thing giving safety, security, or comfort: *Grandmother was Mary's refuge when the other children teased her.* *n.*

ref·u·gee (ref′yə jē′) a person who flees for refuge or safety, especially to a foreign country, in time of war, persecution, or disaster: *Many refugees came from Europe to Canada. The homeless refugees from the*

hat, āge, fär; let, ēqual, tėrm; it, īce
hot, ōpen, ôrder; oil, out; cup, pu̇t, rüle
əbove, takən, pencəl, lemən, circəs
ch, child; ng, long; sh, ship
th, thin; ᴛʜ, then; zh, measure

flooded town were helped by the Red Cross. *n.*

re·fund (ri fund′ for 1, rē′fund for 2 and 3) **1** pay back: *If these shoes do not wear well, the shop will refund your money.* **2** the return of money paid. **3** the money paid back. 1 *v.,* 2, 3 *n.*

re·fus·al (ri fyü′zəl) refusing: *His refusal to play provoked the other boys.* *n.*

re·fuse[1] (ri fyüz′) **1** say 'no' to; reject: *He refuses the offer. She refused him when he asked her to marry him.* **2** say 'no': *She is free to refuse.* **3** say one will not do it, give it, etc.: *He refuses to obey.* *v.,* **re·fused, re·fus·ing.**

ref·use[2] (ref′yüs) useless stuff; waste; rubbish: *The street-cleaning department took away all refuse from the streets.* *n.*

re·fute (ri fyüt′) prove a claim, opinion, or argument to be false or incorrect: *How would you refute the statement that the cow jumped over the moon?* *v.,* **re·fut·ed, re·fut·ing.**

re·gain (ri gān′) **1** get again; recover: *to regain health.* **2** get back to; reach again: *You can regain the main road by turning left two kilometres ahead.* *v.*

re·gal (rē′gəl) **1** belonging to a king; royal: *The regal power descends from father to son.* **2** such as kings have; fit for a king; stately; splendid; magnificent: *It was a regal banquet.* *adj.*

re·gale (ri gāl′) **1** entertain very well; delight with something pleasing: *The old sailor regaled the boys with sea stories.* **2** feast: *The children regaled themselves with ice cream and candy.* *v.,* **re·galed, re·gal·ing.**

re·gard (ri gärd′) **1** think of; consider: *He is regarded as the best doctor in town.* **2** care for; respect: *She always regards her parents' wishes.* **3** thoughtfulness for others and their feelings; care: *Have regard for the feelings of others.* **4** look at; look closely at; watch: *The cat regarded me anxiously when I picked up her kittens.* **5** a look; a steady look: *The man's regard seemed fixed upon some distant object.* **6** good opinion; esteem: *The teacher has high regard for Ron's ability.* **7 regards,** *pl.* good wishes or an expression of esteem: *He sends his regards.* 1, 2, 4 *v.,* 3, 5–7 *n.*

as regards, with respect to; concerning: *As regards money, I have enough.*

in regard to or **with regard to,** concerning; about; regarding: *The teacher spoke to me in regard to being late.*

re·gard·ing (ri gär′ding) concerning; about: *A letter regarding the boy's conduct was sent to his father.* *prep.*

re·gard·less (ri gärd′lis) with no heed; careless: *Regardless of grammar, he said, 'Him and I have went.'* *adj., adv.*

re·gat·ta (ri gat′ə) a boat race; a series of boat races: *the annual regatta of the yacht club.* *n.*

re·gent (rē′jənt) a person who rules when the regular ruler is absent or unfit: *The mother of the boy king acted as regent until he grew up.* *n.*

re·gime (ri zhēm′ or rā zhēm′) **1** a system of government or rule: *Under the old regime women could not vote.* **2** a system of living: *Baby's regime includes two naps a day.* *n.*

reg·i·ment (rej′ə mənt) **1** a unit of an army made up of several companies of soldiers organized into one large group. **2** a large number. **3** form into a regiment or organized group. **4** treat in a strict or uniform manner: *A dictatorship regiments its citizens.* 1, 2 *n.,* 3, 4 *v.*

re·gion (rē′jən) **1** any large part of the earth's surface: *the arctic region.* **2** a place; space; area: *an unhealthful region, a mountainous region, the Maritime region.* **3** a part of the body: *the region of the heart.* **4** a field of thought or action: *the region of modern art, the region of the imagination.* **5** *Cdn.* in Ontario, a geographical division for purposes of government, having wider powers than those of a county. *n.*

re·gion·al (rē′jə nəl) of or in a particular region: *a regional storm.* *adj.*

reg·is·ter (rej′is tər) **1** a list; a record: *A register of attendance is kept in our school.* **2** a book in which a list or record is kept: *Look up his record in the register. He signed the hotel register.* **3** write in a list or record: *Register the names of the new pupils.* **4** have one's name written in a list or record: *You must register if you want to attend the conference.* **5** anything that records: *A cash register shows the amount of money taken in.* **6** indicate; record: *The thermometer registers 20 degrees.* **7** have a letter, package, etc. recorded in the post office, paying extra postage for special care in delivering: *He registered the letter containing the cheque.* **8** show surprise, joy, anger, etc. by the expression on one's face or by actions. **9** the range of a voice or an instrument. **10** an opening with a device to regulate the amount of heated or cooled air passing through from a furnace or ventilator. 1, 2, 5, 9, 10 *n.,* 3, 4, 6–8 *v.*

reg·is·tra·tion (rej′is trā′shən) **1** the act of registering. **2** an entry in a register. **3** the number of people registered: *Registration for camp is higher this year than last.* *n.*

re·gret (ri gret′) **1** feel sorry for or about: *We regretted his absence.* **2** feel sorry; mourn: *He wrote, regretting that he could not visit us.* **3** the feeling of being sorry; sorrow; a sense of loss: *It is a matter of regret that I could not see my mother before leaving.* **4 regrets,** *pl.* a polite reply declining an invitation: *She could not come to the party, but she sent regrets.* 1, 2 *v.,* **re·gret·ted, re·gret·ting;** 3, 4 *n.*

re·gret·ful (ri gret′fəl) sorry; sorrowful; feeling or expressing regret. *adj.*

re·gret·ta·ble (re gret′ə bəl) that should be or is regretted. *adj.*

reg·u·lar (reg′yə lər) **1** fixed by custom or rule; usual: *Our regular sleeping place is in a bedroom.* **2** following some rule or principle; according to rule: *A period is the regular ending for a sentence.* **3** coming, acting, or done again and again at the same time: *Saturday is a regular holiday.* **4** steady; habitual: *regular customers.* **5** well-balanced; even in size, spacing, or speed: *regular teeth, regular breathing.* **6** orderly; methodical: *a regular life.* **7** *Informal.* thorough; complete: *a regular bore.* **8** a full-time member of a group: *The fire department was made up of regulars and volunteers.* **9** a person who is a usual or steady customer, player on a team, etc. 1–7 *adj.,* 8, 9 *n.* **—reg′u·lar·ly,** *adv.*

reg·u·lar·i·ty (reg′yə lar′ə tē or reg′yə ler′ə tē) order; system; steadiness; the state or condition of being regular. *n.*

reg·u·late (reg′yə lāt′) **1** control by rule, principle, or system: *Accidents happen even in the best regulated families.* **2** put in condition to work properly: *My watch is losing time; I will have to have it regulated.* **3** keep at some standard: *This instrument regulates the temperature of the room. v.,* **reg·u·lat·ed, reg·u·lat·ing.**

reg·u·la·tion (reg′yə lā′shən) **1** control by rule, principle, or system. **2** a rule or law: *traffic regulations.* **3** required by some rule: *Soldiers wear a regulation uniform. n.*

re·hears·al (ri hėr′səl) the act of rehearsing; a performance beforehand for practice or drill. *n.*

re·hearse (ri hėrs′) **1** practise for a public performance: *We rehearsed our parts for the school play.* **2** tell in detail; repeat: *The child rehearsed the happenings of the day to his father. v.,* **re·hearsed, re·hears·ing.**

reign (rān) **1** the period of power of a ruler: *The queen's reign lasted fifty years.* **2** to rule: *A king reigns over his kingdom.* **3** ruling; royal power: *The reign of a wise ruler benefits his country.* **4** exist everywhere; prevail: *Silence reigned on the lake, except for the sound of our paddles in the water.* 1, 3 *n.,* 2, 4 *v.*

☛ **Reign, rain,** and **rein** are pronounced the same.

rein (rān) **1** a long, narrow strap or line fastened to the bit of a bridle, by which to guide and control an animal: *A driver or rider of a horse holds the reins in his hands.* See **harness** for picture. **2** a means of control and direction: *The king's oldest son took the reins of government.* **3** to guide and control: *He reined his horse well. Rein your tongue.* 1, 2 *n.,* 3 *v.*

give rein to, let move or act freely without guidance: *give rein to one's feelings.*

☛ **Rein, rain,** and **reign** are pronounced the same.

rein·deer (rān′dēr′) a kind of large deer, with branching antlers, living in northern regions: *The caribou is a North American reindeer.* See **caribou** for picture. *n., pl.* **rein·deer.**

re·in·force (rē′in fôrs′) **1** strengthen with new force or materials: *to reinforce an army or a fleet, to reinforce a garment with an extra thickness of cloth, to reinforce a wall or a bridge.* **2** strengthen: *to reinforce an argument, to reinforce a plea, to reinforce a supply, etc. v.,* **re·in·forced, re·in·forc·ing.**

re·in·force·ment (rē′in fôrs′mənt) **1** strengthening or being strengthened. **2** something that strengthens. **3 reinforcements,** *pl.* extra men and equipment, especially soldiers, warships, planes, etc.: *Reinforcements were sent to the battle front. n.*

re·it·er·ate (rē it′ər āt′) repeat again; say or do several times: *The boy did not move, though the teacher reiterated her command. v.,* **re·it·er·at·ed, re·it·er·at·ing.**

re·ject (ri jekt′ for 1 and 2, rē′jekt for 3) **1** refuse to take, use, believe, consider, grant, etc.: *He rejected our offer of help.* **2** throw away as useless or unsatisfactory: *All the spotted apples were rejected.* **3** anything discarded as unsatisfactory: *The rejects were sold at a lower price.* 1, 2 *v.,* 3 *n.*

re·jec·tion (ri jek′shən) **1** rejecting or being rejected: *He ordered the rejection of the faulty parts.* **2** the thing rejected: *All rejections will be destroyed at once. n.*

re·joice (ri jois′) **1** be glad: *Mother rejoiced at our success.* **2** make glad. *v.,* **re·joiced, re·joic·ing.**

re·join[1] (rē′join′) **1** join again; unite again: *The members of our family will rejoin at Thanksgiving.* **2** join the company of again: *The sailor will rejoin his comrades. v.*

re·join[2] (ri join′) answer; reply: *'Not on your life,' he rejoined. v.*

re·lapse (ri laps′) **1** fall or slip back into a former state or way of acting: *After one cry of surprise, she relapsed into silence.* **2** falling or slipping back into a former state or way of acting: *He seemed to be getting over his illness but had a relapse.* 1 *v.,* **re·lapsed, re·laps·ing;** 2 *n.*

re·late (ri lāt′) **1** give an account of; tell: *The traveller related his adventures.* **2** connect in thought or meaning: *'Better' and 'best' are related to 'good.'* **3** be connected in any way: *We are interested in what relates to ourselves. v.,* **re·lat·ed, re·lat·ing.**

re·lat·ed (ri lā′tid) **1** connected in any way. **2** belonging to the same family; connected by common origin: *Cousins are related. adj.*

re·la·tion (ri lā′shən) **1** the act of telling; an account: *We were interested by his relation of his adventures.* **2** a connection in thought or meaning: *Part of your answer has no relation to the question.* **3** connections or dealings between persons, groups, countries, etc.: *The relation between master and servant has changed greatly during the last century. The relation of mother and child is the closest in the world.* **4 relations,** *pl.* dealings; affairs: *Our firm has business relations with his firm.* **5** a person who belongs to the same family as another, such as a father, brother, aunt, nephew, cousin, etc.; a relative. *n.*

in relation to or **with relation to,** about; concerning: *We must plan in relation to the future.*

re·la·tion·ship (ri lā′shən ship′) **1** connection: *What is the relationship of clouds to rain?* **2** belonging to the same family. *n.*

rel·a·tive (rel′ə tiv) **1** a person who belongs to the same family as another, such as a father, brother, aunt, nephew, cousin, etc. **2** compared to each other: *Before ordering our dinner, we considered the relative merits of chicken and roast beef.* **3** depending for meaning on a relation to something else: *East is a relative term; for example, Regina is east of Vancouver but west of Toronto.* 1 *n.,* 2, 3 *adj.* **—rel′a·tive·ly,** *adv.*

relative to, a about; concerning: *The teacher asked me some questions relative to my plans for the summer.* **b** in comparison with; in proportion to; for: *He is strong relative to his size. A tugboat is broad, relative to its length.*

re·lax (ri laks′) **1** loosen up; make or become less stiff or firm: *Relax your muscles to rest them. Relax when you dance.* **2** make or become less strict or severe; lessen in force: *Discipline is relaxed on the last day of school.* **3** relieve or be relieved from work or effort; give or take recreation or amusement: *Take a vacation and relax.* **4** weaken: *Don't relax your efforts because the examinations are over. v.*

re·lax·a·tion (rē′lak sā′shən) **1** loosening: *the relaxation of the muscles.* **2** a lessening of strictness, severity, force, etc.: *the relaxation of discipline.*

hat, āge, fär; let, ēqual, tėrm; it, īce
hot, ōpen, ôrder; oil, out; cup, pu̇t, rüle
əbove, takən, pencəl, lemən, circəs
ch, child; ng, long; sh, ship
th, thin; ᴛʜ, then; zh, measure

3 recreation; amusement: *Walking and reading are relaxations.* *n.*

re·lay (rē′lā for 1 and 3, ri lā′ or rē′lā for 2) **1** a fresh supply: *New relays of men were sent to the battle front.* **2** take and carry farther: *Messengers will relay your message.* **3** relay race. 1, 3 *n.*, 2 *v.*, **re·layed, re·lay·ing.**

re·lay race (rē′lā) a race in which each member of a team runs, swims, etc. only a certain part of the distance.

re·lease (ri lēs′) **1** let go: *Release the catch and the box will open.* **2** let loose; set free: *She released him from his promise.* **3** relieve: *The nurse will be released from duty at seven o'clock.* **4** letting go; setting free: *The end of the war brought the release of the prisoners.* **5** freedom; relief: *This medicine will give you a release from pain.* **6** a device for releasing a part or parts of a mechanism. 1–3 *v.*, **re·leased, re·leas·ing;** 4–6 *n.*

re·lent (ri lent′) become less harsh; be more tender and merciful: *After hours of questioning the suspect, the police relented and allowed him to rest.* *v.*

re·lent·less (ri lent′lis) without pity; not relenting; harsh: *The storm raged with relentless fury.* *adj.*

rel·e·vance (rel′ə vəns) being to the point; being relevant: *The relevance of his question was doubtful.* *n.*

rel·e·van·cy (rel′ə vən sē) relevance. *n.*

rel·e·vant (rel′ə vənt) bearing upon or connected with the matter in hand; to the point: *relevant questions.* *adj.*

re·li·a·ble (ri lī′ə bəl) worthy of trust; that can be depended on: *Send John to the bank for the money; he is a reliable boy.* *adj.*

re·li·ance (ri lī′əns) trust; dependence; confidence: *A child has reliance on his mother.* *n.*

re·li·ant (ri lī′ənt) trusting or depending; relying. *adj.*

rel·ic (rel′ik) **1** something left from the past: *This ruined bridge is a relic of pioneer days.* **2** something belonging to a holy person, kept as a sacred memorial. *n.*

re·lied (ri līd′) See **rely.** *v.*

Reliefs (def. 8). In the low relief at the left, the figure is almost flat; in the high relief at the right, the figure is much more rounded.

re·lief (ri lēf′) **1** the lessening of, or freeing from, a pain, burden, difficulty, etc.: *His relief from pain was noticeable as the medicine began to work.* **2** something that lessens or frees from pain, burden, difficulty, etc.; aid; help: *Relief was quickly sent to the sufferers from the great fire.* **3** help given to poor people from public funds. **4** something that makes a pleasing change or lessens strain. **5** freedom from a post of duty: *This nurse is on duty from seven in the morning until seven at night, with only two hours' relief.* **6** a change of persons on duty. **7** the persons who relieve others from duty; a person who does this: *The nurse's relief arrives at seven.* **8** the projection of figures and designs from a flat surface in sculpture, drawing, or painting. **9** differences in height between the summits and lowlands of a region. *n.*

in relief, standing out from a surface.

on relief, receiving money to live on from public funds.

relief map a map that shows the different heights of a surface by using shading, colors, etc. or solid materials such as clay.

re·lieve (ri lēv′) **1** make less; make easier; reduce the pain or trouble of: *What will relieve a headache?* **2** set free: *Your coming relieves me of the bother of writing a long letter.* **3** free a person on duty by taking his place. **4** bring aid to; help: *Soldiers were sent to relieve the fort.* **5** give variety to: *The black dress was relieved by red trimmings.* *v.*, **re·lieved, re·liev·ing.**

re·li·gion (ri lij′ən) **1** belief in and worship of God or gods. **2** a particular system of faith and worship: *the Christian religion, the Moslem religion.* **3** a matter of conscience or great personal importance: *She makes a religion of keeping her house neat.* *n.*

re·li·gious (ri lij′əs) **1** of religion; connected with religion: *religious meetings, religious books, religious differences.* **2** much interested in religion; devoted to religion: *She is very religious and goes to church every day.* **3** a monk, nun, friar, etc.; a member of a religious order: *There are six religious teaching in this school.* **4** strict; very careful: *We paid religious attention to the doctor's orders.* 1, 2, 4 *adj.*, 3 *n.*, *pl.* **re·li·gious.**

re·lin·quish (ri ling′kwish) give up; let go: *The small dog relinquished his bone to the big dog. She has relinquished all hope of going to Europe this year.* *v.*

rel·ish (rel′ish) **1** a pleasant taste; a good flavor: *Hunger gives relish to simple food.* **2** something to add flavor to food: *Olives and pickles are relishes.* **3** a kind of pickle made of chopped cucumbers: *She put some relish on her hamburger.* **4** a liking; appetite; enjoyment: *The hungry boy ate with a great relish. The teacher has no relish for old jokes.* **5** like the taste of; like; enjoy: *That cat relishes cream. He did not relish the prospect of staying after school.* 1–4 *n.*, 5 *v.*

re·luc·tance (ri luk′təns) unwillingness; slowness in action because of unwillingness: *She was tired and took part in the game with reluctance.* *n.*

re·luc·tant (ri luk′tənt) unwilling; slow to act because unwilling: *I am reluctant to go out in very cold weather.* *adj.*

re·ly (ri lī′) depend; trust: *Rely on your own efforts. I relied upon your promise.* *v.*, **re·lied, re·ly·ing.**

re·main (ri mān′) **1** continue in a place; stay: *We shall remain at the lake till September.* **2** continue; last; keep on: *The town remains the same year after year.* **3** be left: *A few apples remain on the tree. If you take 2 from 5, 3 remains.* **4 remains,** *pl.* **a** what is left: *The remains of the meal were fed to the dog.* **b** a dead body: *His remains were lowered into the grave.* 1–3 v., 4 *n.*

re·main·der (ri mān′dər) 1 the part left over; the rest: *After studying an hour, she spent the remainder of the afternoon in play.* 2 in arithmetic: **a** a number left over after subtracting one number from another: *In 9 - 2, the remainder is 7.* **b** a number left over after dividing one number by another: *In 14 ÷ 3, the quotient is 4 with a remainder of 2.* *n.*

re·mark (ri märk′) 1 say; speak; comment: *Mother remarked that John's hands would be better for a wash.* 2 something said in a few words; a short statement: *The president made a few remarks.* 3 observe or notice: *Did you remark that oddly shaped cloud?* 1, 3 *v.*, 2 *n.*

re·mark·a·ble (ri mär′kə bəl) worthy of notice; unusual: *a remarkable memory.* *adj.* **—re·mark′a·bly,** *adv.*

re·me·di·al (ri mē′dē əl) intended as a remedy or cure; curing; helping. *adj.*

rem·e·dy (rem′ə dē) 1 anything used to cure or relieve illness: *Aspirin and a mustard plaster are two old cold remedies.* 2 anything intended to put right something bad or wrong: *The free movie was a remedy for the children's bad spirits.* 3 make right; put right; cure: *A thorough cleaning remedied the trouble.* 1, 2 *n.*, **rem·e·dies;** 3 *v.*, **rem·e·died, rem·e·dy·ing.**

re·mem·ber (ri mem′ber) 1 call back to mind: *I can't remember that man's name.* 2 have something return to the mind: *Then I remembered where I was.* 3 keep in mind; take care not to forget: *Remember me when I am gone.* 4 keep in mind as deserving a reward, gift, etc.; make a gift to: *My uncle remembered us in his will.* 5 mention a person as sending friendly greetings: *She asked to be remembered to Sue's sister.* *v.*

re·mem·brance (ri mem′brəns) 1 the act of remembering; a memory. 2 a keepsake; any thing or action that makes a person remember someone else; souvenir: *We treasured the remembrance of our visit.* *n.*

Remembrance Day November 11, the day set aside to honor the memory of those killed in World Wars I and II.

re·mind (ri mīnd′) make one think of something; cause to remember: *This picture reminds me of a story I heard.* *v.*

re·mind·er (ri mīn′dər) something to help one remember. *n.*

re·miss (ri mis′) careless or slack in doing what one should: *A policeman who fails to report a crime is remiss in his duties.* *adj.*

re·mit (ri mit′) 1 send money to a person or place: *Enclosed is our bill; please remit.* 2 refrain from carrying out; cancel: *The king is remitting the prisoner's punishment.* 3 pardon; forgive: *Christ gave His disciples power to remit sins.* 4 make less; decrease: *After we had rowed the boat into calm water, we remitted our efforts.* *v.*, **re·mit·ted, re·mit·ting.**

re·mit·tance (ri mit′əns) 1 sending money to someone at a distance: *The remittance was made by letter.* 2 the money sent. *n.*

remittance man someone who lives abroad on money sent from his relatives at home.

rem·nant (rem′nənt) a small part left: *She bought a remnant of fine silk at the sale.* *This town has only a remnant of its former population.* *n.*

re·mod·el (rē mod′əl) make over; change or alter: *They are remodelling the old barn into a house.* *v.*, **re·mod·elled** or **re·mod·eled, re·mod·el·ling** or **re·mod·el·ing.**

re·mon·strance (ri mon′strəns) a protest; complaint. *n.*

re·mon·strate (ri mon′strāt) speak, reason, or plead in complaint or protest: *The teacher remonstrated with the boy about his low grades.* *v.*, **re·mon·strat·ed, re·mon·strat·ing.**

re·morse (ri môrs′) deep, painful regret for having done wrong: *Because the thief felt remorse for his crime, he confessed.* *n.*

re·morse·less (ri môrs′lis) 1 without remorse. 2 pitiless; cruel: *The remorseless master hit and kicked his dog.* *adj.*

re·mote (ri mōt′) 1 far away from a given place or time: *Dinosaurs lived in remote ages.* 2 out of the way; secluded: *Mail comes to this remote village only once a week.* 3 distantly related or connected: *He is a remote relative.* 4 slight; faint: *I haven't the remotest idea what you mean.* *adj.*, **re·mot·er, re·mot·est.**

remote control control from a distance of a machine, operation, etc., usually by electrical impulses or radio signals: *Some model airplanes can be flown by remote control.*

re·mov·al (ri müv′əl) 1 taking away: *He paid ten dollars for garbage removal.* 2 a change of place: *The store announced its removal to larger quarters.* 3 a dismissal from an office or position. *n.*

re·move (ri müv′) 1 move from a place or position; take off; take away: *Remove your hat.* 2 get rid of; put an end to: *An experiment removed all our doubt about the fact that water is made up of two gases.* 3 dismiss from an office or position: *The council voted to remove the city engineer.* 4 go away; move oneself to another place. 5 moving away. 6 a step or degree of distance: *At every remove the mountain seemed smaller.* 1–4 *v.*, **re·moved, re·mov·ing;** 5, 6 *n.*

rend (rend) 1 pull apart violently; tear: *Wolves will rend a lamb in pieces.* 2 split: *Lightning rent the tree.* 3 disturb violently: *He was rent by a wish to keep the money he found and the knowledge that he ought to return it.* 4 remove with force or violence: *He rent the sword from the knight's hand.* *v.*, **rent, rend·ing.**

ren·der (ren′dər) 1 cause to become; make: *An accident has rendered him helpless.* 2 give; do: *Can I render any aid?* *What service has he rendered to the school?* 3 hand in; report: *The treasurer rendered an account of all the money spent.* 4 pay as due: *The conquered rendered tribute to the conqueror.* 5 bring out the meaning of; represent; perform: *The actor rendered the part of the villain well.* *v.*

ren·dez·vous (ron′də vü) 1 an appointment to meet at a fixed place or time; a meeting by agreement. 2 a meeting place; a gathering place: *The family had two favorite rendezvous, the living room and the lawn.* *n.*, *pl.* **ren·dez·vous** (ron′də vüz).

ren·e·gade (ren′ə gād′) a deserter from a religious faith, a political party, etc.; traitor. *n.*

re·new (ri nyü′ or ri nü′) 1 make new again; make like new; restore: *Rain restores the greenness of the fields.* 2 begin again; say, do, or give again: *He renewed his efforts to open the window.* 3 replace by new material or a new thing of the same sort; fill again:

hat, āge, fär; let, ēqual, tėrm; it, īce
hot, ōpen, ôrder; oil, out; cup, pu̇t, rüle
əbove, takən, pencəl, lemən, circəs
ch, child; ng, long; sh, ship
th, thin; ᴛʜ, then; zh, measure

She renewed the sleeves of her dress. The well renews itself no matter how much water is taken away. **4** give or get for a new period: *We renewed the lease for another year.* *v.*

re·new·al (ri nyü′əl or ri nü′əl) renewing or being renewed: *When hot weather comes, there will be a renewal of interest in swimming.* *n.*

re·nounce (ri nouns′) **1** give up; declare that one gives up: *He renounced his claim to the money.* **2** cast off; refuse to recognize as one's own: *He renounced his wicked son.* *v.,* **re·nounced, re·nounc·ing.**

ren·o·vate (ren′ə vāt′) make like new; restore to good condition: *to renovate a house.* *v.,* **ren·o·vat·ed, ren·o·vat·ing.**

re·nown (ri noun′) the condition of being well-known; fame: *A hero in war wins renown.* *n.*

re·nowned (ri nound′) famous. *adj.*

rent[1] (rent) **1** a regular payment for the use of property. **2** pay at regular times for the use of property: *We rent a house from Mr. Smith.* **3** receive regular pay for the use of property: *He rents several other houses.* **4** be rented: *This farm rents for $1200 a year.* 1 *n.,* 2–4 *v.*

for rent, available in return for rent paid: *That vacant apartment is for rent.*

rent[2] (rent) **1** a tear; a torn place; a split. **2** See **rend.** *The tree was rent by the wind.* 1 *n.,* 2 *v.*

rent·al (ren′təl) **1** an amount received or paid as rent: *The yearly rental of Mrs. Smith's house is $1800.* **2** something rented or able to be rented: *a rental car.* *n.*

re·o·pen (rē ō′pən) **1** open again: *School will reopen in September.* **2** bring up again for discussion: *The case is settled and cannot be reopened.* *v.*

re·paid (ri pād′) See **repay.** *He repaid the money he had borrowed. All debts should be repaid.* *v.*

re·pair[1] (ri per′) **1** put in good condition again; mend: *He repairs shoes.* **2** the act or work of repairing: *Repairs on the school building are made during the summer.* **3** an instance or piece of repairing. **4** a condition fit to be used: *Keeping highways in repair is the responsibility of the provinces.* **5** a condition with regard to the need for repairs: *The house was in very bad repair.* **6** make up for: *How can I repair the harm done?* 1, 6 *v.,* 2–5 *n.*

re·pair[2] (ri per′) go to a place: *After dinner we repaired to the porch.* *v.*

re·past (ri past′) a meal; food: *Breakfast at our house is a light repast.* *n.*

re·pay (ri pā′) **1** pay back; give back: *He repaid the money he had borrowed.* **2** make return for: *No thanks can repay such kindness.* **3** make return to: *The boy's success repaid the teacher for her efforts.* *v.,* **re·paid, re·pay·ing.**

re·peal (ri pēl′) **1** take back; withdraw; do away with: *The law was repealed because it no longer seemed just.* **2** the act of repealing; withdrawal or abolition: *He voted for the repeal of that law.* 1 *v.,* 2 *n.*

re·peat (ri pēt′) **1** do or make again: *to repeat an error.* **2** say again: *to repeat a word for emphasis.* **3** say over; recite: *She can repeat many poems from memory.* **4** say after another says: *Repeat the words after me.* **5** tell to anyone else: *Promise not to repeat this.* **6** a repeating. **7** the thing repeated: *We saw the repeat on television.* 1–5 *v.,* 6, 7 *n.*

re·peat·ed (ri pēt′id) said, done, made, or happening a number of times: *Her repeated efforts at last won success.* *adj.* **—re·peat′ed·ly,** *adv.*

re·pel (ri pel′) **1** force back; drive back; drive away: *They repelled the enemy. We can repel bad thoughts.* **2** keep off or out; fail to mix with: *Oil and water repel each other. This tent repels moisture.* **3** force apart or away by some inherent force: *The positive poles of two magnets repel each other.* **4** be displeasing to; cause dislike in: *Spiders and worms repel some children.* *v.,* **re·pelled, re·pel·ling.**

re·pel·lent (ri pel′ənt) **1** disagreeable; unattractive: *He has a cold, repellent manner.* **2** anything that repels: *We sprayed insect repellent on our arms and legs to keep the mosquitoes away.* 1 *adj.,* 2 *n.*

re·pent (ri pent′) **1** feel sorry for sin: *He repented after he had done wrong.* **2** feel sorry for; regret: *She bought the red hat and has repented her choice.* *v.*

re·pent·ance (ri pen′təns) sorrow for doing wrong; regret. *n.*

re·pent·ant (ri pen′tənt) repenting; feeling regret; sorry for doing wrong. *adj.*

rep·er·toire (rep′ər twär′) the list of plays, operas, parts, pieces, etc., that a company, an actor, a musician, or a singer is prepared to perform. *n.*

rep·e·ti·tion (rep′ə tish′ən) **1** repeating; doing or saying again: *Repetition helps learning. Any repetition of the offence will be punished.* **2** a repeated occurrence; the thing repeated. *n.*

re·place (ri plās′) **1** fill or take the place of: *Dave replaced Don as captain.* **2** get another in place of: *I will replace the cup I broke.* **3** put back; put in place again: *Replace the books on the shelves.* *v.,* **re·placed, re·plac·ing.**

re·place·ment (ri plās′mənt) **1** replacing or being replaced: *The company agreed to the replacement of all wooden desks with steel ones.* **2** something or someone that replaces. *n.*

re·plen·ish (ri plen′ish) fill again; provide a new supply for: *Her supply of towels needs replenishing. You had better replenish the fire.* *v.*

rep·li·ca (rep′lə kə) a copy; reproduction: *The artist made a replica of his picture. He is a replica of his father in looks.* *n.*

re·ply (ri plī′) **1** respond or answer: *She replied that she was tired. I will reply to the letter next week.* **2** an answer: *When can I expect a reply?* 1 *v.,* **re·plied, re·ply·ing;** 2 *n., pl.* **re·plies.**

re·port (ri pôrt′) **1** an account or statement of facts: *a school report, a report of a traffic accident.* **2** give an account of something; make a report; state formally: *Our treasurer reports that all dues are paid up.* **3** repeat or give an account of; describe; tell: *The radio reports the news and weather.* **4** present oneself: *Report for work at eight o'clock.* **5** the sound of a shot or an explosion:

the report of a gun. 6 common talk; rumor: *Report has it that our neighbors are leaving town.* 1, 5, 6 *n.*, 2–4 *v.*

report card a report sent regularly by a school to parents or guardians showing the quality of a student's work.

re·port·er (ri pôr′tər) a person who gathers news for a newspaper, magazine, radio station, etc. *n.*

re·pose[1] (ri pōz′) 1 rest or sleep: *Do not disturb her repose.* 2 lie at rest: *The cat reposed upon the cushion.* 3 quietness; ease: *She has repose of manner.* 1, 3 *n.*, 2 *v.*, **re·posed, re·pos·ing.**

re·pose[2] (ri pōz′) put; place: *We repose complete confidence in his honesty.* *v.*, **re·posed, re·pos·ing.**

rep·re·sent (rep′ri zent′) 1 stand for; be a sign or symbol of: *The stars on this map represent cities.* 2 act in place of; speak and act for: *We chose a committee to represent us.* 3 act the part of: *Each child will represent an animal at the party.* 4 show in a picture, statue, carving, etc.; give a likeness of; portray: *This painting represents the Fathers of Confederation.* 5 describe; set forth: *He represented the plan as safe, but it was not.* 6 bring before the mind; make one think of: *Images in the mind represent real objects.* *v.*

rep·re·sen·ta·tion (rep′ri zen tā′shən) 1 representing or being represented: *'Taxation without representation is tyranny.'* 2 a likeness or model; picture. 3 the performance of a play; presentation: *A representation of the story of Robin Hood will be given today.* 4 account; statement: *They deceived us by false representations.* *n.*

rep·re·sent·a·tive (rep′ri zen′tə tiv) 1 a person appointed or elected to act or speak for others: *He attended the meeting as the representative of his company.* 2 having its citizens represented by chosen persons: *a representative government.* 3 representing: *Images representative of animals were made by the children out of clay.* 4 a typical example; a type: *The tiger is a representative of the cat family.* 5 serving as an example of; typical: *Oak, birch, and maple are representative North American hardwoods.* 1, 4 *n.*, 2, 3, 5 *adj.*

re·press (ri pres′) 1 prevent from acting; check: *She repressed her desire to laugh.* 2 keep down; put down; suppress: *The government repressed a revolt.* *v.*

re·pres·sion (ri presh′ən) 1 repressing: *The repression of a laugh made him choke.* 2 being repressed: *Repression made her behave worse.* *n.*

re·prieve (ri prēv′) 1 delay the execution of a person condemned to death. 2 a delay in carrying out punishment, especially the death penalty. 3 postpone something unpleasant or unwanted. 4 the temporary delay or postponement of something unpleasant or unwanted; a respite: *We had a reprieve of two days, and then the rain started again.* 1, 3 *v.*, **re·prieved, re·priev·ing**; 2, 4 *n.*

rep·ri·mand (rep′rə mand′) 1 a formal or official scolding. 2 find fault with formally or officially: *The principal reprimanded the boys for smoking.* 1 *n.*, 2 *v.*

re·proach (ri prōch′) 1 blame or censure: *Bad people bring reproach on their families.* 2 scold or blame; find fault with: *Father reproached me for being late.* 3 a cause of blame or disgrace: *A coward is a reproach to a regiment.* 1, 3 *n.*, 2 *v.*

re·proach·ful (ri prōch′fəl) full of reproach; expressing reproach. *adj.*

re·pro·duce (rē′prə dyüs′ or rē′prə düs′) 1 produce again: *A radio reproduces sounds.* 2 make a copy of: *He took the picture to the printer to be reproduced.* 3 produce offspring: *Most plants reproduce by seeds.* *v.*, **re·pro·duced, re·pro·duc·ing.**

re·pro·duc·tion (rē′prə duk′shən) 1 reproducing or being reproduced: *the reproduction of sounds.* 2 a copy. 3 the process by which offspring are produced. *n.*

re·proof (ri prüf′) words of blame or disapproval; blame. *n.*

re·prove (ri prüv′) find fault with; blame: *Reprove the boy for teasing the cat.* *v.*, **re·proved, re·prov·ing.**

rep·tile (rep′tīl) any of the group of cold-blooded animals that creep or crawl: *Snakes, lizards, turtles, alligators, and crocodiles are reptiles.* *n.*

re·pub·lic (ri pub′lik) a nation or state in which the citizens elect representatives to manage the government, which is usually headed by a president rather than a monarch: *The United States and Mexico are republics.* *n.*

re·pub·li·can (ri pub′lə kən) 1 of a republic; like that of a republic: *Many countries have a republican form of government.* 2 a person who favors a republic: *The republicans fought with the royalists.* 1 *adj.*, 2 *n.*

re·pu·di·ate (ri pyü′dē āt′) 1 refuse to accept; reject: *to repudiate a doctrine.* 2 refuse to acknowledge or pay: *to repudiate a debt.* 3 cast off; disown: *to repudiate a son.* *v.*, **re·pu·di·at·ed, re·pu·di·at·ing.**

re·pug·nant (ri pug′nənt) disagreeable or offensive; distasteful: *Work is repugnant to lazy people.* *adj.*

re·pulse (ri puls′) 1 drive back; repel: *Our soldiers repulsed the enemy.* 2 driving back; being driven back: *After the second repulse, the enemy surrendered.* 3 refuse to accept; reject: *She coldly repulsed him.* 4 a refusal; rejection: *The repulse was quite unexpected.* 1, 3 *v.*, **re·pulsed, re·puls·ing**; 2, 4 *n.*

re·pul·sive (ri pul′siv) causing disgust or strong dislike: *Snakes are repulsive to some people.* *adj.*

rep·u·ta·ble (rep′yə tə bəl) having a good reputation; well thought of: *a reputable businessman.* *adj.*

rep·u·ta·tion (rep′yə tā′shən) 1 what people think and say the character of a person or thing is; character in the opinion of others; name: *This store has an excellent reputation for fair dealing.* 2 a good name; a high standing in the opinion of others: *Cheating at the game ruined that player's reputation.* 3 fame: *Some movie actors enjoy a world-wide reputation.* *n.*

re·pute (ri pyüt′) 1 reputation: *This is a district of bad repute because so many robberies occur here.* 2 consider; suppose; generally suppose to be: *He is reputed the richest man in the city.* 1 *n.*, 2 *v.*, **re·put·ed, re·put·ing.**

re·put·ed (ri pyüt′id) generally supposed: *the reputed author of a book.* *adj.*

re·quest (ri kwest′) 1 ask for; ask as a favor: *He requested a loan from the bank.* 2 ask: *He requested her to go with him.* 3 the act of asking: *Your request for a ticket was made too late.* 4 what is asked for: *He granted my request.* 5 being asked for or sought after:

She is such a good dancer that she is in great request. 1, 2 *v.*, 3–5 *n.*

by request, in response to a request: *The school remained open all evening by request of the principal.*

re·quire (ri kwīr′) 1 need: *The government requires more money.* 2 demand; order; command: *The rules required us all to be present.* *v.*, **re·quired, re·quir·ing.**

re·quire·ment (ri kwīr′mənt) 1 a need; the thing needed: *Patience is a requirement in teaching.* 2 a demand; the thing demanded: *He has filled the college's requirements for graduation.* *n.*

req·ui·site (rek′wə zit) 1 required by circumstances; needed; necessary: *the requisite qualities for a leader, the number of votes requisite for election.* 2 a requirement; the thing needed: *Food and air are requisites for life.* 1 *adj.*, 2 *n.*

req·ui·si·tion (rek′wə zish′ən) 1 a demand made, especially a formal written demand: *The officer sent in his requisition for supplies.* 2 demand or take by authority: *to requisition supplies, horses, or labor.* 1 *n.*, 2 *v.*

re·quite (ri kwīt′) 1 pay back; make return for: *The Bible tells us to requite evil with good.* 2 make return to: *The knight requited the boy for his warning.* *v.*, **re·quit·ed, re·quit·ing.**

res·cue (res′kyü) 1 save from danger, capture, harm, etc.; free; deliver: *The dog rescued the child from drowning.* 2 saving or freeing from danger, capture, harm, etc.: *The fireman was praised for his brave rescue of the children in the burning house. A dog was chasing our cat when Ruth came to the rescue.* 1 *v.*, **res·cued, res·cu·ing;** 2 *n.* **—res′cu·er,** *n.*

re·search (ri sėrch′ or rē′sėrch) 1 a careful hunting for facts or truth; inquiry; investigation: *Medical research has done much to lessen disease.* 2 carry out research. 1 *n.*, 2 *v.*

re·sem·blance (ri zem′bləns) a similar appearance; likeness: *Twins often show great resemblance.* *n.*

re·sem·ble (ri zem′bəl) be like; have likeness to in form, figure, or qualities: *An orange resembles a grapefruit.* *v.*, **re·sem·bled, re·sem·bling.**

re·sent (ri zent′) feel injured and angry at; feel indignation at: *She resented being called a baby. Our cat seems to resent having anyone sit in its chair.* *v.*

re·sent·ful (ri zent′fəl) feeling resentment; injured and angry; showing resentment. *adj.*

re·sent·ment (ri zent′mənt) the feeling that one has at being injured or insulted; indignation: *Everyone feels resentment at being treated unfairly.* *n.*

res·er·va·tion (rez′ər vā′shən) 1 keeping back; hiding in part; something not expressed: *She outwardly approved the plan—with the mental reservation that she would change it to suit herself.* 2 a limiting condition: *The committee accepted the plan with reservations plainly stated.* 3 land set aside for a special purpose: *Many Indian bands live on reservations.* 4 an arrangement to keep a thing for a person; the securing of accommodations, etc. in advance: *We make reservations for rooms at a hotel, seats at a theatre or stadium, and passage on a steamship.* *n.*

re·serve (ri zėrv′) 1 keep back; hold back: *Mother reserved her complaint about my messy room until my friend left.* 2 set apart: *He reserves his evenings to spend with his family.* 3 save for use later: *Reserve enough money for your fare home.* 4 something kept

hat, āge, fär; let, ēqual, tėrm; it, īce
hot, ōpen, ôrder; oil, out; cup, pu̇t, rüle
əbove, takən, pencəl, lemən, circəs
ch, child; ng, long; sh, ship
th, thin; ᴛʜ, then; zh, measure

back for future use; a store: *a reserve of energy. Banks must keep a reserve of money.* 5 soldiers kept ready to help in battle: *Reserves will be sent to help the men fighting at the front.* 6 public land set apart for a special purpose: *a timber reserve.* 7 land set apart for the use of Indians. 8 keeping back; holding back; reservation: *You may speak before her without reserve.* 9 self-restraint in action or speech. 10 a silent manner that keeps people from making friends easily. 1–3 *v.*, **re·served, re·serv·ing;** 4–10 *n.*

re·served (ri zėrvd′) 1 kept in reserve; kept by special arrangement: *reserved seats.* 2 set apart. 3 self-restrained in action or speech. *adj.*

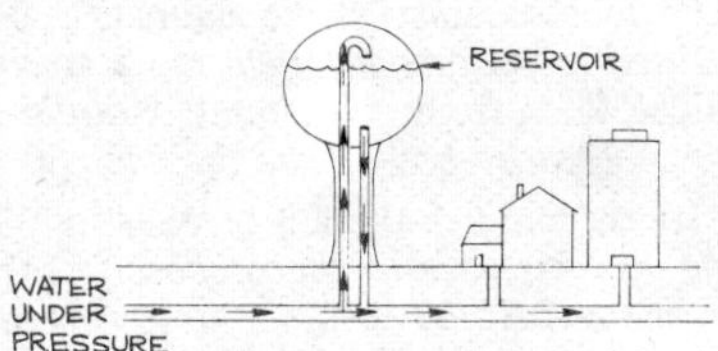

A tank type of reservoir, showing the pipes inside

res·er·voir (rez′ər vwär′ or rez′ər vwôr′) 1 a place where water is collected and stored for use: *This reservoir supplies the entire city.* 2 anything to hold a liquid: *A fountain pen has an ink reservoir.* 3 a place where anything is collected and stored: *His mind was a reservoir of facts.* 4 a great supply: *a reservoir of weapons.* *n.*

re·side (ri zīd′) 1 live in or at for a long time; dwell: *This family has resided in our town for 100 years.* 2 be in; exist in: *Her charm resides in her happy smile.* *v.*, **re·sid·ed, re·sid·ing.**

res·i·dence (rez′ə dəns) 1 a house or home; the place where a person lives. 2 residing; living; dwelling: *Long residence in France made him very fond of the French people.* 3 a building in which students, nurses, etc. live: *A new residence is being built at the university.* *n.*

res·i·dent (rez′ə dənt) 1 a person living in a place, not a visitor: *The residents of the town are proud of its new library.* 2 staying; dwelling in a place: *A resident owner lives on his property. Dr. Jones is a resident physician at the hospital.* 1 *n.*, 2 *adj.*

res·i·den·tial (rez′ə den′shəl) of or having something to do with homes: *a residential district outside the city.* *adj.*

res·i·due (rez′ə dyü′ or rez′ə dü′) what remains after a part is taken; a remainder: *The syrup had dried up, leaving a sticky residue. Mr. Smith's will directed that, after payment of all debts, the residue of his property should go to his son.* *n.*

re·sign (ri zīn′) 1 give up a job, office, or position: *The manager of the football team resigned.* 2 give up: *The M.P. resigned his seat in Parliament.* *v.*

resign oneself, give in or yield, often unwillingly but

without complaint: *He had to resign himself to a week in bed when he hurt his back.*

res·ig·na·tion (rez′ig nā′shən) 1 the act of resigning: *There have been so many resignations from the committee that a new one must be formed.* 2 a written statement giving notice that one resigns. 3 patient acceptance; quiet submission: *She bore the pain with resignation.* *n.*

re·signed (ri zīnd′) accepting what comes without complaint. *adj.*

res·in (rez′ən) a sticky substance that flows from some plants and trees, especially the pine and fir. It is also produced chemically and is used in medicines, varnishes, etc.: *When pine resin is heated, it yields turpentine; the hard, yellow substance that remains is called rosin.* *n.*

res·in·ous (rez′ə nəs) 1 of resin. 2 like resin. 3 containing resin; full of resin. *adj.*

re·sist (ri zist′) 1 act against; strive against; oppose: *The window resisted his efforts to open it.* 2 strive successfully against; keep from; withstand: *I could not resist laughing. A healthy boy resists disease.* *v.*

re·sist·ance (ri zis′təns) 1 the act of resisting: *The bank clerk made no resistance to the robbers.* 2 the power to resist: *She has little resistance to germs and so is often ill.* 3 an opposition; an opposing force; some thing or act that resists: *An airplane can overcome the resistance of the air and go in the desired direction, but an ordinary balloon just drifts.* 4 the power of a conductor to oppose the passage of an electric current and change electric energy into heat: *The elements of electric stoves have a high resistance.* *n.*

re·sist·ant (ri zis′tənt) resisting. *adj.*

res·o·lute (rez′ə lüt′) determined; firm; bold: *He was resolute in his attempt to climb to the top of the mountain. The captain's resolute words cheered the team.* *adj.*

res·o·lu·tion (rez′ə lü′shən) 1 something decided on or determined: *He made a resolution to get up early.* 2 the power of holding firmly to a purpose; determination: *The man's firm resolution overcame the handicap of poverty.* 3 a formal expression of opinion: *The club passed a resolution thanking the teacher for her help.* 4 the act or result of solving; solution: *the resolution of a problem.* *n.*

re·solve (ri zolv′) 1 make up one's mind; determine; decide: *He resolved to do better work in the future.* 2 the thing determined or decided on: *He kept his resolve to stop smoking.* 3 firmness in carrying out a purpose; determination: *The general was a man of great resolve.* 4 decide by vote: *It was resolved that our class should have a picnic.* 5 answer and explain; solve: *His letter resolved all our doubts.* 6 break into parts; break up: *Some chemical compounds can be resolved by heat.* 1, 4–6 *v.*, **re·solved, re·solv·ing;** 2, 3 *n.*

re·solved (ri zolvd′) determined; firm; resolute. *adj.*

res·o·nant (rez′ə nənt) 1 resounding; continuing to sound: *a resonant tone.* 2 tending to increase or prolong sounds: *A guitar has a resonant body.* *adj.*

re·sort (ri zôrt′) 1 go; go often: *Many people resort to the beaches in hot weather.* 2 a place people go to, usually for relaxation and recreation: *There are many summer resorts in the mountains.* 3 turn for help: *The mother resorted to punishment to make the child obey.* 4 turning to for help: *The resort to force is forbidden in this school.* 5 a person or thing turned to for help: *Friends are usually the best resort in trouble.* 1, 3 *v.*, 2, 4, 5 *n.*

re·sound (ri zound′) 1 give back sound; echo: *The hills resounded when we shouted.* 2 sound loudly: *Radios resound from every house.* 3 be filled with sound: *The room resounded with the children's shouts.* 4 be much talked about: *The fame of the first flight across the Atlantic resounded all over the world.* *v.*

re·source (ri zôrs′ or ri sôrs′) 1 any supply that will meet a need: *resources of money, resources of knowledge, resources of strength.* 2 any means of getting success or getting out of trouble: *Climbing a tree is a cat's resource when chased by a dog.* 3 skill in meeting difficulties, getting out of trouble, etc. 4 **natural resources,** *pl.* the things provided by nature that add to a country's wealth: *Canada's natural resources include fish, lumber, oil, and minerals.* *n.*

re·source·ful (ri zôrs′fəl or ri sôrs′fəl) good at thinking of ways to do things: *That resourceful boy mowed lawns all summer to buy a new bicycle.* *adj.*

re·spect (ri spekt′) 1 honor; esteem: *Children should show respect to those who are older and wiser.* 2 feel or show honor or esteem for: *We respect an honest person.* 3 **respects,** *pl.* expressions of respect; regards: *Give her my respects. We must pay our respects to the mayor.* 4 care; consideration: *We should show respect for school buildings, parks, and other public property.* 5 to care for; show consideration for: *Respect the ideas and feelings of others.* 6 a feature; a point or detail: *He is a good boy in every respect.* 7 reference; relation: *We must plan with respect to the future.* 1, 3, 4, 6, 7 *n.*, 2, 5 *v.*

re·spect·a·ble (ri spek′tə bəl) 1 worthy of respect; having a good reputation: *Respectable citizens obey the laws.* 2 fairly good; moderate in size or quality: *His record in school was always respectable, but never brilliant.* 3 good enough to use; fit to be seen: *That dirty dress is not respectable.* *adj.*

re·spect·ful (ri spekt′fəl) showing respect; polite: *He was always respectful to older people.* *adj.*

re·spect·ing (ri spek′ting) regarding; about; concerning: *A discussion arose respecting the merits of different automobiles.* *prep.*

re·spec·tive (ri spek′tiv) belonging to each; particular; individual: *The classes went to their respective rooms.* *adj.*

re·spec·tive·ly (ri spek′tiv lē) as regards each one in his turn or in the order mentioned: *Bob, Dick, and Tom are 6, 8, and 10 years old respectively.* *adv.*

res·pi·ra·tion (res′pə rā′shən) breathing: *Her bad cold hinders respiration.* *n.*

res·pi·ra·to·ry (res′pə rə tô′rē) having to do with breathing: *The lungs are respiratory organs.* *adj.*

res·pite (res′pit or res′pīt) a time of relief and rest; a lull: *A thick cloud brought a respite from the glare of the sun.* *n.*

re·splend·ent (ri splen′dənt) very bright; shining; splendid: *The queen was resplendent with jewels.* *adj.*

re·spond (ri spond′) 1 answer; reply: *He responded briefly to the question.* 2 act in answer; react: *A dog*

hat, āge, fär; let, ēqual, tėrm; it, īce
hot, ōpen, ôrder; oil, out; cup, pu̇t, rüle
əbove, takən, pencəl, lemən, circəs
ch, child; ng, long; sh, ship
th, thin; ᴛʜ, then; zh, measure

responds to kind treatment by loving its master. She responded quickly to the medicine and was well in a few days. v.

re·sponse (ri spons′) 1 an answer by word or act: *Her response to my letter was prompt. She laughed in response to his joke.* 2 a set of words said or sung by the congregation or choir in answer to the minister. 3 the reaction of body or mind to a stimulus. *n.*

re·spon·si·bil·i·ty (ri spon′sə bil′ə tē) 1 being responsible; obligation: *A little child does not feel much responsibility.* 2 something for which one is responsible: *Keeping house and caring for the children are her responsibilities. n., pl.* **re·spon·si·bil·i·ties.**

re·spon·si·ble (ri spon′sə bəl) 1 obliged or expected to account for; accountable; answerable: *Each pupil is responsible for the care of the books given him.* 2 deserving credit or blame: *Rain was responsible for the small attendance.* 3 trustworthy; reliable: *The class chose a responsible pupil to take care of its money.* 4 involving obligation or duties: *The Prime Minister holds one of the most responsible positions in our country. adj.*

re·spon·sive (ri spon′siv) 1 making answer; responding: *a responsive glance.* 2 easily moved; responding readily: *a very friendly person with a responsive nature. adj.*

rest[1] (rest) 1 sleep; repose: *The children had a good night's rest.* 2 be still or quiet; sleep: *My mother rests for an hour every afternoon.* 3 quiet; freedom from work, disturbance, trouble, pain, etc.: *The workmen were allowed an hour for rest. The medicine gave the sick man a short rest from pain.* 4 be free from work, trouble, pain, etc.: *He was able to rest during his holidays.* 5 the absence of motion; stillness: *The driver brought the car to rest. The lake was at rest.* 6 give rest to; refresh by rest: *Stop and rest your horse.* 7 be supported; lean; lie: *The ladder rested against the wall. The roof of the porch rests on columns.* 8 place for support; lay; lean: *to rest one's head in one's hands. He rested his rifle against the wall.* 9 a support; something to lean on. 10 to look; be fixed: *Our eyes rested on the open book.* 11 be at ease: *Don't let Mrs. Smith rest until she promises to visit us.* 12 depend; rely; be based: *Our hope rests on you.* 13 be found; be present; lie: *In a democracy, government rests with the people. A smile rested on the girl's lips.* 14 in music, a pause. 15 a mark to show such a pause. See **bar** for picture. 16 be dead; lie in the grave: *The old man rests with his forefathers in the village cemetery.* 1, 3, 5, 9, 14, 15 *n.*, 2, 4, 6–8, 10–13, 16 *v.*
lay to rest, bury: *Lay his bones to rest.*
☞ **Rest** and **wrest** are pronounced the same.

rest[2] (rest) 1 what is left; those that are left: *The sun was out in the morning but it rained for the rest of the day. One horse was running ahead of the rest.* 2 continue to be; remain: *The final decision rests with Father.* 1 *n.*, 2 *v.*
☞ See note at **rest**[1].

res·tau·rant (res′tə ront or res′tront) a place to buy and eat a meal. *n.*

rest·ful (rest′fəl) 1 full of rest; giving rest: *She had a restful nap.* 2 quiet; peaceful. *adj.*

rest·less (rest′lis) 1 unable to rest; uneasy: *The dog seemed restless, as if he sensed some danger.* 2 without rest or sleep; not restful: *The sick child passed a restless night.* 3 rarely or never still or quiet; always moving: *That nervous boy is very restless. adj.*

res·to·ra·tion (res′tə rā′shən) 1 the act of restoring or being restored; bringing back to a former condition: *the restoration of health, the restoration of a king.* 2 something restored: *The house we slept in was a restoration of a Loyalist mansion. n.*

re·store (ri stôr′) 1 bring back; establish again: *The police restored order.* 2 bring back to a former condition or to a normal condition: *The old house has been restored. He is restored to health.* 3 give back; put back: *The honest boy restored the money to its owner. v.,* **re·stored, re·stor·ing.**

re·strain (ri strān′) hold back; keep down; keep in check; keep within limits: *She could not restrain her curiosity to see what was in the box. He restrained the excited dog when guests came. v.*

re·straint (ri strānt′) 1 restraining or being restrained: *Noisy children sometimes need restraint.* 2 a means of restraining: *A horse's bridle is a restraint.* 3 control of natural feeling; reserve: *He was very angry, but he spoke with restraint. n.*

re·strict (ri strikt′) keep within limits; confine: *Our club membership is restricted to twelve. v.*

re·stric·tion (ri strik′shən) 1 something that restricts; a limiting condition or rule: *The restrictions on the use of the playground are: No fighting; no damaging property.* 2 restricting or being restricted: *This park is open to the public without restriction. n.*

rest room a washroom in a public building, theatre, store, service station, etc.

re·sult (ri zult′) 1 that which happens as the outcome of something: *The result of his fall was a broken leg. We were happy at the result of the hockey game.* 2 a good or useful result: *We want results, not talk.* 3 be a result; follow as a consequence: *Sickness often results from eating too much.* 4 have as a result; end: *Eating too much often results in sickness.* 5 an answer obtained in arithmetic. 1, 2, 5 *n.*, 3, 4 *v.*

re·sume (ri züm′ or ri zyüm′) 1 begin again; go on: *Resume reading where we left off.* 2 get or take again: *Those standing may resume their seats. v.,* **re·sumed, re·sum·ing.**

re·sump·tion (ri zump′shən) resuming: *the resumption of duties after absence. n.*

res·ur·rect (rez′ə rekt′) 1 raise from the dead; bring back to life. 2 bring back to sight or into use: *to resurrect an ancient custom. v.*

res·ur·rec·tion (rez′ə rek′shən) 1 coming to life again; rising from the dead. 2 restoration from decay; revival: *The resurrection of an old plan for rebuilding the city.* 3 **Resurrection,** the rising again of Christ after His death and burial. *n.*

re·sus·ci·tate (ri sus′ə tāt′) bring or come back to life or consciousness; revive: *The doctor resuscitated the man who had nearly drowned. v.*

re·tail (rē′tāl) 1 the sale of goods in small quantities directly to the final consumer: *Most stores sell at retail. This suit costs $110 retail.* 2 selling in small quantities to the final consumer: *Retail merchants usually buy their goods in large quantities from wholesale dealers, who buy directly from the factories.* 3 sell at retail: *This suit retails for $110.* 1 *n.*, 2 *adj.*, 3 *v.*

re·tail·er (rē′tāl ər) a retail merchant or dealer. *n.*

re·tain (ri tān′) 1 continue to have or hold; keep: *China dishes retain heat longer than metal pans do. The old lady has retained all her interest in life.* 2 keep in mind; remember: *She retained the tune but not the words of the song.* 3 employ by payment of a fee: *He retained the best lawyer in the city.* *v.*

re·tain·er (ri tān′ər) a person who serves someone of rank; an attendant or follower: *The king had many retainers.* *n.*

re·tal·i·ate (ri tal′ē āt′) pay back a wrong or injury; to return like for like, usually to return evil for evil: *If we insult people, they will retaliate.* *v.*, **re·tal·i·at·ed, re·tal·i·at·ing.**

re·tard (ri tärd′) make slow; delay the progress of; keep back; hinder: *Lack of education retards progress. Bad roads retarded the car.* *v.*

re·tard·ed (ri tär′dəd) limited in mental development; backward. *adj.*

retch (rech) make efforts to vomit. *v.*

ret·i·na (ret′ə nə) the layer of cells at the back of the eyeball, which is sensitive to light and receives the images of things looked at. See **eye** for picture. *n.*

ret·i·nue (ret′ə nyü′) a group of attendants or retainers; a following: *The king's retinue accompanied him on the journey.* *n.*

re·tire (ri tīr′) 1 give up an office, occupation, etc.: *The teacher expects to retire at 65.* 2 remove from an office, occupation, etc. 3 go away, especially to be quiet: *She retired to a convent.* 4 withdraw; draw back; send back: *The government retires worn or torn dollar bills from use.* 5 go back; retreat: *The enemy retired before the advance of our troops.* 6 go to bed: *We retire early.* 7 in baseball and cricket, to put out a batter or a side. *v.*, **re·tired, re·tir·ing.**

re·tired (ri tīrd′) 1 withdrawn from one's occupation: *a retired sea captain, a retired teacher.* 2 reserved; retiring: *She has a shy, retired nature.* 3 secluded; shut off; hidden: *a retired spot.* *adj.*

re·tire·ment (ri tīr′mənt) 1 retiring or being retired; withdrawal: *The teacher's retirement from teaching was regretted by the whole school. The old man was enjoying his retirement.* 2 a quiet way or place of living: *She lives in retirement, neither making nor receiving visits.* *n.*

re·tir·ing (ri tīr′ing) shrinking from society or publicity; shy: *a retiring nature.* *adj.*

re·tort (ri tôrt′) 1 reply quickly or sharply: *'It's none of your business,' he retorted.* 2 a sharp or witty reply: *'Why are your teeth so sharp?' asked Red Riding Hood. 'The better to eat you with,' was the wolf's retort.* 1 *v.*, 2 *n.*

re·trace (ri trās′) go back over: *We retraced our steps to where we started.* *v.*, **re·traced, re·trac·ing.**

re·tract (ri trakt′) 1 draw back or in: *The kitten retracted her claws and purred when I petted her.* 2 withdraw; take back: *retract an offer or an opinion.* *v.*

re·tread (rē tred′ for 1; rē′tred′ for 2) 1 put a new tread on. 2 a tire that has been retreaded. 1 *v.*, 2 *n.*

re·treat (ri trēt′) 1 go back; move back; withdraw: *Seeing the big dog, the tramp retreated rapidly. He retreated to his cottage at weekends.* 2 going back or withdrawing: *The army's retreat was orderly.* 3 a signal for a retreat: *The drums beat a retreat.* 4 a signal blown on a trumpet or bugle when the flag is lowered at sunset. 5 a safe, quiet place; a place of rest or refuge. 1 *v.*, 2–5 *n.*

beat a retreat, run away; retreat: *We dropped the apples and beat a hasty retreat when the farmer shouted at us.*

re·trieve (ri trēv′) 1 get again; recover: *to retrieve a lost pocketbook.* 2 bring back to a former or better condition; restore: *to retrieve one's fortunes.* 3 make good; make amends for; repair: *A person can retrieve a mistake, a loss, or a defeat.* 4 find and bring to a person: *Some dogs can be trained to retrieve game.* *v.*, **re·trieved, re·triev·ing.**

re·triev·er (ri trēv′ər) a dog trained to find killed or wounded game and bring it to a hunter. *n.*

re·turn (ri tėrn′) 1 go back; come back: *Return home for your report card. Your mother will return in a moment. We'll return to this hard example after doing the easy ones.* 2 going or coming back; happening again: *We look forward all winter to our return to the country. We wish you many happy returns of your birthday.* 3 bring back; give back; send back; put back; pay back: *Return that book to the library. You took his cap; return it at once. She admired my dress, and I returned the compliment.* 4 bringing back; giving back; sending back; putting back; hitting back: *His bad behavior was a poor return for his uncle's kindness.* 5 the thing returned. 6 a profit; an amount received: *The returns from the sale were more than a hundred dollars.* 7 yield; provide: *The concert returned about $50 over expenses.* 8 a report or account: *The election returns are all in.* 9 reply; answer: *'Not I,' he returned crossly.* 10 having something to do with a return: *a return ticket.* 11 sent, given, or done in return: *a return game.* 1, 3, 7, 9 *v.*, 2, 4–6, 8 *n.*, 10, 11 *adj.*

in return, as a return: *If you lend me your skates now, I'll lend you my tennis racket next summer in return.*

re·un·ion (rē yün′yən) coming together again: *a family reunion at Thanksgiving.* *n.*

re·u·nite (rē′ yü nīt′) bring together again; come together again: *Mother and child were reunited after years of separation.* *v.*, **re·u·nit·ed, re·u·nit·ing.**

Rev. Reverend.

re·veal (ri vēl′) 1 make known something hidden or secret: *Promise never to reveal my secret.* 2 display; show: *Her smile revealed her even teeth.* *v.*

re·veil·le (rə val′ē) a signal on a bugle or drum to waken soldiers, sailors, or airmen in the morning: *The bugler blew reveille.* *n.*

rev·el (rev′əl) 1 take great pleasure: *The children revel in country life.* 2 a merrymaking; a noisy good time: *Christmas revels with feasting and dancing were common in England.* 3 make merry. 1, 3 *v.*, **rev·elled** or **rev·eled, rev·el·ling** or **rev·el·ing;** 2 *n.*

rev·e·la·tion (rev′ə lā′shən) 1 making known something hidden or secret: *The revelation of the*

hat, āge, fär; let, ēqual, tėrm; it, īce
hot, ōpen, ôrder; oil, out; cup, pu̇t, rüle
əbove, takən, pencəl, lemən, circəs
ch, child; ng, long; sh, ship
th, thin; ᴛʜ, then; zh, measure

thieves' hiding place resulted in their capture. **2** the thing made known: *I had thought her stupid, so her knowledge of history was a revelation to me.* *n.*

rev·el·ry (rev′əl rē) a boisterous revelling or festivity; a wild merrymaking: *The sound of revelry came from the big house on the hill.* *n., pl.* **rev·el·ries.**

re·venge (ri venj′) **1** hurting or harming someone in return for having been hurt; repaying a wrong: *They vowed to have their revenge.* **2** do harm in return for: *His family vowed to revenge his death.* **3** make up to a person for a wrong suffered by that person: *His father took up arms to revenge him.* **4** a desire to be revenged: *She said nothing, but there was revenge in her heart.* 1, 4 *n.*, 2, 3 *v.*, **re·venged, re·veng·ing.**

be revenged, get revenge: *He swore to be revenged on his brother's murderers.*

revenge oneself on, take revenge: *I'll revenge myself on her for that insult!*

re·venge·ful (ri venj′fəl) feeling or showing a strong desire for revenge. *adj.*

rev·e·nue (rev′ə nyü′) money coming in; income: *The government got much revenue from taxes last year.* *n.*

re·ver·ber·ate (ri vėr′bər āt′) echo back: *His deep, rumbling voice reverberates from the high ceiling.* *v.*, **re·ver·ber·at·ed, re·ver·ber·at·ing.**

re·vere (ri vēr′) love and respect deeply; honor greatly; show reverence for: *People revered the great statesman.* *v.*, **re·vered, re·ver·ing.**

rev·er·ence (rev′ər əns) **1** a feeling of deep respect, mixed with wonder, fear, and love. **2** regard with reverence: *We reverence men of noble lives.* 1 *n.*, 2 *v.*, **rev·er·enced, rev·er·enc·ing.**

rev·er·end (rev′ər ənd) **1** worthy of great respect. **2 Reverend,** a title for clergymen: *the Reverend T. A. Brown.* 1 *adj.*, 2 *n.*

rev·er·ent (rev′ər ənt) feeling reverence; showing reverence: *He gave reverent attention to the sermon.* *adj.*

rev·er·ie (rev′ər ē) dreamy thoughts; a dreamy thinking of pleasant things: *She was so lost in reverie that she did not hear the bell ring. He loved to indulge in reveries about his future.* *n.*

re·verse (ri vėrs′) **1** the opposite or contrary: *She did the reverse of what I ordered.* **2** turned backward; opposite or contrary in position or direction: *Play the reverse side of that record.* **3** to turn the other way; turn inside out; turn upside down: *Reverse that gun; don't point it at me.* **4** an arrangement of gears set so as to move backward: *Put the car in reverse to drive out of the garage.* **5** change to the opposite; repeal: *The court reversed its decree of imprisonment, and the man went free.* **6** the back: *His name is on the reverse of the medal.* **7** a change to bad fortune; a check or defeat: *He used to be rich, but he met with reverses in his business.* 1, 4, 6, 7 *n.*, 2 *adj.*, 3, 5 *v.*, **re·versed, re·vers·ing.**

re·vert (ri vėrt′) go back; return: *After the foreigners left, the people reverted to their traditional customs. My thoughts reverted to the last time that I had seen her.* *v.*

re·view (ri vyü′) **1** study again; look at again: *Please review this lesson for tomorrow.* **2** studying again: *Before the examinations we have a review of the term's work.* **3** look back on: *Before falling asleep, she reviewed the day's happenings.* **4** looking back on; a survey: *A review of the trip was pleasant.* **5** an examination or inspection: *A review of the troops will be held during the general's visit to the camp.* **6** inspect formally: *The Admiral reviewed the fleet.* **7** a critical account of a book, play, movie, etc., giving its merits and faults: *He wrote a review of the movie for the school magazine.* **8** prepare such a critical account: *to review a book.* 1, 3, 6, 8 *v.*, 2, 4, 5, 7 *n.*

re·vile (ri vīl′) call bad names; abuse with words: *The tramp reviled the man who drove him off.* *v.*, **re·viled, re·vil·ing.**

re·vise (ri vīz′) **1** read carefully and correct or improve; look over and change: *She has revised the poem she wrote.* **2** change; alter: *A stubborn person is slow to revise his opinion.* *v.*, **re·vised, re·vis·ing.**

re·vi·sion (ri vizh′ən) **1** the act or work of revising. **2** a revised form: *a revision of a book.* *n.*

re·viv·al (ri vīv′əl) **1** bringing or coming back to life or consciousness. **2** a restoration to vigor or health. **3** bringing or coming back to style or use: *Most Western movies on television are revivals of the motion pictures of years ago.* **4** special services or efforts made to awaken or increase interest in religion. *n.*

re·vive (ri vīv′) **1** bring back or come back to life or consciousness: *He was nearly drowned, but we revived him.* **2** bring or come back to a fresh, lively condition: *The flowers revived in water.* **3** restore; make or become fresh: *Hot coffee revives a cold, tired man.* **4** bring back or come back to notice, use, fashion, memory, activity, etc.: *revive an old song. An old play is sometimes revived on the stage.* *v.*, **re·vived, re·viv·ing.**

re·voke (ri vōk′) take back; cancel; withdraw: *The government revoked the bill before it was voted on.* *v.*, **re·voked, re·vok·ing.**

re·volt (ri vōlt′) **1** turn away from and fight against a leader; rise against the government's authority: *The people revolted against the dictator.* **2** the act or state of rebelling: *The town is in revolt.* **3** turn away with disgust: *to revolt at a bad smell.* **4** to cause to feel disgust: *A dirty house revolts Mother.* 1, 3, 4 *v.*, 2 *n.*

rev·o·lu·tion (rev′ə lü′shən) **1** a complete, often violent, overthrow of a government or political system. **2** a complete change: *Plastics have brought about a revolution in industry.* **3** a movement in a circle or curve around some point: *One revolution of the earth around the sun takes a year.* **4** a turning round a centre; rotation: *The revolution of the earth causes day and night.* **5** a single complete turn around a centre: *The wheel of the motor turns at a rate of more than one thousand revolutions a minute.* *n.*

rev·o·lu·tion·ar·y (rev′ə lü′shən er′ē) **1** of a revolution; connected with a revolution (defs. 1 and 2). **2** bringing or causing great changes. **3** a person in favor of or taking part in a revolution. 1, 2 *adj.*, 3 *n.*

rev·o·lu·tion·ize (rev′ə lü′shən īz′) change

completely; produce a very great change in: *Mechanization revolutionized farm life. The new chief of police says he will revolutionize that department.* *v.,* **rev·o·lu·tion·ized, rev·o·lu·tion·iz·ing.**

re·volve (ri volv′) 1 move in a circle; move in a curve round a point: *The moon revolves around the earth.* 2 turn round a centre; rotate: *The wheels of a moving car revolve.* 3 turn over in the mind; consider from many points of view: *He wishes to revolve the problem before giving an answer.* *v.,* **re·volved, re·volv·ing.**

re·volv·er (ri vol′vər) a pistol with a revolving cylinder in which the cartridges are contained. It can be fired several times without reloading. See **pistol** for picture. *n.*

re·vue (ri vyü′) a humorous theatrical entertainment with singing, dancing, etc. *n.*

re·ward (ri wôrd′) 1 a return made for something done. 2 a money payment given or offered: *Rewards are sometimes given for the capture of criminals and the return of lost property.* 3 give a reward to. 4 give a reward for. 1, 2 *n.,* 3, 4 *v.*

rhe·a (rē′ə) any of several large birds of South America that resemble the ostrich, but are smaller and have three toes instead of two. *n.*

rheu·mat·ic (rü mat′ik) 1 of or having rheumatism. 2 a person who has rheumatism. 1 *adj.,* 2 *n.*

rheu·ma·tism (rü′mə tiz′əm) a disease that causes inflammation, swelling, and stiffness of the joints. *n.*

A black rhinoceros of Africa — about 175 cm high at the shoulder and about 3 m long

rhi·noc·er·os (rī nos′ər əs) a large, thick-skinned animal of Africa and Asia having one or two upright horns on the snout. *n., pl.* **rhi·noc·er·os·es** or **rhi·noc·er·os.**

☛ **Rhinoceros** comes from Greek *rhis,* meaning 'nose,' and *keras,* meaning 'horn.'

rho·do·den·dron (rō′də den′drən) an evergreen shrub having beautiful pink, purple, or white flowers. *n.*

rhu·barb (rü′bärb) a garden plant having very large leaves, whose sour stalks are used for making sauce, pies, etc. *n.*

rhyme (rīm) 1 sound alike in the last part: *'Long' and 'song' rhyme. 'Go to bed' rhymes with 'sleepy head.'* 2 a word or line having the same last sound as another: *'Cat' is a rhyme for 'mat.' 'Hey! diddle, diddle' and 'The cat and the fiddle' are rhymes.* 3 verses or poetry with some of the lines ending in similar sounds. 4 make a rhyme: *to rhyme 'love' and 'dove.' He enjoys rhyming.* 1, 4 *v.,* **rhymed, rhym·ing;** 2, 3 *n.* Also spelled **rime.**

rhythm (riᴛʜ′əm) a movement having a regular repetition of a beat, accent, rise and fall, or the like: *the rhythm of dancing, the rhythm of music, the rhythm of the tides.* *n.*

rhyth·mic (riᴛʜ′mik) rhythmical. *adj.*

rhyth·mi·cal (riᴛʜ′mə kəl) having rhythm; of rhythm. *adj.*

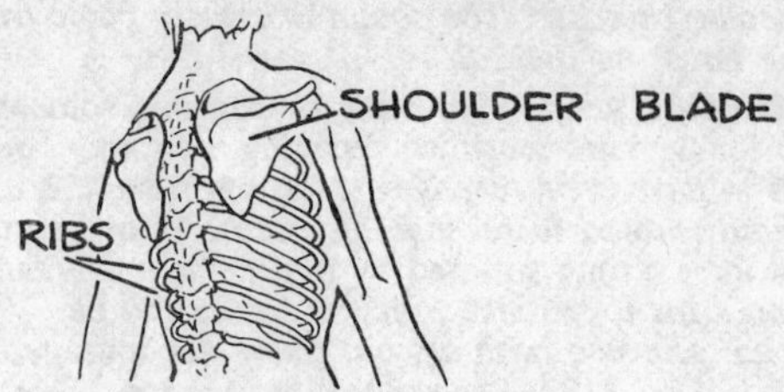

rib (rib) 1 one of the curved bones extending round the chest from the backbone to the front of the body. 2 something like a rib: *The curved timbers in a ship's frame are called ribs. An umbrella has ribs.* 3 a ridge in cloth, knitting, etc. 4 *Informal.* tease. 1–3 *n.,* 4 *v.*

rib·bon (rib′ən) 1 a strip or band of silk, satin, velvet, etc.: *Bows for the hair, belts, and badges are often made of ribbon.* 2 anything like such a strip: *a typewriter ribbon.* 3 **ribbons,** *pl.* torn pieces; shreds: *Her dress was torn to ribbons by the thorns she had come through.* *n.*

rice (rīs) the edible seeds or grain of a plant grown in warm climates: *Rice is an important food in India, China, and Japan.* *n.*

rich (rich) 1 having much money, land, goods, etc. 2 abounding; well supplied: *Canada is rich in oil and nickel.* 3 fertile; producing much: *a rich soil, a rich mine.* 4 valuable; having great worth: *a rich harvest, a rich suggestion.* 5 costly; elegant: *rich dresses, rich jewels, rich carpets.* 6 containing plenty of butter, eggs, flavoring, etc.: *a rich fruit cake.* 7 of colors, sounds, smells, etc., deep; full: *a rich red, a rich tone.* 8 **the rich,** *pl.* rich people. 1–7 *adj.,* 8 *n.* **—rich′ness,** *n.*

rich·es (rich′iz) wealth; abundance of property; much money, land, goods, etc. *n. pl.*

rick·ets (rik′its) a disease of childhood, caused by lack of proper food or sunshine: *Rickets results in softening, and sometimes bending, of the bones.* *n.*

rick·et·y (rik′ə tē) weak; liable to fall or break down; shaky: *a rickety old chair.* *adj.*

A rickshaw

rick·shaw or **rick·sha** (rik′sho or rik′shô) a small, two-wheeled, hooded carriage drawn by one or more men, used in the Orient. *n.*

ric·o·chet (rik′ə shā′) 1 the skipping or jumping motion of an object as it goes along a flat surface: *the ricochet of a stone thrown along the surface of water.* 2 to move in this way: *The bullets struck the ground and ricocheted through the grass.* 1 *n.,* 2 *v.,* **ric·o·chetted** or **ric·o·cheted** (rik′ə shād′), **ric·o·chet·ting** or **ric·o·chet·ing** (rik′ə shā′ing).

hat, āge, fär; let, ēqual, tėrm; it, īce
hot, ōpen, ôrder; oil, out; cup, pu̇t, rüle
əbove, takən, pencəl, lemən, circəs
ch, child; ng, long; sh, ship
th, thin; ᴛʜ, then; zh, measure

rid (rid) make free: *What will rid a house of rats?* *v.*, **rid** or **rid·ded, rid·ding.**
be rid of, be freed from.
get rid of, **a** get free from: *I can't get rid of this cold.* **b** to do away with: *Poison will get rid of the rats in the barn.*

rid·dance (rid′əns) clearing away or out; removal. *n.*
good riddance, an exclamation expressing relief that something or somebody has been removed.

rid·den (rid′ən) See **ride.** *The horseman had ridden all day.* *v.*

rid·dle¹ (rid′əl) **1** a puzzling question, statement, problem, etc. *Example:* When is a door not a door? *Answer:* When it's ajar. **2** a person or thing that is hard to understand, explain, etc. *n.*

rid·dle² (rid′əl) make many holes in: *The door of the fort was riddled with bullets.* *v.*, **rid·dled, rid·dling.**

ride (rīd) **1** sit on a horse and make it go. **2** sit on something and make it go: *to ride a camel, to ride a bicycle.* **3** be carried along by anything: *to ride on a train, to ride in a car.* **4** ride over, along, or through: *He likes to ride the mountain trail.* **5** be carried on: *The eagle rides the wind.* **6** move or float on the water: *The ship rides at anchor.* **7** a trip on horseback, in an automobile, on a train, etc.: *On Sundays we take a ride into the country.* **8** a mechanical amusement, such as a merry-go-round, Ferris wheel, roller coaster, etc.: *Most children enjoy the rides on the midway.* **9** a turn on a merry-go-round, Ferris wheel, roller coaster, etc.: *My brother enjoyed his ride on the merry-go-round.* 1–6 *v.*, **rode, rid·den, rid·ing;** 7–9 *n.* **—rid′er,** *n.*
ride down, **a** knock down. **b** overcome. **c** overtake by riding.
ride out, endure successfully: *The small boat rode out the storm without damage.*

ridge (rij) **1** the long and narrow upper part of something: *the ridge of an animal's back.* **2** the line where two upward sloping surfaces meet: *the ridge of a roof.* **3** a long, narrow chain of hills or mountains. **4** any raised narrow strip: *the ridges in ploughed ground, the ridges on corduroy cloth.* *n.*

ridge·pole (rij′pōl′) the horizontal timber along the top of a roof or tent. See **frame** for picture. *n.*

rid·i·cule (rid′ə kyül′) **1** laugh at; make fun of: *Sometimes boys ridicule their sisters' friends.* **2** laughter in mockery; words or actions that make fun of somebody or something: *Silly mistakes and strange clothes often invite ridicule.* 1 *v.*, **rid·i·culed, rid·i·cul·ing;** 2 *n.*

ri·dic·u·lous (ri dik′yə ləs) deserving ridicule; absurd; laughable: *It would be ridiculous to walk backward all the time.* *adj.*

rid·ing (rīd′ing) *Cdn.* a political division represented by a Member of Parliament or a Member of the Legislative Assembly; a constituency: *He votes in the riding of Hull.* *n.*

rife (rīf) **1** happening often; common; numerous; widespread: *Sudden noises, so rife in the big city, bothered the visitor from the country.* **2** well supplied; full; abounding: *The land was rife with rumors of war.* *adj.*

ri·fle¹ (rī′fəl) **1** a gun having spiral grooves in its barrel that spin or twist the bullet as it is shot. **2** cut such grooves in a gun. 1 *n.*, 2 *v.*, **ri·fled, ri·fling.**

ri·fle² (rī′fəl) **1** search and rob; ransack and rob. **2** steal; take away. **3** strip bare: *The boys had rifled the apple tree.* *v.*, **ri·fled, ri·fling.**

rift (rift) a split or break; cleft; crack: *There's a rift in the clouds; perhaps the sun will come out soon. The quarrel created a rift between the two friends.* *n.*

rig (rig) **1** equip a ship with masts, sails, ropes, etc.: *The sailor rigged a toy boat for the little boy.* **2** the arrangement of masts, sails, etc. on a ship: *The rig of a schooner is not the same as that of a brig.* **3** *Informal.* dress: *On Halloween the children rig themselves up in funny clothes.* **4** *Informal.* clothes; dress: *His rig consisted of a silk hat and overalls.* **5** fit out; equip: *rig out a football team.* **6** outfit; equipment: *a camper's rig, an oil-drilling rig.* **7** put together in a hurry or by using odds and ends: *The boys rigged up a tent with a rope and a blanket.* **8** arrange in an unfair way: *The race was rigged.* 1, 3, 5, 7, 8 *v.*, **rigged, rig·ging;** 2, 4, 6 *n.*

rig·ging (rig′ing) **1** the ropes, chains, etc. used to support and work the masts, yards, sails, etc. on a ship. **2** tackle; equipment: *Do you need all that rigging for a trip of only two days?* *n.*

right (rīt) **1** good; just; lawful: *He did the right thing when he told the truth.* **2** in a way that is good, just, or lawful: *He acted right when he told the truth.* **3** that which is right, just, good, true: *Do right, not wrong.* **4** a just claim; something that is due to a person: *Each member of the club has a right to vote. He demanded his rights.* **5** correct; true: *the right answer.* **6** correctly; truly: *I guessed right.* **7** fitting; suitable; proper: *Learn to say the right thing at the right time.* **8** properly; well: *It's faster to do a job right the first time.* **9** well; healthy; in good condition: *My head doesn't feel right.* **10** meant to be seen; most important: *the right side of cloth.* **11** make correct; set right: *to right a wrong.* **12** put right; get into the proper position: *The boys righted the boat. The ship righted after the big wave passed.* **13** of the side that is turned to the east when the main side faces north; opposite of left: *You have a right hand and a left hand. Most people eat, write, and work with their right hands.* **14** the right side or hand: *Turn to your right. The school is on the right.* **15** on or to the right: *Turn right.* **16** exactly: *Your cap is right where you left it.* **17** used in some titles, very: *Right Honourable.* **18** in a straight line; directly: *He looked the man right in the eye.* **19** yes; very well: *'Come at once,' his mother called. 'Right,' he replied.* **20** completely: *His hat was knocked right off.* **21** See **right of way.** 1, 5, 7, 9, 10,

13 *adj.*, 2, 6, 8, 15–20 *adv.*, 3, 4, 14, 21 *n.* 11, 12 *v.* **—right·ly,** *adv.*

by rights or **by right,** rightly; properly; correctly.

right away, at once; immediately: *He promised to do it right away.*

right now, immediately; at the present time: *Stop that right now! They're playing in the yard right now.*

to rights, *Informal.* in or into proper condition, order, etc.

☛ **Right, rite, wright,** and **write** are pronounced the same.

right angle an angle that is formed by a line perpendicular to another line; angle of 90 degrees: *The angles in a square or in the capital letters* F, L, *and* T *are right angles.* See **angle** for picture.

right·eous (rī′chəs) 1 virtuous; doing right; behaving justly: *a righteous man.* 2 proper; just; right: *righteous anger. adj.*

right·eous·ness (rī′chəs nis) upright conduct; virtue; the state or condition of being right and just. *n.*

right·ful (rīt′fəl) 1 according to law; by rights: *the rightful owner of this dog.* 2 just and right; proper. *adj.* **—right′ful·ly,** *adv.*

right–hand (rīt′hand′) 1 on or to the right. 2 of, for, or with the right hand. 3 most helpful or useful: *He is the scoutmaster's right-hand man. adj.*

right–handed (rīt′han′did) 1 using the right hand more easily and more readily than the left. 2 done with the right hand. 3 made to be used with the right hand. *adj.*

Right Honourable in Canada, a title given to the Governor General, the Prime Minister, and certain other statesmen.

right·ly (rīt′lē) 1 justly; fairly. 2 correctly: *He rightly guessed that I was safe.* 3 properly; in a suitable manner. *adv.*

right of way 1 the right to go first: *Car drivers must give fire trucks and ambulances the right of way.* 2 the right to pass over property belonging to someone else. 3 a strip of land on which a road, railway, power line, etc. is built.

rig·id (rij′id) 1 stiff; firm; not bending: *Hold your arm rigid.* 2 strict; not changing: *In our home, it is a rigid rule to wash one's hands before eating. adj.*

rig·ma·role (rig′mə rōl′) foolish talk or activity; words or action without meaning; nonsense. *n.*

rig·or or **rig·our** (rig′ər) 1 strictness; severity: *The sergeant trained the recruits with great rigor.* 2 harshness: *the rigor of a long, cold winter.* 3 logical exactness: *the rigor of scientific method. n.*

rig·or·ous (rig′ər əs) 1 very severe; strict: *the rigorous discipline in the army.* 2 harsh: *a rigorous climate.* 3 exact; thoroughly logical and scientific: *the rigorous methods of science. adj.*

rig·our (rig′ər) See **rigor.**

rile (rīl) 1 make water, etc. muddy by stirring up sediment. 2 disturb; irritate. *v.,* **riled, ril·ing.**

rill (ril) a tiny stream; a little brook. *n.*

rim (rim) 1 an edge, border, or margin on or around anything: *the rim of a wheel.* 2 form a rim around: *Wild flowers and grasses rimmed the little pool.* 1 *n.*, 2 *v.*, **rimmed, rim·ming.**

rime[1] (rīm) See **rhyme.** *v.,* **rimed, rim·ing.**

rime[2] (rīm) white frost. *n.*

rind (rīnd) a hard or firm outer covering: *We do not eat the rind of melons and cheese. n.*

ring[1] (ring) 1 a circle: *The fairies danced in a ring. One can tell the age of a tree by counting the rings in a cross-section of its trunk.* 2 a thin circle of metal or other material: *a wedding ring, a key ring, a napkin ring.* 3 put a ring around; enclose; form a circle around. 4 an enclosed space for races or games, circus performances, showing livestock, etc.: *A ring was roped off for the fight.* 5 a group of people combined for a selfish or bad purpose: *A ring of crooks controlled the smuggling operation.* 1, 2, 4, 5 *n.*, 3 *v.*, **ringed, ring·ing.**

☛ **Ring** and **wring** are pronounced the same.

ring[2] (ring) 1 give forth a clear sound, as a bell does: *Did the telephone ring?* 2 cause to give forth a clear, ringing sound: *Ring the bell.* 3 cause a bell or buzzer to sound: *Did you ring?* 4 make a sound by ringing: *The bells rang a joyous peal.* 5 the sound of a bell or buzzer: *Did you hear a ring?* 6 a sound like that of a bell: *On a cold night we can hear the ring of skates on ice.* 7 hear a sound like that of a bell ringing: *My ears are ringing.* 8 sound loudly; resound: *The room rang with shouts and laughter.* 9 echo; give back sound: *The mountains rang with the roll of thunder.* 10 sound: *His words rang true.* 11 a characteristic quality or effect: *There was a ring of sincerity in his voice.* 12 to call up on a telephone: *I'll ring you tomorrow.* 13 a telephone call. 1–4, 7–10, 12 *v.*, **rang, rung, ring·ing;** 5, 6, 11, 13 *n.*

ring off, end a telephone call.

ring up, a record a specific amount on a cash register. **b** call on the telephone.

☛ See note at **ring**[1].

ring·lead·er (ring′lēd′ər) a person who leads others in opposition to authority. *n.*

Ringlets (def. 1)

ring·let (ring′lit) 1 a long curl: *She wears her hair in ringlets.* 2 a little ring: *Drops of rain made ringlets in the pond. n.*

ring·side (ring′sīd′) 1 a place just outside the ring at a circus, fight, etc. 2 a place giving a close view. *n.*

ring·worm (ring′wėrm′) a skin disease caused by fungi: *Athlete's foot is a common type of ringworm. n.*

rink (ringk) 1 a sheet of ice for playing hockey or for pleasure skating. 2 a smooth floor for roller skating. 3 a sheet of ice for curling. 4 a curling team of four players: *Canada's best rinks curled in the bonspiel. n.*

rinse (rins) 1 wash with clean water: *Rinse all the soap out of your hair after you wash it.* 2 washing in clean water: *Give the plate a final rinse in cold water.* 3 wash lightly: *Rinse your mouth with water and soda.* 1, 3 *v.*, **rinsed, rins·ing;** 2 *n.*

ri·ot (rī′ət) 1 a wild, violent public disturbance; disorder caused by an unruly crowd or mob: *The guards stopped several riots in the prison.* 2 behave in a wild,

hat, āge, fär; let, ēqual, tėrm; it, īce
hot, ōpen, ôrder; oil, out; cup, pu̇t, rüle
əbove, takən, pencəl, lemən, circəs
ch, child; ng, long; sh, ship
th, thin; ᴛʜ, then; zh, measure

disorderly way. 3 a bright display: *The garden was a riot of color.* 4 *Informal.* a very amusing person or performance: *He was a riot at the party.* 1, 3, 4 *n.*, 2 *v.*
run riot, a act without restraint. **b** grow wildly and luxuriantly: *The weeds have run riot in our garden.*

ri·ot·ous (rī′ət əs) 1 taking part in a riot. 2 boisterous; disorderly: *He was expelled from school for riotous conduct. Sounds of riotous glee came from the playhouse. adj.*

rip (rip) 1 cut roughly; tear apart; tear off: *Rip the cover off this box.* 2 cut or pull out the stitches in the seams of a garment. 3 a torn place, especially a seam burst in a garment: *Please sew up this rip in my sleeve.* 1, 2 *v.*, **ripped, rip·ping;** 3 *n.*

ripe (rīp) 1 full-grown and ready to be gathered and eaten: *ripe fruit, ripe grain, ripe vegetables.* 2 fully developed; mature: *a ripe cheese, ripe in knowledge.* 3 ready: *ripe for mischief. adj.*, **rip·er, rip·est.**

rip·en (rīp′ən) become ripe; make ripe. *v.*

rip·ple (rip′əl) 1 a very little wave: *Throw a stone into still water and watch the ripples spread in rings.* 2 anything that seems like a little wave: *the ripples in her hair.* 3 a sound that reminds one of little waves: *a ripple of laughter in the crowd.* 4 make little waves on: *A breeze rippled the quiet waters.* 1–3 *n.*, 4 *v.*, **rip·pled, rip·pling.**

rise (rīz) 1 get up from a lying, sitting, or kneeling position; stand up; get up: *Please rise from your seat when you recite.* 2 get up from sleep or rest: *The farmer's wife rises at six every morning.* 3 go up; come up: *The kite rises in the air. Mercury rises in a thermometer on a hot day. Fish rise to the surface.* 4 go higher; increase: *Butter rose five cents in price. The wind rose rapidly. His anger rose at that remark.* 5 going up; an increase: *We watched the rise of the balloon. There has been a great rise in prices since the war.* 6 slope upward: *Hills rise in the distance.* 7 an upward slope: *The rise of the hill is gradual.* 8 a piece of rising or high ground; hill: *The house is situated on a rise.* 9 appear above the horizon: *The sun rises in the morning.* 10 start; begin: *The river rises from a spring. Quarrels often rise from trifles.* 11 an origin; beginning; start: *the rise of a river, the rise of a storm, the rise of a new problem.* 12 become more cheerful; improve: *Our spirits rose at the good news.* 13 advance in importance, rank, etc.: *He rose from errand boy to president of the country.* 14 revolt; rebel: *The slaves rose against their masters.* 15 grow larger and lighter: *Yeast makes dough rise.* 1–4, 6, 9, 10, 12–15 *v.*, **rose, ris·en, ris·ing;** 5, 7, 8, 11 *n.*
give rise to, start; begin; cause: *The circumstances of his disappearance gave rise to the fear that he might have been kidnapped.*

ris·en (riz′ən) See **rise.** *The sun had risen long before I woke up. v.*

risk (risk) 1 a chance of harm or loss; danger: *He rescued the dog at the risk of his own life. If you drive carefully, there is no risk of being fined.* 2 expose to the chance of harm or loss: *Don't risk any money in gambling. You risk your neck trying to climb that tree.* 3 take the risk of: *They risked defeat in fighting the larger army.* 1 *n.*, 2, 3 *v.*
run a risk or **take a risk,** expose oneself to the chance of harm or loss.

risk·y (ris′kē) full of risk; dangerous. *adj.*, **risk·i·er, risk·i·est.**

rite (rīt) a solemn ceremony: *Most churches have rites for baptism, marriage, and burial. Secret societies have their special rites. n.*
☛ **Rite, right, wright,** and **write** are pronounced the same.

rit·u·al (rich′ü əl) a form or system of rites: *The rites of baptism, marriage, and burial are parts of the ritual of most churches. n.*

ri·val (rī′vəl) 1 a person who wants and tries to get the same thing as another; one who tries to equal or do better than another; competitor: *The two boys were rivals for the same class office. They were also rivals in sports.* 2 wanting the same thing as another; competing: *A rival store tried to get our grocer's trade.* 3 try to equal or outdo: *The stores rival each other in beautiful window displays.* 4 equal; match: *The sunset rivalled the sunrise in beauty.* 5 a thing that will bear comparison with something else; equal; match: *Her beauty has no rival.* 1, 5 *n.*, 2 *adj.*, 3, 4 *v.*, **ri·valled** or **ri·valed, ri·val·ling** or **ri·val·ing.**

ri·val·ry (rī′vəl rē) the effort to obtain something another person wants; competition: *There is rivalry among business firms for trade. n., pl.* **ri·val·ries.**

riv·er (riv′ər) 1 a large, natural stream of water that flows into a lake, ocean, etc. 2 any abundant stream or flow: *rivers of blood. n.*

riv·er·side (riv′ər sīd′) 1 the bank of a river: *We walked along the riverside.* 2 beside a river: *The riverside path is much used.* 1 *n.*, 2 *adj.*

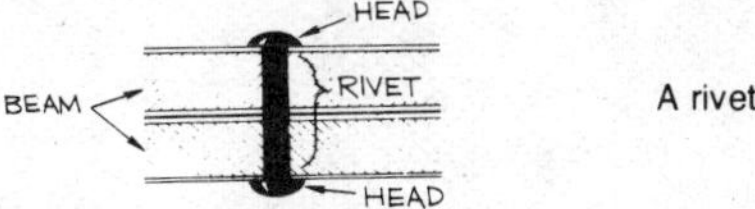

A rivet

riv·et (riv′it) 1 a metal bolt with a head at one end, the other end made to be hammered into a head once it is in position: *Rivets fasten heavy steel beams together.* 2 fasten with a rivet or rivets. 3 fasten firmly; fix firmly: *Their eyes were riveted on the speaker.* 1 *n.*, 2, 3 *v.*

riv·u·let (riv′yə lit) a very small stream. *n.*

roach (rōch) cockroach. *n.*

road (rōd) 1 a way between places; a way made for teams of horses, automobiles, trucks, etc. to travel on: *The road from here to the city is being paved.* 2 a way or route: *Our road went through the woods.* 3 a way: *the road to ruin, a road to peace.* 4 a railway. 5 a place near the shore where ships can anchor. *n.*
on the road, travelling, especially as a salesman.
☛ **Road** and **rode** are pronounced the same.

road·block (rōd′blok′) an obstacle placed across a road: *The police set up a roadblock to stop the car thief. n.*

road·side (rōd′sīd′) 1 the side of a road: *Flowers grew along the roadside.* 2 beside a road: *a roadside inn.* 1 *n.*, 2 *adj.*

road·way (rōd′wā′) 1 a road. 2 the part of a road used by vehicles: *Walk on the path, not in the roadway.* *n.*

roam (rōm) go about with no special plan or aim; wander: *to roam through the fields.* *v.*

roan (rōn) 1 yellowish or reddish brown sprinkled with grey or white. 2 a roan horse. 1 *adj.,* 2 *n.*

roar (rôr) 1 make a loud, deep sound; make a loud noise: *The lions roared. The wind roared at the windows. The audience roared with laughter at the clown.* 2 a loud, deep sound; a loud noise: *the roar of the cannon, a roar of laughter.* 1 *v.,* 2 *n.*

roast (rōst) 1 cook by dry heat; bake: *We roasted meat and potatoes.* 2 a piece of baked meat; a piece of meat to be roasted. 3 an informal outdoor meal, at which some food is cooked over an open fire: *a wiener roast.* 4 roasted: *roast beef, roast pork.* 5 make or become very hot. 1, 5 *v.,* 2 *n.,* 4 *adj.*

rob (rob) 1 take away from by force or threats; plunder; pillage: *Thieves robbed the bank of thousands of dollars. Some boys robbed the orchard. They said they would not rob again.* 2 take away some characteristic; keep from having or doing: *The disease has robbed him of his strength.* *v.,* **robbed, rob·bing.**

rob·ber (rob′ər) a person who robs; thief. *n.*

rob·ber·y (rob′ər ē) an act of robbing; theft: *a bank robbery.* *n., pl.* **rob·ber·ies.**

robe (rōb) 1 a long, loose outer garment: *The priests wore robes.* 2 a garment that shows rank, office, etc.: *a judge's robe, the king's robes of state.* 3 a bathrobe or dressing gown. 4 a covering or wrap: *Put a robe over you when you go on the sleigh ride.* 5 put a robe on; dress. 1–4 *n.,* 5 *v.,* **robed, rob·ing.**

A robin — about 25 cm long with the tail

rob·in (rob′ən) 1 a large North American thrush with a reddish breast. 2 a small European bird having a yellowish-red breast. *n.*

ro·bot (rō′bot) 1 a machine made in imitation of a human being. 2 a person who acts or works in a dull, mechanical way. *n.*

ro·bust (rō bust′ or rō′bust) strong and healthy; sturdy: *a robust person, a robust mind.* *adj.*

rock[1] (rok) 1 a large mass of stone: *The ship was wrecked on the rocks.* 2 a stone: *He threw a rock in the lake.* 3 the mass of mineral matter of which the earth's crust is made up. 4 curling stone. 5 something firm like a rock; a support or defence: *Christ is called the Rock of Ages.* *n.*

rock[2] (rok) 1 move backward and forward, or from side to side; sway: *My chair rocks. The waves rocked the ship. Mother rocked the baby to sleep.* 2 move or shake violently: *The earthquake rocked the houses.* 3 a rocking movement. 4 a kind of lively music with a strong beat. 1, 2 *v.,* 3, 4 *n.*

rock·er (rok′ər) 1 one of the curved pieces on which a cradle, rocking chair, etc. rocks. See **rocking chair** for picture. 2 rocking chair. *n.*

rock·er·y (rok′ər ē) an ornamental garden consisting of an arrangement of rocks and earth for growing plants and flowers; a rock garden: *Rockeries are often built on slopes.* *n., pl.* **rock·er·ies.**

A large rocket which uses liquid fuel

rock·et (rok′it) 1 a projectile consisting of a tube open at one end and filled with some substance that burns rapidly, creating expanding gases that force ahead the tube and whatever is attached to it at great speed: *Some rockets, used for fireworks and signalling, shoot up high in the air and explode into a shower of sparks or stars. Other rockets are used as weapons. Large rockets are used for carrying satellites into outer space.* 2 a spacecraft, missile, etc. propelled by such a projectile. 3 go like a rocket; rise or move extremely fast: *The brilliant scientist rocketed to fame with his discoveries. The racing car rocketed across the finish line to victory.* 1, 2 *n.,* 3 *v.*

rock garden rockery.

Rock·ies (rok′ēz) the Rocky Mountains. *n. pl.*

A rocking chair

rocking chair a chair mounted on rockers, or on springs, so that it can rock back and forth.

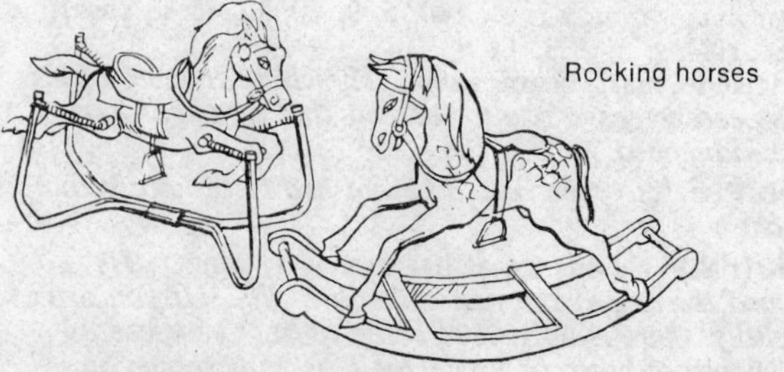

Rocking horses

rocking horse a toy horse on rockers, or sometimes springs, for children to ride.

rock salt common salt as it occurs in the earth in large crystals: *Rock salt is often used to melt ice on roads and sidewalks.*

rock·y[1] (rok′ē) 1 full of rocks: *a rocky shore.* 2 made of rock. 3 like rock; hard; firm. *adj.,* **rock·i·er, rock·i·est.**

hat, āge, fär; let, ēqual, tėrm; it, īce
hot, ōpen, ôrder; oil, out; cup, pu̇t, rüle
əbove, takən, pencəl, lemən, circəs
ch, child; ng, long; sh, ship
th, thin; ᴛʜ, then; zh, measure

rock·y² (rok′ē) shaky; likely to rock: *That table seems a bit rocky to me; put a piece of wood under the short leg.* *adj.*, **rock·i·er, rock·i·est.**

rod (rod) **1** a thin, straight bar of metal or wood: *An atomic furnace is made to operate by rods of some radio-active substance.* **2** a thin, straight stick, either growing or cut off. **3** a stick used to beat or punish: *'Spare the rod and spoil the child.'* **4** a long, springy, tapered piece of wood, metal, plastic, etc. to which a reel may be attached, used for fishing: *His father gave him a rod and reel for Christmas.* **5** a measure of length equal to 5½ yards or 16½ feet (about 5 metres). *n.*

rode (rōd) See **ride.** *We rode all day yesterday.* *v.*

☞ **Rode** and **road** are pronounced the same.

ro·dent (rō′dənt) any of a group of mammals with teeth especially suitable for gnawing: *Rats, mice, and squirrels are rodents.* *n.*

ro·de·o (rō′dē ō or rō dā′ō) **1** a contest or exhibition of skill in roping cattle, riding horses, etc. **2** the driving of cattle together. *n., pl.* **ro·de·os.**

roe¹ (rō) fish eggs. *n.*

☞ **Roe, row¹** and **row²** are pronounced the same.

roe² (rō) a small deer of Europe and Asia. *n., pl.* **roes** or **roe.**

☞ See note at **roe¹**.

roe·buck (rō′buk′) a male roe deer. *n.*

rogue (rōg) **1** a tricky, dishonest, or worthless person; rascal. **2** a mischievous person: *The little rogue has his grandpa's glasses on.* **3** an animal with a savage nature that lives apart from the herd: *An elephant that is a rogue is very dangerous.* *n.*

rogues' gallery a collection of photographs of known criminals.

ro·guish (rō′gish) **1** dishonest; rascally; having to do with rogues. **2** playfully mischievous: *a roguish twinkle in her eyes.* *adj.*

roil (roil) rile. *v.*

role or **rôle** (rōl) **1** an actor's part in a play, motion picture, etc.: *She wished to play the leading role in the school play.* **2** a part played in real life: *a mother's role.* *n.*

☞ **Role** comes from French *rôle,* originally the roll of paper, etc. on which a part was written.

☞ **Role** and **roll** are pronounced the same.

roll (rōl) **1** move along by turning over and over: *Wheels roll. A ball rolls. The child rolls a hoop.* **2** turn round and round on itself or on something else; wrap; be wrapped round: *She rolled the string into a ball. The boy rolled himself up in a blanket.* **3** something rolled up: *a roll of film, a roll of paper.* **4** a rounded or rolled-up mass: *a roll of butter.* **5** move on wheels: *The nurse rolls the baby carriage. The automobile rolls along.* **6** move smoothly; sweep along: *Waves roll in on the beach. The years roll on.* **7** move with a side-to-side motion: *The ship rolled in the waves. The girl rolled her eyes.* **8** the act of rolling; a motion from side to side: *The ship's roll made many people sick.* **9** rise and fall again and again: *rolling country, rolling waves.* **10** make flat or smooth with a roller; spread out with a rolling pin, etc.: *Rolling the grass makes a smooth lawn. Mother rolls the dough for cookies.* **11** make deep, loud sounds: *Thunder rolls.* **12** a deep, loud sound: *the roll of thunder.* **13** beat a drum with rapid, continuous strokes. **14** a rapid, continuous beating on a drum. **15** trill: *to roll your r's.* **16** a list of names; a list: *I will call the roll to find out who is absent.* **17** a kind of bread or cake: *a sweet roll.* 1, 2, 5–7, 9–11, 13, 15 *v.*, 3, 4, 8, 12, 14, 16, 17 *n.*

roll up, pile up or become piled up; increase: *Bills roll up fast.*

☞ **Roll** and **role** are pronounced the same.

roll·er (rōl′ər) **1** anything that rolls, especially a cylinder on which something is rolled along or up: *They used rollers to beach the boat. The window blinds were on rollers.* **2** a cylinder of metal, stone, wood, etc., used for smoothing, pressing, crushing, etc.: *A heavy roller was used to smooth the tennis court.* **3** a long, swelling wave: *Huge rollers broke on the sandy beach.* *n.*

roller coaster a railway set up for amusement at fairs, etc., consisting of tracks along which small cars roll, climb, dip sharply, turn, etc.

A roller for smoothing a lawn

A roller skate

roller skate a skate equipped with small wheels: *Roller skates are used on floors, roads, sidewalks, etc.*

roll·er–skate (rōl′ər skāt′) move on roller skates: *The children roller-skated to the park.* *v.*, **roll·er-skat·ed, roll·er-skat·ing.**

rol·lick·ing (rol′ik ing) frolicking; jolly; lively: *I had a rollicking time at the picnic.* *adj.*

rolling pin a cylinder about thirty centimetres long, used for rolling out dough.

Ro·man (rō′mən) **1** of or having to do with ancient or modern Rome. **2** a person born in or living in Rome. **3** of or having to do with the Roman Catholic Church. **4 roman,** the style of type most used in printing and typewriting: *Most of this dictionary is in roman; this sentence is in italic.* 1, 3 *adj.*, 2, 4 *n.*

Roman Catholic **1** a member of the Christian church that recognizes the Pope as its supreme head. **2** of or having to do with this church.

ro·mance (rō mans′ or rō′mans) **1** a love story. **2** a story of adventure: *'The Arabian Nights' and 'Treasure Island' are romances.* **3** a story or poem telling of heroes: *Have you read the romances about King Arthur and his knights?* **4** real happenings that are like stories of heroes and are full of love, excitement, or noble deeds: *The boy dreamed of travelling in search of romance. The explorer's life was filled with romance.* **5** a love affair. **6** a made-up story: *Nobody believes her romances about the wonderful things that have happened to her.* **7** make up stories or adventures: *Some children* *romance because of their lively imaginations.* 1–6 *n.,* 7 *v.,* **ro·manced, ro·manc·ing.**

ROMAN NUMERALS

ROMAN	I	V	X	L	C	D	M
ARABIC	1	5	10	50	100	500	1000

EXAMPLES: XXIII=23, LVI=56, LXIX=69, MDCCLXI=1761

Roman numerals a system of numerals used by the ancient Romans, based on multiples of five.

ro·man·tic (rō man′tik) **1** characteristic of romances or romance; appealing to fancy and the imagination: *She likes romantic tales of love and war. She thinks it would be romantic to be an actress.* **2** having ideas or feelings suited to romance: *The romantic girl's mind was full of handsome heroes, dances, and fine clothes. adj.*

Rome (rōm) **1** the capital city of modern Italy and of the old Roman Empire. **2** the Roman Empire and the republic that came before it: *Rome once ruled the western world.* **3** the Roman Catholic Church, which has its headquarters in Rome. *n.*

romp (romp) **1** to play in a rough, boisterous way; rush, tumble, and punch in play. **2** a rough, lively play or frolic: *A pillow fight is a romp.* **3** run or go quickly and easily. 1, 3 *v.,* 2 *n.*

romp·ers (rom′pərz) a loose one-piece outer garment, worn by young children. *n. pl.*

roof (rüf) **1** the top covering of a building. **2** something like the roof of a building in shape or position: *the roof of a cave, the roof of a car, the roof of the mouth.* **3** to cover with a roof; form a roof over: *The trees roofed the glade where we camped.* 1, 2 *n.,* 3 *v.*

raise the roof, *Informal.* make a disturbance; create an uproar or confusion.

rook[1] (ru̇k) a European crow that often nests in trees near buildings. *n.*

rook[2] (ru̇k) in chess, a castle. *n.*

rook·ie (ru̇k′ē) *Slang.* a beginner, such as a recruit or a new player on a team. *n.*

room (rüm) **1** a part of a house, or other building, with walls of its own: *a dining room, a schoolroom.* **2** the people in a room: *The whole room laughed.* **3** the space occupied by, or available for, something: *The street was so crowded that the cars did not have room to move. There is room for one more in the boat.* **4** scope; opportunity: *There was room for improvement in his work. There was room for advancement in the newly formed company.* **5** rent a room; live in a room: *Mr. Smith rooms in the grey house. Ethel rooms with Edith in the dormitory.* **6 rooms,** *pl.* lodgings, as in a rooming house. 1–4, 6 *n.,* 5 *v.*

room·i·ness (rüm′ē nis) ample space; an abundance of room. *n.*

rooming house a house with rooms to rent.

room–mate (rüm′māt′) a person who shares a room with another or others. *n.*

room·y (rüm′ē) large; spacious; having plenty of room. *adj.,* **room·i·er, room·i·est.**

roost (rüst) **1** a bar, pole, or perch on which birds rest or sleep. **2** sit as birds do on a roost; settle for the night. **3** a place for birds to roost in. 1, 3 *n.,* 2 *v.*

roost·er (rüs′tər) a male domestic fowl; cock: *We have ten hens and a rooster. n.*

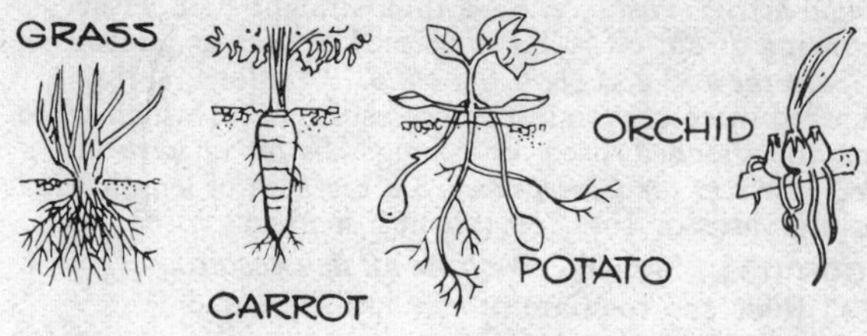

Examples of the four main types of root

root[1] (rüt) **1** the part of a plant that grows down into the soil, holds the plant in place, and feeds it. **2** any underground part of a plant. **3** something like a root in shape, position, or use: *the root of a tooth, the roots of the hair.* **4** a part from which other things grow and develop; a cause; a source: *'The love of money is the root of all evil.'* **5** become fixed in the ground; send out roots and begin to grow: *Some plants root more quickly than others.* **6** fix firmly: *He was rooted to the spot by surprise.* **7** a word from which other words are made: Room *is the root of* roomy *and* roominess. 1–4, 7 *n.,* 5, 6 *v.*

root out or **root up,** get rid of completely.

take root, a send out roots and begin to grow. **b** become firmly fixed.

☛ **Root** and **route** are sometimes pronounced the same.

root[2] (rüt) **1** dig with the snout: *Pigs like to root in gardens.* **2** search; rummage: *She rooted through the closet looking for her old shoes. v.*

☛ See note at **root[1]**.

root[3] (rüt) *Informal.* cheer or support a team or a member of a team enthusiastically. *v.*

☛ See note at **root[1]**.

root beer a soft drink flavored with the juice of the roots of certain plants.

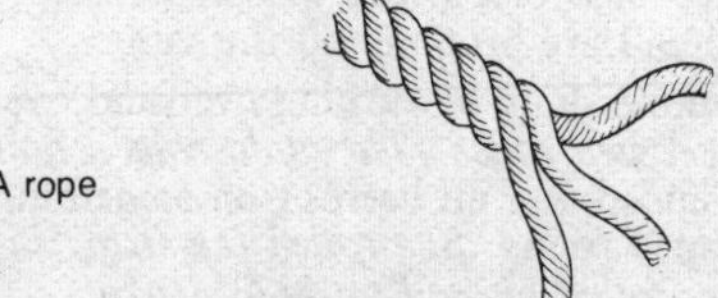

A rope

rope (rōp) **1** a strong, thick line or cord made by twisting smaller cords together. **2** to tie, bind, or fasten with a rope. **3** enclose or mark off with a rope. **4** catch a horse, calf, etc. with a lasso. **5** a number of things twisted or strung together: *a rope of onions, a rope of pearls.* **6** a cord or noose for hanging a person. 1, 5, 6 *n.,* 2–4 *v.,* **roped, rop·ing.**

know the ropes, a know the various ropes of a ship. **b** *Informal.* know about a business or activity.

ro·sa·ry (rō′zə rē) **1** a string of beads for keeping count in saying a series of prayers. **2** a series of prayers. *n., pl.* **ro·sa·ries.**

rose[1] (rōz) **1** a flower that grows on a bush with thorny stems: *Roses are red, pink, white, or yellow, and usually smell very sweet.* **2** the bush itself. **3** pinkish

hat, āge, fär; let, ēqual, tėrm; it, īce
hot, ōpen, ôrder; oil, out; cup, pu̇t, rüle
əbove, takən, pencəl, lemən, circəs
ch, child; ng, long; sh, ship
th, thin; ᴛʜ, then; zh, measure

red: *Her dress was rose.* 4 something shaped like a rose, or suggesting a rose, such as a rosette. 1, 2, 4 *n.*, 3 *adj.*

rose² (rōz) See **rise.** *The cat rose and stretched itself.* *v.*

rose·bud (rōz′bud′) the bud of a rose. *n.*

rose·bush (rōz′bu̇sh′) a shrub or vine that bears roses. *n.*

ro·sette (rō zet′) an ornament shaped like a rose: *Rosettes made of ribbon are given as prizes at livestock shows.* *n.*

ros·in (roz′ən) a hard, yellow substance that remains when turpentine is evaporated from pine resin: *Rosin is rubbed on violin bows, and on the shoes of circus performers and boxers to keep them from slipping.* *n.*

ros·y (rōz′ē) 1 like a rose; rose-red; pinkish-red. 2 bright; cheerful: *a rosy future.* *adj.*, **ros·i·er, ros·i·est.**

rot (rot) 1 decay; spoil: *So much rain will make the fruit rot.* 2 the process of rotting; decay. 3 a disease of plants and animals, especially sheep. 4 *Slang.* nonsense; rubbish. 1 *v.*, **rot·ted, rot·ting;** 2–4 *n.*

☛ **Rot** and **wrought** are sometimes pronounced the same.

ro·ta·ry (rō′tə rē) 1 turning like a top or wheel; rotating. 2 traffic circle. 3 a system in schools by which students move to different rooms and teachers for different subjects: *All classes are on rotary this year.* 1 *adj.*, 2, 3 *n.*

ro·tate (rō tāt′ or rō′tāt) 1 move around a centre or axis; turn in a circle; revolve: *Wheels, tops, and the earth rotate.* 2 change in a regular order; cause to take turns: *Farmers rotate crops. The officials will rotate.* *v.*, **ro·tat·ed, ro·tat·ing.**

ro·ta·tion (rō tā′shən) 1 turning round a centre; turning in a circle: *the rotation of a top. The earth's rotation causes night and day.* 2 a system of taking turns; changing in regular succession: *The job of classroom roll call is done in rotation.* 3 in farming, varying the crops grown in the same field to keep the soil from losing its fertility. *n.*

rote (rōt) a set, mechanical way of doing things. *n.*
by rote, by memory, without thought of the meaning: *learn a lesson by rote.*

☛ **Rote** and **wrote** are pronounced the same.

ro·tis·se·rie (rō tis′ə rē) a rotating spit used in an oven, under a broiler, or over an open fire, for roasting meat or fowl. *n.*

ro·tor (rō′tər) 1 the rotating part of a machine or apparatus. 2 a system of rotating blades by which a helicopter is enabled to fly. See **helicopter** for picture. *n.*

rot·ten (rot′ən) 1 decayed; spoiled: *a rotten egg.* 2 foul; disgusting: *a rotten smell.* 3 not in good condition; unsound; weak: *The rotten ice gave way, and he fell into the water.* 4 corrupt; dishonest: *rotten government.* 5 *Slang.* bad; nasty: *rotten luck, to feel rotten.* *adj.*

ro·tund (rō tund′) 1 round; plump: *a rotund face.* 2 full-toned; sounding rich and full: *a rotund voice.* *adj.*

rouge (rüzh) 1 a red powder, paste, or liquid for coloring the cheeks or lips. 2 to color with rouge. 1 *n.*, 2 *v.*, **rouged, roug·ing.**

rough (ruf) 1 not smooth; not level; not even: *rough boards, the rough bark of oak trees, a rough, rocky hill.* 2 stormy: *rough weather.* 3 likely to hurt others; harsh; not gentle: *rough manners.* 4 without luxury and ease: *a rough life in camp.* 5 without polish or fine finish: *rough diamonds.* 6 not completed; done as a first try; without details: *a rough drawing, a rough idea.* 7 coarse and tangled: *rough fur, a dog with a rough coat of hair.* 8 a coarse, violent person. 9 *Informal.* unpleasant; hard; severe: *He was in for a rough time.* 10 make rough; roughen. 11 treat roughly: *The angry mob roughed up the suspected traitor.* 12 shape or sketch roughly: *rough out a plan, rough in the outlines of a face.* 13 in a rough manner; roughly: *Those boys play too rough for me.* 1–7, 9 *adj.*, 8 *n.*, 10–12 *v.*, 13 *adv.* —**rough′ness,** *n.*
rough it, to live without comforts and conveniences: *'Roughing It in the Bush' is a famous book about pioneer life in Ontario.*

☛ **Rough** and **ruff** are pronounced the same.

rough·age (ruf′ij) the coarser parts or kinds of food which stimulate the movement of food and waste products through the intestines: *Bran, fruit skins, and certain fruits are roughage.* *n.*

rough·en (ruf′ən) make rough or become rough. *v.*

rough·ing (ruf′ing) the rough treatment of another player in hockey, football, and other games: *He got a penalty for roughing.* *n.*

rough·ly (ruf′lē) 1 in a rough manner. 2 approximately: *From Quebec City to Vancouver is roughly five thousand kilometres.* *adv.*

rough·neck (ruf′nek′) *Informal.* a rough, bad-mannered person; a rowdy. *n.*

round (round) 1 shaped like a ball, a ring, a cylinder, or the like; having a circular or curved outline or surface: *a round hoop.* 2 anything shaped like a ball, circle, cylinder, or the like: *The rungs of a ladder are sometimes called rounds.* 3 make or become round: *The carpenter rounded the corners of the table.* 4 making or requiring a circular movement: *The waltz is a round dance.* 5 in a circle; with a whirling motion: *Wheels go round.* 6 on all sides; in every direction; around: *The travellers were compassed round by dangers.* 7 on all sides of: *Bullets whistled round him, but he was not hurt.* 8 in circumference; in distance around: *The huge pumpkin measured* 150 cm *round.* 9 go round; make a turn to the other side of: *The ship rounded Cape Horn.* 10 so as to make a turn to the other side of: *He walked round the corner.* 11 by a longer road or way: *We went round by the candy store on our way home.* 12 to all or various parts of: *We took our cousins round the town.* 13 a fixed course ending where it begins: *The watchman makes his rounds of the building.* 14 a movement in a circle or about an axis: *the earth's yearly round.* 15 from one to another: *A report is going round that the schools will close early.* 16 about; around: *He stood on the hill and looked round.* 17 a series of duties, events, etc.; a routine: *a round of pleasures, a round of duties.* 18 a section of a game or sport: *a round in a boxing match, a round of* *cards.* **19** the firing of a number or group of rifles, guns, etc. at the same time. **20** the powder, bullets, etc. for one such firing, or for a single shot: *The soldier had three rounds of ammunition left in his rifle.* **21** an action that a number of people do together: *a round of applause, a round of cheers.* **22** a dance in which the dancers move in a circle. **23** a short song sung by several persons or groups beginning one after the other: *'Three Blind Mice' is a round.* **24** full; complete: *a round dozen.* **25** large: *a good round sum of money.* **26** general; approximate; to the nearest unit, ten, hundred, etc.: *The cost of the whole trip should be $500 in round figures. 3974 in round numbers would be 4000.* **27** plain-spoken; frank; plainly expressed: *The boy's father scolded him in good round terms.* 1, 4, 24–27 *adj.,* 2, 13, 14, 17–23 *n.,* 3, 9 *v.,* 5, 6, 8, 11, 15, 16 *adv.,* 7, 10, 12 *prep.*

round off, a make round: *round off the corner of a shelf.* **b** complete: *round off a meal with a light dessert.* **c** make a number more simple or less exact by taking to the nearest unit, ten, hundred, etc.; generalize a number: *The total was 361, but he rounded it off to 350. Please round the answer off to two decimal places.*

round out, complete: *round out a paragraph, round out a career.*

round up, drive or bring together: *The cowboys rounded up the cattle.*

round·a·bout (round′ə bout′) indirect: *a roundabout route. I heard about it in a roundabout way. adj.*

round·ish (roun′dish) somewhat round. *adj.*

round·ly (round′lē) plainly; bluntly; severely: *to refuse roundly, to scold roundly. adv.*

round number a number in even tens, hundreds, thousands, etc.

round–shoul·dered (round′shōl′dərd) having the shoulders bent forward. *adj.*

round trip a trip to a place and back again.

round·up (round′up′) **1** driving or bringing cattle or horses together from long distances. **2** the men and horses that round up cattle or horses. **3** any similar gathering: *a roundup of old friends. n.*

rouse (rouz) **1** wake up; arouse: *I was roused by the telephone bell.* **2** stir up; excite: *He was roused to anger by the insult. v.,* **roused, rous·ing.**

rout¹ (rout) **1** the flight in disorder of a defeated army: *The enemy's retreat soon became a rout.* **2** put to flight: *Our soldiers routed the enemy.* **3** a complete defeat. **4** defeat completely: *The team routed its opponents by a score of ten to one.* 1, 3 *n.,* 2, 4 *v.*

☛ **Rout** and **route** are sometimes pronounced the same.

rout² (rout) **1** dig out; get by searching. **2** put or force out: *The farmer routed his sons out of bed at five o'clock.* **3** dig with the snout: *The pigs were routing for nuts under the trees. v.*

☛ See note at **rout¹**.

route (rüt or rout) **1** a way to go; a road: *Will you go to the coast by the northern route?* **2** arrange the route for: *The automobile club routed us on our vacation to the Maritimes.* **3** send by a certain route: *The bus was routed by way of the detour.* **4** a fixed, regular course or area assigned to a person making deliveries, sales, etc.: *a newspaper route.* 1, 4 *n.,* 2, 3 *v.,* **rout·ed, rout·ing.**

☛ **Route** and **root** are sometimes pronounced the same (rhyming with *boot).* **Route** and **rout** are sometimes pronounced the same (rhyming with *out).*

rou·tine (rü tēn′) **1** a fixed, regular method of doing things; a habitual doing of the same things in the same way: *Getting up and going to bed are parts of your daily routine.* **2** using routine: *routine methods, routine questions.* 1 *n.,* 2 *adj.*

rove (rōv) wander; wander about; roam: *He loved to rove through the fields and woods. v.,* **roved, rov·ing.**

rov·er (rōv′ər) **1** a wanderer. **2** a player on a lacrosse team who holds no special position but who may rove over the entire field. **3 Rover,** a member of the senior branch of the Boy Scouts, for boys over 17 years. *n.*

row¹ (rō) a line of people or things: *The children stood in a row in front of the row of chairs. Corn is planted in rows. n.*

☛ **Row¹**, **row²**, and **roe** are pronounced the same.

row² (rō) **1** move a boat by means of oars: *We rowed to the island. Row the boat to the island.* **2** carry in a rowboat: *He rowed us to shore.* **3** a trip in a rowboat: *It's only a short row.* 1, 2 *v.,* 3 *n.*

☛ See note at **row¹**.

row³ (rou) a noisy quarrel; a loud disturbance: *The three children had a row over the bicycle. What's all this row about? n.*

A rowboat

row·boat (rō′bōt′) a boat moved by oars. *n.*

row·dy (rou′dē) **1** a rough, disorderly person. **2** rough; disorderly. 1 *n., pl.* **row·dies;** 2 *adj.,* **row·di·er, row·di·est.**

roy·al (roi′əl) **1** of or having to do with kings or queens: *royal power, a royal command.* **2** of a kingdom or its government. **3** appropriate for a king; splendid: *a royal welcome, a royal feast. adj.* **—roy′al·ly,** *adv.*

Royal Canadian Mounted Police the federal police force of Canada: *In some provinces the Royal Canadian Mounted Police act as provincial police.*

roy·al·ty (roi′əl tē) **1** a royal person; royal persons: *A box in the theatre was reserved for royalty. Kings, queens, princes, and princesses are royalty.* **2** the rank or dignity of a king or queen; royal power: *The crown is the symbol of royalty.* **3** a kingly nature; a royal quality; nobility. **4** a share of income paid to an inventor, writer, etc.: *An author receives royalties from the sale of his books. n.*

rpm or **r.p.m.** revolutions per minute.

R.R. 1 rural route: *His address is R.R. 1, Kingston, Ontario.* **2** railroad.

Rt. Hon. Right Honourable.

rub (rub) **1** move one thing back and forth against another: *He rubbed her hands to warm them. He rubs his hands with soap.* **2** push and press along the surface of: *The nurse rubbed my lame back. That door rubs on the floor.* **3** make or bring by rubbing: *He used* *a special polish to rub the silver clean.* 4 clean, smooth, or polish by moving one thing firmly against another: *Rub out your error with an eraser.* 5 the act of rubbing: *Give the silver a rub with this cloth.* 6 irritate or make sore by rubbing: *The new shoes rubbed his heels.* 7 a difficulty: *The rub came when both boys wanted to sit with the driver.* 1–4, 6 *v.,* **rubbed, rub·bing;** 5, 7 *n.*

rub the wrong way, annoy; irritate.

rub·ber (rub′ər) 1 an elastic substance obtained from the juice of certain tropical plants or by a chemical process: *Rubber will not let air or water through.* 2 made of rubber: *a rubber tire.* 3 something made from this substance: *Pencils often have rubbers for erasing pencil marks.* 4 overshoe. *n.*

rubber band a circular strip of rubber, used to hold things together.

rub·bish (rub′ish) 1 worthless or useless stuff; waste; trash: *Pick up the rubbish and burn it.* 2 silly words and thoughts; nonsense: *Don't talk rubbish.* *n.*

rub·ble (rub′əl) rough, broken stones, bricks, etc.: *the rubble left by an explosion or an earthquake.* *n.*

ru·ble (rü′bəl) the unit of money in the U.S.S.R. *n.*

ru·by (rü′bē) 1 a clear, hard, red precious stone: *Real rubies are very rare.* 2 deep, glowing red: *ruby lips, ruby wine.* 1, 2 *n., pl.* **ru·bies;** 2 *adj.*

ruck·sack (ruk′sak′) a kind of knapsack, usually of canvas with two shoulder straps. *n.*

ruck·us (ruk′əs) *Slang.* a noisy disturbance or uproar; row. *n.*

A rudder on a boat

rud·der (rud′ər) 1 a flat piece of wood or metal hinged vertically to the rear end of a boat and used to steer it. 2 a similar piece on an aircraft. See **airplane** for picture. *n.*

rud·dy (rud′ē) 1 red or reddish: *the ruddy glow of a fire.* 2 having a fresh, healthy, red look: *ruddy cheeks.* *adj.,* **rud·di·er, rud·di·est.**

rude (rüd) 1 impolite; not courteous: *It is rude to stare at people or to point.* 2 rough in manner or behavior; violent: *Rude hands seized the man and threw him into the car.* *Bill had a rude shock when the other boys poured a pail of water on him.* 3 roughly made or done; coarse; rough; crude; without finish or polish: *He made a rude bed from the branches of evergreen trees.* *The savage made rude ornaments from shells and pebbles.* 4 not having learned much; rather wild; barbarous: *Life is rude in tribes that have few tools.* *adj.,* **rud·er, rud·est. —rude′ness,** *n.*

ru·di·ment (rü′də mənt) 1 a part to be learned first; a beginning: *the rudiments of arithmetic.* 2 something in an early stage: *the rudiments of wings on a baby chick.* *n.*

ru·di·men·ta·ry (rü′də men′tə rē or rü′də men′trē) 1 to be learned or studied first; elementary: *rudimentary facts.* 2 in an early stage of development: *The wings on a baby chick are only rudimentary.* *adj.*

hat, āge, fär; let, ēqual, tėrm; it, īce
hot, ōpen, ôrder; oil, out; cup, pu̇t, rüle
əbove, takən, pencəl, lemən, circəs
ch, child; ng, long; sh, ship
th, thin; ᴛʜ, then; zh, measure

rue¹ (rü) be sorry for; repent; regret: *She will soon rue the day she insulted your mother.* *v.,* **rued, ru·ing.**

rue² (rü) a bitter herb. *n.*

rue·ful (rü′fəl) 1 sorrowful; unhappy; mournful: *a rueful expression.* 2 causing sorrow or pity: *a rueful sight.* *adj.*

A ruff

ruff (ruf) 1 a deep frill, stiff enough to stand out, worn around the neck by men and women in the 16th century. 2 a collar-like growth of long or specially marked feathers or hairs on the neck of a bird or other animal. *n.*

☛ **Ruff** and **rough** are pronounced the same.

ruffed grouse a North American game bird with a tuft of feathers on each side of the neck. See **grouse** for picture.

ruf·fi·an (ruf′ē ən) 1 a rough, brutal, or cruel person. 2 rough; cruel. *n.*

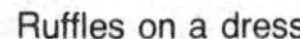

Ruffles on a dress

ruf·fle (ruf′əl) 1 make rough or uneven; to wrinkle: *A breeze ruffled the lake.* *The hen ruffled her feathers at the sight of the dog.* 2 a strip of cloth, ribbon, or lace gathered along one edge and used for trimming. 3 gather into a ruffle. 4 disturb; annoy: *Nothing can ruffle her calm temper.* 1, 3, 4 *v.,* **ruf·fled, ruf·fling;** 2 *n.*

rug (rug) 1 a heavy floor covering: *a fur rug, a rag rug.* 2 a thick, warm cloth used as a covering: *He wrapped the woollen rug around him.* *n.*

rug·by (rug′bē) 1 in Canada, a game played by teams of twelve men who carry, pass, or kick an oval ball toward the opposing team's goal; football. 2 rugger. *n.*

☛ Named after *Rugby,* a famous school for boys in Rugby, England, where the game was first played.

rug·ged (rug′id) 1 covered with rough edges; rough and uneven: *rugged rocks, rugged ground.* 2 sturdy and vigorous; able to do and endure much: *The pioneers were rugged people.* 3 strong and irregular: *rugged features.* 4 harsh; stern: *rugged times.* 5 stormy: *rugged weather.* *adj.*

rug·ger (rug′ər) a game played by teams of fifteen men who kick or pass an oval ball toward the opposing team's goal. *n.*

ru·in (rü′ən) 1 a building, wall, etc. that has fallen to pieces: *That ruin was once a famous castle.* 2 very great damage; destruction; overthrow: *The ruin of property caused by the earthquake was enormous. His enemies planned the duke's ruin.* 3 a fallen or decayed condition: *The house had gone to ruin from neglect.* 4 the cause of destruction, decay, or downfall: *Gambling was his ruin.* 5 bring to ruin; destroy; spoil: *The rain has ruined my new dress.* 6 **ruins,** *pl.* that which is left after destruction, decay, or downfall, especially of a building, wall, etc. that has fallen to pieces: *the ruins of an ancient city.* 1–4, 6 *n.,* 5 *v.*

ru·in·ous (rü′ə nəs) 1 bringing ruin; causing destruction: *The heavy frost was ruinous to the crops.* 2 fallen into ruins; ruined: *a building in a ruinous condition. adj.*

rule (rül) 1 a statement of what to do and what not to do; a principle governing conduct, action, etc.: *Obey the rules of the game.* 2 a custom or habit: *Different kinds of monks live under different rules.* 3 make a rule; decide: *The judge ruled against them.* 4 to control; govern: *The majority rules in a democracy.* 5 control; government: *In a democracy the people have the rule.* 6 a period of power of a ruler; reign: *The B.N.A. Act was passed during the rule of Queen Victoria.* 7 a regular method; what usually happens or is done; what is usually true: *Fair weather is the rule in June.* 8 ruler (def. 2). 9 to mark with lines: *He used a ruler to rule the paper.* 1, 2, 5–8 *n.,* 3, 4, 9 *v.,* **ruled, rul·ing.**
as a rule, usually; normally.
rule out, decide against; exclude.

rul·er (rü′lər) 1 a person who rules. 2 a straight strip of wood, metal, etc. marked in units such as centimetres, used in drawing lines or in measuring. *n.*

rul·ing (rü′ling) a decision of a judge or court: *The ruling was that her evidence could not be accepted. n.*

rum (rum) an alcoholic liquor made from sugar cane, molasses, etc. *n.*

rum·ble (rum′bəl) 1 make a deep, heavy, continuous sound. 2 a deep, heavy, continuous sound: *We hear the far-off rumble of thunder.* 3 move with such a sound: *The train rumbled along the track.* 1, 3 *v.,* **rum·bled, rum·bling;** 2 *n.*

ru·mi·nant (rü′mə nənt) an animal that chews the cud: *Cows, sheep, and camels are ruminants. n.*

rum·mage (rum′ij) 1 search thoroughly by moving things about: *I rummaged in my drawer for a pair of gloves.* 2 a thorough search in which things are moved about. 1 *v.,* **rum·maged, rum·mag·ing;** 2 *n.*

rummage sale a sale of odds and ends, old clothing, etc., usually held to raise money for charity.

rum·my (rum′ē) a kind of card game in which points are scored by forming sets of three or more cards. *n.*

ru·mor or **ru·mour** (rü′mər) 1 a story or statement talked of as news without any proof that it is true: *The rumor spread that a new school would be built here.* 2 vague, general talk: *Rumor has it that the new girl went to school in France.* 3 tell or spread by rumor: *It was rumored that the government was going to increase taxes.* 1, 2 *n.,* 3 *v.*

rump (rump) 1 the hind part of the body of an animal, where the legs join the back. 2 a cut of beef from this part. 3 the hind part of the human body; buttocks. *n.*

rum·ple (rum′pəl) crumple; wrinkle; crush: *If you play in your best dress, you'll rumple it. v.,* **rum·pled, rum·pling.**

rum·pus (rum′pəs) *Informal.* a noisy disturbance or uproar; row. *n.*

rumpus room a room where children can romp and play; a recreation room.

run (run) 1 move the legs quickly; go faster than walking: *A horse can run faster than a man.* 2 go in a hurry; hasten: *Run for help.* 3 flee: *Run for your life.* 4 cause to run; cause to move: *to run a horse up and down the track.* 5 do by running: *to run errands.* 6 go; move; keep going: *This train runs to Calgary. Does your watch run well?* 7 go on; proceed: *Prices of hats run as high as $50.* 8 creep; grow; climb: *Vines run along the sides of the road.* 9 stretch; extend: *Shelves run along the walls.* 10 drive; force; thrust: *He ran a splinter into his hand.* 11 flow; flow with: *The street ran oil after an oil truck overturned.* 12 discharge fluid, mucus, or pus: *My nose runs.* 13 get; become: *Never run into debt. The well ran dry.* 14 spread: *The color ran when the dress was washed.* 15 continue; last: *a lease to run two years.* 16 pass or cause to pass quickly: *A thought ran through my mind.* 17 occur; be current: *The story runs that school will close early today.* 18 have a particular character, quality, form, size, etc.: *These potatoes run large.* 19 take part in a race or contest. 20 be a candidate for election: *Mr. Smith will run for mayor.* 21 expose oneself to: *to run a risk of taking cold.* 22 cause to keep operating: *to run a machine.* 23 the act of running: *to set out at a run. The dog came on the run.* 24 a trip, especially a journey over a certain route: *The train makes its run of 170 kilometres in two hours.* 25 a way, track, or path. 26 conduct; manage: *to run a business.* 27 the unit of score in baseball or cricket. 28 a period; a continuous spell or series: *a run of good luck. Our team has had a run of wins.* 29 a succession of performances: *This play has had a run of two years.* 30 an onward movement; progress; a course; a trend: *the run of events.* 31 a sudden demand or series of demands: *There was a run on beef when people feared a price rise.* 32 the usual kind: *the common run of mankind.* 33 freedom to go over or through, or to use: *The guests were given the run of the house.* 34 go about without restraint: *The children were allowed to run the streets.* 35 a number of fish moving together: *a run of salmon.* 36 a stretch of ground or an enclosed place for animals: *a chicken run.* 37 drop stitches; ravel: *Nylon stockings often run.* 38 a place where stitches have slipped out or become undone: *a run in a stocking.* 39 get past or through: *to run a blockade.* 40 publish an advertisement, story, etc. in a newspaper, magazine, etc.: *He ran an ad in the evening paper.* 1–22, 26, 34, 37, 39, 40 *v.,* **ran, run, run·ning;** 23–25, 27–33, 35, 36, 38 *n.*
in the long run, on the whole; in the end.
run across, meet by chance.
run down, a stop going or working: *The clock has run down.* b chase till caught. c speak evil against. d make tired or ill: *She is run down from working too hard.*
run for it, run for safety.

hat, āge, fär; let, ēqual, tėrm; it, īce
hot, ōpen, ôrder; oil, out; cup, pu̇t, rüle
əbove, takən, pencəl, lemən, circəs
ch, child; ng, long; sh, ship
th, thin; ᴛʜ, then; zh, measure

run in, **a** pay a short visit. **b** *Informal.* arrest: *The police ran him in for careless driving.*
run into, **a** meet by chance. **b** crash into.
run out, come to an end; become used up: *Our time has run out. His money soon ran out.*
run out of, use up; have no more.
run over, **a** ride or drive over. **b** overflow: *The waiter filled his cup too full and the coffee ran over into the saucer.* **c** go through quickly: *Please run over these figures to check my addition.*
run through, **a** use up, spend, or consume rapidly or foolishly. **b** pierce. **c** review; rehearse: *The teacher ran through the homework assignment a second time.*

run·a·way (run′ə wā′) a person, horse, etc. that runs out of control: *He jumped into the runaway car and jammed on the brakes.* *n.*

run–down (run′doun′) **1** tired; sick: *The doctor said Mary was in a run-down condition.* **2** falling to pieces; partly ruined: *a run-down building.* *adj.*

run·down (run′doun′) a brief summary: *Give me a rundown on what happened.* *n.*

rung[1] (rung) See **ring**[2]. *The bell has rung.* *v.*
☛ **Rung** and **wrung** are pronounced the same.

rung[2] (rung) **1** a round rod or bar used as a step of a ladder. See **ladder** for picture. **2** a crosspiece set between the legs of a chair or as part of the back or arm of a chair. *n.*
☛ See note at **rung**[1].

run–in (run′in′) *Informal.* a sharp disagreement; argument; quarrel. *n.*

A runner of a strawberry plant

run·ner (run′ər) **1** a person or animal that runs: *A deer is a good runner.* **2** a messenger: *a runner for a bank.* **3** either of the narrow pieces upon which a sleigh or sled slides. **4** the blade of a skate. **5** a long, narrow strip: *We have a runner of carpet in our hall, and runners of linen on our dressers.* **6** a person or ship that tries to evade somebody; a smuggler: *a blockade runner.* **7** a slender stem that grows along the ground and takes root, thus producing new plants: *Strawberry plants spread by runners.* *n.*

run·ner–up (run′ər up′) the person, player, or team that takes second place in a contest. *n.*

run–off (run′of′) **1** a running off of water, as during the spring thaw or after a heavy rain: *The streams are swollen from the run-off.* **2** a final, deciding race or contest. *n.*

run–of–the–mill (run′əv ᴛʜə mil′) average or commonplace; ordinary: *a run-of-the-mill design.* *adj.*

runt (runt) an animal, person, or plant which is smaller than the usual size. *n.*

run·way (run′wā′) **1** a strip having a level surface on which aircraft land and take off. **2** a channel, track, groove, trough, or the like, along which something moves, slides, etc. **3** the beaten track of deer or other animals. **4** an enclosed place for animals to run in. *n.*

rup·ture (rup′chər) **1** a break; breaking: *the rupture of a blood vessel.* **2** a breaking off of friendly relations. **3** the sticking out of some tissue or organ of the body through the wall of the cavity that should hold it in. **4** to break; burst; break off. 1–3 *n.,* 4 *v.,* **rup·tured, rup·tur·ing.**

ru·ral (rür′əl) in the country; belonging to the country; like that of the country: *Rural life is healthful and quiet.* *adj.*

rural route a mail-delivery circuit in the country: *R.R. stands for rural route.*

ruse (rüz) a trick or stratagem. *n.*

rush[1] (rush) **1** move or go with speed and force: *The river rushed past.* **2** send, push, or force with speed or haste: *Rush this order, please.* **3** go or act with great haste: *He rushes into things without knowing anything about them.* **4** to attack with much speed and force: *The soldiers rushed the enemy's trenches.* **5** the act of rushing; a dash: *The rush of the flood swept everything before it.* **6** a hurry: *the rush of city life.* **7** a great or sudden effort of many people to go somewhere or get something: *Few people got rich in the Klondike gold rush.* **8** requiring haste: *A rush order must be filled at once.* 1–4 *v.,* 5–7 *n.,* 8 *adj.*

rush[2] (rush) a grasslike plant with pithy or hollow stems that grows in wet soil or marshy places: *The seats of chairs are sometimes made of rushes.* *n.*

rus·set (rus′it) **1** yellowish brown; reddish brown: *The leaves in the fall are scarlet, yellow, and russet.* **2** a kind of apple having a rough, brownish skin. 1, 2 *n.,* 1 *adj.*

Rus·sian (rush′ən) **1** of or having something to do with Russia, its people, or their language. **2** a person born in or living in Russia. **3** the language of Russia. 1 *adj.,* 2, 3 *n.*

rust (rust) **1** the reddish-brown or orange coating that forms on iron or steel which is exposed to air or moisture. **2** become covered with this coating: *The careless carpenter allowed his tools to rust.* **3** spoil or become spoiled by not being used: *Don't let your mind rust during vacation.* **4** a plant disease that spots leaves and stems. **5** reddish brown or orange. 1, 4, 5 *n.,* 2, 3 *v.,* 5 *adj.*

rus·tic (rus′tik) **1** belonging to the country; rural; suitable for the country. **2** simple; plain; like those of country people: *His rustic speech and ways made him uncomfortable in the city school.* **3** rough; awkward. **4** a country person: *The rustics had gathered at the county fair.* 1–3 *adj.,* 4 *n.*

rus·tle (rus′əl) **1** the sound that leaves make when moved by the wind; a sound like this. **2** make or cause to make this sound: *Leaves rustled in the breeze. The wind rustled the papers.* **3** *Informal.* steal cattle or horses. 1 *n.,* 2, 3 *v.,* **rus·tled, rus·tling.**
rustle up, **a** gather; find. **b** get ready; prepare: *The cook rustled up some food.*

rus·tler (rus′lər) *Informal.* a cattle thief. *n.*

rust·y (rus′tē) **1** covered with rust; rusted: *a rusty* *knife.* 2 made by rust: *a rusty spot.* 3 colored like rust. 4 faded: *a rusty black.* 5 weakened from lack of use or practice: *Mother's arithmetic is rusty, she says.* *adj.,* **rust·i·er, rust·i·est.**

rut (rut) 1 a track made in the ground by wheels. 2 make ruts in. 3 a fixed or established way of acting: *The old man was so set in his ways that everyone said he was in a rut.* 1, 3 *n.,* 2 *v.,* **rut·ted, rut·ting.**

ru·ta·ba·ga (rü′tə bā′gə or rü′tə bag′ə) a kind of large, yellow or white turnip. *n.*

ruth·less (rüth′lis) having no pity; showing no mercy; cruel: *a ruthless tyrant. adj.*

rye (rī) 1 a hardy plant widely grown in cold regions. 2 its seed or grain, used for making flour, as food for livestock, and in making whisky. 3 flour made from this grain: *Some of the people in Germany and Russia eat a great deal of black rye bread.* 4 whisky made from rye. *n.*

☛ **Rye and wry are pronounced the same.**

hat, āge, fär; let, ēqual, tėrm; it, īce
hot, ōpen, ôrder; oil, out; cup, pu̇t, rüle
əbove, takən, pencəl, lemən, circəs
ch, child; ng, long; sh, ship
th, thin; ᴛʜ, then; zh, measure

s or **S** (es) 1 the 19th letter of the alphabet: *There are two* s's *in* sister. 2 anything shaped like an S. 3 shaped like an S: *an S-curve, an S-wrench. n., pl.* **s's** or **S's.**

s second; seconds.

S. or **S** 1 south. 2 southern.

Sab·bath (sab′əth) the day of the week used for rest and worship: *Sunday is the Christian Sabbath. Saturday is the Jewish Sabbath. n.*

sa·ber (sā′bər) See **sabre.**

sa·ble (sā′bəl) 1 a small flesh-eating animal related to the weasel and the mink. 2 its dark-brown, glossy fur: *Sable is one of the most costly furs. n.*

sa·bre or **sa·ber** (sā′bər) a heavy, curved sword with a sharp point and cutting edge. *n.*

sac (sak) a baglike part in an animal or plant, often containing liquids: *the sac of a honeybee. n.*

☛ Sac and **sack** are pronounced the same.

sac·cha·rin (sak′ə rin) a very sweet substance obtained from coal tar, used instead of sugar: *She takes saccharin in her coffee. n.*

sa·chem (sā′chəm) the chief of a North American Indian tribe. *n.*

sack[1] (sak) 1 a large bag made of coarse cloth or strong paper: *Sacks are used for holding grain, flour, potatoes, and coal.* 2 such a bag with what is in it: *He bought two sacks of corn.* 3 *Esp. U.S.* any bag or what is in it: *a sack of candy.* 4 put into a sack or sacks. 1–3 *n.*, 4 *v.*

☛ Sack and **sac** are pronounced the same.

sack[2] (sak) 1 plunder a captured city: *The invaders sacked the town.* 2 a plundering of a captured city: *the sack of Rome by the barbarians.* 1 *v.*, 2 *n.*

☛ See note at **sack**[1].

sac·ra·ment (sak′rə mənt) in Christian churches, any of certain religious ceremonies considered especially sacred: *Baptism is a sacrament. n.*

sa·cred (sā′krid) 1 belonging to God; holy: *A church is a sacred building.* 2 connected with religion; religious: *sacred writings, sacred music.* 3 worthy of reverence: *the sacred memory of a dead hero.* 4 that must not be violated or disregarded: *He made a sacred promise. adj.*

sac·ri·fice (sak′rə fīs′) 1 the act of offering to a god. 2 the thing offered: *The ancient Hebrews killed animals on the altars as sacrifices to God.* 3 give or offer to a god: *They sacrificed oxen, sheep, and doves.* 4 the giving up of one thing for another: *Our teacher does not approve of any sacrifice of studies to sports.* 5 give up: *A mother will sacrifice her life for her children.* 6 a loss from selling something below its value: *He will sell his house at a sacrifice because he needs the money.* 7 sell at a loss. 1, 2, 4, 6 *n.*, 3, 5, 7 *v.*, **sac·ri·ficed, sac·ri·fic·ing.**

sac·ri·lege (sak′rə lij) an intentional injury to anything sacred; disrespectful treatment of anyone or anything sacred: *Robbing the church was a sacrilege. n.*

sad (sad) 1 not happy; full of sorrow: *You feel sad if your best friend goes away. Mary was sad because she lost her money.* 2 causing sorrow: *The death of a pet is a sad loss.* 3 *Informal.* shocking; hopeless: *a sad mess. adj.*, **sad·der, sad·dest.**

sad·den (sad′ən) make or become sad: *The news saddened him. His face saddened at the news. v.*

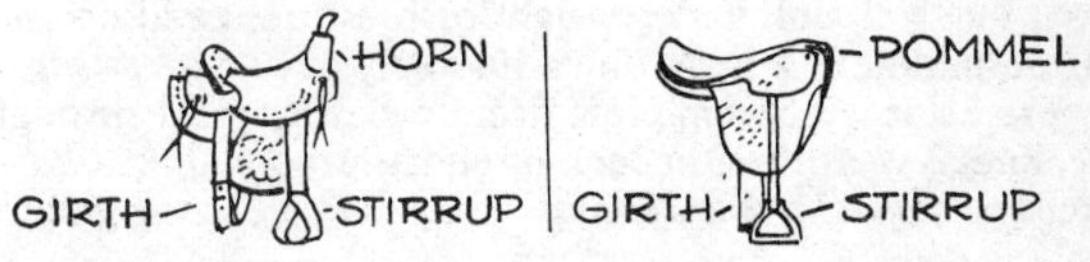

A western saddle An English saddle

sad·dle (sad′əl) 1 a seat for a rider on a horse's back, on a bicycle, etc. 2 anything shaped or used like a saddle: *A ridge between two mountain peaks is called a saddle.* 3 put a saddle on: *Saddle the horse.* 4 to burden: *He is saddled with a big house that he does not need or want.* 5 a cut of mutton, venison, lamb, etc., consisting of the upper back portion of the animal. 1, 2, 5 *n.*, 3, 4 *v.*, **sad·dled, sad·dling.**

in the saddle, in a position of control.

sad·ness (sad′nis) sorrow; grief. *n.*

sa·fa·ri (sə fä′rē) 1 a journey or hunting expedition in eastern Africa. 2 any long trip or expedition. *n.*

safe (sāf) 1 free from harm or danger: *Keep money in a safe place.* 2 not harmed: *He returned from war safe and sound.* 3 out of danger; secure: *We feel safe with the dog in the house.* 4 careful: *a safe guess, a safe move.* 5 that can be depended on: *a safe guide.* 6 a metal container for keeping things safe. 1–5 *adj.*, **saf·er, saf·est;** 6 *n.*

safe·guard (sāf′gärd′) 1 keep safe; guard against hurt or danger; protect: *Food and drug laws safeguard our health.* 2 a protection; a defence: *Keeping clean is a safeguard against disease.* 1 *v.*, 2 *n.*

safe·keep·ing (sāf′kēp′ing) protection; keeping safe; care. *n.*

safe·ty (sāf′tē) 1 freedom from harm or danger: *A bank assures safety for your money. You can cross the street in safety when the policeman holds up his hand to stop the cars.* 2 giving safety; making harm unlikely: *a safety belt, a safety lamp.* 1 *n.*, 2 *adj.*

safety belt 1 a belt used in cars and airplanes to keep a person from falling or being thrown out of his seat in the case of a crash or other accident: *Safety belts in cars often include a strap that passes over the shoulder.* 2 a strap used by window cleaners, loggers, linemen, etc. to keep themselves from falling.

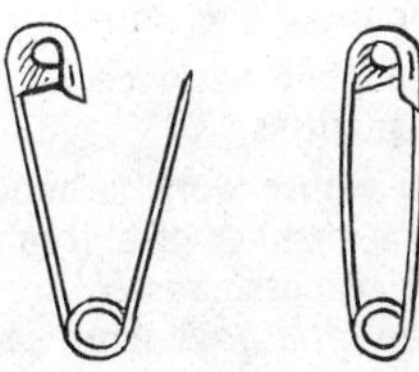

A safety pin, open and closed

safety pin a pin bent back on itself to form a spring

and having a guard that covers the point to prevent accidental unfastening.

saf·fron (saf′rən) 1 an orange-yellow coloring matter obtained from a kind of crocus: *Saffron is used to color and flavor candy, drinks, etc.* 2 orange yellow. 1, 2 *n.,* 2 *adj.*

sag (sag) 1 sink under weight or pressure; bend down in the middle. 2 hang down unevenly: *Your dress sags in the back.* 3 become less firm or elastic; yield through weakness, weariness, or lack of effort; droop; sink: *Our courage sagged.* 4 a sagging. 1–3 *v.,* **sagged, sag·ging;** 4 *n.*

sa·ga (sä′gə) any story of heroic deeds. *n.*

☛ **Saga** comes from an old Norse word meaning a tale or story.

sa·ga·cious (sə gā′shəs) shrewd; wise in a keen, practical way. *adj.*

sa·gac·i·ty (sə gas′ə tē) keen, sound judgment: *Laurier was a man of sagacity. n.*

sage[1] (sāj) 1 wise: *a sage adviser.* 2 wise-looking; grave; solemn: *Owls are sage birds.* 3 a very wise man: *The sage gave advice to the young man.* 1, 2 *adj.,* **sag·er, sag·est;** 3 *n.*

sage[2] (sāj) 1 a plant whose dried leaves are much used in cooking and in medicine. 2 sagebrush. *n.*

sage·brush (sāj′brush′) a greyish-green shrub that smells like sage, common on the dry plains of western North America. *n.*

Sa·har·a (sə her′ə or sə här′ə) the great desert in the north of Africa. *n.*

said (sed) 1 See **say.** *He said he would come. She had said 'No' every time.* 2 named or mentioned before: *the said witness, the said sum of money.* 1 *v.,* 2 *adj.*

sail (sāl) 1 a piece of cloth that catches the wind to make a ship move on the water. See **schooner** for picture. 2 something like a sail, such as the part of a windmill that catches the wind. 3 travel on water by the action of wind on sails. 4 travel on a ship of any kind: *He sailed to England on a steamship.* 5 a trip on a boat with sails: *Let's go for a sail.* 6 a ship; ships: *a fleet numbering 30 sail.* 7 move smoothly like a ship with sails: *The swans sail along the lake. The eagle sailed by. Mrs. Grand sailed into the room.* 8 sail upon, over, or through: *to sail the seas.* 9 manage a ship or boat: *The boys are learning to sail.* 10 begin a trip by water: *She sails from Halifax today.* 1, 2, 5, 6 *n.,* 3, 4, 7–10 *v.*

make sail, a spread out the sails of a ship. **b** begin a trip by water.

set sail, begin a trip by water.

under sail, moving with the sails spread out.

☛ **Sail** and **sale** are pronounced the same.

sail·boat (sāl′bōt′) a boat that is moved by sails. See **schooner** and **sloop** for pictures. *n.*

sail·or (sāl′ər) 1 a person whose work is handling a sailboat or other vessel. 2 a member of a ship's crew. 3 one who sails for pleasure; yachtsman: *He's a keen sailor.* 4 like a sailor's: *The little boys wore sailor suits and sailor caps.* 1–3 *n.,* 4 *adj.*

saint (sānt) 1 a very holy person; a true Christian. 2 a person declared to be a saint by the Roman Catholic Church. 3 a person who is very humble, patient, etc., like a saint. *n.*

Saint Most names beginning with 'Saint' are commonly written with the abbreviation 'St.'

A Saint Bernard — about 75 cm high at the shoulder

Saint Ber·nard (sānt′bər närd′ or sənt bėr′nərd) a big, powerful, tan-and-white dog with a large head: *Saint Bernards are often trained to rescue travellers lost in the snow of the Swiss mountains.*

saint·ly (sānt′lē) like a saint; very holy; very good. *adj.,* **saint·li·er, saint·li·est.**

sake (sāk) 1 benefit; account; interest: *Put yourself to no trouble for our sakes.* 2 purpose; aim: *He moved to the country for the sake of peace and quiet. n.*

for your own sake, on your own account; to help yourself.

sal·a·ble (sāl′ə bəl) that can be sold; fit to be sold; easily sold: *After the fire, few things in the store were salable. adj.* Also spelled **saleable.**

sal·ad (sal′əd) 1 raw vegetables, such as lettuce, green onions, and celery, usually served with a dressing. 2 a prepared course or dish made with raw vegetables or raw fruit, sometimes molded in jelly, and often mixed or served with eggs, seafood, chicken, or other cold meats. *n.*

A spotted salamander — about 15 cm long with the tail

sal·a·man·der (sal′ə man′dər) an animal shaped like a lizard, but belonging to the same family as frogs and toads: *Salamanders live in water or in damp places. n.*

sal·a·ry (sal′ə rē or sal′rē) fixed pay for regular work: *Teachers and clerks receive salaries. n., pl.* **sal·a·ries.**

sale (sāl) 1 the act of selling; the exchange of goods for money: *The sale of his old home made him sad.* 2 the amount sold: *Today's sales were larger than yesterday's.* 3 the chance to sell; the demand: *There is almost no sale for washboards in these days.* 4 selling at lower prices than usual: *This store is having a sale on suits.* 5 an auction. *n.*

for sale, to be sold; available for buying: *That car is for sale.*

on sale, a for sale at lower prices than usual: *All the winter boots are on sale now.* **b** for sale: *Tickets for the concert will be on sale here on Monday.*

☛ **Sale** and **sail** are pronounced the same.

sale·a·ble (sāl′ə bəl) See **salable.**

sales·la·dy (sālz′lā′dē) a woman whose work is selling, especially in a store. *n.*

hat, āge, fär; let, ēqual, tėrm; it, īce
hot, ōpen, ôrder; oil, out; cup, pu̇t, rüle
əbove, takən, pencəl, lemən, circəs
ch, child; ng, long; sh, ship
th, thin; ᴛʜ, then; zh, measure

sales·man (sālz′mən) a man whose work is selling goods or services: *Four salesmen were showing people suits and sweaters.* *n., pl.* **sales·men** (sālz′mən).

sales tax a tax based on the amount received for articles sold.

sales·wom·an (sālz′wu̇m′ən) saleslady. *n., pl.* **sales·wom·en** (sālz′wim′ən).

sa·li·va (sə lī′və) the liquid produced by glands in the mouth to keep it moist, help in chewing, and start digestion. *n.*

sal·i·var·y (sal′ə ver′ē) of or producing saliva: *the salivary glands.* *adj.*

sal·low (sal′ō) of a pallid, yellowish color: *a sallow complexion, a sallow face.* *adj.*

sal·ly (sal′ē) **1** a sudden rushing forth: *The men in the fort made a brave sally and returned with many prisoners.* **2** rush forth suddenly; go out; set out briskly: *We sallied forth at dawn.* **3** a witty remark: *She continued her story undisturbed by the merry sallies of her hearers.* 1, 3 *n., pl.* **sal·lies;** 2 *v.,* **sal·lied, sal·ly·ing.**

salm·on (sam′ən) **1** a large fish with silvery scales and yellowish-pink flesh: *Canned salmon is a tasty food.* **2** yellowish pink. 1, 2 *n., pl.* **salm·on** or **salm·ons;** 2 *adj.*

salm·on·ber·ry (sam′ən ber′ē) **1** a large, red-flowered raspberry bush that bears edible pink fruit. **2** the fruit of this bush. *n.*

sa·lon (sə lon′ or sal′on) a large room for receiving and entertaining guests. *n.*

sa·loon (sə lün′) **1** a place where alcoholic drinks are sold and drunk. **2** a large room for general or public use: *Concerts were often held in the saloon of the steamship. The ship's passengers ate in the dining saloon.* *n.*

salt (solt or sôlt) **1** a white substance found in the earth and in sea water: *Salt is used to season and preserve food.* **2** containing salt: *salt water.* **3** tasting like salt. **4** mix or sprinkle with salt. **5** cure or preserve with salt. **6** cured or preserved with salt. **7** provide or feed with salt: *to salt cattle.* **8** a chemical compound formed by the union of an acid and a base: *Baking soda is a salt.* **9** a sailor: *an old salt.* **10** a small container for salt: *silver salts and peppers.* **11 Take** a statement **with a grain of salt** means to doubt what is stated because it is likely to be either untrue or exaggerated: *The policeman took their story with a grain of salt.* 1, 8–11 *n.,* 2, 3, 6 *adj.,* 4, 5, 7 *v.*

salt away or **salt down, a** pack with salt in order to preserve: *The fish were salted down in a barrel.* **b** *Slang.* store away: *The miser salted a lot of money away.*

salt of the earth, the best people.

worth one's salt, worth one's wages, pay, support, etc.

salt lick a place where natural salt is found on the surface of the ground and where animals go to lick it up.

salt–wa·ter (solt′wo′tər or sôlt′wô′tər) of, containing, or having to do with salt water or the sea: *a salt-water solution, salt-water fishing.* *adj.*

salt·y (sol′tē or sôl′tē) containing salt; tasting of salt: *Sweat and tears are salty.* *adj.,* **salt·i·er, salt·i·est.**

sal·u·tar·y (sal′yə ter′ē) **1** beneficial: *The teacher gave the boy salutary advice.* **2** good for the health: *salutary exercise.* *adj.*

sal·u·ta·tion (sal′yə tā′shən) **1** a greeting; saluting: *The man raised his hat in salutation.* **2** something uttered, written, or done to salute: *You begin a letter with a salutation, such as 'Dear Sir' or 'My dear Mrs. Jones.' A formal bow was her parting salutation.* *n.*

sa·lute (sə lüt′) **1** honor or show respect in a formal manner by raising the hand to the head, by firing guns, by dipping flags, etc.: *The soldier saluted the officer.* **2** meet with kind words, cheers, a bow, a kiss, etc.; greet. **3** the act of saluting; a sign of welcome, farewell, or honor: *The queen gracefully acknowledged the salutes of the crowd.* **4** the position of the hand, rifle, sword, etc. when saluting: *The general held the salute till the troops had marched past.* 1, 2 *v.,* **sa·lut·ed, sa·lut·ing;** 3, 4 *n.*

sal·vage (sal′vij) **1** the act or process of saving a ship or its cargo from wreck or capture. **2** the payment for saving it. **3** the rescue of property from fire, flood, shipwreck, etc. **4** save from fire, flood, shipwreck, etc. **5** the property salvaged. 1–3, 5 *n.,* 4 *v.,* **sal·vaged, sal·vag·ing.**

sal·va·tion (sal vā′shən) **1** a person or thing that saves: *Christians believe that Christ is the salvation of the world. The firefighters were our salvation; they stopped the forest fire before it reached our town.* **2** a saving of the soul; the deliverance from sin and from punishment for sin. *n.*

salve (sav) **1** a soft, greasy ointment put on wounds and sores to soothe or heal them: *Is this salve good for burns?* **2** put salve on. **3** something soothing: *The kind words were a salve to his hurt feelings.* **4** soothe; smooth over: *He salved his conscience by the thought that his lie harmed no one.* 1, 3 *n.,* 2, 4 *v.,* **salved, salv·ing.**

sal·vo (sal′vō) the discharge of several guns at the same time, as a broadside or as a salute. *n.*

same (sām) **1** not another: *We came back the same way we went.* **2** just alike; not different: *Her name and mine are the same.* **3** not changed: *He is the same kind old man.* **4** just spoken of: *The boys were talking about a strange man. This same man wore his hair very long and always dressed in white.* **5** the same person or thing. 1–4 *adj.,* 5 *pron.*

all the same, regardless; nevertheless.

just the same, a in the same manner. **b** nevertheless.

the same, in the same manner: *'Sea' and 'see' are pronounced the same.*

same·ness (sām′nis) **1** being the same: *He was struck by the sameness of the two pictures.* **2** a lack of variety: *The sameness of the food in this cafeteria is depressing.* *n.*

sam·pan (sam′pan) any of various small boats of China, etc.: *A sampan is sculled by one or more oars at the stern; it usually has a single sail.* *n.*

sam·ple (sam′pəl) **1** a part to show what the rest is like; one thing to show what the others are like: *Get samples of blue silk for a new dress. He showed us a sample of his new book.* **2** take a part of; test a part of:

We sampled the cake and found it very good. 1 *n.*, 2 *v.*, **sam·pled, sam·pling.**

san·a·tor·i·um (san′ə tôr′ ē əm) sanitarium. *n.*

sanc·tion (sangk′shən) 1 permission with authority; support; approval: *We have the sanction of the law to play ball in this park.* 2 approve; authorize; allow: *Her conscience does not sanction stealing.* 1 *n.*, 2 *v.*

sanc·ti·ty (sangk′tə tē) 1 saintliness: *the sanctity of a saint.* 2 sacredness; holy character: *the sanctity of a church, the sanctity of the home.* *n., pl.* **sanc·ti·ties.**

sanc·tu·ar·y (sangk′chü er′ē) 1 a sacred place: *A church is a sanctuary.* 2 the part of a church around the altar. 3 a place of refuge or protection: *This island is maintained as a bird sanctuary.* 4 refuge or protection: *The lost travellers found sanctuary in a deserted hut.* *n., pl.* **sanc·tu·ar·ies.**

sand (sand) 1 tiny grains of worn-down or disintegrated rock: *the sands of the seashore, the sands of the desert.* 2 scrape, smooth, polish, or clean with sand or sandpaper. 3 spread sand over: *to sand an icy road.* 1 *n.*, 2, 3 *v.*

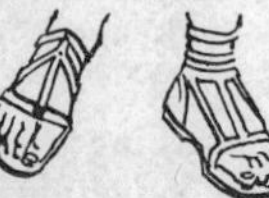

Sandals

san·dal (san′dəl) a kind of shoe made of a sole and a strap or any of various kinds of low-cut shoes, slippers, etc. *n.*

sand bar a ridge of sand in a river or along a shore, formed by the action of tides and currents.

sand·box (sand′boks′) a box for holding sand, especially for children to play in. *n.*

sand·man (sand′man′) in folk tales, a man said to make children sleepy by sprinkling sand in their eyes. *n.*

sand·pa·per (sand′pā′pər) 1 a strong paper with sand or some other rough material glued on it, used for smoothing, cleaning, or polishing. 2 to smooth, clean, or polish with sandpaper. 1 *n.*, 2 *v.*

sand·pip·er (sand′pī′pər) a small bird having a long bill, living on sandy shores. *n.*

sand·stone (sand′stōn′) a kind of rock formed mostly of sand. *n.*

sand·storm (sand′stôrm′) a storm of wind that carries along clouds of sand. *n.*

sand·wich (sand′wich) 1 two or more slices of bread with meat, jelly, cheese, or some other filling between them. 2 put or squeeze in between: *He was sandwiched between two fat women.* 1 *n.*, 2 *v.*

☛ Named after the Earl of *Sandwich* (1718–1792), who supposedly invented it so that he would not have to stop playing cards for meals.

sand·y (san′dē) 1 containing sand; consisting of sand; covered with sand: *to lie in the sun on a sandy beach.* 2 yellowish-red: *sandy hair.* *adj.*, **sand·i·er, sand·i·est.**

sane (sān) 1 having a healthy mind; not crazy. 2 having or showing good sense; sensible: *She has a sane attitude toward studying.* *adj.*, **san·er, san·est.**

☛ **Sane** and **seine** are pronounced the same.

sang (sang) See **sing.** *He sang a solo.* *v.*

san·guine (sang′gwin) 1 naturally cheerful and hopeful: *a sanguine disposition.* 2 confident; hopeful: *sanguine of success.* 3 having a healthy red color; ruddy: *a sanguine complexion.* *adj.*

san·i·tar·i·um (san′ə ter′ē əm) a place for the treatment of the sick, especially people with long-term illnesses or those recovering after illness: *A person with tuberculosis may be sent to a sanitarium.* *n.*

san·i·tar·y (san′ə ter′ē) 1 of health; about health; favorable to health; preventing disease. 2 free from dirt and filth: *Food should be kept in a sanitary place.* *adj.*

san·i·ta·tion (san′ə tā′shən) the working out and practical application of sanitary measures: *Disposal of garbage and government inspection of milk, meat, and other foods are important parts of sanitation.* *n.*

san·i·ty (san′ə tē) 1 soundness of mind; mental health. 2 soundness of judgment. *n.*

sank (sangk) See **sink.** *The ship sank before help reached them.* *v.*

San·ta (san′tə) Santa Claus. *n.*

San·ta Claus (san′tə kloz′ or san′tə klôz′) the spirit or saint of Christmas giving; Saint Nicholas: *Santa Claus is pictured as a jolly old man with a white beard, dressed in a fur-trimmed red suit.*

sap¹ (sap) the liquid that circulates through a plant, carrying water, food, etc., as blood does in animals: *Rising sap carries water and salt from the roots; sap going downward carries sugar, gums, and resins. Maple sugar is made from the sap of certain maple trees.* *n.*

sap² (sap) 1 dig under or wear away the foundation of: *The walls of the boathouse had been sapped by the waves.* 2 weaken; use up: *The extreme heat sapped her strength.* *v.*, **sapped, sap·ping.**

sap·ling (sap′ling) a young tree. *n.*

sap·phire (saf′īr) 1 a bright-blue or colorless precious stone: *A sapphire is hard and clear like a diamond.* 2 bright blue: *a sapphire sky.* 1, 2 *n.*, 2 *adj.*

sap·suck·er (sap′suk′ər) a small American woodpecker that feeds on the sap of trees. *n.*

sap·wood (sap′wu̇d′) the soft, new, living wood between the bark and the hard, inner wood of most trees. *n.*

sar·casm (sär′kaz əm) 1 a sneering or cutting remark that means the opposite of what it says. 2 the act of making fun of a person to hurt his feelings; harsh or bitter irony: *Her sarcasm was obvious when she called the frightened boy a hero.* *n.*

sar·cas·tic (sär kas′tik) using sarcasm; sneering; bitterly cutting: *'Don't hurry!' was his mother's sarcastic comment as he began to dress at his usual slow rate.* *adj.*

sar·dine (sär dēn′) a young or small herring or related fish, often preserved in oil for food. *n., pl.* **sar·dines** or **sar·dine.**

packed like sardines, very much crowded.

sa·ri (sä′rē) a garment, the principal dress of women in India and Pakistan, consisting of a long piece of cotton or silk wound and draped around the body. *n.*

sa·rong (sə rong′) a rectangular piece of cloth, usually a brightly colored, printed material, worn as a skirt by men and women in the East Indies. *n.*

sash¹ (sash) a long, broad strip of cloth or ribbon,

worn as an ornament around the waist or over one shoulder: *She wore a white dress with a blue sash around her waist.* *n.*

sash[2] (sash) the frame which holds the glass in a window or door: *The window sash slipped down and crushed her finger.* See **lintel** for picture. *n.*

Sask. Saskatchewan.

Sas·katch·e·wan·i·an (səs kach′ə won′ē ən) **1** a person born in or living in Saskatchewan. **2** of or having to do with Saskatchewan. 1 *n.*, 2 *adj.*

sas·ka·toon (sas′kə tün′) **1** a bush or small tree bearing large, sweet, purple berries. **2** the fruit of this bush: *Saskatoons are delicious in pies or jam.* *n.*

☛ **Saskatoon** comes from a Cree word meaning 'fruit of the tree of many branches.'

sat (sat) See **sit.** *Yesterday I sat in a train all day. The cat sat at that mouse hole for hours.* *v.*

Sat. Saturday.

Sa·tan (sā′tən) the evil spirit; the enemy of goodness; the Devil. *n.*

satch·el (sach′əl) a small bag for carrying clothes, books, etc. *n.*

sat·el·lite (sat′ə līt′) **1** a heavenly body that revolves around a planet, especially around one of the nine major planets of the solar system: *The moon is a satellite of the earth.* **2** a man-made object shot into space to revolve around the earth or other heavenly body in an orbit. **3** a follower or attendant upon a person of importance. **4** a country that is supposedly independent but is actually under the control of another country: *East Germany is a satellite of the Soviet Union.* *n.*

sat·in (sat′ən) **1** a cloth with one very smooth, glossy side. **2** a smoothness or glossiness like that of satin: *the satin of the baby's skin. The silver bowl had a satin finish.* *n.*

sat·is·fac·tion (sat′is fak′shən) **1** the condition of being satisfied, or pleased and contented: *She felt satisfaction at winning a prize.* **2** anything that makes us feel pleased or contented: *It is a great satisfaction to have things turn out just the way you want.* **3** a fulfilment; satisfying: *The satisfaction of hunger requires food.* *n.*

sat·is·fac·to·ri·ly (sat′is fak′tə rə lē or sat′is fak′trə lē) in a satisfactory manner. *adv.*

sat·is·fac·to·ry (sat′is fak′tə rē or sat′is fak′trē) satisfying; good enough to satisfy; adequate or sufficient: *a satisfactory answer, a satisfactory holiday.* *adj.*

sat·is·fy (sat′is fī′) **1** give enough to; fulfil desires, hopes, or demands; put an end to wants or needs: *He satisfied his hunger with a sandwich.* **2** make contented; please: *Are you satisfied now?* **3** pay; make right: *After the accident he satisfied all claims for the damage he had caused.* **4** convince: *The teacher was satisfied that Jack's statement was true.* *v.*, **sat·is·fied, sat·is·fy·ing.**

A sari

A sarong

hat, āge, fär; let, ēqual, tėrm; it, īce
hot, ōpen, ôrder; oil, out; cup, pu̇t, rüle
əbove, takən, pencəl, lemən, circəs
ch, child; ng, long; sh, ship
th, thin; ᴛʜ, then; zh, measure

sat·u·rate (sach′ə rāt′) soak thoroughly; fill full: *During the fog, the air was saturated with moisture. Saturate the moss with water before planting the bulbs.* *v.*, **sat·u·rat·ed, sat·u·rat·ing.**

Sat·ur·day (sat′ər dē or sat′ər dā′) the seventh day of the week, the day after Friday. *n.*

☛ **Saturday** developed from *Sæterdæg*, the Old English translation of the Latin phrase meaning 'day of Saturn.'

Sat·urn (sat′ərn) **1** the Roman god of agriculture. **2** the second largest planet: *Saturn is encircled by three rings made up of tiny particles of matter.* *n.*

sat·yr (sat′ər or sā′tər) in Greek legends, a creature of the woods, part man and part goat or horse: *The satyrs were followers of Bacchus, the god of wine.* *n.*

sauce (sos or sôs) **1** something, usually a liquid, served with a food to make it taste better: *We eat mint sauce with lamb, egg sauce with fish, and many different sauces with puddings.* **2** stewed fruit. *n.*

sauce·pan (sos′pan′ or sôs′pan′) a deep cooking pan with a handle, used for stewing, boiling, etc. *n.*

sau·cer (so′sər or sô′sər) **1** a shallow dish to set a cup on. **2** a small, round dish with its edge curved up. **3** something round and shallow like a saucer. *n.*

sau·cy (so′sē or sô′sē) **1** showing lack of respect; rude. **2** pert; smart: *She wore a saucy hat.* *adj.*, **sau·ci·er, sau·ci·est.**

sauer·kraut (sour′krout′) cabbage cut fine, salted, and allowed to sour. *n.*

sault (sü) *Cdn.* a falls or rapids. *n.*

saun·ter (son′tər or sôn′tər) **1** walk along slowly and quietly; stroll: *People saunter through the park on summer evenings.* **2** a stroll. 1 *v.*, 2 *n.*

sau·sage (so′sij or sô′sij) chopped pork, beef, or other meats, seasoned and usually stuffed into a thin tube or skin. *n.*

sav·age (sav′ij) **1** wild or rugged: *He likes savage mountain scenery.* **2** not civilized; barbarous: *savage customs.* **3** a member of a primitive, uncivilized people. **4** fierce; cruel; ready to fight: *The savage lion attacked the hunter.* **5** a fierce, brutal, or cruel person. 1, 2, 4 *adj.*, 3, 5 *n.*

sav·age·ry (sav′ij rē) **1** fierceness; cruelty; brutality. **2** wildness. **3** an uncivilized condition. *n.*, *pl.* **sav·age·ries.**

save[1] (sāv) **1** make safe from harm, danger, hurt, loss, etc.; rescue: *The dog saved the boy's life. The woman saved her jewels from the fire.* **2** keep safe from harm, danger, hurt, loss, etc.; protect: *to save one's honor.* **3** lay aside; store up: *to save money. She saves pieces of string.* **4** keep from spending or wasting: *Save your strength.* **5** avoid expense or waste: *She saves in every* *way she can.* 6 prevent; make less: *to save work, to save trouble, to save expense.* 7 treat carefully to lessen wear, weariness, etc.: *Large print saves one's eyes.* 8 set free from sin and its results: *The Christian church teaches that Christ came to save the world.* *v.,* **saved, sav·ing.**

save² (sāv) except; but: *He works every day of the week save Sunday. prep.*

sav·ing (sāv′ing) 1 a way of saving money, time, etc.: *It will be a saving to take this short cut.* 2 **savings,** *pl.* money saved. 3 save; except; with the exception of: *We had eaten nothing all day, saving a few cookies.* 1, 2 *n.,* 3 *prep.*

sav·ior or **sav·iour** (sāv′yər) one who saves or rescues. *n.*

Sav·iour or **Sav·ior** (sāv′yər) Jesus Christ: *In the Christian religion, Christ is the Saviour of mankind. n.*

sa·vor or **sa·vour** (sā′vər) 1 a taste or smell; flavor: *The soup has a savor of onion.* 2 enjoy the taste or smell of: *He savored the soup with pleasure.* 3 have the quality or nature of: *The plot savored of treason.* 1 *n.,* 2, 3 *v.*

sa·vor·y¹ or **sa·vour·y** (sā′vər ē) pleasing in taste or smell: *The savory smell of roasting turkey greeted us as we entered the house. adj.,* **sa·vor·i·er** or **sa·vour·i·er, sa·vor·i·est** or **sa·vour·i·est.**

sa·vor·y² (sā′vər ē) a fragrant herb related to the mint, used for seasoning food. *n.*

saw¹ (so or sô) 1 a tool for cutting, made of a thin blade with sharp teeth on the edge. See the picture. 2 cut with a saw: *The man saws wood.* 3 make with a saw: *Boards are sawed from logs.* 4 use a saw: *Can you saw straight?* 5 be sawed: *Pine saws more easily than oak.* 1 *n.,* 2–5 *v.,* **sawed, sawed** or **sawn, saw·ing.**

saw² (so or sô) See **see¹**. *I saw a robin. v.*

saw³ (so or sô) a wise saying; proverb: *'A stitch in time saves nine' is a familiar saw. n.*

☛ Saw³ comes from an Old English word *sagu,* meaning 'a saying.' It is related to **saga.**

saw·dust (so′dust′ or sô′dust′) the tiny particles of wood that result from sawing. *n.*

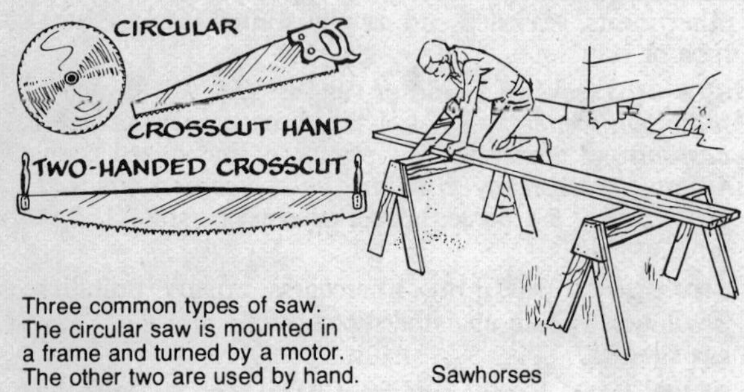

Three common types of saw. The circular saw is mounted in a frame and turned by a motor. The other two are used by hand.

Sawhorses

saw·horse (so′hôrs′ or sô′hôrs′) a frame for holding wood that is being sawed. *n.*

saw·mill (so′mil′ or sô′mil′) a building where machines saw timber into planks, boards, etc. *n.*

sawn (son or sôn) sawed. See **saw¹**. *v.*

A saxophone

sax·o·phone (sak′sə fōn′) a musical wind instrument having a curved metal body with keys for the fingers and a reed mouthpiece. *n.*

☛ Named after Adolphe *Sax* (1814–1894), a Belgian inventor, and Greek *phōnē,* meaning 'sound.'

say (sā) 1 speak: *Mother has taught me always to say 'Please' and 'Thank you.'* 2 put into words; declare: *Say what you think.* 3 recite; repeat: *Say your prayers.* 4 let us suppose or guess: *You can learn to dance in, say, ten lessons.* 5 express an opinion: *It is hard to say which dress is prettier.* 6 what a person says or has to say: *He said his say and left.* 7 the chance to say something: *Everyone will have his say before the meeting ends.* 8 power; authority: *the final say.* 1–5 *v.,* **said, say·ing;** 6–8 *n.*

say·ing (sā′ing) something said, especially a wise statement that is often repeated: *I remember a saying of my father's. 'Haste makes waste' is an old saying. n.* **go without saying,** be too obvious to need mention: *It goes without saying that people need food to keep alive.*

says (sez) See **say.** *He says 'No' to everything. v.*

scab (skab) 1 the crust that forms over a sore or wound as it heals: *A scab formed on the spot where he was vaccinated.* 2 a skin disease in animals, especially sheep. 3 a disease of plants, usually producing spots like crusts: *Scab is caused by a fungus. n.*

scab·bard (skab′ərd) a sheath or case for the blade of a sword, dagger, etc. See **sword** for picture. *n.*

A scaffold

scaf·fold (skaf′əld) 1 a temporary structure for holding workmen and materials. 2 a raised platform used as a base for a gallows or guillotine. *n.*

scald (skold or skôld) 1 burn with hot liquid or steam: *She scalded herself with hot grease.* 2 a burn caused by hot liquid or steam: *The scald on her hand came from lifting a pot cover carelessly.* 3 pour boiling liquid over; use boiling liquid on: *Scald the dishes before drying them.* 4 heat almost to boiling, but not quite: *Scald the milk.* 1, 3, 4 *v.,* 2 *n.*

scale¹ (skāl) 1 one of the thin, flat, hard plates forming the outer covering of some fishes, snakes, and lizards. **2** a thin layer like a scale: *Scales of skin peeled off after she had scarlet fever.* **3** remove scales from: *He scaled the fish with a sharp knife.* **4** come off in scales: *The paint is scaling off the house.* **5** See **scale insect.** 1, 2, 5 *n.*, 3, 4 *v.*, **scaled, scal·ing.**

scale[2] (skāl) **1** the dish or pan of a balance. **2** Usually, **scales,** *pl.* a balance; an instrument for weighing: *She weighed some meat on the scales.* See **balance** for picture. **3** weigh: *He scales 40 kilograms.* 1, 2 *n.*, 3 *v.*, **scaled, scal·ing.**

scale[3] (skāl) **1** a series of steps or degrees; a scheme of graded amounts: *The scale of wages in this factory ranges from twenty dollars to forty dollars a day.* **2** a series of marks made along a line at regular distances, to use in measuring: *A thermometer has a scale.* **3** an instrument marked in this way, used for measuring. **4** the size of a plan, map, drawing, or model compared with what it represents: *The scale of the map is* 1 cm *to* 40 km *on the ground.* **5** a relative size or extent: *That rich woman entertains on a large scale.* **6** change by a certain amount in relation to other amounts: *All prices were scaled down 10 per cent.* **7** in music, a specific series of tones ascending or descending in pitch: *She practises scales on the piano.* **8** climb: *They scaled the wall by ladders.* **9** make according to a scale. 1–5, 7 *n.*, 6, 8, 9 *v.*, **scaled, scal·ing.**

☛ **Scale**[3] comes from the Latin word *scalae,* meaning 'ladder' or 'steps.'

scale insect a small insect, the female of which is covered by a scale or shield: *Scale insects feed on and often destroy plants.*

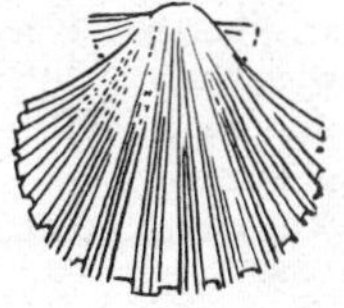

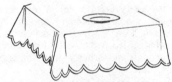

A scallop (def. 1)

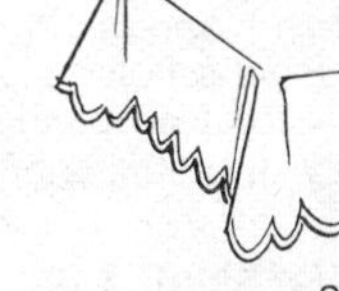

Scallops (def. 3) on a tablecloth

scal·lop (skol′əp or skal′əp) **1** a shellfish resembling a clam but having a fan-shaped shell with ridges that form a wavy edge around the shell: *In some kinds of scallops, the large muscle that opens and closes the shell is good to eat.* **2** this muscle used as food. **3** one of a series of curves that resemble the wavy edge of a scallop shell: *scallops on the edge of a cuff.* **4** finish or decorate with such curves: *The edges of the pillow cases were scalloped and embroidered by hand.* **5** in cooking, bake potatoes, oysters, or other food in a scallop shell or other dish with bread crumbs, cream, butter, etc. 1–3 *n.*, 4, 5 *v.*

scalp (skalp) **1** the skin on the top and back of the head that is usually covered with hair. **2** cut or tear the scalp from. 1 *n.*, 2 *v.*

scal·y (skāl′ē) **1** having scales like a fish. **2** covered with a layer something like scales: *This iron pipe is scaly with rust. adj.*, **scal·i·er, scal·i·est.**

scamp (skamp) **1** a rascal or rogue; a worthless person. **2** a mischievous person, especially a child. *n.*

scam·per (skam′pər) **1** run or move away quickly: *The mice scampered when the cat came.* **2** run about playfully: *The dogs were scampering in the yard.* **3** a playful running about: *Let the dog out for a scamper.* 1, 2 *v.*, 3 *n.*

hat, āge, fär; let, ēqual, tėrm; it, īce
hot, ōpen, ôrder; oil, out; cup, pu̇t, rüle
əbove, takən, pencəl, lemən, circəs
ch, child; ng, long; sh, ship
th, thin; ᴛʜ, then; zh, measure

scan (skan) **1** look at closely; examine with care: *His mother scanned his face to see if he was telling the truth.* **2** *Informal.* glance at; look over hastily. *v.*, **scanned, scan·ning.**

scan·dal (skan′dəl) **1** a shameful action, condition, or event that brings disgrace or shocks public opinion: *It was a scandal for the city treasurer to take tax money for his own use.* **2** damage to someone's reputation; disgrace. **3** public talk about a person that will hurt his reputation; evil gossip; slander. *n.*

scan·dal·ize (skan′dəl īz′) offend by doing something thought to be wrong or improper; shock: *She scandalized her granddaughter by riding a motorcycle. v.*, **scan·dal·ized, scan·dal·iz·ing.**

scan·dal·ous (skan′dəl əs) **1** bringing disgrace; shameful; shocking: *scandalous behavior.* **2** spreading scandal or slander: *a scandalous piece of gossip. adj.*

Scan·di·na·vi·a (skan′də nā′vē ə) **1** the area including Norway, Sweden, Denmark, and sometimes Finland and Iceland. **2** the peninsula on which Norway and Sweden are located. *n.* **—Scan′di·na′vi·an,** *adj.*

scant (skant) **1** not enough in size or quantity: *Her coat was short and scant.* **2** barely enough; barely full; bare: *Use a scant cup of butter in the cake. You have a scant hour in which to pack.* **3** make scant; cut down; limit; stint: *Don't scant the butter if you want a rich cake.* 1, 2 *adj.*, 3 *v.*

scant of, having not enough: *She was scant of breath.*

scant·y (skan′tē) **1** not enough: *His scanty clothing did not keep out the cold.* **2** barely enough; meagre: *a scanty harvest. adj.*, **scant·i·er, scant·i·est.**

scape·goat (skāp′gōt′) a person made to bear the blame for a misfortune or for the mistakes or sins of others: *John came just after the children had broken the window, so they ran away quickly and left him to be the scapegoat. n.*

scar (skär) **1** the mark left by a healed cut, wound, burn, or sore: *a small vaccination scar.* **2** any mark like this: *See the scars your shoes have made on the chair.* **3** make a scar on: *He scarred the door with a hammer.* 1, 2 *n.*, 3 *v.*, **scarred, scar·ring.**

scarce (skers) **1** hard to get; rare: *Good cooks are scarce. Very old stamps are scarce.* **2** scarcely. 1 *adj.*, **scarc·er, scarc·est;** 2 *adv.*

make oneself scarce, *Informal.* **a** go away. **b** stay away.

scarce·ly (skers′lē) **1** barely; not quite: *We could scarcely see the ship through the thick fog. He is scarcely old enough to go to school yet.* **2** decidedly not: *He can scarcely have said that. adv.*

☛ See note at **hardly.**

scar·ci·ty (sker′sə tē) too small a supply; lack; rarity: *There is a scarcity of nurses. n., pl.* **scar·ci·ties.**

scare (sker) **1** frighten: *We were scared and ran away.* **2** a fright. 1 *v.*, **scared, scar·ing;** 2 *n.*

scare up, *Informal.* get; raise: *scare up a few extra blankets on a cold night.*

scare·crow (sker′krō′) **1** a figure of a man dressed in old clothes, set in a field to frighten birds away from growing crops. **2** a person, usually skinny, dressed in ragged clothes. *n.*

scarf (skärf) a piece of silk, wool, etc. worn about the neck, shoulders, or head. *n., pl.* **scarves** (skärvz) or **scarfs**.

scar·let (skär′lit) **1** very bright red. **2** cloth or clothing having this color: *The Mounties look fine in their scarlets.* 1, 2 *n.*, 1 *adj.*

scarlet fever a contagious disease that causes a scarlet rash, a sore throat, and a fever.

scar·y (sker′ē) *Informal.* **1** causing fright or alarm: *She tells scary stories on Halloween.* **2** easily frightened. *adj.*

scat·ter (skat′ər) **1** throw here and there; sprinkle: *The farmer scattered corn for the chickens. Scatter ashes on the icy sidewalk.* **2** separate and drive off in different directions: *The police scattered the disorderly crowd.* **3** separate and go in different directions: *The hens scattered in fright when the car honked at them.* *v.*

scat·ter·brain (skat′ər brān′) a thoughtless, frivolous person. *n.*

scav·en·ger (skav′ən jər) **1** any creature that feeds on dead animals or other decaying matter: *Vultures and jackals are scavengers.* **2** a person who searches through discarded objects for something of value. *n.*

scene (sēn) **1** a view; picture: *The white sailboats in the blue water made a pretty scene.* **2** an action, incident, situation, etc.: *There was an unpleasant scene when the crowd panicked.* **3** a show of anger or bad temper in front of others: *The child kicked and screamed and made such a scene on the train that his mother was ashamed of him.* **4** the time, place, circumstances, etc. of a play or story: *The scene of the book is laid in Quebec City in the year 1775.* **5** the painted screens, hangings, etc. used in a theatre to represent places: *The scene represents a city street.* **6** a part of an act of a play: *The king comes to the castle in Act 1, Scene 2.* **7** a particular incident of a play: *The trial scene is the most exciting one in 'The Merchant of Venice.'* *n.*

behind the scenes, a out of sight of the audience. **b** not publicly; privately; secretly: *A lot of planning for the Festival was done behind the scenes.*

☞ **Scene** comes from a Greek word *skēnē,* which originally meant the tent where actors changed their costumes.

☞ **Scene** and **seen** are pronounced the same.

scen·er·y (sēn′ər ē) **1** the general appearance of a place: *She enjoys mountain scenery very much.* **2** the painted hangings, screens, etc. used in a theatre to represent places: *The scenery pictures a garden.* *n.*

sce·nic (sē′nik) **1** of or having something to do with natural scenery: *the scenic splendors of Lake Louise.* **2** having much fine scenery: *a scenic highway.* *adj.*

scent (sent) **1** a smell: *The scent of roses filled the air.* **2** smell: *The dog scented a rabbit and ran after it.* **3** the sense of smell: *Bloodhounds have a keen scent.* **4** a smell left in passing: *The dogs followed the fox by its scent.* **5** the means by which a thing or person can be traced: *The police are on the scent of the thieves.* **6** have a suspicion of; be aware of: *I scent a trick in his offer.* **7** perfume: *She used too much scent.* **8** fill with odor; perfume: *She uses scented writing paper.* 1, 3–5, 7 *n.*, 2, 6, 8 *v.*

☞ **Scent, cent,** and **sent** are pronounced the same.

scep·tre or **scep·ter** (sep′tər) the rod or staff carried by a ruler as a symbol of royal power or authority. *n.*

sched·ule (skej′ül or shej′ül) **1** a written or printed statement of details; a list: *A timetable is the schedule of the coming and going of trains.* **2** a listing of the games to be played by the teams in a league: *a hockey schedule.* **3** make a schedule of; enter in a schedule; plan or arrange something for a definite time or date: *Schedule the convention for the fall.* 1, 2 *n.*, 3 *v.*, **sched·uled, sched·ul·ing.**

on schedule, at the time or times fixed for doing something, arrival at a place, etc.: *The bus came on schedule.*

scheme (skēm) **1** a program of action; plan: *He has a scheme for extracting salt from sea water.* **2** a plot: *a scheme to cheat the government.* **3** plan; plot: *The men were scheming to cheat the government by bringing the jewels into the country without paying any duty.* **4** a system of connected things, parts, thoughts, etc.: *The color scheme of the room is blue and gold.* 1, 2, 4 *n.*, 3 *v.*, **schemed, schem·ing.**

schol·ar (skol′ər) **1** a learned person; a person having much knowledge: *a famous Latin scholar.* **2** a pupil at school; learner. *n.*

schol·ar·ly (skol′ər lē) **1** of a scholar; like that of a scholar: *scholarly habits. Spectacles gave her a scholarly look.* **2** fit for a scholar. **3** having much knowledge; learned. **4** fond of learning; studious. **5** thorough and orderly in methods of study: *a scholarly book.* *adj.*

schol·ar·ship (skol′ər ship) **1** the possession of knowledge gained by study; the quality of learning and knowledge: *Good scholarship is more important than athletics.* **2** money or other aid given to help a student continue his studies: *He passed his examinations with such high marks that he received a scholarship.* *n.*

school[1] (skül) **1** a place for teaching and learning: *Children go to school to learn.* **2** regular meetings of teachers and pupils for teaching and learning. **3** the pupils who are taught and their teachers: *Our school will be in a new building next fall.* **4** a group of people holding the same beliefs or opinions: *the French school of painting, a gentleman of the old school.* **5** a particular department or group in a university: *a medical school, a law school.* **6** teach; train; discipline: *School yourself to control your temper.* 1–5 *n.*, 6 *v.*

school[2] (skül) a large number of the same kind of fish or water animals swimming together: *a school of mackerel.* *n.*

school board a group of people, usually elected, who manage the schools in a certain area.

school·book (skül′bůk′) a book for study in schools. *n.*

school·boy (skül′boi′) a boy attending school. *n.*

school·fel·low (skül′fel′ō) a companion at school. *n.*

school·girl (skül′gėrl′) a girl attending school. *n.*

hat, āge, fär; let, ēqual, tėrm; it, īce
hot, ōpen, ôrder; oil, out; cup, pu̇t, rüle
əbove, takən, pencəl, lemən, circəs
ch, child; ng, long; sh, ship
th, thin; ᴛʜ, then; zh, measure

school·house (skül′hous′) a building used as a school. *n.*

school·ing (skül′ing) instruction in school; the education received at school. *n.*

school·master (skül′mas′tər) a man who teaches in a school, or is its principal. *n.*

school·mate (skül′māt′) a companion at school. *n.*

school·room (skül′rüm′) a room in which pupils are taught. *n.*

school·teach·er (skül′tēch′ər) a person who teaches in a school. *n.*

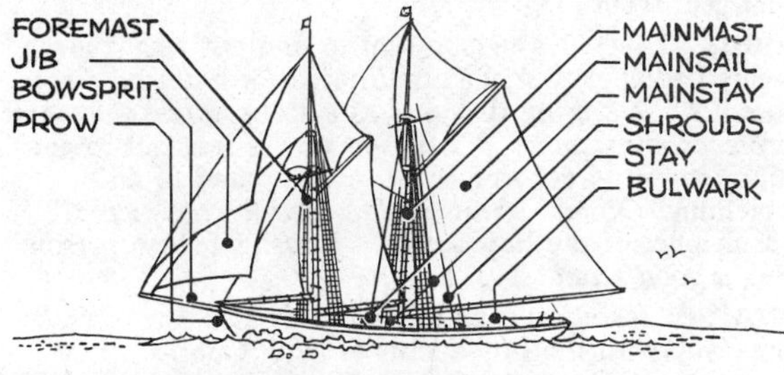

A schooner — the Bluenose

schoon·er (skün′ər) 1 a ship with two or more masts and having sails set lengthwise: *Modern schooners are usually used as yachts and have only two masts.* 2 prairie schooner. *n.*

schwa (shwo or shwä) 1 an unstressed vowel sound such as *a* in *about* or *u* in *circus.* 2 the symbol (ə), used to represent this sound. *n.*

sci·ence (sī′əns) 1 knowledge based on observed facts and tested truths arranged in an orderly system: *the laws of science.* 2 a branch of such knowledge. Biology, chemistry, physics, and astronomy are **natural sciences.** Agriculture and engineering are **applied sciences.** Economics is a **social science.** *n.*

science fiction stories or novels that combine science and fantasy: *Science fiction stories are often about life in the future or on other galaxies and make much use of the latest discoveries of science.*

sci·en·tif·ic (sī′ən tif′ik) 1 using the facts and laws of science: *a scientific method, a scientific farmer.* 2 of or having something to do with science; used in science: *scientific books, scientific instruments. adj.*

sci·en·tist (sī′ən tist) a person who has expert knowledge of some branch of science: *Persons specially trained in and familiar with the facts and laws of such fields of study as biology, chemistry, mathematics, physics, geology, and astronomy are scientists. n.*

scim·i·tar (sim′ə tər) a short, curved sword used by Turks, Persians, and other Oriental peoples. *n.*

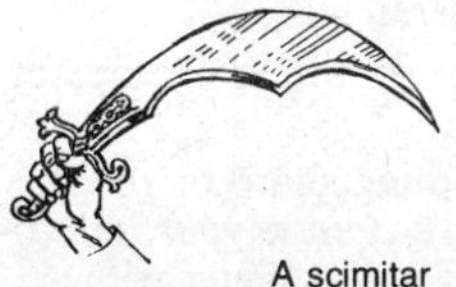
A scimitar

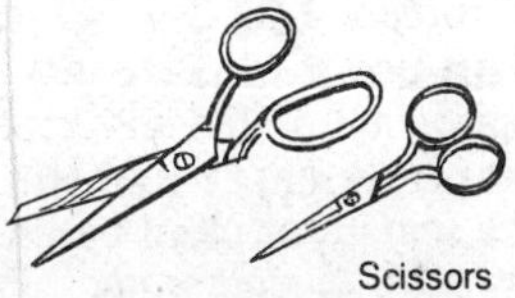
Scissors

scis·sors (siz′ərz) a tool or instrument for cutting that has two sharp blades so fastened that their edges slide against each other. *n. pl.*

scoff (skof) 1 make fun to show that one does not believe something; mock: *We scoffed at the idea of drowning in five centimetres of water.* 2 mocking words or acts. 1 *v.,* 2 *n.*

scold (skōld) 1 find fault with; blame with angry words: *His mother scolded him for tearing his coat in rough play.* 2 find fault; talk angrily: *He scolds so much because he is always bad-tempered.* 3 a person, especially a woman, who makes a habit of scolding: *In olden times, scolds were punished by being ducked in ponds.* 1, 2 *v.,* 3 *n.*

scone (skon or skōn) a thick, flat, round cake cooked on a griddle or in an oven: *Some scones taste much like bread; some are like buns. n.*

scoop (sküp) 1 a tool like a small shovel, having a short handle and a deep, hollow part for dipping out or shovelling up things. 2 the part of a dredge, steam shovel, etc. that holds coal, sand, etc. 3 the amount taken up at one time by a scoop: *She used two scoops of flour and one of sugar.* 4 take up or out with a scoop, or as a scoop does: *Scoop out a kilogram of sugar. The children scooped up the snow with their hands to build a snowman.* 5 hollow out; dig out; make by scooping: *The children scooped holes in the sand.* 6 a movement or process of scooping. 1–3, 6 *n.,* 4, 5 *v.*

scoot (sküt) *Informal.* go quickly; dart: *He scooted out the door. v.*

A child's scooter

scoot·er (sküt′ər) 1 a child's vehicle consisting of a footboard between two wheels, one in front of the other, steered by a handlebar and pushed by one foot. 2 a similar vehicle run by a motor. 3 a sailboat with runners, for use on either water or ice. *n.*

scope (skōp) 1 the amount the mind can take in; the extent of one's view: *Very hard words are not within the scope of a child's understanding.* 2 space; opportunity: *Football gives scope for courage and quick thinking. n.*

scorch (skôrch) 1 burn slightly; burn on the outside: *The cake tastes scorched. The maid scorched the shirt in ironing it.* 2 a slight burn. 3 dry up; wither: *The grass is scorched by so much hot sunshine.* 1, 3 *v.,* 2 *n.*

score (skôr) 1 the record of points made in a game, contest, or test: *The score was 9 to 2 in favor of our school.* 2 make as points in a game, contest, or test: *He scored two runs in the second inning.* 3 make points or a gain; succeed: *He had difficulty getting a job but scored at last.* 4 keep a record of the number of points made in a game or contest: *The teacher will appoint some pupil to score for both sides.* 5 make as an addition to the score; gain; win: *He scored a touchdown in the last minute of the game.* 6 an amount owed; a debt or account: *He paid his score at the inn.* **7** to record; mark; set down: *The innkeeper scored on a slate every meal each person had.* **8** a group or set of twenty: *A score or more were present at the party.* **9 scores,** *pl.* a large number, but less than hundreds: *Scores of people died in the epidemic.* **10** a written or printed piece of music arranged for different instruments or voices: *She was studying the score of the piece she was learning to play.* **11** cut; scratch; mark; line: *Moving the furniture across the floor scores the polish. He scores through the mistakes in red ink.* **12** an account; reason; ground: *Don't worry on that score.* **13 the score,** *Informal.* the truth about anything or things in general; the facts: *The new boy doesn't know the score yet.* 1, 6, 8–10, 12, 13 *n.,* 2–5, 7, 11 *v.,* **scored, scor·ing. —score′less,** *adj.* **—scor′er,** *n.*

scorn (skôrn) **1** look down upon; think of as mean or low; despise: *Honest boys scorn sneaks and liars.* **2** reject or refuse as low or wrong: *The judge scorned to take a bribe.* **3** a feeling that a person or act is mean or low; contempt: *Most pupils feel scorn for those who cheat.* **4** a person, animal, or thing that is scorned or despised: *That coward is the scorn of the school.* 1, 2 *v.,* 3, 4 *n.* **—scorn′ful,** *adj.*

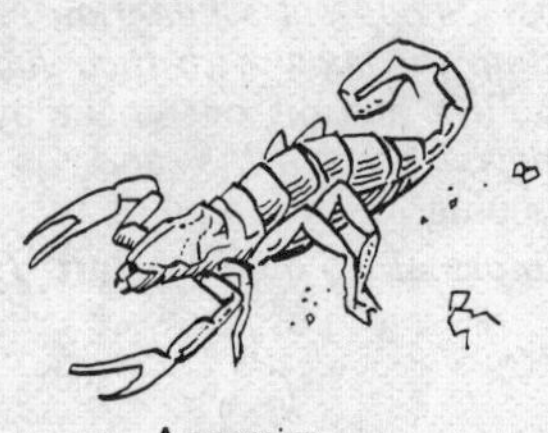

A scorpion — about 7 cm long

scor·pi·on (skôr′pē ən) a small animal belonging to the same group as the spider and having a poisonous sting at the end of its tail. *n.*

Scot (skot) a person born in or living in Scotland, a division of Great Britain. *n.*

Scotch (skoch) **1** Scottish. **2** a kind of whisky made in Scotland. 1 *adj.,* 2 *n.*

scot–free (skot′frē′) free from injury, punishment, penalty, etc.: *The driver was slightly hurt but his passengers got off scot-free. adj.*

Scots (skots) **1** Scottish. **2** plural of **Scot.** 1 *adj.,* 2 *n.*

Scots·man (skots′mən) Scot. *n., pl.* **Scots·men** (skots′mən).

Scot·tish (skot′ish) **1** of or having to do with Scotland, its people, or their language. **2** the people of Scotland. **3** the English spoken by the people of Scotland. 1 *adj.,* 2, 3 *n.*

scoun·drel (skoun′drəl) a very bad person without honor or good principles; a villain; a rascal: *The scoundrel who set fire to the barn has been caught. n.*

scour¹ (skour) **1** clean or polish by hard rubbing: *Mother scours the frying pan with cleanser and the floor with a mop and soap.* **2** remove dirt and grease by washing: *Raw wool is usually scoured before it is made into yarn.* **3** clear of dirt, weeds, etc.: *The current scoured mud and sand out of the channel.* **4** dig or dig out by the action of running water: *The stream had scoured a deep channel.* **5** the act of scouring. 1–4 *v.,* 5 *n.*

scour² (skour) **1** move quickly over: *Men scoured the country round about for the lost child.* **2** go rapidly in search or pursuit. *v.*

scourge (skėrj) **1** a whip. **2** any means of punishment. **3** whip; punish. **4** some person or thing that causes great trouble, misfortune, or suffering: *In former times, an outbreak of disease was called a scourge.* **5** put great hardship or suffering on: *War scourged the country for eight years.* 1, 2, 4 *n.,* 3, 5 *v.,* **scourged, scourg·ing.**

scout (skout) **1** a person sent to find out what the enemy is doing: *A scout usually wears a uniform; a spy does not.* **2** a thing that acts as a scout: *Some ships and airplanes are scouts.* **3** a person who is sent out to get information. **4** act as a scout; hunt around to find something: *Go and scout for firewood for the picnic.* **5** a member of the Boy Scouts. **6** *Slang.* fellow; person: *He's a good scout.* 1–3, 5, 6 *n.,* 4 *v.*

scout·er (skout′ər) an adult who is associated in some way with the Boy Scouts or Wolf Cubs. *n.*

scout·ing (skout′ing) the activities of Boy Scouts. *n.*

scout·mas·ter (skout′mas′tər) the man in charge of a troop of Boy Scouts. *n.*

scow (skou) a large boat with a flat bottom, used to carry freight, and usually either towed or pushed with a pole, like a raft: *The scow was loaded with sand. n.*

scowl (skoul) **1** look angry or sullen by lowering the eyebrows; frown: *The angry man scowled at his son.* **2** an angry, sullen look; a frown. 1 *v.,* 2 *n.*

scram·ble (skram′bəl) **1** make one's way by climbing, crawling, etc.: *The boys scrambled up the steep, rocky hill.* **2** a climb or walk over rough ground: *It was a long scramble through bushes and over rocks to the top of the hill.* **3** struggle with others for something: *The boys scrambled to get the football.* **4** a struggle to possess: *the scramble for wealth and power.* **5** any disorderly struggle or activity: *The pile of boys on the football seemed a wild scramble of arms and legs.* **6** mix together in a confused way. **7** cook eggs with the whites and yolks mixed together. 1, 3, 6, 7 *v.,* **scram·bled, scram·bling;** 2, 4, 5 *n.*

scrap¹ (skrap) **1** a small piece; a little bit; a small part left over: *The cook gave some scraps of meat to the dog. Put the scraps of paper in the waste basket.* **2** make into scraps; break up: *The army scrapped the old tanks.* **3** throw aside as useless or worn out. **4** the material thrown aside; junk: *The garden was full of scrap metal.* 1, 4 *n.,* 2, 3 *v.,* **scrapped, scrap·ping.**

scrap² (skrap) *Informal.* **1** a fight; quarrel; struggle. **2** fight; quarrel; struggle: *He was always scrapping with his brother.* 1 *n.,* 2 *v.,* **scrapped, scrap·ping.**

scrap·book (skrap′bu̇k′) a book in which pictures or clippings are pasted and kept. *n.*

scrape (skrāp) **1** rub with something sharp or rough; make smooth or clean by doing this: *Scrape your muddy shoes with this old knife.* **2** remove by rubbing with something sharp or rough: *The man scraped some paint off the table when he pushed it through the doorway.* **3** scratch or graze by rubbing against something rough: *She fell and scraped her knee on the sidewalk.* **4** the act of scraping. **5** a scraped place. **6** rub with a harsh sound: *Don't scrape your feet on the floor. The branch*

hat, āge, fär; let, ēqual, tėrm; it, īce
hot, ōpen, ôrder; oil, out; cup, pu̇t, rüle
əbove, takən, pencəl, lemən, circəs
ch, child; ng, long; sh, ship
th, thin; ᴛʜ, then; zh, measure

of the tree scraped against the window. **7** give a harsh sound; grate. **8** a harsh, grating sound: *the scrape of the bow of a violin.* **9** dig: *The child scraped a hole in the sand.* **10** collect with difficulty and a little at a time: *He has scraped together enough money to buy a bicycle.* **11** a difficulty; a position hard to get out of: *Boys often get into scrapes.* 1–3, 6, 7, 9, 10 *v.,* **scraped, scrap·ing;** 4, 5, 8, 11 *n.*

scrape along, through, or **by,** barely get through or manage with difficulty: *He thought he had failed, but fortunately he just scraped through.*

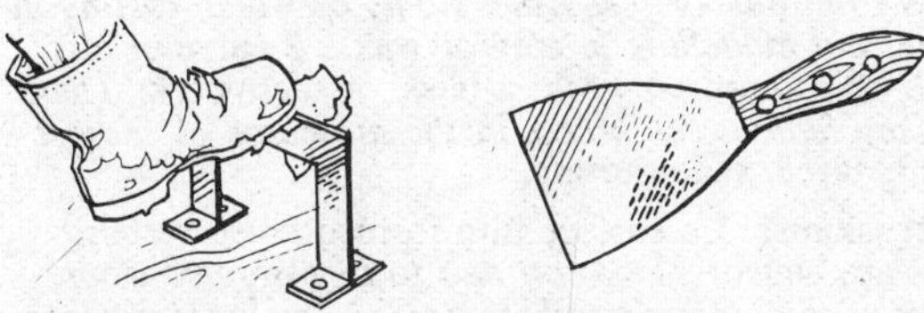

Two kinds of scraper

scrap·er (skrāp′ər) an instrument or tool for scraping: *We removed the loose paint with a scraper.* *n.*

scratch (skrach) **1** mark or cut slightly with something sharp or rough: *Your shoes have scratched the chair.* **2** a mark made by scratching: *There are deep scratches on this desk.* **3** tear or dig with the nails or claws: *The cat scratched him.* **4** a slight cut on the skin: *That scratch on your hand will soon be well.* **5** rub or scrape to relieve itching: *Don't scratch your mosquito bites.* **6** rub with a harsh noise; rub: *He scratched a match on the wall.* **7** the act of scratching. **8** the sound of scratching: *the scratch of a pen.* **9** strike out; draw a line through; cancel. 1, 3, 5, 6, 9 *v.,* 2, 4, 7, 8 *n.*

from scratch, with no advantages; from the beginning: *He lost his notes and so had to start his project again from scratch.*

up to scratch, up to standard; in good condition.

scratch pad a pad of paper for hurried writing.

scrawl (skrol or skrôl) **1** write or draw poorly or carelessly. **2** poor, careless handwriting. 1 *v.,* 2 *n.*

scraw·ny (skro′nē or skrô′nē) *Informal.* lean; thin; skinny: *Turkeys have scrawny necks.* *adj.,* **scraw·ni·er, scraw·ni·est.**

scream (skrēm) **1** make a loud, sharp, piercing cry: *She screamed when she saw the child fall.* **2** a loud, sharp, piercing cry. **3** *Informal.* something or somebody extremely funny. 1 *v.,* 2, 3 *n.*

screech (skrēch) **1** cry out sharply in a high voice; shriek: *'Help! help!' she screeched.* **2** a shrill, harsh scream: *The woman's screeches brought the police.* 1 *v.,* 2 *n.*

screen (skrēn) **1** a covered frame that hides, protects, or separates: *She keeps her trunk behind a screen.* **2** wire woven together with small openings in between the strands: *Screens on the windows keep out flies.* **3** an ornamental partition. **4** anything like a screen: *A screen of trees hides our house from the road.* **5** shelter, protect, or hide with, or as with, a screen: *We have screened our porch to keep out flies. She screened her face from the fire with a fan. The mother tried to screen her guilty son.* **6** a surface on which motion pictures, television images, etc. appear or are shown. **7** show a motion picture on a screen. **8** a sieve for sifting sand, gravel, coal, seed, etc. **9** sift with a screen: *to screen sand.* **10** examine or test very carefully: *Government offices screen people before hiring them.* 1–4, 6, 8 *n.,* 5, 7, 9, 10 *v.*

Screws

screw (skrü) **1** a fastening device like a nail but having a ridge twisted evenly around its length and often a groove across the head: *Turn the screw to the right to tighten it.* **2** anything that turns like a screw or looks like one. **3** a turn of a screw; screwing motion. **4** turn as one turns a screw; twist: *Screw the lid on the jar.* **5** fasten or tighten with a screw or screws: *The carpenter screwed the hinges to the door.* **6** a propeller that moves a boat or ship. 1–3, 6 *n.,* 4, 5 *v.*

screw·driv·er (skrü′drīv′ər) a tool for putting in or taking out screws by turning them. *n.*

scrib·ble (skrib′əl) **1** write or draw carelessly or hastily. **2** make marks that do not mean anything. **3** something scribbled. 1, 2 *v.,* **scrib·bled, scrib·bling;** 3 *n.*

scrib·bler (skrib′lər) a pad of paper or a book in which to make notes, do rough work, etc. *n.*

scribe (skrīb) **1** a person who copies manuscripts: *Before printing was invented, there were many scribes.* **2** a teacher of the Jewish law. *n.*

scrim·mage (skrim′ij) **1** a rough fight or struggle. **2** take part in a rough fight or struggle. **3** in football, the play that takes place when the two teams are lined up and the ball is snapped back. 1, 3 *n.,* 2 *v.,* **scrim·maged, scrim·mag·ing.**

script (skript) **1** handwriting; written letters, figures, signs, etc.: *German script.* **2** a style of printing that looks like handwriting. **3** the manuscript or typewritten copy of a play, of an actor's part, of a radio or television announcer's message, etc. *n.*

Scrip·ture (skrip′chər) **1** the Bible. **2 the Scriptures** or **the Holy Scriptures,** *pl.* the Bible. **3 scripture,** any sacred writing. *n.*

A scroll (def. 1)

scroll (skrōl) **1** a roll of parchment or paper, especially one with writing on it: *He slowly unrolled the scroll as he read it.* **2** an ornament resembling a partly unrolled sheet of paper, or having a spiral or coiled form. *n.*

scrub[1] (skrub) **1** rub hard; wash or clean by rubbing: *She scrubbed the floor with a brush and soapsuds.* **2** a scrubbing: *Give your face and hands a good scrub.* 1 *v.*, **scrubbed, scrub·bing;** 2 *n.*

scrub[2] (skrub) 1 low, stunted trees or shrubs. 2 anything small or below the usual size: *He is a little scrub of a man.* 3 small; poor; inferior: *scrub pine. A scrub team is made up of inferior, substitute, or untrained players.* 1, 2 *n.*, 3 *adj.*

scruff (skruf) the skin at the back of the neck; the back of the neck. *n.*

scruf·fy (skruf′ē) unkempt; slovenly; shabby: *John's brother looks scruffy.* *adj.*

scru·ple (skrü′pəl) 1 a feeling of doubt or uneasiness about what is right that keeps a person from doing something: *No scruple ever holds him back from prompt action. She has scruples about playing cards for money.* 2 hesitate or be unwilling to do something: *A dishonest man does not scruple to deceive others.* 1 *n.*, 2 *v.*, **scru·pled, scru·pling.**

scru·pu·lous (skrü′pyə ləs) 1 very careful to do what is right. 2 attending thoroughly to details; very careful: *A soldier must pay scrupulous attention to orders.* *adj.*

scru·ti·nize (skrü′tə nīz′) examine closely; inspect carefully: *The jeweller scrutinized the diamond for flaws.* *v.*, **scru·ti·nized, scru·ti·niz·ing.**

scru·ti·ny (skrü′tə nē) a close examination; careful inspection: *His work looks all right at first glance, but it will not bear scrutiny.* *n.*, *pl.* **scru·ti·nies.**

scu·ba (skü′bə) portable breathing equipment, including one or more tanks of compressed air, used by underwater swimmers and divers. See **skindiver** for picture. *n.*

☛ **Scuba** is formed from the initials of *self-contained underwater breathing apparatus.*

scud (skud) 1 run or move rapidly: *Clouds scudded across the sky, driven by the high wind.* 2 a scudding. 3 clouds or spray driven by the wind. 1 *v.*, **scud·ded, scud·ding;** 2, 3 *n.*

scuff (skuf) 1 walk without lifting the feet; shuffle. 2 wear or injure the surface of by hard use: *to scuff one's shoes.* *v.*

scuf·fle (skuf′əl) 1 struggle or fight in a rough, confused manner, but not violently: *The children scuffled for first place in the line-up.* 2 a confused rough struggle or fight: *The boy lost his hat in the scuffle.* 1 *v.*, **scuf·fled, scuf·fling;** 2 *n.*

A girl using a scull (def. 1) A man using sculls (def. 2)

scull (skul) 1 an oar worked with a side twist over the end of a boat to make it go. 2 one of a pair of oars used, one on each side, by a single rower. 3 make a boat go by a scull or by sculls. 4 a light racing boat for one or more rowers. 1, 2, 4 *n.*, 3 *v.*

☛ **Scull** and **skull** are pronounced the same.

sculp·tor (skulp′tər) a person who makes figures by carving, modelling, casting, etc.; artist in sculpture: *Sculptors work in marble, wood, bronze, etc.* *n.*

sculp·tress (skulp′tris) a woman sculptor. *n.*

sculp·ture (skulp′chər) 1 the art of carving or modelling figures: *Sculpture includes the cutting of statues from blocks of marble, stone, or wood, casting in bronze, and modelling in clay or wax.* 2 carve or model. 3 sculptured work; a piece of such work: *There are many famous sculptures in the museums.* 1, 3 *n.*, 2 *v.*, **sculp·tured, sculp·tur·ing.**

scum (skum) 1 a surface film formed when certain liquids are boiled: *The scum had to be skimmed from the top of the boiling maple syrup.* 2 the layer of algae or other matter that forms on the top of still water: *Green scum floated on top of the water.* 3 low, worthless people: *the scum of the town.* *n.*

scur·ry (skėr′ē) 1 run quickly; scamper; hurry: *We could hear the mice scurry about in the walls.* 2 a hasty running or hurrying: *With much fuss and scurry, she at last got started.* 1 *v.*, **scur·ried, scur·ry·ing;** 2 *n.*

scur·vy (skėr′vē) 1 a disease caused by a lack of vegetables and fruits and causing swollen and bleeding gums, extreme weakness, and livid spots on the skin: *Scurvy used to be common among sailors when they had little to eat except bread and salt meat.* 2 mean; contemptible; base: *a scurvy fellow, a scurvy trick.* 1 *n.*, 2 *adj.*, **scur·vi·er, scur·vi·est.**

scut·tle[1] (skut′əl) a kind of bucket for holding or carrying coal; a hod. See the picture. *n.*

scut·tle[2] (skut′əl) scamper; scurry: *The dogs scuttled off into the woods.* *v.*, **scut·tled, scut·tling.**

scut·tle[3] (skut′əl) 1 a small opening with a lid or cover, especially in the deck or side of a ship. 2 cut holes through the bottom or sides of a ship to sink it: *After the pirates captured the ship, they scuttled it.* 1 *n.*, 2 *v.*, **scut·tled, scut·tling.**

A scuttle for coal

A scythe

scythe (sīᴛʜ) a long, slightly curved blade on a long handle, used for cutting grass, etc. *n.*

S.E. or **SE** 1 southeast. 2 southeastern.

sea (sē) 1 the great body of salt water that covers almost three fourths of the earth's surface; the ocean. 2 any large body of salt water, smaller than an ocean: *the North Sea, the Mediterranean Sea.* 3 a large lake of fresh water: *the Sea of Galilee.* 4 a large, heavy wave: *A high sea swept away the ship's masts.* 5 the swell of the ocean. 6 an overwhelming amount or vast expanse: *a sea of trouble, a sea of faces.* *n.*

at sea, a out on the sea. **b** puzzled; confused: *His complicated explanation left me even more at sea about the problem.*
follow the sea, be a sailor.
go to sea, a become a sailor. **b** begin a voyage.
☛ **Sea** and **see** are pronounced the same.

sea·board (sē′bôrd′) the land near the sea; the seacoast; the seashore: *Halifax is on the Atlantic seaboard. n.*

sea·coast (sē′kōst′) the land along the sea: *the seacoast of North America. n.*

sea element *Cdn.* the branch of the Canadian Armed Forces having to do with ships of war and their officers and men, formerly known as the Royal Canadian Navy.

sea·far·ing (sē′fer′ing) going, travelling, or working on the sea: *Sailors are seafaring men. adj.*

sea–go·ing (sē′gō′ing) **1** going by sea; seafaring. **2** fit for going to sea: *a sea-going freighter. adj.*

sea gull any gull, especially one living on or near the sea. See **gull** for picture.

A sea horse — about 16 cm long

sea horse a kind of small fish with a head suggesting that of a horse: *A sea horse swims upright.*

seal¹ (sēl) **1** a design stamped on a piece of wax, etc. and used to show ownership or authority: *The official seal of Canada is attached to important government papers.* **2** a stamp for marking things with such a design: *Mabel has a seal with her initials M.B. on it, with which she stamps sealing wax to fasten her letters.* **3** a piece of wax, paper, metal, etc. on which the design is stamped. **4** mark a document with a seal to certify it or make it binding: *The treaty was signed and sealed by both governments.* **5** close very tightly; fasten: *She sealed the letter. She sealed the jars of fruit. His eyes were sealed with sleep. Her promise sealed her lips.* **6** a thing that fastens or closes something tightly. **7** anything that makes something safe, secret, or official: *a seal of secrecy, the seal of authority.* **8** settle; determine: *The judge's words sealed the prisoner's fate.* **9** a special kind of stamp: *Christmas seals.* 1–3, 6, 7, 9 *n.*, 4, 5, 8 *v.*

One kind of seal — about 150 cm long

seal² (sēl) **1** a flesh-eating sea mammal having large flippers, usually living in cold regions: *Some seals have very valuable fur.* **2** its skin or fur. *n., pl.* **seals** or **seal.**

hat, āge, fär; let, ēqual, tėrm; it, īce
hot, ōpen, ôrder; oil, out; cup, pu̇t, rüle
əbove, takən, pencəl, lemən, circəs
ch, child; ng, long; sh, ship
th, thin; ᴛʜ, then; zh, measure

seal·er (sē′lər) **1** a person who hunts seals. **2** a ship used for hunting seals. *n.*

sea level the level of the surface of the sea: *Mountains, plains, ocean beds, etc. are measured as so many metres above or below sea level.*

sealing wax a hard substance, soft when heated, used for sealing letters, packages, etc.: *Sealing wax is made of resin and shellac.*

sea lion a large seal of the Pacific Coast.

seal·skin (sēl′skin′) **1** the skin of the fur seal, prepared for use. **2** a garment made of this fur. *n.*

seam (sēm) **1** the join formed when two pieces of cloth, canvas, leather, etc. are sewn together: *the seams of a coat, the seams of a sail.* **2** any join where edges come together: *The seams of the boat must be filled in or they will leak. The seams of the carpet hardly show.* **3** join with a seam. **4** any mark or line like a seam: *The old sword cut had left a seam in his face.* **5** mark with wrinkles or scars: *Years of worrying have seamed his brow.* **6** a layer within the earth: *a seam of coal.* 1, 2, 4, 6 *n.*, 3, 5 *v.*
☛ **Seam** and **seem** are pronounced the same.

sea·man (sē′mən) **1** a sailor, usually one who sails the ocean. **2** a sailor who is not an officer. *n., pl.* **sea·men** (sē′mən).

seam·stress (sēm′stris) a woman whose work is sewing. *n.*

A seaplane

sea·plane (sē′plān′) an airplane that can rise from and alight on water. *n.*

sea·port (sē′pôrt′) a port or harbor on the seacoast; a city or town with a harbor that ships can reach from the sea: *St. John's and Vancouver are seaports. n.*

sear (sēr) **1** burn the surface of: *The hot iron seared his flesh.* **2** make hard or unfeeling: *His years of cruelty had seared his heart.* **3** dry up; wither. *v.*
☛ **Sear** and **seer** are pronounced the same.

search (sėrch) **1** try to find by looking; seek; look for: *We searched all day for the lost kitten.* **2** look through; go over carefully; examine, especially for something concealed: *The police searched the prisoner to see if he had a gun. The doctor searched the wound for the bullet.* **3** searching; an examination: *He found his book after a long search. 1, 2 v.*, 3 *n.*
in search of, trying to find; looking for: *They went in search of buried treasure.*

search·ing (sėr′ching) **1** examining carefully; thorough: *a searching gaze or look, a searching* *examination.* 2 piercing; penetrating: *a searching wind. adj.*

search·light (sėrch′līt′) a powerful light that can throw a bright beam in any direction. *n.*

sea shell the shell of any sea mollusc, such as an oyster, conch, abalone, etc.

sea·shore (sē′shôr′) the land along the sea; the beach at the seaside. *n.*

sea·sick (sē′sik′) dizzy and sick to the stomach because of a ship's motion. *adj.*

sea·side (sē′sīd′) 1 the seacoast or seashore. 2 beside the sea: *We stayed at a seaside hotel.* 1 *n.*, 2 *adj.*

sea·son (sē′zən) 1 one of the four periods of the year; spring, summer, autumn, or winter. 2 any period of time marked by something special: *the Christmas season, the harvest season.* 3 a suitable or fit time. 4 add flavor to: *Season your egg with salt.* 5 make or become fit for use by a period of keeping or treatment: *Wood is seasoned for building by drying and hardening it.* 6 make less severe; soften: *Season justice with mercy.* 1–3 *n.*, 4–6 *v.*

in season, the right or proper time for picking, eating, hunting, etc.: *Cherries are in season in June.*

sea·son·al (sē′zən əl) having to do with the seasons; depending on a season; happening at regular intervals: *seasonal rains, seasonal unemployment. adj.*

sea·son·ing (sē′zən ing) 1 something that gives an added flavor: *Salt, pepper, and spices are seasonings.* 2 something that gives interest or character: *We like conversation with a seasoning of humor. n.*

seat[1] (sēt) 1 something to sit on: *Chairs, benches, and stools are seats.* 2 a place to sit: *Are there any seats left for the show tonight?* 3 a place in which one has the right to sit: *Our seats are in the fifth row of the first balcony.* 4 that part of a chair, bench, stool, etc. on which one sits: *This bench has a broken seat.* 5 that part of the body on which one sits, or the clothing covering it: *The seat of his trousers was patched.* 6 to set or place on a seat: *He seated himself in the most comfortable chair.* 7 have seats for: *Our school auditorium seats one thousand pupils.* 8 a place in a parliament, a city council, etc.: *The Liberals lost ten seats in the last election.* 1–5, 8 *n.*, 6, 7 *v.*

seat[2] (sēt) an established place or centre: *A university is a seat of learning. The seat of our government is in Ottawa. n.*

seat belt a belt attached to the seat of an automobile or airplane, used to hold a person in place in the event of a crash, jolt, bumps, etc.

sea urchin any of a group of small, round sea animals having spiny shells.

sea·ward (sē′wərd) 1 toward the sea: *a seaward breeze (adj.). Our house faces seaward (adv.).* 2 the direction toward the sea: *The island lies one kilometre to seaward.* 1 *adv., adj.,* 2 *n.*

sea·wards (sē′wərdz) seaward. *adv.*

sea·way (sē′wā′) 1 a way over the sea. 2 an inland waterway that connects with the open sea and is deep enough to permit ocean shipping: *Ocean liners reach Toronto by passing through the St. Lawrence Seaway. n.*

sea·weed (sē′wēd′) any plant or plants growing in the sea. *n.*

sec. second; seconds.

se·clude (si klüd′) keep apart from company; shut off from others: *He secludes himself and sees only his close friends. v.,* **se·clud·ed, se·clud·ing.**

se·clud·ed (si klü′did) shut off from others; undisturbed: *a secluded cottage. adj.*

se·clu·sion (si klü′zhən) 1 keeping apart or being shut off from others; retirement: *She lives in seclusion apart from her friends.* 2 a secluded place. *n.*

sec·ond[1] (sek′ənd) 1 next after the 1st; 2nd: *the second seat from the front.* 2 next below the first in rank, value, etc.: *She refused to buy cloth of second quality.* 3 another; other: *Napoleon has been called a second Caesar. She says her friend Pam is her second self.* 4 a person or thing that is second. 5 an article below first quality: *These stockings are seconds and have some slight defects.* 6 a person who supports or aids another: *The prize fighter had a second.* 7 support; back up; assist: *A man seconded the motion to adjourn.* 1–3 *adj.*, 4–6 *n.*, 7 *v.*

sec·ond[2] (sek′ənd) 1 one of the sixty very short, equal periods of time that make up a minute. Symbol: s 2 a very short time; moment. *n.*

sec·ond·ar·y (sek′ən der′ē) 1 next after the first in order, place, time, or importance: *A high school is a secondary school; a public school is an elementary school.* 2 having less importance: *Reading fast is secondary to reading well. adj.*

secondary accent secondary stress.

secondary stress a stress that is weaker than the strongest stress in a word (primary stress) but stronger than no stress. In *ab·bre′vi·a′tion* there is secondary stress on the second syllable and primary stress on the fourth syllable.

second hand a hand on a clock or watch, pointing to the seconds. It moves around the whole dial once in a minute.

sec·ond–hand (sek′ənd hand′) 1 not original; obtained from another: *second-hand information.* 2 not new; used already by someone else: *second-hand clothes.* 3 dealing in used goods: *a second-hand store. adj.*

sec·ond·ly (sek′ənd lē) in the second place. *adv.*

se·cre·cy (sē′krə sē) 1 the condition or fact of being kept secret: *The meeting was surrounded by secrecy.* 2 the act or habit of keeping things secret: *They relied on her secrecy. n., pl.* **se·cre·cies.**

se·cret (sē′krit) 1 kept from the knowledge of others: *a secret errand, a secret marriage.* 2 keeping to oneself what one knows: *He is as secret as a mouse.* 3 known only to a few: *a secret sign.* 4 kept from sight; hidden: *a secret room, a secret drawer, a secret spring.* 5 working or acting in secret: *secret police.* 6 something secret or hidden: *Can you keep a secret?* 7 a hidden cause or reason: *the secret of his success, the secret of her charm.* 1–5 *adj.*, 6, 7 *n.*

in secret, secretly; privately; not openly.

sec·re·tar·y (sek′rə ter′ē) 1 someone who writes letters, keeps records, etc. for a person, company, club, etc.: *Our club has a secretary who keeps the minutes of the meetings.* 2 a writing desk with a set of drawers, often having shelves for books. *n., pl.* **sec·re·tar·ies.**

se·crete (si krēt′) 1 keep secret; hide. 2 produce

and release: *Glands in the mouth secrete saliva.* *v.*, **se·cret·ed, se·cret·ing.**

se·cre·tion (si krē′shən) 1 a substance that is secreted by some part of an animal or plant: *Bile is the secretion of the liver.* 2 the producing and releasing of such a substance. *n.*

se·cret·ly (sē′krət lē) without the knowledge of others: *Spies do their work secretly.* *adv.*

sect (sekt) a group of people that forms part of a larger religious body but rejects some of the larger body's beliefs or customs: *The Protestant church used to have many different sects.* *n.*

A section of an apple

sec·tion (sek′shən) 1 a part; division; slice: *Mother cut the pie into eight equal sections. She divided the orange into sections.* 2 a division of a book: *Our arithmetic text has several sections on fractions.* 3 a region; a part of a country, city, etc.: *The town has a business section and a residential section.* 4 cut into sections; divide into sections: *section an orange.* 5 a view of a thing as it would appear if cut straight through; cross section. 6 a district or tract of land one mile square (about 259 hectares): *He farms two sections near Regina.* 1–3, 5, 6 *n.*, 4 *v.*

sec·u·lar (sek′yə lər) not religious or sacred; worldly: *secular music, a secular education.* *adj.*

se·cure (si kyür′) 1 safe against loss, attack, escape, etc.: *Keep the prisoner secure within his cell. This is a secure hiding place. Land in a growing city is a secure investment.* 2 make safe; protect: *You cannot secure yourself against all risks and dangers.* 3 sure; certain; that can be counted on: *We know in advance that our victory is secure.* 4 free from care or fear: *He hoped for a secure old age.* 5 firmly fastened; not liable to break or fall: *Are the prisoner's bonds secure? The boards of this bridge do not look secure.* 6 make firm or fast: *Secure the locks on the doors and windows.* 7 get; obtain: *We have secured our tickets for the school play.* 1, 3–5 *adj.*, 2, 6, 7 *v.*, **se·cured, se·cur·ing.**

se·cu·ri·ty (si kyür′ə tē) 1 freedom from danger, care, or fear; the feeling or condition of being safe: *You may cross the street in security when a policeman holds up his hand.* 2 something that secures or makes safe: *My watchdog is a security against burglars. Rubber soles are a security against slipping.* 3 something given as a guarantee that a person will be able to pay back a loan or fulfil a promise or duty: *A life insurance policy may serve as security for a loan.* *n., pl.* **se·cu·ri·ties.**

se·dan (si dan′) 1 a closed automobile with a front and back seat, seating four or more persons. 2 sedan chair. *n.*

A sedan chair

sedan chair a covered chair carried on poles by two

hat, āge, fär; let, ēqual, tėrm; it, īce
hot, ōpen, ôrder; oil, out; cup, pu̇t, rüle
əbove, takən, pencəl, lemən, circəs
ch, child; ng, long; sh, ship
th, thin; ᴛʜ, then; zh, measure

men: *Sedan chairs were much used during the 1600's and 1700's.*

se·date (si dāt′) quiet; calm; serious: *She is very sedate for a child and would rather read or sew than play.* *adj.*

sed·a·tive (sed′ə tiv) a medicine that lessens pain or excitement. *n.*

sedge (sej) a grasslike plant that grows chiefly in wet places. *n.*

sed·i·ment (sed′ə mənt) 1 matter that settles to the bottom of a liquid; dregs. 2 earth, stones, etc. deposited by water, wind, or ice: *Each year the river Nile overflows and deposits sediment on the land.* *n.*

sed·i·men·ta·ry (sed′ə men′tə rē) 1 of sediment; having something to do with sediment. 2 formed by the depositing of sediment: *Shale is a sedimentary rock.* *adj.*

se·duce (si dyüs′ or si düs′) 1 tempt to wrongdoing; persuade to do wrong: *The traitor was seduced by the offer of great wealth to betray his country.* 2 lead away from virtue; lead astray; beguile. *v.*, **se·duced, se·duc·ing.**

see[1] (sē) 1 look at; be aware of by using the eyes: *See that black cloud.* 2 have the power of sight: *The blind do not see.* 3 understand; be aware of with the mind: *I see what you mean.* 4 find out: *See what you can do for him.* 5 take care; make sure: *See that the work is done properly. See that you lock the back door.* 6 have knowledge or experience of: *That coat has seen hard wear.* 7 go with; attend; escort: *He will see you home.* 8 have a talk with; call on; meet: *I went to see a friend.* 9 receive a visit from: *She is too ill to see anyone.* 10 visit; attend: *We saw the Canadian National Exhibition.* *v.*, **saw, seen, see·ing.**

see into, understand the real character or hidden purpose of.

see through, a understand the real character or hidden purpose of. **b** go through with; finish. **c** watch over or help through difficulty: *June's mother saw her through her illness.*

see to, look after; take care of.

☛ See and **sea** are pronounced the same.

see[2] (sē) 1 the position or authority of a bishop. 2 the district under a bishop's authority. *n.*

☛ See note at **see**[1].

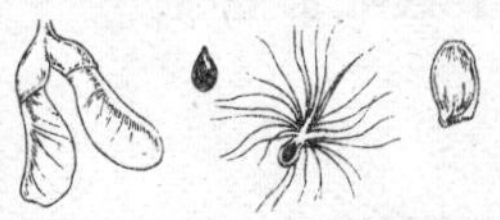
Four kinds of seed

seed (sēd) 1 the thing from which a flower, vegetable, or other plant grows: *We planted seeds in the garden. Part of every crop is saved for seed.* 2 sow with seeds; scatter seeds over: *The farmer seeded the field with corn.* 3 produce seeds; shed seeds: *Dandelions seed themselves.* 4 remove the seeds from: *She seeded the grapes for the salad.* 5 the source or beginning of anything: *the seeds of trouble.* 6 children; descendants: *The Jews are the seed of Abraham.* 1, 5, 6 *n., pl.* **seeds** or **seed;** 2–4 *v.*

go to seed, a come to the time of yielding seeds:

Dandelions go to seed when their heads turn white. **b** come to the end of vigor, good health, usefulness, prosperity, etc.: *After the mines closed, the town went to seed.*

☛ **Seed** and **cede** are pronounced the same.

seed·case (sēd′kās′) any pod, capsule, or other dry, hollow fruit that contains seeds. *n.*

seed·ling (sēd′ling) **1** a young plant grown from seed. **2** a young tree less than one metre high. *n.*

seed·y (sē′dē) **1** full of seed. **2** shabby; no longer fresh or new: *seedy clothes. adj.*

see·ing (sē′ing) in view of the fact; considering: *Seeing that it is 10 o'clock, we will wait no longer. conj.*

seek (sēk) **1** try to find; look for: *The boys are seeking a good camping place.* **2** hunt; search: *to seek for something lost.* **3** try to get: *Most men seek wealth; all men seek happiness. He seeks your advice.* **4** try; attempt: *We sought to make peace between the two boys. v.,* **sought, seek·ing.**

seem (sēm) **1** appear; appear to be: *This apple seemed good but was rotten inside. The dog seemed to like that bone. Does this room seem hot to you?* **2** appear to oneself: *I still seem to hear the music.* **3** appear to exist or be true: *There seems no need to wait longer. It seems likely to rain. v.*

☛ **Seem** and **seam** are pronounced the same.

seem·ing·ly (sēm′ing lē) apparently; as far as appearances go: *This hill is, seemingly, the highest around here. adv.*

seen (sēn) See **see**[1]. *Have you seen William? v.*

☛ **Seen** and **scene** are pronounced the same.

seep (sēp) ooze, trickle, or leak: *Water seeps through sand. v.*

seep·age (sēp′ij) **1** slow leakage; seeping. **2** moisture or liquid that seeps: *two centimetres of seepage in the cellar. n.*

seer (sēr) a person who foresees or foretells future events; prophet. *n.*

☛ **Seer** and **sear** are pronounced the same.

see·saw (sē′so′ or sē′sô) **1** teeter-totter. **2** move up and down or back and forth. **3** moving up and down or back and forth: *the seesaw of a storm-tossed ship.* 1, 2 *v.,* 1, 3 *n.*

seethe (sēᴛʜ) **1** be excited; be disturbed: *The pirate crew was seething with discontent and ready to mutiny.* **2** bubble and foam: *The seething waters carried the light boat down over the falls. v.,* **seethed, seeth·ing.**

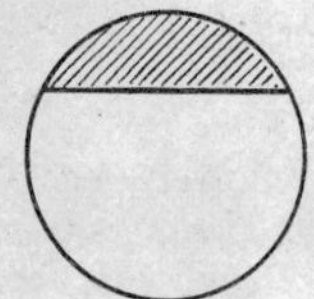

The shaded part is a segment of the circle.

seg·ment (seg′mənt) a piece or part cut off, marked off, or broken off; division; section: *An orange is easily pulled apart into its segments. n.*

seg·re·gate (seg′rə gāt′) **1** separate from others; set apart; isolate: *The doctor segregated the child with mumps to protect the other patients.* **2** separate or keep apart one racial group from another or from the rest of society by maintaining separate schools, separate public facilities, etc. *v.*

seg·re·ga·tion (seg′rə gā′shən) **1** a separation from others; a setting apart; isolation: *the segregation of lepers.* **2** the separation of one racial group from another or from the rest of society, especially in schools, theatres, etc. *n.*

seign·ior or **sei·gneur** (sēn′yər) in French Canada, a person granted a seigniory; landowner. *n.*

seign·ior·y or **sei·gneur·y** (sēn′yər ē) in French Canada, a tract of land or an estate originally granted to an individual by the king of France. *n.*

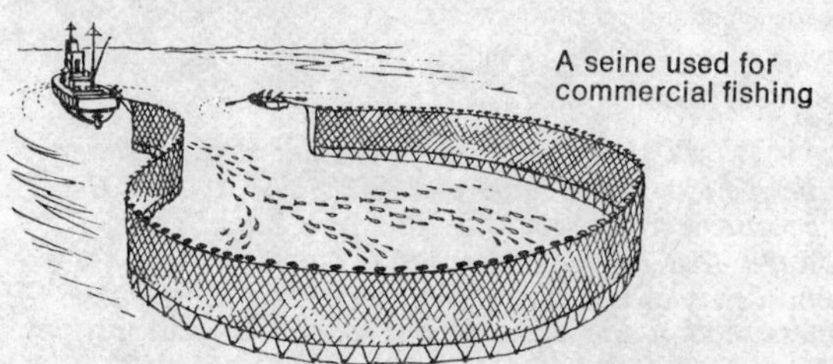

A seine used for commercial fishing

seine (sān) **1** a fishing net that hangs straight down in the water: *A seine has floats at the upper edge and weights at the lower.* **2** fish or catch with a seine. 1 *n.,* 2 *v.* **seined, sein·ing.**

☛ **Seine** and **sane** are pronounced the same.

sein·er (sān′ər) **1** a person who fishes with a seine. **2** a fishing vessel that uses seines. *n.*

seis·mic (sīz′mik or sīs′mik) **1** of earthquakes; having to do with an earthquake. **2** caused by an earthquake. *adj.*

seis·mo·graph (sīz′mə graf′ or sīs′mə graf′) an instrument for recording the direction, intensity, and duration of earthquakes. *n.*

seize (sēz) **1** take hold of suddenly; clutch; grasp: *When she lost her balance, she seized his arm.* **2** take possession of by force: *The soldiers seized the city.* **3** take possession of or come upon suddenly: *a fever seized him. v.,* **seized, seiz·ing.**

sei·zure (sē′zhər) **1** seizing or being seized. **2** a sudden attack of disease: *Our neighbor died of heart seizure. n.*

sel·dom (sel′dəm) rarely; not often: *He is seldom ill. adv.*

se·lect (si lekt′) **1** choose; pick out: *His uncle let him select his own birthday present.* **2** picked as best; chosen specially: *The captain needs a select crew for this dangerous job.* **3** careful in choosing; particular as to friends, company, etc.: *She belongs to a very select club.* 1 *v.,* 2, 3 *adj.*

se·lec·tion (si lek′shən) **1** the act of selecting; choice: *Her selection of a hat took a long time. The shop offered a very good selection of hats.* **2** a person, thing, or group chosen: *The plain blue hat was her selection. n.*

self (self) **1** one's own person: *Your self is you.* **2** one's own welfare or interests: *It is a good thing to think more of others and less of self.* **3** the character of a person; the nature of a person or thing: *She does not seem like her former self. n., pl.* **selves.**

self-ad·dressed (self′ə drest′) addressed to oneself: *a self-addressed envelope. adj.*

hat, āge, fär; let, ēqual, tėrm; it, īce
hot, ōpen, ôrder; oil, out; cup, pu̇t, rüle
əbove, takən, pencəl, lemən, circəs
ch, child; ng, long; sh, ship
th, thin; ᴛʜ, then; zh, measure

self–as·sur·ance (self′ə shůr′əns) self-confidence. *n.*

self–cen·tred or **self–cen·tered** (self′sen′tərd) **1** occupied with one's own interests and affairs. **2** selfish. *adj.*

self–con·fi·dence (self′kon′fə dəns) belief in one's own ability, power, judgment, etc.; confidence in oneself. *n.*

self–con·fi·dent (self′kon′fə dənt) believing in one's own ability, power, judgment, etc. *adj.*

self–con·scious (self′kon′shəs) made conscious of how one is appearing to others; embarrassed, especially by the presence of other people and their attitude toward one; shy. *adj.*

self–con·trol (self′kən trōl′) control of one's own actions, feelings, etc. *n.*

self–de·fence or **self–de·fense** (self′di fens′) defence of one's own person, property, reputation, etc. *n.*

self–dis·ci·pline (self′dis′ə plin) careful control and training of oneself. *n.*

self–ex·pres·sion (self′eks presh′ən) expression of one's personality: *Self-expression is an important part of good writing.* *n.*

self–gov·ern·ment (self′guv′ərn mənt) **1** government of a group by its own members: *We have self-government through our elected representatives.* **2** self-control. *n.*

self–im·por·tant (self′im pôr′tənt) having or showing too great an opinion of one's own importance. *adj.*

self–in·ter·est (self′in′trist or self′in′tər ist) interest in one's own welfare without regard for the welfare of others; selfishness: *His decisions were always determined by self-interest.* *n.*

self·ish (sel′fish) caring too much for oneself; caring too little for others: *A selfish person puts his own interests before the interests of others.* *adj.* **—self′ish·ness,** *n.*

self·less (self′lis) having no regard or thought for self; unselfish. *adj.*

self–made (self′mād′) successful through one's own efforts: *A self-made man is one who succeeds in business, etc. without the usual formal training or education.* *adj.*

self–pos·sessed (self′pə zest′) having or showing control of one's feelings and actions; not excited, embarrassed, or confused; calm: *A self-possessed person knows how to keep his temper.* *adj.*

self–pos·ses·sion (self′pə zesh′ən) the control of one's feelings and actions; calmness. *n.*

self–pro·pelled (self′prə peld′) propelled by an engine, motor, etc. within itself: *a self-propelled missile.* *adj.*

self–re·spect (self′ri spekt′) respect for oneself; proper pride. *n.*

self–re·straint (self′ri strānt′) self-control. *n.*

self·right·eous (self′rī′chəs) thinking that one is more moral than others; thinking that one is very good and pleasing to God. *adj.*

self·same (self′sām′) the very same: *We study the selfsame books that you do.* *adj.*

self–sat·is·fac·tion (self′sat′is fak′shən) satisfaction with oneself. *n.*

self–sat·is·fied (self′sat′is fīd′) pleased with oneself; complacent. *adj.*

self–serv·ice (self′sėr′vis) the act or process of serving oneself in a restaurant, store, etc. *n.*

self–suf·fi·cient (self′sə fish′ənt) **1** asking no help; independent. **2** having too much confidence in one's own resources, power, etc. *adj.*

sell (sel) **1** exchange for money or other payment: *He is going to sell his house.* **2** deal in; keep for sale: *The butcher sells meat.* **3** be sold; get sold: *Strawberries sell at a high price in January.* **4** give up; betray: *The traitor sold his country for money.* *v.,* **sold, sell·ing.**
sell out, a sell all that one has of; get rid of by selling. **b** *Informal.* betray by a secret bargain.
☛ **Sell** and **cell** are pronounced the same.

sell·er (sel′ər) **1** a person who sells: *A druggist is a seller of drugs.* **2** a thing considered with reference to its sale: *This book is a best seller.* *n.*
☛ **Seller** and **cellar** are pronounced the same.

selves (selvz) plural of **self:** *He had two selves—a friendly self and a shy self.* *n. pl.*

Railway semaphores

sem·a·phore (sem′ə fôr) **1** an apparatus for signalling; an upright post or structure with movable arms, or an arrangement of lanterns, flags, etc., used in railway signalling. **2** a system of signals for sending messages by using different positions of the arms or flags, or by using other mechanical devices: *They learned semaphore in the Boy Scouts.* *n.*

sem·blance (sem′bləns) an outward appearance: *His story had the semblance of truth, but was really false.* *n.*

semi– a prefix meaning: **1** half: *semicircle = half circle.* **2** partly; incompletely: *semiskilled = partly skilled.* **3** twice: *semiannually = every half year, or twice a year.*

sem·i·cir·cle (sem′ē sėr′kəl) half a circle: *We sat in a semicircle around the fire.* *n.*

sem·i·co·lon (sem′ē kō′lən) a mark of punctuation (;) that shows a break not so complete as that shown by a period. *n.*

sem·i·fi·nal (sem′ē fī′nəl) **1** one of the games, matches, bouts, etc. that come before the final one: *Our lacrosse team was defeated in the semifinal.* **2** of or having to do with such a game, match, bout, etc.: *a semifinal score.* 1 *n.,* 2 *adj.*

sem·i·nar·y (sem′ə ner′ē) a school for training students to be priests, ministers, etc. *n., pl.* **sem·i·nar·ies.**

sem·i·pre·cious (sem′i presh′əs) having value, but not sufficient value to rank as gems: *Amethysts and garnets are semiprecious stones; diamonds and rubies are precious stones. adj.*

sen·ate (sen′it) **1** a governing or lawmaking assembly: *the senate of a university.* **2** the upper and smaller branch of a parliament or assembly that makes laws: *The Canadian Senate, which consists of 102 members, is made up of representatives from each province. n.*

sen·a·tor (sen′ə tər) a member of a senate. *n.*

send (send) **1** cause to go from one place to another: *send a child on an errand, send someone for a doctor.* **2** cause to be carried: *We sent the letter by air mail.* **3** cause to come, occur, or be: *Send help at once. May God send peace.* **4** drive; throw: *send a ball. The volcano sent clouds of smoke into the air. v.,* **sent, send·ing.**

sen·ior (sēn′yər) **1** older: *a senior citizen.* **2** the older; a father whose son has the same given name: *John Parker, Senior is the father of John Parker, Junior.* **3** an older person: *David is his brother's senior by two years.* **4** higher in rank or longer in service: *He is the senior of the firm of Jones and Brown.* **5** a person of higher rank or longer service. **6** a member of the graduating class of a high school or college. **7** of or having to do with a graduating class. 1, 4, 7 *adj.,* 2, 3, 5, 6 *n.*

senior high school a school attended after junior high school.

sen·sa·tion (sen sā′shən) **1** the action of the senses; the power to see, hear, feel, taste, smell, etc.: *A dead body is without sensation.* **2** a feeling: *Ice gives a sensation of coldness; polished wood gives a sensation of smoothness; sugar gives a sensation of sweetness. He says he has a sensation of dizziness when he walks along cliffs.* **3** a strong or excited feeling: *The announcement of war caused a sensation throughout the land.* **4** the cause of such feeling: *The news of the armistice was a great sensation. n.*

sen·sa·tion·al (sen sā′shən əl) **1** exciting; startling: *The player's sensational catch made the crowd cheer wildly.* **2** trying to cause excitement: *a sensational newspaper story. adj.*

sense (sens) **1** one of the special powers of the body by which people and animals become aware of the world around them and of changes within themselves: *The five senses are sight, smell, taste, hearing, and touch.* **2** a sensation felt through one of these senses: *a sense of pain.* **3** a mental feeling: *Planning for the trip gave her a sense of adventure.* **4** feel; understand: *Mother sensed that Father was tired.* **5** an understanding; appreciation: *Everyone thinks he has a good sense of humor.* **6** judgment; intelligence: *He had the good sense to keep out of foolish quarrels.* **7** usually, **senses,** pl. a clear or sound state of mind: *He must be out of his senses to act so.* **8** a meaning: *He is a gentleman in every sense of the word.* 1–3, 5–8 *n.,* 4 *v.,* **sensed, sens·ing.**
in a sense, in some respects; to some degree.
make sense, have a meaning; be understandable; be reasonable: *The statement 'Cow cat bless Monday' doesn't make sense.*

sense·less (sens′lis) **1** unconscious: *A hard blow on the head knocked him senseless.* **2** foolish; stupid: *That was a senseless thing to do. adj.*

sen·si·bil·i·ty (sen′sə bil′ə tē) **1** the ability to feel or perceive: *Some drugs lessen a person's sensibilities.* **2** a fineness of feeling: *She has an unusual sensibility for colors. n., pl.* **sen·si·bil·i·ties.**

sen·si·ble (sen′sə bəl) **1** having good sense; showing good judgment; wise: *She is much too sensible to do anything so foolish.* **2** aware; conscious: *I am sensible of your kindness.* **3** that can be noticed: *There is a sensible difference between yellow and orange. adj.* —**sen′si·bly,** *adv.*

sen·si·tive (sen′sə tiv) **1** receiving impressions readily: *The eye is sensitive to light.* **2** easily affected or influenced: *The mercury in the thermometer is sensitive to changes in temperature.* **3** easily hurt or offended: *He was very sensitive about his failure. adj.*

sen·so·ry (sen′sə rē) of or having to do with sensation or the senses: *The eyes and ears are sensory organs. adj.*

sen·su·al (sen′shü əl) **1** having to do with the bodily senses rather than with the mind or soul: *Gluttons derive sensual pleasure from eating.* **2** caring too much for the pleasures of the senses. *adj.*

sent (sent) See **send.** *They sent the trunks last week. She was sent on an errand. v.*
☛ **Sent, cent** and **scent** are pronounced the same.

sen·tence (sen′təns) **1** a word or group of words making a grammatically complete statement, question, request, command, or exclamation: *'Boys and girls' is not a sentence. 'The boys are here' is a sentence.* **2** a decision by a judge on the punishment of a criminal. **3** the punishment itself. **4** pronounce punishment on: *The judge sentenced the thief to five years in prison.* 1–3 *n.,* 4 *v.,* **sen·tenced, sen·tenc·ing.**

sen·ti·ment (sen′tə mənt) **1** a mixture of thought and feeling: *Admiration, patriotism, and loyalty are sentiments.* **2** feeling, especially tender feeling: *My sister is full of sentiment. n.*

sen·ti·men·tal (sen′tə men′təl) **1** having or showing much tender feeling: *sentimental poetry.* **2** likely to act from feelings rather than from logical thinking; having too much sentiment. **3** of sentiment; dependent on sentiment: *She values her mother's gift for sentimental reasons. adj.*

sen·ti·nel (sen′tə nəl) sentry. *n.*

sen·try (sen′trē) a person, especially a soldier, stationed at a place to keep watch and guard against surprise attacks, etc. *n., pl.* **sen·tries.**
stand sentry, keep watch; guard: *We stood sentry over the sleepers.*

sentry box a small building for sheltering a sentry.

se·pal (sē′pəl) one of the divisions of the calyx, or outer covering, of a flower: *In a carnation, the sepals make a green cup at the base of the flower.* See **flower** for picture. *n.*

sep·a·rate (sep′ə rāt′ for 1, 2, 3, and 4, sep′ə rit for 5) **1** be between; keep apart; divide: *The Atlantic Ocean separates North and South America from Europe.* **2** take apart; divide into parts or groups: *separate a tangle of string.* **3** go, draw, or come apart: *After school the children separated in all directions. The rope separated under the strain.* **4** put apart; take away: *Separate your books from mine.* **5** apart from others;

hat, āge, fär; let, ēqual, tėrm; it, īce
hot, ōpen, ôrder; oil, out; cup, pu̇t, rüle
əbove, takən, pencəl, lemən, circəs
ch, child; ng, long; sh, ship
th, thin; ᴛʜ, then; zh, measure

divided; not joined; individual; single: *in a separate room, separate seats, the separate parts of a machine.* 1–4 *v.,* **sep·a·rat·ed, sep·a·rat·ing;** 5 *adj.* **—sep′a·rate·ly,** *adv.*

separate school 1 *Cdn.* a school for children belonging to a religious minority in a particular district, receiving taxes imposed by its own school board as well as grants from the provincial Department of Education. 2 a Roman Catholic parochial school. 3 sometimes a school that is not part of the public school system; a private or independent school.

sep·a·ra·tion (sep′ə rā′shən) 1 separating, dividing, or taking apart. 2 being apart or being separated. 3 the line or point where things separate: *They soon came to the separation of the path into two tracks.* *n.*

sep·a·ra·tor (sep′ə rā′tor) a person or thing that separates, especially a machine for separating the cream from milk, wheat from chaff or dirt, etc. *n.*

Sept. September.

Sep·tem·ber (sep tem′bər) the ninth month: *September has 30 days.* *n.*

☛ **September** came into English through Old French from the Latin name for this month, *September,* from *septem,* meaning 'seven.' September was the seventh month in the ancient Roman calendar.

sep·tic tank (sep′tik) a tank in which sewage is broken down by the action of bacteria.

sep·ul·chre or **sep·ul·cher** (sep′əl kər) a place for putting the bodies of persons who have died; tomb. *n.*

se·quel (sē′kwəl) 1 something that follows as a result of some earlier happening; a result of something; outcome: *Famine is often the sequel to war.* 2 a complete story continuing an earlier one about the same people: *Robert Louis Stevenson's 'David Balfour' is a sequel to his 'Kidnapped.'* *n.*

se·quence (sē′kwəns) 1 the coming of one thing after another; succession; the order or succession: *Arrange the names in alphabetical sequence.* 2 a connected series: *a sequence of lessons on one subject.* *n.*

se·quoi·a (si kwoi′ə) either of two kinds of very tall evergreen trees of California. *n.*

☛ Named after *Sequoya* (1770?–1843), a Cherokee Indian, who invented an alphabet for his own language.

ser·e·nade (ser′ə nād′) 1 music played or sung outdoors at night, especially by a lover under his lady's window. 2 sing or play to in this way. 1 *n.,* 2 *v.,* **ser·e·nad·ed, ser·e·nad·ing.**

se·rene (sə rēn′) 1 peaceful; calm: *serene happiness, a serene smile.* 2 clear; bright; not cloudy: *a serene sky.* *adj.*

se·ren·i·ty (sə ren′ə tē) 1 peace; calmness. 2 clearness; brightness. *n.*

serf (sėrf) 1 a person who worked on a feudal estate and passed with the land from one owner to another. 2 a person treated almost like a slave; a person who is mistreated, underpaid, etc. *n.*

☛ **Serf** and **surf** are pronounced the same.

ser·geant (sär′jənt) 1 a non-commissioned officer in the armed forces, ranking next above corporal. 2 a police officer usually ranking next above an ordinary policeman. *n.*

se·ri·al (sēr′ē əl) 1 a story presented one part at a time in a magazine or newspaper, or on radio or television. 2 of a series; arranged in a series: *in serial order, a serial number.* 1 *n.,* 2 *adj.*

☛ **Serial** and **cereal** are pronounced the same.

se·ries (sēr′ēz) 1 a number of similar things in a row: *A series of rooms opened off the long hall.* 2 a number of things placed one after another: *in an alphabetical series.* 3 a number of things or events happening one after the other: *A series of rainy days spoiled their vacation.* *n., pl.* **se·ries.**

se·ri·ous (sēr′ē əs) 1 thoughtful; grave: *a serious face.* 2 in earnest; not fooling: *Are you joking or serious?* 3 important; needing thought: *Choice of one's life work is a serious matter.* 4 important because it may do much harm; dangerous: *The badly injured man was in serious condition.* *adj.* **—se′ri·ous·ness,** *n.*

ser·mon (sėr′mən) 1 a public talk on religion or something connected with religion: *Ministers preach sermons in church.* 2 a serious talk about conduct or duty: *The boy got a sermon on table manners from his father.* *n.*

ser·pent (sėr′pənt) 1 a snake, especially a big snake. 2 a sly, treacherous person. *n.*

ser·pen·tine (sėr′pən tīn′) 1 of or like a serpent. 2 winding; twisting: *the serpentine course of a creek.* *adj.*

ser·rate (ser′āt) notched like the edge of a saw; toothed: *a serrate leaf.* *adj.*

se·rum (sēr′əm) 1 the clear, pale-yellow liquid of the blood, which separates from the clot when blood coagulates. 2 a liquid used to prevent or cure a disease, usually obtained from the blood of an animal that has been made immune to the disease: *Polio vaccine is a serum.* *n.*

serv·ant (sėr′vənt) 1 a person employed in a household: *Cooks and nursemaids are servants.* 2 a person employed by another: *Policemen and firemen are public servants.* 3 a person devoted to any service: *Ministers are called servants of God.* *n.*

serve (sėrv) 1 work for; be a servant of: *A slave serves his master. Good citizens serve their country.* 2 give service; perform duties: *The soldier served three years in the army.* 3 wait on at table; bring food to: *The waiter served us.* 4 put food or drink on the table: *The waiter served the soup. Dinner is served.* 5 supply; furnish; supply with something needed: *The dairy serves us with milk. The men were served with a round of ammunition.* 6 supply enough for: *One pie will serve six persons.* 7 deliver; present: *He was served with a notice to appear in court.* 8 be useful; be what is needed; be used: *A flat stone served as a table.* 9 be favorable or suitable; satisfy: *This will serve my purpose.* 10 pass; spend: *The thief served a term in prison.* 11 in tennis and similar games, put the ball in play by hitting it. 12 a serving of the ball. 1–11 *v.,* **served, serv·ing;** 12 *n.* **—serv′er,** *n.*

serve one right, be just what one deserves: *The punishment serves him right.*

serv·ice (sėr′vis) **1** a helpful act or acts; aid; being useful to others: *The man performed many services for his country.* **2** the arrangements for supplying something useful or necessary: *The bus service was good.* **3** occupation or employment as a servant: *She is in service with Mrs. Brown.* **4** Usually, **services,** *pl.* **a** the performance of duties; work: *She no longer needs the services of a doctor.* **b** work in the service of others: *We pay for services such as repairs, maintenance, and utilities.* **5** advantage; benefit; use: *This coat has given me great service. Every available truck was pressed into service.* **6** a department of government or public employment; the persons working in it: *the civil service, the military service.* **7** the armed forces: *We entered the service together.* **8** duty in the armed forces: *He was on active service during the war.* **9** a religious meeting or ceremony: *We attend church services twice a week. The marriage service was performed at the home of the bride.* **10** the manner of serving food; the food served: *The service in this restaurant is excellent.* **11** a set of dishes, etc.: *She has a silver tea service.* **12** make fit for service; keep fit for service: *The mechanic serviced our automobile.* **13** the act or manner of putting the ball in play in tennis and similar games. 1–11, 13 *n.,* 12 *v.,* **serv·iced, serv·ic·ing.**

at one's service, ready to do what one wants.

of service, helpful; useful.

serv·ice·a·ble (sėr′vis ə bəl) **1** useful for a long time; able to stand much use: *He wanted to buy a serviceable second-hand car.* **2** capable of giving good service; useful: *He should make a serviceable goalkeeper. adj.*

service centre a stopping area adjoining an expressway, consisting of a service station, restaurant, toilet facilities, etc.

serv·ice·man (sėr′vis man′ or sėr′vis mən) **1** a member of the armed forces. **2** a person who maintains or repairs machinery or some kind of equipment: *an automobile serviceman. n., pl.* **serv·ice·men** (sėr′vis men′ or sėr′vis mən).

service station a place for supplying gasoline, oil, water, etc. and for automobile maintenance and repairs.

ser·vi·ette (sėr′vē et′) a cloth or paper napkin used at table: *He wiped his fingers on his serviette. n.*

ser·vile (sėr′vīl) **1** like that of slaves; fit for a slave; mean: *servile flattery.* **2** of or having to do with slaves: *a servile revolt, servile work. adj.*

serv·ing (sėr′ving) a portion of food served to a person at one time; helping. *n.*

ser·vi·tude (sėr′və tyüd′ or sėr′və tüd′) **1** slavery; bondage. **2** forced labor as a punishment: *The criminal was sentenced to five years' servitude. n.*

ses·sion (sesh′ən) **1** a sitting or meeting of a court, council, legislature, etc.: *a session of Parliament.* **2** a series of such sittings. **3** a period of meetings, classes, etc.: *He attended the university during the summer session. n.*

in session, meeting: *The teachers were in session all Saturday morning.*

set (set) **1** put in some place; put; place: *Set the box on its end.* **2** put in the right place, position, or condition for use; arrange; put in proper order: *The hunter sets his traps. Set the table for dinner. Set the clock. The doctor will set Tom's broken leg.* **3** put in some condition or relation: *A spark set the woods on fire. The slaves were set free.* **4** fix; arrange; appoint: *If he sets his mind on it, he will do it. The teacher set a time limit for the examination.* **5** fixed or appointed beforehand; established: *a set time, set rules.* **6** provide for others to follow: *to set a good example.* **7** put in a fixed, rigid, or settled state: *to set one's teeth.* **8** fixed; rigid: *a set smile. He has set opinions.* **9** make or become firm or hard; become fixed: *Jelly sets as it cools.* **10** go down; sink: *The sun sets in the west.* **11** a group; a number of things or persons belonging together: *a set of dishes.* **12** in arithmetic, a group of numbers, points, objects, or other elements which are distinguished from all other elements by specific common properties. The numbers from 0 to 10 form a set, and any number in this set is a member of the set. **13** a group of games in tennis. **14** a device for receiving or sending by radio, television, telephone, telegraph, etc. **15** a form; shape; the way a thing is put or placed: *There was a stubborn set to his jaw.* **16** the scenery for a play, act, scene, etc. **17** begin to move; start: *He set out to cross the river.* **18** begin to apply; begin to apply oneself: *Have you set to work?* **19** in music, adapt; fit: *to set the words of a poem to music.* **20** put a hen to sit on eggs to hatch them; place eggs under a hen to be hatched. A **setting hen** is a hen sitting on eggs to hatch them. 1–4, 6, 7, 9, 10, 17–20 *v.,* **set, set·ting;** 5, 8 *adj.,* 11–16 *n.*

set about, start work upon; begin: *Set about your washing.*

set back, stop; hinder; check: *The job was set back because of the accident.*

set down, a deposit or let alight; put down: *set down a suitcase. The bus set him down near town.* **b** put down in writing or printing. **c** consider; ascribe: *Your failure in the test can be set down to too much haste.*

set forth, a make known; express; declare. **b** start to go: *We set forth on our trip.*

set in, a begin: *Winter set in early.* **b** blow or flow toward the shore.

set off, a explode: *He will set off the fire-crackers.* **b** start to go: *set off for home.* **c** emphasize or heighten by contrast: *The green dress set off her red hair.*

set on or **set upon, a** attack: *The dog set on him.* **b** urge to attack.

set to, a begin: *set to work.* **b** begin fighting: *The two boys set to.*

set up, a build: *set up a monument.* **b** begin; start. **c** put up; raise in place, power, pride, etc.: *They set him up above his rivals.*

☛ **Set,** meaning 'to place,' should not be confused with **sit:** *He set a book on the stool. He sat on the stool. A builder sets his bricks carefully. An old man sits carefully.*

set·back (set′bak′) a check to progress; a reverse: *He suffered a serious financial setback. n.*

set·tee (se tē′) a sofa or long bench with a back and, usually, arms. *n.*

set·ter (set′ər) **1** a person who sets or arranges things: *a setter of type, a setter of jewels.* **2** a long-haired hunting dog, trained to stand motionless and point his nose toward the game that he scents. *n.*

set·ting (set′ing) **1** a frame or other thing in which something is set: *The mounting of a jewel is its setting.* **2** the scenery of a play; a set. **3** the place, time, etc. of a play or story. **4** the surroundings; background: *a scenic mountain setting.* **5** the music composed to go with a story, poem, etc. 6 the eggs that a hen sits on for hatching. *n.*

set·tle[1] (set′əl) 1 determine; decide; agree upon: *We bring our disputes to Mother to settle. Have you settled on a day for the picnic?* 2 put or be put in order; arrange: *I must settle all my affairs before going away for the winter.* 3 pay: *He settled all his bills before leaving town. Let us settle up our expenses for the trip.* 4 take up residence in a new country or place: *Our cousin intends to settle in the Yukon.* 5 establish colonies or communities in: *The English settled Newfoundland.* 6 set or be set in a fairly permanent position, place, or way of life: *At last we are settled in our new home.* 7 come to rest in a particular place; become set or fixed: *His cold settled in his lungs.* 8 place in or come to a desired or comfortable position: *The cat settled itself in the chair for a nap.* 9 make or become quiet: *A vacation will settle your nerves.* 10 go down; sink: *Our house has settled eight centimetres since it was built.* *v.,* **set·tled, set·tling.**

settle down, a live a more regular life. b direct steady effort or attention.

set·tle[2] (set′əl) a long, wooden bench with arms and a high back. *n.*

set·tle·ment (set′əl mənt) 1 settling or being settled. 2 putting in order; an arrangement: *No settlement of the dispute is possible unless each side yields some point.* 3 a payment: *Settlement of all claims against the company will be made shortly.* 4 the settling of persons in a new region: *The settlement of the English along the Atlantic Coast of North America gave England claim to that region.* 5 a region settled in this way: *England had many settlements along the Atlantic Coast.* 6 a group of buildings and the people living in them: *The explorers spent the night in an Indian settlement.* *n.*

set·tler (set′lər) a person who settles in a new region: *The early settlers in Canada faced many hardships.* *n.*

sev·en (sev′ən) one more than six; 7. *n., adj.*

seven seas all the oceans of the world, traditionally considered to be the Arctic, Antarctic, North Atlantic, South Atlantic, North Pacific, South Pacific, and Indian Oceans: *sail the seven seas.*

sev·en·teen (sev′ən tēn′) seven more than ten; 17. *n., adj.*

sev·en·teenth (sev′ən tēnth′) 1 next after the 16th; last in a series of seventeen; 17th. 2 one of 17 equal parts. *adj., n.*

sev·enth (sev′ənth) 1 next after the sixth; last in a series of seven; 7th.: *Saturday is the seventh day of the week.* 2 one of seven equal parts: *A day is one seventh of a week.* *adj., n.*

sev·en·ti·eth (sev′ən tē ith) 1 next after the 69th; last in a series of seventy; 70th. 2 one of 70 equal parts. *adj., n.*

sev·en·ty (sev′ən tē) seven times ten; 70. *n., pl.* **sev·en·ties;** *adj.*

sev·er (sev′ər) 1 cut apart; cut off: *The sailor severed the rope with a knife.* 2 part; divide; separate: *The rope severed and the swing fell down.* 3 break off: *The two nations severed friendly relations.* *v.*

sev·er·al (sev′ər əl or sev′rəl) 1 more than two or three but not many; some; a few: *to eat several candies. Several have given their consent.* 2 different; individual: *The boys went their several ways, each minding his own business.* 1, 2 *adj.,* 1 *n.*

hat, āge, fär; let, ēqual, tėrm; it, īce
hot, ōpen, ôrder; oil, out; cup, pu̇t, rüle
əbove, takən, pencəl, lemən, circəs
ch, child; ng, long; sh, ship
th, thin; ᴛʜ, then; zh, measure

se·vere (sə vēr′) 1 very strict; stern; harsh: *The judge imposed a severe sentence on the criminal.* 2 sharp; violent: *I have a severe headache. That was a severe storm.* 3 serious; grave: *a severe manner, a severe illness.* 4 very plain or simple; without ornament: *Her severe dress made her look old.* 5 difficult: *The new gun had to pass a series of severe tests.* *adj.,* **se·ver·er, se·ver·est. —se·vere′ly,** *adv.*

se·ver·i·ty (sə ver′ə tē) 1 strictness; sternness; harshness: *The children feared their neighbor because of his severity.* 2 violence; sharpness: *the severity of storms, the severity of pain, the severity of grief.* 3 a simplicity of style or taste; plainness: *The severity of her dress is becoming.* *n., pl.* **se·ver·i·ties.**

sew (sō) 1 work with a needle and thread: *You can sew by hand or with a machine.* 2 fasten with stitches: *sew on a button. She sewed her new dress neatly.* *v.,* **sewed, sewn** or **sewed, sew·ing.**

sew up, close with stitches: *The doctor sewed up the wound.*

☛ **Sew, so,** and **sow**[1] are pronounced the same.

sew·age (sü′ij) the waste matter that passes through sewers. *n.*

sew·er (sü′ər) a pipe or channel to carry off waste water and refuse: *Sewers are usually underground.* *n.*

sew·ing (sō′ing) 1 work done with a needle and thread. 2 something to be sewn. *n.*

sewn (sōn) See **sew.** *Mother has sewn a new button on your shirt.* *v.*

☛ **Sewn** and **sown** are pronounced the same.

sex (seks) 1 one of the two divisions of human beings or animals: *Men, bulls, and roosters are of the male sex; women, cows, and hens are of the female sex.* 2 the characteristic of being male or female: *People were admitted without regard to age or sex.* *n.*

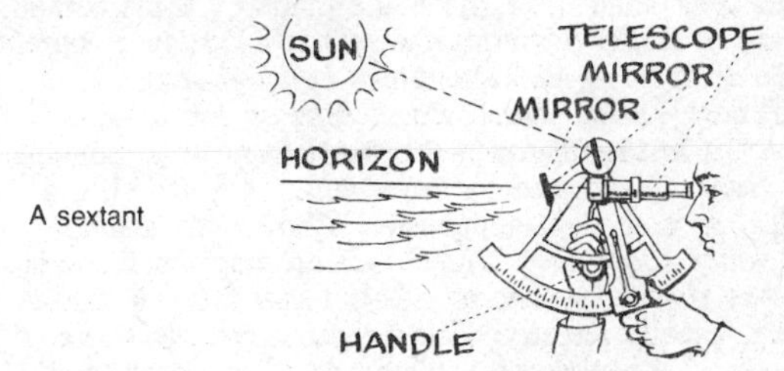

A sextant

sex·tant (seks′tənt) an instrument used by navigators, surveyors, etc. for measuring the angle between two objects: *Sextants are used at sea to measure the altitude of the sun, a star, etc. in order to determine latitude and longitude.* *n.*

sex·ton (seks′tən) a man who takes care of a church building: *The sexton keeps the church clean and warm.* *n.*

sex·u·al (sek′shü əl) of or having to do with sex or the sexes. *adj.*

shab·by (shab′ē) 1 much worn: *His old suit looks shabby.* 2 wearing old or much worn clothes: *She is always shabby.* 3 poor or neglected; run-down: *a shabby old house.* 4 mean; not generous; unfair: *It is shabby not to speak to an old friend because he is poor.* *adj.,* **shab·bi·er, shab·bi·est.**

shack (shak) 1 a roughly built hut or cabin: *The boys made a shack in the back yard.* 2 a house in bad condition: *There are a lot of shacks in that part of town.* *n.*

shack·le (shak′əl) 1 a metal band fastened around the ankle or wrist of a prisoner or slave: *Shackles are usually fastened to each other, the wall, or the floor by chains.* 2 put shackles on. 3 anything that prevents freedom of action or thought. 4 restrain or hamper. 5 something for fastening or coupling. 1, 3, 5 *n.,* 2, 4 *v.,* **shack·led, shack·ling.**

shad (shad) a salt-water fish related to the herring: *The shad, common on the northern Atlantic coast, is a valuable food fish.* *n., pl.* **shad** or **shads.**

shad bush a bush or small tree bearing large, sweet, purple berries: *What is called a 'shad bush' in the Maritimes is called a 'saskatoon' in the West.*

shade (shād) 1 a partly dark place, not in the sunshine: *He sat in the shade of a big tree.* 2 a slight darkness or coolness given by something that cuts off light: *Big trees cast shade.* 3 something that shuts out light; a blind: *Pull down the shades of the windows.* 4 keep light from: *A big hat shades the eyes.* 5 lightness or darkness of color: *I want to see silks in all shades of blue.* 6 make darker than the rest: *A person shades one side of a dish when he draws or paints it.* 7 a very small difference or amount; a little bit: *Your coat is a shade longer than your dress.* 8 show very small differences; change little by little: *This scarf shades from deep rose to pale pink.* 9 ghost; spirit: *the shades of departed heroes.* 1–3, 5, 7, 9 *n.,* 4, 6, 8 *v.,* **shad·ed, shad·ing.**

shad·ing (shād′ing) 1 the use of black with other colors to give the effect of shade or depth in a picture. 2 a slight variation or difference of color, character, etc. *n.*

shad·ow (shad′ō) 1 the shade made by some person, animal, or thing: *Sometimes a person's shadow is much longer than he is, and sometimes much shorter.* 2 darkness; partial shade: *Don't turn on the light; we like to sit in the shadow.* 3 protect from light; shade: *The grass is shadowed by huge oaks.* 4 a little bit; a small degree; a slight suggestion: *There's not a shadow of a doubt about his guilt.* 5 a faint image or likeness: *She was worn to a shadow of her usual self.* 6 follow closely, usually secretly: *The detective shadowed the suspect.* 7 a person who follows another closely and secretly. 1, 2, 4, 5, 7 *n.,* 3, 6 *v.*

shad·ow·y (shad′ō ē) 1 having much shadow or shade; shady: *We went out of the hot sunshine into the cool, shadowy room.* 2 like a shadow; dim; faint: *He saw a shadowy outline that appeared on the window curtains.* *adj.*

shad·y (shād′ē) 1 in the shade. 2 giving shade. 3 *Informal.* of doubtful honesty or character: *That man is a shady character, if not an actual criminal.* *adj.,* **shad·i·er, shad·i·est.**

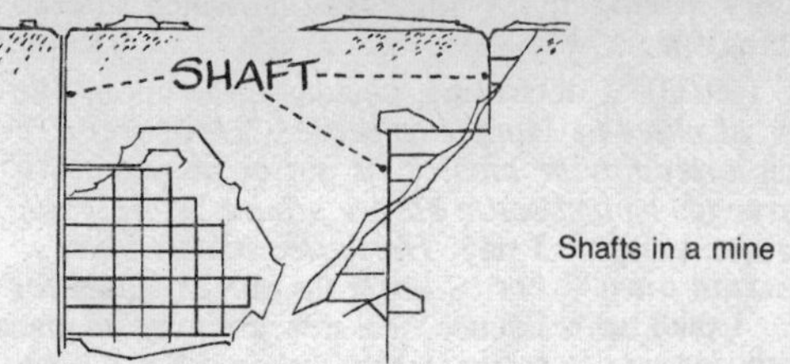

Shafts in a mine

shaft (shaft) 1 in a machine, a bar that turns or that supports turning parts. See **jet engine** for picture. 2 a deep passage sunk down into the earth: *The entrance to a mine is called a shaft.* 3 a passage that is like a well; a deep, narrow space: *an elevator shaft.* 4 the long, straight handle of a hammer, axe, golf club, etc. 5 a ray or beam of light. 6 a wooden pole by means of which a horse is harnessed to a carriage, etc. 7 the main part of a column. See **column** for picture. 8 the long, slender stem of an arrow, spear, lance, etc. 9 an arrow, spear, lance, etc. See **arrow** for picture. *n.*

shag·gy (shag′ē) 1 covered with a thick, rough mass of hair, wool, etc.: *a shaggy dog.* 2 rough, coarse, or unkempt: *the dog had shaggy hair.* *adj.,* **shag·gi·er, shag·gi·est.**

shake (shāk) 1 move quickly backward and forward, up and down, or from side to side: *to shake a rug. The baby shook the rattle. He shook his fist in Tom's face.* 2 bring, throw, or scatter by such movement: *He shook the snow off his clothes.* 3 clasp hands in greeting, congratulating, etc. another: *shake hands.* 4 tremble: *He is shaking with cold.* 5 make tremble: *The explosion shook the town.* 6 disturb; make less firm: *His lie shook my faith in his honesty.* 7 the act of shaking: *A shake of her hand was her only answer.* 8 mix dice before throwing. 1–6, 8 *v.,* **shook, shak·en, shak·ing;** 7 *n.*

shake off, get rid of.

shake up, a shake hard. **b** stir up. **c** jar in body or nerves: *He was much shaken up by the experience.*

shak·y (shāk′ē) 1 shaking: *a shaky voice.* 2 liable to break down; weak: *a shaky porch.* 3 not reliable; not to be depended on: *Joan is going to quit because the firm she works for is shaky.* *adj.,* **shak·i·er, shak·i·est.**

shale (shāl) rock formed from hardened clay or mud in thin layers which split easily. *n.*

shall (shal; *unstressed,* shəl) a word used: 1 in questions with 'I' or 'we' to ask what one is to do: *Shall we go? Shall we wait?* 2 in statements with 'you,' 'he,' 'she,' or 'they' to show that a person has to do something: *You shall pay attention. He shall stay in his room for an hour.* 3 with 'I' and 'we' to indicate simple future time: *I shall go tomorrow if I cannot make it today.* *v.,* **should** (def. 5).

shal·low (shal′ō) 1 not deep: *shallow water, a shallow dish, a shallow mind.* 2 Usually, **shallows,** *pl.* a shallow place: *The boys splashed in the shallows of the pond.* 1 *adj.,* 2 *n.*

sham (sham) 1 a fraud; pretence: *His goodness is all a sham.* 2 false; pretended; being an imitation: *The soldiers had a sham battle for practice.* 3 pretend: *He shammed sickness so he wouldn't have to work.* 1 *n.,* 2 *adj.,* 3 *v.,* **shammed, sham·ming.**

sham·ble (sham′bəl) 1 walk awkwardly or unsteadily: *The tired old man shambles.* 2 a shambling walk. 1 *v.,* **sham·bled, sham·bling;** 2 *n.*

hat, āge, fär; let, ēqual, tėrm; it, īce
hot, ōpen, ôrder; oil, out; cup, pu̇t, rüle
əbove, takən, pencəl, lemən, circəs
ch, child; ng, long; sh, ship
th, thin; ᴛʜ, then; zh, measure

sham·bles (sham′bəlz) *Informal.* confusion; mess; general disorder: *The careless children made a shambles of their room.* *n.*

shame (shām) 1 a painful feeling of having done something wrong, improper, or silly: *The child blushed with shame when he was caught stealing candy.* 2 cause to feel shame: *My silly mistake shamed me.* 3 drive or force by shame: *He was shamed into combing his hair.* 4 disgrace; dishonor: *That young man's arrest has brought shame to a fine family.* 5 bring disgrace upon: *He has shamed his parents by doing wrong.* 6 a fact to be sorry about; pity: *It is a shame to be so wasteful. What a shame you can't come to the party!* 1, 4, 6 *n.*, 2, 3, 5 *v.*, **shamed, sham·ing.**
put to shame, a make ashamed; disgrace. b surpass: *His careful work put all the rest to shame.*

shame·faced (shām′fāst′) showing shame and embarrassment. *adj.*

shame·ful (shām′fəl) causing shame; bring disgrace. *adj.*

shame·less (shām′lis) 1 without shame. 2 not modest. *adj.*

sham·poo (sham pü′) 1 wash the hair, scalp, a rug, etc. with a soapy or oily preparation. 2 a washing of this kind. 3 a preparation used for shampooing. 1 *v.*, **sham·pooed, sham·poo·ing;** 2, 3 *n.*

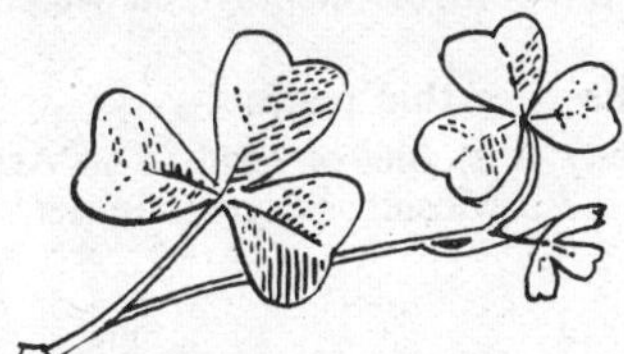

Shamrocks

sham·rock (sham′rok) a plant having a bright green leaf composed of three parts: *The shamrock is the national emblem of Ireland.* *n.*

shank (shangk) 1 the part of the leg between the knee and the ankle. 2 the whole leg. 3 any part like a leg, stem, or shaft: *The shank of a fish-hook is the straight part between hook and loop.* *n.*

shan't (shant) shall not.

shan·ty[1] (shan′tē) *Cdn.* 1 a roughly built hut or cabin. 2 the log-built living quarters of a gang of lumbermen. *n., pl.* **shan·ties.**

☛ **Shanty**[1] comes from the Canadian French word *chantier,* meaning 'lumberjack's headquarters.'

shan·ty[2] (shan′tē) a song sung by sailors in rythm with the motions made during their work. *n., pl.* **shan·ties.** Also spelled **chantey.**

☛ **Shanty**[2], originally *chantey,* comes from a French word *chanter,* meaning 'to sing.'

shape (shāp) 1 the outline or form of a person or thing; figure; appearance: *An apple is different in shape from a banana. A witch could take the shape of a cat or a bat. A white shape stood at his bedside.* 2 form into a shape; mould: *The child shapes clay into balls.* 3 develop; take shape: *His plan is shaping well.* 4 condition: *The athlete exercised to keep himself in good shape.* 5 order; definite form; proper arrangement: *Take time to get your thoughts into shape.* 1, 4, 5 *n.*, 2, 3 *v.*, **shaped, shap·ing.**
take shape, have or take on a definite form.

shape·less (shāp′lis) without definite shape: *She wore a shapeless old hat.* *adj.*

shape·ly (shāp′lē) having a pleasing shape; well-formed. *adj.*, **shape·li·er, shape·li·est.**

share (sher) 1 a part belonging to one person; a part or portion: *The father left each child an equal share of his property. He does more than his share of the work and does not always get his share of the praise.* 2 each of the parts into which the ownership of a company or corporation is divided: *The ownership of this company is divided into several million shares.* 3 use together; enjoy together; have in common: *The sisters share a room.* 4 divide into parts, each taking a part: *John shared his candy with his sister.* 5 have a share; take part: *Everyone shared in making the school picnic a huge success.* 1, 2 *n.*, 3–5 *v.*, **shared, shar·ing.**

A white shark — about 6 m long with the tail

shark (shärk) 1 any of a group of fishes, some of which are large and ferocious: *Certain kinds of sharks are sometimes dangerous to man.* 2 a dishonest person who preys on others. *n.*

sharp (shärp) 1 having a thin cutting edge or a fine point: *a sharp knife, a sharp pin.* 2 having a point; not rounded: *a sharp nose, a sharp corner on a box.* 3 with a sudden change of direction: *a sharp turn.* 4 very cold: *sharp weather, a sharp morning.* 5 severe; biting: *sharp words.* 6 feeling somewhat like a cut or prick; acting keenly on the senses: *a sharp taste, a sharp noise, a sharp pain.* 7 clear; distinct: *the sharp contrast between black and white.* 8 quick; brisk: *a sharp walk or run.* 9 fierce; violent: *a sharp struggle.* 10 keen; eager: *a sharp desire, a sharp appetite.* 11 being aware of things quickly: *a sharp eye, sharp ears.* 12 watchful; wide-awake: *The sentry kept a sharp watch for the enemy.* 13 quick in mind; shrewd; clever: *a sharp boy, a sharp lawyer, sharp at a bargain.* 14 promptly; exactly: *Come at one o'clock sharp.* 15 suddenly: *to pull a horse up sharp.* 16 high in pitch; shrill: *a sharp voice.* 17 in music, above the true pitch: *to sing sharp.* 18 a tone one half step above a given tone. 19 the sign (♯) that stands for such a tone. 1–13, 16, 17 *adj.*, 14, 15, 17 *adv.*, 18, 19 *n.* **—sharp′ness,** *n.*

sharp·en (shär′pən) 1 make sharp: *Sharpen the pencil. Sharpen your wits.* 2 become sharp: *Her voice sharpened as she became angry.* *v.*

sharp·shoot·er (shärp′shüt′ər) a person who shoots very well, especially with a rifle. *n.*

shat·ter (shat′ər) 1 break into pieces: *A stone shattered the window.* 2 destroy; disturb greatly: *Our hopes for a picnic were shattered by the rain.* *v.*

shave (shāv) 1 cut hair from anything with a razor:

Father shaves every day. He shaves his beard. 2 the cutting off of hair with a razor. 3 cut off in thin slices: *She shaved the chocolate.* 4 come very close to; graze: *The car shaved the corner.* 5 a narrow miss or escape: *The shot missed him, but it was a close shave.* 1, 3, 4 *v.,* **shaved, shaved** or **shav·en, shav·ing;** 2, 5 *n.*

shav·en (shāv′ən) 1 shaved. 2 closely cut. 3 See **shave.** 1, 2 *adj.,* 3 *v.*

shav·ing (shāv′ing) a very thin piece or slice: *Shavings of wood are cut off by a plane. n.*

shawl (shol or shôl) a square or oblong piece of cloth worn about the shoulders or head. *n.*

she (shē) 1 the girl, woman, or female animal already referred to and identified: *My sister says she likes to read.* 2 anything thought of as female and already referred to and identified: *She was a fine old ship.* 3 any girl, woman, or female animal: *Is the baby a he or a she?* 1, 2 *pron., pl.* **they;** 3 *n., pl.* **she's.**

sheaf (shēf) 1 a bundle of cut grain bound in the middle for drying, loading, and stacking: *They were bringing sheaves of wheat.* 2 any bundle of things of the same sort: *a sheaf of arrows. n., pl.* **sheaves.**

shear (shēr) 1 cut with shears or scissors. 2 cut the wool or fleece from: *The farmer sheared his sheep.* 3 cut close; cut off; cut. *v.,* **sheared, sheared** or **shorn, shear·ing.**

☛ **Shear** and **sheer** are pronounced the same.

shears (shērz) 1 large scissors: *barber's shears.* 2 any cutting instrument resembling scissors: *grass shears, tin shears. n. pl.*

sheath (shēth) 1 a case or covering for the blade of a sword or knife. 2 any similar covering, especially on an animal or plant. *n., pl.* **sheaths** (shēᴛʜz).

sheathe (shēᴛʜ) 1 put into a sheath. 2 enclose in a case or covering: *a mummy sheathed in linen. The doors were sheathed in metal. v.,* **sheathed, sheath·ing.**

sheaves (shēvz) plural of **sheaf.** *n. pl.*

shed[1] (shed) a building used for shelter, storage, etc., usually having only one storey: *a tool shed, a wagon shed. n.*

shed[2] (shed) 1 pour out; let fall: *The girl shed tears.* 2 throw off; cast aside: *The snake shed its skin. The umbrella sheds water.* 3 scatter abroad; give forth: *The sun sheds light. Flowers shed perfume.* 4 cause to flow: *He shed his enemy's blood. v.,* **shed, shed·ding.**
shed one's blood, sacrifice one's life: *The soldier shed his blood for his country.*

she'd (shēd) 1 she had. 2 she would.

sheen (shēn) brightness; lustre; shine: *Satin and polished silver have a sheen. n.*

A domestic sheep — usually about 90 cm high at the shoulder

sheep (shēp) 1 an animal raised for meat, wool, and skin. 2 a person who is weak, timid, or easily led: *'Are you men or are you sheep?' cried the captain. n., pl.* **sheep.**

sheep·ish (shēp′ish) 1 awkwardly bashful or embarrassed: *a sheepish smile.* 2 like a sheep; timid; weak; stupid. *adj.*

sheep·skin (shēp′skin′) 1 the skin of a sheep, especially with the wool on it. 2 leather or parchment made from the skin of a sheep. *n.*

sheer[1] (shēr) 1 very thin; almost transparent: *Her dress had long, sheer sleeves.* 2 unmixed with anything else; complete: *She fainted from sheer weariness.* 3 straight up or down; steep: *From the top of the wall, there was a sheer drop of 50 metres to the water below.* 4 steeply: *The cliff rose sheer from the river edge.* 1–3 *adj.,* 4 *adv.*

☛ **Sheer** and **shear** are pronounced the same.

sheer[2] (shēr) turn from a course; turn aside; swerve. *v.*

☛ **See note at sheer**[1].

sheet[1] (shēt) 1 a large piece of cloth, usually cotton or partly cotton, used to sleep on or under. 2 a broad, thin piece of anything: *a sheet of glass.* 3 a single piece of paper. 4 a newspaper. 5 a broad, flat surface: *a sheet of water. n.*

sheet[2] (shēt) a rope that controls the angle at which a sail is set. *n.*

sheet iron iron in sheets or thin plates.

sheik or **sheikh** (shēk) 1 a chief or head of an Arab family, village, or tribe. 2 a Moslem religious leader. *n.*

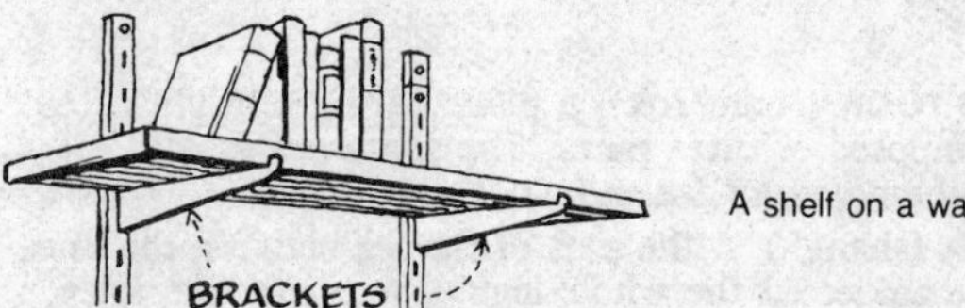

A shelf on a wall

shelf (shelf) 1 a thin, flat piece of wood or other material fastened to a wall or frame to hold things, such as books, dishes, etc. 2 anything like a shelf: *The ship hit a shelf of coral. n., pl.* **shelves.**

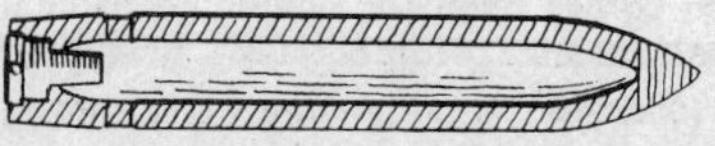

An artillery shell

shell (shel) 1 the hard outside covering of nuts, eggs, certain animals, etc.: *Oysters, turtles, and beetles all have shells.* 2 take out of a shell: *The cook is shelling peas.* 3 something like a shell: *The framework of a house, a very light racing boat, and a hollow case of pastry are all called shells.* 4 a cartridge used in a rifle or shotgun. See **cartridge** for picture. 5 a metal projectile filled with explosives that is fired by artillery and explodes on impact. 6 fire cannon at; bombard with shells: *The enemy shelled the town.* 1, 3–5 *n.,* 2, 6 *v.*
come out of one's shell, stop being shy or reserved; join in conversation, etc. with others.
shell out, *Informal.* **a** give something away: *On Halloween the children cry, 'Shell out!'* **b** pay out: *He shelled out $5.00 for the roses.*

hat, āge, fär; let, ēqual, tėrm; it, īce
hot, ōpen, ôrder; oil, out; cup, pu̇t, rüle
əbove, takən, pencəl, lemən, circəs
ch, child; ng, long; sh, ship
th, thin; ᴛʜ, then; zh, measure

she'll (shēl) **1** she will. **2** she shall.

shel·lac (shə lak′) **1** a liquid for coating wood, metal, etc.: *Shellac hardens to a smooth, shiny, finish.* **2** put shellac on. 1 *n.,* 2 *v.,* **shel·lacked, shel·lack·ing.**

shell·fish (shel′fish′) a water animal having a shell: *Oysters, clams, crabs, and lobsters are called shellfish. n., pl.* **shell·fish** or **shell·fish·es.**

shel·ter (shel′tər) **1** something that covers or protects from weather, danger, or attack: *Trees are a shelter from the sun.* **2** protect; shield; hide: *to shelter runaway slaves.* **3** protection; refuge: *We took shelter from the storm in a barn.* **4** find shelter; take shelter: *The sheep sheltered from the hot sun in the shade of the haystack.* 1, 3 *n.,* 2, 4 *v.*

shelve[1] (shelv) **1** put on a shelf. **2** lay aside: *Let us shelve that argument.* **3** furnish with shelves. *v.,* **shelved, shelv·ing.**

shelve[2] (shelv) slope gradually: *The sandy bottom of the lake shelves down to rock in the middle. v.,* **shelved, shelv·ing.**

shelves (shelvz) plural of **shelf.** *n. pl.*

shep·herd (shep′ərd) **1** person who takes care of sheep. **2** take care of: *He will shepherd his flock.* **3** guide; direct: *The teacher shepherded the children safely out of the burning building.* **4** a person who cares for and protects. 1, 4 *n.,* 2, 3 *v.*

shep·herd·ess (shep′ər dis) a woman who takes care of sheep. *n.*

sher·bet (shėr′bət) a frozen dessert made of fruit juice, sugar, and water or milk. *n.*

sher·iff (sher′if) **1** in Canada, an official whose job is to enforce certain court orders, such as evicting persons for failure to pay rent and escorting convicted persons to prison. **2** in the United States, the most important law-enforcing officer of a county. *n.*

sher·ry (sher′ē) a strong wine: *Sherry ranges in color from pale yellow to brown. n., pl.* **sher·ries.**

she's (shēz) **1** she is. **2** she has.

shied (shīd) See **shy.** *The horse shied and threw the rider. The boy shied a stone at the tree. v.*

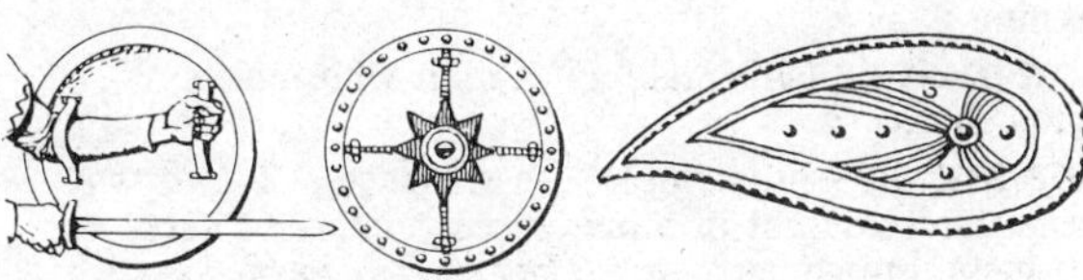

An Anglo-Saxon shield A twelfth-century shield

shield (shēld) **1** a piece of armor carried on the arm to protect the body in battle. **2** any person or thing that protects: *She held up a newspaper as a shield against the sun.* **3** protect; defend: *His mother shielded him from punishment.* 1, 2 *n.,* 3 *v.*

shift (shift) **1** change from one place, position, person, etc. to another; change: *He shifted the heavy bag from one hand to the other. He always tries to shift the blame to someone else. The wind has shifted to the southeast.* **2** a change of direction, position, attitude, etc.: *a shift of the wind, a shift in policy. There are two shifts of work at the factory.* **3** a group of workers who work during the same period of time: *This man is on the night shift.* **4** a way of getting on; a scheme; a trick: *The lazy girl used many shifts to avoid doing her work.* **5** manage to get along: *When his parents died, he had to shift for himself.* **6** change the position of the gears of an automobile. 1, 5, 6 *v.,* 2–4 *n.*

shift·less (shift′lis) lazy; inefficient. *adj.*

shift·y (shif′tē) tricky; not straight-forward; sly. *adj.,* **shift·i·er, shift·i·est.**

shil·ling (shil′ing) a former British silver coin equal to five new pence. *n.*

shim·mer (shim′ər) **1** gleam faintly: *The satin shimmers.* **2** a faint gleam or shine: *Those pearls your mother wears have a beautiful shimmer.* 1 *v.,* 2 *n.*

shin (shin) **1** the front part of the leg from the knee to the ankle. See **leg** for picture. **2** climb up or down a rope, pole, etc. by gripping alternately with the hands and feet: *He shinned up the tree.* 1, *n.,* 2 *v.,* **shinned, shin·ning.**

shine (shīn) **1** give off light; be bright with light; glow: *The sun shines. The light shone in the darkness.* **2** a light; brightness: *the shine of a lamp.* **3** a lustre; polish: *Silk has a shine.* **4** fair weather; sunshine: *He goes to school rain or shine.* **5** do very well; be outstanding: *She shines in school. He is a shining athlete.* **6** make bright; polish: *to shine shoes. We shined the silver.* 1, 5, 6 *v.,* **shone** or **shined, shin·ing;** 2–4 *n.*

shin·er (shīn′ər) **1** a small fresh-water fish with glistening scales. **2** *Slang.* a black eye. *n.*

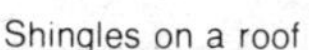
Shingles on a roof

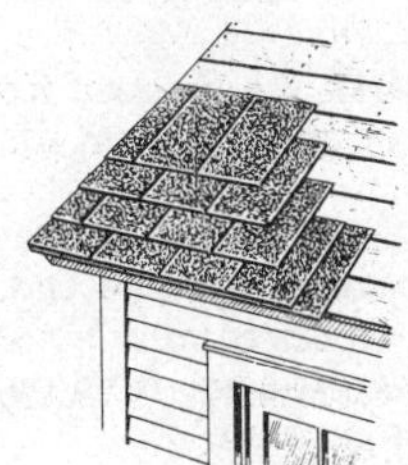

shin·gle (shing′gəl) **1** a thin piece of wood, etc. used to cover roofs, walls, etc.: *Shingles are laid in overlapping rows with the thicker ends showing.* **2** cover with such pieces: *shingle a roof.* 1 *n.,* 2 *v.,* **shin·gled, shin·gling.**

shin·ny[1] (shin′ē) a simple kind of hockey, played on the ice with skates, or without skates on the street or in a field. *n.*

shin·ny[2] (shin′ē) *Informal.* to shin; climb. *v.*

shin·y (shīn′ē) **1** bright; shining: *A new nickel is shiny.* **2** worn to a glossy smoothness: *a coat shiny from hard wear. adj.,* **shin·i·er, shin·i·est.**

ship (ship) **1** any large vessel for travel on water, such as a steamship, frigate, or galley. **2** a large sailing vessel, especially one with three or more masts. **3** an airship, airplane, spacecraft, etc. **4** put or take on board a ship. 5 travel on a ship; sail. 6 send or carry from one place to another by a ship, train, truck, etc.: *Did he ship it by express or by freight?* 7 take a job on a ship: *He shipped as cook.* 8 take in water over the side, as a boat does when the waves break over it. 1–3 *n.,* 4–8 *v.,* **shipped, ship·ping.**

-ship a prefix meaning: 1 the office, position, or occupation of____: *Governorship = office of governor. Authorship = occupation of an author.* 2 the quality or condition of being____: *Partnership = condition of being a partner.* 3 the act, power, or skill of____: *Workmanship = skill of a workman.*

ship·board (ship′bôrd′) **on shipboard,** on or inside a ship. *n.*

ship·load (ship′lōd′) a full load for a ship. *n.*

ship·ment (ship′mənt) 1 the act of shipping goods: *A thousand boxes of oranges were ready for shipment.* 2 goods sent at one time to a person or company: *The last two shipments are still in the warehouse. n.*

ship·per (ship′ər) a person who ships goods. *n.*

ship·ping (ship′ing) 1 the sending of goods by water, rail, etc. 2 ships: *There is a lot of shipping in the harbor.* 3 the ships of a nation, city, or business. *n.*

ship·shape (ship′shāp′) 1 trim; in good order. 2 in a trim, neat manner. 1 *adj.,* 2 *adv.*

ship·wreck (ship′rek′) 1 the destruction or loss of a ship: *Only two people were saved from the shipwreck.* 2 a wrecked ship. 3 destruction; ruin: *The shipwreck of his plans discouraged him.* 4 wreck, ruin, or destroy. 1–3 *n.,* 4 *v.*

ship·yard (ship′yärd′) a place near the water where ships are built or repaired. *n.*

shirk (shėrk) avoid or get out of doing work, a duty, etc.: *He lost his job because he shirked his work. v.* **—shirk′er,** *n.*

shirt (shėrt) 1 a garment for the upper part of a man's body. 2 an undergarment for the upper part of the body. *n.*

keep one's shirt on, *Slang.* stay calm; keep one's temper.

☛ **Shirt** comes from an Old English word *scyrte. Skirt* comes from a Norse word *skyrta.* Both *scyrte* and *skyrta* came from one word that meant 'shirt' or 'short garment.'

shiv·er¹ (shiv′ər) 1 shake with cold, fear, etc.: *He crept shivering into bed.* 2 shaking from cold, fear, etc. 1 *v.,* 2 *n.*

shiv·er² (shiv′ər) 1 break into small pieces: *He shivered the mirror with a hammer.* 2 a small piece; a splinter: *There were shivers of glass on the floor.* 1 *v.,* 2 *n.*

shoal¹ (shōl) 1 a place in a sea, lake, or stream where the water is shallow. 2 a sandbank or sand bar that makes the water shallow: *The ship was wrecked on the shoals. n.*

shoal² (shōl) 1 a large number; crowd: *We saw a shoal of fish in the water.* 2 form into a shoal; crowd together. 1 *n.,* 2 *v.*

shock¹ (shok) 1 a sudden, violent shake, blow, or crash: *Earthquake shocks are often felt in Japan. The two trains collided with a terrible shock.* 2 a sudden, violent, or upsetting disturbance to the mind or feelings: *His death was a great shock to his family.* 3 cause to feel surprise, horror, or disgust: *That child's bad language shocks everyone.* 4 a condition of physical collapse or depression, often resulting in unconsciousness: *Shock may set in after a severe injury, or a sudden emotional disturbance.* 5 a disturbance produced by an electric current passing through the body. 1, 2, 4, 5 *n.,* 3 *v.*

shock² (shok) stook. See **stook** for picture. *n.*

shock³ (shok) a thick, bushy mass: *He has a shock of red hair. n.*

shock·ing (shok′ing) 1 causing intense and painful surprise: *shocking news.* 2 offensive; disgusting: *a shocking sight.* 3 *Informal.* very bad: *shocking manners. adj.*

shod (shod) See **shoe.** *The blacksmith shod the horses. v.*

shod·dy (shod′ē) 1 an inferior kind of wool made of woollen waste, old rags, yarn, etc. 2 pretending to be better than it is: *a shoddy necklace.* 3 mean; shabby: *shoddy treatment, a shoddy trick.* 1 *n.,* 2, 3 *adj.*

Two styles of shoe

shoe (shü) 1 an outer covering for a person's foot: *Shoes are often made of leather.* 2 anything like a shoe in shape or use. 3 a horseshoe. 4 furnish with a shoe or shoes: *A blacksmith shoes horses. Her feet were shod with slippers.* 1–3 *n.,* 4 *v.,* **shod, shoe·ing.**

in another's shoes, in another's place, situation, or circumstances: *I wouldn't like to be in the murderer's shoes right now.*

☛ **Shoe** and **shoo** are pronounced the same.

shoe·lace (shü′lās′) a cord, braid, or leather strip for fastening a shoe. *n.*

shoe·mak·er (shü′māk′ər) a man who makes or repairs shoes. *n.*

shoe·string (shü′string′) 1 a shoelace. 2 *Informal.* a very small amount of money used to start or carry on a business, investment, etc.: *They started in business on a shoestring. n.*

shoe tree a device with a shaped front for keeping a shoe in shape when it is not being worn.

shone (shon) See **shine.** *The sun shone all last week. It has not shone since. v.*

shoo (shü) 1 an exclamation used to scare away hens, birds, etc. 2 scare or drive away: *Shoo those flies away from the sugar.* 1 *interj.,* 2 *v.,* **shooed, shoo·ing.**

☛ **Shoo** and **shoe** are pronounced the same.

shook (shůk) See **shake.** *They shook hands. v.*

shoot (shüt) 1 hit or kill with a bullet, arrow, etc.: *He shot a rabbit.* 2 send with force or swiftly at or as if at a target: *He shot the puck into the open net. A bow shoots an arrow. He shot question after question at us.* 3 fire or use a weapon, such as a gun, bow, catapult, etc.: *The boys shot at the mark.* 4 send a bullet: *This* *gun shoots straight.* 5 move suddenly and rapidly: *A car shot past. We saw flames shoot up from a burning house. Pain shot up his arm from his hurt finger.* 6 pass quickly along, through, over, or under: *The voyageurs shot the rapids.* 7 come forth from the ground; grow; grow rapidly: *Buds shoot forth in the spring. The corn is shooting up in the warm weather.* 8 a new part growing out; a young branch: *See the new shoots on that bush.* 9 take a picture with a camera; photograph. 1–7, 9 *v.*, **shot, shoot·ing;** 8 *n.*

☛ **Shoot** and **chute** are pronounced the same.

shooting star meteor.

shop (shop) 1 a place where things are sold; a store, especially a small one. 2 visit stores to look at or to buy things: *We shopped all morning for new coats.* 3 a place where things are made or repaired: *He works in a carpenter's shop.* 4 a place where a certain kind of work is done: *a barber shop, a beauty shop.* 1, 3, 4 *n.*, 2 *v.*, **shopped, shop·ping.**

set up shop, start work or business.

talk shop, talk about one's work or occupation.

shop·keep·er (shop′kēp′ər) a person who carries on business in a shop or small store. *n.*

shop·lift·ing (shop′lif′ting) stealing goods from a store while pretending to be a customer. *n.*

shop·ping (shop′ing) the visiting of stores to look at or to buy things. *n.*

shopping centre a large block of stores, usually in the suburbs of a city and built as a unit with a large parking lot.

shore[1] (shôr) 1 the land at the edge of a sea, lake, etc.: *They walked along the shore.* 2 the land near a sea: *There is good farmland on the western shore of the island.* 3 land: *foreign shores.* *n.*

off shore, in or on the water, not far from the shore.

shore[2] (shôr) 1 a prop placed against or beneath something to support it. 2 prop up or support with shores. 1 *n.*, 2 *v.*

shorn (shôrn) See **shear.** *The sheep was shorn of its wool.* *v.*

short (shôrt) 1 not long; of small extent from end to end: *a short time, a short life, a short street, short hair.* 2 not tall: *a short man, short grass.* 3 not coming up to the right amount, measure, or standard: *The cashier is short in his accounts.* 4 so brief as to be rude: *He was so short with me that I felt hurt.* 5 in a short manner; suddenly: *He stopped short.* 6 breaking or crumbling easily: *Pastry is made short with lard and butter.* 1–4, 6 *adj.*, 5 *adv.*

cut short, end suddenly.

fall short, a fail to reach. **b** be insufficient.

for short, in order to make shorter: *Robert was called Rob for short.*

in short, briefly.

make short work of, deal with quickly.

run short, a not have enough. **b** not be enough.

short of, a not up to; less than: *Nothing short of your best work will satisfy me.* **b** not having enough of.

short·age (shôr′tij) a lack; too small an amount: *There is a shortage of grain because of poor crops.* *n.*

short cake a sponge cake or biscuit covered or filled with berries or other fruit.

short circuit an electrical circuit, formed accidentally or intentionally, that by-passes the main circuit: *An accidental short circuit, in which worn or faulty wires touch each other, may blow a fuse or cause a fire.*

short–cir·cuit (shôrt′sėr′kit) cause a short circuit in. *v.*

short·com·ing (shôrt′kum′ing) a fault or defect: *Rudeness is a serious shortcoming.* *n.*

short cut a way that is quicker or not so long.

short·en (shôr′tən) 1 make shorter; cut off: *The new highway shortens the trip. She has had all her dresses shortened.* 2 become shorter: *The days shorten in November.* *v.*

short·en·ing (shôr′tən ing) butter, lard, etc. used in baking to make pastry, cake, etc. crisp or crumbly. *n.*

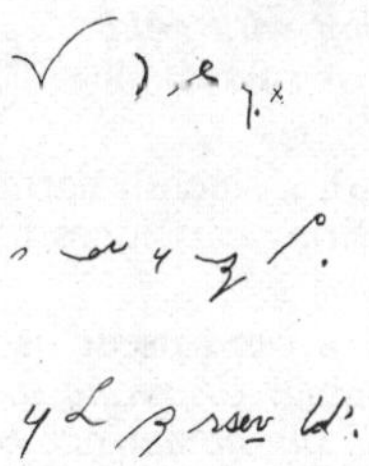

Examples of three systems of shorthand. Each says, "Your letter was received today."

short·hand (shôrt′hand′) 1 a method of rapid writing which uses symbols or a combination of letters and symbols to represent sounds. In the examples, the symbols mean 'Your letter was received today.' 2 writing in such symbols. *n.*

short–hand·ed (shôrt′han′did) 1 not having enough workmen or helpers. 2 in hockey and certain other games, playing without the services of one or more players as a result of penalties. *adj.*

short·horn (shôrt′hôrn′) a breed of cattle with short horns, raised for beef. *n.*

short·ly (shôrt′lē) 1 in a short time; before long; soon: *I will be with you shortly.* 2 in a few words; briefly. *adv.*

shorts (shôrts) 1 short, loose-fitting pants that reach no lower than the knees: *Shorts are worn by players in such games as tennis, soccer, and basketball. Many people like to wear shorts during the hot weather.* 2 a pair of short underpants worn by men or boys. *n. pl.*

short–sight·ed (shôrt′sīt′id) 1 near-sighted; not able to see far. 2 lacking in foresight; not prudent: *a short-sighted plan.* *adj.*

short·stop (shôrt′stop′) a baseball player stationed between second and third base. See **baseball** for diagram. *n.*

short wave a high-frequency radio wave having a wave length of 60 metres or less.

shot[1] (shot) 1 the discharge of a gun or cannon: *He heard two shots.* 2 the act of shooting. 3 tiny balls of lead, steel, etc.; bullets. 4 a single ball of lead, steel, etc. for a gun or cannon. 5 an attempt to hit by

shooting: *That was a good shot, and it hit the mark.* 6 the distance a weapon can shoot; the range: *We were within rifle shot of the fort.* 7 a person who shoots: *He is a good shot.* 8 the act of sending, directing, or propelling with force or swiftly: *His shot is hard for a goalie to stop. The billiard player made a skilful shot.* 9 *Informal.* an injection of a vaccine or drug: *A polio shot is a dose of polio virus to protect against getting infantile paralysis.* 10 a remark aimed at some person or thing. 11 a heavy metal ball thrown in athletic contests. 12 a single picture taken with a camera or a motion picture record of a single scene or subject. 13 the cost: *Father said he would pay the shot.* *n., pl.* **shots** or, for def. 3, **shot.**
a long shot, an attempt at something difficult.
not by a long shot, not at all.
put the shot, in athletics, heave a heavy metal ball as far as one can with one throw.

shot² (shot) 1 See **shoot.** *Many years ago he shot a rival and was himself shot in revenge.* 2 woven so as to show a play of colors: *blue silk shot with gold.* 3 *Slang.* that has been used up, worn out, or ruined. 1 *v.*, 2, 3 *adj.*

shot·gun (shot′gun′) a gun with a smooth barrel or with no grooves in its barrel, for firing cartridges filled with small shot. *n.*

should (shůd; *unstressed,* shəd) a word used: 1 to mean that one ought to do something: *Everyone should learn to swim. I really should do my homework before I go out.* 2 to suggest that the speaker is uncertain about a thing or unwilling to believe something: *I don't see why you should think that. It's strange that they should be so late.* 3 to express a possible action in the future: *If we should go, we'll call you. 'I will be there in an hour' is a promise; 'I should be there in an hour' means that the speaker is not sure and therefore is not willing to promise.* 4 to express a belief: *She should be there by now.* 5 See **shall** (def. 3): *I was afraid I should be late.* *v.*

shoul·der (shōl′dər) 1 the part of the body to which an arm of a man, a foreleg of an animal, or a wing of a bird is attached. 2 the part of a garment that covers a shoulder. 3 **shoulders,** *pl.* the two shoulders and the upper part of the back: *The man carried a trunk on his shoulders.* 4 take upon or support with the shoulder or the shoulders: *to shoulder a tray.* 5 bear a burden, blame, etc.: *He shouldered the responsibility and expense of sending his nephew to college.* 6 something that sticks out like a shoulder: *the shoulder of a hill.* 7 the edge of a road, often unpaved: *Don't drive on the shoulder of the road.* 8 push with the shoulders: *He shouldered his way through the crowded square.* 1–3, 6, 7 *n.*, 4, 5, 8 *v.*
put one's shoulder to the wheel, make a great effort.
straight from the shoulder, frankly; directly.
turn a cold shoulder to, show dislike for; shun; avoid.

shoulder blade the flat triangular bone in the upper back behind either shoulder. See **rib** for picture.

should·n't (shůd′ənt) should not.

shout (shout) 1 call or cry loudly and vigorously: *The drowning boy shouted for help. Somebody shouted 'Fire!' The crowd shouted with laughter.* 2 a loud, vigorous call or cry: *Shouts of joy rang through the halls.* 3 express by a shout or shouts: *The officer shouted his commands.* 1, 3 *v.*, 2 *n.*

shove (shuv) 1 to push; move forward or along by force from behind: *He shoved the bookcase into place.* 2 push roughly or rudely; jostle: *The people shoved to get on the crowded bus.* 3 a push: *He gave the boat a shove that sent it far out into the water.* 1, 2 *v.*, **shoved, shov·ing;** 3 *n.*

A shovel for snow

shov·el (shuv′əl) 1 a tool with a broad blade or scoop, used to lift and throw loose matter: *a snow shovel, a coal shovel. A steam shovel is worked by steam.* 2 lift and throw with a shovel: *The men shovelled the sand into a cart.* 3 make with a shovel: *They shovelled a path through the snow.* 4 as much as a shovel will hold. 5 throw or lift as if with a shovel: *The hungry tramp shovelled the food into his mouth.* 1, 4 *n.*, 2, 3, 5 *v.*, **shov·elled** or **shov·eled, shov·el·ling** or **shov·el·ing.**

show (shō) 1 let be seen; put in sight: *The little girl showed us her dolls. The dog showed his teeth.* 2 be in sight; appear; be seen: *The hole in his sock shows above his shoe. Anger showed in his face.* 3 point out: *A boy showed us the way to town.* 4 direct; guide: *Show him out.* 5 make clear to; explain to: *The teacher showed the children how to do the problem.* 6 grant; give: *to show mercy, to show favor.* 7 a display, especially a display for effect or to impress: *The jewels made a fine show. He put on a show of learning to impress us.* 8 *Informal.* an entertainment, such as a stage play or motion picture. 9 *Informal.* a motion-picture theatre: *I'll meet you in front of the show at six o'clock.* 10 a showing: *The club voted by a show of hands.* 11 an appearance: *There is some show of truth in his excuse.* 12 a pretence; a false appearance: *He hid his treachery by a show of friendship.* 1–6 *v.*, **showed, shown** or **showed, show·ing;** 7–12 *n.*
for show, for effect; to attract attention: *Some houses are furnished for show, not for comfort.*
show off, a to display: *She liked to show off her fine clothes.* **b** make a vain display; to act in such a way as to attract attention: *That boy is always showing off.*
show up, a reveal: *The bright lights showed up cracks in the plaster.* **b** stand out: *He is very tall and shows up in any crowd.* **c** *Informal.* put in an appearance: *The Prime Minister showed up at the first concert.*

show·case (shō′kās′) 1 a glass case used to display articles in a store, museum, etc. 2 any display or exhibit: *Quebec City is a showcase of Canadian history.* *n.*

show·er (shou′ər) 1 a brief fall of rain. 2 wet with a shower; sprinkle; spray. 3 anything like a fall of rain: *a shower of hail, a shower of tears, a shower of sparks from an engine.* 4 come or fall in a shower. 5 send in a shower; give abundantly: *Her rich aunt showered gifts upon her.* 6 a party at which gifts are presented to a woman about to be married or on some other special occasion. 7 a bath in which water pours down on the body from above in small jets: *He takes a shower every morning.* 8 take a bath in this manner. 1, 3, 6, 7 *n.*, 2, 4, 5, 8 *v.*

show·man (shō′mən) 1 a person who manages a show. 2 a person skilled in presenting things in a dramatic and exciting way. *n., pl.* **show·men** (shō′mən).

shown (shōn) See **show.** *The clerk has shown the lady many hats. We were shown many tricks. v.*

show–off (shō′of′) 1 showing off. 2 *Informal.* a person who is always calling attention to himself: *He is a good hockey player, but he's a terrible show-off. n.*

show·y (shō′ē) 1 making a display; likely to attract attention; conspicuous: *A peony is a showy flower.* 2 too bright and gay to be in good taste. *adj.,* **show·i·er, show·i·est.**

shrank (shrangk) See **shrink.** *That shirt shrank in the wash. v.*

shrap·nel (shrap′nəl) 1 a shell filled with fragments of metal and powder, set to explode in the air and scatter the fragments over a wide area. 2 the fragments scattered by such a shell: *He showed us the scars made when he was hit by shrapnel. n.*

☛ Named after Henry *Shrapnel* (1761–1842), a British army officer, who invented it.

shred (shred) 1 a very small piece torn off or cut off; a very narrow strip; scrap: *The wind tore the sail to shreds.* 2 a particle; fragment; bit: *There's not a shred of evidence that he took the money.* 3 tear or cut into small pieces: *Shredded paper is used in packing dishes.* 1, 2 *n.*, 3 *v.,* **shred·ded** or **shred, shred·ding.**

shrew (shrü) 1 a bad-tempered, quarrelsome woman. 2 an animal usually smaller than a mouse, that has a long snout and brownish fur: *Shrews are fierce fighters and will attack animals much larger than themselves. n.*

shrewd (shrüd) having a sharp, practical mind; showing a keen wit; clever: *He is a shrewd businessman. adj.* —**shrewd′ness,** *n.*

shriek (shrēk) 1 a loud, sharp, shrill sound: *the shriek of an engine's whistle.* 2 make such a sound: *People shriek because of terror, anger, pain, or amusement.* 1 *n.*, 2 *v.*

shrike (shrīk) a bird with a strong, hooked beak that feeds on large insects, frogs, and sometimes on other birds. *n.*

shrill (shril) 1 having a high pitch; high and sharp in sound; piercing: *Crickets, locusts, and katydids make shrill noises.* 2 make a shrill sound. 1 *adj.*, 2 *v.* —**shril′ly,** *adv.*

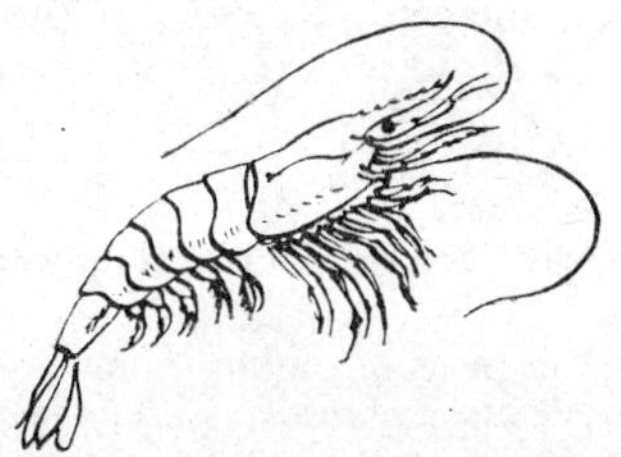

A shrimp — about 5 cm long

shrimp (shrimp) 1 a small shellfish having a long tail: *Some shrimps are edible.* 2 a small or insignificant person. *n., pl.* **shrimps** or, for def. 1, **shrimp.**

shrine (shrīn) 1 a sacred place; a place where sacred

hat, āge, fär; let, ēqual, tėrm; it, īce
hot, ōpen, ôrder; oil, out; cup, pu̇t, rüle
əbove, takən, pencəl, lemən, circəs
ch, child; ng, long; sh, ship
th, thin; ᴛʜ, then; zh, measure

things are kept: *A shrine may be the tomb of a saint, an altar in a church, or a box holding a holy object.* 2 any place or object sacred because of its history; something sacred because of memories connected with it. *n.*

shrink (shringk) 1 draw back: *The dog shrank from the whip. That shy girl shrinks from meeting strangers.* 2 become smaller: *His wool sweater shrank when it was washed.* 3 make smaller: *Hot water shrinks wool. v.,* **shrank** or **shrunk, shrunk** or **shrunk·en, shrink·ing.**

shriv·el (shriv′əl) dry up; wither; shrink and wrinkle: *The hot sunshine shrivelled the grass. v.,* **shriv·elled** or **shriv·eled, shriv·el·ling** or **shriv·el·ing.**

shroud (shroud) 1 a cloth or garment in which a dead person is wrapped for burial. 2 something that covers, conceals, or veils: *The fog was a shroud over the city.* 3 cover; conceal; veil: *The earth is shrouded in darkness.* 4 one of the ropes running from a mast to the side of a ship: *Shrouds help to support the mast.* See **schooner** for picture. 1, 2, 4 *n.*, 3 *v.*

shrub (shrub) a woody plant smaller than a tree, usually with many separate stems starting from or near the ground: *A lilac bush is a shrub. n.*

shrub·ber·y (shrub′ər ē) 1 shrubs. 2 a place planted with shrubs. *n., pl.* **shrub·ber·ies.**

shrug (shrug) 1 raise the shoulders as an expression of dislike, doubt, indifference, or impatience: *He merely shrugged in answer to our request for help.* 2 a raising of the shoulders in this way: *His only answer was a shrug.* 1 *v.,* **shrugged, shrug·ging;** 2 *n.*

shrunk (shrungk) See **shrink.** *His wool socks have shrunk. v.*

shrunk·en (shrung′kən) 1 grown smaller; shrivelled. 2 shrunk. See **shrink.** 1 *adj.*, 2 *v.*

shuck (shuk) 1 a husk or pod. 2 remove the husks or pods from: *Please shuck the corn.* 1 *n.*, 2 *v.*

shud·der (shud′ər) 1 tremble with horror, fear, cold, etc.: *She shudders at the sight of a snake.* 2 a trembling; quivering. 1 *v.*, 2 *n.*

shuf·fle (shuf′əl) 1 walk without lifting the feet: *The old man shuffles feebly along.* 2 a scraping or dragging movement of the feet. 3 mix cards, etc. so as to change the order. 4 a shuffling of cards. 5 push about; thrust or throw with clumsy haste: *He shuffled on his clothes and ran out of the house.* 6 move this way and that: *to shuffle a stack of papers.* 7 a movement this way and that: *After a hasty shuffle of his papers, the speaker began to talk.* 1, 3, 5, 6 *v.,* **shuf·fled, shuf·fling;** 2, 4, 7 *n.*

shun (shun) keep away from; avoid: *She was lazy and shunned work. v.,* **shunned, shun·ning.**

shunt (shunt) 1 move out of the way; turn or put aside. 2 switch a train from one track to another. *v.*

shut (shut) 1 close a container or opening by pushing or pulling a lid, door, or other such part into place: *He shut the doors and windows.* 2 close the eyes, a knife, a book, etc. by bringing parts together: *Shut your eyes.* **3** close tight; close securely; close the doors or other openings of: *After Thanksgiving, we shut our cottage up for the winter.* **4** become closed; be closed. **5** enclose; confine; keep from going out: *Shut the kitten in the basket.* *v.,* **shut, shut·ting.**

shut down, close a factory or stop machinery for a time; stop work.

shut off, close; obstruct; check; bar; turn off: *Shut off the radio.*

shut out, a keep from coming in: *The curtains shut out the light.* **b** defeat a team without allowing it to score.

shut up, *Informal.* stop talking.

shut–down (shut′doun′) shutting down; a closing of a factory, etc. for a time. *n.*

shut–out (shut′out′) the defeat of a team without allowing it to score: *The goalie was credited with five shut-outs during the season.* *n.*

shut·ter (shut′ər) **1** a movable cover for a window: *When we shut up our cottage for the winter, we put shutters on all the windows.* **2** a movable cover, slide, etc. for closing an opening: *The device that opens and closes in front of the film in a camera is the shutter.* *n.*

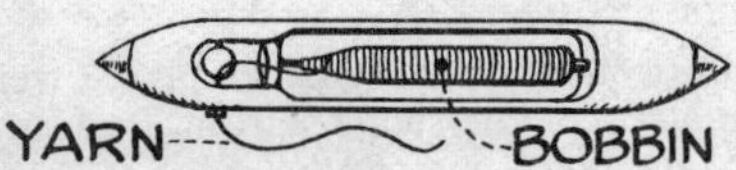

A shuttle for weaving

shut·tle (shut′əl) **1** a device that carries the thread from one side of the web to the other in weaving. **2** move quickly to and fro. **3** a bus, train, airplane, etc. that runs back and forth regularly over a short distance. 1, 3 *n.,* 2 *v.,* **shut·tled, shut·tling.**

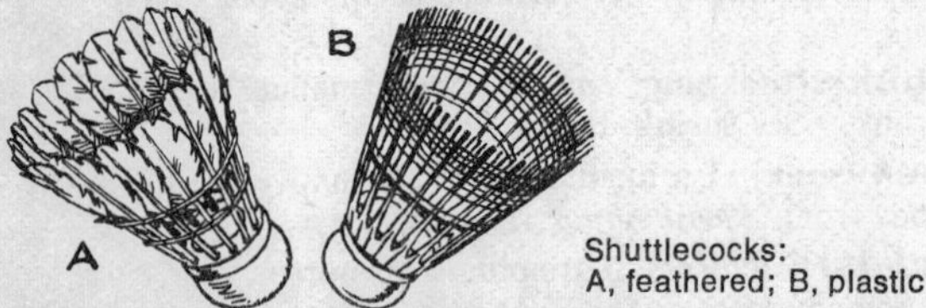

Shuttlecocks: A, feathered; B, plastic

shut·tle·cock (shut′əl kok′) a cone of feathers or light plastic with a cork or similar base, used in the game of badminton. *n.*

shy[1] (shī) **1** uncomfortable in company; bashful: *He is shy and dislikes parties.* **2** easily frightened away; timid: *A deer is a shy animal.* **3** start back or aside suddenly: *The horse shied at the newspaper blowing along the ground.* **4** not having enough; short; scant: *This store is shy on children's clothing.* 1, 2, 4 *adj.,* **shy·er** or **shi·er, shy·est** or **shi·est;** 3 *v.,* **shied, shy·ing.**

fight shy of, keep away from; avoid.

shy[2] (shī) throw; fling: *The boy shied a stone at the tree.* *v.,* **shied, shy·ing.**

shy·ness (shī′nis) shy behavior; the quality or state of being shy. *n.*

Siberian husky one of a breed of dog much used in the North.

sick (sik) **1** in poor health; having some disease; ill. **2** vomiting; inclined to vomit; feeling nausea. **3** for a sick person: *a sick room.* **4 the sick,** sick people: *The sick need special care.* **5** weary; tired: *He is sick of school.* **6** affected with sorrow or longing: *She is sick at heart.* 1–3, 5, 6 *adj.,* 4 *n.*

☛ See note at **ill.**

sick·bed (sik′bed′) the bed of a sick person. *n.*

sick·en (sik′ən) **1** become sick: *The bird sickened when kept in the cage.* **2** make sick: *The sight of blood sickened him.* *v.*

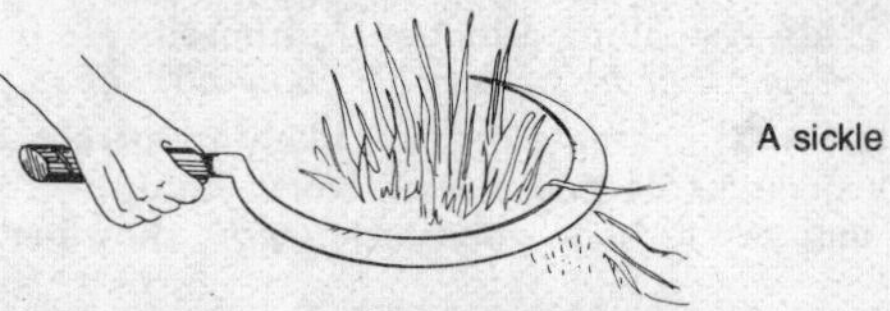

A sickle

sick·le (sik′əl) a tool consisting of a curved blade on a short handle, used for cutting grass, etc. *n.*

sick·ly (sik′lē) **1** often sick; not strong; not healthy. **2** of or having something to do with sickness: *Her skin is a sickly yellow.* **3** causing sickness: *a sickly climate.* **4** faint; weak; pale. *adj.,* **sick·li·er, sick·li·est.**

sick·ness (sik′nis) **1** illness; disease. **2** nausea; vomiting. *n.*

side (sīd) **1** a surface or line bounding a thing: *the sides of a square, a side of a box.* **2** one of the two surfaces of an object that is not the front, back, top, or bottom: *There is a door at the side of the house.* **3** either of the two surfaces of paper, cloth, etc.: *Write only on one side of the paper.* **4** a particular surface: *The outer and inner sides of a hollow ball, the side of the moon turned toward the earth.* **5** either the right or the left part of the body of a person or an animal: *The man was wounded in the side.* **6** the slope of a hill or bank. **7** either the right or the left part of a thing; either part or region beyond a central line: *the east side of a city, our side of the street, to turn to one side.* **8** an aspect or view of someone or something: *the better side of one's nature, the bright side of a difficulty.* **9** a team: *The boys chose sides for a game of softball.* **10** a group of persons who stand up for their beliefs, opinions, ways of doing things, etc. against another group: *The other side is likely to win the election.* **11** the position, course, or part of one person or party against another: *It is pleasant to be on the winning side.* **12** a part of a family; line of descent: *The man is English on his mother's side.* **13** at one side; on one side: *a side door, the side aisles of a theatre.* **14** from one side: *a side view.* **15** toward one side: *a side glance.* **16** less important: *a side issue.* **17 side with,** go along with; support, especially in an argument: *The sisters always side with each other.* 1–12 *n.,* 13–16 *adj.,* 17 *v.,* **sid·ed, sid·ing.**

by one's side, near one.

side by side, beside one another.

take sides, place oneself with one person or group against another.

side·board (sīd′bôrd′) a piece of dining room furniture; a buffet: *A sideboard has drawers and shelves for holding silver and linen.* *n.*

side·burns (sīd′bėrnz′) hair growing down in front of the ears, especially when the chin is shaved. *n. pl.*

☛ **Sideburns** came originally from *burnsides,* named after Ambrose *Burnside* (1824–1881), an American general, who wore such whiskers.

side·line (sīd′līn′) 1 in football, etc., a line that marks the limit of play on the side of the field. 2 **sidelines,** *pl.* the space just outside these lines: *We watched the game from the sidelines.* 3 an additional line of goods or of business. *n.*

side·long (sīd′long′) to one side; toward the side: *a sidelong glance. He glanced sidelong at me. adj., adv.*

side road 1 *Cdn.* in Ontario, a road running at right angles to a concession road or main road. 2 any road that is not a main road.

side show a small show in connection with a principal one: *the side shows of a circus.*

side–step (sīd′step′) 1 step aside. 2 avoid by stepping aside: *to side-step a responsibility. v.,* **side-stepped, side-step·ping.**

side·track (sīd′trak′) 1 a siding. 2 switch a train, etc. to a siding. 3 put aside; turn aside: *The teacher refused to be sidetracked by questions on other subjects.* 1 *n.,* 2, 3 *v.*

side·walk (sīd′wok′ or sīd′wôk′) a place to walk at the side of a street: *Sidewalks are usually paved. n.*

side·ways (sīd′wāz′) 1 to one side; toward one side: *walk sideways.* 2 from one side: *a sideways glimpse.* 3 with one side toward the front: *stand sideways, place a book sideways on a shelf. adv., adj.*

side·wise (sīd′wīz′) sideways. *adv., adj.*

sid·ing (sīd′ing) 1 a short railway track to which cars can be switched from a main track. 2 the boards, shingles, etc. forming the outside walls of a building. *n.*

si·dle (sī′dəl) move sideways, especially shyly or stealthily: *The little boy shyly sidled up to the visitor. v.,* **si·dled, si·dling.**

siege (sēj) 1 the surrounding of a fortified place by an army trying to capture it: *Troy was under a siege for ten years.* 2 any long or persistent effort to overcome resistance; any long-continued attack: *a siege of illness. n.*

lay siege to, a besiege: *The Greeks laid siege to Troy for ten years.* **b** attempt to win or get by long and persistent effort.

si·er·ra (sē er′ə) a chain of hills or mountains whose peaks suggest the teeth of a saw. *n.*

☛ **Sierra** comes from the Spanish word *sierra,* meaning 'a saw.'

si·es·ta (sē es′tə) a nap or rest taken at noon or in the afternoon. *n.*

Sieves

sieve (siv) 1 a utensil having holes that let liquids and smaller pieces pass through, but not the larger pieces: *Shaking flour through a sieve breaks up lumps.* 2 put through a sieve. 1 *n.,* 2 *v.,* **sieved, siev·ing.**

sift (sift) 1 separate large pieces from small by shaking in a sieve: *Sift the gravel and put the larger stones in another pile.* 2 put through a sieve: *Sift sugar onto the top of the cake.* 3 fall through, or as if through, a sieve: *The snow sifted softly down.* 4 examine very carefully: *The jury sifted the evidence to decide if the man was guilty. v.*

hat, āge, fär; let, ēqual, tėrm; it, īce
hot, ōpen, ôrder; oil, out; cup, pu̇t, rüle
əbove, takən, pencəl, lemən, circəs
ch, child; ng, long; sh, ship
th, thin; ᴛʜ, then; zh, measure

sigh (sī) 1 draw in or let out a long, deep, loud breath because one is sad, tired, relieved, etc.: *Mary sighed but didn't quit until the work was done.* 2 the act or sound of sighing: *a sigh of relief.* 3 make a sound like a sigh: *The wind sighed in the treetops.* 4 wish very much; long: *She often sighed for home and friends.* 1, 3, 4 *v.,* 2 *n.*

sight (sīt) 1 the power of seeing: *Birds have better sight than dogs.* 2 the act or fact of seeing; look: *love at first sight.* 3 the range of seeing: *Keep that car in sight. We live in sight of the school.* 4 the thing seen; view; glimpse: *I caught a sight of him running around the corner.* 5 something impressive, startling, or strange to see: *Niagara Falls is one of the sights of the world. She is a sight in that ugly dress.* 6 catch sight of; see: *At last Columbus sighted land.* 7 a device to guide the eye in taking aim or observing: *a bomb sight, the sights on a rifle.* 8 the aim or observation taken by means of such devices. 9 look at through sights; point to; aim at; aim: *The hunter sighted carefully before firing his gun.* 10 a way of looking or thinking; regard: *Dolls are precious in a little girl's sight.* 1–5, 7, 8, 10 *n.,* 6, 9, *v.*

at sight or **on sight,** as soon as seen: *She reads music at sight.*

catch sight of, see: *I caught sight of him.*

in sight of, where one can see or be seen by: *We live in sight of the school.*

out of sight of, a where one cannot see: *Columbus was out of sight of land for several weeks.* **b** where one cannot be seen by: *out of sight of the neighbors.*

☛ **Sight, cite,** and **site** are pronounced the same.

sight·less (sīt′lis) blind. *adj.*

sight·see·ing (sīt′sē′ing) the act of going around to see objects or places of interest: *a weekend of sightseeing. n.*

sign (sīn) 1 any mark or thing used to mean, represent, or point out something: *The signs for add, subtract, multiply, and divide are* +, −, ×, *and* ÷. 2 put one's name on; write one's name: *The man forgot to sign the cheque. Mother signed for the telegram.* 3 a motion or gesture used to mean, represent, or point out something: *She made the sign of the cross. A nod is a sign of agreement.* 4 give a sign to; signal: *The guard signed the visitor to enter.* 5 an inscribed board, space, etc. serving for advertisement, information, etc.: *The sign reads, 'Keep off the grass.'* 6 an indication; trace; evidence: *There were no signs of life about the house. The Star in the East was the sign of Christ's coming.* 1, 3, 5, 6 *n.,* 2, 4 *v.*

sign off, stop broadcasting.

sign on or **sign up, a** accept a job by putting one's name to an agreement: *Twenty men signed on with the company last week.* **b** hire in this way: *The company signed up twenty new men.* **c** enlist in the armed services.

sig·nal (sig′nəl) **1** a sign giving notice of something: *A red light is a signal of danger. The raising of the flag was a signal to advance.* **2** a wave, current, impulse, etc. serving to convey sounds and images in communications by radio, televison, etc. **3** make a signal or signals to: *He signalled the car to stop by raising his hand.* **4** make known by a signal or signals: *A bell signals the end of a school period.* **5** used as a signal or in signalling: *a signal flag.* **6** remarkable; striking: *The airplane was a signal invention.* 1, 2 *n.,* 3, 4 *v.,* **sig·nalled** or **sig·naled, sig·nal·ling** or **sig·nal·ing;** 5, 6 *adj.*

sig·na·ture (sig′nə chər) **1** a person's name written by himself. **2** the signs printed at the beginning of a staff to show the key and time of a piece of music. *n.*

sign·board (sīn′bôrd′) a board having a sign, notice, advertisement, etc. on it. *n.*

sig·net (sig′nit) a small seal: *The order was sealed with the king's signet. n.*

sig·nif·i·cance (sig nif′ə kəns) **1** importance; consequence: *a matter of significance.* **2** the meaning: *She did not understand the significance of my nod. n.*

sig·nif·i·cant (sig nif′ə kənt) **1** full of meaning; important; of consequence: *July 1, 1867, is a significant date for Canadians.* **2** having or expressing a hidden or special meaning: *A significant nod from his friend warned him to stop talking. adj.*

sig·ni·fy (sig′nə fī′) **1** be a sign of; mean: *'Oh!' signifies surprise.* **2** make known by signs, words, or actions: *He signified his consent with a nod.* **3** have importance; be of consequence; matter: *What a fool says does not signify. v.,* **sig·ni·fied, sig·ni·fy·ing.**

sign·post (sīn′pōst′) a post having signs, notices, or directions on it. *n.*

Sikh (sēk) a member of a Hindu sect of northwestern India: *Sikhs are famous as fighters. n.*

si·lage (sī′lij) green fodder for farm animals, preserved and stored in a silo. *n.*

si·lence (sī′ləns) **1** the absence of sound or noise; stillness: *The teacher asked for silence.* **2** a state of keeping still; not talking: *Silence gives consent.* **3** stop the speech or noise of; make silent; quiet: *The nurse silenced the baby's crying.* 1, 2 *n.,* 3 *v.,* **si·lenced, si·lenc·ing.**

in silence, without saying anything: *Mother passed over his foolish remarks in silence.*

si·lent (sī′lənt) **1** quiet; still; noiseless: *a silent house.* **2** not speaking; saying little or nothing: *The stranger was silent about his early life. Pupils must be silent during the study hour.* **3** not spoken; not said out loud: *a silent prayer. The 'l' in 'folk' is a silent letter.* **4** taking no open or active part: *A silent partner in a business has no share in managing the business. adj.*

sil·hou·ette (sil′ü et′) **1** an outline portrait cut out of black paper or filled in with some single color. **2** a dark image outlined against a lighter background. **3** show in outline: *The mountain was silhouetted against the sky.* 1, 2 *n.,* 3 *v.,* **sil·hou·et·ted, sil·hou·et·ting.**

☛ Named after Etienne de *Silhouette* (1709–1767), a French minister of finance, who was scorned for doing such drawings.

silk (silk) **1** a fine, soft, strong fibre spun by silkworms. **2** the cloth made from this fibre. **3** fibre or cloth like silk, made artifically. **4** anything like silk: *corn silk.* **5** of, like, or having to do with silk: *She sewed the silk dress with silk thread.* 1–4 *n.,* 5 *adj.*

silk·en (sil′kən) **1** made of silk: *The king wore silken robes.* **2** like silk; smooth, soft, and glossy: *She has silken hair. adj.*

silk·worm (silk′wėrm′) a caterpillar that spins silk to form a cocoon. *n.*

silk·y (sil′kē) like silk; smooth, soft, and glossy: *A kitten has silky fur. adj.,* **silk·i·er, silk·i·est.**

sill (sil) a piece of wood or stone across the bottom of a door, window, or house frame. See **lintel** for picture. *n.*

sil·ly (sil′ē) without sense or reason; foolish; ridiculous. *adj.,* **sil·li·er, sil·li·est.**

A silo

si·lo (sī′lō) an airtight building or pit in which green fodder for farm animals is preserved. *n., pl.* **si·los.**

silt (silt) **1** earth, sand, etc. carried by moving water and deposited as sediment: *The harbor is being choked up with silt.* **2** to fill or choke up with silt. 1 *n.,* 2 *v.*

sil·ver (sil′vər) **1** a shining, white, precious, metallic element: *Silver is used for making coins, jewellery, cutlery, dishes, etc.* **2** coins, especially those made of silver or having a silvery color: *a handful of silver.* **3** utensils or dishes made from silver; silverware: *table silver.* **4** made of silver or covered with a layer of silver: *a silver spoon.* **5** cover or coat with silver or something like silver: *to silver a mirror.* **6** the color of silver. **7** having the color of silver: *a silver slipper.* 1–3, 6 *n.,* 4, 7 *adj.,* 5 *v.*

silver lining the brighter side of a sad or unfortunate situation: *Every cloud has a silver lining.*

sil·ver·smith (sil′vər smith′) a person who makes articles of silver. *n.*

sil·ver·ware (sil′vər wer′) silver things; utensils or dishes made of or plated with silver or made of stainless steel: *Her silverware consisted of knives, forks, and spoons. n.*

sil·ver·y (sil′vər ē) like silver; like that of silver: *Moonbeams are silvery. The bell has a silvery sound. adj.*

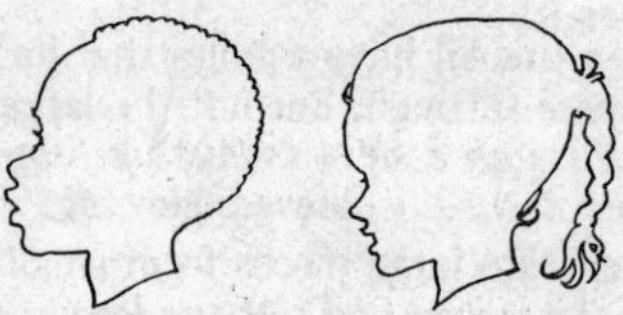

Silhouettes of children's heads

hat, āge, fär; let, ēqual, tėrm; it, īce
hot, ōpen, ôrder; oil, out; cup, put, rüle
əbove, takən, pencəl, lemən, circəs
ch, child; ng, long; sh, ship
th, thin; ꜰʜ, then; zh, measure

sim·i·lar (sim′ə lər) much the same; alike; like: *A creek and a brook are similar.* *adj.*

sim·i·lar·i·ty (sim′ə lar′ə tē or sim′ə ler′ə tē) likeness; resemblance. *n., pl.* **sim·i·lar·i·ties.**

sim·i·le (sim′ə lē) a statement that one thing is like another. Examples: *a face like marble, as brave as a lion.* *n.*

sim·mer (sim′ər) **1** keep or stay just below the boiling point; boil gently. **2** cooking at or just below the boiling point: *Do not let the soup cook faster than a simmer.* **3** be on the point of just bursting or breaking out: *simmering rebellion. He simmered with anger, but he said nothing.* 1, 3 *v.*, 2 *n.*
simmer down, cool off; calm down: *His anger simmered down after a while.*

sim·ple (sim′pəl) **1** easy to do or understand: *a simple problem. This book is in simple language.* **2** not divided into parts; not complex or involved: *An oak leaf is a simple leaf. 'John called his dog' is a simple sentence.* **3** with nothing added; bare; mere: *My answer is the simple truth.* **4** without ornament; not rich or showy; plain: *He eats simple food and wears simple clothing.* **5** natural; not affected; not showing off: *She has a pleasant, simple manner.* **6** common; ordinary: *a simple citizen.* **7** weak in mind; dull; stupid: *'Simple Simon met a pieman.'* *adj.,* **sim·pler, sim·plest.**

sim·ple·ton (sim′pəl tən) a silly person; fool. *n.*

sim·plic·i·ty (sim plis′ə tē) **1** the state of being simple. **2** freedom from difficulty; clearness: *The simplicity of that book makes it suitable for children.* **3** plainness: *A room in a hospital should be furnished with simplicity.* **4** the absence of show or pretence; sincerity. **5** a lack of shrewdness: *He was easily fooled because of his simplicity.* *n., pl.* **sim·plic·i·ties.**

sim·pli·fy (sim′plə fī′) make plainer or easier; make simple or more simple. *v.,* **sim·pli·fied, sim·pli·fy·ing.**

sim·ply (sim′plē) **1** in a simple manner. **2** without much ornament; without pretence or affectation; plainly: *She was simply dressed.* **3** merely; only: *The baby did not simply cry; he yelled.* **4** foolishly: *He acted as simply as an idiot.* **5** absolutely: *simply perfect.* *adv.*

sim·ul·cast (sim′əl kast′ or sī′məl kast′) **1** a broadcast carried over a radio and a TV station or network at the same time. **2** broadcast a program in this way. 1, *n.,* 2 *v.,* **sim·ul·cast** or **sim·ul·cast·ed, sim·ul·cast·ing.**

sim·ul·ta·ne·ous (sim′əl tā′nē əs or sī′məl tā′nē əs) existing, done, or happening at the same time: *simultaneous events. The two simultaneous shots sounded like one.* *adj.*

sin (sin) **1** the breaking of the law of God on purpose. **2** break the law of God. **3** wrongdoing of any kind; an immoral act: *Lying, stealing, dishonesty, and cruelty are sins.* **4** do wrong. 1, 3 *n.,* 2, 4 *v.,* **sinned, sin·ning.**

since (sins) **1** from a past time till now: *We have been up since five.* **2** after the time that; from the time when: *He has been home only once since he went to Ottawa.* **3** from then till now: *He caught cold Saturday and has been in bed ever since.* **4** at some time between then and now: *He at first refused the position, but has since accepted it.* **5** before now; ago: *Old Rover died long since.* **6** because: *Since you feel tired, you should rest.* 1 *prep.,* 2, 6 *conj.,* 3–5 *adv.*

sin·cere (sin sēr′) free from pretence or deceit; genuine; real; honest: *He made a sincere effort to pass his exams.* *adj.,* **sin·cer·er, sin·cer·est.**

sin·cer·i·ty (sin ser′ə tē) freedom from pretence or deceit; honesty: *No one doubted his sincerity.* *n., pl.* **sin·cer·i·ties.**

sin·ew (sin′yü) **1** a tough, strong band or cord that joins muscle to bone; a tendon: *You can see the sinews in this cooked chicken leg.* **2** strength; energy. **3** a means of strength; a source of power: *Men and money are the sinews of war.* *n.*

sin·ew·y (sin′yə wē or sin′yü ē) **1** having strong sinews; strong; powerful: *A blacksmith has sinewy arms.* **2** vigorous; forcible: *His sinewy arguments finally convinced them that he was right.* **3** tough; stringy: *sinewy beef.* *adj.*

sin·ful (sin′fəl) full of sin; wicked; wrong: *The sinful man repented.* *adj.*

sing (sing) **1** make music with the voice: *He sings on television.* **2** make pleasant, musical sounds: *Birds sing.* **3** utter musically: *She sang the song beautifully.* **4** bring, send, or put with or by singing: *The baby was sung to sleep.* **5** tell in song or poetry: *The poet sang of war and heroes.* **6** make a ringing, whistling, humming, or buzzing sound: *The teakettle sang.* *v.,* **sang** or **sung, sung, sing·ing. —sing′er,** *n.*
sing out, call loudly; shout.

singe (sinj) **1** burn a little. **2** a slight burn. 1 *v.,* **singed, singe·ing;** 2 *n.*

sin·gle (sing′gəl) **1** one and no more; only one: *The spider hung by a single thread. Each child spoke a single line of the poem.* **2** for only one; individual: *The sisters share one room with two single beds in it.* **3** not married: *They rent rooms to single men.* **4** having only one on each side: *The knights engaged in single combat.* **5** having only one set of petals: *Most cultivated roses have double flowers with many petals; wild roses have single flowers with five petals.* **6** sincere; honest; genuine: *She showed single devotion to her religion.* **7** pick from others: *The teacher singled him out for praise.* **8** a single thing or person. **9** in baseball, a one-base hit. **10** make a one-base hit: *He singled in the second inning.* 1–6 *adj.,* 7, 10 *v.,* **sin·gled, sin·gling;** 8, 9 *n.*

single file a line of persons or things arranged one behind another: *The Indians moved silently along the trail in single file.*

sin·gle–hand·ed (sing′gəl han′did) without help from others; working alone. *adj.*

sin·gly (sing′glē) **1** by itself; separately: *Let us consider each point singly.* **2** one by one; one at a time: *Misfortunes never come singly.* **3** by one's own efforts; without help. *adv.*

sin·gu·lar (sing′gyə lər) **1** extraordinary; unusual: *'Treasure Island' is a story of singular interest to boys.* **2** strange; queer; peculiar: *The dectectives were puzzled by the singular nature of the crime.* **3** being the only one of its kind: *an event singular in history.* **4** referring to one: *'Boy' is singular; 'boys' is plural.* **5** the form of a word used to show that one is meant: *'Ox' is the singular of 'oxen.'* 1–4 *adj.*, 5 *n.* —**sin′gu·lar·ly,** *adv.*

sin·is·ter (sin′is tər) **1** showing ill will; threatening: *a sinister rumor, a sinister look.* **2** bad; evil; dishonest: *a sinister plan. adj.*

sink (singk) **1** go down; fall slowly; go lower and lower: *She sank to the floor in a faint. The sun is sinking in the west.* **2** make go down; make fall: *Lack of rain sank the water level of the lake by one metre.* **3** go under: *The swimmer is sinking.* **4** make go under: *The submarine sank two ships.* **5** become lower or weaker: *The wind has sunk. His spirits sank.* **6** make lower; reduce: *She sank her voice to a whisper.* **7** go or cause to go deeply: *Let the lessons sink into your mind.* **8** make by digging or drilling: *The men are sinking a well.* **9** a shallow basin or tub with a pipe to drain it: *The dishes are in the kitchen sink.* 1–8 *v.*, **sank** or **sunk, sunk, sink·ing;** 9 *n.*

sink·er (sing′kər) a lead weight for sinking a line or net for fishing. *n.*

sin·ner (sin′ər) a person who sins or does wrong: *The sinner who repented was forgiven. n.*

si·nus (sī′nəs) a cavity or hollow in the body, especially one of the hollows in the bones of the skull that connect with the nose: *Inflamed sinuses can be very painful. n.*

sip (sip) **1** drink little by little: *She sipped her tea.* **2** a very small drink: *She took a sip.* 1 *v.*, **sipped, sip·ping;** 2 *n.*

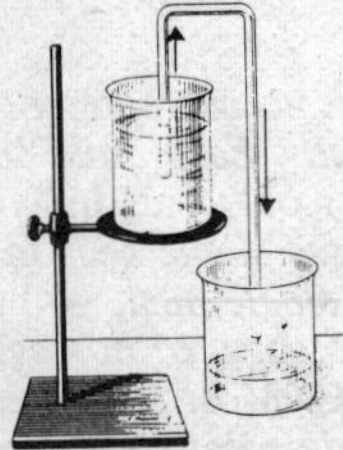

A siphon. The arrows show the direction of flow of the liquid.

si·phon (sī′fən) **1** a bent tube through which liquid can be drawn over the edge of one container into another at a lower level by air pressure. **2** draw off or pass through a siphon: *He siphoned water from the rain barrel onto the garden.* 1 *n.*, 2 *v.* Also spelled **syphon.**

sir (sėr) **1** a respectful or formal term of address used for a man: *Excuse me, sir.* **2 Sir,** the title of a knight or baronet: *Sir Walter Scott. n.*

sire (sīr) **1** a male ancestor. **2** a male parent; father: *The sire of Danger, a great race horse, was Lightning.* **3** be the father of: *Lightning, a great race horse himself, sired the champion Danger.* **4** a title of respect for a king or great noble: *'I am killed, Sire!' said the messenger to Napoleon.* 1, 2, 4 *n.*, 3 *v.*, **sired, sir·ing.**

si·ren (sī′rən) **1** a kind of whistle that makes a loud, piercing sound: *We heard the sirens of the fire engines.* **2** in Greek myths, a woman who, by her sweet singing, lured sailors to destruction upon the rocks. **3** a woman who lures, tempts, or entices. *n.*

sir·up (sėr′əp or sir′əp) See **syrup.**

sis·al (sis′əl or sī′səl) **1** a strong, white fibre, used for making rope, twine, etc. **2** the plant that it comes from. *n.*

sis·sy (sis′ē) *Informal.* **1** sister. **2** a boy or man who behaves too much like a girl. *n.*

sis·ter (sis′tər) **1** a daughter of the same parents: *I have one sister and two brothers.* **2** a woman closely associated with another, such as a member of a club, church, etc. **3** a member of a religious order of women; nun: *Sisters of Charity. n.*

sis·ter–in–law (sis′tər in lo′ or sis′tər in lô′) **1** the sister of one's husband or wife. **2** the wife of one's brother. *n., pl.* **sis·ters-in-law.**

sit (sit) **1** rest on the lower part of the body, with the weight off the feet: *She sat in a chair.* **2** seat; cause to sit: *The woman sat the little boy down hard.* **3** sit on: *He sat his horse well.* **4** have place or position: *The clock has sat on that shelf for years.* **5** have a seat in an assembly; be a member of a council: *to sit in Parliament.* **6** hold a session: *The court sits next month.* **7** place oneself in a position for having one's picture made; pose: *to sit for a portrait.* **8** press or weigh: *Care sat heavy on his brow.* **9** perch: *The birds were sitting on the fence rail.* **10** watch children when parents are away; baby-sit: *She used to sit for the woman next door.* **11** cover eggs so that they will hatch; brood: *The hen will sit until the eggs are ready to hatch.* **12** fit: *Her coat sits well. v.*, **sat, sit·ting.**

sit down, take a seat; put oneself in a sitting position.

sit on or **upon, a** sit in judgment or council on. **b** have a seat on a jury, committee, etc.

sit out, a remain seated during a dance. **b** stay through; wait through: *to sit out a storm. They sat out the performance although the singing was poor.*

sit up, a raise the body to a sitting position. **b** keep such a position. **c** *Informal.* start up in surprise.

☛ See note at **set.**

site (sīt) the position or place of anything: *The big house on the hill has one of the best sites in town. The site for the new school has not yet been chosen. n.*

☛ **Site, cite,** and **sight** are pronounced the same.

sit·ter (sit′ər) baby-sitter. *n.*

sit·ting (sit′ing) **1** a meeting or session of a court, legislature, etc. **2** a time of remaining seated: *He read five chapters at one sitting. n.*

sitting room a room to sit in; a parlor; a living room.

sit·u·at·ed (sich′ü āt′id) placed; located: *The school is so situated that it can be reached easily from all parts of town. Montreal is situated on the St. Lawrence River. adj.*

sit·u·a·tion (sich′ü ā′shən) **1** circumstances; a case; condition: *What would you do in the same situation? It is a very disagreeable situation to be alone and without money in a strange city.* **2** site; position; location: *Our house has a beautiful situation on a hill.* **3** a place to work; job or position: *She is trying to find a situation. n.*

six (siks) **1** one more than five; 6: *She bought six apples.* **2** one of the sections of six into which a pack of Wolf Cubs or Brownies is divided: *John is in the Red six.* 1, 2 *n.*, 1 *adj.*

at sixes and sevens, in confusion or disagreement.

six·er (siks′ər) the leader of a six of Wolf Cubs or Brownies: *A sixer wears two stripes around his left arm. n.*

hat, āge, fär; let, ēqual, tėrm; it, īce
hot, ōpen, ôrder; oil, out; cup, pu̇t, rüle
ə above, takən, pencəl, lemən, circəs
ch, child; ng, long; sh, ship
th, thin; ᴛʜ, then; zh, measure

six·pence (siks′pəns) **1** in Britain, six pennies. **2** a British silver coin equal to 2½ new pence, formerly equal to six pennies. *n.*

six·teen (siks′tēn′) six more than ten; 16. *n., adj.*

six·teenth (siks′tēnth′) **1** next after the 15th; last in a series of sixteen; 16th. **2** one of 16 equal parts: *An ounce is one sixteenth of a pound. adj., n.*

sixth (siksth) **1** next after the 5th; last in a series of six; 6th. **2** one of 6 equal parts. *adj., n.*

six·ti·eth (siks′tē ith) **1** next after the 59th; last in a series of sixty; 60th. **2** one of 60 equal parts. *adj., n.*

six·ty (siks′tē) six times ten; 60. *n., pl.* **six·ties;** *adj.*

siz·a·ble (sīz′ə bəl) fairly large: *a sizable piece of property. adj.* Also spelled **sizeable.**

size[1] (sīz) **1** the amount of surface or space a thing takes up: *The two boys are of the same size. The library contains books of all sizes.* **2** extent; amount; magnitude: *the size of an industry.* **3** one of a series of measures: *I want the larger size, please. His sweater size is medium.* **4** arrange according to size: *Size these nails.* 1–3 *n.,* 4 *v.,* **sized, siz·ing.**

size up, *Informal.* form a judgment or opinion of.

size[2] (sīz) **1** a preparation made from glue or starch and used to cover surfaces about to be painted, to stiffen cloth, and to glaze paper. **2** coat or treat with size; apply size to: *We sized the wall before painting it.* 1 *n.,* 2 *v.,* **sized, siz·ing.**

size·a·ble (sīz′ə bəl) See **sizable.** *adj.*

siz·zle (siz′əl) **1** make a hissing sound, as fat does when it is frying or burning. **2** a hissing sound. 1 *v.,* **siz·zled, siz·zling;** 2 *n.*

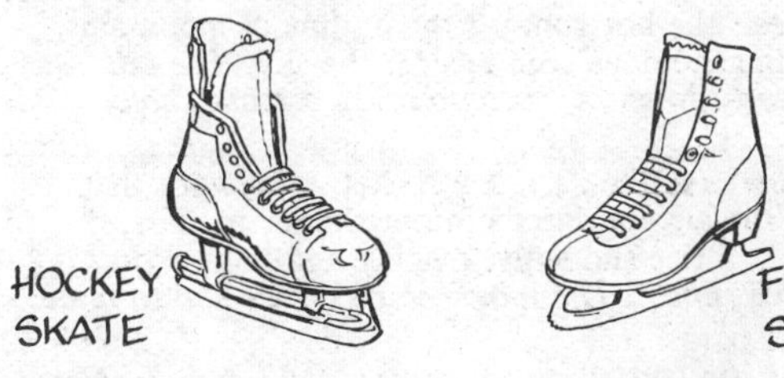

skate[1] (skāt) **1** a frame with a blade fixed to a boot or that can be fastened to a boot so that a person can glide over ice. **2** a roller skate. **3** glide or move along on skates. 1, 2 *n.,* 3 *v.,* **skat·ed, skat·ing.**

☛ **Skate**[1] came through Dutch *schaats* from an old French word *escache,* meaning 'stilt.'

skate[2] (skāt) a kind of broad, flat fish: *A skate is a kind of ray. n.*

☛ **Skate**[2] came from an old Norse word *skata.*

skein (skān) a small bundle of yarn or thread. *n.*

skel·e·ton (skel′ə tən) **1** the bones of a body, fitted together in their natural places: *The skeleton is a frame that supports the muscles, organs, etc.* **2** a frame: *the steel skeleton of a building.* **3** the basic features or elements; outline: *He first thought out the skeleton of the story he was going to write. n.*

skeleton key a key made to open many locks.

sketch (skech) **1** a rough, quickly done drawing, painting, or design. **2** make a sketch of; draw roughly. **3** make sketches: *He sketches in his free time.* **4** an outline; plan. **5** a short description, story, play, etc. 1, 4, 5 *n.,* 2, 3 *v.*

sketch·y (skech′ē) **1** having or giving only outlines or main features. **2** incomplete; slight; imperfect: *a sketchy meal. adj.,* **sketch·i·er, sketch·i·est.**

skew·er (skyü′ər) **1** a long pin of wood or metal for holding meat together while cooking. **2** something shaped or used like a skewer. **3** fasten with a skewer or skewers: *The butcher skewered the roast of beef.* **4** pierce with or as if with a skewer. 1, 2 *n.,* 3, 4 *v.*

ski (skē) **1** one of a pair of long, slender pieces of hard wood, plastic, or metal fastened by straps or special harness to the boots to enable a person to glide over snow. **2** glide over the snow on skis. 1 *n., pl.* **skis;** 2 *v.,* **skied, ski·ing.**

skid (skid) **1** slip or slide sideways while moving: *The car skidded on the slippery road.* **2** slipping or sliding while moving: *The car went into a skid on the icy road.* **3** a piece of wood or metal used to prevent a wheel from turning. **4** slide along without turning, as a wheel does when held by a skid. **5** a piece of timber or a runner on which something heavy may slide: *A stoneboat runs on skids.* **6** a frame on which heavy articles may be piled for moving to another position, often by lifting with a crane. 1, 4 *v.,* **skid·ded, skid·ding;** 2, 3, 5, 6 *n.*

skies (skīz) plural of **sky.** *n. pl.*

skiff (skif) **1** a light rowboat. **2** a small, light boat with a mast for a single triangular sail. *n.*

skil·ful or **skill·ful** (skil′fəl) **1** having skill; expert: *He is a very skilful surgeon.* **2** showing skill: *a skilful piece of work. adj.*

skill (skil) **1** ability gained by practice or knowledge; expertness: *It takes skill to tune a piano.* **2** an ability that can be learned: *One must master the basic language skills. n.*

skilled (skild) **1** having skill; trained; experienced: *A carpenter is a skilled workman.* **2** showing skill; requiring skill: *Plastering is skilled labor. adj.*

skil·let (skil′it) **1** a shallow pan with a handle, used for frying; a frying pan: *He made the pancakes in a skillet.* **2** a long-handled saucepan. *n.*

skill·ful (skil′fəl) See **skilful.**

skim (skim) **1** remove from the top: *The cook skims the cream from the milk and the fat from the soup.* **2** take something from the top of: *She skims the milk to get cream.* **3** move lightly over: *The pebble I threw skimmed the little waves. The skaters were skimming over the ice.* **4** glide along: *The swallows were skimming by.* **5** send skimming: *We made a contest to see who could skim a flat stone over the water the farthest.* **6** read hastily; read with omissions: *It took me an hour to skim the book. v.,* **skimmed, skim·ming.**

skim milk milk from which the cream has been removed.

skimp (skimp) **1** supply in too small an amount: *Don't skimp the butter in making a cake.* **2** be very saving or economical: *She had to skimp to send her son to university. v.*

skimp·y (skim′pē) scanty; not enough: *a skimpy meal.* *adj.,* **skimp·i·er, skimp·i·est.**

skin (skin) 1 the outer layer of tissue of the body in persons and animals: *Cows have thick skins.* 2 a hide or pelt: *The skin of a calf makes soft leather.* 3 any outer surface layer, as the rind of a fruit, a sausage casing, etc. 4 take the skin off: *He skinned his knees when he fell. The hunter skinned the deer.* 5 a container made of skin for holding liquids. 1–3, 5 *n.,* 4 *v.,* **skinned, skin·ning.**
by the skin of one's teeth, very narrowly; barely.

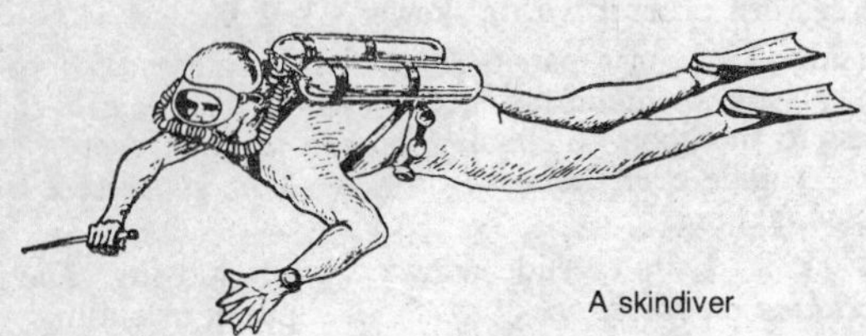
A skindiver

skin·div·er (skin′dīv′ər) a person engaged in skin diving. *n.*

skin diving swimming under water, sometimes at great depth and for long periods of time, equipped with goggles, rubber flippers, a portable breathing device, and sometimes a skin-tight rubber suit.

skin·flint (skin′flint′) a mean, stingy person. *n.*

skin·ny (skin′ē) 1 very thin; very lean. 2 like skin. *adj.,* **skin·ni·er, skin·ni·est.**

skip (skip) 1 leap lightly; spring; jump: *Lambs skip in the fields.* 2 a light spring, jump, or leap: *The child gave a skip of joy.* 3 move along by stepping and hopping first with one foot, then with the other. 4 moving in this way. 5 leap lightly over: *The girls skipped rope.* 6 send bounding along a surface: *Boys like to skip stones on the lake.* 7 pass over; fail to notice; omit: *She skips the hard words when she reads. Answer the questions in order without skipping.* 8 *Informal.* stay away from: *to skip classes.* 9 *Informal.* leave in a hurry: *He skipped town to avoid meeting his enemies.* 1, 3, 5–9 *v.,* **skipped, skip·ping;** 2, 4 *n.*

skip·per (skip′ər) 1 the captain of a ship, especially of a small trading or fishing boat. 2 any captain or leader. *n.*

skir·mish (skėr′mish) 1 a minor fight between small groups of soldiers, ships, aircraft, etc. 2 a slight conflict, argument, contest, etc. 3 take part in a skirmish. 1, 2 *n.,* 3 *v.*

skirt (skėrt) 1 the part of a dress that hangs from the waist. 2 a woman's or girl's garment that hangs from the waist. 3 pass along the border or edge of: *The boys skirted the forest instead of going through it.* 1, 2 *n.,* 3 *v.*
☛ See note at **shirt.**

skit (skit) a short, humorous scene for acting on stage or television: *Our class did a skit on learning to ride a bike.* *n.*

skulk (skulk) 1 keep out of sight to avoid danger, work, or duty; hide or lurk in a cowardly way. 2 move in a stealthy, sneaking way: *The wolf was skulking in the woods near the sheep.* *v.*

skull (skul) the bony framework of the head and face. *n.*
☛ **Skull** and **scull** are pronounced the same.

A striped skunk — about 40 cm long without the tail

skunk (skungk) 1 a black, bushy-tailed animal of North America, about the size of a cat, usually with white stripes along the back: *Skunks give off a very strong, unpleasant smell when frightened or attacked.* 2 the fur of this animal, used on coats, etc. 3 *Informal.* a mean, contemptible person. *n.*

skunk cabbage a perennial herb having wide leaves and thick roots: *Skunk cabbage has a strong, unpleasant smell.*

sky (skī) 1 the space high above the earth, appearing as a great arch or dome covering the world; the region of the clouds or the upper air; the heavens: *a blue sky, a cloudy sky.* 2 heaven. *n., pl.* **skies.**
out of a clear sky, suddenly; unexpectedly.

sky·lark (skī′lärk′) 1 a small bird of Europe that sings very sweetly as it flies toward the sky. 2 play pranks; frolic: *The children were skylarking in the orchard.* 1 *n.,* 2 *v.*

sky·light (skī′līt′) a window in a roof or ceiling. *n.*

sky·line (skī′līn′) 1 the line at which earth and sky seem to meet; the horizon. 2 the outline of mountains, trees, buildings, etc. as seen against the sky: *The tall buildings and towers of Toronto make a remarkable skyline.* *n.*

sky·rock·et (skī′rok′it) 1 a rocket; a firework that goes up in the air and bursts into a shower of stars, sparks, etc. 2 rise suddenly, quickly and high: *Prices were skyrocketing. The movie star skyrocketed to fame.* 1 *n.,* 2 *v.*

sky·scrap·er (skī′skrāp′ər) a very tall building: *New York is famous for its skyscrapers.* *n.*

slab (slab) a broad, flat, thick piece of stone, wood, meat, etc.: *This sidewalk is made of slabs of stone. The hungry boy ate a slab of cheese as big as his hand.* *n.*

slack (slak) 1 not tight or firm; loose: *The rope hung slack.* 2 the part that hangs loose: *He pulled in the slack of the rope.* 3 careless: *She is a slack housekeeper.* 4 slow: *The horse was moving at a slack pace.* 5 not active; not brisk; dull: *Business is slack at this season.* 1, 3–5 *adj.,* 2 *n.*
slack off, a loosen. b lessen one's efforts.
slack up, slow down; go more slowly.

slack·en (slak′ən) 1 make or become slower: *Don't slacken your efforts till the work is done. Work slackens on a hot day.* 2 make or become looser: *Slacken the rope. The rope slackened as the wave sent the boat toward the pier.* *v.*

slacks (slaks) trousers for informal wear. *n. pl.*

slag (slag) the rough, hard waste left after metal is separated from ore by melting it. *n.*

slain (slān) See **slay.** *The sheep were slain by the wolves.* *v.*

slake (slāk) 1 satisfy thirst, revenge, wrath, etc.: *We*

hat, āge, fär; let, ēqual, tėrm; it, īce
hot, ōpen, ôrder; oil, out; cup, pu̇t, rüle
əbove, takən, pencəl, lemən, circəs
ch, child; ng, long; sh, ship
th, thin; ŦH, then; zh, measure

slaked our thirst at the spring. 2 change lime by leaving it in moist air or putting water on it: *Plaster contains slaked lime and sand.* *v.*, **slaked, slak·ing.**

sla·lom (slä′ləm, slal′əm, or slā′ləm) 1 in skiing, a zigzag race downhill on a course set between a series of posts. 2 ski on such a course. 1 *n.*, 2 *v.*

slam (slam) 1 shut with force and noise; close with a bang: *He slammed the window down. The door slammed.* 2 throw, push, hit, or move with force: *He slammed himself down his bed. The car slammed into a truck.* 3 a violent and noisy closing, striking, etc.; a bang: *He threw his books down with a slam.* 1, 2 *v.*, **slammed, slam·ming;** 3 *n.*

slan·der (slan′dər) 1 a false spoken statement meant to do harm to the reputation of another. 2 talk falsely about. 3 the spreading of false reports: *Evil, malicious slander had caused some people to doubt the mayor's honesty.* 1, 3 *n.*, 2 *v.*

slang (slang) 1 words, phrases, meanings, etc. not considered acceptable for use in formal speech and writing: *Slang usually consists of new words, expressions, or meanings that are popular for only a short time. Some words considered slang are entered in this dictionary and labelled 'Slang.'* 2 the special talk of a particular class of people: *Indoor trapping meant 'stealing furs from a warehouse' in the slang of the Canadian fur trade.* *n.*

slant (slant) 1 slope: *Most handwriting slants to the right.* 2 a slope: *Has your roof a sharp slant?* 3 sloping: *a slant roof.* 1 *v.*, 2 *n.*, 3 *adj.*

slap (slap) 1 a blow with the open hand or with something flat. 2 strike with the open hand or with something flat: *He slapped at the fly with a folded newspaper.* 3 put or throw with force: *She slapped the book down on the table.* 1 *n.*, 2, 3 *v.*, **slapped, slap·ping.**

slap·dash (slap′dash′) 1 hastily and carelessly: *He went slapdash at a job.* 2 hasty and careless: *Slapdash people do slapdash work.* 1 *adv.*, 2 *adj.*

slash (slash) 1 cut with a sweeping stroke of a sword, knife, whip, etc.; gash: *He slashed the bark off the tree with his knife.* 2 make a slashing stroke: *He slashed at his enemy with a knife.* 3 a sweeping, slashing stroke: *the slash of a sword, the slash of rain.* 4 a cut or wound made by such a stroke; a gash. 5 cut down severely; reduce a great deal: *His salary was slashed when business became bad.* 1, 2, 5 *v.*, 3, 4 *n.*

slat (slat) a long, thin, narrow piece of wood or metal. *n.*

slate (slāt) 1 a bluish-grey rock that splits easily into thin, smooth layers: *Slate is used to cover roofs.* 2 a thin piece of this rock: *Children used to write on slates, but now they use paper.* 3 dark, bluish grey. 4 a list of candidates, officers, etc. to be considered for appointment, nomination, election, etc. 1–4 *n.*, 3 *adj.*
a clean slate, a record not spoiled by mistakes or faults: *start again with a clean slate.*

slaugh·ter (slo′tər or slô′tər) 1 the killing of an animal or animals for food; butchering: *the slaughter of a steer, to fatten hogs for slaughter.* 2 brutal killing; much or needless killing: *The battle resulted in a frightful slaughter.* 3 kill an animal or animals for food; butcher: *Millions of cattle are slaughtered every year.* 4 kill brutally; massacre. 1, 2 *n.*, 3, 4 *v.*

slaugh·ter·house (slo′tər hous′ or slô′tər hous′) a place where cattle, pigs, sheep, etc. are killed and prepared for sale in meat markets; an abattoir. *n.*

slave (slāv) 1 a person who is the property of another: *Slaves were bought and sold like horses.* 2 a person who is controlled or ruled by some desire, habit, or influence: *A drunkard is a slave of drink.* 3 a person who works like a slave. 4 work like a slave: *Many mothers slave for their children.* 5 of slaves; done by slaves: *slave labor.* 1–3 *n.*, 4 *v.*, **slaved, slav·ing;** 5 *adj.*

slav·er·y (slāv′ər ē) 1 the condition of being a slave: *Many African Negroes were captured and sold into slavery.* 2 the custom of owning slaves: *Where slavery is permitted, certain men own others.* 3 a condition like that of a slave. 4 hard work like that of a slave. *n.*

slav·ish (slāv′ish) 1 of or having something to do with a slave or slaves. 2 like a slave; mean; base: *a slavish person.* 3 weakly submitting: *He is a slavish personality.* 4 like that of slaves; fit for slaves: *We were surprised by his slavish behavior.* 5 lacking originality and independence: *a slavish reproduction.* *adj.*

slay (slā) kill with violence, especially in battle: *Many soldiers were slain on that hill. Jack slew the giant.* *v.*, **slew, slain, slay·ing.**

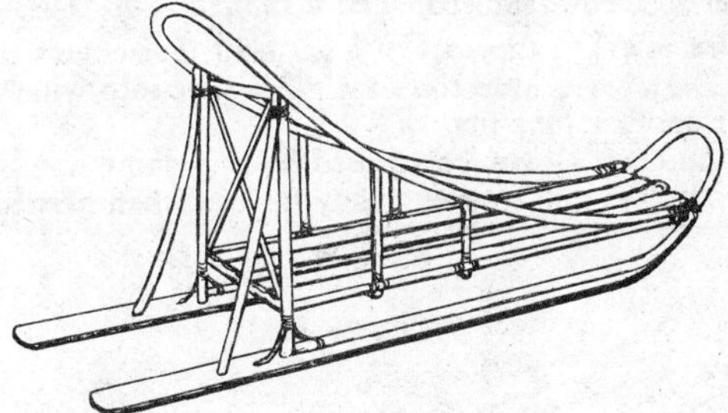

A sled designed to be pulled by a team of dogs

sled (sled) 1 a vehicle having runners instead of wheels, for use on ice or snow: *Sleds pulled by dogs are in common use in the North.* 2 See **sleigh** (def. 2). 3 ride or carry on a sled. 1, 2 *n.*, 3 *v.*

sledge[1] (slej) 1 a heavy sled or sleigh, usually pulled by horses. 2 a sled or sleigh. *n.*

sledge[2] (slej) sledge hammer. *n.*

sledge hammer a large, heavy hammer, usually swung with both hands.

sleek (slēk) 1 soft and glossy; smooth: *sleek hair.* 2 having smooth, soft skin, hair, fur, etc.: *a sleek cat.* 3 having clean lines; trim: *a sleek jet plane.* 4 make smooth and glossy: *He used a brush to sleek down his dog's hair.* 1–3 *adj.*, 4 *v.*

sleep (slēp) 1 rest body and mind; be without ordinary thought or movement: *We sleep at night. Most animals sleep.* 2 a resting of the body and mind occurring naturally and regularly: *Most people need eight hours of sleep a day.* 3 be in a condition like sleep: *The seeds slept in the ground all winter.* 4 a state or condition like sleep. 5 spend in sleeping: *She* *slept the night in peace.* 1, 3, 5 *v.*, **slept, sleep·ing;** 2, 4 *n.*

sleep away, pass or spend in sleeping: *She slept away the whole morning.*

sleep in, a remain in bed later than usual: *We always sleep in on a Sunday morning.* **b** sleep late or oversleep: *He was late for school because he slept in.* **c** sleep at one's place of work: *The maid slept in, but the gardener did not.*

sleep off, get rid of or improve by having a sleep: *His mother told him to go and sleep off his bad humor.*

sleep·er (slēp′ər) a railway car that has berths or small rooms for passengers to sleep in. *n.*

sleeping bag a zippered bag for sleeping in, usually waterproof and warmly lined, used especially when camping.

sleep·less (slēp′lis) without sleep; not sleeping; restless. *adj.*

sleep·walk·ing (slēp′wok′ing or slēp′wôk′ing) walking while asleep. *n.*

sleep·y (slēp′ē) **1** ready to go to sleep; inclined to sleep: *He never gets enough rest and is always sleepy.* **2** quiet; not active: *a sleepy little town.* *adj.*, **sleep·i·er, sleep·i·est.**

sleet (slēt) **1** partly frozen rain; snow or hail mixed with rain. **2** to rain and snow or hail at the same time: *It sleeted; then it snowed; then it rained.* 1 *n.*, 2 *v.*

sleeve (slēv) **1** the part of a garment that covers the arm: *The sleeves were too long.* **2** a tube into which a rod or another tube fits. *n.*

laugh up one's sleeve, be amused but not show it.

up one's sleeve, in reserve; ready for use when needed.

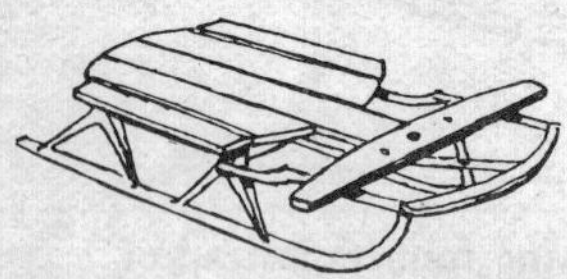

A sleigh (def. 2)

sleigh (slā) **1** a carriage or cart mounted on runners for use on snow or ice: *In some northern countries people use sleighs in winter.* See **cutter** for picture. **2** a plaything consisting of a framework of boards mounted on metal runners, for use on snow or ice: *The children had great fun playing with their sleighs.* **3** travel in or ride on a sleigh. 1, 2 *n.*, 3 *v.*

slen·der (slen′dər) **1** long and thin; not big around: *The ballet dancer was tall and slender. A pencil is a slender piece of wood.* **2** slight; small: *a slender meal, a slender income, a slender hope.* *adj.*

slept (slept) See **sleep.** *The baby has slept soundly for several nights.* *v.*

slew[1] (slü) See **slay.** *Jack slew the giant.* *v.*

☛ Slew and **slough**[1] are sometimes pronounced the same.

slew[2] (slü) *Informal.* a large number or amount; lot: *The new boy quickly gained a slew of friends.* *n.*

☛ See note at **slew**[1].

☛ Slew[2] comes from Irish *sluagh,* meaning 'crowd.'

slice (slīs) **1** a thin, flat, broad piece cut from something, especially food: *a slice of bread, a slice of meat, a slice of cake.* **2** cut into slices: *Slice the bread. We ate sliced peaches.* **3** cut off as a slice. 1 *n.*, 2, 3 *v.*, **sliced, slic·ing.**

slick (slik) **1** sleek; smooth: *slick hair.* **2** make sleek or smooth. **3** slippery; greasy: *a road slick with ice or mud.* **4** *Informal.* smooth in speech or manner, especially in a tricky or deceitful way. 1, 3, 4 *adj.*, 2 *v.*

slick·er (slik′ər) a long, loose waterproof coat. *n.*

slid (slid) See **slide.** *The minutes slid rapidly by.* *v.*

slide (slīd) **1** move smoothly over a surface: *The bureau drawers slide in and out.* **2** move easily, quietly, or secretly: *The thief quickly slid behind the curtains.* **3** slip in an uncontrolled manner. **4** pass by degrees; slip: *He had slid into bad habits.* **5** pass or put quietly or secretly: *He slid a pistol into his pocket.* **6** the act of sliding: *The children each take a slide in turn.* **7** a smooth surface for sliding: *The frozen brook makes a good slide.* **8** a track, rail, etc. on which something slides. **9** a mass of earth, snow, etc. sliding down: *The slide cut off the valley from the rest of the world.* **10** a small, thin sheet of glass on which objects are placed in order to look at them under a microscope. **11** a small transparent photograph made of glass or film: *Slides are put in a projector and shown on a screen.* 1–5 *v.*, **slid, slid** or **slid·den, slid·ing;** 6–11 *n.*

let slide, neglect; not bother about: *He let his business slide so far that he became bankrupt.*

slide fastener zipper.

slight (slīt) **1** not much; not important; small: *One slice of bread is a very slight lunch. I have a slight headache. I hardly felt that slight scratch.* **2** not big around; slender: *She is a slight girl.* **3** pay too little attention to; neglect: *She felt slighted because she was not asked to the party.* **4** slighting treatment; an act showing neglect or lack of respect: *She suffered many slights from her sisters.* 1, 2 *adj.*, 3 *v.*, 4 *n.*

slight·ly (slīt′lē) **1** in a slight manner. **2** to a slight degree; somewhat; a little: *I knew him slightly.* *adv.*

slim (slim) **1** slender; thin: *Many young girls are slim.* **2** small; slight; weak: *Because of the rain, there was a slim attendance at the football game.* **3** make or become thin or slender: *The girl slimmed her figure with a rigid diet.* 1, 2 *adj.*, **slim·mer, slim·mest;** 3 *v.*

slime (slīm) **1** soft, sticky mud or something like it: *His shoes were covered with slime from the swamp.* **2** a sticky substance given off by snails, slugs, fish, etc. **3** disgusting filth. *n.*

slim·y (slīm′ē) **1** covered with slime: *The pond is too slimy to swim in.* **2** of slime; like slime. **3** disgusting; filthy. *adj.*, **slim·i·er, slim·i·est.**

sling (sling) **1** a strip of leather with a string fastened to each end, for throwing stones. **2** throw with a sling. **3** throw; cast; hurl: *The cruel boy slung stones at the cat.* **4** a hanging loop of cloth fastened around the neck to support a hurt arm. **5** a rope, band, or chain by which heavy objects are lifted, carried, or held: *The men lowered the boxes into the cellar by a sling.* **6** hang in a sling; hang so as to swing loosely: *The soldier's gun was slung over his shoulder.* 1, 4, 5 *n.*, 2, 3, 6 *v.*, **slung, sling·ing.**

sling·shot (sling′shot′) a Y-shaped stick with a band

of rubber between its prongs, used to shoot pebbles, etc.; catapult. *n.*

slink (slingk) move in a secret, guilty manner; sneak: *After stealing the meat, the dog slunk away.* *v.,* **slunk, slink·ing.**

slip[1] (slip) **1** go or move smoothly, quietly, easily, or quickly: *She slipped out of the room. Time slips by. The ship slips through the waves.* **2** slide; move out of place: *The knife slipped and cut him.* **3** slide suddenly without wanting to: *He slipped on the icy sidewalk.* **4** the act or fact of slipping: *His broken leg was caused by a slip on a banana peel.* **5** cause to slip; put, pass, or draw smoothly, quietly, or secretly: *He slipped back the bolt on the door. She slipped the ring from her finger. Slip the note into Mary's hand.* **6** put on or take off something easily or quickly: *Slip on your coat and come with us. Slip off your shoes.* **7** a pillowcase. **8** a sleeveless garment worn under a dress: *Grace wore a pink slip under her party dress.* **9** pass without notice; pass through neglect; escape: *Don't let this opportunity slip.* **10** get loose from; get away from; escape from: *The dog has slipped his collar. Your name has slipped my mind.* **11** fall off; decline: *Sales are slipping.* **12** make a mistake or error. **13** a mistake; error: *He makes slips in pronouncing words. That remark was a slip of the tongue.* 1–3, 5, 6, 9–12 *v.,* **slipped, slip·ping;** 4, 7, 8, 13 *n.*

give (someone) **the slip,** *Informal.* escape from or get away from (someone): *The deer gave his hunter the slip.*

let slip, tell without meaning to: *She let the secret slip in a careless moment.*

slip up, *Informal.* make a mistake or error.

slip[2] (slip) **1** a narrow strip of paper, wood, etc. **2** a small branch or twig cut from a plant, used to grow a new plant: *She has promised us slips from that bush.* *n.*

slip knot a knot made to slip along the rope or cord around which it is made. See **knot** for diagram.

slip·per (slip′ər) a light, low shoe that is slipped on easily: *She has pretty dancing slippers and comfortable bedroom slippers.* *n.*

slip·per·y (slip′ər ē) **1** causing or likely to cause slipping: *A wet street is slippery. The steps are slippery with ice.* **2** slipping away easily: *Wet soap is slippery.* **3** not to be depended on; tricky. *adj.,* **slip·per·i·er, slip·per·i·est.**

slip·shod (slip′shod′) careless in dress, habits, speech, etc.; untidy; slovenly. *adj.*

slit (slit) **1** cut or tear along a line; make a long, straight cut or tear in: *to slit cloth into strips.* **2** a straight, narrow cut, tear, or opening: *a slit in a bag.* 1 *v.,* **slit, slit·ting;** 2 *n.*

sliv·er (sliv′ər) **1** a long, thin piece that has been split off, broken off, or cut off; splinter. **2** split or break into slivers. 1 *n.,* 2 *v.*

slob (slob) **1** *Slang.* a stupid, untidy, or clumsy person. **2** *Cdn.* slob ice. *n.*

A sling for lifting

hat, āge, fär; let, ēqual, tėrm; it, īce
hot, ōpen, ôrder; oil, out; cup, pu̇t, rüle
əbove, takən, pencəl, lemən, circəs
ch, child; ng, long; sh, ship
th, thin; ᴛʜ, then; zh, measure

slob·ber (slob′ər) **1** let liquid run out from the mouth; drool. **2** saliva or other liquid running out from the mouth. 1 *v.,* 2 *n.*

slob ice *Cdn.* small pieces of ice crowded together: *The boat pushed its way through the slob ice.*

slo·gan (slō′gən) **1** a word or phrase used by any group, party, class, or business to advertise its purpose; motto: *'Safety First' is our slogan.* **2** a war cry; battle cry. *n.*

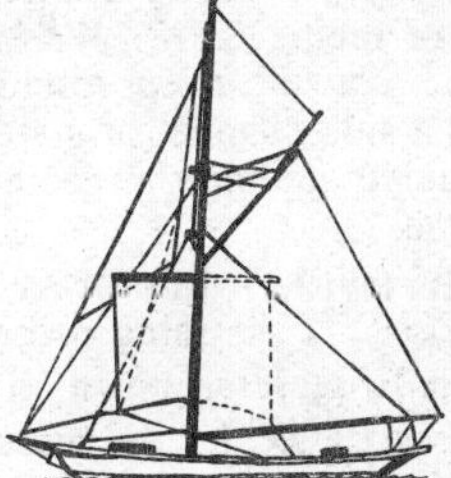

A sloop

sloop (slüp) a sailboat having one mast, a mainsail, a jib, and sometimes other sails: *All sails on a sloop are rigged fore-and-aft.* *n.*

slop (slop) **1** spill liquid upon; spill; splash: *He slopped water on me.* **2** liquid carelessly spilled or splashed about. **3** dirty water; liquid garbage: *the kitchen slops.* **4** a weak liquid food, such as gruel. 1 *v.,* **slopped, slop·ping;** 2–4 *n.*

slope (slōp) **1** go up or down at an angle; slant: *The land slopes toward the sea. That house has a sloping roof.* **2** any line, surface, land, etc. that goes up or down at an angle: *If you roll a ball up a slope, it will roll down again.* **3** the amount of slope: *The floor of the theatre has a slope of one metre from the back seats to the front seats.* 1 *v.,* **sloped, slop·ing;** 2, 3 *n.*

slop·py (slop′ē) **1** very wet; slushy: *sloppy ground, sloppy weather.* **2** *Informal.* careless; slovenly: *to use sloppy language, to do sloppy work.* *adj.,* **slop·pi·er, slop·pi·est.**

slosh (slosh) splash in slush, mud, or water: *He sloshed around in the bathtub and got the floor all wet.* *v.*

slot (slot) **1** a small, narrow opening or groove: *He put a cent in the slot of the gum machine.* **2** make a slot or slots. 1 *n.,* 2 *v.,* **slot·ted, slot·ting.**

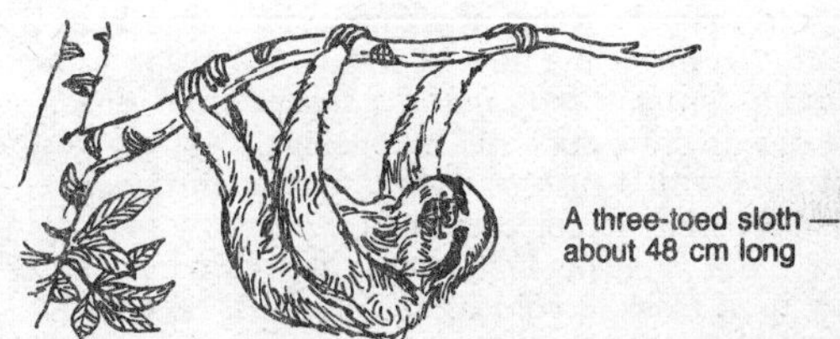

A three-toed sloth — about 48 cm long

sloth (slōth or sloth) **1** unwillingness to work or exert oneself; laziness; idleness: *His sloth keeps him from taking part in sports.* 2 a very slow-moving animal of South America that lives in trees: *Sloths hang upside down from tree branches.* *n.* —**sloth′ful,** *adj.*

slot machine a machine that is worked by dropping a coin into a slot. Some slot machines sell peanuts, sticks of gum, etc.; others are used for gambling.

slouch (slouch) 1 to stand, sit, walk, or move in an awkward, drooping manner: *The weary man slouched along.* 2 droop or bend downward: *He slouched his shoulders.* 3 a bending forward of the head and shoulders; an awkward, drooping way of standing, sitting, or walking. 4 an awkward, slovenly, or inefficient person. 1, 2 *v.,* 3, 4 *n.*

slough[1] (slü or slou) 1 a body of fresh water formed by rain or melted snow: *Wild ducks nest on the prairie sloughs.* 2 a soft, deep, muddy place; a mud hole or bog. 3 a side channel of a stream; snye. *n.*

☛ **Slough**[1] and **slew** are sometimes pronounced the same.

slough[2] (sluf) 1 drop or cast off: *The snake sloughed its old skin.* 2 the thing dropped or cast off. 1 *v.,* 2 *n.*

slov·en·ly (sluv′ən lē) untidy, dirty, or careless in dress, appearance, habits, work, etc. *adj.,* **slov·en·li·er, slov·en·li·est.**

slow (slō) 1 taking a long time; taking longer than usual; not fast or quick: *a slow journey.* 2 behind time; running at less than proper speed: *a slow runner.* 3 showing time earlier than the correct time: *The clock was slow and I was late for school.* 4 make slow or slower; reduce the speed of: *to slow down a car.* 5 become slow; go slower: *Slow up when you drive through a town.* 6 in a slow manner or way; slowly: *Drive slow.* 7 dull; not interesting: *a slow party.* 8 not quick to understand: *a slow pupil.* 1–3, 7, 8 *adj.,* 4, 5 *v.,* 6 *adv.*

slow·poke (slō′pōk′) *Informal.* a very slow person or thing. *n.*

slug[1] (slug) 1 a slow-moving animal like a snail, without a shell or with only a partly developed shell. 2 a caterpillar or larva that looks like a slug. 3 a piece of lead or other metal for firing from a gun. 4 a small disc or other shaped piece of metal: *It is illegal to use slugs instead of coins in a slot machine.* *n.*

slug[2] (slug) *Informal.* 1 hit hard with the fist, a bat, or a blunt-weapon. 2 a hard blow. 1 *v.,* **slugged, slug·ging;** 2 *n.*

slug·gard (slug′ərd) a lazy, idle person. *n.*

slug·gish (slug′ish) slow; lacking energy or vigor: *a sluggish stream, a sluggish mind.* *adj.*

sluice (slüs) 1 a structure with a gate for holding back or controlling the water of a canal, river, or lake. 2 a gate that controls the flow of water: *When the water behind a dam gets too high, the sluices are opened.* 3 let out or draw off water by opening a sluice. 4 flush or cleanse with a rush of water; pour or throw water over. 5 a channel for carrying off overflow or surplus water. 6 a long, sloping trough through which water flows, used to wash gold from sand, dirt, or gravel. 1, 2, 5, 6 *n.,* 3, 4 *v.,* **sluiced, sluic·ing.**

slum (slum) a crowded run-down part of a city or town: *Disease is common in slums.* *n.*

slum·ber (slum′bər) 1 to sleep. 2 a sleep: *He awoke from his slumber.* 3 pass in sleep: *The baby slumbers away the hours.* 4 be inactive: *The volcano had slumbered for years.* 1, 3, 4 *v.,* 2 *n.*

slump (slump) 1 drop heavily; fall suddenly: *The boy's feet slumped repeatedly through the melting ice.* 2 move, walk, sit, etc. in a drooping manner; slouch: *The bored students slumped in their seats.* 3 a heavy or sudden fall: *a slump in prices.* 1, 2 *v.,* 3 *n.*

slung (slung) See **sling.** *They slung some stones and ran away. The boy had slung his books over his shoulder.* *v.*

slunk (slungk) See **slink.** *The dog slunk off.* *v.*

slur (slėr) 1 pass lightly over; go through hurriedly or in a careless way. 2 pronounce in an incomplete or indistinct way: *Many persons slur 'How do you do.'* 3 a slurred pronunciation, sound, etc. 4 a blot or stain upon a reputation; an insulting or slighting remark: *a slur on a person's good name.* 1, 2 *v.,* **slurred, slur·ring;** 3, 4 *n.*

slush (slush) 1 partly melted snow; snow and water mixed. 2 silly, sentimental talk, writing, etc. *n.*

sly (slī) 1 cunning; crafty; tricky: *That girl is as sly as a fox. The sly cat stole the meat while the cook's back was turned. She asked sly questions.* 2 playfully mischievous or knowing: *The week before Christmas the children exchanged many sly looks and smiles.* *adj.,* **sly·er** or **sli·er, sly·est** or **sli·est:** —**sly′ly,** *adv.*
on the sly, in a sly way; secretly.

smack[1] (smak) 1 a slight taste or flavor: *This sauce has a smack of lemon.* 2 a trace; suggestion: *The old sailor still has a smack of the sea about him.* 3 have a taste, trace, or suggestion of: *The speech of the man from Ireland smacked of the Old Country.* 1, 2 *n.,* 3 *v.*

smack[2] (smak) 1 open the lips quickly so as to make a sharp sound. 2 a sharp sound that is made in this way. 3 kiss loudly. 4 slap: *She smacked his face.* 5 a loud kiss, slap, or crack. 1, 3, 4 *v.,* 2, 5 *n.*

smack[3] (smak) a small sailboat with one mast. *n.*

small (smol or smôl) 1 not large; little; not large as compared with other things of the same kind: *A cottage is a small house.* 2 not great in amount, degree, extent, duration, value, or strength: *a small dose, small hope of success. The cent is our smallest coin.* 3 not important: *Don't bother Mother with that small matter now.* 4 of low social position; humble; poor: *People great and small mourned Laurier's death.* 5 having little land or capital: *a small farmer.* 6 mean: *A boy with a small nature is not generous.* 7 that which is small; a small, slender, or narrow part: *the small of the back.* 1–6 *adj.,* 7 *n.*

small change 1 coins of small value, such as nickels, dimes, etc. 2 anything small and unimportant.

small fry 1 babies or children; small or young

A sluice (def. 1)

creatures. 2 people or things having little importance: *He thinks himself too important to talk to small fry like us.*

small hours the early hours of the morning.

small letter an ordinary letter, not a capital.

small·pox (smol′poks′ or smôl′poks′) a contagious disease accompanied by fever and sores on the skin that often leave permanent scars shaped like little pits. *n.*

small talk talk about matters having little importance; chat.

smart (smärt) 1 feel sharp pain: *His eyes smarted.* 2 cause sharp pain: *The cut smarts.* 3 a sharp pain: *The smart of the hurt kept him awake.* 4 feel distress or irritation: *He smarted from the scolding.* 5 sharp; severe: *He gave the horse a smart blow.* 6 keen; active; lively: *They walked at a smart pace.* 7 clever; bright: *He is a smart boy.* 8 fresh and neat; in good order: *the smart uniform of a good soldier.* 9 stylish; fashionable: *Beth has a smart new dress.* 1, 2, 4 *v.*, 3 *n.*, 5–9 *adj.* —**smart′ly,** *adv.* —**smart′ness,** *n.*

smart·en (smär′tən) 1 improve in appearance; brighten: *The new rug smartens up the whole room.* 2 make or become brisker: *He smartened his walk when the sergeant approached.* *v.*

smarten up, *Informal.* move, behave, or work more briskly or efficiently: *The teacher told his idle class to smarten up.*

smash (smash) 1 break into pieces with violence and noise: *The boy smashed a window with a stone.* 2 destroy; shatter; ruin: *to smash a person's hopes.* 3 be broken to pieces: *The dishes smashed as the tray upset.* 4 rush violently; crash: *The car smashed into the tree.* 5 a violent breaking or shattering; crash: *the smash of two automobiles.* 6 the act or sound of a smash or crash: *the smash of broken glass.* 1–4, *v.*, 5, 6 *n.*

smear (smēr) 1 cover or stain with anything sticky, greasy, or dirty: *She smeared her fingers with jam.* 2 rub or spread oil, grease, paint, etc. 3 a mark or stain left by smearing: *There are smears of paint on the wallpaper.* 4 receive a mark or stain; be smeared: *Wet paint smears easily.* 5 harm a person's reputation or character: *His opponents smeared the mayor by spreading rumors about his conduct.* 6 harming a person's reputation; slander: *The rumors were a wicked smear against the mayor.* 1, 2, 4, 5 *v.*, 3, 6, *n.*

smell (smel) 1 detect or recognize by breathing in through the nose: *Can you smell the smoke?* 2 the sense of smelling: *Smell is keener in dogs than in people.* 3 detect or recognize smells: *We smell with our noses.* 4 sniff at: *She picked up a rose and smelled it. The dog smelled at the strange man's legs.* 5 the quality in a thing that affects the sense of smell; odor: *The smell of burning rubber is not pleasant. The smell of roses is delightful.* 6 give out a smell: *The garden smelled of roses.* 7 give out a bad smell: *That dirty, wet dog smells.* 8 a sniff; the act of smelling: *Have a smell of this rose.* 1, 3, 4, 6, 7 *v.*, **smelled** or **smelt, smell·ing;** 2, 5, 8 *n.*

smell·y (smel′ē) having or giving out a strong or unpleasant smell: *Rotten fish are smelly.* *adj.*

smelt[1] (smelt) 1 melt ore in order to get the metal out of it. 2 obtain metal from ore by melting. 3 refine impure metal by melting. *v.*

smelt[2] (smelt) a small food fish with silvery scales. *n., pl.* **smelt** or **smelts.**

hat, āge, fär; let, ēqual, tėrm; it, īce
hot, ōpen, ôrder; oil, out; cup, pu̇t, rüle
əbove, takən, pencəl, lemən, circəs
ch, child; ng, long; sh, ship
th, thin; ᴛʜ, then; zh, measure

smelt[3] (smelt) See **smell.** *v.*

smelt·er (smel′tər) 1 a person whose work or business is smelting ores or metals. 2 a place where ores or metals are melted. 3 a furnace for smelting ores. *n.*

smile (smīl) 1 look pleased or amused; show pleasure, favor, kindness, amusement, etc. by an upward curve of the mouth. 2 show scorn, disdain, etc. by a curve of the mouth: *She smiled bitterly.* 3 bring, put, drive, etc. by smiling: *Smiling your tears away.* 4 express by a smile: *She smiled consent.* 5 the act of smiling: *a friendly smile, a smile of pity.* 1–4 *v.*, **smiled, smil·ing;** 5 *n.*

smirk (smėrk) 1 smile in a knowing, self-satisfied way. 2 a knowing or self-satisfied smile. 1 *v.*, 2 *n.*

smit (smit) See **smite.** *v.*

smite (smīt) strike; strike hard; hit hard: *The hero smites the giant with his sword. His conscience smote him. She was smitten with curiosity about the forbidden room.* *v.*, **smote, smit·ten** or **smit, smit·ing.**

smith (smith) 1 a man who makes or shapes things out of metal: *a goldsmith, a tinsmith.* 2 a blacksmith. *n.*

smith·er·eens (smiᴛʜ′ər ēnz′) *Informal.* small pieces; bits: *smash a chair into smithereens.* *n. pl.*

smith·y (smith′ē or smiᴛʜ′ē) the workshop of a smith, especially a blacksmith: *'Under a spreading chestnut tree the village smithy stands.'* *n., pl.* **smith·ies.**

smit·ten (smit′ən) 1 hard hit; struck: *sudden sparks from smitten steel.* 2 See **smite.** *The giant was smitten by the sword of the knight.* 1 *adj.*, 2 *v.*

smock (smok) a loose outer garment worn to protect clothing. *n.*

smog (smog) a combination in the air of smoke and fog: *Automobile exhaust fumes are one of the major causes of smog.* *n.*

☞ **Smog** is formed from *sm*oke and f*og*.

smoke (smōk) 1 the mixture of gases and carbon that can be seen rising in a cloud from anything burning. 2 something like this. 3 give off smoke or steam, or something like it: *The fireplace smokes. The turkey was brought smoking hot to the table.* 4 draw the smoke from a pipe, cigar, or cigarette into the mouth and puff it out again. 5 the act or period of smoking tobacco. 6 preserve or flavor meat, fish, etc. by exposing to smoke: *People smoke fish to preserve them.* 1, 2, 5 *n.*, 3, 4, 6 *v.*, **smoked, smok·ing.** —**smok′er,** *n.*

smoke out, drive out by smoke: *We tried in vain to smoke the groundhog out of its hole.*

smoke·house (smōk′hous′) a building or place in which meat, fish, etc. are treated with smoke to keep them from spoiling. *n.*

smoke·jump·er (smōk′jump′ər) a man who, especially equipped to fight forest fires, is dropped by parachute into a stricken area: *The smokejumpers got there in time to prevent the fire from spreading.* *n.*

smoke·stack (smōk′stak′) 1 a tall chimney. 2 a pipe that discharges smoke: *The smokestack of a steamship or locomotive. n.*

smok·y (smōk′ē) 1 giving off much smoke: *a smoky fire.* 2 full of smoke. 3 darkened or stained with smoke. 4 like smoke or suggesting smoke: *a smoky grey, a smoky taste. adj.,* **smok·i·er, smok·i·est.**

smol·der (smōl′dər) See **smoulder.**

smooth (smüᴛʜ) 1 having an even surface, like glass, silk, or still water; flat; level: *smooth stones.* 2 free from unevenness or roughness: *smooth sailing, a smooth voyage.* 3 without lumps: *smooth gravy.* 4 easy; flowing; polished; pleasant; polite: *That salesman is a smooth talker.* 5 make smooth or smoother; make flat: *Smooth this dress with a hot iron. He smoothed out the ball of crushed paper and read what was on it.* 6 make easy: *His pleasantness smoothed the way to an agreement.* 1–4 *adj.,* 5, 6 *v.*

smooth away, get rid of troubles or difficulties: *He smoothed away all objections to the plan.*

smooth down, to calm or soothe: *She smoothed down her father's temper after the quarrel.*

smooth over, make something seem less wrong, unpleasant, or noticeable: *The teacher tried to smooth over the argument between the two boys.*

smor·gas·bord (smôr′gəs bôrd′) a buffet meal featuring a large variety of meats, salads, etc. *n.*

☛ **Smorgasbord** comes from a Swedish word *smörgasbord,* meaning 'sandwich table.'

smote (smōt) See **smite.** *God smote the wicked city with fire from heaven. v.*

smoth·er (smuᴛʜ′ər) 1 make unable to get air; kill by depriving of air: *The murderer smothered his victim with a pillow.* 2 deaden or put out by covering thickly: *The fire is smothered by ashes.* 3 be unable to breathe freely; suffocate: *We are smothering in this stuffy room.* 4 cover thickly: *In the fall the grass is smothered with leaves.* 5 keep back; check: *He smothered a sharp reply. His smothered anger suddenly broke out. v.*

smoul·der or **smol·der** (smōl′dər) 1 burn and smoke without flame: *The fire smouldered most of the night.* 2 a slow, smoky burning without flame; smouldering. 3 exist or continue in a suppressed condition: *The people's discontent smouldered for years before it broke out into open rebellion.* 4 show suppressed feeling: *The man's eyes smouldered with anger as he waited for a chance to fight back.* 1, 3, 4 *v.,* 2 *n.*

smudge (smuj) 1 a dirty mark; a smear. 2 smear: *The child's drawing was smudged.* 3 a smoky fire made to drive away insects or to protect fruit and plants from frost. 1, 3 *n.,* 2 *v.,* **smudged, smudg·ing.**

smug (smug) self-satisfied; too pleased with one's own goodness, cleverness, etc.: *Nothing disturbs the smug beliefs of some prim, narrow-minded people. adj.,* **smug·ger, smug·gest.**

smug·gle (smug′əl) 1 bring in or take out of a country secretly and against the law: *They were sentenced to several years in prison for smuggling opium into Canada.* 2 bring, take, put, etc. secretly: *He tried to smuggle his puppy into the house. v.,* **smug·gled, smug·gling. —smug′gler,** *n.*

snack (snak) a light meal: *He eats a snack before going to bed. n.*

snack bar a counter where light meals, coffee, etc. are served.

snag (snag) 1 a tree or branch held fast in a river or lake: *Snags are dangerous to boats.* 2 any sharp or rough projecting point such as the broken end of a branch. 3 a hidden or unexpected obstacle: *He had to drop his plans because of a snag.* 4 a pulled or broken thread in fabric. 5 catch on a snag: *He snagged his coat on a nail.* 1–4 *n.,* 5 *v.,* **snagged, snag·ging.**

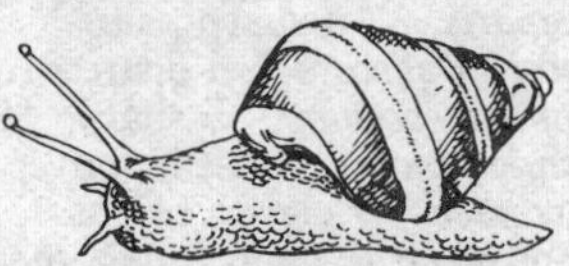

A tree snail found in Florida — about 25 mm long

snail (snāl) a small, soft-bodied animal that crawls very slowly: *Most snails have shells on their backs into which they can pull back for protection. n.*

Snake: a prairie rattlesnake — about 120 cm long

snake (snāk) 1 a long, slender reptile without legs: *Some snakes are poisonous.* 2 a sly, treacherous person. 3 to move, wind, or curve like a snake: *The narrow road snaked through the mountains.* 1, 2 *n.,* 3 *v.,* **snaked, snak·ing.**

snap (snap) 1 make or cause to make a sudden, sharp sound: *This wood snaps as it burns. The teacher snapped her fingers to get our attention.* 2 a quick, sharp sound: *The small box shut with a snap.* 3 move, shut, catch, etc. with a snap: *The latch snapped.* 4 break suddenly or sharply: *The violin string snapped.* 5 a sudden breaking or the sound of breaking: *The blade broke with a snap.* 6 make a sudden, quick bite or snatch: *The dog snapped at the child's hand. The dog snapped up the meat.* 7 seize eagerly: *snap up a bargain. She snapped at the chance to go to visit her uncle.* 8 a quick, sudden bite or snatch: *The dog made a snap at a fly.* 9 speak quickly and sharply: *'Silence!' snapped the captain. Don't snap at him; he doesn't understand what you want.* 10 move quickly and sharply: *The soldiers snapped to attention. Her eyes snapped with anger.* 11 a quick, sharp way: *She moves with snap and energy.* 12 a fastener; a clasp: *One of the snaps of your dress is unfastened.* 13 a thin, crisp cookie: *a vanilla snap.* 14 made or done suddenly: *A snap judgment is likely to be wrong.* 15 take a snapshot of. 16 *Informal.* a snapshot. 17 *Slang.* an easy job, piece of work, etc. 18 in football, the act of passing the ball between the legs by the centre: *That was a bad snap.* 19 pass the ball between the legs in a football game. 20 in football, the player in the middle of the line of scrimmage; the centre. 1, 3, 4, 6, 7, 9, 10, 15, 19 *v.,* **snapped, snap·ping;** 2, 5, 8, 11–13, 16–18, 20 *n.,* 14 *adj.*

cold snap, a few days of cold weather.

snap·drag·on (snap′drag′ən) a garden plant with showy flowers of various colors. *n.*

hat, āge, fär; let, ēqual, tėrm; it, īce
hot, ōpen, ôrder; oil, out; cup, pu̇t, rüle
əbove, takən, pencəl, lemən, circəs
ch, child; ng, long; sh, ship
th, thin; ᴛʜ, then; zh, measure

snapping turtle a large, savage turtle of North American rivers that has powerful jaws with which it snaps at its prey.

snap·py (snap′ē) **1** sharp in speech or manner. **2** snapping or crackling in sound: *a snappy fire.* **3** *Informal.* having snap, smartness, etc.; lively: *a snappy cheese, a snappy sports jacket. adj.,* **snap·pi·er, snap·pi·est.**

snap·shot (snap′shot′) a photograph taken informally with a simple camera. *n.*

snare (sner) **1** a noose for catching small animals and birds: *The boys made snares to catch rabbits.* **2** catch with a snare; trap: *One day they snared a wounded skunk.* 1 *n.,* 2 *v.,* **snared, snar·ing.**

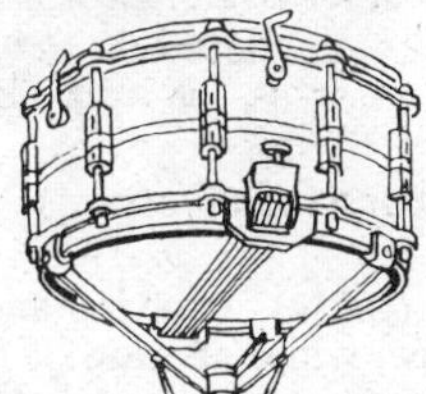

A snare drum, showing the snares on the bottom

snare drum a small drum with strings stretched across the bottom to make a rattling sound.

snarl[1] (snärl) **1** growl sharply and show one's teeth: *The dog snarled at the stranger.* **2** a sharp, angry growl. **3** speak harshly in a sharp, angry tone: *The speaker snarled at the crowd.* **4** say or express with a snarl: *The bully snarled a threat.* **5** a sharp, angry tone or remark: *A snarl was his only reply.* 1, 3, 4 *v.,* 2, 5 *n.*

snarl[2] (snärl) **1** a tangle: *She combed the snarls out of her hair.* **2** confusion: *His business affairs were in a snarl.* **3** tangle or become tangled: *Her hair snarls easily.* **4** confuse. 1, 2 *n.,* 3, 4 *v.*

snatch (snach) **1** seize or grab suddenly: *The hawk snatched the chicken and flew away.* **2** seizing; a sudden, grabbing movement: *The boy made a snatch at the ball.* **3** take suddenly: *He snatched off his hat and bowed.* **4** a short time: *He had a snatch of sleep sitting in his chair.* **5** a small amount; a bit or scrap: *We heard snatches of their conversation as they raised their voices from time to time.* 1, 3 *v.,* 2, 4, 5 *n.*

snatch at, a try to seize or grasp: *He snatched at the rail.* **b** take advantage of eagerly: *He snatched at the chance to travel.*

sneak (snēk) **1** move in a stealthy, sly way: *The man sneaked about the barn watching for a chance to steal the cow.* **2** get, put, pass, etc. in a stealthy, sly way: *The boys sneaked the puppy into the house.* **3** act like a thief or a person who is ashamed to be seen: *He sneaked in by the back way.* **4** a person who sneaks; a sneaking, cowardly person. **5** stealthy; underhand; sneaking: *a sneak thief, a sneak attack.* 1–3 *v.,* 4 *n.,* 5 *adj.*

sneak·ers (snē′kərz) light canvas shoes with rubber soles, used for games, sports, or casual wear. *n. pl.*

sneak·y (snē′kē) sly, mean, or underhand. *adj.*

sneer (snēr) **1** show scorn or contempt by looks or words: *The mean girls sneered at poor Anna's clothes.* **2** a look or words expressing scorn or contempt: *He feared sneers more than blows.* **3** say or express with scorn or contempt: *'Bah!' he sneered with a curl of his lip.* 1, 3 *v.,* 2 *n.*

sneeze (snēz) **1** expel air suddenly and violently through the nose and mouth: *The pepper made her sneeze. A person sneezes when he has a cold.* **2** a sudden, violent expelling of air through the nose and mouth. 1 *v.,* **sneezed, sneez·ing;** 2 *n.*

sneeze at, *Informal.* treat with contempt; despise; scorn: *Ten dollars is not a sum to be sneezed at.*

snick·er (snik′ər) **1** a giggle; a sly or silly laugh. **2** giggle or laugh in a silly way. 1 *n.,* 2 *v.*

snide (snīd) mean or spiteful in a sly way: *a snide remark. adj.*

snies (snīz) a plural of **snye.** *n. pl.*

sniff (snif) **1** draw air through the nose in short, quick breaths that can be heard: *The man who had a cold was sniffing.* **2** smell with sniffs: *The dog sniffed at the stranger.* **3** try the smell of: *He sniffed the medicine before taking a spoonful of it.* **4** draw in through the nose with the breath: *He sniffed steam to clear his head.* **5** the act or sound of sniffing: *He cleared his nose with a loud sniff.* **6** show contempt by sniffing: *She sniffed at the present he gave her.* **7** a single breathing in of something; breath. 1–4, 6 *v.,* 5, 7 *n.*

snif·fle (snif′əl) **1** sniff again and again, as one does from a cold in the head or in trying to stop crying. **2** the act or sound of sniffing. **3 the sniffles,** a slight cold in the head. 1 *v.,* **snif·fled, snif·fling;** 2, 3 *n.*

snip (snip) **1** cut with a small, quick stroke or series of strokes with scissors: *She snipped the thread.* **2** the act of snipping: *With a few snips she cut out a paper doll.* **3** a small piece cut off: *Pick up the snips of cloth and thread from the floor.* 1 *v.,* **snipped, snip·ping;** 2, 3 *n.*

snipe (snīp) **1** a marsh bird with a long bill. **2** shoot as a sniper does. 1 *n.,* 2 *v.,* **snipe** or **snipes, sniped, snip·ing.**

snip·er (snīp′ər) person who shoots from a concealed place at one enemy or target at a time, as a sportsman shoots at game. *n.*

sniv·el (sniv′əl) **1** cry with sniffling. **2** put on a show of grief; whine. *v.,* **sniv·elled** or **sniv·eled, sniv·el·ling** or **sniv·el·ing.**

snob (snob) a person who cares too much for wealth and social position, who tries too hard to please or imitate those above him and who ignores those below him. *n.*

snoop (snüp) *Informal.* **1** go about in a sneaking, prying way; pry: *The old lady snooped into everybody's business.* **2** a person who snoops. 1 *v.,* 2 *n.*

snooze (snüz) *Informal.* **1** sleep; doze; take a nap: *The dog snoozed on the porch in the sun.* **2** a doze; nap. 1 *v.,* **snoozed, snooz·ing;** 2 *n.*

snore (snôr) **1** breathe during sleep with a harsh, rough sound: *People often snore when sleeping on their backs.* **2** the sound made by a person snoring. 1 *v.,* **snored, snor·ing;** 2 *n.*

snor·kel (snôr′kəl) **1** a shaft for taking in air and

discharging gases, which allows submarines to remain under water for a long time. See **submarine** for picture. **2** a curved tube which enables swimmers to breathe under water while swimming near the surface. *n.*

snort (snôrt) **1** force the breath violently through the nose with a loud, harsh sound: *The horse snorted.* **2** make a sound like this: *The engine snorted.* **3** the act or sound of snorting. **4** say with a snort: *'Indeed!' snorted my aunt.* 1, 2, 4 *v.*, 3 *n.*

snout (snout) **1** the long nose of an animal; the nose and mouth of an animal: *Pigs, dogs, and crocodiles have snouts.* **2** anything like an animal's snout. *n.*

snow (snō) **1** frozen water in soft, white flakes that fall to earth and cover it as a white layer: *Rain falls in summer; snow falls in winter.* **2** a fall of snow. **3** fall as snow: *to snow all day.* **4** let fall or scatter as snow: *Petals from the apple blossoms were snowing over the garden.* 1, 2 *n.*, 3, 4 *v.*

snow in or **snow up,** shut in by snow: *The town was snowed in for almost a week.*

snow under, a cover completely with snow. **b** *Informal.* overwhelm: *He is snowed under with work.*

snow·ball (snō′bol′ or snō′bôl′) **1** a ball made of snow pressed together. **2** throw balls of snow at: *They snowballed each other.* **3** a shrub with white flowers in large clusters like balls. **4** increase rapidly by additions like a rolling snowball: *The number of signers of the petition for a swimming pool snowballed.* 1, 3 *n.*, 2, 4 *v.*

snow blindness a temporary or partial blindness caused by the reflection of sunlight from snow or ice.

snow–bound (snō′bound′) shut in by snow; snowed in. *adj.*

snow·drift (snō′drift′) **1** a bank of snow piled up by wind. **2** snow driven before the wind. *n.*

snow·fall (snō′fol′ or snō′fôl′) **1** a fall of snow. **2** the amount of snow falling within a certain time and area: *The snowfall last night was 20 centimetres.* *n.*

snow·flake (snō′flāk′) a small, feathery piece of snow. *n.*

snow goose a type of wild goose, white with black wing tips, that breeds in the Arctic.

snow·man (snō′man′) a mass of snow made into a figure shaped somewhat like a man. *n., pl.* **snow·men** (snō′men′).

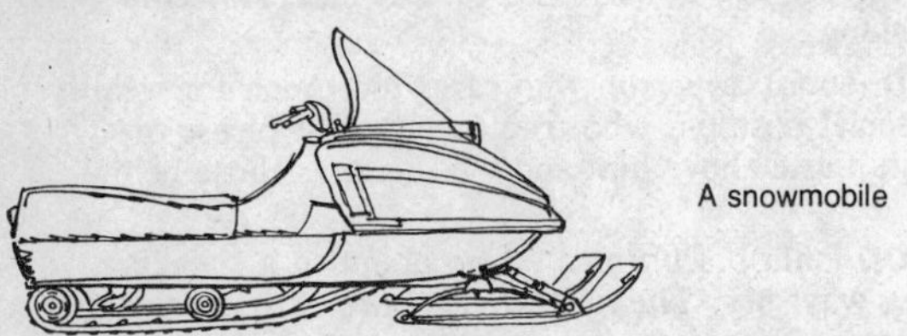

A snowmobile

snow·mo·bile (snō′mə bēl′) a powerful vehicle equipped with caterpillar tracks and used for travelling over snow and ice: *A bombardier is one kind of snowmobile.* *n.*

snow·plough or **snow·plow** (snō′plou′) a machine for clearing away snow from streets, railway tracks, etc. *n.*

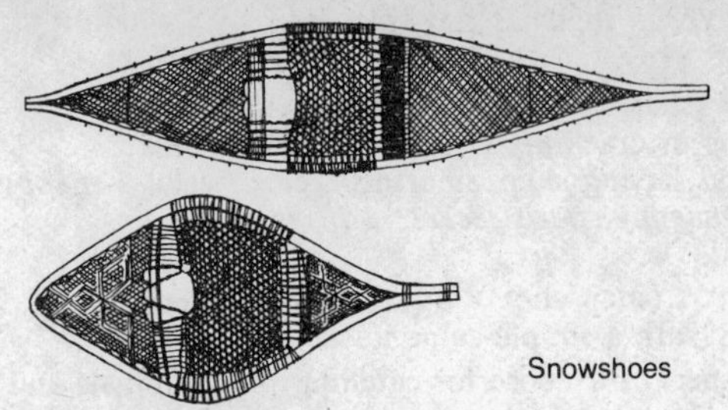

Snowshoes

snow·shoe (snō′shü′) **1** a light, wooden frame with strips of leather stretched across it: *Trappers in the far North wear snowshoes on their feet to keep from sinking in deep, soft snow.* **2** walk or travel on snowshoes. 1 *n.*, 2 *v.*

snow·storm (snō′stôrm′) a storm with much snow. *n.*

snow·y (snō′ē) **1** having snow. **2** covered with snow. **3** like snow; white as snow: *The old lady has snowy hair.* *adj.*, **snow·i·er, snow·i·est.**

snub (snub) **1** treat coldly, scornfully, or with contempt: *The wealthy widow snubbed her poor cousin.* **2** cold, scornful, or disdainful treatment. **3** short and turned up at the tip: *a snub nose.* 1 *v.*, **snubbed, snub·bing;** 2, 3 *adj.*

snuff[1] (snuf) **1** draw in through the nose; draw up into the nose: *He snuffs up salt and water to cure a cold.* **2** sniff; smell: *The young hound snuffed at the track of the fox.* **3** powdered tobacco that is snuffed into the nose. 1, 2 *v.*, 3 *n.*

up to snuff, *Informal.* in perfect order or condition; as good as expected.

snuff[2] (snuf) **1** cut or pinch off the burned part of the wick of a candle. **2** put out a candle; extinguish. *v.*

snuff out, put an end to suddenly and completely: *The new dictator snuffed out the people's hopes for freedom.*

snug (snug) **1** comfortable; warm; sheltered: *The cat has found a snug corner behind the stove.* **2** neat; trim; compact: *The cabins on the boat are snug.* **3** fitting closely: *That coat is a little too snug.* **4** hidden; concealed: *He lay snug until the searchers passed by.* *adj.*, **snug·ger, snug·gest.**

snug·gle (snug′əl) lie or press closely for warmth or comfort or from affection; nestle; cuddle. *v.*, **snug·gled, snug·gling.**

snye or **sny** (snī) *Cdn.* a side channel of a stream or river: *There are many snyes in the Mackenzie River.* *n., pl.* **snyes** or **snies.**

☛ Snye comes from a Canadian French word *chenail,* meaning 'channel.'

so[1] (sō) **1** in that way; in the same way or degree; in such a way; as stated; as shown: *Hold your pen so. The chair is broken and has been so for a long time. Do not walk so fast. He is not so tall as his brother. She is sick. Is that so?* **2** very: *You are so kind.* **3** very much: *My head aches so!* **4** therefore; accordingly; for that reason: *The dog seemed hungry; so we fed him.* **5** with the result that; in order that: *Go away so I can rest.* **6** So is sometimes used alone to ask a question or to exclaim: *So! Late again! The train is late. So?* 1–3 *adv.*, 4, 5 *conj.*, 6 *interj.*

and so, a likewise; also: *Pete is here, and so is Joe.* **b**

hat, āge, fär; let, ēqual, tėrm; it, īce
hot, ōpen, ôrder; oil, out; cup, pu̇t, rüle
əbove, takən, pencəl, lemən, circəs
ch, child; ng, long; sh, ship
th, thin; ᴛʜ, then; zh, measure

accordingly: *I said I would go, and so I shall.*
or so, more or less: *It came a day or so ago.*
so as, with the aim or purpose: *He goes to bed early so as to get enough sleep.*
so that, with the result or purpose that: *Work so that you will succeed.*
☞ **So, sew,** and **sow**[1] are pronounced the same.

so[2] (sō) the fifth tone of the musical scale; sol. See **do**[2] for picture. *n.*
☞ See note at **so**[1].

soak (sōk) **1** make very wet; wet through: *The rain soaked my clothes.* **2** let remain in water or other liquid until wet through: *Soak the clothes all night before you wash them.* **3** become very wet. **4** the act or process of soaking: *Give the clothes a long soak.* **5** go; enter; make its way: *Water will soak through the earth.* 1–3, 5 *v.,* 4 *n.*
soak up, absorb: *The sponge soaked up the water.*

soap (sōp) **1** a substance used for washing, usually made of a fat and lye. **2** rub with soap: *Soap the dirty shirts well.* 1 *n.,* 2 *v.*

soap·stone (sōp′stōn′) a heavy, soft stone that feels somewhat like soap: *Eskimo carvings are often made of soapstone.* *n.*

soap·suds (sōp′sudz′) bubbles and foam made with soap and water. *n. pl.*

soap·y (sōp′ē) **1** covered with soap or soapsuds. **2** containing soap: *soapy water.* **3** of or like soap: *The water has a soapy taste.* *adj.,* **soap·i·er, soap·i·est.**

soar (sôr) **1** fly at a great height; fly upward: *The eagle soared without flapping its wings.* **2** rise beyond what is common and ordinary: *His hopes soared when he found there was a letter for him. Prices are soaring.* *v.*
☞ **Soar** and **sore** are pronounced the same.

sob (sob) **1** cry or sigh with short, quick breaths: *The child sobbed itself to sleep.* **2** a catching of short, quick breaths because of grief, etc. **3** make a sound like a sob: *The wind sobbed.* **4** say or express with sobs: *She sobbed out her sad story.* 1, 3, 4 *v.,* **sobbed, sob·bing;** 2 *n.*

so·ber (sō′bər) **1** not drunk. **2** temperate; moderate: *The Puritans led sober, hard-working lives.* **3** quiet; serious; solemn: *He looked sober at the thought of missing the picnic.* **4** calm; sensible; free from exaggeration: *The judge's sober opinion was not influenced by prejudice or strong feeling.* **5** make or become sober: *Seeing the car accident sobered us all. The class sobered as the teacher came into the room.* 1–4 *adj.,* 5 *v.*

so–called (sō′kold′ or sō′kôld′) called so, but really not so: *Her so-called friend hasn't even written to her.* *adj.*

soc·cer (sok′ər) a game played between two teams of eleven men each, using a round ball. The ball may be struck with any part of the body except the hands and arms. *n.*

so·cia·ble (sō′shə bəl) **1** liking company; friendly: *They are a sociable family and entertain a great deal.* **2** with conversation and companionship: *We had a sociable gathering.* **3** an informal social gathering. 1, 2 *adj.,* 3 *n.*

so·cial (sō′shəl) **1** of or dealing with human beings in their relations to each other; having to do with the life of human beings in a community or society: *social conditions, social problems.* **2** living or liking to live with others: *Man is a social being.* **3** for companionship or friendliness; having to do with companionship or friendliness: *Ten of us girls have formed a social club.* **4** liking company: *She has a social nature.* **5** connected with fashionable society: *She is the social leader of our town.* **6** a social gathering or party. **7** of animals, living together in communities: *Ants and bees are social insects.* 1–5, 7 *adj.,* 6 *n.* **—so′cial·ly,** *adv.*

Social Credit Party a Canadian political party, founded in Alberta in the 1930's.

social studies school subjects, including history and geography, that deal with the development of peoples, their societies, and the parts of the world in which they live.

social work work directed toward the betterment of social conditions in a community: *Social work includes such services as medical clinics, counselling for families, and recreational activities.*

social worker a person who does social work.

so·ci·e·ty (sə sī′ə tē) **1** all the people; the people of any particular time or place; their activities and customs: *Many organizations work for the good of society. Canadian society benefits from a wide variety of ethnic backgrounds. Magic plays an important part in primitive society.* **2** a group of persons joined together for a common purpose or by common interests: *A club, a fraternity, a lodge, or an association may be called a society.* **3** company; companionship: *I enjoy your society.* **4** fashionable people or their doings: *Her mother is a leader of society.* *n., pl.* **so·ci·e·ties.**

sock (sok) a close-fitting, knitted covering for the foot and lower leg. *n.*

sock·et (sok′it) a hollow part or piece for receiving and holding something: *A candlestick has a socket in which to set a candle. Eyes are set in sockets. An electric lamp has a socket into which a bulb is screwed.* *n.*

sock·eye (sok′ī′) a variety of red salmon found in the North Pacific: *Canned sockeye is a popular food.* *n., pl.* **sock·eye** or **sock·eyes.**

So·cred (sō′kred′) **1** the Social Credit Party. **2** a member of this party. *n.*

sod (sod) **1** ground covered with grass. **2** a piece or layer of such ground containing the grass and its roots: *Some pioneers built houses of sods.* **3** cover with sods: *We must have all the bare spots on our lawn sodded.* 1, 2 *n.,* 3 *v.,* **sod·ded, sod·ding.**

so·da (sō′də) **1** any of several chemical substances containing sodium, such as sodium bicarbonate. **2** soda water. **3** soda water flavored with fruit juice or syrup, and often containing ice cream. *n.*

soda fountain a counter having places for holding soda water, flavored syrups, ice cream, etc.

soda water water charged with carbon dioxide to

make it bubble and fizz, often served with the addition of syrup, ice cream, etc.

sod·den (sod′ən) 1 soaked through: *His clothing was sodden with rain.* 2 heavy and moist: *This bread is sodden because it was not baked well.* *adj.*

so·di·um (sō′dē əm) a soft, silver-white, metallic element which reacts violently with water: *Salt and soda contain sodium.* *n.*

sodium bicarbonate bicarbonate of soda.

so·fa (sō′fə) a long, upholstered seat or couch having a back and arms; chesterfield. *n.*

soft (soft) 1 not hard; not stiff; yielding easily to touch: *Feathers, cotton, and wool are soft.* 2 not hard compared with other things of the same sort: *Pine is softer than oak. Copper and lead are softer than steel.* 3 smooth; pleasant to the touch; not rough or coarse: *the soft hair of a kitten, soft silk.* 4 quietly pleasant; mild: *a soft spring morning, soft air, soft words, the soft light of candles.* 5 gentle; kind; tender: *a soft voice, soft eyes, a soft heart.* 6 weak: *The soldiers had become soft from idleness and luxury.* 7 softly; gently. 8 See **soft water.** 1–6, 8 *adj.*, 7 *adv.* —**soft′ly,** *adv.* —**soft′ness,** *n.*

soft·ball (soft′bol′ or soft′bôl′) 1 a kind of baseball game: *A larger ball and lighter bats are used in softball than in baseball.* 2 the ball used in this game. *n.*

soft coal coal that burns with a yellow, smoky flame; bituminous coal.

soft drink a drink that does not contain alcohol: *Pop is a soft drink.*

soft·en (sof′ən) 1 make softer: *Hand lotion softens the skin.* 2 become softer: *Soap softens in water.* *v.*

soft–heart·ed (sôft′här′tid) gentle; kind; tender. *adj.*

soft palate the fleshy back part of the roof of the mouth.

soft water water containing few or no minerals, in which soapsuds are easily formed and clothes are easily washed.

soft·wood (soft′wůd′) 1 a tree that has needles or does not have broad leaves: *Pine is a softwood; oak is a hardwood.* 2 the wood of such a tree. *n.*

sog·gy (sog′ē) 1 soaked; thoroughly wet. 2 damp and heavy: *soggy bread.* *adj.*, **sog·gi·er, sog·gi·est.**

soil[1] (soil) 1 ground; earth; dirt: *Most plants grow best in rich soil.* 2 one's land or country: *This is my native soil.* *n.*

soil[2] (soil) 1 make dirty: *She soiled her dress.* 2 become dirty: *White gloves soil easily.* 3 to disgrace; to dishonor: *His actions have soiled the family name.* *v.*

so·journ (sō jėrn′ or sō′jėrn for 1, sō′jėrn for 2) 1 dwell for a time: *The Jews sojourned in the land of Egypt.* 2 a brief stay; a stay that is not permanent: *During their sojourn in Turkey, the family learned much about the customs there.* 1 *v.*, 2 *n.*

sol (sōl) the fifth tone of the musical scale. *n.* Also, **so.**

sol·ace (sol′is) 1 comfort; relief: *She found solace from her troubles in music.* 2 to comfort; cheer; relieve: *She solaced herself with a book.* 1 *n.*, 2 *v.*, **sol·aced, sol·ac·ing.**

so·lar (sō′lər) 1 of or having to do with the sun: *a solar eclipse.* 2 See **solar system.** 3 measured or determined by the earth's motion in relation to the sun: *solar time.* 4 working by means of the sun's light or heat: *A solar battery traps sunlight and converts it into electrical energy.* *adj.*

solar system the sun and all the planets, satellites, comets, etc. that revolve around it.

sold (sōld) See **sell.** *He sold it a week ago. He has sold his car.* *v.*

sol·der (sod′ər) 1 a metal or alloy that can be melted and used for joining or mending metal surfaces, parts, etc. 2 fasten, mend, or join with solder: *He soldered the broken wires together.* 1 *n.*, 2 *v.*

sol·dier (sōl′jər) 1 a man who serves in an army. 2 an enlisted man in the army, not a commissioned officer. 3 act or serve as a soldier. 1, 2 *n.*, 3 *v.*

sole[1] (sōl) 1 one and only; single: *He was the sole heir to the fortune when his aunt died.* 2 only: *We three were the sole survivors from the wreck.* *adj.*

sole[2] (sōl) 1 the bottom or under surface of the foot. 2 the bottom of a shoe, slipper, boot, etc. 3 a piece of leather, rubber, etc. cut in the shape of the bottom of a shoe, slipper, boot, etc. 4 put a sole on: *I must have my shoes soled.* 1–3 *n.*, 4 *v.* **soled, sol·ing.**

sole[3] (sōl) a kind of flat fish: *European sole is very good to eat.* *n.*, *pl.* **sole** or **soles.**

sole·ly (sōl′lē) 1 as the only one or ones; alone: *I am solely responsible for providing the lunch.* 2 only; purely; entirely: *He does it solely for convenience.* *adv.*

sol·emn (sol′əm) 1 serious; grave; earnest: *He gave his solemn promise to do better. That minister speaks in a solemn voice.* 2 causing serious thoughts: *The organ played solemn music.* 3 done with form and ceremony: *a solemn procession.* *adj.*

so·lem·ni·ty (sə lem′nə tē) 1 a solemn feeling; seriousness; impressiveness: *The solemnity of the church service was felt even by the children.* 2 a solemn, formal ceremony: *Easter is observed with solemnities.* *n.*, *pl.* **so·lem·ni·ties.**

so·lic·it (sə lis′it) 1 ask earnestly; try to get: *The tailor has sent around cards soliciting trade.* 2 make appeals or requests: *to solicit for contributions to the Red Cross.* *v.*

sol·id (sol′id) 1 not a liquid or a gas: *Water becomes solid when it freezes.* 2 not hollow: *A bar of iron is solid; a pipe is hollow.* 3 hard; firm: *They were glad to leave the boat and put their feet on solid ground.* 4 strongly made or put together: *This is not a very solid table.* 5 alike throughout: *The cloth is a solid blue.* 6 firmly united: *The country was solid for defending itself.* 7 that can be depended on: *He is a solid citizen.* 8 whole; entire: *He spent a solid hour on his arithmetic.* 9 undivided; continuous: *a solid row of houses.* 10 a substance that is not a liquid or a gas: *Iron, wood, and ice are solids.* 11 a body that has length, breadth, and thickness: *A cube is a solid.* 1–9 *adj.*, 10, 11 *n.*

so·lid·i·fy (sə lid′ə fī′) make solid; become solid; harden: *Extreme cold will solidify water into ice.* *v.*, **so·lid·i·fied, so·lid·i·fy·ing.**

sol·i·taire (sol′ə ter′) 1 any of various card games played by one person. 2 a diamond or other gem set by itself. *n.*

sol·i·tar·y (sol′ə ter′ē) 1 alone; single; only: *A solitary rider was seen in the distance.* 2 without companions; away from people; lonely: *He leads a solitary life in his* *hut in the mountains. The house is in a solitary spot miles from a town. adj.*

sol·i·tude (sol′ə tyüd′ or sol′ə tüd′) 1 the state or condition of being alone: *She likes company and hates solitude.* 2 a lonely place: *This forest is a solitude. n.*

so·lo (sō′lō) 1 a piece of music for one voice or instrument: *She sang three solos.* 2 arranged for or performed by one voice or instrument: *a solo part.* 3 without a partner, teacher, etc.; alone: *a solo flight across the ocean.* 1 *n., pl.* **so·los;** 2, 3 *adj.*

so·lo·ist (sō′lō ist) a person who performs a solo. *n.*

so long *Informal.* good-bye; farewell.

sol·stice (sol′stis) either of the two times in the year when the sun is at its greatest distance from the equator. In the Northern Hemisphere, June 21 or 22, the *summer solstice,* is the longest day of the year and December 21 or 22, the *winter solstice,* is the shortest. *n.*

sol·u·ble (sol′yə bəl) 1 that can be dissolved: *Salt is soluble in water.* 2 that can be solved: *soluble puzzles. This problem is soluble. adj.*

so·lu·tion (sə lü′shən) 1 the solving of a problem: *That problem was hard; its solution required many hours.* 2 an answer; explanation: *The police are seeking a solution of the crime.* 3 the process of dissolving; the changing of a solid or gas to a liquid by mixing with a liquid. 4 a liquid or mixture formed by dissolving: *Every time you put sugar in lemonade you are making a solution.* 5 separating into parts. 6 the condition of being dissolved: *Sugar and salt can be held in solution in water. n.*

solve (solv) find the answer to; clear up; explain: *The mystery was never solved. He has solved all the problems in his arithmetic lesson. v.,* **solved, solv·ing.**

sol·vent (sol′vənt) a substance, usually a liquid, that can dissolve other substances: *Water is a solvent of sugar and salt. n.*

som·bre or **som·ber** (som′bər) 1 dark; gloomy: *A cloudy winter day is sombre. It was a sombre room with dark furniture and heavy black hangings.* 2 melancholy; dismal: *His losses made him very sombre. adj.*

A sombrero

som·brer·o (som brer′ō) a broad-brimmed hat worn in the southwestern United States, Mexico, and Spain. *n., pl.* **som·brer·os.**

some (sum) 1 certain or particular, but not known or not named: *Some dogs are large; some are small.* 2 a number of: *Ask some boys to help you. He left the city some years ago.* 3 a quantity of: *Drink some milk.* 4 a certain number or quantity: *He ate some and threw the rest away.* 5 a; any: *Can't you find some kind person who will help you?* 6 about: *Some twenty men asked for work.* 1–3, 5 *adj.,* 4 *pron.,* 6 *adv.*

☛ **Some** and **sum** are pronounced the same.

–some a suffix meaning: tending to, as in *frolicsome, meddlesome.*

some·bod·y (sum′bud′ē or sum′bod′ē) 1 a person not known or not named; some person; someone: *Somebody has taken my pen.* 2 a person of importance: *She acts as if she were somebody since she won the prize.* 1 *pron.,* 2 *n., pl.* **some·bod·ies.**

hat, āge, fär; let, ēqual, tėrm; it, īce
hot, ōpen, ôrder; oil, out; cup, pu̇t, rüle
əbove, takən, pencəl, lemən, circəs
ch, child; ng, long; sh, ship
th, thin; ᴛʜ, then; zh, measure

some·day (sum′dā′) at some future time. *adv.*

some·how (sum′hou′) in a way not known or not stated; in one way or another: *I'll finish this work somehow. adv.*

some·one (sum′wun′) some person; somebody: *Someone has to lock up the house. pron.*

some·place (sum′plās′) in or to some place; somewhere. *adv.*

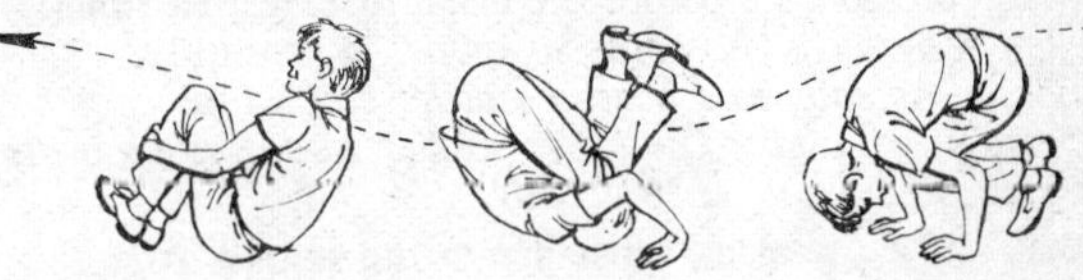

A somersault

som·er·sault (sum′ər solt′ or sum′ər sôlt′) 1 a complete roll of the body, forward or backward, bringing the feet over the head. 2 roll in this way. 1 *n.,* 2 *v.*

some·thing (sum′thing′) 1 some thing; a particular thing not named or not known: *I'm sure I've forgotten something.* 2 a part; a certain amount; a little: *There is something of his father in his smile.* 3 somewhat; to some extent or degree: *He is something like his father.* 4 a thing or person of some value or importance: *He thinks he's something.* 1, 2, 4 *n.,* 3 *adv.*

some·time (sum′tīm′) 1 at one time or another: *come to see us sometime.* 2 at an indefinite point of time: *It happened sometime last March. adv.*

some·times (sum′tīmz′) now and then; at times: *He comes to visit sometimes. adv.*

some·what (sum′wot′ or sum′hwot′) 1 to some extent or degree; slightly: *He has changed somewhat since we last saw him.* 2 some part; some amount: *Somewhat of the fun is lost when you hear a joke a second time.* 1 *adv.,* 2 *n.*

some·where (sum′wer′ or sum′hwer′) 1 in or to some place; in or to one place or another: *He is somewhere about the house.* 2 at some time: *It happened somewhere in the past. adv.*

son (sun) 1 a male child in relation to either or both of his parents: *A boy is the son of his father and mother.* 2 a male descendant. 3 a boy or man attached to a country, cause, etc. as a child is to its parents: *sons of liberty. n.*

☛ **Son** and **sun** are pronounced the same.

so·nar (sō′när) a device for detecting and locating objects under water by the reflection of sound waves. *n.*

☛ **Sonar** is formed from *so*und *na*vigation *r*ange.

so·na·ta (sə nä′tə) a piece of music for one or two instruments, having three or four movements in contrasted rhythms but related keys. *n.*

song (song) 1 something to sing; a short poem set to music. 2 singing: *The canary burst into song.* 3 poetry that has a musical sound. 4 any sound like singing: *the cricket's song, the song of the teakettle. n.*
for a song, very cheaply: *to buy things for a song.*

song·bird (song′bėrd′) a bird that sings. *n.*

song·ster (song′stər) 1 singer. 2 a writer of songs or poems. 3 songbird. *n.*

son–in–law (sun′in lo′ or sun′in lô′) the husband of one's daughter. *n., pl.* **sons-in-law.**

so·no·rous (sə nô′rəs or son′ər əs) 1 giving out or having a deep, loud sound: *a big, sonorous church bell.* 2 full and rich in sound. *adj.*

Sons of Freedom a sect of Doukhobors, located, for the most part, in British Columbia.

soon (sün) 1 in a short time; before long: *I will see you again soon.* 2 before the usual or expected time; early: *Why have you come so soon?* 3 promptly; quickly: *As soon as I hear, I will let you know.* 4 readily; willingly: *The brave soldier would as soon die as yield to such an enemy. adv.*

soot (sůt) the black substance in the smoke from burning coal, wood, oil, etc.: *Soot makes smokes dark and collects on the inside of chimneys. n.*

soothe (süᴛʜ) 1 quiet; calm; comfort: *The mother soothed the crying child.* 2 make less painful; ease: *Heat soothes some aches; cold soothes others. v.,* **soothed, sooth·ing.**

sooth·say·er (süth′sā′ər) a person who claims to foretell the future; a person who makes prophecies. *n.*

sop (sop) 1 dip or soak: *He sopped the bread in milk.* 2 take up water, etc.; wipe; mop: *Please sop up that water with a cloth.* 3 something given to soothe or quiet; bribe. 1, 2 *v.,* **sopped, sop·ping;** 3 *n.*
sopping wet, soaked; drenched.

so·phis·ti·cat·ed (sə fis′tə kāt′id) 1 experienced in worldly ways; informed; knowing; aware. 2 no longer having natural simplicity or frankness. 3 of mechanical or electronic devices, complex and advanced in design: *sophisticated missiles. adj.*

soph·o·more (sof′ə môr′) a student in the second year of college. *n.*

so·pran·o (sə pran′ō) 1 the highest singing voice in women and boys. 2 a singer with such a voice. 3 a part to be sung by a soprano voice. 4 of, for, or having something to do with the soprano. *n., pl.* **so·pran·os.**
☛ **Soprano** comes from an Italian word that developed from Latin *supra,* meaning 'above.'

sor·cer·er (sôr′sər ər) a man who supposedly practises magic with the aid of evil spirits; magician. *n.*

sor·cer·ess (sôr′sər is) a woman who supposedly practises magic with the aid of evil spirits; witch. *n.*

sor·cer·y (sôr′sər ē) magic supposedly performed with the aid of evil spirits; witchcraft: *The prince had been changed into a lion by sorcery. n., pl.* **sor·cer·ies.**

sor·did (sôr′did) 1 dirty; filthy: *The poor family lived in a sordid hut.* 2 mean or base; contemptible: *a sordid trick. adj.*

sore (sôr) 1 painful; aching; tender; smarting: *a sore finger.* 2 a painful place on the body where the skin or flesh is broken or bruised. 3 sad; distressed: *The suffering of the poor makes her heart sore.* 4 *Informal.* offended; angered: *He is sore at missing the game.* 5 causing pain, misery, anger, or offence: *Their defeat is a sore subject with the members of the team.* 6 a cause of pain, sorrow, sadness, anger, offence, etc. 7 severe; distressing: *Your going away is a sore grief to us.* 1, 3–5, 7 *adj.,* **sor·er, sor·est;** 2, 6 *n.* **—sore′ly,** *adv.* **—sore′ness,** *n.*
☛ Sore and **soar** are pronounced the same.

sor·rel[1] (sôr′əl) 1 reddish brown: *a sorrel horse.* 2 a reddish-brown horse. 1 *adj.,* 1, 2 *n.*

sor·rel[2] (sôr′əl) a plant with sour leaves and juice. *n.*

sor·row (sor′ō) 1 grief; sadness; regret: *She felt sorrow at the loss of her kitten. She expressed sorrow at her mistake.* 2 a cause of grief or sadness; trouble; suffering; misfortune: *Her sorrows have aged her.* 3 feel or show grief, sadness, or regret; be sad; feel sorrow: *She sorrowed over the lost money.* 1, 2 *n.,* 3 *v.*

sor·row·ful (sor′ə fəl) 1 full of sorrow; feeling sorrow; sad: *a sorrowful person.* 2 showing sorrow: *a sorrowful smile.* 3 causing sorrow: *a sorrowful occasion. adj.*

sor·ry (sor′ē) 1 feeling pity, regret, or sympathy; sad: *I am sorry that you are sick. We are sorry that we cannot come to the party. Everyone is sorry for a blind man.* 2 wretched; poor; pitiful: *The blind beggar in his ragged clothes was a sorry sight. adj.,* **sor·ri·er, sor·ri·est.**

sort (sôrt) 1 a kind or class: *What sort of work does he do? She is not the sort of person to tell tales.* 2 arrange by kinds or classes; arrange in order: *Sort these cards according to their colors.* 1 *n.,* 2 *v.*
out of sorts, ill, cross, or uncomfortable.
sort of, *Informal.* somewhat; rather: *In spite of her faults I sort of like her.*
sort out, separate from others; put: *The farmer sorted out the best apples for eating.*

SOS (es′ō′es′) 1 a signal of distress consisting of the letters *s o s* of the international Morse code (...---...), used in wireless telegraphy by ships, aircraft, etc. 2 *Informal.* an urgent call for help. *n.*

sought (sot or sôt) See **seek.** *For days she sought a safe hiding place. He was sought and found. v.*

soul (sōl) 1 the spiritual part of man, regarded as the source of thought, feeling, and action, and considered as separate from the body: *Many religions believe that the soul and the body are separated in death and that the soul lives forever.* 2 energy of mind or feelings; spirit: *She puts her whole soul into her work.* 3 the cause of inspiration and energy: *Florence Nightingale was the soul of the movement to reform nursing.* 4 a person: *Don't tell a soul. n.*

sound[1] (sound) 1 what is or can be heard: *the sound of music, the sound of thunder.* 2 the distance within which a noise may be heard: *If you go outside, please stay within sound of the phone bell.* 3 make a sound or noise: *The trumpet sounds for battle. The wind sounds like an animal howling.* 4 pronounce: *Sound each syllable.* 5 be pronounced: *'Rough' and 'ruff' sound just alike.* 6 cause to sound: *Sound the trumpets; beat the drums.* 7 order or direct by a sound: *Sound the retreat.* 8 make known; announce; utter: *The trumpets sounded the call to battle. Everyone sounded his praises.* 9 seem: *That excuse sounds queer.* 1, 2 *n.,* 3–9 *v.*

hat, āge, fär; let, ēqual, tėrm; it, īce
hot, ōpen, ôrder; oil, out; cup, pu̇t, rüle
əbove, takən, pencəl, lemən, circəs
ch, child; ng, long; sh, ship
th, thin; ᴛʜ, then; zh, measure

sound² (sound) 1 healthy; free from disease: *a sound body, a sound mind.* 2 free from injury, decay, or defect: *sound walls, a sound ship, sound fruit.* 3 strong; safe; secure: *a sound business firm.* 4 correct; right; reasonable; reliable: *sound advice, sound religious teaching.* 5 thorough; hearty: *a sound whipping, a sound sleep.* 6 deeply; thoroughly: *He was sound asleep.* 1–5 *adj.,* 6 *adv.* **—sound′ly,** *adv.* **—sound′ness,** *n.*

sound³ (sound) 1 measure the depth of water by letting down a weight fastened on the end of a line. 2 try to find out the views of; test; examine: *We sounded Mother on the subject of a picnic.* 3 go toward the bottom; dive: *The whale sounded. v.*

sound⁴ (sound) 1 a long, narrow strip of water joining two larger bodies of water or separating an island and the mainland: *Queen Charlotte Sound.* 2 an inlet or arm of the sea: *Howe's Sound. n.*

sound barrier a sudden increase in air resistance met by an aircraft or projectile as it nears the speed of sound (about 1190 kilometres per hour at sea level).

sound·proof (sound′prüf′) 1 not letting sound pass through: *a soundproof room or ceiling.* 2 make soundproof: *Father soundproofed his den.* 1 *adj.,* 2 *v.*

sound track a recording of the sounds of words, music, etc., made along one edge of a motion-picture film.

soup (süp) a liquid food made by boiling meat, vegetables, fish, etc. *n.*

sour (sour) 1 having a taste like vinegar or lemon juice; sharp and biting: *This green fruit is sour.* 2 fermented; spoiled: *Sour milk is healthful, but most foods are not good to eat when they have become sour.* 3 disagreeable; bad-tempered; peevish: *a sour face, a sour remark.* 4 make sour; become sour; turn sour: *The milk soured in the heat.* 5 make or become peevish, bad-tempered, or disagreeable. 1–3 *adj.,* 4, 5 *v.*

source (sôrs) 1 a person or place from which anything comes or is obtained: *A newspaper gets news from many sources. Mines are the chief source of diamonds.* 2 the beginning of a river or brook; the fountain or spring. *n.*

south (south) 1 the direction to the left as one faces the setting sun; the direction opposite to north. See **compass** for picture. 2 toward the south; farther toward the south: *Drive south forty kilometres.* 3 coming from the south: *a south wind.* 4 in the south; living in the south. 5 Also, **South,** the part of the world, country, or continent toward the south. 6 **the South,** in the United States, the southern part. 1, 5, 6 *n.,* 2 *adv.,* 3, 4 *adj.*

South African 1 of or having to do with South Africa or its people: *a South African story.* 2 a person born in or living in South Africa.

South American 1 of or having to do with South America or its people: *a South American nation.* 2 a person born in or living in South America.

south·east (south′ēst′) 1 the direction halfway between south and east. 2 a place that is in the southeast part or direction. 3 of, at, in, to, toward, or from the southeast: *a southeast wind (adj.). She walked southeast (adv.).* 1, 2 *n.,* 3 *adj., adv.*

south·east·ern (south′ēs′tərn) of, at, in, to, toward, or from the southeast. *adj.*

south·er·ly (suᴛʜ′ər lē) 1 toward the south: *The windows face southerly.* 2 from the south: *a southerly wind. adv., adj.*

south·ern (suᴛʜ′ərn) 1 toward the south: *a southern view.* 2 from the south: *a southern breeze.* 3 of or in the south: *He has travelled in southern countries. adj.*

South·ern·er (suᴛʜ′ər nər) a person born in or living in the South. *n.*

south·paw (south′po′ or south′pô′) *Slang.* 1 a left-handed baseball pitcher. 2 any left-handed person. *n.*

South Pole the southern end of the earth's axis.

south·ward (south′wərd) toward the south; south: *He walked southward. The orchard is on the southward slope of the hill. adv., adj.*

south·wards (south′wərdz) southward. *adv.*

south·west (south′west′) 1 the direction halfway between south and west. 2 a place that is in the southwest part or direction. 3 of, at, in, to, toward, or from the southwest: *a southwest wind (adj.). They walked southwest (adv.).* 1, 2 *n.,* 3 *adj., adv.*

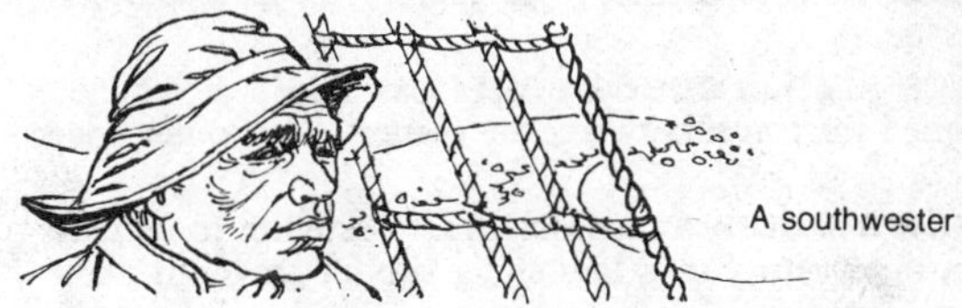
A southwester

south·west·er (south′wes′tər or sou′wes′tər) 1 a wind or storm from the southwest. 2 a waterproof hat with a broad brim at the back to protect the neck. *n.*

south·west·ern (south′wes′tərn) of, at, in, to, toward, or from the southwest. *adj.*

sou·ve·nir (sü′və nēr′ or sü′və nēr′) something given or kept for remembrance; a remembrance; a keepsake: *Father bought us cowboy boots as a souvenir of our holiday in Alberta. n.*

sou′west·er (sou′wes′tər) southwester. *n.*

sov·er·eign (sov′rən) 1 a supreme ruler; a king or queen; a monarch: *Queen Victoria was the sovereign of Great Britain from 1837 to 1901.* 2 greatest in rank or power: *a sovereign court.* 3 above all others; supreme; greatest: *Character is of sovereign importance.* 4 independent of the control of other governments. 5 a former British gold coin, worth one pound. 1, 5 *n.,* 2–4 *adj.*

sov·er·eign·ty (sov′rən tē) 1 supreme power or authority: *The French Revolution resulted in the ending of the king's sovereignty.* 2 freedom from outside control; independence in exercising power or authority: *Countries that are satellites lack full sovereignty.* 3 a state, territory, community, etc. that is independent or sovereign. *n., pl.* **sov·er·eign·ties.**

sow¹ (sō) 1 scatter seed on the ground; plant seed: *He sows more wheat than oats.* 2 plant seed in: *The farmer sowed the field.* 3 scatter anything; spread about: *The enemy tried to sow discontent among our men.* *v.,* **sowed, sown** or **sowed, sow·ing.**

☛ **Sow**[1], **sew,** and **so** are pronounced the same.

sow² (sou) a fully grown female pig. *n.*

sown (sōn) See **sow**[1]. *The field had been sown with oats.* *v.*

☛ **Sown** and **sewn** are pronounced the same.

soy·bean (soi′bēn′) a bean widely grown in Asia and North America: *Soybeans are used in making flour, oil, etc. and as a food.* *n.*

space (spās) 1 the unlimited room or expanse extending in all directions and in which all things exist: *Our earth moves through space.* 2 a limited place or area: *This brick fits a space* 20.32 cm × 6.35 cm. *Is there space in the car for another person?* 3 an extent or area of ground, surface, etc.: *The trees covered acres of space.* 4 See **outer space.** 5 a distance: *The road is bad for a space of five kilometres. The trees are set at equal spaces apart.* 6 a length of time: *Many changes occur within the space of one man's life.* 7 separate by spaces: *Space your words evenly when you write.* 1–6 *n.,* 7 *v.,* **spaced, spac·ing.**

space·craft (spās′kraft′) a vehicle used for flight in outer space. *n.*

space·man (spās′mən) astronaut. *n., pl.* **space·men** (spās′mən).

space ship or **space·ship** (spās′ship′) a vehicle designed for travel between the planets or in outer space. *n.*

space station an artificial earth satellite to be used as an observatory or a launching site for travel in outer space.

spa·cious (spā′shəs) containing much space; with plenty of room; vast: *The rooms of the palace were spacious.* *adj.*

A spade

spade¹ (spād) 1 a tool for digging having a blade which can be pressed into the ground with the foot, and a long handle with a grip or crosspiece at the top. 2 dig with a spade: *Spade up the garden.* 1 *n.,* 2 *v.,* **spad·ed, spad·ing.**

call a spade a spade, call a thing by its real name; speak plainly and frankly.

spade² (spād) 1 a playing card marked with one or more black figures like this: ♠. 2 **spades,** *pl.* the suit of such playing cards. *n.*

spa·ghet·ti (spə get′ē) a food consisting of a mixture of flour and water made into long, slender sticks that are cooked in water: *Spaghetti is thinner than macaroni.* *n.*

spake (spāk) an old form of **spoke.** *Thus spake the Lord.* *v.*

span¹ (span) 1 the part between two supports: *That bridge consists of a single span.* 2 a period of time: *His span of life is nearly over.* 3 extend over: *A bridge spanned the river.* 4 measure by the hand spread out: *This post can be spanned by one's two hands.* 5 the distance between the tip of a man's thumb and the tip of his little finger when the hand is spread out; about 23 centimetres. 1, 2, 5 *n.,* 3, 4 *v.,* **spanned, span·ning.**

span² (span) a pair of horses or other animals harnessed and driven together. *n.*

span·gle (spang′gəl) 1 a small piece of glittering metal used for decoration: *The dress was covered with spangles.* 2 any small, bright bit: *This rock shows spangles of gold.* 3 decorate with spangles: *The dress was spangled with gold.* 1, 2 *n.,* 3 *v.,* **span·gled, span·gling.**

Span·iard (span′yərd) a person born in or living in Spain. *n.*

span·iel (span′yəl) a dog, usually of small or medium size, with long, silky hair and drooping ears: *Spaniels are very gentle and affectionate.* *n.*

Span·ish (span′ish) 1 of or having to do with Spain, a country in southwestern Europe. 2 the people of Spain. 3 the language of Spain and of most countries in Latin America. 1 *adj.,* 2, 3 *n.*

spank (spangk) 1 strike with the open hand, a slipper, etc.: *The father spanked his naughty child.* 2 a blow with the open hand, a slipper, etc.; a slap. 1 *v.,* 2 *n.*

spank·ing (spang′king) 1 brisk; lively; vigorous: *a spanking breeze.* 2 *Informal.* unusually fine, great, large, etc. 3 slapping with the open hand, a slipper, etc.: *The naughty boy was given a spanking.* 1, 2 *adj.,* 3 *n.*

spar¹ (spär) a stout pole used to support or extend the sails of a ship; a mast, yard, boom, etc. of a ship. *n.*

spar² (spär) 1 make motions of attack and defence with the arms and fists; box. 2 argue; dispute. *v.,* **sparred, spar·ring.**

spare (sper) 1 show mercy to; refrain from harming or destroying: *He spared his enemy. Her cruel tongue spares nobody.* 2 show consideration for; save from labor, pain, etc.: *She washed the dishes to spare her mother.* 3 get along without; omit; do without: *Father couldn't spare the car; so Dick had to walk. 'Spare the rod and spoil the child.'* 4 use in small quantities or not at all; be saving of: *Spare no expense.* 5 have free or available for use: *Can you spare the time? I have no money to spare.* 6 extra; in reserve: *a spare tire.* 7 a spare thing, part, tire, etc. 8 thin; lean: *The minister was a tall, spare man.* 9 small in quantity; scanty: *a spare diet.* 1–5 *v.,* **spared, spar·ing;** 6, 8, 9 *adj.,* **spar·er, spar·est;** 7 *n.*

spare·rib (sper′rib′) a rib of meat, especially pork, having less meat than the ribs near the loins. *n.*

spar·ing (sper′ing) avoiding waste; economical; frugal: *a sparing use of sugar.* *adj.* **—spar′ing·ly,** *adv.*

spark (spärk) 1 a small bit of fire: *The burning wood threw off sparks.* 2 a flash given off when electricity jumps across an open space: *An electric spark explodes the gas in the engine of an automobile.* 3 a flash; gleam: *We saw a spark of light through the trees.* 4 a small amount: *I haven't a spark of interest in the plan.* 5 send out small bits of fire; produce sparks. 6 stir to activity, stimulate: *spark a revolt. He sparked the team to victory.* 1–4 *n.,* 5, 6 *v.*

hat, āge, fär; let, ēqual, tėrm; it, īce
hot, ōpen, ôrder; oil, out; cup, put, rüle
əbove, takən, pencəl, lemən, circəs
ch, child; ng, long; sh, ship
th, thin; ᴛʜ, then; zh, measure

spar·kle (spär′kəl) **1** send out little sparks: *The fireworks sparkled.* **2** a little spark. **3** shine; glitter; flash: *The diamonds sparkled.* **4** a gleam; a flash of light: *I like the sparkle of her eyes.* **5** be brilliant; be lively: *His wit sparkles.* **6** brilliance; liveliness: *We admired the sparkle of his wit.* 1, 3, 5 *v.*, **spar·kled, spar·kling;** 2, 4, 6 *n.*

spar·kler (spär′klər) a small wire or stick covered with a substance that, when lighted, throws off showers of sparks: *The children waved their sparklers in the air.* *n.*

spar·row (spar′ō) a small, brownish-grey bird: *English sparrows live near houses; others live in woods and fields.* *n.*

sparse (spärs) thinly scattered; occurring here and there: *a sparse population, sparse hair.* *adj.*, **spars·er, spars·est.**

spasm (spaz′əm) **1** a sudden, involuntary contraction of a muscle or muscles: *A spasm in his leg made him fall.* **2** any sudden, brief fit or spell of unusual energy or activity: *a spasm of temper, a spasm of enthusiasm.* *n.*

spat[1] (spat) a slight quarrel. *n.*

spat[2] (spat) See **spit**[1]. *The cat spat at the dog.* *v.*

spat[3] (spat) Usually, **spats,** *pl.* a cloth or leather covering for the top of the shoe and the ankle. *n.*

spat·ter (spat′ər) **1** scatter or dash in drops: *to spatter mud.* **2** fall in drops: *Rain spatters on the sidewalk.* **3** strike in a shower; strike in a number of places: *Bullets spattered the wall.* **4** a spattering: *a spatter of hail.* **5** splash or spot with mud, paint, etc. 1–3, 5 *v.*, 4 *n.*

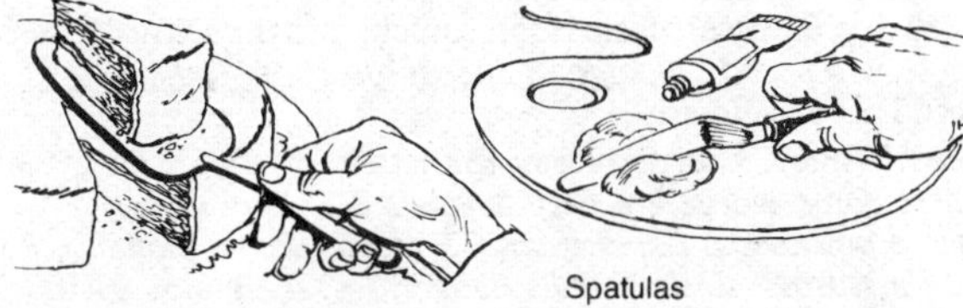
Spatulas

spat·u·la (spach′ů lə) a tool with a broad, flat, flexible blade, used for mixing drugs, in cooking and baking, for spreading paints, etc. *n.*

spawn (spon or spôn) **1** the eggs of fish, frogs, shellfish, etc. **2** young fish, frogs, etc. when newly hatched from these eggs. **3** of fish, etc., produce eggs: *Salmon spawn in the rivers of British Columbia.* **4** give birth to; bring forth in great quantity: *The comedian spent ten minutes spawning poor jokes.* **5** offspring, especially a large number of offspring. 1, 2, 5 *n.*, 3, 4 *v.*

speak (spēk) **1** say words; talk: *A cat cannot speak. Speak distinctly.* **2** make a speech: *The mayor spoke at our club last week.* **3** say; tell; express; make known: *Speak the truth. Her eyes speak of suffering.* **4** use a language: *Do you speak French?* **5** give forth sound: *The guns of the artillery spoke.* *v.*, **spoke, spo·ken, speak·ing.**

speak for, express the opinions of; act as spokesman for: *He spoke for the group that wanted a picnic.*

speak of, mention; refer to: *He spoke of the matter to me. I have no complaints to speak of.*

speak out or **speak up, a** speak loudly and clearly. **b** speak freely and without restraint: *No one dared to speak out against the big bully. The children all spoke up in favor of the teacher's suggestion to have a party.*

speak·er (spēk′ər) **1** a person who speaks, especially one who speaks before an audience. **2** Also, **Speaker,** a person who presides over an assembly: *the Speaker of the House of Commons.* **3** a loudspeaker. *n.*

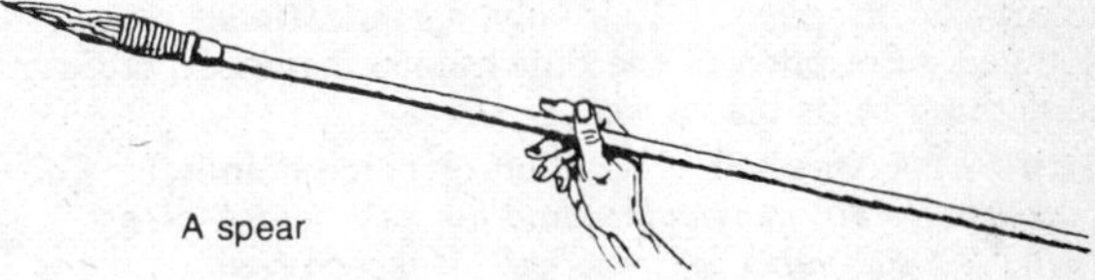
A spear

spear[1] (spēr) **1** a weapon with a long shaft and a sharp-pointed head. **2** pierce with a spear: *The Indian speared a fish.* **3** pierce or stab with anything sharp: *He speared a wiener with the fork.* 1 *n.*, 2, 3 *v.*

spear[2] (spēr) a sprout or shoot of a plant: *a spear of grass.* *n.*

spear·head (spēr′hed′) **1** the sharp-pointed striking end of a spear. **2** the part, person, or group that is first in an attack, undertaking, etc.: *She was the spearhead of the project to make a park here.* **3** go first in an attack, undertaking, etc.: *The tanks spearheaded the army's advance.* 1, 2 *n.*, 3 *v.*

spe·cial (spesh′əl) **1** of a particular kind; distinct from others; not general: *This desk has a special lock. Have you any special color in mind for your new coat?* **2** more than ordinary; unusual; exceptional: *Today's topic is of special interest.* **3** held in unusually high regard; valued in an exceptional way: *a special friend, a special favorite.* **4** for a particular person, thing, purpose, etc.: *The railway ran special trains on holidays. Send the letter by a special messenger.* **5** a special train, car, bus, etc. **6** a product especially featured in a store; bargain: *a weekend special.* **7** a specially produced television show, not part of the regular daily or weekly programs. 1–4 *adj.*, 5–7 *n.* **—spe′cial·ly,** *adv.*

spe·cial·ist (spesh′əl ist) a person who devotes himself to one particular branch of study, business, etc.: *Dr. White is a specialist in diseases of the nose and throat.* *n.*

spe·cial·ize (spesh′əl īz′) **1** pursue some special branch of study, work, etc.: *Some doctors specialize in taking care of children.* **2** adapt to a special function or condition: *Lungs and gills are specialized for breathing.* *v.*, **spe·cial·ized, spe·cial·iz·ing.**

spe·cial·ized (spesh′əl īzd′) designed for or devoted to a particular use or type of work: *An engineer needs much specialized knowledge.* *adj.*

spe·cial·ty (spesh′əl tē) **1** a special study; a special line of work, profession, trade, etc.: *Repairing watches is his specialty.* **2** a product, article, etc. to which special attention is given: *This store makes a specialty of children's clothes.* *n.*, *pl.* **spe·cial·ties.**

spe·cies (spē′sēz or spē′shēz) **1** a group of animals or plants that have certain permanent characteristics in common: *Wheat is a species of grass.* 2 a kind; sort; distinct kind or sort: *The news gave us a species of hope.* *n., pl.* **spe·cies.**

spe·cif·ic (spə sif′ik) 1 definite; precise; particular: *There was no specific reason for the quarrel.* 2 characteristic of; peculiar to: *A scaly skin is a specific feature of snakes.* *adj.*

spec·i·fi·ca·tion (spes′ə fə kā′shən) 1 the act of specifying; a detailed statement of particulars: *Mary made careful specification as to the kinds of cake and candy for her party.* 2 Usually, **specifications,** *pl.* a detailed description of the dimensions, materials, etc. for something to be made. *n.*

spec·i·fy (spes′ə fī′) mention or name definitely: *Did you specify any particular time for us to call? He delivered the paper as specified.* *v.,* **spec·i·fied, spec·i·fy·ing.**

spec·i·men (spes′ə mən) one of a group or class taken to show what the others are like; sample: *He collects specimens of all kinds of rocks and minerals.* *n.*

speck (spek) 1 a small spot; stain: *Can you clean the specks off this wallpaper?* 2 a tiny bit; particle: *a speck in the eye.* 3 mark with specks: *This fruit is specked.* 1, 2 *n.,* 3 *v.*

speck·le (spek′əl) 1 a small spot or mark: *This hen is grey with white speckles.* 2 mark with speckles: *The boy is speckled with freckles.* 1 *n.,* 2 *v.,* **speck·led, speck·ling.**

spec·ta·cle (spek′tə kəl) 1 something to look at; a sight: *The children at play among the flowers made a charming spectacle. A quarrel is an unpleasant spectacle.* 2 a public show or display: *The big parade was a fine spectacle.* *n.*

Spectacles

spec·ta·cles (spek′tə kəlz) a pair of glasses to help a person's sight or to protect his eyes. *n. pl.*

spec·tac·u·lar (spek tak′yə lər) 1 making a great display: *The television program included a spectacular scene of a storm.* 2 a spectacular display or show. 1 *adj.,* 2 *n.*

spec·ta·tor (spek′tā tər or spek tā′tər) a person who looks on without taking part: *There were many spectators at the game.* *n.*

spec·tre or **spec·ter** (spek′tər) ghost. *n.*

spec·trum (spek′trəm) the band of colors formed when a beam of light is broken up by being passed through a prism or by some other means: *A rainbow has all the colors of the spectrum: red, orange, yellow, green, blue, indigo, and violet.* *n., pl.* **spec·tra** (spek′trə) or **spec·trums.**

spec·u·late (spek′yə lāt′) 1 reflect; meditate; consider: *The philosopher speculated about time and space.* 2 guess; conjecture: *She refused to speculate about the possible winner.* 3 buy or sell when there is a large risk, with the hope of making a profit from future price changes. *v.,* **spec·u·lat·ed, spec·u·lat·ing.**

spec·u·la·tion (spek′yə lā′shən) 1 reflection; thought: *Former speculations about electricity were often mere guesses.* 2 guessing; conjecture: *His estimates of the cost were based on speculation.* 3 buying or selling when there is a large risk, with the hope of making a profit from future price changes. *n.*

sped (sped) See **speed.** *The police car sped down the road.* *v.*

speech (spēch) 1 the act of speaking; talk. 2 the power of speaking: *Animals lack speech.* 3 a manner of speaking: *His speech showed that he was a Newfoundlander.* 4 what is said; the words spoken: *We made the usual farewell speeches.* 5 a public talk: *The mayor gave an excellent speech.* 6 language: *His native speech was French.* *n.*

speech·less (spēch′lis) 1 not able to speak: *Animals are speechless. He was speechless with anger.* 2 silent: *Her frown gave a speechless message.* *adj.*

speed (spēd) 1 swift or rapid movement. 2 go fast: *The boat sped over the water.* 3 make go fast: *Let's all help speed the work.* 4 a rate of movement: *The boys ran at full speed.* 5 go faster than is safe or lawful: *The car was caught speeding near the school zone.* 1, 4 *n.,* 2, 3, 5 *v.,* **sped** or **speed·ed, speed·ing.**

speed up, go or cause to go faster; increase in speed.

speed·i·ly (spēd′ə lē) quickly; with speed; soon. *adv.*

speed limit the top speed at which vehicles are allowed to travel on a particular road.

speed·om·e·ter (spēd om′ə tər or spi dom′ə tər) an instrument to indicate the speed of an automobile or other vehicle, and often the distance travelled. *n.*

speed·y (spēd′ē) fast; rapid; quick; swift: *speedy workers, a speedy change, a speedy decision.* *adj.,* **speed·i·er, speed·i·est.**

spell¹ (spel) 1 write or say the letters of a word in order: *Some words are easy to spell.* 2 make up or form a word: *C-a-t spells cat.* 3 mean: *Those clouds spell a storm. Delay spells danger.* *v.,* **spelled** or **spelt, spell·ing.**

spell² (spel) 1 a word or set of words supposed to have magic power. 2 fascination; charm: *The beautiful music cast a spell over the audience.* *n.*

under a spell, controlled by a spell; spellbound: *The explorer's story held the children under a spell.*

spell³ (spel) 1 a period of work or duty: *The sailor's spell at the wheel was four hours.* 2 a period or time of anything: *The child has spells of coughing. There was a long spell of rainy weather in August.* 3 *Informal.* work in place of another person for a while: *I'll spell you at cutting the grass.* 1, 2 *n.,* 3 *v.,* **spelled, spell·ing.**

spell·bound (spel′bound′) too interested to move; fascinated; enchanted: *The children were spellbound by the circus performance.* *adj.*

spell·er (spel′ər) a book for teaching spelling. *n.*

spell·ing (spel′ing) 1 the writing or saying of the letters of a word in order: *He is poor at spelling.* 2 the way in which a word is spelled: *'Grey' has two spellings, 'grey' and 'gray.'* *n.*

spelling bee a spelling contest.

spelt (spelt) spelled. See **spell¹.** *v.*

spend (spend) 1 pay out: *She spent ten dollars today.* 2 pay out money: *Earn before you spend.* 3 use; use

hat, āge, fär; let, ēqual, tėrm; it, īce
hot, ōpen, ôrder; oil, out; cup, pu̇t, rüle
 əbove, takən, pencəl, lemən, circəs
ch, child; ng, long; sh, ship
th, thin; ᴛʜ, then; zh, measure

up: *Don't spend any more time on that lesson.* **4** pass: *We spent last summer at the seashore.* **5** wear out: *The storm has spent its force.* *v.,* **spent, spend·ing.**

spend·thrift (spend′thrift′) **1** a person who wastes money. **2** wasteful: *his spendthrift ways.* 1 *n.,* 2 *adj.*

spent (spent) **1** See **spend.** *Saturday was spent in playing. How have you spent your time today?* **2** used up. **3** worn out; tired: *a spent swimmer, a spent horse.* 1 *v.,* 2, 3 *adj.*

sperm whale (spėrm) a large whale having a square head from which valuable oil is obtained. See **whale** for picture.

sphere (sfēr) **1** a round body whose surface is at all points equally distant from the centre; a ball or globe: *The sun, moon, earth, and stars are spheres. A baseball is a sphere.* **2** the place or field in which a person or thing exists, acts, or works: *Her sphere is advertising.* **3** a range, extent, or region: *England's sphere of influence.* *n.*

spher·i·cal (sfer′ə kəl) shaped like a sphere. *adj.*

An Egyptian sphinx

The Sphinx of Greek mythology

sphinx (sfingks) **1** a statue of a lion's body with the head of a man, ram, or hawk: *There are many sphinxes in Egypt.* **2 Sphinx,** in Greek myths, a monster with the head of a woman, the body of a lion, and wings: *The Sphinx proposed a riddle to every passer-by and killed those unable to guess the answer.* **3** a puzzling or mysterious person. *n.*

spice (spīs) **1** any of various seasonings obtained from plants and used to flavor food: *Pepper, cinnamon, cloves, ginger, and nutmeg are common spices.* **2** put spice in; season: *spiced peaches, spiced pickles.* **3** something that adds flavor or interest: *'Variety is the spice of life.'* **4** add flavor or interest to: *The principal spiced his speech with stories and jokes.* 1, 3 *n.,* 2, 4 *v.,* **spiced, spic·ing.**

spick–and–span (spik′ən span′) new; fresh; spruce; smart; neat and clean: *The room looked spick-and-span.* *adj.*

spic·y (spī′sē) **1** flavored with spice: *The cookies were rich and spicy.* **2** having a taste or smell like that of spice: *spicy apples.* *adj.,* **spic·i·er, spic·i·est.**

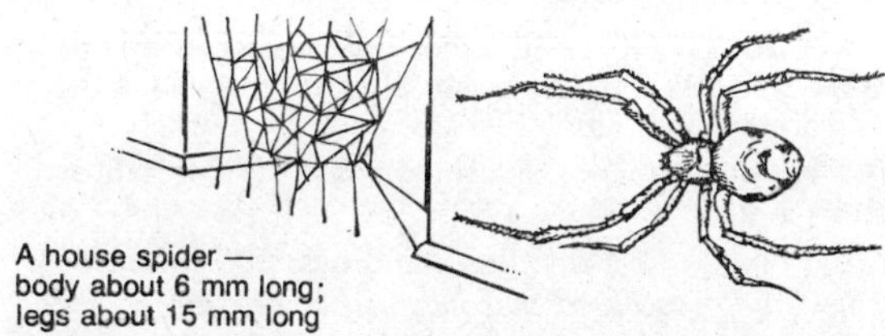

A house spider — body about 6 mm long; legs about 15 mm long

spi·der (spī′dər) **1** a small animal with eight legs and no wings: *Many spiders spin webs to catch insects for food.* **2** something like or suggesting a spider. **3** a kind of frying pan with a handle. *n.*

spied (spīd) See **spy.** *The hunter spied a stag in the distance. Who had spied on us?* *v.*

spig·ot (spig′ət) a tap or faucet. *n.*

spike[1] (spīk) **1** a large, strong nail. **2** fasten with spikes: *The men spiked the rails to the ties when laying the track.* **3** a sharp-pointed piece or part: *The baseball players wore shoes with spikes.* **4** provide or equip with spikes: *The runners wore spiked shoes to keep from slipping.* **5** pierce or injure with a spike. **6** make a cannon useless by driving a spike into the opening where the powder is set off. **7** put an end or stop to; make useless; block: *The extra guard spiked the spy's attempt to escape.* 1, 3 *n.,* 2, 4–7 *v.,* **spiked, spik·ing.**

A spike of wheat and a flower spike

spike[2] (spīk) **1** an ear or head of grain. **2** a long, pointed flower cluster: *gladiolus spikes.* *n.*

spile (spīl) **1** a peg or plug of wood used to stop the small hole of a cask or barrel. **2** a spout for drawing off sap from sugar maple trees. *n.*

spill (spil) **1** let liquid or any matter in loose pieces run or fall: *to spill milk, to spill salt.* **2** fall or flow out: *Water spilled from the pail.* **3** *Informal.* cause to fall from a horse, car, boat, etc.: *The boat upset and spilled the boys into the water.* **4** *Informal.* such a fall: *He got a bad spill trying to ride that horse.* 1–3 *v.,* **spilled** or **spilt, spill·ing;** 4 *n.*

spill·way (spil′wā′) a channel or passage for the escape of surplus water from a dam, river, etc. *n.*

spilt (spilt) See **spill.** *v.*

spin (spin) **1** turn around rapidly: *The wheel spun round.* **2** make turn around rapidly: *The boy spins his top.* **3** feel as if one were whirling around; feel dizzy: *My head is spinning.* **4** draw out and twist cotton, flax, or wool into thread. **5** make a thread, web, or cocoon by giving out from the body sticky material that hardens into thread: *A spider spins a web.* **6** produce; draw out; tell: *The old sailor used to spin yarns about his adventures at sea.* **7** the act of spinning. **8** a ride, run, or drive, especially a short one: *Come for a spin on your bicycle.* **9** run, ride, or drive rapidly: *They were spinning along in my father's car.* **10** a rapid turning around of an airplane as it falls. 1–6, 9 *v.,* **spun, spin·ning;** 7, 8, 10 *n.*

spin out, make long and slow; draw out; prolong: *Try not to spin out your story.*

spin·ach (spin′ich or spin′ij) a plant whose green leaves are used as a vegetable. *n.*

spi·nal (spī′nəl) of or having to do with the backbone. *adj.*

spinal column the spine; the backbone.

spinal cord the thick, whitish cord of nerve tissue that extends from the brain down through most of the backbone and from which nerves to various parts of the body branch off.

spin·dle (spin′dəl) 1 the rod or pin used in spinning to twist, wind, and hold thread. See the picture below. 2 any rod or pin that turns around or on which something turns: *Axles and shafts are spindles.* 3 grow very long and thin. 1, 2 *n.*, 3 *v.*, **spin·dled, spin·dling.**

spin·dly (spin′dlē) very long and slender; too tall and thin: *spindly legs, a spindly plant. adj.*, **spin·dli·er, spin·dli·est.**

spine (spīn) 1 backbone. 2 a stiff, sharp-pointed growth on plants or animals; a thorn or something like it. See **cactus** and **porcupine** for pictures. *n.*

spine·less (spīn′lis) 1 having no backbone: *All insects are spineless.* 2 without courage: *A spineless person will not stand up for his beliefs.* 3 having no spines: *a spineless cactus. adj.*

A spinning wheel. The large wheel causes the smaller one to turn, and this revolves the horizontal spindle, twisting the thread and winding it up at the same time.

spinning wheel a large wheel with a spindle, arranged for spinning cotton, flax, or wool into thread or yarn.

spin·ster (spin′stər) an unmarried woman. *n.*

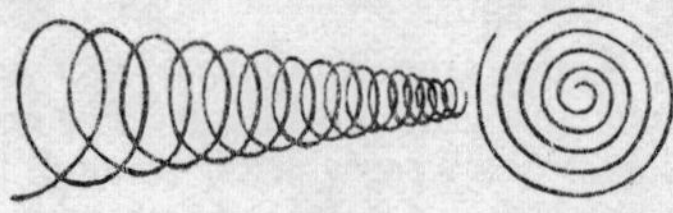

Spirals

spi·ral (spī′rəl) 1 a winding and gradually widening coil: *The spring of a watch is a spiral.* 2 coiled; coiling: *a spiral staircase, a spiral spring, the spiral stripes on a barber's pole.* 3 move in a spiral: *The flaming airplane spiralled to earth.* 1 *n.*, 2 *adj.*, 3 *v.*, **spi·ralled** or **spi·raled, spi·ral·ling** or **spi·ral·ing.**

spire (spīr) 1 the top part of a tower or steeple that narrows to a point. See **steeple** for picture. 2 anything tapering and pointed: *the rocky spires of mountains. A blade of grass is sometimes called a spire of grass. n.*

spir·it (spir′it) 1 the soul: *Many religions teach that at death the spirit leaves the body.* 2 man's moral, religious, or emotional nature. 3 a supernatural being: *God is a spirit. Ghosts and fairies are spirits.* 4 Often, **spirits,** *pl.* a state of mind; disposition; temper: *He is in good spirits.* 5 a person; personality: *He is a brave spirit. He was one of the leading spirits of the revolution.* 6 an influence that stirs up and rouses: *A spirit of progress is good for people.* 7 courage; vigor; liveliness: *A race horse must have spirit.* 8 what is really meant as opposed to what is said or written: *The spirit of a law is more important than its words.* 9 Often, **spirits,** *pl.* an alcoholic drink made by distilling the juice of certain fruits, grains, roots, etc.; liquor: *Whisky and brandy are called spirits. He drinks beer but no spirits.* 10 carry off secretly: *The child has been spirited away.* 1–9 *n.*, 10 *v.*

out of spirits, sad; gloomy.

spir·it·ed (spir′ə tid) full of energy and spirit; lively; dashing; brave: *a spirited race horse. adj.*

spir·i·tu·al (spir′i chü əl) 1 of or having to do with the spirit (defs. 1 and 2) or spirits (def. 3). 2 sacred; religious. 3 a religious song, especially one which originated among the Negroes of the southern United States. 1, 2 *adj.*, 3 *n.*

spit[1] (spit) 1 eject saliva from the mouth. 2 throw out: *The gun spits fire. He spat curses.* 3 the liquid produced in the mouth; saliva. 4 make a spitting sound: *The cat spits when angry.* 1, 2, 4 *v.*, **spat** or **spit, spit·ting;** 3 *n.*

spit[2] (spit) 1 a pointed, slender rod or bar on which meat is roasted: *The spit turns so that the meat is cooked evenly.* 2 run a spit through; pierce; stab: *The hunters spitted two rabbits.* 3 a narrow point of land running into the water. 1, 3 *n.*, 2 *v.*, **spit·ted, spit·ting.**

spite (spīt) 1 ill will; a grudge: *She ruined his flowers out of spite.* 2 show ill will toward; annoy: *He left his yard dirty to spite the people who lived next door.* 1 *n.*, 2 *v.*, **spit·ed, spit·ing.**

in spite of, not prevented by; notwithstanding: *The children went to school in spite of the rain.*

spite·ful (spīt′fəl) full of spite; eager to annoy; behaving with ill will and malice: *The spiteful little girl tore up her older sister's papers. adj.*

splake (splāk) *Cdn.* a game fish that is part speckled trout and part lake trout. *n.*

splash (splash) 1 cause water, mud, etc. to fly about. 2 dash liquid about: *The baby likes to splash in his tub.* 3 dash in scattered masses or drops: *The waves splashed on the beach.* 4 to wet, spatter, or soil: *Our car is all splashed with mud.* 5 the act or sound of splashing; splashing: *The splash of the wave knocked him over. The boat upset with a loud splash.* 6 a spot of liquid splashed on something: *She has splashes of grease on her dress.* 7 a spot; a patch: *The dog is white with brown splashes.* 1–4 *v.*, 5–7 *n.*

splash·down (splash′doun′) the landing of a capsule or other spacecraft in the ocean after re–entry into the earth's atmosphere. *n.*

splat·ter (splat′ər) 1 splash; spatter. 2 a splash or spatter. 1 *v.*, 2 *n.*

spleen (splēn) 1 a ductless gland near the stomach: *The spleen stores blood and helps filter foreign substances from the blood.* 2 bad temper; spite; anger. *n.*

splen·did (splen′did) 1 brilliant; glorious;

magnificent; grand: *a splendid sunset, splendid jewels, a splendid victory.* **2** very good; fine; excellent: *a splendid chance. adj.*

splen·dor or **splen·dour** (splen′dər) **1** a great brightness; a brilliant light: *The sun set in a golden splendor.* **2** a magnificent show; pomp; glory. *n.*

A splice in a rope

splice (splīs) **1** join together ropes or wires by weaving together ends that have been pulled out into separate strands. **2** join together two pieces of timber by overlapping. **3** join together film, tape, wire, etc. by gluing or cementing the ends. **4** a joining of ropes, timbers, film, etc. by splicing: *How neat a splice can you make?* 1–3 *v.,* **spliced, splic·ing;** 4 *n.*

splint (splint) **1** a rigid arrangement of wood, metal, etc. to hold a broken bone in place until it heals. **2** a thin strip of wood, such as is used in making baskets. *n.*

splin·ter (splin′tər) **1** a thin, sharp piece of wood, bone, glass, etc.: *He got a splinter in his hand. The mirror broke into splinters.* **2** split or break into splinters: *The mirror splintered.* 1 *n.,* 2 *v.*

split (split) **1** break or cut from end to end or in layers: *The man is splitting wood. She split the cake and filled it with jelly.* **2** separate into parts; divide: *The huge tree split when it was struck by lightning. The two men split the cost of the dinner between them.* **3** a division in a group, party, etc.: *There was a split in the church for a time, but harmony was soon restored.* **4** a splitting; a break; crack: *Frost caused the split in the rock.* **5** broken or cut from end to end; divided. **6** divide a molecule into two or more individual smaller parts. **7** Often, **splits,** *pl.* an exercise in which one lands on the floor with the legs stretched out in opposite directions. 1, 2, 6 *v.,* **split, split·ting;** 3, 4, 7 *n.,* 5 *adj.*
split hairs, make distinctions that are too fussy: *It is splitting hairs to complain of having just 59 minutes instead of an hour in the pool.*

splotch (sploch) **1** a large, irregular spot; splash. **2** make splotches on. 1 *n.,* 2 *v.*

splut·ter (splut′ər) **1** talk in a hasty, confused way: *People sometimes splutter when they are excited.* **2** sputter; make spitting or popping noises: *The baked apples were spluttering in the oven.* **3** a sputter; spluttering. 1, 2 *v.,* 3 *n.*

spoil (spoil) **1** damage; injure; destroy: *He spoils a dozen pieces of paper before he writes a letter. The rain spoiled the picnic.* **2** be damaged; become bad or unfit for use: *The fruit spoiled because I kept it too long.* **3** injure the character or disposition of, especially by being too kind, generous, etc.: *That child is being spoiled by too much attention.* **4** steal; take by force; plunder: *The Romans spoiled the Egyptians.* **5** **spoils,** *pl.* things taken by force; things won: *The soldiers carried off the spoils of war.* 1–4 *v.,* **spoiled** or **spoilt, spoil·ing;** 5 *n.*

spoilt (spoilt) See **spoil.** *v.*

spoke[1] (spōk) See **speak.** *She spoke about that yesterday. v.*

spoke[2] (spōk) one of the bars going from the centre of a wheel to the rim. See **wheel** for picture. *n.*

spo·ken (spō′kən) **1** See **speak.** *They have often spoken about having a picnic.* **2** expressed with the mouth; uttered; told: *A child understands a spoken direction better than a written one.* 1 *v.,* 2 *adj.*

hat, āge, fär; let, ēqual, tėrm; it, īce
hot, ōpen, ôrder; oil, out; cup, pu̇t, rüle
əbove, takən, pencəl, lemən, circəs
ch, child; ng, long; sh, ship
th, thin; ᴛʜ, then; zh, measure

spokes·man (spōks′mən) a person who speaks for another or others: *He was the spokesman for the factory workers. n., pl.* **spokes·men** (spōks′mən).

sponge (spunj) **1** a kind of sea animal that attaches itself to rocks and has a light, tough skeleton or framework. **2** the light, porous framework of any of these animals, used for soaking up water in bathing or cleaning. **3** a similar article made artificially of rubber or plastic. **4** wipe or rub with a wet sponge; make clean or damp in this way: *Sponge the mud spots off the car. Sponge up the spilled water.* **5** something like a sponge, such as a pad of gauze used by doctors, bread dough, a kind of cake, a kind of pudding, etc. **6** *Informal.* live or profit at the expense of another in a mean way: *That lazy man won't work; he just sponges on his family.* 1–3, 5 *n.,* 4, 6 *v.,* **sponged, spong·ing.**

spon·gy (spun′jē) like a sponge; soft, light, and full of holes: *spongy moss, spongy dough. adj.,* **spon·gi·er, spon·gi·est.**

spon·sor (spon′sər) **1** a person or group that supports or is responsible for a person or thing: *the sponsor of a law, the sponsor of a student applying for a scholarship.* **2** a person who takes vows for an infant at baptism; a godfather or godmother. **3** a company, store, or organization that for purposes of advertising pays the costs of a radio or television program. **4** act as sponsor for. 1–3 *n.,* 4 *v.*

spon·ta·ne·ous (spon tā′nē əs) **1** caused or happening naturally and without being planned beforehand; not forced: *Both sides burst into spontaneous cheers at the skilful play.* **2** happening without outside cause: *Spontaneous combustion occurs when something starts to burn all by itself. adj.*

spook (spük) *Informal.* a ghost or spectre. *n.*

spook·y (spük′ē) like or suggesting spooks; weird; scary. *adj.*

spool (spül) a cylinder of plastic, wood, or metal on which thread, wire, etc. is wound. *n.*

Spoons

spoon (spün) **1** a utensil consisting of a small, shallow bowl at the end of a handle: *Spoons are used to take up or stir food or drink.* **2** take up in a spoon. **3** a shiny, curved bait having hooks attached for catching fish. 1, 3 *n.,* 2 *v.*

born with a silver spoon in one's mouth, born lucky or rich.

spoon·ful (spün′fùl) as much as a spoon can hold. *n., pl.* **spoon·fuls.**

spoor (spür) the trail or track of a wild animal: *The hunters followed the spoor of the deer. n.*

spore (spôr) a single cell capable of growing into a new plant or animal: *Ferns produce spores. Mould grows from spores. n.*

sport (spôrt) 1 a game, contest, or other pastime requiring some skill and a certain amount of exercise: *Baseball and fishing are outdoor sports; bowling and basketball are indoor sports.* 2 fun; play; amusement: *He spends all his time in sport and play.* 3 amuse oneself; play: *Lambs sport in the fields. The kitten sports with its tail.* 4 playful joking; fun: *The man teased the child in sport.* 5 ridicule: *His clumsy dancing was a source of sport to his classmates.* 6 the object of jokes and ridicule: *His attempts to look grown up are the sport of his brothers and sisters.* 7 sportsman. 8 *Informal.* a person who behaves in a sportsmanlike manner; good fellow: *be a sport.* 1, 2, 4–8 *n.*, 3 *v.*

make sport of, make fun of; laugh at; ridicule: *Don't make sport of my clumsiness.*

sport·ing (spôr′ting) 1 of, interested in, or engaging in sports. 2 playing fair: *Letting the little boy throw first was a sporting gesture.* 3 willing to take a chance. 4 *Informal.* involving risk; uncertain: *He took a sporting chance in crossing the stream by stepping from rock to rock. adj.*

sports·man (spôrts′mən) 1 a person who takes part in sports, especially hunting, fishing, etc. 2 a person who plays fair. *n., pl.* **sports·men** (spôrts′mən).

sports·man·ship (spôrts′mən ship′) the qualities or conduct of a sportsman; fair play: *It is good sportsmanship to shake hands after a game. n.*

spot (spot) 1 a mark, stain, or speck: *You have grease spots on your suit. That spot on her cheek is a bruise.* 2 a blemish or flaw in character or reputation: *His character is without spot.* 3 a small part unlike the rest: *His tie is blue with white spots.* 4 make spots on: *to spot a dress. He spotted his reputation by lying.* 5 become spotted; have spots: *This silk spots from rain.* 6 a place: *From this spot you can see the ocean.* 7 place in a certain spot; scatter in various spots: *Lookouts were spotted all along the coast.* 8 *Informal.* pick out; find out; recognize: *I spotted my sister in the crowd. The teacher spotted every mistake in my paper.* 9 a figure or dot on a playing card, domino, or die to show its kind and value. 1–3, 6, 9 *n.*, 4, 5, 7, 8 *v.*, **spot·ted, spot·ting.**

hit the spot, *Informal.* be just right; be satisfactory.

in a spot, in trouble or difficulty.

on the spot, a at that very place. b at once. c in trouble or difficulty: *He put me on the spot by asking a question I could not answer.*

spot·less (spot′lis) without a spot or blemish: *She wore a spotless white apron. His character was spotless. adj.*

spot·light (spot′līt′) 1 a strong light thrown upon a particular spot or person. 2 the lamp that gives the light: *a spotlight in a theatre.* 3 public notice; anything that focusses attention on a person or thing: *Movie stars are often in the spotlight. n.*

spot·ty (spot′ē) 1 having spots; spotted. 2 not of uniform quality; irregular: *His work was spotty. adj.,* **spot·ti·er, spot·ti·est.**

spouse (spous or spouz) a husband or wife: *Mr. Smith is Mrs. Smith's spouse, and she is his spouse. n.*

spout (spout) 1 throw out a liquid in a stream or spray: *The fountain spouted up high. A whale spouts water when it breathes.* 2 flow out with force: *Water spouted from a break in the pipe.* 3 a stream or jet: *A spout of water shot up from the hole in the pipe.* 4 a pipe for carrying off water: *Rain runs down a spout from our roof to the ground.* 5 a tube or lip by which liquid is poured. 6 *Informal.* speak in loud and very emotional tones: *The old-fashioned actor spouted his lines.* 1, 2, 6 *v.*, 3–5 *n.*

sprain (sprān) 1 injure a joint or muscle by a sudden twist or wrench: *to sprain your ankle.* 2 an injury caused by a sudden twist or wrench: *He got a bad sprain when he missed the lower step.* 1 *v.*, 2 *n.*

sprang (sprang) See **spring.** *The tiger sprang at the man. v.*

sprawl (sprol or sprôl) 1 lie or sit with the limbs spread out, especially ungracefully: *The people sprawled on the beach in their bathing suits.* 2 spread out in an irregular or awkward manner: *handwriting that sprawls across the page.* 3 the act or position of sprawling. 1, 2 *v.*, 3 *n.*

spray[1] (sprā) 1 liquid blown or flying through the air in a mist or small drops: *We were wet with the sea spray.* 2 something like this: *A spray of bullets hit the target.* 3 an instrument that sends a liquid out as spray. 4 sprinkle; scatter a liquid in a mist or small drops: *Spray this paint on the far wall.* 5 scatter spray on or over: *We spray apple trees to keep the fruit free from disease.* 1–3 *n.*, 4, 5 *v.*

spray[2] (sprā) a small branch or piece of some plant with its leaves, flowers, or fruit: *a spray of ivy, a spray of lilies, a spray of fern, a spray of berries. n.*

spread (spred) 1 cover or cause to cover a large or larger area; stretch out; unfold; open out: *to spread rugs on the floor, to spread one's arms, a fan that spreads when shaken. The bird spreads its wings.* 2 move farther apart: *Spread out your fingers.* 3 extend; lie: *Fields of corn spread out before us.* 4 scatter; distribute: *He spread the news. Rats have spread all over the world.* 5 cover with a thin layer: *She spread each slice with butter.* 6 put as a thin layer: *He spread jam on his bread.* 7 the act of spreading: *Doctors fight the spread of disease.* 8 the width or extent; the amount of spreading: *The spread of the airplane's wings was twenty metres.* 9 a covering for a bed or table. 10 *Informal.* the food put on the table; a feast. 11 something to spread on bread, etc.: *Peanut butter is a spread.* 12 the area of land owned by a rancher: *He has* *a big spread near Calgary.* 1–6 *v.,* **spread, spread·ing;** 7–12 *n.*

spree (sprē) a lively frolic; a jolly time. *n.*

sprig (sprig) a shoot, twig, or small branch: *a sprig of lilac. n.*

spright·ly (sprīt′lē) lively and quick: *a sprightly kitten. adj.,* **spright·li·er, spright·li·est.**

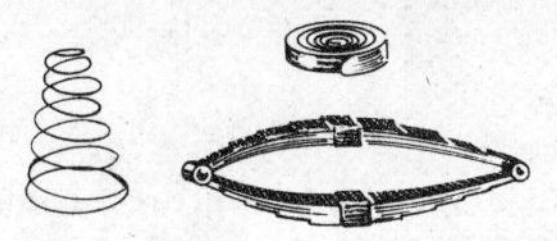

Four kinds of metal spring

spring (spring) **1** move or rise suddenly and lightly; leap or jump: *The dog springs at the thief. The boy sprang to his feet.* **2** a leap or jump: *The boy made a spring over the fence.* **3** fly back or away as if by elastic force: *A bent branch will spring back into place.* **4** cause to spring; cause to act by a spring: *to spring a trap.* **5** a device that returns to its original shape after being pulled or held out of shape: *Beds have wire springs. The spring in a clock makes it go.* **6** an elastic quality: *There is no spring left in these old rubber bands. The old man's knees have lost their spring.* **7** the season after winter when plants begin to grow again. **8** a small stream of water flowing naturally from the earth. **9** come from some source; arise; grow: *A wind sprang up. Plants spring from seeds.* **10** a source or beginning; a cause. **11** bring out, produce, or make suddenly: *to spring a surprise on someone.* **12** to crack, split, warp, bend, strain, or break: *Frost had sprung the rock wall.* 1, 3, 4, 9, 11, 12 *v.,* **sprang** or **sprung, sprung, spring·ing;** 2, 5–8, 10 *n.*

spring a leak, crack and begin to let water through.

spring·board (spring′bôrd′) **1** a flexible board used to give added spring in diving, jumping, or vaulting. **2** anything that gives one a good start toward a goal or purpose: *Hard work was his springboard to success. n.*

spring·time (spring′tīm′) the season of spring: *Flowers bloom in the springtime. n.*

spring·y (spring′ē) **1** yielding; flexible; elastic: *The wet lawn was springy to the feet.* **2** jaunty; full of bounce: *His step was light and springy. adj.,* **spring·i·er, spring·i·est.**

sprin·kle (spring′kəl) **1** scatter in drops or tiny bits: *He sprinkled sand on the icy sidewalk.* **2** spray or cover with small drops: *She sprinkled the flowers with water.* **3** a sprinkling; a small quantity: *The cook put a sprinkle of nuts on the cake.* **4** rain a little. **5** a light rain. 1, 2, 4 *v.,* **sprin·kled, sprin·kling;** 3, 5 *n.* **—sprin′kler,** *n.*

sprin·kling (spring′kling) a small quantity or number scattered here and there: *a sprinkling of grey hairs. n.*

sprint (sprint) **1** run at top speed for a short distance. **2** a short race or dash at top speed. 1 *v.,* 2 *n.*

sprite (sprīt) an elf or fairy; goblin. *n.*

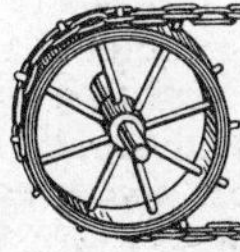

A wheel with sprockets

sprock·et (sprok′it) **1** one of a set of parts sticking out from the rim of a wheel and arranged to fit into the links of a chain. **2** Also **sprocket wheel,** a wheel made with sprockets. *n.*

hat, āge, fär; let, ēqual, tėrm; it, īce
hot, ōpen, ôrder; oil, out; cup, pu̇t, rüle
əbove, takən, pencəl, lemən, circəs
ch, child; ng, long; sh, ship
th, thin; ᴛʜ, then; zh, measure

sprout (sprout) **1** begin to grow; shoot forth: *Seeds sprout. Buds sprout in the spring. Weeds have sprouted in the garden.* **2** cause to grow: *The rain has sprouted the corn.* **3** a shoot or bud of a plant. 1, 2 *v.,* 3 *n.*

A branch of spruce with cones

spruce[1] (sprüs) **1** an evergreen tree having cones and needle-shaped leaves. **2** its wood. *n.*

spruce[2] (sprüs) **1** neat; trim: *He looked very spruce in his new suit.* **2** make or become spruce: *Spruce up before you go back to school. He spruced himself in front of the mirror.* 1 *adj.,* **spruc·er, spruc·est;** 2 *v.,* **spruced, spruc·ing.**

sprung (sprung) See **spring.** *The trap was sprung. v.*

spry (sprī) lively; nimble: *The spry old lady travelled everywhere. adj.,* **spry·er** or **spri·er, spry·est** or **spri·est.**

spun (spun) See **spin.** *The car skidded and spun on the ice. The thread was spun from silk. v.*

spunk (spungk) *Informal.* courage; pluck; spirit: *a little puppy full of spunk. n.*

spur (spėr) **1** a pricking instrument worn on a horseman's heel for urging a horse on. **2** prick with spurs: *The rider spurred his horse on.* **3** something like a spur; a point sticking out: *A spur of rock stuck out from the hill. A rooster has spurs on his legs.* **4** anything that urges on: *Ambition was the spur that made him work.* **5** urge on: *Pride spurred the man to fight.* **6** a ridge sticking out from or smaller than the main body of a mountain or mountain range. **7** any short branch: *a spur of a railway.* 1, 3, 4, 6, 7, *n.,* 2, 5 *v.,* **spurred, spur·ring.**

on the spur of the moment, without previous planning or preparation.

spurn (spėrn) refuse with scorn; scorn: *The judge spurned the bribe. v.*

spurt (spėrt) **1** flow suddenly in a stream or jet; gush out; squirt: *Blood spurted from the wound.* **2** a sudden rushing forth; jet: *Spurts of flame broke out all over the building.* **3** a great increase of effort or activity for a short time: *to put on a spurt.* **4** put forth great energy for a short time; show great activity for a short time: *The runners spurted near the end of the race.* 1, 4 *v.,* 2, 3 *n.*

sput·nik (sput′nik or spu̇t′nik) any of a group of earth satellites put into orbit by the Soviet Union. *n.*
☛ **Sputnik** comes from a Russian word meaning 'satellite.'

sput·ter (sput′ər) **1** make spitting or popping noises: *fat sputtering in the frying pan, sputtering firecrackers.* **2** throw out drops of saliva, bits of food, etc. in excitement or in talking too fast. **3** say words or sounds in haste and confusion. **4** confused talk. **5** a sputtering; sputtering noise. 1–3 *v.,* 4, 5 *n.*

spy (spī) **1** a person who keeps secret watch on the actions of others. **2** a person paid by a government to get secret information about the government plans, military strength, etc. of another country. **3** keep secret watch: *He saw two men spying on him from behind a tree.* **4** act as a spy; be a spy: *The punishment for spying in wartime is death.* **5** catch sight of; see: *He was the first to spy the rescue party in the distance.* 1, 2 *n., pl.* **spies;** 3–5 *v.,* **spies, spied, spy·ing.**
spy out, find out or try to find out by careful observation; search: *She spies out everything that goes on in the neighborhood.*

spy·glass (spī′glas′) a small telescope. *n.*

squab (skwob) a very young bird, especially a young pigeon. *n.*

squab·ble (skwob′əl) **1** a petty, noisy quarrel: *Children's squabbles annoy their parents.* **2** take part in a petty, noisy quarrel: *I won't squabble over three cents.* 1 *n.,* 2 *v.,* **squab·bled, squab·bling.**

squad (skwod) **1** a small number of soldiers grouped for drill, inspection, or work: *The corporal picked a squad for kitchen duty.* **2** any small group of persons working together: *A squad of boys cleaned up the yard.* *n.*

squad·ron (skwod′rən) **1** a part of a naval fleet used for special service: *the Atlantic squadron of the navy.* **2** a number of airplanes that fly or fight together. **3** a formation of armored cars or tanks. **4** a body of cavalry. **5** any group. *n.*

squal·id (skwol′id) wretched; filthy; degraded. *adj.*

squall[1] (skwol or skwôl) a sudden violent gust of wind, often with rain, snow, or sleet. *n.*

squall[2] (skwol or skwôl) **1** cry out loudly; scream violently: *The baby squalled.* **2** a loud, harsh cry: *The parrot's squall was heard all over the house.* 1 *v.,* 2 *n.*

squal·or (skwol′ər) misery and dirt; wretchedness: *There is much squalor in a slum.* *n.*

squan·der (skwon′dər) spend foolishly; waste: *He squanders money in gambling.* *v.*

square (skwer) **1** a figure with four equal sides and four equal angles. See **rectangle** for picture. **2** having this shape: *a square box. A block of stone is usually square.* **3** anything having this shape, or nearly this shape: *The troops were drawn up in a square.* **4** make square in shape: *square a block of granite.* **5** an open space in a city or town bounded by streets on four sides, often planted with grass, trees, etc.: *The soldiers' monument is in the square opposite the city hall.* **6** any similar open space, such as at the meeting of streets. **7** a space in a city or town, bounded by streets on four sides: *This square is filled with stores.* **8** the distance along one side of such a space; a block: *We live three squares from the school.* **9** of a specified length on each side of a square: *a room four metres square.* **10** shape to a right angle. **11** forming a right angle: *a square corner.* **12** an instrument shaped like a T or L, used for drawing right angles and testing the squareness of anything. **13** make straight, level, or even: *square a picture on the wall.* **14** adjust; settle: *Let us square our accounts today.* **15** agree; conform: *His acts do not square with his promises.* **16** just; fair; honest: *You will get a square deal at this shop.* **17** *Informal.* satisfying: *a square meal.* **18** a **square metre** contains the same amount of space as a square measuring one metre on each side: *A rug 1* m × *4* m *and a rug 2* m × *2* m *each cover 4 square metres.* **19** the product obtained when a number is multiplied by itself: *16 is the square of 4.* **20** multiply a number by itself: *25 squared makes 625.* 1, 3, 5–8, 12, 19 *n.,* 2, 9, 11, 16–18 *adj.,* **squar·er, squar·est;** 4, 10, 13–15, 20 *v.,* **squared, squar·ing.**

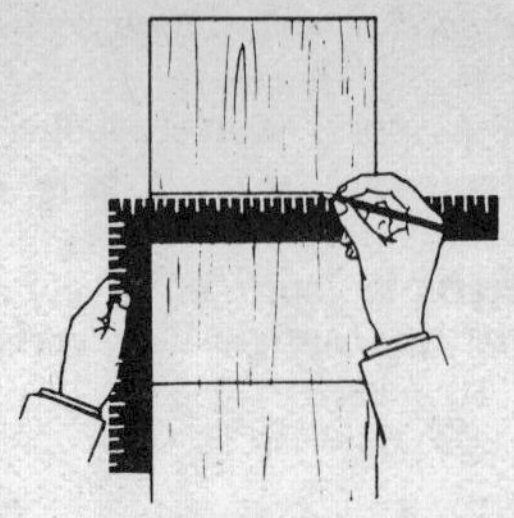
A square for drawing right angles

square dance a dance performed by a set of couples arranged about a square space or in some set form.

square knot a knot firmly joining two loose ends of rope or cord. Each end is formed into a loop which both encloses and passes through the other. See **knot** for picture.

square–rigged (skwer′rigd′) having the principal sails set at right angles across the masts. *adj.*

square root a number that produces a given number when multiplied by itself: *3 is the square root of 9.*

squash[1] (skwosh) **1** press until soft or flat; crush: *The boy squashed the bug. This package was squashed in the mail.* **2** put an end to; stop by force: *The police quickly squashed the riot.* **3** crowd; squeeze. **4** a game resembling handball and tennis, played in a walled court with rackets and a rubber ball. 1–3 *v.,* 4 *n.*
☛ **Squash**[1] comes from early French *esquasser,* which developed from Latin *ex,* meaning 'out,' and *quassare,* meaning 'press.'

squash[2] (skwosh) a vegetable of several varieties that grow on vines on the ground: *Pumpkins and vegetable marrows are two kinds of squash.* *n., pl.* **squash** or **squash·es.**
☛ **Squash**[2] comes from a North American Indian word.

squat (skwot) **1** crouch on the heels. **2** sit on the ground or floor with the legs drawn up closely beneath or in front of the body: *The Indians squatted around the fire.* **3** crouching: *We saw a squat figure in front of the fire.* **4** the act of squatting. **5** settle on another's land without title or right. **6** settle on public land to acquire ownership of it. **7** short and thick; low and broad: *The burglar was a squat, dark man. I like that squat teapot.* 1, 2, 5, 6 *v.,* **squat·ted** or **squat, squat·ting;** 3, 7 *adj.,* 4 *n.*

squaw (skwo or skwô) a North American Indian woman or wife. *n.*

hat, āge, fär; let, ēqual, tėrm; it, īce
hot, ōpen, ôrder; oil, out; cup, pu̇t, rüle
əbove, takən, pencəl, lemən, circəs
ch, child; ng, long; sh, ship
th, thin; ᴛʜ, then; zh, measure

☛ Squaw comes from a North American Indian word. However, many Indians do not use the word and consider it insulting.

squawk (skwok or skwôk) **1** make a loud, harsh sound: *Chickens and ducks squawk when frightened.* **2** a loud, harsh sound. **3** complain loudly. **4** a loud complaint. 1, 3 *v.,* 2, 4 *n.*

squeak (skwēk) **1** make a short, sharp, shrill sound: *A mouse squeaks.* **2** such a sound: *We heard the squeak of the rocking chair.* **3** *Informal.* get or pass (by or through) with difficulty. 1, 3 *v.,* 2 *n.*
narrow squeak, *Informal.* a narrow escape.

squeak·y (skwēk′ē) squeaking: *a squeaky door. adj.,* **squeak·i·er, squeak·i·est.**

squeal (skwēl) **1** make a long, sharp, shrill cry: *A pig squeals when it is hurt.* **2** such a cry. **3** *Informal.* inform on another; tattle. 1, 3 *v.,* 2 *n.*

squeeze (skwēz) **1** press hard: *Don't squeeze the kitten; you will hurt it.* **2** a squeezing; tight pressure: *She gave her sister's arm a squeeze.* **3** hug: *She squeezed her child.* **4** force by pressing: *I can't squeeze another thing into my trunk.* **5** yield to pressure: *Sponges squeeze easily.* **6** force a way: *He squeezed through the crowd.* **7** a crush; crowd: *It's a tight squeeze to get five people in that little car.* 1, 3–6 *v.,* **squeezed, squeez·ing;** 2, 7 *n.*

squid (skwid) a sea creature related to the octopus having a long body, ten arms and a pair of tail fins: *Small squids are used as bait in fishing for cod. n.*

squint (skwint) **1** look with the eyes partly closed. **2** a looking with partly closed eyes. **3** a sidelong look; a hasty look. **4** a defect of the eyes that makes one look sideways or cross-eyed. **5** look sideways or cross-eyed. 1, 5 *v.,* 2–4 *n.*

squire (skwīr) **1** in England, a country gentleman, especially the chief landowner in a district. **2** a young man of noble family who attended a knight till he himself was made a knight. **3** a woman's escort. **4** escort a girl or woman: *He squired his sister to the dance.* 1–3 *n.,* 4 *v.,* **squired, squir·ing.**

squirm (skwėrm) **1** wriggle; writhe; twist: *The restless boy squirmed in his chair.* **2** a wriggle; twist. 1 *v.,* 2 *n.*

A grey squirrel — about 23 cm long without the tail

squir·rel (skwėr′əl or skwir′əl) **1** a small bushy-tailed animal that usually lives in trees. **2** its fur, usually black, grey, dark-brown, or reddish. *n.*

squirt (skwėrt) **1** force out liquid through a narrow opening: *to squirt water through a tube.* **2** come out in a jet or stream: *water squirting from a hose.* **3** wet or soak by shooting liquid in a jet or stream: *The elephant squirted me with its trunk.* **4** a squirting: *The skunk caught the dog with a good squirt.* **5** a jet of liquid: *He dodged a squirt of water from the hose.* **6** *Informal.* an insignificant person who is cheeky or conceited: *a little squirt of a man.* **7** a young boy. 1–3 *v.,* 4–7 *n.*

Sr. senior (def. 2).

St. **1** Street. **2** Saint.

stab (stab) **1** pierce or wound with a pointed weapon. **2** thrust with a pointed weapon; aim a blow. **3** a thrust or blow made with a pointed weapon. **4** a wound made by stabbing. **5** wound someone's feelings sharply or deeply: *The mother was stabbed to the heart by her son's thoughtlessness.* **6** *Informal.* an attempt: *It was a difficult puzzle but he made a stab at it.* 1, 2 5 *v.,* **stabbed, stab·bing;** 3, 4, 6 *n.*

sta·bil·i·ty (stə bil′ə tē) **1** the condition of being fixed in position; firmness: *A concrete wall has more stability than a light wooden fence.* **2** permanence. **3** steadfastness of character or purpose: *the stability of Mackenzie King's character and devotion. n., pl.* **sta·bil·i·ties.**

sta·bi·lize (stā′bə līz′) **1** make stable or firm: *stabilize a government.* **2** prevent changes in; hold steady: *stabilize prices.* **3** keep a ship, aircraft, etc. well-balanced. *v.,* **sta·bi·lized, sta·bi·liz·ing.**

sta·ble[1] (stā′bəl) **1** a building where horses or cattle are kept and fed. **2** a group of animals housed in such a building: *The black horse is one of Mr. Ford's stable.* **3** put or keep in a stable. **4** a group of race horses belonging to one owner. 1, 2, 4 *n.,* 3 *v.,* **sta·bled, sta·bling.**

sta·ble[2] (stā′bəl) **1** not likely to move or change; firm; steady: *Concrete reinforced with steel is stable.* **2** lasting without change; permanent: *The whole world needs a stable peace. adj.*

stac·ca·to (stə kä′tō) in music: **1** with a break between each tone; disconnected; abrupt. **2** in a staccato manner. 1 *adj.,* 2 *adv.*

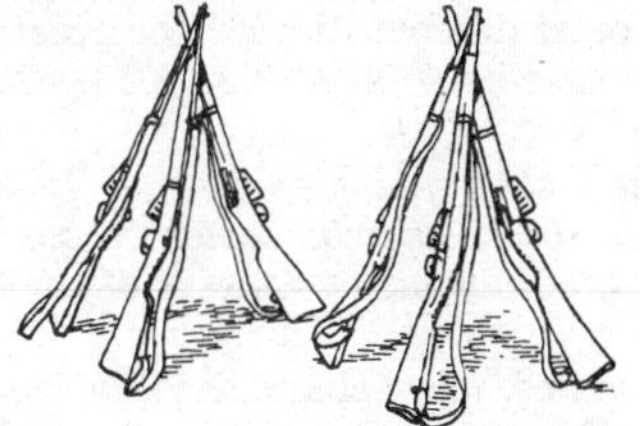
Stacks of rifles

stack (stak) **1** a large pile of hay, straw, etc.: *Haystacks, which are often round, are arranged so as to shed water.* **2** a pile of anything: *a stack of wood.* **3** a number of rifles arranged to form a cone or pyramid. **4** pile or arrange in a stack: *to stack hay, to stack rifles.* **5** a chimney. 1–3, 5 *n.,* 4 *v.*

sta·di·um (stā′dē əm) a place shaped like an oval or a U, consisting of rows of seats around a large, open space for games, concerts, etc.: *The stadium was filled for the final football game of the series. n., pl.* **sta·di·ums** or **sta·di·a** (stā′dē ə).

staff (staf) **1** a stick, pole, or rod used as a support, as an emblem of office, as a weapon, etc.: *The old man leaned on his staff. The flag hangs on a staff.* **2** something that supports or sustains: *Bread is called the staff of life because it will support life.* **3** a group assisting a chief; a group of employees: *Our school has a staff of twenty teachers.* **4** provide with officers or employees. **5** in music, the five lines and four spaces between them on which the notes, rests, etc. are written. See **bar** for picture. 1–3, 5 *n., pl.* **staves** (stāvz) or **staffs** for 1 and 2, **staffs** for 3 and 5; 4 *v.*

stag (stag) **1** a full-grown male deer. **2** for men only: *a stag party.* **3** a party or dinner for men only. 1, 3 *n.*, 2 *adj.*

stage (stāj) **1** one step or degree in a process; a period of development: *Frogs pass through a tadpole stage.* **2** the raised platform in a theatre on which the actors perform. **3** the theatre; the drama; the profession of acting: *Shakespeare wrote for the stage.* **4** a scene of action: *The Plains of Abraham were the stage of a famous battle.* **5** put on a stage or arrange: *The play was very well staged. Mother had staged a surprise for the children's party by hiring a magician.* **6** a stagecoach; bus. **7** a place of rest on a journey; a regular stopping place. **8** platform. 1–4, 6–8 *n.*, 5 *v.*, **staged, stag·ing.**
by or **in easy stages,** a little at a time; slowly; often stopping: *We made the long journey in easy stages.*
on the stage, being an actor or actress.

stage·coach (stāj′kōch′) a coach carrying people, mail, etc. over a regular route. *n.*

stage fright a nervous fear of appearing before an audience.

stag·ger (stag′ər) **1** sway or reel from weakness, a heavy load, or being drunk. **2** make sway or reel: *The blow staggered him for the moment.* **3** a swaying or reeling. **4** become unsteady; waver: *The troops staggered under the severe attack.* **5** hesitate. **6** cause to hesitate or become confused: *The difficulty of the examination staggered him.* **7** confuse or astonish greatly: *We were staggered by the news of the air disaster.* **8** make helpless. **9** arrange in a zigzag order or way. **10** arrange to be at different times: *The times for quitting work were staggered so as to ease the traffic problem.* 1, 2, 4–10 *v.*, 3 *n.*

stag·nant (stag′nənt) **1** not running or flowing; foul from standing still: *stagnant air, stagnant water.* **2** not active; sluggish: *During the summer, business is often stagnant. adj.*

staid (stād) having a settled, quiet character: *We think of Quakers as staid people. adj.*

stain (stān) **1** soil; spot: *The tablecloth is stained where food has been spilled.* **2** a spot; a dirty mark: *He has ink stains on his shirt.* **3** spot by wrongdoing or disgrace; to dishonor: *His crimes stained the family honor.* **4** a mark of disgrace; dishonor: *His character is without stain.* **5** color; dye: *She stained the chair a dark green.* **6** a dye used to color or darken: *She painted the table with a brown stain.* 1, 3, 5 *v.*, 2, 4, 6 *n.* 1, 3, 5 *v.*, 2, 4, 6 *n.*

stair (ster) **1** one of a series of steps for going from one level or floor to another. **2** Also, **stairs,** *pl.* a set of such steps; stairway: *the top of the stairs. n.*
☛ **Stair** and **stare** are pronounced the same.

stair·case (ster′kās′) a flight of stairs with its framework; stairs. *n.*

stair·way (ster′wā′) a way up and down by stairs; a flight or flights of stairs: *the back stairway. n.*

stake¹ (stāk) **1** a stick or post pointed at one end for driving into the ground. **2** fasten to a stake or with a stake. **3** mark with stakes; mark the boundaries of: *The miner staked his claim.* 1 *n.*, 2, 3 *v.*, **staked, stak·ing.**
pull up stakes, *Informal.* move away: *After seven years of drought, they finally pulled up stakes and left the farm.*
☛ **Stake** and **steak** are pronounced the same.

stake² (stāk) **1** risk money or something valuable on the result of a game or on any chance. **2** the money risked; what is staked: *The men played for high stakes.* **3** the prize in a race or contest: *The stakes were divided up among the winners.* **4** something to gain or lose; an interest; a share in a property: *Each of us has a stake in the future of our country.* 1 *v.*, **staked, stak·ing;** 2–4 *n.*
at stake, to be won or lost; risked: *His honor is at stake.*
☛ See note at **stake¹**.

sta·lac·tite (stə lak′tīt or stal′ək tīt′) a formation of lime, shaped like an icicle, hanging from the roof of a cave: *Stalactites are formed by dripping water that contains lime. n.*

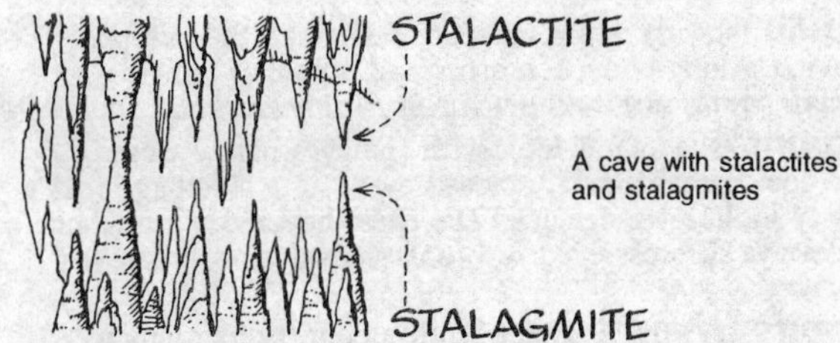

A cave with stalactites and stalagmites

sta·lag·mite (stə lag′mīt or stal′əg mīt′) a formation of lime, shaped like a cone, built up on the floor of a cave: *Stalagmites are formed by water dripping from stalactites. n.*

stale (stāl) **1** not fresh: *stale bread.* **2** no longer new or interesting: *a stale joke.* **3** out of condition: *The horse has gone stale from too much running. adj.*, **stal·er, stal·est.**

stale·mate (stāl′māt′) **1** in the game of chess, a draw which results when a player cannot move any of his pieces. **2** any position in which no action can be taken; complete standstill. *n.*

stalk¹ (stok or stôk) **1** the main stem of a plant. **2** any slender supporting part of a plant or animal: *A flower may have a stalk. The eyes of a lobster are on stalks. n.*
☛ **Stalk** and **stock** are sometimes pronounced the same.

stalk² (stok or stôk) **1** approach or pursue without being seen or heard: *The hunters stalked the lion.* **2** spread silently and steadily: *Disease stalked through the land.* **3** walk proudly or haughtily: *The angry man stalked out of the room.* **4** the act of stalking. 1–3 *v.*, 4 *n.*
☛ See note at **stalk¹**.

stall¹ (stol or stôl) **1** a place in a stable for one animal. **2** a small place for selling things: *At the public market different things were sold in different stalls under one big roof.* **3** a seat in the choir of a church. **4** in

hat, āge, fär; let, ēqual, tėrm; it, īce
hot, ōpen, ôrder; oil, out; cup, pu̇t, rüle
əbove, takən, pencəl, lemən, circəs
ch, child; ng, long; sh, ship
th, thin; ᴛʜ, then; zh, measure

A stall for a horse

Great Britain, a seat in the front part of a theatre. **5** put or keep in a stall: *The horses were safely stalled.* **6** stop or bring to a standstill, usually against one's wish: *He stalled the engine of his automobile.* **7** come to a stop because of too heavy a load or too little fuel: *The truck stalled on the steep hill.* 1–4 *n.*, 5–7 *v.*

stall[2] (stol or stôl) *Informal.* delay: *You have been stalling long enough.* *v.*

stal·lion (stal′yən) a male horse that can be used for breeding. *n.*

stal·wart (stol′wərt or stôl′wərt) **1** strong and brave: *a stalwart knight.* **2** firm; steadfast: *a stalwart friend.* *adj.*

sta·men (stā′mən) one of the parts of a flower that carry the pollen. See **flower** for picture. *n.*

stam·i·na (stam′ə nə) strength; endurance: *A long-distance runner needs stamina.* *n.*

stam·mer (stam′ər) **1** repeat the same sound in an effort to speak; hesitate in speaking: *Example: I s-s-see a d-d-dog.* **2** utter in this manner: *stammer an excuse.* **3** a stammering or stuttering: *He has a nervous stammer.* 1, 2 *v.*, 3 *n.*

stamp (stamp) **1** a small piece of paper with a sticky back, put on letters, papers, parcels, etc., to show that a charge has been paid. **2** a similar piece of paper used for any of various purposes. **3** put a stamp on: *stamp a letter, stamp an official document.* **4** bring down one's foot with force: *He stamped his foot in anger. He stamped on the spider.* **5** the act of stamping. **6** pound; crush; trample; tread: *She stamped out the fire.* **7** an instrument that cuts, shapes, or prints a design on paper, metal, wax, etc.; thing that puts a mark on: *The stamp had her name on it.* **8** mark with such an instrument: *She stamped the papers with the date.* **9** the mark made by such an instrument. **10** a mill or machine that crushes rock, etc. **11** show to be of a certain quality or character: *His speech stamps him as a man of education.* **12** an impression; marks: *Her face bore the stamp of suffering.* 1, 2, 5, 7, 9, 10, 12 *n.*, 3, 4, 6, 8, 11 *v.*

stam·pede (stam pēd′) **1** a sudden scattering or headlong flight of a frightened herd of cattle, horses, etc. **2** any headlong flight of a large group: *a stampede of a frightened crowd from a burning building.* **3** scatter or flee in a stampede. **4** a general rush: *a stampede to newly discovered gold fields.* **5** make a general rush. **6** cause to stampede: *The thunderstorm stampeded the cattle.* **7** *Cdn.* a rodeo, often accompanied by other amusements usually found at a fair: *The Calgary Stampede began with a huge parade.* 1, 2, 4, 7 *n.*, 3, 5, 6 *v.*, **stam·ped·ed, stam·ped·ing.**

stance (stans) the manner of standing; posture: *an erect stance.* *n.*

stanch (stonch) staunch. *v., adj.*

stand (stand) **1** be upright on one's feet: *Don't stand if you are tired, but sit down.* **2** rise to one's feet: *The children stood when the visitor arrived.* **3** be set upright; be placed; be located: *The box stands over there.* **4** set upright: *Stand the box here.* **5** be in a certain place, rank, scale, etc.: *Pillars stand on each side of the door. He stood first in his class for service to the school.* **6** be in a special condition: *He stands innocent of any wrong. The poor man stood in need of food and clothing.* **7** be unchanged; hold good; remain the same: *The rule against being late will stand.* **8** stay in place; last: *The old house has stood for a hundred years.* **9** bear; endure: *Those plants cannot stand cold; they die in the winter.* **10** *Informal.* bear the expense of: *I'll stand you a dinner.* **11** stop moving; halt; stop: *'Stand!' cried the sentry.* **12** a halt; stop: *We made a last stand against the enemy.* **13** a place where a person stands; position: *The policeman took his stand at the street corner.* **14** a raised place where people can sit or stand: *The mayor sat on the reviewing stand at the parade. The crowd in the stands cheered the winning team.* **15** something to put things on or in: *Leave your wet umbrella in the stand in the hall.* **16** a stall, booth, table, etc. for a small business: *a newspaper stand, a fruit stand.* **17** a group of growing trees or plants: *a stand of timber.* 1–11 *v.*, **stood, stand·ing;** 12–17 *n.*

stand by, a be near. **b** side with; help; support: *stand by a friend.* **c** be or get ready for use, action, etc.: *The radio operator was ordered to stand by.*

stand for, a represent; mean: *What does the abbreviation St. stand for?* **b** be on the side of; take the part of; uphold: *Our school stands for fair play.* **c** *Informal.* put up with: *The teacher said she would not stand for talking during class.*

stand out, a project: *His ears stood out.* **b** be noticeable or prominent: *Certain facts stand out.* **c** refuse to yield: *stand out against popular opinion.*

stand up, a get to one's feet; rise: *He stood up and began to speak.* **b** endure; last.

stand up for, take the part of; defend; support: *stand up for a friend.*

stand up to, meet or face boldly: *The young boy stood up to the bully.*

stand·ard (stan′dərd) **1** anything taken as a basis of comparison; a model: *Your work is not up to the class standard.* **2** of the accepted or normal size, amount, power, quality, etc.: *the standard rate of pay.* **3** used as a standard; according to rule: *standard spelling, standard pronunciation.* **4** having recognized excellence or authority: *Scott and Dickens are standard authors.* **5** a flag, emblem, or symbol: *The dragon was the standard of China.* **6** an upright support: *The floor lamp has a long standard.* 1, 5, 6 *n.*, 2–4 *adj.*

stand·ard·ize (stan′dər dīz′) make standard in size, shape, weight, quality, etc.: *The parts of an automobile are standardized.* *v.*, **stand·ard·ized, stand·ard·iz·ing.**

standard time the time normally adopted for a region or country: *Standard time is one hour different from daylight-saving time.*

stand–by (stand′bī′) 1 a person or thing that can be relied upon for support or encouragement. 2 a person or thing held in reserve, especially as a possible replacement or substitute. *n.*

stand–in (stand′in′) a person or thing that takes the place of another; substitute: *Will you be my stand-in at the next meeting? n.*

stand·ing (stan′ding) 1 position; reputation: *men of good standing.* 2 duration: *a feud of long standing between two families.* 3 straight up; erect: *standing timber.* 4 done from an erect position: *a standing broad jump.* 5 established; permanent: *a standing invitation, a standing army.* 6 not flowing; stagnant: *standing water.* 1, 2 *n.,* 3–6 *adj.*

stand–out (stand′out′) *Informal.* a thing or person that is outstanding in appearance or performance. *n.*

stand·point (stand′point′) a point of view; a mental attitude: *From his standpoint, swimming is a waste of time. n.*

stand·still (stand′stil′) a complete stop; a halt or pause. *n.*

stank (stangk) See **stink.** *The dead fish stank. v.*

stan·za (stan′zə) a group of lines of poetry, usually four or more, arranged according to a fixed plan; a verse of a poem: *They sang the first and last stanzas of 'O Canada.' n.*

sta·ple[1] (stā′pəl) 1 a U-shaped piece of metal with pointed ends: *Staples are driven into doors, etc. to hold hooks, pins, or bolts.* 2 a bent piece of wire folded over to fasten papers, etc. or driven into wood, etc. to attach some other material. 3 fasten with a staple or staples. 1, 2 *n.,* 3 *v.,* **sta·pled, sta·pling.**

sta·ple[2] (stā′pəl) 1 the most important or principal article grown or manufactured in a place: *Wheat is the staple in Saskatchewan.* 2 any major article of trade. 3 most important; principal: *Bread is a staple food. The weather is a staple topic of conversation.* 4 a fibre of cotton or wool. 1, 2, 4 *n.,* 3 *adj.*

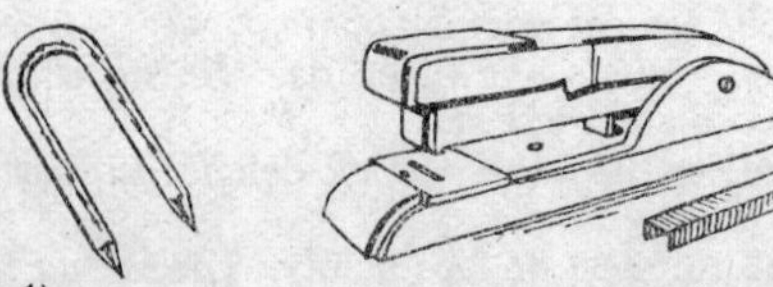

A staple (def. 1) A stapler

sta·pler (stā′plər) a machine for driving wire staples into paper, cardboard, wood, or plaster: *He used a stapler to fasten the pages of the booklet together. n.*

star (stär) 1 any of the heavenly bodies, especially one that is not the moon, a planet, a comet, or a meteor, appearing as bright points seen in the sky at night. 2 a figure having usually five points, sometimes six, like these: ★ ✶. 3 anything having or suggesting this shape. 4 mark or ornament with stars: *Her card was starred for perfect attendance.* 5 a sign like this (∗). 6 mark with such a sign. 7 a person having brilliant qualities: *an athletic star.* 8 a famous person in some art or profession, especially one who plays the lead in a performance: *a movie star.* 9 chief; best; leading; excellent: *the star player on a football team.* 10 be prominent; be a leading performer; excel: *She has starred in many motion pictures.* 1–3, 5, 7, 8 *n.,* 4, 6, 10 *v.,* **starred, star·ring;** 9 *adj.*

star·board (stär′bərd) 1 the right side of a ship or aircraft, when facing forward. See **aft** for picture. 2 on the right side of a ship or aircraft. 1 *n.,* 2 *adj.*

starch (stärch) 1 a white, tasteless food substance. *Potatoes, wheat, rice, and corn contain much starch.* 2 a preparation of this substance used to stiffen clothes, curtains, etc. 3 stiffen clothes, curtains, etc. with starch. 1, 2 *n.,* 3 *v.*

starch·y (stär′chē) 1 like starch; containing starch. 2 stiffened with starch. 3 stiff in manner; formal. *adj.,* **starch·i·er, starch·i·est.**

stare (ster) 1 look long and directly with the eyes wide open: *A person stares in wonder, surprise, stupidity, or curiosity, or from mere rudeness. The little girl stared at the toys in the window.* 2 a long and direct look with the eyes wide open: *The doll's eyes were set in an unchanging stare.* 3 be very striking or glaring: *His eyes stared with anger.* 1, 3 *v.,* **stared, star·ing;** 2 *n.*

stare one in the face, be very evident; force itself on the notice of: *His spelling mistake was staring him in the face.*

☛ **Stare** and **stair** are pronounced the same.

A starfish — about 9 cm across

star·fish (stär′fish′) a star-shaped sea animal: *Starfish are not fish. n., pl.* **star·fish** or **star·fish·es.**

stark (stärk) 1 downright; complete: *That fool is talking stark nonsense.* 2 entirely; completely: *The boys went swimming stark naked.* 3 bare; barren; desolate: *a stark landscape.* 1, 3 *adj.,* 2 *adv.*

star·light (stär′līt′) 1 light from the stars. 2 lighted by the stars. 1 *n.,* 2 *adj.*

star·ling (stär′ling) a common bird having glossy, greenish-black or brownish-black feathers: *Starlings nest about buildings and fly in large flocks. n.*

star·lit (stär′lit′) lighted by the stars: *a starlit night. adj.*

star·ry (stär′ē) 1 lighted by stars; containing many stars: *a starry sky.* 2 shining like stars: *starry eyes. adj.,* **star·ri·er, star·ri·est.**

Stars and Stripes the flag of the United States.

start (stärt) 1 begin to move, go, or act: *The train started on time.* 2 begin: *to start reading a book.* 3 set going; put into action: *I started a fire.* 4 setting in motion. 5 beginning to move, go, or act. 6 move suddenly: *She started in surprise.* 7 a sudden movement; jerk: *On seeing the snake, the man sprang up with a start. I awoke with a start.* 8 come or rise suddenly; spring suddenly: *Tears started from her eyes.* 9 a surprise; fright: *The sudden appearance of the bear gave her quite a start.* 10 a beginning ahead of others; advantage: *He got the start of his rivals.* 11 the place,

line, etc. where a race begins. 1–3, 6, 8 *v.*, 4, 5, 7, 9–11 *n.*
by fits and starts. See **fit**[2].
start in or **start out,** begin to do something.

star·tle (stär′təl) 1 frighten suddenly; surprise: *The dog jumped at the girl and startled her.* 2 cause to make a sudden movement: *The hunters startled the deer.* *v.*, **star·tled, star·tling.**

star·tling (stärt′ling) surprising; frightening: *startling tales.* *adj.*

star·va·tion (stär vā′shən) 1 starving. 2 suffering from extreme hunger; being starved: *Starvation caused his death.* *n.*

starve (stärv) 1 die because of hunger. 2 suffer severely because of hunger. 3 weaken or kill with hunger: *That cruel man half starves his horses.* 4 *Informal.* feel very hungry. *v.*, **starved, starv·ing.**
starve for, suffer from the lack of: *starve for news. That child is starving for affection.*

state (stāt) 1 the condition of a person or thing: *He is in a state of poor health. The house is in a bad state of repair.* 2 the physical condition of a material with regard to its structure, composition, or form: *Ice is water in a solid state.* 3 a political unit consisting of an independent government and the people it represents. 4 one of several such units that together form a nation: *The State of Alaska is one of the United States.* 5 a person's position in life; rank: *He is a man of humble state.* 6 tell in speech or writing; express; say: *State your opinion of the new school rules.* 7 a high style of living; dignity; pomp: *Kings lived in great state.* 8 having to do with special occasions or ceremonies: *state robes.* 1–5, 7 *n.*, 6 *v.*, **stat·ed, stat·ing;** 8 *adj.*
lie in state, lie in a coffin so as to be seen formally and publicly before being buried: *The dead king lay in state for a day in the main hall of the royal palace.*

stat·ed (stāt′id) fixed; settled: *School begins daily at a stated time.* *adj.*

state·ly (stāt′lē) having dignity; imposing; grand; majestic: *Rideau Hall is a stately mansion.* *adj.*, **state·li·er, state·li·est.**

state·ment (stāt′mənt) 1 something stated; an account; report: *His statement was correct.* 2 a manner of stating something; stating: *The statement of an idea helps me to remember it.* *n.*

states·man (stāts′mən) a person skilled in the management of public or national affairs: *Winston Churchill was an outstanding statesman.* *n., pl.* **states·men** (stāts′mən).

states·man·ship (stāts′mən ship′) skill in the management of public affairs. *n.*

stat·ic (stat′ik) 1 at rest; standing still. 2 noises and other interference on radio and television caused by electrical disturbances in the air. 3 having to do with stationary electrical charges that balance each other: *Static electricity can be produced by rubbing a glass rod with a silk cloth.* 1, 3 *adj.*, 2 *n.*

sta·tion (stā′shən) 1 a place to stand in; a place that a person is appointed to occupy in the performance of some duty: *The policeman took his station at the corner.* 2 a building or place used for a definite purpose: *a police station.* 3 a regular stopping place: *She met her at the railway station.* 4 the place or equipment for sending out or receiving programs, messages, etc. by radio or television. 5 give a position or place to; place: *He*

hat, āge, fär; let, ēqual, tėrm; it, īce
hot, ōpen, ôrder; oil, out; cup, pu̇t, rüle
əbove, takən, pencəl, lemən, circəs
ch, child; ng, long; sh, ship
th, thin; ᴛʜ, then; zh, measure

stationed himself outside the hotel. The soldier was stationed at Kingston. 6 social position; rank: *A serf was a man of humble station in life.* 1–4, 6 *n.*, 5 *v.*

sta·tion·ar·y (stā′shən er′ē) 1 having a fixed station or place; not movable: *A factory engine is stationary.* 2 standing still; not moving: *A parked car is stationary.* 3 not changing in size, number, activity, etc.: *The population of this town has been stationary for ten years at about 5000 people.* *adj.*
☞ **Stationary** and **stationery** are pronounced the same.

sta·tion·er·y (stā′shən er′ē) writing materials; paper, cards, and envelopes. *n.*
☞ See note at **stationary.**

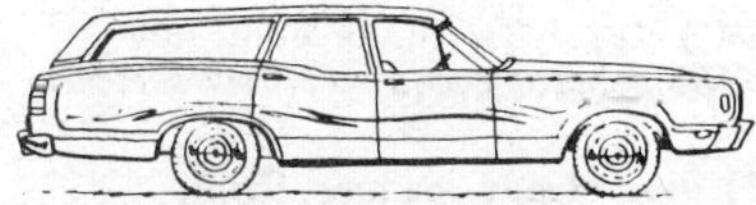
A station wagon

station wagon a kind of automobile that can serve both as a passenger car and as a light truck: *The back end of our station wagon can be opened to permit loading.*

sta·tis·tics (stə tis′tiks) 1 numerical facts about people, business conditions, the weather, etc.: *population statistics.* 2 the science of collecting and classifying such facts in order to show their significance. *n.*

stat·ue (stach′ü) an image of a person or animal carved in stone, wood, etc., cast in bronze, or modelled: *We saw a marble statue of Queen Victoria.* *n.*

stat·ure (stach′ər) 1 height: *A man* 185 cm *tall is above average stature.* 2 reputation or distinction: *He is a man of considerable stature in his line of business.* *n.*

sta·tus (stā′təs or stat′əs) 1 one's social or professional standing; one's position: *the status of a doctor.* 2 the condition or state: *Diplomats are interested in the status of world affairs.* *n.*

stat·ute (stach′üt) a law enacted by a legislative body: *The statutes for Canada are made by Parliament.* *n.*

staunch[1] (stonch or stônch) 1 stop the flow of blood, etc. 2 stop the flow of blood from a wound: *He staunched the wound successfully.* *v.*

staunch[2] (stonch or stônch) 1 strong; firm: *staunch walls, a staunch defence.* 2 loyal; steadfast: *a staunch friend.* 3 watertight: *a staunch boat.* *adj.*

stave (stāv) 1 one of the curved pieces of wood that form the sides of a barrel, tub, etc. 2 a stick or staff. 3 break a hole in a barrel, boat, etc. 4 become smashed or broken in. 5 a verse or stanza of a poem, song, etc. 1, 2, 5 *n.*, 3, 4 *v.*, **staved** or **stove, stav·ing.**
stave off, put off; to keep back, delay, or prevent: *The lost campers ate birds' eggs to stave off starvation.*

staves (stāvz) 1 a plural of **staff.** 2 plural of **stave.** *n.*

stay[1] (stā) 1 remain; continue to be: *Stay still. Stay here till I tell you to move. The cat stayed out all* *night. Shall I go or stay?* **2** live for a while; dwell: *She is staying with her aunt while her mother is ill.* **3** staying; a stop; the time spent: *a pleasant stay at the seashore.* **4** put an end to for a while; satisfy: *He ate some bread and butter to stay his hunger till time for dinner.* **5** put off; hold back; delay: *The teacher stayed judgment till she could hear both sides.* **6** last; endure: *I was unable to stay to the end of the race.* 1, 2, 4–6 *v.*, 3 *n.*

stay[2] (stā) a support, prop, or brace: *The oldest son was the family's stay. n.*

stay[3] (stā) a strong rope, chain, or wire attached to something to steady it: *The mast of a ship is held in place by stays.* See **schooner** for picture. *n.*

stead (sted) place: *Our regular baby-sitter could not come, but sent her sister in her stead. n.*

stand in good stead, be of advantage or service to: *His ability to swim stood him in good stead when the boat upset.*

stead·fast (sted′fast′) firmly fixed; constant; not moving or changing: *The general was a steadfast servant of his country. adj.*

stead·i·ly (sted′ə lē) in a steady manner; firmly; uniformly. *adv.*

stead·i·ness (sted′ē nis) the condition of being steady; firmness. *n.*

stead·y (sted′ē) **1** changing little; uniform; regular: *He is making steady progress at school.* **2** firmly fixed; firm; not swaying or shaking: *This post is steady as a rock. Hold the ladder steady.* **3** not easily excited; calm: *steady nerves.* **4** having good habits; reliable: *He is a steady young man.* **5** make steady; keep steady: *Steady the ladder while I climb to the roof.* **6** become steady: *Our sails filled as the wind steadied from the east.* 1–4 *adj.*, **stead·i·er, stead·i·est;** 5, 6 *v.*, **stead·ied, stead·y·ing.**

go steady, a *Informal.* of a boy or girl, date the same person all the time. **b** go carefully.

steak (stāk) a slice of meat, especially beef, or fish for broiling or frying. *n.*

☛ **Steak** and **stake** are pronounced the same.

steal (stēl) **1** take something that does not belong to one; take dishonestly: *Robbers stole the money.* **2** take, get, or do secretly: *She stole time from her lessons to read a story.* **3** take, get, or win by art, charm, etc.: *The baby stole our hearts.* **4** move secretly or quietly: *She stole softly out of the room.* **5** *Informal.* stealing: *The boy's use of his brother's notes was a steal.* **6** *Informal.* something obtained very cheaply or very easily: *This table is such a bargain it's a steal.* 1–4 *v.*, **stole, sto·len, steal·ing;** 5, 6 *n.*

☛ **Steal** and **steel** are pronounced the same.

stealth (stelth) secret or sly action: *He obtained the letter by stealth, taking it while nobody was in the room. n.*

stealth·y (stel′thē) done in a secret manner; secret; sly: *The cat crept in a stealthy way toward the bird. adj.*, **stealth·i·er, stealth·i·est.**

steam (stēm) **1** water in the form of vapor or gas: *Boiling water gives off steam. Steam is used to heat houses and run engines.* **2** give off steam: *The cup of coffee was steaming.* **3** become covered with steam: *The windshield had steamed up inside the heated car.* **4** rise in the form of steam: *The mist steamed off the lake.* **5** move by steam: *The ship steamed off.* **6** cook, soften, or freshen by steam: *to steam vegetables. She steamed what was left of the pudding.* **7** *Informal.* power; energy; force: *That old man still has a lot of steam left in him.* 1, 7 *n.*, 2–6 *v.*

let off steam, *Informal.* relieve one's feelings.

steam·boat (stēm′bōt′) a boat moved by steam. *n.*

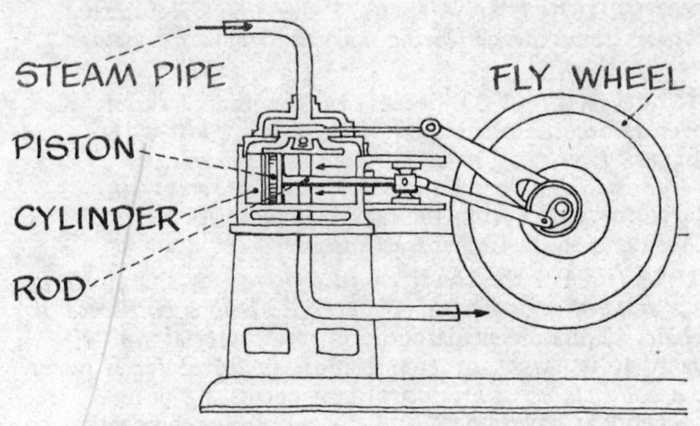

A steam engine. The pressure of the steam forced into the cylinder pushes the piston back and forth. This causes the rod to turn a shaft that passes on motion to wheels or other parts.
The weight of the heavy flywheel attached to the shaft keeps the shaft turning evenly.

steam engine an engine worked by steam. See the picture just above. See also **piston** for picture.

steam·er (stēm′ər) **1** a steamboat; steamship. **2** an engine run by steam. **3** a container in which something is steamed or kept warm. *n.*

steam iron an electric iron in which water is heated to produce steam which is released through holes in its base to dampen cloth while pressing it.

steam roller a heavy roller moved by steam, formerly used to crush and level materials in making roads.

steam·ship (stēm′ship′) a ship moved by steam. *n.*

steam shovel a machine for digging, operated by steam.

steed (stēd) a horse, especially a high-spirited riding horse. *n.*

steel (stēl) **1** iron mixed with carbon so that it is very hard, strong, and tough: *Most tools are made from steel.* **2** something made from steel: *A sword or a piece of steel for sharpening knives can be called a steel.* **3** made of steel. **4** make hard or strong like steel: *He steeled his heart against the sufferings of the poor. The soldiers steeled themselves to withstand the expected attack.* 1–3 *n.*, 4 *v.*

☛ **Steel** and **steal** are pronounced the same.

steel wool fine steel threads or shavings in a pad, etc., used for cleaning or polishing.

steep[1] (stēp) having a sharp slope; almost straight up and down: *The hill is steep. adj.*

steep[2] (stēp) soak: *She steeped the tea in boiling water. His sword was steeped in blood. v.*

steeped in, filled with; permeated by: *ruins steeped in gloom, a mind steeped in hatred.*

hat, āge, fär; let, ēqual, tėrm; it, īce
hot, ōpen, ôrder; oil, out; cup, pu̇t, rüle
əbove, takən, pencəl, lemən, circəs
ch, child; ng, long; sh, ship
th, thin; ᴛʜ, then; zh, measure

stee·ple (stē′pəl) a high tower on a church: *Steeples usually have spires.* See the picture. *n.*

stee·ple·chase (stē′pəl chās′) a horse race over a course having ditches, hedges, and other obstacles. *n.*

steer¹ (stēr) **1** guide the course of: *to steer a car.* **2** be guided: *This car steers easily.* **3** direct one's way or course: *Steer straight for the harbor. Steer away from trouble. v.*

steer² (stēr) **1** a young ox, usually two to four years old. **2** any male of beef cattle. *n.*

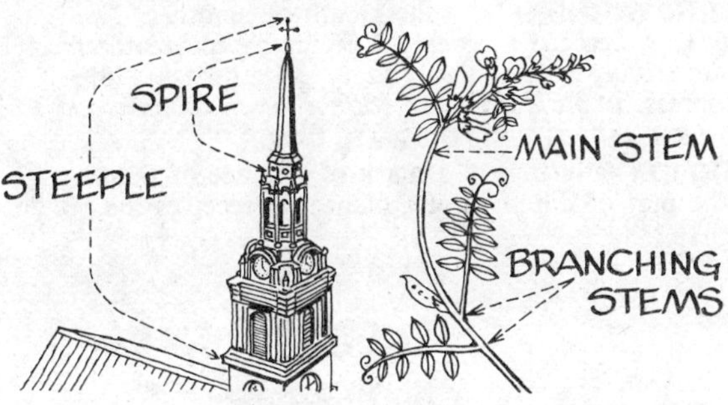

stem¹ (stem) **1** the main part of a plant, usually above the ground: *The stem supports the branches. The trunk of a tree and the stalks of corn are stems.* **2** the part of a flower, a fruit, or a leaf that joins it to the plant or tree. **3** remove the stem from a leaf, fruit, etc. **4** anything like the stem of a plant: *the stem of a goblet, the stem of a pipe.* **5** the bow or front end of a boat. 1, 2, 4, 5 *n.*, 3 *v.*, **stemmed, stem·ming.**
from stem to stern, from one end of a ship to the other.
stem from, come from; have as a source or cause: *The difficulty stems from his failure to plan properly.*

stem² (stem) **1** stop; check; dam up. **2** make progress against: *When you swim upstream, you have to stem the current. v.*, **stemmed, stem·ming.**

stench (stench) a very bad smell; stink: *the stench of a dirty pigsty, the stench of gas. n.*

sten·cil (sten′səl) **1** a thin sheet of metal, paper, etc. having letters or designs cut through it: *When a stencil is laid on a surface and ink or color is spread on, the letters and designs are made on the surface.* **2** the letters and designs so made. **3** mark, paint, or make with a stencil: *The curtains have a stencilled border.* 1, 2 *n.*, 3 *v.*, **sten·cilled, sten·cil·ling.**

ste·nog·ra·pher (stə nog′rə fər) a person whose main work is taking dictation in shorthand and then typing it. *n.*

step (step) **1** a movement made by lifting the foot and putting it down again in a new position; one motion of the leg in walking, running, dancing, etc. **2** the distance covered by one such movement: *She was three steps away when he called her back.* **3** move the legs as in walking, running, dancing, etc.: *Step lively!* **4** a short distance; a little way: *The school is only a step from our house.* **5** walk a short distance: *Step this way.* **6** a way of walking, dancing, etc.: *a quick step, a dance with fancy steps.* **7** put the foot down: *He stepped on a bug.* **8** the sound made by putting the foot down: *I hear steps upstairs.* **9** a place for the foot in going up or coming down: *A stair or a rung of a ladder is a step.* **10** a footprint: *I see steps in the mud.* **11** an action: *The principal took steps to stop needless absence from school.* **12** a degree in a scale; a grade in rank: *A colonel is two steps above a captain.* 1, 2, 4, 6, 8–12 *n.*, 3, 5, 7 *v.*, **stepped, step·ping.**
in step, a making the rhythm of one's steps fit that of another person or persons in marching, walking, or dancing. **b** making one's actions or ideas agree with those of another person or persons; in agreement.
keep step, move at the same pace as another person or persons in time with music.
out of step, not in step; not in agreement with others.
step down, surrender or resign from an office or position.
step off, measure by taking steps: *Step off the distance from the door to the window.*
step up, make go faster, higher, etc.; increase: *to step up the production of automobiles, to step up the pressure in a boiler.*
watch one's step, be careful: *Watch your step when you ride down that steep hill on the bicycle.*

step·child (step′chīld′) a child of one's husband or wife by a former marriage. *n.*

step·fa·ther (step′fo′ᴛʜər) a man who has married one's mother after the death or divorce of one's natural father. *n.*

A stepladder

step·lad·der (step′lad′ər) a ladder having flat steps instead of rungs and, usually, a pair of hinged legs so that it stands by itself. *n.*

step·moth·er (step′muᴛʜ′ər) a woman who has married one's father after the death or divorce of one's natural mother. *n.*

steppe (step) a vast, treeless plain, especially as found in Russia. *n.*

ster·e·o (ster′ē ō′ or stēr′ē ō′) *Informal.* a radio, record player, or tape-recorder equipped with a stereophonic system. *n.*

ster·e·o·phon·ic (ster′ē ə fon′ik or stēr′ē ə fon′ik) giving the effect of lifelike sound by using two or more sets of equipment for recording or broadcasting and two or more sets of receiving equipment. *adj.*

ster·ile (ster′īl or ster′əl) **1** free from living germs: *The doctor kept his instruments sterile.* **2** not producing seed, offspring, crops, etc.; barren; not fertile: *a sterile cow. Sterile land does not produce crops. adj.*

ster·i·lize (ster′ə līz′) **1** make free from living germs: *The water was sterilized by boiling to make it fit to drink.* **2** make unable to produce seed, offspring, crops, etc. *v.*, **ster·i·lized, ster·i·liz·ing.**

ster·ling (stėr′ling) **1** of standard quality for silver; containing 92.5 per cent pure silver: *'Sterling' is stamped* *on solid silver knives, forks, etc.* 2 sterling silver or things made of it. 3 genuine; excellent; reliable: *a man of sterling character.* 4 British money, especially the pound as the standard British unit of money in international trade: *pay in sterling. n.*

stern[1] (stėrn) 1 severe; strict; harsh: *He was a stern master. His stern frown frightened the children.* 2 hard; not yielding; firm: *stern necessity. adj.*

stern[2] (stėrn) the back end of a ship or boat. See **aft** for picture. *n.*

stern–wheel·er (stėrn′wēl′ər or stėrn′hwēl′ər) a steamboat driven by a paddle wheel at the stern or rear. See **paddle wheel** for picture. *n.*

steth·o·scope (steth′ə skōp′) an instrument used by doctors to hear sounds in the lungs, heart, etc. *n.*

stew (styü or stü) 1 cook by slow boiling: *The cook stewed the chicken for a long time.* 2 food cooked by slow boiling: *beef stew.* 3 *Informal.* worry; fret. 4 *Informal.* a state of worry; fret: *She is in a stew over her lost suitcase.* 1, 3 *v.,* 2, 4 *n.*

stew·ard (styü′ərd or stü′ərd) 1 a man who looks after the needs of persons in a club or on a ship, train, aircraft, etc., especially one in charge of food and table service. 2 a man who manages another's property: *He is the steward of that great estate. n.*

stew·ard·ess (styü′ər dis or stü′ər dis) a woman steward, especially one who waits on passengers in an aircraft. *n.*

stick[1] (stik) 1 a long, thin piece of wood: *Put some sticks on the fire.* 2 such a piece of wood shaped for a special use: *a walking stick.* 3 something like a stick in shape: *a stick of candy. n.*

stick[2] (stik) 1 pierce with a pointed instrument; stab: *He stuck his fork into the potato.* 2 fasten by thrusting the point or end into or through something: *He stuck a flower in his buttonhole.* 3 put in a place or position: *He stuck his hands in his pocket. Don't stick your head out of the car window.* 4 be thrust; extend from, out of, through, up, etc.: *His arms stick out of his coat sleeves.* 5 fasten; attach: *Stick a stamp on the letter. Two pages of the book stuck together.* 6 keep on; hold fast: *He sticks to a task until he finishes it.* 7 *Informal.* puzzle: *That problem in arithmetic stuck me.* 8 be or become fastened; become fixed; be at a standstill: *Our car stuck in the mud.* 9 bring to a stop: *Our work was stuck by the power failure. v.,* **stuck, stick·ing.**

stick at, to hesitate at: *He sticks at nothing to get his own way.*

stick by or **stick to,** remain faithful or attached to; refuse to desert: *He sticks by his friends when they are in trouble.*

stick up, *Slang.* hold up; rob.

stick up for, *Informal.* stand up for; support; defend.

stick·er (stik′ər) a gummed label. *n.*

stick·y (stik′ē) 1 that sticks: *sticky glue.* 2 that makes things stick: *sticky flypaper.* 3 hot and damp: *sticky weather.* 4 *Informal.* puzzling; difficult: *a sticky problem. adj.,* **stick·i·er, stick·i·est.**

sties (stīz) plural of **sty**[1] and **sty**[2]. *n.*

stiff (stif) 1 not easily bent: *He wore a stiff collar.* 2 hard to move: *The old hinges on the barn door are stiff.* 3 not able to move easily: *The old man's joints were stiff.* 4 firm: *The jelly is stiff enough to stand alone.* 5 not easy or natural in manner; formal: *He made a stiff bow. He writes in a stiff style.* 6 strong: *A stiff breeze was blowing.* 7 hard to deal with; hard: *The teacher gave us a stiff test.* 8 *Informal.* more than seems suitable: *He asks a stiff price for his house. adj.*

stiff·en (stif′ən) 1 make stiff: *She stiffened the shirt with starch.* 2 become stiff: *The jelly will stiffen as it cools. He stiffened with anger. The wind was stiffening as the storm approached. v.*

sti·fle (stī′fəl) 1 stop the breath of; smother: *The smoke stifled the firemen.* 2 be unable to breathe freely: *I am stifling in this close room.* 3 keep back; stop; suppress: *to stifle a cry, to stifle a yawn, to stifle business activity. v.,* **sti·fled, sti·fling.**

stig·ma (stig′mə) 1 a mark of disgrace or shame. 2 the part of the pistil of a plant that receives the pollen. *n.*

A stile

stile (stīl) 1 a step or steps for getting over a fence or wall. 2 a turnstile. *n.*

☛ **Stile** and **style** are pronounced the same.

still[1] (stil) 1 without motion: *Sit still. The lake is still today.* 2 without noise; quiet: *The room was so still that you could have heard a pin drop.* 3 make calm or quiet: *The mother stilled the crying baby.* 4 become calm or quiet: *The people prayed that the storm might still.* 5 quiet; stillness: *in the still of the night.* 6 even; yet: *You can read still better if you try.* 7 and yet; but yet; nevertheless: *He was hungry; still he would not eat. Though she has new dolls, still she loves her old one best.* 8 even to this time; even to that time: *Was the store still open?* 1, 2 *adj.,* 3, 4 *v.,* 5 *n.,* 6, 8 *adv.,* 7 *conj.*

still[2] (stil) an apparatus for distilling liquids, especially alcoholic liquors. *n.*

still·ness (stil′nis) 1 quiet; silence. 2 the absence of motion; calm. *n.*

stilt (stilt) one of a pair of poles to stand on and hold while walking, each with a support for the foot at some distance above the ground: *Stilts are used in walking through shallow water, or for amusement. n.*

stilt·ed (stil′tid) stiffly dignified: *He has a stilted manner of speaking. adj.*

stim·u·lant (stim′yə lənt) something that excites or stirs or stimulates: *Tea and coffee are bodily stimulants. n.*

stim·u·late (stim′yə lāt′) spur on; stir up; rouse to action: *Praise stimulated her to work hard. v.,* **stim·u·lat·ed, stim·u·lat·ing.**

stim·u·lus (stim′yə ləs) something that stirs to action or effort: *Ambition is a great stimulus. n., pl.* **stim·u·li** (stim′yə lī′).

sting (sting) 1 prick with a sharp-pointed organ: *Bees, wasps, and hornets sting. A bee stung him.* 2 the wound caused by stinging: *He put mud on the sting to take away the pain.* 3 a stinger. 4 hurt sharply: *He was stung by the mockings of the other children.* 5 a

hat, āge, fär; let, ēqual, tėrm; it, īce
hot, ōpen, ôrder; oil, out; cup, pu̇t, rüle
əbove, takən, pencəl, lemən, circəs
ch, child; ng, long; sh, ship
th, thin; ᴛʜ, then; zh, measure

sharp pain: *The ball team felt the sting of defeat.* **6** cause a feeling like that of a prick: *Mustard stings the tongue.* 1, 4, 6 *v.,* **stung, sting·ing;** 2, 3, 5 *n.*

sting·er (sting′ər) the sharp part of an insect or animal that pricks or wounds and often poisons: *The stinger of the mosquito causes itchy swellings. n.*

stin·gi·ness (stin′jē nis) meanness about spending, lending, or giving. *n.*

stin·gy (stin′jē) mean about spending, lending, or giving money: *He tried to save money without being stingy. adj.,* **stin·gi·er, stin·gi·est.**

stink (stingk) **1** a bad smell. **2** have a bad smell: *Decaying fish stink.* **3** *Informal.* have poor quality or be unattractive in some way. 1 *n.,* 2, 3 *v.,* **stank** or **stunk, stunk, stink·ing.**

stint (stint) **1** keep on short allowance; be saving or careful in using or spending; limit: *The parents stinted themselves of food to give it to the children.* **2** limit: *That generous man gives without stint.* **3** a task assigned: *She had to wash the supper dishes as her daily stint.* 1 *v.,* 2, 3 *n.*

stir (stėr) **1** move: *The wind stirs the leaves.* **2** move about: *No one was stirring in the house.* **3** mix by moving around with a spoon, fork, stick, etc.: *He stirs the sugar in his tea with his spoon.* **4** affect strongly; set going; excite: *He stirred up the other children to mischief.* **5** a movement: *There was a stir in the bushes.* **6** excitement: *The coming of the queen caused a great stir.* **7** the act of stirring: *She gave the mixture a hard stir.* 1–4 *v.,* **stirred, stir·ring;** 5–7 *n.*

stir·ring (stėr′ing) **1** moving; active; lively: *stirring times.* **2** rousing; exciting: *a stirring speech. adj.*

stir·rup (stėr′əp or stir′əp) one of a pair of foot supports that hang from a saddle: *The rider stood up in his stirrups.* See **saddle** for picture. *n.*

stitch (stich) **1** in sewing, one complete movement of a threaded needle through cloth: *Take short stitches.* **2** one complete movement in knitting, crocheting, embroidering, etc. **3** a particular method of making stitches: *buttonhole stitch.* **4** the loop of thread, etc. made by a stitch: *Rip out these long stitches. The doctor will take out the stitches of the wound tomorrow.* **5** make stitches in; fasten with stitches: *She stitched his shirt. The doctor stitched the cut.* **6** sew. **7** *Informal.* a small bit: *The lazy boy wouldn't do a stitch of work.* **8** a sudden, sharp pain: *He got a stitch in his side from running.* 1–4, 7, 8 *n.,* 5, 6 *v.*

St. John's Day the anniversary holiday of Newfoundland, held on June 24 to commemorate the landing of John Cabot on that date in 1497.

A man in the stocks

stock (stok) **1** goods for use or for sale; a supply used as it is needed: *This store keeps a large stock of toys.* **2** cattle or other farm animals; livestock: *The farm was sold with all its stock.* **3** lay in a supply of; supply: *Our camp is well stocked with everything we need for a short stay.* **4** keep regularly for use or for sale: *A toy store stocks toys.* **5** kept on hand regularly for use or for sale: *stock sizes of dresses.* **6** in common use; commonplace; everyday: *The weather is a stock subject of conversation.* **7** the shares in a company: *The profits of a company are divided among the owners of stock.* **8** family or race: *she is of United Empire Loyalist stock.* **9** a part used as a support or handle: *the wooden stock of a rifle.* **10** raw material: *Rags are used as a stock for making paper.* **11** water in which meat or fish has been cooked, used as a base for soups, sauces, etc. **12** furnish with livestock: *stock a farm.* **13 the stocks,** a wooden frame having holes for the feet, and sometimes for the hands, in which people were formerly placed in public as a punishment. 1, 2, 6–11, 13 *n.,* 3, 4, 12 *v.,* 5 *adj.*

take stock, a find out how much stock there is on hand. **b** make an estimate or examination.

☛ **Stock** and **stalk** are sometimes pronounced the same.

stock·ade (stok ād′) a defence enclosure made of large, strong upright posts placed closely together in the ground: *A heavy stockade protected the trading post from attack. n.*

stock·bro·ker (stok′brō′kər) a person who buys and sells stocks and bonds for others. *n.*

stock exchange a place where stocks and bonds are bought and sold.

stock·ing (stok′ing) a close-fitting knitted covering of nylon, cotton, wool, etc. for the foot and leg. *n.*

stocking cap tuque (def. 1).

stock market **1** a place where stocks and bonds are bought and sold; stock exchange. **2** the buying and selling in such a place.

stock–still (stok′stil′) motionless. *adj.*

stock·y (stok′ē) having a solid or sturdy form or build; thick for its height: *a stocky little child, a stocky building. adj.,* **stock·i·er, stock·i·est.**

stock·yard (stok′yärd′) a place with pens and sheds for cattle, sheep, hogs, and horses: *Livestock is kept in a stockyard before being slaughtered or sent to market. n.*

stoke (stōk) **1** stir up and feed a fire; tend the fire of a furnace: *His father showed him how to stoke the fire.* **2** tend a fire: *He is busy stoking. v.,* **stoked, stok·ing. —stok′er,** *n.*

stole (stōl) See **steal.** *He stole the money years ago. v.*

sto·len (stō′lən) See **steal.** *The money was stolen by a thief. v.*

stom·ach (stum′ək) **1** the large muscular bag in the body that first receives the food, and that digests some of it before passing it on to the intestines. See **alimentary canal** for picture. **2** the part of the body containing the stomach: *He hit me in the stomach.* **3** appetite. **4** put up with; bear; endure: *He could not* *stomach such an insult.* **5** liking: *I have no stomach for killing harmless creatures.* 1–3, 5 *n.*, 4 *v.*

stomp (stomp) stamp with the foot. *v.*

stone (stōn) **1** a hard mineral matter that is not metal; rock: *Stone is much used in building.* **2** a small piece of rock: *The children threw stones in the lake.* **3** a piece of rock of definite size, shape, etc., used for a particular purpose: *His grave is marked by a fine stone.* **4** made of stone: *a stone wall, a stone house.* **5** having something to do with stone. **6** a gem or jewel: *The queen's diamonds were very fine stones.* **7** throw stones at; drive by throwing stones: *The cruel children stoned the dog.* **8** a hard seed: *peach stones, plum stones.* **9** take stones or seeds out of: *to stone cherries or plums.* **10** made of stoneware or coarse clay. **11** a curling stone. 1–3, 6, 8, 11 *n.*, 4, 5, 10 *adj.*, 7, 9 *v.*, **stoned, ston·ing.**

Stone Age the period when people used tools and weapons made from stone.

stone·boat (stōn′bōt′) a platform on runners, used for transporting stones and other heavy objects short distances. *n.*

stone·ware (stōn′wer′) coarse, hard, glazed pottery. *n.*

ston·y (stōn′ē) **1** having many stones: *The beach is stony.* **2** without expression or feeling: *a stony stare. That cruel man has a stony heart.* *adj.*, **ston·i·er, ston·i·est.**

stood (stůd) See **stand.** *He stood in the corner for five minutes. This building has stood here for many years.* *v.*

Stooks of wheat

stook (stük) **1** an upright arrangement of sheaves of grain intended to speed up drying in the field: *stooks of golden wheat.* **2** build such arrangements of sheaves: *He earned some money stooking on his father's farm.* 1 *n.*, 2 *v.*

stool (stül) **1** a seat without back or arms. **2** any similar article used to rest the feet on, or to kneel on. *n.*

stool pigeon *Slang.* a spy for the police; informer.

stoop[1] (stüp) **1** bend forward: *He stooped to pick up the money. She stoops over her desk.* **2** a forward bend of the head and shoulders: *My uncle walks with a slight stoop.* **3** carry the head and shoulders bent forward: *The old man stoops.* **4** lower oneself; descend: *He stooped to cheating.* 1, 3, 4 *v.*, 2 *n.*

stoop[2] (stüp) a porch or platform at the entrance of a house. *n.*

stop (stop) **1** keep from moving, acting, doing, being, working, etc.: *The men stopped the boys from teasing the cat. I stopped the clock.* **2** put an end to; check: *to stop a noise.* **3** stay: *She stopped at the bank for a few minutes.* **4** come to an end; cease; leave off moving, acting, doing, being, etc.: *The baby stopped crying. The rain is stopping.* **5** close a hole or opening by filling it: *He is going to stop up the rats' holes.* **6** block; obstruct: *A big box stops up the doorway.* **7** stopping; closing; blocking; checking: *We put a stop to his tricks.* **8** a stay or staying; a halt: *We made a stop for lunch.* **9** a place where a stop is made: *a bus stop.* **10** anything that stops, such as a block, a plug, etc. **11** a punctuation mark: *The most used stops are ? ! . , ; : —.* **12** a device that controls the pitch of a musical instrument. 1–6 *v.*, **stopped, stop·ping;** 7–12 *n.*

stop off, *Informal.* stop for a short stay.

stop over, a make a short stay. **b** *Informal.* stop in the course of a trip.

stop·light (stop′līt′) a traffic light or signal. *n.*

stop·o·ver (stop′ō′vər) a stopping over in the course of a journey. *n.*

stop·page (stop′ij) **1** stopping: *The foreman called for a stoppage of operations to oil the machinery.* **2** being stopped: *During the work stoppage, many workers looked for other jobs.* **3** a block; obstruction. *n.*

stop·per (stop′ər) a plug or cork for closing a bottle, tube, etc. *n.*

stop·watch (stop′woch′) a watch which has a hand that can be stopped or started at any instant: *A stopwatch indicates fractions of a second and is used for timing races and contests.* *n.*

stor·age (stôr′ij) **1** the act or fact of storing goods. **2** the condition of being stored. **Cold storage** is used to keep eggs and meat from spoiling. **3** a place for storing: *She has put her furniture in storage.* **4** the cost of storing: *She paid $30 storage on her furniture.* *n.*

storage battery a battery that stores electrical energy and that can be recharged.

store (stôr) **1** a place where goods are kept for sale: *a clothing store.* **2** something put away for use later; a supply or stock: *She puts up stores of preserves and jellies every year.* **3** put away for use later; lay up: *The squirrel stores away nuts. We stored our furs during the summer.* **4** a place where supplies are kept for future use; a storehouse. 1, 2, 4 *n.*, 3 *v.*, **stored, stor·ing.**

set store by, value; esteem: *She sets great store by her father's opinions.*

store·house (stôr′hous′) a place where things are stored: *The factory has many storehouses for its products. A library is a storehouse of information.* *n.*

store·keep·er (stôr′kēp′ər) a person who has charge of a store or stores. *n.*

store·room (stôr′rüm′) a room where things are stored. *n.*

sto·rey or **sto·ry** (stô′rē) a level or floor of a house or other building: *They are now building the second storey of our new house.* *n., pl.* **sto·reys** or **sto·ries.**

White storks — about 105 cm long with the tail

stork (stôrk) a large, long-legged bird having a long

hat, āge, fär; let, ēqual, tėrm; it, īce
hot, ōpen, ôrder; oil, out; cup, pu̇t, rüle
əbove, takən, pencəl, lemən, circəs
ch, child; ng, long; sh, ship
th, thin; ᴛʜ, then; zh, measure

neck and a long bill, found in parts of Europe and Africa: *Storks often nest on rooftops and have been thought to bring good luck.* *n.*

storm (stôrm) 1 a strong wind, usually accompanied by rain, snow, hail, or thunder and lightning: *In deserts there are storms of sand.* 2 a heavy fall of rain, snow, or hail. 3 blow hard; rain; snow; hail. 4 a violent outburst or disturbance: *a storm of tears, a storm of angry words.* 5 be violent; rage: *She stormed at the manager about his high prices.* 6 rush violently: *He stormed out of the room.* 7 attack violently: *The enemy stormed the castle.* 8 a storm window or storm door: *Our house has a complete set of storms and screens.* 1, 2, 4, 8 *n.*, 3, 5–7 *v.*

take by storm, seize or capture by a violent attack: *The castle was taken by storm.*

storm door an extra door outside an ordinary door, to keep out snow, cold winds, etc.

storm window an extra window outside an ordinary window, to keep out snow, cold winds, etc.: *Dad puts the storm windows on in October each year.*

storm·y (stôr′mē) 1 having storms; likely to have storms; troubled by storms: *a stormy sea, stormy weather, a stormy night.* 2 rough and disturbed; violent: *They had stormy quarrels.* *adj.*, **storm·i·er, storm·i·est.**

sto·ry[1] (stô′rē) 1 an account of some happening or group of happenings: *The man told the story of his life.* 2 such an account, either true or made-up, intended to interest the reader or hearer; a tale: *fairy stories, ghost stories, stories of adventure, funny stories.* 3 *Informal.* a falsehood: *That boy is a liar; he tells stories.* *n., pl.* **sto·ries.**

sto·ry[2] (stô′rē) storey. *n., pl.* **sto·ries.**

sto·ry·book (stô′rē bu̇k′) a book containing one or more stories or tales, especially for children. *n.*

stout (stout) 1 fat and large: *That boy could run faster if he weren't so stout.* 2 strongly built; firm; strong: *The fort has stout walls.* 3 brave; bold: *Robin Hood was a stout fellow.* *adj.*

stove[1] (stōv) an apparatus for cooking and heating: *There are wood, coal, gas, oil, and electric stoves.* *n.*

stove[2] (stōv) staved. See **stave.** *That barrel was stove in when it dropped off the truck.* *v.*

stove·pipe (stōv′pīp′) a metal pipe that carries smoke and gases from a stove to a chimney. *n.*

stow (stō) 1 pack: *The cargo was stowed in the ship's hold.* 2 pack things closely in; fill by packing: *The boys stowed the little cabin with supplies for the trip.* *v.*

stow away, hide on a ship, airplane, etc. to avoid paying the fare or to escape.

stow·a·way (stō′ə wā′) a person who hides on a ship, airplane, etc. to get a free passage or to escape. *n.*

strad·dle (strad′əl) 1 walk, stand, or sit with the legs wide apart. 2 have a leg on each side of a horse, bicycle, chair, ditch, etc. *v.*, **strad·dled, strad·dling.**

strag·gle (strag′əl) 1 wander in a scattered fashion: *Cows straggled along the lane.* 2 spread in an irregular, rambling manner: *Vines straggled all over the yard. It was a straggling little town on the side of a hill.* *v.*, **strag·gled, strag·gling.**

straight (strāt) 1 without a bend or curve: *a straight line, a straight path, straight hair.* 2 in a line; directly: *Walk straight. He went straight home.* 3 frank; honest; upright: *a straight answer.* 4 frankly; honestly; uprightly: *Live straight.* 5 in proper order or condition: *Set the room straight. Our accounts are straight.* 6 showing no emotion, humor, etc.: *He kept a straight face, though he wanted to laugh.* 1, 3, 6 *adj.*, 2, 4, 5 *adv.*

☛ **Straight** and **strait** are pronounced the same.

straight·en (strāt′ən) 1 make straight: *He straightened the bent pin. Straighten your shoulders.* 2 become straight. 3 put in the proper order or condition: *to straighten out accounts. Straighten up your room.* *v.*

straight·for·ward (strāt′fôr′wərd) 1 honest; frank: *a straightforward answer.* 2 going straight ahead; direct. *adj.* —**straight′for′ward·ly,** *adv.* —**straight′for′ward·ness, n.**

straight·way (strāt′wā′) at once; immediately: *The captain read the letter and burned it straightway.* *adv.*

strain[1] (strān) 1 draw tight; stretch: *The weight strained the rope.* 2 pull hard: *The dog strained at his leash.* 3 a force or weight that stretches: *The strain on the rope made it break.* 4 stretch more than one should: *She strained the truth in telling that story.* 5 use to the utmost: *He strained every muscle to lift the rock.* 6 make a very great effort. 7 injure by too much effort or by stretching: *The runner strained his heart.* 8 an injury caused by too much effort or by stretching; a sprain: *The doctor said the injury to his ankle was only a slight strain.* 9 any severe or wearing pressure: *The strain of sleepless nights made her ill.* 10 the effect of such pressure on the body or mind. 11 press or pour through a material or device that allows only liquid to pass through it: *Consommée is a soup that has been strained.* 1, 2, 4–7, 11 *v.*, 3, 8–10 *n.* —**strain′er,** *n.*

strain[2] (strān) 1 a line of descent; a race; stock: *He is proud of his Irish strain.* 2 a group of animals or plants that form a part of a breed, race, or variety. 3 an inherited quality: *There is a strain of musical talent in that family.* 4 a trace or streak: *That horse has a mean strain.* 5 a part of a piece of music; a melody; song. 6 a manner or style of doing or speaking: *He wrote in a playful strain.* *n.*

strait (strāt) 1 a narrow channel connecting two larger bodies of water. 2 **straits,** *pl.* difficulty; need; distress: *He was in desperate straits for money.* *n.*

☛ **Strait** and **straight** are pronounced the same.

strait jacket a strong, tight jacket or coat that binds the arms close to the sides: *A strait jacket keeps a violent person from harming himself or others.*

strand[1] (strand) 1 place or leave in a helpless position: *He was stranded a thousand kilometres away with no money.* 2 run aground; drive on the shore: *The ship was stranded on the rocks.* 3 a shore; the land bordering a sea, lake, or river. 1, 2 *v.*, 3 *n.*

strand[2] (strand) 1 one of the threads, strings, or wires that are twisted together to make a rope or cable: *This is a rope of three strands.* 2 a thread or string: *a strand of hair, a strand of pearls. n.*

strange (strānj) 1 unusual; queer; peculiar: *What a strange experience!* 2 not known, seen, or heard of before; not familiar: *She is moving to a strange place. A strange cat is on our steps.* 3 not used to: *He is strange to the work, but he will soon learn.* 4 out of place; not at home: *The poor child felt strange in the palace.* 5 unfamiliar to: *The city was strange to the newcomer. adj.,* **strang·er, strang·est. —strange′ly,** *adv.* **—strange′ness,** *n.*

stran·ger (strān′jər) 1 a person not known, seen, or heard of before: *She is a stranger to us.* 2 a person or thing new to a place: *He is a stranger in Saskatoon.* 3 a person from another country: *The king received the strangers with kindness. n.*

stran·gle (strang′gəl) 1 kill by squeezing the throat to stop the breath: *Hercules strangled a snake with each hand.* 2 choke; suffocate: *His collar seemed to be strangling him. She almost strangled on a piece of meat that caught in her throat.* 3 choke down; suppress; keep back: *He strangled an impulse to cough. v.,* **stran·gled, stran·gling.**

strap (strap) 1 a narrow strip of leather, cloth, or other material that bends easily: *He has a strap around his books. She wore a sun dress with narrow shoulder straps.* 2 fasten with a strap: *We strapped the trunk.* 3 beat with a strap. 1 *n.,* 2, 3 *v.,* **strapped, strap·ping.**

strap·ping (strap′ing) *Informal.* tall, strong, and healthy: *a fine, strapping boy. adj.*

stra·ta (strā′tə or strat′ə) a plural of **stratum.** *n.*

strat·a·gem (strat′ə jəm) a scheme or trick for deceiving the enemy; a trick; an act of trickery: *The spy got into the castle by the stratagem of dressing as a beggar. n.*

stra·te·gic (strə tē′jik) 1 of strategy; based on strategy; useful in strategy: *a strategic retreat.* 2 important in strategy: *Each element of the armed forces is a strategic link in our defence. adj.*

strat·e·gy (strat′ə jē) 1 the planning and directing of military movements and operations. 2 the skilful planning and management of anything: *Strategy is needed to keep the boys at work. n., pl.* **strat·e·gies.**

strat·o·sphere (strat′ə sfēr′) the upper region of the atmosphere, which begins about 11 kilometres above the earth: *In the stratosphere, temperature varies little with changes in altitude, and the winds are chiefly horizontal. n.*

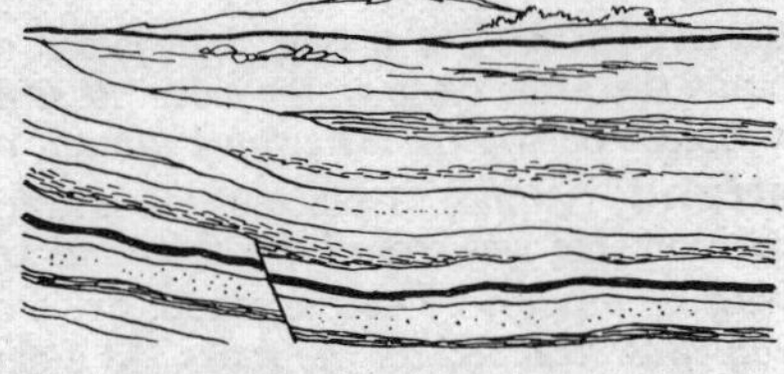
Strata of rock

stra·tum (strā′təm or strat′əm) 1 a layer of material, especially one of several parallel layers placed one upon another: *In digging the well, the men struck first a stratum of sand, then several strata of rock.* 2 a level of society: *Professional people, such as doctors and lawyers, represent one stratum of society. n., pl.* **stra·ta** or **stra·tums.**

stra·tus (strā′təs or strat′əs) a low, horizontal layer of grey cloud that spreads over a large area. *n.*

straw (stro or strô) 1 the stalks or stems of grain after drying and threshing: *Straw is used for bedding for horses and cows, for making hats, and for many other purposes.* 2 a hollow stem or stalk. 3 a tube made of waxed paper, plastic, or glass, used for sucking up drinks. 4 made of straw: *a straw hat.* 5 a bit; trifle: *He doesn't care a straw. n.*

straw·ber·ry (stro′ber′ē or strô′ber′ē) 1 a small, juicy, red fruit that is good to eat. 2 the plant strawberries grow on. *n., pl.* **straw·ber·ries.**

stray (strā) 1 lose one's way; wander; roam: *Our dog has strayed off somewhere.* 2 wandering; lost: *A stray cat is crying at the door.* 3 a wanderer; a lost animal; anything that is lost: *That cat is a stray that we took in.* 4 turn from the right course; go wrong. 5 scattered; here and there: *There were a few stray fishermen's huts along the beach.* 1, 4 *v.,* 2, 5 *adj.,* 3 *n.*

streak (strēk) 1 a long, thin mark or line: *He has a streak of dirt on his face. We saw the streaks of lightning.* 2 a layer: *Side bacon has streaks of fat and streaks of lean.* 3 a vein; a strain; an element: *He has a streak of humor, though he looks very serious.* 4 put long, thin marks or lines on: *The Indians used to streak their faces with paint.* 5 *Informal.* move very fast; go at full speed: *He streaked past the others and over the finish line.* 1–3 *n.,* 4, 5 *v.*

like a streak, *Informal.* very fast: *When the dog saw his master, he ran like a streak across the lawn to greet him.*

stream (strēm) 1 a body of running water; a flow of liquid: *Small rivers and large brooks are both called streams.* 2 any steady flow: *a stream of lava, a stream of light, a stream of words.* 3 flow: *Tears streamed from her eyes.* 4 move steadily; move swiftly: *Soldiers streamed out of the fort.* 5 float or wave: *The flags streamed in the wind.* 1, 2 *n.,* 3–5 *v.*

stream·er (strēm′ər) 1 any long, narrow, flowing thing: *Streamers of ribbon hung from her hat.* 2 a long, narrow flag. *n.*

stream·line (strēm′līn′) 1 having a shape that offers the least possible resistance to air or water: *a streamline train.* 2 give a streamline shape to: *to streamline an airplane.* 3 bring up to date or make more efficient: *a streamlined road-building program.* 1 *adj.,* 2, 3 *v.,* **stream·lined, stream·lin·ing.**

street (strēt) 1 a road in a city or town, usually with buildings on both sides. 2 the people who live in the buildings on a street: *All Oak Street welcomed him. n.*
the man in the street, the typical person or the average person.

street·car (strēt′kär′) an electrically powered car that runs on rails in the streets and carries passengers. *n.*

strength (strength) 1 the quality of being strong; power; force; vigor: *Because of his strength he could lift great weights. The strength of the dog's love for his master is well known.* 2 the power to resist or endure: *the strength of a fort, the strength of a rope.* 3 a degree

of strength or intensity: *Some flavorings lose their strength in cooking.* *n.*
on the strength of, relying or depending on: *Father bought the dog on the strength of Bill's promise to take care of it.*

strength·en (streng′thən) 1 make stronger: *The soldiers strengthened their defences.* 2 grow stronger. *v.*

stren·u·ous (stren′yü əs) 1 very active; requiring much energy: *We had a strenuous day moving into our new house. Running is a strenuous exercise.* 2 full of energy: *The gym teacher is a strenuous man.* *adj.*

stress (stres) 1 pressure; force; strain: *Under the stress of hunger the man stole some food.* 2 emphasis; importance: *That school lays stress upon arithmetic and reading.* 3 treat as important; emphasize: *The principal stressed the importance of safety rules.* 4 the greater force with which a certain syllable in a word is pronounced as compared with other syllables in the same word: *In 'hero,' the stress is on the first syllable.* 5 a mark (′) written or printed to show the spoken force of a syllable, as in *yes′ter day, to day′, to mor′row.* Many words have two stresses, a heavy stress (′) and a light stress (′), as in *accelerator* (ak sel′ər ā′tor). 6 mark with a stress. 7 pronounce with a stress: *'Accept' is stressed on the second syllable.* 1, 2, 4, 5 *n.*, 3, 6, 7 *v.*

stretch (strech) 1 draw out; extend to full length: *The bird stretched its wings. The blow stretched him out on the ground.* 2 extend one's body or limbs: *He arose and stretched.* 3 continue over a distance; extend from one place to another; fill space; spread: *The forest stretches for miles to the west.* 4 reach out; hold out: *He stretched out a hand for the money.* 5 draw out to greater size: *Stretch this shoe a little.* 6 become longer or wider without breaking: *Rubber stretches.* 7 *Informal.* exaggerate: *stretch the truth.* 8 an unbroken length; extent: *A stretch of sand hills lay between the road and the ocean.* 9 the act of stretching or the condition of being stretched: *With a sudden stretch, Don took Frank's cap.* 1–7 *v.*, 8, 9 *n.*

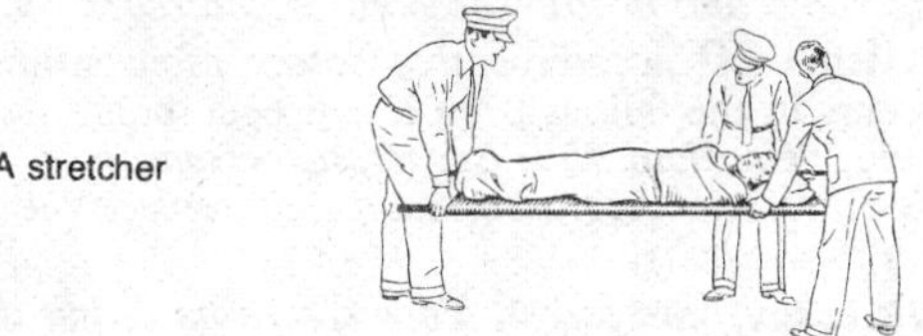
A stretcher

stretch·er (strech′ər) 1 a frame or other device for stretching something: *a glove stretcher.* 2 a frame having a canvas or similar covering and either wheels or carrying handles on which to move the sick, wounded, or dead. *n.*

A streetcar

hat, āge, fär; let, ēqual, tėrm; it, īce
hot, ōpen, ôrder; oil, out; cup, pu̇t, rüle
əbove, takən, pencəl, lemən, circəs
ch, child; ng, long; sh, ship
th, thin; ᴛʜ, then; zh, measure

strew (strü) 1 scatter; sprinkle: *She strewed seeds in her garden.* 2 cover with something scattered or sprinkled: *The ground was strewn with leaves.* *v.*, **strewed, strewn** or **strewed, strew·ing.**

strewn (strün) See **strew.** *v.*

strick·en (strik′ən) 1 hit, wounded, or affected by wounds, diseases, trouble, sorrows, etc.: *The stricken man was taken to a hospital. Help was rushed to the fire-stricken city.* 2 See **strike.** 1 *adj.*, 2 *v.*

strict (strikt) 1 very careful in following a rule or in making others follow it: *Our teacher is strict but fair.* 2 harsh; severe: *Cinderella's stepmother was very strict with her.* 3 exact; precise: *He told the strict truth.* 4 perfect; complete; absolute: *The secret was told in strict confidence.* *adj.*

strid·den (strid′ən) See **stride.** *He had stridden away angrily.* *v.*

stride (strīd) 1 walk with long steps: *The tall man strides rapidly down the street.* 2 pass with one long step: *He strode over the brook.* 3 a long step: *The child could not keep up with his father's stride.* 4 sit or stand with one leg on each side of: *to stride a fence.* 1, 2, 4 *v.*, **strode, strid·den, strid·ing;** 3 *n.*
hit one's stride, reach one's regular speed or normal activity.
make great or **rapid strides,** make great progress; advance rapidly.
take in one's stride, do or take without difficulty, hesitation, or special effort.

stri·dent (strī′dənt) making or having a harsh sound; creaking; grating; shrill: *strident sounds at the start of a motor race.* *adj.*

strife (strīf) a struggle; quarrelling or fighting: *bitter strife between rivals.* *n.*

strike (strīk) 1 hit: *He struck his enemy. The car struck a fence. Lightning struck the barn.* 2 give; deal forth or out: *He struck a blow in self-defence.* 3 make by stamping, printing, etc.: *They will strike a medal in memory of the great victory.* 4 set or be set on fire by hitting or rubbing: *Strike a match.* 5 appear to affect the mind or feelings of; impress: *The plan strikes me as silly.* 6 sound: *The clock strikes twelve times at noon. The clock strikes the hour and the half hour.* 7 overcome by death, disease, suffering, terror, fear, etc.: *All were struck with terror at her wild cry.* 8 attack; make an attack: *The enemy will strike at dawn.* 9 an attack: *a strike by bombers on a target.* 10 occur to: *She smiled as an amusing thought struck her.* 11 find or come upon ore, oil, etc.: *The miner struck gold.* 12 the act or fact of finding rich ore, oil, etc.; sudden success: *He made a rich strike in Yukon.* 13 stop work to get better pay, shorter hours, etc.: *The coal miners struck.* 14 stopping work to get more pay, better hours, etc.: *There was a strike at the steel plant last year.* 15 cross; rub: *strike his name off the list.* 16 advance; go: *We will walk along the road a little, then strike out across the fields.* 17 make; decide; enter upon: *The* *employer and the workmen have struck an agreement.* **18** lower or take down a sail, flag, tent, etc.: *The ship struck her flag as a sign of surrender.* **19** in baseball, a failure of the batter to make a proper hit. **20** in bowling, an upsetting of all the pins with the first ball bowled. 1–8, 10, 11, 13, 15–18 *v.,* **struck, struck** or **strick·en, strik·ing;** 9, 12, 14, 19, 20 *n.*

on strike, stopping work to get more pay, shorter hours, etc.: *Most of the workers voted to go on strike.*

strike out, a cross out or rub out. **b** in baseball, fail to hit three times: *The batter struck out.* **c** cause a batter to fail to hit three times: *The pitcher struck him out.*

strike up, begin: *The two boys struck up a friendship.*

strik·ing (strīk′ing) attracting attention; very noticeable: *There was a striking oil painting on the wall.* *adj.* **—strik′ing·ly,** *adv.*

string (string) **1** a small cord or very thin rope: *The package is tied with red string.* **2** a cord or thread with things on it: *She wore a string of beads around her neck.* **3** put on a string: *The child is stringing beads.* **4** a length of wire or catgut for a musical instrument: *the strings of a violin.* **5 strings,** *pl.* in an orchestra, violins, cellos, and other stringed instruments. **6** to furnish with strings: *He had his tennis racket strung.* **7** anything used for tying: *shoestrings, apron strings.* **8** tie with string or rope; hang with a string or rope: *We dry herbs by stringing them from rafters in the barn.* **9** extend or stretch from one point to another: *string a cable.* **10** remove strings from: *String the beans.* **11** form into a string or strings: *to string beads.* **12** a number of things in a line or row: *A string of cars came down the street.* 1, 2, 4, 5, 7, 12 *n.,* 3, 6, 8–11 *v.,* **strung, string·ing.**

string along, *Informal.* **a** fool; hoax. **b** go along with; agree.

string out, stretch or extent: *The program was strung out too long.*

stringed instrument (stringd) a musical instrument having strings, played with a bow, by striking, or by plucking: *A violin, a piano, a harp, and a guitar are stringed instruments.*

string·y (string′ē) **1** like a string or strings. **2** having tough fibres: *stringy meat.* *adj.,* **string·i·er, string·i·est.**

strip[1] (strip) **1** make bare or naked; undress. **2** take off the covering of: *The boy stripped the skin from a banana.* **3** remove; pull off: *The boys stripped the fruit from the trees.* **4** rob: *Thieves stripped the house of everything valuable.* *v.,* **stripped, strip·ping.**

strip[2] (strip) **1** a long, narrow, flat piece of cloth, paper, bark, etc. **2** a long, narrow runway for airplanes to take off from and land on. *n.*

stripe (strīp) **1** a long, narrow band distinct from its background: *A tiger has stripes. The uniform had a red stripe down the side of each leg.* **2** in the armed services, a badge or symbol of rank: *A corporal wears two stripes, a sergeant three.* **3** mark with stripes. 1, 2 *n.,* 3 *v.,* **striped, strip·ing.**

striped (strīpt) having stripes; marked with stripes: *Zebras are striped.* *adj.*

strip·ling (strip′ling) a boy just coming into manhood; a youth; lad. *n.*

strive (strīv) **1** try hard; work hard: *Strive to succeed.* **2** struggle; fight: *The swimmer strove against the tide.* *v.,* **strove** or **strived, striv·en, striv·ing.**

striv·en (striv′ən) See **strive.** *She has striven hard to make the party a success.* *v.*

strode (strōd) See **stride.** *He strode over the ditch.* *v.*

stroke[1] (strōk) **1** something sudden or painful like a blow: *He drove in the nail with one stroke of the hammer. The house was hit by a stroke of lightning.* **2** a sound made by striking: *We arrived at the stroke of three o'clock.* **3** a piece of luck, fortune, etc.: *a stroke of bad luck.* **4** a single, complete movement to be made again and again: *He rowed with a strong stroke of the oars. He swims a fast stroke.* **5** in a game such as tennis and golf, the hitting of a ball. **6** a movement or mark made by a pen, pencil, brush, etc.: *He writes with a heavy down stroke.* **7** a very successful effort; feat: *a stroke of genius.* **8** a single effort; an act: *The lazy boy hasn't done a stroke of work all week.* **9** a sudden attack of certain illnesses or disease: *a stroke of paralysis.* *n.*

stroke[2] (strōk) **1** move the hand gently along: *She likes to stroke her kitten.* **2** such a movement: *She brushed away the crumbs with one stroke.* 1 *v.,* **stroked, strok·ing;** 2 *n.*

stroll (strōl) **1** take a quiet walk for pleasure; walk. **2** a leisurely walk: *We went for a stroll in the park.* **3** go from place to place: *strolling gypsies.* 1, 3 *v.,* 2 *n.*

strong (strong) **1** having much force or power: *A strong man can lift heavy things. A strong wind blew down the trees. A strong nation is one that has many able citizens and great resources.* **2** able to last, endure, resist, etc.: *a strong fort, a strong rope.* **3** having a particular quality or property in high degree: *strong perfume. A strong acid is one that contains much acid and little water.* *adj.*

strong·hold (strong′hōld′) a fort; a strong place; a safe place: *The robbers have a stronghold in the mountains.* *n.*

stron·ti·um (stron′tē əm or stron′shē əm) a soft silver-white, metallic element which occurs only in combination with other elements: *Strontium is used in making alloys and in fireworks and signal flares.* *n.*

strontium 90 a radio-active isotope of strontium that occurs in the fallout from a hydrogen bomb explosion: *Strontium 90 is dangerous because it is absorbed by bones and tissues and may replace the calcium in the body.*

strove (strōv) See **strive.** *They strove hard, but did not win the game.* *v.*

struck (struk) See **strike.** *The clock struck four. The barn was struck by lightning.* *v.*

struc·ture (struk′chər) **1** a building; something built: *The city hall is a large stone structure.* **2** anything composed of parts arranged together: *The human body is a wonderful structure.* **3** the way parts are put together; the manner of building; the construction: *The structure of the schoolhouse was excellent.* **4** the arrangement of parts: *the structure of an atom, the structure of a flower.* *n.*

strug·gle (strug′əl) **1** make great efforts with the body; try hard; work hard against difficulties: *The poor have to struggle for a living. The swimmer struggled against the tide. She struggled to keep back the tears.* **2** get, move, or make one's way with great effort: *The old man struggled to his feet.* **3** great effort; hard work:

hat, āge, fär; let, ēqual, tėrm; it, īce
hot, ōpen, ôrder; oil, out; cup, pu̇t, rüle
əbove, takən, pencəl, lemən, circəs
ch, child; ng, long; sh, ship
th, thin; ᴛʜ, then; zh, measure

Making him eat vegetables is a struggle. **4** fighting; a conflict: *The struggle between the two countries went on for years.* 1, 2 *v.,* **strug·gled, strug·gling;** 3, 4 *n.*

strum (strum) play by running the fingers lightly or carelessly across the strings or keys: *strum a guitar, strum on the piano.* *n.*

strung (strung) See **string.** *The children strung out in a line after the teacher. The vines were strung on poles.* *v.*

strut¹ (strut) **1** walk in a stiff, erect manner, suggesting vanity or self-importance: *He strutted about the room in his new jacket.* **2** a strutting walk. 1 *v.,* **strut·ted, strut·ting;** 2 *n.*

strut² (strut) a supporting piece; brace. See **truss** for picture. *n.*

stub (stub) **1** a short piece that is left: *the stub of a pencil, the stub of a cigarette.* **2** the short piece of each leaf in a cheque book, etc. kept as a record. **3** the stump of a tree, a broken tooth, etc. **4** strike the toe against something: *He stubbed his toe on a rock.* **5** put out a cigarette or cigar by crushing the fire out. 1–3 *n.,* 4, 5 *v.,* **stubbed, stub·bing.**

stub·ble (stub′əl) **1** the lower ends of stalks of grain that are left in the ground after the grain is cut: *The stubble hurt the boy's bare feet.* **2** any short, rough growth: *There was a dark stubble of beard on his face.* *n.*

stub·born (stub′ərn) **1** fixed in purpose or opinion; not giving in to argument or requests: *The stubborn boy refused to listen to reasons for not going out in the rain.* **2** hard to deal with or manage: *a stubborn cough.* *adj.* ☛ See note at **obstinate.**

stub·by (stub′ē) short and thick: *stubby fingers.* *adj.*

stuc·co (stuk′ō) **1** a rough, strong plaster for covering the outer walls of buildings. **2** cover with stucco: *We had our house stuccoed last year.* 1 *n., pl.* **stuc·coes** or **stuc·cos;** 2 *v.,* **stuc·coed, stuc·co·ing.**

stuck (stuk) See **stick².** *She stuck out her tongue. We were stuck in the mud.* *v.*

stuck–up (stuk′up′) *Informal.* too proud; conceited; haughty. *adj.*

stud¹ (stud) **1** a head of a nail, a knob, etc. sticking out from a surface: *The belt was ornamented with silver studs.* **2** set with studs or something like studs: *He planned to stud the sword hilt with jewels.* **3** be set or scattered over: *Little islands studded the harbor.* **4** a kind of small button used in men's shirts. **5** set like studs: *Stooks of wheat were studded over the field.* **6** one of a row of upright posts, usually wooden, which form part of the frame to which boards or laths are nailed in making a wall of a building. See **frame** for picture. 1, 4, 6 *n.,* 2, 3, 5 *v.,* **stud·ded, stud·ding.**

stud² (stud) **1** a collection of horses kept for breeding, hunting, racing, etc. **2** a male horse kept for breeding; stallion. **3** any male animal kept for breeding. *n.*

stu·dent (styü′dənt or stü′dənt) **1** a person who is studying in a school, college, or university: *That high school has 3000 students.* **2** a person who studies: *She is a student of birds.* *n.*

stud·ied (stud′ēd) **1** See **study.** *She studied the lesson carefully.* **2** carefully planned; done on purpose: *What she said to me was a studied insult.* 1 *v.,* 2 *adj.*

stu·di·o (styü′dē ō or stü′dē ō) **1** the workroom of a painter, sculptor, photographer, etc. **2** a place where motion pictures are made. **3** a place from which a radio or television program is broadcast. *n., pl.* **stu·di·os.**

stu·di·ous (styü′dē əs or stü′dē əs) **1** fond of study: *That studious boy likes school.* **2** careful; thoughtful; showing careful consideration: *The clerk made a studious effort to please customers. She is always studious of her mother's comfort.* *adj.*

stud·y (stud′ē) **1** the effort to learn by reading or thinking: *After an hour's hard study he knew his lesson.* **2** try to learn: *She studied her spelling lesson for half an hour. He is studying to be a doctor.* **3** a careful examination; investigation. **4** examine carefully: *We studied the map to find the shortest road home.* **5** a subject that is studied; a branch of learning: *History, music, and law are studies.* **6** a room for study, reading, or writing: *The minister was reading in his study.* **7** consider with care; think out; plan: *The prisoner studied ways to escape.* **8** deep thought; reverie: *The judge was absorbed in study about the case.* 1, 3, 5, 6, 8 *n., pl.* **stud·ies;** 2, 4, 7 *v.,* **stud·ied, stud·y·ing.**

stuff (stuf) **1** what a thing is made of; material: *She bought some white stuff for curtains. That boy has good stuff in him.* **2** a thing or things; substance: *The doctor rubbed some kind of stuff on the burn.* **3** goods; belongings: *He was told to move his stuff out of the room.* **4** pack full; fill: *She stuffed the pillow with feathers.* **5** stop or block up: *My head is stuffed up by a cold.* **6** fill the skin of a dead animal to make it look as it did when alive: *We saw many stuffed birds at the museum.* **7** fill a chicken, turkey, etc. with stuffing. **8** eat too much: *He stuffed himself with candy.* 1–3 *n.,* 4–8 *v.*

stuff and nonsense, silly words and thoughts.

stuff·ing (stuf′ing) **1** any material used to fill or pack something. **2** seasoned breadcrumbs, etc. used to stuff a chicken, turkey, etc. before cooking. *n.*

stuff·y (stuf′ē) **1** lacking fresh air: *a stuffy room.* **2** lacking freshness or interest; dull: *a stuffy speech.* **3** stopped up: *A cold makes my head feel stuffy.* *adj.,* **stuff·i·er, stuff·i·est.**

stum·ble (stum′bəl) **1** trip by striking the foot against something: *He stumbled over the stool in the dark kitchen.* **2** walk in an unsteady way: *The tired soldiers stumbled along.* **3** speak, act, etc. in a clumsy or hesitating way: *The boy made many blunders as he stumbled through his recitation.* **4** come by accident or chance: *While in the country, she stumbled upon some fine old pieces of furniture.* **5** the act of stumbling. 1–4 *v.,* **stum·bled, stum·bling;** 5 *n.*

stumbling block an obstacle; hindrance.

stump (stump) **1** the lower end of a tree or plant left after the main part is cut off: *We sat on top of a stump.* **2** anything left after the main or important part is removed: *The dog wagged his stump of a tail.* **3** walk in a stiff, clumsy way: *The lame man stumped along.*

4 go about, or travel through an area, making speeches: *The candidates for parliament will stump their ridings before the election.* **5** *Informal.* make unable to answer, do, etc.: *The unexpected question stumped him.* 1, 2 *n.*, 3–5 *v.*

stun (stun) **1** make senseless; knock unconscious: *He was stunned by the fall.* **2** bewilder; shock; overwhelm: *She was stunned by the news of her friend's death.* *v.*, **stunned, stun·ning.**

stung (stung) See **sting.** *A wasp stung him. He was stung on the neck.* *v.*

stunk (stungk) See **stink.** *The garbage dump stunk.* *v.*

stun·ning (stun′ing) *Informal.* excellent; very attractive; good-looking: *a stunning girl.* *adj.*

stunt[1] (stunt) check in growth or development: *Lack of proper food stunts a child.* *v.*

stunt[2] (stunt) *Informal.* **1** a feat or act intended to thrill an audience or to attract attention; an act showing boldness or skill: *The circus performers did all sorts of stunts.* **2** perform such feats: *The aviators like to stunt.* 1 *n.*, 2 *v.*

stu·pe·fy (styü′pə fī′ or stü′pə fī′) **1** make stupid, dull, or senseless: *stupefied by a drug.* **2** overwhelm with shock or amazement; astound: *They were stupefied by the calamity.* *v.*, **stu·pe·fied, stu·pe·fy·ing.**

stu·pen·dous (styü pen′dəs or stü pen′dəs) amazing; marvellous; immense: *Niagara Falls is a stupendous sight.* *adj.*

stu·pid (styü′pid or stü′pid) **1** not intelligent; dull: *a stupid person, a stupid remark.* **2** not interesting; boring: *a stupid book.* *adj.*

stu·pid·i·ty (styü pid′ə tē or stü pid′ə tē) **1** lack of intelligence. **2** a stupid act, idea, etc. *n.*, *pl.* **stu·pid·i·ties.**

stu·por (styü′pər or stü′pər) a loss or lessening of the power to feel or act: *The injured man lay in a stupor, unable to tell what had happened to him.* *n.*

stur·dy (stėr′dē) **1** strong; stout: *sturdy legs.* **2** firm; not yielding: *sturdy resistance, sturdy defenders.* *adj.*, **stur·di·er, stur·di·est.**

stur·geon (stėr′jən) a large food fish whose body has a tough skin with rows of bony plates. *n.*, *pl.* **stur·geon** or **stur·geons.**

stut·ter (stut′ər) **1** repeat the same sound in an effort to speak. *Example: C-c-c-c-can't th–th-th-they c-c-c-come?* **2** utter in this manner: *stutter a reply.* **3** the act or habit of stuttering. 1, 2 *v.*, 3 *n.*

sty[1] (stī) **1** a pen for pigs. **2** any filthy place. *n.*, *pl.* **sties.**

sty[2] or **stye** (stī) a small, painful swelling on the edge of the eyelid: *A sty is like a small boil.* *n.*, *pl.* **sties** or **styes.**

style (stīl) **1** fashion: *Paris, London, and New York set the style in dress for the world. Her dress is out of style.* **2** a manner; method; way: *She learned several styles of swimming.* **3** a way of writing or speaking: *Books for children should have a clear, easy style.* **4** a manner or way considered fashionable or excellent: *She dresses in style.* **5** design or make to suit an approved manner or fashion. **6** name; call: *Joan of Arc was styled 'the Maid of Orleans.'* 1–4 *n.*, 5, 6 *v.*, **styled, styl·ing.**

☛ **Style** and **stile** are pronounced the same.

styl·ish (stīl′ish) having style; in the current fashion; fashionable: *She wears stylish clothes.* *adj.*

suave (swäv) smoothly agreeable or polite: *the suave manner of the ambassador.* *adj.*

sub– a prefix meaning: **1** under; below, as in *subway, submarine.* **2** down; further; again, as in *subdivide.* **3** near; nearly, as in *subarctic.* **4** lower; subordinate; assistant, as in *subcommittee.*

sub·arc·tic (sub′ärk′tik or sub är′tik) near or just below the arctic region; having to do with or occurring in regions just south of the Arctic. *adj.*

sub·di·vide (sub′də vīd′) divide again; divide into smaller parts: *A builder bought the farm, subdivided it into lots, and built homes on them.* *v.*, **sub·di·vid·ed, sub·di·vid·ing.**

sub·di·vi·sion (sub′də vizh′ən) **1** a division into smaller parts. **2** a part of a part. **3** a tract of land divided into building lots. *n.*

sub·due (səb dyü′ or səb dü′) **1** conquer; overcome: *Our army subdued the enemy.* **2** keep down; hold back: *We subdued a desire to laugh.* **3** tone down; soften: *The window curtains give the room a subdued light.* *v.*, **sub·dued, sub·du·ing.**

sub·ject (sub′jikt for 1, 2, 3, 4, and 6, səb jekt′ for 5 and 7) **1** something thought about, discussed, etc.: *The subject for our composition was 'An Exciting Moment.'* **2** something learned or taught; course of study in some branch of knowledge: *Arithmetic and science are two of the subjects we take in school.* **3** a person who is under the power, control, or influence of another: *The people are the subjects of the king.* **4** under some power or influence: *the subject nations of an empire.* **5** bring under some power or influence: *Rome subjected all Italy to her rule.* **6** the word or words with which the verb is said to agree: *The subject often indicates the performer of the action, as in 'The boy trains dogs' and 'The boys train dogs.'* **7** cause to undergo or experience something: *The savages subjected their captives to torture.* 1–3, 6 *n.*, 4 *adj.*, 5, 7 *v.*

subject to, a under the power or influence of: *We are subject to our country's laws.* **b** likely to have: *I am subject to colds. Japan is subject to earthquakes.* **c** depending on; on the condition of: *I bought the car subject to your approval.*

sub·lime (sə blīm′) lofty; noble; majestic; grand: *Mountain scenery is often sublime.* *adj.*

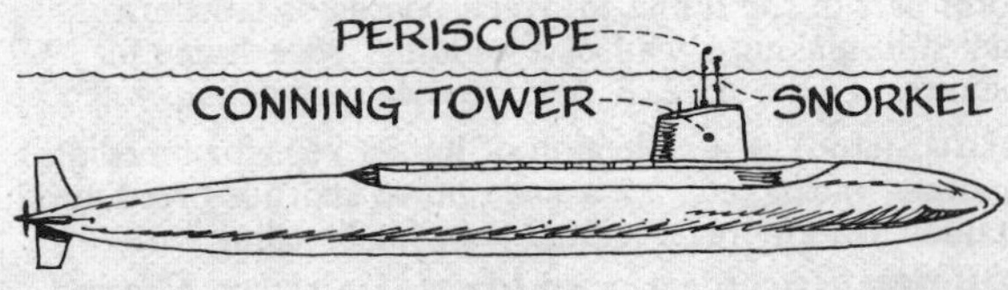

A submarine

sub·ma·rine (sub′mə rēn′ for 1, sub′mə rēn′ for 2) **1** a boat that can go under water: *Submarines are used in warfare for discharging torpedoes, etc.* **2** placed, growing, or used below the surface of the sea: *submarine plants.* 1 *n.*, 2 *adj.*

☛ See note at **U-boat.**

hat, āge, fär; let, ēqual, tėrm; it, īce
hot, ōpen, ôrder; oil, out; cup, pu̇t, rüle
əbove, takən, pencəl, lemən, circəs
ch, child; ng, long; sh, ship
th, thin; ᴛʜ, then; zh, measure

sub·merge (səb mėrj′) 1 put under water; cover with water: *At high tide this path is submerged. A big wave submerged us.* 2 cover; bury: *His talent was submerged by his shyness.* 3 go below the surface of the water: *The submarine submerged to escape being destroyed.* *v.*, **sub·merged, sub·merg·ing.**

sub·mis·sion (səb mish′ən) 1 yielding to power, control, or authority of another: *The defeated general showed his submission by giving up his sword.* 2 humble obedience: *He bowed in submission to the king's order.* 3 a petition; a formal request: *The submission of the teachers was approved by the principal.* *n.*

sub·mis·sive (səb mis′iv) yielding to the power, control, or authority of another; obedient; humble. *adj.*

sub·mit (səb mit′) 1 yield to the power, control, or authority of some person or group; surrender; yield: *The thief submitted to arrest by the police.* 2 refer to the consideration or judgment of another or others: *The secretary submitted a report of the last meeting.* *v.*, **sub·mit·ted, sub·mit·ting.**

sub·or·di·nate (sə bôr′də nit for 1, 2, and 3, sə bôr′də nāt′ for 4) 1 in a lower order or rank: *In the armed forces, lieutenants are subordinate to captains.* 2 having less importance; secondary; dependent: *An errand boy has a subordinate position.* 3 a subordinate person or thing. 4 place in a lower order or rank; make subject to or dependent on: *We must subordinate our wishes to his this time.* 1, 2 *adj.*, 3 *n.*, 4 *v.*, **sub·or·di·nat·ed, sub·or·di·nat·ing.**

sub·scribe (səb skrīb′) 1 promise to give or pay a sum of money: *He subscribed $5 to the hospital fund.* 2 promise to accept and pay for: *We subscribe to a few magazines.* 3 write one's name at the end of a document, etc.; sign one's name: *The men who subscribed to the peace treaty are now famous.* 4 give one's consent or approval; agree: *He could not subscribe to their unfair plan.* *v.*, **sub·scribed, sub·scrib·ing.**

sub·scrib·er (səb skrīb′ər) a person who subscribes: *The magazine made a special offer to new subscribers.* *n.*

sub·scrip·tion (səb skrip′shən) 1 subscribing. 2 the money subscribed; a contribution: *His subscription to the Fresh Air Fund was $5.* 3 the right obtained for the money: *His subscription to the newspaper expires next week.* 4 a sum of money raised by a number of persons: *We are raising a subscription for the new hospital.* *n.*

sub·se·quent (sub′sə kwənt) coming after; following after; later: *Subsequent events proved that he was right. The story will be continued in subsequent chapters.* *adj.* —**sub′se·quent·ly,** *adv.*

sub·set (sub′set′) in mathematics, a set, each of whose members is a member of a second set: *The set of numbers from 2 through 5 is a subset of the set of numbers from 0 through 10.* *n.*

sub·side (səb sīd′) 1 sink to a lower level: *After the rain stopped, the flood waters subsided.* 2 grow less; die down; become less active: *The waves subsided when the wind stopped. Her fever subsided after she took the medicine.* *v.*, **sub·sid·ed, sub·sid·ing.**

sub·si·dize (sub′sə dīz′) aid or assist with a grant of money: *The government subsidizes airlines that carry mail.* *v.*

sub·si·dy (sub′sə dē) a grant or contribution of money, especially one made by a government: *a subsidy for school lunches.* *n.*

sub·sist (səb sist′) 1 keep alive; live: *While the hikers were stranded they subsisted on berries.* 2 continue to be; exist: *A club cannot subsist without members.* *v.*

sub·sist·ence (səb sis′təns) 1 keeping alive; living: *Selling papers was the crippled man's only means of subsistence.* 2 a means of keeping alive; livelihood: *The sea provides a subsistence for fishermen.* *n.*

sub·soil (sub′soil′) the layer of earth that lies just under the surface soil: *In our backyard, we have clay subsoil under a thin layer of loam.* *n.*

sub·stance (sub′stəns) 1 what a thing consists of; matter; material: *Ice and water are the same substance in different forms.* 2 the real, main, or important part of anything: *The substance of an education is its effect on your life, not just learning lessons.* 3 the real meaning: *Give the substance of the speech in your own words.* 4 a solid quality; body: *Pea soup has more substance than water.* 5 wealth; property: *a man of substance.* *n.*

sub·stan·tial (səb stan′shəl) 1 real; actual: *People and things are substantial; dreams and ghosts are not.* 2 strong; firm; solid: *That house is substantial enough to last a hundred years.* 3 large; important; ample: *He made a substantial improvement in arithmetic.* 4 well-to-do; wealthy. 5 in the main; in substance: *The stories told by the two boys were in substantial agreement.* *adj.* —**sub·stan′tial·ly,** *adv.*

sub·sti·tute (sub′stə tyüt′ or sub′stə tüt′) 1 something used instead of something else; a person taking the place of another: *A substitute taught our class today.* 2 put in the place of another: *We substituted brown sugar for molasses in these cookies.* 3 take the place of another: *She substituted for Miss Brown, who is ill.* 1 *n.*, 2, 3 *v.*, **sub·sti·tut·ed, sub·sti·tut·ing.**

sub·sti·tu·tion (sub′stə tyü′shən or sub′stə tü′shən) the use of one thing for another; the putting of one person or thing in the place of another; taking the place of another. *n.*

sub·ter·ra·ne·an (sub′tə rā′nē ən) underground: *A subterranean passage led from the castle to a cave.* *adj.*

sub·ti·tle (sub′tī′təl) 1 an additional or subordinate title of a book, article, etc. 2 a word or words shown on a motion-picture screen; caption. *n.*

sub·tle (sut′əl) 1 delicate; thin; fine: *Some subtle odors are hard to recognize. Subtle jokes are hard to understand.* 2 faint; mysterious: *a subtle smile.* 3 having a keen, quick mind; discerning; acute: *She is a subtle observer of slight differences in things.* 4 sly; crafty; tricky: *a subtle scheme to get money.* *adj.* —**sub′tly,** *adv.*

sub·tle·ty (sut′əl tē) 1 a subtle quality. 2 something subtle. *n., pl.* **sub·tle·ties.**

sub·tract (səb trakt′) take away: *Subtract 2 from 10 and you have 8. Symbol:* – *v.*

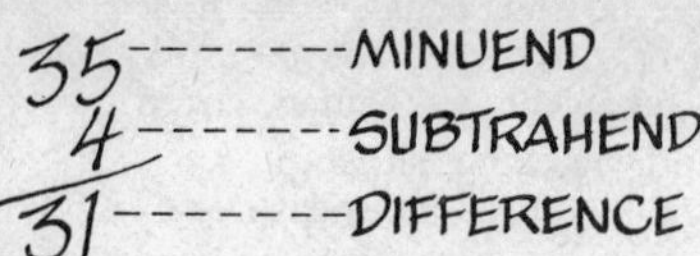

The parts of a subtraction problem

sub·trac·tion (səb trak′shən) the process of taking one number or quantity from another; the process of finding the difference between two numbers or quantities: *10 – 2 = 8 is a simple subtraction. n.*

sub·tra·hend (sub′trə hend′) a number or quantity to be subtracted from another: *In 10 – 2 = 8, the subtrahend is 2. n.*

sub·urb (sub′ėrb) **1** a district, town, or village just outside or near a city or town. **2 the suburbs,** the residential section or sections near a city or town: *Many people who work in the city live in the suburbs. n.*

☛ **Suburb** comes from Latin *suburbium,* made up of *sub-,* meaning 'below,' and *urbs,* meaning 'city.'

sub·ur·ban (sə bėr′bən) of, in, or to a suburb or the suburbs: *a suburban town, a suburban train service. adj.*

sub·way (sub′wā′) **1** an electric railway running mainly beneath the surface of the streets in a city. **2** an underground passage. **3** a road running under another road or under a railway track; underpass: *The subway was flooded during the storm. n.*

suc·ceed (sək sēd′) **1** turn out well; do well; have success: *The general's plans succeeded.* **2** come next after; follow; take the place of: *Diefenbaker succeeded St. Laurent as Prime Minister of Canada. v.*

succeed to, come into possession of an office, power, property, etc. through right of birth, by election, etc.: *The Prince of Wales succeeds to the throne of England.*

suc·cess (sək ses′) **1** a favorable result; a wished-for ending; good fortune: *Success in school comes from intelligence and work.* **2** a person or thing that succeeds: *The circus was a great success.* **3** the result; outcome; fortune: *What success did you have in finding a new apartment? n.* **—suc·cess′ful,** *adj.*

suc·ces·sion (sək sesh′ən) **1** a group of things happening one after another; a series: *A succession of accidents spoiled our automobile trip.* **2** the coming of one person or thing after another. **3** the right of succeeding to an office, property, or rank: *There was a dispute about the rightful succession to the throne.* **4** the order of persons having such a right: *The king's oldest son is next in succession to the throne. n.*

in succession, one after another: *We visited our sick friend several days in succession.*

suc·ces·sive (sək ses′iv) coming one after another; following in order: *It has rained for three successive days. adj.* **—suc·ces′sive·ly,** *adv.*

suc·ces·sor (sək ses′ər) one that follows or succeeds another in office, position, or ownership or property; anything that comes after another in a series: *Elizabeth II was her father's successor on the throne. n.*

suc·cor or **suc·cour** (suk′ər) **1** assist; help; aid. **2** assistance; help or aid. 1 *v.,* 2 *n.*

suc·cu·lent (suk′yə lənt) juicy: *a ripe and succulent peach. adj.*

suc·cumb (sə kum′) **1** give way; yield: *He succumbed to the temptation and stole the jewellery.* **2** die. *v.*

such (such) **1** of that kind; of the same kind or degree: *Such men are rare. The child had such a fever that he nearly died.* **2** of the kind already spoken of or suggested: *The ladies took only tea and coffee and such drinks.* **3** so great, so bad, so good, etc.: *He is such a liar! Such weather!* **4** one or more persons or things of a certain kind: *The box contains blankets and towels and such.* 1–3 *adj.,* 4 *pron.*

such as, a the kind or degree that; of a particular kind: *Her behavior was such as might be expected of a young child.* **b** of a particular character or kind: *The food, such as it was, was plentiful.* **c** for example: *members of the dog family, such as the wolf, fox, and jackal.*

suck (suk) **1** draw into the mouth: *Lemonade can be sucked through a straw.* **2** draw something from with the mouth: *to suck oranges.* **3** drink; take; absorb: *Plants suck up moisture from the earth. A sponge sucks in water.* **4** hold in the mouth and lick: *The child sucked a lollipop.* **5** the act of sucking: *The baby took one suck at the bottle and pushed it away.* 1–4 *v.,* 5 *n.*

suck·er (suk′ər) **1** a fish that sucks in food or has a mouth suggesting that it does so. **2** an organ in some animals for sucking or holding fast by a sucking force. **3** a shoot growing from an underground stem or root. **4** a lump of hard candy, usually on a stick: *Lollipops are suckers.* **5** *Slang.* a person easily fooled. *n.*

suc·tion (suk′shən) **1** the process of drawing liquids or gases into a space by sucking out or otherwise removing part of the air: *We draw lemonade through a straw by suction. Some pumps work by suction.* **2** causing a suction; working by suction: *a suction valve. n.*

sud·den (sud′ən) **1** not expected: *a sudden attack.* **2** quick; rapid: *The cat made a sudden jump at the mouse. adj.* **—sud′den·ly,** *adv.*

all of a sudden, unexpectedly or quickly.

suds (sudz) **1** soapy water. **2** the bubbles and foam on soapy water. *n. pl.*

sue (sü) **1** start a lawsuit against: *He sued the railway because his cow was killed by the engine.* **2** take legal action: *He decided to sue for damages.* **3** beg or ask for; plead: *Messengers came suing for peace. v.,* **sued, su·ing.**

suede (swād) a kind of soft leather that has a velvety nap on one or both sides: *suede shoes. n.*

su·et (sü′it) the hard fat of cattle or sheep. *n.*

suf·fer (suf′ər) **1** have pain, grief, injury, etc.: *She suffers from headaches.* **2** feel; experience; endure: *He suffered harm from being out in the storm.* **3** experience harm or loss: *His business suffered greatly during the war.* **4** allow; permit: *Jesus said 'Suffer little children to come unto me.'* **5** bear with patiently; endure: *I will not suffer such insults. v.*

suf·fer·ing (suf′ər ing) pain, trouble, or distress: *Hunger causes suffering. n.*

suf·fice (sə fīs′) **1** be enough; be sufficient: *Fifty dollars will suffice to buy that coat.* **2** satisfy; make content: *A small amount of cake sufficed the baby. v.,* **suf·ficed, suf·fic·ing.**

suf·fi·cient (sə fish′ənt) as much as is needed; enough: *The poor child did not have sufficient clothing for the winter. adj.* **—suf·fi′cient·ly,** *adv.*

suf·fix (suf′iks) a syllable or syllables put at the end

hat, āge, fär; let, ēqual, tėrm; it, īce
hot, ōpen, ôrder; oil, out; cup, pu̇t, rüle
 əbove, takən, pencəl, lemən, circəs
ch, child; ng, long; sh, ship
th, thin; ᴛʜ, then; zh, measure

of a word to change its meaning or to make another word, as *-ly* in *badly, -ness* in *goodness,* and *-ful* in *spoonful.* *n.*

suf·fo·cate (suf′ə kāt′) 1 kill by stopping the breath. 2 keep from breathing; hinder in breathing. 3 die for lack of air: *The child suffocated in the smoke-filled bedroom.* *v.,* **suf·fo·cat·ed, suf·fo·cat·ing.**

suf·fo·ca·tion (suf′ə kā′shən) suffocating or being suffocated. *n.*

suf·frage (suf′rij) the right to vote: *Alberta granted the suffrage to women in 1916.* *n.*

sug·ar (shu̇g′ər) 1 a sweet substance made chiefly from sugar cane or sugar beets. 2 put sugar in; sweeten with sugar: *She sugared her tea.* 3 cover with sugar; sprinkle with sugar: *to sugar doughnuts.* 4 form crystals of sugar: *Honey sugars if kept too long.* 5 cause to seem pleasant or agreeable: *He sugared his criticism of the team with some praise for the individual players.* 1 *n.,* 2–5 *v.*

sugar beet a large beet with a white root that yields sugar.

Sugar cane

sugar cane a very tall grass with a strong, jointed stem and flat leaves, growing in warm regions: *Sugar cane is one of the chief sources of sugar.*

sugar maple a maple tree yielding a sweet sap from which maple sugar and maple syrup are made.

sug·gest (sə jest′ or səg jest′) 1 bring to mind; call up the thought of: *The thought of summer suggests swimming and hot weather.* 2 propose: *He suggested a swim, and we all agreed.* 3 show in an indirect way; hint: *His yawns suggested that he would like to go to bed.* *v.*

sug·ges·tion (sə jes′chən or səg jes′chən) 1 suggesting: *The suggestion of a swim made the children jump with joy.* 2 the thing suggested: *The picnic was her suggestion.* 3 a very small amount; a slight trace: *There was a suggestion of anger in Father's voice when he had to call us in from play for the third time.* *n.*

sug·ges·tive (sə jes′tiv or səg jes′tiv) 1 tending to suggest ideas, acts, or feelings: *Summer is suggestive of swimming.* 2 tending to suggest something improper. *adj.*

su·i·cide (sü′ə sīd′) 1 killing oneself on purpose. 2 a person who kills or tries to kill himself on purpose. *n.*
commit suicide, kill oneself on purpose.

suit (süt) 1 a set of clothes to be worn together: *A man's suit consists of a coat, trousers, and, sometimes, a vest. The knight wore a suit of armor.* 2 a case in a law court: *He started a suit to collect damages for his injuries in the automobile accident.* 3 make suitable; make fit: *The teacher suited the punishment to the fault by making him sweep the room after he threw bits of paper on the floor.* 4 be good for; agree with: *A cold climate suits apples and wheat, but not oranges and tea.* 5 be agreeable or convenient to; please; satisfy: *Which date suits you best?* 6 be becoming to: *Her blue hat suits her fair skin.* 7 request; an asking; a wooing: *The prince's suit was successful, and Cinderella married him.* 8 one of the four sets of playing cards in a deck: *Spades, hearts, diamonds, and clubs are the four suits.* 1, 2, 7, 8 *n.,* 3–6 *v.*
follow suit, a play a card of the same suit as that first played. **b** follow the example of another.
suit oneself, do as one pleases.

suit·a·ble (süt′ə bəl) right for the occasion; fitting; proper: *A simple dress is suitable for school wear. The park gives the children a suitable playground.* *adj.*

suit·case (süt′kās′) a flat, rectangular travelling bag. *n.*

suit coat or **suit·coat** (süt′kōt′) the long-sleeved upper part, or jacket, of a suit. *n.*

suite (swēt) 1 a set of connected rooms to be used by one person or family: *She has a suite of rooms at the hotel—a living room, bedroom, and bath.* 2 a set of furniture that matches. 3 any set or series of like things. 4 a group of attendants: *The queen travelled with a suite of twelve.* 5 an apartment. *n.*
☛ **Suite** and **sweet** are pronounced the same.

suit·or (süt′ər) 1 a man who is courting a woman: *The princess had many suitors.* 2 a person bringing a suit in a law court. 3 anyone who sues or petitions. *n.*

sul·fur (sul′fər) See **sulphur.**

sulk (sulk) 1 be sulky. 2 a fit of sulking; a sulky mood. 3 **the sulks,** bad humor shown by sulking: *The baby seems to have a fit of the sulks.* 1 *v.,* 2, 3 *n.*

sulk·y[1] (sul′kē) silent because of bad humor; sullen: *He gets sulky and won't play if he can't be leader.* *adj.,* **sulk·i·er, sulk·i·est.**

A sulky for racing

sulk·y[2] (sul′kē) a light one-horse carriage with two wheels, for one person, commonly used in trotting races. *n., pl.* **sulk·ies.**

sul·len (sul′ən) 1 silent because of bad humor or

anger: *The boy becomes sullen if he is punished.* 2 gloomy; dismal: *The sullen skies threatened rain.* *adj.*

sul·phur or **sul·fur** (sul′fər) a light-yellow substance that burns with a blue flame and a stifling smell: *Sulphur is used in making matches, paper pulp, fertilizers, etc.* *n.*

sul·tan (sul′tən) the ruler of certain Moslem countries: *Turkey was ruled by a sultan until 1922.* *n.*

sul·try (sul′trē) 1 hot, close, and moist: *We expect some sultry weather during July.* 2 hot or fiery: *a sultry sun.* *adj.* **sul·tri·er, sul·tri·est.**

sum (sum) 1 an amount of money: *He paid a huge sum for that bicycle.* 2 the number or quantity obtained by adding two or more numbers or quantities together: *The sum of 2 and 3 and 4 is 9.* See **addition** for picture. 3 a problem in arithmetic: *He can do easy sums in his head, but he has to use pencil and paper for hard ones.* 4 the whole amount; the total amount: *That boy reached the sum of his happiness when he became captain of the football team.* 5 **sum up,** express or tell briefly: *Sum up the main points of the lesson in three sentences. The judge summed up the evidence.* 1–4 *n.*, 5 *v.*, **summed, sum·ming.**

☛ **Sum** and **some** are pronounced the same.

su·mac or **su·mach** (shü′mak or sü′mak) a shrub or small tree having long clusters of red and white fruit, and leaves that turn scarlet in the autumn. *n.*

sum·ma·rize (sum′ə rīz′) make a summary of; give only the main points of; express briefly: *summarize the story of a book.* *v.*, **sum·ma·rized, sum·ma·riz·ing.**

sum·ma·ry (sum′ə rē) 1 a brief statement giving the main points: *This history book has a summary at the end of each chapter.* 2 brief; short. 3 direct and prompt; without delay: *The soldier took summary vengeance by killing both his enemies.* 1 *n.*, *pl.* **sum·ma·ries;** 2, 3 *adj.*

sum·mer (sum′ər) 1 the warmest season of the year; the season of the year between spring and autumn. 2 of or having to do with summer: *summer heat, summer clothes, summer holidays.* 3 pass the summer: *to summer at the seashore.* 1 *n.*, 2 *adj.*, 3 *v.*

sum·mer·time (sum′ər tīm′) the summer season; summer. *n.*

sum·mit (sum′it) the highest point; the top: *We could see the summit of the mountain twenty-five kilometres away. The summit of her ambition was to be an actress.* *n.*

sum·mon (sum′ən) 1 call with authority; order to come; send for: *The church bells summon people to worship. A telegram summoned him home.* 2 stir to action; rouse: *He summoned his courage and entered the deserted house.* *v.*

sum·mons (sum′ənz) 1 an order to appear at a certain place, especially in a law court: *He received a summons to be at the traffic court at 10 a.m., October 5.* 2 an urgent call; a command, message, or signal: *I hurried in response to my friend's summons for help.* *n.*

sump (sump) a pit or reservoir for collecting water, oil, sewage, etc. *n.*

sump·tu·ous (sump′chü əs) costly; magnificient; rich: *The king gave a sumptuous banquet.* *adj.*

sun (sun) 1 the star around which the earth and the other planets revolve: *The sun lights and warms the earth.* 2 the light and warmth of the sun: *The cat likes to sit in the sun.* 3 put in the light and warmth of the sun; expose to the sun's rays: *The swimmers sunned themselves on the beach.* 4 any heavenly body like the sun: *Many stars are suns and have their worlds that travel around them.* 5 something like the sun in brightness or splendor. 1, 2, 4, 5 *n.*, 3 *v.*, **sunned, sun·ning.**

☛ **Sun** and **son** are pronounced the same.

Sun. Sunday.

sun·beam (sun′bēm′) a ray of sunlight: *A sunbeam brightened the child's hair to gold.* *n.*

sun·bon·net (sun′bon′it) a large bonnet that shades the face and neck. *n.*

sun·burn (sun′bėrn′) 1 a burning of the skin by the sun's rays: *A sunburn is often red and painful.* 2 burn the skin by the sun's rays: *He is sunburned from a day on the beach.* 3 become burned by the sun: *Her skin sunburns quickly.* 1 *n.*, 2, 3 *v.*, **sun·burned** or **sun·burnt, sun·burn·ing.**

sun·burnt (sun′bėrnt′) See **sunburn.** *v.*

sun·dae (sun′dē or sun′dā′) a serving of ice cream with syrup, crushed fruit, nuts, etc. on it. *n.*

☛ **Sundae** and **Sunday** are sometimes pronounced the same.

Sun·day (sun′dē or sun′dā′) the first day of the week; the day of worship among most Christians. *n.*

☛ See note at **sundae.**

☛ **Sunday** developed from Old English *sunnandæg,* meaning 'day of the sun.'

Sunday school 1 a school held on Sunday for teaching religion. 2 its members.

sun·der (sun′dər) separate; part; divide; split: *Time often sunders friends.* *v.*

in sunder, apart: *Lightning tore the tree in sunder.*

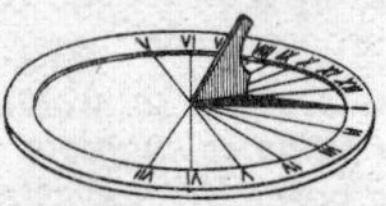

A sundial

sun·di·al (sun′dī′əl or sun′dīl′) an instrument for telling the time of day by the position of a shadow cast by the sun. *n.*

sun·down (sun′doun′) sunset: *We'll be home by sundown.* *n.*

sun·dries (sun′drēz) sundry things; items not named; odds and ends: *We spent almost ten dollars for sundries.* *n. pl.*

sun·dry (sun′drē) several; various: *From sundry hints, he guessed he was to be given a bicycle for his birthday.* *adj.*

sun·flow·er (sun′flou′ər) a tall plant having large, yellow flowers with brown centres and seeds that are rich in oil. *n.*

sung (sung) See **sing.** *Many songs were sung at the concert.* *v.*

sun·glass·es (sun′glas′iz) spectacles, often made of colored glass, to protect the eyes from the glare of the sun. *n. pl.*

hat, āge, fär; let, ēqual, tėrm; it, īce
hot, ōpen, ôrder; oil, out; cup, pu̇t, rüle
əbove, takən, pencəl, lemən, circəs
ch, child; ng, long; sh, ship
th, thin; ᴛʜ, then; zh, measure

sunk (sungk) See **sink.** *The ship had sunk to the bottom.* *v.*

sunk·en (sungk′ən) 1 sunk: *a sunken ship.* 2 submerged; under water: *a sunken rock.* 3 situated below the general level: *a sunken living room.* 4 fallen in; hollow: *sunken eyes.* *adj.*

sun·light (sun′līt′) the light of the sun. *n.*

sun·lit (sun′lit′) lighted by the sun. *adj.*

sun·ny (sun′ē) 1 having much sunshine: *a sunny day.* 2 lighted or warmed by the sun: *a sunny room.* 3 bright; cheerful; happy: *The baby gave a sunny smile.* *adj.,* **sun·ni·er, sun·ni·est.**

sun·rise (sun′rīz′) 1 the coming up of the sun; the first appearance of the sun in the morning. 2 the time when the sun comes up; the beginning of the day. *n.*

sun·set (sun′set′) 1 the going down of the sun; the last appearance of the sun in the evening. 2 the time when the sun goes down; the close of the day. *n.*

sun·shade (sun′shād′) an umbrella, awning, etc. used to give protection from the sun. *n.*

sun·shine (sun′shīn′) 1 the shining of the sun; light or rays of the sun. 2 brightness; cheerfulness; happiness: *the sunshine of her smile.* *n.*

sun·spot (sun′spot′) one of the dark spots that appear at regular intervals on the surface of the sun. *n.*

sun·stroke (sun′strōk′) a sudden illness caused by too much exposure to the sun's rays or by too much heat. *n.*

sun–up (sun′up′) sunrise. *n.*

sup[1] (sup) eat the evening meal; take supper: *He supped alone on bread and milk.* *v.,* **supped, sup·ping.**

sup[2] (sup) sip. *v.,* **supped, sup·ping;** *n.*

su·per (sü′pər) 1 *Informal.* a superintendent. 2 *Slang.* excellent; wonderful. 1 *n.,* 2 *adj.*

su·perb (su̇ pėrb′) 1 grand; stately; majestic; magnificent; splendid: *Mountain scenery is superb. The queen's jewels are superb.* 2 very fine; first-rate; excellent: *The actor gave a superb performance.* *adj.*

su·per·fi·cial (sü′pər fish′əl) 1 of the surface; on the surface; at the surface: *superficial measurement. His burns were superficial and soon healed.* 2 not thorough; shallow: *Girls used to receive only a superficial education.* *adj.*

su·per·flu·ous (su̇ pėr′flü əs) more than is needed: *The author uses superfluous words.* *adj.*

su·per·hu·man (sü′pər hyü′mən) above or beyond ordinary human power, experience, etc.: *By a superhuman effort, the hunter choked the leopard to death.* *adj.*

su·per·in·tend (sü′pər in tend′) oversee and direct work or workers; manage a place, institution, etc. *v.*

su·per·in·tend·ent (sü′pər in ten′dənt) a person who oversees, directs, or manages; supervisor: *a superintendent of schools, a superintendent of a factory.* *n.*

su·pe·ri·or (sə pēr′ē ər) 1 very good; excellent: *He has a superior mind.* 2 higher in quality; better; greater: *This blend of coffee is not very good; the last one we tried was superior. Our army had to fight off a superior force.* 3 higher in position, rank, or importance: *a superior officer.* 4 a person who is higher in rank or more accomplished than another: *A captain is a lieutenant's superior. As a violin player, he has no superior.* 5 showing a feeling of being above others; proud: *The other girls disliked her superior manner.* 6 the head of a monastery or convent. 1–3, 5 *adj.,* 4, 6 *n.*

superior to, a better than; greater than: *Man considers himself superior to the beasts.* **b** not giving in to; above yielding to: *A wise man is superior to flattery.*

su·pe·ri·or·i·ty (sə pēr′ē ôr′ə tē) a superior state or quality: *Few people doubt the superiority of modern ways of travelling over those of olden times.* *n.*

su·per·la·tive (sə pėr′lə tiv) 1 of the highest kind; above all others; supreme: *Solomon is said to have been a man of superlative wisdom.* 2 the third of three degrees of comparison, used when qualities are being compared: *'Fairest' is the superlative of 'fair.' 'Most quickly' is the superlative of 'quickly.'* 1 *adj.,* 2 *n.*

su·per·man (sü′pər man′) a man having more than human powers. *n., pl.* **su·per·men** (su′pər men′).

su·per·mar·ket (sü′pər mär′kit) a large store for food and household articles in which customers select items from open shelves and pay for them just before leaving. *n.*

su·per·nat·u·ral (sü′pər nach′rəl or sü′pər nach′ə rəl) above or beyond what is natural: *Miracles are considered as supernatural events.* *adj.*

su·per·sede (sü′pər sēd′) 1 take the place of; cause to be set aside; displace: *Gas light has been superseded by electric light.* 2 fill the place of; replace: *A new mayor superseded the old.* *v.,* **su·per·sed·ed, su·per·sed·ing.**

su·per·son·ic (sü′pər son′ik) 1 of or having to do with sound waves beyond the limit of human hearing. 2 of or having a speed greater than that of sound in air (about 1200 kilometres per hour at sea level). *adj.*

su·per·sti·tion (sü′pər stish′ən) 1 unreasoning fear of what is unknown or mysterious; unreasoning expectation: *As knowledge increases, superstition decreases.* 2 a belief or practice founded on ignorant fear or mistaken reverence: *A common superstition considered 13 an unlucky number.* *n.*

su·per·sti·tious (sü′pər stish′əs) full of superstition; likely to believe superstitions; caused by superstition: *He was superstitious about the number 13.* *adj.*

su·per·vise (sü′pər vīz′) look after and direct work or workers, a process, etc.; oversee; manage: *Examinations are supervised by teachers.* *v.,* **su·per·vised, su·per·vis·ing.**

su·per·vi·sion (sü′pər vizh′ən) management; direction; overseeing: *The house was built under the careful supervision of an architect.* *n.*

su·per·vi·sor (sü′pər vī′zər) a person who supervises: *The music supervisor has charge of the school band, chorus, and orchestra.* *n.*

sup·per (sup′ər) the evening meal; a meal eaten early in the evening if dinner is near noon, or late in the evening if dinner is at six or later. *n.*

sup·plant (sə plant′) 1 take the place of: *Machinery has supplanted hand labor in the making of shoes.* 2 take the place of by unfair methods: *The prince plotted to supplant the king.* *v.*

sup·ple (sup′əl) 1 bending easily: *a supple birch tree, supple leather, a supple dancer, supple joints.* 2 readily adapting to different ideas, circumstances, people, etc.; yielding: *She gets along well with people because of her supple nature.* *adj.,* **sup·pler, sup·plest.**

sup·ple·ment (sup′lə mənt for 1, sup′lə ment′ for 2) 1 something added to complete a thing, or to make it larger or better: *a diet supplement. The newspaper has a supplement every Saturday.* 2 add to; complete: *He supplemented his income by taking an extra job on Saturdays.* 1 *n.,* 2 *v.*

sup·pli·ca·tion (sup′lə kā′shən) a humble, earnest request or prayer: *Supplications to God arose from all the churches.* *n.*

sup·ply (sə plī′) 1 furnish; provide: *The school supplies books for the children. He is supplying us with ice.* 2 a quantity ready for use; stock; store: *Our school gets its supply of paper from the city. Alberta has very large supplies of coal and oil.* 3 **supplies,** *pl.* the food, equipment, etc. necessary for an army, expedition, or the like. 4 make up for a loss, lack, absence, etc.; fill: *Rocks and stumps supplied the place of chairs at the picnic.* 5 satisfy a want, need, etc.: *There was just enough to supply the demand.* 1, 4, 5 *v.,* **sup·plied, sup·ply·ing;** 2, 3 *n., pl.* **sup·plies.**

sup·port (sə pôrt′) 1 keep from falling; hold up: *Walls support the roof.* 2 give strength or courage to; keep up; help: *Hope supports us in trouble.* 3 provide for: *A healthy man should support his family.* 4 be in favor of; back: *He supports the Liberals.* 5 help prove; bear out: *The facts support his claim.* 6 put up with; bear; endure: *She couldn't support life without friends.* 7 assistance; help or aid: *He needs the support of a scholarship.* 8 a person or thing that supports; a prop: *The neck is the support of the head.* 1–6 *v.,* 7, 8 *n.* **—sup·port′er,** *n.*

sup·pose (sə pōz′) 1 consider as possible: *Let's suppose we have three wishes. Suppose we are late, what will the teacher say?* 2 believe; think; imagine: *I suppose she will come as usual.* *v.,* **sup·posed, sup·pos·ing.**

sup·posed (sə pōzd′) 1 considered as possible or probable; accepted as true; assumed: *The supposed beggar was really a prince.* *adj.*
supposed to, obliged to; expected to: *You're not supposed to jump on the bed. I was supposed to bring the cake, but I forgot.*

sup·pos·ing (sə pōz′ing) in the event that; if: *Supposing it rains, shall we go?* *conj.*

sup·press (sə pres′) 1 put an end to; put down; stop by force: *The soldiers suppressed a riot by firing over the heads of the mob.* 2 keep in; hold back; check: *She suppressed a yawn.* 3 hide; refuse to make known: *The government was accused of suppressing important facts.* *v.*

sup·pres·sion (sə presh′ən) 1 putting down by force or authority; the act of putting an end to: *Troops were used in the suppression of the revolt.* 2 keeping in; holding back: *suppression of an impulse to cough.* 3 hiding; refusal to make known: *The suppression of facts may be as dishonest as the telling of lies.* *n.*

su·prem·a·cy (sə prem′ə sē) 1 the condition of being supreme. 2 supreme authority or power. *n.*

su·preme (sə prēm′) 1 highest in rank or authority: *a supreme ruler, a supreme court.* 2 highest in degree or quality; greatest; utmost: *With supreme courage she snatched the baby from in front of the car.* *adj.*

Supreme Court 1 the highest court in Canada, located in Ottawa. 2 the highest court in each province, located in the provincial capital. 3 a similar court in other countries.

sure (shür) 1 free from doubt; certain: *Are you sure you locked the door? Make sure you have the key.* 2 safe; reliable; to be trusted: *You can trust him; he is a sure messenger.* 3 never missing, slipping, failing, etc.; unerring: *a sure aim.* 4 certain to be or to happen: *The army faced sure defeat. He is sure to win the prize.* 5 firm: *to stand on sure ground.* 6 *Informal.* surely; certainly. 1–5 *adj.,* **sur·er, sur·est;** 6 *adv.*
for sure, *Informal.* certainly; undoubtedly.

sure–foot·ed (shür′fůt′id) not liable to stumble, slip, or fall. *adj.*

sure·ly (shür′lē) 1 certainly: *Half a loaf is surely better than none at all.* 2 firmly; without mistake; without missing, slipping, etc.: *The goat leaped surely from rock to rock.* *adv.*

sur·e·ty (shür′ə tē) 1 security against loss, damage, or failure to do something: *An insurance company gives surety against loss by fire.* 2 a person who agrees to be responsible for another: *He was surety for his brother's appearance in court on the day set for the trial.* *n., pl.* **sur·e·ties.**

surf (sėrf) 1 the waves or swell of the sea breaking on the shore: *The surf is high just after a storm.* 2 travel or ride on the crest of such a wave, especially with a surfboard. 1 *n.,* 2 *v.*
☛ **Surf** and **serf** are pronounced the same.

sur·face (sėr′fis) 1 the outside of anything: *the surface of a mountain. An egg has a smooth surface.* 2 any face or side of a thing: *A cube has six surfaces. The upper surface of the plate has pictures on it.* 3 the outward appearance: *He seems rough, but you will find him very kind below the surface.* 4 of the surface; on the surface; having to do with the surface: *a surface view, surface travel.* 5 put a surface on; make smooth: *to surface a road.* 6 rise to the surface of the water: *The submarine surfaced.* 1–3 *n.,* 4 *adj.,* 5, 6 *v.,* **sur·faced, sur·fac·ing.**

surf·board (sėrf′bôrd′) a long, narrow board for riding the surf. *n.*

surge (sėrj) 1 rise and fall; move like waves: *A great wave surged over us. The crowd surged through the streets.* 2 a swelling wave; a sweep or rush of waves: *Our boat was upset by a surge.* 3 something like a wave: *A surge of anger rushed over him.* 1 *v.,* **surged, surg·ing;** 2, 3 *n.*

sur·geon (sėr′jən) a doctor who performs operations: *A surgeon removed my tonsils.* *n.*

sur·ger·y (sėr′jər ē) treating disease and injury by means of operations: *Malaria can be cured by medicine, but cancer usually requires surgery.* *n.*

sur·gi·cal (sėr′jə kəl) 1 of surgery; having to do with surgery: *a surgical specialist.* 2 used in surgery: *surgical instruments.* *adj.*

hat, āge, fär; let, ēqual, tėrm; it, īce
hot, ōpen, ôrder; oil, out; cup, pu̇t, rüle
əbove, takən, pencəl, lemən, circəs
ch, child; ng, long; sh, ship
th, thin; ŦH, then; zh, measure

sur·ly (sėr′lē) bad-tempered and unfriendly; rude; gruff: *The surly dog growled at the child. The grouchy old man grumbled a surly reply.* *adj.*, **sur·li·er, sur·li·est.**

sur·mise (sər mīz′) **1** guessing; a guess: *His guilt was a matter of surmise; there was no proof.* **2** to guess: *We surmised that the delay was caused by some accident.* 1 *n.*, 2 *v.*, **sur·mised, sur·mis·ing.**

sur·mount (sər mount′) **1** rise above: *Mt. Robson surmounts all the peaks near it.* **2** be above or on top of: *A statue surmounts the monument.* **3** overcome: *The committee surmounted many difficulties before they finally developed a workable plan.* *v.*

sur·name (sėr′nām′) **1** a last name; a family name: *Smith is the surname of John Smith.* **2** give an added name to: *Simon was surnamed Peter.* 1 *n.*, 2 *v.*, **sur·named, sur·nam·ing.**

sur·pass (sər pas′) **1** do better than; be greater than; excel: *She surpasses her sister in arithmetic.* **2** be too much or too great for; go beyond; exceed: *The glory of heaven surpasses description. Helen of Troy was of surpassing beauty.* *v.*

sur·plus (sėr′pləs) **1** an amount over and above what is needed; an extra quantity left over; an excess: *The store was selling off its surplus of fresh fruit.* **2** more than is needed; extra; excess: *Surplus wheat is put in storage.* 1 *n.*, 2 *adj.*

sur·prise (sər prīz′) **1** a feeling caused by something unexpected: *His face showed surprise at the news.* **2** something unexpected: *Mother always has a surprise for the children on holidays.* **3** catching unprepared; coming upon suddenly: *The fort was captured by surprise.* **4** catch unprepared; come upon suddenly: *Our army surprised the enemy while they were sleeping.* **5** cause to feel surprised; astonish: *The victory surprised us.* **6** surprising; that is not expected; coming as a surprise: *a surprise party, a surprise visit.* **7** lead or bring a person, etc. unawares: *The news surprised her into tears.* 1–3 *n.*, 4, 5, 7 *v.*, **sur·prised, sur·pris·ing;** 6 *adj.*

sur·pris·ing (sər prīz′ing) causing surprise or wonder: *a surprising recovery.* *adj.*

sur·ren·der (sə ren′dər) **1** give up; give oneself or itself up; yield: *The captain had to surrender to the enemy. As the storm increased, the men on the raft surrendered all hope. He surrendered himself to bitter grief.* **2** the act of surrendering: *The surrender of the soldiers saved them from being shot.* 1 *v.*, 2 *n.*

sur·rey (sėr′ē) a light, four-wheeled, horse-drawn carriage having two seats and sometimes a top. *n.*, *pl.* **sur·reys.**

sur·round (sə round′) shut in on all sides; be around; extend around: *A high fence surrounds the field. They surrounded the sick girl with every comfort.* *v.*

sur·round·ings (sə roun′dingz) surrounding things, conditions, etc.: *The poor child had never had cheerful surroundings.* *n. pl.*

sur·vey (sər vā′ for 1 and 4, sėr′vā or sər vā′ for 2, 3, 5, and 6) **1** look over; view; examine: *Grandma surveyed her with a stern look. The buyers surveyed the goods offered for sale.* **2** a general look; a view; examination or inspection: *We were pleased with our first survey of the house.* **3** a formal or official inspection, study, poll, etc.: *a survey of public opinion.* **4** measure for size, shape, position, boundaries, etc.: *Men are surveying the land before it is divided into house lots.* **5** a careful measurement: *A survey showed that the northern boundary was not correct.* **6** a plan or description of such a measurement: *He pointed out the route of the railway on the government survey.* 1, 4 *v.*, 2, 3, 5, 6 *n.*, *pl.* **sur·veys.**

sur·vey·ing (sər vā′ing) the business of making surveys of land. *n.*

sur·vey·or (sər vā′ər) a person who surveys, especially land: *The surveyor set up his instruments and began to make a survey of the road.* *n.*

sur·viv·al (sər vī′vəl) **1** surviving; a continuance of life; the fact of living or lasting longer than others. **2** a person, thing, custom, belief, etc. that has lasted from an earlier time: *Belief in the evil eye is a survival of ancient magic.* *n.*

sur·vive (sər vīv′) **1** live longer than; remain alive after: *The old man survived his wife by three years. Only ten of the crew survived the shipwreck.* **2** live through or after; outlast: *The crops survived the drought.* **3** continue to exist; remain: *Books have survived from the time of the Ancient Greeks.* *v.*, **sur·vived, sur·viv·ing.**

sur·viv·or (sər vī′vər) a person, animal, or plant that remains alive; anything that continues to exist: *He is the only survivor of a family of nine. There were two survivors from the plane crash.* *n.*

sus·cep·ti·ble (sə sep′tə bəl) easily influenced by feelings or emotions; very sensitive: *Poetry appealed to his susceptible nature.* *adj.*

susceptible of, capable of receiving, undergoing, or being affected by: *Oak is susceptible of a high polish.*

susceptible to, easily affected by; especially liable to; open to: *Vain people are susceptible to flattery. Young children are susceptible to many diseases.*

sus·pect (səs pekt′ for 1, 2, and 3, sus′pekt for 4, sus′pekt or səs pekt′ for 5) **1** imagine to be so; think likely: *The mouse suspected danger and did not touch the trap. I suspect that some accident has delayed him.* **2** believe guilty, false, bad, etc. without proof: *The policeman suspected the thief of lying.* **3** feel no confidence in; doubt: *The judge suspected the truth of the thief's excuse.* **4** a person suspected: *The police have arrested two suspects in connection with the bank robbery.* **5** open to or viewed with suspicion; suspected: *That version of the story is suspect.* 1–3 *v.*, 4 *n.*, 5 *adj.*

sus·pend (səs pend′) **1** hang down by attaching to something above: *The lamp was suspended from the ceiling.* **2** hold or stay in place as if by hanging: *We saw the smoke suspended in the still air.* **3** stop for a while: *We suspended building operations during the winter.* **4** remove or exclude for a while from some privilege or job: *He was suspended from school for a week for bad conduct.* **5** keep undecided; put off: *Let us suspend judgment until we know all the facts.* *v.*

sus·pend·ers (səs pen′dərz) **1** straps worn over the shoulders to hold up the trousers; braces. **2** garters worn by men to hold up their socks. *n. pl.*

sus·pense (sə pens′) 1 the condition of being uncertain: *The detective story kept me in suspense until the last chapter.* 2 anxious uncertainty; anxiety: *Parents feel suspense when their children are sick.* *n.*

sus·pen·sion (sə pen′shən) suspending or being suspended: *the suspension of a boy from school for bad conduct.* *n.*

The suspension bridge at Dunvegan, Alberta

suspension bridge a bridge hung on cables or chains between towers.

sus·pi·cion (sə pish′ən) 1 the state of mind of a person who suspects; suspecting: *My suspicion of the stranger was well-founded.* 2 the condition of being suspected: *The real thief tried to turn suspicion toward the others.* 3 a very small amount; a slight trace; a suggestion: *She spoke with a suspicion of spite in her voice.* *n.*

above suspicion, so honorable as not to be suspected of wrongdoing: *Our old servants are all above suspicion.*

on suspicion, because of being suspected: *He was arrested on suspicion of robbery.*

under suspicion, suspected; believed guilty but not proven to be so.

sus·pi·cious (sə pish′əs) 1 causing one to suspect: *A man was loitering near the house in a suspicious manner.* 2 feeling suspicion; suspecting: *The dog is suspicious of strangers.* 3 showing suspicion: *The dog gave suspicious sniffs at my leg.* *adj.*

sus·tain (sə tān′) 1 keep up; keep going: *Hope sustains him in his misery. She eats barely enough to sustain life.* 2 hold up; support: *Arches sustain the weight of the roof.* 3 bear; endure: *The sea wall sustains the shock of the waves.* 4 suffer; experience: *She sustained a great loss in the death of her husband.* 5 allow; admit; favor: *The court sustained his claim.* 6 agree with; confirm: *The facts sustain his theory.* *v.*

sus·te·nance (sus′tə nəns) 1 a means of sustaining life; food or provisions: *He has gone for a week without sustenance.* 2 the means of living; support: *He gave money for the sustenance of a poor family.* *n.*

SW, S.W., or **s.w.** 1 southwest. 2 southwestern.

swab (swob) 1 a mop for cleaning decks, floors, etc. 2 a bit of sponge, cloth, or cotton for cleansing some part of the body or for applying medicine to it. 3 clean with a swab; apply a swab to: *to swab a person's throat.* 1, 2 *n.,* 3 *v.,* **swabbed, swab·bing.**

swad·dle (swod′əl) bind a baby with long, narrow strips of cloth; wrap tightly with clothes, bandages, etc. *v.,* **swad·dled, swad·dling.**

swag·ger (swag′ər) 1 walk with a bold, rude, or superior air; strut about or show off in a vain or insolent way: *The bully swaggered into the yard.* 2 a swaggering way of walking or acting: *The pirate captain moved among his prisoners with a swagger.* 1 *v.,* 2 *n.*

swal·low[1] (swol′ō) 1 take into the stomach through the throat: *We swallow all our food and drink.* 2 take in; absorb: *The waves swallowed up the swimmer.* 3 *Informal.* believe too easily; accept without question or suspicion: *He will swallow any story.* 4 put up with; take meekly: *He swallowed the insults of the bully without saying anything.* 5 keep back; keep from expressing: *She swallowed her displeasure and smiled.* 6 a swallowing: *He took the medicine at one swallow.* 7 an amount that is or can be swallowed at one time: *There are only about four swallows of water left in the bottle.* 1–5 *v.,* 6, 7 *n.*

swal·low[2] (swol′ō) a small bird that can fly very fast: *The barn swallow has a deeply forked tail.* *n.*

swam (swam) See **swim.** *When the boat sank, we swam to shore.* *v.*

swamp (swomp) 1 wet, soft land: *The farmer will drain the swamp so that he can plant crops there.* 2 sink in a swamp or in water: *The horses were swamped in the stream.* 3 fill with water and sink: *Their boat swamped. The waves swamped the boat.* 4 overwhelm as by a flood; make or become helpless: *The rich man was swamped with letters asking for money. That factory is swamped with orders it cannot fill.* 1 *n.,* 2–4 *v.*

swamp·y (swom′pē) 1 like a swamp; soft and wet: *The front yard is swampy from the heavy rain.* 2 containing swamps: *swampy meadow land.* *adj.,* **swamp·i·er, swamp·i·est.**

One kind of swan — about 150 cm long with the tail; wingspread about 275 cm

swan (swon) a large, graceful water bird having a long, slender, curving neck: *The grown male swan is usually pure white.* *n.*

swap (swop) *Informal.* 1 exchange or trade: *He swapped his penknife for a hockey stick.* 2 an exchange or trade. 1 *v.,* **swapped, swap·ping;** 2 *n.*

swarm (swôrm) 1 a group of bees that leave a hive and fly off together to start a new colony. 2 fly off together to start a new colony. 3 a group of bees settled together in a hive. 4 a large group of insects, animals, people, etc. moving about together: *Swarms of children were playing in the park.* 5 fly or move about in a swarm; move about in great numbers; be in very great numbers: *The mosquitoes swarmed about us.* 6 be crowded; crowd: *The swamp swarms with mosquitoes and gnats.* 1, 3, 4 *n.,* 2, 5, 6 *v.*

swarth·y (swôr′ᴛʜē) having a dark skin: *The sailor was swarthy from the sun of the tropics.* *adj.,* **swarth·i·er, swarth·i·est.**

swat (swot) *Informal.* 1 hit sharply or violently: *to swat a fly.* 2 a sharp or violent blow. 1 *v.,* **swat·ted, swat·ting;** 2 *n.*

sway (swā) 1 swing back and forth; swing from side

to side, or to one side: *She swayed and fell in a faint. The pail swayed in his hands as he ran.* **2** make move; cause to sway: *The wind sways the grass.* **3** a swinging back and forth or from side to side: *The sway of the pail caused some milk to spill out.* **4** move to one side; turn aside: *The horse swayed against the barn.* **5** change in opinion or feeling: *Nothing could sway him after he had made up his mind.* **6** influence; control; rule: *The speaker's words swayed his audience.* **7** an influence, control, or rule: *Few countries are now under the sway of kings.* 1, 2, 4–6 *v.*, 3, 7 *n.*

swear (swer) **1** make a solemn promise before a judge, coroner, etc.: *A witness at a trial has to swear to tell the truth.* **2** bind by an oath; require to promise: *Members of the club were sworn to secrecy.* **3** promise on oath or solemnly to observe or do something; vow: *The knights had sworn to be true to their king.* **4** use profane language; curse: *The pirate raged and swore when he was captured.* *v.*, **swore, sworn, swear·ing.**
swear in, admit to office or service by giving an oath: *to swear in a jury.*
swear off, promise to give up: *to swear off smoking.*

sweat (swet) **1** moisture coming through the skin: *He wiped the sweat from his face.* **2** give out moisture through the pores of the skin: *We sweat when it is very hot.* **3** cause to sweat: *He sweated his horse by riding him too hard.* **4** get rid of by sweating or as if by sweating: *to sweat off excess weight, to sweat out a hard test.* **5** a fit or condition of sweating: *He was in a cold sweat from fear.* **6** *Informal.* a condition of anxiety, impatience, or anything that might make a person sweat: *We were all in a sweat over the big test we would get on Monday.* **7** moisture given out by something or gathered on its surface: *The water pipes were covered with sweat.* **8** give out moisture; collect or gather moisture on the surface: *A pitcher of ice water sweats on a hot day.* **9** cause to work hard and under bad conditions: *That employer sweats his workers.* **10** *Informal.* work very hard. 1, 5–7 *n.*, 2–4, 8–10 *v.*, **sweat** or **sweat·ed, sweat·ing.**

sweat·er (swet′ər) a knitted or crocheted outer garment for the upper body, made of wool, nylon, orlon, etc.; a pullover or cardigan. *n.*

Swede (swēd) a person born in or living in Sweden, a country in Europe. *n.*

Swed·ish (swēd′ish) **1** of or having to do with Sweden. **2** the language of Sweden. 1 *adj.*, 2 *n.*

sweep (swēp) **1** clean or clear with a broom or brush; use a broom or something like one to remove dirt: *The campers swept the floor of their cabin every morning.* **2** move, drive, or take away with a broom or as if with a broom, brush, etc.: *They swept the dust into a pan. The wind sweeps the snow into drifts.* **3** remove with a sweeping motion; carry along: *A flood swept away the bridge.* **4** the act of sweeping; clearing away; removing: *He made a clean sweep of all his debts.* **5** pass over with a steady movement: *Her fingers swept the harp strings. His eye swept the sky, searching for signs of rain.* **6** move swiftly; pass swiftly: *Pirates swept down on the town. The wind sweeps through the valley.* **7** a steady, driving motion or swift onward course of something: *The sweep of the wind kept the trees from growing tall.* **8** move with purpose and dignity: *The lady swept out of the room.* **9** move or extend in a long course or curve: *The shore sweeps to the south for several kilometres.* **10** a swinging or curving motion: *He cut the grass with strong sweeps of his scythe.* **11** a curve; bend: *the sweep of a road.* **12** a continuous extent; a stretch: *The house looks upon a wide sweep of farming country.* **13** the reach; range; extent: *The mountain is beyond the sweep of your eye.* **14** a winning of all the games in a series, match, contest, etc.; complete victory. **15** a person who sweeps chimneys, streets, etc. **16** a long oar. **17** a long pole which pivots on a high post and is used to raise or lower a bucket in a well. 1–3, 5, 6, 8, 9 *v.*, **swept, sweep·ing;** 4, 7, 10–17 *n.* —**sweep′er,** *n.*

hat, āge, fär; let, ēqual, tėrm; it, īce
hot, ōpen, ôrder; oil, out; cup, pu̇t, rüle
əbove, takən, pencəl, lemən, circəs
ch, child; ng, long; sh, ship
th, thin; ŧh, then; zh, measure

sweep·ing (swēp′ing) **1** passing over a wide space: *Her sweeping glance took in the whole room.* **2** having wide range: *a sweeping victory, a sweeping statement.* *adj.*

sweep·ings (swēp′ingz) dust, rubbish, scraps, etc. swept out or up. *n. pl.*

sweep·stakes (swēp′stāks′) **1** a system of gambling on horse races, etc. People buy tickets, and the money they pay goes to the holder or holders of winning tickets. **2** the race or contest. *n.*

sweet (swēt) **1** having a taste like sugar or honey: *Pears are much sweeter than lemons.* **2** having a pleasant taste or smell: *Perfume is sweet.* **3** pleasant; agreeable: *a sweet child, a sweet smile, sweet music.* **4** fresh; not sour, salty, bitter, or spoiled: *He drinks sweet milk. Ice helps to keep food sweet.* **5** dear; darling. **6** a dear person. **7** something sweet. **8 sweets,** *pl.* candy or other sweet things. 1–5 *adj.*, 6–8 *n.* —**sweet′ly,** *adv.* —**sweet′ness,** *n.*

☛ **Sweet** and **suite** are pronounced the same.

sweet·en (swēt′ən) **1** make sweet: *He sweetened his coffee with sugar.* **2** become sweet: *Those pears will sweeten as they ripen.* *v.*

sweet·en·ing (swēt′ning) something that sweetens: *Sugar is the most common sweetening.* *n.*

sweet·heart (swēt′härt′) a loved one; lover. *n.*

sweet·ish (swēt′ish) somewhat sweet. *adj.*

sweet·meats (swēt′mēts′) candy; candied fruits; sugar-covered nuts, etc. *n. pl.*

sweet pea a climbing plant with delicate fragrant flowers of various colors.

sweet potato the sweetish, yellow root of a certain vine, used as a vegetable: *Sweet potatoes and yams are very similar.*

sweet tooth fondness for sweet foods.

swell (swel) **1** grow or make larger in size, amount, degree, force, etc.: *Rain swelled the river. His head is swollen where he bumped it. Savings may swell into a fortune. The sound swelled from a murmur to a roar.* **2** be larger or thicker in a particular place; stick out: *A barrel swells in the middle.* **3** the act of swelling; an increase in amount, degree, force, etc. **4** rise above the level: *Rounded hills swell gradually from the village plain.* **5** a long, unbroken wave or waves: *The boat rocked in the swell.* **6** *Informal.* stylish; grand.

7 *Slang.* excellent; very satisfactory: *We had a swell time at the party.* 1, 2, 4 *v.,* **swelled, swelled** or **swol·len, swell·ing;** 3, 5 *n.,* 6, 7 *adj.*

swell·ing (swel′ing) a swollen part: *There is a swelling on his head where he bumped it.* *n.*

swel·ter (swel′tər) suffer from heat. *v.*

swept (swept) See **sweep.** *She swept the room. It was swept clean.* *v.*

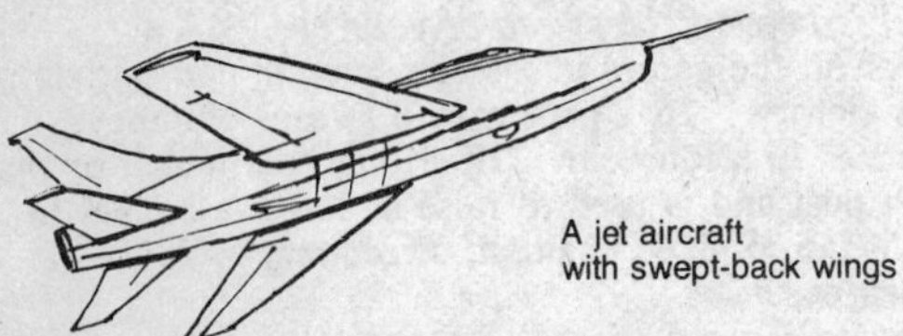

A jet aircraft with swept-back wings

swept–back (swept′bak′) extending outward and sharply backward. *adj.*

swerve (swėrv) **1** turn aside: *The car swerved and hit a tree. Nothing could swerve him from doing his duty.* **2** turning aside: *The swerve of the ball made it hard to hit.* 1 *v.,* **swerved, swerv·ing;** 2 *n.*

swift (swift) **1** moving very fast; able to move very fast: *a swift automobile.* **2** coming or happening quickly: *a swift answer.* **3** quick, rapid, or prompt to act: *He is swift to repay a kindness.* **4** a small bird with long wings: *A swift resembles a swallow when flying, but the two birds are not related.* 1–3 *adj.,* 4 *n.*
—**swift′ness,** *n.*

swig (swig) *Informal.* **1** a big or hearty drink. **2** drink heartily or greedily. 1 *n.,* 2 *v.*

swim (swim) **1** move along in the water by using arms, legs, fins, etc.: *Fish swim. Most boys like to swim.* **2** swim across: *He swam the river.* **3** make swim: *He swam his horse across the stream.* **4** float or appear to float: *The roast lamb was swimming in gravy.* **5** be overflowed or flooded with: *Her eyes were swimming with tears.* **6** the act, time, motion, or distance of swimming: *Her swim had tired her. She had had an hour's swim.* **7** go smoothly; glide: *White clouds swam across the sky.* **8** be dizzy; whirl: *The heat and noise made my head swim.* **9 the swim,** what is going on; the main current: *An active and sociable person likes to be in the swim.* 1–5, 7, 8 *v.,* **swam, swum, swim·ming;** 6, 9 *n.*

swim·mer (swim′ər) a person or animal that swims. *n.*

swim·ming (swim′ing) **1** the practice or sport of swimming: *Tom is expert at both swimming and diving.* **2** the act of swimming: *Can you reach the island by swimming?* *n.*

swim suit a garment worn for swimming.

swin·dle (swin′dəl) **1** cheat; defraud: *Honest merchants do not swindle their customers.* **2** the act of swindling; cheating or defrauding. 1 *v.,* **swin·dled, swin·dling;** 2 *n.*

swin·dler (swin′dlər) a person who cheats or defrauds. *n.*

swine (swīn) **1** a hog or pig. **2** a coarse, beastly person. *n., pl.* **swine.**

A swing

swing (swing) **1** move back and forth, especially with a regular motion: *The hammock swings. He swings his arms as he walks.* **2** move in a curve: *He swings the club twice around his head. He swung the automobile around the corner.* **3** an act or manner of swinging. **4** a swinging blow: *He brought the hammer down with a long swing.* **5** a seat hung from ropes or chains, in which one may sit and swing. **6** hang: *We swung the hammock between two trees.* **7** move with a free, swaying motion: *The soldiers came swinging down the street.* **8** a marked, swinging rhythm: *The song 'Dixie' has a swing.* **9** movement; activity. **10** jazz music with a lively, steady rhythm, in which the players improvise freely on the original melody. **11** *Informal.* manage successfully: *swing a business deal.* 1, 2, 6, 7, 11 *v.,* **swung, swing·ing;** 3–5, 8–10 *n.*
in full swing, going on actively and completely: *By five o'clock the party was in full swing.*

swipe (swīp) **1** *Informal.* a sweeping stroke; hard blow: *He made two swipes at the golf ball without hitting it.* **2** *Informal.* strike with a sweeping blow. **3** *Slang.* steal. 1 *n.,* 2, 3 *v.*

swirl (swėrl) **1** move or drive along with a twisting motion; whirl: *dust swirling in the air, a stream swirling over rocks.* **2** a swirling movement; a whirl; an eddy. **3** a twist; curl: *a swirl of whipped cream on top of a sundae.* 1 *v.,* 2, 3 *n.*

swish (swish) **1** move with a thin, light, hissing or brushing sound: *The whip swished through the air.* **2** make such a sound: *The long gown swished as she danced across the floor.* **3** cause to swish: *The cow swished her tail.* **4** a swishing movement or sound: *the swish of little waves on the shore.* 1–3 *v.,* 4 *n.*

Swiss (swis) **1** of or having to do with Switzerland, a country in Europe. **2** a person born in or living in Switzerland. 1 *adj.,* 2 *n., pl.* **Swiss.**

switch (swich) **1** a slender stick used in whipping. **2** whip; strike: *He switched the boys with a birch stick.* **3** a stroke; lash: *The big dog knocked a vase off the table with a switch of his tail.* **4** move or swing like a switch: *The horse switched his tail to drive off the flies.* **5** a device for making or breaking a connection in an electric circuit: *An electric switch turns the current off or on.* **6** a pair of movable rails by which a train can shift from one track to another. **7** change, turn, or shift by using a switch: *Switch off the light.* **8** change; exchange: *switch places. The boys switched hats.* **9** a change or exchange: *a last-minute switch of plans. He lost the election when his supporters made a switch of their votes to the other candidate.* 1, 3, 5, 6, 9 *n.,* 2, 4, 7, 8 *v.*

switch·board (swich′bôrd′) a panel containing the necessary switches, meters, and other devices for opening, closing, combining, or controlling electric circuits: *A telephone switchboard has plugs or buttons for connecting one line to another.* *n.*

swiv·el (swiv′əl) **1** a fastening that allows the thing fastened to turn round freely upon it. **2** turn on a swivel. **3** swing round; rotate; turn. 1 *n.*, 2, 3 *v.*

swol·len (swō′lən) **1** swelled: *a swollen ankle.* **2** See **swell.** 1 *adj.*, 2 *v.*

swoon (swün) **1** faint: *She swoons at the sight of blood.* **2** a faint: *Cold water will bring her out of the swoon.* 1 *v.*, 2 *n.*

swoop (swüp) **1** come down with a rush, as a hawk does; sweep rapidly down upon in a sudden attack: *The pirates swooped down on the towns.* **2** a rapid downward sweep of a bird of prey upon its victim; a sudden, swift descent or attack: *With one swoop the hawk seized the chicken and flew away.* 1 *v.*, 2 *n.*

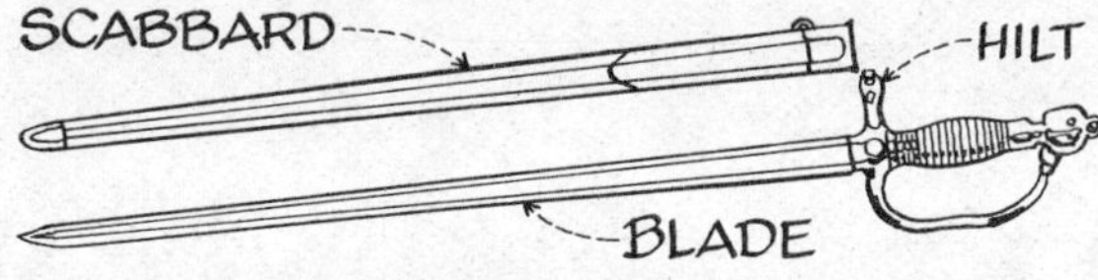

A sword and its scabbard

sword (sôrd) **1** a weapon, usually metal, with a long, sharp blade fixed in a handle or hilt. **2 the sword,** fighting, war, or military power: *'Those that live by the sword shall perish by the sword.' 'The pen is mightier than the sword.'* *n.*
cross swords, fight or quarrel.

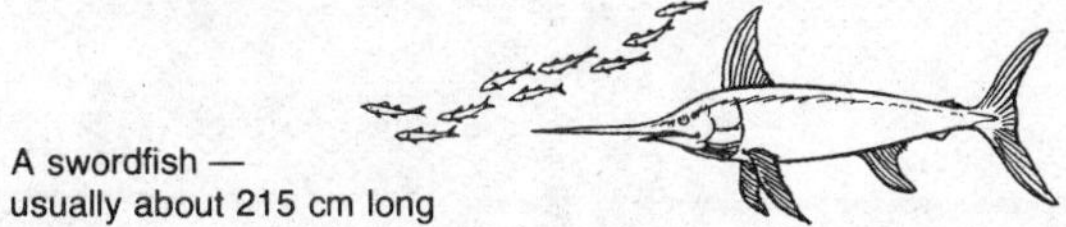
A swordfish — usually about 215 cm long

sword·fish (sôrd′fish′) a very large sea fish that has a swordlike projection from its upper jaw. *n., pl.* **sword·fish** or **sword·fish·es.**

swords·man (sôrdz′mən) **1** a person skilled in using a sword. **2** a person using a sword. *n., pl.* **swords·men** (sôrdz′mən).

swore (swôr) See **swear.** *He swore to be a loyal Canadian when he became a citizen.* *v.*

sworn (swôrn) **1** See **swear.** *A solemn oath of loyalty was sworn by all the knights.* **2** having taken an oath; bound by an oath: *There were ten sworn witnesses.* **3** declared, promised, etc. with an oath: *We have his sworn statement.* 1 *v.*, 2, 3 *adj.*

swum (swum) See **swim.** *He had never swum before.* *v.*

swung (swung) See **swing.** *He swung his arms as he walked. The door had swung open.* *v.*

syc·a·more (sik′ə môr′) a kind of shade tree with large leaves and light-colored bark. *n.*

syl·lab·ic (sə lab′ik) of, having to do with, or consisting of syllables. *adj.*

syl·lab·i·cate (sə lab′ə kāt′) divide into syllables. *v.,* **syl·lab·i·cat·ed, syl·lab·i·cat·ing.**

syl·lab·i·ca·tion (sə lab′ə kā′shən) the process of dividing into syllables; a division into syllables. *n.*

syl·lab·i·fy (sə lab′ə fī′) divide into syllables. *v.,* **syl·lab·i·fied, syl·lab·i·fy·ing.**

hat, āge, fär; let, ēqual, tėrm; it, īce
hot, ōpen, ôrder; oil, out; cup, pu̇t, rüle
əbove, takən, pencəl, lemən, circəs
ch, child; ng, long; sh, ship
th, thin; ᴛʜ, then; zh, measure

syl·la·ble (sil′ə bəl) **1** a part of a word pronounced as a unit that usually consists of a vowel alone or a vowel with one or more consonants: *'Canadian' and 'Manitoba' are words of four syllables; 'do' and 'stretch' are words of one syllable.* **2** in writing and printing, a letter or group of letters representing a syllable. *n.*

syl·van (sil′vən) of the woods; in the woods; having woods: *They lived in a sylvan retreat.* *adj.*

sym·bol (sim′bəl) something that stands for or represents something else: *The lion is the symbol of courage; the lamb, of meekness; the olive branch, of peace; the cross, of Christianity. The marks* $+$, $-$, $\times$, *and* $\div$ *are symbols for add, subtract, multiply, and divide.* *n.*

sym·bol·ic (sim bol′ik) **1** used as a symbol: *The maple leaf is symbolic of Canada.* **2** of a symbol; expressed by a symbol or symbols; using symbols: *Writing is a symbolic form of expression.* *adj.*

sym·bol·ize (sim′bəl īz′) be a symbol of; stand for; represent: *A dove symbolizes peace.* *v.,* **sym·bol·ized, sym·bol·iz·ing.**

sym·met·ri·cal (si met′rə kəl) having symmetry: *symmetrical figures.* *adj.*

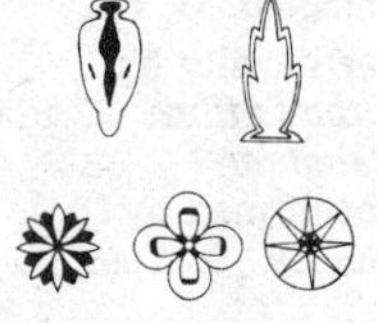
Symmetry. The figures in the top row show symmetry on opposite sides of a line; the figures in the bottom row show symmetry around a central point.

sym·me·try (sim′ə trē) **1** regular, balanced form or arrangement on opposite sides of a line or around a centre. **2** a well-balanced arrangement of parts; harmony: *A swollen cheek spoiled the symmetry of his face.* *n., pl.* **sym·me·tries.**

sym·pa·thet·ic (sim′pə thet′ik) **1** having or showing kind feelings toward others; sympathizing: *She is an unselfish and sympathetic friend.* **2** *Informal.* approving; agreeing: *The teacher was sympathetic to the class's plan for a trip to the museum.* *adj.*

sym·pa·thet·i·cal·ly (sim′pə thet′ik lē) in a sympathetic way; with kindness: *The doctor spoke sympathetically while he bandaged my leg.* *adv.*

sym·pa·thize (sim′pə thīz′) **1** feel or show sympathy: *The girl sympathized with her little brother, who had hurt himself.* **2** share in or agree with a feeling or opinion: *My mother sympathizes with my plan to be a doctor when I grow up.* *v.,* **sym·pa·thized, sym·pa·thiz·ing.**

sym·pa·thy (sim′pə thē) **1** a sharing of another's sorrow or trouble: *Sick people arouse our sympathies.* **2** agreement in feeling; the condition or fact of having the same feeling: *The sympathy between the twins was so great that they always smiled or cried at the same* *things.* 3 agreement; approval; favor: *Mother is in sympathy with my plan.* *n., pl.* **sym·pa·thies.**

sym·pho·ny (sim′fə nē) 1 an elaborate musical composition for an orchestra. 2 a symphony orchestra: *The Vancouver Symphony.* 3 a harmony of sounds. 4 a harmony of colors: *In autumn the woods are a symphony in red, brown, and yellow.* *n., pl.* **sym·pho·nies.**

symphony orchestra a large orchestra for playing symphonies, made up of brass, woodwind, percussion, and stringed instruments.

symp·tom (simp′təm) a sign; indication: *Fever is a symptom of illness.* *n.*

syn·a·gogue (sin′ə gog′) 1 a building used by Jews for religious instruction and worship. 2 an assembly of Jews for religious instruction and worship. *n.*

syn·chro·nize (sing′krə nīz′) 1 move or take place at the same rate and exactly together. 2 make agree in time: *synchronize all the clocks in a building.* *v.,* **syn·chro·nized, syn·chro·niz·ing.**

syn·o·nym (sin′ə nim′) a word that means the same or nearly the same as another word: *Little is a synonym of small.* *n.*

syn·tax (sin′taks) sentence structure; the way in which the words and phrases of a sentence are arranged to show how they relate to each other. *n.*

syn·the·sis (sin′thə sis) a combination of parts or elements into a whole. A compound or complex substance may be produced by the chemical synthesis of various elements or simpler compounds. *n.*

syn·thet·ic (sin thet′ik) 1 made artificially by combining chemicals: *Nylon is a synthetic fibre.* 2 not real or genuine; artificial: *synthetic laughter.* 3 **synthetics,** *pl.* man-made substances formed by chemical synthesis: *Plastics are synthetics.* 1, 2 *adj.,* 3 *n.*

sy·phon (sī′fən) See **siphon.**

sy·ringe (sə rinj′) 1 a narrow tube fitted with a piston or rubber bulb for drawing in a quantity of fluid and then forcing it out in a stream: *Syringes are used for cleaning wounds, injecting fluids into the body etc.* 2 clean, wash, inject, etc. by means of a syringe. 1 *n.,* 2 *v.*

syr·up or **sir·up** (sėr′əp or sir′əp) a sweet, thick liquid: *Sugar boiled with water or fruit juices makes a syrup. Maple syrup is made from the sap of maple trees.* *n.*

sys·tem (sis′təm) 1 a set of things or parts forming a whole: *a mountain system, a railway system, the digestive system.* 2 an ordered group of facts, principles, beliefs, etc.: *a system of government, a system of education.* 3 a plan; scheme; method: *That little boy has a system for always getting a ride home from school.* 4 an orderly way of getting things done: *He works by a system, not by chance.* 5 the body as a whole: *His sickness weakened his entire system.* *n.*

sys·tem·at·ic (sis′tə mat′ik) 1 according to a system; having a system, method, or plan: *systematic work.* 2 orderly in arranging things or in getting things done: *a very systematic person.* *adj.*

sys·tem·at·i·cal·ly (sis′tə mat′ik lē) with system; according to some plan or method. *adv.*

hat, āge, fär; let, ēqual, tėrm; it, īce
hot, ōpen, ôrder; oil, out; cup, put, rüle
əbove, takən, pencəl, lemən, circəs
ch, child; ng, long; sh, ship
th, thin; ᴛʜ, then; zh, measure

t or **T** (tē) the 20th letter of the alphabet: *There are two* t's *in* tablet. *n., pl.* **t's** or **T's.**
to a T, exactly or perfectly: *That suits me to a T.*

t tonne; tonnes.

t. ton; tons.

tab (tab) a small flap, strap, loop, or piece: *He wore a fur cap with tabs over the ears. n.*

tab·by (tab′ē) a grey or tawny cat having dark stripes. *n., pl.* **tab·bies.**

tab·er·nac·le (tab′ər nak′əl) **1** a place of worship, especially a Jewish temple. **2 Tabernacle,** the covered wooden framework carried by the Jews for use as a place of worship during their journey from Egypt to Palestine. *n.*

ta·ble (tā′bəl) **1** a piece of furniture having a smooth, flat top on legs. **2** the food put on a table to be eaten: *Mrs. Brown sets a good table.* **3** the persons seated at a table: *a table of bridge.* **4** information in a very brief form; a list: *a table of contents in the front of a book, the multiplication table, a timetable.* **5** a thin, flat piece of wood, stone, metal, etc.; a tablet: *The Ten Commandments were written on tables of stone.* **6** a flat, raised area of land; a plateau. *n.*
turn the tables, reverse conditions: *The enemy troops had advanced, but our sudden attack turned the tables on them.*

ta·ble·cloth (tā′bəl kloth′) a cloth for covering a table: *Spread the tablecloth and set the table for dinner. n.*

ta·ble·land (tā′bəl land′) a high plain; plateau. *n.*

ta·ble·spoon (tā′bəl spün′) a large spoon (about 15 ml) used for serving food and for measuring: *A tablespoon holds the same amount as three teaspoons. n.*

tab·let (tab′lit) **1** a small, flat sheet of stone, wood, ivory, etc. used to write or draw on: *The ancient Romans used tablets as we use pads of paper.* **2** a number of sheets of writing paper fastened together at one edge. **3** a small, flat surface with an inscription: *The names of the members of the first council are inscribed on a tablet in the city hall.* **4** a small, flat piece of medicine, candy, etc.: *vitamin tablets, sleeping tablets. n.*

table tennis a game played on a table marked somewhat like a tennis court, using small wooden rackets and a light, plastic ball.

ta·boo (tə bü′) forbidden by custom or tradition; banned: *Eating human flesh is taboo in all civilized countries. adj.*

tack (tak) **1** a short, sharp-pointed nail or pin having a broad, flat head: *We bought some carpet tacks.* **2** fasten with tacks: *She tacked mosquito netting over the windows.* **3** sew with temporary stitches. **4** attach; add: *He tacked a postscript to the end of the letter.* **5** sail in a zigzag course against the wind: *The ship was tacking, trying to make the harbor.* **6** the movement of a boat or ship in relation to the direction of the wind: *A ship is on port tack when she has the wind on her left.* **7** the act of zigzagging; a turn from one direction to the next. **8** a course of action or conduct: *To demand what he wanted was the wrong tack to take with his father.* 1, 6–8 *n.,* 2–5 *v.*

tack·le (tak′əl) **1** equipment; apparatus; gear: *Fishing tackle means the rod, line, hooks, etc.* **2** a set of ropes and pulleys for lifting, lowering, or moving heavy things: *The sails of a ship are raised and moved by tackle.* See **block and tackle** for picture. **3** try to deal with: *Everyone has his own problems to tackle.* **4** lay hold of; seize: *John tackled the thief and held him till help arrived.* **5** in football, seize and stop an opponent having the ball by bringing him to the ground. **6** the act of tackling. **7** the player between the guard and the end on either side of the line in football. 1, 2, 6, 7 *n.,* 3–5 *v.,* **tack·led, tack·ling.**

tack·y[1] (tak′ē) sticky. *adj.*

tack·y[2] (tak′ē) *Informal.* shabby; dowdy. *adj.*

tact (takt) the ability to say and do the right things; skill in dealing with people or handling difficult situations: *Mother showed tact in not talking about Jim's failure to get into the school choir. n.*

tact·ful (takt′fəl) **1** having tact: *Mother is a tactful person.* **2** showing tact: *A tactful reply does not hurt a person's feelings. adj.*

tac·tics (tak′tiks) **1** the art or science of managing military or naval forces in action: *All officers should study tactics.* **2** the operations themselves: *The tactics of pretending to cross the river and of making a retreat fooled the enemy.* **3** procedures to gain advantage or success; methods: *When coaxing failed, the little boy changed his tactics and began to cry. n.*

☛ **Tactics** meaning the science (def. 1) is plural in form and singular in use: *Tactics differs from strategy, which refers to the overall plans of a nation at war.* Otherwise, the word is plural in form and use: *The general's tactics were successful.*

An adult frog

A tadpole at different stages of growth

tad·pole (tad′pōl′) a very young frog or toad, at the stage when it has a tail and lives in water. *n.*

taf·fy (taf′ē) a kind of chewy candy made of brown sugar or molasses boiled down, often with butter. *n.* Also **toffee.**

tag[1] (tag) **1** a piece of card, paper, leather, etc. to be tied or fastened to something: *Each coat in a store has a tag with the price marked on it.* **2** a small hanging piece; a loosely attached piece; a loose end: *Mother cut all the tags off the old frayed rug.* **3** a metal or plastic covering for the end of a shoelace. **4** furnish with a tag or tags: *All his trunks and suitcases were tagged with his name and address.* **5** *Informal.* follow closely: *The baby tagged after his brother.* **6** a piece of cardboard, etc., sometimes with a piece of string attached, sold by organizations to raise money: *He bought a tag and tied* *it to his coat lapel.* 7 sell tags: *She tagged for the Cancer Society.* 1–3, 6 *n.,* 4, 5, 7 *v.,* **tagged, tag·ging.**

tag[2] (tag) 1 a children's game in which one child who is 'it' chases the rest of the children until he touches one of them. The one touched is then 'it' and must chase the others. 2 touch or tap with the hand. 1 *n.,* 2 *v.,* **tagged, tag·ging.**

tag day a day on which tags are sold by a charitable organization, such as the Humane Society.

tail (tāl) 1 in certain animals, the part that extends or hangs beyond the rear of the body: *Rabbits have very short tails. Mice have long tails. My dog wags his tail.* 2 something like an animal's tail: *the tail of a kite.* 3 the back part of anything; the back or rear: *The boys fastened their sleighs to the tail of the cart. A crowd of small boys formed the tail of the procession.* 4 follow close behind: *Some boys tailed after the parade.* 5 at the back; coming from behind: *a tail wind.* 6 *Informal.* follow closely and secretly, especially in order to watch or to prevent escaping. 1–3, 5 *n.,* 4, 6 *v.*

tails, a the reverse side of a coin. **b** *Informal.* a coat with long tails worn on formal occasions.

turn tail, run away from danger, trouble, etc.

with one's tail between one's legs, afraid; humiliated.

☛ **Tail** and **tale** are pronounced the same.

tail·gate (tāl′gāt′) 1 a board at the back end of a wagon, truck, station wagon, etc. that can be let down or removed when loading or unloading. 2 drive a vehicle too close to the one ahead of it. 1 *n.,* 2 *v.*

tail–less (tāl′lis) having no tail. *adj.*

tai·lor (tā′lər) 1 a man whose business is making or repairing clothes, especially men's clothes. 2 make clothes, especially clothes that have details of shape and finish: *She wore a tailored suit.* 3 make specially to fit; adjust; adapt: *Mother tailors her menus to suit our likes and dislikes.* 1 *n.,* 2, 3 *v.*

tail spin of an airplane, a downward spin with the nose first.

taint (tānt) 1 a stain or spot; a trace of decay, corruption, or disgrace: *No taint of dishonor ever touched him.* 2 give a taint to; spoil: *Flies sometimes taint what they touch. His reputation was tainted from keeping bad company.* 3 decay; become tainted: *Meat will taint if it is left too long in a warm place.* 1 *n.,* 2, 3 *v.*

take (tāk) 1 lay hold of: *A little child takes its mother's hand in walking.* 2 seize; capture: *Wild animals are taken in traps.* 3 have the proper effect; catch hold; lay hold: *The fire has taken. The medicine seems to be taking; the fever is better.* 4 accept: *Take my advice. The man won't take a cent less for the car.* 5 get; receive: *She took her gifts with a smile of thanks.* 6 win: *Tom took six games. George took first prize.* 7 get; have: *He took a holiday.* 8 use; make use of: *He hates to take medicine. Take care not to fall. We took a train to go to Winnipeg.* 9 submit to; put up with: *take hard punishment.* 10 need; require: *It takes time and patience to learn how to drive an automobile.* 11 choose; select: *Take the shortest way home.* 12 remove: *Please take the waste basket away and empty it.* 13 subtract: *If you take 2 from 7, you have 5.* 14 go with; escort: *He likes to take his dog out for a walk.* 15 carry: *We take flowers to our sick friends.* 16 do; make; obtain by a special method: *Take a walk. Please take my photograph.* 17 feel: *She takes pride in her schoolwork.* 18 of ice, to form; become thick enough to support people: *When the ice takes, cars are driven across the river.* 19 understand; interpret: *How did you take his comment?* 20 regard; consider: *Let us take an example.* 21 engage; hire; lease: *We have taken a cottage for the summer.* 22 receive and pay for regularly; subscribe for: *take a newspaper.* 23 become: *take cold. He took sick.* 24 please; attract; charm: *The song took the fancy of the public.* 25 *Slang.* swindle; cheat. 26 the amount or number taken: *a great take of fish.* 1–25 *v.,* **took, tak·en, tak·ing;** 26 *n.*

take after, be like; resemble: *She takes after her mother.*

take back, withdraw; retract: *I take that comment back; I didn't mean what I said.*

take down, a write down: *take down a speech.* **b** lower the pride of; humble: *take him down a peg.*

take for, suppose to be: *I took him for a wiser man.*

take in, a receive; admit: *take in boarders.* **b** make smaller: *Mother took in the waist of her skirt.* **c** understand. **d** deceive; trick; cheat: *I was taken in by the strange boy's friendly manner; in fact, he wasn't friendly at all.*

take off, a leave the ground or water: *Three airplanes took off at the same time.* **b** rush away: *He took off at the first sign of trouble.* **c** *Informal.* give an amusing imitation of; mimic.

take on, a engage; hire. **b** undertake to deal with: *take on an opponent.*

take to, a form a liking for; become fond of: *Good students take to books.* **b** go to: *The cat took to the woods and became wild.*

take up, a soak up; absorb: *A sponge takes up liquid.* **b** make smaller. **c** begin; undertake: *He took up piano lessons in the summer.* **d** establish a homestead; settle: *He took up land in Alberta.*

tak·en (tāk′ən) See **take.** *I have taken this toy from the shelf.* *v.*

taken aback, suddenly surprised or startled.

take–off (tāk′of′) 1 the leaving of the ground in leaping or in beginning a flight in an aircraft. 2 the place or point at which one takes off. 3 *Informal.* an amusing imitation; mimicking. *n.*

take–o·ver (tāk′ō′vər) taking over; seizure of ownership or control: *a take-over of a country by the army.* *n.*

talc (talk) a soft, smooth substance, used in making face powder, chalk, etc. *n.*

tal·cum powder (tal′kəm) powder made of purified white talc, for use on the face and body.

tale (tāl) 1 a story: *Grandfather told the children tales of his boyhood.* 2 a falsehood or lie. *n.*

tell tales, spread gossip or scandal; tattle.

☛ **Tale** and **tail** are pronounced the same.

tal·ent (tal′ənt) 1 special natural ability; an ability: *She has a talent for music. It is hard to succeed without talent.* 2 a person or persons with talent: *That young singer is a real talent.* 3 an ancient unit of weight or money: *A talent of silver at one time was worth about $2000.* *n.*

tal·ent·ed (tal′ən tid) having natural ability; gifted: *a talented musician.* *adj.*

tal·is·man (tal′is mən or tal′iz mən) a stone, ring, etc. engraved with figures supposed to have magic power; a charm. *n., pl.* **tal·is·mans.**

hat, āge, fär; let, ēqual, tėrm; it, īce
hot, ōpen, ôrder; oil, out; cup, pu̇t, rüle
əbove, takən, pencəl, lemən, circəs
ch, child; ng, long; sh, ship
th, thin; ᴛʜ, then; zh, measure

talk (tok or tôk) 1 use words; speak: *Baby is learning to talk.* 2 use in speaking: *Can you talk French?* 3 the use of words; spoken words; speech; conversation: *The old friends met for a good talk.* 4 an informal speech: *The coach gave the team a talk about the need for more team spirit.* 5 bring, put, drive, influence, etc. by talk: *We talked Joe into joining the club.* 6 discuss: *to talk politics.* 7 spread ideas by other means than speech: *to talk by signs.* 8 gossip; spread rumors: *She talked behind their backs.* 9 gossip or rumor: *There is talk of a quarrel between them.* 10 a subject for talk or gossip: *She is the talk of the town.* 1, 2, 5–8 *v.*, 3, 4, 9, 10 *n.*
talk back, *Informal.* answer rudely or disrespectfully.
talk down to, speak to in a superior tone.

talk·a·tive (tok′ə tiv or tôk′ə tiv) having the habit of talking a great deal; fond of talking: *a talkative old gossip. adj.*

tall (tol or tôl) 1 higher than the average; high: *Toronto has many tall buildings.* 2 having the height of; in height: *The man is 173 centimetres tall. The tree is 30 metres tall.* 3 *Informal.* hard to believe; exaggerated: *That is a pretty tall story. adj.*

tal·low (tal′ō) hard fat from sheep, cows, etc.: *Tallow is used for making candles and soap. n.*

tal·ly (tal′ē) 1 a stick of wood in which notches are cut to represent numbers: *Tallies were formerly used to show the amount of a debt or payment.* 2 anything on which a score or account is kept. 3 a notch or mark made on a tally; a mark made for a certain number of objects in keeping account. 4 to mark on a tally; count up: *to tally a score.* 5 an account; a reckoning; a score: *a tally of a game.* 6 in sports, make scoring points; score: *The hockey team tallied seven goals in their last game.* 7 agree; correspond: *Your account tallied with mine.* 1–3, 5 *n., pl.* **tal·lies;** 4, 6, 7 *v.,* **tal·lied, tal·ly·ing.**

tal·on (tal′ən) the claw of a bird of prey; a claw: *Eagles have talons. n.*

tam (tam) tam-o'-shanter. *n.*

tam·a·rack (tam′ə rak′) an evergreen tree of the larch family; larch. *n.*

tam·bou·rine (tam′bə rēn′) a small drum with jingling metal disks around the side, played by striking it with the knuckles or by shaking it. See the picture. *n.*

tame (tām) 1 taken from the wild state and made obedient: *The man has a tame bear.* 2 gentle; without fear: *The birds are so tame that they will eat from our hands.* 3 make tame; break in: *The lion was tamed for the circus.* 4 become tame: *White rats tame easily.* 5 deprive of courage; tone down; subdue: *Harsh punishment in childhood had tamed him and broken his will.* 6 dull: *a tame story. The party was tame because all the people were sleepy.* 1, 2, 6 *adj.,* **tam·er, tam·est;** 3–5 *v.,* **tamed, tam·ing.**

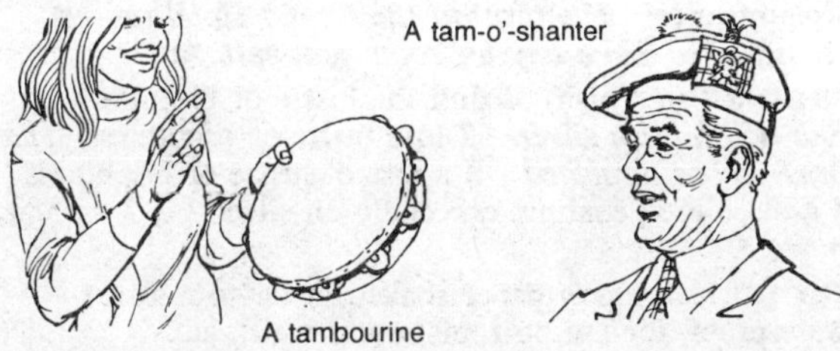

A tam-o'-shanter

A tambourine

tam–o'–shan·ter (tam′ə shan′tər) a hat, usually woollen, that has no brim, is quite loose in the crown, and is often topped with a pompom: *Tam-o'shanters (or tams, as they are usually called) originated in Scotland. n.*

tam·per (tam′pər) meddle; meddle in a bad or improper way: *Do not tamper with the lock. v.*

tan (tan) 1 light yellowish brown: *He wore tan shoes.* 2 the brown color of a person's skin caused by being in the sun and air: *His arms and legs had a dark tan.* 3 make or become brown by exposure to sun and air: *Sun and wind had tanned the sailor's face. If you lie on the beach in the sun, you will tan.* 4 make a hide into leather by soaking in a special liquid. 5 *Informal.* beat or thrash in punishment. 1 *adj.,* 1, 2 *n.,* 3–5 *v.,* **tanned, tan·ning.**

tan·a·ger (tan′ə jər) a kind of small North American bird related to the finches: *Male tanagers are usually brilliantly colored. n.*

tan·dem (tan′dəm) 1 one behind the other: *drive horses tandem, tandem seats.* 2 a bicycle with two seats, one behind the other. 3 a truck or other vehicle with two attached parts, such as a cab for pulling and a trailor to carry the load. 1 *adv., adj.,* 2, 3 *n.*

tang (tang) a strong taste or flavor: *the tang of mustard, the salt tang of sea air. n.*

tan·ge·rine (tan′jə rēn′) a small, reddish-orange fruit resembling an orange but having a very loose peel and segments that separate easily. *n.*

tan·gi·ble (tan′jə bəl) 1 capable of being touched or felt by touch: *Books are tangible; stories are not.* 2 real; actual; definite: *There has been a tangible improvement in his work. adj.*

tan·gle (tang′gəl) 1 twist and twine together in a confused mass: *The kitten had tangled the ball of yarn.* 2 a confused or tangled mass: *The climbing vines are all one tangle and need to be pruned and tied up.* 3 a bewildering confusion; mess: *a tangle of words. Her quick temper gets her into one tangle after another.* 1 *v.,* **tan·gled, tan·gling;** 2, 3 *n.*

tang·y (tang′ē) having a tang. *adj.*

tank (tangk) 1 a large container for liquid or gas: *Our school had a swimming tank. He always kept plenty of gasoline in the tank of his automobile.* 2 put or store in a tank: *The plane tanked up on gas just before taking off.* 3 a self-moving armored vehicle used in war: *Tanks are mounted on tracks so that they can travel over rough ground, fallen trees, and other obstacles.* 1, 3 *n.,* 2 *v.*

tank·ard (tangk′ərd) a large drinking mug with a handle and a hinged cover. *n.*

tank car a railway car with a tank for carrying liquids or gases.

tank·er (tangk′ər) a ship, aircraft, or truck with tanks for carrying oil, gasoline, or other liquid freight. *n.*

tan·ner (tan′ər) a person whose work is tanning hides. *n.*

tan·ner·y (tan′ər ē) a place where hides are tanned. *n.*

tan·ta·lize (tan′tə līz′) torment or tease by keeping something desired in sight but out of reach, or by holding out hopes that are repeatedly disappointed: *He tantalized the hungry dog by pretending to feed him.* *v.,* **tan·ta·lized, tan·ta·liz·ing.**

tan·trum (tan′trəm) *Informal.* a fit of bad temper: *The spoiled child had a tantrum whenever she did not get her own way.* *n.*

tap[1] (tap) **1** strike lightly: *He tapped on the window.* **2** a light blow: *There was a tap at the door.* **3** make, put, etc. by light blows: *to tap a message, to tap a rhythm, to tap time, to tap the ashes out of a pipe.* **4** the sound of a light blow. 1, 3 *v.,* **tapped, tap·ping;** 2, 4 *n.*

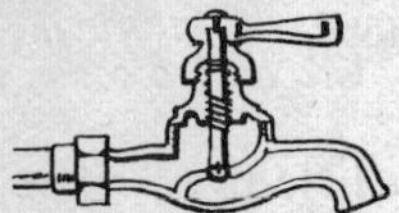
A water tap

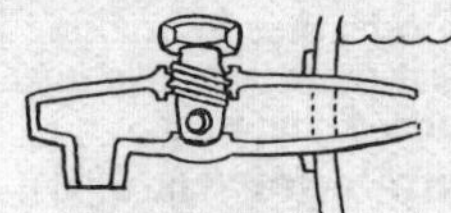
A tap in a cask

tap[2] (tap) **1** a device for turning on and off a flow of liquid from a pipe; faucet: *Most sinks have taps for hot and cold water.* **2** make a hole in to let out liquid: *to tap sugar maples.* **3** make resources, reserves, etc. accessible; penetrate to; open up: *This highway taps a large district.* **4** make a connection on: *tap a telegraph wire to intercept the message.* 1 *n.,* 2–4 *v.,* **tapped, tap·ping.**
on tap, ready for use: *Mother keeps an extra box of stationery on tap so that she won't run out of it unexpectedly.*

tap dance a dance in which the steps are accented by loud taps of the foot, toe, or heel.

tape (tāp) **1** a long, narrow strip of cloth, paper, plastic, etc.: *That candy store uses fancy tape to tie all packages.* **2** something like such a strip: *The strip stretched across the finish line in a race is called a tape. A tape of cloth or steel, marked in centimetres, etc., is used for measuring. Sound may be recorded on a kind of plastic tape.* **3** a strip of material coated with a sticky substance to make it adhere to a surface: *He strengthened his hockey stick by wrapping tape around it.* **4** a strip of plastic that has been magnetized for recording sound or television images and sound. **5** record on tape by means of a tape-recorder: *The program was taped for broadcasting at a later time.* **6** fasten with tape; wrap with tape: *The doctor taped up the wound.* 1–4 *n.,* 5, 6 *v.,* **taped, tap·ing.**

tape measure a long strip of cloth or steel marked in centimetres, etc. for measuring.

tap·er (tā′pər) **1** become gradually smaller toward one end; make gradually smaller toward one end: *The church spire tapers off to a point.* **2** grow less gradually; diminish: *His business tapered to nothing as people moved away.* **3** a very slender candle. 1, 2 *v.,* 3 *n.*
☛ **Taper** and **tapir** are pronounced the same.

tape–re·cord·er (tāp′ri kôr′dər) a machine that records and plays back sound on magnetized plastic or paper tape. *n.*

tap·es·try (tap′is trē) a piece of fabric with pictures or designs woven in it, used to hang on walls, cover furniture, etc. *n., pl.* **tap·es·tries.**

tape·worm (tāp′wėrm′) a long, flat worm that lives in the intestines of people and animals. *n.*

tap·i·o·ca (tap′ē ō′kə) a starchy food obtained from the root of a tropical plant, the cassava: *Tapioca is sometimes used for puddings.* *n.*

ta·pir (tā′pər) a large piglike animal of tropical America that has hoofs and a flexible snout. See the picture. *n.*
☛ **Tapir** and **taper** are pronounced the same.

tap·root (tap′rüt′) a main root growing downward. *n.*

taps (taps) a signal on a bugle or drum to put out lights at night. *n. pl.*

tar[1] (tär) **1** a thick, black, sticky substance obtained from wood or coal: *Tar is used to cover and patch roads and to keep telephone poles and other timbers from rotting.* **2** cover or smear with tar; soak in tar: *a tarred roof.* 1 *n.,* 2 *v.,* **tarred, tar·ring.**
tar and feather, pour heated tar on and cover with feathers as a punishment.

tar[2] (tär) sailor. *n.*

A Malay tapir — about 245 cm long without the tail

Tarantula: a bird spider, one of the world's largest spiders — body about 8 cm long

ta·ran·tu·la (tə ran′chü lə) one of a group of mostly large, hairy spiders, whose bite is painful but usually not serious: *People used to think that the bite of the tarantula caused an uncontrollable desire to dance.* *n.*

tar·dy (tär′dē) **1** behind time; late: *He was tardy for school four times last year.* **2** slow: *The old bus was tardier than ever.* *adj.,* **tar·di·er, tar·di·est.**

tar·get (tär′git) **1** a mark for shooting at; something aimed at: *Although a target is often a circle, anything may be used as a target.* See **arrow** for picture. **2** an object of abuse, scorn, or criticism: *His crazy ideas made him the target of jokes by everyone.* **3** any aim one tries to achieve; goal; objective. *n.*

tar·iff (tar′if) **1** a list of duties or taxes on imports or exports. **2** any duty or tax in such a list: *There is a very high tariff on imported jewellery.* **3** any table or scale of prices: *The tariff at the Grand Hotel ranges from $12 to $23 a day for room and bath.* *n.*

tar·nish (tär′nish) **1** dull the lustre or brightness of: *Salt will tarnish silver.* **2** lose lustre or brightness: *The brass knobs tarnished.* **3** a loss of lustre or brightness. **4** a discolored coating, especially on silver. 1, 2 *v.,* 3, 4 *n.*

tar paper heavy paper soaked in tar to make it waterproof, for use on roofs, outer walls, etc.

tar·pau·lin (tär po′lən or tär pô′lən) a sheet of canvas, or other coarse cloth, made waterproof and used

hat, āge, fär; let, ēqual, tėrm; it, īce
hot, ōpen, ôrder; oil, out; cup, pu̇t, rüle
ǝbove, takǝn, pencǝl, lemǝn, circǝs
ch, child; ng, long; sh, ship
th, thin; ᴛʜ, then; zh, measure

to protect goods against the weather. *n.*

tar·ry[1] (tar′ē) 1 delay leaving; remain; stay: *He tarried at the inn till he felt strong enough to travel.* 2 be tardy; hesitate: *Why do you tarry so long?* *v.,* **tar·ried, tar·ry·ing.**

tar·ry[2] (tär′ē) 1 of tar; like tar: *a tarry smell.* 2 covered with tar: *a tarry road.* *adj.,* **tar·ri·er, tar·ri·est.**

tart[1] (tärt) 1 having a sharp taste; sour: *Some apples are tart.* 2 sharp: *Her reply was too tart to be polite.* *adj.*

tart[2] (tärt) a piece of pastry filled with cooked fruit, jam, etc.: *In Canada and the United States, a tart is small and open at the top; in England, any fruit pie may be called a tart.* *n.*

tar·tan (tär′tǝn) 1 a plaid woollen cloth: *Each Scottish clan has its own pattern of tartan.* 2 the pattern or design itself: *The main color in the Douglas tartan is green.* See **plaid** for picture. *n.*

tar·tar[1] (tär′tǝr) a hard substance that has collected on the teeth. *n.*

tar·tar[2] (tär′tǝr) 1 a bad-tempered person. 2 **Tartar,** a member of a race of people now living in parts of western Asia: *In the Middle Ages, hordes of Tartars swept into Europe, bringing terror and destruction.* *n.*

task (task) 1 work to be done; a piece of work; duty: *Her task is to set the table.* 2 put work on; force to work: *The master tasked his slaves beyond their strength.* 3 burden; strain: *Lifting that trunk would task the strongest man.* 1 *n.,* 2, 3 *v.*
take to task, blame; scold; reprove: *The teacher took him to task for not studying harder.*

tas·sel (tas′ǝl) 1 a hanging bunch of threads, small cords, beads, etc. fastened together at the top end. 2 something like this: *Corn has tassels.* 3 grow tassels: *Corn tassels just before the ears form.* 1, 2 *n.,* 3 *v.,* **tas·selled** or **tas·seled, tas·sel·ling** or **tas·sel·ing.**

taste (tāst) 1 what is special about something to the sense organs of the mouth; flavor: *Sweet, sour, salt, and bitter are four important tastes.* 2 try the flavor of something by taking a little into the mouth: *The cook tastes everything to see if it is right.* 3 the sense by which the flavor of things is perceived: *Her taste is unusually keen.* 4 get the flavor of by the sense of taste: *I taste almond in this cake.* 5 have a particular flavor: *The soup tastes of onion.* 6 eat or drink a little bit of: *The children barely tasted their breakfast the day they went to the circus.* 7 a little bit; sample: *Give me just a taste of the pudding. The snowstorm gave me a taste of northern winter.* 8 to experience; have: *Having tasted freedom, the bird would not return to its cage.* 9 a liking: *Most people have a taste for apple pie.* 10 the ability to perceive and enjoy what is beautiful and excellent: *Good books and pictures appeal to people of taste.* 11 a manner or style that shows such ability: *Her house is furnished in excellent taste.* 1, 3, 7, 9–11 *n.,* 2, 4–6, 8 *v.,* **tast·ed, tast·ing.**

taste bud any of certain groups of cells, most of which are in the outer layer of the tongue, that are sense organs of taste.

taste·ful (tāst′fǝl) 1 having good taste. 2 showing or done in good taste: *The furnishing of the room was tasteful.* *adj.*

taste·less (tāst′lis) 1 without taste: *tasteless food.* 2 without good taste; in poor taste: *a tasteless choice of furniture.* *adj.*

tast·y (tās′tē) of food or drink, tasting good; pleasing to the taste. *adj.,* **tast·i·er, tast·i·est.**

tat·ter (tat′ǝr) 1 a torn piece; rag: *After the storm the flag hung in tatters upon the mast.* 2 wear to pieces; make ragged. 3 **tatters,** *pl.* torn or ragged clothing. 1, 3 *n.,* 2 *v.*

tat·tered (tat′ǝrd) 1 full of tatters; torn or ragged: *a tattered dress.* 2 wearing torn or ragged clothes. *adj.*

tat·tle (tat′ǝl) 1 tell tales or secrets. 2 talk foolishly; gossip. 3 idle or foolish talk; gossip; the telling of tales or secrets. 1, 2 *v.,* **tat·tled, tat·tling;** 3 *n.*

tat·tle·tale (tat′ǝl tāl′) *Informal.* telltale. *n., adj.*

tat·too[1] (ta tü′) 1 a signal on a bugle or drum calling soldiers, sailors, or airmen to their quarters at night. 2 a series of raps, taps, etc.: *The hail beat a loud tattoo on the windowpane.* *n., pl.* **tat·toos.**

☛ **Tattoo**[1] comes from Dutch *taptoe,* made up of *tap,* meaning 'tap of a barrel,' and *toe,* meaning 'shut.' *Taptoe* is used to signal closing time in a 'taproom' or bar.

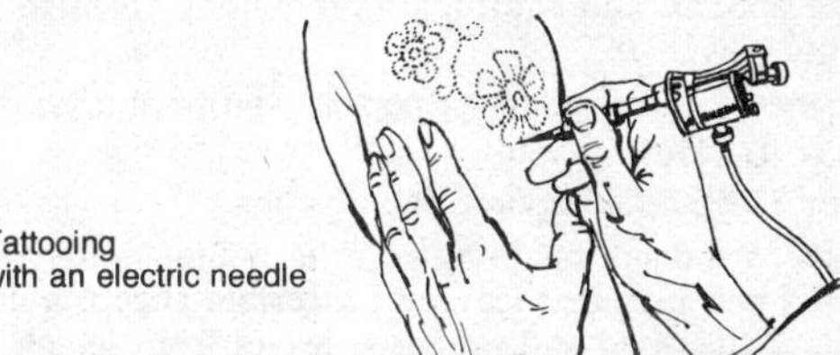
Tattooing
with an electric needle

tat·too[2] (ta tü′) 1 mark the skin with designs or patterns by pricking it and putting in colors: *The sailor had a ship tattooed on his arm.* 2 a mark or design tattooed on the skin. 1 *v.,* **tat·tooed, tat·too·ing;** 2 *n., pl.* **tat·toos.**

☛ **Tattoo**[2] comes from a Polynesian word *tatau.*

taught (tot or tôt) See **teach.** *Miss Jones taught my mother. She has taught arithmetic for many years.* *v.*

☛ **Taught** and **taut** are pronounced the same.

taunt (tont or tônt) 1 jeer at; mock; reproach: *Some mean girls taunted her because she was poor.* 2 a bitter or insulting remark; mocking; jeering. 3 get or drive by taunts: *They taunted him into taking the dare.* 1, 3 *v.,* 2 *n.*

taut (tot or tôt) 1 drawn tight; tense: *a taut rope.* 2 in neat condition; tidy: *The captain insists on a taut ship.* *adj.*

☛ **Taut** and **taught** are pronounced the same.

tav·ern (tav′ǝrn) 1 a place where alcoholic drinks are sold and drunk. 2 an inn: *Hotels have taken the place of the old taverns.* *n.*

taw·dry (to′drē or tô′drē) showy and cheap; gaudy. *adj.*

☛ **Tawdry** is from Sain*t Audrey*'s lace, sold at the fair of St. Audrey in Ely, England.

taw·ny (to′nē or tô′nē) brownish yellow: *A lion has a*

tawny skin. *adj.*, **taw·ni·er, taw·ni·est.**

tax (taks) 1 money paid by people for the support of the government and the cost of public works and services; money regularly collected from people by their rulers: *Our parents pay taxes to the city to pay for our schools.* 2 put a tax on: *People who own property are taxed in order to provide clean streets, paved roads, protection against crime, and free education.* 3 a burden, duty, or demand that oppresses; strain: *Climbing stairs is a tax on a weak heart.* 4 lay a heavy burden on; be hard for: *The work taxed her strength. Reading in a poor light taxes the eyes.* 5 reprove; accuse: *The teacher taxed him with having neglected his work.* 1, 3 *n.*, 2, 4, 5 *v.*

tax·a·tion (taks ā′shən) 1 the act of taxing: *Taxation is necessary to provide roads, schools, and police protection.* 2 the amount people pay for the support of the government; taxes. *n.*

tax·i (tak′sē) 1 an automobile driven for hire, usually having a meter for recording the fare. 2 ride in a taxi. 3 of an aircraft, move across the ground or water under its own power: *The airplane taxied onto the runway.* 1 *n., pl.* **tax·is;** 2, 3 *v.*, **tax·ied, tax·i·ing.**

tax·i·cab (tak′sē kab′) taxi. *n.*

tax·i·der·my (tak′sə dėr′mē) the art of preparing the skins of animals and stuffing and mounting them so that they look alive. *n.*

tax·pay·er (taks′pā′ər) a person who pays a tax or is required by law to do so. *n.*

tbs. or **tbsp.** tablespoon; tablespoons.

tea (tē) 1 a drink made by pouring boiling water over the dried and prepared leaves of a certain shrub: *a cup of tea.* 2 the dried and prepared leaves from which this drink is made: *Mother buys tea at the grocery.* 3 the shrub on which these leaves grow: *Tea is grown chiefly in China, Japan, and India.* 4 a light meal in the late afternoon or early evening, at which tea is served: *The English have afternoon tea.* 5 an afternoon reception at which tea is served. 6 a hot drink made from herbs, meat, etc.: *sage tea, beef tea.* *n.*

☛ Tea and tee are pronounced the same.

tea bag tea leaves in a little bag of thin cloth or paper for easy removal from the cup or pot after use.

teach (tēch) 1 help to learn; show how to do; make understand: *He is teaching his dog to shake hands.* 2 give lessons in: *She teaches music.* 3 give lessons; act as teacher: *She has taught for many years.* *v.*, **taught, teach·ing.**

teach·er (tēch′ər) a person who teaches, especially one who teaches in a school. *n.*

teach·ing (tēch′ing) 1 the work or profession of a teacher. 2 what is taught: *Many Indian superstitions are old teachings of the tribe.* *n.*

tea cosy a hatlike covering for putting over a teapot to keep the tea hot.

tea·cup (tē′kup′) a cup for drinking tea. *n.*
storm in a teacup. See **storm.**

teak (tēk) the hard, yellowish-brown wood of a large tree of the East Indies: *Teak is used for shipbuilding, making fine furniture, etc.* *n.*

tea·ket·tle (tē′ket′əl) a kettle for heating water to make tea, etc. *n.*

teal (tēl) any of several kinds of small fresh-water ducks. *n., pl.* **teal** or **teals.**

team (tēm) 1 a number of people working or acting together, especially one of the sides in a game or match: *a football team, a debating team.* 2 two or more horses or other animals harnessed together to work. 3 join together in a team: *Everybody teamed up to clean the classroom after the party.* 1, 2 *n.*, 3 *v.*

☛ **Team** and **teem** are pronounced the same.

team·mate (tēm′māt′) a fellow member of a team. *n.*

team·ster (tēm′stər) 1 a truck driver. 2 a man who drives a team of horses. *n.*

team·work (tēm′wėrk′) the acting together of a number of people to make the work of the group successful and effective: *Teamwork makes hard jobs easier.* *n.*

tea·pot (tē′pot′) a container with a handle and a spout for making and serving tea. *n.*

tear[1] (tēr) a drop of salty water coming from the eye. *n.*
in tears, shedding tears; crying: *The baby is in tears.*

☛ **Tear**[1] and **tier** are pronounced the same.

tear[2] (ter) 1 pull apart by force: *He tore the page in half.* 2 make by pulling apart: *He tore a hole in his coat.* 3 pull hard; pull violently: *He tore down the enemy's flag.* 4 cut badly; wound: *He tore his hand on a nail.* 5 rend; divide; split: *The family was torn by a serious quarrel.* 6 remove by effort; force away: *He could not tear himself from that spot.* 7 make miserable; distress: *She was torn by sorrow.* 8 become torn: *Lace tears easily.* 9 a torn place: *She has a tear in her dress.* 10 *Informal.* move with great force or haste: *An automobile came tearing down the road.* 1–8, 10 *v.*, **tore, torn, tear·ing;** 9 *n.*

tear·ful (tēr′fəl) 1 full of tears; weeping. 2 causing tears; sad: *Getting lost was a tearful experience.* *adj.*

tease (tēz) 1 vex or worry by jokes, questions, requests, etc.; annoy: *Don't tease the cat by rubbing its fur the wrong way. The other boys teased him about his curly hair.* 2 beg: *That child teases for everything he sees.* 3 a person who teases. 1, 2 *v.*, **teased, teas·ing;** 3 *n.*

teas·er (tē′zər) *Informal.* an annoying problem; puzzling task. *n.*

tea·spoon (tē′spün′) a small spoon (about 5 ml) commonly used to stir tea, coffee, etc. and for measuring: *A teaspoon holds one-third as much as a tablespoon.* *n.*

teat (tēt) the nipple of a breast or udder, from which the young suck milk. *n.*

tech·ni·cal (tek′nə kəl) 1 of or having to do with a mechanical or industrial art or with applied science: *Technical training is needed for many jobs in industry.* 2 of or having to do with the special facts of a science or art: *'Transistor' and 'protein' are technical words.* 3 of or having to do with any art or science: *technical skill in singing.* *adj.*

tech·ni·cian (tek nish′ən) a person experienced or skilled in the technical facts and methods of a subject. *n.*

tech·nique (tek nēk′) a method or way of performing the mechanical details of an art; technical skill. *n.*

hat, āge, fär; let, ēqual, tėrm; it, īce
hot, ōpen, ôrder; oil, out; cup, pu̇t, rüle
ə above, takən, pencəl, lemən, circəs
ch, child; ng, long; sh, ship
th, thin; ᴛʜ, then; zh, measure

tech·nol·o·gy (tek nol′ə jē) the application of scientific knowledge to practical uses: *Engineering is a branch of technology.* *n.*

te·di·ous (tē′dē əs) long and tiring: *A long talk that you cannot understand is tedious.*

tee (tē) in golf: **1** a mark or place from which a player starts in playing each hole. **2** a little mound of sand or dirt or a short wooden or plastic peg on which a ball is placed when a player drives. **3** put a golf ball on a tee. 1, 2 *n.*, 3 *v.*

☞ Tee and **tea** are pronounced the same.

teem[1] (tēm) be full; abound; swarm: *The swamp teemed with mosquitoes.* *v.*

☞ Teem and **team** are pronounced the same.

teem[2] (tēm) pour; come down in torrents: *It simply teemed all afternoon. A teeming rain spoiled the picnic.* *v.*

☞ See note at **teem**[1].

teen–ag·er (tēn′āj′ər) a person in his or her teens. *n.*

teens (tēnz) the years of life from 13 to 19: *The girls were all in their teens.* *n. pl.*

tee·ny (tē′nē) *Informal.* tiny. *adj.*

tee·pee or **te·pee** (tē′pē) a tent of the North American Indians; a wigwam. See **wigwam** for picture. *n.*

tee·ter (tē′tər) **1** a teeter-totter or seesaw. **2** be badly balanced; move unsteadily: *The tightrope walker teetered on the narrow wire.* 1 *n.*, 2 *v.*

tee·ter–tot·ter (tē′tər tot′ər) **1** a plank resting on a support near its middle so that the ends can move up and down; a seesaw. **2** move up and down on such a plank: *The two boys teeter-tottered for hours.* **3** a children's game in which the children sit at opposite ends of such a plank and move alternately up and down. **4** move up and down or back and forth. 1, 3 *n.*, 2, 4 *v.*

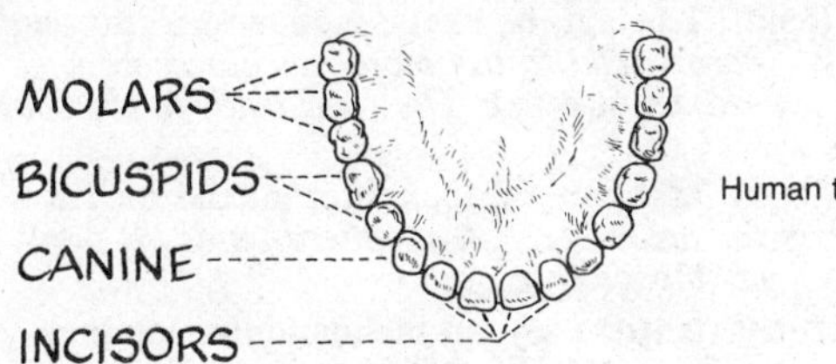

Human teeth

teeth (tēth) plural of **tooth:** *You often show your teeth when you smile.* *n.*
by the skin of one's teeth, just barely: *He escaped by the skin of his teeth.*
in the teeth of, straight against; in the face of: *He advanced in the teeth of the wind.*

teethe (tēᴛʜ) grow teeth, cut teeth: *Baby is teething.* *v.*, **teethed, teeth·ing.**

tee·to·tal·ler or **tee·to·tal·er** (tē tō′təl ər) a person who never drinks alcoholic liquor. *n.*

tel·e·cast (tel′ə kast′) **1** broadcast by televsion. **2** a television broadcast. 1 *v.*, **tel·e·cast** or **tel·e·cast·ed, tel·e·cast·ing;** 2 *n.*

tel·e·gram (tel′ə gram′) a message sent by telegraph: *The telegram arrived last night.* *n.*

tel·e·graph (tel′ə graf′) **1** an apparatus, system, or process for sending and receiving coded messages over electric wires. **2** send a message by telegraph: *Mother telegraphed that she would arrive home by the afternoon plane.* **3** send a message to a person, etc. by telegraph: *She telegraphed us yesterday.* 1 *n.*, 2, 3 *v.*

te·leg·ra·phy (tə leg′rə fē) the making or operating of telegraphs. *n.*

te·lep·a·thy (tə lep′ə thē) the communication of one mind with another without using speech, hearing, sight, or any other sense used normally to communicate. *n.*

tel·e·phone (tel′ə fōn′) **1** an apparatus, system, or process for sending and receiving sound or speech to a distant point over wires: *A man in Vancouver can talk to a man in Halifax by using a telephone.* **2** talk through a telephone; send a message by telephone. **3** make a telephone call to. 1 *n.*, 2, 3 *v.*, **tel·e·phoned, tel·e·phon·ing.**

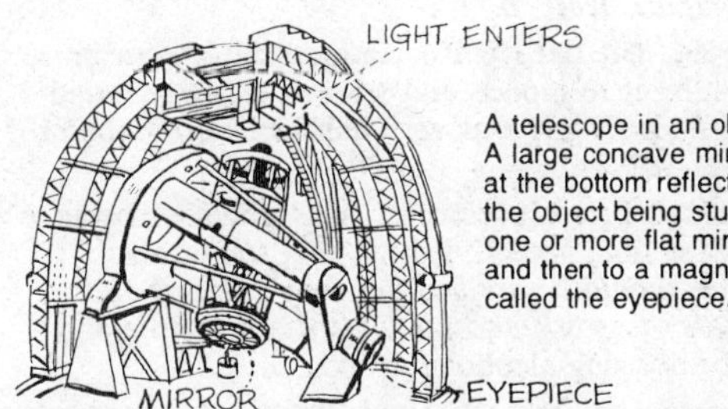

A telescope in an observatory. A large concave mirror at the bottom reflects light from the object being studied to one or more flat mirrors and then to a magnifying lens called the eyepiece.

tel·e·scope (tel′ə skōp′) **1** an instrument for making distant objects appear nearer and larger: *The stars are studied by means of telescopes.* **2** force or be forced together, one inside another, like the sliding tubes of some telescopes: *When the two railway trains crashed into each other, the cars were telescoped.* 1 *n.*, 2 *v.*, **tel·e·scoped, tel·e·scop·ing.**

tel·e·vise (tel′ə vīz′) send by television: *televise a baseball game.* *v.*, **tel·e·vised, tel·e·vis·ing.**

tel·e·vi·sion (tel′ə vizh′ən) **1** the process of sending pictures through the air or over a wire by means of electricity, so that people can see them in many places at once. **2** the apparatus on which these pictures may be seen. *n.*

tell (tel) **1** put in words; say: *Tell us a story. Tell the truth.* **2** tell to; inform: *Tell us about it. Tell him the news.* **3** make known: *Don't tell where the candy is.* **4** recognize; know: *I can't tell which house is yours.* **5** say to; order; command: *Do as you are told.* **6** count; count one by one: *The nun tells her beads.* **7** have effect or force: *Every blow told.* *v.*, **told, tell·ing.**
tell off, a count off; count off and detach for some special duty: *The sergeant told off ten men for special duty.* **b** *Informal.* rebuke strongly: *His father told him off for staying out late.*
tell on, a inform on; tell tales about: *No child likes anyone to tell on him.* **b** have an injurious effect on; break down: *The strain was telling on the man's health.*
tell time, know what time it is by the clock.

tell·er (tel′ər) a cashier in a bank: *A teller in a bank takes in, gives out, and counts money.* *n.*

tell·tale (tel′tāl′) 1 a person who tells tales on others; a person who reveals private or secret matters from malice. 2 telling what is not supposed to be told; revealing: *a telltale fingerprint.* 1 *n.*, 2 *adj.*

tem·per (tem′pər) 1 a state of mind; disposition; condition: *She has a sweet temper. She was in no temper to be kept waiting.* 2 an angry state of mind: *He flies into a temper at trifles.* 3 a calm or controlled state of mind: *He became angry and lost his temper.* 4 moderate; soften: *Temper justice with mercy.* 5 bring to a proper or desired condition of hardness, toughness, etc. by mixing or preparing: *A painter tempers his colors by mixing them with oil. Steel is tempered by heating it and working it till it has the proper degree of hardness and toughness.* 6 the degree of hardness, toughness, etc. of a substance: *The temper of the clay was right for shaping.* 1–3, 6 *n.*, 4, 5 *v.*

tem·per·a·ment (tem′pər ə mənt or tem′prə mənt) a person's nature, make-up, or disposition: *She has a nervous temperament.* *n.*

tem·per·a·men·tal (tem′pər ə men′təl or tem′prə men′təl) subject to moods and whims; easily irritated; sensitive: *The little girl was very temperamental about her clothes.* *adj.*

tem·per·ance (tem′pər əns or tem′prəns) 1 being moderate in action, speech, habits, etc.; self-control: *Temperance should be applied not only to food and drink but also to work and play.* 2 the principle and practice of not using alcoholic drinks. *n.*

tem·per·ate (tem′pər it) 1 not very hot and not very cold: *Much of Canada lies in the North Temperate Zone.* 2 moderate; using self-control: *He spoke in a temperate manner, not favoring either side especially.* 3 moderate in using alcoholic drinks: *A temperate man never drinks too much.* *adj.*

tem·per·a·ture (tem′pər ə chər or tem′prə chər) 1 the degree of heat or cold: *The temperature of freezing water is 0 degrees Celsius.* 2 a body temperature higher than the normal, which is usually about 37 degrees Celsius. *n.*
run a temperature, have a fever; have a body temperature that is higher than normal.

tem·pest (tem′pist) 1 a violent windstorm, usually accompanied by rain, hail, or snow: *The tempest drove the ship on the rocks.* 2 a violent disturbance: *She burst into a tempest of anger.* *n.*

tem·pes·tu·ous (tem pes′chü əs) 1 stormy: *It was a tempestuous night.* 2 violent: *She burst into a tempestuous fit of anger.* *adj.*

tem·ple¹ (tem′pəl) 1 a building used for the service or worship of a god or gods: *Greek temples were beautifully built.* 2 **the Temple,** any of three temples in ancient Jerusalem built at different times by the Jews. 3 any building set apart for Christian worship; church. 4 a synagogue. *n.*

tem·ple² (tem′pəl) the flattened part on either side of the forehead. *n.*

tem·po (tem′pō) 1 in music, the time or rate of movement: *the correct tempo for a dance tune.* 2 rate; speed; pace; characteristic rhythm: *the fast tempo of modern life.* *n.*

tem·po·rar·i·ly (tem′pə rer′ə lē) for a short time; for the present: *They are living in a hotel temporarily.* *adv.*

tem·po·rar·y (tem′pə rer′ē) lasting for a short time only: *The hunter make a temporary shelter out of branches.* *adj.*

tempt (tempt) 1 make, or try to make, a person do something, especially something wrong: *The sight of the food tempted the hungry man to steal.* 2 appeal strongly to; attract: *The candy tempts me.* *v.*
tempt Providence, fate, etc., take a foolish risk; ask for trouble: *It is tempting Providence to go in that old boat.*

temp·ta·tion (temp tā′shən) 1 tempting: *No temptation could make him false to a friend.* 2 being tempted: *The Lord's Prayer says, 'Lead us not into temptation.'* 3 anything that tempts: *Money left carelessly about is a temptation.* *n.*

tempt·ing (temp′ting) that tempts; alluring; inviting: *A party is a tempting idea.* *adj.*

ten (ten) one more than nine; 10: *Five and five make ten.* *n., adj.*

te·na·cious (ti nā′shəs) 1 holding fast: *the tenacious jaws of a bulldog, a person tenacious of his rights, a tenacious memory.* 2 stubborn; persistent: *a tenacious salesman.* *adj.*

te·nac·i·ty (ti nas′ə tē) 1 firmness in holding fast or holding together. 2 stubbornness; persistence. *n.*

ten·ant (ten′ənt) 1 a person paying rent for the temporary use of land or buildings belonging to another person: *That building has apartments for one hundred tenants.* 2 a person or thing that occupies: *Birds are tenants of the trees.* 3 hold or occupy as a tenant; inhabit: *That old house has not been tenanted for many years.* 1, 2 *n.*, 3 *v.*

Ten Commandments in the Bible, the ten rules for living and for worship that God revealed to Moses on Mount Sinai.

tend¹ (tend) 1 be apt; be likely; incline to: *Fruit tends to decay. Farms tend to use more machinery now.* 2 move toward; be directed: *The road tends to the south here.* *v.*

tend² (tend) take care of; look after; attend to: *He tends shop for his father. A shepherd tends his flock. A nurse tends the sick.* *v.*

tend·en·cy (ten′dən sē) an inclination or leaning toward; a trend toward: *Wood has a tendency to swell if it gets wet.* *n., pl.* **tend·en·cies.**

ten·der¹ (ten′dər) 1 not hard or tough; soft: *The meat is tender. Stones hurt the little child's tender feet.* 2 delicate; not strong and hardy: *The leaves in spring are green and tender.* 3 kind; affectionate; loving: *The mother spoke tender words to her baby.* 4 gentle; not rough or crude: *He patted the dog with tender hands.* 5 young: *Two years is a tender age.* 6 sensitive; painful; sore: *a tender wound. Automobiles are a tender subject with Dad since he wrecked his. The elbow joint is a tender spot.* 7 feeling pain or grief easily: *She has a tender heart and would never hurt anyone.* *adj.* **—ten′der·ness,** *n.*

ten·der² (ten′dər) 1 offer formally: *He tendered his thanks.* 2 a formal offer: *She refused his tender of marriage.* 3 the thing offered: *Money that must be accepted as payment for a debt is called legal tender.* 1 *v.*, 2, 3 *n.*

tend·er³ (ten′dər) 1 a person or thing that tends another: *He did not like his job as baby tender.* 2 a

hat, āge, fär; let, ēqual, tėrm; it, īce
hot, ōpen, ôrder; oil, out; cup, pu̇t, rüle
əbove, takən, pencəl, lemən, circəs
ch, child; ng, long; sh, ship
th, thin; ᴛʜ, then; zh, measure

small boat carried or towed by a big one and used for landing passengers. 3 a small ship used for carrying supplies and passengers to and from larger ships. 4 the car attached behind a steam locomotive: *The tender carries coal and water for the locomotive.* *n.*

ten·der·foot (ten′dər fu̇t′) *Informal.* 1 a newcomer to the pioneer life of the West. 2 a person not used to rough living and hardships. 3 an inexperienced person. 4 a beginnning Boy Scout or Girl Guide. *n., pl.* **ten·der·feet.**

ten·don (ten′dən) a tough, strong band or cord of tissue that joins a muscle to a bone or some other part; sinew. *n.*

ten·dril (ten′drəl) 1 a threadlike part of a climbing plant that attaches itself to something and helps support the plant. 2 something similar: *curly tendrils of hair.* *n.*

ten·e·ment (ten′ə mənt) 1 a building, especially in a poor section of a city, divided into sets of rooms for separate families. 2 a dwelling or part of a dwelling occupied by a tenant: *A two-family house has two tenements.* *n.*

ten·fold (ten′fōld′) ten times as much or as many. *adj., adv., n.*

ten·nis (ten′is) a game played by two or four players on a special court, in which a ball is hit back and forth over a net with a racket. *n.*

ten·or (ten′ər) 1 the general tendency; a course: *The calm tenor of her life has never been disturbed by excitement or trouble.* 2 the general meaning: *I understand French well enough to get the tenor of his speech.* 3 the highest adult male voice: *He sings tenor in the choir.* 4 a singer with such a voice. 5 a part sung by, or written for, such a voice. *n.*

ten·pins (ten′pinz′) a bowling game in which a ball is bowled at 10 wooden pins to knock them down. *n.*

tense¹ (tens) 1 stretched tight; strained to stiffness: *a tense rope.* 2 stretch tight; stiffen: *He tensed his muscles for the leap.* 3 strained: *tense nerves, a tense moment.* 1, 3 *adj.,* **tens·er, tens·est;** 2 *v.,* **tensed, tens·ing.**

tense² (tens) a form of the verb that shows the time of the action or state expressed by the verb: *'He obeys' is in the present tense. 'He obeyed' is in the past tense.* *n.*

ten·sion (ten′shən) 1 a stretching. 2 a stretched condition; a taut state: *The tension of the bow gives speed to the arrow.* 3 mental strain: *A mother feels tension when her baby is sick.* 4 a strained condition; an unfriendly or hostile atmosphere: *There was much tension before the meeting started.* *n.*

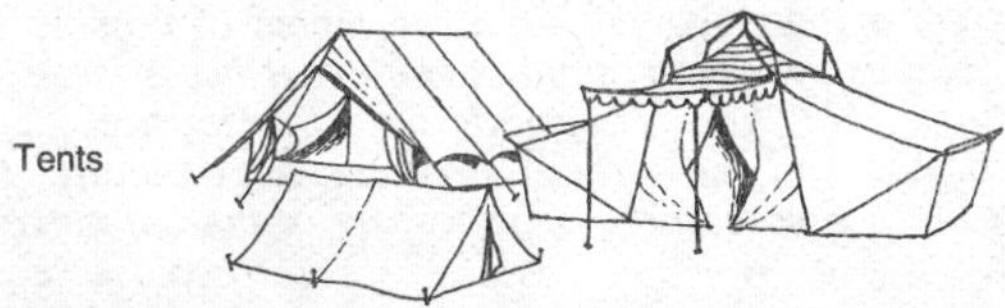
Tents

tent (tent) 1 a movable shelter, usually made of canvas and often supported by one or more poles and ropes or wires. 2 camp out or live in a tent: *We sang 'We are tenting tonight on the old camp ground.'* 1 *n.,* 2 *v.*

ten·ta·cle (ten′tə kəl) 1 a long, slender, flexible growth on the head or around the mouth of an animal, used to touch, hold, or move; a feeler: *An octopus has tentacles.* 2 a sensitive, hairlike growth on a plant. *n.*

tenth (tenth) 1 next after the 9th; last in a series of ten; 10th. 2 one of 10 equal parts: *A dime is a tenth of a dollar.* *adj., n.*

te·pee (tē′pē) See **teepee.**

tep·id (tep′id) slightly warm; lukewarm. *adj.*

term (tėrm) 1 a word or group of words used in connection with some special subject, science, art, or business: *medical terms, terms about radio.* 2 name; call: *He might be termed handsome.* 3 a set period of time: *The mayor's term of office is two years. Most schools have a fall term and a spring term.* 4 **terms,** *pl.* **a** conditions: *The terms of the peace were very hard for the defeated nation.* **b** agreement: *The two rivals keep arguing, but someone will have to make them come to terms.* **c** personal relations: *We are on good terms with the Smiths.* 1, 3, 4 *n.,* 2 *v.*

ter·mi·nal (tėr′mə nəl) 1 at the end; forming the end part: *Terminal buds grow at the end of stems.* 2 the end; the end part: *A railway terminal is the station, sheds, tracks, etc. at either end of the line.* 3 a device for making an electrical connection: *the terminals of a battery.* 1 *adj.,* 2, 3 *n.*

ter·mi·nate (tėr′mə nāt′) 1 bring to an end; put an end to; end: *A policeman terminated the quarrel by sending the boys home.* 2 come to an end: *The evening's entertainment will terminate in a dance.* 3 form the end of; bound; limit. *v.,* **ter·mi·nat·ed, ter·mi·nat·ing.**

ter·mi·na·tion (tėr′mə nā′shən) an ending; end: *the termination of a war.* *n.*

ter·mi·nus (tėr′mə nəs) 1 an end of a railway line, bus line, etc. 2 a boundary; a goal or end. *n., pl.* **ter·mi·nus·es** or **ter·mi·ni** (tėr′mə nī).

ter·mite (tėr′mīt) a kind of insect that has a soft, pale body and lives in colonies: *Termites, which are sometimes called white ants, eat the wood of buildings, furniture, etc.* *n.*

A series of terraces on the side of a mountain

ter·race (ter′is) 1 a flat level of land like a large step, especially one of a series of such levels on a slope. 2 form into a terrace or terraces; furnish with terraces: *a terraced garden.* 3 a paved outdoor space adjoining a house, used for lounging, dining, etc. 1, 3 *n.,* 2 *v.,* **ter·raced, ter·rac·ing.**

ter·rar·i·um (tə rer′ē əm) a glass enclosure in which plants or small land animals are kept. *n., pl.* **ter·rar·i·ums** or **ter·rar·i·a** (tə rer′ē ə).

ter·res·tri·al (tə res′trē əl) **1** of the earth; not of the heavens: *this terrestrial globe.* **2** of land, not water or air: *Islands and continents make up the terrestrial parts of the earth.* **3** living on the ground, not in the air or water or in trees: *Cows, lions, and elephants are terrestrial animals. adj.*

ter·ri·ble (ter′ə bəl) **1** causing great fear; dreadful; awful: *The terrible storm destroyed many lives.* **2** *Informal.* extremely bad; unpleasant: *She has a terrible temper. adj.*

ter·ri·bly (ter′ə blē) **1** in a terrible manner; dreadfully: *She is terribly afraid of lightning.* **2** *Informal.* extremely; very: *I am terribly sorry I stepped on your toes. adv.*

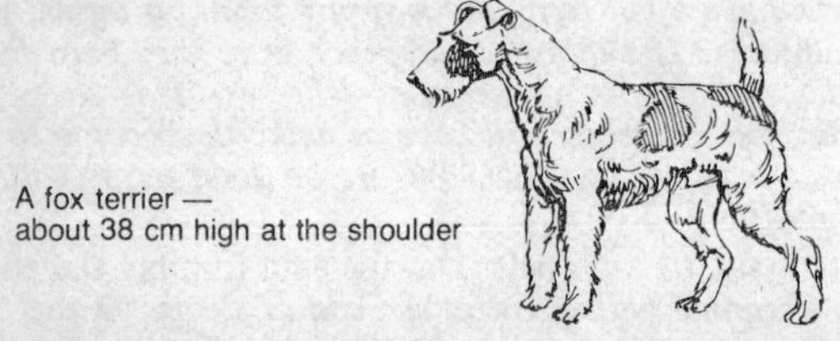

A fox terrier — about 38 cm high at the shoulder

ter·ri·er (ter′ē ər) a kind of small, active, intelligent, and courageous dog formerly used to pursue prey into its burrow: *fox terriers, Irish terriers, Scotch terriers. n.*

ter·rif·ic (tə rif′ik) **1** causing great fear; terrifying: *A terrific earthquake shook Japan.* **2** *Informal.* very unusual; remarkable; extraordinary: *A terrific hot spell ruined many of the crops. adj.*

ter·ri·fy (ter′ə fī′) fill with great fear; frighten very much: *Terrified by the sight of the bear, he ran into the cabin. v.,* **ter·ri·fied, ter·ri·fy·ing.**

ter·ri·to·ry (ter′ə tô′rē) **1** land: *Much territory in the northern part of Africa is desert.* **2** a region; an area of land: *The company leased a large territory for oil exploration.* **3** land under the rule or control of a distant government: *The British Empire included many territories.* **4** in Canada, a region administered by the Federal Governemnt: *Yukon Territory, Northwest Territories.* **5** a region assigned to a salesman or agent. *n., pl.* **ter·ri·to·ries.**

ter·ror (ter′ər) **1** great fear: *The child has a terror of thunder.* **2** a cause of great fear: *Pirates were once the terror of the sea. n.*

ter·ror·ize (ter′ər īz′) **1** fill with terror: *The sight of the growling dog terrorized the little child.* **2** rule or subdue by causing terror: *The village was terrorized by bandits during the revolution. v.,* **ter·ror·ized, ter·ror·iz·ing.**

terse (tèrs) brief and to the point: *'No!' was Father's terse reply when I asked if I could play after bedtime. adj.,* **ters·er, ters·est.**

test (test) **1** an examination; trial: *The teacher gave us a test in arithmetic. People who want a licence to drive an automobile must pass a test.* **2** a means of trial: *Trouble is a test of character.* **3** an examination of a substance to see what it is or what it contains: *A test showed that the water from our well was pure.* **4** put to a test of any kind; try out: *That water was tested for purity.* 1–3 *n.,* 4 *v.*

tes·ta·ment (tes′tə mənt) **1** written instructions telling what to do with a person's property after his death; a will. **2 Testament, a** a main division of the Bible; the Old Testament or the New Testament. **b** *Informal.* the New Testament. *n.*

tes·ti·fy (tes′tə fī′) **1** give evidence or proof: *The excellence of Shakespeare's plays testifies to his genius.* **2** declare or give evidence under oath before a judge, coroner, etc.: *The police testified that the speeding car had crashed into the truck. He hated to testify against a friend. v.,* **tes·ti·fied, tes·ti·fy·ing.**

tes·ti·mo·ny (tes′tə mō′nē) **1** a statement used for evidence or proof: *A witness gave testimony that Mr. Doe was at home all day.* **2** evidence: *The pupils presented their teacher with a watch in testimony of their respect and affection. n., pl.* **tes·ti·mo·nies.**

test tube a thin glass tube closed at one end, used in making chemical tests.

tes·ty (tes′tē) easily irritated; impatient: *a very unpleasant and testy old man. adj.,* **tes·ti·er, tes·ti·est.**

tet·a·nus (tet′ə nəs) a disease that causes violent spasms, stiffness of many muscles, and even death: *You can be protected against tetanus by inoculation. n.*

teth·er (teᴛʜ′ər) **1** a rope or chain for fastening an animal so that it can graze or move only within a certain limit: *The cow had broken its tether and was in the garden.* **2** fasten with a tether: *The horse is tethered to a stake.* 1 *n.,* 2 *v.*

at the end of one's tether, at the end of one's resources or endurance: *After the class had gone wild for an hour, the teacher was at the end of her tether.*

text (tekst) **1** the main body of reading matter in a book: *This history contains 300 pages of text and about 50 pages of notes, explanations, and questions for study.* **2** the original words of a writer: *Always quote the exact words of a text.* **3** a short passage in the Bible used as the subject of a sermon: *The minister preached on the text 'Blessed are the merciful.'* **4** a topic; subject: *Town improvement was the speaker's text.* **5** textbook. *n.*

text·book (tekst′bůk′) a book for regular study by pupils. *n.*

tex·tile (teks′tīl or teks′təl) **1** a woven or knitted fabric; cloth: *Beautiful textiles are sold in Paris.* **2** woven: *Linen is a textile material.* **3** suitable for weaving: *cotton, silk, nylon, and wool are common textile fibres.* **4** of or having something to do with the making, selling, etc. of textiles: *His father has been in the textile business for 20 years.* 1 *n.,* 2–4 *adj.*

tex·ture (teks′chər) **1** an arrangement of threads woven together: *Homespun is cloth that has a loose texture. This linen tablecloth has a fine texture.* **2** the arrangement of the parts of anything; the structure: *Her skin has a fine texture. The texture of marble makes it take a polish. n.*

than (ᴛʜan) **1** in comparison with; compared to that which: *John is taller than his sister. You know better than I do.* **2** except; besides: *How else can we reach the city than by train? conj.*

thank (thangk) **1** say that one is pleased and grateful for something given or done: *She thanked her teacher for helping her.* **2 thanks,** *pl.* **a** I thank you. **b** the act

hat, āge, fär; let, ēqual, tėrm; it, īce
hot, ōpen, ôrder; oil, out; cup, pùt, rüle
əbove, takən, pencəl, lemən, circəs
ch, child; ng, long; sh, ship
th, thin; ᴛʜ, then; zh, measure

of thanking; the expression of pleasure and gratitude. **c** a feeling of kindness received; gratitude: *You have our thanks for everything you have done.* 1 *v.,* 2 *n.*
have oneself to thank, be to blame: *You have yourself to thank if you eat too much.*
thanks to, owing to; because of: *Thanks to his efforts, we won the game.*

thank·ful (thangk′fəl) feeling thanks; grateful: *He is thankful for good health. adj.* **—thank′ful·ly,** *adv.* **—thank′ful·ness,** *n.*

thank·less (thangk′lis) **1** not likely to get thanks: *Giving advice is usually a thankless act.* **2** not feeling thanks; without a desire to do a favor in return: *The thankless woman did nothing for the neighbors who had helped her. adj.*

thanks·giv·ing (thangks giv′ing) **1** the act of giving thanks. **2** an expression of thanks: *They offered thanksgiving to God for their escape.* **3 Thanksgiving,** Thanksgiving Day. *n.*

Thanksgiving Day a day set apart as a holiday on which to give thanks to God, especially for the harvest: *In Canada, Thanksgiving Day is the second Monday in October.*

that (ᴛʜat) **1 That** is used to point out some one person, thing, or idea. We use *this* for the thing nearer us and *that* for the thing farther away from us: *Do you know that boy? Shall we buy this book or that one? I like that better.* **2 That** is also used to connect a group of words: *I know that 6 and 4 are 10.* **3 That** is used to show purpose: *He ran very fast so that he would not be late.* **4 That** is used to show result: *He ran so fast that he was five minutes early.* **5** which; who; whom: *Bring the box that will hold most. Is he the man that sells dogs? She is the girl that you saw in school.* **6** when; at or in which: *It was the day that school began. 1971 was the year that we went to England.* **7** to that extent; to such a degree; so: *The baby cannot stay up that long.* 1 *adj.,* 2–4 *conj.,* 1, 5, 6 *pron,* 7 *adv.*
in that, because: *I prefer his plan to yours, in that I think it is more practical.*
that's that, *Informal.* that is settled or decided.

☞ **That** may be used to refer to people, animals, or things: *The man that talked to you is the new teacher. What happened to the car that was used by the bank robbers?* **Who** and **whom** are used for people and sometimes for animals (especially when thought of as pets): *The man who talked to you is the new teacher. It was Rex, our collie, who got lost in the woods.* **Which** is used only for things and animals: *This is the dog which chased our car yesterday.*

An English house with a roof of thatch

thatch (thach) **1** straw, rushes, or the like, used as a roof or covering. **2** a roof or covering of thatch. **3** *Informal.* the hair covering the head. **4** roof or cover with thatch. 1–3 n., 4 *v.*

that's (ᴛʜats) that is.

thaw (tho or thô) **1** melt ice, snow, or anything frozen; free from frost: *Salt was put on the sidewalk to thaw the ice. It thawed early last spring.* **2** become free of frost, ice, etc.: *The pond thaws in April.* **3** weather above the freezing point (0°C); a time of melting: *The spring thaw came late this year.* **4** make or become less cold, less formal, or less reserved: *His shyness thawed under the teacher's kindness.* 1, 2, 4 *v.,* 3 *n.*

the[1] (ᴛʜə before consonants; before vowels, and when stressed, ᴛʜē) **1 The** is used when referring to a certain or particular thing or things: *The* (ᴛʜə) *tree in our garden is a maple. The* (ᴛʜē) *apples in the basket are snows.* **2** the only one worthy of consideration; the most significant or important: *He claimed that Swain's was the* (ᴛʜē) *restaurant in town.* **3** any one of its kind; any: *The dog is a quadruped. definite article.*

the[2] (ᴛʜə or ᴛʜē) by how much, by that much: *The longer you work, the more you get. The later I sit up, the sleepier I become. adv.*

the·a·tre or **the·a·ter** (thē′ə tər) **1** a place where plays or other stage performances are acted or where motion pictures are shown. **2** a place that looks like a theatre in its arrangement of seats: *The surgeon performed an operation before the medical students in the operating theatre.* **3** a place of action: *France has been the theatre of many wars.* **4** plays; writing, acting in, or producing plays; the drama: *He was interested in the theatre and tried to write plays himself. n.*

the·at·ri·cal (thē at′rə kəl) **1** of or having to do with the theatre or actors: *theatrical performances, a theatrical company.* **2** suggesting a theatre or acting; for display or effect; artificial: *The new girl would have won more friends if she had not had such a theatrical manner. adj.*

thee (ᴛʜē) an old word meaning **you:** *'The Lord bless thee and keep thee.' pron.*

theft (theft) stealing: *The theft of the jewels caused much excitement. People are put in prison for theft. n.*

their (ᴛʜer) of them; belonging to them: *They like their fine, new school. adj.*

☞ **Their, there,** and **they're** are pronounced the same.

☞ **Their, theirs** are the possessive forms of **they. Their** is always followed by a noun: *This is their farm.* **Theirs** stands alone: *This farm is theirs.*

theirs (ᴛʜerz) **1** of them; belonging to them: *Those books are theirs, not mine.* **2** the one or ones belonging to them: *Our house is white; theirs is brown. pron.*

☞ **Theirs** and **there's** are pronounced the same.

☞ See second note at **their.**

them (ᴛʜem) persons, animals, or things already spoken or written about: *The books are new; take care of them. pron.*

theme (thēm) **1** a subject; topic: *Patriotism was the speaker's theme.* **2** a short written composition: *Our school themes must be written in ink and on white paper.* **3** the principal melody in a piece of music. **4** a melody used to identify a particular radio or televison program. *n.*

them·selves (ᴛʜem selvz′) 1 a form used instead of **them** when referring back to the subject of the sentence: *Their boots were muddy, so they washed them and then washed themselves.* 2 a form of **they** or **them** used to make a statement stronger: *The teachers themselves said that the test was too hard.* 3 their normal or usual selves: *The children are sick and are not themselves this morning. pron.*

then (ᴛʜen) 1 at that time: *Father talked of his childhood, and recalled that prices were lower then.* 2 that time: *By then we shall know the result of the election.* 3 being at that time in the past; existing then: *the then Premier.* 4 soon afterward: *The noise stopped and then began again.* 5 next in time or place: *First comes spring, then summer.* 6 also; besides: *The dress seems too good to throw away, and then it is very attractive.* 7 in that case; therefore: *If he broke the window, then he should pay for it.* 1, 4–7 *adv.*, 2 *n.*, 3 *adj.*

thence (thens or ᴛʜens) 1 from that place; from there: *He went to Italy; thence he went to France.* 2 for that reason: *You didn't work; thence you will get no pay.* 3 from that time; from then: *a few years thence. adv.*

the·ol·o·gy (thē ol′ə jē) the study of religion and religious beliefs. *n., pl.* **the·ol·o·gies.**

the·o·rem (thē′ə rəm) 1 a statement or rule in mathematics that has been or is to be proved. *Example: In an isosceles triangle the angles opposite the equal sides are equal.* 2 any statement or rule that can be proved to be true. *n.*

the·o·ry (thē′ə rē) 1 an explanation based on thought; an explanation based on observation and reasoning: *There are several theories about the way in which the fire started. According to one scientific theory of life, the more complicated animals developed from the simple ones.* 2 the principles or methods of a science or art rather than its practice: *the theory of music.* 3 an idea or opinion about something: *I think the fire was started by a careless smoker. What is your theory? n., pl.* **the·o·ries.**

ther·a·py (ther′ə pē) the treatment of diseases or disorders. *n.*

there (ᴛʜer) 1 in that place; at that place; at that point: *Sit there. Finish reading the page and stop there.* 2 to or into that place: *Have you seen the new house? We are going there tomorrow.* 3 that place: *We go to Hamilton first and from there to Windsor.* 4 in that matter: *You are mistaken there.* 5 **There** is used in sentences in which the verb comes before its subject: *There are three new houses on our street. Is there a drugstore near here?* 6 **There** is used to call attention to some person or thing: *There goes the bell.* 7 **There** is used to express some feeling: *There, there! Don't cry.* 1, 2, 4–6 *adv.*, 3 *n.*, 7 *interj.*

☛ **There, their,** and **they're** are pronounced the same.

there·a·bout (ᴛʜer′ə bout′) thereabouts. *adv.*

there·a·bouts (ᴛʜer′ə bouts′) 1 near that place: *She lives downtown, on Main Street or thereabouts.* 2 near that time: *He went home in the late afternoon, at 5 o'clock or thereabouts.* 3 near that number or amount: *The book cost me two dollars or thereabouts. adv.*

there·af·ter (ᴛʜer af′tər) after that; afterward: *He was very ill as a child and was considered delicate thereafter. adv.*

there·at (ᴛʜer at′) 1 when that happened; at that time. 2 because of that; because of it. 3 at that place; there. *adv.*

there·by (ᴛʜer bī′) 1 by means of that; in that way: *He wished to travel and thereby study the customs of other countries.* 2 in connection with that: *George won the game, and thereby hangs a tale.* 3 near there: *A farm lay thereby. adv.*

there·fore (ᴛʜer′fôr) for that reason; as a result of that: *She went to a party and therefore did not study her lessons. adv.*

there·in (ᴛʜer in′) 1 in that place; in it: *God created the sea and all that is therein.* 2 in that matter; in that way; in that respect: *The captain thought all danger was past; therein he made a mistake. adv.*

there·of (ᴛʜer ov′) 1 of that; of it. 2 from it; from that source. *adv.*

there·on (ᴛʜer on′) 1 on that; on it: *Before the window was a table; a huge book lay thereon.* 2 immediately after that: *Jesus touched the sick man; thereon he was healed. adv.*

there's (ᴛʜerz) there is.

☛ **There's** and **theirs** are pronounced the same.

there·to (ᴛʜer tü′) 1 to that; to it: *The castle stands on the hill, and the road thereto is steep and rough.* 2 in addition to that; also: *The king gave his faithful servant rich garments and added thereto a bag of gold. adv.*

there·un·to (ᴛʜer un′tü) to that; to it. *adv.*

there·up·on (ᴛʜer′ə pon′) 1 immediately after that: *The Queen appeared. Thereupon the people clapped.* 2 because of that; therefore: *The stolen jewels were found in his room; thereupon he was put in jail.* 3 on that; on it: *The knight carried a shield with a cross painted thereupon. adv.*

there·with (ᴛʜer wiᴛʜ′ or ᴛʜer with′) 1 with that; with it: *The lady gave him a rose and a smile therewith.* 2 immediately after that; then: *'Avenge me!' said the ghost and therewith disappeared. adv.*

ther·mal (thėr′məl) of or having to do with heat: *Steaming water came from an underground thermal spring. adj.*

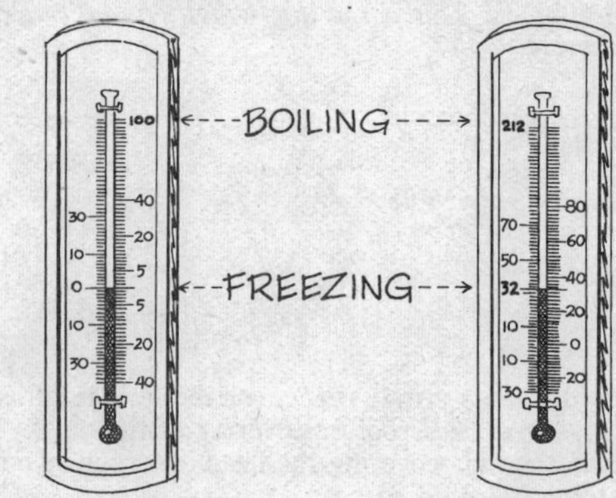

A Celsius thermometer A Fahrenheit thermometer

ther·mom·e·ter (thər mom′ə tər) an instrument for

measuring temperature. *n.*

Ther·mos bot·tle (thėr′məs bot′əl) the trademark for a kind of bottle or jug that will keep its contents at about the same temperature for several hours.

ther·mo·stat (thėr′mə stat′) an automatic device for regulating temperature: *Most furnaces and ovens are controlled by thermostats.* *n.*

the·sau·rus (thi′sô′rəs) a book in which words are classified under certain headings according to their meanings. *n.*

☞ **Thesaurus** comes through Latin from a Greek word *thesauros,* meaning 'treasure' or 'treasure house.'

these (ᴛʜēz) **These** is used to point out persons, things, or ideas that are near the speaker in time, space, or relationship: *These days are cold. These two problems are hard. These are my books.* *adj., pron.*

they (ᴛʜā) **1** persons, animals, things, or ideas already spoken or written about: *I had three books yesterday. Do you know where they are? They are on the table.* **2** *Informal.* some people; any people; persons: *They say we should have a new school.* *pron.*

they'd (ᴛʜād) **1** they had. **2** they would.

they'll (ᴛʜāl) they will.

they're (ᴛʜer) they are.

☞ **They're, their,** and **there** are pronounced the same.

they've (ᴛʜāv) they have.

thick (thik) **1** filling much space from one surface to the other; not thin: *The castle has thick stone walls.* **2** measuring between two opposite surfaces: *This brick is about 20 centimetres long, 10 centimetres wide, and 6.3 centimetres thick.* **3** set close together; dense: *She has thick hair. It is a thick forest.* **4** many and close together; abundant: *The troops were greeted by bullets thick as hail.* **5** like glue or syrup; heavy: *Thick liquids pour much more slowly than thin liquids.* **6** not clear; foggy: *The weather was thick and the airports were shut down.* **7** not clear in sound; hoarse: *She had a thick voice because of a cold.* **8** stupid; dull: *He has a thick head.* **9** thickly: *The field was planted so thick with corn that you could hide among the stalks.* **10** the hardest part; the place where there is the most danger, activity, etc.: *King Arthur was in the thick of the fight.* **11** very friendly; intimate: *The two boys were as thick as thieves.* 1–8, 11 *adj.,* 9 *adv.,* 10 *n.*

thick skin, the ability to take criticism, etc. without being affected by it.

through thick and thin, in good times and bad: *A true friend stays loyal through thick and thin.*

thick·en (thik′ən) make thick or thicker; become thick or thicker: *The cook thickens the gravy with flour. The pudding will thicken as it cools.* *v.*

thick·et (thik′it) shrubs, bushes, or small trees growing close together: *We crawled into the thicket and hid.* *n.*

thick·ly (thik′lē) **1** in a thick manner; closely; densely: *The Toronto district is a thickly settled region.* **2** in great numbers; in abundance: *Weeds grow thickly in the rich soil.* **3** in tones that are hoarse or hard to understand. *adv.*

thick·ness (thik′nis) **1** the state or condition of being thick: *The thickness of the walls shuts out all sound.* **2** the distance between two opposite surfaces; the third measurement of a solid, not length nor breadth: *The length of the board is 3 metres, the width 15 centimetres, the thickness 2 centimetres.* **3** a layer: *The pad was made up of three thicknesses of cloth.* *n.*

hat, āge, fär; let, ēqual, tėrm; it, īce
hot, ōpen, ôrder; oil, out; cup, pu̇t, rüle
əbove, takən, pencəl, lemən, circəs
ch, child; ng, long; sh, ship
th, thin; ᴛʜ, then; zh, measure

thick–set (thik′set′) thick in form or build: *a thick-set man.* *adj.*

thief (thēf) a person who steals, especially one who steals secretly and, usually, without using force: *A thief stole the little boy's bicycle from the yard.* *n., pl.* **thieves.**

thieve (thēv) steal: *He saw a boy thieving at school.* *v.,* **thieved, thiev·ing.**

thieves (thēvz) plural of **thief.** *n. pl.*

thigh (thī) the part of the leg between the hip and the knee. See **leg** for picture. *n.*

thim·ble (thim′bəl) a small cap of metal, bone, plastic, etc. worn on the finger to protect it when pushing the needle in sewing. *n.*

thin (thin) **1** filling little space from one surface to the other; not thick: *thin paper, thin wire. The ice on the pond is too thin for skating.* **2** having little flesh; slender; lean: *a thin man.* **3** not set close together; scanty: *He has thin hair.* **4** not dense: *The air on the tops of high mountains is thin.* **5** few and far apart; not abundant: *The actors played to a thin audience.* **6** like water; not like glue or syrup; not as thick as usual: *This gravy is too thin.* **7** not deep or strong; having little depth, fullness, or intensity: *a thin color. She speaks in a shrill, thin voice.* **8** easily seen through; flimsy: *It was a thin excuse that satisfied no one.* **9** make thin; become thin: *to thin paint.* 1–8 *adj.,* **thin·ner, thin·nest;** 9 *v.,* **thinned, thin·ning.**

thin skin, the condition of being easily affected by criticism, etc.

thine (ᴛʜīn) in old or poetic use: **1** belonging to you; yours: *'The princess shall be thine,' said the king to the knight.* **2** the one or ones belonging to you; yours: *Thine is the swiftest steed.* **3** your; thy (used only before a vowel or *h*): *thine eyes.* 1, 2 *pron.,* 3 *adj.*

thing (thing) **1** any object or substance; what you can see or hear or touch or taste or smell: *All the things in the house were burned. Put these things away.* **2** whatever is spoken or thought of; any act, fact, deed, event, or idea: *It was a good thing to do. A strange thing happened. That is a strange thing to think of.* **3** a matter or affair: *Let's settle this thing between us. How are things going?* **4** a person or animal: *I felt sorry for the poor thing.* **5 things,** *pl.* **a** personal belongings. **b** clothes: *I packed my things and took the train.* *n.*

think (thingk) **1** have ideas; use the mind: *You must learn to think clearly.* **2** have in the mind: *He thought that he would go.* **3** have an opinion; believe: *Do you think it will rain? We thought it might snow.* **4** reflect: *I want to think about that question before I answer it.* **5** consider: *They think their teacher an angel.* *v.,* **thought, think·ing.**

think out, plan, discover or understand by thinking: *Bill thought out the reasons for his dad's anger.*

think over, consider carefully: *Think over our plan*

before you go.
think up, plan or discover by thinking: *We will think up a way to get the candy.*

third (thėrd) **1** next after the 2nd; last in a series of three; 3rd: *C is the third letter of the alphabet.* **2** one of three equal parts: *Mother divided the pizza into thirds. adj., n.*

third·ly (thėrd′lē) in the third place. *adv.*

thirst (thėrst) **1** a dry, uncomfortable feeling in the mouth or throat caused by having had nothing to drink; a desire or need for something to drink: *The traveller in the desert suffered from thirst. He satisfied his thirst at the spring.* **2** feel thirst; be thirsty. **3** a strong desire: *Many children have a thirst for adventure.* **4** have a strong desire. 1, 3 *n.*, 2, 4 *v.*

thirst·y (thėrs′tē) **1** feeling thirst; having thirst: *The dog is thirsty; please give him some water.* **2** without water or moisture; dry: *The land seemed thirstier than a desert. adj.*, **thirst·i·er, thirst·i·est.**

thir·teen (thėr′tēn′) three more than ten; 13: *She thinks thirteen is an unlucky number. n., adj.*

thir·teenth (thėr′tēnth′) **1** next after the 12th; last in a series of thirteen; 13th. **2** one of 13 equal parts. *adj., n.*

thir·ti·eth (thėr′tē ith) **1** next after the 29th; last in a series of thirty; 30th. **2** one of 30 equal parts: *A day is about one thirtieth of a month. adj., n.*

thir·ty (thėr′tē) three times ten; 30. *n., pl.* **thir·ties;** *adj.*

this (ŦHis) **1 This** is used to point out some one person, thing, or idea as present, or near, or spoken of before. We use *that* for the thing farther away from us and *this* for the thing nearer us: *This is my brother. Shall we buy this or that?* **2** present; near; spoken of: *this minute, this child, this idea.* **3** to this degree or extent; so: *You can have this much.* 1 *pron.*, 2 *adj.*, 3 *adv.*

A thistle

this·tle (this′əl) a kind of plant having a prickly stalk and leaves: *The purple thistle is the national flower of Scotland. n.*

thith·er (thiŦH′ər) to that place; toward that place; there. *adv.*

tho′ (ŦHō) *Informal.* though.

thong (thong) **1** a narrow strip of leather, especially one used as a fastening: *The ancient Greeks laced their sandals on with thongs.* **2** a kind of sandal held on the foot by a narrow piece of leather, plastic, etc. that passes between the toes. *n.*

tho·rax (thô′raks) **1** the part of the body between the neck and the abdomen: *A man's chest is his thorax.* **2** the second division of an insect's body, between the head and the abdomen. See **insect** for picture. *n.*

thorn (thôrn) **1** a sharp point on a stem or branch of a tree or plant: *Roses have thorns.* **2** a tree or plant that has thorns on it: *Thorns sprang up and choked the wheat. n.*
thorn in the flesh or **side,** a cause of trouble or annoyance: *My cousin is at our house and he is always a thorn in the flesh.*

thorn·y (thôr′nē) **1** full of thorns: *He scratched his hands on the thorny bush. He tried to make his way through the thorny undergrowth.* **2** troublesome; annoying: *The boys argued over the thorny points in the lesson. adj.*, **thorn·i·er, thorn·i·est.**

thor·ough (thėr′ō or thėr′ə) **1** complete: *Please make a thorough search for the lost money.* **2** doing all that should be done: *The doctor was very thorough in his examination of the sick child. adj.* **—thor′ough·ly,** *adv.*

thor·ough·bred (thėr′ə bred′) **1** of pure breed or stock. **2** a thoroughbred animal, especially a horse. **3** well-bred; thoroughly trained. 1, 3 *adj.*, 2 *n.*

thor·ough·fare (thėr′ə fer′) **1** a passage, road, or street open at both ends. **2** a main road; highway: *The Queen Elizabeth Way is a famous thoroughfare between Toronto and Niagara Falls.* **3** The sign **No Thoroughfare** means that people are not allowed to go through. *n.*

those (ŦHōz) **Those** is used to point out several persons or things that are more or less distant from the speaker in time, space, or relationship: *She owns that dog; the boys own those dogs. These are his books; those are my books. adj., pron.*

thou (ŦHou) an old word meaning **you:** *'Thou art fair,' said the knight to the lady.* God is sometimes addressed as **Thou.** *pron.*

though (ŦHō) **1** in spite of the fact that: *We take our medicine, though we do not like it. Though it was pouring, the girls went to school.* **2** even supposing that: *Though I fail, I shall try again.* **3** however; nevertheless: *I am sorry for our quarrel; you began it, though.* 1, 2 *conj.*, 3 *adv.*
as though, as if: *You look as though you are tired.*

thought (thot or thôt) **1** what a person thinks; an idea or notion: *Her thought was to have a picnic.* **2** the act or power of thinking: *Thought helps us solve problems.* **3** care; attention; regard: *Show some thought for others than yourself.* **4** the characteristic thinking of a particular person, time, or place: *20th-century scientific thought.* **5** See **think.** *We thought it would snow yesterday.* 1–4 *n.*, 5 *v.*

thought·ful (thot′fəl or thôt′fəl) **1** deep in thought; thinking: *He was thoughtful for a while and then replied, 'No.'* **2** careful; showing careful thought: *a thoughtful plan.* **3** careful of others; considerate: *She is always thoughtful of her mother. adj.*

thought·less (thot′lis or thôt′lis) **1** without thought; doing things without thinking; careless: *He is a thoughtless boy and is always making blunders.* **2** showing little or no care or regard for others: *It is thoughtless of her to keep us waiting so long. adj.*

thou·sand (thou′zənd) ten hundred; 1000. *n., adj.*

thou·sandth (thou′zəndth) **1** last in a series of a thousand. **2** one of a thousand equal parts. *adj., n.*

thrall (throl or thrôl) **1** a person in bondage; slave:

hat, āge, fär; let, ēqual, tėrm; it, īce
hot, ōpen, ôrder; oil, out; cup, pu̇t, rüle
əbove, takən, pencəl, lemən, circəs
ch, child; ng, long; sh, ship
th, thin; ᴛʜ, then; zh, measure

The thralls did the work of the castle. 2 bondage; slavery: *An enchantress had the prince in thrall.* *n.*

thrash (thrash) 1 beat: *The man thrashed the boy for stealing apples.* 2 move violently; toss: *The feverish child thrashed about in his bed all night.* 3 thresh. *v.* **thrash out,** settle by thorough discussion: *Let's stay until we thrash out the problem.*

thrash·er (thrash′ər) a bird resembling a thrush. *n.*

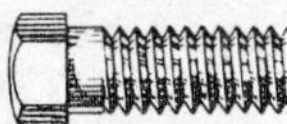
A bolt, showing the thread

thread (thred) 1 cotton, silk, flax, etc. spun out into a fine cord: *Thread is used for sewing.* 2 pass a thread through: *She threaded her needle. She threaded a hundred beads.* 3 something long and slender like a thread: *The spider hung by a thread.* 4 the main thought that connects the parts of a story or speech: *He lost the thread of their conversation when he heard the phone ring.* 5 make one's way; go carefully: *The cat threaded its way among the dishes on the shelf. The path threads through the forest.* 6 the sloping ridge that winds around a bolt, screw, pipe joint, etc.: *The thread of a nut interlocks with the thread of a bolt.* 1, 3, 4, 6 *n.,* 2, 5 *v.*

thread·bare (thred′ber′) 1 having the nap worn off; worn so much that the threads show: *a threadbare coat.* 2 wearing clothes worn to the threads; shabby: *a threadbare beggar.* 3 old and worn: *Saying 'I forgot' is a threadbare excuse.* *adj.*

threat (thret) 1 a statement of what will be done to hurt or punish someone: *They were frightened by the robber's threat to harm them if they shouted.* 2 a sign or cause of possible harm or unpleasantness: *Those black clouds are a threat of rain.* *n.*

threat·en (thret′ən) 1 make a threat against; say what will be done to hurt or punish: *The farmer threatened to shoot any dog that killed one of his sheep. She threatens and scolds too much.* 2 be a sign or warning of possible harm or unpleasantness: *The clouds threaten rain.* 3 be a cause of possible harm or unpleasantness to: *A flood threatened the city.* *v.*

three (thrē) one more than two; 3: *This stool has three legs.* *n., adj.*

three·fold (thrē′fōld′) 1 three times as much or as many. 2 having three parts. 1, 2 *adj.,* 1 *adv.*

three·score (thrē′skôr′) three times twenty; 60. *adj., n.*

thresh (thresh) 1 separate the grain or seeds from wheat, etc.; thrash: *Nowadays most farmers use a machine to thresh their wheat.* 2 toss about; thrash. *v.*

thresh·er (thresh′ər) 1 a person who threshes. 2 a machine used for separating the grain or seeds from the stalks and other parts of wheat, oats, etc. *n.*

thresh·old (thresh′ōld or thresh′hōld) 1 a piece of wood or stone under a door. 2 a doorway. 3 the point of entering; the beginning point: *The scientist was on the threshold of an important discovery.* *n.*

threw (thrü) See **throw.** *He threw a stone and ran away.* *v.*

thrice (thrīs) three times: *He knocked thrice.* *adv.*

thrift (thrift) the absence of waste; economical management; the habit of saving: *By thrift she managed to live on her small salary. A bank account encourages thrift.* *n.*

thrift·y (thrif′tē) careful in spending; economical; saving. *adj.,* **thrift·i·er, thrift·i·est.**

thrill (thril) 1 a shivering, exciting feeling: *She gets thrills from the movies.* 2 give a shivering, exciting feeling to: *Stories of adventure thrilled him.* 3 have a shivering, exciting feeling: *The children thrilled with joy at the sight of the Christmas tree.* 4 tremble: *Her voice thrilled with terror.* 1 *n.,* 2–4 *v.*

thrive (thrīv) 1 grow strong; grow vigorously: *Most flowers will not thrive without sunshine.* 2 be successful; grow rich: *His business is thriving.* *v.,* **throve** or **thrived, thrived** or **thriv·en** (thriv′ən), **thriv·ing.**

throat (thrōt) 1 the front of the neck: *She wore a scarf at her throat.* 2 the passage from the mouth to the stomach or the lungs: *A bone stuck in his throat.* 3 any narrowed opening or passage: *The throat of the valley was blocked by fallen rocks.* *n.*

throb (throb) 1 beat rapidly or strongly: *The long climb up the hill made her heart throb. His wounded arm throbbed with pain.* 2 a rapid or strong beat: *She felt the throb of the little plane's engine.* 1 *v.,* **throbbed, throb·bing;** 2 *n.*

throne (thrōn) 1 the chair on which a king, queen, bishop, or other person of high rank sits during ceremonies. 2 the power of authority of a king, queen, etc.: *The throne commands respect but no longer commands armies.* *n.*

☛ **Throne** and **thrown** are pronounced the same.

throng (throng) 1 a crowd; multitude. 2 to crowd; fill with a crowd: *People thronged the theatre to see the famous actress.* 3 come together in a crowd; go or press in large numbers: *The people thronged to see the Queen.* 1 *n.,* 2, 3 *v.*

throt·tle (throt′əl) 1 a valve for regulating the supply of steam or gasoline to an engine. 2 a lever or pedal working such a valve: *The throttle of a car is called an accelerator.* 3 stop or check by closing such a valve: *to throttle a steam engine.* 4 stop the breath of by pressure on the throat; choke; strangle: *The thief throttled the dog to keep it from barking.* 1, 2 *n.,* 3, 4 *v.,* **throt·tled, throt·tling.**

through (thrü) 1 from end to end of; from side to side of; between the parts of: *The soldiers marched through the town. He had a job through the summer. Fish swim through water. The carpenter bored holes through a board. We look through windows.* 2 from beginning to end; from one side to the other: *She read the book all the way through.* 3 here and there in; over: *We saw many interesting things while travelling through Quebec.* 4 because of; by reason of: *The woman refused help through pride.* 5 by means of: *He became rich through hard work and ability.* 6 completely; thoroughly: *He walked home in the rain and was wet through.* 7 going all the way without change: *a through train from Montreal to Vancouver.*

8 having reached the end of; finished with: *We are through school at three o'clock.* 9 having reached the end; finished: *I will soon be through.* 1, 3–5, 8 *prep.,* 2, 6 *adv.,* 7, 9 *adj.*

through·out (thrü out′) 1 all the way through; through all; in every part of: *Dominion Day is celebrated throughout Canada.* 2 in every part: *The house is well built throughout.* 1 *prep.,* 2 *adv.*

throve (thrōv) See **thrive.** *She throve on hard work.* *v.*

throw (thrō) 1 cast; toss; hurl: *The boy threw the ball. The fire hose threw water on the burning house.* 2 a cast, toss, etc.: *That was a good throw from left field to the catcher.* 3 bring to the ground: *He was thrown by his horse.* 4 put carelessly or in haste: *She threw a cloak over her shoulders.* 5 put into a certain condition: *throw a person into confusion.* 6 turn, direct, or move, especially quickly: *She threw a glance at each car that passed us.* 7 move a lever, etc. that connects or disconnects parts of a switch, clutch, or other mechanism. 1, 3–7 *v.,* **threw, thrown, throw·ing;** 2 *n.*

throw up, a *Informal.* vomit. **b** give up; abandon: *He threw up his chance to go to Europe.*

thrown (thrōn) See **throw.** *She has thrown her old toys out.* *v.*

☞ **Thrown** and **throne** are pronounced the same.

thrush (thrush) any of a large group of songbirds that includes the robin, the bluebird, and the wood thrush. *n.*

thrust (thrust) 1 push with force: *He thrust his hands into his pockets. She thrust past me into the room. A soldier thrusts himself into danger.* 2 a push with force: *With a quick thrust, she hid the book behind the pillow.* 3 stab; pierce: *He thrust the knife into the apple.* 4 a stab: *A thrust with the pin broke the balloon.* 5 an attack. 6 the force of one thing pushing against another: *the thrust of a jet engine.* 1, 3 *v.,* **thrust, thrust·ing;** 2, 4–6 *n.*

thud (thud) 1 a dull sound caused by a blow or a fall: *The book hit the floor with a thud.* 2 hit, move, or strike with a thud: *The heavy box fell and thudded on the floor.* 1 *n.,* 2 *v.,* **thud·ded, thud·ding.**

thumb (thum) 1 the short, thick finger of the hand. See **arm** for picture. 2 the part of a glove, mitten, etc. that covers the thumb: *There was a hole in the thumb of his mitten.* 3 soil or wear by handling with the thumbs: *Some of the books were badly thumbed.* 4 turn the pages of rapidly, with a thumb or as if with a thumb: *He thumbed the book and gave it back to me.* 5 *Informal.* ask for or get a free ride by holding up one's thumb to motorists going in one's direction. 1, 2 *n.,* 3–5 *v.*

all thumbs, very clumsy, awkward, etc.

thumbs down, a sign of disapproval or rejection.

thumbs up, a sign of approval or acceptance.

under the thumb of, under the power or influence of: *The bully tried to keep us all under his thumb, but we outwitted him.*

thumb·tack (thum′tak′) a tack having a broad, flat head, that can be pressed into a wall, board, etc. with the thumb. *n.*

thump (thump) 1 strike with something thick and heavy; pound: *He thumped the table with his fist. He thumped on the piano.* 2 a blow with something thick and heavy; a heavy knock: *He hit the thief a thump on the head.* 3 the dull sound made by a blow, knock, or fall: *We heard the thump as he fell.* 4 make a dull sound: *The hammer thumped against the wood.* 5 beat violently or heavily: *His heart thumped as he walked past the cemetery at night.* 1, 4, 5 *v.,* 2, 3 *n.*

thun·der (thun′dər) 1 the loud noise that accompanies a flash of lightning: *Thunder is caused by a disturbance of the air resulting from the discharge of electricity.* 2 give forth thunder: *It thundered, but no rain fell.* 3 any noise like thunder: *the thunder of Niagara Falls, a thunder of applause.* 4 make a noise like thunder: *The cannon thundered.* 5 utter very loudly; roar: *thunder a reply.* 1, 3 *n.,* 2, 4, 5 *v.*

thun·der·bolt (thun′dər bōlt′) 1 a flash of lightning and the thunder that follows it. 2 something sudden, startling, and terrible: *The news of his death came as a thunderbolt.* *n.*

thun·der·clap (thun′dər klap′) a loud crash of thunder. *n.*

thun·der·cloud (thun′dər kloud′) a dark cloud that brings thunder and lightning. *n.*

thun·der·ous (thun′dər əs) 1 producing thunder. 2 making a noise like thunder: *The famous actor received a thunderous burst of applause.* *adj.*

thun·der·show·er (thun′dər shou′ər) a shower accompanied by thunder and lightning. *n.*

thun·der·storm (thun′dər stôrm′) a storm accompanied by thunder and lightning. *n.*

thun·der·struck (thun′dər struk′) overcome as if by a thunderbolt; astonished; amazed: *We were thunderstruck by the news of war.* *adj.*

Thurs. or **Thur.** Thursday.

Thurs·day (thėrz′dē or thėrz′dā′) the fifth day of the week, following Wednesday. *n.*

☞ **Thursday** developed from Old English *thunresdæg,* originally meaning 'day of Thor'; Thor was the Germanic god of thunder.

thus (ᴛʜus) 1 in this way; in the following manner: *He spoke thus: 'Friends, Romans, Countrymen.'* 2 therefore: *The boy studied hard; thus he got high marks.* 3 to this extent or degree; so: *Thus far may you go and no farther.* *adv.*

thwack (thwak) 1 strike vigorously with a stick or something flat. 2 a sharp blow with a stick or something flat. 1 *v.,* 2 *n.*

thwart (thwôrt) 1 oppose and defeat; keep from doing something: *The boy's lack of money thwarted his plans for a trip. Our army thwarted the enemy attack.* 2 a seat across a boat, on which a rower sits. 3 a brace in a canoe. See **canoe** for picture. 1 *v.,* 2, 3 *n.*

thy (ᴛʜī) an old word meaning **your:** *'Thy kingdom come, Thy will be done.'* *pron., adj.*

thyme (tīm) a small plant that smells like mint: *The sweet-smelling leaves of thyme are often used for seasoning.* *n.*

☞ **Thyme** and **time** are pronounced the same.

thy·roid (thī′roid) a gland in the neck that affects one's physical development and rate of growth. *n.*

thy·self (ᴛʜī self′) an old word meaning **yourself.** *pron.*

hat, āge, fär; let, ēqual, tėrm; it, īce
hot, ōpen, ôrder; oil, out; cup, pu̇t, rüle
əbove, takən, pencəl, lemən, circəs
ch, child; ng, long; sh, ship
th, thin; ᴛʜ, then; zh, measure

ti (tē) the seventh tone of the musical scale. See **do**[2] for picture. *n.*

ti·ar·a (tē ä′rə or tī er′ə) **1** a band of gold, jewels, flowers, etc. worn around the head as an ornament. **2** the triple crown of the Pope. *n.*

tick[1] (tik) **1** a sound made by a clock or watch. **2** make such a sound: *The clock ticked.* **3** a sound like this. **4** mark off: *The clock ticked away the minutes.* **5** a small mark used in checking. We use ✓ or / as a tick: *He put a tick opposite each item on his list.* **6** mark with a tick; check: *He ticked off the items one by one.* **7** *Informal.* function, work, or go: *What makes that gadget tick?* 1, 3, 5 *n.*, 2, 4, 6, 7 *v.*

tick[2] (tik) **1** a tiny eight-legged animal, related to the spider, that attaches itself to humans and animals and sucks their blood. **2** a wingless insect that sucks blood of certain animals, such as sheep, cattle, or deer. *n.*

tick[3] (tik) the cloth covering of a mattress or pillow. *n.*

tick·et (tik′it) **1** a card or piece of paper that gives its holder a right or privilege: *a bus ticket.* **2** *Informal.* a summons to appear in court given by a police officer to a person who has broken a traffic law: *a ticket for speeding, a parking ticket.* **3** a card or piece of paper attached to something to show its price, etc. **4** put a ticket on: *All articles in the store are ticketed with the price.* 1–3 *n.*, 4 *v.*

tick·ing (tik′ing) a strong cotton or linen cloth, used to cover mattresses and pillows and to make tents and awnings. *n.*

tick·le (tik′əl) **1** touch lightly, causing little thrills, shivers, or wriggles: *He tickled the baby's feet and made her laugh.* **2** have a feeling like this: *My nose tickles.* **3** a tingling or itching feeling. **4** amuse; excite pleasantly: *The story tickled him. The child was tickled with his new toys.* 1, 2, 4 *v.*, **tick·led, tick·ling;** 3 *n.*

tick·lish (tik′lish) **1** sensitive to tickling: *The bottoms of the feet are ticklish.* **2** requiring careful handling; delicate; risky: *Repairing the radio was a ticklish job.* **3** easily upset; unstable: *A canoe is a ticklish craft.* **4** easily annoyed or offended: *a proud and ticklish fellow.* *adj.*

tick–tack–toe (tik′tak tō′) a game in which two players alternately put circles or crosses in a figure of nine squares, each player trying to be the first to fill three squares in a row with his mark. *n.*

tid·al (tī′dəl) of tides; having tides; caused by tides: *A tidal river is affected by the ocean's tide.* *adj.*

tidal wave **1** a large wave or sudden increase in the level of water along a shore, caused by unusually strong winds. **2** a destructive ocean wave which is caused by an underwater earthquake.

tid·bit (tid′bit′) a very pleasing bit of food, news, etc. *n.* Also **titbit.**

tid·dly·winks (tid′lē wingks′) a game in which the players try to make small colored disks jump into a cup by pressing on their edges with a larger disk. *n.*

tide (tīd) **1** the rise and fall of the ocean that takes place, in southern Canada, for example, about every twelve hours, caused by the attraction of the moon and the sun: *We go swimming at high tide; at low tide we dig clams.* **2** anything that rises and falls like the tide: *the tide of public opinion.* **3 tide over,** help along for a time: *This money will tide him over his illness.* 1, 2 *n.*, 3 *v.*, **tid·ed, tid·ing.**

ti·di·ly (tī′də lē) in a tidy manner; neatly. *adv.*

ti·di·ness (tī′dē nis) neatness. *n.*

ti·dings (tī′dingz) news; information: *The letter brought tidings from their daughter and her family.* *n. pl.*

ti·dy (tī′dē) **1** neat and in order: *a tidy room.* **2** make neat; put in order: *She tidied the room.* **3** *Informal.* considerable; fairly large: *$500 is a tidy sum of money.* 1, 3 *adj.*, **ti·di·er, ti·di·est;** 2 *v.*, **ti·died, ti·dy·ing.**

tie (tī) **1** fasten with string or the like; bind: *Please tie up this package.* **2** arrange to form a bow or knot: *Mother tied the strings of her apron behind her back.* **3** fasten; form a bow: *That paper ribbon doesn't tie well.* **4** tighten and fasten the string or strings of: *Tie up your shoes.* **5** a necktie: *He always wears a shirt and tie.* **6** anything that ties; a fastening; a bond or connection: *Family ties have kept him at home.* **7** fasten, join, or connect in any way; make a bond or connection. **8** restrain; restrict; limit: *He did not want to be tied to a steady job.* **9** a heavy piece of timber or iron placed crosswise to form a foundation or support: *The rails of a railway track rest on ties placed about* 30 cm *apart.* See **rail**[1] for picture. **10** equality in points, votes, etc.: *The game ended in a tie, 3 to 3.* **11** make the same score; be equal in points: *The two teams tied.* **12** in music, a curved line joining two notes of the same pitch, to show that they are to be played or sung without a break. 1–4, 7, 8, 11 *v.*, **tied, ty·ing;** 5, 6, 9, 10, 12 *n.*

tie up, a tie firmly or tightly. **b** wrap up. **c** hinder; stop: *The stalled truck tied up traffic for half an hour.* **d** invest or place money or property in such a way as to make it unavailable for other uses: *Since his money was tied up in other investments, he was unable to buy the stocks and bonds.* **e** have one's program full; be very busy: *I can't go tomorrow; I'm all tied up.*

tier (tēr) one of a series of rows arranged one above another: *tiers of seats in a football stadium.* *n.*

☞ **Tier** and **tear**[1] are pronounced the same.

tiff (tif) a little quarrel. *n.*

A tiger — about 2 m long without the tail

ti·ger (tī′gər) a large, fierce animal of Asia that has dull-yellow fur striped with black. *n.*

tiger lily a lily that has dull-orange flowers spotted with black.

tight (tīt) **1** firm; held firmly; packed or put together firmly: *a tight knot.* **2** closely; securely; firmly: *The rope was tied too tight.* **3** fitting closely; close: *Since she gained weight, her skirt has a tight fit.* **4** not letting water, air, or gas in or out: *The caulking of the boat is* *tight.* 5 hard to get; scarce: *Money is tight just now.* 6 *Informal.* stingy: *A miser is tight with his money.* 1, 3–6 *adj.,* 2 *adv.*

sit tight, *Informal.* keep the same position, opinion, etc.

tight·en (tīt′ən) 1 make tight: *He tightened his belt.* 2 become tight: *The rope tightened as I pulled it. v.*

tight·rope (tīt′rōp′) a rope stretched tight on which acrobats perform. *n.*

tights (tīts) a close-fitting garment, usually for the legs and the lower part of the body, worn by acrobats, dancers, etc. They are often worn by women and girls in cold weather. *n. pl.*

ti·gress (tī′gris) a female tiger. *n.*

tile (tīl) 1 a thin piece of baked clay: *Tiles are used for covering roofs and floors, and for ornamenting.* 2 a thin square of plastic, rubber, etc. used for surfacing floors, walls, or ceilings: *It took sixty tiles to cover the bathroom floor.* 3 such squares considered together: *We have tile on the ceiling of our classroom.* 4 a pipe for draining land. 5 put tiles on or in; cover with tile: *to tile a bathroom floor.* 1–4 *n.,* 5 *v.,* **tiled, til·ing.**

till[1] (til) 1 up to the time of; until: *The child played till eight.* 2 up to the time when; until: *Walk till you come to a white house.* 1 *prep.,* 2 *conj.*

till[2] (til) cultivate; plough, harrow, etc.: *Farmers till the land. v.*

till[3] (til) 1 a small drawer for money: *The till is under the counter.* 2 a cash register. *n.*

till·er (til′ər) a bar or handle used to turn the rudder in steering a boat. See **rudder** for picture. *n.*

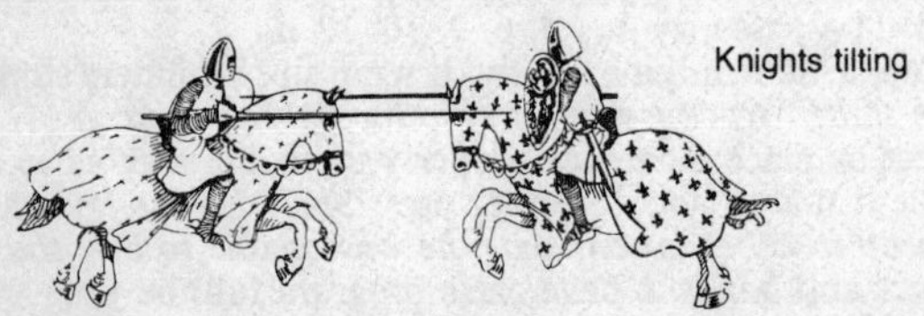
Knights tilting

tilt (tilt) 1 tip or cause to tip; slope or slant: *You tilt your head forward when you bow. You tilt your cup when you drink. This table tilts.* 2 a slope; slant: *This table is on a tilt.* 3 rush, charge, or fight with lances: *Knights used to tilt on horseback.* 4 a fight on horseback with lances. 1, 3 *v.,* 2, 4 *n.*

full tilt, at full speed; with full force: *His car ran full tilt against the tree, but no one was hurt.*

tim·ber (tim′bər) 1 wood for building and making things: *Houses, ships, and furniture are made from timber.* 2 a large piece of wood used in building: *Beams and rafters are timbers.* 3 trees that are growing and suitable for cutting: *Half of his land is covered with timber.* 4 cover, support, or furnish with timbers. 1–3 *n.,* 4 *v.*

timber limit timber line.

timber line on mountains and in the polar regions, a line beyond which trees will not grow because of the cold.

time (tīm) 1 all the days there have been or ever will be; the past, present, and future: *We measure time in years, months, days, hours, minutes, and seconds.* 2 a part of time: *A minute is a short time. A long time ago people lived in caves.* 3 a long time: *What a time it took you!* 4 some point in time: *The time the game begins is two o'clock, November 8. What time is it now?* 5 the right part or point of time: *It is time to go to bed.* 6 an occasion: *This time we will succeed. Do it five times.* 7 a way of reckoning time: *standard time, daylight-saving time.* 8 **times,** *pl.* conditions of life: *War brings hard times.* 9 an experience during a certain time: *Everyone had a good time.* 10 the rate of movement in music; rhythm: *march time, waltz time.* 11 measure the time of: *He timed the horse for each kilometre.* 12 do at regular times; do in rhythm with; set the time of: *The dancers time their steps to the music.* 13 choose the moment or occasion for: *The demonstrators timed their march through the business section so that most shoppers would see them.* 14 **times,** *pl.* multiplied by: *Four times three is twelve. Twenty is five times as much as four. Symbol:* × 1–10, 14 *n.,* 11–13 *v.,* **timed, tim·ing. —tim′er,** *n.*

at times, now and then; once in a while.

behind the times, old-fashioned; out of date.

for the time being, for the present; for now.

from time to time, now and then; once in a while: *From time to time we visited Uncle Jim's fruit farm.*

in good time, a at the right time. **b** soon; quickly.

in no time, shortly; before long: *We hurried and reached the boys in no time.*

in time, a after a while. **b** soon enough: *Will the groceries arrive in time to cook for supper?* **c** in the right rate of movement in music, dancing, marching, etc.

on time, a at the right time; not late. **b** with time in which to pay; on credit: *He bought a car on time.*

time after time or **time and again,** again and again.

☛ **Time** and **thyme** are pronounced the same.

time·ly (tīm′lē) at the right time: *The timely arrival of the police stopped the riot. adj.,* **time·li·er, time·li·est.**

time·piece (tīm′pēs′) a clock or watch. *n.*

time·ta·ble (tīm′tā′bəl) 1 a schedule that shows the times when trains, boats, buses, or airplanes come and go. 2 a student's schedule of classes. *n.*

time zone a geographical region within which the same standard of time is used. The world is divided into 24 time zones, beginning and ending at the International Date Line.

tim·id (tim′id) easily frightened; shy: *The timid child was afraid of the dark. Deer are timid animals. adj.*

ti·mid·i·ty (tə mid′ə tē) timid behavior; shyness. *n.*

tim·or·ous (tim′ər əs) easily frightened; timid: *The timorous rabbit ran away. adj.*

tin (tin) 1 a soft, silver-white metallic element used as a coating on other metals and in making alloys. 2 thin sheets of iron or steel coated with tin. 3 made of or lined with tin: *We cleaned up all the old tin cans.* 4 cover with tin. 5 any can, box, pan, or pot made of or lined with tin: *a pie tin, a tin of peas.* 1, 2, 5 *n.,* 3 *adj.,* 4 *v.,* **tinned, tin·ning.**

tin·der (tin′dər) 1 anything that catches fire easily. 2 material used to catch fire from a spark: *Before matches were invented people carried a box holding tinder, flint, and steel. n.*

tine (tīn) a sharp projecting point or prong: *the tines of a fork. n.*

tin foil a very thin sheet of tin, or tin and lead, used as a wrapping for candy, tobacco, etc.

tinge (tinj) 1 color slightly: *A drop of ink will tinge a*

hat, āge, fär; let, ēqual, tėrm; it, īce
hot, ōpen, ôrder; oil, out; cup, pu̇t, rüle
əbove, takən, pencəl, lemən, circəs
ch, child; ng, long; sh, ship
th, thin; ᴛʜ, then; zh, measure

glass of water. **2** a slight coloring or tint: *There is a tinge of red in her cheeks.* **3** add a trace of some quality to; change a very little: *Her remarks were tinged with envy.* **4** a trace; a very small amount: *She likes just a tinge of lemon in her tea. There was a tinge of envy in his voice.* 1, 3 *v.*, **tinged, tinge·ing** or **ting·ing;** 2, 4 *n.*

tin·gle (ting′gəl) **1** have a pricking or stinging feeling, especially from excitement: *He tingled with delight on his first train trip.* **2** a pricking, stinging feeling: *The cold caused a tingle in my fingers.* 1 *v.*, **tin·gled, tin·gling;** 2 *n.*

tink·er (tingk′ər) **1** a man who mends pots, pans, etc. **2** work or repair in an unskilled or clumsy way: *Somebody has been tinkering with my bicycle.* **3** work or keep busy in a rather useless way: *tinker with a radio, tinker with a new idea.* 1 *n.*, 2, 3 *v.*

tin·kle (ting′kəl) **1** make short, light, ringing sounds: *The sleigh bells tinkled.* **2** cause to tinkle: *The baby tinkled the little bell.* **3** a series of short, light, ringing sounds: *the tinkle of sleigh bells.* 1, 2 *v.*, **tin·kled, tin·kling;** 3 *n.*

tin·sel (tin′səl) **1** glittering copper, brass, etc. in thin sheets, strips, threads, etc.: *Tinsel is used to trim Christmas trees.* **2** something of or like tinsel; showy but not worth much. **3** thin cloth woven with threads of gold, silver, or copper: *She wore a beautiful dress of gold tinsel. n.*

tin·smith (tin′smith′) a person who works with tin or other light metal; a maker of tinware. *n.*

tint (tint) **1** a light variety of a color: *The dress was striped in tints of blue.* **2** a delicate or pale color. **3** put a tint on; color slightly: *The walls were tinted grey.* 1, 2 *n.*, 3 *v.*

tin·ware (tin′wer′) articles made of or lined with tin. *n.*

ti·ny (tī′nē) very small; wee: *a tiny baby chicken. adj.*, **ti·ni·er, ti·ni·est.**

–tion a suffix meaning: **1** the act or process of ____ing: *Addition means the act or process of adding.* **2** the condition of being ____ed: *Exhaustion means the condition of being exhausted.* **3** the result of ____ing: *Reflection means the result of reflecting.*

tip¹ (tip) **1** the end part; end: *the tips of the fingers.* **2** a small piece put on the end of something: *Buy rubber tips to put on the legs of the stool.* **3** put a tip on; furnish with a tip: *spears tipped with steel.* **4** cover or adorn at the tip: *mountains tipped with snow. Sunlight tips the steeple.* 1, 2 *n.*, 3, 4 *v.*, **tipped, tip·ping.**

tip² (tip) **1** slope; slant: *She tipped the table toward her.* **2** a slope or slant: *There is such a tip to that table that everything slips off it.* **3** upset; overturn: *We fell in the water when the canoe tipped.* **4** take off a hat in greeting: *Men used to tip their hats when meeting a lady.* **5** empty out; dump: *She tipped the money from her purse onto the table.* 1, 3–5 *v.*, **tipped, tip·ping;** 2 *n.*

tip³ (tip) **1** a small present of money in return for service: *He gave the waiter a tip.* **2** give a small present of money to: *Did you tip the porter?* **3** a piece of secret information: *He had a tip that the black horse would win the race.* **4** a useful hint, suggestion, etc.: *Father gave me a helpful tip about pitching the tent where trees would shade it.* 1, 3, 4 *n.*, 2 *v.*, **tipped, tip·ping.**
tip off, *Informal.* **a** give secret information to: *They tipped me off about a good bargain.* **b** warn: *Someone tipped off the criminal and he escaped before the police arrived.*

tip·sy (tip′sē) **1** tipping easily; unsteady. **2** somewhat intoxicated but not completely drunk. *adj.*, **tip·si·er, tip·si·est.**

tip·toe (tip′tō′) **1** the tips of the toes. **2** walk on one's toes, without using the heels: *She tiptoed quietly up the stairs.* 1 *n.*, 2 *v.*, **tip·toed, tip·toe·ing.**
on tiptoe a walking on one's toes. **b** eager: *The children were on tiptoe for vacation to begin.* **c** in a secret manner.

tip·top (tip′top′) **1** the very top; the highest point. **2** *Informal.* first-rate; excellent. 1 *n.*, 2 *adj.*

tire¹ (tīr) **1** lower or use up the strength of; make weary: *The long walk tired her.* **2** become weary: *The old lady tires easily.* **3** wear down the patience or interest of: *Dull filing jobs tired the office boy. v.*, **tired, tir·ing.**

tire² (tīr) **1** a circular tube made of rubber, nylon, etc. and filled with air, for placing around the wheel of a truck, plane, bicycle, etc.: *Some tires have inner tubes for holding the air; others are tubeless.* **2** a band of rubber or metal around a wheel: *We had a bumpy ride on a wagon with steel tires. n.*

tired (tīrd) weary; wearied; exhausted: *The team was tired, but each boy continued to play as hard as he could. adj.*
tired of, no longer interested in; bored with: *I'm tired of hearing about their holidays.*

tire·less (tīr′lis) **1** never becoming tired; requiring little rest: *a tireless worker.* **2** never stopping: *tireless efforts. adj.*

tire·some (tīr′səm) tiring because not interesting: *a tiresome speech. adj.*

'tis (tiz) it is.

tis·sue (tish′ü) **1** a mass of similar cells forming some part of an animal or plant: *The teacher showed pictures of muscle tissues, brain tissues, and skin tissues.* **2** a thin, light cloth: *Her dress was of silk tissue.* **3** a web or network: *Her whole story was a tissue of lies.* **4** tissue paper. **5** a thin, soft paper that absorbs moisture easily: *toilet tissue, cleansing tissue.* **6** a piece or a sheet of this paper: *There are 450 tissues in each box. n.*

tissue paper very thin, soft paper used for wrapping or covering things.

tit·bit (tit′bit′) tidbit. *n.*

ti·tle (tī′təl) **1** the name of a book, poem, picture, song, etc. **2** a name showing a person's rank, occupation, or condition in life: *King, Duke, Captain, Doctor, Professor, Madame, and Miss are titles. The first letter in titles is capitalized.* **3** the first-place position; a championship: *He won the tennis title at school.* **4** a legal right to the possession of property: *When a house is sold, the seller gives title to the buyer. n.*

title page the page at the front of a book that gives its title, the name of its author, etc.

tit·ter (tit′ər) 1 laugh or giggle in a partly-checked way: *Some people in the audience tittered nervously when the actor forgot his lines.* 2 such a laugh or giggle: *A titter ran through the classroom.* 3 say with such a laugh or giggle: *'He's got his sweater on inside out,' she tittered.* 1, 3 *v.*, 2 *n.*

to (tü; *unstressed,* tu̇ or tə) 1 in the direction of: *Go to the right.* 2 as far as; until: *This apple is rotten to the core. He was faithful to his country to the end.* 3 for the purpose of; for: *Mother came to the rescue.* 4 into: *She tore the letter to pieces.* 5 along with; with: *He sang to his guitar.* 6 compared with: *Those dogs are as different as black is to white. The score was 9 to 5.* 7 in agreement with: *Going without food is not to my liking.* 8 belonging with; of: *the key to my room.* 9 on; against: *Fasten it to the wall.* 10 about; concerning: *What did he say to that?* 11 in: *four glasses to the litre.* 12 To is used to show action toward: *Give the book to me.* 13 To is used with verbs: *John likes to read.* 14 forward: *He wore his cap wrong side to.* 15 together; touching; closed: *The door slammed to.* 16 to action or work: *We turned to gladly.* 17 to consciousness: *She came to.* 1–13 *prep.,* 14–17 *adv.*
to and fro, first one way and then back again; back and forth.

☛ **To, too,** and **two** are sometimes pronounced the same.

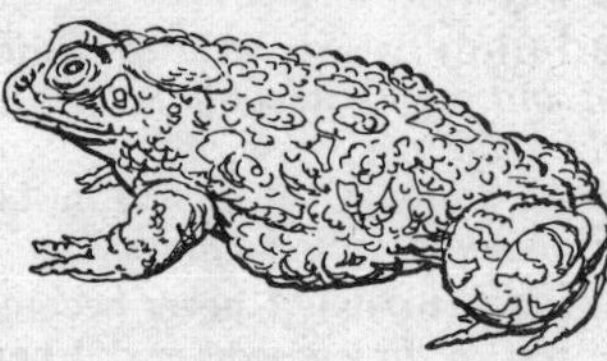
A common toad — usually about 9 cm long

toad (tōd) a small animal somewhat like a frog, that lives most of the time on land rather than in water: *Toads, which are found in gardens, have a rough, brown skin that suggests a lump of earth.* *n.*

toad·stool (tōd′stül′) a mushroom, especially a poisonous mushroom. *n.*

toast¹ (tōst) 1 a slice or slices of bread browned by heat. 2 brown by heat: *We toasted the bread.* 3 heat thoroughly: *He toasted his feet before the open fire.* 1 *n.,* 2, 3 *v.*

toast² (tōst) 1 take a drink and wish good fortune to; drink to the health of: *The men toasted the general.* 2 a person or thing whose health is proposed and drunk: *'The Queen' was the first toast drunk by the officers.* 3 a person having many admirers: *She used to be the toast of the town.* 4 the act of drinking to the health of a person or thing. 1 *v.,* 2–4 *n.*

☛ The word **toast** was first used around 1700 for a lady whose health was drunk. Saying the lady's name was supposed to add to the drink as much flavor as the spices that were often added to hot wine.

toast·er (tōs′tər) a device for toasting bread: *She bought an electric toaster.* *n.*

to·bac·co (tə bak′ō) 1 the prepared leaves of certain plants, used for smoking or chewing or as snuff. 2 one of these plants. *n., pl.* **to·bac·cos** or **to·bac·coes.**

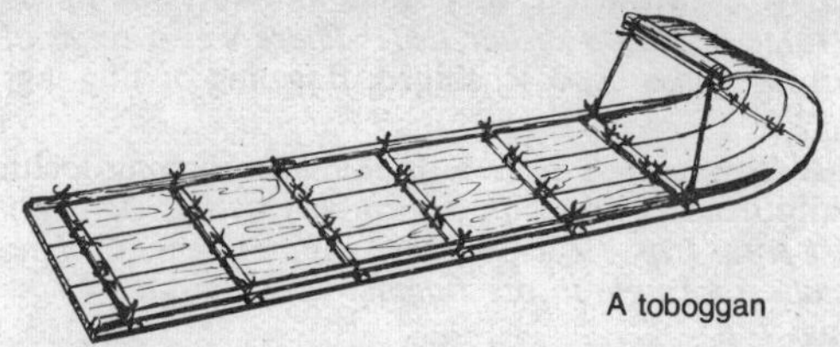
A toboggan

to·bog·gan (tə bog′ən) 1 a long, narrow, flat sled with its front end curved upward and without runners. 2 slide downhill on such a sled: *We all went tobogganing on New Year's Day.* 1 *n.,* 2 *v.*

☛ **Toboggan** came into English from a Canadian French word which was taken from a North American Indian word *tobagun,* meaning 'handsled.'

to·day or **to–day** (tə dā′) 1 this day; the present time: *Today is Wednesday.* 2 on or during this day: *What are you doing today?* 3 at the present time; in these times; now: *Many girls wear their hair cut in short curls today.* 1 *n.,* 2, 3 *adv.*

tod·dle (tod′əl) walk with short, unsteady steps, as a baby does. *v.,* **tod·dled, tod·dling.**

to–do (tə dü′) *Informal.* fuss; flurry; excitement: *There was a great to–do when the new puppy arrived.* *n., pl.* **to-dos.**

toe (tō) 1 one of the five end parts of the foot. 2 the part of a stocking, shoe, etc. that covers the toes. 3 anything like a toe. 4 touch or reach with the toes: *Toe this line.* 1–3 *n.,* 4 *v.,* **toed, toe·ing.**

☛ **Toe** and **tow** are pronounced the same.

toe·nail (tō′nāl′) the nail growing on a toe. *n.*

tof·fee (tof′ē) taffy. *n.*

to·ga (tō′gə) 1 in ancient Rome, the loose, flowing outer garment worn by citizens: *A toga was made of a single piece of cloth with no sleeves or armholes, covering the whole body except for the right arm.* 2 a robe of office. *n.*

to·geth·er (tə geᴛʜ′ər) 1 in company; with each other: *The girls were walking together.* 2 into one gathering, company, mass, or body: *The pastor called the people together. The woman will sew these pieces together and make a dress.* 3 at the same time: *You cannot have day and night together.* 4 without a stop or break; continuously: *He reads for hours together.* *adv.*

togs (togz) *Informal.* clothes. *n. pl.*

toil (toil) 1 hard work; labor: *to succeed finally after years of toil.* 2 work hard: *to toil with one's hands for a living.* 3 move with difficulty, pain, or weariness: *Carrying heavy loads, they toiled up the mountain.* 1 *n.,* 2, 3 *v.*

toi·let (toi′lit) 1 bathroom. 2 a porcelain bowl with a seat attached and with a drain at the bottom to flush the bowl clean: *Waste matter from the body is disposed of in a toilet.* 3 the process of washing, dressing, and grooming oneself: *She took an hour to complete her toilet.* 4 of or for use in the process of dressing and grooming: *Combs and brushes are toilet articles.*

toil·some (toil′səm) requiring hard work; laborious: *a long, toilsome climb up the mountain.* *adj.*

hat, āge, fär; let, ēqual, tėrm; it, īce
hot, ōpen, ôrder; oil, out; cup, pu̇t, rüle
əbove, takən, pencəl, lemən, circəs
ch, child; ng, long; sh, ship
th, thin; ᴛʜ, then; zh, measure

to·ken (tō′kən) **1** a mark or sign of something: *Black is a token of mourning.* **2** a sign of friendship; keepsake: *She received many birthday tokens.* **3** a piece of metal, plastic, etc. stamped for a higher value than that of the material: *Tokens are used on some buses and trains instead of money.* **4** a piece of metal, plastic, etc. indicating a right or privilege: *This token will admit you to the swimming pool.* *n.*

told (tōld) See **tell.** *You told me that last week. We were told to wait.* *v.*

tol·er·a·ble (tol′ər ə bəl) **1** that can be endured: *The pain has become tolerable.* **2** fairly good: *She is in tolerable health.* *adj.*

tol·er·ance (tol′ər əns) willingness to be tolerant and patient toward people whose opinions or ways differ from one's own. *n.*

tol·er·ant (tol′ər ənt) willing to let other people do as they think best; willing to allow beliefs and actions of which one does not approve: *A more tolerant person would not have walked out in the middle of the meeting.* *adj.*

tol·er·ate (tol′ər āt′) **1** allow; permit: *The teacher won't tolerate any disorder.* **2** bear; endure; put up with: *They tolerated the grouchy old man only because he was their employer.* *v.*, **tol·er·at·ed, tol·er·at·ing.**

toll[1] (tōl) **1** sound with single strokes slowly and regularly repeated: *Bells were tolled all over the country at the King's death.* **2** the stroke or sound of a bell being tolled. 1 *v.*, 2 *n.*

toll[2] (tōl) **1** a tax or fee paid for some right or privilege: *We pay a toll when we use that bridge.* **2** a charge for a certain service: *There is a toll on long-distance telephone calls.* **3** something paid, lost, suffered, etc.: *Automobile accidents take a heavy toll of human lives.* *n.*

tom (tom) the male of some animals; male: *a tom turkey. This cat is a tom.* *n.*

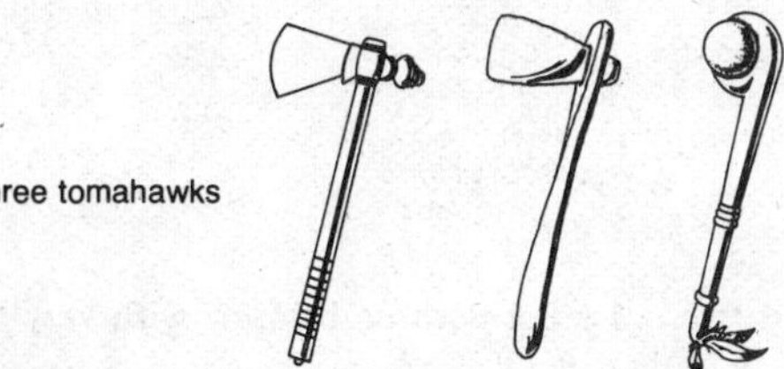
Three tomahawks

tom·a·hawk (tom′ə hok′ or tom′ə hôk′) a light axe used by North American Indians as a weapon and as a tool. *n.*

to·ma·to (tə mā′tō or tə mä′tō) **1** a juicy fruit used as a vegetable: *Most tomatoes are red, but some kinds are yellow.* **2** the plant it grows on: *Tomato plants have hairy leaves and stems, and small, yellow flowers.* *n., pl.* **to·ma·toes.**

tomb (tüm) a grave, vault, etc. for a dead body, often above ground. *n.*

tom·boy (tom′boi′) a girl who is more active and enjoys rougher games than most girls. *n.*

tomb·stone (tüm′stōn′) a stone that marks a tomb or grave. *n.*

tom·cat (tom′kat′) a male cat. *n.*

to·mor·row or **to–mor·row** (tə môr′ō) **1** the day after today. **2** on the day after today. 1 *n.*, 2 *adv.*

tom–tom (tom′tom′) a drum, usually beaten with the hands: *Tom-toms are used to dance to and for sending signals in Africa and among the American Indians.* *n.*

ton (tun) a measure of weight. In Canada and the United States, a ton is 2000 pounds **(short ton),** equal to approximately 907.18 kilograms. In England, a ton is 2240 pounds **(long ton),** equal to approximately 1016.05 kilograms. A **metric ton (tonne)** is 1000 kilograms. *n.*
☛ Ton and tonne are pronounced the same.

tone (tōn) **1** any sound considered with reference to its quality, pitch, strength, source, etc.: *low, angry, or gentle tones, the deep tone of the organ.* **2** the quality of sound: *Her voice was silvery in tone.* **3** in music, **a** a sound of definite pitch and character. **b** the difference in pitch between two notes: *C and D are one tone apart.* **4** a manner of speaking or writing: *We disliked the haughty tone of her letter.* **5** spirit; character; style: *A tone of quiet elegance prevails in her home.* **6** a normal, healthy condition; vigor. **7** the effect of color and of light and shade in a picture: *I like the soft green tone of that painting.* **8** a shade of color: *The room is furnished in tones of brown.* **9** harmonize: *This rug tones in well with the wallpaper and furniture.* 1–8 *n.*, 9 *v.*, **toned, ton·ing.**

tone down, soften: *Tone down your voice. Tone down the colors in that painting.*

tone up, give more sound, color, or vigor to; to strengthen: *Bright curtains would tone up this dull room.*

tongs (tongz) a tool for holding or lifting: *He changed the position of the burning log with the tongs.* See **fireplace** for picture. *n. pl.*

tongue (tung) **1** the movable fleshy organ in the lower part of the mouth: *The tongue is used in tasting and, by people, for talking.* **2** an animal's tongue used as food: *Father likes cold tongue and salad.* **3** the power of speech: *Have you lost your tongue?* **4** a way of speaking; speech; talk: *Beware of that man's flattering tongue.* **5** the language of a people: *the English tongue.* **6** something shaped or used like a tongue: *tongues of flame.* **7** the strip under the laces of a shoe. *n.*

hold one's tongue, keep silent: *Please hold your tongue while I'm speaking!*

on the tip of one's tongue, a almost spoken. **b** ready to be spoken.

tongue–tied (tung′tīd′) unable to speak because of shyness, embarrassment, etc. *adj.*

ton·ic (ton′ik) **1** anything that gives strength; a medicine to give strength: *Cod-liver oil is a tonic.* **2** giving strength; bracing: *The mountain air is tonic.* 1 *n.*, 2 *adj.*

to·night or **to–night** (tə nīt′) **1** the night of this day; this night or evening: *I wish tonight would come.* **2** on or during this night or evening: *Do you think it will snow tonight?* 1 *n.*, 2 *adv.*

ton·nage (tun′ij) **1** the carrying capacity of a ship.

2 the total of ships in tons: *the tonnage of Canada's navy.* 3 weight in tons. *n.*

tonne (tun) a measure of mass, equal to one thousand kilograms. *Symbol:* t *n.*

☛ **Tonne** and **ton** are pronounced the same.

ton·sil (ton′səl) either of the two small, oval masses of tissue on the sides of the throat, just back of the mouth. See **adenoids** for picture. *n.*

ton·sil·li·tis (ton′sə lī′tis) a diseased condition of the tonsils, making them red, swollen, and painful. *n.*

too (tü) 1 also; besides: *The dog is hungry, and thirsty too. We, too, are going away.* 2 more than what is proper or enough: *My dress is too long for you. He ate too much. The summer passed too quickly.* 3 very; exceedingly: *I am only too glad to help you. It doesn't hurt too much. adv.*

☛ **Too** and **two** are pronounced the same. **Two** and **to** are sometimes pronounced the same.

took (tu̇k) See **take.** *She took the car an hour ago. v.*

tool (tül) 1 a knife, hammer, saw, shovel, or any instrument used in doing work: *Plumbers, mechanics, carpenters, and shoemakers need tools.* 2 any thing used to achieve some purpose: *Books are a student's tools.* 3 a person used by another like a tool: *He is a tool of the boss.* 4 use a tool on; work or shape with a tool: *He tooled beautiful designs in the leather with a knife.* 1–3 *n.*, 4 *v.*

toot (tüt) 1 the sound of a horn, whistle, etc. 2 give forth a short blast of sound: *He heard the train toot three times.* 3 sound a horn, whistle, etc. in short blasts. 1 *n.*, 2, 3 *v.*

tooth (tüth) 1 one of the hard, bonelike parts in the mouth, used for biting and chewing. See **teeth** for picture. 2 something like a tooth: *Each one of the projecting parts of a comb, rake, or saw is a tooth. n., pl.* **teeth.**

fight tooth and nail, fight fiercely, with all one's force.

tooth·ache (tüth′āk′) a pain in a tooth or the teeth. *n.*

tooth·brush (tüth′brush′) a small brush for cleaning the teeth. *n.*

tooth·paste (tüth′pāst′) a paste for use in cleaning the teeth. *n.*

tooth·pick (tüth′pik′) a small, pointed piece of wood, plastic, etc. for removing bits of food from between the teeth. *n.*

top[1] (top) 1 the highest point or part: *the top of a mountain.* 2 the upper end or surface: *a shoe top, the top of the table.* 3 the highest or leading place, rank, etc.: *He is at the top of his class.* 4 the highest point, pitch, or degree: *The boy was yelling at the top of his voice.* 5 the part of a plant that grows above ground: *Beet tops are somewhat like spinach.* 6 the head: *She was dressed in brown from top to toe.* 7 having to do with, situated at, or forming the top: *the top shelf.* 8 highest; greatest: *The runners set off at top speed.* 9 put a top on: *to top a box.* 10 be on top of; be the top of: *A church tops the hill.* 11 reach the top of: *Call me when you see a grey car topping the hill.* 12 rise high; rise above: *The sun topped the horizon.* 13 be higher or greater than. 14 do better than; outdo; excel: *His story topped all the rest.* 15 remove the top part of a plant, tree, etc. 1–6 *n.*, 7, 8 *adj.*, 9–15 *v.*, **topped, top·ping.**

Spinning tops

top[2] (top) a toy that spins on a point. *n.*

to·paz (tō′paz) a mineral that occurs in crystals of various forms and colors: *Yellow topaz is used as a gem. n.*

top·ic (top′ik) a subject that people think, write, or talk about: *The main topics at Mother's dinner party were the weather and the election. n.*

top·knot (top′not′) a knot of hair or a tuft of feathers on the top of the head. *n.*

top·mast (top′mast′ or top′məst) the second section of a mast above the deck. *n.*

top·most (top′mōst′) highest: *The best cherries always seem to grow on the topmost branches. adj.*

top·ple (top′əl) 1 fall forward; tumble down: *The chimney toppled over on the roof.* 2 throw over or down; overturn. *v.*, **top·pled, top·pling.**

top·sail (top′sāl′ or top′səl) the second sail above the deck on a mast. *n.*

top·soil (top′soil′) surface soil suitable for growing plants in: *People buy topsoil for gardens and lawns. n.*

top·sy–tur·vy (top′sē tėr′vē) 1 upside down. 2 in confusion or disorder: *Her room was always topsy-turvy because she never put anything away. adv., adj.*

Two kinds of toque

toque (tōk) 1 a hat with no brim or with very little brim. 2 tuque. *n.*

☛ **Toque** comes from a French word of the same spelling, which came through Spanish from a Basque word *tauka,* meaning a certain kind of cap.

to·rah or **to·ra** (tô′rə) 1 in Jewish usage, a doctrine, teaching, or law. 2 **the Torah,** the law of Moses; the first five books of the Old Testament. *n.*

torch (tôrch) 1 a light to be carried around or stuck in a holder on a wall: *A piece of pine wood or anything that burns easily makes a good torch.* 2 a device for producing a very hot flame, used especially to burn off paint, to solder metal, and to melt metal. *n.*

tore (tôr) See **tear**[2]. *Yesterday she tore her dress on a nail. v.*

tor·ment (tôr ment′ for 1 and 4, tôr′ment for 2 and 3) 1 cause very great pain to: *Headaches tormented him.* 2 a cause of very great pain: *A bad burn can be a torment.* 3 very great pain: *He suffered torments from his aching teeth.* 4 worry or annoy very much: *That boy torments with silly questions.* 1, 4 *v.*, 2, 3 *n.*

hat, āge, fär; let, ēqual, tėrm; it, īce
hot, ōpen, ôrder; oil, out; cup, pu̇t, rüle
əbove, takən, pencəl, lemən, circəs
ch, child; ng, long; sh, ship
th, thin; ᴛʜ, then; zh, measure

tor·men·tor or **tor·men·ter** (tôr men′tər) a person who torments. *n.*

torn (tôrn) See **tear**[2]. *He has torn up the plant by the roots. His coat was old and torn. v.*

tor·na·do (tôr nā′dō) a violent and destructive whirlwind: *A tornado moves forward as a whirling funnel extending down from dark clouds. n., pl.* **tor·na·does** or **tor·na·dos.**

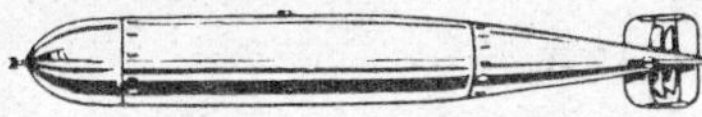

A torpedo. When it is launched from a ship, aircraft, etc., it travels much like a small ship. It contains a motor and devices for controlling its course and depth.

tor·pe·do (tôr pē′dō) **1** a large, cigar-shaped metal tube that contains explosives and travels through water by its own power. **2** attack or destroy with a torpedo or torpedoes. **3** an explosive put on a railway track to make a loud noise as a signal when a wheel of a locomotive runs over it. **4** a kind of firework that explodes when it is thrown against something hard. 1, 3, 4 *n., pl.* **tor·pe·does;** 2 *v.,* **tor·pe·doed, tor·pe·do·ing.**

tor·pid (tôr′pid) **1** inactive; sluggish. **2** not moving or feeling: *Animals that hibernate become torpid in the winter. adj.*

tor·rent (tôr′ənt) **1** a violent, rushing stream of water: *The mountain torrent dashed over the rocks.* **2** any violent, rushing stream; a flood: *a torrent of lava from a volcano, a torrent of questions. n.*

tor·rid (tôr′id) **1** very hot: *July is usually a torrid month.* **2** the **Torrid Zone** is the very warm region between the two temperate zones; the tropics: *The equator divides the Torrid Zone in half.* See **zone** for diagram. *adj.*

tor·toise (tôr′təs) a turtle, especially a land turtle. *n., pl.* **tor·tois·es** or **tor·toise.**

tor·ture (tôr′chər) **1** the act of inflicting very severe pain: *Torture used to be widely used to make people give evidence about crimes, or to make them confess.* **2** very severe pain: *She suffered torture from a toothache.* **3** cause very severe pain to: *That cruel boy tortures animals.* 1, 2 *n.,* 3 *v.,* **tor·tured, tor·tur·ing.**

To·ry (tô′rē) **1** Conversative; Progressive Conservative. **2** of or having to do with a Conservative or the Conservative party: *Tory policies.* 1 *n., pl.* **To·ries;** 2 *adj.*

toss (tos) **1** throw lightly with the palm of the hand upward; cast; fling: *She tossed the ball to the baby.* **2** throw about; roll or pitch about: *The ship is tossed by the waves. He tossed on his bed all night.* **3** lift quickly; throw upward: *She tossed her head. He was tossed by the bull.* **4** mix lightly: *toss a salad.* **5** throw a coin to decide something by the side that falls upward. **6** a throw; tossing: *A toss of a coin decided who should play first.* 1–5 *v.,* 6 *n.*

tot (tot) a little child. *n.*

to·tal (tō′təl) **1** whole; entire: *The total cost of the house and land will be $25 000.* **2** the whole amount: *His expenses reached a total of $100. Add the different sums to get the total.* **3** find the sum of; add: *Total that column of figures.* **4** reach an amount of; amount to: *The money spent yearly on chewing gum totals millions of dollars.* **5** complete; absolute: *The lights went out and we were in total darkness.* 1, 5 *adj.,* 2 *n.,* 3, 4 *v.,* **to·talled** or **to·taled, to·tal·ling** or **to·tal·ing.** —**to′tal·ly,** *adv.*

tote (tōt) *Informal.* carry; haul: *I had to tote all the stuff home by myself. v.,* **tot·ed, tot·ing.**

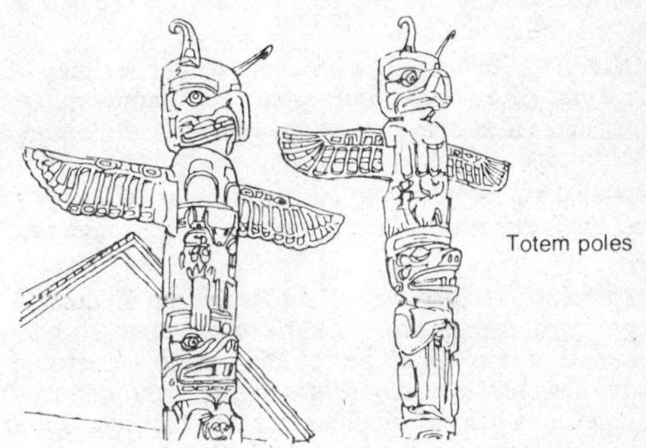

Totem poles

to·tem (tō′təm) **1** a natural object, often an animal, taken as the emblem of a tribe, clan, or family. **2** the image of such an object: *Totems are often carved and painted on poles. n.*

tot·ter (tot′ər) **1** walk with shaky, unsteady steps: *The baby tottered three steps all by herself.* **2** be unsteady; shake as if about to fall: *The old wall tottered in the wind and fell. v.*

touch (tuch) **1** put the hand or some other part of the body on or against and feel: *She touched the pan to see whether it was still hot.* **2** put one thing against another: *He touched the post with his umbrella.* **3** be against; come against: *Your sleeve is touching the butter.* **4** touching or being touched: *A bubble bursts at a touch. The touch of a snake makes her shrink.* **5** the sense by which a person perceives things by feeling, handling, or coming against them: *The blind develop a keen touch.* **6** communication or connection: *A newspaper keeps one in touch with the world. He has been out of touch with his mother since he left home.* **7** a slight amount; a little bit: *We had a touch of frost.* **8** a stroke with a brush, pencil, pen, etc.; a detail: *The artist finished my picture with a few touches.* **9** strike lightly or gently: *She touched the strings of the harp.* **10** injure slightly: *The flowers were touched by the frost.* **11** affect with some feeling: *The poor woman's sad story touched our hearts.* **12** have to do with; concern: *The matter touches your interests.* **13** reach; come up to: *His head almost touches the top of the doorway. Nobody in our class can touch her in music.* **14** the act or manner of playing a musical instrument: *The girl playing the piano has an excellent touch.* **15** a distinctive manner or quality: *The work showed an expert's touch.* 1–3, 9–13 *v.,* 4–8, 14, 15 *n.*

touch down, land an airplane: *The passenger plane*

touched down at Gander airport.
touch on or **upon,** speak of; treat lightly: *Our conversation touched on many subjects.*
touch up, change a little; improve: *He touched up the photograph.*

touch·down (tuch′doun′) **1** in football, the act of a player possessing the ball on or behind the opponents' goal line. **2** the score made in this way. **3** the landing of an aircraft: *The pilot made an unexpected touchdown because of engine trouble. n.*

touch football a game having rules similar to those of football except that the person carrying the ball is touched rather than tackled.

touch·ing (tuch′ing) **1** arousing tender feeling: *'A Christmas Carol' is a touching story.* **2** concerning; about: *He asked many questions touching my home and school. adj.*

touch·y (tuch′ē) apt to take offence at trifles: *He is tired and very touchy this afternoon. adj.,* **touch·i·er, touch·i·est.**

tough (tuf) **1** bending without breaking: *Leather is tough; cardboard is not.* **2** hard to cut, tear, or chew: *The steak was so tough he couldn't eat it.* **3** strong; hardy: *Donkeys are tough little animals and can carry big loads.* **4** hard; difficult: *Dragging the load uphill was tough work for the horses.* **5** hard to influence; stubborn: *a tough customer.* **6** rough; disorderly: *He lived in a tough neighborhood.* **7** a rough person: *A gang of toughs attacked the policeman.* 1–6 *adj.,* 7 *n.*

tough·en (tuf′ən) **1** make tough: *He toughened his muscles by doing exercises.* **2** become tough: *His muscles finally toughened. v.*

tour (tür) **1** travel from place to place: *Many people tour by car every summer.* **2** a long journey: *The family made a tour through Europe.* **3** travel through: *Last year they toured Mexico.* **4** a short journey; a walk around: *The children made a tour of the ship.* **5** walk around in: *The children will tour the museum.* 1, 3, 5 *v.,* 2, 4 *n.*

tour·ist (tür′ist or tůr′ist) a person travelling for pleasure. *n. n.*

tour·na·ment (tėr′nə mənt or tür′nə mənt) **1** a series of contests testing the skill of many persons: *a golf tournament. His uncle won the bridge tournament.* **2** in the Middle Ages, a contest between two groups of knights on horseback who fought for a prize. *n.*

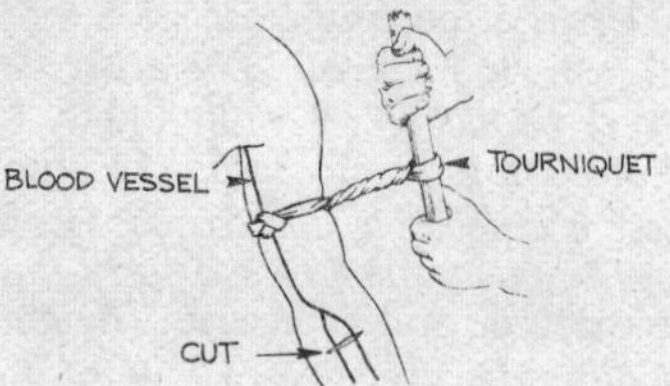

tour·ni·quet (tür′nə ket′ or tür′nə kā′) a device for stopping bleeding by compressing a blood vessel, such as a bandage tightened by twisting with a stick. *n.*

tou·sle (tou′zəl) put into disorder; muss; make untidy: *He tousled his hair in the game. v.,* **tou·sled, tou·sling.**

tow¹ (tō) **1** pull by a rope, chain, etc.: *The tug is towing three barges.* **2** the act of towing. **3** the condition of being towed: *The launch had the sailboat in tow.* **4** what is towed: *Each tug had a tow of three barges.* **5** the rope, chain, etc. used for towing. 1 *v.,* 2–5 *n.*
☛ **Tow** and **toe** are pronounced the same.

tow² (tō) the coarse and broken fibres of flax, hemp, etc., prepared for spinning: *This string is made of tow. n.*
☛ See note at **tow¹**.

to·ward (tôrd or tə wôrd′) **1** in the direction of: *He walked toward the north.* **2** with respect to; about; concerning: *What is his attitude toward war?* **3** near: *It must be toward four o'clock.* **4** as a help to; for: *Will you give something toward our new hospital? prep.*

to·wards (tôrdz or tə wôrdz′) toward. *prep.*

tow·el (tou′əl) a piece of cloth or paper for wiping and drying something wet: *hand towels, bath towels, dish towels. n.*

tow·er (tou′ər) **1** a high structure that may stand alone or form part of a church, castle, or other building: *Some towers are forts or prisons.* **2** a defence; protection. **3** rise high up: *The boy towered over his baby brother.* **4** a person or thing that is like a tower in some way: *The defenceman was a tower of strength to the team.* 1, 2, 4 *n.,* 3 *v.*

tow·er·ing (tou′ər ing) **1** very high: *a towering peak.* **2** very great: *Making electricity from atomic power is a towering achievement.* **3** very violent: *a towering rage. adj.*

town (toun) **1** a large group of houses and other buildings, having fixed boundaries and its own local government: *A town is usually smaller than a city but larger than a village.* **2** any large place with many people living it in: *Father says Moose Jaw is a fine town.* **3** the people of a town: *The whole town was having a holiday. n.*

town hall a building used for a town's business.

town·ship (toun′ship) in Canada and the United States, a part of a county having certain powers of government; municipality. *n.*

tox·ic (tok′sik) poisonous: *Fumes from an automobile exhaust are toxic. adj.*

toy (toi) **1** something for a child to play with; a plaything. **2** something that has little value or importance. **3** of, made as, or like a toy. **4** amuse oneself; play; trifle: *She toyed with her beads. He toyed with the idea of writing a book, but he did nothing about it.* **5** small; tiny: *a toy poodle.* 1, 2 *n.,* 3, 5 *adj.,* 4 *v.*

trace¹ (trās) **1** a sign or evidence of the existence, presence, or action of something in the past: *The explorer found traces of an ancient city.* **2** a footprint or other mark left; track; trail: *We saw traces of rabbits and squirrels on the snow.* **3** follow by means of marks, tracks, or signs: *The dog traced the fox to its den.* **4** follow the course of; follow a trail of evidence to: *He traced the river to its source. He traced his family back through eight generations.* **5** mark out; draw: *The spy traced a plan of the fort.* **6** copy by following the lines of with a pencil or pen: *He put thin paper over the map and traced it.* **7** a very small amount; a little bit: *There was not a trace of color in her cheeks.* 1, 2, 7 *n.,* 3–6 *v.,* **traced, trac·ing.**

hat, āge, fär; let, ēqual, tėrm; it, īce
hot, ōpen, ôrder; oil, out; cup, pu̇t, rüle
əbove, takən, pencəl, lemən, circəs
ch, child; ng, long; sh, ship
th, thin; ŦH, then; zh, measure

trace[2] (trās) either of the two straps, ropes, or chains by which an animal pulls a wagon, carriage, etc. See **harness** for picture. *n.*

tra·che·a (trā′kē ə) the windpipe. *n., pl.* **tra·che·ae** (trā′kē ē).

trac·ing (trās′ing) a copy of something made by putting thin paper over it and following the lines with a pencil or pen. *n.*

track (trak) 1 a line of metal rails for cars to run on: *A railway has tracks.* 2 a mark left: *The dirt road showed many automobile tracks.* 3 a footprint: *We saw a wild animal's tracks near the camp.* 4 follow by means of footprints, marks, smell, etc.: *The hunter tracked the bear and killed it.* 5 trace in any way: *track down a criminal.* 6 make footprints or other marks on: *Don't track the floor with your muddy feet.* 7 a path or trail: *A track runs through the woods to the farmhouse.* 8 a course for running or racing: *a race track, a cinder track.* 9 the sport made up of contests in running: *My older brother has gone out for track this year.* See **track and field.** 10 an endless belt of linked steel treads by which a tank, bulldozer, etc. is driven forward. 1–3, 7–10 *n.,* 4–6 *v.* **—track′less,** *adj.*

keep track of, keep within one's sight, knowledge, or attention: *The noise of the crowd made it difficult to keep track of what was going on.*

make tracks, *Informal.* go very fast; run away.

off the track, wrong; off the subject.

on the track, right; on the subject.

track and field the sports of running, jumping, pole-vaulting, throwing, etc. considered as a group: *John doesn't play hockey, but he's good at track and field. Joan entered several track and field events.*

tract[1] (trakt) 1 a stretch of land, water, etc.; an area: *A tract of desert land has little value to farmers.* 2 a system of related parts or organs in the body: *The stomach and intestines are parts of the digestive tract.* *n.*

tract[2] (trakt) 1 a little book or pamphlet on a religious topic. 2 any book or pamphlet that strongly supports a point of view. *n.*

trac·tion (trak′shən) 1 the power used in drawing or pulling: *Electric traction is used on some railways.* 2 the friction between a body and the surface on which it moves: *Wheels slip on ice because there is too little traction.* *n.*

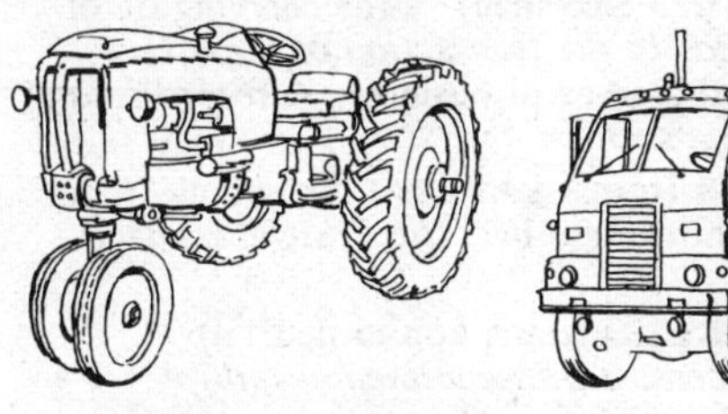

A tractor (def. 1)

A tractor (def. 2)

trac·tor (trak′tər) 1 an engine used to pull wagons, ploughs, etc. on a farm. 2 a powerful truck having a short body and a cab for the driver, used to pull a trailer along the highway. *n.*

trade (trād) 1 the process of buying and selling; the exchange of goods; commerce: *Canada has much trade with foreign countries.* 2 buy and sell; exchange goods; be in commerce: *Some Canadian companies trade all over the world. The settlers traded with the native tribes.* 3 make an exchange: *The boys traded seats. He traded a stick of gum for a ride on her bicycle.* 4 an exchange: *an even trade.* 5 *Informal.* a bargain; deal: *He made a good trade.* 6 a kind of work; a business, especially one requiring skilled work: *He is learning the carpenter's trade.* 1, 4–6 *n.,* 2, 3 *v.,* **trad·ed, trad·ing.**

trade in, give an automobile, radio, etc. as part payment for something.

trade on, take advantage of: *She traded on her father's good name.*

trade–in (trād′in′) something given or accepted as part payment for something else. *n.*

trade·mark (trād′märk′) a mark, picture, name, symbol, or letters owned and used by a manufacturer or merchant to distinguish his goods. *n.*

trad·er (trā′dər) 1 a person who trades: *The trappers sold fur to traders.* 2 a ship used in trading: *a slave trader.* 3 an item of which a collector has another copy; a duplicate: *He offered traders for stamps he didn't have.* *n.*

trades·man (trādz′mən) a storekeeper; shopkeeper. *n., pl.* **trades·men** (trādz′mən).

trade wind a wind blowing steadily toward the equator: *North of the equator, the trade wind blows from the northeast; south of the equator, it blows from the southeast.*

trading post a store or station of a trader, especially in a remote place: *The Hudson's Bay Company operates trading posts in the North.*

tra·di·tion (trə dish′ən) 1 the handing down of beliefs, opinions, customs, stories, etc. from one generation to another. 2 what is handed down in this way: *Many traditions of the past are still kept today.* *n.*

tra·di·tion·al (trə dish′ən əl) 1 of tradition. 2 handed down by tradition: *The coronation is a traditional ceremony.* 3 according to tradition: *traditional furniture.* 4 customary: *It is traditional to have turkey for Thanksgiving dinner.* *adj.*

traf·fic (traf′ik) 1 the people, automobiles, wagons, ships, etc. coming and going along a way of travel: *Police control the traffic in large cities.* 2 the process of buying and selling; commerce; trade. 3 carry on trade; buy; sell; exchange: *The man trafficked with the natives for ivory.* 4 the business done by a railway, a steamship line, or an airline; the number of passengers or amount of freight carried. 1, 2, 4 *n.,* 3 *v.,* **traf·ficked, traf·fick·ing.**

traffic circle a type of intersection in which traffic from different roads moves in a single direction around a circular island.

trag·e·dy (traj′ə dē) 1 a serious play having an unhappy ending: *'Hamlet' is a tragedy.* 2 a very sad or terrible happening: *The father's death was a tragedy to his family.* *n., pl.* **trag·e·dies.**

trag·ic (traj′ik) **1** of tragedy; having to do with tragedy: *a tragic actor, a tragic poet.* **2** very sad; dreadful: *a tragic death, a tragic accident. adj.*

trail (trāl) **1** a path across a wild or unsettled region: *The men had followed mountain trails for days.* **2** a track or smell: *The dogs found the trail of the rabbit.* **3** hunt by track or smell: *The dogs trailed the rabbit.* **4** anything that follows along behind: *The car left a trail of dust behind it.* **5** follow along behind; follow: *The dog trailed its master constantly.* **6** pull or be pulled along behind: *The child trailed a toy horse after him. Her dress trails on the ground.* 1, 2, 4 *n.*, 3, 5, 6 *v.*

trail·blaz·er (trāl′blāz′ər) **1** a person who blazes a trail. **2** a person who pioneers or prepares the way to something new. *n.*

trail·er (trāl′ər) **1** a vehicle designed to be pulled along the highway by a truck, etc. See **tractor** for picture. **2** a vehicle designed to be hauled by an automobile and equipped for people to live in or for a place of business: *The 4-H Club has a trailer at the Fair. n.*

train (trān) **1** a connected line of railway cars pulled by an engine: *a very long freight train of 100 cars.* **2** a line of people, animals, wagons, trucks, etc. moving along together: *A train of snowmobiles sped across the ice.* **3** a part of a cloak or gown that trails behind the wearer: *Two attendants carried the queen's train.* **4** a group of followers: *the rodeo star and his train.* **5** a series; succession: *A train of misfortunes overcame the hero.* **6** bring up; rear; teach: *He trained his sons to respect their parents and teachers.* **7** make skilful by teaching and practice: *train women as nurses. Saint Bernard dogs were trained to hunt for travellers lost in the snow.* **8** make fit by exercise and diet: *The runners trained for races.* **9** point; aim: *to train guns upon a fort.* **10** bring into a particular position: *We trained the vines around the post.* 1–5 *n.*, 6–10 *v.* **—train′er,** *n.*
train of thought, a succession of thoughts passing through one's mind at a particular time: *Now where was I when you interrupted? I seem to have lost my train of thought.*

train·ing (trān′ing) **1** practical education in some art, profession, etc.: *training for teachers.* **2** the development of strength and endurance: *Soldiers undergo constant training to keep fit for action.* **3** a good condition maintained by exercise and care: *The athlete was advised to keep in training. n.*

trait (trāt or trā) a quality of mind or character; a feature; characteristic: *Courage and common sense are desirable traits. n.*

trai·tor (trā′tər) **1** a person who betrays his country or ruler. **2** a person who betrays a trust, a duty, or a friend. *n.*

trai·tor·ous (trā′tər əs) like a traitor; treacherous; faithless. *adj.*

tram (tram) *Esp. British.* streetcar. *n.*

tramp (tramp) **1** walk heavily: *He tramped across the floor in his heavy boots.* **2** step heavily on: *He tramped on the flowers.* **3** the sound of heavy footsteps: *I hear the tramp of the parade.* **4** walk; go on foot: *We tramped all day. It seemed as if we'd tramped for hours.* **5** a long, steady walk; a hike: *The boys took a tramp together over the hills.* **6** a person who goes about on foot, living by begging, doing odd jobs, etc.: *A tramp came to the door and asked for food.* **7** a freight ship that takes a cargo when and where it can. 1, 2, 4 *v.*, 3, 5–7 *n.*

tram·ple (tram′pəl) **1** tread heavily on; crush: *The cattle broke through the fence and trampled the farmer's crops.* **2** the act or sound of tramping: *We heard the trample of many feet.* 1 *v.*, **tram·pled, tram·pling;** 2 *n.*
trample on or **upon,** treat with scorn or cruelty: *The dictator trampled on the rights of his people.*

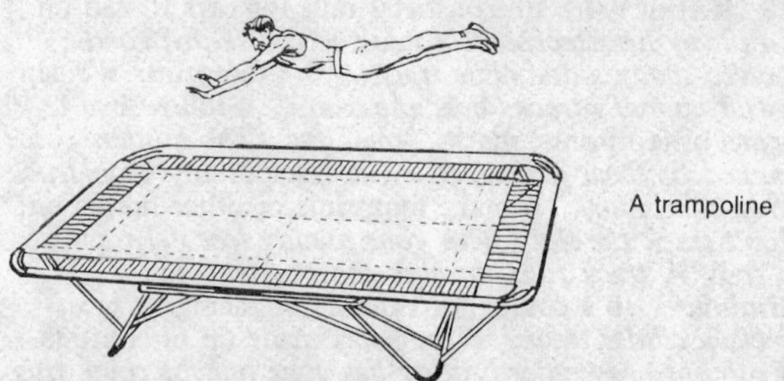
A trampoline

tram·po·line (tram′pə lēn′) an apparatus for tumbling, acrobatics, etc. consisting of a taut piece of canvas or other sturdy fabric attached by springs to a metal frame: *The boy liked to bounce around on the trampoline. n.*

trance (trans) **1** a state of unconsciousness somewhat like sleep: *A person may be in a trance from illness, from the influence of some other person, or from his own will.* **2** a dreamy, absorbed condition that is like a trance: *The old man sat before the fire in a trance, thinking about his past life. n.*

tran·quil (trang′kwəl) calm; peaceful; quiet: *the tranquil evening air. adj.,* **tran·quil·ler** or **tran·quil·er, tran·quil·lest** or **tran·quil·est.**

tran·quil·li·ty or **tran·quil·i·ty** (trang kwil′ə tē) a tranquil condition; calmness; peacefulness; quiet. *n.*

tran·quil·liz·er or **tran·quil·izer** (trang′kwəl īz′ər) any of several drugs for reducing physical or nervous tension, lowering blood pressure, etc. *n.*

trans– a prefix meaning: **1** across, over, or through, as in *transcontinental.* **2** into a different place, condition, etc., as in *transform, transfusion.*

trans·act (tran zakt′) attend to; manage; do; carry on business: *He transacts business with stores all over the country. v.*

trans·ac·tion (tran zak′shən) **1** the carrying on of business: *He attends to the transaction of important matters himself.* **2** a piece of business: *A record is kept of all the firm's transactions. n.*

trans–Can·a·da (trans′ kan′ə də) extending from one end of Canada to the other: *the Trans-Canada Highway. adj.*

trans·con·ti·nen·tal (trans′kon tə nen′təl) **1** crossing a continent: *a transcontinental railway.* **2** a train that crosses a continent: *We went from Halifax to Vancouver on the transcontinental.* **3** on the other side of a continent. 1, 3 *adj.*, 2 *n.*

trans·fer (trans fėr′ for 1, 2, and 5, trans′fėr for 3, 4, and 6) **1** convey or remove from one person or place to another; hand over: *This farm has been transferred from father to son for generations. My trunks were transferred by express.* **2** convey a drawing, design, pattern from one surface to another: *You transfer the embroidery design from the paper to cloth by pressing it*

hat, āge, fär; let, ēqual, tėrm; it, īce
hot, ōpen, ôrder; oil, out; cup, pu̇t, rüle
əbove, takən, pencəl, lemən, circəs
ch, child; ng, long; sh, ship
th, thin; ᴛʜ, then; zh, measure

with a warm iron. **3** transferring or being transferred. **4** a drawing, pattern, etc. printed or to be printed from one surface onto another. **5** change from one streetcar, bus, train, etc. to another, without having to pay another fare. **6** a ticket allowing a passenger to continue his journey on another streetcar, bus, train, etc. 1, 2, 5 *v.*, **trans·ferred, trans·fer·ring;** 3, 4, 6 *n.*

trans·form (trans fôrm′) **1** change in form or appearance: *The blizzard transformed the bushes into glittering mounds of snow.* **2** change in condition, nature, or character: *The witch transformed the men into pigs. A dynamo transforms mechanical energy into electricity.* **3** of electrical current, change to a different voltage or type. *v.*

trans·for·ma·tion (trans′fər mā′shən) transforming or being transformed: *The witch's transformation of the men into pigs was terrifying. We were amazed at the transformation of a thief into an honest man. n.*

trans·form·er (trans fôr′mər) a device for changing the voltage of an electrical current: *In Europe I will have to use a transformer for my record player because the voltage there is higher than in Canada. n.*

trans·fu·sion (trans fyü′zhən) **1** the act or process of causing something to pass from one container or holder to another. **2** the process of transferring blood from one person or animal to another. **3** the blood so transferred: *The wounded soldier was given three transfusions in a week. n.*

trans·gress (trans gres′ or tranz gres′) **1** break a law; act against a command; sin. **2** go beyond a limit or bound: *Her manners transgressed the bounds of good taste. v.*

tran·si·ent (tran′zē ənt) **1** passing soon; fleeting; not lasting: *Joy and sorrow are often transient.* **2** passing through and not staying long: *a transient guest in a hotel.* **3** a visitor or boarder who stays for a short time. 1, 2 *adj.*, 3 *n.*

tran·sis·tor (tran zis′tər) **1** a small electronic device that controls the flow of electricity, used in computers, radios, television sets, etc. **2** a portable radio that has transistors instead of tubes: *She carries her transistor wherever she goes. n.*

tran·sit (tran′sit or tran′zit) **1** passing across or through. **2** carrying or being carried across or through: *The goods were damaged in transit.* **3** transportation by trains, buses, etc.: *All systems of transit are crowded during the rush hour.* **4** an instrument used in surveying to measure angles. *n.*

tran·si·tion (tran zish′ən) a change or passing from one condition, place, thing, etc. to another: *The life of Dick Whittington illustrates a transition from poverty to power. Abrupt transitions in a book confuse the reader. n.*

trans·late (trans lāt′ or tranz lāt′) **1** change from one language into another: *to translate a book from French into English.* **2** explain the meaning of: *He translated his idea into language we could understand.* **3** change from one place, position, or condition to another: *In a second she was translated to the fairy palace. v.*, **trans·lat·ed, trans·lat·ing.**

trans·la·tion (trans lā′shən or tranz lā′shən) **1** translating or being translated: *Her translation of the German novel was very successful. The translation of a promise into a deed is not always easy.* **2** the result of translating; version: *a translation of a French poem. n.*

trans·lu·cent (trans lü′sənt or tranz lü′sənt) letting light through, but not able to be seen through: *Frosted glass is translucent. adj.*

trans·mis·sion (trans mish′ən or tranz mish′ən) **1** sending over; passing or passing along; letting through: *Mosquitoes are the only means of transmission of malaria.* **2** the part of a motor vehicle that transmits power from the engine to the driving axle. **3** the passage through space of radio waves from the transmitting station to the receiving station: *When transmission is good, distant radio stations can be heard. n.*

trans·mit (trans mit′ or tranz mit′) **1** send over; pass on; pass along; let through: *I will transmit the money by special messenger. Rats transmit disease.* **2** send out signals, voice, music, pictures, etc. by radio or television: *Some station is transmitting every hour of the day. v.*, **trans·mit·ted, trans·mit·ting.**

trans·mit·ter (trans mit′ər or tranz mit′ər) a device for transmitting: *a radio transmitter. n.*

tran·som (tran′səm) a window over a door or other window, usually hinged for opening. *n.*

trans·par·en·cy (trans per′ən sē or trans par′ən sē) **1** a transparent quality or condition: *the transparency of a fly's wing, the transparency of her lies.* **2** a photograph, picture, or design on glass or clear plastic, made visible by light shining through from below or behind. *n., pl.* **trans·par·en·cies.**

trans·par·ent (trans per′ənt or trans par′ənt) **1** transmitting light so that something behind or beyond can be distinctly seen: *Window glass is transparent.* **2** easily seen through or detected: *The boy offered a transparent excuse. adj.*

trans·plant (trans plant′ for 1, 2 and 3, trans′plant for 4) **1** plant again in a different place: *We start the flowers indoors and then transplant them to the garden.* **2** remove from one place to another: *The colony was transplanted to a more healthful location.* **3** transfer skin, an organ, etc. from one person or animal to another, or from one part of the body to another: *to transplant a kidney.* **4** the transfer of an organ, etc. from one person or animal to another, or from one part of the body to another: *a heart transplant.* 1–3 *v.*, 4 *n.*

trans·port (trans pôrt′ for 1, 6, and 8, trans′pôrt for 2, 3, 4, 5, and 7) **1** carry from one place to another: *Wheat is transported from the farms to the mills.* **2** carrying from one place to another: *Trucks are much used for transport.* **3** a large truck used to carry freight long distances by road. **4** a ship used to carry men and supplies. **5** an aircraft that transports passengers, mail, freight, etc. **6** carry away by strong feeling: *She was transported with joy by the good news.* **7** a strong feeling: *a transport of rage.* **8** send away to another country as a punishment: *Years ago, England transported many of her criminals to Australia.* 1, 6, 8 *v.*, 2–5, 7 *n.*

trans·por·ta·tion (trans′pər tā′shən) 1 transporting or being transported: *The railway allows free transportation for a certain amount of a passenger's baggage.* 2 a means of transport. 3 the cost of transport; a ticket for transport: *The transportation for our summer trip came to $300.* *n.*

trans·pose (trans pōz′) 1 change the position or order of. 2 change the usual order of letters, words, or numbers. *Example: The wind came up and away went his hat.* 3 in music, change the key of. *v.,* **trans·posed, trans·pos·ing.**

trans·verse (trans vėrs′ or tranz vėrs′) 1 lying across; placed crosswise; crossing from side to side: *The transverse beams in the barn were walnut.* 2 something transverse. 1 *adj.,* 2 *n.*

trap (trap) 1 a device for catching animals, lobsters, birds, etc. 2 a trick or other means for catching someone off guard: *The questions by the police were traps to make the thief tell where the money was.* 3 catch in a trap: *The bear was trapped.* 4 set traps for animals: *Some men make their living by trapping animals for their furs.* 5 trap door. 6 a bend in a pipe for holding a small amount of water to prevent the escape of air, gas, etc. 7 a light, two-wheeled carriage. 8 a device to throw dummy birds, etc. into the air to be shot at. 1, 2, 5–8 *n.,* 3, 4 *v.,* **trapped, trap·ping.**

trap door a door in a floor or roof.

tra·peze (trə pēz′) a short, horizontal bar hung by ropes like a swing, used in gymnasiums and circuses. *n.*

tra·pe·zi·um (trə pē′zē əm) a four-sided plane figure having no sides parallel. *n., pl.* **tra·pe·zi·ums** or **tra·pe·zi·a** (tra pē′zē ə).

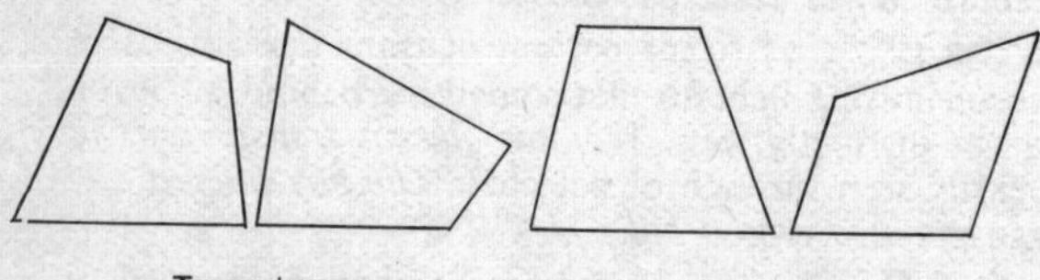

Trapeziums Trapezoids

trap·e·zoid (trap′ə zoid′) a four-sided plane figure having two sides parallel. *n.*

trap·line (trap′līn′) in trapping, the way or route along which traps are set for beaver and other small animals. *n.*

trap·per (trap′ər) a person who traps wild animals for food or for their furs. *n.*

trap·pings (trap′ingz) 1 ornamental coverings for a horse. 2 things worn; ornamental dress: *the trappings of a king and his court.* 3 outward appearances: *He had all the trappings of a cowboy, but he couldn't even ride a horse.* *n. pl.*

trash (trash) 1 twigs, leaves, bits of paper, etc.: *Put the trash in the can.* 2 worthless stuff; rubbish: *When we say that a book is trash, we mean that it contains false and worthless ideas.* 3 a person or persons of worthless character. *n.*

trav·ail (trav′āl) 1 hard work; toil or labor. 2 work hard; toil; labor. 3 trouble or hardship: *It was a time of great travail.* 1, 3 *n.,* 2 *v.*

trav·el (trav′əl) 1 go from one place to another: *She is travelling in Europe this summer.* 2 going in trains, airplanes, ships, cars, etc. from one place to another: *She loves travel.* 3 go from place to place on business: *He travels for a large firm.* 4 move; proceed; pass: *Sound travels in waves.* 1, 3, 4 *v.,* **trav·elled** or **trav·eled, trav·el·ling** or **trav·el·ing;** 2 *n.*

trav·el·ler or **trav·el·er** (trav′əl ər) a person who travels. *n.*

trav·e·logue (trav′ə log′) 1 a lecture describing travel, usually together with pictures. 2 a motion picture about travel. *n.*

☛ **Travelogue** was formed by blending *travel* and *-logue,* as in *dialogue* and *monologue.*

trav·erse (trav′ərs or trə vėrs′) pass across, over, or through: *The caravan traversed the desert.* *v.,* **trav·ersed, trav·ers·ing.**

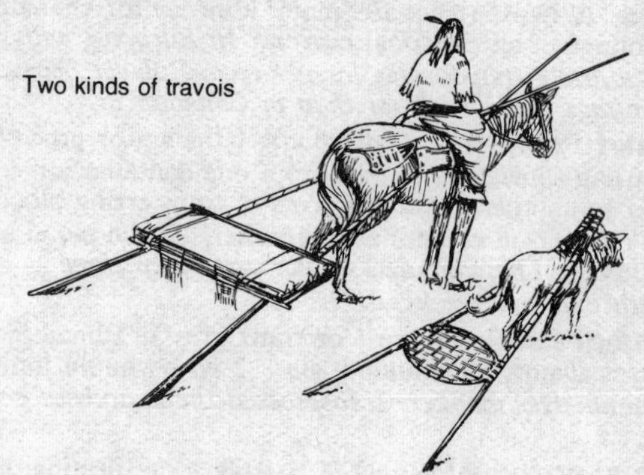

Two kinds of travois

tra·vois (trə voi′ or trav′wo) 1 a simple wheel-less vehicle used by the Prairie Indians and made of two shafts, or poles, to which was attached a platform or net for holding a load: *A travois was dragged by a horse or dog hitched to the shafts.* 2 *Cdn.* a dog sled. *n., pl.* **tra·vois.**

☛ **Travois** comes from a Canadian-French variation of the French word *travail* meaning 'frame,' originally a frame to keep a horse steady in order to shoe it.

trawl (trol or trôl) 1 a net dragged along the bottom of the sea. 2 to fish with such a net. 3 a line supported by buoys and having many short lines with baited hooks attached to it. 4 to fish with such a line. 1, 3 *n.,* 2, 4 *v.*

tray (trā) a flat holder or container with a low rim around it: *The waiter carries the dishes on a tray. Our dentist keeps his instruments in a tray.* *n.*

treach·er·ous (trech′ər əs) 1 not to be trusted; not faithful; not reliable; deceiving: *The treacherous soldier carried reports to the enemy.* 2 having a false appearance of strength, security, etc.: *Thin ice is treacherous.* *adj.*

treach·er·y (trech′ər ē) 1 breaking of faith; treacherous behavior; deceit: *Arthur's kingdom was destroyed by treachery.* 2 treason. *n., pl.* **treach·er·ies.**

trea·cle (trē′kəl) especially in England, molasses. *n.*

tread (tred) 1 walk; step; set the foot down: *Don't tread on the flower beds.* 2 press under the feet; trample; crush: *Tread out the fire before you go away.* 3 make, form, or do by walking: *Cattle had trodden a path to the pond.* 4 the act or sound of treading: *the*

hat, āge, fär; let, ēqual, tėrm; it, īce
hot, ōpen, ôrder; oil, out; cup, pu̇t, rüle
əbove, takən, pencəl, lemən, circəs
ch, child; ng, long; sh, ship
th, thin; ᴛʜ, then; zh, measure

tread of marching feet. 5 a way of walking: *He walks with a heavy tread.* 6 the part of stairs or a ladder that a person steps on: *The stair treads were covered with rubber.* 7 the part of something, such as a wheel or shoe, that touches the ground. 8 the raised pattern on the surface of a tire: *The tread on the back tires is almost gone.* 1–3 *v.*, **trod, trod·den** or **trod, tread·ing;** 4–8 *n.*

tread water, keep afloat in water, remaining upright with one's head above the surface, by slowly moving the legs as if bicycling.

trea·dle (tred′əl) 1 a lever or pedal worked by the foot to make a machine move: *My grandmother's old sewing machine was worked by a treadle.* See **grindstone** for picture. 2 work a treadle. 1 *n.*, 2 *v.*

tread·mill (tred′mil′) 1 an apparatus for producing a turning motion by having a person or animal walk on the moving steps of a wheel or of a sloping, endless belt. 2 any wearisome or monotonous round of work or of life. *n.*

trea·son (trē′zən) the act or fact of betraying one's country or ruler: *Helping the enemies of one's country is treason. n.*

treas·ure (trezh′ər) 1 wealth or riches stored up; valuable things: *The pirates buried treasure along the coast. The palace contains treasures.* 2 any thing or person that is much loved or valued: *The silver teapot was the old lady's chief treasure.* 3 value highly: *She treasures that doll more than all her other toys.* 4 put away for future use; store up. 1, 2 *n.*, 3, 4 *v.*, **treas·ured, treas·ur·ing.**

treas·ur·er (trezh′ər ər) a person in charge of money: *The treasurer of a club pays its bills. n.*

treas·ur·y (trezh′ər ē) 1 a place where money is kept: *The national treasury is in Ottawa.* 2 money owned; funds: *We paid for the party out of the club treasury.* 3 a place where treasure is kept. *n., pl.* **treas·ur·ies.**

treat (trēt) 1 act toward; handle: *He treats his dog gently. My father treats our new car with care.* 2 think of; consider; regard: *He treated the mistake as a joke.* 3 deal with to relieve or cure: *The dentist treated my toothache.* 4 deal with; discuss: *This magazine treats the progress of medicine.* 5 express or deal with in literature or art: *The author treats the characters of his story so that you feel you know them.* 6 discuss terms; arrange terms: *Messengers came to treat for peace.* 7 entertain by giving food, drink, or amusement: *He treated his friends to ice cream.* 8 a gift of food, drink, or amusement: *'This is my treat,' she said, as she paid for the tickets.* 9 anything that gives pleasure: *Being in the country is a treat to her.* 1–7 *v.*, 8, 9 *n.*

treat of, deal with; discuss: *'The Medical Journal' treats of the progress of medicine.*

treat·ment (trēt′mənt) 1 the act or process of treating: *My cold won't respond to treatment.* 2 a way of treating: *This cat has suffered from bad treatment.* 3 something done or used to treat something else, such as a disease. *n.*

trea·ty (trē′tē) 1 an agreement, especially one between nations, signed and approved by each nation. 2 in Canada, an agreement between the federal government and an Indian tribe whereby the tribe gives up its land rights except for reserves and receives an annual payment for each member. *n., pl.* **trea·ties.**

treaty Indian in Canada, a member of certain Indian tribes who live on reserves and receive treaty money and other treaty rights.

treaty money in Canada, annual payments made to treaty Indians.

tre·ble (treb′əl) 1 three times: *His salary is treble mine.* 2 make or become three times as much: *He trebled his money by buying a dog for $25 and selling it for $75.* 3 the highest part in music; soprano: *a treble voice.* 4 shrill; high-pitched: *the treble sounds of children at play.* 1, 4 *adj.*, 2 *v.*, **tre·bled, tre·bling;** 3 *n.*

tree (trē) 1 a large plant with a woody trunk and, usually, branches and leaves on its upper part. 2 a piece of wood used for some special purpose: *a clothes tree.* 3 anything suggesting a tree and its branches. 4 See **family tree.** 5 chase up a tree: *The cat was treed by a dog.* 1–4 *n.*, 5 *v.*, **treed, tree·ing.**

up a tree, *Informal.* in a difficult position.

tree·top (trē′top′) the top part of a tree: *From our place in the treetop, we could see for miles. n.*

trek (trek) 1 travel slowly; travel: *The settlers trekked hundreds of kilometres on foot.* 2 journey, especially a slow or difficult one: *It was a long trek over the mountains.* 1 *v.*, **trekked, trek·king;** 2 *n.*

A trellis

trel·lis (trel′is) a frame of light strips of wood or metal crossing one another with open spaces in between; a lattice, especially one supporting growing vines. *n.*

trem·ble (trem′bəl) 1 shake because of fear, excitement, weakness, cold, etc.: *The old woman's hands trembled. His voice trembled with fear.* 2 move gently: *The leaves trembled in the breeze.* 3 a trembling or quivering: *There was a tremble in her voice as she began to recite.* 1, 2 *v.*, **trem·bled, trem·bling;** 3 *n.*

tre·men·dous (tri men′dəs) 1 dreadful; very severe: *The army suffered a tremendous defeat.* 2 *Informal.* enormous; very great: *That is a tremendous house for a family of three.* 3 *Informal.* especially good: *We saw a tremendous movie yesterday. adj.*

trem·or (trem′ər) 1 an involuntary shaking or trembling: *a nervous tremor in the voice.* 2 a thrill of emotion or excitement. 3 a shaking movement: *An earthquake is called an earth tremor. n.*

trem·u·lous (trem′yə ləs) 1 trembling; quivering: *The child's voice was tremulous with sobs.* 2 timid; feeling or showing fear: *He was shy and tremulous in the presence of strangers. adj.*

trench (trench) **1** a long, narrow ditch with earth thrown up in front to protect soldiers. **2** a deep furrow; ditch: *They dug a trench around the walls of the tent to carry off the rain water.* **3** dig a trench in. 1, 2 *n.*, 3 *v.*

trend (trend) **1** the general direction; a course; tendency: *The hills have a western trend. The trend of modern living is away from the city to the suburbs.* **2** have a general direction; tend; run: *The road trends to the north.* 1 *n.*, 2 *v.*

trep·i·da·tion (trep′ə dā′shən) **1** fear; fright. **2** trembling. *n.*

tres·pass (tres′pəs or tres′pas) **1** go on somebody's property without any right: *The farmer put up 'No Trespassing' signs to keep people off his farm.* **2** go beyond the limits of what is right, proper, or polite: *I won't trespass on your time any longer.* **3** trespassing. **4** do wrong; sin. **5** a wrong; sin: *'Forgive us our trespasses as we forgive those who trespass against us.'* 1, 2, 4 *v.*, 3, 5 *n.*

tress (tres) a lock, curl, or braid of hair: *golden tresses.* *n.*

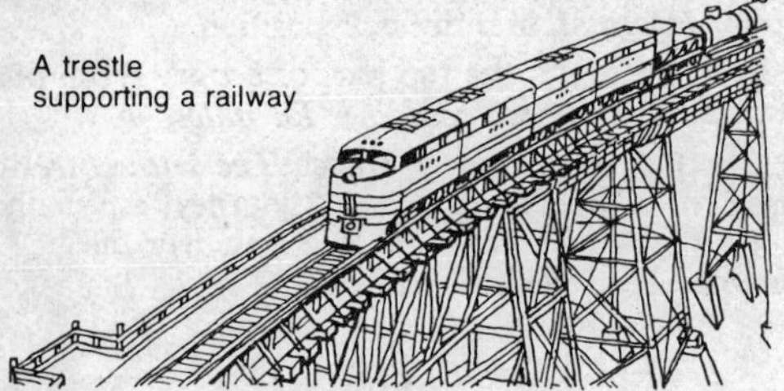
A trestle supporting a railway

tres·tle (tres′əl) **1** a frame that is used as a support. See **sawhorse** for picture. **2** a framework used as a bridge to support a road, railway tracks, etc. *n.*

tri– a prefix meaning 'three' or 'having three': *A triangle has three angles. A tripod is a stand with three feet. A tricycle has three wheels.*

☞ **Tri-** is a form of the Latin word *tres,* meaning 'three.'

tri·al (trī′əl) **1** the process of examining and deciding a case in court: *Many suspected thieves are arrested and brought to trial.* **2** the process of trying or testing: *He gave the machine another trial to see if it would work.* **3** for a try or test: *a trial trip, a trial model.* **4** the condition of being tried or tested: *He is employed on trial.* **5** trouble; hardship: *Her life has been full of trials—sickness, poverty, and loss of loved ones.* **6** a cause of trouble or hardship: *She is a trial to her big sister.* 1, 2, 4–6 *n.*, 3 *adj.*

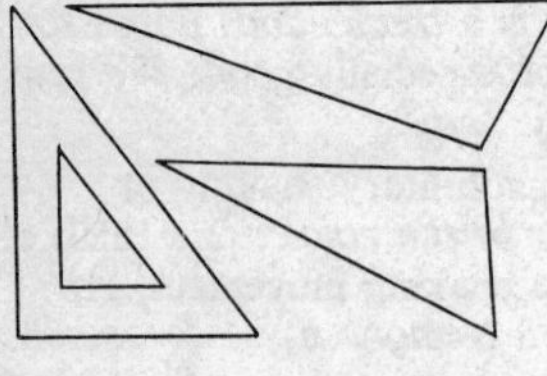
Triangles (def. 1)

A triangle (def. 3)

tri·an·gle (trī′ang′gəl) **1** a figure having three sides and three angles. **2** something shaped like a triangle. **3** a musical instrument made of a triangle of steel, open at one corner, that is struck with a steel rod. *n.*

tri·an·gu·lar (trī ang′gyə lər) shaped like a triangle; three-cornered. *adj.*

trib·al (trī′bəl) of a tribe: *tribal customs.* *adj.*

tribe (trīb) **1** a group of people united by race and customs under the same leaders: *Indian tribes, African tribes.* **2** a group of people having a common interest, profession, etc.: *the tribe of artists, the whole tribe of gossips.* **3** a class, kind, or sort of animals, plants, or other things: *The feathered tribe is a name for birds.* *n.*

tribes·man (trībz′mən) a member of a tribe, especially a man who is a member of a primitive tribe. *n., pl.* **tribes·men** (trībz′mən).

trib·u·la·tion (trib′yə lā′shən) affliction; great trouble; a severe trial: *The early Christians suffered many tribulations.* *n.*

tri·bu·nal (tri byü′nəl or trī byü′nəl) a court of justice; a place of judgement: *He was brought before the tribunal for trial.* *n.*

trib·u·tar·y (trib′yə ter′ē) **1** a stream that flows into a larger stream: *The Ottawa River is one of the tributaries of the St. Lawrence River.* **2** flowing into a larger stream or body of water. **3** paying tribute; required to pay tribute. **4** a person, country, etc. that pays tribute. 1, 4 *n., pl.* **trib·u·tar·ies;** 2, 3 *adj.*

trib·ute (trib′yüt) **1** money paid by one nation to another for peace or protection or because of some agreement. **2** any forced payment: *The pirates demanded tribute from passing ships.* **3** an acknowledgment of thanks or respect; compliment: *Remembrance Day is a tribute to our dead soldiers.* *n.*

trick (trik) **1** something done to deceive or cheat: *The false message was a trick to get him to leave the house.* **2** deceive; cheat: *We were tricked into buying a poor car.* **3** a clever act; a feat of skill: *We enjoyed the tricks of the trained animals.* **4** the best way of doing or dealing with something: *Mother certainly knows the trick of making pies.* **5** a piece of mischief; prank: *Stealing his lunch was a mean trick.* **6** play pranks. **7** a peculiar habit or way of acting: *He has a trick of pulling at his collar.* **8** the cards played in a single round of certain card games. **9** a turn or period of duty at a job, especially at steering a ship. 1, 3–5, 7–9 *n.*, 2, 6 *v.*

trick out or **up,** dress up; ornament: *She was tricked out in her mother's clothes.*

trick·er·y (trik′ər ē) the use of tricks (def. 1); deception; cheating. *n., pl.* **trick·er·ies.**

trick·le (trik′əl) **1** flow or fall in drops or in a small stream: *Tears trickled down her cheeks. The brook trickled through the valley.* **2** come, go, pass, etc. slowly and unevenly: *An hour before the show began, people started to trickle into the theatre. The money trickled away.* **3** a small flow or stream. 1, 2 *v.*, **trick·led, trick·ling;** 3 *n.*

trick·y (trik′ē) **1** full of tricks; deceiving: *A fox is trickier than a sheep.* **2** not reliable; difficult to handle: *Our neighbor's back door has a tricky lock.* *adj.,* **trick·i·er, trick·i·est.**

tri·col·or or **tri·col·our** (trī′kul′ər) **1** having three colors. **2** a flag having three colors: *The tricolor of France has three equal vertical stripes of blue, white,* and red. *The tricolor of Italy is green, white, and red.* 1 *adj.*, 2 *n.*

tri·cy·cle (trī′sə kəl) a three-wheeled vehicle usually worked by pedals attached to the large single wheel in front: *Children often ride tricycles before they are old enough to ride bicycles.* *n.*

tri·dent (trī′dənt) a spear with three prongs. *n.*

tried (trīd) **1** tested; proved: *a man of tried abilities.* **2** See **try.** *I tried to call him last night. I haven't tried this morning.* 1 *adj.*, 2 *v.*

tri·fle (trī′fəl) **1** something that is of very little value or of small importance. **2** a small amount; a little bit: *I am a trifle late.* **3** a small amount of money: *The picture cost only a trifle.* **4** talk or act lightly, not seriously: *Don't trifle with serious matters.* **5** play or toy with: *He trifled with his pen while he was talking to me.* **6** spend time, effort, money, etc. on things having little value: *She had trifled away the whole morning.* **7** a rich dessert made of sponge cake, whipped cream, custard, fruit, wine, etc. 1–3, 7 *n.*, 4–6 *v.*, **tri·fled, tri·fling.**

tri·fler (trī′flər) a frivolous or shallow person. *n.*

tri·fling (trī′fling) **1** having little value; not important; small: *The friends treated their quarrel as only a trifling matter.* **2** frivolous; shallow. *adj.*

trig·ger (trig′ər) **1** the small lever pulled back by the finger in firing a gun. See **pistol** for picture. **2** any lever that releases a spring, catch, etc. when pulled or pressed. **3** set off: *The explosion was triggered by a spark.* **4** cause to start; begin: *The fiery speech triggered an outburst of violence.* 1, 2 *n.*, 3, 4 *v.*

trike (trīk) *Informal.* tricycle. *n.*

trill (tril) **1** sing, play, sound, or speak with a quivering, vibrating sound: *some birds trill their songs.* **2** the act or sound of trilling. **3** a quick alternating of two musical tones. 1 *v.*, 2, 3 *n.*

Trilliums

tril·li·um (tril′ē əm) a plant having three leaves in a whorl, from the centre of which rises a single flower with three petals: *The trillium is the floral emblem of Ontario.* *n.*

trim (trim) **1** put in good order; make neat by cutting away parts: *The lumber has to be trimmed for the carpenter. The gardener trims the hedge.* **2** remove parts that are not needed: *He trims dead leaves off plants.* **3** neat; in good condition or order: *She keeps her desk trim.* **4** good condition or order: *Is our team in trim for the game?* **5** a condition; order: *That ship is in poor trim for a voyage.* **6** decorate: *The children were trimming the Christmas tree.* **7** balance a boat, airplane, etc. by arranging the load carried. **8** arrange the sails of a boat or ship to fit wind and direction. **9** *Informal.* defeat heavily: *We trimmed that team twice last year.* 1, 2, 6–9 *v.*, **trimmed, trim·ming;** 3 *adj.*, **trim·mer, trim·mest;** 4, 5 *n.*

trim·ming (trim′ing) **1** anything used to trim or decorate; ornament: *She bought the trimmings for her costume.* **2** *Informal.* a decisive defeat. **3 trimmings,**

hat, āge, fär; let, ēqual, tėrm; it, īce
hot, ōpen, ôrder; oil, out; cup, pu̇t, rüle
əbove, takən, pencəl, lemən, circəs
ch, child; ng, long; sh, ship
th, thin; ᴛʜ, then; zh, measure

pl. **a** parts cut away in trimming. **b** *Informal.* additions to food: *We ate turkey with all the trimmings.* *n.*

trin·ket (tring′kit) **1** any small, fancy article, bit of jewellery, or the like. **2** a trifle. *n.*

tri·o (trē′ō) **1** a piece of music for three voices or instruments. **2** a group of three singers or players performing together. **3** any group of three. *n., pl.* **tri·os.**

trip (trip) **1** a journey; voyage: *We took a trip to Europe.* **2** stumble: *He tripped on the stairs.* **3** cause to stumble and fall: *The broken stair tripped him.* **4** a loss of footing; a stumble. **5** make a mistake; do something wrong: *He tripped on that difficult question.* **6** cause to make a mistake or blunder: *Father tripped me with that question.* **7** take light, quick steps: *The children came tripping down the path to meet us.* 1, 4 *n.*, 2, 3, 5–7 *v.*, **tripped, trip·ping.**

tripe (trīp) **1** the walls of the first and second stomachs of a steer or cow, used for food: *tripe and onions.* **2** *Slang.* something foolish or worthless. *n.*

tri·ple (trip′əl) **1** including three; having three parts: *the triple petals of the trillium.* **2** three times as much or as many: *She has triple the foreign stamps I have.* **3** a number or amount three times as much or as many: *Nine is the triple of three.* **4** make or become three times as much or as many: *My older brother has tripled his wages in five years.* **5** in baseball, a three-base hit. **6** make a three-base hit: *He tripled in the eighth inning.* 1, 2 *adj.*, 3, 5 *n.*, 4, 6 *v.*, **tri·pled, tri·pling.**

tri·plet (trip′lit) **1** one of three children born at the same time from the same mother. **2** any group of three. *n.*

tri·pod (trī′pod) **1** a support or stand having three legs, as for a camera, telescope, etc. **2** a stool or other article having three legs. *n.*

trite (trīt) ordinary; commonplace; no longer interesting: *The movie turned out to be very trite, so we left early.* *adj.*, **trit·er, trit·est.**

tri·umph (trī′umf) **1** a victory; success: *Atomic energy is a triumph of modern science.* **2** gain victory; win success: *Our team triumphed over theirs.* **3** joy because of victory or success: *We welcomed the team home with cheers of triumph.* **4** rejoice because of victory or success: *They triumphed in their conquest of the enemy.* 1, 3 *n.*, 2, 4 *v.*

tri·um·phal (trī um′fəl) celebrating a victory: *a triumphal march.* *adj.*

tri·um·phant (trī um′fənt) **1** victorious; successful: *a triumphant army.* **2** rejoicing because of victory or success: *The winner of the match spoke in triumphant tones to his supporters.* *adj.*

triv·i·al (triv′ē əl) minor; not important: *Your composition has only a few trivial mistakes.* *adj.*

trod (trod) See **tread.** *He trod on a tack. You have trod on my foot again.* *v.*

trod·den (trod′ən) See **tread.** *The cattle have trodden down the corn.* *v.*

troll[1] (trōl) **1** sing in a full, rolling voice. **2** sing as a round is sung, each person or group starting one after the other. **3** a song whose parts are sung in succession; a round: *'Three Blind Mice' is a well-known troll.* **4** fish with a moving line, usually by trailing the line behind the boat near the surface: *He trolled for bass.* **5** a fishing lure or bait, especially one used for trolling. 1, 2, 4 *v.,* 3, 5 *n.*

troll[2] (trōl) in stories, an ugly giant or dwarf living in caves or underground. *n.*

trol·ley (trol′ē) **1** a pulley moving against a wire to carry electricity to a streetcar, electric engine, etc. See **streetcar** for picture. **2** a streetcar or bus that gets its power in this way. **3** a basket, carriage, etc. suspended from a pulley running on an overhead track. *n., pl.* **trol·leys.**

A trombone

trom·bone (trom′bōn or trom bōn′) a musical wind instrument resembling a trumpet and having either a sliding piece or, less often, valves for varying the notes. *n.*

troop (trüp) **1** a group or band of persons: *a troop of boys.* **2** a herd, flock, or swarm: *a troop of deer.* **3** a formation of cavalry or armored forces smaller than a squadron; a similar group in other army units. **4** a band of Boy Scouts: *He belongs to the 4th Kingston Troop.* **5** gather in troops or bands; move together: *The children trooped around the teacher.* **6** walk; go; go away: *The young boys trooped off after the older ones.* **7 troops,** *pl.* soldiers: *The government sent troops to put down the revolt.* 1–4, 7 *n.,* 5, 6 *v.*

☛ **Troop** and **troupe** are pronounced the same.

troop·er (trüp′ər) **1** a soldier in a cavalry regiment or an armored regiment. **2** *U.S.* a motorized or mounted policeman: *State troopers patrolled the roads near the prison.* *n.*

tro·phy (trō′fē) **1** something taken or won in war, hunting, etc., especially if displayed as a memorial or souvenir: *The hunter kept the lion's skin as a trophy.* **2** a prize, cup, etc. awarded to a victorious person or team: *He kept his tennis trophy on the mantelpiece.* *n., pl.* **tro·phies.**

trop·i·cal (trop′ə kəl) of the tropics: *Bananas are tropical fruit.* *adj.*

trop·ics or **Trop·ics** (trop′iks) the regions near the equator, between about 23½ degrees north and 23½ degrees south of it; the Torrid Zone: *The hottest parts of the earth are in the tropics.* *n. pl.*

trot (trot) **1** of horses, go by lifting the right forefoot and the left hind foot at about the same time and then the other two feet in the same way: *Some horses gallop more smoothly than they trot.* **2** the motion of a trotting horse. **3** ride a horse at a trot. **4** make a horse trot. **5** run, but not fast: *The child trotted along after his mother.* **6** a slow running. 1, 3–5 *v.,* **trot·ted, trot·ting;** 2, 6 *n.*

troth (troth or trōth) **1** faithfulness; loyalty. **2** a promise. *n.*

plight one's troth, a promise to marry. **b** promise to be faithful.

trou·ble (trub′əl) **1** distress; worry; difficulty: *That boy makes trouble for his teachers.* **2** cause trouble to; disturb: *She is troubled by headaches. That boy's poor grades trouble his parents.* **3** disturbance; disorder: *political troubles.* **4** extra work; bother; effort: *Take the trouble to do careful work. If she won't take the trouble to answer our letters, we shall stop writing.* **5** require extra work or effort of: *May I trouble you to do something for me?* **6** cause oneself inconvenience: *Don't trouble to come to the door; I can let myself in.* **7** illness; disease: *He has stomach trouble.* 1, 3, 4, 7 *n.,* 2, 5, 6 *v.,* **trou·bled, trou·bling.**

trou·ble·some (trub′əl səm) causing trouble; annoying: *Bullies are troublesome people.* *adj.*

trough (trof) **1** a long, narrow container for holding food or water for animals: *He led the horses to the watering trough.* **2** something shaped like this: *The baker used a trough for kneading dough.* **3** a channel for carrying water; gutter: *A wooden trough under the eaves of the houses carries off rain water.* **4** a long hollow between two ridges: *the trough between two waves.* *n.*

trounce (trouns) **1** beat; thrash. **2** *Informal.* defeat severely in a contest, game, etc.: *The home team was trounced by the visitors.* *v.,* **trounced, trounc·ing.**

troupe (trüp) a troop, band, or company, especially a group of actors, singers, or acrobats. *n.*

☛ **Troupe** and **troop** are pronounced the same.

trou·sers (trou′zərz) a two-legged outer garment reaching from the waist to the ankles: *He has a new suit with two pairs of trousers.* *n. pl.*

trout (trout) any of certain fresh-water food and game fish of the same family as the salmon: *rainbow trout.* *n., pl.* **trout** or **trouts.**

Trowels

trow·el (trou′əl) **1** a tool with a flat blade, used for spreading or smoothing plaster or mortar. **2** a tool with a curved blade, used for taking up plants, loosening dirt, etc. *n.*

troy weight (troi) a standard system of weights used for gems and precious metals: *One pound troy weight equals a little over four fifths of an ordinary pound, or about 370 grams. One pound troy weight equals twelve troy ounces.*

hat, āge, fär; let, ēqual, tėrm; it, īce
hot, ōpen, ôrder; oil, out; cup, pu̇t, rüle
əbove, takən, pencəl, lemən, circəs
ch, child; ng, long; sh, ship
th, thin; ᴛʜ, then; zh, measure

tru·ant (trü′ənt) 1 a student who stays away from school without permission. 2 a person who neglects his duty. 3 guilty of neglecting a duty: *The truant shepherd left his sheep.* 4 wandering: *a truant dog.* 1, 2 *n.*, 3, 4 *adj.*
play truant, a stay away from school without permission. **b** stay away from work or other duties.

truce (trüs) 1 a stop in fighting; peace for a short time: *A truce was declared between the two armies.* 2 a rest from trouble or pain: *The hot weather gave the old man a truce from rheumatism.* *n.*

truck[1] (truk) 1 a strongly built vehicle for carrying heavy loads, especially a motor truck: *There are many trucks on the highways nowadays.* 2 carry on a truck: *The lettuce was trucked to market.* 3 a small vehicle, sometimes with a motor, for carrying trunks, boxes, etc.: *Tim uses a truck in the warehouse. The redcap is coming with a truck.* 4 a frame with two or more pairs of wheels supporting the end of a railway car, locomotive, etc. 1, 3, 4 *n.*, 2 *v.*

truck[2] (truk) 1 vegetables raised for market. 2 *Informal.* rubbish; trash. 3 *Informal.* dealings: *She has no truck with peddlers.* *n.*

truck·er (truk′ər) 1 a person who drives a truck. 2 a person whose business is carrying goods, etc. by trucks. *n.*

trudge (truj) 1 walk. 2 walk wearily or with effort. 3 a hard or weary walk: *It was a long trudge up the hill.* 1, 2 *v.*, **trudged, trudg·ing;** 3 *n.*

true (trü) 1 agreeing with fact; not false: *It is true that 6 and 4 are 10. The story he told is true.* 2 real; genuine: *true gold, true kindness.* 3 faithful; loyal: *my truest friend, true to your promises.* 4 agreeing with a standard; proper; correct; accurate: *This is a true copy of my letter.* 5 rightful; lawful: *the true heir to the property.* 6 in a true manner; truly; exactly: *His words ring true.* *adj.* **tru·er, tru·est.**
come true, happen as expected; become real.

tru·ly (trü′lē) 1 in a true manner; exactly; rightly; faithfully: *Tell me truly what you think.* 2 really; in fact: *It was truly a beautiful sight.* *adv.*

A trumpet

trum·pet (trum′pit) 1 a musical wind instrument having a looped tube that is bell-shaped at one end and has three valves to vary the pitch. 2 anything shaped like a trumpet: *Some people used ear trumpets before small hearing aids were invented.* 3 blow a trumpet. 4 a sound like that of a trumpet. 5 make a sound like a trumpet: *The elephant trumpeted in fright.* 6 proclaim loudly or widely: *She'll trumpet that story all over town.* 1, 2, 4 *n.*, 3, 5, 6 *v.*

trum·pet·er (trum′pə tər) a person who blows a trumpet. *n.*

trun·dle (trun′dəl) 1 roll along; push along: *The workman trundled a wheelbarrow full of cement.* 2 a small wheel. 1 *v.*, **trun·dled, trun·dling;** 2 *n.*

trundle bed a low bed on small wheels: *Each morning he pushes his trundle bed under his brother's big bed.*

trunk (trungk) 1 the main stem of a tree, as distinct from the branches and the roots. 2 the main part of anything: *The marble trunk of the column rested on a granite base.* 3 main; chief: *the trunk line of a railway.* 4 an enclosed compartment in an automobile for storing baggage, tools, etc. 5 a big box used usually for transporting or storing clothes and other personal property. 6 a body considered without the head, arms, and legs. 7 an elephant's snout. 8 **trunks,** *pl.* very short pants worn by male athletes, swimmers, boxers, etc. 1, 2, 4–8 *n.*, 3 *adj.*

A truss supporting a roof

truss (trus) 1 tie; fasten: *We trussed the burglar up and called the police.* 2 fasten the wings or legs of a fowl in preparation for cooking. 3 a framework of beams or other braces for supporting a roof, bridge, etc. 4 a bandage or pad used for support. 1, 2 *v.*, 3, 4 *n.*

trust (trust) 1 a firm belief in the honesty, truthfulness, justice, or power of a person or thing; faith: *A child puts trust in his mother. We have trust in the new hospital.* 2 believe firmly in the honesty, truth, justice, or power of; have faith in: *He is a man you can trust.* 3 rely on; depend on: *A forgetful man should not trust his memory; he should write things down in a notebook.* 4 a person or thing trusted: *God is our trust.* 5 something managed for the benefit of another: *The house is a trust which he holds for his dead brother's children.* 6 the obligation or responsibility imposed on a person who takes charge of another's property: *Mr. Adams will be faithful to his trust.* 7 commit to the care of; leave without fear: *Can I trust the keys to him?* 8 hope; believe: *I trust you will soon feel better.* 9 confident expectation or hope: *Our trust is that she will soon be well.* 1, 4–6, 9 *n.*, 2, 3, 7, 8 *v.*
in trust, as a thing taken charge of for another person or group: *My aunt holds the house in trust.*

trus·tee (trus tē′) 1 a person responsible for the property or affairs of another person, of a company, or of an institution: *A trustee will manage the children's property until they grow up.* 2 a person elected to a board or committee that is responsible for the schools in a district; school trustee. *n.*

trust·ful (trust′fəl) ready to confide; ready to have faith; believing: *That trustful boy would lend money to any of his friends.* *adj.*

trust·wor·thy (trust′wėr′ᴛʜē) that can be depended on; reliable: *The class chose a trustworthy boy for treasurer.* *adj.*

trust·y (trus′tē) **1** that can be depended on; reliable: *The master left his money with a trusty servant.* **2** a convict who is given special privileges because of his good behavior: *The trusties were allowed to work on the gardens outside the prison walls.* 1 *adj.,* **trust·i·er, trust·i·est;** 2 *n., pl.* **trust·ies.**

truth (trüth) **1** that which is true: *Tell the truth.* **2** a fixed or established principle, law, etc.; proven doctrine: *a scientific truth.* **3** the quality of being true or exact: *the truth of a statement or belief. n.*
in truth, truly; really; in fact.

truth·ful (trüth′fəl) **1** telling the truth: *He is a truthful boy and will tell what really happened.* **2** conforming to truth; agreeing with the facts: *You can count on him for a truthful report of the accident. adj.*

try (trī) **1** attempt; make an effort: *If at first you don't succeed, try, try again.* **2** test; put to a test; find out about by using or experimenting: *Try this candy and see if you like it. We try each car before we sell it.* **3** an attempt: *Each boy had three tries at the high jump.* **4** investigate in a law court: *The man was tried and found guilty of robbery.* **5** put to severe test; strain: *Don't try your eyes by reading in a poor light. Her mistakes try my patience.* 1, 2, 4, 5 *v.,* **tried, try·ing;** 3 *n.*
try on, put on to test the fit, looks, etc.: *She tried on her new dress.*
try out, a test or sample: *Try out this new recipe for apple pie.* **b** be tested; take a test: *He tried out for the hockey team.*

try·ing (trī′ing) hard to endure; annoying; distressing: *a trying day. adj.*

try·out (trī′out′) *Informal.* a test made to determine fitness for a specific purpose: *Tryouts for our football team will start a week after school opens. n.*

tsar (zär) See **czar.**

tsa·ri·na (zä rē′nə) See **czarina.**

T-shirt (tē′shėrt′) a light, knitted sport shirt or undershirt having no collar and, usually, short sleeves. *n.*

tsp. teaspoon; teaspoons.

tub (tub) **1** a large, open container for washing clothes, etc. **2** a tub for bathing in. **3** *Informal.* a bath: *He takes a cold tub every morning.* **4** a round, wooden container for holding butter, lard, etc. *n.*

A tuba

tu·ba (tyü′bə or tü′bə) a very large horn having a low pitch. *n.*

tube (tyüb or tüb) **1** a long pipe of metal, glass, rubber, etc.: *Tubes are mostly used to hold or carry liquids or gases.* **2** a small cylinder of thin, easily bent metal or plastic with a cap that screws on the open end, used for holding toothpaste, ointment, etc. **3** a pipe or tunnel through which something travels: *The subway runs under the city through a tube.* **4** anything like a tube: *the bronchial tubes.* **5** a sealed glass or metal container used in television sets, radar, etc. to control the flow of electric currents. *n.*

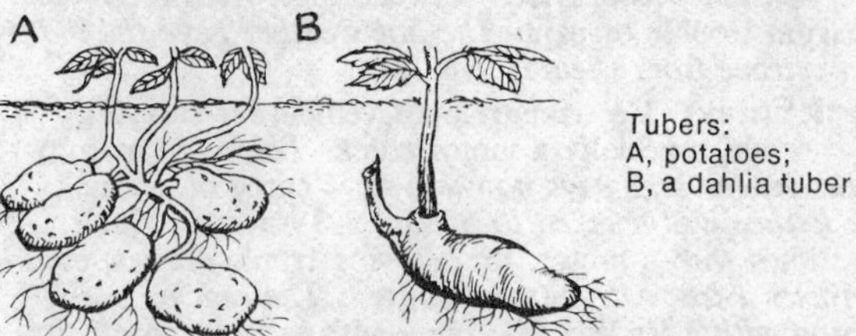

Tubers: A, potatoes; B, a dahlia tuber

tu·ber (tyü′bər or tü′bər) the thick part of an underground stem: *A potato is a tuber. n.*

tu·ber·cu·lo·sis (tyü bėr′kyə lō′sis or tü bėr′kyə lō′sis) a disease affecting various tissues of the body, but most often the lungs. *n.*

tuck (tuk) **1** thrust into some narrow space or into some out-of-the-way place: *She tucked her purse under her arm. He tucked the letter in his pocket. The little cottage is tucked away under the hill.* **2** thrust the edge or end of something closely into place: *Tuck your shirt in. He tucked a serviette under his chin.* **3** draw close together; fold: *He tucked up his sleeves before washing his hands.* **4** a fold sewn in a garment: *Since the dress was too big, Mother put a tuck in it.* **5** sew a fold in a garment for trimming or to make it shorter or tighter: *The baby's dress was beautifully tucked with tiny stitches.* 1–3, 5 *v.,* 4 *n.*
tuck away, a put away; hide. **b** eat heartily: *He tucked away a big meal.*
tuck in, a cover snugly: *Mother comes every night to tuck us in bed.* **b** eat heartily.

Tues. Tuesday.

Tues·day (tyüz′dē or tüz′dē, tyüz′dā′ or tüz′dā′) the third day of the week, following Monday. *n.*
☛ **Tuesday** developed from Old English *Tīwesdæg,* meaning 'day of Tīw'; Tīw was the Germanic god of war.

tuft (tuft) **1** a bunch of feathers, hair, grass, etc. growing or held close together at one end: *A goat has a tuft of hair on its chin.* **2** a clump of bushes, trees, etc. **3** a cluster of threads, sewn tightly through a comforter, mattress, etc. so as to keep the padding in place. **4** put tufts on; divide into tufts. 1–3 *n.,* 4 *v.*

tug (tug) **1** pull with force or effort; pull hard: *We tugged the boat in to shore. The child tugged at his mother's hand.* **2** a hard pull: *The baby gave a tug at her hair.* **3** a hard strain, struggle, effort, or contest. **4** tugboat. **5** tow by a tugboat. **6** one of a pair of long leather straps by which a horse pulls a wagon, cart, etc. See **harness** for picture. 1, 5 *v.,* **tugged, tug·ging;** 2–4, 6 *n.*

tug·boat (tug′bōt′) a small, powerful boat used to tow or push other boats; a tug. *n.*

tug–of–war (tug′əv wôr′) **1** a contest between two teams pulling at the ends of a rope, each trying to drag the other over a line marked between them. **2** any hard struggle. *n.*

tu·i·tion (tyü ish′ən or tü ish′ən) **1** teaching;

hat, āge, fär; let, ēqual, tėrm; it, īce
hot, ōpen, ôrder; oil, out; cup, pu̇t, rüle
əbove, takən, pencəl, lemən, circəs
ch, child; ng, long; sh, ship
th, thin; ᴛʜ, then; zh, measure

instruction: *He pays for his son's tuition at college.* **2** money paid for instruction: *His yearly tuition is $500.* *n.*

A tulip

tu·lip (tyü′lip or tü′lip) any of certain plants of the lily family, which grow from bulbs and have large cup-shaped flowers of various colors. *n.*

tum·ble (tum′bəl) **1** fall: *The child tumbled down the stairs.* **2** a fall: *The tumble hurt him badly.* **3** throw over or down; cause to fall: *The earthquake tumbled the tall buildings.* **4** roll or toss about: *The sick child tumbled restlessly in his bed.* **5** move in a hurried or awkward way: *He tumbled out of bed.* **6** perform leaps, springs, somersaults, etc. **7** turn over; rumple: *tumble clothes in a drier.* 1, 3–7 *v.,* **tum·bled, tum·bling;** 2 *n.*

tum·ble–down (tum′bəl doun′) ready to fall down; not in good condition: *a tumble-down shack in the mountains. adj.*

tum·bler (tum′blər) **1** a person who performs leaps or springs; acrobat. **2** a drinking glass. **3** the amount a glass will hold: *to drink a tumbler of water.* *n.*

tum·ble·weed (tum′bəl wēd′) a plant that after drying out in the fall is broken off from its roots and blown about by the wind: *The Russian thistle of the Prairies is one kind of tumbleweed.* *n.*

tum·my (tum′ē) *Informal.* stomach. *n., pl.* **tum·mies.**

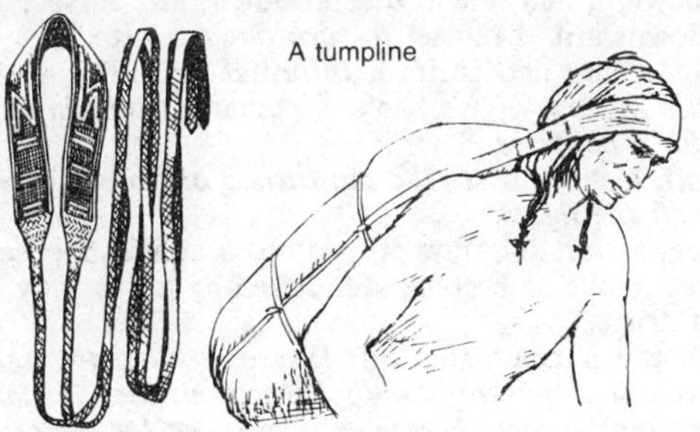
A tumpline

tump·line (tump′līn′) a strap used for carrying, when it is placed around the forehead, or for pulling, when it is placed around the chest. *n.*

tu·mult (tyü′mult or tü′mult) **1** a violent disturbance or disorder; uproar: *We heard the tumult of the storm. The shout of 'Fire!' caused a tumult in the theatre.* **2** a disturbance of mind or feeling; confusion; excitement: *I was in a state of tumult after the policeman's questions.* *n.*

tu·mul·tu·ous (tyü mul′chü əs or tü mul′chü əs) **1** very noisy or disorderly; violent: *The football team celebrated its victory in a tumultuous fashion.* **2** greatly disturbed. **3** rough; stormy: *Tumultuous waves beat upon the rocks. adj.*

tu·na (tü′nə or tyü′nə) a large sea fish, valued for food and for the sport of fishing: *The tuna sometimes grows to a length of three metres.* *n., pl.* **tu·na** or **tu·nas.**

tun·dra (tun′drə) a vast, level, treeless plain in the arctic regions: *The ground beneath the surface of the tundra is frozen even in summer.* *n.*

tune (tyün or tün) **1** a piece of music; an air or melody: *hymn tunes.* **2** the proper pitch: *The piano is out of tune. He can't sing in tune.* **3** mood or manner; tone: *He'll soon change his tune.* **4** agreement; harmony: *A person out of tune with his surroundings is unhappy.* **5** adjust to the proper pitch; put in tune: *A man is tuning the piano.* 1–4 *n.,* 5 *v.,* **tuned, tun·ing.**
in or **out of tune,** in or out of harmony or agreement with some person or thing: *She won't be elected because she's out of tune with the times.*
tune in, adjust a radio or television set to the desired station or channel.
tune up, put an engine, etc. into good working order.

tune–up (tyün′up′ or tün′up′) putting into good running order: *He took his car in for an engine tune-up.* *n.*

tung·sten (tung′stən) a rare metal used in making steel and for the filaments of electric lamps: *Tungsten has the highest melting point of all metals.* *n.*

A Roman tunic

tu·nic (tyü′nik or tü′nik) **1** a garment like a shirt or gown, worn by the ancient Greeks and Romans. **2** any garment like this, especially a sleeveless one worn by girls or women, usually over a blouse. **3** a short, close-fitting coat, part of the uniform worn by soldiers, policemen, etc. *n.*

A tuning fork

tuning fork a small steel instrument that sounds a fixed tone when struck: *Anne uses a tuning fork to help us begin our song in tune.*

tun·nel (tun′əl) **1** any underground passage, such as an underground way for a railway, a horizontal passage in a mine, or an animal's burrow. **2** make a tunnel: *The mole tunnelled in the ground. The workmen are* *tunnelling under the river.* 1 *n.,* 2 *v.,* **tun·nelled** or **tun·neled, tun·nel·ling** or **tun·nel·ing.**

tun·ny (tun′ē) tuna. *n., pl.* **tun·ny** or **tun·nies.**

tuque (tük or tyük) *Cdn.* **1** a knitted cap resembling a long stocking, usually knotted at one end: *Tuques are popular at the winter carnival.* **2** a tight-fitting, short knitted cap often having a round tassel on top. *n.*

☛ **Tuque** comes from a Canadian-French variation of the French word *toque,* meaning 'cap.' See the note at **toque.**

Two styles of tuque A turban

tur·ban (tėr′bən) **1** a scarf wound around the head or around a cap, worn by men in parts of India and in some other countries. **2** any head-dress resembling this, such as a small brimless hat worn by women or a big handkerchief tied around the head. *n.*

tur·bine (tėr′bīn) an engine or motor in which a wheel with blades is made to revolve by the force of water, steam, or air: *Turbines are used to turn dynamos that produce electric power.* See **jet engine** for picture. *n.*

tur·bu·lent (tėr′byə lənt) **1** causing disturbance; unruly; violent: *A turbulent mob rushed into the store.* **2** greatly disturbed; stormy: *turbulent weather, turbulent water. adj.*

tu·reen (tů rēn′) a deep, covered dish for serving soup, etc. *n.*

turf (tėrf) **1** grass with its roots; sod: *We cut some turfs from a field and covered bare spots in the lawn with them.* **2** Usually, **the turf, a** a race track for horses. **b** horse racing. *n., pl.* **turfs.**

Turk (tėrk) a person born in or living in Turkey, a country in the Middle East. *n.*

A wild turkey — about 120 cm long with the tail

tur·key (tėr′kē) a large fowl raised for food. *n., pl.* **tur·keys.**

Turk·ish (tėr′kish) **1** of or having to do with Turkey or the Turks. **2** the language of Turkey. 1 *adj.,* 2 *n.*

tur·moil (tėr′moil) a commotion; disturbance; tumult: *Six robberies in one night put our village in a turmoil. n.*

turn (tėrn) **1** move round as a wheel does; rotate: *The merry-go-round turned.* **2** cause to move round as a wheel does: *I turned the crank three times.* **3** a motion like that of a wheel: *At each turn the screw goes in further.* **4** move part way around; change from one side to the other: *Turn over on your back.* **5** cause to move around in order to open, close, raise, lower, or tighten: *She turned the key in the lock.* **6** take a new direction: *The road turns to the north here.* **7** give a new direction to: *He turned his steps to the north.* **8** a change of direction: *A turn to the left brought him in front of us.* **9** change in direction or position; invert; reverse: *turn a page.* **10** change so as to become: *She turned pale.* **11** a change in affairs, conditions, or circumstances: *The sick man has taken a turn for the better.* **12** change for or to a worse condition; spoil; sour: *Hot weather turns milk.* **13** become sour or spoiled: *That milk has turned.* **14** give form to; make: *He can turn pretty compliments.* **15** a form; style: *A scholar often has a serious turn of mind.* **16** put out of order; unsettle: *Too much praise turned his head.* **17** depend: *The success of the picnic turns on the weather.* **18** move to the other side of; go round; get beyond: *turn the corner.* **19** a twist; bend: *Give that rope a few more turns around the tree.* **20** a time or chance to do something; opportunity: *It is his turn to read.* **21** a deed or act: *One good turn deserves another.* **22** a walk, drive, or ride: *We all enjoyed a turn in the park before dinner.* 1, 2, 4–7, 9, 10, 12–14, 16–18 *v.,* 3, 8, 11, 15, 19–22 *n.*

by turns, one after another.

in turn, in proper order.

out of turn, a not in proper order. **b** at an inappropriate time, stage, etc.: *He was tactless to speak out of turn.*

take turns, play, act, etc., one after another in proper order.

to a turn, to just the right degree: *meat done to a turn.*

turn down, a fold down. **b** bend downward. **c** place with face downward. **d** refuse: *to turn down a plan.*

turn in, a turn and go in. **b** *Informal.* go to bed: *I think I'll turn in now.* **c** give back. **d** exchange: *turn in an old bike for a new one.*

turn off, a shut off: *Is the tap turned off?* **b** put out: *Turn off the lights.*

turn on, a start the flow of; put on. **b** attack; oppose. **c** *Slang.* make or become stimulated by, or as if by, the use of drugs.

turn out, a put out; shut off: *Please turn out the light.* **b** drive out: *The army finally turned out the invaders.* **c** come out; go out: *Everyone turned out for the circus.* **d** make; produce: *That factory turns out good shoes.* **e** result: *How did the game turn out?* **f** be found or known: *He turned out to be a good club president.*

turn over, a give; hand over; transfer: *He turned the job over to his assistant.* **b** think carefully about; consider in different ways: *I will turn the idea over in my mind.*

turn·coat (tėrn′kōt′) a person who changes his political party or principles; a person who goes over to the opposing side. *n.*

tur·nip (tėr′nip) **1** a plant with a large, roundish root. **2** its root, used as a vegetable. *n.*

turn·out (tėrn′out′) a gathering of people for a special purpose or event: *There was a good turnout at the dance. n.*

turn·o·ver (tėrn′ō′vər) **1** a small pie made by placing jam, mincemeat, or some other filling on one half of a piece of pastry, and then folding the other half over. **2** the total amount of business done in a given time: *He made a profit of $6000 on a turnover of $90 000.* **3** in football, an instance where a ball changes hands other than by punting, as through a pass interception or an unrecovered fumble: *We lost the game because of the turnover just before the end when our team fumbled the ball and their team picked it up.* *n.*

turn·pike (tėrn′pīk′) **1** a road on which a toll is or used to be charged. **2** a gate or booth where toll is paid. *n.*

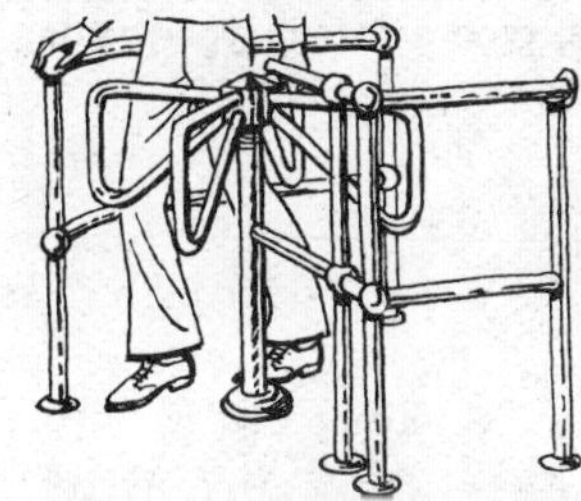

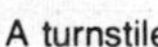
A turnstile

turn·stile (tėrn′stīl′) an entrance barrier consisting of a post with two crossed bars, or of several rods set in a revolving centre: *Only one person at a time can pass through a turnstile.* *n.*

turn·ta·ble (tėrn′tā′bəl) **1** on a record player, the revolving disk on which a record is placed to be played. **2** any similar disk or platform that revolves: *We saw some beautiful dolls on a turntable in the store window.* *n.*

tur·pen·tine (tėr′pən tīn′) **1** a mixture of oil and resin obtained from various cone-bearing trees. **2** an oil distilled from this mixture: *Turpentine is used in mixing paints and varnishes, in medicine, etc.* *n.*

tur·quoise (tėr′koiz or tėr′kwoiz) **1** a sky-blue or greenish-blue mineral which is used as a gem. **2** sky blue; greenish blue. 1, 2 *n.*, 2 *adj.*

tur·ret (tėr′it) **1** a small tower, often on the corner of a building. **2** any of various low, rotating armored structures in which guns are mounted: *The big guns of battleships are mounted in turrets.* *n.*

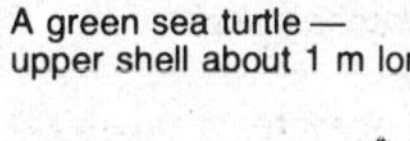
A green sea turtle — upper shell about 1 m long

tur·tle (tėr′təl) an animal having a soft body enclosed in a hard shell into which it can draw its head and legs: *Turtles live in fresh water, in salt water, or on land; those living on land are often called tortoises.* *n.*
turn turtle, turn bottom side up.

tusk (tusk) a very long, pointed, projecting tooth: *Elephants, walruses, and wild boars have tusks.* See **elephant** and **walrus** for picture. *n.*

tus·sle (tus′əl) **1** a struggle; argument; conflict: *We had a long tussle before we agreed on a new schedule.*

hat, āge, fär; let, ēqual, tėrm; it, īce
hot, ōpen, ôrder; oil, out; cup, pu̇t, rüle
əbove, takən, pencəl, lemən, circəs
ch, child; ng, long; sh, ship
th, thin; ᴛʜ, then; zh, measure

2 struggle or wrestle; scuffle about: *Boys like to tussle with one another.* 1 *n.*, 2 *v.*, **tus·sled, tus·sling.**

tu·tor (tyü′tər or tü′tər) **1** a private teacher: *The children of rich people or members of the nobility sometimes have tutors.* **2** teach; instruct: *Ann was tutored at home during her long illness.* 1 *n.*, 2 *v.*

TV or **T.V.** television.

twang (twang) **1** a sharp, ringing sound: *The bow made a twang when I shot the arrow.* **2** make or cause to make a sharp, ringing sound: *The banjos twanged.* **3** a sharp, nasal tone: *Some Nova Scotians speak with a twang.* **4** speak with a sharp, nasal tone. 1, 3 *n.*, 2, 4 *v.*

'twas (twoz or twuz) it was: *'Twas the night before Christmas.*

tweak (twēk) **1** pull sharply and twist with the fingers: *She tweaked her little brother's ear and made him cry.* **2** a sharp pull and twist: *His mother told him to give his sister's ear a tweak in return.* 1 *v.*, 2 *n.*

tweed (twēd) **1** a woollen cloth with a rough surface: *Tweed is sometimes made of wool and cotton, and usually has two or more colors.* **2 tweeds,** *pl.* clothes made of tweed. *n.*

twelfth (twelfth) **1** next after the 11th; last in a series of twelve; 12th: *The final game will be played on February twelfth.* **2** one of 12 equal parts: *Two is a twelfth of twenty-four.* *adj., n.*

twelve (twelv) one more than 11; 12: *There are twelve months in a year.* *n., adj.*

twelve·month (twelv′munth′) a period of twelve months; a year. *n.*

twen·ti·eth (twen′tē ith) **1** next after the 19th; last in a series of twenty; 20th. **2** one of 20 equal parts. *adj., n.*

twen·ty (twen′tē) two times ten; 20. *n., pl.* **twen·ties;** *adj.*

'twere (twėr or twer) it were.

twice (twīs) **1** two times: *Twice two is four.* **2** doubly: *twice as much.* *adv.*

twid·dle (twid′əl) **1** twirl: *twiddle one's pencil.* **2** play with idly. *v.*, **twid·dled, twid·dling.**
twiddle one's thumbs, do nothing; be idle.

twig (twig) a slender shoot of a tree or other plant; a very small branch: *Dry twigs are good to start a fire with.* *n.*

twi·light (twī′līt′) **1** the faint light reflected from the sky before the sun rises and after it sets. **2** the period during which this exists, especially after sunset. *n.*

twill (twil) cloth woven in raised diagonal lines: *Denim is a twill.* *n.*

'twill (twil) it will.

twin (twin) **1** one of two children or animals born at the same time from the same mother: *Twins sometimes look just alike. Have you met my twin sister?* **2** one of two persons or things very much or exactly alike: *twin beds. This table is the twin of the one we have at home.* *n.*

twine (twīn) **1** a strong thread or string made of two or more strands twisted together. **2** twist together: *She twined holly into wreaths.* **3** wind or wrap around: *The vine twines around the tree.* 1 *n.,* 2, 3 *v.,* **twined, twin·ing.**

twinge (twinj) a sudden, sharp pain: *a twinge of rheumatism, a twinge of remorse.* *n.*

twin·kle (twing′kəl) **1** shine with quick little gleams: *The stars twinkled. His eyes twinkled when he laughed.* **2** a twinkling; a sparkle; gleam: *Santa Claus has a merry twinkle in his eye.* **3** move quickly: *The dancer's feet twinkled.* 1, 3 *v.,* **twin·kled, twin·kling;** 2 *n.*

twin·kling (twing′kling) a very short period of time; instant: *When I called my dog, he was there in a twinkling.* *n.*

twirl (twėrl) **1** revolve rapidly; spin; whirl. **2** turn round and round idly: *He twirled the ends of his mustache.* **3** a spin; whirl; turn: *a twirl in a dance.* 1, 2 *v.,* 3 *n.*

twist (twist) **1** turn; wind: *She twisted the ring on her finger.* **2** wind together; twine: *This rope is twisted from many threads. She twisted flowers into a wreath.* **3** curve; crook; bend: *The path twists in and out among the rocks.* **4** a curve; crook; bend: *The road is full of twists and turns.* **5** force out of shape or place: *His face was twisted with pain.* **6** injure by a sudden turn or wrench: *He twisted his ankle.* **7** change the meaning of: *Don't twist what I say into something different.* **8** twisting; being twisted. **9** a peculiar bias or tendency: *a mental twist.* **10** an unexpected change or variation: *A new twist in the plot kept us in suspense.* 1–3, 5–7 *v.,* 4, 8–10 *n.*

twist·er (twis′tər) *Informal.* a whirlwind; cyclone or tornado. *n.*

twit (twit) tease; jeer at; taunt: *They twitted me because I wouldn't play.* *v.,* **twit·ted, twit·ting.**

twitch (twich) **1** move with a quick jerk: *The child's mouth twitched as if she were about to cry.* **2** a quick, jerky movement of some part of the body. **3** pull with a sudden tug or jerk; pull at: *She twitched the curtain aside.* **4** a short, sudden pull or jerk: *He felt a twitch at his watch chain.* 1, 3 *v.,* 2, 4 *n.*

twit·ter (twit′ər) **1** a sound made by birds; chirping. **2** make such a sound: *Birds begin to twitter just before sunrise.* **3** an excited condition: *My nerves are in a twitter when I have to sing in public.* **4** tremble with excitement. 1, 3 *n.,* 2, 4 *v.*

two (tü) one more than one; 2: *We have two arms and two legs.* *adj., n., pl.* **twos.**

in two, in two parts or pieces: *She broke the cookie in two.*

☛ **Two** and **too** are pronounced the same. **Two** and **to** are sometimes pronounced the same.

two·fold (tü′fōld′) **1** two times as much or as many; double. **2** having two parts: *a twofold shipment, part coming now and the rest later.* 1, 2 *adj.,* 1 *adv.*

'twould (twu̇d) it would.

ty·ing (tī′ing) See **tie.** *He is tying his shoes.* *v.*

tyke (tīk) *Informal.* a small child. *n.*

type (tīp) **1** a kind, class, or group alike in some important way: *She is a woman of the motherly type; her heart goes out to every child she sees.* **2** a person or thing having the characteristics of a kind, class, or group; representative; symbol: *He is a fine type of schoolboy.* **3** the general form, style, or character of some kind, class, or group: *She is above the ordinary type of student.* **4** a piece of metal or wood having on its upper surface a raised letter or figure for use in printing. **5** a collection of such pieces: *to set the manuscript for a book in type.* **6** printed letters or figures: *a small or large type.* **7** write with a typewriter: *She typed a letter.* 1–6 *n.,* 7 *v.,* **typed, typ·ing.**

type·write (tīp′rīt′) write with a typewriter. *v.,* **type·wrote, type·writ·ten, type·writ·ing.**

A typewriter

type·writ·er (tīp′rīt′ər) a machine for writing which reproduces letters and figures similar to printed ones: *My mother uses a typewriter for most of her letters.* *n.*

ty·phoid fever (tī′foid fē′vər) an infectious, often fatal, fever with intestinal inflammation, caused by a germ taken into the body with food or drink: *People can be inoculated against typhoid fever.*

ty·phoon (tī fün′) a hurricane occurring in the western Pacific Ocean and the China Sea. *n.*

ty·phus (tī′fəs) an infectious disease that produces high fever, dark-red spots on the skin, and extreme weakness: *Typhus is carried by lice and fleas, and used to occur in epidemics in which many people died.* *n.*

typ·i·cal (tip′ə kəl) **1** very much like others of its kind or type; representative: *The typical Thanksgiving dinner always includes turkey.* **2** of or having to do with a type; characteristic: *the hospitality typical of the pioneer.* *adj.*

typ·i·fy (tip′ə fī′) **1** be a symbol of: *The dove typifies peace.* **2** have the common characteristics of: *Alexander Mackenzie typifies the adventurous explorer.* *v.,* **typ·i·fied, typ·i·fy·ing.**

typ·ist (tīp′ist) a person who operates a typewriter, especially one who earns a living by typewriting. *n.*

ty·ran·ni·cal (tə ran′ə kəl) of a tyrant; like a tyrant; arbitrary; cruel; unjust: *a tyrannical king.* *adj.*

tyr·an·ny (tir′ə nē) **1** the cruel or unjust use of power: *The boy ran away to sea to escape his father's tyranny.* **2** a tyrannical act: *He had suffered many tyrannies.* **3** government by an absolute ruler. *n., pl.* **tyr·an·nies.**

ty·rant (tī′rənt) **1** a person who uses his power cruelly or unjustly: *A good teacher is never a tyrant.* **2** a cruel or unjust ruler. **3** a ruler with absolute power: *Some tyrants in ancient Greece were kind and just rulers.* *n.*

ty·ro (tī′rō) a beginner in learning anything; novice: *Much practice changed the tyro into an expert.* *n.*

hat, āge, fär; let, ēqual, tėrm; it, īce
hot, ōpen, ôrder; oil, out; cup, pu̇t, rüle
ə above, takən, pencəl, lemən, circəs
ch, child; ng, long; sh, ship
th, thin; ᴛʜ, then; zh, measure

u or **U** (yü) the 21st letter of the alphabet: *There are two* u's *in* usual. *n., pl.* **u's** or **U's.**

U–boat (yü′bōt′) a German submarine: *U-boats were first used during World War I. n.*

☛ **U-boat** is an abbreviation of the German word *Unterseeboot,* meaning 'under-sea boat.' The English word **submarine** also means 'under-sea' but was made from Latin *sub,* meaning 'under,' and *marinus,* meaning 'of the sea.'

ud·der (ud′ər) of cows, sheep, goats, etc., the gland from which milk comes. *n.*

U.E.L. United Empire Loyalist.

ugh (u̇h or u) an exclamation expressing disgust or horror. *interj.*

ug·li·ness (ug′lē nis) an ugly quality or appearance; being ugly. *n.*

ug·ly (ug′lē) **1** unpleasant to look at: *an ugly house, an ugly face.* **2** disagreeable; unpleasant; bad; offensive: *an ugly task, an ugly scowl, ugly language.* **3** threatening; dangerous: *ugly clouds. The wound looked sore and ugly.* **4** *Informal.* cross; bad-tempered; quarrelsome: *an ugly dog. adj.,* **ug·li·er, ug·li·est.**

U.K. United Kingdom.

U·krain·i·an (yü krān′ē ən) **1** of or having to do with the Ukraine, its peoples, or their language. **2** a person born in or living in the Ukraine. **3** the language of the Ukraine, closely related to Russian. 1 *adj.,* 2, 3 *n.*

u·ku·le·le (yü′kə lā′lē) a small guitar-shaped musical instrument having four strings. *n.*

☛ **Ukulele,** meaning 'small, quick person,' was the nickname given in Hawaii to a British army officer, Edward Purvis, who made this instrument popular there in the 1880's. **Ukulele** comes from Hawaiian *uku,* meaning 'flea,' and *lele,* meaning 'jumping.'

ul·cer (ul′sər) an open sore found on the skin or, inside the body, on a mucous membrane: *Ulcers most often appear in the mouth or in the stomach. n.*

ul·te·ri·or (ul tēr′ē ər) beyond what is seen or expressed; hidden, especially for a bad purpose: *He had an ulterior motive in inviting my sister: he wanted to make another girl jealous. adj.*

ul·ti·mate (ul′tə mit) **1** last; final: *Most people who drive too fast never consider that the ultimate result might be death in an accident.* **2** basic: *Hard work is the ultimate source of success. adj.* **—ul′ti·mate·ly,** *adv.*

ultra– a prefix meaning: **1** beyond, as in *ultraviolet.* **2** very; extremely; unusually, as in *ultra-ambitious, ultramodest, ultraradical.*

ul·tra·son·ic (ul′trə son′ik) of or having to do with sound waves beyond human hearing. *adj.*

ul·tra·vi·o·let (ul′trə vī′ə lit) of or having to do with the invisible light waves just beyond the violet part of the color spectrum: *Ultraviolet rays are present in sunlight. adj.*

u·lu (ü′lü) See **ooloo.**

um·bi·li·cal cord (um bil′i kəl) a cordlike structure connecting an unborn mammal to its mother, through which it receives food: *The umbilical cord is attached to the abdomen of the baby and the womb of the mother.*

um·brel·la (um brel′ə) a light, folding frame covered with cloth or plastic, used as a protection against rain or sun. *n.*

☛ **Umbrella** comes from an Italian word *ombrella,* meaning 'shade.' The first umbrellas were used to protect people from the sun. Compare **parasol.**

u·mi·ak (ü′mē ak) See **oomiak.**

um·pire (um′pīr) **1** a person who rules on the plays in a game: *The umpire called the ball a foul.* **2** a person chosen to settle a dispute. **3** act as umpire in a game, dispute, etc. 1, 2 *n.,* 3 *v.,* **um·pired, um·pir·ing.**

UN or **U.N.** United Nations.

un– a prefix meaning: **1** not____or the opposite of____: *Unfair means not fair, the opposite of fair. Unhappily means not happily, the opposite of happily.* **2** do the opposite of____: *Untie means do the opposite of tie.*

un·a·ble (un ā′bəl) not able: *A newborn baby is unable to walk or talk. adj.*

un·ac·cent·ed (un ak′sen tid or un′ək sent′əd) not stressed: *In 'upward' the second syllable is unaccented. adj.*

un·ac·count·a·ble (un′ə koun′tə bəl) **1** that cannot be accounted for or explained. **2** not able to account for or explain: *A madman is unaccountable for his actions. adj.*

un·ac·cus·tomed (un′ə kus′təmd) **1** not used to; not accustomed: *John did not like his new job at first because he was unaccustomed to the routines.* **2** not familiar; unusual or strange: *The unaccustomed heat made us all very tired. adj.*

un·aid·ed (un ād′id) not aided; without help. *adj.*

u·nan·i·mous (yü nan′ə məs) **1** in complete accord or agreement; agreed: *The children were unanimous in their wish to ride to the beach.* **2** showing complete accord: *He was elected by a unanimous vote. adj.* **—u·nan′i·mous·ly,** *adv.*

un·armed (un ärmd′) without weapons; without armor: *an unarmed robber. adj.*

un·as·sum·ing (un′ə süm′ing or un′ə syüm′ing) modest; not putting on airs: *The people were delighted by the duke's unassuming manner. adj.*

un·at·tend·ed (un′ə ten′did) **1** without attendants; alone. **2** not accompanied. **3** not taken care of; not attended to: *The switchboard was left unattended while the receptionist took a coffee break. adj.*

un·a·vail·ing (un′ə vāl′ing) not successful; useless: *His attempt to climb the fence was unavailing. adj.*

un·a·void·a·ble (un′ə void′ə bəl) that cannot be avoided: *an unavoidable delay. adj.*

An umbrella

un·a·ware (un′ə wer′) 1 not aware; unconscious: *The child was unaware of any danger from the snake.* 2 without knowing; unawares. 1 *adj.*, 2 *adv.*

un·a·wares (un′ə werz′) 1 without being expected; by surprise: *The police caught the burglar unawares.* 2 without knowing or being aware: *We made the error unawares.* *adv.*

un·bear·a·ble (un ber′ə bəl) that cannot be endured: *The pain from a severe toothache is almost unbearable.* *adj.*

un·be·com·ing (un′bi kum′ing) 1 not becoming; not appropriate: *unbecoming clothes.* 2 not proper: *unbecoming behavior.* *adj.*

un·be·known (un′bi nōn′) *Informal.* not known: *He arrived unbeknown to anyone.* *adj.*

un·be·liev·ing (un′bi lēv′ing) not believing; doubting. *adj.*

un·bend (un bend′) relax: *The judge unbent and behaved like a boy.* *v.*, **un·bent** or **un·bend·ed**, **un·bend·ing.**

un·bind (un bīnd′) release from bonds or restraints; untie; unfasten: *The cowboys unbound the calf and let it go.* *v.*, **un·bound, un·bind·ing.**

un·born (un bôrn′) not yet born; still to come; of the future: *unborn generations.* *adj.*

un·bos·om (un bůz′əm or un büz′əm) disclose; reveal. *v.*

unbosom oneself, tell one's feelings, thoughts, or secrets.

un·bound (un bound′) 1 not fastened or bound together: *Unbound sheets of music were scattered about the room.* 2 See **unbind.** 1 *adj.*, 2 *v.*

un·bound·ed (un boun′did) not bounded; without bounds or limits; very great: *His unbounded good spirits cheered all of us up.* *adj.*

un·break·a·ble (un brā′kə bəl) not breakable; that cannot be easily broken: *This toy was supposed to be unbreakable, but the baby broke it in two days.* *adj.*

un·bro·ken (un brō′kən) 1 not broken; whole: *There was only one unbroken cup left in the whole set.* 2 continuous; not interrupted: *He had eight hours of unbroken sleep.* 3 not tamed: *an unbroken colt.* *adj.*

un·buck·le (un buk′əl) unfasten the buckle or buckles of: *She unbuckled her shoes and took them off.* *v.*, **un·buck·led, un·buck·ling.**

un·but·ton (un but′ən) unfasten the button or buttons of. *v.*

un·called–for (un kold′fôr′ or un kôld′fôr′) unnecesary and improper: *an uncalled-for remark.* *adj.*

un·can·ny (un kan′ē) 1 strange and mysterious; weird: *The trees seemed to have uncanny shapes in the half darkness.* 2 seeming to have powers beyond what is expected or normal: *an uncanny knack for solving riddles, an uncanny sense of time.* *adj.*

un·ceas·ing (un sēs′ing) continual. *adj.*

un·cer·tain (un sėr′tən) 1 not certain; doubtful: *She came so late that she was uncertain of her welcome.* 2 likely to change; not to be depended on: *This dog has an uncertain temper.* *adj.*

un·cer·tain·ly (un sėr′tən lē) in an uncertain way: *He spoke slowly and uncertainly.* *adv.*

un·cer·tain·ty (un sėr′tən tē) 1 an uncertain state or condition; doubt. 2 something uncertain: *Our trip is still an uncertainty.* *n.*, *pl.* **un·cer·tain·ties.**

un·chain (un chān′) let loose; set free. *v.*

un·changed (un chānjd′) not changed; the same: *unchanged tradition.* *adj.*

un·civ·i·lized (un siv′ə līzd′) not civilized; barbarous; savage: *The cave men of Europe were uncivilized hunters and fishermen of the Stone Age.* *adj.*

un·clasp (un klasp′) 1 unfasten. 2 release from a clasp or grasp. *v.*

un·cle (ung′kəl) 1 a brother of one's father or mother. 2 the husband of one's aunt. *n.*

un·clean (un klēn′) 1 dirty; not clean. 2 not pure morally; evil. *adj.*

Uncle Sam the government or people of the United States.

☛ **Uncle Sam** comes from the initial letters of the United States. It was first used in an unfriendly way during the War of 1812, but it later became a popular nickname for the United States government. In 1961 **Uncle Sam** became an official national symbol.

un·coil (un koil′) unwind. *v.*

un·com·fort·a·ble (un kum′fər tə bəl) 1 not comfortable: *I am uncomfortable in this chair.* 2 uneasy: *I feel uncomfortable at formal dinners.* 3 disagreeable; causing discomfort: *This is an uncomfortable chair.* *adj.*

un·com·mon (un kom′ən) 1 rare; unusual. 2 remarkable. *adj.* **—un·com′mon·ly,** *adv.*

un·com·pro·mis·ing (un kom′prə mīz′ing) unyielding; firm: *His uncompromising attitude makes him very hard to deal with.* *adj.*

un·con·cerned (un′kən sėrnd′) not concerned; not interested; free from care or anxiety; indifferent. *adj.*

un·con·di·tion·al (un′kən dish′ən əl) without conditions; absolute: *The victorious general demanded unconditional surrender of the enemy.* *adj.* **—un′con·di′tion·al·ly,** *adv.*

un·con·quer·a·ble (un kong′kər ə bəl) that cannot be conquered. *adj.*

un·con·scious (un kon′shəs) 1 not conscious; not able to feel or think: *He was knocked unconscious when the car struck him.* 2 not aware: *The general was unconscious of being followed by a spy.* 3 not meant; not intended: *unconscious neglect.* *adj.*

un·con·scious·ly (un kon′shəs lē) without consciousness; without being aware of what one is doing. *adv.*

un·con·sti·tu·tion·al (un′kon stə tyü′shən əl or un′kon stə tü′shən əl) contrary to the constitution; not constitutional. *adj.*

un·con·trol·la·ble (un′kən trōl′ə bəl) not controllable; that cannot be controlled or held back: *I had to leave quickly because I felt an uncontrollable desire to laugh.* *adj.* **—un′con·trol′la·bly,** *adv.*

un·con·trolled (un′kən trōld′) without control; not restrained: *Because its uncontrolled behavior on the street was a nuisance, the dog was finally shut up in the back yard.* *adj.*

un·couth (un küth′) 1 awkward; clumsy; crude: *uncouth manners.* 2 unusual and unpleasant; strange: *The idiot made uncouth noises.* *adj.*

hat, āge, fär; let, ēqual, tėrm; it, īce
hot, ōpen, ôrder; oil, out; cup, pu̇t, rüle
əbove, takən, pencəl, lemən, circəs
ch, child; ng, long; sh, ship
th, thin; ᴛʜ, then; zh, measure

un·cov·er (un kuv′ər) 1 remove the cover from. 2 reveal; expose; make known: *The plot was uncovered when the letter was found.* 3 remove one's hat or cap in respect: *The men uncovered as the flag passed by.* *v.*

un·cul·ti·vat·ed (un kul′tə vāt′id) not cultivated; wild; undeveloped. *adj.*

un·curl (un kėrl′) straighten out. *v.*

un·daunt·ed (un don′tid or un dôn′tid) not afraid; not discouraged; fearless: *an undaunted leader. The kitten was undaunted by the size of the Newfoundland dog.* *adj.*

un·de·cid·ed (un′di sīd′id) 1 not decided; not settled. 2 not having one's mind made up. *adj.*

un·de·ni·a·ble (un′di nī′ə bəl) that cannot be denied. *adj.*

un·der (un′dər) 1 below; beneath: *The book fell under the table (prep.). The swimmer went under (adv.).* 2 below the surface of: *under the sea.* 3 lower than; lower down than; not so high as: *He hit me under the belt.* 4 less than: *The coat will cost under fifty dollars.* 5 during the rule or time of: *England under King John.* 6 in the condition or position of being affected by: *under the new rules. We learned a great deal under her teaching.* 7 because of: *Under these conditions we must cancel the picnic.* 8 according to: *under the law. The soldiers acted under orders.* 9 included in a particular group, category, or class: *In this library, books on gymnastics are under sports.* 1–9 *prep.,* 1 *adv.*

under– a prefix meaning: 1 on the underside; below; beneath, as in *underline, underarm.* 2 being or worn beneath, as in *underwear.* 3 lower in position, as in *underlip.* 4 lower in rank, as in *undersecretary.* 5 not enough, as in *underfed.* 6 below normal, as in *undersized.*

un·der·brush (un′dər brush′) bushes and small trees growing under large trees in woods or forests; undergrowth. *n.*

un·der·clothes (un′dər klōz′ or un′dər klōᴛʜz′) clothes worn under outer clothing; underwear. *n. pl.*

un·der·dog (un′dər dog′) one who is expected to lose; a person getting the worst of any struggle: *We've been the underdogs for the last few years, but this year our school is going to win.* *n.*

un·der·foot (un′dər fu̇t′) 1 under one's feet; on the ground; underneath. 2 in the way: *That dog is always underfoot.* *adv.*

un·der·gar·ment (un′dər gär′mənt) any garment worn under outer clothing. *n.*

un·der·go (un′dər gō′) 1 go through; pass through; be subjected to: *The town is undergoing many changes as more and more people are moving in.* 2 endure; suffer: *Soldiers undergo many hardships.* *v.,* **un·der·went, un·der·gone, un·der·go·ing.**

un·der·gone (un′dər gon′) See **undergo.** *He has undergone much pain during his illness.* *v.*

un·der·ground (un′dər ground′) 1 beneath the surface of the ground: *Miners work underground.* 2 being, working, or used beneath the surface of the ground. 3 a place or space beneath the surface of the ground. 4 in or into secrecy or concealment: *The thieves went underground after the robbery.* 5 secret: *The revolt against the government was an underground plot.* 6 a secret organization working against an unpopular government: *The French underground was active during the Second World War.* 1, 4 *adv.,* 2, 5 *adj.,* 3, 6 *n.*

un·der·growth (un′dər grōth′) bushes and small trees growing under large trees in woods or forests. *n.*

un·der·hand (un′dər hand′) 1 secret; sly; not open or honest. 2 secretly; slyly. 3 with an upward movement of the hand: *an underhand pitch (adj.), throw a ball underhand (adv.).* 1, 3 *adj.,* 2, 3 *adv.*

un·der·hand·ed (un′dər han′did) underhand; secret; sly: *an underhanded trick.* *adj.*

un·der·line (un′dər līn′) 1 draw a line under: *In writing, we underline titles of books.* 2 make emphatic or more emphatic; emphasize: *His speech underlined the importance of co-operation.* *v.,* **un·der·lined, un·der·lin·ing.**

un·der·mine (un′dər mīn′) 1 dig under; make a passage or hole under: *The soldiers undermined the wall.* 2 wear away the foundations of: *The cliff was undermined by the waves.* 3 weaken by secret or unfair means: *Some people tried to undermine the missionary's influence by spreading lies about him.* 4 weaken or destroy gradually: *Many severe colds had undermined her health.* *v.,* **un·der·mined, un·der·min·ing.**

un·der·neath (un′dər nēth′) beneath; below; under: *We can sit underneath this tree. He was pushing up from underneath.* *prep., adv.*

un·der·pass (un′dər pas′) a path underneath; a road under railway tracks or under another road. *n.*

un·der·rate (un′dər rāt′) rate or estimate too low; put too low a value on. *v.,* **un·der·rat·ed, un·der·rat·ing.**

un·der·sea (un′dər sē′) being, working, or used beneath the surface of the sea: *an undersea cable, undersea explorations.* *adj.*

un·der·shirt (un′dər shėrt′) a collarless shirt worn next to the skin under other clothing. *n.*

un·der·side (un′dər sīd′) the surface lying underneath; the bottom side: *The underside of the stone was covered with ants.* *n.*

un·der·stand (un′dər stand′) 1 get the meaning of; comprehend: *Now I understand the teacher's question.* 2 get the meaning: *People listen but often do not understand.* 3 know well; know how to deal with: *A good teacher understands children.* 4 be informed; learn: *I understand that he is leaving town.* 5 take as a fact; believe: *It is understood that you will come.* 6 supply in the mind. In 'He hit the tree harder than I,' the word *did* is understood after *I.* *v.,* **un·der·stood, un·der·stand·ing.**

un·der·stand·ing (un′dər stan′ding) 1 comprehension; knowledge: *a clear understanding of the problem.* 2 intelligence; the ability to learn and know: *The doctor was a man of understanding.* 3 intelligent and sympathetic: *an understanding reply.* 4 knowledge of each other's meaning and wishes: *True friendship is based on understanding.* 5 an agreement: *You and I must come to an understanding.* 1, 2, 4, 5 *n.,* 3 *adj.*

un·der·stood (un′dər stůd′) See **understand.** *I understood what he said. Have you understood the lesson?* *v.*

un·der·stud·y (un′dər stud′ē) a person who is ready to substitute in an emergency for an actor or any other regular performer. *n., pl.* **un·der·stud·ies.**

un·der·take (un′dər tāk′) 1 try; attempt: *Don't undertake what you can't finish.* 2 agree to do; promise: *I will undertake to feed your dogs while you are away.* *v.,* **un·der·took, un·der·tak·en, un·der·tak·ing.**

un·der·tak·er (un′dər tāk′ər) a person who prepares the dead for burial and takes charge of funerals; a funeral director. *n.*

un·der·tak·ing (un′dər tāk′ing) 1 something undertaken; task; enterprise. 2 a promise; pledge. *n.*

un·der·tone (un′dər tōn′) 1 a low or very quiet tone: *to talk in undertones.* 2 a subdued color; a color seen through other colors: *There was an undertone of brown beneath all the gold and crimson of autumn.* 3 a quality or feeling that is beneath the surface: *an undertone of sadness in her gaiety.* *n.*

un·der·took (un′dər tůk′) See **undertake.** *He failed because he undertook more than he could do.* *v.*

un·der·wa·ter (un′dər wo′tər or un′dər wô′tər for 1, un′dər wo′tər or un′dər wô′tər for 2) 1 growing, done, or used below the surface of the water: *underwater plants. A submarine is an underwater ship.* 2 below the surface of the water: *She stayed underwater for two minutes.* 1 *adj.,* 2 *adv.*

un·der·wear (un′dər wer′) clothing worn next to the skin, under one's outer clothes; underclothes. *n.*

un·der·went (un′dər went′) See **undergo.** *Transportation underwent a great change with the development of the automobile.* *v.*

un·der·world (un′dər wėrld′) 1 the criminal part of society. 2 in Roman myths, the world of the dead. *n.*

un·de·sir·a·ble (un′di zīr′ə bəl) 1 objectionable; disagreeable: *That drug was taken off the market because it was found to have undesirable effects.* 2 a person who is not wanted. 1 *adj.,* 2 *n.*

un·did (un did′) See **undo.** *He undid his shoes. The fire in the artist's studio undid many years of work.* *v.*

un·dig·ni·fied (un dig′nə fīd′) not dignified; lacking dignity. *adj.*

un·dis·put·ed (un′dis pyüt′id) not disputed; not doubted. *adj.*

un·dis·turbed (un′dis tėrbd′) not disturbed; not troubled; calm. *adj.*

un·do (un dü′) 1 unfasten; untie: *Please undo the package. I undid the string.* 2 do away with; cancel or reverse: *We mended the roof, but a heavy storm undid our work.* 3 bring to ruin; spoil; destroy. *v.,* **un·did, un·done, un·do·ing.**

un·do·ing (un dü′ing) a cause of destruction or ruin: *Drink was his undoing.* *n.*

un·done (un dun′) 1 not done; not finished: *I left all my homework undone and went to a movie.* 2 See **undo.** 1 *adj.,* 2 *v.*

un·doubt·ed (un dout′id) not doubted; accepted as true. *adj.*

un·doubt·ed·ly (un dout′id lē) beyond doubt; surely; certainly. *adv.*

un·dress (un dres′) take the clothes off; strip. *v.*

un·due (un dyü′ or un dü′) 1 not fitting; improper; not right: *He made undue remarks about those around him.* 2 too great; too much: *A miser gives undue importance to money.* *adj.*

un·du·late (un′jə lāt′ or un′dyə lāt′) 1 move in waves: *undulating water.* 2 have a wavy form or surface: *an undulating prairie.* *v.,* **un·du·lat·ed, un·du·lat·ing.**

un·du·ly (un dyü′lē or un dü′lē) 1 improperly: *He was punished unduly.* 2 excessively; too much: *unduly harsh, unduly optimistic.* *adv.*

un·dy·ing (un dī′ing) deathless; immortal; eternal: *undying beauty.* *adj.*

un·earth (un ėrth′) 1 dig up: *to unearth a buried city.* 2 discover; find out: *to unearth a plot.* *v.*

un·earth·ly (un ėrth′lē) 1 not of this world; supernatural. 2 strange; wild; weird; ghostly. *adj.*

un·eas·i·ness (un ēz′ē nis) a lack of ease or comfort; restlessness; anxiety: *His uneasiness grew as midnight drew nearer.* *n.*

un·eas·y (un ēz′ē) 1 restless; disturbed; anxious. 2 not comfortable. 3 not easy in manner; awkward. *adj.,* **un·eas·i·er, un·eas·i·est.**

un·em·ployed (un′em ploid′) 1 not employed; not in use: *an unemployed skill.* 2 not having a job; having no work: *an unemployed person.* 3 **the unemployed,** people out of work: *Some of the unemployed receive aid from the government.* 1, 2 *adj.,* 3 *n.*

un·em·ploy·ment (un′em ploi′mənt) a lack of employment; being out of work. *n.*

un·end·ing (un en′ding) continuing; endless. *adj.*

un·e·qual (un ē′kwəl) 1 not the same in amount, size, number, or value: *unequal sums of money.* 2 not fair; one-sided: *an unequal contest.* 3 not enough; not adequate: *His strength was unequal to the task.* *adj.*

un·e·qualled or **un·e·qualed** (un ē′kwəld) that has no equal or superior; matchless: *unequalled speed.* *adj.*

un·err·ing (un ėr′ing or un er′ing) making no mistakes; exactly right: *He shot with unerring accuracy.* *adj.*

un·e·ven (un ē′vən) 1 not level: *uneven ground.* 2 not equal; one-sided: *an uneven contest.* 3 of a number, leaving a remainder of 1 when divided by 2; odd: *The numbers 27 and 9 are uneven.* *adj.*

un·e·vent·ful (un′i vent′fəl) without important or striking occurrences: *an uneventful day.* *adj.*

un·ex·pect·ed (un′eks pek′tid) not expected: *an unexpected visit from my aunt.* *adj.* **—un′ex·pect′ed·ly,** *adv.*

un·fail·ing (un fāl′ing) 1 never failing; always ready when needed; loyal: *an unfailing friend.* 2 never running short: *an unfailing supply of water.* *adj.*

un·fair (un fer′) not fair; unjust: *It was unfair of him to trick his little brother into giving him all the candy.* *adj.*

un·faith·ful (un fāth′fəl) not faithful; not true to duty or one's promises: faithless. *adj.*

un·fa·mil·iar (un′fə mil′yər) 1 not well known; strange: *That face is unfamiliar to me.* 2 not

hat, āge, fär; let, ēqual, tėrm; it, īce
hot, ōpen, ôrder; oil, out; cup, pu̇t, rüle
əbove, takən, pencəl, lemən, circəs
ch, child; ng, long; sh, ship
th, thin; ᴛʜ, then; zh, measure

acquainted: *He is unfamiliar with the Greek language.* *adj.*

un·fas·ten (un fas′ən) undo; loosen; untie; open. *v.*

un·fa·vor·a·ble or **un·fa·vour·a·ble** (unfā′vər ə bəl) not favorable; adverse; harmful. *adj.*

un·feel·ing (un fēl′ing) **1** hard-hearted; cruel: *a cold, unfeeling person.* **2** not able to feel: *numb, unfeeling hands.* *adj.*

un·fin·ished (un fin′isht) **1** not finished; not complete: *unfinished homework.* **2** without some special finish; rough; not polished; not painted: *unfinished furniture.* *adj.*

un·fit (un fit′) **1** not fit; not suitable. **2** not good enough. *adj.*

un·flinch·ing (un flin′ching) not drawing back from difficulty, danger, or pain; firm; resolute: *unflinching courage.* *adj.*

un·fold (un fōld′) **1** open the folds of; spread out: *to unfold a napkin.* **2** reveal; show; explain: *unfold the plot of a story.* **3** open; develop: *Buds unfold into flowers.* *v.*

un·fore·seen (un′fôr sēn′) not known beforehand; unexpected: *They had to change their plans because of an unforeseen crisis.* *adj.*

un·for·get·ta·ble (un′fər get′ə bəl) that can never be forgotten. *adj.*

un·for·tu·nate (un fôr′chə nit) **1** not lucky; having bad luck. **2** not suitable; not fitting: *The child's outburst of temper was an unfortunate thing for the guest to see.* **3** an unfortunate person. 1, 2 *adj.*, 3 *n.*

un·found·ed (un foun′did) without foundation; without reason: *an unfounded complaint.* *adj.*

un·friend·ly (un frend′lē) **1** not friendly: *an unfriendly dog.* **2** not favorable: *unfriendly weather.* *adj.*

un·furl (un fėrl′) spread out; shake out; unfold: *Unfurl the sail. The flag unfurled.* *v.*

un·fur·nished (un fėr′nisht) not furnished; without furniture. *adj.*

un·gain·ly (un gān′lē) awkward; clumsy: *The boy's long arms and large hands give him an ungainly appearance.* *adj.*

un·god·ly (un god′lē) **1** not religious. **2** wicked; sinful. **3** *Informal.* very annoying; shocking: *an ungodly noise.* *adj.*

un·gra·cious (un grā′shəs) not polite; rude. *adj.*

un·guard·ed (un gär′did) **1** not protected: *an unguarded camp.* **2** careless: *In an unguarded moment, she gave away the secret.* *adj.*

un·guent (ung′gwənt) an ointment for sores, burns, etc.; salve. *n.*

un·hap·py (un hap′ē) **1** sad; sorrowful: *an unhappy face.* **2** unlucky: *an unhappy accident.* **3** not suitable: *an unhappy selection of colors.* *adj.*, **un·hap·pi·er, un·hap·pi·est.** —**un·hap′pi·ly,** *adv.* —**un·hap′pi·ness,** *n.*

un·health·y (un hel′thē) **1** not possessing good health; not well: *an unhealthy child.* **2** coming from or showing poor health: *an unhealthy paleness.* **3** harmful to health; unwholesome: *an unhealthy climate.* *adj.*

un·heard (un hėrd′) **1** not listened to; not heard: *unheard music.* **2** not given a hearing: *condemn a person unheard.* *adj.*

un·heard–of (un hėrd′ov′) **1** never heard of; unknown: *The electric light was unheard-of 200 years ago.* **2** not known before: *A price of $2 a dozen for eggs is unheard-of.* *adj.*

un·heed·ed (un hēd′id) not heeded; disregarded; unnoticed. *adj.*

un·heed·ing (un hēd′ing) not heeding; not attentive. *adj.*

un·hes·i·tat·ing (un hez′i tāt′ing) ready; prompt; immediate: *His unhesitating acceptance of the job surprised us all, for it was not an easy one.* *adj.* —**un·hes′i·tat′ing·ly,** *adv.*

un·hinge (un hinj′) **1** take a door, etc. off its hinges. **2** unsettle; upset: *Trouble has unhinged this poor man's mind.* *v.*, **un·hinged, un·hing·ing.**

un·hook (un hu̇k′) **1** loosen from a hook. **2** undo by loosening a hook or hooks. **3** become unhooked; become undone. *v.*

un·horse (un hôrs′) pull or knock from a horse's back; cause to fall from a horse: *The knight was unhorsed by the sharp thrust of his opponent's lance.* *v.*, **un·horsed, un·hors·ing.**

un·hurt (un hėrt′) not hurt; not harmed: *The other people involved in the accident are in the hospital, but she was unhurt.* *adj.*

U·NI·CEF (yü′ni sef′) United Nations International Children's Emergency Fund. *n.*

A unicorn.
This animal was once thought to have the body of a horse, the head of a stag, the feet of an elephant, and the tail of a boar.

u·ni·corn (yü′nə kôrn′) a legendary animal like a horse, but having a single long horn in the middle of its forehead. *n.*

u·ni·form (yü′nə fôrm′) **1** always the same; not changing: *The earth turns around at a uniform rate.* **2** all alike; not varying: *All the bricks have a uniform size.* **3** the clothes worn by the members of a group when on duty, by which they may be recognized as belonging to that group: *Soldiers, policemen, and nurses wear uniforms.* 1, 2 *adj.*, 3 *n.*

u·ni·form·i·ty (yü′nə fôr′mə tē) a uniform condition or character; a sameness throughout. *n.*, *pl.* **u·ni·form·i·ties.**

u·ni·form·ly (yü′nə fôrm′lē) always; regularly; in all cases. *adv.*

u·ni·fy (yü′nə fī′) unite; make or form into one: *Several small states were unified into one nation.* *v.*, **u·ni·fied, u·ni·fy·ing.**

un·im·por·tant (un′im pôr′tənt) not important; insignificant; trifling. *adj.*

un·in·hab·it·ed (un′in hab′ə tid) not lived in; without inhabitants: *an uninhabited wilderness. adj.*

un·in·tel·li·gi·ble (un′in tel′ə jə bəl) that cannot be understood: *There was so much static on the radio that the program was unintelligible. adj.*

un·ion (yün′yən) 1 united or being united: *The United States was formed by the union of thirteen former colonies of Great Britain.* 2 something formed by combining two or more members or parts: *The ten provinces of Canada form a union.* 3 a group of workers joined together to protect and promote their interests; labor union or trade union. *n.*

The Union Jack

Union Jack the red, white, and blue flag of the United Kingdom, formed by combining the crosses of St. George, St. Andrew, and St. Patrick, for England, Scotland, and Ireland.

u·nique (yü nēk′) 1 having no like or equal; being the only one of its kind: *He discovered a unique specimen of rock in the cave.* 2 *Informal.* rare; unusual: *His style of singing is rather unique. adj.*

u·ni·son (yü′nə sən) 1 agreement: *There was unison among the club members on the question of increasing fees.* 2 the agreement in pitch of two or more tones, voices, etc.; sounding together at the same pitch: *The children sang 'Happy Birthday' in unison. n.*

u·nit (yü′nit) 1 a single thing or person. 2 any group of things or persons considered as one: *The family is a social unit.* 3 one of the individuals or groups of which a whole is composed: *The body consists of units called cells.* 4 a standard quantity or amount, used as a basis for measuring: *A metre is a unit of length; a minute is a unit of time.* 5 the smallest whole number; 1. *n.*

U·ni·tar·i·an (yü′ni ter′ē ən) a member of a group that believes that God exists as one being, and is not at the same time the Father, the Son, and the Holy Spirit: *Unitarians accept the moral teachings of Jesus but do not believe that He was the Son of God. n.*

u·nite (yü nīt′) 1 join together; make one; combine: *Bricks united by mortar make a strong wall.* 2 bring together; join in action, interest, opinion, etc.: *Several firms were united to form one company. All the tennis clubs in Winnipeg will unite to plan the provincial tournament. v.,* **u·nit·ed, u·nit·ing.**

United Church of Canada a Christian church formed by the union of former Methodists, Presbyterian, and other churches.

United Empire Loyalist one of the persons who came to Canada during and after the American Revolution of 1776: *The United Empire Loyalists left the United States because they preferred to remain British subjects.*

United Nations 1 a world-wide organization devoted to establishing world peace and promoting economic and social welfare: *The United Nations charter was put into effect on October 24, 1945.* 2 the nations that belong to this organization: *Canada is one of the United Nations.*

u·ni·ty (yü′nə tē) 1 oneness; being united: *A circle has more unity than a row of dots. A nation has more unity than a group of tribes.* 2 harmony: *Brothers and sisters should live together in unity.* 3 an arrangement and choice of material to give a single effect, main idea, etc.: *A pleasing picture has unity; so has a good written composition. n., pl.* **u·ni·ties.**

u·ni·ver·sal (yü′nə vėr′səl) 1 of all; belonging to all; concerning all; done by all: *Food, fire, and shelter are universal needs.* 2 existing everywhere: *The law of gravity is universal. adj.* **—u′ni·ver′sal·ly,** *adv.*

u·ni·verse (yü′nə vėrs′) all things; everything there is: *Our world is but a small part of the universe. n.*

u·ni·ver·si·ty (yü′nə vėr′sə tē) an educational institution attended after secondary school for studies leading to a degree: *Universities offer advanced courses in general subjects such as literature, history, and science, and also often have schools of law, medicine, business, etc. n., pl.* **u·ni·ver·si·ties.**

un·just (un just′) not just; not fair. *adj.* **—un·just′ly,** *adv.*

un·kempt (un kempt′) 1 not combed. 2 neglected; untidy: *the unkempt clothes of a tramp. adj.*

un·kind (un kīnd′) harsh; cruel. *adj.*

un·kind·ly (un kīnd′lē) 1 harsh; unkind. 2 in an unkind way; harshly. 1 *adj.,* 2 *adv.*

un·kind·ness (un kīnd′nis) 1 harsh treatment; cruelty. 2 an unkind act. *n.*

un·known (un nōn′) 1 not known; not familiar; strange; unexplored: *an unknown country, an unknown number.* 2 a person or thing that is unknown: *The diver descended into the unknown. The main actor in this movie is an unknown.* 1 *adj.,* 2 *n.*

un·lace (un lās′) undo the laces of. *v.,* **un·laced, un·lac·ing.**

un·law·ful (un lo′fəl or un lô′fəl) contrary to the law; against the law; forbidden; illegal. *adj.*

un·learn·ed (un lėr′nid for 1, un lėrnd′ for 2) 1 not educated; ignorant: *The man was unlearned and could not write his name.* 2 not learned; known without being learned: *A baby's ability to suck is unlearned. adj.*

un·less (un les′) if it were not that; if not: *We shall go unless it rains. conj.*

un·like (un līk′) 1 not like; different: *The two problems are quite unlike.* 2 different from: *to act unlike others. adj.*

un·like·ly (un līk′lē) 1 not likely; not probable: *He is unlikely to win the race.* 2 not likely to succeed: *an unlikely undertaking. adj.*

un·like·ness (un līk′nis) difference. *n.*

un·lim·it·ed (un lim′ə tid) 1 without limits; boundless: *The boy seems to have unlimited energy.* 2 not restrained; not restricted: *a government of unlimited power. adj.*

un·load (un lōd′) 1 remove a load: *We unloaded as soon as we got home.* 2 take the load from: *Please help us unload the car.* 3 get rid of: *She began to unload* *her troubles onto her mother.* 4 remove powder, shot, bullets, or shells from a gun. 5 discharge a cargo: *The ship is unloading.* *v.*

un·lock (un lok′) 1 open the lock of; open anything firmly closed. 2 disclose; reveal: *Science has unlocked the mystery of the atom.* *v.*

un·looked–for (un lu̇kt′fôr′) unexpected; unforeseen. *adj.*

un·loose (un lüs′) let loose; set free; release. *v.,* **un·loosed, un·loos·ing.**

un·luck·y (un luk′ē) 1 not lucky; unfortunate. 2 bringing or thought to bring bad luck: *The number 13 is unlucky.* *adj.*

un·mar·ried (un mar′ēd or un mer′ēd) not married; single. *adj.*

un·mask (un mask′) 1 remove a mask or disguise: *The guests unmasked at midnight.* 2 take off a mask or disguise from: *The police caught the burglar and unmasked him.* 3 show the real nature of; expose: *We unmasked the coward.* *v.*

un·mind·ful (un mīnd′fəl) regardless; heedless; careless: *He went ahead despite our warning and unmindful of the results.* *adj.*

un·mis·tak·a·ble (un′mis tāk′ə bəl) that cannot be mistaken or misunderstood; clear; plain; evident. *adj.*

un·mixed (un mikst′) not mixed; pure. *adj.*

un·mo·lest·ed (un′mə les′tid) not molested; undisturbed. *adj.*

un·moved (un müvd′) 1 not moved; firm. 2 not disturbed; indifferent: *He was unmoved by the scenes of horror.* *adj.*

un·nat·u·ral (un nach′rəl or un nach′ə rəl) 1 not natural; artificial. 2 not normal; strange: *Unnatural cruelty is seen in horror movies.* *adj.*

un·nec·es·sar·y (un nes′ə ser′ē) not necessary; needless. *adj.* **—un·nec′es·sar′i·ly,** *adv.*

un·nerve (un nėrv′) deprive of firmness or self-control: *The sight of blood unnerves her.* *v.,* **un·nerved, un·nerv·ing.**

un·num·bered (un num′bərd) 1 not numbered; not counted: *The pages of this composition have been left unnumbered.* 2 too many to count: *There are unnumbered fish in the ocean.* *adj.*

un·oc·cu·pied (un ok′yə pīd′) 1 not occupied; vacant: *The driver pulled his car into the one unoccupied parking space.* 2 not in action or use; idle: *an unoccupied mind.* *adj.*

un·pack (un pak′) 1 take out things packed in a box, trunk, etc.: *to unpack your clothes.* 2 take things out of: *to unpack a trunk.* *v.*

un·paid (un pād′) not paid: *His unpaid bills amounted to $200. Candystripers are unpaid workers.* *adj.*

un·par·al·leled (un par′ə leld′ or un per′ə leld′) having no parallel; unequalled; matchless: *an unparalleled achievement.* *adj.*

un·pleas·ant (un plez′ənt) not pleasant; disagreeable. *adj.* **—un·pleas′ant·ly,** *adv.*

un·pop·u·lar (un pop′yə lər) not generally liked; disliked. *adj.*

un·prec·e·dent·ed (un pres′ə den′tid or unprē′sə den′tid) having no precedent; never done before; never known before: *an unprecedented event took place in 1961, when a human being travelled in outer space.* *adj.*

un·pre·pared (un′pri perd′) 1 not made ready; not worked out ahead: *an unprepared speech.* 2 not ready: *a person unprepared to answer.* *adj.*

un·prin·ci·pled (un prin′sə pəld) lacking good moral principles; bad. *adj.*

un·ques·tion·a·ble (un kwes′chən ə bəl) beyond dispute or doubt; certain: *It is an unquestionable advantage to know several languages.* *adj.* **—un·ques′tion·a·bly,** *adv.*

un·rav·el (un rav′əl) 1 separate the threads of: *The kitten unravelled Grandma's knitting.* 2 come apart; ravel: *My knitted gloves are unravelling at the wrist.* 3 bring or come out of a tangled state; clear up: *to unravel a mystery.* *v.,* **un·rav·elled** or **un·rav·eled, un·rav·el·ling** or **un·rav·el·ing.**

un·re·al (un rē′əl or un rēl′) not real; imaginary; fanciful. *adj.*

un·re·al·i·ty (un′rē al′ə tē) 1 a lack of reality; imaginary or fanciful quality. 2 something unreal: *Unrealities such as elves and goblins, are fun to imagine.* *n., pl.* **un·re·al·i·ties.**

un·rea·son·a·ble (un rē′zən ə bəl) 1 not reasonable; not sensible: *The little boy was very timid and had an unreasonable fear of the dark.* 2 not moderate; excessive: *$50 is an unreasonable price for that pair of shoes.* *adj.*

un·rea·son·a·bly (un rē′zən ə blē) 1 in a way that is not reasonable; contrary to reason; foolishly. 2 extremely: *August often has some unreasonably hot days.* *adv.*

un·rest (un rest′) 1 restlessness; a lack of ease and quiet. 2 agitation or disturbance amounting almost to rebellion. *n.*

un·re·strained (un′ri strānd′) not held back; not checked: *unrestrained laughter, unrestrained freedom.* *adj.*

un·ri·valled or **un·ri·valed** (un rī′vəld) having no rival; without an equal. *adj.*

un·roll (un rōl′) 1 open or spread out something rolled. 2 become spread out. 3 reveal; display: *He soon unrolled the story of the burglary.* 4 become revealed or displayed: *As the story unrolled, everyone became interested.* *v.*

un·ru·ly hard to rule or control; lawless: *an unruly horse, a disobedient and unruly child, an unruly section of a country.* *adj.*

un·sad·dle (un sad′əl) 1 take the saddle off a horse. 2 cause to fall from a horse. *v.,* **un·sad·dled, un·sad·dling.**

un·safe (un sāf′) dangerous. *adj.*

un·said (un sed′) 1 not said: *Everything he had meant to say remained unsaid.* 2 See **unsay.** 1 *adj.,* 2 *v.*

un·sat·is·fac·to·ry (un′sat is fak′tə rē) not good

enough to satisfy. *adj.*

un·sat·is·fied (un sat′is fīd′) not satisfied; not contented. *adj.*

un·say (un sā′) take back or cancel something said: *What is said cannot be unsaid.* *v.,* **un·said, un·say·ing.**

un·screw (un skrü′) **1** take out the screw or screws from. **2** loosen or take off by turning: *unscrew an electric light bulb.* *v.*

un·scru·pu·lous (un skrü′pyə ləs) not careful about right and wrong; without principles: *The unscrupulous boys cheated on the test.* *adj.*

un·seal (un sēl′) **1** break or remove the seal of: *to unseal a letter.* **2** open: *The threat of punishment unsealed her lips.* *v.*

un·seat (un sēt′) **1** displace from a seat: *The bronco unseated everyone who tried to ride it.* **2** remove from office: *unseat the mayor. Our previous M.P. was unseated in the last election.* *v.*

un·seem·ly (un sēm′lē) not proper; not suitable: *His unseemly laughter annoyed the rest of the audience.* *adj.*

un·seen (un sēn′) **1** not seen: *an unseen error.* **2** not visible: *an unseen spirit.* *adj.*

un·self·ish (un sel′fish) caring for others; generous. *adj.*

un·set·tle (un set′əl) disturb; make or become unstable; shake; weaken: *The shock unsettled his mind.* *v.,* **un·set·tled, un·set·tling.**

un·set·tled (un set′əld) **1** disordered; not in proper condition or order: *Our house is still unsettled after our move.* **2** liable to change; uncertain: *The weather is unsettled.* **3** not adjusted or disposed of: *an unsettled estate, an unsettled bill.* **4** not determined or decided: *an unsettled question.* **5** not inhabited: *Large parts of Canada are still unsettled.* *adj.*

un·shak·en (un shāk′ən) not shaken; firm: *He still had an unshaken belief in Santa Claus.* *adj.*

un·sheathe (un shēTH′) draw a sword, knife, or the like from a sheath. *v.,* **un·sheathed, un·sheath·ing.**

un·shod (un shod′) without shoes. *adj.*

un·sight·ly (un sīt′lē) ugly or unpleasant to look at: *His cluttered room was an unsightly mess.* *adj.*

un·skilled (un skild′) **1** not skilled; not trained; not expert: *Unskilled workers usually earn less than skilled workers.* **2** not requiring special skills or training: *unskilled labor.* *adj.*

un·so·phis·ti·cat·ed (un′sə fis′tə kāt′id) not sophisticated; simple; natural. *adj.*

un·sound (un sound′) **1** not sound; not in good condition: *A diseased mind or body is unsound. Unsound walls are not firm. An unsound business is not reliable.* **2** not based on truth or fact: *an unsound doctrine, an unsound theory.* **3** not restful; disturbed: *an unsound sleep.* *adj.*

un·speak·a·ble (un spēk′ə bəl) **1** that cannot be expressed in words: *unspeakable joy, an unspeakable loss.* **2** extremely bad; so bad that it can hardly be spoken of: *That was an unspeakable thing to do!* *adj.* —**un·speak′a·bly,** *adv.*

un·sta·ble (un stā′bəl) not firmly fixed; easily moved, shaken, or overthrown. *adj.*

un·stead·y (un sted′ē) **1** not steady; shaky: *an unsteady voice, an unsteady flame.* **2** likely to change; not reliable: *unsteady winds.* *adj.*

un·stressed (un strest′) not pronounced with force: *In 'unattended' the second and fourth syllables are unstressed.* *adj.*

un·suc·cess·ful (un′sək ses′fəl) not successful; having no success. *adj.*

un·suit·a·ble (un süt′ə bəl) not suitable; unfit. *adj.*

un·sus·pect·ed (un′səs pek′tid) **1** not suspected: *He had already committed several burglaries but was still unsuspected.* **2** not thought of: *an unsuspected danger.* *adj.*

un·think·a·ble (un thingk′ə bəl) that can hardly be imagined: *It is unthinkable that she could be a thief.* *adj.*

un·think·ing (un thingk′ing) thoughtless; heedless; careless: *An unthinking comment can sometimes cause a lot of trouble.* *adj.*

un·ti·dy (un tī′dē) not neat; not in order: *an untidy house.* *adj.*

un·tie (un tī′) **1** unfasten; undo: *She was untying bundles.* **2** make free; release: *She untied her horse.* *v.,* **un·tied, un·ty·ing.**

un·til (un til′) **1** up to the time of: *It was cold from Christmas until April.* **2** up to the time when: *He waited until the sun had set.* **3** before: *She did not leave until morning.* **4** to the point or stage that: *He worked until he was too tired to do more.* 1, 3 *prep.,* 2, 4 *conj.*

un·time·ly (un tīm′lē) **1** at a wrong time or season: *Snow in May is untimely.* **2** too early; too soon: *an untimely death.* 1, 2 *adj.,* 2 *adv.*

un·tir·ing (un tīr′ing) tireless: *an untiring runner.* *adj.*

un·to (un′tü) to: *The soldier was faithful unto death.* *prep.*

un·told (un tōld′) **1** not told; not revealed: *an untold secret.* **2** too many to be counted; countless: *There are untold stars in the sky.* **3** not counted; immense: *untold wealth. Wars do untold harm.* *adj.*

un·touched (un tucht′) not touched: *The cat left the milk untouched. The miser was untouched by the poor man's story.* *adj.*

un·to·ward (un tôrd′ or un′tə wôrd′) **1** unfavorable; unfortunate: *an untoward wind, an untoward accident.* **2** perverse; stubborn; willful: *The untoward child was very hard to manage.* *adj.*

un·trained (un trānd′) not trained; without discipline or education: *The company was not willing to hire untrained people.* *adj.*

un·tried (un trīd′) not tried; not tested: *an untried plan.* *adj.*

un·true (un trü′) **1** false; incorrect. **2** not faithful. *adj.*

un·truth (un trüth′) **1** a lack of truth; falseness. **2** a lie; falsehood. *n.*

un·used (un yüzd′) **1** not in use: *an unused room.* **2** never having been used: *We'll keep the unused paper cups for our next picnic.* *adj.*

unused to (un yüst′tü), not accustomed to: *The actor's hands were unused to manual labor.*

un·u·su·al (un yü′zhü əl) not in common use; not

common; rare; beyond the ordinary. *adj.* **—un·u′su·al·ly,** *adv.*

un·ut·ter·a·ble (un ut′ər ə bəl) unspeakable; that cannot be expressed. *adj.*

un·veil (un vāl′) 1 remove a veil from; uncover; disclose; reveal: *The statue was unveiled the day the graduating class presented it to the school.* 2 take off one's veil; reveal oneself: *The princess unveiled.* *v.*

un·war·y (un wer′ē) not cautious; unguarded; not careful. *adj.*

un·wel·come (un wel′kəm) not welcome; not wanted: *The bees were unwelcome guests at our picnic.* *adj.*

un·well (un wel′) ailing; ill; sick. *adj.*

un·whole·some (un hōl′səm) not wholesome; unhealthy; bad for the body or the mind: *a damp, unwholesome climate. Trashy reading is unwholesome.* *adj.*

un·wield·y (un wēl′dē) hard to handle or manage; not easy to use or control because of size, shape, or weight; bulky and clumsy: *The armor worn by knights seems unwieldy to us today.* *adj.*

un·will·ing (un wil′ing) not willing; not consenting. *adj.* **—un·will′ing·ly,** *adv.* **—un·will′ing·ness,** *n.*

un·wind (un wīnd′) 1 wind off; take from a spool, ball, etc. 2 become unwound. *v.,* **un·wound, un·wind·ing.**

un·wise (un wīz′) not wise; not showing good judgment; foolish: *It is unwise to delay going to the doctor if you are sick.* *adj.* **—un·wise′ly,** *adv.*

un·wit·ting·ly (un wit′ing lē) not knowingly; unconsciously; not intentionally: *He unwittingly gave away our secret.* *adv.*

un·wor·thy (un wėr′ᴛʜē) 1 not worthy; not deserving: *Such a silly story is unworthy of belief.* 2 base; shameful: *unworthy conduct.* *adj.*

un·wound (un wound′) See **unwind.** *v.*

un·wrap (un rap′) 1 remove a wrapping from; open. 2 become opened. *v.,* **un·wrapped, un·wrap·ping.**

un·yield·ing (un yēl′ding) firm; not giving in: *The crippled man learned to walk again because of his unyielding determination.* *adj.*

up (up) 1 to a higher place or condition: *The bird flew up.* 2 in a higher place or condition: *He stayed up in the mountains several days.* 3 to or at a higher place on or in something: *The cat ran up the tree.* 4 to the top of; near the top of; at the top of: *He went up the hill to get a good view.* 5 from a smaller to a larger amount: *Prices have gone up.* 6 along; through: *She walked up the street.* 7 to, near, or at the upper part of: *We sailed up the river. He lives up the road.* 8 above the horizon: *The sun is up.* 9 in an erect position: *Stand up.* 10 above the ground: *The wheat is up.* 11 out of bed: *Please get up or you will be late (adv.). The children were up at dawn (adj.).* 12 completely; entirely: *The paper burned up in a few minutes. My eraser is almost used up.* 13 at an end; over: *His time is up now.* 14 in or into being or action: *Don't stir up trouble.* 15 together: *Add these numbers up.* 16 to or in an even position; not behind: *to catch up in a race. Keep up with the times.* 17 ahead of an opponent by a certain number: *We are three games up.* 18 in or into view, notice, or consideration: *bring up a new topic.* 19 with much knowledge or skill: *The engineer is up on the newest methods.* 20 into storage or a safe place; aside; by: *Squirrels lay up nuts for the winter.* 21 *Informal.* a period of good luck, prosperity or happiness: *Her life is full of ups and downs.* 22 *Informal.* put, lift, or get up. 23 *Informal.* increase: *They upped the price of eggs.* 1, 2, 5, 8–16, 18, 20 *adv.,* 3, 4, 6, 7 *prep,* 8, 10, 11, 16, 17, 19 *adj.,* 21 *n.,* 22, 23 *v.,* **upped, up·ping.**

hat, āge, fär; let, ēqual, tėrm; it, īce
hot, ōpen, ôrder; oil, out; cup, pu̇t, rüle
əbove, takən, pencəl, lemən, circəs
ch, child; ng, long; sh, ship
th, thin; ᴛʜ, then; zh, measure

up to, a doing; about to do: *She is up to some mischief.* **b** equal to; capable of doing: *Do you feel up to going out so soon after being sick?* **c** *Informal.* before a person as a duty or task to be done: *It's up to the judge to decide.*

up·braid (up brād′) blame; reprove; find fault with: *The captain upbraided his men for falling asleep.* *v.*

up·heav·al (up hē′vəl) heaving up or being heaved up; a great disturbance: *Geologists say that the Rocky Mountains were formed by an upheaval of the earth's crust. The sale of the family business caused a great upheaval.* *n.*

up·held (up held′) See **uphold.** *v.*

up·hill (up′hil′ for 1 and 3, up′hil′ for 2) 1 up the slope of a hill; upward: *It is an uphill road all the way.* 2 upward: *We walked a mile uphill.* 3 difficult: *an uphill fight.* 1, 3 *adj.,* 2 *adv.*

up·hold (up hōld′) 1 give support to; confirm: *The principal upheld the teacher's decision.* 2 hold up; not let down: *We uphold the good name of our school.* *v.,* **up·held, up·hold·ing.**

up·hol·ster (up hōl′stər) provide furniture with coverings, cushions, springs, stuffing, etc. *v.*

up·hol·ster·y (up hōl′stər ē) 1 coverings for furniture; curtains, cushions, carpets, and hangings. 2 the business of upholstering. *n., pl.* **up·hol·ster·ies.**

up·keep (up′kēp′) 1 maintenance: *The upkeep of a house.* 2 the cost of operating and repair: *The upkeep of a big car is expensive.* *n.*

up·land (up′lənd or up′land′) 1 high land. 2 of high land; living or growing on high land: *upland meadow, upland flowers.* 1 *n.,* 2 *adj.*

up·lift (up lift′ for 1 and 3, up′lift′ for 2 and 4) 1 lift up; raise; elevate. 2 the act of lifting up. 3 improve mentally, socially, or morally: *The reformer wanted to uplift all the guests at the party.* 4 mental, social, or moral improvement or a movement toward it: *Good music gives her an uplift when she is discouraged.* 1, 3 *v.,* 2, 4 *n.*

up·on (ə pon′) on. *prep.*

up·per (up′ər) higher: *the upper lip, the upper floor, the upper range of a singer's voice.* *adj.*

upper hand, control; advantage: *Do what the doctor says, or that cold may get the upper hand.*

Upper Canada an older name for that part of Canada now called Ontario: *Upper Canada was farther up the St. Lawrence River than Lower Canada.*

Upper House or **upper house** in a legislature having two branches, the branch that has the smaller number of members. In some countries, the members of the Upper House are elected, as in the United States; in others they are appointed, as in Canada: *The Senate is the Upper House of the Canadian Parliament.*

Upper Lakes the most northerly of the Great lakes; Lakes Superior and Huron and, sometimes, Lake Michigan.

up·per·most (up′ər mōst′) **1** highest; topmost. **2** most prominent; having the most force or influence. **3** in, at, or near the top. **4** first: *The safety of her children came uppermost in the mother's mind.* 1, 2 *adj.*, 3, 4 *adv.*

up·raise (up rāz′) raise; lift up. *v.*, **up·raised, up·rais·ing.**

up·right (up′rīt′) **1** standing up straight; erect: *an upright post.* **2** straight up: *Hold yourself upright.* **3** something standing erect; a vertical part or piece: *The boards for the fence were nailed across the uprights.* **4** good; honest: *an upright man.* 1, 4 *adj.*, 2 *adv.*, 3 *n.* —**up′right′ness,** *n.*

up·ris·ing (up′rīz′ing) a revolt; rebellion: *The revolution began with small uprisings in several towns.* *n.*

up·roar (up′rôr′) **1** a noisy or violent disturbance: *The crowd was in an uproar when the lion escaped during the circus parade.* **2** a loud or confused noise. *n.*

up·root (up rüt′) **1** tear up the roots: *The storm uprooted many trees.* **2** force away from: *Famine uprooted many families from their homes in Ireland during the 1840's.* *v.*

up·set (up set′ for 1, 4, and 7, up′set′ for 2, 3, 5, 6, and 8) **1** tip over; overturn: *He upset the milk pitcher. Moving about in a boat may upset it.* **2** tipping over; an overturn. **3** tipped over; overturned. **4** disturb greatly; disorder: *Rain upset our plans. The shock upset Mother's nerves.* **5** a great disturbance; disorder. **6** greatly disturbed; disordered: *an upset stomach.* **7** overthrow; defeat: *The young candidate upset the mayor in the election.* **8** a defeat: *The hockey team suffered an upset.* 1, 4, 7 *v*, **up·set, up·set·ting;** 2, 5, 8 *n.*, 3, 6 *adj.*

up·shot (up′shot′) conclusion; result: *The upshot of the affair was favorable to everyone.* *n.*

up·side (up′sīd′) the upper side. *n.*

upside down **1** having at the bottom what should be on top: *The slice of bread and butter fell upside down on the floor.* **2** in or into complete disorder: *The room was upside down. The children turned the house upside down.*

up·stairs (up′sterz′) **1** up the stairs: *The boy ran upstairs.* **2** on or of an upper floor: *She lives upstairs (adv.). He is waiting in an upstairs hall (adj.).* **3** the upper storey or storeys: *That small cottage has no upstairs.* 1, 2 *adv.*, 2 *adj.*, 3 *n.*

up·stand·ing (up stan′ding) **1** standing up; erect: *short, upstanding hair.* **2** honorable: *a fine, upstanding young man.* *adj.*

up·start (up′stärt′) **1** a person who has suddenly risen from a humble position to wealth, power, or importance. **2** an unpleasant and conceited person who puts himself forward too much. *n.*

up·stream (up′strēm′) against the current of a stream; up a stream: *It is hard to swim upstream. They stopped at an upstream camping site.* *adv., adj.*

up–to–date (up′tə dāt′) **1** extending to the present time: *an up-to-date record of sales.* **2** keeping up with the times in style, ideas, and methods; modern: *an up-to-date store.* *adj.*

up·turn (up tėrn′ for 1, up′tėrn′ for 2 and 3) **1** turn up. **2** an upward turn: *The airplane made a sudden upturn to avoid the mountain.* **3** an improvement: *As business improved, his income took an upturn.* 1 *v.*, 2, 3 *n.*

up·ward (up′wərd) **1** toward a higher place: *He climbed upward till he reached the apple.* **2** directed or moving toward a higher place; in a higher position: *an upward course, an upward flight.* **3** toward a higher or greater rank, amount, age, etc.: *From public school upward she had studied French.* **4** above; more: *Children of twelve years and upward must pay full fare.* 1, 3, 4 *adv.*, 2 *adj.*

upward of, more than: *Repairs to the car will cost upward of $100.*

up·wards (up′wərdz) upward. *adv.*

u·ra·ni·um (yü rā′nē əm) a heavy, white, radio-active metallic element: *Uranium is a source of atomic energy.* *n.*

U·ra·nus (yü rā′nəs or yür′ə nəs) **1** a Greek god, the father of the Titans and the Cyclopes. **2** one of the larger planets, seventh in order from the sun. *n.*

ur·ban (ėr′bən) **1** of or having to do with cities or towns: *an urban district, urban planning.* **2** living in cities: *the urban population.* *adj.*

ur·chin (ėr′chin) **1** a small boy. **2** a mischievous boy. **3** a poor, ragged child: *Urchins played in the street.* *n.*

urge (ėrj) **1** push; force; drive: *The rider urged on his horse with whip and spurs. Hunger urged him to steal.* **2** a driving force or impulse: *The urge of hunger made him beg.* **3** ask earnestly; plead with: *She urged us to stay longer.* **4** plead or argue earnestly for; recommend strongly: *His doctor urges a change of climate.* 1, 3, 4 *v.*, **urged, urg·ing;** 2 *n.*

ur·gen·cy (ėr′jən sē) **1** need for immediate attention or action: *They said it was a matter of urgency so I came right away.* **2** pressing or forceful quality: *The urgency of his request made it impossible to refuse him.* *n., pl.* **ur·gen·cies.**

ur·gent (ėr′jənt) demanding immediate action or attention; pressing: *an urgent duty, an urgent message.* *adj.*

u·ri·nate (yür′ə nāt′) discharge urine from the body. *v.*, **u·ri·nat·ed, u·ri·nat·ing.**

u·rine (yür′ən) the fluid that is produced by the kidneys, passed from there to the bladder, and then discharged from the body. *n.*

urn (ėrn) **1** a kind of vase with a base or pedestal: *Urns were used in Greece and Rome to hold the ashes of the dead.* **2** a large coffee pot or teapot with a tap. *n.*

☛ **Urn** and **earn** are pronounced the same.

us (us; *unstressed,* əs) **We** and **us** mean the person speaking plus the person or persons addressed or spoken about: *We learn because our teacher helps us. Mother went with us to the theatre.* *pron.*

U.S. United States.

hat, āge, fär; let, ēqual, tėrm; it, īce
hot, ōpen, ôrder; oil, out; cup, pu̇t, rüle
əbove, takən, pencəl, lemən, circəs
ch, child; ng, long; sh, ship
th, thin; ᴛʜ, then; zh, measure

U.S.A. or **USA** United States of America.

us·a·ble (yüz′ə bəl) that can be used; fit for use. *adj.*

us·age (yüs′ij or yüz′ij) **1** a manner or way of using; treatment: *This car had rough usage.* **2** a habit; custom; a customary use; long-continued practice: *Travellers should learn many of the usages of the countries they visit.* **3** the customary way of using words: *The usage of the best writers and speakers determines what is good English.* *n.*

use (yüz for 1–3, yüs for 4–10) **1** put into action or service: *We use our legs in walking. We use spoons to eat soup. May I use your telephone?* **2** act toward; treat: *Use others as you would have them use you.* **3** consume or expend by using: *He uses tobacco. Most of the money you gave me has been used.* **4** using: *the use of tools.* **5** being used: *methods long out of use.* **6** usefulness: *a thing of no practical use.* **7** the purpose that a thing is used for: *to find a new use for something.* **8** a way of using: *poor use of materials.* **9** need; occasion: *He had no further use for it.* **10** the power, right, or privilege of using: *He had the use of his friend's boat last summer.* 1–3 *v.,* **used, us·ing;** 4–10 *n.*
used to (yüst′tü), **a** accustomed to: *Eskimos are used to cold weather.* **b** formerly did: *'You used to come at ten o'clock, but now you come at noon.'*
use up, consume or expend entirely: *use up all the money.*

used (yüzd) not new; that has belonged to someone else: *a used car.* *adj.*

use·ful (yüs′fəl) of use; giving service; helpful: *The guide made himself useful.* *adj.* **—use′ful·ly,** *adv.* **—use′ful·ness,** *n.*

use·less (yüs′lis) of no use; worthless: *My television set would be useless in a house without electricity.* *adj.*

ush·er (ush′ər) **1** a person who shows people to their seats in a church, theatre, etc. **2** to conduct; escort; show: *The footman ushered the visitors to the door.* 1 *n.,* 2 *v.*

ush·er·ette (ush′ər et′) a female usher in a theatre. *n.*

U.S.S.R. Union of Soviet Socialist Republics.

u·su·al (yü′zhü əl) in common use; customary; ordinary: *Snow is usual in most of Canada during winter.* *adj.* **—u′su·al·ly,** *adv.*
as usual, in the usual manner, at the usual time, or in the usual way.

u·surp (yü zėrp′ or yü sėrp′) seize and hold power, position, or authority by force or without right: *The king's wicked brother usurped the throne.* *v.*

u·ten·sil (yü ten′səl) **1** a container or implement used for practical purposes: *Pots and pans are kitchen utensils.* **2** an instrument or tool used for some special purpose: *Pens and pencils are writing utensils.* *n.*

An urn (def. 1)

An urn (def. 2)

u·ter·us (yü′tər əs) womb. *n.*

u·til·i·ty (yü til′ə tē) **1** usefulness: *A fur coat has more utility in winter than in summer.* **2** a useful thing. **3** a company that performs a public service: *Railways, buslines, and gas and electric companies are utilities.* *n., pl.* **u·til·i·ties.**

u·ti·lize (yü′tə līz′) make use of; put to some practical use: *Mother will utilize the bones for soup.* *v.,* **u·ti·lized, u·ti·liz·ing.**

ut·most (ut′mōst′) **1** greatest possible; greatest; highest: *Sunshine is of the utmost importance to health.* **2** farthest; extreme: *He walked to the utmost edge of the cliff.* **3** the extreme limit; the most that is possible: *He enjoyed himself to the utmost at the circus.* 1, 2 *adj.,* 3 *n.*

ut·ter[1] (ut′ər) complete; total; absolute: *utter surprise, utter darkness.* *adj.* **—ut′ter·ly,** *adv.*

ut·ter[2] (ut′ər) **1** speak; make known; express: *'We must fight on to victory' were the last words uttered by the dying soldier.* **2** give out or forth: *She uttered a cry of pain.* *v.*

ut·ter·ance (ut′ər əns) **1** expression in words or sounds: *The child gave utterance to his grief.* **2** a way of speaking: *Stammering hinders clear utterance.* **3** something uttered; a spoken word or words. *n.*

ut·ter·most (ut′ər mōst′) utmost. *adj., n.*

v or **V** (vē) 1 the 22nd letter of the alphabet: *There are two* v's *in* vivid. 2 the Roman numeral for 5. *n., pl.* **v's** or **V's.**

va·can·cy (vā′kən sē) 1 the state of being unoccupied or empty. 2 an unoccupied position: *The death of two policemen made two vacancies in our police force.* 3 a room, space, or apartment for rent: *There was a vacancy in the motel.* 4 empty space: *He stared into the vacancy of the night.* *n., pl.* **va·can·cies.**

va·cant (vā′kənt) 1 empty; not occupied or filled: *a vacant chair, vacant house, vacant space.* 2 empty of thought or intelligence: *a vacant smile.* *adj.*

va·cate (və kāt′ or vā′kāt) go away from and leave empty; make vacant: *They will vacate the house at the end of the month.* *v.,* **va·cat·ed, va·cat·ing.**

va·ca·tion (və kā′shən or vā kā′shən) 1 freedom from school, business, or other duties: *There is a vacation from school every year at Christmas.* 2 holidays: *She spent her vacation at the family cottage on Lake Erie.* 3 take a vacation. 1, 2 *n.,* 3 *v.*

vac·ci·nate (vak′sə nāt′) inoculate with vaccine as a protection against smallpox or other diseases. *v.,* **vac·ci·nat·ed, vac·ci·nat·ing.**

vac·ci·na·tion (vak′sə nā′shən) 1 the act or process of vaccinating: *Vaccination has made smallpox a very rare disease.* 2 the sore or the scar formed where vaccine was injected. *n.*

vac·cine (vak′sēn or vak sēn′) a preparation, often made of weakened viruses of a disease, used to inoculate a person in order to protect him from that disease: *Salk vaccine is used against polio.* *n.*

☛ **Vaccine** comes from the Latin word *vaccinus,* which means 'having to do with cows.' The word first referred to the mild disease called 'cowpox.' The virus of this disease became the first vaccine when it was found to protect people against the much more serious smallpox.

vac·il·late (vas′ə lāt′) 1 move first one way and then another; waver. 2 waver in mind or opinion: *He vacillated too long about which car to buy.* *v.,* **vac·il·lat·ed, vac·il·lat·ing.**

vac·u·um (vak′yü əm) 1 an empty space without even air in it. 2 an enclosed space from which almost all air or gas has been removed. 3 an empty space; void: *His wife's death left a vacuum in his life.* 4 clean with a vacuum cleaner: *Mother vacuumed the rugs yesterday.* 5 vacuum cleaner. 1–3, 5 *n.,* 4 *v.*

vacuum bottle or **vacuum flask** a bottle made with a space between its inner and outer walls from which almost all the air has been removed, so that the contents of the bottle will stay hot or cold for a long time.

vacuum cleaner an apparatus for cleaning carpets, curtains, floors, etc. by suction.

vag·a·bond (vag′ə bond′) 1 a wanderer; an idle wanderer; tramp. 2 wandering: *The gypsies lead a vagabond life.* 1 *n.,* 2 *adj.*

va·grant (vā′grənt) 1 an idle wanderer; tramp. 2 moving in no definite direction or course; wandering: *Gypsies are vagrant people.* 1 *n.,* 2 *adj.*

vague (vāg) not definite; not clear; not distinct: *In a fog everything looks vague. His vague statement confused them.* *adj.,* **va·guer, va·guest.**

vain (vān) 1 having too much pride in one's looks, ability, etc.: *She is vain of her beauty.* 2 of no use; without effect or success: *I made vain attempts to reach her by telephone.* 3 of no value or importance; worthless; empty: *a vain boast.* *adj.* **—vain′ly,** *adv.* **in vain,** without effect or success: *The drowning man shouted in vain, for no one was near.*

☛ **Vain, vane,** and **vein** are pronounced the same.

vale (vāl) valley. *n.*

☛ **Vale** and **veil** are pronounced the same.

val·en·tine (val′ən tīn′) 1 a greeting card or small gift sent or given on Saint Valentine's Day, February 14: *Some valentines make fun of the person to whom they are sent.* 2 a sweetheart chosen on this day. *n.*

val·et (val′it or val′ā) a male servant or a hotel worker who gives personal service and takes care of the cleaning and pressing of clothes. *n.*

val·i·ant (val′ē ənt) brave; courageous: *a valiant soldier, a valiant deed.* *adj.*

val·id (val′id) 1 supported by facts or authority; sound; true: *a valid argument.* 2 having force in law: *A contract made by an insane man is not valid.* *adj.*

va·lise (və lēs′) a travelling bag to hold clothes, etc. *n.*

val·ley (val′ē) 1 low land between hills or mountains: *Most large valleys have rivers running through them.* 2 a wide region drained by a great river system: *the Ottawa Valley.* *n., pl.* **val·leys.**

val·or or **val·our** (val′ər) bravery; courage. *n.*

val·u·a·ble (val′yə bəl or val′yü ə bəl) 1 having value; being worth something: *valuable information, a valuable friend.* 2 worth much money: *a valuable ring. He has a valuable stamp collection.* 3 Usually, **valuables,** *pl.* articles of value: *She keeps her jewellery and other valuables in a safe.* 1, 2 *adj.,* 3 *n.*

val·u·a·tion (val′yü ā′shən) 1 the value estimated or determined: *The jeweller's valuation of the necklace was $10 000.* 2 an estimating or determining of the value of something. *n.*

val·ue (val′yü) 1 worth; excellence; usefulness; importance: *the value of education, the value of milk as a food.* 2 the real worth; the proper price: *He bought the house for less than its value.* 3 rate at a certain value or price; estimate the value of: *The land is valued at $5000.* 4 think highly of; regard highly: *We all value our teacher's opinion of our work.* 1, 2 *n.,* 3, 4 *v.,* **val·ued, val·u·ing.**

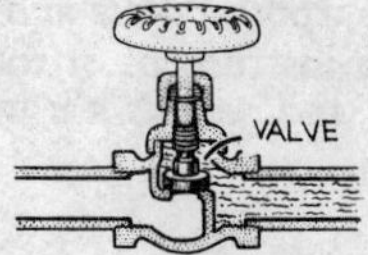

A valve

valve (valv) 1 a movable part that controls the flow of a liquid or gas through a pipe by opening and closing the passage: *A tap is one kind of valve.* 2 a part of the body that works like a valve: *The valves of the heart are membranes that control the flow of blood into and out of the heart.* 3 one of the two halves of the shell of an oyster, clam, etc. *n.*

vam·pire (vam′pīr) 1 an imaginary creature believed to be a corpse that comes back to life at night and sucks the blood of people while they sleep. 2 a person who ruthlessly takes advantage of others. *n.*

van[1] (van) the front part of an army, fleet, or other advancing group; vanguard. *n.*

☛ **Van**[1] comes from the first syllable of *vanguard.*

van[2] (van) a covered truck or wagon for moving furniture, etc. *n.*

☛ **Van**[2] comes from the last syllable of *caravan.*

van·dal (van′dəl) a person who destroys or damages things on purpose, especially beautiful or valuable things. *n.*

☛ The words **vandal** and **vandalism** come from the name of a Germanic tribe, the Vandals, who plundered and destroyed towns in western Europe and North Africa. In A.D. 455 the Vandals sacked Rome.

van·dal·ism (van′dəl iz′əm) destroying or damaging things on purpose, especially beautiful or valuable things: *The destruction of that painting was an act of senseless vandalism. n.*

☛ See note at **vandal.**

vane (vān) 1 a movable device to show which way the wind is blowing. 2 a blade, wing, or similar part attached to an axis, wheel, etc. so as to be turned by a current of air or liquid or to produce a current when turned: *The vanes of a windmill are turned by the wind; the vanes of an electric fan produce air currents as they turn.* See **propeller** for picture. *n.*

☛ **Vane, vain,** and **vein** are pronounced the same.

van·guard (van′gärd′) 1 a body of soldiers going ahead of the main part of an army to clear the way and guard against surprise. 2 the foremost or leading position. 3 the leaders of a movement. *n.*

va·nil·la (və nil′ə) a food flavoring made from the beanlike pods of a tropical plant. *n.*

van·ish (van′ish) 1 disappear; disappear suddenly: *The sun vanished behind a cloud.* 2 pass away; cease to be: *Dinosaurs have vanished from the earth. v.*

van·i·ty (van′ə tē) 1 too much pride in one's looks, ability, etc.: *The girl's vanity made her look in the mirror often.* 2 a lack of real value: *the vanity of wealth.* 3 a table or built-in counter with a mirror, in a bathroom or bedroom: *Mother was delighted with the vanity in the new house. n., pl.* **van·i·ties.**

van·quish (vang′kwish) conquer; defeat; overcome. *v.*

va·por or **va·pour** (vā′pər) 1 steam from boiling water; moisture in the air that can be seen; fog; mist. 2 a gas formed from a substance that is usually a liquid or a solid: *We could smell the gasoline vapor as the gas tank of the car was being filled. n.*

va·por·ize (vā′pər īz′) change from a solid or liquid to a vapor: *To distil water, we first have to vaporize it. v.,* **va·por·ized, va·por·iz·ing.**

var·i·a·ble (ver′ē ə bəl or var′ē ə bəl) 1 apt to change; changeable; uncertain: *The weather is more variable in Toronto that it is in Regina.* 2 that can be varied: *This curtain rod is of variable length.* 3 a thing, quality, or quantity that varies: *Temperature and rainfall are variables.* 1, 2 *adj.,* 3 *n.*

var·i·ance (ver′ē əns or var′ē əns) 1 a difference or disagreement. 2 varying; a change. *n.*
at variance, in disagreement: *His actions are at variance with his promises.*

hat, āge, fär; let, ēqual, tėrm; it, īce
hot, ōpen, ôrder; oil, out; cup, pu̇t, rüle
əbove, takən, pencəl, lemən, circəs
ch, child; ng, long; sh, ship
th, thin; ᴛʜ, then; zh, measure

var·i·ant (ver′ē ənt or var′ē ənt) 1 a somewhat different form, especially a less common one: *These are variants of the original design.* 2 varying; different: *'Catalog' is a variant spelling of 'catalogue.'* 1 *n.,* 2 *adj.*

var·i·a·tion (ver′ē ā′shən or var′ē ā′shən) 1 varying; a change. 2 the amount of change: *There was a variation of 12 degrees in the temperature yesterday.* 3 a varied or changed form. *n.*

var·ied (ver′ēd or var′ēd) 1 of different kinds; having variety: *a varied assortment of candies.* 2 changed; altered. *adj.*

va·ri·e·ty (və rī′ə tē) 1 a lack of sameness; a difference or change: *Variety is the spice of life.* 2 a number of different kinds: *This shop has a variety of toys.* 3 a kind or sort: *Which varieties of cake did you buy? n., pl.* **va·ri·e·ties.**

var·i·ous (ver′e əs or var′ē əs) 1 different; differing from one another: *There have been various opinions as to the best way to train a pet.* 2 several; many: *We have looked at various houses, but have decided to buy this one. adj.*

var·let (vär′lit) an old word meaning a low fellow; a rascal. *n.*

var·nish (vär′nish) 1 a liquid that gives a smooth, glossy appearance to wood, metal, etc.: *Varnish is often made from substances like resin dissolved in oil or alcohol.* 2 the smooth, hard surface made by this liquid when it dries: *The varnish on the table has been scratched.* 3 put varnish on. 4 a false or deceiving appearance; pretence: *She covers her selfishness with a varnish of good manners.* 5 give a false or deceiving appearance to: *to varnish over the truth with a lie.* 1, 2, 4 *n.,* 3, 5 *v.*

var·y (ver′ē or var′ē) 1 change; make or become different: *The driver can vary the speed of an automobile. The weather varies.* 2 be different; differ: *Stars vary in brightness. v.,* **var·ied, var·y·ing.**

☛ **Vary** and **very** are sometimes pronounced the same.

vase (vāz, väz, or voz) a holder or container used for ornament or for holding flowers. *n.*

vas·sal (vas′əl) in former times, a person who held land from a lord or superior, to whom in return he gave help in war or some other service: *A great noble could be a vassal of the king and have many other men as his vassals. n.*

vast (vast) extremely large; immense: *Ontario and Quebec are vast provinces. A billion dollars is a vast amount of money. adj.* **—vast′ness,** *n.*

vast·ly (vast′lē) very greatly; to a vast extent; to a vast degree. *adv.*

vat (vat) a tank; a large container for liquids: *a vat of dye. n.*

Vat·i·can (vat′ə kən) 1 in Vatican City, the buildings of the Roman Catholic Church and the palace of the Pope. 2 the government, office, or authority of the Pope. *n.*

Vatican City an independent state inside the city of Rome: *Vatican City is ruled by the Pope.*

vau·de·ville (vo′də vil′ or vô′də vil′) theatrical entertainment consisting of a variety of acts, such as singing, dancing, juggling, short plays, and animal acts. *n.*

vault[1] (volt or vôlt) **1** an arched roof or ceiling; a series of arches. **2** an arched space or passage. **3** something like an arched roof. The **vault of heaven** means the sky. **4** make in the form of a vault: *The roof was vaulted.* **5** cover with a vault. **6** an underground cellar or storehouse. **7** a place for storing valuable things and keeping them safe: *Vaults are often made of steel.* **8** a place of burial. 1–3, 6–8 *n.*, 4, 5 *v.*

Vaults in the Houses of Parliament, Ottawa

A man vaulting with a pole

vault[2] (volt or vôlt) **1** to jump or leap over by using the hands or a pole: *He vaulted the fence.* **2** such a jump or leap. 1 *v.*, 2 *n.*

V.C. **1** Victoria Cross. **2** a person who has won a Victoria Cross: *There were several V.C.'s at the reunion.*

veal (vēl) the flesh of a calf, used for food: *a veal chop. n.*

veer (vēr) change in direction; shift; turn: *The wind veered to the south. The talk veered to ghosts. v.*

veg·e·ta·ble (vej′tə bəl or vej′ə tə bəl) **1** a part of a plant, such as leaves, seeds, or roots, used for food and usually eaten with the main part of the meal. **2** a plant producing such food. **3** any plant. **4** of, having to do with, or like plants: *the vegetable kingdom, vegetable life. 1–3 n.*, 4 *adj.*

vegetable marrow an oblong vegetable of the squash family, having a light-yellow skin when ripe.

veg·e·tar·i·an (vej′ə ter′ē ən) **1** a person who eats vegetable foods but no meat, fish, or other animal products. **2** eating vegetables but no meat. **3** containing no meat: *a vegetarian diet.* 1 *n.*, 2, 3 *adj.*

veg·e·ta·tion (vej′ə tā′shən) plant life; growing plants: *There is not much vegetation in deserts. n.*

ve·he·mence (vē′ə məns) strong personal feelings; passionate force or excitement: *The two brothers argued loudly and with vehemence. n.*

ve·he·ment (vē′ə mənt) having or showing strong feeling. *adj.*

ve·hi·cle (vē′ə kəl) **1** a carriage, cart, wagon, automobile, sled, or any other conveyance used on land. **2** any form of conveyance or transportation: *a space vehicle.* **3** a means by which something is communicated, shown, done, etc.: *Language is the vehicle of thought. n.*

veil (vāl) **1** a piece of very thin material worn to protect or hide the face, or as an ornament. **2** a piece of material worn so as to fall over the head and shoulders. **3** cover with a veil: *Moslem women used to veil their faces before going out in public.* **4** anything that screens or hides: *A veil of clouds hid the sun.* **5** cover, screen, or hide: *Fog veiled the shore. The spy veiled his plans in secrecy.* 1, 2, 4 *n.*, 3, 5 *v.*
take the veil, become a nun.

☛ **Veil** and **vale** are pronounced the same.

vein (vān) **1** one of the blood vessels or tubes that carry blood to the heart from all parts of the body. **2** a rib of an insect's wing. **3** one of the bundles of tubes and fibres that carry food and water through a leaf and form its main framework. **4** a crack or seam in rock filled with a different mineral: *a vein of copper.* **5** any streak or marking of a different shade or color in wood, marble, etc. **6** a strain or streak of some quality in character, conduct, writing, etc.: *There is a vein of fun in these poems. He has a vein of cruelty. n.*

☛ **Vein, vain,** and **vane** are pronounced the same.

veldt or **veld** (velt or felt) in South Africa, open country having grass or bushes but few trees. *n.*

vel·lum (vel′əm) **1** the finest kind of parchment, once used instead of paper for books: *Some very expensive books are still bound with vellum.* **2** paper imitating such parchment: *A college diploma is usually made of vellum. n.*

ve·loc·i·ty (və los′ə tē) **1** speed; swiftness; quickness of motion: *to fly with the velocity of a bird.* **2** the rate of motion: *The velocity of light is nearly 300 000 kilometres per second. n., pl.* **ve·loc·i·ties.**

vel·vet (vel′vit) **1** cloth with a thick, soft pile usually made of silk, rayon, or cotton. **2** smoothness or softness like that of velvet: *Our kitten has velvet paws. n.*

vel·vet·een (vel′və tēn′) a cotton fabric resembling velvet. *n.*

vel·vet·y (vel′və tē) smooth and soft like velvet. *adj.*

vend (vend) sell; peddle: *He vends fruit from a cart. v.*

vending machine a coin-operated machine from which one may obtain candy, stamps, etc.

ven·dor or **vend·er** (ven′dər) a seller; a peddler. *n.*

ve·neer (və nēr′) **1** a thin layer of fine wood or other material covering a cheaper grade of wood, fibreboard, etc.: *We bought a pine desk with a walnut veneer.* **2** cover with veneer. **3** surface appearance or show: *a veneer of honesty.* 1, 3 *n.*, 2 *v.*

ven·er·a·ble (ven′ər ə bəl) worthy of reverence; deserving respect because of age, character, or importance: *a venerable priest, venerable customs. adj.*

ven·er·ate (ven′ər āt′) regard with reverence; revere: *He venerates his father's memory. v.,* **ven·er·at·ed, ven·er·at·ing.**

ven·er·a·tion (ven′ər ā′shən) deep respect; reverence. *n.*

Ve·ne·tian blind (və nē′shən) a window blind made of horizontal wooden, plastic, or metal slats that can be turned by a cord to shut out or let in light or air.

venge·ance (ven′jəns) revenge; punishment in return for a wrong: *He swore vengeance against the men who murdered his father. n.*

hat, āge, fär; let, ēqual, tėrm; it, īce
hot, ōpen, ôrder; oil, out; cup, pu̇t, rüle
əbove, takən, pencəl, lemən, circəs
ch, child; ng, long; sh, ship
th, thin; ᴛʜ, then; zh, measure

with a vengeance, with great force or violence: *By six o'clock it was raining with a vengeance.*

ven·i·son (ven′ə sən) deer meat; the flesh of a deer, used for food. *n.*

ven·om (ven′əm) 1 the poison of snakes, spiders, etc. 2 spite; malice: *Her enemies had learned to fear the venom of her tongue.* *n.*

ven·om·ous (ven′əm əs) 1 poisonous: *a venomous snake.* 2 spiteful; malicious. *adj.*

vent[1] (vent) 1 a hole; opening: *He used a pencil to make air vents in the box top so the frog could breathe.* 2 an outlet; a way out: *Her grief found vent in tears.* 3 let out; express freely: *He vented his anger on the dog.* 1, 2 *n.,* 3 *v.*

vent[2] (vent) a slit or opening in a garment: *His new leather jacket has side vents.* *n.*

ven·ti·late (ven′tə lāt′) 1 change the air in: *We ventilate a room by opening windows.* 2 purify by fresh air: *The lungs ventilate the blood.* 3 make known publicly; discuss openly: *We were glad of the chance to ventilate our opinions.* *v.,* **ven·ti·lat·ed, ven·ti·lat·ing.**

ven·ti·la·tion (ven′tə lā′shən) 1 a change of air; the act or process of supplying with fresh air. 2 the means of supplying fresh air: *That small window is the only ventilation in the building.* *n.*

ven·ti·la·tor (ven′tə lā′tər) any apparatus or means for changing or improving the air in an enclosed space. *n.*

ven·tril·o·quist (ven tril′ə kwist) a person who can make his voice seem to come from another place: *A ventriloquist can talk almost without moving his lips.* *n.*

☛ **Ventriloquist** comes from Latin *ventriloquus,* a combination of *venter* meaning 'belly' and *loqui* meaning 'speak.'

ven·ture (ven′chər) 1 a risky or daring undertaking: *A lucky venture in oil stock made him a rich man.* 2 expose to risk or danger: *Men venture their lives in war.* 3 dare: *No one ventured to interrupt the speaker.* 4 dare to say or make: *He ventured an objection.* 1 *n.,* 2–4 *v.,* **ven·tured, ven·tur·ing.**

ven·ture·some (ven′chər səm) 1 inclined to take risks; rash; daring: *a venturesome explorer.* 2 risky: *A trip to the moon is a venturesome journey.* *adj.*

Ve·nus (vē′nəs) 1 the Roman goddess of love and beauty. 2 the most brilliant planet, second in distance from the sun and coming closest to the earth. *n.*

ve·ran·da or **ve·ran·dah** (və ran′də) a large covered porch along one or more sides of a house. See **porch** for picture. *n.*

verb (vėrb) a word that tells what is or what is done; the part of speech that expresses action or being. *Examples:* do, go, come, be, sit, think, know, eat. *n.*

ver·bal (vėr′bəl) 1 in words; of words: *A description is a verbal picture.* 2 expressed in spoken words; oral: *a verbal message, a verbal promise.* 3 word for word; literal: *a verbal translation from the French.* 4 of, relating to, or derived from a verb: *a verbal noun.* *adj.* —**ver′bal·ly,** *adv.*

ver·be·na (vər bē′nə) a low growing garden plant with spikes of flowers having various colors. *n.*

ver·dant (vėr′dənt) green: *The fields are covered with verdant grass.* *adj.*

ver·dict (vėr′dikt) 1 the decision of a jury: *The jury returned a verdict of 'Not Guilty.'* 2 any decision or judgment: *the public's verdict, the verdict of history.* *n.*

verge[1] (vėrj) 1 the point at which something begins or happens; brink: *His business is on the verge of ruin.* 2 be on the verge; border: *His talk was so poorly prepared that it verged on the ridiculous.* 1 *n.,* 2 *v.,* **verged, verg·ing.**

verge[2] (vėrj) tend; incline: *She was plump, verging on fatness.* *v.,* **verged, verg·ing.**

ver·i·fy (ver′ə fī′) 1 prove to be true; confirm: *The driver's report of the accident was verified by two women who had seen it happen.* 2 find out the truth of; test the correctness of: *You can verify the spelling of a word by looking in a dictionary.* *v.,* **ver·i·fied, ver·i·fy·ing.**

ver·i·ly (ver′ə lē) in truth; truly; really. *adv.*

ver·i·ta·ble (ver′ə tə bəl) true or real; actual. *adj.*

ver·mil·ion (vər mil′yən) 1 bright red. 2 a bright-red coloring matter. 1, 2 *n.,* 1 *adj.*

ver·min (vėr′mən) 1 small, troublesome, or destructive animals: *Fleas, lice, wasps, rats, and mice are vermin.* 2 a very unpleasant and troublesome person or persons. *n.*

ver·sa·tile (vėr′sə tīl′ or vėr′sə təl) able to do many things well: *She is a very versatile girl; she plays tennis, works with computers, and writes good plays.* *adj.*

verse (vėrs) 1 lines of words with a regularly repeated stress and often with rhyme. 2 a single line of poetry. 3 a group of lines of poetry: *Sing the first verse of 'O Canada.'* 4 in the Bible, a short division of a chapter. *n.*

versed (vėrst) experienced; practised; skilled: *Our doctor is well versed in medicine.* *adj.*

ver·sion (vėr′zhən or vėr′shən) 1 a translation from one language to another: *a version of the Bible.* 2 a statement or description from a particular point of view: *Each of the three boys gave his own version of the quarrel.* *n.*

ver·sus (vėr′səs) against: *In this year's Grey Cup game, it will be the Ottawa Roughriders versus the Edmonton Eskimos.* *prep.*

ver·te·bra (vėr′tə brə) one of the bones of the backbone. See **backbone** for picture. *n., pl.* **ver·te·brae** (vėr′tə brā′ or vėr′tə brē′) or **ver·te·bras.**

ver·te·brate (vėr′tə brāt′ or vėr′tə brit) any animal that has a backbone: *Fish, amphibians, reptiles, birds, and mammals are all vertebrates.* *n.*

ver·tex (vėr′teks) 1 the highest point; the top. 2 the point opposite the base of a triangle, pyramid, etc. *n.*

ver·ti·cal (vėr′tə kəl) 1 straight up and down; perpendicular to a level surface: *A person standing up straight is in a vertical position.* See **horizontal** for picture. 2 a vertical line, circle, position, part, etc. 1 *adj,* 2 *n.*

ver·y (ver′ē) 1 much; greatly; extremely: *The sunshine is very hot in July.* 2 absolutely; exactly: *He stood in the very same place for an hour.* 3 same: *The very* *people who used to love her hate her now.* **4** even; mere; sheer: *The very thought of blood makes her sick. She wept from very joy.* 1, 2 *adv.,* 3, 4 *adj.,* **ver·i·er, ver·i·est.**

☛ **Very** and **vary** are sometimes pronounced the same.

ves·pers or **Ves·pers** (ves′pərz) a church service held in the late afternoon or early evening. *n. pl.*

ves·sel (ves′əl) **1** a ship; a large boat. **2** a hollow holder or container: *Cups, bowls, pitchers, bottles, barrels, and tubs are vessels.* **3** a tube carrying blood or some other fluid: *Veins and arteries are blood vessels. n.*

vest (vest) **1** a short sleeveless garment worn by men or boys under a suit coat. **2** a similar garment worn by women. **3** an undershirt. **4** clothe or robe: *The vested priest stood before the altar.* **5** furnish with powers, authority, rights, etc.: *Parliament is vested with the power to declare war.* **6** put in the possession or control of a person or persons: *The management of the hospital is vested in a board of trustees.* 1–3 *n.,* 4–6 *v.*

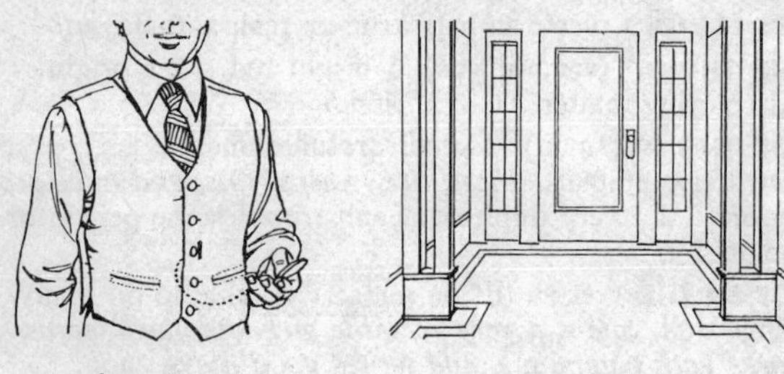

A man's vest A vestibule

ves·ti·bule (ves′tə byül′) **1** a passage or hall between the outer door and the inside of a building. **2** the enclosed space at the end of a railway passenger car. *n.*

ves·tige (ves′tij) all that remains; a trace: *A charred stump was a vestige of the fire. n.*

vest·ment (vest′mənt) a garment, especially one for ceremonial wear or one worn by a clergyman in performing sacred duties. *n.*

vet[1] (vet) *Informal.* veterinarian. *n.*

vet[2] (vet) *Informal.* veteran. *n.*

vet·er·an (vet′ər ən or vet′rən) **1** a person who has served in the armed services, especially during wartime: *There are thousands of Canadian veterans from the Second World War and the Korean War.* **2** a person having had much experience in war: *Veteran troops fought side by side with the young soldiers.* **3** a person who has had much experience in some position, occupation, etc.: *a veteran farmer, a veteran of the stage. n.*

vet·er·i·nar·i·an (vet′ər ə ner′ē ən) a doctor who treats animals. *n.*

vet·er·i·nar·y (vet′ər ə ner′ē) **1** having to do with the medical or surgical treatment of animals. **2** veterinarian. 1 *adj.,* 2 *n., pl.* **vet·er·i·nar·ies.**

ve·to (vē′tō) **1** the power or right to forbid or prevent: *The Senate has the power of veto over most bills passed in the House of Commons.* **2** use the power of veto against; refuse to consent to: *Father vetoed our plan to buy a big snake.* **3** a prohibition; a refusal of consent: *Our plan met with three vetoes, from Father, Mother, and the teacher.* 1, 3 *n., pl.* **ve·toes;** 2 *v.,* **ve·toed, ve·to·ing.**

vex (veks) **1** annoy; anger by trifles; provoke: *It is vexing to have to wait for anyone.* **2** disturb; trouble: *Cape Sable, in Nova Scotia, is much vexed by storms. v.*

vex·a·tion (veks ā′shən) **1** vexing or being vexed: *His face showed his vexation at the delay.* **2** something that vexes: *Rain on Saturday was a vexation to the children. n.*

vi·a (vī′ə or vē′ə) by way of; by a route that passes through: *He is going from Montreal to Toronto via the St. Lawrence Seaway. prep.*

☛ **Via** comes from *via,* meaning 'by way of,' which was originally a form of Latin *via,* meaning 'road' or 'way.'

vi·a·ble (vī′ə bəl) **1** able to stay alive: *a viable animal or plant.* **2** able to keep operating or functioning: *Our program for improving the community seems to be viable, so we ought to continue it. adj.*

vi·a·duct (vī′ə dukt′) a bridge for carrying a road or railway over a valley, a part of a city, etc. *n.*

vi·al (vī′əl) a small bottle, especially a glass bottle for holding medicines, perfumes, etc. *n.*

☛ **Vial** and **viol** are pronounced the same.

vi·and (vī′ənd or vē′ənd) an article of food, especially one of choice quality. *n.*

vi·brant (vī′brənt) **1** vibrating. **2** resounding; resonant. **3** throbbing with vitality, enthusiasm, etc. *adj.*

vi·brate (vī′brāt) **1** move or cause to move rapidly to and fro: *A snake's tongue vibrates. A piano string vibrates and makes a sound when a key is struck.* **2** thrill; respond with feeling: *The crowd vibrated to the sound of the music.* **3** resound: *The clanging vibrated in his ears. v.,* **vi·brat·ed, vi·brat·ing.**

vi·bra·tion (vī brā′shən) a rapid movement to and fro; a quivering motion; vibrating: *The buses shake the house so much that we feel the vibration. n.*

vic·ar (vik′ər) **1** in the Anglican church, a clergyman who carries out the duties of a parish but is not officially the rector: *A rector may be responsible for several parishes, with a different vicar representing him in each one.* **2** in the Roman Catholic church, a deputy or representative of another official: *The cardinal vicar of Rome is appointed to represent the pope.* **3** any person who takes the place of another; a substitute or representative. *n.*

vice[1] (vīs) **1** evil; wickedness. **2** a fault; a bad habit: *He said that his horse had no vices. n.*

☛ **Vice** and **vise** are pronounced the same.

vice[2] (vīs) See **vise.**

☛ See note at **vice**[1].

vice–pres·i·dent (vīz′prez′ə dənt) an official next in rank to a president: *A vice-president takes the president's place when necessary. n.*

vice·re·gal (vīs′rē′gəl) of or having to do with a viceroy. *adj.*

vice·roy (vīs′roi) a person ruling as the deputy of the sovereign. *n.*

vice ver·sa (vī′sə vėr′sə or vīs′vėr′sə) the other way round: *John blamed Harry, and vice versa (Harry blamed John).*

vi·cin·i·ty (və sin′ə tē) **1** a region near or about a place; a neighborhood: *There are no houses for sale in this vicinity.* 2 nearness in place; closeness: *The vicinity of the school to the house was an advantage on rainy days.* *n., pl.* **vi·cin·i·ties.**

hat, āge, fär; let, ēqual, tėrm; it, īce
hot, ōpen, ôrder; oil, out; cup, pu̇t, rüle
əbove, takən, pencəl, lemən, circəs
ch, child; ng, long; sh, ship
th, thin; ᴛʜ, then; zh, measure

vi·cious (vish′əs) 1 evil; wicked: *The drunkard led a vicious life.* 2 having bad habits or a bad disposition: *a vicious horse.* 3 spiteful; malicious: *I won't listen to such vicious gossip.* 4 *Informal.* unpleasantly severe: *a vicious headache.* *adj.*

vicious circle two or more bad things, each of which keeps causing the other: *It's a vicious circle: the more you scratch a flea bite, the more it itches.*

vic·tim (vik′təm) 1 a person or animal sacrificed, injured, or destroyed: *victims of war, victims of a disease, victims of an accident.* 2 a person badly treated by another: *the victim of a swindler.* 3 a person or animal offered as a sacrifice to a god. *n.*

vic·tor (vik′tər) a winner; conqueror. *n.*

Victoria Cross a medal in the shape of a cross, awarded to servicemen for outstanding valor in the presence of the enemy: *The Victoria Cross is the highest award given for bravery in the armed forces of the Commonwealth.*

Victoria Day in Canada, a national holiday falling on the Monday before or on the 24th of May, the birthday of Queen Victoria.

vic·to·ri·ous (vik tô′rē əs) conquering; having won a victory: *a victorious army.* *adj.*

vic·to·ry (vik′tə rē) success in a contest; a defeat of an enemy or opponent: *The game ended in a victory for our school.* *n., pl.* **vic·to·ries.**

vict·ual (vit′əl) 1 Usually, **victuals,** *pl.* food. 2 supply with food or provisions: *The captain victualled his ship for the voyage.* 1 *n.,* 2 *v.,* **vict·ualled** or **vict·ualed, vict·ual·ling** or **vict·ual·ing.**

vi·cu·ña (vi kün′yə or vi kyü′nə) 1 a wild animal of South Ameria, related to the llama, having soft, delicate wool. 2 cloth made from this wool. *n.*

vid·e·o (vid′ē ō′) 1 of or used in the transmission or reception of images in television. 2 television. 1 *adj.,* 2 *n.*

☛ **Video** comes from the Latin word *video,* meaning 'I see.'

vid·e·o·tape (vid′ē ō tāp′) 1 a wide, magnetized tape that records and reproduces both sound and picture for television. 2 to record on videotape. 1 *n.,* 2 *v.,* **vid·e·o·taped, vid·e·o·tap·ing.**

vie (vī) strive for superiority; contend in rivalry; compete: *The children vied with each other to be first in line.* *v.,* **vied, vy·ing.**

view (vyü) 1 an act of seeing; a sight: *It was our first view of the ocean.* 2 the power of seeing; the range of vision: *A ship came into view.* 3 see; look at: *They viewed the scene with pleasure.* 4 something seen; scene: *The view from our house is beautiful.* 5 a picture of some scene: *Various views of the coast hung on the walls.* 6 a mental picture; idea: *This book will give you a general view of the way the pioneers lived.* 7 a way of looking at or considering a matter; opinion: *A child's view of school is different from a teacher's.* 8 consider; regard: *The plan for having classes on Saturdays was not viewed with favor by the students.* 1, 2, 4–7 *n.,* 3, 8 *v.*
in view, a in sight: *As the noise grew louder, the airplane came in view.* **b** under consideration: *Keep the teacher's advice in view as you try to improve your work.* **c** as a purpose or intention: *He works hard and has a definite aim in view.*
in view of, considering; because of.
on view, to be seen; open for people to see: *The exhibit is on view from 9 a.m. to 5 p.m.*
with a view to, a with the purpose or intention of: *He worked hard after school with a view to earning money for a new bicycle.* **b** with a hope of; expecting to.

view·point (vyü′point′) 1 the place from which one looks at something. 2 an attitude of mind; a point of view: *A heavy rain that is good from the viewpoint of farmers may be bad from the viewpoint of tourists.* *n.*

vig·il (vij′əl) 1 staying awake for some purpose; an act of watching; a watch: *All night the mother kept vigil over the sick child.* 2 the day and night before a religious festival. *n.*

vig·i·lance (vij′ə ləns) watchfulness; alertness; caution: *The cat watched the mouse hole with vigilance.* *n.*

vig·i·lant (vij′ə lənt) watchful; alert; wide-awake: *The watchdog was vigilant.* *adj.*

vig·i·lan·te (vij′ə lan′tē) a member of a group of citizens organized informally in a community or district for protection when there is no effective police force. *n.*

vig·or or **vig·our** (vig′ər) 1 active strength or force: *The principal argued with vigor that the new school should have a bigger library.* 2 healthy energy or power: *The old woman had kept the full vigor of her mind.* *n.*

vig·or·ous (vig′ər əs) full of vigor; strong and active; energetic; forceful: *The old man is still vigorous and lively. Doctors wage a vigorous war against disease.* *adj.* —**vig′or·ous·ly,** *adv.*

Vi·king or **vi·king** (vī′king) one of the daring adventurers and pirates from Norway, Denmark and Sweden who raided the coasts of Europe from the eighth to the tenth century. *n.*

vile (vīl) 1 very unpleasant; disgusting: *Old garbage has a vile smell. The weather today was vile—rainy, windy, and cold.* 2 evil; immoral: *The murderer's vile way of life was made public at his trial.* *adj.,* **vil·er, vil·est.**

vil·la (vil′ə) a house in the country or suburbs, sometimes at the seashore: *A villa is usually a large and elegant residence.* *n.*

vil·lage (vil′ij) 1 a group of houses and other buildings, usually in a rural area, having fixed boundaries and some local powers of government: *In Canada, a village is the smallest community that can have its own local government.* 2 the people of a village: *The whole village was out to see the fire.* *n.*

vil·lag·er (vil′ij ər) a person who lives in a village. *n.*

vil·lain (vil′ən) a very wicked person: *The villain stole the box and put the blame on me.* *n.*

vil·lain·ous (vil′ən əs) 1 very wicked. 2 extremely bad; nasty: *a villainous temper.* *adj.*

vil·lain·y (vil′ən ē) 1 great wickedness. 2 a very wicked act; crime. *n., pl.* **vil·lain·ies.**

vim (vim) force; energy; vigor: *The campers were full of vim after a good night's sleep. n.*

vin·di·cate (vin′də kāt′) 1 clear from suspicion, dishonor, or any charge of wrongdoing: *The verdict of 'Not guilty' vindicated him.* 2 defend successfully against opposition; uphold; justify: *He vindicated his claim to his uncle's fortune. v.,* **vin·di·cat·ed, vin·di·cat·ing.**

vin·di·ca·tion (vin′də kā′shən) 1 the act or process of clearing from any charge of wrongdoing. 2 justification: *The success of his invention was a vindication of his new idea. n.*

vin·dic·tive (vin dik′tiv) 1 bearing a grudge; wanting revenge: *He is so vindictive that he never forgives anybody.* 2 showing a strong tendency toward revenge: *Vindictive acts rarely do much good. adj.*

vine (vīn) 1 a plant having a long, slender stem that grows along the ground or that climbs by attaching itself to a wall, tree, or other support: *Melons and pumpkins grow on vines. Ivy is a vine.* 2 a grapevine. *n.*

vin·e·gar (vin′ə gər) a sour liquid produced by the fermenting of cider, wine, etc.: *Vinegar is used to flavor and to preserve food. n.*

☛ **Vinegar** came into English in the Middle Ages from a French word made up of *vin,* meaning 'wine,' and *aigre,* meaning 'sour.'

vine·yard (vin′yərd) a place planted with grapevines. *n.*

vin·tage (vin′tij) 1 the wine or grapes from a certain crop: *The finest vintages cost much more than others.* 2 the season of gathering grapes and making wine. 3 *Informal.* the crop or output of anything at some particular time: *Her bike is of the 1950 vintage.* 4 excellent; outstanding: *a vintage year, a vintage crop.* 1–3 *n.,* 4 *adj.*

vi·nyl (vī′nil) a tough, man-made plastic used to make floor and furniture coverings, toys, phonograph records, and other articles. *n.*

vi·ol (vī′əl) one of several musical instruments, similar to the violin but usually having six strings and played with a curved bow. *n.*

☛ **Viol** and **vial** are pronounced the same.

vi·o·la (vē ō′lə or vī ō′lə) a stringed musical instrument shaped like a violin, but slightly larger and having a lower tone. *n.*

vi·o·late (vī′ə lāt′) 1 break a law, rule, agreement, promise, etc.; act contrary to: *Speeding violates the traffic regulations.* 2 break in upon; disturb: *The sound of the explosion violated the usual calm of Sunday morning.* 3 treat with disrespect or contempt: *The soldiers violated the church by using it as a stable. v.,* **vi·o·lat·ed, vi·o·lat·ing.**

vi·o·la·tion (vī′ə lā′shən) 1 a breaking of a law, rule, agreement, promise, etc.: *He was fined $10 for his violation of the traffic law.* 2 an interruption or disturbance. 3 the treatment of a holy thing with disrespect or contempt. *n.*

vi·o·la·tor (vī′ə lā′tər) one who violates. *n.*

vi·o·lence (vī′ə ləns) 1 rough force in action: *He slammed the door with violence.* 2 rough or harmful action or treatment: *The policeman had to use violence in arresting the gunman.* 3 harm; injury: *It would do violence to her principles to work on Sunday.* 4 strength of feeling: *We were shocked by the violence of her hate. n.*

vi·o·lent (vī′ə lənt) 1 acting or done with strong, rough force: *a violent blow.* 2 caused by strong, rough force: *a violent death.* 3 showing or caused by very strong feeling, action, etc.: *violent language.* 4 severe; extreme; very great: *a violent pain, violent heat. adj.* **—vi′o·lent·ly,** *adv.*

vi·o·let (vī′ə lit) 1 a small plant with purple, blue, yellow, or white flowers: *Many common violets grow wild and bloom in the spring.* 2 bluish purple: *Violet is red and blue mixed.* 1, 2 *n.,* 2 *adj.*

A violin

vi·o·lin (vī′ə lin′) a small musical instrument having four strings, played by drawing a bow across the strings: *The violin has a tone of great variety and richness. n.*

vi·o·lin·ist (vī′ə lin′ist) a person skilled in playing the violin. *n.*

vi·o·lon·cel·lo (vī′ə lən chel′ō) cello. *n., pl.* **vi·o·lon·cel·los.**

vi·per (vī′pər) 1 a poisonous snake having a pair of large, hollow fangs: *Rattlesnakes are vipers.* 2 a spiteful, treacherous person. *n.*

vir·gin (vėr′jən) 1 a maiden; an unmarried woman. 2 pure; spotless: *Virgin snow is newly fallen snow.* 3 not changed or used by man: *virgin soil, virgin forest.* 1 *n.,* 2, 3 *adj.*

vir·tu·al (vėr′chü əl) real; actual; being something in effect, though not so in name; for all practical purposes: *He is the virtual president, though his title is secretary. The battle was won with so great a loss of soldiers that it was a virtual defeat. adj.* **—vir′tu·al·ly,** *adv.*

vir·tue (vėr′chü) 1 goodness; moral excellence: *Her virtue is shown in her many good deeds.* 2 a particular kind of goodness: *Justice and kindness are virtues.* 3 a good quality: *He praised the virtues of his car.* 4 the power to produce good results: *There is little virtue in that medicine. n.*

by or **in virtue of,** because of; on account of: *By virtue of getting to the theatre early, they got the best seats.*

vir·tu·ous (vėr′chü əs) good; moral; righteous: *virtuous conduct, a virtuous life, a virtuous person. adj.*

vi·rus (vī′rəs) 1 any one of a group of substances that cause certain infectious diseases: *Viruses are so small that they cannot be seen through most microscopes.* 2 something that poisons the mind or morals: *the virus of prejudice. n.*

vis·age (viz′ij) the face: *a grim visage, a visage of despair. n.*

☛ The words **visage, visible, visibility, vision, visionary, visit, visitor, visor, vista,** and **visual** came into English from Latin, French, and Italian words

hat, āge, fär; let, ēqual, tėrm; it, īce
hot, ōpen, ôrder; oil, out; cup, pu̇t, rüle
əbove, takən, pencəl, lemən, circəs
ch, child; ng, long; sh, ship
th, thin; ᴛʜ, then; zh, measure

which all developed from one Latin word, the verb *videre*, meaning 'to see.'

vis·count (vī′kount) a nobleman ranking next below an earl or count and next above a baron. *n.*

vis·count·ess (vī′koun tis) 1 the wife or widow of a viscount. 2 a woman who holds in her own right a rank equal to that of a viscount. *n.*

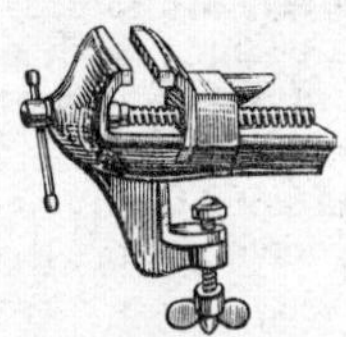

A vise. It can be fastened to a carpenter's bench by the screw at the bottom.

vise or **vice** (vīs) a tool having two jaws moved by a screw, used to hold an object firmly while work is being done on it. *n.*

☛ **Vise** and **vice** are pronounced the same.

vis·i·bil·i·ty (viz′ə bil′ə tē) the distance at which things are visible: *Fog and rain decreased visibility to about 12 metres.* *n.*

☛ See note at **visage.**

vis·i·ble (viz′ə bəl) 1 that can be seen: *The shore was barely visible through the fog.* 2 apparent; obvious: *The tramp had no visible means of support.* *adj.*

☛ See note at **visage.**

vis·i·bly (viz′ə blē) so as to be visible; plainly: *After the hike over the mountain the boys were visibly weary.* *adv.*

vi·sion (vizh′ən) 1 the power of seeing; the sense of sight: *The old man wears glasses because his vision is poor.* 2 the act or fact of seeing; sight: *The vision of the table loaded with food made our mouths water.* 3 the power of perceiving by the imagination or by clear thinking: *the vision of a prophet, a man of great vision.* 4 something seen in the imagination, in a dream, etc.: *The beggar had visions of great wealth.* *n.*

☛ See note at **visage.**

vi·sion·ar·y (vizh′ən er′ē) a person who is not practical; dreamer: *Many great scientists have been visionaries.* 2 not practicable; fanciful: *visionary plans for travelling to the stars.* 1 *n., pl.* **vi·sion·ar·ies;** 2 *adj.*

☛ See note at **visage.**

vis·it (viz′it) 1 go to see; come to see: *Would you like to visit Victoria?* 2 make a call on; stay with; make a stay; be a guest of: *I shall visit my aunt next week.* 3 the act of visiting; a short stay: *My aunt paid us a visit last week.* 4 come upon; afflict: *The poor old man was visited by many troubles.* 1, 2, 4 *v.*, 3 *n.*

☛ See note at **visage.**

vis·i·tor (viz′ə tər) a person who visits or is visiting; guest: *Visitors from the East arrived last night.* *n.*

☛ See note at **visage.**

vi·sor or **vi·zor** (vī′zər) 1 the movable front part of a helmet, covering the face. See **armor** for picture. 2 a projecting part, such as the peak of a cap, intended to protect the eyes from bright sun or other strong light. 3 a small movable shade attached at the top of an automobile windshield. *n.*

☛ See note at **visage.**

vis·ta (vis′tə) 1 a view seen through a narrow opening or passage: *The opening between the two rows of trees afforded a vista of the lake.* 2 such an opening or passage itself: *a shady vista of elms.* 3 a mental view: *Education should open up new vistas.* *n.*

☛ See note at **visage.**

vis·u·al (vizh′ü əl) of, having to do with, or used in sight or vision: *Being near-sighted is a visual defect. The teacher used diagrams and motion pictures as visual aids to help us learn the safety rules.* *adj.*

☛ See note at **visage.**

vis·u·al·ize (vizh′ü əl īz′) form a mental picture of: *I can visualize his reaction when he hears the news.* *v.*, **vis·u·al·ized, vis·u·al·iz·ing.**

vi·tal (vī′təl) 1 of life; having to do with life: *vital forces.* 2 necessary to life: *Eating is a vital function. The heart is a vital organ.* 3 **vitals,** *pl.* **a** parts of organs necessary to life: *The brain, heart, lungs, and stomach are vitals.* **b** the essential parts or features. 4 essential; very important: *The education of young people is vital to the future of our country.* 5 causing death, failure, or ruin: *a vital wound, a vital blow to an industry.* 6 full of life and spirit; lively: *What a vital boy he is—never idle, never dull!* 1, 2, 4–6 *adj.*, 3 *n.*

☛ **Vital** and **vitality** came into English in the Middle Ages from the Latin adjective *vitalis,* meaning 'of life.'

vi·tal·i·ty (vī tal′ə tē) 1 vital force; the power to live: *Her vitality was lessened by illness.* 2 the power to endure and act: *Canada has great vitality.* 3 strength; vigor of mind or body: *There is little vitality in his weak efforts to cope with his problems.* *n., pl.* **vi·tal·i·ties.**

☛ See note at **vital.**

vi·ta·min (vī′tə min) 1 any of certain substances necessary for the normal growth and proper nourishment of the body, found especially in milk, butter, raw fruits and vegetables, cod-liver oil, and the outside part of wheat and other grains: *Lack of vitamins causes certain diseases as well as general poor health.* 2 of or containing vitamins: *He protected himself against vitamin deficiency by taking vitamin tablets.* 1 *n.*, 2 *adj.*

vi·va·cious (vi vā′shəs or vī vā′shəs) lively; sprightly; animated; gay: *The girl had a vivacious smile.* *adj.*

vi·vac·i·ty (vi vas′ə tē or vī vas′ə tē) liveliness; gaiety. *n., pl.* **vi·vac·i·ties.**

viv·id (viv′id) 1 strikingly bright; brilliant; strong and clear: *Dandelions are a vivid yellow.* 2 lively; full of life: *Her description of the party was so vivid that I almost felt I had been there.* 3 strong and distinct: *I have a vivid memory of the fire.* *adj.*

vix·en (vik′sən) 1 a female fox. 2 a bad-tempered or quarrelsome woman. *n.*

vi·zier or **vi·zir** (vi zēr′) a high official in Moslem countries; a minister of state. *n.*

vi·zor (vī′zər) See visor.

vo·cab·u·lar·y (vō kab′yə ler′ē) 1 the stock of words used by a person or group of people: *Reading will increase your vocabulary. The vocabulary of science has grown tremendously in the past 20 years.* 2 a list of words, usually arranged in alphabetical order, with their translations or meanings: *There is a vocabulary in the back of our French book.* *n., pl.* **vo·cab·u·lar·ies.**

vo·cal (vō′kəl) **1** of, by, for, with, or having to do with the voice: *The tongue is a vocal organ. I like vocal music better than instrumental.* **2** having a voice; giving forth sound: *Men are vocal beings. The zoo was vocal with the roar of the lions.* **3** aroused to speech; inclined to talk freely: *He became vocal with anger.* *adj.*
☛ See note at **voice.**

vocal cords either of two pairs of membranes in the larynx: *The lower pair of vocal cords are relaxed when one whispers, but otherwise they are drawn tight and made to vibrate when one utters vowel sounds and most consonant sounds.*

vo·cal·ist (vō′kəl ist) singer. *n.*

vo·ca·tion (vō kā′shən) **1** an occupation, business, profession, or trade: *She chose teaching as her vocation.* **2** an inclination or summons to a particular activity, especially to religious work: *Since childhood she felt a vocation for nursing.* *n.*

vo·ca·tion·al (və kā′shən əl or vō kā′shən əl) of or having to do with some occupation, trade, etc.: *Trades such as carpentry, stenography, and printing are taught in vocational schools.* *adj.*

vo·cif·er·ous (və sif′ər əs or vō sif′ər əs) loud and noisy; shouting; clamoring: *a vociferous person, vociferous cheers.* *adj.*

vod·ka (vod′kə) an alcoholic liquor made from potatoes, rye, barley, or corn. *n.*
☛ **Vodka** comes from the Russian name for this drink, which developed from Russian *voda,* meaning 'water.'

vogue (vōg) **1** the fashion: *Hoop skirts were the vogue many years ago.* **2** popularity or acceptance: *That song had a great vogue at one time.* *n.*

voice (vois) **1** the sound or sounds human beings make in speaking, singing, laughing, etc.: *The voices of the children could be heard coming from the playground.* **2** the power to make such sounds: *His voice was gone because of a sore throat.* **3** anything like speech or song: *the voice of the wind.* **4** express; utter: *They voiced their approval of the plan.* **5** expression: *They gave voice to their joy.* **6** an expressed opinion or choice: *His voice was for compromise.* **7** the right to express an opinion or choice: *We had no voice in the matter.* 1–3, 5–7 *n.,* 4 *v.,* **voiced, voic·ing.**
☛ Both **voice** and **vocal** came originally from the Latin word *vox,* meaning 'voice.' However, **voice** came into English through Old French *vois,* meaning 'voice'; **vocal** came into English later directly from Latin **vocalis,** meaning 'with the sound of the voice.'

void (void) **1** an empty space: *The death of his dog left an aching void in Bill's heart.* **2** empty; vacant: *a void space.* **3** without force; not binding in law: *Any contract made by a twelve-year-old boy is void.* **4** make of no force or effect in law: *The contract was voided by the court.* **5** to empty out. 1 *n.,* 2, 3 *adj.,* 4, 5 *v.*

vol·a·tile (vol′ə tīl′ or vol′ə təl) **1** evaporating rapidly; changing into vapor easily: *Gasoline is volatile.* **2** changing rapidly from one mood or interest to another: *He has a volatile disposition; he changes very quickly from being happy to being sad.* *adj.*

vol·can·ic (vol kan′ik) **1** of or caused by a volcano; having to do with volcanoes: *a volcanic eruption.* **2** like a volcano; liable to break out violently: *a volcanic temper.* *adj.*

vol·ca·no (vol kā′nō) **1** an opening in the earth's crust through which steam, ashes, and lava are forced out. **2** a hill or mountain around this opening, built up of the material that is forced out. *n., pl.* **vol·ca·noes** or **vol·ca·nos.**

vole (vōl) an animal belonging to the same family as rats and mice, but usually heavier and having short legs and tail. *n.*

vol·ley (vol′ē) **1** a shower of stones, bullets, arrows, etc.: *A volley of arrows rained down from the walls upon the attacking troops.* **2** the discharge of a number of guns at once. **3** discharge or be discharged in a volley: *Cannon volleyed on all sides.* **4** a burst or outpouring of words, shouts, cheers, etc. 1, 2, 4 *n., pl.* **vol·leys;** 3 *v.,* **vol·leyed, vol·ley·ing.**

vol·ley·ball (vol′ē bol′ or vol′ē bôl′) **1** a game played with a large ball and a high net: *In volleyball, the players try to hit the ball with their hands so that it goes back and forth across the net without touching the ground.* **2** the ball used in this game. *n.*

volt (vōlt) the unit of electric pressure, used to measure the ability of any source of electricity to make an electric current flow between two points: *The electric pressure between the two terminals of this lantern battery is 6 volts. Symbol:* V *n.*
☛ Named after an Italian physicist, Count Alessandro *Volta* (1745–1827), who invented the electric battery.

vol·tage (vōl′tij) the strength of electric pressure, measured in volts: *A current of high voltage is used in transmitting electric power over long distances.* *n.*

vol·u·ble (vol′yə bəl) **1** ready to talk much; talkative. **2** having an easy rapid flow of words. *adj.*

vol·ume (vol′yəm or vol′yüm) **1** a book: *We own a library of five hundred volumes.* **2** a book forming part of a set or series: *You can find what you want to know in the ninth volume of this encyclopedia.* **3** the space occupied: *The storeroom has a volume of 12 cubic metres.* **4** an amount; quantity: *Volumes of smoke poured from the chimneys of the factory.* **5** an amount or loudness of sound; a fullness of tone: *A pipe organ has more volume than a violin or flute.* *n.*

vo·lu·mi·nous (və lü′mə nəs) **1** forming or filling a large book or many books: *a voluminous report.* **2** of great size; very bulky: *A voluminous cloak covered the horseman from top to toe.* *adj.*

vol·un·tar·i·ly (vol′ən ter′ə lē) of one's own choice; without force or compulsion: *Did you do that voluntarily, or did someone force you to do it by threats?* *adv.*

vol·un·tar·y (vol′ən ter′ē) **1** acting, done, made, given, etc. of one's choice; not forced; not compelled: *The thief's confession was voluntary. The church is supported by voluntary contributions.* **2** in law, intended; done on purpose: *voluntary manslaughter.* **3** controlled by the will: *Speaking and walking are voluntary; breathing is only partly so.* *adj.*

vol·un·teer (vol′ən tēr′) **1** a person who enters any service by his own choice; one who is not drafted: *Some*

hat, āge, fär; let, ēqual, tėrm; it, īce
hot, ōpen, ôrder; oil, out; cup, pu̇t, rüle
əbove, takən, pencəl, lemən, circəs
ch, child; ng, long; sh, ship
th, thin; ᴛʜ, then; zh, measure

soldiers are volunteers. **2** a person who serves without pay: *In some towns, the firemen are volunteers.* **3** offer one's services: *As soon as war was declared, many men volunteered for the army.* **4** offer of one's own free will: *He volunteered to carry the water.* **5** made up of volunteers: *Our village has a volunteer fire department.* 1, 2 *n.*, 3, 4 *v.*, 5 *adj.*

vom·it (vom′it) **1** expel the contents of the stomach through the mouth; throw up what has been eaten. **2** the substance thrown up from the stomach. **3** throw out with force: *The chimneys vomited smoke.* 1, 3 *v.*, 2 *n.*

vo·ra·cious (və rā′shəs) **1** eating much; greedy in eating; ravenous: *voracious sharks.* **2** very eager; unable to be satisfied: *He is a voracious reader of history.* *adj.*

vor·tex (vôr′teks) a whirling mass of water, air, etc. that sucks everything near it into its centre: *A whirlpool is a kind of vortex.* *n.*

vote (vōt) **1** a formal expression of a wish or choice: *In an election, the person receiving the most votes is elected.* **2** the right to give such an expression: *In federal elections, we don't have the vote until we are 19 years old. In our club, those who have not paid their fees do not have the vote.* **3** a ballot: *More than a million votes were cast.* **4** votes considered together: *the labor vote, the vote of the people.* **5** give a vote: *He voted for the new school.* **6** pass, determine, or grant by a vote: *Money for a new school was voted by the board.* **7** declare: *The children all voted the trip a great success.* 1–4 *n.*, 5–7 *v.*, **vot·ed, vot·ing.**

vot·er (vōt′ər) a person who has the right to vote. *n.*

vouch (vouch) be responsible; give a guarantee: *I can vouch for the truth of the story. The principal vouched for Bill's honesty.* *v.*

vouch·safe (vouch sāf′) be willing to grant or give; deign to do or give: *The proud boy vouchsafed no reply when we told him we had not meant to hurt his feelings.* *v.*, **vouch·safed, vouch·saf·ing.**

vow (vou) **1** a solemn promise: *a vow of secrecy, marriage vows.* **2** a promise made to God: *a nun's vows.* **3** make a vow: *She vowed not to tell the secret.* **4** declare earnestly or emphatically: *She vowed she would never shop there again.* 1, 2 *n.*, 3, 4 *v.*

vow·el (vou′əl) **1** a speech sound in which the breath is not stopped at any point by the tongue, teeth, or lips: *When you say 'awe,' you are uttering a vowel.* **2** a letter representing such a sound: *There are five vowels used in writing, a, e, i, o, and u.* *n.*

voy·age (voi′ij) **1** a journey by water: *We had a pleasant voyage to England.* **2** a journey through the air or through space: *an airplane voyage, the earth's voyage around the sun.* **3** make or take a voyage; travel by water or air: *Columbus voyaged on unknown seas.* 1, 2 *n.*, 3 *v.*, **voy·aged, voy·ag·ing. —voy′ag·er,** *n.*

vo·ya·geur (voi′ə zhėr′) *Cdn.* **1** a boatman, especially a French Canadian, in the service of the early fur-trading companies. **2** a boatman or woodsman of the Canadian forests, especially in the North. *n.*

vs. versus.

vul·gar (vul′gər) **1** showing poor manners, taste, etc.; not refined; coarse: *The tramp used vulgar words.* **2** of the common people: *Modern French, Italian, Portuguese, and Spanish developed from vulgar varieties of Latin.* *adj.*

☛ **Vulgar** came into English in the Middle Ages from Latin *vulgaris,* meaning 'of the people,' 'ordinary,' which in turn was formed from *vulgus,* meaning 'a crowd,' 'the common people,' 'the public.'

vul·gar·i·ty (vul gar′ə tē or vul ger′ə tē) **1** lack of refinement; lack of good training, manners, taste, etc.: *Talking loudly in a bus and chewing gum at a dance are signs of vulgarity.* **2** something done or said that shows vulgarity; a vulgar act or word: *His vulgarities made him unwelcome in our home.* *n.*, *pl.* **vul·gar·i·ties.**

vul·ner·a·ble (vul′nər ə bəl) capable of being wounded or injured; open to attack: *Your head is vulnerable when you play hockey–wear a helmet, please.* *adj.*

vulnerable to, sensitive to; offended or influenced by: *Most people are vulnerable to ridicule.*

vul·ture (vul′chər) **1** a large bird of prey, related to eagles and hawks, that eats the flesh of dead animals. **2** a greedy, ruthless person: *Misers, swindlers, and other vultures are not welcome here.* *n.*

vy·ing (vī′ing) See **vie.** *The boys were vying with each other for a position on the baseball team.* *v.*

w or **W** (dub′əl yü′) the 23rd letter of the alphabet: *There are two* w's *in* window. *n., pl.* **w's** or **W's.**

W. or **W** 1 west. 2 western.

wab·ble (wob′əl) See **wobble.** *v.,* **wab·bled, wab·bling.**

wad (wod) 1 a small, soft mass: *He used wads of cotton to plug his ears.* 2 a tight roll; compact bundle or mass: *a wad of bills.* 3 make into a wad; press into a wad: *He wadded up the paper and threw it on the floor.* 4 a round plug of cloth, cardboard, etc., used to hold the powder and shot in place in a gun or cartridge. 5 stuff with a wad. 1, 2, 4 *n.,* 3, 5 *v.,* **wad·ded, wad·ding.**

wad·dle (wod′əl) 1 walk with short steps and an awkward, swaying motion, as a duck does: *A very fat man with very fat legs waddled across the street.* 2 an awkward, swaying gait: *It made us laugh to see his waddle.* 1 *v.,* **wad·dled, wad·dling;** 2 *n.*

wade (wād) 1 walk through water, snow, sand, mud, or anything that hinders free motion. 2 make one's way with difficulty: *Must I wade through that dull book?* 3 get across or pass through by wading: *The soldiers waded the stream when they saw the bridge had been destroyed. v.,* **wad·ed, wad·ing.**
wade into, *Informal.* attack, go at, or go to work on vigorously: *She wades into every activity we plan.*

wa·fer (wā′fər) 1 a very thin cake, biscuit, or candy: *a soda wafer, a mint wafer.* 2 in some churches, the thin, round piece of bread used in the Communion. *n.*

waf·fle (wof′əl) a light, crisp cake made from a batter and cooked in a waffle iron. *n.*

A waffle iron and waffles

waffle iron a utensil in which waffles are cooked, consisting of two hinged parts having projections on the inside.

waft (waft or woft) 1 carry over water or through air: *The waves wafted the boat to shore.* 2 a breath or puff of air, wind, etc.: *A waft of fresh air came through the open window.* 3 a waving movement: *a waft of the hand.* 1 *v.,* 2, 3 *n.*

wag (wag) 1 move from side to side or up and down: *The dog wagged its tail. Its tail wagged back and forth.* 2 a wagging motion: *He refused with a wag of his head.* 3 a person who is fond of making jokes. 1 *v.,* **wagged, wag·ging;** 2, 3 *n.*

wage (wāj) 1 an amount paid for work: *His wages are $4.50 an hour.* 2 something given in return: *His illness taught him the wages of poor eating.* 3 carry on: *Doctors wage war against disease.* 1, 2 *n.,* 3 *v.,* **waged, wag·ing.**

wa·ger (wā′jər) 1 make a bet; bet: *I'll wager $10 that the black horse will win the race. He doesn't often wager.* 2 a bet: *The wager of $10 was promptly paid.* 1 *v.,* 2 *n.*

wag·gish (wag′ish) 1 fond of making jokes. 2 funny; humorous: *He had a waggish look as he told about the practical joke. adj.*

wag·gle (wag′əl) 1 move quickly and repeatedly from side to side; wag. 2 a wagging motion. 1 *v.,* **wag·gled, wag·gling;** 2 *n.*

wag·on (wag′ən) a four-wheeled vehicle, especially one for carrying loads: *a tea wagon, a toy wagon, a station wagon. n.* Also spelled **waggon.**

waif (wāf) 1 a person without home or friends, especially a homeless or neglected child. 2 anything without an owner; a stray thing, animal, etc. *n.*

wail (wāl) 1 cry loud and long because of grief or pain: *The baby wailed.* 2 a long cry of grief or pain. 3 a sound like such a cry: *the wail of a hungry coyote.* 4 make a mournful sound: *The wind wailed around the old house.* 1, 4 *v.,* 2, 3 *n.*

☛ **Wail** and **whale** are sometimes pronounced the same.

wain·scot (wān′skot or wān′skət) a lining of wood on the walls of a room: *A wainscot usually has panels. n.*

waist (wāst) 1 the part of a person's body between the ribs and the hips. 2 waistline. 3 a garment or part of a garment covering the body from the neck or shoulders to the hips. 4 a narrow middle part: *the waist of a violin. n.*

☛ **Waist** and **waste** are pronounced the same.

waist·coat (wāst′kōt′ or wes′kət) a man's vest. See **vest** for picture. *n.*

waist·line (wāst′līn′) 1 an imaginary line around the body at the smallest part of the waist. 2 in a garment, the seam joining the top and bottom sections, usually at or near the smallest part of the waist: *Higher waistlines are the fashion this year. n.*

wait (wāt) 1 stay or stop doing something till someone comes or something happens: *Let's wait in the shade.* 2 *Informal.* delay or put off: *Mother waited dinner for us.* 3 the act or time of waiting: *He had a long wait at the doctor's office.* 4 be ready; look forward: *He is waiting impatiently for his holidays.* 5 act as a servant; change plates, pass food, etc. at table. 1, 2, 4, 5 *v.,* 3 *n.*
lie in wait, stay hidden, ready to attack: *Robbers lay in wait for the travellers.*
wait on or **wait upon, a** be a servant to. **b** call on to pay a respectful visit: *The victorious general waited upon the king.*

☛ **Wait** and **weight** are pronounced the same.

wait·er (wāt′ər) a man who waits on tables in a hotel, restaurant, etc. *n.*

wait·ing (wāt′ing) 1 that waits: *The waiting crowd rushed to the train as soon as it was ready.* 2 used to wait in: *a waiting room. adj.*
in waiting, in attendance on a king, queen, prince, princess, etc.

wait·ress (wāt′ris) a woman who waits on tables in a hotel, restaurant, etc. *n.*

waive (wāv) give up; refrain from pressing or claiming; renounce: *The lawyer waived her right to cross-examine the witness. v.,* **waived, waiv·ing.**

☛ **Waive** and **wave** are pronounced the same.

hat, āge, fär; let, ēqual, tėrm; it, īce
hot, ōpen, ôrder; oil, out; cup, pu̇t, rüle
əbove, takən, pencəl, lemən, circəs
ch, child; ng, long; sh, ship
th, thin; ᴛʜ, then; zh, measure

wake[1] (wāk) **1** stop sleeping: *I usually wake at dawn.* **2** cause to stop sleeping: *The noise will wake the baby.* **3** be awake; stay awake: *all his waking hours.* **4** become alive or active: *Flowers wake in the spring.* **5** make alive or active: *He needs some interest to wake him up.* **6** a watching over the body of a dead person before its burial. **7** keep watch. 1–5, 7 *v.,* **woke** or **waked, wak·ing;** 6 *n.*

wake[2] (wāk) **1** the track left behind a moving ship. **2** a track left behind anything. *n.*
in the wake of, behind; after: *Floods came in the wake of the hurricane.*

wake·ful (wāk′fəl) **1** not able to sleep. **2** without sleep. **3** watchful. *adj.* **—wake′ful·ness,** *n.*

wak·en (wāk′ən) stop sleeping or cause to stop sleeping; wake. *v.*

walk (wok or wôk) **1** go on foot: *Walk down to the post office with me. In walking, a person always has one foot on the ground.* **2** go over, on, or through on foot: *The man walked the floor in pain from toothache.* **3** cause to walk; make go step by step: *The rider walked his horse up the hill.* **4** the act of walking, especially for pleasure or exercise: *The children went for a walk.* **5** a distance to walk: *It is a short walk from our house to the school.* **6** a manner or way of walking; gait: *We knew the man was a sailor from his rolling walk.* **7** a route, sidewalk, or path for walking: *We always preferred the walk down by the river. I shovelled the snow off the walk. There are many pretty walks in the park.* **8** occupation; social position: *A doctor and a street cleaner are in different walks of life.* 1–3 *v.,* 4–8 *n.*

walk·ie–talk·ie (wok′ē tok′ē or wôk′ē tôk′ē) a small, portable, two-way radio set: *Two people using very strong walkie-talkies can talk to each other at a distance of six kilometres. n., pl.* **walk·ie-talk·ies.**

walk·o·ver (wok′ō′vər or wôk′ō′vər) *Informal.* an easy victory. *n.*

wall (wol or wôl) **1** the side of a house, room, or other hollow thing. **2** stone, brick, or other material built up to enclose, divide, support, or protect: *Cities used to be surrounded by high walls to keep out enemies.* **3** something like a wall in looks or use: *The flood came in a wall of water five metres high. The soldiers kept their ranks a solid wall.* **4** enclose, divide, protect, or fill with a wall: *The garden is walled. Workmen walled up the doorway.* 1–3 *n.,* 4 *v.*
drive to the wall, make desperate or helpless: *His debts drove him to the wall and he finally became bankrupt.*

wal·let (wol′it) a small, flat, folding case, often made of leather, for carrying money, cards, etc. in one's pocket. *n.*

wal·lop (wol′əp) *Informal.* **1** beat soundly; thrash. **2** hit very hard. **3** a very hard blow: *The wallop knocked him out.* **4** the power to hit very hard blows: *He's got a real wallop! My arm still hurts.* **5** defeat thoroughly, as in a game. 1, 2, 5 *v.,* 3, 4 *n.*

wal·low (wol′ō) **1** roll about; flounder: *The pigs wallowed in the mud. The boat wallowed helplessly in the stormy sea.* **2** indulge oneself excessively in some pleasure, state of mind, way of living, etc.: *wallow in luxury. She wallowed for hours in the music of her favorite records.* **3** the act of wallowing. **4** a place where an animal wallows: *There used to be many buffalo wallows on the prairies.* 1, 2 *v.,* 3, 4 *n.*

wall·pa·per (wol′pā′pər or wôl′pā′pər) **1** paper, usually printed with a pattern in color, for pasting on and covering walls. **2** put wallpaper on. 1 *n.,* 2 *v.*

wal·nut (wol′nut′ or wôl′nut′) **1** a rather large, almost round nut with a division between its two halves: *The meat of the walnut is good to eat.* **2** the tree it grows on. **3** the wood of this tree: *Some kinds of walnut are used in making furniture. n.*

☛ **Walnut** developed from the Old English word *wealhhnutu,* from *wealh,* meaning 'foreign' and *hnutu,* meaning 'nut.'

A walrus — about 3.5 m long

wal·rus (wol′rəs or wôl′rəs) a large sea animal of the arctic regions, resembling a seal but having long tusks: *Walrus hide is made into leather for luggage. n., pl.* **wal·rus** or **wal·rus·es.**

waltz (wolts or wôlts) **1** a smooth, even, gliding dance. **2** the music for such a dance. **3** dance a waltz. 1, 2 *n.,* 3 *v.*

Wampum

wam·pum (wom′pəm) beads made from shells, formerly used by North American Indians as money or for ornament. *n.*

wan (won) **1** pale: *Her face looked wan after her long illness.* **2** faint; weak; looking worn or tired: *The sick boy gave the doctor a wan smile. adj.,* **wan·ner, wan·nest.**

wand (wond) a slender stick or rod: *The magician waved his wand and a rabbit popped out of the hat. n.*

wan·der (won′dər) **1** move about without any special purpose: *We wandered through the stores without buying anything.* **2** go from the right way; stray: *The dog wandered off and got lost.* **3** talk or think in an unreasonable way; ramble: *Fever made his mind wander. She wanders away from her subject when she talks. v.* **—wan′der·er,** *n.*

wane (wān) **1** lose size; become smaller gradually:

The moon wanes after it has become full. **2** lose strength, power, or importance: *Her influence in the club has waned.* *v.,* **waned, wan·ing.**
on the wane, growing less; waning: *The power of the president was on the wane.*

wan·gle (wang′gəl) *Informal.* manage to get by schemes, tricks, or persuasion: *She wangled an invitation to the party.* *v.,* **wan·gled, wan·gling.**

wan·i·gan (won′ə gən) **1** a lumberman's chest or trunk. **2** *Cdn.* a tracked vehicle used for carrying troops and supplies in the North. *n.*

☛ **Wanigan** comes from a North American Indian word *waniigan,* meaning 'trap' or 'place for stray objects.'

want (wont) **1** wish for; wish: *The child wants his dinner. He wants to become an engineer.* **2** something desired or needed: *He is a man of few wants and is happy with simple pleasures.* **3** lack; be without: *The fund for a new church wants only a few hundred dollars of the sum needed.* **4** a lack; being without something desired or needed: *The plant died for want of water.* **5** to need: *That plant wants water.* **6** a need: *The water supplied a want that had been felt for many days.* **7** poverty: *There is want in many parts of the city.* **8** wish to see, speak to, or use a person: *Call me if you want me.* 1, 3, 5, 8 *v.,* 2, 4, 6, 7 *n.*
want for, lack: *They are wealthy people and want for nothing.*

want ad *Informal.* a notice in a newspaper that an employee, an apartment, an article of some kind, etc. is wanted, or is for sale or rent.

want·ing (won′ting) **1** lacking; missing: *The machine had some of its parts wanting.* **2** not satisfactory; not coming up to a standard or need: *The stranger was wanting in courtesy. The vegetables were weighed and found wanting.* *adj.*

wan·ton (won′tən) **1** done in a reckless, heartless, or pointless way; done without reason or excuse: *a wanton attack, wanton mischief. That boy hurts animals from wanton cruelty.* **2** not moral; not chaste: *a wanton woman.* **3** a person who is not moral or not chaste. **4** playful not restrained: *a wanton mood, a wanton child, a wanton breeze.* 1, 2, 4 *adj.,* 3 *n.*

wap·i·ti (wop′i tē) the North American elk, a deer having long branched antlers. *n., pl.* **wap·i·ti** or **wap·i·tis.**

war (wôr) **1** fighting carried on by armed force between nations or parts of a nation. **2** any struggle; strife; conflict: *Doctors carry on war against disease. There is always a war between his gang and mine.* **3** the occupation or art of fighting with weapons: *Soldiers are trained for war.* **4** fight; make war: *war against poverty. Germany warred against France.* 1–3 *n.,* 4 *v.,* **warred, war·ring.**

☛ **War** and **wore** are pronounced the same.

war·ble (wôr′bəl) **1** sing with trills, quavers, etc.: *Birds warbled in the trees.* **2** make a sound something like a bird warbling: *the warbling brook.* **3** a bird's song or a sound like it. 1, 2 *v.,* **war·bled, war·bling;** 3 *n.*

war·bler (wôr′blər) any of several kinds of small songbirds, often brightly colored. *n.*

war cry a word or phrase shouted in fighting.

ward (wôrd) **1** a division of a hospital or prison. **2** a district of a city or town, especially one represented by an alderman. **3** a person under the care of a guardian or of a court. **4** guard: *The soldiers kept watch and ward over the castle.* 1–3 *n.,* 4 *v.*
ward off, keep away or turn aside: *He warded off the blow with his arm.*

ward·en (wôr′dən) **1** an official who enforces certain laws or rules: *a fire warden.* **2** the person in charge of a prison. **3** an officer in certain colleges, churches, or other institutions. **4** *Cdn.* the chief officer in the municipal government of a county: *The office of warden does not exist in all provinces.* *n.*

☛ **Warden** and **guardian** came into English in the Middle Ages from different French dialects; both these French words came from the same Germanic word for 'guard.'

ward·er (wôr′dər) **1** a guard or watchman. **2** jailer. *n.*

ward·robe (wôrd′rōb′) **1** a stock of clothes: *She is shopping for her spring wardrobe.* **2** a room, closet, or piece of furniture for holding clothes. *n.*

ware (wer) **1** Usually, **wares,** *pl.* articles for sale; manufactured goods: *The peddler sold his wares from door to door.* **2** pottery; earthenware: *Mother bought some lovely blue-and-white ware when we were travelling in Quebec last summer.* *n.*

☛ **Ware** and **wear** are pronounced the same. **Ware** and **where** are sometimes pronounced the same.

ware·house (wer′hous′) a place where goods are kept; storehouse. *n.*

war·fare (wôr′fer′) war; fighting. *n.*

war·i·ly (wer′ə lē) cautiously; with care: *The soldiers climbed warily up the dangerous path.* *adv.*

war·i·ness (wer′ē nis) caution; care. *n.*

war·like (wôr′līk′) **1** fit for war; ready for war; fond of war: *warlike tribes.* **2** threatening war: *a warlike speech.* **3** of or having to do with war: *warlike discipline.* *adj.*

warm (wôrm) **1** more hot than cold; having some heat; giving forth some heat: *a warm fire. She sat in the warm sunshine.* **2** that makes or keeps warm: *a warm coat.* **3** quick to show irritation or anger: *a warm temper.* **4** showing irritation or anger: *a warm dispute.* **5** having or showing affection, enthusiasm, etc.: *a warm welcome, a warm friend, a warm heart.* **6** suggesting heat: *Red, orange, and yellow are warm colors.* **7** *Informal.* in games, treasure hunts, etc., near what one is searching for. **8** make or become warm: *to warm a room.* **9** make or become cheered, interested, or friendly: *The speaker warmed to his subject. Her happiness warms my heart.* 1–7 *adj.,* 8, 9 *v.*
warm up, a heat: *My supper is ready for me to warm up when I get home.* **b** make or become more interested, friendly, etc. **c** practise or exercise for a few minutes before entering a game, contest, etc.

warm–blood·ed (wôrm′blud′id) having warm blood that stays about the same temperature regardless of the surrounding air or water: *The temperature of warm-blooded animals is between 36 degrees and 44 degrees Celsius. Cats are warm-blooded; snakes are cold-blooded.* *adj.*

war·mon·ger (wôr′mung′gər) a person who is in favor of war or who attempts to bring about war. *n.*

warmth (wôrmth) **1** the condition or state of being

hat, āge, fär; let, ēqual, tėrm; it, īce
hot, ōpen, ôrder; oil, out; cup, pu̇t, rüle
əbove, takən, pencəl, lemən, circəs
ch, child; ng, long; sh, ship
th, thin; ŧʜ, then; zh, measure

warm: *We enjoyed the warmth of the open fire.* 2 a warm or friendly feeling: *the warmth of our host's welcome.* 3 liveliness of feelings or emotions: *He spoke with warmth of the natural beauty of the mountains.* *n.*

warn (wôrn) 1 give notice to in advance; put on guard against unpleasantness or danger: *The clouds warned us that a storm was coming up.* 2 inform; give notice of something that requires attention or action: *Mother warned us that we would have to leave at eight.*

warn·ing (wôr′ning) something that warns; notice given in advance. *n.*

warp (wôrp) 1 bend or twist out of shape: *This old floor has warped so that it is not level.* 2 mislead; cause not to work as it should: *Prejudice warps our judgment.* 3 a bend or twist. 4 the threads running lengthwise in a fabric: *The warp is crossed by the woof.* See **weave** for picture. 5 move a ship, etc. by pulling on a rope fastened at one end to a fixed object. 6 a rope used in this way. 1, 2, 5 *v.*, 3, 4, 6 *n.*

war·path (wôr′path′) a way taken by a fighting expedition of North American Indians. *n.*
on the warpath, a ready for war. b looking for a fight; angry.

war·rant (wôr′ənt) 1 that which gives a right; authority: *He had no warrant for using the bike.* 2 a written order giving authority for something: *a warrant to search the house, a warrant for a man's arrest, a warrant for the payment of money.* 3 a guarantee; promise; good and sufficient reason: *There was no warrant for believing she would be chosen.* 4 justify: *Nothing can warrant such rudeness.* 5 give one's word for; guarantee; promise: *The storekeeper warranted the quality of the eggs and the milk.* 1–3 *n.*, 4, 5 *v.*

warrant officer a senior non-commissioned officer in the armed forces, ranking next above a sergeant.

war·ren (wôr′ən) 1 a piece of land having many burrows where rabbits live, or where they are raised. 2 a building or district having many people living in it. *n.*

war·ri·or (wôr′ē ər) a fighting man; an experienced soldier. *n.*

war·ship (wôr′ship′) a ship used in fighting; a ship designed to be used in war. *n.*

wart (wôrt) 1 a small, hard lump on the skin. 2 a similar lump on a plant or tree. *n.*

war·y (wer′ē) 1 on one's guard against danger or deception: *a wary fox.* 2 cautious; careful: *He gave wary answers to all of the stranger's questions.* *adj.*, **war·i·er, war·i·est.**
wary of, cautious about; careful about: *Be wary of gossip.*

was (wuz or woz; *unstressed,* wəz) a form of the verb **be,** used with *I, he, she, it* or any singular noun when speaking of past time: *Once there was a king. I was an hour late for school yesterday. The candy was all gone.* *v.*

wash (wosh) 1 clean with water: *to wash one's face, to wash dishes, to wash clothes.* 2 remove dirt, stains, etc. by or as by scrubbing with soap and water: *Can you wash that spot out?* 3 wash oneself; wash one's face and hands: *You should always wash before eating.* 4 wash clothes: *Mother usually washes on Monday.* 5 washing or being washed: *This floor needs a good wash.* 6 a quantity of clothes washed or to be washed: *She hung the wash on the line.* 7 undergo washing without damage: *Some silks wash perfectly.* 8 carry or be carried along or away by water or other liquid: *Wood is often washed ashore by waves.* 9 the material carried along by moving water and then deposited as sediment: *A delta is formed by the wash of a river.* 10 wear by water or other liquid: *The cliffs are being washed away by waves.* 11 the motion, rush, or sound of water: *We listened to the wash of the waves against the boat.* 12 make wet: *The rose is washed with dew.* 13 a liquid for special use: *a mouth wash, a hair wash.* 14 a thin coating of color or metal: *He began his watercolor with a wash of blue for the sky.* 15 cover with a thin coating of color or of metal: *The walls were washed with blue.* 16 the rough or broken water left just behind by a moving ship. 17 a disturbance in air made by a moving aircraft. 1–4, 7, 8, 10, 12, 15 *v.*, 5, 6, 9, 11, 13, 14, 16, 17 *n.*
wash up, a wash the hands and face, as before meals. b wash the dishes after meals: *We washed up right after supper.*

wash·cloth (wosh′kloth′) a small cloth for washing oneself. *n.*

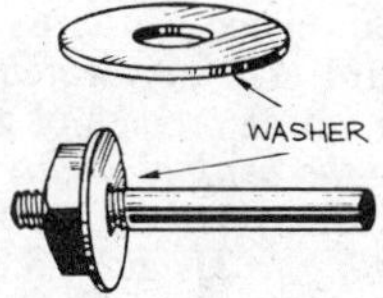

A washer for a bolt

wash·er (wosh′ər) 1 a machine that washes. 2 a flat ring of metal, rubber, leather, etc., used with bolts or nuts, to make joints tight. *n.*

wash·ing (wosh′ing) clothes, etc. washed or to be washed: *to hang washing out today, to send washing to the laundry.* *n.*

wash·out (wosh′out′) 1 a break in a road or railway track caused by floods or storms. 2 *Slang.* a failure; disappointment: *The party was a complete washout.* *n.*

wash·room (wash′rüm′) 1 a room equipped with a toilet and sink, especially such a room in a public building: *Most restaurants and gas stations have washrooms for their customers.* 2 a room for washing. *n.*

was·n't (wuz′ənt or woz′ənt) was not.

wasp (wosp) a flying insect that has a slender body and a powerful sting: *A hornet is a kind of wasp.* See **insect** for picture. *n.*

waste (wāst) 1 make poor use of; spend uselessly; fail to get full value or benefit from: *Don't waste time or money. We try not to waste food.* 2 a failure to use well; poor use: *Buying that suit was a waste of money; it is already starting to wear out.* 3 thrown away as useless or worthless: *a pile of waste lumber.* 4 useless or worthless material; stuff to be thrown away: *Garbage* *or sewage is waste.* **5** left over; not used: *waste food.* **6** stuff that is left over: *Bunches of cotton waste are used to clean machinery.* **7** not cultivated; bare; wild: *waste land.* **8** bare or wild land; desert; wilderness: *We travelled through treeless wastes. Before us stretched a waste of snow and ice.* **9** wearing down little by little; gradual destruction or loss: *Both waste and repair are constantly going on in our bodies.* **10** wear down little by little; destroy or lose gradually: *The sick man was wasted by disease.* **11** spoil; ruin; destroy: *The soldiers wasted the fields and towns of the enemy.* 1, 10, 11 *v.,* **wast·ed, wast·ing;** 2, 4, 6, 8, 9 *n.,* 3, 5, 7 *adj.*

lay waste, damage greatly; destroy: *The invading army laid waste the countryside.*

☛ **Waste** and **waist** are pronounced the same.

waste·bas·ket (wāst′bas′kit) a bucket or other container for paper that is thrown away. *n.*

waste·ful (wāst′fəl) using or spending too much. *adj.*

waste·land (wāst′land′) barren, uncultivated land; land in its natural state. *n.*

watch (woch) **1** look carefully; observe closely: *The medical students watched while the surgeon performed the operation.* **2** look at; observe; view: *Are you watching the show on television? We watched the kittens play.* **3** look or wait with care and attention; be very careful: *The boy watched for a chance to cross the busy street.* **4** a careful looking; attitude of attention: *Be on the watch for cars when you cross the street.* **5** keep guard over; guard: *The dog watches over his master's house.* **6** the act or process of guarding: *A man keeps watch over the bank at night.* **7** a person or persons kept to guard: *The man's cry aroused the town watch, who came running to his aid.* **8** a period of time for guarding: *a watch in the night.* **9** stay awake for some purpose: *The nurse watched with her patient.* **10** staying awake for some purpose. **11** a device for telling time, small enough to be carried in a pocket or worn on the wrist. **12** the time of duty of one part of a ship's crew: *A watch usually lasts four hours.* **13** the part of a ship's crew on duty at the same time. 1–3, 5, 9 *v.,* 4, 6–8, 10–13 *n.*

watch out, be on guard; be careful: *Watch out for cars. Watch out! the tree is falling.*

watch·dog (woch′dog′) a dog kept to guard property. *n.*

watch·ful (woch′fəl) on the lookout; wide-awake; watching carefully: *You should always be watchful for cars when you cross the street. adj.*

watch·man (woch′mən) a man who keeps watch: *A watchman guards the bank at night. n., pl.* **watch·men** (woch′mən).

watch·tow·er (woch′tou′ər) a tower from which a person watches for enemies, fires, ships, etc. *n.*

watch·word (woch′wėrd′) **1** a secret word that allows a person to pass a guard; password: *We gave the watchword, and the sentinel let us pass.* **2** a motto or slogan: *'Forward' is our watchword. n.*

wa·ter (wo′tər or wô′tər) **1** the colorless, tasteless, and odorless liquid that fills the oceans, lakes, etc. and falls as rain: *We use water for drinking and washing.* **2** a liquid like or containing water: *rose water. When you cry, water runs from your eyes.* **3** sprinkle or wet with water: *to water a street, to water grass.* **4** supply or provide with water: *water the horses. Our valley is well watered by rivers and brooks.* **5** weaken by adding water: *It is against the law to sell watered milk.* **6** fill with water; discharge water: *Strong sunlight will make your eyes water. The boy's mouth watered when he saw the cake.* 1, 2 *n.,* 3–6 *v.*

throw cold water on, discourage: *Father will throw cold water on your plan to camp in the mountains.*

tread water, keep afloat in water, remaining upright with one's head above the surface, by slowly moving the legs as if bicycling.

water bird a bird that swims or wades in water.

water buffalo the common buffalo of Asia and the Philippines.

water color or **water colour** **1** paint mixed with water instead of oil. **2** the art or skill of painting with water colors: *He's good at water color.* **3** a picture painted with water colors.

wa·ter·course (wo′tər kôrs′ or wô′tər kôrs′) **1** a stream of water; a river or brook. **2** a channel or bed of a stream of water: *In the summer many watercourses dry up. n.*

wa·ter·cress (wo′tər kres′ or wô′tər kres′) a plant that grows in running water and has crisp leaves, often used in salads. *n.*

wa·ter·fall (wo′tər fol′ or wô′tər fôl′) a fall of water from a high place. *n.*

wa·ter·fowl (wo′tər foul′ or wô′tər foul′) a water bird. *n., pl.* **wa·ter·fowls** or **wa·ter·fowl.**

wa·ter·front or **water front** (wo′tər frunt′ or wô′tər frunt′) the land at the water's edge, especially the part of a city beside a river, lake, or harbor. *n.*

water hole a hole in the ground where water collects; a small pond; a pool.

Water lilies

water lily a water plant having flat, floating leaves and showy fragrant flowers: *The flowers of the common North American water lily are white, or sometimes pink.*

wa·ter–logged (wo′tər logd′ or wô′tər logd′) **1** of a boat, etc., so full of water that it will barely float. **2** completely soaked with water. *adj.*

water main a large pipe for carrying water.

wa·ter·mel·on (wo′tər mel′ən or wô′tər mel′ən) a large, juicy melon with red or pink pulp and hard, green rind. *n.*

water polo a game played in a swimming pool by two teams of seven players who try to throw or push an inflated ball into the opponent's goal.

water power the power from flowing or falling water, used to drive machinery and make electricity.

wa·ter·proof (wo′tər prüf′ or wô′tər prüf′) **1** that will not let water through: *An umbrella should be* *waterproof.* 2 a waterproof coat; raincoat. 3 make waterproof: *These hiking shoes have been waterproofed.* 1 *adj.,* 2 *n.,* 3 *v.*

wa·ter·shed (wo′tər shed′ or wô′tər shed′) 1 a high ridge that divides two areas drained by different river systems; a divide (def. 5): *On one side of a watershed, rivers and streams flow in one direction; on the other side, they flow in a different direction.* 2 the region drained by one river system. *n.*

water ski a ski, usually one of a pair, for gliding over the water while being towed by a boat.

wa·ter–ski (wo′tər skē′ or wô′tər skē′) glide over the water on water skis. *v.,* **wa·ter-skied, wa·ter-ski·ing.**

wa·ter·tight (wo′tər tīt′ or wô′tər tīt′) 1 so tight that no water can get in or out: *Large ships are often divided into watertight compartments by watertight partitions.* 2 leaving no opening for misunderstanding, criticism, etc.; perfect: *a watertight argument. adj.*

wa·ter·way (wo′tər wā′ or wô′tər wā′) 1 a river, canal, or other body of water that ships can go on. 2 a channel for water. *n.*

water wheel a wheel turned by water, usually to supply power: *The grindstones of grain mills used to be run by water wheels.*

wa·ter·works (wo′tər wėrks′ or wô′tər wėrks′) a system of pipes, reservoirs, pumps, etc. for supplying a city or town with water. *n.*

wa·ter·y (wo′tər ē or wô′tər ē) 1 full of water; wet: *watery soil.* 2 containing too much water; too thin: *watery soup.* 3 full of tears; tearful: *watery eyes.* 4 like water: *a watery fluid.* 5 of water: *a watery grave. adj.*

watt (wot) a unit for measuring electric power: *My lamp uses 60 watts; my toaster uses 1000 watts.* *Symbol:* W *n.*

☞ **Watt** and **what** are sometimes pronounced the same.

☞ Named in honor of the Scottish engineer and inventor, James **Watt** (1736–1819).

wave (wāv) 1 a moving ridge or swell of water: *The raft rose and fell on the waves.* 2 any movement like this, especially of light, heat, and sound. 3 a swell or sudden increase of some condition, emotion, etc.: *A cold wave is sweeping over the country. The announcement brought a wave of enthusiasm.* 4 move as waves do; move up and down or back and forth; sway: *The tall grass waved in the breeze. I waved my flag when the Governor General arrived.* 5 signal or direct by waving: *The policeman waved the speeding driver to the side of the road.* 6 a waving, especially of something, as a signal: *a wave of the hand.* 7 a curve or series of curves: *the waves in a girl's hair.* 8 give a wavelike form to: *Girls wave their hair.* 1–3, 6, 7 *n.,* 4, 5, 8 *v,* **waved, wav·ing.**

☞ **Wave** and **waive** are pronounced the same.

wave length or **wave–length** (wāv′length′) in science, the distance between one peak or crest of a wave of sound or light and the next: *The wave lengths of radio waves are measured in metres. n.*

wa·ver (wā′vər) 1 move to and fro; flutter: *a wavering voice.* 2 vary in intensity; flicker: *a wavering light.* 3 be undecided; hesitate: *She is still wavering between staying for another week and having us visit her in town for a week.* 4 become unsteady; begin to give way: *The battle line wavered and broke.* 5 a wavering. 1–4 *v.,* 5 *n.*

hat, āge, fär; let, ēqual, tėrm; it, īce
hot, ōpen, ôrder; oil, out; cup, pu̇t, rüle
əbove, takən, pencəl, lemən, circəs
ch, child; ng, long; sh, ship
th, thin; ᴛʜ, then; zh, measure

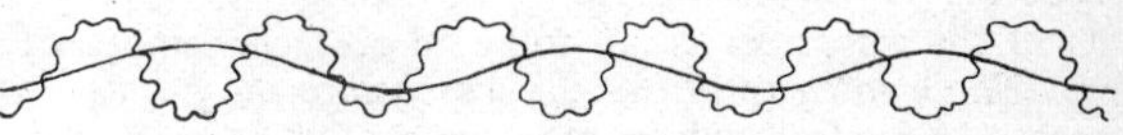

Wavy lines

wav·y (wāv′ē) 1 having waves; having many waves: *a wavy line, wavy hair.* 2 moving with a wavelike motion: *We saw acres of wavy fields of wheat. adj.,* **wav·i·er, wav·i·est.**

wax[1] (waks) 1 a yellowish substance made by bees for constructing their honeycomb: *Wax is hard when cold, but can be easily shaped when warm.* 2 any substance like this: *Most of the wax used for candles, for keeping air from jelly, etc. is really paraffin. Sealing wax and floor wax are other common waxes.* 3 rub, stiffen, polish, etc. with wax or something like wax: *We wax that floor once a month.* 1, 2 *n.,* 3 *v.*

wax[2] (waks) 1 grow bigger or greater; increase: *The moon waxes till it becomes full, and then it wanes.* 2 become: *The party waxed merry. v.*

wax·en (wak′sən) 1 made of wax. 2 like wax; smooth, soft, and pale: *Her skin was waxen. adj.*

wax paper or **waxed paper** paper coated with a waxy substance such as paraffin, used mostly for wrapping food.

wax·wing (waks′wing′) any of several small brown-and-grey birds having a large crest on the head and often having small, red, waxlike tips on the wings. The **cedar waxwing** is found in all provinces of Canada; the **bohemian waxwing** is found only in the northern and western part of Canada. *n.*

wax·work (waks′wėrk′) 1 a figure or figures made of wax. 2 **waxworks,** *pl.* an exhibition of such figures, especially one showing figures of historical or famous people. *n.*

way (wā) 1 a manner or style: *She is wearing her hair in a new way.* 2 a means or method: *Scientists are trying to find new ways to prevent disease.* 3 a point or feature; detail; respect: *The plan is bad in several ways.* 4 a direction: *Look this way.* 5 movement or progress along a course: *The guide led the way.* 6 a distance: *The sun is a long way off.* 7 a road; path; street; course: *The hunter found a way through the forest.* 8 a space for passing or going ahead: *Automobiles must make way for a fire engine.* 9 a habit or custom: *Don't mind his teasing; it's only his way.* 10 one's wish or will: *A spoiled child wants his own way all the time.* 11 *Informal.* a condition or state: *That sick man is in a bad way.* 12 movement; forward motion: *The boat slowly gathered way as it slid through the water.* 13 *Informal.* at or to a great distance; far: *The cloud of smoke stretched way out to the pier.* 1–12 *n.,* 13 *adv.*

by way of, a by the route of; through. **b** as; for: *By way of an answer he just nodded.*

give way, a retreat; yield. **b** break down or fall: *Several*

people were hurt when the platform gave way. **c** abandon oneself to emotion: *give way to tears.*
in the way, being an obstacle, hindrance, etc.
make one's way, a go: *They made their way through the bushes to the road.* **b** get ahead; succeed: *He's sure to make his way in the world.*
out of the way, a so as not to be an obstacle, hindrance, etc.: *She wanted us out of the way before the guests arrived.* **b** far from where most people live or go. **c** unusual, strange: *His clothes seemed out of the way to us.*
under way, going on; in motion; in progress: *The program is under way.*

☛ **Way** and **weigh** are pronounced the same. **Way** and **whey** are sometimes pronounced the same.

way·far·er (wā′fer′ər) traveller. *n.*

way·far·ing (wā′fer′ing) travelling. *n.*

way·laid (wā′lād′) See **waylay.** *I waylaid him when he entered the meeting. v.*

way·lay (wā′lā′) **1** lie in wait for; attack on the way: *Robin Hood waylaid rich travellers and robbed them.* **2** stop a person on his way: *Newspaper reporters waylaid the famous actor and asked him many questions. v.,* **way·laid, way·lay·ing.**

way·side (wā′sīd′) **1** the edge of a road or path: *We ate lunch on the wayside.* **2** along the edge of the road or path: *We slept in a wayside inn.* 1 *n.,* 2 *adj.*

way·ward (wā′wərd) **1** turning from the right way; disobedient; willful: *In a wayward mood, he ran away from home.* **2** irregular; unsteady. *adj.*

we (wē) **1** the speaker plus the person or persons spoken to or spoken about: *We will all go in the one bus.* **2** a person speaking or writing formally or officially: *An author, a sovereign, a judge, or a newspaper editor sometimes uses* we *when others would say* I. *pron.*

☛ **We** and **wee** are pronounced the same.

weak (wēk) **1** that can easily be broken, crushed, overcome, torn, etc.; not strong: *a weak board in a floor. A weak fort can be easily captured.* **2** not having bodily strength or health: *The weak old man tottered as he walked.* **3** lacking power, authority, or force: *a weak law.* **4** lacking moral strength: *a weak character.* **5** lacking mental power: *a weak mind.* **6** lacking or poor in amount, volume, loudness, taste, etc.: *Weak tea has less flavor than strong tea.* **7** lacking or poor in something specified: *She is still a little weak in spelling. adj.*

☛ **Weak** and **week** are pronounced the same.

weak·en (wēk′ən) **1** make weak or weaker: *You can weaken tea by adding water.* **2** become weak or weaker: *We are almost to the top of the mountain; let's not weaken now. v.*

weak·ling (wēk′ling) a weak person or animal. *n.*

weak·ly (wēk′lē) **1** weak; feeble; sickly. **2** in a weak manner. 1 *adj.,* **weak·li·er, weak·li·est;** 2 *adv.*

weak–mind·ed (wēk′mīn′did) **1** having or showing little intelligence. **2** lacking firmness of mind: *Because she was so shy, she appeared weak-minded and unsure of herself. adj.*

weak·ness (wēk′nis) **1** the condition of being weak; lack of power, force, or vigor: *Weakness kept him in bed.* **2** a weak point; a slight fault: *Putting things off is her weakness.* **3** fondness: *She has a weakness for candy. n.*

wealth (welth) **1** riches; many valuable possessions; property: *a man of wealth.* **2** all things that have money value; resources: *The wealth of our country includes its mines and forests as well as its factories.* **3** an abundance; a large quantity: *a wealth of hair, a wealth of words. n.*

wealth·y (wel′thē) having wealth; rich. *adj.,* **wealth·i·er, wealth·i·est.**

wean (wēn) **1** accustom a child or young animal to food other than its mother's milk. **2** accustom a person to do without something; cause to turn away: *He was sent away to school to wean him from bad companions. v.*

weap·on (wep′ən) anything used in fighting; means of attack or defence: *Swords, spears, arrows, clubs, guns, and shields are weapons. Animals use claws, horns, teeth, and stings as weapons. Drugs are effective weapons against many diseases. n.*

wear (wer) **1** have on the body: *Men wear coats, hats, collars, watches, beards. She wears black since her husband died.* **2** have; show: *The house wore an air of sadness.* **3** wearing; being worn: *Clothing for summer wear is being shown in the shops. This suit has been in constant wear for two years.* **4** clothing; things worn or to be worn: *summer wear. Children's wear is sold in this store.* **5** last long; give good service: *This coat has worn well. A friendship wears well if you like a person better the longer you know him.* **6** lasting quality; good service: *There is still much wear in these shoes.* **7** use up; be used up: *The pencil is worn to a stub. The paint wears off the house.* **8** cause loss or damage to by using: *These shoes are badly worn.* **9** cause or make by rubbing, scraping, or washing away: *Walking wore a hole in my shoe. Water wore the stones smooth.* **10** tire: *She is worn out by too much work. Teaching is wearing work.* **11** pass or go gradually: *It became hotter as the day wore on.* 1, 2, 5, 7–11 *v.,* **wore, worn, wear·ing;** 3, 4, 6 *n.* **—wear′er,** *n.*

☛ **Wear** and **ware** are pronounced the same. **Wear** and **where** are sometimes pronounced the same.

wea·ri·ly (wēr′ə lē) in a weary manner: *We all walked wearily home after our long hike. adv.*

wea·ri·ness (wēr′ē nis) a weary condition; a tired feeling: *After tramping all day the hikers were overcome with weariness. n.*

wea·ri·some (wēr′ē səm) wearying; tiring; tiresome: *a long and wearisome tale. adj.*

wea·ry (wēr′ē) **1** tired: *weary feet, a weary brain.* **2** causing tiredness; tiring: *a weary wait.* **3** having one's patience or liking exhausted: *She was weary of his stupid jokes.* **4** make weary; tire: *Walking up hill wearied Grandfather.* **5** become weary. 1–3 *adj.,* **wea·ri·er, wea·ri·est;** 4, 5 *v.,* **wea·ried, wea·ry·ing.**

A long-tailed weasel — about 30 cm long without the tail

wea·sel (wē′zəl) a small, quick animal with a long, slender body and short legs: *Weasels eat rats, mice, birds, and eggs. n.*

hat, āge, fär; let, ēqual, tėrm; it, īce
hot, ōpen, ôrder; oil, out; cup, pu̇t, rüle
əbove, takən, pencəl, lemən, circəs
ch, child; ng, long; sh, ship
th, thin; ᴛʜ, then; zh, measure

weath·er (weᴛʜ′ər) **1** the condition of the air with respect to temperature, moisture, cloudiness, etc.: *hot weather. We have had a lot of windy weather lately.* **2** expose to the weather; wear or discolor by sun, rain, frost, etc.: *Wood turns grey if weathered for a long time.* **3** go or come through safely: *The ship weathered the storm.* 1 *n.,* 2, 3 *v.*
under the weather, *Informal.* sick; ailing: *She was under the weather and missed the Brownie meeting.*
☛ **Weather** and **whether** are sometimes pronounced the same.

weath·er–beat·en (weᴛʜ′ər bēt′ən) worn or hardened by the wind, rain, and other forces of the weather: *an old farmer's weather-beaten face, a weather-beaten old ship. adj.*

weath·er·cock (weᴛʜ′ər kok′) a device to show which way the wind is blowing, especially one in the shape of a rooster. *n.*

weath·er·proof (weᴛʜ′ər prüf′) **1** protected against rain, snow, or wind; able to stand exposure to all kinds of weather: *They built a small weatherproof cabin and lived there all winter.* **2** make weatherproof: *I'm looking for something that will weatherproof my boots.* 1 *adj.,* 2 *v.*

weather vane weathercock.

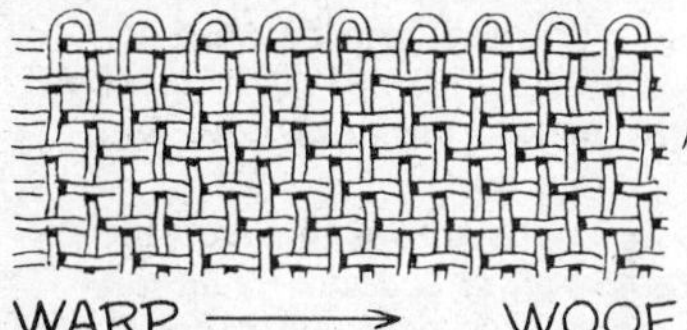

A basic pattern of weaving

weave (wēv) **1** form threads or strips into a thing or fabric; interlace: *People weave thread into cloth, straw into hats, and reeds into baskets.* **2** make out of thread, strips, etc.: *She is weaving a rug.* **3** a method or pattern of weaving: *Homespun is a cloth of coarse weave.* **4** combine into a whole: *The author wove three plots together into one story.* **5** make by combining parts: *The story he wove was exciting.* **6** go by twisting and turning: *We weaved around beds and boxes to the back door.* 1, 2, 4–6 *v.,* **wove** or **weaved, wo·ven** or **weav·ing;** 3 *n.* **—weav′er,** *n.*
☛ **Weave** and **we've** are pronounced the same.

web (web) **1** something woven: *A spider spins a web.* See **spider** for picture. **2** a whole piece of cloth while being woven or after being taken from the loom. **3** any complicated network, especially one that entangles as a cobweb: *His story seems to be a web of lies.* **4** the skin joining the toes of swimming birds and certain other water animals. *n.*

webbed (webd) **1** formed like a web or with a web. **2** having the toes joined by a web: *Ducks have webbed feet.* See **duck** for picture. *adj.*

wed (wed) **1** marry. **2** unite. *v.,* **wed·ded, wed·ded** or **wed, wed·ding.**

we'd (wēd) **1** we had. **2** we would.
☛ **We'd** and **weed** are pronounced the same.

Wed. Wednesday.

wed·ding (wed′ing) **1** a marriage ceremony. **2** an anniversary of this ceremony. A **golden wedding** is the fiftieth anniversary of a marriage. *n.*

Wedges

wedge (wej) **1** a piece of wood or metal with a thin edge used in splitting, separating, etc. **2** something shaped like a wedge: *We cut the big pie into ten wedges.* **3** something used like a wedge to make an opening or opportunity: *Her grand party was a wedge for her entry into society.* **4** thrust or pack in tightly; squeeze: *He wedged himself through the narrow window. His foot was wedged between the rocks.* **5** split or separate with a wedge. **6** fasten or tighten with a wedge. 1–3 *n.,* 4–6 *v.,* **wedged, wedg·ing.**

wed·lock (wed′lok) married life; marriage. *n.*

Wednes·day (wenz′dē or wenz′dā′) the fourth day of the week, following Tuesday. *n.*
☛ **Wednesday** developed from Old English *Wōdnesdæg,* meaning 'day of Woden'; Woden, or Odin, was the chief Germanic god.

wee (wē) very small; tiny. *adj.,* **we·er, we·est.**
☛ **Wee** and **we** are pronounced the same.

weed (wēd) **1** a useless or troublesome plant: *Weeds choked out the vegetables and flowers.* **2** take weeds out of: *Please weed the garden now.* **3** take out weeds: *I spent all morning weeding.* 1 *n.,* 2, 3 *v.*
weed out, remove or discard as not wanted: *The weak players were weeded out before the first game was played.*
☛ **Weed** and **we'd** are pronounced the same.

weeds (wēdz) mourning garments: *a widow's weeds. n. pl.*

weed·y (wēd′ē) **1** full of weeds: *a weedy garden.* **2** thin and lanky. *adj.,* **weed·i·er, weed·i·est.**

week (wēk) **1** seven days, one after another. **2** the time from Sunday through Saturday: *This is the last week of holidays.* **3** the working days of a seven-day period: *A school week is usually five days. n.*
☛ **Week** and **weak** are pronounced the same.

week·day (wēk′dā′) **1** any day of the week except Sunday. **2** any day of the week except Saturday and Sunday. *n.*

week·end (wēk′end′) **1** Saturday and Sunday as a time for recreation, visiting, etc.; the time between the end of one week of work or school and the beginning of the next: *a weekend in the country, Thanksgiving weekend.* **2** spend a weekend: *They are weekending at their cottage.* 1 *n.,* 2 *v.*

week·ly (wēk′lē) **1** of a week; for a week; lasting a

week: *His weekly wage is $150.* 2 done or happening once a week: *She writes a weekly letter to her grandmother.* 3 once each week; every week: *The clerks in the store are paid weekly.* 4 a newspaper or magazine published once a week. 1, 2 *adj.*, 3 *adv.*, 4 *n.*, *pl.* **week·lies.**

weep (wēp) 1 cry; shed tears: *she wept for joy when she won the award.* 2 shed tears for; mourn. 3 be very damp; drip: *That basement wall sometimes weeps.* *v.*, **wept, weep·ing.**

wee·vil (wē′vəl) a small beetle whose larvae eat grain, nuts, fruit, etc.: *Weevils do much damage to the corn and cotton crops.* *n.*

weft (weft) the threads running from side to side across a fabric; the woof. See **weave** for picture. *n.*

weigh (wā) 1 find the mass of: *I weighed myself this morning.* 2 have as a measure of mass: *I weigh 45 kilograms.* 3 measure a quantity of something by mass: *The grocer weighed out two kilograms of potatoes.* 4 find out how heavy a thing is at a certain altitude. 5 have as a measure of weight (def. 3): *Things weigh much less on the moon than on earth.* 6 bend by weight; burden: *The boughs of the apple tree are weighed down with fruit.* 7 bear down; be a burden: *The mistake weighed heavily upon his mind.* 8 have importance or influence: *The amount of his salary does not weigh with him at all, because he is a very rich man.* 9 balance in the mind; consider carefully: *He weighs his words before speaking.* 10 lift up an anchor: *The ship weighed anchor and sailed away.* *v.*

☛ **Weigh** and **way** are pronounced the same. **Weigh** and **whey** are sometimes pronounced the same.

weight (wāt) 1 mass (def. 7): *The dog's weight is 20 kilograms.* 2 a piece of metal having a particular mass, used to weigh (def. 1) something on a balance: *a 50 gram weight.* 3 how heavy a thing is; the quality of anything that makes it tend toward the centre of the earth: *Gas has hardly any weight at all. Your weight is a little less on a mountain than at sea level.* 4 a heavy thing or mass: *A weight keeps the papers in place.* 5 a load; burden: *The pillars support the weight of the roof. She sank under the weight of her troubles.* 6 load down; burden: *The manager was weighted with troubles.* 7 add weight to; put weight on: *The elevator is weighted too heavily.* 8 influence; importance; value: *What he says carries weight with me.* 1–5, 8 *n.*, 6, 7 *v.*

pull one's weight, do one's part or share: *We will finish the job quickly if we all pull our weight.*

☛ **Weight** and **wait** are pronounced the same.

weight·less (wāt′lis) 1 appearing to have no weight: *The snow was weightless on my shoulders.* 2 being free from the pull of gravity: *In outer space, all things are weightless.* *adj.*

weight·y (wāt′ē) 1 heavy. 2 too heavy; burdensome: *The old king could no longer deal with the weighty cares of state.* 3 important; influential: *a weighty speaker.* *adj.*, **weight·i·er, weight·i·est.**

weir (wēr) 1 a dam in a river. 2 a fence of stakes or broken branches put in a stream or channel to catch fish. *n.*

weird (wērd) 1 unearthly; mysterious; wild; strange: *The witches moved in a weird dance. We were awakened by a weird shriek.* 2 *Informal.* odd; fantastic; queer: *The shadows made weird figures on the wall.* *adj.*

wel·come (wel′kəm) 1 greet kindly: *We always welcome guests at our house.* 2 a kind reception: *You will always have a welcome here.* 3 receive gladly: *We welcome new ideas and suggestions.* 4 gladly received; pleasing: *a welcome visitor, a welcome letter, a welcome rest.* 5 gladly or freely permitted: *Everybody is welcome to walk in the public park.* 6 as a reply to thanks, free to have or do something, to enjoy some favor, etc.: *You are quite welcome.* 7 an exclamation of friendly greeting: *Welcome!* 1, 3 *v.*, **wel·comed, wel·com·ing;** 2 *n.*, 4–6 *adj.*, 7 *interj.*

weld (weld) 1 join together metal, plastic, etc. by hammering or pressing while hot and soft: *He welded the broken rod.* 2 a welded joint. 3 unite closely: *Working together for a month welded them into a strong team.* 4 become welded or be capable of being welded: *Steel welds; wood does not.* 1, 3, 4 *v.*, 2 *n.*

wel·fare (wel′fer′) health, happiness, and prosperity; a condition of being or doing well: *Uncle Charles asked about the welfare of everyone in our family.* *n.*

on welfare, receiving benefits from the government or from some organization to provide a basic standard of living: *There was no harvest, and many families were on welfare.*

welfare work work done to improve the lives and living conditions of people who need help because of poverty, sickness, family problems, etc.: *Welfare work is carried on by governments, private organizations, and sometimes individuals.*

well[1] (wel) 1 all right; in a satisfactory or favorable manner: *Is everything going well at school? The job was well done.* 2 good; right: *It is well you came along.* 3 thoroughly: *He knew the lesson well. Shake the medicine well before taking it.* 4 much; to a considerable degree: *The fair brought in well over a hundred dollars.* 5 fairly; reasonably: *You can't well argue today for what you were against yesterday.* 6 in good health: *He is well.* 7 an expression used to show mild surprise or merely to fill in: *Well! well! Here's Jack. Well, I'm not sure.* 1, 3–5 *adv.*, **bet·ter, best;** 2, 6 *adj.*, 7 *interj.*

as well, a also; besides. **b** equally.

as well as, a in addition to; besides. **b** as much as.

well[2] (wel) 1 a hole dug or bored in the ground to get water, oil, gas, etc.: *The farmer pumped all his water from a well.* 2 a fountain or source: *Our class president is a well of ideas.* 3 something like a well in shape or use: *The reservoir of a fountain pen is a well.* 4 a shaft for light, or for stairs or an elevator, extending vertically through the floors of a building. 5 spring; rise; gush: *Water wells from a spring beneath the rock. Tears welled up in her eyes.* 1–4 *n.*, 5 *v.*

we'll (wēl) we will; we shall.

☛ **We'll** and **wheel** are sometimes pronounced the same.

well–be·ing (wel′bē′ing) welfare; health and happiness. *n.*

well–bred (wel′bred′) well brought up; having or showing good manners. *adj.*

well–known (wel′nōn′) generally or widely known. *adj.*

well–nigh (wel′nī′) very nearly; almost. *adv.*

well–off (wel′of′) 1 in a good condition or position: *Your whole family is healthy, so you should consider* yourself well-off. 2 fairly rich; prosperous: *Her family is well-off but not wealthy.* *adj.*

well–to–do (wel′tə dü′) having enough money to live well; prosperous. *adj.*

Welsh (welsh) 1 of or having to do with Wales, a division of Great Britain. 2 the people of Wales. 3 their native language. 1 *adj.*, 2, 3 *n.*

welt (welt) 1 a streak or ridge made on the skin by a stick or whip. 2 a strip of leather between the upper part and the sole of a shoe. *n.*

wel·ter (wel′tər) 1 roll or tumble about; wallow. 2 a surging or confused mass: *All we saw was a welter of arms, legs, and bodies.* 1 *v.*, 2 *n.*

wench (wench) 1 a girl or young woman. 2 a woman servant. *n.*

wend (wend) 1 direct one's way: *We wended our way home.* 2 go. *v.*

wen·di·go (wen′di gō′) 1 an evil spirit. 2 a kind of trout; splake. *n., pl.* **wen·di·gos** for 1, **wen·di·go** or **wen·di·gos** for 2.

went (went) See **go.** *I went home promptly after school.* *v.*

wept (wept) See **weep.** *She wept for hours. She has often wept.* *v.*

were (wėr; *unstressed,* wər) a form of the verb **be:** *The officer's orders were obeyed. If I were you I wouldn't tease that dog.*

we're (wēr) we are.

weren't (wėrnt or wernt) were not.

were·wolf (wēr′wůlf′ or wėr′wůlf′) in folk tales, a man who has been changed into a wolf, or who can change himself into a wolf, while keeping his human intelligence. *n., pl.* **were·wolves.**

☛ Werewolf has developed from an Old English word made up of *wer,* meaning 'a man,' and *wulf,* meaning 'wolf.'

west (west) 1 the direction of the sunset. See **compass** for picture. 2 toward the west; farther toward the west: *Walk west three blocks.* 3 from the west: *a warm west wind.* 4 in the west: *the west wing of a house.* 5 Also, **West,** the part of the world, country or continent toward the west. 6 **the West, a** in Canada, the western part of Canada or the United States. **b** the countries in Europe and America as distinguished from those in Asia. 1, 5, 6 *n.*, 2 *adv.*, 3, 4 *adj.*

west of, farther west than: *Alberta is west of Saskatchewan.*

west·er·ly (wes′tər lē) 1 toward the west. 2 from the west: *a westerly wind.* *adj., adv.*

west·ern (wes′tərn) 1 toward the west. 2 from the west. 3 of or in the west; of or in the western part of the country. 4 *Informal.* a story, motion picture, or television show about life in the western part of North America, especially about cowboy life in the United States. 1–3 *adj.*, 4 *n.*

west·ward (west′wərd) toward the west; west: *He walked westward. The orchard is on the westward slope of the hill.* *adv., adj.*

west·wards (west′wərdz) westward. *adv.*

wet (wet) 1 covered or soaked with water or other liquid: *wet hands, a wet sponge.* 2 watery: *Her eyes were wet with tears.* 3 not yet dry: *Don't touch the wet paint.* 4 make or become wet: *Wet the cloth before you wipe off the window.* 5 water or other liquid: *I dropped my scarf in the wet.* 6 rainy: *wet weather.*

hat, āge, fär; let, ēqual, tėrm; it, īce
hot, ōpen, ôrder; oil, out; cup, pů t, rüle
əbove, takən, pencəl, lemən, circəs
ch, child; ng, long; sh, ship
th, thin; ᴛʜ, then; zh, measure

7 wetness; rain: *Come in out of the wet.* 1–3, 6 *adj.*, **wet·ter, wet·test;** 4 *v.*, **wet** or **wet·ted, wet·ting;** 5, 7 *n.*

☛ **Wet** and **whet** are sometimes pronounced the same.

wet blanket *Informal.* a person who has a discouraging or depressing effect: *He's really a wet blanket; when we were planning our picnic he said it would probably be cold, and besides, we'd get bugs in our food.*

wet·ness (wet′nis) a wet condition. *n.*

we've (wēv) we have.

☛ **We've** and **weave** are pronounced the same.

whack (wak or hwak) 1 *Informal.* a sharp, resounding blow. 2 *Informal.* strike with such a blow: *The batter whacked the ball out of the park.* 3 *Slang.* a trial or attempt: *I'd like to have a whack at flying in a glider to see what it's like.* 1, 3 *n.*, 2 *v.*

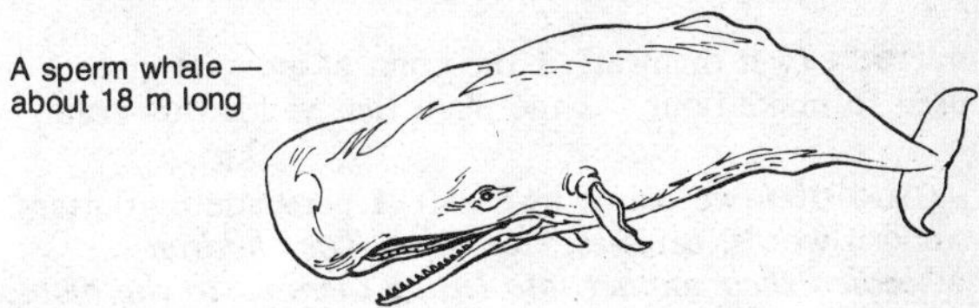

A sperm whale — about 18 m long

whale (wāl or hwāl) 1 an animal shaped like a huge fish and living in the sea: *Men hunt whales for oil and whalebone.* 2 hunt and catch whales. 1 *n., pl.* **whales** or **whale;** 2 *v.*, **whaled, whal·ing.**

a whale of, *Informal.* a very big or impressive kind of: *a whale of a car, a whale of a good time.*

☛ **Whale** and **wail** are sometimes pronounced the same.

whal·er (wāl′ər or hwāl′ər) 1 a hunter of whales. 2 a ship used for hunting whales. *n.*

wharf (wôrf or hwôrf) a platform built on the shore or out from the shore, beside which ships can load and unload. See **dock** for picture. *n., pl.* **wharves** (wôrvz or hwôrvz) or **wharfs.**

what (wut or wot, hwut or hwot) 1 a word used in asking questions about persons or things: *What is your name (pron.)? What time is it (adj.)?* 2 that which: *I know what you mean (pron.). Give me what paper you don't use (adj.).* 3 whatever; anything that; any that: *Do what you please (pron.). Take what supplies you will need (adj.).* 4 how much; how: *What does it matter?* 5 having regard to; taking into account: *What with the wind and the rain, our picnic was spoiled.* 6 a word used to show surprise, liking, anger, or to add emphasis: *What a mistake! What a pity! What a good time we had! What! are you late again?* 1–3 *pron.*, 1–3, 6 *adj.*, 4–6 *adv.*, 6 *interj.*

what if, what would happen if: *What if it rains on the day of the game?*

what's what, *Informal.* the true state of affairs: *That boy knows what's what.*

☛ **What** and **watt** are sometimes pronounced the same.

what·ev·er (wət ev′ər or wot ev′ər, hwət ev′er or hwot ev′ər) **1** anything that: *Do whatever you like.* **2** any that: *Ask whatever girls you like to the party.* **3** no matter who; at all: *Any person whatever can tell you the way.* **4** no matter what: *Do it, whatever happens.* **5** *Informal.* a word used for emphasis instead of *what*: *Whatever do you mean?* 1, 4, 5 *pron*, 2, 3 *adj.*

what's (wuts or wots, hwuts or hwots) **1** what is: *What's the latest news?* **2** what has: *What's been going on here lately?*

what·so·ev·er (wut′sō ev′ər or wot′sō ev′ər, hwut′sō ev′ər or hwot′sō ev′ər) whatever. *pron., adj.*

Wheat

wheat (wēt or hwēt) **1** the grain of a cereal grass, used to make flour. **2** the plant that yields this grain. *n.*

whee·dle (wē′dəl or hwē′dəl) **1** persuade by flattery, smooth words, caresses, etc.; coax: *The children wheedled their mother into letting them go to the picnic.* **2** get by wheedling: *They wheedled the secret out of him.* *v.*, **whee·dled, whee·dling.**

wheel (wēl or hwēl) **1** a round frame or disk that can turn on a pin or shaft in its centre. **2** any instrument, machine, apparatus, etc. shaped or moving like a wheel: *A ship's wheel is used in steering. Clay is shaped into dishes, etc. on a potter's wheel.* **3** *Informal.* bicycle. **4** any force thought of as moving or propelling: *The wheels of government began to turn. A turn of fortune's wheel made her father rich.* **5** turn: *The rider wheeled his horse about. He wheeled around suddenly.* **6** move on wheels: *The workman was wheeling a load of bricks on a wheelbarrow.* 1–4 *n.*, 5, 6 *v.*

at the wheel, a at the steering wheel. **b** in control: *The variety night is bound to be a success with Peter at the wheel.*

☛ **Wheel** and **we'll** are sometimes pronounced the same.

Two kinds of wheel A wheelbarrow

wheel·bar·row (wēl′bar′ō or wēl′ber′ō, hwēl′bar′ō or hwēl′ber′ō) a small vehicle for carrying loads, having one wheel at the front and two handles at the back. *n.*

wheel chair a chair mounted on wheels so that it can be pushed from behind or moved by the person sitting in it: *Wheel chairs are used by invalids and people who are paralysed.*

wheeze (wēz or hwēz) **1** breathe with difficulty and with a whistling sound. **2** a whistling sound caused by difficult breathing. **3** make a sound like this: *The old engine wheezed.* 1, 3 *v.*, **wheezed, wheez·ing;** 2 *n.*

The shell of a whelk — about 7 cm long

whelk (welk or hwelk) a small sea animal with a spiral shell, used for food in Europe. *n.*

whelp (welp or hwelp) **1** a puppy or cub; a young dog, wolf, bear, lion, tiger, etc. **2** give birth to whelps. **3** a good-for-nothing boy or young man. 1, 3 *n.*, 2 *v.*

when (wen or hwen) **1** at what time: *When does school close?* **2** at the time that: *Stand up when your name is called.* **3** at any time that: *The dog comes when he is called.* **4** at which time; and then: *The dog growled till his master spoke, when he gave a joyful bark.* **5** although: *We have only three books when we need five.* **6** what time; which time: *Since when have they had a new car?* **7** the time or occasion: *the when and where of an act.* 1 *adv.*, 2–5 *conj.*, 6 *pron.*, 7 *n.*

whence (wens or hwens) from what place, source, or cause; from where: *Whence do you come? Whence has he learned so much about our affairs? Let him return to that land whence he came.* *adv., conj.*

when·ev·er (wen ev′ər or hwen ev′ər) at whatever time; when; at any time that: *Please come whenever you wish. He played chess whenever possible.* *adv., conj.*

where (wer or wher) **1** in what place; at what place: *Where do you live? Where is he?* **2** to what place: *Where are you going?* **3** from what place: *Where did you get that story?* **4** what place: *Where did he come from?* **5** in which; at which: *That is the house where he was born.* **6** to the place to which: *I will go where you go.* **7** in the place in which; at the place at which: *Your coat is where you left it.* **8** the place or scene: *the when and the where of it.* 1–3, 5 *adv.*, 4 *pron*, 6, 7 *conj.*, 8 *n.*

☛ **Where** is sometimes pronounced the same as **ware** and **wear.**

where·a·bouts (wer′ə bouts′ or hwer′ə bouts′) **1** where; near what place: *Whereabouts are my books?* **2** the place where a person or thing is: *Do you know the whereabouts of the cottage?* 1 *adv., conj.* 2 *n.*

where·as (wer az′ or hwer az′) **1** but; while; on the contrary: *Some children like school, whereas others do not.* **2** considering that; since: *Whereas there is need for a swimming pool in the community, we hereby request that money be made available for this project.* *conj.*

where·at (wer at′ or hwer at′) at what; at which. *adv., conj.*

where·by (wer bī′ or hwer bī′) by what; by which: *There is no other way whereby he can be saved.* *adv., conj.*

hat, āge, fär; let, ēqual, tėrm; it, īce
hot, ōpen, ôrder; oil, out; cup, pu̇t, rüle
əbove, takən, pencəl, lemən, circəs
ch, child; ng, long; sh, ship
th, thin; ᴛʜ, then; zh, measure

where·fore (wer′fôr or hwer′fôr) 1 for what reason; why: *Wherefore do you weep?* 2 for which reason; therefore; so: *He has been found guilty, wherefore he must be banished.* 3 for what reason; why: *I think I know wherefore he is angry.* 4 a reason: *I don't want to hear all the whys and wherefores.* 1, 2 *adv.*, 3 *conj.*, 4 *n.*

where·in (wer in′ or hwer in′) in what; in which; how. *adv., conj.*

where·of (wer uv′ or wer ov′, hwer uv′ or hwer ov′) of what; of which; of whom: *Solomon knew whereof he spoke. adv., conj.*

where·on (wer on′ or hwer on′) on which; on what. *adv., conj.*

where·so·ev·er (wer′sō ev′ər or hwer′sō ev′ər) wherever. *conj., adv.*

where·un·to (wer un′tü or hwer un′tü) 1 to which; where. 2 for what purpose; why. *adv., conj.*

where·up·on (wer′ə pon′ or hwer′ə pon′) 1 upon what; upon which. 2 at which; after which: *The prince kissed the Sleeping Beauty, whereupon she awoke. adv., conj.*

where·ev·er (wer ev′ər or hwer ev′ər) where; to whatever place; in whatever place: *He goes wherever he wishes. Sit wherever you like. conj., adv.*

where·with (wer wiᴛʜ′ or wer with′, hwer wiᴛʜ′ or hwer with′) with what; with which: *Wherewith shall we be fed? adv., conj.*

where·with·al (wer′wiᴛʜ ol′ or hwer′wiᴛʜ ol′, wer′wiᴛʜ ôl′ or hwer′wiᴛʜ ôl′) the means, supplies, or money needed: *Has she the wherewithal to pay for the trip? n.*

whet (wet or hwet) 1 sharpen by rubbing: *to whet a knife.* 2 stir up; awaken: *The smell of food whetted my appetite. An exciting story whets your interest. v.*, **whet·ted, whet·ting.**

☛ **Whet** and **wet** are sometimes pronounced the same.

wheth·er (weᴛʜ′ər or hweᴛʜ′ər) 1 a word used in expressing a choice or an alternative: *Whether we go or whether we stay matters very little. He does not know whether to go to the shop or not.* 2 if: *He asked whether he should finish the work.* 3 either: *Whether sick or well, she is always cheerful. conj.*

☛ **Whether** and **weather** are sometimes pronounced the same.

whet·stone (wet′stōn′ or hwet′stōn′) a stone for sharpening knives or tools. *n.*

whew (hwyü) a word expressing surprise, dismay, etc.: *Whew! it's cold! interj.*

whey (wā or hwā) the watery part of milk that separates from the curd when milk sours or when cheese is made. *n.*

☛ **Whey** is sometimes pronounced the same as **way** and **weigh.**

which (wich or hwich) a word used: 1 in asking questions about one or more persons or things from a group: *Which boy won the prize (adj.)? Which books are yours (adj.)? Which seems the best plan (pron.)?* 2 in connecting a group of words with some other word in the sentence: *Read the book which is on the desk (pron.). The house was very expensive, for which reason they did not buy it (adj.).* 3 in making statements about one or more persons or things from a group: *I don't know which dress to wear (adj.). Tell me which is best (pron.). adj., pron.*

☛ **Which** and **witch** are sometimes pronounced the same.

☛ See note at **that.**

which·ev·er (wich ev′ər or hwich ev′ər) 1 any one; any that: *Take whichever you want (pron.). Buy whichever hat you like (adj.).* 2 no matter which: *Whichever you take will be all right (pron.). Whichever side wins, I shall be satisfied (adj.). pron., adj.*

whiff (wif or hwif) 1 a slight gust; puff; breath: *A whiff of fresh air cleared his head.* 2 breathe in or out gently. 3 a slight smell; a puff of air having an odor. 1, 3 *n.*, 2 *v.*

while (wīl or hwīl) 1 a time; a space of time: *He kept us waiting a long while. The postman came a while ago.* 2 during the time that; in the time that: *While I was speaking, he said nothing. Summer is pleasant while it lasts.* 3 although: *While I like the color of the hat, I do not like its shape.* 4 **while away,** pass or spend in some easy or pleasant manner: *The children while away many afternoons on the beach.* 1 *n.*, 2, 3 *conj.*, 4 *v.*, **whiled, whil·ing.**

worth while, worth time, attention, or effort: *All this fussing about such a small matter is hardly worth while.*

☛ **While** and **wile** are sometimes pronounced the same.

whilst (wīlst or hwīlst) while. *conj.*

whim (wim or hwim) a sudden fancy or notion: *She has a whim for gardening, but it won't last. n.*

whim·per (wim′pər or hwim′pər) 1 cry with soft, broken sounds, in the way that a sick child or dog does. 2 a whimpering cry. 3 complain in a peevish, childish way; whine. 1, 3 *v.*, 2 *n.*

whim·sey (wim′zē or hwim′zē) See **whimsy.**

whim·si·cal (wim′zə kəl or hwim′zə kəl) having many odd notions or fancies; fanciful; odd. *adj.*

whim·sy (wim′zē or hwim′zē) 1 an odd or fanciful idea: *It was just one of her whimsies; don't take it seriously.* 2 odd or fanciful humor; quaintness: *'Alice in Wonderland' is full of whimsy. n., pl.* **whim·sies.** Also spelled **whimsey.**

whine (wīn or hwīn) 1 make a soft, drawn-out complaining cry or sound: *The dog whined to go out with us.* 2 a soft, drawn-out complaining cry or sound. 3 complain in a peevish, childish way: *Some people are always whining about trifles.* 4 say with a whine. 1, 3, 4 *v.*, **whined, whin·ing;** 2 *n.*

☛ **Whine** and **wine** are sometimes pronounced the same.

whin·ny (win′ē or hwin′ē) 1 the sound that a horse makes. 2 make such a sound. 1 *n., pl.* **whin·nies;** 2 *v.*, **whin·nied, whin·ny·ing.**

whip (wip or hwip) 1 a thing to strike or beat with, usually a stick with a cord at the end. 2 strike or beat with or as with a whip; lash: *He whipped the horse to make it go faster.* 3 move, put, or pull quickly and suddenly: *He whipped off his coat and whipped out his knife.* 4 *Informal.* defeat in a fight, contest, etc.: *The* *mayor whipped his opponent in the election.* **5** beat cream, eggs, etc. to a froth. **6** rouse; incite: *He whipped the crowd into a state of frenzy.* 1 *n.,* 2–6 *v.,* **whipped, whip·ping.**

whip up, a prepare or make quickly: *She whipped up some masks for us to wear on Halloween.* **b** stir up: *We are trying to whip up some interest in speed skating.*

whip·pet (wip′ət or hwip′ət) a swift racing dog that resembles a greyhound. *n.*

whip–poor–will (wip′ər wil′ or hwip′ər wil′) a North American bird whose call sounds somewhat like its name: *The whip-poor-will is active at night or in the twilight. n.*

whir or **whirr** (wėr or hwėr) **1** a buzzing noise, as of something turning at high speed: *the whir of a small machine.* **2** operate or move with such a noise: *The motor whirs.* 1 *n.,* 2 *v.,* **whirred, whir·ring.**

whirl (wėrl or hwėrl) **1** turn or swing round and round; spin: *The leaves whirled in the wind.* **2** move round and round: *We whirled about the room. He whirled the club.* **3** move or carry quickly: *We were whirled away in an airplane.* **4** a whirling movement: *The dancer suddenly made a whirl.* **5** a confused condition: *His thoughts are in a whirl.* **6** great activity; a rapid round of happenings, parties, etc.: *We had a rest after the whirl of Christmas holidays.* 1–3 *v.,* 4–6 *n.*

☛ **Whirl** and **whorl** are sometimes pronounced the same.

whirl·pool (wėrl′pül′ or hwėrl′pül′) water whirling round and round rapidly and violently: *The swimmer caught in the whirlpool had hard work to keep from drowning. n.*

whirl·wind (wėrl′wind′ or hwėrl′wind′) air whirling violently round and round; a whirling storm of wind. *n.*

whirr (wėr or hwėr) See **whir.**

whisk (wisk or hwisk) **1** sweep; brush: *She whisked the crumbs from the table.* **2** a quick sweep: *She brushed away the dirt with a few whisks of her broom.* **3** move quickly: *The mouse whisked into its hole. She whisked the letter out of sight.* **4** a light, quick movement. **5** a small brush or broom: *We brushed our coats with a whisk.* **6** beat or whip to a froth. 1, 3, 6 *v.,* 2, 4, 5 *n.*

whisk·er (wis′kər or hwis′kər) **1** Usually, **whiskers,** *pl.* the hair growing on a man's face, especially that on his cheeks and chin. **2** one of the hairs growing on a man's face. **3** a long, stiff hair growing near the mouth of a cat, rat, etc. *n.*

whis·ky or **whis·key** (wis′kē or hwis′kē) a strong, intoxicating liquor made from grain: *Whisky is about half alcohol. n., pl.* **whis·kies** or **whis·keys.**

whis·ky–jack (wis′kē jak′ or hwis′kē jak′) *Cdn.* the Canada jay. *n.*

☛ **Whisky-jack** is a variation of the older word *whisky-john,* which was taken from a North American Indian name for this bird. The word may have come from the Cree *weskuchanis.* To English speakers, the word sounded like *whisky-john.*

whis·per (wis′pər or hwis′pər) **1** speak very softly. **2** a very soft, low spoken sound. **3** speak to in a whisper. **4** tell secretly or privately: *It is widely whispered that his business is failing.* **5** something told secretly or privately: *No whisper about having a new teacher has come to our ears.* **6** make a soft, rustling sound: *The wind whispered in the pines.* **7** a soft, rustling sound: *The wind was so gentle that we could hear the whisper of the leaves.* 1, 3, 4, 6 *v.,* 2, 5, 7 *n.*

whis·tle (wis′əl or hwis′əl) **1** make a clear, shrill sound by forcing breath through one's teeth or lips: *The boy whistled and his dog ran to him quickly.* **2** the sound made by whistling. **3** an instrument for making whistling sounds. **4** blow a whistle: *The policeman whistled for the automobile to stop.* **5** produce by whistling: *to whistle a tune.* **6** move with a shrill sound: *The wind whistled around the house.* 1, 4–6 *v.,* **whis·tled, whis·tling;** 2, 3 *n.*

whis·tler (wis′lər or hwis′lər) **1** any of several whistling birds. **2** an animal related to the groundhog and gopher, found in the mountainous parts of western Canada. *n.*

whit (wit or hwit) a very small bit: *The sick man is not a whit better. n.*

☛ **Whit** and **wit** are sometimes pronounced the same.

white (wīt or hwīt) **1** the color of snow or salt. **2** having this color or one approaching it: *Grandmother has white hair.* **3** white clothing. **4** a part that is white or whitish: *Take the whites of four eggs.* **5** pale: *She turned white with fear.* **6** light-colored: *a white wine, white meat.* **7** having a light-colored skin; not black, brown, or yellow. **8** a member of a light-skinned race. **9** spotless; pure; innocent. 1, 3, 4, 8 *n.,* 2, 5–7, 9 *adj.,* **whit·er, whit·est.**

white ant a termite: *White ants eat wood and are very destructive to buildings.*

white·cap (wīt′kap′ or hwīt′kap′) a wave with a foaming white crest. *n.*

white elephant anything that is expensive and troublesome to keep and take care of.

white flag a plain white flag used as a sign of truce or surrender.

white lie a lie about some small matter, especially one told to avoid being rude or hurting someone's feelings: *I was very tempted to tell a white lie and say that I liked her ugly dress.*

whit·en (wīt′ən or hwīt′ən) make or become white: *She used bleach to whiten the sheets. He whitened when he heard the bad news. v.*

white·wash (wīt′wosh′ or hwīt′wosh′) **1** a liquid for whitening walls, woodwork, etc.: *Whitewash is usually made of lime and water.* **2** whiten with whitewash. **3** cover up the faults or mistakes of. **4** a covering up of faults or mistakes. **5** *Informal.* defeat in a game without a score for the loser: *We whitewashed our opponents 7–0.* **6** *Informal.* a defeat of this kind. 1, 4, 6 *n.,* 2, 3, 5 *v.*

whith·er (wiᴛʜ′ər or hwiᴛʜ′ər) where; to what place; to which place: *He did not know whither she had gone. adv., conj.*

☛ **Whither** and **wither** are sometimes pronounced the same.

whit·ish (wīt′ish or hwīt′ish) almost white. *adj.*

whit·tle (wit′əl or hwit′əl) **1** cut shavings or chips from wood, etc. with a knife. **2** shape wood with a knife; carve: *The old sailor whittled a boat for Paul. v.,* **whit·tled, whit·tling.**

whittle down or **away,** cut down little by little: *We tried to whittle down our expenses.*

hat, āge, fär; let, ēqual, tėrm; it, īce
hot, ōpen, ôrder; oil, out; cup, pu̇t, rüle
ə above, takən, pencəl, lemən, circəs
ch, child; ng, long; sh, ship
th, thin; ᴛʜ, then; zh, measure

whiz or **whizz** (wiz or hwiz) **1** a humming or hissing sound. **2** move or rush with such a sound: *An arrow whizzed past.* 1 *n.,* 2 *v.,* **whizzed, whiz·zing.**

who (hü) a word used: **1** in asking questions about a person or persons: *Who goes there? Who is your friend? Who told you?* **2** in connecting a group of words with some previous word in the sentence: *The girl who spoke is my best friend. We saw men who were working in the fields.* **3** in making statements about a person or persons: *We know who is coming. pron.*

☛ **Who** is used as a subject; **whom** is used only as an object. *The woman who spoke at the meeting is a friend of my parents. The woman whom you heard at the meeting is a friend of my parents.* However, in informal English, **who** is very often used for either subject or object: *Who gave you the book?* (**Who** is the subject.) *Who were you talking to?* (**Who** is the object.) If a preposition comes first, then **whom** must be used: *To whom were you talking?*

☛ **Whose** is always used for people, but it can also be used for things, to make a long written or spoken sentence smoother. For instance, it is easier to read the second of the following sentences than the first: *The plant has three new generators, the combined capacity of which is greater than that of the five we had before. The plant has three new generators whose combined capacity is greater than that of the five we had before.*

☛ See note at **that.**

whoa (wō or hwō) stop! *'Whoa there!' said the farmer to his horse. interj.*

☛ **Whoa** is sometimes pronounced the same as **woe.**

who·ev·er (hü ev′ər) **1** who; any person that: *Whoever wants the book may have it.* **2** no matter who: *Whoever else goes hungry, he won't. pron.*

whole (hōl) **1** having all its parts; complete: *He gave her a whole set of dishes.* **2** all of a thing; the total: *Three thirds make a whole.* **3** full; entire: *He worked the whole day.* **4** anything complete in itself; a system. **5** not injured or broken: *He came out of the fight with a whole skin.* **6** in one piece: *The dog swallowed the meat whole.* **7** well; healthy. 1, 3, 5–7 *adj.,* 2, 4 *n.*
on the whole, a considering everything. **b** for the most part.

☛ **Whole** and **hole** are pronounced the same.

whole–heart·ed (hōl′här′tid) sincere; hearty; without reserve or hesitation: *The returning soldiers were given a whole-hearted welcome. adj.*

whole number a number denoting zero or one or more whole things or units; a number that does not contain a fraction: *0, 1, 2, 3, 15, and 106 are whole numbers; ½, ¾, and ⅞ are fractions; 1⅜ and 2½ are mixed numbers.*

whole·sale (hōl′sāl′) **1** the sale of goods in large quantities at a time, usually to store-keepers or others who will in turn sell them to users: *He buys at wholesale and sells at retail.* **2** in large lots or quantities: *The wholesale price of this dress is $20; the retail price is $30 (adj.). He bought the team sweaters wholesale (adv.).* **3** selling in large quantities: *a wholesale fruit business.* **4** sell or be sold in large quantities: *They wholesale these jackets at $10 each. Such jackets usually wholesale for much less.* 1 *n.,* 2, 3 *adj.,* 2 *adv.,* 4 *v.,* **whole·saled, whole·sal·ing.**

whole·some (hōl′səm) **1** healthful; good for the health: *Milk is a wholesome food.* **2** healthy-looking; suggesting health: *She has a clean, wholesome face.* **3** good for the mind or morals: *He reads only wholesome books. adj.*

who'll (hül) who will; who shall.

whol·ly (hōl′ē) completely; entirely; totally: *The boy was wholly cured. adv.*

☛ **Wholly** and **holy** are pronounced the same.

whom (hüm) what person; which person: *Whom do you like best? He does not know whom to believe. The girl to whom I spoke is my cousin. pron.*

☛ See the note at **that** and the first note at **who.**

whoop (hüp, wüp, or hwüp) **1** a loud cry or shout: *When land was sighted, the sailor let out a whoop of joy.* **2** shout loudly. **3** the loud, gasping sound a person makes when he has whooping cough. **4** make this noise. 1, 3 *n.,* 2, 4 *v.*

☛ **Whoop** and **hoop** are sometimes pronounced the same.

whooping cough (hüp′ing kof′) an infectious disease of children and, rarely, of adults, which causes fits or coughing that end with a loud, gasping sound.

Whooping cranes — about 135 cm long with the tail; height about 120 cm

whooping crane a very large, white bird having a long neck and long legs, with black wing tips and a red patch on the face: *The whooping crane is the tallest of Canadian birds.*

whorl (wėrl or wôrl, hwėrl or hwôrl) **1** a circle of leaves or flowers round the stem of a plant. **2** one of the turns of a spiral shell. **3** anything that circles or turns on or around something else: *A person can be identified by the whorls of his fingerprints. n.*

☛ **Whorl** and **whirl** are sometimes pronounced the same.

whose (hüz) of whom; of which: *The girl whose work got the prize is the youngest in her class. Whose book is this? pron.*

☛ See the second note at **who.**

why (wī or hwī) **1** for what reason: *Why did the baby cry? He does not know why he failed.* **2** because of which: *The reason why he failed was his laziness.* **3** the cause; reason: *I can't understand the whys and wherefores of her behavior.* **4** an expression used to show surprise, doubt, etc. or just to fill in, without adding any important meaning to what is said: *Why!*

The cage is empty! Why, yes, I will if you wish. 1, 2 *adv.*, 3 *n.*, *pl.* **whys;** 4 *interj.*

wick (wik) the part of an oil lamp or candle that is lighted, usually a loosely-twisted cord through which oil or melted wax is drawn up and burned. *n.*

wick·ed (wik′id) **1** bad; evil; sinful: *a wicked old witch, wicked deeds.* **2** mischievous; playfully sly: *a wicked smile.* **3** *Informal.* unpleasant; severe: *A wicked storm swept through the northern part of the province.* *adj.*

wick·ed·ness (wik′id nis) **1** the state of being wicked. **2** a wicked thing or act; something evil. *n.*

wick·er (wik′ər) slender, easily bent branches or twigs that can be woven together: *Wicker is used to make furniture and baskets.* *n.*

A croquet wicket A cricket wicket — 71 cm high and 23 cm wide

wick·et (wik′it) **1** a small door or gate: *The big door has a wicket in it.* **2** a small window, often protected by a screen or grating: *Buy your tickets at this wicket.* **3** in croquet, a wire arch stuck in the ground to knock the ball through. **4** in cricket, either of the two sets of sticks that one side tries to hit with the ball. *n.*

wide (wīd) **1** filling much space from side to side; broad; not narrow: *a wide street. Columbus sailed across the wide ocean. They went forth into the wide world.* **2** extending a certain distance from side to side, measured at right angles to length: *The door is 90 centimetres wide.* **3** over an extensive space: *travel far and wide.* **4** having great range; including many different things: *A trip around the world gives wide experience. Wide reading gives wide understanding of other times and places.* **5** far open: *The child stared with wide eyes.* **6** to the full extent: *Open your mouth wide. The gates stand wide open.* 1, 2, 4, 5 *adj.*, **wid·er, wid·est;** 3, 6 *adv.*

wide of, far from: *His guess was wide of the truth. The shot was wide of the mark.*

wide–a·wake (wīd′ə wāk′) **1** fully awake; with the eyes wide open. **2** alert; keen; knowing: *A watchdog must be a wide-awake guard against danger.* *adj.*

wide–eyed (wīd′īd′) with the eyes wide open: *The baby gazed at the Christmas tree with wide-eyed surprise.* *adj.*

wide·ly (wīd′lē) **1** to a wide extent: *a widely distributed plant, a man who is widely known, to be widely read.* **2** very; extremely: *The boys gave two widely different accounts of the quarrel.* *adv.*

wid·en (wīd′ən) make or become wide or wider: *He widened the path through the forest. The river widens as it flows.* *v.*

wide·spread (wīd′spred′) **1** spread widely or fully: *widespread wings.* **2** spread over a wide space: *a widespread flood.* **3** occurring in many places or among many persons far apart: *a widespread belief.* *adj.*

wid·ow (wid′ō) **1** a woman whose husband is dead and who has not married again. **2** make a widow or widower of: *She was widowed when she was only thirty years old.* 1 *n.*, 2 *v.*

wid·ow·er (wid′ō ər) a man whose wife is dead and who has not married again. *n.*

width (width) **1** how wide a thing is; the distance across; breadth: *The width of the room is three metres.* **2** a piece of a certain width: *Two widths of cloth will make the curtains.* *n.*

wield (wēld) hold and use; manage; control: *The soldier wielded his sword well. A writer wields the pen. The people wield the power in a democracy.* *v.*

wie·ner (wē′nər) a reddish sausage, usually made of pork and beef; frankfurter: *Wieners in buns are called hot dogs.* *n.*

wiener roast an outdoor social function at which wieners are roasted or boiled over an open fire.

wife (wīf) a married woman, especially when thought of in connection with her husband: *Joan is Tom's wife.* *n.*, *pl.* **wives.**

wig (wig) an artificial covering of hair, or of something that imitates hair, for the head: *a doll's wig. The bald man wore a wig. British judges wear wigs in court.* *n.*

wig·gle (wig′əl) **1** wriggle; move with short, quick movements from side to side: *The restless child wiggled in his chair.* **2** such a movement. 1 *v.*, **wig·gled, wig·gling;** 2 *n.*

wig·gly (wig′lē) **1** wiggling: *a wiggly little caterpillar.* **2** wavy: *He drew a wiggly line under the heading.* *adj.*, **wig·gli·er, wig·gli·est.**

wig·wag (wig′wag′) **1** move to and fro. **2** signal by movements of arms, flags, or lights, according to a code. **3** such signalling. 1, 2 *v.*, **wig·wagged, wig·wag·ging;** 3 *n.*

A wigwam

wig·wam (wig′wom) a hut built of poles covered with bark, mats, or skins, made by North American Indians. *n.*

wild (wīld) **1** living or growing in the forests or fields; not tamed; not cultivated: *The tiger is a wild animal. The daisy is a wild flower.* **2** with no people living in it: *Airplanes fly from Edmonton to Europe over the wild region of the North.* **3 wilds,** *pl.* wild country. **4** not civilized; savage: *He is reading about the wild tribes of ancient times in Europe.* **5** not checked; not restrained: *a wild rush for the ball.* **6** violently excited; frantic: *wild with rage, wild with joy.* **7** violent: *a wild storm.* **8** rash; crazy: *a wild scheme.* 1, 2, 4–8 *adj.*, 3 *n.*

wild·cat (wīld′kat′) **1** any of several kinds of wild animal related to the common cat, but larger: *The cougar and the lynx are two kinds of wildcat.* **2** bobcat. **3** a fierce fighter. **4** a well drilled for oil or gas in a region where none has been found before. **5** drill wells in regions not known to contain oil. **6** not authorized by proper union officials: *a wildcat strike.* 1–4 *n.*, 5 *v.*, **wild·cat·ted, wild·cat·ting;** 6 *adj.*

hat, āge, fär; let, ēqual, tėrm; it, īce
hot, ōpen, ôrder; oil, out; cup, pu̇t, rüle
əbove, takən, pencəl, lemən, circəs
ch, child; ng, long; sh, ship
th, thin; ᴛʜ, then; zh, measure

wil·der·ness (wil′dər nis) a wild or desolate region with few or no people living in it. *n.*

wild·fire (wīld′fīr′) a substance that burns fiercely and is hard to put out, formerly used in warfare. *n.*
like wildfire, very rapidly: *The news spread like wildfire.*

wild flower 1 any uncultivated flowering plant that grows in the woods, fields, etc. 2 a flower of such a plant.

wild·fowl (wīld′foul′) birds ordinarily hunted, such as wild ducks or geese, partridges, quail, and pheasants. *n.*

wild·life (wīld′līf′) wild animals as a group, usually those native to a particular area: *the northern wildlife.* *n.*

wile (wīl) 1 a trick to deceive; a cunning way: *The witch by her wiles persuaded the prince to go with her.* 2 coax; lure; entice: *The sunshine wiled me from my work.* 1 *n.,* 2 *v.,* **wiled, wil·ing.**
☞ **Wile** and **while** are sometimes pronounced the same.

wil·ful (wil′fəl) See **willful.** *adj.*

will[1] (wil; *unstressed,* wəl) a word used: 1 to express a promise: *'I will come at 4 o'clock' means that the speaker has made a definite appointment. The doctor will see you now.* 2 to refer to future happenings: *The train will be late. If they leave now, they will arrive in time for dinner.* 3 to introduce a polite request: *Will you please hand me that book?* 4 to express a capacity or power that something has: *This pail will hold eight litres.* 5 to refer to something done again and again: *She will read for hours at a time.* 6 with 'you' to mean that a person has to do something: *Don't argue with me; you will do it at once!* *v.,* **would.**

will[2] (wil) 1 the power of the mind to decide and do: *A good leader must have a strong will.* 2 decide by using this power; use the will: *She willed to keep awake.* 3 determine: *Fate has willed it otherwise.* 4 purpose; determination: *the will to live.* 5 wish; desire: *'Thy will be done.'* 6 a legal statement of a person's wishes about what shall be done with his property after he is dead. 7 give by such a statement: *He willed all his property to his two daughters.* 8 a feeling toward another: *Most people feel good will toward their friends and ill will toward their enemies.* 1, 4–6, 8 *n.,* 2, 3, 7 *v.,* **willed, will·ing.**
at will, whenever one wishes.

will·ful or **wil·ful** (wil′fəl) 1 wanting or taking one's own way; stubborn: *The willful child would not eat his supper.* 2 intended; done on purpose: *willful murder, willful waste.* *adj.* **—will′ful·ly** or **wil′ful·ly,** *adv.*

wil·lies (wil′ēz) *Informal.* a feeling of nervousness and uneasiness: *The movie gave me the willies—I won't go to that kind of show again.* *n.*

WILDCATS
A Canada lynx — about 80 cm long without the tail
A cougar — about 183 cm long without the tail

will·ing (wil′ing) 1 ready; consenting: *He is willing to wait.* 2 cheerfully ready: *willing obedience.* *adj.* **—will′ing·ly,** *adv.* **—will′ing·ness,** *n.*

wil·low (wil′ō) 1 a kind of tree or shrub having tough, slender branches and narrow leaves: *The branches of most willows bend easily and are used to make furniture, baskets, etc.* 2 the wood of this tree. *n.*

wil·low·y (wil′ə wē) 1 like a willow; slender; supple; graceful: *That tall, willowy girl should be good at gymnastics.* 2 having many willows: *We walked along the willowy bank of the river.* *adj.*

wilt (wilt) 1 become limp and drooping; wither: *Flowers wilt when they do not get enough water.* 2 lose strength and vigor. 3 cause to wilt: *The early frost wilted the plant's leaves.* *v.*

wil·y (wīl′ē) tricky; cunning; crafty; sly: *a wily thief. The wily fox got away.* *adj.,* **wil·i·er, wil·i·est.**

win (win) 1 be successful over others; get victory or success: *The tortoise won in the end. We all hope our team will win.* 2 get victory or success in: *He won the race.* 3 *Informal.* a success; victory: *We had five wins and no defeats.* 4 get by effort, ability, or skill; gain: *to win fame, to win a prize.* 5 gain the favor of; persuade: *The speaker soon won his audience. Mary has completely won Mother over to her side.* 1, 2, 4, 5 *v.,* **won, win·ning;** 3 *n.*

wince (wins) 1 draw back suddenly; flinch slightly: *The boy winced when the dentist's drill touched his tooth.* 2 the act of wincing: *When he saw the wince, the dentist stopped drilling for a moment.* 1 *v.,* **winced, winc·ing;** 2 *n.*

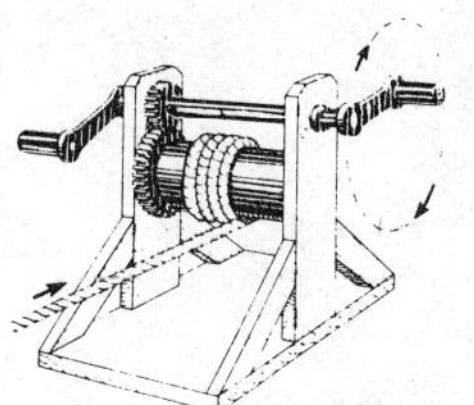
A winch or windlass. The arrows show the way the handles and rope go.

winch (winch) a machine for lifting or pulling, having a roller around which a rope or cable is wound: *The crank of a winch is turned by hand or by an engine.* *n.*

wind[1] (wind) 1 air in motion: *The wind bends the branches. The wind varies in force from a slight breeze to a strong gale.* 2 air filled with some smell: *The deer caught the wind of the hunter and ran off.* 3 smell; follow by scent. 4 the breath; the power of breathing: *A runner needs good wind.* 5 gas in the stomach or bowels. 6 put out of breath; cause difficulty in breathing: *The fat man was winded by walking up the steep hill.* 1, 2, 4, 5 *n.,* 3, 6 *v.,* **wind·ed, wind·ing.**
get wind of, a find out about; get a hint of: *Don't let*

Mother get wind of our plans. **b** smell: *The deer soon got wind of the hunter.*

in the wind, happening; about to happen: *There's an election in the wind.*

wind[2] (wīnd) **1** move this way and that; go in a crooked way; change direction; turn: *A brook winds through the woods. We wound our way through the narrow streets.* **2** fold, wrap, or place about something: *The mother wound her arms about the child.* **3** cover with something put, wrapped, or folded around: *The man's arm is wound with bandages.* **4** roll into a ball or on a spool: *Grandma was winding yarn. Thread comes wound on spools.* **5** a bend; turn; twist. **6** twist or turn around something: *The vine winds around a pole.* **7** make some machine go by turning some part of it: *to wind a clock.* 1–4, 6, 7 *v.,* **wound, wind·ing;** 5 *n.*

wind up, a end; settle; conclude: *We expect to wind up the project tomorrow.* **b** in baseball, make swinging and twisting movements of the arm and body just before pitching the ball.

wind[3] (wīnd) blow: *The hunter winds his horn. v.,* **wind·ed** or **wound, wind·ing.**

wind·break (wind′brāk′) **1** a shelter from the wind: *The high stone wall served as a windbreak.* **2** *Cdn.* a row or clump of trees planted to afford protection from the wind. *n.*

wind·break·er (wind′brāk′ər) a short jacket having close-fitting cuffs and waistband, used for outdoor wear. *n.*

wind·fall (wind′fol′ or wind′fôl′) **1** fruit blown down by the wind. **2** an unexpected piece of good luck. *n.*

wind instrument a musical instrument sounded by blowing air into it: *Horns and flutes are wind instruments.*

wind·lass (wind′ləs) a machine for pulling or lifting things; winch. See **winch** for picture. *n.*

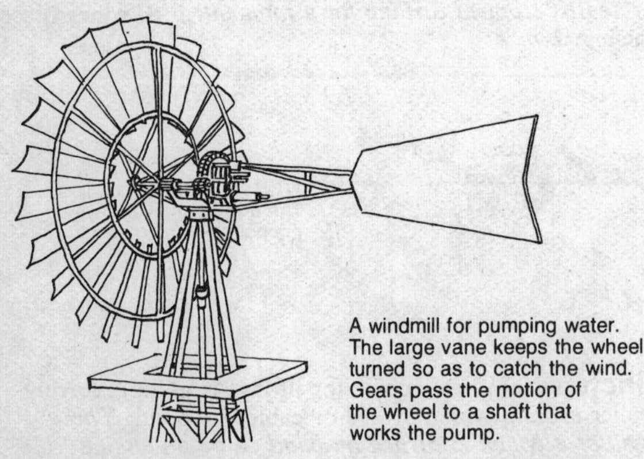

A windmill for pumping water. The large vane keeps the wheel turned so as to catch the wind. Gears pass the motion of the wheel to a shaft that works the pump.

wind·mill (wind′mil′) a mill or machine worked by the action of the wind upon a wheel of vanes or sails mounted on a tower: *Windmills are mostly used to pump water. n.*

win·dow (win′dō) **1** an opening in a wall or roof to let in light or air. **2** such an opening with its frame and glass. *n.*

☛ **Window** came into English in the Middle Ages from an Old Norse word *vindauga* (literally, 'wind eye'), a compound of *vindr,* meaning 'wind,' and *auga,* meaning 'eye.'

win·dow·pane (win′dō pān′) a piece of glass in a window. *n.*

window sill a piece of wood or stone across the bottom of a window.

wind·pipe (wind′pīp′) the passage by which air is carried from the throat to the lungs; trachea. See **larynx** for picture. *n.*

wind·shield (wind′shēld′) a sheet of glass, etc. to keep off the wind: *Automobiles have windshields. n.*

wind·storm (wind′stôrm′) a storm with much wind but little or no rain. *n.*

wind–up (wīnd′up′) **1** an ending; close; conclusion: *As a wind-up to the evening we all went for a swim.* **2** in baseball, a series of movements made by a pitcher just before throwing the ball. *n.*

wind·ward (wind′wərd) **1** on the side toward the wind. **2** in the direction from which the wind is blowing. **3** the direction from which the wind is blowing: *They saw a ship to windward.* 1 *adj.,* 2 *adv.,* 3 *n.*

wind·y (win′dē) **1** having much wind: *a windy street, windy weather.* **2** talking a great deal; voluble: *Those two are windy and we won't have a chance to say much. adj.,* **wind·i·er, wind·i·est.**

wine (wīn) **1** the juice of grapes, when it is fermented and contains alcohol. **2** the fermented juice of other fruits or plants: *currant wine, dandelion wine.* **3** entertain with wine: *We wined and dined our guests.* 1, 2 *n.,* 3 *v.,* **wined, win·ing.**

☛ **Wine** and **whine** are sometimes pronounced the same.

wing (wing) **1** the part of a bird, insect, or bat used in flying, or a corresponding part of a bird or insect that does not fly. **2** anything like a wing in shape or use: *the wings of an airplane.* **3** a part that sticks out from the main part or body: *The house has a wing at each side.* **4** either of the side portions of an army or fleet ready for battle. **5** either of the spaces to the right or left of the stage in a theatre. **6** a part of an organization: *The left wing of the party opposed the new policy.* **7** fly: *The bird wings its way to the south.* **8** make able to fly; give speed to: *Terror winged his steps as the bull drew nearer.* **9** wound in the wing or arm: *The bullet winged the bird but did not kill it.* 1–6 *n.,* 7–9 *v.* **—wing′less,** *adj.*

take wing, fly away: *The bird took wing when the cat came near.*

under the wing of, under the protection of.

winged (wingd or wing′id) **1** having wings. **2** swift; rapid: *a winged messenger. adj.*

wing·spread (wing′spred′) the distance between the tips of the wings when they are spread out. *n.*

wink (wingk) **1** close the eyes and open them again quickly: *The bright light made him wink.* **2** close and open one eye on purpose as a hint or signal: *Father winked at him to keep still.* **3** a winking. **4** a hint or signal given by winking. **5** twinkle: *The stars winked.* **6** a very short time: *I can go back in a wink. I didn't sleep a wink.* 1, 2, 5 *v.,* 3, 4, 6 *n.*

wink at, pretend not to see: *Mother knows we help ourselves to cookies now and then, but she winks at it.*

win·ner (win′ər) a person or thing that wins: *The winner got a prize. n.*

hat, āge, fär; let, ēqual, tėrm; it, īce
hot, ōpen, ôrder; oil, out; cup, pu̇t, rüle
əbove, takən, pencəl, lemən, circəs
ch, child; ng, long; sh, ship
th, thin; ᴛʜ, then; zh, measure

win·ning (win′ing) 1 that wins: *a winning team.* 2 charming; attractive: *She has a very winning smile.* 3 **winnings,** *pl.* what is won; money won: *He pocketed his winnings.* 1, 2 *adj.,* 3 *n.*

Winnipeg couch a kind of couch having no arms or back and opening out into a double bed.

Winnipeg goldeye goldeye.

win·now (win′ō) 1 blow off the chaff from grain; drive or blow away chaff. 2 separate; sift; sort out: *to winnow truth from lies.* *v.*

win·some (win′səm) charming; attractive; pleasing: *a winsome girl.* *adj.*

win·ter (win′tər) 1 the coldest of the four seasons; the time of the year between fall and spring. 2 of or for the winter; like that of winter: *winter clothes, winter weather.* 3 pass the winter: *Robins winter in the South.* 4 keep or feed during winter: *We wintered our cattle in the warm valley.* 1 *n.,* 2 *adj.,* 3, 4 *v.*

win·ter·green (win′tər grēn′) 1 a small evergreen plant with bright-red berries: *An oil made from leaves of wintergreen is used in medicine and as a flavoring.* 2 the oil of this plant. 3 its flavor. *n.*

win·ter·time (win′tər tīm′) the season of winter. *n.*

win·try (win′trē) 1 of or having to do with winter; like winter: *wintry weather, a wintry sky.* 2 not warm or friendly; chilly: *a wintry manner, a wintry smile, a wintry greeting.* *adj.,* **win·tri·er, win·tri·est.**

wipe (wīp) 1 rub in order to clean or dry: *We wipe our shoes on the mat. We wipe the dishes with a towel.* 2 take away, off, or out by rubbing: *Wipe away your tears. She wiped off the dust.* 3 the act of wiping: *He gave his face a hasty wipe.* 1, 2 *v.,* **wiped, wip·ing;** 3 *n.*
wipe out, destroy completely: *The pollution in the river has wiped out all the fish.*

wire (wīr) 1 metal drawn out into a thin, flexible rod or thread: *telephone wire.* 2 a piece of such metal: *Use wire to connect these two batteries.* 3 made of wire: *a wire fence.* 4 furnish with wire: *to wire a house for electricity.* 5 fasten with wire: *He wired the two pieces together.* 6 telegraph: *He sent a message by wire.* 7 to telegraph: *Please wire your answer at once.* 8 *Informal.* telegram: *The news of his arrival came in a wire.* 1, 2, 6, 8 *n.,* 3 *adj.,* 4, 5, 7 *v.,* **wired, wir·ing.**

wire·less (wīr′lis) 1 using no wires; transmitting by radio waves instead of by electric wires: *wireless telegraphy.* 2 *Esp. British.* radio. 1 *adj.,* 2 *n.*

wir·ing (wīr′ing) a system of wires to carry an electric current. *n.*

wir·y (wīr′ē) 1 made of wire. 2 like wire. 3 lean, strong, and tough: *The athlete had a wiry body.* *adj.,* **wir·i·er, wir·i·est.**

wis·dom (wiz′dəm) 1 knowledge and good judgment based on experience. 2 wise conduct; wise words: *His wisdom guided us.* *n.*

wisdom tooth the back tooth on either side of the upper and lower jaw, ordinarily appearing between the ages of 17 and 25.

wise[1] (wīz) 1 having or showing knowledge and good judgment: *a wise judge, wise advice, wise plans.* 2 having knowledge or information: *We are none the wiser for his explanations.* *adj.,* **wis·er, wis·est.**

wise[2] (wīz) way; manner: *He is in no wise a bad boy, but he is often a little mischievous.* *n.*

-wise a suffix meaning: 1 in ___ manner: *Likewise means in like manner.* 2 in the normal way of: *Clockwise means in the normal way of a clock.* 3 in the ___ respect or case: *Otherwise means in the other case.* 4 in the direction of ___: *Lengthwise means in the direction of length.* 5 with regard to ___: *Businesswise means with regard to business.*

wise·crack (wīz′krak′) *Slang.* 1 a smart remark; a quick, witty answer. 2 make wisecracks. 1 *n.,* 2 *v.*

wish (wish) 1 have a need or longing for; desire; want: *Do you wish to go home?* 2 have a desire; express a hope: *He wished for a new house. I wish that I had enough money to buy that model boat.* 3 a wishing; a desire: *What is your wish? He had no wish to be king.* 4 the saying of a wish: *Please give her my best wishes for a Happy New Year.* 5 wish something for someone; have a hope for: *We wish peace for all mankind. I wish you a Happy New Year.* 6 the thing wished for: *She got her wish.* 1, 2, 5 *v.,* 3, 4, 6 *n.*

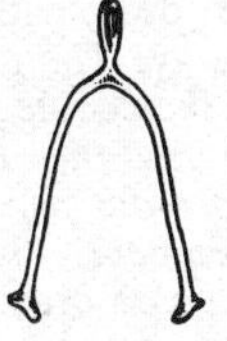
A wishbone

wish·bone (wish′bōn′) the forked bone in the front of the breast in poultry and other birds. *n.*

wish·ful (wish′fəl) having or expressing a wish; desiring; desirous: *His boast about winning the race was only wishful thinking.* *adj.*

wisp (wisp) 1 a small bundle; small bunch: *a wisp of hay.* 2 a small portion of anything; a little bit: *a wisp of hair, a wisp of smoke.* 3 a little thing: *a wisp of a girl.* *n.*

wis·tar·i·a (wis ter′ē ə or wis tar′ē ə) a climbing shrub having large clusters of purple or white flowers. *n.* Also spelled **wisteria** (wis tēr′ē ə).

wist·ful (wist′fəl) longing; yearning: *A child stood looking with wistful eyes at the toys in the window.* *adj.*

wit (wit) 1 the power to perceive quickly and express cleverly ideas that are unusual, striking, and amusing: *His wit made even troubles seem amusing.* 2 a person with such power: *Stephen Leacock was a wit.* 3 the power of understanding; mind; sense: *People with quick wits learn easily. The child was out of his wits with fright. That poor man hasn't wit enough to earn a living.* *n.*

☛ **Wit** and **whit** are sometimes pronounced the same.

witch (wich) 1 a woman supposed to have magic power: *Witches were thought to use their power to do evil.* 2 an ugly old woman. 3 *Informal.* a fascinating girl or woman. *n.*

☛ **Witch** and **which** are sometimes pronounced the same.

witch·craft (witch′kraft′) what a witch does or is supposed to be able to do; magic power. *n.*

witch·er·y (wich′ər ē) 1 witchcraft; magic. 2 charm; fascination: *There was witchery in the moonlit scene. n., pl.* **witch·er·ies.**

with (wiᴛʜ or with) 1 in the company of: *Come with me.* 2 among: *They will mix with the crowd.* 3 having, wearing, carrying, etc.: *He is a man with brains. She received a telegram with good news.* 4 by means of: *The man cut the meat with a knife.* 5 using; showing: *Work with care.* 6 added to: *Do you want sugar with your tea?* 7 in relation to: *They are friendly with us.* 8 in regard to: *We are pleased with the house.* 9 in proportion to: *The army's power increases with its size.* 10 because of: *The man almost died with thirst. The child is shaking with cold.* 11 in the keeping or service of: *Leave the dog with me.* 12 at the same time as: *With this event the field day ended.* 13 on the side of; for: *They are with us in our plan.* 14 from: *I hate to part with my favorite things.* 15 against: *We fought with that gang. prep.*

with·al (wiᴛʜ ol′ or wiᴛʜ ôl′, with ol′ or with ôl′) with it all; also; as well; besides: *The lady is rich and fair and wise withal. adv.*

with·draw (wiᴛʜ dro′ or wiᴛʜ drô′, with dro′ or with drô′) 1 draw back; draw away: *The guilty child quickly withdrew his hand from the cookie jar.* 2 take back; remove: *He agreed to withdraw the charge of theft if they returned the money. Worn-out paper money is withdrawn from use by the government.* 3 go away: *She withdrew from the room. v.,* **with·drew, with·drawn, with·draw·ing.**

with·draw·al (wiᴛʜ dro′əl or wiᴛʜ drô′əl, with dro′əl or with drô′əl) drawing back or taking back; taking away or going away: *The chairman noticed her withdrawal from the meeting. n.*

with·drawn (wiᴛʜ dron′ or wiᴛʜ drôn′, with dron′ or with drôn′) 1 See **withdraw.** *He notified the secretary that he had withdrawn from the club.* 2 shy; of a retiring nature: *People who are too sensitive to what others think of them are often withdrawn.* 1 *v.,* 2 *adj.*

with·drew (wiᴛʜ drü′ or with drü′) See **withdraw.** *The coach withdrew the player from the game when he was hurt. v.*

with·er (wiᴛʜ′ər) 1 make or become dry and lifeless; dry up; fade: *The hot sun withers the grass. Flowers wither after they are cut. Age had withered the old lady's face.* 2 cause to feel ashamed or confused: *She blushed under her aunt's withering look. v.*

☛ **Wither** and **whither** are sometimes pronounced the same.

with·held (with held′) See **withhold.** *The witness withheld information from the police. v.*

with·hold (with hōld′) 1 refuse to give: *There will be no school play if the principal withholds his consent.* 2 hold back; keep back: *The general withheld two regiments from the attack. v.,* **with·held, with·hold·ing.**

with·in (wiᴛʜ in′ or with in′) 1 not beyond; inside the limits of: *The task was within the man's powers. He guessed my mass within two kilograms.* 2 in or into the inner part of; inside of: *By the use of X rays, doctors can see within the body.* 3 in or into the inner part; inside: *The house has been painted within and without. The curtains were white without and green within.* 1, 2 *prep.,* 3 *adv.*

with·out (wiᴛʜ out′ or with out′) 1 with no; not having; lacking; free from: *A cat walks without noise. He drinks tea without sugar.* 2 so as to leave out, avoid, or neglect: *She walked past without noticing us.* 3 outside of; beyond: *Soldiers are camped within and without the city walls.* 4 outside; on the outside: *The house is painted without and within.* 1–3 *prep.,* 4 *adv.*

do or **go without,** remain in want of something; manage in spite of not having a certain thing: *Either cook your own supper or go without.*

with·stand (with stand′ or wiᴛʜ stand′) stand against; hold out against; resist; oppose especially successfully; endure: *Soldiers have to withstand hardships. These shoes will withstand hard wear. v.,* **with·stood, with·stand·ing.**

with·stood (with stu̇d′ or wiᴛʜ stu̇d′) See **withstand.** *The soldiers withstood the attack. These shoes have withstood three years of hard wear. v.*

wit·less (wit′lis) lacking sense; stupid; foolish: *Walking into the street without looking is a witless thing to do. adj.*

wit·ness (wit′nis) 1 a person who saw something happen; spectator: *He started the fight in the presence of several witnesses.* 2 see: *He witnessed the accident.* 3 a person who gives evidence or testifies under oath before a judge, coroner, etc. 4 evidence; testimony: *This document is witness to my honesty.* 5 testify to; give evidence of: *Her whole manner witnessed her surprise.* 6 a person who signs a document to show that another person's signature on it is genuine. 7 sign a document as witness: *to witness a will.* 1, 3, 4, 6 *n.,* 2, 5, 7 *v.*

bear witness, be evidence; give evidence; testify: *The thief's fingerprints bore witness to his guilt.*

wit·ty (wit′ē) full of wit; clever and amusing: *A witty person makes witty remarks. adj.,* **wit·ti·er, wit·ti·est.**

wives (wīvz) plural of **wife.** *n.*

wiz·ard (wiz′ərd) 1 a man supposed to have magic power. 2 *Informal.* a very clever person; expert: *Edison was a wizard at invention. n.*

wiz·ened (wiz′ənd) dried up; withered; shrivelled: *a wizened face, a wizened apple. adj.*

wk. week.

wob·ble (wob′əl) 1 move unsteadily from side to side; shake; tremble: *The front wheel on her bicycle wobbles.* 2 waver; be uncertain, unsteady, or changeable. 3 a wobbling motion. *1, 2 v.,* **wob·bled, wob·bling;** 3 *n.* Also spelled **wabble.**

wob·bly (wob′lē) unsteady; shaky; wavering. *adj.*

woe (wō) great grief, trouble, or distress: *Sickness and poverty are common woes. n.*

☛ **Woe** and **whoa** are sometimes pronounced the same.

woe·ful (wō′fəl) 1 full of woe; sad; sorrowful; wretched: *a woeful expression.* 2 pitiful: *a woeful sight. adj.*

woke (wōk) See **wake**[1]. *He woke before we did. v.*

wolf (wu̇lf) 1 a wild animal resembling a large dog and having a bushy tail and erect ears. 2 a cruel, greedy person. 3 eat greedily: *The starving men wolfed down the food.* 1, 2 *n., pl.* **wolves;** 3 *v.*

cry wolf, give a false alarm.

keep the wolf from the door, keep safe from hunger or poverty.

hat, āge, fär; let, ēqual, tėrm; it, īce
hot, ōpen, ôrder; oil, out; cup, pu̇t, rüle
əbove, takən, pencəl, lemən, circəs
ch, child; ng, long; sh, ship
th, thin; ᴛʜ, then; zh, measure

Wolf Cub a member of the junior branch of the Boy Scouts.

wolf·hound (wu̇lf′hound′) one of various breeds of large dog once used in hunting wolves. *n.*

wolf·ish (wu̇l′fish) **1** like a wolf: *a wolfish looking dog.* **2** greedy: *He ate with wolfish impatience. adj.*

A wolverine — about 75 cm long without the tail

wol·ver·ine or **wol·ver·ene** (wu̇l′vər ēn′ or wu̇l′vər ēn′) a very powerful, heavily built, meat-eating animal related to the badger and the skunk: *The wolverine is found in Canada and the northern United States. n.*

wolves (wu̇lvz) plural of **wolf.** *n.*

wom·an (wu̇m′ən) **1** an adult female human being: *A woman is a girl who has grown up.* **2** women as a group; the average woman: *a magazine designed for the modern woman.* **3** a female servant: *The princess always travelled with her woman. n., pl.* **wom·en.** (wim′ən)
☛ See note at **lady.**

wom·an·hood (wu̇m′ən hu̇d′) **1** the condition or time of being a woman. **2** the character or qualities of a woman. **3** women as a group: *Marie Curie was an honor to womanhood. n.*

wom·an·kind (wu̇m′ən kīnd′) women as a group. *n.*

wom·an·ly (wu̇m′ən lē) **1** like or typical of a woman: *a womanly nature. She is a very womanly person—gentle, capable, and sympathetic.* **2** proper or suitable for a woman: *Grandma says that hockey is not a womanly sport. adj.*

womb (wüm) in female mammals, the organ of the body that holds and provides food for the young until birth; uterus. *n.*

wom·en (wim′ən) plural of **woman.** *n.*

wom·en·folk (wim′ən fōk′) women. *n. pl.*

won (wun) See **win.** *Which side won yesterday? We have won four games. v.*
☛ **Won** and **one** are pronounced the same.

won·der (wun′dər) **1** a strange and surprising thing or event: *The pyramids are one of the wonders of the world. It is a wonder that he refused such a good offer. No wonder that child is sick; he eats too much candy.* **2** the feeling caused by what is strange and surprising: *The baby looked with wonder at the Christmas tree.* **3** feel wonder: *We wonder at the splendor of the stars.* **4** be surprised or astonished: *I wonder that you came at all. I shouldn't wonder if he wins the prize.* **5** be curious about; wish to know: *I wonder what time it is. I wonder when she got her new hat.* 1, 2 *n.*, 3–5 *v.*

A timber wolf — about 70 cm high at the shoulder

won·der·ful (wun′dər fəl) **1** causing wonder; marvellous; remarkable: *The works of God are wonderful. The explorer had wonderful adventures.* **2** *Informal.* excellent; splendid; fine: *We had a wonderful time at the party. adj.*

won·der·ment (wun′dər mənt) wonder; surprise: *He stared at the huge bear in wonderment. n.*

won·drous (wun′drəs) wonderful. *adj.*

wont (wōnt) **1** accustomed: *He was wont to read the paper at breakfast.* **2** a custom or habit: *He rose early, as was his wont.* 1 *adj.*, 2 *n.*
☛ **Wont** and **won't** are pronounced the same.

won't (wōnt) will not.
☛ See note at **wont.**

woo (wü) **1** make love to; seek to marry. **2** seek to win; try to get: *Some people woo fame; some woo riches.* **3** try to persuade; urge. *v.*

wood (wu̇d) **1** the hard substance beneath the bark of trees and shrubs: *Wood is used for making houses, boats, boxes, and furniture.* **2** trees cut up for use: *The carpenter brought wood to build a playhouse. Put some wood on the fire.* **3** made of wood; wooden: *a wood house.* **4** used for or on wood: *We have a wood basket for the fireplace.* **5** a large number of growing trees; a woods (def. 1): *The children go to the wood behind the farm for wild flowers and for nuts.* **6** See **woods** (def. 2). 1, 2, 5, 6 *n.*, 3, 4 *adj.*
out of the woods, out of the danger or difficulty.
☛ **Wood** and **would** are pronounced the same.
☛ See note at **woods.**

wood·bine (wu̇d′bīn′) **1** the honeysuckle. **2** the Virginia creeper, a climbing vine that has leaves with five leaflets and bluish-black berries. *n.*

wood·chuck (wu̇d′chuk′) a small, thick-bodied North American animal with short legs and a bushy tail; groundhog: *Woodchucks sleep in their holes all winter.* See **groundhog** for picture. *n.*
☛ **Woodchuck** comes from a North American Indian name for this animal. It may have come from the Cree word, *ochāk.* To English speakers, the first syllable sounded like *wood.*

wood·cock (wu̇d′kok′) a small game bird with a long bill and short legs. *n., pl.* **wood·cocks** or **wood·cock.**

wood·craft (wu̇d′kraft′) **1** knowledge about how to get food and shelter in the woods; skill in hunting, trapping, finding one's way, etc. **2** the making or carving of objects in wood. *n.*

wood·cut·ter (wu̇d′kut′ər) a man who cuts down trees or chops wood. *n.*

wood·ed (wu̇d′id) covered with trees: *The house stood on a wooded hill overlooking the lake. adj.*

wood·en (wu̇d′ən) **1** made of wood. **2** stiff as wood; awkward: *The boy gave a wooden bow and left the stage.* **3** dull; stupid. *adj.*

wood·land (wůd′lənd) land covered with trees: *sounds of the woodland, woodland animals. n.*

wood lot a piece of land on which trees are grown and cut; a bush lot.

wood·man (wůd′mən) **1** a man who cuts down trees. **2** a person who lives in the woods. *n., pl.* **wood·men** (wůd′mən).

A downy woodpecker — about 17 cm long with the tail

wood·peck·er (wůd′pek′ər) a bird with a hard, pointed bill for pecking holes in trees to get insects. *n.*

woods (wůdz) **1** a place having a number of trees growing wild; a small forest: *There is a woods behind the farm.* **2** a forest; an area covered by forests: *Many people hunt in the Ontario woods. n.*

☛ **Woods** is plural in form but may be singular in meaning. We speak of *a woods* but ordinarily use a plural verb with *the woods: The woods are pretty in the fall.*

wood·shed (wůd′shed′) a shed for storing wood. *n.*

woods·man (wůdz′mən) **1** a man used to life in the woods and skilled in hunting, fishing, trapping, etc. **2** a man whose work is cutting down trees; lumberjack. *n., pl.* **woods·men** (wůdz′mən).

wood thrush a thrush common in the thickets and woods of eastern North America.

wood·wind (wůd′wind′) **1 woodwinds,** *pl.* the wind instruments of an orchestra, including clarinets, oboes, etc. **2** any such instrument: *Woodwinds were formerly made of wood but some are now often made of metal. n.*

wood·work (wůd′wėrk′) things made of wood, especially the doors, stairs, mouldings, etc. inside a house. *n.*

wood·work·ing (wůd′wėr′king) making or shaping things of wood. *n.*

wood·y (wůd′ē) **1** having many trees; covered with trees: *a woody hillside.* **2** consisting of wood: *the woody parts of a shrub.* **3** like wood: *Turnips become woody when they are left in the ground too long. adj.,* **wood·i·er, wood·i·est.**

woof (wüf) **1** the threads running from side to side across a woven fabric: *The woof crosses the warp.* See **weave** for picture. **2** woven fabric or its texture. *n.*

wool (wůl) **1** the soft hair or fur of sheep and some other animals. **2** short, thick, curly hair. **3** something like wool: *Glass wool for insulation is made from fibres of glass.* **4** yarn, cloth, or garments made of wool: *We wear wool in winter. n.*

pull the wool over someone's eyes, *Informal.* deceive or trick someone.

wool·len or **wool·en** (wůl′ən) **1** made of wool: *a woollen suit.* **2 woollens** or **woolens,** *pl.* cloth or clothing made of wool: *Mother puts our woollens in plastic bags every summer to protect them against moths.* **3** of or having to do with wool or cloth made of wool: *a woollen mill.* 1, 3 *adj.,* 2 *n.*

wool·ly or **wool·y** (wůl′ē) **1** consisting of wool: *the woolly coat of a sheep.* **2** like wool. **3** covered with wool or something like it. *adj.,* **wool·li·er** or **wool·i·er, wool·li·est** or **wool·i·est.**

word (wėrd) **1** a sound or a group of sounds that has meaning and is a unit of speech: *She answered one word, 'No.'* **2** the writing or printing that stands for a word: *This page is filled with words.* **3** a brief expression or comment: *The teacher gave us a word of advice.* **4** speech: *He is honest in word and deed.* **5** a command; order: *We have to wait till she gives the word.* **6** a promise: *The boy kept his word.* **7** news: *No word has come from the battle front.* **8 words,** *pl.* angry talk; a quarrel or dispute: *They had words about whose fault it was.* **9** put into words: *He worded his message clearly.* 1–8 *n.,* 9 *v.*

eat one's words, take back what one has said.

word·ing (wėr′ding) the way of saying a thing; the choice or use of words: *Careful wording helps you make clear to others what you really mean. n.*

word·y (wėr′dē) using too many words. *adj.,* **word·i·er, word·i·est.**

wore (wôr) See **wear.** *He wore out his shoes in two months. v.*

☛ **Wore** and **war** are pronounced the same.

work (wėrk) **1** the effort of doing or making something: *Few people like hard work.* **2** something to do; an occupation; employment: *The man is out of work.* **3** something made or done, especially something creative; the result of effort: *The artist considers that picture to be his greatest work.* **4** that on which effort is put: *The dressmaker took her work on the porch.* **5 works,** *pl.* **a** a factory or other place for doing some kind of work: *His first job was in the boiler works.* **b** the moving parts of a machine: *the works of a watch.* **c** actions; deeds: *good works.* **6** do work; labor: *Most people must work to live.* **7** work for pay; be employed: *He works in a bank.* **8** put one's effort or labor into; perform a required or expected activity on or in: *He worked his farm with success. The policeman was working his beat.* **9** act; operate: *This pump will not work. The plan worked well.* **10** form; shape: *He worked a piece of copper into a tray.* **11** cause to do work: *He works his men long hours.* **12** make, get, do, or bring about by effort: *The injured man worked his way across the room on his hands and knees. He worked his way through college.* **13** bring about; cause; do: *The plan worked harm.* **14** go or do slowly or with effort: *The ship worked to windward. Work the cork loose.* **15** gradually become: *The window catch has worked loose.* **16** ferment: *Yeast makes the brew work.* 1–5 *n.,* 6–16 *v.,* **worked** or sometimes (for defs. 10, 13) **wrought, work·ing.**

work out, a plan; develop. **b** solve; find out. **c** give exercise to; practise.

work up, a plan; develop. **b** excite; stir up.

work·bench (wėrk′bench′) a table at which a carpenter, mechanic, etc. works. *n.*

work·book (wėrk′bůk′) **1** a book containing outlines for the study of some subject, questions to be answered,

hat, āge, fär; let, ēqual, tėrm; it, īce
hot, ōpen, ôrder; oil, out; cup, pu̇t, rüle
əbove, takən, pencəl, lemən, circəs
ch, child; ng, long; sh, ship
th, thin; ŦH, then; zh, measure

etc. 2 a book in which a student does parts of his written work. *n.*

work·er (wėr′kər) 1 a person who works with his or her hands or with machines. 2 a person who works hard. 3 one of the insects in a colony of bees, ants, wasps, etc. that do the work in their community. *n.*

work·ing (wėr′king) 1 the method or manner of work; operation; action: *Do you understand the working of this machine?* 2 that works: *The class constructed a working model of a helicopter.* 3 of, for, or used in working: *working hours, working clothes.* 1 *n.*, 2, 3 *adj.*

work·ing·man (wėr′king man′) a man who works for wages, especially one who works with his hands or with machines. *n., pl.* **work·ing·men** (wėr′king men′).

work·man (wėrk′mən) 1 workingman. 2 a man skilled in his trade or craft. *n., pl.* **work·men** (wėrk′mən).

work·man·like (wėrk′mən līk′) skilful; done well: *a workmanlike job. adj.*

work·man·ship (wėrk′mən ship′) the art or skill in a worker or his work: *Good workmanship deserves good pay. n.*

work·out (wėrk′out′) *Informal.* 1 an exercise; practice: *The team had a good workout before the game.* 2 a trial or test: *The mechanic gave the car a thorough workout after repairing it. n.*

work·room (wėrk′rüm′) a room set aside for working in: *We have a workroom in the basement. n.*

work·shop (wėrk′shop′) 1 a room or building where work, especially manual work, is done. 2 a meeting of people for discussion, study, etc. of a particular subject: *The hockey coaches for the League had a workshop in September. n.*

world (wėrld) 1 the earth: *Ships can sail around the world.* 2 all of certain parts, people, or things of the earth: *the insect world, a woman's world. The* **Old World** *is Europe, Asia, and Africa. The* **New World** *is North America and South America.* 3 a sphere of interest, activity, thought, etc.: *the world of music.* 4 all people; the public: *The whole world knows it.* 5 the things of this life and the people devoted to them: *Monks and nuns live apart from the world.* 6 a star or planet, especially when considered inhabited. 7 all things; everything; the universe. 8 a great deal; very much; a large amount: *Sunshine does children a world of good. n.*

on top of the world, in high spirits: *I was on top of the world when I found out I had won.*

out of this world, *Informal.* great; wonderful; distinctive: *Our plans for the decorations are out of this world.*

world·ly (wėrld′lē) 1 of this world; not of heaven: *worldly wealth.* 2 caring much for the interests and pleasures of this world. *adj.,* **world·li·er, world·li·est.**

world–wide (wėrld′wīd′) spread throughout the world: *Gasoline now has world-wide use. adj.*

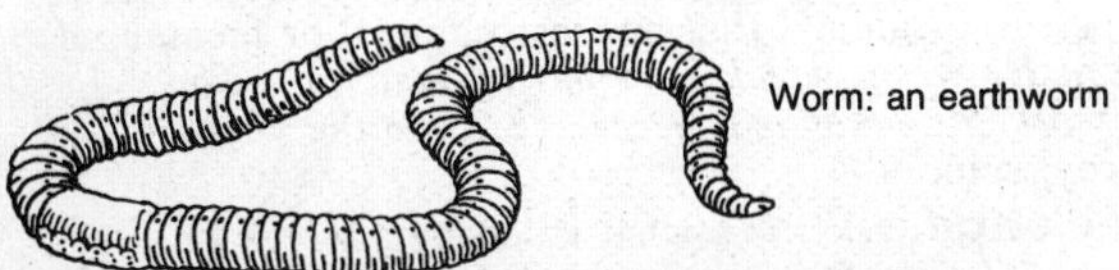
Worm: an earthworm

worm (wėrm) 1 a small, slender crawling or creeping animal: *Most worms have soft bodies and no legs.* 2 **worms,** *pl.* a disease caused by worms in the body: *Our dog had worms, but he is fine now.* 3 something like a worm in shape or movement, such as the thread of a screw. 4 move like a worm; crawl or creep like a worm: *The soldiers wormed their way through the tall grass toward the enemy's camp. We wormed under the high fence.* 5 work or get by persistent and secret means: *He wormed himself into our confidence. He tried to worm the secret out of me.* 6 a person who deserves contempt or pity. 1–3, 6 *n.*, 4, 5 *v.*

worm·y (wėr′mē) 1 having worms; containing many worms: *some wormy apples.* 2 damaged by worms: *wormy wood. adj.,* **worm·i·er, worm·i·est.**

worn (wôrn) 1 See **wear.** *He has worn that suit for two years.* 2 damaged by use: *worn rugs.* 3 tired; wearied: *a worn face.* 1 *v.*, 2, 3 *adj.*

worn–out (wôrn′out′) 1 used until no longer fit for use: *You should throw those worn-out shoes away.* 2 very tired; exhausted: *I'm worn-out after all that running. adj.*

wor·ry (wėr′ē) 1 feel anxious; be uneasy: *She worries about little things. She will worry if we are late.* 2 make anxious; trouble: *The problem worried him.* 3 care; anxiety; trouble; uneasiness: *Worry kept her awake.* 4 annoy; bother; vex: *Don't worry your father with so many questions.* 5 seize and shake with the teeth; bite at; snap at: *The dog worried the rat.* 1, 2, 4, 5 *v.,* **wor·ries, wor·ried, wor·ry·ing;** 3 *n.*

worse (wėrs) 1 more ill: *The sick man seems even worse today.* 2 more bad; more evil: *He is dishonest enough, but his brother is much worse.* 3 in a more severe or evil manner or degree: *It is raining worse than ever today.* 4 that which is worse: *The weather has been bad, but we can expect even worse tonight.* 1, 2 *adj.*, 3 *adv.*, 4 *n.*

wor·sen (wėr′sən) make or become worse: *You will only worsen the situation if you talk about it. She was taken to hospital, but her condition worsened through the night. v.*

wor·ship (wėr′ship) 1 great honor and respect paid to someone or something regarded as sacred: *the worship of God, idol worship.* 2 pay great honor and respect to: *People go to church to worship God.* 3 ceremonies or services in which one pays such respect: *Prayers and hymns are part of worship.* 4 take part in a religious service. 5 great love and admiration: *hero worship.* 6 consider extremely precious; hold very dear; adore: *A miser worships money. She worships her mother.* 1, 3, 5 *n.*, 2, 4, 6 *v.,* **wor·shipped** or **wor·shiped, wor·ship·ping** or **wor·ship·ing. —wor′ship·per** or **wor′ship·er,** *n.*

wor·ship·ful (wėr′ship fəl) 1 honorable: *We beg you, worshipful gentlemen, to grant our request.* 2 worshipping: *The dog watches his master with worshipful eyes. adj.*

worst (wėrst) 1 most ill: *This is the worst I've been since I got sick.* 2 most bad; most evil: *None of them are good, but he's the worst of the lot.* 3 in the worst manner or degree: *He acts worst when he's tired.*

4 that which is worst: *Yesterday was bad, but the worst is yet to come.* **5** beat; defeat: *He has worsted his enemies.* 1, 2 *adj.*, 3 *adv.*, 4 *n.*, 5 *v.*

wor·sted (wėr′stid or wu̇s′tid) **1** firmly twisted woollen thread or yarn. **2** cloth made from such thread or yarn. *n.*

☛ The word **worsted** comes from the name of the town in England where this kind of cloth was first made.

worth (wėrth) **1** good or important enough for; deserving of: *That book is worth reading. Vancouver is a city worth visiting.* **2** merit; usefulness; importance: *We should read books of real worth.* **3** value in money: *He needed money and had to sell his car for less than its worth.* **4** the quantity that a certain amount will buy: *He bought a dollar's worth of stamps.* **5** equal in value to: *This book is worth five dollars. That toy is worth little.* **6** having property that amounts to: *That man is worth a million dollars.* 1, 5, 6 *adj.*, 2–4 *n.*

wor·thi·ness (wėr′ᴛʜē nis) worth; merit: *Nobody in our town doubts the worthiness of that fine young teacher.* *n.*

worth·less (wėrth′lis) without worth; good-for-nothing; useless: *Throw those worthless broken toys away. Don't read that worthless book.* *adj.*

worth·while (wėrth′ wīl′ or wėrth′hwīl′) worth time, attention, or effort; having real merit: *He ought to spend his time on some worthwhile reading.* *adj.*

wor·thy (wėr′ᴛʜē) **1** having worth or merit. **2** deserving; meriting: *His courage was worthy of high praise. Bad acts are worthy of punishment.* **3** a person of great merit; an admirable person: *Winston Churchill stands very high among English worthies.* 1, 2 *adj.*, **wor·thi·er, wor·thi·est;** 3 *n.*, *pl.* **wor·thies.**

would (wu̇d; *unstressed,* wəd) a word used: **1** to introduce a very polite request: *Would you please close the window?* **2** to soften a statement or express uncertainty: *I wouldn't like to ask him.* **3** to express an unlikely or an impossible condition: *If I asked whether I could go, she would say no. If I knew the way, I would tell you.* **4** to express action done again and again: *When we were small, we would spend hours playing in the sand.* **5** See **will**[1]. *v.*

☛ **Would** as the past tense of **will** is used most often in reported speech. Compare *He said, 'I will come'* with *He said that he would come.*

☛ **Would** and **wood** are pronounced the same.

would·n't (wu̇d′ənt) would not.

wound[1] (wünd) **1** a hurt or injury caused by cutting, stabbing, shooting, etc.: *The man has a knife wound in his arm.* **2** injure by cutting, stabbing, shooting, etc.; hurt: *The hunter wounded the deer.* **3** any hurt or injury to feelings, reputation, etc.: *The loss of his job was a wound to his pride.* **4** injure in feelings, reputation, etc.: *His unkind words wounded her.* 1, 3 *n.*, 2, 4 *v.*

wound[2] (wound) See **wind**[2]. *She wound the string into a ball some time ago. It is wound too loosely.* *v.*

wound[3] (wound) See **wind**[3]. *v.*

wove (wōv) See **weave.** *The spider wove a new web after the first was destroyed.* *v.*

wo·ven (wō′vən) See **weave.** *This cloth is closely woven.* *v.*

wow (wou) *Slang.* **1** an exclamation of delight, admiration, etc. **2** a complete success; a hit: *The clown's act was a wow!* **3** dazzle or impress: *My father really wowed everyone with his new suit.* 1, 2 *n.*, 3 *v.*

wraith (rāth) **1** the ghost of a person seen before or soon after his death. **2** a ghost; spectre. *n.*

wran·gle (rang′gəl) **1** argue or dispute in a noisy or angry way; quarrel: *The children wrangled about who should sit on the front seat.* **2** a noisy dispute; an angry quarrel. **3** in the western United States and Canada, herd or tend horses, cattle, etc. on the range. 1, 3 *v.*, **wran·gled, wran·gling;** 2 *n.* **—wran′gler,** *n.*

wrap (rap) **1** cover by winding or folding something around: *She wrapped herself in a shawl.* **2** wind or fold as a covering: *Wrap a shawl around yourself.* **3** cover with paper and tie up or fasten: *Have you wrapped all the presents?* **4** cover; envelop; hide: *The mountain peak is wrapped in clouds.* **5** an outer covering: *Shawls, scarfs, coats, and furs are wraps.* 1–4 *v.*, **wrapped** or **wrapt, wrap·ping;** 5 *n.*

wrapped up in, devoted to; thinking of: *She is wrapped up in her children.*

☛ **Wrap** and **rap** are pronounced the same.

wrap·per (rap′ər) a covering or cover: *Some magazines are mailed in paper wrappers.* *n.*

wrap·ping (rap′ing) the paper or other material in which something is wrapped. *n.*

wrapt (rapt) See **wrap.** *v.*

wrath (rath or roth) very great anger; rage. *n.*

wrath·ful (rath′fəl or roth′fəl) very angry; showing wrath: *The wrathful lion turned on the hunters. His wrathful eyes flashed.* *adj.*

wreak (rēk) **1** give expression to; work off feelings, desires, etc.: *The cruel boy wreaked his temper on his dog.* **2** inflict: *The hurricane wreaked havoc on the city.* *v.*

☛ **Wreak** and **reek** are pronounced the same.

wreath (rēth) **1** a ring of flowers or leaves twisted together: *We hang wreaths in the windows at Christmas.* **2** something suggesting a wreath: *a wreath of smoke.* *n.*, *pl.* **wreaths** (rēᴛʜz).

wreathe (rēᴛʜ) **1** make into a wreath: *The children wreathed flowers to put on the soldiers' graves.* **2** decorate or adorn with wreaths: *The inside of the schoolhouse was wreathed with Christmas greens.* **3** make a ring around; encircle: *Mist wreathes the hills.* *v.*, **wreathed, wreath·ing.**

wreck (rek) **1** the destruction of a ship, building, train, automobile, or aircraft: *The hurricane caused many wrecks. Careless driving causes many wrecks on the highway.* **2** any destruction or serious injury: *Heavy rains caused the wreck of many crops.* **3** what is left of anything that has been destroyed or much injured: *The wreck of a ship was cast upon the shore by the waves.* **4** a person or animal that has lost physical or mental health: *He was a wreck after having malaria. The overworked donkey is a wreck.* **5** cause the wreck of; destroy; ruin. 1–4 *n.*, 5 *v.*

wreck·age (rek′ij) **1** what is left by a wreck or wrecks: *The shore was covered with the wreckage of ships.* **2** wrecking or being wrecked: *She wept at the wreckage of her hopes.* *n.*

wreck·er (rek′ər) **1** a person or machine that tears

down buildings: *John operates the wrecker that is demolishing the vacant building.* **2** a person, car, train, or machine that removes wrecks. **3** a person or ship that recovers wrecked or disabled ships or their cargoes. *n.*

wren (ren) a small brown or grey songbird having a slender bill and a short tail, often held erect: *Wrens often build their nests near houses.* *n.*

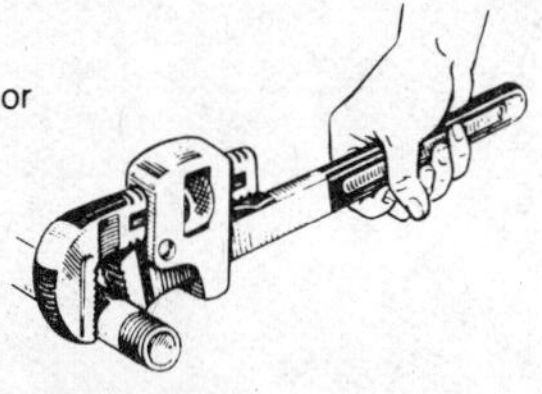

A wrench. The jaws have ridged surfaces for gripping. They can be moved together or apart by means of a screw.

wrench (rench) **1** a violent twist or twisting pull: *He broke the branch off the tree with a sudden wrench. He gave his ankle a wrench when he jumped off the bus.* **2** twist or pull violently: *He wrenched the knob off when he was trying to open the door. The policeman wrenched the gun out of the man's hand.* **3** injure by twisting: *He wrenched his back in wrestling.* **4** an injury caused by twisting: *He was suffering from a wrench in the back.* **5** a source of grief or sorrow: *It was a wrench to leave our old home.* **6** a tool to hold and turn nuts, bolts, etc. 1, 4–6 *n.*, 2, 3 *v.*

wrest (rest) **1** twist, pull, or tear away with force; wrench away: *He bravely wrested the knife from the insane man.* **2** take by force: *An enemy wrested the power from the duke.* *v.*

☛ **Wrest** and **rest** are pronounced the same.

wres·tle (res′əl) **1** try to throw or force an opponent to the ground: *The rules for wrestling do not allow using the fists or certain holds on the body.* **2** a wrestling match. **3** a struggle. **4** to struggle: *I have been wrestling with this problem for an hour.* 1, 4 *v.*, **wres·tled, wres·tling;** 2, 3 *n.* **—wres′tler,** *n.*

wres·tling (res′ling) a sport or contest in which each of two opponents tries to throw or force the other to the ground. *n.*

wretch (rech) **1** a very unfortunate or unhappy person. **2** a very bad person. *n.*

wretch·ed (rech′id) **1** very unfortunate or unhappy. **2** very unsatisfactory; miserable: *a wretched hut.* **3** very bad: *a wretched traitor.* *adj.* **—wretch′ed·ness,** *n.*

wrig·gle (rig′əl) **1** twist and turn: *Children wriggle when they are restless.* **2** move by twisting and turning: *The worm wriggled out of my hand when I tried to put it on the hook.* **3** make one's way by tricks, excuses, etc.: *That boy can wriggle out of any difficulty.* **4** the act of wriggling: *With one wriggle, he was under the bed.* 1–3 *v.*, **wrig·gled, wrig·gling;** 4 *n.*

wright (rīt) used mostly in compounds, a maker or author of something: *A wheelwright makes wheels. A playwright writes plays for the theatre.* *n.*

☛ **Wright, right, rite,** and **write** are pronounced the same.

wring (ring) **1** twist with force; squeeze hard: *Do wring your wet bathing suit. His soul was wrung with grief.* **2** get by twisting or squeezing; force out: *The hikers wrung water from their soaking clothes.* **3** get by force, effort, or persuasion: *The old beggar could wring money from a miser with his sad story.* **4** clasp and hold firmly: *He wrung his old friend's hand in joy at*

hat, āge, fär; let, ēqual, tėrm; it, īce
hot, ōpen, ôrder; oil, out; cup, pu̇t, rüle
əbove, takən, pencəl, lemən, circəs
ch, child; ng, long; sh, ship
th, thin; ᴛʜ, then; zh, measure

seeing him. **5** cause pain or pity in: *Their poverty wrung his heart.* **6** a twisting or squeezing: *Give the bathing suits a wring, please.* 1–5 *v.*, **wrung, wring·ing;** 6 *n.*

wring out, squeeze so as to remove water from: *He wrung out his wet socks.*

☛ **Wring** and **ring** are pronounced the same.

wring·er (ring′ər) a machine for squeezing water from clothes. *n.*

wrin·kle[1] (ring′kəl) **1** an irregular ridge or fold; crease: *The old man's face has wrinkles. I must press out the wrinkles in this dress.* **2** make a wrinkle or wrinkles in: *He wrinkled his forehead.* **3** have wrinkles; acquire wrinkles: *This shirt will not wrinkle.* 1 *n.*, 2, 3 *v.*, **wrin·kled, wrin·kling.**

wrin·kle[2] (ring′kəl) *Informal.* a useful hint or idea; clever trick: *She will give you some wrinkles for using empty cartons to make toys.* *n.*

wrist (rist) the joint connecting hand and arm. See **arm** for picture. *n.*

wrist·band (rist′band′) the band of a sleeve fitting around the wrist. *n.*

wrist·watch (rist′woch′) a small watch worn on a strap around the wrist. *n.*

writ (rit) **1** something written; a writing: *The Bible is Holy Writ.* **2** a formal order directing a person to do or not do something: *A writ from the judge ordered the man's release from jail.* **3** an old form meaning **written:** *Their names are writ in gold.* 1, 2 *n.*, 3 *v.*

write (rīt) **1** make letters or words with pen, pencil, chalk, etc.: *You can read and write.* **2** mark with letters or words: *He had to write a cheque.* **3** put down the letters or words of: *Write your name.* **4** make up stories, books, etc.; compose: *He writes for the magazine.* **5** write a letter: *She writes to her mother every week.* **6** show plainly: *Fear was written on his face.* *v.*, **wrote, writ·ten, writ·ing.**

write down, put into writing: *Many early folk songs were never written down.*

write out, a put into writing. **b** write in full: *She made quick notes during the interview and wrote out her report later.*

write up, a write a description or account of. **b** write in detail.

☛ **Write, right, rite,** and **wright** are pronounced the same.

writ·er (rīt′ər) a person whose occupation is writing; author. *n.*

writhe (rīᴛʜ) **1** twist; twist out of shape; twist about: *The snake writhed along the branch. The wounded man writhed with pain.* **2** suffer mentally; be very uncomfortable: *We writhed when we heard the angry man insult our friend.* *v.*, **writhed, writh·ing.**

writ·ing (rīt′ing) **1** written form: *Put your ideas in writing.* **2** handwriting: *His writing is hard to read.* **3** something written; a letter, paper, document, etc. **4** a literary work; a book or other literary production: *the writings of Judge Haliburton.* *n.*

writ·ten (rit′ən) See **write.** *He has written a letter.* *v.*

wrong (rong) **1** not right; bad: *Stealing is wrong.* **2** not true; not correct; not what it should be: *He gave the wrong answer.* **3** not proper; not fit; unsuitable: *Heavy boots would be the wrong thing to wear for tennis.* **4** out of order: *Something is wrong with the car.* **5** in a wrong manner; ill; badly: *You've done it all wrong.* **6** anything not right; a wrong thing or action: *Two wrongs do not make a right.* **7** injury; harm: *You do an honest man a wrong if you call him a liar or a thief.* **8** do wrong to; treat unfairly; injure: *He forgave those who had wronged him.* **9** not meant to be seen or shown: *The wrong side of cloth.* 1–4, 9 *adj.,* 5 *adv.,* 6, 7 *n.,* 8 *v.*

go wrong, a turn out badly: *Everything went wrong today.* **b** stop being good and become bad.

in the wrong, at fault; guilty.

wrong·do·ing (rong′dü′ing) the doing of wrong; bad acts: *The thief was guilty of wrongdoing.* *n.*

wrong·ful (rong′fəl) wrong. *adj.*

wrote (rōt) See **write.** *He wrote his mother a long letter last week.* *n.*

☛ **Wrote** and **rote** are pronounced the same.

wroth (roth) angry. *adj.*

wrought (rot or rôt) **1** See **work** (defs. 10, 13). *The gate was wrought with great skill.* **2** of metals, formed by hammering: *wrought iron.* 1 *v.,* 2 *adj.*

☛ **Wrought** and **rot** are sometimes pronounced the same.

wrought iron a tough, durable form of iron that is soft enough to be easily forged and welded, but that will not break as easily as cast iron: *Wrought iron is often used for decorative furniture, gates, or railings.*

wrought–up (rot′up′ or rôt′up′) stirred up; excited: *After all the work of planning, she was too wrought-up to enjoy the party.* *adj.*

wrung (rung) See **wring.** *She wrung out the wet cloth and hung it up. Her heart is wrung with pity for the poor.* *v.*

☛ **Wrung** and **rung** are pronounced the same.

wry (rī) **1** twisted; turned to one side: *She made a wry face to show her disgust.* **2** showing clever or grim irony: *wry humor.* *adj.,* **wri·er, wri·est.**

☛ **Wry** and **rye** are pronounced the same.

wt. weight.

x or **X** (eks) **1** the 24th letter of the alphabet: *There are very few words that begin with* x. **2** an unknown quantity. **3** anything shaped like an x. **4** the Roman numeral for 10. *n., pl.* **x's** or **X's.**

Xmas (kris′məs) *Informal.* Christmas. *n.*

Xer·ox (zēr′oks) **1** a trademark for a process for making copies of writing, printing, black-and-white pictures, etc. **2** a copying machine using this process. **3** make copies by this process. 1, 2 *n.,* 3 *v.*

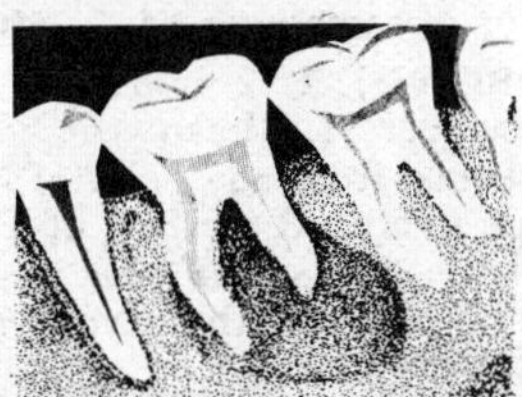

An X ray of an abscessed tooth. The abscess is shown by the dark area around the roots of the tooth.

X ray **1** a ray which can go through substances that ordinary rays of light cannot penetrate, but which will act in the same way as light does on photographic films or plates to produce a picture: *X rays are used to locate breaks in bones or bullets lodged in the body, and to treat certain diseases.* **2** a picture made by means of X rays.

X–ray (eks′rā′) **1** examine, photograph, or treat with X rays: *The doctor X-rayed my knee to see if any bones had been broken by my fall.* **2** of, by, or having to do with X rays: *an X-ray examination of one's teeth.* 1 *v.,* 2 *adj.*

A xylophone

xy·lo·phone (zī′lə fōn′) a musical instrument consisting of two rows of wooden bars of varying lengths, which are sounded by striking them with wooden hammers. *n.*

hat, āge, fär; let, ēqual, tėrm; it, īce
hot, ōpen, ôrder; oil, out; cup, pu̇t, rüle
əbove, takən, pencəl, lemən, circəs
ch, child; ng, long; sh, ship
th, thin; ᴛʜ, then; zh, measure

y or **Y** (wī) **1** the 25th letter of the alphabet: *There are two* y's *in* yearly. **2** anything shaped like the letter Y. *n., pl.* **y's** or **Y's.**

–y[1] a suffix meaning: **1** full of, made of, or having: *Watery means full of water.* **2** like; resembling: *Icy means like ice.* **3** inclined to ___: *Fidgety means inclined to fidget.*

–y[2] a suffix used to indicate that someone or something is considered as small and attractive, thought of with affection, etc.: *doggy, dolly, mummy.*

yacht (yot) **1** a boat for pleasure trips or for racing. **2** to sail or race on a yacht. 1 *n.*, 2 *v.*

yacht·ing (yot′ing) **1** the art of sailing a yacht. **2** the pastime of sailing on a yacht. *n.*

yachts·man (yots′mən) a person who owns or sails a yacht. *n., pl.* **yachts·men** (yots′mən).

yak (yak) a large, long-haired animal of central Asia, related to the North American buffalo and to cattle: *Yaks are often domesticated and used for food and as beasts of burden. n.*

yam (yam) **1** a kind of sweet potato: *We often have candied yams with ham.* **2** the starchy root of a vine grown for food in warm countries. *n.*

yank (yangk) *Informal.* **1** pull with a sudden motion; jerk: *You almost yanked my arm off!* **2** a sudden pull; jerk: *He gave the door a yank.* 1 *v.*, 2 *n.*

yank out, take out with a jerk.

Yank (yangk) *Slang.* Yankee. *n.*

Yan·kee (yang′kē) *Informal.* **1** a native of one of the six New England states of the north-eastern part of the United States. **2** a native of any of the northern states of the United States. **3** a person born in or living in the United States; an American. *n.*

yap (yap) **1** a snappish bark; a yelp. **2** bark in a snappish way; yelp: *Her little dog yaps at strangers.* 1 *n.*, 2 *v.*, **yapped, yap·ping.**

yard[1] (yärd) **1** a piece of ground near or around a house, barn, school, etc.: *He is in the back yard.* **2** a piece of enclosed ground for some special purpose or business: *a chicken yard, a junk yard.* **3** a space with tracks where railway cars are stored, shifted around, etc.: *My brother works at the CN yards. n.*

yard[2] (yärd) **1** a measure of length equal to 36 inches or 3 feet, or about 91 centimetres: *The football player ran 40 yards for a touchdown.* **2** a beam or pole fastened across a mast, used to support a sail. See **brig** for picture. *n.*

yard·arm (yärd′ärm′) either end of the beam or pole that supports a square sail. *n.*

yard·stick (yärd′stik′) **1** a stick one yard long, used for measuring. **2** a standard of judgment or comparison: *What yardstick do you use to decide whether your conduct is right or wrong? n.*

yarn (yärn) **1** any spun thread, especially that prepared for weaving or knitting: *This yarn is soft enough for baby clothes.* **2** *Informal.* a tale; story: *The old sailor made up his yarns as he told them. n.*

yawl (yol or yôl) **1** a boat having a large mast near the bow and a small mast near the stern: *A yawl has its sails rigged fore-and-aft.* **2** a ship's boat rowed by four or six oars. *n.*

yawn (yon or yôn) **1** open the mouth wide because one is sleepy, tired, or bored. **2** the act of doing so. **3** open wide: *The canyon yawned beneath our feet.* 1, 3 *v.*, 2 *n.*

☛ **Yawn** and **yon** are sometimes pronounced the same.

yd. yard; yards.

yds. yards.

ye (yē) an old form of **you:** *'Come, all ye faithful.' pron.*

yea (yā) **1** yes. **2** indeed; truly. **3** a vote or voter in favor of something. 1, 2 *adv.*, 3 *n.*

year (yēr) **1** 12 months or 365 days; January 1 to December 31. Leap year has 366 days. **2** 12 months reckoned from any point: *I will see you again a year from today.* **3** the part of a year spent in a certain activity: *Our school year is nine months.* **4** the exact period of the earth's revolution around the sun, about 365¼ days. *n.*

year in, year out, always, continuously: *He has always worked hard, year in, year out.*

year·book (yēr′bu̇k′) a book or report published every year: *Yearbooks often report events of the year. n.*

year·ling (yēr′ling) an animal one year old: *a yearling colt. The rancher decided to sell his yearlings. n.*

year·ly (yēr′lē) **1** once a year; in every year: *He takes a yearly trip to Toronto (adj.). A new volume comes out yearly (adv.).* **2** lasting a year: *The earth makes a yearly revolution around the sun.* **3** for a year: *She is paid $700 a month, or $8400 yearly.* 1, 2 *adj.*, 1, 3 *adv.*

yearn (yėrn) **1** feel a longing or desire; desire earnestly: *He yearns for home.* **2** feel pity; have tender feelings: *Her kind heart yearned for the homeless children. v.*

yearn·ing (yėr′ning) an earnest or strong desire; longing. *n.*

year–round (yēr′round′) throughout the year: *Our town has many summer visitors but few year-round residents. adj., adv.*

yeast (yēst) **1** the substance that causes bread dough to rise and beer to ferment: *Yeast consists of very small plants or cells that grow quickly in a liquid containing sugar.* **2** a product containing yeast, often in a small pressed block or cake made by mixing flour or meal with yeast: *We need either a package of yeast particles or a yeast cake to make this bread. n.*

yell (yel) **1** cry out with a strong, loud sound: *He yelled with pain.* **2** a strong, loud cry. **3** say with a yell: *We yelled our goodbyes to our friends as the bus moved away.* **4** a special shout or cheer especially one used by a school or college to encourage its sports teams. 1, 3 *v.*, 2, 4 *n.*

yel·low (yel′ō) **1** the color of gold, butter, or ripe lemons. **2** having this color. **3** become yellow: *Paper yellows with age.* **4** make yellow: *Buttercups yellowed the field.* **5** having a yellowish-brown skin. **6** something yellow, especially the yolk of an egg: *We used the whites of six eggs for cake and the yellows for custards.* **7** *Informal.* cowardly. 1, 6 *n.*, 2, 5, 7 *adj.*, 3, 4 *v.*

yellow fever a disease of warm climates, spread by a kind of mosquito.

yellow jacket a wasp or hornet marked with bright yellow.

yelp (yelp) **1** a quick, sharp bark or cry: *The yelps of* *the small puppy didn't bother the Newfoundland dog.* **2** make such a bark or cry: *I yelped when the rock fell on my toe.* 1 *n.*, 2 *v.*

yen[1] (yen) a unit of money of Japan. *n., pl.* **yen.**

yen[2] *Informal.* a fanciful desire: *I've always had a yen to travel all over the world. n.*

yeo·man (yō′mən) **1** especially in England, a person who owns land, but not a large amount, and usually farms it himself. **2** formerly, a servant or attendant of a lord or king. *n., pl.* **yeo·men** (yō′mən).
yeoman service or **yeoman's service,** extremely valuable service or assistance.

yeo·man·ry (yō′mən rē) yeomen as a group. *n.*

yes (yes) **1** a word used to indicate that one can or will, or that something is so; a word used to affirm, accept, or agree: *'Yes, five and two are seven,' said Bob. Will you go? Yes.* **2** agreement; acceptance; consent: *You have my yes to that.* **3** and what is more: *'Your work is good, yes, very good,' said the teacher.* 1, 3 *adv.*, 2 *n., pl.* **yes·es.**

yes·ter·day (yes′tər dē or yes′tər dā′) **1** the day before today: *Yesterday was cold.* **2** on the day before today. **3** the recent past: *The fashions of yesterday amuse us now.* 1, 3 *n.*, 2 *adv.*

yet (yet) **1** up to the present time; thus far: *The work is not yet finished.* **2** now; at this time: *Don't go yet.* **3** then; at that time: *It was not yet dark.* **4** still; even now: *It is yet light. She is talking yet.* **5** sometime: *I may yet get rich.* **6** also; again: *Yet once more I forbid you to go.* **7** even: *He spoke yet more loudly when asked to be quiet.* **8** but; nevertheless; however: *The story was strange, yet true (adv.). The work is good, yet it could be better (conj.).* 1–8 *adv.*, 8 *conj.*
as yet, up to now: *As yet we have no news of him.*

yew (yü) **1** an evergreen tree of Europe and Asia: *Some kinds of yew are now widely grown in Canada as shrubs.* **2** the wood of this tree: *Bows used to be made of a kind of yew that grows in England. n.*
☛ **Yew** and **ewe** are pronounced the same. **Yew** and **you** are sometimes pronounced the same.

Yid·dish (yid′ish) a language that developed from a German dialect of the Middle Ages, nowadays containing many Hebrew and Slavic words and written in Hebrew letters: *Yiddish is spoken especially by Jews in eastern and central Europe. n.*

yield (yēld) **1** produce; bear: *This land yields good crops. Mines yield ore.* **2** the amount yielded; the product: *This year's yield from the silver mine was very large.* **3** give; grant: *Her mother yielded her consent to the plan.* **4** give up; submit; surrender: *The enemy yielded to our soldiers. I yielded to temptation and ate all the candy.* **5** give way: *The door yielded to his touch.* **6** give place: *We yield to nobody in love of freedom.* 1, 3–6 *v.*, 2 *n.*

yield·ing (yēl′ding) **1** submissive; not resisting: *He loses most arguments because of his yielding nature.* **2** soft; giving way under weight or force: *We lay back in the yielding grass. adj.*

Y.M.C.A. Young Men's Christian Association.

yo·del (yō′dəl) **1** sing or call with frequent, sudden changes from the ordinary voice pitch to a much higher pitch: *The Swiss mountaineer was yodelling as we came up the valley.* **2** the act or sound of yodelling. 1 *v.*, **yo·delled** or **yo·deled, yo·del·ling** or **yo·del·ing;** 2 *n.*

yo·ga or **Yo·ga** (yō′gə) a system to help the body, mind, and spirit to grow and develop by means of slow, rhythmic body movements and by complete relaxation of the body and mind: *Yoga originated in India about 6000 years ago. n.*

hat, āge, fär; let, ēqual, tėrm; it, īce
hot, ōpen, ôrder; oil, out; cup, pu̇t, rüle
əbove, takən, pencəl, lemən, circəs
ch, child; ng, long; sh, ship
th, thin; ᴛʜ, then; zh, measure

yo·gurt (yō′gėrt) a kind of thickened, fermented liquid food made from milk: *Yogurt can be eaten plain or with fruit or sugar. n.*

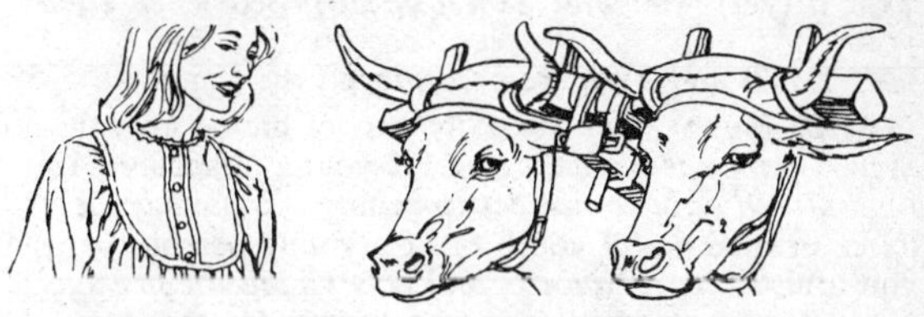
A yoke on a nightgown A yoke for oxen

yoke (yōk) **1** a wooden frame which fits around the neck of two work animals to fasten them together for pulling a plough or vehicle. **2** a pair fastened together by a yoke: *The plough was drawn by a yoke of oxen.* **3** any frame connecting two other parts: *The man carried two buckets on a yoke, one at each end.* **4** put a yoke on; fasten with a yoke. **5** harness or fasten a work animal or animals to: *The farmer yoked his plough.* **6** a part of a garment fitted closely to the shoulders. **7** the top piece to a skirt, fitting the hips. **8** something that binds together: *the yoke of marriage.* **9** something that holds people in slavery or submission: *Throw off your yoke and be free.* **10** rule; dominion: *Slaves are under the yoke of their masters.* 1–3, 6–10 *n.*, 4, 5 *v.*, **yoked, yok·ing.**

yo·kel (yō′kəl) a person from the country, especially one who is unused to city ways: *Some city people look down on country folk and call them yokels. n.*

yolk (yōk) the yellow part of an egg. *n.*

Yom Kip·pur (yom kip′ər) an annual Jewish day of fasting and atoning for sins, observed on the tenth day after the Jewish New Year.

yon (yon) yonder: *The frightened chickens ran hither and yon. adv., adj.*
☛ **Yon** and **yawn** are sometimes pronounced the same.

yon·der (yon′dər) **1** over there; within sight, but not near: *Look at that wild duck yonder! The sky is getting black yonder in the west.* **2** situated over there; being within sight, but not near: *On yonder hill stands a ruined castle.* 1 *adv.*, 2 *adj.*

yore (yôr) **of yore,** of long ago; formerly; in the past: *in days of yore, tales of yore. adv.*

A York boat

York boat *Cdn.* formerly, a type of heavy freight

canoe developed by the Hudson's Bay Company at York Factory on Hudson Bay.

York·shire pudding (yôrk′shir) a batter that is baked and often served with roast beef.

you (yü; *unstressed* yə) 1 the person or persons spoken to: *Are you ready? Then you may go.* 2 one; anybody: *You never can tell. You can push this button to get a light. His sermons put you to sleep. pron.*

☞ **You** is sometimes pronounced the same as **ewe** and **yew.**

you'd (yüd) 1 you had: *You'd better go quickly.* 2 you would: *You'd like this story.*

you'll (yül) you will: *You'll be surprised when I tell you.*

☞ **You'll** and **Yule** are pronounced the same.

young (yung) 1 in the early part of life or growth; not old: *A puppy is a young dog.* 2 young offspring: *An animal will fight to protect its young.* 3 having the looks or qualities of youth or of a young person; youthful; lively: *She looks and acts young for her age.* 4 without much experience or practice: *He was too young in the business.* 5 **the young,** young people. 1, 3, 4 *adj.,* **young·er** (yung′gər), **young·est** (yung′gist); 2, 5 *n.*

young·ster (yung′stər) 1 a child: *He is a lively youngster.* 2 a young person: *The old farmer was as spry as a youngster. n.*

your (yür; *unstressed,* yər) 1 of you; belonging to you: *Wash your hands.* 2 having to do with you; made or done by you: *We enjoyed your visit. We saw your paintings at the art gallery.* 3 **Your** is used as part of a title: *Your Highness, Your Lordship, Your Honor. adj.*

☞ **Your** and **you're** are pronounced the same.

you're (yür; *unstressed,* yər) you are.

☞ See note at **your.**

yours (yürz; *unstressed, yərz)* 1 of you; belonging to you: *The red book is yours.* 2 the one or ones belonging to or having something to do with you: *My hands are clean; yours are dirty. I like ours better than yours. pron.*

your·self (yür self′; *unstressed,* yər self′) 1 a form used instead of **you** when referring back to the subject of the sentence: *Did you hurt yourself? Try to do it by yourself.* 2 a form of **you** used to make a statement stronger: *You yourself know the story is not true.* 3 your real or true self: *Now that your cold is better, you'll feel like yourself again. pron., pl.* **your·selves.**

your·selves (yür selvz′; *unstressed,* yər selvs′) See **yourself.** *You can all see for yourselves that the room is empty. pron. pl.*

youth (yüth) 1 the fact or quality of being young: *He has the vigor of youth. She keeps her youth well.* 2 the time between childhood and manhood or womanhood. 3 a young man. 4 young people. 5 the first or early stage of anything: *Many of the things we believe in go back to the youth of this country. n., pl.* **youths** (yüths or yüᴛʜz).

youth·ful (yüth′fəl) 1 young. 2 of youth; suitable for young people: *youthful faults, youthful energy, youthful pleasures.* 3 having the looks or qualities of youth; fresh; lively: *The old man had a very happy and youthful spirit. adj.* —**youth′ful·ly,** *adv.* —**youth′ful·ness,** *n.*

you've (yüv; *unstressed,* yəv) you have: *You've gone too far.*

yowl (youl) 1 a long, distressful, or dismal cry; a howl. 2 howl: *That dog is always yowling.* 1 *n.,* 2 *v.*

yo–yo (yō′yō) a small, wheel-shaped toy made up of two disks, usually wooden, joined by a central peg to which is attached a long string. The string is held by one hand, and the toy is spun out and reeled in on the string. *n., pl.* **yo-yos.**

yr. year; years.

yrs. years.

Y.T. Yukon Territory.

yuc·ca (yuk′ə) a plant having sword-shaped evergreen leaves and a cluster of large, white lily-like flowers on a tall stalk: *The yucca plant has an edible, potato-like root, widely used in Central and South America as a vegetable. n.*

Yule or **yule** (yül) 1 Christmas. 2 Yuletide. *n.*

☞ **Yule** and **you'll** are pronounced the same.

Yule log a large log burned at Christmas.

Yule·tide or **yule·tide** (yül′tīd′) Christmas time; the Christmas season. *n.*

Y.W.C.A. Young Women's Christian Association.

hat, āge, fär; let, ēqual, tėrm; it, īce
hot, ōpen, ôrder; oil, out; cup, pu̇t, rüle
əbove, takən, pencəl, lemən, circəs
ch, child; ng, long; sh, ship
th, thin; ᴛʜ, then; zh, measure

z or **Z** (zed) the 26th and last letter of the alphabet: *There are two* z's *in* zigzag. *n., pl.* **z's** or **Z's.**

za·ny (zā'nē) **1** foolish; comical; ridiculous: *His zany stories make everyone laugh.* **2** a fool. 1 *adj.,* 2 *n.*

zeal (zēl) eager desire or effort; earnest enthusiasm: *A good citizen works with zeal for his country's interests.* *n.*

zeal·ot (zel'ət) a person who shows too much zeal; a fanatic. *n.*

zeal·ous (zel'əs) full of zeal; eager; earnest: *The children made zealous efforts to clean up the house for the party. That salesman seems zealous to please.* *adj.*

A zebra — about 125 cm high at the shoulder

ze·bra (zē'brə or zeb'rə) a wild animal of Africa, related to the horse and donkey, but striped with dark bands on white. *n.*

zen·ith (zen'ith or zē'nith) **1** the point in the heavens directly overhead. **2** the highest or greatest point: *At the zenith of its power Rome dominated all the known world.* *n.*

zeph·yr (zef'ər) **1** the west wind. **2** any soft, gentle wind; a mild breeze. **3** a fine, soft yarn. *n.*

Zep·pe·lin or **zep·pe·lin** (zep'ə lən or zep'lən) a type of airship shaped like a cigar with pointed ends and having compartments for gas, engines, passengers, etc. See **dirigible** for picture. *n.*

☛ Named after Count Ferdinand von *Zeppelin* (1838–1917), a German pioneer in the design of such aircraft.

ze·ro (zēr'ō) **1** nought; the figure 0: *There are three zeros in 40 006.* **2** the point marked as 0 on the scale of a thermometer, etc: *A thermometer reads up and down from zero.* **3** the temperature that corresponds to zero on the scale of a thermometer: *The forecast is zero. Water freezes at zero.* **4** of or at zero: *a zero score.* **5** nothing: *The other team's score was zero.* **6** not any; none at all: *The weather station at the airport announced zero visibility.* **7** the lowest point: *The team's spirit sank to zero after its third defeat.* 1–3, 5, 7 *n., pl.* **ze·ros** or **ze·roes;** 4, 6 *adj.*

☛ **Zero** came into English from an Italian word which in turn was taken from the Arabic word *sifr,* meaning 'empty.' It is related to *cipher.*

zest (zest) **1** keen enjoyment; relish: *The hungry man ate with zest.* **2** a pleasant or exciting quality or flavor: *Wit gives zest to conversation.* *n.*

Zeus (züs) the chief god of the ancient Greeks, called Jupiter by the Romans. *n.*

zig·zag (zig'zag') **1** with short, sharp turns from one side to the other: *go in a zigzag direction (adj.). The path ran zigzag up the hill (adv.).* **2** move in a zigzag way: *Lightning zigzagged across the sky.* **3** a zigzag line or course. **4** one of the short, sharp turns of a zigzag. 1 *adj., adv.,* 2 *v.,* **zig·zagged, zig·zag·ging;** 3, 4 *n.*

zinc (zingk) a bluish-white metal very little affected by air and moisture: *Zinc is used as a roofing material, in electric batteries, in paint, in medicine, and for coating some metals.* *n.*

zing (zing) **1** a sharp, humming sound. **2** *Slang.* spirit; liveliness; zest: *Put more zing in your story; it's too dull.* **3** make a sharp, humming sound, especially in going fast: *A fly zinged past my ear.* 1, 2 *n.,* 3 *v.*

Zinnias

zin·ni·a (zin'ē ə) a garden plant grown for its showy flowers of many colors. *n.*

☛ Named in honor of a German botanist, Johann *Zinn* (1727–1759).

Zi·on (zī'ən) **1** a hill in Jerusalem on which the royal palace and the temple (def. 2) were built. **2** Israel; the people of Israel. **3** heaven; the heavenly city. *n.*

☛ **Zion** developed from an Old English word which came through Latin and Greek from the Hebrew word *tsīyōn,* meaning 'hill.'

Zi·on·ism (zī'ən iz'əm) a movement, begun in the late 19th century, to make modern Palestine (now Israel) a Jewish national state. *n.*

Zi·on·ist (zī'ən ist) a supporter of Zionism. *n.*

zip (zip) **1** a sudden, brief hissing sound, as of a flying bullet. **2** make such a sound. **3** *Informal.* energy or vim. **4** *Informal.* proceed with energy. **5** fasten or close with a zipper: *He zipped up his jacket.* 1, 3 *n.,* 2, 4, 5 *v.,* **zipped, zip·ping.**

zip·per (zip'ər) **1** a sliding fastener for clothes, purses, etc.: *He has a zipper on his windbreaker.* **2** do up a zipper: *Zipper up your coat before you go out in the cold.* 1 *n.,* 2 *v.*

zir·con (zėr'kon) a mineral that occurs in crystals of many forms and colors: *Transparent zircon is used as a gemstone.* *n.*

zith·er (zith'ər) a musical instrument having 30 to 40 strings, played with the fingers and a pick (def. 10). *n.*

☛ See note at **guitar.**

zo·di·ac (zō'dē ak') **1** an imaginary belt of the heavens divided into 12 equal parts, called signs, named

A zigzag design

after 12 groups of stars. **2** a diagram representing the zodiac, used in astrology. *n.*

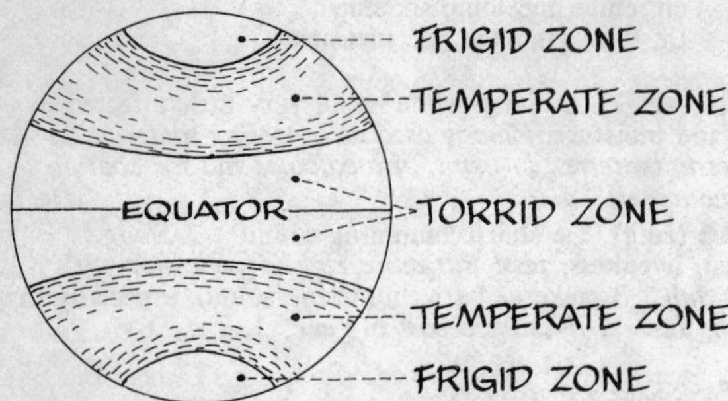

zone (zōn) **1** any of the five great divisions of the earth's surface, bounded by imaginary lines going around the earth parallel to the equator. **2** any region, district, or section especially considered or set off: *a hospital zone. A combat zone is an area where fighting is going on. There were two houses here before it was designated a zone for industry. Alberta, B.C., and the Yukon are in the same postal rate zone.* **3** set an area or areas apart for a special purpose, especially in a city or town: *This area is zoned for apartment buildings.* 1, 2 *n.*, 3 *v.*, **zoned, zon·ing.**

zoo (zü) a place where animals are kept and shown; zoological garden: *We saw lions and tigers in the zoo.* *n.*

☛ See note at **zoology.**

zo·o·log·i·cal (zō′ə loj′ə kəl or zü′ə loj′ə kəl) **1** of animals and animal life. **2** having to do with zoology. *adj.*

☛ See note at **zoology.**

zoological garden zoo.

zo·ol·o·gist (zō ol′ə jist or zü ol′ə jist) a person skilled or trained in zoology. *n.*

☛ See note at **zoology.**

zo·ol·o·gy (zō ol′ə jē or zü ol′ə jē) the science of animals; the study of animals and animal life: *Zoology is a branch of biology.* *n.*

☛ **Zoology, zoological,** and **zoologist** all came into English in the seventeenth century from the ancient Greek word *zōion,* meaning 'animal.' The word **zoo** was created in the nineteenth century as an abbreviation for *zoological garden.*

zoom (züm) **1** move suddenly upward: *The airplane zoomed.* **2** a sudden upward flight: *The airplane made a zoom and left the mountain far below.* **3** travel or move with a humming or buzzing sound. 1, 3 *v.*, 2 *n.*

zuc·chi·ni (zü kē′nē) a kind of dark-green squash shaped like a cucumber: *Zucchini is eaten as a cooked vegetable.* *n.*

zwie·back (tswē′bäk′) a kind of bread cut into slices and toasted dry in an oven. *n.*

☛ **Zwieback** comes from the German word *Zwieback,* formed from a translation of an Italian word which developed from Latin *bis coctus,* meaning 'twice cooked.' Our word **biscuit** comes from a French word which developed from the same Latin expression.

Grammar Key

n.	noun	*pron.*	pronoun
v.	verb	*prep.*	preposition
adj.	adjective	*conj.*	conjunction
adv.	adverb	*interj.*	interjection

Word History Key

Names of languages from which English words have come are given in full. The following need special explanation:

Middle English — the language spoken by the English people from about A.D. 1100 to about 1450.

Old English — the language spoken by the English people until about A.D. 1100. It developed from the Germanic speech brought to England after about A.D. 450.

Old French — the language spoken by the French people from about A.D. 800 to about 1100.

Old Norse — the language spoken by the people of Scandinavia from about A.D. 700 to about 1300.